The
HOLY
BIBLE

NEW INTERNATIONAL VERSION

WORDS OF LIFE EDITION

The HOLY BIBLE

NEW INTERNATIONAL VERSION

WORDS OF LIFE EDITION

Hodder & Stoughton
LONDON SYDNEY AUCKLAND

Preface

THE NEW INTERNATIONAL VERSION is a completely new translation of the Holy Bible made by over a hundred scholars working directly from the best available Hebrew, Aramaic and Greek texts. It had its beginning in 1965 when, after several years of exploratory study by committees from the Christian Reformed Church and the National Association of Evangelicals, a group of scholars met at Palos Heights, Illinois, and concurred in the need for a new translation of the Bible in contemporary English. This group, though not made up of official church representatives, was transdenominational. Its conclusion was endorsed by a large number of leaders from many denominations who met in Chicago in 1966.

Responsibility for the new version was delegated by the Palos Heights group to a self-governing body of fifteen, the Committee on Bible Translation, composed for the most part of biblical scholars from colleges, universities and seminaries. In 1967 the New York Bible Society (now the International Bible Society) generously undertook the financial sponsorship of the project – a sponsorship that made it possible to enlist the help of many distinguished scholars. The fact that participants from the United States, Great Britain, Canada, Australia and New Zealand worked together gave the project its international scope. That they were from many denominations – including Anglican, Assemblies of God, Baptist, Brethren, Christian Reformed, Church of Christ, Evangelical Free, Lutheran, Mennonite, Methodist, Nazarene, Presbyterian, Wesleyan and other churches – helped to safeguard the translation from sectarian bias.

How it was made helps to give the New International Version its distinctiveness. The translation of each book was assigned to a team of scholars. Next, one of the Intermediate Editorial Committees revised the initial translation, with constant reference to the Hebrew, Aramaic or Greek. Their work then went to one of the General Editorial Committees, which checked it in detail and made another thorough revision. This revision in turn was carefully reviewed by the Committee on Bible Translation, which made further changes and then released the final version for publication. In this way the entire Bible underwent three revisions, during each of which the translation was examined for its faithfulness to the original languages and for its English style.

All this involved many thousands of hours of research and discussion regarding the meaning of the texts and the precise way of putting them into English. It may well be that no other translation has been made by a more thorough process of review and revision from committee to committee than this one.

From the beginning of the project, the Committee on Bible Translation held to certain goals for the New International Version: that it would be an accurate translation and one that would have clarity and literary quality and so prove suitable for public and private reading, teaching, preaching, memorising and liturgical use. The Committee also sought to preserve some measure of continuity with the long tradition of translating the Scriptures into English.

In working towards these goals, the translators were united in their commitment to the authority and infallibility of the Bible as God's Word in written form. They believe that it contains the divine answer to the deepest needs of humanity, that it sheds unique light on our path in a dark world, and that it sets forth the way to our eternal well-being.

The first concern of the translators has been the accuracy of the translation and its fidelity to the thought of the biblical writers. They have weighed the significance of the lexical and grammatical details of the Hebrew, Aramaic and Greek texts. At the same time, they have striven for more than a word-for-word translation. Because thought patterns and syntax differ from language to language, faithful communication of the meaning of the writers of the Bible demands frequent modifications in sentence structure and constant regard for the contextual meanings of words.

A sensitive feeling for style does not always accompany scholarship. Accordingly the Committee on Bible Translation submitted the developing version to a number of stylistic consultants. Two of them read every book of both Old and New Testaments twice – once before and once after the last major revision – and made invaluable suggestions. Samples of the translation were tested for clarity and ease of reading by various kinds of people – young and old, highly educated and less well educated, ministers and laymen.

Concern for clear and natural English – that the New International Version sould be idiomatic but not idiosyncratic, contemporary but not dated – motivated the translators and consultants. At the same time, they tried to reflect the differing styles of the biblical writers. In view of the international use of English, the translators sought to avoid obvious Americanisms on the one hand and obvious Anglicisms on the other. A British edition reflects the comparatively few differences of significant idiom and of spelling.

As for the traditional pronouns "thou", "thee" and "thine" in reference to the Deity, the translators judged that to use these archaisms (along with old verb forms such as "doest", "wouldest" and "hadst") would violate accuracy in translation. Neither Hebrew, Aramaic nor Greek uses special pronouns for the persons of the Godhead. A present-day translation is not enhanced by forms that in the time of the King James Version were used in everyday speech, whether referring to God or man.

For the Old Testament the standard Hebrew text, the Masoretic Text as published in the latest edition of *Biblia Hebraica*, was used throughout. The Dead Sea Scrolls contain material bearing on an earlier stage of the Hebrew text. They were consulted, as were the Samaritan Pentateuch and the ancient scribal traditions relating to textual changes. Sometimes a variant Hebrew reading in the margin of the Masoretic tradition, are not specified by footnotes. In rare cases, words in the consonantal text were divided different from the way they appear in the Masoretic Text. Footnotes indicate this. The translators also consulted the more important early versions – the Septuagint; Aquila, Symmachus and Theodotion; the Vulgate; the Syriac Peshitta; the Targums; and for the Psalms the *Juxta Hebraica* of Jerome. Readings from these versions were occasionally followed where the Masoretic Text seemed doubtful and where accepted principles of textual criticism showed that one or more of these textual witnesses appeared to provide the correct reading. Such instances are footnoted. Sometimes vowel letters and vowel signs did not, in the judgment of the translators, represent the correct vowels for the original consonantal text. Accordingly some words were read with a different set of vowels. These instances are usually not indicated by footnotes.

The Greek text used in translating the New Testament was an eclectic one. No other piece of ancient literature has such an abundance of manuscript witnesses as does the New Testament. Where existing manuscripts differ, the translators made their choice of readings according to accepted principles of New Testament textual criticism. Footnotes call attention to places where there was uncertainty about what the original text was. The best current printed texts of the Greek New Testament were used.

There is a sense in which the work of translation is never wholly finished. This applies to all great literature and uniquely so to the Bible. In 1973 the New Testament in the New International Version was published. Since then, suggestions for corrections and revisions have been received from various sources. The Committee on Bible Translation carefully considered the suggestions and adopted a number of them. These were incorporated in the first printing of the entire Bible in 1978. Additional revisions were made by the Committee on Bible Translation in 1983 and appear in printings after that date.

As in other ancient documents, the precise meaning of the biblical texts is sometimes uncertain. This is more often the case with the Hebrew and Aramaic texts than with the Greek text. Although archaeological and linguistic discoveries in this century aid in understanding difficult passages, some uncertainties remain. The more significant of these have been called to the reader's attention in the footnotes.

In regard to the divine name *YHWH*, commonly referred to as the *Tetragrammaton*, the translators adopted the device used in most English versions of rendering that name as "Lord" in capital letters to distinguish it from *Adonai*, another Hebrew word rendered "Lord", for which small letters are used. Wherever the two names stand together in the Old Testament as a compound name of God, they are rendered "Sovereign Lord".

Because for most readers today the phrases, "the Lord of hosts" and "God of hosts" have little meaning, this version renders them "the Lord Almighty" and "God Almighty". These renderings convey the sense of the Hebrew, namely, "he who is sovereign over all the 'hosts' (powers) in heaven and on earth, especially over the 'hosts' (armies) of Israel." For readers unacquainted with Hebrew this does not make clear the distinction between *Sabaoth* ("hosts" or "Almighty") and *Shaddai* (which can also be translated "Almighty"), but the latter occurs infrequently and is always footnoted. When *Adonai* and *YHWH Sabaoth* occur together, they are rendered "the Lord, the Lord Almighty."

As for the other proper nouns, the familiar spellings of the Authorised Version are generally retained. Names traditionally spelled with "ch", except where it is final, are usually spelled in this translation with "k" or "c", since the biblical languages do not have the sound that "ch" frequently indicates in English – for example, in *chant*. For well-known names such as Zechariah, however, the traditional spelling has been retained. Variation in the spelling of names in the original languages has usually not been indicated. Where a person or place has two or more different names in the Hebrew, Aramaic or Greek texts, the more familiar one has generally been used, with footnotes where needed.

To achieve clarity the translators sometimes supplied words not in the original texts but required by the context. If there was uncertainty about such material, it is enclosed in brackets. Also for the sake of clarity or style, nouns, including some proper nouns, are sometimes substituted for pronouns, and vice versa. And though the Hebrew writers often shifted back and forth between first, second and third personal pronouns without change of antecedent, this translation often makes them uniform, in accordance with English style and without the use of footnotes.

Poetical passages are printed as poetry, that is, with indentation of lines and with separate stanzas. These are generally designed to reflect the structure of Hebrew poetry. This poetry is normally characterised by parallelism in balanced lines. Most of the poetry in the Bible is in the Old Testament, and scholars differ regarding the scansion of Hebrew lines. The translators determined the stanza divisions for the most part by analysis of the subject matter. The stanzas therefore serve as poetic paragraphs.

As an aid to the reader, italicised sectional headings are inserted in most of the books. They are not to be regarded as part of the NIV text, are not for oral reading, and are not intended to dictate the interpretation of the sections they head.

The footnotes in this version are of several kinds, most of which need no explanation. Those giving alternative translations begin with "Or" and generally introduce the alternative with the last word proceeding it in the text, except when it is a single-word alternative; in poetry quoted in a footnote a slant mark indicates a line division. Footnotes introduced by "Or" do not have uniform significance. In some cases two possible translations were considered to have about equal validity. In other cases, though the translators were convinced that the translation in the text was correct, they judged that another interpretation was possible and of sufficient importance to be represented in a footnote.

In the New Testament, footnotes that refer to uncertainty regarding the original text are introduced by "Some manuscripts" or similar expressions. In the Old Testament, evidence for the reading chosen is given first and evidence for the alternative is added after a semicolon (for example: Septuagint; Hebrew *father*). In such notes the term "Hebrew" refers to the Masoretic Text.

It should be noted that minerals, flora and fauna, architectural details, articles of clothing and jewellery, musical instruments and other articles cannot always be identified with precision. Also measures of capacity in the biblical period are particularly uncertain (see the table of weights and measures following the text).

Like all translations of the Bible, made as they are by imperfect man, this one undoubtedly falls short of its goals. Yet we are grateful to God for the extent to which he has enabled us to realise these goals and for the strength he has given us and our colleagues to complete our task. We offer this version of the Bible to him in whose name and for whose glory it has been made. We pray that it will lead many into a better understanding of the Holy Scripture and a fuller knowledge of Jesus Christ the incarnate Word, of whom the Scriptures so faithfully testify.

The Committee on Bible Translation

June 1978
(Revised August 1983)

Names of the translators and editors may be secured
from the International Bible Society,
translation sponsors of the New International Version,
1820 Jet Stream Drive, Colorado Springs, CO 80921-3696, USA.

Foreword

God intended Christianity to be relevant. As Christ related himself to the needs of the world to which he came, so the Church which is his body (cf. Eph 4:11–13) is faced with a challenge of relevance. These are, therefore, exciting days for men and women of faith. God, who stands behind the Scriptures (1 Ti 3:16), uses his word, the *word of life* (Phm 2:16), to point us to the *Word of Life* which is Jesus (1 John 1:1). In consequence, the Scriptures are alive with insight, throb with power, and are vital to the well-being of all Christians.

The NIV WORDS OF LIFE BIBLE is a natural development from the daily devotional book which began as *The Soldier's Armoury*, becoming more recently the *Words of Life* devotional notes. From its commencement it has been gladly received by a wide range of churches and worshipping groups across the world. Successive editions have maintained a high standard of sound scholarship, without losing sight of the challenge to grow in Christ, and fulfil the great commission to make disciples of all nations (Mt 28:19).

This NIV WORDS OF LIFE BIBLE makes available the New International Version, now the most popular of modern English translations, with daily comments which combine a panoramic view of Scripture with important biblical insights. These insights help us to understand God more, and better interpret his bold, imaginative and totally effective strategy of sending first Christ, and then the Holy Spirit, into our world. This new Bible has also been fashioned to foster our devotional life. How else can we be strong in our faith, match our hopes for spiritual maturity, put life into perspective, unless we have meaningful times of meditation? We can be sure that the Holy Spirit who illuminates these pages will make this NIV WORDS OF LIFE BIBLE a resource of infinite worth and satisfaction to us.

Commissioner Harry Read
The Salvation Army

How to Use This Bible

There are three ways to read this Bible in order to make the most of the special WORDS OF LIFE daily reading pages:

1 Bible Overview
Starting with the first WORDS OF LIFE reading on page 5, you follow the arrow at the bottom of each page which will direct you to your next reading. There are 312 readings, one for each weekday and one for the weekend, giving a guide for readings for a whole year. These daily notes will highlight significant Bible passages and events, providing a good overview of the Bible.

2 One-Year Reading Plan
This plan can be found at the back of the Bible, and lists longer Bible passages to read each day so that you can read the whole Bible in one year. You will come across, and gain extra insight from, the WORDS OF LIFE notes in the course of your reading.

3 Readings by Subject or Special Seasons of the Year
The *Subject Index* and list of readings for *Special Seasons of the Year* can be found at the back of the Bible. Using these, you can look up WORDS OF LIFE readings which deal with particular subjects that interest you, or which are relevant to your current situation; and you can also find Bible readings which are appropriate to special times of the year. This allows for flexibility in your Bible reading.

Contents

THE
OLD TESTAMENT

Genesis

The Beginning

1 In the beginning God created the heavens and the earth. ²Now the earth was*ᵃ* formless and empty, darkness was over the surface of the deep, and the Spirit of God was hovering over the waters.

³And God said, "Let there be light," and there was light. ⁴God saw that the light was good, and he separated the light from the darkness. ⁵God called the light "day", and the darkness he called "night". And there was evening, and there was morning—the first day.

⁶And God said, "Let there be an expanse between the waters to separate water from water." ⁷So God made the expanse and separated the water under the expanse from the water above it. And it was so. ⁸God called the expanse "sky". And there was evening, and there was morning—the second day.

⁹And God said, "Let the water under the sky be gathered to one place, and let dry ground appear." And it was so. ¹⁰God called the dry ground "land", and the gathered waters he called "seas". And God saw that it was good.

¹¹Then God said, "Let the land produce vegetation: seed-bearing plants and trees on the land that bear fruit with seed in it, according to their various kinds." And it was so. ¹²The land produced vegetation: plants bearing seed according to their kinds and trees bearing fruit with seed in it according to their kinds. And God saw that it was good. ¹³And there was evening, and there was morning—the third day.

¹⁴And God said, "Let there be lights in the expanse of the sky to separate the day from the night, and let them serve as signs to mark seasons and days and years, ¹⁵and let them be lights in the expanse of the sky to give light on the earth." And it was so. ¹⁶God made two great lights—the greater light to govern the day and the lesser light to govern the night. He also made the stars. ¹⁷God set them in the expanse of the sky to give light on the earth, ¹⁸to govern the day and the night, and to separate light from darkness. And God saw that it was good. ¹⁹And there was evening, and there was morning—the fourth day.

²⁰And God said, "Let the water teem with living creatures, and let birds fly above the earth across the expanse of the sky." ²¹So God created the great creatures of the sea and every living and moving thing with which the water teems, according to their kinds, and every winged bird according to its kind. And God saw that it was good. ²²God blessed them and said, "Be fruitful and increase in number and fill the water in the seas, and let the birds increase on the earth." ²³And there was evening, and there was morning—the fifth day.

²⁴And God said, "Let the land produce living creatures according to their kinds: livestock, creatures that move along the ground, and wild animals, each according to its kind." And it was so. ²⁵God made the wild animals according to their kinds, the livestock according to their kinds, and all the creatures that move along the ground according to their kinds. And God saw that it was good.

²⁶Then God said, "Let us make man in our image, in our likeness, and let them rule over the fish of the sea and the birds of the air, over the livestock, over all the earth,*ᵇ* and over all the creatures that move along the ground."

²⁷So God created man
  in his own image,
  in the image of God
  he created him;
male and female
  he created them.

²⁸God blessed them and said to them, "Be fruitful and increase in number; fill the earth and subdue it. Rule over the fish of the sea and the birds of the air and over every living creature that moves on the ground."

²⁹Then God said, "I give you every seed-bearing plant on the face of the whole earth and every tree that has fruit with seed in it. They will be yours for

---

*ᵃ2 Or possibly *became*   *ᵇ26 Hebrew; Syriac *all the wild animals* food. [30]And to all the beasts of the earth and all the birds of the air and all the creatures that move on the ground—everything that has the breath of life in it—I give every green plant for food.'' And it was so.

[31]God saw all that he had made, and it was very good. And there was evening, and there was morning—the sixth day.

2 Thus the heavens and the earth were completed in all their vast array.

[2]By the seventh day God had finished the work he had been doing; so on the seventh day he rested[a] from all his work. [3]And God blessed the seventh day and made it holy, because on it he rested from all the work of creating that he had done.

Adam and Eve

[4]This is the account of the heavens and the earth when they were created.

When the LORD God made the earth and the heavens—[5]and no shrub of the field had yet appeared on the earth[b] and no plant of the field had yet sprung up, for the LORD God had not sent rain on the earth[b] and there was no man to work the ground, [6]but streams[c] came up from the earth and watered the whole surface of the ground—[7]the LORD God formed the man[d] from the dust of the ground and breathed into his nostrils the breath of life, and the man became a living being.

[8]Now the LORD God had planted a garden in the east, in Eden; and there he put the man he had formed. [9]And the LORD God made all kinds of trees grow out of the ground—trees that were pleasing to the eye and good for food. In the middle of the garden were the tree of life and the tree of the knowledge of good and evil.

[10]A river watering the garden flowed from Eden; from there it was separated into four headwaters. [11]The name of the first is the Pishon; it winds through the entire land of Havilah, where there is gold. [12](The gold of that land is good; aromatic resin[e] and onyx are also there.) [13]The name of the second river is the Gihon; it winds through the entire land of Cush.[f] [14]The name of the third river is the Tigris; it runs along the east side of Asshur. And the fourth river is the Euphrates.

[15]The LORD God took the man and put him in the Garden of Eden to work it and take care of it. [16]And the LORD God commanded the man, ''You are free to eat from any tree in the garden; [17]but you must not eat from the tree of the knowledge of good and evil, for when you eat of it you will surely die.''

[18]The LORD God said, ''It is not good for the man to be alone. I will make a helper suitable for him.''

[19]Now the LORD God had formed out of the ground all the beasts of the field and all the birds of the air. He brought them to the man to see what he would name them; and whatever the man called each living creature, that was its name. [20]So the man gave names to all the livestock, the birds of the air and all the beasts of the field.

But for Adam[g] no suitable helper was found. [21]So the LORD God caused the man to fall into a deep sleep; and while he was sleeping, he took one of the man's ribs[h] and closed up the place with flesh. [22]Then the LORD God made a woman from the rib[i] he had taken out of the man, and he brought her to the man.

[23]The man said,

''This is now bone of my bones
    and flesh of my flesh;
she shall be called 'woman',[j]
    for she was taken out of man.''

[24]For this reason a man will leave his father and mother and be united to his wife, and they will become one flesh.

[25]The man and his wife were both naked, and they felt no shame.

The Fall of Man

3 Now the serpent was more crafty than any of the wild animals the LORD God had made. He said to the woman, ''Did God really say, 'You must not eat from any tree in the garden'?''

[2]The woman said to the serpent, ''We may eat fruit from the trees in the garden, [3]but God did say, 'You must not eat fruit from the tree that is in the middle of the garden, and you must not touch it, or you will die.' ''

[4]''You will not surely die,'' the serpent said to the woman. [5]''For God knows that when you eat of it your eyes will be opened, and you will be like God, knowing good and evil.''

[6]When the woman saw that the fruit of the tree was good for food and pleasing to the eye, and also desirable for gaining wisdom, she took some and ate it. She also gave some to her husband, who was with her, and he ate it. [7]Then the eyes of both of them were opened, and they realised that they were naked; so they sewed fig leaves together and made coverings for themselves.

[8]Then the man and his wife heard the sound of the LORD God as he was walking in the garden in the cool of the day, and they hid from the LORD God among the trees of the garden. [9]But the LORD God called to the man, ''Where are you?''

[10]He answered, ''I heard you in the garden, and I was afraid because I was naked; so I hid.''

[11]And he said, ''Who told you that you were naked? Have you eaten from the tree from which I commanded you not to eat?''

---

[a]2 Or *ceased*; also in verse 3   [b]5 Or *land*; also in verse 6   [c]6 Or *mist*
[d]7 The Hebrew for *man* (*adam*) sounds like and may be related to the Hebrew for *ground* (*adamah*); it is also the name *Adam* (see Gen. 2:20).   [e]12 Or *good; pearls*   [f]13 Possibly south-east Mesopotamia
[g]20 Or *the man*   [h]21 Or *took part of the man's side*   [i]22 Or *part*
[j]23 The Hebrew for *woman* sounds like the Hebrew for *man*.

GENESIS 1:1–2
'In the beginning God created . . . Now the earth was formless and empty' (vv. 1a, 2a,).

UNBLEMISHED MATERIALS. Unlike other creation stories the biblical account of creation affirms God started with a clean sheet. The earth was formless and void. It was not already marred. The clarity of the words 'formless' and 'void' or 'empty' are particularly useful for our study today. Some modern translations lose this by using terms like 'chaos' to describe the empty void, giving an unfortunate impression that matter was already corrupt.

God was not forced to use corrupt materials. Genesis contains no story like the creation myths of surrounding nations, where the earth is produced out of conflict between good and evil forces. The Babylonian creation myth – which may have been known to the writer of Genesis – involves Marduk killing the monster Tiamat by forcing the storm wind down her throat and piercing her heart with a dart. An old European myth tells of the earth being formed from the corpse of a giant Ymir, who was murdered by Odin. In Helmut Thielicke's words, such a story would mean that 'the world has a gruesome origin and at its beginning there was an unutterable outrage.'

Genesis contains no such outrage. God created out of nothing. Along with his world we, too, come directly from his hand, and one day God will want us, his creatures, back with himself. Luther said – and with this we can agree – 'God created the world out of nothing. As long as you are not yet nothing God cannot make something out of you.'

May we surrender to God fully and allow him to continue his creative work in us.

GENESIS 2:15–17, 3:1–7
'When the woman saw that the fruit of the tree was good for food and pleasing to the eye, and also desirable for gaining wisdom, she took some and ate it' (v. 6a).

DON'T BLAME EVE. The story of the Fall is a masterpiece. It sums up the way of temptation perfectly. The tempter does not just set out to persuade us to do wrong. He is no mass advertiser, appealing to our baser instincts. He knows it is easier to appeal to base thoughts after he has already gained control of our finer instincts. He convinces us what we are doing is not wrong at all. See how he approaches Eve. He almost becomes God's champion.

'You will not die, Eve, you will be like God, knowing good and evil.' Now it is a perfectly good thing to strive after godliness. And those who do not know the difference between good and evil are in a sorry state indeed. They are the only people who cannot be forgiven (Mark 3: 28–29). So poor Eve is caught. She hardly has a chance. Satan has convinced her that the thing forbidden is actually the way through to life and knowledge itself.

Satan tried the same ploy with Jesus, but our Lord saw through the deception. Jesus' mind was tuned towards God, not to himself. Eve, and Adam too, were self-centred, so they missed what Satan was up to. Concerned for their own wisdom and knowledge, they failed to centre on God. Many take such risks today, and they need our prayers.

God defend me from myself. (Spanish Proverb)

→9

¹²The man said, "The woman you put here with me—she gave me some fruit from the tree, and I ate it."

¹³Then the LORD God said to the woman, "What is this you have done?"

The woman said, "The serpent deceived me, and I ate."

¹⁴So the LORD God said to the serpent, "Because you have done this,

"Cursed are you above all the livestock
　and all the wild animals!
You will crawl on your belly
　and you will eat dust
　all the days of your life.
¹⁵And I will put enmity
　between you and the woman,
　and between your offspring[a] and hers;
he will crush[b] your head,
　and you will strike his heel."

¹⁶To the woman he said,

"I will greatly increase your pains in
　childbearing;
　with pain you will give birth to children.
Your desire will be for your husband,
　and he will rule over you."

¹⁷To Adam he said, "Because you listened to your wife and ate from the tree about which I commanded you, 'You must not eat of it,'

"Cursed is the ground because of you;
　through painful toil you will eat of it
　all the days of your life.
¹⁸It will produce thorns and thistles for you,
　and you will eat the plants of the field.
¹⁹By the sweat of your brow
　you will eat your food
until you return to the ground,
　since from it you were taken;
for dust you are
　and to dust you will return."

²⁰Adam[c] named his wife Eve,[d] because she would become the mother of all the living.

²¹The LORD God made garments of skin for Adam and his wife and clothed them. ²²And the LORD God said, "The man has now become like one of us, knowing good and evil. He must not be allowed to reach out his hand and take also from the tree of life and eat, and live for ever." ²³So the LORD God banished him from the Garden of Eden to work the ground from which he had been taken. ²⁴After he drove the man out, he placed on the east side[e] of the Garden of Eden cherubim and a flaming sword flashing back and forth to guard the way to the tree of life.

Cain and Abel

4 Adam[a] lay with his wife Eve, and she became pregnant and gave birth to Cain.[b] She said, "With the help of the LORD I have brought forth[c] a man." ²Later she gave birth to his brother Abel.

Now Abel kept flocks, and Cain worked the soil. ³In the course of time Cain brought some of the fruits of the soil as an offering to the LORD. ⁴But Abel brought fat portions from some of the firstborn of his flock. The LORD looked with favour on Abel and his offering, ⁵but on Cain and his offering he did not look with favour. So Cain was very angry, and his face was downcast.

⁶Then the LORD said to Cain, "Why are you angry? Why is your face downcast? ⁷If you do what is right, will you not be accepted? But if you do not do what is right, sin is crouching at your door; it desires to have you, but you must master it."

⁸Now Cain said to his brother Abel, "Let's go out to the field."[d] And while they were in the field, Cain attacked his brother Abel and killed him.

⁹Then the LORD said to Cain, "Where is your brother Abel?"

"I don't know," he replied. "Am I my brother's keeper?"

¹⁰The LORD said, "What have you done? Listen! Your brother's blood cries out to me from the ground. ¹¹Now you are under a curse and driven from the ground, which opened its mouth to receive your brother's blood from your hand. ¹²When you work the ground, it will no longer yield its crops for you. You will be a restless wanderer on the earth."

¹³Cain said to the LORD, "My punishment is more than I can bear. ¹⁴Today you are driving me from the land, and I will be hidden from your presence; I will be a restless wanderer on the earth, and whoever finds me will kill me."

¹⁵But the LORD said to him, "Not so;[e] if anyone kills Cain, he will suffer vengeance seven times over." Then the LORD put a mark on Cain so that no-one who found him would kill him. ¹⁶So Cain went out from the LORD's presence and lived in the land of Nod,[f] east of Eden.

¹⁷Cain lay with his wife, and she became pregnant and gave birth to Enoch. Cain was then building a city, and he named it after his son Enoch. ¹⁸To Enoch was born Irad, and Irad was the father of Mehujael, and Mehujael was the father of Methushael, and Methushael was the father of Lamech.

¹⁹Lamech married two women, one named Adah and the other Zillah. ²⁰Adah gave birth to Jabal; he was the father of those who live in tents and raise livestock. ²¹His brother's name was Jubal; he was the father of all who play the harp and flute. ²²Zillah also had a son, Tubal-Cain, who forged all kinds of tools out of[g] bronze and iron. Tubal-Cain's sister was Naamah.

²³Lamech said to his wives,

---

[a]15 Or seed　[b]15 Or strike　[c]20 Or The man　[d]20 Eve probably means living.　[e]24 Or placed in front
[a]1 Or The man　[b]1 Cain sounds like the Hebrew for brought forth or acquired.
[c]1 Or have acquired
[d]8 Samaritan Pentateuch, Septuagint, Vulgate and Syriac; Masoretic Text does not have "Let's go out to the field."
[e]15 Septuagint, Vulgate and Syriac; Hebrew Very well
[f]16 Nod means wandering (see verses 12 and 14).　　[g]22 Or who instructed all who work in

"Adah and Zillah, listen to me;
    wives of Lamech, hear my words.
I have killed*h* a man for wounding me,
    a young man for injuring me.
24If Cain is avenged seven times,
    then Lamech seventy-seven times.''

25Adam lay with his wife again, and she gave birth to a son and named him Seth,*i* saying, ''God has granted me another child in place of Abel, since Cain killed him.'' 26Seth also had a son, and he named him Enosh.

At that time men began to call on*j* the name of the LORD.

From Adam to Noah

5 This is the written account of Adam's line.

When God created man, he made him in the likeness of God. 2He created them male and female and blessed them. And when they were created, he called them ''man''.*a*

3When Adam had lived 130 years, he had a son in his own likeness, in his own image; and he named him Seth. 4After Seth was born, Adam lived 800 years and had other sons and daughters. 5Altogether, Adam lived 930 years, and then he died.

6When Seth had lived 105 years, he became the father*b* of Enosh. 7And after he became the father of Enosh, Seth lived 807 years and had other sons and daughters. 8Altogether, Seth lived 912 years, and then he died.

9When Enosh had lived 90 years, he became the father of Kenan. 10And after he became the father of Kenan, Enosh lived 815 years and had other sons and daughters. 11Altogether, Enosh lived 905 years, and then he died.

12When Kenan had lived 70 years, he became the father of Mahalalel. 13And after he became the father of Mahalalel, Kenan lived 840 years and had other sons and daughters. 14Altogether, Kenan lived 910 years, and then he died.

15When Mahalalel had lived 65 years, he became the father of Jared. 16And after he became the father of Jared, Mahalalel lived 830 years and had other sons and daughters. 17Altogether, Mahalalel lived 895 years, and then he died.

18When Jared had lived 162 years, he became the father of Enoch. 19And after he became the father of Enoch, Jared lived 800 years and had other sons and daughters. 20Altogether, Jared lived 962 years, and then he died.

21When Enoch had lived 65 years, he became the father of Methuselah. 22And after he became the father of Methuselah, Enoch walked with God 300 years and had other sons and daughters. 23Altogether, Enoch lived 365 years. 24Enoch walked with God;

then he was no more, because God took him away.

25When Methuselah had lived 187 years, he became the father of Lamech. 26And after he became the father of Lamech, Methuselah lived 782 years and had other sons and daughters. 27Altogether, Methuselah lived 969 years, and then he died.

28When Lamech had lived 182 years, he had a son. 29He named him Noah*c* and said, ''He will comfort us in the labour and painful toil of our hands caused by the ground the LORD has cursed.'' 30After Noah was born, Lamech lived 595 years and had other sons and daughters. 31Altogether, Lamech lived 777 years, and then he died.

32After Noah was 500 years old, he became the father of Shem, Ham and Japheth.

The Flood

6 When men began to increase in number on the earth and daughters were born to them, 2the sons of God saw that the daughters of men were beautiful, and they married any of them they chose. 3Then the LORD said, ''My Spirit will not contend with*a* man for ever, for he is mortal;*b* his days will be a hundred and twenty years.''

4The Nephilim were on the earth in those days—and also afterwards—when the sons of God went to the daughters of men and had children by them. They were the heroes of old, men of renown.

5The LORD saw how great man's wickedness on the earth had become, and that every inclination of the thoughts of his heart was only evil all the time. 6The LORD was grieved that he had made man on the earth, and his heart was filled with pain. 7So the LORD said, ''I will wipe mankind, whom I have created, from the face of the earth—men and animals, and creatures that move along the ground, and birds of the air—for I am grieved that I have made them.'' 8But Noah found favour in the eyes of the LORD.

9This is the account of Noah.

Noah was a righteous man, blameless among the people of his time, and he walked with God. 10Noah had three sons: Shem, Ham and Japheth.

11Now the earth was corrupt in God's sight and was full of violence. 12God saw how corrupt the earth had become, for all the people on earth had corrupted their ways. 13So God said to Noah, ''I am going to put an end to all people, for the earth is filled with violence because of them. I am surely going to destroy both them and the earth. 14So make yourself an ark of cypress*c* wood; make rooms in it and coat it with pitch inside and out. 15This is how you are to build it: The ark is to be 450 feet long, 75 feet wide and 45 feet high.*d* 16Make a roof for it and finish*e* the ark

---

h23 Or *I will kill*   *i25 Seth* probably means *granted.*   *j26* Or *to proclaim*
a2 Hebrew *adam*   *b6 Father* may mean *ancestor;* also in verses 7–26.
c29 Noah sounds like the Hebrew for *comfort.*   *a3* Or *My spirit will not remain in*
b3 Or *corrupt*   *c14* The meaning of the Hebrew for this word is uncertain.
d15 Hebrew *300 cubits long, 50 cubits wide and 30 cubits high* (about 140 metres long, 23 metres wide and 13.5 metres high)   *e16* Or *Make an opening for light by finishing*

GENESIS 6:9–22

'But I will establish my covenant with you, and you will enter the ark . . . You are to bring into the ark two of all living creatures, male and female, to keep them alive with you' (vv. 18, 19).

GOD'S COVENANT WITH HIS WHOLE CREATION. We look at the first promise of a unique *covenant* with Noah.

Notice how general the covenant will be. In spite of God's agreement being made with just one individual the covenant will extend to his family, to his descendants – amongst whom we are all numbered in the eyes of the author – and to the wider family of creation. The mind boggles at the idea of an ark to contain two specimens of all God's living creatures – and the command (7:3) to take in seven of every clean animal as well. It would be larger than any seagoing vessel ever built, but the instruction is only to build an ark less than a tenth the size of a modern oil tanker! Two points stand out for us today.

1. Noah's faith against the odds. To Noah the ark was not a symbol of security in the way that some churchmen talk of the 'Ark of the Church'. It was not a safe haven from the storm but a venture of incredible faith, taking God at his word in spite of ridicule from all around.

2. Animals are included. People's responsibility is to all God's creation. The covenant with Noah reinforces the need for care of the environment.

Let us never forget that we share with animals the unique blessing *of God (Gen. 1:22), and treat them accordingly.*

→10

GENESIS 8:1–14

'He waited seven more days and again sent out the dove from the ark. When the dove returned to him in the evening, there in its beak was a freshly plucked olive leaf!' (vv. 10, 11a).

A SYMBOL OF PEACE. Following the storms and the Flood, the dove finally confirmed that peace had returned to the earth, albeit a limited peace which did not last long. The dove still symbolizes peace. It is used in logos recognized the world over. But does the symbol ever become reality? Reconciliations so often just seem to provide a lull before hostilities break out again.

The editor of Genesis Chapters 7 and 8 achieves a wonderful reconciliation in producing the finished account of the Flood. Careful reading may reveal two stories interwoven. One account says two of each animal (6:20), the other has seven of each 'clean' species (7:2). In one the flood lasts forty days, in the other 150. It is noticeable in Chapter 8, with a split between verses 5 and 6. Other differences are so cleverly reconciled we scarcely see them, and many people are convinced the whole thing is a single story after all.

That kind of reconciliation is possible. Some differences remain. The drama as a whole functions perfectly. The symbolism is all there, and the best elements of each story retained. Reconciling human beings in conflict is much harder.

Let us pray that all who work for reconciliation here on earth will be as successful as the genius who edited Genesis 7 and 8.

to within 18 inches*f* of the top. Put a door in the side of the ark and make lower, middle and upper decks. ¹⁷I am going to bring floodwaters on the earth to destroy all life under the heavens, every creature that has the breath of life in it. Everything on earth will perish. ¹⁸But I will establish my covenant with you, and you will enter the ark—you and your sons and your wife and your sons' wives with you. ¹⁹You are to bring into the ark two of all living creatures, male and female, to keep them alive with you. ²⁰Two of every kind of bird, of every kind of animal and of every kind of creature that moves along the ground will come to you to be kept alive. ²¹You are to take every kind of food that is to be eaten and store it away as food for you and for them.''

²²Noah did everything just as God commanded him.

7 The Lord then said to Noah, ''Go into the ark, you and your whole family, because I have found you righteous in this generation. ²Take with you seven*a* of every kind of clean animal, a male and its mate, and two of every kind of unclean animal, a male and its mate, ³and also seven of every kind of bird, male and female, to keep their various kinds alive throughout the earth. ⁴Seven days from now I will send rain on the earth for forty days and forty nights, and I will wipe from the face of the earth every living creature I have made.''

⁵And Noah did all that the Lord commanded him.

⁶Noah was six hundred years old when the floodwaters came on the earth. ⁷And Noah and his sons and his wife and his sons' wives entered the ark to escape the waters of the flood. ⁸Pairs of clean and unclean animals, of birds and of all creatures that move along the ground, ⁹male and female, came to Noah and entered the ark, as God had commanded Noah. ¹⁰And after the seven days the floodwaters came on the earth.

¹¹In the six hundredth year of Noah's life, on the seventeenth day of the second month —on that day all the springs of the great deep burst forth, and the floodgates of the heavens were opened. ¹²And rain fell on the earth for forty days and forty nights.

¹³On that very day Noah and his sons, Shem, Ham and Japheth, together with his wife and the wives of his three sons, entered the ark. ¹⁴They had with them every wild animal according to its kind, all livestock according to their kinds, every creature that moves along the ground according to its kind and every bird according to its kind, everything with wings. ¹⁵Pairs of all creatures that have the breath of life in them came to Noah and entered the ark. ¹⁶The animals going in were male and female of every living thing, as God had commanded Noah. Then the Lord shut him in.

¹⁷For forty days the flood kept coming on the earth, and as the waters increased they lifted the ark high above the earth. ¹⁸The waters rose and increased greatly on the earth, and the ark floated on the surface of the water. ¹⁹They rose greatly on the earth, and all the high mountains under the entire heavens were covered. ²⁰The waters rose and covered the mountains to a depth of more than twenty feet.*b,c* ²¹Every living thing that moved on the earth perished—birds, livestock, wild animals, all the creatures that swarm over the earth, and all mankind. ²²Everything on dry land that had the breath of life in its nostrils died. ²³Every living thing on the face of the earth was wiped out; men and animals and the creatures that move along the ground and the birds of the air were wiped from the earth. Only Noah was left, and those with him in the ark.

²⁴The waters flooded the earth for a hundred and fifty days.

8 But God remembered Noah and all the wild animals and the livestock that were with him in the ark, and he sent a wind over the earth, and the waters receded. ²Now the springs of the deep and the floodgates of the heavens had been closed, and the rain had stopped falling from the sky. ³The water receded steadily from the earth. At the end of the hundred and fifty days the water had gone down, ⁴and on the seventeenth day of the seventh month the ark came to rest on the mountains of Ararat. ⁵The waters continued to recede until the tenth month, and on the first day of the tenth month the tops of the mountains became visible.

⁶After forty days Noah opened the window he had made in the ark ⁷and sent out a raven, and it kept flying back and forth until the water had dried up from the earth. ⁸Then he sent out a dove to see if the water had receded from the surface of the ground. ⁹But the dove could find no place to set its feet because there was water over all the surface of the earth; so it returned to Noah in the ark. He reached out his hand and took the dove and brought it back to himself in the ark. ¹⁰He waited seven more days and again sent out the dove from the ark. ¹¹When the dove returned to him in the evening, there in its beak was a freshly plucked olive leaf! Then Noah knew that the water had receded from the earth. ¹²He waited seven more days and sent the dove out again, but this time it did not return to him.

¹³By the first day of the first month of Noah's six hundred and first year, the water had dried up from the earth. Noah then removed the covering from the ark and saw that the surface of the ground was dry. ¹⁴By the twenty-seventh day of the second month the earth was completely dry.

¹⁵Then God said to Noah, ¹⁶''Come out of the ark, you and your wife and your sons and their wives. ¹⁷Bring out every kind of living creature that is with you—the birds, the animals, and all the creatures that move along the ground—so they can multiply on

---

f16 Hebrew a cubit (about 0.5 metre)　　a2 Or seven pairs; also in verse 3
b20 Hebrew fifteen cubits (about 6.9 metres)
c20 Or rose more than twenty feet, and the mountains were covered

the earth and be fruitful and increase in number upon it."

¹⁸So Noah came out, together with his sons and his wife and his sons' wives. ¹⁹All the animals and all the creatures that move along the ground and all the birds—everything that moves on the earth—came out of the ark, one kind after another.

²⁰Then Noah built an altar to the LORD and, taking some of all the clean animals and clean birds, he sacrificed burnt offerings on it. ²¹The LORD smelled the pleasing aroma and said in his heart: "Never again will I curse the ground because of man, even though*a* every inclination of his heart is evil from childhood. And never again will I destroy all living creatures, as I have done.

²²"As long as the earth endures,
    seedtime and harvest,
    cold and heat,
    summer and winter,
    day and night
    will never cease."

God's Covenant With Noah

9 Then God blessed Noah and his sons, saying to them, "Be fruitful and increase in number and fill the earth. ²The fear and dread of you will fall upon all the beasts of the earth and all the birds of the air, upon every creature that moves along the ground, and upon all the fish of the sea; they are given into your hands. ³Everything that lives and moves will be food for you. Just as I gave you the green plants, I now give you everything.

⁴"But you must not eat meat that has its lifeblood still in it. ⁵And for your lifeblood I will surely demand an accounting. I will demand an accounting from every animal. And from each man, too, I will demand an accounting for the life of his fellow man.

⁶"Whoever sheds the blood of man,
    by man shall his blood be shed;
for in the image of God
    has God made man.

⁷As for you, be fruitful and increase in number; multiply on the earth and increase upon it."

⁸Then God said to Noah and to his sons with him: ⁹"I now establish my covenant with you and with your descendants after you ¹⁰and with every living creature that was with you—the birds, the livestock and all the wild animals, all those that came out of the ark with you—every living creature on earth. ¹¹I establish my covenant with you: Never again will all life be cut off by the waters of a flood; never again will there be a flood to destroy the earth."

¹²And God said, "This is the sign of the covenant I am making between me and you and every living creature with you, a covenant for all generations to come: ¹³I have

set my rainbow in the clouds, and it will be the sign of the covenant between me and the earth. ¹⁴Whenever I bring clouds over the earth and the rainbow appears in the clouds, ¹⁵I will remember my covenant between me and you and all living creatures of every kind. Never again will the waters become a flood to destroy all life. ¹⁶Whenever the rainbow appears in the clouds, I will see it and remember the everlasting covenant between God and all living creatures of every kind on earth."

¹⁷So God said to Noah, "This is the sign of the covenant I have established between me and all life on the earth."

The Sons of Noah

¹⁸The sons of Noah who came out of the ark were Shem, Ham and Japheth. (Ham was the father of Canaan.) ¹⁹These were the three sons of Noah, and from them came the people who were scattered over the earth.

²⁰Noah, a man of the soil, proceeded*a* to plant a vineyard. ²¹When he drank some of its wine, he became drunk and lay uncovered inside his tent. ²²Ham, the father of Canaan, saw his father's nakedness and told his two brothers outside. ²³But Shem and Japheth took a garment and laid it across their shoulders; then they walked in backwards and covered their father's nakedness. Their faces were turned the other way so that they would not see their father's nakedness.

²⁴When Noah awoke from his wine and found out what his youngest son had done to him, ²⁵he said,

"Cursed be Canaan!
    The lowest of slaves
    will he be to his brothers."

²⁶He also said,

"Blessed be the LORD, the God of Shem!
    May Canaan be the slave of Shem.*b*
²⁷May God extend the territory of Japheth;*c*
    may Japheth live in the tents of Shem,
    and may Canaan be his*d* slave."

²⁸After the flood Noah lived 350 years. ²⁹Altogether, Noah lived 950 years, and then he died.

The Table of Nations

10 This is the account of Shem, Ham and Japheth, Noah's sons, who themselves had sons after the flood.

The Japhethites

²The sons*a* of Japheth:
    Gomer, Magog, Madai, Javan, Tubal,
    Meshech and Tiras.
³The sons of Gomer:
    Ashkenaz, Riphath and Togarmah.
⁴The sons of Javan:
    Elishah, Tarshish, the Kittim and the
    Rodanim.*b* ⁵(From these the maritime

---

*a*21 Or *man, for*   *a*20 Or *soil, was the first*   *b*26 Or *be his slave*
*c*27 *Japheth* sounds like the Hebrew for *extend.*   *d*27 Or *their*
*a*2 *Sons* may mean *descendants* or *successors* or *nations*; also in verses 3, 4, 6, 7, 20–23, 29 and 31.
*b*4 Some manuscripts of the Masoretic Text and Samaritan Pentateuch (see also Septuagint and 1 Chron. 1:7); most manuscripts of the Masoretic Text *Dodanim*

GENESIS 11:1–9
'The Lord said, "If as one people speaking the same language they have begun to do this, then nothing they plan to do will be impossible for them" ' (v. 6).

ONE LANGUAGE has been a pipe dream of people for many centuries. But whenever one language has spread over large areas of the earth, it has been a result of military conquest or violent occupation. Alexander spread Greek; Romans – Latin; Muslims – Arabic, and more recently the British spread English.

Today things are slightly different. A common language is required in some limited areas, such as air traffic control. Electronic communications also bring people together in a way similar to using a common language. But such unifying factors apply only to small minorities of the world's population, and we are still divided, as in the time of Babel.

Is it God's intention this should be so? Today's story gives that impression, but

> From the rest of the Bible it is clear the God does not suffer from fear or envy, as we do. He wants men to grow more responsible and to develop the resources of the earth. But he hates to see men behaving as if they had no need of him. This is because he cares greatly for them and because he knows they need him. It is not because he is envious. (John Hargreaves)

From the beginning of Christ's mission he still had to say (John 3:19), 'men loved darkness instead of light.'

May Christ rescue us from that love of darkness, from the Babel of confusion.

GENESIS 16:1–10

'[Sarai] said to Abram, "The LORD has kept me from having children. Go, sleep with my maidservant; perhaps I can build a family through her" ' (v. 2).

DIFFICULTIES SURROUNDING surrogate motherhood are not new. The custom described here may sound strange, but is it very different from modern attempts at surrogate motherhood? There was no possibility of artificial insemination in Abraham's day to 'sanitize' the proceedings. But the purpose was the same. A childless wife wanted another to bear a child on her behalf.

By ancient Hebrew custom the couple adopted the slave-girl's child. The slave was paid in kind, by being looked after – as natural mother of the family's heir, and given honoured status. The custom was not unique to Hebrews. Ancient tablets from Nuzi show

> it was a custom for childless people to adopt a son to serve them as long as they lived, to bury and mourn for them when they died. As compensation the adopted son was made heir to the possessions of the childless couple. If, however, the couple had a son of their own after the adoption, the actual son would assume the right of heir.

(H. A. Hoffner, *The Hittites and Hurrians*)

Genesis 16 shows clearly the dangers of surrogacy, even where it is strictly controlled and legislated for. Today's commercial surrogacy is not an accepted social custom in the way that Sarai's deal with Hagar was. Tensions and jealousies, the impossibility of enforcing the contract, the sheer immorality of exploiting another woman's body – all lead us to conclude that surrogacy is not the answer to overcoming the very real stigma of childlessness in today's society.

Surrogacy is not the answer to childlessness. Rather we need to discover the real problems of childlessness, and remove the stigma which surrounds it – an enormous task, which would involve great changes in society.

peoples spread out into their territories by their clans within their nations, each with its own language.)

The Hamites

6The sons of Ham:
Cush, Mizraim,c Put and Canaan.
7The sons of Cush:
Seba, Havilah, Sabtah, Raamah and Sabteca.
The sons of Raamah:
Sheba and Dedan.

8Cush was the fatherd of Nimrod, who grew to be a mighty warrior on the earth. 9He was a mighty hunter before the LORD; that is why it is said, "Like Nimrod, a mighty hunter before the LORD." 10The first centres of his kingdom were Babylon, Erech, Akkad and Calneh, ine Shinar.f 11From that land he went to Assyria, where he built Nineveh, Rehoboth Ir,g Calah 12and Resen, which is between Nineveh and Calah; that is the great city.

13Mizraim was the father of
the Ludites, Anamites, Lehabites, Naphtuhites, 14Pathrusites, Casluhites (from whom the Philistines came) and Caphtorites.

15Canaan was the father of
Sidon his firstborn,h and of the Hittites, 16Jebusites, Amorites, Girgashites, 17Hivites, Arkites, Sinites, 18Arvadites, Zemarites and Hamathites.

Later the Canaanite clans scattered 19and the borders of Canaan reached from Sidon towards Gerar as far as Gaza, and then towards Sodom, Gomorrah, Admah and Zeboiim, as far as Lasha.
20These are the sons of Ham by their clans and languages, in their territories and nations.

The Semites

21Sons were also born to Shem, whose older brother wasi Japheth; Shem was the ancestor of all the sons of Eber.

22The sons of Shem:
Elam, Asshur, Arphaxad, Lud and Aram.
23The sons of Aram:
Uz, Hul, Gether and Meshech.j
24Arphaxad was the father ofk Shelah, and Shelah the father of Eber.
25Two sons were born to Eber:
One was named Peleg,l because in his time the earth was divided; his brother was named Joktan.

26Joktan was the father of
Almodad, Sheleph, Hazarmaveth, Jerah, 27Hadoram, Uzal, Diklah, 28Obal, Abimael, Sheba, 29Ophir, Havilah and Jobab. All these were sons of Joktan.

30The region where they lived stretched from Mesha towards Sephar, in the eastern hill country.
31These are the sons of Shem by their clans and languages, in their territories and nations.

32These are the clans of Noah's sons, according to their lines of descent, within their nations. From these the nations spread out over the earth after the flood.

The Tower of Babel

11 Now the whole world had one language and a common speech. 2As men moved eastward,a they found a plain in Shinarb and settled there.
3They said to each other, "Come, let's make bricks and bake them thoroughly." They used brick instead of stone, and bitumen for mortar. 4Then they said, "Come, let us build ourselves a city, with a tower that reaches to the heavens, so that we may make a name for ourselves and not be scattered over the face of the whole earth."

5But the LORD came down to see the city and the tower that the men were building. 6The LORD said, "If as one people speaking the same language they have begun to do this, then nothing they plan to do will be impossible for them. 7Come, let us go down and confuse their language so they will not understand each other."

8So the LORD scattered them from there over all the earth, and they stopped building the city. 9That is why it was called Babelc —because there the LORD confused the language of the whole world. From there the LORD scattered them over the face of the whole earth.

From Shem to Abram

10This is the account of Shem.

Two years after the flood, when Shem was 100 years old, he became the fatherd of Arphaxad. 11And after he became the father of Arphaxad, Shem lived 500 years and had other sons and daughters.

12When Arphaxad had lived 35 years, he became the father of Shelah. 13And after he became the father of Shelah, Arphaxad lived 403 years and had other sons and daughters.e

c6 That is, Egypt; also in verse 13
d8 Father may mean ancestor or predecessor or founder; also in verses 13, 15, 24 and 26.
e10 Or Erech and Akkad—all of them in   f10 That is, Babylonia   g11 Or Nineveh with its city squares
h15 Or of the Sidonians, the foremost   i21 Or Shem, the older brother of
j23 See Septuagint and 1 Chron. 1:17; Hebrew Mash.
k24 Hebrew; Septuagint father of Cainan, and Cainan was the father of   l25 Peleg means division.
a2 Or from the east; or in the east   b2 That is, Babylonia
c9 That is, Babylon; Babel sounds like the Hebrew for confused.
d10 Father may mean ancestor; also in verses 11–25.
e12,13 Hebrew; Septuagint (see also Luke 3:35, 36 and note at Gen. 10:24) 35 years, he became the father of Cainan.
13And after he became the father of Cainan, Arphaxad lived 430 years and had other sons and daughters, and then he died. When Cainan had lived 130 years, he became the father of Shelah. And after he became the father of Shelah, Cainan lived 330 years and had other sons and daughters

¹⁴When Shelah had lived 30 years, he became the father of Eber. ¹⁵And after he became the father of Eber, Shelah lived 403 years and had other sons and daughters.

¹⁶When Eber had lived 34 years, he became the father of Peleg. ¹⁷And after he became the father of Peleg, Eber lived 430 years and had other sons and daughters.

¹⁸When Peleg had lived 30 years, he became the father of Reu. ¹⁹And after he became the father of Reu, Peleg lived 209 years and had other sons and daughters.

²⁰When Reu had lived 32 years, he became the father of Serug. ²¹And after he became the father of Serug, Reu lived 207 years and had other sons and daughters.

²²When Serug had lived 30 years, he became the father of Nahor. ²³And after he became the father of Nahor, Serug lived 200 years and had other sons and daughters.

²⁴When Nahor had lived 29 years, he became the father of Terah. ²⁵And after he became the father of Terah, Nahor lived 119 years and had other sons and daughters.

²⁶After Terah had lived 70 years, he became the father of Abram, Nahor and Haran.

²⁷This is the account of Terah.

Terah became the father of Abram, Nahor and Haran. And Haran became the father of Lot. ²⁸While his father Terah was still alive, Haran died in Ur of the Chaldeans, in the land of his birth. ²⁹Abram and Nahor both married. The name of Abram's wife was Sarai, and the name of Nahor's wife was Milcah; she was the daughter of Haran, the father of both Milcah and Iscah. ³⁰Now Sarai was barren; she had no children.

³¹Terah took his son Abram, his grandson Lot son of Haran, and his daughter-in-law Sarai, the wife of his son Abram, and together they set out from Ur of the Chaldeans to go to Canaan. But when they came to Haran, they settled there.

³²Terah lived 205 years, and he died in Haran.

The Call of Abram

12 The LORD had said to Abram, "Leave your country, your people and your father's household and go to the land I will show you.

²"I will make you into a great nation
    and I will bless you;
I will make your name great,
    and you will be a blessing.
³I will bless those who bless you,
    and whoever curses you I will curse;
and all peoples on earth
    will be blessed through you."

⁴So Abram left, as the LORD had told him; and Lot went with him. Abram was seventy-five years old when he set out from Haran. ⁵He took his wife Sarai, his nephew Lot, all the possessions they had accumulated and the people they had acquired in Haran, and they set out for the land of Canaan, and they arrived there.

⁶Abram travelled through the land as far as the site of the great tree of Moreh at Shechem. At that time the Canaanites were in the land. ⁷The LORD appeared to Abram and said, "To your offspring*ᵃ* I will give this land." So he built an altar there to the LORD, who had appeared to him.

⁸From there he went on towards the hills east of Bethel and pitched his tent, with Bethel on the west and Ai on the east. There he built an altar to the LORD and called on the name of the LORD. ⁹Then Abram set out and continued towards the Negev.

Abram in Egypt

¹⁰Now there was a famine in the land, and Abram went down to Egypt to live there for a while because the famine was severe. ¹¹As he was about to enter Egypt, he said to his wife Sarai, "I know what a beautiful woman you are. ¹²When the Egyptians see you, they will say, 'This is his wife.' Then they will kill me but will let you live. ¹³Say you are my sister, so that I will be treated well for your sake and my life will be spared because of you."

¹⁴When Abram came to Egypt, the Egyptians saw that she was a very beautiful woman. ¹⁵And when Pharaoh's officials saw her, they praised her to Pharaoh, and she was taken into his palace. ¹⁶He treated Abram well for her sake, and Abram acquired sheep and cattle, male and female donkeys, menservants and maidservants, and camels.

¹⁷But the LORD inflicted serious diseases on Pharaoh and his household because of Abram's wife Sarai. ¹⁸So Pharaoh summoned Abram. "What have you done to me?" he said. "Why didn't you tell me she was your wife? ¹⁹Why did you say, 'She is my sister,' so that I took her to be my wife? Now then, here is your wife. Take her and go!" ²⁰Then Pharaoh gave orders about Abram to his men, and they sent him on his way, with his wife and everything he had.

Abram and Lot Separate

13 So Abram went up from Egypt to the Negev, with his wife and everything he had, and Lot went with him. ²Abram had become very wealthy in livestock and in silver and gold.

³From the Negev he went from place to place until he came to Bethel, to the place between Bethel and Ai where his tent had been earlier ⁴and where he had first built an altar. There Abram called on the name of the LORD.

⁵Now Lot, who was moving about with Abram, also had flocks and herds and tents. ⁶But the land could not support them while they stayed together, for their possessions were so great that they were not able to stay together. ⁷And quarrelling arose between Abram's herdsmen and the herdsmen of Lot. The Canaanites and Perizzites were also living in the land at that time.

⁸So Abram said to Lot, "Let's not have

ᵃ7 Or seed

any quarrelling between you and me, or between your herdsmen and mine, for we are brothers. ⁹Is not the whole land before you? Let's part company. If you go to the left, I'll go to the right; if you go to the right, I'll go to the left."

¹⁰Lot looked up and saw that the whole plain of the Jordan was well watered, like the garden of the LORD, like the land of Egypt, towards Zoar. (This was before the LORD destroyed Sodom and Gomorrah.) ¹¹So Lot chose for himself the whole plain of the Jordan and set out towards the east. The two men parted company: ¹²Abram lived in the land of Canaan, while Lot lived among the cities of the plain and pitched his tents near Sodom. ¹³Now the men of Sodom were wicked and were sinning greatly against the LORD.

¹⁴The LORD said to Abram after Lot had parted from him, "Lift up your eyes from where you are and look north and south, east and west. ¹⁵All the land that you see I will give to you and your offspring^a for ever. ¹⁶I will make your offspring like the dust of the earth, so that if anyone could count the dust, then your offspring could be counted. ¹⁷Go, walk through the length and breadth of the land, for I am giving it to you."

¹⁸So Abram moved his tents and went to live near the great trees of Mamre at Hebron, where he built an altar to the LORD.

Abram Rescues Lot

14 At this time Amraphel king of Shinar,^a Arioch king of Ellasar, Kedorlaomer king of Elam and Tidal king of Goiim ²went to war against Bera king of Sodom, Birsha king of Gomorrah, Shinab king of Admah, Shemeber king of Zeboiim, and the king of Bela (that is, Zoar). ³All these latter kings joined forces in the Valley of Siddim (the Salt Sea^b). ⁴For twelve years they had been subject to Kedorlaomer, but in the thirteenth year they rebelled.

⁵In the fourteenth year, Kedorlaomer and the kings allied with him went out and defeated the Rephaites in Ashteroth Karnaim, the Zuzites in Ham, the Emites in Shaveh Kiriathaim ⁶and the Horites in the hill country of Seir, as far as El Paran near the desert. ⁷Then they turned back and went to En Mishpat (that is, Kadesh), and they conquered the whole territory of the Amalekites, as well as the Amorites who were living in Hazezon Tamar.

⁸Then the king of Sodom, the king of Gomorrah, the king of Admah, the king of Zeboiim and the king of Bela (that is, Zoar) marched out and drew up their battle lines in the Valley of Siddim ⁹against Kedorlaomer king of Elam, Tidal king of Goiim, Amraphel king of Shinar and Arioch king of Ellasar —four kings against five. ¹⁰Now the Valley of Siddim was full of tar pits, and when the kings of Sodom and Gomorrah fled, some of the men fell into them and the rest fled to the hills. ¹¹The four kings seized all the goods of Sodom and Gomorrah and all their food; then they went away. ¹²They also carried off Abram's nephew Lot and his possessions, since he was living in Sodom.

¹³One who had escaped came and reported this to Abram the Hebrew. Now Abram was living near the great trees of Mamre the Amorite, a brother^c of Eshcol and Aner, all of whom were allied with Abram. ¹⁴When Abram heard that his relative had been taken captive, he called out the 318 trained men born in his household and went in pursuit as far as Dan. ¹⁵During the night Abram divided his men to attack them and he routed them, pursuing them as far as Hobah, north of Damascus. ¹⁶He recovered all the goods and brought back his relative Lot and his possessions, together with the women and the other people.

¹⁷After Abram returned from defeating Kedorlaomer and the kings allied with him, the king of Sodom came out to meet him in the Valley of Shaveh (that is, the King's Valley).

¹⁸Then Melchizedek king of Salem^d brought out bread and wine. He was priest of God Most High, ¹⁹and he blessed Abram, saying,

"Blessed be Abram by God Most High,
    Creator^e of heaven and earth.
²⁰And blessed be^f God Most High,
    who delivered your enemies into your
        hand."

Then Abram gave him a tenth of everything.

²¹The king of Sodom said to Abram, "Give me the people and keep the goods for yourself."

²²But Abram said to the king of Sodom, "I have raised my hand to the LORD, God Most High, Creator of heaven and earth, and have taken an oath ²³that I will accept nothing belonging to you, not even a thread or the thong of a sandal, so that you will never be able to say, 'I made Abram rich.' ²⁴I will accept nothing but what my men have eaten and the share that belongs to the men who went with me—to Aner, Eshcol and Mamre. Let them have their share."

God's Covenant With Abram

15 After this, the word of the LORD came to Abram in a vision:

"Do not be afraid, Abram.
    I am your shield,^a
    your very great reward."^b

²But Abram said, "O Sovereign LORD, what can you give me since I remain childless and the one who will inherit^c my estate is Eliezer of Damascus?" ³And Abram said, "You have given me no children; so a servant in my household will be my heir."

---

^a15 Or *seed*; also in verse 16   ^a1 That is, Babylonia; also in verse 9   ^b3 That is, the Dead Sea
^c13 Or *a relative*; or *an ally*   ^d18 That is, Jerusalem   ^e19 Or *Possessor*; also in verse 22
^f20 Or *And praise be to*   ^a1 Or *sovereign*   ^b1 Or *shield*; *l your reward will be very great*
^c2 The meaning of the Hebrew for this phrase is uncertain.

4Then the word of the LORD came to him: "This man will not be your heir, but a son coming from your own body will be your heir." 5He took him outside and said, "Look up at the heavens and count the stars—if indeed you can count them." Then he said to him, "So shall your offspring be."

6Abram believed the LORD, and he credited it to him as righteousness.

7He also said to him, "I am the LORD, who brought you out of Ur of the Chaldeans to give you this land to take possession of it."

8But Abram said, "O Sovereign LORD, how can I know that I shall gain possession of it?"

9So the LORD said to him, "Bring me a heifer, a goat and a ram, each three years old, along with a dove and a young pigeon."

10Abram brought all these to him, cut them in two and arranged the halves opposite each other; the birds, however, he did not cut in half. 11Then birds of prey came down on the carcasses, but Abram drove them away.

12As the sun was setting, Abram fell into a deep sleep, and a thick and dreadful darkness came over him. 13Then the LORD said to him, "Know for certain that your descendants will be strangers in a country not their own, and they will be enslaved and ill-treated four hundred years. 14But I will punish the nation they serve as slaves, and afterwards they will come out with great possessions. 15You, however, will go to your fathers in peace and be buried at a good old age. 16In the fourth generation your descendants will come back here, for the sin of the Amorites has not yet reached its full measure."

17When the sun had set and darkness had fallen, a smoking brazier with a blazing torch appeared and passed between the pieces. 18On that day the LORD made a covenant with Abram and said, "To your descendants I give this land, from the river*d* of Egypt to the great river, the Euphrates—19the land of the Kenites, Kenizzites, Kadmonites, 20Hittites, Perizzites, Rephaites, 21Amorites, Canaanites, Girgashites and Jebusites."

Hagar and Ishmael

16 Now Sarai, Abram's wife, had borne him no children. But she had an Egyptian maidservant named Hagar; 2so she said to Abram, "The LORD has kept me from having children. Go, sleep with my maidservant; perhaps I can build a family through her."

Abram agreed to what Sarai said. 3So after Abram had been living in Canaan ten years, Sarai his wife took her Egyptian maidservant Hagar and gave her to her husband to be his wife. 4He slept with Hagar, and she conceived.

When she knew she was pregnant, she began to despise her mistress. 5Then Sarai said to Abram, "You are responsible for the wrong I am suffering. I put my servant in your arms, and now that she knows she is pregnant, she despises me. May the LORD judge between you and me."

6"Your servant is in your hands," Abram said. "Do with her whatever you think best." Then Sarai ill-treated Hagar; so she fled from her.

7The angel of the LORD found Hagar near a spring in the desert; it was the spring that is beside the road to Shur. 8And he said, "Hagar, servant of Sarai, where have you come from, and where are you going?"

"I'm running away from my mistress Sarai," she answered.

9Then the angel of the LORD told her, "Go back to your mistress and submit to her." 10The angel added, "I will so increase your descendants that they will be too numerous to count."

11The angel of the LORD also said to her:

"You are now with child
    and you will have a son.
You shall name him Ishmael,*a*
    for the LORD has heard of your misery.
12He will be a wild donkey of a man;
    his hand will be against everyone
    and everyone's hand against him,
and he will live in hostility
    towards*b* all his brothers."

13She gave this name to the LORD who spoke to her: "You are the God who sees me," for she said, "I have now seen*c* the One who sees me." 14That is why the well was called Beer Lahai Roi;*d* it is still there, between Kadesh and Bered.

15So Hagar bore Abram a son, and Abram gave the name Ishmael to the son she had borne. 16Abram was eighty-six years old when Hagar bore him Ishmael.

The Covenant of Circumcision

17 When Abram was ninety-nine years old, the LORD appeared to him and said, "I am God Almighty;*a* walk before me and be blameless. 2I will confirm my covenant between me and you and will greatly increase your numbers."

3Abram fell face down, and God said to him, 4"As for me, this is my covenant with you: You will be the father of many nations. 5No longer will you be called Abram;*b* your name will be Abraham,*c* for I have made you a father of many nations. 6I will make you very fruitful; I will make nations of you, and kings will come from you. 7I will establish my covenant as an everlasting covenant between me and you and your descendants after you for the generations to come, to be your God and the God of your descendants after you. 8The whole land of Canaan, where you are now an alien, I will give as an everlasting possession to you and your descendants after you; and I will be their God."

9Then God said to Abraham, "As for you, you must keep my covenant, you and your descendants after you for the generations to

---

*d*18 Or *Wadi*   *a*11 *Ishmael* means *God hears.*   *b*12 Or *live to the east*l *of*   *c*13 Or *seen the back of*
*d*14 *Beer Lahai Roi* means *well of the Living One who sees me.*   *a*1 Hebrew *El-Shaddai*
*b*5 *Abram* means *exalted father.*   *c*5 *Abraham* means *father of many.*

GENESIS 18:20–33
'Then Abraham approached him and said: "Will you sweep away the righteous with the wicked? What if there are fifty righteous people in the city? Will you really sweep it away and not spare the place for the sake of the fifty righteous people in it?" ' (vv. 23, 24).

THE NOBILITY OF COMPASSION shines through these verses. Abraham has travelled a long way from the impersonal coldness and paganism of Ur of the Chaldees. His faith and obedience to a God of great power and great compassion have shaped his judgements and finely tuned his feelings. Sodom and Gomorrah deserved their destruction. Abram's rejection of the King of Sodom earlier was on valid grounds, but Abraham knew that in addition to Lot and his family there were probably other righteous people in the city and he pleaded with God accordingly.

The manner of Abraham's pleading is tender and impressive. He now had a relationship with God of such warmth and familiarity that he felt he could presume on God's patience. His 'bargaining' approach had dignity and confident expectation. 'Will not the Judge of all the earth do right?' Abraham knew that the compassions of God exceed by far the compassions of men. Had he not believed this he would not have stayed with the figure of ten righteous souls. He would have reduced the figure at least to make sure that Lot and his family would be saved.

Intercession is one of the problem areas of faith. If God is all compassion, why does he need our prayers for others? And yet such intercessions are required of us. We are commanded to pray for those who persecute us. We are also commanded to pray for the saints. The dynamics of intercession are a mystery to us, but intercessory prayer is effective.

I am at my noblest and best when I am praying for others.

→20

GENESIS 21:1–14

'Sarah said, "God has brought me laughter". . . . Sarah saw that the son whom Hagar the Egyptian had borne to Abraham was mocking, and she said to Abraham, "Get rid of that slave woman and her son" ' (vv. 6a, 9, 10a).

THE BOUNDARY BETWEEN LAUGHTER AND TEARS is narrow. It may be hard to tell if someone is laughing or crying. Laughter itself can be joyous, harmonious and jolly – or it can be hollow, mocking and sad.

Sarai, now renamed Sarah, laughed before, (18:12) a mocking laugh when she heard she would bear a child. After the birth, all was happiness, a full-throated laughter of joy. Yet how that changed! Looking after a baby, even with fine resources like Sarah had, is no picnic, especially in older age. Maturity of years hardly seems to fit one better to bring up a first child. Young and old parents alike make similar mistakes. They look at others with older children, who seem to cope well, and tend to feel *they* are not coping. We can understand how, with Hagar's fine young son Ishmael around, and a crying baby at her own breast. Sarah felt inadequate. And when Ishmael played – and laughed? – with the baby boy her feelings of jealousy got the better of her. Always a rather unpleasant character, under the stress of dealing with her infant son, Sarah turned on Hagar and demanded Abraham should send her away.

What a difference laughter makes! It relieves tension, makes relationships easier, and brings lightness and fun to an otherwise heavy situation. It can also raise spectres of envy, mockery and spite. How careful we must be that our laughter is wholesome! But even innocent laughter can have unexpected results, as witness Ishmael playing with baby Isaac.

Praise God for wholesome laughter, despite its dangers.

come. [10]This is my covenant with you and your descendants after you, the covenant you are to keep: Every male among you shall be circumcised. [11]You are to undergo circumcision, and it will be the sign of the covenant between me and you. [12]For the generations to come every male among you who is eight days old must be circumcised, including those born in your household or bought with money from a foreigner—those who are not your offspring. [13]Whether born in your household or bought with your money, they must be circumcised. My covenant in your flesh is to be an everlasting covenant. [14]Any uncircumcised male, who has not been circumcised in the flesh, will be cut off from his people; he has broken my covenant."

[15]God also said to Abraham, "As for Sarai your wife, you are no longer to call her Sarai; her name will be Sarah. [16]I will bless her and will surely give you a son by her. I will bless her so that she will be the mother of nations; kings of peoples will come from her."

[17]Abraham fell face down; he laughed and said to himself, "Will a son be born to a man a hundred years old? Will Sarah bear a child at the age of ninety?" [18]And Abraham said to God, "If only Ishmael might live under your blessing!"

[19]Then God said, "Yes, but your wife Sarah will bear you a son, and you will call him Isaac.[d] I will establish my covenant with him as an everlasting covenant for his descendants after him. [20]And as for Ishmael, I have heard you: I will surely bless him; I will make him fruitful and will greatly increase his numbers. He will be the father of twelve rulers, and I will make him into a great nation. [21]But my covenant I will establish with Isaac, whom Sarah will bear to you by this time next year." [22]When he had finished speaking with Abraham, God went up from him.

[23]On that very day Abraham took his son Ishmael and all those born in his household or bought with his money, every male in his household, and circumcised them, as God told him. [24]Abraham was ninety-nine years old when he was circumcised, [25]and his son Ishmael was thirteen; [26]Abraham and his son Ishmael were both circumcised on that same day. [27]And every male in Abraham's household, including those born in his household or bought from a foreigner, was circumcised with him.

The Three Visitors

18 The LORD appeared to Abraham near the great trees of Mamre while he was sitting at the entrance to his tent in the heat of the day. [2]Abraham looked up and saw three men standing nearby. When he saw them, he hurried from the entrance of his tent to meet them and bowed low to the ground.

[3]He said, "If I have found favour in your eyes, my lord,[a] do not pass your servant by.

[4]Let a little water be brought, and then you may all wash your feet and rest under this tree. [5]Let me get you something to eat, so you can be refreshed and then go on your way—now that you have come to your servant."

"Very well," they answered, "do as you say."

[6]So Abraham hurried into the tent to Sarah. "Quick," he said, "get three seahs[b] of fine flour and knead it and bake some bread."

[7]Then he ran to the herd and selected a choice, tender calf and gave it to a servant, who hurried to prepare it. [8]He then brought some curds and milk and the calf that had been prepared, and set these before them. While they ate, he stood near them under a tree.

[9]"Where is your wife Sarah?" they asked him.

"There, in the tent," he said.

[10]Then the LORD[c] said, "I will surely return to you about this time next year, and Sarah your wife will have a son."

Now Sarah was listening at the entrance to the tent, which was behind him. [11]Abraham and Sarah were already old and well advanced in years, and Sarah was past the age of childbearing. [12]So Sarah laughed to herself as she thought, "After I am worn out and my master[d] is old, will I now have this pleasure?"

[13]Then the LORD said to Abraham, "Why did Sarah laugh and say, 'Will I really have a child, now that I am old?' [14]Is anything too hard for the LORD? I will return to you at the appointed time next year and Sarah will have a son."

[15]Sarah was afraid, so she lied and said, "I did not laugh."

But he said, "Yes, you did laugh."

Abraham Pleads for Sodom

[16]When the men got up to leave, they looked down towards Sodom, and Abraham walked along with them to see them on their way. [17]Then the LORD said, "Shall I hide from Abraham what I am about to do? [18]Abraham will surely become a great and powerful nation, and all nations on earth will be blessed through him. [19]For I have chosen him, so that he will direct his children and his household after him to keep the way of the LORD by doing what is right and just, so that the LORD will bring about for Abraham what he has promised him."

[20]Then the LORD said, "The outcry against Sodom and Gomorrah is so great and their sin so grievous [21]that I will go down and see if what they have done is as bad as the outcry that has reached me. If not, I will know."

[22]The men turned away and went towards Sodom, but Abraham remained standing before the LORD.[e] [23]Then Abraham approached him and said: "Will you sweep away the righteous with the wicked? [24]What if there

---

[d]19 Isaac means he laughs.   [a]3 Or O Lord   [b]6 That is, probably about 39 pints (about 22 litres)
[c]10 Hebrew Then he   [d]12 Or husband
[e]22 Masoretic Text; an ancient Hebrew scribal tradition but the LORD remained standing before Abraham

are fifty righteous people in the city? Will you really sweep it away and not spare*f* the place for the sake of the fifty righteous people in it? 25Far be it from you to do such a thing—to kill the righteous with the wicked, treating the righteous and the wicked alike. Far be it from you! Will not the Judge*g* of all the earth do right?"

26The LORD said, "If I find fifty righteous people in the city of Sodom, I will spare the whole place for their sake."

27Then Abraham spoke up again: "Now that I have been so bold as to speak to the Lord, though I am nothing but dust and ashes, 28what if the number of the righteous is five less than fifty? Will you destroy the whole city because of five people?"

"If I find forty-five there," he said, "I will not destroy it."

29Once again he spoke to him, "What if only forty are found there?"

He said, "For the sake of forty, I will not do it."

30Then he said, "May the Lord not be angry, but let me speak. What if only thirty can be found there?"

He answered, "I will not do it if I find thirty there."

31Abraham said, "Now that I have been so bold as to speak to the Lord, what if only twenty can be found there?"

He said, "For the sake of twenty, I will not destroy it."

32Then he said, "May the Lord not be angry, but let me speak just once more. What if only ten can be found there?"

He answered, "For the sake of ten, I will not destroy it."

33When the LORD had finished speaking with Abraham, he left, and Abraham returned home.

Sodom and Gomorrah Destroyed

19 The two angels arrived at Sodom in the evening, and Lot was sitting in the gateway of the city. When he saw them, he got up to meet them and bowed down with his face to the ground. 2"My lords," he said, "please turn aside to your servant's house. You can wash your feet and spend the night and then go on your way early in the morning."

"No," they answered, "we will spend the night in the square."

3But he insisted so strongly that they did go with him and entered his house. He prepared a meal for them, baking bread without yeast, and they ate. 4Before they had gone to bed, all the men from every part of the city of Sodom—both young and old—surrounded the house. 5They called to Lot, "Where are the men who came to you tonight? Bring them out to us so that we can have sex with them."

6Lot went outside to meet them and shut the door behind him 7and said, "No, my friends. Don't do this wicked thing. 8Look, I have two daughters who have never slept

with a man. Let me bring them out to you, and you can do what you like with them. But don't do anything to these men, for they have come under the protection of my roof."

9"Get out of our way," they replied. And they said, "This fellow came here as an alien, and now he wants to play the judge! We'll treat you worse than them." They kept bringing pressure on Lot and moved forward to break down the door.

10But the men inside reached out and pulled Lot back into the house and shut the door. 11Then they struck the men who were at the door of the house, young and old, with blindness so that they could not find the door.

12The two men said to Lot, "Do you have anyone else here—sons-in-law, sons or daughters, or anyone else in the city who belongs to you? Get them out of here, 13because we are going to destroy this place. The outcry to the LORD against its people is so great that he has sent us to destroy it."

14So Lot went out and spoke to his sons-in-law, who were pledged to marry*a* his daughters. He said, "Hurry and get out of this place, because the LORD is about to destroy the city!" But his sons-in-law thought he was joking.

15With the coming of dawn, the angels urged Lot, saying, "Hurry! Take your wife and your two daughters who are here, or you will be swept away when the city is punished."

16When he hesitated, the men grasped his hand and the hands of his wife and of his two daughters and led them safely out of the city, for the LORD was merciful to them. 17As soon as they had brought them out, one of them said, "Flee for your lives! Don't look back, and don't stop anywhere in the plain! Flee to the mountains or you will be swept away!"

18But Lot said to them, "No, my lords,*b* please! 19Your*c* servant has found favour in your*c* eyes, and you*c* have shown great kindness to me in sparing my life. But I can't flee to the mountains; this disaster will overtake me, and I'll die. 20Look, here is a town near enough to run to, and it is small. Let me flee to it—it is very small, isn't it? Then my life will be spared."

21He said to him, "Very well, I will grant this request too; I will not overthrow the town you speak of. 22But flee there quickly, because I cannot do anything until you reach it." (That is why the town was called Zoar.*d*)

23By the time Lot reached Zoar, the sun had risen over the land. 24Then the LORD rained down burning sulphur on Sodom and Gomorrah—from the LORD out of the heavens. 25Thus he overthrew those cities and the entire plain, including all those living in the cities—and also the vegetation in the land. 26But Lot's wife looked back, and she became a pillar of salt.

27Early the next morning Abraham got up and returned to the place where he had stood before the LORD. 28He looked down towards Sodom and Gomorrah, towards all the land

---

f24 Or *forgive*; also in verse 26   *g25* Or *Ruler*   *a14* Or *were married to*
b18 Or *No, Lord*; or *No, my lord*   *c19* The Hebrew is singular.   *d22 Zoar* means *small*.

of the plain, and he saw dense smoke rising from the land, like smoke from a furnace.

²⁹So when God destroyed the cities of the plain, he remembered Abraham, and he brought Lot out of the catastrophe that overthrew the cities where Lot had lived.

Lot and His Daughters

³⁰Lot and his two daughters left Zoar and settled in the mountains, for he was afraid to stay in Zoar. He and his two daughters lived in a cave. ³¹One day the older daughter said to the younger, "Our father is old, and there is no man around here to lie with us, as is the custom all over the earth. ³²Let's get our father to drink wine and then lie with him and preserve our family line through our father."

³³That night they got their father to drink wine, and the older daughter went in and lay with him. He was not aware of it when she lay down or when she got up.

³⁴The next day the older daughter said to the younger, "Last night I lay with my father. Let's get him to drink wine again tonight, and you go in and lie with him so we can preserve our family line through our father." ³⁵So they got their father to drink wine that night also, and the younger daughter went and lay with him. Again he was not aware of it when she lay down or when she got up.

³⁶So both of Lot's daughters became pregnant by their father. ³⁷The older daughter had a son, and she named him Moab;ᵉ he is the father of the Moabites of today. ³⁸The younger daughter also had a son, and she named him Ben-Ammi;ᶠ he is the father of the Ammonites of today.

Abraham and Abimelech

20 Now Abraham moved on from there into the region of the Negev and lived between Kadesh and Shur. For a while he stayed in Gerar, ²and there Abraham said of his wife Sarah, "She is my sister." Then Abimelech king of Gerar sent for Sarah and took her.

³But God came to Abimelech in a dream one night and said to him, "You are as good as dead because of the woman you have taken; she is a married woman."

⁴Now Abimelech had not gone near her, so he said, "Lord, will you destroy an innocent nation? ⁵Did he not say to me, 'She is my sister,' and didn't she also say, 'He is my brother'? I have done this with a clear conscience and clean hands."

⁶Then God said to him in the dream, "Yes, I know you did this with a clear conscience, and so I have kept you from sinning against me. That is why I did not let you touch her. ⁷Now return the man's wife, for he is a prophet, and he will pray for you and you will live. But if you do not return her, you may be sure that you and all yours will die."

⁸Early the next morning Abimelech summoned all his officials, and when he told them all that had happened, they were very much afraid. ⁹Then Abimelech called Abraham in and said, "What have you done to us? How have I wronged you that you have brought such great guilt upon me and my kingdom? You have done things to me that should not be done." ¹⁰And Abimelech asked Abraham, "What was your reason for doing this?"

¹¹Abraham replied, "I said to myself, 'There is surely no fear of God in this place, and they will kill me because of my wife.' ¹²Besides, she really is my sister, the daughter of my father though not of my mother; and she became my wife. ¹³And when God caused me to wander from my father's household, I said to her, 'This is how you can show your love to me: Everywhere we go, say of me, "He is my brother." ' "

¹⁴Then Abimelech brought sheep and cattle and male and female slaves and gave them to Abraham, and he returned Sarah his wife to him. ¹⁵And Abimelech said, "My land is before you; live wherever you like."

¹⁶To Sarah he said, "I am giving your brother a thousand shekelsᵃ of silver. This is to cover the offence against you before all who are with you; you are completely vindicated."

¹⁷Then Abraham prayed to God, and God healed Abimelech, his wife and his slave girls so they could have children again, ¹⁸for the LORD had closed up every womb in Abimelech's household because of Abraham's wife Sarah.

The Birth of Isaac

21 Now the LORD was gracious to Sarah as he had said, and the LORD did for Sarah what he had promised. ²Sarah became pregnant and bore a son to Abraham in his old age, at the very time God had promised him. ³Abraham gave the name Isaacᵃ to the son Sarah bore him. ⁴When his son Isaac was eight days old, Abraham circumcised him, as God commanded him. ⁵Abraham was a hundred years old when his son Isaac was born to him.

⁶Sarah said, "God has brought me laughter, and everyone who hears about this will laugh with me." ⁷And she added, "Who would have said to Abraham that Sarah would nurse children? Yet I have borne him a son in his old age."

Hagar and Ishmael Sent Away

⁸The child grew and was weaned, and on the day Isaac was weaned Abraham held a great feast. ⁹But Sarah saw that the son whom Hagar the Egyptian had borne to Abraham was mocking, ¹⁰and she said to Abraham, "Get rid of that slave woman and her son, for that slave woman's son will never share in the inheritance with my son Isaac."

¹¹The matter distressed Abraham greatly because it concerned his son. ¹²But God said to him, "Do not be so distressed about the boy and your maidservant. Listen to whatever Sarah tells you, because it is through

---

ᵉ37 *Moab* sounds like the Hebrew for *from father.*   ᶠ38 *Ben-Ammi* means *son of my people.*
ᵃ16 That is, about 25 pounds (about 11.5 kilograms)   ᵃ3 *Isaac* means *he laughs.*

Isaac that your offspring[b] will be reckoned. ¹³I will make the son of the maidservant into a nation also, because he is your offspring."

¹⁴Early the next morning Abraham took some food and a skin of water and gave them to Hagar. He set them on her shoulders and then sent her off with the boy. She went on her way and wandered in the desert of Beersheba.

¹⁵When the water in the skin was gone, she put the boy under one of the bushes. ¹⁶Then she went off and sat down nearby, about a bow-shot away, for she thought, "I cannot watch the boy die." And as she sat there nearby, she[c] began to sob.

¹⁷God heard the boy crying, and the angel of God called to Hagar from heaven and said to her, "What is the matter, Hagar? Do not be afraid; God has heard the boy crying as he lies there. ¹⁸Lift the boy up and take him by the hand, for I will make him into a great nation."

¹⁹Then God opened her eyes and she saw a well of water. So she went and filled the skin with water and gave the boy a drink.

²⁰God was with the boy as he grew up. He lived in the desert and became an archer. ²¹While he was living in the Desert of Paran, his mother got a wife for him from Egypt.

The Treaty at Beersheba

²²At that time Abimelech and Phicol the commander of his forces said to Abraham, "God is with you in everything you do. ²³Now swear to me here before God that you will not deal falsely with me or my children or my descendants. Show to me and the country where you are living as an alien the same kindness that I have shown to you."

²⁴Abraham said, "I swear it."

²⁵Then Abraham complained to Abimelech about a well of water that Abimelech's servants had seized. ²⁶But Abimelech said, "I don't know who has done this. You did not tell me, and I heard about it only today."

²⁷So Abraham brought sheep and cattle and gave them to Abimelech, and the two men made a treaty. ²⁸Abraham set apart seven ewe lambs from the flock, ²⁹and Abimelech asked Abraham, "What is the meaning of these seven ewe lambs you have set apart by themselves?"

³⁰He replied, "Accept these seven lambs from my hand as a witness that I dug this well."

³¹So that place was called Beersheba,[d] because the two men swore an oath there.

³²After the treaty had been made at Beersheba, Abimelech and Phicol the commander of his forces returned to the land of the Philistines. ³³Abraham planted a tamarisk tree in Beersheba, and there he called upon the name of the LORD, the Eternal God. ³⁴And Abraham stayed in the land of the Philistines for a long time.

Abraham Tested

22 Some time later God tested Abraham. He said to him, "Abraham!"

"Here I am," he replied.

²Then God said, "Take your son, your only son, Isaac, whom you love, and go to the region of Moriah. Sacrifice him there as a burnt offering on one of the mountains I will tell you about."

³Early the next morning Abraham got up and saddled his donkey. He took with him two of his servants and his son Isaac. When he had cut enough wood for the burnt offering, he set out for the place God had told him about. ⁴On the third day Abraham looked up and saw the place in the distance. ⁵He said to his servants, "Stay here with the donkey while I and the boy go over there. We will worship and then we will come back to you."

⁶Abraham took the wood for the burnt offering and placed it on his son Isaac, and he himself carried the fire and the knife. As the two of them went on together, ⁷Isaac spoke up and said to his father Abraham, "Father?"

"Yes, my son?" Abraham replied.

"The fire and wood are here," Isaac said, "but where is the lamb for the burnt offering?"

⁸Abraham answered, "God himself will provide the lamb for the burnt offering, my son." And the two of them went on together.

⁹When they reached the place God had told him about, Abraham built an altar there and arranged the wood on it. He bound his son Isaac and laid him on the altar, on top of the wood. ¹⁰Then he reached out his hand and took the knife to slay his son. ¹¹But the angel of the LORD called out to him from heaven, "Abraham! Abraham!"

"Here I am," he replied.

¹²"Do not lay a hand on the boy," he said. "Do not do anything to him. Now I know that you fear God, because you have not withheld from me your son, your only son."

¹³Abraham looked up and there in a thicket he saw a ram[a] caught by its horns. He went over and took the ram and sacrificed it as a burnt offering instead of his son. ¹⁴So Abraham called that place The LORD Will Provide. And to this day it is said, "On the mountain of the LORD it will be provided."

¹⁵The angel of the LORD called to Abraham from heaven a second time ¹⁶and said, "I swear by myself, declares the LORD, that because you have done this and have not withheld your son, your only son, ¹⁷I will surely bless you and make your descendants as numerous as the stars in the sky and as the sand on the seashore. Your descendants will take possession of the cities of their enemies, ¹⁸and through your offspring[b] all nations on earth will be blessed, because you have obeyed me."

¹⁹Then Abraham returned to his servants, and they set off together for Beersheba. And Abraham stayed in Beersheba.

---

[b]12 Or *seed*   [c]16 Hebrew; Septuagint *the child*   [d]31 *Beersheba* can mean *well of seven* or *well of the oath*.
[a]13 Many manuscripts of the Masoretic Text, Samaritan Pentateuch, Septuagint and Syriac; most manuscripts of the Masoretic Text *a ram behind* ⌞*him*⌟   [b]18 Or *seed*

GENESIS 22:1–2
'Some time later God tested Abraham. He said to him, "Abraham!" "Here I am," he replied' (v. 1).

SOONER OR LATER GOD TESTS or allows his people to be tested. The sheer simplicity and beauty of this narrative, added to our knowledge of the happy ending, could easily dull our perceptions concerning the enormity, the unreasonableness, of God's demand that Isaac should be sacrificed. For years the promise had been made: 'You will have a son.' Abraham had thought that the son Hagar bore him might be the answer, but God decreed otherwise. Sarah and he had rejoiced with wide-eyed wonder at the birth of Isaac and now, he whose name meant laughter and who had brought so much joy, was to die, not by accident but seemingly by the direct command of the God who had declared his strategy that through Isaac Abraham would father a nation.

God was determined that Abraham would be a man of faith. He wanted Abraham to serve him for his own sake, not because he had made promises, the fulfilment of which increased Abraham's feelings of self-worth, his standing with his peers and other leaders. Was Abraham God's man unconditionally? The answer was 'yes' and had great consequences.

Others have expressed that same strength of faith in God. Job stated clearly: 'Though he slay me, yet will I trust in him.' The prophet Habakkuk also envisaged everything going wrong that could go wrong and responded, 'Yet I will rejoice in the Lord.' Our Lord made a statement of universal application: 'For whoever wants to save his life will lose it, but whoever loses his life for me and for the gospel will save it.'

Faith is refined, sometimes painfully, in the crucible of life, but that is the kind of faith God looks for in each of us.

GENESIS 25:21–34

'But Jacob said, "Swear to me first." So he swore an oath to him, selling his birthright to Jacob' (v. 33).

THE PROXY WOOING of Rebekah and her subsequent marriage to Isaac make us expect better of their offspring than the records show. The overtones of divine guidance, the confidence of the faithful servant, the natural grace in Rebekah's response and Isaac's apparent love at first sight all lead us to expect that from this idyllic marriage will issue ideal children. Not so, however. Problems with children are not new!

Rebekah knew that Jacob, the youngest, was to occupy the position of first-born. Had she told Isaac, Isaac might well have leaned Jacob's way rather than towards Esau. As it was, Esau the hunter appealed to Isaac more than Jacob the home-lover.

The grasping hand of Jacob on Esau's heel at birth was to be an indication of Jacob's nature and his later relationship with Esau. Following an abortive hunting trip, the hungry and exhausted Esau begged Jacob for some of the stew he was cooking, and the opportunistic Jacob made Esau surrender his birthright in exchange. The birthright of the first-born conferred a double portion of the inheritance. Isaac may have been so wealthy in Esau's judgement that a single portion of the inheritance would suffice, but the ease with which he submitted to Jacob's condition condemned him.

The writer to the Hebrews has a most serious view of Esau. He uses him as an example of those who, through their godlessness, surrender their spiritual birthright. God's judgement is therefore on him and others like him, for God is a consuming fire.

'If you belong to Christ, then you are Abraham's seed, and heirs according to the promise.' Thank you, Lord. Amen.

Nahor's Sons

20Some time later Abraham was told, "Milcah is also a mother; she has borne sons to your brother Nahor: 21Uz the firstborn, Buz his brother, Kemuel (the father of Aram), 22Kesed, Hazo, Pildash, Jidlaph and Bethuel." 23Bethuel became the father of Rebekah. Milcah bore these eight sons to Abraham's brother Nahor. 24His concubine, whose name was Reumah, also had sons: Tebah, Gaham, Tahash and Maacah.

The Death of Sarah

23 Sarah lived to be a hundred and twenty-seven years old. 2She died at Kiriath Arba (that is, Hebron) in the land of Canaan, and Abraham went to mourn for Sarah and to weep over her.

3Then Abraham rose from beside his dead wife and spoke to the Hittites.*a* He said, 4"I am an alien and a stranger among you. Sell me some property for a burial site here so that I can bury my dead."

5The Hittites replied to Abraham, 6"Sir, listen to us. You are a mighty prince among us. Bury your dead in the choicest of our tombs. None of us will refuse you his tomb for burying your dead."

7Then Abraham rose and bowed down before the people of the land, the Hittites. 8He said to them, "If you are willing to let me bury my dead, then listen to me and intercede with Ephron son of Zohar on my behalf 9so that he will sell me the cave of Machpelah, which belongs to him and is at the end of his field. Ask him to sell it to me for the full price as a burial site among you."

10Ephron the Hittite was sitting among his people and he replied to Abraham in the hearing of all the Hittites who had come to the gate of his city. 11"No, my lord," he said. "Listen to me; I give*b* you the field, and I give*b* you the cave that is in it. I give*b* it to you in the presence of my people. Bury your dead."

12Again Abraham bowed down before the people of the land 13and he said to Ephron in their hearing, "Listen to me, if you will. I will pay the price of the field. Accept it from me so that I can bury my dead there."

14Ephron answered Abraham, 15"Listen to me, my lord; the land is worth four hundred shekels*c* of silver, but what is that between me and you? Bury your dead."

16Abraham agreed to Ephron's terms and weighed out for him the price he had named in the hearing of the Hittites: four hundred shekels of silver, according to the weight current among the merchants.

17So Ephron's field in Machpelah near Mamre—both the field and the cave in it, and all the trees within the borders of the field —was legally made over 18to Abraham as his property in the presence of all the Hittites who had come to the gate of the city. 19Afterwards Abraham buried his wife Sarah in the cave in the field of Machpelah near

Mamre (which is at Hebron) in the land of Canaan. 20So the field and the cave in it were legally made over to Abraham by the Hittites as a burial site.

Isaac and Rebekah

24 Abraham was now old and well advanced in years, and the Lord had blessed him in every way. 2He said to the chief*a* servant in his household, the one in charge of all that he had, "Put your hand under my thigh. 3I want you to swear by the Lord, the God of heaven and the God of earth, that you will not get a wife for my son from the daughters of the Canaanites, among whom I am living, 4but will go to my country and my own relatives and get a wife for my son Isaac."

5The servant asked him, "What if the woman is unwilling to come back with me to this land? Shall I then take your son back to the country you came from?"

6"Make sure that you do not take my son back there," Abraham said. 7"The Lord, the God of heaven, who brought me out of my father's household and my native land and who spoke to me and promised me on oath, saying, 'To your offspring*b* I will give this land'—he will send his angel before you so that you can get a wife for my son from there. 8If the woman is unwilling to come back with you, then you will be released from this oath of mine. Only do not take my son back there." 9So the servant put his hand under the thigh of his master Abraham and swore an oath to him concerning this matter.

10Then the servant took ten of his master's camels and left, taking with him all kinds of good things from his master. He set out for Aram Naharaim*c* and made his way to the town of Nahor. 11He made the camels kneel down near the well outside the town; it was towards evening, the time the women go out to draw water.

12Then he prayed, "O Lord, God of my master Abraham, give me success today, and show kindness to my master Abraham. 13See, I am standing beside this spring, and the daughters of the townspeople are coming out to draw water. 14May it be that when I say to a girl, 'Please let down your jar that I may have a drink,' and she says, 'Drink, and I'll water your camels too'—let her be the one you have chosen for your servant Isaac. By this I will know that you have shown kindness to my master."

15Before he had finished praying, Rebekah came out with her jar on her shoulder. She was the daughter of Bethuel son of Milcah, who was the wife of Abraham's brother Nahor. 16The girl was very beautiful, a virgin; no man had ever lain with her. She went down to the spring, filled her jar and came up again.

17The servant hurried to meet her and said, "Please give me a little water from your jar."

18"Drink, my lord," she said, and quickly

---

*a*3 Or *the sons of Heth*; also in verses 5, 7, 10, 16, 18 and 20   *b*11 Or *sell*
*c*15 That is, about 10 pounds (about 4.5 kilograms)   *a*2 Or *oldest*   *b*7 Or *seed*
*c*10 That is, North-west Mesopotamia

lowered the jar to her hands and gave him a drink.

¹⁹After she had given him a drink, she said, "I'll draw water for your camels too, until they have finished drinking." ²⁰So she quickly emptied her jar into the trough, ran back to the well to draw more water, and drew enough for all his camels. ²¹Without saying a word, the man watched her closely to learn whether or not the LORD had made his journey successful.

²²When the camels had finished drinking, the man took out a gold nose ring weighing a beka*ᵈ* and two gold bracelets weighing ten shekels.*ᵉ* ²³Then he asked, "Whose daughter are you? Please tell me, is there room in your father's house for us to spend the night?"

²⁴She answered him, "I am the daughter of Bethuel, the son that Milcah bore to Nahor." ²⁵And she added, "We have plenty of straw and fodder, as well as room for you to spend the night."

²⁶Then the man bowed down and worshipped the LORD, ²⁷saying, "Praise be to the LORD, the God of my master Abraham, who has not abandoned his kindness and faithfulness to my master. As for me, the LORD has led me on the journey to the house of my master's relatives."

²⁸The girl ran and told her mother's household about these things. ²⁹Now Rebekah had a brother named Laban, and he hurried out to the man at the spring. ³⁰As soon as he had seen the nose ring, and the bracelets on his sister's arms, and had heard Rebekah tell what the man said to her, he went out to the man and found him standing by the camels near the spring. ³¹"Come, you who are blessed by the LORD," he said. "Why are you standing out here? I have prepared the house and a place for the camels."

³²So the man went to the house, and the camels were unloaded. Straw and fodder were brought for the camels, and water for him and his men to wash their feet. ³³Then food was set before him, but he said, "I will not eat until I have told you what I have to say."

"Then tell us," Laban said.

³⁴So he said, "I am Abraham's servant. ³⁵The LORD has blessed my master abundantly, and he has become wealthy. He has given him sheep and cattle, silver and gold, menservants and maidservants, and camels and donkeys. ³⁶My master's wife Sarah has borne him a son in her*ᶠ* old age, and he has given him everything he owns. ³⁷And my master made me swear an oath, and said, 'You must not get a wife for my son from the daughters of the Canaanites, in whose land I live, ³⁸but go to my father's family and to my own clan, and get a wife for my son.'

³⁹"Then I asked my master, 'What if the woman will not come back with me?'

⁴⁰"He replied, 'The LORD, before whom I have walked, will send his angel with you and make your journey a success, so that you can get a wife for my son from my own clan and

from my father's family. ⁴¹Then, when you go to my clan, you will be released from my oath even if they refuse to give her to you —you will be released from my oath.'

⁴²"When I came to the spring today, I said, 'O LORD, God of my master Abraham, if you will, please grant success to the journey on which I have come. ⁴³See, I am standing beside this spring; if a maiden comes out to draw water and I say to her, "Please let me drink a little water from your jar," ⁴⁴and if she says to me, "Drink, and I'll draw water for your camels too," let her be the one the LORD has chosen for my master's son.'

⁴⁵"Before I finished praying in my heart, Rebekah came out, with her jar on her shoulder. She went down to the spring and drew water, and I said to her, 'Please give me a drink.'

⁴⁶"She quickly lowered her jar from her shoulder and said, 'Drink, and I'll water your camels too.' So I drank, and she watered the camels also.

⁴⁷"I asked her, 'Whose daughter are you?'

"She said, 'The daughter of Bethuel son of Nahor, whom Milcah bore to him.'

"Then I put the ring in her nose and the bracelets on her arms, ⁴⁸and I bowed down and worshipped the LORD. I praised the LORD, the God of my master Abraham, who had led me on the right road to get the granddaughter of my master's brother for his son. ⁴⁹Now if you will show kindness and faithfulness to my master, tell me; and if not, tell me, so I may know which way to turn."

⁵⁰Laban and Bethuel answered, "This is from the LORD; we can say nothing to you one way or the other. ⁵¹Here is Rebekah; take her and go, and let her become the wife of your master's son, as the LORD has directed."

⁵²When Abraham's servant heard what they said, he bowed down to the ground before the LORD. ⁵³Then the servant brought out gold and silver jewellery and articles of clothing and gave them to Rebekah; he also gave costly gifts to her brother and to her mother. ⁵⁴Then he and the men who were with him ate and drank and spent the night there.

When they got up the next morning, he said, "Send me on my way to my master."

⁵⁵But her brother and her mother replied, "Let the girl remain with us ten days or so; then you*ᵍ* may go."

⁵⁶But he said to them, "Do not detain me, now that the LORD has granted success to my journey. Send me on my way so I may go to my master."

⁵⁷Then they said, "Let's call the girl and ask her about it." ⁵⁸So they called Rebekah and asked her, "Will you go with this man?"

"I will go," she said.

⁵⁹So they sent their sister Rebekah on her way, along with her nurse and Abraham's servant and his men. ⁶⁰And they blessed Rebekah and said to her,

ᵈ22 That is, about ⅕ ounce (about 6 grams)   *ᵉ22* That is, about 4 ounces (about 115 grams)
ᶠ36 Or *his*   *ᵍ55* Or *she*

"Our sister, may you increase
   to thousands upon thousands;
may your offspring possess
   the gates of their enemies."

61Then Rebekah and her maids got ready and mounted their camels and went back with the man. So the servant took Rebekah and left.

62Now Isaac had come from Beer Lahai Roi, for he was living in the Negev. 63He went out to the field one evening to meditate,h and as he looked up, he saw camels approaching. 64Rebekah also looked up and saw Isaac. She got down from her camel 65and asked the servant, "Who is that man in the field coming to meet us?"

"He is my master," the servant answered. So she took her veil and covered herself.

66Then the servant told Isaac all he had done. 67Isaac brought her into the tent of his mother Sarah, and he married Rebekah. So she became his wife, and he loved her; and Isaac was comforted after his mother's death.

The Death of Abraham

25 Abraham tooka another wife, whose name was Keturah. 2She bore him Zimran, Jokshan, Medan, Midian, Ishbak and Shuah. 3Jokshan was the father of Sheba and Dedan; the descendants of Dedan were the Asshurites, the Letushites and the Leummites. 4The sons of Midian were Ephah, Epher, Hanoch, Abida and Eldaah. All these were descendants of Keturah.

5Abraham left everything he owned to Isaac. 6But while he was still living, he gave gifts to the sons of his concubines and sent them away from his son Isaac to the land of the east.

7Altogether, Abraham lived a hundred and seventy-five years. 8Then Abraham breathed his last and died at a good old age, an old man and full of years; and he was gathered to his people. 9His sons Isaac and Ishmael buried him in the cave of Machpelah near Mamre, in the field of Ephron son of Zohar the Hittite, 10the field Abraham had bought from the Hittites.b There Abraham was buried with his wife Sarah. 11After Abraham's death, God blessed his son Isaac, who then lived near Beer Lahai Roi.

Ishmael's Sons

12This is the account of Abraham's son Ishmael, whom Sarah's maidservant, Hagar the Egyptian, bore to Abraham.

13These are the names of the sons of Ishmael, listed in the order of their birth: Nebaioth the firstborn of Ishmael, Kedar, Adbeel, Mibsam, 14Mishma, Dumah, Massa, 15Hadad, Tema, Jetur, Naphish and Kedemah. 16These were the sons of Ishmael, and these are the names of the twelve tribal rulers according to their settlements and camps.

17Altogether, Ishmael lived a hundred and thirty-seven years. He breathed his last and died, and he was gathered to his people. 18His descendants settled in the area from Havilah to Shur, near the border of Egypt, as you go towards Asshur. And they lived in hostility towardsc all their brothers.

Jacob and Esau

19This is the account of Abraham's son Isaac.

Abraham became the father of Isaac, 20and Isaac was forty years old when he married Rebekah daughter of Bethuel the Aramean from Paddan Aramd and sister of Laban the Aramean.

21Isaac prayed to the LORD on behalf of his wife, because she was barren. The LORD answered his prayer, and his wife Rebekah became pregnant. 22The babies jostled each other within her, and she said, "Why is this happening to me?" So she went to enquire of the LORD.

23The LORD said to her,

"Two nations are in your womb,
   and two peoples from within you will be
      separated;
one people will be stronger than the other,
   and the older will serve the younger."

24When the time came for her to give birth, there were twin boys in her womb. 25The first to come out was red, and his whole body was like a hairy garment; so they named him Esau.e 26After this, his brother came out, with his hand grasping Esau's heel; so he was named Jacob.f Isaac was sixty years old when Rebekah gave birth to them.

27The boys grew up, and Esau became a skilful hunter, a man of the open country, while Jacob was a quiet man, staying among the tents. 28Isaac, who had a taste for wild game, loved Esau, but Rebekah loved Jacob.

29Once when Jacob was cooking some stew, Esau came in from the open country, famished. 30He said to Jacob, "Quick, let me have some of that red stew! I'm famished!" (That is why he was also called Edom.g)

31Jacob replied, "First sell me your birthright."

32"Look, I am about to die," Esau said. "What good is the birthright to me?"

33But Jacob said, "Swear to me first." So he swore an oath to him, selling his birthright to Jacob.

34Then Jacob gave Esau some bread and some lentil stew. He ate and drank, and then got up and left.

So Esau despised his birthright.

Isaac and Abimelech

26 Now there was a famine in the land —besides the earlier famine of Abraham's time—and Isaac went to Abimelech king of the Philistines in Gerar. 2The LORD

---

h63 The meaning of the Hebrew for this word is uncertain.   a1 Or had taken
b10 Or the sons of Heth   c18 Or lived to the east of   d20 That is, North-west Mesopotamia
e25 Esau may mean hairy; he was also called Edom, which means red.
f26 Jacob means he grasps the heel (figuratively, he deceives).   g30 Edom means red.

appeared to Isaac and said, "Do not go down to Egypt; live in the land where I tell you to live. [3]Stay in this land for a while, and I will be with you and will bless you. For to you and your descendants I will give all these lands and will confirm the oath I swore to your father Abraham. [4]I will make your descendants as numerous as the stars in the sky and will give them all these lands, and through your offspring[a] all nations on earth will be blessed, [5]because Abraham obeyed me and kept my requirements, my commands, my decrees and my laws." [6]So Isaac stayed in Gerar.

[7]When the men of that place asked him about his wife, he said, "She is my sister," because he was afraid to say, "She is my wife." He thought, "The men of this place might kill me on account of Rebekah, because she is beautiful."

[8]When Isaac had been there a long time, Abimelech king of the Philistines looked down from a window and saw Isaac caressing his wife Rebekah. [9]So Abimelech summoned Isaac and said, "She is really your wife! Why did you say, 'She is my sister'?"

Isaac answered him, "Because I thought I might lose my life on account of her."

[10]Then Abimelech said, "What is this you have done to us? One of the men might well have slept with your wife, and you would have brought guilt upon us."

[11]So Abimelech gave orders to all the people: "Anyone who molests this man or his wife shall surely be put to death."

[12]Isaac planted crops in that land and the same year reaped a hundredfold, because the LORD blessed him. [13]The man became rich, and his wealth continued to grow until he became very wealthy. [14]He had so many flocks and herds and servants that the Philistines envied him. [15]So all the wells that his father's servants had dug in the time of his father Abraham, the Philistines stopped up, filling them with earth.

[16]Then Abimelech said to Isaac, "Move away from us; you have become too powerful for us."

[17]So Isaac moved away from there and encamped in the Valley of Gerar and settled there. [18]Isaac reopened the wells that had been dug in the time of his father Abraham, which the Philistines had stopped up after Abraham died, and he gave them the same names his father had given them.

[19]Isaac's servants dug in the valley and discovered a well of fresh water there. [20]But the herdsmen of Gerar quarrelled with Isaac's herdsmen and said, "The water is ours!" So he named the well Esek,[b] because they disputed with him. [21]Then they dug another well, but they quarrelled over that one also; so he named it Sitnah.[c] [22]He moved on from there and dug another well, and no-one quarrelled over it. He named it Rehoboth,[d] saying, "Now the LORD has given us room and we will flourish in the land."

[23]From there he went up to Beersheba.

[24]That night the LORD appeared to him and said, "I am the God of your father Abraham. Do not be afraid, for I am with you; I will bless you and will increase the number of your descendants for the sake of my servant Abraham."

[25]Isaac built an altar there and called on the name of the LORD. There he pitched his tent, and there his servants dug a well.

[26]Meanwhile, Abimelech had come to him from Gerar, with Ahuzzath his personal adviser and Phicol the commander of his forces. [27]Isaac asked them, "Why have you come to me, since you were hostile to me and sent me away?"

[28]They answered, "We saw clearly that the LORD was with you; so we said, 'There ought to be a sworn agreement between us' —between us and you. Let us make a treaty with you [29]that you will do us no harm, just as we did not molest you but always treated you well and sent you away in peace. And now you are blessed by the LORD."

[30]Isaac then made a feast for them, and they ate and drank. [31]Early the next morning the men swore an oath to each other. Then Isaac sent them on their way, and they left him in peace.

[32]That day Isaac's servants came and told him about the well they had dug. They said, "We've found water!" [33]He called it Shibah,[e] and to this day the name of the town has been Beersheba.[f]

[34]When Esau was forty years old, he married Judith daughter of Beeri the Hittite, and also Basemath daughter of Elon the Hittite. [35]They were a source of grief to Isaac and Rebekah.

Jacob Gets Isaac's Blessing

27 When Isaac was old and his eyes were so weak that he could no longer see, he called for Esau his older son and said to him, "My son."

"Here I am," he answered.

[2]Isaac said, "I am now an old man and don't know the day of my death. [3]Now then, get your weapons—your quiver and bow —and go out to the open country to hunt some wild game for me. [4]Prepare me the kind of tasty food I like and bring it to me to eat, so that I may give you my blessing before I die."

[5]Now Rebekah was listening as Isaac spoke to his son Esau. When Esau left for the open country to hunt game and bring it back, [6]Rebekah said to her son Jacob, "Look, I overheard your father say to your brother Esau, [7]'Bring me some game and prepare me some tasty food to eat, so that I may give you my blessing in the presence of the LORD before I die.' [8]Now, my son, listen carefully and do what I tell you: [9]Go out to the flock and bring me two choice young goats, so that I can prepare some tasty food for your father, just the way he likes it. [10]Then take it to your father to eat, so that he may give you his blessing before he dies."

[11]Jacob said to Rebekah his mother, "But

---

[a]4 Or seed   [b]20 Esek means dispute.   [c]21 Sitnah means opposition.   [d]22 Rehoboth means room.
[e]33 Shibah can mean oath or seven.   [f]33 Beersheba can mean well of the oath or well of seven.

my brother Esau is a hairy man, and I'm a man with smooth skin. [12]What if my father touches me? I would appear to be tricking him and would bring down a curse on myself rather than a blessing."

[13]His mother said to him, "My son, let the curse fall on me. Just do what I say; go and get them for me."

[14]So he went and got them and brought them to his mother, and she prepared some tasty food, just the way his father liked it. [15]Then Rebekah took the best clothes of Esau her older son, which she had in the house, and put them on her younger son Jacob. [16]She also covered his hands and the smooth part of his neck with the goatskins. [17]Then she handed to her son Jacob the tasty food and the bread she had made.

[18]He went to his father and said, "My father."

"Yes, my son," he answered. "Who is it?"

[19]Jacob said to his father, "I am Esau your firstborn. I have done as you told me. Please sit up and eat some of my game so that you may give me your blessing."

[20]Isaac asked his son, "How did you find it so quickly, my son?"

"The LORD your God gave me success," he replied.

[21]Then Isaac said to Jacob, "Come near so I can touch you, my son, to know whether you really are my son Esau or not."

[22]Jacob went close to his father Isaac, who touched him and said, "The voice is the voice of Jacob, but the hands are the hands of Esau." [23]He did not recognise him, for his hands were hairy like those of his brother Esau; so he blessed him. [24]"Are you really my son Esau?" he asked.

"I am," he replied.

[25]Then he said, "My son, bring me some of your game to eat, so that I may give you my blessing."

Jacob brought it to him and he ate; and he brought some wine and he drank. [26]Then his father Isaac said to him, "Come here, my son, and kiss me."

[27]So he went to him and kissed him. When Isaac caught the smell of his clothes, he blessed him and said,

"Ah, the smell of my son
    is like the smell of a field
    that the LORD has blessed.
[28]May God give you of heaven's dew
    and of earth's richness—
    an abundance of grain and new wine.
[29]May nations serve you
    and peoples bow down to you.
Be lord over your brothers,
    and may the sons of your mother bow
        down to you.
May those who curse you be cursed
    and those who bless you be blessed."

[30]After Isaac finished blessing him and Jacob had scarcely left his father's presence, his brother Esau came in from hunting. [31]He too prepared some tasty food and brought it to his father. Then he said to him, "My father, sit up and eat some of my game, so that you may give me your blessing."

[32]His father Isaac asked him, "Who are you?"

"I am your son," he answered, "your firstborn, Esau."

[33]Isaac trembled violently and said, "Who was it, then, that hunted game and brought it to me? I ate it just before you came and I blessed him—and indeed he will be blessed!"

[34]When Esau heard his father's words, he burst out with a loud and bitter cry and said to his father, "Bless me—me too, my father!"

[35]But he said, "Your brother came deceitfully and took your blessing."

[36]Esau said, "Isn't he rightly named Jacob?[a] He has deceived me these two times: He took my birthright, and now he's taken my blessing!" Then he asked, "Haven't you reserved any blessing for me?"

[37]Isaac answered Esau, "I have made him lord over you and have made all his relatives his servants, and I have sustained him with grain and new wine. So what can I possibly do for you, my son?"

[38]Esau said to his father, "Do you have only one blessing, my father? Bless me too, my father!" Then Esau wept aloud.

[39]His father Isaac answered him,

"Your dwelling will be
    away from the earth's richness,
    away from the dew of heaven above.
[40]You will live by the sword
    and you will serve your brother.
But when you grow restless,
    you will throw his yoke
    from off your neck."

Jacob Flees to Laban

[41]Esau held a grudge against Jacob because of the blessing his father had given him. He said to himself, "The days of mourning for my father are near; then I will kill my brother Jacob."

[42]When Rebekah was told what her older son Esau had said, she sent for her younger son Jacob and said to him, "Your brother Esau is consoling himself with the thought of killing you. [43]Now then, my son, do what I say: Flee at once to my brother Laban in Haran. [44]Stay with him for a while until your brother's fury subsides. [45]When your brother is no longer angry with you and forgets what you did to him, I'll send word for you to come back from there. Why should I lose both of you in one day?"

[46]Then Rebekah said to Isaac, "I'm disgusted with living because of these Hittite women. If Jacob takes a wife from among the women of this land, from Hittite women like these, my life will not be worth living."

28 So Isaac called for Jacob and blessed[a] him and commanded him: "Do not marry a Canaanite woman. [2]Go at once to

---

[a]36 *Jacob* means *he grasps the heel* (figuratively, *he deceives*).   [a]1 Or *greeted*

Paddan Aram,[b] to the house of your mother's father Bethuel. Take a wife for yourself there, from among the daughters of Laban, your mother's brother. [3]May God Almighty[c] bless you and make you fruitful and increase your numbers until you become a community of peoples. [4]May he give you and your descendants the blessing given to Abraham, so that you may take possession of the land where you now live as an alien, the land God gave to Abraham.'' [5]Then Isaac sent Jacob on his way, and he went to Paddan Aram, to Laban son of Bethuel the Aramean, the brother of Rebekah, who was the mother of Jacob and Esau.

[6]Now Esau learned that Isaac had blessed Jacob and had sent him to Paddan Aram to take a wife from there, and that when he blessed him he commanded him, ''Do not marry a Canaanite woman,'' [7]and that Jacob had obeyed his father and mother and had gone to Paddan Aram. [8]Esau then realised how displeasing the Canaanite women were to his father Isaac; [9]so he went to Ishmael and married Mahalath, the sister of Nebaioth and daughter of Ishmael son of Abraham, in addition to the wives he already had.

Jacob's Dream at Bethel

[10]Jacob left Beersheba and set out for Haran. [11]When he reached a certain place, he stopped for the night because the sun had set. Taking one of the stones there, he put it under his head and lay down to sleep. [12]He had a dream in which he saw a stairway[d] resting on the earth, with its top reaching to heaven, and the angels of God were ascending and descending on it. [13]There above it[e] stood the LORD, and he said: ''I am the LORD, the God of your father Abraham and the God of Isaac. I will give you and your descendants the land on which you are lying. [14]Your descendants will be like the dust of the earth, and you will spread out to the west and to the east, to the north and to the south. All peoples on earth will be blessed through you and your offspring. [15]I am with you and will watch over you wherever you go, and I will bring you back to this land. I will not leave you until I have done what I have promised you.''

[16]When Jacob awoke from his sleep, he thought, ''Surely the LORD is in this place, and I was not aware of it.'' [17]He was afraid and said, ''How awesome is this place! This is none other than the house of God; this is the gate of heaven.''

[18]Early the next morning Jacob took the stone he had placed under his head and set it up as a pillar and poured oil on top of it. [19]He called that place Bethel,[f] though the city used to be called Luz. [20]Then Jacob made a vow, saying, ''If God will be with me and will watch over me on this journey I am taking and will give me food to eat and clothes to wear [21]so that I return safely to my father's house, then the LORD[g]

will be my God [22]and[h] this stone that I have set up as a pillar will be God's house, and of all that you give me I will give you a tenth.''

Jacob Arrives in Paddan Aram

29 Then Jacob continued on his journey and came to the land of the eastern peoples. [2]There he saw a well in the field, with three flocks of sheep lying near it because the flocks were watered from that well. The stone over the mouth of the well was large. [3]When all the flocks were gathered there, the shepherds would roll the stone away from the well's mouth and water the sheep. Then they would return the stone to its place over the mouth of the well.

[4]Jacob asked the shepherds, ''My brothers, where are you from?''

''We're from Haran,'' they replied.

[5]He said to them, ''Do you know Laban, Nahor's grandson?''

''Yes, we know him,'' they answered.

[6]Then Jacob asked them, ''Is he well?''

''Yes, he is,'' they said, ''and here comes his daughter Rachel with the sheep.''

[7]''Look,'' he said, ''the sun is still high; it is not time for the flocks to be gathered. Water the sheep and take them back to pasture.''

[8]''We can't,'' they replied, ''until all the flocks are gathered and the stone has been rolled away from the mouth of the well. Then we will water the sheep.''

[9]While he was still talking with them, Rachel came with her father's sheep, for she was a shepherdess. [10]When Jacob saw Rachel daughter of Laban, his mother's brother, and Laban's sheep, he went over and rolled the stone away from the mouth of the well and watered his uncle's sheep. [11]Then Jacob kissed Rachel and began to weep aloud. [12]He had told Rachel that he was a relative of her father and a son of Rebekah. So she ran and told her father.

[13]As soon as Laban heard the news about Jacob, his sister's son, he hurried to meet him. He embraced him and kissed him and brought him to his home, and there Jacob told him all these things. [14]Then Laban said to him, ''You are my own flesh and blood.''

Jacob Marries Leah and Rachel

After Jacob had stayed with him for a whole month, [15]Laban said to him, ''Just because you are a relative of mine, should you work for me for nothing? Tell me what your wages should be.''

[16]Now Laban had two daughters; the name of the older was Leah, and the name of the younger was Rachel. [17]Leah had weak[a] eyes, but Rachel was lovely in form, and beautiful. [18]Jacob was in love with Rachel and said, ''I'll work for you seven years in return for your younger daughter Rachel.''

[19]Laban said, ''It's better that I give her to you than to some other man. Stay here with me.'' [20]So Jacob served seven years to get

[b]2 That is, North-west Mesopotamia; also in verses 5, 6 and 7   [c]3 Hebrew El-Shaddai
[d]12 Or ladder   [e]13 Or There beside him   [f]19 Bethel means house of God.
[g]20,21 Or Since God . . . father's house, the LORD   [h]21,22 Or house, and the LORD will be my God, [22] then
[a]17 Or delicate

GENESIS 28:16–22
'He was afraid and said, "How awesome is this place! This is none other than the house of God; this is the gate of heaven" ' (v. 17).

THE PLACE WHERE Jacob had slept was no less desolate, his pillow was no less hard than when he laid himself down to rest, but suddenly it had become the house of God, the gateway to heaven itself. A sense of the presence of God always achieves that kind of transformation. The fear which Jacob experienced at Bethel turned to awe, that sense of the mysterious which is a compound of apprehension, attraction to all that is holy and profound reverence.

There are all too infrequent moments in a Christian's life when God is so strongly apprehended by the senses that one feels as though to reach out would be to touch him. Those rare moments are unforgettable and are enormously treasured. Not that our feelings are the true barometer of our spiritual life: we can feel less than good, but if forgiveness is real and we are trusting the Lord, then our spiritual life is sound. We live by faith, not feelings. But occasionally, God grants us a sense of being overwhelmed by him and those moments are precious indeed.

God does not bypass desolate places. He makes himself known there also and that place becomes the house of God. An unintended symbol of this truth is observed by visitors to the Holy Land. A church stands over the rock at which Christ prayed in Gethsemane, another stands over the assumed place of Calvary itself.

God comes to us in the desolate places of loneliness, illness, bereavement, rejection, hardship and despair. The occasion should be valued and marked in some way: it will be a constant encouragement. Jacob marked it with a pillar of stone.

'I am with you and will watch over you wherever you go.' Thank you, Lord. Amen.

GENESIS 32:22–32

'Then the man said, "Let me go, for it is daybreak." But Jacob replied, "I will not let you go unless you bless me" ' (v. 26).

'HE WHO WOULD HAVE POWER with men must first have power with God,' is a self-evident truth and Jacob underwent a mighty experience to qualify as a man of power. Bethel was a great occasion and this event could not have happened without it, but Peniel far exceeded Bethel in significance.

God used the occasion to change Jacob's nature and, for good measure, he changed his name to Israel. The given meaning of the new name is 'he struggles with God'. In keeping with a long-established custom, Jacob, now Israel, gave the place the name of Peniel, which means 'face of God', because 'I saw God face to face, and yet my life was spared.'

Persistent, urgent prayer is defined as the prayer of importunity. Jesus told the story of the man who sought bread from his friend at midnight. The friend was reluctant to rise from his bed at that hour, but the caller persisted and our Lord said, 'Though he will not get up and give him the bread because he is his friend, yet because of the man's persistence he will get up and give him as much as he needs.' Jesus went on, 'Ask and it will be given to you; seek and you will find; knock and the door will be opened to you.' God is not reluctant to give, but there are times when our basic desires and faith need to be deepened and proved. Jacob's example has been followed by many.

There were no losers in this struggle. Jacob won because he received the blessing he sought. God won because he changed Jacob's nature. Jacob's example is of value to us today.

'For everyone who asks receives; he who seeks finds; and to him who knocks, the door will be opened.'

Rachel, but they seemed like only a few days to him because of his love for her.

²¹Then Jacob said to Laban, "Give me my wife. My time is completed, and I want to lie with her."

²²So Laban brought together all the people of the place and gave a feast. ²³But when evening came, he took his daughter Leah and gave her to Jacob, and Jacob lay with her. ²⁴And Laban gave his servant girl Zilpah to his daughter as her maidservant.

²⁵When morning came, there was Leah! So Jacob said to Laban, "What is this you have done to me? I served you for Rachel, didn't I? Why have you deceived me?"

²⁶Laban replied, "It is not our custom here to give the younger daughter in marriage before the older one. ²⁷Finish this daughter's bridal week; then we will give you the younger one also, in return for another seven years of work."

²⁸And Jacob did so. He finished the week with Leah, and then Laban gave him his daughter Rachel to be his wife. ²⁹Laban gave his servant girl Bilhah to his daughter Rachel as her maidservant. ³⁰Jacob lay with Rachel also, and he loved Rachel more than Leah. And he worked for Laban another seven years.

Jacob's Children

³¹When the Lord saw that Leah was not loved, he opened her womb, but Rachel was barren. ³²Leah became pregnant and gave birth to a son. She named him Reuben,ᵇ for she said, "It is because the Lord has seen my misery. Surely my husband will love me now."

³³She conceived again, and when she gave birth to a son she said, "Because the Lord heard that I am not loved, he gave me this one too." So she named him Simeon.ᶜ

³⁴Again she conceived, and when she gave birth to a son she said, "Now at last my husband will become attached to me, because I have borne him three sons." So he was named Levi.ᵈ

³⁵She conceived again, and when she gave birth to a son she said, "This time I will praise the Lord." So she named him Judah.ᵉ Then she stopped having children.

30 When Rachel saw that she was not bearing Jacob any children, she became jealous of her sister. So she said to Jacob, "Give me children, or I'll die!"

²Jacob became angry with her and said, "Am I in the place of God, who has kept you from having children?"

³Then she said, "Here is Bilhah, my maidservant. Sleep with her so that she can bear children for me and that through her I too can build a family."

⁴So she gave him her servant Bilhah as a wife. Jacob slept with her, ⁵and she became pregnant and bore him a son. ⁶Then Rachel said, "God has vindicated me; he has listened to my plea and given me a son." Because of this she named him Dan.ᵃ

⁷Rachel's servant Bilhah conceived again and bore Jacob a second son. ⁸Then Rachel said, "I have had a great struggle with my sister, and I have won." So she named him Naphtali.ᵇ

⁹When Leah saw that she had stopped having children, she took her maidservant Zilpah and gave her to Jacob as a wife. ¹⁰Leah's servant Zilpah bore Jacob a son. ¹¹Then Leah said, "What good fortune!"ᶜ So she named him Gad.ᵈ

¹²Leah's servant Zilpah bore Jacob a second son. ¹³Then Leah said, "How happy I am! The women will call me happy." So she named him Asher.ᵉ

¹⁴During wheat harvest, Reuben went out into the fields and found some mandrake plants, which he brought to his mother Leah. Rachel said to Leah, "Please give me some of your son's mandrakes."

¹⁵But she said to her, "Wasn't it enough that you took away my husband? Will you take my son's mandrakes too?"

"Very well," Rachel said, "he can sleep with you tonight in return for your son's mandrakes."

¹⁶So when Jacob came in from the fields that evening, Leah went out to meet him. "You must sleep with me," she said. "I have hired you with my son's mandrakes." So he slept with her that night.

¹⁷God listened to Leah, and she became pregnant and bore Jacob a fifth son. ¹⁸Then Leah said, "God has rewarded me for giving my maidservant to my husband." So she named him Issachar.ᶠ

¹⁹Leah conceived again and bore Jacob a sixth son. ²⁰Then Leah said, "God has presented me with a precious gift. This time my husband will treat me with honour, because I have borne him six sons." So she named him Zebulun.ᵍ

²¹Some time later she gave birth to a daughter and named her Dinah.

²²Then God remembered Rachel; he listened to her and opened her womb. ²³She became pregnant and gave birth to a son and said, "God has taken away my disgrace." ²⁴She named him Joseph,ʰ and said, "May the Lord add to me another son."

Jacob's Flocks Increase

²⁵After Rachel gave birth to Joseph, Jacob said to Laban, "Send me on my way so that I can go back to my own homeland. ²⁶Give me my wives and children, for whom I have served you, and I will be on my way. You know how much work I've done for you."

ᵇ32 *Reuben* sounds like the Hebrew for *he has seen my misery*; the name means *see, a son.*
ᶜ33 *Simeon* probably means *one who hears.*
ᵈ34 *Levi* sounds like and may be derived from the Hebrew for *attached.*
ᵉ35 *Judah* sounds like and may be derived from the Hebrew for *praise.*
ᵃ6 *Dan* here means *he has vindicated.*   ᵇ8 *Naphtali* means *my struggle.*   ᶜ11 Or *"A troop is coming!"*
ᵈ11 *Gad* can mean *good fortune* or *a troop.*   ᵉ13 *Asher* means *happy.*
ᶠ18 *Issachar* sounds like the Hebrew for *reward.*   ᵍ20 *Zebulun* probably means *honour.*
ʰ24 *Joseph* means *may he add.*

27But Laban said to him, "If I have found favour in your eyes, please stay. I have learned by divination that*i* the Lord has blessed me because of you." 28He added, "Name your wages, and I will pay them."

29Jacob said to him, "You know how I have worked for you and how your livestock has fared under my care. 30The little you had before I came has increased greatly, and the Lord has blessed you wherever I have been. But now, when may I do something for my own household?"

31"What shall I give you?" he asked.

"Don't give me anything," Jacob replied. "But if you will do this one thing for me, I will go on tending your flocks and watching over them: 32Let me go through all your flocks today and remove from them every speckled or spotted sheep, every dark-coloured lamb and every spotted or speckled goat. They will be my wages. 33And my honesty will testify for me in the future, whenever you check on the wages you have paid me. Any goat in my possession that is not speckled or spotted, or any lamb that is not dark-coloured, will be considered stolen."

34"Agreed," said Laban. "Let it be as you have said." 35That same day he removed all the male goats that were streaked or spotted, and all the speckled or spotted female goats (all that had white on them) and all the dark-coloured lambs, and he placed them in the care of his sons. 36Then he put a three-day journey between himself and Jacob, while Jacob continued to tend the rest of Laban's flocks.

37Jacob, however, took fresh-cut branches from poplar, almond and plane trees and made white stripes on them by peeling the bark and exposing the white inner wood of the branches. 38Then he placed the peeled branches in all the watering troughs, so that they would be directly in front of the flocks when they came to drink. When the flocks were in heat and came to drink, 39they mated in front of the branches. And they bore young that were streaked or speckled or spotted. 40Jacob set apart the young of the flock by themselves, but made the rest face the streaked and dark-coloured animals that belonged to Laban. Thus he made separate flocks for himself and did not put them with Laban's animals. 41Whenever the stronger females were in heat, Jacob would place the branches in the troughs in front of the animals so that they would mate near the branches, 42but if the animals were weak, he would not place them there. So the weak animals went to Laban and the strong ones to Jacob. 43In this way the man grew exceedingly prosperous and came to own large flocks, and maidservants and menservants, and camels and donkeys.

Jacob Flees From Laban

31 Jacob heard that Laban's sons were saying, "Jacob has taken everything our father owned and has gained all this wealth from what belonged to our father."

2And Jacob noticed that Laban's attitude towards him was not what it had been.

3Then the Lord said to Jacob, "Go back to the land of your fathers and to your relatives, and I will be with you."

4So Jacob sent word to Rachel and Leah to come out to the fields where his flocks were. 5He said to them, "I see that your father's attitude towards me is not what it was before, but the God of my father has been with me. 6You know that I've worked for your father with all my strength, 7yet your father has cheated me by changing my wages ten times. However, God has not allowed him to harm me. 8If he said, 'The speckled ones will be your wages,' then all the flocks gave birth to speckled young; and if he said, 'The streaked ones will be your wages,' then all the flocks bore streaked young. 9So God has taken away your father's livestock and has given them to me.

10"In the breeding season I once had a dream in which I looked up and saw that the male goats mating with the flock were streaked, speckled or spotted. 11The angel of God said to me in the dream, 'Jacob.' I answered, 'Here I am.' 12And he said, 'Look up and see that all the male goats mating with the flock are streaked, speckled or spotted, for I have seen all that Laban has been doing to you. 13I am the God of Bethel, where you anointed a pillar and where you made a vow to me. Now leave this land at once and go back to your native land.' "

14Then Rachel and Leah replied, "Do we still have any share in the inheritance of our father's estate? 15Does he not regard us as foreigners? Not only has he sold us, but he has used up what was paid for us. 16Surely all the wealth that God took away from our father belongs to us and our children. So do whatever God has told you."

17Then Jacob put his children and his wives on camels, 18and he drove all his livestock ahead of him, along with all the goods he had accumulated in Paddan Aram,*a* to go to his father Isaac in the land of Canaan.

19When Laban had gone to shear his sheep, Rachel stole her father's household gods. 20Moreover, Jacob deceived Laban the Aramean by not telling him he was running away. 21So he fled with all he had, and crossing the River,*b* he headed for the hill country of Gilead.

Laban Pursues Jacob

22On the third day Laban was told that Jacob had fled. 23Taking his relatives with him, he pursued Jacob for seven days and caught up with him in the hill country of Gilead. 24Then God came to Laban the Aramean in a dream at night and said to him, "Be careful not to say anything to Jacob, either good or bad."

25Jacob had pitched his tent in the hill country of Gilead when Laban overtook him, and Laban and his relatives camped there too. 26Then Laban said to Jacob, "What have you done? You've deceived me, and you've

---

*i*27 Or possibly *have become rich and*   *a*18 That is, North-west Mesopotamia   *b*21 That is, the Euphrates carried off my daughters like captives in war. ²⁷Why did you run off secretly and deceive me? Why didn't you tell me, so that I could send you away with joy and singing to the music of tambourines and harps? ²⁸You didn't even let me kiss my grandchildren and my daughters good-bye. You have done a foolish thing. ²⁹I have the power to harm you; but last night the God of your father said to me, 'Be careful not to say anything to Jacob, either good or bad.' ³⁰Now you have gone off because you longed to return to your father's house. But why did you steal my gods?"

³¹Jacob answered Laban, "I was afraid, because I thought you would take your daughters away from me by force. ³²But if you find anyone who has your gods, he shall not live. In the presence of our relatives, see for yourself whether there is anything of yours here with me; and if so, take it." Now Jacob did not know that Rachel had stolen the gods.

³³So Laban went into Jacob's tent and into Leah's tent and into the tent of the two maidservants, but he found nothing. After he came out of Leah's tent, he entered Rachel's tent. ³⁴Now Rachel had taken the household gods and put them inside her camel's saddle and was sitting on them. Laban searched through everything in the tent but found nothing.

³⁵Rachel said to her father, "Don't be angry, my lord, that I cannot stand up in your presence; I'm having my period." So he searched but could not find the household gods.

³⁶Jacob was angry and took Laban to task. "What is my crime?" he asked Laban. "What sin have I committed that you hunt me down? ³⁷Now that you have searched through all my goods, what have you found that belongs to your household? Put it here in front of your relatives and mine, and let them judge between the two of us.

³⁸"I have been with you for twenty years now. Your sheep and goats have not miscarried, nor have I eaten rams from your flocks. ³⁹I did not bring you animals torn by wild beasts; I bore the loss myself. And you demanded payment from me for whatever was stolen by day or night. ⁴⁰This was my situation: The heat consumed me in the daytime and the cold at night, and sleep fled from my eyes. ⁴¹It was like this for the twenty years I was in your household. I worked for you fourteen years for your two daughters and six years for your flocks, and you changed my wages ten times. ⁴²If the God of my father, the God of Abraham and the Fear of Isaac, had not been with me, you would surely have sent me away empty-handed. But God has seen my hardship and the toil of my hands, and last night he rebuked you."

⁴³Laban answered Jacob, "The women are my daughters, the children are my children, and the flocks are my flocks. All you see is mine. Yet what can I do today about these daughters of mine, or about the children they have borne? ⁴⁴Come now, let's make a covenant, you and I, and let it serve as a witness between us."

⁴⁵So Jacob took a stone and set it up as a pillar. ⁴⁶He said to his relatives, "Gather some stones." So they took stones and piled them in a heap, and they ate there by the heap. ⁴⁷Laban called it Jegar Sahadutha,ᶜ and Jacob called it Galeed.ᵈ

⁴⁸Laban said, "This heap is a witness between you and me today." That is why it was called Galeed. ⁴⁹It was also called Mizpah,ᵉ because he said, "May the LORD keep watch between you and me when we are away from each other. ⁵⁰If you ill-treat my daughters or if you take any wives besides my daughters, even though no-one is with us, remember that God is a witness between you and me."

⁵¹Laban also said to Jacob, "Here is this heap, and here is this pillar I have set up between you and me. ⁵²This heap is a witness, and this pillar is a witness, that I will not go past this heap to your side to harm you and that you will not go past this heap and pillar to my side to harm me. ⁵³May the God of Abraham and the God of Nahor, the God of their father, judge between us."

So Jacob took an oath in the name of the Fear of his father Isaac. ⁵⁴He offered a sacrifice there in the hill country and invited his relatives to a meal. After they had eaten, they spent the night there.

⁵⁵Early the next morning Laban kissed his grandchildren and his daughters and blessed them. Then he left and returned home.

Jacob Prepares to Meet Esau

32 Jacob also went on his way, and the angels of God met him. ²When Jacob saw them, he said, "This is the camp of God!" So he named that place Mahanaim.ᵃ

³Jacob sent messengers ahead of him to his brother Esau in the land of Seir, the country of Edom. ⁴He instructed them: "This is what you are to say to my master Esau: 'Your servant Jacob says, I have been staying with Laban and have remained there till now. ⁵I have cattle and donkeys, sheep and goats, menservants and maidservants. Now I am sending this message to my lord, that I may find favour in your eyes.'"

⁶When the messengers returned to Jacob, they said, "We went to your brother Esau, and now he is coming to meet you, and four hundred men are with him."

⁷In great fear and distress Jacob divided the people who were with him into two groups,ᵇ and the flocks and herds and camels as well. ⁸He thought, "If Esau comes and attacks one group,ᶜ the groupᶜ that is left may escape."

⁹Then Jacob prayed, "O God of my father Abraham, God of my father Isaac, O LORD, who said to me, 'Go back to your country and your relatives, and I will make you prosper,'

ᶜ47 The Aramaic *Jegar Sahadutha* means *witness heap.*   ᵈ47 The Hebrew *Galeed* means *witness heap.*
ᵉ49 *Mizpah* means *watchtower.*   ᵃ2 *Mahanaim* means *two camps.*   ᵇ7 Or *camps*; also in verse 10
ᶜ8 Or *camp*

10I am unworthy of all the kindness and faithfulness you have shown your servant. I had only my staff when I crossed this Jordan, but now I have become two groups. 11Save me, I pray, from the hand of my brother Esau, for I am afraid he will come and attack me, and also the mothers with their children. 12But you have said, 'I will surely make you prosper and will make your descendants like the sand of the sea, which cannot be counted.'"

13He spent the night there, and from what he had with him he selected a gift for his brother Esau: 14two hundred female goats and twenty male goats, two hundred ewes and twenty rams, 15thirty female camels with their young, forty cows and ten bulls, and twenty female donkeys and ten male donkeys. 16He put them in the care of his servants, each herd by itself, and said to his servants, "Go ahead of me, and keep some space between the herds."

17He instructed the one in the lead: "When my brother Esau meets you and asks, 'To whom do you belong, and where are you going, and who owns all these animals in front of you?' 18then you are to say, 'They belong to your servant Jacob. They are a gift sent to my lord Esau, and he is coming behind us.'"

19He also instructed the second, the third and all the others who followed the herds: "You are to say the same thing to Esau when you meet him. 20And be sure to say, 'Your servant Jacob is coming behind us.'" For he thought, "I will pacify him with these gifts I am sending on ahead; later, when I see him, perhaps he will receive me." 21So Jacob's gifts went on ahead of him, but he himself spent the night in the camp.

Jacob Wrestles with God

22That night Jacob got up and took his two wives, his two maidservants and his eleven sons and crossed the ford of the Jabbok. 23After he had sent them across the stream, he sent over all his possessions. 24So Jacob was left alone, and a man wrestled with him till daybreak. 25When the man saw that he could not overpower him, he touched the socket of Jacob's hip so that his hip was wrenched as he wrestled with the man. 26Then the man said, "Let me go, for it is daybreak."

But Jacob replied, "I will not let you go unless you bless me."

27The man asked him, "What is your name?"

"Jacob," he answered.

28Then the man said, "Your name will no longer be Jacob, but Israel,d because you have struggled with God and with men and have overcome."

29Jacob said, "Please tell me your name."

But he replied, "Why do you ask my name?" Then he blessed him there.

30So Jacob called the place Peniel,e saying,

"It is because I saw God face to face, and yet my life was spared."

31The sun rose above him as he passed Peniel,f and he was limping because of his hip. 32Therefore to this day the Israelites do not eat the tendon attached to the socket of the hip, because the socket of Jacob's hip was touched near the tendon.

Jacob Meets Esau

33 Jacob looked up and there was Esau, coming with his four hundred men; so he divided the children among Leah, Rachel and the two maidservants. 2He put the maidservants and their children in front, Leah and her children next, and Rachel and Joseph in the rear. 3He himself went on ahead and bowed down to the ground seven times as he approached his brother.

4But Esau ran to meet Jacob and embraced him; he threw his arms around his neck and kissed him. And they wept. 5Then Esau looked up and saw the women and children. "Who are these with you?" he asked.

Jacob answered, "They are the children God has graciously given your servant."

6Then the maidservants and their children approached and bowed down. 7Next, Leah and her children came and bowed down. Last of all came Joseph and Rachel, and they too bowed down.

8Esau asked, "What do you mean by all these droves I met?"

"To find favour in your eyes, my lord," he said.

9But Esau said, "I already have plenty, my brother. Keep what you have for yourself."

10"No, please!" said Jacob. "If I have found favour in your eyes, accept this gift from me. For to see your face is like seeing the face of God, now that you have received me favourably. 11Please accept the present that was brought to you, for God has been gracious to me and I have all I need." And because Jacob insisted, Esau accepted it.

12Then Esau said, "Let us be on our way; I'll accompany you."

13But Jacob said to him, "My lord knows that the children are tender and that I must care for the ewes and cows that are nursing their young. If they are driven hard just one day, all the animals will die. 14So let my lord go on ahead of his servant, while I move along slowly at the pace of the droves before me and that of the children, until I come to my lord in Seir."

15Esau said, "Then let me leave some of my men with you."

"But why do that?" Jacob asked. "Just let me find favour in the eyes of my lord."

16So that day Esau started on his way back to Seir. 17Jacob, however, went to Succoth, where he built a place for himself and made shelters for his livestock. That is why the place is called Succoth.a

18After Jacob came from Paddan Aram,b he arrived safely at thec city of Shechem in

---

d28 Israel means he struggles with God.   e30 Peniel means face of God.
f31 Hebrew Penuel, a variant of Peniel   a17 Succoth means shelters.
b18 That is, North-west Mesopotamia   c18 Or arrived at Shalem, a

Canaan and camped within sight of the city. [19]For a hundred pieces of silver,[d] he bought from the sons of Hamor, the father of Shechem, the plot of ground where he pitched his tent. [20]There he set up an altar and called it El Elohe Israel.[e]

Dinah and the Shechemites

34 Now Dinah, the daughter Leah had borne to Jacob, went out to visit the women of the land. [2]When Shechem son of Hamor the Hivite, the ruler of that area, saw her, he took her and raped her. [3]His heart was drawn to Dinah daughter of Jacob, and he loved the girl and spoke tenderly to her. [4]And Shechem said to his father Hamor, "Get me this girl as my wife."

[5]When Jacob heard that his daughter Dinah had been defiled, his sons were in the fields with his livestock; so he kept quiet about it until they came home.

[6]Then Shechem's father Hamor went out to talk with Jacob. [7]Now Jacob's sons had come in from the fields as soon as they heard what had happened. They were filled with grief and fury, because Shechem had done a disgraceful thing in[a] Israel by lying with Jacob's daughter—a thing that should not be done.

[8]But Hamor said to them, "My son Shechem has his heart set on your daughter. Please give her to him as his wife. [9]Intermarry with us; give us your daughters and take our daughters for yourselves. [10]You can settle among us; the land is open to you. Live in it, trade[b] in it, and acquire property in it."

[11]Then Shechem said to Dinah's father and brothers, "Let me find favour in your eyes, and I will give you whatever you ask. [12]Make the price for the bride and the gift I am to bring as great as you like, and I'll pay whatever you ask me. Only give me the girl as my wife."

[13]Because their sister Dinah had been defiled, Jacob's sons replied deceitfully as they spoke to Shechem and his father Hamor. [14]They said to them, "We can't do such a thing; we can't give our sister to a man who is not circumcised. That would be a disgrace to us. [15]We will give our consent to you on one condition only: that you become like us by circumcising all your males. [16]Then we will give you our daughters and take your daughters for ourselves. We'll settle among you and become one people with you. [17]But if you will not agree to be circumcised, we'll take our sister[c] and go."

[18]Their proposal seemed good to Hamor and his son Shechem. [19]The young man, who was the most honoured of all his father's household, lost no time in doing what they said, because he was delighted with Jacob's daughter. [20]So Hamor and his son Shechem went to the gate of their city to speak to their fellow townsmen. [21]"These men are friendly towards us," they said. "Let them live in our

land and trade in it; the land has plenty of room for them. We can marry their daughters and they can marry ours. [22]But the men will consent to live with us as one people only on the condition that our males be circumcised, as they themselves are. [23]Won't their livestock, their property and all their other animals become ours? So let us give our consent to them, and they will settle among us."

[24]All the men who went out of the city gate agreed with Hamor and his son Shechem, and every male in the city was circumcised.

[25]Three days later, while all of them were still in pain, two of Jacob's sons, Simeon and Levi, Dinah's brothers, took their swords and attacked the unsuspecting city, killing every male. [26]They put Hamor and his son Shechem to the sword and took Dinah from Shechem's house and left. [27]The sons of Jacob came upon the dead bodies and looted the city where[d] their sister had been defiled. [28]They seized their flocks and herds and donkeys and everything else of theirs in the city and out in the fields. [29]They carried off all their wealth and all their women and children, taking as plunder everything in the houses.

[30]Then Jacob said to Simeon and Levi, "You have brought trouble on me by making me a stench to the Canaanites and Perizzites, the people living in this land. We are few in number, and if they join forces against me and attack me, I and my household will be destroyed."

[31]But they replied, "Should he have treated our sister like a prostitute?"

Jacob Returns to Bethel

35 Then God said to Jacob, "Go up to Bethel and settle there, and build an altar there to God, who appeared to you when you were fleeing from your brother Esau."

[2]So Jacob said to his household and to all who were with him, "Get rid of the foreign gods you have with you, and purify yourselves and change your clothes. [3]Then come, let us go up to Bethel, where I will build an altar to God, who answered me in the day of my distress and who has been with me wherever I have gone." [4]So they gave Jacob all the foreign gods they had and the rings in their ears, and Jacob buried them under the oak at Shechem. [5]Then they set out, and the terror of God fell upon the towns all around them so that no-one pursued them.

[6]Jacob and all the people with him came to Luz (that is, Bethel) in the land of Canaan. [7]There he built an altar, and he called the place El Bethel,[a] because it was there that God revealed himself to him when he was fleeing from his brother.

[8]Now Deborah, Rebekah's nurse, died and was buried under the oak below Bethel. So it was named Allon Bacuth.[b]

[9]After Jacob returned from Paddan Aram,[c]

---

[d]19 Hebrew *hundred kesitahs*; a kesitah was a unit of money of unknown weight and value.
[e]20 *El Elohe Israel* can mean *God, the God of Israel* or *mighty is the God of Israel.*   [a]7 Or *against*
[b]10 Or *move about freely*; also in verse 21   [c]17 Hebrew *daughter*   [d]27 Or *because*
[a]7 *El Bethel* means *God of Bethel.*   [b]8 *Allon Bacuth* means *oak of weeping.*
[c]9 That is, North-west Mesopotamia; also in verse 26

God appeared to him again and blessed him. [10]God said to him, "Your name is Jacob,[d] but you will no longer be called Jacob; your name will be Israel."[e] So he named him Israel.

[11]And God said to him, "I am God Almighty;[f] be fruitful and increase in number. A nation and a community of nations will come from you, and kings will come from your body. [12]The land I gave to Abraham and Isaac I also give to you, and I will give this land to your descendants after you." [13]Then God went up from him at the place where he had talked with him.

[14]Jacob set up a stone pillar at the place where God had talked with him, and he poured out a drink offering on it; he also poured oil on it. [15]Jacob called the place where God had talked with him Bethel.[g]

The Deaths of Rachel and Isaac

[16]Then they moved on from Bethel. While they were still some distance from Ephrath, Rachel began to give birth and had great difficulty. [17]And as she was having great difficulty in childbirth, the midwife said to her, "Don't be afraid, for you have another son." [18]As she breathed her last—for she was dying—she named her son Ben-Oni.[h] But his father named him Benjamin.[i]

[19]So Rachel died and was buried on the way to Ephrath (that is, Bethlehem). [20]Over her tomb Jacob set up a pillar, and to this day that pillar marks Rachel's tomb.

[21]Israel moved on again and pitched his tent beyond Migdal Eder. [22]While Israel was living in that region, Reuben went in and slept with his father's concubine Bilhah, and Israel heard of it.

Jacob had twelve sons:
[23]The sons of Leah:
Reuben the firstborn of Jacob,
Simeon, Levi, Judah, Issachar and Zebulun.
[24]The sons of Rachel:
Joseph and Benjamin.
[25]The sons of Rachel's maidservant Bilhah:
Dan and Naphtali.
[26]The sons of Leah's maidservant Zilpah:
Gad and Asher.
These were the sons of Jacob, who were born to him in Paddan Aram.

[27]Jacob came home to his father Isaac in Mamre, near Kiriath Arba (that is, Hebron), where Abraham and Isaac had stayed. [28]Isaac lived a hundred and eighty years. [29]Then he breathed his last and died and was gathered to his people, old and full of years. And his sons Esau and Jacob buried him.

Esau's Descendants

36 This is the account of Esau (that is, Edom).

[2]Esau took his wives from the women of Canaan: Adah daughter of Elon the Hittite, and Oholibamah daughter of Anah and granddaughter of Zibeon the Hivite— [3]also Basemath daughter of Ishmael and sister of Nebaioth.

[4]Adah bore Eliphaz to Esau, Basemath bore Reuel, [5]and Oholibamah bore Jeush, Jalam and Korah. These were the sons of Esau, who were born to him in Canaan.

[6]Esau took his wives and sons and daughters and all the members of his household, as well as his livestock and all his other animals and all the goods he had acquired in Canaan, and moved to a land some distance from his brother Jacob. [7]Their possessions were too great for them to remain together; the land where they were staying could not support them both because of their livestock. [8]So Esau (that is, Edom) settled in the hill country of Seir.

[9]This is the account of Esau the father of the Edomites in the hill country of Seir.

[10]These are the names of Esau's sons:
Eliphaz, the son of Esau's wife Adah, and Reuel, the son of Esau's wife Basemath.
[11]The sons of Eliphaz:
Teman, Omar, Zepho, Gatam and Kenaz.
[12]Esau's son Eliphaz also had a concubine named Timna, who bore him Amalek. These were grandsons of Esau's wife Adah,
[13]The sons of Reuel:
Nahath, Zerah, Shammah and Mizzah. These were grandsons of Esau's wife Basemath.
[14]The sons of Esau's wife Oholibamah daughter of Anah and granddaughter of Zibeon, whom she bore to Esau:
Jeush, Jalam and Korah.

[15]These were the chiefs among Esau's descendants:
The sons of Eliphaz the firstborn of Esau:
Chiefs Teman, Omar, Zepho, Kenaz, [16]Korah,[a] Gatam and Amalek. These were the chiefs descended from Eliphaz in Edom; they were grandsons of Adah.
[17]The sons of Esau's son Reuel:
Chiefs Nahath, Zerah, Shammah and Mizzah. These were the chiefs descended from Reuel in Edom; they were grandsons of Esau's wife Basemath.
[18]The sons of Esau's wife Oholibamah:
Chiefs Jeush, Jalam and Korah. These were the chiefs descended from Esau's wife Oholibamah daughter of Anah.
[19]These were the sons of Esau (that is, Edom), and these were their chiefs.

---

[d]10 *Jacob* means *he grasps the heel* (figuratively, *he deceives*).
[f]11 Hebrew *El-Shaddai*   [g]15 *Bethel* means *house of God*.
[i]18 *Benjamin* means *son of my right hand*.
[a]16 Masoretic Text; Samaritan Pentateuch (see also Gen. 36:11 and 1 Chron. 1:36) does not have *Korah*.
[e]10 *Israel* means *he struggles with God*.
[h]18 *Ben-Oni* means *son of my trouble*.

20These were the sons of Seir the Horite, who were living in the region:

Lotan, Shobal, Zibeon, Anah, 21Dishon, Ezer and Dishan. These sons of Seir in Edom were Horite chiefs.

22The sons of Lotan:

Hori and Homam.*b* Timna was Lotan's sister.

23The sons of Shobal:

Alvan, Manahath, Ebal, Shepho and Onam.

24The sons of Zibeon:

Aiah and Anah. This is the Anah who discovered the hot springs*c* in the desert while he was grazing the donkeys of his father Zibeon.

25The children of Anah:

Dishon and Oholibamah daughter of Anah.

26The sons of Dishon:*d*

Hemdan, Eshban, Ithran and Keran.

27The sons of Ezer:

Bilhan, Zaavan and Akan.

28The sons of Dishan:

Uz and Aran.

29These were the Horite chiefs:

Lotan, Shobal, Zibeon, Anah, 30Dishon, Ezer and Dishan. These were the Horite chiefs, according to their divisions, in the land of Seir.

The Rulers of Edom

31These were the kings who reigned in Edom before any Israelite king reigned:*e*

32Bela son of Beor became king of Edom. His city was named Dinhabah.

33When Bela died, Jobab son of Zerah from Bozrah succeeded him as king.

34When Jobab died, Husham from the land of the Temanites succeeded him as king.

35When Husham died, Hadad son of Bedad, who defeated Midian in the country of Moab, succeeded him as king. His city was named Avith.

36When Hadad died, Samlah from Masrekah succeeded him as king.

37When Samlah died, Shaul from Rehoboth on the river*f* succeeded him as king.

38When Shaul died, Baal-Hanan son of Acbor succeeded him as king.

39When Baal-Hanan son of Acbor died, Hadad*g* succeeded him as king. His city was named Pau, and his wife's name was Mehetabel daughter of Matred, the daughter of Me-Zahab.

40These were the chiefs descended from Esau, by name, according to their clans and regions:

Timna, Alvah, Jetheth, 41Oholibamah, Elah, Pinon, 42Kenaz,

Teman, Mibzar, 43Magdiel and Iram. These were the chiefs of Edom, according to their settlements in the land they occupied.

This was Esau the father of the Edomites.

Joseph's Dreams

37 Jacob lived in the land where his father had stayed, the land of Canaan.

2This is the account of Jacob.

Joseph, a young man of seventeen, was tending the flocks with his brothers, the sons of Bilhah and the sons of Zilpah, his father's wives, and he brought their father a bad report about them.

3Now Israel loved Joseph more than any of his other sons, because he had been born to him in his old age; and he made a richly ornamented*a* robe for him. 4When his brothers saw that their father loved him more than any of them, they hated him and could not speak a kind word to him.

5Joseph had a dream, and when he told it to his brothers, they hated him all the more. 6He said to them, "Listen to this dream I had: 7We were binding sheaves of corn out in the field when suddenly my sheaf rose and stood upright, while your sheaves gathered round mine and bowed down to it."

8His brothers said to him, "Do you intend to reign over us? Will you actually rule us?" And they hated him all the more because of his dream and what he had said.

9Then he had another dream, and he told it to his brothers. "Listen," he said, "I had another dream, and this time the sun and moon and eleven stars were bowing down to me."

10When he told his father as well as his brothers, his father rebuked him and said, "What is this dream you had? Will your mother and I and your brothers actually come and bow down to the ground before you?" 11His brothers were jealous of him, but his father kept the matter in mind.

Joseph Sold by His Brothers

12Now his brothers had gone to graze their father's flocks near Shechem, 13and Israel said to Joseph, "As you know, your brothers are grazing the flocks near Shechem. Come, I am going to send you to them."

"Very well," he replied.

14So he said to him, "Go and see if all is well with your brothers and with the flocks, and bring word back to me." Then he sent him off from the Valley of Hebron.

When Joseph arrived at Shechem, 15a man found him wandering around in the fields and asked him, "What are you looking for?"

16He replied, "I'm looking for my

---

b22 Hebrew *Hemam*, a variant of *Homam* (see 1 Chron. 1:39)
c24 Vulgate; Syriac *discovered water*; the meaning of the Hebrew for this word is uncertain.
d26 Hebrew *Dishan*, a variant of *Dishon*   *e31* Or *before an Israelite king reigned over them*
f37 Possibly the Euphrates
g39 Many manuscripts of the Masoretic Text, Samaritan Pentateuch and Syriac (see also 1 Chron. 1:50); most manuscripts of the Masoretic Text *Hadar*
a3 The meaning of the Hebrew for *richly ornamented* is uncertain; also in verses 23 and 32.

brothers. Can you tell me where they are grazing their flocks?''

17"They have moved on from here,'' the man answered. ''I heard them say, 'Let's go to Dothan.'''

So Joseph went after his brothers and found them near Dothan. 18But they saw him in the distance, and before he reached them, they plotted to kill him.

19"Here comes that dreamer!'' they said to each other. 20"Come now, let's kill him and throw him into one of these cisterns and say that a ferocious animal devoured him. Then we'll see what comes of his dreams.''

21When Reuben heard this, he tried to rescue him from their hands. ''Let's not take his life,'' he said. 22"Don't shed any blood. Throw him into this cistern here in the desert, but don't lay a hand on him.'' Reuben said this to rescue him from them and take him back to his father.

23So when Joseph came to his brothers, they stripped him of his robe—the richly ornamented robe he was wearing—24and they took him and threw him into the cistern. Now the cistern was empty; there was no water in it.

25As they sat down to eat their meal, they looked up and saw a caravan of Ishmaelites coming from Gilead. Their camels were loaded with spices, balm and myrrh, and they were on their way to take them down to Egypt.

26Judah said to his brothers, ''What will we gain if we kill our brother and cover up his blood? 27Come, let's sell him to the Ishmaelites and not lay our hands on him; after all, he is our brother, our own flesh and blood.'' His brothers agreed.

28So when the Midianite merchants came by, his brothers pulled Joseph up out of the cistern and sold him for twenty shekels*b* of silver to the Ishmaelites, who took him to Egypt.

29When Reuben returned to the cistern and saw that Joseph was not there, he tore his clothes. 30He went back to his brothers and said, ''The boy isn't there! Where can I turn now?''

31Then they got Joseph's robe, slaughtered a goat and dipped the robe in the blood. 32They took the ornamented robe back to their father and said, ''We found this. Examine it to see whether it is your son's robe.''

33He recognised it and said, ''It is my son's robe! Some ferocious animal has devoured him. Joseph has surely been torn to pieces.''

34Then Jacob tore his clothes, put on sackcloth and mourned for his son many days. 35All his sons and daughters came to comfort him, but he refused to be comforted. ''No,'' he said, ''in mourning will I go down to the grave*c* to my son.'' So his father wept for him.

36Meanwhile, the Midianites*d* sold Joseph in Egypt to Potiphar, one of Pharaoh's officials, the captain of the guard.

Judah and Tamar

38 At that time, Judah left his brothers and went down to stay with a man of Adullam named Hirah. 2There Judah met the daughter of a Canaanite man named Shua. He married her and lay with her; 3she became pregnant and gave birth to a son, who was named Er. 4She conceived again and gave birth to a son and named him Onan. 5She gave birth to still another son and named him Shelah. It was at Kezib that she gave birth to him.

6Judah got a wife for Er, his firstborn, and her name was Tamar. 7But Er, Judah's firstborn, was wicked in the LORD's sight; so the LORD put him to death.

8Then Judah said to Onan, ''Lie with your brother's wife and fulfil your duty to her as a brother-in-law to produce offspring for your brother.'' 9But Onan knew that the offspring would not be his; so whenever he lay with his brother's wife, he spilled his semen on the ground to keep from producing offspring for his brother. 10What he did was wicked in the LORD's sight; so he put him to death also.

11Judah then said to his daughter-in-law Tamar, ''Live as a widow in your father's house until my son Shelah grows up.'' For he thought, ''He may die too, just like his brothers.'' So Tamar went to live in her father's house.

12After a long time Judah's wife, the daughter of Shua, died. When Judah had recovered from his grief, he went up to Timnah, to the men who were shearing his sheep, and his friend Hirah the Adullamite went with him.

13When Tamar was told, ''Your father-in-law is on his way to Timnah to shear his sheep,'' 14she took off her widow's clothes, covered herself with a veil to disguise herself, and then sat down at the entrance to Enaim, which is on the road to Timnah. For she saw that, though Shelah had now grown up, she had not been given to him as his wife.

15When Judah saw her, he thought she was a prostitute, for she had covered her face. 16Not realising that she was his daughter-in-law, he went over to her by the roadside and said, ''Come now, let me sleep with you.''

''And what will you give me to sleep with you?'' she asked.

17"I'll send you a young goat from my flock,'' he said.

''Will you give me something as a pledge until you send it?'' she asked.

18He said, ''What pledge should I give you?''

''Your seal and its cord, and the staff in your hand,'' she answered. So he gave them to her and slept with her, and she became pregnant by him. 19After she left, she took off her veil and put on her widow's clothes again.

20Meanwhile Judah sent the young goat by his friend the Adullamite in order to get his

b28 That is, about 8 ounces (about 0.2 kilogram)
c35 Hebrew *Sheol*
d36 Samaritan Pentateuch, Septuagint, Vulgate and Syriac (see also verse 28); Masoretic Text *Medanites*

GENESIS 37:5–11

'Joseph had a dream, and when he told it to his brothers, they hated him all the more' (v. 5).

WE ARE DREAMERS ALL. Some dreams we share and some we do not. Some, long forgotten, have fallen to the ground, nourishing the soil out of which more dreams have sprung. Other dreams have come to some degree of fulfilment. Without our dreams life would be drab and our achievements minimal. 'We are such stuff,' said Shakespeare, 'as dreams are made on.' He was right, of course.

Grand dreams were in Joseph's bloodstream. God gave his great-grandfather Abraham a dream of a new faith, a new land, and a new people: a dream which was to change world history. The genes were dormant in Joseph's grandfather Isaac but came to life again with his father Jacob, who was given a dream at Bethel, which was to change his own life and help fulfill Abraham's dream. Now Joseph, the teenager, was dreaming. His unsought dreams were of power and influence over his family and he was unwise enough to share them with his brothers who, not unnaturally, were resentful, and who sarcastically dubbed him the 'master-dreamer'. His father also lacked appreciation, but he bore the dreams in mind, possibly speculating on Joseph's place in the furtherance of Abraham's dream.

Literature abounds on the subject of dreams, their significance and interpretation, but we do well to sidestep that complex and not always wholesome material. The dreams God gives us are positive. They relate to our spiritual awakening and development and are to the advantage of others. We need more of such dreams.

> *Dream-maker God, give me the eyes to see*
> *And share your vision for humanity.*
> *Let me but dream of conquest over wrong,*
> *Of this weak soul of mine, by Christ made strong,*
> *Then will my dream be one of destiny.*

→44

GENESIS 41:25–45

'The dreams of Pharaoh are one and the same. God has revealed to Pharaoh what he is about to do . . . Seven years of great abundance are coming throughout the land of Egypt, but seven years of famine will follow them. Then all the abundance in Egypt will be forgotten' (vv. 25, 29, 30).

THE CYCLE OF PLENTY then famine, boom then recession, is not new. It is not new to build grain mountains against the years of famine. What is new is our modern ability to produce and store grain, meat, milk and other commodities wildly in excess of our own needs while the rest of the world goes hungry.

In biblical times there were rich nations and poor nations, well-fed and hungry peoples. There were traders who threw away food cargoes in order to keep prices up. Ruthless men used famine to grab the land of others. The big difference was in communications. While it may have been known that others went hungry, the slowness of travel and the relatively limited resources of even the richest nations meant that although the will to help might be present, little could be done to improve the situation.

All people could do was to store and hope. Egypt was fortunate. Her dry climate meant easy storage. Grain keeps for years, when properly stored in such an environment. It was natural to put Joseph in charge of the storage scheme. Not only could he interpret Pharaoh's dreams, but he had already shown his ability as an administrator in a large household, and in prison.

Dreams brought Joseph to the attention of Pharaoh, but his prison experience kept him in favour. Others might have withdrawn into embittered inactivity. With industry and enthusiasm Joseph took every opportunity open to him. The administrative skills finely tuned in prison were put to good use in running the country afterwards!

pledge back from the woman, but he did not find her. [21]He asked the men who lived there, "Where is the shrine-prostitute who was beside the road at Enaim?"

"There hasn't been any shrine-prostitute here," they said.

[22]So he went back to Judah and said, "I didn't find her. Besides, the men who lived there said, 'There hasn't been any shrine-prostitute here.'"

[23]Then Judah said, "Let her keep what she has, or we will become a laughing-stock. After all, I did send her this young goat, but you didn't find her."

[24]About three months later Judah was told, "Your daughter-in-law Tamar is guilty of prostitution, and as a result she is now pregnant."

Judah said, "Bring her out and have her burned to death!"

[25]As she was being brought out, she sent a message to her father-in-law. "I am pregnant by the man who owns these," she said. And she added, "See if you recognise whose seal and cord and staff these are."

[26]Judah recognised them and said, "She is more righteous than I, since I wouldn't give her to my son Shelah." And he did not sleep with her again.

[27]When the time came for her to give birth, there were twin boys in her womb. [28]As she was giving birth, one of them put out his hand; so the midwife took a scarlet thread and tied it on his wrist and said, "This one came out first." [29]But when he drew back his hand, his brother came out, and she said, "So this is how you have broken out!" And he was named Perez.[a] [30]Then his brother, who had the scarlet thread on his wrist, came out and he was given the name Zerah.[b]

Joseph and Potiphar's Wife

39 Now Joseph had been taken down to Egypt. Potiphar, an Egyptian who was one of Pharaoh's officials, the captain of the guard, bought him from the Ishmaelites who had taken him there.

[2]The LORD was with Joseph and he prospered, and he lived in the house of his Egyptian master. [3]When his master saw that the LORD was with him and that the LORD gave him success in everything he did, [4]Joseph found favour in his eyes and became his attendant. Potiphar put him in charge of his household, and he entrusted to his care everything he owned. [5]From the time he put him in charge of his household and of all that he owned, the LORD blessed the household of the Egyptian because of Joseph. The blessing of the LORD was on everything Potiphar had, both in the house and in the field. [6]So he left in Joseph's care everything he had; with Joseph in charge, he did not concern himself with anything except the food he ate.

Now Joseph was well-built and handsome, [7]and after a while his master's wife took notice of Joseph and said, "Come to bed with me!"

[8]But he refused. "With me in charge," he told her, "my master does not concern himself with anything in the house; everything he owns he has entrusted to my care. [9]No-one is greater in this house than I am. My master has withheld nothing from me except you, because you are his wife. How then could I do such a wicked thing and sin against God?" [10]And though she spoke to Joseph day after day, he refused to go to bed with her or even to be with her.

[11]One day he went into the house to attend to his duties, and none of the household servants was inside. [12]She caught him by his cloak and said, "Come to bed with me!" But he left his cloak in her hand and ran out of the house.

[13]When she saw that he had left his cloak in her hand and had run out of the house, [14]she called her household servants. "Look," she said to them, "this Hebrew has been brought to us to make sport of us! He came in here to sleep with me, but I screamed. [15]When he heard me scream for help, he left his cloak beside me and ran out of the house."

[16]She kept his cloak beside her until his master came home. [17]Then she told him this story: "That Hebrew slave you brought us came to me to make sport of me. [18]But as soon as I screamed for help, he left his cloak beside me and ran out of the house."

[19]When his master heard the story his wife told him, saying, "This is how your slave treated me," he burned with anger. [20]Joseph's master took him and put him in prison, the place where the king's prisoners were confined.

But while Joseph was there in the prison, [21]the LORD was with him; he showed him kindness and granted him favour in the eyes of the prison warder. [22]So the warder put Joseph in charge of all those held in the prison, and he was made responsible for all that was done there. [23]The warder paid no attention to anything under Joseph's care, because the LORD was with Joseph and gave him success in whatever he did.

The Cupbearer and the Baker

40 Some time later, the cupbearer and the baker of the king of Egypt offended their master, the king of Egypt. [2]Pharaoh was angry with his two officials, the chief cupbearer and the chief baker, [3]and put them in custody in the house of the captain of the guard, in the same prison where Joseph was confined. [4]The captain of the guard assigned them to Joseph, and he attended them.

After they had been in custody for some time, [5]each of the two men—the cupbearer and the baker of the king of Egypt, who were being held in prison—had a dream the same night, and each dream had a meaning of its own.

[6]When Joseph came to them the next morning, he saw that they were dejected. [7]So he asked Pharaoh's officials who were in custody with him in his master's house, "Why are your faces so sad today?"

[a]29 Perez means breaking out.   [b]30 Zerah can mean scarlet or brightness.

8"We both had dreams," they answered, "but there is no-one to interpret them."

Then Joseph said to them, "Do not interpretations belong to God? Tell me your dreams."

9So the chief cupbearer told Joseph his dream. He said to him, "In my dream I saw a vine in front of me, 10and on the vine were three branches. As soon as it budded, it blossomed, and its clusters ripened into grapes. 11Pharaoh's cup was in my hand, and I took the grapes, squeezed them into Pharaoh's cup and put the cup in his hand."

12"This is what it means," Joseph said to him. "The three branches are three days. 13Within three days Pharaoh will lift up your head and restore you to your position, and you will put Pharaoh's cup in his hand, just as you used to do when you were his cupbearer. 14But when all goes well with you, remember me and show me kindness; mention me to Pharaoh and get me out of this prison. 15For I was forcibly carried off from the land of the Hebrews, and even here I have done nothing to deserve being put in a dungeon."

16When the chief baker saw that Joseph had given a favourable interpretation, he said to Joseph, "I too had a dream: On my head were three baskets of bread.*a* 17In the top basket were all kinds of baked goods for Pharaoh, but the birds were eating them out of the basket on my head."

18"This is what it means," Joseph said. "The three baskets are three days. 19Within three days Pharaoh will lift off your head and hang you on a tree.*b* And the birds will eat away your flesh."

20Now the third day was Pharaoh's birthday, and he gave a feast for all his officials. He lifted up the heads of the chief cupbearer and the chief baker in the presence of his officials: 21He restored the chief cupbearer to his position, so that he once again put the cup into Pharaoh's hand, 22but he hanged*c* the chief baker, just as Joseph had said to them in his interpretation.

23The chief cupbearer, however, did not remember Joseph; he forgot him.

Pharaoh's Dreams

41 When two full years had passed, Pharaoh had a dream: He was standing by the Nile, 2when out of the river there came up seven cows, sleek and fat, and they grazed among the reeds. 3After them, seven other cows, ugly and gaunt, came up out of the Nile and stood beside those on the riverbank. 4And the cows that were ugly and gaunt ate up the seven sleek, fat cows. Then Pharaoh woke up.

5He fell asleep again and had a second dream: Seven ears of corn, healthy and good, were growing on a single stalk. 6After them, seven other ears of corn sprouted—thin and scorched by the east wind. 7The thin ears of corn swallowed up the seven healthy, full ears. Then Pharaoh woke up; it had been a dream.

8In the morning his mind was troubled, so he sent for all the magicians and wise men of Egypt. Pharaoh told them his dreams, but no-one could interpret them for him.

9Then the chief cupbearer said to Pharaoh, "Today I am reminded of my shortcomings. 10Pharaoh was once angry with his servants, and he imprisoned me and the chief baker in the house of the captain of the guard. 11Each of us had a dream the same night, and each dream had a meaning of its own. 12Now a young Hebrew was there with us, a servant of the captain of the guard. We told him our dreams, and he interpreted them for us, giving each man the interpretation of his dream. 13And things turned out exactly as he interpreted them to us: I was restored to my position, and the other man was hanged."*a*

14So Pharaoh sent for Joseph, and he was quickly brought from the dungeon. When he had shaved and changed his clothes, he came before Pharaoh.

15Pharaoh said to Joseph, "I had a dream, and no-one can interpret it. But I have heard it said of you that when you hear a dream you can interpret it."

16"I cannot do it," Joseph replied to Pharaoh, "but God will give Pharaoh the answer he desires."

17Then Pharaoh said to Joseph, "In my dream I was standing on the bank of the Nile, 18when out of the river there came up seven cows, fat and sleek, and they grazed among the reeds. 19After them, seven other cows came up—scrawny and very ugly and lean. I had never seen such ugly cows in all the land of Egypt. 20The lean, ugly cows ate up the seven fat cows that came up first. 21But even after they ate them, no-one could tell that they had done so; they looked just as ugly as before. Then I woke up.

22"In my dreams I also saw seven ears of corn, full and good, growing on a single stalk. 23After them, seven other ears sprouted—withered and thin and scorched by the east wind. 24The thin ears of corn swallowed up the seven good ears. I told this to the magicians, but none could explain it to me."

25Then Joseph said to Pharaoh, "The dreams of Pharaoh are one and the same. God has revealed to Pharaoh what he is about to do. 26The seven good cows are seven years, and the seven good ears of corn are seven years; it is one and the same dream. 27The seven lean, ugly cows that came up afterwards are seven years, and so are the seven worthless ears of corn scorched by the east wind: They are seven years of famine.

28"It is just as I said to Pharaoh: God has shown Pharaoh what he is about to do. 29Seven years of great abundance are coming throughout the land of Egypt, 30but seven years of famine will follow them. Then all the abundance in Egypt will be forgotten, and the famine will ravage the land. 31The abundance in the land will not be remembered, because the famine that follows it will be so severe. 32The reason the dream was given to Pharaoh in two forms is that the matter has been firmly decided by God, and God will do it soon.

---

*a*16 Or *three wicker baskets*   *b*19 Or *and impale you on a pole*   *c*22 Or *impaled*   *a*13 Or *impaled*

33"And now let Pharaoh look for a discerning and wise man and put him in charge of the land of Egypt. 34Let Pharaoh appoint commissioners over the land to take a fifth of the harvest of Egypt during the seven years of abundance. 35They should collect all the food of these good years that are coming and store up the grain under the authority of Pharaoh, to be kept in the cities for food. 36This food should be held in reserve for the country, to be used during the seven years of famine that will come upon Egypt, so that the country may not be ruined by the famine."

37The plan seemed good to Pharaoh and to all his officials. 38So Pharaoh asked them, "Can we find anyone like this man, one in whom is the spirit of God?"[b]

39Then Pharaoh said to Joseph, "Since God has made all this known to you, there is no-one so discerning and wise as you. 40You shall be in charge of my palace, and all my people are to submit to your orders. Only with respect to the throne will I be greater than you."

Joseph in Charge of Egypt

41So Pharaoh said to Joseph, "I hereby put you in charge of the whole land of Egypt." 42Then Pharaoh took his signet ring from his finger and put it on Joseph's finger. He dressed him in robes of fine linen and put a gold chain around his neck. 43He had him ride in a chariot as his second-in-command,[c] and men shouted before him, "Make way!"[d] Thus he put him in charge of the whole land of Egypt.

44Then Pharaoh said to Joseph, "I am Pharaoh, but without your word no-one will lift hand or foot in all Egypt." 45Pharaoh gave Joseph the name Zaphenath-Paneah and gave him Asenath daughter of Potiphera, priest of On,[e] to be his wife. And Joseph went throughout the land of Egypt.

46Joseph was thirty years old when he entered the service of Pharaoh king of Egypt. And Joseph went out from Pharaoh's presence and travelled throughout Egypt. 47During the seven years of abundance the land produced plentifully. 48Joseph collected all the food produced in those seven years of abundance in Egypt and stored it in the cities. In each city he put the food grown in the fields surrounding it. 49Joseph stored up huge quantities of grain, like the sand of the sea; it was so much that he stopped keeping records because it was beyond measure.

50Before the years of famine came, two sons were born to Joseph by Asenath daughter of Potiphera, priest of On. 51Joseph named his firstborn Manasseh[f] and said, "It is because God has made me forget all my trouble and all my father's household." 52The second son he named Ephraim[g] and said, "It is because God has made me fruitful in the land of my suffering."

53The seven years of abundance in Egypt came to an end, 54and the seven years of

famine began, just as Joseph had said. There was famine in all the other lands, but in the whole land of Egypt there was food. 55When all Egypt began to feel the famine, the people cried to Pharaoh for food. Then Pharaoh told all the Egyptians, "Go to Joseph and do what he tells you."

56When the famine had spread over the whole country, Joseph opened the storehouses and sold grain to the Egyptians, for the famine was severe throughout Egypt. 57And all the countries came to Egypt to buy grain from Joseph, because the famine was severe in all the world.

Joseph's Brothers Go to Egypt

42 When Jacob learned that there was grain in Egypt, he said to his sons, "Why do you just keep looking at each other?" 2He continued, "I have heard that there is grain in Egypt. Go down there and buy some for us, so that we may live and not die."

3Then ten of Joseph's brothers went down to buy grain from Egypt. 4But Jacob did not send Benjamin, Joseph's brother, with the others, because he was afraid that harm might come to him. 5So Israel's sons were among those who went to buy grain, for the famine was in the land of Canaan also.

6Now Joseph was the governor of the land, the one who sold grain to all its people. So when Joseph's brothers arrived, they bowed down to him with their faces to the ground. 7As soon as Joseph saw his brothers, he recognised them, but he pretended to be a stranger and spoke harshly to them. "Where do you come from?" he asked.

"From the land of Canaan," they replied, "to buy food."

8Although Joseph recognised his brothers, they did not recognise him. 9Then he remembered his dreams about them and said to them, "You are spies! You have come to see where our land is unprotected."

10"No, my lord," they answered. "Your servants have come to buy food. 11We are all the sons of one man. Your servants are honest men, not spies."

12"No!" he said to them. "You have come to see where our land is unprotected."

13But they replied, "Your servants were twelve brothers, the sons of one man, who lives in the land of Canaan. The youngest is now with our father, and one is no more."

14Joseph said to them, "It is just as I told you: You are spies! 15And this is how you will be tested: As surely as Pharaoh lives, you will not leave this place unless your youngest brother comes here. 16Send one of your number to get your brother; the rest of you will be kept in prison, so that your words may be tested to see if you are telling the truth. If you are not, then as surely as Pharaoh lives, you are spies!" 17And he put them all in custody for three days.

18On the third day, Joseph said to them,

[b]38 Or of the gods   [c]43 Or in the chariot of his second-in-command; or in his second chariot
[d]43 Or Bow down   [e]45 That is, Heliopolis; also in verse 50
[f]51 Manasseh sounds like and may be derived from the Hebrew for forget.
[g]52 Ephraim sounds like the Hebrew for twice fruitful.

"Do this and you will live, for I fear God: ¹⁹If you are honest men, let one of your brothers stay here in prison, while the rest of you go and take grain back for your starving households. ²⁰But you must bring your youngest brother to me, so that your words may be verified and that you may not die." This they proceeded to do.

²¹They said to one another, "Surely we are being punished because of our brother. We saw how distressed he was when he pleaded with us for his life, but we would not listen; that's why this distress has come upon us."

²²Reuben replied, "Didn't I tell you not to sin against the boy? But you wouldn't listen! Now we must give an accounting for his blood." ²³They did not realise that Joseph could understand them, since he was using an interpreter.

²⁴He turned away from them and began to weep, but then turned back and spoke to them again. He had Simeon taken from them and bound before their eyes.

²⁵Joseph gave orders to fill their bags with grain, to put each man's silver back in his sack, and to give them provisions for their journey. After this was done for them, ²⁶they loaded their grain on their donkeys and left.

²⁷At the place where they stopped for the night one of them opened his sack to get feed for his donkey, and he saw his silver in the mouth of his sack. ²⁸"My silver has been returned," he said to his brothers. "Here it is in my sack."

Their hearts sank and they turned to each other trembling and said, "What is this that God has done to us?"

²⁹When they came to their father Jacob in the land of Canaan, they told him all that had happened to them. They said, ³⁰"The man who is lord over the land spoke harshly to us and treated us as though we were spying on the land. ³¹But we said to him, 'We are honest men; we are not spies. ³²We were twelve brothers, sons of one father. One is no more, and the youngest is now with our father in Canaan.'

³³"Then the man who is lord over the land said to us, 'This is how I will know whether you are honest men: Leave one of your brothers here with me, and take food for your starving households and go. ³⁴But bring your youngest brother to me so I will know that you are not spies but honest men. Then I will give your brother back to you, and you can trade*ᵃ* in the land.'"

³⁵As they were emptying their sacks, there in each man's sack was his pouch of silver! When they and their father saw the money pouches, they were frightened. ³⁶Their father Jacob said to them, "You have deprived me of my children. Joseph is no more and Simeon is no more, and now you want to take Benjamin. Everything is against me!"

³⁷Then Reuben said to his father, "You may put both of my sons to death if I do not bring him back to you. Entrust him to my care, and I will bring him back."

³⁸But Jacob said, "My son will not go down there with you; his brother is dead and he is the only one left. If harm comes to him on the journey you are taking, you will bring my grey head down to the grave*ᵇ* in sorrow."

The Second Journey to Egypt

43 Now the famine was still severe in the land. ²So when they had eaten all the grain they had brought from Egypt, their father said to them, "Go back and buy us a little more food."

³But Judah said to him, "The man warned us solemnly, 'You will not see my face again unless your brother is with you.' ⁴If you will send our brother along with us, we will go down and buy food for you. ⁵But if you will not send him, we will not go down, because the man said to us, 'You will not see my face again unless your brother is with you.'"

⁶Israel asked, "Why did you bring this trouble on me by telling the man you had another brother?"

⁷They replied, "The man questioned us closely about ourselves and our family. 'Is your father still living?' he asked us. 'Do you have another brother?' We simply answered his questions. How were we to know he would say, 'Bring your brother down here'?"

⁸Then Judah said to Israel his father, "Send the boy along with me and we will go at once, so that we and you and our children may live and not die. ⁹I myself will guarantee his safety; you can hold me personally responsible for him. If I do not bring him back to you and set him here before you, I will bear the blame before you all my life. ¹⁰As it is, if we had not delayed, we could have gone and returned twice."

¹¹Then their father Israel said to them, "If it must be, then do this: Put some of the best products of the land in your bags and take them down to the man as a gift—a little balm and a little honey, some spices and myrrh, some pistachio nuts and almonds. ¹²Take double the amount of silver with you, for you must return the silver that was put back into the mouths of your sacks. Perhaps it was a mistake. ¹³Take your brother also and go back to the man at once. ¹⁴And may God Almighty*ᵃ* grant you mercy before the man so that he will let your other brother and Benjamin come back with you. As for me, if I am bereaved, I am bereaved."

¹⁵So the men took the gifts and double the amount of silver, and Benjamin also. They hurried down to Egypt and presented themselves to Joseph. ¹⁶When Joseph saw Benjamin with them, he said to the steward of his house, "Take these men to my house, slaughter an animal and prepare dinner; they are to eat with me at noon."

¹⁷The man did as Joseph told him and took the men to Joseph's house. ¹⁸Now the men were frightened when they were taken to his house. They thought, "We were brought here because of the silver that was put back into our sacks the first time. He wants to

---

ᵃ34 Or move about freely   ᵇ38 Hebrew Sheol   ᵃ14 Hebrew El-Shaddai attack us and overpower us and seize us as slaves and take our donkeys."

¹⁹So they went up to Joseph's steward and spoke to him at the entrance to the house. ²⁰"Please, sir," they said, "we came down here the first time to buy food. ²¹But at the place where we stopped for the night we opened our sacks and each of us found his silver—the exact weight—in the mouth of his sack. So we have brought it back with us. ²²We have also brought additional silver with us to buy food. We don't know who put our silver in our sacks."

²³"It's all right," he said. "Don't be afraid. Your God, the God of your father, has given you treasure in your sacks; I received your silver." Then he brought Simeon out to them.

²⁴The steward took the men into Joseph's house, gave them water to wash their feet and provided fodder for their donkeys. ²⁵They prepared their gifts for Joseph's arrival at noon, because they had heard that they were to eat there.

²⁶When Joseph came home, they presented to him the gifts they had brought into the house, and they bowed down before him to the ground. ²⁷He asked them how they were, and then he said, "How is your aged father you told me about? Is he still living?"

²⁸They replied, "Your servant our father is still alive and well." And they bowed low to pay him honour.

²⁹As he looked about and saw his brother Benjamin, his own mother's son, he asked, "Is this your youngest brother, the one you told me about?" And he said, "God be gracious to you, my son." ³⁰Deeply moved at the sight of his brother, Joseph hurried out and looked for a place to weep. He went into his private room and wept there.

³¹After he had washed his face, he came out and, controlling himself, said, "Serve the food."

³²They served him by himself, the brothers by themselves, and the Egyptians who ate with him by themselves, because Egyptians could not eat with Hebrews, for that is detestable to Egyptians. ³³The men had been seated before him in the order of their ages, from the firstborn to the youngest; and they looked at each other in astonishment. ³⁴When portions were served to them from Joseph's table, Benjamin's portion was five times as much as anyone else's. So they feasted and drank freely with him.

A Silver Cup in a Sack

44 Now Joseph gave these instructions to the steward of his house: "Fill the men's sacks with as much food as they can carry, and put each man's silver in the mouth of his sack. ²Then put my cup, the silver one, in the mouth of the youngest one's sack, along with the silver for his grain." And he did as Joseph said.

³As morning dawned, the men were sent on their way with their donkeys. ⁴They had not gone far from the city when Joseph said to his steward, "Go after those men at once, and when you catch up with them, say to them, 'Why have you repaid good with evil? ⁵Isn't this the cup my master drinks from and also uses for divination? This is a wicked thing you have done.'"

⁶When he caught up with them, he repeated these words to them. ⁷But they said to him, "Why does my lord say such things? Far be it from your servants to do anything like that! ⁸We even brought back to you from the land of Canaan the silver we found inside the mouths of our sacks. So why would we steal silver or gold from your master's house? ⁹If any of your servants is found to have it, he will die; and the rest of us will become my lord's slaves."

¹⁰"Very well, then," he said, "let it be as you say. Whoever is found to have it will become my slave; the rest of you will be free from blame."

¹¹Each of them quickly lowered his sack to the ground and opened it. ¹²Then the steward proceeded to search, beginning with the oldest and ending with the youngest. And the cup was found in Benjamin's sack. ¹³At this, they tore their clothes. Then they all loaded their donkeys and returned to the city.

¹⁴Joseph was still in the house when Judah and his brothers came in, and they threw themselves to the ground before him. ¹⁵Joseph said to them, "What is this you have done? Don't you know that a man like me can find things out by divination?"

¹⁶"What can we say to my lord?" Judah replied. "What can we say? How can we prove our innocence? God has uncovered your servants' guilt. We are now my lord's slaves—we ourselves and the one who was found to have the cup."

¹⁷But Joseph said, "Far be it from me to do such a thing! Only the man who was found to have the cup will become my slave. The rest of you, go back to your father in peace."

¹⁸Then Judah went up to him and said: "Please, my lord, let your servant speak a word to my lord. Do not be angry with your servant, though you are equal to Pharaoh himself. ¹⁹My lord asked his servants, 'Do you have a father or a brother?' ²⁰And we answered, 'We have an aged father, and there is a young son born to him in his old age. His brother is dead, and he is the only one of his mother's sons left, and his father loves him.'

²¹"Then you said to your servants, 'Bring him down to me so I can see him for myself.' ²²And we said to my lord, 'The boy cannot leave his father; if he leaves him, his father will die.' ²³But you told your servants, 'Unless your youngest brother comes down with you, you will not see my face again.' ²⁴When we went back to your servant my father, we told him what my lord had said.

²⁵"Then our father said, 'Go back and buy a little more food.' ²⁶But we said, 'We cannot go down. Only if our youngest brother is with us will we go. We cannot see the man's face unless our youngest brother is with us.'

²⁷"Your servant my father said to us, 'You know that my wife bore me two sons. ²⁸One of them went away from me, and I said, "He has surely been torn to pieces." And I have

not seen him since. ²⁹If you take this one from me too and harm comes to him, you will bring my grey head down to the grave^a in misery.'

³⁰"So now, if the boy is not with us when I go back to your servant my father and if my father, whose life is closely bound up with the boy's life, ³¹sees that the boy isn't there, he will die. Your servants will bring the grey head of our father down to the grave in sorrow. ³²Your servant guaranteed the boy's safety to my father. I said, 'If I do not bring him back to you, I will bear the blame before you, my father, all my life!'

³³"Now then, please let your servant remain here as my lord's slave in place of the boy, and let the boy return with his brothers. ³⁴How can I go back to my father if the boy is not with me? No! Do not let me see the misery that would come upon my father."

Joseph Makes Himself Known

45 Then Joseph could no longer control himself before all his attendants, and he cried out, "Make everyone leave my presence!" So there was no-one with Joseph when he made himself known to his brothers. ²And he wept so loudly that the Egyptians heard him, and Pharaoh's household heard about it.

³Joseph said to his brothers, "I am Joseph! Is my father still living?" But his brothers were not able to answer him, because they were terrified at his presence.

⁴Then Joseph said to his brothers, "Come close to me." When they had done so, he said, "I am your brother Joseph, the one you sold into Egypt! ⁵And now, do not be distressed and do not be angry with yourselves for selling me here, because it was to save lives that God sent me ahead of you. ⁶For two years now there has been famine in the land, and for the next five years there will not be ploughing and reaping. ⁷But God sent me ahead of you to preserve for you a remnant on earth and to save your lives by a great deliverance.^a

⁸"So then, it was not you who sent me here, but God. He made me father to Pharaoh, lord of his entire household and ruler of all Egypt. ⁹Now hurry back to my father and say to him, 'This is what your son Joseph says: God has made me lord of all Egypt. Come down to me; don't delay. ¹⁰You shall live in the region of Goshen and be near me—you, your children and grandchildren, your flocks and herds, and all you have. ¹¹I will provide for you there, because five years of famine are still to come. Otherwise you and your household and all who belong to you will become destitute.'

¹²"You can see for yourselves, and so can my brother Benjamin, that it is really I who am speaking to you. ¹³Tell my father about all the honour accorded me in Egypt and about everything you have seen. And bring my father down here quickly."

¹⁴Then he threw his arms around his brother Benjamin and wept, and Benjamin embraced him, weeping. ¹⁵And he kissed all his brothers and wept over them. Afterwards his brothers talked with him.

¹⁶When the news reached Pharaoh's palace that Joseph's brothers had come, Pharaoh and all his officials were pleased. ¹⁷Pharaoh said to Joseph, "Tell your brothers, 'Do this: Load your animals and return to the land of Canaan, ¹⁸and bring your father and your families back to me. I will give you the best of the land of Egypt and you can enjoy the fat of the land.'

¹⁹"You are also directed to tell them, 'Do this: Take some carts from Egypt for your children and your wives, and get your father and come. ²⁰Never mind about your belongings, because the best of all Egypt will be yours.'"

²¹So the sons of Israel did this. Joseph gave them carts, as Pharaoh had commanded, and he also gave them provisions for their journey. ²²To each of them he gave new clothing, but to Benjamin he gave three hundred shekels^b of silver and five sets of clothes. ²³And this is what he sent to his father: ten donkeys loaded with the best things of Egypt, and ten female donkeys loaded with grain and bread and other provisions for his journey. ²⁴Then he sent his brothers away, and as they were leaving he said to them, "Don't quarrel on the way!"

²⁵So they went up out of Egypt and came to their father Jacob in the land of Canaan. ²⁶They told him, "Joseph is still alive! In fact, he is ruler of all Egypt." Jacob was stunned; he did not believe them. ²⁷But when they told him everything Joseph had said to them, and when he saw the carts Joseph had sent to carry him back, the spirit of their father Jacob revived. ²⁸And Israel said, "I'm convinced! My son Joseph is still alive. I will go and see him before I die."

Jacob Goes to Egypt

46 So Israel set out with all that was his, and when he reached Beersheba, he offered sacrifices to the God of his father Isaac.

²And God spoke to Israel in a vision at night and said, "Jacob! Jacob!"

"Here I am," he replied.

³"I am God, the God of your father," he said. "Do not be afraid to go down to Egypt, for I will make you into a great nation there. ⁴I will go down to Egypt with you, and I will surely bring you back again. And Joseph's own hand will close your eyes."

⁵Then Jacob left Beersheba, and Israel's sons took their father Jacob and their children and their wives in the carts that Pharaoh had sent to transport him. ⁶They also took with them their livestock and the possessions they had acquired in Canaan, and Jacob and all his offspring went to Egypt. ⁷He took with him to Egypt his sons and grandsons and

^a29 Hebrew *Sheol*; also in verse 31　^a7 Or *save you as a great band of survivors*
^b22 That is, about 7½ pounds (about 3.5 kilograms)

his daughters and granddaughters—all his offspring.

8These are the names of the sons of Israel (Jacob and his descendants) who went to Egypt:

Reuben the firstborn of Jacob.
9The sons of Reuben:
　Hanoch, Pallu, Hezron and Carmi.
10The sons of Simeon:
　Jemuel, Jamin, Ohad, Jakin, Zohar
　and Shaul the son of a Canaanite
　woman.
11The sons of Levi:
　Gershon, Kohath and Merari.
12The sons of Judah:
　Er, Onan, Shelah, Perez and Zerah
　(but Er and Onan had died in the land
　of Canaan).
　The sons of Perez:
　　Hezron and Hamul.
13The sons of Issachar:
　Tola, Puah,a Jashubb and Shimron.
14The sons of Zebulun:
　Sered, Elon and Jahleel.
15These were the sons Leah bore to Jacob in Paddan Aram,c besides his daughter Dinah. These sons and daughters of his were thirty-three in all.

16The sons of Gad:
　Zephon,d Haggi, Shuni, Ezbon, Eri,
　Arodi and Areli.
17The sons of Asher:
　Imnah, Ishvah, Ishvi and Beriah.
　Their sister was Serah.
　The sons of Beriah:
　　Heber and Malkiel.
18These were the children born to Jacob by Zilpah, whom Laban had given to his daughter Leah—sixteen in all.

19The sons of Jacob's wife Rachel:
　Joseph and Benjamin. 20In Egypt,
　Manasseh and Ephraim were born to
　Joseph by Asenath daughter of
　Potiphera, priest of On.e
21The sons of Benjamin:
　Bela, Beker, Ashbel, Gera, Naaman,
　Ehi, Rosh, Muppim, Huppim and
　Ard.
22These were the sons of Rachel who were born to Jacob—fourteen in all.

23The son of Dan:
　Hushim.
24The sons of Naphtali:
　Jahziel, Guni, Jezer and Shillem.
25These were the sons born to Jacob by Bilhah, whom Laban had given to his daughter Rachel—seven in all.

26All those who went to Egypt with Jacob —those who were his direct descendants, not counting his sons' wives—numbered sixty-six persons. 27With the two sonsf who had been born to Joseph in Egypt, the members of Jacob's family, which went to Egypt, were seventyg in all.

28Now Jacob sent Judah ahead of him to Joseph to get directions to Goshen. When they arrived in the region of Goshen, 29Joseph had his chariot made ready and went to Goshen to meet his father Israel. As soon as Joseph appeared before him, he threw his arms around his fatherh and wept for a long time.

30Israel said to Joseph, "Now I am ready to die, since I have seen for myself that you are still alive."

31Then Joseph said to his brothers and to his father's household, "I will go up and speak to Pharaoh and will say to him, 'My brothers and my father's household, who were living in the land of Canaan, have come to me. 32The men are shepherds; they tend livestock, and they have brought along their flocks and herds and everything they own.' 33When Pharaoh calls you in and asks, 'What is your occupation?' 34you should answer, 'Your servants have tended livestock from our boyhood on, just as our fathers did.' Then you will be allowed to settle in the region of Goshen, for all shepherds are detestable to the Egyptians."

47 Joseph went and told Pharaoh, "My father and brothers, with their flocks and herds and everything they own, have come from the land of Canaan and are now in Goshen." 2He chose five of his brothers and presented them before Pharaoh.

3Pharaoh asked the brothers, "What is your occupation?"

"Your servants are shepherds," they replied to Pharaoh, "just as our fathers were." 4They also said to him, "We have come to live here awhile, because the famine is severe in Canaan and your servants' flocks have no pasture. So now, please let your servants settle in Goshen."

5Pharaoh said to Joseph, "Your father and your brothers have come to you, 6and the land of Egypt is before you; settle your father and your brothers in the best part of the land. Let them live in Goshen. And if you know of any among them with special ability, put them in charge of my own livestock."

7Then Joseph brought his father Jacob in and presented him before Pharaoh. After Jacob blesseda Pharaoh, 8Pharaoh asked him, "How old are you?"

9And Jacob said to Pharaoh, "The years of my pilgrimage are a hundred and thirty. My years have been few and difficult, and they do not equal the years of the pilgrimage of my fathers." 10Then Jacob blessedb Pharaoh and went out from his presence.

a13 Samaritan Pentateuch and Syriac (see also 1 Chron. 7:1); Masoretic Text Puvah
b13 Samaritan Pentateuch and some Septuagint manuscripts (see also Num. 26:24 and 1 Chron. 7:1); Masoretic Text Job　　c15 That is, North-west Mesopotamia
d16 Samaritan Pentateuch and Septuagint (see also Num. 26:15); Masoretic Text Ziphion
e20 That is, Heliopolis　　f27 Hebrew; Septuagint the nine children
g27 Hebrew (see also Exodus 1:5 and footnote); Septuagint (see also Acts 7:14) seventy-five
h29 Hebrew around him　　a7 Or greeted　　b10 Or said farewell to

¹¹So Joseph settled his father and his brothers in Egypt and gave them property in the best part of the land, the district of Rameses, as Pharaoh directed. ¹²Joseph also provided his father and his brothers and all his father's household with food, according to the number of their children.

Joseph and the Famine

¹³There was no food, however, in the whole region because the famine was severe; both Egypt and Canaan wasted away because of the famine. ¹⁴Joseph collected all the money that was to be found in Egypt and Canaan in payment for the grain they were buying, and he brought it to Pharaoh's palace. ¹⁵When the money of the people of Egypt and Canaan was gone, all Egypt came to Joseph and said, "Give us food. Why should we die before your eyes? Our money is used up."

¹⁶"Then bring your livestock," said Joseph. "I will sell you food in exchange for your livestock, since your money is gone." ¹⁷So they brought their livestock to Joseph, and he gave them food in exchange for their horses, their sheep and goats, their cattle and donkeys. And he brought them through that year with food in exchange for all their livestock.

¹⁸When that year was over, they came to him the following year and said, "We cannot hide from our lord the fact that since our money is gone and our livestock belongs to you, there is nothing left for our lord except our bodies and our land. ¹⁹Why should we perish before your eyes—we and our land as well? Buy us and our land in exchange for food, and we with our land will be in bondage to Pharaoh. Give us seed so that we may live and not die, and that the land may not become desolate."

²⁰So Joseph bought all the land in Egypt for Pharaoh. The Egyptians, one and all, sold their fields, because the famine was too severe for them. The land became Pharaoh's, ²¹and Joseph reduced the people to servitude,^{c} from one end of Egypt to the other. ²²However, he did not buy the land of the priests, because they received a regular allotment from Pharaoh and had food enough from the allotment Pharaoh gave them. That is why they did not sell their land.

²³Joseph said to the people, "Now that I have bought you and your land today for Pharaoh, here is seed for you so you can plant the ground. ²⁴But when the crop comes in, give a fifth of it to Pharaoh. The other four-fifths you may keep as seed for the fields and as food for yourselves and your households and your children."

²⁵"You have saved our lives," they said. "May we find favour in the eyes of our lord; we will be in bondage to Pharaoh."

²⁶So Joseph established it as a law concerning land in Egypt—still in force today—that a fifth of the produce belongs to Pharaoh. It was only the land of the priests that did not become Pharaoh's.

²⁷Now the Israelites settled in Egypt in the region of Goshen. They acquired property there and were fruitful and increased greatly in number.

²⁸Jacob lived in Egypt seventeen years, and the years of his life were a hundred and forty-seven. ²⁹When the time drew near for Israel to die, he called for his son Joseph and said to him, "If I have found favour in your eyes, put your hand under my thigh and promise that you will show me kindness and faithfulness. Do not bury me in Egypt, ³⁰but when I rest with my fathers, carry me out of Egypt and bury me where they are buried."

"I will do as you say," he said.

³¹"Swear to me," he said. Then Joseph swore to him, and Israel worshipped as he leaned on the top of his staff.^{d}

Manasseh and Ephraim

48 Some time later Joseph was told, "Your father is ill." So he took his two sons Manasseh and Ephraim along with him. ²When Jacob was told, "Your son Joseph has come to you," Israel rallied his strength and sat up on the bed.

³Jacob said to Joseph, "God Almighty^a appeared to me at Luz in the land of Canaan, and there he blessed me ⁴and said to me, 'I am going to make you fruitful and will increase your numbers. I will make you a community of peoples, and I will give this land as an everlasting possession to your descendants after you.'

⁵"Now then, your two sons born to you in Egypt before I came to you here will be reckoned as mine; Ephraim and Manasseh will be mine, just as Reuben and Simeon are mine. ⁶Any children born to you after them will be yours; in the territory they inherit they will be reckoned under the names of their brothers. ⁷As I was returning from Paddan,^{b} to my sorrow Rachel died in the land of Canaan while we were still on the way, a little distance from Ephrath. So I buried her there beside the road to Ephrath" (that is, Bethlehem).

⁸When Israel saw the sons of Joseph, he asked, "Who are these?"

⁹"They are the sons God has given me here," Joseph said to his father.

Then Israel said, "Bring them to me so that I may bless them."

¹⁰Now Israel's eyes were failing because of old age, and he could hardly see. So Joseph brought his sons close to him, and his father kissed them and embraced them.

¹¹Israel said to Joseph, "I never expected to see your face again, and now God has allowed me to see your children too."

¹²Then Joseph removed them from Israel's knees and bowed down with his face to the ground. ¹³And Joseph took both of them, Ephraim on his right towards Israel's left hand and Manasseh on his left towards

---

^{c}21 Samaritan Pentateuch and Septuagint (see also Vulgate); Masoretic Text *and he moved the people into the cities* ^{d}31 Or *Israel bowed down at the head of his bed* ^{a}3 Hebrew *El-Shaddai*
^{b}7 That is, North-west Mesopotamia

Israel's right hand, and brought them close to him. ¹⁴But Israel reached out his right hand and put it on Ephraim's head, though he was the younger, and crossing his arms, he put his left hand on Manasseh's head, even though Manasseh was the firstborn. ¹⁵Then he blessed Joseph and said,

"May the God before whom my fathers
    Abraham and Isaac walked,
the God who has been my shepherd
    all my life to this day,
¹⁶the Angel who has delivered me from all
        harm
    —may he bless these boys.
May they be called by my name
    and the names of my fathers Abraham
        and Isaac,
and may they increase greatly
    upon the earth."

¹⁷When Joseph saw his father placing his right hand on Ephraim's head he was displeased; so he took hold of his father's hand to move it from Ephraim's head to Manasseh's head. ¹⁸Joseph said to him, "No, my father, this one is the firstborn; put your right hand on his head."

¹⁹But his father refused and said, "I know, my son, I know. He too will become a people, and he too will become great. Nevertheless, his younger brother will be greater than he, and his descendants will become a group of nations." ²⁰He blessed them that day and said,

"In your*c* name will Israel pronounce this
        blessing:
    'May God make you like Ephraim and
        Manasseh.'"

So he put Ephraim ahead of Manasseh.

²¹Then Israel said to Joseph, "I am about to die, but God will be with you*d* and take you*d* back to the land of your*d* fathers. ²²And to you, as one who is over your brothers, I give the ridge of land*e* I took from the Amorites with my sword and my bow."

Jacob Blesses His Sons

49 Then Jacob called for his sons and said: "Gather round so that I can tell you what will happen to you in days to come.

²"Assemble and listen, sons of Jacob;
    listen to your father Israel.

³"Reuben, you are my firstborn,
    my might, the first sign of my strength,
    excelling in honour, excelling in power.
⁴Turbulent as the waters, you will no longer
        excel,
    for you went up onto your father's bed,
    onto my couch and defiled it.

⁵"Simeon and Levi are brothers—
    their swords*a* are weapons of violence.
⁶Let me not enter their council,
    let me not join their assembly,
for they have killed men in their anger
    and hamstrung oxen as they pleased.
⁷Cursed be their anger, so fierce,
    and their fury, so cruel!
I will scatter them in Jacob
    and disperse them in Israel.

⁸"Judah,*b* your brothers will praise you;
    your hand will be on the neck of your
        enemies;
    your father's sons will bow down to
        you.
⁹You are a lion's cub, O Judah;
    you return from the prey, my son.
Like a lion he crouches and lies down,
    like a lioness—who dares to rouse
        him?
¹⁰The sceptre will not depart from Judah,
    nor the ruler's staff from between his
        feet,
until he comes to whom it belongs*c*
    and the obedience of the nations is his.
¹¹He will tether his donkey to a vine,
    his colt to the choicest branch;
he will wash his garments in wine,
    his robes in the blood of grapes.
¹²His eyes will be darker than wine,
    his teeth whiter than milk.*d*

¹³"Zebulun will live by the seashore
    and become a haven for ships;
    his border will extend towards Sidon.

¹⁴"Issachar is a scrawny*e* donkey
    lying down between two saddlebags.*f*
¹⁵When he sees how good is his resting place
    and how pleasant is his land,
he will bend his shoulder to the burden
    and submit to forced labour.

¹⁶"Dan*g* will provide justice for his people
    as one of the tribes of Israel.
¹⁷Dan will be a serpent by the roadside,
    a viper along the path,
that bites the horse's heels
    so that its rider tumbles backwards.

¹⁸"I look for your deliverance, O LORD.

¹⁹"Gad*h* will be attacked by a band of
        raiders,
    but he will attack them at their heels.

²⁰"Asher's food will be rich;
    he will provide delicacies fit for a
        king.

²¹"Naphtali is a doe set free
    that bears beautiful fawns.*i*

---

*c*20 The Hebrew is singular.   *d*21 The Hebrew is plural.
*e*22 Or *And to you I give one portion more than to your brothers—the portion*
*a*5 The meaning of the Hebrew for this word is uncertain.
*b*8 *Judah* sounds like and may be derived from the Hebrew for *praise.*
*c*10 Or *until Shiloh comes;* or *until he comes to whom tribute belongs*
*d*12 Or *will be dull from wine,* / *his teeth white from milk*   *e*14 Or *strong*   *f*14 Or *campfires*
*g*16 *Dan* here means *he provides justice.*   *h*19 *Gad* can mean *attack* and *band of raiders.*
*i*21 Or *free;* / *he utters beautiful words*

22"Joseph is a fruitful vine,
a fruitful vine near a spring,
whose branches climb over a wall.*j*
23With bitterness archers attacked him;
they shot at him with hostility.
24But his bow remained steady,
his strong arms stayed*k* supple,
because of the hand of the Mighty One of
Jacob,
because of the Shepherd, the Rock of
Israel,
25because of your father's God, who helps
you,
because of the Almighty,*l* who blesses
you
with blessings of the heavens above,
blessings of the deep that lies below,
blessings of the breast and womb.
26Your father's blessings are greater
than the blessings of the ancient
mountains,
than*m* the bounty of the age-old hills.
Let all these rest on the head of Joseph,
on the brow of the prince among*n* his
brothers.

27"Benjamin is a ravenous wolf;
in the morning he devours the prey,
in the evening he divides the plunder."

28All these are the twelve tribes of Israel,
and this is what their father said to them
when he blessed them, giving each the blessing appropriate to him.

The Death of Jacob

29Then he gave them these instructions: "I
am about to be gathered to my people. Bury
me with my fathers in the cave in the field
of Ephron the Hittite, 30the cave in the field of
Machpelah, near Mamre in Canaan, which
Abraham bought as a burial place from
Ephron the Hittite, along with the field.
31There Abraham and his wife Sarah were
buried, there Isaac and his wife Rebekah
were buried, and there I buried Leah. 32The
field and the cave in it were bought from
the Hittites."*o*
33When Jacob had finished giving instructions to his sons, he drew his feet up into the
bed, breathed his last and was gathered to his
people.

50 Joseph threw himself upon his father
and wept over him and kissed him.
2Then Joseph directed the physicians in his
service to embalm his father Israel. So the
physicians embalmed him, 3taking a full forty
days, for that was the time required for
embalming. And the Egyptians mourned for
him seventy days.
4When the days of mourning had passed,
Joseph said to Pharaoh's court, "If I have
found favour in your eyes, speak to Pharaoh
for me. Tell him, 5'My father made me swear
an oath and said, "I am about to die; bury me

in the tomb I dug for myself in the land of
Canaan." Now let me go up and bury my
father; then I will return.' "
6Pharaoh said, "Go up and bury your
father, as he made you swear to do."
7So Joseph went up to bury his father. All
Pharaoh's officials accompanied him—the
dignitaries of his court and all the dignitaries
of Egypt—8besides all the members of
Joseph's household and his brothers and
those belonging to his father's household.
Only their children and their flocks and herds
were left in Goshen. 9Chariots and horsemen*a* also went up with him. It was a very
large company.
10When they reached the threshing-floor of
Atad, near the Jordan, they lamented loudly
and bitterly; and there Joseph observed a
seven-day period of mourning for his father.
11When the Canaanites who lived there saw
the mourning at the threshing-floor of Atad,
they said, "The Egyptians are holding a
solemn ceremony of mourning." That is why
that place near the Jordan is called Abel
Mizraim.*b*
12So Jacob's sons did as he had commanded them: 13They carried him to the land of
Canaan and buried him in the cave in the field
of Machpelah, near Mamre, which Abraham
had bought as a burial place from Ephron the
Hittite, along with the field. 14After burying
his father, Joseph returned to Egypt,
together with his brothers and all the others
who had gone with him to bury his father.

Joseph Reassures His Brothers

15When Joseph's brothers saw that their
father was dead, they said, "What if Joseph
holds a grudge against us and pays us back
for all the wrongs we did to him?" 16So they
sent word to Joseph, saying, "Your father
left these instructions before he died: 17'This
is what you are to say to Joseph: I ask you to
forgive your brothers the sins and the wrongs
they committed in treating you so badly.'
Now please forgive the sins of the servants of
the God of your father." When their message
came to him, Joseph wept.
18His brothers then came and threw themselves down before him. "We are your
slaves," they said.
19But Joseph said to them, "Don't be
afraid. Am I in the place of God? 20You
intended to harm me, but God intended it for
good to accomplish what is now being done,
the saving of many lives. 21So then, don't be
afraid. I will provide for you and your children." And he reassured them and spoke
kindly to them.

The Death of Joseph

22Joseph stayed in Egypt, along with all his
father's family. He lived a hundred and ten
years 23and saw the third generation of

*j*22 Or *Joseph is a wild colt, | a wild colt near a spring, | a wild donkey on a terraced hill*
*k*23,24 Or *archers will attack . . . will shoot . . . will remain . . . will stay*   *l*25 Hebrew *Shaddai*
*m*26 Or *of my progenitors, | as great as*   *n*26 Or *the one separated from*   *o*32 Or *the sons of Heth*
*a*9 Or *charioteers*   *b*11 *Abel Mizraim* means *mourning of the Egyptians.*

GENESIS 45:1–13

'But God sent me ahead of you to preserve for you a remnant on earth and to save your lives by a great deliverance. So then, it was not you who sent me here, but God' (vv. 7, 8a).

HUMAN TRAGEDY is transformed by the touch of God. Again this is easier to say than to accept. Sometimes we may feel the burdens we carry are too great for us. Often we are amazed at the suffering others are asked to bear. Always at the back of our mind there lurks the question 'Where is God in all of this?'

We may ask the same question concerning Joseph's story. Where was God when Joseph was cast into the pit? Where was he when Joseph tormented his brothers to distraction? What divine mercy would put Jacob through the misery of losing sons and facing famine at the same time?

When we put the matter like this, and look at Joseph saying 'do not feel upset or blame yourselves,' we could be forgiven for thinking that God himself was entirely responsible for it all. In one sense he is. He plans everything. Words like these of Anna Waring strike a chord in us

> *Father, I know that all my life is portioned out for me;*
> *The changes that will surely come I do not fear to see.*

But the brothers are still guilty. Joseph is still answerable for his revengeful actions. Jacob is the victim, not of God, but of his sons, guilty actions and the vagaries of the weather.

Genesis shows how God uses even the wrongful actions of his people to bring about his own purposes. But that does not mean we can excuse ourselves because God has used our wrongdoing. We can indeed agree with Joseph 'It was really God who sent me' – but we cannot, on that basis, excuse the brothers.

Despite Joseph's words his brothers' guilt remains, and can only be wiped out by the mercy of God himself.

→56

EXODUS 2:1–4
'Now a man of the house of Levi married a Levite woman' (v. 1).

GOD DEMONSTRATED his infinite wisdom when he ordained that human beings, the peak of his creation (Gen. 1:27), should live in families. Within an ideal family grouping, there is all that a child needs for care, nurturing, sustenance and training for life's adventures and demands. The family of Moses illustrates this admirably. In spite of Pharaoh's requirement that all male Hebrew babies should be killed, Moses' life was saved by his loving and resourceful mother (vv. 3, 4), shrewdly assisted by Miriam, his elder sister (vv. 4, 7, 9). Miriam, the oldest child, and Aaron, who was senior to Moses by three years (7:7), were nurtured and assisted to develop their considerable potential by the quality of their home life. The whole world has reason to be glad of the home created by Amram and Jochabed (6:20).

An ideal home life is not always possible and many single parents have brought up their children to be fulfilled, responsible citizens. A tremendous achievement indeed. There are also instances of children from difficult home backgrounds, or even no home at all, who have still made good, but these instances support rather than detract from the ideal of a stable family unit.

God said important things about the family when he described himself as 'Father' (Jer. 31:9) and had his Son born into a Jewish home. Even though the family history revealed royal connections, it was still a working-class home to which he came (Luke 2:39, 40). It was as though God was setting a seal on the home, and on family relationships. Home, and work, have been hallowed because Christ lived a pure life in both situations. We lose that sense of sanctity and love in our homes at our peril. We must do all we can to maintain Christian family life.

> *O Lord, come to our hearts and homes again,*
> *Come in as guest, forever to remain,*
> *Come in as king, and then forever reign.*

→69

Ephraim's children. Also the children of Makir son of Manasseh were placed at birth on Joseph's knees.[c]

24Then Joseph said to his brothers, "I am about to die. But God will surely come to your aid and take you up out of this land to the land he promised on oath to Abraham,

Isaac and Jacob." 25And Joseph made the sons of Israel swear an oath and said, "God will surely come to your aid, and then you must carry my bones up from this place."

26So Joseph died at the age of a hundred and ten. And after they embalmed him, he was placed in a coffin in Egypt.

---

[c]23 That is, were counted as his

Exodus

The Israelites Oppressed

1 These are the names of the sons of Israel who went to Egypt with Jacob, each with his family: ²Reuben, Simeon, Levi and Judah; ³Issachar, Zebulun and Benjamin; ⁴Dan and Naphtali; Gad and Asher. ⁵The descendants of Jacob numbered seventy*a* in all; Joseph was already in Egypt.

⁶Now Joseph and all his brothers and all that generation died, ⁷but the Israelites were fruitful and multiplied greatly and became exceedingly numerous, so that the land was filled with them.

⁸Then a new king, who did not know about Joseph, came to power in Egypt. ⁹"Look," he said to his people, "the Israelites have become much too numerous for us. ¹⁰Come, we must deal shrewdly with them or they will become even more numerous and, if war breaks out, will join our enemies, fight against us and leave the country."

¹¹So they put slave masters over them to oppress them with forced labour, and they built Pithom and Rameses as store cities for Pharaoh. ¹²But the more they were oppressed, the more they multiplied and spread; so the Egyptians came to dread the Israelites ¹³and worked them ruthlessly. ¹⁴They made their lives bitter with hard labour in brick and mortar and with all kinds of work in the fields; in all their hard labour the Egyptians used them ruthlessly.

¹⁵The king of Egypt said to the Hebrew midwives, whose names were Shiphrah and Puah, ¹⁶"When you help the Hebrew women in childbirth and observe them on the delivery stool, if it is a boy, kill him; but if it is a girl, let her live." ¹⁷The midwives, however, feared God and did not do what the king of Egypt had told them to do; they let the boys live. ¹⁸Then the king of Egypt summoned the midwives and asked them, "Why have you done this? Why have you let the boys live?"

¹⁹The midwives answered Pharaoh, "Hebrew women are not like Egyptian women; they are vigorous and give birth before the midwives arrive."

²⁰So God was kind to the midwives and the people increased and became even more numerous. ²¹And because the midwives feared God, he gave them families of their own.

²²Then Pharaoh gave this order to all his people: "Every boy that is born*b* you must throw into the Nile, but let every girl live."

The Birth of Moses

2 Now a man of the house of Levi married a Levite woman, ²and she became pregnant and gave birth to a son. When she saw that he was a fine child, she hid him for three months. ³But when she could hide him no longer, she got a papyrus basket for him and coated it with tar and pitch. Then she placed the child in it and put it among the reeds along the bank of the Nile. ⁴His sister stood at a distance to see what would happen to him.

⁵Then Pharaoh's daughter went down to the Nile to bathe, and her attendants were walking along the river bank. She saw the basket among the reeds and sent her slave girl to get it. ⁶She opened it and saw the baby. He was crying, and she felt sorry for him. "This is one of the Hebrew babies," she said.

⁷Then his sister asked Pharaoh's daughter, "Shall I go and get one of the Hebrew women to nurse the baby for you?"

⁸"Yes, go," she answered. And the girl went and got the baby's mother. ⁹Pharaoh's daughter said to her, "Take this baby and nurse him for me, and I will pay you." So the woman took the baby and nursed him. ¹⁰When the child grew older, she took him to Pharaoh's daughter and he became her son. She named him Moses,*a* saying, "I drew him out of the water."

Moses Flees to Midian

¹¹One day, after Moses had grown up, he went out to where his own people were and watched them at their hard labour. He saw an Egyptian beating a Hebrew, one of his own people. ¹²Glancing this way and that and seeing no-one, he killed the Egyptian and hid him in the sand. ¹³The next day he went out and saw two Hebrews fighting. He asked the one in the wrong, "Why are you hitting your fellow Hebrew?"

¹⁴The man said, "Who made you ruler and

---

*a*5 Masoretic Text (see also Gen. 46:27); Dead Sea Scrolls and Septuagint (see also Acts 7:14 and note at Gen. 46:27) *seventy-five*
*b*22 Masoretic Text; Samaritan Pentateuch, Septuagint and Targums *born to the Hebrews*
*a*10 *Moses* sounds like the Hebrew for *draw out*.

judge over us? Are you thinking of killing me as you killed the Egyptian?'' Then Moses was afraid and thought, ''What I did must have become known.''

¹⁵When Pharaoh heard of this, he tried to kill Moses, but Moses fled from Pharaoh and went to live in Midian, where he sat down by a well. ¹⁶Now a priest of Midian had seven daughters, and they came to draw water and fill the troughs to water their father's flock. ¹⁷Some shepherds came along and drove them away, but Moses got up and came to their rescue and watered their flock.

¹⁸When the girls returned to Reuel their father, he asked them, ''Why have you returned so early today?''

¹⁹They answered, ''An Egyptian rescued us from the shepherds. He even drew water for us and watered the flock.''

²⁰''And where is he?'' he asked his daughters. ''Why did you leave him? Invite him to have something to eat.''

²¹Moses agreed to stay with the man, who gave his daughter Zipporah to Moses in marriage. ²²Zipporah gave birth to a son, and Moses named him Gershom,ᵇ saying, ''I have become an alien in a foreign land.''

²³During that long period, the king of Egypt died. The Israelites groaned in their slavery and cried out, and their cry for help because of their slavery went up to God. ²⁴God heard their groaning and he remembered his covenant with Abraham, with Isaac and with Jacob. ²⁵So God looked on the Israelites and was concerned about them.

Moses and the Burning Bush

3 Now Moses was tending the flock of Jethro his father-in-law, the priest of Midian, and he led the flock to the far side of the desert and came to Horeb, the mountain of God. ²There the angel of the LORD appeared to him in flames of fire from within a bush. Moses saw that though the bush was on fire it did not burn up. ³So Moses thought, ''I will go over and see this strange sight—why the bush does not burn up.''

⁴When the LORD saw that he had gone over to look, God called to him from within the bush, ''Moses! Moses!''

And Moses said, ''Here I am.''

⁵''Do not come any closer,'' God said. ''Take off your sandals, for the place where you are standing is holy ground.'' ⁶Then he said, ''I am the God of your father, the God of Abraham, the God of Isaac and the God of Jacob.'' At this, Moses hid his face, because he was afraid to look at God.

⁷The LORD said, ''I have indeed seen the misery of my people in Egypt. I have heard them crying out because of their slave drivers, and I am concerned about their suffering. ⁸So I have come down to rescue them from the hand of the Egyptians and to bring them up out of that land into a good and spacious land, a land flowing with milk and honey—the home of the Canaanites,

Hittites, Amorites, Perizzites, Hivites and Jebusites. ⁹And now the cry of the Israelites has reached me, and I have seen the way the Egyptians are oppressing them. ¹⁰So now, go. I am sending you to Pharaoh to bring my people the Israelites out of Egypt.''

¹¹But Moses said to God, ''Who am I, that I should go to Pharaoh and bring the Israelites out of Egypt?''

¹²And God said, ''I will be with you. And this will be the sign to you that it is I who have sent you: When you have brought the people out of Egypt, youᵃ will worship God on this mountain.''

¹³Moses said to God, ''Suppose I go to the Israelites and say to them, 'The God of your fathers has sent me to you,' and they ask me, 'What is his name?' Then what shall I tell them?''

¹⁴God said to Moses, ''I AM WHO I AM.ᵇ This is what you are to say to the Israelites: 'I AM has sent me to you.' ''

¹⁵God also said to Moses, ''Say to the Israelites, 'The LORD,ᶜ the God of your fathers—the God of Abraham, the God of Isaac and the God of Jacob—has sent me to you.' This is my name for ever, the name by which I am to be remembered from generation to generation.

¹⁶''Go, assemble the elders of Israel and say to them, 'The LORD, the God of your fathers—the God of Abraham, Isaac and Jacob—appeared to me and said: I have watched over you and have seen what has been done to you in Egypt. ¹⁷And I have promised to bring you up out of your misery in Egypt into the land of the Canaanites, Hittites, Amorites, Perizzites, Hivites and Jebusites—a land flowing with milk and honey.'

¹⁸''The elders of Israel will listen to you. Then you and the elders are to go to the king of Egypt and say to him, 'The LORD, the God of the Hebrews, has met with us. Let us take a three-day journey into the desert to offer sacrifices to the LORD our God.' ¹⁹But I know that the king of Egypt will not let you go unless a mighty hand compels him. ²⁰So I will stretch out my hand and strike the Egyptians with all the wonders that I will perform among them. After that, he will let you go.

²¹''And I will make the Egyptians favourably disposed towards this people, so that when you leave you will not go empty-handed. ²²Every woman is to ask her neighbour and any woman living in her house for articles of silver and gold and for clothing, which you will put on your sons and daughters. And so you will plunder the Egyptians.''

Signs for Moses

4 Moses answered, ''What if they do not believe me or listen to me and say, 'The LORD did not appear to you'?''

²Then the LORD said to him, ''What is that in your hand?''

ᵇ22 *Gershom* sounds like the Hebrew for *an alien there*.
ᵃ12 The Hebrew is plural.   ᵇ14 Or *I WILL BE WHAT I WILL BE*
ᶜ15 The Hebrew for *LORD* sounds like and may be derived from the Hebrew for *I AM* in verse 14.

"A staff," he replied.

3The LORD said, "Throw it on the ground."

Moses threw it on the ground and it became a snake, and he ran from it. 4Then the LORD said to him, "Reach out your hand and take it by the tail." So Moses reached out and took hold of the snake and it turned back into a staff in his hand. 5"This," said the LORD, "is so that they may believe that the LORD, the God of their fathers—the God of Abraham, the God of Isaac and the God of Jacob —has appeared to you."

6Then the LORD said, "Put your hand inside your cloak." So Moses put his hand into his cloak, and when he took it out, it was leprous,a like snow.

7"Now put it back into your cloak," he said. So Moses put his hand back into his cloak, and when he took it out, it was restored, like the rest of his flesh.

8Then the LORD said, "If they do not believe you or pay attention to the first miraculous sign, they may believe the second. 9But if they do not believe these two signs or listen to you, take some water from the Nile and pour it on the dry ground. The water you take from the river will become blood on the ground."

10Moses said to the LORD, "O Lord, I have never been eloquent, neither in the past nor since you have spoken to your servant. I am slow of speech and tongue."

11The LORD said to him, "Who gave man his mouth? Who makes him deaf or mute? Who gives him sight or makes him blind? Is it not I, the LORD? 12Now go; I will help you speak and will teach you what to say."

13But Moses said, "O Lord, please send someone else to do it."

14Then the LORD's anger burned against Moses and he said, "What about your brother, Aaron the Levite? I know he can speak well. He is already on his way to meet you, and his heart will be glad when he sees you. 15You shall speak to him and put words in his mouth; I will help both of you speak and will teach you what to do. 16He will speak to the people for you, and it will be as if he were your mouth and as if you were God to him. 17But take this staff in your hand so that you can perform miraculous signs with it."

Moses Returns to Egypt

18Then Moses went back to Jethro his father-in-law and said to him, "Let me go back to my own people in Egypt to see if any of them are still alive."

Jethro said, "Go, and I wish you well."

19Now the LORD had said to Moses in Midian, "Go back to Egypt, for all the men who wanted to kill you are dead." 20So Moses took his wife and sons, put them on a donkey and started back to Egypt. And he took the staff of God in his hand.

21The LORD said to Moses, "When you return to Egypt, see that you perform before Pharaoh all the wonders I have given you the power to do. But I will harden his heart so that he will not let the people go. 22Then say to Pharaoh, 'This is what the LORD says: Israel is my firstborn son, 23and I told you, "Let my son go, so that he may worship me." But you refused to let him go; so I will kill your firstborn son.'"

24At a lodging place on the way, the LORD met‚Mosesb and was about to kill him. 25But Zipporah took a flint knife, cut off her son's foreskin and touched‚Moses'‚feet with it.c "Surely you are a bridegroom of blood to me," she said. 26So the LORD let him alone. (At that time she said "bridegroom of blood", referring to circumcision.)

27The LORD said to Aaron, "Go into the desert to meet Moses." So he met Moses at the mountain of God and kissed him. 28Then Moses told Aaron everything the LORD had sent him to say, and also about all the miraculous signs he had commanded him to perform.

29Moses and Aaron brought together all the elders of the Israelites, 30and Aaron told them everything the LORD had said to Moses. He also performed the signs before the people, 31and they believed. And when they heard that the LORD was concerned about them and had seen their misery, they bowed down and worshipped.

Bricks Without Straw

5 Afterwards Moses and Aaron went to Pharaoh and said, "This is what the LORD, the God of Israel, says: 'Let my people go, so that they may hold a festival to me in the desert.'"

2Pharaoh said, "Who is the LORD, that I should obey him and let Israel go? I do not know the LORD and I will not let Israel go."

3Then they said, "The God of the Hebrews has met with us. Now let us take a three-day journey into the desert to offer sacrifices to the LORD our God, or he may strike us with plagues or with the sword."

4But the king of Egypt said, "Moses and Aaron, why are you taking the people away from their labour? Get back to your work!" 5Then Pharaoh said, "Look, the people of the land are now numerous, and you are stopping them from working."

6That same day Pharaoh gave this order to the slave drivers and foremen in charge of the people: 7"You are no longer to supply the people with straw for making bricks; let them go and gather their own straw. 8But require them to make the same number of bricks as before; don't reduce the quota. They are lazy; that is why they are crying out, 'Let us go and sacrifice to our God.' 9Make the work harder for the men so that they keep working and pay no attention to lies."

10Then the slave drivers and the foremen went out and said to the people, "This is what Pharaoh says: 'I will not give you any more straw. 11Go and get your own straw wherever you can find it, but your work will

a6 The Hebrew word was used for various diseases affecting the skin—not necessarily leprosy.
b24 Or Moses' son; Hebrew him   c25 Or and drew near‚Moses'‚feet

not be reduced at all.' " 12So the people scattered all over Egypt to gather stubble to use for straw. 13The slave drivers kept pressing them, saying, "Complete the work required of you for each day, just as when you had straw." 14The Israelite foremen appointed by Pharaoh's slave drivers were beaten and were asked, "Why didn't you meet your quota of bricks yesterday or today, as before?"

15Then the Israelite foremen went and appealed to Pharaoh: "Why have you treated your servants this way? 16Your servants are given no straw, yet we are told, 'Make bricks!' Your servants are being beaten, but the fault is with your own people."

17Pharaoh said, "Lazy, that's what you are—lazy! That is why you keep saying, 'Let us go and sacrifice to the LORD.' 18Now get to work. You will not be given any straw, yet you must produce your full quota of bricks."

19The Israelite foremen realised they were in trouble when they were told, "You are not to reduce the number of bricks required of you for each day." 20When they left Pharaoh, they found Moses and Aaron waiting to meet them, 21and they said, "May the LORD look upon you and judge you! You have made us a stench to Pharaoh and his officials and have put a sword in their hand to kill us."

God Promises Deliverance

22Moses returned to the LORD and said, "O Lord, why have you brought trouble upon this people? Is this why you sent me? 23Ever since I went to Pharaoh to speak in your name, he has brought trouble upon this people, and you have not rescued your people at all."

6 Then the LORD said to Moses, "Now you will see what I will do to Pharaoh: Because of my mighty hand he will let them go; because of my mighty hand he will drive them out of his country."

2God also said to Moses, "I am the LORD. 3I appeared to Abraham, to Isaac and to Jacob as God Almighty,[a] but by my name the LORD[b] I did not make myself known to them.[c] 4I also established my covenant with them to give them the land of Canaan, where they lived as aliens. 5Moreover, I have heard the groaning of the Israelites, whom the Egyptians are enslaving, and I have remembered my covenant.

6"Therefore, say to the Israelites: 'I am the LORD, and I will bring you out from under the yoke of the Egyptians. I will free you from being slaves to them, and I will redeem you with an outstretched arm and with mighty acts of judgment. 7I will take you as my own people, and I will be your God. Then you will know that I am the LORD your God, who brought you out from under the yoke of the Egyptians. 8And I will bring you to the land I swore with uplifted hand to give to Abraham, to Isaac and to Jacob. I will give it to you as a possession. I am the LORD.' "

9Moses reported this to the Israelites, but they did not listen to him because of their discouragement and cruel bondage.

10Then the LORD said to Moses, 11"Go, tell Pharaoh king of Egypt to let the Israelites go out of his country."

12But Moses said to the LORD, "If the Israelites will not listen to me, why would Pharaoh listen to me, since I speak with faltering lips?"[d]

Family Record of Moses and Aaron

13Now the LORD spoke to Moses and Aaron about the Israelites and Pharaoh king of Egypt, and he commanded them to bring the Israelites out of Egypt.

14These were the heads of their families:[e]

The sons of Reuben the firstborn son of Israel were Hanoch and Pallu, Hezron and Carmi. These were the clans of Reuben.

15The sons of Simeon were Jemuel, Jamin, Ohad, Jakin, Zohar and Shaul the son of a Canaanite woman. These were the clans of Simeon.

16These were the names of the sons of Levi according to their records: Gershon, Kohath and Merari. Levi lived 137 years.

17The sons of Gershon, by clans, were Libni and Shimei.

18The sons of Kohath were Amram, Izhar, Hebron and Uzziel. Kohath lived 133 years.

19The sons of Merari were Mahli and Mushi.

These were the clans of Levi according to their records.

20Amram married his father's sister Jochebed, who bore him Aaron and Moses. Amram lived 137 years.

21The sons of Izhar were Korah, Nepheg and Zicri.

22The sons of Uzziel were Mishael, Elzaphan and Sithri.

23Aaron married Elisheba, daughter of Amminadab and sister of Nahshon, and she bore him Nadab and Abihu, Eleazar and Ithamar.

24The sons of Korah were Assir, Elkanah and Abiasaph. These were the Korahite clans.

25Eleazar son of Aaron married one of the daughters of Putiel, and she bore him Phinehas.

These were the heads of the Levite families, clan by clan.

26It was this same Aaron and Moses to whom the LORD said, "Bring the Israelites out of Egypt by their divisions." 27They were the ones who spoke to Pharaoh king of Egypt

---

[a]3 Hebrew El-Shaddai   [b]3 See note at Exodus 3:15.
[c]3 Or Almighty, and by my name the LORD did I not let myself be known to them?
[d]12 Hebrew I am uncircumcised of lips; also in verse 30
[e]14 The Hebrew for families here and in verse 25 refers to units larger than clans.

about bringing the Israelites out of Egypt. It was the same Moses and Aaron.

Aaron to Speak for Moses

28Now when the LORD spoke to Moses in Egypt, 29he said to him, "I am the LORD. Tell Pharaoh king of Egypt everything I tell you."

30But Moses said to the LORD, "Since I speak with faltering lips, why would Pharaoh listen to me?"

7 Then the LORD said to Moses, "See, I have made you like God to Pharaoh, and your brother Aaron will be your prophet. 2You are to say everything I command you, and your brother Aaron is to tell Pharaoh to let the Israelites go out of his country. 3But I will harden Pharaoh's heart, and though I multiply my miraculous signs and wonders in Egypt, 4he will not listen to you. Then I will lay my hand on Egypt and with mighty acts of judgment I will bring out my divisions, my people the Israelites. 5And the Egyptians will know that I am the LORD when I stretch out my hand against Egypt and bring the Israelites out of it."

6Moses and Aaron did just as the LORD commanded them. 7Moses was eighty years old and Aaron eighty-three when they spoke to Pharaoh.

Aaron's Staff Becomes a Snake

8The LORD said to Moses and Aaron, 9"When Pharaoh says to you, 'Perform a miracle,' then say to Aaron, 'Take your staff and throw it down before Pharaoh,' and it will become a snake."

10So Moses and Aaron went to Pharaoh and did just as the LORD commanded. Aaron threw his staff down in front of Pharaoh and his officials, and it became a snake. 11Pharaoh then summoned the wise men and sorcerers, and the Egyptian magicians also did the same things by their secret arts: 12Each one threw down his staff and it became a snake. But Aaron's staff swallowed up their staffs. 13Yet Pharaoh's heart became hard and he would not listen to them, just as the LORD had said.

The Plague of Blood

14Then the LORD said to Moses, "Pharaoh's heart is unyielding; he refuses to let the people go. 15Go to Pharaoh in the morning as he goes out to the water. Wait on the bank of the Nile to meet him, and take in your hand the staff that was changed into a snake. 16Then say to him, 'The LORD, the God of the Hebrews, has sent me to say to you: Let my people go, so that they may worship me in the desert. But until now you have not listened. 17This is what the LORD says: By this you will know that I am the LORD: With the staff that is in my hand I will strike the water of the Nile, and it will be changed into blood. 18The fish in the Nile will die, and the river will stink; the Egyptians will not be able to drink its water.'"

19The LORD said to Moses, "Tell Aaron, 'Take your staff and stretch out your hand over the waters of Egypt—over the streams and canals, over the ponds and all the reservoirs'—and they will turn to blood. Blood will be everywhere in Egypt, even in the wooden buckets and stone jars.'"

20Moses and Aaron did just as the LORD had commanded. He raised his staff in the presence of Pharaoh and his officials and struck the water of the Nile, and all the water was changed into blood. 21The fish in the Nile died, and the river smelled so bad that the Egyptians could not drink its water. Blood was everywhere in Egypt.

22But the Egyptian magicians did the same things by their secret arts, and Pharaoh's heart became hard; he would not listen to Moses and Aaron, just as the LORD had said. 23Instead, he turned and went into his palace, and did not take even this to heart. 24And all the Egyptians dug along the Nile to get drinking water, because they could not drink the water of the river.

The Plague of Frogs

25Seven days passed after the LORD struck the Nile. 1Then the LORD said to Moses, 8 "Go to Pharaoh and say to him, 'This is what the LORD says: Let my people go, so that they may worship me. 2If you refuse to let them go, I will plague your whole country with frogs. 3The Nile will teem with frogs. They will come up into your palace and your bedroom and onto your bed, into the houses of your officials and on your people, and into your ovens and kneading troughs. 4The frogs will go up on you and your people and all your officials.'"

5Then the LORD said to Moses, "Tell Aaron, 'Stretch out your hand with your staff over the streams and canals and ponds, and make frogs come up on the land of Egypt.'"

6So Aaron stretched out his hand over the waters of Egypt, and the frogs came up and covered the land. 7But the magicians did the same things by their secret arts; they also made frogs come up on the land of Egypt.

8Pharaoh summoned Moses and Aaron and said, "Pray to the LORD to take the frogs away from me and my people, and I will let your people go to offer sacrifices to the LORD."

9Moses said to Pharaoh, "I leave to you the honour of setting the time for me to pray for you and your officials and your people that you and your houses may be rid of the frogs, except for those that remain in the Nile."

10"Tomorrow," Pharaoh said.

Moses replied, "It will be as you say, so that you may know there is no-one like the LORD our God. 11The frogs will leave you and your houses, your officials and your people; they will remain only in the Nile."

12After Moses and Aaron left Pharaoh, Moses cried out to the LORD about the frogs he had brought on Pharaoh. 13And the LORD did what Moses asked. The frogs died in the houses, in the courtyards and in the fields. 14They were piled into heaps, and the land reeked of them. 15But when Pharaoh saw that there was relief, he hardened his heart and would not listen to Moses and Aaron, just as the LORD had said.

The Plague of Gnats

16Then the LORD said to Moses, "Tell Aaron, 'Stretch out your staff and strike the dust of the ground,' and throughout the land of Egypt the dust will become gnats." 17They did this, and when Aaron stretched out his hand with the staff and struck the dust of the ground, gnats came upon men and animals. All the dust throughout the land of Egypt became gnats. 18But when the magicians tried to produce gnats by their secret arts, they could not. And the gnats were on men and animals.

19The magicians said to Pharaoh, "This is the finger of God." But Pharaoh's heart was hard and he would not listen, just as the LORD had said.

The Plague of Flies

20Then the LORD said to Moses, "Get up early in the morning and confront Pharaoh as he goes to the water and say to him, 'This is what the LORD says: Let my people go, so that they may worship me. 21If you do not let my people go, I will send swarms of flies on you and your officials, on your people and into your houses. The houses of the Egyptians will be full of flies, and even the ground where they are.

22"'But on that day I will deal differently with the land of Goshen, where my people live; no swarms of flies will be there, so that you will know that I, the LORD, am in this land. 23I will make a distinction[a] between my people and your people. This miraculous sign will occur tomorrow.'"

24And the LORD did this. Dense swarms of flies poured into Pharaoh's palace and into the houses of his officials, and throughout Egypt the land was ruined by the flies.

25Then Pharaoh summoned Moses and Aaron and said, "Go, sacrifice to your God here in the land."

26But Moses said, "That would not be right. The sacrifices we offer the LORD our God would be detestable to the Egyptians. And if we offer sacrifices that are detestable in their eyes, will they not stone us? 27We must take a three-day journey into the desert to offer sacrifices to the LORD our God, as he commands us."

28Pharaoh said, "I will let you go to offer sacrifices to the LORD your God in the desert, but you must not go very far. Now pray for me."

29Moses answered, "As soon as I leave you, I will pray to the LORD, and tomorrow the flies will leave Pharaoh and his officials and his people. Only be sure that Pharaoh does not act deceitfully again by not letting the people go to offer sacrifices to the LORD."

30Then Moses left Pharaoh and prayed to the LORD, 31and the LORD did what Moses asked: The flies left Pharaoh and his officials and his people; not a fly remained. 32But this time also Pharaoh hardened his heart and would not let the people go.

The Plague on Livestock

9 Then the LORD said to Moses, "Go to Pharaoh and say to him, 'This is what the LORD, the God of the Hebrews, says: "Let my people go, so that they may worship me." 2If you refuse to let them go and continue to hold them back, 3the hand of the LORD will bring a terrible plague on your livestock in the field—on your horses and donkeys and camels and on your cattle and sheep and goats. 4But the LORD will make a distinction between the livestock of Israel and that of Egypt, so that no animal belonging to the Israelites will die.'"

5The LORD set a time and said, "Tomorrow the LORD will do this in the land." 6And the next day the LORD did it: All the livestock of the Egyptians died, but not one animal belonging to the Israelites died. 7Pharaoh sent men to investigate and found that not even one of the animals of the Israelites had died. Yet his heart was unyielding and he would not let the people go.

The Plague of Boils

8Then the LORD said to Moses and Aaron, "Take handfuls of soot from a furnace and have Moses toss it into the air in the presence of Pharaoh. 9It will become fine dust over the whole land of Egypt, and festering boils will break out on men and animals throughout the land."

10So they took soot from a furnace and stood before Pharaoh. Moses tossed it into the air, and festering boils broke out on men and animals. 11The magicians could not stand before Moses because of the boils that were on them and on all the Egyptians. 12But the LORD hardened Pharaoh's heart and he would not listen to Moses and Aaron, just as the LORD had said to Moses.

The Plague of Hail

13Then the LORD said to Moses, "Get up early in the morning, confront Pharaoh and say to him, 'This is what the LORD, the God of the Hebrews, says: Let my people go, so that they may worship me, 14or this time I will send the full force of my plagues against you and against your officials and your people, so you may know that there is no-one like me in all the earth. 15For by now I could have stretched out my hand and struck you and your people with a plague that would have wiped you off the earth. 16But I have raised you up[a] for this very purpose, that I might show you my power and that my name might be proclaimed in all the earth. 17You still set yourself against my people and will not let them go. 18Therefore, at this time tomorrow I will send the worst hailstorm that has ever fallen on Egypt, from the day it was founded till now. 19Give an order now to bring your livestock and everything you have in the field to a place of shelter, because the hail will fall on every man and animal that has not been brought in and is still out in the field, and they will die.'"

---

[a]23 Septuagint and Vulgate; Hebrew will put a deliverance
[a]16 Or have spared you

²⁰Those officials of Pharaoh who feared the word of the LORD hurried to bring their slaves and their livestock inside. ²¹But those who ignored the word of the LORD left their slaves and livestock in the field.

²²Then the LORD said to Moses, "Stretch out your hand towards the sky so that hail will fall all over Egypt—on men and animals and on everything growing in the fields of Egypt." ²³When Moses stretched out his staff towards the sky, the LORD sent thunder and hail, and lightning flashed down to the ground. So the LORD rained hail on the land of Egypt; ²⁴hail fell and lightning flashed back and forth. It was the worst storm in all the land of Egypt since it had become a nation. ²⁵Throughout Egypt hail struck everything in the fields—both men and animals; it beat down everything growing in the fields and stripped every tree. ²⁶The only place it did not hail was the land of Goshen, where the Israelites were.

²⁷Then Pharaoh summoned Moses and Aaron. "This time I have sinned," he said to them. "The LORD is in the right, and I and my people are in the wrong. ²⁸Pray to the LORD, for we have had enough thunder and hail. I will let you go; you don't have to stay any longer."

²⁹Moses replied, "When I have gone out of the city, I will spread out my hands in prayer to the LORD. The thunder will stop and there will be no more hail, so you may know that the earth is the LORD's. ³⁰But I know that you and your officials still do not fear the LORD God."

³¹(The flax and barley were destroyed, since the barley was in the ear and the flax was in bloom. ³²The wheat and spelt, however, were not destroyed, because they ripen later.)

³³Then Moses left Pharaoh and went out of the city. He spread out his hands towards the LORD; the thunder and hail stopped, and the rain no longer poured down on the land. ³⁴When Pharaoh saw that the rain and hail and thunder had stopped, he sinned again: He and his officials hardened their hearts. ³⁵So Pharaoh's heart was hard and he would not let the Israelites go, just as the LORD had said through Moses.

The Plague of Locusts

10 Then the LORD said to Moses, "Go to Pharaoh, for I have hardened his heart and the hearts of his officials so that I may perform these miraculous signs of mine among them ²that you may tell your children and grandchildren how I dealt harshly with the Egyptians and how I performed my signs among them, and that you may know that I am the LORD."

³So Moses and Aaron went to Pharaoh and said to him, "This is what the LORD, the God of the Hebrews, says: 'How long will you refuse to humble yourself before me? Let my people go, so that they may worship me. ⁴If you refuse to let them go, I will bring locusts into your country tomorrow. ⁵They will cover the face of the ground so that it cannot be seen. They will devour what little you have left after the hail, including every tree that is growing in your fields. ⁶They will fill your houses and those of all your officials and all the Egyptians—something neither your fathers nor your forefathers have ever seen from the day they settled in this land till now.'" Then Moses turned and left Pharaoh.

⁷Pharaoh's officials said to him, "How long will this man be a snare to us? Let the people go, so that they may worship the LORD their God. Do you not yet realise that Egypt is ruined?"

⁸Then Moses and Aaron were brought back to Pharaoh. "Go, worship the LORD your God," he said. "But just who will be going?"

⁹Moses answered, "We will go with our young and old, with our sons and daughters, and with our flocks and herds, because we are to celebrate a festival to the LORD."

¹⁰Pharaoh said, "The LORD be with you—if I let you go, along with your women and children! Clearly you are bent on evil.^a ¹¹No! Let only the men go; and worship the LORD, since that's what you have been asking for." Then Moses and Aaron were driven out of Pharaoh's presence.

¹²And the LORD said to Moses, "Stretch out your hand over Egypt so that locusts will swarm over the land and devour everything growing in the fields, everything left by the hail."

¹³So Moses stretched out his staff over Egypt, and the LORD made an east wind blow across the land all that day and all that night. By morning the wind had brought the locusts; ¹⁴they invaded all Egypt and settled down in every area of the country in great numbers. Never before had there been such a plague of locusts, nor will there ever be again. ¹⁵They covered all the ground until it was black. They devoured all that was left after the hail—everything growing in the fields and the fruit on the trees. Nothing green remained on tree or plant in all the land of Egypt.

¹⁶Pharaoh quickly summoned Moses and Aaron and said, "I have sinned against the LORD your God and against you. ¹⁷Now forgive my sin once more and pray to the LORD your God to take this deadly plague away from me."

¹⁸Moses then left Pharaoh and prayed to the LORD. ¹⁹And the LORD changed the wind to a very strong west wind, which caught up the locusts and carried them into the Red Sea.^b Not a locust was left anywhere in Egypt. ²⁰But the LORD hardened Pharaoh's heart, and he would not let the Israelites go.

The Plague of Darkness

²¹Then the LORD said to Moses, "Stretch out your hand towards the sky so that darkness will spread over Egypt—darkness that can be felt." ²²So Moses stretched out his hand towards the sky, and total darkness covered all Egypt for three days. ²³No-one

---

^a10 Or *Be careful, trouble is in store for you!*   ^b19 Hebrew *Yam Suph*; that is, Sea of Reeds

could see anyone else or leave his place for three days. Yet all the Israelites had light in the places where they lived.

²⁴Then Pharaoh summoned Moses and said, "Go, worship the LORD. Even your women and children may go with you; only leave your flocks and herds behind."

²⁵But Moses said, "You must allow us to have sacrifices and burnt offerings to present to the LORD our God. ²⁶Our livestock too must go with us; not a hoof is to be left behind. We have to use some of them in worshipping the LORD our God, and until we get there we will not know what we are to use to worship the LORD."

²⁷But the LORD hardened Pharaoh's heart, and he was not willing to let them go. ²⁸Pharaoh said to Moses, "Get out of my sight! Make sure you do not appear before me again! The day you see my face you will die."

²⁹"Just as you say," Moses replied, "I will never appear before you again."

The Plague on the Firstborn

11 Now the LORD said to Moses, "I will bring one more plague on Pharaoh and on Egypt. After that, he will let you go from here, and when he does, he will drive you out completely. ²Tell the people that men and women alike are to ask their neighbours for articles of silver and gold." ³(The LORD made the Egyptians favourably disposed towards the people, and Moses himself was highly regarded in Egypt by Pharaoh's officials and by the people.)

⁴So Moses said, "This is what the LORD says: 'About midnight I will go throughout Egypt. ⁵Every firstborn son in Egypt will die, from the firstborn son of Pharaoh, who sits on the throne, to the firstborn son of the slave girl, who is at her hand mill, and all the firstborn of the cattle as well. ⁶There will be loud wailing throughout Egypt—worse than there has ever been or ever will be again. ⁷But among the Israelites not a dog will bark at any man or animal.' Then you will know that the LORD makes a distinction between Egypt and Israel. ⁸All these officials of yours will come to me, bowing down before me and saying, 'Go, you and all the people who follow you!' After that I will leave." Then Moses, hot with anger, left Pharaoh.

⁹The LORD had said to Moses, "Pharaoh will refuse to listen to you—so that my wonders may be multiplied in Egypt." ¹⁰Moses and Aaron performed all these wonders before Pharaoh, but the LORD hardened Pharaoh's heart, and he would not let the Israelites go out of his country.

The Passover

12 The LORD said to Moses and Aaron in Egypt, ²"This month is to be for you the first month, the first month of your year. ³Tell the whole community of Israel that on the tenth day of this month each man is to take a lamb*a* for his family, one for each household. ⁴If any household is too small for

a whole lamb, they must share one with their nearest neighbour, having taken into account the number of people there are. You are to determine the amount of lamb needed in accordance with what each person will eat. ⁵The animals you choose must be year-old males without defect, and you may take them from the sheep or the goats. ⁶Take care of them until the fourteenth day of the month, when all the people of the community of Israel must slaughter them at twilight. ⁷Then they are to take some of the blood and put it on the sides and tops of the door-frames of the houses where they eat the lambs. ⁸That same night they are to eat the meat roasted over the fire, along with bitter herbs, and bread made without yeast. ⁹Do not eat the meat raw or cooked in water, but roast it over the fire—head, legs and inner parts. ¹⁰Do not leave any of it till morning; if some is left till morning, you must burn it. ¹¹This is how you are to eat it: with your cloak tucked into your belt, your sandals on your feet and your staff in your hand. Eat it in haste; it is the LORD's Passover.

¹²"On that same night I will pass through Egypt and strike down every firstborn—both men and animals—and I will bring judgment on all the gods of Egypt. I am the LORD. ¹³The blood will be a sign for you on the houses where you are; and when I see the blood, I will pass over you. No destructive plague will touch you when I strike Egypt.

¹⁴"This is a day you are to commemorate; for the generations to come you shall celebrate it as a festival to the LORD—a lasting ordinance. ¹⁵For seven days you are to eat bread made without yeast. On the first day remove the yeast from your houses, for whoever eats anything with yeast in it from the first day until the seventh must be cut off from Israel. ¹⁶On the first day hold a sacred assembly, and another one on the seventh day. Do no work at all on these days, except to prepare food for everyone to eat—that is all you may do.

¹⁷"Celebrate the Feast of Unleavened Bread, because it was on this very day that I brought your divisions out of Egypt. Celebrate this day as a lasting ordinance for the generations to come. ¹⁸In the first month you are to eat bread made without yeast, from the evening of the fourteenth day until the evening of the twenty-first day. ¹⁹For seven days no yeast is to be found in your houses. And whoever eats anything with yeast in it must be cut off from the community of Israel, whether he is an alien or native-born. ²⁰Eat nothing made with yeast. Wherever you live, you must eat unleavened bread."

²¹Then Moses summoned all the elders of Israel and said to them, "Go at once and select the animals for your families and slaughter the Passover lamb. ²²Take a bunch of hyssop, dip it into the blood in the basin and put some of the blood on the top and on both sides of the door-frame. Not one of you shall go out of the door of his house until morning. ²³When the LORD goes through the

---

a3 The Hebrew word can mean *lamb* or *kid*; also in verse 4.

land to strike down the Egyptians, he will see the blood on the top and sides of the door-frame and will pass over that doorway, and he will not permit the destroyer to enter your houses and strike you down.

24"Obey these instructions as a lasting ordinance for you and your descendants. 25When you enter the land that the LORD will give you as he promised, observe this ceremony. 26And when your children ask you, 'What does this ceremony mean to you?' 27then tell them, 'It is the Passover sacrifice to the LORD, who passed over the houses of the Israelites in Egypt and spared our homes when he struck down the Egyptians.'" Then the people bowed down and worshipped. 28The Israelites did just what the LORD commanded Moses and Aaron.

29At midnight the LORD struck down all the firstborn in Egypt, from the firstborn of Pharaoh, who sat on the throne, to the firstborn of the prisoner, who was in the dungeon, and the firstborn of all the livestock as well. 30Pharaoh and all his officials and all the Egyptians got up during the night, and there was loud wailing in Egypt, for there was not a house without someone dead.

The Exodus

31During the night Pharaoh summoned Moses and Aaron and said, "Up! Leave my people, you and the Israelites! Go, worship the LORD as you have requested. 32Take your flocks and herds, as you have said, and go. And also bless me."

33The Egyptians urged the people to hurry and leave the country. "For otherwise," they said, "we will all die!" 34So the people took their dough before the yeast was added, and carried it on their shoulders in kneading troughs wrapped in clothing. 35The Israelites did as Moses instructed and asked the Egyptians for articles of silver and gold and for clothing. 36The LORD had made the Egyptians favourably disposed towards the people, and they gave them what they asked for; so they plundered the Egyptians.

37The Israelites journeyed from Rameses to Succoth. There were about six hundred thousand men on foot, besides women and children. 38Many other people went up with them, as well as large droves of livestock, both flocks and herds. 39With the dough they had brought from Egypt, they baked cakes of unleavened bread. The dough was without yeast because they had been driven out of Egypt and did not have time to prepare food for themselves.

40Now the length of time the Israelite people lived in Egypt*b* was 430 years. 41At the end of the 430 years, to the very day, all the LORD's divisions left Egypt. 42Because the LORD kept vigil that night to bring them out of Egypt, on this night all the Israelites are to keep vigil to honour the LORD for the generations to come.

Passover Restrictions

43The LORD said to Moses and Aaron, "These are the regulations for the Passover:

"No foreigner is to eat of it. 44Any slave you have bought may eat of it after you have circumcised him, 45but a temporary resident and a hired worker may not eat of it.

46"It must be eaten inside one house; take none of the meat outside the house. Do not break any of the bones. 47The whole community of Israel must celebrate it.

48"An alien living among you who wants to celebrate the LORD's Passover must have all the males in his household circumcised; then he may take part like one born in the land. No uncircumcised male may eat of it. 49The same law applies to the native-born and to the alien living among you."

50All the Israelites did just what the LORD had commanded Moses and Aaron. 51And on that very day the LORD brought the Israelites out of Egypt by their divisions.

Consecration of the Firstborn

13 The LORD said to Moses, 2"Consecrate to me every firstborn male. The first offspring of every womb among the Israelites belongs to me, whether man or animal."

3Then Moses said to the people, "Commemorate this day, the day you came out of Egypt, out of the land of slavery, because the LORD brought you out of it with a mighty hand. Eat nothing containing yeast. 4Today, in the month of Abib, you are leaving. 5When the LORD brings you into the land of the Canaanites, Hittites, Amorites, Hivites and Jebusites—the land he swore to your forefathers to give you, a land flowing with milk and honey—you are to observe this ceremony in this month: 6For seven days eat bread made without yeast and on the seventh day hold a festival to the LORD. 7Eat unleavened bread during those seven days; nothing with yeast in it is to be seen among you, nor shall any yeast be seen anywhere within your borders. 8On that day tell your son, 'I do this because of what the LORD did for me when I came out of Egypt.' 9This observance will be for you like a sign on your hand and a reminder on your forehead that the law of the LORD is to be on your lips. For the LORD brought you out of Egypt with his mighty hand. 10You must keep this ordinance at the appointed time year after year.

11"After the LORD brings you into the land of the Canaanites and gives it to you, as he promised on oath to you and your forefathers, 12you are to give over to the LORD the first offspring of every womb. All the firstborn males of your livestock belong to the LORD. 13Redeem with a lamb every firstborn donkey, but if you do not redeem it, break its neck. Redeem every firstborn among your sons.

14"In days to come when your son asks you, 'What does this mean?' say to him, 'With a mighty hand the LORD brought us out of Egypt, out of the land of slavery. 15When Pharaoh stubbornly refused to let us go, the LORD killed every firstborn in Egypt, both man and animal. This is why I sacrifice to the

b40 Masoretic Text; Samaritan Pentateuch and Septuagint Egypt and Canaan

LORD the first male offspring of every womb and redeem each of my firstborn sons.' [16]And it will be like a sign on your hand and a symbol on your forehead that the LORD brought us out of Egypt with his mighty hand."

Crossing the Sea

[17]When Pharaoh let the people go, God did not lead them on the road through the Philistine country, though that was shorter. For God said, "If they face war, they might change their minds and return to Egypt." [18]So God led the people around by the desert road towards the Red Sea.[a] The Israelites went up out of Egypt armed for battle.

[19]Moses took the bones of Joseph with him because Joseph had made the sons of Israel swear an oath. He had said, "God will surely come to your aid, and then you must carry my bones up with you from this place."[b]

[20]After leaving Succoth they camped at Etham on the edge of the desert. [21]By day the LORD went ahead of them in a pillar of cloud to guide them on their way and by night in a pillar of fire to give them light, so that they could travel by day or night. [22]Neither the pillar of cloud by day nor the pillar of fire by night left its place in front of the people.

14 Then the LORD said to Moses, [2]"Tell the Israelites to turn back and camp near Pi Hahiroth, between Migdol and the sea. They are to camp by the sea, directly opposite Baal Zephon. [3]Pharaoh will think, 'The Israelites are wandering around the land in confusion, hemmed in by the desert.' [4]And I will harden Pharaoh's heart, and he will pursue them. But I will gain glory for myself through Pharaoh and all his army, and the Egyptians will know that I am the LORD." So the Israelites did this.

[5]When the king of Egypt was told that the people had fled, Pharaoh and his officials changed their minds about them and said, "What have we done? We have let the Israelites go and have lost their services!" [6]So he had his chariot made ready and took his army with him. [7]He took six hundred of the best chariots, along with all the other chariots of Egypt, with officers over all of them. [8]The LORD hardened the heart of Pharaoh king of Egypt, so that he pursued the Israelites, who were marching out boldly. [9]The Egyptians—all Pharaoh's horses and chariots, horsemen[a] and troops—pursued the Israelites and overtook them as they camped by the sea near Pi Hahiroth, opposite Baal Zephon.

[10]As Pharaoh approached, the Israelites looked up, and there were the Egyptians, marching after them. They were terrified and cried out to the LORD. [11]They said to Moses, "Was it because there were no graves in Egypt that you brought us to the desert to die? What have you done to us by bringing us out of Egypt? [12]Didn't we say to you in Egypt, 'Leave us alone; let us serve the

Egyptians'? It would have been better for us to serve the Egyptians than to die in the desert!"

[13]Moses answered the people, "Do not be afraid. Stand firm and you will see the deliverance the LORD will bring you today. The Egyptians you see today you will never see again. [14]The LORD will fight for you; you need only to be still."

[15]Then the LORD said to Moses, "Why are you crying out to me? Tell the Israelites to move on. [16]Raise your staff and stretch out your hand over the sea to divide the water so that the Israelites can go through the sea on dry ground. [17]I will harden the hearts of the Egyptians so that they will go in after them. And I will gain glory through Pharaoh and all his army, through his chariots and his horsemen. [18]The Egyptians will know that I am the LORD when I gain glory through Pharaoh, his chariots and his horsemen."

[19]Then the angel of God, who had been travelling in front of Israel's army, withdrew and went behind them. The pillar of cloud also moved from in front and stood behind them, [20]coming between the armies of Egypt and Israel. Throughout the night the cloud brought darkness to the one side and light to the other; so neither went near the other all night long.

[21]Then Moses stretched out his hand over the sea, and all that night the LORD drove the sea back with a strong east wind and turned it into dry land. The waters were divided, [22]and the Israelites went through the sea on dry ground, with a wall of water on their right and on their left.

[23]The Egyptians pursued them, and all Pharaoh's horses and chariots and horsemen followed them into the sea. [24]During the last watch of the night the LORD looked down from the pillar of fire and cloud at the Egyptian army and threw it into confusion. [25]He made the wheels of their chariots come off[b] so that they had difficulty driving. And the Egyptians said, "Let's get away from the Israelites! The LORD is fighting for them against Egypt."

[26]Then the LORD said to Moses, "Stretch out your hand over the sea so that the waters may flow back over the Egyptians and their chariots and horsemen." [27]Moses stretched out his hand over the sea, and at daybreak the sea went back to its place. The Egyptians were fleeing towards[c] it, and the LORD swept them into the sea. [28]The water flowed back and covered the chariots and horsemen—the entire army of Pharaoh that had followed the Israelites into the sea. Not one of them survived.

[29]But the Israelites went through the sea on dry ground, with a wall of water on their right and on their left. [30]That day the LORD saved Israel from the hands of the Egyptians, and Israel saw the Egyptians lying dead on the shore. [31]And when the Israelites saw the great power the LORD displayed against

---

[a]18 Hebrew *Yam Suph;* that is, Sea of Reeds   [b]19 See Gen. 50:25.
[a]9 Or *charioteers;* also in verses 17, 18, 23, 26 and 28
[b]25 Or *He jammed the wheels of their chariots* (see Samaritan Pentateuch, Septuagint and Syriac)   [c]27 Or *from*

the Egyptians, the people feared the LORD and put their trust in him and in Moses his servant.

The Song of Moses and Miriam

15 Then Moses and the Israelites sang this song to the LORD:

"I will sing to the LORD,
   for he is highly exalted.
The horse and its rider
   he has hurled into the sea.
[2]The LORD is my strength and my song;
   he has become my salvation.
He is my God, and I will praise him,
   my father's God, and I will exalt him.
[3]The LORD is a warrior;
   the LORD is his name.
[4]Pharaoh's chariots and his army
   he has hurled into the sea.
The best of Pharaoh's officers
   are drowned in the Red Sea.[a]
[5]The deep waters have covered them;
   they sank to the depths like a stone.

[6]"Your right hand, O LORD,
   was majestic in power.
Your right hand, O LORD,
   shattered the enemy.
[7]In the greatness of your majesty
   you threw down those who opposed
      you.
You unleashed your burning anger;
   it consumed them like stubble.
[8]By the blast of your nostrils
   the waters piled up.
The surging waters stood firm like a wall;
   the deep waters congealed in the heart
      of the sea.

[9]"The enemy boasted,
   'I will pursue, I will overtake them.
I will divide the spoils;
   I will gorge myself on them.
I will draw my sword
   and my hand will destroy them.'
[10]But you blew with your breath,
   and the sea covered them.
They sank like lead
   in the mighty waters.

[11]"Who among the gods is like you, O
      LORD?
Who is like you—
   majestic in holiness,
   awesome in glory,
   working wonders?
[12]You stretched out your right hand
   and the earth swallowed them.

[13]"In your unfailing love you will lead
   the people you have redeemed.
In your strength you will guide them
   to your holy dwelling.
[14]The nations will hear and tremble;
   anguish will grip the people of Philistia.
[15]The chiefs of Edom will be terrified,
   the leaders of Moab will be seized with
      trembling,

the people[b] of Canaan will melt away;
[16] terror and dread will fall upon them.
By the power of your arm
   they will be as still as a stone—
until your people pass by, O LORD,
   until the people you bought[c] pass by.
[17]You will bring them in and plant them
   on the mountain of your inheritance—
the place, O LORD, you made for your
      dwelling,
   the sanctuary, O Lord, your hands
      established.
[18]The LORD will reign
   for ever and ever."

[19]When Pharaoh's horses, chariots and horsemen[d] went into the sea, the LORD brought the waters of the sea back over them, but the Israelites walked through the sea on dry ground. [20]Then Miriam the prophetess, Aaron's sister, took a tambourine in her hand, and all the women followed her, with tambourines and dancing. [21]Miriam sang to them:

"Sing to the LORD,
   for he is highly exalted.
The horse and its rider
   he has hurled into the sea."

The Waters of Marah and Elim

[22]Then Moses led Israel from the Red Sea and they went into the Desert of Shur. For three days they travelled in the desert without finding water. [23]When they came to Marah, they could not drink its water because it was bitter. (That is why the place is called Marah.[e]) [24]So the people grumbled against Moses, saying, "What are we to drink?"

[25]Then Moses cried out to the LORD, and the LORD showed him a piece of wood. He threw it into the water, and the water became sweet.

There the LORD made a decree and a law for them, and there he tested them. [26]He said, "If you listen carefully to the voice of the LORD your God and do what is right in his eyes, if you pay attention to his commands and keep all his decrees, I will not bring on you any of the diseases I brought on the Egyptians, for I am the LORD, who heals you."

[27]Then they came to Elim, where there were twelve springs and seventy palm trees, and they camped there near the water.

Manna and Quail

16 The whole Israelite community set out from Elim and came to the Desert of Sin, which is between Elim and Sinai, on the fifteenth day of the second month after they had come out of Egypt. [2]In the desert the whole community grumbled against Moses and Aaron. [3]The Israelites said to them, "If only we had died by the LORD's hand in Egypt! There we sat round pots of meat and ate all the food we wanted, but you

---

[a]4 Hebrew *Yam Suph*; that is, Sea of Reeds; also in verse 22   [b]15 Or *rulers*
[c]16 Or *created*   [d]19 Or *charioteers*   [e]23 *Marah* means bitter.

EXODUS 15:1–5

'The LORD is my strength and my song; he has become my salvation. He is my God, and I will praise him, my father's God, and I will exalt him' (v. 2).

SOME SONGS are born out of great historical events. It is not only the French who are stirred by the singing of the *Marseillaise* or the Americans by the 'Battle Hymn of the Republic' or the British by Rudyard Kipling's 'Recessional'. Presumably, all nations have a song which touches the nerve of patriotism and nationhood. As the Israelites marvelled at their rescue from the pursuing Egyptians, their fear turned to joy, and spontaneously they sang of the deliverance which God had effected for them.

Instead of suffering carnage, they had witnessed one of history's outstanding miracles. Today, some people question the miracle and almost dismiss it as a natural event. But God had many options before him, and if he chose to use the east wind to achieve his ends we need not doubt the miracle. He owned the wind. And the timing, so crucial to success, revealed a divine precision. The Hebrews sang because of a miracle of deliverance, not a coincidence. They sang to God's glory. Although it was Moses who had stretched his hand over the sea, he only did so because God commanded him. In their song the Israelites happily linked themselves with their ancestors to whom God had revealed himself as a caring, promise-making God.

The Church has many songs of praise, written to celebrate a deliverance as significant on a personal level as that which Israel celebrated as a nation on the northern shore of the Red Sea.

> *Then sings my soul, my Saviour God, to thee:*
> *How great thou art! How great thou art!*
> *Then sings my soul, my Saviour God, to thee:*
> *How great thou art! How great thou art!*

> (*Carl Boberg, trs. Stuart K. Hine*)

→70

EXODUS 17:1–7
'They tested the LORD saying, "Is the LORD among us or not?" ' (v. 7b).

IT WAS CRISIS TIME AGAIN. The Israelites had moved steadily towards Rephidim. Because the name means 'resting places' they had expectations that a water supply would be available to them, but found instead that the wells or streams were dry. Immediately they complained, even questioning whether God was with them or not. How often difficulties affect the memory! They had experienced the Passover, the crossing of the Red Sea, the sweetening of the water at Marah, the provision of manna, and they could still believe that God had deserted them. John Newton's words indicate for us a better reaction:

> *Though dark be my way,*
> *Since he is my guide,*
> *'Tis mine to obey,*
> *'Tis his to provide.*

God told Moses to take some of the elders with him and directed him to a rock which, when struck, immediately gushed out water enough for all the people. As with the manna, the striking of the rock and provision of water had associations far greater than merely meeting a temporary need. Paul affirmed the supernatural nature of the food and of the water, linking the rock and the water with Christ. Our Lord, with the Samaritan woman at the well-side, and at the Feast of Tabernacles, claimed that he was the source of the water of everlasting life.

Even on the darkest of days, we can be sure that God is with us every step of the way, giving us all the grace we need.

> *All the rivers of thy grace I claim,*
> *Over every promise write my name.*

> (*Herbert Howard Booth*)

→75

have brought us out into this desert to starve this entire assembly to death.''

⁴Then the LORD said to Moses, ''I will rain down bread from heaven for you. The people are to go out each day and gather enough for that day. In this way I will test them and see whether they will follow my instructions. ⁵On the sixth day they are to prepare what they bring in, and that is to be twice as much as they gather on the other days.''

⁶So Moses and Aaron said to all the Israelites, ''In the evening you will know that it was the LORD who brought you out of Egypt, ⁷and in the morning you will see the glory of the LORD, because he has heard your grumbling against him. Who are we, that you should grumble against us?'' ⁸Moses also said, ''You will know that it was the LORD when he gives you meat to eat in the evening and all the bread you want in the morning, because he has heard your grumbling against him. Who are we? You are not grumbling against us, but against the LORD.''

⁹Then Moses told Aaron, ''Say to the entire Israelite community, 'Come before the LORD, for he has heard your grumbling.' ''

¹⁰While Aaron was speaking to the whole Israelite community, they looked towards the desert, and there was the glory of the LORD appearing in the cloud.

¹¹The LORD said to Moses, ¹²''I have heard the grumbling of the Israelites. Tell them, 'At twilight you will eat meat, and in the morning you will be filled with bread. Then you will know that I am the LORD your God.' ''

¹³That evening quail came and covered the camp, and in the morning there was a layer of dew around the camp. ¹⁴When the dew was gone, thin flakes like frost on the ground appeared on the desert floor. ¹⁵When the Israelites saw it, they said to each other, ''What is it?'' For they did not know what it was.

Moses said to them, ''It is the bread the LORD has given you to eat. ¹⁶This is what the LORD has commanded: 'Each one is to gather as much as he needs. Take an omerᵃ for each person you have in your tent.' ''

¹⁷The Israelites did as they were told; some gathered much, some little. ¹⁸And when they measured it by the omer, he who gathered much did not have too much, and he who gathered little did not have too little. Each one gathered as much as he needed.

¹⁹Then Moses said to them, ''No-one is to keep any of it until morning.''

²⁰However, some of them paid no attention to Moses; they kept part of it until morning, but it was full of maggots and began to smell. So Moses was angry with them.

²¹Each morning everyone gathered as much as he needed, and when the sun grew hot, it melted away. ²²On the sixth day, they gathered twice as much—two omersᵇ for each person—and the leaders of the community came and reported this to Moses. ²³He said to them, ''This is what the LORD

commanded: 'Tomorrow is to be a day of rest, a holy Sabbath to the LORD. So bake what you want to bake and boil what you want to boil. Save whatever is left and keep it until morning.' ''

²⁴So they saved it until morning, as Moses commanded, and it did not stink or get maggots in it. ²⁵''Eat it today,'' Moses said, ''because today is a Sabbath to the LORD. You will not find any of it on the ground today. ²⁶Six days you are to gather it, but on the seventh day, the Sabbath, there will not be any.''

²⁷Nevertheless, some of the people went out on the seventh day to gather it, but they found none. ²⁸Then the LORD said to Moses, ''How long will youᶜ refuse to keep my commands and my instructions? ²⁹Bear in mind that the LORD has given you the Sabbath; that is why on the sixth day he gives you bread for two days. Everyone is to stay where he is on the seventh day; no-one is to go out.'' ³⁰So the people rested on the seventh day.

³¹The people of Israel called the bread manna.ᵈ It was white like coriander seed and tasted like wafers made with honey. ³²Moses said, ''This is what the LORD has commanded: 'Take an omer of manna and keep it for the generations to come, so they can see the bread I gave you to eat in the desert when I brought you out of Egypt.' ''

³³So Moses said to Aaron, ''Take a jar and put an omer of manna in it. Then place it before the LORD to be kept for the generations to come.''

³⁴As the LORD commanded Moses, Aaron put the manna in front of the Testimony, that it might be kept. ³⁵The Israelites ate manna for forty years, until they came to a land that was settled; they ate manna until they reached the border of Canaan.

³⁶(An omer is one tenth of an ephah.)

Water From the Rock

17 The whole Israelite community set out from the Desert of Sin, travelling from place to place as the LORD commanded. They camped at Rephidim, but there was no water for the people to drink. ²So they quarrelled with Moses and said, ''Give us water to drink.''

Moses replied, ''Why do you quarrel with me? Why do you put the LORD to the test?''

³But the people were thirsty for water there, and they grumbled against Moses. They said, ''Why did you bring us up out of Egypt to make us and our children and livestock die of thirst?''

⁴Then Moses cried out to the LORD, ''What am I to do with these people? They are almost ready to stone me.''

⁵The LORD answered Moses, ''Walk on ahead of the people. Take with you some of the elders of Israel and take in your hand the staff with which you struck the Nile, and go. ⁶I will stand there before you by the rock at Horeb. Strike the rock, and water will come

---

ᵃ16 That is, probably about 4 pints (about 2 litres); also in verses 18, 32, 33 and 36
ᵇ22 That is, probably about 7½ pints (about 4.5 litres)   ᶜ28 The Hebrew is plural.
ᵈ31 *Manna* means *What is it?* (see verse 15).

out of it for the people to drink." So Moses did this in the sight of the elders of Israel. [7]And he called the place Massah[a] and Meribah[b] because the Israelites quarrelled and because they tested the LORD saying, "Is the LORD among us or not?"

The Amalekites Defeated

[8]The Amalekites came and attacked the Israelites at Rephidim. [9]Moses said to Joshua, "Choose some of our men and go out to fight the Amalekites. Tomorrow I will stand on top of the hill with the staff of God in my hands."

[10]So Joshua fought the Amalekites as Moses had ordered, and Moses, Aaron and Hur went to the top of the hill. [11]As long as Moses held up his hands, the Israelites were winning, but whenever he lowered his hands, the Amalekites were winning. [12]When Moses' hands grew tired, they took a stone and put it under him and he sat on it. Aaron and Hur held his hands up—one on one side, one on the other—so that his hands remained steady till sunset. [13]So Joshua overcame the Amalekite army with the sword.

[14]Then the LORD said to Moses, "Write this on a scroll as something to be remembered and make sure that Joshua hears it, because I will completely blot out the memory of Amalek from under heaven."

[15]Moses built an altar and called it The LORD is my Banner. [16]He said, "For hands were lifted up to the throne of the LORD. The[c] LORD will be at war against the Amalekites from generation to generation."

Jethro Visits Moses

18 Now Jethro, the priest of Midian and father-in-law of Moses, heard of everything God had done for Moses and for his people Israel, and how the LORD had brought Israel out of Egypt.

[2]After Moses had sent away his wife Zipporah, his father-in-law Jethro received her [3]and her two sons. One son was named Gershom,[a] for Moses said, "I have become an alien in a foreign land"; [4]and the other was named Eliezer,[b] for he said, "My father's God was my helper; he saved me from the sword of Pharaoh."

[5]Jethro, Moses' father-in-law, together with Moses' sons and wife, came to him in the desert, where he was camped near the mountain of God. [6]Jethro had sent word to him, "I, your father-in-law Jethro, am coming to you with your wife and her two sons."

[7]So Moses went out to meet his father-in-law and bowed down and kissed him. They greeted each other and then went into the tent. [8]Moses told his father-in-law about everything the LORD had done to Pharaoh and the Egyptians for Israel's sake and about all the hardships they had met along the way and how the LORD had saved them.

[9]Jethro was delighted to hear about all the good things the LORD had done for Israel in rescuing them from the hand of the Egyptians. [10]He said, "Praise be to the LORD, who rescued you from the hand of the Egyptians and of Pharaoh, and who rescued the people from the hand of the Egyptians. [11]Now I know that the LORD is greater than all other gods, for he did this to those who had treated Israel arrogantly." [12]Then Jethro, Moses' father-in-law, brought a burnt offering and other sacrifices to God, and Aaron came with all the elders of Israel to eat bread with Moses' father-in-law in the presence of God.

[13]The next day Moses took his seat to serve as judge for the people, and they stood round him from morning till evening. [14]When his father-in-law saw all that Moses was doing for the people, he said, "What is this you are doing for the people? Why do you alone sit as judge, while all these people stand round you from morning till evening?"

[15]Moses answered him, "Because the people come to me to seek God's will. [16]Whenever they have a dispute, it is brought to me, and I decide between the parties and inform them of God's decrees and laws."

[17]Moses' father-in-law replied, "What you are doing is not good. [18]You and these people who come to you will only wear yourselves out. The work is too heavy for you; you cannot handle it alone. [19]Listen now to me and I will give you some advice, and may God be with you. You must be the people's representative before God and bring their disputes to him. [20]Teach them the decrees and laws, and show them the way to live and the duties they are to perform. [21]But select capable men from all the people—men who fear God, trustworthy men who hate dishonest gain—and appoint them as officials over thousands, hundreds, fifties and tens. [22]Have them serve as judges for the people at all times, but have them bring every difficult case to you; the simple cases they can decide themselves. That will make your load lighter, because they will share it with you. [23]If you do this and God so commands, you will be able to stand the strain, and all these people will go home satisfied."

[24]Moses listened to his father-in-law and did everything he said. [25]He chose capable men from all Israel and made them leaders of the people, officials over thousands, hundreds, fifties and tens. [26]They served as judges for the people at all times. The difficult cases they brought to Moses, but the simple ones they decided themselves.

[27]Then Moses sent his father-in-law on his way, and Jethro returned to his own country.

At Mount Sinai

19 In the third month after the Israelites left Egypt—on the very day—they came to the Desert of Sinai. [2]After they set out from Rephidim, they entered the Desert of Sinai, and Israel camped there in the desert in front of the mountain.

[3]Then Moses went up to God, and the

---

[a]7 Massah means testing.   [b]7 Meribah means quarrelling.
[c]16 Or "Because a hand was against the throne of the LORD, the
[a]3 Gershom sounds like the Hebrew for an alien there.   [b]4 Eliezer means my God is helper.

LORD called to him from the mountain and said, "This is what you are to say to the house of Jacob and what you are to tell the people of Israel: 4'You yourselves have seen what I did to Egypt, and how I carried you on eagles' wings and brought you to myself. 5Now if you obey me fully and keep my covenant, then out of all nations you will be my treasured possession. Although the whole earth is mine, 6you*a* will be for me a kingdom of priests and a holy nation.' These are the words you are to speak to the Israelites."

7So Moses went back and summoned the elders of the people and set before them all the words the LORD had commanded him to speak. 8The people all responded together, "We will do everything the LORD has said." So Moses brought their answer back to the LORD.

9The LORD said to Moses, "I am going to come to you in a dense cloud, so that the people will hear me speaking with you and will always put their trust in you." Then Moses told the LORD what the people had said.

10And the LORD said to Moses, "Go to the people and consecrate them today and tomorrow. Make them wash their clothes 11and be ready by the third day, because on that day the LORD will come down on Mount Sinai in the sight of all the people. 12Put limits for the people around the mountain and tell them, 'Be careful that you do not go up the mountain or touch the foot of it. Whoever touches the mountain shall surely be put to death. 13He shall surely be stoned or shot with arrows; not a hand is to be laid on him. Whether man or animal, he shall not be permitted to live.' Only when the ram's horn sounds a long blast may they go up to the mountain."

14After Moses had gone down the mountain to the people, he consecrated them, and they washed their clothes. 15Then he said to the people, "Prepare yourselves for the third day. Abstain from sexual relations."

16On the morning of the third day there was thunder and lightning, with a thick cloud over the mountain, and a very loud trumpet blast. Everyone in the camp trembled. 17Then Moses led the people out of the camp to meet with God, and they stood at the foot of the mountain. 18Mount Sinai was covered with smoke, because the LORD descended on it in fire. The smoke billowed up from it like smoke from a furnace, the whole mountain*b* trembled violently, 19and the sound of the trumpet grew louder and louder. Then Moses spoke and the voice of God answered him.*c*

20The LORD descended to the top of Mount Sinai and called Moses to the top of the mountain. So Moses went up 21and the LORD said to him, "Go down and warn the people so they do not force their way through to see the LORD and many of them perish. 22Even the priests, who approach the LORD, must

consecrate themselves, or the LORD will break out against them."

23Moses said to the LORD, "The people cannot come up Mount Sinai, because you yourself warned us, 'Put limits around the mountain and set it apart as holy.'"

24The LORD replied, "Go down and bring Aaron up with you. But the priests and the people must not force their way through to come up to the LORD, or he will break out against them."

25So Moses went down to the people and told them.

The Ten Commandments

20 And God spoke all these words:

2"I am the LORD your God, who brought you out of Egypt, out of the land of slavery.

3"You shall have no other gods before*a* me.

4"You shall not make for yourself an idol in the form of anything in heaven above or on the earth beneath or in the waters below. 5You shall not bow down to them or worship them; for I, the LORD your God, am a jealous God, punishing the children for the sin of the fathers to the third and fourth generation of those who hate me, 6but showing love to a thousand ⌊generations⌋ of those who love me and keep my commandments.

7"You shall not misuse the name of the LORD your God, for the LORD will not hold anyone guiltless who misuses his name.

8"Remember the Sabbath day by keeping it holy. 9Six days you shall labour and do all your work, 10but the seventh day is a Sabbath to the LORD your God. On it you shall not do any work, neither you, nor your son or daughter, nor your manservant or maidservant, nor your animals, nor the alien within your gates. 11For in six days the LORD made the heavens and the earth, the sea, and all that is in them, but he rested on the seventh day. Therefore the LORD blessed the Sabbath day and made it holy.

12"Honour your father and your mother, so that you may live long in the land the LORD your God is giving you.

13"You shall not murder.

14"You shall not commit adultery.

15"You shall not steal.

16"You shall not give false testimony against your neighbour.

17"You shall not covet your neighbour's house. You shall not covet your neighbour's wife, or his manservant or maidservant, his ox or

---

a5,6 Or *possession, for the whole earth is mine.* 6*You*
b18 Most Hebrew manuscripts; a few Hebrew manuscripts and Septuagint *all the people*
c19 Or *and God answered him with thunder*   *a3* Or *besides*

donkey, or anything that belongs to your neighbour.''

18When the people saw the thunder and lightning and heard the trumpet and saw the mountain in smoke, they trembled with fear. They stayed at a distance 19and said to Moses, ''Speak to us yourself and we will listen. But do not have God speak to us or we will die.''

20Moses said to the people, ''Do not be afraid. God has come to test you, so that the fear of God will be with you to keep you from sinning.''

21The people remained at a distance, while Moses approached the thick darkness where God was.

Idols and Altars

22Then the LORD said to Moses, ''Tell the Israelites this: 'You have seen for yourselves that I have spoken to you from heaven: 23Do not make any gods to be alongside me; do not make for yourselves gods of silver or gods of gold.

24'' 'Make an altar of earth for me and sacrifice on it your burnt offerings and fellowship offerings,b your sheep and goats and your cattle. Wherever I cause my name to be honoured, I will come to you and bless you. 25If you make an altar of stones for me, do not build it with dressed stones, for you will defile it if you use a tool on it. 26And do not go up to my altar on steps, lest your nakedness be exposed on it.'

21 ''These are the laws you are to set before them:

Hebrew Servants

2''If you buy a Hebrew servant, he is to serve you for six years. But in the seventh year, he shall go free, without paying anything. 3If he comes alone, he is to go free alone; but if he has a wife when he comes, she is to go with him. 4If his master gives him a wife and she bears him sons or daughters, the woman and her children shall belong to her master, and only the man shall go free.

5''But if the servant declares, 'I love my master and my wife and children and do not want to go free,' 6then his master must take him before the judges.a He shall take him to the door or the door-post and pierce his ear with an awl. Then he will be his servant for life.

7''If a man sells his daughter as a servant, she is not to go free as menservants do. 8If she does not please the master who has selected her for himself,b he must let her be redeemed. He has no right to sell her to foreigners, because he has broken faith with her. 9If he selects her for his son, he must grant her the rights of a daughter. 10If he marries another woman, he must not deprive the first one of her food, clothing and marital rights. 11If he does not provide her with these

three things, she is to go free, without any payment of money.

Personal Injuries

12''Anyone who strikes a man and kills him shall surely be put to death. 13However, if he does not do it intentionally, but God lets it happen, he is to flee to a place I will designate. 14But if a man schemes and kills another man deliberately, take him away from my altar and put him to death.

15''Anyone who attacksc his father or his mother must be put to death.

16''Anyone who kidnaps another and either sells him or still has him when he is caught must be put to death.

17''Anyone who curses his father or mother must be put to death.

18''If men quarrel and one hits the other with a stone or with his fistd and he does not die but is confined to bed, 19the one who struck the blow will not be held responsible if the other gets up and walks around outside with his staff; however, he must pay the injured man for the loss of his time and see that he is completely healed.

20''If a man beats his male or female slave with a rod and the slave dies as a direct result, he must be punished, 21but he is not to be punished if the slave gets up after a day or two, since the slave is his property.

22''If men who are fighting hit a pregnant woman and she gives birth prematurelye but there is no serious injury, the offender must be fined whatever the woman's husband demands and the court allows. 23But if there is serious injury, you are to take life for life, 24eye for eye, tooth for tooth, hand for hand, foot for foot, 25burn for burn, wound for wound, bruise for bruise.

26''If a man hits a manservant or maidservant in the eye and destroys it, he must let the servant go free to compensate for the eye. 27And if he knocks out the tooth of a manservant or maidservant, he must let the servant go free to compensate for the tooth.

28''If a bull gores a man or a woman to death, the bull must be stoned to death, and its meat must not be eaten. But the owner of the bull will not be held responsible. 29If, however, the bull has had the habit of goring and the owner has been warned but has not kept it penned up and it kills a man or woman, the bull must be stoned and the owner also must be put to death. 30However, if payment is demanded of him, he may redeem his life by paying whatever is demanded. 31This law also applies if the bull gores a son or a daughter. 32If the bull gores a male or female slave, the owner must pay thirty shekelsf of silver to the master of the slave, and the bull must be stoned.

33''If a man uncovers a pit or digs one and fails to cover it and an ox or a donkey falls into it, 34the owner of the pit must pay for the loss; he must pay its owner, and the dead animal will be his.

b24 Traditionally peace offerings   a6 Or before God   b8 Or master so that he does not choose her
c15 Or kills   d18 Or with a tool   e22 Or she has a miscarriage
f32 That is, about 12 ounces (about 0.3 kilogram)

EXODUS 20:13–21

'You shall not covet your neighbour's house. You shall not covet your neighbour's wife, or his manservant or maidservant, his ox or donkey, or anything that belongs to your neighbour' (v. 17).

THE LAWS related to murder, adultery, stealing and lying (primarily, though not exclusively, to giving false witness), probably carry the judgement of the vast majority of people, even though they are the laws most commonly broken today. Violence, immorality, theft and dishonesty keep the legal systems of countries, large and small, in a constant state of overwork.

The tenth commandment, the law against coveting, serves to bring the commandments right home to the heart. A legalistic person could claim to have obeyed the Mosaic Law completely, and be proud of that achievement, were it not for this last law which makes for an inwardness of appeal not found in the others. The prophets knew of the deceitfulness of the heart, but it was left to our Lord to state that it was out of the heart that all ills came. The list is comprehensive and frightening. But coveting, that sin of desiring something or someone which rightly belongs to another, is probably the most readily identifiable source of human lawlessness. It is possibly the sin which insinuates itself most easily into our conscious thought.

The negative wording of the laws only emphasizes their positive nature. They are basic laws, the first four relating us to God and the last six to each other. We still cannot do without them.

> *Deepen in me thy work of grace,*
> *Teach me to do thy will,*
> *Help me to live a spotless life,*
> *Thy holy laws fulfil.*

(*William Henry Hutchings*)

→76

EXODUS 26:1–30

'Set up the tabernacle according to the plan shown you on the mountain' (v. 30).

THE DETAILS of the building of the tabernacle can be tedious, but we cannot afford to overlook the great design. It must be remembered that Israel was a pilgrim people at this time, in slow, laborious and dangerous transit from Egypt, the land of bondage, to Canaan, the land of promise. God was determined to establish them as a nation, subject to him and his law, and the tabernacle was a crucial element in his strategy. The entire structure consisted of a courtyard, measuring 150 by 75 feet, with an entrance at the eastern end. Immediately facing the entrance was the altar of burnt offering. Beyond that was the basin, where the priests washed hands and feet before engaging in the ceremonies. Beyond the basin stood the tabernacle itself, consisting of the holy place which housed, on the right, the table of shewbread, and on the left, the golden lampstand. Beyond them, immediately in front of the veil and centrally placed, was the altar of incense. Behind the veil was the Holy of Holies with the Ark of the Covenant and the mercy seat. Solomon's temple (*c.* 960 BC) was much more elaborate than the pilgrim tabernacle.

The structure and procedures ensured that the people could not rush into the presence of God. From the moment they entered the courtyard they were confronted by symbols which reminded them of their sinfulness and the need for cleansing. The fact that God dwelt in the tabernacle imparted a deep sense of awe, generating within sensitive souls a spirit of worship and thanksgiving.

> *Praise to the holiest in the height.*
> *And in the depth be praise,*
> *In all his words most wonderful,*
> *Most sure in all his ways.*

(John Henry Newman)

35"If a man's bull injures the bull of another and it dies, they are to sell the live one and divide both the money and the dead animal equally. 36However, if it was known that the bull had the habit of goring, yet the owner did not keep it penned up, the owner must pay, animal for animal, and the dead animal will be his.

Protection of Property

22 "If a man steals an ox or a sheep and slaughters it or sells it, he must pay back five head of cattle for the ox and four sheep for the sheep.

2"If a thief is caught breaking in and is struck so that he dies, the defender is not guilty of bloodshed; 3but if it happens[a] after sunrise, he is guilty of bloodshed.

"A thief must certainly make restitution, but if he has nothing, he must be sold to pay for his theft.

4"If the stolen animal is found alive in his possession—whether ox or donkey or sheep —he must pay back double.

5"If a man grazes his livestock in a field or vineyard and lets them stray and they graze in another man's field, he must make restitution from the best of his own field or vineyard.

6"If a fire breaks out and spreads into thornbushes so that it burns shocks of grain or standing corn or the whole field, the one who started the fire must make restitution.

7"If a man gives his neighbour silver or goods for safekeeping and they are stolen from the neighbour's house, the thief, if he is caught, must pay back double. 8But if the thief is not found, the owner of the house must appear before the judges[b] to determine whether he has laid his hands on the other man's property. 9In all cases of illegal possession of an ox, a donkey, a sheep, a garment, or any other lost property about which somebody says, 'This is mine,' both parties are to bring their cases before the judges. The one whom the judges declare[c] guilty must pay back double to his neighbour.

10"If a man gives a donkey, an ox, a sheep or any other animal to his neighbour for safekeeping and it dies or is injured or is taken away while no-one is looking, 11the issue between them will be settled by the taking of an oath before the LORD that the neighbour did not lay hands on the other person's property. The owner is to accept this, and no restitution is required. 12But if the animal was stolen from the neighbour, he must make restitution to the owner. 13If it was torn to pieces by a wild animal, he shall bring in the remains as evidence and he will not be required to pay for the torn animal.

14"If a man borrows an animal from his neighbour and it is injured or dies while the owner is not present, he must make restitution. 15But if the owner is with the animal, the borrower will not have to pay. If the animal was hired, the money paid for the hire covers the loss.

Social Responsibility

16"If a man seduces a virgin who is not pledged to be married and sleeps with her, he must pay the bride-price, and she shall be his wife. 17If her father absolutely refuses to give her to him, he must still pay the bride-price for virgins.

18"Do not allow a sorceress to live.

19"Anyone who has sexual relations with an animal must be put to death.

20"Whoever sacrifices to any god other than the LORD must be destroyed.[d]

21"Do not ill-treat an alien or oppress him, for you were aliens in Egypt.

22"Do not take advantage of a widow or an orphan. 23If you do and they cry out to me, I will certainly hear their cry. 24My anger will be aroused, and I will kill you with the sword; your wives will become widows and your children fatherless.

25"If you lend money to one of my people among you who is needy, do not be like a money-lender; charge him no interest.[e] 26If you take your neighbour's cloak as a pledge, return it to him by sunset, 27because his cloak is the only covering he has for his body. What else will he sleep in? When he cries out to me, I will hear, for I am compassionate.

28"Do not blaspheme God[f] or curse the ruler of your people.

29"Do not hold back offerings from your granaries or your vats.[g]

"You must give me the firstborn of your sons. 30Do the same with your cattle and your sheep. Let them stay with their mothers for seven days, but give them to me on the eighth day.

31"You are to be my holy people. So do not eat the meat of an animal torn by wild beasts; throw it to the dogs.

Laws of Justice and Mercy

23 "Do not spread false reports. Do not help a wicked man by being a malicious witness.

2"Do not follow the crowd in doing wrong. When you give testimony in a lawsuit, do not pervert justice by siding with the crowd, 3and do not show favouritism to a poor man in his lawsuit.

4"If you come across your enemy's ox or donkey wandering off, be sure to take it back to him. 5If you see the donkey of someone who hates you fallen down under its load, do not leave it there; be sure you help him with it.

6"Do not deny justice to your poor people in their lawsuits. 7Have nothing to do with a false charge and do not put an innocent or honest person to death, for I will not acquit the guilty.

8"Do not accept a bribe, for a bribe blinds those who see and twists the words of the righteous.

---

a3 Or if he strikes him   b8 Or before God; also in verse 9   c9 Or whom God declares
d20 The Hebrew term refers to the irrevocable giving over of things or persons to the LORD, often by totally destroying them.   e25 Or excessive interest   f28 Or Do not revile the judges
g29 The meaning of the Hebrew for this phrase is uncertain.

9"Do not oppress an alien; you yourselves know how it feels to be aliens, because you were aliens in Egypt.

Sabbath Laws

10"For six years you are to sow your fields and harvest the crops, 11but during the seventh year let the land lie unploughed and unused. Then the poor among your people may get food from it, and the wild animals may eat what they leave. Do the same with your vineyard and your olive grove.

12"Six days do your work, but on the seventh day do not work, so that your ox and your donkey may rest and the slave born in your household, and the alien as well, may be refreshed.

13"Be careful to do everything I have said to you. Do not invoke the names of other gods; do not let them be heard on your lips.

The Three Annual Festivals

14"Three times a year you are to celebrate a festival to me.

15"Celebrate the Feast of Unleavened Bread; for seven days eat bread made without yeast, as I commanded you. Do this at the appointed time in the month of Abib, for in that month you came out of Egypt.

"No-one is to appear before me empty-handed.

16"Celebrate the Feast of Harvest with the firstfruits of the crops you sow in your field.

"Celebrate the Feast of Ingathering at the end of the year, when you gather in your crops from the field.

17"Three times a year all the men are to appear before the Sovereign LORD.

18"Do not offer the blood of a sacrifice to me along with anything containing yeast.

"The fat of my festival offerings must not be kept until morning.

19"Bring the best of the firstfruits of your soil to the house of the LORD your God.

"Do not cook a young goat in its mother's milk.

God's Angel to Prepare the Way

20"See, I am sending an angel ahead of you to guard you along the way and to bring you to the place I have prepared. 21Pay attention to him and listen to what he says. Do not rebel against him; he will not forgive your rebellion, since my Name is in him. 22If you listen carefully to what he says and do all that I say, I will be an enemy to your enemies and will oppose those who oppose you. 23My angel will go ahead of you and bring you into the land of the Amorites, Hittites, Perizzites, Canaanites, Hivites and Jebusites, and I will wipe them out. 24Do not bow down before their gods or worship them or follow their practices. You must demolish them and break their sacred stones to pieces. 25Worship the LORD your God, and his blessing will be on your food and water. I will take away sickness from among you, 26and none will miscarry or be barren in your land. I will give you a full life span.

27"I will send my terror ahead of you and throw into confusion every nation you encounter. I will make all your enemies turn their backs and run. 28I will send the hornet ahead of you to drive the Hivites, Canaanites and Hittites out of your way. 29But I will not drive them out in a single year, because the land would become desolate and the wild animals too numerous for you. 30Little by little I will drive them out before you, until you have increased enough to take possession of the land.

31"I will establish your borders from the Red Sea*a* to the Sea of the Philistines,*b* and from the desert to the River.*c* I will hand over to you the people who live in the land and you will drive them out before you. 32Do not make a covenant with them or with their gods. 33Do not let them live in your land, or they will cause you to sin against me, because the worship of their gods will certainly be a snare to you."

The Covenant Confirmed

24 Then he said to Moses, "Come up to the LORD, you and Aaron, Nadab and Abihu, and seventy of the elders of Israel. You are to worship at a distance, 2but Moses alone is to approach the LORD; the others must not come near. And the people may not come up with him."

3When Moses went and told the people all the LORD's words and laws, they responded with one voice, "Everything the LORD has said we will do." 4Moses then wrote down everything the LORD had said.

He got up early the next morning and built an altar at the foot of the mountain and set up twelve stone pillars representing the twelve tribes of Israel. 5Then he sent young Israelite men, and they offered burnt offerings and sacrificed young bulls as fellowship offerings*a* to the LORD. 6Moses took half of the blood and put it in bowls, and the other half he sprinkled on the altar. 7Then he took the Book of the Covenant and read it to the people. They responded, "We will do everything the LORD has said; we will obey."

8Moses then took the blood, sprinkled it on the people and said, "This is the blood of the covenant that the LORD has made with you in accordance with all these words."

9Moses and Aaron, Nadab and Abihu, and the seventy elders of Israel went up 10and saw the God of Israel. Under his feet was something like a pavement made of sapphire,*b* clear as the sky itself. 11But God did not raise his hand against these leaders of the Israelites; they saw God, and they ate and drank.

12The LORD said to Moses, "Come up to me on the mountain and stay here, and I will give you the tablets of stone, with the law and commands I have written for their instruction."

---

a31 Hebrew *Yam Suph*; that is, Sea of Reeds   *b31* That is, the Mediterranean   *c31* That is, the Euphrates
a5 Traditionally *peace offerings*   *b10* Or *lapis lazuli*

[13]Then Moses set out with Joshua his assistant, and Moses went up on the mountain of God. [14]He said to the elders, "Wait here for us until we come back to you. Aaron and Hur are with you, and anyone involved in a dispute can go to them."

[15]When Moses went up on the mountain, the cloud covered it, [16]and the glory of the LORD settled on Mount Sinai. For six days the cloud covered the mountain, and on the seventh day the LORD called to Moses from within the cloud. [17]To the Israelites the glory of the LORD looked like a consuming fire on top of the mountain. [18]Then Moses entered the cloud as he went on up the mountain. And he stayed on the mountain forty days and forty nights.

Offerings for the Tabernacle

25 The LORD said to Moses, [2]"Tell the Israelites to bring me an offering. You are to receive the offering for me from each man whose heart prompts him to give. [3]These are the offerings you are to receive from them: gold, silver and bronze; [4]blue, purple and scarlet yarn and fine linen; goat hair; [5]ram skins dyed red and hides of sea cows;[a] acacia wood; [6]olive oil for the light; spices for the anointing oil and for the fragrant incense; [7]and onyx stones and other gems to be mounted on the ephod and breastpiece.

[8]"Then have them make a sanctuary for me, and I will dwell among them. [9]Make this tabernacle and all its furnishings exactly like the pattern I will show you.

The Ark

[10]"Have them make a chest of acacia wood—two and a half cubits long, a cubit and a half wide, and a cubit and a half high.[b] [11]Overlay it with pure gold, both inside and out, and make a gold moulding around it. [12]Cast four gold rings for it and fasten them to its four feet, with two rings on one side and two rings on the other. [13]Then make poles of acacia wood and overlay them with gold. [14]Insert the poles into the rings on the sides of the chest to carry it. [15]The poles are to remain in the rings of this ark; they are not to be removed. [16]Then put in the ark the Testimony, which I will give you.

[17]"Make an atonement cover[c] of pure gold —two and a half cubits long and a cubit and a half wide.[d] [18]And make two cherubim out of hammered gold at the ends of the cover. [19]Make one cherub on one end and the second cherub on the other; make the cherubim of one piece with the cover, at the two ends. [20]The cherubim are to have their wings spread upwards, overshadowing the cover with them. The cherubim are to face each other, looking towards the cover. [21]Place the cover on top of the ark and put in the ark the

Testimony, which I will give you. [22]There, above the cover between the two cherubim that are over the ark of the Testimony, I will meet with you and give you all my commands for the Israelites.

The Table

[23]"Make a table of acacia wood—two cubits long, a cubit wide and a cubit and a half high.[e] [24]Overlay it with pure gold and make a gold moulding around it. [25]Also make around it a rim a handbreadth[f] wide and put a gold moulding on the rim. [26]Make four gold rings for the table and fasten them to the four corners, where the four legs are. [27]The rings are to be close to the rim to hold the poles used in carrying the table. [28]Make the poles of acacia wood, overlay them with gold and carry the table with them. [29]And make its plates and dishes of pure gold, as well as its pitchers and bowls for the pouring out of offerings. [30]Put the bread of the Presence on this table to be before me at all times.

The Lampstand

[31]"Make a lampstand of pure gold and hammer it out, base and shaft; its flowerlike cups, buds and blossoms shall be of one piece with it. [32]Six branches are to extend from the sides of the lampstand—three on one side and three on the other. [33]Three cups shaped like almond flowers with buds and blossoms are to be on one branch, three on the next branch, and the same for all six branches extending from the lampstand. [34]And on the lampstand there are to be four cups shaped like almond flowers with buds and blossoms. [35]One bud shall be under the first pair of branches extending from the lampstand, a second bud under the second pair, and a third bud under the third pair—six branches in all. [36]The buds and branches shall all be of one piece with the lampstand, hammered out of pure gold.

[37]"Then make its seven lamps and set them up on it so that they light the space in front of it. [38]Its wick trimmers and trays are to be of pure gold. [39]A talent[g] of pure gold is to be used for the lampstand and all these accessories. [40]See that you make them according to the pattern shown you on the mountain.

The Tabernacle

26 "Make the tabernacle with ten curtains of finely twisted linen and blue, purple and scarlet yarn, with cherubim worked into them by a skilled craftsman. [2]All the curtains are to be the same size—twenty-eight cubits long and four cubits wide.[a] [3]Join five of the curtains together, and do the same with the other five. [4]Make loops of blue material along the edge of the end curtain in one set, and do the same with the end curtain

---

[a]5 That is, large aquatic mammals
[b]10 That is, about 3¾ feet (about 1.1 metres) long and 2¼ feet (about 0.7 metre) wide and high
[c]17 Traditionally *a mercy seat*
[d]17 That is, about 3¾ feet (about 1.1 metres) long and 2¼ feet (about 0.7 metre) wide
[e]23 That is, about 3 feet (about 0.9 metre) long and 1½ feet (about 0.5 metre) wide and 2¼ feet (about 0.7 metre) high
[f]25 That is, about 3 inches (about 8 centimetres)   [g]39 That is, about 75 pounds (about 34 kilograms)
[a]2 That is, about 42 feet (about 13 metres) long and 6 feet (about 1.8 metres) wide

in the other set. ⁵Make fifty loops on one curtain and fifty loops on the end curtain of the other set, with the loops opposite each other. ⁶Then make fifty gold clasps and use them to fasten the curtains together so that the tabernacle is a unit.

⁷"Make curtains of goat hair for the tent over the tabernacle—eleven altogether. ⁸All eleven curtains are to be the same size—thirty cubits long and four cubits wide.ᵇ ⁹Join five of the curtains together into one set and the other six into another set. Fold the sixth curtain double at the front of the tent. ¹⁰Make fifty loops along the edge of the end curtain in one set and also along the edge of the end curtain in the other set. ¹¹Then make fifty bronze clasps and put them in the loops to fasten the tent together as a unit. ¹²As for the additional length of the tent curtains, the half curtain that is left over is to hang down at the rear of the tabernacle. ¹³The tent curtains will be a cubitᶜ longer on both sides; what is left will hang over the sides of the tabernacle so as to cover it. ¹⁴Make for the tent a covering of ram skins dyed red, and over that a covering of hides of sea cows.ᵈ

¹⁵"Make upright frames of acacia wood for the tabernacle. ¹⁶Each frame is to be ten cubits long and a cubit and a half wide,ᵉ ¹⁷with two projections set parallel to each other. Make all the frames of the tabernacle in this way. ¹⁸Make twenty frames for the south side of the tabernacle ¹⁹and make forty silver bases to go under them—two bases for each frame, one under each projection. ²⁰For the other side, the north side of the tabernacle, make twenty frames ²¹and forty silver bases—two under each frame. ²²Make six frames for the far end, that is, the west end of the tabernacle, ²³and make two frames for the corners at the far end. ²⁴At these two corners they must be double from the bottom all the way to the top, and fitted into a single ring; both shall be like that. ²⁵So there will be eight frames and sixteen silver bases—two under each frame.

²⁶"Also make crossbars of acacia wood: five for the frames on one side of the tabernacle, ²⁷five for those on the other side, and five for the frames on the west, at the far end of the tabernacle. ²⁸The centre crossbar is to extend from end to end at the middle of the frames. ²⁹Overlay the frames with gold and make gold rings to hold the crossbars. Also overlay the crossbars with gold.

³⁰"Set up the tabernacle according to the plan shown you on the mountain.

³¹"Make a curtain of blue, purple and scarlet yarn and finely twisted linen, with cherubim worked into it by a skilled craftsman. ³²Hang it with gold hooks on four posts of acacia wood overlaid with gold and standing on four silver bases. ³³Hang the curtain from the clasps and place the ark of the Testimony

behind the curtain. The curtain will separate the Holy Place from the Most Holy Place. ³⁴Put the atonement cover on the ark of the Testimony in the Most Holy Place. ³⁵Place the table outside the curtain on the north side of the tabernacle and put the lampstand opposite it on the south side.

³⁶"For the entrance to the tent make a curtain of blue, purple and scarlet yarn and finely twisted linen—the work of an embroiderer. ³⁷Make gold hooks for this curtain and five posts of acacia wood overlaid with gold. And cast five bronze bases for them.

The Altar of Burnt Offering

27 "Build an altar of acacia wood, three cubitsᵃ high; it is to be square, five cubits long and five cubits wide.ᵇ ²Make a horn at each of the four corners, so that the horns and the altar are of one piece, and overlay the altar with bronze. ³Make all its utensils of bronze—its pots to remove the ashes, and its shovels, sprinkling bowls, meat forks and firepans. ⁴Make a grating for it, a bronze network, and make a bronze ring at each of the four corners of the network. ⁵Put it under the ledge of the altar so that it is halfway up the altar. ⁶Make poles of acacia wood for the altar and overlay them with bronze. ⁷The poles are to be inserted into the rings so they will be on two sides of the altar when it is carried. ⁸Make the altar hollow, out of boards. It is to be made just as you were shown on the mountain.

The Courtyard

⁹"Make a courtyard for the tabernacle. The south side shall be a hundred cubitsᶜ long and is to have curtains of finely twisted linen, ¹⁰with twenty posts and twenty bronze bases and with silver hooks and bands on the posts. ¹¹The north side shall also be a hundred cubits long and is to have curtains, with twenty posts and twenty bronze bases and with silver hooks and bands on the posts. ¹²The west end of the courtyard shall be fifty cubitsᵈ wide and have curtains, with ten posts and ten bases. ¹³On the east end, towards the sunrise, the courtyard shall also be fifty cubits wide. ¹⁴Curtains fifteen cubitsᵉ long are to be on one side of the entrance, with three posts and three bases, ¹⁵and curtains fifteen cubits long are to be on the other side, with three posts and three bases.

¹⁶"For the entrance to the courtyard, provide a curtain twenty cubitsᶠ long, of blue, purple and scarlet yarn and finely twisted linen—the work of an embroiderer—with four posts and four bases. ¹⁷All the posts around the courtyard are to have silver bands and hooks, and bronze bases. ¹⁸The courtyard shall be a hundred cubits long and fifty

---

ᵇ8 That is, about 45 feet (about 13.5 metres) long and 6 feet (about 1.8 metres) wide
ᶜ13 That is, about 1½ feet (about 0.5 metre)   ᵈ14 That is, large aquatic mammals
ᵉ16 That is, about 15 feet (about 4.5 metres) long and 2¼ feet (about 0.7 metre) wide
ᵃ1 That is, about 4½ feet (about 1.4 metres)   ᵇ1 That is, about 7½ feet (about 2.3 metres) long and wide
ᶜ9 That is, about 150 feet (about 46 metres); also in verse 11
ᵈ12 That is, about 75 feet (about 23 metres); also in verse 13
ᵉ14 That is, about 22½ feet (about 6.9 metres); also in verse 15   ᶠ16 That is, about 30 feet (about 9 metres)

cubits wide,[g] with curtains of finely twisted linen five cubits[h] high, and with bronze bases. 19All the other articles used in the service of the tabernacle, whatever their function, including all the tent pegs for it and those for the courtyard, are to be of bronze.

Oil for the Lampstand

20"Command the Israelites to bring you clear oil of pressed olives for the light so that the lamps may be kept burning. 21In the Tent of Meeting, outside the curtain that is in front of the Testimony, Aaron and his sons are to keep the lamps burning before the LORD from evening till morning. This is to be a lasting ordinance among the Israelites for the generations to come.

The Priestly Garments

28 "Have Aaron your brother brought to you from among the Israelites, with his sons Nadab and Abihu, Eleazar and Ithamar, so that they may serve me as priests. 2Make sacred garments for your brother Aaron, to give him dignity and honour. 3Tell all the skilled men to whom I have given wisdom in such matters that they are to make garments for Aaron, for his consecration, so that he may serve me as priest. 4These are the garments they are to make: a breastpiece, an ephod, a robe, a woven tunic, a turban and a sash. They are to make these sacred garments for your brother Aaron and his sons, so that they may serve me as priests. 5Make them use gold, and blue, purple and scarlet yarn, and fine linen.

The Ephod

6"Make the ephod of gold, and of blue, purple and scarlet yarn, and of finely twisted linen—the work of a skilled craftsman. 7It is to have two shoulder pieces attached to two of its corners, so that it can be fastened. 8Its skilfully woven waistband is to be like it—of one piece with the ephod and made with gold, and with blue, purple and scarlet yarn, and with finely twisted linen.

9"Take two onyx stones and engrave on them the names of the sons of Israel 10in the order of their birth—six names on one stone and the remaining six on the other. 11Engrave the names of the sons of Israel on the two stones the way a gem cutter engraves a seal. Then mount the stones in gold filigree settings 12and fasten them on the shoulder pieces of the ephod as memorial stones for the sons of Israel. Aaron is to bear the names on his shoulders as a memorial before the LORD. 13Make gold filigree settings 14and two braided chains of pure gold, like a rope, and attach the chains to the settings.

The Breastpiece

15"Fashion a breastpiece for making decisions—the work of a skilled craftsman. Make it like the ephod: of gold, and of blue, purple and scarlet yarn, and of finely twisted

linen. 16It is to be square—a span[a] long and a span wide—and folded double. 17Then mount four rows of precious stones on it. In the first row there shall be a ruby, a topaz and a beryl; 18in the second row a turquoise, a sapphire[b] and an emerald; 19in the third row a jacinth, an agate and an amethyst; 20in the fourth row a chrysolite, an onyx and a jasper.[c] Mount them in gold filigree settings. 21There are to be twelve stones, one for each of the names of the sons of Israel, each engraved like a seal with the name of one of the twelve tribes.

22"For the breastpiece make braided chains of pure gold, like a rope. 23Make two gold rings for it and fasten them to two corners of the breastpiece. 24Fasten the two gold chains to the rings at the corners of the breastpiece, 25and the other ends of the chains to the two settings, attaching them to the shoulder pieces of the ephod at the front. 26Make two gold rings and attach them to the other two corners of the breastpiece on the inside edge next to the ephod. 27Make two more gold rings and attach them to the bottom of the shoulder pieces on the front of the ephod, close to the seam just above the waistband of the ephod. 28The rings of the breastpiece are to be tied to the rings of the ephod with blue cord, connecting it to the waistband, so that the breastpiece will not swing out from the ephod.

29"Whenever Aaron enters the Holy Place, he will bear the names of the sons of Israel over his heart on the breastpiece of decision as a continuing memorial before the LORD. 30Also put the Urim and the Thummim in the breastpiece, so they may be over Aaron's heart whenever he enters the presence of the LORD. Thus Aaron will always bear the means of making decisions for the Israelites over his heart before the LORD.

Other Priestly Garments

31"Make the robe of the ephod entirely of blue cloth, 32with an opening for the head in its centre. There shall be a woven edge like a collar[d] around this opening, so that it will not tear. 33Make pomegranates of blue, purple and scarlet yarn around the hem of the robe, with gold bells between them. 34The gold bells and the pomegranates are to alternate around the hem of the robe. 35Aaron must wear it when he ministers. The sound of the bells will be heard when he enters the Holy Place before the LORD and when he comes out, so that he will not die.

36"Make a plate of pure gold and engrave on it as on a seal: HOLY TO THE LORD. 37Fasten a blue cord to it to attach it to the turban; it is to be on the front of the turban. 38It will be on Aaron's forehead, and he will bear the guilt involved in the sacred gifts the Israelites consecrate, whatever their gifts may be. It will be on Aaron's forehead continually so that they will be acceptable to the LORD.

---

[g]18 That is, about 150 feet (about 46 metres) long and 75 feet (about 23 metres) wide
[h]18 That is, about 7½ feet (about 2.3 metres)   [a]16 That is, about 9 inches (about 23 centimetres)
[b]18 Or lapis lazuli   [c]20 The precise identification of some of these precious stones is uncertain.
[d]32 The meaning of the Hebrew for this word is uncertain.

39"Weave the tunic of fine linen and make the turban of fine linen. The sash is to be the work of an embroiderer. 40Make tunics, sashes and headbands for Aaron's sons, to give them dignity and honour. 41After you put these clothes on your brother Aaron and his sons, anoint and ordain them. Consecrate them so they may serve me as priests.

42"Make linen undergarments as a covering for the body, reaching from the waist to the thigh. 43Aaron and his sons must wear them whenever they enter the Tent of Meeting or approach the altar to minister in the Holy Place, so that they will not incur guilt and die.

"This is to be a lasting ordinance for Aaron and his descendants.

Consecration of the Priests

29 "This is what you are to do to consecrate them, so that they may serve me as priests: Take a young bull and two rams without defect. 2And from fine wheat flour, without yeast, make bread, and cakes mixed with oil, and wafers spread with oil. 3Put them in a basket and present them in it —along with the bull and the two rams. 4Then bring Aaron and his sons to the entrance to the Tent of Meeting and wash them with water. 5Take the garments and dress Aaron with the tunic, the robe of the ephod, the ephod itself and the breastpiece. Fasten the ephod on him by its skilfully woven waistband. 6Put the turban on his head and attach the sacred diadem to the turban. 7Take the anointing oil and anoint him by pouring it on his head. 8Bring his sons and dress them in tunics 9and put headbands on them. Then tie sashes on Aaron and his sons.*a* The priesthood is theirs by a lasting ordinance. In this way you shall ordain Aaron and his sons.

10"Bring the bull to the front of the Tent of Meeting, and Aaron and his sons shall lay their hands on its head. 11Slaughter it in the LORD's presence at the entrance to the Tent of Meeting. 12Take some of the bull's blood and put it on the horns of the altar with your finger, and pour out the rest of it at the base of the altar. 13Then take all the fat around the inner parts, the covering of the liver, and both kidneys with the fat on them, and burn them on the altar. 14But burn the bull's flesh and its hide and its offal outside the camp. It is a sin offering.

15"Take one of the rams, and Aaron and his sons shall lay their hands on its head. 16Slaughter it and take the blood and sprinkle it against the altar on all sides. 17Cut the ram into pieces and wash the inner parts and the legs, putting them with the head and the other pieces. 18Then burn the entire ram on the altar. It is a burnt offering to the LORD, a pleasing aroma, an offering made to the LORD by fire.

19"Take the other ram, and Aaron and his sons shall lay their hands on its head. 20Slaughter it, take some of its blood and put it on the lobes of the right ears of Aaron and

his sons, on the thumbs of their right hands, and on the big toes of their right feet. Then sprinkle blood against the altar on all sides. 21And take some of the blood on the altar and some of the anointing oil and sprinkle it on Aaron and his garments and on his sons and their garments. Then he and his sons and their garments will be consecrated.

22"Take from this ram the fat, the fat tail, the fat around the inner parts, the covering of the liver, both kidneys with the fat on them, and the right thigh. (This is the ram for the ordination.) 23From the basket of bread made without yeast, which is before the LORD, take a loaf, and a cake made with oil, and a wafer. 24Put all these in the hands of Aaron and his sons and wave them before the LORD as a wave offering. 25Then take them from their hands and burn them on the altar along with the burnt offering for a pleasing aroma to the LORD, an offering made to the LORD by fire. 26After you take the breast of the ram for Aaron's ordination, wave it before the LORD as a wave offering, and it will be your share.

27"Consecrate those parts of the ordination ram that belong to Aaron and his sons: the breast that was waved and the thigh that was presented. 28This is always to be the regular share from the Israelites for Aaron and his sons. It is the contribution the Israelites are to make to the LORD from their fellowship offerings.*b*

29"Aaron's sacred garments will belong to his descendants so that they can be anointed and ordained in them. 30The son who succeeds him as priest and comes to the Tent of Meeting to minister in the Holy Place is to wear them seven days.

31"Take the ram for the ordination and cook the meat in a sacred place. 32At the entrance to the Tent of Meeting, Aaron and his sons are to eat the meat of the ram and the bread that is in the basket. 33They are to eat these offerings by which atonement was made for their ordination and consecration. But no-one else may eat them, because they are sacred. 34And if any of the meat of the ordination ram or any bread is left over till morning, burn it up. It must not be eaten, because it is sacred.

35"Do for Aaron and his sons everything I have commanded you, taking seven days to ordain them. 36Sacrifice a bull each day as a sin offering to make atonement. Purify the altar by making atonement for it, and anoint it to consecrate it. 37For seven days make atonement for the altar and consecrate it. Then the altar will be most holy, and whatever touches it will be holy.

38"This is what you are to offer on the altar regularly each day: two lambs a year old. 39Offer one in the morning and the other at twilight. 40With the first lamb offer a tenth of an ephah*c* of fine flour mixed with a quarter of a hin*d* of oil from pressed olives, and a quarter of a hin of wine as a drink offering. 41Sacrifice the other lamb at twilight with the same grain offering and its drink offering as in

---

a9 Hebrew; Septuagint *on them*   *b28* Traditionally *peace offerings*
c40 That is, probably about 4 pints (about 2 litres)   *d40* That is, probably about 1½ pints (about 1 litre)

the morning—a pleasing aroma, an offering made to the LORD by fire.

42"For the generations to come this burnt offering is to be made regularly at the entrance to the Tent of Meeting before the LORD. There I will meet you and speak to you; 43there also I will meet with the Israelites, and the place will be consecrated by my glory.

44"So I will consecrate the Tent of Meeting and the altar and will consecrate Aaron and his sons to serve me as priests. 45Then I will dwell among the Israelites and be their God. 46They will know that I am the LORD their God, who brought them out of Egypt so that I might dwell among them. I am the LORD their God.

The Altar of Incense

30 "Make an altar of acacia wood for burning incense. 2It is to be square, a cubit long and a cubit wide, and two cubits high*a*—its horns of one piece with it. 3Overlay the top and all the sides and the horns with pure gold, and make a gold moulding around it. 4Make two gold rings for the altar below the moulding—two on opposite sides—to hold the poles used to carry it. 5Make the poles of acacia wood and overlay them with gold. 6Put the altar in front of the curtain that is before the ark of the Testimony—before the atonement cover that is over the Testimony—where I will meet with you.

7"Aaron must burn fragrant incense on the altar every morning when he tends the lamps. 8He must burn incense again when he lights the lamps at twilight so that incense will burn regularly before the LORD for the generations to come. 9Do not offer on this altar any other incense or any burnt offering or grain offering, and do not pour a drink offering on it. 10Once a year Aaron shall make atonement on its horns. This annual atonement must be made with the blood of the atoning sin offering for the generations to come. It is most holy to the LORD."

Atonement Money

11Then the LORD said to Moses, 12"When you take a census of the Israelites to count them, each one must pay the LORD a ransom for his life at the time he is counted. Then no plague will come on them when you number them. 13Each one who crosses over to those already counted is to give a half shekel,*b* according to the sanctuary shekel, which weighs twenty gerahs. This half shekel is an offering to the LORD. 14All who cross over, those twenty years old or more, are to give an offering to the LORD. 15The rich are not to give more than a half shekel and the poor are not to give less when you make the offering to the LORD to atone for your lives. 16Receive the atonement money from the Israelites and use it for the service of the Tent of Meeting. It will be a memorial for the Israelites

before the LORD, making atonement for your lives."

Basin for Washing

17Then the LORD said to Moses, 18"Make a bronze basin, with its bronze stand, for washing. Place it between the Tent of Meeting and the altar, and put water in it. 19Aaron and his sons are to wash their hands and feet with water from it. 20Whenever they enter the Tent of Meeting, they shall wash with water so that they will not die. Also, when they approach the altar to minister by presenting an offering made to the LORD by fire, 21they shall wash their hands and feet so that they will not die. This is to be a lasting ordinance for Aaron and his descendants for the generations to come."

Anointing Oil

22Then the LORD said to Moses, 23"Take the following fine spices: 500 shekels*c* of liquid myrrh, half as much (that is, 250 shekels) of fragrant cinnamon, 250 shekels of fragrant cane, 24500 shekels of cassia—all according to the sanctuary shekel—and a hin*d* of olive oil. 25Make these into a sacred anointing oil, a fragrant blend, the work of a perfumer. It will be the sacred anointing oil. 26Then use it to anoint the Tent of Meeting, the ark of the Testimony, 27the table and all its articles, the lampstand and its accessories, the altar of incense, 28the altar of burnt offering and all its utensils, and the basin with its stand. 29You shall consecrate them so they will be most holy, and whatever touches them will be holy.

30"Anoint Aaron and his sons and consecrate them so they may serve me as priests. 31Say to the Israelites, 'This is to be my sacred anointing oil for the generations to come. 32Do not pour it on men's bodies and do not make any oil with the same formula. It is sacred, and you are to consider it sacred. 33Whoever makes perfume like it and whoever puts it on anyone other than a priest must be cut off from his people.'"

Incense

34Then the LORD said to Moses, "Take fragrant spices—gum resin, onycha and galbanum—and pure frankincense, all in equal amounts, 35and make a fragrant blend of incense, the work of a perfumer. It is to be salted and pure and sacred. 36Grind some of it to powder and place it in front of the Testimony in the Tent of Meeting, where I will meet with you. It shall be most holy to you. 37Do not make any incense with this formula for yourselves; consider it holy to the LORD. 38Whoever makes any like it to enjoy its fragrance must be cut off from his people."

Bezalel and Oholiab

31 Then the LORD said to Moses, 2"See I have chosen Bezalel son of Uri, the son of Hur, of the tribe of Judah, 3and I have

---

*a*2 That is, about 1½ feet (about 0.5 metre) long and wide and about 3 feet (about 0.9 metre) high
*b*13 That is, about ⅓ ounce (about 6 grams); also in verse 15   *c*23 That is, about 12½ pounds (about 6 kilograms)
*d*24 That is, probably about 6½ pints (about 4 litres)

filled him with the Spirit of God, with skill, ability and knowledge in all kinds of crafts —⁴to make artistic designs for work in gold, silver and bronze, ⁵to cut and set stones, to work in wood, and to engage in all kinds of craftsmanship. ⁶Moreover, I have appointed Oholiab son of Ahisamach, of the tribe of Dan, to help him. Also I have given skill to all the craftsmen to make everything I have commanded you: ⁷the Tent of Meeting, the ark of the Testimony with the atonement cover on it, and all the other furnishings of the tent—⁸the table and its articles, the pure gold lampstand and all its accessories, the altar of incense, ⁹the altar of burnt offering and all its utensils, the basin with its stand —¹⁰and also the woven garments, both the sacred garments for Aaron the priest and the garments for his sons when they serve as priests, ¹¹and the anointing oil and fragrant incense for the Holy Place. They are to make them just as I commanded you.''

The Sabbath

¹²Then the LORD said to Moses, ¹³''Say to the Israelites, 'You must observe my Sabbaths. This will be a sign between me and you for the generations to come, so that you may know that I am the LORD, who makes you holy.ᵃ

¹⁴'' 'Observe the Sabbath, because it is holy to you. Anyone who desecrates it must be put to death; whoever does any work on that day must be cut off from his people. ¹⁵For six days, work is to be done, but the seventh day is a Sabbath of rest, holy to the LORD. Whoever does any work on the Sabbath day must be put to death. ¹⁶The Israelites are to observe the Sabbath, celebrating it for the generations to come as a lasting covenant. ¹⁷It will be a sign between me and the Israelites for ever, for in six days the LORD made the heavens and the earth, and on the seventh day he abstained from work and rested.' ''

¹⁸When the LORD finished speaking to Moses on Mount Sinai, he gave him the two tablets of the Testimony, the tablets of stone inscribed by the finger of God.

The Golden Calf

32 When the people saw that Moses was so long in coming down from the mountain, they gathered round Aaron and said, ''Come, make us godsᵃ who will go before us. As for this fellow Moses who brought us up out of Egypt, we don't know what has happened to him.''

²Aaron answered them, ''Take off the gold ear-rings that your wives, your sons and your daughters are wearing, and bring them to me.'' ³So all the people took off their ear-rings and brought them to Aaron. ⁴He took what they handed him and made it into an idol cast in the shape of a calf, fashioning it with a tool. Then they said, ''These are your gods,ᵇ O Israel, who brought you up out of Egypt.''

⁵When Aaron saw this, he built an altar in front of the calf and announced, ''Tomorrow there will be a festival to the LORD.'' ⁶So the next day the people rose early and sacrificed burnt offerings and presented fellowship offerings.ᶜ Afterwards they sat down to eat and drink and got up to indulge in revelry.

⁷Then the LORD said to Moses, ''Go down, because your people, whom you brought up out of Egypt, have become corrupt. ⁸They have been quick to turn away from what I commanded them and have made themselves an idol cast in the shape of a calf. They have bowed down to it and sacrificed to it and have said, 'These are your gods, O Israel, who brought you up out of Egypt.'

⁹''I have seen these people,'' the LORD said to Moses, ''and they are a stiff-necked people. ¹⁰Now leave me alone so that my anger may burn against them and that I may destroy them. Then I will make you into a great nation.''

¹¹But Moses sought the favour of the LORD his God. ''O LORD,'' he said, ''why should your anger burn against your people, whom you brought out of Egypt with great power and a mighty hand? ¹²Why should the Egyptians say, 'It was with evil intent that he brought them out, to kill them in the mountains and to wipe them off the face of the earth'? Turn from your fierce anger; relent and do not bring disaster on your people. ¹³Remember your servants Abraham, Isaac and Israel, to whom you swore by your own self: 'I will make your descendants as numerous as the stars in the sky and I will give your descendants all this land I promised them, and it will be their inheritance for ever.' '' ¹⁴Then the LORD relented and did not bring on his people the disaster he had threatened.

¹⁵Moses turned and went down the mountain with the two tablets of the Testimony in his hands. They were inscribed on both sides, front and back. ¹⁶The tablets were the work of God; the writing was the writing of God, engraved on the tablets.

¹⁷When Joshua heard the noise of the people shouting, he said to Moses, ''There is the sound of war in the camp.''

¹⁸Moses replied:

''It is not the sound of victory,
  it is not the sound of defeat;
  it is the sound of singing that I hear.''

¹⁹When Moses approached the camp and saw the calf and the dancing, his anger burned and he threw the tablets out of his hands, breaking them to pieces at the foot of the mountain. ²⁰And he took the calf they had made and burned it in the fire; then he ground it to powder, scattered it on the water and made the Israelites drink it.

²¹He said to Aaron, ''What did these people do to you, that you led them into such great sin?''

²²''Do not be angry, my lord,'' Aaron answered. ''You know how prone these

ᵃ13 Or who sanctifies you; or who sets you apart as holy   ᵃ1 Or a god; also in verses 23 and 31
ᵇ4 Or This is your god; also in verse 8   ᶜ6 Traditionally peace offerings

EXODUS 32:1–6

'He took what they handed him and made it into an idol cast in the shape of a calf, fashioning it with a tool. Then they said, "These are your gods, O Israel, who brought you up out of Egypt" ' (v. 4).

MOSES WAS WITH GOD on the mountain top for almost six weeks. For him, the time must have seemed brief, but for his people it was a very long time. We assume they thought he had died in the cloud of smoke and fire at the summit of Sinai, and with his death, their commitment to obey God had also died. Quite obviously, Aaron was a man of little influence. As brother and spokesman for Moses, his standing in the community should have been high, but status without moral authority is not of much worth. To all intents and purposes the people were leaderless, and they reverted to the old ways of Egypt.

Whether Aaron was hoping that his demand for their gold earrings would make them consider that the cost of an idol was too great, causing them to cancel their request, we do not know, but they happily paid the price. Aaron made the golden calf, a bull calf, a symbol of fertility, and it was acclaimed as their god. Aaron clearly sought to redeem the situation by building an altar and declaring a festival to the Lord. However, the people sacrificed and made their offerings to the Lord and followed it by revelry which had pagan overtones.

The sorry incident illustrates how lack of strength and purpose leads to disaster. How important faithfulness is.

> *Arm me with jealous care,*
> *As in thy sight to live;*
> *And O thy servant, Lord, prepare*
> *A strict account to give!*

(*Charles Wesley*)

EXODUS 33:17–21
'Then Moses said, "Now show me your glory" ' (v. 18).

THE MORE WE HAVE of God the more our hungering souls desire. Moses had received so much already from God's hand. Because of his importunity, the people had been saved from disaster. He had prevailed upon God to restore the promise of his presence. He had also asked to be initiated into the ways of God. Now he made the supreme prayer which was not answered on earth until he stood on the mount of transfiguration with Elijah, and witnessed the glory of Jesus. How God must have loved Moses for that prayer! If, as George Matheson suggests, the true measure of a man is found in his aspiration, Moses had reached an unprecedented height. His longing for God and his standing with God were strong enough for him to make that prayer. Of his own volition God revealed his glory when Christ became flesh. 'We have seen his glory,' said John and, in seeing his glory, the world has seen the Father's glory.

Moses was not ready for the glory of God to be revealed, but we observe how graciously and tenderly God handled him. God proposed that he would let his goodness pass by Moses. Because this was more than Moses could bear, God would shelter him in a cleft of the rock, shading him further with his hand as he passed, only removing his hand when the full glory had abated. With the same tenderness our heavenly Father handles us. How he must long for his people to make big prayers, and if the time is not ripe for a full answer, he will give whatever response is fitting and, at least, the reassurance of his favour.

> *He hideth my soul in the cleft of the rock*
> *That shadows a dry, thirsty land;*
> *He hideth my life in the depths of his love,*
> *And covers me there with his hand.*

(Fanny Crosby)

people are to evil. 23They said to me, 'Make us gods who will go before us. As for this fellow Moses who brought us up out of Egypt, we don't know what has happened to him.' 24So I told them, 'Whoever has any gold jewellery, take it off.' Then they gave me the gold, and I threw it into the fire, and out came this calf!''

25Moses saw that the people were running wild and that Aaron had let them get out of control and so become a laughing-stock to their enemies. 26So he stood at the entrance to the camp and said, ''Whoever is for the LORD, come to me.'' And all the Levites rallied to him.

27Then he said to them, ''This is what the LORD, the God of Israel, says: 'Each man strap a sword to his side. Go back and forth through the camp from one end to the other, each killing his brother and friend and neighbour.' '' 28The Levites did as Moses commanded, and that day about three thousand of the people died. 29Then Moses said, ''You have been set apart to the LORD today, for you were against your own sons and brothers, and he has blessed you this day.''

30The next day Moses said to the people, ''You have committed a great sin. But now I will go up to the LORD; perhaps I can make atonement for your sin.''

31So Moses went back to the LORD and said, ''Oh, what a great sin these people have committed! They have made themselves gods of gold. 32But now, please forgive their sin—but if not, then blot me out of the book you have written.''

33The LORD replied to Moses, ''Whoever has sinned against me I will blot out of my book. 34Now go, lead the people to the place I spoke of, and my angel will go before you. However, when the time comes for me to punish, I will punish them for their sin.''

35And the LORD struck the people with a plague because of what they did with the calf Aaron had made.

33 Then the LORD said to Moses, ''Leave this place, you and the people you brought up out of Egypt, and go up to the land I promised on oath to Abraham, Isaac and Jacob, saying, 'I will give it to your descendants.' 2I will send an angel before you and drive out the Canaanites, Amorites, Hittites, Perizzites, Hivites and Jebusites. 3Go up to the land flowing with milk and honey. But I will not go with you, because you are a stiff-necked people and I might destroy you on the way.''

4When the people heard these distressing words, they began to mourn and no-one put on any ornaments. 5For the LORD had said to Moses, ''Tell the Israelites, 'You are a stiff-necked people. If I were to go with you even for a moment, I might destroy you. Now take off your ornaments and I will decide what to do with you.' '' 6So the Israelites stripped off their ornaments at Mount Horeb.

The Tent of Meeting

7Now Moses used to take a tent and pitch it outside the camp some distance away, calling it the ''tent of meeting''. Anyone enquiring of the LORD would go to the tent of meeting outside the camp. 8And whenever Moses went out to the tent, all the people rose and stood at the entrances to their tents, watching Moses until he entered the tent. 9As Moses went into the tent, the pillar of cloud would come down and stay at the entrance, while the LORD spoke with Moses. 10Whenever the people saw the pillar of cloud standing at the entrance to the tent, they all stood and worshipped, each at the entrance to his tent. 11The LORD would speak to Moses face to face, as a man speaks with his friend. Then Moses would return to the camp, but his young assistant Joshua son of Nun did not leave the tent.

Moses and the Glory of the LORD

12Moses said to the LORD, ''You have been telling me, 'Lead these people,' but you have not let me know whom you will send with me. You have said, 'I know you by name and you have found favour with me.' 13If you are pleased with me, teach me your ways so I may know you and continue to find favour with you. Remember that this nation is your people.''

14The LORD replied, ''My Presence will go with you, and I will give you rest.''

15Then Moses said to him, ''If your Presence does not go with us, do not send us up from here. 16How will anyone know that you are pleased with me and with your people unless you go with us? What else will distinguish me and your people from all the other people on the face of the earth?''

17And the LORD said to Moses, ''I will do the very thing you have asked, because I am pleased with you and I know you by name.''

18Then Moses said, ''Now show me your glory.''

19And the LORD said, ''I will cause all my goodness to pass in front of you, and I will proclaim my name, the LORD, in your presence. I will have mercy on whom I will have mercy, and I will have compassion on whom I will have compassion. 20But,'' he said, ''you cannot see my face, for no-one may see me and live.''

21Then the LORD said, ''There is a place near me where you may stand on a rock. 22When my glory passes by, I will put you in a cleft in the rock and cover you with my hand until I have passed by. 23Then I will remove my hand and you will see my back; but my face must not be seen.''

The New Stone Tablets

34 The LORD said to Moses, ''Chisel out two stone tablets like the first ones, and I will write on them the words that were on the first tablets, which you broke. 2Be ready in the morning, and then come up on Mount Sinai. Present yourself to me there on top of the mountain. 3No-one is to come with you or be seen anywhere on the mountain; not even the flocks and herds may graze in front of the mountain.''

4So Moses chiselled out two stone tablets like the first ones and went up Mount Sinai early in the morning, as the LORD had commanded him; and he carried the two stone tablets in his hands. [5]Then the LORD came down in the cloud and stood there with him and proclaimed his name, the LORD. [6]And he passed in front of Moses, proclaiming, "The LORD, the LORD, the compassionate and gracious God, slow to anger, abounding in love and faithfulness, [7]maintaining love to thousands, and forgiving wickedness, rebellion and sin. Yet he does not leave the guilty unpunished; he punishes the children and their children for the sin of the fathers to the third and fourth generation."

[8]Moses bowed to the ground at once and worshipped. [9]"O Lord, if I have found favour in your eyes," he said, "then let the Lord go with us. Although this is a stiff-necked people, forgive our wickedness and our sin, and take us as your inheritance."

[10]Then the LORD said: "I am making a covenant with you. Before all your people I will do wonders never before done in any nation in all the world. The people you live among will see how awesome is the work that I, the LORD, will do for you. [11]Obey what I command you today. I will drive out before you the Amorites, Canaanites, Hittites, Perizzites, Hivites and Jebusites. [12]Be careful not to make a treaty with those who live in the land where you are going, or they will be a snare among you. [13]Break down their altars, smash their sacred stones and cut down their Asherah poles.[a] [14]Do not worship any other god, for the LORD, whose name is Jealous, is a jealous God.

[15]"Be careful not to make a treaty with those who live in the land; for when they prostitute themselves to their gods and sacrifice to them, they will invite you and you will eat their sacrifices. [16]And when you choose some of their daughters as wives for your sons and those daughters prostitute themselves to their gods, they will lead your sons to do the same.

[17]"Do not make cast idols.

[18]"Celebrate the Feast of Unleavened Bread. For seven days eat bread made without yeast, as I commanded you. Do this at the appointed time in the month of Abib, for in that month you came out of Egypt.

[19]"The first offspring of every womb belongs to me, including all the firstborn males of your livestock, whether from herd or flock. [20]Redeem the firstborn donkey with a lamb, but if you do not redeem it, break its neck. Redeem all your firstborn sons.

"No-one is to appear before me empty-handed.

[21]"Six days you shall labour, but on the seventh day you shall rest; even during the ploughing season and harvest you must rest.

[22]"Celebrate the Feast of Weeks with the firstfruits of the wheat harvest, and the Feast of Ingathering at the turn of the year.[b] [23]Three times a year all your men are to appear before the Sovereign LORD, the God of Israel. [24]I will drive out nations before you

and enlarge your territory, and no-one will covet your land when you go up three times each year to appear before the LORD your God.

[25]"Do not offer the blood of a sacrifice to me along with anything containing yeast, and do not let any of the sacrifice from the Passover Feast remain until morning.

[26]"Bring the best of the firstfruits of your soil to the house of the LORD your God.

"Do not cook a young goat in its mother's milk."

[27]Then the LORD said to Moses, "Write down these words, for in accordance with these words I have made a covenant with you and with Israel." [28]Moses was there with the LORD forty days and forty nights without eating bread or drinking water. And he wrote on the tablets the words of the covenant —the Ten Commandments.

The Radiant Face of Moses

[29]When Moses came down from Mount Sinai with the two tablets of the Testimony in his hands, he was not aware that his face was radiant because he had spoken with the LORD. [30]When Aaron and all the Israelites saw Moses, his face was radiant, and they were afraid to come near him. [31]But Moses called to them; so Aaron and all the leaders of the community came back to him, and he spoke to them. [32]Afterwards all the Israelites came near him, and he gave them all the commands the LORD had given him on Mount Sinai.

[33]When Moses finished speaking to them, he put a veil over his face. [34]But whenever he entered the LORD's presence to speak with him, he removed the veil until he came out. And when he came out and told the Israelites what he had been commanded, [35]they saw that his face was radiant. Then Moses would put the veil back over his face until he went in to speak with the LORD.

Sabbath Regulations

35 Moses assembled the whole Israelite community and said to them, "These are the things the LORD has commanded you to do: [2]For six days, work is to be done, but the seventh day shall be your holy day, a Sabbath of rest to the LORD. Whoever does any work on it must be put to death. [3]Do not light a fire in any of your dwellings on the Sabbath day."

Materials for the Tabernacle

[4]Moses said to the whole Israelite community, "This is what the LORD has commanded: [5]From what you have, take an offering for the LORD. Everyone who is willing is to bring to the LORD an offering of gold, silver and bronze; [6]blue, purple and scarlet yarn and fine linen; goat hair; [7]ram skins dyed red and hides of sea cows;[a] acacia wood; [8]olive oil for the light; spices for the anointing oil and for the fragrant incense; [9]and onyx

---

[a]13 That is, symbols of the goddess Asherah   [b]22 That is, in the autumn
[a]7 That is, large aquatic mammals; also in verse 23

stones and other gems to be mounted on the ephod and breastpiece.

10"All who are skilled among you are to come and make everything the LORD has commanded: 11the tabernacle with its tent and its covering, clasps, frames, crossbars, posts and bases; 12the ark with its poles and the atonement cover and the curtain that shields it; 13the table with its poles and all its articles and the bread of the Presence; 14the lampstand that is for light with its accessories, lamps and oil for the light; 15the altar of incense with its poles, the anointing oil and the fragrant incense; the curtain for the doorway at the entrance to the tabernacle; 16the altar of burnt offering with its bronze grating, its poles and all its utensils; the bronze basin with its stand; 17the curtains of the courtyard with its posts and bases, and the curtain for the entrance to the courtyard; 18the tent pegs for the tabernacle and for the courtyard, and their ropes; 19the woven garments worn for ministering in the sanctuary—both the sacred garments for Aaron the priest and the garments for his sons when they serve as priests."

20Then the whole Israelite community withdrew from Moses' presence, 21and everyone who was willing and whose heart moved him came and brought an offering to the LORD for the work on the Tent of Meeting, for all its service, and for the sacred garments. 22All who were willing, men and women alike, came and brought gold jewellery of all kinds: brooches, ear-rings, rings and ornaments. They all presented their gold as a wave offering to the LORD. 23Everyone who had blue, purple or scarlet yarn or fine linen, or goat hair, ram skins dyed red or hides of sea cows brought them. 24Those presenting an offering of silver or bronze brought it as an offering to the LORD, and everyone who had acacia wood for any part of the work brought it. 25Every skilled woman spun with her hands and brought what she had spun—blue, purple or scarlet yarn or fine linen. 26And all the women who were willing and had the skill spun the goat hair. 27The leaders brought onyx stones and other gems to be mounted on the ephod and breastpiece. 28They also brought spices and olive oil for the light and for the anointing oil and for the fragrant incense. 29All the Israelite men and women who were willing brought to the LORD freewill offerings for all the work the LORD through Moses had commanded them to do.

Bezalel and Oholiab

30Then Moses said to the Israelites, "See, the LORD has chosen Bezalel son of Uri, the son of Hur, of the tribe of Judah, 31and he has filled him with the Spirit of God, with skill, ability and knowledge in all kinds of crafts —32to make artistic designs for work in gold, silver and bronze, 33to cut and set stones, to work in wood and to engage in all kinds of

artistic craftsmanship. 34And he has given both him and Oholiab son of Ahisamach, of the tribe of Dan, the ability to teach others. 35He has filled them with skill to do all kinds of work as craftsmen, designers, embroiderers in blue, purple and scarlet yarn and fine linen, and weavers—all of them master craftsmen and designers. 1So Bezalel, Oholiab and every skilled person to whom the LORD has given skill and ability to know how to carry out all the work of constructing the sanctuary are to do the work just as the LORD has commanded."

36

2Then Moses summoned Bezalel and Oholiab and every skilled person to whom the LORD had given ability and who was willing to come and do the work. 3They received from Moses all the offerings the Israelites had brought to carry out the work of constructing the sanctuary. And the people continued to bring freewill offerings morning after morning. 4So all the skilled craftsmen who were doing all the work on the sanctuary left their work 5and said to Moses, "The people are bringing more than enough for doing the work the LORD commanded to be done."

6Then Moses gave an order and they sent this word throughout the camp: "No man or woman is to make anything else as an offering for the sanctuary." And so the people were restrained from bringing more, 7because what they already had was more than enough to do all the work.

The Tabernacle

8All the skilled men among the workmen made the tabernacle with ten curtains of finely twisted linen and blue, purple and scarlet yarn, with cherubim worked into them by a skilled craftsman. 9All the curtains were the same size—twenty-eight cubits long and four cubits wide.a 10They joined five of the curtains together and did the same with the other five. 11Then they made loops of blue material along the edge of the end curtain in one set, and the same was done with the end curtain in the other set. 12They also made fifty loops on one curtain and fifty loops on the end curtain of the other set, with the loops opposite each other. 13Then they made fifty gold clasps and used them to fasten the two sets of curtains together so that the tabernacle was a unit.

14They made curtains of goat hair for the tent over the tabernacle—eleven altogether. 15All eleven curtains were the same size— thirty cubits long and four cubits wide.b 16They joined five of the curtains into one set and the other six into another set. 17Then they made fifty loops along the edge of the end curtain in one set and also along the edge of the end curtain in the other set. 18They made fifty bronze clasps to fasten the tent together as a unit. 19Then they made for the tent a covering of ram skins dyed red, and over that a covering of hides of sea cows.c 20They made upright frames of acacia

---

a9 That is, about 42 feet (about 13 metres) long and 6 feet (about 1.8 metres) wide
b15 That is, about 45 feet (about 13.5 metres) long and 6 feet (about 1.8 metres) wide
c19 That is, large aquatic mammals

wood for the tabernacle. 21Each frame was ten cubits long and a cubit and a half wide,*d* 22with two projections set parallel to each other. They made all the frames of the tabernacle in this way. 23They made twenty frames for the south side of the tabernacle 24and made forty silver bases to go under them—two bases for each frame, one under each projection. 25For the other side, the north side of the tabernacle, they made twenty frames 26and forty silver bases—two under each frame. 27They made six frames for the far end, that is, the west end of the tabernacle, 28and two frames were made for the corners of the tabernacle at the far end. 29At these two corners the frames were double from the bottom all the way to the top and fitted into a single ring; both were made alike. 30So there were eight frames and sixteen silver bases—two under each frame.

31They also made crossbars of acacia wood: five for the frames on one side of the tabernacle, 32five for those on the other side, and five for the frames on the west, at the far end of the tabernacle. 33They made the centre crossbar so that it extended from end to end at the middle of the frames. 34They overlaid the frames with gold and made gold rings to hold the crossbars. They also overlaid the crossbars with gold.

35They made the curtain of blue, purple and scarlet yarn and finely twisted linen, with cherubim worked into it by a skilled craftsman. 36They made four posts of acacia wood for it and overlaid them with gold. They made gold hooks for them and cast their four silver bases. 37For the entrance to the tent they made a curtain of blue, purple and scarlet yarn and finely twisted linen—the work of an embroiderer; 38and they made five posts with hooks for them. They overlaid the tops of the posts and their bands with gold and made their five bases of bronze.

The Ark

37 Bezalel made the ark of acacia wood —two and a half cubits long, a cubit and a half wide, and a cubit and a half high.*a* 2He overlaid it with pure gold, both inside and out, and made a gold moulding around it. 3He cast four gold rings for it and fastened them to its four feet, with two rings on one side and two rings on the other. 4Then he made poles of acacia wood and overlaid them with gold. 5And he inserted the poles into the rings on the sides of the ark to carry it.

6He made the atonement cover of pure gold—two and a half cubits long and a cubit and a half wide.*b* 7Then he made two cherubim out of hammered gold at the ends of the cover. 8He made one cherub on one end and the second cherub on the other; at the two ends he made them of one piece with the cover. 9The cherubim had their wings spread upwards, overshadowing the cover with them. The cherubim faced each other, looking towards the cover.

The Table

10They*c* made the table of acacia wood —two cubits long, a cubit wide, and a cubit and a half high.*d* 11Then they overlaid it with pure gold and made a gold moulding around it. 12They also made around it a rim a handbreadth*e* wide and put a gold moulding on the rim. 13They cast four gold rings for the table and fastened them to the four corners, where the four legs were. 14The rings were put close to the rim to hold the poles used in carrying the table. 15The poles for carrying the table were made of acacia wood and were overlaid with gold. 16And they made from pure gold the articles for the table—its plates and dishes and bowls and its pitchers for the pouring out of drink offerings.

The Lampstand

17They made the lampstand of pure gold and hammered it out, base and shaft; its flowerlike cups, buds and blossoms were of one piece with it. 18Six branches extended from the sides of the lampstand—three on one side and three on the other. 19Three cups shaped like almond flowers with buds and blossoms were on one branch, three on the next branch and the same for all six branches extending from the lampstand. 20And on the lampstand were four cups shaped like almond flowers with buds and blossoms. 21One bud was under the first pair of branches extending from the lampstand, a second bud under the second pair, and a third bud under the third pair—six branches in all. 22The buds and the branches were all of one piece with the lampstand, hammered out of pure gold.

23They made its seven lamps, as well as its wick trimmers and trays, of pure gold. 24They made the lampstand and all its accessories from one talent*f* of pure gold.

The Altar of Incense

25They made the altar of incense out of acacia wood. It was square, a cubit long and a cubit wide, and two cubits high*g*—its horns of one piece with it. 26They overlaid the top and all the sides and the horns with pure gold, and made a gold moulding around it. 27They made two gold rings below the moulding —two on opposite sides—to hold the poles used to carry it. 28They made the poles of acacia wood and overlaid them with gold.

29They also made the sacred anointing oil and the pure, fragrant incense—the work of a perfumer.

---

d21 That is, about 15 feet (about 4.5 metres) long and 2¼ feet (about 0.7 metre) wide
a1 That is, about 3¾ feet (about 1.1 metres) long and 2¼ feet (about 0.7 metre) wide and high
b6 That is, about 3¾ feet (about 1.1 metres) long and 2¼ feet (about 0.7 metre) wide
c10 Or *He*; also in verses 11–29
d10 That is, about 3 feet (about 0.9 metre) long, 1½ feet (about 0.5 metre) wide, and 2¼ feet (about 0.7 metre) high
e12 That is, about 3 inches (about 8 centimetres)   *f24* That is, about 75 pounds (about 34 kilograms)
g25 That is, about 1½ feet (about 0.5 metre) long and wide, and about 3 feet (about 0.9 metre) high

The Altar of Burnt Offering

38 They[a] built the altar of burnt offering of acacia wood, three cubits[b] high; it was square, five cubits long and five cubits wide.[c] 2They made a horn at each of the four corners, so that the horns and the altar were of one piece, and they overlaid the altar with bronze. 3They made all its utensils of bronze —its pots, shovels, sprinkling bowls, meat forks and firepans. 4They made a grating for the altar, a bronze network, to be under its ledge, halfway up the altar. 5They cast bronze rings to hold the poles for the four corners of the bronze grating. 6They made the poles of acacia wood and overlaid them with bronze. 7They inserted the poles into the rings so they would be on the sides of the altar for carrying it. They made it hollow, out of boards.

Basin for Washing

8They made the bronze basin and its bronze stand from the mirrors of the women who served at the entrance to the Tent of Meeting.

The Courtyard

9Next they made the courtyard. The south side was a hundred cubits[d] long and had curtains of finely twisted linen, 10with twenty posts and twenty bronze bases, and with silver hooks and bands on the posts. 11The north side was also a hundred cubits long and had twenty posts and twenty bronze bases, with silver hooks and bands on the posts.

12The west end was fifty cubits[e] wide and had curtains, with ten posts and ten bases, with silver hooks and bands on the posts. 13The east end, towards the sunrise, was also fifty cubits wide. 14Curtains fifteen cubits[f] long were on one side of the entrance, with three posts and three bases, 15and curtains fifteen cubits long were on the other side of the entrance to the courtyard, with three posts and three bases. 16All the curtains around the courtyard were of finely twisted linen. 17The bases for the posts were bronze. The hooks and bands on the posts were silver, and their tops were overlaid with silver; so all the posts of the courtyard had silver bands.

18The curtain for the entrance to the courtyard was of blue, purple and scarlet yarn and finely twisted linen—the work of an embroiderer. It was twenty cubits[g] long and, like the curtains of the courtyard, five cubits[h] high, 19with four posts and four bronze bases. Their hooks and bands were silver, and their tops were overlaid with silver. 20All the tent pegs of the tabernacle and of the surrounding courtyard were bronze.

The Materials Used

21These are the amounts of the materials used for the tabernacle, the tabernacle of the Testimony, which were recorded at Moses' command by the Levites under the direction of Ithamar son of Aaron, the priest. 22(Bezalel son of Uri, the son of Hur, of the tribe of Judah, made everything the LORD commanded Moses; 23with him was Oholiab son of Ahisamach, of the tribe of Dan—a craftsman and designer, and an embroiderer in blue, purple and scarlet yarn and fine linen.) 24The total amount of the gold from the wave offering used for all the work on the sanctuary was 29 talents and 730 shekels,[i] according to the sanctuary shekel.

25The silver obtained from those of the community who were counted in the census was 100 talents and 1,775 shekels,[j] according to the sanctuary shekel—26one beka per person, that is, half a shekel,[k] according to the sanctuary shekel, from everyone who had crossed over to those counted, twenty years old or more, a total of 603,550 men. 27The 100 talents[l] of silver were used to cast the bases for the sanctuary and for the curtain—100 bases from the 100 talents, one talent for each base. 28They used the 1,775 shekels[m] to make the hooks for the posts, to overlay the tops of the posts, and to make their bands.

29The bronze from the wave offering was 70 talents and 2,400 shekels.[n] 30They used it to make the bases for the entrance to the Tent of Meeting, the bronze altar with its bronze grating and all its utensils, 31the bases for the surrounding courtyard and those for its entrance and all the tent pegs for the tabernacle and those for the surrounding courtyard.

The Priestly Garments

39 From the blue, purple and scarlet yarn they made woven garments for ministering in the sanctuary. They also made sacred garments for Aaron, as the LORD commanded Moses.

The Ephod

2They[a] made the ephod of gold, and of blue, purple and scarlet yarn, and of finely twisted linen. 3They hammered out thin sheets of gold and cut strands to be worked into the blue, purple and scarlet yarn and fine linen—the work of a skilled craftsman. 4They made shoulder pieces for the ephod, which were attached to two of its corners, so that it could be fastened. 5Its skilfully woven waistband was like it—of one piece with the ephod and made with gold, and with blue, purple and scarlet yarn, and with finely twisted linen, as the LORD commanded Moses.

---

[a]1 Or *He*; also in verses 2–9   [b]1 That is, about 4½ feet (about 1.4 metres)
[c]1 That is, about 7½ feet (about 2.3 metres) long and wide   [d]9 That is, about 150 feet (about 46 metres)
[e]12 That is, about 75 feet (about 23 metres)   [f]14 That is, about 22½ feet (about 6.9 metres)
[g]18 That is, about 30 feet (about 9 metres)   [h]18 That is, about 7½ feet (about 2.3 metres)
[i]24 The weight of the gold was about one ton (about 1 metric ton).
[j]25 The weight of the silver was a little over 3⅓ tons (about 3.4 metric tons).
[k]26 That is, about ⅕ ounce (about 6 grams)   [l]27 That is, about 3⅓ tons (about 3.4 metric tons)
[m]28 That is, about 45 pounds (about 20 kilograms)
[n]29 The weight of the bronze was about 2⅓ tons (about 2.4 metric tons).   [a]2 Or *He*; also in verses 7, 8 and 22

⁶They mounted the onyx stones in gold filigree settings and engraved them like a seal with the names of the sons of Israel. ⁷Then they fastened them on the shoulder pieces of the ephod as memorial stones for the sons of Israel, as the LORD commanded Moses.

The Breastpiece

⁸They fashioned the breastpiece—the work of a skilled craftsman. They made it like the ephod: of gold, and of blue, purple and scarlet yarn, and of finely twisted linen. ⁹It was square—a span*b* long and a span wide—and folded double. ¹⁰Then they mounted four rows of precious stones on it. In the first row there was a ruby, a topaz and a beryl; ¹¹in the second row a turquoise, a sapphire*c* and an emerald; ¹²in the third row a jacinth, an agate and an amethyst; ¹³in the fourth row a chrysolite, an onyx and a jasper.*d* They were mounted in gold filigree settings. ¹⁴There were twelve stones, one for each of the names of the sons of Israel, each engraved like a seal with the name of one of the twelve tribes.

¹⁵For the breastpiece they made braided chains of pure gold, like a rope. ¹⁶They made two gold filigree settings and two gold rings, and fastened the rings to two of the corners of the breastpiece. ¹⁷They fastened the two gold chains to the rings at the corners of the breastpiece, ¹⁸and the other ends of the chains to the two settings, attaching them to the shoulder pieces of the ephod at the front. ¹⁹They made two gold rings and attached them to the other two corners of the breastpiece on the inside edge next to the ephod. ²⁰Then they made two more gold rings and attached them to the bottom of the shoulder pieces on the front of the ephod, close to the seam just above the waistband of the ephod. ²¹They tied the rings of the breastpiece to the rings of the ephod with blue cord, connecting it to the waistband so that the breastpiece would not swing out from the ephod—as the LORD commanded Moses.

Other Priestly Garments

²²They made the robe of the ephod entirely of blue cloth—the work of a weaver—²³with an opening in the centre of the robe like the opening of a collar,*e* and a band around this opening, so that it would not tear. ²⁴They made pomegranates of blue, purple and scarlet yarn and finely twisted linen around the hem of the robe. ²⁵And they made bells of pure gold and attached them around the hem between the pomegranates. ²⁶The bells and pomegranates alternated around the hem of the robe to be worn for ministering, as the LORD commanded Moses.

²⁷For Aaron and his sons, they made tunics of fine linen—the work of a weaver—²⁸and the turban of fine linen, the linen headbands and the undergarments of finely twisted linen. ²⁹The sash was of finely twisted linen and blue, purple and scarlet yarn—the work of an embroiderer—as the LORD commanded Moses.

³⁰They made the plate, the sacred diadem, out of pure gold and engraved on it, like an inscription on a seal: HOLY TO THE LORD. ³¹Then they fastened a blue cord to it to attach it to the turban, as the LORD commanded Moses.

Moses Inspects the Tabernacle

³²So all the work on the tabernacle, the Tent of Meeting, was completed. The Israelites did everything just as the LORD commanded Moses. ³³Then they brought the tabernacle to Moses: the tent and all its furnishings, its clasps, frames, crossbars, posts and bases; ³⁴the covering of ram skins dyed red, the covering of hides of sea cows*f* and the shielding curtain; ³⁵the ark of the Testimony with its poles and the atonement cover; ³⁶the table with all its articles and the bread of the Presence; ³⁷the pure gold lampstand with its row of lamps and all its accessories, and the oil for the light; ³⁸the gold altar, the anointing oil, the fragrant incense, and the curtain for the entrance to the tent; ³⁹the bronze altar with its bronze grating, its poles and all its utensils; the basin with its stand; ⁴⁰the curtains of the courtyard with its posts and bases, and the curtain for the entrance to the courtyard; the ropes and tent pegs for the courtyard; all the furnishings for the tabernacle, the Tent of Meeting; ⁴¹and the woven garments worn for ministering in the sanctuary, both the sacred garments for Aaron the priest and the garments for his sons when serving as priests.

⁴²The Israelites had done all the work just as the LORD had commanded Moses. ⁴³Moses inspected the work and saw that they had done it just as the LORD had commanded. So Moses blessed them.

Setting Up the Tabernacle

40 Then the LORD said to Moses: ²"Set up the tabernacle, the Tent of Meeting, on the first day of the first month. ³Place the ark of the Testimony in it and shield the ark with the curtain. ⁴Bring in the table and set out what belongs on it. Then bring in the lampstand and set up its lamps. ⁵Place the gold altar of incense in front of the ark of the Testimony and put the curtain at the entrance to the tabernacle.

⁶"Place the altar of burnt offering in front of the entrance to the tabernacle, the Tent of Meeting; ⁷place the basin between the Tent of Meeting and the altar and put water in it. ⁸Set up the courtyard around it and put the curtain at the entrance to the courtyard.

⁹"Take the anointing oil and anoint the tabernacle and everything in it; consecrate it and all its furnishings, and it will be holy. ¹⁰Then anoint the altar of burnt offering and all its utensils; consecrate the altar, and it will be most holy. ¹¹Anoint the basin and its stand and consecrate them.

---

b9 That is, about 9 inches (about 23 centimetres)   *c11* Or *lapis lazuli*
d13 The precise identification of some of these precious stones is uncertain.
e23 The meaning of the Hebrew for this word is uncertain.   *f34* That is, large aquatic mammals

EXODUS 40:1–38
'Then the cloud covered the Tent of Meeting, and the glory of the LORD filled the tabernacle' (v. 34).

THE GREAT DAY had arrived. The various parts of the tabernacle had been completed and were ready to be assembled (39:42, 43). Moses was directed to establish the tabernacle on the first day of the first month (vv. 1, 2). We can well imagine his feelings of satisfaction as the various parts of the tabernacle, given to him in such detail on Sinai (25: 8ff.), began to take shape. God had given the directions, he had given the skills to the workmen (35:30–36:5), soon he was to set his seal upon the undertaking.

After the manual work was done, the cloud, which represented the presence of God and which had hovered over the temporary tent of meeting, moved to the new tabernacle and the glory of the Lord filled it so powerfully that not even Moses, no stranger to that glory, could enter at that time (v. 35).

The presence of God also guarantees guidance. He who is the source of all wisdom and compassion, is always ready to guide. The Israelites learned quickly that if the cloud of the presence moved, then they moved, and if it remained, they remained also (vv. 36–38). We are not vouchsafed so clear and obvious a guide, but, even better, we have the Scriptures and we have the Holy Spirit who is our personal teacher (John 14:26) and guide (John 16:13). We also know that our bodies have become tabernacles in which the glory of God should dwell (1 Cor. 3:16). The ancient tabernacle, which housed the glory of God for a pilgrim people, foreshadowed the glory of God indwelling each pilgrim heart. What glory that is!

> *Thou hast my flesh, thy hallowed shrine,*
> *Devoted solely to thy will;*
> *Here let thy light forever shine,*
> *This house still let thy presence fill;*
> *O Source of life, live, dwell and move*
> *In me, till all my life be love!*

(Joachim Lange, trs. John Wesley)

Pray for a deeper awareness of the indwelling Spirit.

→94

LEVITICUS 16:1–17

'He shall then slaughter the goat for the sin offering for the people and take its blood behind the curtain and do with it as he did with the bull's blood: he shall sprinkle it on the atonement cover and in front of it' (v. 15).

ONCE A YEAR on the Day of Atonement, the High Priest entered the Holy of Holies to make an atonement for his own sins and the sins of his people. First, he sacrificed a bull and sprinkled the blood on the mercy seat for his own and his household's sins, following which he sacrificed a goat for the people's sins, again sprinkling the blood on the mercy seat. The mercy seat was the place where atonement, an at-one-ment, was made between a sinful people and a holy, just God.

The original Hebrew word for 'mercy seat' meant a covering, hence the NIV translation 'atonement cover'. It was intended to convey the idea of forgiveness and the covering of human sin. Very powerfully, and most significantly, the Greek equivalent word for 'mercy seat' is used by Paul and John to describe the redemptive work of Jesus. The same word is used in Hebrews to describe the mercy seat. In many versions the English word used is 'propitiation'. Lack of space precludes a discussion on that word, but it is sufficient to say that through the sacrifice of Jesus, when we exercise faith in him, our sins have been dealt with. He has made full atonement for us. In fact, as Paul and John have indicated, he, Jesus, has become our mercy seat. The symbol of the Ark of the Covenant has become a glorious reality in Christ Jesus.

> *There is welcome for the sinner,*
> *And more graces for the good;*
> *There is mercy with the Saviour;*
> *There is healing in his blood.*

(*Frederick William Faber*)

¹²"Bring Aaron and his sons to the entrance to the Tent of Meeting and wash them with water. ¹³Then dress Aaron in the sacred garments, anoint him and consecrate him so that he may serve me as priest. ¹⁴Bring his sons and dress them in tunics. ¹⁵Anoint them just as you anointed their father, so that they may serve me as priests. Their anointing will be to a priesthood that will continue for all generations to come." ¹⁶Moses did everything just as the LORD commanded him.

¹⁷So the tabernacle was set up on the first day of the first month in the second year. ¹⁸When Moses set up the tabernacle, he put the bases in place, erected the frames, inserted the crossbars and set up the posts. ¹⁹Then he spread the tent over the tabernacle and put the covering over the tent, as the LORD commanded him.

²⁰He took the Testimony and placed it in the ark, attached the poles to the ark and put the atonement cover over it. ²¹Then he brought the ark into the tabernacle and hung the shielding curtain and shielded the ark of the Testimony, as the LORD commanded him.

²²Moses placed the table in the Tent of Meeting on the north side of the tabernacle outside the curtain ²³and set out the bread on it before the LORD, as the LORD commanded him.

²⁴He placed the lampstand in the Tent of Meeting opposite the table on the south side of the tabernacle ²⁵and set up the lamps before the LORD, as the LORD commanded him.

²⁶Moses placed the gold altar in the Tent of Meeting in front of the curtain ²⁷and burned fragrant incense on it, as the LORD commanded him. ²⁸Then he put up the curtain at the entrance to the tabernacle.

²⁹He set the altar of burnt offering near the entrance to the tabernacle, the Tent of Meeting, and offered on it burnt offerings and grain offerings, as the LORD commanded him.

³⁰He placed the basin between the Tent of Meeting and the altar and put water in it for washing, ³¹and Moses and Aaron and his sons used it to wash their hands and feet. ³²They washed whenever they entered the Tent of Meeting or approached the altar, as the LORD commanded Moses.

³³Then Moses set up the courtyard around the tabernacle and altar and put up the curtain at the entrance to the courtyard. And so Moses finished the work.

The Glory of the LORD

³⁴Then the cloud covered the Tent of Meeting, and the glory of the LORD filled the tabernacle. ³⁵Moses could not enter the Tent of Meeting because the cloud had settled upon it, and the glory of the LORD filled the tabernacle.

³⁶In all the travels of the Israelites, whenever the cloud lifted from above the tabernacle, they would set out; ³⁷but if the cloud did not lift, they did not set out—until the day it lifted. ³⁸So the cloud of the LORD was over the tabernacle by day, and fire was in the cloud by night, in the sight of all the house of Israel during all their travels.

Leviticus

The Burnt Offering

1 The LORD called to Moses and spoke to him from the Tent of Meeting. He said, 2"Speak to the Israelites and say to them: 'When any of you brings an offering to the LORD, bring as your offering an animal from either the herd or the flock.

3"'If the offering is a burnt offering from the herd, he is to offer a male without defect. He must present it at the entrance to the Tent of Meeting so that it*a* will be acceptable to the LORD. 4He is to lay his hand on the head of the burnt offering, and it will be accepted on his behalf to make atonement for him. 5He is to slaughter the young bull before the LORD, and then Aaron's sons the priests shall bring the blood and sprinkle it against the altar on all sides at the entrance to the Tent of Meeting. 6He is to skin the burnt offering and cut it into pieces. 7The sons of Aaron the priest are to put fire on the altar and arrange wood on the fire. 8Then Aaron's sons the priests shall arrange the pieces, including the head and the fat, on the burning wood that is on the altar. 9He is to wash the inner parts and the legs with water, and the priest is to burn all of it on the altar. It is a burnt offering, an offering made by fire, an aroma pleasing to the LORD.

10"'If the offering is a burnt offering from the flock, from either the sheep or the goats, he is to offer a male without defect. 11He is to slaughter it at the north side of the altar before the LORD, and Aaron's sons the priests shall sprinkle its blood against the altar on all sides. 12He is to cut it into pieces, and the priest shall arrange them, including the head and the fat, on the burning wood that is on the altar. 13He is to wash the inner parts and the legs with water, and the priest is to bring all of it and burn it on the altar. It is a burnt offering, an offering made by fire, an aroma pleasing to the LORD.

14"'If the offering to the LORD is a burnt offering of birds, he is to offer a dove or a young pigeon. 15The priest shall bring it to the altar, wring off the head and burn it on the altar; its blood shall be drained out on the side of the altar. 16He is to remove the crop with its contents*b* and throw it to the east side of the altar, where the ashes are.

17He shall tear it open by the wings, not severing it completely, and then the priest shall burn it on the wood that is on the fire on the altar. It is a burnt offering, an offering made by fire, an aroma pleasing to the LORD.

The Grain Offering

2 "'When someone brings a grain offering to the LORD, his offering is to be of fine flour. He is to pour oil on it, put incense on it 2and take it to Aaron's sons the priests. The priest shall take a handful of the fine flour and oil, together with all the incense, and burn this as a memorial portion on the altar, an offering made by fire, an aroma pleasing to the LORD. 3The rest of the grain offering belongs to Aaron and his sons; it is a most holy part of the offerings made to the LORD by fire.

4"'If you bring a grain offering baked in an oven, it is to consist of fine flour: cakes made without yeast and mixed with oil, or*a* wafers made without yeast and spread with oil. 5If your grain offering is prepared on a griddle, it is to be made of fine flour mixed with oil, and without yeast. 6Crumble it and pour oil on it; it is a grain offering. 7If your grain offering is cooked in a pan, it is to be made of fine flour and oil. 8Bring the grain offering made of these things to the LORD; present it to the priest, who shall take it to the altar. 9He shall take out the memorial portion from the grain offering and burn it on the altar as an offering made by fire, an aroma pleasing to the LORD. 10The rest of the grain offering belongs to Aaron and his sons; it is a most holy part of the offerings made to the LORD by fire.

11"'Every grain offering you bring to the LORD must be made without yeast, for you are not to burn any yeast or honey in an offering made to the LORD by fire. 12You may bring them to the LORD as an offering of the firstfruits, but they are not to be offered on the altar as a pleasing aroma. 13Season all your grain offerings with salt. Do not leave the salt of the covenant of your God out of your grain offerings; add salt to all your offerings.

14"'If you bring a grain offering of firstfruits to the LORD, offer crushed heads of new grain roasted in the fire. 15Put oil and

---

a3 Or *he*   *b16* Or *crop and the feathers;* the meaning of the Hebrew for this word is uncertain.
a4 Or *and*

incense on it; it is a grain offering. [16]The priest shall burn the memorial portion of the crushed grain and the oil, together with all the incense, as an offering made to the LORD by fire.

The Fellowship Offering

3 "'If someone's offering is a fellowship offering,[a] and he offers an animal from the herd, whether male or female, he is to present before the LORD an animal without defect. [2]He is to lay his hand on the head of his offering and slaughter it at the entrance to the Tent of Meeting. Then Aaron's sons the priests shall sprinkle the blood against the altar on all sides. [3]From the fellowship offering he is to bring a sacrifice made to the LORD by fire: all the fat that covers the inner parts or is connected to them, [4]both kidneys with the fat on them near the loins, and the covering of the liver, which he will remove with the kidneys. [5]Then Aaron's sons are to burn it on the altar on top of the burnt offering that is on the burning wood, as an offering made by fire, an aroma pleasing to the LORD.

[6]"'If he offers an animal from the flock as a fellowship offering to the LORD, he is to offer a male or female without defect. [7]If he offers a lamb, he is to present it before the LORD. [8]He is to lay his hand on the head of his offering and slaughter it in front of the Tent of Meeting. Then Aaron's sons shall sprinkle its blood against the altar on all sides. [9]From the fellowship offering he is to bring a sacrifice made to the LORD by fire: its fat, the entire fat tail cut off close to the backbone, all the fat that covers the inner parts or is connected to them, [10]both kidneys with the fat on them near the loins, and the covering of the liver, which he will remove with the kidneys. [11]The priest shall burn them on the altar as food, an offering made to the LORD by fire.

[12]"'If his offering is a goat, he is to present it before the LORD. [13]He is to lay his hand on its head and slaughter it in front of the Tent of Meeting. Then Aaron's sons shall sprinkle its blood against the altar on all sides. [14]From what he offers he is to make this offering to the LORD by fire: all the fat that covers the inner parts or is connected to them, [15]both kidneys with the fat on them near the loins, and the covering of the liver, which he will remove with the kidneys. [16]The priest shall burn them on the altar as food, an offering made by fire, a pleasing aroma. All the fat is the LORD's.

[17]"'This is a lasting ordinance for the generations to come, wherever you live: You must not eat any fat or any blood.'"

The Sin Offering

4 The LORD said to Moses, [2]"Say to the Israelites: 'When anyone sins unintentionally and does what is forbidden in any of the LORD's commands—

[3]"'If the anointed priest sins, bringing guilt on the people, he must bring to the LORD

a young bull without defect as a sin offering for the sin he has committed. [4]He is to present the bull at the entrance to the Tent of Meeting before the LORD. He is to lay his hand on its head and slaughter it before the LORD. [5]Then the anointed priest shall take some of the bull's blood and carry it into the Tent of Meeting. [6]He is to dip his finger into the blood and sprinkle some of it seven times before the LORD, in front of the curtain of the sanctuary. [7]The priest shall then put some of the blood on the horns of the altar of fragrant incense that is before the LORD in the Tent of Meeting. The rest of the bull's blood he shall pour out at the base of the altar of burnt offering at the entrance to the Tent of Meeting. [8]He shall remove all the fat from the bull of the sin offering—the fat that covers the inner parts or is connected to them, [9]both kidneys with the fat on them near the loins, and the covering of the liver, which he will remove with the kidneys—[10]just as the fat is removed from the ox[a] sacrificed as a fellowship offering.[b] Then the priest shall burn them on the altar of burnt offering. [11]But the hide of the bull and all its flesh, as well as the head and legs, the inner parts and offal—[12]that is, all the rest of the bull—he must take outside the camp to a place ceremonially clean, where the ashes are thrown, and burn it in a wood fire on the ash heap.

[13]"'If the whole Israelite community sins unintentionally and does what is forbidden in any of the LORD's commands, even though the community is unaware of the matter, they are guilty. [14]When they become aware of the sin they committed, the assembly must bring a young bull as a sin offering and present it before the Tent of Meeting. [15]The elders of the community are to lay their hands on the bull's head before the LORD, and the bull shall be slaughtered before the LORD. [16]Then the anointed priest is to take some of the bull's blood into the Tent of Meeting. [17]He shall dip his finger into the blood and sprinkle it before the LORD seven times in front of the curtain. [18]He is to put some of the blood on the horns of the altar that is before the LORD in the Tent of Meeting. The rest of the blood he shall pour out at the base of the altar of burnt offering at the entrance to the Tent of Meeting. [19]He shall remove all the fat from it and burn it on the altar, [20]and do with this bull just as he did with the bull for the sin offering. In this way the priest will make atonement for them, and they will be forgiven. [21]Then he shall take the bull outside the camp and burn it as he burned the first bull. This is the sin offering for the community.

[22]"'When a leader sins unintentionally and does what is forbidden in any of the commands of the LORD his God, he is guilty. [23]When he is made aware of the sin he committed, he must bring as his offering a male goat without defect. [24]He is to lay his hand on the goat's head and slaughter it at the place

---

[a]1 Traditionally *peace offering*; also in verses 3, 6 and 9
[a]10 The Hebrew word can include both male and female.
[b]10 Traditionally *peace offering*; also in verses 26, 31 and 35

where the burnt offering is slaughtered before the LORD. It is a sin offering. ²⁵Then the priest shall take some of the blood of the sin offering with his finger and put it on the horns of the altar of burnt offering and pour out the rest of the blood at the base of the altar. ²⁶He shall burn all the fat on the altar as he burned the fat of the fellowship offering. In this way the priest will make atonement for the man's sin, and he will be forgiven.

²⁷"'If a member of the community sins unintentionally and does what is forbidden in any of the LORD's commands, he is guilty. ²⁸When he is made aware of the sin he committed, he must bring as his offering for the sin he committed a female goat without defect. ²⁹He is to lay his hand on the head of the sin offering and slaughter it at the place of the burnt offering. ³⁰Then the priest is to take some of the blood with his finger and put it on the horns of the altar of burnt offering and pour out the rest of the blood at the base of the altar. ³¹He shall remove all the fat, just as the fat is removed from the fellowship offering, and the priest shall burn it on the altar as an aroma pleasing to the LORD. In this way the priest will make atonement for him, and he will be forgiven.

³²"'If he brings a lamb as his sin offering, he is to bring a female without defect. ³³He is to lay his hand on its head and slaughter it for a sin offering at the place where the burnt offering is slaughtered. ³⁴Then the priest shall take some of the blood of the sin offering with his finger and put it on the horns of the altar of burnt offering and pour out the rest of the blood at the base of the altar. ³⁵He shall remove all the fat, just as the fat is removed from the lamb of the fellowship offering, and the priest shall burn it on the altar on top of the offerings made to the LORD by fire. In this way the priest will make atonement for him for the sin he has committed, and he will be forgiven.

5 "'If a person sins because he does not speak up when he hears a public charge to testify regarding something he has seen or learned about, he will be held responsible.

²"'Or if a person touches anything ceremonially unclean—whether the carcasses of unclean wild animals or of unclean livestock or of unclean creatures that move along the ground—even though he is unaware of it, he has become unclean and is guilty.

³"'Or if he touches human uncleanness —anything that would make him unclean —even though he is unaware of it, when he learns of it he will be guilty.

⁴"'Or if a person thoughtlessly takes an oath to do anything, whether good or evil —in any matter one might carelessly swear about—even though he is unaware of it, in any case when he learns of it he will be guilty.

⁵"'When anyone is guilty in any of these ways, he must confess in what way he has sinned ⁶and, as a penalty for the sin he has

committed, he must bring to the LORD a female lamb or goat from the flock as a sin offering; and the priest shall make atonement for him for his sin.

⁷"'If he cannot afford a lamb, he is to bring two doves or two young pigeons to the LORD as a penalty for his sin—one for a sin offering and the other for a burnt offering. ⁸He is to bring them to the priest, who shall first offer the one for the sin offering. He is to wring its head from its neck, not severing it completely, ⁹and is to sprinkle some of the blood of the sin offering against the side of the altar; the rest of the blood must be drained out at the base of the altar. It is a sin offering. ¹⁰The priest shall then offer the other as a burnt offering in the prescribed way and make atonement for him for the sin he has committed, and he will be forgiven.

¹¹"'If, however, he cannot afford two doves or two young pigeons, he is to bring as an offering for his sin a tenth of an ephah*a* of fine flour for a sin offering. He must not put oil or incense on it, because it is a sin offering. ¹²He is to bring it to the priest, who shall take a handful of it as a memorial portion and burn it on the altar on top of the offerings made to the LORD by fire. It is a sin offering. ¹³In this way the priest will make atonement for him for any of these sins he has committed, and he will be forgiven. The rest of the offering will belong to the priest, as in the case of the grain offering.'"

The Guilt Offering

¹⁴The LORD said to Moses: ¹⁵"When a person commits a violation and sins unintentionally in regard to any of the LORD's holy things, he is to bring to the LORD as a penalty a ram from the flock, one without defect and of the proper value in silver, according to the sanctuary shekel.*b* It is a guilt offering. ¹⁶He must make restitution for what he has failed to do in regard to the holy things, add a fifth of the value to that and give it all to the priest, who will make atonement for him with the ram as a guilt offering, and he will be forgiven.

¹⁷"If a person sins and does what is forbidden in any of the LORD's commands, even though he does not know it, he is guilty and will be held responsible. ¹⁸He is to bring to the priest as a guilt offering a ram from the flock, one without defect and of the proper value. In this way the priest will make atonement for him for the wrong he has committed unintentionally, and he will be forgiven. ¹⁹It is a guilt offering; he has been guilty of*c* wrongdoing against the LORD."

6 The LORD said to Moses: ²"If anyone sins and is unfaithful to the LORD by deceiving his neighbour about something entrusted to him or left in his care or stolen, or if he cheats him, ³or if he finds lost property and lies about it, or if he swears falsely, or if he commits any such sin that people may do—⁴when he thus sins and becomes guilty, he must return what he has stolen or taken by

---

a11 That is, probably about 4 pints (about 2 litres)   *b15* That is, about ⅖ ounce (about 11.5 grams)
c19 Or *has made full expiation for his*

extortion, or what was entrusted to him, or the lost property he found, [5]or whatever it was he swore falsely about. He must make restitution in full, add a fifth of the value to it and give it all to the owner on the day he presents his guilt offering. [6]And as a penalty he must bring to the priest, that is, to the LORD, his guilt offering, a ram from the flock, one without defect and of the proper value. [7]In this way the priest will make atonement for him before the LORD, and he will be forgiven for any of these things he did that made him guilty."

The Burnt Offering

[8]The LORD said to Moses: [9]"Give Aaron and his sons this command: 'These are the regulations for the burnt offering: The burnt offering is to remain on the altar hearth throughout the night, till morning, and the fire must be kept burning on the altar. [10]The priest shall then put on his linen clothes, with linen undergarments next to his body, and shall remove the ashes of the burnt offering that the fire has consumed on the altar and place them beside the altar. [11]Then he is to take off these clothes and put on others, and carry the ashes outside the camp to a place that is ceremonially clean. [12]The fire on the altar must be kept burning; it must not go out. Every morning the priest is to add firewood and arrange the burnt offering on the fire and burn the fat of the fellowship offerings[a] on it. [13]The fire must be kept burning on the altar continuously; it must not go out.

The Grain Offering

[14]"'These are the regulations for the grain offering: Aaron's sons are to bring it before the LORD, in front of the altar. [15]The priest is to take a handful of fine flour and oil, together with all the incense on the grain offering, and burn the memorial portion on the altar as an aroma pleasing to the LORD. [16]Aaron and his sons shall eat the rest of it, but it is to be eaten without yeast in a holy place; they are to eat it in the courtyard of the Tent of Meeting. [17]It must not be baked with yeast; I have given it as their share of the offerings made to me by fire. Like the sin offering and the guilt offering, it is most holy. [18]Any male descendant of Aaron may eat it. It is his regular share of the offerings made to the LORD by fire for the generations to come. Whatever touches it will become holy.'"[b]

[19]The LORD also said to Moses, [20]"This is the offering Aaron and his sons are to bring to the LORD on the day he[c] is anointed: a tenth of an ephah[d] of fine flour as a regular grain offering, half of it in the morning and half in the evening. [21]Prepare it with oil on a griddle; bring it well-mixed and present the grain offering broken[e] in pieces as an aroma pleasing to the LORD. [22]The son who is to succeed him as anointed priest shall prepare it. It is the LORD's regular share and is to be burned completely. [23]Every grain offering of a priest

shall be burned completely; it must not be eaten."

The Sin Offering

[24]The LORD said to Moses, [25]"Say to Aaron and his sons: 'These are the regulations for the sin offering: The sin offering is to be slaughtered before the LORD in the place where the burnt offering is slaughtered; it is most holy. [26]The priest who offers it shall eat it; it is to be eaten in a holy place, in the courtyard of the Tent of Meeting. [27]Whatever touches any of the flesh will become holy, and if any of the blood is spattered on a garment, you must wash it in a holy place. [28]The clay pot that the meat is cooked in must be broken; but if it is cooked in a bronze pot, the pot is to be scoured and rinsed with water. [29]Any male in a priest's family may eat it; it is most holy. [30]But any sin offering whose blood is brought into the Tent of Meeting to make atonement in the Holy Place must not be eaten; it must be burned.

The Guilt Offering

7 "'These are the regulations for the guilt offering, which is most holy: [2]The guilt offering is to be slaughtered in the place where the burnt offering is slaughtered, and its blood is to be sprinkled against the altar on all sides. [3]All its fat shall be offered: the fat tail and the fat that covers the inner parts, [4]both kidneys with the fat on them near the loins, and the covering of the liver, which is to be removed with the kidneys. [5]The priest shall burn them on the altar as an offering made to the LORD by fire. It is a guilt offering. [6]Any male in a priest's family may eat it, but it must be eaten in a holy place; it is most holy.

[7]"'The same law applies to both the sin offering and the guilt offering: They belong to the priest who makes atonement with them. [8]The priest who offers a burnt offering for anyone may keep its hide for himself. [9]Every grain offering baked in an oven or cooked in a pan or on a griddle belongs to the priest who offers it, [10]and every grain offering, whether mixed with oil or dry, belongs equally to all the sons of Aaron.

The Fellowship Offering

[11]"'These are the regulations for the fellowship offering[a] a person may present to the LORD:

[12]"'If he offers it as an expression of thankfulness, then along with this thank-offering he is to offer cakes of bread made without yeast and mixed with oil, wafers made without yeast and spread with oil, and cakes of fine flour well-kneaded and mixed with oil. [13]Along with his fellowship offering of thanksgiving he is to present an offering with cakes of bread made with yeast. [14]He is to bring one of each kind as an offering, a contribution to the LORD; it belongs to

---

[a]12 Traditionally *peace offerings*   [b]18 Or *Whoever touches them must be holy*; similarly in verse 27
[c]20 Or *each*   [d]20 That is, probably about 4 pints (about 2 litres)
[e]21 The meaning of the Hebrew for this word is uncertain.   [a]11 Traditionally *peace offering*; also in verses 13–37

the priest who sprinkles the blood of the fellowship offerings. [15]The meat of his fellowship offering of thanksgiving must be eaten on the day it is offered; he must leave none of it till morning.

[16]"'If, however, his offering is the result of a vow or is a freewill offering, the sacrifice shall be eaten on the day he offers it, but anything left over may be eaten on the next day. [17]Any meat of the sacrifice left over till the third day must be burned up. [18]If any meat of the fellowship offering is eaten on the third day, it will not be accepted. It will not be credited to the one who offered it, for it is impure; the person who eats any of it will be held responsible.

[19]"'Meat that touches anything ceremonially unclean must not be eaten; it must be burned up. As for other meat, anyone ceremonially clean may eat it. [20]But if anyone who is unclean eats any meat of the fellowship offering belonging to the LORD, that person must be cut off from his people. [21]If anyone touches something unclean— whether human uncleanness or an unclean animal or any unclean, detestable thing— and then eats any of the meat of the fellowship offering belonging to the LORD, that person must be cut off from his people.'"

Eating Fat and Blood Forbidden

[22]The LORD said to Moses, [23]"Say to the Israelites: 'Do not eat any of the fat of cattle, sheep or goats. [24]The fat of an animal found dead or torn by wild animals may be used for any other purpose, but you must not eat it. [25]Anyone who eats the fat of an animal from which an offering by fire may be[b] made to the LORD must be cut off from his people. [26]And wherever you live, you must not eat the blood of any bird or animal. [27]If anyone eats blood, that person must be cut off from his people.'"

The Priests' Share

[28]The LORD said to Moses, [29]"Say to the Israelites: 'Anyone who brings a fellowship offering to the LORD is to bring part of it as his sacrifice to the LORD. [30]With his own hands he is to bring the offering made to the LORD by fire; he is to bring the fat, together with the breast, and wave the breast before the LORD as a wave offering. [31]The priest shall burn the fat on the altar, but the breast belongs to Aaron and his sons. [32]You are to give the right thigh of your fellowship offerings to the priest as a contribution. [33]The son of Aaron who offers the blood and the fat of the fellowship offering shall have the right thigh as his share. [34]From the fellowship offerings of the Israelites, I have taken the breast that is waved and the thigh that is presented and have given them to Aaron the priest and his sons as their regular share from the Israelites.'"

[35]This is the portion of the offerings made to the LORD by fire that were allotted to Aaron and his sons on the day they were presented to serve the LORD as priests. [36]On the day they were anointed, the LORD commanded that the Israelites give this to them as their regular share for the generations to come.

[37]These, then, are the regulations for the burnt offering, the grain offering, the sin offering, the guilt offering, the ordination offering and the fellowship offering, [38]which the LORD gave Moses on Mount Sinai on the day he commanded the Israelites to bring their offerings to the LORD, in the Desert of Sinai.

The Ordination of Aaron and His Sons

8 The LORD said to Moses, [2]"Bring Aaron and his sons, their garments, the anointing oil, the bull for the sin offering, the two rams and the basket containing bread made without yeast, [3]and gather the entire assembly at the entrance to the Tent of Meeting." [4]Moses did as the LORD commanded him, and the assembly gathered at the entrance to the Tent of Meeting.

[5]Moses said to the assembly, "This is what the LORD has commanded to be done." [6]Then Moses brought Aaron and his sons forward and washed them with water. [7]He put the tunic on Aaron, tied the sash around him, clothed him with the robe and put the ephod on him. He also tied the ephod to him by its skilfully woven waistband; so it was fastened on him. [8]He placed the breastpiece on him and put the Urim and Thummim in the breastpiece. [9]Then he placed the turban on Aaron's head and set the gold plate, the sacred diadem, on the front of it, as the LORD commanded Moses.

[10]Then Moses took the anointing oil and anointed the tabernacle and everything in it, and so consecrated them. [11]He sprinkled some of the oil on the altar seven times, anointing the altar and all its utensils and the basin with its stand, to consecrate them. [12]He poured some of the anointing oil on Aaron's head and anointed him to consecrate him. [13]Then he brought Aaron's sons forward, put tunics on them, tied sashes around them and put headbands on them, as the LORD commanded Moses.

[14]He then presented the bull for the sin offering, and Aaron and his sons laid their hands on its head. [15]Moses slaughtered the bull and took some of the blood, and with his finger he put it on all the horns of the altar to purify the altar. He poured out the rest of the blood at the base of the altar. So he consecrated it to make atonement for it. [16]Moses also took all the fat around the inner parts, the covering of the liver, and both kidneys and their fat, and burned it on the altar. [17]But the bull with its hide and its flesh and its offal he burned up outside the camp, as the LORD commanded Moses.

[18]He then presented the ram for the burnt offering, and Aaron and his sons laid their hands on its head. [19]Then Moses slaughtered the ram and sprinkled the blood against the altar on all sides. [20]He cut the ram into pieces

and burned the head, the pieces and the fat.
21He washed the inner parts and the legs with
water and burned the whole ram on the altar
as a burnt offering, a pleasing aroma, an
offering made to the LORD by fire, as the LORD
commanded Moses.

22He then presented the other ram, the ram
for the ordination, and Aaron and his sons
laid their hands on its head. 23Moses slaughtered the ram and took some of its blood and
put it on the lobe of Aaron's right ear, on the
thumb of his right hand and on the big toe of
his right foot. 24Moses also brought Aaron's
sons forward and put some of the blood on
the lobes of their right ears, on the thumbs of
their right hands and on the big toes of their
right feet. Then he sprinkled blood against
the altar on all sides. 25He took the fat, the fat
tail, all the fat around the inner parts, the
covering of the liver, both kidneys and their
fat and the right thigh. 26Then from the basket
of bread made without yeast, which was
before the LORD, he took a cake of bread, and
one made with oil, and a wafer; he put these
on the fat portions and on the right thigh.
27He put all these in the hands of Aaron and
his sons and waved them before the LORD as
a wave offering. 28Then Moses took them
from their hands and burned them on the
altar on top of the burnt offering as an
ordination offering, a pleasing aroma, an
offering made to the LORD by fire. 29He also
took the breast—Moses' share of the ordination ram—and waved it before the LORD
as a wave offering, as the LORD commanded
Moses.

30Then Moses took some of the anointing
oil and some of the blood from the altar and
sprinkled them on Aaron and his garments
and on his sons and their garments. So he
consecrated Aaron and his garments and his
sons and their garments.

31Moses then said to Aaron and his sons,
"Cook the meat at the entrance to the Tent of
Meeting and eat it there with the bread from
the basket of ordination offerings, as I commanded, saying,ᵃ 'Aaron and his sons are to
eat it.' 32Then burn up the rest of the meat
and the bread. 33Do not leave the entrance to
the Tent of Meeting for seven days, until the
days of your ordination are completed, for
your ordination will last seven days. 34What
has been done today was commanded by the
LORD to make atonement for you. 35You must
stay at the entrance to the Tent of Meeting
day and night for seven days and do what the
LORD requires, so that you will not die; for
that is what I have been commanded." 36So
Aaron and his sons did everything the LORD
commanded through Moses.

The Priests Begin Their Ministry

9 On the eighth day Moses summoned
Aaron and his sons and the elders of
Israel. 2He said to Aaron, "Take a bull calf
for your sin offering and a ram for your burnt
offering, both without defect, and present
them before the LORD. 3Then say to the

Israelites: 'Take a male goat for a sin offering, a calf and a lamb—both a year old and
without defect—for a burnt offering, 4and an
oxᵃ and a ram for a fellowship offeringᵇ to
sacrifice before the LORD, together with a
grain offering mixed with oil. For today the
LORD will appear to you.'''

5They took the things Moses commanded
to the front of the Tent of Meeting, and
the entire assembly came near and stood
before the LORD. 6Then Moses said, "This
is what the LORD has commanded you to do,
so that the glory of the LORD may appear to
you."

7Moses said to Aaron, "Come to the altar
and sacrifice your sin offering and your burnt
offering and make atonement for yourself
and the people; sacrifice the offering that is
for the people and make atonement for them,
as the LORD has commanded."

8So Aaron came to the altar and slaughtered the calf as a sin offering for himself.
9His sons brought the blood to him, and he
dipped his finger into the blood and put it on
the horns of the altar; the rest of the blood he
poured out at the base of the altar. 10On the
altar he burned the fat, the kidneys and the
covering of the liver from the sin offering, as
the LORD commanded Moses; 11the flesh and
the hide he burned up outside the camp.

12Then he slaughtered the burnt offering.
His sons handed him the blood, and he
sprinkled it against the altar on all sides.
13They handed him the burnt offering piece
by piece, including the head, and he burned
them on the altar. 14He washed the inner
parts and the legs and burned them on top of
the burnt offering on the altar.

15Aaron then brought the offering that was
for the people. He took the goat for the
people's sin offering and slaughtered it and
offered it for a sin offering as he did with the
first one.

16He brought the burnt offering and offered
it in the prescribed way. 17He also brought
the grain offering, took a handful of it and
burned it on the altar in addition to the morning's burnt offering.

18He slaughtered the ox and the ram as the
fellowship offering for the people. His sons
handed him the blood, and he sprinkled it
against the altar on all sides. 19But the fat
portions of the ox and the ram—the fat tail,
the layer of fat, the kidneys and the covering
of the liver—20these they laid on the breasts,
and then Aaron burned the fat on the altar.
21Aaron waved the breasts and the right thigh
before the LORD as a wave offering, as Moses
commanded.

22Then Aaron lifted his hands towards the
people and blessed them. And having sacrificed the sin offering, the burnt offering and
the fellowship offering, he stepped down.

23Moses and Aaron then went into the Tent
of Meeting. When they came out, they blessed the people; and the glory of the LORD
appeared to all the people. 24Fire came out
from the presence of the LORD and consumed

ᵃ31 Or I was commanded: ᵃ4 The Hebrew word can include both male and female; also in verses 18 and 19.
ᵇ4 Traditionally peace offering; also in verses 18 and 22

the burnt offering and the fat portions on the altar. And when all the people saw it, they shouted for joy and fell face down.

The Death of Nadab and Abihu

10 Aaron's sons Nadab and Abihu took their censers, put fire in them and added incense; and they offered unauthorised fire before the Lord, contrary to his command. ²So fire came out from the presence of the Lord and consumed them, and they died before the Lord. ³Moses then said to Aaron, "This is what the Lord spoke of when he said:

"'Among those who approach me
I will show myself holy;
in the sight of all the people
I will be honoured.'"

Aaron remained silent.
⁴Moses summoned Mishael and Elzaphan, sons of Aaron's uncle Uzziel, and said to them, "Come here; carry your cousins outside the camp, away from the front of the sanctuary." ⁵So they came and carried them, still in their tunics, outside the camp, as Moses ordered.
⁶Then Moses said to Aaron and his sons Eleazar and Ithamar, "Do not let your hair become unkempt,*a* and do not tear your clothes, or you will die and the Lord will be angry with the whole community. But your relatives, all the house of Israel, may mourn for those the Lord has destroyed by fire. ⁷Do not leave the entrance to the Tent of Meeting or you will die, because the Lord's anointing oil is on you." So they did as Moses said.
⁸Then the Lord said to Aaron, ⁹"You and your sons are not to drink wine or other fermented drink whenever you go into the Tent of Meeting, or you will die. This is a lasting ordinance for the generations to come. ¹⁰You must distinguish between the holy and the common, between the unclean and the clean, ¹¹and you must teach the Israelites all the decrees the Lord has given them through Moses."
¹²Moses said to Aaron and his remaining sons, Eleazar and Ithamar, "Take the grain offering left over from the offerings made to the Lord by fire and eat it prepared without yeast beside the altar, for it is most holy. ¹³Eat it in a holy place, because it is your share and your sons' share of the offerings made to the Lord by fire; for so I have been commanded. ¹⁴But you and your sons and your daughters may eat the breast that was waved and the thigh that was presented. Eat them in a ceremonially clean place; they have been given to you and your children as your share of the Israelites' fellowship offerings.*b* ¹⁵The thigh that was presented and the breast that was waved must be brought with the fat portions of the offerings made by fire, to be waved before the Lord as a wave offering. This will be the regular share for you and your children, as the Lord has commanded."

¹⁶When Moses enquired about the goat of the sin offering and found that it had been burned up, he was angry with Eleazar and Ithamar, Aaron's remaining sons, and asked, ¹⁷"Why didn't you eat the sin offering in the sanctuary area? It is most holy; it was given to you to take away the guilt of the community by making atonement for them before the Lord. ¹⁸Since its blood was not taken into the Holy Place, you should have eaten the goat in the sanctuary area, as I commanded."
¹⁹Aaron replied to Moses, "Today they sacrificed their sin offering and their burnt offering before the Lord, but such things as this have happened to me. Would the Lord have been pleased if I had eaten the sin offering today?" ²⁰When Moses heard this, he was satisfied.

Clean and Unclean Food

11 The Lord said to Moses and Aaron, ²"Say to the Israelites: 'Of all the animals that live on land, these are the ones you may eat: ³You may eat any animal that has a split hoof completely divided and that chews the cud.
⁴"'There are some that only chew the cud or only have a split hoof, but you must not eat them. The camel, though it chews the cud, does not have a split hoof; it is ceremonially unclean for you. ⁵The coney,*a* though it chews the cud, does not have a split hoof; it is unclean for you. ⁶The rabbit, though it chews the cud, does not have a split hoof; it is unclean for you. ⁷And the pig, though it has a split hoof completely divided, does not chew the cud; it is unclean for you. ⁸You must not eat their meat or touch their carcasses; they are unclean for you.
⁹"'Of all the creatures living in the water of the seas and the streams, you may eat any that have fins and scales. ¹⁰But all creatures in the seas or streams that do not have fins and scales—whether among all the swarming things or among all the other living creatures in the water—you are to detest. ¹¹And since you are to detest them, you must not eat their meat and you must detest their carcasses. ¹²Anything living in the water that does not have fins and scales is to be detestable to you.
¹³"'These are the birds you are to detest and not eat because they are detestable: the eagle, the vulture, the black vulture, ¹⁴the red kite, any kind of black kite, ¹⁵any kind of raven, ¹⁶the horned owl, the screech owl, the gull, any kind of hawk, ¹⁷the little owl, the cormorant, the great owl, ¹⁸the white owl, the desert owl, the osprey, ¹⁹the stork, any kind of heron, the hoopoe and the bat.*b*
²⁰"'All flying insects that walk on all fours are to be detestable to you. ²¹There are, however, some winged creatures that walk on all fours that you may eat: those that have jointed legs for hopping on the ground. ²²Of these you may eat any kind of locust, katydid, cricket or grasshopper. ²³But all other winged creatures that have four legs you are to detest.

---

*a*6 Or *Do not uncover your heads*   *b*14 Traditionally *peace offerings*   *a*5 That is, the hyrax or rock badger
*b*19 The precise identification of some of the birds, insects and animals in this chapter is uncertain.

²⁴"'You will make yourselves unclean by these; whoever touches their carcasses will be unclean till evening. ²⁵Whoever picks up one of their carcasses must wash his clothes, and he will be unclean till evening.

²⁶"'Every animal that has a split hoof not completely divided or that does not chew the cud is unclean for you; whoever touches the carcass of any of them will be unclean. ²⁷Of all the animals that walk on all fours, those that walk on their paws are unclean for you; whoever touches their carcasses will be unclean till evening. ²⁸Anyone who picks up their carcasses must wash his clothes, and he will be unclean till evening. They are unclean for you.

²⁹"'Of the animals that move about on the ground, these are unclean for you: the weasel, the rat, any kind of great lizard, ³⁰the gecko, the monitor lizard, the wall lizard, the skink and the chameleon. ³¹Of all those that move along the ground, these are unclean for you. Whoever touches them when they are dead will be unclean till evening. ³²When one of them dies and falls on something, that article, whatever its use, will be unclean, whether it is made of wood, cloth, hide or sackcloth. Put it in water; it will be unclean till evening, and then it will be clean. ³³If one of them falls into a clay pot, everything in it will be unclean, and you must break the pot. ³⁴Any food that could be eaten but has water on it from such a pot is unclean, and any liquid that could be drunk from it is unclean. ³⁵Anything that one of their carcasses falls on becomes unclean; an oven or cooking pot must be broken up. They are unclean, and you are to regard them as unclean. ³⁶A spring, however, or a cistern for collecting water remains clean, but anyone who touches one of these carcasses is unclean. ³⁷If a carcass falls on any seeds that are to be planted, they remain clean. ³⁸But if water has been put on the seed and a carcass falls on it, it is unclean for you.

³⁹"'If an animal that you are allowed to eat dies, anyone who touches the carcass will be unclean till evening. ⁴⁰Anyone who eats some of the carcass must wash his clothes, and he will be unclean till evening. Anyone who picks up the carcass must wash his clothes, and he will be unclean till evening.

⁴¹"'Every creature that moves about on the ground is detestable; it is not to be eaten. ⁴²You are not to eat any creature that moves about on the ground, whether it moves on its belly or walks on all fours or on many feet; it is detestable. ⁴³Do not defile yourselves by any of these creatures. Do not make yourselves unclean by means of them or be made unclean by them. ⁴⁴I am the LORD your God; consecrate yourselves and be holy, because I am holy. Do not make yourselves unclean by any creature that moves about on the ground. ⁴⁵I am the LORD who brought you up out of Egypt to be your God; therefore be holy, because I am holy.

⁴⁶"'These are the regulations concerning animals, birds, every living thing that moves in the water and every creature that moves about on the ground. ⁴⁷You must distinguish between the unclean and the clean, between living creatures that may be eaten and those that may not be eaten.'"

Purification After Childbirth

12 The LORD said to Moses, ²"Say to the Israelites: 'A woman who becomes pregnant and gives birth to a son will be ceremonially unclean for seven days, just as she is unclean during her monthly period. ³On the eighth day the boy is to be circumcised. ⁴Then the woman must wait thirty-three days to be purified from her bleeding. She must not touch anything sacred or go to the sanctuary until the days of her purification are over. ⁵If she gives birth to a daughter, for two weeks the woman will be unclean, as during her period. Then she must wait sixty-six days to be purified from her bleeding.

⁶"'When the days of her purification for a son or daughter are over, she is to bring to the priest at the entrance to the Tent of Meeting a year-old lamb for a burnt offering and a young pigeon or a dove for a sin offering. ⁷He shall offer them before the LORD to make atonement for her, and then she will be ceremonially clean from her flow of blood.

"'These are the regulations for the woman who gives birth to a boy or a girl. ⁸If she cannot afford a lamb, she is to bring two doves or two young pigeons, one for a burnt offering and the other for a sin offering. In this way the priest will make atonement for her, and she will be clean.'"

Regulations About Infectious Skin Diseases

13 The LORD said to Moses and Aaron, ²"When anyone has a swelling or a rash or a bright spot on his skin that may become an infectious skin disease,ᵃ he must be brought to Aaron the priest or to one of his sonsᵇ who is a priest. ³The priest is to examine the sore on his skin, and if the hair in the sore has turned white and the sore appears to be more than skin deep,ᶜ it is an infectious skin disease. When the priest examines him, he shall pronounce him ceremonially unclean. ⁴If the spot on his skin is white but does not appear to be more than skin deep and the hair in it has not turned white, the priest is to put the infected person in isolation for seven days. ⁵On the seventh day the priest is to examine him, and if he sees that the sore is unchanged and has not spread in the skin, he is to keep him in isolation another seven days. ⁶On the seventh day the priest is to examine him again, and if the sore has faded and has not spread in the skin, the priest shall pronounce him clean; it is only a rash. The man must wash his clothes, and he will be clean. ⁷But if

---

ᵃ2 Traditionally *leprosy*; the Hebrew word was used for various diseases affecting the skin—not necessarily leprosy; also elsewhere in this chapter.   ᵇ2 Or *descendants*
ᶜ3 Or *be lower than the rest of the skin*; also elsewhere in this chapter

the rash does spread in his skin after he has shown himself to the priest to be pronounced clean, he must appear before the priest again. [8]The priest is to examine him, and if the rash has spread in the skin, he shall pronounce him unclean; it is an infectious disease.

[9]"When anyone has an infectious skin disease, he must be brought to the priest. [10]The priest is to examine him, and if there is a white swelling in the skin that has turned the hair white and if there is raw flesh in the swelling, [11]it is a chronic skin disease and the priest shall pronounce him unclean. He is not to put him in isolation, because he is already unclean.

[12]"If the disease breaks out all over his skin and, so far as the priest can see, it covers all the skin of the infected person from head to foot, [13]the priest is to examine him, and if the disease has covered his whole body, he shall pronounce that person clean. Since it has all turned white, he is clean. [14]But whenever raw flesh appears on him, he will be unclean. [15]When the priest sees the raw flesh, he shall pronounce him unclean. The raw flesh is unclean; he has an infectious disease. [16]Should the raw flesh change and turn white, he must go to the priest. [17]The priest is to examine him, and if the sores have turned white, the priest shall pronounce the infected person clean; then he will be clean.

[18]"When someone has a boil on his skin and it heals, [19]and in the place where the boil was, a white swelling or reddish-white spot appears, he must present himself to the priest. [20]The priest is to examine it, and if it appears to be more than skin deep and the hair in it has turned white, the priest shall pronounce him unclean. It is an infectious skin disease that has broken out where the boil was. [21]But if, when the priest examines it, there is no white hair in it and it is not more than skin deep and has faded, then the priest is to put him in isolation for seven days. [22]If it is spreading in the skin, the priest shall pronounce him unclean; it is infectious. [23]But if the spot is unchanged and has not spread, it is only a scar from the boil, and the priest shall pronounce him clean.

[24]"When someone has a burn on his skin and a reddish-white or white spot appears in the raw flesh of the burn, [25]the priest is to examine the spot, and if the hair in it has turned white, and it appears to be more than skin deep, it is an infectious disease that has broken out in the burn. The priest shall pronounce him unclean; it is an infectious skin disease. [26]But if the priest examines it and there is no white hair in the spot and if it is not more than skin deep and has faded, then the priest is to put him in isolation for seven days. [27]On the seventh day the priest is to examine him, and if it is spreading in the skin, the priest shall pronounce him unclean; it is an infectious skin disease. [28]If, however, the spot is unchanged and has not spread in the skin but has faded, it is a swelling from the burn, and the priest shall pronounce him clean; it is only a scar from the burn.

[29]"If a man or woman has a sore on the head or on the chin, [30]the priest is to examine the sore, and if it appears to be more than skin deep and the hair in it is yellow and thin, the priest shall pronounce that person unclean; it is an itch, an infectious disease of the head or chin. [31]But if, when the priest examines this kind of sore, it does not seem to be more than skin deep and there is no black hair in it, then the priest is to put the infected person in isolation for seven days. [32]On the seventh day the priest is to examine the sore, and if the itch has not spread and there is no yellow hair in it and it does not appear to be more than skin deep, [33]he must be shaved except for the diseased area, and the priest is to keep him in isolation another seven days. [34]On the seventh day the priest is to examine the itch, and if it has not spread in the skin and appears to be no more than skin deep, the priest shall pronounce him clean. He must wash his clothes, and he will be clean. [35]But if the itch does spread in the skin after he is pronounced clean, [36]the priest is to examine him, and if the itch has spread in the skin, the priest does not need to look for yellow hair; the person is unclean. [37]If, however, in his judgment it is unchanged and black hair has grown in it, the itch is healed. He is clean, and the priest shall pronounce him clean.

[38]"When a man or woman has white spots on the skin, [39]the priest is to examine them, and if the spots are dull white, it is a harmless rash that has broken out on the skin; that person is clean.

[40]"When a man has lost his hair and is bald, he is clean. [41]If he has lost his hair from the front of his scalp and has a bald forehead, he is clean. [42]But if he has a reddish-white sore on his bald head or forehead, it is an infectious disease breaking out on his head or forehead. [43]The priest is to examine him, and if the swollen sore on his head or forehead is reddish-white like an infectious skin disease, [44]the man is diseased and is unclean. The priest shall pronounce him unclean because of the sore on his head.

[45]"The person with such an infectious disease must wear torn clothes, let his hair be unkempt,[d] cover the lower part of his face and cry out, 'Unclean! Unclean!' [46]As long as he has the infection he remains unclean. He must live alone; he must live outside the camp.

Regulations About Mildew

[47]"If any clothing is contaminated with mildew—any woollen or linen clothing, [48]any woven or knitted material of linen or wool, any leather or anything made of leather —[49]and if the contamination in the clothing, or leather, or woven or knitted material, or any leather article, is greenish or reddish, it is a spreading mildew and must be shown to the priest. [50]The priest is to examine the mildew and isolate the affected article for seven days. [51]On the seventh day he is to examine it, and if the mildew has spread in the clothing, or the woven or knitted material, or the

leather, whatever its use, it is a destructive mildew; the article is unclean. [52]He must burn up the clothing, or the woven or knitted material of wool or linen, or any leather article that has the contamination in it, because the mildew is destructive; the article must be burned up.

[53]"But if, when the priest examines it, the mildew has not spread in the clothing, or the woven or knitted material, or the leather article, [54]he shall order that the contaminated article be washed. Then he is to isolate it for another seven days. [55]After the affected article has been washed, the priest is to examine it, and if the mildew has not changed its appearance, even though it has not spread, it is unclean. Burn it with fire, whether the mildew has affected one side or the other. [56]If, when the priest examines it, the mildew has faded after the article has been washed, he is to tear the contaminated part out of the clothing, or the leather, or the woven or knitted material. [57]But if it reappears in the clothing, or in the woven or knitted material, or in the leather article, it is spreading, and whatever has the mildew must be burned with fire. [58]The clothing, or the woven or knitted material, or any leather article that has been washed and is rid of the mildew, must be washed again, and it will be clean."

[59]These are the regulations concerning contamination by mildew in woollen or linen clothing, woven or knitted material, or any leather article, for pronouncing them clean or unclean.

Cleansing From Infectious Skin Diseases

14 The Lord said to Moses, [2]"These are the regulations for the diseased person at the time of his ceremonial cleansing, when he is brought to the priest: [3]The priest is to go outside the camp and examine him. If the person has been healed of his infectious skin disease,[a] [4]the priest shall order that two live clean birds and some cedar wood, scarlet yarn and hyssop be brought for the one to be cleansed. [5]Then the priest shall order that one of the birds be killed over fresh water in a clay pot. [6]He is then to take the live bird and dip it, together with the cedar wood, the scarlet yarn and the hyssop, into the blood of the bird that was killed over the fresh water. [7]Seven times he shall sprinkle the one to be cleansed of the infectious disease and pronounce him clean. Then he is to release the live bird in the open fields.

[8]"The person to be cleansed must wash his clothes, shave off all his hair and bathe with water; then he will be ceremonially clean. After this he may come into the camp, but he must stay outside his tent for seven days. [9]On the seventh day he must shave off all his hair; he must shave his head, his beard, his eyebrows and the rest of his hair. He must wash his clothes and bathe himself with water, and he will be clean.

[10]"On the eighth day he must bring two male lambs and one ewe lamb a year old, each without defect, along with three-tenths of an ephah[b] of fine flour mixed with oil for a grain offering, and one log[c] of oil. [11]The priest who pronounces him clean shall present both the one to be cleansed and his offerings before the Lord at the entrance to the Tent of Meeting.

[12]"Then the priest is to take one of the male lambs and offer it as a guilt offering, along with the log of oil; he shall wave them before the Lord as a wave offering. [13]He is to slaughter the lamb in the holy place where the sin offering and the burnt offering are slaughtered. Like the sin offering, the guilt offering belongs to the priest; it is most holy. [14]The priest is to take some of the blood of the guilt offering and put it on the lobe of the right ear of the one to be cleansed, on the thumb of his right hand and on the big toe of his right foot. [15]The priest shall then take some of the log of oil, pour it in the palm of his own left hand, [16]dip his right forefinger into the oil in his palm, and with his finger sprinkle some of it before the Lord seven times. [17]The priest is to put some of the oil remaining in his palm on the lobe of the right ear of the one to be cleansed, on the thumb of his right hand and on the big toe of his right foot, on top of the blood of the guilt offering. [18]The rest of the oil in his palm the priest shall put on the head of the one to be cleansed and make atonement for him before the Lord.

[19]"Then the priest is to sacrifice the sin offering and make atonement for the one to be cleansed from his uncleanness. After that, the priest shall slaughter the burnt offering [20]and offer it on the altar, together with the grain offering, and make atonement for him, and he will be clean.

[21]"If, however, he is poor and cannot afford these, he must take one male lamb as a guilt offering to be waved to make atonement for him, together with a tenth of an ephah[d] of fine flour mixed with oil for a grain offering, a log of oil, [22]and two doves or two young pigeons, which he can afford, one for a sin offering and the other for a burnt offering.

[23]"On the eighth day he must bring them for his cleansing to the priest at the entrance to the Tent of Meeting, before the Lord. [24]The priest is to take the lamb for the guilt offering, together with the log of oil, and wave them before the Lord as a wave offering. [25]He shall slaughter the lamb for the guilt offering and take some of its blood and put it on the lobe of the right ear of the one to be cleansed, on the thumb of his right hand and on the big toe of his right foot. [26]The priest is to pour some of the oil into the palm of his own left hand, [27]and with his right forefinger sprinkle some of the oil from his palm seven times before the Lord. [28]Some of the oil in his palm he is to put on the same places he put the blood of the guilt offering—on the lobe of the right ear of the one to be cleansed, on the

---

[a]3 Traditionally *leprosy*; the Hebrew word was used for various diseases affecting the skin—not necessarily leprosy; also elsewhere in this chapter.   [b]10 That is, probably about 11½ pints (about 6.5 litres)
[c]10 That is, probably about ½ pint (about 0.3 litre); also in verses 12, 15, 21 and 24
[d]21 That is, probably about 4 pints (about 2 litres)

thumb of his right hand and on the big toe of his right foot. ²⁹The rest of the oil in his palm the priest shall put on the head of the one to be cleansed, to make atonement for him before the LORD. ³⁰Then he shall sacrifice the doves or the young pigeons, which the person can afford, ³¹one*ᵉ* as a sin offering and the other as a burnt offering, together with the grain offering. In this way the priest will make atonement before the LORD on behalf of the one to be cleansed.''

³²These are the regulations for anyone who has an infectious skin disease and who cannot afford the regular offerings for his cleansing.

Cleansing From Mildew

³³The LORD said to Moses and Aaron, ³⁴''When you enter the land of Canaan, which I am giving you as your possession, and I put a spreading mildew in a house in that land, ³⁵the owner of the house must go and tell the priest, 'I have seen something that looks like mildew in my house.' ³⁶The priest is to order the house to be emptied before he goes in to examine the mildew, so that nothing in the house will be pronounced unclean. After this the priest is to go in and inspect the house. ³⁷He is to examine the mildew on the walls, and if it has greenish or reddish depressions that appear to be deeper than the surface of the wall, ³⁸the priest shall go out of the doorway of the house and close it up for seven days. ³⁹On the seventh day the priest shall return to inspect the house. If the mildew has spread on the walls, ⁴⁰he is to order that the contaminated stones be torn out and thrown into an unclean place outside the town. ⁴¹He must have all the inside walls of the house scraped and the material that is scraped off dumped into an unclean place outside the town. ⁴²Then they are to take other stones to replace these and take new clay and plaster the house.

⁴³''If the mildew reappears in the house after the stones have been torn out and the house scraped and plastered, ⁴⁴the priest is to go and examine it and, if the mildew has spread in the house, it is a destructive mildew; the house is unclean. ⁴⁵It must be torn down—its stones, timbers and all the plaster —and taken out of the town to an unclean place.

⁴⁶''Anyone who goes into the house while it is closed up will be unclean till evening. ⁴⁷Anyone who sleeps or eats in the house must wash his clothes.

⁴⁸''But if the priest comes to examine it and the mildew has not spread after the house has been plastered, he shall pronounce the house clean, because the mildew is gone. ⁴⁹To purify the house he is to take two birds and some cedar wood, scarlet yarn and hyssop. ⁵⁰He shall kill one of the birds over fresh water in a clay pot. ⁵¹Then he is to take the cedar wood, the hyssop, the scarlet yarn and the live bird, dip them into the blood of the dead bird and the fresh water, and sprinkle the house seven times. ⁵²He shall purify the house with the bird's blood, the fresh water, the live bird, the cedar wood, the hyssop and the scarlet yarn. ⁵³Then he is to release the live bird in the open fields outside the town. In this way he will make atonement for the house, and it will be clean.''

⁵⁴These are the regulations for any infectious skin disease, for an itch, ⁵⁵for mildew in clothing or in a house, ⁵⁶and for a swelling, a rash or a bright spot, ⁵⁷to determine when something is clean or unclean.

These are the regulations for infectious skin diseases and mildew.

Discharges Causing Uncleanness

15 The LORD said to Moses and Aaron, ²''Speak to the Israelites and say to them: 'When any man has a bodily discharge, the discharge is unclean. ³Whether it continues flowing from his body or is blocked, it will make him unclean. This is how his discharge will bring about uncleanness:

⁴'''Any bed the man with a discharge lies on will be unclean, and anything he sits on will be unclean. ⁵Anyone who touches his bed must wash his clothes and bathe with water, and he will be unclean till evening. ⁶Whoever sits on anything that the man with a discharge sat on must wash his clothes and bathe with water, and he will be unclean till evening.

⁷'''Whoever touches the man who has a discharge must wash his clothes and bathe with water, and he will be unclean till evening.

⁸'''If the man with the discharge spits on someone who is clean, that person must wash his clothes and bathe with water, and he will be unclean till evening.

⁹'''Everything the man sits on when riding will be unclean, ¹⁰and whoever touches any of the things that were under him will be unclean till evening; whoever picks up those things must wash his clothes and bathe with water, and he will be unclean till evening.

¹¹'''Anyone the man with a discharge touches without rinsing his hands with water must wash his clothes and bathe with water, and he will be unclean till evening.

¹²'''A clay pot that the man touches must be broken, and any wooden article is to be rinsed with water.

¹³'''When a man is cleansed from his discharge, he is to count off seven days for his ceremonial cleansing; he must wash his clothes and bathe himself with fresh water, and he will be clean. ¹⁴On the eighth day he must take two doves or two young pigeons and come before the LORD to the entrance to the Tent of Meeting and give them to the priest. ¹⁵The priest is to sacrifice them, the one for a sin offering and the other for a burnt offering. In this way he will make atonement before the LORD for the man because of his discharge.

¹⁶'''When a man has an emission of semen, he must bathe his whole body with water, and he will be unclean till evening. ¹⁷Any clothing or leather that has semen on it must

be washed with water, and it will be unclean till evening. [18]When a man lies with a woman and there is an emission of semen, both must bathe with water, and they will be unclean till evening.

[19]"When a woman has her regular flow of blood, the impurity of her monthly period will last seven days, and anyone who touches her will be unclean till evening.

[20]"Anything she lies on during her period will be unclean, and anything she sits on will be unclean. [21]Whoever touches her bed must wash his clothes and bathe with water, and he will be unclean till evening. [22]Whoever touches anything she sits on must wash his clothes and bathe with water, and he will be unclean till evening. [23]Whether it is the bed or anything she was sitting on, when anyone touches it, he will be unclean till evening.

[24]"If a man lies with her and her monthly flow touches him, he will be unclean for seven days; any bed he lies on will be unclean.

[25]"When a woman has a discharge of blood for many days at a time other than her monthly period or has a discharge that continues beyond her period, she will be unclean as long as she has the discharge, just as in the days of her period. [26]Any bed she lies on while her discharge continues will be unclean, as is her bed during her monthly period, and anything she sits on will be unclean, as during her period. [27]Whoever touches them will be unclean; he must wash his clothes and bathe with water, and he will be unclean till evening.

[28]"When she is cleansed from her discharge, she must count off seven days, and after that she will be ceremonially clean. [29]On the eighth day she must take two doves or two young pigeons and bring them to the priest at the entrance to the Tent of Meeting. [30]The priest is to sacrifice one for a sin offering and the other for a burnt offering. In this way he will make atonement for her before the LORD for the uncleanness of her discharge.

[31]"You must keep the Israelites separate from things that make them unclean, so they will not die in their uncleanness for defiling my dwelling-place,[a] which is among them.'"

[32]These are the regulations for a man with a discharge, for anyone made unclean by an emission of semen, [33]for a woman in her monthly period, for a man or a woman with a discharge, and for a man who lies with a woman who is ceremonially unclean.

The Day of Atonement

16 The LORD spoke to Moses after the death of the two sons of Aaron who died when they approached the LORD. [2]The LORD said to Moses: "Tell your brother Aaron not to come whenever he chooses into the Most Holy Place behind the curtain in front of the atonement cover on the ark, or else he will die, because I appear in the cloud over the atonement cover.

[3]"This is how Aaron is to enter the sanctuary area: with a young bull for a sin offering and a ram for a burnt offering. [4]He is to put on the sacred linen tunic, with linen undergarments next to his body; he is to tie the linen sash around him and put on the linen turban. These are sacred garments; so he must bathe himself with water before he puts them on. [5]From the Israelite community he is to take two male goats for a sin offering and a ram for a burnt offering.

[6]"Aaron is to offer the bull for his own sin offering to make atonement for himself and his household. [7]Then he is to take the two goats and present them before the LORD at the entrance to the Tent of Meeting. [8]He is to cast lots for the two goats—one lot for the LORD and the other for the scapegoat.[a] [9]Aaron shall bring the goat whose lot falls to the LORD and sacrifice it for a sin offering. [10]But the goat chosen by lot as the scapegoat shall be presented alive before the LORD to be used for making atonement by sending it into the desert as a scapegoat.

[11]"Aaron shall bring the bull for his own sin offering to make atonement for himself and his household, and he is to slaughter the bull for his own sin offering. [12]He is to take a censer full of burning coals from the altar before the LORD and two handfuls of finely ground fragrant incense and take them behind the curtain. [13]He is to put the incense on the fire before the LORD, and the smoke of the incense will conceal the atonement cover above the Testimony, so that he will not die. [14]He is to take some of the bull's blood and with his finger sprinkle it on the front of the atonement cover; then he shall sprinkle some of it with his finger seven times before the atonement cover.

[15]"He shall then slaughter the goat for the sin offering for the people and take its blood behind the curtain and do with it as he did with the bull's blood: He shall sprinkle it on the atonement cover and in front of it. [16]In this way he will make atonement for the Most Holy Place because of the uncleanness and rebellion of the Israelites, whatever their sins have been. He is to do the same for the Tent of Meeting, which is among them in the midst of their uncleanness. [17]No-one is to be in the Tent of Meeting from the time Aaron goes in to make atonement in the Most Holy Place until he comes out, having made atonement for himself, his household and the whole community of Israel.

[18]"Then he shall come out to the altar that is before the LORD and make atonement for it. He shall take some of the bull's blood and some of the goat's blood and put it on all the horns of the altar. [19]He shall sprinkle some of the blood on it with his finger seven times to cleanse it and consecrate it from the uncleanness of the Israelites.

[20]"When Aaron has finished making atonement for the Most Holy Place, the Tent of Meeting and the altar, he shall bring forward the live goat. [21]He is to lay both hands on the head of the live goat and confess over

---

[a]31 Or *my tabernacle*　　[a]8 That is, the goat of removal; Hebrew *azazel*; also in verses 10 and 26

it all the wickedness and rebellion of the Israelites—all their sins—and put them on the goat's head. He shall send the goat away into the desert in the care of a man appointed for the task. [22]The goat will carry on itself all their sins to a solitary place; and the man shall release it in the desert.

[23]"Then Aaron is to go into the Tent of Meeting and take off the linen garments he put on before he entered the Most Holy Place, and he is to leave them there. [24]He shall bathe himself with water in a holy place and put on his regular garments. Then he shall come out and sacrifice the burnt offering for himself and the burnt offering for the people, to make atonement for himself and for the people. [25]He shall also burn the fat of the sin offering on the altar.

[26]"The man who releases the goat as a scapegoat must wash his clothes and bathe himself with water; afterwards he may come into the camp. [27]The bull and the goat for the sin offerings, whose blood was brought into the Most Holy Place to make atonement, must be taken outside the camp; their hides, flesh and offal are to be burned up. [28]The man who burns them must wash his clothes and bathe himself with water; afterwards he may come into the camp.

[29]"This is to be a lasting ordinance for you: On the tenth day of the seventh month you must deny yourselves[b] and not do any work —whether native-born or an alien living among you—[30]because on this day atonement will be made for you, to cleanse you. Then, before the LORD, you will be clean from all your sins. [31]It is a sabbath of rest, and you must deny yourselves; it is a lasting ordinance. [32]The priest who is anointed and ordained to succeed his father as high priest is to make atonement. He is to put on the sacred linen garments [33]and make atonement for the Most Holy Place, for the Tent of Meeting and the altar, and for the priests and all the people of the community.

[34]"This is to be a lasting ordinance for you: Atonement is to be made once a year for all the sins of the Israelites."

And it was done, as the LORD commanded Moses.

Eating Blood Forbidden

17 The LORD said to Moses, [2]"Speak to Aaron and his sons and to all the Israelites and say to them: 'This is what the LORD has commanded: [3]Any Israelite who sacrifices an ox,[a] a lamb or a goat in the camp or outside of it [4]instead of bringing it to the entrance to the Tent of Meeting to present it as an offering to the LORD in front of the tabernacle of the LORD—that man shall be considered guilty of bloodshed; he has shed blood and must be cut off from his people. [5]This is so that the Israelites will bring to the LORD the sacrifices they are now making in the open fields. They must bring them to the priest, that is, to the LORD, at the entrance to the Tent of Meeting and sacrifice them

as fellowship offerings.[b] [6]The priest is to sprinkle the blood against the altar of the LORD at the entrance to the Tent of Meeting and burn the fat as an aroma pleasing to the LORD. [7]They must no longer offer any of their sacrifices to the goat idols[c] to whom they prostitute themselves. This is to be a lasting ordinance for them and for the generations to come.'

[8]"Say to them: 'Any Israelite or any alien living among them who offers a burnt offering or sacrifice [9]and does not bring it to the entrance to the Tent of Meeting to sacrifice it to the LORD—that man must be cut off from his people.

[10]"'Any Israelite or any alien living among them who eats any blood—I will set my face against that person who eats blood and will cut him off from his people. [11]For the life of a creature is in the blood, and I have given it to you to make atonement for yourselves on the altar; it is the blood that makes atonement for one's life. [12]Therefore I say to the Israelites, "None of you may eat blood, nor may an alien living among you eat blood."

[13]"'Any Israelite or any alien living among you who hunts any animal or bird that may be eaten must drain out the blood and cover it with earth, [14]because the life of every creature is its blood. That is why I have said to the Israelites, "You must not eat the blood of any creature, because the life of every creature is its blood; anyone who eats it must be cut off."

[15]"'Anyone, whether native-born or alien, who eats anything found dead or torn by wild animals must wash his clothes and bathe with water, and he will be ceremonially unclean till evening; then he will be clean. [16]But if he does not wash his clothes and bathe himself, he will be held responsible.'"

Unlawful Sexual Relations

18 The LORD said to Moses, [2]"Speak to the Israelites and say to them: 'I am the LORD your God. [3]You must not do as they do in Egypt, where you used to live, and you must not do as they do in the land of Canaan, where I am bringing you. Do not follow their practices. [4]You must obey my laws and be careful to follow my decrees. I am the LORD your God. [5]Keep my decrees and laws, for the man who obeys them will live by them. I am the LORD.

[6]"'No-one is to approach any close relative to have sexual relations. I am the LORD.

[7]"'Do not dishonour your father by having sexual relations with your mother. She is your mother; do not have relations with her.

[8]"'Do not have sexual relations with your father's wife; that would dishonour your father.

[9]"'Do not have sexual relations with your sister, either your father's daughter or your mother's daughter, whether she was born in the same home or elsewhere.

[10]"'Do not have sexual relations with your

---

[b]29 Or *must fast*; also in verse 31   [a]3 The Hebrew word can include both male and female.
[b]5 Traditionally *peace offerings*   [c]7 Or *demons*

son's daughter or your daughter's daughter; that would dishonour you.

¹¹"'Do not have sexual relations with the daughter of your father's wife, born to your father; she is your sister.

¹²"'Do not have sexual relations with your father's sister; she is your father's close relative.

¹³"'Do not have sexual relations with your mother's sister, because she is your mother's close relative.

¹⁴"'Do not dishonour your father's brother by approaching his wife to have sexual relations; she is your aunt.

¹⁵"'Do not have sexual relations with your daughter-in-law. She is your son's wife; do not have relations with her.

¹⁶"'Do not have sexual relations with your brother's wife; that would dishonour your brother.

¹⁷"'Do not have sexual relations with both a woman and her daughter. Do not have sexual relations with either her son's daughter or her daughter's daughter; they are her close relatives. That is wickedness.

¹⁸"'Do not take your wife's sister as a rival wife and have sexual relations with her while your wife is living.

¹⁹"'Do not approach a woman to have sexual relations during the uncleanness of her monthly period.

²⁰"'Do not have sexual relations with your neighbour's wife and defile yourself with her.

²¹"'Do not give any of your children to be sacrificed*a* to Molech, for you must not profane the name of your God. I am the LORD.

²²"'Do not lie with a man as one lies with a woman; that is detestable.

²³"'Do not have sexual relations with an animal and defile yourself with it. A woman must not present herself to an animal to have sexual relations with it; that is a perversion.

²⁴"'Do not defile yourselves in any of these ways, because this is how the nations that I am going to drive out before you became defiled. ²⁵Even the land was defiled; so I punished it for its sin, and the land vomited out its inhabitants. ²⁶But you must keep my decrees and my laws. The native-born and the aliens living among you must not do any of these detestable things, ²⁷for all these things were done by the people who lived in the land before you, and the land became defiled. ²⁸And if you defile the land, it will vomit you out as it vomited out the nations that were before you.

²⁹"'Everyone who does any of these detestable things—such persons must be cut off from their people. ³⁰Keep my requirements and do not follow any of the detestable customs that were practised before you came and do not defile yourselves with them. I am the LORD your God.'"

Various Laws

19 The LORD said to Moses, ²"Speak to the entire assembly of Israel and say to them: 'Be holy because I, the LORD your God, am holy.

³"'Each of you must respect his mother and father, and you must observe my Sabbaths. I am the LORD your God.

⁴"'Do not turn to idols or make gods of cast metal for yourselves. I am the LORD your God.

⁵"'When you sacrifice a fellowship offering*a* to the LORD, sacrifice it in such a way that it will be accepted on your behalf. ⁶It shall be eaten on the day you sacrifice it or on the next day; anything left over until the third day must be burned up. ⁷If any of it is eaten on the third day, it is impure and will not be accepted. ⁸Whoever eats it will be held responsible because he has desecrated what is holy to the LORD; that person must be cut off from his people.

⁹"'When you reap the harvest of your land, do not reap to the very edges of your field or gather the gleanings of your harvest. ¹⁰Do not go over your vineyard a second time or pick up the grapes that have fallen. Leave them for the poor and the alien. I am the LORD your God.

¹¹"'Do not steal.

"'Do not lie.

"'Do not deceive one another.

¹²"'Do not swear falsely by my name and so profane the name of your God. I am the LORD.

¹³"'Do not defraud your neighbour or rob him.

"'Do not hold back the wages of a hired man overnight.

¹⁴"'Do not curse the deaf or put a stumbling-block in front of the blind, but fear your God. I am the LORD.

¹⁵"'Do not pervert justice; do not show partiality to the poor or favouritism to the great, but judge your neighbour fairly.

¹⁶"'Do not go about spreading slander among your people.

"'Do not do anything that endangers your neighbour's life. I am the LORD.

¹⁷"'Do not hate your brother in your heart. Rebuke your neighbour frankly so that you will not share in his guilt.

¹⁸"'Do not seek revenge or bear a grudge against one of your people, but love your neighbour as yourself. I am the LORD.

¹⁹"'Keep my decrees.

"'Do not mate different kinds of animals.

"'Do not plant your field with two kinds of seed.

"'Do not wear clothing woven of two kinds of material.

²⁰"'If a man sleeps with a woman who is a slave girl promised to another man but who has not been ransomed or given her freedom, there must be due punishment. Yet they are not to be put to death, because she had not been freed. ²¹The man, however, must bring a ram to the entrance to the Tent of Meeting for a guilt offering to the LORD. ²²With the ram of the guilt offering the priest is to make atonement for him before the LORD for the sin he has committed, and his sin will be forgiven.

²³"'When you enter the land and plant any

---

a21 Or *to be passed through ⌊the fire⌋*   *a5* Traditionally *peace offering* kind of fruit tree, regard its fruit as forbidden.[b] For three years you are to consider it forbidden;[b] it must not be eaten. 24In the fourth year all its fruit will be holy, an offering of praise to the LORD. 25But in the fifth year you may eat its fruit. In this way your harvest will be increased. I am the LORD your God.

26"'Do not eat any meat with the blood still in it.

"'Do not practise divination or sorcery. 27"'Do not cut the hair at the sides of your head or clip off the edges of your beard.

28"'Do not cut your bodies for the dead or put tattoo marks on yourselves. I am the LORD.

29"'Do not degrade your daughter by making her a prostitute, or the land will turn to prostitution and be filled with wickedness.

30"'Observe my Sabbaths and have reverence for my sanctuary. I am the LORD.

31"'Do not turn to mediums or seek out spiritists, for you will be defiled by them. I am the LORD your God.

32"'Rise in the presence of the aged, show respect for the elderly and revere your God. I am the LORD.

33"'When an alien lives with you in your land, do not ill-treat him. 34The alien living with you must be treated as one of your native-born. Love him as yourself, for you were aliens in Egypt. I am the LORD your God.

35"'Do not use dishonest standards when measuring length, weight or quantity. 36Use honest scales and honest weights, an honest ephah[c] and an honest hin.[d] I am the LORD your God, who brought you out of Egypt.

37"'Keep all my decrees and all my laws and follow them. I am the LORD.'"

Punishments for Sin

20 The LORD said to Moses, 2"Say to the Israelites: 'Any Israelite or any alien living in Israel who gives[a] any of his children to Molech must be put to death. The people of the community are to stone him. 3I will set my face against that man and I will cut him off from his people; for by giving his children to Molech, he has defiled my sanctuary and profaned my holy name. 4If the people of the community close their eyes when that man gives one of his children to Molech and they fail to put him to death, 5I will set my face against that man and his family and will cut off from their people both him and all who follow him in prostituting themselves to Molech.

6"'I will set my face against the person who turns to mediums and spiritists to prostitute himself by following them, and I will cut him off from his people.

7"'Consecrate yourselves and be holy, because I am the LORD your God. 8Keep my decrees and follow them. I am the LORD, who makes you holy.[b]

9"'If anyone curses his father or mother, he must be put to death. He has cursed his father or his mother, and his blood will be on his own head.

10"'If a man commits adultery with another man's wife—with the wife of his neighbour—both the adulterer and the adulteress must be put to death.

11"'If a man sleeps with his father's wife, he has dishonoured his father. Both the man and the woman must be put to death; their blood will be on their own heads.

12"'If a man sleeps with his daughter-in-law, both of them must be put to death. What they have done is a perversion; their blood will be on their own heads.

13"'If a man lies with a man as one lies with a woman, both of them have done what is detestable. They must be put to death; their blood will be on their own heads.

14"'If a man marries both a woman and her mother, it is wicked. Both he and they must be burned in the fire, so that no wickedness will be among you.

15"'If a man has sexual relations with an animal, he must be put to death, and you must kill the animal.

16"'If a woman approaches an animal to have sexual relations with it, kill both the woman and the animal. They must be put to death; their blood will be on their own heads.

17"'If a man marries his sister, the daughter of either his father or his mother, and they have sexual relations, it is a disgrace. They must be cut off before the eyes of their people. He has dishonoured his sister and will be held responsible.

18"'If a man lies with a woman during her monthly period and has sexual relations with her, he has exposed the source of her flow, and she has also uncovered it. Both of them must be cut off from their people.

19"'Do not have sexual relations with the sister of either your mother or your father, for that would dishonour a close relative; both of you would be held responsible.

20"'If a man sleeps with his aunt, he has dishonoured his uncle. They will be held responsible; they will die childless.

21"'If a man marries his brother's wife, it is an act of impurity; he has dishonoured his brother. They will be childless.

22"'Keep all my decrees and laws and follow them, so that the land where I am bringing you to live may not vomit you out. 23You must not live according to the customs of the nations I am going to drive out before you. Because they did all these things, I abhorred them. 24But I said to you, "You will possess their land; I will give it to you as an inheritance, a land flowing with milk and honey." I am the LORD your God, who has set you apart from the nations.

25"'You must therefore make a distinction between clean and unclean animals and between unclean and clean birds. Do not defile yourselves by any animal or bird or anything that moves along the ground—those which I have set apart as unclean for you. 26You are

---

[b]23 Hebrew *uncircumcised*   [c]36 An ephah was a dry measure.   [d]36 A hin was a liquid measure.
[a]2 Or *sacrifices*; also in verses 3 and 4   [b]8 Or *who sanctifies you*; or *who sets you apart as holy*

to be holy to me[c] because I, the LORD, am holy, and I have set you apart from the nations to be my own.

27"'A man or woman who is a medium or spiritist among you must be put to death. You are to stone them; their blood will be on their own heads.'"

Rules for Priests

21 The LORD said to Moses, "Speak to the priests, the sons of Aaron, and say to them: 'A priest must not make himself ceremonially unclean for any of his people who die, ²except for a close relative, such as his mother or father, his son or daughter, his brother, ³or an unmarried sister who is dependent on him since she has no husband —for her he may make himself unclean. ⁴He must not make himself unclean for people related to him by marriage,[a] and so defile himself.

5"'Priests must not shave their heads or shave off the edges of their beards or cut their bodies. ⁶They must be holy to their God and must not profane the name of their God. Because they present the offerings made to the LORD by fire, the food of their God, they are to be holy.

7"'They must not marry women defiled by prostitution or divorced from their husbands, because priests are holy to their God. ⁸Regard them as holy, because they offer up the food of your God. Consider them holy, because I the LORD am holy—I who make you holy.[b]

9"'If a priest's daughter defiles herself by becoming a prostitute, she disgraces her father; she must be burned in the fire.

10"'The high priest, the one among his brothers who has had the anointing oil poured on his head and who has been ordained to wear the priestly garments, must not let his hair become unkempt[c] or tear his clothes. ¹¹He must not enter a place where there is a dead body. He must not make himself unclean, even for his father or mother, ¹²nor leave the sanctuary of his God or desecrate it, because he has been dedicated by the anointing oil of his God. I am the LORD.

13"'The woman he marries must be a virgin. ¹⁴He must not marry a widow, a divorced woman, or a woman defiled by prostitution, but only a virgin from his own people, ¹⁵so that he will not defile his offspring among his people. I am the LORD, who makes him holy.'"[d]

16The LORD said to Moses, 17"Say to Aaron: 'For the generations to come none of your descendants who has a defect may come near to offer the food of his God. ¹⁸No man who has any defect may come near: no man who is blind or lame, disfigured or deformed; ¹⁹no man with a crippled foot or hand, ²⁰or who is hunchbacked or dwarfed, or who has any eye defect, or who

has festering or running sores or damaged testicles. ²¹No descendant of Aaron the priest who has any defect is to come near to present the offerings made to the LORD by fire. He has a defect; he must not come near to offer the food of his God. ²²He may eat the most holy food of his God, as well as the holy food; ²³yet because of his defect, he must not go near the curtain or approach the altar, and so desecrate my sanctuary. I am the LORD, who makes them holy.[e]'"

24So Moses told this to Aaron and his sons and to all the Israelites.

22 The LORD said to Moses, ²"Tell Aaron and his sons to treat with respect the sacred offerings the Israelites consecrate to me, so that they will not profane my holy name. I am the LORD.

3"Say to them: 'For the generations to come, if any of your descendants is ceremonially unclean and yet comes near the sacred offerings that the Israelites consecrate to the LORD, that person must be cut off from my presence. I am the LORD.

4"'If a descendant of Aaron has an infectious skin disease[a] or a bodily discharge, he may not eat the sacred offerings until he is cleansed. He will also be unclean if he touches something defiled by a corpse or by anyone who has an emission of semen, ⁵or if he touches any crawling thing that makes him unclean, or any person who makes him unclean, whatever the uncleanness may be. ⁶The one who touches any such thing will be unclean till evening. He must not eat any of the sacred offerings unless he has bathed himself with water. ⁷When the sun goes down, he will be clean, and after that he may eat the sacred offerings, for they are his food. ⁸He must not eat anything found dead or torn by wild animals, and so become unclean through it. I am the LORD.

9"'The priests are to keep my requirements so that they do not become guilty and die for treating them with contempt. I am the LORD, who makes them holy.[b]

10"'No-one outside a priest's family may eat the sacred offering, nor may the guest of a priest or his hired worker eat it. ¹¹But if a priest buys a slave with money, or if a slave is born in his household, that slave may eat his food. ¹²If a priest's daughter marries anyone other than a priest, she may not eat any of the sacred contributions. ¹³But if a priest's daughter becomes a widow or is divorced, yet has no children, and she returns to live in her father's house as in her youth, she may eat of her father's food. No unauthorised person, however, may eat any of it.

14"'If anyone eats a sacred offering by mistake, he must make restitution to the priest for the offering and add a fifth of the value to it. ¹⁵The priests must not desecrate the sacred offerings the Israelites present to the LORD ¹⁶by allowing them to eat the sacred

---

c26 Or *be my holy ones*   a4 Or *unclean as a leader among his people*
b8 Or *who sanctify you*; or *who set you apart as holy*   c10 Or *not uncover his head*
d15 Or *who sanctifies him*; or *who sets him apart as holy*   e23 Or *who sanctifies them*; or *who sets them apart as holy*
a4 Traditionally *leprosy*; the Hebrew word was used for various diseases affecting the skin—not necessarily leprosy.
b9 Or *who sanctifies them*; or *who sets them apart as holy*; also in verse 16

offerings and so bring upon them guilt requiring payment. I am the LORD, who makes them holy.'"

Unacceptable Sacrifices

17The LORD said to Moses, 18"Speak to Aaron and his sons and to all the Israelites and say to them: 'If any of you—either an Israelite or an alien living in Israel—presents a gift for a burnt offering to the LORD, either to fulfil a vow or as a freewill offering, 19you must present a male without defect from the cattle, sheep or goats in order that it may be accepted on your behalf. 20Do not bring anything with a defect, because it will not be accepted on your behalf. 21When anyone brings from the herd or flock a fellowship offeringc to the LORD to fulfil a special vow or as a freewill offering, it must be without defect or blemish to be acceptable. 22Do not offer to the LORD the blind, the injured or the maimed, or anything with warts or festering or running sores. Do not place any of these on the altar as an offering made to the LORD by fire. 23You may, however, present as a freewill offering an oxd or a sheep that is deformed or stunted, but it will not be accepted in fulfilment of a vow. 24You must not offer to the LORD an animal whose testicles are bruised, crushed, torn or cut. You must not do this in your own land, 25and you must not accept such animals from the hand of a foreigner and offer them as the food of your God. They will not be accepted on your behalf, because they are deformed and have defects.'"

26The LORD said to Moses, 27"When a calf, a lamb or a goat is born, it is to remain with its mother for seven days. From the eighth day on, it will be acceptable as an offering made to the LORD by fire. 28Do not slaughter a cow or a sheep and its young on the same day.

29"When you sacrifice a thank-offering to the LORD, sacrifice it in such a way that it will be accepted on your behalf. 30It must be eaten that same day; leave none of it till morning. I am the LORD.

31"Keep my commands and follow them. I am the LORD. 32Do not profane my holy name. I must be acknowledged as holy by the Israelites. I am the LORD, who makese you holyf 33and who brought you out of Egypt to be your God. I am the LORD."

23 The LORD said to Moses, 2"Speak to the Israelites and say to them: 'These are my appointed feasts, the appointed feasts of the LORD, which you are to proclaim as sacred assemblies.

The Sabbath

3"'There are six days when you may work, but the seventh day is a Sabbath of rest, a day of sacred assembly. You are not to do any work; wherever you live, it is a Sabbath to the LORD.

The Passover and Unleavened Bread

4"'These are the LORD's appointed feasts, the sacred assemblies you are to proclaim at their appointed times: 5The LORD's Passover begins at twilight on the fourteenth day of the first month. 6On the fifteenth day of that month the LORD's Feast of Unleavened Bread begins; for seven days you must eat bread made without yeast. 7On the first day hold a sacred assembly and do no regular work. 8For seven days present an offering made to the LORD by fire. And on the seventh day hold a sacred assembly and do no regular work.'"

Firstfruits

9The LORD said to Moses, 10"Speak to the Israelites and say to them: 'When you enter the land I am going to give you and you reap its harvest, bring to the priest a sheaf of the first grain you harvest. 11He is to wave the sheaf before the LORD so that it will be accepted on your behalf; the priest is to wave it on the day after the Sabbath. 12On the day you wave the sheaf, you must sacrifice as a burnt offering to the LORD a lamb a year old without defect, 13together with its grain offering of two-tenths of an ephaha of fine flour mixed with oil—an offering made to the LORD by fire, a pleasing aroma—and its drink offering of a quarter of a hinb of wine. 14You must not eat any bread, or roasted or new grain, until the very day you bring this offering to your God. This is to be a lasting ordinance for the generations to come, wherever you live.

Feast of Weeks

15"'From the day after the Sabbath, the day you brought the sheaf of the wave offering, count off seven full weeks. 16Count off fifty days up to the day after the seventh Sabbath, and then present an offering of new grain to the LORD. 17From wherever you live, bring two loaves made of two-tenths of an ephah of fine flour, baked with yeast, as a wave offering of firstfruits to the LORD. 18Present with this bread seven male lambs, each a year old and without defect, one young bull and two rams. They will be a burnt offering to the LORD, together with their grain offerings and drink offerings—an offering made by fire, an aroma pleasing to the LORD. 19Then sacrifice one male goat for a sin offering and two lambs, each a year old, for a fellowship offering.c 20The priest is to wave the two lambs before the LORD as a wave offering, together with the bread of the firstfruits. They are a sacred offering to the LORD for the priest. 21On that same day you are to proclaim a sacred assembly and do no regular work. This is to be a lasting ordinance for the generations to come, wherever you live.

22"'When you reap the harvest of your land, do not reap to the very edges of your

---

c21 Traditionally *peace offering*   d23 The Hebrew word can include both male and female.
e32 Or *made*   f32 Or *who sanctifies you*; or *who sets you apart as holy*
a13 That is, probably about 7½ pints (about 4.5 litres); also in verse 17
b13 That is, probably about 1½ pints (about 1 litre)   c19 Traditionally *peace offering*

field or gather the gleanings of your harvest.
Leave them for the poor and the alien. I am
the LORD your God.'''

Feast of Trumpets

23The LORD said to Moses, 24"Say to the
Israelites: 'On the first day of the seventh
month you are to have a day of rest, a sacred
assembly commemorated with trumpet
blasts. 25Do no regular work, but present an
offering made to the LORD by fire.'''

Day of Atonement

26The LORD said to Moses, 27"The tenth
day of this seventh month is the Day of
Atonement. Hold a sacred assembly and
deny yourselves,d and present an offering
made to the LORD by fire. 28Do no work on
that day, because it is the Day of Atonement,
when atonement is made for you before the
LORD your God. 29Anyone who does not
deny himself on that day must be cut off from
his people. 30I will destroy from among his
people anyone who does any work on that
day. 31You shall do no work at all. This is to
be a lasting ordinance for the generations to
come, wherever you live. 32It is a sabbath of
rest for you, and you must deny yourselves.
From the evening of the ninth day of the
month until the following evening you are to
observe your sabbath."

Feast of Tabernacles

33The LORD said to Moses, 34"Say to the
Israelites: 'On the fifteenth day of the
seventh month the LORD's Feast of Tabernacles begins, and it lasts for seven days. 35The
first day is a sacred assembly; do no regular
work. 36For seven days present offerings
made to the LORD by fire, and on the eighth
day hold a sacred assembly and present an
offering made to the LORD by fire. It is the
closing assembly; do no regular work.
37("'These are the LORD's appointed
feasts, which you are to proclaim as sacred
assemblies for bringing offerings made to the
LORD by fire—the burnt offerings and grain
offerings, sacrifices and drink offerings required for each day. 38These offerings are in
addition to those for the LORD's Sabbaths
ande in addition to your gifts and whatever
you have vowed and all the freewill offerings
you give to the LORD.)
39"'So beginning with the fifteenth day of
the seventh month, after you have gathered
the crops of the land, celebrate the festival
to the LORD for seven days; the first day is a
day of rest, and the eighth day also is a day of
rest. 40On the first day you are to take choice
fruit from the trees, and palm fronds, leafy
branches and poplars, and rejoice before the
LORD your God for seven days. 41Celebrate
this as a festival to the LORD for seven days
each year. This is to be a lasting ordinance for
the generations to come; celebrate it in the
seventh month. 42Live in booths for seven
days: All native-born Israelites are to live in

booths 43so that your descendants will know
that I made the Israelites live in booths when
I brought them out of Egypt. I am the LORD
your God.'''
44So Moses announced to the Israelites the
appointed feasts of the LORD.

Oil and Bread Set Before the LORD

24 The LORD said to Moses,
2"Command the Israelites to bring
you clear oil of pressed olives for the light so
that the lamps may be kept burning continually. 3Outside the curtain of the Testimony in the Tent of Meeting, Aaron is to tend
the lamps before the LORD from evening till
morning, continually. This is to be a lasting
ordinance for the generations to come. 4The
lamps on the pure gold lampstand before the
LORD must be tended continually.
5"Take fine flour and bake twelve loaves of
bread, using two-tenths of an ephaha for each
loaf. 6Set them in two rows, six in each row,
on the table of pure gold before the LORD.
7Along each row put some pure incense as a
memorial portion to represent the bread and
to be an offering made to the LORD by fire.
8This bread is to be set out before the LORD
regularly, Sabbath after Sabbath, on behalf
of the Israelites, as a lasting covenant. 9It
belongs to Aaron and his sons, who are to eat
it in a holy place, because it is a most holy
part of their regular share of the offerings
made to the LORD by fire."

A Blasphemer Stoned

10Now the son of an Israelite mother and
an Egyptian father went out among the
Israelites, and a fight broke out in the camp
between him and an Israelite. 11The son of
the Israelite woman blasphemed the Name
with a curse; so they brought him to Moses.
(His mother's name was Shelomith, the
daughter of Dibri the Danite.) 12They put him
in custody until the will of the LORD should be
made clear to them.
13Then the LORD said to Moses: 14"Take
the blasphemer outside the camp. All those
who heard him are to lay their hands on his
head, and the entire assembly is to stone him.
15Say to the Israelites: 'If anyone curses his
God, he will be held responsible; 16anyone
who blasphemes the name of the LORD must
be put to death. The entire assembly must
stone him. Whether an alien or native-born,
when he blasphemes the Name, he must be
put to death.
17"'If anyone takes the life of a human
being, he must be put to death. 18Anyone
who takes the life of someone's animal must
make restitution—life for life. 19If anyone
injures his neighbour, whatever he has done
must be done to him: 20fracture for fracture,
eye for eye, tooth for tooth. As he has injured
the other, so he is to be injured. 21Whoever
kills an animal must make restitution, but
whoever kills a man must be put to death.
22You are to have the same law for the alien

d27 Or and fast; also in verses 29 and 32
e38 Or These feasts are in addition to the LORD's Sabbaths, and these offerings are
a5 That is, probably about 7½ pints (about 4.5 litres)

and the native-born. I am the LORD your God.'"

23Then Moses spoke to the Israelites, and they took the blasphemer outside the camp and stoned him. The Israelites did as the LORD commanded Moses.

The Sabbath Year

25 The LORD said to Moses on Mount Sinai, 2"Speak to the Israelites and say to them: 'When you enter the land I am going to give you, the land itself must observe a sabbath to the LORD. 3For six years sow your fields, and for six years prune your vineyards and gather their crops. 4But in the seventh year the land is to have a sabbath of rest, a sabbath to the LORD. Do not sow your fields or prune your vineyards. 5Do not reap what grows of itself or harvest the grapes of your untended vines. The land is to have a year of rest. 6Whatever the land yields during the sabbath year will be food for you —for yourself, your manservant and maidservant, and the hired worker and temporary resident who live among you, 7as well as for your livestock and the wild animals in your land. Whatever the land produces may be eaten.

The Year of Jubilee

8"'Count off seven sabbaths of years— seven times seven years—so that the seven sabbaths of years amount to a period of forty-nine years. 9Then have the trumpet sounded everywhere on the tenth day of the seventh month; on the Day of Atonement sound the trumpet throughout your land. 10Consecrate the fiftieth year and proclaim liberty throughout the land to all its inhabitants. It shall be a jubilee for you; each one of you is to return to his family property and each to his own clan. 11The fiftieth year shall be a jubilee for you; do not sow and do not reap what grows of itself or harvest the untended vines. 12For it is a jubilee and is to be holy for you; eat only what is taken directly from the fields.

13"'In this Year of Jubilee everyone is to return to his own property.

14"'If you sell land to one of your countrymen or buy any from him, do not take advantage of each other. 15You are to buy from your countryman on the basis of the number of years since the Jubilee. And he is to sell to you on the basis of the number of years left for harvesting crops. 16When the years are many, you are to increase the price, and when the years are few, you are to decrease the price, because what he is really selling you is the number of crops. 17Do not take advantage of each other, but fear your God. I am the LORD your God.

18"'Follow my decrees and be careful to obey my laws, and you will live safely in the land. 19Then the land will yield its fruit, and you will eat your fill and live there in safety. 20You may ask, "What will we eat in the seventh year if we do not plant or harvest our crops?" 21I will send you such a blessing in the sixth year that the land will yield enough

for three years. 22While you plant during the eighth year, you will eat from the old crop and will continue to eat from it until the harvest of the ninth year comes in.

23"'The land must not be sold permanently, because the land is mine and you are but aliens and my tenants. 24Throughout the country that you hold as a possession, you must provide for the redemption of the land.

25"'If one of your countrymen becomes poor and sells some of his property, his nearest relative is to come and redeem what his countryman has sold. 26If, however, a man has no-one to redeem it for him but he himself prospers and acquires sufficient means to redeem it, 27he is to determine the value for the years since he sold it and refund the balance to the man to whom he sold it; he can then go back to his own property. 28But if he does not acquire the means to repay him, what he sold will remain in the possession of the buyer until the Year of Jubilee. It will be returned in the Jubilee, and he can then go back to his property.

29"'If a man sells a house in a walled city, he retains the right of redemption a full year after its sale. During that time he may redeem it. 30If it is not redeemed before a full year has passed, the house in the walled city shall belong permanently to the buyer and his descendants. It is not to be returned in the Jubilee. 31But houses in villages without walls round them are to be considered as open country. They can be redeemed, and they are to be returned in the Jubilee.

32"'The Levites always have the right to redeem their houses in the Levitical towns, which they possess. 33So the property of the Levites is redeemable—that is, a house sold in any town they hold—and is to be returned in the Jubilee, because the houses in the towns of the Levites are their property among the Israelites. 34But the pasture-land belonging to their towns must not be sold; it is their permanent possession.

35"'If one of your countrymen becomes poor and is unable to support himself among you, help him as you would an alien or a temporary resident, so that he can continue to live among you. 36Do not take interest of any kindᵃ from him, but fear your God, so that your countryman may continue to live among you. 37You must not lend him money at interest or sell him food at a profit. 38I am the LORD your God, who brought you out of Egypt to give you the land of Canaan and to be your God.

39"'If one of your countrymen becomes poor among you and sells himself to you, do not make him work as a slave. 40He is to be treated as a hired worker or a temporary resident among you; he is to work for you until the Year of Jubilee. 41Then he and his children are to be released, and he will go back to his own clan and to the property of his forefathers. 42Because the Israelites are my servants, whom I brought out of Egypt, they must not be sold as slaves. 43Do not rule over them ruthlessly, but fear your God.

ᵃ36 Or take excessive interest; similarly in verse 37

44"'Your male and female slaves are to come from the nations around you; from them you may buy slaves. 45You may also buy some of the temporary residents living among you and members of their clans born in your country, and they will become your property. 46You can will them to your children as inherited property and can make them slaves for life, but you must not rule over your fellow Israelites ruthlessly.

47"'If an alien or a temporary resident among you becomes rich and one of your countrymen becomes poor and sells himself to the alien living among you or to a member of the alien's clan, 48he retains the right of redemption after he has sold himself. One of his relatives may redeem him: 49An uncle or a cousin or any blood-relative in his clan may redeem him. Or if he prospers, he may redeem himself. 50He and his buyer are to count the time from the year he sold himself up to the Year of Jubilee. The price for his release is to be based on the rate paid to a hired man for that number of years. 51If many years remain, he must pay for his redemption a larger share of the price paid for him. 52If only a few years remain until the Year of Jubilee, he is to compute that and pay for his redemption accordingly. 53He is to be treated as a man hired from year to year; you must see to it that his owner does not rule over him ruthlessly.

54"'Even if he is not redeemed in any of these ways, he and his children are to be released in the Year of Jubilee, 55for the Israelites belong to me as servants. They are my servants, whom I brought out of Egypt. I am the LORD your God.

Reward for Obedience

26 "'Do not make idols or set up an image or a sacred stone for yourselves, and do not place a carved stone in your land to bow down before it. I am the LORD your God.

2"'Observe my Sabbaths and have reverence for my sanctuary. I am the LORD.

3"'If you follow my decrees and are careful to obey my commands, 4I will send you rain in its season, and the ground will yield its crops and the trees of the field their fruit. 5Your threshing will continue until grape harvest and the grape harvest will continue until planting, and you will eat all the food you want and live in safety in your land.

6"'I will grant peace in the land, and you will lie down and no-one will make you afraid. I will remove savage beasts from the land, and the sword will not pass through your country. 7You will pursue your enemies, and they will fall by the sword before you. 8Five of you will chase a hundred, and a hundred of you will chase ten thousand, and your enemies will fall by the sword before you.

9"'I will look on you with favour and make you fruitful and increase your numbers, and I will keep my covenant with you. 10You will still be eating last year's harvest when you

will have to move it out to make room for the new. 11I will put my dwelling-place[a] among you, and I will not abhor you. 12I will walk among you and be your God, and you will be my people. 13I am the LORD your God, who brought you out of Egypt so that you would no longer be slaves to the Egyptians; I broke the bars of your yoke and enabled you to walk with heads held high.

Punishment for Disobedience

14"'But if you will not listen to me and carry out all these commands, 15and if you reject my decrees and abhor my laws and fail to carry out all my commands and so violate my covenant, 16then I will do this to you: I will bring upon you sudden terror, wasting diseases and fever that will destroy your sight and drain away your life. You will plant seed in vain, because your enemies will eat it. 17I will set my face against you so that you will be defeated by your enemies; those who hate you will rule over you, and you will flee even when no-one is pursuing you.

18"'If after all this you will not listen to me, I will punish you for your sins seven times over. 19I will break down your stubborn pride and make the sky above you like iron and the ground beneath you like bronze. 20Your strength will be spent in vain, because your soil will not yield its crops, nor will the trees of the land yield their fruit.

21"'If you remain hostile towards me and refuse to listen to me, I will multiply your afflictions seven times over, as your sins deserve. 22I will send wild animals against you, and they will rob you of your children, destroy your cattle and make you so few in number that your roads will be deserted.

23"'If in spite of these things you do not accept my correction but continue to be hostile towards me, 24I myself will be hostile towards you and will afflict you for your sins seven times over. 25And I will bring the sword upon you to avenge the breaking of the covenant. When you withdraw into your cities, I will send a plague among you, and you will be given into enemy hands. 26When I cut off your supply of bread, ten women will be able to bake your bread in one oven, and they will dole out the bread by weight. You will eat, but you will not be satisfied.

27"'If in spite of this you still do not listen to me but continue to be hostile towards me, 28then in my anger I will be hostile towards you, and I myself will punish you for your sins seven times over. 29You will eat the flesh of your sons and the flesh of your daughters. 30I will destroy your high places, cut down your incense altars and pile your dead bodies on the lifeless forms of your idols, and I will abhor you. 31I will turn your cities into ruins and lay waste your sanctuaries, and I will take no delight in the pleasing aroma of your offerings. 32I will lay waste the land, so that your enemies who live there will be appalled. 33I will scatter you among the nations and will draw out my sword and pursue you. Your land will be laid waste, and your cities will lie

a11 Or my tabernacle

in ruins. 34Then the land will enjoy its sabbath years all the time that it lies desolate and you are in the country of your enemies; then the land will rest and enjoy its sabbaths. 35All the time that it lies desolate, the land will have the rest it did not have during the sabbaths you lived in it.

36"'As for those of you who are left, I will make their hearts so fearful in the lands of their enemies that the sound of a wind-blown leaf will put them to flight. They will run as though fleeing from the sword, and they will fall, even though no-one is pursuing them. 37They will stumble over one another as though fleeing from the sword, even though no-one is pursuing them. So you will not be able to stand before your enemies. 38You will perish among the nations; the land of your enemies will devour you. 39Those of you who are left will waste away in the lands of their enemies because of their sins; also because of their fathers' sins they will waste away.

40"'But if they will confess their sins and the sins of their fathers—their treachery against me and their hostility towards me, 41which made me hostile towards them so that I sent them into the land of their enemies —then when their uncircumcised hearts are humbled and they pay for their sin, 42I will remember my covenant with Jacob and my covenant with Isaac and my covenant with Abraham, and I will remember the land. 43For the land will be deserted by them and will enjoy its sabbaths while it lies desolate without them. They will pay for their sins because they rejected my laws and abhorred my decrees. 44Yet in spite of this, when they are in the land of their enemies, I will not reject them or abhor them so as to destroy them completely, breaking my covenant with them. I am the LORD their God. 45But for their sake I will remember the covenant with their ancestors whom I brought out of Egypt in the sight of the nations to be their God. I am the LORD.'"

46These are the decrees, the laws and the regulations that the LORD established on Mount Sinai between himself and the Israelites through Moses.

Redeeming What Is the LORD's

27 The LORD said to Moses, 2"Speak to the Israelites and say to them: 'If anyone makes a special vow to dedicate persons to the LORD by giving equivalent values, 3set the value of a male between the ages of twenty and sixty at fifty shekels^a of silver, according to the sanctuary shekel;^{b} 4and if it is a female, set her value at thirty shekels.^{c} 5If it is a person between the ages of five and twenty, set the value of a male at twenty shekels^d and of a female at ten shekels.^{e} 6If it is a person between one month and five years, set the value of a male at five shekels^f of silver and that of a female at three shekels^g

of silver. 7If it is a person sixty years old or more, set the value of a male at fifteen shekels^h and of a female at ten shekels. 8If anyone making the vow is too poor to pay the specified amount, he is to present the person to the priest, who will set the value for him according to what the man making the vow can afford.

9"'If what he vowed is an animal that is acceptable as an offering to the LORD, such an animal given to the LORD becomes holy. 10He must not exchange it or substitute a good one for a bad one, or a bad one for a good one; if he should substitute one animal for another, both it and the substitute become holy. 11If what he vowed is a ceremonially unclean animal—one that is not acceptable as an offering to the LORD—the animal must be presented to the priest, 12who will judge its quality as good or bad. Whatever value the priest then sets, that is what it will be. 13If the owner wishes to redeem the animal, he must add a fifth to its value.

14"'If a man dedicates his house as something holy to the LORD, the priest will judge its quality as good or bad. Whatever value the priest then sets, so it will remain. 15If the man who dedicates his house redeems it, he must add a fifth to its value, and the house will again become his.

16"'If a man dedicates to the LORD part of his family land, its value is to be set according to the amount of seed required for it—fifty shekels of silver to a homer^i of barley seed. 17If he dedicates his field during the Year of Jubilee, the value that has been set remains. 18But if he dedicates his field after the Jubilee, the priest will determine the value according to the number of years that remain until the next Year of Jubilee, and its set value will be reduced. 19If the man who dedicates the field wishes to redeem it, he must add a fifth to its value, and the field will again become his. 20If, however, he does not redeem the field, or if he has sold it to someone else, it can never be redeemed. 21When the field is released in the Jubilee, it will become holy, like a field devoted to the LORD; it will become the property of the priests.^{j}

22"'If a man dedicates to the LORD a field he has bought, which is not part of his family land, 23the priest will determine its value up to the Year of Jubilee, and the man must pay its value on that day as something holy to the LORD. 24In the Year of Jubilee the field will revert to the person from whom he bought it, the one whose land it was. 25Every value is to be set according to the sanctuary shekel, twenty gerahs to the shekel.

26"'No-one, however, may dedicate the firstborn of an animal, since the firstborn already belongs to the LORD; whether an ox^k or a sheep, it is the LORD's. 27If it is one of the unclean animals, he may buy it back at its set value, adding a fifth of the value to it. If he

---

^{a}3 That is, about 1¼ pounds (about 0.6 kilogram); also in verse 16
^{b}3 That is, about ⅖ ounce (about 11.5 grams); also in verse 25 ^{c}4 That is, about 12 ounces (about 0.3 kilogram)
^{d}5 That is, about 8 ounces (about 0.2 kilogram) ^{e}5 That is, about 4 ounces (about 115 grams); also in verse 7
^{f}6 That is, about 2 ounces (about 55 grams) ^{g}6 That is, about 1¼ ounces (about 35 grams)
^{h}7 That is, about 6 ounces (about 170 grams) ^{i}16 That is, probably about 6 bushels (about 220 litres)
^{j}21 Or priest ^{k}26 The Hebrew word can include both male and female.

does not redeem it, it is to be sold at its set value.

28"'But nothing that a man owns and devotes*l* to the LORD—whether man or animal or family land—may be sold or redeemed; everything so devoted is most holy to the LORD.

29"'No person devoted to destruction*m* may be ransomed; he must be put to death.

30"'A tithe of everything from the land, whether grain from the soil or fruit from the trees, belongs to the LORD; it is holy to the LORD. 31If a man redeems any of his tithe, he must add a fifth of the value to it. 32The entire tithe of the herd and flock—every tenth animal that passes under the shepherd's rod —will be holy to the LORD. 33He must not pick out the good from the bad or make any substitution. If he does make a substitution, both the animal and its substitute become holy and cannot be redeemed.'"

34These are the commands the LORD gave Moses on Mount Sinai for the Israelites.

---

l28 The Hebrew term refers to the irrevocable giving over of things or persons to the LORD.
m29 The Hebrew term refers to the irrevocable giving over of things or persons to the LORD, often by totally destroying them.

Numbers

The Census

1 The LORD spoke to Moses in the Tent of Meeting in the Desert of Sinai on the first day of the second month of the second year after the Israelites came out of Egypt. He said: 2"Take a census of the whole Israelite community by their clans and families, listing every man by name, one by one. 3You and Aaron are to number by their divisions all the men in Israel twenty years old or more who are able to serve in the army. 4One man from each tribe, each the head of his family, is to help you. 5These are the names of the men who are to assist you:

from Reuben, Elizur son of Shedeur;
6from Simeon, Shelumiel son of Zurishaddai;
7from Judah, Nahshon son of Amminadab;
8from Issachar, Nethanel son of Zuar;
9from Zebulun, Eliab son of Helon;
10from the sons of Joseph:
    from Ephraim, Elishama son of Ammihud;
    from Manasseh, Gamaliel son of Pedahzur;
11from Benjamin, Abidan son of Gideoni;
12from Dan, Ahiezer son of Ammishaddai;
13from Asher, Pagiel son of Ocran;
14from Gad, Eliasaph son of Deuel;
15from Naphtali, Ahira son of Enan."

16These were the men appointed from the community, the leaders of their ancestral tribes. They were the heads of the clans of Israel.

17Moses and Aaron took these men whose names had been given, 18and they called the whole community together on the first day of the second month. The people indicated their ancestry by their clans and families, and the men twenty years old or more were listed by name, one by one, 19as the LORD commanded Moses. And so he counted them in the Desert of Sinai:

20From the descendants of Reuben the firstborn son of Israel:
    All the men twenty years old or more who were able to serve in the army were listed by name, one by one, according to the records of their clans and families. 21The number from the tribe of Reuben was 46,500.

22From the descendants of Simeon:
    All the men twenty years old or more who were able to serve in the army were counted and listed by name, one by one, according to the records of their clans and families. 23The number from the tribe of Simeon was 59,300.

24From the descendants of Gad:
    All the men twenty years old or more who were able to serve in the army were listed by name, according to the records of their clans and families. 25The number from the tribe of Gad was 45,650.

26From the descendants of Judah:
    All the men twenty years old or more who were able to serve in the army were listed by name, according to the records of their clans and families. 27The number from the tribe of Judah was 74,600.

28From the descendants of Issachar:
    All the men twenty years old or more who were able to serve in the army were listed by name, according to the records of their clans and families. 29The number from the tribe of Issachar was 54,400.

30From the descendants of Zebulun:
    All the men twenty years old or more who were able to serve in the army were listed by name, according to the records of their clans and families. 31The number from the tribe of Zebulun was 57,400.

32From the sons of Joseph:
From the descendants of Ephraim:
    All the men twenty years old or more who were able to serve in the army were listed by name, according to the records of their clans and families. 33The number from the tribe of Ephraim was 40,500.

34From the descendants of Manasseh:
    All the men twenty years old or more who were able to serve in the army were listed by name, according to the records of their clans and families.

[35]The number from the tribe of Manasseh was 32,200.

[36]From the descendants of Benjamin:
All the men twenty years old or more who were able to serve in the army were listed by name, according to the records of their clans and families. [37]The number from the tribe of Benjamin was 35,400.

[38]From the descendants of Dan:
All the men twenty years old or more who were able to serve in the army were listed by name, according to the records of their clans and families. [39]The number from the tribe of Dan was 62,700.

[40]From the descendants of Asher:
All the men twenty years old or more who were able to serve in the army were listed by name, according to the records of their clans and families. [41]The number from the tribe of Asher was 41,500.

[42]From the descendants of Naphtali:
All the men twenty years old or more who were able to serve in the army were listed by name, according to the records of their clans and families. [43]The number from the tribe of Naphtali was 53,400.

[44]These were the men counted by Moses and Aaron and the twelve leaders of Israel, each one representing his family. [45]All the Israelites twenty years old or more who were able to serve in Israel's army were counted according to their families. [46]The total number was 603,550.

[47]The families of the tribe of Levi, however, were not counted along with the others. [48]The LORD had said to Moses: [49]"You must not count the tribe of Levi or include them in the census of the other Israelites. [50]Instead, appoint the Levites to be in charge of the tabernacle of the Testimony—over all its furnishings and everything belonging to it. They are to carry the tabernacle and all its furnishings; they are to take care of it and encamp round it. [51]Whenever the tabernacle is to move, the Levites are to take it down, and whenever the tabernacle is to be set up, the Levites shall do it. Anyone else who goes near it shall be put to death. [52]The Israelites are to set up their tents by divisions, each man in his own camp under his own standard. [53]The Levites, however, are to set up their tents round the tabernacle of the Testimony so that wrath will not fall on the Israelite community. The Levites are to be responsible for the care of the tabernacle of the Testimony."

[54]The Israelites did all this just as the LORD commanded Moses.

The Arrangement of the Tribal Camps

2 The LORD said to Moses and Aaron: [2]"The Israelites are to camp round the Tent of Meeting some distance from it, each man under his standard with the banners of his family."

[3]On the east, towards the sunrise, the divisions of the camp of Judah are to encamp under their standard. The leader of the people of Judah is Nahshon son of Amminadab. [4]His division numbers 74,600.

[5]The tribe of Issachar will camp next to them. The leader of the people of Issachar is Nethanel son of Zuar. [6]His division numbers 54,400.

[7]The tribe of Zebulun will be next. The leader of the people of Zebulun is Eliab son of Helon. [8]His division numbers 57,400.

[9]All the men assigned to the camp of Judah, according to their divisions, number 186,400. They will set out first.

[10]On the south will be the divisions of the camp of Reuben under their standard. The leader of the people of Reuben is Elizur son of Shedeur. [11]His division numbers 46,500.

[12]The tribe of Simeon will camp next to them. The leader of the people of Simeon is Shelumiel son of Zurishaddai. [13]His division numbers 59,300.

[14]The tribe of Gad will be next. The leader of the people of Gad is Eliasaph son of Deuel.[a] [15]His division numbers 45,650.

[16]All the men assigned to the camp of Reuben, according to their divisions, number 151,450. They will set out second.

[17]Then the Tent of Meeting and the camp of the Levites will set out in the middle of the camps. They will set out in the same order as they encamp, each in his own place under his standard.

[18]On the west will be the divisions of the camp of Ephraim under their standard. The leader of the people of Ephraim is Elishama son of Ammihud. [19]His division numbers 40,500.

[20]The tribe of Manasseh will be next to them. The leader of the people of Manasseh is Gamaliel son of Pedahzur. [21]His division numbers 32,200.

[22]The tribe of Benjamin will be next. The leader of the people of Benjamin is Abidan son of Gideoni. [23]His division numbers 35,400.

[24]All the men assigned to the camp of Ephraim, according to their divisions, number 108,100. They will set out third.

[25]On the north will be the divisions of the camp of Dan, under their standard.

---

[a]14 Many manuscripts of the Masoretic Text, Samaritan Pentateuch and Vulgate (see also Num. 1:14); most manuscripts of the Masoretic Text Reuel

The leader of the people of Dan is Ahiezer son of Ammishaddai. [26]His division numbers 62,700.

[27]The tribe of Asher will camp next to them. The leader of the people of Asher is Pagiel son of Ocran. [28]His division numbers 41,500.

[29]The tribe of Naphtali will be next. The leader of the people of Naphtali is Ahira son of Enan. [30]His division numbers 53,400.

[31]All the men assigned to the camp of Dan number 157,600. They will set out last, under their standards.

[32]These are the Israelites, counted according to their families. All those in the camps, by their divisions, number 603,550. [33]The Levites, however, were not counted along with the other Israelites, as the LORD commanded Moses.

[34]So the Israelites did everything the LORD commanded Moses; that is the way they encamped under their standards, and that is the way they set out, each with his clan and family.

The Levites

3 This is the account of the family of Aaron and Moses at the time the LORD talked with Moses on Mount Sinai.

[2]The names of the sons of Aaron were Nadab the firstborn and Abihu, Eleazar and Ithamar. [3]Those were the names of Aaron's sons, the anointed priests, who were ordained to serve as priests. [4]Nadab and Abihu, however, fell dead before the LORD when they made an offering with unauthorised fire before him in the Desert of Sinai. They had no sons; so only Eleazar and Ithamar served as priests during the lifetime of their father Aaron.

[5]The LORD said to Moses, [6]"Bring the tribe of Levi and present them to Aaron the priest to assist him. [7]They are to perform duties for him and for the whole community at the Tent of Meeting by doing the work of the tabernacle. [8]They are to take care of all the furnishings of the Tent of Meeting, fulfilling the obligations of the Israelites by doing the work of the tabernacle. [9]Give the Levites to Aaron and his sons; they are the Israelites who are to be given wholly to him.[a] [10]Appoint Aaron and his sons to serve as priests; anyone else who approaches the sanctuary must be put to death."

[11]The LORD also said to Moses, [12]"I have taken the Levites from among the Israelites in place of the first male offspring of every Israelite woman. The Levites are mine, [13]for all the firstborn are mine. When I struck down all the firstborn in Egypt, I set apart for myself every firstborn in Israel, whether man or animal. They are to be mine. I am the LORD."

[14]The LORD said to Moses in the Desert of Sinai, [15]"Count the Levites by their families and clans. Count every male a month old or more." [16]So Moses counted them, as he was commanded by the word of the LORD.

[17]These were the names of the sons of Levi:
Gershon, Kohath and Merari.
[18]These were the names of the Gershonite clans:
Libni and Shimei.
[19]The Kohathite clans:
Amram, Izhar, Hebron and Uzziel.
[20]The Merarite clans:
Mahli and Mushi.
These were the Levite clans, according to their families.

[21]To Gershon belonged the clans of the Libnites and Shimeites; these were the Gershonite clans. [22]The number of all the males a month old or more who were counted was 7,500. [23]The Gershonite clans were to camp on the west, behind the tabernacle. [24]The leader of the families of the Gershonites was Eliasaph son of Lael. [25]At the Tent of Meeting the Gershonites were responsible for the care of the tabernacle and tent, its coverings, the curtain at the entrance to the Tent of Meeting, [26]the curtains of the courtyard, the curtain at the entrance to the courtyard surrounding the tabernacle and altar, and the ropes—and everything related to their use.

[27]To Kohath belonged the clans of the Amramites, Izharites, Hebronites and Uzzielites; these were the Kohathite clans. [28]The number of all the males a month old or more was 8,600.[b] The Kohathites were responsible for the care of the sanctuary. [29]The Kohathite clans were to camp on the south side of the tabernacle. [30]The leader of the families of the Kohathite clans was Elizaphan son of Uzziel. [31]They were responsible for the care of the ark, the table, the lampstand, the altars, the articles of the sanctuary used in ministering, the curtain, and everything related to their use. [32]The chief leader of the Levites was Eleazar son of Aaron, the priest. He was appointed over those who were responsible for the care of the sanctuary.

[33]To Merari belonged the clans of the Mahlites and the Mushites; these were the Merarite clans. [34]The number of all the males a month old or more who were counted was 6,200. [35]The leader of the families of the Merarite clans was Zuriel son of Abihail; they were to camp on the north side of the tabernacle. [36]The Merarites were appointed to take care of the frames of the tabernacle, its crossbars, posts, bases, all its equipment, and everything related to their use, [37]as well as the posts of the surrounding courtyard with their bases, tent pegs and ropes.

[38]Moses and Aaron and his sons were to camp to the east of the tabernacle, towards

---

[a]9 Most manuscripts of the Masoretic Text; some manuscripts of the Masoretic Text, Samaritan Pentateuch and Septuagint (see also Num. 8:16) *to me*   [b]28 Hebrew; some Septuagint manuscripts *8,300*

the sunrise, in front of the Tent of Meeting. They were responsible for the care of the sanctuary on behalf of the Israelites. Anyone else who approached the sanctuary was to be put to death.

39The total number of Levites counted at the LORD's command by Moses and Aaron according to their clans, including every male a month old or more, was 22,000.

40The LORD said to Moses, "Count all the firstborn Israelite males who are a month old or more and make a list of their names. 41Take the Levites for me in place of all the firstborn of the Israelites, and the livestock of the Levites in place of all the firstborn of the livestock of the Israelites. I am the LORD."

42So Moses counted all the firstborn of the Israelites, as the LORD commanded him. 43The total number of firstborn males a month old or more, listed by name, was 22,273.

44The LORD also said to Moses, 45"Take the Levites in place of all the firstborn of Israel, and the livestock of the Levites in place of their livestock. The Levites are to be mine. I am the LORD. 46To redeem the 273 firstborn Israelites who exceed the number of the Levites, 47collect five shekels[c] for each one, according to the sanctuary shekel, which weighs twenty gerahs. 48Give the money for the redemption of the additional Israelites to Aaron and his sons."

49So Moses collected the redemption money from those who exceeded the number redeemed by the Levites. 50From the firstborn of the Israelites he collected silver weighing 1,365 shekels,[d] according to the sanctuary shekel. 51Moses gave the redemption money to Aaron and his sons, as he was commanded by the word of the LORD.

The Kohathites

4 The LORD said to Moses and Aaron: 2"Take a census of the Kohathite branch of the Levites by their clans and families. 3Count all the men from thirty to fifty years of age who come to serve in the work in the Tent of Meeting.

4"This is the work of the Kohathites in the Tent of Meeting: the care of the most holy things. 5When the camp is to move, Aaron and his sons are to go in and take down the shielding curtain and cover the ark of the Testimony with it. 6Then they are to cover this with hides of sea cows,[a] spread a cloth of solid blue over that and put the poles in place.

7"Over the table of the Presence they are to spread a blue cloth and put on it the plates, dishes and bowls, and the jars for drink offerings; the bread that is continually there is to remain on it. 8Over these they are to spread a scarlet cloth, cover that with hides of sea cows and put its poles in place.

9"They are to take a blue cloth and cover the lampstand that is for light, together with its lamps, its wick trimmers and trays, and all its jars for the oil used to supply it. 10Then they are to wrap it and all its accessories in a covering of hides of sea cows and put it on a carrying frame.

11"Over the gold altar they are to spread a blue cloth and cover that with hides of sea cows and put its poles in place.

12"They are to take all the articles used for ministering in the sanctuary, wrap them in a blue cloth, cover that with hides of sea cows and put them on a carrying frame.

13"They are to remove the ashes from the bronze altar and spread a purple cloth over it. 14Then they are to place on it all the utensils used for ministering at the altar, including the firepans, meat forks, shovels and sprinkling bowls. Over it they are to spread a covering of hides of sea cows and put its poles in place.

15"After Aaron and his sons have finished covering the holy furnishings and all the holy articles, and when the camp is ready to move, the Kohathites are to come to do the carrying. But they must not touch the holy things or they will die. The Kohathites are to carry those things that are in the Tent of Meeting.

16"Eleazar son of Aaron, the priest, is to have charge of the oil for the light, the fragrant incense, the regular grain offering and the anointing oil. He is to be in charge of the entire tabernacle and everything in it, including its holy furnishings and articles."

17The LORD said to Moses and Aaron, 18"See that the Kohathite tribal clans are not cut off from the Levites. 19So that they may live and not die when they come near the most holy things, do this for them: Aaron and his sons are to go into the sanctuary and assign to each man his work and what he is to carry. 20But the Kohathites must not go in to look at the holy things, even for a moment, or they will die."

The Gershonites

21The LORD said to Moses, 22"Take a census also of the Gershonites by their families and clans. 23Count all the men from thirty to fifty years of age who come to serve in the work at the Tent of Meeting.

24"This is the service of the Gershonite clans as they work and carry burdens: 25They are to carry the curtains of the tabernacle, the Tent of Meeting, its covering and the outer covering of hides of sea cows, the curtains for the entrance to the Tent of Meeting, 26the curtains of the courtyard surrounding the tabernacle and altar, the curtain for the entrance, the ropes and all the equipment used in its service. The Gershonites are to do all that needs to be done with these things. 27All their service, whether carrying or doing other work, is to be done under the direction of Aaron and his sons. You shall assign to them as their responsibility all they are to carry. 28This is the service of the Gershonite clans at the Tent of Meeting. Their duties are to be under the direction of Ithamar son of Aaron, the priest.

c47 That is, about 2 ounces (about 55 grams)   d50 That is, about 35 pounds (about 15.5 kilograms)
a6 That is, large aquatic mammals; also elsewhere in this chapter

The Merarites

29"Count the Merarites by their clans and families. 30Count all the men from thirty to fifty years of age who come to serve in the work at the Tent of Meeting. 31This is their duty as they perform service at the Tent of Meeting: to carry the frames of the tabernacle, its crossbars, posts and bases, 32as well as the posts of the surrounding courtyard with their bases, tent pegs, ropes, all their equipment and everything related to their use. Assign to each man the specific things he is to carry. 33This is the service of the Merarite clans as they work at the Tent of Meeting under the direction of Ithamar son of Aaron, the priest."

The Numbering of the Levite Clans

34Moses, Aaron and the leaders of the community counted the Kohathites by their clans and families. 35All the men from thirty to fifty years of age who came to serve in the work in the Tent of Meeting, 36counted by clans, were 2,750. 37This was the total of all those in the Kohathite clans who served in the Tent of Meeting. Moses and Aaron counted them according to the LORD's command through Moses.

38The Gershonites were counted by their clans and families. 39All the men from thirty to fifty years of age who came to serve in the work at the Tent of Meeting, 40counted by their clans and families, were 2,630. 41This was the total of those in the Gershonite clans who served at the Tent of Meeting. Moses and Aaron counted them according to the LORD's command.

42The Merarites were counted by their clans and families. 43All the men from thirty to fifty years of age who came to serve in the work at the Tent of Meeting, 44counted by their clans, were 3,200. 45This was the total of those in the Merarite clans. Moses and Aaron counted them according to the LORD's command through Moses.

46So Moses, Aaron and the leaders of Israel counted all the Levites by their clans and families. 47All the men from thirty to fifty years of age who came to do the work of serving and carrying the Tent of Meeting 48numbered 8,580. 49At the LORD's command through Moses, each was assigned his work and told what to carry.

Thus they were counted, as the LORD commanded Moses.

The Purity of the Camp

5 The LORD said to Moses, 2"Command the Israelites to send away from the camp anyone who has an infectious skin disease*a* or a discharge of any kind, or who is ceremonially unclean because of a dead body. 3Send away male and female alike; send them outside the camp so that they will not defile their camp, where I dwell among them." 4The Israelites did this; they sent

them outside the camp. They did just as the LORD had instructed Moses.

Restitution for Wrongs

5The LORD said to Moses, 6"Say to the Israelites: 'When a man or woman wrongs another in any way*b* and so is unfaithful to the LORD, that person is guilty 7and must confess the sin he has committed. He must make full restitution for his wrong, add one fifth to it and give it all to the person he has wronged. 8But if that person has no close relative to whom restitution can be made for the wrong, the restitution belongs to the LORD and must be given to the priest, along with the ram with which atonement is made for him. 9All the sacred contributions the Israelites bring to a priest will belong to him. 10Each man's sacred gifts are his own, but what he gives to the priest will belong to the priest.'"

The Test for an Unfaithful Wife

11Then the LORD said to Moses, 12"Speak to the Israelites and say to them: 'If a man's wife goes astray and is unfaithful to him 13by sleeping with another man, and this is hidden from her husband and her impurity is undetected (since there is no witness against her and she has not been caught in the act), 14and if feelings of jealousy come over her husband and he suspects his wife and she is impure —or if he is jealous and suspects her even though she is not impure—15then he is to take his wife to the priest. He must also take an offering of a tenth of an ephah*c* of barley flour on her behalf. He must not pour oil on it or put incense on it, because it is a grain offering for jealousy, a reminder offering to draw attention to guilt.

16"'The priest shall bring her and make her stand before the LORD. 17Then he shall take some holy water in a clay jar and put some dust from the tabernacle floor into the water. 18After the priest has made the woman stand before the LORD, he shall loosen her hair and place in her hands the reminder offering, the grain offering for jealousy, while he himself holds the bitter water that brings a curse. 19Then the priest shall put the woman under oath and say to her, "If no other man has slept with you and you have not gone astray and become impure while married to your husband, may this bitter water that brings a curse not harm you. 20But if you have gone astray while married to your husband and you have defiled yourself by sleeping with a man other than your husband"—21here the priest is to put the woman under this curse of the oath—"may the LORD cause your people to curse and denounce you when he causes your thigh to waste away and your abdomen to swell.*d* 22May this water that brings a curse enter your body so that your abdomen swells and your thigh wastes away."*e*

"'Then the woman is to say, "Amen. So be it."

---

a2 Traditionally *leprosy*; the Hebrew word was used for various diseases affecting the skin—not necessarily leprosy.
b6 Or *woman commits any wrong common to mankind*   *c15* That is, probably about 4 pints (about 2 litres)
d21 Or *causes you to have a miscarrying womb and barrenness*
e22 Or *body and cause you to be barren and have a miscarrying womb*

NUMBERS 6:22–27

'The LORD said to Moses, "Tell Aaron and his sons, 'This is how you are to bless the Israelites. Say to them:

> **"The LORD bless you and keep you;**
> **the LORD make his face shine upon you**
> **and be gracious to you;**
> **the LORD turn his face towards you**
> **and give you peace" ' " ' (vv. 22–26).**

DOWN THROUGH the centuries this blessing, known as the Aaronic blessing, has comforted and uplifted God's people. Gloriously simple and equally gloriously profound, these strong and tender words rarely fail to impart grace. Behind the words lies the sure and dynamic name of God. The threefold repetition of the Lord's name has made many people conclude that the blessing conveys the grace of God the Father, God the Son and God the Holy Spirit. It is a powerful blessing.

The shining face expresses approval, acceptance and pleasure. The turning of the face means that God is taking notice with the intention of fulfilling a gracious act, and that act is the gift of peace. The *shalom*, which means so much more than a conventional greeting of peace, desirable though that is, is meant to bestow all that is necessary and good to the recipient.

The blessing is a positive act of good will by God towards man and behind the word 'keep' lie the thoughts of hedging around, guarding, and attention to needs. A marvellous blessing indeed.

> *What a fellowship, what a joy divine,*
> *Leaning on the everlasting arms;*
> *What a blessèdness, what a peace is mine,*
> *Leaning on the everlasting arms.*

(*Elisha Albright Hoffman*)

→124

NUMBERS 21:6–9
'The LORD said to Moses, "Make a snake and put it up on a pole; anyone who is bitten can look at it and live" ' (v. 8).

GOD PUNISHED the people for their complaining spirit by sending fiery snakes, the bite of which was fatal. Not unexpectedly, repentance came quickly with a deputation to Moses confessing their sin, and asking that the Lord might grant them relief from the snakes. God's response was immediate. A bronze snake was to be made: upon being lifted up on a pole, all those who looked upon it would be healed.

Quite why God should choose this method of healing we do not know, especially since later generations of Israelites used the bronze snake as an object of worship. However, our Lord used the incident to good purpose when he said to Nicodemus, a Pharisee who would be aware of all the nuances of the story, 'Just as Moses lifted up the snake in the desert, so the Son of Man must be lifted up, that everyone who believes in him may have eternal life.' The Old Testament event points to God as the healer. He alone can heal the people of their sins and the consequences of that sin. In like manner, the New Testament portrays Christ as the healer. A. M. Toplady helps us to sing the confident prayer:

> *Be of sin the double cure,*
> *Cleanse me from its guilt and power.*

Lifted up, the serpent was the means whereby those Israelites who looked at it were healed. Lifted high on his cross, Christ is the means whereby the whole world may be saved from every sin.

> *There is life for a look at the crucified one,*
> *There is life at this moment for thee.*

(Amelia Matilda Hull)

23"'The priest is to write these curses on a scroll and then wash them off into the bitter water. 24He shall make the woman drink the bitter water that brings a curse, and this water will enter her and cause bitter suffering. 25The priest is to take from her hands the grain offering for jealousy, wave it before the LORD and bring it to the altar. 26The priest is then to take a handful of the grain offering as a memorial offering and burn it on the altar; after that, he is to make the woman drink the water. 27If she has defiled herself and been unfaithful to her husband, then when she is made to drink the water that brings a curse, it will go into her and cause bitter suffering; her abdomen will swell and her thigh waste away,*f* and she will become accursed among her people. 28If, however, the woman has not defiled herself and is free from impurity, she will be cleared of guilt and will be able to have children.

29"'This, then, is the law of jealousy when a woman goes astray and defiles herself while married to her husband, 30or when feelings of jealousy come over a man because he suspects his wife. The priest is to make her stand before the LORD and is to apply this entire law to her. 31The husband will be innocent of any wrongdoing, but the woman will bear the consequences of her sin.'"

The Nazirite

6 The LORD said to Moses, 2"Speak to the Israelites and say to them: 'If a man or woman wants to make a special vow, a vow of separation to the LORD as a Nazirite, 3he must abstain from wine and other fermented drink and must not drink vinegar made from wine or from other fermented drink. He must not drink grape juice or eat grapes or raisins. 4As long as he is a Nazirite, he must not eat anything that comes from the grapevine, not even the seeds or skins.

5"'During the entire period of his vow of separation no razor may be used on his head. He must be holy until the period of his separation to the LORD is over; he must let the hair of his head grow long. 6Throughout the period of his separation to the LORD he must not go near a dead body. 7Even if his own father or mother or brother or sister dies, he must not make himself ceremonially unclean on account of them, because the symbol of his separation to God is on his head. 8Throughout the period of his separation he is consecrated to the LORD.

9"'If someone dies suddenly in his presence, thus defiling the hair he has dedicated, he must shave his head on the day of his cleansing—the seventh day. 10Then on the eighth day he must bring two doves or two young pigeons to the priest at the entrance to the Tent of Meeting. 11The priest is to offer one as a sin offering and the other as a burnt offering to make atonement for him because he sinned by being in the presence of the dead body. That same day he is to consecrate his head. 12He must dedicate himself to the LORD

for the period of his separation and must bring a year-old male lamb as a guilt offering. The previous days do not count, because he became defiled during his separation.

13"'Now this is the law for the Nazirite when the period of his separation is over. He is to be brought to the entrance to the Tent of Meeting. 14There he is to present his offerings to the LORD: a year-old male lamb without defect for a burnt offering, a year-old ewe lamb without defect for a sin offering, a ram without defect for a fellowship offering,*a* 15together with their grain offerings and drink offerings, and a basket of bread made without yeast—cakes made of fine flour mixed with oil, and wafers spread with oil.

16"'The priest is to present them before the LORD and make the sin offering and the burnt offering. 17He is to present the basket of unleavened bread and is to sacrifice the ram as a fellowship offering to the LORD, together with its grain offering and drink offering.

18"'Then at the entrance to the Tent of Meeting, the Nazirite must shave off the hair that he dedicated. He is to take the hair and put it in the fire that is under the sacrifice of the fellowship offering.

19"'After the Nazirite has shaved off the hair of his dedication, the priest is to place in his hands a boiled shoulder of the ram, and a cake and a wafer from the basket, both made without yeast. 20The priest shall then wave them before the LORD as a wave offering; they are holy and belong to the priest, together with the breast that was waved and the thigh that was presented. After that, the Nazirite may drink wine.

21"'This is the law of the Nazirite who vows his offering to the LORD in accordance with his separation, in addition to whatever else he can afford. He must fulfil the vow he has made, according to the law of the Nazirite.'"

The Priestly Blessing

22The LORD said to Moses, 23"Tell Aaron and his sons, 'This is how you are to bless the Israelites. Say to them:

24"'"The LORD bless you
    and keep you;
25the LORD make his face shine upon you
    and be gracious to you;
26the LORD turn his face towards you
    and give you peace."'"

27"So they will put my name on the Israelites, and I will bless them."

Offerings at the Dedication of the Tabernacle

7 When Moses finished setting up the tabernacle, he anointed it and consecrated it and all its furnishings. He also anointed and consecrated the altar and all its utensils. 2Then the leaders of Israel, the heads of families who were the tribal leaders

---

f27 Or *suffering; she will have barrenness and a miscarrying womb*
a14 Traditionally *peace offering*; also in verses 17 and 18

in charge of those who were counted, made offerings. ³They brought as their gifts before the LORD six covered carts and twelve oxen—an ox from each leader and a cart from every two. These they presented before the tabernacle.

⁴The LORD said to Moses, ⁵"Accept these from them, that they may be used in the work at the Tent of Meeting. Give them to the Levites as each man's work requires."

⁶So Moses took the carts and oxen and gave them to the Levites. ⁷He gave two carts and four oxen to the Gershonites, as their work required, ⁸and he gave four carts and eight oxen to the Merarites, as their work required. They were all under the direction of Ithamar son of Aaron, the priest. ⁹But Moses did not give any to the Kohathites, because they were to carry on their shoulders the holy things, for which they were responsible.

¹⁰When the altar was anointed, the leaders brought their offerings for its dedication and presented them before the altar. ¹¹For the LORD had said to Moses, "Each day one leader is to bring his offering for the dedication of the altar."

¹²The one who brought his offering on the first day was Nahshon son of Amminadab of the tribe of Judah.

¹³His offering was one silver plate weighing a hundred and thirty shekels,ᵃ and one silver sprinkling bowl weighing seventy shekels,ᵇ both according to the sanctuary shekel, each filled with fine flour mixed with oil as a grain offering; ¹⁴one gold dish weighing ten shekels,ᶜ filled with incense; ¹⁵one young bull, one ram and one male lamb a year old, for a burnt offering; ¹⁶one male goat for a sin offering; ¹⁷and two oxen, five rams, five male goats and five male lambs a year old, to be sacrificed as a fellowship offering.ᵈ This was the offering of Nahshon son of Amminadab.

¹⁸On the second day Nethanel son of Zuar, the leader of Issachar, brought his offering.

¹⁹The offering he brought was one silver plate weighing a hundred and thirty shekels, and one silver sprinkling bowl weighing seventy shekels, both according to the sanctuary shekel, each filled with fine flour mixed with oil as a grain offering; ²⁰one gold dish weighing ten shekels, filled with incense; ²¹one young bull, one ram and one male lamb a year old, for a burnt offering; ²²one male goat for a sin offering; ²³and two oxen, five rams, five male goats and five male lambs a year old, to be sacrificed as a fellowship offering. This was the offering of Nethanel son of Zuar.

²⁴On the third day, Eliab son of Helon, the leader of the people of Zebulun, brought his offering.

²⁵His offering was one silver plate weighing a hundred and thirty shekels, and one silver sprinkling bowl weighing seventy shekels, both according to the sanctuary shekel, each filled with fine flour mixed with oil as a grain offering; ²⁶one gold dish weighing ten shekels, filled with incense; ²⁷one young bull, one ram and one male lamb a year old, for a burnt offering; ²⁸one male goat for a sin offering; ²⁹and two oxen, five rams, five male goats and five male lambs a year old, to be sacrificed as a fellowship offering. This was the offering of Eliab son of Helon.

³⁰On the fourth day Elizur son of Shedeur, the leader of the people of Reuben, brought his offering.

³¹His offering was one silver plate weighing a hundred and thirty shekels, and one silver sprinkling bowl weighing seventy shekels, both according to the sanctuary shekel, each filled with fine flour mixed with oil as a grain offering; ³²one gold dish weighing ten shekels, filled with incense; ³³one young bull, one ram and one male lamb a year old, for a burnt offering; ³⁴one male goat for a sin offering; ³⁵and two oxen, five rams, five male goats and five male lambs a year old, to be sacrificed as a fellowship offering. This was the offering of Elizur son of Shedeur.

³⁶On the fifth day Shelumiel son of Zurishaddai, the leader of the people of Simeon, brought his offering.

³⁷His offering was one silver plate weighing a hundred and thirty shekels, and one silver sprinkling bowl weighing seventy shekels, both according to the sanctuary shekel, each filled with fine flour mixed with oil as a grain offering; ³⁸one gold dish weighing ten shekels, filled with incense; ³⁹one young bull, one ram and one male lamb a year old, for a burnt offering; ⁴⁰one male goat for a sin offering; ⁴¹and two oxen, five rams, five male goats and five male lambs a year old, to be sacrificed as a fellowship offering. This was the offering of Shelumiel son of Zurishaddai.

⁴²On the sixth day Eliasaph son of Deuel, the leader of the people of Gad, brought his offering.

⁴³His offering was one silver plate weighing a hundred and thirty shekels, and one silver sprinkling bowl weighing seventy shekels, both according to the sanctuary shekel, each filled with fine flour mixed with oil as a grain offering; ⁴⁴one gold dish weighing ten shekels, filled with incense; ⁴⁵one young bull, one ram and one male lamb a year old, for a burnt offering; ⁴⁶one male goat for a sin

---

ᵃ13 That is, about 3¼ pounds (about 1.5 kilograms); also elsewhere in this chapter
ᵇ13 That is, about 1¾ pounds (about 0.8 kilogram); also elsewhere in this chapter
ᶜ14 That is, about 4 ounces (about 115 grams); also elsewhere in this chapter
ᵈ17 Traditionally *peace offering*; also elsewhere in this chapter

offering; [47]and two oxen, five rams, five male goats and five male lambs a year old, to be sacrificed as a fellowship offering. This was the offering of Eliasaph son of Deuel.

[48]On the seventh day Elishama son of Ammihud, the leader of the people of Ephraim, brought his offering.

[49]His offering was one silver plate weighing a hundred and thirty shekels, and one silver sprinkling bowl weighing seventy shekels, both according to the sanctuary shekel, each filled with fine flour mixed with oil as a grain offering; [50]one gold dish weighing ten shekels, filled with incense; [51]one young bull, one ram and one male lamb a year old, for a burnt offering; [52]one male goat for a sin offering; [53]and two oxen, five rams, five male goats and five male lambs a year old, to be sacrificed as a fellowship offering. This was the offering of Elishama son of Ammihud.

[54]On the eighth day Gamaliel son of Pedahzur, the leader of the people of Manasseh, brought his offering.

[55]His offering was one silver plate weighing a hundred and thirty shekels, and one silver sprinkling bowl weighing seventy shekels, both according to the sanctuary shekel, each filled with fine flour mixed with oil as a grain offering; [56]one gold dish weighing ten shekels, filled with incense; [57]one young bull, one ram and one male lamb a year old, for a burnt offering; [58]one male goat for a sin offering; [59]and two oxen, five rams, five male goats and five male lambs a year old, to be sacrificed as a fellowship offering. This was the offering of Gamaliel son of Pedahzur.

[60]On the ninth day Abidan son of Gideoni, the leader of the people of Benjamin, brought his offering.

[61]His offering was one silver plate weighing a hundred and thirty shekels, and one silver sprinkling bowl weighing seventy shekels, both according to the sanctuary shekel, each filled with fine flour mixed with oil as a grain offering; [62]one gold dish weighing ten shekels, filled with incense; [63]one young bull, one ram and one male lamb a year old, for a burnt offering; [64]one male goat for a sin offering; [65]and two oxen, five rams, five male goats and five male lambs a year old, to be sacrificed as a fellowship offering. This was the offering of Abidan son of Gideoni.

[66]On the tenth day Ahiezer son of Ammishaddai, the leader of the people of Dan, brought his offering.

[67]His offering was one silver plate weighing a hundred and thirty shekels, and one silver sprinkling bowl weighing seventy shekels, both according to the sanctuary shekel, each filled with fine flour mixed with oil as a grain offering; [68]one gold dish weighing ten shekels, filled with incense; [69]one young bull, one ram and one male lamb a year old, for a burnt offering; [70]one male goat for a sin offering; [71]and two oxen, five rams, five male goats and five male lambs a year old, to be sacrificed as a fellowship offering. This was the offering of Ahiezer son of Ammishaddai.

[72]On the eleventh day Pagiel son of Ocran, the leader of the people of Asher, brought his offering.

[73]His offering was one silver plate weighing a hundred and thirty shekels, and one silver sprinkling bowl weighing seventy shekels, both according to the sanctuary shekel, each filled with fine flour mixed with oil as a grain offering; [74]one gold dish weighing ten shekels, filled with incense; [75]one young bull, one ram and one male lamb a year old, for a burnt offering; [76]one male goat for a sin offering; [77]and two oxen, five rams, five male goats and five male lambs a year old, to be sacrificed as a fellowship offering. This was the offering of Pagiel son of Ocran.

[78]On the twelfth day Ahira son of Enan, the leader of the people of Naphtali, brought his offering.

[79]His offering was one silver plate weighing a hundred and thirty shekels, and one silver sprinkling bowl weighing seventy shekels, both according to the sanctuary shekel, each filled with fine flour mixed with oil as a grain offering; [80]one gold dish weighing ten shekels, filled with incense; [81]one young bull, one ram and one male lamb a year old, for a burnt offering; [82]one male goat for a sin offering; [83]and two oxen, five rams, five male goats and five male lambs a year old, to be sacrificed as a fellowship offering. This was the offering of Ahira son of Enan.

[84]These were the offerings of the Israelite leaders for the dedication of the altar when it was anointed: twelve silver plates, twelve silver sprinkling bowls and twelve gold dishes. [85]Each silver plate weighed a hundred and thirty shekels, and each sprinkling bowl seventy shekels. Altogether, the silver dishes weighed two thousand four hundred shekels,[e] according to the sanctuary shekel. [86]The twelve gold dishes filled with incense weighed ten shekels each, according to the sanctuary shekel. Altogether, the gold dishes weighed a hundred and twenty shekels.[f] [87]The total number of animals for the burnt offering came to twelve young bulls, twelve rams and twelve male lambs a year old, together with their grain offering. Twelve male goats were used for the sin offering.

[e]85 That is, about 61 pounds (about 28 kilograms)   [f]86 That is, about 3 pounds (about 1.4 kilograms)

88The total number of animals for the sacrifice of the fellowship offering came to twenty-four oxen, sixty rams, sixty male goats and sixty male lambs a year old. These were the offerings for the dedication of the altar after it was anointed.

89When Moses entered the Tent of Meeting to speak with the LORD, he heard the voice speaking to him from between the two cherubim above the atonement cover on the ark of the Testimony. And he spoke with him.

Setting Up the Lamps

8 The LORD said to Moses, 2"Speak to Aaron and say to him, 'When you set up the seven lamps, they are to light the area in front of the lampstand.'"

3Aaron did so; he set up the lamps so that they faced forward on the lampstand, just as the LORD commanded Moses. 4This is how the lampstand was made: It was made of hammered gold—from its base to its blossoms. The lampstand was made exactly like the pattern the LORD had shown Moses.

The Setting Apart of the Levites

5The LORD said to Moses: 6"Take the Levites from among the other Israelites and make them ceremonially clean. 7To purify them, do this: Sprinkle the water of cleansing on them; then make them shave their whole bodies and wash their clothes, and so purify themselves. 8Make them take a young bull with its grain offering of fine flour mixed with oil; then you are to take a second young bull for a sin offering. 9Bring the Levites to the front of the Tent of Meeting and assemble the whole Israelite community. 10You are to bring the Levites before the LORD, and the Israelites are to lay their hands on them. 11Aaron is to present the Levites before the LORD as a wave offering from the Israelites, so that they may be ready to do the work of the LORD.

12"After the Levites lay their hands on the heads of the bulls, use the one for a sin offering to the LORD and the other for a burnt offering, to make atonement for the Levites. 13Make the Levites stand in front of Aaron and his sons and then present them as a wave offering to the LORD. 14In this way you are to set the Levites apart from the other Israelites, and the Levites will be mine.

15"After you have purified the Levites and presented them as a wave offering, they are to come to do their work at the Tent of Meeting. 16They are the Israelites who are to be given wholly to me. I have taken them as my own in place of the firstborn, the first male offspring from every Israelite woman. 17Every firstborn male in Israel, whether man or animal, is mine. When I struck down all the firstborn in Egypt, I set them apart for myself. 18And I have taken the Levites in place of all the firstborn sons in Israel. 19Of all the Israelites, I have given the Levites as gifts to Aaron and his sons to do the work at the Tent of Meeting on behalf of the Israelites and to make atonement for them so that no plague will strike the Israelites when they go near the sanctuary."

20Moses, Aaron and the whole Israelite community did with the Levites just as the LORD commanded Moses. 21The Levites purified themselves and washed their clothes. Then Aaron presented them as a wave offering before the LORD and made atonement for them to purify them. 22After that, the Levites came to do their work at the Tent of Meeting under the supervision of Aaron and his sons. They did with the Levites just as the LORD commanded Moses.

23The LORD said to Moses, 24"This applies to the Levites: Men twenty-five years old or more shall come to take part in the work at the Tent of Meeting, 25but at the age of fifty, they must retire from their regular service and work no longer. 26They may assist their brothers in performing their duties at the Tent of Meeting, but they themselves must not do the work. This, then, is how you are to assign the responsibilities of the Levites."

The Passover

9 The LORD spoke to Moses in the Desert of Sinai in the first month of the second year after they came out of Egypt. He said, 2"Make the Israelites celebrate the Passover at the appointed time. 3Celebrate it at the appointed time, at twilight on the fourteenth day of this month, in accordance with all its rules and regulations."

4So Moses told the Israelites to celebrate the Passover, 5and they did so in the Desert of Sinai at twilight on the fourteenth day of the first month. The Israelites did everything just as the LORD commanded Moses.

6But some of them could not celebrate the Passover on that day because they were ceremonially unclean on account of a dead body. So they came to Moses and Aaron that same day 7and said to Moses, "We have become unclean because of a dead body, but why should we be kept from presenting the LORD's offering with the other Israelites at the appointed time?"

8Moses answered them, "Wait until I find out what the LORD commands concerning you."

9Then the LORD said to Moses, 10"Tell the Israelites: 'When any of you or your descendants are unclean because of a dead body or are away on a journey, they may still celebrate the LORD's Passover. 11They are to celebrate it on the fourteenth day of the second month at twilight. They are to eat the lamb, together with unleavened bread and bitter herbs. 12They must not leave any of it till morning or break any of its bones. When they celebrate the Passover, they must follow all the regulations. 13But if a man who is ceremonially clean and not on a journey fails to celebrate the Passover, that person must be cut off from his people because he did not present the LORD's offering at the appointed time. That man will bear the consequences of his sin.

14"'An alien living among you who wants to celebrate the LORD's Passover must do so in accordance with its rules and regulations. You must have the same regulations for the alien and the native-born.'"

The Cloud Above the Tabernacle

15On the day the tabernacle, the Tent of the Testimony, was set up, the cloud covered it. From evening till morning the cloud above the tabernacle looked like fire. 16That is how it continued to be; the cloud covered it, and at night it looked like fire. 17Whenever the cloud lifted from above the Tent, the Israelites set out; wherever the cloud settled, the Israelites encamped. 18At the LORD's command the Israelites set out, and at his command they encamped. As long as the cloud stayed over the tabernacle, they remained in camp. 19When the cloud remained over the tabernacle a long time, the Israelites obeyed the LORD's order and did not set out. 20Sometimes the cloud was over the tabernacle only a few days; at the LORD's command they would encamp, and then at his command they would set out. 21Sometimes the cloud stayed only from evening till morning, and when it lifted in the morning, they set out. Whether by day or by night, whenever the cloud lifted, they set out. 22Whether the cloud stayed over the tabernacle for two days or a month or a year, the Israelites would remain in camp and not set out; but when it lifted, they would set out. 23At the LORD's command they encamped, and at the LORD's command they set out. They obeyed the LORD's order, in accordance with his command through Moses.

The Silver Trumpets

10 The LORD said to Moses: 2"Make two trumpets of hammered silver, and use them for calling the community together and for having the camps set out. 3When both are sounded, the whole community is to assemble before you at the entrance to the Tent of Meeting. 4If only one is sounded, the leaders —the heads of the clans of Israel—are to assemble before you. 5When a trumpet blast is sounded, the tribes camping on the east are to set out. 6At the sounding of a second blast, the camps on the south are to set out. The blast will be the signal for setting out. 7To gather the assembly, blow the trumpets, but not with the same signal.

8"The sons of Aaron, the priests, are to blow the trumpets. This is to be a lasting ordinance for you and the generations to come. 9When you go into battle in your own land against an enemy who is oppressing you, sound a blast on the trumpets. Then you will be remembered by the LORD your God and rescued from your enemies. 10Also at your times of rejoicing—your appointed feasts and New Moon festivals—you are to sound the trumpets over your burnt offerings and fellowship offerings,*a* and they will be a memorial for you before your God. I am the LORD your God."

The Israelites Leave Sinai

11On the twentieth day of the second month of the second year, the cloud lifted from above the tabernacle of the Testimony. 12Then the Israelites set out from the Desert of Sinai and travelled from place to place until the cloud came to rest in the Desert of Paran. 13They set out, this first time, at the LORD's command through Moses.

14The divisions of the camp of Judah went first, under their standard. Nahshon son of Amminadab was in command. 15Nethanel son of Zuar was over the division of the tribe of Issachar, 16and Eliab son of Helon was over the division of the tribe of Zebulun. 17Then the tabernacle was taken down, and the Gershonites and Merarites, who carried it, set out.

18The divisions of the camp of Reuben went next, under their standard. Elizur son of Shedeur was in command. 19Shelumiel son of Zurishaddai was over the division of the tribe of Simeon, 20and Eliasaph son of Deuel was over the division of the tribe of Gad. 21Then the Kohathites set out, carrying the holy things. The tabernacle was to be set up before they arrived.

22The divisions of the camp of Ephraim went next, under their standard. Elishama son of Ammihud was in command. 23Gamaliel son of Pedahzur was over the division of the tribe of Manasseh, 24and Abidan son of Gideoni was over the division of the tribe of Benjamin.

25Finally, as the rear guard for all the units, the divisions of the camp of Dan set out, under their standard. Ahiezer son of Ammishaddai was in command. 26Pagiel son of Ocran was over the division of the tribe of Asher, 27and Ahira son of Enan was over the division of the tribe of Naphtali. 28This was the order of march for the Israelite divisions as they set out.

29Now Moses said to Hobab son of Reuel the Midianite, Moses' father-in-law, "We are setting out for the place about which the LORD said, 'I will give it to you.' Come with us and we will treat you well, for the LORD has promised good things to Israel."

30He answered, "No, I will not go; I am going back to my own land and my own people."

31But Moses said, "Please do not leave us. You know where we should camp in the desert, and you can be our eyes. 32If you come with us, we will share with you whatever good things the LORD gives us."

33So they set out from the mountain of the LORD and travelled for three days. The ark of the covenant of the LORD went before them during those three days to find them a place to rest. 34The cloud of the LORD was over them by day when they set out from the camp. 35Whenever the ark set out, Moses said,

"Rise up, O LORD!
   May your enemies be scattered;
   may your foes flee before you."

36Whenever it came to rest, he said,

"Return, O LORD,
   to the countless thousands of Israel."

---

a10 Traditionally *peace offerings*

Fire From the LORD

11 Now the people complained about their hardships in the hearing of the LORD, and when he heard them his anger was aroused. Then fire from the LORD burned among them and consumed some of the outskirts of the camp. ²When the people cried out to Moses, he prayed to the LORD and the fire died down. ³So that place was called Taberah,ᵃ because fire from the LORD had burned among them.

Quail From the LORD

⁴The rabble with them began to crave other food, and again the Israelites started wailing and said, "If only we had meat to eat! ⁵We remember the fish we ate in Egypt at no cost—also the cucumbers, melons, leeks, onions and garlic. ⁶But now we have lost our appetite; we never see anything but this manna!"

⁷The manna was like coriander seed and looked like resin. ⁸The people went around gathering it, and then ground it in a hand mill or crushed it in a mortar. They cooked it in a pot or made it into cakes. And it tasted like something made with olive oil. ⁹When the dew settled on the camp at night, the manna also came down.

¹⁰Moses heard the people of every family wailing, each at the entrance to his tent. The LORD became exceedingly angry, and Moses was troubled. ¹¹He asked the LORD, "Why have you brought this trouble on your servant? What have I done to displease you that you put the burden of all these people on me? ¹²Did I conceive all these people? Did I give them birth? Why do you tell me to carry them in my arms, as a nurse carries an infant, to the land you promised on oath to their forefathers? ¹³Where can I get meat for all these people? They keep wailing to me, 'Give us meat to eat!' ¹⁴I cannot carry all these people by myself; the burden is too heavy for me. ¹⁵If this is how you are going to treat me, put me to death right now—if I have found favour in your eyes—and do not let me face my own ruin."

¹⁶The LORD said to Moses: "Bring me seventy of Israel's elders who are known to you as leaders and officials among the people. Make them come to the Tent of Meeting, that they may stand there with you. ¹⁷I will come down and speak with you there, and I will take of the Spirit that is on you and put the Spirit on them. They will help you carry the burden of the people so that you will not have to carry it alone.

¹⁸"Tell the people: 'Consecrate yourselves in preparation for tomorrow, when you will eat meat. The LORD heard you when you wailed, "If only we had meat to eat! We were better off in Egypt!" Now the LORD will give you meat, and you will eat it. ¹⁹You will not eat it for just one day, or two days, or five, ten or twenty days, ²⁰but for a whole month—until it comes out of your nostrils

and you loathe it—because you have rejected the LORD, who is among you, and have wailed before him, saying, "Why did we ever leave Egypt?"'"

²¹But Moses said, "Here I am among six hundred thousand men on foot, and you say, 'I will give them meat to eat for a whole month!' ²²Would they have enough if flocks and herds were slaughtered for them? Would they have enough if all the fish in the sea were caught for them?"

²³The LORD answered Moses, "Is the LORD's arm too short? You will now see whether or not what I say will come true for you."

²⁴So Moses went out and told the people what the LORD had said. He brought together seventy of their elders and made them stand round the Tent. ²⁵Then the LORD came down in the cloud and spoke with him, and he took of the Spirit that was on him and put the Spirit on the seventy elders. When the Spirit rested on them, they prophesied, but they did not do so again.ᵇ

²⁶However, two men, whose names were Eldad and Medad, had remained in the camp. They were listed among the elders, but did not go out to the Tent. Yet the Spirit also rested on them, and they prophesied in the camp. ²⁷A young man ran and told Moses, "Eldad and Medad are prophesying in the camp."

²⁸Joshua son of Nun, who had been Moses' assistant since youth, spoke up and said, "Moses, my lord, stop them!"

²⁹But Moses replied, "Are you jealous for my sake? I wish that all the LORD's people were prophets and that the LORD would put his Spirit on them!" ³⁰Then Moses and the elders of Israel returned to the camp.

³¹Now a wind went out from the LORD and drove quail in from the sea. It brought themᶜ down all around the camp to about three feetᵈ above the ground, as far as a day's walk in any direction. ³²All that day and night and all the next day the people went out and gathered quail. No-one gathered less than ten homers.ᵉ Then they spread them out all around the camp. ³³But while the meat was still between their teeth and before it could be consumed, the anger of the LORD burned against the people, and he struck them with a severe plague. ³⁴Therefore the place was named Kibroth Hattaavah,ᶠ because there they buried the people who had craved other food.

³⁵From Kibroth Hattaavah the people travelled to Hazeroth and stayed there.

Miriam and Aaron Oppose Moses

12 Miriam and Aaron began to talk against Moses because of his Cushite wife, for he had married a Cushite. ²"Has the LORD spoken only through Moses?" they asked. "Hasn't he also spoken through us?" And the LORD heard this.

³(Now Moses was a very humble man,

ᵃ3 *Taberah* means *burning.*   ᵇ25 Or *prophesied and continued to do so*   ᶜ31 Or *They flew*
ᵈ31 Hebrew *two cubits* (about 0.9 metre)   ᵉ32 That is, probably about 60 bushels (about 2.2 kilolitres)
ᶠ34 *Kibroth Hattaavah* means *graves of craving.*

more humble than anyone else on the face of the earth.)

⁴At once the LORD said to Moses, Aaron and Miriam, "Come out to the Tent of Meeting, all three of you." So the three of them came out. ⁵Then the LORD came down in a pillar of cloud; he stood at the entrance to the Tent and summoned Aaron and Miriam. When both of them stepped forward, ⁶he said, "Listen to my words:

"When a prophet of the LORD is among you,
    I reveal myself to him in visions,
    I speak to him in dreams.
⁷But this is not true of my servant Moses;
    he is faithful in all my house.
⁸With him I speak face to face,
    clearly and not in riddles;
    he sees the form of the LORD.
Why then were you not afraid
    to speak against my servant Moses?"

⁹The anger of the LORD burned against them, and he left them.

¹⁰When the cloud lifted from above the Tent, there stood Miriam—leprous,ᵃ like snow. Aaron turned towards her and saw that she had leprosy; ¹¹and he said to Moses, "Please, my lord, do not hold against us the sin we have so foolishly committed. ¹²Do not let her be like a stillborn infant coming from its mother's womb with its flesh half eaten away."

¹³So Moses cried out to the LORD, "O God, please heal her!"

¹⁴The LORD replied to Moses, "If her father had spat in her face, would she not have been in disgrace for seven days? Confine her outside the camp for seven days; after that she can be brought back." ¹⁵So Miriam was confined outside the camp for seven days, and the people did not move on till she was brought back.

¹⁶After that, the people left Hazeroth and encamped in the Desert of Paran.

Exploring Canaan

13 The LORD said to Moses, ²"Send some men to explore the land of Canaan, which I am giving to the Israelites. From each ancestral tribe send one of its leaders."

³So at the LORD's command Moses sent them out from the Desert of Paran. All of them were leaders of the Israelites. ⁴These are their names:

from the tribe of Reuben, Shammau son of Zaccur;
⁵from the tribe of Simeon, Shaphat son of Hori;
⁶from the tribe of Judah, Caleb son of Jephunneh;
⁷from the tribe of Issachar, Igal son of Joseph;
⁸from the tribe of Ephraim, Hoshea son of Nun;

⁹from the tribe of Benjamin, Palti son of Raphu;
¹⁰from the tribe of Zebulun, Gaddiel son of Sodi;
¹¹from the tribe of Manasseh (a tribe of Joseph), Gaddi son of Susi;
¹²from the tribe of Dan, Ammiel son of Gemalli;
¹³from the tribe of Asher, Sethur son of Michael;
¹⁴from the tribe of Naphtali, Nahbi son of Vophsi;
¹⁵from the tribe of Gad, Geuel son of Maki.

¹⁶These are the names of the men Moses sent to explore the land. (Moses gave Hoshea son of Nun the name Joshua.)

¹⁷When Moses sent them to explore Canaan, he said, "Go up through the Negev and on into the hill country. ¹⁸See what the land is like and whether the people who live there are strong or weak, few or many. ¹⁹What kind of land do they live in? Is it good or bad? What kind of towns do they live in? Are they unwalled or fortified? ²⁰How is the soil? Is it fertile or poor? Are there trees on it or not? Do your best to bring back some of the fruit of the land." (It was the season for the first ripe grapes.)

²¹So they went up and explored the land from the Desert of Zin as far as Rehob, towards Leboᵃ Hamath. ²²They went up through the Negev and came to Hebron, where Ahiman, Sheshai and Talmai, the descendants of Anak, lived. (Hebron had been built seven years before Zoan in Egypt.) ²³When they reached the Valley of Eshcol,ᵇ they cut off a branch bearing a single cluster of grapes. Two of them carried it on a pole between them, along with some pomegranates and figs. ²⁴That place was called the Valley of Eshcol because of the cluster of grapes the Israelites cut off there. ²⁵At the end of forty days they returned from exploring the land.

Report on the Exploration

²⁶They came back to Moses and Aaron and the whole Israelite community at Kadesh in the Desert of Paran. There they reported to them and to the whole assembly and showed them the fruit of the land. ²⁷They gave Moses this account: "We went into the land to which you sent us, and it does flow with milk and honey! Here is its fruit. ²⁸But the people who live there are powerful, and the cities are fortified and very large. We even saw descendants of Anak there. ²⁹The Amalekites live in the Negev; the Hittites, Jebusites and Amorites live in the hill country; and the Canaanites live near the sea and along the Jordan."

³⁰Then Caleb silenced the people before Moses and said, "We should go up and take possession of the land, for we can certainly do it."

³¹But the men who had gone up with him

ᵃ10 The Hebrew word was used for various diseases affecting the skin—not necessarily leprosy.
ᵃ21 Or towards the entrance to   ᵇ23 Eshcol means cluster; also in verse 24.

said, "We can't attack those people; they are stronger than we are." 32And they spread among the Israelites a bad report about the land they had explored. They said, "The land we explored devours those living in it. All the people we saw there are of great size. 33We saw the Nephilim there (the descendants of Anak come from the Nephilim). We seemed like grasshoppers in our own eyes, and we looked the same to them."

The People Rebel

14 That night all the people of the community raised their voices and wept aloud. 2All the Israelites grumbled against Moses and Aaron, and the whole assembly said to them, "If only we had died in Egypt! Or in this desert! 3Why is the LORD bringing us to this land only to let us fall by the sword? Our wives and children will be taken as plunder. Wouldn't it be better for us to go back to Egypt?" 4And they said to each other, "We should choose a leader and go back to Egypt."

5Then Moses and Aaron fell face down in front of the whole Israelite assembly gathered there. 6Joshua son of Nun and Caleb son of Jephunneh, who were among those who had explored the land, tore their clothes 7and said to the entire Israelite assembly, "The land we passed through and explored is exceedingly good. 8If the LORD is pleased with us, he will lead us into that land, a land flowing with milk and honey, and will give it to us. 9Only do not rebel against the LORD. And do not be afraid of the people of the land, because we will swallow them up. Their protection is gone, but the LORD is with us. Do not be afraid of them."

10But the whole assembly talked about stoning them. Then the glory of the LORD appeared at the Tent of Meeting to all the Israelites. 11The LORD said to Moses, "How long will these people treat me with contempt? How long will they refuse to believe in me, in spite of all the miraculous signs I have performed among them? 12I will strike them down with a plague and destroy them, but I will make you into a nation greater and stronger than they."

13Moses said to the LORD, "Then the Egyptians will hear about it! By your power you brought these people up from among them. 14And they will tell the inhabitants of this land about it. They have already heard that you, O LORD, are with these people and that you, O LORD, have been seen face to face, that your cloud stays over them, and that you go before them in a pillar of cloud by day and a pillar of fire by night. 15If you put these people to death all at one time, the nations who have heard this report about you will say, 16'The LORD was not able to bring these people into the land he promised them on oath; so he slaughtered them in the desert.'

17"Now may the Lord's strength be displayed, just as you have declared: 18'The LORD is slow to anger, abounding in love and forgiving sin and rebellion. Yet he does not leave the guilty unpunished; he punishes the children for the sin of the fathers to the third and fourth generation.' 19In accordance with your great love, forgive the sin of these people, just as you have pardoned them from the time they left Egypt until now."

20The LORD replied, "I have forgiven them, as you asked. 21Nevertheless, as surely as I live and as surely as the glory of the LORD fills the whole earth, 22not one of the men who saw my glory and the miraculous signs I performed in Egypt and in the desert but who disobeyed me and tested me ten times—23not one of them will ever see the land I promised on oath to their forefathers. No-one who has treated me with contempt will ever see it. 24But because my servant Caleb has a different spirit and follows me wholeheartedly, I will bring him into the land he went to, and his descendants will inherit it. 25Since the Amalekites and Canaanites are living in the valleys, turn back tomorrow and set out towards the desert along the route to the Red Sea."[a]

26The LORD said to Moses and Aaron: 27"How long will this wicked community grumble against me? I have heard the complaints of these grumbling Israelites. 28So tell them, 'As surely as I live, declares the LORD, I will do to you the very things I heard you say: 29In this desert your bodies will fall —every one of you twenty years old or more who was counted in the census and who has grumbled against me. 30Not one of you will enter the land I swore with uplifted hand to make your home, except Caleb son of Jephunneh and Joshua son of Nun. 31As for your children that you said would be taken as plunder, I will bring them in to enjoy the land you have rejected. 32But you—your bodies will fall in this desert. 33Your children will be shepherds here for forty years, suffering for your unfaithfulness, until the last of your bodies lies in the desert. 34For forty years —one year for each of the forty days you explored the land—you will suffer for your sins and know what it is like to have me against you.' 35I, the LORD, have spoken, and I will surely do these things to this whole wicked community, which has banded together against me. They will meet their end in this desert; here they will die."

36So the men Moses had sent to explore the land, who returned and made the whole community grumble against him by spreading a bad report about it—37these men responsible for spreading the bad report about the land were struck down and died of a plague before the LORD. 38Of the men who went to explore the land, only Joshua son of Nun and Caleb son of Jephunneh survived.

39When Moses reported this to all the Israelites, they mourned bitterly. 40Early the next morning they went up towards the high hill country. "We have sinned," they said. "We will go up to the place the LORD promised."

41But Moses said, "Why are you disobeying the LORD's command? This will not

---

*a*25 Hebrew *Yam Suph*; that is, Sea of Reeds

succeed! ⁴²Do not go up, because the LORD
is not with you. You will be defeated by
your enemies, ⁴³for the Amalekites and
Canaanites will face you there. Because you
have turned away from the LORD, he will not
be with you and you will fall by the sword."

⁴⁴Nevertheless, in their presumption they
went up towards the high hill country, though
neither Moses nor the ark of the LORD's
covenant moved from the camp. ⁴⁵Then the
Amalekites and Canaanites who lived in that
hill country came down and attacked them
and beat them down all the way to Hormah.

Supplementary Offerings

15 The LORD said to Moses, ²"Speak to
the Israelites and say to them: 'After
you enter the land I am giving you as a home
³and you present to the LORD offerings made
by fire, from the herd or the flock, as an
aroma pleasing to the LORD—whether burnt
offerings or sacrifices, for special vows or
freewill offerings or festival offerings—⁴then
the one who brings his offering shall present
to the LORD a grain offering of a tenth of an
ephah*ᵃ* of fine flour mixed with a quarter of a
hin*ᵇ* of oil. ⁵With each lamb for the burnt
offering or the sacrifice, prepare a quarter of
a hin of wine as a drink offering.

⁶"'With a ram prepare a grain offering of
two-tenths of an ephah*ᶜ* of fine flour mixed
with a third of a hin*ᵈ* of oil, ⁷and a third of a
hin of wine as a drink offering. Offer it as an
aroma pleasing to the LORD.

⁸"'When you prepare a young bull as a
burnt offering or sacrifice, for a special vow
or a fellowship offering*ᵉ* to the LORD, ⁹bring
with the bull a grain offering of three-tenths
of an ephah*ᶠ* of fine flour mixed with half a
hin*ᵍ* of oil. ¹⁰Also bring half a hin of wine as a
drink offering. It will be an offering made by
fire, an aroma pleasing to the LORD. ¹¹Each
bull or ram, each lamb or young goat, is to be
prepared in this manner. ¹²Do this for each
one, for as many as you prepare.

¹³"'Everyone who is native-born must do
these things in this way when he brings an
offering made by fire as an aroma pleasing to
the LORD. ¹⁴For the generations to come,
whenever an alien or anyone else living
among you presents an offering made by fire
as an aroma pleasing to the LORD, he must do
exactly as you do. ¹⁵The community is to
have the same rules for you and for the alien
living among you; this is a lasting ordinance
for the generations to come. You and the
alien shall be the same before the LORD:
¹⁶The same laws and regulations will apply
both to you and to the alien living among
you.'"

¹⁷The LORD said to Moses, ¹⁸"Speak to the
Israelites and say to them: 'When you enter
the land to which I am taking you ¹⁹and you
eat the food of the land, present a portion as
an offering to the LORD. ²⁰Present a cake from

the first of your ground meal and present
it as an offering from the threshing-floor.
²¹Throughout the generations to come you
are to give this offering to the LORD from the
first of your ground meal.

Offerings for Unintentional Sins

²²"'Now if you unintentionally fail to keep
any of these commands the LORD gave Moses
—²³any of the LORD's commands to you
through him, from the day the LORD gave
them and continuing through the generations
to come—²⁴and if this is done unintentionally
without the community being aware of it,
then the whole community is to offer a young
bull for a burnt offering as an aroma pleasing
to the LORD, along with its prescribed grain
offering and drink offering, and a male goat
for a sin offering. ²⁵The priest is to make
atonement for the whole Israelite community, and they will be forgiven, for it was not
intentional and they have brought to the
LORD for their wrong an offering made by fire
and a sin offering. ²⁶The whole Israelite community and the aliens living among them will
be forgiven, because all the people were
involved in the unintentional wrong.

²⁷"'But if just one person sins unintentionally, he must bring a year-old female goat
for a sin offering. ²⁸The priest is to make
atonement before the LORD for the one who
erred by sinning unintentionally, and when
atonement has been made for him, he will be
forgiven. ²⁹One and the same law applies to
everyone who sins unintentionally, whether
he is a native-born Israelite or an alien.

³⁰"'But anyone who sins defiantly,
whether native-born or alien, blasphemes the
LORD, and that person must be cut off from
his people. ³¹Because he has despised the
LORD's word and broken his commands, that
person must surely be cut off; his guilt remains on him.'"

The Sabbath-Breaker Put to Death

³²While the Israelites were in the desert, a
man was found gathering wood on the Sabbath day. ³³Those who found him gathering
wood brought him to Moses and Aaron and
the whole assembly, ³⁴and they kept him in
custody, because it was not clear what
should be done to him. ³⁵Then the LORD said
to Moses, "The man must die. The whole
assembly must stone him outside the camp."
³⁶So the assembly took him outside the camp
and stoned him to death, as the LORD commanded Moses.

Tassels on Garments

³⁷The LORD said to Moses, ³⁸"Speak to the
Israelites and say to them: 'Throughout the
generations to come you are to make tassels
on the corners of your garments, with a blue
cord on each tassel. ³⁹You will have these
tassels to look at and so you will remember

ᵃ4 That is, probably about 4 pints (about 2 litres)
ᵇ4 That is, probably about 1½ pints (about 1 litre); also in verse 5
ᶜ6 That is, probably about 7½ pints (about 4.5 litres)
ᵈ6 That is, probably about 2¼ pints (about 1.2 litres); also in verse 7
ᵉ8 Traditionally *peace offering*   *ᶠ9* That is, probably about 11½ pints (about 6.5 litres)
ᵍ9 That is, probably about 3 pints (about 2 litres); also in verse 10

all the commands of the LORD, that you may obey them and not prostitute yourselves by going after the lusts of your own hearts and eyes. ⁴⁰Then you will remember to obey all my commands and will be consecrated to your God. ⁴¹I am the LORD your God, who brought you out of Egypt to be your God. I am the LORD your God.'"

Korah, Dathan and Abiram

16 Korah son of Izhar, the son of Kohath, the son of Levi, and certain Reubenites—Dathan and Abiram, sons of Eliab, and On son of Peleth—became insolent*a* ²and rose up against Moses. With them were 250 Israelite men, well-known community leaders who had been appointed members of the council. ³They came as a group to oppose Moses and Aaron and said to them, "You have gone too far! The whole community is holy, every one of them, and the LORD is with them. Why then do you set yourselves above the LORD's assembly?"

⁴When Moses heard this, he fell face down. ⁵Then he said to Korah and all his followers: "In the morning the LORD will show who belongs to him and who is holy, and he will make that person come near him. The man he chooses he will cause to come near him. ⁶You, Korah, and all your followers are to do this: Take censers ⁷and tomorrow put fire and incense in them before the LORD. The man the LORD chooses will be the one who is holy. You Levites have gone too far!"

⁸Moses also said to Korah, "Now listen, you Levites! ⁹Isn't it enough for you that the God of Israel has separated you from the rest of the Israelite community and brought you near himself to do the work at the LORD's tabernacle and to stand before the community and minister to them? ¹⁰He has brought you and all your fellow Levites near himself, but now you are trying to get the priesthood too. ¹¹It is against the LORD that you and all your followers have banded together. Who is Aaron that you should grumble against him?"

¹²Then Moses summoned Dathan and Abiram, the sons of Eliab. But they said, "We will not come! ¹³Isn't it enough that you have brought us up out of a land flowing with milk and honey to kill us in the desert? And now you also want to lord it over us? ¹⁴Moreover, you haven't brought us into a land flowing with milk and honey or given us an inheritance of fields and vineyards. Will you gouge out the eyes of*b* these men? No, we will not come!"

¹⁵Then Moses became very angry and said to the LORD, "Do not accept their offering. I have not taken so much as a donkey from them, nor have I wronged any of them."

¹⁶Moses said to Korah, "You and all your followers are to appear before the LORD tomorrow—you and they and Aaron. ¹⁷Each man is to take his censer and put incense in it—250 censers in all—and present it before the LORD. You and Aaron are to present your censers also." ¹⁸So each man took his censer, put fire and incense in it, and stood with Moses and Aaron at the entrance to the Tent of Meeting. ¹⁹When Korah had gathered all his followers in opposition to them at the entrance to the Tent of Meeting, the glory of the LORD appeared to the entire assembly. ²⁰The LORD said to Moses and Aaron, ²¹"Separate yourselves from this assembly so that I can put an end to them at once."

²²But Moses and Aaron fell face down and cried out, "O God, God of the spirits of all mankind, will you be angry with the entire assembly when only one man sins?"

²³Then the LORD said to Moses, ²⁴"Say to the assembly, 'Move away from the tents of Korah, Dathan and Abiram.'"

²⁵Moses got up and went to Dathan and Abiram, and the elders of Israel followed him. ²⁶He warned the assembly, "Move back from the tents of these wicked men! Do not touch anything belonging to them, or you will be swept away because of all their sins." ²⁷So they moved away from the tents of Korah, Dathan and Abiram. Dathan and Abiram had come out and were standing with their wives, children and little ones at the entrances to their tents.

²⁸Then Moses said, "This is how you will know that the LORD has sent me to do all these things and that it was not my idea: ²⁹If these men die a natural death and experience only what usually happens to men, then the LORD has not sent me. ³⁰But if the LORD brings about something totally new, and the earth opens its mouth and swallows them, with everything that belongs to them, and they go down alive into the grave,*c* then you will know that these men have treated the LORD with contempt."

³¹As soon as he finished saying all this, the ground under them split apart ³²and the earth opened its mouth and swallowed them, with their households and all Korah's men and all their possessions. ³³They went down alive into the grave, with everything they owned; the earth closed over them, and they perished and were gone from the community. ³⁴At their cries, all the Israelites around them fled, shouting, "The earth is going to swallow us too!"

³⁵And fire came out from the LORD and consumed the 250 men who were offering the incense.

³⁶The LORD said to Moses, ³⁷"Tell Eleazar son of Aaron, the priest, to take the censers out of the smouldering remains and scatter the coals some distance away, for the censers are holy—³⁸the censers of the men who sinned at the cost of their lives. Hammer the censers into sheets to overlay the altar, for they were presented before the LORD and have become holy. Let them be a sign to the Israelites."

³⁹So Eleazar the priest collected the bronze censers brought by those who had been burned up, and he had them hammered out to overlay the altar, ⁴⁰as the LORD directed him through Moses. This was to

---

a1 Or *Peleth—took ⌐men⌐*   *b14* Or *you make slaves of;* or *you deceive*   *c30* Hebrew *Sheol;* also in verse 33 remind the Israelites that no-one except a descendant of Aaron should come to burn incense before the LORD, or he would become like Korah and his followers.

⁴¹The next day the whole Israelite community grumbled against Moses and Aaron. "You have killed the LORD's people," they said.

⁴²But when the assembly gathered in opposition to Moses and Aaron and turned towards the Tent of Meeting, suddenly the cloud covered it and the glory of the LORD appeared. ⁴³Then Moses and Aaron went to the front of the Tent of Meeting, ⁴⁴and the LORD said to Moses, ⁴⁵"Get away from this assembly so that I can put an end to them at once." And they fell face down.

⁴⁶Then Moses said to Aaron, "Take your censer and put incense in it, along with fire from the altar, and hurry to the assembly to make atonement for them. Wrath has come out from the LORD; the plague has started." ⁴⁷So Aaron did as Moses said, and ran into the midst of the assembly. The plague had already started among the people, but Aaron offered the incense and made atonement for them. ⁴⁸He stood between the living and the dead, and the plague stopped. ⁴⁹But 14,700 people died from the plague, in addition to those who had died because of Korah. ⁵⁰Then Aaron returned to Moses at the entrance to the Tent of Meeting, for the plague had stopped.

The Budding of Aaron's Staff

17 The LORD said to Moses, ²"Speak to the Israelites and get twelve staffs from them, one from the leader of each of their ancestral tribes. Write the name of each man on his staff. ³On the staff of Levi write Aaron's name, for there must be one staff for the head of each ancestral tribe. ⁴Place them in the Tent of Meeting in front of the Testimony, where I meet with you. ⁵The staff belonging to the man I choose will sprout, and I will rid myself of this constant grumbling against you by the Israelites."

⁶So Moses spoke to the Israelites, and their leaders gave him twelve staffs, one for the leader of each of their ancestral tribes, and Aaron's staff was among them. ⁷Moses placed the staffs before the LORD in the Tent of the Testimony.

⁸The next day Moses entered the Tent of the Testimony and saw that Aaron's staff, which represented the house of Levi, had not only sprouted but had budded, blossomed and produced almonds. ⁹Then Moses brought out all the staffs from the LORD's presence to all the Israelites. They looked at them, and each man took his own staff.

¹⁰The LORD said to Moses, "Put back Aaron's staff in front of the Testimony, to be kept as a sign to the rebellious. This will put an end to their grumbling against me, so that they will not die." ¹¹Moses did just as the LORD commanded him.

¹²The Israelites said to Moses, "We shall die! We are lost, we are all lost! ¹³Anyone who even comes near the tabernacle of the LORD will die. Are we all going to die?"

Duties of Priests and Levites

18 The LORD said to Aaron, "You, your sons and your father's family are to bear the responsibility for offences against the sanctuary, and you and your sons alone are to bear the responsibility for offences against the priesthood. ²Bring your fellow Levites from your ancestral tribe to join you and assist you when you and your sons minister before the Tent of the Testimony. ³They are to be responsible to you and are to perform all the duties of the Tent, but they must not go near the furnishings of the sanctuary or the altar, or both they and you will die. ⁴They are to join you and be responsible for the care of the Tent of Meeting—all the work at the Tent—and no-one else may come near where you are.

⁵"You are to be responsible for the care of the sanctuary and the altar, so that wrath will not fall on the Israelites again. ⁶I myself have selected your fellow Levites from among the Israelites as a gift to you, dedicated to the LORD to do the work at the Tent of Meeting. ⁷But only you and your sons may serve as priests in connection with everything at the altar and inside the curtain. I am giving you the service of the priesthood as a gift. Anyone else who comes near the sanctuary must be put to death."

Offerings for Priests and Levites

⁸Then the LORD said to Aaron, "I myself have put you in charge of the offerings presented to me; all the holy offerings the Israelites give me I give to you and your sons as your portion and regular share. ⁹You are to have the part of the most holy offerings that is kept from the fire. From all the gifts they bring me as most holy offerings, whether grain or sin or guilt offerings, that part belongs to you and your sons. ¹⁰Eat it as something most holy; every male shall eat it. You must regard it as holy.

¹¹"This also is yours: whatever is set aside from the gifts of all the wave offerings of the Israelites. I give this to you and your sons and daughters as your regular share. Everyone in your household who is ceremonially clean may eat it.

¹²"I give you all the finest olive oil and all the finest new wine and grain they give to the LORD as the firstfruits of their harvest. ¹³All the land's firstfruits that they bring to the LORD will be yours. Everyone in your household who is ceremonially clean may eat it.

¹⁴"Everything in Israel that is devoted*a* to the LORD is yours. ¹⁵The first offspring of every womb, both man and animal, that is offered to the LORD is yours. But you must redeem every firstborn son and every firstborn male of unclean animals. ¹⁶When they are a month old, you must redeem them at the redemption price set at five shekels*b* of

---

a14 The Hebrew term refers to the irrevocable giving over of things or persons to the LORD.
b16 That is, about 2 ounces (about 55 grams)

silver, according to the sanctuary shekel, which weighs twenty gerahs.

17"But you must not redeem the firstborn of an ox, a sheep or a goat; they are holy. Sprinkle their blood on the altar and burn their fat as an offering made by fire, an aroma pleasing to the LORD. 18Their meat is to be yours, just as the breast of the wave offering and the right thigh are yours. 19Whatever is set aside from the holy offerings the Israelites present to the LORD I give to you and your sons and daughters as your regular share. It is an everlasting covenant of salt before the LORD for both you and your offspring."

20The LORD said to Aaron, "You will have no inheritance in their land, nor will you have any share among them; I am your share and your inheritance among the Israelites.

21"I give to the Levites all the tithes in Israel as their inheritance in return for the work they do while serving at the Tent of Meeting. 22From now on the Israelites must not go near the Tent of Meeting, or they will bear the consequences of their sin and will die. 23It is the Levites who are to do the work at the Tent of Meeting and bear the responsibility for offences against it. This is a lasting ordinance for the generations to come. They will receive no inheritance among the Israelites. 24Instead, I give to the Levites as their inheritance the tithes that the Israelites present as an offering to the LORD. That is why I said concerning them: 'They will have no inheritance among the Israelites.'"

25The LORD said to Moses, 26"Speak to the Levites and say to them: 'When you receive from the Israelites the tithe I give you as your inheritance, you must present a tenth of that tithe as the LORD's offering. 27Your offering will be reckoned to you as grain from the threshing-floor or juice from the winepress. 28In this way you also will present an offering to the LORD from all the tithes you receive from the Israelites. From these tithes you must give the LORD's portion to Aaron the priest. 29You must present as the LORD's portion the best and holiest part of everything given to you.'

30"Say to the Levites: 'When you present the best part, it will be reckoned to you as the product of the threshing-floor or the winepress. 31You and your households may eat the rest of it anywhere, for it is your wages for your work at the Tent of Meeting. 32By presenting the best part of it you will not be guilty in this matter; then you will not defile the holy offerings of the Israelites, and you will not die.'"

The Water of Cleansing

19 The LORD said to Moses and Aaron: 2"This is a requirement of the law that the LORD has commanded: Tell the Israelites to bring you a red heifer without defect or blemish and that has never been under a yoke. 3Give it to Eleazar the priest; it is to be taken outside the camp and slaughtered in his presence. 4Then Eleazar the priest is to take some of its blood on his finger and sprinkle it seven times towards the front of the Tent of Meeting. 5While he watches, the heifer is to

be burned—its hide, flesh, blood and offal. 6The priest is to take some cedar wood, hyssop and scarlet wool and throw them onto the burning heifer. 7After that, the priest must wash his clothes and bathe himself with water. He may then come into the camp, but he will be ceremonially unclean till evening. 8The man who burns it must also wash his clothes and bathe with water, and he too will be unclean till evening.

9"A man who is clean shall gather up the ashes of the heifer and put them in a ceremonially clean place outside the camp. They shall be kept by the Israelite community for use in the water of cleansing; it is for purification from sin. 10The man who gathers up the ashes of the heifer must also wash his clothes, and he too will be unclean till evening. This will be a lasting ordinance both for the Israelites and for the aliens living among them.

11"Whoever touches the dead body of anyone will be unclean for seven days. 12He must purify himself with the water on the third day and on the seventh day; then he will be clean. But if he does not purify himself on the third and seventh days, he will not be clean. 13Whoever touches the dead body of anyone and fails to purify himself defiles the LORD's tabernacle. That person must be cut off from Israel. Because the water of cleansing has not been sprinkled on him, he is unclean; his uncleanness remains on him.

14"This is the law that applies when a person dies in a tent: Anyone who enters the tent and anyone who is in it will be unclean for seven days, 15and every open container without a lid fastened on it will be unclean.

16"Anyone out in the open who touches someone who has been killed with a sword or someone who has died a natural death, or anyone who touches a human bone or a grave, will be unclean for seven days.

17"For the unclean person, put some ashes from the burned purification offering into a jar and pour fresh water over them. 18Then a man who is ceremonially clean is to take some hyssop, dip it in the water and sprinkle the tent and all the furnishings and the people who were there. He must also sprinkle anyone who has touched a human bone or a grave or someone who has been killed or someone who has died a natural death. 19The man who is clean is to sprinkle the unclean person on the third and seventh days, and on the seventh day he is to purify him. The person being cleansed must wash his clothes and bathe with water, and that evening he will be clean. 20But if a person who is unclean does not purify himself, he must be cut off from the community, because he has defiled the sanctuary of the LORD. The water of cleansing has not been sprinkled on him, and he is unclean. 21This is a lasting ordinance for them.

"The man who sprinkles the water of cleansing must also wash his clothes, and anyone who touches the water of cleansing will be unclean till evening. 22Anything that an unclean person touches becomes unclean, and anyone who touches it becomes unclean till evening.''

Water From the Rock

20 In the first month the whole Israelite community arrived at the Desert of Zin, and they stayed at Kadesh. There Miriam died and was buried.

²Now there was no water for the community, and the people gathered in opposition to Moses and Aaron. ³They quarrelled with Moses and said, ''If only we had died when our brothers fell dead before the LORD! ⁴Why did you bring the LORD's community into this desert, that we and our livestock should die here? ⁵Why did you bring us up out of Egypt to this terrible place? It has no grain or figs, grapevines or pomegranates. And there is no water to drink!''

⁶Moses and Aaron went from the assembly to the entrance to the Tent of Meeting and fell face down, and the glory of the LORD appeared to them. ⁷The LORD said to Moses, ⁸''Take the staff, and you and your brother Aaron gather the assembly together. Speak to that rock before their eyes and it will pour out its water. You will bring water out of the rock for the community so that they and their livestock can drink.''

⁹So Moses took the staff from the LORD's presence, just as he commanded him. ¹⁰He and Aaron gathered the assembly together in front of the rock and Moses said to them, ''Listen, you rebels, must we bring you water out of this rock?'' ¹¹Then Moses raised his arm and struck the rock twice with his staff. Water gushed out, and the community and their livestock drank.

¹²But the LORD said to Moses and Aaron, ''Because you did not trust in me enough to honour me as holy in the sight of the Israelites, you will not bring this community into the land I give them.''

¹³These were the waters of Meribah,ᵃ where the Israelites quarrelled with the LORD and where he showed himself holy among them.

Edom Denies Israel Passage

¹⁴Moses sent messengers from Kadesh to the king of Edom, saying:

''This is what your brother Israel says: You know about all the hardships that have come upon us. ¹⁵Our forefathers went down into Egypt, and we lived there many years. The Egyptians ill-treated us and our fathers, ¹⁶but when we cried out to the LORD, he heard our cry and sent an angel and brought us out of Egypt.

''Now we are here at Kadesh, a town on the edge of your territory. ¹⁷Please let us pass through your country. We will not go through any field or vineyard, or drink water from any well. We will travel along the king's highway and not turn to the right or to the left until we have passed through your territory.''

¹⁸But Edom answered:

''You may not pass through here; if you try, we will march out and attack you with the sword.''

¹⁹The Israelites replied:

''We will go along the main road, and if we or our livestock drink any of your water, we will pay for it. We only want to pass through on foot—nothing else.''

²⁰Again they answered:

''You may not pass through.''

Then Edom came out against them with a large and powerful army. ²¹Since Edom refused to let them go through their territory, Israel turned away from them.

The Death of Aaron

²²The whole Israelite community set out from Kadesh and came to Mount Hor. ²³At Mount Hor, near the border of Edom, the LORD said to Moses and Aaron, ²⁴''Aaron will be gathered to his people. He will not enter the land I give the Israelites, because both of you rebelled against my command at the waters of Meribah. ²⁵Call Aaron and his son Eleazar and take them up Mount Hor. ²⁶Remove Aaron's garments and put them on his son Eleazar, for Aaron will be gathered to his people; he will die there.''

²⁷Moses did as the LORD commanded: They went up Mount Hor in the sight of the whole community. ²⁸Moses removed Aaron's garments and put them on his son Eleazar. And Aaron died there on top of the mountain. Then Moses and Eleazar came down from the mountain, ²⁹and when the whole community learned that Aaron had died, the entire house of Israel mourned for him thirty days.

Arad Destroyed

21 When the Canaanite king of Arad, who lived in the Negev, heard that Israel was coming along the road to Atharim, he attacked the Israelites and captured some of them. ²Then Israel made this vow to the LORD: ''If you will deliver these people into our hands, we will totally destroyᵃ their cities.'' ³The LORD listened to Israel's plea and gave the Canaanites over to them. They completely destroyed them and their towns; so the place was named Hormah.ᵇ

The Bronze Snake

⁴They travelled from Mount Hor along the route to the Red Sea,ᶜ to go round Edom. But the people grew impatient on the way; ⁵they spoke against God and against Moses, and

---

ᵃ13 *Meribah* means *quarrelling.*
ᵃ2 The Hebrew term refers to the irrevocable giving over of things or persons to the LORD, often by totally destroying them; also in verse 3.   ᵇ3 *Hormah* means *destruction.*   ᶜ4 Hebrew *Yam Suph*; that is, Sea of Reeds

said, "Why have you brought us up out of Egypt to die in the desert? There is no bread! There is no water! And we detest this miserable food!"

6Then the LORD sent venomous snakes among them; they bit the people and many Israelites died. 7The people came to Moses and said, "We sinned when we spoke against the LORD and against you. Pray that the LORD will take the snakes away from us." So Moses prayed for the people.

8The LORD said to Moses, "Make a snake and put it up on a pole; anyone who is bitten can look at it and live." 9So Moses made a bronze snake and put it up on a pole. Then when anyone was bitten by a snake and looked at the bronze snake, he lived.

The Journey to Moab

10The Israelites moved on and camped at Oboth. 11Then they set out from Oboth and camped in Iye Abarim, in the desert that faces Moab towards the sunrise. 12From there they moved on and camped in the Zered Valley. 13They set out from there and camped alongside the Arnon, which is in the desert extending into Amorite territory. The Arnon is the border of Moab, between Moab and the Amorites. 14That is why the Book of the Wars of the LORD says:

". . . Waheb in Suphah*d* and the ravines,
  the Arnon 15and*e* the slopes of the
    ravines
  that lead to the site of Ar
  and lie along the border of Moab."

16From there they continued on to Beer, the well where the LORD said to Moses, "Gather the people together and I will give them water."

17Then Israel sang this song:

"Spring up, O well!
  Sing about it,
18about the well that the princes dug,
  that the nobles of the people sank—
  the nobles with sceptres and staffs."

Then they went from the desert to Mattanah, 19from Mattanah to Nahaliel, from Nahaliel to Bamoth, 20and from Bamoth to the valley in Moab where the top of Pisgah overlooks the wasteland.

Defeat of Sihon and Og

21Israel sent messengers to say to Sihon king of the Amorites:

22"Let us pass through your country. We will not turn aside into any field or vineyard, or drink water from any well. We will travel along the king's highway until we have passed through your territory."

23But Sihon would not let Israel pass through his territory. He mustered his entire

army and marched out into the desert against Israel. When he reached Jahaz, he fought with Israel. 24Israel, however, put him to the sword and took over his land from the Arnon to the Jabbok, but only as far as the Ammonites, because their border was fortified. 25Israel captured all the cities of the Amorites and occupied them, including Heshbon and all its surrounding settlements. 26Heshbon was the city of Sihon king of the Amorites, who had fought against the former king of Moab and had taken from him all his land·as far as the Arnon.

27That is why the poets say:

"Come to Heshbon and let it be rebuilt;
  let Sihon's city be restored.

28"Fire went out from Heshbon,
  a blaze from the city of Sihon.
It consumed Ar of Moab,
  the citizens of Arnon's heights.
29Woe to you, O Moab!
  You are destroyed, O people of Che-
    mosh!
He has given up his sons as fugitives
  and his daughters as captives
  to Sihon king of the Amorites.

30"But we have overthrown them;
  Heshbon is destroyed all the way to
    Dibon.
We have demolished them as far as
    Nophah,
  which extends to Medeba."

31So Israel settled in the land of the Amorites.

32After Moses had sent spies to Jazer, the Israelites captured its surrounding settlements and drove out the Amorites who were there. 33Then they turned and went up along the road towards Bashan, and Og king of Bashan and his whole army marched out to meet them in battle at Edrei.

34The LORD said to Moses, "Do not be afraid of him, for I have handed him over to you, with his whole army and his land. Do to him what you did to Sihon king of the Amorites, who reigned in Heshbon."

35So they struck him down, together with his sons and his whole army, leaving them no survivors. And they took possession of his land.

Balak Summons Balaam

22 Then the Israelites travelled to the plains of Moab and camped along the Jordan across from Jericho.*a*

2Now Balak son of Zippor saw all that Israel had done to the Amorites, 3and Moab was terrified because there were so many people. Indeed, Moab was filled with dread because of the Israelites.

4The Moabites said to the elders of Midian, "This horde is going to lick up everything around us, as an ox licks up the grass of the field."

d14 The meaning of the Hebrew for this phrase is uncertain.
e14,15 Or *'I have been given from Suphah and the ravines / of the Arnon* 15*to*
a1 Hebrew *Jordan of Jericho*; possibly an ancient name for the Jordan River

So Balak son of Zippor, who was king of Moab at that time, [5]sent messengers to summon Balaam son of Beor, who was at Pethor, near the River,[b] in his native land. Balak said:

"A people has come out of Egypt; they cover the face of the land and have settled next to me. [6]Now come and put a curse on these people, because they are too powerful for me. Perhaps then I will be able to defeat them and drive them out of the country. For I know that those you bless are blessed, and those you curse are cursed."

[7]The elders of Moab and Midian left, taking with them the fee for divination. When they came to Balaam, they told him what Balak had said.

[8]"Spend the night here," Balaam said to them, "and I will bring you back the answer the LORD gives me." So the Moabite princes stayed with him.

[9]God came to Balaam and asked, "Who are these men with you?"

[10]Balaam said to God, "Balak son of Zippor, king of Moab, sent me this message: [11]'A people that has come out of Egypt covers the face of the land. Now come and put a curse on them for me. Perhaps then I will be able to fight them and drive them away.'"

[12]But God said to Balaam, "Do not go with them. You must not put a curse on those people, because they are blessed."

[13]The next morning Balaam got up and said to Balak's princes, "Go back to your own country, for the LORD has refused to let me go with you."

[14]So the Moabite princes returned to Balak and said, "Balaam refused to come with us."

[15]Then Balak sent other princes, more numerous and more distinguished than the first. [16]They came to Balaam and said:

"This is what Balak son of Zippor says: Do not let anything keep you from coming to me, [17]because I will reward you handsomely and do whatever you say. Come and put a curse on these people for me."

[18]But Balaam answered them, "Even if Balak gave me his palace filled with silver and gold, I could not do anything great or small to go beyond the command of the LORD my God. [19]Now stay here tonight as the others did, and I will find out what else the LORD will tell me."

[20]That night God came to Balaam and said, "Since these men have come to summon you, go with them, but do only what I tell you."

Balaam's Donkey

[21]Balaam got up in the morning, saddled his donkey and went with the princes of Moab. [22]But God was very angry when he went, and the angel of the LORD stood in the road to oppose him. Balaam was riding on his donkey, and his two servants were with him. [23]When the donkey saw the angel of the LORD standing in the road with a drawn sword in his hand, she turned off the road into a field. Balaam beat her to get her back on the road.

[24]Then the angel of the LORD stood in a narrow path between two vineyards, with walls on both sides. [25]When the donkey saw the angel of the LORD, she pressed close to the wall, crushing Balaam's foot against it. So he beat her again.

[26]Then the angel of the LORD moved on ahead and stood in a narrow place where there was no room to turn, either to the right or to the left. [27]When the donkey saw the angel of the LORD, she lay down under Balaam, and he was angry and beat her with his staff. [28]Then the LORD opened the donkey's mouth, and she said to Balaam, "What have I done to you to make you beat me these three times?"

[29]Balaam answered the donkey, "You have made a fool of me! If I had a sword in my hand, I would kill you right now."

[30]The donkey said to Balaam, "Am I not your own donkey, which you have always ridden, to this day? Have I been in the habit of doing this to you?"

"No," he said.

[31]Then the LORD opened Balaam's eyes, and he saw the angel of the LORD standing in the road with his sword drawn. So he bowed low and fell face down.

[32]The angel of the LORD asked him, "Why have you beaten your donkey these three times? I have come here to oppose you because your path is a reckless one before me.[c] [33]The donkey saw me and turned away from me these three times. If she had not turned away, I would certainly have killed you by now, but I would have spared her."

[34]Balaam said to the angel of the LORD, "I have sinned. I did not realise you were standing in the road to oppose me. Now if you are displeased, I will go back."

[35]The angel of the LORD said to Balaam, "Go with the men, but speak only what I tell you." So Balaam went with the princes of Balak.

[36]When Balak heard that Balaam was coming, he went out to meet him at the Moabite town on the Arnon border, at the edge of his territory. [37]Balak said to Balaam, "Did I not send you an urgent summons? Why didn't you come to me? Am I really not able to reward you?"

[38]"Well, I have come to you now," Balaam replied. "But can I say just anything? I must speak only what God puts in my mouth."

[39]Then Balaam went with Balak to Kiriath Huzoth. [40]Balak sacrificed cattle and sheep, and gave some to Balaam and the princes who were with him. [41]The next morning Balak took Balaam up to Bamoth Baal, and from there he saw part of the people.

Balaam's First Oracle

23 Balaam said, "Build me seven altars here, and prepare seven bulls and seven rams for me." ²Balak did as Balaam said, and the two of them offered a bull and a ram on each altar.

³Then Balaam said to Balak, "Stay here beside your offering while I go aside. Perhaps the LORD will come to meet with me. Whatever he reveals to me I will tell you." Then he went off to a barren height.

⁴God met with him, and Balaam said, "I have prepared seven altars, and on each altar I have offered a bull and a ram."

⁵The LORD put a message in Balaam's mouth and said, "Go back to Balak and give him this message."

⁶So he went back to him and found him standing beside his offering, with all the princes of Moab. ⁷Then Balaam uttered his oracle:

"Balak brought me from Aram,
　　the king of Moab from the eastern
　　　mountains.
'Come,' he said, 'curse Jacob for me;
　　come, denounce Israel.'
⁸How can I curse
　　those whom God has not cursed?
How can I denounce
　　those whom the LORD has not
　　　denounced?
⁹From the rocky peaks I see them,
　　from the heights I view them.
I see people who live apart
　　and do not consider themselves one of
　　　the nations.
¹⁰Who can count the dust of Jacob
　　or number the fourth part of Israel?
Let me die the death of the righteous,
　　and may my end be like theirs!"

¹¹Balak said to Balaam, "What have you done to me? I brought you to curse my enemies, but you have done nothing but bless them!"

¹²He answered, "Must I not speak what the LORD puts in my mouth?"

Balaam's Second Oracle

¹³Then Balak said to him, "Come with me to another place where you can see them; you will see only a part but not all of them. And from there, curse them for me." ¹⁴So he took him to the field of Zophim on the top of Pisgah, and there he built seven altars and offered a bull and a ram on each altar.

¹⁵Balaam said to Balak, "Stay here beside your offering while I meet with him over there."

¹⁶The LORD met with Balaam and put a message in his mouth and said, "Go back to Balak and give him this message."

¹⁷So he went to him and found him standing beside his offering, with the princes of Moab. Balak asked him, "What did the LORD say?"

¹⁸Then he uttered his oracle:

"Arise, Balak, and listen;
　　hear me, son of Zippor.
¹⁹God is not a man, that he should lie,
　　nor a son of man, that he should change
　　　his mind.
Does he speak and then not act?
　　Does he promise and not fulfil?
²⁰I have received a command to bless;
　　he has blessed, and I cannot change it.

²¹"No misfortune is seen in Jacob,
　　no misery observed in Israel.*ᵃ*
The LORD their God is with them;
　　the shout of the King is among them.
²²God brought them out of Egypt;
　　they have the strength of a wild ox.
²³There is no sorcery against Jacob,
　　no divination against Israel.
It will now be said of Jacob
　　and of Israel, 'See what God has done!'
²⁴The people rise like a lioness;
　　they rouse themselves like a lion
that does not rest till he devours his prey
　　and drinks the blood of his victims."

²⁵Then Balak said to Balaam, "Neither curse them at all nor bless them at all!"

²⁶Balaam answered, "Did I not tell you I must do whatever the LORD says?"

Balaam's Third Oracle

²⁷Then Balak said to Balaam, "Come, let me take you to another place. Perhaps it will please God to let you curse them for me from there." ²⁸And Balak took Balaam to the top of Peor, overlooking the wasteland.

²⁹Balaam said, "Build me seven altars here, and prepare seven bulls and seven rams for me." ³⁰Balak did as Balaam had said, and offered a bull and a ram on each altar.

24 Now when Balaam saw that it pleased the LORD to bless Israel, he did not resort to sorcery as at other times, but turned his face towards the desert. ²When Balaam looked out and saw Israel encamped tribe by tribe, the Spirit of God came upon him ³and he uttered his oracle:

"The oracle of Balaam son of Beor,
　　the oracle of one whose eye sees clearly,
⁴the oracle of one who hears the words of
　　　God,
who sees a vision from the Almighty,*ᵃ*
　　who falls prostrate, and whose eyes are
　　　opened:

⁵"How beautiful are your tents, O Jacob,
　　your dwelling-places, O Israel!

⁶"Like valleys they spread out,
　　like gardens beside a river,
like aloes planted by the LORD,
　　like cedars beside the waters.
⁷Water will flow from their buckets;
　　their seed will have abundant water.

"Their king will be greater than Agag;
　　their kingdom will be exalted.

ᵃ21 Or *He has not looked on Jacob's offences / or on the wrongs found in Israel.*
ᵃ4 Hebrew *Shaddai;* also in verse 16

8"God brought them out of Egypt;
 they have the strength of a wild ox.
They devour hostile nations
 and break their bones in pieces;
 with their arrows they pierce them.
9Like a lion they crouch and lie down,
 like a lioness—who dares to rouse
 them?

"May those who bless you be blessed
 and those who curse you be cursed!"

10Then Balak's anger burned against
Balaam. He struck his hands together and
said to him, "I summoned you to curse my
enemies, but you have blessed them these
three times. 11Now leave at once and go
home! I said I would reward you handsomely, but the LORD has kept you from
being rewarded."

12Balaam answered Balak, "Did I not tell
the messengers you sent me, 13'Even if Balak
gave me his palace filled with silver and gold,
I could not do anything of my own accord,
good or bad, to go beyond the command of
the LORD—and I must say only what the
LORD says'? 14Now I am going back to my
people, but come, let me warn you of what
this people will do to your people in days to
come."

Balaam's Fourth Oracle

15Then he uttered his oracle:

"The oracle of Balaam son of Beor,
 the oracle of one whose eye sees clearly,
16the oracle of one who hears the words of
 God,
 who has knowledge from the Most High,
who sees a vision from the Almighty,
 who falls prostrate, and whose eyes are
 opened:

17"I see him, but not now;
 I behold him, but not near.
A star will come out of Jacob;
 a sceptre will rise out of Israel.
He will crush the foreheads of Moab,
 the skulls[b] of[c] all the sons of Sheth.[d]
18Edom will be conquered;
 Seir, his enemy, will be conquered,
 but Israel will grow strong.
19A ruler will come out of Jacob
 and destroy the survivors of the city."

Balaam's Final Oracles

20Then Balaam saw Amalek and uttered
his oracle:

"Amalek was first among the nations,
 but he will come to ruin at last."

21Then he saw the Kenites and uttered his
oracle:

"Your dwelling-place is secure,
 your nest is set in a rock;

22yet you Kenites will be destroyed
 when Asshur takes you captive."

23Then he uttered his oracle:

"Ah, who can live when God does this?[e]
24 Ships will come from the shores of
 Kittim;
 they will subdue Asshur and Eber,
 but they too will come to ruin."

25Then Balaam got up and returned home
and Balak went his own way.

Moab Seduces Israel

25 While Israel was staying in Shittim,
the men began to indulge in sexual
immorality with Moabite women, 2who invited them to the sacrifices to their gods. The
people ate and bowed down before these
gods. 3So Israel joined in worshipping the
Baal of Peor. And the LORD's anger burned
against them.

4The LORD said to Moses, "Take all the
leaders of these people, kill them and expose
them in broad daylight before the LORD, so
that the LORD's fierce anger may turn away
from Israel."

5So Moses said to Israel's judges, "Each
of you must put to death those of your men
who have joined in worshipping the Baal of
Peor."

6Then an Israelite man brought to his family a Midianite woman right before the eyes
of Moses and the whole assembly of Israel
while they were weeping at the entrance to
the Tent of Meeting. 7When Phinehas son of
Eleazar, the son of Aaron, the priest, saw
this, he left the assembly, took a spear in his
hand 8and followed the Israelite into the tent.
He drove the spear through both of them
—through the Israelite and into the woman's
body. Then the plague against the Israelites
was stopped; 9but those who died in the
plague numbered 24,000.

10The LORD said to Moses, 11"Phinehas
son of Eleazar, the son of Aaron, the priest,
has turned my anger away from the
Israelites; for he was as zealous as I am for
my honour among them, so that in my zeal I
did not put an end to them. 12Therefore tell
him I am making my covenant of peace with
him. 13He and his descendants will have a
covenant of a lasting priesthood, because he
was zealous for the honour of his God and
made atonement for the Israelites."

14The name of the Israelite who was killed
with the Midianite woman was Zimri son of
Salu, the leader of a Simeonite family. 15And
the name of the Midianite woman who was
put to death was Cozbi daughter of Zur, a
tribal chief of a Midianite family.

16The LORD said to Moses, 17"Treat the
Midianites as enemies and kill them,
18because they treated you as enemies when
they deceived you in the affair of Peor and
their sister Cozbi, the daughter of a Midianite

b17 Samaritan Pentateuch (see also Jer. 48:45); the meaning of the word in the Masoretic Text is uncertain.
c17 Or possibly Moab, / batter   d17 Or all the noisy boasters
e23 Masoretic Text; with a different word division of the Hebrew A people will gather from the north.

leader, the woman who was killed when the plague came as a result of Peor."

The Second Census

26 After the plague the LORD said to Moses and Eleazar son of Aaron, the priest, ²"Take a census of the whole Israelite community by families—all those twenty years old or more who are able to serve in the army of Israel." ³So on the plains of Moab by the Jordan across from Jericho,ᵃ Moses and Eleazar the priest spoke with them and said, ⁴"Take a census of men twenty years old or more, as the LORD commanded Moses."

These were the Israelites who came out of Egypt:

⁵The descendants of Reuben, the firstborn son of Israel, were:
through Hanoch, the Hanochite clan;
through Pallu, the Palluite clan;
⁶through Hezron, the Hezronite clan;
through Carmi, the Carmite clan.
⁷These were the clans of Reuben; those numbered were 43,730.
⁸The son of Pallu was Eliab, ⁹and the sons of Eliab were Nemuel, Dathan and Abiram. The same Dathan and Abiram were the community officials who rebelled against Moses and Aaron and were among Korah's followers when they rebelled against the LORD. ¹⁰The earth opened its mouth and swallowed them along with Korah, whose followers died when the fire devoured the 250 men. And they served as a warning sign. ¹¹The line of Korah, however, did not die out.

¹²The descendants of Simeon by their clans were:
through Nemuel, the Nemuelite clan;
through Jamin, the Jaminite clan;
through Jakin, the Jakinite clan;
¹³through Zerah, the Zerahite clan;
through Shaul, the Shaulite clan.
¹⁴These were the clans of Simeon; there were 22,200 men.

¹⁵The descendants of Gad by their clans were:
through Zephon, the Zephonite clan;
through Haggi, the Haggite clan;
through Shuni, the Shunite clan;
¹⁶through Ozni, the Oznite clan;
through Eri, the Erite clan;
¹⁷through Arodi,ᵇ the Arodite clan;
through Areli, the Arelite clan.
¹⁸These were the clans of Gad; those numbered were 40,500.

¹⁹Er and Onan were sons of Judah, but they died in Canaan.
²⁰The descendants of Judah by their clans were:
through Shelah, the Shelanite clan;

through Perez, the Perezite clan;
through Zerah, the Zerahite clan.
²¹The descendants of Perez were:
through Hezron, the Hezronite clan;
through Hamul, the Hamulite clan.
²²These were the clans of Judah; those numbered were 76,500.

²³The descendants of Issachar by their clans were:
through Tola, the Tolaite clan;
through Puah, the Puiteᶜ clan;
²⁴through Jashub, the Jashubite clan;
through Shimron, the Shimronite clan.
²⁵These were the clans of Issachar; those numbered were 64,300.

²⁶The descendants of Zebulun by their clans were:
through Sered, the Seredite clan;
through Elon, the Elonite clan;
through Jahleel, the Jahleelite clan.
²⁷These were the clans of Zebulun; those numbered were 60,500.

²⁸The descendants of Joseph by their clans through Manasseh and Ephraim were:

²⁹The descendants of Manasseh:
through Makir, the Makirite clan (Makir was the father of Gilead);
through Gilead, the Gileadite clan.
³⁰These were the descendants of Gilead:
through Iezer, the Iezerite clan;
through Helek, the Helekite clan;
³¹through Asriel, the Asrielite clan;
through Shechem, the Shechemite clan;
³²through Shemida, the Shemidaite clan;
through Hepher, the Hepherite clan.
³³(Zelophehad son of Hepher had no sons; he had only daughters, whose names were Mahlah, Noah, Hoglah, Milcah and Tirzah.)
³⁴These were the clans of Manasseh; those numbered were 52,700.

³⁵These were the descendants of Ephraim by their clans:
through Shuthelah, the Shuthelahite clan;
through Beker, the Bekerite clan;
through Tahan, the Tahanite clan.
³⁶These were the descendants of Shuthelah:
through Eran, the Eranite clan.
³⁷These were the clans of Ephraim; those numbered were 32,500.

These were the descendants of Joseph by their clans.

³⁸The descendants of Benjamin by their clans were:
through Bela, the Belaite clan;
through Ashbel, the Ashbelite clan;
through Ahiram, the Ahiramite clan;
³⁹through Shupham,ᵈ the Shuphamite clan;
through Hupham, the Huphamite clan.

ᵃ3 Hebrew *Jordan of Jericho*; possibly an ancient name for the Jordan River; also in verse 63
ᵇ17 Samaritan Pentateuch and Syriac (see also Gen. 46:16); Masoretic Text *Arod*
ᶜ23 Samaritan Pentateuch, Septuagint, Vulgate and Syriac (see also 1 Chron. 7:1); Masoretic Text *through Puvah, the Punite*
ᵈ39 A few manuscripts of the Masoretic Text, Samaritan Pentateuch, Vulgate and Syriac (see also Septuagint); most manuscripts of the Masoretic Text *Shephupham*

40The descendants of Bela through Ard and Naaman were:

through Ard,*e* the Ardite clan;
through Naaman, the Naamite clan.

41These were the clans of Benjamin; those numbered were 45,600.

42These were the descendants of Dan by their clans:

through Shuham, the Shuhamite clan.

These were the clans of Dan: 43All of them were Shuhamite clans; and those numbered were 64,400.

44The descendants of Asher by their clans were:

through Imnah, the Imnite clan;
through Ishvi, the Ishvite clan;
through Beriah, the Beriite clan;

45and through the descendants of Beriah:

through Heber, the Heberite clan;
through Malkiel, the Malkielite clan.

46(Asher had a daughter named Serah.)

47These were the clans of Asher; those numbered were 53,400.

48The descendants of Naphtali by their clans were:

through Jahzeel, the Jahzeelite clan;
through Guni, the Gunite clan;

49through Jezer, the Jezerite clan;
through Shillem, the Shillemite clan.

50These were the clans of Naphtali; those numbered were 45,400.

51The total number of the men of Israel was 601,730.

52The LORD said to Moses, 53"The land is to be allotted to them as an inheritance based on the number of names. 54To a larger group give a larger inheritance, and to a smaller group a smaller one; each is to receive its inheritance according to the number of those listed. 55Be sure that the land is distributed by lot. What each group inherits will be according to the names for its ancestral tribe. 56Each inheritance is to be distributed by lot among the larger and smaller groups."

57These were the Levites who were counted by their clans:

through Gershon, the Gershonite clan;
through Kohath, the Kohathite clan;
through Merari, the Merarite clan.

58These also were Levite clans:

the Libnite clan,
the Hebronite clan,
the Mahlite clan,
the Mushite clan,
the Korahite clan.

(Kohath was the forefather of Amram; 59the name of Amram's wife was Jochebed, a descendant of Levi, who was born to the Levites*f* in Egypt. To Amram she bore Aaron, Moses and their sister Miriam. 60Aaron was the father of Nadab and Abihu, Eleazar and Ithamar.

61But Nadab and Abihu died when they made an offering before the LORD with unauthorised fire.)

62All the male Levites a month old or more numbered 23,000. They were not counted along with the other Israelites because they received no inheritance among them.

63These are the ones counted by Moses and Eleazar the priest when they counted the Israelites on the plains of Moab by the Jordan across from Jericho. 64Not one of them was among those counted by Moses and Aaron the priest when they counted the Israelites in the Desert of Sinai. 65For the LORD had told those Israelites they would surely die in the desert, and not one of them was left except Caleb son of Jephunneh and Joshua son of Nun.

Zelophehad's Daughters

27 The daughters of Zelophehad son of Hepher, the son of Gilead, the son of Makir, the son of Manasseh, belonged to the clans of Manasseh son of Joseph. The names of the daughters were Mahlah, Noah, Hoglah, Milcah and Tirzah. They approached 2the entrance to the Tent of Meeting and stood before Moses, Eleazar the priest, the leaders and the whole assembly, and said, 3"Our father died in the desert. He was not among Korah's followers, who banded together against the LORD, but he died for his own sin and left no sons. 4Why should our father's name disappear from his clan because he had no son? Give us property among our father's relatives."

5So Moses brought their case before the LORD 6and the LORD said to him, 7"What Zelophehad's daughters are saying is right. You must certainly give them property as an inheritance among their father's relatives and give their father's inheritance over to them.

8"Say to the Israelites, 'If a man dies and leaves no son, give his inheritance over to his daughter. 9If he has no daughter, give his inheritance to his brothers. 10If he has no brothers, give his inheritance to his father's brothers. 11If his father had no brothers, give his inheritance to the nearest relative in his clan, that he may possess it. This is to be a legal requirement for the Israelites, as the LORD commanded Moses.'"

Joshua to Succeed Moses

12Then the LORD said to Moses, "Go up this mountain in the Abarim Range and see the land I have given the Israelites. 13After you have seen it, you too will be gathered to your people, as your brother Aaron was, 14for when the community rebelled at the waters in the Desert of Zin, both of you disobeyed my command to honour me as holy before their eyes." (These were the waters of Meribah Kadesh, in the Desert of Zin.)

---

e40 Samaritan Pentateuch and Vulgate (see also Septuagint); Masoretic Text does not have *through Ard,*
f59 Or *Jochebed, a daughter of Levi, who was born to Levi*

¹⁵Moses said to the LORD, ¹⁶"May the LORD, the God of the spirits of all mankind, appoint a man over this community ¹⁷to go out and come in before them, one who will lead them out and bring them in, so that the LORD's people will not be like sheep without a shepherd."

¹⁸So the LORD said to Moses, "Take Joshua son of Nun, a man in whom is the spirit,[a] and lay your hand on him. ¹⁹Make him stand before Eleazar the priest and the entire assembly and commission him in their presence. ²⁰Give him some of your authority so that the whole Israelite community will obey him. ²¹He is to stand before Eleazar the priest, who will obtain decisions for him by enquiring of the Urim before the LORD. At his command he and the entire community of the Israelites will go out, and at his command they will come in."

²²Moses did as the LORD commanded him. He took Joshua and made him stand before Eleazar the priest and the whole assembly. ²³Then he laid his hands on him and commissioned him, as the LORD instructed through Moses.

Daily Offerings

28 The LORD said to Moses, ²"Give this command to the Israelites and say to them: 'See that you present to me at the appointed time the food for my offerings made by fire, as an aroma pleasing to me.' ³Say to them: 'This is the offering made by fire that you are to present to the LORD: two lambs a year old without defect, as a regular burnt offering each day. ⁴Prepare one lamb in the morning and the other at twilight, ⁵together with a grain offering of a tenth of an ephah[a] of fine flour mixed with a quarter of a hin[b] of oil from pressed olives. ⁶This is the regular burnt offering instituted at Mount Sinai as a pleasing aroma, an offering made to the LORD by fire. ⁷The accompanying drink offering is to be a quarter of a hin of fermented drink with each lamb. Pour out the drink offering to the LORD at the sanctuary. ⁸Prepare the second lamb at twilight, along with the same kind of grain offering and drink offering that you prepare in the morning. This is an offering made by fire, an aroma pleasing to the LORD.

Sabbath Offerings

⁹"'On the Sabbath day, make an offering of two lambs a year old without defect, together with its drink offering and a grain offering of two-tenths of an ephah[c] of fine flour mixed with oil. ¹⁰This is the burnt offering for every Sabbath, in addition to the regular burnt offering and its drink offering.

Monthly Offerings

¹¹"'On the first of every month, present to the LORD a burnt offering of two young bulls, one ram and seven male lambs a year old, all without defect. ¹²With each bull there is to be a grain offering of three-tenths of an ephah[d] of fine flour mixed with oil; with the ram, a grain offering of two-tenths of an ephah of fine flour mixed with oil; ¹³and with each lamb, a grain offering of a tenth of an ephah of fine flour mixed with oil. This is for a burnt offering, a pleasing aroma, an offering made to the LORD by fire. ¹⁴With each bull there is to be a drink offering of half a hin[e] of wine; with the ram, a third of a hin;[f] and with each lamb, a quarter of a hin. This is the monthly burnt offering to be made at each new moon during the year. ¹⁵Besides the regular burnt offering with its drink offering, one male goat is to be presented to the LORD as a sin offering.

The Passover

¹⁶"'On the fourteenth day of the first month the LORD's Passover is to be held. ¹⁷On the fifteenth day of this month there is to be a festival; for seven days eat bread made without yeast. ¹⁸On the first day hold a sacred assembly and do no regular work. ¹⁹Present to the LORD an offering made by fire, a burnt offering of two young bulls, one ram and seven male lambs a year old, all without defect. ²⁰With each bull prepare a grain offering of three-tenths of an ephah of fine flour mixed with oil; with the ram, two-tenths; ²¹and with each of the seven lambs, one-tenth. ²²Include one male goat as a sin offering to make atonement for you. ²³Prepare these in addition to the regular morning burnt offering. ²⁴In this way prepare the food for the offering made by fire every day for seven days as an aroma pleasing to the LORD; it is to be prepared in addition to the regular burnt offering and its drink offering. ²⁵On the seventh day hold a sacred assembly and do no regular work.

Feast of Weeks

²⁶"'On the day of firstfruits, when you present to the LORD an offering of new grain during the Feast of Weeks, hold a sacred assembly and do no regular work. ²⁷Present a burnt offering of two young bulls, one ram and seven male lambs a year old as an aroma pleasing to the LORD. ²⁸With each bull there is to be a grain offering of three-tenths of an ephah of fine flour mixed with oil; with the ram, two-tenths; ²⁹and with each of the seven lambs, one-tenth. ³⁰Include one male goat to make atonement for you. ³¹Prepare these together with their drink offerings, in addition to the regular burnt offering and its grain offering. Be sure the animals are without defect.

Feast of Trumpets

29 "'On the first day of the seventh month hold a sacred assembly and do no regular work. It is a day for you to sound the trumpets. ²As an aroma pleasing to the

---

[a]18 Or *Spirit*   [a]5 That is, probably about 4 pints (about 2 litres); also in verses 13, 21 and 29
[b]5 That is, probably about 1½ pints (about 1 litre); also in verses 7 and 14
[c]9 That is, probably about 7½ pints (about 4.5 litres); also in verses 12, 20 and 28
[d]12 That is, probably about 11½ pints (about 6.5 litres); also in verses 20 and 28
[e]14 That is, probably about 3 pints (about 2 litres)   [f]14 That is, probably about 2¼ pints (about 1.2 litres)

Lord, prepare a burnt offering of one young bull, one ram and seven male lambs a year old, all without defect. ³With the bull prepare a grain offering of three-tenths of an ephah*a* of fine flour mixed with oil; with the ram, two-tenths;*b* ⁴and with each of the seven lambs, one-tenth.*c* ⁵Include one male goat as a sin offering to make atonement for you. ⁶These are in addition to the monthly and daily burnt offerings with their grain offerings and drink offerings as specified. They are offerings made to the Lord by fire—a pleasing aroma.

Day of Atonement

⁷" 'On the tenth day of this seventh month hold a sacred assembly. You must deny yourselves*d* and do no work. ⁸Present as an aroma pleasing to the Lord a burnt offering of one young bull, one ram and seven male lambs a year old, all without defect. ⁹With the bull prepare a grain offering of three-tenths of an ephah of fine flour mixed with oil; with the ram, two-tenths; ¹⁰and with each of the seven lambs, one-tenth. ¹¹Include one male goat as a sin offering, in addition to the sin offering for atonement and the regular burnt offering with its grain offering, and their drink offerings.

Feast of Tabernacles

¹²" 'On the fifteenth day of the seventh month, hold a sacred assembly and do no regular work. Celebrate a festival to the Lord for seven days. ¹³Present an offering made by fire as an aroma pleasing to the Lord, a burnt offering of thirteen young bulls, two rams and fourteen male lambs a year old, all without defect. ¹⁴With each of the thirteen bulls prepare a grain offering of three-tenths of an ephah of fine flour mixed with oil; with each of the two rams, two-tenths; ¹⁵and with each of the fourteen lambs, one-tenth. ¹⁶Include one male goat as a sin offering, in addition to the regular burnt offering with its grain offering and drink offering.

¹⁷" 'On the second day prepare twelve young bulls, two rams and fourteen male lambs a year old, all without defect. ¹⁸With the bulls, rams and lambs, prepare their grain offerings and drink offerings according to the number specified. ¹⁹Include one male goat as a sin offering, in addition to the regular burnt offering with its grain offering, and their drink offerings.

²⁰" 'On the third day prepare eleven bulls, two rams and fourteen male lambs a year old, all without defect. ²¹With the bulls, rams and lambs, prepare their grain offerings and drink offerings according to the number specified. ²²Include one male goat as a sin offering, in addition to the regular burnt offering with its grain offering and drink offering.

²³" 'On the fourth day prepare ten bulls, two rams and fourteen male lambs a year old, all without defect. ²⁴With the bulls, rams and lambs, prepare their grain offerings and drink

offerings according to the number specified. ²⁵Include one male goat as a sin offering, in addition to the regular burnt offering with its grain offering and drink offering.

²⁶" 'On the fifth day prepare nine bulls, two rams and fourteen male lambs a year old, all without defect. ²⁷With the bulls, rams and lambs, prepare their grain offerings and drink offerings according to the number specified. ²⁸Include one male goat as a sin offering, in addition to the regular burnt offering with its grain offering and drink offering.

²⁹" 'On the sixth day prepare eight bulls, two rams and fourteen male lambs a year old, all without defect. ³⁰With the bulls, rams and lambs, prepare their grain offerings and drink offerings according to the number specified. ³¹Include one male goat as a sin offering, in addition to the regular burnt offering with its grain offering and drink offering.

³²" 'On the seventh day prepare seven bulls, two rams and fourteen male lambs a year old, all without defect. ³³With the bulls, rams and lambs, prepare their grain offerings and drink offerings according to the number specified. ³⁴Include one male goat as a sin offering, in addition to the regular burnt offering with its grain offering and drink offering.

³⁵" 'On the eighth day hold an assembly and do no regular work. ³⁶Present an offering made by fire as an aroma pleasing to the Lord, a burnt offering of one bull, one ram and seven male lambs a year old, all without defect. ³⁷With the bull, the ram and the lambs, prepare their grain offerings and drink offerings according to the number specified. ³⁸Include one male goat as a sin offering, in addition to the regular burnt offering with its grain offering and drink offering.

³⁹" 'In addition to what you vow and your freewill offerings, prepare these for the Lord at your appointed feasts: your burnt offerings, grain offerings, drink offerings and fellowship offerings.' "*e*

⁴⁰Moses told the Israelites all that the Lord commanded him.

Vows

30 Moses said to the heads of the tribes of Israel: "This is what the Lord commands: ²When a man makes a vow to the Lord or takes an oath to bind himself by a pledge, he must not break his word but must do everything he said.

³"When a young woman still living in her father's house makes a vow to the Lord or binds herself by a pledge ⁴and her father hears about her vow or pledge but says nothing to her, then all her vows and every pledge by which she bound herself will stand. ⁵But if her father forbids her when he hears about it, none of her vows or the pledges by which she bound herself will stand; the Lord will release her because her father has forbidden her.

⁶"If she marries after she makes a vow or

---

a3 That is, probably about 11½ pints (about 6.5 litres); also in verses 9 and 14
b3 That is, probably about 7½ pints (about 4.5 litres); also in verses 9 and 14
c4 That is, probably about 4 pints (about 2 litres); also in verses 10 and 15
d7 Or *must fast*   *e39* Traditionally *peace offerings*

after her lips utter a rash promise by which she binds herself [7]and her husband hears about it but says nothing to her, then her vows or the pledges by which she bound herself will stand. [8]But if her husband forbids her when he hears about it, he nullifies the vow that binds her or the rash promise by which she binds herself, and the LORD will release her.

[9]"Any vow or obligation taken by a widow or divorced woman will be binding on her.

[10]"If a woman living with her husband makes a vow or binds herself by a pledge under oath [11]and her husband hears about it but says nothing to her and does not forbid her, then all her vows or the pledges by which she bound herself will stand. [12]But if her husband nullifies them when he hears about them, then none of the vows or pledges that came from her lips will stand. Her husband has nullified them, and the LORD will release her. [13]Her husband may confirm or nullify any vow she makes or any sworn pledge to deny herself. [14]But if her husband says nothing to her about it from day to day, then he confirms all her vows or the pledges binding on her. He confirms them by saying nothing to her when he hears about them. [15]If, however, he nullifies them some time after he hears about them, then he is responsible for her guilt."

[16]These are the regulations the LORD gave Moses concerning relationships between a man and his wife, and between a father and his young daughter still living in his house.

Vengeance on the Midianites

31 The LORD said to Moses, [2]"Take vengeance on the Midianites for the Israelites. After that, you will be gathered to your people."

[3]So Moses said to the people, "Arm some of your men to go to war against the Midianites and to carry out the LORD's vengeance on them. [4]Send into battle a thousand men from each of the tribes of Israel." [5]So twelve thousand men armed for battle, a thousand from each tribe, were supplied from the clans of Israel. [6]Moses sent them into battle, a thousand from each tribe, along with Phinehas son of Eleazar, the priest, who took with him articles from the sanctuary and the trumpets for signalling.

[7]They fought against Midian, as the LORD commanded Moses, and killed every man. [8]Among their victims were Evi, Rekem, Zur, Hur and Reba—the five kings of Midian. They also killed Balaam son of Beor with the sword. [9]The Israelites captured the Midianite women and children and took all the Midianite herds, flocks and goods as plunder. [10]They burned all the towns where the Midianites had settled, as well as all their camps. [11]They took all the plunder and spoils, including the people and animals, [12]and brought the captives, spoils and plunder to Moses and Eleazar the priest and the Israelite assembly at their camp on the plains of Moab, by the Jordan across from Jericho.[a]

[13]Moses, Eleazar the priest and all the leaders of the community went to meet them outside the camp. [14]Moses was angry with the officers of the army—the commanders of thousands and commanders of hundreds—who returned from the battle.

[15]"Have you allowed all the women to live?" he asked them. [16]"They were the ones who followed Balaam's advice and were the means of turning the Israelites away from the LORD in what happened at Peor, so that a plague struck the LORD's people. [17]Now kill all the boys. And kill every woman who has slept with a man, [18]but save for yourselves every girl who has never slept with a man.

[19]"All of you who have killed anyone or touched anyone who was killed must stay outside the camp seven days. On the third and seventh days you must purify yourselves and your captives. [20]Purify every garment as well as everything made of leather, goat hair or wood."

[21]Then Eleazar the priest said to the soldiers who had gone into battle, "This is the requirement of the law that the LORD gave Moses: [22]Gold, silver, bronze, iron, tin, lead [23]and anything else that can withstand fire must be put through the fire, and then it will be clean. But it must also be purified with the water of cleansing. And whatever cannot withstand fire must be put through that water. [24]On the seventh day wash your clothes and you will be clean. Then you may come into the camp."

Dividing the Spoils

[25]The LORD said to Moses, [26]"You and Eleazar the priest and the family heads of the community are to count all the people and animals that were captured. [27]Divide the spoils between the soldiers who took part in the battle and the rest of the community. [28]From the soldiers who fought in the battle, set apart as tribute for the LORD one out of every five hundred, whether persons, cattle, donkeys, sheep or goats. [29]Take this tribute from their half share and give it to Eleazar the priest as the LORD's part. [30]From the Israelites' half, select one out of every fifty, whether persons, cattle, donkeys, sheep, goats or other animals. Give them to the Levites, who are responsible for the care of the LORD's tabernacle." [31]So Moses and Eleazar the priest did as the LORD commanded Moses.

[32]The plunder remaining from the spoils that the soldiers took was 675,000 sheep, [33]72,000 cattle, [34]61,000 donkeys [35]and 32,000 women who had never slept with a man.

[36]The half share of those who fought in the battle was:

337,500 sheep, [37]of which the tribute for the LORD was 675;
[38]36,000 cattle, of which the tribute for the LORD was 72;
[39]30,500 donkeys, of which the tribute for the LORD was 61;

---

[a]12 Hebrew *Jordan of Jericho*; possibly an ancient name for the Jordan River

⁴⁰16,000 people, of which the tribute for the LORD was 32.

⁴¹Moses gave the tribute to Eleazar the priest as the LORD's part, as the LORD commanded Moses.

⁴²The half belonging to the Israelites, which Moses set apart from that of the fighting men— ⁴³the community's half—was 337,500 sheep, ⁴⁴436,000 cattle, ⁴⁵30,500 donkeys ⁴⁶and 16,000 people. ⁴⁷From the Israelites' half, Moses selected one out of every fifty persons and animals, as the LORD commanded him, and gave them to the Levites, who were responsible for the care of the LORD's tabernacle.

⁴⁸Then the officers who were over the units of the army—the commanders of thousands and commanders of hundreds—went to Moses ⁴⁹and said to him, "Your servants have counted the soldiers under our command, and not one is missing. ⁵⁰So we have brought as an offering to the LORD the gold articles each of us acquired—armlets, bracelets, signet rings, ear-rings and necklaces—to make atonement for ourselves before the LORD."

⁵¹Moses and Eleazar the priest accepted from them the gold—all the handcrafted articles. ⁵²All the gold from the commanders of thousands and commanders of hundreds that Moses and Eleazar presented as a gift to the LORD weighed 16,750 shekels.ᵇ ⁵³Each soldier had taken plunder for himself. ⁵⁴Moses and Eleazar the priest accepted the gold from the commanders of thousands and commanders of hundreds and brought it into the Tent of Meeting as a memorial for the Israelites before the LORD.

The Transjordan Tribes

32 The Reubenites and Gadites, who had very large herds and flocks, saw that the lands of Jazer and Gilead were suitable for livestock. ²So they came to Moses and Eleazar the priest and to the leaders of the community, and said, ³"Ataroth, Dibon, Jazer, Nimrah, Heshbon, Elealeh, Sebam, Nebo and Beon—⁴the land the LORD subdued before the people of Israel—are suitable for livestock, and your servants have livestock. ⁵If we have found favour in your eyes," they said, "let this land be given to your servants as our possession. Do not make us cross the Jordan."

⁶Moses said to the Gadites and Reubenites, "Shall your countrymen go to war while you sit here? ⁷Why do you discourage the Israelites from going over into the land the LORD has given them? ⁸This is what your fathers did when I sent them from Kadesh Barnea to look over the land. ⁹After they went up to the Valley of Eshcol and viewed the land, they discouraged the Israelites from entering the land the LORD had given them. ¹⁰The LORD's anger was aroused that day and he swore this oath: ¹¹'Because they have not followed me wholeheartedly, not one of the men twenty years old or more who came up

out of Egypt will see the land I promised on oath to Abraham, Isaac and Jacob—¹²not one except Caleb son of Jephunneh the Kenizzite and Joshua son of Nun, for they followed the LORD wholeheartedly.' ¹³The LORD's anger burned against Israel and he made them wander in the desert for forty years, until the whole generation of those who had done evil in his sight was gone.

¹⁴"And here you are, a brood of sinners, standing in the place of your fathers and making the LORD even more angry with Israel. ¹⁵If you turn away from following him, he will again leave all this people in the desert, and you will be the cause of their destruction."

¹⁶Then they came up to him and said, "We would like to build pens here for our livestock and cities for our women and children. ¹⁷But we are ready to arm ourselves and go ahead of the Israelites until we have brought them to their place. Meanwhile our women and children will live in fortified cities, for protection from the inhabitants of the land. ¹⁸We will not return to our homes until every Israelite has received his inheritance. ¹⁹We will not receive any inheritance with them on the other side of the Jordan, because our inheritance has come to us on the east side of the Jordan."

²⁰Then Moses said to them, "If you will do this—if you will arm yourselves before the LORD for battle, ²¹and if all of you will go armed over the Jordan before the LORD until he has driven his enemies out before him —²²then when the land is subdued before the LORD, you may return and be free from your obligation to the LORD and to Israel. And this land will be your possession before the LORD.

²³"But if you fail to do this, you will be sinning against the LORD; and you may be sure that your sin will find you out. ²⁴Build cities for your women and children, and pens for your flocks, but do what you have promised."

²⁵The Gadites and Reubenites said to Moses, "We your servants will do as our lord commands. ²⁶Our children and wives, our flocks and herds will remain here in the cities of Gilead. ²⁷But your servants, every man armed for battle, will cross over to fight before the LORD, just as our lord says."

²⁸Then Moses gave orders about them to Eleazar the priest and Joshua son of Nun and to the family heads of the Israelite tribes. ²⁹He said to them, "If the Gadites and Reubenites, every man armed for battle, cross over the Jordan with you before the LORD, then when the land is subdued before you, give them the land of Gilead as their possession. ³⁰But if they do not cross over with you armed, they must accept their possession with you in Canaan."

³¹The Gadites and Reubenites answered, "Your servants will do what the LORD has said. ³²We will cross over before the LORD into Canaan armed, but the property we inherit will be on this side of the Jordan."

³³Then Moses gave to the Gadites, the

ᵇ52 That is, about 420 pounds (about 190 kilograms)

Reubenites and the half-tribe of Manasseh son of Joseph the kingdom of Sihon king of the Amorites and the kingdom of Og king of Bashan—the whole land with its cities and the territory around them.

³⁴The Gadites built up Dibon, Ataroth, Aroer, ³⁵Atroth Shophan, Jazer, Jogbehah, ³⁶Beth Nimrah and Beth Haran as fortified cities, and built pens for their flocks. ³⁷And the Reubenites rebuilt Heshbon, Elealeh and Kiriathaim, ³⁸as well as Nebo and Baal Meon (these names were changed) and Sibmah. They gave names to the cities they rebuilt.

³⁹The descendants of Makir son of Manasseh went to Gilead, captured it and drove out the Amorites who were there. ⁴⁰So Moses gave Gilead to the Makirites, the descendants of Manasseh, and they settled there. ⁴¹Jair, a descendant of Manasseh, captured their settlements and called them Havvoth Jair.[a] ⁴²And Nobah captured Kenath and its surrounding settlements and called it Nobah after himself.

Stages in Israel's Journey

33 Here are the stages in the journey of the Israelites when they came out of Egypt by divisions under the leadership of Moses and Aaron. ²At the LORD's command Moses recorded the stages in their journey. This is their journey by stages:

³The Israelites set out from Rameses on the fifteenth day of the first month, the day after the Passover. They marched out boldly in full view of all the Egyptians, ⁴who were burying all their firstborn, whom the LORD had struck down among them; for the LORD had brought judgment on their gods.

⁵The Israelites left Rameses and camped at Succoth.

⁶They left Succoth and camped at Etham, on the edge of the desert.

⁷They left Etham, turned back to Pi Hahiroth, to the east of Baal Zephon, and camped near Migdol.

⁸They left Pi Hahiroth[a] and passed through the sea into the desert, and when they had travelled for three days in the Desert of Etham, they camped at Marah.

⁹They left Marah and went to Elim, where there were twelve springs and seventy palm trees, and they camped there.

¹⁰They left Elim and camped by the Red Sea.[b]

¹¹They left the Red Sea and camped in the Desert of Sin.

¹²They left the Desert of Sin and camped at Dophkah.

¹³They left Dophkah and camped at Alush.

¹⁴They left Alush and camped at Rephidim, where there was no water for the people to drink.

¹⁵They left Rephidim and camped in the Desert of Sinai.

¹⁶They left the Desert of Sinai and camped at Kibroth Hattaavah.

¹⁷They left Kibroth Hattaavah and camped at Hazeroth.

¹⁸They left Hazeroth and camped at Rithmah.

¹⁹They left Rithmah and camped at Rimmon Perez.

²⁰They left Rimmon Perez and camped at Libnah.

²¹They left Libnah and camped at Rissah.

²²They left Rissah and camped at Kehelathah.

²³They left Kehelathah and camped at Mount Shepher.

²⁴They left Mount Shepher and camped at Haradah.

²⁵They left Haradah and camped at Makheloth.

²⁶They left Makheloth and camped at Tahath.

²⁷They left Tahath and camped at Terah.

²⁸They left Terah and camped at Mithcah.

²⁹They left Mithcah and camped at Hashmonah.

³⁰They left Hashmonah and camped at Moseroth.

³¹They left Moseroth and camped at Bene Jaakan.

³²They left Bene Jaakan and camped at Hor Haggidgad.

³³They left Hor Haggidgad and camped at Jotbathah.

³⁴They left Jotbathah and camped at Abronah.

³⁵They left Abronah and camped at Ezion Geber.

³⁶They left Ezion Geber and camped at Kadesh, in the Desert of Zin.

³⁷They left Kadesh and camped at Mount Hor, on the border of Edom. ³⁸At the LORD's command Aaron the priest went up Mount Hor, where he died on the first day of the fifth month of the fortieth year after the Israelites came out of Egypt. ³⁹Aaron was a hundred and twenty-three years old when he died on Mount Hor.

⁴⁰The Canaanite king of Arad, who lived in the Negev of Canaan, heard that the Israelites were coming.

⁴¹They left Mount Hor and camped at Zalmonah.

⁴²They left Zalmonah and camped at Punon.

⁴³They left Punon and camped at Oboth.

⁴⁴They left Oboth and camped at Iye Abarim, on the border of Moab.

---

[a]41 Or them the settlements of Jair
[a]8 Many manuscripts of the Masoretic Text, Samaritan Pentateuch and Vulgate; most manuscripts of the Masoretic Text left from before Hahiroth   [b]10 Hebrew Yam Suph; that is, Sea of Reeds; also in verse 11

45They left Iyim[c] and camped at Dibon Gad.

46They left Dibon Gad and camped at Almon Diblathaim.

47They left Almon Diblathaim and camped in the mountains of Abarim, near Nebo.

48They left the mountains of Abarim and camped on the plains of Moab by the Jordan across from Jericho.[d] 49There on the plains of Moab they camped along the Jordan from Beth Jeshimoth to Abel Shittim.

50On the plains of Moab by the Jordan across from Jericho the LORD said to Moses, 51"Speak to the Israelites and say to them: 'When you cross the Jordan into Canaan, 52drive out all the inhabitants of the land before you. Destroy all their carved images and their cast idols, and demolish all their high places. 53Take possession of the land and settle in it, for I have given you the land to possess. 54Distribute the land by lot, according to your clans. To a larger group give a larger inheritance, and to a smaller group a smaller one. Whatever falls to them by lot will be theirs. Distribute it according to your ancestral tribes.

55"'But if you do not drive out the inhabitants of the land, those you allow to remain will become barbs in your eyes and thorns in your sides. They will give you trouble in the land where you will live. 56And then I will do to you what I plan to do to them.'"

Boundaries of Canaan

34 The LORD said to Moses, 2"Command the Israelites and say to them: 'When you enter Canaan, the land that will be allotted to you as an inheritance will have these boundaries:

3"'Your southern side will include some of the Desert of Zin along the border of Edom. On the east, your southern boundary will start from the end of the Salt Sea,[a] 4cross south of Scorpion[b] Pass, continue on to Zin and go south of Kadesh Barnea. Then it will go to Hazar Addar and over to Azmon, 5where it will turn, join the Wadi of Egypt and end at the Sea.[c]

6"'Your western boundary will be the coast of the Great Sea. This will be your boundary on the west.

7"'For your northern boundary, run a line from the Great Sea to Mount Hor 8and from Mount Hor to Lebo[d] Hamath. Then the boundary will go to Zedad, 9continue to Ziphron and end at Hazar Enan. This will be your boundary on the north.

10"'For your eastern boundary, run a line from Hazar Enan to Shepham. 11The boundary will go down from Shepham to Riblah on the east side of Ain and continue along the slopes east of the Sea of Kinnereth.[e] 12Then the boundary will go down along the Jordan and end at the Salt Sea.

"'This will be your land, with its boundaries on every side.'"

13Moses commanded the Israelites: "Assign this land by lot as an inheritance. The LORD has ordered that it be given to the nine and a half tribes, 14because the families of the tribe of Reuben, the tribe of Gad and the half-tribe of Manasseh have received their inheritance. 15These two and a half tribes have received their inheritance on the east side of the Jordan of Jericho,[f] towards the sunrise."

16The LORD said to Moses, 17"These are the names of the men who are to assign the land for you as an inheritance: Eleazar the priest and Joshua son of Nun. 18And appoint one leader from each tribe to help assign the land. 19These are their names:

Caleb son of Jephunneh,
    from the tribe of Judah;
20Shemuel son of Ammihud,
    from the tribe of Simeon;
21Elidad son of Kislon,
    from the tribe of Benjamin;
22Bukki son of Jogli,
    the leader from the tribe of Dan;
23Hanniel son of Ephod,
    the leader from the tribe of Manasseh
    son of Joseph;
24Kemuel son of Shiphtan,
    the leader from the tribe of Ephraim
    son of Joseph;
25Elizaphan son of Parnach,
    the leader from the tribe of Zebulun;
26Paltiel son of Azzan,
    the leader from the tribe of Issachar;
27Ahihud son of Shelomi,
    the leader from the tribe of Asher;
28Pedahel son of Ammihud,
    the leader from the tribe of Naphtali."

29These are the men the LORD commanded to assign the inheritance to the Israelites in the land of Canaan.

Towns for the Levites

35 On the plains of Moab by the Jordan across from Jericho,[a] the LORD said to Moses, 2"Command the Israelites to give the Levites towns to live in from the inheritance the Israelites will possess. And give them pasture-lands around the towns. 3Then they will have towns to live in and pasture-lands for their cattle, flocks and all their other livestock.

4"The pasture-lands around the towns that you give the Levites will extend out fifteen hundred feet[b] from the town wall. 5Outside the town, measure three thousand feet[c] on

c45 That is, Iye Abarim
d48 Hebrew *Jordan of Jericho*; possibly an ancient name for the Jordan River; also in verse 50
a3 That is, the Dead Sea; also in verse 12   b4 Hebrew *Akrabbim*
c5 That is, the Mediterranean; also in verses 6 and 7   d8 Or *to the entrance to*   e11 That is, Galilee
f15 *Jordan of Jericho* was possibly an ancient name for the Jordan River.
a1 Hebrew *Jordan of Jericho*; possibly an ancient name for the Jordan River
b4 Hebrew *a thousand cubits* (about 450 metres)   c5 Hebrew *two thousand cubits* (about 900 metres)

the east side, three thousand on the south side, three thousand on the west and three thousand on the north, with the town in the centre. They will have this area as pasture-land for the towns.

Cities of Refuge

6"Six of the towns you give the Levites will be cities of refuge, to which a person who has killed someone may flee. In addition, give them forty-two other towns. 7In all you must give the Levites forty-eight towns, together with their pasture-lands. 8The towns you give the Levites from the land the Israelites possess are to be given in proportion to the inheritance of each tribe: Take many towns from a tribe that has many, but few from one that has few."

9Then the LORD said to Moses: 10"Speak to the Israelites and say to them: 'When you cross the Jordan into Canaan, 11select some towns to be your cities of refuge, to which a person who has killed someone accidentally may flee. 12They will be places of refuge from the avenger, so that a person accused of murder may not die before he stands trial before the assembly. 13These six towns you give will be your cities of refuge. 14Give three on this side of the Jordan and three in Canaan as cities of refuge. 15These six towns will be a place of refuge for Israelites, aliens and any other people living among them, so that anyone who has killed another accidentally can flee there.

16"'If a man strikes someone with an iron object so that he dies, he is a murderer; the murderer shall be put to death. 17Or if anyone has a stone in his hand that could kill, and he strikes someone so that he dies, he is a murderer; the murderer shall be put to death. 18Or if anyone has a wooden object in his hand that could kill, and he hits someone so that he dies, he is a murderer; the murderer shall be put to death. 19The avenger of blood shall put the murderer to death; when he meets him, he shall put him to death. 20If anyone with malice aforethought pushes another or throws something at him intentionally so that he dies 21or if in hostility he hits him with his fist so that he dies, that person shall be put to death; he is a murderer. The avenger of blood shall put the murderer to death when he meets him.

22"'But if without hostility someone suddenly pushes another or throws something at him unintentionally 23or, without seeing him, drops a stone on him that could kill him, and he dies, then since he was not his enemy and he did not intend to harm him, 24the assembly must judge between him and the avenger of blood according to these regulations. 25The assembly must protect the one accused of murder from the avenger of blood and send him back to the city of refuge to which he fled. He must stay there until the death of the high priest, who was anointed with holy oil.

26"'But if the accused ever goes outside the limits of the city of refuge to which he has fled 27and the avenger of blood finds him

outside the city, the avenger of blood may kill the accused without being guilty of murder. 28The accused must stay in his city of refuge until the death of the high priest; only after the death of the high priest may he return to his own property.

29"'These are to be legal requirements for you throughout the generations to come, wherever you live.

30"'Anyone who kills a person is to be put to death as a murderer only on the testimony of witnesses. But no-one is to be put to death on the testimony of only one witness.

31"'Do not accept a ransom for the life of a murderer, who deserves to die. He must surely be put to death.

32"'Do not accept a ransom for anyone who has fled to a city of refuge and so allow him to go back and live on his own land before the death of the high priest.

33"'Do not pollute the land where you are. Bloodshed pollutes the land, and atonement cannot be made for the land on which blood has been shed, except by the blood of the one who shed it. 34Do not defile the land where you live and where I dwell, for I, the LORD, dwell among the Israelites.'"

Inheritance of Zelophehad's Daughters

36 The family heads of the clan of Gilead son of Makir, the son of Manasseh, who were from the clans of the descendants of Joseph, came and spoke before Moses and the leaders, the heads of the Israelite families. 2They said, "When the LORD commanded my lord to give the land as an inheritance to the Israelites by lot, he ordered you to give the inheritance of our brother Zelophehad to his daughters. 3Now suppose they marry men from other Israelite tribes; then their inheritance will be taken from our ancestral inheritance and added to that of the tribe they marry into. And so part of the inheritance allotted to us will be taken away. 4When the Year of Jubilee for the Israelites comes, their inheritance will be added to that of the tribe into which they marry, and their property will be taken from the tribal inheritance of our forefathers."

5Then at the LORD's command Moses gave this order to the Israelites: "What the tribe of the descendants of Joseph is saying is right. 6This is what the LORD commands for Zelophehad's daughters: They may marry anyone they please as long as they marry within the tribal clan of their father. 7No inheritance in Israel is to pass from tribe to tribe, for every Israelite shall keep the tribal land inherited from his forefathers. 8Every daughter who inherits land in any Israelite tribe must marry someone in her father's tribal clan, so that every Israelite will possess the inheritance of his fathers. 9No inheritance may pass from tribe to tribe, for each Israelite tribe is to keep the land it inherits."

10So Zelophehad's daughters did as the LORD commanded Moses. 11Zelophehad's daughters—Mahlah, Tirzah, Hoglah, Milcah and Noah—married their cousins on their

NUMBERS 35:9–25

'Select some towns to be your cities of refuge, to which a person who has killed someone accidentally may flee' (v. 11).

GOD WAS INTENT upon making a provision whereby those who had inadvertently killed another could be afforded a reasonable trial and measure of security from vengeful kinsmen. The reference to the avenger of blood points to the custom whereby the next of kin avenged a murder, whether the death be wilful or accidental. Little imagination is needed to envisage the dreadful situation where one act of revenge led to another until families and tribes became embroiled in a blood feud of fearsome proportions. To eliminate this, God planned the creation of six cities of refuge.

The cities were to be strategically located to ensure accessibility to any fugitive. Once he arrived in the city, if he was found guilty of murder, then the avenger would carry out the sentence. If, however, he was innocent of murder but guilty of manslaughter, he remained in the city of refuge for life, or until the death of the high priest. Should the fugitive ever leave the city of refuge, it was permissible for the avenger to slay him.

Although vengeance remained in the hands of the next of kin, the establishment of cities of refuge and the judicial assembly acknowledged the seriousness of the crime, the need to apply mercy where possible and to limit the possibility of a blood feud. Where man chooses revenge. God chooses a mercy.

> *Depth of mercy! Can there be*
> *Mercy still reserved for me?*
> *Can my God his wrath forbear?*
> *Me, the chief of sinners, spare?*

(*Charles Wesley*)

DEUTERONOMY 6:1–9

'Hear, O Israel: The LORD our God, the LORD is one. Love the LORD your God with all your heart and with all your soul and with all your strength' (vv. 4, 5).

EAR, HEAR, HEART – AND TALK! Vv. 4–5, with the instructions which follow, form the *Shema* or basic Hebrew statement of belief which is placed in the Mezuzah, a little box attached to doorposts of the houses of devout Jews, and touched as they go in and out – to remind them of the basic tenets of their faith.

It is the verse Jesus quoted to the lawyer (Mark 12:29). And to it Jesus added another Old Testament verse. Leviticus 19:18, 'but love your neighbour as yourself'. Note how Deuteronomy hesitates to take the step of including others within God's care.

'Hearing' these words is vitally important. In Hebrew 'hearing' implies also 'understanding'. That, to some, is quite different, but what is the use of hearing without taking it in and acting on it? From ear to heart, unfortunately, is often a long way and there are many hindrances before impressions on the eardrum are translated into heart-felt action.

One way of making sure the love of God is uppermost in the heart is to talk about it in ordinary conversation. We are told (v.7), to teach our children by talking. Not just by dictating, but by talking to each other, naturally in normal conversation as we do the ordinary things we have to do each day. Sunday has been set aside for such worship and conversation. Do take the opportunity to talk about your Lord – it will then be so much easier also to hear, and to apply what you hear in your heart.

You know, Lord, the pressures and joys of family life: bring your Spirit to bear on our close relationships; help parents teaching children to do so naturally, with compassion and understanding, being ready to listen and learn as well as to teach. May your name always be used in love, never blasphemously.

father's side. [12]They married within the clans of the descendants of Manasseh son of Joseph, and their inheritance remained in their father's clan and tribe.

[13]These are the commands and regulations the LORD gave through Moses to the Israelites on the plains of Moab by the Jordan across from Jericho.[a]

[a]13 Hebrew *Jordan of Jericho*; possibly an ancient name for the Jordan River

Deuteronomy

The Command to Leave Horeb

1 These are the words Moses spoke to all Israel in the desert east of the Jordan —that is, in the Arabah—opposite Suph, between Paran and Tophel, Laban, Hazeroth and Dizahab. ²(It takes eleven days to go from Horeb to Kadesh Barnea by the Mount Seir road.)

³In the fortieth year, on the first day of the eleventh month, Moses proclaimed to the Israelites all that the LORD had commanded him concerning them. ⁴This was after he had defeated Sihon king of the Amorites, who reigned in Heshbon, and at Edrei had defeated Og king of Bashan, who reigned in Ashtaroth.

⁵East of the Jordan in the territory of Moab, Moses began to expound this law, saying:

⁶The LORD our God said to us at Horeb, "You have stayed long enough at this mountain. ⁷Break camp and advance into the hill country of the Amorites; go to all the neighbouring peoples in the Arabah, in the mountains, in the western foothills, in the Negev and along the coast, to the land of the Canaanites and to Lebanon, as far as the great river, the Euphrates. ⁸See, I have given you this land. Go in and take possession of the land that the LORD swore he would give to your fathers—to Abraham, Isaac and Jacob —and to their descendants after them."

The Appointment of Leaders

⁹At that time I said to you, "You are too heavy a burden for me to carry alone. ¹⁰The LORD your God has increased your numbers so that today you are as many as the stars in the sky. ¹¹May the LORD, the God of your fathers, increase you a thousand times and bless you as he has promised! ¹²But how can I bear your problems and your burdens and your disputes all by myself? ¹³Choose some wise, understanding and respected men from each of your tribes, and I will set them over you."

¹⁴You answered me, "What you propose to do is good."

¹⁵So I took the leading men of your tribes, wise and respected men, and appointed them to have authority over you—as commanders of thousands, of hundreds, of fifties and of tens and as tribal officials. ¹⁶And I charged your judges at that time: Hear the disputes between your brothers and judge fairly, whether the case is between brother Israelites or between one of them and an alien. ¹⁷Do not show partiality in judging; hear both small and great alike. Do not be afraid of any man, for judgment belongs to God. Bring me any case too hard for you, and I will hear it. ¹⁸And at that time I told you everything you were to do.

Spies Sent Out

¹⁹Then, as the LORD our God commanded us, we set out from Horeb and went towards the hill country of the Amorites through all that vast and dreadful desert that you have seen, and so we reached Kadesh Barnea. ²⁰Then I said to you, "You have reached the hill country of the Amorites, which the LORD our God is giving us. ²¹See, the LORD your God has given you the land. Go up and take possession of it as the LORD, the God of your fathers, told you. Do not be afraid; do not be discouraged."

²²Then all of you came to me and said, "Let us send men ahead to spy out the land for us and bring back a report about the route we are to take and the towns we will come to."

²³The idea seemed good to me; so I selected twelve of you, one man from each tribe. ²⁴They left and went up into the hill country, and came to the Valley of Eshcol and explored it. ²⁵Taking with them some of the fruit of the land, they brought it down to us and reported, "It is a good land that the LORD our God is giving us."

Rebellion Against the LORD

²⁶But you were unwilling to go up; you rebelled against the command of the LORD your God. ²⁷You grumbled in your tents and said, "The LORD hates us; so he brought us out of Egypt to deliver us into the hands of the Amorites to destroy us. ²⁸Where can we go? Our brothers have made us lose heart. They say, 'The people are stronger and taller than we are; the cities are large, with walls up to the sky. We even saw the Anakites there.'"

²⁹Then I said to you, "Do not be terrified; do not be afraid of them. ³⁰The LORD your God, who is going before you, will fight for you, as he did for you in Egypt, before your

very eyes, [31]and in the desert. There you saw how the LORD your God carried you, as a father carries his son, all the way you went until you reached this place.''

[32]In spite of this, you did not trust in the LORD your God, [33]who went ahead of you on your journey, in fire by night and in a cloud by day, to search out places for you to camp and to show you the way you should go.

[34]When the LORD heard what you said, he was angry and solemnly swore: [35]''Not a man of this evil generation shall see the good land I swore to give your forefathers, [36]except Caleb son of Jephunneh. He will see it, and I will give him and his descendants the land he set his feet on, because he followed the LORD wholeheartedly.''

[37]Because of you the LORD became angry with me also and said, ''You shall not enter it, either. [38]But your assistant, Joshua son of Nun, will enter it. Encourage him, because he will lead Israel to inherit it. [39]And the little ones that you said would be taken captive, your children who do not yet know good from bad—they will enter the land. I will give it to them and they will take possession of it. [40]But as for you, turn round and set out towards the desert along the route to the Red Sea.''[a]

[41]Then you replied, ''We have sinned against the LORD. We will go up and fight, as the LORD our God commanded us.'' So every one of you put on his weapons, thinking it easy to go up into the hill country.

[42]But the LORD said to me, ''Tell them, 'Do not go up and fight, because I will not be with you. You will be defeated by your enemies.' ''

[43]So I told you, but you would not listen. You rebelled against the LORD's command and in your arrogance you marched up into the hill country. [44]The Amorites who lived in those hills came out against you; they chased you like a swarm of bees and beat you down from Seir all the way to Hormah. [45]You came back and wept before the LORD, but he paid no attention to your weeping and turned a deaf ear to you. [46]And so you stayed in Kadesh many days—all the time you spent there.

Wanderings in the Desert

2 Then we turned back and set out towards the desert along the route to the Red Sea,[a] as the LORD had directed me. For a long time we made our way around the hill country of Seir.

[2]Then the LORD said to me, [3]''You have made your way around this hill country long enough; now turn north. [4]Give the people these orders: 'You are about to pass through the territory of your brothers the descendants of Esau, who live in Seir. They will be afraid of you, but be very careful. [5]Do not provoke them to war, for I will not give you any of their land, not even enough to put your foot on. I have given Esau the hill country of Seir as his own. [6]You are to pay them in

silver for the food you eat and the water you drink.' ''

[7]The LORD your God has blessed you in all the work of your hands. He has watched over your journey through this vast desert. These forty years the LORD your God has been with you, and you have not lacked anything.

[8]So we went on past our brothers the descendants of Esau, who live in Seir. We turned from the Arabah road, which comes up from Elath and Ezion Geber, and travelled along the desert road of Moab.

[9]Then the LORD said to me, ''Do not harass the Moabites or provoke them to war, for I will not give you any part of their land. I have given Ar to the descendants of Lot as a possession.''

[10](The Emites used to live there—a people strong and numerous, and as tall as the Anakites. [11]Like the Anakites, they too were considered Rephaites, but the Moabites called them Emites. [12]Horites used to live in Seir, but the descendants of Esau drove them out. They destroyed the Horites from before them and settled in their place, just as Israel did in the land the LORD gave them as their possession.)

[13]And the LORD said, ''Now get up and cross the Zered Valley.'' So we crossed the valley.

[14]Thirty-eight years passed from the time we left Kadesh Barnea until we crossed the Zered Valley. By then, that entire generation of fighting men had perished from the camp, as the LORD had sworn to them. [15]The LORD's hand was against them until he had completely eliminated them from the camp.

[16]Now when the last of these fighting men among the people had died, [17]the LORD said to me, [18]''Today you are to pass by the region of Moab at Ar. [19]When you come to the Ammonites, do not harass them or provoke them to war, for I will not give you possession of any land belonging to the Ammonites. I have given it as a possession to the descendants of Lot.''

[20](That too was considered a land of the Rephaites, who used to live there; but the Ammonites called them Zamzummites. [21]They were a people strong and numerous, and as tall as the Anakites. The LORD destroyed them from before the Ammonites, who drove them out and settled in their place. [22]The LORD had done the same for the descendants of Esau, who lived in Seir, when he destroyed the Horites from before them. They drove them out and have lived in their place to this day. [23]And as for the Avvites who lived in villages as far as Gaza, the Caphtorites coming out from Caphtor[b] destroyed them and settled in their place.)

Defeat of Sihon King of Heshbon

[24]''Set out now and cross the Arnon Gorge. See, I have given into your hand Sihon the Amorite, king of Heshbon, and his country. Begin to take possession of it and engage him in battle. [25]This very day I will

---

[a]40 Hebrew *Yam Suph*; that is, Sea of Reeds   [a]1 Hebrew *Yam Suph*; that is, Sea of Reeds
[b]23 That is, Crete

begin to put the terror and fear of you on all the nations under heaven. They will hear reports of you and will tremble and be in anguish because of you."

26From the desert of Kedemoth I sent messengers to Sihon king of Heshbon offering peace and saying, 27"Let us pass through your country. We will stay on the main road; we will not turn aside to the right or to the left. 28Sell us food to eat and water to drink for their price in silver. Only let us pass through on foot—29as the descendants of Esau, who live in Seir, and the Moabites, who live in Ar, did for us—until we cross the Jordan into the land the LORD our God is giving us." 30But Sihon king of Heshbon refused to let us pass through. For the LORD your God had made his spirit stubborn and his heart obstinate in order to give him into your hands, as he has now done.

31The LORD said to me, "See, I have begun to deliver Sihon and his country over to you. Now begin to conquer and possess his land."

32When Sihon and all his army came out to meet us in battle at Jahaz, 33the LORD our God delivered him over to us and we struck him down, together with his sons and his whole army. 34At that time we took all his towns and completely destroyed[c] them—men, women and children. We left no survivors. 35But the livestock and the plunder from the towns we had captured we carried off for ourselves. 36From Aroer on the rim of the Arnon Gorge, and from the town in the gorge, even as far as Gilead, not one town was too strong for us. The LORD our God gave us all of them. 37But in accordance with the command of the LORD our God, you did not encroach on any of the land of the Ammonites, neither the land along the course of the Jabbok nor that around the towns in the hills.

Defeat of Og King of Bashan

3 Next we turned and went up along the road towards Bashan, and Og king of Bashan with his whole army marched out to meet us in battle at Edrei. 2The LORD said to me, "Do not be afraid of him, for I have handed him over to you with his whole army and his land. Do to him what you did to Sihon king of the Amorites, who reigned in Heshbon."

3So the LORD our God also gave into our hands Og king of Bashan and all his army. We struck them down, leaving no survivors. 4At that time we took all his cities. There was not one of the sixty cities that we did not take from them—the whole region of Argob, Og's kingdom in Bashan. 5All these cities were fortified with high walls and with gates and bars, and there were also a great many unwalled villages. 6We completely destroyed[a] them, as we had done with Sihon king of Heshbon, destroying[a] every city—men,

women and children. 7But all the livestock and the plunder from their cities we carried off for ourselves.

8So at that time we took from these two kings of the Amorites the territory east of the Jordan, from the Arnon Gorge as far as Mount Hermon. 9(Hermon is called Sirion by the Sidonians; the Amorites call it Senir.) 10We took all the towns on the plateau, and all Gilead, and all Bashan as far as Salecah and Edrei, towns of Og's kingdom in Bashan. 11(Only Og king of Bashan was left of the remnant of the Rephaites. His bed[b] was made of iron and was more than thirteen feet long and six feet wide.[c] It is still in Rabbah of the Ammonites.)

Division of the Land

12Of the land that we took over at that time, I gave the Reubenites and the Gadites the territory north of Aroer by the Arnon Gorge, including half the hill country of Gilead, together with its towns. 13The rest of Gilead and also all of Bashan, the kingdom of Og, I gave to the half-tribe of Manasseh. (The whole region of Argob in Bashan used to be known as a land of the Rephaites. 14Jair, a descendant of Manasseh, took the whole region of Argob as far as the border of the Geshurites and the Maacathites; it was named after him, so that to this day Bashan is called Havvoth Jair.[d]) 15And I gave Gilead to Makir. 16But to the Reubenites and the Gadites I gave the territory extending from Gilead down to the Arnon Gorge (the middle of the gorge being the border) and out to the Jabbok River, which is the border of the Ammonites. 17Its western border was the Jordan in the Arabah, from Kinnereth to the Sea of the Arabah (the Salt Sea[e]), below the slopes of Pisgah.

18I commanded you at that time: "The LORD your God has given you this land to take possession of it. But all your able-bodied men, armed for battle, must cross over ahead of your brother Israelites. 19However, your wives, your children and your livestock (I know you have much livestock) may stay in the towns I have given you, 20until the LORD gives rest to your brothers as he has to you, and they too have taken over the land that the LORD your God is giving them, across the Jordan. After that, each of you may go back to the possession I have given you."

Moses Forbidden to Cross the Jordan

21At that time I commanded Joshua: "You have seen with your own eyes all that the LORD your God has done to these two kings. The LORD will do the same to all the kingdoms over there where you are going. 22Do not be afraid of them; the LORD your God himself will fight for you."

---

[c]34 The Hebrew term refers to the irrevocable giving over of things or persons to the LORD, often by totally destroying them.
[a]6 The Hebrew term refers to the irrevocable giving over of things or persons to the LORD, often by totally destroying them.   [b]11 Or sarcophagus
[c]11 Hebrew nine cubits long and four cubits wide (about 4 metres long and 1.8 metres wide)
[d]14 Or called the settlements of Jair   [e]17 That is, the Dead Sea

23At that time I pleaded with the LORD: 24"O Sovereign LORD, you have begun to show to your servant your greatness and your strong hand. For what god is there in heaven or on earth who can do the deeds and mighty works you do? 25Let me go over and see the good land beyond the Jordan—that fine hill country and Lebanon."

26But because of you the LORD was angry with me and would not listen to me. "That is enough," the LORD said. "Do not speak to me any more about this matter. 27Go up to the top of Pisgah and look west and north and south and east. Look at the land with your own eyes, since you are not going to cross this Jordan. 28But commission Joshua, and encourage and strengthen him, for he will lead this people across and will cause them to inherit the land that you will see." 29So we stayed in the valley near Beth Peor.

Obedience Commanded

4 Hear now, O Israel, the decrees and laws I am about to teach you. Follow them so that you may live and may go in and take possession of the land that the LORD, the God of your fathers, is giving you. 2Do not add to what I command you and do not subtract from it, but keep the commands of the LORD your God that I give you.

3You saw with your own eyes what the LORD did at Baal Peor. The LORD your God destroyed from among you everyone who followed the Baal of Peor, 4but all of you who held fast to the LORD your God are still alive today.

5See, I have taught you decrees and laws as the LORD my God commanded me, so that you may follow them in the land you are entering to take possession of it. 6Observe them carefully, for this will show your wisdom and understanding to the nations, who will hear about all these decrees and say, "Surely this great nation is a wise and understanding people." 7What other nation is so great as to have their gods near them the way the LORD our God is near us whenever we pray to him? 8And what other nation is so great as to have such righteous decrees and laws as this body of laws I am setting before you today?

9Only be careful, and watch yourselves closely so that you do not forget the things your eyes have seen or let them slip from your heart as long as you live. Teach them to your children and to their children after them. 10Remember the day you stood before the LORD your God at Horeb, when he said to me, "Assemble the people before me to hear my words so that they may learn to revere me as long as they live in the land and may teach them to their children." 11You came near and stood at the foot of the mountain while it blazed with fire to the very heavens, with black clouds and deep darkness. 12Then the LORD spoke to you out of the fire. You heard the sound of words but saw no form; there was only a voice. 13He declared to you his covenant, the Ten Commandments, which he commanded you to follow and then wrote them on two stone tablets. 14And the LORD directed me at that time to teach you the decrees and laws you are to follow in the land that you are crossing the Jordan to possess.

Idolatry Forbidden

15You saw no form of any kind the day the LORD spoke to you at Horeb out of the fire. Therefore watch yourselves very carefully, 16so that you do not become corrupt and make for yourselves an idol, an image of any shape, whether formed like a man or a woman, 17or like any animal on earth or any bird that flies in the air, 18or like any creature that moves along the ground or any fish in the waters below. 19And when you look up to the sky and see the sun, the moon and the stars —all the heavenly array—do not be enticed into bowing down to them and worshipping things the LORD your God has apportioned to all the nations under heaven. 20But as for you, the LORD took you and brought you out of the iron-smelting furnace, out of Egypt, to be the people of his inheritance, as you now are.

21The LORD was angry with me because of you, and he solemnly swore that I would not cross the Jordan and enter the good land the LORD your God is giving you as your inheritance. 22I will die in this land; I will not cross the Jordan; but you are about to cross over and take possession of that good land. 23Be careful not to forget the covenant of the LORD your God that he made with you; do not make for yourselves an idol in the form of anything the LORD your God has forbidden. 24For the LORD your God is a consuming fire, a jealous God.

25After you have had children and grandchildren and have lived in the land a long time—if you then become corrupt and make any kind of idol, doing evil in the eyes of the LORD your God and provoking him to anger, 26I call heaven and earth as witnesses against you this day that you will quickly perish from the land that you are crossing the Jordan to possess. You will not live there long but will certainly be destroyed. 27The LORD will scatter you among the peoples, and only a few of you will survive among the nations to which the LORD will drive you. 28There you will worship man-made gods of wood and stone, which cannot see or hear or eat or smell. 29But if from there you seek the LORD your God, you will find him if you look for him with all your heart and with all your soul. 30When you are in distress and all these things have happened to you, then in later days you will return to the LORD your God and obey him. 31For the LORD your God is a merciful God; he will not abandon or destroy you or forget the covenant with your forefathers, which he confirmed to them by oath.

The LORD Is God

32Ask now about the former days, long before your time, from the day God created man on the earth; ask from one end of the heavens to the other. Has anything so great as this ever happened, or has anything like it ever been heard of? 33Has any other people heard the voice of God[a] speaking out of fire, as you have, and lived? [34]Has any god ever tried to take for himself one nation out of another nation, by testings, by miraculous signs and wonders, by war, by a mighty hand and an outstretched arm, or by great and awesome deeds, like all the things the LORD your God did for you in Egypt before your very eyes?

[35]You were shown these things so that you might know that the LORD is God; besides him there is no other. [36]From heaven he made you hear his voice to discipline you. On earth he showed you his great fire, and you heard his words from out of the fire. [37]Because he loved your forefathers and chose their descendants after them, he brought you out of Egypt by his Presence and his great strength, [38]to drive out before you nations greater and stronger than you and to bring you into their land to give it to you for your inheritance, as it is today.

[39]Acknowledge and take to heart this day that the LORD is God in heaven above and on the earth below. There is no other. [40]Keep his decrees and commands, which I am giving you today, so that it may go well with you and your children after you and that you may live long in the land the LORD your God gives you for all time.

Cities of Refuge

[41]Then Moses set aside three cities east of the Jordan, [42]to which anyone who had killed a person could flee if he had unintentionally killed his neighbour without malice aforethought. He could flee into one of these cities and save his life. [43]The cities were these: Bezer in the desert plateau, for the Reubenites; Ramoth in Gilead, for the Gadites; and Golan in Bashan, for the Manassites.

Introduction to the Law

[44]This is the law Moses set before the Israelites. [45]These are the stipulations, decrees and laws Moses gave them when they came out of Egypt [46]and were in the valley near Beth Peor east of the Jordan, in the land of Sihon king of the Amorites, who reigned in Heshbon and was defeated by Moses and the Israelites as they came out of Egypt. [47]They took possession of his land and the land of Og king of Bashan, the two Amorite kings east of the Jordan. [48]This land extended from Aroer on the rim of the Arnon Gorge to Mount Siyon[b] (that is, Hermon), [49]and included all the Arabah east of the Jordan, as far as the Sea of the Arabah,[c] below the slopes of Pisgah.

The Ten Commandments

5 Moses summoned all Israel and said:
    Hear, O Israel, the decrees and the laws I declare in your hearing today. Learn them and be sure to follow them. [2]The LORD our God made a covenant with us at Horeb. [3]It was not with our fathers that the LORD made this covenant, but with us, with all of us who are alive here today. [4]The LORD spoke to you face to face out of the fire on the mountain. [5](At that time I stood between the LORD and you to declare to you the word of the LORD, because you were afraid of the fire and did not go up the mountain.) And he said:

[6]"I am the LORD your God, who brought you out of Egypt, out of the land of slavery.

[7]"You shall have no other gods before[a] me.

[8]"You shall not make for yourself an idol in the form of anything in heaven above or on the earth beneath or in the waters below. [9]You shall not bow down to them or worship them; for I, the LORD your God, am a jealous God, punishing the children for the sin of the fathers to the third and fourth generation of those who hate me, [10]but showing love to a thousand ‚generations‚ of those who love me and keep my commandments.

[11]"You shall not misuse the name of the LORD your God, for the LORD will not hold anyone guiltless who misuses his name.

[12]"Observe the Sabbath day by keeping it holy, as the LORD your God has commanded you. [13]Six days you shall labour and do all your work, [14]but the seventh day is a Sabbath to the LORD your God. On it you shall not do any work, neither you, nor your son or daughter, nor your manservant or maidservant, nor your ox, your donkey or any of your animals, nor the alien within your gates, so that your manservant and maidservant may rest, as you do. [15]Remember that you were slaves in Egypt and that the LORD your God brought you out of there with a mighty hand and an outstretched arm. Therefore the LORD your God has commanded you to observe the Sabbath day.

[16]"Honour your father and your mother, as the LORD your God has commanded you, so that you may live long and that it may go well with you in the land the LORD your God is giving you.

[17]"You shall not murder.

[18]"You shall not commit adultery.

[19]"You shall not steal.

[20]"You shall not give false testimony against your neighbour.

[21]"You shall not covet your neighbour's wife. You shall not set your desire on your neighbour's house or land, his manservant or maidservant, his ox or donkey, or anything that belongs to your neighbour."

[22]These are the commandments the LORD proclaimed in a loud voice to your whole assembly there on the mountain from out of

---

[a]33 Or *of a god*   [b]48 Hebrew; Syriac (see also Deut. 3:9) *Sirion*   [c]49 That is, the Dead Sea   [a]7 Or *besides*

DEUTERONOMY 6:10–14

'Be careful that you do not forget the LORD, who brought you out of Egypt, out of the land of slavery' (v. 12).

NO PLACE FOR PRIDE. There was no doubt that the Lord had delivered Israel. But how easily we forget. When people have their vineyards and olive trees, or nowadays factories, farms and fine houses, how easily they forget. The new owner – or old one for that matter – may have worked, built, and laboured for what he has achieved. Inevitably, in doing so he used the skills of others, as well as those God gave him. We can never say 'This is mine, all mine.'

People quickly come to treat things as a right. Sometimes they should be. No one would quarrel about everyone's right to education. But only in the last century has universal education applied even in developed countries, let alone in poorer ones where this right is often still a minority one.

People still deprive others of rights to land, property, even to food and shelter itself. They argue that their own work or skill has brought prosperity, forgetting the sheer chance of where they live; how they were educated; who they belong to; what they know; which either gives or denies them opportunity to use the skills God gave them. Let us pray that Christians will remember God has redeemed them, not for any merit or skill they possess, but just because he loves them. No one is worth more than another. Some skills may be more valued by society. Foolish people may pay inflated salaries, but society is not God and one day rich fools will know their own true worth.

Let me not forget you, Lord.

→160

DEUTERONOMY 14:1–2; 16:16–17, 21–22

'For you are a people holy to the LORD your God. Out of all the peoples on the face of the earth, the LORD has chosen you to be his treasured possession' (14: 2).

ISRAEL'S DISTINCTIVE CALLING was to be a holy people. This meant they were special, chosen, separate from all other peoples. It is not fashionable to approach things in this way. Emphases today are all on equality, sameness, the things which unite us. That is right and proper. Equality is very necessary. Injustices must be brought to light, and resources apportioned more fairly.

But Israel was to be different. They had to be an example to the peoples around. They had a mission to fulfil. That difference came out in the conduct of their ceremonies. Every year they were to celebrate three main festivals which would unite them, give them an identity different from that of the peoples amongst whom they lived, and show that it was possible to worship without the magical, often immoral practices associated with the pagan worship of their day.

In Canaan it was usual for fertility rites to be associated with groves of trees, planted as memorials to Astarte, or Ashteroth, the goddess who was the partner of Baal. Israel must have no part in such ceremonies, and in order to avoid all temptation to copy the Canaanite practice, they were to plant no trees beside their altars.

Christians, too, have a distinctive calling and we are required to avoid actions which will be misunderstood. We are called to purity, a purity which must permeate our everyday activity, as well as our public profile.

→177

the fire, the cloud and the deep darkness; and he added nothing more. Then he wrote them on two stone tablets and gave them to me.

²³When you heard the voice out of the darkness, while the mountain was ablaze with fire, all the leading men of your tribes and your elders came to me. ²⁴And you said, "The LORD our God has shown us his glory and his majesty, and we have heard his voice from the fire. Today we have seen that a man can live even if God speaks with him. ²⁵But now, why should we die? This great fire will consume us, and we will die if we hear the voice of the LORD our God any longer. ²⁶For what mortal man has ever heard the voice of the living God speaking out of fire, as we have, and survived? ²⁷Go near and listen to all that the LORD our God says. Then tell us whatever the LORD our God tells you. We will listen and obey."

²⁸The LORD heard you when you spoke to me and the LORD said to me, "I have heard what this people said to you. Everything they said was good. ²⁹Oh, that their hearts would be inclined to fear me and keep all my commands always, so that it might go well with them and their children for ever!

³⁰"Go, tell them to return to their tents. ³¹But you stay here with me so that I may give you all the commands, decrees and laws that you are to teach them to follow in the land I am giving them to possess."

³²So be careful to do what the LORD your God has commanded you; do not turn aside to the right or to the left. ³³Walk in all the way that the LORD your God has commanded you, so that you may live and prosper and prolong your days in the land that you will possess.

Love the LORD Your God

6 These are the commands, decrees and laws the LORD your God directed me to teach you to observe in the land that you are crossing the Jordan to possess, ²so that you, your children and their children after them may fear the LORD your God as long as you live by keeping all his decrees and commands that I give you, and so that you may enjoy long life. ³Hear, O Israel, and be careful to obey so that it may go well with you and that you may increase greatly in a land flowing with milk and honey, just as the LORD, the God of your fathers, promised you.

⁴Hear, O Israel: The LORD our God, the LORD is one.ᵃ ⁵Love the LORD your God with all your heart and with all your soul and with all your strength. ⁶These commandments that I give you today are to be upon your hearts. ⁷Impress them on your children. Talk about them when you sit at home and when you walk along the road, when you lie down and when you get up. ⁸Tie them as symbols on your hands and bind them on your foreheads. ⁹Write them on the door-frames of your houses and on your gates.

¹⁰When the LORD your God brings you into the land he swore to your fathers, to Abraham, Isaac and Jacob, to give you—a land with large, flourishing cities you did not build, ¹¹houses filled with all kinds of good things you did not provide, wells you did not dig, and vineyards and olive groves you did not plant—then when you eat and are satisfied, ¹²be careful that you do not forget the LORD, who brought you out of Egypt, out of the land of slavery.

¹³Fear the LORD your God, serve him only and take your oaths in his name. ¹⁴Do not follow other gods, the gods of the peoples around you; ¹⁵for the LORD your God, who is among you, is a jealous God and his anger will burn against you, and he will destroy you from the face of the land. ¹⁶Do not test the LORD your God as you did at Massah. ¹⁷Be sure to keep the commands of the LORD your God and the stipulations and decrees he has given you. ¹⁸Do what is right and good in the LORD's sight, so that it may go well with you and you may go in and take over the good land that the LORD promised on oath to your forefathers, ¹⁹thrusting out all your enemies before you, as the LORD said.

²⁰In the future, when your son asks you, "What is the meaning of the stipulations, decrees and laws the LORD our God has commanded you?" ²¹tell him: "We were slaves of Pharaoh in Egypt, but the LORD brought us out of Egypt with a mighty hand. ²²Before our eyes the LORD sent miraculous signs and wonders—great and terrible—upon Egypt and Pharaoh and his whole household. ²³But he brought us out from there to bring us in and give us the land that he promised on oath to our forefathers. ²⁴The LORD commanded us to obey all these decrees and to fear the LORD our God, so that we might always prosper and be kept alive, as is the case today. ²⁵And if we are careful to obey all this law before the LORD our God, as he has commanded us, that will be our righteousness."

Driving Out the Nations

7 When the LORD your God brings you into the land you are entering to possess and drives out before you many nations—the Hittites, Girgashites, Amorites, Canaanites, Perizzites, Hivites and Jebusites, seven nations larger and stronger than you—²and when the LORD your God has delivered them over to you and you have defeated them, then you must destroy them totally.ᵃ Make no treaty with them, and show them no mercy. ³Do not intermarry with them. Do not give your daughters to their sons or take their daughters for your sons, ⁴for they will turn your sons away from following me to serve other gods, and the LORD's anger will burn against you and will quickly destroy you. ⁵This is what you are to do to them: Break down their altars, smash their sacred stones, cut down their Asherah polesᵇ and burn their idols in the fire. ⁶For you are a people holy to

---

ᵃ4 Or *The LORD our God is one LORD*; or *The LORD is our God, the LORD is one*; or *The LORD is our God, the LORD alone*
ᵃ2 The Hebrew term refers to the irrevocable giving over of things or persons to the LORD, often by totally destroying them; also in verse 26.   ᵇ5 That is, symbols of the goddess Asherah; here and elsewhere in Deuteronomy

the LORD your God. The LORD your God has chosen you out of all the peoples on the face of the earth to be his people, his treasured possession.

7The LORD did not set his affection on you and choose you because you were more numerous than other peoples, for you were the fewest of all peoples. 8But it was because the LORD loved you and kept the oath he swore to your forefathers that he brought you out with a mighty hand and redeemed you from the land of slavery, from the power of Pharaoh king of Egypt. 9Know therefore that the LORD your God is God; he is the faithful God, keeping his covenant of love to a thousand generations of those who love him and keep his commands. 10But

> those who hate him he will repay to their
>   face by destruction;
> he will not be slow to repay to their face
>   those who hate him.

11Therefore, take care to follow the commands, decrees and laws I give you today.

12If you pay attention to these laws and are careful to follow them, then the LORD your God will keep his covenant of love with you, as he swore to your forefathers. 13He will love you and bless you and increase your numbers. He will bless the fruit of your womb, the crops of your land—your grain, new wine and oil—the calves of your herds and the lambs of your flocks in the land that he swore to your forefathers to give you. 14You will be blessed more than any other people; none of your men or women will be childless, nor any of your livestock without young. 15The LORD will keep you free from every disease. He will not inflict on you the horrible diseases you knew in Egypt, but he will inflict them on all who hate you. 16You must destroy all the peoples the LORD your God gives over to you. Do not look on them with pity and do not serve their gods, for that will be a snare to you.

17You may say to yourselves, "These nations are stronger than we are. How can we drive them out?" 18But do not be afraid of them; remember well what the LORD your God did to Pharaoh and to all Egypt. 19You saw with your own eyes the great trials, the miraculous signs and wonders, the mighty hand and outstretched arm, with which the LORD your God brought you out. The LORD your God will do the same to all the peoples you now fear. 20Moreover, the LORD your God will send the hornet among them until even the survivors who hide from you have perished. 21Do not be terrified by them, for the LORD your God, who is among you, is a great and awesome God. 22The LORD your God will drive out those nations before you, little by little. You will not be allowed to eliminate them all at once, or the wild animals will multiply around you. 23But the LORD your God will deliver them over to you, throwing them into great confusion until they are destroyed. 24He will give their kings into your hand, and you will wipe out their names from under heaven. No-one will be able to

stand up against you; you will destroy them. 25The images of their gods you are to burn in the fire. Do not covet the silver and gold on them, and do not take it for yourselves, or you will be ensnared by it, for it is detestable to the LORD your God. 26Do not bring a detestable thing into your house or you, like it, will be set apart for destruction. Utterly abhor and detest it, for it is set apart for destruction.

Do Not Forget the LORD

8 Be careful to follow every command I am giving you today, so that you may live and increase and may enter and possess the land that the LORD promised on oath to your forefathers. 2Remember how the LORD your God led you all the way in the desert these forty years, to humble you and to test you in order to know what was in your heart, whether or not you would keep his commands. 3He humbled you, causing you to hunger and then feeding you with manna, which neither you nor your fathers had known, to teach you that man does not live on bread alone but on every word that comes from the mouth of the LORD. 4Your clothes did not wear out and your feet did not swell during these forty years. 5Know then in your heart that as a man disciplines his son, so the LORD your God disciplines you.

6Observe the commands of the LORD your God, walking in his ways and revering him. 7For the LORD your God is bringing you into a good land—a land with streams and pools of water, with springs flowing in the valleys and hills; 8a land with wheat and barley, vines and fig-trees, pomegranates, olive oil and honey; 9a land where bread will not be scarce and you will lack nothing; a land where the rocks are iron and you can dig copper out of the hills.

10When you have eaten and are satisfied, praise the LORD your God for the good land he has given you. 11Be careful that you do not forget the LORD your God, failing to observe his commands, his laws and his decrees that I am giving you this day. 12Otherwise, when you eat and are satisfied, when you build fine houses and settle down, 13and when your herds and flocks grow large and your silver and gold increase and all you have is multiplied, 14then your heart will become proud and you will forget the LORD your God, who brought you out of Egypt, out of the land of slavery. 15He led you through the vast and dreadful desert, that thirsty and waterless land, with its venomous snakes and scorpions. He brought you water out of hard rock. 16He gave you manna to eat in the desert, something your fathers had never known, to humble you and to test you so that in the end it might go well with you. 17You may say to yourself, "My power and the strength of my hands have produced this wealth for me." 18But remember the LORD your God, for it is he who gives you the ability to produce wealth, and so confirms his covenant, which he swore to your forefathers, as it is today.

19If you ever forget the LORD your God and

follow other gods and worship and bow down to them, I testify against you today that you will surely be destroyed. ²⁰Like the nations the LORD destroyed before you, so you will be destroyed for not obeying the LORD your God.

Not Because of Israel's Righteousness

9 Hear, O Israel. You are now about to cross the Jordan to go in and dispossess nations greater and stronger than you, with large cities that have walls up to the sky. ²The people are strong and tall—Anakites! You know about them and have heard it said: "Who can stand up against the Anakites?" ³But be assured today that the LORD your God is the one who goes across ahead of you like a devouring fire. He will destroy them; he will subdue them before you. And you will drive them out and annihilate them quickly, as the LORD has promised you.

⁴After the LORD your God has driven them out before you, do not say to yourself, "The LORD has brought me here to take possession of this land because of my righteousness." No, it is on account of the wickedness of these nations that the LORD is going to drive them out before you. ⁵It is not because of your righteousness or your integrity that you are going in to take possession of their land; but on account of the wickedness of these nations, the LORD your God will drive them out before you, to accomplish what he swore to your fathers, to Abraham, Isaac and Jacob. ⁶Understand, then, that it is not because of your righteousness that the LORD your God is giving you this good land to possess, for you are a stiff-necked people.

The Golden Calf

⁷Remember this and never forget how you provoked the LORD your God to anger in the desert. From the day you left Egypt until you arrived here, you have been rebellious against the LORD. ⁸At Horeb you aroused the LORD's wrath so that he was angry enough to destroy you. ⁹When I went up on the mountain to receive the tablets of stone, the tablets of the covenant that the LORD had made with you, I stayed on the mountain forty days and forty nights; I ate no bread and drank no water. ¹⁰The LORD gave me two stone tablets inscribed by the finger of God. On them were all the commandments the LORD proclaimed to you on the mountain out of the fire, on the day of the assembly.

¹¹At the end of the forty days and forty nights, the LORD gave me the two stone tablets, the tablets of the covenant. ¹²Then the LORD told me, "Go down from here at once, because your people whom you brought out of Egypt have become corrupt. They have turned away quickly from what I commanded them and have made a cast idol for themselves."

¹³And the LORD said to me, "I have seen this people, and they are a stiff-necked people indeed! ¹⁴Let me alone, so that I may destroy them and blot out their name from

under heaven. And I will make you into a nation stronger and more numerous than they."

¹⁵So I turned and went down from the mountain while it was ablaze with fire. And the two tablets of the covenant were in my hands.^a ¹⁶When I looked, I saw that you had sinned against the LORD your God; you had made for yourselves an idol cast in the shape of a calf. You had turned aside quickly from the way that the LORD had commanded you. ¹⁷So I took the two tablets and threw them out of my hands, breaking them to pieces before your eyes.

¹⁸Then once again I fell prostrate before the LORD for forty days and forty nights; I ate no bread and drank no water, because of all the sin you had committed, doing what was evil in the LORD's sight and so provoking him to anger. ¹⁹I feared the anger and wrath of the LORD, for he was angry enough with you to destroy you. But again the LORD listened to me. ²⁰And the LORD was angry enough with Aaron to destroy him, but at that time I prayed for Aaron too. ²¹Also I took that sinful thing of yours, the calf you had made, and burned it in the fire. Then I crushed it and ground it to powder as fine as dust and threw the dust into a stream that flowed down the mountain.

²²You also made the LORD angry at Taberah, at Massah and at Kibroth Hattaavah.

²³And when the LORD sent you out from Kadesh Barnea, he said, "Go up and take possession of the land I have given you." But you rebelled against the command of the LORD your God. You did not trust him or obey him. ²⁴You have been rebellious against the LORD ever since I have known you.

²⁵I lay prostrate before the LORD those forty days and forty nights because the LORD had said he would destroy you. ²⁶I prayed to the LORD and said, "O Sovereign LORD, do not destroy your people, your own inheritance that you redeemed by your great power and brought out of Egypt with a mighty hand. ²⁷Remember your servants Abraham, Isaac and Jacob. Overlook the stubbornness of this people, their wickedness and their sin. ²⁸Otherwise, the country from which you brought us will say, 'Because the LORD was not able to take them into the land he had promised them, and because he hated them, he brought them out to put them to death in the desert.' ²⁹But they are your people, your inheritance that you brought out by your great power and your outstretched arm."

Tablets Like the First Ones

10 At that time the LORD said to me, "Chisel out two stone tablets like the first ones and come up to me on the mountain. Also make a wooden chest.^a ²I will write on the tablets the words that were on the first tablets, which you broke. Then you are to put them in the chest."

³So I made the ark out of acacia wood and chiselled out two stone tablets like the first ones, and I went up on the mountain with the

---

^a15 Or And I had the two tablets of the covenant with me, one in each hand   ^a1 That is, an ark

two tablets in my hands. [4]The LORD wrote on these tablets what he had written before, the Ten Commandments he had proclaimed to you on the mountain, out of the fire, on the day of the assembly. And the LORD gave them to me. [5]Then I came back down the mountain and put the tablets in the ark I had made, as the LORD commanded me, and they are there now.

[6](The Israelites travelled from the wells of the Jaakanites to Moserah. There Aaron died and was buried, and Eleazar his son succeeded him as priest. [7]From there they travelled to Gudgodah and on to Jotbathah, a land with streams of water. [8]At that time the LORD set apart the tribe of Levi to carry the ark of the covenant of the LORD, to stand before the LORD to minister and to pronounce blessings in his name, as they still do today. [9]That is why the Levites have no share or inheritance among their brothers; the LORD is their inheritance, as the LORD your God told them.)

[10]Now I had stayed on the mountain forty days and nights, as I did the first time, and the LORD listened to me at this time also. It was not his will to destroy you. [11]"Go," the LORD said to me, "and lead the people on their way, so that they may enter and possess the land that I swore to their fathers to give them."

Fear the LORD

[12]And now, O Israel, what does the LORD your God ask of you but to fear the LORD your God, to walk in all his ways, to love him, to serve the LORD your God with all your heart and with all your soul, [13]and to observe the LORD's commands and decrees that I am giving you today for your own good?

[14]To the LORD your God belong the heavens, even the highest heavens, the earth and everything in it. [15]Yet the LORD set his affection on your forefathers and loved them, and he chose you, their descendants, above all the nations, as it is today. [16]Circumcise your hearts, therefore, and do not be stiff-necked any longer. [17]For the LORD your God is God of gods and Lord of lords, the great God, mighty and awesome, who shows no partiality and accepts no bribes. [18]He defends the cause of the fatherless and the widow, and loves the alien, giving him food and clothing. [19]And you are to love those who are aliens, for you yourselves were aliens in Egypt. [20]Fear the LORD your God and serve him. Hold fast to him and take your oaths in his name. [21]He is your praise; he is your God, who performed for you those great and awesome wonders you saw with your own eyes. [22]Your forefathers who went down into Egypt were seventy in all, and now the LORD your God has made you as numerous as the stars in the sky.

Love and Obey the LORD

11 Love the LORD your God and keep his requirements, his decrees, his laws and his commands always. [2]Remember today that your children were not the ones who saw and experienced the discipline of the LORD your God: his majesty, his mighty hand, his outstretched arm; [3]the signs he performed and the things he did in the heart of Egypt, both to Pharaoh king of Egypt and to his whole country; [4]what he did to the Egyptian army, to its horses and chariots, how he overwhelmed them with the waters of the Red Sea[a] as they were pursuing you, and how the LORD brought lasting ruin on them. [5]It was not your children who saw what he did for you in the desert until you arrived at this place, [6]and what he did to Dathan and Abiram, sons of Eliab the Reubenite, when the earth opened its mouth right in the middle of all Israel and swallowed them up with their households, their tents and every living thing that belonged to them. [7]But it was your own eyes that saw all these great things the LORD has done.

[8]Observe therefore all the commands I am giving you today, so that you may have the strength to go in and take over the land that you are crossing the Jordan to possess, [9]and so that you may live long in the land that the LORD swore to your forefathers to give to them and their descendants, a land flowing with milk and honey. [10]The land you are entering to take over is not like the land of Egypt, from which you have come, where you planted your seed and irrigated it by foot as in a vegetable garden. [11]But the land you are crossing the Jordan to take possession of is a land of mountains and valleys that drinks rain from heaven. [12]It is a land the LORD your God cares for; the eyes of the LORD your God are continually on it from the beginning of the year to its end.

[13]So if you faithfully obey the commands I am giving you today—to love the LORD your God and to serve him with all your heart and with all your soul—[14]then I will send rain on your land in its season, both autumn and spring rains, so that you may gather in your grain, new wine and oil. [15]I will provide grass in the fields for your cattle, and you will eat and be satisfied.

[16]Be careful, or you will be enticed to turn away and worship other gods and bow down to them. [17]Then the LORD's anger will burn against you, and he will shut the heavens so that it will not rain and the ground will yield no produce, and you will soon perish from the good land the LORD is giving you. [18]Fix these words of mine in your hearts and minds; tie them as symbols on your hands and bind them on your foreheads. [19]Teach them to your children, talking about them when you sit at home and when you walk along the road, when you lie down and when you get up. [20]Write them on the door-frames of your houses and on your gates, [21]so that your days and the days of your children may be many in the land that the LORD swore to give your forefathers, as many as the days that the heavens are above the earth.

[22]If you carefully observe all these commands I am giving you to follow—to love the

---

[a]4 Hebrew *Yam Suph*; that is, Sea of Reeds

LORD your God, to walk in all his ways and to hold fast to him—[23]then the LORD will drive out all these nations before you, and you will dispossess nations larger and stronger than you. [24]Every place where you set your foot will be yours: Your territory will extend from the desert to Lebanon, and from the Euphrates River to the western sea.[b] [25]No man will be able to stand against you. The LORD your God, as he promised you, will put the terror and fear of you on the whole land, wherever you go.

[26]See, I am setting before you today a blessing and a curse—[27]the blessing if you obey the commands of the LORD your God that I am giving you today; [28]the curse if you disobey the commands of the LORD your God and turn from the way that I command you today by following other gods, which you have not known. [29]When the LORD your God has brought you into the land you are entering to possess, you are to proclaim on Mount Gerizim the blessings, and on Mount Ebal the curses. [30]As you know, these mountains are across the Jordan, west of the road,[c] towards the setting sun, near the great trees of Moreh, in the territory of those Canaanites living in the Arabah in the vicinity of Gilgal. [31]You are about to cross the Jordan to enter and take possession of the land the LORD your God is giving you. When you have taken it over and are living there, [32]be sure that you obey all the decrees and laws I am setting before you today.

The One Place of Worship

12 These are the decrees and laws you must be careful to follow in the land that the LORD, the God of your fathers, has given you to possess—as long as you live in the land. [2]Destroy completely all the places on the high mountains and on the hills and under every spreading tree where the nations you are dispossessing worship their gods. [3]Break down their altars, smash their sacred stones and burn their Asherah poles in the fire; cut down the idols of their gods and wipe out their names from those places.

[4]You must not worship the LORD your God in their way. [5]But you are to seek the place the LORD your God will choose from among all your tribes to put his Name there for his dwelling. To that place you must go; [6]there bring your burnt offerings and sacrifices, your tithes and special gifts, what you have vowed to give and your freewill offerings, and the firstborn of your herds and flocks. [7]There, in the presence of the LORD your God, you and your families shall eat and shall rejoice in everything you have put your hand to, because the LORD your God has blessed you.

[8]You are not to do as we do here today, everyone as he sees fit, [9]since you have not yet reached the resting place and the inheritance the LORD your God is giving you. [10]But you will cross the Jordan and settle in the land the LORD your God is giving you as an inheritance, and he will give you rest from all your enemies around you so that you will live in safety. [11]Then to the place the LORD your God will choose as a dwelling for his Name —there you are to bring everything I command you: your burnt offerings and sacrifices, your tithes and special gifts, and all the choice possessions you have vowed to the LORD. [12]And there rejoice before the LORD your God, you, your sons and daughters, your menservants and maidservants, and the Levites from your towns, who have no allotment or inheritance of their own. [13]Be careful not to sacrifice your burnt offerings anywhere you please. [14]Offer them only at the place the LORD will choose in one of your tribes, and there observe everything I command you.

[15]Nevertheless, you may slaughter your animals in any of your towns and eat as much of the meat as you want, as if it were gazelle or deer, according to the blessing the LORD your God gives you. Both the ceremonially unclean and the clean may eat it. [16]But you must not eat the blood; pour it out on the ground like water. [17]You must not eat in your own towns the tithe of your grain and new wine and oil, or the firstborn of your herds and flocks, or whatever you have vowed to give, or your freewill offerings or special gifts. [18]Instead, you are to eat them in the presence of the LORD your God at the place the LORD your God will choose—you, your sons and daughters, your menservants and maidservants, and the Levites from your towns—and you are to rejoice before the LORD your God in everything you put your hand to. [19]Be careful not to neglect the Levites as long as you live in your land.

[20]When the LORD your God has enlarged your territory as he promised you, and you crave meat and say, "I would like some meat," then you may eat as much of it as you want. [21]If the place where the LORD your God chooses to put his Name is too far away from you, you may slaughter animals from the herds and flocks the LORD has given you, as I have commanded you, and in your own towns you may eat as much of them as you want. [22]Eat them as you would gazelle or deer. Both the ceremonially unclean and the clean may eat. [23]But be sure you do not eat the blood, because the blood is the life, and you must not eat the life with the meat. [24]You must not eat the blood; pour it out on the ground like water. [25]Do not eat it, so that it may go well with you and your children after you, because you will be doing what is right in the eyes of the LORD.

[26]But take your consecrated things and whatever you have vowed to give, and go to the place the LORD will choose. [27]Present your burnt offerings on the altar of the LORD your God, both the meat and the blood. The blood of your sacrifices must be poured beside the altar of the LORD your God, but you may eat the meat. [28]Be careful to obey all these regulations I am giving you, so that it may always go well with you and your children after you, because you will be doing

[b]24 That is, the Mediterranean   [c]30 Or Jordan, westward

what is good and right in the eyes of the LORD your God.

29The LORD your God will cut off before you the nations you are about to invade and dispossess. But when you have driven them out and settled in their land, 30and after they have been destroyed before you, be careful not to be ensnared by enquiring about their gods, saying, "How do these nations serve their gods? We will do the same." 31You must not worship the LORD your God in their way, because in worshipping their gods, they do all kinds of detestable things the LORD hates. They even burn their sons and daughters in the fire as sacrifices to their gods.

32See that you do all I command you; do not add to it or take away from it.

Worshipping Other Gods

13 If a prophet, or one who foretells by dreams, appears among you and announces to you a miraculous sign or wonder, 2and if the sign or wonder of which he has spoken takes place, and he says, "Let us follow other gods" (gods you have not known) "and let us worship them," 3you must not listen to the words of that prophet or dreamer. The LORD your God is testing you to find out whether you love him with all your heart and with all your soul. 4It is the LORD your God you must follow, and him you must revere. Keep his commands and obey him; serve him and hold fast to him. 5That prophet or dreamer must be put to death, because he preached rebellion against the LORD your God, who brought you out of Egypt and redeemed you from the land of slavery; he has tried to turn you from the way the LORD your God commanded you to follow. You must purge the evil from among you.

6If your very own brother, or your son or daughter, or the wife you love, or your closest friend secretly entices you, saying, "Let us go and worship other gods" (gods that neither you nor your fathers have known, 7gods of the peoples around you, whether near or far, from one end of the land to the other), 8do not yield to him or listen to him. Show him no pity. Do not spare him or shield him. 9You must certainly put him to death. Your hand must be the first in putting him to death, and then the hands of all the people. 10Stone him to death, because he tried to turn you away from the LORD your God, who brought you out of Egypt, out of the land of slavery. 11Then all Israel will hear and be afraid, and no-one among you will do such an evil thing again.

12If you hear it said about one of the towns the LORD your God is giving you to live in 13that wicked men have arisen among you and have led the people of their town astray, saying, "Let us go and worship other gods" (gods you have not known), 14then you must enquire, probe and investigate it thoroughly. And if it is true and it has been proved that this detestable thing has been done among you, 15you must certainly put to the sword all who live in that town. Destroy it completely,a both its people and its livestock. 16Gather all the plunder of the town into the middle of the public square and completely burn the town and all its plunder as a whole burnt offering to the LORD your God. It is to remain a ruin for ever, never to be rebuilt. 17None of those condemned thingsa shall be found in your hands, so that the LORD will turn from his fierce anger; he will show you mercy, have compassion on you, and increase your numbers, as he promised on oath to your forefathers, 18because you obey the LORD your God, keeping all his commands that I am giving you today and doing what is right in his eyes.

Clean and Unclean Food

14 You are the children of the LORD your God. Do not cut yourselves or shave the front of your heads for the dead, 2for you are a people holy to the LORD your God. Out of all the peoples on the face of the earth, the LORD has chosen you to be his treasured possession.

3Do not eat any detestable thing. 4These are the animals you may eat: the ox, the sheep, the goat, 5the deer, the gazelle, the roe deer, the wild goat, the ibex, the antelope and the mountain sheep.a 6You may eat any animal that has a split hoof divided in two and that chews the cud. 7However, of those that chew the cud or that have a split hoof completely divided you may not eat the camel, the rabbit or the coney.b Although they chew the cud, they do not have a split hoof; they are ceremonially unclean for you. 8The pig is also unclean; although it has a split hoof, it does not chew the cud. You are not to eat their meat or touch their carcasses.

9Of all the creatures living in the water, you may eat any that has fins and scales. 10But anything that does not have fins and scales you may not eat; for you it is unclean.

11You may eat any clean bird. 12But these you may not eat: the eagle, the vulture, the black vulture, 13the red kite, the black kite, any kind of falcon, 14any kind of raven, 15the horned owl, the screech owl, the gull, any kind of hawk, 16the little owl, the great owl, the white owl, 17the desert owl, the osprey, the cormorant, 18the stork, any kind of heron, the hoopoe and the bat.

19All flying insects that swarm are unclean to you; do not eat them. 20But any winged creature that is clean you may eat.

21Do not eat anything you find already dead. You may give it to an alien living in any of your towns, and he may eat it, or you may sell it to a foreigner. But you are a people holy to the LORD your God.

Do not cook a young goat in its mother's milk.

---

a15 The Hebrew term refers to the irrevocable giving over of things or persons to the LORD, often by totally destroying them; also in verse 17.
a5 The precise identification of some of the birds and animals in this chapter is uncertain.
b7 That is, the hyrax or rock badger

Tithes

²²Be sure to set aside a tenth of all that your fields produce each year. ²³Eat the tithe of your grain, new wine and oil, and the firstborn of your herds and flocks in the presence of the LORD your God at the place he will choose as a dwelling for his Name, so that you may learn to revere the LORD your God always. ²⁴But if that place is too distant and you have been blessed by the LORD your God and cannot carry your tithe (because the place where the LORD will choose to put his Name is so far away), ²⁵then exchange your tithe for silver, and take the silver with you and go to the place the LORD your God will choose. ²⁶Use the silver to buy whatever you like: cattle, sheep, wine or other fermented drink, or anything you wish. Then you and your household shall eat there in the presence of the LORD your God and rejoice. ²⁷And do not neglect the Levites living in your towns, for they have no allotment or inheritance of their own.

²⁸At the end of every three years, bring all the tithes of that year's produce and store it in your towns, ²⁹so that the Levites (who have no allotment or inheritance of their own) and the aliens, the fatherless and the widows who live in your towns may come and eat and be satisfied, and so that the LORD your God may bless you in all the work of your hands.

The Year for Cancelling Debts

15 At the end of every seven years you must cancel debts. ²This is how it is to be done: Every creditor shall cancel the loan he has made to his fellow Israelite. He shall not require payment from his fellow Israelite or brother, because the LORD's time for cancelling debts has been proclaimed. ³You may require payment from a foreigner, but you must cancel any debt your brother owes you. ⁴However, there should be no poor among you, for in the land the LORD your God is giving you to possess as your inheritance, he will richly bless you, ⁵if only you fully obey the LORD your God and are careful to follow all these commands I am giving you today. ⁶For the LORD your God will bless you as he has promised, and you will lend to many nations but will borrow from none. You will rule over many nations but none will rule over you.

⁷If there is a poor man among your brothers in any of the towns of the land that the LORD your God is giving you, do not be hard-hearted or tight-fisted towards your poor brother. ⁸Rather be open-handed and freely lend him whatever he needs. ⁹Be careful not to harbour this wicked thought: "The seventh year, the year for cancelling debts, is near," so that you do not show ill will towards your needy brother and give him nothing. He may then appeal to the LORD against you, and you will be found guilty of sin. ¹⁰Give generously to him and do so without a grudging heart; then because of this the LORD your God will bless you in all your work and in everything you put your hand to. ¹¹There will always be poor people in the land. Therefore I command you to be open-handed towards your brothers and towards the poor and needy in your land.

Freeing Servants

¹²If a fellow Hebrew, a man or woman, sells himself to you and serves you six years, in the seventh year you must let him go free. ¹³And when you release him, do not send him away empty-handed. ¹⁴Supply him liberally from your flock, your threshing-floor and your winepress. Give to him as the LORD your God has blessed you. ¹⁵Remember that you were slaves in Egypt and the LORD your God redeemed you. That is why I give you this command today.

¹⁶But if your servant says to you, "I do not want to leave you," because he loves you and your family and is well off with you, ¹⁷then take an awl and push it through his ear lobe into the door, and he will become your servant for life. Do the same for your maidservant.

¹⁸Do not consider it a hardship to set your servant free, because his service to you these six years has been worth twice as much as that of a hired hand. And the LORD your God will bless you in everything you do.

The Firstborn Animals

¹⁹Set apart for the LORD your God every firstborn male of your herds and flocks. Do not put the firstborn of your oxen to work, and do not shear the firstborn of your sheep. ²⁰Each year you and your family are to eat them in the presence of the LORD your God at the place he will choose. ²¹If an animal has a defect, is lame or blind, or has any serious flaw, you must not sacrifice it to the LORD your God. ²²You are to eat it in your own towns. Both the ceremonially unclean and the clean may eat it, as if it were gazelle or deer. ²³But you must not eat the blood; pour it out on the ground like water.

Passover

16 Observe the month of Abib and celebrate the Passover of the LORD your God, because in the month of Abib he brought you out of Egypt by night. ²Sacrifice as the Passover to the LORD your God an animal from your flock or herd at the place the LORD will choose as a dwelling for his Name. ³Do not eat it with bread made with yeast, but for seven days eat unleavened bread, the bread of affliction, because you left Egypt in haste—so that all the days of your life you may remember the time of your departure from Egypt. ⁴Let no yeast be found in your possession in all your land for seven days. Do not let any of the meat you sacrifice on the evening of the first day remain until morning.

⁵You must not sacrifice the Passover in any town the LORD your God gives you ⁶except in the place he will choose as a dwelling for his Name. There you must sacrifice the Passover in the evening, when the

sun goes down, on the anniversary[a] of your departure from Egypt. [7]Roast it and eat it at the place the Lord your God will choose. Then in the morning return to your tents. [8]For six days eat unleavened bread and on the seventh day hold an assembly to the Lord your God and do no work.

Feast of Weeks

[9]Count off seven weeks from the time you begin to put the sickle to the standing corn. [10]Then celebrate the Feast of Weeks to the Lord your God by giving a freewill offering in proportion to the blessings the Lord your God has given you. [11]And rejoice before the Lord your God at the place he will choose as a dwelling for his Name—you, your sons and daughters, your menservants and maidservants, the Levites in your towns, and the aliens, the fatherless and the widows living among you. [12]Remember that you were slaves in Egypt, and follow carefully these decrees.

Feast of Tabernacles

[13]Celebrate the Feast of Tabernacles for seven days after you have gathered the produce of your threshing-floor and your winepress. [14]Be joyful at your Feast—you, your sons and daughters, your menservants and maidservants, and the Levites, the aliens, the fatherless and the widows who live in your towns. [15]For seven days celebrate the Feast to the Lord your God at the place the Lord will choose. For the Lord your God will bless you in all your harvest and in all the work of your hands, and your joy will be complete.

[16]Three times a year all your men must appear before the Lord your God at the place he will choose: at the Feast of Unleavened Bread, the Feast of Weeks and the Feast of Tabernacles. No man should appear before the Lord empty-handed: [17]Each of you must bring a gift in proportion to the way the Lord your God has blessed you.

Judges

[18]Appoint judges and officials for each of your tribes in every town the Lord your God is giving you, and they shall judge the people fairly. [19]Do not pervert justice or show partiality. Do not accept a bribe, for a bribe blinds the eyes of the wise and twists the words of the righteous. [20]Follow justice and justice alone, so that you may live and possess the land the Lord your God is giving you.

Worshipping Other Gods

[21]Do not set up any wooden Asherah pole[b] beside the altar you build to the Lord your God, [22]and do not erect a sacred stone, for these the Lord your God hates.

17 Do not sacrifice to the Lord your God an ox or a sheep that has any defect or flaw in it, for that would be detestable to him.

[2]If a man or woman living among you in one of the towns the Lord gives you is found

doing evil in the eyes of the Lord your God in violation of his covenant, [3]and contrary to my command has worshipped other gods, bowing down to them or to the sun or the moon or the stars of the sky, [4]and this has been brought to your attention, then you must investigate it thoroughly. If it is true and it has been proved that this detestable thing has been done in Israel, [5]take the man or woman who has done this evil deed to your city gate and stone that person to death. [6]On the testimony of two or three witnesses a man shall be put to death, but no-one shall be put to death on the testimony of only one witness. [7]The hands of the witnesses must be the first in putting him to death, and then the hands of all the people. You must purge the evil from among you.

Law Courts

[8]If cases come before your courts that are too difficult for you to judge—whether bloodshed, lawsuits or assaults—take them to the place the Lord your God will choose. [9]Go to the priests, who are Levites, and to the judge who is in office at that time. Enquire of them and they will give you the verdict. [10]You must act according to the decisions they give you at the place the Lord will choose. Be careful to do everything they direct you to do. [11]Act according to the law they teach you and the decisions they give you. Do not turn aside from what they tell you, to the right or to the left. [12]The man who shows contempt for the judge or for the priest who stands ministering there to the Lord your God must be put to death. You must purge the evil from Israel. [13]All the people will hear and be afraid, and will not be contemptuous again.

The King

[14]When you enter the land the Lord your God is giving you and have taken possession of it and settled in it, and you say, "Let us set a king over us like all the nations around us," [15]be sure to appoint over you the king the Lord your God chooses. He must be from among your own brothers. Do not place a foreigner over you, one who is not a brother Israelite. [16]The king, moreover, must not acquire great numbers of horses for himself or make the people return to Egypt to get more of them, for the Lord has told you, "You are not to go back that way again." [17]He must not take many wives, or his heart will be led astray. He must not accumulate large amounts of silver and gold.

[18]When he takes the throne of his kingdom, he is to write for himself on a scroll a copy of this law, taken from that of the priests, who are Levites. [19]It is to be with him, and he is to read it all the days of his life so that he may learn to revere the Lord his God and follow carefully all the words of this law and these decrees [20]and not consider himself better than his brothers and turn from the law to the right or to the left. Then he and his descendants will reign a long time over his kingdom in Israel.

---

[a]6 Or *down, at the time of day*   [b]21 Or *Do not plant any tree dedicated to Asherah*

Offerings for Priests and Levites

18 The priests, who are Levites—indeed the whole tribe of Levi—are to have no allotment or inheritance with Israel. They shall live on the offerings made to the LORD by fire, for that is their inheritance. [2]They shall have no inheritance among their brothers; the LORD is their inheritance, as he promised them.

[3]This is the share due to the priests from the people who sacrifice a bull or a sheep: the shoulder, the jowls and the inner parts. [4]You are to give them the firstfruits of your grain, new wine and oil, and the first wool from the shearing of your sheep, [5]for the LORD your God has chosen them and their descendants out of all your tribes to stand and minister in the LORD's name always.

[6]If a Levite moves from one of your towns anywhere in Israel where he is living, and comes in all earnestness to the place the LORD will choose, [7]he may minister in the name of the LORD his God like all his fellow Levites who serve there in the presence of the LORD. [8]He is to share equally in their benefits even though he has received money from the sale of family possessions.

Detestable Practices

[9]When you enter the land the LORD your God is giving you, do not learn to imitate the detestable ways of the nations there. [10]Let no-one be found among you who sacrifices his son or daughter in[a] the fire, who practises divination or sorcery, interprets omens, engages in witchcraft, [11]or casts spells, or who is a medium or spiritist or who consults the dead. [12]Anyone who does these things is detestable to the LORD, and because of these detestable practices the LORD your God will drive out those nations before you. [13]You must be blameless before the LORD your God.

The Prophet

[14]The nations you will dispossess listen to those who practise sorcery or divination. But as for you, the LORD your God has not permitted you to do so. [15]The LORD your God will raise up for you a prophet like me from among your own brothers. You must listen to him. [16]For this is what you asked of the LORD your God at Horeb on the day of the assembly when you said, "Let us not hear the voice of the LORD our God nor see this great fire any more, or we will die."

[17]The LORD said to me: "What they say is good. [18]I will raise up for them a prophet like you from among their brothers; I will put my words in his mouth, and he will tell them everything I command him. [19]If anyone does not listen to my words that the prophet speaks in my name, I myself will call him to account. [20]But a prophet who presumes to speak in my name anything I have not commanded him to say, or a prophet who speaks in the name of other gods, must be put to death."

[21]You may say to yourselves, "How can we know when a message has not been spoken by the LORD?" [22]If what a prophet proclaims in the name of the LORD does not take place or come true, that is a message the LORD has not spoken. That prophet has spoken presumptuously. Do not be afraid of him.

Cities of Refuge

19 When the LORD your God has destroyed the nations whose land he is giving you, and when you have driven them out and settled in their towns and houses, [2]then set aside for yourselves three cities centrally located in the land the LORD your God is giving you to possess. [3]Build roads to them and divide into three parts the land the LORD your God is giving you as an inheritance, so that anyone who kills a man may flee there.

[4]This is the rule concerning the man who kills another and flees there to save his life —one who kills his neighbour unintentionally, without malice aforethought. [5]For instance, a man may go into the forest with his neighbour to cut wood, and as he swings his axe to fell a tree, the head may fly off and hit his neighbour and kill him. That man may flee to one of these cities and save his life. [6]Otherwise, the avenger of blood might pursue him in a rage, overtake him if the distance is too great, and kill him even though he is not deserving of death, since he did it to his neighbour without malice aforethought. [7]This is why I command you to set aside for yourselves three cities.

[8]If the LORD your God enlarges your territory, as he promised on oath to your forefathers, and gives you the whole land he promised them, [9]because you carefully follow all these laws I command you today—to love the LORD your God and to walk always in his ways—then you are to set aside three more cities. [10]Do this so that innocent blood will not be shed in your land, which the LORD your God is giving you as your inheritance, and so that you will not be guilty of bloodshed.

[11]But if a man hates his neighbour and lies in wait for him, assaults and kills him, and then flees to one of these cities, [12]the elders of his town shall send for him, bring him back from the city, and hand him over to the avenger of blood to die. [13]Show him no pity. You must purge from Israel the guilt of shedding innocent blood, so that it may go well with you.

[14]Do not move your neighbour's boundary stone set up by your predecessors in the inheritance you receive in the land the LORD your God is giving you to possess.

Witnesses

[15]One witness is not enough to convict a man accused of any crime or offence he may have committed. A matter must be established by the testimony of two or three witnesses.

[16]If a malicious witness takes the stand to

---

[a]10 Or *who makes his son or daughter pass through*

accuse a man of a crime, 17the two men involved in the dispute must stand in the presence of the LORD before the priests and the judges who are in office at the time. 18The judges must make a thorough investigation, and if the witness proves to be a liar, giving false testimony against his brother, 19then do to him as he intended to do to his brother. You must purge the evil from among you. 20The rest of the people will hear of this and be afraid, and never again will such an evil thing be done among you. 21Show no pity: life for life, eye for eye, tooth for tooth, hand for hand, foot for foot.

Going to War

20 When you go to war against your enemies and see horses and chariots and an army greater than yours, do not be afraid of them, because the LORD your God, who brought you up out of Egypt, will be with you. 2When you are about to go into battle, the priest shall come forward and address the army. 3He shall say: "Hear, O Israel, today you are going into battle against your enemies. Do not be faint-hearted or afraid; do not be terrified or give way to panic before them. 4For the LORD your God is the one who goes with you to fight for you against your enemies to give you victory."

5The officers shall say to the army: "Has anyone built a new house and not dedicated it? Let him go home, or he may die in battle and someone else may dedicate it. 6Has anyone planted a vineyard and not begun to enjoy it? Let him go home, or he may die in battle and someone else enjoy it. 7Has anyone become pledged to a woman and not married her? Let him go home, or he may die in battle and someone else marry her." 8Then the officers shall add, "Is any man afraid or faint-hearted? Let him go home so that his brothers will not become disheartened too." 9When the officers have finished speaking to the army, they shall appoint commanders over it.

10When you march up to attack a city, make its people an offer of peace. 11If they accept and open their gates, all the people in it shall be subject to forced labour and shall work for you. 12If they refuse to make peace and they engage you in battle, lay siege to that city. 13When the LORD your God delivers it into your hand, put to the sword all the men in it. 14As for the women, the children, the livestock and everything else in the city, you may take these as plunder for yourselves. And you may use the plunder the LORD your God gives you from your enemies. 15This is how you are to treat all the cities that are at a distance from you and do not belong to the nations nearby.

16However, in the cities of the nations the LORD your God is giving you as an inheritance, do not leave alive anything that breathes. 17Completely destroy[a] them—the Hittites, Amorites, Canaanites, Perizzites, Hivites and Jebusites—as the LORD your God has commanded you. 18Otherwise, they will teach you to follow all the detestable things they do in worshipping their gods, and you will sin against the LORD your God.

19When you lay siege to a city for a long time, fighting against it to capture it, do not destroy its trees by putting an axe to them, because you can eat their fruit. Do not cut them down. Are the trees of the field people, that you should besiege them?[b] 20However, you may cut down trees that you know are not fruit trees and use them to build siege works until the city at war with you falls.

Atonement for an Unsolved Murder

21 If a man is found slain, lying in a field in the land the LORD your God is giving you to possess, and it is not known who killed him, 2your elders and judges shall go out and measure the distance from the body to the neighbouring towns. 3Then the elders of the town nearest the body shall take a heifer that has never been worked and has never worn a yoke 4and lead her down to a valley that has not been ploughed or planted and where there is a flowing stream. There in the valley they are to break the heifer's neck. 5The priests, the sons of Levi, shall step forward, for the LORD your God has chosen them to minister and to pronounce blessings in the name of the LORD and to decide all cases of dispute and assault. 6Then all the elders of the town nearest the body shall wash their hands over the heifer whose neck was broken in the valley, 7and they shall declare: "Our hands did not shed this blood, nor did our eyes see it done. 8Accept this atonement for your people Israel, whom you have redeemed, O LORD, and do not hold your people guilty of the blood of an innocent man." And the bloodshed will be atoned for. 9So you will purge from yourselves the guilt of shedding innocent blood, since you have done what is right in the eyes of the LORD.

Marrying a Captive Woman

10When you go to war against your enemies and the LORD your God delivers them into your hands and you take captives, 11if you notice among the captives a beautiful woman and are attracted to her, you may take her as your wife. 12Bring her into your home and make her shave her head, trim her nails 13and put aside the clothes she was wearing when captured. After she has lived in your house and mourned her father and mother for a full month, then you may go to her and be her husband and she shall be your wife. 14If you are not pleased with her, let her go wherever she wishes. You must not sell her or treat her as a slave, since you have dishonoured her.

The Right of the Firstborn

15If a man has two wives, and he loves one but not the other, and both bear him sons but the firstborn is the son of the wife he does not love, 16when he wills his property to his sons,

---

a17 The Hebrew term refers to the irrevocable giving over of things or persons to the LORD, often by totally destroying them.   b19 Or *down to use in the siege, for the fruit trees are for the benefit of man.*

he must not give the rights of the firstborn to the son of the wife he loves in preference to his actual firstborn, the son of the wife he does not love. [17]He must acknowledge the son of his unloved wife as the firstborn by giving him a double share of all he has. That son is the first sign of his father's strength. The right of the firstborn belongs to him.

A Rebellious Son

[18]If a man has a stubborn and rebellious son who does not obey his father and mother and will not listen to them when they discipline him, [19]his father and mother shall take hold of him and bring him to the elders at the gate of his town. [20]They shall say to the elders, "This son of ours is stubborn and rebellious. He will not obey us. He is a profligate and a drunkard." [21]Then all the men of his town shall stone him to death. You must purge the evil from among you. All Israel will hear of it and be afraid.

Various Laws

[22]If a man guilty of a capital offence is put to death and his body is hung on a tree, [23]you must not leave his body on the tree overnight. Be sure to bury him that same day, because anyone who is hung on a tree is under God's curse. You must not desecrate the land the LORD your God is giving you as an inheritance.

22 If you see your brother's ox or sheep straying, do not ignore it but be sure to take it back to him. [2]If the brother does not live near you or if you do not know who he is, take it home with you and keep it until he comes looking for it. Then give it back to him. [3]Do the same if you find your brother's donkey or his cloak or anything he loses. Do not ignore it.

[4]If you see your brother's donkey or his ox fallen on the road, do not ignore it. Help him to get it to its feet.

[5]A woman must not wear men's clothing, nor a man wear women's clothing, for the LORD your God detests anyone who does this.

[6]If you come across a bird's nest beside the road, either in a tree or on the ground, and the mother is sitting on the young or on the eggs, do not take the mother with the young. [7]You may take the young, but be sure to let the mother go, so that it may go well with you and you may have a long life.

[8]When you build a new house, make a parapet around your roof so that you may not bring the guilt of bloodshed on your house if someone falls from the roof.

[9]Do not plant two kinds of seed in your vineyard; if you do, not only the crops you plant but also the fruit of the vineyard will be defiled.[a]

[10]Do not plough with an ox and a donkey yoked together.

[11]Do not wear clothes of wool and linen woven together.

[12]Make tassels on the four corners of the cloak you wear.

Marriage Violations

[13]If a man takes a wife and, after lying with her, dislikes her [14]and slanders her and gives her a bad name, saying, "I married this woman, but when I approached her, I did not find proof of her virginity," [15]then the girl's father and mother shall bring proof that she was a virgin to the town elders at the gate. [16]The girl's father will say to the elders, "I gave my daughter in marriage to this man, but he dislikes her. [17]Now he has slandered her and said, 'I did not find your daughter to be a virgin.' But here is the proof of my daughter's virginity." Then her parents shall display the cloth before the elders of the town, [18]and the elders shall take the man and punish him. [19]They shall fine him a hundred shekels of silver[b] and give them to the girl's father, because this man has given an Israelite virgin a bad name. She shall continue to be his wife; he must not divorce her as long as he lives.

[20]If, however, the charge is true and no proof of the girl's virginity can be found, [21]she shall be brought to the door of her father's house and there the men of her town shall stone her to death. She has done a disgraceful thing in Israel by being promiscuous while still in her father's house. You must purge the evil from among you.

[22]If a man is found sleeping with another man's wife, both the man who slept with her and the woman must die. You must purge the evil from Israel.

[23]If a man happens to meet in a town a virgin pledged to be married and he sleeps with her, [24]you shall take both of them to the gate of that town and stone them to death —the girl because she was in a town and did not scream for help, and the man because he violated another man's wife. You must purge the evil from among you.

[25]But if out in the country a man happens to meet a girl pledged to be married and rapes her, only the man who has done this shall die. [26]Do nothing to the girl; she has committed no sin deserving death. This case is like that of someone who attacks and murders his neighbour, [27]for the man found the girl out in the country, and though the betrothed girl screamed, there was no-one to rescue her.

[28]If a man happens to meet a virgin who is not pledged to be married and rapes her and they are discovered, [29]he shall pay the girl's father fifty shekels of silver.[c] He must marry the girl, for he has violated her. He can never divorce her as long as he lives.

[30]A man is not to marry his father's wife; he must not dishonour his father's bed.

Exclusion From the Assembly

23 No-one who has been emasculated by crushing or cutting may enter the assembly of the LORD.

[2]No-one born of a forbidden marriage[a] nor

---

[a]9 Or *be forfeited to the sanctuary*   [b]19 That is, about 2½ pounds (about 1 kilogram)
[c]29 That is, about 1¼ pounds (about 0.6 kilogram)   [a]2 Or *one of illegitimate birth*

any of his descendants may enter the assembly of the LORD, even down to the tenth generation.

³No Ammonite or Moabite or any of his descendants may enter the assembly of the LORD, even down to the tenth generation. ⁴For they did not come to meet you with bread and water on your way when you came out of Egypt, and they hired Balaam son of Beor from Pethor in Aram Naharaim[b] to pronounce a curse on you. ⁵However, the LORD your God would not listen to Balaam but turned the curse into a blessing for you, because the LORD your God loves you. ⁶Do not seek a treaty of friendship with them as long as you live.

⁷Do not abhor an Edomite, for he is your brother. Do not abhor an Egyptian, because you lived as an alien in his country. ⁸The third generation of children born to them may enter the assembly of the LORD.

Uncleanness in the Camp

⁹When you are encamped against your enemies, keep away from everything impure. ¹⁰If one of your men is unclean because of a nocturnal emission, he is to go outside the camp and stay there. ¹¹But as evening approaches he is to wash himself, and at sunset he may return to the camp.

¹²Designate a place outside the camp where you can go to relieve yourself. ¹³As part of your equipment have something to dig with, and when you relieve yourself, dig a hole and cover up your excrement. ¹⁴For the LORD your God moves about in your camp to protect you and to deliver your enemies to you. Your camp must be holy, so that he will not see among you anything indecent and turn away from you.

Miscellaneous Laws

¹⁵If a slave has taken refuge with you, do not hand him over to his master. ¹⁶Let him live among you wherever he likes and in whatever town he chooses. Do not oppress him.

¹⁷No Israelite man or woman is to become a shrine-prostitute. ¹⁸You must not bring the earnings of a female prostitute or of a male prostitute[c] into the house of the LORD your God to pay any vow, because the LORD your God detests them both.

¹⁹Do not charge your brother interest, whether on money or food or anything else that may earn interest. ²⁰You may charge a foreigner interest, but not a brother Israelite, so that the LORD your God may bless you in everything you put your hand to in the land you are entering to possess.

²¹If you make a vow to the LORD your God, do not be slow to pay it, for the LORD your God will certainly demand it of you and you will be guilty of sin. ²²But if you refrain from making a vow, you will not be guilty. ²³Whatever your lips utter you must be sure to do, because you made your vow freely to the LORD your God with your own mouth.

²⁴If you enter your neighbour's vineyard, you may eat all the grapes you want, but do not put any in your basket. ²⁵If you enter your neighbour's cornfield, you may pick the ears with your hands, but you must not put a sickle to his standing corn.

24 If a man marries a woman who becomes displeasing to him because he finds something indecent about her, and he writes her a certificate of divorce, gives it to her and sends her from his house, ²and if after she leaves his house she becomes the wife of another man, ³and her second husband dislikes her and writes her a certificate of divorce, gives it to her and sends her from his house, or if he dies, ⁴then her first husband, who divorced her, is not allowed to marry her again after she has been defiled. That would be detestable in the eyes of the LORD. Do not bring sin upon the land the LORD your God is giving you as an inheritance.

⁵If a man has recently married, he must not be sent to war or have any other duty laid on him. For one year he is to be free to stay at home and bring happiness to the wife he has married.

⁶Do not take a pair of millstones—not even the upper one—as security for a debt, because that would be taking a man's livelihood as security.

⁷If a man is caught kidnapping one of his brother Israelites and treats him as a slave or sells him, the kidnapper must die. You must purge the evil from among you.

⁸In cases of leprous[a] diseases be very careful to do exactly as the priests, who are Levites, instruct you. You must follow carefully what I have commanded them. ⁹Remember what the LORD your God did to Miriam along the way after you came out of Egypt.

¹⁰When you make a loan of any kind to your neighbour, do not go into his house to get what he is offering as a pledge. ¹¹Stay outside and let the man to whom you are making the loan bring the pledge out to you. ¹²If the man is poor, do not go to sleep with his pledge in your possession. ¹³Return his cloak to him by sunset so that he may sleep in it. Then he will thank you, and it will be regarded as a righteous act in the sight of the LORD your God.

¹⁴Do not take advantage of a hired man who is poor and needy, whether he is a brother Israelite or an alien living in one of your towns. ¹⁵Pay him his wages each day before sunset, because he is poor and is counting on it. Otherwise he may cry to the LORD against you, and you will be guilty of sin.

¹⁶Fathers shall not be put to death for their children, nor children put to death for their fathers; each is to die for his own sin.

¹⁷Do not deprive the alien or the fatherless of justice, or take the cloak of the widow as a pledge. ¹⁸Remember that you were slaves in Egypt and the LORD your God redeemed you

---

[b]4 That is, North-west Mesopotamia   [c]18 Hebrew *of a dog*
[a]8 The Hebrew word was used for various diseases affecting the skin—not necessarily leprosy.

from there. That is why I command you to do this.

¹⁹When you are harvesting in your field and you overlook a sheaf, do not go back to get it. Leave it for the alien, the fatherless and the widow, so that the LORD your God may bless you in all the work of your hands. ²⁰When you beat the olives from your trees, do not go over the branches a second time. Leave what remains for the alien, the fatherless and the widow. ²¹When you harvest the grapes in your vineyard, do not go over the vines again. Leave what remains for the alien, the fatherless and the widow. ²²Remember that you were slaves in Egypt. That is why I command you to do this.

25 When men have a dispute, they are to take it to court and the judges will decide the case, acquitting the innocent and condemning the guilty. ²If the guilty man deserves to be beaten, the judge shall make him lie down and have him flogged in his presence with the number of lashes his crime deserves, ³but he must not give him more than forty lashes. If he is flogged more than that, your brother will be degraded in your eyes.

⁴Do not muzzle an ox while it is treading out the grain.

⁵If brothers are living together and one of them dies without a son, his widow must not marry outside the family. Her husband's brother shall take her and marry her and fulfil the duty of a brother-in-law to her. ⁶The first son she bears shall carry on the name of the dead brother so that his name will not be blotted out from Israel.

⁷However, if a man does not want to marry his brother's wife, she shall go to the elders at the town gate and say, "My husband's brother refuses to carry on his brother's name in Israel. He will not fulfil the duty of a brother-in-law to me." ⁸Then the elders of his town shall summon him and talk to him. If he persists in saying, "I do not want to marry her," ⁹his brother's widow shall go up to him in the presence of the elders, take off one of his sandals, spit in his face and say, "This is what is done to the man who will not build up his brother's family line." ¹⁰That man's line shall be known in Israel as The Family of the Unsandalled.

¹¹If two men are fighting and the wife of one of them comes to rescue her husband from his assailant, and she reaches out and seizes him by his private parts, ¹²you shall cut off her hand. Show her no pity.

¹³Do not have two differing weights in your bag—one heavy, one light. ¹⁴Do not have two differing measures in your house—one large, one small. ¹⁵You must have accurate and honest weights and measures, so that you may live long in the land the LORD your God is giving you. ¹⁶For the LORD your God detests anyone who does these things, anyone who deals dishonestly.

¹⁷Remember what the Amalekites did to you along the way when you came out of Egypt. ¹⁸When you were weary and worn out, they met you on your journey and cut off all who were lagging behind; they had no fear

of God. ¹⁹When the LORD your God gives you rest from all the enemies around you in the land he is giving you to possess as an inheritance, you shall blot out the memory of Amalek from under heaven. Do not forget!

Firstfruits and Tithes

26 When you have entered the land that the LORD your God is giving you as an inheritance and have taken possession of it and settled in it, ²take some of the firstfruits of all that you produce from the soil of the land that the LORD your God is giving you and put them in a basket. Then go to the place that the LORD your God will choose as a dwelling for his Name ³and say to the priest in office at the time, "I declare today to the LORD your God that I have come to the land that the LORD swore to our forefathers to give us." ⁴The priest shall take the basket from your hands and set it down in front of the altar of the LORD your God. ⁵Then you shall declare before the LORD your God: "My father was a wandering Aramean, and he went down into Egypt with a few people and lived there and became a great nation, powerful and numerous. ⁶But the Egyptians ill-treated us and made us suffer, putting us to hard labour. ⁷Then we cried out to the LORD, the God of our fathers, and the LORD heard our voice and saw our misery, toil and oppression. ⁸So the LORD brought us out of Egypt with a mighty hand and an outstretched arm, with great terror and with miraculous signs and wonders. ⁹He brought us to this place and gave us this land, a land flowing with milk and honey; ¹⁰and now I bring the firstfruits of the soil that you, O LORD, have given me." Place the basket before the LORD your God and bow down before him. ¹¹And you and the Levites and the aliens among you shall rejoice in all the good things the LORD your God has given to you and your household.

¹²When you have finished setting aside a tenth of all your produce in the third year, the year of the tithe, you shall give it to the Levite, the alien, the fatherless and the widow, so that they may eat in your towns and be satisfied. ¹³Then say to the LORD your God: "I have removed from my house the sacred portion and have given it to the Levite, the alien, the fatherless and the widow, according to all you commanded. I have not turned aside from your commands nor have I forgotten any of them. ¹⁴I have not eaten any of the sacred portion while I was in mourning, nor have I removed any of it while I was unclean, nor have I offered any of it to the dead. I have obeyed the LORD my God; I have done everything you commanded me. ¹⁵Look down from heaven, your holy dwelling-place, and bless your people Israel and the land you have given us as you promised on oath to our forefathers, a land flowing with milk and honey."

Follow the LORD's Commands

¹⁶The LORD your God commands you this day to follow these decrees and laws; carefully observe them with all your heart and

with all your soul. ¹⁷You have declared this day that the LORD is your God and that you will walk in his ways, that you will keep his decrees, commands and laws, and that you will obey him. ¹⁸And the LORD has declared this day that you are his people, his treasured possession as he promised, and that you are to keep all his commands. ¹⁹He has declared that he will set you in praise, fame and honour high above all the nations he has made and that you will be a people holy to the LORD your God, as he promised.

The Altar on Mount Ebal

27 Moses and the elders of Israel commanded the people: "Keep all these commands that I give you today. ²When you have crossed the Jordan into the land the LORD your God is giving you, set up some large stones and coat them with plaster. ³Write on them all the words of this law when you have crossed over to enter the land the LORD your God is giving you, a land flowing with milk and honey, just as the LORD, the God of your fathers, promised you. ⁴And when you have crossed the Jordan, set up these stones on Mount Ebal, as I command you today, and coat them with plaster. ⁵Build there an altar to the LORD your God, an altar of stones. Do not use any iron tool upon them. ⁶Build the altar of the LORD your God with stones from the field and offer burnt offerings on it to the LORD your God. ⁷Sacrifice fellowship offerings*ᵃ* there, eating them and rejoicing in the presence of the LORD your God. ⁸And you shall write very clearly all the words of this law on these stones you have set up."

Curses From Mount Ebal

⁹Then Moses and the priests, who are Levites, said to all Israel, "Be silent, O Israel, and listen! You have now become the people of the LORD your God. ¹⁰Obey the LORD your God and follow his commands and decrees that I give you today."

¹¹On the same day Moses commanded the people:

¹²When you have crossed the Jordan, these tribes shall stand on Mount Gerizim to bless the people: Simeon, Levi, Judah, Issachar, Joseph and Benjamin. ¹³And these tribes shall stand on Mount Ebal to pronounce curses: Reuben, Gad, Asher, Zebulun, Dan and Naphtali.

¹⁴The Levites shall recite to all the people of Israel in a loud voice:

¹⁵"Cursed is the man who carves an image or casts an idol—a thing detestable to the LORD, the work of the craftsman's hands—and sets it up in secret."
Then all the people shall say,
"Amen!"

¹⁶"Cursed is the man who dishonours his father or his mother."
Then all the people shall say,
"Amen!"

¹⁷"Cursed is the man who moves his neighbour's boundary stone."
Then all the people shall say,
"Amen!"

¹⁸"Cursed is the man who leads the blind astray on the road."
Then all the people shall say,
"Amen!"

¹⁹"Cursed is the man who withholds justice from the alien, the fatherless or the widow."
Then all the people shall say,
"Amen!"

²⁰"Cursed is the man who sleeps with his father's wife, for he dishonours his father's bed."
Then all the people shall say,
"Amen!"

²¹"Cursed is the man who has sexual relations with any animal."
Then all the people shall say,
"Amen!"

²²"Cursed is the man who sleeps with his sister, the daughter of his father or the daughter of his mother."
Then all the people shall say,
"Amen!"

²³"Cursed is the man who sleeps with his mother-in-law."
Then all the people shall say,
"Amen!"

²⁴"Cursed is the man who kills his neighbour secretly."
Then all the people shall say,
"Amen!"

²⁵"Cursed is the man who accepts a bribe to kill an innocent person."
Then all the people shall say,
"Amen!"

²⁶"Cursed is the man who does not uphold the words of this law by carrying them out."
Then all the people shall say,
"Amen!"

Blessings for Obedience

28 If you fully obey the LORD your God and carefully follow all his commands that I give you today, the LORD your God will set you high above all the nations on earth. ²All these blessings will come upon you and accompany you if you obey the LORD your God:

³You will be blessed in the city and blessed in the country.

⁴The fruit of your womb will be blessed, and the crops of your land and the young of your livestock—the calves of your herds and the lambs of your flocks.

⁵Your basket and your kneading trough will be blessed.

⁶You will be blessed when you come in and blessed when you go out.

⁷The LORD will grant that the enemies who rise up against you will be defeated before you. They will come at you from one direction but flee from you in seven.

ᵃ7 Traditionally peace offerings

[8]The LORD will send a blessing on your barns and on everything you put your hand to. The LORD your God will bless you in the land he is giving you.

[9]The LORD will establish you as his holy people, as he promised you on oath, if you keep the commands of the LORD your God and walk in his ways. [10]Then all the peoples on earth will see that you are called by the name of the LORD, and they will fear you. [11]The LORD will grant you abundant prosperity—in the fruit of your womb, the young of your livestock and the crops of your ground—in the land he swore to your forefathers to give you.

[12]The LORD will open the heavens, the storehouse of his bounty, to send rain on your land in season and to bless all the work of your hands. You will lend to many nations but will borrow from none. [13]The LORD will make you the head, not the tail. If you pay attention to the commands of the LORD your God that I give you this day and carefully follow them, you will always be at the top, never at the bottom. [14]Do not turn aside from any of the commands I give you today, to the right or to the left, following other gods and serving them.

Curses for Disobedience

[15]However, if you do not obey the LORD your God and do not carefully follow all his commands and decrees I am giving you today, all these curses will come upon you and overtake you:

[16]You will be cursed in the city and cursed in the country.

[17]Your basket and your kneading trough will be cursed.

[18]The fruit of your womb will be cursed, and the crops of your land, and the calves of your herds and the lambs of your flocks.

[19]You will be cursed when you come in and cursed when you go out.

[20]The LORD will send on you curses, confusion and rebuke in everything you put your hand to, until you are destroyed and come to sudden ruin because of the evil you have done in forsaking him.[a] [21]The LORD will plague you with diseases until he has destroyed you from the land you are entering to possess. [22]The LORD will strike you with wasting disease, with fever and inflammation, with scorching heat and drought, with blight and mildew, which will plague you until you perish. [23]The sky over your head will be bronze, the ground beneath you iron. [24]The LORD will turn the rain of your country into dust and powder; it will come down from the skies until you are destroyed.

[25]The LORD will cause you to be defeated before your enemies. You will come at them from one direction but flee from them in seven, and you will become a thing of horror to all the kingdoms on earth. [26]Your carcasses will be food for all the birds of the air and the beasts of the earth, and there will be no-one to frighten them away. [27]The LORD will afflict you with the boils of Egypt and with tumours, festering sores and the itch, from which you cannot be cured. [28]The LORD will afflict you with madness, blindness and confusion of mind. [29]At midday you will grope about like a blind man in the dark. You will be unsuccessful in everything you do; day after day you will be oppressed and robbed, with no-one to rescue you.

[30]You will be pledged to be married to a woman, but another will take her and ravish her. You will build a house, but you will not live in it. You will plant a vineyard, but you will not even begin to enjoy its fruit. [31]Your ox will be slaughtered before your eyes, but you will eat none of it. Your donkey will be forcibly taken from you and will not be returned. Your sheep will be given to your enemies, and no-one will rescue them. [32]Your sons and daughters will be given to another nation, and you will wear out your eyes watching for them day after day, powerless to lift a hand. [33]A people that you do not know will eat what your land and labour produce, and you will have nothing but cruel oppression all your days. [34]The sights you see will drive you mad. [35]The LORD will afflict your knees and legs with painful boils that cannot be cured, spreading from the soles of your feet to the top of your head.

[36]The LORD will drive you and the king you set over you to a nation unknown to you or your fathers. There you will worship other gods, gods of wood and stone. [37]You will become a thing of horror and an object of scorn and ridicule to all the nations where the LORD will drive you.

[38]You will sow much seed in the field but you will harvest little, because locusts will devour it. [39]You will plant vineyards and cultivate them but you will not drink the wine or gather the grapes, because worms will eat them. [40]You will have olive trees throughout your country but you will not use the oil, because the olives will drop off. [41]You will have sons and daughters but you will not keep them, because they will go into captivity. [42]Swarms of locusts will take over all your trees and the crops of your land.

[43]The alien who lives among you will rise above you higher and higher, but you will sink lower and lower. [44]He will lend to you, but you will not lend to him. He will be the head, but you will be the tail.

[45]All these curses will come upon you. They will pursue you and overtake you until you are destroyed, because you did not obey the LORD your God and observe the commands and decrees he gave you. [46]They will be a sign and a wonder to you and your descendants for ever. [47]Because you did not serve the LORD your God joyfully and gladly in the time of prosperity, [48]therefore in hunger and thirst, in nakedness and dire poverty, you will serve the enemies the LORD sends against you. He will put an iron yoke on your neck until he has destroyed you.

⁴⁹The LORD will bring a nation against you from far away, from the ends of the earth, like an eagle swooping down, a nation whose language you will not understand, ⁵⁰a fierce-looking nation without respect for the old or pity for the young. ⁵¹They will devour the young of your livestock and the crops of your land until you are destroyed. They will leave you no grain, new wine or oil, nor any calves of your herds or lambs of your flocks until you are ruined. ⁵²They will lay siege to all the cities throughout your land until the high fortified walls in which you trust fall down. They will besiege all the cities throughout the land the LORD your God is giving you.

⁵³Because of the suffering that your enemy will inflict on you during the siege, you will eat the fruit of the womb, the flesh of the sons and daughters the LORD your God has given you. ⁵⁴Even the most gentle and sensitive man among you will have no compassion on his own brother or the wife he loves or his surviving children, ⁵⁵and he will not give to one of them any of the flesh of his children that he is eating. It will be all he has left because of the suffering that your enemy will inflict on you during the siege of all your cities. ⁵⁶The most gentle and sensitive woman among you—so sensitive and gentle that she would not venture to touch the ground with the sole of her foot—will begrudge the husband she loves and her own son or daughter ⁵⁷the afterbirth from her womb and the children she bears. For she intends to eat them secretly during the siege and in the distress that your enemy will inflict on you in your cities.

⁵⁸If you do not carefully follow all the words of this law, which are written in this book, and do not revere this glorious and awesome name—the LORD your God—⁵⁹the LORD will send fearful plagues on you and your descendants, harsh and prolonged disasters, and severe and lingering illnesses. ⁶⁰He will bring upon you all the diseases of Egypt that you dreaded, and they will cling to you. ⁶¹The LORD will also bring on you every kind of sickness and disaster not recorded in this Book of the Law, until you are destroyed. ⁶²You who were as numerous as the stars in the sky will be left but few in number, because you did not obey the LORD your God. ⁶³Just as it pleased the LORD to make you prosper and increase in number, so it will please him to ruin and destroy you. You will be uprooted from the land you are entering to possess.

⁶⁴Then the LORD will scatter you among all nations, from one end of the earth to the other. There you will worship other gods—gods of wood and stone, which neither you nor your fathers have known. ⁶⁵Among those nations you will find no repose, no resting place for the sole of your foot. There the LORD will give you an anxious mind, eyes weary with longing, and a despairing heart. ⁶⁶You will live in constant suspense, filled with dread both night and day, never sure of your life. ⁶⁷In the morning you will say, "If only it were evening!" and in the evening, "If only it were morning!"—because of the terror that will fill your hearts and the sights that your eyes will see. ⁶⁸The LORD will send you back in ships to Egypt on a journey I said you should never make again. There you will offer yourselves for sale to your enemies as male and female slaves, but no-one will buy you.

Renewal of the Covenant

29 These are the terms of the covenant the LORD commanded Moses to make with the Israelites in Moab, in addition to the covenant he had made with them at Horeb.

²Moses summoned all the Israelites and said to them:

Your eyes have seen all that the LORD did in Egypt to Pharaoh, to all his officials and to all his land. ³With your own eyes you saw those great trials, those miraculous signs and great wonders. ⁴But to this day the LORD has not given you a mind that understands or eyes that see or ears that hear. ⁵During the forty years that I led you through the desert, your clothes did not wear out, nor did the sandals on your feet. ⁶You ate no bread and drank no wine or other fermented drink. I did this so that you might know that I am the LORD your God.

⁷When you reached this place, Sihon king of Heshbon and Og king of Bashan came out to fight against us, but we defeated them. ⁸We took their land and gave it as an inheritance to the Reubenites, the Gadites and the half-tribe of Manasseh.

⁹Carefully follow the terms of this covenant, so that you may prosper in everything you do. ¹⁰All of you are standing today in the presence of the LORD your God—your leaders and chief men, your elders and officials, and all the other men of Israel, ¹¹together with your children and your wives, and the aliens living in your camps who chop your wood and carry your water. ¹²You are standing here in order to enter into a covenant with the LORD your God, a covenant the LORD is making with you this day and sealing with an oath, ¹³to confirm you this day as his people, that he may be your God as he promised you and as he swore to your fathers, Abraham, Isaac and Jacob. ¹⁴I am making this covenant, with its oath, not only with you ¹⁵who are standing here with us today in the presence of the LORD our God but also with those who are not here today.

¹⁶You yourselves know how we lived in Egypt and how we passed through the countries on the way here. ¹⁷You saw among them their detestable images and idols of wood and stone, of silver and gold. ¹⁸Make sure there is no man or woman, clan or tribe among you today whose heart turns away from the LORD our God to go and worship the gods of those nations; make sure there is no root among you that produces such bitter poison.

¹⁹When such a person hears the words of this oath, he invokes a blessing on himself and therefore thinks, "I will be safe, even though I persist in going my own way." This will bring disaster on the watered land as well

DEUTERONOMY 30:11–20

'No the word is very near you; it is in your mouth and in your heart so that you can may obey it. See, I have set before you today life and prosperity, death and destruction' (vv. 14, 15).

THE THEME OF CHOICE. Israel has been aware of God's presence throughout forty years of wandering. They now face a decision: continue following God, or turn aside to the false gods of Canaan. The Law has been given to help them. It is already written down, about to be deposited beside the ark (31:26) and it will then be as near to them as life itself, rather like Paul's statement in Acts 17:27 about how near God is to us.

They have made choices before. On numerous occasions they have either followed or deserted Moses along the way. They have agreed to accept the covenant (Exod. 24:7), but that agreement has to be renewed again, and again, and again. On God's part it is once-for-all. God does not change. Only our perceptions of him change. For us there is always need for renewal, further thought, and further commitment. We say sincerely, at one moment, I will do this – and in no time at all find ourselves doing something different. That is why we need a continual reminder of our obligations. We so easily forget.

Choice for us is ongoing. We can never say we have arrived, not even when we are, like Israel, actually in the promised land. We may be fulfilling God's call to us. We may be serving him, remaining close to him, but wherever we are and whatever we do, there is no getting away from the active responsibility of choice. At any time we can desert God, in thought, word, or deed.

Let us pray to be kept close to God continually.

→178

JOSHUA 2 (especially vv. 1–14)
'Now then, please swear to me by the LORD that you will show kindness to my family, because I have shown kindness to you' (v. 12).

ALMOST EVERYTHING in the story of Rahab has something unsavoury about it. It is set in a brothel. It contains vulgar double meanings, only fully apparent in the Hebrew text. Rahab's action appears on the face of it to be treachery, bringing about the downfall of her own people. She harboured spies whose one aim was to extract information which would lead to the capture of the city. Even if – as is likely – Rahab herself was a foreigner with no real allegiance to Jericho, the story still shows her biting the hand that fed her.

Two things stand out as redeeming features. The first is her absolute conviction that the Hebrews' God was in control, and had given the land to the Hebrew invaders. This conviction is taken up in the New Testament, so that Rahab is held up as an example of faith.

The other feature is Rahab's noble adherence to the code of her profession. Her brothel was, in a sense, a 'safe house'. Once she had given 'hospitality' to the spies, she felt honour-bound to protect them. She would not betray one of her clients at any cost. Knowing her reputation, the king of Jericho himself accepted her word, and didn't have the premises searched.

And Rahab expected the spies to keep their word to her. Having shown kindness she trusted them to return kindness to her. According to her own rules she had shown strength, nobility and devotion to duty.

> *Be strong in the grace of the Lord,*
> *Be noble and upright and true,*
> *Be valiant for God and the right,*
> *Live daily your duty to do.*
> *Be strong! Be strong!*
> *And God will your courage renew.*

> *(Walter H. Windybank)*

as the dry.*a* 20The LORD will never be willing to forgive him; his wrath and zeal will burn against that man. All the curses written in this book will fall upon him, and the LORD will blot out his name from under heaven. 21The LORD will single him out from all the tribes of Israel for disaster, according to all the curses of the covenant written in this Book of the Law.

22Your children who follow you in later generations and foreigners who come from distant lands will see the calamities that have fallen on the land and the diseases with which the LORD has afflicted it. 23The whole land will be a burning waste of salt and sulphur —nothing planted, nothing sprouting, no vegetation growing on it. It will be like the destruction of Sodom and Gomorrah, Admah and Zeboiim, which the LORD overthrew in fierce anger. 24All the nations will ask: "Why has the LORD done this to this land? Why this fierce, burning anger?"

25And the answer will be: "It is because this people abandoned the covenant of the LORD, the God of their fathers, the covenant he made with them when he brought them out of Egypt. 26They went off and worshipped other gods and bowed down to them, gods they did not know, gods he had not given them. 27Therefore the LORD's anger burned against this land, so that he brought on it all the curses written in this book. 28In furious anger and in great wrath the LORD uprooted them from their land and thrust them into another land, as it is now."

29The secret things belong to the LORD our God, but the things revealed belong to us and to our children for ever, that we may follow all the words of this law.

Prosperity After Turning to the LORD

30 When all these blessings and curses I have set before you come upon you and you take them to heart wherever the LORD your God disperses you among the nations, 2and when you and your children return to the LORD your God and obey him with all your heart and with all your soul according to everything I command you today, 3then the LORD your God will restore your fortunes*a* and have compassion on you and gather you again from all the nations where he scattered you. 4Even if you have been banished to the most distant land under the heavens, from there the LORD your God will gather you and bring you back. 5He will bring you to the land that belonged to your fathers, and you will take possession of it. He will make you more prosperous and numerous than your fathers. 6The LORD your God will circumcise your hearts and the hearts of your descendants, so that you may love him with all your heart and with all your soul, and live. 7The LORD your God will put all these curses on your enemies who hate and persecute you. 8You will again obey the LORD and follow all his commands I am giving you today. 9Then the LORD your God will make you most prosperous in all the work of your hands and in the fruit of your womb, the young of your livestock and the crops of your land. The LORD will again delight in you and make you prosperous, just as he delighted in your fathers, 10if you obey the LORD your God and keep his commands and decrees that are written in this Book of the Law and turn to the LORD your God with all your heart and with all your soul.

The Offer of Life or Death

11Now what I am commanding you today is not too difficult for you or beyond your reach. 12It is not up in heaven, so that you have to ask, "Who will ascend into heaven to get it and proclaim it to us so that we may obey it?" 13Nor is it beyond the sea, so that you have to ask, "Who will cross the sea to get it and proclaim it to us so that we may obey it?" 14No, the word is very near you; it is in your mouth and in your heart so that you may obey it.

15See, I set before you today life and prosperity, death and destruction. 16For I command you today to love the LORD your God, to walk in his ways, and to keep his commands, decrees and laws; then you will live and increase, and the LORD your God will bless you in the land you are entering to possess.

17But if your heart turns away and you are not obedient, and if you are drawn away to bow down to other gods and worship them, 18I declare to you this day that you will certainly be destroyed. You will not live long in the land you are crossing the Jordan to enter and possess.

19This day I call heaven and earth as witnesses against you that I have set before you life and death, blessings and curses. Now choose life, so that you and your children may live 20and that you may love the LORD your God, listen to his voice, and hold fast to him. For the LORD is your life, and he will give you many years in the land he swore to give to your fathers, Abraham, Isaac and Jacob.

Joshua to Succeed Moses

31 Then Moses went out and spoke these words to all Israel: 2"I am now a hundred and twenty years old and I am no longer able to lead you. The LORD has said to me, 'You shall not cross the Jordan.' 3The LORD your God himself will cross over ahead of you. He will destroy these nations before you, and you will take possession of their land. Joshua also will cross over ahead of you, as the LORD said. 4And the LORD will do to them what he did to Sihon and Og, the kings of the Amorites, whom he destroyed along with their land. 5The LORD will deliver them to you, and you must do to them all that I have commanded you. 6Be strong and courageous. Do not be afraid or terrified because of them, for the LORD your God goes with you; he will never leave you nor forsake you."

7Then Moses summoned Joshua and said

a19 Or *way, in order to add drunkenness to thirst."* *a3* Or *will bring you back from captivity* to him in the presence of all Israel, "Be strong and courageous, for you must go with this people into the land that the LORD swore to their forefathers to give them, and you must divide it among them as their inheritance. 8The LORD himself goes before you and will be with you; he will never leave you nor forsake you. Do not be afraid; do not be discouraged."

The Reading of the Law

9So Moses wrote down this law and gave it to the priests, the sons of Levi, who carried the ark of the covenant of the LORD, and to all the elders of Israel. 10Then Moses commanded them: "At the end of every seven years, in the year for cancelling debts, during the Feast of Tabernacles, 11when all Israel comes to appear before the LORD your God at the place he will choose, you shall read this law before them in their hearing. 12Assemble the people—men, women and children, and the aliens living in your towns—so that they can listen and learn to fear the LORD your God and follow carefully all the words of this law. 13Their children, who do not know this law, must hear it and learn to fear the LORD your God as long as you live in the land you are crossing the Jordan to possess."

Israel's Rebellion Predicted

14The LORD said to Moses, "Now the day of your death is near. Call Joshua and present yourselves at the Tent of Meeting, where I will commission him." So Moses and Joshua came and presented themselves at the Tent of Meeting.

15Then the LORD appeared at the Tent in a pillar of cloud, and the cloud stood over the entrance to the Tent. 16And the LORD said to Moses: "You are going to rest with your fathers, and these people will soon prostitute themselves to the foreign gods of the land they are entering. They will forsake me and break the covenant I made with them. 17On that day I will become angry with them and forsake them; I will hide my face from them, and they will be destroyed. Many disasters and difficulties will come upon them, and on that day they will ask, 'Have not these disasters come upon us because our God is not with us?' 18And I will certainly hide my face on that day because of all their wickedness in turning to other gods.

19"Now write down for yourselves this song and teach it to the Israelites and make them sing it, so that it may be a witness for me against them. 20When I have brought them into the land flowing with milk and honey, the land I promised on oath to their forefathers, and when they eat their fill and thrive, they will turn to other gods and worship them, rejecting me and breaking my covenant. 21And when many disasters and difficulties come upon them, this song will testify against them, because it will not be forgotten by their descendants. I know what they are disposed to do, even before I bring them into the land I promised them on oath." 22So Moses wrote down this song that day and taught it to the Israelites.

23The LORD gave this command to Joshua son of Nun: "Be strong and courageous, for you will bring the Israelites into the land I promised them on oath, and I myself will be with you."

24After Moses finished writing in a book the words of this law from beginning to end, 25he gave this command to the Levites who carried the ark of the covenant of the LORD: 26"Take this Book of the Law and place it beside the ark of the covenant of the LORD your God. There it will remain as a witness against you. 27For I know how rebellious and stiff-necked you are. If you have been rebellious against the LORD while I am still alive and with you, how much more will you rebel after I die! 28Assemble before me all the elders of your tribes and all your officials, so that I can speak these words in their hearing and call heaven and earth to testify against them. 29For I know that after my death you are sure to become utterly corrupt and to turn from the way I have commanded you. In days to come, disaster will fall upon you because you will do evil in the sight of the LORD and provoke him to anger by what your hands have made."

The Song of Moses

30And Moses recited the words of this song from beginning to end in the hearing of the whole assembly of Israel:

32 Listen, O heavens, and I will speak;
  hear, O earth, the words of my
    mouth.
2Let my teaching fall like rain
  and my words descend like dew,
like showers on new grass,
  like abundant rain on tender plants.

3I will proclaim the name of the LORD.
  Oh, praise the greatness of our God!
4He is the Rock, his works are perfect,
  and all his ways are just.
A faithful God who does no wrong,
  upright and just is he.

5They have acted corruptly towards him;
  to their shame they are no longer his
    children,
but a warped and crooked generation.*a*
6Is this the way you repay the LORD,
  O foolish and unwise people?
Is he not your Father, your Creator,*b*
  who made you and formed you?

7Remember the days of old;
  consider the generations long past.
Ask your father and he will tell you,
  your elders, and they will explain to
    you.
8When the Most High gave the nations their
    inheritance,
  when he divided all mankind,

---

*a*5 Or *Corrupt are they and not his children, / a generation warped and twisted to their shame*
*b*6 Or *Father, who bought you*

he set up boundaries for the peoples
    according to the number of the sons of
        Israel.^c
⁹For the LORD's portion is his people,
    Jacob his allotted inheritance.

¹⁰In a desert land he found him,
    in a barren and howling waste.
He shielded him and cared for him;
    he guarded him as the apple of his eye,
¹¹like an eagle that stirs up its nest
    and hovers over its young,
that spreads its wings to catch them
    and carries them on its pinions.
¹²The LORD alone led him;
    no foreign god was with him.

¹³He made him ride on the heights of the
       land
    and fed him with the fruit of the fields.
He nourished him with honey from the
       rock,
    and with oil from the flinty crag,
¹⁴with curds and milk from herd and flock
    and with fattened lambs and goats,
with choice rams of Bashan
    and the finest grains of wheat.
You drank the foaming blood of the grape.

¹⁵Jeshurun^d grew fat and kicked;
    filled with food, he became heavy and
       sleek.
He abandoned the God who made him
    and rejected the Rock his Saviour.
¹⁶They made him jealous with their foreign
       gods
    and angered him with their detestable
       idols.
¹⁷They sacrificed to demons, which are not
       God—
    gods they had not known,
    gods that recently appeared,
    gods your fathers did not fear.
¹⁸You deserted the Rock, who fathered you;
    you forgot the God who gave you birth.

¹⁹The LORD saw this and rejected them
    because he was angered by his sons and
       daughters.
²⁰"I will hide my face from them," he said,
    "and see what their end will be;
for they are a perverse generation,
    children who are unfaithful.
²¹They made me jealous by what is no god
    and angered me with their worthless
       idols.
I will make them envious by those who are
       not a people;
I will make them angry by a nation that
       has no understanding.
²²For a fire has been kindled by my wrath,
    one that burns to the realm of death^e
       below.
It will devour the earth and its harvests
    and set on fire the foundations of the
       mountains.

²³"I will heap calamities upon them
    and expend my arrows against them.

²⁴I will send wasting famine against them,
    consuming pestilence and deadly
       plague;
I will send against them the fangs of wild
       beasts,
    the venom of vipers that glide in the
       dust.
²⁵In the street the sword will make them
       childless;
    in their homes terror will reign.
Young men and young women will perish,
    infants and grey-haired men.
²⁶I said I would scatter them
    and blot out their memory from
       mankind,
²⁷but I dreaded the taunt of the enemy,
    lest the adversary misunderstand
and say, 'Our hand has triumphed;
    the LORD has not done all this.' "

²⁸They are a nation without sense,
    there is no discernment in them.
²⁹If only they were wise and would
       understand this
    and discern what their end will be!
³⁰How could one man chase a thousand,
    or two put ten thousand to flight,
unless their Rock had sold them,
    unless the LORD had given them up?
³¹For their rock is not like our Rock,
    as even our enemies concede.
³²Their vine comes from the vine of Sodom
    and from the fields of Gomorrah.
Their grapes are filled with poison,
    and their clusters with bitterness.
³³Their wine is the venom of serpents,
    the deadly poison of cobras.

³⁴"Have I not kept this in reserve
    and sealed it in my vaults?
³⁵It is mine to avenge; I will repay.
    In due time their foot will slip;
their day of disaster is near
    and their doom rushes upon them."

³⁶The LORD will judge his people
    and have compassion on his servants
when he sees their strength is gone
    and no-one is left, slave or free.
³⁷He will say: "Now where are their gods,
    the rock they took refuge in,
³⁸the gods who ate the fat of their sacrifices
    and drank the wine of their drink
       offerings?
Let them rise up to help you!
    Let them give you shelter!

³⁹"See now that I myself am He!
    There is no god besides me.
I put to death and I bring to life,
    I have wounded and I will heal,
    and no-one can deliver out of my hand.
⁴⁰I lift my hand to heaven and declare:
    As surely as I live for ever,
⁴¹when I sharpen my flashing sword
    and my hand grasps it in judgment,
I will take vengeance on my adversaries
    and repay those who hate me.

---

^c8 Masoretic Text; Dead Sea Scrolls (see also Septuagint) *sons of God*
^d15 *Jeshurun* means *the upright one*, that is, Israel.   ^e22 Hebrew *to Sheol*

⁴²I will make my arrows drunk with blood,
   while my sword devours flesh:
the blood of the slain and the captives,
   the heads of the enemy leaders.''

⁴³Rejoice, O nations, with his people,*f,g*
   for he will avenge the blood of his
      servants;
he will take vengeance on his enemies
   and make atonement for his land and
      people.

⁴⁴Moses came with Joshua*h* son of Nun and
spoke all the words of this song in the hearing
of the people. ⁴⁵When Moses finished recit-
ing all these words to all Israel, ⁴⁶he said to
them, "Take to heart all the words I have
solemnly declared to you this day, so that
you may command your children to obey
carefully all the words of this law. ⁴⁷They are
not just idle words for you—they are your
life. By them you will live long in the land you
are crossing the Jordan to possess.''

Moses to Die on Mount Nebo

⁴⁸On that same day the LORD told Moses,
⁴⁹"Go up into the Abarim Range to Mount
Nebo in Moab, across from Jericho, and
view Canaan, the land I am giving the
Israelites as their own possession. ⁵⁰There on
the mountain that you have climbed you will
die and be gathered to your people, just as
your brother Aaron died on Mount Hor and
was gathered to his people. ⁵¹This is because
both of you broke faith with me in the presence of the Israelites at the waters of Meribah
Kadesh in the Desert of Zin and because you
did not uphold my holiness among the
Israelites. ⁵²Therefore, you will see the land
only from a distance; you will not enter the
land I am giving to the people of Israel.''

Moses Blesses the Tribes

33 This is the blessing that Moses the
man of God pronounced on the
Israelites before his death. ²He said:

"The LORD came from Sinai
   and dawned over them from Seir;
   he shone forth from Mount Paran.
He came with*a* myriads of holy ones
   from the south, from his mountain
      slopes.*b*
³Surely it is you who love the people;
   all the holy ones are in your hand.
At your feet they all bow down,
   and from you receive instruction,
⁴the law that Moses gave us,
   the possession of the assembly of Jacob.
⁵He was king over Jeshurun*c*
   when the leaders of the people
      assembled,
   along with the tribes of Israel.

⁶"Let Reuben live and not die,
   nor*d* his men be few.''

⁷And this he said about Judah:

"Hear, O LORD, the cry of Judah;
   bring him to his people.
With his own hands he defends his cause.
   Oh, be his help against his foes!''

⁸About Levi he said:

"Your Thummim and Urim belong
   to the man you favoured.
You tested him at Massah;
   you contended with him at the waters of
      Meribah.
⁹He said of his father and mother,
   'I have no regard for them.'
He did not recognise his brothers
   or acknowledge his own children,
but he watched over your word
   and guarded your covenant.
¹⁰He teaches your precepts to Jacob
   and your law to Israel.
He offers incense before you
   and whole burnt offerings on your altar.
¹¹Bless all his skills, O LORD,
   and be pleased with the work of his
      hands.
Smite the loins of those who rise up
      against him;
   strike his foes till they rise no more.''

¹²About Benjamin he said:

"Let the beloved of the LORD rest secure
      in him,
for he shields him all day long,
   and the one the LORD loves rests
      between his shoulders.''

¹³About Joseph he said:

"May the LORD bless his land
   with the precious dew from heaven
      above
   and with the deep waters that lie
      below;
¹⁴with the best the sun brings forth
   and the finest the moon can yield;
¹⁵with the choicest gifts of the ancient
      mountains
   and the fruitfulness of the everlasting
      hills;
¹⁶with the best gifts of the earth and its
      fulness
   and the favour of him who dwelt in the
      burning bush.
Let all these rest on the head of Joseph,
   on the brow of the prince among*e* his
      brothers.
¹⁷In majesty he is like a firstborn bull;
   his horns are the horns of a wild ox.
With them he will gore the nations,
   even those at the ends of the earth.
Such are the ten thousands of Ephraim;
   such are the thousands of Manasseh.''

---

*f*43 Or *Make his people rejoice, O nations*
*g*43 Masoretic Text; Dead Sea Scrolls (see also Septuagint) *people, / and let all the angels worship him /*
*h*44 Hebrew *Hoshea,* a variant of *Joshua*   *a*2 Or *from*
*b*2 The meaning of the Hebrew for this phrase is uncertain.
*c*5 *Jeshurun* means *the upright one,* that is, Israel; also in verse 26.   *d*6 Or *but let*
*e*16 Or *of the one separated from*

¹⁸About Zebulun he said:

"Rejoice, Zebulun, in your going out,
and you, Issachar, in your tents.
¹⁹They will summon peoples to the
mountain
and there offer sacrifices of
righteousness;
they will feast on the abundance of the
seas,
on the treasures hidden in the sand."

²⁰About Gad he said:

"Blessed is he who enlarges Gad's
domain!
Gad lives there like a lion,
tearing at arm or head.
²¹He chose the best land for himself;
the leader's portion was kept for him.
When the heads of the people assembled,
he carried out the LORD's righteous will,
and his judgments concerning Israel."

²²About Dan he said:

"Dan is a lion's cub,
springing out of Bashan."

²³About Naphtali he said:

"Naphtali is abounding with the favour of
the LORD
and is full of his blessing;
he will inherit southward to the lake."

²⁴About Asher he said:

"Most blessed of sons is Asher;
let him be favoured by his brothers,
and let him bathe his feet in oil.
²⁵The bolts of your gates will be iron and
bronze,
and your strength will equal your days.

²⁶"There is no-one like the God of Jeshurun,
who rides on the heavens to help you
and on the clouds in his majesty.
²⁷The eternal God is your refuge,
and underneath are the everlasting
arms.
He will drive out your enemy before you,

saying, 'Destroy him!'
²⁸So Israel will live in safety alone;
Jacob's spring is secure
in a land of grain and new wine,
where the heavens drop dew.
²⁹Blessed are you, O Israel!
Who is like you,
a people saved by the LORD?
He is your shield and helper
and your glorious sword.
Your enemies will cower before you,
and you will trample down their high
places."^f

The Death of Moses

34 Then Moses climbed Mount Nebo
from the plains of Moab to the top of
Pisgah, across from Jericho. There the LORD
showed him the whole land—from Gilead to
Dan, ²all of Naphtali, the territory of
Ephraim and Manasseh, all the land of Judah
as far as the western sea,^a ³the Negev and the
whole region from the Valley of Jericho, the
City of Palms, as far as Zoar. ⁴Then the LORD
said to him, "This is the land I promised on
oath to Abraham, Isaac and Jacob when I
said, 'I will give it to your descendants.' I
have let you see it with your eyes, but you
will not cross over into it."

⁵And Moses the servant of the LORD died
there in Moab, as the LORD had said. ⁶He
buried him^b in Moab, in the valley opposite
Beth Peor, but to this day no-one knows
where his grave is. ⁷Moses was a hundred
and twenty years old when he died, yet his
eyes were not weak nor his strength gone.
⁸The Israelites grieved for Moses in the
plains of Moab thirty days, until the time of
weeping and mourning was over.

⁹Now Joshua son of Nun was filled with
the spirit^c of wisdom because Moses had laid
his hands on him. So the Israelites listened to
him and did what the LORD had commanded
Moses.

¹⁰Since then, no prophet has risen in Israel
like Moses, whom the LORD knew face to
face, ¹¹who did all those miraculous signs and
wonders the LORD sent him to do in Egypt
—to Pharaoh and to all his officials and to his
whole land. ¹²For no-one has ever shown the
mighty power or performed the awesome
deeds that Moses did in the sight of all Israel.

f 29 Or *will tread upon their bodies*　　*a* 2 That is, the Mediterranean　　*b* 6 Or *He was buried*　　*c* 9 Or *Spirit*

Joshua

The Lord Commands Joshua

1 After the death of Moses the servant of the Lord, the Lord said to Joshua son of Nun, Moses' assistant: 2"Moses my servant is dead. Now then, you and all these people, get ready to cross the Jordan River into the land I am about to give to them—to the Israelites. 3I will give you every place where you set your foot, as I promised Moses. 4Your territory will extend from the desert to Lebanon, and from the great river, the Euphrates—all the Hittite country—to the Great Sea*a* on the west. 5No-one will be able to stand up against you all the days of your life. As I was with Moses, so I will be with you; I will never leave you nor forsake you.

6"Be strong and courageous, because you will lead these people to inherit the land I swore to their forefathers to give them. 7Be strong and very courageous. Be careful to obey all the law my servant Moses gave you; do not turn from it to the right or to the left, that you may be successful wherever you go. 8Do not let this Book of the Law depart from your mouth; meditate on it day and night, so that you may be careful to do everything written in it. Then you will be prosperous and successful. 9Have I not commanded you? Be strong and courageous. Do not be terrified; do not be discouraged, for the Lord your God will be with you wherever you go."

10So Joshua ordered the officers of the people: 11"Go through the camp and tell the people, 'Get your supplies ready. Three days from now you will cross the Jordan here to go in and take possession of the land the Lord your God is giving you for your own.'"

12But to the Reubenites, the Gadites and the half-tribe of Manasseh, Joshua said, 13"Remember the command that Moses the servant of the Lord gave you: 'The Lord your God is giving you rest and has granted you this land.' 14Your wives, your children and your livestock may stay in the land that Moses gave you east of the Jordan, but all your fighting men, fully armed, must cross over ahead of your brothers. You are to help your brothers 15until the Lord gives them rest, as he has done for you, and until they too have taken possession of the land that the Lord your God is giving them. After that,

you may go back and occupy your own land, which Moses the servant of the Lord gave you east of the Jordan towards the sunrise."

16Then they answered Joshua, "Whatever you have commanded us we will do, and wherever you send us we will go. 17Just as we fully obeyed Moses, so we will obey you. Only may the Lord your God be with you as he was with Moses. 18Whoever rebels against your word and does not obey your words, whatever you may command them, will be put to death. Only be strong and courageous!"

Rahab and the Spies

2 Then Joshua son of Nun secretly sent two spies from Shittim. "Go, look over the land," he said, "especially Jericho." So they went and entered the house of a prostitute*a* named Rahab and stayed there.

2The king of Jericho was told, "Look! Some of the Israelites have come here tonight to spy out the land." 3So the king of Jericho sent this message to Rahab: "Bring out the men who came to you and entered your house, because they have come to spy out the whole land."

4But the woman had taken the two men and hidden them. She said, "Yes, the men came to me, but I did not know where they had come from. 5At dusk, when it was time to close the city gate, the men left. I don't know which way they went. Go after them quickly. You may catch up with them." 6(But she had taken them up to the roof and hidden them under the stalks of flax she had laid out on the roof.) 7So the men set out in pursuit of the spies on the road that leads to the fords of the Jordan, and as soon as the pursuers had gone out, the gate was shut.

8Before the spies lay down for the night, she went up on the roof 9and said to them, "I know that the Lord has given this land to you and that a great fear of you has fallen on us, so that all who live in this country are melting in fear because of you. 10We have heard how the Lord dried up the water of the Red Sea*b* for you when you came out of Egypt, and what you did to Sihon and Og, the two kings of the Amorites east of the Jordan, whom you completely destroyed.*c* 11When we heard of

---

a4 That is, the Mediterranean   *a1* Or possibly *an innkeeper*   *b10* Hebrew *Yam Suph*; that is, Sea of Reeds
c10 The Hebrew term refers to the irrevocable giving over of things or persons to the Lord, often by totally destroying them.

it, our hearts sank[d] and everyone's courage failed because of you, for the LORD your God is God in heaven above and on the earth below. [12]Now then, please swear to me by the LORD that you will show kindness to my family, because I have shown kindness to you. Give me a sure sign [13]that you will spare the lives of my father and mother, my brothers and sisters, and all who belong to them, and that you will save us from death."

[14]"Our lives for your lives!" the men assured her. "If you don't tell what we are doing, we will treat you kindly and faithfully when the LORD gives us the land."

[15]So she let them down by a rope through the window, for the house she lived in was part of the city wall. [16]Now she had said to them, "Go to the hills so that the pursuers will not find you. Hide yourselves there three days until they return, and then go on your way."

[17]The men said to her, "This oath you made us swear will not be binding on us [18]unless, when we enter the land, you have tied this scarlet cord in the window through which you let us down, and unless you have brought your father and mother, your brothers and all your family into your house. [19]If anyone goes outside your house into the street, his blood will be on his own head; we will not be responsible. As for anyone who is in the house with you, his blood will be on our head if a hand is laid on him. [20]But if you tell what we are doing, we will be released from the oath you made us swear."

[21]"Agreed," she replied. "Let it be as you say." So she sent them away and they departed. And she tied the scarlet cord in the window.

[22]When they left, they went into the hills and stayed there three days, until the pursuers had searched all along the road and returned without finding them. [23]Then the two men started back. They went down out of the hills, forded the river and came to Joshua son of Nun and told him everything that had happened to them. [24]They said to Joshua, "The LORD has surely given the whole land into our hands; all the people are melting in fear because of us."

Crossing the Jordan

3 Early in the morning Joshua and all the Israelites set out from Shittim and went to the Jordan, where they camped before crossing over. [2]After three days the officers went throughout the camp, [3]giving orders to the people: "When you see the ark of the covenant of the LORD your God, and the priests, who are Levites, carrying it, you are to move out from your positions and follow it. [4]Then you will know which way to go, since you have never been this way before. But keep a distance of about a thousand yards[a] between you and the ark; do not go near it."

[5]Joshua told the people, "Consecrate yourselves, for tomorrow the LORD will do amazing things among you."

[6]Joshua said to the priests, "Take up the ark of the covenant and pass on ahead of the people." So they took it up and went ahead of them.

[7]And the LORD said to Joshua, "Today I will begin to exalt you in the eyes of all Israel, so that they may know that I am with you as I was with Moses. [8]Tell the priests who carry the ark of the covenant: 'When you reach the edge of the Jordan's waters, go and stand in the river.' "

[9]Joshua said to the Israelites, "Come here and listen to the words of the LORD your God. [10]This is how you will know that the living God is among you and that he will certainly drive out before you the Canaanites, Hittites, Hivites, Perizzites, Girgashites, Amorites and Jebusites. [11]See, the ark of the covenant of the Lord of all the earth will go into the Jordan ahead of you. [12]Now then, choose twelve men from the tribes of Israel, one from each tribe. [13]And as soon as the priests who carry the ark of the LORD—the Lord of all the earth—set foot in the Jordan, its waters flowing downstream will be cut off and stand up in a heap."

[14]So when the people broke camp to cross the Jordan, the priests carrying the ark of the covenant went ahead of them. [15]Now the Jordan is in flood all during harvest. Yet as soon as the priests who carried the ark reached the Jordan and their feet touched the water's edge, [16]the water from upstream stopped flowing. It piled up in a heap a great distance away, at a town called Adam in the vicinity of Zarethan, while the water flowing down to the Sea of the Arabah (the Salt Sea[b]) was completely cut off. So the people crossed over opposite Jericho. [17]The priests who carried the ark of the covenant of the LORD stood firm on dry ground in the middle of the Jordan, while all Israel passed by until the whole nation had completed the crossing on dry ground.

4 When the whole nation had finished crossing the Jordan, the LORD said to Joshua, [2]"Choose twelve men from among the people, one from each tribe, [3]and tell them to take up twelve stones from the middle of the Jordan from right where the priests stood and to carry them over with you and put them down at the place where you stay tonight."

[4]So Joshua called together the twelve men he had appointed from the Israelites, one from each tribe, [5]and said to them, "Go over before the ark of the LORD your God into the middle of the Jordan. Each of you is to take up a stone on his shoulder, according to the number of the tribes of the Israelites, [6]to serve as a sign among you. In the future, when your children ask you, 'What do these stones mean?' [7]tell them that the flow of the Jordan was cut off before the ark of the covenant of the LORD. When it crossed the Jordan, the waters of the Jordan were cut off. These stones are to be a memorial to the people of Israel for ever."

d11 Hebrew melted   a4 Hebrew about two thousand cubits (about 900 metres)   b16 That is, the Dead Sea

8So the Israelites did as Joshua commanded them. They took twelve stones from the middle of the Jordan, according to the number of the tribes of the Israelites, as the LORD had told Joshua; and they carried them over with them to their camp, where they put them down. 9Joshua set up the twelve stones that had beena in the middle of the Jordan at the spot where the priests who carried the ark of the covenant had stood. And they are there to this day.

. 10Now the priests who carried the ark remained standing in the middle of the Jordan until everything the LORD had commanded Joshua was done by the people, just as Moses had directed Joshua. The people hurried over, 11and as soon as all of them had crossed, the ark of the LORD and the priests came to the other side while the people watched. 12The men of Reuben, Gad and the half-tribe of Manasseh crossed over, armed, in front of the Israelites, as Moses had directed them. 13About forty thousand armed for battle crossed over before the LORD to the plains of Jericho for war.

14That day the LORD exalted Joshua in the sight of all Israel; and they revered him all the days of his life, just as they had revered Moses.

15Then the LORD said to Joshua, 16"Command the priests carrying the ark of the Testimony to come up out of the Jordan."

17So Joshua commanded the priests, "Come up out of the Jordan."

18And the priests came up out of the river carrying the ark of the covenant of the LORD. No sooner had they set their feet on the dry ground than the waters of the Jordan returned to their place and ran in flood as before.

19On the tenth day of the first month the people went up from the Jordan and camped at Gilgal on the eastern border of Jericho. 20And Joshua set up at Gilgal the twelve stones they had taken out of the Jordan. 21He said to the Israelites, "In the future when your descendants ask their fathers, 'What do these stones mean?' 22tell them, 'Israel crossed the Jordan on dry ground.' 23For the LORD your God dried up the Jordan before you until you had crossed over. The LORD your God did to the Jordan just what he had done to the Red Seab when he dried it up before us until we had crossed over. 24He did this so that all the peoples of the earth might know that the hand of the LORD is powerful and so that you might always fear the LORD your God."

Circumcision at Gilgal

5 Now when all the Amorite kings west of the Jordan and all the Canaanite kings along the coast heard how the LORD had dried up the Jordan before the Israelites until we had crossed over, their hearts sanka and they no longer had the courage to face the Israelites.

2At that time the LORD said to Joshua, "Make flint knives and circumcise the Israelites again." 3So Joshua made flint knives and circumcised the Israelites at Gibeath Haaraloth.b

4Now this is why he did so: All those who came out of Egypt—all the men of military age—died in the desert on the way after leaving Egypt. 5All the people that came out had been circumcised, but all the people born in the desert during the journey from Egypt had not. 6The Israelites had moved about in the desert forty years until all the men who were of military age when they left Egypt had died, since they had not obeyed the LORD. For the LORD had sworn to them that they would not see the land that he had solemnly promised their fathers to give us, a land flowing with milk and honey. 7So he raised up their sons in their place, and these were the ones Joshua circumcised. They were still uncircumcised because they had not been circumcised on the way. 8And after the whole nation had been circumcised, they remained where they were in camp until they were healed.

9Then the LORD said to Joshua, "Today I have rolled away the reproach of Egypt from you." So the place has been called Gilgalc to this day.

10On the evening of the fourteenth day of the month, while camped at Gilgal on the plains of Jericho, the Israelites celebrated the Passover. 11The day after the Passover, that very day, they ate some of the produce of the land: unleavened bread and roasted grain. 12The manna stopped the day afterd they ate this food from the land; there was no longer any manna for the Israelites, but that year they ate of the produce of Canaan.

The Fall of Jericho

13Now when Joshua was near Jericho, he looked up and saw a man standing in front of him with a drawn sword in his hand. Joshua went up to him and asked, "Are you for us or for our enemies?"

14"Neither," he replied, "but as commander of the army of the LORD I have now come." Then Joshua fell face down to the ground in reverence, and asked him, "What message does my Lorde have for his servant?"

15The commander of the LORD's army replied, "Take off your sandals, for the place where you are standing is holy." And Joshua did so.

6 Now Jericho was tightly shut up because of the Israelites. No-one went out and no-one came in.

2Then the LORD said to Joshua, "See, I have delivered Jericho into your hands, along with its king and its fighting men. 3March around the city once with all the armed men. Do this for six days. 4Make seven priests carry trumpets of rams' horns in front of the ark. On the seventh day, march around the city seven times, with the priests

a9 Or Joshua also set up twelve stones   b23 Hebrew Yam Suph; that is, Sea of Reeds
a1 Hebrew melted   b3 Gibeath Haaraloth means hill of foreskins.
c9 Gilgal sounds like the Hebrew for roll.   d12 Or the day   e14 Or lord

JOSHUA 3:5–17
'Joshua told the people, "Consecrate yourselves, for tomorrow the LORD will do amazing things among you" ' (v. 5).

THE RIVER JORDAN was a barrier to the people under Joshua's command. While they remained east of it, they were still in the 'desert' situation of the Exodus, but relatively safe. Once across Jordan they would be in the promised land. At that point there would be no turning back. The only alternatives were to conquer or be defeated. They believed the land had been given to them by God, but even so, they would have to fight hard to take it.

A miracle took them across the river. Unknown to them at this time, a miracle was going to enable them to take Jericho. Crossing Jordan and capturing Jericho would help their morale, but much more than that was needed for victory. Once across the Jordan it took longer to conquer the land than it had taken them to get there. Forty years of wandering in the desert were followed by several decades of struggle.

The book of Joshua gives an impression of victory after victory after victory. Certain hints let us know that the victory was not complete, and the book of Judges tells of continual struggle as the Israelites sought to establish themselves in the land.

The people were called on to consecrate themselves ready for crossing the Jordan. Amazing things were going to happen. But the amazing things were only a start. The future kingdom of Israel would not be built on spectacular, miraculous interventions alone. They were foundations, a starting-point and no more. For the tribes to be built into a people would require a continual consecration.

Crossing Jordan is only a beginning. The real wonders belong to 'tomorrow'.

JOSHUA 5:13–6:11

'Joshua went up to him and asked, "Are you for us or for our enemies?" "Neither," he replied, "but as commander of the army of the LORD I have now come . . . Take off your sandals, for the place where you are standing is holy" ' (vv. 13–15).

GOD IS FOR US. That statement is always true – yet God is never partisan. At the point where it seems that God most favours Israel, the commander of his forces says he is neither for Israel, nor for her enemies. It is a strange statement, for the impression we get throughout the book of Joshua is that God has the interests of Israel, and Israel alone, at heart. But that is never the case. God's interest is for all. Israel is chosen in order to lead others to him. When Israel fails, other instruments are used by God.

It is not in order to glorify Israel that God engineers the conquest of the promised land, but in order that Israel and others will glorify God.

People continue to make the same mistake throughout the ages. They continue to believe God is on their side alone. They pray to him for victory. They claim his hand is with them when they wipe out their enemies. They wage war in his name and commit outrages, believing they have God's blessing.

The author of Joshua certainly believed God was pleased with Israel when they slaughtered whole communities and destroyed everything before them. But this tiny verse, slipped in almost unnoticed, gives the true picture. The conquest does not belong to Israel, but to God. And God's conquests are not military victories. They are conquests of the hearts and minds of men.

The 'holy' ground on which we stand, the area where we live, the part we call 'our own' is not ours at all, but God's. It is up to us to care for it, nourish it, and use it under God's direction.

→203

blowing the trumpets. ⁵When you hear them sound a long blast on the trumpets, make all the people give a loud shout; then the wall of the city will collapse and the people will go up, every man straight in.''

⁶So Joshua son of Nun called the priests and said to them, ''Take up the ark of the covenant of the LORD and make seven priests carry trumpets in front of it.'' ⁷And he ordered the people, ''Advance! March around the city, with the armed guard going ahead of the ark of the LORD.''

⁸When Joshua had spoken to the people, the seven priests carrying the seven trumpets before the LORD went forward, blowing their trumpets, and the ark of the LORD's covenant followed them. ⁹The armed guard marched ahead of the priests who blew the trumpets, and the rear guard followed the ark. All this time the trumpets were sounding. ¹⁰But Joshua had commanded the people, ''Do not give a war cry, do not raise your voices, do not say a word until the day I tell you to shout. Then shout!'' ¹¹So he had the ark of the LORD carried around the city, circling it once. Then the people returned to camp and spent the night there.

¹²Joshua got up early the next morning and the priests took up the ark of the LORD. ¹³The seven priests carrying the seven trumpets went forward, marching before the ark of the LORD and blowing the trumpets. The armed men went ahead of them and the rear guard followed the ark of the LORD, while the trumpets kept sounding. ¹⁴So on the second day they marched around the city once and returned to the camp. They did this for six days.

¹⁵On the seventh day, they got up at daybreak and marched around the city seven times in the same manner, except that on that day they circled the city seven times. ¹⁶The seventh time around, when the priests sounded the trumpet blast, Joshua commanded the people, ''Shout! For the LORD has given you the city! ¹⁷The city and all that is in it are to be devoted^a to the LORD. Only Rahab the prostitute^b and all who are with her in her house shall be spared, because she hid the spies we sent. ¹⁸But keep away from the devoted things, so that you will not bring about your own destruction by taking any of them. Otherwise you will make the camp of Israel liable to destruction and bring trouble on it. ¹⁹All the silver and gold and the articles of bronze and iron are sacred to the LORD and must go into his treasury.''

²⁰When the trumpets sounded, the people shouted, and at the sound of the trumpet, when the people gave a loud shout, the wall collapsed; so every man charged straight in, and they took the city. ²¹They devoted the city to the LORD and destroyed with the sword every living thing in it—men and women, young and old, cattle, sheep and donkeys.

²²Joshua said to the two men who had spied out the land, ''Go into the prostitute's house and bring her out and all who belong to her, in accordance with your oath to her.'' ²³So the young men who had done the spying went in and brought out Rahab, her father and mother and brothers and all who belonged to her. They brought out her entire family and put them in a place outside the camp of Israel.

²⁴Then they burned the whole city and everything in it, but they put the silver and gold and the articles of bronze and iron into the treasury of the LORD's house. ²⁵But Joshua spared Rahab the prostitute, with her family and all who belonged to her, because she hid the men Joshua had sent as spies to Jericho—and she lives among the Israelites to this day.

²⁶At that time Joshua pronounced this solemn oath: ''Cursed before the LORD is the man who undertakes to rebuild this city, Jericho:

''At the cost of his firstborn son
    will he lay its foundations;
at the cost of his youngest
    will he set up its gates.''

²⁷So the LORD was with Joshua, and his fame spread throughout the land.

Achan's Sin

7 But the Israelites acted unfaithfully in regard to the devoted things;^{a} Achan son of Carmi, the son of Zimri,^{b} the son of Zerah, of the tribe of Judah, took some of them. So the LORD's anger burned against Israel.

²Now Joshua sent men from Jericho to Ai, which is near Beth Aven to the east of Bethel, and told them, ''Go up and spy out the region.'' So the men went up and spied out Ai.

³When they returned to Joshua, they said, ''Not all the people will have to go up against Ai. Send two or three thousand men to take it and do not weary all the people, for only a few men are there.'' ⁴So about three thousand men went up; but they were routed by the men of Ai, ⁵who killed about thirty-six of them. They chased the Israelites from the city gate as far as the stone quarries^c and struck them down on the slopes. At this the hearts of the people melted and became like water.

⁶Then Joshua tore his clothes and fell face down to the ground before the ark of the LORD, remaining there till evening. The elders of Israel did the same, and sprinkled dust on their heads. ⁷And Joshua said, ''Ah, Sovereign LORD, why did you ever bring this people across the Jordan to deliver us into the hands of the Amorites to destroy us? If only we had been content to stay on the other side of the Jordan! ⁸O Lord, what can I say, now that Israel has been routed by its enemies? ⁹The Canaanites and the other

---

^{a}17 The Hebrew term refers to the irrevocable giving over of things or persons to the LORD, often by totally destroying them; also in verses 18 and 21. ^{b}17 Or possibly *innkeeper*; also in verses 22 and 25
^{a}1 The Hebrew term refers to the irrevocable giving over of things or persons to the LORD, often by totally destroying them; also in verses 11, 12, 13 and 15.
^{b}1 See Septuagint and 1 Chron. 2:6; Hebrew *Zabdi*; also in verses 17 and 18. ^{c}5 Or *as far as Shebarim*

people of the country will hear about this and they will surround us and wipe out our name from the earth. What then will you do for your own great name?"

¹⁰The LORD said to Joshua, "Stand up! What are you doing down on your face? ¹¹Israel has sinned; they have violated my covenant, which I commanded them to keep. They have taken some of the devoted things; they have stolen, they have lied, they have put them with their own possessions. ¹²That is why the Israelites cannot stand against their enemies; they turn their backs and run because they have been made liable to destruction. I will not be with you any more unless you destroy whatever among you is devoted to destruction.

¹³"Go, consecrate the people. Tell them, 'Consecrate yourselves in preparation for tomorrow; for this is what the LORD, the God of Israel, says: That which is devoted is among you, O Israel. You cannot stand against your enemies until you remove it.

¹⁴"'In the morning, present yourselves tribe by tribe. The tribe that the LORD takes shall come forward clan by clan; the clan that the LORD takes shall come forward family by family; and the family that the LORD takes shall come forward man by man. ¹⁵He who is caught with the devoted things shall be destroyed by fire, along with all that belongs to him. He has violated the covenant of the LORD and has done a disgraceful thing in Israel!'"

¹⁶Early the next morning Joshua had Israel come forward by tribes, and Judah was taken. ¹⁷The clans of Judah came forward, and he took the Zerahites. He had the clan of the Zerahites come forward by families, and Zimri was taken. ¹⁸Joshua had his family come forward man by man, and Achan son of Carmi, the son of Zimri, the son of Zerah, of the tribe of Judah, was taken.

¹⁹Then Joshua said to Achan, "My son, give glory to the LORD,ᵈ the God of Israel, and give him the praise.ᵉ Tell me what you have done; do not hide it from me."

²⁰Achan replied, "It is true! I have sinned against the LORD, the God of Israel. This is what I have done: ²¹When I saw in the plunder a beautiful robe from Babylonia,ᶠ two hundred shekelsᵍ of silver and a wedge of gold weighing fifty shekels,ʰ I coveted them and took them. They are hidden in the ground inside my tent, with the silver underneath."

²²So Joshua sent messengers, and they ran to the tent, and there it was, hidden in his tent, with the silver underneath. ²³They took the things from the tent, brought them to Joshua and all the Israelites and spread them out before the LORD.

²⁴Then Joshua, together with all Israel, took Achan son of Zerah, the silver, the robe, the gold wedge, his sons and daughters, his cattle, donkeys and sheep, his tent and all that he had, to the Valley of Achor. ²⁵Joshua said, "Why have you brought this trouble

on us? The LORD will bring trouble on you today."

Then all Israel stoned him, and after they had stoned the rest, they burned them. ²⁶Over Achan they heaped up a large pile of rocks, which remains to this day. Then the LORD turned from his fierce anger. Therefore that place has been called the Valley of Achorⁱ ever since.

Ai Destroyed

8 Then the LORD said to Joshua, "Do not be afraid; do not be discouraged. Take the whole army with you, and go up and attack Ai. For I have delivered into your hands the king of Ai, his people, his city and his land. ²You shall do to Ai and its king as you did to Jericho and its king, except that you may carry off their plunder and livestock for yourselves. Set an ambush behind the city."

³So Joshua and the whole army moved out to attack Ai. He chose thirty thousand of his best fighting men and sent them out at night ⁴with these orders: "Listen carefully. You are to set an ambush behind the city. Don't go very far from it. All of you be on the alert. ⁵I and all those with me will advance on the city, and when the men come out against us, as they did before, we will flee from them. ⁶They will pursue us until we have lured them away from the city, for they will say, 'They are running away from us as they did before.' So when we flee from them, ⁷you are to rise up from ambush and take the city. The LORD your God will give it into your hand. ⁸When you have taken the city, set it on fire. Do what the LORD has commanded. See to it; you have my orders."

⁹Then Joshua sent them off, and they went to the place of ambush and lay in wait between Bethel and Ai, to the west of Ai—but Joshua spent that night with the people.

¹⁰Early the next morning Joshua mustered his men, and he and the leaders of Israel marched before them to Ai. ¹¹The entire force that was with him marched up and approached the city and arrived in front of it. They set up camp north of Ai, with the valley between them and the city. ¹²Joshua had taken about five thousand men and set them in ambush between Bethel and Ai, to the west of the city. ¹³They had the soldiers take up their positions—all those in the camp to the north of the city and the ambush to the west of it. That night Joshua went into the valley.

¹⁴When the king of Ai saw this, he and all the men of the city hurried out early in the morning to meet Israel in battle at a certain place overlooking the Arabah. But he did not know that an ambush had been set against him behind the city. ¹⁵Joshua and all Israel let themselves be driven back before them, and they fled towards the desert. ¹⁶All the men of Ai were called to pursue them, and they pursued Joshua and were lured away from

ᵈ19 A solemn charge to tell the truth   ᵉ19 Or and confess to him
ᶠ21 Hebrew Shinar   ᵍ21 That is, about 5 pounds (about 2.3 kilograms)
ʰ21 That is, about 1¼ pounds (about 0.6 kilogram)   ⁱ26 Achor means trouble.

the city. ¹⁷Not a man remained in Ai or Bethel who did not go after Israel. They left the city open and went in pursuit of Israel.

¹⁸Then the LORD said to Joshua, "Hold out towards Ai the javelin that is in your hand, for into your hand I will deliver the city." So Joshua held out his javelin towards Ai. ¹⁹As soon as he did this, the men in the ambush rose quickly from their position and rushed forward. They entered the city and captured it and quickly set it on fire.

²⁰The men of Ai looked back and saw the smoke of the city rising against the sky, but they had no chance to escape in any direction, for the Israelites who had been fleeing towards the desert had turned back against their pursuers. ²¹For when Joshua and all Israel saw that the ambush had taken the city and that smoke was going up from the city, they turned round and attacked the men of Ai. ²²The men of the ambush also came out of the city against them, so that they were caught in the middle, with Israelites on both sides. Israel cut them down, leaving them neither survivors nor fugitives. ²³But they took the king of Ai alive and brought him to Joshua.

²⁴When Israel had finished killing all the men of Ai in the fields and in the desert where they had chased them, and when every one of them had been put to the sword, all the Israelites returned to Ai and killed those who were in it. ²⁵Twelve thousand men and women fell that day—all the people of Ai. ²⁶For Joshua did not draw back the hand that held out his javelin until he had destroyed^a all who lived in Ai. ²⁷But Israel did carry off for themselves the livestock and plunder of this city, as the LORD had instructed Joshua.

²⁸So Joshua burned Ai and made it a permanent heap of ruins, a desolate place to this day. ²⁹He hung the king of Ai on a tree and left him there until evening. At sunset, Joshua ordered them to take his body from the tree and throw it down at the entrance of the city gate. And they raised a large pile of rocks over it, which remains to this day.

The Covenant Renewed at Mount Ebal

³⁰Then Joshua built on Mount Ebal an altar to the LORD, the God of Israel, ³¹as Moses the servant of the LORD had commanded the Israelites. He built it according to what is written in the Book of the Law of Moses—an altar of uncut stones, on which no iron tool had been used. On it they offered to the LORD burnt offerings and sacrificed fellowship offerings.^b ³²There, in the presence of the Israelites, Joshua copied on stones the law of Moses, which he had written. ³³All Israel, aliens and citizens alike, with their elders, officials and judges, were standing on both sides of the ark of the covenant of the LORD, facing those who carried it—the priests, who were Levites. Half of the people stood in front of Mount Gerizim and half of them in front of Mount Ebal, as Moses the servant of

the LORD had formerly commanded when he gave instructions to bless the people of Israel.

³⁴Afterwards, Joshua read all the words of the law—the blessings and the curses—just as it is written in the Book of the Law. ³⁵There was not a word of all that Moses had commanded that Joshua did not read to the whole assembly of Israel, including the women and children, and the aliens who lived among them.

The Gibeonite Deception

9 Now when all the kings west of the Jordan heard about these things—those in the hill country, in the western foothills, and along the entire coast of the Great Sea^a as far as Lebanon (the kings of the Hittites, Amorites, Canaanites, Perizzites, Hivites and Jebusites)—²they came together to make war against Joshua and Israel.

³However, when the people of Gibeon heard what Joshua had done to Jericho and Ai, ⁴they resorted to a ruse: They went as a delegation whose donkeys were loaded^b with worn-out sacks and old wineskins, cracked and mended. ⁵The men put worn and patched sandals on their feet and wore old clothes. All the bread of their food supply was dry and mouldy. ⁶Then they went to Joshua in the camp at Gilgal and said to him and the men of Israel, "We have come from a distant country; make a treaty with us."

⁷The men of Israel said to the Hivites, "But perhaps you live near us. How then can we make a treaty with you?"

⁸"We are your servants," they said to Joshua.

But Joshua asked, "Who are you and where do you come from?"

⁹They answered: "Your servants have come from a very distant country because of the fame of the LORD your God. For we have heard reports of him: all that he did in Egypt, ¹⁰and all that he did to the two kings of the Amorites east of the Jordan—Sihon king of Heshbon, and Og king of Bashan, who reigned in Ashtaroth. ¹¹And our elders and all those living in our country said to us, 'Take provisions for your journey; go and meet them and say to them, "We are your servants; make a treaty with us."' ¹²This bread of ours was warm when we packed it at home on the day we left to come to you. But now see how dry and mouldy it is. ¹³And these wineskins that we filled were new, but see how cracked they are. And our clothes and sandals are worn out by the very long journey."

¹⁴The men of Israel sampled their provisions but did not enquire of the LORD. ¹⁵Then Joshua made a treaty of peace with them to let them live, and the leaders of the assembly ratified it by oath.

¹⁶Three days after they made the treaty with the Gibeonites, the Israelites heard that they were neighbours, living near them. ¹⁷So

---

^a26 The Hebrew term refers to the irrevocable giving over of things or persons to the LORD, often by totally destroying them.   ^b31 Traditionally *peace offerings*   ^a1 That is, the Mediterranean
^b4 Most Hebrew manuscripts; some Hebrew manuscripts, Vulgate and Syriac (see also Septuagint) *They prepared provisions and loaded their donkeys*

the Israelites set out and on the third day came to their cities: Gibeon, Kephirah, Beeroth and Kiriath Jearim. 18But the Israelites did not attack them, because the leaders of the assembly had sworn an oath to them by the LORD, the God of Israel.

The whole assembly grumbled against the leaders, 19but all the leaders answered, "We have given them our oath by the LORD, the God of Israel, and we cannot touch them now. 20This is what we will do to them: We will let them live, so that wrath will not fall on us for breaking the oath we swore to them." 21They continued, "Let them live, but let them be woodcutters and water-carriers for the entire community." So the leaders' promise to them was kept.

22Then Joshua summoned the Gibeonites and said, "Why did you deceive us by saying, 'We live a long way from you,' while actually you live near us? 23You are now under a curse: You will never cease to serve as woodcutters and water-carriers for the house of my God."

24They answered Joshua, "Your servants were clearly told how the LORD your God had commanded his servant Moses to give you the whole land and to wipe out all its inhabitants from before you. So we feared for our lives because of you, and that is why we did this. 25We are now in your hands. Do to us whatever seems good and right to you."

26So Joshua saved them from the Israelites, and they did not kill them. 27That day he made the Gibeonites woodcutters and water-carriers for the community and for the altar of the LORD at the place the LORD would choose. And that is what they are to this day.

The Sun Stands Still

10 Now Adoni-Zedek king of Jerusalem heard that Joshua had taken Ai and totally destroyed[a] it, doing to Ai and its king as he had done to Jericho and its king, and that the people of Gibeon had made a treaty of peace with Israel and were living near them. 2He and his people were very much alarmed at this, because Gibeon was an important city, like one of the royal cities; it was larger than Ai, and all its men were good fighters. 3So Adoni-Zedek king of Jerusalem appealed to Hoham king of Hebron, Piram king of Jarmuth, Japhia king of Lachish and Debir king of Eglon. 4"Come up and help me attack Gibeon," he said, "because it has made peace with Joshua and the Israelites."

5Then the five kings of the Amorites—the kings of Jerusalem, Hebron, Jarmuth, Lachish and Eglon—joined forces. They moved up with all their troops and took up positions against Gibeon and attacked it.

6The Gibeonites then sent word to Joshua in the camp at Gilgal: "Do not abandon your servants. Come up to us quickly and save us! Help us, because all the Amorite kings from the hill country have joined forces against us."

7So Joshua marched up from Gilgal with his entire army, including all the best fighting men. 8The LORD said to Joshua, "Do not be afraid of them; I have given them into your hand. Not one of them will be able to withstand you."

9After an all-night march from Gilgal, Joshua took them by surprise. 10The LORD threw them into confusion before Israel, who defeated them in a great victory at Gibeon. Israel pursued them along the road going up to Beth Horon and cut them down all the way to Azekah and Makkedah. 11As they fled before Israel on the road down from Beth Horon to Azekah, the LORD hurled large hailstones down on them from the sky, and more of them died from the hailstones than were killed by the swords of the Israelites.

12On the day the LORD gave the Amorites over to Israel, Joshua said to the LORD in the presence of Israel:

"O sun, stand still over Gibeon,
    O moon, over the Valley of Aijalon."
13So the sun stood still,
    and the moon stopped,
till the nation avenged itself on[b] its
    enemies,

as it is written in the Book of Jashar.

The sun stopped in the middle of the sky and delayed going down about a full day. 14There has never been a day like it before or since, a day when the LORD listened to a man. Surely the LORD was fighting for Israel!

15Then Joshua returned with all Israel to the camp at Gilgal.

Five Amorite Kings Killed

16Now the five kings had fled and hidden in the cave at Makkedah. 17When Joshua was told that the five kings had been found hiding in the cave at Makkedah, 18he said, "Roll large rocks up to the mouth of the cave, and post some men there to guard it. 19But don't stop! Pursue your enemies, attack them from the rear and don't let them reach their cities, for the LORD your God has given them into your hand."

20So Joshua and the Israelites destroyed them completely—almost to a man—but the few who were left reached their fortified cities. 21The whole army then returned safely to Joshua in the camp at Makkedah, and no-one uttered a word against the Israelites.

22Joshua said, "Open the mouth of the cave and bring those five kings out to me." 23So they brought the five kings out of the cave—the kings of Jerusalem, Hebron, Jarmuth, Lachish and Eglon. 24When they had brought these kings to Joshua, he summoned all the men of Israel and said to the army commanders who had come with him, "Come here and put your feet on the necks of these kings." So they came forward and placed their feet on their necks.

25Joshua said to them, "Do not be afraid; do not be discouraged. Be strong and courageous. This is what the LORD will do to

---

[a]1 The Hebrew term refers to the irrevocable giving over of things or persons to the LORD, often by totally destroying them; also in verses 28, 35, 37, 39 and 40.   [b]13 Or *nation triumphed over*

all the enemies you are going to fight."

26Then Joshua struck and killed the kings and hung them on five trees, and they were left hanging on the trees until evening.

27At sunset Joshua gave the order and they took them down from the trees and threw them into the cave where they had been hiding. At the mouth of the cave they placed large rocks, which are there to this day.

28That day Joshua took Makkedah. He put the city and its king to the sword and totally destroyed everyone in it. He left no survivors. And he did to the king of Makkedah as he had done to the king of Jericho.

Southern Cities Conquered

29Then Joshua and all Israel with him moved on from Makkedah to Libnah and attacked it. 30The LORD also gave that city and its king into Israel's hand. The city and everyone in it Joshua put to the sword. He left no survivors there. And he did to its king as he had done to the king of Jericho.

31Then Joshua and all Israel with him moved on from Libnah to Lachish; he took up positions against it and attacked it. 32The LORD handed Lachish over to Israel, and Joshua took it on the second day. The city and everyone in it he put to the sword, just as he had done to Libnah. 33Meanwhile, Horam king of Gezer had come up to help Lachish, but Joshua defeated him and his army—until no survivors were left.

34Then Joshua and all Israel with him moved on from Lachish to Eglon; they took up positions against it and attacked it. 35They captured it that same day and put it to the sword and totally destroyed everyone in it, just as they had done to Lachish.

36Then Joshua and all Israel with him went up from Eglon to Hebron and attacked it. 37They took the city and put it to the sword, together with its king, its villages and every-one in it. They left no survivors. Just as at Eglon, they totally destroyed it and everyone in it.

38Then Joshua and all Israel with him turned round and attacked Debir. 39They took the city, its king and its villages, and put them to the sword. Everyone in it they totally destroyed. They left no survivors. They did to Debir and its king as they had done to Libnah and its king and to Hebron.

40So Joshua subdued the whole region, including the hill country, the Negev, the western foothills and the mountain slopes, together with all their kings. He left no survivors. He totally destroyed all who breathed, just as the LORD, the God of Israel, had commanded. 41Joshua subdued them from Kadesh Barnea to Gaza and from the whole region of Goshen to Gibeon. 42All these kings and their lands Joshua conquered in one campaign, because the LORD, the God of Israel, fought for Israel.

43Then Joshua returned with all Israel to the camp at Gilgal.

Northern Kings Defeated

11 When Jabin king of Hazor heard of this, he sent word to Jobab king of Madon, to the kings of Shimron and Acshaph, 2and to the northern kings who were in the mountains, in the Arabah south of Kinnereth, in the western foothills and in Naphoth Dor*a* on the west; 3to the Canaanites in the east and west; to the Amorites, Hittites, Perizzites and Jebusites in the hill country; and to the Hivites below Hermon in the region of Mizpah. 4They came out with all their troops and a large number of horses and chariots—a huge army, as numerous as the sand on the seashore. 5All these kings joined forces and made camp together at the Waters of Merom, to fight against Israel.

6The LORD said to Joshua, "Do not be afraid of them, because by this time tomorrow I will hand all of them over to Israel, slain. You are to hamstring their horses and burn their chariots."

7So Joshua and his whole army came against them suddenly at the Waters of Merom and attacked them, 8and the LORD gave them into the hand of Israel. They defeated them and pursued them all the way to Greater Sidon, to Misrephoth Maim, and to the Valley of Mizpah on the east, until no survivors were left. 9Joshua did to them as the LORD had directed: He hamstrung their horses and burned their chariots.

10At that time Joshua turned back and captured Hazor and put its king to the sword. (Hazor had been the head of all these kingdoms.) 11Everyone in it they put to the sword. They totally destroyed*b* them, not sparing anything that breathed, and he burned up Hazor itself.

12Joshua took all these royal cities and their kings and put them to the sword. He totally destroyed them, as Moses the servant of the LORD had commanded. 13Yet Israel did not burn any of the cities built on their mounds—except Hazor, which Joshua burned. 14The Israelites carried off for themselves all the plunder and livestock of these cities, but all the people they put to the sword until they completely destroyed them, not sparing anyone that breathed. 15As the LORD commanded his servant Moses, so Moses commanded Joshua, and Joshua did it; he left nothing undone of all that the LORD commanded Moses.

16So Joshua took this entire land: the hill country, all the Negev, the whole region of Goshen, the western foothills, the Arabah and the mountains of Israel with their foothills, 17from Mount Halak, which rises towards Seir, to Baal Gad in the Valley of Lebanon below Mount Hermon. He captured all their kings and struck them down, putting them to death. 18Joshua waged war against all these kings for a long time. 19Except for the Hivites living in Gibeon, not one city made a treaty of peace with the

---

*a*2 Or *in the heights of Dor*
*b*11 The Hebrew term refers to the irrevocable giving over of things or persons to the LORD, often by totally destroying them; also in verses 12, 20 and 21.

Israelites, who took them all in battle. [20]For it was the LORD himself who hardened their hearts to wage war against Israel, so that he might destroy them totally, exterminating them without mercy, as the LORD had commanded Moses.

[21]At that time Joshua went and destroyed the Anakites from the hill country: from Hebron, Debir and Anab, from all the hill country of Judah, and from all the hill country of Israel. Joshua totally destroyed them and their towns. [22]No Anakites were left in Israelite territory; only in Gaza, Gath and Ashdod did any survive. [23]So Joshua took the entire land, just as the LORD had directed Moses, and he gave it as an inheritance to Israel according to their tribal divisions.

Then the land had rest from war.

List of Defeated Kings

12 These are the kings of the land whom the Israelites had defeated and whose territory they took over east of the Jordan, from the Arnon Gorge to Mount Hermon, including all the eastern side of the Arabah:

[2]Sihon king of the Amorites,
who reigned in Heshbon. He ruled from Aroer on the rim of the Arnon Gorge —from the middle of the gorge—to the Jabbok River, which is the border of the Ammonites. This included half of Gilead. [3]He also ruled over the eastern Arabah from the Sea of Kinnereth[a] to the Sea of the Arabah (the Salt Sea[b]), to Beth Jeshimoth, and then southward below the slopes of Pisgah.

[4]And the territory of Og king of Bashan,
one of the last of the Rephaites, who reigned in Ashtaroth and Edrei. [5]He ruled over Mount Hermon, Salecah, all of Bashan to the border of the people of Geshur and Maacah, and half of Gilead to the border of Sihon king of Heshbon.

[6]Moses, the servant of the LORD, and the Israelites conquered them. And Moses the servant of the LORD gave their land to the Reubenites, the Gadites and the half-tribe of Manasseh to be their possession.

[7]These are the kings of the land that Joshua and the Israelites conquered on the west side of the Jordan, from Baal Gad in the Valley of Lebanon to Mount Halak, which rises towards Seir (their lands Joshua gave as an inheritance to the tribes of Israel according to their tribal divisions—[8]the hill country, the western foothills, the Arabah, the mountain slopes, the desert and the Negev—the lands of the Hittites, Amorites, Canaanites, Perizzites, Hivites and Jebusites):

[9]the king of Jericho	one
the king of Ai (near Bethel)	one
[10]the king of Jerusalem	one
the king of Hebron	one
[11]the king of Jarmuth	one
the king of Lachish	one
[12]the king of Eglon	one
the king of Gezer	one
[13]the king of Debir	one
the king of Geder	one
[14]the king of Hormah	one
the king of Arad	one
[15]the king of Libnah	one
the king of Adullam	one
[16]the king of Makkedah	one
the king of Bethel	one
[17]the king of Tappuah	one
the king of Hepher	one
[18]the king of Aphek	one
the king of Lasharon	one
[19]the king of Madon	one
the king of Hazor	one
[20]the king of Shimron Meron	one
the king of Acshaph	one
[21]the king of Taanach	one
the king of Megiddo	one
[22]the king of Kedesh	one
the king of Jokneam in Carmel	one
[23]the king of Dor (in Naphoth Dor[c])	one
the king of Goyim in Gilgal	one
[24]the king of Tirzah	one

thirty-one kings in all.

Land Still to Be Taken

13 When Joshua was old and well advanced in years, the LORD said to him, "You are very old, and there are still very large areas of land to be taken over.

[2]"This is the land that remains: all the regions of the Philistines and Geshurites: [3]from the Shihor River on the east of Egypt to the territory of Ekron on the north, all of it counted as Canaanite (the territory of the five Philistine rulers in Gaza, Ashdod, Ashkelon, Gath and Ekron—that of the Avvites); [4]from the south, all the land of the Canaanites, from Arah of the Sidonians as far as Aphek, the region of the Amorites, [5]the area of the Gebalites;[a] and all Lebanon to the east, from Baal Gad below Mount Hermon to Lebo[b] Hamath.

[6]"As for all the inhabitants of the mountain regions from Lebanon to Misrephoth Maim, that is, all the Sidonians, I myself will drive them out before the Israelites. Be sure to allocate this land to Israel for an inheritance, as I have instructed you, [7]and divide it as an inheritance among the nine tribes and half of the tribe of Manasseh."

Division of the Land East of the Jordan

[8]The other half of Manasseh,[c] the Reubenites and the Gadites had received the inheritance that Moses had given them east of the

---

[a]3 That is, Galilee   [b]3 That is, the Dead Sea   [c]23 Or *in the heights of Dor*   [a]5 That is, the area of Byblos   [b]5 Or *to the entrance to*   [c]8 Hebrew *With it* (that is, with the other half of Manasseh)

Jordan, as he, the servant of the LORD, had assigned it to them.

9It extended from Aroer on the rim of the Arnon Gorge, and from the town in the middle of the gorge, and included the whole plateau of Medeba as far as Dibon, 10and all the towns of Sihon king of the Amorites, who ruled in Heshbon, out to the border of the Ammonites. 11It also included Gilead, the territory of the people of Geshur and Maacah, all of Mount Hermon and all Bashan as far as Salecah—12that is, the whole kingdom of Og in Bashan, who had reigned in Ashtaroth and Edrei and had survived as one of the last of the Rephaites. Moses had defeated them and taken over their land. 13But the Israelites did not drive out the people of Geshur and Maacah, so they continue to live among the Israelites to this day.

14But to the tribe of Levi he gave no inheritance, since the offerings made by fire to the LORD, the God of Israel, are their inheritance, as he promised them.

15This is what Moses had given to the tribe of Reuben, clan by clan:

16The territory from Aroer on the rim of the Arnon Gorge, and from the town in the middle of the gorge, and the whole plateau past Medeba 17to Heshbon and all its towns on the plateau, including Dibon, Bamoth Baal, Beth Baal Meon, 18Jahaz, Kedemoth, Mephaath, 19Kiriathaim, Sibmah, Zereth Shahar on the hill in the valley, 20Beth Peor, the slopes of Pisgah, and Beth Jeshimoth 21—all the towns on the plateau and the entire realm of Sihon king of the Amorites, who ruled at Heshbon. Moses had defeated him and the Midianite chiefs, Evi, Rekem, Zur, Hur and Reba—princes allied with Sihon—who lived in that country. 22In addition to those slain in battle, the Israelites had put to the sword Balaam son of Beor, who practised divination. 23The boundary of the Reubenites was the bank of the Jordan. These towns and their villages were the inheritance of the Reubenites, clan by clan.

24This is what Moses had given to the tribe of Gad, clan by clan:

25The territory of Jazer, all the towns of Gilead and half the Ammonite country as far as Aroer, near Rabbah; 26and from Heshbon to Ramath Mizpah and Betonim, and from Mahanaim to the territory of Debir; 27and in the valley, Beth Haram, Beth Nimrah, Succoth and Zaphon with the rest of the realm of Sihon king of Heshbon (the east side of the Jordan, the territory up to the end of the Sea of Kinnereth*d*). 28These towns and their villages were the inheritance of the Gadites, clan by clan.

29This is what Moses had given to the half-tribe of Manasseh, that is, to half the family of the descendants of Manasseh, clan by clan:

30The territory extending from Mahanaim and including all of Bashan, the entire realm of Og king of Bashan—all the settlements of Jair in Bashan, sixty towns, 31half of Gilead, and Ashtaroth and Edrei (the royal cities of Og in Bashan). This was for the descendants of Makir son of Manasseh—for half of the sons of Makir, clan by clan.

32This is the inheritance Moses had given when he was in the plains of Moab across the Jordan east of Jericho. 33But to the tribe of Levi, Moses had given no inheritance; the LORD, the God of Israel, is their inheritance, as he promised them.

Division of the Land West of the Jordan

14 Now these are the areas the Israelites received as an inheritance in the land of Canaan, which Eleazar the priest, Joshua son of Nun and the heads of the tribal clans of Israel allotted to them. 2Their inheritances were assigned by lot to the nine-and-a-half tribes, as the LORD had commanded through Moses. 3Moses had granted the two-and-a-half tribes their inheritance east of the Jordan but had not granted the Levites an inheritance among the rest, 4for the sons of Joseph had become two tribes—Manasseh and Ephraim. The Levites received no share of the land but only towns to live in, with pasture-lands for their flocks and herds. 5So the Israelites divided the land, just as the LORD had commanded Moses.

Hebron Given to Caleb

6Now the men of Judah approached Joshua at Gilgal, and Caleb son of Jephunneh the Kenizzite said to him, "You know what the LORD said to Moses the man of God at Kadesh Barnea about you and me. 7I was forty years old when Moses the servant of the LORD sent me from Kadesh Barnea to explore the land. And I brought him back a report according to my convictions, 8but my brothers who went up with me made the hearts of the people sink.*a* I, however, followed the LORD my God wholeheartedly. 9So on that day Moses swore to me, 'The land on which your feet have walked will be your inheritance and that of your children for ever, because you have followed the LORD my God wholeheartedly.'*b*

10"Now then, just as the LORD promised, he has kept me alive for forty-five years since the time he said this to Moses, while Israel moved about in the desert. So here I am today, eighty-five years old! 11I am still as strong today as the day Moses sent me out;

I'm just as vigorous to go out to battle now as I was then. ¹²Now give me this hill country that the LORD promised me that day. You yourself heard then that the Anakites were there and their cities were large and fortified, but, the LORD helping me, I will drive them out just as he said.''

¹³Then Joshua blessed Caleb son of Jephunneh and gave him Hebron as his inheritance. ¹⁴So Hebron has belonged to Caleb son of Jephunneh the Kenizzite ever since, because he followed the LORD, the God of Israel, wholeheartedly. ¹⁵(Hebron used to be called Kiriath Arba after Arba, who was the greatest man among the Anakites.)

Then the land had rest from war.

Allotment for Judah

15 The allotment for the tribe of Judah, clan by clan, extended down to the territory of Edom, to the Desert of Zin in the extreme south.

²Their southern boundary started from the bay at the southern end of the Salt Sea,ᵃ ³crossed south of Scorpionᵇ Pass, continued on to Zin and went over to the south of Kadesh Barnea. Then it ran past Hezron up to Addar and curved around to Karka. ⁴It then passed along to Azmon and joined the Wadi of Egypt, ending at the sea. This is theirᶜ southern boundary.

⁵The eastern boundary is the Salt Sea as far as the mouth of the Jordan.

The northern boundary started from the bay of the sea at the mouth of the Jordan, ⁶went up to Beth Hoglah and continued north of Beth Arabah to the Stone of Bohan son of Reuben. ⁷The boundary then went up to Debir from the Valley of Achor and turned north to Gilgal, which faces the Pass of Adummim south of the gorge. It continued along to the waters of En Shemesh and came out at En Rogel. ⁸Then it ran up the Valley of Ben Hinnom along the southern slope of the Jebusite city (that is, Jerusalem). From there it climbed to the top of the hill west of the Hinnom Valley at the northern end of the Valley of Rephaim. ⁹From the hilltop the boundary headed towards the spring of the waters of Nephtoah, came out at the towns of Mount Ephron and went down towards Baalah (that is, Kiriath Jearim). ¹⁰Then it curved westward from Baalah to Mount Seir, ran along the northern slope of Mount Jearim (that is, Kesalon), continued down to Beth Shemesh and crossed to Timnah. ¹¹It went to the northern slope of Ekron, turned towards Shikkeron, passed along to Mount Baalah and reached Jabneel. The boundary ended at the sea.

¹²The western boundary is the coastline of the Great Sea.ᵈ

These are the boundaries around the people of Judah by their clans.

¹³In accordance with the LORD's command to him, Joshua gave to Caleb son of Jephunneh a portion in Judah—Kiriath Arba, that is, Hebron. (Arba was the forefather of Anak.) ¹⁴From Hebron Caleb drove out the three Anakites—Sheshai, Ahiman and Talmai—descendants of Anak. ¹⁵From there he marched against the people living in Debir (formerly called Kiriath Sepher). ¹⁶And Caleb said, "I will give my daughter Acsah in marriage to the man who attacks and captures Kiriath Sepher." ¹⁷Othniel son of Kenaz, Caleb's brother, took it; so Caleb gave his daughter Acsah to him in marriage.

¹⁸One day when she came to Othniel, she urged himᵉ to ask her father for a field. When she got off her donkey, Caleb asked her, "What can I do for you?"

¹⁹She replied, "Do me a special favour. Since you have given me land in the Negev, give me also springs of water." So Caleb gave her the upper and lower springs.

²⁰This is the inheritance of the tribe of Judah, clan by clan:

²¹The southernmost towns of the tribe of Judah in the Negev towards the boundary of Edom were:

Kabzeel, Eder, Jagur, ²²Kinah, Dimonah, Adadah, ²³Kedesh, Hazor, Ithnan, ²⁴Ziph, Telem, Bealoth, ²⁵Hazor Hadattah, Kerioth Hezron (that is, Hazor), ²⁶Amam, Shema, Moladah, ²⁷Hazar Gaddah, Heshmon, Beth Pelet, ²⁸Hazar Shual, Beersheba, Biziothiah, ²⁹Baalah, Iim, Ezem, ³⁰Eltolad, Kesil, Hormah, ³¹Ziklag, Madmannah, Sansannah, ³²Lebaoth, Shilhim, Ain and Rimmon —a total of twenty-nine towns and their villages.

³³In the western foothills:

Eshtaol, Zorah, Ashnah, ³⁴Zanoah, En Gannim, Tappuah, Enam, ³⁵Jarmuth, Adullam, Socoh, Azekah, ³⁶Shaaraim, Adithaim and Gederah (or Gederothaim)ᶠ—fourteen towns and their villages.

³⁷Zenan, Hadashah, Migdal Gad, ³⁸Dilean, Mizpah, Joktheel, ³⁹Lachish, Bozkath, Eglon, ⁴⁰Cabbon, Lahmas, Kitlish, ⁴¹Gederoth, Beth Dagon, Naamah and Makkedah—sixteen towns and their villages.

⁴²Libnah, Ether, Ashan, ⁴³Iphtah, Ashnah, Nezib, ⁴⁴Keilah, Aczib and Mareshah—nine towns and their villages.

⁴⁵Ekron, with its surrounding settlements and villages; ⁴⁶west of Ekron, all that were in the vicinity of Ashdod, together with their villages; ⁴⁷Ashdod, its surrounding settlements and villages;

ᵃ2 That is, the Dead Sea; also in verse 5   ᵇ3 Hebrew Akrabbim
ᶜ4 Hebrew your   ᵈ12 That is, the Mediterranean; also in verse 47
ᵉ18 Hebrew and some Septuagint manuscripts; other Septuagint manuscripts (see also note at Judges 1:14) Othniel, he urged her   ᶠ36 Or Gederah and Gederothaim

and Gaza, its settlements and villages, as far as the Wadi of Egypt and the coastline of the Great Sea.

48In the hill country:
Shamir, Jattir, Socoh, 49Dannah, Kiriath Sannah (that is, Debir), 50Anab, Eshtemoh, Anim, 51Goshen, Holon and Giloh—eleven towns and their villages.

52Arab, Dumah, Eshan, 53Janim, Beth Tappuah, Aphekah, 54Humtah, Kiriath Arba (that is, Hebron) and Zior—nine towns and their villages.

55Maon, Carmel, Ziph, Juttah, 56Jezreel, Jokdeam, Zanoah, 57Kain, Gibeah and Timnah—ten towns and their villages.

58Halhul, Beth Zur, Gedor, 59Maarath, Beth Anoth and Eltekon—six towns and their villages.

60Kiriath Baal (that is, Kiriath Jearim) and Rabbah—two towns and their villages.

61In the desert:
Beth Arabah, Middin, Secacah, 62Nibshan, the City of Salt and En Gedi—six towns and their villages.

63Judah could not dislodge the Jebusites, who were living in Jerusalem; to this day the Jebusites live there with the people of Judah.

Allotment for Ephraim and Manasseh

16 The allotment for Joseph began at the Jordan of Jericho,[a] east of the waters of Jericho, and went up from there through the desert into the hill country of Bethel. 2It went on from Bethel (that is, Luz),[b] crossed over to the territory of the Arkites in Ataroth, 3descended westward to the territory of the Japhletites as far as the region of Lower Beth Horon and on to Gezer, ending at the sea.

4So Manasseh and Ephraim, the descendants of Joseph, received their inheritance.

5This was the territory of Ephraim, clan by clan:
The boundary of their inheritance went from Ataroth Addar in the east to Upper Beth Horon 6and continued to the sea. From Micmethath on the north it curved eastward to Taanath Shiloh, passing by it to Janoah on the east. 7Then it went down from Janoah to Ataroth and Naarah, touched Jericho and came out at the Jordan. 8From Tappuah the border went west to the Kanah Ravine and ended at the sea. This was the inheritance of the tribe of the Ephraimites, clan by clan. 9It also included all the towns and their villages that were set aside for the Ephraimites within the inheritance of the Manassites.

10They did not dislodge the Canaanites living in Gezer; to this day the Canaanites live among the people of Ephraim but are required to do forced labour.

17 This was the allotment for the tribe of Manasseh as Joseph's firstborn, that is, for Makir, Manasseh's firstborn. Makir was the ancestor of the Gileadites, who had received Gilead and Bashan because the Makirites were great soldiers. 2So this allotment was for the rest of the people of Manasseh—the clans of Abiezer, Helek, Asriel, Shechem, Hepher and Shemida. These are the other male descendants of Manasseh son of Joseph by their clans.

3Now Zelophehad son of Hepher, the son of Gilead, the son of Makir, the son of Manasseh, had no sons but only daughters, whose names were Mahlah, Noah, Hoglah, Milcah and Tirzah. 4They went to Eleazar the priest, Joshua son of Nun, and the leaders and said, "The Lord commanded Moses to give us an inheritance among our brothers." So Joshua gave them an inheritance along with the brothers of their father, according to the Lord's command. 5Manasseh's share consisted of ten tracts of land besides Gilead and Bashan east of the Jordan, 6because the daughters of the tribe of Manasseh received an inheritance among the sons. The land of Gilead belonged to the rest of the descendants of Manasseh.

7The territory of Manasseh extended from Asher to Micmethath east of Shechem. The boundary ran southward from there to include the people living at En Tappuah. 8(Manasseh had the land of Tappuah, but Tappuah itself, on the boundary of Manasseh, belonged to the Ephraimites.) 9Then the boundary continued south to the Kanah Ravine. There were towns belonging to Ephraim lying among the towns of Manasseh, but the boundary of Manasseh was the northern side of the ravine and ended at the sea. 10On the south the land belonged to Ephraim, on the north to Manasseh. The territory of Manasseh reached the sea and bordered Asher on the north and Issachar on the east.

11Within Issachar and Asher, Manasseh also had Beth Shan, Ibleam and the people of Dor, Endor, Taanach and Megiddo, together with their surrounding settlements (the third in the list is Naphoth[a]).

12Yet the Manassites were not able to occupy these towns, for the Canaanites were determined to live in that region. 13However, when the Israelites grew stronger, they subjected the Canaanites to forced labour but did not drive them out completely.

14The people of Joseph said to Joshua, "Why have you given us only one allotment and one portion for an inheritance? We are a numerous people and the Lord has blessed us abundantly."

15"If you are so numerous," Joshua answered, "and if the hill country of Ephraim is too small for you, go up into the

---

[a]1 *Jordan of Jericho* was possibly an ancient name for the Jordan River.   [b]2 Septuagint; Hebrew *Bethel to Luz*
[a]11 That is, Naphoth Dor

forest and clear land for yourselves there in the land of the Perizzites and Rephaites.''

16The people of Joseph replied, ''The hill country is not enough for us, and all the Canaanites who live in the plain have iron chariots, both those in Beth Shan and its settlements and those in the Valley of Jezreel.''

17But Joshua said to the house of Joseph —to Ephraim and Manasseh—''You are numerous and very powerful. You will have not only one allotment 18but the forested hill country as well. Clear it, and its farthest limits will be yours; though the Canaanites have iron chariots and though they are strong, you can drive them out.''

Division of the Rest of the Land

18 The whole assembly of the Israelites gathered at Shiloh and set up the Tent of Meeting there. The country was brought under their control, 2but there were still seven Israelite tribes who had not yet received their inheritance.

3So Joshua said to the Israelites: ''How long will you wait before you begin to take possession of the land that the LORD, the God of your fathers, has given you? 4Appoint three men from each tribe. I will send them out to make a survey of the land and to write a description of it, according to the inheritance of each. Then they will return to me. 5You are to divide the land into seven parts. Judah is to remain in its territory on the south and the house of Joseph in its territory on the north. 6After you have written descriptions of the seven parts of the land, bring them here to me and I will cast lots for you in the presence of the LORD our God. 7The Levites, however, do not get a portion among you, because the priestly service of the LORD is their inheritance. And Gad, Reuben and the half-tribe of Manasseh have already received their inheritance on the east side of the Jordan. Moses the servant of the LORD gave it to them.''

8As the men started on their way to map out the land, Joshua instructed them, ''Go and make a survey of the land and write a description of it. Then return to me, and I will cast lots for you here at Shiloh in the presence of the LORD.'' 9So the men left and went through the land. They wrote its description on a scroll, town by town, in seven parts, and returned to Joshua in the camp at Shiloh. 10Joshua then cast lots for them in Shiloh in the presence of the LORD, and there he distributed the land to the Israelites according to their tribal divisions.

Allotment for Benjamin

11The lot came up for the tribe of Benjamin, clan by clan. Their allotted territory lay between the tribes of Judah and Joseph: 12On the north side their boundary began at the Jordan, passed the northern slope of Jericho and headed west into the hill country, coming out at the desert of Beth Aven. 13From there it crossed to the south slope of Luz (that is, Bethel) and went down to Ataroth Addar on the hill south of Lower Beth Horon.

14From the hill facing Beth Horon on the south the boundary turned south along the western side and came out at Kiriath Baal (that is, Kiriath Jearim), a town of the people of Judah. This was the western side.

15The southern side began at the outskirts of Kiriath Jearim on the west, and the boundary came out at the spring of the waters of Nephtoah. 16The boundary went down to the foot of the hill facing the Valley of Ben Hinnom, north of the Valley of Rephaim. It continued down the Hinnom Valley along the southern slope of the Jebusite city and so to En Rogel. 17It then curved north, went to En Shemesh, continued to Geliloth, which faces the Pass of Adummim, and ran down to the Stone of Bohan son of Reuben. 18It continued to the northern slope of Beth Arabah[a] and on down into the Arabah. 19It then went to the northern slope of Beth Hoglah and came out at the northern bay of the Salt Sea,[b] at the mouth of the Jordan in the south. This was the southern boundary.

20The Jordan formed the boundary on the eastern side.

These were the boundaries that marked out the inheritance of the clans of Benjamin on all sides.

21The tribe of Benjamin, clan by clan, had the following cities:

Jericho, Beth Hoglah, Emek Keziz, 22Beth Arabah, Zemaraim, Bethel, 23Avvim, Parah, Ophrah, 24Kephar Ammoni, Ophni and Geba—twelve towns and their villages.

25Gibeon, Ramah, Beeroth, 26Mizpah, Kephirah, Mozah, 27Rekem, Irpeel, Taralah, 28Zelah, Haeleph, the Jebusite city (that is, Jerusalem), Gibeah and Kiriath—fourteen towns and their villages.

This was the inheritance of Benjamin for its clans.

Allotment for Simeon

19 The second lot came out for the tribe of Simeon, clan by clan. Their inheritance lay within the territory of Judah. 2It included:

Beersheba (or Sheba),[a] Moladah, 3Hazar Shual, Balah, Ezem, 4Eltolad, Bethul, Hormah, 5Ziklag, Beth Marcaboth, Hazar Susah, 6Beth Lebaoth and Sharuhen—thirteen towns and their villages;

7Ain, Rimmon, Ether and Ashan— four towns and their villages—8and all the villages around these towns as far as Baalath Beer (Ramah in the Negev).

This was the inheritance of the tribe of the

a18 Septuagint; Hebrew slope facing the Arabah   b19 That is, the Dead Sea
a2 Or Beersheba, Sheba; 1 Chron. 4:28 does not have Sheba.

Simeonites, clan by clan. 9The inheritance of the Simeonites was taken from the share of Judah, because Judah's portion was more than they needed. So the Simeonites received their inheritance within the territory of Judah.

Allotment for Zebulun

10The third lot came up for Zebulun, clan by clan:

The boundary of their inheritance went as far as Sarid. 11Going west it ran to Maralah, touched Dabbesheth, and extended to the ravine near Jokneam. 12It turned east from Sarid towards the sunrise to the territory of Kisloth Tabor and went on to Daberath and up to Japhia. 13Then it continued eastward to Gath Hepher and Eth Kazin; it came out at Rimmon and turned towards Neah. 14There the boundary went round on the north to Hannathon and ended at the Valley of Iphtah El. 15Included were Kattath, Nahalal, Shimron, Idalah and Bethlehem. There were twelve towns and their villages.

16These towns and their villages were the inheritance of Zebulun, clan by clan.

Allotment for Issachar

17The fourth lot came out for Issachar, clan by clan. 18Their territory included:

Jezreel, Kesulloth, Shunem, 19Haph-araim, Shion, Anaharath, 20Rabbith, Kishion, Ebez, 21Remeth, En Gannim, En Haddah and Beth Pazzez. 22The boundary touched Tabor, Shahazumah and Beth Shemesh, and ended at the Jordan. There were sixteen towns and their villages.

23These towns and their villages were the inheritance of the tribe of Issachar, clan by clan.

Allotment for Asher

24The fifth lot came out for the tribe of Asher, clan by clan. 25Their territory included:

Helkath, Hali, Beten, Acshaph, 26Allammelech, Amad and Mishal. On the west the boundary touched Carmel and Shihor Libnath. 27It then turned east towards Beth Dagon, touched Zebulun and the Valley of Iphtah El, and went north to Beth Emek and Neiel, passing Cabul on the left. 28It went to Abdon,b Rehob, Hammon and Kanah, as far as Greater Sidon. 29The boundary then turned back towards Ramah and went to the fortified city of Tyre, turned towards Hosah and came out at the sea in the region of Aczib, 30Ummah, Aphek and Rehob. There were twenty-two towns and their villages.

31These towns and their villages were the inheritance of the tribe of Asher, clan by clan.

Allotment for Naphtali

32The sixth lot came out for Naphtali, clan by clan:

33Their boundary went from Heleph and the large tree in Zaanannim, passing Adami Nekeb and Jabneel to Lakkum and ending at the Jordan. 34The boundary ran west through Aznoth Tabor and came out at Hukkok. It touched Zebulun on the south, Asher on the west and the Jordanc on the east. 35The fortified cities were Ziddim, Zer, Hammath, Rakkath, Kinnereth, 36Adamah, Ramah, Hazor, 37Kedesh, Edrei, En Hazor, 38Iron, Migdal El, Horem, Beth Anath and Beth Shemesh. There were nineteen towns and their villages.

39These towns and their villages were the inheritance of the tribe of Naphtali, clan by clan.

Allotment for Dan

40The seventh lot came out for the tribe of Dan, clan by clan. 41The territory of their inheritance included:

Zorah, Eshtaol, Ir Shemesh, 42Shaalabbin, Aijalon, Ithlah, 43Elon, Timnah, Ekron, 44Eltekeh, Gibbethon, Baalath, 45Jehud, Bene Berak, Gath Rimmon, 46Me Jarkon and Rakkon, with the area facing Joppa.

47(But the Danites had difficulty taking possession of their territory, so they went up and attacked Leshem, took it, put it to the sword and occupied it. They settled in Leshem and named it Dan after their forefather.)

48These towns and their villages were the inheritance of the tribe of Dan, clan by clan.

Allotment for Joshua

49When they had finished dividing the land into its allotted portions, the Israelites gave Joshua son of Nun an inheritance among them, 50as the LORD had commanded. They gave him the town he asked for—Timnath Serahd in the hill country of Ephraim. And he built up the town and settled there.

51These are the territories that Eleazar the priest, Joshua son of Nun and the heads of the tribal clans of Israel assigned by lot at Shiloh in the presence of the LORD at the entrance to the Tent of Meeting. And so they finished dividing the land.

Cities of Refuge

20 Then the LORD said to Joshua: 2"Tell the Israelites to designate the cities of refuge, as I instructed you through Moses, 3so that anyone who kills a person accidentally and unintentionally may flee there and find protection from the avenger of blood.

4"When he flees to one of these cities, he is to stand in the entrance of the city gate and state his case before the elders of that city. Then they are to admit him into their city and

b28 Some Hebrew manuscripts (see also Joshua 21:30); most Hebrew manuscripts Ebron
c34 Septuagint; Hebrew west, and Judah, the Jordan,
d50 Also known as Timnath Heres (see Judges 2:9)

give him a place to live with them. ⁵If the avenger of blood pursues him, they must not surrender the one accused, because he killed his neighbour unintentionally and without malice aforethought. ⁶He is to stay in that city until he has stood trial before the assembly and until the death of the high priest who is serving at that time. Then he may go back to his own home in the town from which he fled."

⁷So they set apart Kedesh in Galilee in the hill country of Naphtali, Shechem in the hill country of Ephraim, and Kiriath Arba (that is, Hebron) in the hill country of Judah. ⁸On the east side of the Jordan of Jericho*a* they designated Bezer in the desert on the plateau in the tribe of Reuben, Ramoth in Gilead in the tribe of Gad, and Golan in Bashan in the tribe of Manasseh. ⁹Any of the Israelites or any alien living among them who killed someone accidentally could flee to these designated cities and not be killed by the avenger of blood prior to standing trial before the assembly.

Towns for the Levites

21 Now the family heads of the Levites approached Eleazar the priest, Joshua son of Nun, and the heads of the other tribal families of Israel ²at Shiloh in Canaan and said to them, "The LORD commanded through Moses that you give us towns to live in, with pasture-lands for our livestock." ³So, as the LORD had commanded, the Israelites gave the Levites the following towns and pasture-lands out of their own inheritance:

⁴The first lot came out for the Kohathites, clan by clan. The Levites who were descendants of Aaron the priest were allotted thirteen towns from the tribes of Judah, Simeon and Benjamin. ⁵The rest of Kohath's descendants were allotted ten towns from the clans of the tribes of Ephraim, Dan and half of Manasseh.

⁶The descendants of Gershon were allotted thirteen towns from the clans of the tribes of Issachar, Asher, Naphtali and the half-tribe of Manasseh in Bashan.

⁷The descendants of Merari, clan by clan, received twelve towns from the tribes of Reuben, Gad and Zebulun.

⁸So the Israelites allotted to the Levites these towns and their pasture-lands, as the LORD had commanded through Moses.

⁹From the tribes of Judah and Simeon they allotted the following towns by name ¹⁰(these towns were assigned to the descendants of Aaron who were from the Kohathite clans of the Levites, because the first lot fell to them): ¹¹They gave them Kiriath Arba (that is, Hebron), with its surrounding pasture-land, in the hill country of Judah. (Arba was the forefather of Anak.) ¹²But the fields and villages around the city they had given to Caleb son of Jephunneh as his possession.

¹³So to the descendants of Aaron the priest they gave Hebron (a city of refuge for one accused of murder), Libnah, ¹⁴Jattir, Eshtemoa, ¹⁵Holon, Debir, ¹⁶Ain, Juttah and Beth Shemesh, together with their pasture-lands—nine towns from these two tribes.

¹⁷And from the tribe of Benjamin they gave them Gibeon, Geba, ¹⁸Anathoth and Almon, together with their pasture-lands—four towns.

¹⁹All the towns for the priests, the descendants of Aaron, were thirteen, together with their pasture-lands.

²⁰The rest of the Kohathite clans of the Levites were allotted towns from the tribe of Ephraim:

²¹In the hill country of Ephraim they were given Shechem (a city of refuge for one accused of murder) and Gezer, ²²Kibzaim and Beth Horon, together with their pasture-lands—four towns.

²³Also from the tribe of Dan they received Eltekeh, Gibbethon, ²⁴Aijalon and Gath Rimmon, together with their pasture-lands—four towns.

²⁵From half the tribe of Manasseh they received Taanach and Gath Rimmon, together with their pasture-lands—two towns.

²⁶All these ten towns and their pasture-lands were given to the rest of the Kohathite clans.

²⁷The Levite clans of the Gershonites were given:

from the half-tribe of Manasseh,
    Golan in Bashan (a city of refuge for one accused of murder) and Be Eshtarah, together with their pasture-lands—two towns;
²⁸from the tribe of Issachar,
    Kishion, Daberath, ²⁹Jarmuth and En Gannim, together with their pasture-lands—four towns;
³⁰from the tribe of Asher,
    Mishal, Abdon, ³¹Helkath and Rehob, together with their pasture-lands—four towns;
³²from the tribe of Naphtali,
    Kedesh in Galilee (a city of refuge for one accused of murder), Hammoth Dor and Kartan, together with their pasture-lands—three towns.
³³All the towns of the Gershonite clans were thirteen, together with their pasture-lands.

³⁴The Merarite clans (the rest of the Levites) were given:
from the tribe of Zebulun,
    Jokneam, Kartah, ³⁵Dimnah and Nahalal, together with their pasture-lands—four towns;
³⁶from the tribe of Reuben,
    Bezer, Jahaz, ³⁷Kedemoth and Mephaath, together with their pasture-lands—four towns;
³⁸from the tribe of Gad,
    Ramoth in Gilead (a city of refuge for one accused of murder), Mahanaim,

---

*a*8 *Jordan of Jericho* was possibly an ancient name for the Jordan River.

39Heshbon and Jazer, together with their pasture-lands—four towns in all. 40All the towns allotted to the Merarite clans, who were the rest of the Levites, were twelve. 41The towns of the Levites in the territory held by the Israelites were forty-eight in all, together with their pasture-lands. 42Each of these towns had pasture-lands surrounding it; this was true for all these towns.

43So the LORD gave Israel all the land he had sworn to give their forefathers, and they took possession of it and settled there. 44The LORD gave them rest on every side, just as he had sworn to their forefathers. Not one of their enemies withstood them; the LORD handed all their enemies over to them. 45Not one of all the LORD's good promises to the house of Israel failed; every one was fulfilled.

Eastern Tribes Return Home

22 Then Joshua summoned the Reubenites, the Gadites and the half-tribe of Manasseh 2and said to them, "You have done all that Moses the servant of the LORD commanded, and you have obeyed me in everything I commanded. 3For a long time now—to this very day—you have not deserted your brothers but have carried out the mission the LORD your God gave you. 4Now that the LORD your God has given your brothers rest as he promised, return to your homes in the land that Moses the servant of the LORD gave you on the other side of the Jordan. 5But be very careful to keep the commandment and the law that Moses the servant of the LORD gave you: to love the LORD your God, to walk in all his ways, to obey his commands, to hold fast to him and to serve him with all your heart and all your soul."

6Then Joshua blessed them and sent them away, and they went to their homes. 7(To the half-tribe of Manasseh Moses had given land in Bashan, and to the other half of the tribe Joshua gave land on the west side of the Jordan with their brothers.) When Joshua sent them home, he blessed them, 8saying, "Return to your homes with your great wealth—with large herds of livestock, with silver, gold, bronze and iron, and a great quantity of clothing—and divide with your brothers the plunder from your enemies."

9So the Reubenites, the Gadites and the half-tribe of Manasseh left the Israelites at Shiloh in Canaan to return to Gilead, their own land, which they had acquired in accordance with the command of the LORD through Moses.

10When they came to Geliloth near the Jordan in the land of Canaan, the Reubenites, the Gadites and the half-tribe of Manasseh built an imposing altar there by the Jordan. 11And when the Israelites heard that they had built the altar on the border of Canaan at Geliloth near the Jordan on the Israelite side, 12the whole assembly of Israel gathered at Shiloh to go to war against them.

13So the Israelites sent Phinehas son of Eleazar, the priest, to the land of Gilead—to Reuben, Gad and the half-tribe of Manasseh. 14With him they sent ten of the chief men, one for each of the tribes of Israel, each the head of a family division among the Israelite clans.

15When they went to Gilead—to Reuben, Gad and the half-tribe of Manasseh—they said to them: 16"The whole assembly of the LORD says: 'How could you break faith with the God of Israel like this? How could you turn away from the LORD and build yourselves an altar in rebellion against him now? 17Was not the sin of Peor enough for us? Up to this very day we have not cleansed ourselves from that sin, even though a plague fell on the community of the LORD! 18And are you now turning away from the LORD?

" 'If you rebel against the LORD today, tomorrow he will be angry with the whole community of Israel. 19If the land you possess is defiled, come over to the LORD's land, where the LORD's tabernacle stands, and share the land with us. But do not rebel against the LORD or against us by building an altar for yourselves, other than the altar of the LORD our God. 20When Achan son of Zerah acted unfaithfully regarding the devoted things,a did not wrath come upon the whole community of Israel? He was not the only one who died for his sin.' "

21Then Reuben, Gad and the half-tribe of Manasseh replied to the heads of the clans of Israel: 22"The Mighty One, God, the LORD! The Mighty One, God, the LORD! He knows! And let Israel know! If this has been in rebellion or disobedience to the LORD, do not spare us this day. 23If we have built our own altar to turn away from the LORD and to offer burnt offerings and grain offerings, or to sacrifice fellowship offeringsb on it, may the LORD himself call us to account.

24"No! We did it for fear that some day your descendants might say to ours, 'What do you have to do with the LORD, the God of Israel? 25The LORD has made the Jordan a boundary between us and you—you Reubenites and Gadites! You have no share in the LORD.' So your descendants might cause ours to stop fearing the LORD.

26"That is why we said, 'Let us get ready and build an altar—but not for burnt offerings or sacrifices.' 27On the contrary, it is to be a witness between us and you and the generations that follow, that we will worship the LORD at his sanctuary with our burnt offerings, sacrifices and fellowship offerings. Then in the future your descendants will not be able to say to ours, 'You have no share in the LORD.'

28"And we said, 'If they ever say this to us, or to our descendants, we will answer: Look at the replica of the LORD's altar, which our fathers built, not for burnt offerings and sacrifices, but as a witness between us and you.'

29"Far be it from us to rebel against the

a20 The Hebrew term refers to the irrevocable giving over of things or persons to the LORD, often by totally destroying them.   b23 Traditionally peace offerings; also in verse 27

LORD and turn away from him today by building an altar for burnt offerings, grain offerings and sacrifices, other than the altar of the LORD our God that stands before his tabernacle.''

30When Phinehas the priest and the leaders of the community—the heads of the clans of the Israelites—heard what Reuben, Gad and Manasseh had to say, they were pleased. 31And Phinehas son of Eleazar, the priest, said to Reuben, Gad and Manasseh, "Today we know that the LORD is with us, because you have not acted unfaithfully towards the LORD in this matter. Now you have rescued the Israelites from the LORD's hand.''

32Then Phinehas son of Eleazar, the priest, and the leaders returned to Canaan from their meeting with the Reubenites and Gadites in Gilead and reported to the Israelites. 33They were glad to hear the report and praised God. And they talked no more about going to war against them to devastate the country where the Reubenites and the Gadites lived.

34And the Reubenites and the Gadites gave the altar this name: A Witness Between Us that the LORD is God.

Joshua's Farewell to the Leaders

23 After a long time had passed and the LORD had given Israel rest from all their enemies around them, Joshua, by then old and well advanced in years, 2summoned all Israel—their elders, leaders, judges and officials—and said to them: "I am old and well advanced in years. 3You yourselves have seen everything the LORD your God has done to all these nations for your sake; it was the LORD your God who fought for you. 4Remember how I have allotted as an inheritance for your tribes all the land of the nations that remain—the nations I conquered —between the Jordan and the Great Sea*a* in the west. 5The LORD your God himself will drive them out of your way. He will push them out before you, and you will take possession of their land, as the LORD your God promised you.

6"Be very strong; be careful to obey all that is written in the Book of the Law of Moses, without turning aside to the right or to the left. 7Do not associate with these nations that remain among you; do not invoke the names of their gods or swear by them. You must not serve them or bow down to them. 8But you are to hold fast to the LORD your God, as you have until now.

9"The LORD has driven out before you great and powerful nations; to this day no-one has been able to withstand you. 10One of you routs a thousand, because the LORD your God fights for you, just as he promised. 11So be very careful to love the LORD your God.

12"But if you turn away and ally yourselves with the survivors of these nations that remain among you and if you intermarry with them and associate with them, 13then you may be sure that the LORD your God will no longer drive out these nations before you.

Instead, they will become snares and traps for you, whips on your backs and thorns in your eyes, until you perish from this good land, which the LORD your God has given you.

14"Now I am about to go the way of all the earth. You know with all your heart and soul that not one of all the good promises the LORD your God gave you has failed. Every promise has been fulfilled; not one has failed. 15But just as every good promise of the LORD your God has come true, so the LORD will bring on you all the evil he has threatened, until he has destroyed you from this good land he has given you. 16If you violate the covenant of the LORD your God, which he commanded you, and go and serve other gods and bow down to them, the LORD's anger will burn against you, and you will quickly perish from the good land he has given you.''

The Covenant Renewed at Shechem

24 Then Joshua assembled all the tribes of Israel at Shechem. He summoned the elders, leaders, judges and officials of Israel, and they presented themselves before God.

2Joshua said to all the people, "This is what the LORD, the God of Israel, says: 'Long ago your forefathers, including Terah the father of Abraham and Nahor, lived beyond the River*a* and worshipped other gods. 3But I took your father Abraham from the land beyond the River and led him throughout Canaan and gave him many descendants. I gave him Isaac, 4and to Isaac I gave Jacob and Esau. I assigned the hill country of Seir to Esau, but Jacob and his sons went down to Egypt.

5"'Then I sent Moses and Aaron, and I afflicted the Egyptians by what I did there, and I brought you out. 6When I brought your fathers out of Egypt, you came to the sea, and the Egyptians pursued them with chariots and horsemen*b* as far as the Red Sea.*c* 7But they cried to the LORD for help, and he put darkness between you and the Egyptians; he brought the sea over them and covered them. You saw with your own eyes what I did to the Egyptians. Then you lived in the desert for a long time.

8"'I brought you to the land of the Amorites who lived east of the Jordan. They fought against you, but I gave them into your hands. I destroyed them from before you, and you took possession of their land. 9When Balak son of Zippor, the king of Moab, prepared to fight against Israel, he sent for Balaam son of Beor to put a curse on you. 10But I would not listen to Balaam, so he blessed you again and again, and I delivered you out of his hand.

11"'Then you crossed the Jordan and came to Jericho. The citizens of Jericho fought against you, as did also the Amorites, Perizzites, Canaanites, Hittites, Girgashites, Hivites and Jebusites, but I gave them into your hands. 12I sent the hornet ahead of you,

---

a4 That is, the Mediterranean   *a2* That is, the Euphrates; also in verses 3, 14 and 15
b6 Or *charioteers*   *c6* Hebrew *Yam Suph*; that is, Sea of Reeds

JOSHUA 23: 1–11

'One of you routs a thousand, because the LORD your God fights for you, just as he promised. So be very careful to love the LORD your God' vv. 10, 11).

JOSHUA'S FAREWELL address to Israel, gathered together at an unnamed place, was a very strongly worded speech. He did not mince matters. He demanded absolute purity of religious worship. Nothing must be allowed to divert attention from God himself.

And one of Joshua's warnings is to be aware of the power of God. With God on your side 'one of you routs a thousand'. It is therefore important, not just to make sure that God alone is worshipped, but to make sure that worship of God is directed to him in love.

The worship of God must never be carried out in order to further our own ends. True worship is worship in love. Love is outward-looking, directed away from the narrow concerns and interests of ourselves and our own small group. If love is turned inwards upon itself it becomes warped and negative. We then risk attempting to use the power of God – the power that 'routs a thousand' for unworthy ends.

Christians run this risk continually. We must continually be on our guard against our own desire to take hold of God's power to serve our own purposes. For us, the example of Christ himself is the one to follow:

> *O the deep, deep love of Jesus,*
>> *Spread his praise from shore to shore;*
> *How he loveth, ever loveth,*
>> *Changeth never, nevermore;*
> *How he watcheth o'er his loved ones,*
>> *Died to call them all his own;*
> *How for them he intercedeth,*
>> *Watcheth o'er them from the throne.*

(Samuel Trevor Francis)

→204

JUDGES 4:3–10
'Deborah, a prophetess, the wife of Lappidoth, was leading Israel at that time'
(v. 4).

SPIRITUAL LEADERSHIP. Deborah was undoubtedly a remarkable woman. She combined the roles of housewife and prophetess, and as a judge in Israel she dealt justice to those who went before her. Her main claim to fame, however, lies in her inspired leadership of Israelite forces when they defeated their enemy Sisera and his dreaded chariots of iron.

The characteristic of the judges that we can observe today is that they were seen to be blessed with the Spirit of the Lord. The Israelites believed that unusual powers or talents were the gift of the Spirit, and it was those who in this way showed the presence of God's Spirit in their lives, or who in times of emergency were raised up by the Spirit, who became the judges. So it did not matter that Deborah was a woman! The one criterion for her leadership of the people of God was that the Spirit of God was upon her. In his Spirit, she delivered her people from their oppressors.

A woman of more recent days who has brought help to many was the Revd Elsie Chamberlain. A member of the then Congregational ministry, she served in a number of churches, was a chaplain in the Royal Air Force, and for seventeen years worked on the staff of the BBC Religious Department. She wrote once of the 'exciting, driving sense of vocation' which God had given her. She too was a spiritual leader – because of the way in which the Spirit of God was working in her life.

Lead me, Lord, and use the gifts you have given me.

which drove them out before you—also the two Amorite kings. You did not do it with your own sword and bow. [13]So I gave you a land on which you did not toil and cities you did not build; and you live in them and eat from vineyards and olive groves that you did not plant.'

[14]"Now fear the LORD and serve him with all faithfulness. Throw away the gods your forefathers worshipped beyond the River and in Egypt, and serve the LORD. [15]But if serving the LORD seems undesirable to you, then choose for yourselves this day whom you will serve, whether the gods your forefathers served beyond the River, or the gods of the Amorites, in whose land you are living. But as for me and my household, we will serve the LORD."

[16]Then the people answered, "Far be it from us to forsake the LORD to serve other gods! [17]It was the LORD our God himself who brought us and our fathers up out of Egypt, from that land of slavery, and performed those great signs before our eyes. He protected us on our entire journey and among all the nations through which we travelled. [18]And the LORD drove out before us all the nations, including the Amorites, who lived in the land. We too will serve the LORD, because he is our God."

[19]Joshua said to the people, "You are not able to serve the LORD. He is a holy God; he is a jealous God. He will not forgive your rebellion and your sins. [20]If you forsake the LORD and serve foreign gods, he will turn and bring disaster on you and make an end of you, after he has been good to you."

[21]But the people said to Joshua, "No! We will serve the LORD."

[22]Then Joshua said, "You are witnesses against yourselves that you have chosen to serve the LORD."

"Yes, we are witnesses," they replied.

[23]"Now then," said Joshua, "throw away the foreign gods that are among you and yield your hearts to the LORD, the God of Israel."

[24]And the people said to Joshua, "We will serve the LORD our God and obey him."

[25]On that day Joshua made a covenant for the people, and there at Shechem he drew up for them decrees and laws. [26]And Joshua recorded these things in the Book of the Law of God. Then he took a large stone and set it up there under the oak near the holy place of the LORD.

[27]"See!" he said to all the people. "This stone will be a witness against us. It has heard all the words the LORD has said to us. It will be a witness against you if you are untrue to your God."

Buried in the Promised Land

[28]Then Joshua sent the people away, each to his own inheritance.

[29]After these things, Joshua son of Nun, the servant of the LORD, died at the age of a hundred and ten. [30]And they buried him in the land of his inheritance, at Timnath Serah[d] in the hill country of Ephraim, north of Mount Gaash.

[31]Israel served the LORD throughout the lifetime of Joshua and of the elders who outlived him and who had experienced everything the LORD had done for Israel.

[32]And Joseph's bones, which the Israelites had brought up from Egypt, were buried at Shechem in the tract of land that Jacob bought for a hundred pieces of silver[e] from the sons of Hamor, the father of Shechem. This became the inheritance of Joseph's descendants.

[33]And Eleazar son of Aaron died and was buried at Gibeah, which had been allotted to his son Phinehas in the hill country of Ephraim.

---

[d]30 Also known as *Timnath Heres* (see Judges 2:9)
[e]32 Hebrew *hundred kesitahs*; a kesitah was a unit of money of unknown weight and value.

Judges

Israel Fights the Remaining Canaanites

1 After the death of Joshua, the Israelites asked the LORD, "Who will be the first to go up and fight for us against the Canaanites?"

²The LORD answered, "Judah is to go; I have given the land into their hands."

³Then the men of Judah said to the Simeonites their brothers, "Come up with us into the territory allotted to us, to fight against the Canaanites. We in turn will go with you into yours." So the Simeonites went with them.

⁴When Judah attacked, the LORD gave the Canaanites and Perizzites into their hands and they struck down ten thousand men at Bezek. ⁵It was there that they found Adoni-Bezek and fought against him, putting to rout the Canaanites and Perizzites. ⁶Adoni-Bezek fled, but they chased him and caught him, and cut off his thumbs and big toes.

⁷Then Adoni-Bezek said, "Seventy kings with their thumbs and big toes cut off have picked up scraps under my table. Now God has paid me back for what I did to them." They brought him to Jerusalem, and he died there.

⁸The men of Judah attacked Jerusalem also and took it. They put the city to the sword and set it on fire.

⁹After that, the men of Judah went down to fight against the Canaanites living in the hill country, the Negev and the western foothills. ¹⁰They advanced against the Canaanites living in Hebron (formerly called Kiriath Arba) and defeated Sheshai, Ahiman and Talmai.

¹¹From there they advanced against the people living in Debir (formerly called Kiriath Sepher). ¹²And Caleb said, "I will give my daughter Acsah in marriage to the man who attacks and captures Kiriath Sepher." ¹³Othniel son of Kenaz, Caleb's younger brother, took it; so Caleb gave his daughter Acsah to him in marriage.

¹⁴One day when she came to Othniel, she urged him*a* to ask her father for a field. When she got off her donkey, Caleb asked her, "What can I do for you?"

¹⁵She replied, "Do me a special favour. Since you have given me land in the Negev, give me also springs of water." Then Caleb gave her the upper and lower springs.

¹⁶The descendants of Moses' father-in-law, the Kenite, went up from the City of Palms*b* with the men of Judah to live among the people of the Desert of Judah in the Negev near Arad.

¹⁷Then the men of Judah went with the Simeonites their brothers and attacked the Canaanites living in Zephath, and they totally destroyed*c* the city. Therefore it was called Hormah.*d* ¹⁸The men of Judah also took*e* Gaza, Ashkelon and Ekron—each city with its territory.

¹⁹The LORD was with the men of Judah. They took possession of the hill country, but they were unable to drive the people from the plains, because they had iron chariots. ²⁰As Moses had promised, Hebron was given to Caleb, who drove from it the three sons of Anak. ²¹The Benjamites, however, failed to dislodge the Jebusites, who were living in Jerusalem; to this day the Jebusites live there with the Benjamites.

²²Now the house of Joseph attacked Bethel, and the LORD was with them. ²³When they sent men to spy out Bethel (formerly called Luz), ²⁴the spies saw a man coming out of the city and they said to him, "Show us how to get into the city and we will see that you are treated well." ²⁵So he showed them, and they put the city to the sword but spared the man and his whole family. ²⁶He then went to the land of the Hittites, where he built a city and called it Luz, which is its name to this day.

²⁷But Manasseh did not drive out the people of Beth Shan or Taanach or Dor or Ibleam or Megiddo and their surrounding settlements, for the Canaanites were determined to live in that land. ²⁸When Israel became strong, they pressed the Canaanites into forced labour but never drove them out completely. ²⁹Nor did Ephraim drive out the Canaanites living in Gezer, but the Canaanites continued to live there among them. ³⁰Neither did Zebulun drive out the Canaanites living in Kitron or Nahalol, who remained among them; but they did subject them to forced labour. ³¹Nor did Asher drive

---

*a*14 Hebrew; Septuagint and Vulgate *Othniel, he urged her*   *b*16 That is, Jericho
*c*17 The Hebrew term refers to the irrevocable giving over of things or persons to the LORD, often by totally destroying them.   *d*17 *Hormah* means *destruction.*   *e*18 Hebrew; Septuagint *Judah did not take*

out those living in Acco or Sidon or Ahlab or Aczib or Helbah or Aphek or Rehob, 32and because of this the people of Asher lived among the Canaanite inhabitants of the land. 33Neither did Naphtali drive out those living in Beth Shemesh or Beth Anath; but the Naphtalites too lived among the Canaanite inhabitants of the land, and those living in Beth Shemesh and Beth Anath became forced labourers for them. 34The Amorites confined the Danites to the hill country, not allowing them to come down into the plain. 35And the Amorites were determined also to hold out in Mount Heres, Aijalon and Shaal-bim, but when the power of the house of Joseph increased, they too were pressed into forced labour. 36The boundary of the Amor-ites was from Scorpion*f* Pass to Sela and beyond.

The Angel of the LORD at Bokim

2 The angel of the LORD went up from Gilgal to Bokim and said, "I brought you up out of Egypt and led you into the land that I swore to give to your forefathers. I said, 'I will never break my covenant with you, 2and you shall not make a covenant with the peo-ple of this land, but you shall break down their altars.' Yet you have disobeyed me. Why have you done this? 3Now therefore I tell you that I will not drive them out before you; they will be ⌊thorns⌋ in your sides and their gods will be a snare to you."

4When the angel of the LORD had spoken these things to all the Israelites, the people wept aloud, 5and they called that place Bokim.*a* There they offered sacrifices to the LORD.

Disobedience and Defeat

6After Joshua had dismissed the Israelites, they went to take possession of the land, each to his own inheritance. 7The people served the LORD throughout the lifetime of Joshua and of the elders who outlived him and who had seen all the great things the LORD had done for Israel.

8Joshua son of Nun, the servant of the LORD, died at the age of a hundred and ten. 9And they buried him in the land of his inheri-tance, at Timnath Heres*b* in the hill country of Ephraim, north of Mount Gaash.

10After that whole generation had been gathered to their fathers, another generation grew up, who knew neither the LORD nor what he had done for Israel. 11Then the Israelites did evil in the eyes of the LORD and served the Baals. 12They forsook the LORD, the God of their fathers, who had brought them out of Egypt. They followed and wor-shipped various gods of the peoples around them. They provoked the LORD to anger 13because they forsook him and served Baal and the Ashtoreths. 14In his anger against Israel the LORD handed them over to raiders who plundered them. He sold them to their enemies all around, whom they were no lon-ger able to resist. 15Whenever Israel went out to fight, the hand of the LORD was against them to defeat them, just as he had sworn to them. They were in great distress.

16Then the LORD raised up judges,*c* who saved them out of the hands of these raiders. 17Yet they would not listen to their judges but prostituted themselves to other gods and worshipped them. Unlike their fathers, they quickly turned from the way in which their fathers had walked, the way of obedience to the LORD's commands. 18Whenever the LORD raised up a judge for them, he was with the judge and saved them out of the hands of their enemies as long as the judge lived; for the LORD had compassion on them as they groaned under those who oppressed and afflicted them. 19But when the judge died, the people returned to ways even more corrupt than those of their fathers, following other gods and serving and worshipping them. They refused to give up their evil practices and stubborn ways.

20Therefore the LORD was very angry with Israel and said, "Because this nation has violated the covenant that I laid down for their forefathers and has not listened to me, 21I will no longer drive out before them any of the nations Joshua left when he died. 22I will use them to test Israel and see whether they will keep the way of the LORD and walk in it as their forefathers did." 23The LORD had allowed those nations to remain; he did not drive them out at once by giving them into the hands of Joshua.

3 These are the nations the LORD left to test all those Israelites who had not ex-perienced any of the wars in Canaan 2(he did this only to teach warfare to the descendants of the Israelites who had not had previous battle experience): 3the five rulers of the Philistines, all the Canaanites, the Sidonians, and the Hivites living in the Lebanon moun-tains from Mount Baal Hermon to Lebo*a* Hamath. 4They were left to test the Israelites to see whether they would obey the LORD's commands, which he had given their fore-fathers through Moses.

5The Israelites lived among the Canaanites, Hittites, Amorites, Perizzites, Hivites and Jebusites. 6They took their daughters in marriage and gave their own daughters to their sons, and served their gods.

Othniel

7The Israelites did evil in the eyes of the LORD; they forgot the LORD their God and served the Baals and the Asherahs. 8The anger of the LORD burned against Israel so that he sold them into the hands of Cushan-Rishathaim king of Aram Naharaim,*b* to whom the Israelites were subject for eight years. 9But when they cried out to the LORD, he raised up for them a deliverer, Othniel son of Kenaz, Caleb's younger brother, who

---

f36 Hebrew *Akrabbim*   *a5 Bokim* means *weepers.*
b9 Also known as *Timnath Serah* (see Joshua 19:50 and 24:30)   *c16* Or *leaders;* similarly in verses 17–19
a3 Or *to the entrance to*   *b8* That is, North-west Mesopotamia

saved them. ¹⁰The Spirit of the LORD came upon him, so that he became Israel's judge*ᶜ* and went to war. The LORD gave Cushan-Rishathaim king of Aram into the hands of Othniel, who overpowered him. ¹¹So the land had peace for forty years, until Othniel son of Kenaz died.

Ehud

¹²Once again the Israelites did evil in the eyes of the LORD, and because they did this evil the LORD gave Eglon king of Moab power over Israel. ¹³Getting the Ammonites and Amalekites to join him, Eglon came and attacked Israel, and they took possession of the City of Palms.*ᵈ* ¹⁴The Israelites were subject to Eglon king of Moab for eighteen years.

¹⁵Again the Israelites cried out to the LORD, and he gave them a deliverer—Ehud, a left-handed man, the son of Gera the Benjamite. The Israelites sent him with tribute to Eglon king of Moab. ¹⁶Now Ehud had made a double-edged sword about a foot and a half*ᵉ* long, which he strapped to his right thigh under his clothing. ¹⁷He presented the tribute to Eglon king of Moab, who was a very fat man. ¹⁸After Ehud had presented the tribute, he sent on their way the men who had carried it. ¹⁹At the idols*ᶠ* near Gilgal he himself turned back and said, "I have a secret message for you, O king."

The king said, "Quiet!" And all his attendants left him.

²⁰Ehud then approached him while he was sitting alone in the upper room of his summer palace*ᵍ* and said, "I have a message from God for you." As the king rose from his seat, ²¹Ehud reached with his left hand, drew the sword from his right thigh and plunged it into the king's belly. ²²Even the handle sank in after the blade, which came out of his back. Ehud did not pull the sword out, and the fat closed in over it. ²³Then Ehud went out to the porch;*ʰ* he shut the doors of the upper room behind him and locked them.

²⁴After he had gone, the servants came and found the doors of the upper room locked. They said, "He must be relieving himself in the inner room of the house." ²⁵They waited to the point of embarrassment, but when he did not open the doors of the room, they took a key and unlocked them. There they saw their lord fallen to the floor, dead.

²⁶While they waited, Ehud got away. He passed by the idols and escaped to Seirah. ²⁷When he arrived there, he blew a trumpet in the hill country of Ephraim, and the Israelites went down with him from the hills, with him leading them.

²⁸"Follow me," he ordered, "for the LORD has given Moab, your enemy, into your hands." So they followed him down and, taking possession of the fords of the Jordan that led to Moab, they allowed no-one to cross over. ²⁹At that time they struck down about ten thousand Moabites, all vigorous

and strong; not a man escaped. ³⁰That day Moab was made subject to Israel, and the land had peace for eighty years.

Shamgar

³¹After Ehud came Shamgar son of Anath, who struck down six hundred Philistines with an ox-goad. He too saved Israel.

Deborah

4 After Ehud died, the Israelites once again did evil in the eyes of the LORD. ²So the LORD sold them into the hands of Jabin, a king of Canaan, who reigned in Hazor. The commander of his army was Sisera, who lived in Harosheth Haggoyim. ³Because he had nine hundred iron chariots and had cruelly oppressed the Israelites for twenty years, they cried to the LORD for help.

⁴Deborah, a prophetess, the wife of Lappidoth, was leading*ᵃ* Israel at that time. ⁵She held court under the Palm of Deborah between Ramah and Bethel in the hill country of Ephraim, and the Israelites came to her to have their disputes decided. ⁶She sent for Barak son of Abinoam from Kedesh in Naphtali and said to him, "The LORD, the God of Israel, commands you: 'Go, take with you ten thousand men of Naphtali and Zebulun and lead the way to Mount Tabor. ⁷I will lure Sisera, the commander of Jabin's army, with his chariots and his troops to the Kishon River and give him into your hands.'"

⁸Barak said to her, "If you go with me, I will go; but if you don't go with me, I won't go."

⁹"Very well," Deborah said, "I will go with you. But because of the way you are going about this,*ᵇ* the honour will not be yours, for the LORD will hand Sisera over to a woman." So Deborah went with Barak to Kedesh, ¹⁰where he summoned Zebulun and Naphtali. Ten thousand men followed him, and Deborah also went with him.

¹¹Now Heber the Kenite had left the other Kenites, the descendants of Hobab, Moses' brother-in-law,*ᶜ* and pitched his tent by the great tree in Zaanannim near Kedesh.

¹²When they told Sisera that Barak son of Abinoam had gone up to Mount Tabor, ¹³Sisera gathered together his nine hundred iron chariots and all the men with him, from Harosheth Haggoyim to the Kishon River.

¹⁴Then Deborah said to Barak, "Go! This is the day the LORD has given Sisera into your hands. Has not the LORD gone ahead of you?" So Barak went down Mount Tabor, followed by ten thousand men. ¹⁵At Barak's advance, the LORD routed Sisera and all his chariots and army by the sword, and Sisera abandoned his chariot and fled on foot. ¹⁶But Barak pursued the chariots and army as far as Harosheth Haggoyim. All the troops of Sisera fell by the sword; not a man was left.

¹⁷Sisera, however, fled on foot to the tent of Jael, the wife of Heber the Kenite, because there were friendly relations between Jabin

---

ᶜ10 Or *leader*   *ᵈ13* That is, Jericho   *ᵉ16* Hebrew *a cubit* (about 0.5 metre)
ᶠ19 Or *the stone quarries;* also in verse 26   *ᵍ20* The meaning of the Hebrew for this phrase is uncertain.
ʰ23 The meaning of the Hebrew for this word is uncertain.   *ᵃ4* Traditionally *judging*
ᵇ9 Or *But on the expedition you are undertaking*   *ᶜ11* Or *father-in-law*

JUDGES 5: 1–7, 19–21
'From the heavens the stars fought, from their courses they fought against Sisera'
(v. 20)

THE GOD WHO SAVES. The Song of Deborah has been described as the 'supreme literary treasure' of Judges, 'a magnificent example of early Hebrew poetry' (G. W. Anderson). A torrential rainstorm caused the River Kishon to overflow its banks, so rendering the chariots of the Canaanites helpless (see verse 21), and the forces of Sisera were then no match for the Israelites who descended on them.

The poem gives a clear witness to Israel's faith. God, for Deborah and her warriors, was God over all. Nature was under his control, as were the events of history, and God was working in the world to further the end he had in view. People could not ultimately defeat his will, and neither could the forces of nature prevail against him. On the contrary, God commanded all that he had created, to serve his purpose (see verse 20 above). So the Israelites held that God was involved in their affairs, and they rejoiced that when they were in distress he came to them with his saving acts.

Some Christians today might describe, for example, the British evacuation from Dunkirk in World War II as 'miraculous'; others might not. But at least all Christians will affirm with the apostle Paul that 'in all things God works for the good of those who love him, who have been called according to his purpose' (Romans 8: 28). In this sense we may sing our songs of praise.

To God belong all things, and his purpose is for good, for salvation.

→210

'Tear down your father's altar to Baal . . . Then build a proper kind of altar of the
to the LORD your God' (vv. 25, 26).

TAKING A STAND. As recorded in these verses, Gideon's response
to God's call did not involve him immediately in challenging the
Midianites. First he was called to witness to the Lord he served – and
to make that witness at home.

Yet our reading also helps us to understand how faith in God affects
every part of life. The Israelites found that when their faith was strong,
they had a spirit within which helped them to triumph over their foes;
but when they allied themselves to the Baal worship practised by their
neighbours, they found it increasingly more difficult to defeat them.

Gideon's overthrow of Baal's altar, thus, was first of all an act
valuable in itself. But then that affirmation of faith in God, coupled
with the evident inability of Baal to defend himself (v. 31), became
powerful in transforming the situation in which the Israelites found
themselves. It helped, surely, in leading Gideon to the point where he
did challenge the Midianites, and it served also to encourage the
Israelites to respond to his summons and join the fight in the name of
the Lord.

The French philosopher Gabriel Marcel said: 'I am obliged to bear
witness because I hold, as it were, a particle of light, and to keep it to
myself would be equivalent to extinguishing it.'

*Bearing witness to the light, as commanded by God, is always a worthy
act; and sometimes it has repercussions beyond our imagining.*

→219

king of Hazor and the clan of Heber the Kenite.

¹⁸Jael went out to meet Sisera and said to him, "Come, my lord, come right in. Don't be afraid." So he entered her tent, and she put a covering over him.

¹⁹"I'm thirsty," he said. "Please give me some water." She opened a skin of milk, gave him a drink, and covered him up.

²⁰"Stand in the doorway of the tent," he told her. "If someone comes by and asks you, 'Is anyone here?' say 'No.'"

²¹But Jael, Heber's wife, picked up a tent peg and a hammer and went quietly to him while he lay fast asleep, exhausted. She drove the peg through his temple into the ground, and he died.

²²Barak came by in pursuit of Sisera, and Jael went out to meet him. "Come," she said, "I will show you the man you're looking for." So he went in with her, and there lay Sisera with the tent peg through his temple—dead.

²³On that day God subdued Jabin, the Canaanite king, before the Israelites. ²⁴And the hand of the Israelites grew stronger and stronger against Jabin, the Canaanite king, until they destroyed him.

The Song of Deborah

5 On that day Deborah and Barak son of Abinoam sang this song:

²"When the princes in Israel take the lead,
when the people willingly offer
    themselves—
  praise the LORD!

³"Hear this, you kings! Listen, you rulers!
  I will sing to*ᵃ* the LORD, I will sing;
  I will make music to*ᵇ* the LORD, the God
    of Israel.

⁴"O LORD, when you went out from Seir,
  when you marched from the land of
    Edom,
the earth shook, the heavens poured,
  the clouds poured down water.
⁵The mountains quaked before the LORD,
    the One of Sinai,
  before the LORD, the God of Israel.

⁶"In the days of Shamgar son of Anath,
  in the days of Jael, the roads were
    abandoned;
  travellers took to winding paths.
⁷Village life*ᶜ* in Israel ceased,
  ceased until I,*ᵈ* Deborah, arose,
  arose a mother in Israel.
⁸When they chose new gods,
  war came to the city gates,
and not a shield or spear was seen
  among forty thousand in Israel.
⁹My heart is with Israel's princes,
  with the willing volunteers among the
    people.
  Praise the LORD!

¹⁰"You who ride on white donkeys,
  sitting on your saddle blankets,
  and you who walk along the road,
consider ¹¹the voice of the singers*ᵉ* at the
    watering places.
They recite the righteous acts of the
    LORD,
  the righteous acts of his warriors*ᶠ* in
    Israel.

"Then the people of the LORD
  went down to the city gates.
¹²"Wake up, wake up, Deborah!
  Wake up, wake up, break out in song!
Arise, O Barak!
  Take captive your captives, O son of
    Abinoam.'

¹³"Then the men who were left
  came down to the nobles;
the people of the LORD
  came to me with the mighty.
¹⁴Some came from Ephraim, whose roots
    were in Amalek;
  Benjamin was with the people who
    followed you.
From Makir captains came down,
  from Zebulun those who bear a
    commander's staff.
¹⁵The princes of Issachar were with
    Deborah;
  yes, Issachar was with Barak,
  rushing after him into the valley.
In the districts of Reuben
  there was much searching of heart.
¹⁶Why did you stay among the campfires*ᵍ*
  to hear the whistling for the flocks?
In the districts of Reuben
  there was much searching of heart.
¹⁷Gilead stayed beyond the Jordan.
  And Dan, why did he linger by the
    ships?
Asher remained on the coast
  and stayed in his coves.
¹⁸The people of Zebulun risked their very
    lives;
  so did Naphtali on the heights of the
    field.

¹⁹"Kings came, they fought;
  the kings of Canaan fought
at Taanach by the waters of Megiddo,
  but they carried off no silver, no
    plunder.
²⁰From the heavens the stars fought,
  from their courses they fought against
    Sisera.
²¹The river Kishon swept them away,
  the age-old river, the river Kishon.
  March on, my soul; be strong!
²²Then thundered the horses' hoofs—
  galloping, galloping go his mighty
    steeds.
²³'Curse Meroz,' said the angel of the LORD.
  'Curse its people bitterly,
because they did not come to help the
    LORD,
  to help the LORD against the mighty.'

---

*ᵃ*3 Or *of*   *ᵇ*3 Or *I with song I will praise*   *ᶜ*7 Or *Warriors*   *ᵈ*7 Or *you*
*ᵉ*11 Or *archers*; the meaning of the Hebrew for this word is uncertain.   *ᶠ*11 Or *villagers*   *ᵍ*16 Or *saddlebags*

24"Most blessed of women be Jael,
   the wife of Heber the Kenite,
   most blessed of tent-dwelling women.
25He asked for water, and she gave him
      milk;
   in a bowl fit for nobles she brought him
      curdled milk.
26Her hand reached for the tent peg,
   her right hand for the workman's
      hammer.
   She struck Sisera, she crushed his head,
   she shattered and pierced his temple.
27At her feet he sank,
   he fell; there he lay.
   At her feet he sank, he fell;
   where he sank, there he fell—dead.

28"Through the window peered Sisera's
      mother;
   behind the lattice she cried out,
   'Why is his chariot so long in coming?
   Why is the clatter of his chariots
      delayed?'
29The wisest of her ladies answer her;
   indeed, she keeps saying to herself,
30'Are they not finding and dividing the
      spoils:
   a girl or two for each man,
   colourful garments as plunder for
      Sisera,
   colourful garments embroidered,
   highly embroidered garments for my
      neck—
   all this as plunder?'

31"So may all your enemies perish, O LORD!
   But may they who love you be like the
      sun
   when it rises in its strength."

Then the land had peace for forty years.

Gideon

6 Again the Israelites did evil in the eyes of
   the LORD, and for seven years he gave
them into the hands of the Midianites.
2Because the power of Midian was so oppressive, the Israelites prepared shelters for
themselves in mountain clefts, caves and
strongholds. 3Whenever the Israelites
planted their crops, the Midianites, Amalekites and other eastern peoples invaded the
country. 4They camped on the land and
ruined the crops all the way to Gaza and did
not spare a living thing for Israel, neither
sheep nor cattle nor donkeys. 5They came up
with their livestock and their tents like
swarms of locusts. It was impossible to count
the men and their camels; they invaded the
land to ravage it. 6Midian so impoverished
the Israelites that they cried out to the LORD
for help.

7When the Israelites cried to the LORD
because of Midian, 8he sent them a prophet,
who said, "This is what the LORD, the God of
Israel, says: I brought you up out of Egypt,
out of the land of slavery. 9I snatched you
from the power of Egypt and from the hand of
all your oppressors. I drove them from before you and gave you their land. 10I said to
you, 'I am the LORD your God; do not
worship the gods of the Amorites, in whose
land you live.' But you have not listened to
me."

11The angel of the LORD came and sat down
under the oak in Ophrah that belonged to
Joash the Abiezrite, where his son Gideon
was threshing wheat in a winepress to keep it
from the Midianites. 12When the angel of the
LORD appeared to Gideon, he said, "The
LORD is with you, mighty warrior."

13"But sir," Gideon replied, "if the LORD
is with us, why has all this happened to us?
Where are all his wonders that our fathers
told us about when they said, 'Did not the
LORD bring us up out of Egypt?' But now
the LORD has abandoned us and put us into
the hand of Midian."

14The LORD turned to him and said, "Go in
the strength you have and save Israel out of
Midian's hand. Am I not sending you?"

15"But Lord,"a Gideon asked, "how can I
save Israel? My clan is the weakest in Manasseh, and I am the least in my family."

16The LORD answered, "I will be with you,
and you will strike down all the Midianites
together."

17Gideon replied, "If now I have found
favour in your eyes, give me a sign that it is
really you talking to me. 18Please do not go
away until I come back and bring my offering
and set it before you."

And the LORD said, "I will wait until you
return."

19Gideon went in, prepared a young goat,
and from an ephahb of flour he made bread
without yeast. Putting the meat in a basket
and its broth in a pot, he brought them out
and offered them to him under the oak.

20The angel of God said to him, "Take the
meat and the unleavened bread, place them
on this rock, and pour out the broth." And
Gideon did so. 21With the tip of the staff that
was in his hand, the angel of the LORD
touched the meat and the unleavened bread.
Fire flared from the rock, consuming the
meat and the bread. And the angel of the
LORD disappeared. 22When Gideon realised
that it was the angel of the LORD, he exclaimed, "Ah, Sovereign LORD! I have seen
the angel of the LORD face to face!"

23But the LORD said to him, "Peace! Do not
be afraid. You are not going to die."

24So Gideon built an altar to the LORD there
and called it The LORD is Peace. To this day it
stands in Ophrah of the Abiezrites.

25That same night the LORD said to him,
"Take the second bull from your father's
herd, the one seven years old.c Tear down
your father's altar to Baal and cut down the
Asherah poled beside it. 26Then build a
proper kind ofe altar to the LORD your God
on the top of this height. Using the wood of
the Asherah pole that you cut down, offer the
secondf bull as a burnt offering."

a15 Or sir   b19 That is, probably about ⅗ bushel (about 22 litres)
c25 Or Take a full-grown, mature bull from your father's herd
d25 That is, a symbol of the goddess Asherah; here and elsewhere in Judges
e26 Or build with layers of stone an   f26 Or full-grown; also in verse 28

²⁷So Gideon took ten of his servants and did as the Lᴏʀᴅ told him. But because he was afraid of his family and the men of the town, he did it at night rather than in the daytime.

²⁸In the morning when the men of the town got up, there was Baal's altar, demolished, with the Asherah pole beside it cut down and the second bull sacrificed on the newly-built altar!

²⁹They asked each other, "Who did this?"

When they carefully investigated, they were told, "Gideon son of Joash did it."

³⁰The men of the town demanded of Joash, "Bring out your son. He must die, because he has broken down Baal's altar and cut down the Asherah pole beside it."

³¹But Joash replied to the hostile crowd around him, "Are you going to plead Baal's cause? Are you trying to save him? Whoever fights for him shall be put to death by morning! If Baal really is a god, he can defend himself when someone breaks down his altar." ³²So that day they called Gideon "Jerub-Baal",ᵍ saying, "Let Baal contend with him," because he broke down Baal's altar.

³³Now all the Midianites, Amalekites and other eastern peoples joined forces and crossed over the Jordan and camped in the Valley of Jezreel. ³⁴Then the Spirit of the Lᴏʀᴅ came upon Gideon, and he blew a trumpet, summoning the Abiezrites to follow him. ³⁵He sent messengers throughout Manasseh, calling them to arms, and also into Asher, Zebulun and Naphtali, so that they too went up to meet them.

³⁶Gideon said to God, "If you will save Israel by my hand as you have promised —³⁷look, I will place a wool fleece on the threshing-floor. If there is dew only on the fleece and all the ground is dry, then I will know that you will save Israel by my hand, as you said." ³⁸And that is what happened. Gideon rose early the next day; he squeezed the fleece and wrung out the dew—a bowlful of water.

³⁹Then Gideon said to God, "Do not be angry with me. Let me make just one more request. Allow me one more test with the fleece. This time make the fleece dry and the ground covered with dew." ⁴⁰That night God did so. Only the fleece was dry; all the ground was covered with dew.

Gideon Defeats the Midianites

7 Early in the morning, Jerub-Baal (that is, Gideon) and all his men camped at the spring of Harod. The camp of Midian was north of them in the valley near the hill of Moreh. ²The Lᴏʀᴅ said to Gideon, "You have too many men for me to deliver Midian into their hands. In order that Israel may not boast against me that her own strength has saved her, ³announce now to the people, 'Anyone who trembles with fear may turn back and leave Mount Gilead.'" So twenty-two thousand men left, while ten thousand remained.

⁴But the Lᴏʀᴅ said to Gideon, "There are still too many men. Take them down to the water, and I will sift them out for you there. If I say, 'This one shall go with you,' he shall go; but if I say, 'This one shall not go with you,' he shall not go."

⁵So Gideon took the men down to the water. There the Lᴏʀᴅ told him, "Separate those who lap the water with their tongues like a dog from those who kneel down to drink." ⁶Three hundred men lapped with their hands to their mouths. All the rest got down on their knees to drink.

⁷The Lᴏʀᴅ said to Gideon, "With the three hundred men that lapped I will save you and give the Midianites into your hands. Let all the other men go, each to his own place." ⁸So Gideon sent the rest of the Israelites to their tents but kept the three hundred, who took over the provisions and trumpets of the others.

Now the camp of Midian lay below him in the valley. ⁹During that night the Lᴏʀᴅ said to Gideon, "Get up, go down against the camp, because I am going to give it into your hands. ¹⁰If you are afraid to attack, go down to the camp with your servant Purah ¹¹and listen to what they are saying. Afterwards, you will be encouraged to attack the camp." So he and Purah his servant went down to the outposts of the camp. ¹²The Midianites, the Amalekites and all the other eastern peoples had settled in the valley, thick as locusts. Their camels could no more be counted than the sand on the seashore.

¹³Gideon arrived just as a man was telling a friend his dream. "I had a dream," he was saying. "A round loaf of barley bread came tumbling into the Midianite camp. It struck the tent with such force that the tent overturned and collapsed."

¹⁴His friend responded, "This can be nothing other than the sword of Gideon son of Joash, the Israelite. God has given the Midianites and the whole camp into his hands."

¹⁵When Gideon heard the dream and its interpretation, he worshipped God. He returned to the camp of Israel and called out, "Get up! The Lᴏʀᴅ has given the Midianite camp into your hands." ¹⁶Dividing the three hundred men into three companies, he placed trumpets and empty jars in the hands of all of them, with torches inside.

¹⁷"Watch me," he told them. "Follow my lead. When I get to the edge of the camp, do exactly as I do. ¹⁸When I and all who are with me blow our trumpets, then from all around the camp blow yours and shout, 'For the Lᴏʀᴅ and for Gideon.'"

¹⁹Gideon and the hundred men with him reached the edge of the camp at the beginning of the middle watch, just after they had changed the guard. They blew their trumpets and broke the jars that were in their hands. ²⁰The three companies blew the trumpets and smashed the jars. Grasping the torches in their left hands and holding in their right hands the trumpets they were to blow, they shouted, "A sword for the Lᴏʀᴅ and for

---

ᵍ32 Jerub-Baal means let Baal contend.

Gideon!'' 21While each man held his position around the camp, all the Midianites ran, crying out as they fled.

22When the three hundred trumpets sounded, the LORD caused the men throughout the camp to turn on each other with their swords. The army fled to Beth Shittah towards Zererah as far as the border of Abel Meholah near Tabbath. 23Israelites from Naphtali, Asher and all Manasseh were called out, and they pursued the Midianites. 24Gideon sent messengers throughout the hill country of Ephraim, saying, ''Come down against the Midianites and seize the waters of the Jordan ahead of them as far as Beth Barah.''

So all the men of Ephraim were called out and they took the waters of the Jordan as far as Beth Barah. 25They also captured two of the Midianite leaders, Oreb and Zeeb. They killed Oreb at the rock of Oreb, and Zeeb at the winepress of Zeeb. They pursued the Midianites and brought the heads of Oreb and Zeeb to Gideon, who was by the Jordan.

Zebah and Zalmunna

8 Now the Ephraimites asked Gideon, ''Why have you treated us like this? Why didn't you call us when you went to fight Midian?'' And they criticised him sharply.

2But he answered them, ''What have I accomplished compared to you? Aren't the gleanings of Ephraim's grapes better than the full grape harvest of Abiezer? 3God gave Oreb and Zeeb, the Midianite leaders, into your hands. What was I able to do compared to you?'' At this, their resentment against him subsided.

4Gideon and his three hundred men, exhausted yet keeping up the pursuit, came to the Jordan and crossed it. 5He said to the men of Succoth, ''Give my troops some bread; they are worn out, and I am still pursuing Zebah and Zalmunna, the kings of Midian.''

6But the officials of Succoth said, ''Do you already have the hands of Zebah and Zalmunna in your possession? Why should we give bread to your troops?''

7Then Gideon replied, ''Just for that, when the LORD has given Zebah and Zalmunna into my hand, I will tear your flesh with desert thorns and briers.''

8From there he went up to Peniel[a] and made the same request of them, but they answered as the men of Succoth had. 9So he said to the men of Peniel, ''When I return in triumph, I will tear down this tower.''

10Now Zebah and Zalmunna were in Karkor with a force of about fifteen thousand men, all that were left of the armies of the eastern peoples; a hundred and twenty thousand swordsmen had fallen. 11Gideon went up by the route of the nomads east of Nobah and Jogbehah and fell upon the unsuspecting army. 12Zebah and Zalmunna, the two kings of Midian, fled, but he pursued them and captured them, routing their entire army.

13Gideon son of Joash then returned from the battle by the Pass of Heres. 14He caught a young man of Succoth and questioned him, and the young man wrote down for him the names of the seventy-seven officials of Succoth, the elders of the town. 15Then Gideon came and said to the men of Succoth, ''Here are Zebah and Zalmunna, about whom you taunted me by saying, 'Do you already have the hands of Zebah and Zalmunna in your possession? Why should we give bread to your exhausted men?' '' 16He took the elders of the town and taught the men of Succoth a lesson by punishing them with desert thorns and briers. 17He also pulled down the tower of Peniel and killed the men of the town.

18Then he asked Zebah and Zalmunna, ''What kind of men did you kill at Tabor?''

''Men like you,'' they answered, ''each one with the bearing of a prince.''

19Gideon replied, ''Those were my brothers, the sons of my own mother. As surely as the LORD lives, if you had spared their lives, I would not kill you.'' 20Turning to Jether, his oldest son, he said, ''Kill them!'' But Jether did not draw his sword, because he was only a boy and was afraid.

21Zebah and Zalmunna said, ''Come, do it yourself. 'As is the man, so is his strength.' '' So Gideon stepped forward and killed them, and took the ornaments off their camels' necks.

Gideon's Ephod

22The Israelites said to Gideon, ''Rule over us—you, your son and your grandson—because you have saved us out of the hand of Midian.''

23But Gideon told them, ''I will not rule over you, nor will my son rule over you. The LORD will rule over you.'' 24And he said, ''I do have one request, that each of you give me an ear-ring from your share of the plunder.'' (It was the custom of the Ishmaelites to wear gold ear-rings.)

25They answered, ''We'll be glad to give them.'' So they spread out a garment, and each man threw a ring from his plunder onto it. 26The weight of the gold rings he asked for came to seventeen hundred shekels,[b] not counting the ornaments, the pendants and the purple garments worn by the kings of Midian or the chains that were on their camels' necks. 27Gideon made the gold into an ephod, which he placed in Ophrah, his town. All Israel prostituted themselves by worshipping it there, and it became a snare to Gideon and his family.

Gideon's Death

28Thus Midian was subdued before the Israelites and did not raise its head again. During Gideon's lifetime, the land enjoyed peace for forty years.

29Jerub-Baal son of Joash went back home to live. 30He had seventy sons of his own, for he had many wives. 31His concubine, who lived in Shechem, also bore him a son, whom

---

[a]8 Hebrew *Penuel*, a variant of *Peniel*; also in verses 9 and 17
[b]26 That is, about 43 pounds (about 19.5 kilograms)

he named Abimelech. ³²Gideon son of Joash died at a good old age and was buried in the tomb of his father Joash in Ophrah of the Abiezrites.

³³No sooner had Gideon died than the Israelites again prostituted themselves to the Baals. They set up Baal-Berith as their god and ³⁴did not remember the LORD their God, who had rescued them from the hands of all their enemies on every side. ³⁵They also failed to show kindness to the family of Jerub-Baal (that is, Gideon) for all the good things he had done for them.

Abimelech

9 Abimelech son of Jerub-Baal went to his mother's brothers in Shechem and said to them and to all his mother's clan, ²"Ask all the citizens of Shechem, 'Which is better for you: to have all seventy of Jerub-Baal's sons rule over you, or just one man?' Remember, I am your flesh and blood."

³When the brothers repeated all this to the citizens of Shechem, they were inclined to follow Abimelech, for they said, "He is our brother." ⁴They gave him seventy shekels[a] of silver from the temple of Baal-Berith, and Abimelech used it to hire reckless adventurers, who became his followers. ⁵He went to his father's home in Ophrah and on one stone murdered his seventy brothers, the sons of Jerub-Baal. But Jotham, the youngest son of Jerub-Baal, escaped by hiding. ⁶Then all the citizens of Shechem and Beth Millo gathered beside the great tree at the pillar in Shechem to crown Abimelech king.

⁷When Jotham was told about this, he climbed up on the top of Mount Gerizim and shouted to them, "Listen to me, citizens of Shechem, so that God may listen to you. ⁸One day the trees went out to anoint a king for themselves. They said to the olive tree, 'Be our king.'

⁹"But the olive tree answered, 'Should I give up my oil, by which both gods and men are honoured, to hold sway over the trees?'

¹⁰"Next, the trees said to the fig-tree, 'Come and be our king.'

¹¹"But the fig-tree replied, 'Should I give up my fruit, so good and sweet, to hold sway over the trees?'

¹²"Then the trees said to the vine, 'Come and be our king.'

¹³"But the vine answered, 'Should I give up my wine, which cheers both gods and men, to hold sway over the trees?'

¹⁴"Finally all the trees said to the thornbush, 'Come and be our king.'

¹⁵"The thornbush said to the trees, 'If you really want to anoint me king over you, come and take refuge in my shade; but if not, then let fire come out of the thornbush and consume the cedars of Lebanon!'

¹⁶"Now if you have acted honourably and in good faith when you made Abimelech king, and if you have been fair to Jerub-Baal and his family, and if you have treated him as

he deserves—¹⁷and to think that my father fought for you, risked his life to rescue you from the hand of Midian ¹⁸(but today you have revolted against my father's family, murdered his seventy sons on a single stone, and made Abimelech, the son of his slave girl, king over the citizens of Shechem because he is your brother)—¹⁹if then you have acted honourably and in good faith towards Jerub-Baal and his family today, may Abimelech be your joy, and may you be his, too! ²⁰But if you have not, let fire come out from Abimelech and consume you, citizens of Shechem and Beth Millo, and let fire come out from you, citizens of Shechem and Beth Millo, and consume Abimelech!"

²¹Then Jotham fled, escaping to Beer, and he lived there because he was afraid of his brother Abimelech.

²²After Abimelech had governed Israel for three years, ²³God sent an evil spirit between Abimelech and the citizens of Shechem, who acted treacherously against Abimelech. ²⁴God did this in order that the crime against Jerub-Baal's seventy sons, the shedding of their blood, might be avenged on their brother Abimelech and on the citizens of Shechem, who had helped him murder his brothers. ²⁵In opposition to him these citizens of Shechem set men on the hilltops to ambush and rob everyone who passed by, and this was reported to Abimelech.

²⁶Now Gaal son of Ebed moved with his brothers into Shechem, and its citizens put their confidence in him. ²⁷After they had gone out into the fields and gathered the grapes and trodden them, they held a festival in the temple of their god. While they were eating and drinking, they cursed Abimelech. ²⁸Then Gaal son of Ebed said, "Who is Abimelech, and who is Shechem, that we should be subject to him? Isn't he Jerub-Baal's son, and isn't Zebul his deputy? Serve the men of Hamor, Shechem's father! Why should we serve Abimelech? ²⁹If only this people were under my command! Then I would get rid of him. I would say to Abimelech, 'Call out your whole army!'"[b]

³⁰When Zebul the governor of the city heard what Gaal son of Ebed said, he was very angry. ³¹Under cover he sent messengers to Abimelech, saying, "Gaal son of Ebed and his brothers have come to Shechem and are stirring up the city against you. ³²Now then, during the night you and your men should come and lie in wait in the fields. ³³In the morning at sunrise, advance against the city. When Gaal and his men come out against you, do whatever your hand finds to do."

³⁴So Abimelech and all his troops set out by night and took up concealed positions near Shechem in four companies. ³⁵Now Gaal son of Ebed had gone out and was standing at the entrance to the city gate just as Abimelech and his soldiers came out from their hiding-place.

³⁶When Gaal saw them, he said to Zebul,

---

[a]4 That is, about 1¾ pounds (about 0.8 kilogram)
[b]29 Septuagint; Hebrew *him." Then he said to Abimelech, "Call out your whole army!"*

"Look, people are coming down from the tops of the mountains!"

Zebul replied, "You mistake the shadows of the mountains for men."

[37]But Gaal spoke up again: "Look, people are coming down from the centre of the land, and a company is coming from the direction of the soothsayers' tree."

[38]Then Zebul said to him, "Where is your big talk now, you who said, 'Who is Abimelech that we should be subject to him?' Aren't these the men you ridiculed? Go out and fight them!"

[39]So Gaal led out[c] the citizens of Shechem and fought Abimelech. [40]Abimelech chased him, and many fell wounded in the flight— all the way to the entrance to the gate. [41]Abimelech stayed in Arumah, and Zebul drove Gaal and his brothers out of Shechem.

[42]The next day the people of Shechem went out to the fields, and this was reported to Abimelech. [43]So he took his men, divided them into three companies and set an ambush in the fields. When he saw the people coming out of the city, he rose to attack them. [44]Abimelech and the companies with him rushed forward to a position at the entrance to the city gate. Then two companies rushed upon those in the fields and struck them down. [45]All that day Abimelech pressed his attack against the city until he had captured it and killed its people. Then he destroyed the city and scattered salt over it.

[46]On hearing this, the citizens in the tower of Shechem went into the stronghold of the temple of El-Berith. [47]When Abimelech heard that they had assembled there, [48]he and all his men went up Mount Zalmon. He took an axe and cut off some branches, which he lifted to his shoulders. He ordered the men with him, "Quick! Do what you have seen me do!" [49]So all the men cut branches and followed Abimelech. They piled them against the stronghold and set it on fire over the people inside. So all the people in the tower of Shechem, about a thousand men and women, also died.

[50]Next Abimelech went to Thebez and besieged it and captured it. [51]Inside the city, however, was a strong tower, to which all the men and women—all the people of the city —fled. They locked themselves in and climbed up on the tower roof. [52]Abimelech went to the tower and stormed it. But as he approached the entrance to the tower to set it on fire, [53]a woman dropped an upper millstone on his head and cracked his skull.

[54]Hurriedly he called to his armour-bearer, "Draw your sword and kill me, so that they can't say, 'A woman killed him.'" So his servant ran him through, and he died. [55]When the Israelites saw that Abimelech was dead, they went home.

[56]Thus God repaid the wickedness that Abimelech had done to his father by murdering his seventy brothers. [57]God also made the men of Shechem pay for all their wickedness.

The curse of Jotham son of Jerub-Baal came on them.

Tola

10 After the time of Abimelech a man of Issachar, Tola son of Puah, the son of Dodo, rose to save Israel. He lived in Shamir, in the hill country of Ephraim. [2]He led[a] Israel for twenty-three years; then he died, and was buried in Shamir.

Jair

[3]He was followed by Jair of Gilead, who led Israel for twenty-two years. [4]He had thirty sons, who rode thirty donkeys. They controlled thirty towns in Gilead, which to this day are called Havvoth Jair.[b] [5]When Jair died, he was buried in Kamon.

Jephthah

[6]Again the Israelites did evil in the eyes of the LORD. They served the Baals and the Ashtoreths, and the gods of Aram, the gods of Sidon, the gods of Moab, the gods of the Ammonites and the gods of the Philistines. And because the Israelites forsook the LORD and no longer served him, [7]he became angry with them. He sold them into the hands of the Philistines and the Ammonites, [8]who that year shattered and crushed them. For eighteen years they oppressed all the Israelites on the east side of the Jordan in Gilead, the land of the Amorites. [9]The Ammonites also crossed the Jordan to fight against Judah, Benjamin and the house of Ephraim; and Israel was in great distress. [10]Then the Israelites cried out to the LORD, "We have sinned against you, forsaking our God and serving the Baals."

[11]The LORD replied, "When the Egyptians, the Amorites, the Ammonites, the Philistines, the Sidonians, the Amalekites and the Maonites[c] oppressed you and you cried to me for help, did I not save you from their hands? [13]But you have forsaken me and served other gods, so I will no longer save you. [14]Go and cry out to the gods you have chosen. Let them save you when you are in trouble!"

[15]But the Israelites said to the LORD, "We have sinned. Do with us whatever you think best, but please rescue us now." [16]Then they got rid of the foreign gods among them and served the LORD. And he could bear Israel's misery no longer.

[17]When the Ammonites were called to arms and camped in Gilead, the Israelites assembled and camped at Mizpah. [18]The leaders of the people of Gilead said to each other, "Whoever will launch the attack against the Ammonites will be the head of all those living in Gilead."

11 Jephthah the Gileadite was a mighty warrior. His father was Gilead; his mother was a prostitute. [2]Gilead's wife also bore him sons, and when they were grown up, they drove Jephthah away. "You are not going to get any inheritance in our family,"

---

[c]39 Or *Gaal went out in the sight of*　[a]2 Traditionally *judged*; also in verse 3
[b]4 Or *called the settlements of Jair*　[c]12 Hebrew; some Septuagint manuscripts *Midianites*

they said, "because you are the son of another woman." ³So Jephthah fled from his brothers and settled in the land of Tob, where a group of adventurers gathered around him and followed him.

⁴Some time later, when the Ammonites made war on Israel, ⁵the elders of Gilead went to get Jephthah from the land of Tob. ⁶"Come," they said, "be our commander, so we can fight the Ammonites."

⁷Jephthah said to them, "Didn't you hate me and drive me from my father's house? Why do you come to me now, when you're in trouble?"

⁸The elders of Gilead said to him, "Nevertheless, we are turning to you now; come with us to fight the Ammonites, and you will be our head over all who live in Gilead."

⁹Jephthah answered, "Suppose you take me back to fight the Ammonites and the LORD gives them to me—will I really be your head?"

¹⁰The elders of Gilead replied, "The LORD is our witness; we will certainly do as you say." ¹¹So Jephthah went with the elders of Gilead, and the people made him head and commander over them. And he repeated all his words before the LORD in Mizpah.

¹²Then Jephthah sent messengers to the Ammonite king with the question: "What do you have against us that you have attacked our country?"

¹³The king of the Ammonites answered Jephthah's messengers, "When Israel came up out of Egypt, they took away my land from the Arnon to the Jabbok, all the way to the Jordan. Now give it back peaceably."

¹⁴Jephthah sent back messengers to the Ammonite king, ¹⁵saying:

"This is what Jephthah says: Israel did not take the land of Moab or the land of the Ammonites. ¹⁶But when they came up out of Egypt, Israel went through the desert to the Red Sea*ᵃ* and on to Kadesh. ¹⁷Then Israel sent messengers to the king of Edom, saying, 'Give us permission to go through your country,' but the king of Edom would not listen. They sent also to the king of Moab, and he refused. So Israel stayed at Kadesh.

¹⁸"Next they travelled through the desert, skirted the lands of Edom and Moab, passed along the eastern side of the country of Moab, and camped on the other side of the Arnon. They did not enter the territory of Moab, for the Arnon was its border.

¹⁹"Then Israel sent messengers to Sihon king of the Amorites, who ruled in Heshbon, and said to him, 'Let us pass through your country to our own place.' ²⁰Sihon, however, did not trust Israel*ᵇ* to pass through his territory. He mustered all his men and encamped at Jahaz and fought with Israel.

²¹"Then the LORD, the God of Israel, gave Sihon and all his men into Israel's hands, and they defeated them. Israel took over all the land of the Amorites who lived in that country, ²²capturing all of it from the Arnon to the Jabbok and from the desert to the Jordan.

²³"Now since the LORD, the God of Israel, has driven the Amorites out before his people Israel, what right have you to take it over? ²⁴Will you not take what your god Chemosh gives you? Likewise, whatever the LORD our God has given us, we will possess. ²⁵Are you better than Balak son of Zippor, king of Moab? Did he ever quarrel with Israel or fight with them? ²⁶For three hundred years Israel occupied Heshbon, Aroer, the surrounding settlements and all the towns along the Arnon. Why didn't you retake them during that time? ²⁷I have not wronged you, but you are doing me wrong by waging war against me. Let the LORD, the Judge,*ᶜ* decide the dispute this day between the Israelites and the Ammonites."

²⁸The king of Ammon, however, paid no attention to the message Jephthah sent him.

²⁹Then the Spirit of the LORD came upon Jephthah. He crossed Gilead and Manasseh, passed through Mizpah of Gilead, and from there he advanced against the Ammonites. ³⁰And Jephthah made a vow to the LORD: "If you give the Ammonites into my hands, ³¹whatever comes out of the door of my house to meet me when I return in triumph from the Ammonites will be the LORD's, and I will sacrifice it as a burnt offering."

³²Then Jephthah went over to fight the Ammonites, and the LORD gave them into his hands. ³³He devastated twenty towns from Aroer to the vicinity of Minnith, as far as Abel Karamim. Thus Israel subdued Ammon.

³⁴When Jephthah returned to his home in Mizpah, who should come out to meet him but his daughter, dancing to the sound of tambourines! She was an only child. Except for her he had neither son nor daughter. ³⁵When he saw her, he tore his clothes and cried, "Oh! My daughter! You have made me miserable and wretched, because I have made a vow to the LORD that I cannot break." ³⁶"My father," she replied, "you have given your word to the LORD. Do to me just as you promised, now that the LORD has avenged you of your enemies, the Ammonites. ³⁷But grant me this one request," she said. "Give me two months to roam the hills and weep with my friends, because I will never marry."

³⁸"You may go," he said. And he let her go for two months. She and the girls went into the hills and wept because she would never marry. ³⁹After the two months, she returned to her father and he did to her as he had vowed. And she was a virgin. From this comes the Israelite custom ⁴⁰that each year the young women of Israel

---

ᵃ16 Hebrew Yam Suph; that is, Sea of Reeds   ᵇ20 Or however, would not make an agreement for Israel   ᶜ27 Or Ruler go out for four days to commemorate the daughter of Jephthah the Gileadite.

Jephthah and Ephraim

12 The men of Ephraim called out their forces, crossed over to Zaphon and said to Jephthah, "Why did you go to fight the Ammonites without calling us to go with you? We're going to burn down your house over your head."

2Jephthah answered, "I and my people were engaged in a great struggle with the Ammonites, and although I called, you didn't save me out of their hands. 3When I saw that you wouldn't help, I took my life in my hands and crossed over to fight the Ammonites, and the LORD gave me the victory over them. Now why have you come up today to fight me?"

4Jephthah then called together the men of Gilead and fought against Ephraim. The Gileadites struck them down because the Ephraimites had said, "You Gileadites are renegades from Ephraim and Manasseh." 5The Gileadites captured the fords of the Jordan leading to Ephraim, and whenever a survivor of Ephraim said, "Let me cross over," the men of Gilead asked him, "Are you an Ephraimite?" If he replied, "No," 6they said, "All right, say 'Shibboleth'." If he said, "Sibboleth," because he could not pronounce the word correctly, they seized him and killed him at the fords of the Jordan. Forty-two thousand Ephraimites were killed at that time.

7Jephthah led[a] Israel for six years. Then Jephthah the Gileadite died, and was buried in a town in Gilead.

Ibzan, Elon and Abdon

8After him, Ibzan of Bethlehem led Israel. 9He had thirty sons and thirty daughters. He gave his daughters away in marriage to those outside his clan, and for his sons he brought in thirty young women as wives from outside his clan. Ibzan led Israel for seven years. 10Then Ibzan died, and was buried in Bethlehem.

11After him, Elon the Zebulunite led Israel for ten years. 12Then Elon died, and was buried in Aijalon in the land of Zebulun.

13After him, Abdon son of Hillel, from Pirathon, led Israel. 14He had forty sons and thirty grandsons, who rode on seventy donkeys. He led Israel for eight years. 15Then Abdon son of Hillel died, and was buried at Pirathon in Ephraim, in the hill country of the Amalekites.

The Birth of Samson

13 Again the Israelites did evil in the eyes of the LORD, so the LORD delivered them into the hands of the Philistines for forty years.

2A certain man of Zorah, named Manoah, from the clan of the Danites, had a wife who was sterile and remained childless. 3The angel of the LORD appeared to her and said, "You are sterile and childless, but you are going to conceive and have a son. 4Now see to it that you drink no wine or other fermented drink and that you do not eat anything unclean, 5because you will conceive and give birth to a son. No razor may be used on his head, because the boy is to be a Nazirite, set apart to God from birth, and he will begin the deliverance of Israel from the hands of the Philistines."

6Then the woman went to her husband and told him, "A man of God came to me. He looked like an angel of God, very awesome. I didn't ask him where he came from, and he didn't tell me his name. 7But he said to me, 'You will conceive and give birth to a son. Now then, drink no wine or other fermented drink and do not eat anything unclean, because the boy will be a Nazirite of God from birth until the day of his death.'"

8Then Manoah prayed to the LORD: "O Lord, I beg you, let the man of God you sent to us come again to teach us how to bring up the boy who is to be born."

9God heard Manoah, and the angel of God came again to the woman while she was out in the field; but her husband Manoah was not with her. 10The woman hurried to tell her husband, "He's here! The man who appeared to me the other day!"

11Manoah got up and followed his wife. When he came to the man, he said, "Are you the one who talked to my wife?"

"I am," he said.

12So Manoah asked him, "When your words are fulfilled, what is to be the rule for the boy's life and work?"

13The angel of the LORD answered, "Your wife must do all that I have told her. 14She must not eat anything that comes from the grapevine, nor drink any wine or other fermented drink nor eat anything unclean. She must do everything I have commanded her."

15Manoah said to the angel of the LORD, "We would like you to stay until we prepare a young goat for you."

16The angel of the LORD replied, "Even though you detain me, I will not eat any of your food. But if you prepare a burnt offering, offer it to the LORD." (Manoah did not realise that it was the angel of the LORD.)

17Then Manoah enquired of the angel of the LORD, "What is your name, so that we may honour you when your word comes true?"

18He replied, "Why do you ask my name? It is beyond understanding."[a] 19Then Manoah took a young goat, together with the grain offering, and sacrificed it on a rock to the LORD. And the LORD did an amazing thing while Manoah and his wife watched: 20As the flame blazed up from the altar towards heaven, the angel of the LORD ascended in the flame. Seeing this, Manoah and his wife fell with their faces to the ground. 21When the angel of the LORD did not show himself again to Manoah and his wife, Manoah realised that it was the angel of the LORD.

22"We are doomed to die!" he said to his wife. "We have seen God!"

---

*a*7 Traditionally *judged*; also in verses 8–14   *a*18 Or *is wonderful*

JUDGES 13:1–7
'The boy is to be a Nazirite, set apart to God from birth' (v. 5).

DEDICATED TO GOD. Samson, like other heroes in the Old Testament, is portrayed as being *the gift of God* to a barren and childless woman. This is the truth which is at the heart of the angel's announcement. The coming of the one who is to help deliver Israel from the Philistines is nothing less than God's gift to his people.

But great emphasis is found in this reading on the place of *human co-operation and obedience*. The mother is told to take no fermented drink and to eat no forbidden food. The boy, furthermore, is to be under a lifelong Nazirite vow (see Numbers 6), and no razor must touch his head. The stress upon the human aspect remains throughout the story, and almost to the end the strength of Samson is related to his obedience.

Here, then, we may see the intertwining of the divine and human elements in life. A church choir or Salvation Army band is a blessing to others as through both prayer and practice it does all it can to make its music a fit offering to God. Similarly, the preachers or Christians whose gifts lie in practical service prove to be a help to their fellows in so far as they are consecrated to God and *cooperating fully with him* in the work they are is given to do. God's gifts to the world do not dispense with the need for our cooperation: *they demand it.*

The gifts of God for our deliverance operate through human co-operation and not apart from it.

→220

JUDGES 16:23–31

'Samson prayed to the LORD' "O Sovereign LORD, remember me. O God, please strengthen me just once more" ' (v. 28).

THE SOURCE OF STRENGTH. Samson has reached the low point of his life. Everything seems to have gone wrong; his strength has left him and he has become an object of curiosity and amusement to his enemies. But it is not the end! The low point proves to be the turning point. It becomes by God's grace the prelude to a final witness to his Lord.

In this final scene there is no mention of Samson's hair or Nazirite vow (16:22). The emphasis instead is upon Samson's prayer to the Lord in humility and repentance. And in this picture – of Samson returning to God – do we not also see the secret of his strength? In the last resort Samson's power did not lie in his hair, or even in his vow; he was strong when he was living in harmony with God. The vow was designed to preserve that harmony.

Samson's story, like others that have been handed down in the tradition of nations, is the story of a country hero who performed feats of incredible strength. He lived in a day far removed from our own, and his actions were not always such as we would commend, but we do well to take careful note of the overriding and final direction of his life. In the end he is found returning to God.

He belonged with God; there lay his strength; and there he could still be of use to his fellows.

23But his wife answered, "If the Lord had meant to kill us, he would not have accepted a burnt offering and grain offering from our hands, nor shown us all these things or now told us this."

24The woman gave birth to a boy and named him Samson. He grew and the Lord blessed him, 25and the Spirit of the Lord began to stir him while he was in Mahaneh Dan, between Zorah and Eshtaol.

Samson's Marriage

14 Samson went down to Timnah and saw there a young Philistine woman. 2When he returned, he said to his father and mother, "I have seen a Philistine woman in Timnah; now get her for me as my wife."

3His father and mother replied, "Isn't there an acceptable woman among your relatives or among all our people? Must you go to the uncircumcised Philistines to get a wife?"

But Samson said to his father, "Get her for me. She's the right one for me." 4(His parents did not know that this was from the Lord, who was seeking an occasion to confront the Philistines; for at that time they were ruling over Israel.) 5Samson went down to Timnah together with his father and mother. As they approached the vineyards of Timnah, suddenly a young lion came roaring towards him. 6The Spirit of the Lord came upon him in power so that he tore the lion apart with his bare hands as he might have torn a young goat. But he told neither his father nor his mother what he had done. 7Then he went down and talked with the woman, and he liked her.

8Some time later, when he went back to marry her, he turned aside to look at the lion's carcass. In it was a swarm of bees and some honey, 9which he scooped out with his hands and ate as he went along. When he rejoined his parents, he gave them some, and they too ate it. But he did not tell them that he had taken the honey from the lion's carcass.

10Now his father went down to see the woman. And Samson made a feast there, as was customary for bridegrooms. 11When he appeared, he was given thirty companions.

12"Let me tell you a riddle," Samson said to them. "If you can give me the answer within the seven days of the feast, I will give you thirty linen garments and thirty sets of clothes. 13If you can't tell me the answer, you must give me thirty linen garments and thirty sets of clothes."

"Tell us your riddle," they said. "Let's hear it."

14He replied,

"Out of the eater, something to eat;
    out of the strong, something sweet."

For three days they could not give the answer.

15On the fourth[a] day, they said to Samson's wife, "Coax your husband into explaining the riddle for us, or we will burn you

and your father's household to death. Did you invite us here to rob us?"

16Then Samson's wife threw herself on him, sobbing, "You hate me! You don't really love me. You've given my people a riddle, but you haven't told me the answer."

"I haven't even explained it to my father or mother," he replied, "so why should I explain it to you?" 17She cried the whole seven days of the feast. So on the seventh day he finally told her, because she continued to press him. She in turn explained the riddle to her people.

18Before sunset on the seventh day the men of the town said to him,

"What is sweeter than honey?
    What is stronger than a lion?"

Samson said to them,

"If you had not ploughed with my heifer,
    you would not have solved my riddle."

19Then the Spirit of the Lord came upon him in power. He went down to Ashkelon, struck down thirty of their men, stripped them of their belongings and gave their clothes to those who had explained the riddle. Burning with anger, he went up to his father's house. 20And Samson's wife was given to the friend who had attended him at his wedding.

Samson's Vengeance on the Philistines

15 Later on, at the time of wheat harvest, Samson took a young goat and went to visit his wife. He said, "I'm going to my wife's room." But her father would not let him go in.

2"I was so sure you thoroughly hated her," he said, "that I gave her to your friend. Isn't her younger sister more attractive? Take her instead."

3Samson said to them, "This time I have a right to get even with the Philistines; I will really harm them." 4So he went out and caught three hundred foxes and tied them tail to tail in pairs. He then fastened a torch to every pair of tails, 5lit the torches and let the foxes loose in the standing corn of the Philistines. He burned up the shocks and standing corn, together with the vineyards and olive groves.

6When the Philistines asked, "Who did this?" they were told, "Samson, the Timnite's son-in-law, because his wife was given to his friend."

So the Philistines went up and burned her and her father to death. 7Samson said to them, "Since you've acted like this, I won't stop until I get my revenge on you." 8He attacked them viciously and slaughtered many of them. Then he went down and stayed in a cave in the rock of Etam.

9The Philistines went up and camped in Judah, spreading out near Lehi. 10The men of Judah asked, "Why have you come to fight us?"

---

a15 Some Septuagint manuscripts and Syriac; Hebrew *seventh*

"We have come to take Samson prisoner," they answered, "to do to him as he did to us."

[11]Then three thousand men from Judah went down to the cave in the rock of Etam and said to Samson, "Don't you realise that the Philistines are rulers over us? What have you done to us?"

He answered, "I merely did to them what they did to me."

[12]They said to him, "We've come to tie you up and hand you over to the Philistines."

Samson said, "Swear to me that you won't kill me yourselves."

[13]"Agreed," they answered. "We will only tie you up and hand you over to them. We will not kill you." So they bound him with two new ropes and led him up from the rock. [14]As he approached Lehi, the Philistines came towards him shouting. The Spirit of the LORD came upon him in power. The ropes on his arms became like charred flax, and the bindings dropped from his hands. [15]Finding a fresh jaw-bone of a donkey, he grabbed it and struck down a thousand men.

[16]Then Samson said,

"With a donkey's jaw-bone
I have made donkeys of them.[a]
With a donkey's jaw-bone
I have killed a thousand men."

[17]When he finished speaking, he threw away the jaw-bone; and the place was called Ramath Lehi.[b]

[18]Because he was very thirsty, he cried out to the LORD, "You have given your servant this great victory. Must I now die of thirst and fall into the hands of the uncircumcised?" [19]Then God opened up the hollow place in Lehi, and water came out of it. When Samson drank, his strength returned and he revived. So the spring was called En Hakkore,[c] and it is still there in Lehi.

[20]Samson led[d] Israel for twenty years in the days of the Philistines.

Samson and Delilah

16 One day Samson went to Gaza, where he saw a prostitute. He went in to spend the night with her. [2]The people of Gaza were told, "Samson is here!" So they surrounded the place and lay in wait for him all night at the city gate. They made no move during the night, saying, "At dawn we'll kill him."

[3]But Samson lay there only until the middle of the night. Then he got up and took hold of the doors of the city gate, together with the two posts, and tore them loose, bar and all. He lifted them to his shoulders and carried them to the top of the hill that faces Hebron.

[4]Some time later, he fell in love with a woman in the Valley of Sorek whose name was Delilah. [5]The rulers of the Philistines went to her and said, "See if you can lure him into showing you the secret of his great strength and how we can overpower him so that we may tie him up and subdue him. Each one of us will give you eleven hundred shekels[a] of silver."

[6]So Delilah said to Samson, "Tell me the secret of your great strength and how you can be tied up and subdued."

[7]Samson answered her, "If anyone ties me with seven fresh thongs[b] that have not been dried, I'll become as weak as any other man."

[8]Then the rulers of the Philistines brought her seven fresh thongs that had not been dried, and she tied him with them. [9]With men hidden in the room, she called to him, "Samson, the Philistines are upon you!" But he snapped the thongs as easily as a piece of string snaps when it comes close to a flame. So the secret of his strength was not discovered.

[10]Then Delilah said to Samson, "You have made a fool of me; you lied to me. Come now, tell me how you can be tied."

[11]He said, "If anyone ties me securely with new ropes that have never been used, I'll become as weak as any other man."

[12]So Delilah took new ropes and tied him with them. Then, with men hidden in the room, she called to him, "Samson, the Philistines are upon you!" But he snapped the ropes off his arms as if they were threads.

[13]Delilah then said to Samson, "Until now, you have been making a fool of me and lying to me. Tell me how you can be tied."

He replied, "If you weave the seven braids of my head into the fabric ⌞on the loom⌟ and tighten it with the pin, I'll become as weak as any other man." So while he was sleeping, Delilah took the seven braids of his head, wove them into the fabric [14]and[c] tightened it with the pin.

Again she called to him, "Samson, the Philistines are upon you!" He awoke from his sleep and pulled up the pin and the loom, with the fabric.

[15]Then she said to him, "How can you say, 'I love you,' when you won't confide in me? This is the third time you have made a fool of me and haven't told me the secret of your great strength." [16]With such nagging she prodded him day after day until he was tired to death.

[17]So he told her everything. "No razor has ever been used on my head," he said, "because I have been a Nazirite set apart to God since birth. If my head were shaved, my strength would leave me, and I would become as weak as any other man."

[18]When Delilah saw that he had told her everything, she sent word to the rulers of the Philistines, "Come back once more; he has told me everything." So the rulers of the Philistines returned with the silver in their hands. [19]Having put him to sleep on her lap, she called a man to shave off the seven braids

---

[a]16 Or *made a heap or two*; the Hebrew for *donkey* sounds like the Hebrew for *heap*.
[b]17 *Ramath Lehi* means *jaw-bone hill*.   [c]19 *En Hakkore* means *caller's spring*.   [d]20 Traditionally *judged*
[a]5 That is, about 28 pounds (about 13 kilograms)   [b]7 Or *bow-strings*; also in verses 8 and 9
[c]13, 14 Some Septuagint manuscripts; Hebrew "⌞*I can*⌟ *if you weave the seven braids of my head into the fabric* ⌞*on the loom*⌟." [14]*So she*

of his hair, and so began to subdue him.*d* And his strength left him.

20Then she called, "Samson, the Philistines are upon you!"

He awoke from his sleep and thought, "I'll go out as before and shake myself free." But he did not know that the LORD had left him.

21Then the Philistines seized him, gouged out his eyes and took him down to Gaza. Binding him with bronze shackles, they set him to grinding in the prison. 22But the hair on his head began to grow again after it had been shaved.

The Death of Samson

23Now the rulers of the Philistines assembled to offer a great sacrifice to Dagon their god and to celebrate, saying, "Our god has delivered Samson, our enemy, into our hands."

24When the people saw him, they praised their god, saying,

"Our god has delivered our enemy
    into our hands,
the one who laid waste our land
    and multiplied our slain."

25While they were in high spirits, they shouted, "Bring out Samson to entertain us." So they called Samson out of the prison, and he performed for them.

When they stood him among the pillars, 26Samson said to the servant who held his hand, "Put me where I can feel the pillars that support the temple, so that I may lean against them." 27Now the temple was crowded with men and women; all the rulers of the Philistines were there, and on the roof were about three thousand men and women watching Samson perform. 28Then Samson prayed to the LORD, "O Sovereign LORD, remember me. O God, please strengthen me just once more, and let me with one blow get revenge on the Philistines for my two eyes." 29Then Samson reached towards the two central pillars on which the temple stood. Bracing himself against them, his right hand on the one and his left hand on the other, 30Samson said, "Let me die with the Philistines!" Then he pushed with all his might, and down came the temple on the rulers and all the people in it. Thus he killed many more when he died than while he lived.

31Then his brothers and his father's whole family went down to get him. They brought him back and buried him between Zorah and Eshtaol in the tomb of Manoah his father. He had led*e* Israel twenty years.

Micah's Idols

17 Now a man named Micah from the hill country of Ephraim 2said to his mother, "The eleven hundred shekels*a* of silver that were taken from you and about

which I heard you utter a curse—I have that silver with me; I took it."

Then his mother said, "The LORD bless you, my son!"

3When he returned the eleven hundred shekels of silver to his mother, she said, "I solemnly consecrate my silver to the LORD for my son to make a carved image and a cast idol. I will give it back to you."

4So he returned the silver to his mother, and she took two hundred shekels*b* of silver and gave them to a silversmith, who made them into the image and the idol. And they were put in Micah's house.

5Now this man Micah had a shrine, and he made an ephod and some idols and installed one of his sons as his priest. 6In those days Israel had no king; everyone did as he saw fit.

7A young Levite from Bethlehem in Judah, who had been living within the clan of Judah, 8left that town in search of some other place to stay. On his way*c* he came to Micah's house in the hill country of Ephraim.

9Micah asked him, "Where are you from?"

"I'm a Levite from Bethlehem in Judah," he said, "and I'm looking for a place to stay."

10Then Micah said to him, "Live with me and be my father and priest, and I'll give you ten shekels*d* of silver a year, your clothes and your food." 11So the Levite agreed to live with him, and the young man was to him like one of his sons. 12Then Micah installed the Levite, and the young man became his priest and lived in his house. 13And Micah said, "Now I know that the LORD will be good to me, since this Levite has become my priest."

Danites Settle in Laish

18 In those days Israel had no king.
And in those days the tribe of the Danites was seeking a place of their own where they might settle, because they had not yet come into an inheritance among the tribes of Israel. 2So the Danites sent five warriors from Zorah and Eshtaol to spy out the land and explore it. These men represented all their clans. They told them, "Go, explore the land."

The men entered the hill country of Ephraim and came to the house of Micah, where they spent the night. 3When they were near Micah's house, they recognised the voice of the young Levite; so they turned in there and asked him, "Who brought you here? What are you doing in this place? Why are you here?"

4He told them what Micah had done for him, and said, "He has hired me and I am his priest."

5Then they said to him, "Please enquire of God to learn whether our journey will be successful."

6The priest answered them, "Go in peace. Your journey has the LORD's approval."

---

d19 Hebrew; some Septuagint manuscripts *and he began to weaken*   *e31* Traditionally *judged*
a2 That is, about 28 pounds (about 13 kilograms)   *b4* That is, about 5 pounds (about 2.3 kilograms)
c8 Or *To carry on his profession*   *d10* That is, about 4 ounces (about 115 grams)

7So the five men left and came to Laish, where they saw that the people were living in safety, like the Sidonians, unsuspecting and secure. And since their land lacked nothing, they were prosperous.*a* Also, they lived a long way from the Sidonians and had no relationship with anyone else.*b*

8When they returned to Zorah and Eshtaol, their brothers asked them, "How did you find things?"

9They answered, "Come on, let's attack them! We have seen that the land is very good. Aren't you going to do something? Don't hesitate to go there and take it over. 10When you get there, you will find an unsuspecting people and a spacious land that God has put into your hands, a land that lacks nothing whatever."

11Then six hundred men from the clan of the Danites, armed for battle, set out from Zorah and Eshtaol. 12On their way they set up camp near Kiriath Jearim in Judah. This is why the place west of Kiriath Jearim is called Mahaneh Dan*c* to this day. 13From there they went on to the hill country of Ephraim and came to Micah's house.

14Then the five men who had spied out the land of Laish said to their brothers, "Do you know that one of these houses has an ephod, other household gods, a carved image and a cast idol? Now you know what to do." 15So they turned in there and went to the house of the young Levite at Micah's place and greeted him. 16The six hundred Danites, armed for battle, stood at the entrance to the gate. 17The five men who had spied out the land went inside and took the carved image, the ephod, the other household gods and the cast idol while the priest and the six hundred armed men stood at the entrance to the gate. 18When these men went into Micah's house and took the carved image, the ephod, the other household gods and the cast idol, the priest said to them, "What are you doing?"

19They answered him, "Be quiet! Don't say a word. Come with us, and be our father and priest. Isn't it better that you serve a tribe and clan in Israel as priest rather than just one man's household?" 20Then the priest was glad. He took the ephod, the other household gods and the carved image and went along with the people. 21Putting their little children, their livestock and their possessions in front of them, they turned away and left.

22When they had gone some distance from Micah's house, the men who lived near Micah were called together and overtook the Danites. 23As they shouted after them, the Danites turned and said to Micah, "What's the matter with you that you called out your men to fight?"

24He replied, "You took the gods I made, and my priest, and went away. What else do I have? How can you ask, 'What's the matter with you?'"

25The Danites answered, "Don't argue with us, or some hot-tempered men will attack you, and you and your family will lose your lives." 26So the Danites went their way, and Micah, seeing that they were too strong for him, turned round and went back home.

27Then they took what Micah had made, and his priest, and went on to Laish, against a peaceful and unsuspecting people. They attacked them with the sword and burned down their city. 28There was no-one to rescue them because they lived a long way from Sidon and had no relationship with anyone else. The city was in a valley near Beth Rehob.

The Danites rebuilt the city and settled there. 29They named it Dan after their forefather Dan, who was born to Israel—though the city used to be called Laish. 30There the Danites set up for themselves the idols, and Jonathan son of Gershom, the son of Moses,*d* and his sons were priests for the tribe of Dan until the time of the captivity of the land. 31They continued to use the idols Micah had made, all the time the house of God was in Shiloh.

A Levite and His Concubine

19 In those days Israel had no king.

Now a Levite who lived in a remote area in the hill country of Ephraim took a concubine from Bethlehem in Judah. 2But she was unfaithful to him. She left him and went back to her father's house in Bethlehem, Judah. After she had been there for four months, 3her husband went to her to persuade her to return. He had with him his servant and two donkeys. She took him into her father's house, and when her father saw him, he gladly welcomed him. 4His father-in-law, the girl's father, prevailed upon him to stay; so he remained with him three days, eating and drinking, and sleeping there.

5On the fourth day they got up early and he prepared to leave, but the girl's father said to his son-in-law, "Refresh yourself with something to eat; then you can go." 6So the two of them sat down to eat and drink together. Afterwards the girl's father said, "Please stay tonight and enjoy yourself." 7And when the man got up to go, his father-in-law persuaded him, so he stayed there that night. 8On the morning of the fifth day, when he rose to go, the girl's father said, "Refresh yourself. Wait till afternoon!" So the two of them ate together.

9Then when the man, with his concubine and his servant, got up to leave, his father-in-law, the girl's father, said, "Now look, it's almost evening. Spend the night here; the day is nearly over. Stay and enjoy yourself. Early tomorrow morning you can get up and be on your way home." 10But, unwilling to stay another night, the man left and went towards Jebus (that is, Jerusalem), with his two saddled donkeys and his concubine. 11When they were near Jebus and the day

---

a7 The meaning of the Hebrew for this clause is uncertain.
b7 Hebrew; some Septuagint manuscripts *with the Arameans* *c12 Mahaneh Dan means Dan's camp.*
d30 An ancient Hebrew scribal tradition, some Septuagint manuscripts and Vulgate; Masoretic Text *Manasseh*

was almost gone, the servant said to his master, "Come, let's stop at this city of the Jebusites and spend the night."

¹²His master replied, "No. We won't go into an alien city, whose people are not Israelites. We will go on to Gibeah." ¹³He added, "Come, let's try to reach Gibeah or Ramah and spend the night in one of those places." ¹⁴So they went on, and the sun set as they neared Gibeah in Benjamin. ¹⁵There they stopped to spend the night. They went and sat in the city square, but no-one took them into his home for the night.

¹⁶That evening an old man from the hill country of Ephraim, who was living in Gibeah (the men of the place were Benjamites), came in from his work in the fields. ¹⁷When he looked and saw the traveller in the city square, the old man asked, "Where are you going? Where did you come from?"

¹⁸He answered, "We are on our way from Bethlehem in Judah to a remote area in the hill country of Ephraim where I live. I have been to Bethlehem in Judah and now I am going to the house of the LORD. No-one has taken me into his house. ¹⁹We have both straw and fodder for our donkeys and bread and wine for ourselves your servants—me, your maidservant, and the young man with us. We don't need anything."

²⁰"You are welcome at my house," the old man said. "Let me supply whatever you need. Only don't spend the night in the square." ²¹So he took him into his house and fed his donkeys. After they had washed their feet, they had something to eat and drink.

²²While they were enjoying themselves, some of the wicked men of the city surrounded the house. Pounding on the door, they shouted to the old man who owned the house, "Bring out the man who came to your house so we can have sex with him."

²³The owner of the house went outside and said to them, "No, my friends, don't be so vile. Since this man is my guest, don't do this disgraceful thing. ²⁴Look, here is my virgin daughter, and his concubine. I will bring them out to you now, and you can use them and do to them whatever you wish. But to this man, don't do such a disgraceful thing."

²⁵But the men would not listen to him. So the man took his concubine and sent her outside to them, and they raped her and abused her throughout the night, and at dawn they let her go. ²⁶At daybreak the woman went back to the house where her master was staying, fell down at the door and lay there until daylight.

²⁷When her master got up in the morning and opened the door of the house and stepped out to continue on his way, there lay his concubine, fallen in the doorway of the house, with her hands on the threshold. ²⁸He said to her, "Get up; let's go." But there was no answer. Then the man put her on his donkey and set out for home.

²⁹When he reached home, he took a knife and cut up his concubine, limb by limb, into twelve parts and sent them into all the areas of Israel. ³⁰Everyone who saw it said, "Such a thing has never been seen or done, not since the day the Israelites came up out of Egypt. Think about it! Consider it! Tell us what to do!"

Israelites Fight the Benjamites

20 Then all the Israelites from Dan to Beersheba and from the land of Gilead came out as one man and assembled before the LORD in Mizpah. ²The leaders of all the people of the tribes of Israel took their places in the assembly of the people of God, four hundred thousand soldiers armed with swords. ³(The Benjamites heard that the Israelites had gone up to Mizpah.) Then the Israelites said, "Tell us how this awful thing happened."

⁴So the Levite, the husband of the murdered woman, said, "I and my concubine came to Gibeah in Benjamin to spend the night. ⁵During the night the men of Gibeah came after me and surrounded the house, intending to kill me. They raped my concubine, and she died. ⁶I took my concubine, cut her into pieces and sent one piece to each region of Israel's inheritance, because they committed this lewd and disgraceful act in Israel. ⁷Now, all you Israelites, speak up and give your verdict."

⁸All the people rose as one man, saying, "None of us will go home. No, not one of us will return to his house. ⁹But now this is what we'll do to Gibeah: We'll go up against it as the lot directs. ¹⁰We'll take ten men out of every hundred from all the tribes of Israel, and a hundred from a thousand, and a thousand from ten thousand, to get provisions for the army. Then, when the army arrives at Gibeah^a in Benjamin, it can give them what they deserve for all this vileness done in Israel." ¹¹So all the men of Israel got together and united as one man against the city.

¹²The tribes of Israel sent men throughout the tribe of Benjamin, saying, "What about this awful crime that was committed among you? ¹³Now surrender those wicked men of Gibeah so that we may put them to death and purge the evil from Israel."

But the Benjamites would not listen to their fellow Israelites. ¹⁴From their towns they came together at Gibeah to fight against the Israelites. ¹⁵At once the Benjamites mobilised twenty-six thousand swordsmen from their towns, in addition to seven hundred chosen men from those living in Gibeah. ¹⁶Among all these soldiers there were seven hundred chosen men who were left-handed, each of whom could sling a stone at a hair and not miss.

¹⁷Israel, apart from Benjamin, mustered four hundred thousand swordsmen, all of them fighting men.

¹⁸The Israelites went up to Bethel^b and enquired of God. They said, "Who of us shall go first to fight against the Benjamites?"

^a10 One Hebrew manuscript; most Hebrew manuscripts *Geba*, a variant of *Gibeah*
^b18 Or *to the house of God*; also in verse 26

The LORD replied, "Judah shall go first."

19The next morning the Israelites got up and pitched camp near Gibeah. 20The men of Israel went out to fight the Benjamites and took up battle positions against them at Gibeah. 21The Benjamites came out of Gibeah and cut down twenty-two thousand Israelites on the battlefield that day. 22But the men of Israel encouraged one another and again took up their positions where they had stationed themselves the first day. 23The Israelites went up and wept before the LORD until evening, and they enquired of the LORD. They said, "Shall we go up again to battle against the Benjamites, our brothers?"

The LORD answered, "Go up against them."

24Then the Israelites drew near to Benjamin the second day. 25This time, when the Benjamites came out from Gibeah to oppose them, they cut down another eighteen thousand Israelites, all of them armed with swords.

26Then the Israelites, all the people, went up to Bethel, and there they sat weeping before the LORD. They fasted that day until evening and presented burnt offerings and fellowship offeringsc to the LORD. 27And the Israelites enquired of the LORD. (In those days the ark of the covenant of God was there, 28with Phinehas son of Eleazar, the son of Aaron, ministering before it.) They asked, "Shall we go up again to battle with Benjamin our brother, or not?"

The LORD responded, "Go, for tomorrow I will give them into your hands."

29Then Israel set an ambush around Gibeah. 30They went up against the Benjamites on the third day and took up positions against Gibeah as they had done before. 31The Benjamites came out to meet them and were drawn away from the city. They began to inflict casualties on the Israelites as before, so that about thirty men fell in the open field and on the roads—the one leading to Bethel and the other to Gibeah.

32While the Benjamites were saying, "We are defeating them as before," the Israelites were saying, "Let's retreat and draw them away from the city to the roads."

33All the men of Israel moved from their places and took up positions at Baal Tamar, and the Israelite ambush charged out of its place on the westd of Gibeah.e 34Then ten thousand of Israel's finest men made a frontal attack on Gibeah. The fighting was so heavy that the Benjamites did not realise how near disaster was. 35The LORD defeated Benjamin before Israel, and on that day the Israelites struck down 25,100 Benjamites, all armed with swords. 36Then the Benjamites saw that they were beaten.

Now the men of Israel had given way before Benjamin, because they relied on the ambush they had set near Gibeah. 37The men who had been in ambush made a sudden dash into Gibeah, spread out and put the whole city to the sword. 38The men of Israel had arranged with the ambush that they should send up a great cloud of smoke from the city, 39and then the men of Israel would turn in the battle.

The Benjamites had begun to inflict casualties on the men of Israel (about thirty), and they said, "We are defeating them as in the first battle." 40But when the column of smoke began to rise from the city, the Benjamites turned and saw the smoke of the whole city going up into the sky. 41Then the men of Israel turned on them, and the men of Benjamin were terrified, because they realised that disaster had come upon them. 42So they fled before the Israelites in the direction of the desert, but they could not escape the battle. And the men of Israel who came out of the towns cut them down there. 43They surrounded the Benjamites, chased them and easilyf overran them in the vicinity of Gibeah on the east. 44Eighteen thousand Benjamites fell, all of them valiant fighters. 45As they turned and fled towards the desert to the rock of Rimmon, the Israelites cut down five thousand men along the roads. They kept pressing after the Benjamites as far as Gidom and struck down two thousand more.

46On that day twenty-five thousand Benjamite swordsmen fell, all of them valiant fighters. 47But six hundred men turned and fled into the desert to the rock of Rimmon, where they stayed for four months. 48The men of Israel went back to Benjamin and put all the towns to the sword, including the animals and everything else they found. All the towns they came across they set on fire.

Wives for the Benjamites

21 The men of Israel had taken an oath at Mizpah: "Not one of us will give his daughter in marriage to a Benjamite."

2The people went to Bethel,a where they sat before God until evening, raising their voices and weeping bitterly. 3"O LORD, the God of Israel," they cried, "why has this happened to Israel? Why should one tribe be missing from Israel today?"

4Early the next day the people built an altar and presented burnt offerings and fellowship offerings.b

5Then the Israelites asked, "Who from all the tribes of Israel has failed to assemble before the LORD?" For they had taken a solemn oath that anyone who failed to assemble before the LORD at Mizpah should certainly be put to death.

6Now the Israelites grieved for their brothers, the Benjamites. "Today one tribe is cut off from Israel," they said. 7"How can we provide wives for those who are left, since we have taken an oath by the LORD not to give them any of our daughters in marriage?" 8Then they asked, "Which one of the

c26 Traditionally *peace offerings*
d33 Some Septuagint manuscripts and Vulgate; the meaning of the Hebrew for this word is uncertain.
e33 Hebrew *Geba*, a variant of *Gibeah*   f43 The meaning of the Hebrew for this word is uncertain.
a2 Or *to the house of God*   b4 Traditionally *peace offerings*

tribes of Israel failed to assemble before the LORD at Mizpah?'' They discovered that no-one from Jabesh Gilead had come to the camp for the assembly. ⁹For when they counted the people, they found that none of the people of Jabesh Gilead were there.

¹⁰So the assembly sent twelve thousand fighting men with instructions to go to Jabesh Gilead and put to the sword those living there, including the women and children. ¹¹"This is what you are to do," they said. "Kill every male and every woman who is not a virgin." ¹²They found among the people living in Jabesh Gilead four hundred young women who had never slept with a man, and they took them to the camp at Shiloh in Canaan.

¹³Then the whole assembly sent an offer of peace to the Benjamites at the rock of Rimmon. ¹⁴So the Benjamites returned at that time and were given the women of Jabesh Gilead who had been spared. But there were not enough for all of them.

¹⁵The people grieved for Benjamin, because the LORD had made a gap in the tribes of Israel. ¹⁶And the elders of the assembly said, "With the women of Benjamin destroyed, how shall we provide wives for the men who are left? ¹⁷The Benjamite survivors must have heirs," they said, "so that a tribe

of Israel will not be wiped out. ¹⁸We can't give them our daughters as wives, since we Israelites have taken this oath: 'Cursed be anyone who gives a wife to a Benjamite.' ¹⁹But look, there is the annual festival of the LORD in Shiloh, to the north of Bethel, and east of the road that goes from Bethel to Shechem, and to the south of Lebonah.''

²⁰So they instructed the Benjamites, saying, "Go and hide in the vineyards ²¹and watch. When the girls of Shiloh come out to join in the dancing, then rush from the vineyards and each of you seize a wife from the girls of Shiloh and go to the land of Benjamin. ²²When their fathers or brothers complain to us, we will say to them, 'Do us a kindness by helping them, because we did not get wives for them during the war, and you are innocent, since you did not give your daughters to them.''

²³So that is what the Benjamites did. While the girls were dancing, each man caught one and carried her off to be his wife. Then they returned to their inheritance and rebuilt the towns and settled in them.

²⁴At that time the Israelites left that place and went home to their tribes and clans, each to his own inheritance.

²⁵In those days Israel had no king; everyone did as he saw fit.

Ruth

Naomi and Ruth

1 In the days when the judges ruled,[a] there was a famine in the land, and a man from Bethlehem in Judah, together with his wife and two sons, went to live for a while in the country of Moab. [2]The man's name was Elimelech, his wife's name Naomi, and the names of his two sons were Mahlon and Kilion. They were Ephrathites from Bethlehem, Judah. And they went to Moab and lived there.

[3]Now Elimelech, Naomi's husband, died, and she was left with her two sons. [4]They married Moabite women, one named Orpah and the other Ruth. After they had lived there about ten years, [5]both Mahlon and Kilion also died, and Naomi was left without her two sons and her husband.

[6]When she heard in Moab that the LORD had come to the aid of his people by providing food for them, Naomi and her daughters-in-law prepared to return home from there. [7]With her two daughters-in-law she left the place where she had been living and set out on the road that would take them back to the land of Judah.

[8]Then Naomi said to her two daughters-in-law, "Go back, each of you, to your mother's home. May the LORD show kindness to you, as you have shown to your dead and to me. [9]May the LORD grant that each of you will find rest in the home of another husband."

Then she kissed them and they wept aloud [10]and said to her, "We will go back with you to your people."

[11]But Naomi said, "Return home, my daughters. Why would you come with me? Am I going to have any more sons, who could become your husbands? [12]Return home, my daughters; I am too old to have another husband. Even if I thought there was still hope for me—even if I had a husband tonight and then gave birth to sons—[13]would you wait until they grew up? Would you remain unmarried for them? No, my daughters. It is more bitter for me than for you, because the LORD's hand has gone out against me!"

[14]At this they wept again. Then Orpah kissed her mother-in-law good-bye, but Ruth clung to her.

[15]"Look," said Naomi, "your sister-in-law is going back to her people and her gods. Go back with her."

[16]But Ruth replied, "Don't urge me to leave you or to turn back from you. Where you go I will go, and where you stay I will stay. Your people will be my people and your God my God. [17]Where you die I will die, and there I will be buried. May the LORD deal with me, be it ever so severely, if anything but death separates you and me." [18]When Naomi realised that Ruth was determined to go with her, she stopped urging her.

[19]So the two women went on until they came to Bethlehem. When they arrived in Bethlehem, the whole town was stirred because of them, and the women exclaimed, "Can this be Naomi?"

[20]"Don't call me Naomi,"[b] she told them. "Call me Mara,[c] because the Almighty[d] has made my life very bitter. [21]I went away full, but the LORD has brought me back empty. Why call me Naomi? The LORD has afflicted[e] me; the Almighty has brought misfortune upon me."

[22]So Naomi returned from Moab accompanied by Ruth the Moabitess, her daughter-in-law, arriving in Bethlehem as the barley harvest was beginning.

Ruth Meets Boaz

2 Now Naomi had a relative on her husband's side from the clan of Elimelech, a man of standing, whose name was Boaz.

[2]And Ruth the Moabitess said to Naomi, "Let me go to the fields and pick up the leftover grain behind anyone in whose eyes I find favour."

Naomi said to her, "Go ahead, my daughter." [3]So she went out and began to glean in the fields behind the harvesters. As it turned out, she found herself working in a field belonging to Boaz, who was from the clan of Elimelech.

[4]Just then Boaz arrived from Bethlehem and greeted the harvesters, "The LORD be with you!"

"The LORD bless you!" they called back.

[5]Boaz asked the foreman of his harvesters, "Whose young woman is that?"

---

[a]1 Traditionally *judged*   [b]20 *Naomi* means *pleasant*; also in verse 21.   [c]20 *Mara* means *bitter*.
[d]20 Hebrew *Shaddai*; also in verse 21   [e]21 Or *has testified against*

RUTH 1:15–22

'Where you go I will go, and where you stay I will stay. Your people will be my people and your God my God. Where you die I will die, and there I will be buried. May the LORD deal with me, be it ever so severely, if anything but death separates you and me' (vv. 16, 17).

RUTH'S VOW is more like a marriage vow than a pledge to a mother-in-law. Her love for Naomi, her sense of obligation, is such that she will not leave her. Today such devotion would be misunderstood. An ulterior motive would be assumed, or some unhealthy aspect in the relationship suspected. But for the author of this delightful book Ruth's motives are entirely pure. He (or she?) describes the strength, power, and beauty of this relationship so perfectly that even Goethe was driven to say that the story of Ruth was the most perfect story he knew.

But Naomi, at this stage, is unaware of Ruth's devotion. She doesn't hear what her daughter-in-law is saying. Like the possessed man who did not want to be free of the devils inside him (Mark 5:10), Naomi, too, wants to cling to her sorrow and emptiness. David Clines writes 'Naomi wishes her daughters-in-law back in Moab and out of her life, so that outwardly also her life may appear to be as empty as she feels it is inwardly. She has not noticed that Ruth is dedicating herself to her . . . she hears only the girl's determination, and knows no words for responding to her love.'

At this point of the story things could have gone tragically wrong. Few of us would have persevered like Ruth did. Just imagine the hurt when Naomi says, 'I went away full, and the Lord has brought me back empty.' Ruth's devotion, her support, her loyalty, her love were all ignored completely by Naomi. The risk was becoming even greater, yet still Ruth persevered.

Thank you, Lord, for those who are willing to care for others even when their care is not appreciated. May they be strengthened in their resolve to go on caring. May they know that you are with them in their task.

→230

RUTH 4:7–12
'This was the method of legalising transactions in Israel' (v. 7b).

THE CUSTOM OF TAKING OFF A SHOE and giving it to another as a sign that a contract has been made, had to be explained for the readers at the time when Ruth was written.

In this passage there are other echoes of the past; Rachel and Leah, and Tamar. By mentioning them the author is recognizing again the potential dangers faced by – or possibly brought about through? – Ruth the Moabitess. Rachel and Leah, sought from afar by Jacob, had little love for each other and caused much domestic upheaval. The unsavoury incident of Tamar's relationship with Judah brought the house of Judah close to complete disaster and disrepute, not through Tamar's own fault, but as a result of Judah's failure to fulfil the requirements of the 'levirate' law.

Ruth's acceptance into the mainstream of life in Israel will not be easy for her. It will not be easy for Israel. Changing one's country and one's loyalties is never easy. There are great potential dangers. But there can also be great rewards. Ruth accepted the challenge so fully that she became the ancestress, not only of David the great king of Israel, but of Christ himself.

How has the life of my own country been enriched by those who have come from other cultures in the past?

⁶The foreman replied, "She is the Moabitess who came back from Moab with Naomi. ⁷She said, 'Please let me glean and gather among the sheaves behind the harvesters.' She went into the field and has worked steadily from morning till now, except for a short rest in the shelter."

⁸So Boaz said to Ruth, "My daughter, listen to me. Don't go and glean in another field and don't go away from here. Stay here with my servant girls. ⁹Watch the field where the men are harvesting, and follow along after the girls. I have told the men not to touch you. And whenever you are thirsty, go and get a drink from the water jars the men have filled."

¹⁰At this, she bowed down with her face to the ground. She exclaimed, "Why have I found such favour in your eyes that you notice me—a foreigner?"

¹¹Boaz replied, "I've been told all about what you have done for your mother-in-law since the death of your husband—how you left your father and mother and your homeland and came to live with a people you did not know before. ¹²May the LORD repay you for what you have done. May you be richly rewarded by the LORD, the God of Israel, under whose wings you have come to take refuge."

¹³"May I continue to find favour in your eyes, my lord," she said. "You have given me comfort and have spoken kindly to your servant—though I do not have the standing of one of your servant girls."

¹⁴At mealtime Boaz said to her, "Come over here. Have some bread and dip it in the wine vinegar."

When she sat down with the harvesters, he offered her some roasted grain. She ate all she wanted and had some left over. ¹⁵As she got up to glean, Boaz gave orders to his men, "Even if she gathers among the sheaves, don't embarrass her. ¹⁶Rather, pull out some stalks for her from the bundles and leave them for her to pick up, and don't rebuke her."

¹⁷So Ruth gleaned in the field until evening. Then she threshed the barley she had gathered, and it amounted to about an ephah.ᵃ ¹⁸She carried it back to town, and her mother-in-law saw how much she had gathered. Ruth also brought out and gave her what she had left over after she had eaten enough.

¹⁹Her mother-in-law asked her, "Where did you glean today? Where did you work? Blessed be the man who took notice of you!"

Then Ruth told her mother-in-law about the one at whose place she had been working. "The name of the man I worked with today is Boaz," she said.

²⁰"The LORD bless him!" Naomi said to her daughter-in-law. "He has not stopped showing his kindness to the living and the dead." She added, "That man is our close relative; he is one of our kinsman-redeemers."

²¹Then Ruth the Moabitess said, "He even said to me, 'Stay with my workers until they finish harvesting all my grain.'"

²²Naomi said to Ruth her daughter-in-law, "It will be good for you, my daughter, to go with his girls, because in someone else's field you might be harmed."

²³So Ruth stayed close to the servant girls of Boaz to glean until the barley and wheat harvests were finished. And she lived with her mother-in-law.

Ruth and Boaz at the Threshing-Floor

3 One day Naomi her mother-in-law said to her, "My daughter, should I not try to find a homeᵃ for you, where you will be well provided for? ²Is not Boaz, with whose servant girls you have been, a kinsman of ours? Tonight he will be winnowing barley on the threshing-floor. ³Wash and perfume yourself, and put on your best clothes. Then go down to the threshing-floor, but don't let him know you are there until he has finished eating and drinking. ⁴When he lies down, note the place where he is lying. Then go and uncover his feet and lie down. He will tell you what to do."

⁵"I will do whatever you say," Ruth answered. ⁶So she went down to the threshing-floor and did everything her mother-in-law told her to do.

⁷When Boaz had finished eating and drinking and was in good spirits, he went over to lie down at the far end of the grain pile. Ruth approached quietly, uncovered his feet and lay down. ⁸In the middle of the night something startled the man, and he turned and discovered a woman lying at his feet.

⁹"Who are you?" he asked.

"I am your servant Ruth," she said. "Spread the corner of your garment over me, since you are a kinsman-redeemer."

¹⁰"The LORD bless you, my daughter," he replied. "This kindness is greater than that which you showed earlier: You have not run after the younger men, whether rich or poor. ¹¹And now, my daughter, don't be afraid. I will do for you all you ask. All my fellow townsmen know that you are a woman of noble character. ¹²Although it is true that I am near of kin, there is a kinsman-redeemer nearer than I. ¹³Stay here for the night, and in the morning if he wants to redeem, good; let him redeem. But if he is not willing, as surely as the LORD lives I will do it. Lie here until morning."

¹⁴So she lay at his feet until morning, but got up before anyone could be recognised; and he said, "Don't let it be known that a woman came to the threshing-floor."

¹⁵He also said, "Bring me the shawl you are wearing and hold it out." When she did so, he poured into it six measures of barley and put it on her. Then heᵇ went back to town.

¹⁶When Ruth came to her mother-in-law, Naomi asked, "How did it go, my daughter?"

Then she told her everything Boaz had done for her [17]and added, "He gave me these six measures of barley, saying, 'Don't go back to your mother-in-law empty-handed.'"

[18]Then Naomi said, "Wait, my daughter, until you find out what happens. For the man will not rest until the matter is settled today."

Boaz Marries Ruth

4 Meanwhile Boaz went up to the town gate and sat there. When the kinsman-redeemer he had mentioned came along, Boaz said, "Come over here, my friend, and sit down." So he went over and sat down.

[2]Boaz took ten of the elders of the town and said, "Sit here," and they did so. [3]Then he said to the kinsman-redeemer, "Naomi, who has come back from Moab, is selling the piece of land that belonged to our brother Elimelech. [4]I thought I should bring the matter to your attention and suggest that you buy it in the presence of these seated here and in the presence of the elders of my people. If you will redeem it, do so. But if you[a] will not, tell me, so that I will know. For no-one has the right to do it except you, and I am next in line."

"I will redeem it," he said.

[5]Then Boaz said, "On the day you buy the land from Naomi and from Ruth the Moabitess, you acquire[b] the dead man's widow, in order to maintain the name of the dead with his property."

[6]At this, the kinsman-redeemer said, "Then I cannot redeem it because I might endanger my own estate. You redeem it yourself. I cannot do it."

[7](Now in earlier times in Israel, for the redemption and transfer of property to become final, one party took off his sandal and gave it to the other. This was the method of legalising transactions in Israel.)

[8]So the kinsman-redeemer said to Boaz, "Buy it yourself." And he removed his sandal.

[9]Then Boaz announced to the elders and all the people, "Today you are witnesses that I have bought from Naomi all the property of Elimelech, Kilion and Mahlon. [10]I have also acquired Ruth the Moabitess, Mahlon's widow, as my wife, in order to maintain the name of the dead with his property, so that his name will not disappear from among his family or from the town records. Today you are witnesses!"

[11]Then the elders and all those at the gate said, "We are witnesses. May the LORD make the woman who is coming into your home like Rachel and Leah, who together built up the house of Israel. May you have standing in Ephrathah and be famous in Bethlehem. [12]Through the offspring the LORD gives you by this young woman, may your family be like that of Perez, whom Tamar bore to Judah."

The Genealogy of David

[13]So Boaz took Ruth and she became his wife. Then he went to her, and the LORD enabled her to conceive, and she gave birth to a son. [14]The women said to Naomi: "Praise be to the LORD, who this day has not left you without a kinsman-redeemer. May he become famous throughout Israel! [15]He will renew your life and sustain you in your old age. For your daughter-in-law, who loves you and who is better to you than seven sons, has given him birth."

[16]Then Naomi took the child, laid him in her lap and cared for him. [17]The women living there said, "Naomi has a son." And they named him Obed. He was the father of Jesse, the father of David.

[18]This, then, is the family line of Perez:

Perez was the father of Hezron,
[19]Hezron the father of Ram,
Ram the father of Amminadab,
[20]Amminadab the father of Nahshon,
Nahshon the father of Salmon,[c]
[21]Salmon the father of Boaz,
Boaz the father of Obed,
[22]Obed the father of Jesse,
and Jesse the father of David.

---

[a]4 Many Hebrew manuscripts, Septuagint, Vulgate and Syriac; most Hebrew manuscripts *he*
[b]5 Hebrew; Vulgate and Syriac *Naomi, you acquire Ruth the Moabitess,*
[c]20 A few Hebrew manuscripts, some Septuagint manuscripts and Vulgate (see also verse 21 and Septuagint of 1 Chron. 2:11); most Hebrew manuscripts *Salma*

1 Samuel

The Birth of Samuel

1 There was a certain man from Ramathaim, a Zuphite[a] from the hill country of Ephraim, whose name was Elkanah son of Jeroham, the son of Elihu, the son of Tohu, the son of Zuph, an Ephraimite. ²He had two wives; one was called Hannah and the other Peninnah. Peninnah had children, but Hannah had none.

³Year after year this man went up from his town to worship and sacrifice to the LORD Almighty at Shiloh, where Hophni and Phinehas, the two sons of Eli, were priests of the LORD. ⁴Whenever the day came for Elkanah to sacrifice, he would give portions of the meat to his wife Peninnah and to all her sons and daughters. ⁵But to Hannah he gave a double portion because he loved her, and the LORD had closed her womb. ⁶And because the LORD had closed her womb, her rival kept provoking her in order to irritate her. ⁷This went on year after year. Whenever Hannah went up to the house of the LORD, her rival provoked her till she wept and would not eat. ⁸Elkanah her husband would say to her, "Hannah, why are you weeping? Why don't you eat? Why are you downhearted? Don't I mean more to you than ten sons?"

⁹Once when they had finished eating and drinking in Shiloh, Hannah stood up. Now Eli the priest was sitting on a chair by the doorpost of the LORD's temple.[b] ¹⁰In bitterness of soul Hannah wept much and prayed to the LORD. ¹¹And she made a vow, saying, "O LORD Almighty, if you will only look upon your servant's misery and remember me, and not forget your servant but give her a son, then I will give him to the LORD for all the days of his life, and no razor will ever be used on his head."

¹²As she kept on praying to the LORD, Eli observed her mouth. ¹³Hannah was praying in her heart, and her lips were moving but her voice was not heard. Eli thought she was drunk ¹⁴and said to her, "How long will you keep on getting drunk? Get rid of your wine."

¹⁵"Not so, my lord," Hannah replied, "I am a woman who is deeply troubled. I have not been drinking wine or beer; I was pouring out my soul to the LORD. ¹⁶Do not take your servant for a wicked woman; I have been praying here out of my great anguish and grief."

¹⁷Eli answered, "Go in peace, and may the God of Israel grant you what you have asked of him."

¹⁸She said, "May your servant find favour in your eyes." Then she went her way and ate something, and her face was no longer downcast.

¹⁹Early the next morning they arose and worshipped before the LORD and then went back to their home at Ramah. Elkanah lay with Hannah his wife, and the LORD remembered her. ²⁰So in the course of time Hannah conceived and gave birth to a son. She named him Samuel,[c] saying, "Because I asked the LORD for him."

Hannah Dedicates Samuel

²¹When the man Elkanah went up with all his family to offer the annual sacrifice to the LORD and to fulfil his vow, ²²Hannah did not go. She said to her husband, "After the boy is weaned, I will take him and present him before the LORD, and he will live there always."

²³"Do what seems best to you," Elkanah her husband told her. "Stay here until you have weaned him; only may the LORD make good his[d] word." So the woman stayed at home and nursed her son until she had weaned him.

²⁴After he was weaned, she took the boy with her, young as he was, along with a three-year-old bull,[e] an ephah[f] of flour and a skin of wine, and brought him to the house of the LORD at Shiloh. ²⁵When they had slaughtered the bull, they brought the boy to Eli, ²⁶and she said to him, "As surely as you live, my lord, I am the woman who stood here beside you praying to the LORD. ²⁷I prayed for this child, and the LORD has granted me what I asked of him. ²⁸So now I give him to the LORD. For his whole life he shall be given

---

a1 Or *from Ramathaim Zuphim*   *b9* That is, tabernacle
c20 *Samuel* sounds like the Hebrew for *heard of God.*
d23 Masoretic Text; Dead Sea Scrolls, Septuagint and Syriac *your*
e24 Dead Sea Scrolls, Septuagint and Syriac; Masoretic Text *with three bulls*
f24 That is, probably about ⅗ bushel (about 22 litres)

over to the LORD.'' And he worshipped the LORD there.

Hannah's Prayer

2 Then Hannah prayed and said:

"My heart rejoices in the LORD;
  in the LORD my horn[a] is lifted high.
My mouth boasts over my enemies,
  for I delight in your deliverance.

[2]"There is no-one holy[b] like the LORD;
  there is no-one besides you;
  there is no Rock like our God.

[3]"Do not keep talking so proudly
  or let your mouth speak such arrogance,
for the LORD is a God who knows,
  and by him deeds are weighed.

[4]"The bows of the warriors are broken,
  but those who stumbled are armed with
    strength.
[5]Those who were full hire themselves out
    for food,
  but those who were hungry hunger no
    more.
She who was barren has borne seven
    children,
  but she who has had many sons pines
    away.

[6]"The LORD brings death and makes alive;
  he brings down to the grave[c] and raises
    up.
[7]The LORD sends poverty and wealth;
  he humbles and he exalts.
[8]He raises the poor from the dust
  and lifts the needy from the ash heap;
he seats them with princes
  and has them inherit a throne of honour.

"For the foundations of the earth are the
    LORD's;
  upon them he has set the world.
[9]He will guard the feet of his saints,
  but the wicked will be silenced in
    darkness.

"It is not by strength that one prevails;
[10] those who oppose the LORD will be
    shattered.
He will thunder against them from heaven;
  the LORD will judge the ends of the
    earth.

"He will give strength to his king
  and exalt the horn of his anointed."

[11]Then Elkanah went home to Ramah, but the boy ministered before the LORD under Eli the priest.

Eli's Wicked Sons

[12]Eli's sons were wicked men; they had no regard for the LORD. [13]Now it was the practice of the priests with the people that whenever anyone offered a sacrifice and while the meat was being boiled, the servant of the priest would come with a three-pronged fork in his hand. [14]He would plunge it into the pan or kettle or cauldron or pot, and the priest would take for himself whatever the fork brought up. This is how they treated all the Israelites who came to Shiloh. [15]But even before the fat was burned, the servant of the priest would come and say to the man who was sacrificing, "Give the priest some meat to roast; he won't accept boiled meat from you, but only raw." [16]If the man said to him, "Let the fat be burned up first, and then take whatever you want," the servant would then answer, "No, hand it over now; if you don't, I'll take it by force."

[17]This sin of the young men was very great in the LORD's sight, for they[d] were treating the LORD's offering with contempt.

[18]But Samuel was ministering before the LORD—a boy wearing a linen ephod. [19]Each year his mother made him a little robe and took it to him when she went up with her husband to offer the annual sacrifice. [20]Eli would bless Elkanah and his wife, saying, "May the LORD give you children by this woman to take the place of the one she prayed for and gave to the LORD." Then they would go home. [21]And the LORD was gracious to Hannah; she conceived and gave birth to three sons and two daughters. Meanwhile, the boy Samuel grew up in the presence of the LORD.

[22]Now Eli, who was very old, heard about everything his sons were doing to all Israel and how they slept with the women who served at the entrance to the Tent of Meeting. [23]So he said to them, "Why do you do such things? I hear from all the people about these wicked deeds of yours. [24]No, my sons; it is not a good report that I hear spreading among the LORD's people. [25]If a man sins against another man, God[e] may mediate for him; but if a man sins against the LORD, who will intercede for him?" His sons, however, did not listen to their father's rebuke, for it was the LORD's will to put them to death.

[26]And the boy Samuel continued to grow in stature and in favour with the LORD and with men.

Prophecy Against the House of Eli

[27]Now a man of God came to Eli and said to him, "This is what the LORD says: 'Did I not clearly reveal myself to your father's house when they were in Egypt under Pharaoh? [28]I chose your father out of all the tribes of Israel to be my priest, to go up to my altar, to burn incense, and to wear an ephod in my presence. I also gave your father's house all the offerings made with fire by the Israelites. [29]Why do you[f] scorn my sacrifice and offering that I prescribed for my dwelling? Why do you honour your sons more than me by fattening yourselves on the choice parts of every offering made by my people Israel?'

[30]"Therefore the LORD, the God of Israel,

---

[a]1 *Horn* here symbolises strength; also in verse 10.   [b]2 Or *no Holy One*   [c]6 Hebrew *Sheol*
[d]17 Or *men*   [e]25 Or *the judges*   [f]29 The Hebrew is plural.

declares: 'I promised that your house and your father's house would minister before me for ever.' But now the LORD declares: 'Far be it from me! Those who honour me I will honour, but those who despise me will be disdained. ³¹The time is coming when I will cut short your strength and the strength of your father's house, so that there will not be an old man in your family line ³²and you will see distress in my dwelling. Although good will be done to Israel, in your family line there will never be an old man. ³³Every one of you that I do not cut off from my altar will be spared only to blind your eyes with tears and to grieve your heart, and all your descendants will die in the prime of life.

³⁴"'And what happens to your two sons, Hophni and Phinehas, will be a sign to you —they will both die on the same day. ³⁵I will raise up for myself a faithful priest, who will do according to what is in my heart and mind. I will firmly establish his house, and he will minister before my anointed one always. ³⁶Then everyone left in your family line will come and bow down before him for a piece of silver and a crust of bread and plead, "Appoint me to some priestly office so that I can have food to eat."'"

The LORD Calls Samuel

3 The boy Samuel ministered before the LORD under Eli. In those days the word of the LORD was rare; there were not many visions.

²One night Eli, whose eyes were becoming so weak that he could barely see, was lying down in his usual place. ³The lamp of God had not yet gone out, and Samuel was lying down in the temple*a* of the LORD, where the ark of God was. ⁴Then the LORD called Samuel.

Samuel answered, "Here I am." ⁵And he ran to Eli and said, "Here I am; you called me."

But Eli said, "I did not call; go back and lie down." So he went and lay down.

⁶Again the LORD called, "Samuel!" And Samuel got up and went to Eli and said, "Here I am; you called me."

"My son," Eli said, "I did not call; go back and lie down."

⁷Now Samuel did not yet know the LORD: The word of the LORD had not yet been revealed to him.

⁸The LORD called Samuel a third time, and Samuel got up and went to Eli and said, "Here I am; you called me."

Then Eli realised that the LORD was calling the boy. ⁹So Eli told Samuel, "Go and lie down, and if he calls you, say, 'Speak, LORD, for your servant is listening.'" So Samuel went and lay down in his place.

¹⁰The LORD came and stood there, calling as at the other times, "Samuel! Samuel!"

Then Samuel said, "Speak, for your servant is listening."

¹¹And the LORD said to Samuel: "See, I am about to do something in Israel that will make the ears of everyone who hears of it tingle. ¹²At that time I will carry out against Eli everything I spoke against his family—from beginning to end. ¹³For I told him that I would judge his family for ever because of the sin he knew about; his sons made themselves contemptible,*b* and he failed to restrain them. ¹⁴Therefore, I swore to the house of Eli, 'The guilt of Eli's house will never be atoned for by sacrifice or offering.'"

¹⁵Samuel lay down until morning and then opened the doors of the house of the LORD. He was afraid to tell Eli the vision, ¹⁶but Eli called him and said, "Samuel, my son."

Samuel answered, "Here I am."

¹⁷"What was it he said to you?" Eli asked. "Do not hide it from me. May God deal with you, be it ever so severely, if you hide from me anything he told you." ¹⁸So Samuel told him everything, hiding nothing from him. Then Eli said, "He is the LORD; let him do what is good in his eyes."

¹⁹The LORD was with Samuel as he grew up, and he let none of his words fall to the ground. ²⁰And all Israel from Dan to Beersheba recognised that Samuel was attested as a prophet of the LORD. ²¹The LORD continued to appear at Shiloh, and there he revealed himself to Samuel through his word.

4 And Samuel's word came to all Israel.

The Philistines Capture the Ark

Now the Israelites went out to fight against the Philistines. The Israelites camped at Ebenezer, and the Philistines at Aphek. ²The Philistines deployed their forces to meet Israel, and as the battle spread, Israel was defeated by the Philistines, who killed about four thousand of them on the battlefield. ³When the soldiers returned to camp, the elders of Israel asked, "Why did the LORD bring defeat upon us today before the Philistines? Let us bring the ark of the LORD's covenant from Shiloh, so that it*a* may go with us and save us from the hand of our enemies."

⁴So the people sent men to Shiloh, and they brought back the ark of the covenant of the LORD Almighty, who is enthroned between the cherubim. And Eli's two sons, Hophni and Phinehas, were there with the ark of the covenant of God.

⁵When the ark of the LORD's covenant came into the camp, all Israel raised such a great shout that the ground shook. ⁶Hearing the uproar, the Philistines asked, "What's all this shouting in the Hebrew camp?"

When they learned that the ark of the LORD had come into the camp, ⁷the Philistines were afraid. "A god has come into the camp," they said. "We're in trouble! Nothing like this has happened before. ⁸Woe to us! Who will deliver us from the hand of these mighty gods? They are the gods who struck the Egyptians with all kinds of plagues in the

---

a3 That is, tabernacle
b13 Masoretic Text; an ancient Hebrew scribal tradition and Septuagint *sons blasphemed God*   *a3* Or *he*

desert. ⁹Be strong, Philistines! Be men, or you will be subject to the Hebrews, as they have been to you. Be men, and fight!''

¹⁰So the Philistines fought, and the Israelites were defeated and every man fled to his tent. The slaughter was very great; Israel lost thirty thousand foot soldiers. ¹¹The ark of God was captured, and Eli's two sons, Hophni and Phinehas, died.

Death of Eli

¹²That same day a Benjamite ran from the battle line and went to Shiloh, his clothes torn and dust on his head. ¹³When he arrived, there was Eli sitting on his chair by the side of the road, watching, because his heart feared for the ark of God. When the man entered the town and told what had happened, the whole town sent up a cry.

¹⁴Eli heard the outcry and asked, ''What is the meaning of this uproar?''

The man hurried over to Eli, ¹⁵who was ninety-eight years old and whose eyes were set so that he could not see. ¹⁶He told Eli, ''I have just come from the battle line; I fled from it this very day.''

Eli asked, ''What happened, my son?''

¹⁷The man who brought the news replied, ''Israel fled before the Philistines, and the army has suffered heavy losses. Also your two sons, Hophni and Phinehas, are dead, and the ark of God has been captured.''

¹⁸When he mentioned the ark of God, Eli fell backwards off his chair by the side of the gate. His neck was broken and he died, for he was an old man and heavy. He had led*ᵇ* Israel for forty years.

¹⁹His daughter-in-law, the wife of Phinehas, was pregnant and near the time of delivery. When she heard the news that the ark of God had been captured and that her father-in-law and her husband were dead, she went into labour and gave birth, but was overcome by her labour pains. ²⁰As she was dying, the women attending her said, ''Don't despair; you have given birth to a son.'' But she did not respond or pay any attention.

²¹She named the boy Ichabod,ᶜ saying, ''The glory has departed from Israel''— because of the capture of the ark of God and the deaths of her father-in-law and her husband. ²²She said, ''The glory has departed from Israel, for the ark of God has been captured.''

The Ark in Ashdod and Ekron

5 After the Philistines had captured the ark of God, they took it from Ebenezer to Ashdod. ²Then they carried the ark into Dagon's temple and set it beside Dagon. ³When the people of Ashdod rose early the next day, there was Dagon, fallen on his face on the ground before the ark of the LORD! They took Dagon and put him back in his place. ⁴But the following morning when they rose, there was Dagon, fallen on his face on the ground before the ark of the LORD! His

head and hands had been broken off and were lying on the threshold; only his body remained. ⁵That is why to this day neither the priests of Dagon nor any others who enter Dagon's temple at Ashdod step on the threshold.

⁶The LORD's hand was heavy upon the people of Ashdod and its vicinity; he brought devastation upon them and afflicted them with tumours.*ᵃ* ⁷When the men of Ashdod saw what was happening, they said, ''The ark of the god of Israel must not stay here with us, because his hand is heavy upon us and upon Dagon our god.'' ⁸So they called together all the rulers of the Philistines and asked them, ''What shall we do with the ark of the god of Israel?''

They answered, ''Have the ark of the god of Israel moved to Gath.'' So they moved the ark of the God of Israel.

⁹But after they had moved it, the LORD's hand was against that city, throwing it into a great panic. He afflicted the people of the city, both young and old, with an outbreak of tumours.*ᵇ* ¹⁰So they sent the ark of God to Ekron.

As the ark of God was entering Ekron, the people of Ekron cried out, ''They have brought the ark of the god of Israel round to us to kill us and our people.'' ¹¹So they called together all the rulers of the Philistines and said, ''Send the ark of the god of Israel away; let it go back to its own place, or itᶜ will kill us and our people.'' For death had filled the city with panic; God's hand was very heavy upon it. ¹²Those who did not die were afflicted with tumours, and the outcry of the city went up to heaven.

The Ark Returned to Israel

6 When the ark of the LORD had been in Philistine territory for seven months, ²the Philistines called for the priests and the diviners and said, ''What shall we do with the ark of the LORD? Tell us how we should send it back to its place.''

³They answered, ''If you return the ark of the god of Israel, do not send it away empty, but by all means send a guilt offering to him. Then you will be healed, and you will know why his hand has not been lifted from you.''

⁴The Philistines asked, ''What guilt offering should we send to him?''

They replied, ''Five gold tumours and five gold rats, according to the number of the Philistine rulers, because the same plague has struck both you and your rulers. ⁵Make models of the tumours and of the rats that are destroying the country, and pay honour to Israel's god. Perhaps he will lift his hand from you and your gods and your land. ⁶Why do you harden your hearts as the Egyptians and Pharaoh did? When heᵃ treated them harshly, did they not send the Israelites out so that they could go on their way?

⁷''Now then, get a new cart ready, with two cows that have calved and have never

---

ᵇ18 Traditionally *judged*   *ᶜ21 Ichabod* means *no glory.*
ᵃ6 Hebrew; Septuagint and Vulgate *tumours. And rats appeared in their land, and death and destruction were throughout the city*   *ᵇ9* Or *with tumours in the groin* (see Septuagint)   *ᶜ11* Or *he*   *ᵃ6* That is, God

been yoked. Hitch the cows to the cart, but take their calves away and pen them up. [8]Take the ark of the LORD and put it on the cart, and in a chest beside it put the gold objects you are sending back to him as a guilt offering. Send it on its way, [9]but keep watching it. If it goes up to its own territory, towards Beth Shemesh, then the LORD has brought this great disaster on us. But if it does not, then we shall know that it was not his hand that struck us and that it happened to us by chance."

[10]So they did this. They took two such cows and hitched them to the cart and penned up their calves. [11]They placed the ark of the LORD on the cart and along with it the chest containing the gold rats and the models of the tumours. [12]Then the cows went straight up towards Beth Shemesh, keeping on the road and lowing all the way; they did not turn to the right or to the left. The rulers of the Philistines followed them as far as the border of Beth Shemesh.

[13]Now the people of Beth Shemesh were harvesting their wheat in the valley, and when they looked up and saw the ark, they rejoiced at the sight. [14]The cart came to the field of Joshua of Beth Shemesh, and there it stopped beside a large rock. The people chopped up the wood of the cart and sacrificed the cows as a burnt offering to the LORD. [15]The Levites took down the ark of the LORD, together with the chest containing the gold objects, and placed them on the large rock. On that day the people of Beth Shemesh offered burnt offerings and made sacrifices to the LORD. [16]The five rulers of the Philistines saw all this and then returned that same day to Ekron.

[17]These are the gold tumours the Philistines sent as a guilt offering to the LORD—one each for Ashdod, Gaza, Ashkelon, Gath and Ekron. [18]And the number of the gold rats was according to the number of Philistine towns belonging to the five rulers—the fortified towns with their country villages. The large rock, on which[b] they set the ark of the LORD, is a witness to this day in the field of Joshua of Beth Shemesh.

[19]But God struck down some of the men of Beth Shemesh, putting seventy[c] of them to death because they had looked into the ark of the LORD. The people mourned because of the heavy blow the LORD had dealt them, [20]and the men of Beth Shemesh asked, "Who can stand in the presence of the LORD, this holy God? To whom will the ark go up from here?" [21]Then they sent messengers to the people of Kiriath Jearim, saying, "The Philistines have returned the ark of the LORD. Come down and take it up to your place."

7 [1]So the men of Kiriath Jearim came and took up the ark of the LORD. They took it to Abinadab's house on the hill and consecrated Eleazar his son to guard the ark of the LORD.

Samuel Subdues the Philistines at Mizpah

[2]It was a long time, twenty years in all, that the ark remained at Kiriath Jearim, and all the people of Israel mourned and sought after the LORD. [3]And Samuel said to the whole house of Israel, "If you are returning to the LORD with all your hearts, then rid yourselves of the foreign gods and the Ashtoreths and commit yourselves to the LORD and serve him only, and he will deliver you out of the hand of the Philistines." [4]So the Israelites put away their Baals and Ashtoreths, and served the LORD only.

[5]Then Samuel said, "Assemble all Israel at Mizpah and I will intercede with the LORD for you." [6]When they had assembled at Mizpah, they drew water and poured it out before the LORD. On that day they fasted and there they confessed, "We have sinned against the LORD." And Samuel was leader[a] of Israel at Mizpah.

[7]When the Philistines heard that Israel had assembled at Mizpah, the rulers of the Philistines came up to attack them. And when the Israelites heard of it, they were afraid because of the Philistines. [8]They said to Samuel, "Do not stop crying out to the LORD our God for us, that he may rescue us from the hand of the Philistines." [9]Then Samuel took a suckling lamb and offered it up as a whole burnt offering to the LORD. He cried out to the LORD on Israel's behalf, and the LORD answered him.

[10]While Samuel was sacrificing the burnt offering, the Philistines drew near to engage Israel in battle. But that day the LORD thundered with loud thunder against the Philistines and threw them into such a panic that they were routed before the Israelites. [11]The men of Israel rushed out of Mizpah and pursued the Philistines, slaughtering them along the way to a point below Beth Car.

[12]Then Samuel took a stone and set it up between Mizpah and Shen. He named it Ebenezer,[b] saying, "Thus far has the LORD helped us." [13]So the Philistines were subdued and did not invade Israelite territory again.

Throughout Samuel's lifetime, the hand of the LORD was against the Philistines. [14]The towns from Ekron to Gath that the Philistines had captured from Israel were restored to her, and Israel delivered the neighbouring territory from the power of the Philistines. And there was peace between Israel and the Amorites.

[15]Samuel continued as judge over Israel all the days of his life. [16]From year to year he went on a circuit from Bethel to Gilgal to Mizpah, judging Israel in all those places. [17]But he always went back to Ramah, where his home was, and there he also judged Israel. And he built an altar there to the LORD.

---

[b]18 A few Hebrew manuscripts (see also Septuagint); most Hebrew manuscripts *villages as far as Greater Abel, where*   [c]19 A few Hebrew manuscripts; most Hebrew manuscripts and Septuagint *50,070*
[a]6 Traditionally *judge*   [b]12 *Ebenezer* means *stone of help.*

Israel Asks for a King

8 When Samuel grew old, he appointed his sons as judges for Israel. [2]The name of his firstborn was Joel and the name of his second was Abijah, and they served at Beersheba. [3]But his sons did not walk in his ways. They turned aside after dishonest gain and accepted bribes and perverted justice.

[4]So all the elders of Israel gathered together and came to Samuel at Ramah. [5]They said to him, "You are old, and your sons do not walk in your ways; now appoint a king to lead[a] us, such as all the other nations have."

[6]But when they said, "Give us a king to lead us," this displeased Samuel; so he prayed to the LORD. [7]And the LORD told him: "Listen to all that the people are saying to you; it is not you they have rejected, but they have rejected me as their king. [8]As they have done from the day I brought them up out of Egypt until this day, forsaking me and serving other gods, so they are doing to you. [9]Now listen to them; but warn them solemnly and let them know what the king who will reign over them will do."

[10]Samuel told all the words of the LORD to the people who were asking him for a king. [11]He said, "This is what the king who will reign over you will do: He will take your sons and make them serve with his chariots and horses, and they will run in front of his chariots. [12]Some he will assign to be commanders of thousands and commanders of fifties, and others to plough his ground and reap his harvest, and still others to make weapons of war and equipment for his chariots. [13]He will take your daughters to be perfumers and cooks and bakers. [14]He will take the best of your fields and vineyards and olive groves and give them to his attendants. [15]He will take a tenth of your grain and of your vintage and give it to his officials and attendants. [16]Your menservants and maidservants and the best of your cattle[b] and donkeys he will take for his own use. [17]He will take a tenth of your flocks, and you yourselves will become his slaves. [18]When that day comes, you will cry out for relief from the king you have chosen, and the LORD will not answer you in that day."

[19]But the people refused to listen to Samuel. "No!" they said. "We want a king over us. [20]Then we shall be like all the other nations, with a king to lead us and to go out before us and fight our battles."

[21]When Samuel heard all that the people said, he repeated it before the LORD. [22]The LORD answered, "Listen to them and give them a king."

Then Samuel said to the men of Israel, "Everyone is to go back to his town."

Samuel Anoints Saul

9 There was a Benjamite, a man of standing, whose name was Kish son of Abiel, the son of Zeror, the son of Becorath, the son of Aphiah of Benjamin. [2]He had a son named Saul, an impressive young man without equal among the Israelites—a head taller than any of the others.

[3]Now the donkeys belonging to Saul's father Kish were lost, and Kish said to his son Saul, "Take one of the servants with you and go and look for the donkeys." [4]So he passed through the hill country of Ephraim and through the area around Shalisha, but they did not find them. They went on into the district of Shaalim, but the donkeys were not there. Then he passed through the territory of Benjamin, but they did not find them.

[5]When they reached the district of Zuph, Saul said to the servant who was with him, "Come, let's go back, or my father will stop thinking about the donkeys and start worrying about us."

[6]But the servant replied, "Look, in this town there is a man of God; he is highly respected, and everything he says comes true. Let's go there now. Perhaps he will tell us what way to take."

[7]Saul said to his servant, "If we go, what can we give the man? The food in our sacks is gone. We have no gift to take to the man of God. What do we have?"

[8]The servant answered him again. "Look," he said, "I have a quarter of a shekel[a] of silver. I will give it to the man of God so that he will tell us what way to take." [9](Formerly in Israel, if a man went to enquire of God, he would say, "Come, let us go to the seer," because the prophet of today used to be called a seer.)

[10]"Good," Saul said to his servant. "Come, let's go." So they set out for the town where the man of God was.

[11]As they were going up the hill to the town, they met some girls coming out to draw water, and they asked them, "Is the seer here?"

[12]"He is," they answered. "He's ahead of you. Hurry now; he has just come to our town today, for the people have a sacrifice at the high place. [13]As soon as you enter the town, you will find him before he goes up to the high place to eat. The people will not begin eating until he comes, because he must bless the sacrifice; afterwards, those who are invited will eat. Go up now; you should find him about this time."

[14]They went up to the town, and as they were entering it, there was Samuel, coming towards them on his way up to the high place.

[15]Now the day before Saul came, the LORD had revealed this to Samuel: [16]"About this time tomorrow I will send you a man from the land of Benjamin. Anoint him leader over my people Israel; he will deliver my people from the hand of the Philistines. I have looked upon my people, for their cry has reached me."

[17]When Samuel caught sight of Saul, the LORD said to him, "This is the man I spoke to you about; he will govern my people."

[18]Saul approached Samuel in the gateway

---

[a]5 Traditionally *judge*; also in verses 6 and 20   [b]16 Septuagint; Hebrew *young men*
[a]8 That is, about 1/10 ounce (about 3 grams)

and asked, "Would you please tell me where the seer's house is?"

¹⁹"I am the seer," Samuel replied. "Go up ahead of me to the high place, for today you are to eat with me, and in the morning I will let you go and will tell you all that is in your heart. ²⁰As for the donkeys you lost three days ago, do not worry about them; they have been found. And to whom is all the desire of Israel turned, if not to you and all your father's family?"

²¹Saul answered, "But am I not a Benjamite, from the smallest tribe of Israel, and is not my clan the least of all the clans of the tribe of Benjamin? Why do you say such a thing to me?"

²²Then Samuel brought Saul and his servant into the hall and seated them at the head of those who were invited—about thirty in number. ²³Samuel said to the cook, "Bring the piece of meat I gave you, the one I told you to lay aside."

²⁴So the cook took up the leg with what was on it and set it in front of Saul. Samuel said, "Here is what has been kept for you. Eat, because it was set aside for you for this occasion, from the time I said, 'I have invited guests.'" And Saul dined with Samuel that day.

²⁵After they came down from the high place to the town, Samuel talked with Saul on the roof of his house. ²⁶They rose about daybreak and Samuel called to Saul on the roof, "Get ready, and I will send you on your way." When Saul got ready, he and Samuel went outside together. ²⁷As they were going down to the edge of the town, Saul said to Saul, "Tell the servant to go on ahead of us"—and the servant did so—"but you stay here awhile, so that I may give you a message from God."

10 Then Samuel took a flask of oil and poured it on Saul's head and kissed him, saying, "Has not the LORD anointed you leader over his inheritance?ᵃ ²When you leave me today, you will meet two men near Rachel's tomb, at Zelzah on the border of Benjamin. They will say to you, 'The donkeys you set out to look for have been found. And now your father has stopped thinking about them and is worried about you. He is asking, "What shall I do about my son?"'

³"Then you will go on from there until you reach the great tree of Tabor. Three men going up to God at Bethel will meet you there. One will be carrying three young goats, another three loaves of bread, and another a skin of wine. ⁴They will greet you and offer you two loaves of bread, which you will accept from them.

⁵"After that you will go to Gibeah of God, where there is a Philistine outpost. As you approach the town, you will meet a procession of prophets coming down from the high place with lyres, tambourines, flutes and harps being played before them, and they will be prophesying. ⁶The Spirit of the LORD will come upon you in power, and you will prophesy with them; and you will be changed into a different person. ⁷Once these signs are fulfilled, do whatever your hand finds to do, for God is with you.

⁸"Go down ahead of me to Gilgal. I will surely come down to you to sacrifice burnt offerings and fellowship offerings,ᵇ but you must wait seven days until I come to you and tell you what you are to do."

Saul Made King

⁹As Saul turned to leave Samuel, God changed Saul's heart, and all these signs were fulfilled that day. ¹⁰When they arrived at Gibeah, a procession of prophets met him; the Spirit of God came upon him in power, and he joined in their prophesying. ¹¹When all those who had formerly known him saw him prophesying with the prophets, they asked each other, "What is this that has happened to the son of Kish? Is Saul also among the prophets?"

¹²A man who lived there answered, "And who is their father?" So it became a saying: "Is Saul also among the prophets?" ¹³After Saul stopped prophesying, he went to the high place.

¹⁴Now Saul's uncle asked him and his servant, "Where have you been?"

"Looking for the donkeys," he said. "But when we saw they were not to be found, we went to Samuel."

¹⁵Saul's uncle said, "Tell me what Samuel said to you."

¹⁶Saul replied, "He assured us that the donkeys had been found." But he did not tell his uncle what Samuel had said about the kingship.

¹⁷Samuel summoned the people of Israel to the LORD at Mizpah ¹⁸and said to them, "This is what the LORD, the God of Israel, says: 'I brought Israel up out of Egypt, and I delivered you from the power of Egypt and all the kingdoms that oppressed you.' ¹⁹But you have now rejected your God, who saves you out of all your calamities and distresses. And you have said, 'No, set a king over us.' So now present yourselves before the LORD by your tribes and clans."

²⁰When Samuel brought all the tribes of Israel near, the tribe of Benjamin was chosen. ²¹Then he brought forward the tribe of Benjamin, clan by clan, and Matri's clan was chosen. Finally Saul son of Kish was chosen. But when they looked for him, he was not to be found. ²²So they enquired further of the LORD, "Has the man come here yet?"

And the LORD said, "Yes, he has hidden himself among the baggage."

²³They ran and brought him out, and as he stood among the people he was a head taller than any of the others. ²⁴Samuel said to all the people, "Do you see the man the LORD has chosen? There is no-one like him among all the people."

ᵃ1 Hebrew; Septuagint and Vulgate *over his people Israel? You will reign over the LORD's people and save them from the power of their enemies round about. And this will be a sign to you that the LORD has anointed you leader over his inheritance:*   ᵇ8 Traditionally *peace offerings*

Then the people shouted, "Long live the king!"

²⁵Samuel explained to the people the regulations of the kingship. He wrote them down on a scroll and deposited it before the LORD. Then Samuel dismissed the people, each to his own home.

²⁶Saul also went to his home in Gibeah, accompanied by valiant men whose hearts God had touched. ²⁷But some troublemakers said, "How can this fellow save us?" They despised him and brought him no gifts. But Saul kept silent.

Saul Rescues the City of Jabesh

11 Nahash the Ammonite went up and besieged Jabesh Gilead. And all the men of Jabesh said to him, "Make a treaty with us, and we will be subject to you."

²But Nahash the Ammonite replied, "I will make a treaty with you only on the condition that I gouge out the right eye of every one of you and so bring disgrace on all Israel."

³The elders of Jabesh said to him, "Give us seven days so that we can send messengers throughout Israel; if no-one comes to rescue us, we will surrender to you."

⁴When the messengers came to Gibeah of Saul and reported these terms to the people, they all wept aloud. ⁵Just then Saul was returning from the fields, behind his oxen, and he asked, "What is wrong with the people? Why are they weeping?" Then they repeated to him what the men of Jabesh had said.

⁶When Saul heard their words, the Spirit of God came upon him in power, and he burned with anger. ⁷He took a pair of oxen, cut them into pieces, and sent the pieces by messengers throughout Israel, proclaiming, "This is what will be done to the oxen of anyone who does not follow Saul and Samuel." Then the terror of the LORD fell on the people, and they turned out as one man. ⁸When Saul mustered them at Bezek, the men of Israel numbered three hundred thousand and the men of Judah thirty thousand.

⁹They told the messengers who had come, "Say to the men of Jabesh Gilead, 'By the time the sun is hot tomorrow, you will be delivered.'" When the messengers went and reported this to the men of Jabesh, they were elated. ¹⁰They said to the Ammonites, "Tomorrow we will surrender to you, and you can do to us whatever seems good to you."

¹¹The next day Saul separated his men into three divisions; during the last watch of the night they broke into the camp of the Ammonites and slaughtered them until the heat of the day. Those who survived were scattered, so that no two of them were left together.

Saul Confirmed as King

¹²The people then said to Samuel, "Who was it that asked, 'Shall Saul reign over us?'

Bring these men to us and we will put them to death."

¹³But Saul said, "No-one shall be put to death today, for this day the LORD has rescued Israel."

¹⁴Then Samuel said to the people, "Come, let us go to Gilgal and there reaffirm the kingship." ¹⁵So all the people went to Gilgal and confirmed Saul as king in the presence of the LORD. There they sacrificed fellowship offerings[a] before the LORD, and Saul and all the Israelites held a great celebration.

Samuel's Farewell Speech

12 Samuel said to all Israel, "I have listened to everything you said to me and have set a king over you. ²Now you have a king as your leader. As for me, I am old and grey, and my sons are here with you. I have been your leader from my youth until this day. ³Here I stand. Testify against me in the presence of the LORD and his anointed. Whose ox have I taken? Whose donkey have I taken? Whom have I cheated? Whom have I oppressed? From whose hand have I accepted a bribe to make me shut my eyes? If I have done any of these, I will make it right."

⁴"You have not cheated or oppressed us," they replied. "You have not taken anything from anyone's hand."

⁵Samuel said to them, "The LORD is witness against you, and also his anointed is witness this day, that you have not found anything in my hand."

"He is witness," they said.

⁶Then Samuel said to the people, "It is the LORD who appointed Moses and Aaron and brought your forefathers up out of Egypt. ⁷Now then, stand here, because I am going to confront you with evidence before the LORD as to all the righteous acts performed by the LORD for you and your fathers.

⁸"After Jacob entered Egypt, they cried to the LORD for help, and the LORD sent Moses and Aaron, who brought your forefathers out of Egypt and settled them in this place.

⁹"But they forgot the LORD their God; so he sold them into the hands of Sisera, the commander of the army of Hazor, and into the hands of the Philistines and the king of Moab, who fought against them. ¹⁰They cried out to the LORD and said, 'We have sinned; we have forsaken the LORD and served the Baals and the Ashtoreths. But now deliver us from the hands of our enemies, and we will serve you.' ¹¹Then the LORD sent Jerub-Baal,[a] Barak,[b] Jephthah and Samuel,[c] and he delivered you from the hands of your enemies on every side, so that you lived securely.

¹²"But when you saw that Nahash king of the Ammonites was moving against you, you said to me, 'No, we want a king to rule over us'—even though the LORD your God was your king. ¹³Now here is the king you have chosen, the one you asked for; see, the LORD

*a15 Traditionally *peace offerings*   *a11 Also called *Gideon*
*b11 Some Septuagint manuscripts and Syriac; Hebrew *Bedan*
*c11 Hebrew; some Septuagint manuscripts and Syriac *Samson*

has set a king over you. 14If you fear the LORD and serve and obey him and do not rebel against his commands, and if both you and the king who reigns over you follow the LORD your God—good! 15But if you do not obey the LORD, and if you rebel against his commands, his hand will be against you, as it was against your fathers.

16"Now then, stand still and see this great thing the LORD is about to do before your eyes! 17Is it not wheat harvest now? I will call upon the LORD to send thunder and rain. And you will realise what an evil thing you did in the eyes of the LORD when you asked for a king."

18Then Samuel called upon the LORD, and that same day the LORD sent thunder and rain. So all the people stood in awe of the LORD and of Samuel.

19The people all said to Samuel, "Pray to the LORD your God for your servants so that we will not die, for we have added to all our other sins the evil of asking for a king."

20"Do not be afraid," Samuel replied. "You have done all this evil; yet do not turn away from the LORD, but serve the LORD with all your heart. 21Do not turn away after useless idols. They can do you no good, nor can they rescue you, because they are useless. 22For the sake of his great name the LORD will not reject his people, because the LORD was pleased to make you his own. 23As for me, far be it from me that I should sin against the LORD by failing to pray for you. And I will teach you the way that is good and right. 24But be sure to fear the LORD and serve him faithfully with all your heart; consider what great things he has done for you. 25Yet if you persist in doing evil, both you and your king will be swept away."

Samuel Rebukes Saul

13 Saul was ₁thirty₁ᵃ years old when he became king, and he reigned over Israel for ₁forty-₁ᵇ two years.

2Saulᶜ chose three thousand men from Israel; two thousand were with him at Michmash and in the hill country of Bethel, and a thousand were with Jonathan at Gibeah in Benjamin. The rest of the men he sent back to their homes.

3Jonathan attacked the Philistine outpost at Geba, and the Philistines heard about it. Then Saul had the trumpet blown throughout the land and said, "Let the Hebrews hear!" 4So all Israel heard the news: "Saul has attacked the Philistine outpost, and now Israel has become an offence to the Philistines." And the people were summoned to join Saul at Gilgal.

5The Philistines assembled to fight Israel, with three thousandᵈ chariots, six thousand charioteers, and soldiers as numerous as the sand on the seashore. They went up and camped at Michmash, east of Beth Aven. 6When the men of Israel saw that their situation was critical and that their army was hard pressed, they hid in caves and thickets, among the rocks, and in pits and cisterns. 7Some Hebrews even crossed the Jordan to the land of Gad and Gilead.

Saul remained at Gilgal, and all the troops with him were quaking with fear. 8He waited for seven days, the time set by Samuel; but Samuel did not come to Gilgal, and Saul's men began to scatter. 9So he said, "Bring me the burnt offering and the fellowship offerings."ᵉ And Saul offered up the burnt offering. 10Just as he finished making the offering, Samuel arrived, and Saul went out to greet him.

11"What have you done?" asked Samuel.

Saul replied, "When I saw that the men were scattering, and that you did not come at the set time, and that the Philistines were assembling at Michmash, 12I thought, 'Now the Philistines will come down against me at Gilgal, and I have not sought the LORD's favour.' So I felt compelled to offer the burnt offering."

13"You acted foolishly," Samuel said. "You have not kept the command the LORD your God gave you; if you had, he would have established your kingdom over Israel for all time. 14But now your kingdom will not endure; the LORD has sought out a man after his own heart and appointed him leader of his people, because you have not kept the LORD's command."

15Then Samuel left Gilgalᶠ and went up to Gibeah in Benjamin, and Saul counted the men who were with him. They numbered about six hundred.

Israel Without Weapons

16Saul and his son Jonathan and the men with them were staying in Gibeahᵍ of Benjamin, while the Philistines camped at Michmash. 17Raiding parties went out from the Philistine camp in three detachments. One turned towards Ophrah in the vicinity of Shual, 18another towards Beth Horon, and the third towards the borderland overlooking the Valley of Zeboim facing the desert.

19Not a blacksmith could be found in the whole land of Israel, because the Philistines had said, "Otherwise the Hebrews will make swords or spears!" 20So all Israel went down to the Philistines to have their ploughshares, mattocks, axes and sicklesʰ sharpened. 21The price was two thirds of a shekelⁱ for sharpening ploughshares and mattocks, and a third of a shekelʲ for sharpening forks and axes and for repointing goads.

22So on the day of the battle not a soldier with Saul and Jonathan had a sword or spear

---

ᵃ1 A few late manuscripts of the Septuagint; Hebrew does not have thirty.
ᵇ1 See the round number in Acts 13:21; Hebrew does not have forty-.
ᶜ1,2 Or and when he had reigned over Israel for two years, ²he
ᵈ5 Some Septuagint manuscripts and Syriac; Hebrew thirty thousand   ᵉ9 Traditionally peace offerings
ᶠ15 Hebrew; Septuagint Gilgal and went his way; the rest of the people went after Saul to meet the army, and they went out of Gilgal   ᵍ16 Two Hebrew manuscripts; most Hebrew manuscripts Geba, a variant of Gibeah
ʰ20 Septuagint; Hebrew ploughshares   ⁱ21 Hebrew pim; that is, about ¼ ounce (about 8 grams)
ʲ21 That is, about ⅛ ounce (about 4 grams)

in his hand; only Saul and his son Jonathan had them.

Jonathan Attacks the Philistines

23Now a detachment of Philistines had gone out to the pass at Michmash.

14 1One day Jonathan son of Saul said to the young man bearing his armour, "Come, let's go over to the Philistine outpost on the other side." But he did not tell his father.

2Saul was staying on the outskirts of Gibeah under a pomegranate tree in Migron. With him were about six hundred men, 3among whom was Ahijah, who was wearing an ephod. He was a son of Ichabod's brother Ahitub son of Phinehas, the son of Eli, the LORD's priest in Shiloh. No-one was aware that Jonathan had left.

4On each side of the pass that Jonathan intended to cross to reach the Philistine outpost was a cliff; one was called Bozez, and the other Seneh. 5One cliff stood to the north towards Michmash, the other to the south towards Geba.

6Jonathan said to his young armour-bearer, "Come, let's go over to the outpost of those uncircumcised fellows. Perhaps the LORD will act on our behalf. Nothing can hinder the LORD from saving, whether by many or by few."

7"Do all that you have in mind," his armour-bearer said. "Go ahead; I am with you heart and soul."

8Jonathan said, "Come, then; we will cross over towards the men and let them see us. 9If they say to us, 'Wait there until we come to you,' we will stay where we are and not go up to them. 10But if they say, 'Come up to us,' we will climb up, because that will be our sign that the LORD has given them into our hands."

11So both of them showed themselves to the Philistine outpost. "Look!" said the Philistines. "The Hebrews are crawling out of the holes they were hiding in." 12The men of the outpost shouted to Jonathan and his armour-bearer, "Come up to us and we'll teach you a lesson."

So Jonathan said to his armour-bearer, "Climb up after me; the LORD has given them into the hand of Israel."

13Jonathan climbed up, using his hands and feet, with his armour-bearer right behind him. The Philistines fell before Jonathan, and his armour-bearer followed and killed behind him. 14In that first attack Jonathan and his armour-bearer killed some twenty men in an area of about half an acre.a

Israel Routs the Philistines

15Then panic struck the whole army—those in the camp and field, and those in the outposts and raiding parties—and the ground shook. It was a panic sent by God.b

16Saul's lookouts at Gibeah in Benjamin saw the army melting away in all directions.

17Then Saul said to the men who were with him, "Muster the forces and see who has left us." When they did, it was Jonathan and his armour-bearer who were not there.

18Saul said to Ahijah, "Bring the ark of God." (At that time it was with the Israelites.)c 19While Saul was talking to the priest, the tumult in the Philistine camp increased more and more. So Saul said to the priest, "Withdraw your hand."

20Then Saul and all his men assembled and went to the battle. They found the Philistines in total confusion, striking each other with their swords. 21Those Hebrews who had previously been with the Philistines and had gone up with them to their camp went over to the Israelites who were with Saul and Jonathan. 22When all the Israelites who had hidden in the hill country of Ephraim heard that the Philistines were on the run, they joined the battle in hot pursuit. 23So the LORD rescued Israel that day, and the battle moved on beyond Beth Aven.

Jonathan Eats Honey

24Now the men of Israel were in distress that day, because Saul had bound the people under an oath, saying, "Cursed be any man who eats food before evening comes, before I have avenged myself on my enemies!" So none of the troops tasted food.

25The entire armyd entered the woods, and there was honey on the ground. 26When they went into the woods, they saw the honey oozing out, yet no-one put his hand to his mouth, because they feared the oath. 27But Jonathan had not heard that his father had bound the people with the oath, so he reached out the end of the staff that was in his hand and dipped it into the honeycomb. He raised his hand to his mouth, and his eyes brightened.e 28Then one of the soldiers told him, "Your father bound the army under a strict oath, saying, 'Cursed be any man who eats food today!' That is why the men are faint."

29Jonathan said, "My father has made trouble for the country. See how my eyes brightenedf when I tasted a little of this honey. 30How much better it would have been if the men had eaten today some of the plunder they took from their enemies. Would not the slaughter of the Philistines have been even greater?"

31That day, after the Israelites had struck down the Philistines from Michmash to Aijalon, they were exhausted. 32They pounced on the plunder and, taking sheep, cattle and calves, they butchered them on the ground and ate them, together with the blood. 33Then someone said to Saul, "Look, the men are sinning against the LORD by eating meat that has blood in it."

"You have broken faith," he said. "Roll a large stone over here at once." 34Then he said, "Go out among the men and tell them, 'Each of you bring me your cattle and sheep,

---

a14 Hebrew half a yoke; a "yoke" was the land ploughed by a yoke of oxen in one day.   b15 Or a terrible panic
c18 Hebrew; Septuagint "Bring the ephod." (At that time he wore the ephod before the Israelites.)
d25 Or Now all the people of the land   e27 Or his strength was renewed   f29 Or my strength was renewed

and slaughter them here and eat them. Do not sin against the LORD by eating meat with blood still in it.'"

So everyone brought his ox that night and slaughtered it there. 35Then Saul built an altar to the LORD; it was the first time he had done this.

36Saul said, "Let us go down after the Philistines by night and plunder them till dawn, and let us not leave one of them alive."

"Do whatever seems best to you," they replied.

But the priest said, "Let us enquire of God here."

37So Saul asked God, "Shall I go down after the Philistines? Will you give them into Israel's hand?" But God did not answer him that day.

38Saul therefore said, "Come here, all you who are leaders of the army, and let us find out what sin has been committed today. 39As surely as the LORD who rescues Israel lives, even if it lies with my son Jonathan, he must die." But not one of the men said a word.

40Saul then said to all the Israelites, "You stand over there; I and Jonathan my son will stand over here."

"Do what seems best to you," the men replied.

41Then Saul prayed to the LORD, the God of Israel, "Give me the right answer."g And Jonathan and Saul were taken by lot, and the men were cleared. 42Saul said, "Cast the lot between me and Jonathan my son." And Jonathan was taken.

43Then Saul said to Jonathan, "Tell me what you have done."

So Jonathan told him, "I merely tasted a little honey with the end of my staff. And now must I die?"

44Saul said, "May God deal with me, be it ever so severely, if you do not die, Jonathan."

45But the men said to Saul, "Should Jonathan die—he who has brought about this great deliverance in Israel? Never! As surely as the LORD lives, not a hair of his head shall fall to the ground, for he did this today with God's help." So the men rescued Jonathan, and he was not put to death.

46Then Saul stopped pursuing the Philistines, and they withdrew to their own land.

47After Saul had assumed rule over Israel, he fought against their enemies on every side: Moab, the Ammonites, Edom, the kingsh of Zobah, and the Philistines. Wherever he turned, he inflicted punishment on them.i 48He fought valiantly and defeated the Amalekites, delivering Israel from the hands of those who had plundered them.

Saul's Family

49Saul's sons were Jonathan, Ishvi and Malki-Shua. The name of his older daughter was Merab, and that of the younger was Michal. 50His wife's name was Ahinoam daughter of Ahimaaz. The name of the commander of Saul's army was Abner son of Ner, and Ner was Saul's uncle. 51Saul's father Kish and Abner's father Ner were sons of Abiel.

52All the days of Saul there was bitter war with the Philistines, and whenever Saul saw a mighty or brave man, he took him into his service.

The LORD Rejects Saul as King

15 Samuel said to Saul, "I am the one the LORD sent to anoint you king over his people Israel; so listen now to the message from the LORD. 2This is what the LORD Almighty says: 'I will punish the Amalekites for what they did to Israel when they waylaid them as they came up from Egypt. 3Now go, attack the Amalekites and totally destroya everything that belongs to them. Do not spare them; put to death men and women, children and infants, cattle and sheep, camels and donkeys.'"

4So Saul summoned the men and mustered them at Telaim—two hundred thousand foot soldiers and ten thousand men from Judah. 5Saul went to the city of Amalek and set an ambush in the ravine. 6Then he said to the Kenites, "Go away, leave the Amalekites so that I do not destroy you along with them; for you showed kindness to all the Israelites when they came up out of Egypt." So the Kenites moved away from the Amalekites.

7Then Saul attacked the Amalekites all the way from Havilah to Shur, to the east of Egypt. 8He took Agag king of the Amalekites alive, and all his people he totally destroyed with the sword. 9But Saul and the army spared Agag and the best of the sheep and cattle, the fat calvesb and lambs—everything that was good. These they were unwilling to destroy completely, but everything that was despised and weak they totally destroyed.

10Then the word of the LORD came to Samuel: 11"I am grieved that I have made Saul king, because he has turned away from me and has not carried out my instructions." Samuel was troubled, and he cried out to the LORD all that night.

12Early in the morning Samuel got up and went to meet Saul, but he was told, "Saul has gone to Carmel. There he has set up a monument in his own honour and has turned and gone on down to Gilgal."

13When Samuel reached him, Saul said, "The LORD bless you! I have carried out the LORD's instructions."

14But Samuel said, "What then is this bleating of sheep in my ears? What is this lowing of cattle that I hear?"

15Saul answered, "The soldiers brought them from the Amalekites; they spared the best of the sheep and cattle to sacrifice to the

---

g41 Hebrew; Septuagint "Why have you not answered your servant today? If the fault is in me or my son Jonathan, respond with Urim, but if the men of Israel are at fault, respond with Thummim."
h47 Masoretic Text; Dead Sea Scrolls and Septuagint king   i47 Hebrew; Septuagint he was victorious
a3 The Hebrew term refers to the irrevocable giving of things or persons to the LORD, often by totally destroying them; also in verses 8, 9, 15, 18, 20 and 21.
b9 Or the grown bulls; the meaning of the Hebrew for this phrase is uncertain.

LORD your God, but we totally destroyed the rest.''

16''Stop!'' Samuel said to Saul. ''Let me tell you what the LORD said to me last night.''

''Tell me,'' Saul replied.

17Samuel said, ''Although you were once small in your own eyes, did you not become the head of the tribes of Israel? The LORD anointed you king over Israel. 18And he sent you on a mission, saying, 'Go and completely destroy those wicked people, the Amalekites; make war on them until you have wiped them out.' 19Why did you not obey the LORD? Why did you pounce on the plunder and do evil in the eyes of the LORD?''

20''But I did obey the LORD,'' Saul said. ''I went on the mission the LORD assigned me. I completely destroyed the Amalekites and brought back Agag their king. 21The soldiers took sheep and cattle from the plunder, the best of what was devoted to God, in order to sacrifice them to the LORD your God at Gilgal.''

22But Samuel replied:

''Does the LORD delight in burnt offerings
　　and sacrifices
　　as much as in obeying the voice of the
　　　LORD?
To obey is better than sacrifice,
　　and to heed is better than the fat of
　　　rams.
23For rebellion is like the sin of divination,
　　and arrogance like the evil of idolatry.
Because you have rejected the word of the
　　LORD,
　　he has rejected you as king.''

24Then Saul said to Samuel, ''I have sinned. I violated the LORD's command and your instructions. I was afraid of the people and so I gave in to them. 25Now I beg you, forgive my sin and come back with me, so that I may worship the LORD.''

26But Samuel said to him, ''I will not go back with you. You have rejected the word of the LORD, and the LORD has rejected you as king over Israel!''

27As Samuel turned to leave, Saul caught hold of the hem of his robe, and it tore. 28Samuel said to him, ''The LORD has torn the kingdom of Israel from you today and has given it to one of your neighbours—to one better than you. 29He who is the Glory of Israel does not lie or change his mind; for he is not a man, that he should change his mind.''

30Saul replied, ''I have sinned. But please honour me before the elders of my people and before Israel; come back with me, so that I may worship the LORD your God.'' 31So Samuel went back with Saul, and Saul worshipped the LORD.

32Then Samuel said, ''Bring me Agag king of the Amalekites.''

Agag came to him confidently,c thinking, ''Surely the bitterness of death is past.''

33But Samuel said,

''As your sword has made women
　　childless,
　　so will your mother be childless among
　　women.''

And Samuel put Agag to death before the LORD at Gilgal.

34Then Samuel left for Ramah, but Saul went up to his home in Gibeah of Saul. 35Until the day Samuel died, he did not go to see Saul again, though Samuel mourned for him. And the LORD was grieved that he had made Saul king over Israel.

Samuel Anoints David

16 The LORD said to Samuel, ''How long will you mourn for Saul, since I have rejected him as king over Israel? Fill your horn with oil and be on your way; I am sending you to Jesse of Bethlehem. I have chosen one of his sons to be king.''

2But Samuel said, ''How can I go? Saul will hear about it and kill me.''

The LORD said, ''Take a heifer with you and say, 'I have come to sacrifice to the LORD.' 3Invite Jesse to the sacrifice, and I will show you what to do. You are to anoint for me the one I indicate.''

4Samuel did what the LORD said. When he arrived at Bethlehem, the elders of the town trembled when they met him. They asked, ''Do you come in peace?''

5Samuel replied, ''Yes, in peace; I have come to sacrifice to the LORD. Consecrate yourselves and come to the sacrifice with me.'' Then he consecrated Jesse and his sons and invited them to the sacrifice.

6When they arrived, Samuel saw Eliab and thought, ''Surely the LORD's anointed stands here before the LORD.''

7But the LORD said to Samuel, 'Do not consider his appearance or his height, for I have rejected him. The LORD does not look at the things man looks at. Man looks at the outward appearance, but the LORD looks at the heart.''

8Then Jesse called Abinadab and made him pass in front of Samuel. But Samuel said, ''The LORD has not chosen this one either.'' 9Jesse then made Shammah pass by, but Samuel said, ''Nor has the LORD chosen this one.'' 10Jesse made seven of his sons pass before Samuel, but Samuel said to him, ''The LORD has not chosen these.'' 11So he asked Jesse, ''Are these all the sons you have?''

''There is still the youngest,'' Jesse answered, ''but he is tending the sheep.''

Samuel said, ''Send for him; we will not sit downd until he arrives.''

12So he sent and had him brought in. He was ruddy, with a fine appearance and handsome features.

Then the LORD said, ''Rise and anoint him; he is the one.''

13So Samuel took the horn of oil and anointed him in the presence of his brothers, and from that day on the Spirit of the LORD came upon David in power. Samuel then went to Ramah.

---

c32 Or him trembling, yet　　d11 Some Septuagint manuscripts; Hebrew not gather round

1 SAMUEL 16:1–13
'The LORD said . . . "Do not consider his appearance or his height . . . The LORD does not look at the things man looks at. Man looks at the outward appearance, but the LORD looks at the heart" ' (v. 7).

CHARACTER COUNTS. The editor of 1 Samuel follows the account of the rejection of Saul (Chapter 15) with a paragraph describing the anointing of a new king. For the remainder of the book David's kingship is not mentioned. At best he is 'a king in waiting', and at worst 'a king in exile', until the death of Saul.

In the choice of David the importance of character is emphasized. Part of Saul's appeal in the eyes of the people had been that he was 'an impressive young man without equal among the Israelites – a head taller than any of the others' (9:2; see also 10:23, 24). Samuel is warned against choosing a new king on these criteria. These qualities may impress men but they are external and do not always match the inner character. God sees beyond appearances and chooses 'a man after his own heart' (13:14).

If this account was intended to make a contrast between David and Saul other factors have to be considered. Saul had also been God's choice (9:16, 17), but was rejected because of his presumption and disobedience (13:13; 15:10).

We are not only warned that external appearances can be deceptive and that what God requires of us is inner integrity; we are also reminded that any genuine promise that we have can be ruined by our arrogance and self-will.

→246

1 SAMUEL 17:1–11, 32–37a
'David said to Saul, "Let no-one lose heart on account of this Philistine; your servant will go and fight him" ' (v. 32.)

CALLED TO COURAGE. The familiar story of David and Goliath needs no expansion here. The first part of this story emphasizes the timidity and lack of resolution which gripped Saul and his army. The challenge of Goliath was to a trial by personal combat (v. 8) and its repetition (v. 10) is a kind of taunt which would only serve to increase the sense of panic in the Israelite ranks.

This story, perhaps more than any other in the Bible, has suffered from a tendency to over-moralize it. However, it contains certain elements which confirm our life experiences. First, it is a fact that inordinate fear results in a kind of paralysis, and the more the cause of that fear is reiterated the stronger the grip of inaction becomes. Second, it is also true that a single act of courage can be enough to break the power of a threat and set others free to act.

The attitude of David was sufficient to show the Israelites that they had forgotten something – they had forgotten God in whose name they were called to act. By his example David showed that they were called to show courage.

The Lord . . . will deliver me.

David in Saul's Service

14Now the Spirit of the LORD had departed from Saul, and an evilb spirit from the LORD tormented him.

15Saul's attendants said to him, "See, an evil spirit from God is tormenting you. 16Let our lord command his servants here to search for someone who can play the harp. He will play when the evil spirit from God comes upon you, and you will feel better."

17So Saul said to his attendants, "Find someone who plays well and bring him to me."

18One of the servants answered, "I have seen a son of Jesse of Bethlehem who knows how to play the harp. He is a brave man and a warrior. He speaks well and is a fine-looking man. And the LORD is with him."

19Then Saul sent messengers to Jesse and said, "Send me your son David, who is with the sheep." 20So Jesse took a donkey loaded with bread, a skin of wine and a young goat and sent them with his son David to Saul.

21David came to Saul and entered his service. Saul liked him very much, and David became one of his armour-bearers. 22Then Saul sent word to Jesse, saying, "Allow David to remain in my service, for I am pleased with him."

23Whenever the spirit from God came upon Saul, David would take his harp and play. Then relief would come to Saul; he would feel better, and the evil spirit would leave him.

David and Goliath

17 Now the Philistines gathered their forces for war and assembled at Socoh in Judah. They pitched camp at Ephes Dammim, between Socoh and Azekah. 2Saul and the Israelites assembled and camped in the Valley of Elah and drew up their battle line to meet the Philistines. 3The Philistines occupied one hill and the Israelites another, with the valley between them.

4A champion named Goliath, who was from Gath, came out of the Philistine camp. He was over nine feeta tall. 5He had a bronze helmet on his head and wore a coat of scale armour of bronze weighing five thousand shekels;b 6on his legs he wore bronze greaves, and a bronze javelin was slung on his back. 7His spear shaft was like a weaver's rod, and its iron point weighed six hundred shekels.c His shield-bearer went ahead of him.

8Goliath stood and shouted to the ranks of Israel, "Why do you come out and line up for battle? Am I not a Philistine, and are you not the servants of Saul? Choose a man and have him come down to me. 9If he is able to fight and kill me, we will become your subjects; but if I overcome him and kill him, you will become our subjects and serve us." 10Then the Philistine said, "This day I defy the ranks of Israel! Give me a man and let us fight each other." 11On hearing the Philistine's words,

Saul and all the Israelites were dismayed and terrified.

12Now David was the son of an Ephrathite named Jesse, who was from Bethlehem in Judah. Jesse had eight sons, and in Saul's time he was old and well advanced in years. 13Jesse's three oldest sons had followed Saul to the war: The firstborn was Eliab; the second, Abinadab; and the third, Shammah. 14David was the youngest. The three oldest followed Saul, 15but David went back and forth from Saul to tend his father's sheep at Bethlehem.

16For forty days the Philistine came forward every morning and evening and took his stand.

17Now Jesse said to his son David, "Take this ephahd of roasted grain and these ten loaves of bread for your brothers and hurry to their camp. 18Take along these ten cheeses to the commander of their unit.e See how your brothers are and bring back some assurancef from them. 19They are with Saul and all the men of Israel in the Valley of Elah, fighting against the Philistines."

20Early in the morning David left the flock with a shepherd, loaded up and set out, as Jesse had directed. He reached the camp as the army was going out to its battle positions, shouting the war cry. 21Israel and the Philistines were drawing up their lines facing each other. 22David left his things with the keeper of supplies, ran to the battle lines and greeted his brothers. 23As he was talking with them, Goliath, the Philistine champion from Gath, stepped out from his lines and shouted his usual defiance, and David heard it. 24When the Israelites saw the man, they all ran from him in great fear.

25Now the Israelites had been saying, "Do you see how this man keeps coming out? He comes out to defy Israel. The king will give great wealth to the man who kills him. He will also give him his daughter in marriage and will exempt his father's family from taxes in Israel."

26David asked the men standing near him, "What will be done for the man who kills this Philistine and removes this disgrace from Israel? Who is this uncircumcised Philistine that he should defy the armies of the living God?"

27They repeated to him what they had been saying and told him, "This is what will be done for the man who kills him."

28When Eliab, David's oldest brother, heard him speaking with the men, he burned with anger at him and asked, "Why have you come down here? And with whom did you leave those few sheep in the desert? I know how conceited you are and how wicked your heart is; you came down only to watch the battle."

29"Now what have I done?" said David. "Can't I even speak?" 30He then turned away to someone else and brought up the same matter, and the men answered him as

---

b14 Or *injurious*; also in verses 15, 16 and 23
b5 That is, about 125 pounds (about 57 kilograms)
d17 That is, probably about ⅗ bushel (about 22 litres)
f18 Or *some token*; or *some pledge of spoils*

a4 Hebrew *was six cubits and a span* (about 3 metres)
c7 That is, about 15 pounds (about 7 kilograms)
e18 Hebrew *thousand*

before. [31]What David said was overheard and reported to Saul, and Saul sent for him.

[32]David said to Saul, "Let no-one lose heart on account of this Philistine; your servant will go and fight him."

[33]Saul replied, "You are not able to go out against this Philistine and fight him; you are only a boy, and he has been a fighting man from his youth."

[34]But David said to Saul, "Your servant has been keeping his father's sheep. When a lion or a bear came and carried off a sheep from the flock, [35]I went after it, struck it and rescued the sheep from its mouth. When it turned on me, I seized it by its hair, struck it and killed it. [36]Your servant has killed both the lion and the bear; this uncircumcised Philistine will be like one of them, because he has defied the armies of the living God. [37]The LORD who delivered me from the paw of the lion and the paw of the bear will deliver me from the hand of this Philistine."

Saul said to David, "Go, and the LORD be with you."

[38]Then Saul dressed David in his own tunic. He put a coat of armour on him and a bronze helmet on his head. [39]David fastened on his sword over the tunic and tried walking around, because he was not used to them.

"I cannot go in these," he said to Saul, "because I am not used to them." So he took them off. [40]Then he took his staff in his hand, chose five smooth stones from the stream, put them in the pouch of his shepherd's bag and, with his sling in his hand, approached the Philistine.

[41]Meanwhile, the Philistine, with his shield-bearer in front of him, kept coming closer to David. [42]He looked David over and saw that he was only a boy, ruddy and handsome, and he despised him. [43]He said to David, "Am I a dog, that you come at me with sticks?" And the Philistine cursed David by his gods. [44]"Come here," he said, "and I'll give your flesh to the birds of the air and the beasts of the field!"

[45]David said to the Philistine, "You come against me with sword and spear and javelin, but I come against you in the name of the LORD Almighty, the God of the armies of Israel, whom you have defied. [46]This day the LORD will hand you over to me, and I'll strike you down and cut off your head. Today I will give the carcasses of the Philistine army to the birds of the air and the beasts of the earth, and the whole world will know that there is a God in Israel. [47]All those gathered here will know that it is not by sword or spear that the LORD saves; for the battle is the LORD's, and he will give all of you into our hands."

[48]As the Philistine moved closer to attack him, David ran quickly towards the battle line to meet him. [49]Reaching into his bag and taking out a stone, he slung it and struck the Philistine on the forehead. The stone sank into his forehead, and he fell face down on the ground.

[50]So David triumphed over the Philistine with a sling and a stone; without a sword in his hand he struck down the Philistine and killed him.

[51]David ran and stood over him. He took hold of the Philistine's sword and drew it from the scabbard. After he killed him, he cut off his head with the sword.

When the Philistines saw that their hero was dead, they turned and ran. [52]Then the men of Israel and Judah surged forward with a shout and pursued the Philistines to the entrance of Gath[g] and to the gates of Ekron. Their dead were strewn along the Shaaraim road to Gath and Ekron. [53]When the Israelites returned from chasing the Philistines, they plundered their camp. [54]David took the Philistine's head and brought it to Jerusalem, and he put the Philistine's weapons in his own tent.

[55]As Saul watched David going out to meet the Philistine, he said to Abner, commander of the army, "Abner, whose son is that young man?"

Abner replied, "As surely as you live, O king, I don't know."

[56]The king said, "Find out whose son this young man is."

[57]As soon as David returned from killing the Philistine, Abner took him and brought him before Saul, with David still holding the Philistine's head.

[58]"Whose son are you, young man?" Saul asked him.

David said, "I am the son of your servant Jesse of Bethlehem."

Saul's Jealousy of David

18 After David had finished talking with Saul, Jonathan became one in spirit with David, and he loved him as himself. [2]From that day Saul kept David with him and did not let him return to his father's house. [3]And Jonathan made a covenant with David because he loved him as himself. [4]Jonathan took off the robe he was wearing and gave it to David, along with his tunic, and even his sword, his bow and his belt.

[5]Whatever Saul sent him to do, David did it so successfully[a] that Saul gave him a high rank in the army. This pleased all the people, and Saul's officers as well.

[6]When the men were returning home after David had killed the Philistine, the women came out from all the towns of Israel to meet King Saul with singing and dancing, with joyful songs and with tambourines and lutes. [7]As they danced, they sang:

"Saul has slain his thousands,
    and David his tens of thousands."

[8]Saul was very angry; this refrain galled him. "They have credited David with tens of thousands," he thought, "but me with only thousands. What more can he get but the kingdom?" [9]And from that time on Saul kept a jealous eye on David.

[10]The next day an evil[b] spirit from God came forcefully upon Saul. He was prophesying in his house, while David was

---

[g]52 Some Septuagint manuscripts; Hebrew *a valley*   [a]5 Or *wisely*   [b]10 Or *injurious*

playing the harp, as he usually did. Saul had a spear in his hand [11]and he hurled it, saying to himself, "I'll pin David to the wall." But David eluded him twice.

[12]Saul was afraid of David, because the LORD was with David but had left Saul. [13]So he sent David away from him and gave him command over a thousand men, and David led the troops in their campaigns. [14]In everything he did he had great success,[c] because the LORD was with him. [15]When Saul saw how successful[d] he was, he was afraid of him. [16]But all Israel and Judah loved David, because he led them in their campaigns.

[17]Saul said to David, "Here is my elder daughter Merab. I will give her to you in marriage; only serve me bravely and fight the battles of the LORD." For Saul said to himself, "I will not raise a hand against him. Let the Philistines do that!"

[18]But David said to Saul, "Who am I, and what is my family or my father's clan in Israel, that I should become the king's son-in-law?" [19]So[e] when the time came for Merab, Saul's daughter, to be given to David, she was given in marriage to Adriel of Meholah.

[20]Now Saul's daughter Michal was in love with David, and when they told Saul about it, he was pleased. [21]"I will give her to him," he thought, "so that she may be a snare to him and so that the hand of the Philistines may be against him." So Saul said to David, "Now you have a second opportunity to become my son-in-law."

[22]Then Saul ordered his attendants: "Speak to David privately and say, 'Look, the king is pleased with you, and his attendants all like you; now become his son-in-law.'"

[23]They repeated these words to David. But David said, "Do you think it is a small matter to become the king's son-in-law? I'm only a poor man and little known."

[24]When Saul's servants told him what David had said, [25]Saul replied, "Say to David, 'The king wants no other price for the bride than a hundred Philistine foreskins, to take revenge on his enemies.'" Saul's plan was to have David fall by the hands of the Philistines.

[26]When the attendants told David these things, he was pleased to become the king's son-in-law. So before the allotted time elapsed, [27]David and his men went out and killed two hundred Philistines. He brought their foreskins and presented the full number to the king so that he might become the king's son-in-law. Then Saul gave him his daughter Michal in marriage.

[28]When Saul realised that the LORD was with David and that his daughter Michal loved David, [29]Saul became still more afraid of him, and he remained his enemy for the rest of his days.

[30]The Philistine commanders continued to go out to battle, and as often as they did, David met with more success[f] than the rest

of Saul's officers, and his name became well known.

Saul Tries to Kill David

19 Saul told his son Jonathan and all the attendants to kill David. But Jonathan was very fond of David [2]and warned him, "My father Saul is looking for a chance to kill you. Be on your guard tomorrow morning; go into hiding and stay there. [3]I will go out and stand with my father in the field where you are. I'll speak to him about you and will tell you what I find out."

[4]Jonathan spoke well of David to Saul his father and said to him, "Let not the king do wrong to his servant David; he has not wronged you, and what he has done has benefited you greatly. [5]He took his life in his hands when he killed the Philistine. The LORD won a great victory for all Israel, and you saw it and were glad. Why then would you do wrong to an innocent man like David by killing him for no reason?"

[6]Saul listened to Jonathan and took this oath: "As surely as the LORD lives, David will not be put to death."

[7]So Jonathan called David and told him the whole conversation. He brought him to Saul, and David was with Saul as before.

[8]Once more war broke out, and David went out and fought the Philistines. He struck them with such force that they fled before him.

[9]But an evil[a] spirit from the LORD came upon Saul as he was sitting in his house with his spear in his hand. While David was playing the harp, [10]Saul tried to pin him to the wall with his spear, but David eluded him as Saul drove the spear into the wall. That night David made good his escape.

[11]Saul sent men to David's house to watch it and to kill him in the morning. But Michal, David's wife, warned him, "If you don't run for your life tonight, tomorrow you'll be killed." [12]So Michal let David down through a window, and he fled and escaped. [13]Then Michal took an idol[b] and laid it on the bed, covering it with a garment and putting some goats' hair at the head.

[14]When Saul sent men to capture David, Michal said, "He is ill."

[15]Then Saul sent the men back to see David and told them, "Bring him up to me in his bed so that I may kill him." [16]But when the men entered, there was the idol in the bed, and at the head was some goats' hair.

[17]Saul said to Michal, "Why did you deceive me like this and send my enemy away so that he escaped?"

Michal told him, "He said to me, 'Let me get away. Why should I kill you?'"

[18]When David had fled[d] and made his escape, he went to Samuel at Ramah and told him all that Saul had done to him. Then he and Samuel went to Naioth and stayed there. [19]Word came to Saul: "David is in Naioth at Ramah"; [20]so he sent men to capture him. But when they saw a group of prophets

---

[c]14 Or *he was very wise* [d]15 Or *wise* [e]19 Or *However,*
[f]30 Or *David acted more wisely* [a]9 Or *injurious* [b]13 Hebrew *teraphim*; also in verse 16

prophesying, with Samuel standing there as their leader, the Spirit of God came upon Saul's men and they also prophesied. ²¹Saul was told about it, and he sent more men, and they prophesied too. Saul sent men a third time, and they also prophesied. ²²Finally, he himself left for Ramah and went to the great cistern at Secu. And he asked, "Where are Samuel and David?"

"Over in Naioth at Ramah," they said.

²³So Saul went to Naioth at Ramah. But the Spirit of God came even upon him, and he walked along prophesying until he came to Naioth. ²⁴He stripped off his robes and also prophesied in Samuel's presence. He lay that way all that day and night. This is why people say, "Is Saul also among the prophets?"

David and Jonathan

20 Then David fled from Naioth at Ramah and went to Jonathan and asked, "What have I done? What is my crime? How have I wronged your father, that he is trying to take my life?"

²"Never!" Jonathan replied. "You are not going to die! Look, my father doesn't do anything, great or small, without confiding in me. Why should he hide this from me? It's not so!"

³But David took an oath and said, "Your father knows very well that I have found favour in your eyes, and he has said to himself, 'Jonathan must not know this or he will be grieved.' Yet as surely as the LORD lives and as you live, there is only a step between me and death."

⁴Jonathan said to David, "Whatever you want me to do, I'll do for you."

⁵So David said, "Look, tomorrow is the New Moon festival, and I am supposed to dine with the king; but let me go and hide in the field until the evening of the day after tomorrow. ⁶If your father misses me at all, tell him, 'David earnestly asked my permission to hurry to Bethlehem, his home town, because an annual sacrifice is being made there for his whole clan.' ⁷If he says, 'Very well,' then your servant is safe. But if he loses his temper, you can be sure that he is determined to harm me. ⁸As for you, show kindness to your servant, for you have brought him into a covenant with you before the LORD. If I am guilty, then kill me yourself! Why hand me over to your father?"

⁹"Never!" Jonathan said. "If I had the least inkling that my father was determined to harm you, wouldn't I tell you?"

¹⁰David asked, "Who will tell me if your father answers you harshly?"

¹¹"Come," Jonathan said, "let's go out into the field." So they went there together.

¹²Then Jonathan said to David: "By the LORD, the God of Israel, I will surely sound out my father by this time the day after tomorrow! If he is favourably disposed towards you, will I not send you word and let you know? ¹³But if my father is inclined to harm you, may the LORD deal with me, be it ever so severely, if I do not let you know and

send you away safely. May the LORD be with you as he has been with my father. ¹⁴But show me unfailing kindness like that of the LORD as long as I live, so that I may not be killed, ¹⁵and do not ever cut off your kindness from my family—not even when the LORD has cut off every one of David's enemies from the face of the earth."

¹⁶So Jonathan made a covenant with the house of David, saying, "May the LORD call David's enemies to account." ¹⁷And Jonathan made David reaffirm his oath out of love for him, because he loved him as he loved himself.

¹⁸Then Jonathan said to David: "Tomorrow is the New Moon festival. You will be missed, because your seat will be empty. ¹⁹The day after tomorrow, towards evening, go to the place where you hid when this trouble began, and wait by the stone Ezel. ²⁰I will shoot three arrows to the side of it, as though I were shooting at a target. ²¹Then I will send a boy and say, 'Go, find the arrows.' If I say to him, 'Look, the arrows are on this side of you; bring them here,' then come, because, as surely as the LORD lives, you are safe; there is no danger. ²²But if I say to the boy, 'Look, the arrows are beyond you,' then you must go, because the LORD has sent you away. ²³And about the matter you and I discussed—remember, the LORD is witness between you and me for ever."

²⁴So David hid in the field, and when the New Moon festival came, the king sat down to eat. ²⁵He sat in his customary place by the wall, opposite Jonathan,ᵃ and Abner sat next to Saul, but David's place was empty. ²⁶Saul said nothing that day, for he thought, "Something must have happened to David to make him ceremonially unclean—surely he is unclean." ²⁷But the next day, the second day of the month, David's place was empty again. Then Saul said to his son Jonathan, "Why hasn't the son of Jesse come to the meal, either yesterday or today?"

²⁸Jonathan answered, "David earnestly asked me for permission to go to Bethlehem. ²⁹He said, 'Let me go, because our family is observing a sacrifice in the town and my brother has ordered me to be there. If I have found favour in your eyes, let me go to see my brothers.' That is why he has not come to the king's table."

³⁰Saul's anger flared up at Jonathan and he said to him, "You son of a perverse and rebellious woman! Don't I know that you have sided with the son of Jesse to your own shame and to the shame of the mother who bore you? ³¹As long as the son of Jesse lives on this earth, neither you nor your kingdom will be established. Now send and bring him to me, for he must die!"

³²"Why should he be put to death? What has he done?" Jonathan asked his father. ³³But Saul hurled his spear at him to kill him. Then Jonathan knew that his father intended to kill David.

³⁴Jonathan got up from the table in fierce anger; on that second day of the month he did

---

ᵃ25 Septuagint; Hebrew *wall. Jonathan arose*

1 SAMUEL 20:1–9

Jonathan said. 'If I had the least inkling that my father was determined to harm you, wouldn't I tell you?' (v. 9).

FRIENDSHIP. Today's reading deals with David's need to escape from Saul's desire to kill him. This account centres around the friendship between Jonathan and David and we notice that Jonathan had no inkling of his father's malicious plans for securing David's death (compare 19:1–5). It seems that the editor of 1 Samuel has woven a second traditional account of this episode in David's life into his narrative.

However, this story gives us a valuable insight into the benefits and problems of friendship. Friends can give each other helpful support during times of crisis, but friendship can also introduce tension into human relationships. Jonathan was loyal to David and because of that their friendship has been regarded as an ideal example, but not all friendships are like that.

Perhaps this is why Christian writers in all ages have been concerned about the quality of friendships. Managing our friendship can be a bit like trying to control two horses at once: riding one and trying to direct the other by means of a halter or rein. The whole enterprise presents little difficulty so long as both animals keep close together and agree to go in the same direction. But when the second horse decides to follow its own course, trouble looms ahead. The rider has to decide at which point he releases the halter, or the control of both animals is lost and he or she ends up in a heap on the ground.

A true friend is one to whom you can tip out all the contents of your heart, chaff and grain together, knowing that the gentlest hands will take it and sift it, keep what is worth keeping, and with the breath of kindness will blow the rest away. (Old Arabic definition)

→252

2 SAMUEL 6:1–11

'David again brought together out of Israel chosen men . . . and . . . set out from Baalah of Judah to bring up from there the ark of God, which is called by . . . the name of the LORD Almighty' (vv. 1, 2).

DANGER: AVOID CONTACT. The Ark of the Covenant (Covenant Box, GNB) was a most important object so far as Hebrew religion was concerned. It had been constructed to most detailed specifications, following the giving of the law at Sinai. The purpose of the Ark was to help the people to appreciate the presence and availability of the invisible God. In Exodus 25:22 we have a statement about the function of the Ark: the presence of God dwelt above the mercy seat, between the two cherubim, and there he and his people could meet.

David saw the importance of the Ark to the religious life of the people, and since he wanted to make Jerusalem the religious centre of the nation, he set out to bring the sacred object to the city. It had remained at Kiriath-Jearim (see 1 Chron. 13:6) since its return from Philistine capture (1 Sam. 6:20–7:1).

The attempt to remove the Ark was not without incident. The death of Uzzah reflects the Hebrew belief that contact with holiness could prove fatal unless proper rituals and safeguards were observed. It has been pointed out that this belief was so strongly held that any transgression of the taboo could lead to terror and death.

We should not attribute Uzzah's death to divine anger, for our Christian view of God sees his love and forgiveness as well as his transcendent holiness.

We should not be careless in our approach to God, but let our awe result in worship and not in terror.

→269

not eat, because he was grieved at his father's shameful treatment of David.

[35]In the morning Jonathan went out to the field for his meeting with David. He had a small boy with him, [36]and he said to the boy, "Run and find the arrows I shoot." As the boy ran, he shot an arrow beyond him. [37]When the boy came to the place where Jonathan's arrow had fallen, Jonathan called out after him, "Isn't the arrow beyond you?" [38]Then he shouted, "Hurry! Go quickly! Don't stop!" The boy picked up the arrow and returned to his master. [39](The boy knew nothing of all this; only Jonathan and David knew.) [40]Then Jonathan gave his weapons to the boy and said, "Go, carry them back to town."

[41]After the boy had gone, David got up from the south side ⌊of the stone⌋ and bowed down before Jonathan three times, with his face to the ground. Then they kissed each other and wept together—but David wept the most.

[42]Jonathan said to David, "Go in peace, for we have sworn friendship with each other in the name of the LORD, saying, 'The LORD is witness between you and me, and between your descendants and my descendants for ever.'" Then David left, and Jonathan went back to the town.

David at Nob

21 David went to Nob, to Ahimelech the priest. Ahimelech trembled when he met him, and asked, "Why are you alone? Why is no-one with you?"

[2]David answered Ahimelech the priest, "The king charged me with a certain matter and said to me, 'No-one is to know anything about your mission and your instructions.' As for my men, I have told them to meet me at a certain place. [3]Now then, what have you to hand? Give me five loaves of bread, or whatever you can find."

[4]But the priest answered David, "I don't have any ordinary bread to hand; however, there is some consecrated bread here—provided the men have kept themselves from women."

[5]David replied, "Indeed women have been kept from us, as usual whenever[a] I set out. The men's things[b] are holy even on missions that are not holy. How much more so to-day!" [6]So the priest gave him the consecrated bread, since there was no bread there except the bread of the Presence that had been removed from before the LORD and replaced by hot bread on the day it was taken away.

[7]Now one of Saul's servants was there that day, detained before the LORD; he was Doeg the Edomite, Saul's head shepherd.

[8]David asked Ahimelech, "Don't you have a spear or sword here? I haven't brought my sword or any other weapon, because the king's business was urgent."

[9]The priest replied, "The sword of Goliath the Philistine, whom you killed in the Valley of Elah, is here; it is wrapped in a cloth behind the ephod. If you want it, take it; there is no sword here but that one."

David said, "There is none like it; give it to me."

David at Gath

[10]That day David fled from Saul and went to Achish king of Gath. [11]But the servants of Achish said to him, "Isn't this David, the king of the land? Isn't he the one they sing about in their dances:

"'Saul has slain his thousands,
    and David his tens of thousands'?"

[12]David took these words to heart and was very much afraid of Achish king of Gath. [13]So he feigned insanity in their presence; and while he was in their hands he acted like a madman, making marks on the doors of the gate and letting saliva run down his beard.

[14]Achish said to his servants, "Look at the man! He is insane! Why bring him to me? [15]Am I so short of madmen that you have to bring this fellow here to carry on like this in front of me? Must this man come into my house?"

David at Adullam and Mizpah

22 David left Gath and escaped to the cave of Adullam. When his brothers and his father's household heard about it, they went down to him there. [2]All those who were in distress or in debt or discontented gathered round him, and he became their leader. About four hundred men were with him.

[3]From there David went to Mizpah in Moab and said to the king of Moab, "Would you let my father and mother come and stay with you until I learn what God will do for me?" [4]So he left them with the king of Moab, and they stayed with him as long as David was in the stronghold.

[5]But the prophet Gad said to David, "Do not stay in the stronghold. Go into the land of Judah." So David left and went to the forest of Hereth.

Saul Kills the Priests of Nob

[6]Now Saul heard that David and his men had been discovered. And Saul, spear in hand, was seated under the tamarisk tree on the hill at Gibeah, with all his officials standing round him. [7]Saul said to them, "Listen, men of Benjamin! Will the son of Jesse give all of you fields and vineyards? Will he make all of you commanders of thousands and commanders of hundreds? [8]Is that why you have all conspired against me? No-one tells me when my son makes a covenant with the son of Jesse. None of you is concerned about me or tells me that my son has incited my servant to lie in wait for me, as he does today."

[9]But Doeg the Edomite, who was standing with Saul's officials, said, "I saw the son of Jesse come to Ahimelech son of Ahitub at Nob. [10]Ahimelech enquired of the LORD for

---

[a]5 Or from us in the past few days since   [b]5 Or bodies

him; he also gave him provisions and the sword of Goliath the Philistine.''

11Then the king sent for the priest Ahimelech son of Ahitub and his father's whole family, who were the priests at Nob, and they all came to the king. 12Saul said, "Listen now, son of Ahitub."

"Yes, my lord," he answered.

13Saul said to him, "Why have you conspired against me, you and the son of Jesse, giving him bread and a sword and enquiring of God for him, so that he has rebelled against me and lies in wait for me, as he does today?"

14Ahimelech answered the king, "Who of all your servants is as loyal as David, the king's son-in-law, captain of your bodyguard and highly respected in your household? 15Was that day the first time I enquired of God for him? Of course not! Let not the king accuse your servant or any of his father's family, for your servant knows nothing at all about this whole affair."

16But the king said, "You shall surely die, Ahimelech, you and your father's whole family."

17Then the king ordered the guards at his side: "Turn and kill the priests of the LORD, because they too have sided with David. They knew he was fleeing, yet they did not tell me."

But the king's officials were not willing to raise a hand to strike the priests of the LORD.

18The king then ordered Doeg, "You turn and strike down the priests." So Doeg the Edomite turned and struck them down. That day he killed eighty-five men who wore the linen ephod. 19He also put to the sword Nob, the town of the priests, with its men and women, its children and infants, and its cattle, donkeys and sheep.

20But Abiathar, son of Ahimelech son of Ahitub, escaped and fled to join David. 21He told David that Saul had killed the priests of the LORD. 22Then David said to Abiathar: "That day, when Doeg the Edomite was there, I knew he would be sure to tell Saul. I am responsible for the death of your father's whole family. 23Stay with me; don't be afraid; the man who is seeking your life is seeking mine also. You will be safe with me."

David Saves Keilah

23 When David was told, "Look, the Philistines are fighting against Keilah and are looting the threshing-floors," 2he enquired of the LORD, saying, "Shall I go and attack these Philistines?"

The LORD answered him, "Go, attack the Philistines and save Keilah."

3But David's men said to him, "Here in Judah we are afraid. How much more, then, if we go to Keilah against the Philistine forces!"

4Once again David enquired of the LORD, and the LORD answered him, "Go down to Keilah, for I am going to give the Philistines into your hand." 5So David and his men went to Keilah, fought the Philistines and carried off their livestock. He inflicted heavy losses on the Philistines and saved the people of Keilah. 6(Now Abiathar son of Ahimelech had brought the ephod down with him when he fled to David at Keilah.)

Saul Pursues David

7Saul was told that David had gone to Keilah, and he said, "God has handed him over to me, for David has imprisoned himself by entering a town with gates and bars." 8And Saul called up all his forces for battle, to go down to Keilah to besiege David and his men.

9When David learned that Saul was plotting against him, he said to Abiathar the priest, "Bring the ephod." 10David said, "O LORD, God of Israel, your servant has heard definitely that Saul plans to come to Keilah and destroy the town on account of me. 11Will the citizens of Keilah surrender me to him? Will Saul come down, as your servant has heard? O LORD, God of Israel, tell your servant."

And the LORD said, "He will."

12Again David asked, "Will the citizens of Keilah surrender me and my men to Saul?"

And the LORD said, "They will."

13So David and his men, about six hundred in number, left Keilah and kept moving from place to place. When Saul was told that David had escaped from Keilah, he did not go there.

14David stayed in the desert strongholds and in the hills of the Desert of Ziph. Day after day Saul searched for him, but God did not give David into his hands.

15While David was at Horesh in the Desert of Ziph, he learned that Saul had come out to take his life. 16And Saul's son Jonathan went to David at Horesh and helped him to find strength in God. 17"Don't be afraid," he said. "My father Saul will not lay a hand on you. You shall be king over Israel, and I will be second to you. Even my father Saul knows this." 18The two of them made a covenant before the LORD. Then Jonathan went home, but David remained at Horesh.

19The Ziphites went up to Saul at Gibeah and said, "Is not David hiding among us in the strongholds at Horesh, on the hill of Hakilah, south of Jeshimon? 20Now, O king, come down whenever it pleases you to do so, and we will be responsible for handing him over to the king."

21Saul replied, "The LORD bless you for your concern for me. 22Go and make further preparation. Find out where David usually goes and who has seen him there. They tell me he is very crafty. 23Find out about all the hiding-places he uses and come back to me with definite information.a Then I will go with you; if he is in the area, I will track him down among all the clans of Judah."

24So they set out and went to Ziph ahead of Saul. Now David and his men were in the Desert of Maon, in the Arabah south of Jeshimon. 25Saul and his men began the search, and when David was told about it, he went

a23 Or me at Nacon

down to the rock and stayed in the Desert of Maon. When Saul heard this, he went into the Desert of Maon in pursuit of David.

26Saul was going along one side of the mountain, and David and his men were on the other side, hurrying to get away from Saul. As Saul and his forces were closing in on David and his men to capture them, 27a messenger came to Saul, saying, "Come quickly! The Philistines are raiding the land." 28Then Saul broke off his pursuit of David and went to meet the Philistines. That is why they call this place Sela Hammahlekoth.b 29And David went up from there and lived in the strongholds of En Gedi.

David Spares Saul's Life

24 After Saul returned from pursuing the Philistines, he was told, "David is in the Desert of En Gedi." 2So Saul took three thousand chosen men from all Israel and set out to look for David and his men near the Crags of the Wild Goats.

3He came to the sheep pens along the way; a cave was there, and Saul went in to relieve himself. David and his men were far back in the cave. 4The men said, "This is the day the LORD spoke of when he saida to you, 'I will give your enemy into your hands for you to deal with as you wish.'" Then David crept up unnoticed and cut off a corner of Saul's robe.

5Afterwards, David was conscience-stricken for having cut off a corner of his robe. 6He said to his men, "The LORD forbid that I should do such a thing to my master, the LORD's anointed, or lift my hand against him; for he is the anointed of the LORD." 7With these words David rebuked his men and did not allow them to attack Saul. And Saul left the cave and went his way.

8Then David went out of the cave and called out to Saul, "My lord the king!" When Saul looked behind him, David bowed down and prostrated himself with his face to the ground. 9He said to Saul, "Why do you listen when men say, 'David is bent on harming you'? 10This day you have seen with your own eyes how the LORD gave you into my hands in the cave. Some urged me to kill you, but I spared you; I said, 'I will not lift my hand against my master, because he is the LORD's anointed.' 11See, my father, look at this piece of your robe in my hand! I cut off the corner of your robe but did not kill you. Now understand and recognise that I am not guilty of wrongdoing or rebellion. I have not wronged you, but you are hunting me down to take my life. 12May the LORD judge between you and me. And may the LORD avenge the wrongs you have done to me, but my hand will not touch you. 13As the old saying goes, 'From evildoers come evil deeds,' so my hand will not touch you.

14"Against whom has the king of Israel come out? Whom are you pursuing? A dead dog? A flea? 15May the LORD be our judge and decide between us. May he consider my cause and uphold it; may he vindicate me by delivering me from your hand."

16When David finished saying this, Saul asked, "Is that your voice, David my son?" And he wept aloud. 17"You are more righteous than I," he said. "You have treated me well, but I have treated you badly. 18You have just now told me of the good you did to me; the LORD gave me into your hands, but you did not kill me. 19When a man finds his enemy, does he let him get away unharmed? May the LORD reward you well for the way you treated me today. 20I know that you will surely be king and that the kingdom of Israel will be established in your hands. 21Now swear to me by the LORD that you will not cut off my descendants or wipe out my name from my father's family."

22So David gave his oath to Saul. Then Saul returned home, but David and his men went up to the stronghold.

David, Nabal and Abigail

25 Now Samuel died, and all Israel assembled and mourned for him; and they buried him at his home in Ramah.

Then David moved down into the Desert of Maon.a 2A certain man in Maon, who had property there at Carmel, was very wealthy. He had a thousand goats and three thousand sheep, which he was shearing in Carmel. 3His name was Nabal and his wife's name was Abigail. She was an intelligent and beautiful woman, but her husband, a Calebite, was surly and mean in his dealings.

4While David was in the desert, he heard that Nabal was shearing sheep. 5So he sent ten young men and said to them, "Go up to Nabal at Carmel and greet him in my name. 6Say to him: 'Long life to you! Good health to you and your household! And good health to all that is yours!

7"'Now I hear that it is sheep-shearing time. When your shepherds were with us, we did not ill-treat them, and the whole time they were at Carmel nothing of theirs was missing. 8Ask your own servants and they will tell you. Therefore be favourable towards my young men, since we come at a festive time. Please give your servants and your son David whatever you can find for them.'"

9When David's men arrived, they gave Nabal this message in David's name. Then they waited.

10Nabal answered David's servants, "Who is this David? Who is this son of Jesse? Many servants are breaking away from their masters these days. 11Why should I take my bread and water, and the meat I have slaughtered for my shearers, and give it to men coming from who knows where?"

12David's men turned round and went back. When they arrived, they reported every word. 13David said to his men, "Put on your swords!" So they put on their swords, and David put on his. About four hundred men went up with David, while two hundred stayed with the supplies.

---

b28 Sela Hammahlekoth means rock of parting.   a4 Or "Today the LORD is saying
a1 Some Septuagint manuscripts; Hebrew Paran

¹⁴One of the servants told Nabal's wife Abigail: "David sent messengers from the desert to give our master his greetings, but he hurled insults at them. ¹⁵Yet these men were very good to us. They did not ill-treat us, and the whole time we were out in the fields near them nothing was missing. ¹⁶Night and day they were a wall around us all the time we were herding our sheep near them. ¹⁷Now think it over and see what you can do, because disaster is hanging over our master and his whole household. He is such a wicked man that no-one can talk to him."

¹⁸Abigail lost no time. She took two hundred loaves of bread, two skins of wine, five dressed sheep, five seahs*b* of roasted grain, a hundred cakes of raisins and two hundred cakes of pressed figs, and loaded them on donkeys. ¹⁹Then she told her servants, "Go on ahead; I'll follow you." But she did not tell her husband Nabal.

²⁰As she came riding her donkey into a mountain ravine, there were David and his men descending towards her, and she met them. ²¹David had just said, "It's been useless—all my watching over this fellow's property in the desert so that nothing of his was missing. He has paid me back evil for good. ²²May God deal with David,*c* be it ever so severely, if by morning I leave alive one male of all who belong to him!"

²³When Abigail saw David, she quickly got off her donkey and bowed down before David with her face to the ground. ²⁴She fell at his feet and said: "My lord, let the blame be on me alone. Please let your servant speak to you; hear what your servant has to say. ²⁵May my lord pay no attention to that wicked man Nabal. He is just like his name —his name is Fool, and folly goes with him. But as for me, your servant, I did not see the men my master sent.

²⁶"Now since the LORD has kept you, my master, from bloodshed and from avenging yourself with your own hands, as surely as the LORD lives and as you live, may your enemies and all who intend to harm my master be like Nabal. ²⁷And let this gift, which your servant has brought to my master, be given to the men who follow you. ²⁸Please forgive your servant's offence, for the LORD will certainly make a lasting dynasty for my master, because he fights the LORD's battles. Let no wrongdoing be found in you as long as you live. ²⁹Even though someone is pursuing you to take your life, the life of my master will be bound securely in the bundle of the living by the LORD your God. But the lives of your enemies he will hurl away as from the pocket of a sling. ³⁰When the LORD has done for my master every good thing he promised concerning him and has appointed him leader over Israel, ³¹my master will not have on his conscience the staggering burden of needless bloodshed or of having avenged himself. And when the LORD has brought my master success, remember your servant."

³²David said to Abigail, "Praise be to the LORD, the God of Israel, who has sent you today to meet me. ³³May you be blessed for your good judgment and for keeping me from bloodshed this day and from avenging myself with my own hands. ³⁴Otherwise, as surely as the LORD, the God of Israel, lives, who has kept me from harming you, if you had not come quickly to meet me, not one male belonging to Nabal would have been left alive by daybreak."

³⁵Then David accepted from her hand what she had brought to him and said, "Go home in peace. I have heard your words and granted your request."

³⁶When Abigail went to Nabal, he was in the house holding a banquet like that of a king. He was in high spirits and very drunk. So she told him nothing until daybreak. ³⁷Then in the morning, when Nabal was sober, his wife told him all these things, and his heart failed him and he became like a stone. ³⁸About ten days later, the LORD struck Nabal and he died.

³⁹When David heard that Nabal was dead, he said, "Praise be to the LORD, who has upheld my cause against Nabal for treating me with contempt. He has kept his servant from doing wrong and has brought Nabal's wrongdoing down on his own head."

Then David sent word to Abigail, asking her to become his wife. ⁴⁰His servants went to Carmel and said to Abigail, "David has sent us to you to take you to become his wife."

⁴¹She bowed down with her face to the ground and said, "Here is your maidservant, ready to serve you and wash the feet of my master's servants." ⁴²Abigail quickly got on a donkey and, attended by her five maids, went with David's messengers and became his wife. ⁴³David had also married Ahinoam of Jezreel, and they both were his wives. ⁴⁴But Saul had given his daughter Michal, David's wife, to Paltiel*d* son of Laish, who was from Gallim.

David Again Spares Saul's Life

26 The Ziphites went to Saul at Gibeah and said, "Is not David hiding on the hill of Hakilah, which faces Jeshimon?"

²So Saul went down to the Desert of Ziph, with his three thousand chosen men of Israel, to search there for David. ³Saul made his camp beside the road on the hill of Hakilah facing Jeshimon, but David stayed in the desert. When he saw that Saul had followed him there, ⁴he sent out scouts and learned that Saul had definitely arrived.*a*

⁵Then David set out and went to the place where Saul had camped. He saw where Saul and Abner son of Ner, the commander of the army, had lain down. Saul was lying inside the camp, with the army encamped around him.

⁶David then asked Ahimelech the Hittite and Abishai son of Zeruiah, Joab's brother,

---

b18 That is, probably about a bushel (about 37 litres)
c22 Some Septuagint manuscripts; Hebrew *with David's enemies*
d44 Hebrew *Palti*, a variant of *Paltiel*   *a4* Or *had come to Nacon*

"Who will go down into the camp with me to Saul?"

"I'll go with you," said Abishai.

⁷So David and Abishai went to the army by night, and there was Saul, lying asleep inside the camp with his spear stuck in the ground near his head. Abner and the soldiers were lying round him.

⁸Abishai said to David, "Today God has given your enemy into your hands. Now let me pin him to the ground with one thrust of my spear; I won't strike him twice."

⁹But David said to Abishai, "Don't destroy him! Who can lay a hand on the LORD's anointed and be guiltless? ¹⁰As surely as the LORD lives," he said, "the LORD himself will strike him; either his time will come and he will die, or he will go into battle and perish. ¹¹But the LORD forbid that I should lay a hand on the LORD's anointed. Now get the spear and water jug that are near his head, and let's go."

¹²So David took the spear and water jug near Saul's head, and they left. No-one saw or knew about it, nor did anyone wake up. They were all sleeping, because the LORD had put them into a deep sleep.

¹³Then David crossed over to the other side and stood on top of the hill some distance away; there was a wide space between them. ¹⁴He called out to the army and to Abner son of Ner, "Aren't you going to answer me, Abner?"

Abner replied, "Who are you who calls to the king?"

¹⁵David said, "You're a man, aren't you? And who is like you in Israel? Why didn't you guard your lord the king? Someone came to destroy your lord the king. ¹⁶What you have done is not good. As surely as the LORD lives, you and your men deserve to die, because you did not guard your master, the LORD's anointed. Look around you. Where are the king's spear and water jug that were near his head?"

¹⁷Saul recognised David's voice and said, "Is that your voice, David my son?"

David replied, "Yes it is, my lord the king." ¹⁸And he added, "Why is my lord pursuing his servant? What have I done, and what wrong am I guilty of? ¹⁹Now let my lord the king listen to his servant's words. If the LORD has incited you against me, then may he accept an offering. If, however, men have done it, may they be cursed before the LORD! They have now driven me from my share in the LORD's inheritance and have said, 'Go, serve other gods.' ²⁰Now do not let my blood fall to the ground far from the presence of the LORD. The king of Israel has come out to look for a flea—as one hunts a partridge in the mountains."

²¹Then Saul said, "I have sinned. Come back, David my son. Because you considered my life precious today, I will not try to harm you again. Surely I have acted like a fool and have erred greatly."

²²"Here is the king's spear," David answered. "Let one of your young men come over and get it. ²³The LORD rewards every man for his righteousness and faithfulness.

The LORD gave you into my hands today, but I would not lay a hand on the LORD's anointed. ²⁴As surely as I valued your life today, so may the LORD value my life and deliver me from all trouble."

²⁵Then Saul said to David, "May you be blessed, my son David; you will do great things and surely triumph."

So David went on his way, and Saul returned home.

David Among the Philistines

27 But David thought to himself, "One of these days I shall be destroyed by the hand of Saul. The best thing I can do is to escape to the land of the Philistines. Then Saul will give up searching for me anywhere in Israel, and I will slip out of his hand."

²So David and the six hundred men with him left and went over to Achish son of Maoch king of Gath. ³David and his men settled in Gath with Achish. Each man had his family with him, and David had his two wives: Ahinoam of Jezreel and Abigail of Carmel, the widow of Nabal. ⁴When Saul was told that David had fled to Gath, he no longer searched for him.

⁵Then David said to Achish, "If I have found favour in your eyes, let a place be assigned to me in one of the country towns, that I may live there. Why should your servant live in the royal city with you?"

⁶So on that day Achish gave him Ziklag, and it has belonged to the kings of Judah ever since. ⁷David lived in Philistine territory for a year and four months.

⁸Now David and his men went up and raided the Geshurites, the Girzites and the Amalekites. (From ancient times these peoples had lived in the land extending to Shur and Egypt.) ⁹Whenever David attacked an area, he did not leave a man or woman alive, but took sheep and cattle, donkeys and camels, and clothes. Then he returned to Achish.

¹⁰When Achish asked, "Where did you go raiding today?" David would say, "Against the Negev of Judah" or "Against the Negev of Jerahmeel" or "Against the Negev of the Kenites." ¹¹He did not leave a man or woman alive to be brought to Gath, for he thought, "They might inform on us and say, 'This is what David did.'" And such was his practice as long as he lived in Philistine territory. ¹²Achish trusted David and said to himself, "He has become so odious to his people, the Israelites, that he will be my servant for ever."

Saul and the Witch of Endor

28 In those days the Philistines gathered their forces to fight against Israel. Achish said to David, "You must understand that you and your men will accompany me in the army."

²David said, "Then you will see for yourself what your servant can do."

Achish replied, "Very well, I will make you my bodyguard for life."

³Now Samuel was dead, and all Israel had mourned for him and buried him in his own

town of Ramah. Saul had expelled the mediums and spiritists from the land.

4The Philistines assembled and came and set up camp at Shunem, while Saul gathered all the Israelites and set up camp at Gilboa. 5When Saul saw the Philistine army, he was afraid; terror filled his heart. 6He enquired of the LORD, but the LORD did not answer him by dreams or Urim or prophets. 7Saul then said to his attendants, "Find me a woman who is a medium, so that I may go and enquire of her."

"There is one in Endor," they said.

8So Saul disguised himself, putting on other clothes, and at night he and two men went to the woman. "Consult a spirit for me," he said, "and bring up for me the one I name."

9But the woman said to him, "Surely you know what Saul has done. He has cut off the mediums and spiritists from the land. Why have you set a trap for my life to bring about my death?"

10Saul swore to her by the LORD, "As surely as the LORD lives, you will not be punished for this."

11Then the woman asked, "Whom shall I bring up for you?"

"Bring up Samuel," he said.

12When the woman saw Samuel, she cried out at the top of her voice and said to Saul, "Why have you deceived me? You are Saul!"

13The king said to her, "Don't be afraid. What do you see?"

The woman said, "I see a spirita coming up out of the ground."

14"What does he look like?" he asked.

"An old man wearing a robe is coming up," she said.

Then Saul knew it was Samuel, and he bowed down and prostrated himself with his face to the ground.

15Samuel said to Saul, "Why have you disturbed me by bringing me up?"

"I am in great distress," Saul said. "The Philistines are fighting against me, and God has turned away from me. He no longer answers me, either by prophets or by dreams. So I have called on you to tell me what to do."

16Samuel said, "Why do you consult me, now that the LORD has turned away from you and become your enemy? 17The LORD has done what he predicted through me. The LORD has torn the kingdom out of your hands and given it to one of your neighbours—to David. 18Because you did not obey the LORD or carry out his fierce wrath against the Amalekites, the LORD has done this to you today. 19The LORD will hand over both Israel and you to the Philistines, and tomorrow you and your sons will be with me. The LORD will also hand over the army of Israel to the Philistines."

20Immediately Saul fell full length on the ground, filled with fear because of Samuel's words. His strength was gone, for he had eaten nothing all that day and night.

21When the woman came to Saul and saw that he was greatly shaken, she said, "Look, your maidservant has obeyed you. I took my life in my hands and did what you told me to do. 22Now please listen to your servant and let me give you some food so that you may eat and have the strength to go on your way."

23He refused and said, "I will not eat."

But his men joined the woman in urging him, and he listened to them. He got up from the ground and sat on the couch.

24The woman had a fattened calf at the house, which she slaughtered at once. She took some flour, kneaded it and baked bread without yeast. 25Then she set it before Saul and his men, and they ate. That same night they got up and left.

Achish Sends David Back to Ziklag

29 The Philistines gathered all their forces at Aphek, and Israel camped by the spring in Jezreel. 2As the Philistine rulers marched with their units of hundreds and thousands, David and his men were marching at the rear with Achish. 3The commanders of the Philistines asked, "What about these Hebrews?"

Achish replied, "Is this not David, who was an officer of Saul king of Israel? He has already been with me for over a year, and from the day he left Saul until now, I have found no fault in him."

4But the Philistine commanders were angry with him and said, "Send the man back, that he may return to the place you assigned him. He must not go with us into battle, or he will turn against us during the fighting. How better could he regain his master's favour than by taking the heads of our own men? 5Isn't this the David they sang about in their dances:

"'Saul has slain his thousands,
    and David his tens of thousands'?"

6So Achish called David and said to him, "As surely as the LORD lives, you have been reliable, and I would be pleased to have you serve with me in the army. From the day you came to me until now, I have found no fault in you, but the rulers don't approve of you. 7Turn back and go in peace; do nothing to displease the Philistine rulers."

8"But what have I done?" asked David. "What have you found against your servant from the day I came to you until now? Why can't I go and fight against the enemies of my lord the king?"

9Achish answered, "I know that you have been as pleasing in my eyes as an angel of God; nevertheless, the Philistine commanders have said, 'He must not go up with us into battle.' 10Now get up early, along with your master's servants who have come with you, and leave in the morning as soon as it is light."

11So David and his men got up early in the morning to go back to the land of the Philistines, and the Philistines went up to Jezreel.

a13 Or see spirits; or see gods

David Destroys the Amalekites

30 David and his men reached Ziklag on the third day. Now the Amalekites had raided the Negev and Ziklag. They had attacked Ziklag and burned it, 2and had taken captive the women and all who were in it, both young and old. They killed none of them, but carried them off as they went on their way.

3When David and his men came to Ziklag, they found it destroyed by fire and their wives and sons and daughters taken captive. 4So David and his men wept aloud until they had no strength left to weep. 5David's two wives had been captured—Ahinoam of Jezreel and Abigail, the widow of Nabal of Carmel. 6David was greatly distressed because the men were talking of stoning him; each one was bitter in spirit because of his sons and daughters. But David found strength in the LORD his God.

7Then David said to Abiathar the priest, the son of Ahimelech, "Bring me the ephod." Abiathar brought it to him, 8and David enquired of the LORD, "Shall I pursue this raiding party? Will I overtake them?"

"Pursue them," he answered. "You will certainly overtake them and succeed in the rescue."

9David and the six hundred men with him came to the Besor Ravine, where some stayed behind, 10for two hundred men were too exhausted to cross the ravine. But David and four hundred men continued the pursuit.

11They found an Egyptian in a field and brought him to David. They gave him water to drink and food to eat—12part of a cake of pressed figs and two cakes of raisins. He ate and was revived, for he had not eaten any food or drunk any water for three days and three nights.

13David asked him, "To whom do you belong, and where do you come from?"

He said, "I am an Egyptian, the slave of an Amalekite. My master abandoned me when I became ill three days ago. 14We raided the Negev of the Kerethites and the territory belonging to Judah and the Negev of Caleb. And we burned Ziklag."

15David asked him, "Can you lead me down to this raiding party?"

He answered, "Swear to me before God that you will not kill me or hand me over to my master, and I will take you down to them."

16He led David down, and there they were, scattered over the countryside, eating, drinking and revelling because of the great amount of plunder they had taken from the land of the Philistines and from Judah. 17David fought them from dusk until the evening of the next day, and none of them got away, except four hundred young men who rode off on camels and fled. 18David recovered everything the Amalekites had taken, including his two wives. 19Nothing was missing: young or old, boy or girl, plunder or anything else they had taken. David brought everything back. 20He took all the flocks and herds, and his men drove them ahead of the other livestock, saying, "This is David's plunder."

21Then David came to the two hundred men who had been too exhausted to follow him and who were left behind at the Besor Ravine. They came out to meet David and the people with him. As David and his men approached, he greeted them. 22But all the evil men and troublemakers among David's followers said, "Because they did not go out with us, we will not share with them the plunder we recovered. However, each man may take his wife and children and go."

23David replied, "No, my brothers, you must not do that with what the LORD has given us. He has protected us and handed over to us the forces that came against us. 24Who will listen to what you say? The share of the man who stayed with the supplies is to be the same as that of him who went down to the battle. All shall share alike." 25David made this a statute and ordinance for Israel from that day to this.

26When David arrived in Ziklag, he sent some of the plunder to the elders of Judah, who were his friends, saying, "Here is a present for you from the plunder of the LORD's enemies."

27He sent it to those who were in Bethel, Ramoth Negev and Jattir; 28to those in Aroer, Siphmoth, Eshtemoa 29and Racal; to those in the towns of the Jerahmeelites and the Kenites; 30to those in Hormah, Bor Ashan, Athach 31and Hebron; and to those in all the other places where David and his men had roamed.

Saul Takes His Life

31 Now the Philistines fought against Israel; the Israelites fled before them, and many fell slain on Mount Gilboa. 2The Philistines pressed hard after Saul and his sons, and they killed his sons Jonathan, Abinadab and Malki-Shua. 3The fighting grew fierce around Saul, and when the archers overtook him, they wounded him critically.

4Saul said to his armour-bearer, "Draw your sword and run me through, or these uncircumcised fellows will come and run me through and abuse me."

But the armour-bearer was terrified and would not do it; so Saul took his own sword and fell on it. 5When the armour-bearer saw that Saul was dead, he too fell on his sword and died with him. 6So Saul and his three sons and his armour-bearer and all his men died together that same day.

7When the Israelites along the valley and those across the Jordan saw that the Israelite army had fled and that Saul and his sons had died, they abandoned their towns and fled. And the Philistines came and occupied them.

8The next day, when the Philistines came to strip the dead, they found Saul and his three sons fallen on Mount Gilboa. 9They cut off his head and stripped off his armour, and they sent messengers throughout the land of the Philistines to proclaim the news in the temple of their idols and among their people. 10They put his armour in the temple of the Ashtoreths and fastened his body to the wall of Beth Shan.

11When the people of Jabesh Gilead heard

of what the Philistines had done to Saul, [12]all their valiant men journeyed through the night to Beth Shan. They took down the bodies of Saul and his sons from the wall of Beth Shan and went to Jabesh, where they burned them. [13]Then they took their bones and buried them under a tamarisk tree at Jabesh, and they fasted seven days.

2 Samuel

David Hears of Saul's Death

1 After the death of Saul, David returned from defeating the Amalekites and stayed in Ziklag two days. ²On the third day a man arrived from Saul's camp, with his clothes torn and with dust on his head. When he came to David, he fell to the ground to pay him honour.

³"Where have you come from?" David asked him.

He answered, "I have escaped from the Israelite camp."

⁴"What happened?" David asked. "Tell me."

He said, "The men fled from the battle. Many of them fell and died. And Saul and his son Jonathan are dead."

⁵Then David said to the young man who brought him the report, "How do you know that Saul and his son Jonathan are dead?"

⁶"I happened to be on Mount Gilboa," the young man said, "and there was Saul, leaning on his spear, with the chariots and riders almost upon him. ⁷When he turned round and saw me, he called out to me, and I said, 'What can I do?'

⁸"He asked me, 'Who are you?'

"'An Amalekite,' I answered.

⁹"Then he said to me, 'Stand over me and kill me! I am in the throes of death, but I'm still alive.'

¹⁰"So I stood over him and killed him, because I knew that after he had fallen he could not survive. And I took the crown that was on his head and the band on his arm and have brought them here to my lord."

¹¹Then David and all the men with him took hold of their clothes and tore them. ¹²They mourned and wept and fasted till evening for Saul and his son Jonathan, and for the army of the LORD and the house of Israel, because they had fallen by the sword.

¹³David said to the young man who brought him the report, "Where are you from?"

"I am the son of an alien, an Amalekite," he answered.

¹⁴David asked him, "Why were you not afraid to lift your hand to destroy the LORD's anointed?"

¹⁵Then David called one of his men and said, "Go, strike him down!" So he struck him down, and he died. ¹⁶For David had said to him, "Your blood be on your own head.

Your own mouth testified against you when you said, 'I killed the LORD's anointed.'"

David's Lament for Saul and Jonathan

¹⁷David took up this lament concerning Saul and his son Jonathan, ¹⁸and ordered that the men of Judah be taught this lament of the bow (it is written in the Book of Jashar):

¹⁹"Your glory, O Israel, lies slain on your heights.
 How the mighty have fallen!

²⁰"Tell it not in Gath,
 proclaim it not in the streets of Ashkelon,
 lest the daughters of the Philistines be glad,
 lest the daughters of the uncircumcised rejoice.

²¹"O mountains of Gilboa,
 may you have neither dew nor rain,
 nor fields that yield offerings ⌊of grain⌋.
 For there the shield of the mighty was defiled,
 the shield of Saul—no longer rubbed with oil.

²²From the blood of the slain,
 from the flesh of the mighty,
 the bow of Jonathan did not turn back,
 the sword of Saul did not return unsatisfied.

²³"Saul and Jonathan—
 in life they were loved and gracious,
 and in death they were not parted.
 They were swifter than eagles,
 they were stronger than lions.

²⁴"O daughters of Israel,
 weep for Saul,
 who clothed you in scarlet and finery,
 who adorned your garments with ornaments of gold.

²⁵"How the mighty have fallen in battle!
 Jonathan lies slain on your heights.
²⁶I grieve for you, Jonathan my brother;
 you were very dear to me.
 Your love for me was wonderful,
 more wonderful than that of women.

²⁷"How the mighty have fallen!
 The weapons of war have perished!"

David Anointed King Over Judah

2 In the course of time, David enquired of the LORD. "Shall I go up to one of the towns of Judah?" he asked.

The LORD said, "Go up."

David asked, "Where shall I go?"

"To Hebron," the LORD answered.

2So David went up there with his two wives, Ahinoam of Jezreel and Abigail, the widow of Nabal of Carmel. 3David also took the men who were with him, each with his family, and they settled in Hebron and its towns. 4Then the men of Judah came to Hebron and there they anointed David king over the house of Judah.

When David was told that it was the men of Jabesh Gilead who had buried Saul, 5he sent messengers to the men of Jabesh Gilead to say to them, "The LORD bless you for showing this kindness to Saul your master by burying him. 6May the LORD now show you kindness and faithfulness, and I too will show you the same favour because you have done this. 7Now then, be strong and brave, for Saul your master is dead, and the house of Judah has anointed me king over them."

War Between the Houses of David and Saul

8Meanwhile, Abner son of Ner, the commander of Saul's army, had taken Ish-Bosheth son of Saul and brought him over to Mahanaim. 9He made him king over Gilead, Ashuri[a] and Jezreel, and also over Ephraim, Benjamin and all Israel.

10Ish-Bosheth son of Saul was forty years old when he became king over Israel, and he reigned two years. The house of Judah, however, followed David. 11The length of time David was king in Hebron over the house of Judah was seven years and six months.

12Abner son of Ner, together with the men of Ish-Bosheth son of Saul, left Mahanaim and went to Gibeon. 13Joab son of Zeruiah and David's men went out and met them at the pool of Gibeon. One group sat down on one side of the pool and one group on the other side.

14Then Abner said to Joab, "Let's have some of the young men get up and fight hand to hand in front of us."

"All right, let them do it," Joab said.

15So they stood up and were counted off —twelve men for Benjamin and Ish-Bosheth son of Saul, and twelve for David. 16Then each man grabbed his opponent by the head and thrust his dagger into his opponent's side, and they fell down together. So that place in Gibeon was called Helkath Hazzurim.[b]

17The battle that day was very fierce, and Abner and the men of Israel were defeated by David's men.

18The three sons of Zeruiah were there: Joab, Abishai and Asahel. Now Asahel was as fleet-footed as a wild gazelle. 19He chased Abner, turning neither to the right nor to the left as he pursued him. 20Abner looked behind him and asked, "Is that you, Asahel?"

"It is," he answered.

21Then Abner said to him, "Turn aside to the right or to the left; take on one of the young men and strip him of his weapons." But Asahel would not stop chasing him.

22Again Abner warned Asahel, "Stop chasing me! Why should I strike you down? How could I look your brother Joab in the face?"

23But Asahel refused to give up the pursuit; so Abner thrust the butt of his spear into Asahel's stomach, and the spear came out through his back. He fell there and died on the spot. And every man stopped when he came to the place where Asahel had fallen and died.

24But Joab and Abishai pursued Abner, and as the sun was setting, they came to the hill of Ammah, near Giah on the way to the wasteland of Gibeon. 25Then the men of Benjamin rallied behind Abner. They formed themselves into a group and took their stand on top of a hill.

26Abner called out to Joab, "Must the sword devour for ever? Don't you realise that this will end in bitterness? How long before you order your men to stop pursuing their brothers?"

27Joab answered, "As surely as God lives, if you had not spoken, the men would have continued the pursuit of their brothers until morning."[c]

28So Joab blew the trumpet, and all the men came to a halt; they no longer pursued Israel, nor did they fight any more.

29All that night Abner and his men marched through the Arabah. They crossed the Jordan, continued through the whole Bithron[d] and came to Mahanaim.

30Then Joab returned from pursuing Abner and assembled all his men. Besides Asahel, nineteen of David's men were found missing. 31But David's men had killed 360 Benjamites who were with Abner. 32They took Asahel and buried him in his father's tomb at Bethlehem. Then Joab and his men marched all night and arrived at Hebron by daybreak.

3 The war between the house of Saul and the house of David lasted a long time. David grew stronger and stronger, while the house of Saul grew weaker and weaker.

2Sons were born to David in Hebron:

His firstborn was Amnon the son of Ahinoam of Jezreel;

3his second, Kileab the son of Abigail the widow of Nabal of Carmel;

the third, Absalom the son of Maacah daughter of Talmai king of Geshur;

4the fourth, Adonijah the son of Haggith;

the fifth, Shephatiah the son of Abital;

5and the sixth, Ithream the son of David's wife Eglah.

These were born to David in Hebron.

---

[a]9 Or Asher   [b]16 Helkath Hazzurim means field of daggers or field of hostilities.
[c]27 Or spoken this morning, the men would not have taken up the pursuit of their brothers; or spoken, the men would have given up the pursuit of their brothers by morning
[d]29 Or morning; or ravine; the meaning of the Hebrew for this word is uncertain.

Abner Goes Over to David

⁶During the war between the house of Saul and the house of David, Abner had been strengthening his own position in the house of Saul. ⁷Now Saul had had a concubine named Rizpah daughter of Aiah. And Ish-Bosheth said to Abner, "Why did you sleep with my father's concubine?"

⁸Abner was very angry because of what Ish-Bosheth said and he answered, "Am I a dog's head—on Judah's side? This very day I am loyal to the house of your father Saul and to his family and friends. I haven't handed you over to David. Yet now you accuse me of an offence involving this woman! ⁹May God deal with Abner, be it ever so severely, if I do not do for David what the LORD promised him on oath ¹⁰and transfer the kingdom from the house of Saul and establish David's throne over Israel and Judah from Dan to Beersheba." ¹¹Ish-Bosheth did not dare to say another word to Abner, because he was afraid of him.

¹²Then Abner sent messengers on his behalf to say to David, "Whose land is it? Make an agreement with me, and I will help you bring all Israel over to you."

¹³"Good," said David. "I will make an agreement with you. But I demand one thing of you: Do not come into my presence unless you bring Michal daughter of Saul when you come to see me." ¹⁴Then David sent messengers to Ish-Bosheth son of Saul, demanding, "Give me my wife Michal, whom I betrothed to myself for the price of a hundred Philistine foreskins."

¹⁵So Ish-Bosheth gave orders and had her taken away from her husband Paltiel son of Laish. ¹⁶Her husband, however, went with her, weeping behind her all the way to Bahurim. Then Abner said to him, "Go back home!" So he went back.

¹⁷Abner conferred with the elders of Israel and said, "For some time you have wanted to make David your king. ¹⁸Now do it! For the LORD promised David, 'By my servant David I will rescue my people Israel from the hand of the Philistines and from the hand of all their enemies.'"

¹⁹Abner also spoke to the Benjamites in person. Then he went to Hebron to tell David everything that Israel and the whole house of Benjamin wanted to do. ²⁰When Abner, who had twenty men with him, came to David at Hebron, David prepared a feast for him and his men. ²¹Then Abner said to David, "Let me go at once and assemble all Israel for my lord the king, so that they may make a compact with you, and that you may rule over all that your heart desires." So David sent Abner away, and he went in peace.

Joab Murders Abner

²²Just then David's men and Joab returned from a raid and brought with them a great deal of plunder. But Abner was no longer with David in Hebron, because David had sent him away, and he had gone in peace. ²³When Joab and all the soldiers with him arrived, he was told that Abner son of Ner had come to the king and that the king had sent him away and that he had gone in peace.

²⁴So Joab went to the king and said, "What have you done? Look, Abner came to you. Why did you let him go? Now he is gone! ²⁵You know Abner son of Ner; he came to deceive you and observe your movements and find out everything you are doing."

²⁶Joab then left David and sent messengers after Abner, and they brought him back from the well of Sirah. But David did not know it. ²⁷Now when Abner returned to Hebron, Joab took him aside into the gateway, as though to speak with him privately. And there, to avenge the blood of his brother Asahel, Joab stabbed him in the stomach, and he died.

²⁸Later, when David heard about this, he said, "I and my kingdom are for ever innocent before the LORD concerning the blood of Abner son of Ner. ²⁹May his blood fall upon the head of Joab and upon all his father's house! May Joab's house never be without someone who has a running sore or leprosy[a] or who leans on a crutch or who falls by the sword or who lacks food."

³⁰(Joab and his brother Abishai murdered Abner because he had killed their brother Asahel in the battle of Gibeon.)

³¹Then David said to Joab and all the people with him, "Tear your clothes and put on sackcloth and walk in mourning in front of Abner." King David himself walked behind the bier. ³²They buried Abner in Hebron, and the king wept aloud at Abner's tomb. All the people wept also.

³³The king sang this lament for Abner:

"Should Abner have died as the lawless die?
³⁴   Your hands were not bound,
    your feet were not fettered.
You fell as one falls before wicked men."

And all the people wept over him again.

³⁵Then they all came and urged David to eat something while it was still day; but David took an oath, saying, "May God deal with me, be it ever so severely, if I taste bread or anything else before the sun sets!"

³⁶All the people took note and were pleased; indeed, everything the king did pleased them. ³⁷So on that day all the people and all Israel knew that the king had no part in the murder of Abner son of Ner.

³⁸Then the king said to his men, "Do you not realise that a prince and a great man has fallen in Israel this day? ³⁹And today, though I am the anointed king, I am weak, and these sons of Zeruiah are too strong for me. May the LORD repay the evildoer according to his evil deeds!"

Ish-Bosheth Murdered

4 When Ish-Bosheth son of Saul heard that Abner had died in Hebron, he lost courage, and all Israel became alarmed. ²Now Saul's son had two men who were leaders of raiding bands. One was named

---

[a]29 The Hebrew word was used for various diseases affecting the skin—not necessarily leprosy.

Baanah and the other Recab; they were sons of Rimmon the Beerothite from the tribe of Benjamin—Beeroth is considered part of Benjamin, ³because the people of Beeroth fled to Gittaim and have lived there as aliens to this day.

⁴(Jonathan son of Saul had a son who was lame in both feet. He was five years old when the news about Saul and Jonathan came from Jezreel. His nurse picked him up and fled, but as she hurried to leave, he fell and became crippled. His name was Mephibosheth.)

⁵Now Recab and Baanah, the sons of Rimmon the Beerothite, set out for the house of Ish-Bosheth, and they arrived there in the heat of the day while he was taking his noonday rest. ⁶They went into the inner part of the house as if to get some wheat, and they stabbed him in the stomach. Then Recab and his brother Baanah slipped away.

⁷They had gone into the house while he was lying on the bed in his bedroom. After they stabbed and killed him, they cut off his head. Taking it with them, they travelled all night by way of the Arabah. ⁸They brought the head of Ish-Bosheth to David at Hebron and said to the king, "Here is the head of Ish-Bosheth son of Saul, your enemy, who tried to take your life. This day the LORD has avenged my lord the king against Saul and his offspring."

⁹David answered Recab and his brother Baanah, the sons of Rimmon the Beerothite, "As surely as the LORD lives, who has delivered me out of all trouble, ¹⁰when a man told me, 'Saul is dead,' and thought he was bringing good news, I seized him and put him to death in Ziklag. That was the reward I gave him for his news! ¹¹How much more—when wicked men have killed an innocent man in his own house and on his own bed—should I not now demand his blood from your hand and rid the earth of you!"

¹²So David gave an order to his men, and they killed them. They cut off their hands and feet and hung the bodies by the pool in Hebron. But they took the head of Ish-Bosheth and buried it in Abner's tomb at Hebron.

David Becomes King Over Israel

5 All the tribes of Israel came to David at Hebron and said, "We are your own flesh and blood. ²In the past, while Saul was king over us, you were the one who led Israel on their military campaigns. And the LORD said to you, 'You shall shepherd my people Israel, and you shall become their ruler.'"

³When all the elders of Israel had come to King David at Hebron, the king made a compact with them at Hebron before the LORD, and they anointed David king over Israel.

⁴David was thirty years old when he became king, and he reigned for forty years. ⁵In Hebron he reigned over Judah for seven years and six months, and in Jerusalem he reigned over all Israel and Judah for thirty-three years.

David Conquers Jerusalem

⁶The king and his men marched to Jerusalem to attack the Jebusites, who lived there. The Jebusites said to David, "You will not get in here; even the blind and the lame can ward you off." They thought, "David cannot get in here." ⁷Nevertheless, David captured the fortress of Zion, the City of David.

⁸On that day, David said, "Anyone who conquers the Jebusites will have to use the water shaft*a* to reach those 'lame and blind' who are David's enemies."*b* That is why they say, "The 'blind and lame' will not enter the palace."

⁹David then took up residence in the fortress and called it the City of David. He built up the area around it, from the supporting terraces*c* inward. ¹⁰And he became more and more powerful, because the LORD God Almighty was with him.

¹¹Now Hiram king of Tyre sent messengers to David, along with cedar logs and carpenters and stonemasons, and they built a palace for David. ¹²And David knew that the LORD had established him as king over Israel and had exalted his kingdom for the sake of his people Israel.

¹³After he left Hebron, David took more concubines and wives in Jerusalem, and more sons and daughters were born to him. ¹⁴These are the names of the children born to him there: Shammua, Shobab, Nathan, Solomon, ¹⁵Ibhar, Elishua, Nepheg, Japhia, ¹⁶Elishama, Eliada and Eliphelet.

David Defeats the Philistines

¹⁷When the Philistines heard that David had been anointed king over Israel, they went up in full force to search for him, but David heard about it and went down to the stronghold. ¹⁸Now the Philistines had come and spread out in the Valley of Rephaim; ¹⁹so David enquired of the LORD, "Shall I go and attack the Philistines? Will you hand them over to me?"

The LORD answered him, "Go, for I will surely hand the Philistines over to you."

²⁰So David went to Baal Perazim, and there he defeated them. He said, "As waters break out, the LORD has broken out against my enemies before me." So that place was called Baal Perazim.*d* ²¹The Philistines abandoned their idols there, and David and his men carried them off.

²²Once more the Philistines came up and spread out in the Valley of Rephaim; ²³so David enquired of the LORD, and he answered, "Do not go straight up, but circle round behind them and attack them in front of the balsam trees. ²⁴As soon as you hear the sound of marching in the tops of the balsam trees, move quickly, because that will mean the LORD has gone out in front of you to strike the Philistine army." ²⁵So David did as the LORD commanded him, and he struck down the Philistines all the way from Gibeon*e* to Gezer.

---

*a*8 Or *use scaling hooks*　　*b*8 Or *are hated by David*　　*c*9 Or *the Millo*
*d*20 *Baal Perazim* means *the lord who breaks out.*　　*e*25 Septuagint (see also 1 Chron. 14:16); Hebrew *Geba*

The Ark Brought to Jerusalem

6 David again brought together out of Israel chosen men, thirty thousand in all. ²He and all his men set out from Baalah of Judah*a* to bring up from there the ark of God, which is called by the Name,*b* the name of the LORD Almighty, who is enthroned between the cherubim that are on the ark. ³They set the ark of God on a new cart and brought it from the house of Abinadab, which was on the hill. Uzzah and Ahio, sons of Abinadab, were guiding the new cart ⁴with the ark of God on it,*c* and Ahio was walking in front of it. ⁵David and the whole house of Israel were celebrating with all their might before the LORD, with songs*d* and with harps, lyres, tambourines, sistrums and with cymbals.

⁶When they came to the threshing-floor of Nacon, Uzzah reached out and took hold of the ark of God, because the oxen stumbled. ⁷The LORD's anger burned against Uzzah because of his irreverent act; therefore God struck him down and he died there beside the ark of God.

⁸Then David was angry because the LORD's wrath had broken out against Uzzah, and to this day that place is called Perez Uzzah.*e*

⁹David was afraid of the LORD that day and said, "How can the ark of the LORD ever come to me?" ¹⁰He was not willing to take the ark of the LORD to be with him in the City of David. Instead, he took it aside to the house of Obed-Edom the Gittite. ¹¹The ark of the LORD remained in the house of Obed-Edom the Gittite for three months, and the LORD blessed him and his entire household.

¹²Now King David was told, "The LORD has blessed the household of Obed-Edom and everything he has, because of the ark of God." So David went down and brought up the ark of God from the house of Obed-Edom to the City of David with rejoicing. ¹³When those who were carrying the ark of the LORD had taken six steps, he sacrificed a bull and a fattened calf. ¹⁴David, wearing a linen ephod, danced before the LORD with all his might, ¹⁵while he and the entire house of Israel brought up the ark of the LORD with shouts and the sound of trumpets.

¹⁶As the ark of the LORD was entering the City of David, Michal daughter of Saul watched from a window. And when she saw King David leaping and dancing before the LORD, she despised him in her heart.

¹⁷They brought the ark of the LORD and set it in its place inside the tent that David had pitched for it, and David sacrificed burnt offerings and fellowship offerings*f* before the LORD. ¹⁸After he had finished sacrificing the burnt offerings and fellowship offerings, he blessed the people in the name of the LORD Almighty. ¹⁹Then he gave a loaf of bread, a cake of dates and a cake of raisins to each person in the whole crowd of Israelites, both men and women. And all the people went to their homes.

²⁰When David returned home to bless his household, Michal daughter of Saul came out to meet him and said, "How the king of Israel has distinguished himself today, disrobing in the sight of the slave girls of his servants as any vulgar fellow would."

²¹David said to Michal, "It was before the LORD, who chose me rather than your father or anyone from his house when he appointed me ruler over the LORD's people Israel—I will celebrate before the LORD. ²²I will become even more undignified than this, and I will be humiliated in my own eyes. But by these slave girls you spoke of, I will be held in honour."

²³And Michal daughter of Saul had no children to the day of her death.

God's Promise to David

7 After the king was settled in his palace and the LORD had given him rest from all his enemies around him, ²he said to Nathan the prophet, "Here I am, living in a palace of cedar, while the ark of God remains in a tent."

³Nathan replied to the king, "Whatever you have in mind, go ahead and do it, for the LORD is with you."

⁴That night the word of the LORD came to Nathan, saying:

⁵"Go and tell my servant David, 'This is what the LORD says: Are you the one to build me a house to dwell in? ⁶I have not dwelt in a house from the day I brought the Israelites up out of Egypt to this day. I have been moving from place to place with a tent as my dwelling. ⁷Wherever I have moved with all the Israelites, did I ever say to any of their rulers whom I commanded to shepherd my people Israel, "Why have you not built me a house of cedar?"'

⁸"Now then, tell my servant David, 'This is what the LORD Almighty says: I took you from the pasture and from following the flock to be ruler over my people Israel. ⁹I have been with you wherever you have gone, and I have cut off all your enemies from before you. Now I will make your name great, like the names of the greatest men of the earth. ¹⁰And I will provide a place for my people Israel and will plant them so that they can have a home of their own and no longer be disturbed. Wicked people shall not oppress them any more, as they did at the beginning ¹¹and have done ever since the time I appointed leaders*a* over my people Israel. I will also give you rest from all your enemies.

---

*a*2 That is, Kiriath Jearim; Hebrew *Baale Judah*, a variant of *Baalah of Judah*
*b*2 Hebrew; Septuagint and Vulgate do not have *the Name*.
*c*3, 4 Dead Sea Scrolls and some Septuagint manuscripts; Masoretic Text *cart* ⁴*and they brought it with the ark of God from the house of Abinadab, which was on the hill*
*d*5 See Dead Sea Scrolls, Septuagint and 1 Chron. 13:8; Masoretic Text *celebrating before the LORD with all kinds of instruments made of pine.*　　*e*8 *Perez Uzzah* means *the outbreak against Uzzah*.
*f*17 Traditionally *peace offerings*; also in verse 18　　*a*11 Traditionally *judges*

'' 'The LORD declares to you that the LORD himself will establish a house for you: ¹²When your days are over and you rest with your fathers, I will raise up your offspring to succeed you, who will come from your own body, and I will establish his kingdom. ¹³He is the one who will build a house for my Name, and I will establish the throne of his kingdom for ever. ¹⁴I will be his father, and he shall be my son. When he does wrong, I will punish him with the rod of men, with floggings inflicted by men. ¹⁵But my love will never be taken away from him, as I took it away from Saul, whom I removed from before you. ¹⁶Your house and your kingdom shall endure for ever before me;ᵇ your throne shall be established for ever.'' '

¹⁷Nathan reported to David all the words of this entire revelation.

David's Prayer

¹⁸Then King David went in and sat before the LORD, and he said:

"Who am I, O Sovereign LORD, and what is my family, that you have brought me this far? ¹⁹And as if this were not enough in your sight, O Sovereign LORD, you have also spoken about the future of the house of your servant. Is this your usual way of dealing with man, O Sovereign LORD?

²⁰"What more can David say to you? For you know your servant, O Sovereign LORD. ²¹For the sake of your word and according to your will, you have done this great thing and made it known to your servant.

²²"How great you are, O Sovereign LORD! There is no-one like you, and there is no God but you, as we have heard with our own ears. ²³And who is like your people Israel—the one nation on earth that God went out to redeem as a people for himself, and to make a name for himself, and to perform great and awesome wonders by driving out nations and their gods from before your people, whom you redeemed from Egypt?ᶜ ²⁴You have established your people Israel as your very own for ever, and you, O LORD, have become their God.

²⁵"And now, LORD God, keep for ever the promise you have made concerning your servant and his house. Do as you promised, ²⁶so that your name will be great for ever. Then men will say, 'The LORD Almighty is God over Israel!' And the house of your servant David will be established before you.

²⁷"O LORD Almighty, God of Israel, you have revealed this to your servant, saying, 'I will build a house for you.' So your servant has found courage to offer you this prayer. ²⁸O Sovereign LORD, you are God! Your words are trustworthy, and you have promised these good things to your servant. ²⁹Now be pleased to bless the house of your servant, that it may continue for ever in your sight; for you, O Sovereign LORD, have spoken, and with your blessing the house of your servant will be blessed for ever."

David's Victories

8 In the course of time, David defeated the Philistines and subdued them, and he took Metheg Ammah from the control of the Philistines.

²David also defeated the Moabites. He made them lie down on the ground and measured them off with a length of cord. Every two lengths of them were put to death, and the third length was allowed to live. So the Moabites became subject to David and brought tribute.

³Moreover, David fought Hadadezer son of Rehob, king of Zobah, when he went to restore his control along the Euphrates River. ⁴David captured a thousand of his chariots, seven thousand charioteersᵃ and twenty thousand foot soldiers. He hamstrung all but a hundred of the chariot horses.

⁵When the Arameans of Damascus came to help Hadadezer king of Zobah, David struck down twenty-two thousand of them. ⁶He put garrisons in the Aramean kingdom of Damascus, and the Arameans became subject to him and brought tribute. The LORD gave David victory wherever he went.

⁷David took the gold shields that belonged to the officers of Hadadezer and brought them to Jerusalem. ⁸From Tebahᵇ and Berothai, towns that belonged to Hadadezer, King David took a great quantity of bronze.

⁹When Touᶜ king of Hamath heard that David had defeated the entire army of Hadadezer, ¹⁰he sent his son Joramᵈ to King David to greet him and congratulate him on his victory in battle over Hadadezer, who had been at war with Tou. Joram brought with him articles of silver and gold and bronze.

¹¹King David dedicated these articles to the LORD, as he had done with the silver and gold from all the nations he had subdued: ¹²Edomᵉ and Moab, the Ammonites and the Philistines, and Amalek. He also dedicated the plunder taken from Hadadezer son of Rehob, king of Zobah.

¹³And David became famous after he returned from striking down eighteen thousand Edomitesᶠ in the Valley of Salt.

ᵇ16 Some Hebrew manuscripts and Septuagint; most Hebrew manuscripts *you*
ᶜ23 See Septuagint and 1 Chron. 17:21; Hebrew *wonders for your land and before your people, whom you redeemed from Egypt, from the nations and their gods.*
ᵃ4 Septuagint (see also Dead Sea Scrolls and 1 Chron. 18:4); Masoretic Text *captured seventeen hundred of his charioteers* ᵇ8 See some Septuagint manuscripts (see also 1 Chron. 18:8); Hebrew *Betah.*
ᶜ9 Hebrew *Toi*, a variant of *Tou*; also in verse 10 ᵈ10 A variant of *Hadoram*
ᵉ12 Some Hebrew manuscripts, Septuagint and Syriac (see also 1 Chron. 18:11); most Hebrew manuscripts *Aram*
ᶠ13 A few Hebrew manuscripts, Septuagint and Syriac (see also 1 Chron. 18:12); most Hebrew manuscripts *Aram* (that is, Arameans)

14He put garrisons throughout Edom, and all the Edomites became subject to David. The Lord gave David victory wherever he went.

David's Officials

15David reigned over all Israel, doing what was just and right for all his people. 16Joab son of Zeruiah was over the army; Jehoshaphat son of Ahilud was recorder; 17Zadok son of Ahitub and Ahimelech son of Abiathar were priests; Seraiah was secretary; 18Benaiah son of Jehoiada was over the Kerethites and Pelethites; and David's sons were royal advisers.g

David and Mephibosheth

9 David asked, "Is there anyone still left of the house of Saul to whom I can show kindness for Jonathan's sake?"

2Now there was a servant of Saul's household named Ziba. They called him to appear before David, and the king said to him, "Are you Ziba?"

"Your servant," he replied.

3The king asked, "Is there no-one still left of the house of Saul to whom I can show God's kindness?"

Ziba answered the king, "There is still a son of Jonathan; he is crippled in both feet."

4"Where is he?" the king asked.

Ziba answered, "He is at the house of Makir son of Ammiel in Lo Debar."

5So King David had him brought from Lo Debar, from the house of Makir son of Ammiel.

6When Mephibosheth son of Jonathan, the son of Saul, came to David, he bowed down to pay him honour.

David said, "Mephibosheth!"

"Your servant," he replied.

7"Don't be afraid," David said to him, "for I will surely show you kindness for the sake of your father Jonathan. I will restore to you all the land that belonged to your grandfather Saul, and you will always eat at my table."

8Mephibosheth bowed down and said, "What is your servant, that you should notice a dead dog like me?"

9Then the king summoned Ziba, Saul's servant, and said to him, "I have given your master's grandson everything that belonged to Saul and his family. 10You and your sons and your servants are to farm the land for him and bring in the crops, so that your master's grandson may be provided for. And Mephibosheth, grandson of your master, will always eat at my table." (Now Ziba had fifteen sons and twenty servants.)

11Then Ziba said to the king, "Your servant will do whatever my lord the king commands his servant to do." So Mephibosheth ate at David'sa table like one of the king's sons.

12Mephibosheth had a young son named Mica, and all the members of Ziba's household were servants of Mephibosheth. 13And Mephibosheth lived in Jerusalem, because he always ate at the king's table, and he was crippled in both feet.

David Defeats the Ammonites

10 In the course of time, the king of the Ammonites died, and his son Hanun succeeded him as king. 2David thought, "I will show kindness to Hanun son of Nahash, just as his father showed kindness to me." So David sent a delegation to express his sympathy to Hanun concerning his father.

When David's men came to the land of the Ammonites, 3the Ammonite nobles said to Hanun their lord, "Do you think David is honouring your father by sending men to you to express sympathy? Hasn't David sent them to you to explore the city and spy it out and overthrow it?" 4So Hanun seized David's men, shaved off half of each man's beard, cut off their garments in the middle at the buttocks, and sent them away.

5When David was told about this, he sent messengers to meet the men, for they were greatly humiliated. The king said, "Stay at Jericho till your beards have grown, and then come back."

6When the Ammonites realised that they had become an offence to David's nostrils, they hired twenty thousand Aramean foot soldiers from Beth Rehob and Zobah, as well as the king of Maacah with a thousand men, and also twelve thousand men from Tob.

7On hearing this, David sent Joab out with the entire army of fighting men. 8The Ammonites came out and drew up in battle formation at the entrance to their city gate, while the Arameans of Zobah and Rehob and the men of Tob and Maacah were by themselves in the open country.

9Joab saw that there were battle lines in front of him and behind him; so he selected some of the best troops in Israel and deployed them against the Arameans. 10He put the rest of the men under the command of Abishai his brother and deployed them against the Ammonites. 11Joab said, "If the Arameans are too strong for me, then you are to come to my rescue; but if the Ammonites are too strong for you, then I will come to rescue you. 12Be strong and let us fight bravely for our people and the cities of our God. The Lord will do what is good in his sight."

13Then Joab and the troops with him advanced to fight the Arameans, and they fled before him. 14When the Ammonites saw that the Arameans were fleeing, they fled before Abishai and went inside the city. So Joab returned from fighting the Ammonites and came to Jerusalem.

15After the Arameans saw that they had been routed by Israel, they regrouped. 16Hadadezer had Arameans brought from beyond the River;a they went to Helam, with Shobach the commander of Hadadezer's army leading them.

17When David was told of this, he gathered all Israel, crossed the Jordan and went to Helam. The Arameans formed their battle

---

g18 Or were priests   a11 Septuagint; Hebrew my   a16 That is, the Euphrates lines to meet David and fought against him. [18]But they fled before Israel, and David killed seven hundred of their charioteers and forty thousand of their foot soldiers.[b] He also struck down Shobach the commander of their army, and he died there. [19]When all the kings who were vassals of Hadadezer saw that they had been defeated by Israel, they made peace with the Israelites and became subject to them.

So the Arameans were afraid to help the Ammonites any more.

David and Bathsheba

11 In the spring, at the time when kings go off to war, David sent Joab out with the king's men and the whole Israelite army. They destroyed the Ammonites and besieged Rabbah. But David remained in Jerusalem.

[2]One evening David got up from his bed and walked around on the roof of the palace. From the roof he saw a woman bathing. The woman was very beautiful, [3]and David sent someone to find out about her. The man said, "Isn't this Bathsheba, the daughter of Eliam and the wife of Uriah the Hittite?" [4]Then David sent messengers to get her. She came to him, and he slept with her. (She had purified herself from her uncleanness.) Then[a] she went back home. [5]The woman conceived and sent word to David, saying, "I am pregnant."

[6]So David sent this word to Joab: "Send me Uriah the Hittite." And Joab sent him to David. [7]When Uriah came to him, David asked him how Joab was, how the soldiers were and how the war was going. [8]Then David said to Uriah, "Go down to your house and wash your feet." So Uriah left the palace, and a gift from the king was sent after him. [9]But Uriah slept at the entrance to the palace with all his master's servants and did not go down to his house.

[10]When David was told, "Uriah did not go home," he asked him, "Haven't you just come from a distance? Why didn't you go home?"

[11]Uriah said to David, "The ark and Israel and Judah are staying in tents, and my master Joab and my lord's men are camped in the open fields. How could I go to my house to eat and drink and lie with my wife? As surely as you live, I will not do such a thing!"

[12]Then David said to him, "Stay here one more day, and tomorrow I will send you back." So Uriah remained in Jerusalem that day and the next. [13]At David's invitation, he ate and drank with him, and David made him drunk. But in the evening Uriah went out to sleep on his mat among his master's servants; he did not go home.

[14]In the morning David wrote a letter to Joab and sent it with Uriah. [15]In it he wrote, "Put Uriah in the front line where the fighting is fiercest. Then withdraw from him so that he will be struck down and die."

[16]So while Joab had the city under siege, he put Uriah at a place where he knew the strongest defenders were. [17]When the men of the city came out and fought against Joab, some of the men in David's army fell; moreover, Uriah the Hittite died.

[18]Joab sent David a full account of the battle. [19]He instructed the messenger: "When you have finished giving the king this account of the battle, [20]the king's anger may flare up, and he may ask you, 'Why did you get so close to the city to fight? Didn't you know they would shoot arrows from the wall? [21]Who killed Abimelech son of Jerub-Besheth?[b] Didn't a woman throw an upper millstone on him from the wall, so that he died in Thebez? Why did you get so close to the wall?' If he asks you this, then say to him, 'Also, your servant Uriah the Hittite is dead.'"

[22]The messenger set out, and when he arrived he told David everything Joab had sent him to say. [23]The messenger said to David, "The men overpowered us and came out against us in the open, but we drove them back to the entrance to the city gate. [24]Then the archers shot arrows at your servants from the wall, and some of the king's men died. Moreover, your servant Uriah the Hittite is dead."

[25]David told the messenger, "Say this to Joab: 'Don't let this upset you; the sword devours one as well as another. Press the attack against the city and destroy it.' Say this to encourage Joab."

[26]When Uriah's wife heard that her husband was dead, she mourned for him. [27]After the time of mourning was over, David had her brought to his house, and she became his wife and bore him a son. But the thing David had done displeased the LORD.

Nathan Rebukes David

12 The LORD sent Nathan to David. When he came to him, he said, "There were two men in a certain town, one rich and the other poor. [2]The rich man had a very large number of sheep and cattle, [3]but the poor man had nothing except one little ewe lamb that he had bought. He raised it, and it grew up with him and his children. It shared his food, drank from his cup and even slept in his arms. It was like a daughter to him.

[4]"Now a traveller came to the rich man, but the rich man refrained from taking one of his own sheep or cattle to prepare a meal for the traveller who had come to him. Instead, he took the ewe lamb that belonged to the poor man and prepared it for the one who had come to him."

[5]David burned with anger against the man and said to Nathan, "As surely as the LORD lives, the man who did this deserves to die! [6]He must pay for that lamb four times over, because he did such a thing and had no pity."

[7]Then Nathan said to David, "You are the man! This is what the LORD, the God of Israel, says: 'I anointed you king over Israel,

b18 Some Septuagint manuscripts (see also 1 Chron. 19:18); Hebrew, *horsemen*
a4 Or *with her. When she purified herself from her uncleanness,*   b21 Also known as *Jerub-Baal* (that is, Gideon)

2 SAMUEL 11:2–17, 25–27
'The thing David had done displeased the LORD' (v. 27).

FRAIL STRENGTH. The Bible describes a number of instances which show David's fine character and generosity. However, that was not the whole story. Like us, he was a mixture of the splendid and the frail.

The Bible does not seek to hide the sins of its heroes and this episode records a catalogue of adultery, intrigue and murder on the part of David. But if we simply dismiss the whole affair as disgusting, we shall miss much that can speak to our human condition.

David's sin begins with what may be described as a chance encounter. He catches sight of Bathsheba bathing (v. 2) and allows his mind to dwell on the sight to the extent that he sends for her and commits adultery with her (vv. 4, 5).

How often sin follows this course. A chance meeting or a thought becomes a means of temptation, the temptation is savoured and sin results. That applies to more than sexual sins. As in the case of David, one sin then leads to another, innocent people are hurt and we are caught up in our own intrigue. The vicious circle can be broken only when we are willing to acknowledge our sin and seek forgiveness: a painful and restorative experience which we avoid at our peril.

Lust, adultery, murder all start in the human heart. Lord, make my heart whole and pure.

→270

2 SAMUEL 12:1–15

' "As surely as the LORD lives, the man who did this deserves to die!" . . . Then Nathan said to David, "You are the man!" ' (vv. 5, 7).

SIGHT WITHOUT INSIGHT. The prophets of the Old Testament often thundered out their message but in Nathan's parable of the ewe lamb we have an example of a gentler approach.

Nathan was dealing with the king and David seemed to be adopting some of the customs of surrounding monarchs. They tended to take what they wanted without scruple and that is what David had done in the matter of Uriah and Bathsheba. Would he now take the same unscrupulous attitude with anyone who dared to rebuke him? Whatever the reason, Nathan used his parable with such skill that David condemned himself (v. 5). Then with great courage the prophet exposed David's sin (vv. 7–9).

It has to be said that David accepted the rebuke and was brought back to the understanding that to be king in Israel meant that he must rule under God. His repentance was met with the assurance of divine forgiveness (v. 13). Nathan could assure David that he was forgiven, but he could not assure him that there would be no consequence of his sin.

To be forgiven is to begin a journey with new hope and new life, but one in which we often meet the consequences of our previous evil influence. Then it is often the most difficult thing to forgive ourselves.

→277

and I delivered you from the hand of Saul. ⁸I gave your master's house to you, and your master's wives into your arms. I gave you the house of Israel and Judah. And if all this had been too little, I would have given you even more. ⁹Why did you despise the word of the LORD by doing what is evil in his eyes? You struck down Uriah the Hittite with the sword and took his wife to be your own. You killed him with the sword of the Ammonites. ¹⁰Now, therefore, the sword shall never depart from your house, because you despised me and took the wife of Uriah the Hittite to be your own.'

¹¹'This is what the LORD says: 'Out of your own household I am going to bring calamity upon you. Before your very eyes I will take your wives and give them to one who is close to you, and he will lie with your wives in broad daylight. ¹²You did it in secret, but I will do this thing in broad daylight before all Israel.''

¹³Then David said to Nathan, "I have sinned against the LORD."

Nathan replied, "The LORD has taken away your sin. You are not going to die. ¹⁴But because by doing this you have made the enemies of the LORD show utter contempt,ᵃ the son born to you will die."

¹⁵After Nathan had gone home, the LORD struck the child that Uriah's wife had borne to David, and he became ill. ¹⁶David pleaded with God for the child. He fasted and went into his house and spent the nights lying on the ground. ¹⁷The elders of his household stood beside him to get him up from the ground, but he refused, and he would not eat any food with them.

¹⁸On the seventh day the child died. David's servants were afraid to tell him that the child was dead, for they thought, "While the child was still living, we spoke to David but he would not listen to us. How can we tell him the child is dead? He may do something desperate."

¹⁹David noticed that his servants were whispering among themselves and he realised that the child was dead. "Is the child dead?" he asked.

"Yes," they replied, "he is dead."

²⁰Then David got up from the ground. After he had washed, put on lotions and changed his clothes, he went into the house of the LORD and worshipped. Then he went to his own house, and at his request they served him food, and he ate.

²¹His servants asked him, "Why are you acting in this way? While the child was alive, you fasted and wept, but now that the child is dead, you get up and eat!"

²²He answered, "While the child was still alive, I fasted and wept. I thought, 'Who knows? The LORD may be gracious to me and let the child live.' ²³But now that he is dead, why should I fast? Can I bring him back again? I will go to him, but he will not return to me."

²⁴Then David comforted his wife Bathsheba, and he went to her and lay with her. She gave birth to a son, and they named him Solomon. The LORD loved him; ²⁵and because the LORD loved him, he sent word through Nathan the prophet to name him Jedidiah.ᵇ

²⁶Meanwhile Joab fought against Rabbah of the Ammonites and captured the royal citadel. ²⁷Joab then sent messengers to David, saying, "I have fought against Rabbah and taken its water supply. ²⁸Now muster the rest of the troops and besiege the city and capture it. Otherwise I shall take the city, and it will be named after me."

²⁹So David mustered the entire army and went to Rabbah, and attacked and captured it. ³⁰He took the crown from the head of their kingᶜ—its weight was a talentᵈ of gold, and it was set with precious stones—and it was placed on David's head. He took a great quantity of plunder from the city ³¹and brought out the people who were there, consigning them to labour with saws and with iron picks and axes, and he made them work at brickmaking.ᵉ He did this to all the Ammonite towns. Then David and his entire army returned to Jerusalem.

Amnon and Tamar

13 In the course of time, Amnon son of David fell in love with Tamar, the beautiful sister of Absalom son of David.

²Amnon became frustrated to the point of illness on account of his sister Tamar, for she was a virgin, and it seemed impossible for him to do anything to her.

³Now Amnon had a friend named Jonadab son of Shimeah, David's brother. Jonadab was a very shrewd man. ⁴He asked Amnon, "Why do you, the king's son, look so haggard morning after morning? Won't you tell me?"

Amnon said to him, "I'm in love with Tamar, my brother Absalom's sister."

⁵"Go to bed and pretend to be ill," Jonadab said. "When your father comes to see you, say to him, 'I would like my sister Tamar to come and give me something to eat. Let her prepare the food in my sight so that I may watch her and then eat it from her hand.'"

⁶So Amnon lay down and pretended to be ill. When the king came to see him, Amnon said to him, "I would like my sister Tamar to come and make some special bread in my sight, so that I may eat from her hand."

⁷David sent word to Tamar at the palace: "Go to the house of your brother Amnon and prepare some food for him." ⁸So Tamar went to the house of her brother Amnon, who was lying down. She took some dough, kneaded it, made the bread in his sight and baked it. ⁹Then she took the pan and served him the bread, but he refused to eat.

"Send everyone out of here," Amnon said. So everyone left him. ¹⁰Then Amnon said to Tamar, "Bring the food here into my bedroom so that I may eat from your hand." And Tamar took the bread she had prepared and brought it to her brother Amnon in his bedroom. [11]But when she took it to him to eat, he grabbed her and said, "Come to bed with me, my sister."

[12]"Don't, my brother!" she said to him. "Don't force me. Such a thing should not be done in Israel! Don't do this wicked thing. [13]What about me? Where could I get rid of my disgrace? And what about you? You would be like one of the wicked fools in Israel. Please speak to the king; he will not keep me from being married to you." [14]But he refused to listen to her, and since he was stronger than she, he raped her.

[15]Then Amnon hated her with intense hatred. In fact, he hated her more than he had loved her. Amnon said to her, "Get up and get out!"

[16]"No!" she said to him. "Sending me away would be a greater wrong than what you have already done to me."

But he refused to listen to her. [17]He called his personal servant and said, "Get this woman out of here and bolt the door after her." [18]So his servant put her out and bolted the door after her. She was wearing a richly ornamented[a] robe, for this was the kind of garment the virgin daughters of the king wore. [19]Tamar put ashes on her head and tore the ornamented robe she was wearing. She put her hand on her head and went away, weeping aloud as she went.

[20]Her brother Absalom said to her, "Has that Amnon, your brother, been with you? Be quiet now, my sister; he is your brother. Don't take this thing to heart." And Tamar lived in her brother Absalom's house, a desolate woman.

[21]When King David heard all this, he was furious. [22]Absalom never said a word to Amnon, either good or bad; he hated Amnon because he had disgraced his sister Tamar.

Absalom Kills Amnon

[23]Two years later, when Absalom's sheep-shearers were at Baal Hazor near the border of Ephraim, he invited all the king's sons to come there. [24]Absalom went to the king and said, "Your servant has had shearers come. Will the king and his officials please join me?"

[25]"No, my son," the king replied. "All of us should not go; we would only be a burden to you." Although Absalom urged him, he still refused to go, but gave him his blessing.

[26]Then Absalom said, "If not, please let my brother Amnon come with us."

The king asked him, "Why should he go with you?" [27]But Absalom urged him, so he sent with him Amnon and the rest of the king's sons.

[28]Absalom ordered his men, "Listen! When Amnon is in high spirits from drinking wine and I say to you, 'Strike Amnon down,'

then kill him. Don't be afraid. Have not I given you this order? Be strong and brave." [29]So Absalom's men did to Amnon what Absalom had ordered. Then all the king's sons got up, mounted their mules and fled.

[30]While they were on their way, the report came to David: "Absalom has struck down all the king's sons; not one of them is left." [31]The king stood up, tore his clothes and lay down on the ground; and all his servants stood by with their clothes torn.

[32]But Jonadab son of Shimeah, David's brother, said, "My lord should not think that they killed all the princes; only Amnon is dead. This has been Absalom's expressed intention ever since the day that Amnon raped his sister Tamar. [33]My lord the king should not be concerned about the report that all the king's sons are dead. Only Amnon is dead."

[34]Meanwhile, Absalom had fled.

Now the man standing watch looked up and saw many people on the road west of him, coming down the side of the hill. The watchman went and told the king, "I see men in the direction of Horonaim, on the side of the hill."[b]

[35]Jonadab said to the king, "See, the king's sons are here; it has happened just as your servant said."

[36]As he finished speaking, the king's sons came in, wailing loudly. The king, too, and all his servants wept very bitterly.

[37]Absalom fled and went to Talmai son of Ammihud, the king of Geshur. But King David mourned for his son every day.

[38]After Absalom fled and went to Geshur, he stayed there for three years. [39]And the spirit of the king[c] longed to go to Absalom, for he was consoled concerning Amnon's death.

Absalom Returns to Jerusalem

14 Joab son of Zeruiah knew that the king's heart longed for Absalom. [2]So Joab sent someone to Tekoa and had a wise woman brought from there. He said to her, "Pretend you are in mourning. Dress in mourning clothes, and don't use any cosmetic lotions. Act like a woman who has spent many days grieving for the dead. [3]Then go to the king and speak these words to him." And Joab put the words in her mouth.

[4]When the woman from Tekoa went[a] to the king, she fell with her face to the ground to pay him honour, and she said, "Help me, O king!"

[5]The king asked her, "What is troubling you?"

She said, "I am indeed a widow; my husband is dead. [6]I your servant had two sons. They got into a fight with each other in the field, and no-one was there to separate them. One struck the other and killed him. [7]Now the whole clan has risen up against your servant; they say, 'Hand over the one who struck his brother down, so that we may put

[a]18 The meaning of the Hebrew for this phrase is uncertain; also in verse 19.
[b]34 Septuagint; Hebrew does not have this sentence.
[c]39 Dead Sea Scrolls and some Septuagint manuscripts; Masoretic Text But ⌊the spirit of ⌋ David the king
[a]4 Many Hebrew manuscripts, Septuagint, Vulgate and Syriac; most Hebrew manuscripts spoke

him to death for the life of his brother whom he killed; then we will get rid of the heir as well.' They would put out the only burning coal I have left, leaving my husband neither name nor descendant on the face of the earth.''

8The king said to the woman, "Go home, and I will issue an order on your behalf.''

9But the woman from Tekoa said to him, "My lord the king, let the blame rest on me and on my father's family, and let the king and his throne be without guilt.''

10The king replied, "If anyone says anything to you, bring him to me, and he will not bother you again.''

11She said, "Then let the king invoke the LORD his God to prevent the avenger of blood from adding to the destruction, so that my son shall not be destroyed.''

"As surely as the LORD lives," he said, "not one hair of your son's head will fall to the ground.''

12Then the woman said, "Let your servant speak a word to my lord the king.''

"Speak," he replied.

13The woman said, "Why then have you devised a thing like this against the people of God? When the king says this, does he not convict himself, for the king has not brought back his banished son? 14Like water spilled on the ground, which cannot be recovered, so we must die. But God does not take away life; instead, he devises ways so that a banished person may not remain estranged from him.

15"And now I have come to say this to my lord the king because the people have made me afraid. Your servant thought, 'I will speak to the king; perhaps he will do what his servant asks. 16Perhaps the king will agree to deliver his servant from the hand of the man who is trying to cut off both me and my son from the inheritance God gave us.'

17"And now your servant says, 'May the word of my lord the king bring me rest, for my lord the king is like an angel of God in discerning good and evil. May the LORD your God be with you.'''

18Then the king said to the woman, "Do not keep from me the answer to what I am going to ask you.''

"Let my lord the king speak," the woman said.

19The king asked, "Isn't the hand of Joab with you in all this?''

The woman answered, "As surely as you live, my lord the king, no-one can turn to the right or to the left from anything my lord the king says. Yes, it was your servant Joab who instructed me to do this and who put all these words into the mouth of your servant. 20Your servant Joab did this to change the present situation. My lord has wisdom like that of an angel of God—he knows everything that happens in the land.''

21The king said to Joab, "Very well, I will do it. Go, bring back the young man Absalom.''

22Joab fell with his face to the ground to pay him honour, and he blessed the king. Joab said, "Today your servant knows that he has found favour in your eyes, my lord the king, because the king has granted his servant's request.''

23Then Joab went to Geshur and brought Absalom back to Jerusalem. 24But the king said, "He must go to his own house; he must not see my face.'' So Absalom went to his own house and did not see the face of the king.

25In all Israel there was not a man so highly praised for his handsome appearance as Absalom. From the top of his head to the sole of his foot there was no blemish in him. 26Whenever he cut the hair of his head—he used to cut his hair from time to time when it became too heavy for him—he would weigh it, and its weight was two hundred shekels*b* by the royal standard.

27Three sons and a daughter were born to Absalom. The daughter's name was Tamar, and she became a beautiful woman.

28Absalom lived for two years in Jerusalem without seeing the king's face. 29Then Absalom sent for Joab in order to send him to the king, but Joab refused to come to him. So he sent a second time, but he refused to come. 30Then he said to his servants, "Look, Joab's field is next to mine, and he has barley there. Go and set it on fire.'' So Absalom's servants set the field on fire.

31Then Joab did go to Absalom's house and he said to him, "Why have your servants set my field on fire?''

32Absalom said to Joab, "Look, I sent word to you and said, 'Come here so that I can send you to the king to ask, "Why have I come from Geshur? It would be better for me if I were still there!"' Now then, I want to see the king's face, and if I am guilty of anything, let him put me to death.''

33So Joab went to the king and told him this. Then the king summoned Absalom, and he came in and bowed down with his face to the ground before the king. And the king kissed Absalom.

Absalom's Conspiracy

15 In the course of time, Absalom provided himself with a chariot and horses and with fifty men to run ahead of him. 2He would get up early and stand by the side of the road leading to the city gate. Whenever anyone came with a complaint to be placed before the king for a decision, Absalom would call out to him, "What town are you from?'' He would answer, "Your servant is from one of the tribes of Israel.'' 3Then Absalom would say to him, "Look, your claims are valid and proper, but there is no representative of the king to hear you.'' 4And Absalom would add, "If only I were appointed judge in the land! Then everyone who has a complaint or case could come to me and I would see that he receives justice.''

5Also, whenever anyone approached him to bow down before him, Absalom would reach out his hand, take hold of him and kiss

b26 That is, about 5 pounds (about 2.3 kilograms)

him. [6]Absalom behaved in this way towards all the Israelites who came to the king asking for justice, and so he stole the hearts of the men of Israel.

[7]At the end of four[a] years, Absalom said to the king, "Let me go to Hebron and fulfil a vow I made to the LORD. [8]While your servant was living at Geshur in Aram, I made this vow: 'If the LORD takes me back to Jerusalem, I will worship the LORD in Hebron.'"[b]

[9]The king said to him, "Go in peace." So he went to Hebron.

[10]Then Absalom sent secret messengers throughout the tribes of Israel to say, "As soon as you hear the sound of the trumpets, then say, 'Absalom is king in Hebron.'" [11]Two hundred men from Jerusalem had accompanied Absalom. They had been invited as guests and went quite innocently, knowing nothing about the matter. [12]While Absalom was offering sacrifices, he also sent for Ahithophel the Gilonite, David's counsellor, to come from Giloh, his home town. And so the conspiracy gained strength, and Absalom's following kept on increasing.

David Flees

[13]A messenger came and told David, "The hearts of the men of Israel are with Absalom."

[14]Then David said to all his officials who were with him in Jerusalem, "Come! We must flee, or none of us will escape from Absalom. We must leave immediately, or he will move quickly to overtake us and bring ruin upon us and put the city to the sword."

[15]The king's officials answered him, "Your servants are ready to do whatever our lord the king chooses."

[16]The king set out, with his entire household following him; but he left ten concubines to take care of the palace. [17]So the king set out, with all the people following him, and they halted at a place some distance away. [18]All his men marched past him, along with all the Kerethites and Pelethites; and all the six hundred Gittites who had accompanied him from Gath marched before the king.

[19]The king said to Ittai the Gittite, "Why should you come along with us? Go back and stay with King Absalom. You are a foreigner, an exile from your homeland. [20]You came only yesterday. And today shall I make you wander about with us, when I do not know where I am going? Go back, and take your countrymen. May kindness and faithfulness be with you."

[21]But Ittai replied to the king, "As surely as the LORD lives, and as my lord the king lives, wherever my lord the king may be, whether it means life or death, there will your servant be."

[22]David said to Ittai, "Go ahead, march on." So Ittai the Gittite marched on with all his men and the families that were with him.

[23]The whole countryside wept aloud as all the people passed by. The king also crossed the Kidron Valley, and all the people moved on towards the desert.

[24]Zadok was there, too, and all the Levites who were with him were carrying the ark of the covenant of God. They set down the ark of God, and Abiathar offered sacrifices[c] until all the people had finished leaving the city.

[25]Then the king said to Zadok, "Take the ark of God back into the city. If I find favour in the LORD's eyes, he will bring me back and let me see it and his dwelling-place again. [26]But if he says, 'I am not pleased with you,' then I am ready; let him do to me whatever seems good to him."

[27]The king also said to Zadok the priest, "Aren't you a seer? Go back to the city in peace, with your son Ahimaaz and Jonathan son of Abiathar. You and Abiathar take your two sons with you. [28]I will wait at the fords in the desert until word comes from you to inform me." [29]So Zadok and Abiathar took the ark of God back to Jerusalem and stayed there.

[30]But David continued up the Mount of Olives, weeping as he went; his head was covered and he was barefoot. All the people with him covered their heads too and were weeping as they went up. [31]Now David had been told, "Ahithophel is among the conspirators with Absalom." So David prayed, "O LORD, turn Ahithophel's counsel into foolishness."

[32]When David arrived at the summit, where people used to worship God, Hushai the Arkite was there to meet him, his robe torn and dust on his head. [33]David said to him, "If you go with me, you will be a burden to me. [34]But if you return to the city and say to Absalom, 'I will be your servant, O king; I was your father's servant in the past, but now I will be your servant,' then you can help me by frustrating Ahithophel's advice. [35]Won't the priests Zadok and Abiathar be there with you? Tell them anything you hear in the king's palace. [36]Their two sons, Ahimaaz son of Zadok and Jonathan son of Abiathar, are there with them. Send them to me with anything you hear."

[37]So David's friend Hushai arrived at Jerusalem as Absalom was entering the city.

David and Ziba

16 When David had gone a short distance beyond the summit, there was Ziba, the steward of Mephibosheth, waiting to meet him. He had a string of donkeys saddled and loaded with two hundred loaves of bread, a hundred cakes of raisins, a hundred cakes of figs and a skin of wine.

[2]The king asked Ziba, "Why have you brought these?"

Ziba answered, "The donkeys are for the king's household to ride on, the bread and fruit are for the men to eat, and the wine is to refresh those who become exhausted in the desert."

[3]The king then asked, "Where is your master's grandson?"

---

[a]7 Some Septuagint manuscripts, Syriac and Josephus; Hebrew *forty*
[b]8 Some Septuagint manuscripts; Hebrew does not have *in Hebron*.   [c]24 Or *Abiathar went up*

Ziba said to him, "He is staying in Jerusalem, because he thinks, 'Today the house of Israel will give me back my grandfather's kingdom.'"

4Then the king said to Ziba, "All that belonged to Mephibosheth is now yours."

"I humbly bow," Ziba said. "May I find favour in your eyes, my lord the king."

Shimei Curses David

5As King David approached Bahurim, a man from the same clan as Saul's family came out from there. His name was Shimei son of Gera, and he cursed as he came out. 6He pelted David and all the king's officials with stones, though all the troops and the special guard were on David's right and left. 7As he cursed, Shimei said, "Get out, get out, you man of blood, you scoundrel! 8The LORD has repaid you for all the blood you shed in the household of Saul, in whose place you have reigned. The LORD has handed the kingdom over to your son Absalom. You have come to ruin because you are a man of blood!"

9Then Abishai son of Zeruiah said to the king, "Why should this dead dog curse my lord the king? Let me go over and cut off his head."

10But the king said, "What do you and I have in common, you sons of Zeruiah? If he is cursing because the LORD said to him, 'Curse David,' who can ask, 'Why do you do this?'"

11David then said to Abishai and all his officials, "My son, who is of my own flesh, is trying to take my life. How much more, then, this Benjamite! Leave him alone; let him curse, for the LORD has told him to. 12It may be that the LORD will see my distress and repay me with good for the cursing I am receiving today."

13So David and his men continued along the road while Shimei was going along the hillside opposite him, cursing as he went and throwing stones at him and showering him with dirt. 14The king and all the people with him arrived at their destination exhausted. And there he refreshed himself.

The Advice of Hushai and Ahithophel

15Meanwhile, Absalom and all the men of Israel came to Jerusalem, and Ahithophel was with him. 16Then Hushai the Arkite, David's friend, went to Absalom and said to him, "Long live the king! Long live the king!"

17Absalom asked Hushai, "Is this the love you show your friend? Why didn't you go with your friend?"

18Hushai said to Absalom, "No, the one chosen by the LORD, by these people and by all the men of Israel—his I will be, and I will remain with him. 19Furthermore, whom should I serve? Should I not serve the son? Just as I served your father, so I will serve you."

20Absalom said to Ahithophel, "Give us your advice. What should we do?"

21Ahithophel answered, "Lie with your father's concubines whom he left to take care of the palace. Then all Israel will hear that you have made yourself an offence to your father's nostrils, and the hands of everyone with you will be strengthened." 22So they pitched a tent for Absalom on the roof, and he lay with his father's concubines in the sight of all Israel.

23Now in those days the advice Ahithophel gave was like that of one who enquires of God. That was how both David and Absalom regarded all of Ahithophel's advice.

17 Ahithophel said to Absalom, "I would*a* choose twelve thousand men and set out tonight in pursuit of David. 2I would*b* attack him while he is weary and weak. I would*b* strike him with terror, and then all the people with him will flee. I would*b* strike down only the king 3and bring all the people back to you. The death of the man you seek will mean the return of all; all the people will be unharmed." 4This plan seemed good to Absalom and to all the elders of Israel.

5But Absalom said, "Summon also Hushai the Arkite, so that we can hear what he has to say." 6When Hushai came to him, Absalom said, "Ahithophel has given this advice. Should we do what he says? If not, give us your opinion."

7Hushai replied to Absalom, "The advice Ahithophel has given is not good this time. 8You know your father and his men; they are fighters, and as fierce as a wild bear robbed of her cubs. Besides, your father is an experienced fighter; he will not spend the night with the troops. 9Even now, he is hidden in a cave or some other place. If he should attack your troops first,*c* whoever hears about it will say, 'There has been a slaughter among the troops who follow Absalom.' 10Then even the bravest soldier, whose heart is like the heart of a lion, will melt with fear, for all Israel knows that your father is a fighter and that those with him are brave.

11"So I advise you: Let all Israel, from Dan to Beersheba—as numerous as the sand on the seashore—be gathered to you, with you yourself leading them into battle. 12Then we will attack him wherever he may be found, and we will fall on him as dew settles on the ground. Neither he nor any of his men will be left alive. 13If he withdraws into a city, then all Israel will bring ropes to that city, and we will drag it down to the valley until not even a piece of it can be found."

14Absalom and all the men of Israel said, "The advice of Hushai the Arkite is better than that of Ahithophel." For the LORD had determined to frustrate the good advice of Ahithophel in order to bring disaster on Absalom.

15Hushai told Zadok and Abiathar, the priests, "Ahithophel has advised Absalom and the elders of Israel to do such and such, but I have advised them to do so and so. 16Now send a message immediately and tell David, 'Do not spend the night at the fords in the desert; cross over without fail, or the king

---

a1 Or Let me　　b2 Or will　　c9 Or When some of the men fall at the first attack and all the people with him will be swallowed up.'"

17Jonathan and Ahimaaz were staying at En Rogel. A servant girl was to go and inform them, and they were to go and tell King David, for they could not risk being seen entering the city. 18But a young man saw them and told Absalom. So the two of them left quickly and went to the house of a man in Bahurim. He had a well in his courtyard, and they climbed down into it. 19His wife took a covering and spread it out over the opening of the well and scattered grain over it. No-one knew anything about it.

20When Absalom's men came to the woman at the house, they asked, "Where are Ahimaaz and Jonathan?"

The woman answered them, "They crossed over the brook."*d* The men searched but found no-one, so they returned to Jerusalem.

21After the men had gone, the two climbed out of the well and went to inform King David. They said to him, "Set out and cross the river at once; Ahithophel has advised such and such against you." 22So David and all the people with him set out and crossed the Jordan. By daybreak, no-one was left who had not crossed the Jordan.

23When Ahithophel saw that his advice had not been followed, he saddled his donkey and set out for his house in his home town. He put his house in order and then hanged himself. So he died and was buried in his father's tomb.

24David went to Mahanaim, and Absalom crossed the Jordan with all the men of Israel. 25Absalom had appointed Amasa over the army in place of Joab. Amasa was the son of a man named Jether,*e* an Israelite*f* who had married Abigail,*g* the daughter of Nahash and sister of Zeruiah the mother of Joab. 26The Israelites and Absalom camped in the land of Gilead.

27When David came to Mahanaim, Shobi son of Nahash from Rabbah of the Ammonites, and Makir son of Ammiel from Lo Debar, and Barzillai the Gileadite from Rogelim 28brought bedding and bowls and articles of pottery. They also brought wheat and barley, flour and roasted grain, beans and lentils,*h* 29honey and curds, sheep, and cheese from cows' milk for David and his people to eat. For they said, "The people have become hungry and tired and thirsty in the desert."

Absalom's Death

18 David mustered the men who were with him and appointed over them commanders of thousands and commanders of hundreds. 2David sent the troops out—a third under the command of Joab, a third under Joab's brother Abishai son of Zeruiah, and a third under Ittai the Gittite. The king told the troops, "I myself will surely march out with you."

3But the men said, "You must not go out; if we are forced to flee, they won't care about us. Even if half of us die, they won't care; but you are worth ten thousand of us.*a* It would be better now for you to give us support from the city."

4The king answered, "I will do whatever seems best to you."

So the king stood beside the gate while all the men marched out in units of hundreds and of thousands. 5The king commanded Joab, Abishai and Ittai, "Be gentle with the young man Absalom for my sake." And all the troops heard the king giving orders concerning Absalom to each of the commanders.

6The army marched into the field to fight Israel, and the battle took place in the forest of Ephraim. 7There the army of Israel was defeated by David's men, and the casualties that day were great—twenty thousand men. 8The battle spread out over the whole countryside, and the forest claimed more lives that day than the sword.

9Now Absalom happened to meet David's men. He was riding his mule, and as the mule went under the thick branches of a large oak, Absalom's head got caught in the tree. He was left hanging in mid-air, while the mule he was riding kept on going.

10When one of the men saw this, he told Joab, "I have just seen Absalom hanging in an oak tree."

11Joab said to the man who had told him this, "What! You saw him? Why didn't you strike him to the ground right there? Then I would have had to give you ten shekels*b* of silver and a warrior's belt."

12But the man replied, "Even if a thousand shekels*c* were weighed out into my hands, I would not lift my hand against the king's son. In our hearing the king commanded you and Abishai and Ittai, 'Protect the young man Absalom for my sake.'*d* 13And if I had put my life in jeopardy*e*—and nothing is hidden from the king—you would have kept your distance from me."

14Joab said, "I am not going to wait like this for you." So he took three javelins in his hand and plunged them into Absalom's heart while Absalom was still alive in the oak tree. 15And ten of Joab's armour-bearers surrounded Absalom, struck him and killed him.

16Then Joab sounded the trumpet, and the troops stopped pursuing Israel, for Joab halted them. 17They took Absalom, threw him into a big pit in the forest and piled up a large heap of rocks over him. Meanwhile, all the Israelites fled to their homes.

18During his life-time Absalom had taken a

d20 Or *"They passed by the sheep pen towards the water."*   *e25* Hebrew *Ithra*, a variant of *Jether*
f25 Hebrew and some Septuagint manuscripts; other Septuagint manuscripts (see also 1 Chron. 2:17) *Ishmaelite* or *Jezreelite*   *g25* Hebrew *Abigal*, a variant of *Abigail*
h28 Most Septuagint manuscripts and Syriac; Hebrew *lentils, and roasted grain*
a3 Two Hebrew manuscripts, some Septuagint manuscripts and Vulgate; most Hebrew manuscripts *care; for now there are ten thousand like us*   *b11* That is, about 4 ounces (about 115 grams)
c12 That is, about 25 pounds (about 11 kilograms)
d12 A few Hebrew manuscripts, Septuagint, Vulgate and Syriac; most Hebrew manuscripts may be translated *Absalom, whoever you may be.*   *e13* Or *Otherwise, if I had acted treacherously towards him*

'The king commanded Joab, Abishai and Ittai, "Be gentle with . . . Absalom for my sake" . . . Joab . . . took three javelins . . . and plunged them into Absalom's heart' (vv. 5, 14).

SENTIMENTALIST AND REALIST. Commenting on this incident William McKane writes: 'In his dealings with his children David loses all sense of proportion and Joab has deliberately ignored his instructions (v. 5). Nor is he slow in justifying his decision, for he has no time for a king who allows his private feelings to destroy his political judgement.' That sums up the essential difference between David and Joab.

David was quite unjust in dealing with the misconduct of his own family. He allowed sentiment to govern his actions. We may conclude that it is natural for parents to react in this way. In fact, parents often follow one of *two* extreme courses. Either they fail to see any wrong in the behaviour of their children or they demand unrealistic standards of behaviour of their offspring. Both these extremes are dangerous so far as the child's development is concerned. David fell into the first of these traps with consequent disaster for his children and much misery for himself.

Joab was a realist. He had previously acted and pleaded for Absalom's restoration to the court (Chapter 14) but he would not support the rebellion which sought to wrest power from David. Absalom in exile would be too much of a political risk. So in spite of David's instructions Joab killed the usurper.

Today, a growing number of people would reject the idea that realism demands the extreme remedy administered by Joab.

Without a strong application of justice, violence and extremism can threaten society.

1 KINGS 3:1–15
'So give your servant a discerning heart to govern your people and to distinguish between right and wrong' (v. 9).

THE WISDOM OF SOLOMON. In later Hebrew history Solomon's name became synonymous with wisdom and he may have founded a school of wisdom during his reign. J. C. Rylaarsdam comments, 'He was himself, by virtue of his kingship, the one through whom divine counsel and wisdom were, in principle, mediated to men.' The account of Solomon's vision at Gibeon provides an idealized picture of the origins of his reputation.

David Stacey has observed that Solomon's 'reputation for magnificence was more merited than his reputation for wisdom. He was . . . a diplomat and an administrator.' We have to recognize that it was that kind of practical shrewdness which was highly valued and admired by the Orientals of Solomon's time. The biblical account does not recognize the limitations of Solomon until the end of his life (1 Kings 11) but if we examine his policies and organisation we see that they had short-term aims. Once the powerful influence of Solomon was removed the structure which he had built around himself rather than around God, quickly disintegrated.

It is sometimes difficult for us to come to terms with ideas which challenge traditional views but such evidence as we have of Solomon's life reveals him as a cunning ruler rather than a man of spiritual wisdom. It is important for our own lives that we understand the difference between these two qualities.

Wisdom without innocence . . . is cynicism, innocence without wisdom is naivety (Fred Brown).

pillar and erected it in the King's Valley as a monument to himself, for he thought, "I have no son to carry on the memory of my name." He named the pillar after himself, and it is called Absalom's Monument to this day.

David Mourns

19Now Ahimaaz son of Zadok said, "Let me run and take the news to the king that the LORD has delivered him from the hand of his enemies."

20"You are not the one to take the news today," Joab told him. "You may take the news another time, but you must not do so today, because the king's son is dead."

21Then Joab said to a Cushite, "Go, tell the king what you have seen." The Cushite bowed down before Joab and ran off.

22Ahimaaz son of Zadok again said to Joab, "Come what may, please let me run behind the Cushite."

But Joab replied, "My son, why do you want to go? You don't have any news that will bring you a reward."

23He said, "Come what may, I want to run."

So Joab said, "Run!" Then Ahimaaz ran by way of the plain*f* and outran the Cushite.

24While David was sitting between the inner and outer gates, the watchman went up to the roof of the gateway by the wall. As he looked out, he saw a man running alone. 25The watchman called out to the king and reported it.

The king said, "If he is alone, he must have good news." And the man came closer and closer.

26Then the watchman saw another man running, and he called down to the gatekeeper, "Look, another man running alone!"

The king said, "He must be bringing good news, too."

27The watchman said, "It seems to me that the first one runs like Ahimaaz son of Zadok."

"He's a good man," the king said. "He comes with good news."

28Then Ahimaaz called out to the king, "All is well!" He bowed down before the king with his face to the ground and said, "Praise be to the LORD your God! He has delivered up the men who lifted their hands against my lord the king."

29The king asked, "Is the young man Absalom safe?"

Ahimaaz answered, "I saw great confusion just as Joab was about to send the king's servant and me, your servant, but I don't know what it was."

30The king said, "Stand aside and wait here." So he stepped aside and stood there.

31Then the Cushite arrived and said, "My lord the king, hear the good news! The LORD has delivered you today from all who rose up against you."

32The king asked the Cushite, "Is the young man Absalom safe?"

The Cushite replied, "May the enemies of my lord the king and all who rise up to harm you be like that young man."

33The king was shaken. He went up to the room over the gateway and wept. As he went, he said: "O my son Absalom! My son, my son Absalom! If only I had died instead of you—O Absalom, my son, my son!"

19 Joab was told, "The king is weeping and mourning for Absalom." 2And for the whole army the victory that day was turned into mourning, because on that day the troops heard it said, "The king is grieving for his son." 3The men stole into the city that day as men steal in who are ashamed when they flee from battle. 4The king covered his face and cried aloud, "O my son Absalom! O Absalom, my son, my son!"

5Then Joab went into the house to the king and said, "Today you have humiliated all your men, who have just saved your life and the lives of your sons and daughters and the lives of your wives and concubines. 6You love those who hate you and hate those who love you. You have made it clear today that the commanders and their men mean nothing to you. I see that you would be pleased if Absalom were alive today and all of us were dead. 7Now go out and encourage your men. I swear by the LORD that if you don't go out, not a man will be left with you by nightfall. This will be worse for you than all the calamities that have come upon you from your youth till now."

8So the king got up and took his seat in the gateway. When the men were told, "The king is sitting in the gateway," they all came before him.

David Returns to Jerusalem

Meanwhile, the Israelites had fled to their homes. 9Throughout the tribes of Israel, the people were all arguing with each other, saying, "The king delivered us from the hand of our enemies; he is the one who rescued us from the hand of the Philistines. But now he has fled the country because of Absalom; 10and Absalom, whom we anointed to rule over us, has died in battle. So why do you say nothing about bringing the king back?"

11King David sent this message to Zadok and Abiathar, the priests: "Ask the elders of Judah, 'Why should you be the last to bring the king back to his palace, since what is being said throughout Israel has reached the king at his quarters? 12You are my brothers, my own flesh and blood. So why should you be the last to bring back the king?' 13And say to Amasa, 'Are you not my own flesh and blood? May God deal with me, be it ever so severely, if from now on you are not the commander of my army in place of Joab.'"

14He won over the hearts of all the men of Judah as though they were one man. They sent word to the king, "Return, you and all your men." 15Then the king returned and went as far as the Jordan.

Now the men of Judah had come to Gilgal to go out and meet the king and bring him

f23 That is, the plain of the Jordan

across the Jordan. ¹⁶Shimei son of Gera, the Benjamite from Bahurim, hurried down with the men of Judah to meet King David. ¹⁷With him were a thousand Benjamites, along with Ziba, the steward of Saul's household, and his fifteen sons and twenty servants. They rushed to the Jordan, where the king was. ¹⁸They crossed at the ford to take the king's household over and to do whatever he wished.

When Shimei son of Gera crossed the Jordan, he fell prostrate before the king ¹⁹and said to him, "May my lord not hold me guilty. Do not remember how your servant did wrong on the day my lord the king left Jerusalem. May the king put it out of his mind. ²⁰For I your servant know that I have sinned, but today I have come here as the first of the whole house of Joseph to come down and meet my lord the king."

²¹Then Abishai son of Zeruiah said, "Shouldn't Shimei be put to death for this? He cursed the LORD's anointed."

²²David replied, "What do you and I have in common, you sons of Zeruiah? This day you have become my adversaries! Should anyone be put to death in Israel today? Do I not know that today I am king over Israel?" ²³So the king said to Shimei, "You shall not die." And the king promised him on oath.

²⁴Mephibosheth, Saul's grandson, also went down to meet the king. He had not taken care of his feet or trimmed his moustache or washed his clothes from the day the king left until the day he returned safely. ²⁵When he came from Jerusalem to meet the king, the king asked him, "Why didn't you go with me, Mephibosheth?"

²⁶He said, "My lord the king, since I your servant am lame, I said, 'I will have my donkey saddled and will ride on it, so that I can go with the king.' But Ziba my servant betrayed me. ²⁷And he has slandered your servant to my lord the king. My lord the king is like an angel of God; so do whatever pleases you. ²⁸All my grandfather's descendants deserved nothing but death from my lord the king, but you gave your servant a place among those who sat at your table. So what right do I have to make any more appeals to the king?"

²⁹The king said to him, "Why say more? I order you and Ziba to divide the fields."

³⁰Mephibosheth said to the king, "Let him take everything, now that my lord the king has arrived home safely."

³¹Barzillai the Gileadite also came down from Rogelim to cross the Jordan with the king and to send him on his way from there. ³²Now Barzillai was a very old man, eighty years of age. He had provided for the king during his stay in Mahanaim, for he was a very wealthy man. ³³The king said to Barzillai, "Cross over with me and stay with me in Jerusalem, and I will provide for you."

³⁴But Barzillai answered the king, "How many more years shall I live, that I should go up to Jerusalem with the king? ³⁵I am now eighty years old. Can I tell the difference between what is good and what is not? Can your servant taste what he eats and drinks?

Can I still hear the voices of men and women singers? Why should your servant be an added burden to my lord the king? ³⁶Your servant will cross over the Jordan with the king for a short distance, but why should the king reward me in this way? ³⁷Let your servant return, that I may die in my own town near the tomb of my father and mother. But here is your servant Kimham. Let him cross over with my lord the king. Do for him whatever pleases you."

³⁸The king said, "Kimham shall cross over with me, and I will do for him whatever pleases you. And anything you desire from me I will do for you."

³⁹So all the people crossed the Jordan, and then the king crossed over. The king kissed Barzillai and gave him his blessing, and Barzillai returned to his home.

⁴⁰When the king crossed over to Gilgal, Kimham crossed with him. All the troops of Judah and half the troops of Israel had taken the king over.

⁴¹Soon all the men of Israel were coming to the king and saying to him, "Why did our brothers, the men of Judah, steal the king away and bring him and his household across the Jordan, together with all his men?"

⁴²All the men of Judah answered the men of Israel, "We did this because the king is closely related to us. Why are you angry about it? Have we eaten any of the king's provisions? Have we taken anything for ourselves?"

⁴³Then the men of Israel answered the men of Judah, "We have ten shares in the king; and besides, we have a greater claim on David than you have. So why do you treat us with contempt? Were we not the first to speak of bringing back our king?"

But the men of Judah responded even more harshly than the men of Israel.

Sheba Rebels Against David

20 Now a troublemaker named Sheba son of Bicri, a Benjamite, happened to be there. He sounded the trumpet and shouted,

"We have no share in David,
    no part in Jesse's son!
Every man to his tent, O Israel!"

²So all the men of Israel deserted David to follow Sheba son of Bicri. But the men of Judah stayed by their king all the way from the Jordan to Jerusalem.

³When David returned to his palace in Jerusalem, he took the ten concubines he had left to take care of the palace and put them in a house under guard. He provided for them, but did not lie with them. They were kept in confinement till the day of their death, living as widows.

⁴Then the king said to Amasa, "Summon the men of Judah to come to me within three days, and be here yourself." ⁵But when Amasa went to summon Judah, he took longer than the time the king had set for him.

⁶David said to Abishai, "Now Sheba son of Bicri will do us more harm than Absalom

did. Take your master's men and pursue him, or he will find fortified cities and escape from us." ⁷So Joab's men and the Kerethites and Pelethites and all the mighty warriors went out under the command of Abishai. They marched out from Jerusalem to pursue Sheba son of Bicri.

⁸While they were at the great rock in Gibeon, Amasa came to meet them. Joab was wearing his military tunic, and strapped over it at his waist was a belt with a dagger in its sheath. As he stepped forward, it dropped out of its sheath.

⁹Joab said to Amasa, "How are you, my brother?" Then Joab took Amasa by the beard with his right hand to kiss him. ¹⁰Amasa was not on his guard against the dagger in Joab's hand, and Joab plunged it into his belly, and his intestines spilled out on the ground. Without being stabbed again, Amasa died. Then Joab and his brother Abishai pursued Sheba son of Bicri.

¹¹One of Joab's men stood beside Amasa and said, "Whoever favours Joab, and whoever is for David, let him follow Joab!" ¹²Amasa lay wallowing in his blood in the middle of the road, and the man saw that all the troops came to a halt there. When he realised that everyone who came up to Amasa stopped, he dragged him from the road into a field and threw a garment over him. ¹³After Amasa had been removed from the road, all the men went on with Joab to pursue Sheba son of Bicri.

¹⁴Sheba passed through all the tribes of Israel to Abel Beth Maacah*a* and through the entire region of the Berites, who gathered together and followed him. ¹⁵All the troops with Joab came and besieged Sheba in Abel Beth Maacah. They built a siege ramp up to the city, and it stood against the outer fortifications. While they were battering the wall to bring it down, ¹⁶a wise woman called from the city, "Listen! Listen! Tell Joab to come here so that I can speak to him." ¹⁷He went towards her, and she asked, "Are you Joab?"

"I am," he answered.

She said, "Listen to what your servant has to say."

"I'm listening," he said.

¹⁸She continued, "Long ago they used to say, 'Get your answer at Abel,' and that settled it. ¹⁹We are the peaceful and faithful in Israel. You are trying to destroy a city that is a mother in Israel. Why do you want to swallow up the LORD's inheritance?"

²⁰"Far be it from me!" Joab replied, "Far be it from me to swallow up or destroy! ²¹That is not the case. A man named Sheba son of Bicri, from the hill country of Ephraim, has lifted up his hand against the king, against David. Hand over this one man, and I'll withdraw from the city."

The woman said to Joab, "His head will be thrown to you from the wall."

²²Then the woman went to all the people with her wise advice, and they cut off the head of Sheba son of Bicri and threw it to Joab. So he sounded the trumpet, and his men dispersed from the city, each returning to his home. And Joab went back to the king in Jerusalem.

²³Joab was over Israel's entire army; Benaiah son of Jehoiada was over the Kerethites and Pelethites; ²⁴Adoniram*b* was in charge of forced labour; Jehoshaphat son of Ahilud was recorder; ²⁵Sheva was secretary; Zadok and Abiathar were priests; ²⁶and Ira the Jairite was David's priest.

The Gibeonites Avenged

21 During the reign of David, there was a famine for three successive years; so David sought the face of the LORD. The LORD said, "It is on account of Saul and his blood-stained house; it is because he put the Gibeonites to death."

²The king summoned the Gibeonites and spoke to them. (Now the Gibeonites were not a part of Israel but were survivors of the Amorites; the Israelites had sworn to ⌊spare⌋ them, but Saul in his zeal for Israel and Judah had tried to annihilate them.) ³David asked the Gibeonites, "What shall I do for you? How shall I make amends so that you will bless the LORD's inheritance?"

⁴The Gibeonites answered him, "We have no right to demand silver or gold from Saul or his family, nor do we have the right to put anyone in Israel to death."

"What do you want me to do for you?" David asked.

⁵They answered the king, "As for the man who destroyed us and plotted against us so that we have been decimated and have no place anywhere in Israel, ⁶let seven of his male descendants be given to us to be killed and exposed before the LORD at Gibeah of Saul—the LORD's chosen one."

So the king said, "I will give them to you."

⁷The king spared Mephibosheth son of Jonathan, the son of Saul, because of the oath before the LORD between David and Jonathan son of Saul. ⁸But the king took Armoni and Mephibosheth, the two sons of Aiah's daughter Rizpah, whom she had borne to Saul, together with the five sons of Saul's daughter Merab,*a* whom she had borne to Adriel son of Barzillai the Meholathite. ⁹He handed them over to the Gibeonites, who killed and exposed them on a hill before the LORD. All seven of them fell together; they were put to death during the first days of harvest, just as the barley harvest was beginning.

¹⁰Rizpah daughter of Aiah took sackcloth and spread it out for herself on a rock. From the beginning of the harvest till the rain poured down from the heavens on the bodies, she did not let the birds of the air touch them by day or the wild animals by night. ¹¹When David was told what Aiah's daughter Rizpah, Saul's concubine, had

---

a14 Or Abel, even Beth Maacah; also in verse 15
b24 Some Septuagint manuscripts (see also 1 Kings 4:6 and 5:14); Hebrew Adoram
a8 Two Hebrew manuscripts, some Septuagint manuscripts and Syriac (see also 1 Samuel 18:19); most Hebrew and Septuagint manuscripts Michal

done, [12]he went and took the bones of Saul and his son Jonathan from the citizens of Jabesh Gilead. (They had taken them secretly from the public square at Beth Shan, where the Philistines had hung them after they struck Saul down on Gilboa.) [13]David brought the bones of Saul and his son Jonathan from there, and the bones of those who had been killed and exposed were gathered up.

[14]They buried the bones of Saul and his son Jonathan in the tomb of Saul's father Kish, at Zela in Benjamin, and did everything the king commanded. After that, God answered prayer on behalf of the land.

Wars Against the Philistines

[15]Once again there was a battle between the Philistines and Israel. David went down with his men to fight against the Philistines, and he became exhausted. [16]And Ishbi-Benob, one of the descendants of Rapha, whose bronze spearhead weighed three hundred shekels[b] and who was armed with a new ⌊sword⌋, said he would kill David. [17]But Abishai son of Zeruiah came to David's rescue; he struck the Philistine down and killed him. Then David's men swore to him, saying, "Never again will you go out with us to battle, so that the lamp of Israel will not be extinguished."

[18]In the course of time, there was another battle with the Philistines, at Gob. At that time Sibbecai the Hushathite killed Saph, one of the descendants of Rapha.

[19]In another battle with the Philistines at Gob, Elhanan son of Jaare-Oregim[c] the Bethlehemite killed Goliath[d] the Gittite, who had a spear with a shaft like a weaver's rod.

[20]In still another battle, which took place at Gath, there was a huge man with six fingers on each hand and six toes on each foot —twenty-four in all. He also was descended from Rapha. [21]When he taunted Israel, Jonathan son of Shimeah, David's brother, killed him.

[22]These four were descendants of Rapha in Gath, and they fell at the hands of David and his men.

David's Song of Praise

22 David sang to the LORD the words of this song when the LORD delivered him from the hand of all his enemies and from the hand of Saul. [2]He said:

"The LORD is my rock, my fortress and my deliverer;
[3]   my God is my rock, in whom I take refuge,
   my shield and the horn[a] of my salvation.
He is my stronghold, my refuge and my saviour—
   from violent men you save me.

[4]I call to the LORD, who is worthy of praise,
   and I am saved from my enemies.

[5]"The waves of death swirled about me;
   the torrents of destruction overwhelmed me.
[6]The cords of the grave[b] coiled around me;
   the snares of death confronted me.
[7]In my distress I called to the LORD;
   I called out to my God.
From his temple he heard my voice;
   my cry came to his ears.

[8]"The earth trembled and quaked,
   the foundations of the heavens[c] shook;
   they trembled because he was angry.
[9]Smoke rose from his nostrils;
   consuming fire came from his mouth,
   burning coals blazed out of it.
[10]He parted the heavens and came down;
   dark clouds were under his feet.
[11]He mounted the cherubim and flew;
   he soared[d] on the wings of the wind.
[12]He made darkness his canopy around him—
   the dark[e] rain clouds of the sky.
[13]Out of the brightness of his presence
   bolts of lightning blazed forth.
[14]The LORD thundered from heaven;
   the voice of the Most High resounded.
[15]He shot arrows and scattered ⌊the enemies⌋,
   bolts of lightning and routed them.
[16]The valleys of the sea were exposed
   and the foundations of the earth laid bare
at the rebuke of the LORD,
   at the blast of breath from his nostrils.

[17]"He reached down from on high and took hold of me;
   he drew me out of deep waters.
[18]He rescued me from my powerful enemy,
   from my foes, who were too strong for me.
[19]They confronted me in the day of my disaster,
   but the LORD was my support.
[20]He brought me out into a spacious place;
   he rescued me because he delighted in me.

[21]"The LORD has dealt with me according to my righteousness;
   according to the cleanness of my hands he has rewarded me.
[22]For I have kept the ways of the LORD;
   I have not done evil by turning from my God.
[23]All his laws are before me;
   I have not turned away from his decrees.
[24]I have been blameless before him
   and have kept myself from sin.

---

[b]16 That is, about 7½ pounds (about 3.5 kilograms)   [c]19 Or son of Jair the weaver
[d]19 Hebrew and Septuagint; 1 Chron. 20:5 son of Jair killed Lahmi the brother of Goliath
[a]3 Horn here symbolises strength.   [b]6 Hebrew Sheol
[c]8 Hebrew; Vulgate and Syriac (see also Psalm 18:7) mountains
[d]11 Many Hebrew manuscripts (see also Psalm 18:10); most Hebrew manuscripts appeared
[e]12 Septuagint and Vulgate (see also Psalm 18:11); Hebrew massed

25The LORD has rewarded me according to
    my righteousness,
  according to my cleanness*f* in his sight.

26"To the faithful you show yourself
    faithful,
  to the blameless you show yourself
    blameless,
27to the pure you show yourself pure,
  but to the crooked you show yourself
    shrewd.
28You save the humble,
  but your eyes are on the haughty to
    bring them low.
29You are my lamp, O LORD;
  the LORD turns my darkness into light.
30With your help I can advance against a
    troop;*g*
  with my God I can scale a wall.

31"As for God, his way is perfect;
  the word of the LORD is flawless.
He is a shield
  for all who take refuge in him.
32For who is God besides the LORD?
  And who is the Rock except our God?
33It is God who arms me with strength*h*
  and makes my way perfect.
34He makes my feet like the feet of a deer;
  he enables me to stand on the heights.
35He trains my hands for battle;
  my arms can bend a bow of bronze.
36You give me your shield of victory;
  you stoop down to make me great.
37You broaden the path beneath me,
  so that my ankles do not turn over.

38"I pursued my enemies and crushed them;
  I did not turn back till they were
    destroyed.
39I crushed them completely, and they could
    not rise;
  they fell beneath my feet.
40You armed me with strength for battle;
  you made my adversaries bow at my
    feet.
41You made my enemies turn their backs in
    flight,
  and I destroyed my foes.
42They cried for help, but there was no-one
    to save them—
  to the LORD, but he did not answer.
43I beat them as fine as the dust of the earth;
  I pounded and trampled them like mud
    in the streets.

44"You have delivered me from the attacks
    of my people;
  you have preserved me as the head of
    nations.
People I did not know are subject to me,
45 and foreigners come cringing to me;

as soon as they hear me, they obey me.
46They all lose heart;
  they come trembling*i* from their
    strongholds.

47"The LORD lives! Praise be to my Rock!
  Exalted be God, the Rock, my Saviour!
48He is the God who avenges me,
  who puts the nations under me,
49 who sets me free from my enemies.
You exalted me above my foes;
  from violent men you rescued me.
50Therefore I will praise you, O LORD,
    among the nations;
  I will sing praises to your name.
51He gives his king great victories;
  he shows unfailing kindness to his
    anointed,
  to David and his descendants for ever."

The Last Words of David

23 These are the last words of David:

"The oracle of David son of Jesse,
  the oracle of the man exalted by the
    Most High,
the man anointed by the God of Jacob,
  Israel's singer of songs:*a*

2"The Spirit of the LORD spoke through me;
  his word was on my tongue.
3The God of Israel spoke,
  the Rock of Israel said to me:
'When one rules over men in
    righteousness,
  when he rules in the fear of God,
4he is like the light of morning at sunrise
  on a cloudless morning,
like the brightness after rain
  that brings the grass from the earth.'

5"Is not my house right with God?
  Has he not made with me an everlasting
    covenant,
  arranged and secured in every part?
Will he not bring to fruition my salvation
  and grant me my every desire?
6But evil men are all to be cast aside like
    thorns,
  which are not gathered with the hand.
7Whoever touches thorns
  uses a tool of iron or the shaft of a spear;
  they are burned up where they lie."

David's Mighty Men

8These are the names of David's mighty
men:
  Josheb-Basshebeth,*b* a Tahkemonite,*c* was
chief of the Three; he raised his spear against
eight hundred men, whom he killed*d* in one
encounter.
  9Next to him was Eleazar son of Dodai the

---

f25 Hebrew; Septuagint and Vulgate (see also Psalm 18:24) *to the cleanness of my hands*
g30 Or *can run through a barricade*
h33 Dead Sea Scrolls, some Septuagint manuscripts, Vulgate and Syriac (see also Psalm 18:32); Masoretic Text *who is my strong refuge*
i46 Some Septuagint manuscripts and Vulgate (see also Psalm 18:45); Masoretic Text *they arm themselves.*
a1 Or *Israel's beloved singer*
b8 Hebrew; some Septuagint manuscripts suggest *Ish-Bosheth*, that is, *Esh-Baal* (see also 1 Chron. 11:11 *Jashobeam*).   *c8* Probably a variant of *Hacmonite* (see 1 Chron. 11:11)
d8 Some Septuagint manuscripts (see also 1 Chron. 11:11); Hebrew and other Septuagint manuscripts *Three; it was Adino the Eznite who killed eight hundred men*

Ahohite. As one of the three mighty men, he was with David when they taunted the Philistines gathered ₗat Pas Dammimₗ*e* for battle. Then the men of Israel retreated, ¹⁰but he stood his ground and struck down the Philistines till his hand grew tired and froze to the sword. The LORD brought about a great victory that day. The troops returned to Eleazar, but only to strip the dead.

¹¹Next to him was Shammah son of Agee the Hararite. When the Philistines banded together at a place where there was a field full of lentils, Israel's troops fled from them. ¹²But Shammah took his stand in the middle of the field. He defended it and struck the Philistines down, and the LORD brought about a great victory.

¹³During harvest time, three of the thirty chief men came down to David at the cave of Adullam, while a band of Philistines was encamped in the Valley of Rephaim. ¹⁴At that time David was in the stronghold, and the Philistine garrison was at Bethlehem. ¹⁵David longed for water and said, "Oh, that someone would get me a drink of water from the well near the gate of Bethlehem!" ¹⁶So the three mighty men broke through the Philistine lines, drew water from the well near the gate of Bethlehem and carried it back to David. But he refused to drink it; instead, he poured it out before the LORD. ¹⁷"Far be it from me, O LORD, to do this!" he said. "Is it not the blood of men who went at the risk of their lives?" And David would not drink it.

Such were the exploits of the three mighty men.

¹⁸Abishai the brother of Joab son of Zeruiah was chief of the Three.*f* He raised his spear against three hundred men, whom he killed, and so he became as famous as the Three. ¹⁹Was he not held in greater honour than the Three? He became their commander, even though he was not included among them.

²⁰Benaiah son of Jehoiada was a valiant fighter from Kabzeel, who performed great exploits. He struck down two of Moab's best men. He also went down into a pit on a snowy day and killed a lion. ²¹And he struck down a huge Egyptian. Although the Egyptian had a spear in his hand, Benaiah went against him with a club. He snatched the spear from the Egyptian's hand and killed him with his own spear. ²²Such were the exploits of Benaiah son of Jehoiada; he too was as famous as the three mighty men. ²³He was held in greater honour than any of the Thirty, but he was not included among the Three. And David put him in charge of his bodyguard.

²⁴Among the Thirty were:
Asahel the brother of Joab,

Elhanan son ₒf Dodo from Bethlehem,
²⁵Shammah the Harodite,
Elika the Harodite,
²⁶Helez the Paltite,
Ira son of Ikkesh from Tekoa,
²⁷Abiezer from Anathoth,
Mebunnai*g* the Hushathite,
²⁸Zalmon the Ahohite,
Maharai the Netophathite,
²⁹Heled*h* son of Baanah the Netophathite,
Ithai son of Ribai from Gibeah in Benjamin,
³⁰Benaiah the Pirathonite,
Hiddai*i* from the ravines of Gaash,
³¹Abi-Albon the Arbathite,
Azmaveth the Barhumite,
³²Eliahba the Shaalbonite,
the sons of Jashen,
Jonathan ³³son of*j* Shammah the Hararite,
Ahiam son of Sharar*k* the Hararite,
³⁴Eliphelet son of Ahasbai the Maacathite,
Eliam son of Ahithophel the Gilonite,
³⁵Hezro the Carmelite,
Paarai the Arbite,
³⁶Igal son of Nathan from Zobah,
the son of Hagri,*l*
³⁷Zelek the Ammonite,
Naharai the Beerothite, the armourbearer of Joab son of Zeruiah,
³⁸Ira the Ithrite,
Gareb the Ithrite
³⁹and Uriah the Hittite.
There are thirty-seven in all.

David Counts the Fighting Men

24 Again the anger of the LORD burned against Israel, and he incited David against them, saying, "Go and take a census of Israel and Judah."

²So the king said to Joab and the army commanders*a* with him, "Go throughout the tribes of Israel from Dan to Beersheba and enrol the fighting men, so that I may know how many there are."

³But Joab replied to the king, "May the LORD your God multiply the troops a hundred times over, and may the eyes of my lord the king see it. But why does my lord the king want to do such a thing?"

⁴The king's word, however, overruled Joab and the army commanders; so they left the presence of the king to enrol the fighting men of Israel.

⁵After crossing the Jordan, they camped near Aroer, south of the town in the gorge, and then went through Gad and on to Jazer. ⁶They went to Gilead and the region of Tahtim Hodshi, and on to Dan Jaan and around towards Sidon. ⁷Then they went towards the fortress of Tyre and all the towns

---

e9 See 1 Chron. 11:13; Hebrew *gathered there.*
f18 Most Hebrew manuscripts (see also 1 Chron. 11:20); two Hebrew manuscripts and Syriac *Thirty*
g27 Hebrew; some Septuagint manuscripts (see also 1 Chron. 11:29) *Sibbecai*
h29 Some Hebrew manuscripts and Vulgate (see also 1 Chron. 11:30); most Hebrew manuscripts *Heleb*
i30 Hebrew; some Septuagint manuscripts (see also 1 Chron. 11:32) *Hurai*
j33 Some Septuagint manuscripts (see also 1 Chron. 11:34); Hebrew does not have *son of.*
k33 Hebrew; some Septuagint manuscripts (see also 1 Chron. 11:35) *Sacar*
l36 Some Septuagint manuscripts (see also 1 Chron. 11:38); Hebrew *Haggadi*
a2 Septuagint (see also verse 4 and 1 Chron. 21:2); Hebrew *Joab the army commander*

of the Hivites and Canaanites. Finally, they went on to Beersheba in the Negev of Judah.

[8]After they had gone through the entire land, they came back to Jerusalem at the end of nine months and twenty days.

[9]Joab reported the number of the fighting men to the king: In Israel there were eight hundred thousand able-bodied men who could handle a sword, and in Judah five hundred thousand.

[10]David was conscience-stricken after he had counted the fighting men, and he said to the LORD, "I have sinned greatly in what I have done. Now, O LORD, I beg you, take away the guilt of your servant. I have done a very foolish thing."

[11]Before David got up the next morning, the word of the LORD had come to Gad the prophet, David's seer: [12]"Go and tell David, 'This is what the LORD says: I am giving you three options. Choose one of them for me to carry out against you.'"

[13]So Gad went to David and said to him, "Shall there come upon you three[b] years of famine in your land? Or three months of fleeing from your enemies while they pursue you? Or three days of plague in your land? Now then, think it over and decide how I should answer the one who sent me."

[14]David said to Gad, "I am in deep distress. Let us fall into the hands of the LORD, for his mercy is great; but do not let me fall into the hands of men."

[15]So the LORD sent a plague on Israel from that morning until the end of the time designated, and seventy thousand of the people from Dan to Beersheba died. [16]When the angel stretched out his hand to destroy Jerusalem, the LORD was grieved because of the calamity and said to the angel who was afflicting the people, "Enough! Withdraw your hand." The angel of the LORD was then at the threshing-floor of Araunah the Jebusite.

[17]When David saw the angel who was striking down the people, he said to the LORD, "I am the one who has sinned and done wrong. These are but sheep. What have they done? Let your hand fall upon me and my family."

David Builds an Altar

[18]On that day Gad went to David and said to him, "Go up and build an altar to the LORD on the threshing-floor of Araunah the Jebusite." [19]So David went up, as the LORD had commanded through Gad. [20]When Araunah looked and saw the king and his men coming towards him, he went out and bowed down before the king with his face to the ground.

[21]Araunah said, "Why has my lord the king come to his servant?"

"To buy your threshing-floor," David answered, "so that I can build an altar to the LORD, that the plague on the people may be stopped."

[22]Araunah said to David, "Let my lord the king take whatever pleases him and offer it up. Here are oxen for the burnt offering, and here are threshing-sledges and ox yokes for the wood. [23]O king, Araunah gives all this to the king." Araunah also said to him, "May the LORD your God accept you."

[24]But the king replied to Araunah, "No, I insist on paying you for it. I will not sacrifice to the LORD my God burnt offerings that cost me nothing."

So David bought the threshing-floor and the oxen and paid fifty shekels[c] of silver for them. [25]David built an altar to the LORD there and sacrificed burnt offerings and fellowship offerings.[d] Then the LORD answered prayer on behalf of the land, and the plague on Israel was stopped.

---

b13 Septuagint (see also 1 Chron. 21:12); Hebrew *seven*　　*c24* That is, about 1¼ pounds (about 0.6 kilogram)
d25 Traditionally *peace offerings*

1 Kings

Adonijah Sets Himself Up as King

1 When King David was old and well advanced in years, he could not keep warm even when they put covers over him. ²So his servants said to him, "Let us look for a young virgin to attend the king and take care of him. She can lie beside him so that our lord the king may keep warm."

³Then they searched throughout Israel for a beautiful girl and found Abishag, a Shunammite, and brought her to the king. ⁴The girl was very beautiful; she took care of the king and waited on him, but the king had no intimate relations with her.

⁵Now Adonijah, whose mother was Haggith, put himself forward and said, "I will be king." So he got chariots and horses*ᵃ* ready, with fifty men to run ahead of him. ⁶(His father had never interfered with him by asking, "Why do you behave as you do?" He was also very handsome and was born next after Absalom.)

⁷Adonijah conferred with Joab son of Zeruiah and with Abiathar the priest, and they gave him their support. ⁸But Zadok the priest, Benaiah son of Jehoiada, Nathan the prophet, Shimei and Rei*ᵇ* and David's special guard did not join Adonijah.

⁹Adonijah then sacrificed sheep, cattle and fattened calves at the Stone of Zoheleth near En Rogel. He invited all his brothers, the king's sons, and all the men of Judah who were royal officials, ¹⁰but he did not invite Nathan the prophet or Benaiah or the special guard or his brother Solomon.

¹¹Then Nathan asked Bathsheba, Solomon's mother, "Have you not heard that Adonijah, the son of Haggith, has become king without our lord David's knowing it? ¹²Now then, let me advise you how you can save your own life and the life of your son Solomon. ¹³Go in to King David and say to him, 'My lord the king, did you not swear to me your servant: "Surely Solomon your son shall be king after me, and he will sit on my throne"? Why then has Adonijah become king?' ¹⁴While you are still there talking to the king, I will come in and confirm what you have said."

¹⁵So Bathsheba went to see the aged king in his room, where Abishag the Shunammite was attending him. ¹⁶Bathsheba bowed low and knelt before the king.

"What is it you want?" the king asked.

¹⁷She said to him, "My lord, you yourself swore to me your servant by the LORD your God: 'Solomon your son shall become king after me, and he will sit on my throne.' ¹⁸But now Adonijah has become king, and you, my lord the king, do not know about it. ¹⁹He has sacrificed great numbers of cattle, fattened calves, and sheep, and has invited all the king's sons, Abiathar the priest and Joab the commander of the army, but he has not invited Solomon your servant. ²⁰My lord the king, the eyes of all Israel are on you, to learn from you who will sit on the throne of my lord the king after him. ²¹Otherwise, as soon as my lord the king is laid to rest with his fathers, I and my son Solomon will be treated as criminals."

²²While she was still speaking with the king, Nathan the prophet arrived. ²³And they told the king, "Nathan the prophet is here." So he went before the king and bowed with his face to the ground.

²⁴Nathan said, "Have you, my lord the king, declared that Adonijah shall be king after you, and that he will sit on your throne? ²⁵Today he has gone down and sacrificed great numbers of cattle, fattened calves, and sheep. He has invited all the king's sons, the commanders of the army and Abiathar the priest. At this very moment they are eating and drinking with him and saying, 'Long live King Adonijah!' ²⁶But me your servant, and Zadok the priest, and Benaiah son of Jehoiada, and your servant Solomon he did not invite. ²⁷Is this something my lord the king has done without letting his servants know who should sit on the throne of my lord the king after him?"

David Makes Solomon King

²⁸Then King David said, "Call in Bathsheba." So she came into the king's presence and stood before him.

²⁹The king then took an oath: "As surely as the LORD lives, who has delivered me out of every trouble, ³⁰I will surely carry out today what I swore to you by the LORD, the God of Israel: Solomon your son shall be king after

---

ᵃ5 Or charioteers   ᵇ8 Or and his friends

me, and he will sit on my throne in my place."

31Then Bathsheba bowed low with her face to the ground and, kneeling before the king, said, "May my lord King David live for ever!"

32King David said, "Call in Zadok the priest, Nathan the prophet and Benaiah son of Jehoiada." When they came before the king, 33he said to them: "Take your lord's servants with you and set Solomon my son on my own mule and take him down to Gihon. 34There shall Zadok the priest and Nathan the prophet anoint him king over Israel. Blow the trumpet and shout, 'Long live King Solomon!' 35Then you are to go up with him, and he is to come and sit on my throne and reign in my place. I have appointed him ruler over Israel and Judah."

36Benaiah son of Jehoiada answered the king, "Amen! May the LORD, the God of my lord the king, so declare it. 37As the LORD was with my lord the king, so may he be with Solomon to make his throne even greater than the throne of my lord King David!"

38So Zadok the priest, Nathan the prophet, Benaiah son of Jehoiada, the Kerethites and the Pelethites went down and put Solomon on King David's mule and escorted him to Gihon. 39Zadok the priest took the horn of oil from the sacred tent and anointed Solomon. Then they sounded the trumpet and all the people shouted, "Long live King Solomon!" 40And all the people went up after him, playing flutes and rejoicing greatly, so that the ground shook with the sound.

41Adonijah and all the guests who were with him heard it as they were finishing their feast. On hearing the sound of the trumpet, Joab asked, "What's the meaning of all the noise in the city?"

42Even as he was speaking, Jonathan son of Abiathar the priest arrived. Adonijah said, "Come in. A worthy man like you must be bringing good news."

43"Not at all!" Jonathan answered. "Our lord King David has made Solomon king. 44The king has sent with him Zadok the priest, Nathan the prophet, Benaiah son of Jehoiada, the Kerethites and the Pelethites, and they have put him on the king's mule, 45and Zadok the priest and Nathan the prophet have anointed him king at Gihon. From there they have gone up cheering, and the city resounds with it. That's the noise you hear. 46Moreover, Solomon has taken his seat on the royal throne. 47Also, the royal officials have come to congratulate our lord King David, saying, 'May your God make Solomon's name more famous than yours and his throne greater than yours!' And the king bowed in worship on his bed 48and said, 'Praise be to the LORD, the God of Israel, who has allowed my eyes to see a successor on my throne today.'"

49At this, all Adonijah's guests rose in alarm and dispersed. 50But Adonijah, in fear of Solomon, went and took hold of the horns

of the altar. 51Then Solomon was told, "Adonijah is afraid of King Solomon and is clinging to the horns of the altar. He says, 'Let King Solomon swear to me today that he will not put his servant to death with the sword.'"

52Solomon replied, "If he shows himself to be a worthy man, not a hair of his head will fall to the ground; but if evil is found in him, he will die." 53Then King Solomon sent men, and they brought him down from the altar. And Adonijah came and bowed down to King Solomon, and Solomon said, "Go to your home."

David's Charge to Solomon

2 When the time drew near for David to die, he gave a charge to Solomon his son.

2"I am about to go the way of all the earth," he said. "So be strong, show yourself a man, 3and observe what the LORD your God requires: Walk in his ways, and keep his decrees and commands, his laws and requirements, as written in the Law of Moses, so that you may prosper in all you do and wherever you go, 4and that the LORD may keep his promise to me: 'If your descendants watch how they live, and if they walk faithfully before me with all their heart and soul, you will never fail to have a man on the throne of Israel.'

5"Now you yourself know what Joab son of Zeruiah did to me—what he did to the two commanders of Israel's armies, Abner son of Ner and Amasa son of Jether. He killed them, shedding their blood in peacetime as if in battle, and with that blood stained the belt round his waist and the sandals on his feet. 6Deal with him according to your wisdom, but do not let his grey head go down to the grave*a* in peace.

7"But show kindness to the sons of Barzillai of Gilead and let them be among those who eat at your table. They stood by me when I fled from your brother Absalom.

8"And remember, you have with you Shimei son of Gera, the Benjamite from Bahurim, who called down bitter curses on me the day I went to Mahanaim. When he came down to meet me at the Jordan, I swore to him by the LORD: 'I will not put you to death by the sword.' 9But now, do not consider him innocent. You are a man of wisdom; you will know what to do to him. Bring his grey head down to the grave in blood."

10Then David rested with his fathers and was buried in the City of David. 11He had reigned for forty years over Israel—seven years in Hebron and thirty-three in Jerusalem. 12So Solomon sat on the throne of his father David, and his rule was firmly established.

Solomon's Throne Established

13Now Adonijah, the son of Haggith, went to Bathsheba, Solomon's mother. Bathsheba asked him, "Do you come peacefully?"

*a*6 Hebrew *Sheol*; also in verse 9

He answered, "Yes, peacefully." ¹⁴Then he added, "I have something to say to you." "You may say it," she replied.

¹⁵"As you know," he said, "the kingdom was mine. All Israel looked to me as their king. But things changed, and the kingdom has gone to my brother; for it has come to him from the LORD. ¹⁶Now I have one request to make of you. Do not refuse me."

"You may make it," she said.

¹⁷So he continued, "Please ask King Solomon—he will not refuse you—to give me Abishag the Shunammite as my wife."

¹⁸"Very well," Bathsheba replied, "I will speak to the king for you."

¹⁹When Bathsheba went to King Solomon to speak to him for Adonijah, the king stood up to meet her, bowed down to her and sat down on his throne. He had a throne brought for the king's mother, and she sat down at his right hand.

²⁰"I have one small request to make of you," she said. "Do not refuse me."

The king replied, "Make it, my mother; I will not refuse you."

²¹So she said, "Let Abishag the Shunammite be given in marriage to your brother Adonijah."

²²King Solomon answered his mother, "Why do you request Abishag the Shunammite for Adonijah? You might as well request the kingdom for him—after all, he is my older brother—yes, for him and for Abiathar the priest and Joab son of Zeruiah!"

²³Then King Solomon swore by the LORD: "May God deal with me, be it ever so severely, if Adonijah does not pay with his life for this request! ²⁴And now, as surely as the LORD lives—he who has established me securely on the throne of my father David and has founded a dynasty for me as he promised—Adonijah shall be put to death today!" ²⁵So King Solomon gave orders to Benaiah son of Jehoiada, and he struck down Adonijah and he died.

²⁶To Abiathar the priest the king said, "Go back to your fields in Anathoth. You deserve to die, but I will not put you to death now, because you carried the ark of the Sovereign LORD before my father David and shared all my father's hardships." ²⁷So Solomon removed Abiathar from the priesthood of the LORD, fulfilling the word the LORD had spoken at Shiloh about the house of Eli.

²⁸When the news reached Joab, who had conspired with Adonijah though not with Absalom, he fled to the tent of the LORD and took hold of the horns of the altar. ²⁹King Solomon was told that Joab had fled to the tent of the LORD and was beside the altar. Then Solomon ordered Benaiah son of Jehoiada, "Go, strike him down!"

³⁰So Benaiah entered the tent of the LORD and said to Joab, "The king says, 'Come out!'"

But he answered, "No, I will die here."

Benaiah reported to the king, "This is how Joab answered me."

³¹Then the king commanded Benaiah, "Do as he says. Strike him down and bury him, and so clear me and my father's house of the guilt of the innocent blood that Joab shed. ³²The LORD will repay him for the blood he shed, because without the knowledge of my father David he attacked two men and killed them with the sword. Both of them—Abner son of Ner, commander of Israel's army, and Amasa son of Jether, commander of Judah's army—were better men and more upright than he. ³³May the guilt of their blood rest on the head of Joab and his descendants for ever. But on David and his descendants, his house and his throne, may there be the LORD's peace for ever."

³⁴So Benaiah son of Jehoiada went up and struck down Joab and killed him, and he was buried on his own land*b* in the desert. ³⁵The king put Benaiah son of Jehoiada over the army in Joab's position and replaced Abiathar with Zadok the priest.

³⁶Then the king sent for Shimei and said to him, "Build yourself a house in Jerusalem and live there, but do not go anywhere else. ³⁷The day you leave and cross the Kidron Valley, you can be sure you will die; your blood will be on your own head."

³⁸Shimei answered the king, "What you say is good. Your servant will do as my lord the king has said." And Shimei stayed in Jerusalem for a long time.

³⁹But three years later, two of Shimei's slaves ran off to Achish son of Maacah, king of Gath, and Shimei was told, "Your slaves are in Gath." ⁴⁰At this, he saddled his donkey and went to Achish at Gath in search of his slaves. So Shimei went away and brought the slaves back from Gath.

⁴¹When Solomon was told that Shimei had gone from Jerusalem to Gath and had returned, ⁴²the king summoned Shimei and said to him, "Did I not make you swear by the LORD and warn you, 'On the day you leave to go anywhere else, you can be sure you will die'? At that time you said to me, 'What you say is good. I will obey.' ⁴³Why then did you not keep your oath to the LORD and obey the command I gave you?"

⁴⁴The king also said to Shimei, "You know in your heart all the wrong you did to my father David. Now the LORD will repay you for your wrongdoing. ⁴⁵But King Solomon will be blessed, and David's throne will remain secure before the LORD for ever."

⁴⁶Then the king gave the order to Benaiah son of Jehoiada, and he went out and struck Shimei down and killed him.

The kingdom was now firmly established in Solomon's hands.

Solomon Asks for Wisdom

3 Solomon made an alliance with Pharaoh king of Egypt and married his daughter. He brought her to the City of David until he finished building his palace and the temple of the LORD, and the wall around Jerusalem. ²The people, however, were still sacrificing at the high places, because a temple had not yet been built for the Name of the LORD.

b34 Or buried in his tomb

³Solomon showed his love for the LORD by walking according to the statutes of his father David, except that he offered sacrifices and burned incense on the high places.

⁴The king went to Gibeon to offer sacrifices, for that was the most important high place, and Solomon offered a thousand burnt offerings on that altar. ⁵At Gibeon the LORD appeared to Solomon during the night in a dream, and God said, "Ask for whatever you want me to give you."

⁶Solomon answered, "You have shown great kindness to your servant, my father David, because he was faithful to you and righteous and upright in heart. You have continued this great kindness to him and have given him a son to sit on his throne this very day.

⁷"Now, O LORD my God, you have made your servant king in place of my father David. But I am only a little child and do not know how to carry out my duties. ⁸Your servant is here among the people you have chosen, a great people, too numerous to count or number. ⁹So give your servant a discerning heart to govern your people and to distinguish between right and wrong. For who is able to govern this great people of yours?"

¹⁰The Lord was pleased that Solomon had asked for this. ¹¹So God said to him, "Since you have asked for this and not for long life or wealth for yourself, nor have asked for the death of your enemies but for discernment in administering justice, ¹²I will do what you have asked. I will give you a wise and discerning heart, so that there will never have been anyone like you, nor will there ever be. ¹³Moreover, I will give you what you have not asked for—both riches and honour—so that in your lifetime you will have no equal among kings. ¹⁴And if you walk in my ways and obey my statutes and commands as David your father did, I will give you a long life." ¹⁵Then Solomon awoke—and he realised it had been a dream.

He returned to Jerusalem, stood before the ark of the Lord's covenant and sacrificed burnt offerings and fellowship offerings.ᵃ Then he gave a feast for all his court.

A Wise Ruling

¹⁶Now two prostitutes came to the king and stood before him. ¹⁷One of them said, "My lord, this woman and I live in the same house. I had a baby while she was there with me. ¹⁸The third day after my child was born, this woman also had a baby. We were alone; there was no-one in the house but the two of us.

¹⁹"During the night this woman's son died because she lay on him. ²⁰So she got up in the middle of the night and took my son from my side while I your servant was asleep. She put him by her breast and put her dead son by my breast. ²¹The next morning, I got up to nurse my son—and he was dead! But when I looked at him closely in the morning light, I saw that it wasn't the son I had borne."

²²The other woman said, "No! The living one is my son; the dead one is yours."

But the first one insisted, "No! The dead one is yours; the living one is mine." And so they argued before the king.

²³The king said, "This one says, 'My son is alive and your son is dead,' while that one says, 'No! Your son is dead and mine is alive.'"

²⁴Then the king said, "Bring me a sword." So they brought a sword for the king. ²⁵He then gave an order: "Cut the living child in two and give half to one and half to the other."

²⁶The woman whose son was alive was filled with compassion for her son and said to the king, "Please, my lord, give her the living baby! Don't kill him!"

But the other said, "Neither I nor you shall have him. Cut him in two!"

²⁷Then the king gave his ruling: "Give the living baby to the first woman. Do not kill him; she is his mother."

²⁸When all Israel heard the verdict the king had given, they held the king in awe, because they saw that he had wisdom from God to administer justice.

Solomon's Officials and Governors

4 So King Solomon ruled over all Israel.
²And these were his chief officials:

Azariah son of Zadok—the priest;
³Elihoreph and Ahijah, sons of Shisha
  —secretaries;
Jehoshaphat son of Ahilud—recorder;
⁴Benaiah son of Jehoiada—commander-in-chief;
Zadok and Abiathar—priests;
⁵Azariah son of Nathan—in charge of the
  district officers;
Zabud son of Nathan—a priest and
  personal adviser to the king;
⁶Ahishar—in charge of the palace;
Adoniram son of Abda—in charge of
  forced labour.

⁷Solomon also had twelve district governors over all Israel, who supplied provisions for the king and the royal household. Each one had to provide supplies for one month in the year. ⁸These are their names:

Ben-Hur—in the hill country of
  Ephraim;
⁹Ben-Deker—in Makaz, Shaalbim, Beth
  Shemesh and Elon Bethhanan;
¹⁰Ben-Hesed—in Arubboth (Socoh and
  all the land of Hepher were his);
¹¹Ben-Abinadab—in Naphoth Dorᵃ (he
  was married to Taphath daughter of
  Solomon);
¹²Baana son of Ahilud—in Taanach and
  Megiddo, and in all of Beth Shan next
  to Zarethan below Jezreel, from
  Beth Shan to Abel Meholah across to
  Jokmeam;
¹³Ben-Geber—in Ramoth Gilead (the
  settlements of Jair son of Manasseh in

ᵃ15 Traditionally *peace offerings*   ᵃ11 Or *in the heights of Dor*

Gilead were his, as well as the district of Argob in Bashan and its sixty large walled cities with bronze gate bars);

¹⁴Ahinadab son of Iddo—in Mahanaim;

¹⁵Ahimaaz—in Naphtali (he had married Basemath daughter of Solomon);

¹⁶Baana son of Hushai—in Asher and in Aloth;

¹⁷Jehoshaphat son of Paruah—in Issachar;

¹⁸Shimei son of Ela—in Benjamin;

¹⁹Geber son of Uri—in Gilead (the country of Sihon king of the Amorites and the country of Og king of Bashan). He was the only governor over the district.

Solomon's Daily Provisions

²⁰The people of Judah and Israel were as numerous as the sand on the seashore; they ate, they drank and they were happy. ²¹And Solomon ruled over all the kingdoms from the River*b* to the land of the Philistines, as far as the border of Egypt. These countries brought tribute and were Solomon's subjects all his life.

²²Solomon's daily provisions were thirty cors*c* of fine flour and sixty cors*d* of meal, ²³ten head of stall-fed cattle, twenty of pasture-fed cattle and a hundred sheep and goats, as well as deer, gazelles, roebucks and choice fowl. ²⁴For he ruled over all the kingdoms west of the River, from Tiphsah to Gaza, and had peace on all sides. ²⁵During Solomon's lifetime Judah and Israel, from Dan to Beersheba, lived in safety, each man under his own vine and fig-tree.

²⁶Solomon had four*e* thousand stalls for chariot horses, and twelve thousand horses.*f*

²⁷The district officers, each in his month, supplied provisions for King Solomon and all who came to the king's table. They saw to it that nothing was lacking. ²⁸They also brought to the proper place their quotas of barley and straw for the chariot horses and the other horses.

Solomon's Wisdom

²⁹God gave Solomon wisdom and very great insight, and a breadth of understanding as measureless as the sand on the seashore. ³⁰Solomon's wisdom was greater than the wisdom of all the men of the East, and greater than all the wisdom of Egypt. ³¹He was wiser than any other man, including Ethan the Ezrahite—wiser than Heman, Calcol and Darda, the sons of Mahol. And his fame spread to all the surrounding nations. ³²He spoke three thousand proverbs and his songs numbered a thousand and five. ³³He described plant life, from the cedar of Lebanon to the hyssop that grows out of walls. He also taught about animals and birds, reptiles and fish. ³⁴Men of all nations came to listen to Solomon's wisdom, sent by all the kings of the world, who had heard of his wisdom.

Preparations for Building the Temple

5 When Hiram king of Tyre heard that Solomon had been anointed king to succeed his father David, he sent his envoys to Solomon, because he had always been on friendly terms with David. ²Solomon sent back this message to Hiram:

³"You know that because of the wars waged against my father David from all sides, he could not build a temple for the Name of the LORD his God until the LORD put his enemies under his feet. ⁴But now the LORD my God has given me rest on every side, and there is no adversary or disaster. ⁵I intend, therefore, to build a temple for the Name of the LORD my God, as the LORD told my father David, when he said, 'Your son whom I will put on the throne in your place will build the temple for my Name.'

⁶"So give orders that cedars of Lebanon be cut for me. My men will work with yours, and I will pay you for your men whatever wages you set. You know that we have no-one so skilled in felling timber as the Sidonians."

⁷When Hiram heard Solomon's message, he was greatly pleased and said, "Praise be to the LORD today, for he has given David a wise son to rule over this great nation."

⁸So Hiram sent word to Solomon:

"I have received the message you sent me and will do all you want in providing the cedar and pine logs. ⁹My men will haul them down from Lebanon to the sea, and I will float them in rafts by sea to the place you specify. There I will separate them and you can take them away. And you are to grant my wish by providing food for my royal household."

¹⁰In this way Hiram kept Solomon supplied with all the cedar and pine logs he wanted, ¹¹and Solomon gave Hiram twenty thousand cors*a* of wheat as food for his household, in addition to twenty thousand baths*b,c* of pressed olive oil. Solomon continued to do this for Hiram year after year. ¹²The LORD gave Solomon wisdom, just as he had promised him. There were peaceful relations between Hiram and Solomon, and the two of them made a treaty.

¹³King Solomon conscripted labourers from all Israel—thirty thousand men. ¹⁴He sent them off to Lebanon in shifts of ten thousand a month, so that they spent one month in Lebanon and two months at home. Adoniram was in charge of the forced labour.

---

b21 That is, the Euphrates; also in verse 24   *c22* That is, probably about 180 bushels (about 6.6 kilolitres)
d22 That is, probably about 365 bushels (about 13.2 kilolitres)
e26 Some Septuagint manuscripts (see also 2 Chron. 9:25); Hebrew *forty*   *f26* Or *charioteers*
a11 That is, probably about 121,000 bushels (about 4,400 kilolitres)
b11 Septuagint (see also 2 Chron. 2:10); Hebrew *twenty cors*
c11 That is, about 97,000 gallons (about 440 kilolitres)

¹⁵Solomon had seventy thousand carriers and eighty thousand stonecutters in the hills, ¹⁶as well as thirty-three hundred[d] foremen who supervised the project and directed the workmen. ¹⁷At the king's command they removed from the quarry large blocks of quality stone to provide a foundation of dressed stone for the temple. ¹⁸The craftsmen of Solomon and Hiram and the men of Gebal[e] cut and prepared the timber and stone for the building of the temple.

Solomon Builds the Temple

6 In the four hundred and eightieth[a] year after the Israelites had come out of Egypt, in the fourth year of Solomon's reign over Israel, in the month of Ziv, the second month, he began to build the temple of the LORD.

²The temple that King Solomon built for the LORD was sixty cubits long, twenty wide and thirty high.[b] ³The portico at the front of the main hall of the temple extended the width of the temple, that is twenty cubits,[c] and projected ten cubits[d] from the front of the temple. ⁴He made narrow clerestory windows in the temple. ⁵Against the walls of the main hall and inner sanctuary he built a structure around the building, in which there were side rooms. ⁶The lowest floor was five cubits[e] wide, the middle floor six cubits[f] and the third floor seven.[g] He made offset ledges around the outside of the temple so that nothing would be inserted into the temple walls.

⁷In building the temple, only blocks dressed at the quarry were used, and no hammer, chisel or any other iron tool was heard at the temple site while it was being built.

⁸The entrance to the lowest[h] floor was on the south side of the temple; a stairway led up to the middle level and from there to the third. ⁹So he built the temple and completed it, roofing it with beams and cedar planks. ¹⁰And he built the side rooms all along the temple. The height of each was five cubits, and they were attached to the temple by beams of cedar.

¹¹The word of the LORD came to Solomon: ¹²"As for this temple you are building, if you follow my decrees, carry out my regulations and keep all my commands and obey them, I will fulfil through you the promise I gave to David your father. ¹³And I will live among the Israelites and will not abandon my people Israel."

¹⁴So Solomon built the temple and completed it. ¹⁵He lined its interior walls with cedar boards, panelling them from the floor of the temple to the ceiling, and covered the floor of the temple with planks of pine. ¹⁶He partitioned off twenty cubits[i] at the rear of the temple with cedar boards from floor to ceiling to form within the temple an inner sanctuary, the Most Holy Place. ¹⁷The main hall in front of this room was forty cubits[j] long. ¹⁸The inside of the temple was cedar, carved with gourds and open flowers. Everything was cedar; no stone was to be seen.

¹⁹He prepared the inner sanctuary within the temple to set the ark of the covenant of the LORD there. ²⁰The inner sanctuary was twenty cubits long, twenty wide and twenty high.[k] He overlaid the inside with pure gold, and he also overlaid the altar of cedar. ²¹Solomon covered the inside of the temple with pure gold, and he extended gold chains across the front of the inner sanctuary, which was overlaid with gold. ²²So he overlaid the whole interior with gold. He also overlaid with gold the altar that belonged to the inner sanctuary.

²³In the inner sanctuary he made a pair of cherubim of olive wood, each ten cubits[l] high. ²⁴One wing of the first cherub was five cubits long, and the other wing five cubits —ten cubits from wing tip to wing tip. ²⁵The second cherub also measured ten cubits, for the two cherubim were identical in size and shape. ²⁶The height of each cherub was ten cubits. ²⁷He placed the cherubim inside the innermost room of the temple, with their wings spread out. The wing of one cherub touched one wall, while the wing of the other touched the other wall, and their wings touched each other in the middle of the room. ²⁸He overlaid the cherubim with gold.

²⁹On the walls all round the temple, in both the inner and outer rooms, he carved cherubim, palm trees and open flowers. ³⁰He also covered the floors of both the inner and outer rooms of the temple with gold.

³¹For the entrance of the inner sanctuary he made doors of olive wood with five-sided jambs. ³²And on the two olive wood doors he carved cherubim, palm trees and open flowers, and overlaid the cherubim and palm trees with beaten gold. ³³In the same way he made four-sided jambs of olive wood for the entrance to the main hall. ³⁴He also made two pine doors, each having two leaves that turned in sockets. ³⁵He carved cherubim, palm trees and open flowers on them and overlaid them with gold hammered evenly over the carvings.

³⁶And he built the inner courtyard of three courses of dressed stone and one course of trimmed cedar beams.

³⁷The foundation of the temple of the LORD was laid in the fourth year, in the month of Ziv. ³⁸In the eleventh year in the month of Bul, the eighth month, the temple was finished in all its details according to its specifications. He had spent seven years building it.

---

d16 Hebrew; some Septuagint manuscripts (see also 2 Chron. 2:2, 18) *thirty-six hundred*   *e18* That is, Byblos
a1 Hebrew; Septuagint *four hundred and fortieth*
b2 That is, about 90 feet (about 27 metres) long and 30 feet (about 9 metres) wide and 45 feet (about 13.5 metres) high
c3 That is, about 30 feet (about 9 metres)   *d3* That is, about 15 feet (about 4.5 metres)
e6 That is, about 7½ feet (about 2.3 metres); also in verses 10 and 24   *f6* That is, about 9 feet (about 2.7 metres)
g6 That is, about 10½ feet (about 3.2 metres)   *h8* Septuagint; Hebrew *middle*
i16 That is, about 30 feet (about 9 metres)   *j17* That is, about 60 feet (about 18 metres)
k20 That is, about 30 feet (about 9 metres) long, wide and high   *l23* That is, about 15 feet (about 4.5 metres)

Solomon Builds His Palace

7 It took Solomon thirteen years, however, to complete the construction of his palace. ²He built the Palace of the Forest of Lebanon a hundred cubits long, fifty wide and thirty high,ᵃ with four rows of cedar columns supporting trimmed cedar beams. ³It was roofed with cedar above the beams that rested on the columns—forty-five beams, fifteen to a row. ⁴Its windows were placed high in sets of three, facing each other. ⁵All the doorways had rectangular frames; they were in the front part in sets of three, facing each other.ᵇ

⁶He made a colonnade fifty cubits long and thirty wide.ᶜ In front of it was a portico, and in front of that were pillars and an overhanging roof.

⁷He built the throne hall, the Hall of Justice, where he was to judge, and he covered it with cedar from floor to ceiling.ᵈ ⁸And the palace in which he was to live, set farther back, was similar in design. Solomon also made a palace like this hall for Pharaoh's daughter, whom he had married.

⁹All these structures, from the outside to the great courtyard and from foundation to eaves, were made of blocks of high-grade stone cut to size and trimmed with a saw on their inner and outer faces. ¹⁰The foundations were laid with large stones of good quality, some measuring ten cubitsᵉ and some eight.ᶠ ¹¹Above were high-grade stones, cut to size, and cedar beams. ¹²The great courtyard was surrounded by a wall of three courses of dressed stone and one course of trimmed cedar beams, as was the inner courtyard of the temple of the LORD with its portico.

The Temple's Furnishings

¹³King Solomon sent to Tyre and brought Huram,ᵍ ¹⁴whose mother was a widow from the tribe of Naphtali and whose father was a man of Tyre and a craftsman in bronze. Huram was highly skilled and experienced in all kinds of bronze work. He came to King Solomon and did all the work assigned to him.

¹⁵He cast two bronze pillars, each eighteen cubits high and twelve cubits round,ʰ by line. ¹⁶He also made two capitals of cast bronze to set on the tops of the pillars; each capital was five cubitsⁱ high. ¹⁷A network of interwoven chains festooned the capitals on top of the pillars, seven for each capital. ¹⁸He made pomegranates in two rowsʲ encircling each network to decorate the capitals on top of the pillars.ᵏ He did the same for each capital. ¹⁹The capitals on top of the pillars in the portico were in the shape of lilies, four cubitsˡ high. ²⁰On the capitals of both pillars, above the bowl-shaped part next to the network, were the two hundred pomegranates in rows all around. ²¹He erected the pillars at the portico of the temple. The pillar to the south he named Jakinᵐ and the one to the north Boaz.ⁿ ²²The capitals on top were in the shape of lilies. And so the work on the pillars was completed.

²³He made the Sea of cast metal, circular in shape, measuring ten cubitsᵒ from rim to rim and five cubits high. It took a line of thirty cubitsᵖ to measure round it. ²⁴Below the rim, gourds encircled it—ten to a cubit. The gourds were cast in two rows in one piece with the Sea.

²⁵The Sea stood on twelve bulls, three facing north, three facing west, three facing south and three facing east. The Sea rested on top of them, and their hindquarters were towards the centre. ²⁶It was a handbreadth�q in thickness, and its rim was like the rim of a cup, like a lily blossom. It held two thousand baths.ʳ

²⁷He also made ten movable stands of bronze; each was four cubits long, four wide and three high.ˢ ²⁸This is how the stands were made: They had side panels attached to uprights. ²⁹On the panels between the uprights were lions, bulls and cherubim—and on the uprights as well. Above and below the lions and bulls were wreaths of hammered work. ³⁰Each stand had four bronze wheels with bronze axles, and each had a basin resting on four supports, cast with wreaths on each side. ³¹On the inside of the stand there was an opening that had a circular frame one cubitᵗ deep. This opening was round, and with its basework it measured a cubit and a half.ᵘ Around its opening there was engraving. The panels of the stands were square, not round. ³²The four wheels were under the panels, and the axles of the wheels were attached to the stand. The diameter of each wheel was a cubit and a half. ³³The wheels were made like chariot wheels; the axles, rims, spokes and hubs were all of cast metal.

³⁴Each stand had four handles, one on each corner, projecting from the stand. ³⁵At the top of the stand there was a circular band half a cubitᵛ deep. The supports and panels were attached to the top of the stand. ³⁶He engraved cherubim, lions and palm trees on the

---

ᵃ2 That is, about 150 feet (about 46 metres) long, 75 feet (about 23 metres) wide and 45 feet (about 13.5 metres) high
ᵇ5 The meaning of the Hebrew for this verse is uncertain.
ᶜ6 That is, about 75 feet (about 23 metres) long and 45 feet (about 13.5 metres) wide
ᵈ7 Vulgate and Syriac; Hebrew *floor*   ᵉ10 That is, about 15 feet (about 4.5 metres)
ᶠ10 That is, about 12 feet (about 3.7 metres)   ᵍ13 Hebrew *Hiram*, a variant of *Huram*; also in verses 40 and 45
ʰ15 That is, about 27 feet (about 8.2 metres) high and 18 feet (about 5.5 metres) round
ⁱ16 That is, about 7½ feet (about 2.3 metres); also in verse 23
ʲ18 Two Hebrew manuscripts and Septuagint; most Hebrew manuscripts *made the pillars, and there were two rows*
ᵏ18 Many Hebrew manuscripts and Syriac; most Hebrew manuscripts *pomegranates*
ˡ19 That is, about 6 feet (about 1.8 metres); also in verse 38   ᵐ21 *Jakin* probably means *he establishes*.
ⁿ21 *Boaz* probably means *in him is strength*.   ᵒ23 That is, about 15 feet (about 4.6 metres)
ᵖ23 That is, about 45 feet (about 13.7 metres)   �q26 That is, about 3 inches (about 8 centimetres)
ʳ26 That is, probably about 9,700 gallons (about 44 kilolitres); the Septuagint does not have this sentence.
ˢ27 That is, about 6 feet (about 1.8 metres) long and wide and about 4½ feet (about 1.4 metres) high
ᵗ31 That is, about 1½ feet (about 0.5 metre)   ᵘ31 That is, about 2¼ feet (about 0.7 metre); also in verse 32
ᵛ35 That is about ¾ foot (about 0.2 metre)

1 KINGS 8:22–30
'But will God really dwell on earth? The heavens, even the highest heaven, cannot contain you. How much less this temple I have built!' (v. 27).

GOD EVERYWHERE. This is a record of a more formal prayer which Solomon offered at the dedication of the temple. Notice the similarity between verses 15 and 23 in this chapter, where the king acknowledges that God is one who keeps his covenant and is faithful to his promises.

There is still a degree of self-interest in this prayer – the reminder that God had promised to preserve a descendant of David as king. Solomon looks to that promise because it means one of his own descendants will reign after him (vv. 25, 26). If we stopped to analyse our own prayers it is likely that most of them would be tainted by self-interest. In this there is nothing unusual about Solomon.

The prayer also contains some remarkable insights. Even the universe itself cannot contain God, how, then, could a temple be adequate for him? Solomon does not come to the concept of God filling all things. His idea is that God would *choose* to dwell in the temple and this is mixed with the idea that the Lord would make regular sorties from his dwelling place in heaven, to meet the worshippers in his temple (vv. 29, 30).

Our view of God should be bigger than that of Solomon. We do not wait for him to come, he confronts us in every place and situation of life. We have to learn to be awake to his presence.

→294

1 KINGS 9:1–9

'But if you or your sons turn away from me and do not observe the commands and decrees I have given you . . . then I will cut off Israel' (vv. 6, 7).

CONTINUING SALVATION. This second appearance of the Lord to Solomon (see 3:5) assured him that his prayer had been answered (v. 3). He was reminded that God's promise regarding the continuation of rulers of Davidic descent was conditional upon there being continued obedience (vv. 4, 5).

At verse 6 a grammatical change takes place in the Hebrew and the word 'you' suddenly becomes plural. The context suggests that the warnings of verses 6 to 9 are addressed not only to Solomon but to the whole nation. The necessity of faithfulness to their covenant with God is stressed. Unfaithfulness will end in national disaster; they will be 'cut off' and they 'will then become a byword and an object of ridicule among all peoples' (vv. 6, 7). There will also be spiritual consequences of disobedience – the temple will be no more than an empty shrine because the glory of God's presence will be withdrawn (v. 7).

Our experience of the peril of a broken relationship with God is less material than these verses suggest. Prosperity is not always a casualty of religious disaffection – in some instances the opposite seems to be true. But to the spiritually sensitive – those who are truly the people of God – deliberate disobedience creates inner turmoil. The sense of God's blessing and of his presence disappears, and cold and darkness shroud the whole personality.

There is no doubt that continuing spiritual health requires continuing obedience to God.

surfaces of the supports and on the panels, in every available space, with wreaths all around. 37This is the way he made the ten stands. They were all cast in the same moulds and were identical in size and shape.

38He then made ten bronze basins, each holding forty baths[w] and measuring four cubits across, one basin to go on each of the ten stands. 39He placed five of the stands on the south side of the temple and five on the north. He placed the Sea on the south side, at the south-east corner of the temple. 40He also made the basins and shovels and sprinkling bowls.

So Huram finished all the work he had undertaken for King Solomon in the temple of the LORD:

41the two pillars;

the two bowl-shaped capitals on top of the pillars;

the two sets of network decorating the two bowl-shaped capitals on top of the pillars;

42the four hundred pomegranates for the two sets of network (two rows of pomegranates for each network, decorating the bowl-shaped capitals on top of the pillars);

43the ten stands with their ten basins;

44the Sea and the twelve bulls under it;

45the pots, shovels and sprinkling bowls.

All these objects that Huram made for King Solomon for the temple of the LORD were of burnished bronze. 46The king had them cast in clay moulds in the plain of the Jordan between Succoth and Zarethan. 47Solomon left all these things unweighed, because there were so many; the weight of the bronze was not determined.

48Solomon also made all the furnishings that were in the LORD's temple:

the golden altar;

the golden table on which was the bread of the Presence;

49the lampstands of pure gold (five on the right and five on the left, in front of the inner sanctuary);

the gold floral work and lamps and tongs;

50the pure gold dishes, wick trimmers, sprinkling bowls, dishes and censers;

and the gold sockets for the doors of the innermost room, the Most Holy Place, and also for the doors of the main hall of the temple.

51When all the work King Solomon had done for the temple of the LORD was finished, he brought in the things his father David had dedicated—the silver and gold and the furnishings—and he placed them in the treasuries of the LORD's temple.

The Ark Brought to the Temple

8 Then King Solomon summoned into his presence at Jerusalem the elders of Israel, all the heads of the tribes and the chiefs of the Israelite families, to bring up the ark of the LORD's covenant from Zion, the City of David. 2All the men of Israel came together to King Solomon at the time of the festival in the month of Ethanim, the seventh month.

3When all the elders of Israel had arrived, the priests took up the ark, 4and they brought up the ark of the LORD and the Tent of Meeting and all the sacred furnishings in it. The priests and Levites carried them up, 5and King Solomon and the entire assembly of Israel that had gathered about him were before the ark, sacrificing so many sheep and cattle that they could not be recorded or counted.

6The priests then brought the ark of the LORD's covenant to its place in the inner sanctuary of the temple, the Most Holy Place, and put it beneath the wings of the cherubim. 7The cherubim spread their wings over the place of the ark and overshadowed the ark and its carrying poles. 8These poles were so long that their ends could be seen from the Holy Place in front of the inner sanctuary, but not from outside the Holy Place; and they are still there today. 9There was nothing in the ark except the two stone tablets that Moses had placed in it at Horeb, where the LORD made a covenant with the Israelites after they came out of Egypt.

10When the priests withdrew from the Holy Place, the cloud filled the temple of the LORD. 11And the priests could not perform their service because of the cloud, for the glory of the LORD filled his temple.

12Then Solomon said, "The LORD has said that he would dwell in a dark cloud; 13I have indeed built a magnificent temple for you, a place for you to dwell for ever."

14While the whole assembly of Israel was standing there, the king turned round and blessed them. 15Then he said:

"Praise be to the LORD, the God of Israel, who with his own hand has fulfilled what he promised with his own mouth to my father David. For he said, 16'Since the day I brought my people Israel out of Egypt, I have not chosen a city in any tribe of Israel to have a temple built for my Name to be there, but I have chosen David to rule my people Israel.'

17"My father David had it in his heart to build a temple for the Name of the LORD, the God of Israel. 18But the LORD said to my father David, 'Because it was in your heart to build a temple for my Name, you did well to have this in your heart. 19Nevertheless, you are not the one to build the temple, but your son, who is your own flesh and blood—he is the one who will build the temple for my Name.'

20"The LORD has kept the promise he made: I have succeeded David my father and now I sit on the throne of Israel, just as the LORD promised, and I have built

---

[w]38 That is, about 195 gallons (about 880 litres)

the temple for the Name of the LORD, the God of Israel. 21I have provided a place there for the ark, in which is the covenant of the LORD that he made with our fathers when he brought them out of Egypt.''

Solomon's Prayer of Dedication

22Then Solomon stood before the altar of the LORD in front of the whole assembly of Israel, spread out his hands towards heaven 23and said:

"O LORD, God of Israel, there is no God like you in heaven above or on earth below—you who keep your covenant of love with your servants who continue wholeheartedly in your way. 24You have kept your promise to your servant David my father; with your mouth you have promised and with your hand you have fulfilled it—as it is today.

25"Now LORD, God of Israel, keep for your servant David my father the promises you made to him when you said, 'You shall never fail to have a man to sit before me on the throne of Israel, if only your sons are careful in all they do to walk before me as you have done.' 26And now, O God of Israel, let your word that you promised your servant David my father come true.

27"But will God really dwell on earth? The heavens, even the highest heaven, cannot contain you. How much less this temple I have built! 28Yet give attention to your servant's prayer and his plea for mercy, O LORD my God. Hear the cry and the prayer that your servant is praying in your presence this day. 29May your eyes be open towards this temple night and day, this place of which you said, 'My Name shall be there,' so that you will hear the prayer your servant prays towards this place. 30Hear the supplication of your servant and of your people Israel when they pray towards this place. Hear from heaven, your dwelling-place, and when you hear, forgive.

31"When a man wrongs his neighbour and is required to take an oath and he comes and swears the oath before your altar in this temple, 32then hear from heaven and act. Judge between your servants, condemning the guilty and bringing down on his own head what he has done. Declare the innocent not guilty, and so establish his innocence.

33"When your people Israel have been defeated by an enemy because they have sinned against you, and when they turn back to you and confess your name, praying and making supplication to you in this temple, 34then hear from heaven and forgive the sin of your people Israel and bring them back to the land you gave to their fathers.

35"When the heavens are shut up and there is no rain because your people have sinned against you, and when they pray towards this place and confess your name and turn from their sin because you have afflicted them, 36then hear from heaven and forgive the sin of your servants, your people Israel. Teach them the right way to live, and send rain on the land you gave your people for an inheritance.

37"When famine or plague comes to the land, or blight or mildew, locusts or grasshoppers, or when an enemy besieges them in any of their cities, whatever disaster or disease may come, 38and when a prayer or plea is made by any of your people Israel—each one aware of the afflictions of his own heart, and spreading out his hands towards this temple—39then hear from heaven, your dwelling-place. Forgive and act; deal with each man according to all he does, since you know his heart (for you alone know the hearts of all men), 40so that they will fear you all the time they live in the land you gave our fathers.

41"As for the foreigner who does not belong to your people Israel but has come from a distant land because of your name—42for men will hear of your great name and your mighty hand and your outstretched arm—when he comes and prays towards this temple, 43then hear from heaven, your dwelling-place, and do whatever the foreigner asks of you, so that all the peoples of the earth may know your name and fear you, as do your own people Israel, and may know that this house I have built bears your Name.

44"When your people go to war against their enemies, wherever you send them, and when they pray to the LORD towards the city you have chosen and the temple I have built for your Name, 45then hear from heaven their prayer and their plea, and uphold their cause.

46"When they sin against you—for there is no-one who does not sin—and you become angry with them and give them over to the enemy, who takes them captive to his own land, far away or near; 47and if they have a change of heart in the land where they are held captive, and repent and plead with you in the land of their conquerors and say, 'We have sinned, we have done wrong, we have acted wickedly'; 48and if they turn back to you with all their heart and soul in the land of their enemies who took them captive, and pray to you towards the land you gave their fathers, towards the city you have chosen and the temple I have built for your Name; 49then from heaven, your dwelling-place, hear their prayer and their plea, and uphold their cause. 50And forgive your people, who have sinned against you; forgive all the offences they have committed against you, and cause their conquerors to show them mercy; 51for they are your people and your inheritance, whom you brought out of Egypt, out of that iron-smelting furnace.

[52]"May your eyes be open to your servant's plea and to the plea of your people Israel, and may you listen to them whenever they cry out to you. [53]For you singled them out from all the nations of the world to be your own inheritance, just as you declared through your servant Moses when you, O Sovereign LORD, brought our fathers out of Egypt."

[54]When Solomon had finished all these prayers and supplications to the LORD, he rose from before the altar of the LORD, where he had been kneeling with his hands spread out towards heaven. [55]He stood and blessed the whole assembly of Israel in a loud voice, saying:

[56]"Praise be to the LORD, who has given rest to his people Israel just as he promised. Not one word has failed of all the good promises he gave through his servant Moses. [57]May the LORD our God be with us as he was with our fathers; may he never leave us nor forsake us. [58]May he turn our hearts to him, to walk in all his ways and to keep the commands, decrees and regulations he gave our fathers. [59]And may these words of mine, which I have prayed before the LORD, be near to the LORD our God day and night, that he may uphold the cause of his servant and the cause of his people Israel according to each day's need, [60]so that all the peoples of the earth may know that the LORD is God and that there is no other. [61]But your hearts must be fully committed to the LORD our God, to live by his decrees and obey his commands, as at this time."

The Dedication of the Temple

[62]Then the king and all Israel with him offered sacrifices before the LORD. [63]Solomon offered a sacrifice of fellowship offerings[a] to the LORD: twenty-two thousand cattle and a hundred and twenty thousand sheep and goats. So the king and all the Israelites dedicated the temple of the LORD.

[64]On that same day the king consecrated the middle part of the courtyard in front of the temple of the LORD, and there he offered burnt offerings, grain offerings and the fat of the fellowship offerings, because the bronze altar before the LORD was too small to hold the burnt offerings, the grain offerings and the fat of the fellowship offerings.

[65]So Solomon observed the festival at that time, and all Israel with him—a vast assembly, people from Lebo[b] Hamath to the Wadi of Egypt. They celebrated it before the LORD our God for seven days and seven days more, fourteen days in all. [66]On the following day he sent the people away. They blessed the king and then went home, joyful and glad in heart for all the good things the LORD had done for his servant David and his people Israel.

The LORD Appears to Solomon

9 When Solomon had finished building the temple of the LORD and the royal palace, and had achieved all he had desired to do, [2]the LORD appeared to him a second time, as he had appeared to him at Gibeon. [3]The LORD said to him:

"I have heard the prayer and plea you have made before me; I have consecrated this temple, which you have built, by putting my Name there for ever. My eyes and my heart will always be there.

[4]"As for you, if you walk before me in integrity of heart and uprightness, as David your father did, and do all I command and observe my decrees and laws, [5]I will establish your royal throne over Israel for ever, as I promised David your father when I said, 'You shall never fail to have a man on the throne of Israel.'

[6]"But if you[a] or your sons turn away from me and do not observe the commands and decrees I have given you[a] and go off to serve other gods and worship them, [7]then I will cut off Israel from the land I have given them and will reject this temple I have consecrated for my Name. Israel will then become a byword and an object of ridicule among all peoples. [8]And though this temple is now imposing, all who pass by will be appalled and will scoff and say, 'Why has the LORD done such a thing to this land and to this temple?' [9]People will answer, 'Because they have forsaken the LORD their God, who brought their fathers out of Egypt, and have embraced other gods, worshipping and serving them—that is why the LORD brought all this disaster on them.'"

Solomon's Other Activities

[10]At the end of twenty years, during which Solomon built these two buildings—the temple of the LORD and the royal palace—[11]King Solomon gave twenty towns in Galilee to Hiram king of Tyre, because Hiram had supplied him with all the cedar and pine and gold he wanted. [12]But when Hiram went from Tyre to see the towns that Solomon had given him, he was not pleased with them. [13]"What kind of towns are these you have given me, my brother?" he asked. And he called them the Land of Cabul,[b] a name they have to this day. [14]Now Hiram had sent to the king 120 talents[c] of gold.

[15]Here is the account of the forced labour King Solomon conscripted to build the LORD's temple, his own palace, the supporting terraces,[d] the wall of Jerusalem, and Hazor, Megiddo and Gezer. [16](Pharaoh king

---

[a]63 Traditionally *peace offerings*; also in verse 64   [b]65 Or *from the entrance to*   [a]6 The Hebrew is plural.
[b]13 *Cabul* sounds like the Hebrew for *good-for-nothing*.   [c]14 That is, about 4 tons (about 4 metric tons)
[d]15 Or *the Millo*; also in verse 24

of Egypt had attacked and captured Gezer. He had set it on fire. He killed its Canaanite inhabitants, and then gave it as a wedding gift to his daughter, Solomon's wife. ¹⁷And Solomon rebuilt Gezer.) He built up Lower Beth Horon, ¹⁸Baalath, and Tadmor^e in the desert, within his land, ¹⁹as well as all his store cities and the towns for his chariots and for his horses^f—whatever he desired to build in Jerusalem, in Lebanon and throughout all the territory he ruled.

²⁰All the people left from the Amorites, Hittites, Perizzites, Hivites and Jebusites (these peoples were not Israelites), ²¹that is, their descendants remaining in the land, whom the Israelites could not exterminate^g —these Solomon conscripted for his slave labour force, as it is to this day. ²²But Solomon did not make slaves of any of the Israelites; they were his fighting men, his government officials, his officers, his captains, and the commanders of his chariots and charioteers. ²³They were also the chief officials in charge of Solomon's projects— 550 officials supervising the men who did the work.

²⁴After Pharaoh's daughter had come up from the City of David to the palace Solomon had built for her, he constructed the supporting terraces.

²⁵Three times a year Solomon sacrificed burnt offerings and fellowship offerings^h on the altar he had built for the Lord, burning incense before the Lord along with them, and so fulfilled the temple obligations.

²⁶King Solomon also built ships at Ezion Geber, which is near Elath in Edom, on the shore of the Red Sea.ⁱ ²⁷And Hiram sent his men—sailors who knew the sea—to serve in the fleet with Solomon's men. ²⁸They sailed to Ophir and brought back 420 talents^j of gold, which they delivered to King Solomon.

The Queen of Sheba Visits Solomon

10 When the queen of Sheba heard about the fame of Solomon and his relation to the name of the Lord, she came to test him with hard questions. ²Arriving at Jerusalem with a very great caravan—with camels carrying spices, large quantities of gold, and precious stones—she came to Solomon and talked with him about all that she had on her mind. ³Solomon answered all her questions; nothing was too hard for the king to explain to her. ⁴When the queen of Sheba saw all the wisdom of Solomon and the palace he had built, ⁵the food on his table, the seating of his officials, the attending servants in their robes, his cupbearers, and the burnt offerings he made at^a the temple of the Lord, she was overwhelmed.

⁶She said to the king, "The report I heard in my own country about your achievements and your wisdom is true. ⁷But I did not believe these things until I came and saw with my own eyes. Indeed, not even half was told me; in wisdom and wealth you have far exceeded the report I heard. ⁸How happy your men must be! How happy your officials, who continually stand before you and hear your wisdom! ⁹Praise be to the Lord your God, who has delighted in you and placed you on the throne of Israel. Because of the Lord's eternal love for Israel, he has made you king, to maintain justice and righteousness."

¹⁰And she gave the king 120 talents^b of gold, large quantities of spices, and precious stones. Never again were so many spices brought in as those the queen of Sheba gave to King Solomon.

¹¹(Hiram's ships brought gold from Ophir; and from there they brought great cargoes of almug-wood^c and precious stones. ¹²The king used the almug-wood to make supports for the temple of the Lord and for the royal palace, and to make harps and lyres for the musicians. So much almug-wood has never been imported or seen since that day.)

¹³King Solomon gave the queen of Sheba all she desired and asked for, besides what he had given her out of his royal bounty. Then she left and returned with her retinue to her own country.

Solomon's Splendour

¹⁴The weight of the gold that Solomon received yearly was 666 talents,^d ¹⁵not including the revenues from merchants and traders and from all the Arabian kings and the governors of the land.

¹⁶King Solomon made two hundred large shields of hammered gold; six hundred bekas^e of gold went into each shield. ¹⁷He also made three hundred small shields of hammered gold, with three minas^f of gold in each shield. The king put them in the Palace of the Forest of Lebanon.

¹⁸Then the king made a great throne inlaid with ivory and overlaid with fine gold. ¹⁹The throne had six steps, and its back had a rounded top. On both sides of the seat were armrests, with a lion standing beside each of them. ²⁰Twelve lions stood on the six steps, one at either end of each step. Nothing like it had ever been made for any other kingdom. ²¹All King Solomon's goblets were gold, and all the household articles in the Palace of the Forest of Lebanon were pure gold. Nothing was made of silver, because silver was considered of little value in Solomon's days. ²²The king had a fleet of trading ships^g at sea along with the ships of Hiram. Once every three years it returned carrying gold, silver and ivory, and apes and baboons.

²³King Solomon was greater in riches and wisdom than all the other kings of the earth. ²⁴The whole world sought audience with Solomon to hear the wisdom God had put in

---

^e18 The Hebrew may also be read *Tamar*. ^f19 Or *charioteers*
^g21 The Hebrew term refers to the irrevocable giving over of things or persons to the Lord, often by totally destroying them. ^h25 Traditionally *peace offerings* ⁱ26 Hebrew *Yam Suph*; that is, Sea of Reeds
^j28 That is, about 14 tons (about 14.5 metric tons) ^a5 Or *the ascent by which he went up to*
^b10 That is, about 4 tons (about 4 metric tons) ^c11 Probably a variant of *algum-wood*; also in verse 12
^d14 That is, about 22½ tons (about 23 metric tons) ^e16 That is, about 7½ pounds (about 3.5 kilograms)
^f17 That is, about 3¾ pounds (about 1.7 kilograms) ^g22 Hebrew *of ships of Tarshish*

1 KINGS 10:1–13

'The queen of Sheba . . . came to Solomon and talked with him about all that she had on her mind. Solomon answered all her questions; nothing was too hard for the king to explain' (vv. 1, 2, 3).

ADMIRATION AND REALITY. If we read this account in our daily newspaper certain suspicions would be aroused. What kind of reporter would produce such a bland description of events? Solomon the wise, has now become Solomon the infallible.

Solomon's splendour, his lavish hospitality, and his shrewdness are not in doubt. However, the suggestion that he answered every question and nothing was too hard for him indicates either that the Queen of Sheba's 'hard questions' (v. 1) were not all that hard, or that there was a certain naivety in the reporting.

Was this a trade mission or a state visit? On the evidence of these verses, the probable answer is that it was a mixture of the two. The caravan mentioned in verse 2, and the quantity and value of goods described in verse 10 suggest that some form of trade was involved (see also v. 13). The queen probably took the opportunity to visit a monarch whose name was becoming a byword in the trading circles of the Near East.

The excessive admiration of verses 6–9 may be accounted for as the kind of overstatement which was typical of oriental courtesy.

A totally uncritical approach to life is as dangerous as being over critical. Such an attitude leads to complacency and unreality, dangers which should be avoided by Christians.

→300

I KINGS 17:15–24
'Then the woman said to Elijah, "Now I know that you are a man of God and that the word of the LORD from your mouth is the truth" ' (v. 24).

WHAT MUST SOMEONE DO to prove they are God's person? Keep to their word, certainly. Elijah had reassured the widow that her jar of flour and jug of oil would not run out. The implication is obviously that a miracle took place. We are not told! It *could* just be that Elijah paid his way, so the widow and her son could continue to fill the vessels. For remember that they were right on the border of Palestine, almost out of range of the drought. Food – at a price – was possibly available.

However, even if we wonder whether the jar of flour and jug of oil implies a miracle, we cannot doubt that today's story of raising the widow's son to life shows Elijah's miraculous power. According to the author of Kings, Elijah's miracle convinced the widow that he was God's man. Miracles in themselves are not proof that someone is from God.

What, then, must someone do to prove their godliness? The simple answer is – nothing! Notice how troubled the widow was at first, when her son died. She immediately thought Elijah had been sent to judge her. She had already heard he was a man of God. Live close to God, as Elijah did, and your actions will speak for themselves. Miracles may not convince others of the truth of your words. Reliability, consistency, compassion even, may not by themselves. But they are the hallmarks of God's people, which will shine through.

Once we set out to 'prove' our goodness, instead of God shining through, it is our self that speaks.

→309

his heart. ²⁵Year after year, everyone who came brought a gift—articles of silver and gold, robes, weapons and spices, and horses and mules.

²⁶Solomon accumulated chariots and horses; he had fourteen hundred chariots and twelve thousand horses,ʰ which he kept in the chariot cities and also with him in Jerusalem. ²⁷The king made silver as common in Jerusalem as stones, and cedar as plentiful as sycamore-fig trees in the foothills. ²⁸Solomon's horses were imported from Egyptⁱ and from Kueʲ—the royal merchants purchased them from Kue.ʲ ²⁹They imported a chariot from Egypt for six hundred shekelsᵏ of silver, and a horse for a hundred and fifty.ˡ They also exported them to all the kings of the Hittites and of the Arameans.

Solomon's Wives

11 King Solomon, however, loved many foreign women besides Pharaoh's daughter—Moabites, Ammonites, Edomites, Sidonians and Hittites. ²They were from nations about which the LORD had told the Israelites, "You must not intermarry with them, because they will surely turn your hearts after their gods." Nevertheless, Solomon held fast to them in love. ³He had seven hundred wives of royal birth and three hundred concubines, and his wives led him astray. ⁴As Solomon grew old, his wives turned his heart after other gods, and his heart was not fully devoted to the LORD his God, as the heart of David his father had been. ⁵He followed Ashtoreth the goddess of the Sidonians, and Molechᵃ the detestable god of the Ammonites. ⁶So Solomon did evil in the eyes of the LORD; he did not follow the LORD completely, as David his father had done.

⁷On a hill east of Jerusalem, Solomon built a high place for Chemosh the detestable god of Moab, and for Molech the detestable god of the Ammonites. ⁸He did the same for all his foreign wives, who burned incense and offered sacrifices to their gods.

⁹The LORD became angry with Solomon because his heart had turned away from the LORD, the God of Israel, who had appeared to him twice. ¹⁰Although he had forbidden Solomon to follow other gods, Solomon did not keep the LORD's command. ¹¹So the LORD said to Solomon, "Since this is your attitude and you have not kept my covenant and my decrees, which I commanded you, I will most certainly tear the kingdom away from you and give it to one of your subordinates. ¹²Nevertheless, for the sake of David your father, I will not do it during your lifetime. I will tear it out of the hand of your son. ¹³Yet I will not tear the whole kingdom from him, but will give him one tribe for the sake of David my servant and for the sake of Jerusalem, which I have chosen."

Solomon's Adversaries

¹⁴Then the LORD raised up against Solomon an adversary, Hadad the Edomite, from the royal line of Edom. ¹⁵Earlier when David was fighting with Edom, Joab the commander of the army, who had gone up to bury the dead, had struck down all the men in Edom. ¹⁶Joab and all the Israelites stayed there for six months, until they had destroyed all the men in Edom. ¹⁷But Hadad, still only a boy, fled to Egypt with some Edomite officials who had served his father. ¹⁸They set out from Midian and went to Paran. Then taking men from Paran with them, they went to Egypt, to Pharaoh king of Egypt, who gave Hadad a house and land and provided him with food.

¹⁹Pharaoh was so pleased with Hadad that he gave him a sister of his own wife, Queen Tahpenes, in marriage. ²⁰The sister of Tahpenes bore him a son named Genubath, whom Tahpenes brought up in the royal palace. There Genubath lived with Pharaoh's own children.

²¹While he was in Egypt, Hadad heard that David rested with his fathers and that Joab the commander of the army was also dead. Then Hadad said to Pharaoh, "Let me go, so that I may return to my own country."

²²"What have you lacked here that you want to go back to your own country?" Pharaoh asked.

"Nothing," Hadad replied, "but do let me go!"

²³And God raised up against Solomon another adversary, Rezon son of Eliada, who had fled from his master, Hadadezer king of Zobah. ²⁴He gathered men around him and became the leader of a band of rebels when David destroyed the forcesᵇ ˌof Zobahˌ; the rebels went to Damascus, where they settled and took control. ²⁵Rezon was Israel's adversary as long as Solomon lived, adding to the trouble caused by Hadad. So Rezon ruled in Aram and was hostile towards Israel.

Jeroboam Rebels Against Solomon

²⁶Also, Jeroboam son of Nebat rebelled against the king. He was one of Solomon's officials, an Ephraimite from Zeredah, and his mother was a widow named Zeruah.

²⁷Here is the account of how he rebelled against the king: Solomon had built the supporting terracesᶜ and had filled in the gap in the wall of the city of David his father. ²⁸Now Jeroboam was a man of standing, and when Solomon saw how well the young man did his work, he put him in charge of the whole labour force of the house of Joseph.

²⁹About that time Jeroboam was going out of Jerusalem, and Ahijah the prophet of Shiloh met him on the way, wearing a new cloak. The two of them were alone out in the country, ³⁰and Ahijah took hold of the new cloak he was wearing and tore it into twelve pieces. ³¹Then he said to Jeroboam, "Take ten

ʰ26 Or charioteers   ⁱ28 Or possibly Muzur, a region in Cilicia; also in verse 29
ʲ28 Probably Cilicia   ᵏ29 That is, about 15 pounds (about 7 kilograms)
ˡ29 That is, about 3¾ pounds (about 1.7 kilograms)   ᵃ5 Hebrew Milcom; also in verse 33
ᵇ24 Hebrew destroyed them   ᶜ27 Or the Millo

pieces for yourself, for this is what the LORD, the God of Israel, says: 'See, I am going to tear the kingdom out of Solomon's hand and give you ten tribes. ³²But for the sake of my servant David and the city of Jerusalem, which I have chosen out of all the tribes of Israel, he will have one tribe. ³³I will do this because they have*d* forsaken me and worshipped Ashtoreth the goddess of the Sidonians, Chemosh the god of the Moabites, and Molech the god of the Ammonites, and have not walked in my ways, nor done what is right in my eyes, nor kept my statutes and laws as David, Solomon's father, did.

³⁴'''But I will not take the whole kingdom out of Solomon's hand; I have made him ruler all the days of his life for the sake of David my servant, whom I chose and who observed my commands and statutes. ³⁵I will take the kingdom from his son's hands and give you ten tribes. ³⁶I will give one tribe to his son so that David my servant may always have a lamp before me in Jerusalem, the city where I chose to put my Name. ³⁷However, as for you, I will take you, and you will rule over all that your heart desires; you will be king over Israel. ³⁸If you do whatever I command you and walk in my ways and do what is right in my eyes by keeping my statutes and commands, as David my servant did, I will be with you. I will build you a dynasty as enduring as the one I built for David and will give Israel to you. ³⁹I will humble David's descendants because of this, but not for ever.'''

⁴⁰Solomon tried to kill Jeroboam, but Jeroboam fled to Egypt, to Shishak the king, and stayed there until Solomon's death.

Solomon's Death

⁴¹As for the other events of Solomon's reign—all he did and the wisdom he displayed—are they not written in the book of the annals of Solomon? ⁴²Solomon reigned in Jerusalem over all Israel for forty years. ⁴³Then he rested with his fathers and was buried in the city of David his father. And Rehoboam his son succeeded him as king.

Israel Rebels Against Rehoboam

12 Rehoboam went to Shechem, for all the Israelites had gone there to make him king. ²When Jeroboam son of Nebat heard this (he was still in Egypt, where he had fled from King Solomon), he returned from*a* Egypt. ³So they sent for Jeroboam, and he and the whole assembly of Israel went to Rehoboam and said to him: ⁴'''Your father put a heavy yoke on us, but now lighten the harsh labour and the heavy yoke he put on us, and we will serve you.''

⁵Rehoboam answered, ''Go away for three days and then come back to me.'' So the people went away.

⁶Then King Rehoboam consulted the elders who had served his father Solomon during his lifetime. ''How would you advise me to answer these people?'' he asked.

⁷They replied, ''If today you will be a servant to these people and serve them and give them a favourable answer, they will always be your servants.''

⁸But Rehoboam rejected the advice the elders gave him and consulted the young men who had grown up with him and were serving him. ⁹He asked them, ''What is your advice? How should we answer these people who say to me, 'Lighten the yoke your father put on us'?''

¹⁰The young men who had grown up with him replied, ''Tell these people who have said to you, 'Your father put a heavy yoke on us, but make our yoke lighter'—tell them, 'My little finger is thicker than my father's waist. ¹¹My father laid on you a heavy yoke; I will make it even heavier. My father scourged you with whips; I will scourge you with scorpions.'''

¹²Three days later Jeroboam and all the people returned to Rehoboam, as the king had said, ''Come back to me in three days.'' ¹³The king answered the people harshly. Rejecting the advice given him by the elders, ¹⁴he followed the advice of the young men and said, ''My father made your yoke heavy; I will make it even heavier. My father scourged you with whips; I will scourge you with scorpions.'' ¹⁵So the king did not listen to the people, for this turn of events was from the LORD, to fulfil the word the LORD had spoken to Jeroboam son of Nebat through Ahijah the Shilonite.

¹⁶When all Israel saw that the king refused to listen to them, they answered the king:

''What share do we have in David,
   what part in Jesse's son?
To your tents, O Israel!
   Look after your own house, O David!''

So the Israelites went home. ¹⁷But as for the Israelites who were living in the towns of Judah, Rehoboam still ruled over them.

¹⁸King Rehoboam sent out Adoniram,*b* who was in charge of forced labour, but all Israel stoned him to death. King Rehoboam, however, managed to get into his chariot and escape to Jerusalem. ¹⁹So Israel has been in rebellion against the house of David to this day.

²⁰When all the Israelites heard that Jeroboam had returned, they sent and called him to the assembly and made him king over all Israel. Only the tribe of Judah remained loyal to the house of David.

²¹When Rehoboam arrived in Jerusalem, he mustered the whole house of Judah and the tribe of Benjamin—a hundred and eighty thousand fighting men—to make war against the house of Israel and to regain the kingdom for Rehoboam son of Solomon.

²²But this word of God came to Shemaiah the man of God: ²³'''Say to Rehoboam son of Solomon king of Judah, to the whole house of Judah and Benjamin, and to the rest of the people, ²⁴'This is what the LORD says: Do not go up to fight against your brothers, the

---

*d33 Hebrew; Septuagint, Vulgate and Syriac because he has   a2 Or he remained in
b18 Some Septuagint manuscripts and Syriac (see also 1 Kings 4:6 and 5:14); Hebrew Adoram*

Israelites. Go home, every one of you, for this is my doing.'" So they obeyed the word of the LORD and went home again, as the LORD had ordered.

Golden Calves at Bethel and Dan

²⁵Then Jeroboam fortified Shechem in the hill country of Ephraim and lived there. From there he went out and built up Peniel.ᶜ

²⁶Jeroboam thought to himself, "The kingdom is now likely to revert to the house of David. ²⁷If these people go up to offer sacrifices at the temple of the LORD in Jerusalem, they will again give their allegiance to their lord, Rehoboam king of Judah. They will kill me and return to King Rehoboam."

²⁸After seeking advice, the king made two golden calves. He said to the people, "It is too much for you to go up to Jerusalem. Here are your gods, O Israel, who brought you up out of Egypt." ²⁹One he set up in Bethel, and the other in Dan. ³⁰And this thing became a sin; the people went even as far as Dan to worship the one there.

³¹Jeroboam built shrines on high places and appointed priests from all sorts of people, even though they were not Levites. ³²He instituted a festival on the fifteenth day of the eighth month, like the festival held in Judah, and offered sacrifices on the altar. This he did in Bethel, sacrificing to the calves he had made. And at Bethel he also installed priests at the high places he had made. ³³On the fifteenth day of the eighth month, a month of his own choosing, he offered sacrifices on the altar he had built at Bethel. So he instituted the festival for the Israelites and went up to the altar to make offerings.

The Man of God From Judah

13 By the word of the LORD a man of God came from Judah to Bethel, as Jeroboam was standing by the altar to make an offering. ²He cried out against the altar by the word of the LORD: "O altar, altar! This is what the LORD says: 'A son named Josiah will be born to the house of David. On you he will sacrifice the priests of the high places who now make offerings here, and human bones will be burned on you.'" ³That same day the man of God gave a sign: "This is the sign the LORD has declared: The altar will be split apart and the ashes on it will be poured out."

⁴When King Jeroboam heard what the man of God cried out against the altar at Bethel, he stretched out his hand from the altar and said, "Seize him!" But the hand he stretched out towards the man shrivelled up, so that he could not pull it back. ⁵Also, the altar was split apart and its ashes poured out according to the sign given by the man of God by the word of the LORD.

⁶Then the king said to the man of God, "Intercede with the LORD your God and pray for me that my hand may be restored." So the man of God interceded with the LORD, and the king's hand was restored and became as it was before.

⁷The king said to the man of God, "Come home with me and have something to eat, and I will give you a gift."

⁸But the man of God answered the king, "Even if you were to give me half your possessions, I would not go with you, nor would I eat bread or drink water here. ⁹For I was commanded by the word of the LORD: 'You must not eat bread or drink water or return by the way you came.'" ¹⁰So he took another road and did not return by the way he had come to Bethel.

¹¹Now there was a certain old prophet living in Bethel, whose sons came and told him all that the man of God had done there that day. They also told their father what he had said to the king. ¹²Their father asked them, "Which way did he go?" And his sons showed him which road the man of God from Judah had taken. ¹³So he said to his sons, "Saddle the donkey for me." And when they had saddled the donkey for him, he mounted it ¹⁴and rode after the man of God. He found him sitting under an oak tree and asked, "Are you the man of God who came from Judah?"

"I am," he replied.

¹⁵So the prophet said to him, "Come home with me and eat."

¹⁶The man of God said, "I cannot turn back and go with you, nor can I eat bread or drink water with you in this place. ¹⁷I have been told by the word of the LORD: 'You must not eat bread or drink water there or return by the way you came.'"

¹⁸The old prophet answered, "I too am a prophet, as you are. And an angel said to me by the word of the LORD: 'Bring him back with you to your house so that he may eat bread and drink water.'" (But he was lying to him.) ¹⁹So the man of God returned with him and ate and drank in his house.

²⁰While they were sitting at the table, the word of the LORD came to the old prophet who had brought him back. ²¹He cried out to the man of God who had come from Judah, "This is what the LORD says: 'You have defied the word of the LORD and have not kept the command the LORD your God gave you. ²²You came back and ate bread and drank water in the place where he told you not to eat or drink. Therefore your body will not be buried in the tomb of your fathers.'"

²³When the man of God had finished eating and drinking, the prophet who had brought him back saddled his donkey for him. ²⁴As he went on his way, a lion met him on the road and killed him, and his body was thrown down on the road, with both the donkey and the lion standing beside it. ²⁵Some people who passed by saw the body thrown down there, with the lion standing beside the body, and they went and reported it in the city where the old prophet lived.

²⁶When the prophet who had brought him back from his journey heard of it, he said, "It is the man of God who defied the word of the LORD. The LORD has given him over to the lion, which has mauled him and killed him, as the word of the LORD had warned him."

²⁷The prophet said to his sons, "Saddle the

ᶜ25 Hebrew *Penuel*, a variant of *Peniel*

donkey for me," and they did so. ²⁸Then he went out and found the body thrown down on the road, with the donkey and the lion standing beside it. The lion had neither eaten the body nor mauled the donkey. ²⁹So the prophet picked up the body of the man of God, laid it on the donkey, and brought it back to his own city to mourn for him and bury him. ³⁰Then he laid the body in his own tomb, and they mourned over him and said, "Oh, my brother!"

³¹After burying him, he said to his sons, "When I die, bury me in the grave where the man of God is buried; lay my bones beside his bones. ³²For the message he declared by the word of the LORD against the altar in Bethel and against all the shrines on the high places in the towns of Samaria will certainly come true."

³³Even after this, Jeroboam did not change his evil ways, but once more appointed priests for the high places from all sorts of people. Anyone who wanted to become a priest he consecrated for the high places. ³⁴This was the sin of the house of Jeroboam that led to its downfall and to its destruction from the face of the earth.

Ahijah's Prophecy Against Jeroboam

14 At that time Abijah son of Jeroboam became ill, ²and Jeroboam said to his wife, "Go, disguise yourself, so that you won't be recognised as the wife of Jeroboam. Then go to Shiloh. Ahijah the prophet is there—the one who told me I would be king over this people. ³Take ten loaves of bread with you, some cakes and a jar of honey, and go to him. He will tell you what will happen to the boy." ⁴So Jeroboam's wife did what he said and went to Ahijah's house in Shiloh.

Now Ahijah could not see; his sight was gone because of his age. ⁵But the LORD had told Ahijah, "Jeroboam's wife is coming to ask you about her son, for he is ill, and you are to give her such and such an answer. When she arrives, she will pretend to be someone else."

⁶So when Ahijah heard the sound of her footsteps at the door, he said, "Come in, wife of Jeroboam. Why this pretence? I have been sent to you with bad news. ⁷Go, tell Jeroboam that this is what the LORD, the God of Israel, says: 'I raised you up from among the people and made you a leader over my people Israel. ⁸I tore the kingdom away from the house of David and gave it to you, but you have not been like my servant David, who kept my commands and followed me with all his heart, doing only what was right in my eyes. ⁹You have done more evil than all who lived before you. You have made for yourself other gods, idols of metal; you have provoked me to anger and thrust me behind your back.

¹⁰"'Because of this, I am going to bring disaster on the house of Jeroboam. I will cut off from Jeroboam every last male in Israel —slave or free. I will burn up the house of Jeroboam as one burns dung, until it is all gone. ¹¹Dogs will eat those belonging to Jeroboam who die in the city, and the birds of the air will feed on those who die in the country. The LORD has spoken!'

¹²"As for you, go back home. When you set foot in your city, the boy will die. ¹³All Israel will mourn for him and bury him. He is the only one belonging to Jeroboam who will be buried, because he is the only one in the house of Jeroboam in whom the LORD, the God of Israel, has found anything good.

¹⁴"The LORD will raise up for himself a king over Israel who will cut off the family of Jeroboam. This is the day! What? Yes, even now.^a ¹⁵And the LORD will strike Israel, so that it will be like a reed swaying in the water. He will uproot Israel from this good land that he gave to their forefathers and scatter them beyond the River,^b because they provoked the LORD to anger by making Asherah poles.^c ¹⁶And he will give Israel up because of the sins Jeroboam has committed and has caused Israel to commit."

¹⁷Then Jeroboam's wife got up and left and went to Tirzah. As soon as she stepped over the threshold of the house, the boy died. ¹⁸They buried him, and all Israel mourned for him, as the LORD had said through his servant the prophet Ahijah.

¹⁹The other events of Jeroboam's reign, his wars and how he ruled, are written in the book of the annals of the kings of Israel. ²⁰He reigned for twenty-two years and then rested with his fathers. And Nadab his son succeeded him as king.

Rehoboam King of Judah

²¹Rehoboam son of Solomon was king in Judah. He was forty-one years old when he became king, and he reigned for seventeen years in Jerusalem, the city the LORD had chosen out of all the tribes of Israel in which to put his Name. His mother's name was Naamah; she was an Ammonite. ²²Judah did evil in the eyes of the LORD. By the sins they committed they stirred up his jealous anger more than their fathers had done. ²³They also set up for themselves high places, sacred stones and Asherah poles on every high hill and under every spreading tree. ²⁴There were even male shrine-prostitutes in the land; the people engaged in all the detestable practices of the nations the LORD had driven out before the Israelites.

²⁵In the fifth year of King Rehoboam, Shishak king of Egypt attacked Jerusalem. ²⁶He carried off the treasures of the temple of the LORD and the treasures of the royal palace. He took everything, including all the gold shields Solomon had made. ²⁷So King Rehoboam made bronze shields to replace them and assigned these to the commanders of the guard on duty at the entrance to the royal palace. ²⁸Whenever the king went to the LORD's temple, the guards bore the shields, and afterwards they returned them to the guardroom.

---

^a14 The meaning of the Hebrew for this sentence is uncertain.   ^b15 That is, the Euphrates
^c15 That is, symbols of the goddess Asherah; here and elsewhere in 1 Kings

²⁹As for the other events of Rehoboam's reign, and all he did, are they not written in the book of the annals of the kings of Judah? ³⁰There was continual warfare between Rehoboam and Jeroboam. ³¹And Rehoboam rested with his fathers and was buried with them in the City of David. His mother's name was Naamah; she was an Ammonite. And Abijah*d* his son succeeded him as king.

Abijah King of Judah

15 In the eighteenth year of the reign of Jeroboam son of Nebat, Abijah*a* became king of Judah, ²and he reigned in Jerusalem for three years. His mother's name was Maacah daughter of Abishalom.*b*

³He committed all the sins his father had done before him; his heart was not fully devoted to the LORD his God, as the heart of David his forefather had been. ⁴Nevertheless, for David's sake the LORD his God gave him a lamp in Jerusalem by raising up a son to succeed him and by making Jerusalem strong. ⁵For David had done what was right in the eyes of the LORD and had not failed to keep any of the LORD's commands all the days of his life—except in the case of Uriah the Hittite.

⁶There was war between Rehoboam*c* and Jeroboam throughout ⌊Abijah's⌋ lifetime. ⁷As for the other events of Abijah's reign, and all he did, are they not written in the book of the annals of the kings of Judah? There was war between Abijah and Jeroboam. ⁸And Abijah rested with his fathers and was buried in the City of David. And Asa his son succeeded him as king.

Asa King of Judah

⁹In the twentieth year of Jeroboam king of Israel, Asa became king of Judah, ¹⁰and he reigned in Jerusalem for forty-one years. His grandmother's name was Maacah daughter of Abishalom.

¹¹Asa did what was right in the eyes of the LORD, as his father David had done. ¹²He expelled the male shrine-prostitutes from the land and got rid of all the idols his fathers had made. ¹³He even deposed his grandmother Maacah from her position as queen mother, because she had made a repulsive Asherah pole. Asa cut the pole down and burned it in the Kidron Valley. ¹⁴Although he did not remove the high places, Asa's heart was fully committed to the LORD all his life. ¹⁵He brought into the temple of the LORD the silver and gold and the articles that he and his father had dedicated.

¹⁶There was war between Asa and Baasha king of Israel throughout their reigns. ¹⁷Baasha king of Israel went up against Judah and fortified Ramah to prevent anyone from leaving or entering the territory of Asa king of Judah.

¹⁸Asa then took all the silver and gold that was left in the treasuries of the LORD's temple and of his own palace. He entrusted it to his officials and sent them to Ben-Hadad son of Tabrimmon, the son of Hezion, the king of Aram, who was ruling in Damascus. ¹⁹"Let there be a treaty between me and you," he said, "as there was between my father and your father. See, I am sending you a gift of silver and gold. Now break your treaty with Baasha king of Israel so that he will withdraw from me."

²⁰Ben-Hadad agreed with King Asa and sent the commanders of his forces against the towns of Israel. He conquered Ijon, Dan, Abel Beth Maacah and all Kinnereth in addition to Naphtali. ²¹When Baasha heard this, he stopped building Ramah and withdrew to Tirzah. ²²Then King Asa issued an order to all Judah—no-one was exempt—and they carried away from Ramah the stones and timber Baasha had been using there. With them King Asa built up Geba in Benjamin, and also Mizpah.

²³As for all the other events of Asa's reign, all his achievements, all he did and the cities he built, are they not written in the book of the annals of the kings of Judah? In his old age, however, his feet became diseased. ²⁴Then Asa rested with his fathers and was buried with them in the city of his father David. And Jehoshaphat his son succeeded him as king.

Nadab King of Israel

²⁵Nadab son of Jeroboam became king of Israel in the second year of Asa king of Judah, and he reigned over Israel for two years. ²⁶He did evil in the eyes of the LORD, walking in the ways of his father and in his sin, which he had caused Israel to commit.

²⁷Baasha son of Ahijah of the house of Issachar plotted against him, and he struck him down at Gibbethon, a Philistine town, while Nadab and all Israel were besieging it. ²⁸Baasha killed Nadab in the third year of Asa king of Judah and succeeded him as king.

²⁹As soon as he began to reign, he killed Jeroboam's whole family. He did not leave Jeroboam anyone that breathed, but destroyed them all, according to the word of the LORD given through his servant Ahijah the Shilonite—³⁰because of the sins Jeroboam had committed and had caused Israel to commit, and because he provoked the LORD, the God of Israel, to anger.

³¹As for the other events of Nadab's reign, and all he did, are they not written in the book of the annals of the kings of Israel? ³²There was war between Asa and Baasha king of Israel throughout their reigns.

Baasha King of Israel

³³In the third year of Asa king of Judah, Baasha son of Ahijah became king of all Israel in Tirzah, and he reigned for twenty-four years. ³⁴He did evil in the eyes of the LORD, walking in the ways of Jeroboam and in his sin, which he had caused Israel to commit.

---

d31 Some Hebrew manuscripts and Septuagint (see also 2 Chron. 12:16); most Hebrew manuscripts *Abijam*
a1 Some Hebrew manuscripts and Septuagint (see also 2 Chron. 12:16); most Hebrew manuscripts *Abijam*; also in verses 7 and 8   *b2* A variant of *Absalom*; also in verse 10
c6 Most Hebrew manuscripts; some Hebrew manuscripts and Syriac *Abijam* (that is, Abijah)

16 Then the word of the LORD came to Jehu son of Hanani against Baasha: 2"I lifted you up from the dust and made you leader of my people Israel, but you walked in the ways of Jeroboam and caused my people Israel to sin and to provoke me to anger by their sins. 3So I am about to consume Baasha and his house, and I will make your house like that of Jeroboam son of Nebat. 4Dogs will eat those belonging to Baasha who die in the city, and the birds of the air will feed on those who die in the country."

5As for the other events of Baasha's reign, what he did and his achievements, are they not written in the book of the annals of the kings of Israel? 6Baasha rested with his fathers and was buried in Tirzah. And Elah his son succeeded him as king.

7Moreover, the word of the LORD came through the prophet Jehu son of Hanani to Baasha and his house, because of all the evil he had done in the eyes of the LORD, provoking him to anger by the things he did, and becoming like the house of Jeroboam—and also because he destroyed it.

Elah King of Israel

8In the twenty-sixth year of Asa king of Judah, Elah son of Baasha became king of Israel, and he reigned in Tirzah for two years.

9Zimri, one of his officials, who had command of half his chariots, plotted against him. Elah was in Tirzah at the time, getting drunk in the home of Arza, the man in charge of the palace at Tirzah. 10Zimri came in, struck him down and killed him in the twenty-seventh year of Asa king of Judah. Then he succeeded him as king.

11As soon as he began to reign and was seated on the throne, he killed off Baasha's whole family. He did not spare a single male, whether relative or friend. 12So Zimri destroyed the whole family of Baasha, in accordance with the word of the LORD spoken against Baasha through the prophet Jehu —13because of all the sins Baasha and his son Elah had committed and had caused Israel to commit, so that they provoked the LORD, the God of Israel, to anger by their worthless idols.

14As for the other events of Elah's reign, and all he did, are they not written in the book of the annals of the kings of Israel?

Zimri King of Israel

15In the twenty-seventh year of Asa king of Judah, Zimri reigned in Tirzah for seven days. The army was encamped near Gibbethon, a Philistine town. 16When the Israelites in the camp heard that Zimri had plotted against the king and murdered him, they proclaimed Omri, the commander of the army, king over Israel that very day there in the camp. 17Then Omri and all the Israelites with him withdrew from Gibbethon and laid siege to Tirzah. 18When Zimri saw that the city was taken, he went into the citadel of the royal palace and set the palace on fire around him. So he died, 19because of the sins he had

committed, doing evil in the eyes of the LORD and walking in the ways of Jeroboam and in the sin he had committed and had caused Israel to commit.

20As for the other events of Zimri's reign, and the rebellion he carried out, are they not written in the book of the annals of the kings of Israel?

Omri King of Israel

21Then the people of Israel were split into two factions; half supported Tibni son of Ginath for king, and the other half supported Omri. 22But Omri's followers proved stronger than those of Tibni son of Ginath. So Tibni died and Omri became king.

23In the thirty-first year of Asa king of Judah, Omri became king of Israel, and he reigned for twelve years, six of them in Tirzah. 24He bought the hill of Samaria from Shemer for two talents*a* of silver and built a city on the hill, calling it Samaria, after Shemer, the name of the former owner of the hill.

25But Omri did evil in the eyes of the LORD and sinned more than all those before him. 26He walked in all the ways of Jeroboam son of Nebat and in his sin, which he had caused Israel to commit, so that they provoked the LORD, the God of Israel, to anger by their worthless idols.

27As for the other events of Omri's reign, what he did and the things he achieved, are they not written in the book of the annals of the kings of Israel? 28Omri rested with his fathers and was buried in Samaria. And Ahab his son succeeded him as king.

Ahab Becomes King of Israel

29In the thirty-eighth year of Asa king of Judah, Ahab son of Omri became king of Israel, and he reigned in Samaria over Israel for twenty-two years. 30Ahab son of Omri did more evil in the eyes of the LORD than any of those before him. 31He not only considered it trivial to commit the sins of Jeroboam son of Nebat, but he also married Jezebel daughter of Ethbaal king of the Sidonians, and began to serve Baal and worship him. 32He set up an altar for Baal in the temple of Baal that he built in Samaria. 33Ahab also made an Asherah pole and did more to provoke the LORD, the God of Israel, to anger than did all the kings of Israel before him.

34In Ahab's time, Hiel of Bethel rebuilt Jericho. He laid its foundations at the cost of his firstborn son Abiram, and he set up its gates at the cost of his youngest son Segub, in accordance with the word of the LORD spoken by Joshua son of Nun.

Elijah Fed by Ravens

17 Now Elijah the Tishbite, from Tishbe*a* in Gilead, said to Ahab, "As the LORD, the God of Israel, lives, whom I serve, there will be neither dew nor rain in the next few years except at my word."

2Then the word of the LORD came to Elijah: 3"Leave here, turn eastward and hide in the

---

a24 That is, about 150 pounds (about 70 kilograms)   *a1* Or *Tishbite, of the settlers*

Kerith Ravine, east of the Jordan. ⁴You will drink from the brook, and I have ordered the ravens to feed you there."

⁵So he did what the LORD had told him. He went to the Kerith Ravine, east of the Jordan, and stayed there. ⁶The ravens brought him bread and meat in the morning and bread and meat in the evening, and he drank from the brook.

The Widow at Zarephath

⁷Some time later the brook dried up because there had been no rain in the land. ⁸Then the word of the LORD came to him: ⁹"Go at once to Zarephath of Sidon and stay there. I have commanded a widow in that place to supply you with food." ¹⁰So he went to Zarephath. When he came to the town gate, a widow was there gathering sticks. He called to her and asked, "Would you bring me a little water in a jar so I may have a drink?" ¹¹As she was going to get it, he called, "And bring me, please, a piece of bread."

¹²"As surely as the LORD your God lives," she replied, "I don't have any bread—only a handful of flour in a jar and a little oil in a jug. I am gathering a few sticks to take home and make a meal for myself and my son, that we may eat it—and die."

¹³Elijah said to her, "Don't be afraid. Go home and do as you have said. But first make a small cake of bread for me from what you have and bring it to me, and then make something for yourself and your son. ¹⁴For this is what the LORD, the God of Israel, says: 'The jar of flour will not be used up and the jug of oil will not run dry until the day the LORD gives rain on the land.'"

¹⁵She went away and did as Elijah had told her. So there was food every day for Elijah and for the woman and her family. ¹⁶For the jar of flour was not used up and the jug of oil did not run dry, in keeping with the word of the LORD spoken by Elijah.

¹⁷Some time later the son of the woman who owned the house became ill. He grew worse and worse, and finally stopped breathing. ¹⁸She said to Elijah, "What do you have against me, man of God? Did you come to remind me of my sin and kill my son?"

¹⁹"Give me your son," Elijah replied. He took him from her arms, carried him to the upper room where he was staying, and laid him on his bed. ²⁰Then he cried out to the LORD, "O LORD my God, have you brought tragedy also upon this widow I am staying with, by causing her son to die?" ²¹Then he stretched himself out on the boy three times and cried to the LORD, "O LORD my God, let this boy's life return to him!"

²²The LORD heard Elijah's cry, and the boy's life returned to him, and he lived. ²³Elijah picked up the child and carried him down from the room into the house. He gave him to his mother and said, "Look, your son is alive!"

²⁴Then the woman said to Elijah, "Now I know that you are a man of God and that the word of the LORD from your mouth is the truth."

Elijah and Obadiah

18 After a long time, in the third year, the word of the LORD came to Elijah: "Go and present yourself to Ahab, and I will send rain on the land." ²So Elijah went to present himself to Ahab.

Now the famine was severe in Samaria, ³and Ahab had summoned Obadiah, who was in charge of his palace. (Obadiah was a devout believer in the LORD. ⁴While Jezebel was killing off the LORD's prophets, Obadiah had taken a hundred prophets and hidden them in two caves, fifty in each, and had supplied them with food and water.) ⁵Ahab had said to Obadiah, "Go through the land to all the springs and valleys. Maybe we can find some grass to keep the horses and mules alive so we will not have to kill any of our animals." ⁶So they divided the land they were to cover, Ahab going in one direction and Obadiah in another.

⁷As Obadiah was walking along, Elijah met him. Obadiah recognised him, bowed down to the ground, and said, "Is it really you, my lord Elijah?"

⁸"Yes," he replied. "Go tell your master, 'Elijah is here.'"

⁹"What have I done wrong," asked Obadiah, "that you are handing your servant over to Ahab to be put to death? ¹⁰As surely as the LORD your God lives, there is not a nation or kingdom where my master has not sent someone to look for you. And whenever a nation or kingdom claimed you were not there, he made them swear they could not find you. ¹¹But now you tell me to go to my master and say, 'Elijah is here.' ¹²I don't know where the Spirit of the LORD may carry you when I leave you. If I go and tell Ahab and he doesn't find you, he will kill me. Yet I your servant have worshipped the LORD since my youth. ¹³Haven't you heard, my lord, what I did while Jezebel was killing the prophets of the LORD? I hid a hundred of the LORD's prophets in two caves, fifty in each, and supplied them with food and water. ¹⁴And now you tell me to go to my master and say, 'Elijah is here.' He will kill me!"

¹⁵Elijah said, "As the LORD Almighty lives, whom I serve, I will surely present myself to Ahab today."

Elijah on Mount Carmel

¹⁶So Obadiah went to meet Ahab and told him, and Ahab went to meet Elijah. ¹⁷When he saw Elijah, he said to him, "Is that you, you troubler of Israel?"

¹⁸"I have not made trouble for Israel," Elijah replied. "But you and your father's family have. You have abandoned the LORD's commands and have followed the Baals. ¹⁹Now summon the people from all over Israel to meet me on Mount Carmel. And bring the four hundred and fifty prophets of Baal and the four hundred prophets of Asherah, who eat at Jezebel's table."

²⁰So Ahab sent word throughout all Israel and assembled the prophets on Mount Carmel. ²¹Elijah went before the people and said, "How long will you waver between two

opinions? If the LORD is God, follow him; but if Baal is God, follow him.''

But the people said nothing.

²²Then Elijah said to them, "I am the only one of the LORD's prophets left, but Baal has four hundred and fifty prophets. ²³Get two bulls for us. Let them choose one for themselves, and let them cut it into pieces and put it on the wood but not set fire to it. I will prepare the other bull and put it on the wood but not set fire to it. ²⁴Then you call on the name of your god, and I will call on the name of the LORD. The god who answers by fire —he is God.''

Then all the people said, "What you say is good.''

²⁵Elijah said to the prophets of Baal, "Choose one of the bulls and prepare it first, since there are so many of you. Call on the name of your god, but do not light the fire.'' ²⁶So they took the bull given them and prepared it.

Then they called on the name of Baal from morning till noon. "O Baal, answer us!'' they shouted. But there was no response; no-one answered. And they danced around the altar they had made.

²⁷At noon Elijah began to taunt them. "Shout louder!'' he said. "Surely he is a god! Perhaps he is deep in thought, or busy, or travelling. Maybe he is sleeping and must be awakened.'' ²⁸So they shouted louder and slashed themselves with swords and spears, as was their custom, until their blood flowed. ²⁹Midday passed, and they continued their frantic prophesying until the time for the evening sacrifice. But there was no response, no-one answered, no-one paid attention.

³⁰Then Elijah said to all the people, "Come here to me.'' They came to him, and he repaired the altar of the LORD, which was in ruins. ³¹Elijah took twelve stones, one for each of the tribes descended from Jacob, to whom the word of the LORD had come, saying, "Your name shall be Israel.'' ³²With the stones he built an altar in the name of the LORD, and he dug a trench round it large enough to hold two seahs*a* of seed. ³³He arranged the wood, cut the bull into pieces and laid it on the wood. Then he said to them, "Fill four large jars with water and pour it on the offering and on the wood.''

³⁴"Do it again,'' he said, and they did it again.

"Do it a third time,'' he ordered, and they did it the third time. ³⁵The water ran down around the altar and even filled the trench.

³⁶At the time of sacrifice, the prophet Elijah stepped forward and prayed: "O LORD, God of Abraham, Isaac and Israel, let it be known today that you are God in Israel and that I am your servant and have done all these things at your command. ³⁷Answer me, O LORD, answer me, so these people will know that you, O LORD, are God, and that you are turning their hearts back again.''

³⁸Then the fire of the LORD fell and burned up the sacrifice, the wood, the stones and the soil, and also licked up the water in the trench.

³⁹When all the people saw this, they fell prostrate and cried, "The LORD—he is God! The LORD—he is God!''

⁴⁰Then Elijah commanded them, "Seize the prophets of Baal. Don't let anyone get away!'' They seized them, and Elijah had them brought down to the Kishon Valley and slaughtered there.

⁴¹And Elijah said to Ahab, "Go, eat and drink, for there is the sound of a heavy rain.'' ⁴²So Ahab went off to eat and drink, but Elijah climbed to the top of Carmel, bent down to the ground and put his face between his knees.

⁴³"Go and look towards the sea,'' he told his servant. And he went up and looked.

"There is nothing there,'' he said.

Seven times Elijah said, "Go back.''

⁴⁴The seventh time the servant reported, "A cloud as small as a man's hand is rising from the sea.''

So Elijah said, "Go and tell Ahab, 'Hitch up your chariot and go down before the rain stops you.' ''

⁴⁵Meanwhile, the sky grew black with clouds, the wind rose, a heavy rain came on and Ahab rode off to Jezreel. ⁴⁶The power of the LORD came upon Elijah and, tucking his cloak into his belt, he ran ahead of Ahab all the way to Jezreel.

Elijah Flees to Horeb

19 Now Ahab told Jezebel everything Elijah had done and how he had killed all the prophets with the sword. ²So Jezebel sent a messenger to Elijah to say, "May the gods deal with me, be it ever so severely, if by this time tomorrow I do not make your life like that of one of them.''

³Elijah was afraid*a* and ran for his life. When he came to Beersheba in Judah, he left his servant there, ⁴while he himself went a day's journey into the desert. He came to a broom tree, sat down under it and prayed that he might die. "I have had enough, LORD,'' he said. "Take my life; I am no better than my ancestors.'' ⁵Then he lay down under the tree and fell asleep.

All at once an angel touched him and said, "Get up and eat.'' ⁶He looked around, and there by his head was a cake of bread baked over hot coals, and a jar of water. He ate and drank and then lay down again.

⁷The angel of the LORD came back a second time and touched him and said, "Get up and eat, for the journey is too much for you.'' ⁸So he got up and ate and drank. Strengthened by that food, he travelled for forty days and forty nights until he reached Horeb, the mountain of God. ⁹There he went into a cave and spent the night.

The LORD Appears to Elijah

And the word of the LORD came to him: "What are you doing here, Elijah?''

¹⁰He replied, "I have been very zealous for the LORD God Almighty. The Israelites have

---

*a*32 That is, probably about 26 pints (about 15 litres)   *a*3 Or *Elijah saw*

I KINGS 19:9–18
'I am the only one left, and now they are trying to kill me too' (v. 10b).

ELIJAH HAD ILLUSIONS of grandeur. He thought he was the only true follower of Yahweh left alive. No such luck! He wasn't alone at all. There were seven thousand others in Israel who had never acknowledged Baal. He did not know them. He simply assumed they were not there. How tragic! Elijah had indeed been brave, but he had been supported throughout by seven thousand people unknown to him who were praying for him to succeed.

Even without God, to whom he ultimately owed the victory, Elijah could still not have claimed all the credit for himself. These seven thousand would also deserve some credit – perhaps a blow to Elijah's pride? He had to be prepared to hear that he was not the only one. That preparation came by means of a most unusual vision, now so well known to us that it is hard to grasp quite how unexpected the still, small voice must have been. But that still, small voice sustained Elijah in a way that the bombastic conquest of the prophets of Baal could never have done. E. W. Heaton writes 'Through a profound spiritual experience, Elijah learns that prophecy is not a matter of using word and action to call down God's power, but rather, a matter of responding in word and action to God's own self disclosure.'

Lord, show people who feel isolated that they aren't alone. Help them to find fellowship with other believers as yet unknown to them.

→310

I KINGS 22

'Finally, a spirit came forward, stood before the LORD and said, "I will entice him" . . . "I will go out and be a lying spirit in the mouths of all his prophets" ' (vv. 21, 22).

ELIJAH WAS NOT ALONE. There was also another true prophet of the Lord, still prophesying while Ahab was on the throne. He was Micaiah, son of Imlah, who is quite unknown to us outside of this chapter, and the parallel chapter recounting the same incidents. We find here a contrast between Micaiah and the 'institutional' prophets, who were in the pay of the king, and whose livelihood depended on giving encouraging words to their employer. Indeed, it comes through here even more strongly than is the case with Elijah. For the king's prophets in this story are not prophets of Baal, but prophets who claim allegiance to Yahweh, Jehovah, the God of Israel.

There is also an interesting sidelight on the way that people in those days thought about God and the spirits who surrounded him. Like the heavenly council depicted in Job and elsewhere the scene here is of God surrounded by spirits who make suggestions about how things are to be run on earth. So one spirit suggests leading the institutional prophets astray, giving them false information about what is going to happen, in order to lead Ahab to his death. It is all very strange.

But Micaiah, like Elijah his contemporary, and like the later prophets from Amos onwards, cannot be corrupted in that way. He is so close to God himself that he cannot be deceived by the lying spirit, that we call Satan. Such closeness to God calls for an independent mind, independent of the corrupt influences around us. It is an independence that few achieve.

What is the role of the Christian community in helping to foster independence of mind?

rejected your covenant, broken down your altars, and put your prophets to death with the sword. I am the only one left, and now they are trying to kill me too."

[11]The LORD said, "Go out and stand on the mountain in the presence of the LORD, for the LORD is about to pass by."

Then a great and powerful wind tore the mountains apart and shattered the rocks before the LORD, but the LORD was not in the wind. After the wind there was an earthquake, but the LORD was not in the earthquake. [12]After the earthquake came a fire, but the LORD was not in the fire. And after the fire came a gentle whisper. [13]When Elijah heard it, he pulled his cloak over his face and went out and stood at the mouth of the cave.

Then a voice said to him, "What are you doing here, Elijah?"

[14]He replied, "I have been very zealous for the LORD God Almighty. The Israelites have rejected your covenant, broken down your altars, and put your prophets to death with the sword. I am the only one left, and now they are trying to kill me too."

[15]The LORD said to him, "Go back the way you came, and go to the Desert of Damascus. When you get there, anoint Hazael king over Aram. [16]Also, anoint Jehu son of Nimshi king over Israel, and anoint Elisha son of Shaphat from Abel Meholah to succeed you as prophet. [17]Jehu will put to death any who escape the sword of Hazael, and Elisha will put to death any who escape the sword of Jehu. [18]Yet I reserve seven thousand in Israel—all whose knees have not bowed down to Baal and all whose mouths have not kissed him."

The Call of Elisha

[19]So Elijah went from there and found Elisha son of Shaphat. He was ploughing with twelve yoke of oxen, and he himself was driving the twelfth pair. Elijah went up to him and threw his cloak around him. [20]Elisha then left his oxen and ran after Elijah. "Let me kiss my father and mother good-bye," he said, "and then I will come with you."

"Go back," Elijah replied. "What have I done to you?"

[21]So Elisha left him and went back. He took his yoke of oxen and slaughtered them. He burned the ploughing equipment to cook the meat and gave it to the people, and they ate. Then he set out to follow Elijah and became his attendant.

Ben-Hadad Attacks Samaria

20 Now Ben-Hadad king of Aram mustered his entire army. Accompanied by thirty-two kings with their horses and chariots, he went up and besieged Samaria and attacked it. [2]He sent messengers into the city to Ahab king of Israel, saying, "This is what Ben-Hadad says: [3]'Your silver and gold are mine, and the best of your wives and children are mine.'"

[4]The king of Israel answered, "Just as you say, my lord the king. I and all I have are yours."

[5]The messengers came again and said, "This is what Ben-Hadad says: 'I sent to demand your silver and gold, your wives and your children. [6]But about this time tomorrow I am going to send my officials to search your palace and the houses of your officials. They will seize everything you value and carry it away.'"

[7]The king of Israel summoned all the elders of the land and said to them, "See how this man is looking for trouble! When he sent for my wives and my children, my silver and my gold, I did not refuse him."

[8]The elders and the people all answered, "Don't listen to him or agree to his demands."

[9]So he replied to Ben-Hadad's messengers, "Tell my lord the king, 'Your servant will do all you demanded the first time, but this demand I cannot meet.'" They left and took the answer back to Ben-Hadad.

[10]Then Ben-Hadad sent another message to Ahab: "May the gods deal with me, be it ever so severely, if enough dust remains in Samaria to give each of my men a handful."

[11]The king of Israel answered, "Tell him: 'One who puts on his armour should not boast like one who takes it off.'"

[12]Ben-Hadad heard this message while he and the kings were drinking in their tents,[a] and he ordered his men: "Prepare to attack." So they prepared to attack the city.

Ahab Defeats Ben-Hadad

[13]Meanwhile a prophet came to Ahab king of Israel and announced, "This is what the LORD says: 'Do you see this vast army? I will give it into your hand today, and then you will know that I am the LORD.'"

[14]"But who will do this?" asked Ahab.

The prophet replied, "This is what the LORD says: 'The young officers of the provincial commanders will do it.'"

"And who will start the battle?" he asked.

The prophet answered, "You will."

[15]So Ahab summoned the young officers of the provincial commanders, 232 men. Then he assembled the rest of the Israelites, 7,000 in all. [16]They set out at noon while Ben-Hadad and the 32 kings allied with him were in their tents getting drunk. [17]The young officers of the provincial commanders went out first.

Now Ben-Hadad had dispatched scouts, who reported, "Men are advancing from Samaria."

[18]He said, "If they have come out for peace, take them alive; if they have come out for war, take them alive."

[19]The young officers of the provincial commanders marched out of the city with the army behind them [20]and each one struck down his opponent. At that, the Arameans fled, with the Israelites in pursuit. But Ben-Hadad king of Aram escaped on horseback with some of his horsemen. [21]The king of Israel advanced and overpowered the horses

[a]12 Or in Succoth; also in verse 16

and chariots and inflicted heavy losses on the Arameans.

²²Afterwards, the prophet came to the king of Israel and said, "Strengthen your position and see what must be done, because next spring the king of Aram will attack you again."

²³Meanwhile, the officials of the king of Aram advised him, "Their gods are gods of the hills. That is why they were too strong for us. But if we fight them on the plains, surely we will be stronger than they. ²⁴Do this: Remove all the kings from their commands and replace them with other officers. ²⁵You must also raise an army like the one you lost—horse for horse and chariot for chariot—so we can fight Israel on the plains. Then surely we will be stronger than they." He agreed with them and acted accordingly.

²⁶The next spring Ben-Hadad mustered the Arameans and went up to Aphek to fight against Israel. ²⁷When the Israelites were also mustered and given provisions, they marched out to meet them. The Israelites camped opposite them like two small flocks of goats, while the Arameans covered the countryside.

²⁸The man of God came up and told the king of Israel, "This is what the LORD says: 'Because the Arameans think the LORD is a god of the hills and not a god of the valleys, I will deliver this vast army into your hands, and you will know that I am the LORD.'"

²⁹For seven days they camped opposite each other, and on the seventh day the battle was joined. The Israelites inflicted a hundred thousand casualties on the Aramean foot soldiers in one day. ³⁰The rest of them escaped to the city of Aphek, where the wall collapsed on twenty-seven thousand of them. And Ben-Hadad fled to the city and hid in an inner room.

³¹His officials said to him, "Look, we have heard that the kings of the house of Israel are merciful. Let us go to the king of Israel with sackcloth round our waists and ropes round our heads. Perhaps he will spare your life."

³²Wearing sackcloth round their waists and ropes round their heads, they went to the king of Israel and said, "Your servant Ben-Hadad says: 'Please let me live.'"

The king answered, "Is he still alive? He is my brother."

³³The men took this as a good sign and were quick to pick up his word. "Yes, your brother Ben-Hadad!" they said.

"Go and get him," the king said. When Ben-Hadad came out, Ahab had him come up into his chariot.

³⁴"I will return the cities my father took from your father," Ben-Hadad offered. "You may set up your own market areas in Damascus, as my father did in Samaria."

Ahab said, "On the basis of a treaty I will set you free." So he made a treaty with him, and let him go.

A Prophet Condemns Ahab

³⁵By the word of the LORD one of the sons of the prophets said to his companion, "Strike me with your weapon," but the man refused.

³⁶So the prophet said, "Because you have not obeyed the LORD, as soon as you leave me a lion will kill you." And after the man went away, a lion found him and killed him.

³⁷The prophet found another man and said, "Strike me, please." So the man struck him and wounded him. ³⁸Then the prophet went and stood by the road waiting for the king. He disguised himself with his headband down over his eyes. ³⁹As the king passed by, the prophet called out to him, "Your servant went into the thick of the battle, and someone came to me with a captive and said, 'Guard this man. If he is missing, it will be your life for his life, or you must pay a talent*b* of silver.' ⁴⁰While your servant was busy here and there, the man disappeared."

"That is your sentence," the king of Israel said. "You have pronounced it yourself."

⁴¹Then the prophet quickly removed the headband from his eyes, and the king of Israel recognised him as one of the prophets. ⁴²He said to the king, "This is what the LORD says: 'You have set free a man I had determined should die.*c* Therefore it is your life for his life, your people for his people.'"

⁴³Sullen and angry, the king of Israel went to his palace in Samaria.

Naboth's Vineyard

21 Some time later there was an incident involving a vineyard belonging to Naboth the Jezreelite. The vineyard was in Jezreel, close to the palace of Ahab king of Samaria. ²Ahab said to Naboth, "Let me have your vineyard to use for a vegetable garden, since it is close to my palace. In exchange I will give you a better vineyard or, if you prefer, I will pay you whatever it is worth."

³But Naboth replied, "The LORD forbid that I should give you the inheritance of my fathers."

⁴So Ahab went home, sullen and angry because Naboth the Jezreelite had said, "I will not give you the inheritance of my fathers." He lay on his bed sulking and refused to eat.

⁵His wife Jezebel came in and asked him, "Why are you so sullen? Why won't you eat?"

⁶He answered her, "Because I said to Naboth the Jezreelite, 'Sell me your vineyard; or if you prefer, I will give you another vineyard in its place.' But he said, 'I will not give you my vineyard.'"

⁷Jezebel his wife said, "Is this how you act as king over Israel? Get up and eat! Cheer up. I'll get you the vineyard of Naboth the Jezreelite."

⁸So she wrote letters in Ahab's name, placed his seal on them, and sent them to the

---

b39 That is, about 75 pounds (about 34 kilograms)
c42 The Hebrew term refers to the irrevocable giving over of things or persons to the LORD, often by totally destroying them.

elders and nobles who lived in Naboth's city with him. 9In those letters she wrote:

"Proclaim a day of fasting and seat Naboth in a prominent place among the people. 10But seat two scoundrels opposite him and have them testify that he has cursed both God and the king. Then take him out and stone him to death."

11So the elders and nobles who lived in Naboth's city did as Jezebel directed in the letters she had written to them. 12They proclaimed a fast and seated Naboth in a prominent place among the people. 13Then two scoundrels came and sat opposite him and brought charges against Naboth before the people, saying, "Naboth has cursed both God and the king." So they took him outside the city and stoned him to death. 14Then they sent word to Jezebel: "Naboth has been stoned and is dead."

15As soon as Jezebel heard that Naboth had been stoned to death, she said to Ahab, "Get up and take possession of the vineyard of Naboth the Jezreelite that he refused to sell you. He is no longer alive, but dead." 16When Ahab heard that Naboth was dead, he got up and went down to take possession of Naboth's vineyard.

17Then the word of the LORD came to Elijah the Tishbite: 18"Go down to meet Ahab king of Israel, who rules in Samaria. He is now in Naboth's vineyard, where he has gone to take possession of it. 19Say to him, 'This is what the LORD says: Have you not murdered a man and seized his property?' Then say to him, 'This is what the LORD says: In the place where dogs licked up Naboth's blood, dogs will lick up your blood—yes, yours!'"

20Ahab said to Elijah, "So you have found me, my enemy!"

"I have found you," he answered, "because you have sold yourself to do evil in the eyes of the LORD. 21'I am going to bring disaster on you. I will consume your descendants and cut off from Ahab every last male in Israel—slave or free. 22I will make your house like that of Jeroboam son of Nebat and that of Baasha son of Ahijah, because you have provoked me to anger and have caused Israel to sin.'

23"And also concerning Jezebel the LORD says: 'Dogs will devour Jezebel by the wall ofᵃ Jezreel.'

24"Dogs will eat those belonging to Ahab who die in the city, and the birds of the air will feed on those who die in the country."

25(There was never a man like Ahab, who sold himself to do evil in the eyes of the LORD, urged on by Jezebel his wife. 26He behaved in the vilest manner by going after idols, like the Amorites the LORD drove out before Israel.)

27When Ahab heard these words, he tore his clothes, put on sackcloth and fasted. He lay in sackcloth and went around meekly.

28Then the word of the LORD came to Elijah the Tishbite: 29"Have you noticed how Ahab

has humbled himself before me? Because he has humbled himself, I will not bring this disaster in his day, but I will bring it on his house in the days of his son."

Micaiah Prophesies Against Ahab

22 For three years there was no war between Aram and Israel. 2But in the third year Jehoshaphat king of Judah went down to see the king of Israel. 3The king of Israel had said to his officials, "Don't you know that Ramoth Gilead belongs to us and yet we are doing nothing to retake it from the king of Aram?"

4So he asked Jehoshaphat, "Will you go with me to fight against Ramoth Gilead?"

Jehoshaphat replied to the king of Israel, "I am as you are, my people as your people, my horses as your horses." 5But Jehoshaphat also said to the king of Israel, "First seek the counsel of the LORD."

6So the king of Israel brought together the prophets—about four hundred men—and asked them, "Shall I go to war against Ramoth Gilead, or shall I refrain?"

"Go," they answered, "for the Lord will give it into the king's hand."

7But Jehoshaphat asked, "Is there not a prophet of the LORD here whom we can enquire of?"

8The king of Israel answered Jehoshaphat, "There is still one man through whom we can enquire of the LORD, but I hate him because he never prophesies anything good about me, but always bad. He is Micaiah son of Imlah."

"The king should not say that," Jehoshaphat replied.

9So the king of Israel called one of his officials and said, "Bring Micaiah son of Imlah at once."

10Dressed in their royal robes, the king of Israel and Jehoshaphat king of Judah were sitting on their thrones at the threshing-floor by the entrance of the gate of Samaria, with all the prophets prophesying before them. 11Now Zedekiah son of Kenaanah had made iron horns and he declared, "This is what the LORD says: 'With these you will gore the Arameans until they are destroyed.'"

12All the other prophets were prophesying the same thing. "Attack Ramoth Gilead and be victorious," they said, "for the LORD will give it into the king's hand."

13The messenger who had gone to summon Micaiah said to him, "Look, as one man the other prophets are predicting success for the king. Let your word agree with theirs, and speak favourably."

14But Micaiah said, "As surely as the LORD lives, I can tell him only what the LORD tells me."

15When he arrived, the king asked him, "Micaiah, shall we go to war against Ramoth Gilead, or shall I refrain?"

"Attack and be victorious," he answered, "for the LORD will give it into the king's hand."

16The king said to him, "How many times

ᵃ23 Most Hebrew manuscripts; a few Hebrew manuscripts, Vulgate and Syriac (see also 2 Kings 9:26) *the plot of ground at* must I make you swear to tell me nothing but the truth in the name of the LORD?"

¹⁷Then Micaiah answered, "I saw all Israel scattered on the hills like sheep without a shepherd, and the LORD said, 'These people have no master. Let each one go home in peace.'"

¹⁸The king of Israel said to Jehoshaphat, "Didn't I tell you that he never prophesies anything good about me, but only bad?"

¹⁹Micaiah continued, "Therefore hear the word of the LORD: I saw the LORD sitting on his throne with all the host of heaven standing round him on his right and on his left. ²⁰And the LORD said, 'Who will entice Ahab into attacking Ramoth Gilead and going to his death there?'

"One suggested this, and another that. ²¹Finally, a spirit came forward, stood before the LORD and said, 'I will entice him.'

²²"'By what means?' the LORD asked.

"'I will go out and be a lying spirit in the mouths of all his prophets,' he said.

"'You will succeed in enticing him,' said the LORD. 'Go and do it.'

²³"So now the LORD has put a lying spirit in the mouths of all these prophets of yours. The LORD has decreed disaster for you."

²⁴Then Zedekiah son of Kenaanah went up and slapped Micaiah in the face. "Which way did the spirit from[a] the LORD go when he went from me to speak to you?" he asked.

²⁵Micaiah replied, "You will find out on the day you go to hide in an inner room."

²⁶The king of Israel then ordered, "Take Micaiah and send him back to Amon the ruler of the city and to Joash the king's son ²⁷and say, 'This is what the king says: Put this fellow in prison and give him nothing but bread and water until I return safely.'"

²⁸Micaiah declared, "If you ever return safely, the LORD has not spoken through me." Then he added, "Mark my words, all you people!"

Ahab Killed at Ramoth Gilead

²⁹So the king of Israel and Jehoshaphat king of Judah went up to Ramoth Gilead. ³⁰The king of Israel said to Jehoshaphat, "I will enter the battle in disguise, but you wear your royal robes." So the king of Israel disguised himself and went into battle.

³¹Now the king of Aram had ordered his thirty-two chariot commanders, "Do not fight with anyone, small or great, except the king of Israel." ³²When the chariot commanders saw Jehoshaphat, they thought, "Surely this is the king of Israel." So they turned to attack him, but when Jehoshaphat cried out, ³³the chariot commanders saw that he was not the king of Israel and stopped pursuing him.

³⁴But someone drew his bow at random and hit the king of Israel between the sections of his armour. The king told his chariot driver, "Wheel round and get me out of the fighting. I've been wounded." ³⁵All day

long the battle raged, and the king was propped up in his chariot facing the Arameans. The blood from his wound ran onto the floor of the chariot, and that evening he died. ³⁶As the sun was setting, a cry spread through the army: "Every man to his town; everyone to his land!"

³⁷So the king died and was brought to Samaria, and they buried him there. ³⁸They washed the chariot at a pool in Samaria (where the prostitutes bathed),[b] and the dogs licked up his blood, as the word of the LORD had declared.

³⁹As for the other events of Ahab's reign, including all he did, the palace he built and inlaid with ivory, and the cities he fortified, are they not written in the book of the annals of the kings of Israel? ⁴⁰Ahab rested with his fathers. And Ahaziah his son succeeded him as king.

Jehoshaphat King of Judah

⁴¹Jehoshaphat son of Asa became king of Judah in the fourth year of Ahab king of Israel. ⁴²Jehoshaphat was thirty-five years old when he became king, and he reigned in Jerusalem for twenty-five years. His mother's name was Azubah daughter of Shilhi. ⁴³In everything he walked in the ways of his father Asa and did not stray from them; he did what was right in the eyes of the LORD. The high places, however, were not removed, and the people continued to offer sacrifices and burn incense there. ⁴⁴Jehoshaphat was also at peace with the king of Israel.

⁴⁵As for the other events of Jehoshaphat's reign, the things he achieved and his military exploits, are they not written in the book of the annals of the kings of Judah? ⁴⁶He rid the land of the rest of the male shrine-prostitutes who remained there even after the reign of his father Asa. ⁴⁷There was then no king in Edom; a deputy ruled.

⁴⁸Now Jehoshaphat built a fleet of trading ships[c] to go to Ophir for gold, but they never set sail—they were wrecked at Ezion Geber. ⁴⁹At that time Ahaziah son of Ahab said to Jehoshaphat, "Let my men sail with your men," but Jehoshaphat refused.

⁵⁰Then Jehoshaphat rested with his fathers and was buried with them in the city of David his father. And Jehoram his son succeeded him.

Ahaziah King of Israel

⁵¹Ahaziah son of Ahab became king of Israel in Samaria in the seventeenth year of Jehoshaphat king of Judah, and he reigned over Israel for two years. ⁵²He did evil in the eyes of the LORD, because he walked in the ways of his father and mother and in the ways of Jeroboam son of Nebat, who caused Israel to sin. ⁵³He served and worshipped Baal and provoked the LORD, the God of Israel, to anger, just as his father had done.

---

[a]24 Or *Spirit of*   [b]38 Or *Samaria and cleaned the weapons*   [c]48 Hebrew *of ships of Tarshish*

2 Kings

The LORD's Judgment on Ahaziah

1 After Ahab's death, Moab rebelled against Israel. ²Now Ahaziah had fallen through the lattice of his upper room in Samaria and injured himself. So he sent messengers, saying to them, "Go and consult Baal-Zebub, the god of Ekron, to see if I will recover from this injury."

³But the angel of the LORD said to Elijah the Tishbite, "Go up and meet the messengers of the king of Samaria and ask them, 'Is it because there is no God in Israel that you are going off to consult Baal-Zebub, the god of Ekron?' ⁴Therefore this is what the LORD says: 'You will not leave the bed you are lying on. You will certainly die!'" So Elijah went.

⁵When the messengers returned to the king, he asked them, "Why have you come back?"

⁶"A man came to meet us," they replied. "And he said to us, 'Go back to the king who sent you and tell him, "This is what the LORD says: Is it because there is no God in Israel that you are sending men to consult Baal-Zebub, the god of Ekron? Therefore you will not leave the bed you are lying on. You will certainly die!"'"

⁷The king asked them, "What kind of man was it who came to meet you and told you this?"

⁸They replied, "He was a man with a garment of hair and with a leather belt round his waist."

The king said, "That was Elijah the Tishbite."

⁹Then he sent to Elijah a captain with his company of fifty men. The captain went up to Elijah, who was sitting on the top of a hill, and said to him, "Man of God, the king says, 'Come down!'"

¹⁰Elijah answered the captain, "If I am a man of God, may fire come down from heaven and consume you and your fifty men!" Then the fire fell from heaven and consumed the captain and his men.

¹¹At this the king sent to Elijah another captain with his fifty men. The captain said to him, "Man of God, this is what the king says, 'Come down at once!'"

¹²"If I am a man of God," Elijah replied, "may fire come down from heaven and consume you and your fifty men!" Then the fire of God fell from heaven and consumed him and his fifty men.

¹³So the king sent a third captain with his fifty men. This third captain went up and fell on his knees before Elijah. "Man of God," he begged, "please have respect for my life and the lives of these fifty men, your servants! ¹⁴See, fire has fallen from heaven and consumed the first two captains and all their men. But now have respect for my life!"

¹⁵The angel of the LORD said to Elijah, "Go down with him; do not be afraid of him." So Elijah got up and went down with him to the king.

¹⁶He told the king, "This is what the LORD says: Is it because there is no God in Israel for you to consult that you have sent messengers to consult Baal-Zebub, the god of Ekron? Because you have done this, you will never leave the bed you are lying on. You will certainly die!" ¹⁷So he died, according to the word of the LORD that Elijah had spoken.

Because Ahaziah had no son, Joram*ᵃ* succeeded him as king in the second year of Jehoram son of Jehoshaphat king of Judah. ¹⁸As for all the other events of Ahaziah's reign, and what he did, are they not written in the book of the annals of the kings of Israel?

Elijah Taken Up to Heaven

2 When the LORD was about to take Elijah up to heaven in a whirlwind, Elijah and Elisha were on their way from Gilgal. ²Elijah said to Elisha, "Stay here; the LORD has sent me to Bethel."

But Elisha said, "As surely as the LORD lives and as you live, I will not leave you." So they went down to Bethel.

³The company of the prophets at Bethel came out to Elisha and asked, "Do you know that the LORD is going to take your master from you today?"

"Yes, I know," Elisha replied, "but do not speak of it."

⁴Then Elijah said to him, "Stay here, Elisha; the LORD has sent me to Jericho."

And he replied, "As surely as the LORD lives and as you live, I will not leave you." So they went to Jericho.

ᵃ17 Hebrew *Jehoram*, a variant of *Joram*

5The company of the prophets at Jericho went up to Elisha and asked him, "Do you know that the LORD is going to take your master from you today?"

"Yes, I know," he replied, "but do not speak of it."

6Then Elijah said to him, "Stay here; the LORD has sent me to the Jordan."

And he replied, "As surely as the LORD lives and as you live, I will not leave you." So the two of them walked on.

7Fifty men of the company of the prophets went and stood at a distance, facing the place where Elijah and Elisha had stopped at the Jordan. 8Elijah took his cloak, rolled it up and struck the water with it. The water divided to the right and to the left, and the two of them crossed over on dry ground.

9When they had crossed, Elijah said to Elisha, "Tell me, what can I do for you before I am taken from you?"

"Let me inherit a double portion of your spirit," Elisha replied.

10"You have asked a difficult thing," Elijah said, "yet if you see me when I am taken from you, it will be yours—otherwise not."

11As they were walking along and talking together, suddenly a chariot of fire and horses of fire appeared and separated the two of them, and Elijah went up to heaven in a whirlwind. 12Elisha saw this and cried out, "My father! My father! The chariots and horsemen of Israel!" And Elisha saw him no more. Then he took hold of his own clothes and tore them apart.

13He picked up the cloak that had fallen from Elijah and went back and stood on the bank of the Jordan. 14Then he took the cloak that had fallen from him and struck the water with it. "Where now is the LORD, the God of Elijah?" he asked. When he struck the water, it divided to the right and to the left, and he crossed over.

15The company of the prophets from Jericho, who were watching, said, "The spirit of Elijah is resting on Elisha." And they went to meet him and bowed to the ground before him. 16"Look," they said, "we your servants have fifty able men. Let them go and look for your master. Perhaps the Spirit of the LORD has picked him up and set him down on some mountain or in some valley."

"No," Elisha replied, "do not send them."

17But they persisted until he was too ashamed to refuse. So he said, "Send them." And they sent fifty men, who searched for three days but did not find him. 18When they returned to Elisha, who was staying in Jericho, he said to them, "Didn't I tell you not to go?"

Healing of the Water

19The men of the city said to Elisha, "Look, our lord, this town is well situated, as you can see, but the water is bad and the land is unproductive."

20"Bring me a new bowl," he said, "and put salt in it." So they brought it to him.

21Then he went out to the spring and threw the salt into it, saying, "This is what the LORD says: 'I have healed this water. Never again will it cause death or make the land unproductive.'" 22And the water has remained wholesome to this day, according to the word Elisha had spoken.

Elisha Is Jeered

23From there Elisha went up to Bethel. As he was walking along the road, some youths came out of the town and jeered at him. "Go on up, you baldhead!" they said. "Go on up, you baldhead!" 24He turned round, looked at them and called down a curse on them in the name of the LORD. Then two bears came out of the woods and mauled forty-two of the youths. 25And he went on to Mount Carmel and from there returned to Samaria.

Moab Revolts

3 Joram[a] son of Ahab became king of Israel in Samaria in the eighteenth year of Jehoshaphat king of Judah, and he reigned for twelve years. 2He did evil in the eyes of the LORD, but not as his father and mother had done. He got rid of the sacred stone of Baal that his father had made. 3Nevertheless he clung to the sins of Jeroboam son of Nebat, which he had caused Israel to commit; he did not turn away from them.

4Now Mesha king of Moab raised sheep, and he had to supply the king of Israel with a hundred thousand lambs and with the wool of a hundred thousand rams. 5But after Ahab died, the king of Moab rebelled against the king of Israel. 6So at that time King Joram set out from Samaria and mobilised all Israel. 7He also sent this message to Jehoshaphat king of Judah: "The king of Moab has rebelled against me. Will you go with me to fight against Moab?"

"I will go with you," he replied. "I am as you are, my people as your people, my horses as your horses."

8"By what route shall we attack?" he asked.

"Through the Desert of Edom," he answered.

9So the king of Israel set out with the king of Judah and the king of Edom. After a roundabout march of seven days, the army had no more water for themselves or for the animals with them.

10"What!" exclaimed the king of Israel. "Has the LORD called us three kings together only to hand us over to Moab?"

11But Jehoshaphat asked, "Is there no prophet of the LORD here, that we may enquire of the LORD through him?"

An officer of the king of Israel answered, "Elisha son of Shaphat is here. He used to pour water on the hands of Elijah."[b]

12Jehoshaphat said, "The word of the LORD is with him." So the king of Israel and Jehoshaphat and the king of Edom went down to him.

---

a1 Hebrew Jehoram, a variant of Joram; also in verse 6　　b11 That is, he was Elijah's personal servant.

[13]Elisha said to the king of Israel, "What do we have to do with each other? Go to the prophets of your father and the prophets of your mother."

"No," the king of Israel answered, "because it was the LORD who called us three kings together to hand us over to Moab."

[14]Elisha said, "As surely as the LORD Almighty lives, whom I serve, if I did not have respect for the presence of Jehoshaphat king of Judah, I would not look at you or even notice you. [15]But now bring me a harpist."

While the harpist was playing, the hand of the LORD came upon Elisha [16]and he said, "This is what the LORD says: Make this valley full of ditches. [17]For this is what the LORD says: You will see neither wind nor rain, yet this valley will be filled with water, and you, your cattle and your other animals will drink. [18]This is an easy thing in the eyes of the LORD; he will also hand Moab over to you. [19]You will overthrow every fortified city and every major town. You will cut down every good tree, stop up all the springs, and ruin every good field with stones."

[20]The next morning, about the time for offering the sacrifice, there it was—water flowing from the direction of Edom! And the land was filled with water.

[21]Now all the Moabites had heard that the kings had come to fight against them; so every man, young and old, who could bear arms was called up and stationed on the border. [22]When they got up early in the morning, the sun was shining on the water. To the Moabites across the way, the water looked red—like blood. [23]"That's blood!" they said. "Those kings must have fought and slaughtered each other. Now to the plunder, Moab!"

[24]But when the Moabites came to the camp of Israel, the Israelites rose up and fought them until they fled. And the Israelites invaded the land and slaughtered the Moabites. [25]They destroyed the towns, and each man threw a stone on every good field until it was covered. They stopped up all the springs and cut down every good tree. Only Kir Hareseth was left with its stones in place, but men armed with slings surrounded it and attacked it as well.

[26]When the king of Moab saw that the battle had gone against him, he took with him seven hundred swordsmen to break through to the king of Edom, but they failed. [27]Then he took his firstborn son, who was to succeed him as king, and offered him as a sacrifice on the city wall. The fury against Israel was great; they withdrew and returned to their own land.

The Widow's Oil

4 The wife of a man from the company of the prophets cried out to Elisha, "Your servant my husband is dead, and you know that he revered the LORD. But now his creditor is coming to take my two boys as his slaves."

[2]Elisha replied to her, "How can I help you? Tell me, what do you have in your house?"

"Your servant has nothing there at all," she said, "except a little oil."

[3]Elisha said, "Go round and ask all your neighbours for empty jars. Don't ask for just a few. [4]Then go inside and shut the door behind you and your sons. Pour oil into all the jars, and as each is filled, put it to one side."

[5]She left him and afterwards shut the door behind her and her sons. They brought the jars to her and she kept pouring. [6]When all the jars were full, she said to her son, "Bring me another one."

But he replied, "There is not a jar left." Then the oil stopped flowing.

[7]She went and told the man of God, and he said, "Go, sell the oil and pay your debts. You and your sons can live on what is left."

The Shunammite's Son Restored to Life

[8]One day Elisha went to Shunem. And a well-to-do woman was there, who urged him to stay for a meal. So whenever he came by, he stopped there to eat. [9]She said to her husband, "I know that this man who often comes our way is a holy man of God. [10]Let's make a small room on the roof and put in it a bed and a table, a chair and a lamp for him. Then he can stay there whenever he comes to us."

[11]One day when Elisha came, he went up to his room and lay down there. [12]He said to his servant Gehazi, "Call the Shunammite." So he called her, and she stood before him. [13]Elisha said to him, "Tell her, 'You have gone to all this trouble for us. Now what can be done for you? Can we speak on your behalf to the king or the commander of the army?'"

She replied, "I have a home among my own people."

[14]"What can be done for her?" Elisha asked.

Gehazi said, "Well, she has no son and her husband is old."

[15]Then Elisha said, "Call her." So he called her, and she stood in the doorway. [16]"About this time next year," Elisha said, "you will hold a son in your arms."

"No, my lord," she objected. "Don't mislead your servant, O man of God!"

[17]But the woman became pregnant, and the next year about that same time she gave birth to a son, just as Elisha had told her.

[18]The child grew, and one day he went out to his father, who was with the reapers. [19]"My head! My head!" he said to his father.

His father told a servant, "Carry him to his mother." [20]After the servant had lifted him up and carried him to his mother, the boy sat on her lap until noon, and then he died. [21]She went up and laid him on the bed of the man of God, then shut the door and went out.

[22]She called her husband and said, "Please send me one of the servants and a donkey so I can go to the man of God quickly and return."

[23]"Why go to him today?" he asked. "It's not the New Moon or the Sabbath."

"It's all right," she said.

[24]She saddled the donkey and said to her

servant, "Lead on; don't slow down for me unless I tell you." ²⁵So she set out and came to the man of God at Mount Carmel.

When he saw her in the distance, the man of God said to his servant Gehazi, "Look! There's the Shunammite! ²⁶Run to meet her and ask her, 'Are you all right? Is your husband all right? Is your child all right?'"

"Everything is all right," she said.

²⁷When she reached the man of God at the mountain, she took hold of his feet. Gehazi came over to push her away, but the man of God said, "Leave her alone! She is in bitter distress, but the LORD has hidden it from me and has not told me why."

²⁸"Did I ask you for a son, my lord?" she said. "Didn't I tell you, 'Don't raise my hopes'?"

²⁹Elisha said to Gehazi, "Tuck your cloak into your belt, take my staff in your hand and run. If you meet anyone, do not greet him, and if anyone greets you, do not answer. Lay my staff on the boy's face."

³⁰But the child's mother said, "As surely as the LORD lives and as you live, I will not leave you." So he got up and followed her.

³¹Gehazi went on ahead and laid the staff on the boy's face, but there was no sound or response. So Gehazi went back to meet Elisha and told him, "The boy has not awakened."

³²When Elisha reached the house, there was the boy lying dead on his couch. ³³He went in, shut the door on the two of them and prayed to the LORD. ³⁴Then he got on the bed and lay upon the boy, mouth to mouth, eyes to eyes, hands to hands. As he stretched himself out upon him, the boy's body grew warm. ³⁵Elisha turned away and walked back and forth in the room and then got onto the bed and stretched out upon him once more. The boy sneezed seven times and opened his eyes.

³⁶Elisha summoned Gehazi and said, "Call the Shunammite." And he did. When she came, he said, "Take your son." ³⁷She came in, fell at his feet and bowed to the ground. Then she took her son and went out.

Death in the Pot

³⁸Elisha returned to Gilgal and there was a famine in that region. While the company of the prophets was meeting with him, he said to his servant, "Put on the large pot and cook some stew for these men."

³⁹One of them went out into the fields to gather herbs and found a wild vine. He gathered some of its gourds and filled the fold of his cloak. When he returned, he cut them up into the pot of stew, though no-one knew what they were. ⁴⁰The stew was poured out for the men, but as they began to eat it, they cried out, "O man of God, there is death in the pot!" And they could not eat it.

⁴¹Elisha said, "Get some flour." He put it into the pot and said, "Serve it to the people to eat." And there was nothing harmful in the pot.

Feeding of a Hundred

⁴²A man came from Baal Shalishah, bringing the man of God twenty loaves of barley bread baked from the first ripe corn, along with some ears of new corn. "Give it to the people to eat," Elisha said.

⁴³"How can I set this before a hundred men?" his servant asked.

But Elisha answered, "Give it to the people to eat. For this is what the LORD says: 'They will eat and have some left over.'" ⁴⁴Then he set it before them, and they ate and had some left over, according to the word of the LORD.

Naaman Healed of Leprosy

5 Now Naaman was commander of the army of the king of Aram. He was a great man in the sight of his master and highly regarded, because through him the LORD had given victory to Aram. He was a valiant soldier, but he had leprosy.ᵃ

²Now bands from Aram had gone out and had taken captive a young girl from Israel, and she served Naaman's wife. ³She said to her mistress, "If only my master would see the prophet who is in Samaria! He would cure him of his leprosy."

⁴Naaman went to his master and told him what the girl from Israel had said. ⁵"By all means, go," the king of Aram replied. "I will send a letter to the king of Israel." So Naaman left, taking with him ten talentsᵇ of silver, six thousand shekelsᶜ of gold and ten sets of clothing. ⁶The letter that he took to the king of Israel read: "With this letter I am sending my servant Naaman to you so that you may cure him of his leprosy."

⁷As soon as the king of Israel read the letter, he tore his robes and said, "Am I God? Can I kill and bring back to life? Why does this fellow send someone to me to be cured of his leprosy? See how he is trying to pick a quarrel with me!"

⁸When Elisha the man of God heard that the king of Israel had torn his robes, he sent him this message: "Why have you torn your robes? Make the man come to me and he will know that there is a prophet in Israel." ⁹So Naaman went with his horses and chariots and stopped at the door of Elisha's house. ¹⁰Elisha sent a messenger to say to him, "Go, wash yourself seven times in the Jordan, and your flesh will be restored and you will be cleansed."

¹¹But Naaman went away angry and said, "I thought that he would surely come out to me and stand and call on the name of the LORD his God, wave his hand over the spot and cure me of my leprosy. ¹²Are not Abana and Pharpar, the rivers of Damascus, better than any of the waters of Israel? Couldn't I wash in them and be cleansed?" So he turned and went off in a rage.

¹³Naaman's servants went to him and said, "My father, if the prophet had told you to do some great thing, would you not have done it? How much more, then, when he tells you,

---

ᵃ1 The Hebrew word was used for various diseases affecting the skin—not necessarily leprosy; also in verses 3, 6, 7, 11 and 27.   ᵇ5 That is, about 750 pounds (about 340 kilograms)   ᶜ5 That is, about 150 pounds (about 70 kilograms)

2 KINGS 4:1–7
' "Go, sell the oil and pay your debts" ' (v. 7).

THE SAME KIND OF STORIES are told about Elisha, as about his master Elijah. The widow described here reminds us very much of the widow of Zarephath who looked after Elijah in the drought. The miraculous element is very similar, even though the details are different. Sometimes, at special moments God does indeed work in such a miraculous fashion. More often he works in the ordinary and the everyday to provide the treasures of life.

An old fable tells of a man who left some treasure to his sons. All they knew about this treasure was, it was hidden in a barren field. After the man's death each son in turn tried to find the treasure. First one dug, then another, after that a third and so on, until the whole field was turned over. They found no precious stones, but the crops which grew provided the treasure, more lasting than any precious stone or jewel they might have found.

Few of us have an Elisha to come along and keep the oil flowing until all our debts are paid. But many of us have resources which we don't fully use. We fail to see the potential in a person who could be asked to do something positive in the community or church. We fail to ask those who would be willing to help. We fail to encourage others who seem reluctant to help when asked. In such ways we deny ourselves access to the miraculous power of God – who will always multiply resources beyond our imagining when we ask him in faith.

Extend the resources available to you today by prayerfully asking help from someone you have not had faith enough to ask to help you before.

→320

2 KINGS 5:1–14
' "Go, wash yourself seven times in the Jordan, and your flesh will be restored and you will be cleansed" ' (v. 10).

LEPROSY IS CURABLE. World Leprosy Day is held on the last Sunday in January. Posters proclaim the message 'leprosy is curable'. It no longer requires a miracle to cure leprosy – or does it?

Naaman despised the simple thing he was being asked to do. He would have been happy to do something great and spectacular. But no, all he was asked to do was to go and wash in the Jordan.

The miracle required today is also a miracle of motivation. Given application of simple resources, and a strong enough will to ensure medicine and vaccine gets to the people who need it, the miracle of wiping leprosy from the face of the earth could be effected, just as surely as smallpox was eradicated earlier. The difficulties with leprosy are:

1. Its onset is so gradual.
2. There is so much stigma attached to it.
3. It is not very infectious, so doesn't command the urgency that smallpox did. Some people can be in contact with lepers for long periods without contracting the disease.
4. It is most prevalent in poor, remote areas.

Convincing people they can be cured is one thing. Convincing authorities it is worth spending massive resources is another. In Malawi, expenditure of something over half a million pounds a year reduced the number of leprosy cases in the eighties by a tenth. That would need multiplying many times over in other similarly poor countries to eradicate this scourge of humanity.

It can be done. Pray, work and give so that it will be done.

'Wash and be cleansed'?" [14]So he went down and dipped himself in the Jordan seven times, as the man of God had told him, and his flesh was restored and became clean like that of a young boy.

[15]Then Naaman and all his attendants went back to the man of God. He stood before him and said, "Now I know that there is no God in all the world except in Israel. Please accept now a gift from your servant."

[16]The prophet answered, "As surely as the LORD lives, whom I serve, I will not accept a thing." And even though Naaman urged him, he refused.

[17]"If you will not," said Naaman, "please let me, your servant, be given as much earth as a pair of mules can carry, for your servant will never again make burnt offerings and sacrifices to any other god but the LORD. [18]But may the LORD forgive your servant for this one thing: When my master enters the temple of Rimmon to bow down and he is leaning on my arm and I bow there also —when I bow down in the temple of Rimmon, may the LORD forgive your servant for this."

[19]"Go in peace," Elisha said.

After Naaman had travelled some distance, [20]Gehazi, the servant of Elisha the man of God, said to himself, "My master was too easy on Naaman, this Aramean, by not accepting from him what he brought. As surely as the LORD lives, I will run after him and get something from him."

[21]So Gehazi hurried after Naaman. When Naaman saw him running towards him, he got down from the chariot to meet him. "Is everything all right?" he asked.

[22]"Everything is all right," Gehazi answered. "My master sent me to say, 'Two young men from the company of the prophets have just come to me from the hill country of Ephraim. Please give them a talent[d] of silver and two sets of clothing.'"

[23]"By all means, take two talents," said Naaman. He urged Gehazi to accept them, and then tied up the two talents of silver in two bags, with two sets of clothing. He gave them to two of his servants, and they carried them ahead of Gehazi. [24]When Gehazi came to the hill, he took the things from the servants and put them away in the house. He sent the men away and they left. [25]Then he went in and stood before his master Elisha.

"Where have you been, Gehazi?" Elisha asked.

"Your servant didn't go anywhere," Gehazi answered.

[26]But Elisha said to him, "Was not my spirit with you when the man got down from his chariot to meet you? Is this the time to take money, or to accept clothes, olive groves, vineyards, flocks, herds, or menservants and maidservants? [27]Naaman's leprosy will cling to you and to your descendants for ever." Then Gehazi went from Elisha's presence and he was leprous, as white as snow.

An Axe-Head Floats

6 The company of the prophets said to Elisha, "Look, the place where we meet with you is too small for us. [2]Let us go to the Jordan, where each of us can get a pole; and let us build a place there for us to live."

And he said, "Go."

[3]Then one of them said, "Won't you please come with your servants?"

"I will," Elisha replied. [4]And he went with them.

They went to the Jordan and began to cut down trees. [5]As one of them was cutting down a tree, the iron axe-head fell into the water. "Oh, my lord," he cried out, "it was borrowed!"

[6]The man of God asked, "Where did it fall?" When he showed him the place, Elisha cut a stick and threw it there, and made the iron float. [7]"Lift it out," he said. Then the man reached out his hand and took it.

Elisha Traps Blinded Arameans

[8]Now the king of Aram was at war with Israel. After conferring with his officers, he said, "I will set up my camp in such and such a place."

[9]The man of God sent word to the king of Israel: "Beware of passing that place, because the Arameans are going down there." [10]So the king of Israel checked on the place indicated by the man of God. Time and again Elisha warned the king, so that he was on his guard in such places.

[11]This enraged the king of Aram. He summoned his officers and demanded of them, "Will you not tell me which of us is on the side of the king of Israel?"

[12]"None of us, my lord the king," said one of his officers, "but Elisha, the prophet who is in Israel, tells the king of Israel the very words you speak in your bedroom."

[13]"Go, find out where he is," the king ordered, "so that I can send men and capture him." The report came back: "He is in Dothan." [14]Then he sent horses and chariots and a strong force there. They went by night and surrounded the city.

[15]When the servant of the man of God got up and went out early the next morning, an army with horses and chariots had surrounded the city. "Oh, my lord, what shall we do?" the servant asked.

[16]"Don't be afraid," the prophet answered. "Those who are with us are more than those who are with them."

[17]And Elisha prayed, "O LORD, open his eyes so that he may see." Then the LORD opened the servant's eyes, and he looked and saw the hills full of horses and chariots of fire all round Elisha.

[18]As the enemy came down towards him, Elisha prayed to the LORD, "Strike these people with blindness." So he struck them with blindness, as Elisha had asked.

[19]Elisha told them, "This is not the road and this is not the city. Follow me, and I will lead you to the man you are looking for." And he led them to Samaria.

[d]22 That is, about 75 pounds (about 34 kilograms)

²⁰After they entered the city, Elisha said, "LORD, open the eyes of these men so that they can see." Then the LORD opened their eyes and they looked, and there they were, inside Samaria.

²¹When the king of Israel saw them, he asked Elisha, "Shall I kill them, my father? Shall I kill them?"

²²"Do not kill them," he answered. "Would you kill men you have captured with your own sword or bow? Set food and water before them so that they may eat and drink and then go back to their master." ²³So he prepared a great feast for them, and after they had finished eating and drinking, he sent them away, and they returned to their master. So the bands from Aram stopped raiding Israel's territory.

Famine in Besieged Samaria

²⁴Some time later, Ben-Hadad king of Aram mobilised his entire army and marched up and laid siege to Samaria. ²⁵There was a great famine in the city; the siege lasted so long that a donkey's head sold for eighty shekels*a* of silver, and a quarter of a cab*b* of seed pods*c* for five shekels.*d*

²⁶As the king of Israel was passing by on the wall, a woman cried to him, "Help me, my lord the king!"

²⁷The king replied, "If the LORD does not help you, where can I get help for you? From the threshing-floor? From the winepress?" ²⁸Then he asked her, "What's the matter?"

She answered, "This woman said to me, 'Give up your son so that we may eat him today, and tomorrow we'll eat my son.' ²⁹So we cooked my son and ate him. The next day I said to her, 'Give up your son so that we may eat him,' but she had hidden him."

³⁰When the king heard the woman's words, he tore his robes. As he went along the wall, the people looked, and there, underneath, he had sackcloth on his body. ³¹He said, "May God deal with me, be it ever so severely, if the head of Elisha son of Shaphat remains on his shoulders today!"

³²Now Elisha was sitting in his house, and the elders were sitting with him. The king sent a messenger ahead, but before he arrived, Elisha said to the elders, "Don't you see how this murderer is sending someone to cut off my head? Look, when the messenger comes, shut the door and hold it shut against him. Is not the sound of his master's footsteps behind him?"

³³While he was still talking to them, the messenger came down to him. And the king said, "This disaster is from the LORD. Why should I wait for the LORD any longer?"

7 Elisha said, "Hear the word of the LORD. This is what the LORD says: About this time tomorrow, a seah*a* of flour will sell for a shekel*b* and two seahs*c* of barley for a shekel at the gate of Samaria."

²The officer on whose arm the king was leaning said to the man of God, "Look, even if the LORD should open the floodgates of the heavens, could this happen?"

"You will see it with your own eyes," answered Elisha, "but you will not eat any of it!"

The Siege Lifted

³Now there were four men with leprosy*d* at the entrance of the city gate. They said to each other, "Why stay here until we die? ⁴If we say, 'We'll go into the city'—the famine is there, and we will die. And if we stay here, we will die. So let's go over to the camp of the Arameans and surrender. If they spare us, we live; if they kill us, then we die."

⁵At dusk they got up and went to the camp of the Arameans. When they reached the edge of the camp, not a man was there, ⁶for the Lord had caused the Arameans to hear the sound of chariots and horses and a great army, so that they said to one another, "Look, the king of Israel has hired the Hittite and Egyptian kings to attack us!" ⁷So they got up and fled in the dusk and abandoned their tents and their horses and donkeys. They left the camp as it was and ran for their lives.

⁸The men who had leprosy reached the edge of the camp and entered one of the tents. They ate and drank, and carried away silver, gold and clothes, and went off and hid them. They returned and entered another tent and took some things from it and hid them also.

⁹Then they said to each other, "We're not doing right. This is a day of good news and we are keeping it to ourselves. If we wait until daylight, punishment will overtake us. Let's go at once and report this to the royal palace."

¹⁰So they went and called out to the city gatekeepers and told them, "We went into the Aramean camp and not a man was there —not a sound of anyone—only tethered horses and donkeys, and the tents left just as they were." ¹¹The gatekeepers shouted the news, and it was reported within the palace.

¹²The king got up in the night and said to his officers, "I will tell you what the Arameans have done to us. They know we are starving; so they have left the camp to hide in the countryside, thinking, 'They will surely come out, and then we will take them alive and get into the city.'"

¹³One of his officers answered, "Make some men take five of the horses that are left in the city. Their plight will be like that of all the Israelites left here—yes, they will only be like all these Israelites who are doomed. So let us send them to find out what happened."

¹⁴So they selected two chariots with their horses, and the king sent them after the Aramean army. He commanded the drivers,

---

*a*25 That is, about 2 pounds (about 1 kilogram)   *b*25 That is, probably about ½ pint (about 0.3 litre)
*c*25 Or *of dove's dung*   *d*25 That is, about 2 ounces (about 55 grams)
*a*1 That is, probably about 13 pints (about 7.3 litres); also in verses 16 and 18
*b*1 That is, about ⅔ ounce (about 11 grams); also in verses 16 and 18
*c*1 That is, probably about 13 quarts (about 15 litres); also in verses 16 and 18
*d*3 The Hebrew word is used for various diseases affecting the skin, not necessarily leprosy; also in verse 8.

"Go and find out what has happened."
15They followed them as far as the Jordan,
and they found the whole road strewn with
the clothing and equipment the Arameans
had thrown away in their headlong flight. So
the messengers returned and reported to the
king. 16Then the people went out and plundered the camp of the Arameans. So a seah of
flour sold for a shekel, and two seahs of
barley sold for a shekel, as the LORD had said.

17Now the king had put the officer on
whose arm he leaned in charge of the gate,
and the people trampled him in the gateway,
and he died, just as the man of God had
foretold when the king came down to his
house. 18It happened as the man of God had
said to the king: "About this time tomorrow,
a seah of flour will sell for a shekel and two
seahs of barley for a shekel at the gate of
Samaria."

19The officer had said to the man of God,
"Look, even if the LORD should open the
floodgates of the heavens, could this happen?" The man of God had replied, "You
will see it with your own eyes, but you will
not eat any of it!" 20And that is exactly what
happened to him, for the people trampled
him in the gateway, and he died.

The Shunammite's Land Restored

8 Now Elisha had said to the woman
whose son he had restored to life, "Go
away with your family and stay for a while
wherever you can, because the LORD has
decreed a famine in the land that will last
seven years." 2The woman proceeded to do
as the man of God said. She and her family
went away and stayed in the land of the
Philistines for seven years.

3At the end of the seven years she came
back from the land of the Philistines and went
to the king to beg for her house and land.
4The king was talking to Gehazi, the servant
of the man of God, and had said, "Tell me
about all the great things Elisha has done."
5Just as Gehazi was telling the king how
Elisha had restored the dead to life, the
woman whose son Elisha had brought back
to life came to beg the king for her house and
land.

Gehazi said, "This is the woman, my lord
the king, and this is her son whom Elisha
restored to life." 6The king asked the woman
about it, and she told him.

Then he assigned an official to her case and
said to him, "Give back everything that belonged to her, including all the income from
her land from the day she left the country
until now."

Hazael Murders Ben-Hadad

7Elisha went to Damascus, and Ben-
Hadad king of Aram was ill. When the king
was told, "The man of God has come all the
way up here," 8he said to Hazael, "Take a
gift with you and go to meet the man of God.
Consult the LORD through him; ask him, 'Will
I recover from this illness?'"

9Hazael went to meet Elisha, taking with
him as a gift forty camel-loads of all the finest
wares of Damascus. He went in and stood
before him, and said, "Your son Ben-Hadad
king of Aram has sent me to ask, 'Will I
recover from this illness?'"

10Elisha answered, "Go and say to him,
'You will certainly recover'; but*a* the LORD
has revealed to me that he will in fact die."
11He stared at him with a fixed gaze until
Hazael felt ashamed. Then the man of God
began to weep.

12"Why is my lord weeping?" asked
Hazael.

"Because I know the harm you will do to
the Israelites," he answered. "You will set
fire to their fortified places, kill their young
men with the sword, dash their little children
to the ground, and rip open their pregnant
women."

13Hazael said, "How could your servant, a
mere dog, accomplish such a feat?"

"The LORD has shown me that you will
become king of Aram," answered Elisha.

14Then Hazael left Elisha and returned to
his master. When Ben-Hadad asked, "What
did Elisha say to you?" Hazael replied, "He
told me that you would certainly recover."
15But the next day he took a thick cloth,
soaked it in water and spread it over the
king's face, so that he died. Then Hazael
succeeded him as king.

Jehoram King of Judah

16In the fifth year of Joram son of Ahab
king of Israel, when Jehoshaphat was king of
Judah, Jehoram son of Jehoshaphat began
his reign as king of Judah. 17He was thirty-
two years old when he became king, and he
reigned in Jerusalem for eight years. 18He
walked in the ways of the kings of Israel, as
the house of Ahab had done, for he married a
daughter of Ahab. He did evil in the eyes of
the LORD. 19Nevertheless, for the sake of his
servant David, the LORD was not willing to
destroy Judah. He had promised to maintain
a lamp for David and his descendants for
ever.

20In the time of Jehoram, Edom rebelled
against Judah and set up its own king. 21So
Jehoram*b* went to Zair with all his chariots.
The Edomites surrounded him and his chariot commanders, but he rose up and broke
through by night; his army, however, fled
back home. 22To this day Edom has been in
rebellion against Judah. Libnah revolted at
the same time.

23As for the other events of Jehoram's
reign, and all he did, are they not written in
the book of the annals of the kings of Judah?
24Jehoram rested with his fathers and was
buried with them in the City of David. And
Ahaziah his son succeeded him as king.

Ahaziah King of Judah

25In the twelfth year of Joram son of Ahab
king of Israel, Ahaziah son of Jehoram king
of Judah began to reign. 26Ahaziah was

---

a10 The Hebrew may also be read *Go and say, 'You will certainly not recover,' for.*
b21 Hebrew *Joram*, a variant of *Jehoram*; also in verses 23 and 24

twenty-two years old when he became king, and he reigned in Jerusalem for one year. His mother's name was Athaliah, a granddaughter of Omri king of Israel. 27He walked in the ways of the house of Ahab and did evil in the eyes of the LORD, as the house of Ahab had done, for he was related by marriage to Ahab's family.

28Ahaziah went with Joram son of Ahab to war against Hazael king of Aram at Ramoth Gilead. The Arameans wounded Joram; 29so King Joram returned to Jezreel to recover from the wounds the Arameans had inflicted on him at Ramoth*c* in his battle with Hazael king of Aram.

Then Ahaziah son of Jehoram king of Judah went down to Jezreel to see Joram son of Ahab, because he had been wounded.

Jehu Anointed King of Israel

9 The prophet Elisha summoned a man from the company of the prophets and said to him, "Tuck your cloak into your belt, take this flask of oil with you and go to Ramoth Gilead. 2When you get there, look for Jehu son of Jehoshaphat, the son of Nimshi. Go to him, get him away from his companions and take him into an inner room. 3Then take the flask and pour the oil on his head and declare, 'This is what the LORD says: I anoint you king over Israel.' Then open the door and run; don't delay!"

4So the young man, the prophet, went to Ramoth Gilead. 5When he arrived, he found the army officers sitting together. "I have a message for you, commander," he said.

"For which of us?" asked Jehu.

"For you, commander," he replied.

6Jehu got up and went into the house. Then the prophet poured the oil on Jehu's head and declared, "This is what the LORD, the God of Israel, says: 'I anoint you king over the LORD's people Israel. 7You are to destroy the house of Ahab your master, and I will avenge the blood of my servants the prophets and the blood of all the LORD's servants shed by Jezebel. 8The whole house of Ahab will perish. I will cut off from Ahab every last male in Israel—slave or free. 9I will make the house of Ahab like the house of Jeroboam son of Nebat and like the house of Baasha son of Ahijah. 10As for Jezebel, dogs will devour her on the plot of ground at Jezreel, and no-one will bury her.' " Then he opened the door and ran.

11When Jehu went out to his fellow officers, one of them asked him, "Is everything all right? Why did this madman come to you?"

"You know the man and the sort of things he says," Jehu replied.

12"That's not true!" they said. "Tell us."

Jehu said, "Here is what he told me: 'This is what the LORD says: I anoint you king over Israel.' "

13They hurried and took their cloaks and spread them under him on the bare steps.

Then they blew the trumpet and shouted, "Jehu is king!"

Jehu Kills Joram and Ahaziah

14So Jehu son of Jehoshaphat, the son of Nimshi, conspired against Joram. (Now Joram and all Israel had been defending Ramoth Gilead against Hazael king of Aram, 15but King Joram*a* had returned to Jezreel to recover from the wounds the Arameans had inflicted on him in the battle with Hazael king of Aram.) Jehu said, "If this is the way you feel, don't let anyone slip out of the city to go and tell the news in Jezreel." 16Then he got into his chariot and rode to Jezreel, because Joram was resting there and Ahaziah king of Judah had gone down to see him.

17When the lookout standing on the tower in Jezreel saw Jehu's troops approaching, he called out, "I see some troops coming."

"Get a horseman," Joram ordered. "Send him to meet them and ask, 'Do you come in peace?' "

18The horseman rode off to meet Jehu and said, "This is what the king says: 'Do you come in peace?' "

"What do you have to do with peace?" Jehu replied. "Fall in behind me."

The lookout reported, "The messenger has reached them, but he isn't coming back."

19So the king sent out a second horseman. When he came to them he said, "This is what the king says: 'Do you come in peace?' "

Jehu replied, "What do you have to do with peace? Fall in behind me."

20The lookout reported, "He has reached them, but he isn't coming back either. The driving is like that of Jehu son of Nimshi—he drives like a madman."

21"Hitch up my chariot," Joram ordered. And when it was hitched up, Joram king of Israel and Ahaziah king of Judah rode out, each in his own chariot, to meet Jehu. They met him at the plot of ground that had belonged to Naboth the Jezreelite. 22When Joram saw Jehu he asked, "Have you come in peace, Jehu?"

"How can there be peace," Jehu replied, "as long as all the idolatry and witchcraft of your mother Jezebel abound?"

23Joram turned about and fled, calling out to Ahaziah, "Treachery, Ahaziah!"

24Then Jehu drew his bow and shot Joram between the shoulders. The arrow pierced his heart and he slumped down in his chariot. 25Jehu said to Bidkar, his chariot officer, "Pick him up and throw him on the field that belonged to Naboth the Jezreelite. Remember how you and I were riding together in chariots behind Ahab his father when the LORD made this prophecy about him: 26'Yesterday I saw the blood of Naboth and the blood of his sons, declares the LORD, and I will surely make you pay for it on this plot of ground, declares the LORD.'*b* Now then, pick him up and throw him on that plot, in accordance with the word of the LORD."

*c*29 Hebrew *Ramah*, a variant of *Ramoth*
*a*15 Hebrew *Jehoram*, a variant of *Joram*; also in verses 17 and 21–24
*b*26 See 1 Kings 21:19.

²⁷When Ahaziah king of Judah saw what had happened, he fled up the road to Beth Haggan.ᶜ Jehu chased him, shouting, "Kill him too!" They wounded him in his chariot on the way up to Gur near Ibleam, but he escaped to Megiddo and died there. ²⁸His servants took him by chariot to Jerusalem and buried him with his fathers in his tomb in the City of David. ²⁹(In the eleventh year of Joram son of Ahab, Ahaziah had become king of Judah.)

Jezebel Killed

³⁰Then Jehu went to Jezreel. When Jezebel heard about it, she painted her eyes, arranged her hair and looked out of a window. ³¹As Jehu entered the gate, she asked, "Have you come in peace, Zimri, you murderer of your master?"ᵈ

³²He looked up at the window and called out, "Who is on my side? Who?" Two or three eunuchs looked down at him. ³³"Throw her down!" Jehu said. So they threw her down, and some of her blood spattered the wall and the horses as they trampled her underfoot.

³⁴Jehu went in and ate and drank. "Take care of that cursed woman," he said, "and bury her, for she was a king's daughter." ³⁵But when they went out to bury her, they found nothing except her skull, her feet and her hands. ³⁶They went back and told Jehu, who said, "This is the word of the Lord that he spoke through his servant Elijah the Tishbite: On the plot of ground at Jezreel dogs will devour Jezebel's flesh.ᵉ ³⁷Jezebel's body will be like refuse on the ground in the plot at Jezreel, so that no-one will be able to say, 'This is Jezebel.'"

Ahab's Family Killed

10 Now there were in Samaria seventy sons of the house of Ahab. So Jehu wrote letters and sent them to Samaria: to the officials of Jezreel,ᵃ to the elders and to the guardians of Ahab's children. He said, ²"As soon as this letter reaches you, since your master's sons are with you and you have chariots and horses, a fortified city and weapons, ³choose the best and most worthy of your master's sons and set him on his father's throne. Then fight for your master's house."

⁴But they were terrified and said, "If two kings could not resist him, how can we?"

⁵So the palace administrator, the city governor, the elders and the guardians sent this message to Jehu: "We are your servants and we will do anything you say. We will not appoint anyone as king; you do whatever you think best."

⁶Then Jehu wrote them a second letter, saying, "If you are on my side and will obey me, take the heads of your master's sons and come to me in Jezreel by this time tomorrow."

Now the royal princes, seventy of them, were with the leading men of the city, who were bringing them up. ⁷When the letter arrived, these men took the princes and slaughtered all seventy of them. They put their heads in baskets and sent them to Jehu in Jezreel. ⁸When the messenger arrived, he told Jehu, "They have brought the heads of the princes."

Then Jehu ordered, "Put them in two piles at the entrance of the city gate until morning."

⁹The next morning Jehu went out. He stood before all the people and said, "You are innocent. It was I who conspired against my master and killed him, but who killed all these? ¹⁰Know then, that not a word the Lord has spoken against the house of Ahab will fail. The Lord has done what he promised through his servant Elijah." ¹¹So Jehu killed everyone in Jezreel who remained of the house of Ahab, as well as all his chief men, his close friends and his priests, leaving him no survivor.

¹²Jehu then set out and went towards Samaria. At Beth Eked of the Shepherds, ¹³he met some relatives of Ahaziah king of Judah and asked, "Who are you?"

They said, "We are relatives of Ahaziah, and we have come down to greet the families of the king and of the queen mother."

¹⁴"Take them alive!" he ordered. So they took them alive and slaughtered them by the well of Beth Eked—forty-two men. He left no survivor.

¹⁵After he left there, he came upon Jehonadab son of Recab, who was on his way to meet him. Jehu greeted him and said, "Are you in accord with me, as I am with you?"

"I am," Jehonadab answered.

"If so," said Jehu, "give me your hand." So he did, and Jehu helped him up into the chariot. ¹⁶Jehu said, "Come with me and see my zeal for the Lord." Then he made him ride in his chariot.

¹⁷When Jehu came to Samaria, he killed all who were left there of Ahab's family; he destroyed them, according to the word of the Lord spoken to Elijah.

Ministers of Baal Killed

¹⁸Then Jehu brought all the people together and said to them, "Ahab served Baal a little; Jehu will serve him much. ¹⁹Now summon all the prophets of Baal, all his ministers and all his priests. See that no-one is missing, because I am going to hold a great sacrifice for Baal. Anyone who fails to come will no longer live." But Jehu was acting deceptively in order to destroy the ministers of Baal.

²⁰Jehu said, "Call an assembly in honour of Baal." So they proclaimed it. ²¹Then he sent word throughout Israel, and all the ministers of Baal came; not one stayed away. They crowded into the temple of Baal until it was full from one end to the other. ²²And Jehu said to the keeper of the wardrobe, "Bring robes for all the ministers of Baal." So he brought out robes for them.

ᶜ27 Or fled by way of the garden house   ᵈ31 Or "Did Zimri have peace, who murdered his master?"
ᵉ36 See 1 Kings 21:23.   ᵃ1 Hebrew; some Septuagint manuscripts and Vulgate of the city

²³Then Jehu and Jehonadab son of Recab went into the temple of Baal. Jehu said to the ministers of Baal, "Look around and see that no servants of the LORD are here with you —only ministers of Baal." ²⁴So they went in to make sacrifices and burnt offerings. Now Jehu had posted eighty men outside with this warning: "If one of you lets any of the men I am placing in your hands escape, it will be your life for his life."

²⁵As soon as Jehu had finished making the burnt offering, he ordered the guards and officers: "Go in and kill them; let no-one escape." So they cut them down with the sword. The guards and officers threw the bodies out and then entered the inner shrine of the temple of Baal. ²⁶They brought the sacred stone out of the temple of Baal and burned it. ²⁷They demolished the sacred stone of Baal and tore down the temple of Baal, and people have used it for a latrine to this day.

²⁸So Jehu destroyed Baal worship in Israel. ²⁹However, he did not turn away from the sins of Jeroboam son of Nebat, which he had caused Israel to commit—the worship of the golden calves at Bethel and Dan.

³⁰The LORD said to Jehu, "Because you have done well in accomplishing what is right in my eyes and have done to the house of Ahab all I had in mind to do, your descendants will sit on the throne of Israel to the fourth generation." ³¹Yet Jehu was not careful to keep the law of the LORD, the God of Israel, with all his heart. He did not turn away from the sins of Jeroboam, which he had caused Israel to commit.

³²In those days the LORD began to reduce the size of Israel. Hazael overpowered the Israelites throughout their territory ³³east of the Jordan in all the land of Gilead (the region of Gad, Reuben and Manasseh), from Aroer by the Arnon Gorge through Gilead to Bashan.

³⁴As for the other events of Jehu's reign, all he did, and all his achievements, are they not written in the book of the annals of the kings of Israel?

³⁵Jehu rested with his fathers and was buried in Samaria. And Jehoahaz his son succeeded him as king. ³⁶The time that Jehu reigned over Israel in Samaria was twenty-eight years.

Athaliah and Joash

11 When Athaliah the mother of Ahaziah saw that her son was dead, she proceeded to destroy the whole royal family. ²But Jehosheba, the daughter of King Jehoram[a] and sister of Ahaziah, took Joash son of Ahaziah and stole him away from among the royal princes, who were about to be murdered. She put him and his nurse in a bedroom to hide him from Athaliah; so he was not killed. ³He remained hidden with his nurse at the temple of the LORD for six years while Athaliah ruled the land.

⁴In the seventh year Jehoiada sent for the commanders of units of a hundred, the Carites and the guards and had them brought to him at the temple of the LORD. He made a covenant with them and put them under oath at the temple of the LORD. Then he showed them the king's son. ⁵He commanded them, saying, "This is what you are to do: You who are in the three companies that are going on duty on the Sabbath—a third of you guarding the royal palace, ⁶a third at the Sur Gate, and a third at the gate behind the guard, who take turns guarding the temple—⁷and you who are in the other two companies that normally go off Sabbath duty are all to guard the temple for the king. ⁸Station yourselves round the king, each man with his weapon in his hand. Anyone who approaches your ranks[b] must be put to death. Stay close to the king wherever he goes."

⁹The commanders of units of a hundred did just as Jehoiada the priest ordered. Each one took his men—those who were going on duty on the Sabbath and those who were going off duty—and came to Jehoiada the priest. ¹⁰Then he gave the commanders the spears and shields that had belonged to King David and that were in the temple of the LORD. ¹¹The guards, each with his weapon in his hand, stationed themselves round the king —near the altar and the temple, from the south side to the north side of the temple.

¹²Jehoiada brought out the king's son and put the crown on him; he presented him with a copy of the covenant and proclaimed him king. They anointed him, and the people clapped their hands and shouted, "Long live the king!"

¹³When Athaliah heard the noise made by the guards and the people, she went to the people at the temple of the LORD. ¹⁴She looked and there was the king, standing by the pillar, as the custom was. The officers and the trumpeters were beside the king, and all the people of the land were rejoicing and blowing trumpets. Then Athaliah tore her robes and called out, "Treason! Treason!"

¹⁵Jehoiada the priest ordered the commanders of units of a hundred, who were in charge of the troops: "Bring her out between the ranks[c] and put to the sword anyone who follows her." For the priest had said, "She must not be put to death in the temple of the LORD." ¹⁶So they seized her as she reached the place where the horses enter the palace grounds, and there she was put to death.

¹⁷Jehoiada then made a covenant between the LORD and the king and people that they would be the LORD's people. He also made a covenant between the king and the people. ¹⁸All the people of the land went to the temple of Baal and tore it down. They smashed the altars and idols to pieces and killed Mattan the priest of Baal in front of the altars.

Then Jehoiada the priest posted guards at the temple of the LORD. ¹⁹He took with him the commanders of hundreds, the Carites, the guards and all the people of the land, and together they brought the king down from the temple of the LORD and went into the palace, entering by way of the gate of the guards. The

---

*a*2 Hebrew *Joram*, a variant of *Jehoram*   *b*8 Or *approaches the precincts*   *c*15 Or *out from the precincts* king then took his place on the royal throne, [20]and all the people of the land rejoiced. And the city was quiet, because Athaliah had been slain with the sword at the palace.

[21]Joash[d] was seven years old when he began his reign.

Joash Repairs the Temple

12 In the seventh year of Jehu, Joash[a] became king, and he reigned in Jerusalem for forty years. His mother's name was Zibiah; she was from Beersheba. [2]Joash did what was right in the eyes of the LORD all the years Jehoiada the priest instructed him. [3]The high places, however, were not removed; the people continued to offer sacrifices and burn incense there.

[4]Joash said to the priests, "Collect all the money that is brought as sacred offerings to the temple of the LORD—the money collected in the census, the money received from personal vows and the money brought voluntarily to the temple. [5]Let every priest receive the money from one of the treasurers, and let it be used to repair whatever damage is found in the temple."

[6]But by the twenty-third year of King Joash the priests still had not repaired the temple. [7]Therefore King Joash summoned Jehoiada the priest and the other priests and asked them, "Why aren't you repairing the damage done to the temple? Take no more money from your treasurers, but hand it over for repairing the temple." [8]The priests agreed that they would not collect any more money from the people and that they would not repair the temple themselves.

[9]Jehoiada the priest took a chest and bored a hole in its lid. He placed it beside the altar, on the right side as one enters the temple of the LORD. The priests who guarded the entrance put into the chest all the money that was brought to the temple of the LORD. [10]Whenever they saw that there was a large amount of money in the chest, the royal secretary and the high priest came, counted the money that had been brought into the temple of the LORD and put it into bags. [11]When the amount had been determined, they gave the money to the men appointed to supervise the work on the temple. With it they paid those who worked on the temple of the LORD—the carpenters and builders, [12]the masons and stonecutters. They purchased timber and dressed stone for the repair of the temple of the LORD, and met all the other expenses of restoring the temple.

[13]The money brought into the temple was not spent for making silver basins, wick trimmers, sprinkling bowls, trumpets or any other articles of gold or silver for the temple of the LORD; [14]it was paid to the workmen, who used it to repair the temple. [15]They did not require an accounting from those to whom they gave the money to pay the workers, because they acted with complete honesty. [16]The money from the guilt offerings and sin offerings was not brought into the temple of the LORD; it belonged to the priests.

[17]About this time Hazael king of Aram went up and attacked Gath and captured it. Then he turned to attack Jerusalem. [18]But Joash king of Judah took all the sacred objects dedicated by his fathers—Jehoshaphat, Jehoram and Ahaziah, the kings of Judah—and the gifts he himself had dedicated and all the gold found in the treasuries of the temple of the LORD and of the royal palace, and he sent them to Hazael king of Aram, who then withdrew from Jerusalem.

[19]As for the other events of the reign of Joash, and all he did, are they not written in the book of the annals of the kings of Judah? [20]His officials conspired against him and assassinated him at Beth Millo, on the road down to Silla. [21]The officials who murdered him were Jozabad son of Shimeath and Jehozabad son of Shomer. He died and was buried with his fathers in the City of David. And Amaziah his son succeeded him as king.

Jehoahaz King of Israel

13 In the twenty-third year of Joash son of Ahaziah king of Judah, Jehoahaz son of Jehu became king of Israel in Samaria, and he reigned for seventeen years. [2]He did evil in the eyes of the LORD by following the sins of Jeroboam son of Nebat, which he had caused Israel to commit, and he did not turn away from them. [3]So the LORD's anger burned against Israel, and for a long time he kept them under the power of Hazael king of Aram and Ben-Hadad his son.

[4]Then Jehoahaz sought the LORD's favour, and the LORD listened to him, for he saw how severely the king of Aram was oppressing Israel. [5]The LORD provided a deliverer for Israel, and they escaped from the power of Aram. So the Israelites lived in their own homes as they had before. [6]But they did not turn away from the sins of the house of Jeroboam, which he had caused Israel to commit; they continued in them. Also, the Asherah pole[a] remained standing in Samaria.

[7]Nothing had been left of the army of Jehoahaz except fifty horsemen, ten chariots and ten thousand foot soldiers, for the king of Aram had destroyed the rest and made them like the dust at threshing time.

[8]As for the other events of the reign of Jehoahaz, all he did and his achievements, are they not written in the book of the annals of the kings of Israel? [9]Jehoahaz rested with his fathers and was buried in Samaria. And Jehoash[b] his son succeeded him as king.

Jehoash King of Israel

[10]In the thirty-seventh year of Joash king of Judah, Jehoash son of Jehoahaz became king of Israel in Samaria, and he reigned for sixteen years. [11]He did evil in the eyes of the LORD and did not turn away from any of the sins of Jeroboam son of Nebat, which he

---

d21 Hebrew *Jehoash*, a variant of *Joash*　　*a1* Hebrew *Jehoash*, a variant of *Joash*; also in verses 2, 4, 6, 7 and 18
a6 That is, a symbol of the goddess Asherah; here and elsewhere in 2 Kings
b9 Hebrew *Joash*, a variant of *Jehoash*; also in verses 12–14 and 25

had caused Israel to commit; he continued in them.

12As for the other events of the reign of Jehoash, all he did and his achievements, including his war against Amaziah king of Judah, are they not written in the book of the annals of the kings of Israel? 13Jehoash rested with his fathers, and Jeroboam succeeded him on the throne. Jehoash was buried in Samaria with the kings of Israel.

14Now Elisha was suffering from the illness from which he died. Jehoash king of Israel went down to see him and wept over him. "My father! My father!" he cried. "The chariots and horsemen of Israel!"

15Elisha said, "Get a bow and some arrows," and he did so. 16"Take the bow in your hands," he said to the king of Israel. When he had taken it, Elisha put his hands on the king's hands.

17"Open the east window," he said, and he opened it. "Shoot!" Elisha said, and he shot. "The LORD's arrow of victory, the arrow of victory over Aram!" Elisha declared. "You will completely destroy the Arameans at Aphek."

18Then he said, "Take the arrows," and the king took them. Elisha told him, "Strike the ground." He struck it three times and stopped. 19The man of God was angry with him and said, "You should have struck the ground five or six times; then you would have defeated Aram and completely destroyed it. But now you will defeat it only three times."

20Elisha died and was buried.

Now Moabite raiders used to enter the country every spring. 21Once while some Israelites were burying a man, suddenly they saw a band of raiders; so they threw the man's body into Elisha's tomb. When the body touched Elisha's bones, the man came to life and stood up on his feet.

22Hazael king of Aram oppressed Israel throughout the reign of Jehoahaz. 23But the LORD was gracious to them and had compassion and showed concern for them because of his covenant with Abraham, Isaac and Jacob. To this day he has been unwilling to destroy them or banish them from his presence.

24Hazael king of Aram died, and Ben-Hadad his son succeeded him as king. 25Then Jehoash son of Jehoahaz recaptured from Ben-Hadad son of Hazael the towns he had taken in battle from his father Jehoahaz. Three times Jehoash defeated him, and so he recovered the Israelite towns.

Amaziah King of Judah

14 In the second year of Jehoash[a] son of Jehoahaz king of Israel, Amaziah son of Joash king of Judah began to reign. 2He was twenty-five years old when he became king, and he reigned in Jerusalem for twenty-nine years. His mother's name was Jehoaddin; she was from Jerusalem. 3He did what was right in the eyes of the LORD, but not as his father David had done. In everything he followed the example of his father Joash. 4The high places, however, were not removed; the people continued to offer sacrifices and burn incense there.

5After the kingdom was firmly in his grasp, he executed the officials who had murdered his father the king. 6Yet he did not put the sons of the assassins to death, in accordance with what is written in the Book of the Law of Moses where the LORD commanded: "Fathers shall not be put to death for their children, nor children put to death for their fathers; each is to die for his own sins."[b]

7He was the one who defeated ten thousand Edomites in the Valley of Salt and captured Sela in battle, calling it Joktheel, the name it has to this day.

8Then Amaziah sent messengers to Jehoash son of Jehoahaz, the son of Jehu, king of Israel, with the challenge: "Come, meet me face to face."

9But Jehoash king of Israel replied to Amaziah king of Judah: "A thistle in Lebanon sent a message to a cedar in Lebanon, 'Give your daughter to my son in marriage.' Then a wild beast in Lebanon came along and trampled the thistle underfoot. 10You have indeed defeated Edom and now you are arrogant. Glory in your victory, but stay at home! Why ask for trouble and cause your own downfall and that of Judah also?"

11Amaziah, however, would not listen, so Jehoash king of Israel attacked. He and Amaziah king of Judah faced each other at Beth Shemesh in Judah. 12Judah was routed by Israel, and every man fled to his home. 13Jehoash king of Israel captured Amaziah king of Judah, the son of Joash, the son of Ahaziah, at Beth Shemesh. Then Jehoash went to Jerusalem and broke down the wall of Jerusalem from the Ephraim Gate to the Corner Gate—a section about six hundred feet long.[c] 14He took all the gold and silver and all the articles found in the temple of the LORD and in the treasuries of the royal palace. He also took hostages and returned to Samaria.

15As for the other events of the reign of Jehoash, what he did and his achievements, including his war against Amaziah king of Judah, are they not written in the book of the annals of the kings of Israel? 16Jehoash rested with his fathers and was buried in Samaria with the kings of Israel. And Jeroboam his son succeeded him as king.

17Amaziah son of Joash king of Judah lived for fifteen years after the death of Jehoash son of Jehoahaz king of Israel. 18As for the other events of Amaziah's reign, are they not written in the book of the annals of the kings of Judah?

19They conspired against him in Jerusalem, and he fled to Lachish, but they sent men after him to Lachish and killed him there. 20He was brought back by horse and was buried in Jerusalem with his fathers, in the City of David.

---

[a]1 Hebrew Joash, a variant of Jehoash; also in verses 13, 23 and 27　　[b]6 Deut. 24:16
[c]13 Hebrew four hundred cubits (about 180 metres)

²¹Then all the people of Judah took Azariah,*d* who was sixteen years old, and made him king in place of his father Amaziah. ²²He was the one who rebuilt Elath and restored it to Judah after Amaziah rested with his fathers.

Jeroboam II King of Israel

²³In the fifteenth year of Amaziah son of Joash king of Judah, Jeroboam son of Jehoash king of Israel became king in Samaria, and he reigned for forty-one years. ²⁴He did evil in the eyes of the LORD and did not turn away from any of the sins of Jeroboam son of Nebat, which he had caused Israel to commit. ²⁵He was the one who restored the boundaries of Israel from Lebo*e* Hamath to the Sea of the Arabah,*f* in accordance with the word of the LORD, the God of Israel, spoken through his servant Jonah son of Amittai, the prophet from Gath Hepher. ²⁶The LORD had seen how bitterly everyone in Israel, whether slave or free, was suffering; there was no-one to help them. ²⁷And since the LORD had not said he would blot out the name of Israel from under heaven, he saved them by the hand of Jeroboam son of Jehoash.

²⁸As for the other events of Jeroboam's reign, all he did, and his military achievements, including how he recovered for Israel both Damascus and Hamath, which had belonged to Yaudi,*g* are they not written in the book of the annals of the kings of Israel? ²⁹Jeroboam rested with his fathers, the kings of Israel. And Zechariah his son succeeded him as king.

Azariah King of Judah

15 In the twenty-seventh year of Jeroboam king of Israel, Azariah son of Amaziah king of Judah began to reign. ²He was sixteen years old when he became king, and he reigned in Jerusalem for fifty-two years. His mother's name was Jecoliah; she was from Jerusalem. ³He did what was right in the eyes of the LORD, just as his father Amaziah had done. ⁴The high places, however, were not removed; the people continued to offer sacrifices and burn incense there.

⁵The LORD afflicted the king with leprosy*a* until the day he died, and he lived in a separate house.*b* Jotham the king's son had charge of the palace and governed the people of the land.

⁶As for the other events of Azariah's reign, and all he did, are they not written in the book of the annals of the kings of Judah? ⁷Azariah rested with his fathers and was buried near them in the City of David. And Jotham his son succeeded him as king.

Zechariah King of Israel

⁸In the thirty-eighth year of Azariah king of Judah, Zechariah son of Jeroboam became king of Israel in Samaria, and he reigned for six months. ⁹He did evil in the eyes of the LORD, as his fathers had done. He did not turn away from the sins of Jeroboam son of Nebat, which he had caused Israel to commit.

¹⁰Shallum son of Jabesh conspired against Zechariah. He attacked him in front of the people,*c* assassinated him and succeeded him as king. ¹¹The other events of Zechariah's reign are written in the book of the annals of the kings of Israel. ¹²So the word of the LORD spoken to Jehu was fulfilled: "Your descendants will sit on the throne of Israel to the fourth generation."*d*

Shallum King of Israel

¹³Shallum son of Jabesh became king in the thirty-ninth year of Uzziah king of Judah, and he reigned in Samaria for one month. ¹⁴Then Menahem son of Gadi went from Tirzah up to Samaria. He attacked Shallum son of Jabesh in Samaria, assassinated him and succeeded him as king.

¹⁵The other events of Shallum's reign, and the conspiracy he led, are written in the book of the annals of the kings of Israel.

¹⁶At that time Menahem, starting out from Tirzah, attacked Tiphsah and everyone in the city and its vicinity, because they refused to open their gates. He sacked Tiphsah and ripped open all the pregnant women.

Menahem King of Israel

¹⁷In the thirty-ninth year of Azariah king of Judah, Menahem son of Gadi became king of Israel, and he reigned in Samaria for ten years. ¹⁸He did evil in the eyes of the LORD. During his entire reign he did not turn away from the sins of Jeroboam son of Nebat, which he had caused Israel to commit.

¹⁹Then Pul*e* king of Assyria invaded the land, and Menahem gave him a thousand talents*f* of silver to gain his support and strengthen his own hold on the kingdom. ²⁰Menahem exacted this money from Israel. Every wealthy man had to contribute fifty shekels*g* of silver to be given to the king of Assyria. So the king of Assyria withdrew and stayed in the land no longer.

²¹As for the other events of Menahem's reign, and all he did, are they not written in the book of the annals of the kings of Israel? ²²Menahem rested with his fathers. And Pekahiah his son succeeded him as king.

Pekahiah King of Israel

²³In the fiftieth year of Azariah king of Judah, Pekahiah son of Menahem became king of Israel in Samaria, and he reigned for two years. ²⁴Pekahiah did evil in the eyes of the LORD. He did not turn away from the sins of Jeroboam son of Nebat, which he had caused Israel to commit. ²⁵One of his chief officers, Pekah son of Remaliah, conspired against him. Taking fifty men of Gilead with

---

*d*21 Also called *Uzziah*   *e*25 Or *from the entrance to*   *f*25 That is, the Dead Sea   *g*28 Or *Judah*
*a*5 The Hebrew word was used for various diseases affecting the skin—not necessarily leprosy.
*b*5 Or *in a house where he was relieved of responsibility*   *c*10 Hebrew; some Septuagint manuscripts *in Ibleam*
*d*12 2 Kings 10:30   *e*19 Also called *Tiglath-Pileser*   *f*19 That is, about 34 tons (about 34 metric tons)
*g*20 That is, about 1¼ pounds (about 0.6 kilogram)

him, he assassinated Pekahiah, along with Argob and Arieh, in the citadel of the royal palace at Samaria. So Pekah killed Pekahiah and succeeded him as king.

26The other events of Pekahiah's reign, and all he did, are written in the book of the annals of the kings of Israel.

Pekah King of Israel

27In the fifty-second year of Azariah king of Judah, Pekah son of Remaliah became king of Israel in Samaria, and he reigned for twenty years. 28He did evil in the eyes of the LORD. He did not turn away from the sins of Jeroboam son of Nebat, which he had caused Israel to commit.

29In the time of Pekah king of Israel, Tiglath-Pileser king of Assyria came and took Ijon, Abel Beth Maacah, Janoah, Kedesh and Hazor. He took Gilead and Galilee, including all the land of Naphtali, and deported the people to Assyria. 30Then Hoshea son of Elah conspired against Pekah son of Remaliah. He attacked and assassinated him, and then succeeded him as king in the twentieth year of Jotham son of Uzziah.

31As for the other events of Pekah's reign, and all he did, are they not written in the book of the annals of the kings of Israel?

Jotham King of Judah

32In the second year of Pekah son of Remaliah king of Israel, Jotham son of Uzziah king of Judah began to reign. 33He was twenty-five years old when he became king, and he reigned in Jerusalem for sixteen years. His mother's name was Jerusha daughter of Zadok. 34He did what was right in the eyes of the LORD, just as his father Uzziah had done. 35The high places, however, were not removed; the people continued to offer sacrifices and burn incense there. Jotham rebuilt the Upper Gate of the temple of the LORD.

36As for the other events of Jotham's reign, and what he did, are they not written in the book of the annals of the kings of Judah? 37(In those days the LORD began to send Rezin king of Aram and Pekah son of Remaliah against Judah.) 38Jotham rested with his fathers and was buried with them in the City of David, the city of his father. And Ahaz his son succeeded him as king.

Ahaz King of Judah

16 In the seventeenth year of Pekah son of Remaliah, Ahaz son of Jotham king of Judah began to reign. 2Ahaz was twenty years old when he became king, and he reigned in Jerusalem for sixteen years. Unlike David his father, he did not do what was right in the eyes of the LORD his God. 3He walked in the ways of the kings of Israel and even sacrificed his son in^a the fire, following the detestable ways of the nations the LORD had driven out before the Israelites. 4He offered sacrifices and burned incense at the

high places, on the hilltops and under every spreading tree.

5Then Rezin king of Aram and Pekah son of Remaliah king of Israel marched up to fight against Jerusalem and besieged Ahaz, but they could not overpower him. 6At that time, Rezin king of Aram recovered Elath for Aram by driving out the men of Judah. Edomites then moved into Elath and have lived there to this day.

7Ahaz sent messengers to say to Tiglath-Pileser king of Assyria, "I am your servant and vassal. Come up and save me out of the hand of the king of Aram and of the king of Israel who are attacking me." 8And Ahaz took the silver and gold found in the temple of the LORD and in the treasuries of the royal palace and sent it as a gift to the king of Assyria. 9The king of Assyria complied by attacking Damascus and capturing it. He deported its inhabitants to Kir and put Rezin to death.

10Then King Ahaz went to Damascus to meet Tiglath-Pileser king of Assyria. He saw an altar in Damascus and sent to Uriah the priest a sketch of the altar, with detailed plans for its construction. 11So Uriah the priest built an altar in accordance with all the plans that King Ahaz had sent from Damascus and finished it before King Ahaz returned. 12When the king came back from Damascus and saw the altar, he approached it and presented offerings^b on it. 13He offered up his burnt offering and grain offering, poured out his drink offering, and sprinkled the blood of his fellowship offerings^c on the altar. 14The bronze altar that stood before the LORD he brought from the front of the temple —from between the new altar and the temple of the LORD—and put it on the north side of the new altar.

15King Ahaz then gave these orders to Uriah the priest: "On the large new altar, offer the morning burnt offering and the evening grain offering, the king's burnt offering and his grain offering, and the burnt offering of all the people of the land, and their grain offering and their drink offering. Sprinkle on the altar all the blood of the burnt offerings and sacrifices. But I will use the bronze altar for seeking guidance." 16And Uriah the priest did just as King Ahaz had ordered.

17King Ahaz took away the side panels and removed the basins from the movable stands. He removed the Sea from the bronze bulls that supported it and set it on a stone base. 18He took away the Sabbath canopy^d that had been built at the temple and removed the royal entrance outside the temple of the LORD, in deference to the king of Assyria.

19As for the other events of the reign of Ahaz, and what he did, are they not written in the book of the annals of the kings of Judah? 20Ahaz rested with his fathers and was buried with them in the City of David. And Hezekiah his son succeeded him as king.

^{a}3 Or even made his son pass through ^{b}12 Or and went up ^{c}13 Traditionally peace offerings
^{d}18 Or the dais of his throne (see Septuagint)

Hoshea Last King of Israel

17 In the twelfth year of Ahaz king of Judah, Hoshea son of Elah became king of Israel in Samaria, and he reigned for nine years. [2]He did evil in the eyes of the LORD, but not like the kings of Israel who preceded him.

[3]Shalmaneser king of Assyria came up to attack Hoshea, who had been Shalmaneser's vassal and had paid him tribute. [4]But the king of Assyria discovered that Hoshea was a traitor, for he had sent envoys to So[a] king of Egypt, and he no longer paid tribute to the king of Assyria, as he had done year by year. Therefore Shalmaneser seized him and put him in prison. [5]The king of Assyria invaded the entire land, marched against Samaria and laid siege to it for three years. [6]In the ninth year of Hoshea, the king of Assyria captured Samaria and deported the Israelites to Assyria. He settled them in Halah, in Gozan on the Habor River and in the towns of the Medes.

Israel Exiled Because of Sin

[7]All this took place because the Israelites had sinned against the LORD their God, who had brought them out of Egypt from under the power of Pharaoh king of Egypt. They worshipped other gods [8]and followed the practices of the nations the LORD had driven out before them, as well as the practices that the kings of Israel had introduced. [9]The Israelites secretly did things against the LORD their God that were not right. From watchtower to fortified city they built themselves high places in all their towns. [10]They set up sacred stones and Asherah poles on every high hill and under every spreading tree. [11]At every high place they burned incense, as the nations whom the LORD had driven out before them had done. They did wicked things that provoked the LORD to anger. [12]They worshipped idols, though the LORD had said, "You shall not do this."[b] [13]The LORD warned Israel and Judah through all his prophets and seers: "Turn from your evil ways. Observe my commands and decrees, in accordance with the entire Law that I commanded your fathers to obey and that I delivered to you through my servants the prophets."

[14]But they would not listen and were as stiff-necked as their fathers, who did not trust in the LORD their God. [15]They rejected his decrees and the covenant he had made with their fathers and the warnings he had given them. They followed worthless idols and themselves became worthless. They imitated the nations around them although the LORD had ordered them, "Do not do as they do," and they did the things the LORD had forbidden them to do.

[16]They forsook all the commands of the LORD their God and made for themselves two idols cast in the shape of calves, and an Asherah pole. They bowed down to all the starry hosts, and they worshipped Baal. [17]They sacrificed their sons and daughters in[c] the fire. They practised divination and sorcery and sold themselves to do evil in the eyes of the LORD, provoking him to anger.

[18]So the LORD was very angry with Israel and removed them from his presence. Only the tribe of Judah was left, [19]and even Judah did not keep the commands of the LORD their God. They followed the practices Israel had introduced. [20]Therefore the LORD rejected all the people of Israel; he afflicted them and gave them into the hands of plunderers, until he thrust them from his presence.

[21]When he tore Israel away from the house of David, they made Jeroboam son of Nebat their king. Jeroboam enticed Israel away from following the LORD and caused them to commit a great sin. [22]The Israelites persisted in all the sins of Jeroboam and did not turn away from them [23]until the LORD removed them from his presence, as he had warned through all his servants the prophets. So the people of Israel were taken from their homeland into exile in Assyria, and they are still there.

Samaria Resettled

[24]The king of Assyria brought people from Babylon, Cuthah, Avva, Hamath and Sepharvaim and settled them in the towns of Samaria to replace the Israelites. They took over Samaria and lived in its towns. [25]When they first lived there, they did not worship the LORD; so he sent lions among them and they killed some of the people. [26]It was reported to the king of Assyria: "The people you deported and resettled in the towns of Samaria do not know what the god of that country requires. He has sent lions among them, which are killing them off, because the people do not know what he requires."

[27]Then the king of Assyria gave this order: "Make one of the priests you took captive from Samaria go back to live there and teach the people what the god of the land requires." [28]So one of the priests who had been exiled from Samaria came to live in Bethel and taught them how to worship the LORD.

[29]Nevertheless, each national group made its own gods in the several towns where they settled, and set them up in the shrines the people of Samaria had made at the high places. [30]The men from Babylon made Succoth Benoth, the men from Cuthah made Nergal, and the men from Hamath made Ashima; [31]the Avvites made Nibhaz and Tartak, and the Sepharvites burned their children in the fire as sacrifices to Adrammelech and Anammelech, the gods of Sepharvaim. [32]They worshipped the LORD, but they also appointed all sorts of their own people to officiate for them as priests in the shrines at the high places. [33]They worshipped the LORD, but they also served their own gods in accordance with the customs of the nations from which they had been brought.

[34]To this day they persist in their former practices. They neither worship the LORD nor adhere to the decrees and ordinances, the

---

[a]4 Or *to Sais, to the*; *So* is possibly an abbreviation for *Osorkon*.   [b]12 Exodus 20:4, 5
[c]17 Or *They made their sons and daughters pass through*

laws and commands that the LORD gave the descendants of Jacob, whom he named Israel. 35When the LORD made a covenant with the Israelites, he commanded them: "Do not worship any other gods or bow down to them, serve them or sacrifice to them. 36But the LORD, who brought you up out of Egypt with mighty power and outstretched arm, is the one you must worship. To him you shall bow down and to him offer sacrifices. 37You must always be careful to keep the decrees and ordinances, the laws and commands he wrote for you. Do not worship other gods. 38Do not forget the covenant I have made with you, and do not worship other gods. 39Rather, worship the LORD your God; it is he who will deliver you from the hand of all your enemies."

40They would not listen, however, but persisted in their former practices. 41Even while these people were worshipping the LORD, they were serving their idols. To this day their children and grandchildren continue to do as their fathers did.

Hezekiah King of Judah

18 In the third year of Hoshea son of Elah king of Israel, Hezekiah son of Ahaz king of Judah began to reign. 2He was twenty-five years old when he became king, and he reigned in Jerusalem for twenty-nine years. His mother's name was Abijah*a* daughter of Zechariah. 3He did what was right in the eyes of the LORD, just as his father David had done. 4He removed the high places, smashed the sacred stones and cut down the Asherah poles. He broke into pieces the bronze snake Moses had made, for up to that time the Israelites had been burning incense to it. (It was called*b* Nehushtan.*c*)

5Hezekiah trusted in the LORD, the God of Israel. There was no-one like him among all the kings of Judah, either before him or after him. 6He held fast to the LORD and did not cease to follow him; he kept the commands the LORD had given Moses. 7And the LORD was with him; he was successful in whatever he undertook. He rebelled against the king of Assyria and did not serve him. 8From watch-tower to fortified city, he defeated the Philistines, as far as Gaza and its territory.

9In King Hezekiah's fourth year, which was the seventh year of Hoshea son of Elah king of Israel, Shalmaneser king of Assyria marched against Samaria and laid siege to it. 10At the end of three years the Assyrians took it. So Samaria was captured in Hezekiah's sixth year, which was the ninth year of Hoshea king of Israel. 11The king of Assyria deported Israel to Assyria and settled them in Halah, in Gozan on the Habor River, and in towns of the Medes. 12This happened because they had not obeyed the LORD their God, but had violated his covenant—all that Moses the servant of the LORD commanded. They neither listened to the commands nor carried them out.

13In the fourteenth year of King Hezekiah's reign, Sennacherib king of Assyria attacked all the fortified cities of Judah and captured them. 14So Hezekiah king of Judah sent this message to the king of Assyria at Lachish: "I have done wrong. Withdraw from me, and I will pay whatever you demand of me." The king of Assyria exacted from Hezekiah king of Judah three hundred talents*d* of silver and thirty talents*e* of gold. 15So Hezekiah gave him all the silver that was found in the temple of the LORD and in the treasuries of the royal palace.

16At this time Hezekiah king of Judah stripped off the gold with which he had covered the doors and doorposts of the temple of the LORD, and gave it to the king of Assyria.

Sennacherib Threatens Jerusalem

17The king of Assyria sent his supreme commander, his chief officer and his field commander with a large army, from Lachish to King Hezekiah at Jerusalem. They came up to Jerusalem and stopped at the aqueduct of the Upper Pool, on the road to the Washerman's Field. 18They called for the king; and Eliakim son of Hilkiah the palace administrator, Shebna the secretary, and Joah son of Asaph the recorder went out to them.

19The field commander said to them, "Tell Hezekiah:

"'This is what the great king, the king of Assyria, says: On what are you basing this confidence of yours? 20You say you have strategy and military strength—but you speak only empty words. On whom are you depending, that you rebel against me? 21Look now, you are depending on Egypt, that splintered reed of a staff, which pierces a man's hand and wounds him if he leans on it! Such is Pharaoh king of Egypt to all who depend on him. 22And if you say to me, "We are depending on the LORD our God"—isn't he the one whose high places and altars Hezekiah removed, saying to Judah and Jerusalem, "You must worship before this altar in Jerusalem"?

23"'Come now, make a bargain with my master, the king of Assyria: I will give you two thousand horses—if you can put riders on them! 24How can you repulse one officer of the least of my master's officials, even though you are depending on Egypt for chariots and horsemen?*f* 25Furthermore, have I come to attack and destroy this place without word from the LORD? The LORD himself told me to march against this country and destroy it.'"

26Then Eliakim son of Hilkiah, and Shebna and Joah said to the field commander, "Please speak to your servants in Aramaic, since we understand it. Don't speak to us in

a2 Hebrew Abi, a variant of Abijah   b4 Or He called it
c4 Nehushtan sounds like the Hebrew for bronze and snake and unclean thing.
d14 That is, about 10 tons (about 10 metric tons)   e14 That is, about 1 ton (about 1 metric ton)
f24 Or charioteers

Hebrew in the hearing of the people on the wall."

²⁷But the commander replied, "Was it only to your master and you that my master sent me to say these things, and not to the men sitting on the wall—who, like you, will have to eat their own filth and drink their own urine?"

²⁸Then the commander stood and called out in Hebrew: "Hear the word of the great king, the king of Assyria! ²⁹This is what the king says: Do not let Hezekiah deceive you. He cannot deliver you from my hand. ³⁰Do not let Hezekiah persuade you to trust in the LORD when he says, 'The LORD will surely deliver us; this city will not be given into the hand of the king of Assyria.'

³¹"Do not listen to Hezekiah. This is what the king of Assyria says: Make peace with me and come out to me. Then every one of you will eat from his own vine and fig-tree and drink water from his own cistern, ³²until I come and take you to a land like your own, a land of grain and new wine, a land of bread and vineyards, a land of olive trees and honey. Choose life and not death!

"Do not listen to Hezekiah, for he is misleading you when he says, 'The LORD will deliver us.' ³³Has the god of any nation ever delivered his land from the hand of the king of Assyria? ³⁴Where are the gods of Hamath and Arpad? Where are the gods of Sepharvaim, Hena and Ivvah? Have they rescued Samaria from my hand? ³⁵Who of all the gods of these countries has been able to save his land from me? How then can the LORD deliver Jerusalem from my hand?"

³⁶But the people remained silent and said nothing in reply, because the king had commanded, "Do not answer him."

³⁷Then Eliakim son of Hilkiah the palace administrator, Shebna the secretary and Joah son of Asaph the recorder went to Hezekiah, with their clothes torn, and told him what the field commander had said.

Jerusalem's Deliverance Foretold

19 When King Hezekiah heard this, he tore his clothes and put on sackcloth and went into the temple of the LORD. ²He sent Eliakim the palace administrator, Shebna the secretary and the leading priests, all wearing sackcloth, to the prophet Isaiah son of Amoz. ³They told him, "This is what Hezekiah says: This day is a day of distress and rebuke and disgrace, as when children come to the point of birth and there is no strength to deliver them. ⁴It may be that the LORD your God will hear all the words of the field commander, whom his master, the king of Assyria, has sent to ridicule the living God, and that he will rebuke him for the words the LORD your God has heard. Therefore pray for the remnant that still survives."

⁵When King Hezekiah's officials came to Isaiah, ⁶Isaiah said to them, "Tell your master, 'This is what the LORD says: Do not be afraid of what you have heard—those words with which the underlings of the king of

Assyria have blasphemed me. ⁷Listen! I am going to put such a spirit in him that when he hears a certain report, he will return to his own country, and there I will have him cut down with the sword.'"

⁸When the field commander heard that the king of Assyria had left Lachish, he withdrew and found the king fighting against Libnah.

⁹Now Sennacherib received a report that Tirhakah, the Cushite[a] king of Egypt, was marching out to fight against him. So he again sent messengers to Hezekiah with this word: ¹⁰"Say to Hezekiah king of Judah: Do not let the god you depend on deceive you when he says, 'Jerusalem will not be handed over to the king of Assyria.' ¹¹Surely you have heard what the kings of Assyria have done to all the countries, destroying them completely. And will you be delivered? ¹²Did the gods of the nations that were destroyed by my forefathers deliver them: the gods of Gozan, Haran, Rezeph and the people of Eden who were in Tel Assar? ¹³Where is the king of Hamath, the king of Arpad, the king of the city of Sepharvaim, or of Hena or Ivvah?"

Hezekiah's Prayer

¹⁴Hezekiah received the letter from the messengers and read it. Then he went up to the temple of the LORD and spread it out before the LORD. ¹⁵And Hezekiah prayed to the LORD: "O LORD, God of Israel, enthroned between the cherubim, you alone are God over all the kingdoms of the earth. You have made heaven and earth. ¹⁶Give ear, O LORD, and hear; open your eyes, O LORD, and see; listen to the words Sennacherib has sent to insult the living God.

¹⁷"It is true, O LORD, that the Assyrian kings have laid waste these nations and their lands. ¹⁸They have thrown their gods into the fire and destroyed them, for they were not gods but only wood and stone, fashioned by men's hands. ¹⁹Now, O LORD our God, deliver us from his hand, so that all kingdoms on earth may know that you alone, O LORD, are God."

Isaiah Prophesies Sennacherib's Fall

²⁰Then Isaiah son of Amoz sent a message to Hezekiah: "This is what the LORD, the God of Israel, says: I have heard your prayer concerning Sennacherib king of Assyria. ²¹This is the word that the LORD has spoken against him:

"'The Virgin Daughter of Zion
    despises you and mocks you.
The Daughter of Jerusalem
    tosses her head as you flee.
²²Who is it you have insulted and
    blasphemed?
    Against whom have you raised your
    voice
and lifted your eyes in pride?
    Against the Holy One of Israel!
²³By your messengers
    you have heaped insults on the Lord.

---

a9 That is, from the upper Nile region

And you have said,
"With my many chariots
I have ascended the heights of the
mountains,
the utmost heights of Lebanon.
I have cut down its tallest cedars,
the choicest of its pines.
I have reached its remotest parts,
the finest of its forests.
24I have dug wells in foreign lands
and drunk the water there.
With the soles of my feet
I have dried up all the streams of
Egypt.''

25'' 'Have you not heard?
Long ago I ordained it.
In days of old I planned it;
now I have brought it to pass,
that you have turned fortified cities
into piles of stone.
26Their people, drained of power,
are dismayed and put to shame.
They are like plants in the field,
like tender green shoots,
like grass sprouting on the roof,
scorched before it grows up.

27'' 'But I know where you stay
and when you come and go
and how you rage against me.
28Because you rage against me
and your insolence has reached my ears,
I will put my hook in your nose
and my bit in your mouth,
and I will make you return
by the way you came.'

29''This will be the sign for you, O Hezekiah:

This year you will eat what grows by itself,
and the second year what springs from
that.
But in the third year sow and reap,
plant vineyards and eat their fruit.
30Once more a remnant of the house of
Judah
will take root below and bear fruit
above.
31For out of Jerusalem will come a remnant,
and out of Mount Zion a band of
survivors.

The zeal of the LORD Almighty will accomplish this.

32''Therefore this is what the LORD says
concerning the king of Assyria:

''He will not enter this city
or shoot an arrow here.
He will not come before it with shield
or build a siege ramp against it.
33By the way that he came he will return;
he will not enter this city,
declares the LORD.
34I will defend this city and save it,
for my sake and for the sake of David
my servant.''

35That night the angel of the LORD went out
and put to death a hundred and eighty-five
thousand men in the Assyrian camp. When
the people got up the next morning—there
were all the dead bodies! 36So Sennacherib
king of Assyria broke camp and withdrew.
He returned to Nineveh and stayed there.

37One day, while he was worshipping in the
temple of his god Nisroch, his sons Adrammelech and Sharezer cut him down with the
sword, and they escaped to the land of Ararat. And Esarhaddon his son succeeded him
as king.

Hezekiah's Illness

20 In those days Hezekiah became ill
and was at the point of death. The
prophet Isaiah son of Amoz went to him and
said, ''This is what the LORD says: Put your
house in order, because you are going to die;
you will not recover.''

2Hezekiah turned his face to the wall and
prayed to the LORD, 3''Remember, O LORD,
how I have walked before you faithfully and
with wholehearted devotion and have done
what is good in your eyes.'' And Hezekiah
wept bitterly.

4Before Isaiah had left the middle court,
the word of the LORD came to him: 5''Go back
and tell Hezekiah, the leader of my people,
'This is what the LORD, the God of your
father David, says: I have heard your prayer
and seen your tears; I will heal you. On the
third day from now you will go up to the
temple of the LORD. 6I will add fifteen years to
your life. And I will deliver you and this city
from the hand of the king of Assyria. I will
defend this city for my sake and for the sake
of my servant David.''

7Then Isaiah said, ''Prepare a poultice of
figs.'' They did so and applied it to the boil,
and he recovered.

8Hezekiah had asked Isaiah, ''What will be
the sign that the LORD will heal me and that I
will go up to the temple of the LORD on the
third day from now?''

9Isaiah answered, ''This is the LORD's sign
to you that the LORD will do what he has
promised: Shall the shadow go forward ten
steps, or shall it go back ten steps?''

10''It is a simple matter for the shadow
to go forward ten steps,'' said Hezekiah.
''Rather, have it go back ten steps.''

11Then the prophet Isaiah called upon the
LORD, and the LORD made the shadow go
back the ten steps it had gone down on the
stairway of Ahaz.

Envoys From Babylon

12At that time Merodach-Baladan son of
Baladan king of Babylon sent Hezekiah letters and a gift, because he had heard of
Hezekiah's illness. 13Hezekiah received the
messengers and showed them all that was in
his storehouses—the silver, the gold, the
spices and the fine oil—his armoury and
everything found among his treasures. There
was nothing in his palace or in all his kingdom
that Hezekiah did not show them.

14Then Isaiah the prophet went to King

Hezekiah and asked, "What did those men say, and where did they come from?"

"From a distant land," Hezekiah replied. "They came from Babylon."

[15]The prophet asked, "What did they see in your palace?"

"They saw everything in my palace," Hezekiah said. "There is nothing among my treasures that I did not show them."

[16]Then Isaiah said to Hezekiah, "Hear the word of the LORD: [17]The time will surely come when everything in your palace, and all that your fathers have stored up until this day, will be carried off to Babylon. Nothing will be left, says the LORD. [18]And some of your descendants, your own flesh and blood, that will be born to you, will be taken away, and they will become eunuchs in the palace of the king of Babylon."

[19]"The word of the LORD you have spoken is good," Hezekiah replied. For he thought, "Will there not be peace and security in my lifetime?"

[20]As for the other events of Hezekiah's reign, all his achievements and how he made the pool and the tunnel by which he brought water into the city, are they not written in the book of the annals of the kings of Judah? [21]Hezekiah rested with his fathers. And Manasseh his son succeeded him as king.

Manasseh King of Judah

21 Manasseh was twelve years old when he became king, and he reigned in Jerusalem for fifty-five years. His mother's name was Hephzibah. [2]He did evil in the eyes of the LORD, following the detestable practices of the nations the LORD had driven out before the Israelites. [3]He rebuilt the high places his father Hezekiah had destroyed; he also erected altars to Baal and made an Asherah pole, as Ahab king of Israel had done. He bowed down to all the starry hosts and worshiped them. [4]He built altars in the temple of the LORD, of which the LORD had said, "In Jerusalem I will put my Name." [5]In both courts of the temple of the LORD, he built altars to all the starry hosts. [6]He sacrificed his own son in[a] the fire, practised sorcery and divination, and consulted mediums and spiritists. He did much evil in the eyes of the LORD, provoking him to anger.

[7]He took the carved Asherah pole he had made and put it in the temple, of which the LORD had said to David and to his son Solomon, "In this temple and in Jerusalem, which I have chosen out of all the tribes of Israel, I will put my Name for ever. [8]I will not again make the feet of the Israelites wander from the land I gave their forefathers, if only they will be careful to do everything I commanded them and will keep the whole Law that my servant Moses gave them." [9]But the people did not listen. Manasseh led them astray, so that they did more evil than the nations the LORD had destroyed before the Israelites.

[10]The LORD said through his servants the prophets: [11]"Manasseh king of Judah has committed these detestable sins. He has done more evil than the Amorites who preceded him and has led Judah into sin with his idols. [12]Therefore this is what the LORD, the God of Israel, says: I am going to bring such disaster on Jerusalem and Judah that the ears of everyone who hears of it will tingle. [13]I will stretch out over Jerusalem the measuring line used against Samaria and the plumb-line used against the house of Ahab. I will wipe out Jerusalem as one wipes out a dish, wiping it and turning it upside-down. [14]I will forsake the remnant of my inheritance and hand them over to their enemies. They will be looted and plundered by all their foes, [15]because they have done evil in my eyes and have provoked me to anger from the day their forefathers came out of Egypt until this day."

[16]Moreover, Manasseh also shed so much innocent blood that he filled Jerusalem from end to end—besides the sin that he had caused Judah to commit, so that they did evil in the eyes of the LORD.

[17]As for the other events of Manasseh's reign, and all he did, including the sin he committed, are they not written in the book of the annals of the kings of Judah? [18]Manasseh rested with his fathers and was buried in his palace garden, the garden of Uzza. And Amon his son succeeded him as king.

Amon King of Judah

[19]Amon was twenty-two years old when he became king, and he reigned in Jerusalem for two years. His mother's name was Meshullemeth daughter of Haruz; she was from Jotbah. [20]He did evil in the eyes of the LORD, as his father Manasseh had done. [21]He walked in all the ways of his father; he worshipped the idols his father had worshipped, and bowed down to them. [22]He forsook the LORD, the God of his fathers, and did not walk in the way of the LORD.

[23]Amon's officials conspired against him and assassinated the king in his palace. [24]Then the people of the land killed all who had plotted against King Amon, and they made Josiah his son king in his place.

[25]As for the other events of Amon's reign, and what he did, are they not written in the book of the annals of the kings of Judah? [26]He was buried in his grave in the garden of Uzza. And Josiah his son succeeded him as king.

The Book of the Law Found

22 Josiah was eight years old when he became king, and he reigned in Jerusalem for thirty-one years. His mother's name was Jedidah daughter of Adaiah; she was from Bozkath. [2]He did what was right in the eyes of the LORD and walked in all the ways of his father David, not turning aside to the right or to the left.

[3]In the eighteenth year of his reign, King Josiah sent the secretary, Shaphan son of Azaliah, the son of Meshullam, to the temple of the LORD. He said: [4]"Go up to Hilkiah the

---

[a]6 Or *He made his own son pass through*

high priest and make him get ready the money that has been brought into the temple of the LORD, which the doorkeepers have collected from the people. 5Make them entrust it to the men appointed to supervise the work on the temple. And make these men pay the workers who repair the temple of the LORD—6the carpenters, the builders and the masons. Also make them purchase timber and dressed stone to repair the temple. 7But they need not account for the money entrusted to them, because they are acting faithfully.''

8Hilkiah the high priest said to Shaphan the secretary, ''I have found the Book of the Law in the temple of the LORD.'' He gave it to Shaphan, who read it. 9Then Shaphan the secretary went to the king and reported to him: ''Your officials have paid out the money that was in the temple of the LORD and have entrusted it to the workers and supervisors at the temple.'' 10Then Shaphan the secretary informed the king, ''Hilkiah the priest has given me a book.'' And Shaphan read from it in the presence of the king.

11When the king heard the words of the Book of the Law, he tore his robes. 12He gave these orders to Hilkiah the priest, Ahikam son of Shaphan, Acbor son of Micaiah, Shaphan the secretary and Asaiah the king's attendant: 13''Go and enquire of the LORD for me and for the people and for all Judah about what is written in this book that has been found. Great is the LORD's anger that burns against us because our fathers have not obeyed the words of this book; they have not acted in accordance with all that is written there concerning us.''

14Hilkiah the priest, Ahikam, Acbor, Shaphan and Asaiah went to speak to the prophetess Huldah, who was the wife of Shallum son of Tikvah, the son of Harhas, keeper of the wardrobe. She lived in Jerusalem, in the Second District.

15She said to them, ''This is what the LORD, the God of Israel, says: Tell the man who sent you to me, 16'This is what the LORD says: I am going to bring disaster on this place and its people, according to everything written in the book the king of Judah has read. 17Because they have forsaken me and burned incense to other gods and provoked me to anger by all the idols their hands have made,a my anger will burn against this place and will not be quenched.' 18Tell the king of Judah, who sent you to enquire of the LORD, 'This is what the LORD, the God of Israel, says concerning the words you heard: 19Because your heart was responsive and you humbled yourself before the LORD when you heard what I have spoken against this place and its people, that they would become accursed and laid waste, and because you tore your robes and wept in my presence, I have heard you, declares the LORD. 20Therefore I will gather you to your fathers, and you will be buried in peace. Your eyes will not see all the disaster I am going to bring on this place.' ''

So they took her answer back to the king.

Josiah Renews the Covenant

23 Then the king called together all the elders of Judah and Jerusalem. 2He went up to the temple of the LORD with the men of Judah, the people of Jerusalem, the priests and the prophets—all the people from the least to the greatest. He read in their hearing all the words of the Book of the Covenant, which had been found in the temple of the LORD. 3The king stood by the pillar and renewed the covenant in the presence of the LORD—to follow the LORD and keep his commands, regulations and decrees with all his heart and all his soul, thus confirming the words of the covenant written in this book. Then all the people pledged themselves to the covenant.

4The king ordered Hilkiah the high priest, the priests next in rank and the doorkeepers to remove from the temple of the LORD all the articles made for Baal and Asherah and all the starry hosts. He burned them outside Jerusalem in the fields of the Kidron Valley and took the ashes to Bethel. 5He did away with the pagan priests appointed by the kings of Judah to burn incense on the high places of the towns of Judah and on those around Jerusalem—those who burned incense to Baal, to the sun and moon, to the constellations and to all the starry hosts. 6He took the Asherah pole from the temple of the LORD to the Kidron Valley outside Jerusalem and burned it there. He ground it to powder and scattered the dust over the graves of the common people. 7He also tore down the quarters of the male shrine-prostitutes, which were in the temple of the LORD and where women did weaving for Asherah.

8Josiah brought all the priests from the towns of Judah and desecrated the high places, from Geba to Beersheba, where the priests had burned incense. He broke down the shrinesa at the gates—at the entrance to the Gate of Joshua, the city governor, which is on the left of the city gate. 9Although the priests of the high places did not serve at the altar of the LORD in Jerusalem, they ate unleavened bread with their fellow priests.

10He desecrated Topheth, which was in the Valley of Ben Hinnom, so no-one could use it to sacrifice his son or daughter inb the fire to Molech. 11He removed from the entrance to the temple of the LORD the horses that the kings of Judah had dedicated to the sun. They were in the court near the room of an official named Nathan-Melech. Josiah then burned the chariots dedicated to the sun.

12He pulled down the altars the kings of Judah had erected on the roof near the upper room of Ahaz, and the altars Manasseh had built in the two courts of the temple of the LORD. He removed them from there, smashed them to pieces and threw the rubble into the Kidron Valley. 13The king also desecrated the high places that were east of Jerusalem on the south of the Hill of Corruption—the ones Solomon king of Israel had built for Ashtoreth the vile goddess of the Sidonians, for Chemosh the vile god of

a17 Or by everything they have done   a8 Or high places   b10 Or to make his son or daughter pass through

Moab, and for Molech[c] the detestable god of the people of Ammon. [14]Josiah smashed the sacred stones and cut down the Asherah poles and covered the sites with human bones.

[15]Even the altar at Bethel, the high place made by Jeroboam son of Nebat, who had caused Israel to sin—even that altar and high place he demolished. He burned the high place and ground it to powder, and burned the Asherah pole also. [16]Then Josiah looked around, and when he saw the tombs that were there on the hillside, he had the bones removed from them and burned on the altar to defile it, in accordance with the word of the LORD proclaimed by the man of God who foretold these things.

[17]The king asked, "What is that tombstone I see?"

The men of the city said, "It marks the tomb of the man of God who came from Judah and pronounced against the altar of Bethel the very things you have done to it."

[18]"Leave it alone," he said. "Don't let anyone disturb his bones." So they spared his bones and those of the prophet who had come from Samaria.

[19]Just as he had done at Bethel, Josiah removed and defiled all the shrines at the high places that the kings of Israel had built in the towns of Samaria that had provoked the LORD to anger. [20]Josiah slaughtered all the priests of those high places on the altars and burned human bones on them. Then he went back to Jerusalem.

[21]The king gave this order to all the people: "Celebrate the Passover to the LORD your God, as it is written in this Book of the Covenant." [22]Not since the days of the judges who led Israel, nor throughout the days of the kings of Israel and the kings of Judah, had any such Passover been observed. [23]But in the eighteenth year of King Josiah, this Passover was celebrated to the LORD in Jerusalem.

[24]Furthermore, Josiah got rid of the mediums and spiritists, the household gods, the idols and all the other detestable things seen in Judah and Jerusalem. This he did to fulfil the requirements of the law written in the book that Hilkiah the priest had discovered in the temple of the LORD. [25]Neither before nor after Josiah was there a king like him who turned to the LORD as he did—with all his heart and with all his soul and with all his strength, in accordance with all the Law of Moses.

[26]Nevertheless, the LORD did not turn away from the heat of his fierce anger, which burned against Judah because of all that Manasseh had done to provoke him to anger. [27]So the LORD said, "I will remove Judah also from my presence as I removed Israel, and I will reject Jerusalem, the city I chose, and this temple, about which I said, 'There shall my Name be.'[d]"

[28]As for the other events of Josiah's reign, and all he did, are they not written in the book of the annals of the kings of Judah?

[29]While Josiah was king, Pharaoh Neco king of Egypt went up to the Euphrates River to help the king of Assyria. King Josiah marched out to meet him in battle, but Neco faced him and killed him at Megiddo. [30]Josiah's servants brought his body in a chariot from Megiddo to Jerusalem and buried him in his own tomb. And the people of the land took Jehoahaz son of Josiah and anointed him and made him king in place of his father.

Jehoahaz King of Judah

[31]Jehoahaz was twenty-three years old when he became king, and he reigned in Jerusalem for three months. His mother's name was Hamutal daughter of Jeremiah; she was from Libnah. [32]He did evil in the eyes of the LORD, just as his fathers had done. [33]Pharaoh Neco put him in chains at Riblah in the land of Hamath[e] so that he might not reign in Jerusalem, and he imposed on Judah a levy of a hundred talents[f] of silver and a talent[g] of gold. [34]Pharaoh Neco made Eliakim son of Josiah king in place of his father Josiah and changed Eliakim's name to Jehoiakim. But he took Jehoahaz and carried him off to Egypt, and there he died. [35]Jehoiakim paid Pharaoh Neco the silver and gold he demanded. In order to do so, he taxed the land and exacted the silver and gold from the people of the land according to their assessments.

Jehoiakim King of Judah

[36]Jehoiakim was twenty-five years old when he became king, and he reigned in Jerusalem for eleven years. His mother's name was Zebidah daughter of Pedaiah; she was from Rumah. [37]And he did evil in the eyes of the LORD, just as his fathers had done.

24 During Jehoiakim's reign, Nebuchadnezzar king of Babylon invaded the land, and Jehoiakim became his vassal for three years. But then he changed his mind and rebelled against Nebuchadnezzar. [2]The LORD sent Babylonian,[a] Aramean, Moabite and Ammonite raiders against him. He sent them to destroy Judah, in accordance with the word of the LORD proclaimed by his servants the prophets. [3]Surely these things happened to Judah according to the LORD's command, in order to remove them from his presence because of the sins of Manasseh and all he had done, [4]including the shedding of innocent blood. For he had filled Jerusalem with innocent blood, and the LORD was not willing to forgive.

[5]As for the other events of Jehoiakim's reign, and all he did, are they not written in the book of the annals of the kings of Judah? [6]Jehoiakim rested with his fathers. And Jehoiachin his son succeeded him as king.

[7]The king of Egypt did not march out from his own country again, because the king of

---

[c]13 Hebrew *Milcom*   [d]27 1 Kings 8:29
[e]33 Hebrew; Septuagint (see also 2 Chron. 36:3) *Neco at Riblah in Hamath removed him*
[f]33 That is, about 3½ tons (about 3.4 metric tons)   [g]33 That is, about 75 pounds (about 34 kilograms)
[a]2 Or *Chaldean*

Babylon had taken all his territory, from the Wadi of Egypt to the Euphrates River.

Jehoiachin King of Judah

[8]Jehoiachin was eighteen years old when he became king, and he reigned in Jerusalem for three months. His mother's name was Nehushta daughter of Elnathan; she was from Jerusalem. [9]He did evil in the eyes of the LORD, just as his father had done.

[10]At that time the officers of Nebuchadnezzar king of Babylon advanced on Jerusalem and laid siege to it, [11]and Nebuchadnezzar himself came up to the city while his officers were besieging it. [12]Jehoiachin king of Judah, his mother, his attendants, his nobles and his officials all surrendered to him.

In the eighth year of the reign of the king of Babylon, he took Jehoiachin prisoner. [13]As the LORD had declared, Nebuchadnezzar removed all the treasures from the temple of the LORD and from the royal palace, and took away all the gold articles that Solomon king of Israel had made for the temple of the LORD. [14]He carried into exile all Jerusalem: all the officers and fighting men, and all the craftsmen and artisans—a total of ten thousand. Only the poorest people of the land were left.

[15]Nebuchadnezzar took Jehoiachin captive to Babylon. He also took from Jerusalem to Babylon the king's mother, his wives, his officials and the leading men of the land. [16]The king of Babylon also deported to Babylon the entire force of seven thousand fighting men, strong and fit for war, and a thousand craftsmen and artisans. [17]He made Mattaniah, Jehoiachin's uncle, king in his place and changed his name to Zedekiah.

Zedekiah King of Judah

[18]Zedekiah was twenty-one years old when he became king, and he reigned in Jerusalem for eleven years. His mother's name was Hamutal daughter of Jeremiah; she was from Libnah. [19]He did evil in the eyes of the LORD, just as Jehoiakim had done. [20]It was because of the LORD's anger that all this happened to Jerusalem and Judah, and in the end he thrust them from his presence.

The Fall of Jerusalem

Now Zedekiah rebelled against the king of Babylon.

25 So in the ninth year of Zedekiah's reign, on the tenth day of the tenth month, Nebuchadnezzar king of Babylon marched against Jerusalem with his whole army. He encamped outside the city and built siege works all around it. [2]The city was kept under siege until the eleventh year of King Zedekiah. [3]By the ninth day of the ˌfourthˌ[a] month the famine in the city had become so severe that there was no food for the people to eat. [4]Then the city wall was broken through, and the whole army fled at night through the gate between the two walls near the king's garden, though the Babylonians[b]

were surrounding the city. They fled towards the Arabah,[c] [5]but the Babylonian[d] army pursued the king and overtook him in the plains of Jericho. All his soldiers were separated from him and scattered, [6]and he was captured. He was taken to the king of Babylon at Riblah, where sentence was pronounced on him. [7]They killed the sons of Zedekiah before his eyes. Then they put out his eyes, bound him with bronze shackles and took him to Babylon.

[8]On the seventh day of the fifth month, in the nineteenth year of Nebuchadnezzar king of Babylon, Nebuzaradan commander of the imperial guard, an official of the king of Babylon, came to Jerusalem. [9]He set fire to the temple of the LORD, the royal palace and all the houses of Jerusalem. Every important building he burned down. [10]The whole Babylonian army, under the commander of the imperial guard, broke down the walls around Jerusalem. [11]Nebuzaradan the commander of the guard carried into exile the people who remained in the city, along with the rest of the populace and those who had gone over to the king of Babylon. [12]But the commander left behind some of the poorest people of the land to work the vineyards and fields.

[13]The Babylonians broke up the bronze pillars, the movable stands and the bronze Sea that were at the temple of the LORD and they carried the bronze to Babylon. [14]They also took away the pots, shovels, wick trimmers, dishes and all the bronze articles used in the temple service. [15]The commander of the imperial guard took away the censers and sprinkling bowls—all that were made of pure gold or silver.

[16]The bronze from the two pillars, the Sea and the movable stands, which Solomon had made for the temple of the LORD, was more than could be weighed. [17]Each pillar was twenty-seven feet[e] high. The bronze capital on top of one pillar was four and a half feet[f] high and was decorated with a network and pomegranates of bronze all around. The other pillar, with its network, was similar.

[18]The commander of the guard took as prisoners Seraiah the chief priest, Zephaniah the priest next in rank and the three doorkeepers. [19]Of those still in the city, he took the officer in charge of the fighting men and five royal advisers. He also took the secretary who was chief officer in charge of conscripting the people of the land and sixty of his men who were found in the city. [20]Nebuzaradan the commander took them all and brought them to the king of Babylon at Riblah. [21]There at Riblah, in the land of Hamath, the king had them executed.

So Judah went into captivity, away from her land.

[22]Nebuchadnezzar king of Babylon appointed Gedaliah son of Ahikam, the son of Shaphan, to be over the people he had left behind in Judah. [23]When all the army officers

---

[a]3 See Jer. 52:6.   [b]4 Or *Chaldeans*; also in verses 13, 25 and 26   [c]4 Or *the Jordan Valley*
[d]5 Or *Chaldean*; also in verses 10 and 24   [e]17 Hebrew *eighteen cubits* (about 8.2 metres)
[f]17 Hebrew *three cubits* (about 1.4 metres)

and their men heard that the king of Babylon had appointed Gedaliah as governor, they came to Gedaliah at Mizpah—Ishmael son of Nethaniah, Johanan son of Kareah, Seraiah son of Tanhumeth the Netophathite, Jaazaniah the son of the Maacathite, and their men. [24]Gedaliah took an oath to reassure them and their men. "Do not be afraid of the Babylonian officials," he said. "Settle down in the land and serve the king of Babylon, and it will go well with you."

[25]In the seventh month, however, Ishmael son of Nethaniah, the son of Elishama, who was of royal blood, came with ten men and assassinated Gedaliah and also the men of Judah and the Babylonians who were with him at Mizpah. [26]At this, all the people from the least to the greatest, together with the army officers, fled to Egypt for fear of the Babylonians.

Jehoiachin Released

[27]In the thirty-seventh year of the exile of Jehoiachin king of Judah, in the year Evil-Merodach[g] became king of Babylon, he released Jehoiachin from prison on the twenty-seventh day of the twelfth month. [28]He spoke kindly to him and gave him a seat of honour higher than those of the other kings who were with him in Babylon. [29]So Jehoiachin put aside his prison clothes and for the rest of his life ate regularly at the king's table. [30]Day by day the king gave Jehoiachin a regular allowance as long as he lived.

---

[g]27 Also called *Amel-Marduk*

1 Chronicles

Historical Records From Adam to Abraham

To Noah's Sons

1 Adam, Seth, Enosh, ²Kenan, Mahalalel, Jared, ³Enoch, Methuselah, Lamech, Noah.

⁴The sons of Noah:ᵃ
Shem, Ham and Japheth.

The Japhethites

⁵The sonsᵇ of Japheth:
Gomer, Magog, Madai, Javan, Tubal, Meshech and Tiras.
⁶The sons of Gomer:
Ashkenaz, Riphathᶜ and Togarmah.
⁷The sons of Javan:
Elishah, Tarshish, the Kittim and the Rodanim.

The Hamites

⁸The sons of Ham:
Cush, Mizraim,ᵈ Put and Canaan.
⁹The sons of Cush:
Seba, Havilah, Sabta, Raamah and Sabteca.
The sons of Raamah:
Sheba and Dedan.
¹⁰Cush was the fatherᵉ of
Nimrod, who grew to be a mighty warrior on earth.
¹¹Mizraim was the father of
the Ludites, Anamites, Lehabites, Naphtuhites, ¹²Pathrusites, Casluhites (from whom the Philistines came) and Caphtorites.
¹³Canaan was the father of
Sidon his firstborn,ᶠ and of the Hittites, ¹⁴Jebusites, Amorites, Girgashites, ¹⁵Hivites, Arkites, Sinites, ¹⁶Arvadites, Zemarites and Hamathites.

The Semites

¹⁷The sons of Shem:
Elam, Asshur, Arphaxad, Lud and Aram.
The sons of Aram:ᵍ
Uz, Hul, Gether and Meshech.
¹⁸Arphaxad was the father of Shelah, and Shelah the father of Eber.
¹⁹Two sons were born to Eber:
One was named Peleg,ʰ because in his time the earth was divided; his brother was named Joktan.
²⁰Joktan was the father of
Almodad, Sheleph, Hazarmaveth, Jerah, ²¹Hadoram, Uzal, Diklah, ²²Obal,ⁱ Abimael, Sheba, ²³Ophir, Havilah and Jobab. All these were sons of Joktan.

²⁴Shem, Arphaxad,ʲ Shelah,
²⁵Eber, Peleg, Reu,
²⁶Serug, Nahor, Terah
²⁷and Abram (that is, Abraham).

The Family of Abraham

²⁸The sons of Abraham:
Isaac and Ishmael.

Descendants of Hagar

²⁹These were their descendants:
Nebaioth the firstborn of Ishmael, Kedar, Adbeel, Mibsam, ³⁰Mishma, Dumah, Massa, Hadad, Tema, ³¹Jetur, Naphish and Kedemah. These were the sons of Ishmael.

Descendants of Keturah

³²The sons born to Keturah,
Abraham's concubine:
Zimran, Jokshan, Medan, Midian, Ishbak and Shuah.
The sons of Jokshan:
Sheba and Dedan.

ᵃ4 Septuagint; Hebrew does not have *The sons of Noah:*
ᵇ5 *Sons* may mean *descendants* or *successors* or *nations*; also in verses 6–10, 17 and 20.
ᶜ6 Many Hebrew manuscripts and Vulgate (see also Septuagint and Gen. 10:3); most Hebrew manuscripts *Diphath*
ᵈ8 That is, Egypt; also in verse 11
ᵉ10 *Father* may mean *ancestor* or *predecessor* or *founder*; also in verses 11, 13, 18 and 20.
ᶠ13 Or *of the Sidonians, the foremost*
ᵍ17 One Hebrew manuscript and some Septuagint manuscripts (see also Gen. 10:23); most Hebrew manuscripts do not have this line.   ʰ19 *Peleg* means *division*.
ⁱ22 Some Hebrew manuscripts and Syriac (see also Gen. 10:28); most Hebrew manuscripts *Ebal*
ʲ24 Hebrew; some Septuagint manuscripts *Arphaxad, Cainan* (see also note at Gen. 11:10)

33The sons of Midian:
Ephah, Epher, Hanoch, Abida and Eldaah.

All these were descendants of Keturah.

Descendants of Sarah

34Abraham was the father of Isaac.

The sons of Isaac:
Esau and Israel.

Esau's Sons

35The sons of Esau:
Eliphaz, Reuel, Jeush, Jalam and Korah.

36The sons of Eliphaz:
Teman, Omar, Zepho,k Gatam and Kenaz;
by Timna: Amalek.l

37The sons of Reuel:
Nahath, Zerah, Shammah and Mizzah.

The People of Seir in Edom

38The sons of Seir:
Lotan, Shobal, Zibeon, Anah, Dishon, Ezer and Dishan.

39The sons of Lotan:
Hori and Homam. Timna was Lotan's sister.

40The sons of Shobal:
Alvan,m Manahath, Ebal, Shepho and Onam.

The sons of Zibeon:
Aiah and Anah.

41The son of Anah:
Dishon.

The sons of Dishon:
Hemdan,n Eshban, Ithran and Keran.

42The sons of Ezer:
Bilhan, Zaavan and Akan.o

The sons of Dishan:p
Uz and Aran.

The Rulers of Edom

43These were the kings who reigned in Edom before any Israelite king reigned:q
Bela son of Beor, whose city was named Dinhabah.

44When Bela died, Jobab son of Zerah from Bozrah succeeded him as king.

45When Jobab died, Husham from the land of the Temanites succeeded him as king.

46When Husham died, Hadad son of Bedad, who defeated Midian in the country of Moab, succeeded him as king. His city was named Avith.

47When Hadad died, Samlah from Masrekah succeeded him as king.

48When Samlah died, Shaul from Rehoboth on the riverr succeeded him as king.

49When Shaul died, Baal-Hanan son of Acbor succeeded him as king.

50When Baal-Hanan died, Hadad succeeded him as king. His city was named Pau,s and his wife's name was Mehetabel daughter of Matred, the daughter of Me-Zahab. 51Hadad also died.

The chiefs of Edom were:
Timna, Alvah, Jetheth, 52Oholibamah, Elah, Pinon, 53Kenaz, Teman, Mibzar, 54Magdiel and Iram. These were the chiefs of Edom.

Israel's Sons

2 These were the sons of Israel:
Reuben, Simeon, Levi, Judah, Issachar, Zebulun, 2Dan, Joseph, Benjamin, Naphtali, Gad and Asher.

Judah

To Hezron's Sons

3The sons of Judah:
Er, Onan and Shelah. These three were born to him by a Canaanite woman, the daughter of Shua. Er, Judah's firstborn, was wicked in the LORD's sight; so the LORD put him to death. 4Tamar, Judah's daughter-in-law, bore him Perez and Zerah. Judah had five sons in all.

5The sons of Perez:
Hezron and Hamul.

6The sons of Zerah:
Zimri, Ethan, Heman, Calcol and Dardaa—five in all.

7The son of Carmi:
Achar,b who brought trouble on Israel by violating the ban on taking devoted things.c

8The son of Ethan:
Azariah.

9The sons born to Hezron were:
Jerahmeel, Ram and Caleb.d

From Ram Son of Hezron

10Ram was the father of
Amminadab, and Amminadab the father of Nahshon, the leader of the

---

k36 Many Hebrew manuscripts, some Septuagint manuscripts and Syriac (see also Gen. 36:11); most Hebrew manuscripts *Zephi*

l36 Some Septuagint manuscripts (see also Gen. 36:12); Hebrew *Gatam, Kenaz, Timna and Amalek*

m40 Many Hebrew manuscripts and some Septuagint manuscripts (see also Gen. 36:23); most Hebrew manuscripts *Alian*

n41 Many Hebrew manuscripts and some Septuagint manuscripts (see also Gen. 36:26); most Hebrew manuscripts *Hamran*

o42 Many Hebrew and Septuagint manuscripts (see also Gen. 36:27); most Hebrew manuscripts *Zaavan, Jaakan*

p42 Hebrew *Dishon,* a variant of *Dishan*   q43 Or *before an Israelite king reigned over them*

r48 Possibly the Euphrates

s50 Many Hebrew manuscripts, some Septuagint manuscripts, Vulgate and Syriac (see also Gen. 36:39); most Hebrew manuscripts *Pai*

a6 Many Hebrew manuscripts, some Septuagint manuscripts and Syriac (see also 1 Kings 4:31); most Hebrew manuscripts *Dara*   b7 *Achar* means *trouble; Achar* is called *Achan* in Joshua.

c7 The Hebrew term refers to the irrevocable giving over of things or persons to the LORD, often by totally destroying them.   d9 Hebrew *Kelubai,* a variant of *Caleb* people of Judah. [11]Nahshon was the father of Salmon,[e] Salmon the father of Boaz, [12]Boaz the father of Obed and Obed the father of Jesse.

[13]Jesse was the father of

Eliab his firstborn; the second son was Abinadab, the third Shimea, [14]the fourth Nethanel, the fifth Raddai, [15]the sixth Ozem and the seventh David. [16]Their sisters were Zeruiah and Abigail. Zeruiah's three sons were Abishai, Joab and Asahel. [17]Abigail was the mother of Amasa, whose father was Jether the Ishmaelite.

Caleb Son of Hezron

[18]Caleb son of Hezron had children by his wife Azubah (and by Jerioth). These were her sons: Jesher, Shobab and Ardon. [19]When Azubah died, Caleb married Ephrath, who bore him Hur. [20]Hur was the father of Uri, and Uri the father of Bezalel.

[21]Later, Hezron lay with the daughter of Makir the father of Gilead (he had married her when he was sixty years old), and she bore him Segub. [22]Segub was the father of Jair, who controlled twenty-three towns in Gilead. [23](But Geshur and Aram captured Havvoth Jair,[f] as well as Kenath with its surrounding settlements—sixty towns.) All these were descendants of Makir the father of Gilead.

[24]After Hezron died in Caleb Ephrathah, Abijah the wife of Hezron bore him Ashhur the father[g] of Tekoa.

Jerahmeel Son of Hezron

[25]The sons of Jerahmeel the firstborn of Hezron:

Ram his firstborn, Bunah, Oren, Ozem and[h] Ahijah. [26]Jerahmeel had another wife, whose name was Atarah; she was the mother of Onam.

[27]The sons of Ram the firstborn of Jerahmeel:

Maaz, Jamin and Eker.

[28]The sons of Onam:

Shammai and Jada.

The sons of Shammai:

Nadab and Abishur.

[29]Abishur's wife was named Abihail, who bore him Ahban and Molid.

[30]The sons of Nadab:

Seled and Appaim. Seled died without children.

[31]The son of Appaim:

Ishi, who was the father of Sheshan.

Sheshan was the father of Ahlai.

[32]The sons of Jada, Shammai's brother:

Jether and Jonathan. Jether died without children.

[33]The sons of Jonathan:

Peleth and Zaza.

These were the descendants of Jerahmeel.

[34]Sheshan had no sons—only daughters.

He had an Egyptian servant named Jarha. [35]Sheshan gave his daughter in marriage to his servant Jarha, and she bore him Attai.

[36]Attai was the father of Nathan,

Nathan the father of Zabad,

[37]Zabad the father of Ephlal,

Ephlal the father of Obed,

[38]Obed the father of Jehu,

Jehu the father of Azariah,

[39]Azariah the father of Helez,

Helez the father of Eleasah,

[40]Eleasah the father of Sismai,

Sismai the father of Shallum,

[41]Shallum the father of Jekamiah, and Jekamiah the father of Elishama.

The Clans of Caleb

[42]The sons of Caleb the brother of Jerahmeel:

Mesha his firstborn, who was the father of Ziph, and his son Mareshah,[i] who was the father of Hebron.

[43]The sons of Hebron:

Korah, Tappuah, Rekem and Shema.

[44]Shema was the father of Raham, and Raham the father of Jorkeam. Rekem was the father of Shammai. [45]The son of Shammai was Maon, and Maon was the father of Beth Zur.

[46]Caleb's concubine Ephah was the mother of Haran, Moza and Gazez. Haran was the father of Gazez.

[47]The sons of Jahdai:

Regem, Jotham, Geshan, Pelet, Ephah and Shaaph.

[48]Caleb's concubine Maacah was the mother of Sheber and Tirhanah. [49]She also gave birth to Shaaph the father of Madmannah and to Sheva the father of Macbenah and Gibea. Caleb's daughter was Acsah. [50]These were the descendants of Caleb.

The sons of Hur the firstborn of Ephrathah:

Shobal the father of Kiriath Jearim, [51]Salma the father of Bethlehem, and Hareph the father of Beth Gader.

[52]The descendants of Shobal the father of Kiriath Jearim were:

Haroeh, half the Manahathites, [53]and the clans of Kiriath Jearim: the Ithrites, Puthites, Shumathites and Mishraites. From these descended the Zorathites and Eshtaolites.

[54]The descendants of Salma:

Bethlehem, the Netophathites, Atroth Beth Joab, half the Manahathites, the Zorites, [55]and the clans of scribes[j] who lived at Jabez: the Tirathites, Shimeathites and Sucathites. These are the Kenites who came

---

[e]11 Septuagint (see also Ruth 4:21); Hebrew *Salma*   [f]23 Or *captured the settlements of Jair*
[g]24 *Father* may mean *civic leader* or *military leader*; also in verses 42, 45, 49–52 and possibly elsewhere.
[h]25 Or *Oren and Ozem, by*   [i]42 The meaning of the Hebrew for this phrase is uncertain.
[j]55 Or *of the Sopherites*

from Hammath, the father of the house of Recab.*k*

The Sons of David

3 These were the sons of David born to him in Hebron:

The firstborn was Amnon the son of Ahinoam of Jezreel;

the second, Daniel the son of Abigail of Carmel;

²the third, Absalom the son of Maacah daughter of Talmai king of Geshur;

the fourth, Adonijah the son of Haggith;

³the fifth, Shephatiah the son of Abital; and the sixth, Ithream, by his wife Eglah.

⁴These six were born to David in Hebron, where he reigned for seven years and six months.

David reigned in Jerusalem for thirty-three years, ⁵and these were the children born to him there:

Shammua,*a* Shobab, Nathan and Solomon. These four were by Bathsheba*b* daughter of Ammiel. ⁶There were also Ibhar, Elishua,*c* Eliphelet, ⁷Nogah, Nepheg, Japhia, ⁸Elishama, Eliada and Eliphelet—nine in all. ⁹All these were the sons of David, besides his sons by his concubines. And Tamar was their sister.

The Kings of Judah

¹⁰Solomon's son was Rehoboam,
Abijah his son,
Asa his son,
Jehoshaphat his son,
¹¹Jehoram*d* his son,
Ahaziah his son,
Joash his son,
¹²Amaziah his son,
Azariah his son,
Jotham his son,
¹³Ahaz his son,
Hezekiah his son,
Manasseh his son,
¹⁴Amon his son,
Josiah his son.
¹⁵The sons of Josiah:
Johanan the firstborn,
Jehoiakim the second son,
Zedekiah the third,
Shallum the fourth.
¹⁶The successors of Jehoiakim:
Jehoiachin*e* his son,
and Zedekiah.

The Royal Line After the Exile

¹⁷The descendants of Jehoiachin the captive:

Shealtiel his son, ¹⁸Malkiram, Pedaiah, Shenazzar, Jekamiah, Hoshama and Nedabiah.

¹⁹The sons of Pedaiah:
Zerubbabel and Shimei.

The sons of Zerubbabel:
Meshullam and Hananiah.
Shelomith was their sister.
²⁰There were also five others:
Hashubah, Ohel, Berekiah, Hasadiah and Jushab-Hesed.

²¹The descendants of Hananiah:
Pelatiah and Jeshaiah, and the sons of Rephaiah, of Arnan, of Obadiah and of Shecaniah.

²²The descendants of Shecaniah:
Shemaiah and his sons:
Hattush, Igal, Bariah, Neariah and Shaphat—six in all.

²³The sons of Neariah:
Elioenai, Hizkiah and Azrikam—three in all.

²⁴The sons of Elioenai:
Hodaviah, Eliashib, Pelaiah, Akkub, Johanan, Delaiah and Anani—seven in all.

Other Clans of Judah

4 The descendants of Judah:
Perez, Hezron, Carmi, Hur and Shobal.

²Reaiah son of Shobal was the father of Jahath, and Jahath the father of Ahumai and Lahad. These were the clans of the Zorathites.

³These were the sons*a* of Etam:
Jezreel, Ishma and Idbash. Their sister was named Hazzelelponi. ⁴Penuel was the father of Gedor, and Ezer the father of Hushah.

These were the descendants of Hur, the firstborn of Ephrathah and father*b* of Bethlehem.

⁵Ashhur the father of Tekoa had two wives, Helah and Naarah.

⁶Naarah bore him Ahuzzam, Hepher, Temeni and Haahashtari. These were the descendants of Naarah.

⁷The sons of Helah:
Zereth, Zohar, Ethnan, ⁸and Koz, who was the father of Anub and Hazzobebah and of the clans of Aharhel son of Harum.

⁹Jabez was more honourable than his brothers. His mother had named him Jabez,*c* saying, "I gave birth to him in pain." ¹⁰Jabez cried out to the God of Israel, "Oh, that you would bless me and enlarge my territory! Let your hand be with me, and keep me from harm so that I will be free from pain." And God granted his request.

¹¹Kelub, Shuhah's brother, was the father of Mehir, who was the father of Eshton. ¹²Eshton was the father of Beth Rapha, Paseah and Tehinnah the

---

*k*55 Or *father of Beth Recab*   *a*5 Hebrew *Shimea*, a variant of *Shammua*
*b*5 One Hebrew manuscript and Vulgate (see also Septuagint and 2 Sam. 11:3); most Hebrew manuscripts *Bathshua*
*c*6 Two Hebrew manuscripts (see also 2 Sam. 5:15 and 1 Chron. 14:5); most Hebrew manuscripts *Elishama*
*d*11 Hebrew *Joram*, a variant of *Jehoram*   *e*16 Hebrew *Jeconiah*, a variant of *Jehoiachin*; also in verse 17
*a*3 Some Septuagint manuscripts (see also Vulgate); Hebrew *father*
*b*4 *Father* may mean *civic leader* or *military leader*; also in verses 12, 14, 17, 18 and possibly elsewhere.
*c*9 *Jabez* sounds like the Hebrew for *pain*.

father of Ir Nahash.*d* These were the men of Recah.

¹³The sons of Kenaz:
　Othniel and Seraiah.
　The sons of Othniel:
　　Hathath and Meonothai.*e* ¹⁴Meonothai was the father of Ophrah.
　Seraiah was the father of Joab,
　　the father of Ge Harashim.*f* It was called this because its people were craftsmen.
¹⁵The sons of Caleb son of Jephunneh:
　Iru, Elah and Naam.
　The son of Elah:
　　Kenaz.
¹⁶The sons of Jehallelel:
　Ziph, Ziphah, Tiria and Asarel.
¹⁷The sons of Ezrah:
　Jether, Mered, Epher and Jalon. One of Mered's wives gave birth to Miriam, Shammai and Ishbah the father of Eshtemoa. ¹⁸(His Judean wife gave birth to Jered the father of Gedor, Heber the father of Soco, and Jekuthiel the father of Zanoah.) These were the children of Pharaoh's daughter Bithiah, whom Mered had married.
¹⁹The sons of Hodiah's wife, the sister of Naham:
　the father of Keilah the Garmite, and Eshtemoa the Maacathite.
²⁰The sons of Shimon:
　Amnon, Rinnah, Ben-Hanan and Tilon.
　The descendants of Ishi:
　　Zoheth and Ben-Zoheth.
²¹The sons of Shelah son of Judah:
　Er the father of Lecah, Laadah the father of Mareshah and the clans of the linen workers at Beth Ashbea, ²²Jokim, the men of Cozeba, and Joash and Saraph, who ruled in Moab and Jashubi Lehem. (These records are from ancient times.) ²³They were the potters who lived at Netaim and Gederah; they stayed there and worked for the king.

Simeon

²⁴The descendants of Simeon:
　Nemuel, Jamin, Jarib, Zerah and Shaul;
²⁵Shallum was Shaul's son, Mibsam his son and Mishma his son.
²⁶The descendants of Mishma:
　Hammuel his son, Zaccur his son and Shimei his son.
²⁷Shimei had sixteen sons and six daughters, but his brothers did not have many children; so their entire clan did not become as numerous as the people of Judah. ²⁸They lived in Beersheba, Moladah, Hazar Shual, ²⁹Bilhah, Ezem, Tolad, ³⁰Bethuel, Hormah,

Ziklag, ³¹Beth Marcaboth, Hazar Susim, Beth Biri and Shaaraim. These were their towns until the reign of David. ³²Their surrounding villages were Etam, Ain, Rimmon, Token and Ashan—five towns—³³and all the villages around these towns as far as Baalath.*g* These were their settlements. And they kept a genealogical record.

³⁴Meshobab, Jamlech, Joshah son of Amaziah, ³⁵Joel, Jehu son of Joshibiah, the son of Seraiah, the son of Asiel, ³⁶also Elioenai, Jaakobah, Jeshohaiah, Asaiah, Adiel, Jesimiel, Benaiah, ³⁷and Ziza son of Shiphi, the son of Allon, the son of Jedaiah, the son of Shimri, the son of Shemaiah.

³⁸The men listed above by name were leaders of their clans. Their families increased greatly, ³⁹and they went to the outskirts of Gedor to the east of the valley in search of pasture for their flocks. ⁴⁰They found rich, good pasture, and the land was spacious, peaceful and quiet. Some Hamites had lived there formerly.

⁴¹The men whose names were listed came in the days of Hezekiah king of Judah. They attacked the Hamites in their dwellings and also the Meunites who were there and completely destroyed*h* them, as is evident to this day. Then they settled in their place, because there was pasture for their flocks. ⁴²And five hundred of these Simeonites, led by Pelatiah, Neariah, Rephaiah and Uzziel, the sons of Ishi, invaded the hill country of Seir. ⁴³They killed the remaining Amalekites who had escaped, and they have lived there to this day.

Reuben

5 The sons of Reuben the firstborn of Israel (he was the firstborn, but when he defiled his father's marriage bed, his rights as firstborn were given to the sons of Joseph son of Israel; so he could not be listed in the genealogical record in accordance with his birthright, ²and though Judah was the strongest of his brothers and a ruler came from him, the rights of the firstborn belonged to Joseph)—³the sons of Reuben the firstborn of Israel:
　Hanoch, Pallu, Hezron and Carmi.
⁴The descendants of Joel:
　Shemaiah his son, Gog his son,
　Shimei his son, ⁵Micah his son,
　Reaiah his son, Baal his son,
　⁶and Beerah his son, whom Tiglath-Pileser*a* king of Assyria took into exile. Beerah was a leader of the Reubenites.
⁷Their relatives by clans, listed according to their genealogical records:
　Jeiel the chief, Zechariah, ⁸and Bela son of Azaz, the son of Shema, the son

---

d12 Or of the city of Nahash
e13 Some Septuagint manuscripts and Vulgate; Hebrew does not have and Meonothai.
f14 Ge Harashim means valley of craftsmen.
g33 Some Septuagint manuscripts (see also Joshua 19:8); Hebrew Baal
h41 The Hebrew term refers to the irrevocable giving over of things or persons to the LORD, often by totally destroying them.   a6 Hebrew Tilgath-Pilneser, a variant of Tiglath-Pileser; also in verse 26

of Joel. They settled in the area from Aroer to Nebo and Baal Meon. ⁹To the east they occupied the land up to the edge of the desert that extends to the Euphrates River, because their livestock had increased in Gilead.

¹⁰During Saul's reign they waged war against the Hagrites, who were defeated at their hands; they occupied the dwellings of the Hagrites throughout the entire region east of Gilead.

Gad

¹¹The Gadites lived next to them in Bashan, as far as Salecah:

¹²Joel was the chief, Shapham the second, then Janai and Shaphat, in Bashan.

¹³Their relatives, by families, were:
Michael, Meshullam, Sheba, Jorai, Jacan, Zia and Eber—seven in all. ¹⁴These were the sons of Abihail son of Huri, the son of Jaroah, the son of Gilead, the son of Michael, the son of Jeshishai, the son of Jahdo, the son of Buz.

¹⁵Ahi son of Abdiel, the son of Guni, was head of their family.

¹⁶The Gadites lived in Gilead, in Bashan and its outlying villages, and on all the pasture-lands of Sharon as far as they extended.

¹⁷All these were entered in the genealogical records during the reigns of Jotham king of Judah and Jeroboam king of Israel.

¹⁸The Reubenites, the Gadites and the half-tribe of Manasseh had 44,760 men ready for military service—able-bodied men who could handle shield and sword, who could use a bow, and who were trained for battle. ¹⁹They waged war against the Hagrites, Jetur, Naphish and Nodab. ²⁰They were helped in fighting them, and God handed the Hagrites and all their allies over to them, because they cried out to him during the battle. He answered their prayers, because they trusted in him. ²¹They seized the livestock of the Hagrites—fifty thousand camels, two hundred and fifty thousand sheep and two thousand donkeys. They also took one hundred thousand people captive, ²²and many others fell slain, because the battle was God's. And they occupied the land until the exile.

The Half-Tribe of Manasseh

²³The people of the half-tribe of Manasseh were numerous; they settled in the land from Bashan to Baal Hermon, that is, to Senir (Mount Hermon).

²⁴These were the heads of their families: Epher, Ishi, Eliel, Azriel, Jeremiah, Hodaviah and Jahdiel. They were brave warriors, famous men, and heads of their families. ²⁵But they were unfaithful to the God of their fathers and prostituted themselves to the gods of the peoples of the land, whom God

had destroyed before them. ²⁶So the God of Israel stirred up the spirit of Pul king of Assyria (that is, Tiglath-Pileser king of Assyria), who took the Reubenites, the Gadites and the half-tribe of Manasseh into exile. He took them to Halah, Habor, Hara and the river of Gozan, where they are to this day.

Levi

6 The sons of Levi:
Gershon, Kohath and Merari.
²The sons of Kohath:
Amram, Izhar, Hebron and Uzziel.
³The children of Amram:
Aaron, Moses and Miriam.
The sons of Aaron:
Nadab, Abihu, Eleazar and Ithamar.
⁴Eleazar was the father of Phinehas,
Phinehas the father of Abishua,
⁵Abishua the father of Bukki,
Bukki the father of Uzzi,
⁶Uzzi the father of Zerahiah,
Zerahiah the father of Meraioth,
⁷Meraioth the father of Amariah,
Amariah the father of Ahitub,
⁸Ahitub the father of Zadok,
Zadok the father of Ahimaaz,
⁹Ahimaaz the father of Azariah,
Azariah the father of Johanan,
¹⁰Johanan the father of Azariah (it was he who served as priest in the temple Solomon built in Jerusalem),
¹¹Azariah the father of Amariah,
Amariah the father of Ahitub,
¹²Ahitub the father of Zadok,
Zadok the father of Shallum,
¹³Shallum the father of Hilkiah,
Hilkiah the father of Azariah,
¹⁴Azariah the father of Seraiah,
and Seraiah the father of Jehozadak.

¹⁵Jehozadak was deported when the LORD sent Judah and Jerusalem into exile by the hand of Nebuchadnezzar.

¹⁶The sons of Levi:
Gershon,ᵃ Kohath and Merari.
¹⁷These are the names of the sons of Gershon:
Libni and Shimei.
¹⁸The sons of Kohath:
Amram, Izhar, Hebron and Uzziel.
¹⁹The sons of Merari:
Mahli and Mushi.
These are the clans of the Levites listed according to their fathers:
²⁰Of Gershon:
Libni his son, Jehath his son,
Zimmah his son, ²¹Joah his son,
Iddo his son, Zerah his son
and Jeatherai his son.
²²The descendants of Kohath:
Amminadab his son, Korah his son,
Assir his son, ²³Elkanah his son,
Ebiasaph his son, Assir his son,
²⁴Tahath his son, Uriel his son,
Uzziah his son and Shaul his son.
²⁵The descendants of Elkanah:
Amasai, Ahimoth,

ᵃ16 Hebrew *Gershom*, a variant of *Gershon*; also in verses 17, 20, 43, 62 and 71

²⁶Elkanah his son,ᵇ Zophai his son,
Nahath his son, ²⁷Eliab his son,
Jeroham his son, Elkanah his son
and Samuel his son.ᶜ

²⁸The sons of Samuel:
Joelᵈ the firstborn
and Abijah the second son.

²⁹The descendants of Merari:
Mahli, Libni his son,
Shimei his son, Uzzah his son,

³⁰Shimea his son, Haggiah his son
and Asaiah his son.

The Temple Musicians

³¹These are the men David put in charge of
the music in the house of the LORD after the
ark came to rest there. ³²They ministered
with music before the tabernacle, the Tent of
Meeting, until Solomon built the temple of
the LORD in Jerusalem. They performed their
duties according to the regulations laid down
for them.

³³Here are the men who served, together
with their sons:
From the Kohathites:
Heman, the musician,
the son of Joel, the son of Samuel,

³⁴the son of Elkanah, the son of Jeroham,
the son of Eliel, the son of Toah,

³⁵the son of Zuph, the son of Elkanah,
the son of Mahath, the son of Amasai,

³⁶the son of Elkanah, the son of Joel,
the son of Azariah, the son of Zephaniah,

³⁷the son of Tahath, the son of Assir,
the son of Ebiasaph, the son of Korah,

³⁸the son of Izhar, the son of Kohath,
the son of Levi, the son of Israel;

³⁹and Heman's associate Asaph, who
served at his right hand: Asaph son of
Berekiah, the son of Shimea,

⁴⁰the son of Michael, the son of
Baaseiah,ᵉ
the son of Malkijah, ⁴¹the son of
Ethni,
the son of Zerah, the son of Adaiah,

⁴²the son of Ethan, the son of Zimmah,
the son of Shimei, ⁴³the son of Jahath,
the son of Gershon, the son of Levi;

⁴⁴and from their associates, the Merarites,
at his left hand:
Ethan son of Kishi, the son of Abdi,
the son of Malluch, ⁴⁵the son of
Hashabiah,
the son of Amaziah, the son of Hilkiah,

⁴⁶the son of Amzi, the son of Bani,
the son of Shemer, ⁴⁷the son of Mahli,
the son of Mushi, the son of Merari,
the son of Levi.

⁴⁸Their fellow Levites were assigned to all
the other duties of the tabernacle, the house
of God. ⁴⁹But Aaron and his descendants
were the ones who presented offerings on the
altar of burnt offering and on the altar of
incense in connection with all that was done
in the Most Holy Place, making atonement
for Israel, in accordance with all that Moses
the servant of God had commanded.

⁵⁰These were the descendants of Aaron:
Eleazar his son, Phinehas his son,
Abishua his son, ⁵¹Bukki his son,
Uzzi his son, Zerahiah his son,

⁵²Meraioth his son, Amariah his son,
Ahitub his son, ⁵³Zadok his son
and Ahimaaz his son.

⁵⁴These were the locations of their settlements allotted as their territory (they were
assigned to the descendants of Aaron who
were from the Kohathite clan, because the
first lot was for them):

⁵⁵They were given Hebron in Judah
with its surrounding pasture-lands.

⁵⁶But the fields and villages around
the city were given to Caleb son of
Jephunneh.

⁵⁷So the descendants of Aaron were
given Hebron (a city of refuge), and
Libnah,ᶠ Jattir, Eshtemoa, ⁵⁸Hilen, Debir, ⁵⁹Ashan, Juttahᵍ and Beth Shemesh,
together with their pasture-lands. ⁶⁰And
from the tribe of Benjamin they were
given Gibeon,ʰ Geba, Alemeth and
Anathoth, together with their pasture-
lands.

These towns, which were distributed
among the Kohathite clans, were thirteen in all.

⁶¹The rest of Kohath's descendants were
allotted ten towns from the clans of half the
tribe of Manasseh.

⁶²The descendants of Gershon, clan by
clan, were allotted thirteen towns from the
tribes of Issachar, Asher and Naphtali, and
from the part of the tribe of Manasseh that is
in Bashan.

⁶³The descendants of Merari, clan by clan,
were allotted twelve towns from the tribes of
Reuben, Gad and Zebulun.

⁶⁴So the Israelites gave the Levites these
towns and their pasture-lands. ⁶⁵From the
tribes of Judah, Simeon and Benjamin they
allotted the previously named towns.

⁶⁶Some of the Kohathite clans were given
as their territory towns from the tribe of
Ephraim.

⁶⁷In the hill country of Ephraim they
were given Shechem (a city of refuge),
and Gezer,ⁱ ⁶⁸Jokmeam, Beth Horon,

ᵇ26 Some Hebrew manuscripts, Septuagint and Syriac; most Hebrew manuscripts *Ahimoth* ²⁶*and Elkanah. The sons of Elkanah:*
ᶜ27 Some Septuagint manuscripts (see also 1 Sam. 1:19, 20 and 1 Chron. 6:33, 34); Hebrew does not have *and Samuel his son.*
ᵈ28 Some Septuagint manuscripts and Syriac (see also 1 Sam. 8:2 and 1 Chron. 6:33); Hebrew does not have *Joel.*
ᵉ40 Most Hebrew manuscripts; some Hebrew manuscripts, one Septuagint manuscript and Syriac *Maaseiah*
ᶠ57 See Joshua 21:13; Hebrew *given the cities of refuge: Hebron, Libnah.*
ᵍ59 Syriac (see also Septuagint and Joshua 21:16); Hebrew does not have *Juttah.*
ʰ60 See Joshua 21:17; Hebrew does not have *Gibeon.*
ⁱ67 See Joshua 21:21; Hebrew *given the cities of refuge: Shechem, Gezer.*

⁶⁹Aijalon and Gath Rimmon, together with their pasture-lands.

⁷⁰And from half the tribe of Manasseh the Israelites gave Aner and Bileam, together with their pasture-lands, to the rest of the Kohathite clans.

⁷¹The Gershonites received the following:
From the clan of the half-tribe of Manasseh
they received Golan in Bashan and also Ashtaroth, together with their pasture-lands;
⁷²from the tribe of Issachar
they received Kedesh, Daberath, ⁷³Ramoth and Anem, together with their pasture-lands;
⁷⁴from the tribe of Asher
they received Mashal, Abdon, ⁷⁵Hukok and Rehob, together with their pasture-lands;
⁷⁶and from the tribe of Naphtali
they received Kedesh in Galilee, Hammon and Kiriathaim, together with their pasture-lands.

⁷⁷The Merarites (the rest of the Levites) received the following:
From the tribe of Zebulun
they received Jokneam, Kartah, Rimmono and Tabor, together with their pasture-lands;
⁷⁸from the tribe of Reuben across the Jordan east of Jericho
they received Bezer in the desert, Jahzah, ⁷⁹Kedemoth and Mephaath, together with their pasture-lands;
⁸⁰and from the tribe of Gad
they received Ramoth in Gilead, Mahanaim, ⁸¹Heshbon and Jazer, together with their pasture-lands.

Issachar

7 The sons of Issachar:
Tola, Puah, Jashub and Shimron— four in all.
²The sons of Tola:
Uzzi, Rephaiah, Jeriel, Jahmai, Ibsam and Samuel—heads of their families. During the reign of David, the descendants of Tola listed as fighting men in their genealogy numbered 22,600.
³The son of Uzzi:
Izrahiah.
The sons of Izrahiah:
Michael, Obadiah, Joel and Isshiah. All five of them were chiefs. ⁴According to their family genealogy, they had 36,000 men ready for battle, for they had many wives and children.
⁵The relatives who were fighting men belonging to all the clans of Issachar, as listed in their genealogy, were 87,000 in all.

Benjamin

⁶Three sons of Benjamin:
Bela, Beker and Jediael.

⁷The sons of Bela:
Ezbon, Uzzi, Uzziel, Jerimoth and Iri, heads of families—five in all. Their genealogical record listed 22,034 fighting men.
⁸The sons of Beker:
Zemirah, Joash, Eliezer, Elioenai, Omri, Jeremoth, Abijah, Anathoth and Alemeth. All these were the sons of Beker. ⁹Their genealogical record listed the heads of families and 20,200 fighting men.
¹⁰The son of Jediael:
Bilhan.
The sons of Bilhan:
Jeush, Benjamin, Ehud, Kenaanah, Zethan, Tarshish and Ahishahar. ¹¹All these sons of Jediael were heads of families. There were 17,200 fighting men ready to go out to war.
¹²The Shuppites and Huppites were the descendants of Ir, and the Hushites the descendants of Aher.

Naphtali

¹³The sons of Naphtali:
Jahziel, Guni, Jezer and Shillem[a] —the descendants of Bilhah.

Manasseh

¹⁴The descendants of Manasseh:
Asriel was his descendant through his Aramean concubine. She gave birth to Makir the father of Gilead. ¹⁵Makir took a wife from among the Huppites and Shuppites. His sister's name was Maacah.
Another descendant was named Zelophehad, who had only daughters.
¹⁶Makir's wife Maacah gave birth to a son and named him Peresh. His brother was named Sheresh, and his sons were Ulam and Rakem.
¹⁷The son of Ulam:
Bedan.
These were the sons of Gilead son of Makir, the son of Manasseh. ¹⁸His sister Hammoleketh gave birth to Ishhod, Abiezer and Mahlah.
¹⁹The sons of Shemida were:
Ahian, Shechem, Likhi and Aniam.

Ephraim

²⁰The descendants of Ephraim:
Shuthelah, Bered his son,
Tahath his son, Eleadah his son,
Tahath his son, ²¹Zabad his son
and Shuthelah his son.
Ezer and Elead were killed by the native-born men of Gath, when they went down to seize their livestock. ²²Their father Ephraim mourned for them many days, and his relatives came to comfort him. ²³Then he lay with his wife again, and she became pregnant and gave birth to a son. He named him Beriah,[b] because there had been misfortune in his family. ²⁴His daughter was

---

77 See Septuagint and Joshua 21:34; Hebrew does not have *Jokneam, Kartah.*
a13 Some Hebrew and Septuagint manuscripts (see also Gen. 46:24 and Num. 26:49); most Hebrew manuscripts *Shallum*   *b23 Beriah* sounds like the Hebrew for *misfortune.*

Sheerah, who built Lower and Upper
Beth Horon as well as Uzzen Sheerah.
25Rephah was his son, Resheph his son,[c]
Telah his son, Tahan his son,
26Ladan his son, Ammihud his son,
Elishama his son, 27Nun his son
and Joshua his son.

28Their lands and settlements included
Bethel and its surrounding villages, Naaran
to the east, Gezer and its villages to the west,
and Shechem and its villages all the way to
Ayyah and its villages. 29Along the borders of
Manasseh were Beth Shan, Taanach, Megiddo and Dor, together with their villages.
The descendants of Joseph son of Israel lived
in these towns.

Asher

30The sons of Asher:
Imnah, Ishvah, Ishvi and Beriah.
Their sister was Serah.
31The sons of Beriah:
Heber and Malkiel, who was the
father of Birzaith.
32Heber was the father of Japhlet, Shomer
and Hotham and of their sister Shua.
33The sons of Japhlet:
Pasach, Bimhal and Ashvath. These
were Japhlet's sons.
34The sons of Shomer:
Ahi, Rohgah,[d] Hubbah and Aram.
35The sons of his brother Helem:
Zophah, Imna, Shelesh and Amal.
36The sons of Zophah:
Suah, Harnepher, Shual, Beri, Imrah,
37Bezer, Hod, Shamma, Shilshah,
Ithran[e] and Beera.
38The sons of Jether:
Jephunneh, Pispah and Ara.
39The sons of Ulla:
Arah, Hanniel and Rizia.
40All these were descendants of Asher—
heads of families, choice men, brave warriors and outstanding leaders. The number
of men ready for battle, as listed in their
genealogy, was 26,000.

The Genealogy of Saul the Benjamite

8 Benjamin was the father of Bela his
firstborn,
Ashbel the second son, Aharah the
third,
2Nohah the fourth and Rapha the fifth.
3The sons of Bela were:
Addar, Gera, Abihud,[a] 4Abishua,
Naaman, Ahoah, 5Gera, Shephuphan
and Huram.
6These were the descendants of Ehud,
who were heads of families of those
living in Geba and were deported to
Manahath:
7Naaman, Ahijah and Gera, who deported them and who was the father of
Uzza and Ahihud.
8Sons were born to Shaharaim in Moab

after he had divorced his wives
Hushim and Baara. 9By his wife
Hodesh he had Jobab, Zibia, Mesha,
Malcam, 10Jeuz, Sakia and Mirmah.
These were his sons, heads of fami-
lies. 11By Hushim he had Abitub and
Elpaal.

12The sons of Elpaal:
Eber, Misham, Shemed (who built
Ono and Lod with its surrounding villages), 13and Beriah and Shema, who
were heads of families of those living
in Aijalon and who drove out the inhabitants of Gath.

14Ahio, Shashak, Jeremoth, 15Zebadiah,
Arad, Eder, 16Michael, Ishpah and
Joha were the sons of Beriah.
17Zebadiah, Meshullam, Hizki, Heber,
18Ishmerai, Izliah and Jobab were the
sons of Elpaal.
19Jakim, Zicri, Zabdi, 20Elienai, Zillethai,
Eliel, 21Adaiah, Beraiah and Shimrath
were the sons of Shimei.
22Ishpan, Eber, Eliel, 23Abdon, Zicri,
Hanan, 24Hananiah, Elam, Anthothi-
jah, 25Iphdeiah and Penuel were the
sons of Shashak.
26Shamsherai, Shehariah, Athaliah,
27Jaareshiah, Elijah and Zicri were the
sons of Jeroham.

28All these were heads of families, chiefs as
listed in their genealogy, and they lived in
Jerusalem.

29Jeiel[b] the father[c] of Gibeon lived in
Gibeon.
His wife's name was Maacah, 30and
his firstborn son was Abdon, followed
by Zur, Kish, Baal, Ner,[d] Nadab,
31Gedor, Ahio, Zeker 32and Mikloth, who was the father of Shimeah.
They too lived near their relatives in
Jerusalem.
33Ner was the father of Kish, Kish the
father of Saul, and Saul the father of
Jonathan, Malki-Shua, Abinadab and
Esh-Baal.[e]
34The son of Jonathan:
Merib-Baal,[f] who was the father of
Micah.
35The sons of Micah:
Pithon, Melech, Tarea and Ahaz.
36Ahaz was the father of Jehoaddah,
Jehoaddah was the father of Alemeth,
Azmaveth and Zimri, and Zimri was
the father of Moza. 37Moza was the
father of Binea; Raphah was his son,
Eleasah his son and Azel his son.
38Azel had six sons, and these were their
names:
Azrikam, Bokeru, Ishmael, Sheariah,
Obadiah and Hanan. All these were
the sons of Azel.
39The sons of his brother Eshek:
Ulam his firstborn, Jeush the second

---

c25 Some Septuagint manuscripts; Hebrew does not have *his son.*   d34 Or *of his brother Shomer: Rohgah*
e37 Possibly a variant of *Jether*   a3 Or *Gera the father of Ehud*
b29 Some Septuagint manuscripts (see also 1 Chron. 9:35); Hebrew does not have *Jeiel.*
c29 *Father* may mean *civic leader* or *military leader.*
d30 Some Septuagint manuscripts (see also 1 Chron. 9:36); Hebrew does not have *Ner.*
e33 Also known as *Ish-Bosheth*   f34 Also known as *Mephibosheth*

son and Eliphelet the third. ⁴⁰The sons of Ulam were brave warriors who could handle the bow. They had many sons and grandsons—150 in all.

All these were descendants of Benjamin.

9 All Israel was listed in the genealogies in the book of the kings of Israel.

The People in Jerusalem

The people of Judah were taken captive to Babylon because of their unfaithfulness. ²Now the first to resettle on their own property in their own towns were some Israelites, priests, Levites and temple servants.

³Those from Judah, from Benjamin, and from Ephraim and Manasseh who lived in Jerusalem were:

⁴Uthai son of Ammihud, the son of Omri, the son of Imri, the son of Bani, a descendant of Perez son of Judah.

⁵Of the Shilonites:

Asaiah the firstborn and his sons.

⁶Of the Zerahites:

Jeuel.

The people from Judah numbered 690.

⁷Of the Benjamites:

Sallu son of Meshullam, the son of Hodaviah, the son of Hassenuah;

⁸Ibneiah son of Jeroham; Elah son of Uzzi, the son of Micri; and Meshullam son of Shephatiah, the son of Reuel, the son of Ibnijah.

⁹The people from Benjamin, as listed in their genealogy, numbered 956. All these men were heads of their families.

¹⁰Of the priests:

Jedaiah; Jehoiarib; Jakin;

¹¹Azariah son of Hilkiah, the son of Meshullam, the son of Zadok, the son of Meraioth, the son of Ahitub, the official in charge of the house of God;

¹²Adaiah son of Jeroham, the son of Pashhur, the son of Malkijah; and Maasai son of Adiel, the son of Jahzerah, the son of Meshullam, the son of Meshillemith, the son of Immer.

¹³The priests, who were heads of families, numbered 1,760. They were able men, responsible for ministering in the house of God.

¹⁴Of the Levites:

Shemaiah son of Hasshub, the son of Azrikam, the son of Hashabiah, a Merarite; ¹⁵Bakbakkar, Heresh, Galal and Mattaniah son of Mica, the son of Zicri, the son of Asaph; ¹⁶Obadiah son of Shemaiah, the son of Galal, the son of Jeduthun; and Berekiah son of Asa, the son of Elkanah, who lived in the villages of the Netophathites.

¹⁷The gatekeepers:

Shallum, Akkub, Talmon, Ahiman and their brothers, Shallum their chief ¹⁸being stationed at the King's Gate on the east, up to the present time.

These were the gatekeepers belonging to the camp of the Levites. ¹⁹Shallum son of Kore, the son of Ebiasaph, the son of Korah, and his fellow gatekeepers from his family (the Korahites) were responsible for guarding the thresholds of the Tent*a* just as their fathers had been responsible for guarding the entrance to the dwelling of the LORD. ²⁰In earlier times Phinehas son of Eleazar was in charge of the gatekeepers, and the LORD was with him.

²¹Zechariah son of Meshelemiah was the gatekeeper at the entrance to the Tent of Meeting.

²²Altogether, those chosen to be gatekeepers at the thresholds numbered 212. They were registered by genealogy in their villages. The gatekeepers had been assigned to their positions of trust by David and Samuel the seer. ²³They and their descendants were in charge of guarding the gates of the house of the LORD—the house called the Tent. ²⁴The gatekeepers were on the four sides: east, west, north and south. ²⁵Their brothers in their villages had to come from time to time and share their duties for seven-day periods. ²⁶But the four principal gatekeepers, who were Levites, were entrusted with the responsibility for the rooms and treasuries in the house of God. ²⁷They would spend the night stationed round the house of God, because they had to guard it; and they had charge of the key for opening it each morning.

²⁸Some of them were in charge of the articles used in the temple service; they counted them when they were brought in and when they were taken out. ²⁹Others were assigned to take care of the furnishings and all the other articles of the sanctuary, as well as the flour and wine, and the oil, incense and spices. ³⁰But some of the priests took care of mixing the spices. ³¹A Levite named Mattithiah, the firstborn son of Shallum the Korahite, was entrusted with the responsibility for baking the offering bread. ³²Some of their Kohathite brothers were in charge of preparing for every Sabbath the bread set out on the table.

³³Those who were musicians, heads of Levite families, stayed in the rooms of the temple and were exempt from other duties because they were responsible for the work day and night.

³⁴All these were heads of Levite families, chiefs as listed in their genealogy, and they lived in Jerusalem.

The Genealogy of Saul

³⁵Jeiel the father*b* of Gibeon lived in Gibeon.

His wife's name was Maacah, ³⁶and his firstborn son was Abdon, followed by Zur, Kish, Baal, Ner, Nadab, ³⁷Gedor, Ahio, Zechariah and Mikloth. ³⁸Mikloth was the father of

---

a19 That is, the temple; also in verses 21 and 23   *b35 Father may mean civic leader or military leader.*

Shimeam. They too lived near their relatives in Jerusalem.

39Ner was the father of Kish, Kish the father of Saul, and Saul the father of Jonathan, Malki-Shua, Abinadab and Esh-Baal.[c]

40The son of Jonathan:

Merib-Baal,[d] who was the father of Micah.

41The sons of Micah:

Pithon, Melech, Tahrea and Ahaz.[e]

42Ahaz was the father of Jadah, Jadah[f] was the father of Alemeth, Azmaveth and Zimri, and Zimri was the father of Moza. 43Moza was the father of Binea; Rephaiah was his son, Eleasah his son and Azel his son.

44Azel had six sons, and these were their names:

Azrikam, Bokeru, Ishmael, Sheariah, Obadiah and Hanan. These were the sons of Azel.

Saul Takes His Life

10 Now the Philistines fought against Israel; the Israelites fled before them, and many fell slain on Mount Gilboa. 2The Philistines pressed hard after Saul and his sons, and they killed his sons Jonathan, Abinadab and Malki-Shua. 3The fighting grew fierce around Saul, and when the archers overtook him, they wounded him.

4Saul said to his armour-bearer, "Draw your sword and run me through, or these uncircumcised fellows will come and abuse me."

But his armour-bearer was terrified and would not do it; so Saul took his own sword and fell on it. 5When the armour-bearer saw that Saul was dead, he too fell on his sword and died. 6So Saul and his three sons died, and all his house died together.

7When all the Israelites in the valley saw that the army had fled and that Saul and his sons had died, they abandoned their towns and fled. And the Philistines came and occupied them.

8The next day, when the Philistines came to strip the dead, they found Saul and his sons fallen on Mount Gilboa. 9They stripped him and took his head and his armour, and sent messengers throughout the land of the Philistines to proclaim the news among their idols and their people. 10They put his armour in the temple of their gods and hung up his head in the temple of Dagon.

11When all the inhabitants of Jabesh Gilead heard of everything the Philistines had done to Saul, 12all their valiant men went and took the bodies of Saul and his sons and brought them to Jabesh. Then they buried their bones under the great tree in Jabesh, and they fasted seven days.

13Saul died because he was unfaithful to the LORD; he did not keep the word of the LORD, and even consulted a medium for guidance, 14and did not enquire of the LORD. So the LORD put him to death and turned the kingdom over to David son of Jesse.

David Becomes King Over Israel

11 All Israel came together to David at Hebron and said, "We are your own flesh and blood. 2In the past, even while Saul was king, you were the one who led Israel on their military campaigns. And the LORD your God said to you, 'You will shepherd my people Israel, and you will become their ruler.'"

3When all the elders of Israel had come to King David at Hebron, he made a compact with them at Hebron before the LORD, and they anointed David king over Israel, as the LORD had promised through Samuel.

David Conquers Jerusalem

4David and all the Israelites marched to Jerusalem (that is, Jebus). The Jebusites who lived there 5said to David, "You will not get in here." Nevertheless, David captured the fortress of Zion, the City of David.

6David had said, "Whoever leads the attack on the Jebusites will become commander-in-chief." Joab son of Zeruiah went up first, and so he received the command.

7David then took up residence in the fortress, and so it was called the City of David. 8He built up the city around it, from the supporting terraces[a] to the surrounding wall, while Joab restored the rest of the city. 9And David became more and more powerful, because the LORD Almighty was with him.

David's Mighty Men

10These were the chiefs of David's mighty men—they, together with all Israel, gave his kingship strong support to extend it over the whole land, as the LORD had promised— 11this is the list of David's mighty men:

Jashobeam,[b] a Hacmonite, was chief of the officers;[c] he raised his spear against three hundred men, whom he killed in one encounter.

12Next to him was Eleazar son of Dodai the Ahohite, one of the three mighty men. 13He was with David at Pas Dammim when the Philistines gathered there for battle. At a place where there was a field full of barley, the troops fled from the Philistines. 14But they took their stand in the middle of the field. They defended it and struck the Philistines down, and the LORD brought about a great victory.

15Three of the thirty chiefs came down to David to the rock at the cave of Adullam, while a band of Philistines was encamped in the Valley of Rephaim. 16At that time David was in the stronghold, and the Philistine garrison was at Bethlehem. 17David longed for water and said, "Oh, that someone would get me a drink of water from the well near the gate of Bethlehem!" 18So the Three broke

---

[c]39 Also known as *Ish-Bosheth*   [d]40 Also known as *Mephibosheth*
[e]41 Vulgate and Syriac (see also Septuagint and 1 Chron. 8:35); Hebrew does not have *and Ahaz*.
[f]42 Some Hebrew manuscripts and Septuagint (see also 1 Chron. 8:36); most Hebrew manuscripts *Jarah, Jarah*
[a]8 Or *the Millo*   [b]11 Possibly a variant of *Jashob-Baal*
[c]11 Or *Thirty*; some Septuagint manuscripts *Three* (see also 2 Sam. 23:8)

through the Philistine lines, drew water from the well near the gate of Bethlehem and carried it back to David. But he refused to drink it; instead, he poured it out before the LORD. [19]"God forbid that I should do this!" he said. "Should I drink the blood of these men who went at the risk of their lives?" Because they risked their lives to bring it back, David would not drink it.

Such were the exploits of the three mighty men.

[20]Abishai the brother of Joab was chief of the Three. He raised his spear against three hundred men, whom he killed, and so he became as famous as the Three. [21]He was doubly honoured above the Three and became their commander, even though he was not included among them.

[22]Benaiah son of Jehoiada was a valiant fighter from Kabzeel, who performed great exploits. He struck down two of Moab's best men. He also went down into a pit on a snowy day and killed a lion. [23]And he struck down an Egyptian who was seven and a half feet[d] tall. Although the Egyptian had a spear like a weaver's rod in his hand, Benaiah went against him with a club. He snatched the spear from the Egyptian's hand and killed him with his own spear. [24]Such were the exploits of Benaiah son of Jehoiada; he too was as famous as the three mighty men. [25]He was held in greater honour than any of the Thirty, but he was not included among the Three. And David put him in charge of his bodyguard.

[26]The mighty men were:
Asahel the brother of Joab,
Elhanan son of Dodo from Bethlehem,
[27]Shammoth the Harorite,
Helez the Pelonite,
[28]Ira son of Ikkesh from Tekoa,
Abiezer from Anathoth,
[29]Sibbecai the Hushathite,
Ilai the Ahohite,
[30]Maharai the Netophathite,
Heled son of Baanah the Netophathite,
[31]Ithai son of Ribai from Gibeah in Benjamin,
Benaiah the Pirathonite,
[32]Hurai from the ravines of Gaash,
Abiel the Arbathite,
[33]Azmaveth the Baharumite,
Eliahba the Shaalbonite,
[34]the sons of Hashem the Gizonite,
Jonathan son of Shagee the Hararite,
[35]Ahiam son of Sacar the Hararite,
Eliphal son of Ur,
[36]Hepher the Mekerathite,
Ahijah the Pelonite,
[37]Hezro the Carmelite,
Naarai son of Ezbai,
[38]Joel the brother of Nathan,
Mibhar son of Hagri,
[39]Zelek the Ammonite,
Naharai the Berothite, the armour-bearer of Joab son of Zeruiah,

[40]Ira the Ithrite,
Gareb the Ithrite,
[41]Uriah the Hittite,
Zabad son of Ahlai,
[42]Adina son of Shiza the Reubenite, who was chief of the Reubenites, and the thirty with him,
[43]Hanan son of Maacah,
Joshaphat the Mithnite,
[44]Uzzia the Ashterathite,
Shama and Jeiel the sons of Hotham the Aroerite,
[45]Jediael son of Shimri,
his brother Joha the Tizite,
[46]Eliel the Mahavite,
Jeribai and Joshaviah the sons of Elnaam,
Ithmah the Moabite,
[47]Eliel, Obed and Jaasiel the Mezobaite.

Warriors Join David

12 These were the men who came to David at Ziklag, while he was banished from the presence of Saul son of Kish (they were among the warriors who helped him in battle; [2]they were armed with bows and were able to shoot arrows or to sling stones right-handed or left-handed; they were kinsmen of Saul from the tribe of Benjamin):

[3]Ahiezer their chief and Joash the sons of Shemaah the Gibeathite; Jeziel and Pelet the sons of Azmaveth; Beracah, Jehu the Anathothite, [4]and Ishmaiah the Gibeonite, a mighty man among the Thirty, who was a leader of the Thirty; Jeremiah, Jahaziel, Johanan, Jozabad the Gederathite, [5]Eluzai, Jerimoth, Bealiah, Shemariah and Shephatiah the Haruphite; [6]Elkanah, Isshiah, Azarel, Joezer and Jashobeam the Korahites; [7]and Joelah and Zebadiah the sons of Jeroham from Gedor.

[8]Some Gadites defected to David at his stronghold in the desert. They were brave warriors, ready for battle and able to handle the shield and spear. Their faces were the faces of lions, and they were as swift as gazelles in the mountains.
[9]Ezer was the chief,
Obadiah the second in command, Eliab the third,
[10]Mishmannah the fourth, Jeremiah the fifth,
[11]Attai the sixth, Eliel the seventh,
[12]Johanan the eighth, Elzabad the ninth,
[13]Jeremiah the tenth and Macbannai the eleventh.

[14]These Gadites were army commanders; the least was a match for a hundred, and the greatest for a thousand. [15]It was they who crossed the Jordan in the first month when it was overflowing all its banks, and they put to flight everyone living in the valleys, to the east and to the west.
[16]Other Benjamites and some men from

Judah also came to David in his stronghold. ¹⁷David went out to meet them and said to them, "If you have come to me in peace, to help me, I am ready to have you unite with me. But if you have come to betray me to my enemies when my hands are free from violence, may the God of our fathers see it and judge you."

¹⁸Then the Spirit came upon Amasai, chief of the Thirty, and he said:

"We are yours, O David!
We are with you, O son of Jesse!
Success, success to you,
and success to those who help you,
for your God will help you."

So David received them and made them leaders of his raiding bands.

¹⁹Some of the men of Manasseh defected to David when he went with the Philistines to fight against Saul. (He and his men did not help the Philistines because, after consultation, their rulers sent him away. They said, "It will cost us our heads if he deserts to his master Saul.") ²⁰When David went to Ziklag, these were the men of Manasseh who defected to him: Adnah, Jozabad, Jediael, Michael, Jozabad, Elihu and Zillethai, leaders of units of a thousand in Manasseh. ²¹They helped David against raiding bands, for all of them were brave warriors, and they were commanders in his army. ²²Day after day men came to help David, until he had a great army, like the army of God.ᵃ

Others Join David at Hebron

²³These are the numbers of the men armed for battle who came to David at Hebron to turn Saul's kingdom over to him, as the LORD had said:

²⁴men of Judah, carrying shield and spear —6,800 armed for battle;
²⁵men of Simeon, warriors ready for battle —7,100;
²⁶men of Levi—4,600, ²⁷including Jehoiada, leader of the family of Aaron with 3,700 men, ²⁸and Zadok, a brave young warrior, with 22 officers from his family;
²⁹men of Benjamin, Saul's kinsmen— 3,000, most of whom had remained loyal to Saul's house until then;
³⁰men of Ephraim, brave warriors, famous in their own clans—20,800;
³¹men of half the tribe of Manasseh, designated by name to come and make David king—18,000;
³²men of Issachar, who understood the times and knew what Israel should do—200 chiefs, with all their relatives under their command;
³³men of Zebulun, experienced soldiers prepared for battle with every type of weapon, to help David with undivided loyalty—50,000;
³⁴men of Naphtali—1,000 officers, together with 37,000 men carrying shields and spears;
³⁵men of Dan, ready for battle—28,600;
³⁶men of Asher, experienced soldiers prepared for battle—40,000;
³⁷and from east of the Jordan, men of Reuben, Gad, and the half-tribe of Manasseh, armed with every type of weapon—120,000.

³⁸All these were fighting men who volunteered to serve in the ranks. They came to Hebron fully determined to make David king over all Israel. All the rest of the Israelites were also of one mind to make David king. ³⁹The men spent three days there with David, eating and drinking, for their families had supplied provisions for them. ⁴⁰Also, their neighbours from as far away as Issachar, Zebulun and Naphtali came bringing food on donkeys, camels, mules and oxen. There were plentiful supplies of flour, fig cakes, raisin cakes, wine, oil, cattle and sheep, for there was joy in Israel.

Bringing Back the Ark

13 David conferred with each of his officers, the commanders of thousands and commanders of hundreds. ²He then said to the whole assembly of Israel, "If it seems good to you and if it is the will of the LORD our God, let us send word far and wide to the rest of our brothers throughout the territories of Israel, and also to the priests and Levites who are with them in their towns and pasture-lands, to come and join us. ³Let us bring the ark of our God back to us, for we did not enquire ofᵃ itᵇ during the reign of Saul." ⁴The whole assembly agreed to do this, because it seemed right to all the people.

⁵So David assembled all the Israelites, from the Shihor River in Egypt to Leboᶜ Hamath, to bring the ark of God from Kiriath Jearim. ⁶David and all the Israelites with him went to Baalah of Judah (Kiriath Jearim) to bring up from there the ark of God the LORD, who is enthroned between the cherubim— the ark that is called by the Name.

⁷They moved the ark of God from Abinadab's house on a new cart, with Uzzah and Ahio guiding it. ⁸David and all the Israelites were celebrating with all their might before God, with songs and with harps, lyres, tambourines, cymbals and trumpets.

⁹When they came to the threshing-floor of Kidon, Uzzah reached out his hand to steady the ark, because the oxen stumbled. ¹⁰The LORD's anger burned against Uzzah, and he struck him down because he had put his hand on the ark. So he died there before God.

¹¹Then David was angry because the LORD's wrath had broken out against Uzzah, and to this day that place is called Perez Uzzah.ᵈ

¹²David was afraid of God that day and asked, "How can I ever bring the ark of God to me?" ¹³He did not take the ark to be with him in the City of David. Instead, he took it

---

ᵃ22 Or a great and mighty army.   ᵃ3 Or we neglected   ᵇ3 Or him   ᶜ5 Or to the entrance to
ᵈ11 Perez Uzzah means outbreak against Uzzah.

aside to the house of Obed-Edom the Gittite. ¹⁴The ark of God remained with the family of Obed-Edom in his house for three months, and the Lᴏʀᴅ blessed his household and everything he had.

David's House and Family

14 Now Hiram king of Tyre sent messengers to David, along with cedar logs, stonemasons and carpenters to build a palace for him. ²And David knew that the Lᴏʀᴅ had established him as king over Israel and that his kingdom had been highly exalted for the sake of his people Israel.

³In Jerusalem David took more wives and became the father of more sons and daughters. ⁴These are the names of the children born to him there: Shammua, Shobab, Nathan, Solomon, ⁵Ibhar, Elishua, Elpelet, ⁶Nogah, Nepheg, Japhia, ⁷Elishama, Beeliada*ᵃ* and Eliphelet.

David Defeats the Philistines

⁸When the Philistines heard that David had been anointed king over all Israel, they went up in full force to search for him, but David heard about it and went out to meet them. ⁹Now the Philistines had come and raided the Valley of Rephaim; ¹⁰so David enquired of God: "Shall I go and attack the Philistines? Will you hand them over to me?"

The Lᴏʀᴅ answered him, "Go, I will hand them over to you."

¹¹So David and his men went up to Baal Perazim, and there he defeated them. He said, "As waters break out, God has broken out against my enemies by my hand." So that place was called Baal Perazim.*ᵇ* ¹²The Philistines had abandoned their gods there, and David gave orders to burn them in the fire.

¹³Once more the Philistines raided the valley; ¹⁴so David enquired of God again, and God answered him, "Do not go straight up, but circle round them and attack them in front of the balsam trees. ¹⁵As soon as you hear the sound of marching in the tops of the balsam trees, move out to battle, because that will mean God has gone out in front of you to strike the Philistine army." ¹⁶So David did as God commanded him, and they struck down the Philistine army, all the way from Gibeon to Gezer.

¹⁷So David's fame spread throughout every land, and the Lᴏʀᴅ made all the nations fear him.

The Ark Brought to Jerusalem

15 After David had constructed buildings for himself in the City of David, he prepared a place for the ark of God and pitched a tent for it. ²Then David said, "No-one but the Levites may carry the ark of God, because the Lᴏʀᴅ chose them to carry the ark of the Lᴏʀᴅ and to minister before him for ever."

³David assembled all Israel in Jerusalem to bring up the ark of the Lᴏʀᴅ to the place he had prepared for it. ⁴He called together the descendants of Aaron and the Levites:

⁵From the descendants of Kohath,
  Uriel the leader and 120 relatives;
⁶from the descendants of Merari,
  Asaiah the leader and 220 relatives;
⁷from the descendants of Gershon,*ᵃ*
  Joel the leader and 130 relatives;
⁸from the descendants of Elizaphan,
  Shemaiah the leader and 200 relatives;
⁹from the descendants of Hebron,
  Eliel the leader and 80 relatives;
¹⁰from the descendants of Uzziel,
  Amminadab the leader and 112 relatives.

¹¹Then David summoned Zadok and Abiathar the priests, and Uriel, Asaiah, Joel, Shemaiah, Eliel and Amminadab the Levites. ¹²He said to them, "You are the heads of the Levitical families; you and your fellow Levites are to consecrate yourselves and bring up the ark of the Lᴏʀᴅ, the God of Israel, to the place I have prepared for it. ¹³It was because you, the Levites, did not bring it up the first time that the Lᴏʀᴅ our God broke out in anger against us. We did not enquire of him about how to do it in the prescribed way." ¹⁴So the priests and Levites consecrated themselves in order to bring up the ark of the Lᴏʀᴅ, the God of Israel. ¹⁵And the Levites carried the ark of God with the poles on their shoulders, as Moses had commanded in accordance with the word of the Lᴏʀᴅ.

¹⁶David told the leaders of the Levites to appoint their brothers as singers to sing joyful songs, accompanied by musical instruments: lyres, harps and cymbals.

¹⁷So the Levites appointed Heman son of Joel; from his brothers, Asaph son of Berekiah; and from their brothers the Merarites, Ethan son of Kushaiah; ¹⁸and with them their brothers next in rank: Zechariah,*ᵇ* Jaaziel, Shemiramoth, Jehiel, Unni, Eliab, Benaiah, Maaseiah, Mattithiah, Eliphelehu, Mikneiah, Obed-Edom and Jeiel,*ᶜ* the gatekeepers. ¹⁹The musicians Heman, Asaph and Ethan were to sound the bronze cymbals; ²⁰Zechariah, Aziel, Shemiramoth, Jehiel, Unni, Eliab, Maaseiah and Benaiah were to play the lyres according to *alamoth*,*ᵈ* ²¹and Mattithiah, Eliphelehu, Mikneiah, Obed-Edom, Jeiel and Azariah were to play the harps, directing according to *sheminith*.*ᵉ* ²²Kenaniah the head Levite was in charge of the singing; that was his responsibility because he was skilful at it.

²³Berekiah and Elkanah were to be doorkeepers for the ark. ²⁴Shebaniah, Joshaphat, Nethanel, Amasai, Zechariah, Benaiah and Eliezer the priests were to blow trumpets before the ark of God. Obed-Edom and

---

*ᵃ7 A variant of *Eliada*   *ᵇ11 *Baal Perazim* means *the lord who breaks out.*
*ᵃ7 Hebrew *Gershom*, a variant of *Gershon*
*ᵇ18 Three Hebrew manuscripts and most Septuagint manuscripts (see also verse 20 and 1 Chron. 16:5); most Hebrew manuscripts *Zechariah son and* or *Zechariah, Ben and*
*ᶜ18 Hebrew; Septuagint (see also verse 21) *Jeiel and Azaziah*   *ᵈ20 Probably a musical term
*ᵉ21 Probably a musical term

Jehiah were also to be doorkeepers for the ark.

25So David and the elders of Israel and the commanders of units of a thousand went to bring up the ark of the covenant of the LORD from the house of Obed-Edom, with rejoicing. 26Because God had helped the Levites who were carrying the ark of the covenant of the LORD, seven bulls and seven rams were sacrificed. 27Now David was clothed in a robe of fine linen, as were all the Levites who were carrying the ark, and as were the singers, and Kenaniah, who was in charge of the singing of the choirs. David also wore a linen ephod. 28So all Israel brought up the ark of the covenant of the LORD with shouts, with the sounding of rams' horns and trumpets, and of cymbals, and the playing of lyres and harps.

29As the ark of the covenant of the LORD was entering the City of David, Michal daughter of Saul watched from a window. And when she saw King David dancing and celebrating, she despised him in her heart.

16 They brought the ark of God and set it inside the tent that David had pitched for it, and they presented burnt offerings and fellowship offerings*a* before God. 2After David had finished sacrificing the burnt offerings and fellowship offerings, he blessed the people in the name of the LORD. 3Then he gave a loaf of bread, a cake of dates and a cake of raisins to each Israelite man and woman.

4He appointed some of the Levites to minister before the ark of the LORD, to make petition, to give thanks, and to praise the LORD, the God of Israel: 5Asaph was the chief, Zechariah second, then Jeiel, Shemiramoth, Jehiel, Mattithiah, Eliab, Benaiah, Obed-Edom and Jeiel. They were to play the lyres and harps, Asaph was to sound the cymbals, 6and Benaiah and Jahaziel the priests were to blow the trumpets regularly before the ark of the covenant of God.

David's Psalm of Thanks

7That day David first committed to Asaph and his associates this psalm of thanks to the LORD:

8Give thanks to the LORD, call on his name;
    make known among the nations what he
      has done.
9Sing to him, sing praise to him;
    tell of all his wonderful acts.
10Glory in his holy name;
    let the hearts of those who seek the
      LORD rejoice.
11Look to the LORD and his strength;
    seek his face always.
12Remember the wonders he has done,
    his miracles, and the judgments he
      pronounced,
13O descendants of Israel his servant,
    O sons of Jacob, his chosen ones.

14He is the LORD our God;
    his judgments are in all the earth.
15He remembers*b* his covenant for ever,
    the word he commanded, for a thousand
      generations,
16the covenant he made with Abraham,
    the oath he swore to Isaac.
17He confirmed it to Jacob as a decree,
    to Israel as an everlasting covenant:
18"To you I will give the land of Canaan
    as the portion you will inherit."

19When they were but few in number,
    few indeed, and strangers in it,
20they*c* wandered from nation to nation,
    from one kingdom to another.
21He allowed no man to oppress them;
    for their sake he rebuked kings:
22"Do not touch my anointed ones;
    do my prophets no harm."

23Sing to the LORD, all the earth;
    proclaim his salvation day after day.
24Declare his glory among the nations,
    his marvellous deeds among all peoples.
25For great is the LORD and most worthy of
      praise;
    he is to be feared above all gods.
26For all the gods of the nations are idols,
    but the LORD made the heavens.
27Splendour and majesty are before him;
    strength and joy in his dwelling-place.
28Ascribe to the LORD, O families of nations,
    ascribe to the LORD glory and strength,
29   ascribe to the LORD the glory due to his
      name.
Bring an offering and come before him;
    worship the LORD in the splendour of
      his*d* holiness.
30Tremble before him, all the earth!
    The world is firmly established; it
      cannot be moved.
31Let the heavens rejoice, let the earth be
      glad;
    let them say among the nations, "The
      LORD reigns!"
32Let the sea resound, and all that is in it;
    let the fields be jubilant, and everything
      in them!
33Then the trees of the forest will sing,
    they will sing for joy before the LORD,
    for he comes to judge the earth.

34Give thanks to the LORD, for he is good;
    his love endures for ever.
35Cry out, "Save us, O God our Saviour;
    gather us and deliver us from the
      nations,
that we may give thanks to your holy
      name,
    that we may glory in your praise."
36Praise be to the LORD, the God of Israel,
    from everlasting to everlasting.

Then all the people said "Amen" and "Praise the LORD."

---

a1 Traditionally *peace offerings*; also in verse 2
b15 Some Septuagint manuscripts (see also Psalm 105:8); Hebrew *Remember*
c18–20 One Hebrew manuscript, Septuagint and Vulgate (see also Psalm 105:12); most Hebrew manuscripts *inherit,* / *19* *though you are but few in number,* / *few indeed, and strangers in it."* / *20* *They*
d29 Or LORD *with the splendour of*

1 CHRONICLES 16:23–33
'Ascribe to the LORD the glory due his name. Bring an offering and come before him; worship the LORD in the splendour of his holiness' (v. 29).

AGAIN, WE LINK OURSELVES with the world Church. Across the world today, new Christians and old Christians join in expressions of worship to the God and Father of our Lord Jesus Christ, who is also the God and Father of us all (John 1:12). Some Christians worship freely, others are oppressed either by political or religious systems, or by both. Some are in desperate need materially, others are prosperous. Some are members of enormous congregations, some are not. Some, through force of circumstances, worship in isolation. Whatever our circumstances God, through his Spirit, who overwhelms all barriers of geography, race, culture, tradition, class or circumstance in order to fulfil his role, binds us all together in Christ Jesus (Eph. 4:3–6).

We are to ascribe to God the glory due to him. He is creator (v. 26), but he is essentially a God for people, faithfully maintaining his convenant (v. 15), performing marvellous deeds among his people (v. 24), and, above all, he is a God of love (v. 34). We give him all praise and glory even though our words are inadequate.

You are worthy, our Lord and God, to receive glory and honour and power, for you created all things, and by your will they were created and have their being. (Rev. 4:11)

Lord, we bring to you an offering. We offer ourselves as a living sacrifice, as a spiritual act of worship, which we believe is pleasing to you. (Rom. 12:1)

Lord, how I love you,
    You have done so much for me . . .
So very, very much for me

(*Keith Banks*)

Grant, Lord, today, that we your people might offer you that worship which is totally acceptable to you. Amen.

→356

1 CHRONICLES 29:10–16

'Yours, O LORD, is the greatness and the power and the glory and the majesty and the splendour, for everything in heaven and earth is yours. Yours, O LORD is the kingdom' (v. 11).

FIRST CHRONICLES describes the charge David gave to his son, Solomon, when it was clear Solomon would soon succeed him as king.

What David handed over was not his own. It was God's. We have no title to anything here on earth. We are 'strangers . . . and sojourners'. The power, the glory, the kingdom itself are all God's. Our stewardship is only temporary.

This theme is taken up in the best known of all prayers, the Lord's Prayer. It, too, makes clear that we have no power of our own. All is God's. The power, the glory and the kingdom all belong to him.

Yet every generation tries to leave something for the next. Our purpose is not simply to 'eat drink and be merry, for tomorrow we die'. We are motivated to leave something better for our children, and their children, with varying degrees of success. Some generations simply seem to leave a legacy of conflict. It is hardly ever possible to look forward and say we *know* our children will find this world a better place than we did. Yet for so many that is so. The labour of earlier generations, their questioning and explorations, their sheer determination and refusal to be beaten, have left resources for us.

The more clearly we recognize that what we own is not ours, the more our children will benefit.

[37]David left Asaph and his associates before the ark of the covenant of the LORD to minister there regularly, according to each day's requirements. [38]He also left Obed-Edom and his sixty-eight associates to minister with them. Obed-Edom son of Jeduthun, and also Hosah, were gatekeepers.

[39]David left Zadok the priest and his fellow priests before the tabernacle of the LORD at the high place in Gibeon [40]to present burnt offerings to the LORD on the altar of burnt offering regularly, morning and evening, in accordance with everything written in the Law of the LORD, which he had given Israel. [41]With them were Heman and Jeduthun and the rest of those chosen and designated by name to give thanks to the LORD, "for his love endures for ever." [42]Heman and Jeduthun were responsible for the sounding of the trumpets and cymbals and for the playing of the other instruments for sacred song. The sons of Jeduthun were stationed at the gate.

[43]Then all the people left, each for his own home, and David returned home to bless his family.

God's Promise to David

17 After David was settled in his palace, he said to Nathan the prophet, "Here I am, living in a palace of cedar, while the ark of the covenant of the LORD is under a tent."

[2]Nathan replied to David, "Whatever you have in mind, do it, for God is with you."

[3]That night the word of God came to Nathan, saying:

[4]"Go and tell my servant David, 'This is what the LORD says: You are not the one to build me a house to dwell in. [5]I have not dwelt in a house from the day I brought Israel up out of Egypt to this day. I have moved from one tent site to another, from one dwelling-place to another. [6]Wherever I have moved with all the Israelites, did I ever say to any of their leaders[a] whom I commanded to shepherd my people, "Why have you not built me a house of cedar?" '

[7]"Now then, tell my servant David, 'This is what the LORD Almighty says: I took you from the pasture and from following the flock, to be ruler over my people Israel. [8]I have been with you wherever you have gone, and I have cut off all your enemies from before you. Now I will make your name like the names of the greatest men of the earth. [9]And I will provide a place for my people Israel and will plant them so that they can have a home of their own and no longer be disturbed. Wicked people will not oppress them any more, as they did at the beginning [10]and have done ever since the time I appointed leaders over my people Israel. I will also subdue all your enemies.

"'I declare to you that the LORD will build a house for you: [11]When your days are over and you go to be with your fathers, I will raise up your offspring to succeed you, one of your own sons, and I will establish his kingdom. [12]He is the one who will build a house for me, and I will establish his throne for ever. [13]I will be his father, and he will be my son. I will never take my love away from him, as I took it away from your predecessor. [14]I will set him over my house and my kingdom for ever; his throne will be established for ever.' "

[15]Nathan reported to David all the words of this entire revelation.

David's Prayer

[16]Then King David went in and sat before the LORD, and he said:

"Who am I, O LORD God, and what is my family, that you have brought me this far? [17]And as if this were not enough in your sight, O God, you have spoken about the future of the house of your servant. You have looked on me as though I were the most exalted of men, O LORD God.

[18]"What more can David say to you for honouring your servant? For you know your servant, [19]O LORD. For the sake of your servant and according to your will, you have done this great thing and made known all these great promises.

[20]"There is no-one like you, O LORD, and there is no God but you, as we have heard with our own ears. [21]And who is like your people Israel—the one nation on earth whose God went out to redeem a people for himself, and to make a name for yourself, and to perform great and awesome wonders by driving out nations from before your people, whom you redeemed from Egypt? [22]You made your people Israel your very own for ever, and you, O LORD, have become their God.

[23]"And now, LORD, let the promise you have made concerning your servant and his house be established for ever. Do as you promised, [24]so that it will be established and that your name will be great for ever. Then men will say, 'The LORD Almighty, the God over Israel, is Israel's God!' And the house of your servant David will be established before you.

[25]"You, my God, have revealed to your servant that you will build a house for him. So your servant has found courage to pray to you. [26]O LORD, you are God! You have promised these good things to your servant. [27]Now you have been pleased to bless the house of your servant, that it may continue for ever in your sight; for you, O LORD, have blessed it, and it will be blessed for ever."

[a]6 Traditionally *judges*; also in verse 10

David's Victories

18 In the course of time, David defeated the Philistines and subdued them, and he took Gath and its surrounding villages from the control of the Philistines.

²David also defeated the Moabites, and they became subject to him and brought tribute.

³Moreover, David fought Hadadezer king of Zobah, as far as Hamath, when he went to establish his control along the Euphrates River. ⁴David captured a thousand of his chariots, seven thousand charioteers and twenty thousand foot soldiers. He hamstrung all but a hundred of the chariot horses.

⁵When the Arameans of Damascus came to help Hadadezer king of Zobah, David struck down twenty-two thousand of them. ⁶He put garrisons in the Aramean kingdom of Damascus, and the Arameans became subject to him and brought tribute. The LORD gave David victory everywhere he went.

⁷David took the gold shields carried by the officers of Hadadezer and brought them to Jerusalem. ⁸From Tebah*a* and Cun, towns that belonged to Hadadezer, David took a great quantity of bronze, which Solomon used to make the bronze Sea, the pillars and various bronze articles.

⁹When Tou king of Hamath heard that David had defeated the entire army of Hadadezer king of Zobah, ¹⁰he sent his son Hadoram to King David to greet him and congratulate him on his victory in battle over Hadadezer, who had been at war with Tou. Hadoram brought all kinds of articles of gold and silver and bronze.

¹¹King David dedicated these articles to the LORD, as he had done with the silver and gold he had taken from all these nations: Edom and Moab, the Ammonites and the Philistines, and Amalek.

¹²Abishai son of Zeruiah struck down eighteen thousand Edomites in the Valley of Salt. ¹³He put garrisons in Edom, and all the Edomites became subject to David. The LORD gave David victory everywhere he went.

David's Officials

¹⁴David reigned over all Israel, doing what was just and right for all his people. ¹⁵Joab son of Zeruiah was over the army; Jehoshaphat son of Ahilud was recorder; ¹⁶Zadok son of Ahitub and Ahimelech*b* son of Abiathar were priests; Shavsha was secretary; ¹⁷Benaiah son of Jehoiada was over the Kerethites and Pelethites; and David's sons were chief officials at the king's side.

The Battle Against the Ammonites

19 In the course of time, Nahash king of the Ammonites died, and his son succeeded him as king. ²David thought, "I will show kindness to Hanun son of Nahash, because his father showed kindness to me."

So David sent a delegation to express his sympathy to Hanun concerning his father.

When David's men came to Hanun in the land of the Ammonites to express sympathy to him, ³the Ammonite nobles said to Hanun, "Do you think David is honouring your father by sending men to you to express sympathy? Haven't his men come to you to explore and spy out the country and overthrow it?" ⁴So Hanun seized David's men, shaved them, cut off their garments in the middle at the buttocks, and sent them away.

⁵When someone came and told David about the men, he sent messengers to meet them, for they were greatly humiliated. The king said, "Stay at Jericho till your beards have grown, and then come back."

⁶When the Ammonites realised that they had become an offence to David's nostrils, Hanun and the Ammonites sent a thousand talents*a* of silver to hire chariots and charioteers from Aram Naharaim,*b* Aram Maacah and Zobah. ⁷They hired thirty-two thousand chariots and charioteers, as well as the king of Maacah with his troops, who came and camped near Medeba, while the Ammonites were mustered from their towns and moved out for battle.

⁸On hearing this, David sent Joab out with the entire army of fighting men. ⁹The Ammonites came out and drew up in battle formation at the entrance to their city, while the kings who had come were by themselves in the open country.

¹⁰Joab saw that there were battle lines in front of him and behind him; so he selected some of the best troops in Israel and deployed them against the Arameans. ¹¹He put the rest of the men under the command of Abishai his brother, and they were deployed against the Ammonites. ¹²Joab said, "If the Arameans are too strong for me, then you are to rescue me; but if the Ammonites are too strong for you, then I will rescue you. ¹³Be strong and let us fight bravely for our people and the cities of our God. The LORD will do what is good in his sight."

¹⁴Then Joab and the troops with him advanced to fight the Arameans, and they fled before him. ¹⁵When the Ammonites saw that the Arameans were fleeing, they too fled before his brother Abishai and went inside the city. So Joab went back to Jerusalem.

¹⁶After the Arameans saw that they had been routed by Israel, they sent messengers and had Arameans brought from beyond the River,*c* with Shophach the commander of Hadadezer's army leading them.

¹⁷When David was told of this, he gathered all Israel and crossed the Jordan; he advanced against them and formed his battle lines opposite them. David formed his lines to meet the Arameans in battle, and they fought against him. ¹⁸But they fled before Israel, and David killed seven thousand of their charioteers and forty thousand of their

---

a8 Hebrew *Tibhath,* a variant of *Tebah*
b16 Some Hebrew manuscripts, Vulgate and Syriac (see also 2 Sam. 8:17); most Hebrew manuscripts *Abimelech*
a6 That is, about 34 tons (about 34 metric tons)   *b6* That is, North-west Mesopotamia
c16 That is, the Euphrates

foot soldiers. He also killed Shophach the commander of their army.

¹⁹When the vassals of Hadadezer saw that they had been defeated by Israel, they made peace with David and became subject to him.

So the Arameans were not willing to help the Ammonites any more.

The Capture of Rabbah

20 In the spring, at the time when kings go off to war, Joab led out the armed forces. He laid waste the land of the Ammonites and went to Rabbah and besieged it, but David remained in Jerusalem. Joab attacked Rabbah and left it in ruins. ²David took the crown from the head of their king*ᵃ*—its weight was found to be a talent*ᵇ* of gold, and it was set with precious stones—and it was placed on David's head. He took a great quantity of plunder from the city ³and brought out the people who were there, consigning them to labour with saws and with iron picks and axes. David did this to all the Ammonite towns. Then David and his entire army returned to Jerusalem.

War With the Philistines

⁴In the course of time, war broke out with the Philistines, at Gezer. At that time Sibbecai the Hushathite killed Sippai, one of the descendants of the Rephaites, and the Philistines were subjugated.

⁵In another battle with the Philistines, Elhanan son of Jair killed Lahmi the brother of Goliath the Gittite, who had a spear with a shaft like a weaver's rod.

⁶In still another battle, which took place at Gath, there was a huge man with six fingers on each hand and six toes on each foot —twenty-four in all. He also was descended from Rapha. ⁷When he taunted Israel, Jonathan son of Shimea, David's brother, killed him.

⁸These were descendants of Rapha in Gath, and they fell at the hands of David and his men.

David Numbers the Fighting Men

21 Satan rose up against Israel and incited David to take a census of Israel. ²So David said to Joab and the commanders of the troops, "Go and count the Israelites from Beersheba to Dan. Then report back to me so that I may know how many there are."

³But Joab replied, "May the LORD multiply his troops a hundred times over. My lord the king, are they not all my lord's subjects? Why does my lord want to do this? Why should he bring guilt on Israel?"

⁴The king's word, however, overruled Joab; so Joab left and went throughout Israel and then came back to Jerusalem. ⁵Joab reported the number of the fighting men to David: In all Israel there were one million one hundred thousand men who could handle a sword, including four hundred and seventy thousand in Judah.

⁶But Joab did not include Levi and Benjamin in the numbering, because the king's command was repulsive to him. ⁷This command was also evil in the sight of God; so he punished Israel.

⁸Then David said to God, "I have sinned greatly by doing this. Now, I beg you, take away the guilt of your servant. I have done a very foolish thing."

⁹The LORD said to Gad, David's seer, ¹⁰"Go and tell David, 'This is what the LORD says: I am giving you three options. Choose one of them for me to carry out against you.'"

¹¹So Gad went to David and said to him, "This is what the LORD says: 'Take your choice: ¹²three years of famine, three months of being swept away*ᵃ* before your enemies, with their swords overtaking you, or three days of the sword of the LORD—days of plague in the land with the angel of the LORD ravaging every part of Israel.' Now then, decide how I should answer the one who sent me."

¹³David said to Gad, "I am in deep distress. Let me fall into the hands of the LORD, for his mercy is very great; but do not let me fall into the hands of men."

¹⁴So the LORD sent a plague on Israel, and seventy thousand men of Israel fell dead. ¹⁵And God sent an angel to destroy Jerusalem. But as the angel was doing so, the LORD saw it and was grieved because of the calamity and said to the angel who was destroying the people, "Enough! Withdraw your hand." The angel of the LORD was then standing at the threshing-floor of Araunah*ᵇ* the Jebusite.

¹⁶David looked up and saw the angel of the LORD standing between heaven and earth, with a drawn sword in his hand extended over Jerusalem. Then David and the elders, clothed in sackcloth, fell face down.

¹⁷David said to God, "Was it not I who ordered the fighting men to be counted? I am the one who has sinned and done wrong. These are but sheep. What have they done? O LORD my God, let your hand fall upon me and my family, but do not let this plague remain on your people."

¹⁸Then the angel of the LORD ordered Gad to tell David to go up and build an altar to the LORD on the threshing-floor of Araunah the Jebusite. ¹⁹So David went up in obedience to the word that Gad had spoken in the name of the LORD.

²⁰While Araunah was threshing wheat, he turned and saw the angel; his four sons who were with him hid themselves. ²¹Then David approached, and when Araunah looked and saw him, he left the threshing-floor and bowed down before David with his face to the ground.

²²David said to him, "Let me have the site of your threshing-floor so that I can build an altar to the LORD, that the plague on the

---

*ᵃ*2 Or *of Milcom*, that is, Molech   *ᵇ*2 That is, about 75 pounds (about 34 kilograms)
*ᵃ*12 Hebrew; Septuagint and Vulgate (see also 2 Sam. 24:13) *of fleeing*
*ᵇ*15 Hebrew *Ornan*, a variant of *Araunah*; also in verses 18–28

people may be stopped. Sell it to me at the full price.''

23Araunah said to David, "Take it! Let my lord the king do whatever pleases him. Look, I will give the oxen for the burnt offerings, the threshing-sledges for the wood, and the wheat for the grain offering. I will give all this.''

24But King David replied to Araunah. "No, I insist on paying the full price. I will not take for the LORD what is yours, or sacrifice a burnt offering that costs me nothing.''

25So David paid Araunah six hundred shekels*c* of gold for the site. 26David built an altar to the LORD there and sacrificed burnt offerings and fellowship offerings.*d* He called on the LORD, and the LORD answered him with fire from heaven on the altar of burnt offering.

27Then the LORD spoke to the angel, and he put his sword back into its sheath. 28At that time, when David saw that the LORD had answered him on the threshing-floor of Araunah the Jebusite, he offered sacrifices there. 29The tabernacle of the LORD, which Moses had made in the desert, and the altar of burnt offering were at that time on the high place at Gibeon. 30But David could not go before it to enquire of God, because he was afraid of the sword of the angel of the LORD.

22 Then David said, "The house of the LORD God is to be here, and also the altar of burnt offering for Israel.''

Preparations for the Temple

2So David gave orders to assemble the aliens living in Israel, and from among them he appointed stonecutters to prepare dressed stone for building the house of God. 3He provided a large amount of iron to make nails for the doors of the gateways and for the fittings, and more bronze than could be weighed. 4He also provided more cedar logs than could be counted, for the Sidonians and Tyrians had brought large numbers of them to David.

5David said, "My son Solomon is young and inexperienced, and the house to be built for the LORD should be of great magnificence and fame and splendour in the sight of all the nations. Therefore I will make preparations for it.'' So David made extensive preparations before his death.

6Then he called for his son Solomon and charged him to build a house for the LORD, the God of Israel. 7David said to Solomon: "My son, I had it in my heart to build a house for the Name of the LORD my God. 8But this word of the LORD came to me: 'You have shed much blood and have fought many wars. You are not to build a house for my Name, because you have shed much blood on the earth in my sight. 9But you will have a son who will be a man of peace and rest, and I will give him rest from all his enemies on every side. His name will be Solomon,*a* and I will grant Israel peace and quiet during his

reign. 10He is the one who will build a house for my Name. He will be my son, and I will be his father. And I will establish the throne of his kingdom over Israel for ever.'

11"Now, my son, the LORD be with you, and may you have success and build the house of the LORD your God, as he said you would. 12May the LORD give you discretion and understanding when he puts you in command over Israel, so that you may keep the law of the LORD your God. 13Then you will have success if you are careful to observe the decrees and laws that the LORD gave to Moses for Israel. Be strong and courageous. Do not be afraid or discouraged.

14"I have taken great pains to provide for the temple of the LORD a hundred thousand talents*b* of gold, a million talents*c* of silver, quantities of bronze and iron too great to be weighed, and wood and stone. And you may add to them. 15You have many workmen: stonecutters, masons and carpenters, as well as men skilled in every kind of work 16in gold and silver, bronze and iron—craftsmen beyond number. Now begin the work, and the LORD be with you.''

17Then David ordered all the leaders of Israel to help his son Solomon. 18He said to them, "Is not the LORD your God with you? And has he not granted you rest on every side? For he has handed the inhabitants of the land over to me, and the land is subject to the LORD and to his people. 19Now devote your heart and soul to seeking the LORD your God. Begin to build the sanctuary of the LORD God, so that you may bring the ark of the covenant of the LORD and the sacred articles belonging to God into the temple that will be built for the Name of the LORD.''

The Levites

23 When David was old and full of years, he made his son Solomon king over Israel.

2He also gathered together all the leaders of Israel, as well as the priests and Levites. 3The Levites thirty years old or more were counted, and the total number of men was thirty-eight thousand. 4David said, "Of these, twenty-four thousand are to supervise the work of the temple of the LORD and six thousand are to be officials and judges. 5Four thousand are to be gatekeepers and four thousand are to praise the LORD with the musical instruments I have provided for that purpose.''

6David divided the Levites into groups corresponding to the sons of Levi: Gershon, Kohath and Merari.

Gershonites

7Belonging to the Gershonites:
   Ladan and Shimei.
8The sons of Ladan:
   Jehiel the first, Zetham and Joel—three in all.

---

c25 That is, about 15 pounds (about 7 kilograms)   *d26 Traditionally peace offerings*
a9 Solomon sounds like and may be derived from the Hebrew for peace.
b14 That is, about 3,395 tons (about 3,450 metric tons)
c14 That is, about 33,950 tons (about 34,500 metric tons)

9The sons of Shimei:

Shelomoth, Haziel and Haran—three in all.

These were the heads of the families of Ladan.

10And the sons of Shimei:

Jahath, Ziza,*a* Jeush and Beriah.

These were the sons of Shimei—four in all.

11Jahath was the first and Ziza the second, but Jeush and Beriah did not have many sons; so they were counted as one family with one assignment.

Kohathites

12The sons of Kohath:

Amram, Izhar, Hebron and Uzziel —four in all.

13The sons of Amram:

Aaron and Moses.

Aaron was set apart, he and his descendants for ever, to consecrate the most holy things, to offer sacrifices before the LORD, to minister before him and to pronounce blessings in his name for ever. 14The sons of Moses the man of God were counted as part of the tribe of Levi.

15The sons of Moses:

Gershom and Eliezer.

16The descendants of Gershom:

Shubael was the first.

17The descendants of Eliezer:

Rehabiah was the first.

Eliezer had no other sons, but the sons of Rehabiah were very numerous.

18The sons of Izhar:

Shelomith was the first.

19The sons of Hebron:

Jeriah the first, Amariah the second, Jahaziel the third and Jekameam the fourth.

20The sons of Uzziel:

Micah the first and Isshiah the second.

Merarites

21The sons of Merari:

Mahli and Mushi.

The sons of Mahli:

Eleazar and Kish.

22Eleazar died without having sons: he had only daughters. Their cousins, the sons of Kish, married them.

23The sons of Mushi:

Mahli, Eder and Jerimoth—three in all.

24These were the descendants of Levi by their families—the heads of families as they were registered under their names and counted individually, that is, the workers twenty years old or more who served in the temple of the LORD. 25For David had said, "Since the LORD, the God of Israel, has granted rest to his people and has come to dwell in Jerusalem for ever, 26the Levites no longer need to carry the tabernacle or any of the articles used in its service." 27According to the last instructions of David, the Levites were counted from those twenty years old or more.

28The duty of the Levites was to help Aaron's descendants in the service of the temple of the LORD: to be in charge of the courtyards, the side rooms, the purification of all sacred things and the performance of other duties at the house of God. 29They were in charge of the bread set out on the table, the flour for the grain offerings, the unleavened wafers, the baking and the mixing, and all measurements of quantity and size. 30They were also to stand every morning to thank and praise the LORD. They were to do the same in the evening 31and whenever burnt offerings were presented to the LORD on Sabbaths and at New Moon festivals and at appointed feasts. They were to serve before the LORD regularly in the proper number and in the way prescribed for them.

32And so the Levites carried out their responsibilities for the Tent of Meeting, for the Holy Place and, under their brothers the descendants of Aaron, for the service of the temple of the LORD.

The Divisions of Priests

24 These were the divisions of the sons of Aaron:

The sons of Aaron were Nadab, Abihu, Eleazar and Ithamar. 2But Nadab and Abihu died before their father did, and they had no sons; so Eleazar and Ithamar served as the priests. 3With the help of Zadok a descendant of Eleazar and Ahimelech a descendant of Ithamar, David separated them into divisions for their appointed order of ministering. 4A larger number of leaders were found among Eleazar's descendants than among Ithamar's, and they were divided accordingly: sixteen heads of families from Eleazar's descendants and eight heads of families from Ithamar's descendants. 5They divided them impartially by drawing lots, for there were officials of the sanctuary and officials of God among the descendants of both Eleazar and Ithamar.

6The scribe Shemaiah son of Nethanel, a Levite, recorded their names in the presence of the king and of the officials: Zadok the priest, Ahimelech son of Abiathar and the heads of families of the priests and of the Levites—one family being taken from Eleazar and then one from Ithamar.

7The first lot fell to Jehoiarib,
the second to Jedaiah,
8the third to Harim,
the fourth to Seorim,
9the fifth to Malkijah,
the sixth to Mijamin,
10the seventh to Hakkoz,
the eighth to Abijah,
11the ninth to Jeshua,
the tenth to Shecaniah,
12the eleventh to Eliashib,
the twelfth to Jakim,

a10 One Hebrew manuscript, Septuagint and Vulgate (see also verse 11); most Hebrew manuscripts *Zina*

13the thirteenth to Huppah,
  the fourteenth to Jeshebeab,
14the fifteenth to Bilgah,
  the sixteenth to Immer,
15the seventeenth to Hezir,
  the eighteenth to Happizzez,
16the nineteenth to Pethahiah,
  the twentieth to Jehezkel,
17the twenty-first to Jakin,
  the twenty-second to Gamul,
18the twenty-third to Delaiah
  and the twenty-fourth to Maaziah.

19This was their appointed order of
ministering when they entered the temple of
the LORD, according to the regulations prescribed for them by their forefather Aaron, as
the LORD, the God of Israel, had commanded
him.

The Rest of the Levites

20As for the rest of the descendants of Levi:
  from the sons of Amram: Shubael;
  from the sons of Shubael: Jehdeiah.
21As for Rehabiah, from his sons:
  Isshiah was the first.
22From the Izharites: Shelomoth;
  from the sons of Shelomoth: Jahath.
23The sons of Hebron: Jeriah the first,a
  Amariah the second, Jahaziel the
  third and Jekameam the fourth.
24The son of Uzziel: Micah;
  from the sons of Micah: Shamir.
25The brother of Micah: Isshiah;
  from the sons of Isshiah: Zechariah.
26The sons of Merari: Mahli and Mushi.
  The son of Jaaziah: Beno.
27The sons of Merari:
  from Jaaziah: Beno, Shoham, Zaccur
  and Ibri.
28From Mahli: Eleazar, who had no sons.
29From Kish: the son of Kish: Jerahmeel.
30And the sons of Mushi: Mahli, Eder and
  Jerimoth.

These were the Levites, according to their
families. 31They also cast lots, just as their
brothers the descendants of Aaron did, in the
presence of King David and of Zadok,
Ahimelech, and the heads of families of the
priests and of the Levites. The families of the
eldest brother were treated the same as those
of the youngest.

The Singers

25 David, together with the commanders
of the army, set apart some of the
sons of Asaph, Heman and Jeduthun for the
ministry of prophesying, accompanied by
harps, lyres and cymbals. Here is the list of
the men who performed this service:

2From the sons of Asaph:
  Zaccur, Joseph, Nethaniah and
  Asarelah. The sons of Asaph were under

the supervision of Asaph, who prophesied under the king's supervision.
3As for Jeduthun, from his sons:
  Gedaliah, Zeri, Jeshaiah, Shimei,a
  Hashabiah and Mattithiah, six in all,
  under the supervision of their father
  Jeduthun, who prophesied, using the
  harp in thanking and praising the LORD.
4As for Heman, from his sons:
  Bukkiah, Mattaniah, Uzziel, Shubael
  and Jerimoth; Hananiah, Hanani,
  Eliathah, Giddalti and Romamti-Ezer;
  Joshbekashah, Mallothi, Hothir and
  Mahazioth. 5All these were sons of Heman the king's seer. They were given to
  him through the promises of God to exalt
  him.b God gave Heman fourteen sons
  and three daughters.

6All these men were under the supervision
of their fathers for the music of the temple of
the LORD, with cymbals, lyres and harps, for
the ministry at the house of God. Asaph,
Jeduthun and Heman were under the supervision of the king. 7Along with their relatives
—all of them trained and skilled in music for
the LORD—they numbered 288. 8Young and
old alike, teacher as well as student, cast lots
for their duties.

9The first lot, which was for
  Asaph, fell to Joseph,
  his sons and relatives,c
	12d

the second to Gedaliah,
  he and his relatives
  and sons,
	12

10the third to Zaccur, his sons and relatives,	12
11the fourth to Izri,e his sons and relatives,	12
12the fifth to Nethaniah, his sons and relatives,	12
13the sixth to Bukkiah, his sons and relatives,	12
14the seventh to Jesarelah,f his sons and relatives,	12
15the eighth to Jeshaiah, his sons and relatives,	12
16the ninth to Mattaniah, his sons and relatives,	12
17the tenth to Shimei, his sons and relatives,	12
18the eleventh to Azarel,g his sons and relatives,	12
19the twelfth to Hashabiah, his sons and relatives,	12
20the thirteenth to Shubael, his sons and relatives,	12

21the fourteenth to
  Mattithiah,
  his sons and relatives,
	12

22the fifteenth to Jerimoth, his sons and relatives,	12
23the sixteenth to Hananiah, his sons and relatives,	12

---

a23 Two Hebrew manuscripts and some Septuagint manuscripts (see also 1 Chron. 23:19); most Hebrew manuscripts
The sons of Jeriah.
a3 One Hebrew manuscript and some Septuagint manuscripts (see also verse 17); most Hebrew manuscripts do not
have *Shimei.*   b5 Hebrew *exalt the horn*   c9 See Septuagint; Hebrew does not have *his sons and relatives.*
d9 See the total in verse 7; Hebrew does not have *twelve.*   e11 A variant of *Zeri*   f14 A variant of *Asarelah*
g18 A variant of *Uzziel*

24the seventeenth to Joshbakashah,
his sons and relatives,   12
25the eighteenth to Hanani,
his sons and relatives,   12
26the nineteenth to Mallothi,
his sons and relatives,   12
27the twentieth to Eliathah,
his sons and relatives,   12
28the twenty-first to Hothir,
his sons and relatives,   12
29the twenty-second to Giddalti,
his sons and relatives,   12
30the twenty-third to Mahazioth,
his sons and relatives,   12
31the twenty-fourth to Romamti-Ezer,
his sons and relatives,   12

The Gatekeepers

26 The divisions of the gatekeepers:

From the Korahites: Meshelemiah son of Kore, one of the sons of Asaph.

2Meshelemiah had sons:
Zechariah the firstborn,
Jediael the second,
Zebadiah the third,
Jathniel the fourth,
3Elam the fifth,
Jehohanan the sixth
and Eliehoenai the seventh.

4Obed-Edom also had sons:
Shemaiah the firstborn,
Jehozabad the second,
Joah the third,
Sacar the fourth,
Nethanel the fifth,
5Ammiel the sixth,
Issachar the seventh
and Peullethai the eighth.
(For God had blessed Obed-Edom.)

6His son Shemaiah also had sons, who were leaders in their father's family because they were very capable men. 7The sons of Shemaiah: Othni, Rephael, Obed and Elzabad; his relatives Elihu and Semakiah were also able men. 8All these were descendants of Obed-Edom; they and their sons and their relatives were capable men with the strength to do the work —descendants of Obed-Edom, 62 in all.

9Meshelemiah had sons and relatives, who were able men—18 in all.

10Hosah the Merarite had sons: Shimri the first (although he was not the first-born, his father had appointed him the first), 11Hilkiah the second, Tabaliah the third and Zechariah the fourth. The sons and relatives of Hosah were 13 in all.

12These divisions of the gatekeepers, through their chief men, had duties for ministering in the temple of the LORD, just as their relatives had. 13Lots were cast for each gate, according to their families, young and old alike.

14The lot for the East Gate fell to Shelemiah.a Then lots were cast for his son Zechariah, a wise counsellor, and the lot for the North Gate fell to him. 15The lot for the South Gate fell to Obed-Edom, and the lot for the storehouse fell to his sons. 16The lots for the West Gate and the Shalleketh Gate on the upper road fell to Shuppim and Hosah.

Guard was alongside guard: 17There were six Levites a day on the east, four a day on the north, four a day on the south and two at a time at the storehouse. 18As for the court to the west, there were four at the road and two at the court itself.

19These were the divisions of the gate-keepers who were descendants of Korah and Merari.

The Treasurers and Other Officials

20Their fellow Levites wereb in charge of the treasuries of the house of God and the treasuries for the dedicated things.

21The descendants of Ladan, who were Gershonites through Ladan and who were heads of families belonging to Ladan the Gershonite, were Jehieli, 22the sons of Jehieli, Zetham and his brother Joel. They were in charge of the treasuries of the temple of the LORD.

23From the Amramites, the Izharites, the Hebronites and the Uzzielites:

24Shubael, a descendant of Gershom son of Moses, was the officer in charge of the treasuries. 25His relatives through Eliezer: Rehabiah his son, Jeshaiah his son, Joram his son, Zicri his son and Shelomith his son. 26Shelomith and his relatives were in charge of all the treasuries for the things dedicated by King David, by the heads of families who were the commanders of thousands and commanders of hundreds, and by the other army commanders. 27Some of the plunder taken in battle they dedicated for the repair of the temple of the LORD. 28And everything dedicated by Samuel the seer and by Saul son of Kish, Abner son of Ner and Joab son of Zeruiah, and all the other dedicated things were in the care of Shelomith and his relatives.

29From the Izharites: Kenaniah and his sons were assigned duties away from the temple, as officials and judges over Israel.

30From the Hebronites: Hashabiah and his relatives—seventeen hundred able men—were responsible in Israel west of the Jordan for all the work of the LORD and for the king's service. 31As for the Hebronites, Jeriah was their chief according to the genealogical records of their families. In the

---

a14 A variant of *Meshelemiah*   b20 Septuagint; Hebrew *As for the Levites, Ahijah was* fortieth year of David's reign a search was made in the records, and capable men among the Hebronites were found at Jazer in Gilead. [32]Jeriah had two thousand seven hundred relatives, who were able men and heads of families, and King David put them in charge of the Reubenites, the Gadites and the half-tribe of Manasseh for every matter pertaining to God and for the affairs of the king.

Army Divisions

27 This is the list of the Israelites—heads of families, commanders of thousands and commanders of hundreds, and their officers, who served the king in all that concerned the army divisions that were on duty month by month throughout the year. Each division consisted of 24,000 men.

[2]In charge of the first division, for the first month, was Jashobeam son of Zabdiel. There were 24,000 men in his division. [3]He was a descendant of Perez and chief of all the army officers for the first month. [4]In charge of the division for the second month was Dodai the Ahohite; Mikloth was the leader of his division. There were 24,000 men in his division. [5]The third army commander, for the third month, was Benaiah son of Jehoiada the priest. He was chief and there were 24,000 men in his division. [6]This was the Benaiah who was a mighty man among the Thirty and was over the Thirty. His son Ammizabad was in charge of his division. [7]The fourth, for the fourth month, was Asahel the brother of Joab; his son Zebadiah was his successor. There were 24,000 men in his division. [8]The fifth, for the fifth month, was the commander Shamhuth the Izrahite. There were 24,000 men in his division. [9]The sixth, for the sixth month, was Ira the son of Ikkesh the Tekoite. There were 24,000 men in his division. [10]The seventh, for the seventh month, was Helez the Pelonite, an Ephraimite. There were 24,000 men in his division. [11]The eighth, for the eighth month, was Sibbecai the Hushathite, a Zerahite. There were 24,000 men in his division. [12]The ninth, for the ninth month, was Abiezer the Anathothite, a Benjamite. There were 24,000 men in his division. [13]The tenth, for the tenth month, was Maharai the Netophathite, a Zerahite. There were 24,000 men in his division. [14]The eleventh, for the eleventh month, was Benaiah the Pirathonite, an Ephraimite. There were 24,000 men in his division. [15]The twelfth, for the twelfth month, was Heldai the Netophathite, from the family of Othniel. There were 24,000 men in his division.

Officers of the Tribes

[16]The officers over the tribes of Israel:

over the Reubenites: Eliezer son of Zicri;

over the Simeonites: Shephatiah son of Maacah;

[17]over Levi: Hashabiah son of Kemuel;

over Aaron: Zadok;

[18]over Judah: Elihu, a brother of David;

over Issachar: Omri son of Michael;

[19]over Zebulun: Ishmaiah son of Obadiah;

over Naphtali: Jerimoth son of Azriel;

[20]over the Ephraimites: Hoshea son of Azaziah;

over half the tribe of Manasseh: Joel son of Pedaiah;

[21]over the half-tribe of Manasseh in Gilead: Iddo son of Zechariah;

over Benjamin: Jaasiel son of Abner;

[22]over Dan: Azarel son of Jeroham.

These were the officers over the tribes of Israel.

[23]David did not take the number of the men twenty years old or less, because the LORD had promised to make Israel as numerous as the stars in the sky. [24]Joab son of Zeruiah began to count the men but did not finish. Wrath came on Israel on account of this numbering, and the number was not entered in the book[a] of the annals of King David.

The King's Overseers

[25]Azmaveth son of Adiel was in charge of the royal storehouses.

Jonathan son of Uzziah was in charge of the storehouses in the outlying districts, in the towns, the villages and the watchtowers. [26]Ezri son of Kelub was in charge of the field workers who farmed the land. [27]Shimei the Ramathite was in charge of the vineyards.

Zabdi the Shiphmite was in charge of the produce of the vineyards for the wine vats. [28]Baal-Hanan the Gederite was in charge of the olive and sycamore-fig trees in the western foothills.

Joash was in charge of the supplies of olive oil. [29]Shitrai the Sharonite was in charge of the herds grazing in Sharon.

Shaphat son of Adlai was in charge of the herds in the valleys. [30]Obil the Ishmaelite was in charge of the camels.

Jehdeiah the Meronothite was in charge of the donkeys. [31]Jaziz the Hagrite was in charge of the flocks.

All these were the officials in charge of King David's property.

[32]Jonathan, David's uncle, was a counsellor, a man of insight and a scribe. Jehiel son of Hacmoni took care of the king's sons. [33]Ahithophel was the king's counsellor. Hushai the Arkite was the king's friend.

[a]24 Septuagint; Hebrew *number*

³⁴Ahithophel was succeeded by Jehoiada son of Benaiah and by Abiathar.

Joab was the commander of the royal army.

David's Plans for the Temple

28 David summoned all the officials of Israel to assemble at Jerusalem: the officers over the tribes, the commanders of the divisions in the service of the king, the commanders of thousands and commanders of hundreds, and the officials in charge of all the property and livestock belonging to the king and his sons, together with the palace officials, the mighty men and all the brave warriors.

²King David rose to his feet and said: "Listen to me, my brothers and my people. I had it in my heart to build a house as a place of rest for the ark of the covenant of the LORD, for the footstool of our God, and I made plans to build it. ³But God said to me, 'You are not to build a house for my Name, because you are a warrior and have shed blood.'

⁴"Yet the LORD, the God of Israel, chose me from my whole family to be king over Israel for ever. He chose Judah as leader, and from the house of Judah he chose my family, and from my father's sons he was pleased to make me king over all Israel. ⁵Of all my sons—and the LORD has given me many—he has chosen my son Solomon to sit on the throne of the kingdom of the LORD over Israel. ⁶He said to me, 'Solomon your son is the one who will build my house and my courts, for I have chosen him to be my son, and I will be his father. ⁷I will establish his kingdom for ever if he is unswerving in carrying out my commands and laws, as is being done at this time.'

⁸"So now I charge you in the sight of all Israel and of the assembly of the LORD, and in the hearing of our God: Be careful to follow all the commands of the LORD your God, that you may possess this good land and pass it on as an inheritance to your descendants for ever.

⁹"And you, my son Solomon, acknowledge the God of your father, and serve him with wholehearted devotion and with a willing mind, for the LORD searches every heart and understands every motive behind the thoughts. If you seek him, he will be found by you; but if you forsake him, he will reject you for ever. ¹⁰Consider now, for the LORD has chosen you to build a temple as a sanctuary. Be strong and do the work."

¹¹Then David gave his son Solomon the plans for the portico of the temple, its buildings, its storerooms, its upper parts, its inner rooms and the place of atonement. ¹²He gave him the plans of all that the Spirit had put in his mind for the courts of the temple of the LORD and all the surrounding rooms, for the treasuries of the temple of God and for the treasuries for the dedicated things. ¹³He gave him instructions for the divisions of the priests and Levites, and for all the work of serving in the temple of the LORD, as well as for all the articles to be used in its service. ¹⁴He designated the weight of gold for all the gold articles to be used in various kinds of service, and the weight of silver for all the silver articles to be used in various kinds of service: ¹⁵the weight of gold for the gold lampstands and their lamps, with the weight for each lampstand and its lamps; and the weight of silver for each silver lampstand and its lamps, according to the use of each lampstand; ¹⁶the weight of gold for each table for consecrated bread; the weight of silver for the silver tables; ¹⁷the weight of pure gold for the forks, sprinkling bowls and pitchers; the weight of gold for each gold dish; the weight of silver for each silver dish; ¹⁸and the weight of the refined gold for the altar of incense. He also gave him the plan for the chariot, that is, the cherubim of gold that spread their wings and shelter the ark of the covenant of the LORD.

¹⁹"All this," David said, "I have in writing from the hand of the LORD upon me, and he gave me understanding in all the details of the plan."

²⁰David also said to Solomon his son, "Be strong and courageous, and do the work. Do not be afraid or discouraged, for the LORD God, my God, is with you. He will not fail you or forsake you until all the work for the service of the temple of the LORD is finished. ²¹The divisions of the priests and Levites are ready for all the work on the temple of God, and every willing man skilled in any craft will help you in all the work. The officials and all the people will obey your every command."

Gifts for Building the Temple

29 Then King David said to the whole assembly: "My son Solomon, the one whom God has chosen, is young and inexperienced. The task is great, because this palatial structure is not for man but for the LORD God. ²With all my resources I have provided for the temple of my God—gold for the gold work, silver for the silver, bronze for the bronze, iron for the iron and wood for the wood, as well as onyx for the settings, turquoise,ᵃ stones of various colours, and all kinds of fine stone and marble—all of these in large quantities. ³Besides, in my devotion to the temple of my God I now give my personal treasures of gold and silver for the temple of my God, over and above everything I have provided for this holy temple: ⁴three thousand talentsᵇ of gold (gold of Ophir) and seven thousand talentsᶜ of refined silver, for the overlaying of the walls of the buildings, ⁵for the gold work and the silver work, and for all the work to be done by the craftsmen. Now, who is willing to consecrate himself today to the LORD?"

⁶Then the leaders of families, the officers of the tribes of Israel, the commanders of thousands and commanders of hundreds, and the officials in charge of the king's work

---

ᵃ2 The meaning of the Hebrew for this word is uncertain.   ᵇ4 That is, about 100 tons (about 100 metric tons)
ᶜ4 That is, about 240 tons (about 240 metric tons)

gave willingly. [7]They gave towards the work on the temple of God five thousand talents[d] and ten thousand darics[e] of gold, ten thousand talents[f] of silver, eighteen thousand talents[g] of bronze and a hundred thousand talents[h] of iron. [8]Any who had precious stones gave them to the treasury of the temple of the LORD in the custody of Jehiel the Gershonite. [9]The people rejoiced at the willing response of their leaders, for they had given freely and wholeheartedly to the LORD. David the king also rejoiced greatly.

David's Prayer

[10]David praised the LORD in the presence of the whole assembly, saying,

"Praise be to you, O LORD,
    God of our father Israel,
    from everlasting to everlasting.
[11]Yours, O LORD, is the greatness and the power
    and the glory and the majesty and the splendour,
    for everything in heaven and earth is yours.
Yours, O LORD, is the kingdom;
    you are exalted as head over all.
[12]Wealth and honour come from you;
    you are the ruler of all things.
In your hands are strength and power
    to exalt and give strength to all.
[13]Now, our God, we give you thanks,
    and praise your glorious name.

[14]"But who am I, and who are my people, that we should be able to give as generously as this? Everything comes from you, and we have given you only what comes from your hand. [15]We are aliens and strangers in your sight, as were all our forefathers. Our days on earth are like a shadow, without hope. [16]O LORD our God, as for all this abundance that we have provided for building you a temple for your Holy Name, it comes from your hand, and all of it belongs to you. [17]I know, my God, that you test the heart and are pleased with integrity. All these things have I given willingly and with honest intent. And now I have seen with joy how willingly your people who are here have given to you. [18]O LORD, God of our fathers Abraham, Isaac

and Israel, keep this desire in the hearts of your people for ever, and keep their hearts loyal to you. [19]And give my son Solomon the wholehearted devotion to keep your commands, requirements and decrees and to do everything to build the palatial structure for which I have provided."

[20]Then David said to the whole assembly, "Praise the LORD your God." So they all praised the LORD, the God of their fathers; they bowed low and fell prostrate before the LORD and the king.

Solomon Acknowledged as King

[21]The next day they made sacrifices to the LORD and presented burnt offerings to him: a thousand bulls, a thousand rams and a thousand male lambs, together with their drink offerings, and other sacrifices in abundance for all Israel. [22]They ate and drank with great joy in the presence of the LORD that day.

Then they acknowledged Solomon son of David as king a second time, anointing him before the LORD to be ruler and Zadok to be priest. [23]So Solomon sat on the throne of the LORD as king in place of his father David. He prospered and all Israel obeyed him. [24]All the officers and mighty men, as well as all of King David's sons, pledged their submission to King Solomon.

[25]The LORD highly exalted Solomon in the sight of all Israel and bestowed on him royal splendour such as no king over Israel ever had before.

The Death of David

[26]David son of Jesse was king over all Israel. [27]He ruled over Israel for forty years —seven in Hebron and thirty-three in Jerusalem. [28]He died at a good old age, having enjoyed long life, wealth and honour. His son Solomon succeeded him as king.

[29]As for the events of King David's reign, from beginning to end, they are written in the records of Samuel the seer, the records of Nathan the prophet and the records of Gad the seer, [30]together with the details of his reign and power, and the circumstances that surrounded him and Israel and the kingdoms of all the other lands.

---

[d]7 That is, about 170 tons (about 170 metric tons)   [e]7 That is, about 185 pounds (about 84 kilograms)
[f]7 That is, about 340 tons (about 345 metric tons)   [g]7 That is, about 610 tons (about 620 metric tons)
[h]7 That is, about 3,400 tons (about 3,450 metric tons)

2 Chronicles

Solomon Asks for Wisdom

1 Solomon son of David established himself firmly over his kingdom, for the LORD his God was with him and made him exceedingly great.

²Then Solomon spoke to all Israel—to the commanders of thousands and commanders of hundreds, to the judges and to all the leaders in Israel, the heads of families—³and Solomon and the whole assembly went to the high place at Gibeon, for God's Tent of Meeting was there, which Moses the LORD's servant had made in the desert. ⁴Now David had brought up the ark of God from Kiriath Jearim to the place he had prepared for it, because he had pitched a tent for it in Jerusalem. ⁵But the bronze altar that Bezalel son of Uri, the son of Hur, had made was in Gibeon in front of the tabernacle of the LORD; so Solomon and the assembly enquired of him there. ⁶Solomon went up to the bronze altar before the LORD in the Tent of Meeting and offered a thousand burnt offerings on it.

⁷That night God appeared to Solomon and said to him, "Ask for whatever you want me to give you."

⁸Solomon answered God, "You have shown great kindness to David my father and have made me king in his place. ⁹Now, LORD God, let your promise to my father David be confirmed, for you have made me king over a people who are as numerous as the dust of the earth. ¹⁰Give me wisdom and knowledge, that I may lead this people, for who is able to govern this great people of yours?"

¹¹God said to Solomon, "Since this is your heart's desire and you have not asked for wealth, riches or honour, nor for the death of your enemies, and since you have not asked for a long life but for wisdom and knowledge to govern my people over whom I have made you king, ¹²therefore wisdom and knowledge will be given you. And I will also give you wealth, riches and honour, such as no king who was before you ever had and none after you will have."

¹³Then Solomon went to Jerusalem from the high place at Gibeon, from before the Tent of Meeting. And he reigned over Israel.

¹⁴Solomon accumulated chariots and horses; he had fourteen hundred chariots and twelve thousand horses,ᵃ which he kept in the chariot cities and also with him in Jerusalem. ¹⁵The king made silver and gold as common in Jerusalem as stones, and cedar as plentiful as sycamore-fig trees in the foothills. ¹⁶Solomon's horses were imported from Egyptᵇ and from Kueᶜ—the royal merchants purchased them from Kue. ¹⁷They imported a chariot from Egypt for six hundred shekelsᵈ of silver, and a horse for a hundred and fifty.ᵉ They also exported them to all the kings of the Hittites and of the Arameans.

Preparations for Building the Temple

2 Solomon gave orders to build a temple for the Name of the LORD and a royal palace for himself. ²He conscripted seventy thousand men as carriers and eighty thousand as stonecutters in the hills and thirty-six hundred as foremen over them.

³Solomon sent this message to Hiramᵃ king of Tyre:

"Send me cedar logs as you did for my father David when you sent him cedar to build a palace to live in. ⁴Now I am about to build a temple for the Name of the LORD my God and to dedicate it to him for burning fragrant incense before him, for setting out the consecrated bread regularly, and for making burnt offerings every morning and evening and on Sabbaths and New Moons and at the appointed feasts of the LORD our God. This is a lasting ordinance for Israel.

⁵"The temple I am going to build will be great, because our God is greater than all other gods. ⁶But who is able to build a temple for him, since the heavens, even the highest heavens, cannot contain him? Who then am I to build a temple for him, except as a place to burn sacrifices before him?

⁷"Send me, therefore, a man skilled to work in gold and silver, bronze and iron, and in purple, crimson and blue yarn, and experienced in the art of engraving, to work in Judah and Jerusalem with my

---

ᵃ14 Or charioteers   ᵇ16 Or possibly Muzur, a region in Cilicia; also in verse 17
ᶜ16 Probably Cilicia   ᵈ17 That is, about 15 pounds (about 7 kilograms)
ᵉ17 That is, about 3¾ pounds (about 1.7 kilograms)
ᵃ3 Hebrew Huram, a variant of Hiram; also in verses 11 and 12

skilled craftsmen, whom my father David provided.

8"Send me also cedar, pine and algum*b* logs from Lebanon, for I know that your men are skilled in cutting timber there. My men shall work with yours 9to provide me with plenty of timber, because the temple I build must be large and magnificent. 10I will give your servants, the woodsmen who cut the timber, twenty thousand cors*c* of ground wheat, twenty thousand cors of barley, twenty thousand baths*d* of wine and twenty thousand baths of olive oil."

11Hiram king of Tyre replied by letter to Solomon:

"Because the LORD loves his people, he has made you their king."

12And Hiram added:

"Praise be to the LORD, the God of Israel, who made heaven and earth! He has given King David a wise son, endowed with intelligence and discernment, who will build a temple for the LORD and a palace for himself.

13"I am sending you Huram-Abi, a man of great skill, 14whose mother was from Dan and whose father was from Tyre. He is trained to work in gold and silver, bronze and iron, stone and wood, and with purple and blue and crimson yarn and fine linen. He is experienced in all kinds of engraving and can execute any design given to him. He will work with your craftsmen and with those of my lord, David your father.

15"Now let my lord send his servants the wheat and barley and the olive oil and wine he promised, 16and we will cut all the logs from Lebanon that you need and will float them in rafts by sea down to Joppa. You can then take them up to Jerusalem."

17Solomon took a census of all the aliens who were in Israel, after the census his father David had taken; and they were found to be 153,600. 18He assigned 70,000 of them to be carriers and 80,000 to be stonecutters in the hills, with 3,600 foremen over them to keep the people working.

Solomon Builds the Temple

3 Then Solomon began to build the temple of the LORD in Jerusalem on Mount Moriah, where the LORD had appeared to his father David. It was on the threshing-floor of Araunah*a* the Jebusite, the place provided by David. 2He began building on the second day of the second month in the fourth year of his reign.

3The foundation Solomon laid for building the temple of God was sixty cubits long and twenty cubits wide*b* (using the cubit of the old standard). 4The portico at the front of the temple was twenty cubits*c* long across the width of the building and twenty cubits*d* high.

He overlaid the inside with pure gold. 5He panelled the main hall with pine and covered it with fine gold and decorated it with palm tree and chain designs. 6He adorned the temple with precious stones. And the gold he used was gold of Parvaim. 7He overlaid the ceiling beams, door-frames, walls and doors of the temple with gold, and he carved cherubim on the walls.

8He built the Most Holy Place, its length corresponding to the width of the temple —twenty cubits long and twenty cubits wide. He overlaid the inside with six hundred talents*e* of fine gold. 9The gold nails weighed fifty shekels.*f* He also overlaid the upper parts with gold.

10In the Most Holy Place he made a pair of sculptured cherubim and overlaid them with gold. 11The total wing-span of the cherubim was twenty cubits. One wing of the first cherub was five cubits*g* long and touched the temple wall, while its other wing, also five cubits long, touched the wing of the other cherub. 12Similarly one wing of the second cherub was five cubits long and touched the other temple wall, and its other wing, also five cubits long, touched the wing of the first cherub. 13The wings of these cherubim extended twenty cubits. They stood on their feet, facing the main hall.*h*

14He made the curtain of blue, purple and crimson yarn and fine linen, with cherubim worked into it.

15In the front of the temple he made two pillars, which ⌊together⌋ were thirty-five cubits*i* long, each with a capital on top measuring five cubits. 16He made interwoven chains*j* and put them on top of the pillars. He also made a hundred pomegranates and attached them to the chains. 17He erected the pillars in the front of the temple, one to the south and one to the north. The one to the south he named Jakin*k* and the one to the north Boaz.*l*

The Temple's Furnishings

4 He made a bronze altar twenty cubits long, twenty cubits wide and ten cubits high.*a* 2He made the Sea of cast metal, circular in shape, measuring ten cubits from rim to

---

*b*8 Probably a variant of *almug*; possibly juniper
*c*10 That is, probably about 120,000 bushels (about 4,400 kilolitres)
*d*10 That is, probably about 95,000 gallons (about 440 kilolitres)   *a*1 Hebrew *Ornan*, a variant of *Araunah*
*b*3 That is, about 90 feet (about 27 metres) long and 30 feet (about 9 metres) wide
*c*4 That is, about 30 feet (about 9 metres); also in verses 8, 11 and 13
*d*4 Some Septuagint and Syriac manuscripts; Hebrew *and a hundred and twenty*
*e*8 That is, about 20 tons (about 21 metric tons)   *f*9 That is, about 1¼ pounds (about 0.6 kilogram)
*g*11 That is, about 7½ feet (about 2.3 metres); also in verse 15   *h*13 Or *facing inward*
*i*15 That is, about 52 feet (about 16 metres)
*j*16 Or possibly *made chains in the inner sanctuary*; the meaning of the Hebrew for this phrase is uncertain.
*k*17 *Jakin* probably means *he establishes*.   *l*17 *Boaz* probably means *in him is strength*.
*a*1 That is, about 30 feet (about 9 metres) long and wide, and about 15 feet (about 4.5 metres) high

rim and five cubits[b] high. It took a line of thirty cubits[c] to measure round it. [3]Below the rim, figures of bulls encircled it—ten to a cubit.[d] The bulls were cast in two rows in one piece with the Sea.

[4]The Sea stood on twelve bulls, three facing north, three facing west, three facing south and three facing east. The Sea rested on top of them, and their hindquarters were towards the centre. [5]It was a handbreadth[e] in thickness, and its rim was like the rim of a cup, like a lily blossom. It held three thousand baths.[f]

[6]He then made ten basins for washing and placed five on the south side and five on the north. In them the things to be used for the burnt offerings were rinsed, but the Sea was to be used by the priests for washing.

[7]He made ten gold lampstands according to the specifications for them and placed them in the temple, five on the south side and five on the north.

[8]He made ten tables and placed them in the temple, five on the south side and five on the north. He also made a hundred gold sprinkling bowls.

[9]He made the courtyard of the priests, and the large court and the doors for the court, and overlaid the doors with bronze. [10]He placed the Sea on the south side, at the south-east corner.

[11]He also made the pots and shovels and sprinkling bowls.

So Huram finished the work he had undertaken for King Solomon in the temple of God:

[12]the two pillars;
the two bowl-shaped capitals on top of the pillars;
the two sets of network decorating the two bowl-shaped capitals on top of the pillars;
[13]the four hundred pomegranates for the two sets of network (two rows of pomegranates for each network, decorating the bowl-shaped capitals on top of the pillars);
[14]the stands with their basins;
[15]the Sea and the twelve bulls under it;
[16]the pots, shovels, meat forks and all related articles.

All the objects that Huram-Abi made for King Solomon for the temple of the LORD were of polished bronze. [17]The king had them cast in clay moulds in the plain of the Jordan between Succoth and Zarethan.[g] [18]All these things that Solomon made amounted to so much that the weight of the bronze was not determined.

[19]Solomon also made all the furnishings that were in God's temple:

the golden altar;
the tables on which was the bread of the Presence;

[20]the lampstands of pure gold with their lamps, to burn in front of the inner sanctuary as prescribed;
[21]the gold floral work and lamps and tongs (they were solid gold);
[22]the pure gold wick trimmers, sprinkling bowls, dishes and censers; and the gold doors of the temple: the inner doors to the Most Holy Place and the doors of the main hall.

5 When all the work Solomon had done for the temple of the LORD was finished, he brought in the things his father David had dedicated—the silver and gold and all the furnishings—and he placed them in the treasuries of God's temple.

The Ark Brought to the Temple

[2]Then Solomon summoned to Jerusalem the elders of Israel, all the heads of the tribes and the chiefs of the Israelite families, to bring up the ark of the LORD's covenant from Zion, the City of David. [3]And all the men of Israel came together to the king at the time of the festival in the seventh month.

[4]When all the elders of Israel had arrived, the Levites took up the ark, [5]and they brought up the ark and the Tent of Meeting and all the sacred furnishings in it. The priests, who were Levites, carried them up; [6]and King Solomon and the entire assembly of Israel that had gathered about him were before the ark, sacrificing so many sheep and cattle that they could not be recorded or counted.

[7]The priests then brought the ark of the LORD's covenant to its place in the inner sanctuary of the temple, the Most Holy Place, and put it beneath the wings of the cherubim. [8]The cherubim spread their wings over the place of the ark and covered the ark and its carrying poles. [9]These poles were so long that their ends, extending from the ark, could be seen from in front of the inner sanctuary, but not from outside the Holy Place; and they are still there today. [10]There was nothing in the ark except the two tablets that Moses had placed in it at Horeb, where the LORD made a covenant with the Israelites after they came out of Egypt.

[11]The priests then withdrew from the Holy Place. All the priests who were there had consecrated themselves, regardless of their divisions. [12]All the Levites who were musicians—Asaph, Heman, Jeduthun and their sons and relatives—stood on the east side of the altar, dressed in fine linen and playing cymbals, harps and lyres. They were accompanied by 120 priests sounding trumpets. [13]The trumpeters and singers joined in unison, as with one voice, to give praise and thanks to the LORD. Accompanied by trumpets, cymbals and other instruments, they raised their voices in praise to the LORD and sang:

---

[b]2 That is, about 7½ feet (about 2.3 metres)   [c]2 That is, about 45 feet (about 13.5 metres)
[d]3 That is, about 1½ feet (about 0.5 metre)   [e]5 That is, about 3 inches (about 8 centimetres)
[f]5 That is, about 14,500 gallons (about 66 kilolitres)   [g]17 Hebrew Zeredatha, a variant of Zarethan

"He is good;
his love endures for ever."

Then the temple of the LORD was filled with a cloud, 14and the priests could not perform their service because of the cloud, for the glory of the LORD filled the temple of God.

6 Then Solomon said, "The LORD has said that he would dwell in a dark cloud; 2I have built a magnificent temple for you, a place for you to dwell for ever."

3While the whole assembly of Israel was standing there, the king turned round and blessed them. 4Then he said:

"Praise be to the LORD, the God of Israel, who with his hands has fulfilled what he promised with his mouth to my father David. For he said, 5'Since the day I brought my people out of Egypt, I have not chosen a city in any tribe of Israel to have a temple built for my Name to be there, nor have I chosen anyone to be the leader over my people Israel. 6But now I have chosen Jerusalem for my Name to be there, and I have chosen David to rule my people Israel.'

7"My father David had it in his heart to build a temple for the Name of the LORD, the God of Israel. 8But the LORD said to my father David, 'Because it was in your heart to build a temple for my Name, you did well to have this in your heart. 9Nevertheless, you are not the one to build the temple, but your son, who is your own flesh and blood—he is the one who will build the temple for my Name.'

10"The LORD has kept the promise he made. I have succeeded David my father and now I sit on the throne of Israel, just as the LORD promised, and I have built the temple for the Name of the LORD, the God of Israel. 11There I have placed the ark, in which is the covenant of the LORD that he made with the people of Israel."

Solomon's Prayer of Dedication

12Then Solomon stood before the altar of the LORD in front of the whole assembly of Israel and spread out his hands. 13Now he had made a bronze platform, five cubits*a* long, five cubits wide and three cubits*b* high, and had placed it in the centre of the outer court. He stood on the platform and then knelt down before the whole assembly of Israel and spread out his hands towards heaven. 14He said:

"O LORD, God of Israel, there is no God like you in heaven or on earth—you who keep your covenant of love with your servants who continue whole-heartedly in your way. 15You have kept your promise to your servant David my father; with your mouth you have promised and with your hand you have fulfilled it—as it is today.

16"Now LORD, God of Israel, keep for your servant David my father the promises you made to him when you said, 'You shall never fail to have a man to sit before me on the throne of Israel, if only your sons are careful in all they do to walk before me according to my law, as you have done.' 17And now, O LORD, God of Israel, let your word that you promised your servant David come true.

18"But will God really dwell on earth with men? The heavens, even the highest heavens, cannot contain you. How much less this temple that I have built! 19Yet give attention to your servant's prayer and his plea for mercy, O LORD my God. Hear the cry and the prayer that your servant is praying in your presence. 20May your eyes be open towards this temple day and night, this place of which you said you would put your Name there. May you hear the prayer your servant prays towards this place. 21Hear the supplications of your servant and of your people Israel when they pray towards this place. Hear from heaven, your dwelling-place; and when you hear, forgive.

22"When a man wrongs his neighbour and is required to take an oath and he comes and swears the oath before your altar in this temple, 23then hear from heaven and act. Judge between your servants, repaying the guilty by bringing down on his own head what he has done. Declare the innocent not guilty and so establish his innocence.

24"When your people Israel have been defeated by an enemy because they have sinned against you and when they turn back and confess your name, praying and making supplication before you in this temple, 25then hear from heaven and forgive the sin of your people Israel and bring them back to the land you gave to them and their fathers.

26"When the heavens are shut up and there is no rain because your people have sinned against you, and when they pray towards this place and confess your name and turn from their sin because you have afflicted them, 27then hear from heaven and forgive the sin of your servants, your people Israel. Teach them the right way to live, and send rain on the land that you gave your people for an inheritance.

28"When famine or plague comes to the land, or blight or mildew, locusts or grasshoppers, or when enemies besiege them in any of their cities, whatever disaster or disease may come, 29and when a prayer or plea is made by any of your people Israel—each one aware of his afflictions and pains, and spreading out his hands towards this temple—30then hear from heaven, your dwelling-place. Forgive, and deal with each man according to all he does, since you know

---

*a*13 That is, about 7½ feet (about 2.3 metres)   *b*13 That is, about 4½ feet (about 1.4 metres)

2 CHRONICLES 6:3–11

'My father David had it in his heart to build a temple for the Name of the LORD, the God of Israel. But the LORD said to my father David, "Because it was in your heart to build a temple for my Name, you did well to have this in your heart. Nevertheless, you are not the one to build the temple" ' (vv. 7–9a).

GENERATION FOLLOWS GENERATION. David, the warrior, wanted to leave a legacy of peace to his son Solomon. He knew the Lord could not bless anything which spoke of war. David, one of the greatest warriors of all time, knew deep down that his warlike activity was ultimately against the will of God.

We do well to remember David's confession at the end of a long life of military action. 'God . . . has forbidden me to do it because I am a soldier and have shed too much blood.'

Maintaining unity in a peaceful society is much harder than within one which is engaged in war against a recognizable external enemy. There is something in our human nature which seems to need an external enemy. We need to blame something for our own failings. Fighting an enemy is a natural way of taking attention away from wrong things within ourselves and our own society.

Recent lessening of tensions between East and West, particularly between USA and the former USSR, should prove a great blessing. But it has dangers. It is easier for a nation fighting against an 'evil empire' to be united, than it is for one newly co-operating with people so long regarded as beyond the pale. In a situation where no external enemy was available, Solomon's successors found it impossible to maintain unity. Let us pray that things will be different in our generation.

Unity between nations requires more effort to maintain than unity against other nations.

→372

2 CHRONICLES 9:1–12

'Solomon answered all her questions; nothing was too hard for him to explain to her. When the queen of Sheba saw the wisdom of Solomon, as well as the palace he had built, the food on his table, the seating of his officials, the attending servants . . . she was overwhelmed' (vv. 2–4).

THE QUEEN had made a long and perilous journey. She was the nearest ancient equivalent to a modern oil sheikh. Her kingdom lay to the south east of Israel, some distance into Arabia. Her wealth would be based on trade in incense, one of the most precious commodities of the ancient world. Incense came from trees which only prospered in certain areas of Arabia. It commanded high prices. In modern terms it was a multi-billion dollar trade. The queen of Sheba was at its source.

Wisdom or wealth? Which really impressed the queen of Sheba most? It is difficult to tell from this passage, for the two things seem so closely bound together. It is tempting to think the two do go together, particularly now, when even Solomon's riches have been far, far surpassed. Neither he nor the queen of Sheba could ever have dreamt of the resources that would one day be available to people.

Despite those material resources, turning theoretical wisdom into practical politics is as hard as ever it was. Solving riddles; finding clever answers to trick questions; making astute appointments to give great happiness and security to 'officials' who will then be dependent on their clever leader – none of this can substitute for dedicated service to one's people; grafting away at the problems; seeking long-term solutions which will bring health to future generations.

God requires more than either wealth or wisdom. He requires dedication, to himself and to all his people.

→397

his heart (for you alone know the hearts of men), ³¹so that they will fear you and walk in your ways all the time they live in the land that you gave our fathers.

³²"As for the foreigner who does not belong to your people Israel but has come from a distant land because of your great name and your mighty hand and your outstretched arm—when he comes and prays towards this temple, ³³then hear from heaven, your dwelling-place, and do whatever the foreigner asks of you, so that all the peoples of the earth may know your name and fear you, as do your own people Israel, and may know that this house that I have built bears your Name.

³⁴"When your people go to war against their enemies, wherever you send them, and when they pray to you towards this city you have chosen and the temple I have built for your Name, ³⁵then hear from heaven their prayer and their plea, and uphold their cause.

³⁶"When they sin against you—for there is no-one who does not sin—and you become angry with them and give them over to the enemy, who takes them captive to a land far away or near; ³⁷and if they have a change of heart in the land where they are held captive, and repent and plead with you in the land of their captivity and say, 'We have sinned, we have done wrong and acted wickedly'; ³⁸and if they turn back to you with all their heart and soul in the land of their captivity where they were taken, and pray towards the land that you gave their fathers, towards the city you have chosen and towards the temple that I have built for your Name; ³⁹then from heaven, your dwelling-place, hear their prayer and their pleas, and uphold their cause. And forgive your people, who have sinned against you.

⁴⁰"Now, my God, may your eyes be open and your ears attentive to the prayers offered in this place.

⁴¹"Now arise, O LORD God, and come to your resting place,
  you and the ark of your might.
May your priests, O LORD God, be clothed with salvation,
  may your saints rejoice in your goodness.
⁴²O LORD God, do not reject your anointed one.
  Remember the great love promised to David your servant."

The Dedication of the Temple

7 When Solomon finished praying, fire came down from heaven and consumed the burnt offering and the sacrifices, and the glory of the LORD filled the temple. ²The priests could not enter the temple of the LORD because the glory of the LORD filled it. ³When all the Israelites saw the fire coming down

and the glory of the LORD above the temple, they knelt on the pavement with their faces to the ground, and they worshipped and gave thanks to the LORD, saying,

  "He is good;
    his love endures for ever."

⁴Then the king and all the people offered sacrifices before the LORD. ⁵And King Solomon offered a sacrifice of twenty-two thousand head of cattle and a hundred and twenty thousand sheep and goats. So the king and all the people dedicated the temple of God. ⁶The priests took their positions, as did the Levites with the LORD's musical instruments, which King David had made for praising the LORD and which were used when he gave thanks, saying, "His love endures for ever." Opposite the Levites, the priests blew their trumpets, and all the Israelites were standing.

⁷Solomon consecrated the middle part of the courtyard in front of the temple of the LORD, and there he offered burnt offerings and the fat of the fellowship offerings,ᵃ because the bronze altar he had made could not hold the burnt offerings, the grain offerings and the fat portions.

⁸So Solomon observed the festival at that time for seven days, and all Israel with him —a vast assembly, people from Leboᵇ Hamath to the Wadi of Egypt. ⁹On the eighth day they held an assembly, for they had celebrated the dedication of the altar for seven days and the festival for seven days more. ¹⁰On the twenty-third day of the seventh month he sent the people to their homes, joyful and glad in heart for the good things the LORD had done for David and Solomon and for his people Israel.

The LORD Appears to Solomon

¹¹When Solomon had finished the temple of the LORD and the royal palace, and had succeeded in carrying out all he had in mind to do in the temple of the LORD and in his own palace, ¹²the LORD appeared to him at night and said:

  "I have heard your prayer and have chosen this place for myself as a temple for sacrifices.
  ¹³"When I shut up the heavens so that there is no rain, or command locusts to devour the land or send a plague among my people, ¹⁴if my people, who are called by my name, will humble themselves and pray and seek my face and turn from their wicked ways, then will I hear from heaven and will forgive their sin and will heal their land. ¹⁵Now my eyes will be open and my ears attentive to the prayers offered in this place. ¹⁶I have chosen and consecrated this temple so that my Name may be there for ever. My eyes and my heart will always be there.

ᵃ7 Traditionally *peace offerings*   ᵇ8 Or *from the entrance to*

17"'As for you, if you walk before me as David your father did, and do all I command, and observe my decrees and laws, 18I will establish your royal throne, as I covenanted with David your father when I said, 'You shall never fail to have a man to rule over Israel.'

19"'But if you[c] turn away and forsake the decrees and commands I have given you[c] and go off to serve other gods and worship them, 20then I will uproot Israel from my land, which I have given them, and will reject this temple which I have consecrated for my Name. I will make it a byword and an object of ridicule among all peoples. 21And though this temple is now so imposing, all who pass by will be appalled and say, 'Why has the LORD done such a thing to this land and to this temple?' 22People will answer, 'Because they have forsaken the LORD, the God of their fathers, who brought them out of Egypt, and have embraced other gods, worshipping and serving them—that is why he brought all this disaster on them.'"

Solomon's Other Activities

8 At the end of twenty years, during which Solomon built the temple of the LORD and his own palace, 2Solomon rebuilt the villages that Hiram[a] had given him, and settled Israelites in them. 3Solomon then went to Hamath Zobah and captured it. 4He also built up Tadmor in the desert and all the store cities he had built in Hamath. 5He rebuilt Upper Beth Horon and Lower Beth Horon as fortified cities, with walls and with gates and bars, 6as well as Baalath and all his store cities, and all the cities for his chariots and for his horses[b]—whatever he desired to build in Jerusalem, in Lebanon and throughout all the territory that he ruled.

7All the people left from the Hittites, Amorites, Perizzites, Hivites and Jebusites (these peoples were not Israelites), 8that is, their descendants remaining in the land, whom the Israelites had not destroyed—these Solomon conscripted for his slave labour force, as it is to this day. 9But Solomon did not make slaves of the Israelites for his work; they were his fighting men, commanders of his captains, and commanders of his chariots and charioteers. 10They were also King Solomon's chief officials—two hundred and fifty officials supervising the men.

11Solomon brought Pharaoh's daughter up from the City of David to the palace he had built for her, for he said, "My wife must not live in the palace of David king of Israel, because the places the ark of the LORD has entered are holy."

12On the altar of the LORD that he had built in front of the portico, Solomon sacrificed burnt offerings to the LORD, 13according to the daily requirement for offerings commanded by Moses for Sabbaths, New Moons and the three annual feasts—the Feast of Unleavened Bread, the Feast of Weeks and the Feast of Tabernacles. 14In keeping with the ordinance of his father David, he appointed the divisions of the priests for their duties and the Levites to lead the praise and to assist the priests according to each day's requirement. He also appointed the gatekeepers by divisions for the various gates, because this was what David the man of God had ordered. 15They did not deviate from the king's commands to the priests or to the Levites in any matter, including that of the treasuries.

16All Solomon's work was carried out, from the day the foundation of the temple of the LORD was laid until its completion. So the temple of the LORD was finished.

17Then Solomon went to Ezion Geber and Elath on the coast of Edom. 18And Hiram sent him ships commanded by his own officers, men who knew the sea. These with Solomon's men, sailed to Ophir and brought back four hundred and fifty talents[c] of gold, which they delivered to King Solomon.

The Queen of Sheba Visits Solomon

9 When the queen of Sheba heard of Solomon's fame, she came to Jerusalem to test him with hard questions. Arriving with a very great caravan—with camels carrying spices, large quantities of gold, and precious stones—she came to Solomon and talked with him about all she had on her mind. 2Solomon answered all her questions; nothing was too hard for him to explain to her. 3When the queen of Sheba saw the wisdom of Solomon, as well as the palace he had built, 4the food on his table, the seating of his officials, the attending servants in their robes, the cupbearers in their robes and the burnt offerings he made at[a] the temple of the LORD, she was overwhelmed.

5She said to the king, "The report I heard in my own country about your achievements and your wisdom is true. 6But I did not believe what they said until I came and saw with my own eyes. Indeed, not even half the greatness of your wisdom was told me; you have far exceeded the report I heard. 7How happy your men must be! How happy your officials, who continually stand before you and hear your wisdom! 8Praise be to the LORD your God, who has delighted in you and placed you on his throne as king to rule for the LORD your God. Because of the love of your God for Israel and his desire to uphold them for ever, he has made you king over them, to maintain justice and righteousness."

9Then she gave the king 120 talents[b] of gold, large quantities of spices, and precious stones. There had never been such spices as those the queen of Sheba gave to King Solomon.

10(The men of Hiram and the men of Solomon brought gold from Ophir; they also brought algum-wood[c] and precious stones.

---

c19 The Hebrew is plural.   a2 Hebrew *Huram*, a variant of *Hiram*; also in verse 18   b6 Or *charioteers*
c18 That is, about 17 tons (about 16 metric tons)   a4 Or *the ascent by which he went up to*
b9 That is, about 4 tons (about 4 metric tons)   c10 Probably a variant of *almug-wood*

11The king used the algum-wood to make steps for the temple of the LORD and for the royal palace, and to make harps and lyres for the musicians. Nothing like them had ever been seen in Judah.)

12King Solomon gave the queen of Sheba all she desired and asked for; he gave her more than she had brought to him. Then she left and returned with her retinue to her own country.

Solomon's Splendour

13The weight of the gold that Solomon received yearly was 666 talents,*d* 14not including the revenues brought in by merchants and traders. Also all the kings of Arabia and the governors of the land brought gold and silver to Solomon.

15King Solomon made two hundred large shields of hammered gold; six hundred bekas*e* of hammered gold went into each shield. 16He also made three hundred small shields of hammered gold, with three hundred bekas*f* of gold in each shield. The king put them in the Palace of the Forest of Lebanon.

17Then the king made a great throne inlaid with ivory and overlaid with pure gold. 18The throne had six steps, and a footstool of gold was attached to it. On both sides of the seat were armrests, with a lion standing beside each of them. 19Twelve lions stood on the six steps, one at either end of each step. Nothing like it had ever been made for any other kingdom. 20All King Solomon's goblets were gold, and all the household articles in the Palace of the Forest of Lebanon were pure gold. Nothing was made of silver, because silver was considered of little value in Solomon's day. 21The king had a fleet of trading ships*g* manned by Hiram's*h* men. Once every three years it returned, carrying gold, silver and ivory, and apes and baboons.

22King Solomon was greater in riches and wisdom than all the other kings of the earth. 23All the kings of the earth sought audience with Solomon to hear the wisdom God had put in his heart. 24Year after year, everyone who came brought a gift—articles of silver and gold, and robes, weapons and spices, and horses and mules.

25Solomon had four thousand stalls for horses and chariots, and twelve thousand horses,*i* which he kept in the chariot cities and also with him in Jerusalem. 26He ruled over all the kings from the River*j* to the land of the Philistines, as far as the border of Egypt. 27The king made silver as common in Jerusalem as stones, and cedar as plentiful as sycamore-fig trees in the foothills. 28Solomon's horses were imported from Egypt*k* and from all other countries.

Solomon's Death

29As for the other events of Solomon's reign, from beginning to end, are they not written in the records of Nathan the prophet, in the prophecy of Ahijah the Shilonite and in the visions of Iddo the seer concerning Jeroboam son of Nebat? 30Solomon reigned in Jerusalem over all Israel for forty years. 31Then he rested with his fathers and was buried in the city of David his father. And Rehoboam his son succeeded him as king.

Israel Rebels Against Rehoboam

10 Rehoboam went to Shechem, for all the Israelites had gone there to make him king. 2When Jeroboam son of Nebat heard this (he was in Egypt, where he had fled from King Solomon), he returned from Egypt. 3So they sent for Jeroboam, and he and all Israel went to Rehoboam and said to him: 4"Your father put a heavy yoke on us, but now lighten the harsh labour and the heavy yoke he put on us, and we will serve you."

5Rehoboam answered, "Come back to me in three days." So the people went away.

6Then King Rehoboam consulted the elders who had served his father Solomon during his lifetime. "How would you advise me to answer these people?" he asked.

7They replied, "If you will be kind to these people and please them and give them a favourable answer, they will always be your servants."

8But Rehoboam rejected the advice the elders gave him and consulted the young men who had grown up with him and were serving him. 9He asked them, "What is your advice? How should we answer these people who say to me, 'Lighten the yoke your father put on us'?"

10The young men who had grown up with him replied, "Tell the people who have said to you, 'Your father put a heavy yoke on us, but make our yoke lighter'—tell them, 'My little finger is thicker than my father's waist. 11My father laid on you a heavy yoke; I will make it even heavier. My father scourged you with whips; I will scourge you with scorpions.'"

12Three days later Jeroboam and all the people returned to Rehoboam, as the king had said, "Come back to me in three days." 13The king answered them harshly. Rejecting the advice of the elders, 14he followed the advice of the young men and said, "My father made your yoke heavy; I will make it even heavier. My father scourged you with whips; I will scourge you with scorpions." 15So the king did not listen to the people, for this turn of events was from God, to fulfil the word that the LORD had spoken to Jeroboam son of Nebat through Ahijah the Shilonite.

16When all Israel saw that the king refused to listen to them, they answered the king:

"What share do we have in David,
    what part in Jesse's son?
To your tents, O Israel!
    Look after your own house, O David!"

---

d13 That is, about 23 tons (about 23 metric tons)   *e15* That is, about 7½ pounds (about 3.5 kilograms)
f16 That is, about 3¾ pounds (about 1.7 kilograms)   *g21* Hebrew *of ships that could go to Tarshish*
h21 Hebrew *Huram,* a variant of *Hiram*   *i25* Or *charioteers*   *j26* That is, the Euphrates
k28 Or possibly *Muzur,* a region in Cilicia

So all the Israelites went home. [17]But as for the Israelites who were living in the towns of Judah, Rehoboam still ruled over them.

[18]King Rehoboam sent out Adoniram,[a] who was in charge of forced labour, but the Israelites stoned him to death. King Rehoboam, however, managed to get into his chariot and escape to Jerusalem. [19]So Israel has been in rebellion against the house of David to this day.

11 When Rehoboam arrived in Jerusalem, he mustered the house of Judah and Benjamin—a hundred and eighty thousand fighting men—to make war against Israel and to regain the kingdom for Rehoboam.

[2]But this word of the LORD came to Shemaiah the man of God: [3]"Say to Rehoboam son of Solomon king of Judah and to all the Israelites in Judah and Benjamin, [4]'This is what the LORD says: Do not go up to fight against your brothers. Go home, every one of you, for this is my doing.'" So they obeyed the words of the LORD and turned back from marching against Jeroboam.

Rehoboam Fortifies Judah

[5]Rehoboam lived in Jerusalem and built up towns for defence in Judah: [6]Bethlehem, Etam, Tekoa, [7]Beth Zur, Soco, Adullam, [8]Gath, Mareshah, Ziph, [9]Adoraim, Lachish, Azekah, [10]Zorah, Aijalon and Hebron. These were fortified cities in Judah and Benjamin. [11]He strengthened their defences and put commanders in them, with supplies of food, olive oil and wine. [12]He put shields and spears in all the cities, and made them very strong. So Judah and Benjamin were his.

[13]The priests and Levites from all their districts throughout Israel sided with him. [14]The Levites even abandoned their pasturelands and property, and came to Judah and Jerusalem because Jeroboam and his sons had rejected them as priests of the LORD. [15]And he appointed his own priests for the high places and for the goat and calf idols he had made. [16]Those from every tribe of Israel who set their hearts on seeking the LORD, the God of Israel, followed the Levites to Jerusalem to offer sacrifices to the LORD, the God of their fathers. [17]They strengthened the kingdom of Judah and supported Rehoboam son of Solomon for three years, walking in the ways of David and Solomon during this time.

Rehoboam's Family

[18]Rehoboam married Mahalath, who was the daughter of David's son Jerimoth and of Abihail, the daughter of Jesse's son Eliab. [19]She bore him sons: Jeush, Shemariah and Zaham. [20]Then he married Maacah daughter of Absalom, who bore him Abijah, Attai, Ziza and Shelomith. [21]Rehoboam loved Maacah daughter of Absalom more than any of his other wives and concubines. In all he had eighteen wives and sixty concubines, twenty-eight sons and sixty daughters.

[22]Rehoboam appointed Abijah son of Maacah to be the chief prince among his brothers, in order to make him king. [23]He acted wisely, dispersing some of his sons throughout the districts of Judah and Benjamin, and to all the fortified cities. He gave them abundant provisions and took many wives for them.

Shishak Attacks Jerusalem

12 After Rehoboam's position as king was established and he had become strong, he and all Israel[a] with him abandoned the law of the LORD. [2]Because they had been unfaithful to the LORD, Shishak king of Egypt attacked Jerusalem in the fifth year of King Rehoboam. [3]With twelve hundred chariots and sixty thousand horsemen and the innumerable troops of Libyans, Sukkites and Cushites[b] that came with him from Egypt, [4]he captured the fortified cities of Judah and came as far as Jerusalem.

[5]Then the prophet Shemaiah came to Rehoboam and to the leaders of Judah who had assembled in Jerusalem for fear of Shishak, and he said to them, "This is what the LORD says: 'You have abandoned me; therefore I now abandon you to Shishak.'"

[6]The leaders of Israel and the king humbled themselves and said, "The LORD is just."

[7]When the LORD saw that they humbled themselves, this word of the LORD came to Shemaiah: "Since they have humbled themselves, I will not destroy them but will soon give them deliverance. My wrath will not be poured out on Jerusalem through Shishak. [8]They will, however, become subject to him, so that they may learn the difference between serving me and serving the kings of other lands."

[9]When Shishak king of Egypt attacked Jerusalem, he carried off the treasures of the temple of the LORD and the treasures of the royal palace. He took everything, including the gold shields that Solomon had made. [10]So King Rehoboam made bronze shields to replace them and assigned these to the commanders of the guard on duty at the entrance to the royal palace. [11]Whenever the king went to the LORD's temple, the guards went with him, bearing the shields, and afterwards they returned them to the guardroom.

[12]Because Rehoboam humbled himself, the LORD's anger turned from him, and he was not totally destroyed. Indeed, there was some good in Judah.

[13]King Rehoboam established himself firmly in Jerusalem and continued as king. He was forty-one years old when he became king, and he reigned for seventeen years in Jerusalem, the city the LORD had chosen out of all the tribes of Israel in which to put his Name. His mother's name was Naamah; she was an Ammonite. [14]He did evil because he had not set his heart on seeking the LORD.

[15]As for the events of Rehoboam's reign, from beginning to end, are they not written in

---

[a]18 Hebrew *Hadoram*, a variant of *Adoniram*   [a]1 That is, Judah, as frequently in 2 Chronicles
[b]3 That is, people from the upper Nile region

the records of Shemaiah the prophet and of Iddo the seer that deal with genealogies? There was continual warfare between Rehoboam and Jeroboam. ¹⁶Rehoboam rested with his fathers and was buried in the City of David. And Abijah his son succeeded him as king.

Abijah King of Judah

13 In the eighteenth year of the reign of Jeroboam, Abijah became king of Judah, ²and he reigned in Jerusalem for three years. His mother's name was Maacah,ᵃ a daughterᵇ of Uriel of Gibeah.

There was war between Abijah and Jeroboam. ³Abijah went into battle with a force of four hundred thousand able fighting men, and Jeroboam drew up a battle line against him with eight hundred thousand able troops.

⁴Abijah stood on Mount Zemaraim, in the hill country of Ephraim, and said, "Jeroboam and all Israel, listen to me! ⁵Don't you know that the LORD, the God of Israel, has given the kingship of Israel to David and his descendants for ever by a covenant of salt? ⁶Yet Jeroboam son of Nebat, an official of Solomon son of David, rebelled against his master. ⁷Some worthless scoundrels gathered around him and opposed Rehoboam son of Solomon when he was young and indecisive and not strong enough to resist them.

⁸"And now you plan to resist the kingdom of the LORD, which is in the hands of David's descendants. You are indeed a vast army and have with you the golden calves that Jeroboam made to be your gods. ⁹But didn't you drive out the priests of the LORD, the sons of Aaron, and the Levites, and make priests of your own as the peoples of other lands do? Whoever comes to consecrate himself with a young bull and seven rams may become a priest of what are not gods.

¹⁰"As for us, the LORD is our God, and we have not forsaken him. The priests who serve the LORD are sons of Aaron, and the Levites assist them. ¹¹Every morning and evening they present burnt offerings and fragrant incense to the LORD. They set out the bread on the ceremonially clean table and light the lamps on the gold lampstand every evening. We are observing the requirements of the LORD our God. But you have forsaken him. ¹²God is with us; he is our leader. His priests with their trumpets will sound the battle cry against you. Men of Israel, do not fight against the LORD, the God of your fathers, for you will not succeed."

¹³Now Jeroboam had sent troops round to the rear, so that while he was in front of Judah the ambush was behind them. ¹⁴Judah turned and saw that they were being attacked at both front and rear. Then they cried out to the LORD. The priests blew their trumpets ¹⁵and the men of Judah raised the battle cry. At the sound of their battle cry, God routed Jeroboam and all Israel before Abijah and Judah. ¹⁶The Israelites fled before Judah, and God delivered them into their hands. ¹⁷Abijah and his men inflicted heavy losses on them, so that there were five hundred thousand casualties among Israel's able men. ¹⁸The men of Israel were subdued on that occasion, and the men of Judah were victorious because they relied on the LORD, the God of their fathers.

¹⁹Abijah pursued Jeroboam and took from him the towns of Bethel, Jeshanah and Ephron, with their surrounding villages. ²⁰Jeroboam did not regain power during the time of Abijah. And the LORD struck him down and he died.

²¹But Abijah grew in strength. He married fourteen wives and had twenty-two sons and sixteen daughters.

²²The other events of Abijah's reign, what he did and what he said, are written in the annotations of the prophet Iddo.

14 And Abijah rested with his fathers and was buried in the City of David. Asa his son succeeded him as king, and in his days the country was at peace for ten years.

Asa King of Judah

²Asa did what was good and right in the eyes of the LORD his God. ³He removed the foreign altars and the high places, smashed the sacred stones and cut down the Asherah poles.ᵃ ⁴He commanded Judah to seek the LORD, the God of their fathers, and to obey his laws and commands. ⁵He removed the high places and incense altars in every town in Judah, and the kingdom was at peace under him. ⁶He built up the fortified cities of Judah, since the land was at peace. No-one was at war with him during those years, for the LORD gave him rest.

⁷"Let us build up these towns," he said to Judah, "and put walls round them, with towers, gates and bars. The land is still ours, because we have sought the LORD our God; we sought him and he has given us rest on every side." So they built and prospered.

⁸Asa had an army of three hundred thousand men from Judah, equipped with large shields and with spears, and two hundred and eighty thousand from Benjamin, armed with small shields and with bows. All these were brave fighting men.

⁹Zerah the Cushite marched out against them with a vast armyᵇ and three hundred chariots, and came as far as Mareshah. ¹⁰Asa went out to meet him, and they took up battle positions in the Valley of Zephathah near Mareshah.

¹¹Then Asa called to the LORD his God and said, "LORD, there is no-one like you to help the powerless against the mighty. Help us, O LORD our God, for we rely on you, and in your name we have come against this vast army. O LORD, you are our God; do not let man prevail against you."

¹²The LORD struck down the Cushites before Asa and Judah. The Cushites fled, ¹³and

---

ᵃ2 Most Septuagint manuscripts and Syriac (see also 2 Chron. 11:20 and 1 Kings 15:2); Hebrew *Micaiah*
ᵇ2 Or *granddaughter*   ᵃ3 That is, symbols of the goddess Asherah; here and elsewhere in 2 Chronicles
ᵇ9 Hebrew *with an army of a thousand thousands* or *with an army of thousands upon thousands*

Asa and his army pursued them as far as Gerar. Such a great number of Cushites fell that they could not recover; they were crushed before the LORD and his forces. The men of Judah carried off a large amount of plunder. [14]They destroyed all the villages around Gerar, for the terror of the LORD had fallen upon them. They plundered all these villages, since there was much booty there. [15]They also attacked the camps of the herdsmen and carried off droves of sheep and goats and camels. Then they returned to Jerusalem.

Asa's Reform

15 The Spirit of God came upon Azariah son of Oded. [2]He went out to meet Asa and said to him, "Listen to me, Asa and all Judah and Benjamin. The LORD is with you when you are with him. If you seek him, he will be found by you, but if you forsake him, he will forsake you. [3]For a long time Israel was without the true God, without a priest to teach and without the law. [4]But in their distress they turned to the LORD, the God of Israel, and sought him, and he was found by them. [5]In those days it was not safe to travel about, for all the inhabitants of the lands were in great turmoil. [6]One nation was being crushed by another and one city by another, because God was troubling them with every kind of distress. [7]But as for you, be strong and do not give up, for your work will be rewarded."

[8]When Asa heard these words and the prophecy of Azariah son of[a] Oded the prophet, he took courage. He removed the detestable idols from the whole land of Judah and Benjamin and from the towns he had captured in the hills of Ephraim. He repaired the altar of the LORD that was in front of the portico of the LORD's temple.

[9]Then he assembled all Judah and Benjamin and the people from Ephraim, Manasseh and Simeon who had settled among them, for large number; had come over to him from Israel when they saw that the LORD his God was with him.

[10]They assembled at Jerusalem in the third month of the fifteenth year of Asa's reign. [11]At that time they sacrificed to the LORD seven hundred head of cattle and seven thousand sheep and goats from the plunder they had brought back. [12]They entered into a covenant to seek the LORD, the God of their fathers, with all their heart and soul. [13]All who would not seek the LORD, the God of Israel, were to be put to death, whether small or great, man or woman. [14]They took an oath to the LORD with loud acclamation, with shouting and with trumpets and horns. [15]All Judah rejoiced about the oath because they had sworn it wholeheartedly. They sought God eagerly, and he was found by them. So the LORD gave them rest on every side.

[16]King Asa also deposed his grandmother Maacah from her position as queen mother, because she had made a repulsive Asherah

pole. Asa cut the pole down, broke it up and burned it in the Kidron Valley. [17]Although he did not remove the high places from Israel, Asa's heart was fully committed to the LORD all his life. [18]He brought into the temple of God the silver and gold and the articles that he and his father had dedicated.

[19]There was no more war until the thirty-fifth year of Asa's reign.

Asa's Last Years

16 In the thirty-sixth year of Asa's reign Baasha king of Israel went up against Judah and fortified Ramah to prevent anyone from leaving or entering the territory of Asa king of Judah.

[2]Asa then took the silver and gold out of the treasuries of the LORD's temple and of his own palace and sent it to Ben-Hadad king of Aram, who was ruling in Damascus. [3]"Let there be a treaty between me and you," he said, "as there was between my father and your father. See, I am sending you silver and gold. Now break your treaty with Baasha king of Israel so that he will withdraw from me."

[4]Ben-Hadad agreed with King Asa and sent the commanders of his forces against the towns of Israel. They conquered Ijon, Dan, Abel Maim[a] and all the store cities of Naphtali. [5]When Baasha heard this, he stopped building Ramah and abandoned his work. [6]Then King Asa brought all the men of Judah, and they carried away from Ramah the stones and timber Baasha had been using. With them he built up Geba and Mizpah.

[7]At that time Hanani the seer came to Asa king of Judah and said to him: "Because you relied on the king of Aram and not on the LORD your God, the army of the king of Aram has escaped from your hand. [8]Were not the Cushites[b] and Libyans a mighty army with great numbers of chariots and horsemen[c]? Yet when you relied on the LORD, he delivered them into your hand. [9]For the eyes of the LORD range throughout the earth to strengthen those whose hearts are fully committed to him. You have done a foolish thing, and from now on you will be at war."

[10]Asa was angry with the seer because of this; he was so enraged that he put him in prison. At the same time Asa brutally oppressed some of the people.

[11]The events of Asa's reign, from beginning to end, are written in the book of the kings of Judah and Israel. [12]In the thirty-ninth year of his reign Asa was afflicted with a disease in his feet. Though his disease was severe, even in his illness he did not seek help from the LORD, but only from the physicians. [13]Then in the forty-first year of his reign Asa died and rested with his fathers. [14]They buried him in the tomb that he had cut out for himself in the City of David. They laid him on a bier covered with spices and various blended perfumes, and they made a huge fire in his honour.

---

[a]8 Vulgate and Syriac (see also Septuagint and verse 1); Hebrew does not have *Azariah son of.*
[a]4 Also known as *Abel Beth Maacah*   [b]8 That is, people from the upper Nile region   [c]8 Or *charioteers*

Jehoshaphat King of Judah

17 Jehoshaphat his son succeeded him as king and strengthened himself against Israel. ²He stationed troops in all the fortified cities of Judah and put garrisons in Judah and in the towns of Ephraim that his father Asa had captured.

³The LORD was with Jehoshaphat because in his early years he walked in the ways that his father David had followed. He did not consult the Baals ⁴but sought the God of his father and followed his commands rather than the practices of Israel. ⁵The LORD established the kingdom under his control; and all Judah brought gifts to Jehoshaphat, so that he had great wealth and honour. ⁶His heart was devoted to the ways of the LORD; furthermore, he removed the high places and the Asherah poles from Judah.

⁷In the third year of his reign he sent his officials Ben-Hail, Obadiah, Zechariah, Nethanel and Micaiah to teach in the towns of Judah. ⁸With them were certain Levites—Shemaiah, Nethaniah, Zebadiah, Asahel, Shemiramoth, Jehonathan, Adonijah, Tobijah and Tob-Adonijah—and the priests Elishama and Jehoram. ⁹They taught throughout Judah, taking with them the Book of the Law of the LORD; they went round to all the towns of Judah and taught the people.

¹⁰The fear of the LORD fell on all the kingdoms of the lands surrounding Judah, so that they did not make war with Jehoshaphat. ¹¹Some Philistines brought Jehoshaphat gifts and silver as tribute, and the Arabs brought him flocks: seven thousand seven hundred rams and seven thousand seven hundred goats.

¹²Jehoshaphat became more and more powerful; he built forts and store cities in Judah ¹³and had large supplies in the towns of Judah. He also kept experienced fighting men in Jerusalem. ¹⁴Their enrolment by families was as follows:

From Judah, commanders of units of 1,000:

Adnah the commander, with 300,000 fighting men;

¹⁵next, Jehohanan the commander, with 280,000;

¹⁶next, Amasiah son of Zicri, who volunteered himself for the service of the LORD, with 200,000.

¹⁷From Benjamin:

Eliada, a valiant soldier, with 200,000 men armed with bows and shields;

¹⁸next, Jehozabad, with 180,000 men armed for battle.

¹⁹These were the men who served the king, besides those he stationed in the fortified cities throughout Judah.

Micaiah Prophesies Against Ahab

18 Now Jehoshaphat had great wealth and honour, and he allied himself with Ahab by marriage. ²Some years later he went down to visit Ahab in Samaria. Ahab slaughtered many sheep and cattle for him and the people with him and urged him to attack Ramoth Gilead. ³Ahab king of Israel asked Jehoshaphat king of Judah, "Will you go with me against Ramoth Gilead?"

Jehoshaphat replied, "I am as you are, and my people as your people; we will join you in the war." ⁴But Jehoshaphat also said to the king of Israel, "First seek the counsel of the LORD."

⁵So the king of Israel brought together the prophets—four hundred men—and asked them, "Shall we go to war against Ramoth Gilead, or shall I refrain?"

"Go," they answered, "for God will give it into the king's hand."

⁶But Jehoshaphat asked, "Is there not a prophet of the LORD here whom we can enquire of?"

⁷The king of Israel answered Jehoshaphat, "There is still one man through whom we can enquire of the LORD, but I hate him because he never prophesies anything good about me, but always bad. He is Micaiah son of Imlah."

"The king should not say that," Jehoshaphat replied.

⁸So the king of Israel called one of his officials and said, "Bring Micaiah son of Imlah at once."

⁹Dressed in their royal robes, the king of Israel and Jehoshaphat king of Judah were sitting on their thrones at the threshing-floor by the entrance to the gate of Samaria, with all the prophets prophesying before them. ¹⁰Now Zedekiah son of Kenaanah had made iron horns, and he declared, "This is what the LORD says: 'With these you will gore the Arameans until they are destroyed.'"

¹¹All the other prophets were prophesying the same thing. "Attack Ramoth Gilead and be victorious," they said, "for the LORD will give it into the king's hand."

¹²The messenger who had gone to summon Micaiah said to him, "Look, as one man the other prophets are predicting success for the king. Let your word agree with theirs, and speak favourably."

¹³But Micaiah said, "As surely as the LORD lives, I can tell him only what my God says."

¹⁴When he arrived, the king asked him, "Micaiah, shall we go to war against Ramoth Gilead, or shall I refrain?"

"Attack and be victorious," he answered, "for they will be given into your hand."

¹⁵The king said to him, "How many times must I make you swear to tell me nothing but the truth in the name of the LORD?"

¹⁶Then Micaiah answered, "I saw all Israel scattered on the hills like sheep without a shepherd, and the LORD said, 'These people have no master. Let each one go home in peace.'"

¹⁷The king of Israel said to Jehoshaphat, "Didn't I tell you that he never prophesies anything good about me, but only bad?"

¹⁸Micaiah continued, "Therefore hear the word of the LORD: I saw the LORD sitting on his throne with all the host of heaven standing on his right and on his left. ¹⁹And the LORD said, 'Who will entice Ahab king of Israel into attacking Ramoth Gilead and going to his death there?'

"One suggested this, and another that.

20Finally, a spirit came forward, stood before the LORD and said, 'I will entice him.'

"'By what means?' the LORD asked.

21"'I will go and be a lying spirit in the mouths of all his prophets,' he said.

"'You will succeed in enticing him,' said the LORD. 'Go and do it.'

22"So now the LORD has put a lying spirit in the mouths of these prophets of yours. The LORD has decreed disaster for you."

23Then Zedekiah son of Kenaanah went up and slapped Micaiah in the face. "Which way did the spirit from*a* the LORD go when he went from me to speak to you?" he asked.

24Micaiah replied, "You will find out on the day you go to hide in an inner room."

25The king of Israel then ordered, "Take Micaiah and send him back to Amon the ruler of the city and to Joash the king's son, 26and say, 'This is what the king says: Put this fellow in prison and give him nothing but bread and water until I return safely.'"

27Micaiah declared, "If you ever return safely, the LORD has not spoken through me." Then he added, "Mark my words, all you people!"

Ahab Killed at Ramoth Gilead

28So the king of Israel and Jehoshaphat king of Judah went up to Ramoth Gilead. 29The king of Israel said to Jehoshaphat, "I will enter the battle in disguise, but you wear your royal robes." So the king of Israel disguised himself and went into battle.

30Now the king of Aram had ordered his chariot commanders, "Do not fight with anyone, small or great, except the king of Israel." 31When the chariot commanders saw Jehoshaphat, they thought, "This is the king of Israel." So they turned to attack him, but Jehoshaphat cried out, and the LORD helped him. God drew them away from him, 32for when the chariot commanders saw that he was not the king of Israel, they stopped pursuing him.

33But someone drew his bow at random and hit the king of Israel between the sections of his armour. The king told the chariot driver, "Wheel around and get me out of the fighting. I've been wounded." 34All day long the battle raged, and the king of Israel propped himself up in his chariot facing the Arameans until evening. Then at sunset he died.

19 When Jehoshaphat king of Judah returned safely to his palace in Jerusalem, 2Jehu the seer, the son of Hanani, went out to meet him and said to the king, "Should you help the wicked and love*a* those who hate the LORD? Because of this, the wrath of the LORD is upon you. 3There is, however, some good in you, for you have rid the land of the Asherah poles and have set your heart on seeking God."

Jehoshaphat Appoints Judges

4Jehoshaphat lived in Jerusalem, and he went out again among the people from Beersheba to the hill country of Ephraim and turned them back to the LORD, the God of their fathers. 5He appointed judges in the land, in each of the fortified cities of Judah. 6He told them, "Consider carefully what you do, because you are not judging for man but for the LORD, who is with you whenever you give a verdict. 7Now let the fear of the LORD be upon you. Judge carefully, for with the LORD our God there is no injustice or partiality or bribery."

8In Jerusalem also, Jehoshaphat appointed some of the Levites, priests and heads of Israelite families to administer the law of the LORD and to settle disputes. And they lived in Jerusalem. 9He gave them these orders: "You must serve faithfully and wholeheartedly in the fear of the LORD. 10In every case that comes before you from your fellow countrymen who live in the cities—whether bloodshed or other concerns of the law, commands, decrees or ordinances—you are to warn them not to sin against the LORD; otherwise his wrath will come on you and your brothers. Do this, and you will not sin.

11"Amariah the chief priest will be over you in any matter concerning the LORD, and Zebadiah son of Ishmael, the leader of the tribe of Judah, will be over you in any matter concerning the king, and the Levites will serve as officials before you. Act with courage, and may the LORD be with those who do well."

Jehoshaphat Defeats Moab and Ammon

20 After this, the Moabites and Ammonites with some of the Meunites*a* came to make war on Jehoshaphat.

2Some men came and told Jehoshaphat, "A vast army is coming against you from Edom,*b* from the other side of the Sea.*c* It is already in Hazazon Tamar" (that is, En Gedi). 3Alarmed, Jehoshaphat resolved to enquire of the LORD, and he proclaimed a fast for all Judah. 4The people of Judah came together to seek help from the LORD; indeed, they came from every town in Judah to seek him.

5Then Jehoshaphat stood up in the assembly of Judah and Jerusalem at the temple of the LORD in the front of the new courtyard 6and said:

"O LORD, God of our fathers, are you not the God who is in heaven? You rule over all the kingdoms of the nations. Power and might are in your hand, and no-one can withstand you. 7O our God, did you not drive out the inhabitants of this land before your people Israel and give it for ever to the descendants of Abraham your friend? 8They have lived in it and have built in it a sanctuary for your Name, saying, 9'If calamity comes upon us, whether the sword of judgment, or plague or famine, we will stand in your presence before this temple that

---

*a23 Or Spirit of   a2 Or and make alliances with   a1 Some Septuagint manuscripts; Hebrew Ammonites
b2 One Hebrew manuscript; most Hebrew manuscripts, Septuagint and Vulgate Aram   c2 That is, the Dead Sea*

bears your Name and will cry out to you in our distress, and you will hear us and save us.'

10"But now here are men from Ammon, Moab and Mount Seir, whose territory you would not allow Israel to invade when they came from Egypt; so they turned away from them and did not destroy them. 11See how they are repaying us by coming to drive us out of the possession you gave us as an inheritance. 12O our God, will you not judge them? For we have no power to face this vast army that is attacking us. We do not know what to do, but our eyes are upon you."

13All the men of Judah, with their wives and children and little ones, stood there before the Lord.

14Then the Spirit of the Lord came upon Jahaziel son of Zechariah, the son of Benaiah, the son of Jeiel, the son of Mattaniah, a Levite and descendant of Asaph, as he stood in the assembly.

15He said, "Listen, King Jehoshaphat and all who live in Judah and Jerusalem! This is what the Lord says to you: 'Do not be afraid or discouraged because of this vast army. For the battle is not yours, but God's. 16Tomorrow march down against them. They will be climbing up by the Pass of Ziz, and you will find them at the end of the gorge in the Desert of Jeruel. 17You will not have to fight this battle. Take up your positions; stand firm and see the deliverance the Lord will give you, O Judah and Jerusalem. Do not be afraid; do not be discouraged. Go out to face them tomorrow, and the Lord will be with you.'"

18Jehoshaphat bowed with his face to the ground, and all the people of Judah and Jerusalem fell down in worship before the Lord. 19Then some Levites from the Kohathites and Korahites stood up and praised the Lord, the God of Israel, with a very loud voice.

20Early in the morning they left for the Desert of Tekoa. As they set out, Jehoshaphat stood and said, "Listen to me, Judah and people of Jerusalem! Have faith in the Lord your God and you will be upheld; have faith in his prophets and you will be successful." 21After consulting the people, Jehoshaphat appointed men to sing to the Lord and to praise him for the splendour of hisd holiness as they went out at the head of the army, saying:

"Give thanks to the Lord,
    for his love endures for ever."

22As they began to sing and praise, the Lord set ambushes against the men of Ammon and Moab and Mount Seir who were invading Judah, and they were defeated. 23The men of Ammon and Moab rose up against the men from Mount Seir to destroy and annihilate them. After they finished slaughtering the men from Seir, they helped to destroy one another.

24When the men of Judah came to the place that overlooks the desert and looked towards the vast army, they saw only dead bodies lying on the ground; no-one had escaped. 25So Jehoshaphat and his men went to carry off their plunder, and they found among them a great amount of equipment and clothinge and also articles of value—more than they could take away. There was so much plunder that it took three days to collect it. 26On the fourth day they assembled in the Valley of Beracah, where they praised the Lord. This is why it is called the Valley of Beracahf to this day.

27Then, led by Jehoshaphat, all the men of Judah and Jerusalem returned joyfully to Jerusalem, for the Lord had given them cause to rejoice over their enemies. 28They entered Jerusalem and went to the temple of the Lord with harps and lutes and trumpets.

29The fear of God came upon all the kingdoms of the countries when they heard how the Lord had fought against the enemies of Israel. 30And the kingdom of Jehoshaphat was at peace, for his God had given him rest on every side.

The End of Jehoshaphat's Reign

31So Jehoshaphat reigned over Judah. He was thirty-five years old when he became king of Judah, and he reigned in Jerusalem for twenty-five years. His mother's name was Azubah daughter of Shilhi. 32He walked in the ways of his father Asa and did not stray from them; he did what was right in the eyes of the Lord. 33The high places, however, were not removed, and the people still had not set their hearts on the God of their fathers.

34The other events of Jehoshaphat's reign, from beginning to end, are written in the annals of Jehu son of Hanani, which are recorded in the book of the kings of Israel.

35Later, Jehoshaphat king of Judah made an alliance with Ahaziah king of Israel, who was guilty of wickedness. 36He agreed with him to construct a fleet of trading ships.g After these were built at Ezion Geber, 37Eliezer son of Dodavahu of Mareshah prophesied against Jehoshaphat, saying, "Because you have made an alliance with Ahaziah, the Lord will destroy what you have made." The ships were wrecked and were not able to set sail to trade.h

21 Then Jehoshaphat rested with his fathers and was buried with them in the City of David. And Jehoram his son succeeded him as king. 2Jehoram's brothers, the sons of Jehoshaphat, were Azariah, Jehiel, Zechariah, Azariahu, Michael and Shephatiah. All these were sons of Jehoshaphat king of Israel.a 3Their father had given them many gifts of silver and gold and

---

d21 Or him with the splendour of
e25 Some Hebrew manuscripts and Vulgate; most Hebrew manuscripts corpses
f26 Beracah means praise.
g36 Hebrew of ships that could go to Tarshish   h37 Hebrew sail for Tarshish
a2 That is, Judah, as frequently in 2 Chronicles

articles of value, as well as fortified cities in Judah, but he had given the kingdom to Jehoram because he was his firstborn son.

Jehoram King of Judah

⁴When Jehoram established himself firmly over his father's kingdom, he put all his brothers to the sword along with some of the princes of Israel. ⁵Jehoram was thirty-two years old when he became king, and he reigned in Jerusalem for eight years. ⁶He walked in the ways of the kings of Israel, as the house of Ahab had done, for he married a daughter of Ahab. He did evil in the eyes of the LORD. ⁷Nevertheless, because of the covenant the LORD had made with David, the LORD was not willing to destroy the house of David. He had promised to maintain a lamp for him and his descendants for ever.

⁸In the time of Jehoram, Edom rebelled against Judah and set up its own king. ⁹So Jehoram went there with his officers and all his chariots. The Edomites surrounded him and his chariot commanders, but he rose up and broke through by night. ¹⁰To this day Edom has been in rebellion against Judah.

Libnah revolted at the same time, because Jehoram had forsaken the LORD, the God of his fathers. ¹¹He had also built high places on the hills of Judah and had caused the people of Jerusalem to prostitute themselves and had led Judah astray.

¹²Jehoram received a letter from Elijah the prophet, which said:

"This is what the LORD, the God of your father David, says: 'You have not walked in the ways of your father Jehoshaphat or of Asa king of Judah. ¹³But you have walked in the ways of the kings of Israel, and you have led Judah and the people of Jerusalem to prostitute themselves, just as the house of Ahab did. You have also murdered your own brothers, members of your father's house, men who were better than you. ¹⁴So now the LORD is about to strike your people, your sons, your wives and everything that is yours, with a heavy blow. ¹⁵You yourself will be very ill with a lingering disease of the bowels, until the disease causes your bowels to come out.'"

¹⁶The LORD aroused against Jehoram the hostility of the Philistines and of the Arabs who lived near the Cushites. ¹⁷They attacked Judah, invaded it and carried off all the goods found in the king's palace, together with his sons and wives. Not a son was left to him except Ahaziah,ᵇ the youngest.

¹⁸After all this, the LORD afflicted Jehoram with an incurable disease of the bowels. ¹⁹In the course of time, at the end of the second year, his bowels came out because of the disease, and he died in great pain. His people

made no fire in his honour, as they had for his fathers.

²⁰Jehoram was thirty-two years old when he became king, and he reigned in Jerusalem for eight years. He passed away, to no-one's regret, and was buried in the City of David, but not in the tombs of the kings.

Ahaziah King of Judah

22 The people of Jerusalem made Ahaziah, Jehoram's youngest son, king in his place, since the raiders, who came with the Arabs into the camp, had killed all the older sons. So Ahaziah son of Jehoram king of Judah began to reign.

²Ahaziah was twenty-twoᵃ years old when he became king, and he reigned in Jerusalem for one year. His mother's name was Athaliah, a granddaughter of Omri.

³He too walked in the ways of the house of Ahab, for his mother encouraged him in doing wrong. ⁴He did evil in the eyes of the LORD, as the house of Ahab had done, for after his father's death they became his advisers, to his undoing. ⁵He also followed their counsel when he went with Joramᵇ son of Ahab king of Israel to war against Hazael king of Aram at Ramoth Gilead. The Arameans wounded Joram; ⁶so he returned to Jezreel to recover from the wounds they had inflicted on him at Ramothᶜ in his battle with Hazael king of Aram.

Then Ahaziahᵈ son of Jehoram king of Judah went down to Jezreel to see Joram son of Ahab because he had been wounded.

⁷Through Ahaziah's visit to Joram, God brought about Ahaziah's downfall. When Ahaziah arrived, he went out with Joram to meet Jehu son of Nimshi, whom the LORD had anointed to destroy the house of Ahab. ⁸While Jehu was executing judgment on the house of Ahab, he found the princes of Judah and the sons of Ahaziah's relatives, who had been attending Ahaziah, and he killed them. ⁹He then went in search of Ahaziah, and his men captured him while he was hiding in Samaria. He was brought to Jehu and put to death. They buried him, for they said, "He was a son of Jehoshaphat, who sought the LORD with all his heart." So there was no-one in the house of Ahaziah powerful enough to retain the kingdom.

Athaliah and Joash

¹⁰When Athaliah the mother of Ahaziah saw that her son was dead, she proceeded to destroy the whole royal family of the house of Judah. ¹¹But Jehosheba,ᵉ the daughter of King Jehoram, took Joash son of Ahaziah and stole him away from among the royal princes who were about to be murdered and put him and his nurse in a bedroom. Because Jehosheba,ᵉ the daughter of King Jehoram and wife of the priest Jehoiada, was Ahaziah's sister, she hid the child from Athaliah so that she could not kill him. ¹²He remained

---

ᵇ17 Hebrew Jehoahaz, a variant of Ahaziah
ᵃ2 Some Septuagint manuscripts and Syriac (see also 2 Kings 8:26); Hebrew forty-two
ᵇ5 Hebrew Jehoram, a variant of Joram; also in verses 6 and 7   ᶜ6 Hebrew Ramah, a variant of Ramoth
ᵈ6 Some Hebrew manuscripts, Septuagint, Vulgate and Syriac (see also 2 Kings 8:29); most Hebrew manuscripts Azariah   ᵉ11 Hebrew Jehoshabeath, a variant of Jehosheba

hidden with them at the temple of God for six years while Athaliah ruled the land.

23 In the seventh year Jehoiada showed his strength. He made a covenant with the commanders of units of a hundred: Azariah son of Jeroham, Ishmael son of Jehohanan, Azariah son of Obed, Maaseiah son of Adaiah, and Elishaphat son of Zicri. ²They went throughout Judah and gathered the Levites and the heads of Israelite families from all the towns. When they came to Jerusalem, ³the whole assembly made a covenant with the king at the temple of God.

Jehoiada said to them, "The king's son shall reign, as the LORD promised concerning the descendants of David. ⁴Now this is what you are to do: A third of you priests and Levites who are going on duty on the Sabbath are to keep watch at the doors, ⁵a third of you at the royal palace and a third at the Foundation Gate, and all the other men are to be in the courtyards of the temple of the LORD. ⁶No-one is to enter the temple of the LORD except the priests and Levites on duty; they may enter because they are consecrated, but all the other men are to guard what the LORD has assigned to them.ᵃ ⁷The Levites are to station themselves round the king, each man with his weapons in his hand. Anyone who enters the temple must be put to death. Stay close to the king wherever he goes."

⁸The Levites and all the men of Judah did just as Jehoiada the priest ordered. Each one took his men—those who were going on duty on the Sabbath and those who were going off duty—for Jehoiada the priest had not released any of the divisions. ⁹Then he gave the commanders of units of a hundred the spears and the large and small shields that had belonged to King David and that were in the temple of God. ¹⁰He stationed all the men, each with his weapon in his hand, round the king—near the altar and the temple, from the south side to the north side of the temple.

¹¹Jehoiada and his sons brought out the king's son and put the crown on him; they presented him with a copy of the covenant and proclaimed him king. They anointed him and shouted, "Long live the king!"

¹²When Athaliah heard the noise of the people running and cheering the king, she went to them at the temple of the LORD. ¹³She looked, and there was the king, standing by his pillar at the entrance. The officers and the trumpeters were beside the king, and all the people of the land were rejoicing and blowing trumpets, and singers with musical instruments were leading the praises. Then Athaliah tore her robes and shouted, "Treason! Treason!"

¹⁴Jehoiada the priest sent out the commanders of units of a hundred, who were in charge of the troops, and said to them: "Bring her out between the ranks,ᵇ and put to the sword anyone who follows her." For the priest had said, "Do not put her to death at the temple of the LORD." ¹⁵So they seized her

as she reached the entrance of the Horse Gate on the palace grounds, and there they put her to death.

¹⁶Jehoiada then made a covenant that he and the people and the kingᶜ would be the LORD's people. ¹⁷All the people went to the temple of Baal and tore it down. They smashed the altars and idols and killed Mattan the priest of Baal in front of the altars.

¹⁸Then Jehoiada placed the oversight of the temple of the LORD in the hands of the priests, who were Levites, to whom David had made assignments in the temple, to present the burnt offerings of the LORD as written in the Law of Moses, with rejoicing and singing, as David had ordered. ¹⁹He also stationed doorkeepers at the gates of the LORD's temple so that no-one who was in any way unclean might enter.

²⁰He took with him the commanders of hundreds, the nobles, the rulers of the people and all the people of the land and brought the king down from the temple of the LORD. They went into the palace through the Upper Gate and seated the king on the royal throne, ²¹and all the people of the land rejoiced. And the city was quiet, because Athaliah had been slain with the sword.

Joash Repairs the Temple

24 Joash was seven years old when he became king, and he reigned in Jerusalem for forty years. His mother's name was Zibiah; she was from Beersheba. ²Joash did what was right in the eyes of the LORD all the years of Jehoiada the priest. ³Jehoiada chose two wives for him, and he had sons and daughters.

⁴Some time later Joash decided to restore the temple of the LORD. ⁵He called together the priests and Levites and said to them, "Go to the towns of Judah and collect the money due annually from all Israel, to repair the temple of your God. Do it now." But the Levites did not act at once.

⁶Therefore the king summoned Jehoiada the chief priest and said to him, "Why haven't you required the Levites to bring in from Judah and Jerusalem the tax imposed by Moses the servant of the LORD and by the assembly of Israel for the Tent of the Testimony?"

⁷Now the sons of that wicked woman Athaliah had broken into the temple of God and had used even its sacred objects for the Baals.

⁸At the king's command, a chest was made and placed outside, at the gate of the temple of the LORD. ⁹A proclamation was then issued in Judah and Jerusalem that they should bring to the LORD the tax that Moses the servant of God required of Israel in the desert. ¹⁰All the officials and all the people brought their contributions gladly, dropping them into the chest until it was full. ¹¹Whenever the chest was brought in by the Levites to the king's officials and they saw that there was a large amount of money, the

---

ᵃ6 Or *to observe the LORD's command ₍not to enter₎*   ᵇ14 Or *out from the precincts*
ᶜ16 Or *covenant between ₍the LORD₎ and the people and the king that they* (see 2 Kings 11:17)

royal secretary and the officer of the chief priest would come and empty the chest and carry it back to its place. They did this regularly and collected a great amount of money. [12]The king and Jehoiada gave it to the men who carried out the work required for the temple of the LORD. They hired masons and carpenters to restore the LORD's temple, and also workers in iron and bronze to repair the temple.

[13]The men in charge of the work were diligent, and the repairs progressed under them. They rebuilt the temple of God according to its original design and reinforced it. [14]When they had finished, they brought the rest of the money to the king and Jehoiada, and with it were made articles for the LORD's temple: articles for the service and for the burnt offerings, and also dishes and other objects of gold and silver. As long as Jehoiada lived, burnt offerings were presented continually in the temple of the LORD.

[15]Now Jehoiada was old and full of years, and he died at the age of a hundred and thirty. [16]He was buried with the kings in the City of David, because of the good he had done in Israel for God and his temple.

The Wickedness of Joash

[17]After the death of Jehoiada, the officials of Judah came and paid homage to the king, and he listened to them. [18]They abandoned the temple of the LORD, the God of their fathers, and worshiped Asherah poles and idols. Because of their guilt, God's anger came upon Judah and Jerusalem. [19]Although the LORD sent prophets to the people to bring them back to him, and though they testified against them, they would not listen.

[20]Then the Spirit of God came upon Zechariah son of Jehoiada the priest. He stood before the people and said, "This is what God says: 'Why do you disobey the LORD's commands? You will not prosper. Because you have forsaken the LORD, he has forsaken you.'"

[21]But they plotted against him, and by order of the king they stoned him to death in the courtyard of the LORD's temple. [22]King Joash did not remember the kindness Zechariah's father Jehoiada had shown him but killed his son, who said as he lay dying, "May the LORD see this and call you to account."

[23]At the turn of the year,[a] the army of Aram marched against Joash; it invaded Judah and Jerusalem and killed all the leaders of the people. They sent all the plunder to their king in Damascus. [24]Although the Aramean army had come with only a few men, the LORD delivered into their hands a much larger army. Because Judah had forsaken the LORD, the God of their fathers, judgment was executed on Joash. [25]When the Arameans withdrew, they left Joash severely wounded. His officials conspired against him for murdering the son of Jehoiada the priest, and

they killed him in his bed. So he died and was buried in the City of David, but not in the tombs of the kings.

[26]Those who conspired against him were Zabad,[b] son of Shimeath an Ammonite woman, and Jehozabad, son of Shimrith[c] a Moabite woman. [27]The account of his sons, the many prophecies about him, and the record of the restoration of the temple of God are written in the annotations on the book of the kings. And Amaziah his son succeeded him as king.

Amaziah King of Judah

25 Amaziah was twenty-five years old when he became king, and he reigned in Jerusalem for twenty-nine years. His mother's name was Jehoaddin;[a] she was from Jerusalem. [2]He did what was right in the eyes of the LORD, but not wholeheartedly. [3]After the kingdom was firmly in his control, he executed the officials who had murdered his father the king. [4]Yet he did not put their sons to death, but acted in accordance with what is written in the Law, in the Book of Moses, where the LORD commanded: "Fathers shall not be put to death for their children, nor children put to death for their fathers; each is to die for his own sins."[b]

[5]Amaziah called the people of Judah together and assigned them according to their families to commanders of thousands and commanders of hundreds for all Judah and Benjamin. He then mustered those twenty years old or more and found that there were three hundred thousand men ready for military service, able to handle the spear and shield. [6]He also hired a hundred thousand fighting men from Israel for a hundred talents[c] of silver.

[7]But a man of God came to him and said, "O king, these troops from Israel must not march with you, for the LORD is not with Israel—not with any of the people of Ephraim. [8]Even if you go and fight courageously in battle, God will overthrow you before the enemy, for God has the power to help or to overthrow."

[9]Amaziah asked the man of God, "But what about the hundred talents I paid for these Israelite troops?"

The man of God replied, "The LORD can give you much more than that."

[10]So Amaziah dismissed the troops who had come to him from Ephraim and sent them home. They were furious with Judah and left for home in a great rage.

[11]Amaziah then marshalled his strength and led his army to the Valley of Salt, where he killed ten thousand men of Seir. [12]The army of Judah also captured ten thousand men alive, took them to the top of a cliff and threw them down so that all were dashed to pieces.

[13]Meanwhile the troops that Amaziah had sent back and had not allowed to take part in the war raided Judean towns from Samaria

---

[a]23 Probably in the spring   [b]26 A variant of *Jozabad*   [c]26 A variant of *Shomer*
[a]1 Hebrew *Jehoaddan*, a variant of *Jehoaddin*   [b]4 Deut. 24:16
[c]6 That is, about 3⅓ tons (about 3.4 metric tons); also in verse 9

to Beth Horon. They killed three thousand people and carried off great quantities of plunder.

¹⁴When Amaziah returned from slaughtering the Edomites, he brought back the gods of the people of Seir. He set them up as his own gods, bowed down to them and burned sacrifices to them. ¹⁵The anger of the LORD burned against Amaziah, and he sent a prophet to him, who said, "Why do you consult this people's gods, which could not save their own people from your hand?"

¹⁶While he was still speaking, the king said to him, "Have we appointed you an adviser to the king? Stop! Why be struck down?"

So the prophet stopped but said, "I know that God has determined to destroy you, because you have done this and have not listened to my counsel."

¹⁷After Amaziah king of Judah consulted his advisers, he sent this challenge to Jehoash*d* son of Jehoahaz, the son of Jehu, king of Israel: "Come, meet me face to face."

¹⁸But Jehoash king of Israel replied to Amaziah king of Judah, "A thistle in Lebanon sent a message to a cedar in Lebanon, 'Give your daughter to my son in marriage.' Then a wild beast in Lebanon came along and trampled the thistle underfoot. ¹⁹You say to yourself that you have defeated Edom, and now you are arrogant and proud. But stay at home! Why ask for trouble and cause your own downfall and that of Judah also?"

²⁰Amaziah, however, would not listen, for God so worked that he might hand them over to Jehoash*j*, because they sought the gods of Edom. ²¹So Jehoash king of Israel attacked. He and Amaziah king of Judah faced each other at Beth Shemesh in Judah. ²²Judah was routed by Israel, and every man fled to his home. ²³Jehoash king of Israel captured Amaziah king of Judah, the son of Joash, the son of Ahaziah,*e* at Beth Shemesh. Then Jehoash brought him to Jerusalem and broke down the wall of Jerusalem from the Ephraim Gate to the Corner Gate—a section about six hundred feet*f* long. ²⁴He took all the gold and silver and all the articles found in the temple of God that had been in the care of Obed-Edom, together with the palace treasures and the hostages, and returned to Samaria.

²⁵Amaziah son of Joash king of Judah lived for fifteen years after the death of Jehoash son of Jehoahaz king of Israel. ²⁶As for the other events of Amaziah's reign, from beginning to end, are they not written in the book of the kings of Judah and Israel? ²⁷From the time that Amaziah turned away from following the LORD, they conspired against him in Jerusalem and he fled to Lachish, but they sent men after him to Lachish and killed him there. ²⁸He was brought back by horse and was buried with his fathers in the City of Judah.

Uzziah King of Judah

26 Then all the people of Judah took Uzziah,*a* who was sixteen years old, and made him king in place of his father Amaziah. ²He was the one who rebuilt Elath and restored it to Judah after Amaziah rested with his fathers.

³Uzziah was sixteen years old when he became king, and he reigned in Jerusalem for fifty-two years. His mother's name was Jecoliah; she was from Jerusalem. ⁴He did what was right in the eyes of the LORD, just as his father Amaziah had done. ⁵He sought God during the days of Zechariah, who instructed him in the fear*b* of God. As long as he sought the LORD, God gave him success.

⁶He went to war against the Philistines and broke down the walls of Gath, Jabneh and Ashdod. He then rebuilt towns near Ashdod and elsewhere among the Philistines. ⁷God helped him against the Philistines and against the Arabs who lived in Gur Baal and against the Meunites. ⁸The Ammonites brought tribute to Uzziah, and his fame spread as far as the border of Egypt, because he had become very powerful.

⁹Uzziah built towers in Jerusalem at the Corner Gate, at the Valley Gate and at the angle of the wall, and he fortified them. ¹⁰He also built towers in the desert and dug many cisterns, because he had much livestock in the foothills and in the plain. He had people working his fields and vineyards in the hills and in the fertile lands, for he loved the soil.

¹¹Uzziah had a well-trained army, ready to go out by divisions according to their numbers as mustered by Jeiel the secretary and Maaseiah the officer under the direction of Hananiah, one of the royal officials. ¹²The total number of family leaders over the fighting men was 2,600. ¹³Under their command was an army of 307,500 men trained for war, a powerful force to support the king against his enemies. ¹⁴Uzziah provided shields, spears, helmets, coats of armour, bows and slingstones for the entire army. ¹⁵In Jerusalem he made machines designed by skilful men for use on the towers and on the corner defences to shoot arrows and hurl large stones. His fame spread far and wide, for he was greatly helped until he became powerful.

¹⁶But after Uzziah became powerful, his pride led to his downfall. He was unfaithful to the LORD his God, and entered the temple of the LORD to burn incense on the altar of incense. ¹⁷Azariah the priest with eighty other courageous priests of the LORD followed him in. ¹⁸They confronted him and said, "It is not right for you, Uzziah, to burn incense to the LORD. That is for the priests, the descendants of Aaron, who have been consecrated to burn incense. Leave the sanctuary, for you have been unfaithful; and you will not be honoured by the LORD God."

¹⁹Uzziah, who had a censer in his hand

---

d17 Hebrew Joash, a variant of *Jehoash*; also in verses 18, 21, 23 and 25
e23 Hebrew Jehoahaz, a variant of *Ahaziah*
f23 Hebrew four hundred cubits (about 180 metres)
a1 Also called Azariah
b5 Many Hebrew manuscripts, Septuagint and Syriac; other Hebrew manuscripts vision

ready to burn incense, became angry. While he was raging at the priests in their presence before the incense altar in the LORD's temple, leprosy[c] broke out on his forehead. [20]When Azariah the chief priest and all the other priests looked at him, they saw that he had leprosy on his forehead, so they hurried him out. Indeed, he himself was eager to leave, because the LORD had afflicted him.

[21]King Uzziah had leprosy until the day he died. He lived in a separate house[d]—leprous, and excluded from the temple of the LORD. Jotham his son had charge of the palace and governed the people of the land.

[22]The other events of Uzziah's reign, from beginning to end, are recorded by the prophet Isaiah son of Amoz. [23]Uzziah rested with his fathers and was buried near them in a field for burial that belonged to the kings, for people said, "He had leprosy." And Jotham his son succeeded him as king.

Jotham King of Judah

27 Jotham was twenty-five years old when he became king, and he reigned in Jerusalem for sixteen years. His mother's name was Jerusha daughter of Zadok. [2]He did what was right in the eyes of the LORD, just as his father Uzziah had done, but unlike him he did not enter the temple of the LORD. The people, however, continued their corrupt practices. [3]Jotham rebuilt the Upper Gate of the temple of the LORD and did extensive work on the wall at the hill of Ophel. [4]He built towns in the Judean hills and forts and towers in the wooded areas.

[5]Jotham made war on the king of the Ammonites and conquered them. That year the Ammonites paid him a hundred talents[a] of silver, ten thousand cors[b] of wheat and ten thousand cors of barley. The Ammonites brought him the same amount also in the second and third years.

[6]Jotham grew powerful because he walked steadfastly before the LORD his God.

[7]The other events in Jotham's reign, including all his wars and the other things he did, are written in the book of the kings of Israel and Judah. [8]He was twenty-five years old when he became king, and he reigned in Jerusalem for sixteen years. [9]Jotham rested with his fathers and was buried in the City of David. And Ahaz his son succeeded him as king.

Ahaz King of Judah

28 Ahaz was twenty years old when he became king, and he reigned in Jerusalem for sixteen years. Unlike David his father, he did not do what was right in the eyes of the LORD. [2]He walked in the ways of the kings of Israel and also made cast idols for worshiping the Baals. [3]He burned sacrifices in the Valley of Ben Hinnom and sacrificed his sons in the fire, following the detestable ways of the nations that the LORD had driven out before the Israelites. [4]He offered sacrifices and burned incense at the high places, on the hilltops and under every spreading tree.

[5]Therefore the LORD his God handed him over to the king of Aram. The Arameans defeated him and took many of his people as prisoners and brought them to Damascus.

He was also given into the hands of the king of Israel, who inflicted heavy casualties on him. [6]In one day Pekah son of Remaliah killed a hundred and twenty thousand soldiers in Judah—because Judah had forsaken the LORD, the God of their fathers. [7]Zicri, an Ephraimite warrior, killed Maaseiah the king's son, Azrikam the officer in charge of the palace, and Elkanah, second to the king. [8]The Israelites took captive from their kinsmen two hundred thousand wives, sons and daughters. They also took a great deal of plunder, which they carried back to Samaria.

[9]But a prophet of the LORD named Oded was there, and he went out to meet the army when it returned to Samaria. He said to them, "Because the LORD, the God of your fathers, was angry with Judah, he gave them into your hand. But you have slaughtered them in a rage that reaches to heaven. [10]And now you intend to make the men and women of Judah and Jerusalem your slaves. But aren't you also guilty of sins against the LORD your God? [11]Now listen to me! Send back your fellow countrymen that you have taken as prisoners, for the LORD's fierce anger rests on you."

[12]Then some of the leaders in Ephraim—Azariah son of Jehohanan, Berekiah son of Meshillemoth, Jehizkiah son of Shallum, and Amasa son of Hadlai—confronted those who were arriving from the war. [13]"You must not bring those prisoners here," they said, "or we will be guilty before the LORD. Do you intend to add to our sin and guilt? For our guilt is already great, and his fierce anger rests on Israel."

[14]So the soldiers gave up the prisoners and plunder in the presence of the officials and all the assembly. [15]The men designated by name took the prisoners, and from the plunder they clothed all who were naked. They provided them with clothes and sandals, food and drink, and healing balm. All those who were weak they put on donkeys. So they took them back to their fellow countrymen at Jericho, the City of Palms, and returned to Samaria.

[16]At that time King Ahaz sent to the king[a] of Assyria for help. [17]The Edomites had again come and attacked Judah and carried away prisoners, [18]while the Philistines had raided towns in the foothills and in the Negev of Judah. They captured and occupied Beth Shemesh, Aijalon and Gederoth, as well as Soco, Timnah and Gimzo, with their surrounding villages. [19]The LORD had humbled

[c]19 The Hebrew word was used for various diseases affecting the skin—not necessarily leprosy; also in verses 20, 21 and 23.   [d]21 Or *in a house where he was relieved of responsibilities*
[a]5 That is, about 3½ tons (about 3.4 metric tons)
[b]5 That is, probably about 60,500 bushels (about 2,200 kilolitres)
[a]16 One Hebrew manuscript, Septuagint and Vulgate (see also 2 Kings 16:7); most Hebrew manuscripts *kings*

Judah because of Ahaz king of Israel,[b] for he had promoted wickedness in Judah and had been most unfaithful to the LORD. [20]Tiglath-Pileser[c] king of Assyria came to him, but gave him trouble instead of help. [21]Ahaz took some of the things from the temple of the LORD and from the royal palace and from the princes and presented them to the king of Assyria, but that did not help him.

[22]In his time of trouble King Ahaz became even more unfaithful to the LORD. [23]He offered sacrifices to the gods of Damascus, who had defeated him; for he thought, "Since the gods of the kings of Aram have helped them, I will sacrifice to them so that they will help me." But they were his downfall and the downfall of all Israel.

[24]Ahaz gathered together the furnishings from the temple of God and took them away.[d] He shut the doors of the LORD's temple and set up altars at every street corner in Jerusalem. [25]In every town in Judah he built high places to burn sacrifices to other gods and provoked the LORD, the God of his fathers, to anger.

[26]The other events of his reign and all his ways, from beginning to end, are written in the book of the kings of Judah and Israel. [27]Ahaz rested with his fathers and was buried in the city of Jerusalem, but he was not placed in the tombs of the kings of Israel. And Hezekiah his son succeeded him as king.

Hezekiah Purifies the Temple

29 Hezekiah was twenty-five years old when he became king, and he reigned in Jerusalem for twenty-nine years. His mother's name was Abijah daughter of Zechariah. [2]He did what was right in the eyes of the LORD, just as his father David had done.

[3]In the first month of the first year of his reign, he opened the doors of the temple of the LORD and repaired them. [4]He brought in the priests and the Levites, assembled them in the square on the east side [5]and said, "Listen to me, Levites! Consecrate yourselves now and consecrate the temple of the LORD, the God of your fathers. Remove all defilement from the sanctuary. [6]Our fathers were unfaithful; they did evil in the eyes of the LORD our God and forsook him. They turned their faces away from the LORD's dwelling-place and turned their backs on him. [7]They also shut the doors of the portico and put out the lamps. They did not burn incense or present any burnt offerings at the sanctuary to the God of Israel. [8]Therefore, the anger of the LORD has fallen on Judah and Jerusalem; he has made them an object of dread and horror and scorn, as you can see with your own eyes. [9]This is why our fathers have fallen by the sword and why our sons and daughters and our wives are in captivity. [10]Now I intend to make a covenant with the LORD, the God of Israel, so that his fierce anger will turn away from us. [11]My sons, do

not be negligent now, for the LORD has chosen you to stand before him and serve him, to minister before him and to burn incense."

[12]Then these Levites set to work:

from the Kohathites,
  Mahath son of Amasai and Joel son of Azariah;
from the Merarites,
  Kish son of Abdi and Azariah son of Jehallel;
from the Gershonites,
  Joah son of Zimmah and Eden son of Joah;
[13]from the descendants of Elizaphan,
  Shimri and Jeiel;
from the descendants of Asaph,
  Zechariah and Mattaniah;
[14]from the descendants of Heman,
  Jehiel and Shimei;
from the descendants of Jeduthun,
  Shemaiah and Uzziel.

[15]When they had assembled their brothers and consecrated themselves, they went in to purify the temple of the LORD, as the king had ordered, following the word of the LORD. [16]The priests went into the sanctuary of the LORD to purify it. They brought out to the courtyard of the LORD's temple everything unclean that they found in the temple of the LORD. The Levites took it and carried it out to the Kidron Valley. [17]They began the consecration on the first day of the first month, and by the eighth day of the month they reached the portico of the LORD. For eight more days they consecrated the temple of the LORD itself, finishing in the sixteenth day of the first month.

[18]Then they went in to King Hezekiah and reported: "We have purified the entire temple of the LORD, the altar of burnt offering with all its utensils, and the table for setting out the consecrated bread, with all its articles. [19]We have prepared and consecrated all the articles that King Ahaz removed in his unfaithfulness while he was king. They are now in front of the LORD's altar."

[20]Early the next morning King Hezekiah gathered the city officials together and went up to the temple of the LORD. [21]They brought seven bulls, seven rams, seven male lambs and seven male goats as a sin offering for the kingdom, for the sanctuary and for Judah. The king commanded the priests, the descendants of Aaron, to offer these on the altar of the LORD. [22]So they slaughtered the bulls, and the priests took the blood and sprinkled it on the altar; next they slaughtered the rams and sprinkled their blood on the altar; then they slaughtered the lambs and sprinkled their blood on the altar. [23]The goats for the sin offering were brought before the king and the assembly, and they laid their hands on them. [24]The priests then slaughtered the goats and presented their blood on the altar for a sin offering to atone for all Israel, because the king had ordered the burnt offering and the sin offering for all Israel.

---

[b]19 That is, Judah, as frequently in 2 Chronicles   [c]20 Hebrew *Tilgath-Pilneser*, a variant of *Tiglath-Pileser*
[d]24 Or *and cut them up*

²⁵He stationed the Levites in the temple of the LORD with cymbals, harps and lyres in the way prescribed by David and Gad the king's seer and Nathan the prophet; this was commanded by the LORD through his prophets. ²⁶So the Levites stood ready with David's instruments, and the priests with their trumpets.

²⁷Hezekiah gave the order to sacrifice the burnt offering on the altar. As the offering began, singing to the LORD began also, accompanied by trumpets and the instruments of David king of Israel. ²⁸The whole assembly bowed in worship, while the singers sang and the trumpeters played. All this continued until the sacrifice of the burnt offering was completed.

²⁹When the offerings were finished, the king and everyone present with him knelt down and worshipped. ³⁰King Hezekiah and his officials ordered the Levites to praise the LORD with the words of David and of Asaph the seer. So they sang praises with gladness and bowed their heads and worshipped.

³¹Then Hezekiah said, "You have now dedicated yourselves to the LORD. Come and bring sacrifices and thank-offerings to the temple of the LORD." So the assembly brought sacrifices and thank-offerings, and all whose hearts were willing brought burnt offerings.

³²The number of burnt offerings the assembly brought was seventy bulls, a hundred rams and two hundred male lambs—all of them for burnt offerings to the LORD. ³³The animals consecrated as sacrifices amounted to six hundred bulls and three thousand sheep and goats. ³⁴The priests, however, were too few to skin all the burnt offerings; so their kinsmen the Levites helped them until the task was finished and until other priests had been consecrated, for the Levites had been more conscientious in consecrating themselves than the priests had been. ³⁵There were burnt offerings in abundance, together with the fat of the fellowship offerings[a] and the drink offerings that accompanied the burnt offerings.

So the service of the temple of the LORD was re-established. ³⁶Hezekiah and all the people rejoiced at what God had brought about for his people, because it was done so quickly.

Hezekiah Celebrates the Passover

30 Hezekiah sent word to all Israel and Judah and also wrote letters to Ephraim and Manasseh, inviting them to come to the temple of the LORD in Jerusalem and celebrate the Passover to the LORD, the God of Israel. ²The king and his officials and the whole assembly in Jerusalem decided to celebrate the Passover in the second month. ³They had not been able to celebrate it at the regular time because not enough priests had consecrated themselves and the people had not assembled in Jerusalem. ⁴The plan seemed right both to the king and to the whole assembly. ⁵They decided to send a proclamation throughout Israel, from Beersheba to Dan, calling the people to come to Jerusalem and celebrate the Passover to the LORD, the God of Israel. It had not been celebrated in large numbers according to what was written.

⁶At the king's command, couriers went throughout Israel and Judah with letters from the king and from his officials, which read:

"People of Israel, return to the LORD, the God of Abraham, Isaac and Israel, that he may return to you who are left, who have escaped from the hand of the kings of Assyria. ⁷Do not be like your fathers and brothers, who were unfaithful to the LORD, the God of their fathers, so that he made them an object of horror, as you see. ⁸Do not be stiff-necked, as your fathers were; submit to the LORD. Come to the sanctuary, which he has consecrated for ever. Serve the LORD your God, so that his fierce anger will turn away from you. ⁹If you return to the LORD, then your brothers and your children will be shown compassion by their captors and will come back to this land, for the LORD your God is gracious and compassionate. He will not turn his face from you if you return to him."

¹⁰The couriers went from town to town in Ephraim and Manasseh, as far as Zebulun, but the people scorned and ridiculed them. ¹¹Nevertheless, some men of Asher, Manasseh and Zebulun humbled themselves and went to Jerusalem. ¹²Also in Judah the hand of God was on the people to give them unity of mind to carry out what the king and his officials had ordered, following the word of the LORD.

¹³A very large crowd of people assembled in Jerusalem to celebrate the Feast of Unleavened Bread in the second month. ¹⁴They removed the altars in Jerusalem and cleared away the incense altars and threw them into the Kidron Valley.

¹⁵They slaughtered the Passover lamb on the fourteenth day of the second month. The priests and the Levites were ashamed and consecrated themselves and brought burnt offerings to the temple of the LORD. ¹⁶Then they took up their regular positions as prescribed in the Law of Moses the man of God. The priests sprinkled the blood handed to them by the Levites. ¹⁷Since many in the crowd had not consecrated themselves, the Levites had to kill the Passover lambs for all those who were not ceremonially clean and could not consecrate ˻their lambs˼ to the LORD. ¹⁸Although most of the many people who came from Ephraim, Manasseh, Issachar and Zebulun had not purified themselves, yet they ate the Passover, contrary to what was written. But Hezekiah prayed for them, saying, "May the LORD, who is good, pardon everyone ¹⁹who sets his heart on seeking God—the LORD, the God of his fathers—even if he is not clean according to

---

ᵃ35 Traditionally *peace offerings*

the rules of the sanctuary." [20]And the LORD heard Hezekiah and healed the people.

[21]The Israelites who were present in Jerusalem celebrated the Feast of Unleavened Bread for seven days with great rejoicing, while the Levites and priests sang to the LORD every day, accompanied by the LORD's instruments of praise.[a]

[22]Hezekiah spoke encouragingly to all the Levites, who showed good understanding of the service of the LORD. For the seven days they ate their assigned portion and offered fellowship offerings[b] and praised the LORD, the God of their fathers.

[23]The whole assembly then agreed to celebrate the festival seven more days; so for another seven days they celebrated joyfully. [24]Hezekiah king of Judah provided a thousand bulls and seven thousand sheep and goats for the assembly, and the officials provided them with a thousand bulls and ten thousand sheep and goats. A great number of priests consecrated themselves. [25]The entire assembly of Judah rejoiced, along with the priests and Levites and all who had assembled from Israel, including the aliens who had come from Israel and those who lived in Judah. [26]There was great joy in Jerusalem, for since the days of Solomon son of David king of Israel there had been nothing like this in Jerusalem. [27]The priests and the Levites stood to bless the people, and God heard them, for their prayer reached heaven, his holy dwelling-place.

31 When all this had ended, the Israelites who were there went out to the towns of Judah, smashed the sacred stones and cut down the Asherah poles. They destroyed the high places and the altars throughout Judah and Benjamin and in Ephraim and Manasseh. After they had destroyed all of them, the Israelites returned to their own towns and to their own property.

Contributions for Worship

[2]Hezekiah assigned the priests and Levites to divisions—each of them according to their duties as priests or Levites—to offer burnt offerings and fellowship offerings,[a] to minister, to give thanks and to sing praises at the gates of the LORD's dwelling. [3]The king contributed from his own possessions for the morning and evening burnt offerings and for the burnt offerings on the Sabbaths, New Moons and appointed feasts as written in the Law of the LORD. [4]He ordered the people living in Jerusalem to give the portion due to the priests and Levites so that they could devote themselves to the Law of the LORD. [5]As soon as the order went out, the Israelites generously gave the firstfruits of their grain, new wine, oil and honey and all that the fields produced. They brought a great amount, a tithe of everything. [6]The men of Israel and Judah who lived in the towns of Judah also brought a tithe of their herds and flocks and a tithe of the holy things dedicated to the LORD their God, and they piled them in heaps.

[7]They began doing this in the third month and finished in the seventh month. [8]When Hezekiah and his officials came and saw the heaps, they praised the LORD and blessed his people Israel.

[9]Hezekiah asked the priests and Levites about the heaps; [10]and Azariah the chief priest, from the family of Zadok, answered, "Since the people began to bring their contributions to the temple of the LORD, we have had enough to eat and plenty to spare, because the LORD has blessed his people, and this great amount is left over."

[11]Hezekiah gave orders to prepare storerooms in the temple of the LORD, and this was done. [12]Then they faithfully brought in the contributions, tithes and dedicated gifts. Conaniah, a Levite, was in charge of these things, and his brother Shimei was next in rank. [13]Jehiel, Azaziah, Nahath, Asahel, Jerimoth, Jozabad, Eliel, Ismakiah, Mahath and Benaiah were supervisors under Conaniah and Shimei his brother, by appointment of King Hezekiah and Azariah the official in charge of the temple of God.

[14]Kore son of Imnah the Levite, keeper of the East Gate, was in charge of the freewill offerings given to God, distributing the contributions made to the LORD and also the consecrated gifts. [15]Eden, Miniamin, Jeshua, Shemaiah, Amariah and Shecaniah assisted him faithfully in the towns of the priests, distributing to their fellow priests according to their divisions, old and young alike.

[16]In addition, they distributed to the males three years old or more whose names were in the genealogical records—all who would enter the temple of the LORD to perform the daily duties of their various tasks, according to their responsibilities and their divisions. [17]And they distributed to the priests enrolled by their families in the genealogical records and likewise to the Levites twenty years old or more, according to their responsibilities and their divisions. [18]They included all the little ones, the wives, and the sons and daughters of the whole community listed in these genealogical records. For they were faithful in consecrating themselves.

[19]As for the priests, the descendants of Aaron, who lived on the farm lands around their towns or in any other towns, men were designated by name to distribute portions to every male among them and to all who were recorded in the genealogies of the Levites.

[20]This is what Hezekiah did throughout Judah, doing what was good and right and faithful before the LORD his God. [21]In everything that he undertook in the service of God's temple and in obedience to the law and the commands, he sought his God and worked wholeheartedly. And so he prospered.

Sennacherib Threatens Jerusalem

32 After all that Hezekiah had so faithfully done, Sennacherib king of Assyria came and invaded Judah. He laid

---

[a]21 Or *priests praised the LORD every day with resounding instruments belonging to the LORD.*
[b]22 Traditionally *peace offerings*   [a]2 Traditionally *peace offerings*

siege to the fortified cities, thinking to conquer them for himself. [2]When Hezekiah saw that Sennacherib had come and that he intended to make war on Jerusalem, [3]he consulted with his officials and military staff about blocking off the water from the springs outside the city, and they helped him. [4]A large force of men assembled, and they blocked all the springs and the stream that flowed through the land. "Why should the kings[a] of Assyria come and find plenty of water?" they said. [5]Then he worked hard repairing all the broken sections of the wall and building towers on it. He built another wall outside that one and reinforced the supporting terraces[b] of the City of David. He also made large numbers of weapons and shields.

[6]He appointed military officers over the people and assembled them before him in the square at the city gate and encouraged them with these words: [7]"Be strong and courageous. Do not be afraid or discouraged because of the king of Assyria and the vast army with him, for there is a greater power with us than with him. [8]With him is only the arm of flesh, but with us is the LORD our God to help us and to fight our battles." And the people gained confidence from what Hezekiah the king of Judah said.

[9]Later, when Sennacherib king of Assyria and all his forces were laying siege to Lachish, he sent his officers to Jerusalem with this message for Hezekiah king of Judah and for all the people of Judah who were there:

[10]"This is what Sennacherib king of Assyria says: On what are you basing your confidence, that you remain in Jerusalem under siege? [11]When Hezekiah says, 'The LORD our God will save us from the hand of the king of Assyria,' he is misleading you, to let you die of hunger and thirst. [12]Did not Hezekiah himself remove this god's high places and altars, saying to Judah and Jerusalem, 'You must worship before one altar and burn sacrifices on it'?

[13]"Do you not know what I and my fathers have done to all the peoples of the other lands? Were the gods of those nations ever able to deliver their land from my hand? [14]Who of all the gods of these nations that my fathers destroyed has been able to save his people from me? How then can your god deliver you from my hand? [15]Now do not let Hezekiah deceive you and mislead you like this. Do not believe him, for no god of any nation or kingdom has been able to deliver his people from my hand or the hand of my fathers. How much less will your god deliver you from my hand!"

[16]Sennacherib's officers spoke further against the LORD God and against his servant Hezekiah. [17]The king also wrote letters insulting the LORD, the God of Israel, and saying this against him: "Just as the gods of the peoples of the other lands did not rescue their people from my hand, so the god of Hezekiah will not rescue his people from my hand." [18]Then they called out in Hebrew to the people of Jerusalem who were on the wall, to terrify them and make them afraid in order to capture the city. [19]They spoke about the God of Jerusalem as they did about the gods of the other peoples of the world—the work of men's hands.

[20]King Hezekiah and the prophet Isaiah son of Amoz cried out in prayer to heaven about this. [21]And the LORD sent an angel, who annihilated all the fighting men and the leaders and officers in the camp of the Assyrian king. So he withdrew to his own land in disgrace. And when he went into the temple of his god, some of his sons cut him down with the sword.

[22]So the LORD saved Hezekiah and the people of Jerusalem from the hand of Sennacherib king of Assyria and from the hand of all others. He took care of them[c] on every side. [23]Many brought offerings to Jerusalem for the LORD and valuable gifts for Hezekiah king of Judah. From then on he was highly regarded by all the nations.

Hezekiah's Pride, Success and Death

[24]In those days Hezekiah became ill and was at the point of death. He prayed to the LORD, who answered him and gave him a miraculous sign. [25]But Hezekiah's heart was proud and he did not respond to the kindness shown him; therefore the LORD's wrath was on him and on Judah and Jerusalem. [26]Then Hezekiah repented of the pride of his heart, as did the people of Jerusalem; therefore the LORD's wrath did not come upon them during the days of Hezekiah.

[27]Hezekiah had very great riches and honour, and he made treasuries for his silver and gold and for his precious stones, spices, shields and all kinds of valuables. [28]He also made buildings to store the harvest of grain, new wine and oil; and he made stalls for various kinds of cattle, and pens for the flocks. [29]He built villages and acquired great numbers of flocks and herds, for God had given him very great riches.

[30]It was Hezekiah who blocked the upper outlet of the Gihon spring and channelled the water down to the west side of the City of David. He succeeded in everything he undertook. [31]But when envoys were sent by the rulers of Babylon to ask him about the miraculous sign that had occurred in the land, God left him to test him and to know everything that was in his heart.

[32]The other events of Hezekiah's reign and his acts of devotion are written in the vision of the prophet Isaiah son of Amoz in the book of the kings of Judah and Israel. [33]Hezekiah rested with his fathers and was buried on the hill where the tombs of David's descendants are. All Judah and the people of Jerusalem

---

[a]4 Hebrew; Septuagint and Syriac *king*   [b]5 Or *the Millo*
[c]22 Hebrew; Septuagint and Vulgate *He gave them rest*

honoured him when he died. And Manasseh his son succeeded him as king.

Manasseh King of Judah

33 Manasseh was twelve years old when he became king, and he reigned in Jerusalem for fifty-five years. ²He did evil in the eyes of the LORD, following the detestable practices of the nations the LORD had driven out before the Israelites. ³He rebuilt the high places his father Hezekiah had demolished; he also erected altars to the Baals and made Asherah poles. He bowed down to all the starry hosts and worshipped them. ⁴He built altars in the temple of the LORD, of which the LORD had said, "My Name will remain in Jerusalem for ever." ⁵In both courts of the temple of the LORD, he built altars to all the starry hosts. ⁶He sacrificed his sons in*a* the fire in the Valley of Ben Hinnom, practised sorcery, divination and witchcraft, and consulted mediums and spiritists. He did much evil in the eyes of the LORD, provoking him to anger.

⁷He took the carved image he had made and put it in God's temple, of which God had said to David and to his son Solomon, "In this temple and in Jerusalem, which I have chosen out of all the tribes of Israel, I will put my Name for ever. ⁸I will not again make the feet of the Israelites leave the land I assigned to your forefathers, if only they will be careful to do everything that I commanded them concerning all the laws, decrees and ordinances given through Moses." ⁹But Manasseh led Judah and the people of Jerusalem astray, so that they did more evil than the nations the LORD had destroyed before the Israelites.

¹⁰The LORD spoke to Manasseh and his people, but they paid no attention. ¹¹So the LORD brought against them the army commanders of the king of Assyria, who took Manasseh prisoner, put a hook in his nose, bound him with bronze shackles and took him to Babylon. ¹²In his distress he sought the favour of the LORD his God and humbled himself greatly before the God of his fathers. ¹³And when he prayed to him, the LORD was moved by his entreaty and listened to his plea; so he brought him back to Jerusalem and to his kingdom. Then Manasseh knew that the LORD is God.

¹⁴Afterwards he rebuilt the outer wall of the City of David, west of the Gihon spring in the valley, as far as the entrance of the Fish Gate and encircling the hill of Ophel; he also made it much higher. He stationed military commanders in all the fortified cities in Judah.

¹⁵He got rid of the foreign gods and removed the image from the temple of the LORD, as well as all the altars he had built on the temple hill and in Jerusalem; and he threw them out of the city. ¹⁶Then he restored the altar of the LORD and sacrificed fellowship offerings*b* and thank-offerings on

it, and told Judah to serve the LORD, the God of Israel. ¹⁷The people, however, continued to sacrifice at the high places, but only to the LORD their God.

¹⁸The other events of Manasseh's reign, including his prayer to his God and the words the seers spoke to him in the name of the LORD, the God of Israel, are written in the annals of the kings of Israel.*c* ¹⁹His prayer and how God was moved by his entreaty, as well as all his sins and unfaithfulness, and the sites where he built high places and set up Asherah poles and idols before he humbled himself—all are written in the records of the seers.*d* ²⁰Manasseh rested with his fathers and was buried in his palace. And Amon his son succeeded him as king.

Amon King of Judah

²¹Amon was twenty-two years old when he became king, and he reigned in Jerusalem for two years. ²²He did evil in the eyes of the LORD, as his father Manasseh had done. Amon worshipped and offered sacrifices to all the idols Manasseh had made. ²³But unlike his father Manasseh, he did not humble himself before the LORD; Amon increased his guilt.

²⁴Amon's officials conspired against him and assassinated him in his palace. ²⁵Then the people of the land killed all who had plotted against King Amon, and they made Josiah his son king in his place.

Josiah's Reforms

34 Josiah was eight years old when he became king, and he reigned in Jerusalem for thirty-one years. ²He did what was right in the eyes of the LORD and walked in the ways of his father David, not turning aside to the right or to the left.

³In the eighth year of his reign, while he was still young, he began to seek the God of his father David. In his twelfth year he began to purge Judah and Jerusalem of high places, Asherah poles, carved idols and cast images. ⁴Under his direction the altars of the Baals were torn down; he cut to pieces the incense altars that were above them, and smashed the Asherah poles, the idols and the images. These he broke to pieces and scattered over the graves of those who had sacrificed to them. ⁵He burned the bones of the priests on their altars, and so he purged Judah and Jerusalem. ⁶In the towns of Manasseh, Ephraim and Simeon, as far as Naphtali, and in the ruins around them, ⁷he tore down the altars and the Asherah poles and crushed the idols to powder and cut to pieces all the incense altars throughout Israel. Then he went back to Jerusalem.

⁸In the eighteenth year of Josiah's reign, to purify the land and the temple, he sent Shaphan son of Azaliah and Maaseiah the ruler of the city, with Joah son of Joahaz, the recorder, to repair the temple of the LORD his God.

---

*a*6 Or *He made his sons pass through*   *b*16 Traditionally *peace offerings*
*c*18 That is, Judah, as frequently in 2 Chronicles
*d*19 One Hebrew manuscript and Septuagint; most Hebrew manuscripts *of Hozai*

⁹They went to Hilkiah the high priest and gave him the money that had been brought into the temple of God, which the Levites who were the doorkeepers had collected from the people of Manasseh, Ephraim and the entire remnant of Israel and from all the people of Judah and Benjamin and the inhabitants of Jerusalem. ¹⁰Then they entrusted it to the men appointed to supervise the work on the LORD's temple. These men paid the workers who repaired and restored the temple. ¹¹They also gave money to the carpenters and builders to purchase dressed stone, and timber for joists and beams for the buildings that the kings of Judah had allowed to fall into ruin.

¹²The men did the work faithfully. Over them to direct them were Jahath and Obadiah, Levites descended from Merari, and Zechariah and Meshullam, descended from Kohath. The Levites—all who were skilled in playing musical instruments—¹³had charge of the labourers and supervised all the workers from job to job. Some of the Levites were secretaries, scribes and doorkeepers.

The Book of the Law Found

¹⁴While they were bringing out the money that had been taken into the temple of the LORD, Hilkiah the priest found the Book of the Law of the LORD that had been given through Moses. ¹⁵Hilkiah said to Shaphan the secretary, "I have found the Book of the Law in the temple of the LORD." He gave it to Shaphan.

¹⁶Then Shaphan took the book to the king and reported to him: "Your officials are doing everything that has been committed to them. ¹⁷They have paid out the money that was in the temple of the LORD and have entrusted it to the supervisors and workers." ¹⁸Then Shaphan the secretary informed the king, "Hilkiah the priest has given me a book." And Shaphan read from it in the presence of the king.

¹⁹When the king heard the words of the Law, he tore his robes. ²⁰He gave these orders to Hilkiah, Ahikam son of Shaphan, Abdon son of Micah,ᵃ Shaphan the secretary and Asaiah the king's attendant: ²¹"Go and enquire of the LORD for me and for the remnant in Israel and Judah about what is written in this book that has been found. Great is the LORD's anger that is poured out on us because our fathers have not kept the word of the LORD; they have not acted in accordance with all that is written in this book."

²²Hilkiah and those the king had sent with himᵇ went to speak to the prophetess Huldah, who was the wife of Shallum son of Tokhath,ᶜ the son of Hasrah,ᵈ keeper of the wardrobe. She lived in Jerusalem, in the Second District.

²³She said to them, "This is what the LORD, the God of Israel, says: Tell the man who sent you to me, ²⁴'This is what the LORD says: I am going to bring disaster on this place and its

people—all the curses written in the book that has been read in the presence of the king of Judah. ²⁵Because they have forsaken me and burned incense to other gods and provoked me to anger by all that their hands have made,ᵉ my anger will be poured out on this place and will not be quenched.' ²⁶Tell the king of Judah, who sent you to enquire of the LORD, 'This is what the LORD, the God of Israel, says concerning the words you heard: ²⁷Because your heart was responsive and you humbled yourself before God when you heard what he spoke against this place and its people, and because you humbled yourself before me and tore your robes and wept in my presence, I have heard you, declares the LORD. ²⁸Now I will gather you to your fathers, and you will be buried in peace. Your eyes will not see all the disaster I am going to bring on this place and on those who live here.'"

So they took her answer back to the king.

²⁹Then the king called together all the elders of Judah and Jerusalem. ³⁰He went up to the temple of the LORD with the men of Judah, the people of Jerusalem, the priests and the Levites—all the people from the least to the greatest. He read in their hearing all the words of the Book of the Covenant, which had been found in the temple of the LORD. ³¹The king stood by his pillar and renewed the covenant in the presence of the LORD—to follow the LORD and keep his commands, regulations and decrees with all his heart and all his soul, and to obey the words of the covenant written in this book.

³²Then he made everyone in Jerusalem and Benjamin pledge themselves to it; the people of Jerusalem did this in accordance with the covenant of God, the God of their fathers.

³³Josiah removed all the detestable idols from all the territory belonging to the Israelites, and he made all who were present in Israel serve the LORD their God. As long as he lived, they did not fail to follow the LORD, the God of their fathers.

Josiah Celebrates the Passover

35 Josiah celebrated the Passover to the LORD in Jerusalem, and the Passover lamb was slaughtered on the fourteenth day of the first month. ²He appointed the priests to their duties and encouraged them in the service of the LORD's temple. ³He said to the Levites, who instructed all Israel and who had been consecrated to the LORD: "Put the sacred ark in the temple that Solomon son of David king of Israel built. It is not to be carried about on your shoulders. Now serve the LORD your God and his people Israel. ⁴Prepare yourselves by families in your divisions, according to the directions written by David king of Israel and by his son Solomon.

⁵"Stand in the holy place with a group of Levites for each sub-division of the families of your fellow countrymen, the lay people. ⁶Slaughter the Passover lambs, consecrate

ᵃ20 Also called *Acbor son of Micaiah*
ᵇ22 One Hebrew manuscript, Vulgate and Syriac; most Hebrew manuscripts do not have *had sent with him*.
ᶜ22 Also called *Tikvah*   ᵈ22 Also called *Harhas*   ᵉ25 Or *by everything they have done*

yourselves and prepare ιthe lambsⱼ for your fellow countrymen, doing what the LORD commanded through Moses."

⁷Josiah provided for all the lay people who were there a total of thirty thousand sheep and goats for the Passover offerings, and also three thousand cattle—all from the king's own possessions.

⁸His officials also contributed voluntarily to the people and the priests and Levites. Hilkiah, Zechariah and Jehiel, the administrators of God's temple, gave the priests two thousand six hundred Passover offerings and three hundred cattle. ⁹Also Conaniah along with Shemaiah and Nethanel, his brothers, and Hashabiah, Jeiel and Jozabad, the leaders of the Levites, provided five thousand Passover offerings and five hundred head of cattle for the Levites.

¹⁰The service was arranged and the priests stood in their places with the Levites in their divisions as the king had ordered. ¹¹The Passover lambs were slaughtered, and the priests sprinkled the blood handed to them, while the Levites skinned the animals. ¹²They set aside the burnt offerings to give them to the sub-divisions of the families of the people to offer to the LORD, as is written in the Book of Moses. They did the same with the cattle. ¹³They roasted the Passover animals over the fire as prescribed, and boiled the holy offerings in pots, cauldrons and pans and served them quickly to all the people. ¹⁴After this, they made preparations for themselves and for the priests, because the priests, the descendants of Aaron, were sacrificing the burnt offerings and the fat portions until nightfall. So the Levites made preparations for themselves and for the Aaronic priests.

¹⁵The musicians, the descendants of Asaph, were in the places prescribed by David, Asaph, Heman and Jeduthun the king's seer. The gatekeepers at each gate did not need to leave their posts, because their fellow Levites made the preparations for them.

¹⁶So at that time the entire service of the LORD was carried out for the celebration of the Passover and the offering of burnt offerings on the altar of the LORD, as King Josiah had ordered. ¹⁷The Israelites who were present celebrated the Passover at that time and observed the Feast of Unleavened Bread for seven days. ¹⁸The Passover had not been observed like this in Israel since the days of the prophet Samuel; and none of the kings of Israel had ever celebrated such a Passover as did Josiah, with the priests, the Levites and all Judah and Israel who were there with the people of Jerusalem. ¹⁹This Passover was celebrated in the eighteenth year of Josiah's reign.

The Death of Josiah

²⁰After all this, when Josiah had set the temple in order, Neco king of Egypt went up to fight at Carchemish on the Euphrates, and

Josiah marched out to meet him in battle. ²¹But Neco sent messengers to him saying, "What quarrel is there between you and me, O king of Judah? It is not you I am attacking at this time, but the house with which I am at war. God has told me to hurry; so stop opposing God, who is with me, or he will destroy you."

²²Josiah, however, would not turn away from him, but disguised himself to engage him in battle. He would not listen to what Neco had said at God's command but went to fight him on the plain of Megiddo.

²³Archers shot King Josiah, and he told his officers, "Take me away; I am badly wounded." ²⁴So they took him out of his chariot, put him in the other chariot he had and brought him to Jerusalem, where he died. He was buried in the tombs of his fathers, and all Judah and Jerusalem mourned for him.

²⁵Jeremiah composed laments for Josiah, and to this day all the men and women singers commemorate Josiah in the laments. These became a tradition in Israel and are written in the Laments.

²⁶The other events of Josiah's reign and his acts of devotion, according to what is written in the Law of the LORD—²⁷all the events, from beginning to end, are written in the book of the kings of Israel and Judah. ¹And the people of the land took Jehoahaz son of Josiah and made him king in Jerusalem in place of his father.

Jehoahaz King of Judah

²Jehoahaz*ᵃ* was twenty-three years old when he became king, and he reigned in Jerusalem for three months. ³The king of Egypt dethroned him in Jerusalem and imposed on Judah a levy of a hundred talents*ᵇ* of silver and a talent*ᶜ* of gold. ⁴The king of Egypt made Eliakim, a brother of Jehoahaz, king over Judah and Jerusalem and changed Eliakim's name to Jehoiakim. But Neco took Eliakim's brother Jehoahaz and carried him off to Egypt.

Jehoiakim King of Judah

⁵Jehoiakim was twenty-five years old when he became king, and he reigned in Jerusalem for eleven years. He did evil in the eyes of the LORD his God. ⁶Nebuchadnezzar king of Babylon attacked him and bound him with bronze shackles to take him to Babylon. ⁷Nebuchadnezzar also took to Babylon articles from the temple of the LORD and put them in his temple*ᵈ* there.

⁸The other events of Jehoiakim's reign, the detestable things he did and all that was found against him, are written in the book of the kings of Israel and Judah. And Jehoiachin his son succeeded him as king.

Jehoiachin King of Judah

⁹Jehoiachin was eighteen*ᵉ* years old when he became king, and he reigned in Jerusalem

---

ᵃ2 Hebrew *Joahaz*, a variant of *Jehoahaz*; also in verse 4   *ᵇ3* That is, about 3⅓ tons (about 3.4 metric tons)
ᶜ3 That is, about 75 pounds (about 34 kilograms)   *ᵈ7* Or *palace*
ᵉ9 One Hebrew manuscript, some Septuagint manuscripts and Syriac (see also 2 Kings 24:8); most Hebrew manuscripts *eight*

for three months and ten days. He did evil in the eyes of the LORD. [10]In the spring, King Nebuchadnezzar sent for him and brought him to Babylon, together with articles of value from the temple of the LORD, and he made Jehoiachin's uncle,*f* Zedekiah, king over Judah and Jerusalem.

Zedekiah King of Judah

[11]Zedekiah was twenty-one years old when he became king, and he reigned in Jerusalem for eleven years. [12]He did evil in the eyes of the LORD his God and did not humble himself before Jeremiah the prophet, who spoke the word of the LORD. [13]He also rebelled against King Nebuchadnezzar, who had made him take an oath in God's name. He became stiff-necked and hardened his heart and would not turn to the LORD, the God of Israel. [14]Furthermore, all the leaders of the priests and the people became more and more unfaithful, following all the detestable practices of the nations and defiling the temple of the LORD, which he had consecrated in Jerusalem.

The Fall of Jerusalem

[15]The LORD, the God of their fathers, sent word to them through his messengers again and again, because he had pity on his people and on his dwelling-place. [16]But they mocked God's messengers, despised his words and scoffed at his prophets until the wrath of the LORD was aroused against his people and there was no remedy. [17]He brought up against them the king of the Babylonians,*g* who killed their young men with the sword in the sanctuary, and spared neither young man nor young woman, old man or aged. God handed all of them over to Nebuchadnezzar. [18]He carried to Babylon all the articles from the temple of God, both large and small, and the treasures of the LORD's temple and the treasures of the king and his officials. [19]They set fire to God's temple and broke down the wall of Jerusalem; they burned all the palaces and destroyed everything of value there.

[20]He carried into exile to Babylon the remnant who escaped from the sword, and they became servants to him and his sons until the kingdom of Persia came to power. [21]The land enjoyed its sabbath rests; all the time of its desolation it rested, until the seventy years were completed in fulfilment of the word of the LORD spoken by Jeremiah.

[22]In the first year of Cyrus king of Persia, in order to fulfil the word of the LORD spoken by Jeremiah, the LORD moved the heart of Cyrus king of Persia to make a proclamation throughout his realm and to put it in writing:

[23]"This is what Cyrus king of Persia says:

"'The LORD, the God of heaven, has given me all the kingdoms of the earth and he has appointed me to build a temple for him at Jerusalem in Judah. Anyone of his people among you—may the LORD his God be with him, and let him go up.'"

---

*f*10 Hebrew *brother*, that is, relative (see 2 Kings 24:17)   *g*17 Or *Chaldeans*

Ezra

Cyrus Helps the Exiles to Return

1 In the first year of Cyrus king of Persia, in order to fulfil the word of the LORD spoken by Jeremiah, the LORD moved the heart of Cyrus king of Persia to make a proclamation throughout his realm and to put it in writing:

2 "This is what Cyrus king of Persia says:

"'The LORD, the God of heaven, has given me all the kingdoms of the earth and he has appointed me to build a temple for him at Jerusalem in Judah. 3 Anyone of his people among you—may his God be with him, and let him go up to Jerusalem in Judah and build the temple of the LORD, the God of Israel, the God who is in Jerusalem. 4 And the people of any place where survivors may now be living are to provide him with silver and gold, with goods and livestock, and with freewill offerings for the temple of God in Jerusalem.'"

5 Then the family heads of Judah and Benjamin, and the priests and Levites—everyone whose heart God had moved—prepared to go up and build the house of the LORD in Jerusalem. 6 All their neighbours assisted them with articles of silver and gold, with goods and livestock, and with valuable gifts, in addition to all the freewill offerings. 7 Moreover, King Cyrus brought out the articles belonging to the temple of the LORD, which Nebuchadnezzar had carried away from Jerusalem and had placed in the temple of his god.[a] 8 Cyrus king of Persia had them brought by Mithredath the treasurer, who counted them out to Sheshbazzar the prince of Judah.

9 This was the inventory:

gold dishes	30
silver dishes	1,000
silver pans[b]	29
10 gold bowls	30
matching silver bowls	410
other articles	1,000

11 In all, there were 5,400 articles of gold and of silver. Sheshbazzar brought all these along when the exiles came up from Babylon to Jerusalem.

The List of the Exiles Who Returned

2 Now these are the people of the province who came up from the captivity of the exiles, whom Nebuchadnezzar king of Babylon had taken captive to Babylon (they returned to Jerusalem and Judah, each to his own town, 2 in company with Zerubbabel, Jeshua, Nehemiah, Seraiah, Reelaiah, Mordecai, Bilshan, Mispar, Bigvai, Rehum and Baanah):

The list of the men of the people of Israel:

3 the descendants of Parosh	2,172
4 of Shephatiah	372
5 of Arah	775
6 of Pahath-Moab (through the line of Jeshua and Joab)	2,812
7 of Elam	1,254
8 of Zattu	945
9 of Zaccai	760
10 of Bani	642
11 of Bebai	623
12 of Azgad	1,222
13 of Adonikam	666
14 of Bigvai	2,056
15 of Adin	454
16 of Ater (through Hezekiah)	98
17 of Bezai	323
18 of Jorah	112
19 of Hashum	223
20 of Gibbar	95
21 the men of Bethlehem	123
22 of Netophah	56
23 of Anathoth	128
24 of Azmaveth	42
25 of Kiriath Jearim,[a] Kephirah and Beeroth	743
26 of Ramah and Geba	621
27 of Michmash	122
28 of Bethel and Ai	223
29 of Nebo	52
30 of Magbish	156
31 of the other Elam	1,254
32 of Harim	320
33 of Lod, Hadid and Ono	725
34 of Jericho	345
35 of Senaah	3,630

36The priests:

the descendants of Jedaiah
    (through the family of Jeshua)   973
37of Immer   1,052
38of Pashhur   1,247
39of Harim   1,017

40The Levites:

the descendants of Jeshua
    and Kadmiel (through
    the line of Hodaviah)   74

41The singers:

the descendants of Asaph   128

42The gatekeepers of the temple:

the descendants of
    Shallum, Ater, Talmon,
    Akkub, Hatita and Shobai   139

43The temple servants:

the descendants of
    Ziha, Hasupha, Tabbaoth,
44Keros, Siaha, Padon,
45Lebanah, Hagabah, Akkub,
46Hagab, Shalmai, Hanan,
47Giddel, Gahar, Reaiah,
48Rezin, Nekoda, Gazzam,
49Uzza, Paseah, Besai,
50Asnah, Meunim, Nephussim,
51Bakbuk, Hakupha, Harhur,
52Bazluth, Mehida, Harsha,
53Barkos, Sisera, Temah,
54Neziah and Hatipha

55The descendants of the servants of
Solomon:

the descendants of
    Sotai, Hassophereth, Peruda,
56Jaala, Darkon, Giddel,
57Shephatiah, Hattil,
    Pokereth-Hazzebaim and Ami

58The temple servants and
    the descendants of the
    servants of Solomon   392

59The following came up from the
towns of Tel Melah, Tel Harsha, Kerub,
Addon and Immer, but they could not
show that their families were descended
from Israel:

60The descendants of
    Delaiah, Tobiah and
    Nekoda   652

61And from among the priests:

The descendants of
    Hobaiah, Hakkoz and Barzillai (a
    man who had married a daughter of
Barzillai the Gileadite and was called
by that name).
62These searched for their family records, but they could not find them and so
were excluded from the priesthood as
unclean. 63The governor ordered them
not to eat any of the most sacred food
until there was a priest ministering with
the Urim and Thummim.

64The whole company numbered
42,360, 65besides their 7,337 menservants and maidservants; and they
also had 200 men and women singers.
66They had 736 horses, 245 mules, 67435
camels and 6,720 donkeys.

68When they arrived at the house of the
LORD in Jerusalem, some of the heads of the
families gave freewill offerings towards
the rebuilding of the house of God on its site.
69According to their ability they gave to the
treasury for this work 61,000 drachmasb of
gold, 5,000 minasc of silver and 100 priestly
garments.
70The priests, the Levites, the singers, the
gatekeepers and the temple servants settled
in their own towns, along with some of the
other people, and the rest of the Israelites
settled in their towns.

Rebuilding the Altar

3 When the seventh month came and the
    Israelites had settled in their towns, the
people assembled as one man in Jerusalem.
2Then Jeshua son of Jozadak and his fellow
priests and Zerubbabel son of Shealtiel and
his associates began to build the altar of the
God of Israel to sacrifice burnt offerings on it,
in accordance with what is written in the Law
of Moses the man of God. 3Despite their fear
of the peoples around them, they built the
altar on its foundation and sacrificed burnt
offerings on it to the LORD, both the morning
and evening sacrifices. 4Then in accordance
with what is written, they celebrated the
Feast of Tabernacles with the required number of burnt offerings prescribed for each
day. 5After that, they presented the regular
burnt offerings, the New Moon sacrifices and
the sacrifices for all the appointed sacred
feasts of the LORD, as well as those brought as
freewill offerings to the LORD. 6On the first
day of the seventh month they began to offer
burnt offerings to the LORD, though the
foundation of the LORD's temple had not yet
been laid.

Rebuilding the Temple

7Then they gave money to the masons and
carpenters, and gave food and drink and oil
to the people of Sidon and Tyre, so that they
would bring cedar logs by sea from Lebanon
to Joppa, as authorised by Cyrus king of
Persia.
8In the second month of the second year
after their arrival at the house of God in
Jerusalem, Zerubbabel son of Shealtiel,
Jeshua son of Jozadak and the rest of their

b69 That is, about 1,100 pounds (about 500 kilograms)   c69 That is, about 2⅖ tons (about 2.9 metric tons)

EZRA 3:1–6
'Despite their fear of the peoples around them, they built the altar on its foundation and sacrificed burnt offerings on it to the LORD' (v. 3).

BUILDING AN ALTAR was a symbolic gesture. The returned exiles were in no position to do more. Surrounded by hostile forces, far from their patron back in Babylon, the cares of everyday life would soon press in upon them, but at the very beginning of their mission they knew they must make a stand.

Lawrence Smith, a young Salvationist, was called up to the forces in 1940. Some wise person had advised the lad to 'start as he meant to go on'. In fear and trembling Lawrence turned up at the training camp in his Salvation Army uniform. He was met by a massive military policeman who thundered at him rather unexpectedly, 'A . . . good idea. Everybody'll know where you stand.' That action was the start of a distinguished military career which lasted throughout the war, and a Christian ministry which has endured for over half a century, not just in the difficult conditions of military service, but in situations as widely different as the City of London (Lawrence is now a freeman of the City) and as a salvationist chaplain in Her Majesty's prisons.

Do people know where I stand? Dare I witness against the odds?

> *Fear not to enter his courts in the slenderness*
> *Of the poor wealth thou would'st reckon as thine;*
> *Truth in its beauty, and love in its tenderness,*
> *These are the offerings to lay on his shrine.*
>
> *These, though we bring them in trembling and fearfulness,*
> *He will accept for the name that is dear;*
> *Mornings of joy give for evenings of tearfulness,*
> *Trust for our trembling, and hope for our fear.*

(J. S. B. Monsell)

→398

NEHEMIAH 3:1–5 and selected verses

'Eliashib the high priest and his fellow priests went to work and rebuilt the Sheep Gate . . . The next section was repaired by the men of Tekoa, but their nobles would not put their shoulders to the work . . . Harumaph made repairs opposite his house . . . Shallum . . . repaired the next section with the help of his daughters' (vv. 1, 5, [10, 12,]).

REPAIRING THE WALLS was a massive task, involving every able-bodied person. It was carefully organized. In the main, people living close to the wall repaired the section next to their houses, in their own districts (vv. 10, 17, 18, 23, 28, 30). They knew the area. They knew the resources available. The rubble which hindered Nehemiah (2:14) could now be put to good use.

Women also worked. Shallum's daughters get special mention (v. 12). This detailed account of the work takes us right into Nehemiah's thinking. He covered every last detail. Even now it is possible to reconstruct the line of Nehemiah's wall almost entirely from details in this chapter.

Skilled craftsmen, specialist goldsmiths, perfume-makers and others left their crafts to become building labourers. They were not afraid to risk injury and harm to the delicately skilled hands which earned them their living.

Only one criticism is made – of the nobles of Tekoa. They wouldn't get on with things 'under their supervisors'. What a pity! The whole operation might have foundered because they, the nobles, were unwilling to be supervised by craftsmen who knew what they were doing.

Lord, you know how people can sometimes be inspired to put great energy into a project. Producing something visible and worthwhile can motivate us to fine effort. Seeing a great work take shape is very satisfying. Help us, Lord, in the difficult tasks of cooperating with others on a daily basis, serving when we see no visible result, working keenly when we do not feel it is appreciated, knowing that everything we do in your name has its own reward.

brothers (the priests and the Levites and all who had returned from the captivity to Jerusalem) began the work, appointing Levites twenty years of age and older to supervise the building of the house of the LORD. 9Jeshua and his sons and brothers and Kadmiel and his sons (descendants of Hodaviah*a*) and the sons of Henadad and their sons and brothers —all Levites—joined together in supervising those working on the house of God.

10When the builders laid the foundation of the temple of the LORD, the priests in their vestments and with trumpets, and the Levites (the sons of Asaph) with cymbals, took their places to praise the LORD, as prescribed by David king of Israel. 11With praise and thanksgiving they sang to the LORD:

"He is good;
    his love to Israel endures for ever."

And all the people gave a great shout of praise to the LORD, because the foundation of the house of the LORD was laid. 12But many of the older priests and Levites and family heads, who had seen the former temple, wept aloud when they saw the foundation of this temple being laid, while many others shouted for joy. 13No-one could distinguish the sound of the shouts of joy from the sound of weeping, because the people made so much noise. And the sound was heard far away.

Opposition to the Rebuilding

4 When the enemies of Judah and Benjamin heard that the exiles were building a temple for the LORD, the God of Israel, 2they came to Zerubbabel and to the heads of the families and said, "Let us help you build because, like you, we seek your God and have been sacrificing to him since the time of Esarhaddon king of Assyria, who brought us here."

3But Zerubbabel, Jeshua and the rest of the heads of the families of Israel answered, "You have no part with us in building a temple to our God. We alone will build it for the LORD, the God of Israel, as King Cyrus, the king of Persia, commanded us."

4Then the peoples around them set out to discourage the people of Judah and make them afraid to go on building.*a* 5They hired counsellors to work against them and frustrate their plans during the entire reign of Cyrus king of Persia and down to the reign of Darius king of Persia.

Later Opposition Under Xerxes and Artaxerxes

6At the beginning of the reign of Xerxes,*b* they lodged an accusation against the people of Judah and Jerusalem.

7And in the days of Artaxerxes king of Persia, Bishlam, Mithredath, Tabeel and the rest of his associates wrote a letter to Artaxerxes. The letter was written in Aramaic script and in the Aramaic language.*c,d*

8Rehum the commanding officer and Shimshai the secretary wrote a letter against Jerusalem to Artaxerxes the king as follows:

9Rehum the commanding officer and Shimshai the secretary, together with the rest of their associates—the judges and officials over the men from Tripolis, Persia,*e* Erech and Babylon, the Elamites of Susa, 10and the other people whom the great and honourable Ashurbanipal*f* deported and settled in the city of Samaria and elsewhere in Trans-Euphrates.

11(This is a copy of the letter they sent him.)

To King Artaxerxes,

From your servants, the men of Trans-Euphrates:

12The king should know that the Jews who came up to us from you have gone to Jerusalem and are rebuilding that rebellious and wicked city. They are restoring the walls and repairing the foundations.

13Furthermore, the king should know that if this city is built and its walls are restored, no more taxes, tribute or duty will be paid, and the royal revenues will suffer. 14Now since we are under obligation to the palace and it is not proper for us to see the king dishonoured, we are sending this message to inform the king, 15so that a search may be made in the archives of your predecessors. In these records you will find that this city is a rebellious city, troublesome to kings and provinces, a place of rebellion from ancient times. That is why this city was destroyed. 16We inform the king that if this city is built and its walls are restored, you will be left with nothing in Trans-Euphrates.

17The king sent this reply:

To Rehum the commanding officer, Shimshai the secretary and the rest of their associates living in Samaria and elsewhere in Trans-Euphrates:

Greetings.

18The letter you sent us has been read and translated in my presence. 19I issued an order and a search was made, and it was found that this city has a long history of revolt against kings and has been a place of rebellion and sedition. 20Jerusalem has had powerful kings ruling over the whole of Trans-Euphrates, and taxes, tribute and duty were paid to them. 21Now issue an order to these men

---

*a*9 Hebrew *Yehudah*, probably a variant of *Hodaviah*
*b*6 Hebrew *Ahasuerus*, a variant of Xerxes' Persian name
*d*7 The text of Ezra 4:8–6:18 is in Aramaic.
*f*10 Aramaic *Osnappar*, a variant of *Ashurbanipal*

*a*4 Or *and troubled them as they built*
*c*7 Or *written in Aramaic and translated*
*e*9 Or *officials, magistrates and governors over the men from*

to stop work, so that this city will not be rebuilt until I so order. ²²Be careful not to neglect this matter. Why let this threat grow, to the detriment of the royal interests?

²³As soon as the copy of the letter of King Artaxerxes was read to Rehum and Shimshai the secretary and their associates, they went immediately to the Jews in Jerusalem and compelled them by force to stop.

²⁴Thus the work on the house of God in Jerusalem came to a standstill until the second year of the reign of Darius king of Persia.

Tattenai's Letter to Darius

5 Now Haggai the prophet and Zechariah the prophet, a descendant of Iddo, prophesied to the Jews in Judah and Jerusalem in the name of the God of Israel, who was over them. ²Then Zerubbabel son of Shealtiel and Jeshua son of Jozadak set to work to rebuild the house of God in Jerusalem. And the prophets of God were with them, helping them.

³At that time Tattenai, governor of Trans-Euphrates, and Shethar-Bozenai and their associates went to them and asked, "Who authorised you to rebuild this temple and restore this structure?" ⁴They also asked, "What are the names of the men constructing this building?"^a ⁵But the eye of their God was watching over the elders of the Jews, and they were not stopped until a report could go to Darius and his written reply be received.

⁶This is a copy of the letter that Tattenai, governor of Trans-Euphrates, and Shethar-Bozenai and their associates, the officials of Trans-Euphrates, sent to King Darius. ⁷The report they sent him read as follows:

To King Darius:

Cordial greetings.

⁸The king should know that we went to the district of Judah, to the temple of the great God. The people are building it with large stones and placing the timbers in the walls. The work is being carried on with diligence and is making rapid progress under their direction.

⁹We questioned the elders and asked them, "Who authorised you to rebuild this temple and restore this structure?" ¹⁰We also asked them their names, so that we could write down the names of their leaders for your information.

¹¹This is the answer they gave us:

"We are the servants of the God of heaven and earth, and we are rebuilding the temple that was built many years ago, one that a great king of Israel built and finished. ¹²But because our fathers angered the God of heaven, he handed them over to Nebuchadnezzar the Chaldean, king of Babylon, who destroyed this temple and deported the people to Babylon.

¹³"However, in the first year of Cyrus king of Babylon, King Cyrus issued a decree to rebuild this house of God. ¹⁴He even removed from the temple^b of Babylon the gold and silver articles of the house of God, which Nebuchadnezzar had taken from the temple in Jerusalem and brought to the temple^b in Babylon.

"Then King Cyrus gave them to a man named Sheshbazzar, whom he had appointed governor, ¹⁵and he told him, 'Take these articles and go and deposit them in the temple in Jerusalem. And rebuild the house of God on its site.' ¹⁶So this Sheshbazzar came and laid the foundations of the house of God in Jerusalem. From that day to the present it has been under construction but is not yet finished."

¹⁷Now if it pleases the king, let a search be made in the royal archives of Babylon to see if King Cyrus did in fact issue a decree to rebuild this house of God in Jerusalem. Then let the king send us his decision in this matter.

The Decree of Darius

6 King Darius then issued an order, and they searched in the archives stored in the treasury at Babylon. ²A scroll was found in the citadel of Ecbatana in the province of Media, and this was written on it:

Memorandum:

³In the first year of King Cyrus, the king issued a decree concerning the temple of God in Jerusalem:

Let the temple be rebuilt as a place to present sacrifices, and let its foundations be laid. It is to be ninety feet^a high and ninety feet wide, ⁴with three courses of large stones and one of timbers. The costs are to be paid by the royal treasury. ⁵Also, the gold and silver articles of the house of God, which Nebuchadnezzar took from the temple in Jerusalem and brought to Babylon, are to be returned to their places in the temple in Jerusalem; they are to be deposited in the house of God.

⁶Now then, Tattenai, governor of Trans-Euphrates, and Shethar-Bozenai and you, their fellow officials of that province, stay away from there. ⁷Do not interfere with the work on this temple of God. Let the governor of the Jews and the Jewish elders rebuild this house of God on its site.

⁸Moreover, I hereby decree what you are to do for these elders of the Jews in the construction of this house of God:

---

^a4 See Septuagint; Aramaic ⁴We told them the names of the men constructing this building.
^b14 Or *palace*   ^a3 Aramaic *sixty cubits* (about 27 metres)

The expenses of these men are to be fully paid out of the royal treasury, from the revenues of Trans-Euphrates, so that the work will not stop. [9]Whatever is needed—young bulls, rams, male lambs for burnt offerings to the God of heaven, and wheat, salt, wine and oil, as requested by the priests in Jerusalem—must be given them daily without fail, [10]so that they may offer sacrifices pleasing to the God of heaven and pray for the well-being of the king and his sons.

[11]Furthermore, I decree that if anyone changes this edict, a beam is to be pulled from his house and he is to be lifted up and impaled on it. And for this crime his house is to be made a pile of rubble. [12]May God, who has caused his Name to dwell there, overthrow any king or people who lifts a hand to change this decree or to destroy this temple in Jerusalem.

I Darius have decreed it. Let it be carried out with diligence.

Completion and Dedication of the Temple

[13]Then, because of the decree King Darius had sent, Tattenai, governor of Trans-Euphrates, and Shethar-Bozenai and their associates carried it out with diligence. [14]So the elders of the Jews continued to build and prosper under the preaching of Haggai the prophet and Zechariah, a descendant of Iddo. They finished building the temple according to the command of the God of Israel and the decrees of Cyrus, Darius and Artaxerxes, kings of Persia. [15]The temple was completed on the third day of the month Adar, in the sixth year of the reign of King Darius.

[16]Then the people of Israel—the priests, the Levites and the rest of the exiles—celebrated the dedication of the house of God with joy. [17]For the dedication of this house of God they offered a hundred bulls, two hundred rams, four hundred male lambs and, as a sin offering for all Israel, twelve male goats, one for each of the tribes of Israel. [18]And they installed the priests in their divisions and the Levites in their groups for the service of God at Jerusalem, according to what is written in the Book of Moses.

The Passover

[19]On the fourteenth day of the first month, the exiles celebrated the Passover. [20]The priests and Levites had purified themselves and were all ceremonially clean. The Levites slaughtered the Passover lamb for all the exiles, for their brothers the priests and for themselves. [21]So the Israelites who had returned from the exile ate it, together with all who had separated themselves from the unclean practices of their Gentile neighbours in order to seek the LORD, the God of Israel. [22]For seven days they celebrated with joy the Feast of Unleavened Bread, because the LORD had filled them with joy by changing the attitude of the king of Assyria, so that

he assisted them in the work on the house of God, the God of Israel.

Ezra Comes to Jerusalem

7 After these things, during the reign of Artaxerxes king of Persia, Ezra son of Seraiah, the son of Azariah, the son of Hilkiah, [2]the son of Shallum, the son of Zadok, the son of Ahitub, [3]the son of Amariah, the son of Azariah, the son of Meraioth, [4]the son of Zerahiah, the son of Uzzi, the son of Bukki, [5]the son of Abishua, the son of Phinehas, the son of Eleazar, the son of Aaron the chief priest—[6]this Ezra came up from Babylon. He was a teacher well versed in the Law of Moses, which the LORD, the God of Israel, had given. The king had granted him everything he asked, for the hand of the LORD his God was on him. [7]Some of the Israelites, including priests, Levites, singers, gatekeepers and temple servants, also came up to Jerusalem in the seventh year of King Artaxerxes.

[8]Ezra arrived in Jerusalem in the fifth month of the seventh year of the king. [9]He had begun his journey from Babylon on the first day of the first month, and he arrived in Jerusalem on the first day of the fifth month, for the gracious hand of his God was on him. [10]For Ezra had devoted himself to the study and observance of the Law of the LORD, and to teaching its decrees and laws in Israel.

King Artaxerxes' Letter to Ezra

[11]This is a copy of the letter King Artaxerxes had given to Ezra the priest and teacher, a man learned in matters concerning the commands and decrees of the LORD for Israel:

[12][a]Artaxerxes, king of kings,

To Ezra the priest, a teacher of the Law of the God of heaven:

Greetings.

[13]Now I decree that any of the Israelites in my kingdom, including priests and Levites, who wish to go to Jerusalem with you, may go. [14]You are sent by the king and his seven advisers to enquire about Judah and Jerusalem with regard to the Law of your God, which is in your hand. [15]Moreover, you are to take with you the silver and gold that the king and his advisers have freely given to the God of Israel, whose dwelling is in Jerusalem, [16]together with all the silver and gold you may obtain from the province of Babylon, as well as the freewill offerings of the people and priests for the temple of their God in Jerusalem. [17]With this money be sure to buy bulls, rams and male lambs, together with their grain offerings and drink offerings, and sacrifice them on the altar of the temple of your God in Jerusalem.

[a]12 The text of Ezra 7:12–26 is in Aramaic.

¹⁸You and your brother Jews may then do whatever seems best with the rest of the silver and gold, in accordance with the will of your God. ¹⁹Deliver to the God of Jerusalem all the articles entrusted to you for worship in the temple of your God. ²⁰And anything else needed for the temple of your God that you may have occasion to supply, you may provide from the royal treasury.

²¹Now I, King Artaxerxes, order all the treasurers of Trans-Euphrates to provide with diligence whatever Ezra the priest, a teacher of the Law of the God of heaven, may ask of you—²²up to a hundred talents*b* of silver, a hundred cors*c* of wheat, a hundred baths*d* of wine, a hundred baths*d* of olive oil, and salt without limit. ²³Whatever the God of heaven has prescribed, let it be done with diligence for the temple of the God of heaven. Why should there be wrath against the realm of the king and of his sons? ²⁴You are also to know that you have no authority to impose taxes, tribute or duty on any of the priests, Levites, singers, gatekeepers, temple servants or other workers at this house of God.

²⁵And you, Ezra, in accordance with the wisdom of your God, which you possess, appoint magistrates and judges to administer justice to all the people of Trans-Euphrates—all who know the laws of your God. And you are to teach any who do not know them. ²⁶Whoever does not obey the law of your God and the law of the king must surely be punished by death, banishment, confiscation of property, or imprisonment.

²⁷Praise be to the LORD, the God of our fathers, who has put it into the king's heart to bring honour to the house of the LORD in Jerusalem in this way ²⁸and who has extended his good favour to me before the king and his advisers and all the king's powerful officials. Because the hand of the LORD my God was on me, I took courage and gathered leading men from Israel to go up with me.

List of the Family Heads Returning With Ezra

8 These are the family heads and those registered with them who came up with me from Babylon during the reign of King Artaxerxes:

²of the descendants of Phinehas, Gershom;
of the descendants of Ithamar, Daniel;
of the descendants of David, Hattush ³of the descendants of Shecaniah;

of the descendants of Parosh, Zechariah, and with him were registered 150 men;

⁴of the descendants of Pahath-Moab, Eliehoenai son of Zerahiah, and with him 200 men;

⁵of the descendants of Zattu,*a* Shecaniah son of Jahaziel, and with him 300 men;

⁶of the descendants of Adin, Ebed son of Jonathan, and with him 50 men;

⁷of the descendants of Elam, Jeshaiah son of Athaliah, and with him 70 men;

⁸of the descendants of Shephatiah, Zebadiah son of Michael, and with him 80 men;

⁹of the descendants of Joab, Obadiah son of Jehiel, and with him 218 men;

¹⁰of the descendants of Bani,*b* Shelomith son of Josiphiah, and with him 160 men;

¹¹of the descendants of Bebai, Zechariah son of Bebai, and with him 28 men;

¹²of the descendants of Azgad, Johanan son of Hakkatan, and with him 110 men;

¹³of the descendants of Adonikam, the last ones, whose names were Eliphelet, Jeuel and Shemaiah, and with them 60 men;

¹⁴of the descendants of Bigvai, Uthai and Zaccur, and with them 70 men.

The Return to Jerusalem

¹⁵I assembled them at the canal that flows towards Ahava, and we camped there three days. When I checked among the people and the priests, I found no Levites there. ¹⁶So I summoned Eliezer, Ariel, Shemaiah, Elnathan, Jarib, Elnathan, Nathan, Zechariah and Meshullam, who were leaders, and Joiarib and Elnathan, who were men of learning, ¹⁷and I sent them to Iddo, the leader in Casiphia. I told them what to say to Iddo and his kinsmen, the temple servants in Casiphia, so that they might bring attendants to us for the house of our God. ¹⁸Because the gracious hand of our God was on us, they brought us Sherebiah, a capable man, from the descendants of Mahli son of Levi, the son of Israel, and Sherebiah's sons and brothers, 18 men; ¹⁹and Hashabiah, together with Jeshaiah from the descendants of Merari, and his brothers and nephews, 20 men. ²⁰They also brought 220 of the temple servants—a body that David and the officials had established to assist the Levites. All were registered by name.

²¹There, by the Ahava Canal, I proclaimed a fast, so that we might humble ourselves before our God and ask him for a safe journey for us and our children, with all our possessions. ²²I was ashamed to ask the king for soldiers and horsemen to protect us from enemies on the road, because we had told the king, "The gracious hand of our God is on everyone who looks to him, but his great anger is against all who forsake him." ²³So we fasted and petitioned our God about this, and he answered our prayer.

²⁴Then I set apart twelve of the leading

---

b22 That is, about 3⅓ tons (about 3.4 metric tons)   *c22* That is, about 600 bushels (about 22 kilolitres)
d22 That is, probably about 500 gallons (about 2.2 kilolitres)
a5 Some Septuagint manuscripts (also 1 Esdras 8:32); Hebrew does not have *Zattu*.
b10 Some Septuagint manuscripts (also 1 Esdras 8:36); Hebrew does not have *Bani*.

priests, together with Sherebiah, Hashabiah and ten of their brothers, ²⁵and I weighed out to them the offering of silver and gold and the articles that the king, his advisers, his officials and all Israel present there had donated for the house of our God. ²⁶I weighed out to them 650 talents*c* of silver, silver articles weighing 100 talents,*d* 100 talents*d* of gold, ²⁷20 bowls of gold valued at 1,000 darics,*e* and two fine articles of polished bronze, as precious as gold.

²⁸I said to them, "You as well as these articles are consecrated to the Lord. The silver and gold are a freewill offering to the Lord, the God of your fathers. ²⁹Guard them carefully until you weigh them out in the chambers of the house of the Lord in Jerusalem before the leading priests and the Levites and the family heads of Israel." ³⁰Then the priests and Levites received the silver and gold and sacred articles that had been weighed out to be taken to the house of our God in Jerusalem.

³¹On the twelfth day of the first month we set out from the Ahava Canal to go to Jerusalem. The hand of our God was on us, and he protected us from enemies and bandits along the way. ³²So we arrived in Jerusalem, where we rested three days.

³³On the fourth day, in the house of our God, we weighed out the silver and gold and the sacred articles into the hands of Meremoth son of Uriah, the priest. Eleazar son of Phinehas was with him, and so were the Levites Jozabad son of Jeshua and Noadiah son of Binnui. ³⁴Everything was accounted for by number and weight, and the entire weight was recorded at that time.

³⁵Then the exiles who had returned from captivity sacrificed burnt offerings to the God of Israel: twelve bulls for all Israel, ninety-six rams, seventy-seven male lambs and, as a sin offering, twelve male goats. All this was a burnt offering to the Lord. ³⁶They also delivered the king's orders to the royal satraps and to the governors of Trans-Euphrates who then gave assistance to the people and to the house of God.

Ezra's Prayer About Intermarriage

9 After these things had been done, the leaders came to me and said, "The people of Israel, including the priests and the Levites, have not kept themselves separate from the neighbouring peoples with their detestable practices, like those of the Canaanites, Hittites, Perizzites, Jebusites, Ammonites, Moabites, Egyptians and Amorites. ²They have taken some of their daughters as wives for themselves and their sons, and have mingled the holy race with the peoples around them. And the leaders and officials have led the way in this unfaithfulness."

³When I heard this, I tore my tunic and cloak, pulled hair from my head and beard and sat down appalled. ⁴Then everyone who trembled at the words of the God of Israel gathered round me because of this unfaithfulness of the exiles. And I sat there appalled until the evening sacrifice.

⁵Then, at the evening sacrifice, I rose from my self-abasement, with my tunic and cloak torn, and fell on my knees with my hands spread out to the Lord my God ⁶and prayed:

"O my God, I am too ashamed and disgraced to lift up my face to you, my God, because our sins are higher than our heads and our guilt has reached to the heavens. ⁷From the days of our forefathers until now, our guilt has been great. Because of our sins, we and our kings and our priests have been subjected to the sword and captivity, to pillage and humiliation at the hand of foreign kings, as it is today.

⁸"But now, for a brief moment, the Lord our God has been gracious in leaving us a remnant and giving us a firm place in his sanctuary, and so our God gives light to our eyes and a little relief in our bondage. ⁹Though we are slaves, our God has not deserted us in our bondage. He has shown us kindness in the sight of the kings of Persia: He has granted us new life to rebuild the house of our God and repair its ruins, and he has given us a wall of protection in Judah and Jerusalem.

¹⁰"But now, O our God, what can we say after this? For we have disregarded the commands ¹¹you gave through your servants the prophets when you said: 'The land you are entering to possess is a land polluted by the corruption of its peoples. By their detestable practices they have filled it with their impurity from one end to the other. ¹²Therefore, do not give your daughters in marriage to their sons or take their daughters for your sons. Do not seek a treaty of friendship with them at any time, that you may be strong and eat the good things of the land and leave it to your children as an everlasting inheritance.'

¹³"What has happened to us is a result of our evil deeds and our great guilt, and yet, our God, you have punished us less than our sins have deserved and have given us a remnant like this. ¹⁴Shall we again break your commands and intermarry with the peoples who commit such detestable practices? Would you not be angry enough with us to destroy us, leaving us no remnant or survivor? ¹⁵O Lord, God of Israel, you are righteous! We are left this day as a remnant. Here we are before you in our guilt, though because of it not one of us can stand in your presence."

The People's Confession of Sin

10 While Ezra was praying and confessing, weeping and throwing himself down before the house of God, a large crowd

---

*c*26 That is, about 22 tons (about 22 metric tons)   *d*26 That is, about 3⅓ tons (about 3.4 metric tons)
*e*27 That is, about 19 pounds (about 8.5 kilograms)

of Israelites—men, women and children—gathered round him. They too wept bitterly. [2]Then Shecaniah son of Jehiel, one of the descendants of Elam, said to Ezra, "We have been unfaithful to our God by marrying foreign women from the peoples around us. But in spite of this, there is still hope for Israel. [3]Now let us make a covenant before our God to send away all these women and their children, in accordance with the counsel of my lord and of those who fear the commands of our God. Let it be done according to the Law. [4]Rise up; this matter is in your hands. We will support you, so take courage and do it."

[5]So Ezra rose up and put the leading priests and Levites and all Israel under oath to do what had been suggested. And they took the oath. [6]Then Ezra withdrew from before the house of God and went to the room of Jehohanan son of Eliashib. While he was there, he ate no food and drank no water, because he continued to mourn over the unfaithfulness of the exiles.

[7]A proclamation was then issued throughout Judah and Jerusalem for all the exiles to assemble in Jerusalem. [8]Anyone who failed to appear within three days would forfeit all his property, in accordance with the decision of the officials and elders, and would himself be expelled from the assembly of the exiles.

[9]Within the three days, all the men of Judah and Benjamin had gathered in Jerusalem. And on the twentieth day of the ninth month, all the people were sitting in the square before the house of God, greatly distressed by the occasion and because of the rain. [10]Then Ezra the priest stood up and said to them, "You have been unfaithful; you have married foreign women, adding to Israel's guilt. [11]Now make confession to the LORD, the God of your fathers, and do his will. Separate yourselves from the peoples around you and from your foreign wives."

[12]The whole assembly responded with a loud voice: "You are right! We must do as you say. [13]But there are many people here and it is the rainy season; so we cannot stand outside. Besides, this matter cannot be taken care of in a day or two, because we have sinned greatly in this thing. [14]Let our officials act for the whole assembly. Then let everyone in our towns who has married a foreign woman come at a set time, along with the elders and judges of each town, until the fierce anger of our God in this matter is turned away from us." [15]Only Jonathan son of Asahel and Jahzeiah son of Tikvah, supported by Meshullam and Shabbethai the Levite, opposed this.

[16]So the exiles did as was proposed. Ezra the priest selected men who were family heads, one from each family division, and all of them designated by name. On the first day of the tenth month they sat down to investigate the cases, [17]and by the first day of the first month they finished dealing with all the men who had married foreign women.

Those Guilty of Intermarriage

[18]Among the descendants of the priests, the following had married foreign women:

From the descendants of Jeshua son of Jozadak, and his brothers: Maaseiah, Eliezer, Jarib and Gedaliah. [19](They all gave their hands in pledge to put away their wives, and for their guilt they each presented a ram from the flock as a guilt offering.)

[20]From the descendants of Immer: Hanani and Zebadiah.

[21]From the descendants of Harim: Maaseiah, Elijah, Shemaiah, Jehiel and Uzziah.

[22]From the descendants of Pashhur: Elioenai, Maaseiah, Ishmael, Nethanel, Jozabad and Elasah.

[23]Among the Levites:

Jozabad, Shimei, Kelaiah (that is Kelita), Pethahiah, Judah and Eliezer.

[24]From the singers: Eliashib.

From the gatekeepers: Shallum, Telem and Uri.

[25]And among the other Israelites:

From the descendants of Parosh: Ramiah, Izziah, Malkijah, Mijamin, Eleazar, Malkijah and Benaiah.

[26]From the descendants of Elam: Mattaniah, Zechariah, Jehiel, Abdi, Jeremoth and Elijah.

[27]From the descendants of Zattu: Elioenai, Eliashib, Mattaniah, Jeremoth, Zabad and Aziza.

[28]From the descendants of Bebai: Jehohanan, Hananiah, Zabbai and Athlai.

[29]From the descendants of Bani: Meshullam, Malluch, Adaiah, Jashub, Sheal and Jeremoth.

[30]From the descendants of Pahath-Moab: Adna, Kelal, Benaiah, Maaseiah, Mattaniah, Bezalel, Binnui and Manasseh.

[31]From the descendants of Harim: Eliezer, Ishijah, Malkijah, Shemaiah, Shimeon, [32]Benjamin, Malluch and Shemariah.

[33]From the descendants of Hashum: Mattenai, Mattattah, Zabad, Eliphelet, Jeremai, Manasseh and Shimei.

[34]From the descendants of Bani: Maadai, Amram, Uel, [35]Benaiah, Bedeiah, Keluhi, [36]Vaniah, Meremoth, Eliashib, [37]Mattaniah, Mattenai and Jaasu.

[38]From the descendants of Binnui:[a]
Shimei, [39]Shelemiah, Nathan,
Adaiah, [40]Macnadebai, Shashai,
Sharai, [41]Azarel, Shelemiah, Shemariah, [42]Shallum, Amariah and Joseph.
[43]From the descendants of Nebo:

Jeiel, Mattithiah, Zabad, Zebina, Jaddai, Joel and Benaiah.

[44]All these had married foreign women,
and some of them had children by these
wives.[b]

Nehemiah

Nehemiah's Prayer

1 The words of Nehemiah son of Hacaliah:

In the month of Kislev in the twentieth year, while I was in the citadel of Susa, ²Hanani, one of my brothers, came from Judah with some other men, and I questioned them about the Jewish remnant that survived the exile, and also about Jerusalem.

³They said to me, "Those who survived the exile and are back in the province are in great trouble and disgrace. The wall of Jerusalem is broken down, and its gates have been burned with fire."

⁴When I heard these things, I sat down and wept. For some days I mourned and fasted and prayed before the God of heaven. ⁵Then I said:

"O LORD, God of heaven, the great and awesome God, who keeps his covenant of love with those who love him and obey his commands, ⁶let your ear be attentive and your eyes open to hear the prayer your servant is praying before you day and night for your servants, the people of Israel. I confess the sins we Israelites, including myself and my father's house, have committed against you. ⁷We have acted very wickedly towards you. We have not obeyed the commands, decrees and laws you gave your servant Moses.

⁸"Remember the instruction you gave your servant Moses, saying, 'If you are unfaithful, I will scatter you among the nations, ⁹but if you return to me and obey my commands, then even if your exiled people are at the farthest horizon, I will gather them from there and bring them to the place I have chosen as a dwelling for my Name.'

¹⁰"They are your servants and your people, whom you redeemed by your great strength and your mighty hand. ¹¹O Lord, let your ear be attentive to the prayer of this your servant and to the prayer of your servants who delight in revering your name. Give your servant success today by granting him favour in the presence of this man."

I was cupbearer to the king.

Artaxerxes Sends Nehemiah to Jerusalem

2 In the month of Nisan in the twentieth year of King Artaxerxes, when wine was brought for him, I took the wine and gave it to the king. I had not been sad in his presence before; ²so the king asked me, "Why does your face look so sad when you are not ill? This can be nothing but sadness of heart."

I was very much afraid, ³but I said to the king, "May the king live for ever! Why should my face not look sad when the city where my fathers are buried lies in ruins, and its gates have been destroyed by fire?"

⁴The king said to me, "What is it you want?"

Then I prayed to the God of heaven, ⁵and I answered the king, "If it pleases the king and if your servant has found favour in his sight, let him send me to the city in Judah where my fathers are buried so that I can rebuild it."

⁶Then the king, with the queen sitting beside him, asked me, "How long will your journey take, and when will you get back?" It pleased the king to send me; so I set a time.

⁷I also said to him, "If it pleases the king, may I have letters to the governors of Trans-Euphrates, so that they will provide me safe-conduct until I arrive in Judah? ⁸And may I have a letter to Asaph, keeper of the king's forest, so he will give me timber to make beams for the gates of the citadel by the temple and for the city wall and for the residence I will occupy?" And because the gracious hand of my God was upon me, the king granted my requests. ⁹So I went to the governors of Trans-Euphrates and gave them the king's letters. The king had also sent army officers and cavalry with me.

¹⁰When Sanballat the Horonite and Tobiah the Ammonite official heard about this, they were very much disturbed that someone had come to promote the welfare of the Israelites.

Nehemiah Inspects Jerusalem's Walls

¹¹I went to Jerusalem, and after staying there three days ¹²I set out during the night with a few men. I had not told anyone what my God had put in my heart to do for Jerusalem. There were no mounts with me except the one I was riding on.

¹³By night I went out through the Valley

Gate towards the Jackal[a] Well and the Dung Gate, examining the walls of Jerusalem, which had been broken down, and its gates, which had been destroyed by fire. [14]Then I moved on towards the Fountain Gate and the King's Pool, but there was not enough room for my mount to get through; [15]so I went up the valley by night, examining the wall. Finally, I turned back and re-entered through the Valley Gate. [16]The officials did not know where I had gone or what I was doing, because as yet I had said nothing to the Jews or the priests or nobles or officials or any others who would be doing the work.

[17]Then I said to them, "You see the trouble we are in: Jerusalem lies in ruins, and its gates have been burned with fire. Come, let us rebuild the wall of Jerusalem, and we will no longer be in disgrace." [18]I also told them about the gracious hand of my God upon me and what the king had said to me.

They replied, "Let us start rebuilding." So they began this good work.

[19]But when Sanballat the Horonite, Tobiah the Ammonite official and Geshem the Arab heard about it, they mocked and ridiculed us. "What is this you are doing?" they asked. "Are you rebelling against the king?"

[20]I answered them by saying, "The God of heaven will give us success. We his servants will start rebuilding, but as for you, you have no share in Jerusalem or any claim or historic right to it."

Builders of the Wall

3 Eliashib the high priest and his fellow priests went to work and rebuilt the Sheep Gate. They dedicated it and set its doors in place, building as far as the Tower of the Hundred, which they dedicated, and as far as the Tower of Hananel. [2]The men of Jericho built the adjoining section, and Zaccur son of Imri built next to them.

[3]The Fish Gate was rebuilt by the sons of Hassenaah. They laid its beams and put its doors and bolts and bars in place. [4]Meremoth son of Uriah, the son of Hakkoz, repaired the next section. Next to him Meshullam son of Berekiah, the son of Meshezabel, made repairs, and next to him Zadok son of Baana also made repairs. [5]The next section was repaired by the men of Tekoa, but their nobles would not put their shoulders to the work under their supervisors.[a]

[6]The Jeshanah[b] Gate was repaired by Joiada son of Paseah and Meshullam son of Besodeiah. They laid its beams and put its doors and bolts and bars in place. [7]Next to them, repairs were made by men from Gibeon and Mizpah—Melatiah of Gibeon and Jadon of Meronoth—places under the authority of the governor of Trans-Euphrates. [8]Uzziel son of Harhaiah, one of the goldsmiths, repaired the next section; and Hananiah, one of the perfume-makers,

made repairs next to that. They restored[c] Jerusalem as far as the Broad Wall. [9]Rephaiah son of Hur, ruler of a half-district of Jerusalem, repaired the next section. [10]Adjoining this, Jedaiah son of Harumaph made repairs opposite his house, and Hattush son of Hashabneiah made repairs next to him. [11]Malkijah son of Harim and Hasshub son of Pahath-Moab repaired another section and the Tower of the Ovens. [12]Shallum son of Hallohesh, ruler of a half-district of Jerusalem, repaired the next section with the help of his daughters.

[13]The Valley Gate was repaired by Hanun and the residents of Zanoah. They rebuilt it and put its doors and bolts and bars in place. They also repaired five hundred yards[d] of the wall as far as the Dung Gate.

[14]The Dung Gate was repaired by Malkijah son of Recab, ruler of the district of Beth Hakkerem. He rebuilt it and put its doors and bolts and bars in place.

[15]The Fountain Gate was repaired by Shallun son of Col-Hozeh, ruler of the district of Mizpah. He rebuilt it, roofing it over and putting its doors and bolts and bars in place. He also repaired the wall of the Pool of Siloam,[e] by the King's Garden, as far as the steps going down from the City of David. [16]Beyond him, Nehemiah son of Azbuk, ruler of a half-district of Beth Zur, made repairs up to a point opposite the tombs[f] of David, as far as the artificial pool and the House of the Heroes.

[17]Next to him, the repairs were made by the Levites under Rehum son of Bani. Beside him, Hashabiah, ruler of half the district of Keilah, carried out repairs for his district. [18]Next to him, the repairs were made by their countrymen under Binnui[g] son of Henadad, ruler of the other half-district of Keilah. [19]Next to him, Ezer son of Jeshua, ruler of Mizpah, repaired another section, from a point facing the ascent to the armoury as far as the angle. [20]Next to him, Baruch son of Zabbai zealously repaired another section, from the angle to the entrance of the house of Eliashib the high priest. [21]Next to him, Meremoth son of Uriah, the son of Hakkoz, repaired another section, from the entrance of Eliashib's house to the end of it.

[22]The repairs next to him were made by the priests from the surrounding region. [23]Beyond them, Benjamin and Hasshub made repairs in front of their house; and next to them, Azariah son of Maaseiah, the son of Ananiah, made repairs beside his house. [24]Next to him, Binnui son of Henadad repaired another section, from Azariah's house to the angle and the corner, [25]and Palal son of Uzai worked opposite the angle and the tower projecting from the upper palace near the court of the guard. Next to him, Pedaiah

---

[a]13 Or *Serpent* or *Fig*   [a]5 Or *their Lord* or *the governor*   [b]6 Or *Old*   [c]8 Or *They left out part of*
[d]13 Hebrew *a thousand cubits* (about 450 metres)   [e]15 Hebrew *Shelah*, a variant of *Shiloah*, that is, *Siloam*
[f]16 Hebrew; Septuagint, some Vulgate manuscripts and Syriac *tomb*
[g]18 Two Hebrew manuscripts and Syriac (see also Septuagint and verse 24); most Hebrew manuscripts *Bavvai*

son of Parosh [26]and the temple servants living on the hill of Ophel made repairs up to a point opposite the Water Gate towards the east and the projecting tower. [27]Next to them, the men of Tekoa repaired another section, from the great projecting tower to the wall of Ophel.

[28]Above the Horse Gate, the priests made repairs, each in front of his own house. [29]Next to them, Zadok son of Immer made repairs opposite his house. Next to him, Shemaiah son of Shecaniah, the guard at the East Gate, made repairs. [30]Next to him, Hananiah son of Shelemiah, and Hanun, the sixth son of Zalaph, repaired another section. Next to them, Meshullam son of Berekiah made repairs opposite his living quarters. [31]Next to him, Malkijah, one of the goldsmiths, made repairs as far as the house of the temple servants and the merchants, opposite the Inspection Gate, and as far as the room above the corner; [32]and between the room above the corner and the Sheep Gate the goldsmiths and merchants made repairs.

Opposition to the Rebuilding

4 When Sanballat heard that we were rebuilding the wall, he became angry and was greatly incensed. He ridiculed the Jews, [2]and in the presence of his associates and the army of Samaria, he said, "What are those feeble Jews doing? Will they restore their wall? Will they offer sacrifices? Will they finish in a day? Can they bring the stones back to life from those heaps of rubble—burned as they are?"

[3]Tobiah the Ammonite, who was at his side, said, "What they are building—if even a fox climbed up on it, he would break down their wall of stones!"

[4]Hear us, O our God, for we are despised. Turn their insults back on their own heads. Give them over as plunder in a land of captivity. [5]Do not cover up their guilt or blot out their sins from your sight, for they have thrown insults in the face of[a] the builders.

[6]So we rebuilt the wall till all of it reached half its height, for the people worked with all their heart.

[7]But when Sanballat, Tobiah, the Arabs, the Ammonites and the men of Ashdod heard that the repairs to Jerusalem's walls had gone ahead and that the gaps were being closed, they were very angry. [8]They all plotted together to come and fight against Jerusalem and stir up trouble against it. [9]But we prayed to our God and posted a guard day and night to meet this threat.

[10]Meanwhile, the people in Judah said, "The strength of the labourers is giving out, and there is so much rubble that we cannot rebuild the wall."

[11]Also our enemies said, "Before they know it or see us, we will be right there among them and will kill them and put an end to the work."

[12]Then the Jews who lived near them came and told us ten times over, "Wherever you turn, they will attack us."

[13]Therefore I stationed some of the people behind the lowest points of the wall at the exposed places, posting them by families, with their swords, spears and bows. [14]After I looked things over, I stood up and said to the nobles, the officials and the rest of the people, "Don't be afraid of them. Remember the Lord, who is great and awesome, and fight for your brothers, your sons and your daughters, your wives and your homes."

[15]When our enemies heard that we were aware of their plot and that God had frustrated it, we all returned to the wall, each to his own work.

[16]From that day on, half of my men did the work, while the other half were equipped with spears, shields, bows and armour. The officers posted themselves behind all the people of Judah [17]who were building the wall. Those who carried materials did their work with one hand and held a weapon in the other, [18]and each of the builders wore his sword at his side as he worked. But the man who sounded the trumpet stayed with me.

[19]Then I said to the nobles, the officials and the rest of the people, "The work is extensive and spread out, and we are widely separated from each other along the wall. [20]Wherever you hear the sound of the trumpet, join us there. Our God will fight for us!"

[21]So we continued the work with half the men holding spears, from the first light of dawn till the stars came out. [22]At that time I also said to the people, "Have every man and his helper stay inside Jerusalem at night, so that they can serve us as guards by night and workmen by day." [23]Neither I nor my brothers nor my men nor the guards with me took off our clothes; each had his weapon, even when he went for water.[b]

Nehemiah Helps the Poor

5 Now the men and their wives raised a great outcry against their Jewish brothers. [2]Some were saying, "We and our sons and daughters are numerous; in order for us to eat and stay alive, we must get grain."

[3]Others were saying, "We are mortgaging our fields, our vineyards and our homes to get grain during the famine."

[4]Still others were saying, "We have had to borrow money to pay the king's tax on our fields and vineyards. [5]Although we are of the same flesh and blood as our countrymen and though our sons are as good as theirs, yet we have to subject our sons and our daughters to slavery. Some of our daughters have already been enslaved, but we are powerless, because our fields and our vineyards belong to others."

[6]When I heard their outcry and these charges, I was very angry. [7]I pondered them in my mind and then accused the nobles and

---

[a]5 Or *have provoked you to anger before*   [b]23 The meaning of the Hebrew for this clause is uncertain.

NEHEMIAH 5:14–19

'In spite of all this, I never demanded the food allotted to the governor, because the demands were heavy on these people' (v. 18b).

LEADERS ARE VULNERABLE to criticism. They have to exercise care in the way they use their resources. Usually their great responsibilities lead to great rewards. Naturally, governors of Judah were entitled to a generous allowance, authorized by the Persian Emperor, and obtained by levying a local community tax. Previous governors had levied this allowance – and possibly more.

Nehemiah, like his predecessors, had a right to the governor's allowance, but he did not use it. Instead he demonstrated that his efforts on behalf of the people were a labour of love. He used his own resources to fulfil the governor's obligations, and more besides.

It is true that only a rich man could afford to do this. Recently a British Prime Minister decided to forgo a salary increase so as to set a good example. Few people were impressed. Few believed it was a real sacrifice. Nehemiah, in one sense, was in a similar position. He had been the chief palace servant of a great emperor. He was wealthy. But he broke the normal pattern, which is for rich men to move every sinew to become richer. Few people are satisfied with what they have, especially when they have more than enough.

Nehemiah really was different. He was not out to impress people. Instead he was motivated by the desire to submit to the will of God. What sounds like boasting is in fact the prelude to prayer. He does not ask the *people* to remember him kindly. He simply leaves his actions with the Lord.

For Nehemiah the power of example was greater than the power of riches.

→410

ESTHER 4

'For if you remain silent at this time, relief and deliverance for the Jews will arise from another place . . . who knows but that you have come to royal position for such a time as this?' (v. 14).

WHEN WE ARE AT OUR WIT'S END, only God can take over. Usually he takes over by using a person. Esther was the person chosen to save her people on this occasion. But notice, too, that the author says if Esther had been unwilling, then God would have raised up another to undertake the task of salvation. Sometimes it appears that salvation is never going to come. Many, indeed, throughout history have perished while waiting for salvation. Have they died because those who had been chosen to save them were unwilling to hear, or if they heard, were unwilling to act?

How many monks in the fourteenth and fifteenth centuries had come to the same conclusions as Luther, yet did not have the courage to make their views public in the way that he did? Did people perish because of that?

How many ship's captains were sickened by the slave trade in the eighteenth century? Even John Newton continued with that trade for some time after his conversion before speaking out against it. Surely people perished because of that.

How many people saw the deprivation in Victorian England before Barnardo, Shaftesbury and Booth, yet held back from speaking out? Did thousands perish because of that?

More recently, how many people saw the rottenness of the Shah's regime in Iran, yet failed to speak out? Surely thousands have since perished because of that. And so we could go on.

Speaking out demands the courage Esther had, the courage to risk reputation, even life itself. Only then will God intervene to save, so dare we, even for a moment face the responsibility of not *speaking out?*

officials. I told them, "You are exacting usury from your own countrymen!" So I called together a large meeting to deal with them [8]and said: "As far as possible, we have bought back our Jewish brothers who were sold to the Gentiles. Now you are selling your brothers, only for them to be sold back to us!" They kept quiet, because they could find nothing to say.

[9]So I continued, "What you are doing is not right. Shouldn't you walk in the fear of our God to avoid the reproach of our Gentile enemies? [10]I and my brothers and my men are also lending the people money and grain. But let the exacting of usury stop! [11]Give back to them immediately their fields, vineyards, olive groves and houses, and also the usury you are charging them—the hundredth part of the money, grain, new wine and oil."

[12]"We will give it back," they said. "And we will not demand anything more from them. We will do as you say."

Then I summoned the priests and made the nobles and officials take an oath to do what they had promised. [13]I also shook out the folds of my robe and said, "In this way may God shake out of his house and possessions every man who does not keep this promise. So may such a man be shaken out and emptied!"

At this the whole assembly said, "Amen," and praised the LORD. And the people did as they had promised.

[14]Moreover, from the twentieth year of King Artaxerxes, when I was appointed to be their governor in the land of Judah, until his thirty-second year—twelve years—neither I nor my brothers ate the food allotted to the governor. [15]But the earlier governors—those preceding me—placed a heavy burden on the people and took forty shekels[a] of silver from them in addition to food and wine. Their assistants also lorded it over the people. But out of reverence for God I did not act like that. [16]Instead, I devoted myself to the work on this wall. All my men were assembled there for the work; we[b] did not acquire any land.

[17]Furthermore, a hundred and fifty Jews and officials ate at my table, as well as those who came to us from the surrounding nations. [18]Each day one ox, six choice sheep and some poultry were prepared for me, and every ten days an abundant supply of wine of all kinds. In spite of all this, I never demanded the food allotted to the governor, because the demands were heavy on these people.

[19]Remember me with favour, O my God, for all I have done for these people.

Further Opposition to the Rebuilding

6 When word came to Sanballat, Tobiah, Geshem the Arab and the rest of our enemies that I had rebuilt the wall and not a gap was left in it—though up to that time I had not set the doors in the gates—[2]Sanballat and Geshem sent me this message: "Come, let us meet together in one of the villages[a] on the plain of Ono."

But they were scheming to harm me; [3]so I sent messengers to them with this reply: "I am carrying on a great project and cannot go down. Why should the work stop while I leave it and go down to you?" [4]Four times they sent me the same message, and each time I gave them the same answer.

[5]Then, the fifth time, Sanballat sent his assistant to me with the same message, and in his hand was an unsealed letter [6]in which was written:

"It is reported among the nations— and Geshem[b] says it is true—that you and the Jews are plotting to revolt, and therefore you are building the wall. Moreover, according to these reports you are about to become their king [7]and have even appointed prophets to make this proclamation about you in Jerusalem: 'There is a king in Judah!' Now this report will get back to the king; so come, let us confer together."

[8]I sent him this reply: "Nothing like what you are saying is happening; you are just making it up out of your head."

[9]They were all trying to frighten us, thinking, "Their hands will get too weak for the work, and it will not be completed."

⌐But I prayed,⌐ "Now strengthen my hands."

[10]One day I went to the house of Shemaiah son of Delaiah, the son of Mehetabel, who was shut in at his home. He said, "Let us meet in the house of God, inside the temple, and let us close the temple doors, because men are coming to kill you—by night they are coming to kill you."

[11]But I said, "Should a man like me run away? Or should one like me go into the temple to save his life? I will not go!" [12]I realised that God had not sent him, but that he had prophesied against me because Tobiah and Sanballat had hired him. [13]He had been hired to intimidate me so that I would commit a sin by doing this, and then they would give me a bad name to discredit me.

[14]Remember Tobiah and Sanballat, O my God, because of what they have done; remember also the prophetess Noadiah and the rest of the prophets who have been trying to intimidate me.

The Completion of the Wall

[15]So the wall was completed on the twenty-fifth of Elul, in fifty-two days. [16]When all our enemies heard about this, all the surrounding nations were afraid and lost their self-confidence, because they realised that this work had been done with the help of our God.

---

[a]15 That is, about 1 pound (about 0.5 kilogram)
[b]16 Most Hebrew manuscripts; some Hebrew manuscripts, Septuagint, Vulgate and Syriac *I*
[a]2 Or *in Kephirim*　[b]6 Hebrew *Gashmu*, a variant of *Geshem*

¹⁷Also, in those days the nobles of Judah were sending many letters to Tobiah, and replies from Tobiah kept coming to them. ¹⁸For many in Judah were under oath to him, since he was son-in-law to Shecaniah son of Arah, and his son Jehohanan had married the daughter of Meshullam son of Berekiah. ¹⁹Moreover, they kept reporting to me his good deeds and then telling him what I said. And Tobiah sent letters to intimidate me.

7 After the wall had been rebuilt and I had set the doors in place, the gatekeepers and the singers and the Levites were appointed. ²I put in charge of Jerusalem my brother Hanani, along with*a* Hananiah the commander of the citadel, because he was a man of integrity and feared God more than most men do. ³I said to them, "The gates of Jerusalem are not to be opened until the sun is hot. While the gatekeepers are still on duty, make them shut the doors and bar them. Also appoint residents of Jerusalem as guards, some at their posts and some near their own houses."

The List of the Exiles Who Returned

⁴Now the city was large and spacious, but there were few people in it, and the houses had not yet been rebuilt. ⁵So my God put it into my heart to assemble the nobles, the officials and the common people for registration by families. I found the genealogical record of those who had been the first to return. This is what I found written there:

⁶These are the people of the province who came up from the captivity of the exiles whom Nebuchadnezzar king of Babylon had taken captive (they returned to Jerusalem and Judah, each to his own town, ⁷in company with Zerubbabel, Jeshua, Nehemiah, Azariah, Raamiah, Nahamani, Mordecai, Bilshan, Mispereth, Bigvai, Nehum and Baanah):

The list of the men of Israel:

⁸the descendants of Parosh	2,172
⁹of Shephatiah	372
¹⁰of Arah	652
¹¹of Pahath-Moab (through the line of Jeshua and Joab)	2,818
¹²of Elam	1,254
¹³of Zattu	845
¹⁴of Zaccai	760
¹⁵of Binnui	648
¹⁶of Bebai	628
¹⁷of Azgad	2,322
¹⁸of Adonikam	667
¹⁹of Bigvai	2,067
²⁰of Adin	655
²¹of Ater (through Hezekiah)	98
²²of Hashum	328
²³of Bezai	324
²⁴of Hariph	112
²⁵of Gibeon	95
²⁶the men of Bethlehem and Netophah	188
²⁷of Anathoth	128
²⁸of Beth Azmaveth	42
²⁹of Kiriath Jearim, Kephirah and Beeroth	743
³⁰of Ramah and Geba	621
³¹of Michmash	122
³²of Bethel and Ai	123
³³of the other Nebo	52
³⁴of the other Elam	1,254
³⁵of Harim	320
³⁶of Jericho	345
³⁷of Lod, Hadid and Ono	721
³⁸of Senaah	3,930

³⁹The priests:

the descendants of Jedaiah (through the family of Jeshua)	973
⁴⁰of Immer	1,052
⁴¹of Pashhur	1,247
⁴²of Harim	1,017

⁴³The Levites:

the descendants of Jeshua (through Kadmiel through the line of Hodaviah)	74

⁴⁴The singers:

the descendants of Asaph	148

⁴⁵The gatekeepers:

the descendants of Shallum, Ater, Talmon, Akkub, Hatita and Shobai	138

⁴⁶The temple servants:

the descendants of
Ziha, Hasupha, Tabbaoth,
⁴⁷Keros, Sia, Padon,
⁴⁸Lebana, Hagaba, Shalmai,
⁴⁹Hanan, Giddel, Gahar,
⁵⁰Reaiah, Rezin, Nekoda,
⁵¹Gazzam, Uzza, Paseah,
⁵²Besai, Meunim, Nephussim,
⁵³Bakbuk, Hakupha, Harhur,
⁵⁴Bazluth, Mehida, Harsha,
⁵⁵Barkos, Sisera, Temah,
⁵⁶Neziah and Hatipha

⁵⁷The descendants of the servants of Solomon:

the descendants of
Sotai, Sophereth, Perida,
⁵⁸Jaala, Darkon, Giddel,
⁵⁹Shephatiah, Hattil, Pokereth-Hazzebaim and Amon

⁶⁰The temple servants and the descendants of the servants of Solomon	392

⁶¹The following came up from the towns of Tel Melah, Tel Harsha, Kerub, Addon and Immer, but they could not

*a*2 Or *Hanani, that is,*

show that their families were descended from Israel:

62the descendants of
Delaiah, Tobiah and Nekoda   642

63And from among the priests:

the descendants of
Hobaiah, Hakkoz and Barzillai (a man who had married a daughter of Barzillai the Gileadite and was called by that name).
64These searched for their family records, but they could not find them and so were excluded from the priesthood as unclean. 65The governor, therefore, ordered them not to eat any of the most sacred food until there should be a priest ministering with the Urim and Thummim.

66The whole company numbered 42,360, 67besides their 7,337 menservants and maidservants; and they also had 245 men and women singers. 68There were 736 horses, 245 mules,b 69435 camels and 6,720 donkeys.

70Some of the heads of the families contributed to the work. The governor gave to the treasury 1,000 drachmasc of gold, 50 bowls and 530 garments for priests. 71Some of the heads of the families gave to the treasury for the work 20,000 drachmasd of gold and 2,200 minase of silver. 72The total given by the rest of the people was 20,000 drachmas of gold, 2,000 minasf of silver and 67 garments for priests.
73The priests, the Levites, the gatekeepers, the singers and the temple servants, along with certain of the people and the rest of the Israelites, settled in their own towns.

Ezra Reads the Law

8 When the seventh month came and the Israelites had settled in their towns, 1all the people assembled as one man in the square before the Water Gate. They told Ezra the scribe to bring out the Book of the Law of Moses, which the LORD had commanded for Israel.

2So on the first day of the seventh month, Ezra the priest brought the Law before the assembly, which was made up of men and women and all who were able to understand. 3He read it aloud from daybreak till noon as he faced the square before the Water Gate in the presence of the men, women and others who could understand. And all the people listened attentively to the Book of the Law.

4Ezra the scribe stood on a high wooden platform built for the occasion. Beside him on his right stood Mattithiah, Shema, Anaiah, Uriah, Hilkiah and Maaseiah; and on his left were Pedaiah, Mishael, Malkijah, Hashum, Hashbaddanah, Zechariah and Meshullam.

5Ezra opened the book. All the people could see him because he was standing above them; and as he opened it, the people all stood up. 6Ezra praised the LORD, the great God; and all the people lifted their hands and responded, "Amen! Amen!" Then they bowed down and worshipped the LORD with their faces to the ground.

7The Levites—Jeshua, Bani, Sherebiah, Jamin, Akkub, Shabbethai, Hodiah, Maaseiah, Kelita, Azariah, Jozabad, Hanan and Pelaiah—instructed the people in the Law while the people were standing there. 8They read from the Book of the Law of God, making it cleara and giving the meaning so that the people could understand what was being read.

9Then Nehemiah the governor, Ezra the priest and scribe, and the Levites who were instructing the people said to them all, "This day is sacred to the LORD your God. Do not mourn or weep." For all the people had been weeping as they listened to the words of the Law.

10Nehemiah said, "Go and enjoy choice food and sweet drinks, and send some to those who have nothing prepared. This day is sacred to our Lord. Do not grieve, for the joy of the LORD is your strength."

11The Levites calmed all the people saying, "Be still, for this is a sacred day. Do not grieve."

12Then all the people went away to eat and drink, to send portions of food and to celebrate with great joy, because they had now understood the words that had been made known to them.

13On the second day of the month, the heads of all the families, along with the priests and the Levites, gathered round Ezra the scribe to give attention to the words of the Law. 14They found written in the Law, which the LORD had commanded through Moses, that the Israelites were to live in booths during the feast of the seventh month 15and that they should proclaim this word and spread it throughout their towns and in Jerusalem: "Go out into the hill country and bring back branches from olive and wild olive trees, and from myrtles, palms and shade trees, to make booths"—as it is written.b

16So the people went out and brought back branches and built themselves booths on their own roofs, in their courtyards, in the courts of the house of God and in the square by the Water Gate and the one by the Gate of Ephraim. 17The whole company that had returned from exile built booths and lived in them. From the days of Joshua son of Nun until that day, the Israelites had not celebrated it like this. And their joy was very great.

---

b68 Some Hebrew manuscripts (see also Ezra 2:66); most Hebrew manuscripts do not have this verse.
c70 That is, about 19 pounds (about 8.5 kilograms)
d71 That is, about 375 pounds (about 170 kilograms); also in verse 72
e71 That is, about 1¼ tons (about 1.3 metric tons)   f72 That is, about 1 ton (about 1.1 metric tons)
a8 Or God, translating it   b15 See Lev. 23:37–40.

18Day after day, from the first day to the last, Ezra read from the Book of the Law of God. They celebrated the feast for seven days, and on the eighth day, in accordance with the regulation, there was an assembly.

The Israelites Confess Their Sins

9 On the twenty-fourth day of the same month, the Israelites gathered together, fasting and wearing sackcloth and having dust on their heads. 2Those of Israelite descent had separated themselves from all foreigners. They stood in their places and confessed their sins and the wickedness of their fathers. 3They stood where they were and read from the Book of the Law of the LORD their God for a quarter of the day, and spent another quarter in confession and in worshipping the LORD their God. 4Standing on the stairs were the Levites—Jeshua, Bani, Kadmiel, Shebaniah, Bunni, Sherebiah, Bani and Kenani—who called with loud voices to the LORD their God. 5And the Levites—Jeshua, Kadmiel, Bani, Hashabneiah, Sherebiah, Hodiah, Shebaniah and Pethahiah—said: "Stand up and praise the LORD your God, who is from everlasting to everlasting."*a*

"Blessed be your glorious name, and may it be exalted above all blessing and praise. 6You alone are the LORD. You made the heavens, even the highest heavens, and all their starry host, the earth and all that is on it, the seas and all that is in them. You give life to everything, and the multitudes of heaven worship you.

7"You are the LORD God, who chose Abram and brought him out of Ur of the Chaldeans and named him Abraham. 8You found his heart faithful to you, and you made a covenant with him to give to his descendants the land of the Canaanites, Hittites, Amorites, Perizzites, Jebusites and Girgashites. You have kept your promise because you are righteous.

9"You saw the suffering of our forefathers in Egypt; you heard their cry at the Red Sea.*b* 10You sent miraculous signs and wonders against Pharaoh, against all his officials and all the people of his land, for you knew how arrogantly the Egyptians treated them. You made a name for yourself, which remains to this day. 11You divided the sea before them, so that they passed through it on dry ground, but you hurled their pursuers into the depths, like a stone into mighty waters. 12By day you led them with a pillar of cloud, and by night with a pillar of fire to give them light on the way they were to take.

13"You came down on Mount Sinai; you spoke to them from heaven. You gave them regulations and laws that are just and right, and decrees and commands that are good. 14You made known to them your holy Sabbath and gave them commands, decrees and laws through your servant Moses. 15In their hunger you gave them bread from heaven and in their thirst you brought them water from the rock; you told them to go in and take possession of the land you had sworn with uplifted hand to give them.

16"But they, our forefathers, became arrogant and stiff-necked, and did not obey your commands. 17They refused to listen and failed to remember the miracles you performed among them. They became stiff-necked and in their rebellion appointed a leader in order to return to their slavery. But you are a forgiving God, gracious and compassionate, slow to anger and abounding in love. Therefore you did not desert them, 18even when they cast for themselves an image of a calf and said, 'This is your god, who brought you up out of Egypt,' or when they committed awful blasphemies.

19"Because of your great compassion you did not abandon them in the desert. By day the pillar of cloud did not cease to guide them on their path, nor the pillar of fire by night to shine on the way they were to take. 20You gave your good Spirit to instruct them. You did not withhold your manna from their mouths, and you gave them water for their thirst. 21For forty years you sustained them in the desert; they lacked nothing, their clothes did not wear out nor did their feet become swollen.

22"You gave them kingdoms and nations, allotting to them even the remotest frontiers. They took over the country of Sihon*c* king of Heshbon and the country of Og king of Bashan. 23You made their sons as numerous as the stars in the sky, and you brought them into the land that you told their fathers to enter and possess. 24Their sons went in and took possession of the land. You subdued before them the Canaanites, who lived in the land; you handed the Canaanites over to them, along with their kings and the peoples of the land, to deal with them as they pleased. 25They captured fortified cities and fertile land; they took possession of houses filled with all kinds of good things, wells already dug, vineyards, olive groves and fruit trees in abundance. They ate to the full and were well-nourished; they revelled in your great goodness.

26"But they were disobedient and rebelled against you; they put your law behind their backs. They killed your prophets, who had admonished them in order to turn them back to you; they committed awful blasphemies. 27So you handed them over to their enemies, who

*a5 Or God for ever and ever   b9 Hebrew Yam Suph; that is, Sea of Reeds
c22 One Hebrew manuscript and Septuagint; most Hebrew manuscripts Sihon, that is, the country of the*

oppressed them. But when they were oppressed they cried out to you. From heaven you heard them, and in your great compassion you gave them deliverers, who rescued them from the hand of their enemies.

28"But as soon as they were at rest, they again did what was evil in your sight. Then you abandoned them to the hand of their enemies so that they ruled over them. And when they cried out to you again, you heard from heaven, and in your compassion you delivered them time after time.

29"You warned them to return to your law, but they became arrogant and disobeyed your commands. They sinned against your ordinances, by which a man will live if he obeys them. Stubbornly they turned their backs on you, became stiff-necked and refused to listen. 30For many years you were patient with them. By your Spirit you admonished them through your prophets. Yet they paid no attention, so you handed them over to the neighbouring peoples. 31But in your great mercy you did not put an end to them or abandon them, for you are a gracious and merciful God.

32"Now therefore, O our God, the great, mighty and awesome God, who keeps his covenant of love, do not let all this hardship seem trifling in your eyes —the hardship that has come upon us, upon our kings and leaders, upon our priests and prophets, upon our fathers and all your people, from the days of the kings of Assyria until today. 33In all that has happened to us, you have been just; you have acted faithfully, while we did wrong. 34Our kings, our leaders, our priests and our fathers did not follow your law; they did not pay attention to your commands or the warnings you gave them. 35Even while they were in their kingdom, enjoying your great goodness to them in the spacious and fertile land you gave them, they did not serve you or turn from their evil ways.

36"But see, we are slaves today, slaves in the land you gave our forefathers so that they could eat its fruit and the other good things it produces. 37Because of our sins, its abundant harvest goes to the kings you have placed over us. They rule over our bodies and our cattle as they please. We are in great distress.

The Agreement of the People

38"In view of all this, we are making a binding agreement, putting it in writing, and our leaders, our Levites and our priests are affixing their seals to it."

10 Those who sealed it were:

Nehemiah the governor, the son of Hacaliah.

Zedekiah, 2Seraiah, Azariah, Jeremiah,
3Pashhur, Amariah, Malkijah,
4Hattush, Shebaniah, Malluch,
5Harim, Meremoth, Obadiah,
6Daniel, Ginnethon, Baruch,
7Meshullam, Abijah, Mijamin,
8Maaziah, Bilgai and Shemaiah.

These were the priests.

9The Levites:

Jeshua son of Azaniah,
Binnui of the sons of Henadad,
Kadmiel,
10and their associates:
Shebaniah, Hodiah, Kelita,
Pelaiah, Hanan,
11Mica, Rehob, Hashabiah,
12Zaccur, Sherebiah, Shebaniah,
13Hodiah, Bani and Beninu.

14The leaders of the people:

Parosh, Pahath-Moab, Elam, Zattu, Bani,
15Bunni, Azgad, Bebai,
16Adonijah, Bigvai, Adin,
17Ater, Hezekiah, Azzur,
18Hodiah, Hashum, Bezai,
19Hariph, Anathoth, Nebai,
20Magpiash, Meshullam, Hezir,
21Meshezabel, Zadok, Jaddua,
22Pelatiah, Hanan, Anaiah,
23Hoshea, Hananiah, Hasshub,
24Hallohesh, Pilha, Shobek,
25Rehum, Hashabnah, Maaseiah,
26Ahiah, Hanan, Anan,
27Malluch, Harim and Baanah.

28"The rest of the people—priests, Levites, gatekeepers, singers, temple servants and all who separated themselves from the neighbouring peoples for the sake of the Law of God, together with their wives and all their sons and daughters who are able to understand —29all these now join their brothers the nobles, and bind themselves with a curse and an oath to follow the Law of God given through Moses the servant of God and to obey carefully all the commands, regulations and decrees of the LORD our Lord.

30"We promise not to give our daughters in marriage to the peoples around us or take their daughters for our sons.

31"When the neighbouring peoples bring merchandise or grain to sell on the Sabbath, we will not buy from them on the Sabbath or on any holy day. Every seventh year we will forgo working the land and will cancel all debts.

32"We assume the responsibility for carrying out the commands to give a third of a shekel[a] each year for the service of the house of our God: 33for the bread set out on the table; for the regular grain offerings and burnt offerings; for

---

[a]32 That is, about 1/8 ounce (about 4 grams)

the offerings on the Sabbaths, New Moon festivals and appointed feasts; for the holy offerings; for sin offerings to make atonement for Israel; and for all the duties of the house of our God.

34"We—the priests, the Levites and the people—have cast lots to determine when each of our families is to bring to the house of our God at set times each year a contribution of wood to burn on the altar of the LORD our God, as it is written in the Law.

35"We also assume responsibility for bringing to the house of the LORD each year the firstfruits of our crops and of every fruit tree.

36"As it is also written in the Law, we will bring the firstborn of our sons and of our cattle, of our herds and of our flocks to the house of our God, to the priests ministering there.

37"Moreover, we will bring to the storerooms of the house of our God, to the priests, the first of our ground meal, of our ᵣgrainᵣ offerings, of the fruit of all our trees and of our new wine and oil. And we will bring a tithe of our crops to the Levites, for it is the Levites who collect the tithes in all the towns where we work. 38A priest descended from Aaron is to accompany the Levites when they receive the tithes, and the Levites are to bring a tenth of the tithes up to the house of our God, to the storerooms of the treasury. 39The people of Israel, including the Levites, are to bring their contributions of grain, new wine and oil to the storerooms where the articles for the sanctuary are kept and where the ministering priests, the gatekeepers and the singers stay.

"We will not neglect the house of our God."

The New Residents of Jerusalem

11 Now the leaders of the people settled in Jerusalem, and the rest of the people cast lots to bring one out of every ten to live in Jerusalem, the holy city, while the remaining nine were to stay in their own towns. 2The people commended all the men who volunteered to live in Jerusalem.

3These are the provincial leaders who settled in Jerusalem (now some Israelites, priests, Levites, temple servants and descendants of Solomon's servants lived in the towns of Judah, each on his own property in the various towns, 4while other people from both Judah and Benjamin lived in Jerusalem):

From the descendants of Judah:

Athaiah son of Uzziah, the son of Zechariah, the son of Amariah, the son of Shephatiah, the son of Mahalalel, a descendant of Perez; 5and Maaseiah son of Baruch, the son of Col-Hozeh, the son of Hazaiah, the son of Adaiah, the son of Joiarib, the son of Zechariah, a descendant of Shelah. 6The descendants of Perez who lived in Jerusalem totalled 468 able men.

7From the descendants of Benjamin:

Sallu son of Meshullam, the son of Joed, the son of Pedaiah, the son of Kolaiah, the son of Maaseiah, the son of Ithiel, the son of Jeshaiah, 8and his followers, Gabbai and Sallai—928 men. 9Joel son of Zicri was their chief officer, and Judah son of Hassenuah was over the Second District of the city.

10From the priests:

Jedaiah; the son of Joiarib; Jakin; 11Seraiah son of Hilkiah, the son of Meshullam, the son of Zadok, the son of Meraioth, the son of Ahitub, supervisor in the house of God, 12and their associates, who carried on work for the temple —822 men; Adaiah son of Jeroham, the son of Pelaliah, the son of Amzi, the son of Zechariah, the son of Pashhur, the son of Malkijah, 13and his associates, who were heads of families—242 men; Amashsai son of Azarel, the son of Ahzai, the son of Meshillemoth, the son of Immer, 14and hisᵃ associates, who were able men—128 men. Their chief officer was Zabdiel son of Haggedolim.

15From the Levites:

Shemaiah son of Hasshub, the son of Azrikam, the son of Hashabiah, the son of Bunni; 16Shabbethai and Jozabad, two of the heads of the Levites, who had charge of the outside work of the house of God; 17Mattaniah son of Mica, the son of Zabdi, the son of Asaph, the director who led in thanksgiving and prayer; Bakbukiah, second among his associates; and Abda son of Shammua, the son of Galal, the son of Jeduthun. 18The Levites in the holy city totalled 284.

19The gatekeepers:

Akkub, Talmon and their associates, who kept watch at the gates—172 men.

20The rest of the Israelites, with the priests and Levites, were in all the towns of Judah, each on his ancestral property.

21The temple servants lived on the hill of Ophel, and Ziha and Gishpa were in charge of them.

22The chief officer of the Levites in Jerusalem was Uzzi son of Bani, the son of Hashabiah, the son of Mattaniah, the son of Mica. Uzzi was one of Asaph's descendants, who were the singers responsible for the service of the house of God. 23The singers were under the king's orders, which regulated their daily activity.

24Pethahiah son of Meshezabel, one of the

ᵃ14 Most Septuagint manuscripts; Hebrew *their*

descendants of Zerah son of Judah, was the king's agent in all affairs relating to the people.

25As for the villages with their fields, some of the people of Judah lived in Kiriath Arba and its surrounding settlements, in Dibon and its settlements, in Jekabzeel and its villages, 26in Jeshua, in Moladah, in Beth Pelet, 27in Hazar Shual, in Beersheba and its settlements, 28in Ziklag, in Meconah and its settlements, 29in En Rimmon, in Zorah, in Jarmuth, 30Zanoah, Adullam and their villages, in Lachish and its fields, and in Azekah and its settlements. So they were living all the way from Beersheba to the Valley of Hinnom.

31The descendants of the Benjamites from Geba lived in Michmash, Aija, Bethel and its settlements, 32in Anathoth, Nob and Ananiah, 33in Hazor, Ramah and Gittaim, 34in Hadid, Zeboim and Neballat, 35in Lod and Ono, and in the Valley of the Craftsmen.

36Some of the divisions of the Levites of Judah settled in Benjamin.

Priests and Levites

12 These were the priests and Levites who returned with Zerubbabel son of Shealtiel and with Jeshua:

Seraiah, Jeremiah, Ezra,
2Amariah, Malluch, Hattush,
3Shecaniah, Rehum, Meremoth,
4Iddo, Ginnethon,a Abijah,
5Mijamin,b Moadiah, Bilgah,
6Shemaiah, Joiarib, Jedaiah,
7Sallu, Amok, Hilkiah and Jedaiah.

These were the leaders of the priests and their associates in the days of Jeshua.

8The Levites were Jeshua, Binnui, Kadmiel, Sherebiah, Judah, and also Mattaniah, who, together with his associates, was in charge of the songs of thanksgiving. 9Bakbukiah and Unni, their associates, stood opposite them in the services.

10Jeshua was the father of Joiakim, Joiakim the father of Eliashib, Eliashib the father of Joiada, 11Joiada the father of Jonathan, and Jonathan the father of Jaddua.

12In the days of Joiakim, these were the heads of the priestly families:
of Seraiah's family, Meraiah;
of Jeremiah's, Hananiah;
13of Ezra's, Meshullam;
of Amariah's, Jehohanan;
14of Malluch's, Jonathan;
of Shecaniah's,c Joseph;
15of Harim's, Adna;
of Meremoth's,d Helkai;
16of Iddo's, Zechariah;
of Ginnethon's, Meshullam;
17of Abijah's, Zicri;
of Miniamin's and of Moadiah's, Piltai;
18of Bilgah's, Shammua;
of Shemaiah's, Jehonathan;
19of Joiarib's, Mattenai;
of Jedaiah's, Uzzi;
20of Sallu's, Kallai;
of Amok's, Eber;
21of Hilkiah's, Hashabiah;
of Jedaiah's, Nethanel.

22The family heads of the Levites in the days of Eliashib, Joiada, Johanan and Jaddua, as well as those of the priests, were recorded in the reign of Darius the Persian. 23The family heads among the descendants of Levi up to the time of Johanan son of Eliashib were recorded in the book of the annals. 24And the leaders of the Levites were Hashabiah, Sherebiah, Jeshua son of Kadmiel, and their associates, who stood opposite them to give praise and thanksgiving, one section responding to the other, as prescribed by David the man of God.

25Mattaniah, Bakbukiah, Obadiah, Meshullam, Talmon and Akkub were gatekeepers who guarded the storerooms at the gates. 26These served in the days of Joiakim son of Jeshua, the son of Jozadak, and in the days of Nehemiah the governor and of Ezra the priest and scribe.

Dedication of the Wall of Jerusalem

27At the dedication of the wall of Jerusalem, the Levites were sought out from where they lived and were brought to Jerusalem to celebrate joyfully the dedication with songs of thanksgiving and with the music of cymbals, harps and lyres. 28The singers also were brought together from the region around Jerusalem—from the villages of the Netophathites, 29from Beth Gilgal, and from the area of Geba and Azmaveth, for the singers had built villages for themselves around Jerusalem. 30When the priests and Levites had purified themselves ceremonially, they purified the people, the gates and the wall.

31I had the leaders of Judah go up on tope of the wall. I also assigned two large choirs to give thanks. One was to proceed on topf of the wall to the right, towards the Dung Gate. 32Hoshaiah and half the leaders of Judah followed them, 33along with Azariah, Ezra, Meshullam, 34Judah, Benjamin, Shemaiah, Jeremiah, 35as well as some priests with trumpets, and also Zechariah son of Jonathan, the son of Shemaiah, the son of Mattaniah, the son of Micaiah, the son of Zaccur, the son of Asaph, 36and his associates—Shemaiah, Azarel, Milalai, Gilalai, Maai, Nethanel, Judah and Hanani—with musical instruments ⌞prescribed by⌟ David the man of God. Ezra the scribe led the procession. 37At the Fountain Gate they continued directly up the steps of the City of David on the ascent to the wall and passed above the house of David to the Water Gate on the east.

38The second choir proceeded in the opposite direction. I followed them on topg of the wall, together with half the people—past the Tower of the Ovens to the Broad Wall, 39over the Gate of Ephraim, the Jeshanahh Gate, the

---

a4 Many Hebrew manuscripts and Vulgate (see also Neh. 12:16); most Hebrew manuscripts Ginnethoi
b5 A variant of Miniamin
c14 Very many Hebrew manuscripts, some Septuagint manuscripts and Syriac (see also Neh. 12:3); most Hebrew manuscripts Shebaniah's   d15 Some Septuagint manuscripts (see also Neh. 12:3); Hebrew Meraioth's
e31 Or go alongside   f31 Or proceed alongside   g38 Or them alongside   h39 Or Old

Fish Gate, the Tower of Hananel and the Tower of the Hundred, as far as the Sheep Gate. At the Gate of the Guard they stopped.

40The two choirs that gave thanks then took their places in the house of God; so did I, together with half the officials, 41as well as the priests—Eliakim, Maaseiah, Miniamin, Micaiah, Elioenai, Zechariah and Hananiah with their trumpets—42and also Maaseiah, Shemaiah, Eleazar, Uzzi, Jehohanan, Malkijah, Elam and Ezer. The choirs sang under the direction of Jezrahiah. 43And on that day they offered great sacrifices, rejoicing because God had given them great joy. The women and children also rejoiced. The sound of rejoicing in Jerusalem could be heard far away.

44At that time men were appointed to be in charge of the storerooms for the contributions, firstfruits and tithes. From the fields around the towns they were to bring into the storerooms the portions required by the Law for the priests and the Levites, for Judah was pleased with the ministering priests and Levites. 45They performed the service of their God and the service of purification, as did also the singers and gatekeepers, according to the commands of David and his son Solomon. 46For long ago, in the days of David and Asaph, there had been directors for the singers and for the songs of praise and thanksgiving to God. 47So in the days of Zerubbabel and of Nehemiah, all Israel contributed the daily portions for the singers and gatekeepers. They also set aside the portion for the other Levites, and the Levites set aside the portion for the descendants of Aaron.

Nehemiah's Final Reforms

13 On that day the Book of Moses was read aloud in the hearing of the people and there it was found written that no Ammonite or Moabite should ever be admitted into the assembly of God, 2because they had not met the Israelites with food and water but had hired Balaam to call a curse down on them. (Our God, however, turned the curse into a blessing.) 3When the people heard this law, they excluded from Israel all who were of foreign descent.

4Before this, Eliashib the priest had been put in charge of the storerooms of the house of our God. He was closely associated with Tobiah, 5and he had provided him with a large room formerly used to store the grain offerings and incense and temple articles, and also the tithes of grain, new wine and oil prescribed for the Levites, singers and gatekeepers, as well as the contributions for the priests.

6But while all this was going on, I was not in Jerusalem, for in the thirty-second year of Artaxerxes king of Babylon I had returned to the king. Some time later I asked his permission 7and came back to Jerusalem. Here I learned about the evil thing Eliashib had done in providing Tobiah a room in the courts of the house of God. 8I was greatly displeased and threw all Tobiah's household goods out of the room. 9I gave orders to purify the rooms, and then I put back into them the equipment of the house of God, with the grain offerings and the incense.

10I also learned that the portions assigned to the Levites had not been given to them, and that all the Levites and singers responsible for the service had gone back to their own fields. 11So I rebuked the officials and asked them, "Why is the house of God neglected?" Then I called them together and stationed them at their posts.

12All Judah brought the tithes of grain, new wine and oil into the storerooms. 13I put Shelemiah the priest, Zadok the scribe, and a Levite named Pedaiah in charge of the storerooms and made Hanan son of Zaccur, the son of Mattaniah, their assistant, because these men were considered trustworthy. They were made responsible for distributing the supplies to their brothers.

14Remember me for this, O my God, and do not blot out what I have so faithfully done for the house of my God and its services.

15In those days I saw men in Judah treading winepresses on the Sabbath and bringing in grain and loading it on donkeys, together with wine, grapes, figs and all other kinds of loads. And they were bringing all this into Jerusalem on the Sabbath. Therefore I warned them against selling food on that day. 16Men from Tyre who lived in Jerusalem were bringing in fish and all kinds of merchandise and selling them in Jerusalem on the Sabbath to the people of Judah. 17I rebuked the nobles of Judah and said to them, "What is this wicked thing you are doing—desecrating the Sabbath day? 18Didn't your forefathers do the same things, so that our God brought all this calamity upon us and upon this city? Now you are stirring up more wrath against Israel by desecrating the Sabbath."

19When evening shadows fell on the gates of Jerusalem before the Sabbath, I ordered the doors to be shut and not opened until the Sabbath was over. I stationed some of my own men at the gates so that no load could be brought in on the Sabbath day. 20Once or twice the merchants and sellers of all kinds of goods spent the night outside Jerusalem. 21But I warned them and said, "Why do you spend the night by the wall? If you do this again, I will lay hands on you." From that time on they no longer came on the Sabbath. 22Then I commanded the Levites to purify themselves and go and guard the gates in order to keep the Sabbath day holy.

Remember me for this also, O my God, and show mercy to me according to your great love.

23Moreover, in those days I saw men of Judah who had married women from Ashdod, Ammon and Moab. 24Half of their children spoke the language of Ashdod or the language of one of the other peoples, and did not know how to speak the language of Judah. 25I rebuked them and called curses down on them. I beat some of the men and pulled out their hair. I made them take an oath in God's name and said: "You are not to give your daughters in marriage to their sons, nor are you to take their daughters in marriage for your sons or for yourselves. [26]Was it not because of marriages like these that Solomon king of Israel sinned? Among the many nations there was no king like him. He was loved by his God, and God made him king over all Israel, but even he was led into sin by foreign women. [27]Must we hear now that you too are doing all this terrible wickedness and are being unfaithful to our God by marrying foreign women?"

[28]One of the sons of Joiada son of Eliashib the high priest was son-in-law to Sanballat the Horonite. And I drove him away from me.

[29]Remember them, O my God, because they defiled the priestly office and the covenant of the priesthood and of the Levites.

[30]So I purified the priests and the Levites of everything foreign, and assigned them duties, each to his own task. [31]I also made provision for contributions of wood at designated times, and for the firstfruits.

Remember me with favour, O my God.

Esther

Queen Vashti Deposed

1 This is what happened during the time of Xerxes,[a] the Xerxes who ruled over 127 provinces stretching from India to Cush:[b] ²At that time King Xerxes reigned from his royal throne in the citadel of Susa, ³and in the third year of his reign he gave a banquet for all his nobles and officials. The military leaders of Persia and Media, the princes, and the nobles of the provinces were present.

⁴For a full 180 days he displayed the vast wealth of his kingdom and the splendour and glory of his majesty. ⁵When these days were over, the king gave a banquet, lasting seven days, in the enclosed garden of the king's palace, for all the people from the least to the greatest, who were in the citadel of Susa. ⁶The garden had hangings of white and blue linen, fastened with cords of white linen and purple material to silver rings on marble pillars. There were couches of gold and silver on a mosaic pavement of porphyry, marble, mother-of-pearl and other costly stones. ⁷Wine was served in goblets of gold, each one different from the other, and the royal wine was abundant, in keeping with the king's liberality. ⁸By the king's command each guest was allowed to drink in his own way, for the king instructed all the wine stewards to serve each man what he wished.

⁹Queen Vashti also gave a banquet for the women in the royal palace of King Xerxes.

¹⁰On the seventh day, when King Xerxes was in high spirits from wine, he commanded the seven eunuchs who served him— Mehuman, Biztha, Harbona, Bigtha, Abagtha, Zethar and Carcas—¹¹to bring before him Queen Vashti, wearing her royal crown, in order to display her beauty to the people and nobles, for she was lovely to look at. ¹²But when the attendants delivered the king's command, Queen Vashti refused to come. Then the king became furious and burned with anger.

¹³Since it was customary for the king to consult experts in matters of law and justice, he spoke with the wise men who understood the times ¹⁴and were closest to the king— Carshena, Shethar, Admatha, Tarshish, Meres, Marsena and Memucan, the seven nobles of Persia and Media who had special access to the king and were highest in the kingdom.

¹⁵"According to law, what must be done to Queen Vashti?" he asked. "She has not obeyed the command of King Xerxes that the eunuchs have taken to her."

¹⁶Then Memucan replied in the presence of the king and the nobles, "Queen Vashti has done wrong, not only against the king but also against all the nobles and the peoples of all the provinces of King Xerxes. ¹⁷For the queen's conduct will become known to all the women, and so they will despise their husbands and say, 'King Xerxes commanded Queen Vashti to be brought before him, but she would not come.' ¹⁸This very day the Persian and Median women of the nobility who have heard about the queen's conduct will respond to all the king's nobles in the same way. There will be no end of disrespect and discord.

¹⁹"Therefore, if it pleases the king, let him issue a royal decree and let it be written in the laws of Persia and Media, which cannot be repealed, that Vashti is never again to enter the presence of King Xerxes. Also let the king give her royal position to someone else who is better than she. ²⁰Then when the king's edict is proclaimed throughout all his vast realm, all the women will respect their husbands, from the least to the greatest."

²¹The king and his nobles were pleased with this advice, so the king did as Memucan proposed. ²²He sent despatches to all parts of the kingdom, to each province in its own script and to each people in its own language, proclaiming in each people's tongue that every man should be ruler over his own household.

Esther Made Queen

2 Later when the anger of King Xerxes had subsided, he remembered Vashti and what she had done and what he had decreed about her. ²Then the king's personal attendants proposed, "Let a search be made for beautiful young virgins for the king. ³Let the king appoint commissioners in every province of his realm to bring all these beautiful girls into the harem at the citadel of Susa. Let them be placed under the care of Hegai,

---

[a]1 Hebrew Ahasuerus, a variant of Xerxes' Persian name; here and throughout Esther
[b]1 That is, the upper Nile region

the king's eunuch, who is in charge of the women; and let beauty treatments be given to them. [4]Then let the girl who pleases the king be queen instead of Vashti." This advice appealed to the king, and he followed it.

[5]Now there was in the citadel of Susa a Jew of the tribe of Benjamin, named Mordecai son of Jair, the son of Shimei, the son of Kish, [6]who had been carried into exile from Jerusalem by Nebuchadnezzar king of Babylon, among those taken captive with Jehoiachin[a] king of Judah. [7]Mordecai had a cousin named Hadassah, whom he had brought up because she had neither father nor mother. This girl, who was also known as Esther, was lovely in form and features, and Mordecai had taken her as his own daughter when her father and mother died.

[8]When the king's order and edict had been proclaimed, many girls were brought to the citadel of Susa and put under the care of Hegai. Esther also was taken to the king's palace and entrusted to Hegai, who had charge of the harem. [9]The girl pleased him and won his favour. Immediately he provided her with her beauty treatments and special food. He assigned to her seven maids selected from the king's palace and moved her and her maids into the best place in the harem.

[10]Esther had not revealed her nationality and family background, because Mordecai had forbidden her to do so. [11]Every day he walked to and fro near the courtyard of the harem to find out how Esther was and what was happening to her.

[12]Before a girl's turn came to go in to King Xerxes, she had to complete twelve months of beauty treatments prescribed for the women, six months with oil of myrrh and six with perfumes and cosmetics. [13]And this is how she would go to the king: Anything she wanted was given to her to take with her from the harem to the king's palace. [14]In the evening she would go there and in the morning return to another part of the harem to the care of Shaashgaz, the king's eunuch who was in charge of the concubines. She would not return to the king unless he was pleased with her and summoned her by name.

[15]When the turn came for Esther (the girl Mordecai had adopted, the daughter of his uncle Abihail) to go to the king, she asked for nothing other than what Hegai, the king's eunuch who was in charge of the harem, suggested. And Esther won the favour of everyone who saw her. [16]She was taken to King Xerxes in the royal residence in the tenth month, the month of Tebeth, in the seventh year of his reign.

[17]Now the king was attracted to Esther more than to any of the other women, and she won his favour and approval more than any of the other virgins. So he set a royal crown on her head and made her queen instead of Vashti. [18]And the king gave a great banquet, Esther's banquet, for all his nobles and officials. He proclaimed a holiday throughout the provinces and distributed gifts with royal liberality.

Mordecai Uncovers a Conspiracy

[19]When the virgins were assembled a second time, Mordecai was sitting at the king's gate. [20]But Esther had kept secret her family background and nationality just as Mordecai had told her to do, for she continued to follow Mordecai's instructions as she had done when he was bringing her up.

[21]During the time Mordecai was sitting at the king's gate, Bigthana[b] and Teresh, two of the king's officers who guarded the doorway, became angry and conspired to assassinate King Xerxes. [22]But Mordecai found out about the plot and told Queen Esther, who in turn reported it to the king, giving credit to Mordecai. [23]And when the report was investigated and found to be true, the two officials were hanged on a gallows.[c] All this was recorded in the book of the annals in the presence of the king.

Haman's Plot to Destroy the Jews

3 After these events, King Xerxes honoured Haman son of Hammedatha, the Agagite, elevating him and giving him a seat of honour higher than that of all the other nobles. [2]All the royal officials at the king's gate knelt down and paid honour to Haman, for the king had commanded this concerning him. But Mordecai would not kneel down or pay him honour.

[3]Then the royal officials at the king's gate asked Mordecai, "Why do you disobey the king's command?" [4]Day after day they spoke to him but he refused to comply. Therefore they told Haman about it to see whether Mordecai's behaviour would be tolerated, for he had told them he was a Jew.

[5]When Haman saw that Mordecai would not kneel down or pay him honour, he was enraged. [6]Yet having learned who Mordecai's people were, he scorned the idea of killing only Mordecai. Instead Haman looked for a way to destroy all Mordecai's people, the Jews, throughout the whole kingdom of Xerxes.

[7]In the twelfth year of King Xerxes, in the first month, the month of Nisan, they cast the *pur* (that is, the lot) in the presence of Haman to select a day and month. And the lot fell on[a] the twelfth month, the month of Adar.

[8]Then Haman said to King Xerxes, "There is a certain people dispersed and scattered among the peoples in all the provinces of your kingdom whose customs are different from those of all other people and who do not obey the king's laws; it is not in the king's best interest to tolerate them. [9]If it pleases the king, let a decree be issued to destroy them, and I will put ten thousand talents[b] of silver into the royal treasury for the men who carry out this business."

[10]So the king took his signet ring from his

---

[a]6 Hebrew *Jeconiah*, a variant of *Jehoiachin*   [b]21 Hebrew *Bigthan*, a variant of *Bigthana*
[c]23 Or *were hung* (or *impaled*) *on poles*; similarly elsewhere in Esther   [a]7 Septuagint; Hebrew does not have *And the lot fell on*.   [b]9 That is, about 340 tons (about 345 metric tons)

finger and gave it to Haman son of Hamme-datha, the Agagite, the enemy of the Jews. ¹¹"Keep the money," the king said to Ha-man, "and do with the people as you please."

¹²Then on the thirteenth day of the first month the royal secretaries were summoned. They wrote out in the script of each province and in the language of each people all Haman's orders to the king's satraps, the governors of the various provinces and the nobles of the various peoples. These were written in the name of King Xerxes himself and sealed with his own ring. ¹³Dispatches were sent by couriers to all the king's prov-inces with the order to destroy, kill and an-nihilate all the Jews—young and old, women and little children—on a single day, the thir-teenth day of the twelfth month, the month of Adar, and to plunder their goods. ¹⁴A copy of the text of the edict was to be issued as law in every province and made known to the peo-ple of every nationality so that they would be ready for that day.

¹⁵Spurred on by the king's command, the couriers went out, and the edict was issued in the citadel of Susa. The king and Haman sat down to drink, but the city of Susa was bewildered.

Mordecai Persuades Esther to Help

4 When Mordecai learned of all that had been done, he tore his clothes, put on sackcloth and ashes, and went out into the city, wailing loudly and bitterly. ²But he went only as far as the king's gate, because no-one clothed in sackcloth was allowed to enter it. ³In every province to which the edict and order of the king came, there was great mourning among the Jews, with fasting, weeping and wailing. Many lay in sackcloth and ashes.

⁴When Esther's maids and eunuchs came and told her about Mordecai, she was in great distress. She sent clothes for him to put on instead of his sackcloth, but he would not accept them. ⁵Then Esther summoned Hathach, one of the king's eunuchs assigned to attend her, and ordered him to find out what was troubling Mordecai and why.

⁶So Hathach went out to Mordecai in the open square of the city in front of the king's gate. ⁷Mordecai told him everything that had happened to him, including the exact amount of money Haman had promised to pay into the royal treasury for the destruction of the Jews. ⁸He also gave him a copy of the text of the edict for their annihilation, which had been published in Susa, to show to Esther and explain it to her, and he told him to urge her to go into the king's presence to beg for mercy and plead with him for her people.

⁹Hathach went back and reported to Esther what Mordecai had said. ¹⁰Then she instructed him to say to Mordecai, ¹¹"All the king's officials and the people of the royal provinces know that for any man or woman who approaches the king in the inner court without being summoned the king has but one law: that he be put to death. The only exception to this is for the king to extend the gold sceptre to him and spare his life. But thirty days have passed since I was called to go to the king."

¹²When Esther's words were reported to Mordecai, ¹³he sent back this answer: "Do not think that because you are in the king's house you alone of all the Jews will escape. ¹⁴For if you remain silent at this time, relief and deliverance for the Jews will arise from another place, but you and your father's family will perish. And who knows but that you have come to royal position for such a time as this?"

¹⁵Then Esther sent this reply to Mordecai: ¹⁶"Go, gather together all the Jews who are in Susa, and fast for me. Do not eat or drink for three days, night or day. I and my maids will fast as you do. When this is done, I will go to the king, even though it is against the law. And if I perish, I perish."

¹⁷So Mordecai went away and carried out all of Esther's instructions.

Esther's Request to the King

5 On the third day Esther put on her royal robes and stood in the inner court of the palace, in front of the king's hall. The king was sitting on his royal throne in the hall, facing the entrance. ²When he saw Queen Esther standing in the court, he was pleased with her and held out to her the gold sceptre that was in his hand. So Esther approached and touched the tip of the sceptre.

³Then the king asked, "What is it, Queen Esther? What is your request? Even up to half the kingdom, it will be given you."

⁴"If it pleases the king," replied Esther, "let the king, together with Haman, come today to a banquet I have prepared for him."

⁵"Bring Haman at once," the king said, "so that we may do what Esther asks."

So the king and Haman went to the ban-quet Esther had prepared. ⁶As they were drinking wine, the king again asked Esther, "Now what is your petition? It will be given you. And what is your request? Even up to half the kingdom, it will be granted."

⁷Esther replied, "My petition and my re-quest is this: ⁸If the king regards me with favour and if it pleases the king to grant my petition and fulfil my request, let the king and Haman come tomorrow to the banquet I will prepare for them. Then I will answer the king's question."

Haman's Rage Against Mordecai

⁹Haman went out that day happy and in high spirits. But when he saw Mordecai at the king's gate and observed that he neither rose nor showed fear in his presence, he was filled with rage against Mordecai. ¹⁰Nevertheless, Haman restrained himself and went home. Calling together his friends and Zeresh, his wife, ¹¹Haman boasted to them about his vast wealth, his many sons, and all the ways the king had honoured him and how he had el-evated him above the other nobles and of-ficials. ¹²"And that's not all," Haman added. "I'm the only person Queen Esther invited to accompany the king to the banquet she gave. And she has invited me along with the king

tomorrow. [13]But all this gives me no satisfaction as long as I see that Jew Mordecai sitting at the king's gate."

[14]His wife Zeresh and all his friends said to him, "Have a gallows built, seventy-five feet[a] high, and ask the king in the morning to have Mordecai hanged on it. Then go with the king to the dinner and be happy." This suggestion delighted Haman, and he had the gallows built.

Mordecai Honoured

6 That night the king could not sleep; so he ordered the book of the chronicles, the record of his reign, to be brought in and read to him. [2]It was found recorded there that Mordecai had exposed Bigthana and Teresh, two of the king's officers who guarded the doorway, who had conspired to assassinate King Xerxes.

[3]"What honour and recognition has Mordecai received for this?" the king asked.

"Nothing has been done for him," his attendants answered.

[4]The king said, "Who is in the court?" Now Haman had just entered the outer court of the palace to speak to the king about hanging Mordecai on the gallows he had erected for him.

[5]His attendants answered, "Haman is standing in the court."

"Bring him in," the king ordered.

[6]When Haman entered, the king asked him, "What should be done for the man the king delights to honour?"

Now Haman thought to himself, "Who is there that the king would rather honour than me?" [7]So he answered the king, "For the man the king delights to honour, [8]have them bring a royal robe the king has worn and a horse the king has ridden, one with a royal crest placed on its head. [9]Then let the robe and horse be entrusted to one of the king's most noble princes. Let them robe the man the king delights to honour, and lead him on the horse through the city streets, proclaiming before him, 'This is what is done for the man the king delights to honour!'"

[10]"Go at once," the king commanded Haman. "Get the robe and the horse and do just as you have suggested for Mordecai the Jew, who sits at the king's gate. Do not neglect anything you have recommended."

[11]So Haman got the robe and the horse. He robed Mordecai, and led him on horseback through the city streets, proclaiming before him, "This is what is done for the man the king delights to honour!"

[12]Afterwards Mordecai returned to the king's gate. But Haman rushed home, with his head covered, in grief, [13]and told Zeresh his wife and all his friends everything that had happened to him.

His advisers and his wife Zeresh said to him, "Since Mordecai, before whom your downfall has started, is of Jewish origin, you cannot stand against him—you will surely come to ruin!" [14]While they were still talking with him, the king's eunuchs arrived and hurried Haman away to the banquet Esther had prepared.

Haman Hanged

7 So the king and Haman went to dine with Queen Esther, [2]and as they were drinking wine on that second day, the king again asked, "Queen Esther, what is your petition? It will be given you. What is your request? Even up to half the kingdom, it will be granted."

[3]Then Queen Esther answered, "If I have found favour with you, O king, and if it pleases your majesty, grant me my life—this is my petition. And spare my people—this is my request. [4]For I and my people have been sold for destruction and slaughter and annihilation. If we had merely been sold as male and female slaves, I would have kept quiet, because no such distress would justify disturbing the king."[a]

[5]King Xerxes asked Queen Esther, "Who is he? Where is the man who has dared to do such a thing?"

[6]Esther said, "The adversary and enemy is this vile Haman."

Then Haman was terrified before the king and queen. [7]The king got up in a rage, left his wine and went out into the palace garden. But Haman, realising that the king had already decided his fate, stayed behind to beg Queen Esther for his life.

[8]Just as the king returned from the palace garden to the banquet hall, Haman was falling on the couch where Esther was reclining.

The king exclaimed, "Will he even molest the queen while she is with me in the house?"

As soon as the word left the king's mouth, they covered Haman's face. [9]Then Harbona, one of the eunuchs attending the king, said, "A gallows seventy-five feet[b] high stands by Haman's house. He had it made for Mordecai, who spoke up to help the king."

The king said, "Hang him on it!" [10]So they hanged Haman on the gallows he had prepared for Mordecai. Then the king's fury subsided.

The King's Edict on Behalf of the Jews

8 That same day King Xerxes gave Queen Esther the estate of Haman, the enemy of the Jews. And Mordecai came into the presence of the king, for Esther had told how he was related to her. [2]The king took off his signet ring, which he had reclaimed from Haman, and presented it to Mordecai. And Esther appointed him over Haman's estate.

[3]Esther again pleaded with the king, falling at his feet and weeping. She begged him to put an end to the evil plan of Haman the Agagite, which he had devised against the Jews. [4]Then the king extended the gold sceptre to Esther and she arose and stood before him.

[5]"If it pleases the king," she said, "and if

---

[a]14 Hebrew *fifty cubits* (about 23 metres)
[a]4 Or *quiet, but the compensation our adversary offers cannot be compared with the loss the king would suffer*
[b]9 Hebrew *fifty cubits* (about 23 metres)

he regards me with favour and thinks it the right thing to do, and if he is pleased with me, let an order be written overruling the dispatches that Haman son of Hammedatha, the Agagite, devised and wrote to destroy the Jews in all the king's provinces. 6For how can I bear to see disaster fall on my people? How can I bear to see the destruction of my family?"

7King Xerxes replied to Queen Esther and to Mordecai the Jew, "Because Haman attacked the Jews, I have given his estate to Esther, and they have hanged him on the gallows. 8Now write another decree in the king's name on behalf of the Jews as seems best to you, and seal it with the king's signet ring—for no document written in the king's name and sealed with his ring can be revoked."

9At once the royal secretaries were summoned—on the twenty-third day of the third month, the month of Sivan. They wrote out all Mordecai's orders to the Jews, and to the satraps, governors and nobles of the 127 provinces stretching from India to Cush.[a] These orders were written in the script of each province and the language of each people and also to the Jews in their own script and language. 10Mordecai wrote in the name of King Xerxes, sealed the dispatches with the king's signet ring, and sent them by mounted couriers, who rode fast horses especially bred for the king.

11The king's edict granted the Jews in every city the right to assemble and protect themselves; to destroy, kill and annihilate any armed force of any nationality or province that might attack them and their women and children; and to plunder the property of their enemies. 12The day appointed for the Jews to do this in all the provinces of King Xerxes was the thirteenth day of the twelfth month, the month of Adar. 13A copy of the text of the edict was to be issued as law in every province and made known to the people of every nationality so that the Jews would be ready on that day to avenge themselves on their enemies.

14The couriers, riding the royal horses, raced out, spurred on by the king's command. And the edict was also issued in the citadel of Susa.

15Mordecai left the king's presence wearing royal garments of blue and white, a large crown of gold and a purple robe of fine linen. And the city of Susa held a joyous celebration. 16For the Jews it was a time of happiness and joy, gladness and honour. 17In every province and in every city, wherever the edict of the king went, there was joy and gladness among the Jews, with feasting and celebrating. And many people of other nationalities became Jews because fear of the Jews had seized them.

Triumph of the Jews

9 On the thirteenth day of the twelfth month, the month of Adar, the edict commanded by the king was to be carried out. On this day the enemies of the Jews had hoped to overpower them, but now the tables were turned and the Jews got the upper hand over those who hated them. 2The Jews assembled in their cities in all the provinces of King Xerxes to attack those seeking their destruction. No-one could stand against them, because the people of all the other nationalities were afraid of them. 3And all the nobles of the provinces, the satraps, the governors and the king's administrators helped the Jews, because fear of Mordecai had seized them. 4Mordecai was prominent in the palace; his reputation spread throughout the provinces, and he became more and more powerful.

5The Jews struck down all their enemies with the sword, killing and destroying them, and they did what they pleased to those who hated them. 6In the citadel of Susa, the Jews killed and destroyed five hundred men. 7They also killed Parshandatha, Dalphon, Aspatha, 8Poratha, Adalia, Aridatha, 9Parmashta, Arisai, Aridai and Vaizatha, 10the ten sons of Haman son of Hammedatha, the enemy of the Jews. But they did not lay their hands on the plunder.

11The number of those slain in the citadel of Susa was reported to the king that same day. 12The king said to Queen Esther, "The Jews have killed and destroyed five hundred men and the ten sons of Haman in the citadel of Susa. What have they done in the rest of the king's provinces? Now what is your petition? It will be given you. What is your request? It will also be granted."

13"If it pleases the king," Esther answered, "give the Jews in Susa permission to carry out this day's edict tomorrow also, and let Haman's ten sons be hanged on gallows."

14So the king commanded that this be done. An edict was issued in Susa, and they hanged the ten sons of Haman. 15The Jews in Susa came together on the fourteenth day of the month of Adar, and they put to death in Susa three hundred men, but they did not lay their hands on the plunder.

16Meanwhile, the remainder of the Jews who were in the king's provinces also assembled to protect themselves and get relief from their enemies. They killed seventy-five thousand of them but did not lay their hands on the plunder. 17This happened on the thirteenth day of the month of Adar, and on the fourteenth they rested and made it a day of feasting and joy.

Purim Celebrated

18The Jews in Susa, however, had assembled on the thirteenth and fourteenth, and then on the fifteenth they rested and made it a day of feasting and joy.

19That is why rural Jews—those living in villages—observe the fourteenth of the month of Adar as a day of joy and feasting, a day for giving presents to each other.

20Mordecai recorded these events, and he sent letters to all the Jews throughout the

---

[a]9 That is, the upper Nile region

provinces of King Xerxes, near and far, [21]to have them celebrate annually the fourteenth and fifteenth days of the month of Adar [22]as the time when the Jews got relief from their enemies, and as the month when their sorrow was turned into joy and their mourning into a day of celebration. He wrote to them to observe the days as days of feasting and joy and giving presents of food to one another and gifts to the poor.

[23]So the Jews agreed to continue the celebration they had begun, doing what Mordecai had written to them. [24]For Haman son of Hammedatha, the Agagite, the enemy of all the Jews, had plotted against the Jews to destroy them and had cast the *pur* (that is, the lot) for their ruin and destruction. [25]But when the plot came to the king's attention,[a] he issued written orders that the evil scheme Haman had devised against the Jews should come back on to his own head, and that he and his sons should be hanged on the gallows. [26](Therefore these days were called Purim, from the word *pur*.) Because of everything written in this letter and because of what they had seen and what had happened to them, [27]the Jews took it upon themselves to establish the custom that they and their descendants and all who join them should without fail observe these two days every year, in the way prescribed and at the time appointed. [28]These days should be remembered and observed in every generation by every family, and in every province and in every city. And these days of Purim should never cease to be celebrated by the Jews, nor should the memory of them die out among their descendants.

[29]So Queen Esther, daughter of Abihail, along with Mordecai the Jew, wrote with full authority to confirm this second letter concerning Purim. [30]And Mordecai sent letters to all the Jews in the 127 provinces of the kingdom of Xerxes—words of goodwill and assurance—[31]to establish these days of Purim at their designated times, as Mordecai the Jew and Queen Esther had decreed for them, and as they had established for themselves and their descendants in regard to their times of fasting and lamentation. [32]Esther's decree confirmed these regulations about Purim, and it was written down in the records.

The Greatness of Mordecai

10 King Xerxes imposed tribute throughout the empire, to its distant shores. [2]And all his acts of power and might, together with a full account of the greatness of Mordecai to which the king had raised him, are they not written in the book of the annals of the kings of Media and Persia? [3]Mordecai the Jew was second in rank to King Xerxes, pre-eminent among the Jews, and held in high esteem by his many fellow Jews, because he worked for the good of his people and spoke up for the welfare of all the Jews.

[a]25 Or *when Esther came before the king*

Job

Prologue

1 In the land of Uz there lived a man whose name was Job. This man was blameless and upright; he feared God and shunned evil. ²He had seven sons and three daughters, ³and he owned seven thousand sheep, three thousand camels, five hundred yoke of oxen and five hundred donkeys, and had a large number of servants. He was the greatest man among all the people of the East.

⁴His sons used to take turns holding feasts in their homes, and they would invite their three sisters to eat and drink with them. ⁵When a period of feasting had run its course, Job would send and have them purified. Early in the morning he would sacrifice a burnt offering for each of them, thinking, "Perhaps my children have sinned and cursed God in their hearts." This was Job's regular custom.

Job's First Test

⁶One day the angels*a* came to present themselves before the LORD, and Satan*b* also came with them. ⁷The LORD said to Satan, "Where have you come from?"

Satan answered the LORD, "From roaming through the earth and going to and fro in it."

⁸Then the LORD said to Satan, "Have you considered my servant Job? There is no-one on earth like him; he is blameless and upright, a man who fears God and shuns evil."

⁹"Does Job fear God for nothing?" Satan replied. ¹⁰"Have you not put a hedge around him and his household and everything he has? You have blessed the work of his hands, so that his flocks and herds are spread throughout the land. ¹¹But stretch out your hand and strike everything he has, and he will surely curse you to your face."

¹²The LORD said to Satan, "Very well, then, everything he has is in your hands, but on the man himself do not lay a finger."

Then Satan went out from the presence of the LORD.

¹³One day when Job's sons and daughters were feasting and drinking wine at the oldest brother's house, ¹⁴a messenger came to Job and said, "The oxen were ploughing and the donkeys were grazing nearby, ¹⁵and the Sabeans attacked and carried them off. They put the servants to the sword, and I am the only one who has escaped to tell you!"

¹⁶While he was still speaking, another messenger came and said, "The fire of God fell from the sky and burned up the sheep and the servants, and I am the only one who has escaped to tell you!"

¹⁷While he was still speaking, another messenger came and said, "The Chaldeans formed three raiding parties and swept down on your camels and carried them off. They put the servants to the sword, and I am the only one who has escaped to tell you!"

¹⁸While he was still speaking, yet another messenger came and said, "Your sons and daughters were feasting and drinking wine at the oldest brother's house, ¹⁹when suddenly a mighty wind swept in from the desert and struck the four corners of the house. It collapsed on them and they are dead, and I am the only one who has escaped to tell you!"

²⁰At this, Job got up and tore his robe and shaved his head. Then he fell to the ground in worship ²¹and said:

"Naked I came from my mother's womb,
    and naked I shall depart.*c*
The LORD gave and the LORD has taken
    away;
    may the name of the LORD be praised."

²²In all this, Job did not sin by charging God with wrongdoing.

Job's Second Test

2 On another day the angels*a* came to present themselves before the LORD, and Satan also came with them to present himself before him. ²And the LORD said to Satan, "Where have you come from?"

Satan answered the LORD, "From roaming through the earth and going to and fro in it."

³Then the LORD said to Satan, "Have you considered my servant Job? There is no-one on earth like him; he is blameless and upright, a man who fears God and shuns evil. And he still maintains his integrity, though you incited me against him to ruin him without any reason."

---

a6 Hebrew *the sons of God*   *b6* Satan means *accuser.*
a1 Hebrew *the sons of God*   *c21* Or *shall return there*

JOB 1:1–7

'This man was blameless and upright; he feared God and shunned evil . . . he would sacrifice a burnt offering for each of them, thinking, "Perhaps my children have sinned and cursed God in their hearts" ' (vv. 1b, 5b).

PURE WITHOUT, WITHIN. The point of Job's experience is that it happened to a blameless man. It does not matter where Job lived, or whether Uz was a real place. It does not matter when the events occurred, whether before, after or in the middle of Hebrew history. The only thing that really matters is the goodness of Job.

Job's goodness was not just a matter of outward show, as verse 5 makes clear. He realized how easy it was to appear righteous. Even his own sons and daughters might curse God in their hearts, so he makes sacrifices on their behalf.

The translation 'curse' is interesting, for the word standing in the Hebrew text is 'bless'. Two points can be made about this. First, some scholars believe that 'bless' is there in order to avoid putting the word 'curse' next to the name of God. It is a matter of reverence and Jewish religious custom. But second we should notice that the dividing line between blessing and cursing is a very narrow one indeed. Most curses are simply irreverent or blasphemous uses of words of blessing – taking the name of God in vain.

We must therefore be doubly careful. Outward appearance is no guide to inward purity. Words of blessing insincerely uttered are no better, indeed are worse than curses.

Let us be like Job, pure and upright, with real concern for others.

→428

'Job . . . sat among the ashes . . . Then they sat on the ground with him for seven days and seven nights. No-one said a word to him, because they saw how great his suffering was' (vv. 8, 13).

MUCH MALIGNED. Who has a good word to say about Job's comforters? 'Job's comforter' is nearly a term of abuse, but in the prologue, before they speak, we can see why they were truly described as Job's three friends (2:11).

Look at where they went for him. He was sitting among the ashes. That means on a dunghill, among the excrement, both human and animal, surrounded by rubbish of all kinds. It was the only place for someone afflicted like Job. No ordinary person would come near him, covered as he was with sores, unclean in every sense of the word. They would throw him a few scraps before putting their own rubbish on the heap, and hope that could be set down as their good deed for the day. But Job's friends went right to the rubbish tip. Even from the distance (v. 12) what they saw caused them to weep, but they did not remain in the distance weeping, they came right up to him.

Look at what they did for him. They sat in silence for seven whole days. Jurgen Moltmann's words bear repeating. 'Anyone who responds to pain merely with activity, to suffering simply with offers of help, and to grief with attempts at distraction . . . merely increases the loneliness of the victim.'

For seven days and seven nights – imagine it! – Job's friends responded in exactly the right way. They were there, with him, suffering, their silence more eloquent than speech.

Thank you for those sensitive souls who seem, naturally, to know what other people need. Help us each one to cultivate powers of listening to, caring for, and accepting people as they are. Thank you for the example of Jesus who used these powers to the full and gave us such a wonderful pattern to follow.

→439

4"'Skin for skin!'' Satan replied. ''A man will give all he has for his own life. 5But stretch out your hand and strike his flesh and bones, and he will surely curse you to your face.''

6The LORD said to Satan, ''Very well, then, he is in your hands; but you must spare his life.''

7So Satan went out from the presence of the LORD and afflicted Job with painful sores from the soles of his feet to the top of his head. 8Then Job took a piece of broken pottery and scraped himself with it as he sat among the ashes.

9His wife said to him, ''Are you still holding on to your integrity? Curse God and die!''

10He replied, ''You are talking like a foolish*b* woman. Shall we accept good from God, and not trouble?''

In all this, Job did not sin in what he said.

Job's Three Friends

11When Job's three friends, Eliphaz the Temanite, Bildad the Shuhite and Zophar the Naamathite, heard about all the troubles that had come upon him, they set out from their homes and met together by agreement to go and sympathise with him and comfort him. 12When they saw him from a distance, they could hardly recognise him; they began to weep aloud, and they tore their robes and sprinkled dust on their heads. 13Then they sat on the ground with him for seven days and seven nights. No-one said a word to him, because they saw how great his suffering was.

Job Speaks

3 After this, Job opened his mouth and cursed the day of his birth. 2He said:

3''May the day of my birth perish,
    and the night it was said, 'A boy is
        born!'
4That day—may it turn to darkness;
    may God above not care about it;
    may no light shine upon it.
5May darkness and deep shadow*a* claim it
        once more;
    may a cloud settle over it;
    may blackness overwhelm its light.
6That night—may thick darkness seize it;
    may it not be included among the days
        of the year
    nor be entered in any of the months.
7May that night be barren;
    may no shout of joy be heard in it.
8May those who curse days*b* curse that day,
    those who are ready to rouse Leviathan.
9May its morning stars become dark;
    may it wait for daylight in vain
    and not see the first rays of dawn,
10for it did not shut the doors of the womb
        on me
    to hide trouble from my eyes.

11''Why did I not perish at birth,
    and die as I came from the womb?

12Why were there knees to receive me
    and breasts that I might be nursed?
13For now I would be lying down in peace;
    I would be asleep and at rest
14with kings and counsellors of the earth,
    who built for themselves places now
        lying in ruins,
15with rulers who had gold,
    who filled their houses with silver.
16Or why was I not hidden in the ground like
        a stillborn child,
    like an infant who never saw the light of
        day?
17There the wicked cease from turmoil,
    and there the weary are at rest.
18Captives also enjoy their ease;
    they no longer hear the slave driver's
        shout.
19The small and the great are there,
    and the slave is freed from his master.

20''Why is light given to those in misery,
    and life to the bitter of soul,
21to those who long for death that does not
        come,
    who search for it more than for hidden
        treasure,
22who are filled with gladness
    and rejoice when they reach the grave?
23Why is life given to a man
    whose way is hidden,
    whom God has hedged in?
24For sighing comes to me instead of food;
    my groans pour out like water.
25What I feared has come upon me;
    what I dreaded has happened to me.
26I have no peace, no quietness;
    I have no rest, but only turmoil.''

Eliphaz

4 Then Eliphaz the Temanite replied:

2''If someone ventures a word with you,
        will you be impatient?
    But who can keep from speaking?
3Think how you have instructed many,
    how you have strengthened feeble
        hands.
4Your words have supported those who
        stumbled;
    you have strengthened faltering knees.
5But now trouble comes to you, and you
        are discouraged;
    it strikes you, and you are dismayed.
6Should not your piety be your confidence
    and your blameless ways your hope?

7''Consider now: Who, being innocent, has
        ever perished?
    Where were the upright ever destroyed?
8As I have observed, those who plough evil
    and those who sow trouble reap it.
9At the breath of God they are destroyed;
    at the blast of his anger they perish.
10The lions may roar and growl,
    yet the teeth of the great lions are
        broken.

---

*b*10 The Hebrew word rendered *foolish* denotes moral deficiency.   *a*5 Or *and the shadow of death*
*b*8 Or *the sea*

11The lion perishes for lack of prey,
and the cubs of the lioness are scattered.

12"A word was secretly brought to me,
my ears caught a whisper of it.
13Amid disquieting dreams in the night,
when deep sleep falls on men,
14fear and trembling seized me
and made all my bones shake.
15A spirit glided past my face,
and the hair on my body stood on end.
16It stopped,
but I could not tell what it was.
A form stood before my eyes,
and I heard a hushed voice:
17'Can a mortal be more righteous than
God?
Can a man be more pure than his
Maker?
18If God places no trust in his servants,
if he charges his angels with error,
19how much more those who live in houses
of clay,
whose foundations are in the dust,
who are crushed more readily than a
moth!
20Between dawn and dusk they are broken
to pieces;
unnoticed, they perish for ever.
21Are not the cords of their tent pulled up,
so that they die without wisdom?'*a*

5 "Call if you will, but who will answer
you?
To which of the holy ones will you turn?
2Resentment kills a fool,
and envy slays the simple.
3I myself have seen a fool taking root,
but suddenly his house was cursed.
4His children are far from safety,
crushed in court without a defender.
5The hungry consume his harvest,
taking it even from among thorns,
and the thirsty pant after his wealth.
6For hardship does not spring from the soil,
nor does trouble sprout from the
ground.
7Yet man is born to trouble
as surely as sparks fly upward.

8"But if it were I, I would appeal to God;
I would lay my cause before him.
9He performs wonders that cannot be
fathomed,
miracles that cannot be counted.
10He bestows rain on the earth;
he sends water upon the countryside.
11The lowly he sets on high,
and those who mourn are lifted to
safety.
12He thwarts the plans of the crafty,
so that their hands achieve no success.
13He catches the wise in their craftiness,
and the schemes of the wily are swept
away.
14Darkness comes upon them in the
daytime;
at noon they grope as in the night.

15He saves the needy from the sword in their
mouth;
he saves them from the clutches of the
powerful.
16So the poor have hope,
and injustice shuts its mouth.

17"Blessed is the man whom God corrects;
so do not despise the discipline of the
Almighty.*a*
18For he wounds, but he also binds up;
he injures, but his hands also heal.
19From six calamities he will rescue you;
in seven no harm will befall you.
20In famine he will ransom you from death,
and in battle from the stroke of the
sword.
21You will be protected from the lash of the
tongue,
and need not fear when destruction
comes.
22You will laugh at destruction and famine,
and need not fear the beasts of the earth.
23For you will have a covenant with the
stones of the field,
and the wild animals will be at peace
with you.
24You will know that your tent is secure;
you will take stock of your property and
find nothing missing.
25You will know that your children will be
many,
and your descendants like the grass of
the earth.
26You will come to the grave in full vigour,
like sheaves gathered in season.

27"We have examined this, and it is true.
So hear it and apply it to yourself."

Job

6 Then Job replied:

2"If only my anguish could be weighed
and all my misery be placed on the
scales!
3It would surely outweigh the sand of the
seas—
no wonder my words have been
impetuous.
4The arrows of the Almighty are in me,
my spirit drinks in their poison;
God's terrors are marshalled against
me.
5Does a wild donkey bray when it has
grass,
or an ox bellow when it has fodder?
6Is tasteless food eaten without salt,
or is there flavour in the white of an
egg?*a*
7I refuse to touch it;
such food makes me ill.

8"Oh, that I might have my request,
that God would grant what I hope for,
9that God would be willing to crush me,
to let loose his hand and cut me off!
10Then I would still have this consolation—
my joy in unrelenting pain—

---

a21 Some interpreters end the quotation after verse 17.
a6 The meaning of the Hebrew for this phrase is uncertain.

a17 Hebrew *Shaddai*; here and throughout Job

that I had not denied the words of the Holy One.

11"What strength do I have, that I should still hope?
What prospects, that I should be patient?
12Do I have the strength of stone?
Is my flesh bronze?
13Do I have any power to help myself, now that success has been driven from me?

14"A despairing man should have the devotion of his friends,
even though he forsakes the fear of the Almighty.
15But my brothers are as undependable as intermittent streams,
as the streams that overflow
16when darkened by thawing ice and swollen with melting snow,
17but that cease to flow in the dry season, and in the heat vanish from their channels.
18Caravans turn aside from their routes; they go up into the wasteland and perish.
19The caravans of Tema look for water, the travelling merchants of Sheba look in hope.
20They are distressed, because they had been confident;
they arrive there, only to be disappointed.
21Now you too have proved to be of no help;
you see something dreadful and are afraid.
22Have I ever said, 'Give something on my behalf,
pay a ransom for me from your wealth,
23deliver me from the hand of the enemy, ransom me from the clutches of the ruthless'?

24"Teach me, and I will be quiet; show me where I have been wrong.
25How painful are honest words!
But what do your arguments prove?
26Do you mean to correct what I say, and treat the words of a despairing man as wind?
27You would even cast lots for the fatherless and barter away your friend.

28"But now be so kind as to look at me. Would I lie to your face?
29Relent, do not be unjust; reconsider, for my integrity is at stake.*b*
30Is there any wickedness on my lips? Can my mouth not discern malice?

7 "Does not man have hard service on earth?
Are not his days like those of a hired man?
2Like a slave longing for the evening shadows,

or a hired man waiting eagerly for his wages,
3so I have been allotted months of futility, and nights of misery have been assigned to me.
4When I lie down I think, 'How long before I get up?'
The night drags on, and I toss till dawn.
5My body is clothed with worms and scabs, my skin is broken and festering.

6"My days are swifter than a weaver's shuttle,
and they come to an end without hope.
7Remember, O God, that my life is but a breath;
my eyes will never see happiness again.
8The eye that now sees me will see me no longer;
you will look for me, but I will be no more.
9As a cloud vanishes and is gone, so he who goes down to the grave*a* does not return.
10He will never come to his house again; his place will know him no more.

11"Therefore I will not keep silent; I will speak out in the anguish of my spirit,
I will complain in the bitterness of my soul.
12Am I the sea, or the monster of the deep, that you put me under guard?
13When I think my bed will comfort me and my couch will ease my complaint,
14even then you frighten me with dreams and terrify me with visions,
15so that I prefer strangling and death, rather than this body of mine.
16I despise my life; I would not live for ever.
Let me alone; my days have no meaning.

17"What is man that you make so much of him,
that you give him so much attention?
18that you examine him every morning and test him every moment?
19Will you never look away from me, or let me alone even for an instant?
20If I have sinned, what have I done to you, O watcher of men?
Why have you made me your target?
Have I become a burden to you?*b*
21Why do you not pardon my offences and forgive my sins?
For I shall soon lie down in the dust; you will search for me, but I shall be no more."

Bildad

8 Then Bildad the Shuhite replied:

2"How long will you say such things?
Your words are a blustering wind.
3Does God pervert justice?

---

b29 Or my righteousness still stands   a9 Hebrew Sheol
b20 A few manuscripts of the Masoretic Text, an ancient Hebrew scribal tradition and Septuagint; most manuscripts of the Masoretic Text I have become a burden to myself.

Does the Almighty pervert what is
     right?
⁴When your children sinned against him,
     he gave them over to the penalty of their
       sin.
⁵But if you will look to God
     and plead with the Almighty,
⁶if you are pure and upright,
     even now he will rouse himself on your
       behalf
     and restore you to your rightful place.
⁷Your beginnings will seem humble,
     so prosperous will your future be.

⁸"Ask the former generations
     and find out what their fathers learned,
⁹for we were born only yesterday and know
       nothing,
     and our days on earth are but a shadow.
¹⁰Will they not instruct you and tell you?
     Will they not bring forth words from
       their understanding?
¹¹Can papyrus grow tall where there is no
       marsh?
     Can reeds thrive without water?
¹²While still growing and uncut,
     they wither more quickly than grass.
¹³Such is the destiny of all who forget God;
     so perishes the hope of the godless.
¹⁴What he trusts in is fragile;ᵃ
     what he relies on is a spider's web.
¹⁵He leans on his web, but it gives way;
     he clings to it, but it does not hold.
¹⁶He is like a well-watered plant in the
       sunshine,
     spreading its shoots over the garden;
¹⁷it entwines its roots around a pile of rocks
     and looks for a place among the stones.
¹⁸But when it is torn from its spot,
     that place disowns it and says, 'I never
       saw you.'
¹⁹Surely its life withers away,
     andᵇ from the soil other plants grow.

²⁰"Surely God does not reject a blameless
       man
     or strengthen the hands of evildoers.
²¹He will yet fill your mouth with laughter
     and your lips with shouts of joy.
²²Your enemies will be clothed in shame,
     and the tents of the wicked will be no
       more."

Job

9 Then Job replied:

²"Indeed, I know that this is true.
     But how can a mortal be righteous
       before God?
³Though one wished to dispute with him,
     he could not answer him one time out of
       a thousand.
⁴His wisdom is profound, his power is vast.
     Who has resisted him and come out
       unscathed?
⁵He moves mountains without their
       knowing
     and overturns them in his anger.

⁶He shakes the earth from its place
     and makes its pillars tremble.
⁷He speaks to the sun and it does not shine;
     he seals off the light of the stars.
⁸He alone stretches out the heavens
     and treads on the waves of the sea.
⁹He is the Maker of the Bear and Orion,
     the Pleiades and the constellations of
       the south.
¹⁰He performs wonders that cannot be
       fathomed,
     miracles that cannot be counted.
¹¹When he passes me, I cannot see him;
     when he goes by, I cannot perceive him.
¹²If he snatches away, who can stop him?
     Who can say to him, 'What are you
       doing?'
¹³God does not restrain his anger;
     even the cohorts of Rahab cowered at
       his feet.

¹⁴"How then can I dispute with him?
     How can I find words to argue with him?
¹⁵Though I were innocent, I could not
       answer him;
     I could only plead with my Judge for
       mercy.
¹⁶Even if I summoned him and he
       responded,
     I do not believe he would give me a
       hearing.
¹⁷He would crush me with a storm
     and multiply my wounds for no reason.
¹⁸He would not let me regain my breath
     but would overwhelm me with misery.
¹⁹If it is a matter of strength, he is mighty!
     And if it is a matter of justice, who will
       summon him?ᵃ
²⁰Even if I were innocent, my mouth would
       condemn me;
     if I were blameless, it would pronounce
       me guilty.

²¹"Although I am blameless,
     I have no concern for myself;
     I despise my own life.
²²It is all the same; that is why I say,
     'He destroys both the blameless and the
       wicked.'
²³When a scourge brings sudden death,
     he mocks the despair of the innocent.
²⁴When a land falls into the hands of the
       wicked,
     he blindfolds its judges.
     If it is not he, then who is it?

²⁵"My days are swifter than a runner;
     they fly away without a glimpse of joy.
²⁶They skim past like boats of papyrus,
     like eagles swooping down on their
       prey.
²⁷If I say, 'I will forget my complaint,
     I will change my expression, and smile,'
²⁸I still dread all my sufferings,
     for I know you will not hold me
       innocent.
²⁹Since I am already found guilty,
     why should I struggle in vain?

ᵃ14 The meaning of the Hebrew for this word is uncertain.
ᵃ19 See Septuagint; Hebrew *me*.

ᵇ19 Or *Surely all the joy it has / is that*

³⁰Even if I washed myself with soap[b]
  and my hands with washing soda,
³¹you would plunge me into a slime pit
  so that even my clothes would detest
  me.

³²"He is not a man like me that I might
  answer him,
  that we might confront each other in
  court.
³³If only there were someone to arbitrate
  between us,
  to lay his hand upon us both,
³⁴someone to remove God's rod from me,
  so that his terror would frighten me no
  more.
³⁵Then I would speak up without fear of
  him,
  but as it now stands with me, I cannot.

10 "I loathe my very life;
  therefore I will give free rein to my
  complaint
  and speak out in the bitterness of my
  soul.
²I will say to God: Do not condemn me,
  but tell me what charges you have
  against me.
³Does it please you to oppress me,
  to spurn the work of your hands,
  while you smile on the schemes of the
  wicked?
⁴Do you have eyes of flesh?
  Do you see as a mortal sees?
⁵Are your days like those of a mortal
  or your years like those of a man,
⁶that you must search out my faults
  and probe after my sin—
⁷though you know that I am not guilty
  and that no-one can rescue me from
  your hand?

⁸"Your hands shaped me and made me.
  Will you now turn and destroy me?
⁹Remember that you moulded me like clay.
  Will you now turn me to dust again?
¹⁰Did you not pour me out like milk
  and curdle me like cheese,
¹¹clothe me with skin and flesh
  and knit me together with bones and
  sinews?
¹²You gave me life and showed me kindness,
  and in your providence watched over
  my spirit.

¹³"But this is what you concealed in your
  heart,
  and I know that this was in your mind:
¹⁴If I sinned, you would be watching me
  and would not let my offence go
  unpunished.
¹⁵If I am guilty—woe to me!
  Even if I am innocent, I cannot lift my
  head,
  for I am full of shame
  and drowned in[a] my affliction.
¹⁶If I hold my head high, you stalk me like a
  lion

and again display your awesome power
  against me.
¹⁷You bring new witnesses against me
  and increase your anger towards me;
  your forces come against me wave upon
  wave.

¹⁸"Why then did you bring me out of the
  womb?
  I wish I had died before any eye saw me.
¹⁹If only I had never come into being,
  or had been carried straight from the
  womb to the grave!
²⁰Are not my few days almost over?
  Turn away from me so that I can have a
  moment's joy
²¹before I go to the place of no return,
  to the land of gloom and deep shadow,[b]
²²to the land of deepest night,
  of deep shadow and disorder,
  where even the light is like darkness."

Zophar

11 Then Zophar the Naamathite replied:

²"Are all these words to go unanswered?
  Is this talker to be vindicated?
³Will your idle talk reduce men to silence?
  Will no-one rebuke you when you
  mock?
⁴You say to God, 'My beliefs are flawless
  and I am pure in your sight.'
⁵Oh, how I wish that God would speak,
  that he would open his lips against you
⁶and disclose to you the secrets of wisdom,
  for true wisdom has two sides.
  Know this: God has even forgotten
  some of your sin.

⁷"Can you fathom the mysteries of God?
  Can you probe the limits of the
  Almighty?
⁸They are higher than the heavens—what
  can you do?
  They are deeper than the depths of the
  grave[a]—what can you know?
⁹Their measure is longer than the earth
  and wider than the sea.

¹⁰"If he comes along and confines you in
  prison
  and convenes a court, who can oppose
  him?
¹¹Surely he recognises deceitful men;
  and when he sees evil, does he not take
  note?
¹²But a witless man can no more become
  wise
  than a wild donkey's colt can be born a
  man.[b]

¹³"Yet if you devote your heart to him
  and stretch out your hands to him,
¹⁴if you put away the sin that is in your hand
  and allow no evil to dwell in your tent,
¹⁵then you will lift up your face without
  shame;
  you will stand firm and without fear.

b30 Or *snow*   a15 Or *and aware of*   b21 Or *and the shadow of death*; also in verse 22
a8 Hebrew *than Sheol*   b12 Or *wild donkey can be born tame*

¹⁶You will surely forget your trouble,
  recalling it only as waters gone by.
¹⁷Life will be brighter than noonday,
  and darkness will become like morning.
¹⁸You will be secure, because there is hope;
  you will look about you and take your
  rest in safety.
¹⁹You will lie down, with no-one to make
  you afraid,
  and many will court your favour.
²⁰But the eyes of the wicked will fail,
  and escape will elude them;
  their hope will become a dying gasp.''

Job

12

Then Job replied:

²''Doubtless you are the people,
  and wisdom will die with you!
³But I have a mind as well as you;
  I am not inferior to you.
  Who does not know all these things?

⁴''I have become a laughing-stock to my
  friends,
  though I called upon God and he
  answered—
  a mere laughing-stock, though righteous
  and blameless!
⁵Men at ease have contempt for misfortune
  as the fate of those whose feet are
  slipping.
⁶The tents of marauders are undisturbed,
  and those who provoke God are
  secure—
  those who carry their god in their
  hands.^a

⁷''But ask the animals, and they will teach
  you,
  or the birds of the air, and they will tell
  you;
⁸or speak to the earth, and it will teach you,
  or let the fish of the sea inform you.
⁹Which of all these does not know
  that the hand of the LORD has done this?
¹⁰In his hand is the life of every creature
  and the breath of all mankind.
¹¹Does not the ear test words
  as the tongue tastes food?
¹²Is not wisdom found among the aged?
  Does not long life bring understanding?

¹³''To God belong wisdom and power;
  counsel and understanding are his.
¹⁴What he tears down cannot be rebuilt;
  the man he imprisons cannot be
  released.
¹⁵If he holds back the waters, there is
  drought;
  if he lets them loose, they devastate the
  land.
¹⁶To him belong strength and victory;
  both deceived and deceiver are his.
¹⁷He leads counsellors away stripped
  and makes fools of judges.
¹⁸He takes off the shackles put on by kings
  and ties a loincloth^b round their waist.

¹⁹He leads priests away stripped
  and overthrows men long established.
²⁰He silences the lips of trusted advisers
  and takes away the discernment of
  elders.
²¹He pours contempt on nobles
  and disarms the mighty.
²²He reveals the deep things of darkness
  and brings deep shadows into the light.
²³He makes nations great, and destroys
  them;
  he enlarges nations, and disperses them.
²⁴He deprives the leaders of the earth of
  their reason;
  he sends them wandering through a
  trackless waste.
²⁵They grope in darkness with no light;
  he makes them stagger like drunkards.

13

''My eyes have seen all this,
  my ears have heard and understood
  it.
²What you know, I also know;
  I am not inferior to you.
³But I desire to speak to the Almighty
  and to argue my case with God.
⁴You, however, smear me with lies;
  you are worthless physicians, all of you!
⁵If only you would be altogether silent!
  For you, that would be wisdom.
⁶Hear now my argument;
  listen to the plea of my lips.
⁷Will you speak wickedly on God's behalf?
  Will you speak deceitfully for him?
⁸Will you show him partiality?
  Will you argue the case for God?
⁹Would it turn out well if he examined you?
  Could you deceive him as you might
  deceive men?
¹⁰He would surely rebuke you
  if you secretly showed partiality.
¹¹Would not his splendour terrify you?
  Would not the dread of him fall on you?
¹²Your maxims are proverbs of ashes;
  your defences are defences of clay.

¹³''Keep silent and let me speak;
  then let come to me what may.
¹⁴Why do I put myself in jeopardy
  and take my life in my hands?
¹⁵Though he slay me, yet will I hope in him;
  I will surely^a defend my ways to his
  face.
¹⁶Indeed, this will turn out for my
  deliverance,
  for no godless man would dare come
  before him!
¹⁷Listen carefully to my words;
  let your ears take in what I say.
¹⁸Now that I have prepared my case,
  I know I will be vindicated.
¹⁹Can anyone bring charges against me?
  If so, I will be silent and die.

²⁰''Only grant me these two things, O God,
  and then I will not hide from you:
²¹Withdraw your hand far from me,

^a6 Or *secure | in what God's hand brings them*   ^b18 Or *shackles of kings | and ties a belt*
^a15 Or *He will surely slay me; I have no hope— | yet I will*

and stop frightening me with your
 terrors.
²²Then summon me and I will answer,
 or let me speak, and you reply.
²³How many wrongs and sins have I
  committed?
 Show me my offence and my sin.
²⁴Why do you hide your face
 and consider me your enemy?
²⁵Will you torment a wind-blown leaf?
 Will you chase after dry chaff?
²⁶For you write down bitter things against
  me
 and make me inherit the sins of my
  youth.
²⁷You fasten my feet in shackles;
 you keep close watch on all my paths
 by putting marks on the soles of my feet.

²⁸"So man wastes away like something
  rotten,
 like a garment eaten by moths.

14 "Man born of woman
    is of few days and full of trouble.
²He springs up like a flower and withers
  away;
 like a fleeting shadow, he does not
  endure.
³Do you fix your eye on such a one?
 Will you bring him^a before you for
  judgment?
⁴Who can bring what is pure from the
  impure?
 No-one!
⁵Man's days are determined;
 you have decreed the number of his
  months
 and have set limits he cannot exceed.
⁶So look away from him and let him alone,
 till he has put in his time like a hired man.

⁷"At least there is hope for a tree:
 If it is cut down, it will sprout again,
 and its new shoots will not fail.
⁸Its roots may grow old in the ground
 and its stump die in the soil,
⁹yet at the scent of water it will bud
 and put forth shoots like a plant.
¹⁰But man dies and is laid low;
 he breathes his last and is no more.
¹¹As water disappears from the sea
 or a river bed becomes parched and dry,
¹²so man lies down and does not rise;
 till the heavens are no more, men will
  not awake
 or be roused from their sleep.

¹³"If only you would hide me in the grave^b
 and conceal me till your anger has
  passed!
 If only you would set me a time
 and then remember me!
¹⁴If a man dies, will he live again?
 All the days of my hard service
 I will wait for my renewal^c to come.
¹⁵You will call and I will answer you;
 you will long for the creature your hands
  have made.

¹⁶Surely then you will count my steps
 but not keep track of my sin.
¹⁷My offences will be sealed up in a bag;
 you will cover over my sin.

¹⁸"But as a mountain erodes and crumbles
 and as a rock is moved from its place,
¹⁹as water wears away stones
 and torrents wash away the soil,
 so you destroy man's hope.
²⁰You overpower him once for all, and he is
  gone;
 you change his countenance and send
  him away.
²¹If his sons are honoured, he does not know
  it;
 if they are brought low, he does not see
  it.
²²He feels but the pain of his own body
 and mourns only for himself."

Eliphaz

15 Then Eliphaz the Temanite replied:

²"Would a wise man answer with empty
  notions
 or fill his belly with the hot east wind?
³Would he argue with useless words,
 with speeches that have no value?
⁴But you even undermine piety
 and hinder devotion to God.
⁵Your sin prompts your mouth;
 you adopt the tongue of the crafty.
⁶Your own mouth condemns you, not
  mine;
 your own lips testify against you.

⁷"Are you the first man ever born?
 Were you brought forth before the hills?
⁸Do you listen in on God's council?
 Do you limit wisdom to yourself?
⁹What do you know that we do not know?
 What insights do you have that we do
  not have?
¹⁰The grey-haired and the aged are on our
  side,
 men even older than your father.
¹¹Are God's consolations not enough for
  you,
 words spoken gently to you?
¹²Why has your heart carried you away,
 and why do your eyes flash,
¹³so that you vent your rage against God
 and pour out such words from your
  mouth?

¹⁴"What is man, that he could be pure,
 or one born of woman, that he could be
  righteous?
¹⁵If God places no trust in his holy ones,
 if even the heavens are not pure in his
  eyes,
¹⁶how much less man, who is vile and
  corrupt,
 who drinks up evil like water!

¹⁷"Listen to me and I will explain to you;
 let me tell you what I have seen,
¹⁸what wise men have declared,

---

^a3 Septuagint, Vulgate and Syriac; Hebrew *me* ^b13 Hebrew *Sheol* ^c14 Or *release*

hiding nothing received from their
fathers

19(to whom alone the land was given
when no alien passed among them):

20All his days the wicked man suffers
torment,
the ruthless through all the years stored
up for him.

21Terrifying sounds fill his ears;
when all seems well, marauders attack
him.

22He despairs of escaping the darkness;
he is marked for the sword.

23He wanders about—food for vultures;[a]
he knows the day of darkness is at hand.

24Distress and anguish fill him with terror;
they overwhelm him, like a king poised
to attack,

25because he shakes his fist at God
and vaunts himself against the
Almighty,

26defiantly charging against him
with a thick, strong shield.

27"Though his face is covered with fat
and his waist bulges with flesh,

28he will inhabit ruined towns
and houses where no-one lives,
houses crumbling to rubble.

29He will no longer be rich and his wealth
will not endure,
nor will his possessions spread over the
land.

30He will not escape the darkness;
a flame will wither his shoots,
and the breath of God's mouth will carry
him away.

31Let him not deceive himself by trusting
what is worthless,
for he will get nothing in return.

32Before his time he will be paid in full,
and his branches will not flourish.

33He will be like a vine stripped of its unripe
grapes,
like an olive tree shedding its blossoms.

34For the company of the godless will be
barren,
and fire will consume the tents of those
who love bribes.

35They conceive trouble and give birth to
evil;
their womb fashions deceit.''

Job

16 Then Job replied:

2"I have heard many things like these;
miserable comforters are you all!

3Will your long-winded speeches never
end?
What ails you that you keep on arguing?

4I also could speak like you,
if you were in my place;
I could make fine speeches against you
and shake my head at you.

5But my mouth would encourage you;
comfort from my lips would bring you
relief.

6"Yet if I speak, my pain is not relieved;
and if I refrain, it does not go away.

7Surely, O God, you have worn me out;
you have devastated my entire
household.

8You have bound me—and it has become a
witness;
my gauntness rises up and testifies
against me.

9God assails me and tears me in his anger
and gnashes his teeth at me;
my opponent fastens on me his piercing
eyes.

10Men open their mouths to jeer at me;
they strike my cheek in scorn
and unite together against me.

11God has turned me over to evil men
and thrown me into the clutches of the
wicked.

12All was well with me, but he shattered me;
he seized me by the neck and crushed
me.
He has made me his target;

13 his archers surround me.
Without pity, he pierces my kidneys
and spills my gall on the ground.

14Again and again he bursts upon me;
he rushes at me like a warrior.

15"I have sewed sackcloth over my skin
and buried my brow in the dust.

16My face is red with weeping,
deep shadows ring my eyes;

17yet my hands have been free of violence
and my prayer is pure.

18"O earth, do not cover my blood;
may my cry never be laid to rest!

19Even now my witness is in heaven;
my advocate is on high.

20My intercessor is my friend[a]
as my eyes pour out tears to God;

21on behalf of a man he pleads with God
as a man pleads for his friend.

22"Only a few years will pass
before I go on the journey of no return.

17 1My spirit is broken,
my days are cut short,
the grave awaits me.

2Surely mockers surround me;
my eyes must dwell on their hostility.

3"Give me, O God, the pledge you
demand.
Who else will put up security for me?

4You have closed their minds to
understanding;
therefore you will not let them triumph.

5If a man denounces his friends for reward,
the eyes of his children will fail.

6"God has made me a byword to everyone,
a man in whose face people spit.

7My eyes have grown dim with grief;
my whole frame is but a shadow.

8Upright men are appalled at this;
the innocent are aroused against the
ungodly.

---

[a]23 Or *about, looking for food*   [a]20 Or *My friends treat me with scorn*

⁹Nevertheless, the righteous will hold to
    their ways,
  and those with clean hands will grow
    stronger.

¹⁰"But come on, all of you, try again!
  I will not find a wise man among you.
¹¹My days have passed, my plans are
    shattered,
  and so are the desires of my heart.
¹²These men turn night into day;
  in the face of darkness they say, 'Light
    is near.'
¹³If the only home I hope for is the grave,ᵃ
  if I spread out my bed in darkness,
¹⁴if I say to corruption, 'You are my father,'
  and to the worm, 'My mother' or 'My
    sister',
¹⁵where then is my hope?
  Who can see any hope for me?
¹⁶Will it go down to the gates of death?ᵇ
  Will we descend together into the
    dust?"

Bildad

18 Then Bildad the Shuhite replied:

²"When will you end these speeches?
  Be sensible, and then we can talk.
³Why are we regarded as cattle
  and considered stupid in your sight?
⁴You who tear yourself to pieces in your
    anger,
  is the earth to be abandoned for your
    sake?
  Or must the rocks be moved from their
    place?

⁵"The lamp of the wicked is snuffed out;
  the flame of his fire stops burning.
⁶The light in his tent becomes dark;
  the lamp beside him goes out.
⁷The vigour of his step is weakened;
  his own schemes throw him down.
⁸His feet thrust him into a net
  and he wanders into its mesh.
⁹A trap seizes him by the heel;
  a snare holds him fast.
¹⁰A noose is hidden for him on the ground;
  a trap lies in his path.
¹¹Terrors startle him on every side
  and dog his every step.
¹²Calamity is hungry for him;
  disaster is ready for him when he falls.
¹³It eats away parts of his skin;
  death's firstborn devours his limbs.
¹⁴He is torn from the security of his tent
  and marched off to the king of terrors.
¹⁵Fire residesᵃ in his tent;
  burning sulphur is scattered over his
    dwelling.
¹⁶His roots dry up below
  and his branches wither above.
¹⁷The memory of him perishes from the
    earth;
  he has no name in the land.
¹⁸He is driven from light into darkness
  and is banished from the world.

¹⁹He has no offspring or descendants among
    his people,
  no survivor where once he lived.
²⁰Men of the west are appalled at his fate;
  men of the east are seized with horror.
²¹Surely such is the dwelling of an evil man;
  such is the place of one who knows not
    God."

Job

19 Then Job replied:

²"How long will you torment me
  and crush me with words?
³Ten times now you have reproached me;
  shamelessly you attack me.
⁴If it is true that I have gone astray,
  my error remains my concern alone.
⁵If indeed you would exalt yourselves
    above me
  and use my humiliation against me,
⁶then know that God has wronged me
  and drawn his net around me.

⁷"Though I cry, 'I've been wronged!' I get
    no response;
  though I call for help, there is no justice.
⁸He has blocked my way so that I cannot
    pass;
  he has shrouded my paths in darkness.
⁹He has stripped me of my honour
  and removed the crown from my head.
¹⁰He tears me down on every side till I am
    gone;
  he uproots my hope like a tree.
¹¹His anger burns against me;
  he counts me among his enemies.
¹²His troops advance in force;
  they build a siege ramp against me
  and encamp around my tent.

¹³"He has alienated my brothers from me;
  my acquaintances are completely
    estranged from me.
¹⁴My kinsmen have gone away;
  my friends have forgotten me.
¹⁵My guests and my maidservants count me
    a stranger;
  they look upon me as an alien.
¹⁶I summon my servant, but he does not
    answer,
  though I beg him with my own mouth.
¹⁷My breath is offensive to my wife;
  I am loathsome to my own brothers.
¹⁸Even the little boys scorn me;
  when I appear, they ridicule me.
¹⁹All my intimate friends detest me;
  those I love have turned against me.
²⁰I am nothing but skin and bones;
  I have escaped by only the skin of my
    teeth.ᵃ

²¹"Have pity on me, my friends, have pity,
  for the hand of God has struck me.
²²Why do you pursue me as God does?
  Will you never get enough of my flesh?

²³"Oh, that my words were recorded,
  that they were written on a scroll,

ᵃ13 Hebrew Sheol   ᵇ16 Hebrew to Sheol   ᵃ15 Or Nothing he had remains   ᵃ20 Or only my gums

²⁴that they were inscribed with an iron tool
on*ᵇ* lead,
or engraved in rock for ever!
²⁵I know that my Redeemer*ᶜ* lives,
and that in the end he will stand upon
the earth.*ᵈ*
²⁶And after my skin has been destroyed,
yet*ᵉ* in*ᶠ* my flesh I will see God;
²⁷I myself will see him
with my own eyes—I, and not another.
How my heart yearns within me!

²⁸''If you say, 'How we will hound him,
since the root of the trouble lies in him,'*ᵍ*
²⁹you should fear the sword yourselves;
for wrath will bring punishment by the
sword,
and then you will know that there is
judgment.''*ʰ*

Zophar

20 Then Zophar the Naamathite replied:

²''My troubled thoughts prompt me to
answer
because I am greatly disturbed.
³I hear a rebuke that dishonours me,
and my understanding inspires me to
reply.

⁴''Surely you know how it has been from of
old,
ever since man*ᵃ* was placed on the
earth,
⁵that the mirth of the wicked is brief,
the joy of the godless lasts but a
moment.
⁶Though his pride reaches to the heavens
and his head touches the clouds,
⁷he will perish for ever, like his own dung;
those who have seen him will say,
'Where is he?'
⁸Like a dream he flies away, no more to be
found,
banished like a vision of the night.
⁹The eye that saw him will not see him
again;
his place will look on him no more.
¹⁰His children must make amends to the
poor;
his own hands must give back his
wealth.
¹¹The youthful vigour that fills his bones
will lie with him in the dust.

¹²''Though evil is sweet in his mouth
and he hides it under his tongue,
¹³though he cannot bear to let it go
and keeps it in his mouth,
¹⁴yet his food will turn sour in his stomach;
it will become the venom of serpents
within him.
¹⁵He will spit out the riches he swallowed;
God will make his stomach vomit them
up.

¹⁶He will suck the poison of serpents;
the fangs of an adder will kill him.
¹⁷He will not enjoy the streams,
the rivers flowing with honey and
cream.
¹⁸What he toiled for he must give back
uneaten;
he will not enjoy the profit from his
trading.
¹⁹For he has oppressed the poor and left
them destitute;
he has seized houses he did not build.

²⁰''Surely he will have no respite from his
craving;
he cannot save himself by his treasure.
²¹Nothing is left for him to devour;
his prosperity will not endure.
²²In the midst of his plenty, distress will
overtake him;
the full force of misery will come upon
him.
²³When he has filled his belly,
God will vent his burning anger against
him
and rain down his blows upon him.
²⁴Though he flees from an iron weapon,
a bronze-tipped arrow pierces him.
²⁵He pulls it out of his back,
the gleaming point out of his liver.
Terrors will come over him;
²⁶   total darkness lies in wait for his
treasures.
A fire unfanned will consume him
and devour what is left in his tent.
²⁷The heavens will expose his guilt;
the earth will rise up against him.
²⁸A flood will carry off his house,
rushing waters*ᵇ* on the day of God's
wrath.
²⁹Such is the fate God allots the wicked,
the heritage appointed for them by
God.''

Job

21 Then Job replied:

²''Listen carefully to my words;
let this be the consolation you give me.
³Bear with me while I speak,
and after I have spoken, mock on.

⁴''Is my complaint directed to man?
Why should I not be impatient?
⁵Look at me and be astonished;
clap your hand over your mouth.
⁶When I think about this, I am terrified;
trembling seizes my body.
⁷Why do the wicked live on,
growing old and increasing in power?
⁸They see their children established around
them,
their offspring before their eyes.
⁹Their homes are safe and free from fear;
the rod of God is not upon them.

ᵇ24 Or *and*   *ᶜ25* Or *defender*   *ᵈ25* Or *upon my grave*
ᵉ26 Or *And after I awake, / though this ,body, has been destroyed, / then*   *ᶠ26* Or */ apart from*
ᵍ28 Many Hebrew manuscripts, Septuagint and Vulgate; most Hebrew manuscripts *me*
ʰ29 Or */ that you may come to know the Almighty*   *ᵃ4* Or *Adam*
ᵇ28 Or *The possessions in his house will be carried off, / washed away*

JOB 19:23–29
'I know that my Redeemer lives, and that in the end he will stand upon the earth
. . . in my flesh I will see God' (vv. 25, 26).

DARKNESS MUST YIELD TO TRUTH. Verse 25, well known due
to its incorporation in Handel's *Messiah*, is indeed the climax of all
Job's deliberations. His plight is not yet relieved, yet sublime understanding has come. The glimmer of light is now a powerful shaft,
piercing the darkness of Job's thought.

Wilfred Kitching, then Divisional Commander of The Salvation
Army in East London, wrote a children's song towards the end of the
Second World War.

> *Brighter days are dawning,*
> *Soon will come the morning,*
> *Darkness must yield to truth.*
> *Earthly joys are taken,*
> *But a rock unshaken,*
> *Waits to bear the feet of youth.*

Hope like that sustained whole populations through the dark days of
war. Today in areas of desperate need – where war brings misery, even
famine, to millions – there is hope that ultimately truth will triumph.

It is often harder for young people to sustain this hope than for
those who are older. The young become discouraged for they so rarely
see any change in us. When they suffer it is all too easy for them –
especially if they have never experienced the good side of life which Job
had enjoyed; if they have only seen others enjoying from a distance – to
feel that there is no hope for them, and their generation. Let us pray
that young people throughout the world will be given hope, hope for a
brighter future in which God himself will be revealed to them.

Dear Father in heaven, we pray for all young people who have lost hope.

→440

JOB 38:1–18
'Where were you when I laid the earth's foundation? Tell me, if you understand. Who marked off its dimensions? Surely you know! Who stretched a measuring line across it?' (vv. 4, 5).

GOD ANSWERS! OR DOES HE? Following Elihu's interruption, in Chapter 38 God's voice thunders from the heavens. We expect an answer, a happy ending, some comfort. Instead we get more magnificent questions. Paul Scherer says 'God seems deliberately intent on overawing Job . . . the very thing Job was sure God would not do, had pleaded that he might not.'

We can compare God's relationship with Job to that between a caring mother and her child. The child is on its own. Mother seems far away, and many, many fears seem very, very close. The child does something stupid, endangering its very existence and once back home is exposed to parental wrath. Mum shouts and hollers, and son or daughter, hopefully, never does it again. Any good reaction results from her care. The child hears nothing new, has probably heard it all before, but the way it is said, with passion, conviction and in sheer desperation, gets the message home. The mother has been suffering and worrying through every step the child takes.

So it is with Job. God is there though he seems distant. In Job's suffering he is there. When Job despairs and blasphemes and hollers, God is there. William Clark's verse, to a catchy tune often sung by Salvationist youngsters, sums it up:

Is there a God?
Does he really care?
This is my question, Is he really there?
I've read all the answers in the Bible on the shelf
But I want to know, really know for myself.

Dear God, who treats us as a mother does her child, we bring before you in prayer mothers everywhere who are worried about their children. Children absent from home, whose whereabouts are unknown. Children surrounded by harmful influences in this modern world. Hungry children. Despondent children, Handicapped children. Sick children. Strengthen them, we pray, and all who support them.

→453

¹⁰Their bulls never fail to breed;
　their cows calve and do not miscarry.
¹¹They send forth their children as a flock;
　their little ones dance about.
¹²They sing to the music of tambourine and
　harp;
　they make merry to the sound of the
　flute.
¹³They spend their years in prosperity
　and go down to the grave*a* in peace.*b*
¹⁴Yet they say to God, 'Leave us alone!
　We have no desire to know your ways.
¹⁵Who is the Almighty, that we should serve
　him?
　What would we gain by praying to him?'
¹⁶But their prosperity is not in their own
　hands,
　so I stand aloof from the counsel of the
　wicked.

¹⁷'Yet how often is the lamp of the wicked
　snuffed out?
　How often does calamity come upon
　them,
　the fate God allots in his anger?
¹⁸How often are they like straw before the
　wind,
　like chaff swept away by a gale?
¹⁹It is said, 'God stores up a man's
　punishment for his sons.'
　Let him repay the man himself, so that
　he will know it!
²⁰Let his own eyes see his destruction;
　let him drink of the wrath of the
　Almighty.*c*
²¹For what does he care about the family he
　leaves behind
　when his allotted months come to an
　end?

²²'Can anyone teach knowledge to God,
　since he judges even the highest?
²³One man dies in full vigour,
　completely secure and at ease,
²⁴his body*d* well nourished,
　his bones rich with marrow.
²⁵Another man dies in bitterness of soul,
　never having enjoyed anything good.
²⁶Side by side they lie in the dust,
　and worms cover them both.

²⁷'I know full well what you are thinking,
　the schemes by which you would wrong
　me.
²⁸You say, 'Where now is the great man's
　house,
　the tents where wicked men lived?'
²⁹Have you never questioned those who
　travel?
　Have you paid no regard to their
　accounts—
³⁰that the evil man is spared from the day of
　calamity,
　that he is delivered from*e* the day of
　wrath?
³¹Who denounces his conduct to his face?

Who repays him for what he has done?
³²He is carried to the grave,
　and watch is kept over his tomb.
³³The soil in the valley is sweet to him;
　all men follow after him,
　and a countless throng goes*f* before him.

³⁴'So how can you console me with your
　nonsense?
　Nothing is left of your answers but
　falsehood!'

Eliphaz

22 Then Eliphaz the Temanite replied:

²'Can a man be of benefit to God?
　Can even a wise man benefit him?
³What pleasure would it give the Almighty
　if you were righteous?
　What would he gain if your ways were
　blameless?

⁴'Is it for your piety that he rebukes you
　and brings charges against you?
⁵Is not your wickedness great?
　Are not your sins endless?
⁶You demanded security from your
　brothers for no reason;
　you stripped men of their clothing,
　leaving them naked.
⁷You gave no water to the weary
　and you withheld food from the hungry,
⁸though you were a powerful man, owning
　land—
　an honoured man, living on it.
⁹And you sent widows away empty-handed
　and broke the strength of the fatherless.
¹⁰That is why snares are all around you,
　why sudden peril terrifies you,
¹¹why it is so dark that you cannot see,
　and why a flood of water covers you.

¹²'Is not God in the heights of heaven?
　And see how lofty are the highest stars!
¹³Yet you say, 'What does God know?
　Does he judge through such darkness?
¹⁴Thick clouds veil him, so he does not see
　us
　as he goes about in the vaulted
　heavens.'
¹⁵Will you keep to the old path
　that evil men have trod?
¹⁶They were carried off before their time,
　their foundations washed away by a
　flood.
¹⁷They said to God, 'Leave us alone!
　What can the Almighty do to us?'
¹⁸Yet it was he who filled their houses with
　good things,
　so I stand aloof from the counsel of the
　wicked.

¹⁹'The righteous see their ruin and rejoice;
　the innocent mock them, saying,
²⁰'Surely our foes are destroyed,
　and fire devours their wealth.'

---

a13 Hebrew *Sheol*　　*b13* Or *in an instant*
c17–20 Verses 17 and 18 may be taken as exclamations and 19 and 20 as declarations.
d24 The meaning of the Hebrew for this word is uncertain.
e30 Or *man is reserved for the day of calamity, / that he is brought forth to*
f33 Or / *as a countless throng went*

²¹"Submit to God and be at peace with him;
  in this way prosperity will come to you.
²²Accept instruction from his mouth
  and lay up his words in your heart.
²³If you return to the Almighty, you will be
    restored:
  If you remove wickedness far from your
    tent
²⁴and assign your nuggets to the dust,
  your gold of Ophir to the rocks in the
    ravines,
²⁵then the Almighty will be your gold,
  the choicest silver for you.
²⁶Surely then you will find delight in the
    Almighty
  and will lift up your face to God.
²⁷You will pray to him, and he will hear you,
  and you will fulfil your vows.
²⁸What you decide on will be done,
  and light will shine on your ways.
²⁹When men are brought low and you say,
    'Lift them up!'
  then he will save the downcast.
³⁰He will deliver even one who is not
    innocent,
  who will be delivered through the
    cleanness of your hands.''

Job

23 Then Job replied:

²"Even today my complaint is bitter;
  his hand*ᵃ* is heavy in spite of*ᵇ* my
    groaning.
³If only I knew where to find him;
  if only I could go to his dwelling!
⁴I would state my case before him
  and fill my mouth with arguments.
⁵I would find out what he would answer
    me,
  and consider what he would say.
⁶Would he oppose me with great power?
  No, he would not press charges against
    me.
⁷There an upright man could present his
    case before him,
  and I would be delivered for ever from
    my judge.

⁸"But if I go to the east, he is not there;
  if I go to the west, I do not find him.
⁹When he is at work in the north, I do not
    see him;
  when he turns to the south, I catch no
    glimpse of him.
¹⁰But he knows the way that I take;
  when he has tested me, I shall come
    forth as gold.
¹¹My feet have closely followed his steps;
  I have kept to his way without turning
    aside.
¹²I have not departed from the commands of
    his lips;
  I have treasured the words of his mouth
    more than my daily bread.

¹³"But he stands alone, and who can oppose
    him?

He does whatever he pleases.
¹⁴He carries out his decree against me,
  and many such plans he still has in
    store.
¹⁵That is why I am terrified before him;
  when I think of all this, I fear him.
¹⁶God has made my heart faint;
  the Almighty has terrified me.
¹⁷Yet I am not silenced by the darkness,
  by the thick darkness that covers my
    face.

24 "Why does the Almighty not set
    times for judgment?
  Why must those who know him look in
    vain for such days?
²Men move boundary stones;
  they pasture flocks they have stolen.
³They drive away the orphan's donkey
  and take the widow's ox in pledge.
⁴They thrust the needy from the path
  and force all the poor of the land into
    hiding.
⁵Like wild donkeys in the desert,
  the poor go about their labour of
    foraging food;
  the wasteland provides food for their
    children.
⁶They gather fodder in the fields
  and glean in the vineyards of the
    wicked.
⁷Lacking clothes, they spend the night
    naked;
  they have nothing to cover themselves
    in the cold.
⁸They are drenched by mountain rains
  and hug the rocks for lack of shelter.
⁹The fatherless child is snatched from the
    breast;
  the infant of the poor is seized for a
    debt.
¹⁰Lacking clothes, they go about naked;
  they carry the sheaves, but still go
    hungry.
¹¹They crush olives among the terraces;*ᵃ*
  they tread the winepresses, yet suffer
    thirst.
¹²The groans of the dying rise from the city,
  and the souls of the wounded cry out for
    help.
  But God charges no-one with
    wrongdoing.

¹³"There are those who rebel against the
    light,
  who do not know its ways
  or stay in its paths.
¹⁴When daylight is gone, the murderer rises
    up
  and kills the poor and needy;
  in the night he steals forth like a thief.
¹⁵The eye of the adulterer watches for
    dusk;
  he thinks, 'No eye will see me,'
  and he keeps his face concealed.
¹⁶In the dark, men break into houses,
  but by day they shut themselves in;
  they want nothing to do with the light.

ᵃ2 Septuagint and Syriac; Hebrew / *the hand on me*   *ᵇ2* Or *heavy on me in*
ᵃ11 Or *olives between the millstones*; the meaning of the Hebrew for this word is uncertain.

17For all of them, deep darkness is their
    morning;*b*
  they make friends with the terrors of
    darkness.*c*

18"Yet they are foam on the surface of the
    water;
  their portion of the land is cursed,
  so that no-one goes to the vineyards.
19As heat and drought snatch away the
    melted snow,
  so the grave*d* snatches away those who
    have sinned.
20The womb forgets them,
  the worm feasts on them;
evil men are no longer remembered
  but are broken like a tree.
21They prey on the barren and childless
    woman,
  and to the widow show no kindness.
22But God drags away the mighty by his
    power;
  though they become established, they
    have no assurance of life.
23He may let them rest in a feeling of
    security,
  but his eyes are on their ways.
24For a little while they are exalted, and then
    they are gone;
  they are brought low and gathered up
    like all others;
  they are cut off like ears of corn.

25"If this is not so, who can prove me false
    and reduce my words to nothing?"

Bildad

25 Then Bildad the Shuhite replied:

2"Dominion and awe belong to God;
  he establishes order in the heights of
    heaven.
3Can his forces be numbered?
  Upon whom does his light not rise?
4How then can a man be righteous before
    God?
  How can one born of woman be pure?
5If even the moon is not bright
  and the stars are not pure in his eyes,
6how much less man, who is but a
    maggot—
  a son of man, who is only a worm!"

Job

26 Then Job replied:

2"How you have helped the powerless!
  How you have saved the arm that is
    feeble!
3What advice you have offered to one
    without wisdom!
  And what great insight you have
    displayed!
4Who has helped you utter these words?
  And whose spirit spoke from your
    mouth?

5"The dead are in deep anguish,
  those beneath the waters and all that
    live in them.
6Death*a* is naked before God;
  Destruction*b* lies uncovered.
7He spreads out the northern ⌊skies⌋ over
    empty space;
  he suspends the earth over nothing.
8He wraps up the waters in his clouds,
  yet the clouds do not burst under their
    weight.
9He covers the face of the full moon,
  spreading his clouds over it.
10He marks out the horizon on the face of
    the waters
  for a boundary between light and
    darkness.
11The pillars of the heavens quake,
  aghast at his rebuke.
12By his power he churned up the sea;
  by his wisdom he cut Rahab to pieces.
13By his breath the skies became fair;
  his hand pierced the gliding serpent.
14And these are but the outer fringe of his
    works;
  how faint the whisper we hear of him!
  Who then can understand the thunder of
    his power?"

27 And Job continued his discourse:

2"As surely as God lives, who has denied
    me justice,
  the Almighty, who has made me taste
    bitterness of soul,
3as long as I have life within me,
  the breath of God in my nostrils,
4my lips will not speak wickedness,
  and my tongue will utter no deceit.
5I will never admit you are in the right;
  till I die, I will not deny my integrity.
6I will maintain my righteousness and never
    let go of it;
  my conscience will not reproach me as
    long as I live.

7"May my enemies be like the wicked,
  my adversaries like the unjust!
8For what hope has the godless when he is
    cut off,
  when God takes away his life?
9Does God listen to his cry
  when distress comes upon him?
10Will he find delight in the Almighty?
  Will he call upon God at all times?

11"I will teach you about the power of God;
  the ways of the Almighty I will not
    conceal.
12You have all seen this yourselves.
  Why then this meaningless talk?

13"Here is the fate God allots to the wicked,
  the heritage a ruthless man receives
    from the Almighty:
14However many his children, their fate is
    the sword;
  his offspring will never have enough to
    eat.

---

*b*17 Or *them, their morning is like the shadow of death*   *c*17 Or *of the shadow of death*   *d*19 Hebrew *Sheol*
*a*6 Hebrew *Sheol*   *b*6 Hebrew *Abaddon*

15The plague will bury those who survive
	him,
	and their widows will not weep for
	them.
16Though he heaps up silver like dust
	and clothes like piles of clay,
17what he lays up the righteous will wear,
	and the innocent will divide his silver.
18The house he builds is like a moth's
	cocoon,
	like a hut made by a watchman.
19He lies down wealthy, but will do so no
	more;
	when he opens his eyes, all is gone.
20Terrors overtake him like a flood;
	a tempest snatches him away in the
	night.
21The east wind carries him off, and he is
	gone;
	it sweeps him out of his place.
22It hurls itself against him without mercy
	as he flees headlong from its power.
23It claps its hands in derision
	and hisses him out of his place.

28 　"There is a mine for silver
	and a place where gold is refined.
2Iron is taken from the earth,
	and copper is smelted from ore.
3Man puts an end to the darkness;
	he searches the farthest recesses
	for ore in the blackest darkness.
4Far from where people dwell he cuts a
	shaft,
	in places forgotten by the foot of man;
	far from men he dangles and sways.
5The earth, from which food comes,
	is transformed below as by fire;
6sapphires*a* come from its rocks,
	and its dust contains nuggets of gold.
7No bird of prey knows that hidden path,
	no falcon's eye has seen it.
8Proud beasts do not set foot on it,
	and no lion prowls there.
9Man's hand assaults the flinty rock
	and lays bare the roots of the
	mountains.
10He tunnels through the rock;
	his eyes see all its treasures.
11He searches*b* the sources of the rivers
	and brings hidden things to light.

12"But where can wisdom be found?
	Where does understanding dwell?
13Man does not comprehend its worth;
	it cannot be found in the land of the
	living.
14The deep says, 'It is not in me';
	the sea says, 'It is not with me.'
15It cannot be bought with the finest gold,
	nor can its price be weighed in silver.
16It cannot be bought with the gold of Ophir,
	with precious onyx or sapphires.
17Neither gold nor crystal can compare with
	it,
	nor can it be had for jewels of gold.
18Coral and jasper are not worthy of
	mention;

	the price of wisdom is beyond rubies.
19The topaz of Cush cannot compare with it;
	it cannot be bought with pure gold.

20"Where then does wisdom come from?
	Where does understanding dwell?
21It is hidden from the eyes of every living
	thing,
	concealed even from the birds of the air.
22Destruction*c* and Death say,
	'Only a rumour of it has reached our
	ears.'
23God understands the way to it
	and he alone knows where it dwells,
24for he views the ends of the earth
	and sees everything under the heavens.
25When he established the force of the wind
	and measured out the waters,
26when he made a decree for the rain
	and a path for the thunderstorm,
27then he looked at wisdom and appraised it;
	he confirmed it and tested it.
28And he said to man,
	'The fear of the Lord—that is wisdom,
	and to shun evil is understanding.' "

29 　Job continued his discourse:

2"How I long for the months gone by,
	for the days when God watched over
	me,
3when his lamp shone upon my head
	and by his light I walked through
	darkness!
4Oh, for the days when I was in my prime,
	when God's intimate friendship blessed
	my house,
5when the Almighty was still with me
	and my children were around me,
6when my path was drenched with cream
	and the rock poured out for me streams
	of olive oil.

7"When I went to the gate of the city
	and took my seat in the public square,
8the young men saw me and stepped aside
	and the old men rose to their feet;
9the chief men refrained from speaking
	and covered their mouths with their
	hands;
10the voices of the nobles were hushed,
	and their tongues stuck to the roof of
	their mouths.
11Whoever heard me spoke well of me,
	and those who saw me commended me,
12because I rescued the poor who cried for
	help,
	and the fatherless who had none to
	assist him.
13The man who was dying blessed me;
	I made the widow's heart sing.
14I put on righteousness as my clothing;
	justice was my robe and my turban.
15I was eyes to the blind
	and feet to the lame.
16I was a father to the needy;
	I took up the case of the stranger.

*a*6 Or *lapis lazuli*; also in verse 16　　*b*11 Septuagint, Aquila and Vulgate; Hebrew *He dams up*
*c*22 Hebrew *Abaddon*

17I broke the fangs of the wicked
　and snatched the victims from their
　　teeth.

18"I thought, 'I shall die in my own house,
　my days as numerous as the grains of
　　sand.
19My roots will reach to the water,
　and the dew will lie all night on my
　　branches.
20My glory will remain fresh in me,
　the bow ever new in my hand.'

21"Men listened to me expectantly,
　waiting in silence for my counsel.
22After I had spoken, they spoke no more;
　my words fell gently on their ears.
23They waited for me as for showers
　and drank in my words as the spring
　　rain.
24When I smiled at them, they scarcely
　believed it;
　the light of my face was precious to
　　them.a
25I chose the way for them and sat as their
　chief;
　I dwelt as a king among his troops;
　I was like one who comforts mourners.

30

"But now they mock me,
　men younger than I,
whose fathers I would have disdained
　to put with my sheep dogs.
2Of what use was the strength of their
　hands to me,
　since their vigour had gone from them?
3Haggard from want and hunger,
　they roameda the parched land
　in desolate wastelands at night.
4In the brush they gathered salt herbs,
　and their foodb was the root of the
　　broom tree.
5They were banished from their
　fellow-men,
　shouted at as if they were thieves.
6They were forced to live in the dry stream
　beds,
　among the rocks and in holes in the
　　ground.
7They brayed among the bushes
　and huddled in the undergrowth.
8A base and nameless brood,
　they were driven out of the land.

9"And now their sons mock me in song;
　I have become a byword among them.
10They detest me and keep their distance;
　they do not hesitate to spit in my face.
11Now that God has unstrung my bow and
　afflicted me,
　they throw off restraint in my presence.
12On my right the tribec attacks;
　they lay snares for my feet,
　they build their siege ramps against me.
13They break up my road;
　they succeed in destroying me—
　without anyone's helping them.d

14They advance as through a gaping breach;
　amid the ruins they come rolling in.
15Terrors overwhelm me;
　my dignity is driven away as by the
　　wind,
　my safety vanishes like a cloud.

16"And now my life ebbs away;
　days of suffering grip me.
17Night pierces my bones;
　my gnawing pains never rest.
18In his great power ⌊God⌋ becomes like
　clothing to me;e
　he binds me like the neck of my
　　garment.
19He throws me into the mud,
　and I am reduced to dust and ashes.

20"I cry out to you, O God, but you do not
　answer;
　I stand up, but you merely look at me.
21You turn on me ruthlessly;
　with the might of your hand you attack
　　me.
22You snatch me up and drive me before the
　wind;
　you toss me about in the storm.
23I know you will bring me down to death,
　to the place appointed for all the living.

24"Surely no-one lays a hand on a broken
　man
　when he cries for help in his distress.
25Have I not wept for those in trouble?
　Has not my soul grieved for the poor?
26Yet when I hoped for good, evil came;
　when I looked for light, then came
　　darkness.
27The churning inside me never stops;
　days of suffering confront me.
28I go about blackened, but not by the sun;
　I stand up in the assembly and cry for
　　help.
29I have become a brother of jackals,
　a companion of owls.
30My skin grows black and peels;
　my body burns with fever.
31My harp is tuned to mourning,
　and my flute to the sound of wailing.

31

"I made a covenant with my eyes
　not to look lustfully at a girl.
2For what is man's lot from God above,
　his heritage from the Almighty on high?
3Is it not ruin for the wicked,
　disaster for those who do wrong?
4Does he not see my ways
　and count my every step?

5"If I have walked in falsehood
　or my foot has hurried after deceit—
6let God weigh me in honest scales
　and he will know that I am blameless—
7if my steps have turned from the path,
　if my heart has been led by my eyes,
　or if my hands have been defiled,
8then may others eat what I have sown,
　and may my crops be uprooted.

---

a24 The meaning of the Hebrew for this clause is uncertain.　　a3 Or gnawed
b4 Or fuel　　c12 The meaning of the Hebrew for this word is uncertain.
d13 Or me. / 'No-one can help him,' ⌊they say⌋　　e18 Hebrew; Septuagint ⌊God⌋ grasps my clothing

⁹"If my heart has been enticed by a woman,
or if I have lurked at my neighbour's door,
¹⁰then may my wife grind another man's grain,
and may other men sleep with her.
¹¹For that would have been shameful,
a sin to be judged.
¹²It is a fire that burns to Destruction;ᵃ
it would have uprooted my harvest.

¹³"If I have denied justice to my menservants and maidservants
when they had a grievance against me,
¹⁴what will I do when God confronts me?
What will I answer when called to account?
¹⁵Did not he who made me in the womb make them?
Did not the same one form us both within our mothers?

¹⁶"If I have denied the desires of the poor
or let the eyes of the widow grow weary,
¹⁷if I have kept my bread to myself,
not sharing it with the fatherless—
¹⁸but from my youth I reared him as would a father,
and from my birth I guided the widow—
¹⁹if I have seen anyone perishing for lack of clothing,
or a needy man without a garment,
²⁰and his heart did not bless me
for warming him with the fleece from my sheep,
²¹if I have raised my hand against the fatherless,
knowing that I had influence in court,
²²then let my arm fall from the shoulder,
let it be broken off at the joint.
²³For I dreaded destruction from God,
and for fear of his splendour I could not do such things.

²⁴"If I have put my trust in gold
or said to pure gold, 'You are my security,'
²⁵if I have rejoiced over my great wealth,
the fortune my hands had gained,
²⁶if I have regarded the sun in its radiance
or the moon moving in splendour,
²⁷so that my heart was secretly enticed
and my hand offered them a kiss of homage,
²⁸then these also would be sins to be judged,
for I would have been unfaithful to God on high.

²⁹"If I have rejoiced at my enemy's misfortune
or gloated over the trouble that came to him—
³⁰I have not allowed my mouth to sin
by invoking a curse against his life—
³¹if the men of my household have never said,

'Who has not had his fill of Job's meat?'—
³²but no stranger had to spend the night in the street,
for my door was always open to the traveller—
³³if I have concealed my sin as men do,ᵇ
by hiding my guilt in my heart
³⁴because I so feared the crowd
and so dreaded the contempt of the clans
that I kept silent and would not go outside—

³⁵("Oh, that I had someone to hear me!
I sign now my defence—let the Almighty answer me;
let my accuser put his indictment in writing.
³⁶Surely I would wear it on my shoulder,
I would put it on like a crown.
³⁷I would give him an account of my every step;
like a prince I would approach him.)—

³⁸"if my land cries out against me
and all its furrows are wet with tears,
³⁹if I have devoured its yield without payment
or broken the spirit of its tenants,
⁴⁰then let briers come up instead of wheat
and weeds instead of barley."

The words of Job are ended.

Elihu

32 So these three men stopped answering Job, because he was righteous in his own eyes. ²But Elihu son of Barakel the Buzite, of the family of Ram, became very angry with Job for justifying himself rather than God. ³He was also angry with the three friends, because they had found no way to refute Job, and yet had condemned him.ᵃ ⁴Now Elihu had waited before speaking to Job because they were older than he. ⁵But when he saw that the three men had nothing more to say, his anger was aroused.

⁶So Elihu son of Barakel the Buzite said:

"I am young in years,
and you are old;
that is why I was fearful,
not daring to tell you what I know.
⁷I thought, 'Age should speak;
advanced years should teach wisdom.'
⁸But it is the spiritᵇ in a man,
the breath of the Almighty, that gives him understanding.
⁹It is not only the oldᶜ who are wise,
not only the aged who understand what is right.

¹⁰"Therefore I say: Listen to me;
I too will tell you what I know.
¹¹I waited while you spoke,
I listened to your reasoning;
while you were searching for words,

ᵃ12 Hebrew *Abaddon* ᵇ33 Or *as Adam did*
ᵃ3 Masoretic Text; an ancient Hebrew scribal tradition *Job, and so had condemned God*
ᵇ8 Or *Spirit*; also in verse 18 ᶜ9 Or *many*; or *great*

¹² I gave you my full attention.
But not one of you has proved Job wrong;
  none of you has answered his
  arguments.
¹³Do not say, 'We have found wisdom;
  let God refute him, not man.'
¹⁴But Job has not marshalled his words
  against me,
  and I will not answer him with your
  arguments.

¹⁵"They are dismayed and have no more to
  say;
  words have failed them.
¹⁶Must I wait, now that they are silent,
  now that they stand there with no reply?
¹⁷I too will have my say;
  I too will tell what I know.
¹⁸For I am full of words,
  and the spirit within me compels me;
¹⁹inside I am like bottled-up wine,
  like new wineskins ready to burst.
²⁰I must speak and find relief;
  I must open my lips and reply.
²¹I will show partiality to no-one,
  nor will I flatter any man;
²²for if I were skilled in flattery,
  my Maker would soon take me away.

33 "But now, Job, listen to my words;
  pay attention to everything I say.
²I am about to open my mouth;
  my words are on the tip of my tongue.
³My words come from an upright heart;
  my lips sincerely speak what I know.
⁴The Spirit of God has made me;
  the breath of the Almighty gives me life.
⁵Answer me then, if you can;
  prepare yourself and confront me.
⁶I am just like you before God;
  I too have been taken from clay.
⁷No fear of me should alarm you,
  nor should my hand be heavy upon you.

⁸"But you have said in my hearing—
  I heard the very words—
⁹'I am pure and without sin;
  I am clean and free from guilt.
¹⁰Yet God has found fault with me;
  he considers me his enemy.
¹¹He fastens my feet in shackles;
  he keeps close watch on all my paths.

¹²"But I tell you, in this you are not right,
  for God is greater than man.
¹³Why do you complain to him
  that he answers none of man's words?^a
¹⁴For God does speak—now one way, now
  another—
  though man may not perceive it.
¹⁵In a dream, in a vision of the night,
  when deep sleep falls on men
  as they slumber in their beds,
¹⁶he may speak in their ears
  and terrify them with warnings,
¹⁷to turn man from wrongdoing
  and keep him from pride,

¹⁸to preserve his soul from the pit,^b
  his life from perishing by the sword.^c
¹⁹Or a man may be chastened on a bed of
  pain
  with constant distress in his bones,
²⁰so that his very being finds food repulsive
  and his soul loathes the choicest meal.
²¹His flesh wastes away to nothing,
  and his bones, once hidden, now stick
  out.
²²His soul draws near to the pit,^d
  and his life to the messengers of death.^e

²³"Yet if there is an angel on his side
  as a mediator, one out of a thousand,
  to tell a man what is right for him,
²⁴to be gracious to him and say,
  'Spare him from going down to the pit;^f
  I have found a ransom for him'—
²⁵then his flesh is renewed like a child's;
  it is restored as in the days of his youth.
²⁶He prays to God and finds favour with
  him,
  he sees God's face and shouts for joy;
  he is restored by God to his righteous
  state.
²⁷Then he comes to men and says,
  'I have sinned, and perverted what was
  right,
  but I did not get what I deserved.
²⁸He redeemed my soul from going down to
  the pit,^g
  and I shall live to enjoy the light.'

²⁹"God does all these things to a man—
  twice, even three times—
³⁰to turn back his soul from the pit,^h
  that the light of life may shine on him.

³¹"Pay attention, Job, and listen to me;
  be silent, and I will speak.
³²If you have anything to say, answer me;
  speak up, for I want you to be cleared.
³³But if not, then listen to me;
  be silent, and I will teach you wisdom."

34 Then Elihu said:

²"Hear my words, you wise men;
  listen to me, you men of learning.
³For the ear tests words
  as the tongue tastes food.
⁴Let us discern for ourselves what is right;
  let us learn together what is good.

⁵"Job says, 'I am innocent,
  but God denies me justice.
⁶Although I am right,
  I am considered a liar;
  although I am guiltless,
  his arrow inflicts an incurable wound.'
⁷What man is like Job,
  who drinks scorn like water?
⁸He keeps company with evildoers;
  he associates with wicked men.
⁹For he says, 'It profits a man nothing
  when he tries to please God.'

---

^a13 Or *that he does not answer for any of his actions*   ^b18 Or *preserve him from the grave*
^c18 Or *from crossing the River*   ^d22 Or *He draws near to the grave*   ^e22 Or *to the dead*   ^f24 Or *grave*
^g28 Or *redeemed me from going down to the grave*   ^h30 Or *turn him back from the grave*

10"So listen to me, you men of
  understanding.
    Far be it from God to do evil,
    from the Almighty to do wrong.
11He repays a man for what he has done;
    he brings upon him what his conduct
    deserves.
12It is unthinkable that God would do
  wrong,
    that the Almighty would pervert
    justice.
13Who appointed him over the earth?
    Who put him in charge of the whole
    world?
14If it were his intention
    and he withdrew his spirit*a* and breath,
15all mankind would perish together
    and man would return to the dust.

16"If you have understanding, hear this;
    listen to what I say.
17Can he who hates justice govern?
    Will you condemn the just and mighty
    One?
18Is he not the One who says to kings, 'You
  are worthless,'
    and to nobles, 'You are wicked,'
19who shows no partiality to princes
    and does not favour the rich over the
    poor,
    for they are all the work of his hands?
20They die in an instant, in the middle of the
  night;
    the people are shaken and they pass
    away;
    the mighty are removed without human
    hand.

21"His eyes are on the ways of men;
    he sees their every step.
22There is no dark place, no deep shadow,
    where evildoers can hide.
23God has no need to examine men further,
    that they should come before him for
    judgment.
24Without enquiry he shatters the mighty
    and sets up others in their place.
25Because he takes note of their deeds,
    he overthrows them in the night and
    they are crushed.
26He punishes them for their wickedness
    where everyone can see them,
27because they turned from following him
    and had no regard for any of his ways.
28They caused the cry of the poor to come
    before him,
    so that he heard the cry of the needy.
29But if he remains silent, who can condemn
    him?
    If he hides his face, who can see him?
    Yet he is over man and nation alike,
30   to keep a godless man from ruling,
    from laying snares for the people.

31"Suppose a man says to God,
    'I am guilty but will offend no more.

32Teach me what I cannot see;
    if I have done wrong, I will not do so
    again.'
33Should God then reward you on your
  terms,
    when you refuse to repent?
    You must decide, not I;
    so tell me what you know.

34"Men of understanding declare,
    wise men who hear me say to me,
35'Job speaks without knowledge;
    his words lack insight.'
36Oh, that Job might be tested to the utmost
    for answering like a wicked man!
37To his sin he adds rebellion;
    scornfully he claps his hands among us
    and multiplies his words against God."

35 Then Elihu said:

2"Do you think this is just?
    You say, 'I shall be cleared by God.'*a*
3Yet you ask him, 'What profit is it to me,*b*
    and what do I gain by not sinning?'

4"I would like to reply to you
    and to your friends with you.
5Look up at the heavens and see;
    gaze at the clouds so high above you.
6If you sin, how does that affect him?
    If your sins are many, what does that do
    to him?
7If you are righteous, what do you give to
  him,
    or what does he receive from your
    hand?
8Your wickedness affects only a man like
  yourself,
    and your righteousness only the sons of
    men.

9"Men cry out under a load of oppression;
    they plead for relief from the arm of the
    powerful.
10But no-one says, 'Where is God my
  Maker,
    who gives songs in the night,
11who teaches more to us than to*c* the beasts
    of the earth
    and makes us wiser than*d* the birds of
    the air?'
12He does not answer when men cry out
    because of the arrogance of the wicked.
13Indeed, God does not listen to their empty
  plea;
    the Almighty pays no attention to it.
14How much less, then, will he listen
    when you say that you do not see him,
    that your case is before him
    and you must wait for him,
15and further, that his anger never punishes
    and he does not take the least notice of
    wickedness.*e*
16So Job opens his mouth with empty talk;
    without knowledge he multiplies
    words."

*a*14 Or *Spirit*   *a*2 Or *My righteousness is more than God's*   *b*3 Or *you*
*c*11 Or *teaches us by*   *d*11 Or *us wise by*
*e*15 Symmachus, Theodotion and Vulgate; the meaning of the Hebrew for this word is uncertain.

36 Elihu continued:

2"Bear with me a little longer and I will
show you
that there is more to be said on God's
behalf.
3I get my knowledge from afar;
I will ascribe justice to my Maker.
4Be assured that my words are not false;
one perfect in knowledge is with you.

5"God is mighty, but does not despise men;
he is mighty, and firm in his purpose.
6He does not keep the wicked alive
but gives the afflicted their rights.
7He does not take his eyes off the
righteous;
he enthrones them with kings
and exalts them for ever.
8But if men are bound in chains,
held fast by cords of affliction,
9he tells them what they have done—
that they have sinned arrogantly.
10He makes them listen to correction
and commands them to repent of their
evil.
11If they obey and serve him,
they will spend the rest of their days in
prosperity
and their years in contentment.
12But if they do not listen,
they will perish by the sword*a*
and die without knowledge.

13"The godless in heart harbour resentment;
even when he fetters them, they do not
cry for help.
14They die in their youth,
among male prostitutes of the shrines.
15But those who suffer he delivers in their
suffering;
he speaks to them in their affliction.

16"He is wooing you from the jaws of
distress
to a spacious place free from restriction,
to the comfort of your table laden with
choice food.
17But now you are laden with the judgment
due to the wicked;
judgment and justice have taken hold of
you.
18Be careful that no-one entices you by
riches;
do not let a large bribe turn you aside.
19Would your wealth
or even all your mighty efforts
sustain you so you would not be in
distress?
20Do not long for the night,
to drag people away from their homes.*b*
21Beware of turning to evil,
which you seem to prefer to affliction.

22"God is exalted in his power.
Who is a teacher like him?
23Who has prescribed his ways for him,

or said to him, 'You have done wrong'?
24Remember to extol his work,
which men have praised in song.
25All mankind has seen it;
men gaze on it from afar.
26How great is God—beyond our
understanding!
The number of his years is past finding
out.

27"He draws up the drops of water,
which distil as rain to the streams;*c*
28the clouds pour down their moisture
and abundant showers fall on mankind.
29Who can understand how he spreads out
the clouds,
how he thunders from his pavilion?
30See how he scatters his lightning about
him,
bathing the depths of the sea.
31This is the way he governs*d* the nations
and provides food in abundance.
32He fills his hands with lightning
and commands it to strike its mark.
33His thunder announces the coming storm;
even the cattle make known its
approach.*e*

37 "At this my heart pounds
and leaps from its place.
2Listen! Listen to the roar of his voice,
to the rumbling that comes from his
mouth.
3He unleashes his lightning beneath the
whole heaven
and sends it to the ends of the earth.
4After that comes the sound of his roar;
he thunders with his majestic voice.
When his voice resounds,
he holds nothing back.
5God's voice thunders in marvellous ways;
he does great things beyond our
understanding.
6He says to the snow, 'Fall on the earth,'
and to the rain shower, 'Be a mighty
downpour.'
7So that all men he has made may know his
work,
he stops every man from his labour.*a*
8The animals take cover;
they remain in their dens.
9The tempest comes out from its chamber,
the cold from the driving winds.
10The breath of God produces ice,
and the broad waters become frozen.
11He loads the clouds with moisture;
he scatters his lightning through them.
12At his direction they swirl around
over the face of the whole earth
to do whatever he commands them.
13He brings the clouds to punish men,
or to water his earth*b* and show his love.

14"Listen to this, Job;
stop and consider God's wonders.
15Do you know how God controls the clouds
and makes his lightning flash?

---

*a*12 Or *will cross the River*   *b*20 The meaning of the Hebrew for verses 18–20 is uncertain.
*c*27 Or *distil from the mist as rain*   *d*31 Or *nourishes*
*e*33 Or *announces his coming—/ the One zealous against evil*   *a*7 Or / *he fills all men with fear by his power*
*b*13 Or *to favour them*

16Do you know how the clouds hang poised,
  those wonders of him who is perfect in
    knowledge?
17You who swelter in your clothes
  when the land lies hushed under the
    south wind,
18can you join him in spreading out the
    skies,
  hard as a mirror of cast bronze?

19"Tell us what we should say to him;
  we cannot draw up our case because of
    our darkness.
20Should he be told that I want to speak?
  Would any man ask to be swallowed up?
21Now no-one can look at the sun,
  bright as it is in the skies
after the wind has swept them clean.
22Out of the north he comes in golden
    splendour;
  God comes in awesome majesty.
23The Almighty is beyond our reach and
    exalted in power;
  in his justice and great righteousness, he
    does not oppress.
24Therefore, men revere him,
  for does he not have regard for all the
    wise in heart?"c

The Lord Speaks

38 Then the Lord answered Job out of
the storm. He said:

2"Who is this that darkens my counsel
  with words without knowledge?
3Brace yourself like a man;
  I will question you,
  and you shall answer me.

4"Where were you when I laid the earth's
    foundation?
  Tell me, if you understand.
5Who marked off its dimensions? Surely
    you know!
  Who stretched a measuring line across
    it?
6On what were its footings set,
  or who laid its cornerstone—
7while the morning stars sang together
  and all the angelsa shouted for joy?

8"Who shut up the sea behind doors
  when it burst forth from the womb,
9when I made the clouds its garment
  and wrapped it in thick darkness,
10when I fixed limits for it
  and set its doors and bars in place,
11when I said, 'This far you may come and
    no farther;
  here is where your proud waves halt'?

12"Have you ever given orders to the
    morning,
  or shown the dawn its place,
13that it might take the earth by the edges
  and shake the wicked out of it?

14The earth takes shape like clay under a
    seal;
  its features stand out like those of a
    garment.
15The wicked are denied their light,
  and their upraised arm is broken.

16"Have you journeyed to the springs of the
    sea
  or walked in the recesses of the deep?
17Have the gates of death been shown to
    you?
  Have you seen the gates of the shadow
    of death?b
18Have you comprehended the vast
    expanses of the earth?
  Tell me, if you know all this.

19"What is the way to the abode of light?
  And where does darkness reside?
20Can you take them to their places?
  Do you know the paths to their
    dwellings?
21Surely you know, for you were already
    born!
  You have lived so many years!

22"Have you entered the storehouses of the
    snow
  or seen the storehouses of the hail,
23which I reserve for times of trouble,
  for days of war and battle?
24What is the way to the place where the
    lightning is dispersed,
  or the place where the east winds are
    scattered over the earth?
25Who cuts a channel for the torrents of rain,
  and a path for the thunderstorm,
26to water a land where no man lives,
  a desert with no-one in it,
27to satisfy a desolate wasteland
  and make it sprout with grass?
28Does the rain have a father?
  Who fathers the drops of dew?
29From whose womb comes the ice?
  Who gives birth to the frost from the
    heavens
30when the waters become hard as stone,
  when the surface of the deep is frozen?

31"Can you bind the beautifulc Pleiades?
  Can you loose the cords of Orion?
32Can you bring forth the constellations in
    their seasonsd
  or lead out the Beare with its cubs?
33Do you know the laws of the heavens?
  Can you set up ⌊God's f⌋ dominion over
    the earth?

34"Can you raise your voice to the clouds
  and cover yourself with a flood of
    water?
35Do you send the lightning bolts on their
    way?
  Do they report to you, 'Here we are'?
36Who endowed the heartg with wisdom
  or gave understanding to the mind?h

---

c24 Or for he does not have regard for any who think they are wise.   a7 Hebrew the sons of God
b17 Or gates of deep shadows   c31 Or the twinkling; or the chains of the
d32 Or the morning star in its season   e32 Or out Leo   f33 Or his; or their
g36 The meaning of the Hebrew for this word is uncertain.
h36 The meaning of the Hebrew for this word is uncertain.

37Who has the wisdom to count the clouds?
Who can tip over the water jars of the
heavens
38when the dust becomes hard
and the clods of earth stick together?

39"Do you hunt the prey for the lioness
and satisfy the hunger of the lions
40when they crouch in their dens
or lie in wait in a thicket?
41Who provides food for the raven
when its young cry out to God
and wander about for lack of food?

39 "Do you know when the mountain
goats give birth?
Do you watch when the doe bears her
fawn?
2Do you count the months till they bear?
Do you know the time they give birth?
3They crouch down and bring forth their
young;
their labour pains are ended.
4Their young thrive and grow strong in the
wilds;
they leave and do not return.

5"Who let the wild donkey go free?
Who untied his ropes?
6I gave him the wasteland as his home,
the salt flats as his habitat.
7He laughs at the commotion in the town;
he does not hear a driver's shout.
8He ranges the hills for his pasture
and searches for any green thing.

9"Will the wild ox consent to serve you?
Will he stay by your manger at night?
10Can you hold him to the furrow with a
harness?
Will he till the valleys behind you?
11Will you rely on him for his great strength?
Will you leave your heavy work to him?
12Can you trust him to bring in your grain
and gather it to your threshing-floor?

13"The wings of the ostrich flap joyfully,
but they cannot compare with the
pinions and feathers of the stork.
14She lays her eggs on the ground
and lets them warm in the sand,
15unmindful that a foot may crush them,
that some wild animal may trample
them.
16She treats her young harshly, as if they
were not hers;
she cares not that her labour was in
vain,
17for God did not endow her with wisdom
or give her a share of good sense.
18Yet when she spreads her feathers to run,
she laughs at horse and rider.

19"Do you give the horse his strength
or clothe his neck with a flowing mane?
20Do you make him leap like a locust,
striking terror with his proud snorting?
21He paws fiercely, rejoicing in his strength,
and charges into the fray.

22He laughs at fear, afraid of nothing;
he does not shy away from the sword.
23The quiver rattles against his side,
along with the flashing spear and lance.
24In frenzied excitement he eats up the
ground;
he cannot stand still when the trumpet
sounds.
25At the blast of the trumpet he snorts,
'Aha!'
He catches the scent of battle from afar,
the shout of commanders and the battle
cry.

26"Does the hawk take flight by your
wisdom
and spread his wings towards the south?
27Does the eagle soar at your command
and build his nest on high?
28He dwells on a cliff and stays there at
night;
a rocky crag is his stronghold.
29From there he seeks out his food;
his eyes detect it from afar.
30His young ones feast on blood,
and where the slain are, there is he."

40 The LORD said to Job:

2"Will the one who contends with the
Almighty correct him?
Let him who accuses God answer him!"

3Then Job answered the LORD:

4"I am unworthy—how can I reply to you?
I put my hand over my mouth.
5I spoke once, but I have no answer—
twice, but I will say no more."

6Then the LORD spoke to Job out of the
storm:

7"Brace yourself like a man;
I will question you,
and you shall answer me.

8"Would you discredit my justice?
Would you condemn me to justify
yourself?
9Do you have an arm like God's,
and can your voice thunder like his?
10Then adorn yourself with glory and
splendour,
and clothe yourself in honour and
majesty.
11Unleash the fury of your wrath,
look at every proud man and bring him
low,
12look at every proud man and humble him,
crush the wicked where they stand.
13Bury them all in the dust together;
shroud their faces in the grave.
14Then I myself will admit to you
that your own right hand can save you.

15"Look at the behemoth,a
which I made along with you
and which feeds on grass like an ox.

---

a15 Possibly the hippopotamus or the elephant

16What strength he has in his loins,
   what power in the muscles of his belly!
17His tail*b* sways like a cedar;
   the sinews of his thighs are close-knit.
18His bones are tubes of bronze,
   his limbs like rods of iron.
19He ranks first among the works of God,
   yet his Maker can approach him with his
      sword.
20The hills bring him their produce,
   and all the wild animals play nearby.
21Under the lotus plant he lies,
   hidden among the reeds in the marsh.
22The lotuses conceal him in their shadow;
   the poplars by the stream surround him.
23When the river rages, he is not alarmed;
   he is secure, though the Jordan should
      surge against his mouth.
24Can anyone capture him by the eyes,*c*
   or trap him and pierce his nose?

41 "Can you pull in the leviathan*a* with a
   fishhook
   or tie down his tongue with a rope?
2Can you put a cord through his nose
   or pierce his jaw with a hook?
3Will he keep begging you for mercy?
   Will he speak to you with gentle words?
4Will he make an agreement with you
   for you to take him as your slave for
      life?
5Can you make a pet of him like a bird
   or put him on a leash for your girls?
6Will traders barter for him?
   Will they divide him up among the
      merchants?
7Can you fill his hide with harpoons
   or his head with fishing spears?
8If you lay a hand on him,
   you will remember the struggle and
      never do it again!
9Any hope of subduing him is false;
   the mere sight of him is overpowering.
10No-one is fierce enough to rouse him.
   Who then is able to stand against me?
11Who has a claim against me that I must
      pay?
   Everything under heaven belongs to me.

12"I will not fail to speak of his limbs,
   his strength and his graceful form.
13Who can strip off his outer coat?
   Who would approach him with a bridle?
14Who dares open the doors of his mouth,
   ringed about with his fearsome teeth?
15His back has*b* rows of shields
   tightly sealed together;
16each is so close to the next
   that no air can pass between.
17They are joined fast to one another;
   they cling together and cannot be
      parted.
18His snorting throws out flashes of light;
   his eyes are like the rays of dawn.
19Firebrands stream from his mouth;
   sparks of fire shoot out.
20Smoke pours from his nostrils
   as from a boiling pot over a fire of reeds.

21His breath sets coals ablaze,
   and flames dart from his mouth.
22Strength resides in his neck;
   dismay goes before him.
23The folds of his flesh are tightly joined;
   they are firm and immovable.
24His chest is hard as rock,
   hard as a lower millstone.
25When he rises up, the mighty are terrified;
   they retreat before his thrashing.
26The sword that reaches him has no effect,
   nor does the spear or the dart or the
      javelin.
27Iron he treats like straw
   and bronze like rotten wood.
28Arrows do not make him flee;
   slingstones are like chaff to him.
29A club seems to him but a piece of straw;
   he laughs at the rattling of the lance.
30His undersides are jagged potsherds,
   leaving a trail in the mud like a
      threshing-sledge.
31He makes the depths churn like a boiling
      cauldron
   and stirs up the sea like a pot of
      ointment.
32Behind him he leaves a glistening wake;
   one would think the deep had white hair.
33Nothing on earth is his equal—
   a creature without fear.
34He looks down on all that are haughty;
   he is king over all that are proud.''

Job

42 Then Job replied to the LORD:

2"I know that you can do all things;
   no plan of yours can be thwarted.
3You asked, 'Who is this that obscures
      my counsel without knowledge?'
   Surely I spoke of things I did not
      understand,
   things too wonderful for me to know.

4"You said, 'Listen now, and I will
      speak;
   I will question you,
   and you shall answer me.'
5My ears had heard of you
   but now my eyes have seen you.
6Therefore I despise myself
   and repent in dust and ashes.''

Epilogue

7After the LORD had said these things to
Job, he said to Eliphaz the Temanite, ''I am
angry with you and your two friends, because you have not spoken of me what is
right, as my servant Job has. 8So now take
seven bulls and seven rams and go to my
servant Job and sacrifice a burnt offering for
yourselves. My servant Job will pray for you,
and I will accept his prayer and not deal with
you according to your folly. You have not
spoken of me what is right, as my servant Job
has.'' 9So Eliphaz the Temanite, Bildad the
Shuhite and Zophar the Naamathite did what
the LORD told them; and the LORD accepted
Job's prayer.

---

*b*17 Possibly trunk   *c*24 Or *by a water hole*   *a*1 Possibly the crocodile   *b*15 Or *His pride is his*

JOB 40:3–5; 42:1–6
'Surely I spoke of things I did not understand . . . My ears had heard of you but now my eyes have seen you. Therefore I despise myself and repent in dust and ashes' (42:3, 5, 6).

GOD ANSWERS, YES HE DOES. Job's response to God's revelation of himself to Job is found in these two short passages. Job has not received pat, easy answers to his problem. His questionings are in large part still unresolved. He has not found a universal cure for all the world's suffering. He still has a lot of searching to do.

Job realized all along, correctly, that the conventional wisdom of his day – prosperity for the righteous, poverty for the wicked – did not square with the facts of his situation. His honesty prevented him from shutting his eyes to the facts. Absolutely correctly he refused to accept, parrot fashion, the tradition as he had been taught it. Where he went wrong was in confusing that tradition with God. He realized, dimly, that God was too great for him to understand – and he let that lead him not only to doubt. but to wholesale disbelief. He went astray because he could not, for the moment, find the narrow way of truth.

When God came he did not just bring an answer. He brought himself. As Clifford Kew says 'a direct vision of God, a first-hand awareness of the reality that is in him . . . will not explain all, but the experience of his present, powerful personality will bring an awareness of ultimate truth and of the relative unimportance of unresolved mental conflicts.

God grant me 'a direct vision of God'.

→454

JOB 42:7–17
'The LORD made him prosperous again' (v. 10).

WHAT AN ANTI-CLIMAX! People sometimes look at the end, to see how a story finishes, before reading the rest of a book. Most of us don't have to do that with Job. We know his fortunes will be restored. Does that detract from the point of the work? Job's revelation of God, and peace with God, come before his restoration. Without these last few verses the book would still be true. Whether or not Job is brought back to favour seems irrelevant.

It is true to say that Job's temptation, after being brought back to favour, could be to side with the 'friends' and the accepted wisdom. We can be sure he did not do that. On the contrary, he prayed for his friends (v. 10), offering sacrifices on their behalf – and through Job's intercession the friends also were restored to favour. There are further hints of New Testament salvation theology here; the suffering of one on behalf of another; the intercession of one who is right with God on behalf of those who are not.

Without his suffering, without rejection by his friends, Job would never have been thrown back on God so completely, would never have learnt to know him in this new way, not just by the understanding of the mind, but in the adversity of the heart. Few of us have such traumas as Job, but we all have our sorrows. In them, though we may doubt and question, let us never despair – for God is with us.

God is far and away beyond our understanding, yet closer to us than the air we breathe.

→459

[10]After Job had prayed for his friends, the LORD made him prosperous again and gave him twice as much as he had before. [11]All his brothers and sisters and everyone who had known him before came and ate with him in his house. They comforted and consoled him over all the trouble the LORD had brought upon him, and each one gave him a piece of silver[a] and a gold ring.

[12]The LORD blessed the latter part of Job's life more than the first. He had fourteen thousand sheep, six thousand camels, a thousand yoke of oxen and a thousand donkeys. [13]And he also had seven sons and three daughters. [14]The first daughter he named Jemimah, the second Keziah and the third Keren-Happuch. [15]Nowhere in all the land were there found women as beautiful as Job's daughters, and their father granted them an inheritance along with their brothers.

[16]After this, Job lived a hundred and forty years; he saw his children and their children to the fourth generation. [17]And so he died, old and full of years.

---

[a]11 Hebrew *him a kesitah*; a kesitah was a unit of money of unknown weight and value.

Psalms

BOOK I

Psalms 1–41

Psalm 1

¹Blessed is the man
 who does not walk in the counsel of the
  wicked
 or stand in the way of sinners
 or sit in the seat of mockers.
²But his delight is in the law of the LORD,
 and on his law he meditates day and
  night.
³He is like a tree planted by streams of
  water,
 which yields its fruit in season
and whose leaf does not wither.
 Whatever he does prospers.

⁴Not so the wicked!
 They are like chaff
 that the wind blows away.
⁵Therefore the wicked will not stand in the
  judgment,
 nor sinners in the assembly of the
  righteous.

⁶For the LORD watches over the way of the
  righteous,
 but the way of the wicked will perish.

Psalm 2

¹Why do the nations conspire*ᵃ*
 and the peoples plot in vain?
²The kings of the earth take their stand
 and the rulers gather together against
  the LORD
 and against his Anointed One.*ᵇ*
³"Let us break their chains," they say,
 "and throw off their fetters."

⁴The One enthroned in heaven laughs;
 the Lord scoffs at them.
⁵Then he rebukes them in his anger
 and terrifies them in his wrath, saying,
⁶"I have installed my King*ᶜ*
 on Zion, my holy hill."

⁷I will proclaim the decree of the LORD:

He said to me, "You are my Son;*ᵈ*
 today I have become your Father.*ᵉ*
⁸Ask of me,
 and I will make the nations your
  inheritance,
 the ends of the earth your possession.*ᶠ*
⁹You will rule them with an iron sceptre;*ᶠ*
 you will dash them to pieces like
  pottery."

¹⁰Therefore, you kings, be wise;
 be warned, you rulers of the earth.
¹¹Serve the LORD with fear
 and rejoice with trembling.
¹²Kiss the Son, lest he be angry
 and you be destroyed in your way,
 for his wrath can flare up in a moment.
 Blessed are all who take refuge in him.

Psalm 3

*A psalm of David. When he fled from his son
Absalom.*

¹O LORD, how many are my foes!
 How many rise up against me!
²Many are saying of me,
 "God will not deliver him."   *Selahᵃ*

³But you are a shield around me, O LORD;
 you bestow glory on me and lift*ᵇ* up my
  head.
⁴To the LORD I cry aloud,
 and he answers me from his holy hill.
  Selah

⁵I lie down and sleep;
 I wake again, because the LORD sustains
  me.
⁶I will not fear the tens of thousands
 drawn up against me on every side.

⁷Arise, O LORD!
 Deliver me, O my God!
Strike all my enemies on the jaw;
 break the teeth of the wicked.

⁸From the LORD comes deliverance.
 May your blessing be on your people.
  Selah

ᵃ1 Hebrew; Septuagint *rage*   *ᵇ2* Or *anointed one*   *ᶜ6* Or *king*   *ᵈ7* Or *son*; also in verse 12
ᵉ7 Or *have begotten you*   *ᶠ9* Or *will break them with a rod of iron*
ᵃ2 A word of uncertain meaning, occurring frequently in the Psalms; possibly a musical term
ᵇ3 Or *LORD, / my Glorious One, who lifts*

Psalm 4

For the director of music. With stringed
instruments. A psalm of David.

[1]Answer me when I call to you,
O my righteous God.
Give me relief from my distress;
be merciful to me and hear my prayer.

[2]How long, O men, will you turn my glory
into shame?[a]
How long will you love delusions and
seek false gods?[b]   *Selah*
[3]Know that the LORD has set apart the
godly for himself;
the LORD will hear when I call to him.

[4]In your anger do not sin;
when you are on your beds,
search your hearts and be silent.   *Selah*
[5]Offer right sacrifices
and trust in the LORD.

[6]Many are asking, "Who can show us any
good?"
Let the light of your face shine upon us,
O LORD.
[7]You have filled my heart with greater joy
than when their grain and new wine
abound.
[8]I will lie down and sleep in peace,
for you alone, O LORD,
make me dwell in safety.

Psalm 5

For the director of music. For flutes.
A psalm of David.

[1]Give ear to my words, O LORD,
consider my sighing.
[2]Listen to my cry for help,
my King and my God,
for to you I pray.
[3]In the morning, O LORD, you hear my
voice;
in the morning I lay my requests before
you
and wait in expectation.

[4]You are not a God who takes pleasure in
evil;
with you the wicked cannot dwell.
[5]The arrogant cannot stand in your
presence;
you hate all who do wrong.
[6]You destroy those who tell lies;
bloodthirsty and deceitful men
the LORD abhors.

[7]But I, by your great mercy,
will come into your house;
in reverence will I bow down
towards your holy temple.
[8]Lead me, O LORD, in your righteousness
because of my enemies—
make straight your way before me.

[9]Not a word from their mouth can be
trusted;
their heart is filled with destruction.

Their throat is an open grave;
with their tongue they speak deceit.
[10]Declare them guilty, O God!
Let their intrigues be their downfall.
Banish them for their many sins,
for they have rebelled against you.

[11]But let all who take refuge in you be glad;
let them ever sing for joy.
Spread your protection over them,
that those who love your name may
rejoice in you.
[12]For surely, O LORD, you bless the
righteous;
you surround them with your favour as
with a shield.

Psalm 6

For the director of music. With stringed
instruments. According to *sheminith*.[a]
A psalm of David.

[1]O LORD, do not rebuke me in your anger
or discipline me in your wrath.
[2]Be merciful to me, LORD, for I am faint;
O LORD, heal me, for my bones are in
agony.
[3]My soul is in anguish.
How long, O LORD, how long?

[4]Turn, O LORD, and deliver me;
save me because of your unfailing love.
[5]No-one remembers you when he is dead.
Who praises you from his grave?[b]

[6]I am worn out from groaning;
all night long I flood my bed with
weeping
and drench my couch with tears.
[7]My eyes grow weak with sorrow;
they fail because of all my foes.

[8]Away from me, all you who do evil,
for the LORD has heard my weeping.
[9]The LORD has heard my cry for mercy;
the LORD accepts my prayer.
[10]All my enemies will be ashamed and
dismayed;
they will turn back in sudden disgrace.

Psalm 7

A *shiggaion*[a] of David, which he sang to the
LORD concerning Cush, a Benjamite.

[1]O LORD my God, I take refuge in you;
save and deliver me from all who pursue
me,
[2]or they will tear me like a lion
and rip me to pieces with no-one to
rescue me.

[3]O LORD my God, if I have done this
and there is guilt on my hands—
[4]if I have done evil to him who is at peace
with me
or without cause have robbed my foe—
[5]then let my enemy pursue and overtake
me;
let him trample my life to the ground
and make me sleep in the dust.   *Selah*

a2 Or you dishonour my Glorious One   b2 Or seek lies   aTitle: Probably a musical term
b5 Hebrew Sheol   aTitle: Probably a literary or musical term

6Arise, O LORD, in your anger;
  rise up against the rage of my enemies.
  Awake, my God; decree justice.
7Let the assembled peoples gather round
      you.
  Rule over them from on high;
8   let the LORD judge the peoples.
  Judge me, O LORD, according to my
      righteousness,
  according to my integrity, O Most High.
9O righteous God,
  who searches minds and hearts,
  bring to an end the violence of the wicked
  and make the righteous secure.

10My shield*b* is God Most High,
  who saves the upright in heart.
11God is a righteous judge,
  a God who expresses his wrath every
      day.
12If he does not relent,
  he*c* will sharpen his sword;
  he will bend and string his bow.
13He has prepared his deadly weapons;
  he makes ready his flaming arrows.

14He who is pregnant with evil
  and conceives trouble gives birth to
      disillusionment.
15He who digs a hole and scoops it out
  falls into the pit he has made.
16The trouble he causes recoils on himself;
  his violence comes down on his own
      head.

17I will give thanks to the LORD because of
      his righteousness
  and will sing praise to the name of the
      LORD Most High.

Psalm 8

For the director of music. According to *gittith.*ᵃ
A psalm of David.

1O LORD, our Lord,
  how majestic is your name in all the
      earth!

  You have set your glory
  above the heavens.
2From the lips of children and infants
  you have ordained praise*b*
  because of your enemies,
  to silence the foe and the avenger.

3When I consider your heavens,
  the work of your fingers,
  the moon and the stars,
  which you have set in place,
4what is man that you are mindful of him,
  the son of man that you care for him?
5You made him a little lower than the
      heavenly beings*c*
  and crowned him with glory and
      honour.

6You made him ruler over the works of
  your hands;

  you put everything under his feet:
7all flocks and herds,
  and the beasts of the field,
8the birds of the air,
  and the fish of the sea,
  all that swim the paths of the seas.

9O LORD, our Lord,
  how majestic is your name in all the
      earth!

Psalm 9ᵃ

For the director of music. To ⌞the tune of⌟ "The
Death of the Son". A psalm of David.

1I will praise you, O LORD, with all my
      heart;
  I will tell of all your wonders.
2I will be glad and rejoice in you;
  I will sing praise to your name, O Most
      High.

3My enemies turn back;
  they stumble and perish before you.
4For you have upheld my right and my
      cause;
  you have sat on your throne, judging
      righteously.
5You have rebuked the nations and
      destroyed the wicked;
  you have blotted out their name for ever
      and ever.
6Endless ruin has overtaken the enemy,
  you have uprooted their cities;
  even the memory of them has perished.

7The LORD reigns for ever;
  he has established his throne for
      judgment.
8He will judge the world in righteousness;
  he will govern the peoples with justice.
9The LORD is a refuge for the oppressed,
  a stronghold in times of trouble.
10Those who know your name will trust in
      you,
  for you, LORD, have never forsaken
      those who seek you.

11Sing praises to the LORD, enthroned in
      Zion;
  proclaim among the nations what he has
      done.
12For he who avenges blood remembers;
  he does not ignore the cry of the
      afflicted.

13O LORD, see how my enemies persecute
      me!
  Have mercy and lift me up from the
      gates of death,
14that I may declare your praises
  in the gates of the Daughter of Zion
  and there rejoice in your salvation.
15The nations have fallen into the pit they
      have dug;
  their feet are caught in the net they have
      hidden.

---

*b10 Or sovereign   *c12 Or If a man does not repent, / God
*b2 Or strength   *c5 Or than God
*ᵃPsalms 9 and 10 may have been originally a single acrostic poem, the stanzas of which begin with the successive
letters of the Hebrew alphabet. In the Septuagint they constitute one psalm.   *ᵃTitle: Probably a musical term

PSALM 9 (especially vv. 1, 2, 15–20)
'The needy will not always be forgotten, nor the hope of the afflicted ever perish' (v. 18).

THE PSALMISTS are often preoccupied by the idea that justice is a long time coming. Over and again they complain that the wicked prosper and the righteous suffer. They look forward to a day when God will judge, and the wicked get what they deserve. But that judgement is delayed. It does not come as soon as we would hope and expect.

Why does it not come? God, says the psalmist, 'forgets'. 'The idea of forgetting is one of the figures of speech adopted by the psalmist in order to express the "delayed action" of God.' (Norman Snaith)

This delayed action also appears in Psalm 10, which Leonard Griffith entitles 'God hides'. Such expressions remind us of the many situations where God appears to be absent. Often we think he is absent when we're in trouble. It is then that so many of us call on him and complain. But when things go well materially there are just as many for whom God appears to be absent. Exceptions occur, of course, and the USA with its high proportion of churchgoers may be one. Or is it such an exception? Is God really present amongst those who call on his name in prosperity? Or is he simply delaying judgement?

We have the Pharisees in the New Testament, and also many prosperous, self-satisfied people in the Old Testament to cite as examples. It may appear that God 'remembers' those who prosper and who worship him loudly, but take heed of the psalmist's words:

> 'The needy shall not always be forgotten,
> and the hope of the poor shall not perish for ever.'

It is not always those who make most noise about their belief in God who are closest to him.

→460

PSALM 23
'The LORD is my shepherd, I shall not be in want' (v. 1).

UNFAILING CARE. This must be the best known psalm in the whole psalter. Because of that, there must be also a great danger of allowing the words to pass through the mind without finding any lodging place in thought.

Although it is frequently referred to as the 'shepherd psalm' it will be noticed that only verses 1–4 are concerned with that theme. Verse 5 describes what a generous host prepares for a guest and the last verse sums up the psalmist's confidence in God. The whole psalm speaks of God's care and protection and it is that aspect which has endeared it to readers throughout the ages. To quote Alexander MacLaren, 'The world could spare many a large book better than this sunny little psalm. It has dried many tears and supplied the mould into which many hearts have poured their peaceful faith.'

The psalmist is not chiefly concerned with his troubles and afflictions but they do become part of the poem that he writes. That is important, for it stresses the fact that God's presence provides succour in suffering and not immunity from it.

To help us reflect upon this divine care it might be helpful to consider some aspects of a shepherd's work as described in Isaiah 40:11: 'He gathers the lambs in his arms and carries them close to his heart; he gently leads those that have young.'

The ultimate in divine protection is seen in Jesus who said, 'I am the good shepherd. The good shepherd lays down his life for the sheep' (John 10:11).

To such care we can confidently commit ourselves.

→471

¹⁶The LORD is known by his justice;
  the wicked are ensnared by the work of
    their hands.   *Higgaion.^b Selah*

¹⁷The wicked return to the grave,^c
  all the nations that forget God.
¹⁸But the needy will not always be forgotten,
  nor the hope of the afflicted ever perish.

¹⁹Arise, O LORD, let not man triumph;
  let the nations be judged in your
    presence.
²⁰Strike them with terror, O LORD;
  let the nations know they are but men.
              Selah

Psalm 10^a

¹Why, O LORD, do you stand far off?
  Why do you hide yourself in times of
    trouble?

²In his arrogance the wicked man hunts
    down the weak,
  who are caught in the schemes he
    devises.
³He boasts of the cravings of his heart;
  he blesses the greedy and reviles the
    LORD.
⁴In his pride the wicked does not seek him;
  in all his thoughts there is no room for
    God.
⁵His ways are always prosperous;
  he is haughty and your laws are far from
    him;
  he sneers at all his enemies.
⁶He says to himself, "Nothing will shake
    me;
  I'll always be happy and never have
    trouble."
⁷His mouth is full of curses and lies and
    threats;
  trouble and evil are under his tongue.
⁸He lies in wait near the villages;
  from ambush he murders the innocent,
  watching in secret for his victims.
⁹He lies in wait like a lion in cover;
  he lies in wait to catch the helpless;
  he catches the helpless and drags them
    off in his net.
¹⁰His victims are crushed, they collapse;
  they fall under his strength.
¹¹He says to himself, "God has forgotten;
  he covers his face and never sees."

¹²Arise, LORD! Lift up your hand, O God.
  Do not forget the helpless.
¹³Why does the wicked man revile God?
  Why does he say to himself,
    "He won't call me to account"?
¹⁴But you, O God, do see trouble and grief;
  you consider it to take it in hand.
  The victim commits himself to you;
  you are the helper of the fatherless.
¹⁵Break the arm of the wicked and evil man;
  call him to account for his wickedness
  that would not be found out.

¹⁶The LORD is King for ever and ever;
  the nations will perish from his land.
¹⁷You hear, O LORD, the desire of the
    afflicted;
  you encourage them, and you listen to
    their cry,
¹⁸defending the fatherless and the
    oppressed,
  in order that man, who is of the earth,
  may terrify no more.

Psalm 11

For the director of music. Of David.

¹In the LORD I take refuge.
  How then can you say to me:
    "Flee like a bird to your mountain.
²For look, the wicked bend their bows;
  they set their arrows against the strings
  to shoot from the shadows
    at the upright in heart.
³When the foundations are being
    destroyed,
  what can the righteous do?"^a

⁴The LORD is in his holy temple;
  the LORD is on his heavenly throne.
  He observes the sons of men;
  his eyes examine them.
⁵The LORD examines the righteous,
  but the wicked^b and those who love
    violence
  his soul hates.
⁶On the wicked he will rain
  fiery coals and burning sulphur;
  a scorching wind will be their lot.

⁷For the LORD is righteous,
  he loves justice;
  upright men will see his face.

Psalm 12

For the director of music. According to
sheminith.^a A psalm of David.

¹Help, LORD, for the godly are no more;
  the faithful have vanished from among
    men.
²Everyone lies to his neighbour;
  their flattering lips speak with
    deception.

³May the LORD cut off all flattering lips
  and every boastful tongue
⁴that says, "We will triumph with our
    tongues;
  we own our lips^b—who is our master?"

⁵"Because of the oppression of the weak
  and the groaning of the needy,
  I will now arise," says the LORD.
    "I will protect them from those who
    malign them."
⁶And the words of the LORD are flawless,
  like silver refined in a furnace of clay,
  purified seven times.

---

^b16 Or *Meditation*; possibly a musical notation   ^c17 Hebrew *Sheol*
^aPsalms 9 and 10 may have been originally a single acrostic poem, the stanzas of which begin with the successive letters of the Hebrew alphabet. In the Septuagint they constitute one psalm.
^a3 Or *what is the Righteous One doing*   ^b5 Or *The LORD, the Righteous One, examines the wicked,/*
^aTitle: Probably a musical term   ^b4 Or / *our lips are our ploughshares*

⁷O Lᴏʀᴅ, you will keep us safe
    and protect us from such people for
      ever.
⁸The wicked freely strut about
    when what is vile is honoured among
      men.

Psalm 13

For the director of music. A psalm of David.

¹How long, O Lᴏʀᴅ? Will you forget me for
    ever?
    How long will you hide your face from
      me?
²How long must I wrestle with my thoughts
    and every day have sorrow in my heart?
    How long will my enemy triumph over
      me?

³Look on me and answer, O Lᴏʀᴅ my God.
    Give light to my eyes, or I will sleep in
      death;
⁴my enemy will say, "I have overcome
    him,"
    and my foes will rejoice when I fall.

⁵But I trust in your unfailing love;
    my heart rejoices in your salvation.
⁶I will sing to the Lᴏʀᴅ,
    for he has been good to me.

Psalm 14

For the director of music. Of David.

¹The fool[a] says in his heart,
    "There is no God."
They are corrupt, their deeds are vile;
    there is no-one who does good.

²The Lᴏʀᴅ looks down from heaven
    on the sons of men
to see if there are any who understand,
    any who seek God.
³All have turned aside,
    they have together become corrupt;
there is no-one who does good,
    not even one.

⁴Will evildoers never learn—
    those who devour my people as men eat
      bread
    and who do not call on the Lᴏʀᴅ?
⁵There they are, overwhelmed with dread,
    for God is present in the company of the
      righteous.
⁶You evildoers frustrate the plans of the
    poor,
    but the Lᴏʀᴅ is their refuge.

⁷Oh, that salvation for Israel would come
    out of Zion!
    When the Lᴏʀᴅ restores the fortunes of
      his people,
    let Jacob rejoice and Israel be glad!

Psalm 15

A psalm of David.

¹Lᴏʀᴅ, who may dwell in your sanctuary?
    Who may live on your holy hill?

²He whose walk is blameless
    and who does what is righteous,
who speaks the truth from his heart
³ and has no slander on his tongue,
who does his neighbour no wrong
    and casts no slur on his fellow-man,
⁴who despises a vile man
    but honours those who fear the Lᴏʀᴅ,
who keeps his oath
    even when it hurts,
⁵who lends his money without usury
    and does not accept a bribe against the
      innocent.

He who does these things
    will never be shaken.

Psalm 16

A miktam[a] of David.

¹Keep me safe, O God,
    for in you I take refuge.

²I said to the Lᴏʀᴅ, "You are my Lord;
    apart from you I have no good thing."
³As for the saints who are in the land,
    they are the glorious ones in whom is all
      my delight.[b]
⁴The sorrows of those will increase
    who run after other gods.
I will not pour out their libations of blood
    or take up their names on my lips.

⁵Lᴏʀᴅ, you have assigned me my portion
    and my cup;
    you have made my lot secure.
⁶The boundary lines have fallen for me in
    pleasant places;
    surely I have a delightful inheritance.

⁷I will praise the Lᴏʀᴅ, who counsels me;
    even at night my heart instructs me.
⁸I have set the Lᴏʀᴅ always before me.
    Because he is at my right hand,
    I shall not be shaken.

⁹Therefore my heart is glad and my tongue
    rejoices;
    my body also will rest secure,
¹⁰because you will not abandon me to the
    grave,[c]
    nor will you let your Holy One[d] see
      decay.
¹¹You have made known[e] to me the path of
    life;
    you will fill me with joy in your
      presence,
    with eternal pleasures at your right
      hand.

Psalm 17

A prayer of David.

¹Hear, O Lᴏʀᴅ, my righteous plea;
    listen to my cry.
Give ear to my prayer—
    it does not rise from deceitful lips.
²May my vindication come from you;
    may your eyes see what is right.

---

[a]1 The Hebrew words rendered *fool* in Psalms denote one who is morally deficient.
[a]Title: Probably a literary or musical term
[b]3 Or *As for the pagan priests who are in the land / and the nobles in whom all delight, I said:*
[c]10 Hebrew *Sheol*   [d]10 Or *your faithful one*   [e]11 Or *You will make known*

³Though you probe my heart and examine
me at night,
though you test me, you will find
nothing;
I have resolved that my mouth will not
sin.
⁴As for the deeds of men—
by the word of your lips
I have kept myself
from the ways of the violent.
⁵My steps have held to your paths;
my feet have not slipped.

⁶I call on you, O God, for you will answer
me;
give ear to me and hear my prayer.
⁷Show the wonder of your great love,
you who save by your right hand
those who take refuge in you from their
foes.
⁸Keep me as the apple of your eye;
hide me in the shadow of your wings
⁹from the wicked who assail me,
from my mortal enemies who surround
me.

¹⁰They close up their callous hearts,
and their mouths speak with arrogance.
¹¹They have tracked me down, they now
surround me,
with eyes alert, to throw me to the
ground.
¹²They are like a lion hungry for prey,
like a great lion crouching in cover.

¹³Rise up, O LORD, confront them, bring
them down;
rescue me from the wicked by your
sword.
¹⁴O LORD, by your hand save me from such
men,
from men of this world whose reward is
in this life.

You still the hunger of those you cherish;
their sons have plenty,
and they store up wealth for their
children.
¹⁵And I—in righteousness I shall see your
face;
when I awake, I shall be satisfied with
seeing your likeness.

Psalm 18

For the director of music. Of David the servant
of the LORD. He sang to the LORD the words of
this song when the LORD delivered him from the
hand of all his enemies and from the hand of
Saul. He said:
¹I love you, O LORD, my strength.

²The LORD is my rock, my fortress and my
deliverer;
my God is my rock, in whom I take
refuge.
He is my shield and the horn*ᵃ* of my
salvation, my stronghold.

³I call to the LORD, who is worthy of praise,
and I am saved from my enemies.

⁴The cords of death entangled me;
the torrents of destruction overwhelmed
me.
⁵The cords of the grave*ᵇ* coiled around me;
the snares of death confronted me.
⁶In my distress I called to the LORD;
I cried to my God for help.
From his temple he heard my voice;
my cry came before him, into his ears.

⁷The earth trembled and quaked,
and the foundations of the mountains
shook;
they trembled because he was angry.
⁸Smoke rose from his nostrils;
consuming fire came from his mouth,
burning coals blazed out of it.
⁹He parted the heavens and came down;
dark clouds were under his feet.
¹⁰He mounted the cherubim and flew;
he soared on the wings of the wind.
¹¹He made darkness his covering, his
canopy around him—
the dark rain clouds of the sky.
¹²Out of the brightness of his presence
clouds advanced,
with hailstones and bolts of lightning.
¹³The LORD thundered from heaven;
the voice of the Most High resounded.*ᶜ*
¹⁴He shot his arrows and scattered ⌐the
enemies⌐,
great bolts of lightning and routed them.
¹⁵The valleys of the sea were exposed
and the foundations of the earth laid
bare
at your rebuke, O LORD,
at the blast of breath from your nostrils.

¹⁶He reached down from on high and took
hold of me;
he drew me out of deep waters.
¹⁷He rescued me from my powerful enemy,
from my foes, who were too strong for
me.
¹⁸They confronted me in the day of my
disaster,
but the LORD was my support.
¹⁹He brought me out into a spacious place;
he rescued me because he delighted in
me.

²⁰The LORD has dealt with me according to
my righteousness;
according to the cleanness of my hands
he has rewarded me.
²¹For I have kept the ways of the LORD;
I have not done evil by turning from my
God.
²²All his laws are before me;
I have not turned away from his
decrees.
²³I have been blameless before him
and have kept myself from sin.

ᵃ2 Horn here symbolises strength.   ᵇ5 Hebrew Sheol
*ᶜ13 Some Hebrew manuscripts and Septuagint (see also 2 Samuel 22:14); most Hebrew manuscripts resounded, /
amid hailstones and bolts of lightning*

²⁴The LORD has rewarded me according to
my righteousness,
according to the cleanness of my hands
in his sight.

²⁵To the faithful you show yourself faithful,
to the blameless you show yourself
blameless,
²⁶to the pure you show yourself pure,
but to the crooked you show yourself
shrewd.
²⁷You save the humble
but bring low those whose eyes are
haughty.
²⁸You, O LORD, keep my lamp burning;
my God turns my darkness into light.
²⁹With your help I can advance against a
troop;ᵈ
with my God I can scale a wall.

³⁰As for God, his way is perfect;
the word of the LORD is flawless.
He is a shield
for all who take refuge in him.
³¹For who is God besides the LORD?
And who is the Rock except our God?
³²It is God who arms me with strength
and makes my way perfect.
³³He makes my feet like the feet of a deer;
he enables me to stand on the heights.
³⁴He trains my hands for battle;
my arms can bend a bow of bronze.
³⁵You give me your shield of victory,
and your right hand sustains me;
you stoop down to make me great.
³⁶You broaden the path beneath me,
so that my ankles do not turn over.

³⁷I pursued my enemies and overtook them;
I did not turn back till they were
destroyed.
³⁸I crushed them so that they could not rise;
they fell beneath my feet.
³⁹You armed me with strength for battle;
you made my adversaries bow at my
feet.
⁴⁰You made my enemies turn their backs in
flight,
and I destroyed my foes.
⁴¹They cried for help, but there was no-one
to save them—
to the LORD, but he did not answer.
⁴²I beat them as fine as dust borne on the
wind;
I poured them out like mud in the
streets.

⁴³You have delivered me from the attacks of
the people;
you have made me the head of nations;
people I did not know are subject to
me.
⁴⁴As soon as they hear me, they obey me;
foreigners cringe before me.
⁴⁵They all lose heart;
they come trembling from their
strongholds.

⁴⁶The LORD lives! Praise be to my Rock!
Exalted be God my Saviour!
⁴⁷He is the God who avenges me,
who subdues nations under me,
⁴⁸ who saves me from my enemies.
You exalted me above my foes;
from violent men you rescued me.
⁴⁹Therefore I will praise you among the
nations, O LORD;
I will sing praises to your name.
⁵⁰He gives his king great victories;
he shows unfailing kindness to his
anointed,
to David and his descendants for ever.

Psalm 19

For the director of music. A psalm of David.

¹The heavens declare the glory of God;
the skies proclaim the work of his
hands.
²Day after day they pour forth speech;
night after night they display
knowledge.
³There is no speech or language
where their voice is not heard.ᵃ
⁴Their voiceᵇ goes out into all the earth,
their words to the ends of the world.

In the heavens he has pitched a tent for the
sun,
⁵ which is like a bridegroom coming forth
from his pavilion,
like a champion rejoicing to run his
course.
⁶It rises at one end of the heavens
and makes its circuit to the other;
nothing is hidden from its heat.

⁷The law of the LORD is perfect,
reviving the soul.
The statutes of the LORD are trustworthy,
making wise the simple.
⁸The precepts of the LORD are right,
giving joy to the heart.
The commands of the LORD are radiant,
giving light to the eyes.
⁹The fear of the LORD is pure,
enduring for ever.
The ordinances of the LORD are sure
and altogether righteous.
¹⁰They are more precious than gold,
than much pure gold;
they are sweeter than honey,
than honey from the comb.
¹¹By them is your servant warned;
in keeping them there is great reward.

¹²Who can discern his errors?
Forgive my hidden faults.
¹³Keep your servant also from wilful sins;
may they not rule over me.
Then will I be blameless,
innocent of great transgression.

¹⁴May the words of my mouth and the
meditation of my heart
be pleasing in your sight,
O LORD, my Rock and my Redeemer.

ᵈ29 Or can run through a barricade
ᵃ3 Or They have no speech, there are no words; I no sound is heard from them
ᵇ4 Septuagint, Jerome and Syriac; Hebrew line

Psalm 20

For the director of music. A psalm of David.

¹May the LORD answer you when you are in distress;
may the name of the God of Jacob protect you.
²May he send you help from the sanctuary and grant you support from Zion.
³May he remember all your sacrifices and accept your burnt offerings. *Selah*
⁴May he give you the desire of your heart and make all your plans succeed.
⁵We will shout for joy when you are victorious
and will lift up our banners in the name of our God.

May the LORD grant all your requests.

⁶Now I know that the LORD saves his anointed;
he answers him from his holy heaven with the saving power of his right hand.
⁷Some trust in chariots and some in horses, but we trust in the name of the LORD our God.
⁸They are brought to their knees and fall, but we rise up and stand firm.

⁹O LORD, save the king!
Answer*a* us when we call!

Psalm 21

For the director of music. A psalm of David.

¹O LORD, the king rejoices in your strength.
How great is his joy in the victories you give!
²You have granted him the desire of his heart
and have not withheld the request of his lips. *Selah*
³You welcomed him with rich blessings and placed a crown of pure gold on his head.
⁴He asked you for life, and you gave it to him—
length of days, for ever and ever.
⁵Through the victories you gave, his glory is great;
you have bestowed on him splendour and majesty.
⁶Surely you have granted him eternal blessings
and made him glad with the joy of your presence.
⁷For the king trusts in the LORD;
through the unfailing love of the Most High
he will not be shaken.

⁸Your hand will lay hold on all your enemies;
your right hand will seize your foes.
⁹At the time of your appearing
you will make them like a fiery furnace.
In his wrath the LORD will swallow them up,
and his fire will consume them.

¹⁰You will destroy their descendants from the earth,
their posterity from mankind.
¹¹Though they plot evil against you and devise wicked schemes, they cannot succeed;
¹²for you will make them turn their backs when you aim at them with drawn bow.

¹³Be exalted, O LORD, in your strength;
we will sing and praise your might.

Psalm 22

For the director of music. To ⌊the tune of⌋ "The Doe of the Morning". A psalm of David.

¹My God, my God, why have you forsaken me?
Why are you so far from saving me,
so far from the words of my groaning?
²O my God, I cry out by day, but you do not answer,
by night, and am not silent.

³Yet you are enthroned as the Holy One;
you are the praise of Israel.*a*
⁴In you our fathers put their trust;
they trusted and you delivered them.
⁵They cried to you and were saved;
in you they trusted and were not disappointed.

⁶But I am a worm and not a man,
scorned by men and despised by the people.
⁷All who see me mock me;
they hurl insults, shaking their heads:
⁸"He trusts in the LORD;
let the LORD rescue him.
Let him deliver him,
since he delights in him."

⁹Yet you brought me out of the womb;
you made me trust in you
even at my mother's breast.
¹⁰From birth I was cast upon you;
from my mother's womb you have been my God.
¹¹Do not be far from me,
for trouble is near
and there is no-one to help.

¹²Many bulls surround me;
strong bulls of Bashan encircle me.
¹³Roaring lions tearing their prey
open their mouths wide against me.
¹⁴I am poured out like water,
and all my bones are out of joint.
My heart has turned to wax;
it has melted away within me.
¹⁵My strength is dried up like a potsherd,
and my tongue sticks to the roof of my mouth;
you lay me*b* in the dust of death.
¹⁶Dogs have surrounded me;
a band of evil men has encircled me,
they have pierced*c* my hands and my feet.
¹⁷I can count all my bones;
people stare and gloat over me.

a9 Or *save! / O King, answer*   *a3* Or *Yet you are holy, / enthroned on the praises of Israel*   *b15* Or *I am laid*
c16 Some Hebrew manuscripts, Septuagint and Syriac; most Hebrew manuscripts / *like the lion,*

18They divide my garments among them
    and cast lots for my clothing.

19But you, O LORD, be not far off;
    O my Strength, come quickly to help
        me.
20Deliver my life from the sword,
    my precious life from the power of the
        dogs.
21Rescue me from the mouth of the lions;
    saved me from the horns of the wild
        oxen.

22I will declare your name to my brothers;
    in the congregation I will praise you.
23You who fear the LORD, praise him!
    All you descendants of Jacob, honour
        him!
    Revere him, all you descendants of
        Israel!
24For he has not despised or disdained
    the suffering of the afflicted one;
he has not hidden his face from him
    but has listened to his cry for help.

25From you comes the theme of my praise in
    the great assembly;
    before those who fear youe will I fulfil
        my vows.
26The poor will eat and be satisfied;
    they who seek the LORD will praise
        him—
    may your hearts live for ever!
27All the ends of the earth
    will remember and turn to the LORD,
    and all the families of the nations
    will bow down before him,
28for dominion belongs to the LORD
    and he rules over the nations.

29All the rich of the earth will feast and
    worship;
    all who go down to the dust will kneel
        before him—
    those who cannot keep themselves
        alive.
30Posterity will serve him;
    future generations will be told about the
        Lord.
31They will proclaim his righteousness
    to a people yet unborn—
    for he has done it.

Psalm 23

A psalm of David.

1The LORD is my shepherd, I shall not be in
    want.
2 He makes me lie down in green
        pastures,
he leads me beside quiet waters,
3   he restores my soul.
He guides me in paths of righteousness
    for his name's sake.
4Even though I walk
    through the valley of the shadow of
        death,a
I will fear no evil,
    for you are with me;

your rod and your staff,
    they comfort me.

5You prepare a table before me
    in the presence of my enemies.
You anoint my head with oil;
    my cup overflows.
6Surely goodness and love will follow me
    all the days of my life,
and I will dwell in the house of the LORD
    for ever.

Psalm 24

Of David. A psalm.

1The earth is the LORD's, and everything
    in it,
    the world, and all who live in it;
2for he founded it upon the seas
    and established it upon the waters.

3Who may ascend the hill of the LORD?
    Who may stand in his holy place?
4He who has clean hands and a pure heart,
    who does not lift up his soul to an idol
    or swear by what is false.a
5He will receive blessing from the LORD
    and vindication from God his Saviour.
6Such is the generation of those who seek
        him,
    who seek your face, O God of Jacob.b
                                        Selah

7Lift up your heads, O you gates;
    be lifted up, you ancient doors,
    that the King of glory may come in.
8Who is this King of glory?
    The LORD strong and mighty,
    the LORD mighty in battle.
9Lift up your heads, O you gates;
    lift them up, you ancient doors,
    that the King of glory may come in.
10Who is he, this King of glory?
    The LORD Almighty—
    he is the King of glory.   Selah

Psalm 25a

Of David.

1To you, O LORD, I lift up my soul;
2   in you I trust, O my God.
Do not let me be put to shame,
    nor let my enemies triumph over me.
3No-one whose hope is in you
    will ever be put to shame,
but they will be put to shame
    who are treacherous without excuse.

4Show me your ways, O LORD,
    teach me your paths;
5guide me in your truth and teach me,
    for you are God my Saviour,
    and my hope is in you all day long.
6Remember, O LORD, your great mercy and
        love,
    for they are from of old.
7Remember not the sins of my youth
    and my rebellious ways;

d21 Or / you have heard   e25 Hebrew him   a4 Or through the darkest valley   a4 Or swear falsely
b6 Two Hebrew manuscripts and Syriac (see also Septuagint); most Hebrew manuscripts face, Jacob
aThis psalm is an acrostic poem, the verses of which begin with the successive letters of the Hebrew alphabet.

according to your love remember me,
for you are good, O LORD.

⁸Good and upright is the LORD;
therefore he instructs sinners in his
ways.
⁹He guides the humble in what is right
and teaches them his way.
¹⁰All the ways of the LORD are loving and
faithful
for those who keep the demands of his
covenant.
¹¹For the sake of your name, O LORD,
forgive my iniquity, though it is great.
¹²Who, then, is the man that fears the LORD?
He will instruct him in the way chosen
for him.
¹³He will spend his days in prosperity,
and his descendants will inherit the land.
¹⁴The LORD confides in those who fear him;
he makes his covenant known to them.
¹⁵My eyes are ever on the LORD,
for only he will release my feet from the
snare.

¹⁶Turn to me and be gracious to me,
for I am lonely and afflicted.
¹⁷The troubles of my heart have multiplied;
free me from my anguish.
¹⁸Look upon my affliction and my distress
and take away all my sins.
¹⁹See how my enemies have increased
and how fiercely they hate me!
²⁰Guard my life and rescue me;
let me not be put to shame,
for I take refuge in you.
²¹May integrity and uprightness protect me,
because my hope is in you.

²²Redeem Israel, O God,
from all their troubles!

Psalm 26
Of David.

¹Vindicate me, O LORD,
for I have led a blameless life;
I have trusted in the LORD
without wavering.
²Test me, O LORD, and try me,
examine my heart and my mind;
³for your love is ever before me,
and I walk continually in your truth.
⁴I do not sit with deceitful men,
nor do I consort with hypocrites;
⁵I abhor the assembly of evildoers
and refuse to sit with the wicked.
⁶I wash my hands in innocence,
and go about your altar, O LORD,
⁷proclaiming aloud your praise
and telling of all your wonderful deeds.
⁸I love the house where you live, O LORD,
the place where your glory dwells.

⁹Do not take away my soul along with
sinners,
my life with bloodthirsty men,
¹⁰in whose hands are wicked schemes,
whose right hands are full of bribes.
¹¹But I lead a blameless life;
redeem me and be merciful to me.

¹²My feet stand on level ground;
in the great assembly I will praise the
LORD.

Psalm 27
Of David.

¹The LORD is my light and my salvation—
whom shall I fear?
The LORD is the stronghold of my life—
of whom shall I be afraid?
²When evil men advance against me
to devour my flesh,ᵃ
when my enemies and my foes attack me,
they will stumble and fall.
³Though an army besiege me,
my heart will not fear;
though war break out against me,
even then will I be confident.

⁴One thing I ask of the LORD,
this is what I seek:
that I may dwell in the house of the LORD
all the days of my life,
to gaze upon the beauty of the LORD
and to seek him in his temple.
⁵For in the day of trouble
he will keep me safe in his dwelling;
he will hide me in the shelter of his
tabernacle
and set me high upon a rock.
⁶Then my head will be exalted
above the enemies who surround me;
at his tabernacle will I sacrifice with
shouts of joy;
I will sing and make music to the LORD.

⁷Hear my voice when I call, O LORD;
be merciful to me and answer me.
⁸My heart says of you, "Seek hisᵇ face!"
Your face, LORD, I will seek.
⁹Do not hide your face from me,
do not turn your servant away in anger;
you have been my helper.
Do not reject me or forsake me,
O God my Saviour.
¹⁰Though my father and mother forsake me,
the LORD will receive me.
¹¹Teach me your way, O LORD;
lead me in a straight path
because of my oppressors.
¹²Do not hand me over to the desire of my
foes,
for false witnesses rise up against me,
breathing out violence.

¹³I am still confident of this:
I will see the goodness of the LORD
in the land of the living.
¹⁴Wait for the LORD;
be strong and take heart
and wait for the LORD.

Psalm 28
Of David.

¹To you I call, O LORD my Rock;
do not turn a deaf ear to me.
For if you remain silent,
I shall be like those who have gone
down to the pit.

ᵃ2 Or to slander me   ᵇ8 Or To you, O my heart, he has said, "Seek my

²Hear my cry for mercy
  as I call to you for help,
as I lift up my hands
  towards your Most Holy Place.

³Do not drag me away with the wicked,
  with those who do evil,
who speak cordially with their neighbours
  but harbour malice in their hearts.
⁴Repay them for their deeds
  and for their evil work;
repay them for what their hands have done
  and bring back upon them what they
    deserve.
⁵Since they show no regard for the works of
    the LORD
  and what his hands have done,
he will tear them down
  and never build them up again.

⁶Praise be to the LORD,
  for he has heard my cry for mercy.
⁷The LORD is my strength and my shield;
  my heart trusts in him, and I am helped.
My heart leaps for joy
  and I will give thanks to him in song.

⁸The LORD is the strength of his people,
  a fortress of salvation for his anointed
    one.
⁹Save your people and bless your
    inheritance;
  be their shepherd and carry them for
    ever.

Psalm 29
A psalm of David.

¹Ascribe to the LORD, O mighty ones,
  ascribe to the LORD glory and strength.
²Ascribe to the LORD the glory due to his
    name;
  worship the LORD in the splendour of
    his*a* holiness.

³The voice of the LORD is over the waters;
  the God of glory thunders,
  the LORD thunders over the mighty
    waters.
⁴The voice of the LORD is powerful;
  the voice of the LORD is majestic.
⁵The voice of the LORD breaks the cedars;
  the LORD breaks in pieces the cedars of
    Lebanon.
⁶He makes Lebanon skip like a calf,
  Sirion*b* like a young wild ox.
⁷The voice of the LORD strikes
  with flashes of lightning.
⁸The voice of the LORD shakes the desert;
  the LORD shakes the Desert of Kadesh.
⁹The voice of the LORD twists the oaks*c*
  and strips the forests bare.
And in his temple all cry, ''Glory!''

¹⁰The LORD sits*d* enthroned over the flood;
  the LORD is enthroned as King for ever.
¹¹The LORD gives strength to his people;
  the LORD blesses his people with peace.

Psalm 30
A psalm. A song. For the dedication of the
temple.*a* Of David.

¹I will exalt you, O LORD,
  for you lifted me out of the depths
  and did not let my enemies gloat over
    me.
²O LORD my God, I called to you for help
  and you healed me.
³O LORD, you brought me up from the
    grave;*b*
  you spared me from going down into the
    pit.

⁴Sing to the LORD, you saints of his;
  praise his holy name.
⁵For his anger lasts only a moment,
  but his favour lasts a lifetime;
weeping may remain for a night,
  but rejoicing comes in the morning.

⁶When I felt secure, I said,
  ''I shall never be shaken.''
⁷O LORD, when you favoured me,
  you made my mountain*c* stand firm;
but when you hid your face,
  I was dismayed.

⁸To you, O LORD, I called;
  to the Lord I cried for mercy:
⁹''What gain is there in my destruction,*d*
  in my going down into the pit?
Will the dust praise you?
  Will it proclaim your faithfulness?
¹⁰Hear, O LORD, and be merciful to me;
  O LORD, be my help.''

¹¹You turned my wailing into dancing;
  you removed my sackcloth and clothed
    me with joy,
¹²that my heart may sing to you and not be
    silent.
  O LORD my God, I will give you thanks
    for ever.

Psalm 31
For the director of music. A psalm of David.

¹In you, O LORD, I have taken refuge;
  let me never be put to shame;
  deliver me in your righteousness.
²Turn your ear to me,
  come quickly to my rescue;
be my rock of refuge,
  a strong fortress to save me.
³Since you are my rock and my fortress,
  for the sake of your name lead and guide
    me.
⁴Free me from the trap that is set for me,
  for you are my refuge.
⁵Into your hands I commit my spirit;
  redeem me, O LORD, the God of truth.

⁶I hate those who cling to worthless idols;
  I trust in the LORD.
⁷I will be glad and rejoice in your love,
  for you saw my affliction

---

*a*2 Or LORD with the splendour of   *b*6 That is, Mount Hermon   *c*9 Or LORD makes the deer give birth
*d*10 Or sat   *a*Title: Or palace   *b*3 Hebrew Sheol   *c*7 Or hill country
*d*9 Or there if I am silenced

and knew the anguish of my soul.
⁸You have not handed me over to the
    enemy
  but have set my feet in a spacious place.

⁹Be merciful to me, O Lord, for I am in
    distress;
  my eyes grow weak with sorrow,
  my soul and my body with grief.
¹⁰My life is consumed by anguish
    and my years by groaning;
  my strength fails because of my affliction,ᵃ
  and my bones grow weak.
¹¹Because of all my enemies,
  I am the utter contempt of my
    neighbours;
  I am a dread to my friends—
    those who see me on the street flee from
    me.
¹²I am forgotten by them as though I were
    dead;
  I have become like broken pottery.
¹³For I hear the slander of many;
    there is terror on every side;
  they conspire against me
    and plot to take my life.

¹⁴But I trust in you, O Lord;
  I say, "You are my God."
¹⁵My times are in your hands;
  deliver me from my enemies
    and from those who pursue me.
¹⁶Let your face shine on your servant;
  save me in your unfailing love.
¹⁷Let me not be put to shame, O Lord,
    for I have cried out to you;
  but let the wicked be put to shame
    and lie silent in the grave.ᵇ
¹⁸Let their lying lips be silenced,
  for with pride and contempt
    they speak arrogantly against the
    righteous.

¹⁹How great is your goodness,
    which you have stored up for those who
    fear you,
  which you bestow in the sight of men
    on those who take refuge in you.
²⁰In the shelter of your presence you hide
    them
    from the intrigues of men;
  in your dwelling you keep them safe
    from accusing tongues.

²¹Praise be to the Lord,
  for he showed his wonderful love to me
    when I was in a besieged city.
²²In my alarm I said,
  "I am cut off from your sight!"
  Yet you heard my cry for mercy
    when I called to you for help.

²³Love the Lord, all his saints!
  The Lord preserves the faithful,
    but the proud he pays back in full.
²⁴Be strong and take heart,
  all you who hope in the Lord.

Psalm 32
Of David. A *maskil.*ᵃ

¹Blessed is he
  whose transgressions are forgiven,
  whose sins are covered.
²Blessed is the man
  whose sin the Lord does not count
    against him
  and in whose spirit is no deceit.

³When I kept silent,
  my bones wasted away
    through my groaning all day long.
⁴For day and night
  your hand was heavy upon me;
  my strength was sapped
    as in the heat of summer.   *Selah*
⁵Then I acknowledged my sin to you
  and did not cover up my iniquity.
  I said, "I will confess
    my transgressions to the Lord"—
  and you forgave
    the guilt of my sin.   *Selah*

⁶Therefore let everyone who is godly pray
    to you
    while you may be found;
  surely when the mighty waters rise,
    they will not reach him.
⁷You are my hiding-place;
  you will protect me from trouble
  and surround me with songs of
    deliverance.   *Selah*

⁸I will instruct you and teach you in the
    way you should go;
  I will counsel you and watch over you.
⁹Do not be like the horse or the mule,
    which have no understanding
  but must be controlled by bit and bridle
    or they will not come to you.
¹⁰Many are the woes of the wicked,
  but the Lord's unfailing love
    surrounds the man who trusts in him.

¹¹Rejoice in the Lord and be glad, you
    righteous;
  sing, all you who are upright in heart!

Psalm 33
¹Sing joyfully to the Lord, you righteous;
  it is fitting for the upright to praise him.
²Praise the Lord with the harp;
  make music to him on the ten-stringed
    lyre.
³Sing to him a new song;
  play skilfully, and shout for joy.

⁴For the word of the Lord is right and true;
  he is faithful in all he does.
⁵The Lord loves righteousness and justice;
  the earth is full of his unfailing love.

⁶By the word of the Lord were the heavens
    made,
  their starry host by the breath of his
    mouth.

ᵃ10 Or *guilt*   ᵇ17 Hebrew *Sheol*   ᵃTitle: Probably a literary or musical term

⁷He gathers the waters of the sea into jars;ᵃ
    he puts the deep into storehouses.
⁸Let all the earth fear the LORD;
    let all the people of the world revere
        him.
⁹For he spoke, and it came to be;
    he commanded, and it stood firm.
¹⁰The LORD foils the plans of the nations;
    he thwarts the purposes of the peoples.
¹¹But the plans of the LORD stand firm for
        ever,
    the purposes of his heart through all
        generations.

¹²Blessed is the nation whose God is the
        LORD,
    the people he chose for his inheritance.
¹³From heaven the LORD looks down
    and sees all mankind;
¹⁴from his dwelling-place he watches
    all who live on earth—
¹⁵he who forms the hearts of all,
    who considers everything they do.
¹⁶No king is saved by the size of his army;
    no warrior escapes by his great strength.
¹⁷A horse is a vain hope for deliverance;
    despite all its great strength it cannot
        save.
¹⁸But the eyes of the LORD are on those who
        fear him,
    on those whose hope is in his unfailing
        love,
¹⁹to deliver them from death
    and keep them alive in famine.

²⁰We wait in hope for the LORD;
    he is our help and our shield.
²¹In him our hearts rejoice,
    for we trust in his holy name.
²²May your unfailing love rest upon us, O
        LORD,
    even as we put our hope in you.

Psalm 34ᵃ

Of David. When he pretended to be insane
before Abimelech, who drove him away,
and he left.

¹I will extol the LORD at all times;
    his praise will always be on my lips.
²My soul will boast in the LORD;
    let the afflicted hear and rejoice.
³Glorify the LORD with me:
    let us exalt his name together.

⁴I sought the LORD, and he answered me;
    he delivered me from all my fears.
⁵Those who look to him are radiant;
    their faces are never covered with
        shame.
⁶This poor man called, and the LORD heard
        him;
    he saved him out of all his troubles.
⁷The angel of the LORD encamps around
        those who fear him,
    and he delivers them.

⁸Taste and see that the LORD is good;
    blessed is the man who takes refuge in
        him.
⁹Fear the LORD, you his saints,
    for those who fear him lack nothing.
¹⁰The lions may grow weak and hungry,
    but those who seek the LORD lack no
        good thing.

¹¹Come, my children, listen to me;
    I will teach you the fear of the LORD.
¹²Whoever of you loves life
    and desires to see many good days,
¹³keep your tongue from evil
    and your lips from speaking lies.
¹⁴Turn from evil and do good;
    seek peace and pursue it.

¹⁵The eyes of the LORD are on the righteous
    and his ears are attentive to their cry;
¹⁶the face of the LORD is against those who
        do evil,
    to cut off the memory of them from the
        earth.

¹⁷The righteous cry out, and the LORD hears
        them;
    he delivers them from all their troubles.
¹⁸The LORD is close to the broken-hearted
    and saves those who are crushed in
        spirit.

¹⁹A righteous man may have many troubles,
    but the LORD delivers him from them all;
²⁰he protects all his bones,
    not one of them will be broken.

²¹Evil will slay the wicked;
    the foes of the righteous will be
        condemned.
²²The LORD redeems his servants;
    no-one will be condemned who takes
        refuge in him.

Psalm 35

Of David.

¹Contend, O LORD, with those who contend
        with me;
    fight against those who fight against me.
²Take up shield and buckler;
    arise and come to my aid.
³Brandish spear and javelinᵃ
    against those who pursue me.
Say to my soul,
    "I am your salvation."

⁴May those who seek my life
    be disgraced and put to shame;
    may those who plot my ruin
    be turned back in dismay.
⁵May they be like chaff before the wind,
    with the angel of the LORD driving them
        away;
⁶may their path be dark and slippery,
    with the angel of the LORD pursuing
        them.

ᵃ7 Or *sea as into a heap*
ᵃThis psalm is an acrostic poem, the verses of which begin with the successive letters of the Hebrew alphabet.
ᵃ3 Or *and block the way*

PSALM 34:15–22
'The eyes of the LORD are on the righteous and his ears are attentive to their cry' (v. 15).

THE GOAL OF THE RIGHTEOUS. There are hints here that believers do not live untroubled lives. Verse 17 recognizes that God's people can experience troubles, whilst verse 18 speaks of them being discouraged and having lost hope.

In the midst of all these trials the psalmist tells of God's unfailing care. He rescues, saves, sustains, and preserves his people. It is the wicked, especially those who persecute the righteous, who will suffer ultimate punishment.

This psalm was written and its promises conceived in the context of Judaism, a climate so different from that of our own, but it is the addition of the Christian dimension which gives these assurances their true meaning.

It is frequently stated in the New Testament that Jesus is the 'true pattern of the suffering righteous' (J. H. Eaton). That being so, we have to recognize that Jesus was not rescued from trial, suffering, and death. He was rescued through God's eternal purpose which transcended death and resulted in the resurrection. At the same time we should note that he was not defeated by his suffering even though it threatened his earthly life.

It is that sense of the eternal nature of God's purpose expressed in Jesus, which has sustained Christians in all ages. That is our hope whatever the nature of our trials.

Almighty God, who through thy Son Jesus Christ hast opened unto us the gate of eternal life, grant that with open hearts we may receive thy gift of life and be renewed in mind and body; and that thy power may work in us to do thy will. Amen. (Source unknown)

→472

PSALM 40:1–3
'I waited patiently for the LORD; he turned to me and heard my cry' (v. 1).

FAR FROM WAITING patiently, the psalmist (G. A. F. Knight suggests in *The Daily Study Bible*) was waiting impatiently. Kirkpatrick, in the *Century Commentary*, offers, 'I waited, yea I waited'; the NEB translates, 'I waited, waited for the Lord.' While Knox in the JB underlines the duration with: 'I waited and waited for Yahweh, now at last he has stooped to me.' Experience teaches us that sometimes God does not appear to respond promptly to our cries for help. Out of his own deep experience the psalmist touches a tender nerve in many hearts.

Why God sometimes appears to come with leaden footsteps is a mystery to us. It could relate to the need for time to break down certain resistances we have built up over the years, an essential preliminary to the cleansing, refining and infilling by the Holy Spirit. Perhaps God is using time to increase our sense of need, or to ensure that in the end our faith is going to be stronger than if he responded the moment we cried out to him. Of this we can be sure: even though we feel him distant, he is nevertheless near, and full of love for us (Acts 9:3–19).

> *How long, O Lord, how long wilt thou delay*
> *And leave my soul despairing and exposed?*
> *My cries to thee but add to my dismay,*
> *Why are those once attentive ears now closed?*

> *How long, O Lord, before I hear the sound*
> *Of thy redeeming, liberating voice,*
> *Before thy mercies my poor heart surround*
> *And once again in thee I can rejoice?*

> *'HE TURNED TO ME AND HEARD MY CRY',*

> *Now thou hast come! I need no longer wait.*
> *And my once burdened heart can celebrate.*

→479

[7] Since they hid their net for me without
cause
and without cause dug a pit for me,
[8] may ruin overtake them by surprise—
may the net they hid entangle them,
may they fall into the pit, to their ruin.
[9] Then my soul will rejoice in the LORD
and delight in his salvation.
[10] My whole being will exclaim,
"Who is like you, O LORD?
You rescue the poor from those too strong
for them,
the poor and needy from those who rob
them."

[11] Ruthless witnesses come forward;
they question me on things I know
nothing about.
[12] They repay me evil for good
and leave my soul forlorn.
[13] Yet when they were ill, I put on sackcloth
and humbled myself with fasting.
When my prayers returned to me
unanswered,
[14] I went about mourning
as though for my friend or brother.
I bowed my head in grief
as though weeping for my mother.
[15] But when I stumbled, they gathered in
glee;
attackers gathered against me when I
was unaware.
They slandered me without ceasing.
[16] Like the ungodly they maliciously
mocked;[b]
they gnashed their teeth at me.
[17] O Lord, how long will you look on?
Rescue my life from their ravages,
my precious life from these lions.
[18] I will give you thanks in the great
assembly;
among throngs of people I will praise
you.

[19] Let not those gloat over me
who are my enemies without cause;
let not those who hate me without reason
maliciously wink the eye.
[20] They do not speak peaceably,
but devise false accusations
against those who live quietly in the
land.
[21] They gape at me and say, "Aha! Aha!
With our own eyes we have seen it."

[22] O LORD, you have seen this; be not silent.
Do not be far from me, O Lord.
[23] Awake, and rise to my defence!
Contend for me, my God and Lord.
[24] Vindicate me in your righteousness, O
LORD my God;
do not let them gloat over me.
[25] Do not let them think, "Aha, just what we
wanted!"
or say, "We have swallowed him up."

[26] May all who gloat over my distress
be put to shame and confusion;

may all who exalt themselves over me
be clothed with shame and disgrace.
[27] May those who delight in my vindication
shout for joy and gladness;
may they always say, "The LORD be
exalted,
who delights in the well-being of his
servant."
[28] My tongue will speak of your
righteousness
and of your praises all day long.

Psalm 36

For the director of music. Of David the servant
of the LORD.

[1] An oracle is within my heart
concerning the sinfulness of the
wicked:[a]
There is no fear of God
before his eyes.
[2] For in his own eyes he flatters himself
too much to detect or hate his sin.
[3] The words of his mouth are wicked and
deceitful;
he has ceased to be wise and to do good.
[4] Even on his bed he plots evil;
he commits himself to a sinful course
and does not reject what is wrong.

[5] Your love, O LORD, reaches to the
heavens,
your faithfulness to the skies.
[6] Your righteousness is like the mighty
mountains,
your justice like the great deep.
O LORD, you preserve both man and beast.
[7] How priceless is your unfailing love!
Both high and low among men
find[b] refuge in the shadow of your
wings.
[8] They feast in the abundance of your
house;
you give them drink from your river of
delights.
[9] For with you is the fountain of life;
in your light we see light.

[10] Continue your love to those who know
you,
your righteousness to the upright in
heart.
[11] May the foot of the proud not come against
me,
nor the hand of the wicked drive me
away.
[12] See how the evildoers lie fallen—
thrown down, not able to rise!

Psalm 37[a]

Of David.

[1] Do not fret because of evil men
or be envious of those who do wrong;
[2] for like the grass they will soon wither,
like green plants they will soon die
away.

[3] Trust in the LORD and do good;
dwell in the land and enjoy safe pasture.

[b]16 Septuagint; Hebrew may mean *ungodly circle of mockers.*   [a]1 Or *heart: / Sin proceeds from the wicked.*
[b]7 Or *love, O God! / Men find;* or *love! / Both heavenly beings and men / find*
[a]This psalm is an acrostic poem, the stanzas of which begin with the successive letters of the Hebrew alphabet.

4Delight yourself in the LORD
and he will give you the desires of your
heart.

5Commit your way to the LORD;
trust in him and he will do this:
6He will make your righteousness shine like
the dawn,
the justice of your cause like the
noonday sun.

7Be still before the LORD and wait patiently
for him;
do not fret when men succeed in their
ways,
when they carry out their wicked
schemes.

8Refrain from anger and turn from wrath;
do not fret—it leads only to evil.
9For evil men will be cut off,
but those who hope in the LORD will
inherit the land.

10A little while, and the wicked will be no
more;
though you look for them, they will not
be found.
11But the meek will inherit the land
and enjoy great peace.

12The wicked plot against the righteous
and gnash their teeth at them;
13but the Lord laughs at the wicked,
for he knows their day is coming.

14The wicked draw the sword
and bend the bow
to bring down the poor and needy,
to slay those whose ways are upright.
15But their swords will pierce their own
hearts,
and their bows will be broken.

16Better the little that the righteous have
than the wealth of many wicked;
17for the power of the wicked will be broken,
but the LORD upholds the righteous.

18The days of the blameless are known to
the LORD,
and their inheritance will endure for
ever.
19In times of disaster they will not wither;
in days of famine they will enjoy plenty.

20But the wicked will perish:
The LORD's enemies will be like the
beauty of the fields,
they will vanish—vanish like smoke.

21The wicked borrow and do not repay,
but the righteous give generously;
22those the LORD blesses will inherit the
land,
but those he curses will be cut off.

23If the LORD delights in a man's way,
he makes his steps firm;

24though he stumble, he will not fall,
for the LORD upholds him with his hand.

25I was young and now I am old,
yet I have never seen the righteous
forsaken
or their children begging bread.
26They are always generous and lend freely;
their children will be blessed.

27Turn from evil and do good;
then you will dwell in the land for ever.
28For the LORD loves the just
and will not forsake his faithful ones.

They will be protected for ever,
but the offspring of the wicked will be
cut off;
29the righteous will inherit the land
and dwell in it for ever.

30The mouth of the righteous man utters
wisdom,
and his tongue speaks what is just.
31The law of his God is in his heart;
his feet do not slip.

32The wicked lie in wait for the righteous,
seeking their very lives;
33but the LORD will not leave them in their
power
or let them be condemned when brought
to trial.

34Wait for the LORD
and keep his way.
He will exalt you to inherit the land;
when the wicked are cut off, you will see
it.

35I have seen a wicked and ruthless man
flourishing like a green tree in its native
soil,
36but he soon passed away and was no more;
though I looked for him, he could not be
found.

37Consider the blameless, observe the
upright;
there is a future^b for the man of peace.
38But all sinners will be destroyed;
the future^c of the wicked will be cut off.

39The salvation of the righteous comes from
the LORD;
he is their stronghold in time of trouble.
40The LORD helps them and delivers them;
he delivers them from the wicked and
saves them,
because they take refuge in him.

Psalm 38

A psalm of David. A petition.

1O LORD, do not rebuke me in your anger
or discipline me in your wrath.
2For your arrows have pierced me,
and your hand has come down upon me.
3Because of your wrath there is no health in
my body;

b37 Or there will be posterity   c38 Or posterity

my bones have no soundness because of
    my sin.
[4]My guilt has overwhelmed me
    like a burden too heavy to bear.

[5]My wounds fester and are loathsome
    because of my sinful folly.
[6]I am bowed down and brought very low;
    all day long I go about mourning.
[7]My back is filled with searing pain;
    there is no health in my body.
[8]I am feeble and utterly crushed;
    I groan in anguish of heart.

[9]All my longings lie open before you, O
    Lord;
    my sighing is not hidden from you.
[10]My heart pounds, my strength fails me;
    even the light has gone from my eyes.
[11]My friends and companions avoid me
    because of my wounds;
    my neighbours stay far away.
[12]Those who seek my life set their traps,
    those who would harm me talk of my
    ruin;
    all day long they plot deception.

[13]I am like a deaf man, who cannot hear,
    like a mute, who cannot open his mouth;
[14]I have become like a man who does not
    hear,
    whose mouth can offer no reply.
[15]I wait for you, O LORD;
    you will answer, O Lord my God.
[16]For I said, "Do not let them gloat
    or exalt themselves over me when my
    foot slips."

[17]For I am about to fall,
    and my pain is ever with me.
[18]I confess my iniquity;
    I am troubled by my sin.
[19]Many are those who are my vigorous
    enemies;
    those who hate me without reason are
    numerous.
[20]Those who repay my good with evil
    slander me when I pursue what is good.

[21]O LORD, do not forsake me;
    be not far from me, O my God.
[22]Come quickly to help me,
    O Lord my Saviour.

Psalm 39

For the director of music. For Jeduthun.
A psalm of David.

[1]I said, "I will watch my ways
    and keep my tongue from sin;
    I will put a muzzle on my mouth
    as long as the wicked are in my
    presence."
[2]But when I was silent and still,
    not even saying anything good,
    my anguish increased.
[3]My heart grew hot within me,
    and as I meditated, the fire burned;
    then I spoke with my tongue:

[4]"Show me, O LORD, my life's end
    and the number of my days;
    let me know how fleeting is my life.
[5]You have made my days a mere
    handbreadth;
    the span of my years is as nothing before
    you.
    Each man's life is but a breath.   Selah
[6]Man is a mere phantom as he goes to and
    fro:
    He bustles about, but only in vain;
    he heaps up wealth, not knowing who
    will get it.

[7]"But now, Lord, what do I look for?
    My hope is in you.
[8]Save me from all my transgressions;
    do not make me the scorn of fools.
[9]I was silent; I would not open my mouth,
    for you are the one who has done this.
[10]Remove your scourge from me;
    I am overcome by the blow of your
    hand.
[11]You rebuke and discipline men for their
    sin;
    you consume their wealth like a moth—
    each man is but a breath.   Selah

[12]"Hear my prayer, O LORD,
    listen to my cry for help;
    be not deaf to my weeping.
    For I dwell with you as an alien,
    a stranger, as all my fathers were.
[13]Look away from me, that I may rejoice
    again
    before I depart and am no more."

Psalm 40

For the director of music. Of David. A psalm.

[1]I waited patiently for the LORD;
    he turned to me and heard my cry.
[2]He lifted me out of the slimy pit,
    out of the mud and mire;
    he set my feet on a rock
    and gave me a firm place to stand.
[3]He put a new song in my mouth,
    a hymn of praise to our God.
    Many will see and fear
    and put their trust in the LORD.

[4]Blessed is the man
    who makes the LORD his trust,
    who does not look to the proud,
    to those who turn aside to false gods.[a]
[5]Many, O LORD my God,
    are the wonders you have done.
    The things you planned for us
    no-one can recount to you;
    were I to speak and tell of them,
    they would be too many to declare.

[6]Sacrifice and offering you did not desire,
    but my ears you have pierced;[b,c]
    burnt offerings and sin offerings
    you did not require.
[7]Then I said, "Here I am, I have come—
    it is written about me in the scroll.[d]

[a]4 Or to falsehood
[b]6 Hebrew; Septuagint but a body you have prepared for me (see also Symmachus and Theodotion)
[c]6 Or opened   [d]7 Or come / with the scroll written for me

⁸I desire to do your will, O my God;
 your law is within my heart.''

⁹I proclaim righteousness in the great
 assembly;
 I do not seal my lips,
 as you know, O LORD.
¹⁰I do not hide your righteousness in my
 heart;
 I speak of your faithfulness and
 salvation.
 I do not conceal your love and your truth
 from the great assembly.

¹¹Do not withhold your mercy from me, O
 LORD;
 may your love and your truth always
 protect me.
¹²For troubles without number surround me;
 my sins have overtaken me, and I
 cannot see.
 They are more than the hairs of my head,
 and my heart fails within me.

¹³Be pleased, O LORD, to save me;
 O LORD, come quickly to help me.
¹⁴May all who seek to take my life
 be put to shame and confusion;
 may all who desire my ruin
 be turned back in disgrace.
¹⁵May those who say to me, ''Aha! Aha!''
 be appalled at their own shame.
¹⁶But may all who seek you
 rejoice and be glad in you;
 may those who love your salvation always
 say,
 ''The LORD be exalted!''

¹⁷Yet I am poor and needy;
 may the Lord think of me.
 You are my help and my deliverer;
 O my God, do not delay.

Psalm 41

For the director of music. A psalm of David.
¹Blessed is he who has regard for the weak;
 the LORD delivers him in times of
 trouble.
²The LORD will protect him and preserve
 his life;
 he will bless him in the land
 and not surrender him to the desire of
 his foes.
³The LORD will sustain him on his sick-bed
 and restore him from his bed of illness.

⁴I said, ''O LORD, have mercy on me;
 heal me, for I have sinned against you.''
⁵My enemies say of me in malice,
 ''When will he die and his name
 perish?''
⁶Whenever one comes to see me,
 he speaks falsely, while his heart
 gathers slander;
 then he goes out and spreads it abroad.

⁷All my enemies whisper together against
 me;
 they imagine the worst for me, saying,
⁸''A vile disease has beset him;
 he will never get up from the place
 where he lies.''
⁹Even my close friend, whom I trusted,
 he who shared my bread,
 has lifted up his heel against me.

¹⁰But you, O LORD, have mercy on me;
 raise me up, that I may repay them.
¹¹I know that you are pleased with me,
 for my enemy does not triumph over
 me.
¹²In my integrity you uphold me
 and set me in your presence for ever.

¹³Praise be to the LORD, the God of Israel,
 from everlasting to everlasting.
 Amen and Amen.

BOOK II

Psalms 42–72

Psalm 42ᵃ

For the director of music. A *maskil*ᵇ of the
Sons of Korah.

¹As the deer pants for streams of water,
 so my soul pants for you, O God.
²My soul thirsts for God, for the living God.
 When can I go and meet with God?
³My tears have been my food
 day and night,
 while men say to me all day long,
 ''Where is your God?''
⁴These things I remember
 as I pour out my soul:
 how I used to go with the multitude,
 leading the procession to the house of
 God,
 with shouts of joy and thanksgiving
 among the festive throng.

⁵Why are you downcast, O my soul?
 Why so disturbed within me?
 Put your hope in God,
 for I will yet praise him,
 my Saviour and ⁶my God.

Myᶜ soul is downcast within me;
 therefore I will remember you
 from the land of the Jordan,
 the heights of Hermon—from Mount
 Mizar.
⁷Deep calls to deep
 in the roar of your waterfalls;
 all your waves and breakers
 have swept over me.

⁸By day the LORD directs his love,
 at night his song is with me—
 a prayer to the God of my life.

ᵃIn many Hebrew manuscripts Psalms 42 and 43 constitute one psalm.
ᵇTitle: Probably a literary or musical term
ᶜ5, 6 A few Hebrew manuscripts, Septuagint and Syriac; most Hebrew manuscripts *praise him for his saving help.* /
⁶*O my God, my*

⁹I say to God my Rock,
  "Why have you forgotten me?
Why must I go about mourning,
  oppressed by the enemy?"
¹⁰My bones suffer mortal agony
  as my foes taunt me,
saying to me all day long,
  "Where is your God?"

¹¹Why are you downcast, O my soul?
  Why so disturbed within me?
Put your hope in God,
  for I will yet praise him,
  my Saviour and my God.

Psalm 43[a]

¹Vindicate me, O God,
  and plead my cause against an ungodly
    nation;
  rescue me from deceitful and wicked
    men.
²You are God my stronghold.
  Why have you rejected me?
Why must I go about mourning,
  oppressed by the enemy?
³Send forth your light and your truth,
  let them guide me;
let them bring me to your holy mountain,
  to the place where you dwell.
⁴Then will I go to the altar of God,
  to God, my joy and my delight.
I will praise you with the harp,
  O God, my God.

⁵Why are you downcast, O my soul?
  Why so disturbed within me?
Put your hope in God,
  for I will yet praise him,
  my Saviour and my God.

Psalm 44

For the director of music. Of the Sons of Korah.
A *maskil*.[a]

¹We have heard with our ears, O God;
  our fathers have told us
what you did in their days,
  in days long ago.
²With your hand you drove out the nations
  and planted our fathers;
you crushed the peoples
  and made our fathers flourish.
³It was not by their sword that they won the
    land,
  nor did their arm bring them victory;
it was your right hand, your arm,
  and the light of your face, for you loved
    them.

⁴You are my King and my God,
  who decrees[b] victories for Jacob.
⁵Through you we push back our enemies;
  through your name we trample our foes.
⁶I do not trust in my bow,
  my sword does not bring me victory;
⁷but you give us victory over our enemies,
  you put our adversaries to shame.
⁸In God we make our boast all day long,
  and we will praise your name for ever.
                                          Selah

⁹But now you have rejected and humbled
    us;
  you no longer go out with our armies.
¹⁰You made us retreat before the enemy,
  and our adversaries have plundered us.
¹¹You gave us up to be devoured like sheep
  and have scattered us among the
    nations.
¹²You sold your people for a pittance,
  gaining nothing from their sale.

¹³You have made us a reproach to our
    neighbours,
  the scorn and derision of those around
    us.
¹⁴You have made us a byword among the
    nations;
  the peoples shake their heads at us.
¹⁵My disgrace is before me all day long,
  and my face is covered with shame
¹⁶at the taunts of those who reproach and
    revile me,
  because of the enemy, who is bent on
    revenge.

¹⁷All this happened to us,
  though we had not forgotten you
  or been false to your covenant.
¹⁸Our hearts had not turned back;
  our feet had not strayed from your path.
¹⁹But you crushed us and made us a haunt
    for jackals
  and covered us over with deep
    darkness.

²⁰If we had forgotten the name of our God
  or spread out our hands to a foreign god,
²¹would not God have discovered it,
  since he knows the secrets of the heart?
²²Yet for your sake we face death all day
    long;
  we are considered as sheep to be
    slaughtered.

²³Awake, O Lord! Why do you sleep?
  Rouse yourself! Do not reject us for
    ever.
²⁴Why do you hide your face
  and forget our misery and oppression?

²⁵We are brought down to the dust;
  our bodies cling to the ground.
²⁶Rise up and help us;
  redeem us because of your unfailing
    love.

Psalm 45

For the director of music. To ⌊the tune of⌋
"Lilies". Of the Sons of Korah. A *maskil*.[a]
A wedding song.

¹My heart is stirred by a noble theme
  as I recite my verses for the king;
  my tongue is the pen of a skilful writer.

²You are the most excellent of men
  and your lips have been anointed with
    grace,
  since God has blessed you for ever.

---

[a]In many Hebrew manuscripts Psalms 42 and 43 constitute one psalm.
[a]Title: Probably a literary or musical term   [b]4 Septuagint, Aquila and Syriac; Hebrew *King, O God; I command*
[a]Title: Probably a literary or musical term

³Gird your sword upon your side, O mighty
   one;
   clothe yourself with splendour and
      majesty.
⁴In your majesty ride forth victoriously
   on behalf of truth, humility and
      righteousness;
   let your right hand display awesome
      deeds.
⁵Let your sharp arrows pierce the hearts of
   the king's enemies;
   let the nations fall beneath your feet.
⁶Your throne, O God, will last for ever and
   ever;
   a sceptre of justice will be the sceptre of
      your kingdom.
⁷You love righteousness and hate
   wickedness;
   therefore God, your God, has set you
      above your companions
   by anointing you with the oil of joy.
⁸All your robes are fragrant with myrrh and
   aloes and cassia;
   from palaces adorned with ivory
   the music of the strings makes you glad.
⁹Daughters of kings are among your
   honoured women;
   at your right hand is the royal bride in
      gold of Ophir.

¹⁰Listen, O daughter, consider and give ear:
   Forget your people and your father's
      house.
¹¹The king is enthralled by your beauty;
   honour him, for he is your lord.
¹²The Daughter of Tyre will come with a
   gift,^b
   men of wealth will seek your favour.

¹³All glorious is the princess within ⌐her
   chamber⌐;
   her gown is interwoven with gold.
¹⁴In embroidered garments she is led to the
   king;
   her virgin companions follow her
   and are brought to you.
¹⁵They are led in with joy and gladness;
   they enter the palace of the king.

¹⁶Your sons will take the place of your
   fathers;
   you will make them princes throughout
      the land.
¹⁷I will perpetuate your memory through all
   generations;
   therefore the nations will praise you for
      ever and ever.

Psalm 46

For the director of music. Of the Sons of Korah.
   According to *alamoth*.^a A song.
¹God is our refuge and strength,
   an ever-present help in trouble.
²Therefore we will not fear, though the
   earth give way
   and the mountains fall into the heart of
      the sea,

³though its waters roar and foam
   and the mountains quake with their
      surging.   *Selah*

⁴There is a river whose streams make glad
   the city of God,
   the holy place where the Most High
      dwells.
⁵God is within her, she will not fall;
   God will help her at break of day.
⁶Nations are in uproar, kingdoms fall;
   he lifts his voice, the earth melts.

⁷The LORD Almighty is with us;
   the God of Jacob is our fortress.   *Selah*

⁸Come and see the works of the LORD,
   the desolations he has brought on the
      earth.
⁹He makes wars cease to the ends of the
   earth;
   he breaks the bow and shatters the
      spear,
   he burns the shields^b with fire.
¹⁰"Be still, and know that I am God;
   I will be exalted among the nations,
   I will be exalted in the earth."

¹¹The LORD Almighty is with us;
   the God of Jacob is our fortress.   *Selah*

Psalm 47

For the director of music. Of the Sons of Korah.
   A psalm.
¹Clap your hands, all you nations;
   shout to God with cries of joy.
²How awesome is the LORD Most High,
   the great King over all the earth!
³He subdued nations under us,
   peoples under our feet.
⁴He chose our inheritance for us,
   the pride of Jacob, whom he loved.
                                       Selah

⁵God has ascended amid shouts of joy,
   the LORD amid the sounding of
      trumpets.
⁶Sing praises to God, sing praises;
   sing praises to our King, sing praises.

⁷For God is the King of all the earth;
   sing to him a psalm^a of praise.
⁸God reigns over the nations;
   God is seated on his holy throne.
⁹The nobles of the nations assemble
   as the people of the God of Abraham,
   for the kings^b of the earth belong to God;
   he is greatly exalted.

Psalm 48

A song. A psalm of the Sons of Korah.
¹Great is the LORD, and most worthy of
   praise,
   in the city of our God, his holy
      mountain.
²It is beautiful in its loftiness,
   the joy of the whole earth.

---

^b12 Or *A Tyrian robe is among the gifts*   ^aTitle: Probably a musical term   ^b9 Or *chariots*
^a7 Or *a maskil* (probably a literary or musical term)   ^b9 Or *shields*

PSALM 46:1–11
'Be still, and know that I am God' (v. 10a).

CLAMOUR, NOISE, HUSTLE AND BUSTLE characterize the everyday activity of most of us. This seemingly ceaseless activity contributes substantially to our feelings of stress, even of insecurity. The psalmist refreshed himself with the reminder that God is a refuge and is ever near (v. 1), and although catastrophes may occur, we have no need to fear (v. 2). He reminds us that wherever God dwells there is total security (vv. 4, 5). He invites us to observe the works of the Lord (vv. 8, 9). We are left to deduce that if God's achievements are of this magnitude we can have total confidence in him.

The psalmist invites us to be still (v. 10). There is therapy in such quietness. Our thoughts assume a better perspective. Our problems either find answers or become bearable. Our spirits lift, endurance is reinforced and courage returns. Let us, therefore, be still before him.

> *I would be quiet and still before thee, Lord,*
> *As still as water on a spring-time dawn,*
> *As still as mountains when the snow has roared,*
> *As still as dew upon the cloistered lawn.*
>
> *For in that stillness I can hear thy voice,*
> *And in that stillness I can feel thee near,*
> *And, in me, all my senses can rejoice,*
> *For thou art God and thou art with me here.*
>
> *The language of the silent heart I know,*
> *Experience has built its forms of speech,*
> *And truth when felt, with eloquence can glow*
> *And in its yearnings can the Father reach.*
>
> *This is the 'deep which calleth unto deep',*
> *And silent hearts alone its mysteries keep.*
>
> *Thank you, Lord. Amen.*

→480

PSALM 51:1–5

'I know my transgressions, and my sin is always before me. Against you, you only, have I sinned and done what is evil in your sight' (vv. 3, 4a).

PSALM 51 STANDS ON ITS OWN amongst the psalms, for it deals with sin and sin alone. Many psalms concern themselves with praising God or bemoaning the fact that God sends trouble – but the trouble of Psalm 51 is entirely man-made, caused by sin.

Some people complain that the Church pays too much attention to sin. Today we prefer to stress people's positive qualities. We are called upon to encourage the development of positive characteristics. That is right and proper. But positive development is enhanced, not hindered, by correct understanding of our sinful condition.

Christian worship rightly gives prominence to confession. Who can take part in the general confession and remain unaware of the depth of human sinfulness and the need for forgiveness? Equally, can anyone who has made that confession sincerely, fail to grasp that forgiveness comes from God alone, through Jesus Christ?

Dependence on God for forgiveness comes through strongly in David's psalm. We may not share the grossness of his sin. Our lust has probably not led to murder – yet we each share his confession. We each know our transgressions, and our sin is always before us. We know how we have hurt and injured others. David points us to what may not be so obvious. The injury and hurt we bring to others is also, entirely, an offence against God.

How marvellous when friends or enemies alike forgive us for the hurt we have inflicted on them! But every offence against others is also an offence against God. How wonderful that, whether others forgive us or not, God in his mercy will wipe out all our guilt!

→487

Like the utmost heights of Zaphon[a] is
   Mount Zion,
   the[b] city of the Great King.
[3]God is in her citadels;
   he has shown himself to be her fortress.

[4]When the kings joined forces,
   when they advanced together,
[5]they saw ⌊her⌋ and were astounded;
   they fled in terror.
[6]Trembling seized them there,
   pain like that of a woman in labour.
[7]You destroyed them like ships of Tarshish
   shattered by an east wind.

[8]As we have heard,
   so have we seen
in the city of the LORD Almighty,
   in the city of our God:
   God makes her secure for ever.   *Selah*

[9]Within your temple, O God,
   we meditate on your unfailing love.
[10]Like your name, O God,
   your praise reaches to the ends of the
      earth;
   your right hand is filled with
      righteousness.
[11]Mount Zion rejoices,
   the villages of Judah are glad
   because of your judgments.

[12]Walk about Zion, go round her,
   count her towers,
[13]consider well her ramparts,
   view her citadels,
   that you may tell of them to the next
      generation.
[14]For this God is our God for ever and ever;
   he will be our guide even to the end.

Psalm 49

For the director of music. Of the Sons of Korah.
A psalm.
[1]Hear this, all you peoples;
   listen, all who live in this world,
[2]both low and high,
   rich and poor alike:
[3]My mouth will speak words of wisdom;
   the utterance from my heart will give
      understanding.
[4]I will turn my ear to a proverb;
   with the harp I will expound my riddle:

[5]Why should I fear when evil days come,
   when wicked deceivers surround me—
[6]those who trust in their wealth
   and boast of their great riches?
[7]No man can redeem the life of another
   or give to God a ransom for him—
[8]the ransom for a life is costly,
   no payment is ever enough—
[9]that he should live on for ever
   and not see decay.

[10]For all can see that wise men die;
   the foolish and the senseless alike perish
   and leave their wealth to others.
[11]Their tombs will remain their houses[a] for
      ever,
   their dwellings for endless generations,
   though they had[b] named lands after
      themselves.

[12]But man, despite his riches, does not
      endure;
   he is[c] like the beasts that perish.

[13]This is the fate of those who trust in
      themselves,
   and of their followers, who approve
      their sayings.   *Selah*
[14]Like sheep they are destined for the
      grave,[d]
   and death will feed on them.
The upright will rule over them in the
      morning;
   their forms will decay in the grave,[d]
   far from their princely mansions.
[15]But God will redeem my life[e] from the
      grave;
   he will surely take me to himself.   *Selah*

[16]Do not be overawed when a man grows
      rich,
   when the splendour of his house
      increases;
[17]for he will take nothing with him when he
      dies,
   his splendour will not descend with him.
[18]Though while he lived he counted himself
      blessed—
   and men praise you when you prosper—
[19]he will join the generation of his fathers,
   who will never see the light ⌊of life⌋.

[20]A man who has riches without
      understanding
   is like the beasts that perish.

Psalm 50

A psalm of Asaph.
[1]The Mighty One, God, the LORD,
   speaks and summons the earth
   from the rising of the sun to the place
      where it sets.
[2]From Zion, perfect in beauty,
   God shines forth.
[3]Our God comes and will not be silent;
   a fire devours before him,
   and around him a tempest rages.
[4]He summons the heavens above,
   and the earth, that he may judge his
      people:
[5]"Gather to me my consecrated ones,
   who made a covenant with me by
      sacrifice."
[6]And the heavens proclaim his
      righteousness,
   for God himself is judge.   *Selah*

---

[a]2 *Zaphon* can refer to a sacred mountain or the direction north.
[b]2 Or *earth, / Mount Zion, on the northern side / of the*
[a]11 Septuagint and Syriac; Hebrew *In their thoughts their houses will remain*
[b]11 Or */ for they have*   [c]12 Hebrew; Septuagint and Syriac read verse 12 the same as verse 20.
[d]14 Hebrew *Sheol*; also in verse 15   [e]15 Or *soul*

7"Hear, O my people, and I will speak,
   O Israel, and I will testify against you:
   I am God, your God.
8I do not rebuke you for your sacrifices
   or your burnt offerings, which are ever
   before me.
9I have no need of a bull from your stall
   or of goats from your pens,
10for every animal of the forest is mine,
   and the cattle on a thousand hills.
11I know every bird in the mountains,
   and the creatures of the field are mine.
12If I were hungry I would not tell you,
   for the world is mine, and all that is in it.
13Do I eat the flesh of bulls
   or drink the blood of goats?
14Sacrifice thank-offerings to God,
   fulfil your vows to the Most High,
15and call upon me in the day of trouble;
   I will deliver you, and you will honour
   me."

16But to the wicked, God says:

"What right have you to recite my laws
   or take my covenant on your lips?
17You hate my instruction
   and cast my words behind you.
18When you see a thief, you join with him;
   you throw in your lot with adulterers.
19You use your mouth for evil
   and harness your tongue to deceit.
20You speak continually against your
   brother
   and slander your own mother's son.
21These things you have done and I kept
   silent;
   you thought I was altogether^a like you.
But I will rebuke you
   and accuse you to your face.

22"Consider this, you who forget God,
   or I will tear you to pieces, with none to
   rescue;
23He who sacrifices thank-offerings honours
   me,
   and he prepares the way
   so that I may show him^b the salvation of
   God."

Psalm 51

For the director of music. A psalm of David.
When the prophet Nathan came to him after
David had committed adultery with Bathsheba.

1Have mercy on me, O God,
   according to your unfailing love;
   according to your great compassion
   blot out my transgressions.
2Wash away all my iniquity
   and cleanse me from my sin.

3For I know my transgressions,
   and my sin is always before me.
4Against you, you only, have I sinned
   and done what is evil in your sight,
so that you are proved right when you
   speak

and justified when you judge.
5Surely I was sinful at birth,
   sinful from the time my mother
   conceived me.
6Surely you desire truth in the inner parts;^{a}
   you teach^b me wisdom in the inmost
   place.

7Cleanse me with hyssop, and I shall be
   clean;
   wash me, and I shall be whiter than
   snow.
8Let me hear joy and gladness;
   let the bones you have crushed rejoice.
9Hide your face from my sins
   and blot out all my iniquity.

10Create in me a pure heart, O God,
   and renew a steadfast spirit within me.
11Do not cast me from your presence
   or take your Holy Spirit from me.
12Restore to me the joy of your salvation
   and grant me a willing spirit, to sustain
   me.

13Then I will teach transgressors your ways,
   and sinners will turn back to you.
14Save me from bloodguilt, O God,
   the God who saves me,
   and my tongue will sing of your
   righteousness.
15O Lord, open my lips,
   and my mouth will declare your praise.
16You do not delight in sacrifice, or I would
   bring it;
   you do not take pleasure in burnt
   offerings.
17The sacrifices of God are^c a broken spirit;
   a broken and contrite heart,
   O God, you will not despise.

18In your good pleasure make Zion prosper;
   build up the walls of Jerusalem.
19Then there will be righteous sacrifices,
   whole burnt offerings to delight you;
   then bulls will be offered on your altar.

Psalm 52

For the director of music. A maskil^a of David.
When Doeg the Edomite had gone to Saul and
   told him: "David has gone to the house of
   Ahimelech."

1Why do you boast of evil, you mighty
   man?
   Why do you boast all day long,
   you who are a disgrace in the eyes of
   God?
2Your tongue plots destruction;
   it is like a sharpened razor,
   you who practise deceit.
3You love evil rather than good,
   falsehood rather than speaking the
   truth.   Selah
4You love every harmful word,
   O you deceitful tongue!

5Surely God will bring you down to
   everlasting ruin:

---

^{a}21 Or thought the 'I AM' was ^{b}23 Or and to him who considers his way / I will show
^{a}6 The meaning of the Hebrew for this phrase is uncertain. ^{b}6 Or you desired . . . ; / you taught
^{c}17 Or My sacrifice, O God, is ^{a}Title: Probably a literary or musical term

He will snatch you up and tear you from
    your tent;
he will uproot you from the land of the
    living.   *Selah*
6The righteous will see and fear;
    they will laugh at him, saying,
7"Here now is the man
    who did not make God his stronghold
but trusted in his great wealth
    and grew strong by destroying others!''

8But I am like an olive tree
    flourishing in the house of God;
I trust in God's unfailing love
    for ever and ever.
9I will praise you for ever for what you
    have done;
    in your name I will hope, for your name
        is good.
I will praise you in the presence of your
    saints.

Psalm 53

For the director of music. According to
    mahalath.[a] A *maskil*[b] of David.
1The fool says in his heart,
    "There is no God."
They are corrupt, and their ways are vile;
    there is no-one who does good.

2God looks down from heaven
    on the sons of men
to see if there are any who understand,
    any who seek God.
3Everyone has turned away,
    they have together become corrupt;
there is no-one who does good,
    not even one.

4Will the evildoers never learn—
    those who devour my people as men eat
        bread
    and who do not call on God?
5There they were, overwhelmed with
        dread,
    where there was nothing to dread.
God scattered the bones of those who
        attacked you;
    you put them to shame, for God
        despised them.

6Oh, that salvation for Israel would come
    out of Zion!
When God restores the fortunes of his
    people,
let Jacob rejoice and Israel be glad!

Psalm 54

For the director of music. With stringed
instruments. A *maskil*[a] of David. When the
Ziphites had gone to Saul and said, "Is not
    David hiding among us?"
1Save me, O God, by your name;
    vindicate me by your might.
2Hear my prayer, O God;
    listen to the words of my mouth.

3Strangers are attacking me;
    ruthless men seek my life—
    men without regard for God.   *Selah*

4Surely God is my help;
    the Lord is the one who sustains me.

5Let evil recoil on those who slander me;
    in your faithfulness destroy them.

6I will sacrifice a freewill offering to you;
    I will praise your name, O Lord,
    for it is good.
7For he has delivered me from all my
    troubles,
    and my eyes have looked in triumph on
    my foes.

Psalm 55

For the director of music. With stringed
    instruments. A *maskil*[a] of David.
1Listen to my prayer, O God,
    do not ignore my plea;
2 hear me and answer me.
My thoughts trouble me and I am
    distraught
3 at the voice of the enemy,
    at the stares of the wicked;
for they bring down suffering upon me
    and revile me in their anger.

4My heart is in anguish within me;
    the terrors of death assail me.
5Fear and trembling have beset me;
    horror has overwhelmed me.
6I said, "Oh, that I had the wings of a dove!
    I would fly away and be at rest—
7I would flee far away
    and stay in the desert;   *Selah*
8I would hurry to my place of shelter,
    far from the tempest and storm.''

9Confuse the wicked, O Lord, confound
    their speech,
for I see violence and strife in the city.
10Day and night they prowl about on its
    walls;
    malice and abuse are within it.
11Destructive forces are at work in the city;
    threats and lies never leave its streets.

12If an enemy were insulting me,
    I could endure it;
if a foe were raising himself against me,
    I could hide from him.
13But it is you, a man like myself,
    my companion, my close friend,
14with whom I once enjoyed sweet
    fellowship
    as we walked with the throng at the
    house of God.

15Let death take my enemies by surprise;
    let them go down alive to the grave,[b]
    for evil finds lodging among them.

16But I call to God,
    and the Lord saves me.

17Evening, morning and noon
    I cry out in distress,
    and he hears my voice.
18He ransoms me unharmed
    from the battle waged against me,
    even though many oppose me.
19God, who is enthroned for ever,
    will hear them and afflict them—   *Selah*
men who never change their ways
    and have no fear of God.

20My companion attacks his friends;
    he violates his covenant.
21His speech is smooth as butter,
    yet war is in his heart;
his words are more soothing than oil,
    yet they are drawn swords.

22Cast your cares on the LORD
    and he will sustain you;
    he will never let the righteous fall.
23But you, O God, will bring down the
        wicked
    into the pit of corruption;
bloodthirsty and deceitful men
    will not live out half their days.

But as for me, I trust in you.

Psalm 56

For the director of music. To ⌊the tune of⌋ "A
    Dove on Distant Oaks". Of David. A *miktam.*[a]
    When the Philistines had seized him in Gath.

1Be merciful to me, O God, for men hotly
        pursue me;
    all day long they press their attack.
2My slanderers pursue me all day long;
    many are attacking me in their pride.

3When I am afraid,
    I will trust in you.
4In God, whose word I praise,
    in God I trust; I will not be afraid.
    What can mortal man do to me?

5All day long they twist my words;
    they are always plotting to harm me.
6They conspire, they lurk,
    they watch my steps,
    eager to take my life.

7On no account let them escape;
    in your anger, O God, bring down the
        nations.
8Record my lament;
    list my tears on your scroll[b]—
    are they not in your record?

9Then my enemies will turn back
    when I call for help.
    By this I will know that God is for me.
10In God, whose word I praise,
    in the LORD, whose word I praise—
11in God I trust; I will not be afraid.
    What can man do to me?

12I am under vows to you, O God;
    I will present my thank-offerings to you.

13For you have delivered me[c] from death
    and my feet from stumbling,
that I may walk before God
    in the light of life.[d]

Psalm 57

For the director of music. ⌊To the tune of⌋ "Do
    Not Destroy". Of David. A *miktam.*[a] When he
    had fled from Saul into the cave.

1Have mercy on me, O God, have mercy on
        me,
    for in you my soul takes refuge.
I will take refuge in the shadow of your
        wings
    until the disaster has passed.

2I cry out to God Most High,
    to God, who fulfils ⌊his purpose⌋ for me.
3He sends from heaven and saves me,
    rebuking those who hotly pursue me;
                                    Selah
    God sends his love and his faithfulness.

4I am in the midst of lions;
    I lie among ravenous beasts—
men whose teeth are spears and arrows,
    whose tongues are sharp swords.

5Be exalted, O God, above the heavens;
    let your glory be over all the earth.

6They spread a net for my feet—
    I was bowed down in distress.
They dug a pit in my path—
    but they have fallen into it themselves.
                                    Selah

7My heart is steadfast, O God,
    my heart is steadfast;
    I will sing and make music.
8Awake, my soul!
    Awake, harp and lyre!
    I will awaken the dawn.

9I will praise you, O Lord, among the
        nations;
    I will sing of you among the peoples.
10For great is your love, reaching to the
        heavens;
    your faithfulness reaches to the skies.

11Be exalted, O God, above the heavens;
    let your glory be over all the earth.

Psalm 58

For the director of music. ⌊To the tune of⌋ "Do
    Not Destroy". Of David. A *miktam.*[a]

1Do you rulers indeed speak justly?
    Do you judge uprightly among men?
2No, in your heart you devise injustice,
    and your hands mete out violence on the
        earth.
3Even from birth the wicked go astray;
    from the womb they are wayward and
        speak lies.
4Their venom is like the venom of a snake,
    like that of a cobra that has stopped its
        ears,

---

[a]Title: Probably a literary or musical term   [b]8 Or / *put my tears in your wineskin*
[c]13 Or *my soul*   [d]13 Or *the land of the living*
[a]Title: Probably a literary or musical term   [a]Title: Probably a literary or musical term

[5]that will not heed the tune of the charmer,
   however skilful the enchanter may be.

[6]Break the teeth in their mouths, O God;
   tear out, O LORD, the fangs of the lions!
[7]Let them vanish like water that flows
      away;
   when they draw the bow, let their
      arrows be blunted.
[8]Like a slug melting away as it moves
      along,
   like a stillborn child, may they not see
      the sun.

[9]Before your pots can feel ⌊the heat of⌋ the
      thorns—
   whether they be green or dry—the
      wicked will be swept away.[b]
[10]The righteous will be glad when they are
      avenged,
   when they bathe their feet in the blood
      of the wicked.
[11]Then men will say,
   "Surely the righteous still are rewarded;
      surely there is a God who judges the
      earth."

Psalm 59

For the director of music. ⌊To the tune of⌋ "Do
Not Destroy". Of David. A *miktam.*[a] When
Saul had sent men to watch David's house in
order to kill him.

[1]Deliver me from my enemies, O God;
   protect me from those who rise up
      against me.
[2]Deliver me from evildoers
   and save me from bloodthirsty men.

[3]See how they lie in wait for me!
   Fierce men conspire against me
   for no offence or sin of mine, O LORD.
[4]I have done no wrong, yet they are ready
      to attack me.
   Arise to help me; look on my plight!
[5]O LORD God Almighty, the God of Israel,
   rouse yourself to punish all the nations;
   show no mercy to wicked traitors. *Selah*

[6]They return at evening,
   snarling like dogs,
   and prowl about the city.
[7]See what they spew from their mouths—
   they spew out swords from their lips,
   and they say, "Who can hear us?"
[8]But you, O LORD, laugh at them;
   you scoff at all those nations.

[9]O my Strength, I watch for you;
   you, O God, are my fortress, [10]my
      loving God.

God will go before me
   and will let me gloat over those who
      slander me.
[11]But do not kill them, O Lord our shield,[b]
   or my people will forget.
In your might make them wander about,
   and bring them down.

[12]For the sins of their mouths,
   for the words of their lips,
   let them be caught in their pride.
For the curses and lies they utter,
[13]   consume them in wrath,
   consume them till they are no more.
Then it will be known to the ends of the
      earth
   that God rules over Jacob.   *Selah*

[14]They return at evening,
   snarling like dogs,
   and prowl about the city.
[15]They wander about for food
   and howl if not satisfied.
[16]But I will sing of your strength,
   in the morning I will sing of your love;
for you are my fortress,
   my refuge in times of trouble.

[17]O my Strength, I sing praise to you;
   you, O God, are my fortress, my loving
      God.

Psalm 60

For the director of music. To ⌊the tune of⌋ "The
Lily of the Covenant". A *miktam*[a] of David. For
teaching. When he fought Aram Naharaim[b] and
Aram Zobah,[c] and when Joab returned and
struck down twelve thousand Edomites in the
Valley of Salt.

[1]You have rejected us, O God, and burst
      forth upon us;
   you have been angry—now restore us!
[2]You have shaken the land and torn it
      open;
   mend its fractures, for it is quaking.
[3]You have shown your people desperate
      times;
   you have given us wine that makes us
      stagger.
[4]But for those who fear you, you have
      raised a banner
   to be unfurled against the bow.   *Selah*

[5]Save us and help us with your right hand,
   that those you love may be delivered.
[6]God has spoken from his sanctuary:
   "In triumph I will parcel out Shechem
   and measure off the Valley of Succoth.
[7]Gilead is mine, and Manasseh is mine;
   Ephraim is my helmet,
   Judah my sceptre.
[8]Moab is my washbasin,
   upon Edom I toss my sandal;
   over Philistia I shout in triumph."

[9]Who will bring me to the fortified city?
   Who will lead me to Edom?
[10]Is it not you, O God, you who have
      rejected us
   and no longer go out with our armies?
[11]Give us aid against the enemy,
   for the help of man is worthless.
[12]With God we shall gain the victory,
   and he will trample down our enemies.

[b]9 The meaning of the Hebrew for this verse is uncertain.
[b]11 Or *sovereign*   [a]Title: Probably a literary or musical term
[b]Title: That is, Arameans of North-west Mesopotamia

[a]Title: Probably a literary or musical term
[c]Title: That is, Arameans of central Syria

Psalm 61

For the director of music. With stringed
instruments. Of David.

[1]Hear my cry, O God;
   listen to my prayer.

[2]From the ends of the earth I call to you,
   I call as my heart grows faint;
   lead me to the rock that is higher than I.
[3]For you have been my refuge,
   a strong tower against the foe.

[4]I long to dwell in your tent for ever
   and take refuge in the shelter of your
      wings.   *Selah*
[5]For you have heard my vows, O God;
   you have given me the heritage of those
      who fear your name.

[6]Increase the days of the king's life,
   his years for many generations.
[7]May he be enthroned in God's presence
      for ever;
   appoint your love and faithfulness to
      protect him.

[8]Then will I ever sing praise to your name
   and fulfil my vows day after day.

Psalm 62

For the director of music. For Jeduthun.
A psalm of David.

[1]My soul finds rest in God alone;
   my salvation comes from him.
[2]He alone is my rock and my salvation;
   he is my fortress, I shall never be
      shaken.

[3]How long will you assault a man?
   Would all of you throw him down—
   this leaning wall, this tottering fence?
[4]They fully intend to topple him
   from his lofty place;
   they take delight in lies.
With their mouths they bless,
   but in their hearts they curse.   *Selah*

[5]Find rest, O my soul, in God alone;
   my hope comes from him.
[6]He alone is my rock and my salvation;
   he is my fortress, I shall not be shaken.
[7]My salvation and my honour depend on
      God;[a]
   he is my mighty rock, my refuge.
[8]Trust in him at all times, O people;
   pour out your hearts to him,
   for God is our refuge.   *Selah*

[9]Lowborn men are but a breath,
   the highborn are but a lie;
   if weighed on a balance, they are nothing;
   together they are only a breath.
[10]Do not trust in extortion
   or take pride in stolen goods;
   though your riches increase,
   do not set your heart on them.

[11]One thing God has spoken,
   two things have I heard:
that you, O God, are strong,
[12]   and that you, O Lord, are loving.
Surely you will reward each person
   according to what he has done.

Psalm 63

A psalm of David. When he was in the
Desert of Judah.

[1]O God, you are my God,
   earnestly I seek you;
my soul thirsts for you,
   my body longs for you,
in a dry and weary land
   where there is no water.

[2]I have seen you in the sanctuary
   and beheld your power and your glory.
[3]Because your love is better than life,
   my lips will glorify you.
[4]I will praise you as long as I live,
   and in your name I will lift up my hands.
[5]My soul will be satisfied as with the richest
      of foods;
   with singing lips my mouth will praise
      you.

[6]On my bed I remember you;
   I think of you through the watches of the
      night.
[7]Because you are my help,
   I sing in the shadow of your wings.
[8]My soul clings to you;
   your right hand upholds me.

[9]They who seek my life will be destroyed;
   they will go down to the depths of the
      earth.
[10]They will be given over to the sword
   and become food for jackals.

[11]But the king will rejoice in God;
   all who swear by God's name will praise
      him,
   while the mouths of liars will be
      silenced.

Psalm 64

For the director of music. A psalm of David.

[1]Hear me, O God, as I voice my complaint;
   protect my life from the threat of the
      enemy.
[2]Hide me from the conspiracy of the
      wicked,
   from that noisy crowd of evildoers.

[3]They sharpen their tongues like swords
   and aim their words like deadly arrows.
[4]They shoot from ambush at the innocent
      man;
   they shoot at him suddenly, without
      fear.

[5]They encourage each other in evil plans,
   they talk about hiding their snares;
   they say, "Who will see them?"[a]

---

[a]7 Or / God Most High is my salvation and my honour   [a]5 Or us

PSALM 61

'From the ends of the earth I call to you, I call as my heart grows faint; lead me to the rock that is higher than I' (v. 2).

THE ROCK THAT IS HIGHER THAN I! What a picture of the coming king, and his kingdom! A rock is solid, enduring, strong.

The idea of height, of something to strive for, of a goal to attain, has inspired countless people throughout the ages. Egyptians built pyramids, Babylonians built great 'ziggurats,' enormous brick buildings with an outside, zigzag staircase which led in a spiral, higher and higher, until people thought they were in the very presence of God himself. Architects in the Middle Ages built tall spires in their fine cathedrals.

People have climbed mountains to put their temples at the summits, to come nearer to God. There is a lot to be said for this picture of a rock that is higher than I, leading me up towards God and the things of heaven.

Yet for Christians, the rock that is higher than I is also a tiny babe, born in a manger, something so fragile that one blow from an animal's hoof, or one stroke of a soldier's sword, could end his life. There are similar contrasts in the parables of Jesus. Not just building upon a rock (Matt. 7:24–29) but also growing from a tiny seed, blown by the wind and scorched by the sun.

The dependability of God is found in that fragile life, just as much as in the solid rock. The infant Messiah is protected by God's 'love and faithfulness' so he can be 'enthroned in God's presence for ever' (v. 7). Such protection can be shared by each of us, giving us strength greater than the strength of any rock.

> O come to my heart, Lord Jesus;
> There is room in my heart for thee.

> (*Emily Elliott*)

→488

PSALM 75:1–3
'We give thanks to you, O God, we give thanks, for your Name is near; men tell of your wonderful deeds' (v. 1).

THE PSALMIST was moved to praise and gratitude because God's great deeds proved that he was with them. The divine Name was among them in power, honour, character and authority (cf. Isa. 30:26, 27) and he was deeply conscious of God's presence. We are reminded again of the revelation of the name Immanuel – 'God with us', also recorded by Isaiah (7:14).

It was with joy they recounted the deeds of God. What, we wonder, were those deeds? Did their hearts not become lighter as they rehearsed the evidences of God's goodness? Presumably, life for them was not without its problems such as sickness, injury, poverty and the same wide range of stresses which affect us today; even so, they counted their blessings. If you are reading this alone, could you pause to list some of God's blessings towards you? If you are sharing the reading, could you not share also evidences of God's goodness, further stimulating each other in prayer and praise to God?

I do not have the words to thank you, Lord;
I do not have the gift of gracious speech;
When all is said, my word is just a word
With real communication past my reach.

If only I had thoughts which would reveal
The depth of my indebtedness to you;
If only I could tell you how I feel
About the love you show, the things you do.

But then, you are a God who reads the heart;
Beyond my graceless words your eyes can see
Emotions void of verbal counterpart,
Those feelings which extol your love for me.

I open up my heart, Lord, to your gaze
Believing you will see a heart of praise.

→525

⁶They plot injustice and say,
  "We have devised a perfect plan!"
  Surely the mind and heart of man are
    cunning.

⁷But God will shoot them with arrows;
  suddenly they will be struck down.
⁸He will turn their own tongues against
    them
  and bring them to ruin;
  all who see them will shake their heads
    in scorn.

⁹All mankind will fear;
  they will proclaim the works of God
  and ponder what he has done.
¹⁰Let the righteous rejoice in the LORD
  and take refuge in him;
  let all the upright in heart praise him!

Psalm 65

For the director of music. A psalm of David.
A song.

¹Praise awaits*ᵃ* you, O God, in Zion;
  to you our vows will be fulfilled.
²O you who hear prayer,
  to you all men will come.
³When we were overwhelmed by sins,
  you forgave*ᵇ* our transgressions.
⁴Blessed are those you choose
  and bring near to live in your courts!
We are filled with the good things of your
    house,
  of your holy temple.

⁵You answer us with awesome deeds of
    righteousness,
  O God our Saviour,
the hope of all the ends of the earth
  and of the farthest seas,
⁶who formed the mountains by your power,
  having armed yourself with strength,
⁷who stilled the roaring of the seas,
  the roaring of their waves,
  and the turmoil of the nations.
⁸Those living far away fear your wonders;
  where morning dawns and evening fades
  you call forth songs of joy.

⁹You care for the land and water it;
  you enrich it abundantly.
The streams of God are filled with water
  to provide the people with corn,
  for so you have ordained it.*ᶜ*
¹⁰You drench its furrows
  and level its ridges;
you soften it with showers
  and bless its crops.
¹¹You crown the year with your bounty,
  and your carts overflow with
    abundance.
¹²The grasslands of the desert overflow;
  the hills are clothed with gladness.
¹³The meadows are covered with flocks
  and the valleys are mantled with corn;
  they shout for joy and sing.

Psalm 66

For the director of music. A song. A psalm.

¹Shout with joy to God, all the earth!
² Sing the glory of his name;
  make his praise glorious!
³Say to God, "How awesome are your
    deeds!
So great is your power
  that your enemies cringe before you.
⁴All the earth bows down to you;
  they sing praise to you,
  they sing praise to your name."   *Selah*

⁵Come and see what God has done,
  how awesome his works on man's
    behalf!
⁶He turned the sea into dry land,
  they passed through the waters on
    foot—
  come, let us rejoice in him.
⁷He rules for ever by his power,
  his eyes watch the nations—
  let not the rebellious rise up against him.
                                  Selah

⁸Praise our God, O peoples,
  let the sound of his praise be heard;
⁹he has preserved our lives
  and kept our feet from slipping.
¹⁰For you, O God, tested us;
  you refined us like silver.
¹¹You brought us into prison
  and laid burdens on our backs.
¹²You let men ride over our heads;
  we went through fire and water,
  but you brought us to a place of
    abundance.

¹³I will come to your temple with burnt
    offerings
  and fulfil my vows to you—
¹⁴vows my lips promised and my mouth
    spoke
  when I was in trouble.
¹⁵I will sacrifice fat animals to you
  and an offering of rams;
  I will offer bulls and goats.   *Selah*

¹⁶Come and listen, all you who fear God;
  let me tell you what he has done for me.
¹⁷I cried out to him with my mouth;
  his praise was on my tongue.
¹⁸If I had cherished sin in my heart,
  the Lord would not have listened;
¹⁹but God has surely listened
  and heard my voice in prayer.
²⁰Praise be to God,
  who has not rejected my prayer
  or withheld his love from me!

Psalm 67

For the director of music. With stringed
instruments. A psalm. A song.

¹May God be gracious to us and bless us
  and make his face shine upon us,   *Selah*
²that your ways may be known on earth,
  your salvation among all nations.

ᵃ1 Or befits; the meaning of the Hebrew for this word is uncertain.
ᵇ3 Or made atonement for   ᶜ9 Or for that is how you prepare the land

³May the peoples praise you, O God;
  may all the peoples praise you.
⁴May the nations be glad and sing for joy,
  for you rule the peoples justly
  and guide the nations of the earth. *Selah*
⁵May the peoples praise you, O God;
  may all the peoples praise you.

⁶Then the land will yield its harvest,
  and God, our God, will bless us.
⁷God will bless us,
  and all the ends of the earth will fear
    him.

Psalm 68

For the director of music. Of David. A psalm.
A song.

¹May God arise, may his enemies be
    scattered;
  may his foes flee before him.
²As smoke is blown away by the wind,
  may you blow them away;
  as wax melts before the fire,
  may the wicked perish before God.
³But may the righteous be glad
  and rejoice before God;
  may they be happy and joyful.

⁴Sing to God, sing praise to his name,
  extol him who rides on the clouds*ª*—
  his name is the LORD—
  and rejoice before him.
⁵A father to the fatherless, a defender of
    widows,
  is God in his holy dwelling.
⁶God sets the lonely in families,*ᵇ*
  he leads forth the prisoners with singing;
  but the rebellious live in a sun-scorched
    land.

⁷When you went out before your people, O
    God,
  when you marched through the
    wasteland,   *Selah*
⁸the earth shook,
  the heavens poured down rain,
  before God, the One of Sinai,
  before God, the God of Israel.
⁹You gave abundant showers, O God;
  you refreshed your weary inheritance.
¹⁰Your people settled in it,
  and from your bounty, O God, you
    provided for the poor.

¹¹The Lord announced the word,
  and great was the company of those who
    proclaimed it:
¹²"Kings and armies flee in haste;
  in the camps men divide the plunder.
¹³Even while you sleep among the
    campfires,*ᶜ*
  the wings of ⌊my⌋ dove are sheathed
    with silver,
  its feathers with shining gold."
¹⁴When the Almighty*ᵈ* scattered the kings in
    the land,
  it was like snow fallen on Zalmon.

¹⁵The mountains of Bashan are majestic
    mountains;
  rugged are the mountains of Bashan.
¹⁶Why gaze in envy, O rugged mountains,
  at the mountain where God chooses to
    reign,
  where the LORD himself will dwell for
    ever?
¹⁷The chariots of God are tens of thousands
    and thousands of thousands;
  the Lord ⌊has come⌋ from Sinai into his
    sanctuary.
¹⁸When you ascended on high,
  you led captives in your train;
  you received gifts from men,
  even from*ᵉ* the rebellious—
    that you,*ᶠ* O LORD God, might dwell
    there.

¹⁹Praise be to the Lord, to God our Saviour,
  who daily bears our burdens.   *Selah*
²⁰Our God is a God who saves;
  from the Sovereign LORD comes escape
    from death.

²¹Surely God will crush the heads of his
    enemies,
  the hairy crowns of those who go on in
    their sins.
²²The Lord says, "I will bring them from
    Bashan;
  I will bring them from the depths of the
    sea,
²³that you may plunge your feet in the blood
    of your foes,
  while the tongues of your dogs have
    their share."

²⁴Your procession has come into view, O
    God,
  the procession of my God and King into
    the sanctuary.
²⁵In front are the singers, after them the
    musicians;
  with them are the maidens playing
    tambourines.
²⁶Praise God in the great congregation;
  praise the LORD in the assembly of
    Israel.
²⁷There is the little tribe of Benjamin,
    leading them,
  there the great throng of Judah's
    princes,
  and there the princes of Zebulun and of
    Naphtali.

²⁸Summon your power, O God;*ᵍ*
  show us your strength, O God, as you
    have done before.
²⁹Because of your temple at Jerusalem
  kings will bring you gifts.
³⁰Rebuke the beast among the reeds,
  the herd of bulls among the calves of the
    nations.
  Humbled, may it bring bars of silver.
  Scatter the nations who delight in war.

[31]Envoys will come from Egypt;
Cush[h] will submit herself to God.

[32]Sing to God, O kingdoms of the earth,
sing praise to the Lord, *Selah*
[33]to him who rides the ancient skies above,
who thunders with mighty voice.
[34]Proclaim the power of God,
whose majesty is over Israel,
whose power is in the skies.
[35]You are awesome, O God, in your
sanctuary;
the God of Israel gives power and
strength to his people.

Praise be to God!

Psalm 69

For the director of music. To ⌊the tune of⌋
"Lilies". Of David.

[1]Save me, O God,
for the waters have come up to my neck.
[2]I sink in the miry depths,
where there is no foothold.
I have come into the deep waters;
the floods engulf me.
[3]I am worn out calling for help;
my throat is parched.
My eyes fail,
looking for my God.
[4]Those who hate me without reason
outnumber the hairs of my head;
many are my enemies without cause,
those who seek to destroy me.
I am forced to restore
what I did not steal.

[5]You know my folly, O God;
my guilt is not hidden from you.

[6]May those who hope in you
not be disgraced because of me,
O Lord, the Lord Almighty;
may those who seek you
not be put to shame because of me,
O God of Israel.
[7]For I endure scorn for your sake,
and shame covers my face.
[8]I am a stranger to my brothers,
an alien to my own mother's sons;
[9]for zeal for your house consumes me,
and the insults of those who insult you
fall on me.
[10]When I weep and fast,
I must endure scorn;
[11]when I put on sackcloth,
people make sport of me.
[12]Those who sit at the gate mock me,
and I am the song of the drunkards.

[13]But I pray to you, O Lord,
in the time of your favour;
in your great love, O God,
answer me with your sure salvation.
[14]Rescue me from the mire,
do not let me sink;
deliver me from those who hate me,
from the deep waters.

[15]Do not let the floodwaters engulf me
or the depths swallow me up
or the pit close its mouth over me.
[16]Answer me, O Lord, out of the goodness
of your love;
in your great mercy turn to me.
[17]Do not hide your face from your servant;
answer me quickly, for I am in trouble.
[18]Come near and rescue me;
redeem me because of my foes.

[19]You know how I am scorned, disgraced
and shamed;
all my enemies are before you.
[20]Scorn has broken my heart
and has left me helpless;
I looked for sympathy, but there was
none,
for comforters, but I found none.
[21]They put gall in my food
and gave me vinegar for my thirst.

[22]May the table set before them become a
snare;
may it become retribution and[a] a trap.
[23]May their eyes be darkened so that they
cannot see,
and their backs be bent for ever.
[24]Pour out your wrath on them;
let your fierce anger overtake them.
[25]May their place be deserted;
let there be no-one to dwell in their
tents.
[26]For they persecute those you wound
and talk about the pain of those you
hurt.
[27]Charge them with crime upon crime;
do not let them share in your salvation.
[28]May they be blotted out of the book of life
and not be listed with the righteous.

[29]I am in pain and distress;
may your salvation, O God, protect me.

[30]I will praise God's name in song
and glorify him with thanksgiving.
[31]This will please the Lord more than an ox,
more than a bull with its horns and
hoofs.
[32]The poor will see and be glad—
you who seek God, may your hearts
live!
[33]The Lord hears the needy
and does not despise his captive people.

[34]Let heaven and earth praise him,
the seas and all that move in them,
[35]for God will save Zion
and rebuild the cities of Judah.
Then people will settle there and possess
it;
[36] the children of his servants will inherit
it,
and those who love his name will dwell
there.

Psalm 70

For the director of music. Of David. A petition.
[1]Hasten, O God, to save me;
O Lord, come quickly to help me.

---

[h]31 That is, the upper Nile region [a]22 Or *snare / and their fellowship become*

²May those who seek my life
be put to shame and confusion;
may all who desire my ruin
be turned back in disgrace.
³May those who say to me, "Aha! Aha!"
turn back because of their shame.
⁴But may all who seek you
rejoice and be glad in you;
may those who love your salvation always
say,
"Let God be exalted!"

⁵Yet I am poor and needy;
come quickly to me, O God.
You are my help and my deliverer;
O LORD, do not delay.

Psalm 71

¹In you, O LORD, I have taken refuge;
let me never be put to shame.
²Rescue me and deliver me in your
righteousness;
turn your ear to me and save me.
³Be my rock of refuge,
to which I can always go;
give the command to save me,
for you are my rock and my fortress.
⁴Deliver me, O my God, from the hand of
the wicked,
from the grasp of evil and cruel men.

⁵For you have been my hope, O Sovereign
LORD,
my confidence since my youth.
⁶From my birth I have relied on you;
you brought me forth from my mother's
womb.
I will ever praise you.
⁷I have become like a portent to many,
but you are my strong refuge.
⁸My mouth is filled with your praise,
declaring your splendour all day long.

⁹Do not cast me away when I am old;
do not forsake me when my strength is
gone.
¹⁰For my enemies speak against me;
those who wait to kill me conspire
together.
¹¹They say, "God has forsaken him;
pursue him and seize him,
for no-one will rescue him."
¹²Be not far from me, O God;
come quickly, O my God, to help me.
¹³May my accusers perish in shame;
may those who want to harm me
be covered with scorn and disgrace.

¹⁴But as for me, I shall always have hope;
I will praise you more and more.
¹⁵My mouth will tell of your righteousness,
of your salvation all day long,
though I know not its measure.
¹⁶I will come and proclaim your mighty acts,
O Sovereign LORD;
I will proclaim your righteousness,
yours alone.

¹⁷Since my youth, O God, you have taught
me,
and to this day I declare your
marvellous deeds.
¹⁸Even when I am old and grey,
do not forsake me, O God,
till I declare your power to the next
generation,
your might to all who are to come.

¹⁹Your righteousness reaches to the skies, O
God,
you who have done great things.
Who, O God, is like you?
²⁰Though you have made me see troubles,
many and bitter,
you will restore my life again;
from the depths of the earth
you will again bring me up.
²¹You will increase my honour
and comfort me once again.

²²I will praise you with the harp
for your faithfulness, O my God;
I will sing praise to you with the lyre,
O Holy One of Israel.
²³My lips will shout for joy
when I sing praise to you—
I, whom you have redeemed.
²⁴My tongue will tell of your righteous acts
all day long,
for those who wanted to harm me
have been put to shame and confusion.

Psalm 72

Of Solomon.

¹Endow the king with your justice, O God,
the royal son with your righteousness.
²He will*ª* judge your people in
righteousness,
your afflicted ones with justice.
³The mountains will bring prosperity to the
people,
the hills the fruit of righteousness.
⁴He will defend the afflicted among the
people
and save the children of the needy;
he will crush the oppressor.

⁵He will endure*ᵇ* as long as the sun,
as long as the moon, through all
generations.
⁶He will be like rain falling on a mown field,
like showers watering the earth.
⁷In his days the righteous will flourish;
prosperity will abound till the moon is
no more.

⁸He will rule from sea to sea
and from the River*ᶜ* to the ends of the
earth.*ᵈ*
⁹The desert tribes will bow before him
and his enemies will lick the dust.
¹⁰The kings of Tarshish and of distant shores
will bring tribute to him;
the kings of Sheba and Seba
will present him gifts.

ª2 Or *May he*; similarly in verses 3–11 and 17   *ᵇ5* Septuagint; Hebrew *You will be feared*
ᶜ8 That is, the Euphrates   *ᵈ8* Or *the end of the land*

11All kings will bow down to him
   and all nations will serve him.

12For he will deliver the needy who cry out,
   the afflicted who have no-one to help.
13He will take pity on the weak and the
   needy
   and save the needy from death.
14He will rescue them from oppression and
   violence,
   for precious is their blood in his sight.

15Long may he live!
   May gold from Sheba be given to him.
May people ever pray for him
   and bless him all day long.
16Let corn abound throughout the land;
   on the tops of the hills may it sway.
Let its fruit flourish like Lebanon;
   let it thrive like the grass of the field.
17May his name endure for ever;
   may it continue as long as the sun.

All nations will be blessed through him,
   and they will call him blessed.

18Praise be to the Lord God, the God of
   Israel,
   who alone does marvellous deeds.
19Praise be to his glorious name for ever;
   may the whole earth be filled with his
   glory.
            Amen and Amen.

20This concludes the prayers of David son of
   Jesse.

BOOK III

Psalms 73–89

Psalm 73

A psalm of Asaph.
1Surely God is good to Israel,
   to those who are pure in heart.

2But as for me, my feet had almost slipped;
   I had nearly lost my foothold.
3For I envied the arrogant
   when I saw the prosperity of the
   wicked.

4They have no struggles;
   their bodies are healthy and strong.*a*
5They are free from the burdens common to
   man;
   they are not plagued by human ills.
6Therefore pride is their necklace;
   they clothe themselves with violence.
7From their callous hearts comes iniquity;*b*
   the evil conceits of their minds know no
   limits.
8They scoff, and speak with malice;
   in their arrogance they threaten
   oppression.
9Their mouths lay claim to heaven,

and their tongues take possession of the
   earth.
10Therefore their people turn to them
   and drink up waters in abundance.*c*
11They say, ''How can God know?
   Does the Most High have knowledge?''

12This is what the wicked are like—
   always carefree, they increase in
   wealth.

13Surely in vain have I kept my heart pure;
   in vain have I washed my hands in
   innocence.
14All day long I have been plagued;
   I have been punished every morning.

15If I had said, ''I will speak thus,''
   I would have betrayed your children.
16When I tried to understand all this,
   it was oppressive to me
17till I entered the sanctuary of God;
   then I understood their final destiny.

18Surely you place them on slippery ground;
   you cast them down to ruin.
19How suddenly are they destroyed,
   completely swept away by terrors!
20As a dream when one awakes,
   so when you arise, O Lord,
   you will despise them as fantasies.

21When my heart was grieved
   and my spirit embittered,
22I was senseless and ignorant;
   I was a brute beast before you.

23Yet I am always with you;
   you hold me by my right hand.
24You guide me with your counsel,
   and afterwards you will take me into
   glory.
25Whom have I in heaven but you?
   And earth has nothing I desire besides
   you.
26My flesh and my heart may fail,
   but God is the strength of my heart
   and my portion for ever.

27Those who are far from you will perish;
   you destroy all who are unfaithful to
   you.
28But as for me, it is good to be near God.
   I have made the Sovereign Lord my
   refuge;
   I will tell of all your deeds.

Psalm 74

A *maskil*a of Asaph.
1Why have you rejected us for ever, O
   God?
   Why does your anger smoulder against
   the sheep of your pasture?
2Remember the people you purchased of
   old,
   the tribe of your inheritance, whom you
   redeemed—
   Mount Zion, where you dwelt.

---

a4 With a different word division of the Hebrew; Masoretic Text *struggles at their death; / their bodies are healthy*
b7 Syriac (see also Septuagint); Hebrew *Their eyes bulge with fat*
c10 The meaning of the Hebrew for this verse is uncertain.   *a*Title: Probably a literary or musical term

³Turn your steps towards these everlasting
ruins,
all this destruction the enemy has
brought on the sanctuary.

⁴Your foes roared in the place where you
met with us;
they set up their standards as signs.
⁵They behaved like men wielding axes
to cut through a thicket of trees.
⁶They smashed all the carved panelling
with their axes and hatchets.
⁷They burned your sanctuary to the
ground;
they defiled the dwelling-place of your
Name.
⁸They said in their hearts, "We will crush
them completely!"
They burned every place where God
was worshipped in the land.
⁹We are given no miraculous signs;
no prophets are left,
and none of us knows how long this will
be.

¹⁰How long will the enemy mock you, O
God?
Will the foe revile your name for
ever?
¹¹Why do you hold back your hand, your
right hand?
Take it from the folds of your garment
and destroy them!

¹²But you, O God, are my king from of old;
you bring salvation upon the earth.
¹³It was you who split open the sea by your
power;
you broke the heads of the monster in
the waters.
¹⁴It was you who crushed the heads of
Leviathan
and gave him as food to the creatures of
the desert.
¹⁵It was you who opened up springs and
streams;
you dried up the ever-flowing rivers.
¹⁶The day is yours, and yours also the
night;
you established the sun and moon.
¹⁷It was you who set all the boundaries of
the earth;
you made both summer and winter.

¹⁸Remember how the enemy has mocked
you, O LORD,
how foolish people have reviled your
name.
¹⁹Do not hand over the life of your dove to
wild beasts;
do not forget the lives of your afflicted
people for ever.
²⁰Have regard for your covenant,
because haunts of violence fill the dark
places of the land.
²¹Do not let the oppressed retreat in
disgrace;
may the poor and needy praise your
name.

²²Rise up, O God, and defend your cause;
remember how fools mock you all day
long.
²³Do not ignore the clamour of your
adversaries,
the uproar of your enemies, which rises
continually.

Psalm 75

For the director of music. To the tune of, "Do
Not Destroy". A psalm of Asaph. A song.

¹We give thanks to you, O God,
we give thanks, for your Name is near;
men tell of your wonderful deeds.

²You say, "I choose the appointed time;
it is I who judge uprightly.
³When the earth and all its people quake,
it is I who hold its pillars firm.   *Selah*
⁴To the arrogant I say, 'Boast no more,'
and to the wicked, 'Do not lift up your
horns.
⁵Do not lift your horns against heaven;
do not speak with outstretched neck.' "

⁶No-one from the east or the west
or from the desert can exalt a man.
⁷But it is God who judges:
He brings one down, he exalts another.
⁸In the hand of the LORD is a cup
full of foaming wine mixed with spices;
he pours it out, and all the wicked of the
earth
drink it down to its very dregs.

⁹As for me, I will declare this for ever;
I will sing praise to the God of Jacob.
¹⁰I will cut off the horns of all the wicked,
but the horns of the righteous shall be
lifted up.

Psalm 76

For the director of music. With stringed
instruments. A psalm of Asaph. A song.

¹In Judah God is known;
his name is great in Israel.
²His tent is in Salem,
his dwelling-place in Zion.
³There he broke the flashing arrows,
the shields and the swords, the weapons
of war.   *Selah*

⁴You are resplendent with light,
more majestic than mountains rich with
game.
⁵Valiant men lie plundered,
they sleep their last sleep;
not one of the warriors
can lift his hands.
⁶At your rebuke, O God of Jacob,
both horse and chariot lie still.
⁷You alone are to be feared.
Who can stand before you when you are
angry?
⁸From heaven you pronounced judgment,
and the land feared and was quiet—

9when you, O God, rose up to judge,
  to save all the afflicted of the land.
                                                    Selah
10Surely your wrath against men brings you
    praise,
  and the survivors of your wrath are
    restrained.[a]

11Make vows to the LORD your God and fulfil
    them;
  let all the neighbouring lands
    bring gifts to the One to be feared.
12He breaks the spirit of rulers;
  he is feared by the kings of the earth.

Psalm 77

For the director of music. For Jeduthun. Of
Asaph. A psalm.

1I cried out to God for help;
  I cried out to God to hear me.
2When I was in distress, I sought the Lord;
  at night I stretched out untiring hands
  and my soul refused to be comforted.

3I remembered you, O God, and I groaned;
  I mused, and my spirit grew faint. *Selah*
4You kept my eyes from closing;
  I was too troubled to speak.
5I thought about the former days,
  the years of long ago;
6I remembered my songs in the night.
  My heart mused and my spirit enquired:

7"Will the Lord reject for ever?
  Will he never show his favour again?
8Has his unfailing love vanished for ever?
  Has his promise failed for all time?
9Has God forgotten to be merciful?
  Has he in anger withheld his
    compassion?"
                                                    Selah

10Then I thought, "To this I will appeal:
    the years of the right hand of the Most
    High."
11I will remember the deeds of the LORD;
  yes, I will remember your miracles of
    long ago.
12I will meditate on all your works
  and consider all your mighty deeds.

13Your ways, O God, are holy.
  What god is so great as our God?
14You are the God who performs miracles;
  you display your power among the
    peoples.
15With your mighty arm you redeemed your
    people,
  the descendants of Jacob and Joseph.
                                                    Selah

16The waters saw you, O God,
  the waters saw you and writhed;
  the very depths were convulsed.
17The clouds poured down water,
  the skies resounded with thunder;
  your arrows flashed back and forth.
18Your thunder was heard in the whirlwind,
  your lightning lit up the world;

the earth trembled and quaked.
19Your path led through the sea,
  your way through the mighty waters,
  though your footprints were not seen.

20You led your people like a flock
  by the hand of Moses and Aaron.

Psalm 78

A *maskil*[a] of Asaph.

1O my people, hear my teaching;
  listen to the words of my mouth.
2I will open my mouth in parables,
  I will utter hidden things, things from of
    old—
3what we have heard and known,
  what our fathers have told us.
4We will not hide them from their children;
  we will tell the next generation
  the praiseworthy deeds of the LORD,
  his power, and the wonders he has
    done.
5He decreed statutes for Jacob
  and established the law in Israel,
  which he commanded our forefathers
    to teach their children,
6so that the next generation would know
    them,
  even the children yet to be born,
  and they in turn would tell their
    children.
7Then they would put their trust in God
  and would not forget his deeds
  but would keep his commands.
8They would not be like their forefathers—
  a stubborn and rebellious generation,
  whose hearts were not loyal to God,
  whose spirits were not faithful to him.

9The men of Ephraim, though armed with
    bows,
  turned back on the day of battle;
10they did not keep God's covenant
  and refused to live by his law.
11They forgot what he had done,
  the wonders he had shown them.
12He did miracles in the sight of their fathers
  in the land of Egypt, in the region of
    Zoan.
13He divided the sea and led them through;
  he made the water stand firm like a wall.
14He guided them with the cloud by day
  and with light from the fire all night.
15He split the rocks in the desert
  and gave them water as abundant as the
    seas;
16he brought streams out of a rocky crag
  and made water flow down like rivers.

17But they continued to sin against him,
  rebelling in the desert against the Most
    High.
18They wilfully put God to the test
  by demanding the food they craved.
19They spoke against God, saying,
  "Can God spread a table in the desert?
20When he struck the rock, water gushed
    out,
  and streams flowed abundantly.

---

[a]10 Or *Surely the wrath of men brings you praise, / and with the remainder of wrath you arm yourself*
[a]Title: Probably a literary or musical term

But can he also give us food?
Can he supply meat for his people?''
21When the LORD heard them, he was very
angry;
his fire broke out against Jacob,
and his wrath rose against Israel,
22for they did not believe in God
or trust in his deliverance.
23Yet he gave a command to the skies above
and opened the doors of the heavens;
24he rained down manna for the people to
eat,
he gave them the grain of heaven.
25Men ate the bread of angels;
he sent them all the food they could eat.
26He let loose the east wind from the
heavens
and led forth the south wind by his
power.
27He rained meat down on them like dust,
flying birds like sand on the seashore.
28He made them come down inside their
camp,
all around their tents.
29They ate till they had more than enough,
for he had given them what they craved.
30But before they turned from the food they
craved,
even while it was still in their mouths,
31God's anger rose against them;
he put to death the sturdiest among
them,
cutting down the young men of Israel.

32In spite of all this, they kept on sinning;
in spite of his wonders, they did not
believe.
33So he ended their days in futility
and their years in terror.
34Whenever God slew them, they would
seek him;
they eagerly turned to him again.
35They remembered that God was their
Rock,
that God Most High was their
Redeemer.
36But then they would flatter him with their
mouths,
lying to him with their tongues;
37their hearts were not loyal to him,
they were not faithful to his covenant.
38Yet he was merciful;
he forgave their iniquities
and did not destroy them.
Time after time he restrained his anger
and did not stir up his full wrath.
39He remembered that they were but flesh,
a passing breeze that does not return.

40How often they rebelled against him in the
desert
and grieved him in the wasteland!
41Again and again they put God to the test;
they vexed the Holy One of Israel.
42They did not remember his power—
the day he redeemed them from the
oppressor,
43the day he displayed his miraculous signs
in Egypt,
his wonders in the region of Zoan.
44He turned their rivers to blood;

they could not drink from their streams.
45He sent swarms of flies that devoured
them,
and frogs that devastated them.
46He gave their crops to the grasshopper,
their produce to the locust.
47He destroyed their vines with hail
and their sycamore-figs with sleet.
48He gave over their cattle to the hail,
their livestock to bolts of lightning.
49He unleashed against them his hot anger,
his wrath, indignation and hostility—
a band of destroying angels.
50He prepared a path for his anger;
he did not spare them from death
but gave them over to the plague.
51He struck down all the firstborn of Egypt,
the firstfruits of manhood in the tents of
Ham.
52But he brought his people out like a flock;
he led them like sheep through the
desert.
53He guided them safely, so they were
unafraid;
but the sea engulfed their enemies.
54Thus he brought them to the border of his
holy land,
to the hill country his right hand had
taken.
55He drove out nations before them
and allotted their lands to them as an
inheritance;
he settled the tribes of Israel in their
homes.

56But they put God to the test
and rebelled against the Most High;
they did not keep his statutes.
57Like their fathers they were disloyal and
faithless,
as unreliable as a faulty bow.
58They angered him with their high places;
they aroused his jealousy with their
idols.
59When God heard them, he was very angry;
he rejected Israel completely.
60He abandoned the tabernacle of Shiloh,
the tent he had set up among men.
61He sent ˌthe ark ofˌ his might into
captivity,
his splendour into the hands of the
enemy.
62He gave his people over to the sword;
he was very angry with his inheritance.
63Fire consumed their young men,
and their maidens had no wedding
songs;
64their priests were put to the sword,
and their widows could not weep.

65Then the Lord awoke as from sleep,
as a man wakes from the stupor of wine.
66He beat back his enemies;
he put them to everlasting shame.
67Then he rejected the tents of Joseph,
he did not choose the tribe of Ephraim;
68but he chose the tribe of Judah,
Mount Zion, which he loved.
69He built his sanctuary like the heights,
like the earth that he established for
ever.

70He chose David his servant
    and took him from the sheep pens;
71from tending the sheep he brought him
    to be the shepherd of his people Jacob,
    of Israel his inheritance.
72And David shepherded them with integrity
    of heart;
    with skilful hands he led them.

Psalm 79

A psalm of Asaph.

1O God, the nations have invaded your
    inheritance;
    they have defiled your holy temple,
    they have reduced Jerusalem to rubble.
2They have given the dead bodies of your
    servants
    as food to the birds of the air,
    the flesh of your saints to the beasts of
    the earth.
3They have poured out blood like water
    all around Jerusalem,
    and there is no-one to bury the dead.
4We are objects of reproach to our
    neighbours,
    of scorn and derision to those around
    us.

5How long, O LORD? Will you be angry for
    ever?
    How long will your jealousy burn like
    fire?
6Pour out your wrath on the nations
    that do not acknowledge you,
    on the kingdoms
    that do not call on your name;
7for they have devoured Jacob
    and destroyed his homeland.
8Do not hold against us the sins of the
    fathers;
    may your mercy come quickly to meet
    us,
    for we are in desperate need.

9Help us, O God our Saviour,
    for the glory of your name;
    deliver us and forgive our sins
    for your name's sake.
10Why should the nations say,
    "Where is their God?"
    Before our eyes, make known among the
    nations
    that you avenge the outpoured blood of
    your servants.
11May the groans of the prisoners come
    before you;
    by the strength of your arm
    preserve those condemned to die.

12Pay back into the laps of our neighbours
    seven times
    the reproach they have hurled at you, O
    Lord.
13Then we your people, the sheep of your
    pasture,
    will praise you for ever;
    from generation to generation
    we will recount your praise.

Psalm 80

For the director of music. To the tune of "The
Lilies of the Covenant". Of Asaph. A psalm.

1Hear us, O Shepherd of Israel,
    you who lead Joseph like a flock;
    you who sit enthroned between the
    cherubim, shine forth
2   before Ephraim, Benjamin and
    Manasseh.
Awaken your might;
    come and save us.

3Restore us, O God;
    make your face shine upon us,
    that we may be saved.

4O LORD God Almighty,
    how long will your anger smoulder
    against the prayers of your people?
5You have fed them with the bread of
    tears;
    you have made them drink tears by the
    bowlful.
6You have made us a source of contention
    to our neighbours,
    and our enemies mock us.

7Restore us, O God Almighty;
    make your face shine upon us,
    that we may be saved.

8You brought a vine out of Egypt;
    you drove out the nations and
    planted it.
9You cleared the ground for it,
    and it took root and filled the land.
10The mountains were covered with its
    shade,
    the mighty cedars with its branches.
11It sent out its boughs to the Sea,a
    its shoots as far as the River.b

12Why have you broken down its walls
    so that all who pass by pick its grapes?
13Boars from the forest ravage it
    and the creatures of the field feed on it.
14Return to us, O God Almighty!
    Look down from heaven and see!
    Watch over this vine,
15   the root your right hand has planted,
    the sonc you have raised up for
    yourself.

16Your vine is cut down, it is burned with
    fire;
    at your rebuke your people perish.
17Let your hand rest on the man at your right
    hand,
    the son of man you have raised up for
    yourself.
18Then we will not turn away from you;
    revive us, and we will call on your
    name.

19Restore us, O LORD God Almighty;
    make your face shine upon us,
    that we may be saved.

a11 Probably the Mediterranean   b11 That is, the Euphrates   c15 Or branch

Psalm 81

For the director of music. According to *gittith*.[a]
Of Asaph.

1 Sing for joy to God our strength;
   shout aloud to the God of Jacob!
2 Begin the music, strike the tambourine,
   play the melodious harp and lyre.

3 Sound the ram's horn at the New Moon,
   and when the moon is full, on the day of
     our Feast;
4 this is a decree for Israel,
   an ordinance of the God of Jacob.
5 He established it as a statute for Joseph
   when he went out against Egypt,
   where we heard a language we did not
     understand.[b]

6 He says, "I removed the burden from
     their shoulders;
   their hands were set free from the
     basket.
7 In your distress you called and I rescued
     you,
   I answered you out of a thundercloud;
   I tested you at the waters of Meribah.
                Selah

8 "Hear, O my people, and I will warn
     you—
   if you would but listen to me, O Israel!
9 You shall have no foreign god among you;
   you shall not bow down to an alien god.
10 I am the LORD your God,
   who brought you up out of Egypt.
   Open wide your mouth and I will fill it.

11 "But my people would not listen to me;
   Israel would not submit to me.
12 So I gave them over to their stubborn
     hearts
   to follow their own devices.

13 "If my people would but listen to me,
   if Israel would follow my ways,
14 how quickly would I subdue their enemies
   and turn my hand against their foes!
15 Those who hate the LORD would cringe
     before him,
   and their punishment would last for
     ever.
16 But you would be fed with the finest of
     wheat;
   with honey from the rock I would satisfy
     you."

Psalm 82

A psalm of Asaph.

1 God presides in the great assembly;
   he gives judgment among the "gods":

2 "How long will you[a] defend the unjust
   and show partiality to the wicked?
                Selah
3 Defend the cause of the weak and
     fatherless;
   maintain the rights of the poor and
     oppressed.

4 Rescue the weak and needy;
   deliver them from the hand of the
     wicked.

5 "They know nothing, they understand
     nothing.
   They walk about in darkness;
   all the foundations of the earth are
     shaken.

6 "I said, 'You are "gods";
   you are all sons of the Most High.'
7 But you will die like mere men;
   you will fall like every other ruler."

8 Rise up, O God, judge the earth,
   for all the nations are your inheritance.

Psalm 83

A song. A psalm of Asaph.

1 O God, do not keep silent;
   be not quiet, O God, be not still.
2 See how your enemies are astir,
   how your foes rear their heads.
3 With cunning they conspire against your
     people;
   they plot against those you cherish.
4 "Come," they say, "let us destroy them
     as a nation,
   that the name of Israel be remembered
     no more."

5 With one mind they plot together;
   they form an alliance against you—
6 the tents of Edom and the Ishmaelites,
   of Moab and the Hagrites,
7 Gebal,[a] Ammon and Amalek,
   Philistia, with the people of Tyre.
8 Even Assyria has joined them
   to lend strength to the descendants of
     Lot.   *Selah*

9 Do to them as you did to Midian,
   as you did to Sisera and Jabin at the
     river Kishon,
10 who perished at Endor
   and became like refuse on the ground.
11 Make their nobles like Oreb and Zeeb,
   all their princes like Zebah and
     Zalmunna,
12 who said, "Let us take possession
   of the pasture-lands of God."

13 Make them like tumble-weed, O my God,
   like chaff before the wind.
14 As fire consumes the forest
   or a flame sets the mountains ablaze,
15 so pursue them with your tempest
   and terrify them with your storm.
16 Cover their faces with shame
   so that men will seek your name, O
     LORD.

17 May they ever be ashamed and dismayed;
   may they perish in disgrace.
18 Let them know that you, whose name is
     the LORD—
   that you alone are the Most High over
     all the earth.

---

[a] Title: Probably a musical term   [b] 5 Or / and we heard a voice we had not known
[a] 2 The Hebrew is plural.   [a] 7 That is, Byblos

Psalm 84

For the director of music. According to *gittith.ᵃ*
Of the Sons of Korah. A psalm.

¹How lovely is your dwelling-place,
  O LORD Almighty!
²My soul yearns, even faints,
  for the courts of the LORD;
my heart and my flesh cry out
  for the living God.

³Even the sparrow has found a home,
  and the swallow a nest for herself,
  where she may have her young—
a place near your altar,
  O LORD Almighty, my King and my
    God.
⁴Blessed are those who dwell in your
    house;
  they are ever praising you.   *Selah*

⁵Blessed are those whose strength is in
    you,
  who have set their hearts on pilgrimage.
⁶As they pass through the Valley of Baca,
  they make it a place of springs;
  the autumn rains also cover it with
    pools.ᵇ
⁷They go from strength to strength,
  till each appears before God in Zion.

⁸Hear my prayer, O LORD God Almighty;
  listen to me, O God of Jacob.   *Selah*
⁹Look upon our shield,ᶜ O God;
  look with favour on your anointed one.

¹⁰Better is one day in your courts
  than a thousand elsewhere;
I would rather be a doorkeeper in the
    house of my God
than dwell in the tents of the wicked.
¹¹For the LORD God is a sun and shield;
  the LORD bestows favour and honour;
no good thing does he withhold
  from those whose walk is blameless.

¹²O LORD Almighty,
  blessed is the man who trusts in you.

Psalm 85

For the director of music. Of the Sons of Korah.
A psalm.

¹You showed favour to your land, O LORD;
  you restored the fortunes of Jacob.
²You forgave the iniquity of your people
  and covered all their sins.   *Selah*
³You set aside all your wrath
  and turned from your fierce anger.

⁴Restore us again, O God our Saviour,
  and put away your displeasure towards
    us.
⁵Will you be angry with us for ever?
  Will you prolong your anger through all
    generations?
⁶Will you not revive us again,
  that your people may rejoice in you?
⁷Show us your unfailing love, O LORD,
  and grant us your salvation.

⁸I will listen to what God the LORD will say;
  he promises peace to his people, his
    saints—
  but let them not return to folly.
⁹Surely his salvation is near those who fear
    him,
  that his glory may dwell in our land.

¹⁰Love and faithfulness meet together;
  righteousness and peace kiss each other.
¹¹Faithfulness springs forth from the earth,
  and righteousness looks down from
    heaven.
¹²The LORD will indeed give what is good,
  and our land will yield its harvest.
¹³Righteousness goes before him
  and prepares the way for his steps.

Psalm 86

A prayer of David.

¹Hear, O LORD, and answer me,
  for I am poor and needy.
²Guard my life, for I am devoted to you.
  You are my God; save your servant
  who trusts in you.
³Have mercy on me, O Lord,
  for I call to you all day long.
⁴Bring joy to your servant,
  for to you, O Lord,
  I lift up my soul.

⁵You are forgiving and good, O Lord,
  abounding in love to all who call to you.
⁶Hear my prayer, O LORD;
  listen to my cry for mercy.
⁷In the day of my trouble I will call to you,
  for you will answer me.

⁸Among the gods there is none like you, O
    Lord;
  no deeds can compare with yours.
⁹All the nations you have made
  will come and worship before you, O
    Lord;
  they will bring glory to your name.
¹⁰For you are great and do marvellous
    deeds;
  you alone are God.

¹¹Teach me your way, O LORD,
  and I will walk in your truth;
give me an undivided heart,
  that I may fear your name.
¹²I will praise you, O Lord my God, with all
    my heart;
  I will glorify your name for ever.
¹³For great is your love towards me;
  you have delivered me from the depths
    of the grave.ᵃ

¹⁴The arrogant are attacking me, O God;
  a band of ruthless men seeks my life—
  men without regard for you.
¹⁵But you, O Lord, are a compassionate and
    gracious God,
  slow to anger, abounding in love and
    faithfulness.

ᵃTitle: Probably a musical term   ᵇ6 Or *blessings*   ᶜ9 Or *sovereign*   ᵃ13 Hebrew *Sheol*

16Turn to me and have mercy on me;
    grant your strength to your servant
    and save the son of your maidservant.*b*
17Give me a sign of your goodness,
    that my enemies may see it and be put to
        shame,
    for you, O LORD, have helped me and
        comforted me.

Psalm 87

Of the Sons of Korah. A psalm. A song.

1He has set his foundation on the holy
    mountain;
2   the LORD loves the gates of Zion
    more than all the dwellings of Jacob.
3Glorious things are said of you,
    O city of God: *Selah*
4"I will record Rahab*a* and Babylon
    among those who acknowledge me—
    Philistia too, and Tyre, along with
        Cush*b*—
    and will say, 'This*c* one was born in
        Zion.'"

5Indeed, of Zion it will be said,
    "This one and that one were born in
        her,
    and the Most High himself will establish
        her."
6The LORD will write in the register of the
    peoples:
    "This one was born in Zion."   *Selah*
7As they make music they will sing,
    "All my fountains are in you."

Psalm 88

A song. A psalm of the Sons of Korah. For the
    director of music. According to *mahalath
    leannoth.a* A *maskilb* of Heman the Ezrahite.

1O LORD, the God who saves me,
    day and night I cry out before you.
2May my prayer come before you;
    turn your ear to my cry.

3For my soul is full of trouble
    and my life draws near the grave.*c*
4I am counted among those who go down to
    the pit;
    I am like a man without strength.
5I am set apart with the dead,
    like the slain who lie in the grave,
    whom you remember no more,
    who are cut off from your care.

6You have put me in the lowest pit,
    in the darkest depths.
7Your wrath lies heavily upon me;
    you have overwhelmed me with all your
        waves.   *Selah*
8You have taken from me my closest
        friends
    and have made me repulsive to them.
    I am confined and cannot escape;
9   my eyes are dim with grief.

I call to you, O LORD, every day;
    I spread out my hands to you.

10Do you show your wonders to the dead?
    Do those who are dead rise up and
        praise you?   *Selah*
11Is your love declared in the grave,
    your faithfulness in Destruction?*d*
12Are your wonders known in the place of
        darkness,
    or your righteous deeds in the land of
        oblivion?

13But I cry to you for help, O LORD;
    in the morning my prayer comes before
        you.
14Why, O LORD, do you reject me
    and hide your face from me?

15From my youth I have been afflicted and
        close to death;
    I have suffered your terrors and am in
        despair.
16Your wrath has swept over me;
    your terrors have destroyed me.
17All day long they surround me like a flood;
    they have completely engulfed me.
18You have taken my companions and loved
        ones from me;
    the darkness is my closest friend.

Psalm 89

A *maskila* of Ethan the Ezrahite.

1I will sing of the LORD's great love for
        ever;
    with my mouth I will make your
        faithfulness known through all
        generations.
2I will declare that your love stands firm for
        ever,
    that you established your faithfulness in
        heaven itself.

3You said, "I have made a covenant with
        my chosen one,
    I have sworn to David my servant,
4'I will establish your line for ever
    and make your throne firm through all
        generations.'"   *Selah*

5The heavens praise your wonders, O
        LORD,
    your faithfulness too, in the assembly of
        the holy ones.
6For who in the skies above can compare
        with the LORD?
    Who is like the LORD among the
        heavenly beings?
7In the council of the holy ones God is
        greatly feared;
    he is more awesome than all who
        surround him.
8O LORD God Almighty, who is like you?
    You are mighty, O LORD, and your
        faithfulness surrounds you.

9You rule over the surging sea;
    when its waves mount up, you still
        them.

---

b16 Or *save your faithful son*   *a4* A poetic name for Egypt   *b4* That is, the upper Nile region
c4 Or *"O Rahab and Babylon, / Philistia, Tyre and Cush, / I will record concerning those who acknowledge me: / 'This*
*a*Title: Possibly a tune, "The Suffering of Affliction"   *b*Title: Probably a literary or musical term
c3 Hebrew *Sheol*   *d11* Hebrew *Abaddon*   *a*Title: Probably a literary or musical term

10You crushed Rahab like one of the slain;
    with your strong arm you scattered your
    enemies.
11The heavens are yours, and yours also the
    earth;
    you founded the world and all that is in
    it.
12You created the north and the south;
    Tabor and Hermon sing for joy at your
    name.
13Your arm is endued with power;
    your hand is strong, your right hand
    exalted.

14Righteousness and justice are the
    foundation of your throne;
    love and faithfulness go before you.
15Blessed are those who have learned to
    acclaim you,
    who walk in the light of your presence,
    O LORD.
16They rejoice in your name all day long;
    they exult in your righteousness.
17For you are their glory and strength,
    and by your favour you exalt our horn.b
18Indeed, our shieldc belongs to the LORD,
    our king to the Holy One of Israel.

19Once you spoke in a vision,
    to your faithful people you said:
"I have bestowed strength on a warrior;
    I have exalted a young man from among
    the people.
20I have found David my servant;
    with my sacred oil I have anointed him.
21My hand will sustain him;
    surely my arm will strengthen him.
22No enemy will subject him to tribute;
    no wicked man will oppress him.
23I will crush his foes before him
    and strike down his adversaries.
24My faithful love will be with him,
    and through my name his hornd will be
    exalted.
25I will set his hand over the sea,
    his right hand over the rivers.
26He will call out to me, 'You are my Father,
    my God, the Rock my Saviour.'
27I will also appoint him my firstborn,
    the most exalted of the kings of the
    earth.
28I will maintain my love to him for ever,
    and my covenant with him will never
    fail.
29I will establish his line for ever,
    his throne as long as the heavens
    endure.

30"If his sons forsake my law
    and do not follow my statutes,
31if they violate my decrees
    and fail to keep my commands,
32I will punish their sin with the rod,
    their iniquity with flogging;
33but I will not take my love from him,
    nor will I ever betray my faithfulness.
34I will not violate my covenant
    or alter what my lips have uttered.

35Once for all, I have sworn by my
    holiness—
    and I will not lie to David—
36that his line will continue for ever
    and his throne endure before me like the
    sun;
37it will be established for ever like the
    moon,
    the faithful witness in the sky."   Selah

38But you have rejected, you have spurned,
    you have been very angry with your
    anointed one.
39You have renounced the covenant with
    your servant
    and have defiled his crown in the dust.
40You have broken through all his walls
    and reduced his strongholds to ruins.
41All who pass by have plundered him;
    he has become the scorn of his
    neighbours.
42You have exalted the right hand of his
    foes;
    you have made all his enemies rejoice.
43You have turned back the edge of his
    sword
    and have not supported him in battle.
44You have put an end to his splendour
    and cast his throne to the ground.
45You have cut short the days of his youth;
    you have covered him with a mantle of
    shame.   Selah

46How long, O LORD? Will you hide yourself
    for ever?
    How long will your wrath burn like fire?
47Remember how fleeting is my life.
    For what futility you have created all
    men!
48What man can live and not see death,
    or save himself from the power of the
    grave?e   Selah
49O Lord, where is your former great love,
    which in your faithfulness you swore to
    David?
50Remember, Lord, how your servant hasf
    been mocked,
    how I bear in my heart the taunts of all
    the nations,
51the taunts with which your enemies have
    mocked, O LORD,
    with which they have mocked every
    step of your anointed one.

52Praise be to the LORD for ever!
    Amen and Amen.

BOOK IV

Psalms 90–106

Psalm 90

A prayer of Moses the man of God.
1Lord, you have been our dwelling-place
    throughout all generations.
2Before the mountains were born

b17 *Horn* here symbolises strong one.   c18 Or *sovereign*   d24 *Horn* here symbolises strength.
e48 Hebrew *Sheol*   f50 Or *your servants have*

or you brought forth the earth and the
world,
from everlasting to everlasting you are
God.

³You turn men back to dust,
saying, "Return to dust, O sons of
men."
⁴For a thousand years in your sight
are like a day that has just gone by,
or like a watch in the night.
⁵You sweep men away in the sleep of
death;
they are like the new grass of the
morning—
⁶though in the morning it springs up new,
by evening it is dry and withered.

⁷We are consumed by your anger
and terrified by your indignation.
⁸You have set our iniquities before you,
our secret sins in the light of your
presence.
⁹All our days pass away under your wrath;
we finish our years with a moan.
¹⁰The length of our days is seventy years—
or eighty, if we have the strength;
yet their span*a* is but trouble and sorrow,
for they quickly pass, and we fly away.

¹¹Who knows the power of your anger?
For your wrath is as great as the fear
that is due to you.
¹²Teach us to number our days aright,
that we may gain a heart of wisdom.

¹³Relent, O LORD! How long will it be?
Have compassion on your servants.
¹⁴Satisfy us in the morning with your
unfailing love,
that we may sing for joy and be glad all
our days.
¹⁵Make us glad for as many days as you have
afflicted us,
for as many years as we have seen
trouble.
¹⁶May your deeds be shown to your
servants,
your splendour to their children.

¹⁷May the favour*b* of the Lord our God rest
upon us;
establish the work of our hands for us—
yes, establish the work of our hands.

Psalm 91

¹He who dwells in the shelter of the Most
High
will rest in the shadow of the Almighty.*a*
²I will say*b* of the LORD, "He is my refuge
and my fortress,
my God, in whom I trust."

³Surely he will save you from the fowler's
snare
and from the deadly pestilence.
⁴He will cover you with his feathers,
and under his wings you will find refuge;

his faithfulness will be your shield and
rampart.
⁵You will not fear the terror of night,
nor the arrow that flies by day,
⁶nor the pestilence that stalks in the
darkness,
nor the plague that destroys at midday.
⁷A thousand may fall at your side,
ten thousand at your right hand,
but it will not come near you.
⁸You will only observe with your eyes
and see the punishment of the wicked.

⁹If you make the Most High your
dwelling—
even the LORD, who is my refuge—
¹⁰then no harm will befall you,
no disaster will come near your tent.
¹¹For he will command his angels
concerning you
to guard you in all your ways;
¹²they will lift you up in their hands,
so that you will not strike your foot
against a stone.
¹³You will tread upon the lion and the cobra;
you will trample the great lion and the
serpent.

¹⁴"Because he loves me," says the LORD, "I
will rescue him;
I will protect him, for he acknowledges
my name.
¹⁵He will call upon me, and I will answer
him;
I will be with him in trouble,
I will deliver him and honour him.
¹⁶With long life will I satisfy him
and show him my salvation."

Psalm 92

A psalm. A song. For the Sabbath day.

¹It is good to praise the LORD
and make music to your name, O Most
High,
²to proclaim your love in the morning
and your faithfulness at night,
³to the music of the ten-stringed lyre
and the melody of the harp.

⁴For you make me glad by your deeds, O
LORD;
I sing for joy at the work of your hands.
⁵How great are your works, O LORD,
how profound your thoughts!
⁶The senseless man does not know,
fools do not understand,
⁷that though the wicked spring up like grass
and all evildoers flourish,
they will be for ever destroyed.

⁸But you, O LORD, are exalted for ever.

⁹For surely your enemies, O LORD,
surely your enemies will perish;
all evildoers will be scattered.
¹⁰You have exalted my horn*a* like that of a
wild ox;
fine oils have been poured upon me.

---

*a*10 Or *yet the best of them*   *b*17 Or *beauty*   *a*1 Hebrew *Shaddai*   *b*2 Or *He says*
*a*10 *Horn* here symbolises strength.

¹¹My eyes have seen the defeat of my
   adversaries;
   my ears have heard the rout of my
     wicked foes.

¹²The righteous will flourish like a palm tree,
   they will grow like a cedar of Lebanon;
¹³planted in the house of the LORD,
   they will flourish in the courts of our
     God.
¹⁴They will still bear fruit in old age,
   they will stay fresh and green,
¹⁵proclaiming, ''The LORD is upright;
   he is my Rock, and there is no
     wickedness in him.''

Psalm 93

¹The LORD reigns, he is robed in majesty;
   the LORD is robed in majesty
   and is armed with strength.
The world is firmly established;
   it cannot be moved.
²Your throne was established long ago;
   you are from all eternity.

³The seas have lifted up, O LORD,
   the seas have lifted up their voice;
   the seas have lifted up their pounding
     waves.
⁴Mightier than the thunder of the great
     waters,
   mightier than the breakers of the sea—
   the LORD on high is mighty.

⁵Your statutes stand firm;
   holiness adorns your house
   for endless days, O LORD.

Psalm 94

¹O LORD, the God who avenges,
   O God who avenges, shine forth.
²Rise up, O Judge of the earth;
   pay back to the proud what they
     deserve.
³How long will the wicked, O LORD,
   how long will the wicked be jubilant?

⁴They pour out arrogant words;
   all the evildoers are full of boasting.
⁵They crush your people, O LORD;
   they oppress your inheritance.
⁶They slay the widow and the alien;
   they murder the fatherless.
⁷They say, ''The LORD does not see;
   the God of Jacob pays no heed.''

⁸Take heed, you senseless ones among the
     people;
   you fools, when will you become wise?
⁹Does he who implanted the ear not hear?
   Does he who formed the eye not see?
¹⁰Does he who disciplines nations not
     punish?
   Does he who teaches man lack
     knowledge?
¹¹The LORD knows the thoughts of man;
   he knows that they are futile.

¹²Blessed is the man you discipline, O LORD,
   the man you teach from your law;
¹³you grant him relief from days of trouble,
   till a pit is dug for the wicked.
¹⁴For the LORD will not reject his people;
   he will never forsake his inheritance.
¹⁵Judgment will again be founded on
     righteousness,
   and all the upright in heart will follow it.

¹⁶Who will rise up for me against the
     wicked?
   Who will take a stand for me against
     evildoers?
¹⁷Unless the LORD had given me help,
   I would soon have dwelt in the silence of
     death.
¹⁸When I said, ''My foot is slipping,''
   your love, O LORD, supported me.
¹⁹When anxiety was great within me,
   your consolation brought joy to my soul.

²⁰Can a corrupt throne be allied with you—
   one that brings on misery by its decrees?
²¹They band together against the righteous
   and condemn the innocent to death.
²²But the LORD has become my fortress,
   and my God the rock in whom I take
     refuge.
²³He will repay them for their sins
   and destroy them for their wickedness;
   the LORD our God will destroy them.

Psalm 95

¹Come, let us sing for joy to the LORD;
   let us shout aloud to the Rock of our
     salvation.
²Let us come before him with thanksgiving
   and extol him with music and song.

³For the LORD is the great God,
   the great King above all gods.
⁴In his hand are the depths of the earth,
   and the mountain peaks belong to him.
⁵The sea is his, for he made it,
   and his hands formed the dry land.

⁶Come, let us bow down in worship,
   let us kneel before the LORD our Maker;
⁷for he is our God
   and we are the people of his pasture,
   the flock under his care.

Today, if you hear his voice,
⁸   do not harden your hearts as you did at
     Meribah,*ᵃ*
   as you did that day at Massah*ᵇ* in the
     desert,
⁹where your fathers tested and tried me,
   though they had seen what I did.
¹⁰For forty years I was angry with that
     generation;
   I said, ''They are a people whose hearts
     go astray,
   and they have not known my ways.''
¹¹So I declared on oath in my anger,
   ''They shall never enter my rest.''

ᵃ8 Meribah means quarrelling.   ᵇ8 Massah means testing.

Psalm 96

[1]Sing to the LORD a new song;
  sing to the LORD, all the earth.
[2]Sing to the LORD, praise his name;
  proclaim his salvation day after day.
[3]Declare his glory among the nations,
  his marvellous deeds among all peoples.

[4]For great is the LORD and most worthy of
    praise;
  he is to be feared above all gods.
[5]For all the gods of the nations are idols,
  but the LORD made the heavens.
[6]Splendour and majesty are before him;
  strength and glory are in his sanctuary.

[7]Ascribe to the LORD, O families of nations,
  ascribe to the LORD glory and strength.
[8]Ascribe to the LORD the glory due to his
    name;
  bring an offering and come into his
    courts.
[9]Worship the LORD in the splendour of his*a*
    holiness;
  tremble before him, all the earth.

[10]Say among the nations, "The LORD
    reigns."
  The world is firmly established, it
    cannot be moved;
  he will judge the peoples with equity.
[11]Let the heavens rejoice, let the earth be
    glad;
  let the sea resound, and all that is in it;
[12] let the fields be jubilant, and everything
    in them.
  Then all the trees of the forest will sing for
    joy;
[13] they will sing before the LORD, for he
    comes,
  he comes to judge the earth.
  He will judge the world in righteousness
  and the peoples in his truth.

Psalm 97

[1]The LORD reigns, let the earth be glad;
  let the distant shores rejoice.

[2]Clouds and thick darkness surround him;
  righteousness and justice are the
    foundation of his throne.
[3]Fire goes before him
  and consumes his foes on every side.
[4]His lightning lights up the world;
  the earth sees and trembles.
[5]The mountains melt like wax before the
    LORD,
  before the Lord of all the earth.
[6]The heavens proclaim his righteousness,
  and all the peoples see his glory.

[7]All who worship images are put to shame,
  those who boast in idols—
  worship him, all you gods!

[8]Zion hears and rejoices
  and the villages of Judah are glad
  because of your judgments, O LORD.

[9]For you, O LORD, are the Most High over
    all the earth;
  you are exalted far above all gods.

[10]Let those who love the LORD hate evil,
  for he guards the lives of his faithful
    ones
  and delivers them from the hand of the
    wicked.
[11]Light is shed upon the righteous
  and joy on the upright in heart.
[12]Rejoice in the LORD, you who are
    righteous,
  and praise his holy name.

Psalm 98

A psalm.

[1]Sing to the LORD a new song,
  for he has done marvellous things;
  his right hand and his holy arm
  have worked salvation for him.
[2]The LORD has made his salvation known
  and revealed his righteousness to the
    nations.
[3]He has remembered his love
  and his faithfulness to the house of
    Israel;
  all the ends of the earth have seen
  the salvation of our God.

[4]Shout for joy to the LORD, all the earth,
  burst into jubilant song with music;
[5]make music to the LORD with the harp,
  with the harp and the sound of singing,
[6]with trumpets and the blast of the ram's
    horn—
  shout for joy before the LORD, the King.

[7]Let the sea resound, and everything in it,
  the world, and all who live in it.
[8]Let the rivers clap their hands,
  let the mountains sing together for joy;
[9]let them sing before the LORD,
  for he comes to judge the earth.
  He will judge the world in righteousness
  and the peoples with equity.

Psalm 99

[1]The LORD reigns,
  let the nations tremble;
  he sits enthroned between the cherubim,
  let the earth shake.
[2]Great is the LORD in Zion;
  he is exalted over all the nations.
[3]Let them praise your great and awesome
    name—
  he is holy.

[4]The King is mighty, he loves justice—
  you have established equity;
  in Jacob you have done
  what is just and right.
[5]Exalt the LORD our God
  and worship at his footstool;
  he is holy.

[6]Moses and Aaron were among his priests,
  Samuel was among those who called on
    his name;

---

*a*9 Or LORD with the splendour of

they called on the LORD
and he answered them.
7He spoke to them from the pillar of cloud;
they kept his statutes and the decrees he
gave them.

8O LORD our God,
you answered them;
you were to Israel[a] a forgiving God,
though you punished their misdeeds.[b]
9Exalt the LORD our God
and worship at his holy mountain,
for the LORD our God is holy.

Psalm 100

A psalm. For giving thanks.

1Shout for joy to the LORD, all the earth.
2   Worship the LORD with gladness;
come before him with joyful songs.
3Know that the LORD is God.
It is he who made us, and we are his;[a]
we are his people, the sheep of his
pasture.

4Enter his gates with thanksgiving
and his courts with praise;
give thanks to him and praise his name.
5For the LORD is good and his love endures
for ever;
his faithfulness continues through all
generations.

Psalm 101

Of David. A psalm.

1I will sing of your love and justice;
to you, O LORD, I will sing praise.
2I will be careful to lead a blameless life—
when will you come to me?

I will walk in my house
with blameless heart.
3I will set before my eyes
no vile thing.

The deeds of faithless men I hate;
they shall not cling to me.
4Men of perverse heart shall be far from
me;
I will have nothing to do with evil.

5Whoever slanders his neighbour in secret,
him will I put to silence;
whoever has haughty eyes and a proud
heart,
him will I not endure.

6My eyes will be on the faithful in the land,
that they may dwell with me;
he whose walk is blameless
will minister to me.

7No-one who practises deceit
will dwell in my house;
no-one who speaks falsely
will stand in my presence.

8Every morning I will put to silence
all the wicked in the land;

I will cut off every evildoer
from the city of the LORD.

Psalm 102

*A prayer of an afflicted man. When he is faint
and pours out his lament before the LORD.*

1Hear my prayer, O LORD;
let my cry for help come to you.
2Do not hide your face from me
when I am in distress.
Turn your ear to me;
when I call, answer me quickly.

3For my days vanish like smoke;
my bones burn like glowing embers.
4My heart is blighted and withered like
grass;
I forget to eat my food.
5Because of my loud groaning
I am reduced to skin and bones.
6I am like a desert owl,
like an owl among the ruins.
7I lie awake; I have become
like a bird alone on a roof.
8All day long my enemies taunt me;
those who rail against me use my name
as a curse.
9For I eat ashes as my food
and mingle my drink with tears
10because of your great wrath,
for you have taken me up and thrown
me aside.
11My days are like the evening shadow;
I wither away like grass.

12But you, O LORD, sit enthroned for ever;
your renown endures through all
generations.
13You will arise and have compassion on
Zion,
for it is time to show favour to her;
the appointed time has come.
14For her stones are dear to your servants;
her very dust moves them to pity.
15The nations will fear the name of the LORD,
all the kings of the earth will revere your
glory.
16For the LORD will rebuild Zion
and appear in his glory.
17He will respond to the prayer of the
destitute;
he will not despise their plea.

18Let this be written for a future generation,
that a people not yet created may praise
the LORD:
19"The LORD looked down from his
sanctuary on high,
from heaven he viewed the earth,
20to hear the groans of the prisoners
and release those condemned to death."
21So the name of the LORD will be declared
in Zion
and his praise in Jerusalem
22when the peoples and the kingdoms
assemble to worship the LORD.

23In the course of my life[a] he broke my
strength;
he cut short my days.

---

a8 Hebrew them   b8 Or / an avenger of the wrongs done to them
a3 Or and not we ourselves   a23 Or By his power

24So I said:
"Do not take me away, O my God, in
the midst of my days;
your years go on through all
generations.
25In the beginning you laid the foundations
of the earth,
and the heavens are the work of your
hands.
26They will perish, but you remain;
they will all wear out like a garment.
Like clothing you will change them
and they will be discarded.
27But you remain the same,
and your years will never end.
28The children of your servants will live in
your presence;
their descendants will be established
before you."

Psalm 103

Of David.

1Praise the LORD, O my soul;
all my inmost being, praise his holy
name.
2Praise the LORD, O my soul,
and forget not all his benefits—
3who forgives all your sins
and heals all your diseases,
4who redeems your life from the pit
and crowns you with love and
compassion,
5who satisfies your desires with good things
so that your youth is renewed like the
eagle's.

6The LORD works righteousness
and justice for all the oppressed.

7He made known his ways to Moses,
his deeds to the people of Israel:
8The LORD is compassionate and gracious,
slow to anger, abounding in love.
9He will not always accuse,
nor will he harbour his anger for ever;
10he does not treat us as our sins deserve
or repay us according to our iniquities.
11For as high as the heavens are above the
earth,
so great is his love for those who fear
him;
12as far as the east is from the west,
so far has he removed our
transgressions from us.
13As a father has compassion on his
children,
so the LORD has compassion on those
who fear him;
14for he knows how we are formed,
he remembers that we are dust.
15As for man, his days are like grass,
he flourishes like a flower of the field;
16the wind blows over it and it is gone,
and its place remembers it no more.
17But from everlasting to everlasting
the LORD's love is with those who fear
him,
and his righteousness with their
children's children—

18with those who keep his covenant
and remember to obey his precepts.

19The LORD has established his throne in
heaven,
and his kingdom rules over all.

20Praise the LORD, you his angels,
you mighty ones who do his bidding,
who obey his word.
21Praise the LORD, all his heavenly hosts,
you his servants who do his will.
22Praise the LORD, all his works
everywhere in his dominion.

Praise the LORD, O my soul.

Psalm 104

1Praise the LORD, O my soul.

O LORD my God, you are very great;
you are clothed with splendour and
majesty.
2He wraps himself in light as with a
garment;
he stretches out the heavens like a tent
3 and lays the beams of his upper
chambers on their waters.
He makes the clouds his chariot
and rides on the wings of the wind.
4He makes winds his messengers,[a]
flames of fire his servants.

5He set the earth on its foundations;
it can never be moved.
6You covered it with the deep as with a
garment;
the waters stood above the mountains.
7But at your rebuke the waters fled,
at the sound of your thunder they took
to flight;
8they flowed over the mountains,
they went down into the valleys,
to the place you assigned for them.
9You set a boundary they cannot cross;
never again will they cover the earth.

10He makes springs pour water into the
ravines;
it flows between the mountains.
11They give water to all the beasts of the
field;
the wild donkeys quench their thirst.
12The birds of the air nest by the waters;
they sing among the branches.
13He waters the mountains from his upper
chambers;
the earth is satisfied by the fruit of his
work.
14He makes grass grow for the cattle,
and plants for man to cultivate—
bringing forth food from the earth:
15wine that gladdens the heart of man,
oil to make his face shine,
and bread that sustains his heart.
16The trees of the LORD are well watered,
the cedars of Lebanon that he planted.
17There the birds make their nests;
the stork has its home in the pine trees.

a4 Or angels

¹⁸The high mountains belong to the wild
    goats;
  the crags are a refuge for the conies.ᵇ

¹⁹The moon marks off the seasons,
  and the sun knows when to go down.
²⁰You bring darkness, it becomes night,
  and all the beasts of the forest prowl.
²¹The lions roar for their prey
  and seek their food from God.
²²The sun rises, and they steal away;
  they return and lie down in their dens.
²³Then man goes out to his work,
  to his labour until evening.

²⁴How many are your works, O LORD!
  In wisdom you made them all;
  the earth is full of your creatures.
²⁵There is the sea, vast and spacious,
  teeming with creatures beyond
    number—
  living things both large and small.
²⁶There the ships go to and fro,
  and the leviathan, which you formed to
    frolic there.

²⁷These all look to you
  to give them their food at the proper
    time.
²⁸When you give it to them,
  they gather it up;
  when you open your hand,
  they are satisfied with good things.
²⁹When you hide your face,
  they are terrified;
  when you take away their breath,
  they die and return to the dust.
³⁰When you send your Spirit,
  they are created,
  and you renew the face of the earth.

³¹May the glory of the LORD endure for ever;
  may the LORD rejoice in his works—
³²he who looks at the earth, and it trembles,
  who touches the mountains, and they
    smoke.

³³I will sing to the LORD all my life;
  I will sing praise to my God as long as I
    live.
³⁴May my meditation be pleasing to him,
  as I rejoice in the LORD.
³⁵But may sinners vanish from the earth
  and the wicked be no more.

Praise the LORD, O my soul.

Praise the LORD.ᶜ

Psalm 105

¹Give thanks to the LORD, call on his name;
  make known among the nations what he
    has done.
²Sing to him, sing praise to him;
  tell of all his wonderful acts.
³Glory in his holy name;
  let the hearts of those who seek the
    LORD rejoice.

⁴Look to the LORD and his strength;
  seek his face always.

⁵Remember the wonders he has done,
  his miracles, and the judgments he
    pronounced,
⁶O descendants of Abraham his servant,
  O sons of Jacob, his chosen ones.
⁷He is the LORD our God;
  his judgments are in all the earth.

⁸He remembers his covenant for ever,
  the word he commanded, for a thousand
    generations,
⁹the covenant he made with Abraham,
  the oath he swore to Isaac.
¹⁰He confirmed it to Jacob as a decree,
  to Israel as an everlasting covenant:
¹¹"To you I will give the land of Canaan
  as the portion you will inherit."

¹²When they were but few in number,
  few indeed, and strangers in it,
¹³they wandered from nation to nation,
  from one kingdom to another.
¹⁴He allowed no-one to oppress them;
  for their sake he rebuked kings:
¹⁵"Do not touch my anointed ones;
  do my prophets no harm."

¹⁶He called down famine on the land
  and destroyed all their supplies of food;
¹⁷and he sent a man before them—
  Joseph, sold as a slave.
¹⁸They bruised his feet with shackles,
  his neck was put in irons,
¹⁹till what he foretold came to pass,
  till the word of the LORD proved him
    true.
²⁰The king sent and released him,
  the ruler of peoples set him free.
²¹He made him master of his household,
  ruler over all he possessed,
²²to instruct his princes as he pleased
  and teach his elders wisdom.

²³Then Israel entered Egypt;
  Jacob lived as an alien in the land of
    Ham.
²⁴The LORD made his people very fruitful;
  he made them too numerous for their
    foes,
²⁵whose hearts he turned to hate his people,
  to conspire against his servants.
²⁶He sent Moses his servant,
  and Aaron, whom he had chosen.
²⁷They performed his miraculous signs
    among them,
  his wonders in the land of Ham.
²⁸He sent darkness and made the land
    dark—
  for had they not rebelled against his
    words?
²⁹He turned their waters into blood,
  causing their fish to die.
³⁰Their land teemed with frogs,
  which went up into the bedrooms of
    their rulers.

ᵇ18 That is, the hyrax or rock badger
ᶜ35 Hebrew Hallelu Yah; in the Septuagint this line stands at the beginning of Psalm 105.

³¹He spoke, and there came swarms of flies,
and gnats throughout their country.
³²He turned their rain into hail,
with lightning throughout their land;
³³he struck down their vines and fig-trees
and shattered the trees of their country.
³⁴He spoke, and the locusts came,
grasshoppers without number;
³⁵they ate up every green thing in their land,
ate up the produce of their soil.
³⁶Then he struck down all the firstborn in
their land,
the firstfruits of all their manhood.

³⁷He brought out Israel, laden with silver
and gold,
and from among their tribes no-one
faltered.
³⁸Egypt was glad when they left,
because dread of Israel had fallen on
them.
³⁹He spread out a cloud as a covering,
and a fire to give light at night.
⁴⁰They asked, and he brought them quail
and satisfied them with the bread of
heaven.
⁴¹He opened the rock, and water gushed
out;
like a river it flowed in the desert.

⁴²For he remembered his holy promise
given to his servant Abraham.
⁴³He brought out his people with rejoicing,
his chosen ones with shouts of joy;
⁴⁴he gave them the lands of the nations,
and they fell heir to what others had
toiled for—
⁴⁵that they might keep his precepts
and observe his laws.

Praise the LORD.ᵃ

Psalm 106

¹Praise the LORD.ᵃ

Give thanks to the LORD, for he is good;
his love endures for ever.
²Who can proclaim the mighty acts of the
LORD
or fully declare his praise?
³Blessed are they who maintain justice,
who constantly do what is right.
⁴Remember me, O LORD, when you show
favour to your people,
come to my aid when you save them,
⁵that I may enjoy the prosperity of your
chosen ones,
that I may share in the joy of your nation
and join your inheritance in giving
praise.

⁶We have sinned, even as our fathers did;
we have done wrong and acted
wickedly.
⁷When our fathers were in Egypt,
they gave no thought to your miracles;
they did not remember your many
kindnesses,

and they rebelled by the sea, the Red
Sea.ᵇ
⁸Yet he saved them for his name's sake,
to make his mighty power known.
⁹He rebuked the Red Sea, and it dried up;
he led them through the depths as
through a desert.
¹⁰He saved them from the hand of the foe;
from the hand of the enemy he
redeemed them.
¹¹The waters covered their adversaries;
not one of them survived.
¹²Then they believed his promises
and sang his praise.

¹³But they soon forgot what he had done
and did not wait for his counsel.
¹⁴In the desert they gave in to their craving;
in the wasteland they put God to the
test.
¹⁵So he gave them what they asked for,
but sent a wasting disease upon them.

¹⁶In the camp they grew envious of Moses
and of Aaron, who was consecrated to
the LORD.
¹⁷The earth opened up and swallowed
Dathan;
it buried the company of Abiram.
¹⁸Fire blazed among their followers;
a flame consumed the wicked.

¹⁹At Horeb they made a calf
and worshipped an idol cast from metal.
²⁰They exchanged their Glory
for an image of a bull, which eats grass.
²¹They forgot the God who saved them,
who had done great things in Egypt,
²²miracles in the land of Ham
and awesome deeds by the Red Sea.
²³So he said he would destroy them—
had not Moses, his chosen one,
stood in the breach before him
to keep his wrath from destroying them.

²⁴Then they despised the pleasant land;
they did not believe his promise.
²⁵They grumbled in their tents
and did not obey the LORD.
²⁶So he swore to them with uplifted hand
that he would make them fall in the
desert,
²⁷make their descendants fall among the
nations
and scatter them throughout the lands.

²⁸They yoked themselves to the Baal of Peor
and ate sacrifices offered to lifeless
gods;
²⁹they provoked the LORD to anger by their
wicked deeds;
and a plague broke out among them.
³⁰But Phinehas stood up and intervened,
and the plague was checked.
³¹This was credited to him as righteousness
for endless generations to come.

³²By the waters of Meribah they angered the
LORD,

ᵃ45 Hebrew *Hallelu Yah*   ᵃ1 Hebrew *Hallelu Yah*; also in verse 48
ᵇ7 Hebrew *Yam Suph*; that is, Sea of Reeds; also in verses 9 and 22

and trouble came to Moses because of
  them;
³³for they rebelled against the Spirit of God,
  and rash words came from Moses' lips.^c

³⁴They did not destroy the peoples
  as the LORD had commanded them,
³⁵but they mingled with the nations
  and adopted their customs.
³⁶They worshipped their idols,
  which became a snare to them.
³⁷They sacrificed their sons
  and their daughters to demons.
³⁸They shed innocent blood,
  the blood of their sons and daughters,
  whom they sacrificed to the idols of
    Canaan,
  and the land was desecrated by their
    blood.
³⁹They defiled themselves by what they did;
  by their deeds they prostituted
    themselves.

⁴⁰Therefore the LORD was angry with his
    people
  and abhorred his inheritance.
⁴¹He handed them over to the nations,
  and their foes ruled over them.
⁴²Their enemies oppressed them
  and subjected them to their power.
⁴³Many times he delivered them,
  but they were bent on rebellion
  and they wasted away in their sin.

⁴⁴But he took note of their distress
  when he heard their cry;
⁴⁵for their sake he remembered his covenant
  and out of his great love he relented.
⁴⁶He caused them to be pitied
  by all who held them captive.

⁴⁷Save us, O LORD our God,
  and gather us from the nations,
  that we may give thanks to your holy name
  and glory in your praise.

⁴⁸Praise be to the LORD, the God of Israel,
  from everlasting to everlasting.
  Let all the people say, ''Amen!''

Praise the LORD.

BOOK V

Psalms 107–150

Psalm 107

¹Give thanks to the LORD, for he is good;
  his love endures for ever.
²Let the redeemed of the LORD say this—
  those he redeemed from the hand of the
    foe,
³those he gathered from the lands,
  from east and west, from north and
    south.^a

⁴Some wandered in desert wastelands,
  finding no way to a city where they
    could settle.

⁵They were hungry and thirsty,
  and their lives ebbed away.
⁶Then they cried out to the LORD in their
    trouble,
  and he delivered them from their
    distress.
⁷He led them by a straight way
  to a city where they could settle.
⁸Let them give thanks to the LORD for his
    unfailing love
  and his wonderful deeds for men,
⁹for he satisfies the thirsty
  and fills the hungry with good things.

¹⁰Some sat in darkness and the deepest
    gloom,
  prisoners suffering in iron chains,
¹¹for they had rebelled against the words of
    God
  and despised the counsel of the Most
    High.
¹²So he subjected them to bitter labour;
  they stumbled, and there was no-one to
    help.
¹³Then they cried to the LORD in their
    trouble,
  and he saved them from their distress.
¹⁴He brought them out of darkness and the
    deepest gloom
  and broke away their chains.
¹⁵Let them give thanks to the LORD for his
    unfailing love
  and his wonderful deeds for men,
¹⁶for he breaks down gates of bronze
  and cuts through bars of iron.

¹⁷Some became fools through their
    rebellious ways
  and suffered affliction because of their
    iniquities.
¹⁸They loathed all food
  and drew near the gates of death.
¹⁹Then they cried to the LORD in their
    trouble,
  and he saved them from their distress.
²⁰He sent forth his word and healed them;
  he rescued them from the grave.
²¹Let them give thanks to the LORD for his
    unfailing love
  and his wonderful deeds for men.
²²Let them sacrifice thank-offerings
  and tell of his works with songs of joy.

²³Others went out on the sea in ships;
  they were merchants on the mighty
    waters.
²⁴They saw the works of the LORD,
  his wonderful deeds in the deep.
²⁵For he spoke and stirred up a tempest
  that lifted high the waves.
²⁶They mounted up to the heavens and went
    down to the depths;
  in their peril their courage melted away.
²⁷They reeled and staggered like drunken
    men;
  they were at their wits' end.
²⁸Then they cried out to the LORD in their
    trouble,
  and he brought them out of their
    distress.

^c33 Or *against his spirit, | and rash words came from his lips*   ^a3 Hebrew *north and the sea*

29He stilled the storm to a whisper;
   the waves of the sea were hushed.
30They were glad when it grew calm,
   and he guided them to their desired
      haven.
31Let them give thanks to the LORD for his
      unfailing love
   and his wonderful deeds for men.
32Let them exalt him in the assembly of the
      people
   and praise him in the council of the
      elders.

33He turned rivers into a desert,
   flowing springs into thirsty ground,
34and fruitful land into a salt waste,
   because of the wickedness of those who
      lived there.
35He turned the desert into pools of water
   and the parched ground into flowing
      springs;
36there he brought the hungry to live,
   and they founded a city where they
      could settle.
37They sowed fields and planted vineyards
   that yielded a fruitful harvest;
38he blessed them, and their numbers greatly
      increased,
   and he did not let their herds diminish.

39Then their numbers decreased, and they
      were humbled
   by oppression, calamity and sorrow;
40he who pours contempt on nobles
   made them wander in a trackless waste.
41But he lifted the needy out of their
      affliction
   and increased their families like flocks.
42The upright see and rejoice,
   but all the wicked shut their mouths.

43Whoever is wise, let him heed these things
   and consider the great love of the LORD.

Psalm 108

A song. A psalm of David.

1My heart is steadfast, O God;
   I will sing and make music with all my
      soul.
2Awake, harp and lyre!
   I will awaken the dawn.
3I will praise you, O LORD, among the
      nations;
   I will sing of you among the peoples.
4For great is your love, higher than the
      heavens;
   your faithfulness reaches to the skies.
5Be exalted, O God, above the heavens,
   and let your glory be over all the earth.

6Save us and help us with your right hand,
   that those you love may be delivered.
7God has spoken from his sanctuary:
   "In triumph I will parcel out Shechem
   and measure off the Valley of Succoth.
8Gilead is mine, Manasseh is mine;
   Ephraim is my helmet,
   Judah my sceptre.

9Moab is my washbasin,
   upon Edom I toss my sandal;
   over Philistia I shout in triumph.''

10Who will bring me to the fortified city?
   Who will lead me to Edom?
11Is it not you, O God, you who have
      rejected us
   and no longer go out with our armies?
12Give us aid against the enemy,
   for the help of man is worthless.
13With God we shall gain the victory,
   and he will trample down our enemies.

Psalm 109

For the director of music. Of David. A psalm.

1O God, whom I praise,
   do not remain silent,
2for wicked and deceitful men
   have opened their mouths against me;
   they have spoken against me with lying
      tongues.
3With words of hatred they surround me;
   they attack me without cause.
4In return for my friendship they accuse me,
   but I am a man of prayer.
5They repay me evil for good,
   and hatred for my friendship.

6Appoint*a* an evil man*b* to oppose him;
   let an accuser*c* stand at his right hand.
7When he is tried, let him be found guilty,
   and may his prayers condemn him.
8May his days be few;
   may another take his place of
      leadership.
9May his children be fatherless
   and his wife a widow.
10May his children be wandering beggars;
   may they be driven*d* from their ruined
      homes.
11May a creditor seize all he has;
   may strangers plunder the fruits of his
      labour.
12May no-one extend kindness to him
   or take pity on his fatherless children.
13May his descendants be cut off,
   their names blotted out from the next
      generation.
14May the iniquity of his fathers be
      remembered before the LORD;
   may the sin of his mother never be
      blotted out.
15May their sins always remain before the
      LORD,
   that he may cut off the memory of them
      from the earth.

16For he never thought of doing a kindness,
   but hounded to death the poor
   and the needy and the broken-hearted.
17He loved to pronounce a curse—
   may it*e* come on him;
   he found no pleasure in blessing—
   may it be*f* far from him.
18He wore cursing as his garment;
   it entered into his body like water,
   into his bones like oil.

---

*a*6 Or , *They say:* , *''Appoint* (with quotation marks at the end of verse 19)   *b*6 Or *the Evil One*
*c*6 Or *let Satan*   *d*10 Septuagint; Hebrew *sought*   *e*17 Or *curse, / and it has*   *f*17 Or *blessing, / and it is*

¹⁹May it be like a cloak wrapped about him,
    like a belt tied for ever round him.
²⁰May this be the LORD's payment to my
    accusers,
    to those who speak evil of me.

²¹But you, O Sovereign LORD,
    deal well with me for your name's sake;
    out of the goodness of your love, deliver
    me.
²²For I am poor and needy,
    and my heart is wounded within me.
²³I fade away like an evening shadow;
    I am shaken off like a locust.
²⁴My knees give way from fasting;
    my body is thin and gaunt.
²⁵I am an object of scorn to my accusers;
    when they see me, they shake their
    heads.

²⁶Help me, O LORD my God;
    save me in accordance with your love.
²⁷Let them know that it is your hand,
    that you, O LORD, have done it.
²⁸They may curse, but you will bless;
    when they attack they will be put to
    shame,
    but your servant will rejoice.
²⁹My accusers will be clothed with disgrace
    and wrapped in shame as in a cloak.

³⁰With my mouth I will greatly extol the
    LORD;
    in the great throng I will praise him.
³¹For he stands at the right hand of the
    needy one,
    to save his life from those who condemn
    him.

Psalm 110
Of David. A psalm.

¹The LORD says to my Lord:
    "Sit at my right hand
until I make your enemies
    a footstool for your feet."

²The LORD will extend your mighty sceptre
    from Zion;
    you will rule in the midst of your
    enemies.
³Your troops will be willing
    on your day of battle.
Arrayed in holy majesty,
    from the womb of the dawn
    you will receive the dew of your youth.ᵃ

⁴The LORD has sworn
    and will not change his mind:
    "You are a priest for ever,
    in the order of Melchizedek."

⁵The Lord is at your right hand;
    he will crush kings on the day of his
    wrath.
⁶He will judge nations, heaping up the dead

and crushing the rulers of the whole
    earth.
⁷He will drink from a brook beside the
    way;ᵇ
    therefore he will lift up his head.

Psalm 111ᵃ

¹Praise the LORD.ᵇ

I will extol the LORD with all my heart
    in the council of the upright and in the
    assembly.

²Great are the works of the LORD;
    they are pondered by all who delight in
    them.
³Glorious and majestic are his deeds,
    and his righteousness endures for ever.
⁴He has caused his wonders to be
    remembered;
    the LORD is gracious and
    compassionate.
⁵He provides food for those who fear him;
    he remembers his covenant for ever.
⁶He has shown his people the power of his
    works,
    giving them the lands of other nations.
⁷The works of his hands are faithful and
    just;
    all his precepts are trustworthy.
⁸They are steadfast for ever and ever,
    done in faithfulness and uprightness.
⁹He provided redemption for his people;
    he ordained his covenant for ever—
    holy and awesome is his name.

¹⁰The fear of the LORD is the beginning of
    wisdom;
    all who follow his precepts have good
    understanding.
    To him belongs eternal praise.

Psalm 112ᵃ

¹Praise the LORD.ᵇ

Blessed is the man who fears the LORD,
    who finds great delight in his
    commands.

²His children will be mighty in the land;
    the generation of the upright will be
    blessed.
³Wealth and riches are in his house,
    and his righteousness endures for ever.
⁴Even in darkness light dawns for the
    upright,
    for the gracious and compassionate and
    righteous man.ᶜ
⁵Good will come to him who is generous
    and lends freely,
    who conducts his affairs with justice.
⁶Surely he will never be shaken;
    a righteous man will be remembered for
    ever.

ᵃ3 Or / your young men will come to you like the dew
ᵇ7 Or / The One who grants succession will set him in authority
ᵃThis psalm is an acrostic poem, the lines of which begin with the successive letters of the Hebrew alphabet.
ᵇ1 Hebrew Hallelu Yah
ᵃThis psalm is an acrostic poem, the lines of which begin with the successive letters of the Hebrew alphabet.
ᵇ1 Hebrew Hallelu Yah   ᶜ4 Or / for ⌐the LORD⌐ is gracious and compassionate and righteous

⁷He will have no fear of bad news;
  his heart is steadfast, trusting in the
    LORD.
⁸His heart is secure, he will have no fear;
  in the end he will look in triumph on his
    foes.
⁹He has scattered abroad his gifts to the
    poor,
  his righteousness endures for ever;
  his horn*d* will be lifted high in honour.

¹⁰The wicked man will see and be vexed,
  he will gnash his teeth and waste away;
  the longings of the wicked will come to
    nothing.

Psalm 113

¹Praise the LORD.*a*

Praise, O servants of the LORD,
  praise the name of the LORD.
²Let the name of the LORD be praised,
  both now and for evermore.
³From the rising of the sun to the place
    where it sets,
  the name of the LORD is to be praised.

⁴The LORD is exalted over all the nations,
  his glory above the heavens.
⁵Who is like the LORD our God,
  the One who sits enthroned on high,
⁶who stoops down to look
  on the heavens and the earth?

⁷He raises the poor from the dust
  and lifts the needy from the ash heap;
⁸he seats them with princes,
  with the princes of their people.
⁹He settles the barren woman in her home
  as a happy mother of children.

Praise the LORD.

Psalm 114

¹When Israel came out of Egypt,
  the house of Jacob from a people of
    foreign tongue,
²Judah became God's sanctuary,
  Israel his dominion.

³The sea looked and fled,
  the Jordan turned back;
⁴the mountains skipped like rams,
  the hills like lambs.

⁵Why was it, O sea, that you fled,
  O Jordan, that you turned back,
⁶you mountains, that you skipped like
    rams,
  you hills, like lambs?

⁷Tremble, O earth, at the presence of the
    Lord,
  at the presence of the God of Jacob,
⁸who turned the rock into a pool,
  the hard rock into springs of water.

Psalm 115

¹Not to us, O LORD, not to us
  but to your name be the glory,
  because of your love and faithfulness.

²Why do the nations say,
  "Where is their God?"
³Our God is in heaven;
  he does whatever pleases him.
⁴But their idols are silver and gold,
  made by the hands of men.
⁵They have mouths, but cannot speak,
  eyes, but they cannot see;
⁶they have ears, but cannot hear,
  noses, but they cannot smell;
⁷they have hands, but cannot feel,
  feet, but they cannot walk;
  nor can they utter a sound with their
    throats.
⁸Those who make them will be like them,
  and so will all who trust in them.

⁹O house of Israel, trust in the LORD—
  he is their help and shield.
¹⁰O house of Aaron, trust in the LORD—
  he is their help and shield.
¹¹You who fear him, trust in the LORD—
  he is their help and shield.

¹²The LORD remembers us and will bless us:
  He will bless the house of Israel,
  he will bless the house of Aaron,
¹³he will bless those who fear the LORD—
  small and great alike.

¹⁴May the LORD make you increase,
  both you and your children.
¹⁵May you be blessed by the LORD,
  the Maker of heaven and earth.

¹⁶The highest heavens belong to the LORD,
  but the earth he has given to man.
¹⁷It is not the dead who praise the LORD,
  those who go down to silence;
¹⁸it is we who extol the LORD,
  both now and for evermore.

Praise the LORD.*a*

Psalm 116

¹I love the LORD, for he heard my voice;
  he heard my cry for mercy.
²Because he turned his ear to me,
  I will call on him as long as I live.

³The cords of death entangled me,
  the anguish of the grave*a* came upon me;
  I was overcome by trouble and sorrow.
⁴Then I called on the name of the LORD:
  "O LORD, save me!"

⁵The LORD is gracious and righteous;
  our God is full of compassion.
⁶The LORD protects the simple-hearted;
  when I was in great need, he saved me.

⁷Be at rest once more, O my soul,
  for the LORD has been good to you.

⁸For you, O LORD, have delivered my soul
    from death,
  my eyes from tears,
  my feet from stumbling,

---

d9 Horn here symbolises dignity.   *a1* Hebrew *Hallelu Yah*; also in verse 9
a18 Hebrew *Hallelu Yah*   *a3* Hebrew *Sheol*

9that I may walk before the LORD
in the land of the living.
10I believed; therefore[b] I said,
"I am greatly afflicted."
11And in my dismay I said,
"All men are liars."

12How can I repay the LORD
for all his goodness to me?
13I will lift up the cup of salvation
and call on the name of the LORD.
14I will fulfil my vows to the LORD
in the presence of all his people.

15Precious in the sight of the LORD
is the death of his saints.
16O LORD, truly I am your servant;
I am your servant, the son of your
maidservant;[c]
you have freed me from my chains.

17I will sacrifice a thank-offering to you
and call on the name of the LORD.
18I will fulfil my vows to the LORD
in the presence of all his people,
19in the courts of the house of the LORD—
in your midst, O Jerusalem.

Praise the LORD.[d]

Psalm 117

1Praise the LORD, all you nations;
extol him, all you peoples.
2For great is his love towards us,
and the faithfulness of the LORD endures
for ever.

Praise the LORD.[d]

Psalm 118

1Give thanks to the LORD, for he is good;
his love endures for ever.

2Let Israel say:
"His love endures for ever."
3Let the house of Aaron say:
"His love endures for ever."
4Let those who fear the LORD say:
"His love endures for ever."

5In my anguish I cried to the LORD,
and he answered by setting me free.
6The LORD is with me; I will not be afraid.
What can man do to me?
7The LORD is with me; he is my helper.
I will look in triumph on my enemies.

8It is better to take refuge in the LORD
than to trust in man.
9It is better to take refuge in the LORD
than to trust in princes.

10All the nations surrounded me,
but in the name of the LORD I cut them
off.
11They surrounded me on every side,
but in the name of the LORD I cut them
off.

12They swarmed around me like bees,
but they died out as quickly as burning
thorns;
in the name of the LORD I cut them off.

13I was pushed back and about to fall,
but the LORD helped me.
14The LORD is my strength and my song;
he has become my salvation.

15Shouts of joy and victory
resound in the tents of the righteous:
"The LORD's right hand has done mighty
things!
16 The LORD's right hand is lifted high;
the LORD's right hand has done mighty
things!"

17I will not die but live,
and will proclaim what the LORD has
done.
18The LORD has chastened me severely,
but he has not given me over to death.

19Open for me the gates of righteousness;
I will enter and give thanks to the LORD.
20This is the gate of the LORD
through which the righteous may enter.
21I will give you thanks, for you answered
me;
you have become my salvation.

22The stone the builders rejected
has become the capstone;
23the LORD has done this,
and it is marvellous in our eyes.
24This is the day the LORD has made;
let us rejoice and be glad in it.

25O LORD, save us;
O LORD, grant us success.
26Blessed is he who comes in the name of
the LORD.
From the house of the LORD we bless
you.[a]
27The LORD is God,
and he has made his light shine upon us.
With boughs in hand, join in the festal
procession
up[b] to the horns of the altar.

28You are my God, and I will give thanks;
you are my God, and I will exalt you.

29Give thanks to the LORD, for he is good;
his love endures for ever.

Psalm 119[a]

א Aleph

1Blessed are they whose ways are
blameless,
who walk according to the law of the
LORD.
2Blessed are they who keep his statutes
and seek him with all their heart.

[b]10 Or *believed even when*   [c]16 Or *servant, your faithful son*   [d]19, 2 Hebrew *Hallelu Yah*
[a]26 The Hebrew is plural.   [b]27 Or *Bind the festal sacrifice with ropes / and take it*
[a]This psalm is an acrostic poem; the verses of each stanza begin with the same letter of the Hebrew alphabet.

³They do nothing wrong;
  they walk in his ways.
⁴You have laid down precepts
  that are to be fully obeyed.
⁵Oh, that my ways were steadfast
  in obeying your decrees!
⁶Then I would not be put to shame
  when I consider all your commands.
⁷I will praise you with an upright heart
  as I learn your righteous laws.
⁸I will obey your decrees;
  do not utterly forsake me.

ב Beth

⁹How can a young man keep his way pure?
  By living according to your word.
¹⁰I seek you with all my heart;
  do not let me stray from your
  commands.
¹¹I have hidden your word in my heart
  that I might not sin against you.
¹²Praise be to you, O LORD;
  teach me your decrees.
¹³With my lips I recount
  all the laws that come from your mouth.
¹⁴I rejoice in following your statutes
  as one rejoices in great riches.
¹⁵I meditate on your precepts
  and consider your ways.
¹⁶I delight in your decrees;
  I will not neglect your word.

ג Gimel

¹⁷Do good to your servant, and I will live;
  I will obey your word.
¹⁸Open my eyes that I may see
  wonderful things in your law.
¹⁹I am a stranger on earth;
  do not hide your commands from me.
²⁰My soul is consumed with longing
  for your laws at all times.
²¹You rebuke the arrogant, who are cursed
  and who stray from your commands.
²²Remove from me scorn and contempt,
  for I keep your statutes.
²³Though rulers sit together and slander me,
  your servant will meditate on your
  decrees.
²⁴Your statutes are my delight;
  they are my counsellors.

ד Daleth

²⁵I am laid low in the dust;
  preserve my life according to your
  word.
²⁶I recounted my ways and you answered
  me;
  teach me your decrees.
²⁷Let me understand the teaching of your
  precepts;
  then I will meditate on your wonders.
²⁸My soul is weary with sorrow;
  strengthen me according to your word.

²⁹Keep me from deceitful ways;
  be gracious to me through your law.
³⁰I have chosen the way of truth;
  I have set my heart on your laws.
³¹I hold fast to your statutes, O LORD;
  do not let me be put to shame.
³²I run in the path of your commands,
  for you have set my heart free.

ה He

³³Teach me, O LORD, to follow your
  decrees;
  then I will keep them to the end.
³⁴Give me understanding, and I will keep
  your law
  and obey it with all my heart.
³⁵Direct me in the path of your commands,
  for there I find delight.
³⁶Turn my heart towards your statutes
  and not towards selfish gain.
³⁷Turn my eyes away from worthless things;
  preserve my life according to your
  word.^{b}
³⁸Fulfil your promise to your servant,
  so that you may be feared.
³⁹Take away the disgrace I dread,
  for your laws are good.
⁴⁰How I long for your precepts!
  Preserve my life in your righteousness.

ו Waw

⁴¹May your unfailing love come to me, O
  LORD,
  your salvation according to your
  promise;
⁴²then I will answer the one who taunts me,
  for I trust in your word.
⁴³Do not snatch the word of truth from my
  mouth,
  for I have put my hope in your laws.
⁴⁴I will always obey your law,
  for ever and ever.
⁴⁵I will walk about in freedom,
  for I have sought out your precepts.
⁴⁶I will speak of your statutes before kings
  and will not be put to shame,
⁴⁷for I delight in your commands
  because I love them.
⁴⁸I lift up my hands to^c your commands,
  which I love,
  and I meditate on your decrees.

ז Zayin

⁴⁹Remember your word to your servant,
  for you have given me hope.
⁵⁰My comfort in my suffering is this:
  Your promise preserves my life.
⁵¹The arrogant mock me without restraint,
  but I do not turn from your law.
⁵²I remember your ancient laws, O LORD,
  and I find comfort in them.
⁵³Indignation grips me because of the
  wicked,
  who have forsaken your law.

b37 Two manuscripts of the Masoretic Text and Dead Sea Scrolls; most manuscripts of the Masoretic Text *life in your way*   *c48* Or *for*

54Your decrees are the theme of my song
wherever I lodge.
55In the night I remember your name, O
LORD,
and I will keep your law.
56This has been my practice:
I obey your precepts.

ח Heth

57You are my portion, O LORD;
I have promised to obey your words.
58I have sought your face with all my heart;
be gracious to me according to your
promise.
59I have considered my ways
and have turned my steps to your
statutes.
60I will hasten and not delay
to obey your commands.
61Though the wicked bind me with ropes,
I will not forget your law.
62At midnight I rise to give you thanks
for your righteous laws.
63I am a friend to all who fear you,
to all who follow your precepts.
64The earth is filled with your love, O LORD;
teach me your decrees.

ט Teth

65Do good to your servant
according to your word, O LORD.
66Teach me knowledge and good judgment,
for I believe in your commands.
67Before I was afflicted I went astray,
but now I obey your word.
68You are good, and what you do is good;
teach me your decrees.
69Though the arrogant have smeared me
with lies,
I keep your precepts with all my heart.
70Their hearts are callous and unfeeling,
but I delight in your law.
71It was good for me to be afflicted
so that I might learn your decrees.
72The law from your mouth is more precious
to me
than thousands of pieces of silver and
gold.

י Yodh

73Your hands made me and formed me;
give me understanding to learn your
commands.
74May those who fear you rejoice when they
see me,
for I have put my hope in your word.
75I know, O LORD, that your laws are
righteous,
and in faithfulness you have afflicted
me.
76May your unfailing love be my comfort,
according to your promise to your
servant.
77Let your compassion come to me that I
may live,
for your law is my delight.
78May the arrogant be put to shame for
wronging me without cause;

but I will meditate on your precepts.
79May those who fear you turn to me,
those who understand your statutes.
80May my heart be blameless towards your
decrees,
that I may not be put to shame.

כ Kaph

81My soul faints with longing for your
salvation,
but I have put my hope in your word.
82My eyes fail, looking for your promise;
I say, "When will you comfort me?"
83Though I am like a wineskin in the smoke,
I do not forget your decrees.
84How long must your servant wait?
When will you punish my persecutors?
85The arrogant dig pitfalls for me,
contrary to your law.
86All your commands are trustworthy;
help me, for men persecute me without
cause.
87They almost wiped me from the earth,
but I have not forsaken your precepts.
88Preserve my life according to your love,
and I will obey the statutes of your
mouth.

ל Lamedh

89Your word, O LORD, is eternal;
it stands firm in the heavens.
90Your faithfulness continues through all
generations;
you established the earth, and it
endures.
91Your laws endure to this day,
for all things serve you.
92If your law had not been my delight,
I would have perished in my affliction.
93I will never forget your precepts,
for by them you have preserved my life.
94Save me, for I am yours;
I have sought out your precepts.
95The wicked are waiting to destroy me,
but I will ponder your statutes.
96To all perfection I see a limit;
but your commands are boundless.

מ Mem

97Oh, how I love your law!
I meditate on it all day long.
98Your commands make me wiser than my
enemies,
for they are ever with me.
99I have more insight than all my teachers,
for I meditate on your statutes.
100I have more understanding than the
elders,
for I obey your precepts.
101I have kept my feet from every evil path
so that I might obey your word.
102I have not departed from your laws,
for you yourself have taught me.
103How sweet are your words to my taste,
sweeter than honey to my mouth!
104I gain understanding from your precepts;
therefore I hate every wrong path.

נ Nun

105Your word is a lamp to my feet
and a light for my path.
106I have taken an oath and confirmed it,
that I will follow your righteous laws.
107I have suffered much;
preserve my life, O LORD, according to
your word.
108Accept, O LORD, the willing praise of my
mouth,
and teach me your laws.
109Though I constantly take my life in my
hands,
I will not forget your law.
110The wicked have set a snare for me,
but I have not strayed from your
precepts.
111Your statutes are my heritage for ever;
they are the joy of my heart.
112My heart is set on keeping your decrees
to the very end.

ס Samekh

113I hate double-minded men,
but I love your law.
114You are my refuge and my shield;
I have put my hope in your word.
115Away from me, you evildoers,
that I may keep the commands of my
God!
116Sustain me according to your promise,
and I shall live;
do not let my hopes be dashed.
117Uphold me, and I shall be delivered;
I shall always have regard for your
decrees.
118You reject all who stray from your
decrees,
for their deceitfulness is in vain.
119All the wicked of the earth you discard
like dross;
therefore I love your statutes.
120My flesh trembles in fear of you;
I stand in awe of your laws.

ע Ayin

121I have done what is righteous and just;
do not leave me to my oppressors.
122Ensure your servant's well-being;
let not the arrogant oppress me.
123My eyes fail, looking for your salvation,
looking for your righteous promise.
124Deal with your servant according to your
love
and teach me your decrees.
125I am your servant; give me discernment
that I may understand your statutes.
126It is time for you to act, O LORD;
your law is being broken.
127Because I love your commands
more than gold, more than pure gold,
128and because I consider all your precepts
right,
I hate every wrong path.

פ Pe

129Your statutes are wonderful;
therefore I obey them.
130The unfolding of your words gives light;
it gives understanding to the simple.
131I open my mouth and pant,
longing for your commands.
132Turn to me and have mercy on me,
as you always do to those who love your
name.
133Direct my footsteps according to your
word;
let no sin rule over me.
134Redeem me from the oppression of men,
that I may obey your precepts.
135Make your face shine upon your servant
and teach me your decrees.
136Streams of tears flow from my eyes,
for your law is not obeyed.

צ Tsadhe

137Righteous are you, O LORD,
and your laws are right.
138The statutes you have laid down are
righteous;
they are fully trustworthy.
139My zeal wears me out,
for my enemies ignore your words.
140Your promises have been thoroughly
tested,
and your servant loves them.
141Though I am lowly and despised,
I do not forget your precepts.
142Your righteousness is everlasting
and your law is true.
143Trouble and distress have come upon me,
but your commands are my delight.
144Your statutes are for ever right;
give me understanding that I may live.

ק Qoph

145I call with all my heart; answer me, O
LORD,
and I will obey your decrees.
146I call out to you; save me
and I will keep your statutes.
147I rise before dawn and cry for help;
I have put my hope in your word.
148My eyes stay open through the watches of
the night,
that I may meditate on your promises.
149Hear my voice in accordance with your
love;
preserve my life, O LORD, according to
your laws.
150Those who devise wicked schemes are
near,
but they are far from your law.
151Yet you are near, O LORD,
and all your commands are true.
152Long ago I learned from your statutes
that you established them to last for
ever.

ר Resh

153Look upon my suffering and deliver me,
for I have not forgotten your law.

154Defend my cause and redeem me;
  preserve my life according to your
    promise.
155Salvation is far from the wicked,
  for they do not seek out your decrees.
156Your compassion is great, O LORD;
  preserve my life according to your laws.
157Many are the foes who persecute me,
  but I have not turned from your statutes.
158I look on the faithless with loathing,
  for they do not obey your word.
159See how I love your precepts;
  preserve my life, O LORD, according to
    your love.
160All your words are true;
  all your righteous laws are eternal.

▥ Sin and Shin

161Rulers persecute me without cause,
  but my heart trembles at your word.
162I rejoice in your promise
  like one who finds great spoil.
163I hate and abhor falsehood
  but I love your law.
164Seven times a day I praise you
  for your righteous laws.
165Great peace have they who love your law,
  and nothing can make them stumble.
166I wait for your salvation, O LORD,
  and I follow your commands.
167I obey your statutes,
  for I love them greatly.
168I obey your precepts and your statutes,
  for all my ways are known to you.

ת Taw

169May my cry come before you, O LORD;
  give me understanding according to
    your word.
170May my supplication come before you;
  deliver me according to your promise.
171May my lips overflow with praise,
  for you teach me your decrees.
172May my tongue sing of your word,
  for all your commands are righteous.
173May your hand be ready to help me,
  for I have chosen your precepts.
174I long for your salvation, O LORD,
  and your law is my delight.
175Let me live that I may praise you,
  and may your laws sustain me.
176I have strayed like a lost sheep.
  Seek your servant,
  for I have not forgotten your commands.

Psalm 120

A song of ascents.

1I call on the LORD in my distress,
  and he answers me.
2Save me, O LORD, from lying lips
  and from deceitful tongues.

3What will he do to you,
  and what more besides, O deceitful
    tongue?
4He will punish you with a warrior's sharp
    arrows,
  with burning coals of the broom tree.

5Woe to me that I dwell in Meshech,
  that I live among the tents of Kedar!
6Too long have I lived
  among those who hate peace.
7I am a man of peace;
  but when I speak, they are for war.

Psalm 121

A song of ascents.

1I lift up my eyes to the hills—
  where does my help come from?
2My help comes from the LORD,
  the Maker of heaven and earth.

3He will not let your foot slip—
  he who watches over you will not
    slumber;
4indeed, he who watches over Israel
  will neither slumber nor sleep.

5The LORD watches over you—
  the LORD is your shade at your right
    hand;
6the sun will not harm you by day,
  nor the moon by night.

7The LORD will keep you from all harm—
  he will watch over your life;
8the LORD will watch over your coming and
    going
  both now and for evermore.

Psalm 122

A song of ascents. Of David.

1I rejoiced with those who said to me,
  "Let us go to the house of the LORD."
2Our feet are standing
  in your gates, O Jerusalem.

3Jerusalem is built like a city
  that is closely compacted together.
4That is where the tribes go up,
  the tribes of the LORD,
  to praise the name of the LORD
    according to the statute given to Israel.
5There the thrones for judgment stand,
  the thrones of the house of David.

6Pray for the peace of Jerusalem:
  "May those who love you be secure.
7May there be peace within your walls
  and security within your citadels."
8For the sake of my brothers and friends,
  I will say, "Peace be within you."
9For the sake of the house of the LORD our
    God,
  I will seek your prosperity.

Psalm 123

A song of ascents.

1I lift up my eyes to you,
  to you whose throne is in heaven.
2As the eyes of slaves look to the hand of
    their master,
  as the eyes of a maid look to the hand of
    her mistress,
so our eyes look to the LORD our God,
  till he shows us his mercy.

³Have mercy on us, O LORD, have mercy
     on us,
  for we have endured much contempt.
⁴We have endured much ridicule from the
     proud,
  much contempt from the arrogant.

Psalm 124
A song of ascents. Of David.

¹If the LORD had not been on our side—
  let Israel say—
²if the LORD had not been on our side
  when men attacked us,
³when their anger flared against us,
  they would have swallowed us alive;
⁴the flood would have engulfed us,
  the torrent would have swept over us,
⁵the raging waters
  would have swept us away.

⁶Praise be to the LORD,
  who has not let us be torn by their teeth.
⁷We have escaped like a bird
  out of the fowler's snare;
  the snare has been broken,
  and we have escaped.
⁸Our help is in the name of the LORD,
  the Maker of heaven and earth.

Psalm 125
A song of ascents.

¹Those who trust in the LORD are like
     Mount Zion,
  which cannot be shaken but endures for
     ever.
²As the mountains surround Jerusalem,
  so the LORD surrounds his people
  both now and for evermore.

³The sceptre of the wicked will not remain
  over the land allotted to the righteous,
  for then the righteous might use
     their hands to do evil.

⁴Do good, O LORD, to those who are good,
  to those who are upright in heart.
⁵But those who turn to crooked ways
  the LORD will banish with the evildoers.

Peace be upon Israel.

Psalm 126
A song of ascents.

¹When the LORD brought back the captives
     toᵃ Zion,
  we were like men who dreamed.ᵇ
²Our mouths were filled with laughter,
  our tongues with songs of joy.
  Then it was said among the nations,
  "The LORD has done great things for
     them."
³The LORD has done great things for us,
  and we are filled with joy.

⁴Restore our fortunes,ᶜ O LORD,
  like streams in the Negev.
⁵Those who sow in tears
  will reap with songs of joy.

⁶He who goes out weeping,
  carrying seed to sow,
  will return with songs of joy,
  carrying sheaves with him.

Psalm 127
A song of ascents. Of Solomon.

¹Unless the LORD builds the house,
  its builders labour in vain.
  Unless the LORD watches over the city,
  the watchmen stand guard in vain.
²In vain you rise early
  and stay up late,
  toiling for food to eat—
  for he grants sleep toᵃ those he loves.

³Sons are a heritage from the LORD,
  children a reward from him.
⁴Like arrows in the hands of a warrior
  are sons born in one's youth.
⁵Blessed is the man
  whose quiver is full of them.
  They will not be put to shame
  when they contend with their enemies in
     the gate.

Psalm 128
A song of ascents.

¹Blessed are all who fear the LORD,
  who walk in his ways.
²You will eat the fruit of your labour;
  blessings and prosperity will be yours.
³Your wife will be like a fruitful vine
  within your house;
  your sons will be like olive shoots
  round your table.
⁴Thus is the man blessed
  who fears the LORD.

⁵May the LORD bless you from Zion
  all the days of your life;
  may you see the prosperity of Jerusalem,
⁶ and may you live to see your children's
     children.

Peace be upon Israel.

Psalm 129
A song of ascents.

¹They have greatly oppressed me from my
     youth—
  let Israel say—
²they have greatly oppressed me from my
     youth,
  but they have not gained the victory
     over me.
³Ploughmen have ploughed my back
  and made their furrows long.
⁴But the LORD is righteous;
  he has cut me free from the cords of the
     wicked.

⁵May all who hate Zion
  be turned back in shame.
⁶May they be like grass on the roof,
  which withers before it can grow;
⁷with it the reaper cannot fill his hands,
  nor the one who gathers fill his arms.

ᵃ1 Or LORD restored the fortunes of   ᵇ1 Or men restored to health   ᶜ4 Or Bring back our captives
ᵃ2 Or eat—/ for while they sleep he provides for

⁸May those who pass by not say,
  "The blessing of the LORD be upon you;
  we bless you in the name of the LORD."

Psalm 130
A song of ascents.

¹Out of the depths I cry to you, O LORD;
² O Lord, hear my voice.
  Let your ears be attentive
  to my cry for mercy.

³If you, O LORD, kept a record of sins,
  O Lord, who could stand?
⁴But with you there is forgiveness;
  therefore you are feared.

⁵I wait for the LORD, my soul waits,
  and in his word I put my hope.
⁶My soul waits for the Lord
  more than watchmen wait for the
      morning,
  more than watchmen wait for the
      morning.

⁷O Israel, put your hope in the LORD,
  for with the LORD is unfailing love
  and with him is full redemption.
⁸He himself will redeem Israel
  from all their sins.

Psalm 131
A song of ascents. Of David.

¹My heart is not proud, O LORD,
  my eyes are not haughty;
  I do not concern myself with great matters
  or things too wonderful for me.
²But I have stilled and quietened my soul;
  like a weaned child with its mother,
  like a weaned child is my soul within
      me.

³O Israel, put your hope in the LORD
  both now and for evermore.

Psalm 132
A song of ascents.

¹O LORD, remember David
  and all the hardships he endured.

²He swore an oath to the LORD
  and made a vow to the Mighty One of
      Jacob:
³"I will not enter my house
  or go to my bed—
⁴I will allow no sleep to my eyes,
  no slumber to my eyelids,
⁵till I find a place for the LORD,
  a dwelling for the Mighty One of
      Jacob."

⁶We heard it in Ephrathah,
  we came upon it in the fields of Jaar: ᵃ,ᵇ
⁷"Let us go to his dwelling-place;
  let us worship at his footstool—
⁸arise, O LORD, and come to your resting
      place,
  you and the ark of your might.

⁹May your priests be clothed with
      righteousness;
  may your saints sing for joy."

¹⁰For the sake of David your servant,
  do not reject your anointed one.

¹¹The LORD swore an oath to David,
  a sure oath that he will not revoke:
  "One of your own descendants
  I will place on your throne—
¹²if your sons keep my covenant
  and the statutes I teach them,
  then their sons shall sit
  on your throne for ever and ever."

¹³For the LORD has chosen Zion,
  he has desired it for his dwelling:
¹⁴"This is my resting place for ever and
      ever;
  here I will sit enthroned, for I have
      desired it—
¹⁵I will bless her with abundant provisions;
  her poor will I satisfy with food.
¹⁶I will clothe her priests with salvation,
  and her saints shall ever sing for joy.

¹⁷"Here I will make a hornᶜ grow for David
  and set up a lamp for my anointed one.
¹⁸I will clothe his enemies with shame,
  but the crown on his head shall be
      resplendent."

Psalm 133
A song of ascents. Of David.

¹How good and pleasant it is
  when brothers live together in unity!
²It is like precious oil poured on the head,
  running down on the beard,
  running down on Aaron's beard,
  down upon the collar of his robes.
³It is as if the dew of Hermon
  were falling on Mount Zion.
  For there the LORD bestows his blessing,
  even life for evermore.

Psalm 134
A song of ascents.

¹Praise the LORD, all you servants of the
      LORD
  who minister by night in the house of the
      LORD.
²Lift up your hands in the sanctuary
  and praise the LORD.

³May the LORD, the Maker of heaven and
      earth,
  bless you from Zion.

Psalm 135

¹Praise the LORD.ᵃ

  Praise the name of the LORD;
  praise him, you servants of the LORD,
²you who minister in the house of the LORD,
  in the courts of the house of our God.

ᵃ6 That is, Kiriath Jearim
ᵇ6 Or *heard of it in Ephrathah,* / *we found it in the fields of Jaar.* (and no quotation marks around verses 7–9)
ᶜ17 *Horn* here symbolises strong one, that is, king.   ᵃ1 Hebrew *Hallelu Yah*; also in verses 3 and 21

3Praise the LORD, for the LORD is good;
    sing praise to his name, for that is
      pleasant.
4For the LORD has chosen Jacob to be his
    own,
    Israel to be his treasured possession.

5I know that the LORD is great,
    that our Lord is greater than all gods.
6The LORD does whatever pleases him,
    in the heavens and on the earth,
    in the seas and all their depths.
7He makes clouds rise from the ends of the
    earth;
    he sends lightning with the rain
    and brings out the wind from his
      storehouses.

8He struck down the firstborn of Egypt,
    the firstborn of men and animals.
9He sent his signs and wonders into your
    midst, O Egypt,
    against Pharaoh and all his servants.
10He struck down many nations
    and killed mighty kings—
11Sihon king of the Amorites,
    Og king of Bashan
    and all the kings of Canaan—
12and he gave their land as an inheritance,
    an inheritance to his people Israel.

13Your name, O LORD, endures for ever,
    your renown, O LORD, through all
      generations.
14For the LORD will vindicate his people
    and have compassion on his servants.

15The idols of the nations are silver and gold,
    made by the hands of men.
16They have mouths, but cannot speak,
    eyes, but they cannot see;
17they have ears, but cannot hear,
    nor is there breath in their mouths.
18Those who make them will be like them,
    and so will all who trust in them.

19O house of Israel, praise the LORD;
    O house of Aaron, praise the LORD;
20O house of Levi, praise the LORD;
    you who fear him, praise the LORD.
21Praise be to the LORD from Zion,
    to him who dwells in Jerusalem.

Praise the LORD.

Psalm 136

1Give thanks to the LORD, for he is good.
    His love endures for ever.
2Give thanks to the God of gods.
    His love endures for ever.
3Give thanks to the Lord of lords:
    His love endures for ever.

4to him who alone does great wonders,
    His love endures for ever.
5who by his understanding made the
    heavens,
    His love endures for ever.
6who spread out the earth upon the waters,
    His love endures for ever.

7who made the great lights—
    His love endures for ever.
8the sun to govern the day,
    His love endures for ever.
9the moon and stars to govern the night;
    His love endures for ever.

10to him who struck down the firstborn of
    Egypt
    His love endures for ever.
11and brought Israel out from among them
    His love endures for ever.
12with a mighty hand and outstretched arm;
    His love endures for ever.

13to him who divided the Red Sea*a* asunder
    His love endures for ever.
14and brought Israel through the midst of it,
    His love endures for ever.
15but swept Pharaoh and his army into the
    Red Sea;
    His love endures for ever.

16to him who led his people through the
    desert,
    His love endures for ever.
17who struck down great kings,
    His love endures for ever.
18and killed mighty kings—
    His love endures for ever.
19Sihon king of the Amorites
    His love endures for ever.
20and Og king of Bashan—
    His love endures for ever.
21and gave their land as an inheritance,
    His love endures for ever.
22an inheritance to his servant Israel;
    His love endures for ever.

23to the One who remembered us in our low
    estate
    His love endures for ever.
24and freed us from our enemies,
    His love endures for ever.
25and who gives food to every creature.
    His love endures for ever.

26Give thanks to the God of heaven.
    His love endures for ever.

Psalm 137

1By the rivers of Babylon we sat and wept
    when we remembered Zion.
2There on the poplars
    we hung our harps,
3for there our captors asked us for songs,
    our tormentors demanded songs of joy;
    they said, "Sing us one of the songs of
    Zion!"

4How can we sing the songs of the LORD
    while in a foreign land?
5If I forget you, O Jerusalem,
    may my right hand forget ⌊its skill⌋.
6May my tongue cling to the roof of my
    mouth
    if I do not remember you,
    if I do not consider Jerusalem
    my highest joy.

a13 Hebrew *Yam Suph;* that is, Sea of Reeds; also in verse 15

⁷Remember, O LORD, what the Edomites did
　　on the day Jerusalem fell.
"Tear it down," they cried,
　　"tear it down to its foundations!"

⁸O Daughter of Babylon, doomed to destruction,
　　happy is he who repays you
　　for what you have done to us—
⁹he who seizes your infants
　　and dashes them against the rocks.

Psalm 138
Of David.

¹I will praise you, O LORD, with all my heart;
　　before the "gods" I will sing your praise.
²I will bow down towards your holy temple
　　and will praise your name
　　for your love and your faithfulness,
for you have exalted above all things
　　your name and your word.
³When I called, you answered me;
　　you made me bold and stout-hearted.

⁴May all the kings of the earth praise you, O LORD,
　　when they hear the words of your mouth.
⁵May they sing of the ways of the LORD,
　　for the glory of the LORD is great.

⁶Though the LORD is on high, he looks upon the lowly,
　　but the proud he knows from afar.
⁷Though I walk in the midst of trouble,
　　you preserve my life;
you stretch out your hand against the anger of my foes,
　　with your right hand you save me.
⁸The LORD will fulfil ₍his purpose₎ for me;
　　your love, O LORD, endures for ever—
　　do not abandon the works of your hands.

Psalm 139
For the director of music. Of David. A psalm.

¹O LORD, you have searched me
　　and you know me.
²You know when I sit and when I rise;
　　you perceive my thoughts from afar.
³You discern my going out and my lying down;
　　you are familiar with all my ways.
⁴Before a word is on my tongue
　　you know it completely, O LORD.

⁵You hem me in—behind and before;
　　you have laid your hand upon me.
⁶Such knowledge is too wonderful for me,
　　too lofty for me to attain.

⁷Where can I go from your Spirit?
　　Where can I flee from your presence?
⁸If I go up to the heavens, you are there;
　　if I make my bed in the depths,ᵃ you are there.

⁹If I rise on the wings of the dawn,
　　if I settle on the far side of the sea,
¹⁰even there your hand will guide me,
　　your right hand will hold me fast.

¹¹If I say, "Surely the darkness will hide me
　　and the light become night around me,"
¹²even the darkness will not be dark to you;
　　the night will shine like the day,
　　for darkness is as light to you.

¹³For you created my inmost being;
　　you knit me together in my mother's womb.
¹⁴I praise you because I am fearfully and wonderfully made;
　　your works are wonderful,
　　I know that full well.
¹⁵My frame was not hidden from you
　　when I was made in the secret place.
When I was woven together in the depths of the earth,
¹⁶　your eyes saw my unformed body.
All the days ordained for me
　　were written in your book
　　before one of them came to be.

¹⁷How precious toᵇ me are your thoughts, O God!
　　How vast is the sum of them!
¹⁸Were I to count them,
　　they would outnumber the grains of sand.
When I awake,
　　I am still with you.

¹⁹If only you would slay the wicked, O God!
　　Away from me, you bloodthirsty men!
²⁰They speak of you with evil intent;
　　your adversaries misuse your name.
²¹Do I not hate those who hate you, O LORD,
　　and abhor those who rise up against you?
²²I have nothing but hatred for them;
　　I count them my enemies.

²³Search me, O God, and know my heart;
　　test me and know my anxious thoughts.
²⁴See if there is any offensive way in me,
　　and lead me in the way everlasting.

Psalm 140
For the director of music. A psalm of David.

¹Rescue me, O LORD, from evil men;
　　protect me from men of violence,
²who devise evil plans in their hearts
　　and stir up war every day.
³They make their tongues as sharp as a serpent's;
　　the poison of vipers is on their lips.
　　　　　　　　　　　　　　　　Selah

⁴Keep me, O LORD, from the hands of the wicked;
　　protect me from men of violence
　　who plan to trip my feet.
⁵Proud men have hidden a snare for me;
　　they have spread out the cords of their net
and have set traps for me along my path.
　　　　　　　　　　　　　　　　Selah

ᵃ8 Hebrew *Sheol*　　ᵇ17 Or *concerning*

6O LORD, I say to you, "You are my God."
  Hear, O LORD, my cry for mercy.
7O Sovereign LORD, my strong deliverer,
  who shields my head in the day of
    battle—
8do not grant the wicked their desires, O
    LORD;
  do not let their plans succeed,
  or they will become proud.   *Selah*

9Let the heads of those who surround me
  be covered with the trouble their lips
    have caused.
10Let burning coals fall upon them;
  may they be thrown into the fire,
  into miry pits, never to rise.
11Let slanderers not be established in the
    land;
  may disaster hunt down men of
    violence.

12I know that the LORD secures justice for
    the poor
  and upholds the cause of the needy.
13Surely the righteous will praise your name
  and the upright will live before you.

Psalm 141
A psalm of David.

1O LORD, I call to you; come quickly to me.
  Hear my voice when I call to you.
2May my prayer be set before you like
    incense;
  may the lifting up of my hands be like
    the evening sacrifice.

3Set a guard over my mouth, O LORD;
  keep watch over the door of my lips.
4Let not my heart be drawn to what is evil,
  to take part in wicked deeds
with men who are evildoers;
  let me not eat of their delicacies.

5Let a righteous man[a] strike me—it is a
    kindness;
  let him rebuke me—it is oil on my head.
  My head will not refuse it.

Yet my prayer is ever against the deeds of
    evildoers;
6   their rulers will be thrown down from
      the cliffs,
  and the wicked will learn that my words
    were well spoken.
7They will say, "As one ploughs and
    breaks up the earth,
  so our bones have been scattered at the
    mouth of the grave."[b]

8But my eyes are fixed on you, O Sovereign
    LORD;
  in you I take refuge—do not give me
    over to death.
9Keep me from the snares they have laid
    for me,
  from the traps set by evildoers.
10Let the wicked fall into their own nets,
  while I pass by in safety.

Psalm 142
A maskil[a] *of David. When he was in the cave.
A prayer.*

1I cry aloud to the LORD;
  I lift up my voice to the LORD for mercy.
2I pour out my complaint before him;
  before him I tell my trouble.

3When my spirit grows faint within me,
  it is you who know my way.
In the path where I walk
  men have hidden a snare for me.
4Look to my right and see;
  no-one is concerned for me.
I have no refuge;
  no-one cares for my life.

5I cry to you, O LORD;
  I say, "You are my refuge,
  my portion in the land of the living."
6Listen to my cry,
  for I am in desperate need;
rescue me from those who pursue me,
  for they are too strong for me.
7Set me free from my prison,
  that I may praise your name.

Then the righteous will gather about me
  because of your goodness to me.

Psalm 143
A psalm of David.

1O LORD, hear my prayer,
  listen to my cry for mercy;
in your faithfulness and righteousness
  come to my relief.
2Do not bring your servant into judgment,
  for no-one living is righteous before
    you.

3The enemy pursues me,
  he crushes me to the ground;
he makes me dwell in darkness
  like those long dead.
4So my spirit grows faint within me;
  my heart within me is dismayed.

5I remember the days of long ago;
  I meditate on all your works
  and consider what your hands have
    done.
6I spread out my hands to you;
  my soul thirsts for you like a parched
    land.   *Selah*

7Answer me quickly, O LORD;
  my spirit fails.
Do not hide your face from me
  or I will be like those who go down to
    the pit.
8Let the morning bring me word of your
    unfailing love,
  for I have put my trust in you.
Show me the way I should go,
  for to you I lift up my soul.
9Rescue me from my enemies, O LORD,
  for I hide myself in you.

---

*a*5 Or *Let the Righteous One*   *b*7 Hebrew *Sheol*   *a*Title: Probably a literary or musical term

[10]Teach me to do your will,
  for you are my God;
may your good Spirit
  lead me on level ground.

[11]For your name's sake, O LORD, preserve
    my life;
  in your righteousness, bring me out of
    trouble.
[12]In your unfailing love, silence my enemies;
  destroy all my foes,
  for I am your servant.

Psalm 144
Of David.

[1]Praise be to the LORD my Rock,
  who trains my hands for war,
  my fingers for battle.
[2]He is my loving God and my fortress,
  my stronghold and my deliverer,
  my shield, in whom I take refuge,
  who subdues peoples*a* under me.

[3]O LORD, what is man that you care for
    him,
  the son of man that you think of him?
[4]Man is like a breath;
  his days are like a fleeting shadow.

[5]Part your heavens, O LORD, and come
    down;
  touch the mountains, so that they
    smoke.
[6]Send forth lightning and scatter ⌊the
    enemies⌋;
  shoot your arrows and rout them.
[7]Reach down your hand from on high;
  deliver me and rescue me
from the mighty waters,
  from the hands of foreigners
[8]whose mouths are full of lies,
  whose right hands are deceitful.

[9]I will sing a new song to you, O God;
  on the ten-stringed lyre I will make
    music to you,
[10]to the One who gives victory to kings,
  who delivers his servant David from the
    deadly sword.

[11]Deliver me and rescue me
  from the hands of foreigners
whose mouths are full of lies,
  whose right hands are deceitful.

[12]Then our sons in their youth
  will be like well-nurtured plants,
and our daughters will be like pillars
  carved to adorn a palace.
[13]Our barns will be filled
  with every kind of provision.
Our sheep will increase by thousands,
  by tens of thousands in our fields;

[14] our oxen will draw heavy loads.*b*
There will be no breaching of walls,
  no going into captivity,
  no cry of distress in our streets.

[15]Blessed are the people of whom this is
    true;
  blessed are the people whose God is the
    LORD.

Psalm 145*a*
A psalm of praise. Of David.

[1]I will exalt you, my God the King;
  I will praise your name for ever and
    ever.
[2]Every day I will praise you
  and extol your name for ever and ever.

[3]Great is the LORD and most worthy of
    praise;
  his greatness no-one can fathom.
[4]One generation will commend your works
    to another;
  they will tell of your mighty acts.
[5]They will speak of the glorious splendour
    of your majesty,
  and I will meditate on your wonderful
    works.*b*
[6]They will tell of the power of your
    awesome works,
  and I will proclaim your great deeds.
[7]They will celebrate your abundant
    goodness
  and joyfully sing of your righteousness.

[8]The LORD is gracious and compassionate,
  slow to anger and rich in love.
[9]The LORD is good to all;
  he has compassion on all he has made.
[10]All you have made will praise you, O
    LORD;
  your saints will extol you.
[11]They will tell of the glory of your kingdom
  and speak of your might,
[12]so that all men may know of your mighty
    acts
  and the glorious splendour of your
    kingdom.
[13]Your kingdom is an everlasting kingdom,
  and your dominion endures through all
    generations.

The LORD is faithful to all his promises
  and loving towards all he has made.*c*
[14]The LORD upholds all those who fall
  and lifts up all who are bowed down.
[15]The eyes of all look to you,
  and you give them their food at the
    proper time.
[16]You open your hand
  and satisfy the desires of every living
    thing.

---

*a*2 Many manuscripts of the Masoretic Text, Dead Sea Scrolls, Aquila, Jerome and Syriac; most manuscripts of the
Masoretic Text *subdues my people*   *b*14 Or *our chieftains will be firmly established*
*a*This psalm is an acrostic poem, the verses of which (including verse 13b) begin with the successive letters of the
Hebrew alphabet.
*b*5 Dead Sea Scrolls and Syriac (see also Septuagint); Masoretic Text *On the glorious splendour of your majesty / and
on your wonderful works I will meditate*
*c*13 One manuscript of the Masoretic Text, Dead Sea Scrolls and Syriac (see also Septuagint); most manuscripts of
the Masoretic Text do not have the last two lines of verse 13.

¹⁷The LORD is righteous in all his ways
and loving towards all he has made.
¹⁸The LORD is near to all who call on him,
to all who call on him in truth.
¹⁹He fulfils the desires of those who fear
him;
he hears their cry and saves them.
²⁰The LORD watches over all who love him,
but all the wicked he will destroy.

²¹My mouth will speak in praise of the LORD.
Let every creature praise his holy name
for ever and ever.

Psalm 146

¹Praise the LORD.ᵃ

Praise the LORD, O my soul.
²   I will praise the LORD all my life;
I will sing praise to my God as long as I
live.

³Do not put your trust in princes,
in mortal men, who cannot save.
⁴When their spirit departs, they return to
the ground;
on that very day their plans come to
nothing.

⁵Blessed is he whose help is the God of
Jacob,
whose hope is in the LORD his God,
⁶the Maker of heaven and earth,
the sea, and everything in them—
the LORD, who remains faithful for ever.
⁷He upholds the cause of the oppressed
and gives food to the hungry.
The LORD sets prisoners free,
⁸   the LORD gives sight to the blind,
the LORD lifts up those who are bowed
down,
the LORD loves the righteous.
⁹The LORD watches over the alien
and sustains the fatherless and the
widow,
but he frustrates the ways of the wicked.

¹⁰The LORD reigns for ever,
your God, O Zion, for all generations.

Praise the LORD.

Psalm 147

¹Praise the LORD.ᵃ

How good it is to sing praises to our God,
how pleasant and fitting to praise him!

²The LORD builds up Jerusalem;
he gathers the exiles of Israel.
³He heals the broken-hearted
and binds up their wounds.

⁴He determines the number of the stars
and calls them each by name.
⁵Great is our Lord and mighty in power;
his understanding has no limit.
⁶The LORD sustains the humble
but casts the wicked to the ground.

⁷Sing to the LORD with thanksgiving;
make music to our God on the harp.
⁸He covers the sky with clouds;
he supplies the earth with rain
and makes grass grow on the hills.
⁹He provides food for the cattle
and for the young ravens when they call.

¹⁰His pleasure is not in the strength of the
horse,
nor his delight in the legs of a man;
¹¹the LORD delights in those who fear him,
who put their hope in his unfailing love.

¹²Extol the LORD, O Jerusalem;
praise your God, O Zion,
¹³for he strengthens the bars of your gates
and blesses your people within you.
¹⁴He grants peace to your borders
and satisfies you with the finest of
wheat.

¹⁵He sends his command to the earth;
his word runs swiftly.
¹⁶He spreads the snow like wool
and scatters the frost like ashes.
¹⁷He hurls down hail like pebbles.
Who can withstand his icy blast?
¹⁸He sends his word and melts them;
he stirs up his breezes, and the waters
flow.

¹⁹He has revealed his word to Jacob,
his laws and decrees to Israel.
²⁰He has done this for no other nation;
they do not know his laws.

Praise the LORD.

Psalm 148

¹Praise the LORD.ᵃ

Praise the LORD from the heavens,
praise him in the heights above.
²Praise him, all his angels,
praise him, all his heavenly hosts.
³Praise him, sun and moon,
praise him, all you shining stars.
⁴Praise him, you highest heavens
and you waters above the skies.
⁵Let them praise the name of the LORD,
for he commanded and they were
created.
⁶He set them in place for ever and ever;
he gave a decree that will never pass
away.

⁷Praise the LORD from the earth,
you great sea creatures and all ocean
depths,
⁸lightning and hail, snow and clouds,
stormy winds that do his bidding,
⁹you mountains and all hills,
fruit trees and all cedars,
¹⁰wild animals and all cattle,
small creatures and flying birds,
¹¹kings of the earth and all nations,
you princes and all rulers on earth,

ᵃ1 Hebrew *Hallelu Yah*; also in verse 10   ᵃ1 Hebrew *Hallelu Yah*; also in verse 20
ᵃ1 Hebrew *Hallelu Yah*; also in verse 14

PSALM 145:13–21
'The LORD is near to all who call on him, to all who call on him in truth' (v. 18).

TODAY I WILL remind myself of the greatness of God. I lift up my heart in praise to him in company with the Church across the world. His kingdom is glorious and his dominion is without end (v. 13a). Although evil forces in our world are rampant and unashamed, because God is God their days are numbered.

Today I remind myself that God makes promises and keeps them (v. 13b). He promised Christ (Isa. 7:14), and he came (Luke 2:7). He promised the Holy Spirit (Joel 2:28–29), and there was Pentecost (Acts 2:1ff). The promise he gave to Israel of his presence (Exod. 33:14) is true today. I will therefore seek to be aware of him.

Today, because God is near at hand, I will reach out to him, I will reach up to him (v. 18; Acts 17:27). I will make a conscious effort to understand more of his greatness. Although he will ever remain beyond my comprehension there is more of him that I can discover. Although he has given me much, there is still more I can receive. He is waiting to fulfil the deep desires of my heart.

> *Reach out in faith, my soul.*
> *Fulfil that strong desire*
> *Which burns, a gentle fire*
> *To be in God's control.*
>
> *He has so much to give*
> *Of peace, of joy, of grace,*
> *To make a holy place*
> *Just where you move and live.*
>
> *He has so much to teach*
> *About your pilgrim way,*
> *About your need to pray;*
> *Look up my soul – and reach.*

→526

PROVERBS 1:20–28; 2:6–8

'Wisdom calls aloud in the street, she raises her voice in the public squares . . . How long will you simple ones love your simple ways? . . . since you ignored all my advice and would not accept my rebuke, I in turn will laugh at your disaster' (vv. 20, 22, 25, 26, GNB).

WATCH OUT! WISDOM IS CALLING! Wisdom is portrayed as personal in Proverbs. She speaks (v. 20). She laughs and jeers (v. 26). She protects (v. 33). She makes plans (8:14). She loves (8:17), and she was born, the first of all creation (8:22). Today our concern is for the character of wisdom.

In many respects she is portrayed in a similar way to the way Jesus is described in the New Testament. She is deeply moved (v. 22), very like Jesus when he looked over Jerusalem and wept (Luke 19:41–42). She longs to bring everyone within the fold of her protection and security, in similar fashion to Jesus, wanting to find the lost sheep and bring it home (Luke 15:4ff.).

But there is also a great difference. When people reject Wisdom she laughs. She mocks them in a way quite foreign to the New Testament. When men finally turn to her she rejects them, unlike the Saviour who requires us to 'ask . . . seek . . . knock' in a determined manner (Luke 11:9).

Wisdom, then, is not something we can pick up at any time we please. If we go on ignoring, if we persist in despising, we shall find that Wisdom eludes us. Similarly, by seeking Wisdom herself rather than God, the source of Wisdom, we risk being met with hollow laughter, mocking when terror strikes.

Christ is the power of God and the wisdom of God.

→531

¹²young men and maidens,
old men and children.

¹³Let them praise the name of the LORD,
for his name alone is exalted;
his splendour is above the earth and the
heavens.
¹⁴He has raised up for his people a horn,[b]
the praise of all his saints,
of Israel, the people close to his heart.

Praise the LORD.

Psalm 149

¹Praise the LORD.[a]

Sing to the LORD a new song,
his praise in the assembly of the saints.

²Let Israel rejoice in their Maker;
let the people of Zion be glad in their
King.
³Let them praise his name with dancing
and make music to him with tambourine
and harp.
⁴For the LORD takes delight in his people;
he crowns the humble with salvation.
⁵Let the saints rejoice in this honour
and sing for joy on their beds.

⁶May the praise of God be in their mouths

and a double-edged sword in their
hands,
⁷to inflict vengeance on the nations
and punishment on the peoples,
⁸to bind their kings with fetters,
their nobles with shackles of iron,
⁹to carry out the sentence written against
them.
This is the glory of all his saints.

Praise the LORD.

Psalm 150

¹Praise the LORD.[a]

Praise God in his sanctuary;
praise him in his mighty heavens.
²Praise him for his acts of power;
praise him for his surpassing greatness.
³Praise him with the sounding of the
trumpet,
praise him with the harp and lyre,
⁴praise him with tambourine and dancing,
praise him with the strings and flute,
⁵praise him with the clash of cymbals,
praise him with resounding cymbals.

⁶Let everything that has breath praise the
LORD.

Praise the LORD.

---

b14 *Horn* here symbolises strong one, that is, king.   a1 Hebrew *Hallelu Yah*; also in verse 9
a1 Hebrew *Hallelu Yah*; also in verse 6

Proverbs

Prologue: Purpose and Theme

1 The proverbs of Solomon son of David,
king of Israel:

[2] for attaining wisdom and discipline;
for understanding words of insight;
[3] for acquiring a disciplined and prudent
life,
doing what is right and just and fair;
[4] for giving prudence to the simple,
knowledge and discretion to the
young—
[5] let the wise listen and add to their learning,
and let the discerning get guidance—
[6] for understanding proverbs and parables,
the sayings and riddles of the wise.

[7] The fear of the LORD is the beginning of
knowledge,
but fools[a] despise wisdom and
discipline.

Exhortations to Embrace Wisdom

Warning Against Enticement

[8] Listen, my son, to your father's
instruction
and do not forsake your mother's
teaching.
[9] They will be a garland to grace your head
and a chain to adorn your neck.

[10] My son, if sinners entice you,
do not give in to them.
[11] If they say, "Come along with us;
let's lie in wait for someone's blood,
let's waylay some harmless soul;
[12] let's swallow them alive, like the grave,[b]
and whole, like those who go down to
the pit;
[13] we will get all sorts of valuable things
and fill our houses with plunder;
[14] throw in your lot with us,
and we will share a common purse"—
[15] my son, do not go along with them,
do not set foot on their paths;
[16] for their feet rush into sin,
they are swift to shed blood.
[17] How useless to spread a net
in full view of all the birds!

[18] These men lie in wait for their own blood;
they waylay only themselves!
[19] Such is the end of all who go after
ill-gotten gain;
it takes away the lives of those who get
it.

Warning Against Rejecting Wisdom

[20] Wisdom calls aloud in the street,
she raises her voice in the public
squares;
[21] at the head of the noisy streets[c] she cries
out,
in the gateways of the city she makes
her speech:

[22] "How long will you simple ones[d] love
your simple ways?
How long will mockers delight in
mockery
and fools hate knowledge?
[23] If you had responded to my rebuke,
I would have poured out my heart to you
and made my thoughts known to you.
[24] But since you rejected me when I called
and no-one gave heed when I stretched
out my hand,
[25] since you ignored all my advice
and would not accept my rebuke,
[26] I in turn will laugh at your disaster;
I will mock when calamity overtakes
you—
[27] when calamity overtakes you like a storm,
when disaster sweeps over you like a
whirlwind,
when distress and trouble overwhelm
you.

[28] "Then they will call to me but I will not
answer;
they will look for me but will not find
me.
[29] Since they hated knowledge
and did not choose to fear the LORD,
[30] since they would not accept my advice
and spurned my rebuke,
[31] they will eat the fruit of their ways
and be filled with the fruit of their
schemes.

---

[a]7 The Hebrew words rendered *fool* in Proverbs, and often elsewhere in the Old Testament, denote one who is
morally deficient.   [b]12 Hebrew *Sheol*   [c]21 Hebrew; Septuagint / *on the tops of the walls*
[d]22 The Hebrew word rendered *simple* in Proverbs generally denotes one without moral direction and inclined to
evil.

32For the waywardness of the simple will kill
     them,
   and the complacency of fools will
     destroy them;
33but whoever listens to me will live in
     safety
   and be at ease, without fear of harm.''

Moral Benefits of Wisdom

2 My son, if you accept my words
   and store up my commands within
   you,
2turning your ear to wisdom
   and applying your heart to
     understanding,
3and if you call out for insight
   and cry aloud for understanding,
4and if you look for it as for silver
   and search for it as for hidden treasure,
5then you will understand the fear of the
     LORD
   and find the knowledge of God.
6For the LORD gives wisdom,
   and from his mouth come knowledge
     and understanding.
7He holds victory in store for the upright,
   he is a shield to those whose walk is
     blameless,
8for he guards the course of the just
   and protects the way of his faithful ones.

9Then you will understand what is right and
     just
   and fair—every good path.
10For wisdom will enter your heart,
   and knowledge will be pleasant to your
     soul.
11Discretion will protect you,
   and understanding will guard you.

12Wisdom will save you from the ways of
     wicked men,
   from men whose words are perverse,
13who leave the straight paths
   to walk in dark ways,
14who delight in doing wrong
   and rejoice in the perverseness of evil,
15whose paths are crooked
   and who are devious in their ways.

16It will save you also from the adulteress,
   from the wayward wife with her
     seductive words,
17who has left the partner of her youth
   and ignored the covenant she made
     before God.a
18For her house leads down to death
   and her paths to the spirits of the dead.
19None who go to her return
   or attain the paths of life.

20Thus you will walk in the ways of good
     men
   and keep to the paths of the righteous.
21For the upright will live in the land,
   and the blameless will remain in it;
22but the wicked will be cut off from the
     land,
   and the unfaithful will be torn from it.

Further Benefits of Wisdom

3 My son, do not forget my teaching,
   but keep my commands in your heart,
2for they will prolong your life many years
   and bring you prosperity.

3Let love and faithfulness never leave you;
   bind them around your neck,
   write them on the tablet of your heart.
4Then you will win favour and a good name
   in the sight of God and man.

5Trust in the LORD with all your heart
   and lean not on your own
     understanding;
6in all your ways acknowledge him,
   and he will make your paths straight.a

7Do not be wise in your own eyes;
   fear the LORD and shun evil.
8This will bring health to your body
   and nourishment to your bones.

9Honour the LORD with your wealth,
   with the firstfruits of all your crops;
10then your barns will be filled to
     overflowing,
   and your vats will brim over with new
     wine.

11My son, do not despise the LORD's
     discipline
   and do not resent his rebuke,
12because the LORD disciplines those he
     loves,
   as a fatherb the son he delights in.

13Blessed is the man who finds wisdom,
   the man who gains understanding,
14for she is more profitable than silver
   and yields better returns than gold.
15She is more precious than rubies;
   nothing you desire can compare with
     her.
16Long life is in her right hand;
   in her left hand are riches and honour.
17Her ways are pleasant ways,
   and all her paths are peace.
18She is a tree of life to those who embrace
     her;
   those who lay hold of her will be
     blessed.

19By wisdom the LORD laid the earth's
     foundations,
   by understanding he set the heavens in
     place;
20by his knowledge the deeps were divided,
   and the clouds let drop the dew.

21My son, preserve sound judgment and
     discernment,
   do not let them out of your sight;
22they will be life for you,
   an ornament to grace your neck.
23Then you will go on your way in safety,
   and your foot will not stumble;
24when you lie down, you will not be afraid;
   when you lie down, your sleep will be
     sweet.

---

a17 Or covenant of her God   a6 Or will direct your paths   b12 Hebrew; Septuagint / and he punishes

25Have no fear of sudden disaster
  or of the ruin that overtakes the wicked,
26for the LORD will be your confidence
  and will keep your foot from being
    snared.

27Do not withhold good from those who
    deserve it,
  when it is in your power to act.
28Do not say to your neighbour,
  "Come back later; I'll give it
    tomorrow"—
  when you now have it with you.

29Do not plot harm against your neighbour,
  who lives trustfully near you.
30Do not accuse a man for no reason—
  when he has done you no harm.

31Do not envy a violent man
  or choose any of his ways,
32for the LORD detests a perverse man
  but takes the upright into his confidence.

33The LORD's curse is on the house of the
    wicked,
  but he blesses the home of the righteous.
34He mocks proud mockers
  but gives grace to the humble.
35The wise inherit honour,
  but fools he holds up to shame.

Wisdom Is Supreme

4 Listen, my sons, to a father's
  instruction;
  pay attention and gain understanding.
2I give you sound learning,
  so do not forsake my teaching.
3When I was a boy in my father's house,
  still tender, and an only child of my
    mother,
4he taught me and said,
  "Lay hold of my words with all your
    heart;
  keep my commands and you will live.
5Get wisdom, get understanding;
  do not forget my words or swerve from
    them.
6Do not forsake wisdom, and she will
    protect you;
  love her, and she will watch over you.
7Wisdom is supreme; therefore get
    wisdom.
  Though it cost all you have,*a* get
    understanding.
8Esteem her, and she will exalt you;
  embrace her, and she will honour you.
9She will set a garland of grace on your
    head
  and present you with a crown of
    splendour."

10Listen, my son, accept what I say,
  and the years of your life will be many.
11I guide you in the way of wisdom
  and lead you along straight paths.
12When you walk, your steps will not be
    hampered;
  when you run, you will not stumble.

13Hold on to instruction, do not let it go;
  guard it well, for it is your life.
14Do not set foot on the path of the wicked
  or walk in the way of evil men.
15Avoid it, do not travel on it;
  turn from it and go on your way.
16For they cannot sleep till they do evil;
  they are robbed of slumber till they
    make someone fall.
17They eat the bread of wickedness
  and drink the wine of violence.

18The path of the righteous is like the first
    gleam of dawn,
  shining ever brighter till the full light of
    day.
19But the way of the wicked is like deep
    darkness;
  they do not know what makes them
    stumble.

20My son, pay attention to what I say;
  listen closely to my words.
21Do not let them out of your sight,
  keep them within your heart;
22for they are life to those who find them
  and health to a man's whole body.
23Above all else, guard your heart,
  for it is the wellspring of life.
24Put away perversity from your mouth;
  keep corrupt talk far from your lips.
25Let your eyes look straight ahead,
  fix your gaze directly before you.
26Make level*b* paths for your feet
  and take only ways that are firm.
27Do not swerve to the right or the left;
  keep your foot from evil.

Warning Against Adultery

5 My son, pay attention to my wisdom,
  listen well to my words of insight,
2that you may maintain discretion
  and your lips may preserve knowledge.
3For the lips of an adulteress drip honey,
  and her speech is smoother than oil;
4but in the end she is bitter as gall,
  sharp as a double-edged sword.
5Her feet go down to death;
  her steps lead straight to the grave.*a*
6She gives no thought to the way of life;
  her paths are crooked, but she knows it
    not.

7Now then, my sons, listen to me;
  do not turn aside from what I say.
8Keep to a path far from her,
  do not go near the door of her house,
9lest you give your best strength to others
  and your years to one who is cruel,
10lest strangers feast on your wealth
  and your toil enrich another man's
    house.
11At the end of your life you will groan,
  when your flesh and body are spent.
12You will say, "How I hated discipline!
  How my heart spurned correction!
13I would not obey my teachers
  or listen to my instructors.

---

*a*7 Or *Whatever else you get*   *b*26 Or *Consider the*   *a*5 Hebrew *Sheol*

PROVERBS 3:6. 27–32
'In all your ways acknowledge him, and he will make your paths straight . . . Do not say to your neighbour, "Come back later" ' (vv. 6, 28).

PROCRASTINATION IS THE THIEF OF TIME. Time-saving is a modern disease. Washing machines, vacuum cleaners, computers, cars, conveyer belts, planes, fax machines – the list is endless. All exist to 'save time'. What do we do with the time saved?

Sometimes we simply rush on further than before. The beach, inaccessible a generation ago, now beckons at the end of a day trip by car, rather than just as the goal of a long-awaited holiday. Clothes, changed weekly by an older generation, can now be changed every day, thanks to the washing machine. We live further from our work, so take longer travelling. We sit longer at our time-saving machines, so use the time saved in exercise, jogging our lives away. That list is also endless.

There are, however, positive ways of using time. When the odd ten minutes comes along, remember your neighbour who is lonely. Half an hour spent listening is not wasted. In a more 'practical' vein, are your hedge-cutters more effective than those of the old person next door? Use the time saved on your own hedge by doing someone else's.

Such advice may not sound like deep theology, but it is the theology of Jesus. Sense our neighbour's need and we become aware of the Lord. Awareness of our Lord helps us sense a neighbour's need – and act upon it.

'In all your ways acknowledge him, and he will make your paths straight'
(v. 6).

PROVERBS 31:10–18, 30, 31
'She considers a field and buys it; out of her earnings she plants a vineyard . . .
Give her the reward she has earned, and let her works bring her praise at the city
gate' (vv. 16, 31).

FEMINISM – OLD TESTAMENT STYLE. The domestic nature of
this hymn praising the good wife may bring scathing rebuke from
modern feminists, but see how the woman's influence extends. Not just
the house, but also the vineyard and the market place, where she is
entitled to the reward she has earned.

Her husband, it is assumed, sits in judgement at the gate of the city –
the equivalent of a modern law court – so there is scope for improvement. Women were not expected to have power within the legal system
– an area where the judgement of a good woman can make enormous
differences. We must go beyond the ancient wisdom of Proverbs to
fully appreciate the relationship with God and with others now open
to us. We are 'dwarfs on giant's shoulders'. We may not be as wise or
as clever as the giants of the past who gave us Proverbs, but because we
stand on their shoulders we can see further than they did.

How necessary it is for women not only to be accorded a secure
place within society – as envisaged by Proverbs, but for their skills and
abilities to be used throughout society. Such thinking was pioneered
by Catherine Booth in the nineteenth century, yet even today our
world is male dominated.

However, even if full participation by women is still in the future we
do well to ponder the final verse of Proverbs. Don't exploit her. 'Give
her the reward she has earned.' Equal pay for equal work. But even
more importantly, equal opportunity, in education, employment and
power.

'My best men are women.' (William Booth)

→555

¹⁴I have come to the brink of utter ruin
   in the midst of the whole assembly.''

¹⁵Drink water from your own cistern,
   running water from your own well.
¹⁶Should your springs overflow in the
   streets,
   your streams of water in the public
    squares?
¹⁷Let them be yours alone,
   never to be shared with strangers.
¹⁸May your fountain be blessed,
   and may you rejoice in the wife of your
    youth.
¹⁹A loving doe, a graceful deer—
   may her breasts satisfy you always,
   may you ever be captivated by her love.
²⁰Why be captivated, my son, by an
   adulteress?
   Why embrace the bosom of another
    man's wife?

²¹For a man's ways are in full view of the
   LORD,
   and he examines all his paths.
²²The evil deeds of a wicked man ensnare
   him;
   the cords of his sin hold him fast.
²³He will die for lack of discipline,
   led astray by his own great folly.

Warnings Against Folly

6   My son, if you have put up security for
    your neighbour,
   if you have struck hands in pledge for
    another,
²if you have been trapped by what you said,
   ensnared by the words of your mouth,
³then do this, my son, to free yourself,
   since you have fallen into your
    neighbour's hands:
 Go and humble yourself;
   press your plea with your neighbour!
⁴Allow no sleep to your eyes,
   no slumber to your eyelids.
⁵Free yourself, like a gazelle from the hand
   of the hunter,
   like a bird from the snare of the fowler.

⁶Go to the ant, you sluggard;
   consider its ways and be wise!
⁷It has no commander,
   no overseer or ruler,
⁸yet it stores its provisions in summer
   and gathers its food at harvest.

⁹How long will you lie there, you sluggard?
   When will you get up from your sleep?
¹⁰A little sleep, a little slumber,
   a little folding of the hands to rest—
¹¹and poverty will come on you like a bandit
   and scarcity like an armed man.ᵃ

¹²A scoundrel and villain,
   who goes about with a corrupt mouth,
¹³ who winks with his eye,
   signals with his feet
   and motions with his fingers,
¹⁴ who plots evil with deceit in his heart—
   he always stirs up dissension.

¹⁵Therefore disaster will overtake him in an
   instant;
   he will suddenly be destroyed—without
    remedy.

¹⁶There are six things the LORD hates,
   seven that are detestable to him:
17   haughty eyes,
   a lying tongue,
   hands that shed innocent blood,
18   a heart that devises wicked schemes,
   feet that are quick to rush into evil,
19   a false witness who pours out lies
   and a man who stirs up dissension
    among brothers.

Warning Against Adultery

²⁰My son, keep your father's commands
   and do not forsake your mother's
    teaching.
²¹Bind them upon your heart for ever;
   fasten them around your neck.
²²When you walk, they will guide you;
   when you sleep, they will watch over
    you;
   when you awake, they will speak to you.
²³For these commands are a lamp,
   this teaching is a light,
   and the corrections of discipline
   are the way to life,
²⁴keeping you from the immoral woman,
   from the smooth tongue of the wayward
    wife.
²⁵Do not lust in your heart after her beauty
   or let her captivate you with her eyes,
²⁶for the prostitute reduces you to a loaf of
   bread,
   and the adulteress preys upon your very
    life.
²⁷Can a man scoop fire into his lap
   without his clothes being burned?
²⁸Can a man walk on hot coals
   without his feet being scorched?
²⁹So is he who sleeps with another man's
   wife;
   no-one who touches her will go
    unpunished.

³⁰Men do not despise a thief if he steals
   to satisfy his hunger when he is starving.
³¹Yet if he is caught, he must pay sevenfold,
   though it costs him all the wealth of his
    house.
³²But a man who commits adultery lacks
   judgment;
   whoever does so destroys himself.
³³Blows and disgrace are his lot,
   and his shame will never be wiped away;
³⁴for jealousy arouses a husband's fury,
   and he will show no mercy when he
    takes revenge.
³⁵He will not accept any compensation;
   he will refuse the bribe, however great it
    is.

Warning Against the Adulteress

7   My son, keep my words
   and store up my commands within
    you.

ᵃ11 Or like a vagrant / and scarcity like a beggar

²Keep my commands and you will live;
    guard my teachings as the apple of your
      eye.
³Bind them on your fingers;
    write them on the tablet of your heart.
⁴Say to wisdom, "You are my sister,"
    and call understanding your kinsman;
⁵they will keep you from the adulteress,
    from the wayward wife with her
      seductive words.

⁶At the window of my house
    I looked out through the lattice.
⁷I saw among the simple,
    I noticed among the young men,
      a youth who lacked judgment.
⁸He was going down the street near her
      corner,
    walking along in the direction of her
      house
⁹at twilight, as the day was fading,
    as the dark of night set in.

¹⁰Then out came a woman to meet him,
    dressed like a prostitute and with crafty
      intent.
¹¹(She is loud and defiant,
    her feet never stay at home;
¹²now in the street, now in the squares,
    at every corner she lurks.)
¹³She took hold of him and kissed him
    and with a brazen face she said:

¹⁴"I have fellowship offerings[a] at home;
    today I fulfilled my vows.
¹⁵So I came out to meet you;
    I looked for you and have found you!
¹⁶I have covered my bed
    with coloured linens from Egypt.
¹⁷I have perfumed my bed
    with myrrh, aloes and cinnamon.
¹⁸Come, let's drink deep of love till morning;
    let's enjoy ourselves with love!
¹⁹My husband is not at home;
    he has gone on a long journey.
²⁰He took his purse filled with money
    and will not be home till full moon."

²¹With persuasive words she led him astray;
    she seduced him with her smooth talk.
²²All at once he followed her
    like an ox going to the slaughter,
    like a deer[b] stepping into a noose[c]
²³   till an arrow pierces his liver,
    like a bird darting into a snare,
    little knowing it will cost him his life.

²⁴Now then, my sons, listen to me;
    pay attention to what I say.
²⁵Do not let your heart turn to her ways
    or stray into her paths.
²⁶Many are the victims she has brought
      down;
    her slain are a mighty throng.
²⁷Her house is a highway to the grave,[d]
    leading down to the chambers of death.

Wisdom's Call

8 Does not wisdom call out?
    Does not understanding raise her
      voice?
²On the heights along the way,
    where the paths meet, she takes her
      stand;
³beside the gates leading into the city,
    at the entrances, she cries aloud:
⁴"To you, O men, I call out;
    I raise my voice to all mankind.
⁵You who are simple, gain prudence;
    you who are foolish, gain
      understanding.
⁶Listen, for I have worthy things to say;
    I open my lips to speak what is right.
⁷My mouth speaks what is true,
    for my lips detest wickedness.
⁸All the words of my mouth are just;
    none of them is crooked or perverse.
⁹To the discerning all of them are right;
    they are faultless to those who have
      knowledge.
¹⁰Choose my instruction instead of silver,
    knowledge rather than choice gold,
¹¹for wisdom is more precious than rubies,
    and nothing you desire can compare
      with her.

¹²"I, wisdom, dwell together with prudence;
    I possess knowledge and discretion.
¹³To fear the LORD is to hate evil;
    I hate pride and arrogance,
    evil behaviour and perverse speech.
¹⁴Counsel and sound judgment are mine;
    I have understanding and power.
¹⁵By me kings reign
    and rulers make laws that are just;
¹⁶by me princes govern,
    and all nobles who rule on earth.[a]
¹⁷I love those who love me,
    and those who seek me find me.
¹⁸With me are riches and honour,
    enduring wealth and prosperity.
¹⁹My fruit is better than fine gold;
    what I yield surpasses choice silver.
²⁰I walk in the way of righteousness,
    along the paths of justice,
²¹bestowing wealth on those who love me
    and making their treasuries full.

²²"The LORD brought me forth as the first of
    his works,[b,c]
    before his deeds of old;
²³I was appointed[d] from eternity,
    from the beginning, before the world
      began.
²⁴When there were no oceans, I was given
      birth,
    when there were no springs abounding
      with water;
²⁵before the mountains were settled in place,
    before the hills, I was given birth,
²⁶before he made the earth or its fields
    or any of the dust of the world.

---

a14 Traditionally *peace offerings*   b22 Syriac (see also Septuagint); Hebrew *fool*
c22 The meaning of the Hebrew for this line is uncertain.   d27 Hebrew *Sheol*
a16 Many Hebrew manuscripts and Septuagint; most Hebrew manuscripts *and nobles—all righteous rulers*
b22 Or *way*; or *dominion*
c22 Or *The LORD possessed me at the beginning of his work*; or *The LORD brought me forth at the beginning of his
work*   d23 Or *fashioned*

27I was there when he set the heavens in
  place,
    when he marked out the horizon on the
      face of the deep,
28when he established the clouds above
    and fixed securely the fountains of the
      deep,
29when he gave the sea its boundary
    so that the waters would not overstep
      his command,
  and when he marked out the foundations
    of the earth.
30   Then I was the craftsman at his side.
  I was filled with delight day after day,
    rejoicing always in his presence,
31rejoicing in his whole world
    and delighting in mankind.

32"Now then, my sons, listen to me;
    blessed are those who keep my ways.
33Listen to my instruction and be wise;
    do not ignore it.
34Blessed is the man who listens to me,
    watching daily at my doors,
      waiting at my doorway.
35For whoever finds me finds life
    and receives favour from the LORD.
36But whoever fails to find me harms
    himself;
    all who hate me love death."

Invitations of Wisdom and of Folly

9   Wisdom has built her house;
    she has hewn out its seven pillars.
2She has prepared her meat and mixed her
    wine;
    she has also set her table.
3She has sent out her maids, and she calls
    from the highest point of the city.
4"Let all who are simple come in here!"
    she says to those who lack judgment.
5"Come, eat my food
    and drink the wine I have mixed.
6Leave your simple ways and you will live;
    walk in the way of understanding.

7"Whoever corrects a mocker invites
    insult;
    whoever rebukes a wicked man incurs
      abuse.
8Do not rebuke a mocker or he will hate
    you;
    rebuke a wise man and he will love you.
9Instruct a wise man and he will be wiser
    still;
    teach a righteous man and he will add to
      his learning.

10"The fear of the LORD is the beginning of
    wisdom,
    and knowledge of the Holy One is
      understanding.
11For through me your days will be many,
    and years will be added to your life.
12If you are wise, your wisdom will reward
    you;
    if you are a mocker, you alone will
      suffer."

13The woman Folly is loud;
    she is undisciplined and without
      knowledge.
14She sits at the door of her house,
    on a seat at the highest point of the city,
15calling out to those who pass by,
    who go straight on their way.
16"Let all who are simple come in here!"
    she says to those who lack judgment.
17"Stolen water is sweet;
    food eaten in secret is delicious!"
18But little do they know that the dead are
    there,
    that her guests are in the depths of the
      grave.a

Proverbs of Solomon

10   The proverbs of Solomon:

A wise son brings joy to his father,
    but a foolish son grief to his mother.

2Ill-gotten treasures are of no value,
    but righteousness delivers from death.

3The LORD does not let the righteous go
    hungry
    but he thwarts the craving of the
      wicked.

4Lazy hands make a man poor,
    but diligent hands bring wealth.

5He who gathers crops in summer is a wise
    son,
    but he who sleeps during harvest is a
      disgraceful son.

6Blessings crown the head of the righteous,
    but violence overwhelms the mouth of
      the wicked.a

7The memory of the righteous will be a
    blessing,
    but the name of the wicked will rot.

8The wise in heart accept commands,
    but a chattering fool comes to ruin.

9The man of integrity walks securely,
    but he who takes crooked paths will be
      found out.

10He who winks maliciously causes grief,
    and a chattering fool comes to ruin.

11The mouth of the righteous is a fountain of
    life,
    but violence overwhelms the mouth of
      the wicked.

12Hatred stirs up dissension,
    but love covers over all wrongs.

13Wisdom is found on the lips of the
    discerning,
    but a rod is for the back of him who
      lacks judgment.

a18 Hebrew Sheol   a6 Or but the mouth of the wicked conceals violence; also in verse 11

14Wise men store up knowledge,
but the mouth of a fool invites ruin.

15The wealth of the rich is their fortified city,
but poverty is the ruin of the poor.

16The wages of the righteous bring them life,
but the income of the wicked brings
them punishment.

17He who heeds discipline shows the way to
life,
but whoever ignores correction leads
others astray.

18He who conceals his hatred has lying lips,
and whoever spreads slander is a fool.

19When words are many, sin is not absent,
but he who holds his tongue is wise.

20The tongue of the righteous is choice
silver,
but the heart of the wicked is of little
value.

21The lips of the righteous nourish many,
but fools die for lack of judgment.

22The blessing of the LORD brings wealth,
and he adds no trouble to it.

23A fool finds pleasure in evil conduct,
but a man of understanding delights in
wisdom.

24What the wicked dreads will overtake him;
what the righteous desire will be
granted.

25When the storm has swept by, the wicked
are gone,
but the righteous stand firm for ever.

26As vinegar to the teeth and smoke to the
eyes,
so is a sluggard to those who send him.

27The fear of the LORD adds length to life,
but the years of the wicked are cut short.

28The prospect of the righteous is joy,
but the hopes of the wicked come to
nothing.

29The way of the LORD is a refuge for the
righteous,
but it is the ruin of those who do evil.

30The righteous will never be uprooted,
but the wicked will not remain in the
land.

31The mouth of the righteous brings forth
wisdom,
but a perverse tongue will be cut out.

32The lips of the righteous know what is
fitting,
but the mouth of the wicked only what is
perverse.

11 The LORD abhors dishonest scales,
but accurate weights are his delight.

2When pride comes, then comes disgrace,
but with humility comes wisdom.

3The integrity of the upright guides them,
but the unfaithful are destroyed by their
duplicity.

4Wealth is worthless in the day of wrath,
but righteousness delivers from death.

5The righteousness of the blameless makes
a straight way for them,
but the wicked are brought down by
their own wickedness.

6The righteousness of the upright delivers
them,
but the unfaithful are trapped by evil
desires.

7When a wicked man dies, his hope
perishes;
all he expected from his power comes to
nothing.

8The righteous man is rescued from
trouble,
and it comes on the wicked instead.

9With his mouth the godless destroys his
neighbour,
but through knowledge the righteous
escape.

10When the righteous prosper, the city
rejoices;
when the wicked perish, there are
shouts of joy.

11Through the blessing of the upright a city
is exalted,
but by the mouth of the wicked it is
destroyed.

12A man who lacks judgment derides his
neighbour,
but a man of understanding holds his
tongue.

13A gossip betrays a confidence,
but a trustworthy man keeps a secret.

14For lack of guidance a nation falls,
but many advisers make victory sure.

15He who puts up security for another will
surely suffer,
but whoever refuses to strike hands in
pledge is safe.

16A kind-hearted woman gains respect,
but ruthless men gain only wealth.

17A kind man benefits himself,
but a cruel man brings trouble on
himself.

18The wicked man earns deceptive wages,
but he who sows righteousness reaps a
sure reward.

19The truly righteous man attains life,
but he who pursues evil goes to his
death.

20The LORD detests men of perverse heart
but he delights in those whose ways are
blameless.

21Be sure of this: The wicked will not go
unpunished,
but those who are righteous will go free.

22Like a gold ring in a pig's snout
is a beautiful woman who shows no
discretion.

23The desire of the righteous ends only in
good,
but the hope of the wicked only in
wrath.

24One man gives freely, yet gains even
more;
another withholds unduly, but comes to
poverty.

25A generous man will prosper;
he who refreshes others will himself be
refreshed.

26People curse the man who hoards grain,
but blessing crowns him who is willing
to sell.

27He who seeks good finds goodwill,
but evil comes to him who searches for
it.

28Whoever trusts in his riches will fall,
but the righteous will thrive like a green
leaf.

29He who brings trouble on his family will
inherit only wind,
and the fool will be servant to the wise.

30The fruit of the righteous is a tree of life,
and he who wins souls is wise.

31If the righteous receive their due on earth,
how much more the ungodly and the
sinner!

12 Whoever loves discipline loves
knowledge,
but he who hates correction is stupid.

2A good man obtains favour from the LORD,
but the LORD condemns a crafty man.

3A man cannot be established through
wickedness,
but the righteous cannot be uprooted.

4A wife of noble character is her husband's
crown,
but a disgraceful wife is like decay in his
bones.

5The plans of the righteous are just,
but the advice of the wicked is deceitful.

6The words of the wicked lie in wait for
blood,
but the speech of the upright rescues
them.

7Wicked men are overthrown and are no
more,
but the house of the righteous stands
firm.

8A man is praised according to his wisdom,
but men with warped minds are
despised.

9Better to be a nobody and yet have a
servant
than pretend to be somebody and have
no food.

10A righteous man cares for the needs of his
animal,
but the kindest acts of the wicked are
cruel.

11He who works his land will have abundant
food,
but he who chases fantasies lacks
judgment.

12The wicked desire the plunder of evil men,
but the root of the righteous flourishes.

13An evil man is trapped by his sinful talk,
but a righteous man escapes trouble.

14From the fruit of his lips a man is filled
with good things
as surely as the work of his hands
rewards him.

15The way of a fool seems right to him,
but a wise man listens to advice.

16A fool shows his annoyance at once,
but a prudent man overlooks an insult.

17A truthful witness gives honest testimony,
but a false witness tells lies.

18Reckless words pierce like a sword,
but the tongue of the wise brings healing.

19Truthful lips endure for ever,
but a lying tongue lasts only a moment.

20There is deceit in the hearts of those who
plot evil,
but joy for those who promote peace.

21No harm befalls the righteous,
but the wicked have their fill of trouble.

22The LORD detests lying lips,
but he delights in men who are truthful.

23A prudent man keeps his knowledge to
himself,
but the heart of fools blurts out folly.

24Diligent hands will rule,
but laziness ends in slave labour.

²⁵An anxious heart weighs a man down,
  but a kind word cheers him up.

²⁶A righteous man is cautious in friendship,ᵃ
  but the way of the wicked leads them
  astray.

²⁷The lazy man does not roastᵇ his game,
  but the diligent man prizes his
  possessions.

²⁸In the way of righteousness there is life;
  along that path is immortality.

13 A wise son heeds his father's
  instruction,
  but a mocker does not listen to rebuke.

²From the fruit of his lips a man enjoys
  good things,
  but the unfaithful have a craving for
  violence.

³He who guards his lips guards his life,
  but he who speaks rashly will come to
  ruin.

⁴The sluggard craves and gets nothing,
  but the desires of the diligent are fully
  satisfied.

⁵The righteous hate what is false,
  but the wicked bring shame and
  disgrace.

⁶Righteousness guards the man of integrity,
  but wickedness overthrows the sinner.

⁷One man pretends to be rich, yet has
  nothing;
  another pretends to be poor, yet has
  great wealth.

⁸A man's riches may ransom his life,
  but a poor man hears no threat.

⁹The light of the righteous shines brightly,
  but the lamp of the wicked is snuffed
  out.

¹⁰Pride only breeds quarrels,
  but wisdom is found in those who take
  advice.

¹¹Dishonest money dwindles away,
  but he who gathers money little by little
  makes it grow.

¹²Hope deferred makes the heart sick,
  but a longing fulfilled is a tree of life.

¹³He who scorns instruction will pay for it,
  but he who respects a command is
  rewarded.

¹⁴The teaching of the wise is a fountain of
  life,
  turning a man from the snares of death.

¹⁵Good understanding wins favour,
  but the way of the unfaithful is hard.ᵃ

¹⁶Every prudent man acts out of
  knowledge,
  but a fool exposes his folly.

¹⁷A wicked messenger falls into trouble,
  but a trustworthy envoy brings healing.

¹⁸He who ignores discipline comes to
  poverty and shame,
  but whoever heeds correction is
  honoured.

¹⁹A longing fulfilled is sweet to the soul,
  but fools detest turning from evil.

²⁰He who walks with the wise grows wise,
  but a companion of fools suffers harm.

²¹Misfortune pursues the sinner,
  but prosperity is the reward of the
  righteous.

²²A good man leaves an inheritance for his
  children's children,
  but a sinner's wealth is stored up for the
  righteous.

²³A poor man's field may produce abundant
  food,
  but injustice sweeps it away.

²⁴He who spares the rod hates his son,
  but he who loves him is careful to
  discipline him.

²⁵The righteous eat to their hearts' content,
  but the stomach of the wicked goes
  hungry.

14 The wise woman builds her house,
  but with her own hands the foolish
  one tears hers down.

²He whose walk is upright fears the LORD,
  but he whose ways are devious despises
  him.

³A fool's talk brings a rod to his back,
  but the lips of the wise protect them.

⁴Where there are no oxen, the manger is
  empty,
  but from the strength of an ox comes an
  abundant harvest.

⁵A truthful witness does not deceive,
  but a false witness pours out lies.

⁶The mocker seeks wisdom and finds none,
  but knowledge comes easily to the
  discerning.

⁷Stay away from a foolish man,
  for you will not find knowledge on his
  lips.

ᵃ26 Or *man is a guide to his neighbour*   ᵇ27 The meaning of the Hebrew for this word is uncertain.
ᵃ15 Or *unfaithful does not endure*

8The wisdom of the prudent is to give
    thought to their ways,
  but the folly of fools is deception.

9Fools mock at making amends for sin,
  but goodwill is found among the upright.

10Each heart knows its own bitterness,
  and no-one else can share its joy.

11The house of the wicked will be destroyed,
  but the tent of the upright will flourish.

12There is a way that seems right to a man,
  but in the end it leads to death.

13Even in laughter the heart may ache,
  and joy may end in grief.

14The faithless will be fully repaid for their
    ways,
  and the good man rewarded for his.

15A simple man believes anything,
  but a prudent man gives thought to his
    steps.

16A wise man fears the LORD and shuns evil,
  but a fool is hotheaded and reckless.

17A quick-tempered man does foolish things,
  and a crafty man is hated.

18The simple inherit folly,
  but the prudent are crowned with
    knowledge.

19Evil men will bow down in the presence of
    the good,
  and the wicked at the gates of the
    righteous.

20The poor are shunned even by their
    neighbours,
  but the rich have many friends.

21He who despises his neighbour sins,
  but blessed is he who is kind to the
    needy.

22Do not those who plot evil go astray?
  But those who plan what is good find*a*
    love and faithfulness.

23All hard work brings a profit,
  but mere talk leads only to poverty.

24The wealth of the wise is their crown,
  but the folly of fools yields folly.

25A truthful witness saves lives,
  but a false witness is deceitful.

26He who fears the LORD has a secure
    fortress,
  and for his children it will be a refuge.

27The fear of the LORD is a fountain of life,
  turning a man from the snares of death.

28A large population is a king's glory,
  but without subjects a prince is ruined.

29A patient man has great understanding,
  but a quick-tempered man displays folly.

30A heart at peace gives life to the body,
  but envy rots the bones.

31He who oppresses the poor shows
    contempt for their Maker,
  but whoever is kind to the needy
    honours God.

32When calamity comes, the wicked are
    brought down,
  but even in death the righteous have a
    refuge.

33Wisdom reposes in the heart of the
    discerning
  and even among fools she lets herself be
    known.*b*

34Righteousness exalts a nation,
  but sin is a disgrace to any people.

35A king delights in a wise servant,
  but a shameful servant incurs his wrath.

15 A gentle answer turns away wrath,
    but a harsh word stirs up anger.

2The tongue of the wise commends
    knowledge,
  but the mouth of the fool gushes folly.

3The eyes of the LORD are everywhere,
  keeping watch on the wicked and the
    good.

4The tongue that brings healing is a tree of
    life,
  but a deceitful tongue crushes the spirit.

5A fool spurns his father's discipline,
  but whoever heeds correction shows
    prudence.

6The house of the righteous contains great
    treasure,
  but the income of the wicked brings
    them trouble.

7The lips of the wise spread knowledge;
  not so the hearts of fools.

8The LORD detests the sacrifice of the
    wicked,
  but the prayer of the upright pleases
    him.

9The LORD detests the way of the wicked
  but he loves those who pursue
    righteousness.

10Stern discipline awaits him who leaves the
    path;
  he who hates correction will die.

---

*a*22 Or *show*   *b*33 Hebrew; Septuagint and Syriac / *but in the heart of fools she is not known*

[11]Death and Destruction[a] lie open before the
 LORD—
  how much more the hearts of men!

[12]A mocker resents correction;
  he will not consult the wise.

[13]A happy heart makes the face cheerful,
  but heartache crushes the spirit.

[14]The discerning heart seeks knowledge,
  but the mouth of a fool feeds on folly.

[15]All the days of the oppressed are
   wretched,
  but the cheerful heart has a continual
   feast.

[16]Better a little with the fear of the LORD
  than great wealth with turmoil.

[17]Better a meal of vegetables where there is
   love
  than a fattened calf with hatred.

[18]A hot-tempered man stirs up dissension,
  but a patient man calms a quarrel.

[19]The way of the sluggard is blocked with
   thorns,
  but the path of the upright is a highway.

[20]A wise son brings joy to his father,
  but a foolish man despises his mother.

[21]Folly delights a man who lacks judgment,
  but a man of understanding keeps a
   straight course.

[22]Plans fail for lack of counsel,
  but with many advisers they succeed.

[23]A man finds joy in giving an apt reply—
  and how good is a timely word!

[24]The path of life leads upward for the wise
  to keep him from going down to the
   grave.[b]

[25]The LORD tears down the proud man's
   house
  but he keeps the widow's boundaries
   intact.

[26]The LORD detests the thoughts of the
   wicked,
  but those of the pure are pleasing to him.

[27]A greedy man brings trouble to his family,
  but he who hates bribes will live.

[28]The heart of the righteous weighs its
   answers,
  but the mouth of the wicked gushes evil.

[29]The LORD is far from the wicked
  but he hears the prayer of the righteous.

[30]A cheerful look brings joy to the heart,
  and good news gives health to the
   bones.

[31]He who listens to a life-giving rebuke
  will be at home among the wise.

[32]He who ignores discipline despises
   himself,
  but whoever heeds correction gains
   understanding.

[33]The fear of the LORD teaches a man
   wisdom,[c]
  and humility comes before honour.

16 To man belong the plans of the heart,
  but from the LORD comes the reply
   of the tongue.

[2]All a man's ways seem innocent to him,
  but motives are weighed by the LORD.

[3]Commit to the LORD whatever you do,
  and your plans will succeed.

[4]The LORD works out everything for his
   own ends—
  even the wicked for a day of disaster.

[5]The LORD detests all the proud of heart.
  Be sure of this: They will not go
   unpunished.

[6]Through love and faithfulness sin is atoned
   for;
  through the fear of the LORD a man
   avoids evil.

[7]When a man's ways are pleasing to the
   LORD,
  he makes even his enemies live at peace
   with him.

[8]Better a little with righteousness
  than much gain with injustice.

[9]In his heart a man plans his course,
  but the LORD determines his steps.

[10]The lips of a king speak as an oracle,
  and his mouth should not betray justice.

[11]Honest scales and balances are from the
   LORD;
  all the weights in the bag are of his
   making.

[12]Kings detest wrongdoing,
  for a throne is established through
   righteousness.

[13]Kings take pleasure in honest lips;
  they value a man who speaks the truth.

[14]A king's wrath is a messenger of death,
  but a wise man will appease it.

---

[a]11 Hebrew *Sheol* and *Abaddon*   [b]24 Hebrew *Sheol*
[c]33 Or *Wisdom teaches the fear of the* LORD

¹⁵When a king's face brightens, it means life;
his favour is like a rain cloud in spring.

¹⁶How much better to get wisdom than gold,
to choose understanding rather than
silver!

¹⁷The highway of the upright avoids evil;
he who guards his way guards his life.

¹⁸Pride goes before destruction,
a haughty spirit before a fall.

¹⁹Better to be lowly in spirit and among the
oppressed
than to share plunder with the proud.

²⁰Whoever gives heed to instruction
prospers,
and blessed is he who trusts in the LORD.

²¹The wise in heart are called discerning,
and pleasant words promote
instruction.ᵃ

²²Understanding is a fountain of life to those
who have it,
but folly brings punishment to fools.

²³A wise man's heart guides his mouth,
and his lips promote instruction.ᵇ

²⁴Pleasant words are a honeycomb,
sweet to the soul and healing to the
bones.

²⁵There is a way that seems right to a man,
but in the end it leads to death.

²⁶The labourer's appetite works for him;
his hunger drives him on.

²⁷A scoundrel plots evil,
and his speech is like a scorching fire.

²⁸A perverse man stirs up dissension,
and a gossip separates close friends.

²⁹A violent man entices his neighbour
and leads him down a path that is not
good.

³⁰He who winks with his eye is plotting
perversity;
he who purses his lips is bent on evil.

³¹Grey hair is a crown of splendour;
it is attained by a righteous life.

³²Better a patient man than a warrior,
a man who controls his temper than one
who takes a city.

³³The lot is cast into the lap,
but its every decision is from the LORD.

17 Better a dry crust with peace and
quiet
than a house full of feasting,ᵃ with strife.

²A wise servant will rule over a disgraceful
son,
and will share the inheritance as one of
the brothers.

³The crucible for silver and the furnace for
gold,
but the LORD tests the heart.

⁴A wicked man listens to evil lips;
a liar pays attention to a malicious
tongue.

⁵He who mocks the poor shows contempt
for their Maker;
whoever gloats over disaster will not go
unpunished.

⁶Children's children are a crown to the
aged,
and parents are the pride of their
children.

⁷Arrogantᵇ lips are unsuited to a fool—
how much worse lying lips to a ruler!

⁸A bribe is a charm to the one who gives it;
wherever he turns, he succeeds.

⁹He who covers over an offence promotes
love,
but whoever repeats the matter
separates close friends.

¹⁰A rebuke impresses a man of discernment
more than a hundred lashes a fool.

¹¹An evil man is bent only on rebellion;
a merciless official will be sent against
him.

¹²Better to meet a bear robbed of her cubs
than a fool in his folly.

¹³If a man pays back evil for good,
evil will never leave his house.

¹⁴Starting a quarrel is like breaching a dam;
so drop the matter before a dispute
breaks out.

¹⁵Acquitting the guilty and condemning the
innocent—
the LORD detests them both.

¹⁶Of what use is money in the hand of a fool,
since he has no desire to get wisdom?

¹⁷A friend loves at all times,
and a brother is born for adversity.

¹⁸A man lacking in judgment strikes hands in
pledge
and puts up security for his neighbour.

¹⁹He who loves a quarrel loves sin;
he who builds a high gate invites
destruction.

ᵃ21 Or *words make a man persuasive*   ᵇ23 Or *mouth / and makes his lips persuasive*
ᵃ1 Hebrew *sacrifices*   ᵇ7 Or *Eloquent*

²⁰A man of perverse heart does not
prosper;
he whose tongue is deceitful falls into
trouble.

²¹To have a fool for a son brings grief;
there is no joy for the father of a fool.

²²A cheerful heart is good medicine,
but a crushed spirit dries up the bones.

²³A wicked man accepts a bribe in secret
to pervert the course of justice.

²⁴A discerning man keeps wisdom in view,
but a fool's eyes wander to the ends of
the earth.

²⁵A foolish son brings grief to his father
and bitterness to the one who bore him.

²⁶It is not good to punish an innocent man,
or to flog officials for their integrity.

²⁷A man of knowledge uses words with
restraint,
and a man of understanding is
even-tempered.

²⁸Even a fool is thought wise if he keeps
silent,
and discerning if he holds his tongue.

18 An unfriendly man pursues selfish
ends;
he defies all sound judgment.

²A fool finds no pleasure in understanding
but delights in airing his own opinions.

³When wickedness comes, so does
contempt,
and with shame comes disgrace.

⁴The words of a man's mouth are deep
waters,
but the fountain of wisdom is a bubbling
brook.

⁵It is not good to be partial to the wicked
or to deprive the innocent of justice.

⁶A fool's lips bring him strife,
and his mouth invites a beating.

⁷A fool's mouth is his undoing,
and his lips are a snare to his soul.

⁸The words of a gossip are like choice
morsels;
they go down to a man's inmost parts.

⁹One who is slack in his work
is brother to one who destroys.

¹⁰The name of the LORD is a strong tower;
the righteous run to it and are safe.

¹¹The wealth of the rich is their fortified
city;
they imagine it an unscalable wall.

¹²Before his downfall a man's heart is
proud,
but humility comes before honour.

¹³He who answers before listening—
that is his folly and his shame.

¹⁴A man's spirit sustains him in sickness,
but a crushed spirit who can bear?

¹⁵The heart of the discerning acquires
knowledge;
the ears of the wise seek it out.

¹⁶A gift opens the way for the giver
and ushers him into the presence of the
great.

¹⁷The first to present his case seems right,
till another comes forward and
questions him.

¹⁸Casting the lot settles disputes
and keeps strong opponents apart.

¹⁹An offended brother is more unyielding
than a fortified city,
and disputes are like the barred gates of
a citadel.

²⁰From the fruit of his mouth a man's
stomach is filled;
with the harvest from his lips he is
satisfied.

²¹The tongue has the power of life and
death,
and those who love it will eat its fruit.

²²He who finds a wife finds what is good
and receives favour from the LORD.

²³A poor man pleads for mercy,
but a rich man answers harshly.

²⁴A man of many companions may come to
ruin,
but there is a friend who sticks closer
than a brother.

19 Better a poor man whose walk is
blameless
than a fool whose lips are perverse.

²It is not good to have zeal without
knowledge,
nor to be hasty and miss the way.

³A man's own folly ruins his life,
yet his heart rages against the LORD.

⁴Wealth brings many friends,
but a poor man's friend deserts him.

⁵A false witness will not go unpunished,
and he who pours out lies will not go
free.

⁶Many curry favour with a ruler,
and everyone is the friend of a man who
gives gifts.

⁷A poor man is shunned by all his
    relatives—
  how much more do his friends avoid
    him!
Though he pursues them with pleading,
  they are nowhere to be found.ᵃ

⁸He who gets wisdom loves his own soul;
  he who cherishes understanding
    prospers.

⁹A false witness will not go unpunished,
  and he who pours out lies will perish.

¹⁰It is not fitting for a fool to live in luxury—
  how much worse for a slave to rule over
    princes!

¹¹A man's wisdom gives him patience;
  it is to his glory to overlook an offence.

¹²A king's rage is like the roar of a lion,
  but his favour is like dew on the grass.

¹³A foolish son is his father's ruin,
  and a quarrelsome wife is like a constant
    dripping.

¹⁴Houses and wealth are inherited from
    parents,
  but a prudent wife is from the LORD.

¹⁵Laziness brings on deep sleep,
  and the shiftless man goes hungry.

¹⁶He who obeys instructions guards his life,
  but he who is contemptuous of his ways
    will die.

¹⁷He who is kind to the poor lends to the
    LORD,
  and he will reward him for what he has
    done.

¹⁸Discipline your son, for in that there is
    hope;
  do not be a willing party to his death.

¹⁹A hot-tempered man must pay the penalty;
  if you rescue him, you will have to do it
    again.

²⁰Listen to advice and accept instruction,
  and in the end you will be wise.

²¹Many are the plans in a man's heart,
  but it is the LORD's purpose that
    prevails.

²²What a man desires is unfailing love;ᵇ
  better to be poor than a liar.

²³The fear of the LORD leads to life:
  Then one rests content, untouched by
    trouble.

²⁴The sluggard buries his hand in the dish;
  he will not even bring it back to his
    mouth!

²⁵Flog a mocker, and the simple will learn
    prudence;
  rebuke a discerning man, and he will
    gain knowledge.

²⁶He who robs his father and drives out his
    mother
  is a son who brings shame and disgrace.

²⁷Stop listening to instruction, my son,
  and you will stray from the words of
    knowledge.

²⁸A corrupt witness mocks at justice,
  and the mouth of the wicked gulps down
    evil.

²⁹Penalties are prepared for mockers,
  and beatings for the backs of fools.

20 Wine is a mocker and beer a brawler;
    whoever is led astray by them is not
    wise.

²A king's wrath is like the roar of a lion;
  he who angers him forfeits his life.

³It is to a man's honour to avoid strife,
  but every fool is quick to quarrel.

⁴A sluggard does not plough in season;
  so at harvest time he looks but finds
    nothing.

⁵The purposes of a man's heart are deep
    waters,
  but a man of understanding draws them
    out.

⁶Many a man claims to have unfailing love,
  but a faithful man who can find?

⁷The righteous man leads a blameless life;
  blessed are his children after him.

⁸When a king sits on his throne to judge,
  he winnows out all evil with his eyes.

⁹Who can say, "I have kept my heart pure;
  I am clean and without sin"?

¹⁰Differing weights and differing
    measures—
  the LORD detests them both.

¹¹Even a child is known by his actions,
  by whether his conduct is pure and right.

¹²Ears that hear and eyes that see—
  the LORD has made them both.

¹³Do not love sleep or you will grow poor;
  stay awake and you will have food to
    spare.

¹⁴"It's no good, it's no good!" says the
    buyer;
  then off he goes and boasts about his
    purchase.

ᵃ7 The meaning of the Hebrew for this sentence is uncertain.   ᵇ22 Or *A man's greed is his shame*

¹⁵Gold there is, and rubies in abundance,
    but lips that speak knowledge are a rare
      jewel.

¹⁶Take the garment of one who puts up
    security for a stranger;
    hold it in pledge if he does it for a
      wayward woman.

¹⁷Food gained by fraud tastes sweet to a
    man,
    but he ends up with a mouth full of
      gravel.

¹⁸Make plans by seeking advice;
    if you wage war, obtain guidance.

¹⁹A gossip betrays a confidence;
    so avoid a man who talks too much.

²⁰If a man curses his father or mother,
    his lamp will be snuffed out in pitch
      darkness.

²¹An inheritance quickly gained at the
    beginning
    will not be blessed at the end.

²²Do not say, "I'll pay you back for this
    wrong!"
    Wait for the Lord, and he will deliver
      you.

²³The Lord detests differing weights,
    and dishonest scales do not please him.

²⁴A man's steps are directed by the Lord.
    How then can anyone understand his
      own way?

²⁵It is a trap for a man to dedicate something
    rashly
    and only later to consider his vows.

²⁶A wise king winnows out the wicked;
    he drives the threshing wheel over them.

²⁷The lamp of the Lord searches the spirit of
    a man;[a]
    it searches out his inmost being.

²⁸Love and faithfulness keep a king safe;
    through love his throne is made secure.

²⁹The glory of young men is their strength,
    grey hair the splendour of the old.

³⁰Blows and wounds cleanse away evil,
    and beatings purge the inmost being.

21 The king's heart is in the hand of the
    Lord;
he directs it like a watercourse wherever
    he pleases.

²All a man's ways seem right to him,
    but the Lord weighs the heart.

³To do what is right and just
    is more acceptable to the Lord than
      sacrifice.

⁴Haughty eyes and a proud heart,
    the lamp of the wicked, are sin!

⁵The plans of the diligent lead to profit
    as surely as haste leads to poverty.

⁶A fortune made by a lying tongue
    is a fleeting vapour and a deadly snare.[a]

⁷The violence of the wicked will drag them
    away,
    for they refuse to do what is right.

⁸The way of the guilty is devious,
    but the conduct of the innocent is
      upright.

⁹Better to live on a corner of the roof
    than share a house with a quarrelsome
      wife.

¹⁰The wicked man craves evil;
    his neighbour gets no mercy from
      him.

¹¹When a mocker is punished, the simple
    gain wisdom;
    when a wise man is instructed, he gets
      knowledge.

¹²The Righteous One[b] takes note of the
    house of the wicked
    and brings the wicked to ruin.

¹³If a man shuts his ears to the cry of the
    poor,
    he too will cry out and not be
      answered.

¹⁴A gift given in secret soothes anger,
    and a bribe concealed in the cloak
      pacifies great wrath.

¹⁵When justice is done, it brings joy to the
    righteous
    but terror to evildoers.

¹⁶A man who strays from the path of
    understanding
    comes to rest in the company of the
      dead.

¹⁷He who loves pleasure will become poor;
    whoever loves wine and oil will never be
      rich.

¹⁸The wicked become a ransom for the
    righteous,
    and the unfaithful for the upright.

¹⁹Better to live in a desert
    than with a quarrelsome and
      ill-tempered wife.

---

[a]27 Or *The spirit of man is the Lord's lamp*
[a]6 Some Hebrew manuscripts, Septuagint and Vulgate; most Hebrew manuscripts *vapour for those who seek death*
[b]12 Or *The righteous man*

20In the house of the wise are stores of
choice food and oil,
but a foolish man devours all he has.

21He who pursues righteousness and love
finds life, prosperity[c] and honour.

22A wise man attacks the city of the mighty
and pulls down the stronghold in which
they trust.

23He who guards his mouth and his tongue
keeps himself from calamity.

24The proud and arrogant man—"Mocker"
is his name;
he behaves with overweening pride.

25The sluggard's craving will be the death of
him,
because his hands refuse to work.

26All day long he craves for more,
but the righteous give without sparing.

27The sacrifice of the wicked is detestable—
how much more so when brought with
evil intent!

28A false witness will perish,
and whoever listens to him will be
destroyed for ever.[d]

29A wicked man puts up a bold front,
but an upright man gives thought to his
ways.

30There is no wisdom, no insight, no plan
that can succeed against the LORD.

31The horse is made ready for the day of
battle,
but victory rests with the LORD.

22 A good name is more desirable than
great riches;
to be esteemed is better than silver or
gold.

2Rich and poor have this in common:
The LORD is the Maker of them all.

3A prudent man sees danger and takes
refuge,
but the simple keep going and suffer for
it.

4Humility and the fear of the LORD
bring wealth and honour and life.

5In the paths of the wicked lie thorns and
snares,
but he who guards his soul stays far
from them.

6Train[a] a child in the way he should go,
and when he is old he will not turn from
it.

7The rich rule over the poor,
and the borrower is servant to the
lender.

8He who sows wickedness reaps trouble,
and the rod of his fury will be destroyed.

9A generous man will himself be blessed,
for he shares his food with the poor.

10Drive out the mocker, and out goes strife;
quarrels and insults are ended.

11He who loves a pure heart and whose
speech is gracious
will have the king for his friend.

12The eyes of the LORD keep watch over
knowledge,
but he frustrates the words of the
unfaithful.

13The sluggard says, "There is a lion
outside!"
or, "I will be murdered in the streets!"

14The mouth of an adulteress is a deep pit;
he who is under the LORD's wrath will
fall into it.

15Folly is bound up in the heart of a child,
but the rod of discipline will drive it far
from him.

16He who oppresses the poor to increase his
wealth
and he who gives gifts to the rich—both
come to poverty.

Sayings of the Wise

17Pay attention and listen to the sayings of
the wise;
apply your heart to what I teach,
18for it is pleasing when you keep them in
your heart
and have all of them ready on your lips.
19So that your trust may be in the LORD,
I teach you today, even you.
20Have I not written thirty[b] sayings for you,
sayings of counsel and knowledge,
21teaching you true and reliable words,
so that you can give sound answers
to him who sent you?

22Do not exploit the poor because they are
poor
and do not crush the needy in court,
23for the LORD will take up their case
and will plunder those who plunder
them.

24Do not make friends with a hot-tempered
man,
do not associate with one easily
angered,
25or you may learn his ways
and get yourself ensnared.

---

c21 Or righteousness   d28 Or / but the words of an obedient man will live on   a6 Or Start
b20 Or not formerly written; or not written excellent

26Do not be a man who strikes hands in
    pledge
    or puts up security for debts;
27if you lack the means to pay,
    your very bed will be snatched from
    under you.

28Do not move an ancient boundary stone
    set up by your forefathers.

29Do you see a man skilled in his work?
    He will serve before kings;
    he will not serve before obscure men.

23 When you sit to dine with a ruler,
    note well what[a] is before you,
2and put a knife to your throat
    if you are given to gluttony.
3Do not crave his delicacies,
    for that food is deceptive.

4Do not wear yourself out to get rich;
    have the wisdom to show restraint.
5Cast but a glance at riches, and they are
    gone,
    for they will surely sprout wings
    and fly off to the sky like an eagle.

6Do not eat the food of a stingy man,
    do not crave his delicacies;
7for he is the kind of man
    who is always thinking about the cost.[b]
    "Eat and drink," he says to you,
    but his heart is not with you.
8You will vomit up the little you have eaten
    and will have wasted your compliments.

9Do not speak to a fool,
    for he will scorn the wisdom of your
    words.

10Do not move an ancient boundary stone
    or encroach on the fields of the
    fatherless,
11for their Defender is strong;
    he will take up their case against you.

12Apply your heart to instruction
    and your ears to words of knowledge.

13Do not withhold discipline from a child;
    if you punish him with the rod, he will
    not die.
14Punish him with the rod
    and save his soul from death.[c]

15My son, if your heart is wise,
    then my heart will be glad;
16my inmost being will rejoice
    when your lips speak what is right.

17Do not let your heart envy sinners,
    but always be zealous for the fear of the
    LORD.
18There is surely a future hope for you,
    and your hope will not be cut off.

19Listen, my son, and be wise,
    and keep your heart on the right path.
20Do not join those who drink too much
    wine
    or gorge themselves on meat,
21for drunkards and gluttons become poor,
    and drowsiness clothes them in rags.

22Listen to your father, who gave you life,
    and do not despise your mother when
    she is old.
23Buy the truth and do not sell it;
    get wisdom, discipline and
    understanding.
24The father of a righteous man has great
    joy;
    he who has a wise son delights in him.
25May your father and mother be glad;
    may she who gave you birth rejoice!

26My son, give me your heart
    and let your eyes keep to my ways,
27for a prostitute is a deep pit
    and a wayward wife is a narrow well.
28Like a bandit she lies in wait,
    and multiplies the unfaithful among
    men.

29Who has woe? Who has sorrow?
    Who has strife? Who has complaints?
    Who has needless bruises? Who has
    bloodshot eyes?
30Those who linger over wine,
    who go to sample bowls of mixed wine.
31Do not gaze at wine when it is red,
    when it sparkles in the cup,
    when it goes down smoothly!
32In the end it bites like a snake
    and poisons like a viper.
33Your eyes will see strange sights
    and your mind imagine confusing things.
34You will be like one sleeping on the high
    seas,
    lying on top of the rigging.
35"They hit me," you will say, "but I'm not
    hurt!
    They beat me, but I don't feel it!
    When will I wake up
    so I can find another drink?"

24 Do not envy wicked men,
    do not desire their company;
2for their hearts plot violence,
    and their lips talk about making trouble.

3By wisdom a house is built,
    and through understanding it is
    established;
4through knowledge its rooms are filled
    with rare and beautiful treasures.

5A wise man has great power,
    and a man of knowledge increases
    strength;
6for waging war you need guidance,
    and for victory many advisers.

---

[a]1 Or who
[b]7 Or for as he thinks within himself, / so he is; or for as he puts on a feast, / so he is
[c]14 Hebrew Sheol

⁷Wisdom is too high for a fool;
   in the assembly at the gate he has
      nothing to say.

⁸He who plots evil
   will be known as a schemer.
⁹The schemes of folly are sin,
   and men detest a mocker.

¹⁰If you falter in times of trouble,
   how small is your strength!

¹¹Rescue those being led away to death;
   hold back those staggering towards
      slaughter.
¹²If you say, "But we knew nothing about
     this,"
   does not he who weighs the heart
      perceive it?
   Does not he who guards your life know it?
   Will he not repay each person according
      to what he has done?

¹³Eat honey, my son, for it is good;
   honey from the comb is sweet to your
      taste.
¹⁴Know also that wisdom is sweet to your
     soul;
   if you find it, there is a future hope for
     you,
   and your hope will not be cut off.

¹⁵Do not lie in wait like an outlaw against a
     righteous man's house,
   do not raid his dwelling-place;
¹⁶for though a righteous man falls seven
     times, he rises again,
   but the wicked are brought down by
      calamity.

¹⁷Do not gloat when your enemy falls;
   when he stumbles, do not let your heart
      rejoice,
¹⁸or the LORD will see and disapprove
   and turn his wrath away from him.

¹⁹Do not fret because of evil men
   or be envious of the wicked,
²⁰for the evil man has no future hope,
   and the lamp of the wicked will be
      snuffed out.

²¹Fear the LORD and the king, my son,
   and do not join with the rebellious,
²²for those two will send sudden destruction
     upon them,
   and who knows what calamities they
      can bring?

Further Sayings of the Wise
²³These also are sayings of the wise:

To show partiality in judging is not good:
²⁴Whoever says to the guilty, "You are
     innocent"—
   peoples will curse him and nations
      denounce him.

²⁵But it will go well with those who convict
     the guilty,
   and rich blessing will come upon them.

²⁶An honest answer
   is like a kiss on the lips.

²⁷Finish your outdoor work
   and get your fields ready;
   after that, build your house.

²⁸Do not testify against your neighbour
     without cause,
   or use your lips to deceive.
²⁹Do not say, "I'll do to him as he has done
     to me;
   I'll pay that man back for what he did."

³⁰I went past the field of the sluggard,
   past the vineyard of the man who lacks
      judgment;
³¹thorns had come up everywhere,
   the ground was covered with weeds,
   and the stone wall was in ruins.
³²I applied my heart to what I observed
   and learned a lesson from what I saw:
³³A little sleep, a little slumber,
   a little folding of the hands to rest—
³⁴and poverty will come on you like a bandit
   and scarcity like an armed man.ᵃ

More Proverbs of Solomon

25 These are more proverbs of Solomon,
copied by the men of Hezekiah king
of Judah:

²It is the glory of God to conceal a matter;
   to search out a matter is the glory of
      kings.

³As the heavens are high and the earth is
     deep,
   so the hearts of kings are unsearchable.

⁴Remove the dross from the silver,
   and out comes material forᵃ the
      silversmith;
⁵remove the wicked from the king's
     presence,
   and his throne will be established
      through righteousness.

⁶Do not exalt yourself in the king's
     presence,
   and do not claim a place among great
      men;
⁷it is better for him to say to you, "Come
     up here,"
   than for him to humiliate you before a
      nobleman.

What you have seen with your eyes
⁸ do not bringᵇ hastily to court,
   for what will you do in the end
     if your neighbour puts you to shame?

⁹If you argue your case with a neighbour,
   do not betray another man's confidence,

ᵃ34 Or like a vagrant / and scarcity like a beggar   ᵃ4 Or comes a vessel from
ᵇ7, 8 Or nobleman / on whom you had set your eyes. / ⁸Do not go

10or he who hears it may shame you
and you will never lose your bad
reputation.

11A word aptly spoken
is like apples of gold in settings of silver.

12Like an ear-ring of gold or an ornament of
fine gold
is a wise man's rebuke to a listening ear.

13Like the coolness of snow at harvest time
is a trustworthy messenger to those who
send him;
he refreshes the spirit of his masters.

14Like clouds and wind without rain
is a man who boasts of gifts he does not
give.

15Through patience a ruler can be
persuaded,
and a gentle tongue can break a bone.

16If you find honey, eat just enough—
too much of it, and you will vomit.
17Seldom set foot in your neighbour's
house—
too much of you, and he will hate you.

18Like a club or a sword or a sharp arrow
is the man who gives false testimony
against his neighbour.

19Like a bad tooth or a lame foot
is reliance on the unfaithful in times of
trouble.

20Like one who takes away a garment on a
cold day,
or like vinegar poured on soda,
is one who sings songs to a heavy heart.

21If your enemy is hungry, give him food to
eat;
if he is thirsty, give him water to drink.
22In doing this, you will heap burning coals
on his head,
and the LORD will reward you.

23As a north wind brings rain,
so a sly tongue brings angry looks.

24Better to live on a corner of the roof
than share a house with a quarrelsome
wife.

25Like cold water to a weary soul
is good news from a distant land.

26Like a muddied spring or a polluted well
is a righteous man who gives way to the
wicked.

27It is not good to eat too much honey,
nor is it honourable to seek one's own
honour.

28Like a city whose walls are broken down
is a man who lacks self-control.

26 Like snow in summer or rain in
harvest,
honour is not fitting for a fool.

2Like a fluttering sparrow or a darting
swallow,
an undeserved curse does not come to
rest.

3A whip for the horse, a halter for the
donkey,
and a rod for the backs of fools!

4Do not answer a fool according to his
folly,
or you will be like him yourself.

5Answer a fool according to his folly,
or he will be wise in his own eyes.

6Like cutting off one's feet or drinking
violence
is the sending of a message by the hand
of a fool.

7Like a lame man's legs that hang limp
is a proverb in the mouth of a fool.

8Like tying a stone in a sling
is the giving of honour to a fool.

9Like a thornbush in a drunkard's hand
is a proverb in the mouth of a fool.

10Like an archer who wounds at random
is he who hires a fool or any passer-by.

11As a dog returns to its vomit,
so a fool repeats his folly.

12Do you see a man wise in his own eyes?
There is more hope for a fool than for
him.

13The sluggard says, ''There is a lion in the
road,
a fierce lion roaming the streets!''

14As a door turns on its hinges,
so a sluggard turns on his bed.

15The sluggard buries his hand in the dish;
he is too lazy to bring it back to his
mouth.

16The sluggard is wiser in his own eyes
than seven men who answer discreetly.

17Like one who seizes a dog by the ears
is a passer-by who meddles in a quarrel
not his own.

18Like a madman shooting
firebrands or deadly arrows
19is a man who deceives his neighbour
and says, ''I was only joking!''

20Without wood a fire goes out;
without gossip a quarrel dies down.

21As charcoal to embers and as wood to fire,
  so is a quarrelsome man for kindling
    strife.

22The words of a gossip are like choice
    morsels;
  they go down to a man's inmost parts.

23Like a coating of glaze*a* over earthenware
  are fervent lips with an evil heart.

24A malicious man disguises himself with his
    lips,
  but in his heart he harbours deceit.
25Though his speech is charming, do not
    believe him,
  for seven abominations fill his heart.
26His malice may be concealed by
    deception,
  but his wickedness will be exposed in
    the assembly.

27If a man digs a pit, he will fall into it;
  if a man rolls a stone, it will roll back on
    him.

28A lying tongue hates those it hurts,
  and a flattering mouth works ruin.

27 Do not boast about tomorrow,
  for you do not know what a day may
    bring forth.

2Let another praise you, and not your own
    mouth;
  someone else, and not your own lips.

3Stone is heavy and sand a burden,
  but provocation by a fool is heavier than
    both.

4Anger is cruel and fury overwhelming,
  but who can stand before jealousy?

5Better is open rebuke
  than hidden love.

6Wounds from a friend can be trusted,
  but an enemy multiplies kisses.

7He who is full loathes honey,
  but to the hungry even what is bitter
    tastes sweet.

8Like a bird that strays from its nest
  is a man who strays from his home.

9Perfume and incense bring joy to the
    heart,
  and the pleasantness of one's friend
    springs from his earnest counsel.

10Do not forsake your friend and the friend
    of your father,
  and do not go to your brother's house
    when disaster strikes you—
  better a neighbour nearby than a brother
    far away.

11Be wise, my son, and bring joy to my
    heart;
  then I can answer anyone who treats me
    with contempt.

12The prudent see danger and take refuge,
  but the simple keep going and suffer for
    it.

13Take the garment of one who puts up
    security for a stranger;
  hold it in pledge if he does it for a
    wayward woman.

14If a man loudly blesses his neighbour early
    in the morning,
  it will be taken as a curse.

15A quarrelsome wife is like
  a constant dripping on a rainy day;
16restraining her is like restraining
    the wind
  or grasping oil with the hand.

17As iron sharpens iron,
  so one man sharpens another.

18He who tends a fig-tree will eat its fruit,
  and he who looks after his master will be
    honoured.

19As water reflects a face,
  so a man's heart reflects the man.

20Death and Destruction*a* are never
    satisfied,
  and neither are the eyes of man.

21The crucible for silver and the furnace for
    gold,
  but man is tested by the praise he
    receives.

22Though you grind a fool in a mortar,
  grinding him like grain with a pestle,
  you will not remove his folly from
    him.

23Be sure you know the condition of your
    flocks,
  give careful attention to your herds;
24for riches do not endure for ever,
  and a crown is not secure for all
    generations.
25When the hay is removed and new growth
    appears
  and the grass from the hills is gathered
    in,
26the lambs will provide you with clothing,
  and the goats with the price of a field.
27You will have plenty of goats' milk
  to feed you and your family
  and to nourish your servant girls.

28 The wicked man flees
  though no-one pursues,
  but the righteous are as bold as a lion.

a23 With a different word division of the Hebrew; Masoretic Text *of silver dross*
a20 Hebrew *Sheol and Abaddon*

²When a country is rebellious, it has many
        rulers,
    but a man of understanding and
        knowledge maintains order.

³A ruler[a] who oppresses the poor
    is like a driving rain that leaves no
        crops.

⁴Those who forsake the law praise the
        wicked,
    but those who keep the law resist them.

⁵Evil men do not understand justice,
    but those who seek the LORD understand
        it fully.

⁶Better a poor man whose walk is blameless
    than a rich man whose ways are
        perverse.

⁷He who keeps the law is a discerning son,
    but a companion of gluttons disgraces
        his father.

⁸He who increases his wealth by exorbitant
        interest
    amasses it for another, who will be kind
        to the poor.

⁹If anyone turns a deaf ear to the law,
    even his prayers are detestable.

¹⁰He who leads the upright along an evil
        path
    will fall into his own trap,
    but the blameless will receive a good
        inheritance.

¹¹A rich man may be wise in his own eyes,
    but a poor man who has discernment
        sees through him.

¹²When the righteous triumph, there is great
        elation;
    but when the wicked rise to power, men
        go into hiding.

¹³He who conceals his sins does not
        prosper,
    but whoever confesses and renounces
        them finds mercy.

¹⁴Blessed is the man who always fears the
        LORD,
    but he who hardens his heart falls into
        trouble.

¹⁵Like a roaring lion or a charging bear
    is a wicked man ruling over a helpless
        people.

¹⁶A tyrannical ruler lacks judgment,
    but he who hates ill-gotten gain will
        enjoy a long life.

¹⁷A man tormented by the guilt of murder
    will be a fugitive till death;
    let no-one support him.

¹⁸He whose walk is blameless is kept safe,
    but he whose ways are perverse will
        suddenly fall.

¹⁹He who works his land will have abundant
        food,
    but the one who chases fantasies will
        have his fill of poverty.

²⁰A faithful man will be richly blessed,
    but one eager to get rich will not go
        unpunished.

²¹To show partiality is not good—
    yet a man will do wrong for a piece of
        bread.

²²A stingy man is eager to get rich
    and is unaware that poverty awaits
        him.

²³He who rebukes a man will in the end gain
        more favour
    than he who has a flattering tongue.

²⁴He who robs his father or mother
    and says, "It's not wrong"—
    he is partner to him who destroys.

²⁵A greedy man stirs up dissension,
    but he who trusts in the LORD will
        prosper.

²⁶He who trusts in himself is a fool,
    but he who walks in wisdom is kept
        safe.

²⁷He who gives to the poor will lack nothing,
    but he who closes his eyes to them
        receives many curses.

²⁸When the wicked rise to power, people go
        into hiding;
    but when the wicked perish, the
        righteous thrive.

29 A man who remains stiff-necked
        after many rebukes
    will suddenly be destroyed—without
        remedy.

²When the righteous thrive, the people
        rejoice;
    when the wicked rule, the people groan.

³A man who loves wisdom brings joy to his
        father,
    but a companion of prostitutes
        squanders his wealth.

⁴By justice a king gives a country stability,
    but one who is greedy for bribes tears it
        down.

⁵Whoever flatters his neighbour
    is spreading a net for his feet.

⁶An evil man is snared by his own sin,
    but a righteous one can sing and be glad.

[a]3 Or A poor man

⁷The righteous care about justice for the
poor,
but the wicked have no such concern.

⁸Mockers stir up a city,
but wise men turn away anger.

⁹If a wise man goes to court with a fool,
the fool rages and scoffs, and there is no
peace.

¹⁰Bloodthirsty men hate a man of integrity
and seek to kill the upright.

¹¹A fool gives full vent to his anger,
but a wise man keeps himself under
control.

¹²If a ruler listens to lies,
all his officials become wicked.

¹³The poor man and the oppressor have this
in common:
The Lord gives sight to the eyes of both.

¹⁴If a king judges the poor with fairness,
his throne will always be secure.

¹⁵The rod of correction imparts wisdom,
but a child left to himself disgraces his
mother.

¹⁶When the wicked thrive, so does sin,
but the righteous will see their downfall.

¹⁷Discipline your son, and he will give you
peace;
he will bring delight to your soul.

¹⁸Where there is no revelation, the people
cast off restraint;
but blessed is he who keeps the law.

¹⁹A servant cannot be corrected by mere
words;
though he understands, he will not
respond.

²⁰Do you see a man who speaks in haste?
There is more hope for a fool than for
him.

²¹If a man pampers his servant from youth,
he will bring grief[a] in the end.

²²An angry man stirs up dissension,
and a hot-tempered one commits many
sins.

²³A man's pride brings him low,
but a man of lowly spirit gains honour.

²⁴The accomplice of a thief is his own enemy;
he is put under oath and dare not testify.

²⁵Fear of man will prove to be a snare,
but whoever trusts in the Lord is kept
safe.

²⁶Many seek an audience with a ruler,
but it is from the Lord that man gets
justice.

²⁷The righteous detest the dishonest;
the wicked detest the upright.

Sayings of Agur

30 The sayings of Agur son of Jakeh—an
oracle:[a]

This man declared to Ithiel,
to Ithiel and to Ucal:[b]

²"I am the most ignorant of men;
I do not have a man's understanding.
³I have not learned wisdom,
nor have I knowledge of the Holy One.
⁴Who has gone up to heaven and come
down?
Who has gathered up the wind in the
hollow of his hands?
Who has wrapped up the waters in his
cloak?
Who has established all the ends of the
earth?
What is his name, and the name of his son?
Tell me if you know!

⁵"Every word of God is flawless;
he is a shield to those who take refuge in
him.
⁶Do not add to his words,
or he will rebuke you and prove you a
liar.

⁷"Two things I ask of you, O Lord;
do not refuse me before I die:
⁸Keep falsehood and lies far from me;
give me neither poverty nor riches,
but give me only my daily bread.
⁹Otherwise, I may have too much and
disown you
and say, 'Who is the Lord?'
Or I may become poor and steal,
and so dishonour the name of my God.

¹⁰"Do not slander a servant to his master,
or he will curse you, and you will pay for
it.

¹¹"There are those who curse their fathers
and do not bless their mothers;
¹²those who are pure in their own eyes
and yet are not cleansed of their filth;
¹³those whose eyes are ever so haughty,
whose glances are so disdainful;
¹⁴those whose teeth are swords
and whose jaws are set with knives
to devour the poor from the earth,
the needy from among mankind.

¹⁵"The leech has two daughters.
'Give! Give!' they cry.

"There are three things that are never
satisfied,
four that never say, 'Enough!':

---

[a]21 The meaning of the Hebrew for this word is uncertain.   [a]1 Or *Jakeh of Massa*
[b]1 Masoretic Text; with a different word division of the Hebrew *declared, "I am weary, O God; I I am weary, O God, and faint.*

16the grave,*c* the barren womb,
   land, which is never satisfied with water,
   and fire, which never says, 'Enough!'

17"The eye that mocks a father,
      that scorns obedience to a mother,
   will be pecked out by the ravens of the
      valley,
   will be eaten by the vultures.

18"There are three things that are too
      amazing for me,
   four that I do not understand:
19the way of an eagle in the sky,
   the way of a snake on a rock,
   the way of a ship on the high seas,
   and the way of a man with a maiden.

20"This is the way of an adulteress:
   She eats and wipes her mouth
   and says, 'I've done nothing wrong.'

21"Under three things the earth trembles,
   under four it cannot bear up:
22a servant who becomes king,
   a fool who is full of food,
23an unloved woman who is married,
   and a maidservant who displaces her
      mistress.

24"Four things on earth are small,
   yet they are extremely wise:
25Ants are creatures of little strength,
   yet they store up their food in the
      summer;
26conies*d* are creatures of little power,
   yet they make their home in the crags;
27locusts have no king,
   yet they advance together in ranks;
28a lizard can be caught with the hand,
   yet it is found in kings' palaces.

29"There are three things that are stately in
      their stride,
   four that move with stately bearing:
30a lion, mighty among beasts,
   who retreats before nothing;
31a strutting cock, a he-goat,
   and a king with his army around him.*e*

32"If you have played the fool and exalted
      yourself,
   or if you have planned evil,
   clap your hand over your mouth!
33For as churning the milk produces butter,
   and as twisting the nose produces blood,
   so stirring up anger produces strife."

Sayings of King Lemuel

31 The sayings of King Lemuel—an
oracle*a* his mother taught him:

2"O my son, O son of my womb,
   O son of my vows,*b*
3do not spend your strength on women,
   your vigour on those who ruin kings.

4"It is not for kings, O Lemuel—
   not for kings to drink wine,
   not for rulers to crave beer,

5lest they drink and forget what the law
      decrees,
   and deprive all the oppressed of their
      rights.
6Give beer to those who are perishing,
   wine to those who are in anguish;
7let them drink and forget their poverty
   and remember their misery no more.

8"Speak up for those who cannot speak for
      themselves,
   for the rights of all who are destitute.
9Speak up and judge fairly;
   defend the rights of the poor and needy."

Epilogue: The Wife of Noble Character

10c A wife of noble character who can find?
   She is worth far more than rubies.
11Her husband has full confidence in her
   and lacks nothing of value.
12She brings him good, not harm,
   all the days of her life.
13She selects wool and flax
   and works with eager hands.
14She is like the merchant ships,
   bringing her food from afar.
15She gets up while it is still dark;
   she provides food for her family
   and portions for her servant girls.
16She considers a field and buys it;
   out of her earnings she plants a
      vineyard.
17She sets about her work vigorously;
   her arms are strong for her tasks.
18She sees that her trading is profitable,
   and her lamp does not go out at night.
19In her hand she holds the distaff
   and grasps the spindle with her fingers.
20She opens her arms to the poor
   and extends her hands to the needy.
21When it snows, she has no fear for her
      household;
   for all of them are clothed in scarlet.
22She makes coverings for her bed;
   she is clothed in fine linen and purple.
23Her husband is respected at the city gate,
   where he takes his seat among the elders
      of the land.
24She makes linen garments and sells them,
   and supplies the merchants with sashes.
25She is clothed with strength and dignity;
   she can laugh at the days to come.
26She speaks with wisdom,
   and faithful instruction is on her tongue.
27She watches over the affairs of her
      household
   and does not eat the bread of idleness.
28Her children arise and call her blessed;
   her husband also, and he praises her:
29"Many women do noble things,
   but you surpass them all."
30Charm is deceptive, and beauty is fleeting;
   but a woman who fears the Lord is to be
      praised.
31Give her the reward she has earned,
   and let her works bring her praise at the
      city gate.

---

c16 Hebrew *Sheol*   *d26* That is, the hyrax or rock badger   *e31* Or *king secure against revolt*
a1 Or *of Lemuel king of Massa, which*   *b2* Or / *the answer to my prayers*
c10 Verses 10–31 are an acrostic, each verse beginning with a successive letter of the Hebrew alphabet.

Ecclesiastes

Everything Is Meaningless

1 The words of the Teacher,*a* son of David, king of Jerusalem:

2"Meaningless! Meaningless!"
   says the Teacher.
   "Utterly meaningless!
   Everything is meaningless."

3What does man gain from all his labour
   at which he toils under the sun?
4Generations come and generations go,
   but the earth remains for ever.
5The sun rises and the sun sets,
   and hurries back to where it rises.
6The wind blows to the south
   and turns to the north;
round and round it goes,
   ever returning on its course.
7All streams flow into the sea,
   yet the sea is never full.
To the place the streams come from,
   there they return again.
8All things are wearisome,
   more than one can say.
The eye never has enough of seeing,
   nor the ear its fill of hearing.
9What has been will be again,
   what has been done will be done again;
   there is nothing new under the sun.
10Is there anything of which one can say,
   "Look! This is something new"?
It was here already, long ago;
   it was here before our time.
11There is no remembrance of men of old,
   and even those who are yet to come
will not be remembered
   by those who follow.

Wisdom Is Meaningless

12I, the Teacher, was king over Israel in Jerusalem. 13I devoted myself to study and to explore by wisdom all that is done under heaven. What a heavy burden God has laid on men! 14I have seen all the things that are done under the sun; all of them are meaningless, a chasing after the wind.

15What is twisted cannot be straightened;
   what is lacking cannot be counted.

16I thought to myself, "Look, I have grown and increased in wisdom more than anyone who has ruled over Jerusalem before me; I have experienced much of wisdom and knowledge." 17Then I applied myself to the understanding of wisdom, and also of madness and folly, but I learned that this, too, is a chasing after the wind.

18For with much wisdom comes much
      sorrow;
   the more knowledge, the more grief.

Pleasures Are Meaningless

2 I thought in my heart, "Come now, I will test you with pleasure to find out what is good." But that also proved to be meaningless. 2"Laughter," I said, "is foolish. And what does pleasure accomplish?" 3I tried cheering myself with wine, and embracing folly—my mind still guiding me with wisdom. I wanted to see what was worth while for men to do under heaven during the few days of their lives.

4I undertook great projects: I built houses for myself and planted vineyards. 5I made gardens and parks and planted all kinds of fruit trees in them. 6I made reservoirs to water groves of flourishing trees. 7I bought male and female slaves and had other slaves who were born in my house. I also owned more herds and flocks than anyone in Jerusalem before me. 8I amassed silver and gold for myself, and the treasure of kings and provinces. I acquired men and women singers, and a harem*a* as well—the delights of the heart of man. 9I became greater by far than anyone in Jerusalem before me. In all this my wisdom stayed with me.

10I denied myself nothing my eyes desired;
   I refused my heart no pleasure.
My heart took delight in all my work,
   and this was the reward for all my
      labour.
11Yet when I surveyed all that my hands had
      done
   and what I had toiled to achieve,
everything was meaningless, a chasing
      after the wind;
   nothing was gained under the sun.

---

a1 Or *leader of the assembly*; also in verses 2 and 12
a8 The meaning of the Hebrew for this phrase is uncertain.

Wisdom and Folly Are Meaningless

12Then I turned my thoughts to consider
wisdom,
and also madness and folly.
What more can the king's successor do
than what has already been done?
13I saw that wisdom is better than folly,
just as light is better than darkness.
14The wise man has eyes in his head,
while the fool walks in the darkness;
but I came to realise
that the same fate overtakes them both.

15Then I thought in my heart,

"The fate of the fool will overtake me also.
What then do I gain by being wise?"
I said in my heart,
"This too is meaningless."
16For the wise man, like the fool, will not be
long remembered;
in days to come both will be forgotten.
Like the fool, the wise man too must die!

Toil Is Meaningless

17So I hated life, because the work that is
done under the sun was grievous to me. All of
it is meaningless, a chasing after the wind. 18I
hated all the things I had toiled for under the
sun, because I must leave them to the one
who comes after me. 19And who knows
whether he will be a wise man or a fool? Yet
he will have control over all the work into
which I have poured my effort and skill under
the sun. This too is meaningless. 20So my
heart began to despair over all my toilsome
labour under the sun. 21For a man may do his
work with wisdom, knowledge and skill, and
then he must leave all he owns to someone
who has not worked for it. This too is
meaningless and a great misfortune. 22What
does a man get for all the toil and anxious
striving with which he labours under the sun?
23All his days his work is pain and grief; even
at night his mind does not rest. This too is
meaningless.

24A man can do nothing better than to eat
and drink and find satisfaction in his work.
This too, I see, is from the hand of God, 25for
without him, who can eat or find enjoyment?
26To the man who pleases him, God gives
wisdom, knowledge and happiness, but to
the sinner he gives the task of gathering and
storing up wealth to hand it over to the one
who pleases God. This too is meaningless, a
chasing after the wind.

A Time for Everything

3 There is a time for everything,
and a season for every activity under
heaven:

2 a time to be born and a time to die,
a time to plant and a time to uproot,
3 a time to kill and a time to heal,
a time to tear down and a time to build,
4 a time to weep and a time to laugh,
a time to mourn and a time to dance,

5 a time to scatter stones and a time to
gather them,
a time to embrace and a time to refrain,
6 a time to search and a time to give up,
a time to keep and a time to throw away,
7 a time to tear and a time to mend,
a time to be silent and a time to speak,
8 a time to love and a time to hate,
a time for war and a time for peace.

9What does the worker gain from his toil?
10I have seen the burden God has laid on
men. 11He has made everything beautiful in
its time. He has also set eternity in the hearts
of men; yet they cannot fathom what God has
done from beginning to end. 12I know that
there is nothing better for men than to be
happy and do good while they live. 13That
everyone may eat and drink, and find satisfaction in all his toil—this is the gift of God.
14I know that everything God does will endure for ever; nothing can be added to it and
nothing taken from it. God does it so that men
will revere him.

15Whatever is has already been,
and what will be has been before;
and God will call the past to account.a

16And I saw something else under the sun:

In the place of judgment—wickedness was
there,
in the place of justice—wickedness was
there.

17I thought in my heart,

"God will bring to judgment
both the righteous and the wicked,
for there will be a time for every activity,
a time for every deed."

18I also thought, "As for men, God tests
them so that they may see that they are like
the animals. 19Man's fate is like that of the
animals; the same fate awaits them both: As
one dies, so dies the other. All have the same
breath;b man has no advantage over the
animal. Everything is meaningless. 20All go
to the same place; all come from dust, and to
dust all return. 21Who knows if the spirit of
man rises upward and if the spirit of the
animalc goes down into the earth?"
22So I saw that there is nothing better for a
man than to enjoy his work, because that is
his lot. For who can bring him to see what
will happen after him?

Oppression, Toil, Friendlessness

4 Again I looked and saw all the oppression that was taking place under the sun:

I saw the tears of the oppressed—
and they have no comforter;
power was on the side of their
oppressors—
and they have no comforter.

---

a15 Or God calls back the past   b19 Or spirit
c21 Or Who knows the spirit of man, which rises upward, or the spirit of the animal, which

ECCLESIASTES 3:1–8

'There is a time for everything, and a season for every activity under heaven . . . a time to love and a time to hate, a time for war and a time for peace' (vv. 1, 8).

NOTHING IS RANDOM in the world the writer of Ecclesiastes sees around him. However hopeless he feels life's continual round may be, he is assured that God has planned it all, and controls it all. To put it in New Testament terms, the author of Ecclesiastes would have no difficulty with Jesus' statement that even the very hairs of your head are numbered.

Today's poem, a poem of great force and beauty, has a memorable quality. It is read on great occasions, at significant times in our lives. At the end of a school year, the sonorous tones of this reading from Ecclesiastes, coupled with the last chapter, make an indelible impression on the minds of students. The beautiful poem gives a sense of security as they plunge into a threatening, insecure world. It reassures men going into battle, or returning from the front.

How strange! For the rest of the book is an example of human insecurity contrasted with the overwhelming power, and apparently random action of God. Even this poem reflects the author's mood of despair. Every statement is followed immediately by an opposite idea. In Ecclesiastes there is no love without hate, nor peace without war. God's plan, as set out in this poem, makes no allowance for progress.

If everything is set, everything planned, what can we do to alter the course of our lives? What hope have we of improvement, of progress, of developing our relationship with God?

→556

SONG OF SONGS 1:1–4

'Let him kkiss me with the kisses of his mouth – for your love is more delightful than wine. Pleasing is the fragrance of your perfumes; your name is like perfume poured out. No wonder the maidens love you!' (vv. 2–3).

THE TITLE 'SONG OF SONGS' is a Hebrew way of saying the very best song possible. The King of Kings, the Lord of Lords, the Holy of Holies, the vanity of vanities are similar expressions. Such was the power and beauty of this particular set of love songs that it found its way into the Old Testament. That does not mean that it necessarily has a deep religious significance. We find all kinds of writing in the Old Testament. We find horrific history, simple wisdom, love stories, personal reminiscences and a host of other kinds of writing in its pages. Each has its own value.

It is striking that the song opens with the woman talking. She takes just as active a part as the man. There is an equality in this poem which speaks strongly to our twentieth-century mind. There is a freedom of speech which we appreciate. Human love is not one-sided. It is man and woman, woman and man, person to person. The woman's longing for her lover is as great as the man's longing for her. It is equally physical. It is equally spiritual.

Self-love in this context would be a contradiction in terms. Love must have an object. Turned inwards it becomes destructive. When completely one-sided it is less than perfect. For love to be true and complete both lover and loved must respond to each other.

Unrequited love may be pure. Selfless devotion is highly honourable. Neither is complete.

→573

²And I declared that the dead,
who had already died,
are happier than the living,
who are still alive.
³But better than both
is he who has not yet been,
who has not seen the evil
that is done under the sun.

⁴And I saw that all labour and all achievement spring from man's envy of his neighbour. This too is meaningless, a chasing after the wind.

⁵The fool folds his hands
and ruins himself.
⁶Better one handful with tranquillity
than two handfuls with toil
and chasing after the wind.

⁷Again I saw something meaningless under the sun:

⁸There was a man all alone;
he had neither son nor brother.
There was no end to his toil,
yet his eyes were not content with his
wealth.
"For whom am I toiling," he asked,
"and why am I depriving myself of
enjoyment?"
This too is meaningless—
a miserable business!

⁹Two are better than one,
because they have a good return for
their work:
¹⁰If one falls down,
his friend can help him up.
But pity the man who falls
and has no-one to help him up!
¹¹Also, if two lie down together, they will
keep warm.
But how can one keep warm alone?
¹²Though one may be overpowered,
two can defend themselves.
A cord of three strands is not quickly
broken.

Advancement Is Meaningless

¹³Better a poor but wise youth than an old but foolish king who no longer knows how to take warning. ¹⁴The youth may have come from prison to the kingship, or he may have been born in poverty within his kingdom. ¹⁵I saw that all who lived and walked under the sun followed the youth, the king's successor. ¹⁶There was no end to all the people who were before them. But those who came later were not pleased with the successor. This too is meaningless, a chasing after the wind.

Stand in Awe of God

5 Guard your steps when you go to the house of God. Go near to listen rather than to offer the sacrifice of fools, who do not know that they do wrong.

²Do not be quick with your mouth,
do not be hasty in your heart
to utter anything before God.
God is in heaven
and you are on earth,
so let your words be few.
³As a dream comes when there are many
cares,
so the speech of a fool when there are
many words.

⁴When you make a vow to God, do not delay in fulfilling it. He has no pleasure in fools; fulfil your vow. ⁵It is better not to vow than to make a vow and not fulfil it. ⁶Do not let your mouth lead you into sin. And do not protest to the ˌtempleˌ messenger, "My vow was a mistake." Why should God be angry at what you say and destroy the work of your hands? ⁷Much dreaming and many words are meaningless. Therefore stand in awe of God.

Riches Are Meaningless

⁸If you see the poor oppressed in a district, and justice and rights denied, do not be surprised at such things; for one official is eyed by a higher one, and over them both are others higher still. ⁹The increase from the land is taken by all; the king himself profits from the fields.

¹⁰Whoever loves money never has money
enough;
whoever loves wealth is never satisfied
with his income.
This too is meaningless.

¹¹As goods increase,
so do those who consume them.
And what benefit are they to the owner
except to feast his eyes on them?

¹²The sleep of a labourer is sweet,
whether he eats little or much,
but the abundance of a rich man
permits him no sleep.

¹³I have seen a grievous evil under the sun:

wealth hoarded to the harm of its owner,
¹⁴ or wealth lost through some misfortune,
so that when he has a son
there is nothing left for him.
¹⁵Naked a man comes from his mother's
womb,
and as he comes, so he departs.
He takes nothing from his labour
that he can carry in his hand.

¹⁶This too is a grievous evil:

As a man comes, so he departs,
and what does he gain,
since he toils for the wind?
¹⁷All his days he eats in darkness,
with great frustration, affliction and
anger.

¹⁸Then I realised that it is good and proper for a man to eat and drink, and to find satisfaction in his toilsome labour under the sun during the few days of life God has given him—for this is his lot. ¹⁹Moreover, when God gives any man wealth and possessions,

and enables him to enjoy them, to accept his lot and be happy in his work—this is a gift of God. ²⁰He seldom reflects on the days of his life, because God keeps him occupied with gladness of heart.

6 I have seen another evil under the sun, and it weighs heavily on men: ²God gives a man wealth, possessions and honour, so that he lacks nothing his heart desires, but God does not enable him to enjoy them, and a stranger enjoys them instead. This is meaningless, a grievous evil.

³A man may have a hundred children and live many years; yet no matter how long he lives, if he cannot enjoy his prosperity and does not receive proper burial, I say that a stillborn child is better off than he. ⁴It comes without meaning, it departs in darkness, and in darkness its name is shrouded. ⁵Though it never saw the sun or knew anything, it has more rest than does that man—⁶even if he lives a thousand years twice over but fails to enjoy his prosperity. Do not all go to the same place?

⁷All man's efforts are for his mouth,
  yet his appetite is never satisfied.
⁸What advantage has a wise man
    over a fool?
  What does a poor man gain
    by knowing how to conduct himself
      before others?
⁹Better what the eye sees
    than the roving of the appetite.
  This too is meaningless,
    a chasing after the wind.

¹⁰Whatever exists has already been named,
    and what man is has been known;
  no man can contend
    with one who is stronger than he.
¹¹The more the words,
    the less the meaning,
    and how does that profit anyone?

¹²For who knows what is good for a man in life, during the few and meaningless days he passes through like a shadow? Who can tell him what will happen under the sun after he is gone?

Wisdom

7 A good name is better than fine
    perfume,
  and the day of death better than the day
    of birth.
²It is better to go to a house of mourning
    than to go to a house of feasting,
  for death is the destiny of every man;
    the living should take this to heart.
³Sorrow is better than laughter,
    because a sad face is good for the heart.
⁴The heart of the wise is in the house of
    mourning,
  but the heart of fools is in the house of
    pleasure.
⁵It is better to heed a wise man's rebuke
    than to listen to the song of fools.

⁶Like the crackling of thorns under the pot,
    so is the laughter of fools.
  This too is meaningless.

⁷Extortion turns a wise man into a fool,
    and a bribe corrupts the heart.

⁸The end of a matter is better than its
    beginning,
  and patience is better than pride.
⁹Do not be quickly provoked in your spirit,
    for anger resides in the lap of fools.

¹⁰Do not say, ''Why were the old days better
    than these?''
  For it is not wise to ask such questions.

¹¹Wisdom, like an inheritance, is a good
    thing
  and benefits those who see the sun.
¹²Wisdom is a shelter
    as money is a shelter,
  but the advantage of knowledge is this:
    that wisdom preserves the life of its
      possessor.

¹³Consider what God has done:

  Who can straighten
    what he has made crooked?
¹⁴When times are good, be happy;
    but when times are bad, consider:
  God has made the one
    as well as the other.
  Therefore, a man cannot discover
    anything about his future.

¹⁵In this meaningless life of mine I have seen both of these:

  a righteous man perishing in his
    righteousness,
  and a wicked man living long in his
    wickedness.
¹⁶Do not be over-righteous,
    neither be overwise—
    why destroy yourself?
¹⁷Do not be overwicked,
    and do not be a fool—
    why die before your time?
¹⁸It is good to grasp the one
    and not let go of the other.
  The man who fears God will avoid all
    ⌊extremes⌋.ᵃ

¹⁹Wisdom makes one wise man more
    powerful
  than ten rulers in a city.

²⁰There is not a righteous man on earth
    who does what is right and never sins.

²¹Do not pay attention to every word people
    say,
  or you may hear your servant cursing
    you—
²²for you know in your heart
    that many times you yourself have
      cursed others.

ᵃ18 Or will follow them both

23All this I tested by wisdom and I said,

"I am determined to be wise"—
    but this was beyond me.
24Whatever wisdom may be,
    it is far off and most profound—
    who can discover it?
25So I turned my mind to understand,
    to investigate and to search out wisdom
        and the scheme of things
    and to understand the stupidity of
        wickedness
    and the madness of folly.

26I find more bitter than death
    the woman who is a snare,
    whose heart is a trap
        and whose hands are chains.
The man who pleases God will escape her,
    but the sinner she will ensnare.

27"Look," says the Teacher,b "this is
what I have discovered:

"Adding one thing to another to discover
        the scheme of things—
28   while I was still searching
        but not finding—
I found one ⌊upright⌋ man among a
        thousand,
    but not one ⌊upright⌋ woman among
        them all.
29This only have I found:
    God made mankind upright,
    but men have gone in search of many
        schemes."

8 Who is like the wise man?
   Who knows the explanation of things?
Wisdom brightens a man's face
    and changes its hard appearance.

Obey the King

2Obey the king's command, I say, because
you took an oath before God. 3Do not be in a
hurry to leave the king's presence. Do not
stand up for a bad cause, for he will do
whatever he pleases. 4Since a king's word is
supreme, who can say to him, "What are you
doing?"

5Whoever obeys his command will come to
        no harm,
    and the wise heart will know the proper
        time and procedure.
6For there is a proper time and procedure
        for every matter,
    though a man's misery weighs heavily
        upon him.

7Since no man knows the future,
    who can tell him what is to come?
8No man has power over the wind to
        contain it;a
    so no-one has power over the day of his
        death.

As no-one is discharged in time of war,
    so wickedness will not release those
        who practise it.

9All this I saw, as I applied my mind to
everything done under the sun. There is a
time when a man lords it over others to his
ownb hurt. 10Then too, I saw the wicked
buried—those who used to come and go from
the holy place and receive praisec in the city
where they did this. This too is meaningless.
11When the sentence for a crime is not
quickly carried out, the hearts of the people
are filled with schemes to do wrong.
12Although a wicked man commits a hundred
crimes and still lives a long time, I know that
it will go better with God-fearing men, who
are reverent before God. 13Yet because the
wicked do not fear God, it will not go well
with them, and their days will not lengthen
like a shadow.
14There is something else meaningless that
occurs on earth: righteous men who get what
the wicked deserve, and wicked men who get
what the righteous deserve. This too, I say, is
meaningless. 15So I commend the enjoyment
of life, because nothing is better for a man
under the sun than to eat and drink and be
glad. Then joy will accompany him in his
work all the days of the life God has given
him under the sun.

16When I applied my mind to know wisdom
and to observe man's labour on earth—his
eyes not seeing sleep day or night—17then I
saw all that God has done. No-one can comprehend what goes on under the sun. Despite
all his efforts to search it out, man cannot
discover its meaning. Even if a wise man
claims he knows, he cannot really comprehend it.

A Common Destiny for All

9 So I reflected on all this and concluded
   that the righteous and the wise and what
they do are in God's hands, but no man
knows whether love or hate awaits him. 2All
share a common destiny—the righteous and
the wicked, the good and the bad,a the clean
and the unclean, those who offer sacrifices
and those who do not.

As it is with the good man,
    so with the sinner;
as it is with those who take oaths,
    so with those who are afraid to take
        them.

3This is the evil in everything that happens
under the sun: The same destiny overtakes
all. The hearts of men, moreover, are full of
evil and there is madness in their hearts while
they live, and afterwards they join the dead.
4Anyone who is among the living has hopeb
—even a live dog is better off than a dead
lion!

b27 Or *leader of the assembly*   a8 Or *over his spirit to retain it*   b9 Or *to their*
c10 Some Hebrew manuscripts and Septuagint (Aquila); most Hebrew manuscripts *and are forgotten*
a2 Septuagint (Aquila), Vulgate and Syriac; Hebrew does not have *and the bad.*
b4 Or *What then is to be chosen? With all who live, there is hope*

5For the living know that they will die,
  but the dead know nothing;
they have no further reward,
  and even the memory of them is
    forgotten.
6Their love, their hate
  and their jealousy have long since
    vanished;
never again will they have a part
  in anything that happens under the sun.

7Go, eat your food with gladness, and
drink your wine with a joyful heart, for it is
now that God favours what you do. 8Always
be clothed in white, and always anoint your
head with oil. 9Enjoy life with your wife,
whom you love, all the days of this meaningless life that God has given you under the
sun—all your meaningless days. For this is
your lot in life and in your toilsome labour
under the sun. 10Whatever your hand finds to
do, do it with all your might, for in the grave,c
where you are going, there is neither working
nor planning nor knowledge nor wisdom.

11I have seen something else under the sun:

The race is not to the swift
  or the battle to the strong,
nor does food come to the wise
  or wealth to the brilliant
  or favour to the learned;
but time and chance happen to them all.

12Moreover, no man knows when his hour
will come:

As fish are caught in a cruel net,
  or birds are taken in a snare,
so men are trapped by evil times
  that fall unexpectedly upon them.

Wisdom Better Than Folly

13I also saw under the sun this example of
wisdom that greatly impressed me: 14There
was once a small city with only a few people
in it. And a powerful king came against it,
surrounded it and built huge siegeworks
against it. 15Now there lived in that city a man
poor but wise, and he saved the city by his
wisdom. But nobody remembered that poor
man. 16So I said, "Wisdom is better than
strength." But the poor man's wisdom is
despised, and his words are no longer
heeded.

17The quiet words of the wise are more to be
  heeded
  than the shouts of a ruler of fools.
18Wisdom is better than weapons of war,
  but one sinner destroys much good.

10 As dead flies give perfume a bad
    smell,
so a little folly outweighs wisdom and
  honour.
2The heart of the wise inclines to the right,
  but the heart of the fool to the left.

3Even as he walks along the road,
  the fool lacks sense
  and shows everyone how stupid he is.
4If a ruler's anger rises against you,
  do not leave your post;
  calmness can lay great errors to rest.

5There is an evil I have seen under the sun,
  the sort of error that arises from a ruler:
6Fools are put in many high positions,
  while the rich occupy the low ones.
7I have seen slaves on horseback,
  while princes go on foot like slaves.

8Whoever digs a pit may fall into it;
  whoever breaks through a wall may be
    bitten by a snake.
9Whoever quarries stones may be injured
  by them;
  whoever splits logs may be endangered
  by them.

10If the axe is dull
  and its edge unsharpened,
more strength is needed
  but skill will bring success.

11If a snake bites before it is charmed,
  there is no profit for the charmer.

12Words from a wise man's mouth are
  gracious,
  but a fool is consumed by his own lips.
13At the beginning his words are folly;
  at the end they are wicked madness—
14 and the fool multiplies words.

No-one knows what is coming—
  who can tell him what will happen after
    him?

15A fool's work wearies him;
  he does not know the way to town.

16Woe to you, O land whose king was a
  servanta
  and whose princes feast in the morning.
17Blessed are you, O land whose king is of
  noble birth
  and whose princes eat at a proper
    time—
  for strength and not for drunkenness.

18If a man is lazy, the rafters sag;
  if his hands are idle, the house leaks.

19A feast is made for laughter,
  and wine makes life merry,
  but money is the answer for
    everything.

20Do not revile the king even in your
  thoughts,
  or curse the rich in your bedroom,
because a bird of the air may carry your
  words,
  and a bird on the wing may report what
  you say.

c10 Hebrew *Sheol*   a16 Or *king is a child*

Bread Upon the Waters

11 Cast your bread upon the waters,
for after many days you will find it
again.
[2]Give portions to seven, yes to eight,
for you do not know what disaster may
come upon the land.

[3]If clouds are full of water,
they pour rain upon the earth.
Whether a tree falls to the south or to the
north,
in the place where it falls, there will it
lie.
[4]Whoever watches the wind will not plant;
whoever looks at the clouds will not
reap.

[5]As you do not know the path of the wind,
or how the body is formed[a] in a
mother's womb,
so you cannot understand the work of
God,
the Maker of all things.

[6]Sow your seed in the morning,
and at evening let not your hands be
idle,
for you do not know which will succeed,
whether this or that,
or whether both will do equally well.

Remember Your Creator While Young

[7]Light is sweet,
and it pleases the eyes to see the sun.
[8]However many years a man may live,
let him enjoy them all.
But let him remember the days of
darkness,
for they will be many.
Everything to come is meaningless.

[9]Be happy, young man, while you are
young,
and let your heart give you joy in the
days of your youth.
Follow the ways of your heart
and whatever your eyes see,
but know that for all these things
God will bring you to judgment.
[10]So then, banish anxiety from your heart
and cast off the troubles of your body,
for youth and vigour are meaningless.

12 Remember your Creator
in the days of your youth,
before the days of trouble come
and the years approach when you will
say,

"I find no pleasure in them"—
[2]before the sun and the light
and the moon and the stars grow dark,
and the clouds return after the rain;
[3]when the keepers of the house tremble,
and the strong men stoop,
when the grinders cease because they are
few,
and those looking through the windows
grow dim;
[4]when the doors to the street are closed
and the sound of grinding fades;
when men rise up at the sound of birds,
but all their songs grow faint;
[5]when men are afraid of heights
and of dangers in the streets;
when the almond tree blossoms
and the grasshopper drags himself along
and desire is no longer is stirred.
Then man goes to his eternal home
and mourners go about the streets.

[6]Remember him—before the silver cord is
severed,
or the golden bowl is broken;
before the pitcher is shattered at the
spring,
or the wheel broken at the well,
[7]and the dust returns to the ground it came
from,
and the spirit returns to God who gave
it.

[8]"Meaningless! Meaningless!" says the
Teacher.[a]
"Everything is meaningless!"

The Conclusion of the Matter

[9]Not only was the Teacher wise, but also
he imparted knowledge to the people. He
pondered and searched out and set in order
many proverbs. [10]The Teacher searched to
find just the right words, and what he wrote
was upright and true.
[11]The words of the wise are like goads,
their collected sayings like firmly embedded
nails—given by one Shepherd. [12]Be warned,
my son, of anything in addition to them.
Of making many books there is no end, and
much study wearies the body.

[13]Now all has been heard;
here is the conclusion of the matter:
Fear God and keep his commandments,
for this is the whole ⌊duty⌋ of man.
[14]For God will bring every deed into
judgment,
including every hidden thing,
whether it is good or evil.

---

[a]5 Or know how life (or the spirit) / enters the body being formed
[a]8 Or the leader of the assembly; also in verses 9 and 10

Song of Songs

1

Solomon's Song of Songs.

Beloved[a]

²Let him kiss me with the kisses of his
  mouth—
  for your love is more delightful than
  wine.
³Pleasing is the fragrance of your perfumes;
  your name is like perfume poured out.
  No wonder the maidens love you!
⁴Take me away with you—let us hurry!
  Let the king bring me into his chambers.

Friends

  We rejoice and delight in you;[b]
  we will praise your love more than wine.

Beloved

  How right they are to adore you!

⁵Dark am I, yet lovely,
  O daughters of Jerusalem,
  dark like the tents of Kedar,
  like the tent curtains of Solomon.[c]
⁶Do not stare at me because I am dark,
  because I am darkened by the sun.
  My mother's sons were angry with me
  and made me take care of the vineyards;
  my own vineyard I have neglected.
⁷Tell me, you whom I love, where you
  graze your flock
  and where you rest your sheep at
  midday.
  Why should I be like a veiled woman
  beside the flocks of your friends?

Friends

⁸If you do not know, most beautiful of
  women,
  follow the tracks of the sheep
  and graze your young goats
  by the tents of the shepherds.

Lover

⁹I liken you, my darling, to a mare
  harnessed to one of the chariots of
  Pharaoh.
¹⁰Your cheeks are beautiful with ear-rings,
  your neck with strings of jewels.

¹¹We will make you ear-rings of gold,
  studded with silver.

Beloved

¹²While the king was at his table,
  my perfume spread its fragrance.
¹³My lover is to me a sachet of myrrh
  resting between my breasts.
¹⁴My lover is to me a cluster of henna
  blossoms
  from the vineyards of En Gedi.

Lover

¹⁵How beautiful you are, my darling!
  Oh, how beautiful!
  Your eyes are doves.

Beloved

¹⁶How handsome you are, my lover!
  Oh, how charming!
  And our bed is verdant.

Lover

¹⁷The beams of our house are cedars;
  our rafters are firs.

Beloved[a]

2

I am a rose[b] of Sharon,
  a lily of the valleys.

Lover

²Like a lily among thorns
  is my darling among the maidens.

Beloved

³Like an apple tree among the trees of the
  forest
  is my lover among the young men.
  I delight to sit in his shade,
  and his fruit is sweet to my taste.
⁴He has taken me to the banquet hall,
  and his banner over me is love.
⁵Strengthen me with raisins,
  refresh me with apples,
  for I am faint with love.
⁶His left arm is under my head,
  and his right arm embraces me.
⁷Daughters of Jerusalem, I charge you
  by the gazelles and by the does of the
  field:

---

a2 Primarily on the basis of the gender of the Hebrew pronouns used, male and female speakers are indicated in the margins by the captions *Lover* and *Beloved* respectively. The words of others are marked *Friends*. In some instances the divisions and their captions are debatable.　　*b4* The Hebrew is masculine singular.　　*c5* Or *Salma*
a1 Or *Lover*　　*b1* Possibly a member of the crocus family

Do not arouse or awaken love
   until it so desires.

8Listen! My lover!
   Look! Here he comes,
leaping across the mountains,
   bounding over the hills.
9My lover is like a gazelle or a young stag.
   Look! There he stands behind our wall,
   gazing through the windows,
   peering through the lattice.
10My lover spoke and said to me,
   "Arise, my darling,
   my beautiful one, and come with me.
11See! The winter is past;
   the rains are over and gone.
12Flowers appear on the earth;
   the season of singing has come,
   the cooing of doves
   is heard in our land.
13The fig-tree forms its early fruit;
   the blossoming vines spread their
      fragrance.
   Arise, come, my darling;
   my beautiful one, come with me."

Lover
14My dove in the clefts of the rock,
   in the hiding-places on the
      mountainside,
   show me your face,
   let me hear your voice;
   for your voice is sweet,
   and your face is lovely.
15Catch for us the foxes,
   the little foxes
   that ruin the vineyards,
   our vineyards that are in bloom.

Beloved
16My lover is mine and I am his;
   he browses among the lilies.
17Until the day breaks
   and the shadows flee,
turn, my lover,
   and be like a gazelle
or like a young stag
   on the rugged hills.*c*

3 All night long on my bed
   I looked for the one my heart loves;
   I looked for him but did not find him.
2I will get up now and go about the city,
   through its streets and squares;
I will search for the one my heart loves.
   So I looked for him but did not find
      him.
3The watchmen found me
   as they made their rounds in the city.
   "Have you seen the one my heart
      loves?"
4Scarcely had I passed them
   when I found the one my heart loves.
I held him and would not let him go
   till I had brought him to my mother's
      house,
   to the room of the one who conceived
      me.

5Daughters of Jerusalem, I charge you
   by the gazelles and by the does of the
      field:
Do not arouse or awaken love
   until it so desires.

6Who is this coming up from the desert
   like a column of smoke,
perfumed with myrrh and incense
   made from all the spices of the
      merchant?
7Look! It is Solomon's carriage,
   escorted by sixty warriors,
   the noblest of Israel,
8all of them wearing the sword,
   all experienced in battle,
each with his sword at his side,
   prepared for the terrors of the night.
9King Solomon made for himself the
      carriage;
   he made it of wood from Lebanon.
10Its posts he made of silver,
   its base of gold.
Its seat was upholstered with purple,
   its interior lovingly inlaid
   by*a* the daughters of Jerusalem.
11Come out, you daughters of Zion,
   and look at King Solomon wearing the
      crown,
   the crown with which his mother
      crowned him
on the day of his wedding,
   the day his heart rejoiced.

Lover
4 How beautiful you are, my darling!
   Oh, how beautiful!
   Your eyes behind your veil are doves.
Your hair is like a flock of goats
   descending from Mount Gilead.
2Your teeth are like a flock of sheep just
      shorn,
   coming up from the washing.
Each has its twin;
   not one of them is alone.
3Your lips are like a scarlet ribbon;
   your mouth is lovely.
Your temples behind your veil
   are like the halves of a pomegranate.
4Your neck is like the tower of David,
   built with elegance;*a*
on it hang a thousand shields,
   all of them shields of warriors.
5Your two breasts are like two fawns,
   like twin fawns of a gazelle
   that browse among the lilies.
6Until the day breaks
   and the shadows flee,
I will go to the mountain of myrrh
   and to the hill of incense.
7All beautiful you are, my darling;
   there is no flaw in you.

8Come with me from Lebanon, my bride,
   come with me from Lebanon.
Descend from the crest of Amana,
   from the top of Senir, the summit of
      Hermon,

*c*17 Or *the hills of Bether*   *a*10 Or *its inlaid interior a gift of love / from*
*a*4 The meaning of the Hebrew for this word is uncertain.

from the lions' dens
  and the mountain haunts of the
    leopards.
⁹You have stolen my heart, my sister, my
    bride;
  you have stolen my heart
with one glance of your eyes,
  with one jewel of your necklace.
¹⁰How delightful is your love, my sister, my
    bride!
  How much more pleasing is your love
    than wine,
  and the fragrance of your perfume than
    any spice!
¹¹Your lips drop sweetness as the
    honeycomb, my bride;
  milk and honey are under your tongue.
  The fragrance of your garments is like
    that of Lebanon.
¹²You are a garden locked up, my sister, my
    bride;
  you are a spring enclosed, a sealed
    fountain.
¹³Your plants are an orchard of
    pomegranates
  with choice fruits,
  with henna and nard,
¹⁴   nard and saffron,
  calamus and cinnamon,
  with every kind of incense tree,
  with myrrh and aloes
  and all the finest spices.
¹⁵You are*b* a garden fountain,
  a well of flowing water
  streaming down from Lebanon.

Beloved

¹⁶Awake, north wind,
  and come, south wind!
Blow on my garden,
  that its fragrance may spread abroad.
Let my lover come into his garden
  and taste its choice fruits.

Lover

5 I have come into my garden, my sister,
    my bride;
  I have gathered my myrrh with my
    spice.
I have eaten my honeycomb and my
    honey;
  I have drunk my wine and my milk.

Friends

Eat, O friends, and drink;
  drink your fill, O lovers.

Beloved

²I slept but my heart was awake.
  Listen! My lover is knocking:
"Open to me, my sister, my darling,
  my dove, my flawless one.
My head is drenched with dew,
  my hair with the dampness of the
    night."
³I have taken off my robe—
  must I put it on again?
I have washed my feet—
  must I soil them again?

⁴My lover thrust his hand through the
    latch-opening;
  my heart began to pound for him.
⁵I arose to open for my lover,
  and my hands dripped with myrrh,
  my fingers with flowing myrrh,
  on the handles of the lock.
⁶I opened for my lover,
  but my lover had left; he was gone.
  My heart sank at his departure.*a*
I looked for him but did not find him.
  I called him but he did not answer.
⁷The watchmen found me
  as they made their rounds in the city.
They beat me, they bruised me;
  they took away my cloak,
  those watchmen of the walls!
⁸O daughters of Jerusalem, I charge you—
  if you find my lover,
what will you tell him?
  Tell him I am faint with love.

Friends

⁹How is your beloved better than others,
  most beautiful of women?
How is your beloved better than others,
  that you charge us so?

Beloved

¹⁰My lover is radiant and ruddy,
  outstanding among ten thousand.
¹¹His head is purest gold;
  his hair is wavy
  and black as a raven.
¹²His eyes are like doves
  by the water streams,
  washed in milk,
  mounted like jewels.
¹³His cheeks are like beds of spice
  yielding perfume.
His lips are like lilies
  dripping with myrrh.
¹⁴His arms are rods of gold
  set with chrysolite.
His body is like polished ivory
  decorated with sapphires.*b*
¹⁵His legs are pillars of marble
  set on bases of pure gold.
His appearance is like Lebanon,
  choice as its cedars.
¹⁶His mouth is sweetness itself;
  he is altogether lovely.
This is my lover, this my friend,
  O daughters of Jerusalem.

Friends

6 Where has your lover gone,
    most beautiful of women?
Which way did your lover turn,
  that we may look for him with you?

Beloved

²My lover has gone down to his garden,
  to the beds of spices,
to browse in the gardens
  and to gather lilies.
³I am my lover's and my lover is mine;
  he browses among the lilies.

---

b15 Or I am (spoken by the *Beloved*)   *a6 Or heart had gone out to him when he spoke*   *b14 Or lapis lazuli*

Lover

⁴You are beautiful, my darling, as Tirzah,
　lovely as Jerusalem,
　majestic as troops with banners.
⁵Turn your eyes from me;
　they overwhelm me.
　Your hair is like a flock of goats
　descending from Gilead.
⁶Your teeth are like a flock of sheep
　coming up from the washing.
　Each has its twin,
　not one of them is alone.
⁷Your temples behind your veil
　are like the halves of a pomegranate.
⁸Sixty queens there may be,
　and eighty concubines,
　and virgins beyond number;
⁹but my dove, my perfect one, is unique,
　the only daughter of her mother,
　the favourite of the one who bore her.
　The maidens saw her and called her
　blessed;
　the queens and concubines praised her.

Friends

¹⁰Who is this that appears like the dawn,
　fair as the moon, bright as the sun,
　majestic as the stars in procession?

Lover

¹¹I went down to the grove of nut trees
　to look at the new growth in the valley,
　to see if the vines had budded
　or the pomegranates were in bloom.
¹²Before I realised it,
　my desire set me among the royal
　chariots of my people.ᵃ

Friends

¹³Come back, come back, O Shulammite;
　come back, come back, that we may
　gaze on you!

Lover

　Why would you gaze on the Shulammite
　as on the dance of Mahanaim?

7 How beautiful your sandalled feet,
　　O prince's daughter!
　Your graceful legs are like jewels,
　the work of a craftsman's hands.
²Your navel is a rounded goblet
　that never lacks blended wine.
　Your waist is a mound of wheat
　encircled by lilies.
³Your breasts are like two fawns,
　twins of a gazelle.
⁴Your neck is like an ivory tower.
　Your eyes are the pools of Heshbon
　by the gate of Bath Rabbim.
　Your nose is like the tower of Lebanon
　looking towards Damascus.
⁵Your head crowns you like Mount Carmel.
　Your hair is like royal tapestry;
　the king is held captive by its tresses.
⁶How beautiful you are and how pleasing,
　O love, with your delights!

⁷Your stature is like that of the palm,
　and your breasts like clusters of fruit.
⁸I said, "I will climb the palm tree;
　I will take hold of its fruit."
　May your breasts be like the clusters of
　the vine,
　the fragrance of your breath like apples,
⁹　and your mouth like the best wine.

Beloved

　May the wine go straight to my lover,
　flowing gently over lips and teeth.ᵃ
¹⁰I belong to my lover,
　and his desire is for me.
¹¹Come, my lover, let us go to the
　countryside,
　let us spend the night in the villages.ᵇ
¹²Let us go early to the vineyards
　to see if the vines have budded,
　if their blossoms have opened,
　and if the pomegranates are in bloom—
　there I will give you my love.
¹³The mandrakes send out their fragrance,
　and at our door is every delicacy,
　both new and old,
　that I have stored up for you, my lover.

8 If only you were to me like a brother,
　　who was nursed at my mother's
　　breasts!
　Then, if I found you outside,
　I would kiss you,
　and no-one would despise me.
²I would lead you
　and bring you to my mother's house—
　she who has taught me.
　I would give you spiced wine to drink,
　the nectar of my pomegranates.
³His left arm is under my head
　and his right arm embraces me.
⁴Daughters of Jerusalem, I charge you:
　Do not arouse or awaken love
　until it so desires.

Friends

⁵Who is this coming up from the desert
　leaning on her lover?

Beloved

　Under the apple tree I roused you;
　there your mother conceived you,
　there she who was in labour gave you
　birth.
⁶Place me like a seal over your heart,
　like a seal on your arm;
　for love is as strong as death,
　its jealousyᵃ unyielding as the grave.ᵇ
　It burns like blazing fire,
　like a mighty flame.ᶜ
⁷Many waters cannot quench love;
　rivers cannot wash it away.
　If one were to give
　all the wealth of his house for love,
　itᵈ would be utterly scorned.

Friends

⁸We have a young sister,
　and her breasts are not yet grown.

ᵃ12 Or *among the chariots of Amminadab*; or *among the chariots of the people of the prince*
ᵃ9 Septuagint, Aquila, Vulgate and Syriac; Hebrew *lips of sleepers*　　ᵇ11 Or *henna bushes*
ᵃ6 Or *ardour*　　ᵇ6 Hebrew *Sheol*　　ᶜ6 Or / *like the very flame of the* LORD　　ᵈ7 Or *he*

What shall we do for our sister
    for the day she is spoken for?
[9]If she is a wall,
    we will build towers of silver on her.
If she is a door,
    we will enclose her with panels of cedar.

Beloved

[10]I am a wall,
    and my breasts are like towers.
Thus I have become in his eyes
    like one bringing contentment.
[11]Solomon had a vineyard in Baal Hamon;
    he let out his vineyard to tenants.
Each was to bring for its fruit
    a thousand shekels*e* of silver.

[12]But my own vineyard is mine to give;
    the thousand shekels are for you, O
        Solomon,
and two hundred*f* are for those who tend
    its fruit.

Lover

[13]You who dwell in the gardens
    with friends in attendance,
    let me hear your voice!

Beloved

[14]Come away, my lover,
    and be like a gazelle
or like a young stag
    on the spice-laden mountains.

e11 That is, about 25 pounds (about 11.5 kilograms); also in verse 12
f12 That is, about 5 pounds (about 2.3 kilograms)

Isaiah

1

¹ The vision concerning Judah and Jerusalem that Isaiah son of Amoz saw during the reigns of Uzziah, Jotham, Ahaz and
Hezekiah, kings of Judah.

A Rebellious Nation

²Hear, O heavens! Listen, O earth!
  For the LORD has spoken:
"I reared children and brought them up,
  but they have rebelled against me.
³The ox knows his master,
  the donkey his owner's manger,
but Israel does not know,
  my people do not understand."

⁴Ah, sinful nation,
  a people loaded with guilt,
a brood of evildoers,
  children given to corruption!
They have forsaken the LORD;
  they have spurned the Holy One of
    Israel
  and turned their backs on him.

⁵Why should you be beaten any more?
  Why do you persist in rebellion?
Your whole head is injured,
  your whole heart afflicted.
⁶From the sole of your foot to the top of
    your head
  there is no soundness—
only wounds and bruises
  and open sores,
not cleansed or bandaged
  or soothed with oil.

⁷Your country is desolate,
  your cities burned with fire;
your fields are being stripped by foreigners
  right before you,
  laid waste as when overthrown by
    strangers.
⁸The Daughter of Zion is left
  like a shelter in a vineyard,
like a hut in a field of melons,
  like a city under siege.
⁹Unless the LORD Almighty
  had left us some survivors,
we would have become like Sodom,
  we would have been like Gomorrah.

¹⁰Hear the word of the LORD,
  you rulers of Sodom;
listen to the law of our God,
  you people of Gomorrah!
¹¹"The multitude of your sacrifices—
  what are they to me?" says the LORD.
"I have more than enough of burnt
    offerings,
  of rams and the fat of fattened
    animals;
I have no pleasure
  in the blood of bulls and lambs and
    goats.
¹²When you come to appear before me,
  who has asked this of you,
  this trampling of my courts?
¹³Stop bringing meaningless offerings!
  Your incense is detestable to me.
New Moons, Sabbaths and
    convocations—
  I cannot bear your evil assemblies.
¹⁴Your New Moon festivals and your
    appointed feasts
  my soul hates.
They have become a burden to me;
  I am weary of bearing them.
¹⁵When you spread out your hands in
    prayer,
  I will hide my eyes from you;
even if you offer many prayers,
  I will not listen.
Your hands are full of blood;
¹⁶ wash and make yourselves clean.
Take your evil deeds
  out of my sight!
Stop doing wrong,
¹⁷ learn to do right!
Seek justice,
  encourage the oppressed.*ᵃ*
Defend the cause of the fatherless,
  plead the case of the widow.

¹⁸"Come now, let us reason together,"
  says the LORD.
"Though your sins are like scarlet,
  they shall be as white as snow;
though they are red as crimson,
  they shall be like wool.
¹⁹If you are willing and obedient,
  you will eat the best from the land;
²⁰but if you resist and rebel,
  you will be devoured by the sword."
    For the mouth of the LORD has
      spoken.

ᵃ17 Or / rebuke the oppressor

21See how the faithful city
   has become a harlot!
She once was full of justice;
   righteousness used to dwell in her—
   but now murderers!
22Your silver has become dross,
   your choice wine is diluted with water.
23Your rulers are rebels,
   companions of thieves;
they all love bribes
   and chase after gifts.
They do not defend the cause of the
   fatherless;
   the widow's case does not come before
   them.
24Therefore the Lord, the LORD Almighty,
   the Mighty One of Israel, declares:
   "Ah, I will get relief from my foes
   and avenge myself on my enemies.
25I will turn my hand against you;
   I will thoroughly purge away your dross
   and remove all your impurities.
26I will restore your judges as in days of old,
   your counsellors as at the beginning.
Afterwards you will be called
   the City of Righteousness,
   the Faithful City."

27Zion will be redeemed with justice,
   her penitent ones with righteousness.
28But rebels and sinners will both be broken,
   and those who forsake the LORD will
   perish.
29"You will be ashamed because of the
   sacred oaks
   in which you have delighted;
you will be disgraced because of the
   gardens
   that you have chosen.
30You will be like an oak with fading leaves,
   like a garden without water.
31The mighty man will become tinder
   and his work a spark;
both will burn together,
   with no-one to quench the fire.' '

The Mountain of the LORD

2 This is what Isaiah son of Amoz saw
   concerning Judah and Jerusalem:

2In the last days

the mountain of the LORD's temple will be
   established
   as chief among the mountains;
it will be raised above the hills,
   and all nations will stream to it.

3Many peoples will come and say,

"Come, let us go up to the mountain of the
   LORD,
   to the house of the God of Jacob.
He will teach us his ways,
   so that we may walk in his paths.' '
The law will go out from Zion,
   the word of the LORD from Jerusalem.
4He will judge between the nations

and will settle disputes for many
   peoples.
They will beat their swords into
   ploughshares
   and their spears into pruning hooks.
Nation will not take up sword against
   nation,
   nor will they train for war any more.

5Come, O house of Jacob,
   let us walk in the light of the LORD.

The Day of the LORD

6You have abandoned your people,
   the house of Jacob.
They are full of superstitions from the
   East;
they practise divination like the
   Philistines
   and clasp hands with pagans.
7Their land is full of silver and gold;
   there is no end to their treasures.
Their land is full of horses;
   there is no end to the chariots.
8Their land is full of idols;
   they bow down to the work of their
   hands,
   to what their fingers have made.
9So man will be brought low
   and mankind humbled—
   do not forgive them.a

10Go into the rocks,
   hide in the ground
from dread of the LORD
   and the splendour of his majesty!
11The eyes of the arrogant man will be
   humbled
   and the pride of men brought low;
the LORD alone will be exalted in that day.

12The LORD Almighty has a day in store
   for all the proud and lofty,
   for all that is exalted
   (and they will be humbled),
13for all the cedars of Lebanon, tall and
   lofty,
   and all the oaks of Bashan,
14for all the towering mountains
   and all the high hills,
15for every lofty tower
   and every fortified wall,
16for every trading shipb
   and every stately vessel.
17The arrogance of man will be brought low
   and the pride of men humbled;
   the LORD alone will be exalted in that day,
18   and the idols will totally disappear.

19Men will flee to caves in the rocks
   and to holes in the ground
from dread of the LORD
   and the splendour of his majesty,
   when he rises to shake the earth.
20In that day men will throw away
   to the rodents and bats
their idols of silver and idols of gold,
   which they made to worship.

a9 Or not raise them up   b16 Hebrew every ship of Tarshish

21They will flee to caverns in the rocks
    and to the overhanging crags
from dread of the LORD
    and the splendour of his majesty,
    when he rises to shake the earth.

22Stop trusting in man,
    who has but a breath in his nostrils.
Of what account is he?

Judgment on Jerusalem and Judah

3   See now, the Lord,
    the LORD Almighty,
is about to take from Jerusalem and Judah
    both supply and support:
all supplies of food and all supplies of
    water,
2   the hero and warrior,
    the judge and prophet,
    the soothsayer and elder,
3the captain of fifty and man of rank,
    the counsellor, skilled craftsman and
    clever enchanter.

4I will make boys their officials;
    mere children will govern them.
5People will oppress each other—
    man against man, neighbour against
    neighbour.
The young will rise up against the old,
    the base against the honourable.

6A man will seize one of his brothers
    at his father's home, and say,
"You have a cloak, you be our leader;
    take charge of this heap of ruins!"
7But in that day he will cry out,
    "I have no remedy.
I have no food or clothing in my house;
    do not make me the leader of the
    people."

8Jerusalem staggers,
    Judah is falling;
their words and deeds are against the
    LORD,
defying his glorious presence.
9The look on their faces testifies against
    them;
    they parade their sin like Sodom;
    they do not hide it.
Woe to them!
    They have brought disaster upon
    themselves.

10Tell the righteous it will be well with them,
    for they will enjoy the fruit of their
    deeds.
11Woe to the wicked! Disaster is upon them!
    They will be paid back for what their
    hands have done.

12Youths oppress my people,
    women rule over them.
O my people, your guides lead you astray;
    they turn you from the path.

13The LORD takes his place in court;
    he rises to judge the people.

14The LORD enters into judgment
    against the elders and leaders of his
    people:
"It is you who have ruined my vineyard;
    the plunder from the poor is in your
    houses.
15What do you mean by crushing my people
    and grinding the faces of the poor?"
            declares the Lord, the LORD
                            Almighty.

16The LORD says,
    "The women of Zion are haughty,
walking along with outstretched necks,
    flirting with their eyes,
tripping along with mincing steps,
    with ornaments jingling on their
    ankles.
17Therefore the Lord will bring sores on the
    heads of the women of Zion;
    the LORD will make their scalps bald."

18In that day the Lord will snatch away
their finery: the bangles and headbands
and crescent necklaces, 19the ear-rings and
bracelets and veils, 20the head-dresses and
ankle chains and sashes, the perfume bottles
and charms, 21the signet rings and nose rings,
22the fine robes and the capes and cloaks, the
purses 23and mirrors, and the linen garments
and tiaras and shawls.

24Instead of fragrance there will be a
    stench;
    instead of a sash, a rope;
instead of well-dressed hair, baldness;
    instead of fine clothing, sackcloth;
    instead of beauty, branding.
25Your men will fall by the sword,
    your warriors in battle.
26The gates of Zion will lament and
    mourn;
    destitute, she will sit on the ground.

4   In that day seven women will take hold
    of one man
and say, "We will eat our own food
    and provide our own clothes;
only let us be called by your name.
    Take away our disgrace!"

The Branch of the LORD

2In that day the Branch of the LORD will be
beautiful and glorious, and the fruit of the
land will be the pride and glory of the survivors in Israel. 3Those who are left in Zion,
who remain in Jerusalem, will be called holy,
all who are recorded among the living in
Jerusalem. 4The Lord will wash away the
filth of the women of Zion; he will cleanse the
bloodstains from Jerusalem by a spirita of
judgment and a spirita of fire. 5Then the LORD
will create over all of Mount Zion and over
those who assemble there a cloud of smoke
by day and a glow of flaming fire by night;
over all the glory will be a canopy. 6It will be
a shelter and shade from the heat of the day,
and a refuge and hiding-place from the storm
and rain.

a4 Or the Spirit

The Song of the Vineyard

5 I will sing for the one I love
a song about his vineyard:
My loved one had a vineyard
on a fertile hillside.
²He dug it up and cleared it of stones
and planted it with the choicest vines.
He built a watchtower in it
and cut out a winepress as well.
Then he looked for a crop of good grapes,
but it yielded only bad fruit.

³"Now you dwellers in Jerusalem and men
of Judah,
judge between me and my vineyard.
⁴What more could have been done for my
vineyard
than I have done for it?
When I looked for good grapes,
why did it yield only bad?
⁵Now I will tell you
what I am going to do to my vineyard:
I will take away its hedge,
and it will be destroyed;
I will break down its wall,
and it will be trampled.
⁶I will make it a wasteland,
neither pruned nor cultivated,
and briers and thorns will grow there.
I will command the clouds
not to rain on it."

⁷The vineyard of the LORD Almighty
is the house of Israel,
and the men of Judah
are the garden of his delight.
And he looked for justice, but saw
bloodshed;
for righteousness, but heard cries of
distress.

Woes and Judgments

⁸Woe to you who add house to house
and join field to field
till no space is left
and you live alone in the land.

⁹The LORD Almighty has declared in my
hearing:

"Surely the great houses will become
desolate,
the fine mansions left without
occupants.
¹⁰A ten-acre*a* vineyard will produce only a
bath*b* of wine,
a homer*c* of seed only an ephah*d* of
grain."

¹¹Woe to those who rise early in the morning
to run after their drinks,
who stay up late at night
till they are inflamed with wine.
¹²They have harps and lyres at their
banquets,
tambourines and flutes and wine,

but they have no regard for the deeds of
the LORD,
no respect for the work of his hands.
¹³Therefore my people will go into exile
for lack of understanding;
their men of rank will die of hunger
and their masses will be parched with
thirst.
¹⁴Therefore the grave*e* enlarges its appetite
and opens its mouth without limit;
into it will descend their nobles and
masses
with all their brawlers and revellers.
¹⁵So man will be brought low
and mankind humbled,
the eyes of the arrogant humbled.
¹⁶But the LORD Almighty will be exalted by
his justice,
and the holy God will show himself holy
by his righteousness.
¹⁷Then sheep will graze as in their own
pasture;
lambs will feed*f* among the ruins of the
rich.

¹⁸Woe to those who draw sin along with
cords of deceit,
and wickedness as with cart ropes,
¹⁹to those who say, "Let God hurry,
let him hasten his work
so that we may see it.
Let it approach,
let the plan of the Holy One of Israel
come,
so that we may know it."

²⁰Woe to those who call evil good
and good evil,
who put darkness for light
and light for darkness,
who put bitter for sweet
and sweet for bitter.

²¹Woe to those who are wise in their own
eyes
and clever in their own sight.

²²Woe to those who are heroes at drinking
wine
and champions at mixing drinks,
²³who acquit the guilty for a bribe,
but deny justice to the innocent.

²⁴Therefore, as tongues of fire lick up straw
and as dry grass sinks down in the
flames,
so their roots will decay
and their flowers blow away like dust;
for they have rejected the law of the LORD
Almighty
and spurned the word of the Holy One
of Israel.
²⁵Therefore the LORD's anger burns against
his people;
his hand is raised and he strikes them
down.

---

a10 Hebrew *ten-yoke*, that is, the land ploughed by 10 yoke of oxen in one day
b10 That is, probably about 5 gallons (about 22 litres)   *c10* That is, probably about 6 bushels (about 220 litres)
d10 That is, probably about ⅓ bushel (about 22 litres)   *e14* Hebrew *Sheol*
f17 Septuagint; Hebrew / *strangers will eat*

The mountains shake,
  and the dead bodies are like refuse in the
    streets.

Yet for all this, his anger is not turned
    away,
  his hand is still upraised.

26He lifts up a banner for the distant nations,
  he whistles for those at the ends of the
    earth.
Here they come,
  swiftly and speedily!
27Not one of them grows tired or stumbles,
  not one slumbers or sleeps;
not a belt is loosened at the waist,
  not a sandal thong is broken.
28Their arrows are sharp,
  all their bows are strung;
their horses' hoofs seem like flint,
  their chariot wheels like a whirlwind.
29Their roar is like that of the lion,
  they roar like young lions;
they growl as they seize their prey
  and carry it off with no-one to rescue.
30In that day they will roar over it
  like the roaring of the sea.
And if one looks at the land,
  he will see darkness and distress;
  even the light will be darkened by the
    clouds.

Isaiah's Commission

6 In the year that King Uzziah died, I saw
the Lord seated on a throne, high and
exalted, and the train of his robe filled the
temple. 2Above him were seraphs, each with
six wings: With two wings they covered their
faces, with two they covered their feet, and
with two they were flying. 3And they were
calling to one another:

  "Holy, holy, holy is the Lord Almighty;
    the whole earth is full of his glory."

4At the sound of their voices the doorposts
and thresholds shook and the temple was
filled with smoke.
  5"Woe to me!" I cried. "I am ruined! For I
am a man of unclean lips, and I live among a
people of unclean lips, and my eyes have
seen the King, the Lord Almighty."
  6Then one of the seraphs flew to me with a
live coal in his hand, which he had taken with
tongs from the altar. 7With it he touched my
mouth and said, "See, this has touched your
lips; your guilt is taken away and your sin
atoned for."
  8Then I heard the voice of the Lord saying,
"Whom shall I send? And who will go for
us?"
  And I said, "Here am I. Send me!"
  9He said, "Go and tell this people:

  "'Be ever hearing, but never
    understanding;
  be ever seeing, but never perceiving.'

10Make the heart of this people calloused;
  make their ears dull
  and close their eyes.a
Otherwise they might see with their eyes,
  hear with their ears,
  understand with their hearts,
  and turn and be healed."

11Then I said, "For how long, O Lord?"
  And he answered:

  "Until the cities lie ruined
    and without inhabitant,
  until the houses are left deserted
    and the fields ruined and ravaged,
12until the Lord has sent everyone far away
  and the land is utterly forsaken.
13And though a tenth remains in the land,
  it will again be laid waste.
But as the terebinth and oak
  leave stumps when they are cut down,
  so the holy seed will be the stump in the
    land."

The Sign of Immanuel

7 When Ahaz son of Jotham, the son of
Uzziah, was king of Judah, King Rezin
of Aram and Pekah son of Remaliah king of
Israel marched up to fight against Jerusalem,
but they could not overpower it.
  2Now the house of David was told, "Aram
has allied itself witha Ephraim"; so the hearts
of Ahaz and his people were shaken, as the
trees of the forest are shaken by the wind.
  3Then the Lord said to Isaiah, "Go out,
you and your son Shear-Jashub,b to meet
Ahaz at the end of the aqueduct of the Upper
Pool, on the road to the Washerman's Field.
4Say to him, 'Be careful, keep calm and don't
be afraid. Do not lose heart because of these
two smouldering stubs of firewood—because
of the fierce anger of Rezin and Aram and of
the son of Remaliah. 5Aram, Ephraim and
Remaliah's son have plotted your ruin,
saying, 6"Let us invade Judah; let us tear it
apart and divide it among ourselves, and
make the son of Tabeel king over it." 7Yet
this is what the Sovereign Lord says:

  "'It will not take place,
    it will not happen,
8for the head of Aram is Damascus,
  and the head of Damascus is only Rezin.
Within sixty-five years
  Ephraim will be too shattered to be a
    people.
9The head of Ephraim is Samaria,
  and the head of Samaria is only
    Remaliah's son.
If you do not stand firm in your faith,
  you will not stand at all.'"

10Again the Lord spoke to Ahaz, 11"Ask
the Lord your God for a sign, whether in the
deepest depths or in the highest heights."
  12But Ahaz said, "I will not ask; I will not
put the Lord to the test."

a9, 10 Hebrew; Septuagint 'You will be ever hearing, but never understanding; / you will be ever seeing, but never
perceiving.' / 10This people's heart has become calloused; / they hardly hear with their ears, / and they have closed
their eyes   a2 Or has set up camp in   b3 Shear-Jashub means a remnant will return.

¹³Then Isaiah said, "Hear now, you house of David! Is it not enough to try the patience of men? Will you try the patience of my God also? ¹⁴Therefore the Lord himself will give you*c* a sign: The virgin will be with child and will give birth to a son, and*d* will call him Immanuel.*e* ¹⁵He will eat curds and honey when he knows enough to reject the wrong and choose the right. ¹⁶But before the boy knows enough to reject the wrong and choose the right, the land of the two kings you dread will be laid waste. ¹⁷The LORD will bring on you and on your people and on the house of your father a time unlike any since Ephraim broke away from Judah—he will bring the king of Assyria."

¹⁸In that day the LORD will whistle for flies from the distant streams of Egypt and for bees from the land of Assyria. ¹⁹They will all come and settle in the steep ravines and in the crevices in the rocks, on all the thornbushes and at all the water holes. ²⁰In that day the Lord will use a razor hired from beyond the River*f*—the king of Assyria—to shave your head and the hair of your legs, and to take off your beards also. ²¹In that day, a man will keep alive a young cow and two goats. ²²And because of the abundance of the milk they give, he will have curds to eat. All who remain in the land will eat curds and honey. ²³In that day, in every place where there were a thousand vines worth a thousand silver shekels,*g* there will be only briers and thorns. ²⁴Men will go there with bow and arrow, for the land will be covered with briers and thorns. ²⁵As for all the hills once cultivated by the hoe, you will no longer go there for fear of the briers and thorns; they will become places where cattle are turned loose and where sheep run.

Assyria, the LORD's Instrument

8 The LORD said to me, "Take a large scroll and write on it with an ordinary pen: Maher-Shalal-Hash-Baz.*a* ²And I will call in Uriah the priest and Zechariah son of Jeberekiah as reliable witnesses for me."

³Then I went to the prophetess, and she conceived and gave birth to a son. And the LORD said to me, "Name him Maher-Shalal-Hash-Baz. ⁴Before the boy knows how to say 'My father' or 'My mother', the wealth of Damascus and the plunder of Samaria will be carried off by the king of Assyria."

⁵The LORD spoke to me again:

⁶"Because this people has rejected
　the gently flowing waters of Shiloah
and rejoices over Rezin
　and the son of Remaliah,
⁷therefore the Lord is about to bring against
　them
　the mighty floodwaters of the River*b*—
　the king of Assyria with all his pomp.

It will overflow all its channels,
　run over all its banks
⁸and sweep on into Judah, swirling over it,
　passing through it and reaching up to the
　　neck.
Its outspread wings will cover the breadth
　　of your land,
　O Immanuel!"*c*

⁹Raise the war cry,*d* you nations, and be
　shattered!
Listen, all you distant lands.
Prepare for battle, and be shattered!
Prepare for battle, and be shattered!
¹⁰Devise your strategy, but it will be
　thwarted;
　propose your plan, but it will not stand,
for God is with us.*e*

Fear God

¹¹The LORD spoke to me with his strong hand upon me, warning me not to follow the way of this people. He said:

¹²"Do not call conspiracy
　everything that these people call
　　conspiracy;*f*
do not fear what they fear,
　and do not dread it.
¹³The LORD Almighty is the one you are to
　regard as holy,
he is the one you are to fear,
he is the one you are to dread,
¹⁴and he will be a sanctuary;
　but for both houses of Israel he will be
a stone that causes men to stumble
　and a rock that makes them fall.
And for the people of Jerusalem he will be
　a trap and a snare.
¹⁵Many of them will stumble;
　they will fall and be broken,
　they will be snared and captured."

¹⁶Bind up the testimony
　and seal up the law among my disciples.
¹⁷I will wait for the LORD,
　who is hiding his face from the house of
　　Jacob.
I will put my trust in him.

¹⁸Here am I, and the children the LORD has given me. We are signs and symbols in Israel from the LORD Almighty, who dwells on Mount Zion.

¹⁹When men tell you to consult mediums and spiritists, who whisper and mutter, should not a people enquire of their God? Why consult the dead on behalf of the living? ²⁰To the law and to the testimony! If they do not speak according to this word, they have no light of dawn. ²¹Distressed and hungry, they will roam through the land; when they are famished, they will become enraged and, looking upward, will curse their king and their God. ²²Then they will look towards the

c14 The Hebrew is plural.　　*d14* Masoretic Text; Dead Sea Scrolls *and he* or *and they*
e14 Immanuel means *God with us*.　　*f20* That is, the Euphrates
g23 That is, about 25 pounds (about 11.5 kilograms)
a1 Maher-Shalal-Hash-Baz means *quick to the plunder, swift to the spoil*; also in verse 3.
b7 That is, the Euphrates　　*c8 Immanuel* means *God with us*.　　*d9* Or *Do your worst*
e10 Hebrew *Immanuel*　　*f12* Or *Do not call for a treaty / every time these people call for a treaty*

ISAIAH 7:10–17

'Therefore the LORD himself will give you a sign: The virgin will be with child and will give birth to a son, and will call him Immanuel' (v. 14).

ADVENT POINTS TO the coming of Christ. Traditionally, it was observed as a solemn time with an emphasis on penitence. Now, carollers, the buying of gifts, decorations, Advent wreaths and colourful Advent calendars make it a season of joyful anticipation. King Ahaz of Judah could only anticipate the future with foreboding when God challenged him to ask for a sign (v. 11). Jerusalem was under attack from the combined armies of the adjacent states of Ephraim (Israel) and Aram (Syria). Its citizens were terrified. Their future looked bleak (vv. 1–6).

King Ahaz refused to put God to the test, therefore a sign was given through the prophet Isaiah that a virgin would conceive a son and his name would be called Immanuel (vv. 12–14). When this name was applied to Jesus in the Gospels, its meaning, 'God with us', was also included (Matt. 1:23).

Isaiah's prophecy was one of tremendous insight. Although the Hebrew people recognized God as father and witnessed to his presence, few related to him in a personal sense. Even so, they had a much greater awareness of God than many people in the Western world today, where God is not rejected outright, but he is ignored. At most, he is safely in the background to be called upon only in dire emergency.

'God is with us' is the hopeful message of Advent. It is a relevant and necessary message today. The birth of Jesus confirms it and Christian experience bears testimony to it.

O come to us, abide with us.
Our Lord Immanuel.

(*Phillips Brooks*)

→574

ISAIAH 9:2–7

'For to us a child is born, to us a son is given, and the government will be on his shoulders. And he will be called Wonderful Counsellor, Mighty God, Everlasting Father, Prince of Peace' (v. 6).

THE IMAGERY OF LIGHT has long been associated with Christmas. In 350 AD Pope Julius 1 made 25 December the day when 'Christ's Mass' should be celebrated in honour of the birth of Jesus. The date was possibly chosen to counteract a popular feast in honour of Saturn at the time of the winter solstice. In the northern hemisphere Christmas Day is one of the shortest days of the year and decorative lights shine brightly. The sun's return in the spring and summer is anticipated in symbolism which acclaims the birth of one who said, 'I am the light of the world' (John 8:12).

Isaiah prophesied about the despair the survivors of the Assyrian invasion would experience. He paints a picture of utter darkness (8:21–9:1), but that was not the end of the story. He promises that a new Israel would emerge in which farmers would rejoice in their harvest (v. 3) and warring parties would be reconciled (v. 5). This new creation would be governed by a just and righteous ruler. He would come as a child and be given the ceremonial names of a king (v. 6). These names witness to his wisdom, divinity, eternal concern and reign of peace.

For those who first heard the prophet's message, the outlook was anything but peaceful. Their prospects were of a land pillaged by the Assyrians, homes destroyed and the death of innocent victims. They had not lost hope, however, and believed that a messianic kingdom would give them health and wealth. Such is still the vivid experience of people living in today's war-torn areas and urban ghettos. Hopefully, some of them burn Advent candles as a witness to the fact that darkness can be defeated by light.

Lord, help us to bring light where there is darkness, hope where there is despair and peace where there is discord. Help us to promote righteousness as we live for you. Amen.

earth and see only distress and darkness and fearful gloom, and they will be thrust into utter darkness.

To Us a Child Is Born

9 Nevertheless, there will be no more gloom for those who were in distress. In the past he humbled the land of Zebulun and the land of Naphtali, but in the future he will honour Galilee of the Gentiles, by the way of the sea, along the Jordan—

²The people walking in darkness
  have seen a great light;
on those living in the land of the shadow of
    death[a]
  a light has dawned.
³You have enlarged the nation
  and increased their joy;
they rejoice before you
  as people rejoice at the harvest,
as men rejoice
  when dividing the plunder.
⁴For as in the day of Midian's defeat,
  you have shattered
the yoke that burdens them,
  the bar across their shoulders,
  the rod of their oppressor.
⁵Every warrior's boot used in battle
  and every garment rolled in blood
will be destined for burning,
  will be fuel for the fire.
⁶For to us a child is born,
  to us a son is given,
  and the government will be on his
    shoulders.
And he will be called
  Wonderful Counsellor,[b] Mighty God,
  Everlasting Father, Prince of Peace.
⁷Of the increase of his government and
    peace
  there will be no end.
He will reign on David's throne
  and over his kingdom,
establishing and upholding it
  with justice and righteousness
  from that time on and for ever.
The zeal of the LORD Almighty
  will accomplish this.

The LORD's Anger Against Israel

⁸The Lord has sent a message against
    Jacob;
  it will fall on Israel.
⁹All the people will know it—
  Ephraim and the inhabitants of
    Samaria—
who say with pride
  and arrogance of heart,
¹⁰"The bricks have fallen down,
  but we will rebuild with dressed stone;
the fig-trees have been felled,
  but we will replace them with cedars."
¹¹But the LORD has strengthened Rezin's
    foes against them
  and has spurred their enemies on.
¹²Arameans from the east and Philistines
    from the west
  have devoured Israel with open mouth.

Yet for all this, his anger is not turned
    away,
  his hand is still upraised.

¹³But the people have not returned to him
    who struck them,
  nor have they sought the LORD
    Almighty.
¹⁴So the LORD will cut off from Israel both
    head and tail,
  both palm branch and reed in a single
    day;
¹⁵the elders and prominent men are the
    head,
  the prophets who teach lies are the tail.
¹⁶Those who guide this people mislead
    them,
  and those who are guided are led astray.
¹⁷Therefore the Lord will take no pleasure in
    the young men,
  nor will he pity the fatherless and
    widows,
for everyone is ungodly and wicked,
  every mouth speaks vileness.

Yet for all this, his anger is not turned
    away,
  his hand is still upraised.

¹⁸Surely wickedness burns like a fire;
  it consumes briers and thorns,
it sets the forest thickets ablaze,
  so that it rolls upward in a column of
    smoke.
¹⁹By the wrath of the LORD Almighty
  the land will be scorched
and the people will be fuel for the fire;
  no-one will spare his brother.
²⁰On the right they will devour,
  but still be hungry;
on the left they will eat,
  but not be satisfied.
Each will feed on the flesh of his own
    offspring:[c]
²¹ Manasseh will feed on Ephraim, and
    Ephraim on Manasseh;
  together they will turn against Judah.

Yet for all this, his anger is not turned
    away,
  his hand is still upraised.

10 Woe to those who make unjust laws,
  to those who issue oppressive
    decrees,
²to deprive the poor of their rights
  and withhold justice from the oppressed
    of my people,
making widows their prey
  and robbing the fatherless.
³What will you do on the day of reckoning,
  when disaster comes from afar?
To whom will you run for help?
  Where will you leave your riches?
⁴Nothing will remain but to cringe among
    the captives
  or fall among the slain.

Yet for all this, his anger is not turned
away,
his hand is still upraised.

God's Judgment on Assyria

5"Woe to the Assyrian, the rod of my
anger,
in whose hand is the club of my wrath!
6I send him against a godless nation,
I dispatch him against a people who
anger me,
to seize loot and snatch plunder,
and to trample them down like mud in
the streets.
7But this is not what he intends,
this is not what he has in mind;
his purpose is to destroy,
to put an end to many nations.
8'Are not my commanders all kings?' he
says.
9   'Has not Calno fared like Carchemish?
Is not Hamath like Arpad,
and Samaria like Damascus?
10As my hand seized the kingdoms of the
idols,
kingdoms whose images excelled those
of Jerusalem and Samaria—
11shall I not deal with Jerusalem and her
images
as I dealt with Samaria and her idols?' ''

12When the Lord has finished all his work
against Mount Zion and Jerusalem, he will
say, "I will punish the king of Assyria for the
wilful pride of his heart and the haughty look
in his eyes. 13For he says:

" 'By the strength of my hand I have done
this,
and by my wisdom, because I have
understanding.
I removed the boundaries of nations,
I plundered their treasures;
like a mighty one I subdued^a their kings.
14As one reaches into a nest,
so my hand reached for the wealth of the
nations;
as men gather abandoned eggs,
so I gathered all the countries;
not one flapped a wing,
or opened its mouth to chirp.' ' ''

15Does the axe raise itself above him who
swings it,
or the saw boast against him who uses
it?
As if a rod were to wield him who lifts it
up,
or a club brandish him who is not wood!
16Therefore, the Lord, the LORD Almighty,
will send a wasting disease upon his
sturdy warriors;
under his pomp a fire will be kindled
like a blazing flame.
17The Light of Israel will become a fire,
their Holy One a flame;
in a single day it will burn and consume
his thorns and his briers.

18The splendour of his forests and fertile
fields
it will completely destroy,
as when a sick man wastes away.
19And the remaining trees of his forests will
be so few
that a child could write them down.

The Remnant of Israel

20In that day the remnant of Israel,
the survivors of the house of Jacob,
will no longer rely on him
who struck them down
but will truly rely on the LORD,
the Holy One of Israel.
21A remnant will return,^{b} a remnant of Jacob
will return to the Mighty God.
22Though your people, O Israel, be like the
sand by the sea,
only a remnant will return.
Destruction has been decreed,
overwhelming and righteous.
23The Lord, the LORD Almighty, will carry
out
the destruction decreed upon the whole
land.

24Therefore, this is what the Lord, the
LORD Almighty, says:

"O my people who live in Zion,
do not be afraid of the Assyrians,
who beat you with a rod
and lift up a club against you, as Egypt
did.
25Very soon my anger against you will end
and my wrath will be directed to their
destruction."

26The LORD Almighty will lash them with a
whip,
as when he struck down Midian at the
rock of Oreb;
and he will raise his staff over the waters,
as he did in Egypt.
27In that day their burden will be lifted from
your shoulders,
their yoke from your neck;
the yoke will be broken
because you have grown so fat.^{c}

28They enter Aiath;
they pass through Migron;
they store supplies at Michmash.
29They go over the pass, and say,
"We will camp overnight at Geba."
Ramah trembles;
Gibeah of Saul flees.
30Cry out, O Daughter of Gallim!
Listen, O Laishah!
Poor Anathoth!
31Madmenah is in flight;
the people of Gebim take cover.
32This day they will halt at Nob;
they will shake their fist
at the mount of the Daughter of Zion,
at the hill of Jerusalem.

^{a}13 Or / I subdued the mighty, ^{b}21 Hebrew shear-jashub; also in verse 22
^{c}27 Hebrew; Septuagint broken / from your shoulders

ISAIAH 11:1–9

'With righteousness he will judge the needy, with justice he will give decisions for the poor of the earth' (v. 4a).

TENACITY is never better illustrated than when a shoot breaks forth from a stump. It is not difficult to imagine the picture painted by the prophet Isaiah. He uses a metaphor of the felling of cedars in Lebanon to describe the destruction of the Assyrian army (10:33, 34). Then comes the Advent promise. 'A shoot will come up from the stump of Jesse' (v. 1). This could be interpreted as a prophecy pointing towards some future Davidic king, for Jesse was the father of King David. But the following verses describe an ideal king who would have little in common with the fallible rulers of Judah and Israel. His charismatic gifts (v. 2) would enable him to rule wisely and well.

His rule is defined in terms of judgement (vv. 3, 4). This may seem harsh in a pre-Christmas context and yet this topic has been traditionally a focus in worship during the Advent season. This in recognition of the fact that whenever Jesus comes, all things come under judgement in the light of his presence. His righteousness shows up anything corrupt and unjust. We do well to recognize this as we prepare in heart and mind for the celebration of Christmas. We are so easily deceived by appearances and hearsay in our judgement of people and situations. This means we often fail to discern that which is true. The ruler from the stump of Jesse would not suffer such failure in discernment (v. 3).

The justice of his rule would make possible a time when life would be idyllic. Violence would cease, ferocious animals become tame and the earth would be full of the knowledge of the Lord (v. 9).

Lord, as we anticipate the celebration of the birth of Jesus, help us to be like him. Give us a spirit of wisdom so that we may discern the truth in every situation. And, Lord, if that demands we humble ourselves, give us a spirit of meekness. May our demeanour be such that we mediate your peace in every setting of our lives. Amen.

→578

ISAIAH 12:1–6

'Shout aloud and sing for joy, people of Zion, for great is the Holy One of Israel among you' (v. 6).

ONE OF ISAIAH'S PROPHECIES was given in the context of Judah being under attack from its near neighbours, Ephraim and Aram (7:1, 10–17). This was the immediate concern for Israel, but as Isaiah indicated, Assyria was their main enemy (7:16, 17). A constant message in succeeding chapters is that a remnant of Israel would survive the impending crisis and return from all parts of the earth. It would be like a new Exodus (11:16).

In contemplating this, the prophet shares two hymns of thanksgiving to be sung by the returning exiles, like that sung by the people following the exodus from Egypt (Exod. 15:1ff.). In the first hymn (vv. 1, 2) the nation would acknowledge that the God is its salvation and the Lord is its strength. This sounds fine in the context of Scripture, but how many people today would express political strength in such terms? This poses the question: would governments today be more respected and productive if spiritual values were given greater prominence in the political equation?

Prior to the second hymn there is the promise (v. 3) which probably alludes back to God's provision during the time the children of Israel wandered into the wilderness. Then the prophet confirms in the second hymn (vv. 4–6) that Judah would have an obligation to witness to the universality of divine redemption. They were saved to tell others in a spirit of joy.

The Advent season presents the Church with one of its best opportunities to proclaim the gospel. Christians need to be alert to those occasions when a simple word or deed will exalt the name of the Lord and tell of the glorious things he has done.

> *Our glad hosannas, Prince of Peace.*
> *Thy welcome shall proclaim.*
> *And Heaven's eternal arches ring*
> *With thy belovèd name.*

(Philip Doddridge)

→587

³³See, the Lord, the LORD Almighty,
 will lop off the boughs with great power.
The lofty trees will be felled,
 the tall ones will be brought low.
³⁴He will cut down the forest thickets with
  an axe;
 Lebanon will fall before the Mighty
  One.

The Branch From Jesse

11 A shoot will come up from the stump
  of Jesse;
 from his roots a Branch will bear fruit.
²The Spirit of the LORD will rest on him—
 the Spirit of wisdom and of
  understanding,
 the Spirit of counsel and of power,
 the Spirit of knowledge and of the fear
  of the LORD—
³and he will delight in the fear of the LORD.

He will not judge by what he sees with his
  eyes,
 or decide by what he hears with his ears;
⁴but with righteousness he will judge the
  needy,
 with justice he will give decisions for the
  poor of the earth.
He will strike the earth with the rod of his
  mouth;
 with the breath of his lips he will slay the
  wicked.
⁵Righteousness will be his belt
 and faithfulness the sash round his
  waist.

⁶The wolf will live with the lamb,
 the leopard will lie down with the goat,
the calf and the lion and the yearling*ᵃ*
  together;
 and a little child will lead them.
⁷The cow will feed with the bear,
 their young will lie down together,
 and the lion will eat straw like the ox.
⁸The infant will play near the hole of the
  cobra,
 and the young child put his hand into the
  viper's nest.
⁹They will neither harm nor destroy
 on all my holy mountain,
for the earth will be full of the knowledge
  of the LORD
 as the waters cover the sea.

¹⁰In that day the Root of Jesse will stand as
a banner for the peoples; the nations will rally
to him, and his place of rest will be glorious.
¹¹In that day the Lord will reach out his hand
a second time to reclaim the remnant that is
left of his people from Assyria, from Lower
Egypt, from Upper Egypt,*ᵇ* from Cush,*ᶜ*
from Elam, from Babylonia,*ᵈ* from Hamath
and from the islands of the sea.

¹²He will raise a banner for the nations
 and gather the exiles of Israel;
he will assemble the scattered people of
  Judah

from the four quarters of the earth.
¹³Ephraim's jealousy will vanish,
 and Judah's enemies*ᵉ* will be cut off;
Ephraim will not be jealous of Judah,
 nor Judah hostile towards Ephraim.
¹⁴They will swoop down on the slopes of
  Philistia to the west;
 together they will plunder the people to
  the east.
They will lay hands on Edom and Moab,
 and the Ammonites will be subject to
  them.
¹⁵The LORD will dry up
 the gulf of the Egyptian sea;
with a scorching wind he will sweep his
  hand
 over the Euphrates River*ᶠ*
He will break it up into seven streams
 so that men can cross over in sandals.
¹⁶There will be a highway for the remnant of
  his people
 that is left from Assyria,
as there was for Israel
 when they came up from Egypt.

Songs of Praise

12 In that day you will say:

"I will praise you, O LORD.
 Although you were angry with me,
your anger has turned away
 and you have comforted me.
²Surely God is my salvation;
 I will trust and not be afraid.
The LORD, the LORD, is my strength and
  my song;
 he has become my salvation."
³With joy you will draw water
 from the wells of salvation.

⁴In that day you will say:

"Give thanks to the LORD, call on his
  name;
 make known among the nations what he
  has done,
 and proclaim that his name is exalted.
⁵Sing to the LORD, for he has done glorious
  things;
 let this be known to all the world.
⁶Shout aloud and sing for joy, people of
  Zion,
 for great is the Holy One of Israel
  among you."

A Prophecy Against Babylon

13 An oracle concerning Babylon that
  Isaiah son of Amoz saw:

²Raise a banner on a bare hilltop,
 shout to them;
beckon to them
 to enter the gates of the nobles.
³I have commanded my holy ones;
 I have summoned my warriors to carry
  out my wrath—
 those who rejoice in my triumph.

ᵃ6 Hebrew; Septuagint *lion will feed* *ᵇ11* Hebrew *from Pathros* *ᶜ11* That is, the upper Nile region
ᵈ11 Hebrew *Shinar* *ᵉ13* Or *hostility* *ᶠ15* Hebrew *the River*

⁴Listen, a noise on the mountains,
　　like that of a great multitude!
Listen, an uproar among the kingdoms,
　　like nations massing together!
The LORD Almighty is mustering
　　an army for war.
⁵They come from faraway lands,
　　from the ends of the heavens—
the LORD and the weapons of his wrath—
　　to destroy the whole country.

⁶Wail, for the day of the LORD is near;
　　it will come like destruction from the
　　　　Almighty.ᵃ
⁷Because of this, all hands will go limp,
　　every man's heart will melt.
⁸Terror will seize them,
　　pain and anguish will grip them;
　　they will writhe like a woman in labour.
They will look aghast at each other,
　　their faces aflame.

⁹See, the day of the LORD is coming
　　—a cruel day, with wrath and fierce
　　　　anger—
to make the land desolate
　　and destroy the sinners within it.
¹⁰The stars of heaven and their
　　　　constellations
　　will not show their light.
The rising sun will be darkened
　　and the moon will not give its light.
¹¹I will punish the world for its evil,
　　the wicked for their sins.
I will put an end to the arrogance of the
　　　　haughty
　　and will humble the pride of the
　　　　ruthless.
¹²I will make man scarcer than pure gold,
　　more rare than the gold of Ophir.
¹³Therefore I will make the heavens
　　　　tremble;
　　and the earth will shake from its place
at the wrath of the LORD Almighty,
　　in the day of his burning anger.

¹⁴Like a hunted gazelle,
　　like sheep without a shepherd,
each will return to his own people,
　　each will flee to his native land.
¹⁵Whoever is captured will be thrust
　　　　through;
　　all who are caught will fall by the sword.
¹⁶Their infants will be dashed to pieces
　　　　before their eyes;
　　their houses will be looted and their
　　　　wives ravished.
¹⁷See, I will stir up against them the Medes,
　　who do not care for silver
　　and have no delight in gold.
¹⁸Their bows will strike down the young
　　　　men;
　　they will have no mercy on infants
　　nor will they look with compassion on
　　　　children.
¹⁹Babylon, the jewel of kingdoms,
　　the glory of the Babylonians'ᵇ pride,

will be overthrown by God
　　like Sodom and Gomorrah.
²⁰She will never be inhabited
　　or lived in through all generations;
no Arab will pitch his tent there,
　　no shepherd will rest his flocks there.
²¹But desert creatures will lie there,
　　jackals will fill her houses;
there the owls will dwell,
　　and there the wild goats will leap about.
²²Hyenas will howl in her strongholds,
　　jackals in her luxurious palaces.
Her time is at hand,
　　and her days will not be prolonged.

14

The LORD will have compassion on
　　Jacob;
　　once again he will choose Israel
　　and will settle them in their own land.
Aliens will join them
　　and unite with the house of Jacob.
²Nations will take them
　　and bring them to their own place.
And the house of Israel will possess the
　　　　nations
　　as menservants and maidservants in the
　　　　LORD's land.
They will make captives of their captors
　　and rule over their oppressors.

³On the day the LORD gives you relief from
suffering and turmoil and cruel bondage,
⁴you will take up this taunt against the king of
Babylon:

How the oppressor has come to an end!
　　How his furyᵃ has ended!
⁵The LORD has broken the rod of the
　　　　wicked,
　　the sceptre of the rulers,
⁶which in anger struck down peoples
　　with unceasing blows,
and in fury subdued nations
　　with relentless aggression.
⁷All the lands are at rest and at peace;
　　they break into singing.
⁸Even the pine trees and the cedars of
　　　　Lebanon
　　exult over you and say,
"Now that you have been laid low,
　　no woodsman comes to cut us down."

⁹The graveᵇ below is all astir
　　to meet you at your coming;
it rouses the spirits of the departed to greet
　　　　you—
　　all those who were leaders in the world;
it makes them rise from their thrones—
　　all those who were kings over the
　　　　nations.
¹⁰They will all respond,
　　they will say to you,
"You also have become weak, as we are;
　　you have become like us."
¹¹All your pomp has been brought down to
　　　　the grave,
　　along with the noise of your harps;

ᵃ6 Hebrew *Shaddai*　　ᵇ19 Or *Chaldeans'*
ᵃ4 Dead Sea Scrolls, Septuagint and Syriac; the meaning of the word in the Masoretic Text is uncertain.
ᵇ9 Hebrew *Sheol*; also in verses 11 and 15

maggots are spread out beneath you
 and worms cover you.

[12]How you have fallen from heaven,
 O morning star, son of the dawn!
You have been cast down to the earth,
 you who once laid low the nations!
[13]You said in your heart,
 "I will ascend to heaven;
I will raise my throne
 above the stars of God;
I will sit enthroned on the mount of
  assembly,
 on the utmost heights of the sacred
  mountain.[c]
[14]I will ascend above the tops of the clouds;
 I will make myself like the Most High."
[15]But you are brought down to the grave,
 to the depths of the pit.

[16]Those who see you stare at you,
 they ponder your fate:
"Is this the man who shook the earth
 and made kingdoms tremble,
[17]the man who made the world a desert,
 who overthrew its cities
 and would not let his captives go
  home?"

[18]All the kings of the nations lie in state,
 each in his own tomb.
[19]But you are cast out of your tomb
 like a rejected branch;
you are covered with the slain,
 with those pierced by the sword,
 those who descend to the stones of the
  pit.
Like a corpse trampled underfoot,
[20] you will not join them in burial,
for you have destroyed your land
 and killed your people.

The offspring of the wicked
 will never be mentioned again.
[21]Prepare a place to slaughter his sons
 for the sins of their forefathers;
they are not to rise to inherit the land
 and cover the earth with their cities.

[22]"I will rise up against them,"
 declares the LORD Almighty.
"I will cut off from Babylon her name and
  survivors,
her offspring and descendants,"
      declares the LORD.
[23]"I will turn her into a place for owls
 and into swampland;
I will sweep her with the broom of
  destruction,"
 declares the LORD Almighty.

A Prophecy Against Assyria
[24]The LORD Almighty has sworn,

"Surely, as I have planned, so it will be,
 and as I have purposed, so it will stand.
[25]I will crush the Assyrian in my land;
 on my mountains I will trample him
  down.

His yoke will be taken from my people,
 and his burden removed from their
  shoulders."

[26]This is the plan determined for the whole
  world;
 this is the hand stretched out over all
  nations.
[27]For the LORD Almighty has purposed, and
  who can thwart him?
His hand is stretched out, and who can
  turn it back?

A Prophecy Against the Philistines
[28]This oracle came in the year King Ahaz
died:

[29]Do not rejoice, all you Philistines,
 that the rod that struck you is broken;
from the root of that snake will spring up a
  viper,
 its fruit will be a darting, venomous
  serpent.
[30]The poorest of the poor will find pasture,
 and the needy will lie down in safety.
But your root I will destroy by famine;
 it will slay your survivors.

[31]Wail, O gate! Howl, O city!
 Melt away, all you Philistines!
A cloud of smoke comes from the north,
 and there is not a straggler in its ranks.
[32]What answer shall be given
 to the envoys of that nation?
"The LORD has established Zion,
 and in her his afflicted people will find
  refuge."

A Prophecy Against Moab
15 An oracle concerning Moab:

Ar in Moab is ruined,
 destroyed in a night!
Kir in Moab is ruined,
 destroyed in a night!
[2]Dibon goes up to its temple,
 to its high places to weep;
Moab wails over Nebo and Medeba.
Every head is shaved
 and every beard cut off.
[3]In the streets they wear sackcloth;
 on the roofs and in the public squares
they all wail,
 prostrate with weeping.
[4]Heshbon and Elealeh cry out,
 their voices are heard all the way to
  Jahaz.
Therefore the armed men of Moab cry out,
 and their hearts are faint.

[5]My heart cries out over Moab;
 her fugitives flee as far as Zoar,
 as far as Eglath Shelishiyah.
They go up the way to Luhith,
 weeping as they go;
on the road to Horonaim
 they lament their destruction.
[6]The waters of Nimrim are dried up
 and the grass is withered;

[c]13 Or *the north*; Hebrew *Zaphon*

the vegetation is gone
　and nothing green is left.
[7]So the wealth they have acquired and
　　stored up
　they carry away over the Ravine of the
　　Poplars.
[8]Their outcry echoes along the border of
　　Moab;
　their wailing reaches as far as Eglaim,
　their lamentation as far as Beer Elim.
[9]Dimon's[a] waters are full of blood,
　but I will bring still more upon
　　Dimon[a]—
　a lion upon the fugitives of Moab
　and upon those who remain in the land.

16 Send lambs as tribute to the ruler of
　　the land,
　from Sela, across the desert,
　to the mount of the Daughter of Zion.
[2]Like fluttering birds
　pushed from the nest,
　so are the women of Moab
　at the fords of the Arnon.

[3]"Give us counsel,
　render a decision.
Make your shadow like night—
　at high noon.
Hide the fugitives,
　do not betray the refugees.
[4]Let the Moabite fugitives stay with you;
　be their shelter from the destroyer."

The oppressor will come to an end,
　and destruction will cease;
　the aggressor will vanish from the land.
[5]In love a throne will be established;
　in faithfulness a man will sit on it—
　one from the house[a] of David—
one who in judging seeks justice
　and speeds the cause of righteousness.

[6]We have heard of Moab's pride—
　her overweening pride and conceit,
　her pride and her insolence—
　but her boasts are empty.
[7]Therefore the Moabites wail,
　they wail together for Moab.
Lament and grieve
　for the men[b] of Kir Hareseth.
[8]The fields of Heshbon wither,
　the vines of Sibmah also.
The rulers of the nations
　have trampled down the choicest vines,
which once reached Jazer
　and spread towards the desert.
Their shoots spread out
　and went as far as the sea.
[9]So I weep, as Jazer weeps,
　for the vines of Sibmah.
O Heshbon, O Elealeh,
　I drench you with tears!
The shouts of joy over your ripened fruit
　and over your harvests have been
　　stilled.
[10]Joy and gladness are taken away from the
　　orchards;
　no-one sings or shouts in the vineyards;

no-one treads out wine at the presses,
　for I have put an end to the shouting.
[11]My heart laments for Moab like a harp,
　my inmost being for Kir Hareseth.
[12]When Moab appears at her high place,
　she only wears herself out;
when she goes to her shrine to pray,
　it is to no avail.

[13]This is the word the LORD has already
spoken concerning Moab. [14]But now the
LORD says: "Within three years, as a servant
bound by contract would count them,
Moab's splendour and all her many people
will be despised, and her survivors will be
very few and feeble."

An Oracle Against Damascus

17 An oracle concerning Damascus:

"See, Damascus will no longer be a city
　but will become a heap of ruins.
[2]The cities of Aroer will be deserted
　and left to flocks, which will lie down,
　with no-one to make them afraid.
[3]The fortified city will disappear from
　　Ephraim,
　and royal power from Damascus;
the remnant of Aram will be
　like the glory of the Israelites,"
　　　　declares the LORD Almighty.

[4]"In that day the glory of Jacob will fade;
　the fat of his body will waste away.
[5]It will be as when a reaper gathers the
　　standing corn
　and harvests the corn with his arm—
as when a man gleans ears of corn
　in the Valley of Rephaim.
[6]Yet some gleanings will remain,
　as when an olive tree is beaten,
leaving two or three olives on the topmost
　　branches,
　four or five on the fruitful boughs,"
　　　　declares the LORD,
　　　　　　the God of Israel.

[7]In that day men will look to their Maker
　and turn their eyes to the Holy One of
　　Israel.
[8]They will not look to the altars,
　the work of their hands,
and they will have no regard for the
　　Asherah poles[a]
　and the incense altars their fingers have
　　made.

[9]In that day their strong cities, which they
left because of the Israelites, will be like
places abandoned to thickets and undergrowth. And all will be desolation.

[10]You have forgotten God your Saviour;
　you have not remembered the Rock,
　your fortress.
Therefore, though you set out the finest
　　plants
　and plant imported vines,

---

[a]9 Masoretic Text; Dead Sea Scrolls, some Septuagint manuscripts and Vulgate *Dibon*
[a]5 Hebrew *tent*　　[b]7 Or "*raisin cakes*," a word play　　[a]8 That is, symbols of the goddess Asherah

[11]though on the day you set them out, you
    make them grow,
and on the morning when you plant
    them, you bring them to bud,
yet the harvest will be as nothing
    in the day of disease and incurable pain.

[12]Oh, the raging of many nations—
    they rage like the raging sea!
Oh, the uproar of the peoples—
    they roar like the roaring of great
    waters!
[13]Although the peoples roar like the roar of
    surging waters,
when he rebukes them they flee far
    away,
driven before the wind like chaff on the
    hills,
like tumble-weed before a gale.
[14]In the evening, sudden terror!
Before the morning, they are gone!
This is the portion of those who loot us,
    the lot of those who plunder us.

A Prophecy Against Cush

18 Woe to the land of whirring wings[a]
    along the rivers of Cush,[b]
[2]which sends envoys by sea
    in papyrus boats over the water.

Go, swift messengers,
to a people tall and smooth-skinned,
    to a people feared far and wide,
an aggressive nation of strange speech,
    whose land is divided by rivers.
[3]All you people of the world,
    you who live on the earth,
when a banner is raised on the mountains,
    you will see it,
and when a trumpet sounds,
    you will hear it.
[4]This is what the LORD says to me:
    "I will remain quiet and will look on
    from my dwelling-place,
like shimmering heat in the sunshine,
    like a cloud of dew in the heat of
    harvest."
[5]For, before the harvest, when the blossom
    is gone
and the flower becomes a ripening
    grape,
he will cut off the shoots with pruning
    knives,
and cut down and take away the
    spreading branches.
[6]They will all be left to the mountain birds
    of prey
and to the wild animals;
the birds will feed on them all summer,
    the wild animals all winter.

[7]At that time gifts will be brought to the
LORD Almighty

from a people tall and smooth-skinned,
    from a people feared far and wide,
an aggressive nation of strange speech,
    whose land is divided by rivers—

the gifts will be brought to Mount Zion, the
    place of the Name of the LORD Almighty.

A Prophecy About Egypt

19 An oracle concerning Egypt:

See, the LORD rides on a swift cloud
    and is coming to Egypt.
The idols of Egypt tremble before him,
    and the hearts of the Egyptians melt
    within them.

[2]"I will stir up Egyptian against Egyptian—
    brother will fight against brother,
    neighbour against neighbour,
    city against city,
    kingdom against kingdom.
[3]The Egyptians will lose heart,
    and I will bring their plans to nothing;
they will consult the idols and the spirits of
    the dead,
    the mediums and the spiritists.
[4]I will hand the Egyptians over
    to the power of a cruel master,
and a fierce king will rule over them,"
    declares the Lord, the LORD Almighty.

[5]The waters of the river will dry up,
    and the river bed will be parched and
    dry.
[6]The canals will stink;
    the streams of Egypt will dwindle and
    dry up.
The reeds and rushes will wither,
[7] also the plants along the Nile,
    at the mouth of the river.
Every sown field along the Nile
    will become parched, will blow away
    and be no more.
[8]The fishermen will groan and lament,
    all who cast hooks into the Nile;
those who throw nets on the water
    will pine away.
[9]Those who work with combed flax will
    despair,
    the weavers of fine linen will lose hope.
[10]The workers in cloth will be dejected,
    and all the wage earners will be sick at
    heart.

[11]The officials of Zoan are nothing but
    fools;
    the wise counsellors of Pharaoh give
    senseless advice.
How can you say to Pharaoh,
    "I am one of the wise men,
    a disciple of the ancient kings"?

[12]Where are your wise men now?
    Let them show you and make known
what the LORD Almighty
    has planned against Egypt.
[13]The officials of Zoan have become fools,
    the leaders of Memphis[a] are deceived;
the cornerstones of her peoples
    have led Egypt astray.
[14]The LORD has poured into them
    a spirit of dizziness;

they make Egypt stagger in all that she
does,
as a drunkard staggers around in his
vomit.
¹⁵There is nothing Egypt can do—
head or tail, palm branch or reed.

¹⁶In that day the Egyptians will be like
women. They will shudder with fear at the
uplifted hand that the LORD Almighty raises
against them. ¹⁷And the land of Judah will
bring terror to the Egyptians; everyone to
whom Judah is mentioned will be terrified,
because of what the LORD Almighty is planning against them.

¹⁸In that day five cities in Egypt will speak
the language of Canaan and swear allegiance
to the LORD Almighty. One of them will be
called the City of Destruction.ᵇ

¹⁹In that day there will be an altar to the
LORD in the heart of Egypt, and a monument
to the LORD at its border. ²⁰It will be a sign
and witness to the LORD Almighty in the land
of Egypt. When they cry out to the LORD
because of their oppressors, he will send
them a saviour and defender, and he will
rescue them. ²¹So the LORD will make himself
known to the Egyptians, and in that day they
will acknowledge the LORD. They will
worship with sacrifices and grain offerings;
they will make vows to the LORD and keep
them. ²²The LORD will strike Egypt with a
plague; he will strike them and heal them.
They will turn to the LORD, and he will respond to their pleas and heal them.

²³In that day there will be a highway from
Egypt to Assyria. The Assyrians will go
to Egypt and the Egyptians to Assyria. The
Egyptians and Assyrians will worship together. ²⁴In that day Israel will be the third,
along with Egypt and Assyria, a blessing on
the earth. ²⁵The LORD Almighty will bless
them, saying, "Blessed be Egypt my people,
Assyria my handiwork, and Israel my
inheritance."

A Prophecy Against Egypt and Cush

20 In the year that the supreme commander, sent by Sargon king of Assyria,
came to Ashdod and attacked and captured
it— ²at that time the LORD spoke through
Isaiah son of Amoz. He said to him, "Take
off the sackcloth from your body and the
sandals from your feet." And he did so, going
around stripped and barefoot.

³Then the LORD said, "Just as my servant
Isaiah has gone stripped and barefoot for
three years, as a sign and portent against
Egypt and Cush,ᵃ ⁴so the king of Assyria will
lead away stripped and barefoot the Egyptian
captives and Cushite exiles, young and old,
with buttocks bared—to Egypt's shame.
⁵Those who trusted in Cush and boasted in
Egypt will be afraid and put to shame. ⁶In
that day the people who live on this coast will
say, 'See what has happened to those we
relied on, those we fled to for help and

deliverance from the king of Assyria! How
then can we escape?'"

A Prophecy Against Babylon

21 An oracle concerning the Desert by
the Sea:

Like whirlwinds sweeping through the
southland,
an invader comes from the desert,
from a land of terror.

²A dire vision has been shown to me:
The traitor betrays, the looter takes
loot.
Elam, attack! Media, lay siege!
I will bring to an end all the groaning she
caused.

³At this my body is racked with pain,
pangs seize me, like those of a woman in
labour;
I am staggered by what I hear,
I am bewildered by what I see.
⁴My heart falters,
fear makes me tremble;
the twilight I longed for
has become a horror to me.

⁵They set the tables,
they spread the rugs,
they eat, they drink!
Get up, you officers,
oil the shields!

⁶This is what the Lord says to me:

"Go, post a lookout
and have him report what he sees.
⁷When he sees chariots
with teams of horses,
riders on donkeys
or riders on camels,
let him be alert,
fully alert."

⁸And the lookoutᵃ shouted,

"Day after day, my lord, I stand on the
watchtower;
every night I stay at my post.
⁹Look, here comes a man in a chariot
with a team of horses.
And he gives back the answer:
'Babylon has fallen, has fallen!
All the images of its gods
lie shattered on the ground!'"

¹⁰O my people, crushed on the
threshing-floor,
I tell you what I have heard
from the LORD Almighty,
from the God of Israel.

A Prophecy Against Edom

¹¹An oracle concerning Dumah:ᵇ

Someone calls to me from Seir,
"Watchman, what is left of the night?
Watchman, what is left of the night?"

ᵇ18 Most manuscripts of the Masoretic Text; some manuscripts of the Masoretic Text, Dead Sea Scrolls and Vulgate
City of the Sun (that is, Heliopolis)   ᵃ3 That is, the upper Nile region; also in verse 5
ᵃ8 Dead Sea Scrolls and Syriac; Masoretic Text A lion
ᵇ11 Dumah means silence or stillness, a word play on Edom.

¹²The watchman replies,
"Morning is coming, but also the night.
If you would ask, then ask;
and come back yet again."

A Prophecy Against Arabia

¹³An oracle concerning Arabia:

You caravans of Dedanites,
who camp in the thickets of Arabia,
¹⁴ bring water for the thirsty;
you who live in Tema,
bring food for the fugitives.
¹⁵They flee from the sword,
from the drawn sword,
from the bent bow
and from the heat of battle.

¹⁶This is what the Lord says to me: "Within one year, as a servant bound by contract would count it, all the pomp of Kedar will come to an end. ¹⁷The survivors of the bowmen, the warriors of Kedar, will be few." The LORD, the God of Israel, has spoken.

A Prophecy About Jerusalem

22 An oracle concerning the Valley of Vision:

What troubles you now,
that you have all gone up on the roofs,
²O town full of commotion,
O city of tumult and revelry?
Your slain were not killed by the sword,
nor did they die in battle.
³All your leaders have fled together;
they have been captured without using
the bow.
All you who were caught were taken
prisoner together,
having fled while the enemy was still far
away.
⁴Therefore I said, "Turn away from me;
let me weep bitterly.
Do not try to console me
over the destruction of my people."

⁵The Lord, the LORD Almighty, has a day
of tumult and trampling and terror
in the Valley of Vision,
a day of battering down walls
and of crying out to the mountains.
⁶Elam takes up the quiver,
with her charioteers and horses;
Kir uncovers the shield.
⁷Your choicest valleys are full of chariots,
and horsemen are posted at the city
gates;
⁸ the defences of Judah are stripped
away.

And you looked in that day
to the weapons in the Palace of the
Forest;
⁹you saw that the City of David
had many breaches in its defences;
you stored up water
in the Lower Pool.

¹⁰You counted the buildings in Jerusalem
and tore down houses to strengthen the
wall.
¹¹You built a reservoir between the two
walls
for the water of the Old Pool,
but you did not look to the One who made
it,
or have regard for the One who planned
it long ago.

¹²The Lord, the LORD Almighty,
called you on that day
to weep and to wail,
to tear out your hair and put on
sackcloth.
¹³But see, there is joy and revelry,
slaughtering of cattle and killing of
sheep,
eating of meat and drinking of wine!
"Let us eat and drink," you say,
"for tomorrow we die!"

¹⁴The LORD Almighty has revealed this in my hearing: "Till your dying day this sin will not be atoned for," says the Lord, the LORD Almighty.

¹⁵This is what the Lord, the LORD Almighty, says:

"Go, say to this steward,
to Shebna, who is in charge of the
palace:
¹⁶What are you doing here and who gave
you permission
to cut out a grave for yourself here,
hewing your grave on the height
and chiselling your resting place in the
rock?

¹⁷"Beware, the LORD is about to take firm
hold of you
and hurl you away, O you mighty man.
¹⁸He will roll you up tightly like a ball
and throw you into a large country.
There you will die
and there your splendid chariots will
remain—
you disgrace to your master's house!
¹⁹I will depose you from your office,
and you will be ousted from your
position.

²⁰"In that day I will summon my servant, Eliakim son of Hilkiah. ²¹I will clothe him with your robe and fasten your sash around him and hand your authority over to him. He will be a father to those who live in Jerusalem and to the house of Judah. ²²I will place on his shoulder the key to the house of David; what he opens no-one can shut, and what he shuts no-one can open. ²³I will drive him like a peg into a firm place; he will be a seat*ᵃ* of honour for the house of his father. ²⁴All the glory of his family will hang on him: its offspring and offshoots—all its lesser vessels, from the bowls to all the jars.

ᵃ23 Or throne

²⁵"In that day," declares the LORD Almighty, "the peg driven into the firm place will give way; it will be sheared off and will fall, and the load hanging on it will be cut down." The LORD has spoken.

A Prophecy About Tyre

23 An oracle concerning Tyre:

Wail, O ships of Tarshish!
    For Tyre is destroyed
    and left without house or harbour.
From the land of Cyprus^a
    word has come to them.

²Be silent, you people of the island
    and you merchants of Sidon,
    whom the seafarers have enriched.
³On the great waters
    came the grain of the Shihor;
the harvest of the Nile^b was the revenue of
        Tyre,
    and she became the market-place of the
        nations.

⁴Be ashamed, O Sidon, and you, O fortress
        of the sea,
    for the sea has spoken:
"I have neither been in labour nor given
        birth;
    I have neither reared sons nor brought
        up daughters."
⁵When word comes to Egypt,
    they will be in anguish at the report from
        Tyre.

⁶Cross over to Tarshish;
    wail, you people of the island.
⁷Is this your city of revelry,
    the old, old city,
    whose feet have taken her
    to settle in far-off lands?
⁸Who planned this against Tyre,
    the bestower of crowns,
    whose merchants are princes,
    whose traders are renowned in the
        earth?
⁹The LORD Almighty planned it,
    to bring low the pride of all glory
    and to humble all who are renowned on
        the earth.

¹⁰Till^c your land as along the Nile,
    O Daughter of Tarshish,
    for you no longer have a harbour.
¹¹The LORD has stretched out his hand over
        the sea
    and made its kingdoms tremble.
He has given an order concerning
        Phoenicia^d
    that her fortresses be destroyed.
¹²He said, "No more of your revelling,
    O Virgin Daughter of Sidon, now
        crushed!

"Up, cross over to Cyprus;^e
    even there you will find no rest."

¹³Look at the land of the Babylonians,^f
    this people that is now of no account!
The Assyrians have made it
    a place for desert creatures;
    they raised up their siege towers,
    they stripped its fortresses bare
    and turned it into a ruin.

¹⁴Wail, you ships of Tarshish;
    your fortress is destroyed!

¹⁵At that time Tyre will be forgotten for
seventy years, the span of a king's life. But at
the end of these seventy years, it will happen
to Tyre as in the song of the prostitute:

¹⁶"Take up a harp, walk through the city,
    O prostitute forgotten;
play the harp well, sing many a song,
    so that you will be remembered."

¹⁷At the end of seventy years, the LORD
will deal with Tyre. She will return to her hire
as a prostitute and will ply her trade with all
the kingdoms on the face of the earth. ¹⁸Yet
her profit and her earnings will be set apart
for the LORD; they will not be stored up or
hoarded. Her profits will go to those who live
before the LORD, for abundant food and fine
clothes.

The LORD's Devastation of the Earth

24 See, the LORD is going to lay waste
    the earth
    and devastate it;
he will ruin its face
    and scatter its inhabitants—
²it will be the same
    for priests as for people,
    for master as for servant,
    for mistress as for maid,
    for seller as for buyer,
    for borrower as for lender,
    for debtor as for creditor.
³The earth will be completely laid waste
    and totally plundered.
                        The LORD has spoken
                                    this word.

⁴The earth dries up and withers,
    the world languishes and withers,
    the exalted of the earth languish.
⁵The earth is defiled by its people;
    they have disobeyed the laws,
violated the statutes
    and broken the everlasting covenant.
⁶Therefore a curse consumes the earth;
    its people must bear their guilt.
Therefore earth's inhabitants are burned
        up,
    and very few are left.
⁷The new wine dries up and the vine
        withers;
    all the merrymakers groan.
⁸The gaiety of the tambourines is stilled,
    the noise of the revellers has stopped,
    the joyful harp is silent.

^a1 Hebrew Kittim
^b2, 3 Masoretic Text; one Dead Sea Scroll Sidon, / who cross over the sea; / your envoys ³are on the great waters.
The grain of the Shihor, / the harvest of the Nile,
^c10 Dead Sea Scrolls and some Septuagint manuscripts; Masoretic Text Go through
^d11 Hebrew Canaan   ^e12 Hebrew Kittim   ^f13 Or Chaldeans

ISAIAH 25:1–8

'O LORD, you are my God; I will exalt you and praise your name, for in perfect faithfulness you have done marvellous things, things planned long ago' (v. 1).

FROM THE COLLECTION OF ORACLES OF JUDGEMENT against various nations, Isaiah moves into a song of praise which has been described as an Old Testament Magnificat. Isaiah's faith was essentially personal: 'O Lord, you are my God.' He could never escape from the reality of his initial encounter with God in the temple. He served a God who initiated action and who took human beings into partnership with himself. His God worked through historic events, and people not necessarily of the chosen race, to achieve his objectives. His God was determined to produce a people refined and holy, regardless of the cost. His was a God with a global view and global authority.

Only a 'remnant' of the people would pass through these refining processes successfully, but Isaiah was confident that the remnant was part of God's strategy. The determinedly sinful would be cast off. The future would belong to the remnant.

The song looks forward to the day when Jerusalem will be re-established and there will be feasting and great rejoicing. God will be enthroned in the hearts of his own people and also in the hearts of all people. In that glad day death and sorrow will be banished because death itself has been conquered.

Isaiah was strong in this time of national upheaval because his faith was firmly fixed in a living, personal God. He could praise and exalt God, because God had become a way of life to him.

> *O Lord, you are my God*
> *And I belong to you.*
> *Let me today exalt your name*
> *In everything I do. Amen.*

→588

ISAIAH 40:9–11

'He tends his flock like a shepherd: he gathers the lambs in his arms and carries them close to his heart; he gently leads those that have young' (v. 11).

IN A PASTORAL COUNTRY sooner or later the metaphor of the shepherd would be used of a caring God. 'The Lord is my shepherd' is a statement which strikes us by its gentle naturalness and relevance. Ezekiel, on behalf of God, takes the nation's carers to task for their lack of diligence and concern. He then adds more powerfully, 'For this is what the Sovereign Lord says: I myself will search for my sheep . . . I will rescue them . . . I will bring them . . . I will pasture them . . . I will shepherd the flock.' With complete congruity our Lord took the figure to himself and affirmed, 'I am the good shepherd.'

The use of the adjective 'good' is interesting. Westcott points out that it means not only 'good inwardly, but good as perceived. His goodness claims the admiration of all that is generous in man.' Temple follows this line and adds, 'He was "good" in such manner as to draw all men to himself.'

Our Lord further qualified his role by indicating that the good shepherd lays down his life for the sheep. No sacrifice is too great for the shepherd to make for the flock of God. He was soon to prove this statement most agonizingly.

A very special relationship is indicated between the sheep and the good shepherd. This good shepherd knows and is known by the sheep, in the same way that our Lord knows and is known by the Father. The more we know the Lord, the more like him we will become.

> *Thou shepherd Christ, who knowest well my way,*
> *Thy goodness now impart, to this my waiting heart*
> *That I thy given goodness might display.*

→609

⁹No longer do they drink wine with a song;
　　the beer is bitter to its drinkers.
¹⁰The ruined city lies desolate;
　　the entrance to every house is barred.
¹¹In the streets they cry out for wine;
　　all joy turns to gloom,
　　all gaiety is banished from the earth.
¹²The city is left in ruins,
　　its gate is battered to pieces.
¹³So will it be on the earth
　　and among the nations,
　as when an olive tree is beaten,
　　or as when gleanings are left after the
　　　grape harvest.

¹⁴They raise their voices, they shout for joy;
　　from the west they acclaim the LORD's
　　　majesty.
¹⁵Therefore in the east give glory to the
　　　LORD;
　　exalt the name of the LORD, the God of
　　　Israel,
　in the islands of the sea.
¹⁶From the ends of the earth we hear
　　　singing:
　　"Glory to the Righteous One."

But I said, "I waste away, I waste away!
　　Woe to me!
The treacherous betray!
　　With treachery the treacherous betray!"
¹⁷Terror and pit and snare await you,
　　O people of the earth.
¹⁸Whoever flees at the sound of terror
　　will fall into a pit;
whoever climbs out of the pit
　　will be caught in a snare.

The floodgates of the heavens are opened,
　　the foundations of the earth shake.
¹⁹The earth is broken up,
　　the earth is split asunder,
　　the earth is thoroughly shaken.
²⁰The earth reels like a drunkard,
　　it sways like a hut in the wind;
so heavy upon it is the guilt of its rebellion
　　that it falls—never to rise again.

²¹In that day the LORD will punish
　　the powers in the heavens above
　　and the kings on the earth below.
²²They will be herded together
　　like prisoners bound in a dungeon;
they will be shut up in prison
　　and be punished[a] after many days.
²³The moon will be abashed, the sun
　　　ashamed;
　for the LORD Almighty will reign
　on Mount Zion and in Jerusalem,
　　and before its elders, gloriously.

Praise to the LORD

25 O LORD, you are my God;
　　I will exalt you and praise your
　　　name,
for in perfect faithfulness
　　you have done marvellous things,
　　things planned long ago.

²You have made the city a heap of rubble,
　　the fortified town a ruin,
the foreigners' stronghold a city no more;
　　it will never be rebuilt.
³Therefore strong peoples will honour you;
　　cities of ruthless nations will revere you.
⁴You have been a refuge for the poor,
　　a refuge for the needy in his distress,
a shelter from the storm
　　and a shade from the heat.
For the breath of the ruthless
　　is like a storm driving against a wall
⁵　and like the heat of the desert.
You silence the uproar of foreigners;
　　as heat is reduced by the shadow of a
　　　cloud,
　so the song of the ruthless is stilled.

⁶On this mountain the LORD Almighty will
　　　prepare
　a feast of rich food for all peoples,
a banquet of aged wine—
　　the best of meats and the finest of wines.
⁷On this mountain he will destroy
　　the shroud that enfolds all peoples,
the sheet that covers all nations;
⁸　he will swallow up death for ever.
The Sovereign LORD will wipe away the
　　　tears
　from all faces;
he will remove the disgrace of his people
　from all the earth.
　　　　　　　　The LORD has spoken.

⁹In that day they will say,

"Surely this is our God;
　　we trusted in him, and he saved us.
This is the LORD, we trusted in him;
　　let us rejoice and be glad in his
　　　salvation."

¹⁰The hand of the LORD will rest on this
　　　mountain;
but Moab will be trampled under him
　　as straw is trampled down in the
　　　manure.
¹¹They will spread out their hands in it,
　　as a swimmer spreads out his hands to
　　　swim.
God will bring down their pride
　　despite the cleverness[a] of their hands.
¹²He will bring down your high fortified
　　　walls
　and lay them low;
he will bring them down to the ground,
　to the very dust.

A Song of Praise

26 In that day this song will be sung in
　　the land of Judah:

We have a strong city;
　　God makes salvation
　　its walls and ramparts.
²Open the gates
　　that the righteous nation may enter,
　　the nation that keeps faith.

---

a22 Or *released*　　*a11* The meaning of the Hebrew for this word is uncertain.

³You will keep in perfect peace
    him whose mind is steadfast,
    because he trusts in you.
⁴Trust in the LORD for ever,
    for the LORD, the LORD, is the Rock
        eternal.
⁵He humbles those who dwell on high,
    he lays the lofty city low;
he levels it to the ground
    and casts it down to the dust.
⁶Feet trample it down—
    the feet of the oppressed,
    the footsteps of the poor.

⁷The path of the righteous is level;
    O upright One, you make the way of the
        righteous smooth.
⁸Yes, LORD, walking in the way of your
        laws,ᵃ
    we wait for you;
your name and renown
    are the desire of our hearts.
⁹My soul yearns for you in the night;
    in the morning my spirit longs for you.
When your judgments come upon the
        earth,
    the people of the world learn
        righteousness.
¹⁰Though grace is shown to the wicked,
    they do not learn righteousness;
even in a land of uprightness they go on
        doing evil
    and regard not the majesty of the LORD.
¹¹O LORD, your hand is lifted high,
    but they do not see it.
Let them see your zeal for your people and
        be put to shame;
    let the fire reserved for your enemies
        consume them.

¹²LORD, you establish peace for us;
    all that we have accomplished you have
        done for us.
¹³O LORD, our God, other lords besides you
        have ruled over us,
    but your name alone do we honour.
¹⁴They are now dead, they live no more;
    those departed spirits do not rise.
You punished them and brought them to
        ruin;
    you wiped out all memory of them.
¹⁵You have enlarged the nation, O LORD;
    you have enlarged the nation.
You have gained glory for yourself;
    you have extended all the borders of the
        land.

¹⁶LORD, they came to you in their distress;
    when you disciplined them,
    they could barely whisper a prayer.ᵇ
¹⁷As a woman with child and about to give
        birth
    writhes and cries out in her pain,
    so were we in your presence, O LORD.
¹⁸We were with child, we writhed in pain,
    but we gave birth to wind.
We have not brought salvation to the
        earth;

we have not given birth to people of the
        world.

¹⁹But your dead will live;
    their bodies will rise.
You who dwell in the dust,
    wake up and shout for joy.
Your dew is like the dew of the morning;
    the earth will give birth to her dead.

²⁰Go, my people, enter your rooms
    and shut the doors behind you;
hide yourselves for a little while
    until his wrath has passed by.
²¹See, the LORD is coming out of his dwelling
    to punish the people of the earth for
        their sins.
The earth will disclose the blood shed
        upon her;
    she will conceal her slain no longer.

Deliverance of Israel

27 In that day,

the LORD will punish with his sword,
    his fierce, great and powerful sword,
Leviathan the gliding serpent,
    Leviathan the coiling serpent;
he will slay the monster of the sea.

²In that day—

"Sing about a fruitful vineyard:
³   I, the LORD, watch over it;
        I water it continually.
    I guard it day and night
        so that no-one may harm it.
⁴   I am not angry.
    If only there were briers and thorns
            confronting me!
        I would march against them in battle;
        I would set them all on fire.
⁵Or else let them come to me for refuge;
    let them make peace with me,
    yes, let them make peace with me."

⁶In days to come Jacob will take root,
    Israel will bud and blossom
    and fill all the world with fruit.

⁷Has ⌊the LORD⌋ struck her
    as he struck down those who struck
        her?
Has she been killed
    as those were killed who killed her?
⁸By warfareᵃ and exile you contend with
        her—
    with his fierce blast he drives her out,
    as on a day the east wind blows.
⁹By this, then, will Jacob's guilt be atoned
        for,
    and this will be the full fruitage of the
        removal of his sin:
When he makes all the altar stones
    to be like chalk stones crushed to
        pieces,
no Asherah polesᵇ or incense altars
    will be left standing.

ᵃ8 Or judgments   ᵇ16 The meaning of the Hebrew for this clause is uncertain.
ᵃ8 See Septuagint; the meaning of the Hebrew for this word is uncertain.
ᵇ9 That is, symbols of the goddess Asherah

¹⁰The fortified city stands desolate,
  an abandoned settlement, forsaken like
    the desert;
there the calves graze,
  there they lie down;
  they strip its branches bare.
¹¹When its twigs are dry, they are broken off
  and women come and make fires with
    them.
For this is a people without understanding;
  so their Maker has no compassion on
    them,
  and their Creator shows them no favour.

¹²In that day the LORD will thresh from the
flowing Euphrates*c* to the Wadi of Egypt, and
you, O Israelites, will be gathered up one by
one. ¹³And in that day a great trumpet will
sound. Those who were perishing in Assyria
and those who were exiled in Egypt will
come and worship the LORD on the holy
mountain in Jerusalem.

Woe to Ephraim

28 Woe to that wreath, the pride of
    Ephraim's drunkards,
  to the fading flower, his glorious beauty,
set on the head of a fertile valley—
  to that city, the pride of those laid low
    by wine!
²See, the Lord has one who is powerful and
    strong.
  Like a hailstorm and a destructive wind,
like a driving rain and a flooding
    downpour,
  he will throw it forcefully to the ground.
³That wreath, the pride of Ephraim's
    drunkards,
  will be trampled underfoot.
⁴That fading flower, his glorious beauty,
  set on the head of a fertile valley,
will be like a fig ripe before harvest—
  as soon as someone sees it and takes it
    in his hand,
  he swallows it.

⁵In that day the LORD Almighty
  will be a glorious crown,
a beautiful wreath
  for the remnant of his people.
⁶He will be a spirit of justice
  to him who sits in judgment,
a source of strength
  to those who turn back the battle at the
    gate.

⁷And these also stagger from wine
  and reel from beer:
Priests and prophets stagger from beer
  and are befuddled with wine;
they reel from beer,
  they stagger when seeing visions,
  they stumble when rendering decisions.
⁸All the tables are covered with vomit
  and there is not a spot without filth.

⁹"Who is it he is trying to teach?
  To whom is he explaining his message?

To children weaned from their milk,
  to those just taken from the breast?
¹⁰For it is:
  Do and do, do and do,
  rule on rule, rule on rule;*a*
  a little here, a little there.''

¹¹Very well then, with foreign lips and
    strange tongues
  God will speak to this people,
¹²to whom he said,
  "This is the resting-place, let the weary
    rest'';
and, "This is the place of repose''—
  but they would not listen.
¹³So then, the word of the LORD to them will
    become:
  Do and do, do and do,
  rule on rule, rule on rule;
  a little here, a little there—
so that they will go and fall backwards,
  be injured and snared and captured.

¹⁴Therefore hear the word of the LORD, you
    scoffers
  who rule this people in Jerusalem.
¹⁵You boast, "We have entered into a
    covenant with death,
  with the grave*b* we have made an
    agreement.
When an overwhelming scourge sweeps
    by,
  it cannot touch us,
for we have made a lie our refuge
  and falsehood*c* our hiding-place.''

¹⁶So this is what the Sovereign LORD says:

"See, I lay a stone in Zion,
  a tested stone,
a precious cornerstone for a sure
    foundation;
  the one who trusts will never be
    dismayed.
¹⁷I will make justice the measuring line
  and righteousness the plumb-line;
hail will sweep away your refuge, the lie,
  and water will overflow your
    hiding-place.
¹⁸Your covenant with death will be
    annulled;
  your agreement with the grave will not
    stand.
When the overwhelming scourge sweeps
    by,
  you will be beaten down by it.
¹⁹As often as it comes it will carry you away;
  morning after morning, by day and by
    night,
  it will sweep through.''

The understanding of this message
  will bring sheer terror.
²⁰The bed is too short to stretch out on,
  the blanket too narrow to wrap around
    you.
²¹The LORD will rise up as he did at Mount
    Perazim,

---

c12 Hebrew *River*
a10 Hebrew / *sav lasav sav lasav* / *kav lakav kav lakav* (possibly meaningless sounds; perhaps a mimicking of the
prophet's words); also in verse 13   *b15* Hebrew *Sheol*; also in verse 18   *c15* Or *false gods*

he will rouse himself as in the Valley of
 Gibeon—
to do his work, his strange work,
 and perform his task, his alien task.
22Now stop your mocking,
 or your chains will become heavier;
the Lord, the LORD Almighty, has told me
 of the destruction decreed against the
 whole land.

23Listen and hear my voice;
 pay attention and hear what I say.
24When a farmer ploughs for planting, does
 he plough continually?
Does he keep on breaking up and
 harrowing the soil?
25When he has levelled the surface,
 does he not sow caraway and scatter
 cummin?
Does he not plant wheat in its place,*d*
 barley in its plot,*d*
 and spelt in its field?
26His God instructs him
 and teaches him the right way.

27Caraway is not threshed with a sledge,
 nor is a cartwheel rolled over cummin;
caraway is beaten out with a rod,
 and cummin with a stick.
28Grain must be ground to make bread;
 so one does not go on threshing it for
 ever.
Though he drives the wheels of his
 threshing-cart over it,
 his horses do not grind it.
29All this also comes from the LORD
 Almighty,
 wonderful in counsel and magnificent in
 wisdom.

Woe to David's City

29 Woe to you, Ariel, Ariel,
 the city where David settled!
Add year to year
 and let your cycle of festivals go on.
2Yet I will besiege Ariel;
 she will mourn and lament,
 she will be to me like an altar hearth.*a*
3I will encamp against you all around;
 I will encircle you with towers
 and set up my siege works against you.
4Brought low, you will speak from the
 ground;
 your speech will mumble out of the
 dust.
Your voice will come ghostlike from the
 earth;
 out of the dust your speech will whisper.

5But your many enemies will become like
 fine dust,
 the ruthless hordes like blown chaff.
Suddenly, in an instant,
6   the LORD Almighty will come
with thunder and earthquake and great
 noise,
 with windstorm and tempest and flames
 of a devouring fire.

7Then the hordes of all the nations that fight
 against Ariel,
 that attack her and her fortress and
 besiege her,
will be as it is with a dream,
 with a vision in the night—
8as when a hungry man dreams that he is
 eating,
 but he awakens, and his hunger
 remains;
as when a thirsty man dreams that he is
 drinking,
 but he awakens faint, with his thirst
 unquenched.
So will it be with the hordes of all the
 nations
 that fight against Mount Zion.

9Be stunned and amazed,
 blind yourselves and be sightless;
be drunk, but not from wine,
 stagger, but not from beer.
10The LORD has brought over you a deep
 sleep:
 He has sealed your eyes (the prophets);
 he has covered your heads (the seers).

11For you this whole vision is nothing but
words sealed in a scroll. And if you give the
scroll to someone who can read, and say to
him, "Read this, please," he will answer, "I
can't; it is sealed." 12Or if you give the scroll
to someone who cannot read, and say,
"Read this, please," he will answer, "I don't
know how to read."

13The Lord says:

"These people come near to me with their
 mouth
 and honour me with their lips,
 but their hearts are far from me.
Their worship of me
 is made up only of rules taught by men.*b*
14Therefore once more I will astound these
 people
 with wonder upon wonder;
the wisdom of the wise will perish,
 the intelligence of the intelligent will
 vanish."
15Woe to those who go to great depths
 to hide their plans from the LORD,
who do their work in darkness and think,
 "Who sees us? Who will know?"
16You turn things upside down,
 as if the potter were thought to be like
 the clay!
Shall what is formed say to him who
 formed it,
 "He did not make me"?
Can the pot say of the potter,
 "He knows nothing"?

17In a very short time, will not Lebanon be
 turned into a fertile field
 and the fertile field seem like a forest?
18In that day the deaf will hear the words of
 the scroll,

d25 The meaning of the Hebrew for this word is uncertain.
a2 The Hebrew for altar hearth sounds like the Hebrew for Ariel.
b13 Hebrew; Septuagint They worship me in vain; / their teachings are but rules taught by men.

and out of gloom and darkness
the eyes of the blind will see.
¹⁹Once more the humble will rejoice in the
LORD;
the needy will rejoice in the Holy One of
Israel.
²⁰The ruthless will vanish,
the mockers will disappear,
and all who have an eye for evil will be
cut down—
²¹those who with a word make a man out to
be guilty,
who ensnare the defender in court
and with false testimony deprive the
innocent of justice.

²²Therefore this is what the LORD, who
redeemed Abraham, says to the house of
Jacob:

"No longer will Jacob be ashamed;
no longer will their faces grow pale.
²³When they see among them their children,
the work of my hands,
they will keep my name holy;
they will acknowledge the holiness of
the Holy One of Jacob,
and will stand in awe of the God of
Israel.
²⁴Those who are wayward in spirit will gain
understanding;
those who complain will accept
instruction."

Woe to the Obstinate Nation

30 "Woe to the obstinate children,"
declares the LORD,
"to those who carry out plans that are not
mine,
forming an alliance, but not by my Spirit,
heaping sin upon sin;
²who go down to Egypt
without consulting me;
who look for help to Pharaoh's protection,
to Egypt's shade for refuge.
³But Pharaoh's protection will be to your
shame,
Egypt's shade will bring you disgrace.
⁴Though they have officials in Zoan
and their envoys have arrived in Hanes,
⁵everyone will be put to shame
because of a people useless to them,
who bring neither help nor advantage,
but only shame and disgrace."

⁶An oracle concerning the animals of the
Negev:

Through a land of hardship and distress,
of lions and lionesses,
of adders and darting snakes,
the envoys carry their riches on donkeys'
backs,
their treasures on the humps of camels,
to that unprofitable nation,
⁷ to Egypt, whose help is utterly useless.
Therefore I call her
Rahab the Do-Nothing.

⁸Go now, write it on a tablet for them,
inscribe it on a scroll,

that for the days to come
it may be an everlasting witness.
⁹These are rebellious people, deceitful
children,
children unwilling to listen to the LORD's
instruction.
¹⁰They say to the seers,
"See no more visions!"
and to the prophets,
"Give us no more visions of what is
right!
Tell us pleasant things,
prophesy illusions.
¹¹Leave this way,
get off this path,
and stop confronting us
with the Holy One of Israel!"

¹²Therefore, this is what the Holy One of
Israel says:

"Because you have rejected this message,
relied on oppression
and depended on deceit,
¹³this sin will become for you
like a high wall, cracked and bulging,
that collapses suddenly, in an instant.
¹⁴It will break in pieces like pottery,
shattered so mercilessly
that among its pieces not a fragment will
be found
for taking coals from a hearth
or scooping water out of a cistern."

¹⁵This is what the Sovereign LORD, the
Holy One of Israel, says:

"In repentance and rest is your salvation,
in quietness and trust is your strength,
but you would have none of it.
¹⁶You said, 'No, we will flee on horses.'
Therefore you will flee!
You said, 'We will ride off on swift
horses.'
Therefore your pursuers will be swift!
¹⁷A thousand will flee
at the threat of one;
at the threat of five
you will all flee away,
till you are left
like a flagstaff on a mountaintop,
like a banner on a hill."

¹⁸Yet the LORD longs to be gracious to you;
he rises to show you compassion.
For the LORD is a God of justice.
Blessed are all who wait for him!

¹⁹O people of Zion, who live in Jerusalem,
you will weep no more. How gracious he will
be when you cry for help! As soon as he
hears, he will answer you. ²⁰Although the
Lord gives you the bread of adversity and
the water of affliction, your teachers will be
hidden no more; with your own eyes you will
see them. ²¹Whether you turn to the right or
to the left, your ears will hear a voice behind
you, saying, "This is the way; walk in it."
²²Then you will defile your idols overlaid
with silver and your images covered with
gold; you will throw them away like a

menstrual cloth and say to them, ''Away with you!''

23He will also send you rain for the seed you sow in the ground, and the food that comes from the land will be rich and plentiful. In that day your cattle will graze in broad meadows. 24The oxen and donkeys that work the soil will eat fodder and mash, spread out with fork and shovel. 25In the day of great slaughter, when the towers fall, streams of water will flow on every high mountain and every lofty hill. 26The moon will shine like the sun, and the sunlight will be seven times brighter, like the light of seven full days, when the LORD binds up the bruises of his people and heals the wounds he inflicted.

27See, the Name of the LORD comes from
        afar,
    with burning anger and dense clouds of
        smoke;
his lips are full of wrath,
    and his tongue is a consuming fire.
28His breath is like a rushing torrent,
    rising up to the neck.
He shakes the nations in the sieve of
        destruction;
    he places in the jaws of the peoples
    a bit that leads them astray.
29And you will sing
    as on the night you celebrate a holy
        festival;
your hearts will rejoice
    as when people go up with flutes
to the mountain of the LORD,
    to the Rock of Israel.
30The LORD will cause men to hear his
        majestic voice
    and will make them see his arm coming
        down
with raging anger and consuming fire,
    with cloudburst, thunderstorm and hail.
31The voice of the LORD will shatter Assyria;
    with his sceptre he will strike them
        down.
32Every stroke the LORD lays on them
        with his punishing rod
will be to the music of tambourines and
        harps,
    as he fights them in battle with the blows
        of his arm.
33Topheth has long been prepared;
    it has been made ready for the king.
Its fire pit has been made deep and wide,
    with an abundance of fire and wood;
the breath of the LORD,
    like a stream of burning sulphur,
    sets it ablaze.

Woe to Those Who Rely on Egypt

31 Woe to those who go down to Egypt
        for help,
    who rely on horses,
who trust in the multitude of their chariots
    and in the great strength of their
        horsemen,
but do not look to the Holy One of Israel,
    or seek help from the LORD.
2Yet he too is wise and can bring disaster;
    he does not take back his words.
He will rise up against the house of the
        wicked,
    against those who help evildoers.
3But the Egyptians are men and not God;
    their horses are flesh and not spirit.
When the LORD stretches out his hand,
    he who helps will stumble,
    he who is helped will fall;
    both will perish together.

4This is what the LORD says to me:

''As a lion growls,
    a great lion over his prey—
and though a whole band of shepherds
    is called together against him,
he is not frightened by their shouts
    or disturbed by their clamour—
so the LORD Almighty will come down
    to do battle on Mount Zion and on its
        heights.
5Like birds hovering overhead,
    the LORD Almighty will shield
        Jerusalem;
he will shield it and deliver it,
    he will 'pass over' it and will rescue it.''

6Return to him you have so greatly revolted against, O Israelites. 7For in that day every one of you will reject the idols of silver and gold your sinful hands have made.

8''Assyria will fall by a sword that is not of
        man;
    a sword, not of mortals, will devour
        them.
They will flee before the sword
    and their young men will be put to
        forced labour.
9Their stronghold will fall because of
        terror;
    at sight of the battle standard their
        commanders will panic,''
declares the LORD,
    whose fire is in Zion,
    whose furnace is in Jerusalem.

The Kingdom of Righteousness

32 See, a king will reign in
        righteousness
    and rulers will rule with justice.
2Each man will be like a shelter from the
        wind
    and a refuge from the storm,
like streams of water in the desert
    and the shadow of a great rock in a
        thirsty land.

3Then the eyes of those who see will no
        longer be closed,
    and the ears of those who hear will
        listen.
4The mind of the rash will know and
        understand,
    and the stammering tongue will be fluent
        and clear.
5No longer will the fool be called noble
    nor the scoundrel be highly respected.
6For the fool speaks folly,
    his mind is busy with evil:

He practises ungodliness
and spreads error concerning the LORD;
the hungry he leaves empty
and from the thirsty he withholds water.
[7]The scoundrel's methods are wicked,
he makes up evil schemes
to destroy the poor with lies,
even when the plea of the needy is just.
[8]But the noble man makes noble plans,
and by noble deeds he stands.

The Women of Jerusalem

[9]You women who are so complacent,
rise up and listen to me;
you daughters who feel secure,
hear what I have to say!
[10]In little more than a year
you who feel secure will tremble;
the grape harvest will fail,
and the harvest of fruit will not come.
[11]Tremble, you complacent women;
shudder, you daughters who feel secure!
Strip off your clothes,
put sackcloth round your waists.
[12]Beat your breasts for the pleasant fields,
for the fruitful vines
[13]and for the land of my people,
a land overgrown with thorns and
briers—
yes, mourn for all houses of merriment
and for this city of revelry.
[14]The fortress will be abandoned,
the noisy city deserted;
citadel and watchtower will become a
wasteland for ever,
the delight of donkeys, a pasture for
flocks,
[15]till the Spirit is poured upon us from on
high,
and the desert becomes a fertile field,
and the fertile field seems like a forest.
[16]Justice will dwell in the desert
and righteousness live in the fertile field.
[17]The fruit of righteousness will be peace;
the effect of righteousness will be
quietness and confidence for ever.
[18]My people will live in peaceful
dwelling-places,
in secure homes,
in undisturbed places of rest.
[19]Though hail flattens the forest
and the city is levelled completely,
[20]how blessed you will be,
sowing your seed by every stream,
and letting your cattle and donkeys
range free.

Distress and Help

33 Woe to you, O destroyer,
you who have not been destroyed!
Woe to you, O traitor,
you who have not been betrayed!
When you stop destroying,
you will be destroyed;
when you stop betraying,
you will be betrayed.

[2]O LORD, be gracious to us;
we long for you.

Be our strength every morning,
our salvation in time of distress.
[3]At the thunder of your voice, the peoples
flee;
when you rise up, the nations scatter.
[4]Your plunder, O nations, is harvested as
by young locusts;
like a swarm of locusts men pounce
on it.

[5]The LORD is exalted, for he dwells on
high;
he will fill Zion with justice and
righteousness.
[6]He will be the sure foundation for your
times,
a rich store of salvation and wisdom and
knowledge;
the fear of the LORD is the key to this
treasure.[a]

[7]Look, their brave men cry aloud in the
streets;
the envoys of peace weep bitterly.
[8]The highways are deserted,
no travellers are on the roads.
The treaty is broken,
its witnesses[b] are despised,
no-one is respected.
[9]The land mourns[c] and wastes away,
Lebanon is ashamed and withers;
Sharon is like the Arabah,
and Bashan and Carmel drop their
leaves.

[10]"Now will I arise," says the LORD.
"Now will I be exalted;
now will I be lifted up.
[11]You conceive chaff,
you give birth to straw;
your breath is a fire that consumes you.
[12]The peoples will be burned as if to lime;
like cut thornbushes they will be set
ablaze."

[13]You who are far away, hear what I have
done;
you who are near, acknowledge my
power!
[14]The sinners in Zion are terrified;
trembling grips the godless:
"Who of us can dwell with the consuming
fire?
Who of us can dwell with everlasting
burning?"
[15]He who walks righteously
and speaks what is right,
who rejects gain from extortion
and keeps his hand from accepting
bribes,
who stops his ears against plots of murder
and shuts his eyes against contemplating
evil—
[16]this is the man who will dwell on the
heights,
whose refuge will be the mountain
fortress.
His bread will be supplied,
and water will not fail him.

---

[a]6 Or is a treasure from him   [b]8 Dead Sea Scrolls; Masoretic Text / the cities   [c]9 Or dries up

17Your eyes will see the king in his beauty
  and view a land that stretches afar.
18In your thoughts you will ponder the
    former terror:
  ''Where is that chief officer?
  Where is the one who took the revenue?
  Where is the officer in charge of the
    towers?''
19You will see those arrogant people no
    more,
  those people of an obscure speech,
  with their strange, incomprehensible
    tongue.

20Look upon Zion, the city of our festivals;
  your eyes will see Jerusalem,
  a peaceful abode, a tent that will not be
    moved;
 its stakes will never be pulled up,
  nor any of its ropes broken.
21There the LORD will be our Mighty One.
  It will be like a place of broad rivers and
    streams.
 No galley with oars will ride them,
  no mighty ship will sail them.
22For the LORD is our judge,
  the LORD is our lawgiver,
 the LORD is our king;
  it is he who will save us.

23Your rigging hangs loose:
  The mast is not held secure,
  the sail is not spread.
 Then an abundance of spoils will be
    divided
  and even the lame will carry off plunder.
24No-one living in Zion will say, ''I am ill'';
  and the sins of those who dwell there
    will be forgiven.

Judgment Against the Nations

34 Come near, you nations, and listen;
     pay attention, you peoples!
 Let the earth hear, and all that is in it,
  the world, and all that comes out of it!
2The LORD is angry with all nations;
  his wrath is upon all their armies.
 He will totally destroy[a] them,
  he will give them over to slaughter.
3Their slain will be thrown out,
  their dead bodies will send up a stench;
  the mountains will be soaked with their
    blood.
4All the stars of the heavens will be
    dissolved
  and the sky rolled up like a scroll;
 all the starry host will fall
  like withered leaves from the vine,
  like shrivelled figs from the fig-tree.

5My sword has drunk its fill in the heavens;
  see, it descends in judgment on Edom,
  the people I have totally destroyed.
6The sword of the LORD is bathed in blood,
  it is covered with fat—
 the blood of lambs and goats,
  fat from the kidneys of rams.
 For the LORD has a sacrifice in Bozrah
  and a great slaughter in Edom.

7And the wild oxen will fall with them,
  the bull calves and the great bulls.
 Their land will be drenched with blood,
  and the dust will be soaked with fat.

8For the LORD has a day of vengeance,
  a year of retribution, to uphold Zion's
    cause.
9Edom's streams will be turned into pitch,
  her dust into burning sulphur;
  her land will become blazing pitch!
10It will not be quenched night and day;
  its smoke will rise for ever.
 From generation to generation it will lie
    desolate;
  no-one will ever pass through it again.
11The desert owl[b] and screech owl[b] will
    possess it;
  the great owl[b] and the raven will nest
    there.
 God will stretch out over Edom
  the measuring line of chaos
  and the plumb-line of desolation.
12Her nobles will have nothing there to be
    called a kingdom,
  all her princes will vanish away.
13Thorns will overrun her citadels,
  nettles and brambles her strongholds.
 She will become a haunt for jackals,
  a home for owls.
14Desert creatures will meet with hyenas,
  and wild goats will bleat to each other;
  there the night creatures will also repose
  and find for themselves places of rest.
15The owl will nest there and lay eggs,
  she will hatch them, and care for her
    young under the shadow of her
    wings;
  there also the falcons will gather,
  each with its mate.

16Look in the scroll of the LORD and read:

 None of these will be missing,
  not one will lack her mate.
 For it is his mouth that has given the order,
  and his Spirit will gather them together.
17He allots their portions;
  his hand distributes them by measure.
 They will possess it for ever
  and dwell there from generation to
    generation.

Joy of the Redeemed

35 The desert and the parched land will
     be glad;
  the wilderness will rejoice and blossom.
 Like the crocus, 2it will burst into bloom;
  it will rejoice greatly and shout for joy.
 The glory of Lebanon will be given to it,
  the splendour of Carmel and Sharon;
 they will see the glory of the LORD,
  the splendour of our God.

3Strengthen the feeble hands,
  steady the knees that give way;
4say to those with fearful hearts,
  ''Be strong, do not fear;

---

[a]2 The Hebrew term refers to the irrevocable giving over of things or persons to the LORD, often by totally destroying them; also in verse 5.   [b]11 The precise identification of these birds is uncertain.

your God will come,
    he will come with vengeance;
with divine retribution
    he will come to save you.''

5Then will the eyes of the blind be opened
    and the ears of the deaf unstopped.
6Then will the lame leap like a deer,
    and the mute tongue shout for joy.
Water will gush forth in the wilderness
    and streams in the desert.
7The burning sand will become a pool,
    the thirsty ground bubbling springs.
In the haunts where jackals once lay,
    grass and reeds and papyrus will grow.

8And a highway will be there;
    it will be called the Way of Holiness.
The unclean will not journey on it;
    it will be for those who walk in that
    Way;
    wicked fools will not go about on it.a
9No lion will be there,
    nor will any ferocious beast get up on it;
    they will not be found there.
But only the redeemed will walk there,
10   and the ransomed of the LORD will
    return.
They will enter Zion with singing;
    everlasting joy will crown their heads.
Gladness and joy will overtake them,
    and sorrow and sighing will flee away.

Sennacherib Threatens Jerusalem

36 In the fourteenth year of King Hezekiah's reign, Sennacherib king of Assyria attacked all the fortified cities of Judah and captured them. 2Then the king of Assyria sent his field commander with a large army from Lachish to King Hezekiah at Jerusalem. When the commander stopped at the aqueduct of the Upper Pool, on the road to the Washerman's Field, 3Eliakim son of Hilkiah the palace administrator, Shebna the secretary, and Joah son of Asaph the recorder went out to him.

4The field commander said to them, "Tell Hezekiah,

" 'This is what the great king, the king of Assyria, says: On what are you basing this confidence of yours? 5You say you have strategy and military strength—but you speak only empty words. On whom are you depending, that you rebel against me? 6Look now, you are depending on Egypt, that splintered reed of a staff, which pierces a man's hand and wounds him if he leans on it! Such is Pharaoh king of Egypt to all who depend on him. 7And if you say to me, "We are depending on the LORD our God"—isn't he the one whose high places and altars Hezekiah removed, saying to Judah and Jerusalem, "You must worship before this altar"?

8" 'Come now, make a bargain with my master, the king of Assyria: I will give you two thousand horses—if you can put riders on them! 9How then can you repulse one officer of the least of my master's officials, even though you are depending on Egypt for chariots and horsemen? 10Furthermore, have I come to attack and destroy this land without the LORD? The LORD himself told me to march against this country and destroy it.' "

11Then Eliakim, Shebna and Joah said to the field commander, "Please speak to your servants in Aramaic, since we understand it. Don't speak to us in Hebrew in the hearing of the people on the wall."

12But the commander replied, "Was it only to your master and you that my master sent me to say these things, and not to the men sitting on the wall—who, like you, will have to eat their own filth and drink their own urine?"

13Then the commander stood and called out in Hebrew, "Hear the words of the great king, the king of Assyria! 14This is what the king says: Do not let Hezekiah deceive you. He cannot deliver you! 15Do not let Hezekiah persuade you to trust in the LORD when he says, 'The LORD will surely deliver us; this city will not be given into the hand of the king of Assyria.'

16"Do not listen to Hezekiah. This is what the king of Assyria says: Make peace with me and come out to me. Then every one of you will eat from his own vine and fig-tree and drink water from his own cistern, 17until I come and take you to a land like your own—a land of corn and new wine, a land of bread and vineyards.

18"Do not let Hezekiah mislead you when he says, 'The LORD will deliver us.' Has the god of any nation ever delivered his land from the hand of the king of Assyria? 19Where are the gods of Hamath and Arpad? Where are the gods of Sepharvaim? Have they rescued Samaria from my hand? 20Who of all the gods of these countries has been able to save his land from me? How then can the LORD deliver Jerusalem from my hand?"

21But the people remained silent and said nothing in reply, because the king had commanded, "Do not answer him."

22Then Eliakim son of Hilkiah the palace administrator, Shebna the secretary, and Joah son of Asaph the recorder went to Hezekiah, with their clothes torn, and told him what the field commander had said.

Jerusalem's Deliverance Foretold

37 When King Hezekiah heard this, he tore his clothes and put on sackcloth and went into the temple of the LORD. 2He sent Eliakim the palace administrator, Shebna the secretary, and the leading priests, all wearing sackcloth, to the prophet Isaiah son of Amoz. 3They told him, "This is what Hezekiah says: This day is a day of distress and rebuke and disgrace, as when children come to the point of birth and there is no strength to deliver them. 4It may be that

a8 Or / the simple will not stray from it

the LORD your God will hear the words of the field commander, whom his master, the king of Assyria, has sent to ridicule the living God, and that he will rebuke him for the words the LORD your God has heard. Therefore pray for the remnant that still survives.''

5When King Hezekiah's officials came to Isaiah, 6Isaiah said to them, ''Tell your master, 'This is what the LORD says: Do not be afraid of what you have heard—those words with which the underlings of the king of Assyria have blasphemed me. 7Listen! I am going to put a spirit in him so that when he hears a certain report, he will return to his own country, and there I will have him cut down with the sword.'''

8When the field commander heard that the king of Assyria had left Lachish, he withdrew and found the king fighting against Libnah.

9Now Sennacherib received a report that Tirhakah, the Cushite*a* king ,of Egypt ,, was marching out to fight against him. When he heard it, he sent messengers to Hezekiah with this word: 10''Say to Hezekiah king of Judah: Do not let the god you depend on deceive you when he says, 'Jerusalem will not be handed over to the king of Assyria.' 11Surely you have heard what the kings of Assyria have done to all the countries, destroying them completely. And will you be delivered? 12Did the gods of the nations that were destroyed by my forefathers deliver them—the gods of Gozan, Haran, Rezeph and the people of Eden who were in Tel Assar? 13Where is the king of Hamath, the king of Arpad, the king of the city of Sepharvaim, or of Hena or Ivvah?''

Hezekiah's Prayer

14Hezekiah received the letter from the messengers and read it. Then he went up to the temple of the LORD and spread it out before the LORD. 15And Hezekiah prayed to the LORD: 16''O LORD Almighty, God of Israel, enthroned between the cherubim, you alone are God over all the kingdoms of the earth. You have made heaven and earth. 17Give ear, O LORD, and hear; open your eyes, O LORD, and see; listen to all the words Sennacherib has sent to insult the living God.

18''It is true, O LORD, that the Assyrian kings have laid waste all these peoples and their lands. 19They have thrown their gods into the fire and destroyed them, for they were not gods but only wood and stone, fashioned by human hands. 20Now, O LORD our God, deliver us from his hand, so that all kingdoms on earth may know that you alone, O LORD, are God.''*b*

Sennacherib's Fall

21Then Isaiah son of Amoz sent a message to Hezekiah: ''This is what the LORD, the God of Israel, says: Because you have prayed to me concerning Sennacherib king of Assyria, 22this is the word the LORD has spoken against him:

''The Virgin Daughter of Zion
    despises and mocks you.
The Daughter of Jerusalem
    tosses her head as you flee.
23Who is it you have insulted and
        blasphemed?
    Against whom have you raised your
        voice
and lifted your eyes in pride?
    Against the Holy One of Israel!
24By your messengers
    you have heaped insults on the Lord.
And you have said,
    'With my many chariots
I have ascended the heights of the
        mountains,
    the utmost heights of Lebanon.
I have cut down its tallest cedars,
    the choicest of its pines.
I have reached its remotest heights,
    the finest of its forests.
25I have dug wells in foreign lands*c*
    and drunk the water there.
With the soles of my feet
    I have dried up all the streams of Egypt.'

26''Have you not heard?
    Long ago I ordained it.
In days of old I planned it;
    now I have brought it to pass,
that you have turned fortified cities
    into piles of stone.
27Their people, drained of power,
    are dismayed and put to shame.
They are like plants in the field,
    like tender green shoots,
like grass sprouting on the roof,
    scorched*d* before it grows up.

28''But I know where you stay
    and when you come and go
    and how you rage against me.
29Because you rage against me
    and because your insolence has reached
        my ears,
I will put my hook in your nose
    and my bit in your mouth,
and I will make you return
    by the way you came.

30''This will be the sign for you, O Hezekiah:

''This year you will eat what grows by
        itself,
    and the second year what springs from
        that.
But in the third year sow and reap,
    plant vineyards and eat their fruit.
31Once more a remnant of the house of
        Judah
    will take root below and bear fruit
        above.

---

*a*9 That is, from the upper Nile region
*b*20 Dead Sea Scrolls (see also 2 Kings 19:19); Masoretic Text *alone are the LORD*
*c*25 Dead Sea Scrolls (see also 2 Kings 19:24); Masoretic Text does not have *in foreign lands.*
*d*27 Some manuscripts of the Masoretic Text, Dead Sea Scrolls and some Septuagint manuscripts (see also 2 Kings 19:26); most manuscripts of the Masoretic Text *roof / and terraced fields*

32For out of Jerusalem will come a remnant,
  and out of Mount Zion a band of
    survivors.
The zeal of the LORD Almighty
  will accomplish this.

33"Therefore this is what the LORD says concerning the king of Assyria:

"He will not enter this city
  or shoot an arrow here.
He will not come before it with shield
  or build a siege ramp against it.
34By the way that he came he will return;
  he will not enter this city,"
                  declares the LORD.
35"I will defend this city and save it,
  for my sake and for the sake of David
    my servant!"

36Then the angel of the LORD went out and put to death a hundred and eighty-five thousand men in the Assyrian camp. When the people got up the next morning—there were all the dead bodies! 37So Sennacherib king of Assyria broke camp and withdrew. He returned to Nineveh and stayed there.

38One day, while he was worshipping in the temple of his god Nisroch, his sons Adrammelech and Sharezer cut him down with the sword, and they escaped to the land of Ararat. And Esarhaddon his son succeeded him as king.

Hezekiah's Illness

38 In those days Hezekiah became ill and was at the point of death. The prophet Isaiah son of Amoz went to him and said, "This is what the LORD says: Put your house in order, because you are going to die; you will not recover."

2Hezekiah turned his face to the wall and prayed to the LORD, 3"Remember, O LORD, how I have walked before you faithfully and with wholehearted devotion and have done what is good in your eyes." And Hezekiah wept bitterly.

4Then the word of the LORD came to Isaiah: 5"Go and tell Hezekiah, 'This is what the LORD, the God of your father David, says: I have heard your prayer and seen your tears; I will add fifteen years to your life. 6And I will deliver you and this city from the hand of the king of Assyria. I will defend this city.

7"'This is the LORD's sign to you that the LORD will do what he has promised: 8I will make the shadow cast by the sun go back the ten steps it has gone down on the stairway of Ahaz.'" So the sunlight went back the ten steps it had gone down.

9A writing of Hezekiah king of Judah after his illness and recovery:

10I said, "In the prime of my life
  must I go through the gates of death*a*
  and be robbed of the rest of my years?"

11I said, "I will not again see the LORD,
  the LORD, in the land of the living;
no longer will I look on mankind,
  or be with those who now dwell in this
    world.*b*
12Like a shepherd's tent my house
  has been pulled down and taken from
    me.
Like a weaver I have rolled up my life,
  and he has cut me off from the loom;
  day and night you made an end of me.
13I waited patiently till dawn,
  but like a lion he broke all my bones;
  day and night you made an end of me.
14I cried like a swift or thrush,
  I moaned like a mourning dove.
My eyes grew weak as I looked to the
  heavens.
I am troubled; O Lord, come to my
  aid!"

15But what can I say?
  He has spoken to me, and he himself has
    done this.
I will walk humbly all my years
  because of this anguish of my soul.
16Lord, by such things men live;
  and my spirit finds life in them too.
You restored me to health
  and let me live.
17Surely it was for my benefit
  that I suffered such anguish.
In your love you kept me
  from the pit of destruction;
you have put all my sins
  behind your back.
18For the grave*c* cannot praise you,
  death cannot sing your praise;
those who go down to the pit
  cannot hope for your faithfulness.
19The living, the living—they praise you,
  as I am doing today;
fathers tell their children
  about your faithfulness.

20The LORD will save me,
  and we will sing with stringed
    instruments
all the days of our lives
  in the temple of the LORD.

21Isaiah had said, "Prepare a poultice of figs and apply it to the boil, and he will recover."

22Hezekiah had asked, "What will be the sign that I will go up to the temple of the LORD?"

Envoys From Babylon

39 At that time Merodach-Baladan son of Baladan king of Babylon sent Hezekiah letters and a gift, because he had heard of his illness and recovery. 2Hezekiah received the envoys gladly and showed them what was in his storehouses—the silver, the gold, the spices, the fine oil, his entire armoury and everything found among his treasures. There was nothing in his palace or

*a*10 Hebrew *Sheol*   *b*11 A few Hebrew manuscripts; most Hebrew manuscripts *in the place of cessation*
*c*18 Hebrew *Sheol*

in all his kingdom that Hezekiah did not show them.

³Then Isaiah the prophet went to King Hezekiah and asked, "What did those men say, and where did they come from?"

"From a distant land," Hezekiah replied. "They came to me from Babylon."

⁴The prophet asked, "What did they see in your palace?"

"They saw everything in my palace," Hezekiah said. "There is nothing among my treasures that I did not show them."

⁵Then Isaiah said to Hezekiah, "Hear the word of the LORD Almighty: ⁶The time will surely come when everything in your palace, and all that your fathers have stored up until this day, will be carried off to Babylon. Nothing will be left, says the LORD. ⁷And some of your descendants, your own flesh and blood who will be born to you, will be taken away, and they will become eunuchs in the palace of the king of Babylon."

⁸"The word of the LORD you have spoken is good," Hezekiah replied. For he thought, "There will be peace and security in my lifetime."

Comfort for God's People

40 Comfort, comfort my people, says your God. ²Speak tenderly to Jerusalem, and proclaim to her that her hard service has been completed, that her sin has been paid for, that she has received from the LORD's hand double for all her sins.

³A voice of one calling:
"In the desert prepare the way for the LORD;^a
make straight in the wilderness a highway for our God.^b
⁴Every valley shall be raised up, every mountain and hill made low;
the rough ground shall become level, the rugged places a plain.
⁵And the glory of the LORD will be revealed, and all mankind together will see it.
For the mouth of the LORD has spoken."

⁶A voice says, "Cry out."
And I said, "What shall I cry?"

"All men are like grass, and all their glory is like the flowers of the field.
⁷The grass withers and the flowers fall, because the breath of the LORD blows on them.
Surely the people are grass.
⁸The grass withers and the flowers fall, but the word of our God stands for ever."

⁹You who bring good tidings to Zion, go up on a high mountain.
You who bring good tidings to Jerusalem,^c lift up your voice with a shout,
lift it up, do not be afraid;
say to the towns of Judah, "Here is your God!"
¹⁰See, the Sovereign LORD comes with power, and his arm rules for him.
See, his reward is with him, and his recompense accompanies him.
¹¹He tends his flock like a shepherd:
He gathers the lambs in his arms and carries them close to his heart;
he gently leads those that have young.

¹²Who has measured the waters in the hollow of his hand, or with the breadth of his hand marked off the heavens?
Who has held the dust of the earth in a basket, or weighed the mountains on the scales and the hills in a balance?
¹³Who has understood the mind^d of the LORD, or instructed him as his counsellor?
¹⁴Whom did the LORD consult to enlighten him, and who taught him the right way?
Who was it that taught him knowledge or showed him the path of understanding?

¹⁵Surely the nations are like a drop in a bucket;
they are regarded as dust on the scales;
he weighs the islands as though they were fine dust.
¹⁶Lebanon is not sufficient for altar fires, nor its animals enough for burnt offerings.
¹⁷Before him all the nations are as nothing; they are regarded by him as worthless and less than nothing.

¹⁸To whom, then, will you compare God?
What image will you compare him to?
¹⁹As for an idol, a craftsman casts it, and a goldsmith overlays it with gold and fashions silver chains for it.
²⁰A man too poor to present such an offering selects wood that will not rot.
He looks for a skilled craftsman to set up an idol that will not topple.

²¹Do you not know?
Have you not heard?
Has it not been told you from the beginning?
Have you not understood since the earth was founded?
²²He sits enthroned above the circle of the earth, and its people are like grasshoppers.

^a3 Or A voice of one calling in the desert: / "Prepare the way for the LORD
^b3 Hebrew; Septuagint make straight the paths of our God
^c9 Or O Zion, bringer of good tidings, / go up on a high mountain. / O Jerusalem, bringer of good tidings
^d13 Or Spirit; or spirit

He stretches out the heavens like a
  canopy,
    and spreads them out like a tent to live
      in.
23He brings princes to naught
    and reduces the rulers of this world to
      nothing.
24No sooner are they planted,
    no sooner are they sown,
    no sooner do they take root in the
      ground,
  than he blows on them and they wither,
    and a whirlwind sweeps them away like
      chaff.

25"To whom will you compare me?
    Or who is my equal?" says the Holy
      One.
26Lift your eyes and look to the heavens:
    Who created all these?
  He who brings out the starry host one by
    one,
    and calls them each by name.
  Because of his great power and mighty
    strength,
    not one of them is missing.

27Why do you say, O Jacob,
    and complain, O Israel,
  "My way is hidden from the LORD;
    my cause is disregarded by my God"?
28Do you not know?
    Have you not heard?
  The LORD is the everlasting God,
    the Creator of the ends of the earth.
  He will not grow tired or weary,
    and his understanding no-one can
      fathom.
29He gives strength to the weary
    and increases the power of the weak.
30Even youths grow tired and weary,
    and young men stumble and fall;
31but those who hope in the LORD
    will renew their strength.
  They will soar on wings like eagles;
    they will run and not grow weary,
    they will walk and not be faint.

The Helper of Israel

41 "Be silent before me, you islands!
    Let the nations renew their
      strength!
  Let them come forward and speak;
    let us meet together at the place of
      judgment.

2"Who has stirred up one from the east,
    calling him in righteousness to his
      service?[a]
  He hands nations over to him
    and subdues kings before him.
  He turns them to dust with his sword,
    to wind-blown chaff with his bow.
3He pursues them and moves on
    unscathed,
    by a path his feet have not travelled
      before.
4Who has done this and carried it through,

calling forth the generations from the
    beginning?
  I, the LORD—with the first of them
    and with the last—I am he."

5The islands have seen it and fear;
    the ends of the earth tremble.
  They approach and come forward;
6   each helps the other
    and says to his brother, "Be strong!"
7The craftsman encourages the goldsmith,
    and he who smooths with the hammer
    spurs on him who strikes the anvil.
  He says of the welding, "It is good."
    He nails down the idol so that it will not
      topple.

8"But you, O Israel, my servant,
    Jacob, whom I have chosen,
    you descendants of Abraham my friend,
9I took you from the ends of the earth,
    from its farthest corners I called you.
  I said, 'You are my servant';
    I have chosen you and have not rejected
      you.
10So do not fear, for I am with you;
    do not be dismayed, for I am your God.
  I will strengthen you and help you;
    I will uphold you with my righteous right
      hand.

11"All who rage against you
    will surely be ashamed and disgraced;
  those who oppose you
    will be as nothing and perish.
12Though you search for your enemies,
    you will not find them.
  Those who wage war against you
    will be as nothing at all.
13For I am the LORD, your God,
    who takes hold of your right hand
  and says to you, Do not fear;
    I will help you.
14Do not be afraid, O worm Jacob,
    O little Israel,
  for I myself will help you," declares the
    LORD,
    your Redeemer, the Holy One of Israel.
15"See, I will make you into a
    threshing-sledge,
    new and sharp, with many teeth.
  You will thresh the mountains and crush
    them,
    and reduce the hills to chaff.
16You will winnow them, the wind will pick
    them up,
    and a gale will blow them away.
  But you will rejoice in the LORD
    and glory in the Holy One of Israel.

17"The poor and needy search for water,
    but there is none;
    their tongues are parched with thirst.
  But I the LORD will answer them;
    I, the God of Israel, will not forsake
      them.
18I will make rivers flow on barren heights,
    and springs within the valleys.

a2 Or / whom victory meets at every step

I will turn the desert into pools of water,
and the parched ground into springs.
¹⁹I will put in the desert
the cedar and the acacia, the myrtle and
the olive.
I will set pines in the wasteland,
the fir and the cypress together,
²⁰so that people may see and know,
may consider and understand,
that the hand of the LORD has done this,
that the Holy One of Israel has created
it.

²¹"Present your case," says the LORD.
"Set forth your arguments," says
Jacob's King.
²²"Bring in ₍your idols₎ to tell us
what is going to happen.
Tell us what the former things were,
so that we may consider them
and know their final outcome.
Or declare to us the things to come,
²³   tell us what the future holds,
so that we may know you are gods.
Do something, whether good or bad,
so that we will be dismayed and filled
with fear.
²⁴But you are less than nothing
and your works are utterly worthless;
he who chooses you is detestable.

²⁵"I have stirred up one from the north, and
he comes—
one from the rising sun who calls on my
name.
He treads on rulers as if they were mortar,
as if he were a potter treading the clay.
²⁶Who told of this from the beginning, so
that we could know,
or beforehand, so that we could say, 'He
was right'?
No-one told of this,
no-one foretold it,
no-one heard any words from you.
²⁷I was the first to tell Zion, 'Look, here
they are!'
I gave to Jerusalem a messenger of good
tidings.
²⁸I look but there is no-one—
no-one among them to give counsel,
no-one to give answer when I ask them.
²⁹See, they are all false!
Their deeds amount to nothing;
their images are but wind and confusion.

The Servant of the LORD

42 "Here is my servant, whom I
uphold,
my chosen one in whom I delight;
I will put my Spirit on him
and he will bring justice to the nations.
²He will not shout or cry out,
or raise his voice in the streets.
³A bruised reed he will not break,
and a smouldering wick he will not snuff
out.
In faithfulness he will bring forth justice;
⁴   he will not falter or be discouraged
till he establishes justice on earth.
In his law the islands will put their
hope."

⁵This is what God the LORD says—
he who created the heavens and stretched
them out,
who spread out the earth and all that
comes out of it,
who gives breath to its people,
and life to those who walk on it:
⁶"I, the LORD, have called you in
righteousness;
I will take hold of your hand.
I will keep you and will make you
to be a covenant for the people
and a light for the Gentiles,
⁷to open eyes that are blind,
to free captives from prison
and to release from the dungeon those
who sit in darkness.

⁸"I am the LORD; that is my name!
I will not give my glory to another
or my praise to idols.
⁹See, the former things have taken place,
and new things I declare;
before they spring into being
I announce them to you."

Song of Praise to the LORD

¹⁰Sing to the LORD a new song,
his praise from the ends of the earth,
you who go down to the sea, and all that is
in it,
you islands, and all who live in them.
¹¹Let the desert and its towns raise their
voices;
let the settlements where Kedar lives
rejoice.
Let the people of Sela sing for joy;
let them shout from the mountaintops.
¹²Let them give glory to the LORD
and proclaim his praise in the islands.
¹³The LORD will march out like a mighty
man,
like a warrior he will stir up his zeal;
with a shout he will raise the battle cry
and will triumph over his enemies.

¹⁴"For a long time I have kept silent,
I have been quiet and held myself back.
But now, like a woman in childbirth,
I cry out, I gasp and pant.
¹⁵I will lay waste the mountains and hills
and dry up all their vegetation;
I will turn rivers into islands
and dry up the pools.
¹⁶I will lead the blind by ways they have not
known,
along unfamiliar paths I will guide them;
I will turn the darkness into light before
them
and make the rough places smooth.
These are the things I will do;
I will not forsake them.
¹⁷But those who trust in idols,
who say to images, 'You are our gods,'
will be turned back in utter shame.

Israel Blind and Deaf

¹⁸"Hear, you deaf;
look, you blind, and see!
¹⁹Who is blind but my servant,
and deaf like the messenger I send?

Who is blind like the one committed to me,
  blind like the servant of the LORD?
20You have seen many things, but have paid
    no attention;
  your ears are open, but you hear
    nothing.''
21It pleased the LORD
  for the sake of his righteousness
  to make his law great and glorious.
22But this is a people plundered and looted,
  all of them trapped in pits
  or hidden away in prisons.
They have become plunder,
  with no-one to rescue them;
they have been made loot,
  with no-one to say, ''Send them back.''

23Which of you will listen to this
  or pay close attention in time to come?
24Who handed Jacob over to become loot,
  and Israel to the plunderers?
  Was it not the LORD,
    against whom we have sinned?
For they would not follow his ways;
  they did not obey his law.
25So he poured out on them his burning
    anger,
  the violence of war.
It enveloped them in flames, yet they did
    not understand;
  it consumed them, but they did not take
    it to heart.

Israel's Only Saviour

43 But now, this is what the LORD
        says—
  he who created you, O Jacob,
  he who formed you, O Israel:
''Fear not, for I have redeemed you;
  I have summoned you by name; you are
    mine.
2When you pass through the waters,
  I will be with you;
and when you pass through the rivers,
  they will not sweep over you.
When you walk through the fire,
  you will not be burned;
  the flames will not set you ablaze.
3For I am the LORD, your God,
  the Holy One of Israel, your Saviour;
I give Egypt for your ransom,
  Cush[a] and Seba in your stead.
4Since you are precious and honoured in
    my sight,
  and because I love you,
I will give men in exchange for you,
  and people in exchange for your life.
5Do not be afraid, for I am with you;
  I will bring your children from the east
  and gather you from the west.
6I will say to the north, 'Give them up!'
  and to the south, 'Do not hold them
    back.'
Bring my sons from afar
  and my daughters from the ends of the
    earth—
7everyone who is called by my name,
  whom I created for my glory,
  whom I formed and made.''

8Lead out those who have eyes but are
    blind,
  who have ears but are deaf.
9All the nations gather together
  and the peoples assemble.
Which of them foretold this
  and proclaimed to us the former things?
Let them bring in their witnesses to prove
    they were right,
  so that others may hear and say, ''It is
    true.''
10''You are my witnesses,'' declares the
    LORD,
  ''and my servant whom I have chosen,
so that you may know and believe me
  and understand that I am he.
Before me no god was formed,
  nor will there be one after me.
11I, even I, am the LORD,
  and apart from me there is no saviour.
12I have revealed and saved and
    proclaimed—
  I, and not some foreign god among you.
You are my witnesses,'' declares the
  LORD, ''that I am God.
13 Yes, and from ancient days I am he.
No-one can deliver out of my hand.
  When I act, who can reverse it?''

God's Mercy and Israel's Unfaithfulness

14This is what the LORD says—
  your Redeemer, the Holy One of Israel:
''For your sake I will send to Babylon
  and bring down as fugitives all the
    Babylonians,[b]
  in the ships in which they took pride.
15I am the LORD, your Holy One,
  Israel's Creator, your King.''

16This is what the LORD says—
  he who made a way through the sea,
  a path through the mighty waters,
17who drew out the chariots and horses,
  the army and reinforcements together,
and they lay there, never to rise again,
  extinguished, snuffed out like a wick:
18''Forget the former things;
  do not dwell on the past.
19See, I am doing a new thing!
  Now it springs up; do you not perceive
    it?
I am making a way in the desert
  and streams in the wasteland.
20The wild animals honour me,
  the jackals and the owls,
because I provide water in the desert
  and streams in the wasteland,
to give drink to my people, my chosen,
21 the people I formed for myself
  that they may proclaim my praise.

22''Yet you have not called upon me, O
    Jacob,
  you have not wearied yourselves for me,
    O Israel.
23You have not brought me sheep for burnt
    offerings,
  nor honoured me with your sacrifices.

a3 That is, the upper Nile region   b14 Or Chaldeans

I have not burdened you with grain
offerings
nor wearied you with demands for
incense.
24You have not bought any fragrant calamus
for me,
or lavished on me the fat of your
sacrifices.
But you have burdened me with your sins
and wearied me with your offences.

25"I, even I, am he who blots out
your transgressions, for my own sake,
and remembers your sins no more.
26Review the past for me,
let us argue the matter together;
state the case for your innocence.
27Your first father sinned;
your spokesmen rebelled against me.
28So I will disgrace the dignitaries of your
temple,
and I will consign Jacob to destructionᶜ
and Israel to scorn.

Israel the Chosen

44 "But now listen, O Jacob, my
servant,
Israel, whom I have chosen.
2This is what the LORD says—
he who made you, who formed you in
the womb,
and who will help you:
Do not be afraid, O Jacob, my servant,
Jeshurun, whom I have chosen.
3For I will pour water on the thirsty land,
and streams on the dry ground;
I will pour out my Spirit on your offspring,
and my blessing on your descendants.
4They will spring up like grass in a
meadow,
like poplar trees by flowing streams.
5One will say, 'I belong to the LORD';
another will call himself by the name of
Jacob;
still another will write on his hand, 'The
LORD's',
and will take the name Israel.

The LORD, Not Idols

6"This is what the LORD says—
Israel's King and Redeemer, the LORD
Almighty:
I am the first and I am the last;
apart from me there is no God.
7Who then is like me? Let him proclaim it.
Let him declare and lay out before me
what has happened since I established my
ancient people,
and what is yet to come—
yes, let him foretell what will come.
8Do not tremble, do not be afraid.
Did I not proclaim this and foretell it
long ago?
You are my witnesses. Is there any God
besides me?
No, there is no other Rock; I know not
one."

9All who make idols are nothing,
and the things they treasure are
worthless.
Those who would speak up for them are
blind;
they are ignorant, to their own shame.
10Who shapes a god and casts an idol,
which can profit him nothing?
11He and his kind will be put to shame;
craftsmen are nothing but men.
Let them all come together and take their
stand;
they will be brought down to terror and
infamy.

12The blacksmith takes a tool
and works with it in the coals;
he shapes an idol with hammers,
he forges it with the might of his arm.
He gets hungry and loses his strength;
he drinks no water and grows faint.
13The carpenter measures with a line
and makes an outline with a marker;
he roughs it out with chisels
and marks it with compasses.
He shapes it in the form of man,
of man in all his glory,
that it may dwell in a shrine.
14He cut down cedars,
or perhaps took a cypress or oak.
He let it grow among the trees of the
forest,
or planted a pine, and the rain made it
grow.
15It is man's fuel for burning;
some of it he takes and warms himself,
he kindles a fire and bakes bread.
But he also fashions a god and worships it;
he makes an idol and bows down to it.
16Half of the wood he burns in the fire;
over it he prepares his meal,
he roasts his meat and eats his fill.
He also warms himself and says,
"Ah! I am warm; I see the fire."
17From the rest he makes a god, his idol;
he bows down to it and worships.
He prays to it and says,
"Save me; you are my god."
18They know nothing, they understand
nothing;
their eyes are plastered over so that they
cannot see,
and their minds closed so that they
cannot understand.
19No-one stops to think,
no-one has the knowledge or
understanding to say,
"Half of it I used for fuel;
I even baked bread over its coals,
I roasted meat and I ate.
Shall I make a detestable thing from what
is left?
Shall I bow down to a block of wood?"
20He feeds on ashes, a deluded heart
misleads him;
he cannot save himself, or say,
"Is not this thing in my right hand a
lie?"

ᶜ28 The Hebrew term refers to the irrevocable giving over of things or persons to the LORD, often by totally
destroying them.

21"Remember these things, O Jacob,
  for you are my servant, O Israel.
I have made you, you are my servant;
  O Israel, I will not forget you.
22I have swept away your offences like a
    cloud,
  your sins like the morning mist.
Return to me,
  for I have redeemed you."

23Sing for joy, O heavens, for the LORD has
    done this;
  shout aloud, O earth beneath.
Burst into song, you mountains,
  you forests and all your trees,
for the LORD has redeemed Jacob,
  he displays his glory in Israel.

Jerusalem to Be Inhabited

24"This is what the LORD says—
  your Redeemer, who formed you in the
    womb:

I am the LORD,
who has made all things,
who alone stretched out the heavens,
who spread out the earth by myself,

25who foils the signs of false prophets
  and makes fools of diviners,
who overthrows the learning of the wise
  and turns it into nonsense,
26who carries out the words of his servants
  and fulfils the predictions of his
    messengers,

who says of Jerusalem, 'It shall be
    inhabited,'
  of the towns of Judah, 'They shall be
    built,'
  and of their ruins, 'I will restore them,'
27who says to the watery deep, 'Be dry,
  and I will dry up your streams,'
28who says of Cyrus, 'He is my shepherd
  and will accomplish all that I please;
he will say of Jerusalem, "Let it be
    rebuilt,"
  and of the temple, "Let its foundations
    be laid."'

45 "This is what the LORD says to his
    anointed,
  to Cyrus, whose right hand I take hold
    of
to subdue nations before him
  and to strip kings of their armour,
to open doors before him
  so that gates will not be shut:
2I will go before you
  and will level the mountains;[a]
I will break down gates of bronze
  and cut through bars of iron.
3I will give you the treasures of darkness,
  riches stored in secret places,
so that you may know that I am the LORD,
  the God of Israel, who summons you by
    name.

4For the sake of Jacob my servant,
  of Israel my chosen,
I summon you by name
  and bestow on you a title of honour,
  though you do not acknowledge me.
5I am the LORD, and there is no other;
  apart from me there is no God.
I will strengthen you,
  though you have not acknowledged me,
6so that from the rising of the sun
  to the place of its setting
men may know there is none besides me.
  I am the LORD, and there is no other.
7I form the light and create darkness,
  I bring prosperity and create disaster;
  I, the LORD, do all these things.

8"You heavens above, rain down
    righteousness;
  let the clouds shower it down.
Let the earth open wide,
  let salvation spring up,
let righteousness grow with it;
  I, the LORD, have created it.

9"Woe to him who quarrels with his
    Maker,
  to him who is but a potsherd among the
    potsherds on the ground.
Does the clay say to the potter,
  'What are you making?'
Does your work say,
  'He has no hands'?
10Woe to him who says to his father,
  'What have you begotten?'
or to his mother,
  'What have you brought to birth?'

11"This is what the LORD says—
  the Holy One of Israel, and its Maker:
Concerning things to come,
  do you question me about my children,
  or give me orders about the work of my
    hands?
12It is I who made the earth
  and created mankind upon it.
My own hands stretched out the heavens;
  I marshalled their starry hosts.
13I will raise up Cyrus[b] in my righteousness:
  I will make all his ways straight.
He will rebuild my city
  and set my exiles free,
but not for a price or reward,
  says the LORD Almighty."

14This is what the LORD says:

"The products of Egypt and the
    merchandise of Cush,[c]
  and those tall Sabeans—
they will come over to you
  and will be yours;
they will trudge behind you,
  coming over to you in chains.
They will bow down before you
  and plead with you, saying,
'Surely God is with you, and there is no
    other;
  there is no other god.'"

---

[a]2 Dead Sea Scrolls and Septuagint; the meaning of the word in the Masoretic Text is uncertain.
[b]13 Hebrew him   [c]14 That is, the upper Nile region

¹⁵Truly you are a God who hides himself,
   O God and Saviour of Israel.
¹⁶All the makers of idols will be put to shame
      and disgraced;
   they will go off into disgrace together.
¹⁷But Israel will be saved by the LORD
      with an everlasting salvation;
   you will never be put to shame or
      disgraced,
   to ages everlasting.

¹⁸For this is what the LORD says—
   he who created the heavens,
      he is God;
   he who fashioned and made the earth,
      he founded it;
   he did not create it to be empty,
      but formed it to be inhabited—
   he says:
   "I am the LORD,
      and there is no other.
¹⁹I have not spoken in secret,
   from somewhere in a land of darkness;
   I have not said to Jacob's descendants,
      'Seek me in vain.'
   I, the LORD, speak the truth;
      I declare what is right.

²⁰"Gather together and come;
   assemble, you fugitives from the
      nations.
Ignorant are those who carry about idols
      of wood,
   who pray to gods that cannot save.
²¹Declare what is to be, present it—
   let them take counsel together.
Who foretold this long ago,
   who declared it from the distant past?
Was it not I, the LORD?
   And there is no God apart from me,
a righteous God and a Saviour;
   there is none but me.

²²"Turn to me and be saved,
   all you ends of the earth;
   for I am God, and there is no other.
²³By myself I have sworn,
   my mouth has uttered in all integrity
   a word that will not be revoked:
Before me every knee will bow;
   by me every tongue will swear.
²⁴They will say of me, 'In the LORD alone
   are righteousness and strength.'"
All who have raged against him
   will come to him and be put to shame.
²⁵But in the LORD all the descendants of
      Israel
   will be found righteous and will exult.

Gods of Babylon

46 Bel bows down, Nebo stoops low;
   their idols are borne by beasts of
      burden.ᵃ
The images that are carried about are
      burdensome,
   a burden for the weary.
²They stoop and bow down together;
   unable to rescue the burden,
   they themselves go off into captivity.

³"Listen to me, O house of Jacob,
   all you who remain of the house of
      Israel,
you whom I have upheld since you were
      conceived,
   and have carried since your birth.
⁴Even to your old age and grey hairs
   I am he, I am he who will sustain you.
I have made you and I will carry you;
   I will sustain you and I will rescue you.

⁵"To whom will you compare me or count
      me equal?
   To whom will you liken me that we may
      be compared?
⁶Some pour out gold from their bags
   and weigh out silver on the scales;
they hire a goldsmith to make it into a god,
   and they bow down and worship it.
⁷They lift it to their shoulders and carry it;
   they set it up in its place, and there it
      stands.
From that spot it cannot move.
   Though one cries out to it, it does not
      answer;
   it cannot save him from his troubles.

⁸"Remember this, fix it in mind,
   take it to heart, you rebels.
⁹Remember the former things, those of long
      ago;
   I am God, and there is no other;
   I am God, and there is none like me.
¹⁰I make known the end from the beginning,
   from ancient times, what is still to come.
I say: My purpose will stand,
   and I will do all that I please.
¹¹From the east I summon a bird of prey;
   from a far-off land, a man to fulfil my
      purpose.
What I have said, that will I bring about;
   what I have planned, that will I do.
¹²Listen to me, you stubborn-hearted,
   you who are far from righteousness.
¹³I am bringing my righteousness near,
   it is not far away;
   and my salvation will not be delayed.
I will grant salvation to Zion,
   my splendour to Israel.

The Fall of Babylon

47 "Go down, sit in the dust,
   Virgin Daughter of Babylon;
sit on the ground without a throne,
   Daughter of the Babylonians.ᵃ
No more will you be called
   tender or delicate.
²Take millstones and grind flour;
   take off your veil.
Lift up your skirts, bare your legs,
   and wade through the streams.
³Your nakedness will be exposed
   and your shame uncovered.
I will take vengeance;
   I will spare no-one."

⁴Our Redeemer—the LORD Almighty is his
      name—
   is the Holy One of Israel.

ᵃ1 Or *are but beasts and cattle*   ᵃ1 Or *Chaldeans*; also in verse 5

5"Sit in silence, go into darkness,
  Daughter of the Babylonians;
no more will you be called
  queen of kingdoms.
6I was angry with my people
  and desecrated my inheritance;
I gave them into your hand,
  and you showed them no mercy.
Even on the aged
  you laid a very heavy yoke.
7You said, 'I will continue for ever—
  the eternal queen!'
But you did not consider these things
  or reflect on what might happen.

8"Now then, listen, you wanton creature,
  lounging in your security
and saying to yourself,
  'I am, and there is none besides me.
I will never be a widow
  or suffer the loss of children.'
9Both of these will overtake you
  in a moment, on a single day:
loss of children and widowhood.
They will come upon you in full measure,
  in spite of your many sorceries
  and all your potent spells.
10You have trusted in your wickedness
  and have said, 'No-one sees me.'
Your wisdom and knowledge mislead you
  when you say to yourself,
  'I am, and there is none besides me.'
11Disaster will come upon you,
  and you will not know how to conjure it
    away.
A calamity will fall upon you
  that you cannot ward off with a ransom;
a catastrophe you cannot foresee
  will suddenly come upon you.

12"Keep on, then, with your magic spells
  and with your many sorceries,
  which you have laboured at since
    childhood.
Perhaps you will succeed,
  perhaps you will cause terror.
13All the counsel you have received has only
    worn you out!
Let your astrologers come forward,
  those stargazers who make predictions
    month by month,
  let them save you from what is coming
    upon you.
14Surely they are like stubble;
  the fire will burn them up.
They cannot even save themselves
  from the power of the flame.
Here are no coals to warm anyone;
  here is no fire to sit by.
15That is all they can do for you—
  these you have laboured with
  and trafficked with since childhood.
Each of them goes on in his error;
  there is not one that can save you.

Stubborn Israel

48 "Listen to this, O house of Jacob,
     you who are called by the name of
     Israel
   and come from the line of Judah,
you who take oaths in the name of the
    LORD
  and invoke the God of Israel—
  but not in truth or righteousness—
2you who call yourselves citizens of the
    holy city
  and rely on the God of Israel—
  the LORD Almighty is his name:
3I foretold the former things long ago,
  my mouth announced them and I made
    them known;
  then suddenly I acted, and they came to
    pass.
4For I knew how stubborn you were;
  the sinews of your neck were iron,
  your forehead was bronze.
5Therefore I told you these things long ago;
  before they happened I announced them
    to you
so that you could not say,
  'My idols did them;
  my wooden image and metal god
    ordained them.'
6You have heard these things; look at them
    all.
  Will you not admit them?

"From now on I will tell you of new
    things,
  of hidden things unknown to you.
7They are created now, and not long ago;
  you have not heard of them before
    today.
So you cannot say,
  'Yes, I knew of them.'
8You have neither heard nor understood;
  from of old your ear has not been open.
Well do I know how treacherous you are;
  you were called a rebel from birth.
9For my own name's sake I delay my
    wrath;
  for the sake of my praise I hold it back
    from you,
  so as not to cut you off.
10See, I have refined you, though not as
    silver;
  I have tested you in the furnace of
    affliction.
11For my own sake, for my own sake, I do
    this.
  How can I let myself be defamed?
  I will not yield my glory to another.

Israel Freed

12"Listen to me, O Jacob,
  Israel, whom I have called:
I am he;
  I am the first and I am the last.
13My own hand laid the foundations of the
    earth,
  and my right hand spread out the
    heavens;
  when I summon them,
  they all stand up together.

14"Come together, all of you, and listen:
  Which of ⌊the idols⌋ has foretold these
    things?
The LORD's chosen ally
  will carry out his purpose against
    Babylon;

his arm will be against the Babylonians.[a]
15I, even I, have spoken;
    yes, I have called him.
I will bring him,
    and he will succeed in his mission.

16"Come near me and listen to this:

"From the first announcement I have not
        spoken in secret;
    at the time it happens, I am there."

And now the Sovereign LORD has sent me,
    with his Spirit.

17This is what the LORD says—
    your Redeemer, the Holy One of Israel:
"I am the LORD your God,
    who teaches you what is best for you,
    who directs you in the way you should
        go.
18If only you had paid attention to my
        commands,
    your peace would have been like a river,
    your righteousness like the waves of the
        sea.
19Your descendants would have been like
        the sand,
    your children like its numberless grains;
their name would never be cut off
    nor destroyed from before me."

20Leave Babylon,
    flee from the Babylonians!
Announce this with shouts of joy
    and proclaim it.
Send it out to the ends of the earth;
    say, "The LORD has redeemed his
        servant Jacob."
21They did not thirst when he led them
        through the deserts;
    he made water flow for them from the
        rock;
he split the rock
    and water gushed out.

22"There is no peace," says the LORD, "for
    the wicked."

The Servant of the LORD

49 Listen to me, you islands;
        hear this, you distant nations;
Before I was born the LORD called me;
    from my birth he has made mention of
        my name.
2He made my mouth like a sharpened
        sword,
    in the shadow of his hand he hid me;
he made me into a polished arrow
    and concealed me in his quiver.
3He said to me, "You are my servant,
    Israel, in whom I will display my
        splendour."
4But I said, "I have laboured to no
        purpose;
    I have spent my strength in vain and for
        nothing.

Yet what is due to me is in the LORD's
        hand,
    and my reward is with my God."

5And now the LORD says—
    he who formed me in the womb to be his
        servant
to bring Jacob back to him
    and gather Israel to himself,
for I am honoured in the eyes of the LORD
    and my God has been my strength—
6he says:
"It is too small a thing for you to be my
        servant
    to restore the tribes of Jacob
    and bring back those of Israel I have
        kept.
I will also make you a light for the
        Gentiles,
    that you may bring my salvation to the
        ends of the earth."

7This is what the LORD says—
    the Redeemer and Holy One of Israel—
to him who was despised and abhorred by
        the nation,
    to the servant of rulers:
"Kings will see you and rise up,
    princes will see and bow down,
because of the LORD, who is faithful,
    the Holy One of Israel, who has chosen
        you."

Restoration of Israel

8This is what the LORD says:

"In the time of my favour I will answer
        you,
    and in the day of salvation I will help
        you;
I will keep you and will make you
    to be a covenant for the people,
to restore the land
    and to reassign its desolate inheritances,
9to say to the captives, 'Come out,'
    and to those in darkness, 'Be free!'

"They will feed beside the roads
    and find pasture on every barren hill.
10They will neither hunger nor thirst,
    nor will the desert heat or the sun beat
        upon them.
He who has compassion on them will
        guide them
    and lead them beside springs of water.
11I will turn all my mountains into roads,
    and my highways will be raised up.
12See, they will come from afar—
    some from the north, some from the
        west,
    some from the region of Aswan."[a]

13Shout for joy, O heavens;
    rejoice, O earth;
    burst into song, O mountains!
For the LORD comforts his people
    and will have compassion on his
        afflicted ones.

---

[a]14 Or *Chaldeans*; also in verse 20   [a]12 Dead Sea Scrolls; Masoretic Text *Sinim*

ISAIAH 49:13–23

'Can a mother forget the baby at her breast and have no compassion on the child she has borne? Though she may forget, I will not forget you! See, I have engraved you on the palms of my hands' (vv. 15, 16).

THE 'MOTHERHOOD' OF GOD. Some would wish to remove all masculine references to God, on the grounds that they are 'sexist'. Unfortunately, English has no suitable unisex words so the only real alternative is to use neuter gender and make God an 'it'. One woman, claiming forcibly that God was feminine, was asked how she knew. 'She told me so,' was her reply! Such apparently petulant protests do, however, usefully remind us that all our masculine references to God (including 'Father') are purely terms of convenience.

D. H. C. Read writes: 'In an agricultural economy it was inevitable that the poetic imagery for God's tender care . . . should be drawn from the shepherd and his flock. In a patriarchal society where the father-figure was dominant, thoughts of God's relationship to his people would circle round the thought of the Father. What matters . . . is that none of these metaphors and similes should be allowed to freeze our pictures of God, and decorate him with static qualities that delimit his being.'

So the 'motherhood' of God might be a helpful concept so long as we do not use it to partition the Godhead, but only as another metaphor to aid us in more adequately describing him (her?). As far as *creativity* is concerned, the mother giving birth has a much closer link with the child than the father who begets it, and is therefore a better illustration of God's activity in creation. Second, motherhood is synonymous with *caring*. 'Nowhere in all creation is there such a caring,' says Read. Yet even if *that* caring fails. God's does not.

'And you, Jesus, are you not also a mother?' (Anselm)

ISAIAH 50:10–11

'Who among you fears the LORD and obeys the word of his servant? Let him who walks in the dark, who has no light, trust in the name of the LORD and rely on his God' (v. 10).

SOMETIMES THE WAY IS DARK. Even for those who love God and seek to live obediently there are times of uncertainty. It was a fairly common experience among the prophets. Moses, wearied by the complaining Israelites, asked of God: 'If this is how you are going to treat me, put me to death . . . and do not let me face my own ruin.' Elijah, escaping from Jezebel, 'came to a broom tree, sat down under it and prayed that he might die. "I have had enough, Lord," he said. "Take my life: I am no better than my ancestors." ' Jeremiah, overwhelmed by his task, even bemoaned his birth. 'Woe is me, my mother, that you have borne me, a man of strife . . .!' In the darkness of the way there is safety if we rely on God. He will still guide.

For those who choose to light their feeble candles of rationalism, humanism, cultism or materialism, and warm themselves by fires which they themselves have kindled, there is disaster. How readily we look for life's answers apart from God, who is the only source of life. With an unbecoming and unjustified assurance, many people offer light upon life's way. Better far the darkness with God, says the prophet, than the light without him. No merely human resource can take us safely through the inevitable stresses and hazards of life.

> *Thy way, not mine. O Lord,*
> *However dark it be;*
> *Lead me by thine own hand;*
> *Choose out the path for me.*

(Horatio Bonar)

'*Even the darkness will not be dark to you; the night will shine like the day, for darkness is as light to you*'. *(Psalm 139:12)*

¹⁴But Zion said, "The LORD has forsaken
    me,
    the Lord has forgotten me."

¹⁵"Can a mother forget the baby at her
        breast
    and have no compassion on the child she
        has borne?
Though she may forget,
    I will not forget you!
¹⁶See, I have engraved you on the palms of
        my hands;
    your walls are ever before me.
¹⁷Your sons hasten back,
    and those who laid you waste depart
        from you.
¹⁸Lift up your eyes and look around;
    all your sons gather and come to you.
As surely as I live," declares the LORD,
    "you will wear them all as ornaments;
    you will put them on, like a bride.

¹⁹"Though you were ruined and made
        desolate
    and your land laid waste,
now you will be too small for your people,
    and those who devoured you will be far
        away.
²⁰The children born during your
        bereavement
    will yet say in your hearing,
'This place is too small for us;
    give us more space to live in.'
²¹Then you will say in your heart,
    'Who bore me these?
I was bereaved and barren;
    I was exiled and rejected.
Who brought these up?
I was left all alone,
    but these—where have they come
        from?'"

²²This is what the Sovereign LORD says:

"See, I will beckon to the Gentiles,
    I will lift up my banner to the peoples;
they will bring your sons in their arms
    and carry your daughters on their
        shoulders.
²³Kings will be your foster fathers,
    and their queens your nursing mothers.
They will bow down before you with their
        faces to the ground;
    they will lick the dust at your feet.
Then you will know that I am the LORD;
    those who hope in me will not be
        disappointed."

²⁴Can plunder be taken from warriors,
    or captives rescued from the fierce?[b]

²⁵But this is what the LORD says:

"Yes, captives will be taken from
        warriors,
    and plunder retrieved from the fierce;
I will contend with those who contend
        with you,
    and your children I will save.

²⁶I will make your oppressors eat their own
        flesh;
    they will be drunk on their own blood,
        as with wine.
Then all mankind will know
    that I, the LORD, am your Saviour,
    your Redeemer, the Mighty One of
        Jacob."

Israel's Sin and the Servant's Obedience

50 This is what the LORD says:

"Where is your mother's certificate of
        divorce
    with which I sent her away?
Or to which of my creditors
    did I sell you?
Because of your sins you were sold;
    because of your transgressions your
        mother was sent away.
²When I came, why was there no-one?
    When I called, why was there no-one to
        answer?
Was my arm too short to ransom you?
    Do I lack the strength to rescue you?
By a mere rebuke I dry up the sea,
    I turn rivers into a desert;
their fish rot for lack of water
    and die of thirst.
³I clothe the sky with darkness
    and make sackcloth its covering."

⁴The Sovereign LORD has given me an
        instructed tongue,
    to know the word that sustains the
        weary.
He wakens me morning by morning,
    wakens my ear to listen like one being
        taught.
⁵The Sovereign LORD has opened my ears,
    and I have not been rebellious;
    I have not drawn back.
⁶I offered my back to those who beat me,
    my cheeks to those who pulled out my
        beard;
I did not hide my face
    from mocking and spitting.
⁷Because the Sovereign LORD helps me,
    I will not be disgraced.
Therefore have I set my face like flint,
    and I know I will not be put to shame.
⁸He who vindicates me is near.
    Who then will bring charges against
        me?
    Let us face each other!
Who is my accuser?
    Let him confront me!
⁹It is the Sovereign LORD who helps me.
    Who is he who will condemn me?
They will all wear out like a garment;
    the moths will eat them up.

¹⁰Who among you fears the LORD
    and obeys the word of his servant?
Let him who walks in the dark,
    who has no light,
trust in the name of the LORD
    and rely on his God.

---

b24 Dead Sea Scrolls, Vulgate and Syriac (see also Septuagint and verse 25); Masoretic Text *righteous*

¹¹But now, all you who light fires
and provide yourselves with flaming
torches,
go, walk in the light of your fires
and of the torches you have set ablaze.
This is what you shall receive from my
hand:
You will lie down in torment.

Everlasting Salvation for Zion

51 "Listen to me, you who pursue
righteousness
and who seek the LORD:
Look to the rock from which you were cut
and to the quarry from which you were
hewn;
²look to Abraham, your father,
and to Sarah, who gave you birth.
When I called him he was but one,
and I blessed him and made him many.
³The LORD will surely comfort Zion
and will look with compassion on all her
ruins;
he will make her deserts like Eden,
her wastelands like the garden of the
LORD.
Joy and gladness will be found in her,
thanksgiving and the sound of singing.

⁴"Listen to me, my people;
hear me, my nation:
The law will go out from me;
my justice will become a light to the
nations.
⁵My righteousness draws near speedily,
my salvation is on the way,
and my arm will bring justice to the
nations.
The islands will look to me
and wait in hope for my arm.
⁶Lift up your eyes to the heavens,
look at the earth beneath;
the heavens will vanish like smoke,
the earth will wear out like a garment
and its inhabitants die like flies.
But my salvation will last for ever,
my righteousness will never fail.

⁷"Hear me, you who know what is right,
you people who have my law in your
hearts:
Do not fear the reproach of men
or be terrified by their insults.
⁸For the moth will eat them up like a
garment;
the worm will devour them like wool.
But my righteousness will last for ever,
my salvation through all generations."

⁹Awake, awake! Clothe yourself with
strength,
O arm of the LORD;
awake, as in days gone by,
as in generations of old.
Was it not you who cut Rahab to pieces,
who pierced that monster through?
¹⁰Was it not you who dried up the sea,
the waters of the great deep,

who made a road in the depths of the sea
so that the redeemed might cross over?
¹¹The ransomed of the LORD will return.
They will enter Zion with singing;
everlasting joy will crown their heads.
Gladness and joy will overtake them,
and sorrow and sighing will flee away.

¹²"I, even I, am he who comforts you.
Who are you that you fear mortal men,
the sons of men, who are but grass,
¹³that you forget the LORD your Maker,
who stretched out the heavens
and laid the foundations of the earth,
that you live in constant terror every day
because of the wrath of the oppressor,
who is bent on destruction?
For where is the wrath of the oppressor?
¹⁴ The cowering prisoners will soon be set
free;
they will not die in their dungeon,
nor will they lack bread.
¹⁵For I am the LORD your God,
who churns up the sea so that its waves
roar—
the LORD Almighty is his name.
¹⁶I have put my words in your mouth
and covered you with the shadow of my
hand—
I who set the heavens in place,
who laid the foundations of the earth,
and who say to Zion, 'You are my
people.'"

The Cup of the LORD's Wrath

¹⁷Awake, awake!
Rise up, O Jerusalem,
you who have drunk from the hand of the
LORD
the cup of his wrath,
you who have drained to its dregs
the goblet that makes men stagger.
¹⁸Of all the sons she bore
there was none to guide her;
of all the sons she brought up
there was none to take her by the hand.
¹⁹These double calamities have come upon
you—
who can comfort you?—
ruin and destruction, famine and sword—
who can^a console you?
²⁰Your sons have fainted;
they lie at the head of every street,
like antelope caught in a net.
They are filled with the wrath of the LORD
and the rebuke of your God.

²¹Therefore hear this, you afflicted one,
made drunk, but not with wine.
²²This is what your Sovereign LORD says,
your God, who defends his people:
"See, I have taken out of your hand
the cup that made you stagger;
from that cup, the goblet of my wrath,
you will never drink again.
²³I will put it into the hands of your
tormentors,
who said to you,

---

^a19 Dead Sea Scrolls, Septuagint, Vulgate and Syriac; Masoretic Text / how can I

'Fall prostrate that we may walk over
    you.'
And you made your back like the ground,
    like a street to be walked over.''

52 Awake, awake, O Zion,
        clothe yourself with strength.
Put on your garments of splendour,
    O Jerusalem, the holy city.
The uncircumcised and defiled
    will not enter you again.
[2]Shake off your dust;
    rise up, sit enthroned, O Jerusalem.
Free yourself from the chains on your
    neck,
    O captive Daughter of Zion.

[3]For this is what the LORD says:

"You were sold for nothing,
    and without money you will be
        redeemed."

[4]For this is what the Sovereign LORD says:

"At first my people went down to Egypt to
        live;
    lately, Assyria has oppressed them.

[5]"And now what do I have here?" declares the LORD.

"For my people have been taken away for
        nothing,
    and those who rule them mock,"[a]
                        declares the LORD.
"And all day long
    my name is constantly blasphemed.
[6]Therefore my people will know my name;
    therefore in that day they will know
    that it is I who foretold it.
    Yes, it is I."

[7]How beautiful on the mountains
    are the feet of those who bring good
        news,
    who proclaim peace,
    who bring good tidings,
    who proclaim salvation,
    who say to Zion,
    "Your God reigns!"
[8]Listen! Your watchmen lift up their
        voices;
    together they shout for joy.
When the LORD returns to Zion,
    they will see it with their own eyes.
[9]Burst into songs of joy together,
    you ruins of Jerusalem,
for the LORD has comforted his people,
    he has redeemed Jerusalem.
[10]The LORD will lay bare his holy arm
    in the sight of all the nations,
and all the ends of the earth will see
    the salvation of our God.

[11]Depart, depart, go out from there!
    Touch no unclean thing!

Come out from it and be pure,
    you who carry the vessels of the LORD.
[12]But you will not leave in haste
    or go in flight;
for the LORD will go before you,
    the God of Israel will be your rear guard.

The Suffering and Glory of the Servant
[13]See, my servant will act wisely;[b]
    he will be raised and lifted up and highly
        exalted.
[14]Just as there were many who were
        appalled at him[c]—
    his appearance was so disfigured beyond
        that of any man
    and his form marred beyond human
        likeness—
[15]so will he sprinkle many nations,[d]
    and kings will shut their mouths because
        of him.
For what they were not told, they will see,
    and what they have not heard, they will
        understand.

53 Who has believed our message
        and to whom has the arm of the LORD
        been revealed?
[2]He grew up before him like a tender shoot,
    and like a root out of dry ground.
He had no beauty or majesty to attract us
        to him,
    nothing in his appearance that we
        should desire him.
[3]He was despised and rejected by men,
    a man of sorrows, and familiar with
        suffering.
Like one from whom men hide their faces
    he was despised, and we esteemed him
        not.

[4]Surely he took up our infirmities
    and carried our sorrows,
yet we considered him stricken by God,
    smitten by him, and afflicted.
[5]But he was pierced for our transgressions,
    he was crushed for our iniquities;
the punishment that brought us peace was
        upon him,
    and by his wounds we are healed.
[6]We all, like sheep, have gone astray,
    each of us has turned to his own way;
and the LORD has laid on him
    the iniquity of us all.

[7]He was oppressed and afflicted,
    yet he did not open his mouth;
he was led like a lamb to the slaughter,
    and as a sheep before her shearers is
        silent,
so he did not open his mouth.
[8]By oppression[a] and judgment he was
        taken away.
And who can speak of his descendants?
For he was cut off from the land of the
        living;
    for the transgression of my people he
        was stricken.[b]

---

[a]5 Dead Sea Scrolls and Vulgate; Masoretic Text *wail*   [b]13 Or *will prosper*   [c]14 Hebrew *you*
[d]15 Hebrew; Septuagint *so will many nations marvel at him*   [a]8 Or *From arrest*
[b]8 Or *away. / Yet who of his generation considered / that he was cut off from the land of the living / for the transgression of my people, / to whom the blow was due?*

9He was assigned a grave with the wicked,
   and with the rich in his death,
though he had done no violence,
   nor was any deceit in his mouth.

10Yet it was the LORD's will to crush him and
      cause him to suffer,
   and though the LORD makes*c* his life a
      guilt offering,
he will see his offspring and prolong his
      days,
   and the will of the LORD will prosper in
      his hand.
11After the suffering of his soul,
   he will see the light ⌐of life ⌐*d* and be
      satisfied;*e*
by his knowledge*f* my righteous servant
      will justify many,
   and he will bear their iniquities.
12Therefore I will give him a portion among
      the great,*g*
   and he will divide the spoils with the
      strong,*h*
because he poured out his life unto death,
   and was numbered with the
      transgressors.
For he bore the sin of many,
   and made intercession for the
      transgressors.

The Future Glory of Zion

54 "Sing, O barren woman,
   you who never bore a child;
burst into song, shout for joy,
   you who were never in labour;
because more are the children of the
      desolate woman
   than of her who has a husband,"
                              says the LORD.
2"Enlarge the place of your tent,
   stretch your tent curtains wide,
      do not hold back;
lengthen your cords,
   strengthen your stakes.
3For you will spread out to the right and to
      the left;
   your descendants will dispossess
      nations
   and settle in their desolate cities.

4"Do not be afraid; you will not suffer
      shame.
   Do not fear disgrace; you will not be
      humiliated.
You will forget the shame of your youth
   and remember no more the reproach of
      your widowhood.
5For your Maker is your husband—
   the LORD Almighty is his name—
the Holy One of Israel is your Redeemer;
   he is called the God of all the earth.
6The LORD will call you back
   as if you were a wife deserted and
      distressed in spirit—
a wife who married young,
   only to be rejected," says your God.

7"For a brief moment I abandoned you,
   but with deep compassion I will bring
      you back.
8In a surge of anger
   I hid my face from you for a moment,
but with everlasting kindness
   I will have compassion on you,"
   says the LORD your Redeemer.

9"To me this is like the days of Noah,
   when I swore that the waters of Noah
      would never again cover the earth.
So now I have sworn not to be angry with
      you,
   never to rebuke you again.
10Though the mountains be shaken
   and the hills be removed,
yet my unfailing love for you will not be
      shaken
   nor my covenant of peace be removed,"
   says the LORD, who has compassion on
      you.

11"O afflicted city, lashed by storms and not
      comforted,
   I will build you with stones of
      turquoise,*a*
   your foundations with sapphires.*b*
12I will make your battlements of rubies,
   your gates of sparkling jewels,
   and all your walls of precious stones.
13All your sons will be taught by the LORD,
   and great will be your children's
      peace.
14In righteousness you will be established:
   Tyranny will be far from you;
   you will have nothing to fear.
Terror will be far removed;
   it will not come near you.
15If anyone does attack you, it will not be
      my doing;
   whoever attacks you will surrender to
      you.

16"See, it is I who created the blacksmith
   who fans the coals into flame
and forges a weapon fit for its work.
And it is I who have created the destroyer
      to work havoc;
17   no weapon forged against you will
      prevail,
   and you will refute every tongue that
      accuses you.
This is the heritage of the servants of the
      LORD,
   and this is their vindication from me,"
                              declares the LORD.

Invitation to the Thirsty

55 "Come, all you who are thirsty,
   come to the waters;
and you who have no money,
   come, buy and eat!
Come, buy wine and milk
   without money and without cost.

---

*c*10 Hebrew *though you make*
*d*11 Dead Sea Scrolls (see also Septuagint); Masoretic Text does not have *the light ⌐of life ⌐*.
*e*11 Or (with Masoretic Text) *11He will see the result of the suffering of his soul / and be satisfied*
*f*11 Or *by knowledge of him*   *g*12 Or *many*   *h*12 Or *numerous*
*a*11 The meaning of the Hebrew for this word is uncertain.   *b*11 Or *lapis lazuli*

ISAIAH 52:13 to 53:12

'He grew up before him like a tender shoot, and like a root out of dry ground. He had no beauty or majesty to attract us to him, nothing in his appearance that we should desire him. He was despised and rejected by men' (53:2, 3).

THE APPEAL OF THE UNATTRACTIVE. Christmas celebrations, carols, sermons all emphasize the welcome to the Saviour, but for every shepherd or wise man who welcomed him there were thousands who ignored or rejected him. The truth is that the ideal Servant (this is Isaiah's fourth 'servant song') did not come to a welcoming world, does not now come to a welcoming world. And the reason why the millions do not welcome him is that they see him in a very different light from how God sees him. He does not fit into the common view that 'life should consist of a journey from discomfort to comfort, from pain to pleasure, from want to plenty' (D. W. Cleverley Ford).

Isaiah portrays the suffering Servant in a selection of uncomplimentary snapshots: a man unrecognizable because of disfigurement (52:14); an unattractive plant struggling to keep alive in dry ground (53:2 – God sees it as the promise of life, man sees it as the harbinger of death); a dumb animal being led to the slaughterhouse (53:7); a man unjustly accused and executed amid total apathy concerning his fate (53:8). What is there to attract anybody there? Who would believe that this was God's Servant? We are 'amazed', 'dumbfounded', 'speechless' (52:14) and only begin to see his attractiveness when we realize that all his sufferings are really ours (53:4–6 – 'he carried our sorrows' etc.).

Perhaps we should seek out some of the world's unfortunates, the unattractive, the disabled, the oppressed, even though we find them repulsive, and try to see the Christ, the suffering Servant in those who bear more than their share of the world's suffering for which we are all responsible.

→616

JEREMIAH 1:11–12

'The word of the Lord came to me: "What do you see, Jeremiah?" "I see the branch of an almond tree," I replied' (v. 11).

THE FLEDGLING PROPHET with his new gifts was tested by his new master. Part of the prophetic skill is to see the ordinary things we see, but to see them with a divine insight. Jeremiah was to observe two significant things about the almond branch. In Israel, the almond branch was the first to awaken from winter. It is the reminder of the life which continues to exist even though appearances are to the contrary. To the new prophet, aware of the despondency of the times, the fear of great nations, the feelings that God was no longer active, it was the perfect indication that the springtime of God's mercy as well as that of nature, was at hand.

Translation loses for us the second significant point: the sound of the Hebrew word for 'almond' differs by one vowel sound only from the word for 'wakefulness'. This play on words is not trivial, God is not uncaring and lethargic; he is active, watching closely to ensure that his words come to fulfilment.

Happily, not only to the prophet's eye, but to many other sensitive people, there is evidence that even in the darkest days, the Lord God is at work. How else could faith be upheld, goodness be sustained, life's direction be maintained, were it not for the constant watchfulness and care of our loving heavenly Father? God is, surely, never closer to us than when we feel in our distress that he is distant.

> *God is your wisdom, God is your might,*
> *God's ever near you, guiding aright;*
> *He understands you, knows all you need;*
> *Trusting in him you'll surely succeed.*

(*Lucy Milward Booth-Hellberg*)

→631

²Why spend money on what is not bread,
  and your labour on what does not
    satisfy?
Listen, listen to me, and eat what is good,
  and your soul will delight in the richest
    of fare.
³Give ear and come to me;
  hear me, that your soul may live.
I will make an everlasting covenant with
    you,
  my faithful love promised to David.
⁴See, I have made him a witness to the
    peoples,
  a leader and commander of the peoples.
⁵Surely you will summon nations you know
    not,
  and nations that do not know you will
    hasten to you,
because of the LORD your God,
  the Holy One of Israel,
  for he has endowed you with
    splendour.''

⁶Seek the LORD while he may be found;
  call on him while he is near.
⁷Let the wicked forsake his way
  and the evil man his thoughts.
Let him turn to the LORD, and he will have
    mercy on him,
  and to our God, for he will freely
    pardon.

⁸''For my thoughts are not your thoughts,
  neither are your ways my ways,''
                          declares the LORD.
⁹''As the heavens are higher than the earth,
  so are my ways higher than your ways
  and my thoughts than your thoughts.
¹⁰As the rain and the snow
  come down from heaven,
and do not return to it
  without watering the earth
and making it bud and flourish,
  so that it yields seed for the sower and
    bread for the eater,
¹¹so is my word that goes out from my
    mouth:
  It will not return to me empty,
but will accomplish what I desire
  and achieve the purpose for which
    I sent it.
¹²You will go out in joy
  and be led forth in peace;
the mountains and hills
  will burst into song before you,
and all the trees of the field
  will clap their hands.
¹³Instead of the thornbush will grow the pine
    tree,
  and instead of briers the myrtle will
    grow.
This will be for the LORD's renown,
  for an everlasting sign,
  which will not be destroyed.''

Salvation for Others

56 This is what the LORD says:

''Maintain justice
  and do what is right,

for my salvation is close at hand
  and my righteousness will soon be
    revealed.
²Blessed is the man who does this,
  the man who holds it fast,
who keeps the Sabbath without
    desecrating it,
  and keeps his hand from doing any
    evil.''

³Let no foreigner who has bound himself to
    the LORD say,
  ''The LORD will surely exclude me from
    his people.''
And let not any eunuch complain,
  ''I am only a dry tree.''

⁴For this is what the LORD says:

''To the eunuchs who keep my Sabbaths,
  who choose what pleases me
  and hold fast to my covenant—
⁵to them I will give within my temple and
    its walls
  a memorial and a name
  better than sons and daughters;
I will give them an everlasting name
  that will not be cut off.
⁶And foreigners who bind themselves to the
    LORD
  to serve him,
to love the name of the LORD,
  and to worship him,
all who keep the Sabbath without
    desecrating it
  and who hold fast to my covenant—
⁷these I will bring to my holy mountain
  and give them joy in my house of
    prayer.
Their burnt offerings and sacrifices
  will be accepted on my altar;
for my house will be called
  a house of prayer for all nations.''
⁸The Sovereign LORD declares—
  he who gathers the exiles of Israel:
''I will gather still others to them
  besides those already gathered.''

God's Accusation Against the Wicked

⁹Come, all you beasts of the field,
  come and devour, all you beasts of the
    forest!
¹⁰Israel's watchmen are blind,
  they all lack knowledge;
they are all mute dogs,
  they cannot bark;
they lie around and dream,
  they love to sleep.
¹¹They are dogs with mighty appetites;
  they never have enough.
They are shepherds who lack
    understanding;
  they all turn to their own way,
  each seeks his own gain.
¹²''Come,'' each one cries, ''let me get
    wine!
  Let us drink our fill of beer!
And tomorrow will be like today,
  or even far better.''

57

The righteous perish,
  and no-one ponders it in his heart;
devout men are taken away,
  and no-one understands
that the righteous are taken away
  to be spared from evil.
2Those who walk uprightly
  enter into peace;
  they find rest as they lie in death.

3"But you—come here, you sons of a
    sorceress,
  you offspring of adulterers and
    prostitutes!
4Whom are you mocking?
  At whom do you sneer
  and stick out your tongue?
Are you not a brood of rebels,
  the offspring of liars?
5You burn with lust among the oaks
  and under every spreading tree;
you sacrifice your children in the ravines
  and under the overhanging crags.

6⌊The idols⌋ among the smooth stones of
    the ravines are your portion;
  they, they are your lot.
Yes, to them you have poured out drink
    offerings
  and offered grain offerings.
  In the light of these things, should I
    relent?
7You have made your bed on a high and
    lofty hill;
  there you went up to offer your
    sacrifices.
8Behind your doors and your doorposts
  you have put your pagan symbols.
Forsaking me, you uncovered your bed,
  you climbed into it and opened it wide;
you made a pact with those whose beds
    you love,
  and you looked on their nakedness.
9You went to Molech[a] with olive oil
  and increased your perfumes.
You sent your ambassadors[b] far away;
  you descended to the grave[c] itself!
10You were wearied by all your ways,
  but you would not say, 'It is hopeless.'
You found renewal of your strength,
  and so you did not faint.

11"Whom have you so dreaded and feared
  that you have been false to me,
and have neither remembered me
  nor pondered this in your hearts?
Is it not because I have long been silent
  that you do not fear me?
12I will expose your righteousness and your
    works,
  and they will not benefit you.
13When you cry out for help,
  let your collection ⌊of idols⌋ save you!
The wind will carry all of them off,
  a mere breath will blow them away.
But the man who makes me his refuge
  will inherit the land
  and possess my holy mountain."

Comfort for the Contrite

14And it will be said:

  "Build up, build up, prepare the road!
  Remove the obstacles out of the way of
    my people."
15For this is what the high and lofty One
    says—
  he who lives for ever, whose name is
    holy:
  "I live in a high and holy place,
  but also with him who is contrite and
    lowly in spirit,
to revive the spirit of the lowly
  and to revive the heart of the contrite.
16I will not accuse for ever,
  nor will I always be angry,
for then the spirit of man would grow faint
    before me—
  the breath of man that I have created.
17I was enraged by his sinful greed;
  I punished him, and hid my face in
    anger,
  yet he kept on in his wilful ways.
18I have seen his ways, but I will heal him;
  I will guide him and restore comfort to
    him,
19 creating praise on the lips of the
    mourners in Israel.
  Peace, peace, to those far and near,"
  says the LORD. "And I will heal them."
20But the wicked are like the tossing sea,
  which cannot rest,
  whose waves cast up mire and mud.
21"There is no peace," says my God, "for
  the wicked."

True Fasting

58

"Shout it aloud, do not hold back.
  Raise your voice like a trumpet.
Declare to my people their rebellion
  and to the house of Jacob their sins.
2For day after day they seek me out;
  they seem eager to know my ways,
as if they were a nation that does what is
    right
  and has not forsaken the commands of
    its God.
They ask me for just decisions
  and seem eager for God to come near
    them.
3'Why have we fasted,' they say,
  'and you have not seen it?
Why have we humbled ourselves,
  and you have not noticed?'

  "Yet on the day of your fasting, you do as
    you please
  and exploit all your workers.
4Your fasting ends in quarrelling and strife,
  and in striking each other with wicked
    fists.
You cannot fast as you do today
  and expect your voice to be heard on
    high.
5Is this the kind of fast I have chosen,
  only a day for a man to humble himself?
Is it only for bowing one's head like a reed
  and for lying on sackcloth and ashes?

---

[a]9 Or to the king   [b]9 Or idols   [c]9 Hebrew Sheol

Is that what you call a fast,
a day acceptable to the LORD?

6"Is not this the kind of fasting I have
chosen:
to loose the chains of injustice
and untie the cords of the yoke,
to set the oppressed free
and break every yoke?
7Is it not to share your food with the hungry
and to provide the poor wanderer with
shelter—
when you see the naked, to clothe him,
and not to turn away from your own
flesh and blood?
8Then your light will break forth like the
dawn,
and your healing will quickly appear;
then your righteousness[a] will go before
you,
and the glory of the LORD will be your
rear guard.
9Then you will call, and the LORD will
answer;
you will cry for help, and he will say:
Here am I.

"If you do away with the yoke of
oppression,
with the pointing finger and malicious
talk,
10and if you spend yourselves on behalf of
the hungry
and satisfy the needs of the oppressed,
then your light will rise in the darkness,
and your night will become like the
noonday.
11The LORD will guide you always;
he will satisfy your needs in a
sun-scorched land
and will strengthen your frame.
You will be like a well-watered garden,
like a spring whose waters never fail.
12Your people will rebuild the ancient ruins
and will raise up the age-old
foundations;
you will be called Repairer of Broken
Walls,
Restorer of Streets with Dwellings.

13"If you keep your feet from breaking the
Sabbath
and from doing as you please on my holy
day,
if you call the Sabbath a delight
and the LORD's holy day honourable,
and if you honour it by not going your own
way
and not doing as you please or speaking
idle words,
14then you will find your joy in the LORD,
and I will cause you to ride on the
heights of the land
and to feast on the inheritance of your
father Jacob."
The mouth of the LORD
has spoken.

Sin, Confession and Redemption

59 Surely the arm of the LORD is not too
short to save,
nor his ear too dull to hear.
2But your iniquities have separated
you from your God;
your sins have hidden his face from you,
so that he will not hear.
3For your hands are stained with blood,
your fingers with guilt.
Your lips have spoken lies,
and your tongue mutters wicked things.
4No-one calls for justice;
no-one pleads his case with integrity.
They rely on empty arguments and speak
lies;
they conceive trouble and give birth to
evil.
5They hatch the eggs of vipers
and spin a spider's web.
Whoever eats their eggs will die,
and when one is broken, an adder is
hatched.
6Their cobwebs are useless for clothing;
they cannot cover themselves with what
they make.
Their deeds are evil deeds,
and acts of violence are in their hands.
7Their feet rush into sin;
they are swift to shed innocent blood.
Their thoughts are evil thoughts;
ruin and destruction mark their ways.
8The way of peace they do not know;
there is no justice in their paths.
They have turned them into crooked
roads;
no-one who walks in them will know
peace.

9So justice is far from us,
and righteousness does not reach us.
We look for light, but all is darkness;
for brightness, but we walk in deep
shadows.
10Like the blind we grope along the wall,
feeling our way like men without eyes.
At midday we stumble as if it were
twilight;
among the strong, we are like the dead.
11We all growl like bears;
we moan mournfully like doves.
We look for justice, but find none;
for deliverance, but it is far away.

12For our offences are many in your sight,
and our sins testify against us.
Our offences are ever with us,
and we acknowledge our iniquities:
13rebellion and treachery against the LORD,
turning our backs on our God,
fomenting oppression and revolt,
uttering lies our hearts have conceived.
14So justice is driven back,
and righteousness stands at a distance;
truth has stumbled in the streets,
honesty cannot enter.
15Truth is nowhere to be found,
and whoever shuns evil becomes a prey.

[a]8 Or *your righteous One*

The LORD looked and was displeased
   that there was no justice.
16He saw that there was no-one,
   he was appalled that there was no-one to
      intervene;
so his own arm worked salvation for him,
   and his own righteousness sustained
      him.
17He put on righteousness as his breastplate,
   and the helmet of salvation on his head;
he put on the garments of vengeance
   and wrapped himself in zeal as in a
      cloak.
18According to what they have done,
   so will he repay
wrath to his enemies
   and retribution to his foes;
he will repay the islands their due.
19From the west, men will fear the name of
      the LORD,
   and from the rising of the sun, they will
      revere his glory.
For he will come like a pent-up flood
   that the breath of the LORD drives
      along.a

20"The Redeemer will come to Zion,
   to those in Jacob who repent of their
      sins,"

                              declares the LORD.

21"As for me, this is my covenant with
them," says the LORD. "My Spirit, who is on
you, and my words that I have put in your
mouth will not depart from your mouth, or
from the mouths of your children, or from the
mouths of their descendants from this time
on and for ever," says the LORD.

The Glory of Zion

60 "Arise, shine, for your light has
   come,
   and the glory of the LORD rises upon
      you.
2See, darkness covers the earth
   and thick darkness is over the peoples,
but the LORD rises upon you
   and his glory appears over you.
3Nations will come to your light,
   and kings to the brightness of your
      dawn.

4"Lift up your eyes and look about you:
   All assemble and come to you;
your sons come from afar,
   and your daughters are carried on the
      arm.
5Then you will look and be radiant,
   your heart will throb and swell with joy;
the wealth on the seas will be brought to
      you,
   to you the riches of the nations will
      come.
6Herds of camels will cover your land,
   young camels of Midian and Ephah.
And all from Sheba will come,
   bearing gold and incense
   and proclaiming the praise of the LORD.

7All Kedar's flocks will be gathered to you,
   the rams of Nebaioth will serve you;
they will be accepted as offerings on my
      altar,
   and I will adorn my glorious temple.

8"Who are these that fly along like clouds,
   like doves to their nests?
9Surely the islands look to me;
   in the lead are the ships of Tarshish,a
bringing your sons from afar,
   with their silver and gold,
to the honour of the LORD your God,
   the Holy One of Israel,
   for he has endowed you with splendour.

10"Foreigners will rebuild your walls,
   and their kings will serve you.
Though in anger I struck you,
   in favour I will show you compassion.
11Your gates will always stand open,
   they will never be shut, day or night,
so that men may bring you the wealth of
      the nations—
   their kings led in triumphal procession.
12For the nation or kingdom that will not
      serve you will perish;
   it will be utterly ruined.

13"The glory of Lebanon will come to you,
   the pine, the fir and the cypress
      together,
to adorn the place of my sanctuary;
   and I will glorify the place of my feet.
14The sons of your oppressors will come
      bowing before you;
   all who despise you will bow down at
      your feet
and will call you the City of the LORD,
   Zion of the Holy One of Israel.

15"Although you have been forsaken and
      hated,
   with no-one travelling through,
I will make you the everlasting pride
   and the joy of all generations.
16You will drink the milk of nations
   and be nursed at royal breasts.
Then you will know that I, the LORD, am
      your Saviour,
   your Redeemer, the Mighty One of
      Jacob.
17Instead of bronze I will bring you gold,
   and silver in place of iron.
Instead of wood I will bring you bronze,
   and iron in place of stones.
I will make peace your governor
   and righteousness your ruler.
18No longer will violence be heard in your
      land,
   nor ruin or destruction within your
      borders,
but you will call your walls Salvation
   and your gates Praise.
19The sun will no more be your light by day,
   nor will the brightness of the moon shine
      on you,

---

a19 Or *When the enemy comes in like a flood, / the Spirit of the LORD will put him to flight*
a9 Or *the trading ships*

for the LORD will be your everlasting light,
  and your God will be your glory.
²⁰Your sun will never set again,
  and your moon will wane no more;
the LORD will be your everlasting light,
  and your days of sorrow will end.
²¹Then will all your people be righteous
  and they will possess the land for ever.
They are the shoot I have planted,
  the work of my hands,
  for the display of my splendour.
²²The least of you will become a thousand,
  the smallest a mighty nation.
I am the LORD;
  in its time I will do this swiftly.''

The Year of the LORD's Favour

61 The Spirit of the Sovereign LORD is
  on me,
  because the LORD has anointed me
to preach good news to the poor.
He has sent me to bind up the
  broken-hearted,
to proclaim freedom for the captives
  and release from darkness for the
  prisoners,^a
²to proclaim the year of the LORD's favour
  and the day of vengeance of our God,
to comfort all who mourn,
³   and provide for those who grieve in
    Zion—
to bestow on them a crown of beauty
  instead of ashes,
the oil of gladness
  instead of mourning,
and a garment of praise
  instead of a spirit of despair.
They will be called oaks of righteousness,
  a planting of the LORD
  for the display of his splendour.

⁴They will rebuild the ancient ruins
  and restore the places long devastated;
they will renew the ruined cities
  that have been devastated for
  generations.
⁵Aliens will shepherd your flocks;
  foreigners will work your fields and
  vineyards.
⁶And you will be called priests of the LORD,
  you will be named ministers of our God.
You will feed on the wealth of nations,
  and in their riches you will boast.

⁷Instead of their shame
  my people will receive a double portion,
and instead of disgrace
  they will rejoice in their inheritance;
and so they will inherit a double portion in
  their land,
  and everlasting joy will be theirs.

⁸''For I, the LORD, love justice;
  I hate robbery and iniquity.
In my faithfulness I will reward them
  and make an everlasting covenant with
  them.
⁹Their descendants will be known among
  the nations

and their offspring among the peoples.
All who see them will acknowledge
  that they are a people the LORD has
  blessed.''

¹⁰I delight greatly in the LORD;
  my soul rejoices in my God.
For he has clothed me with garments of
  salvation
  and arrayed me in a robe of
  righteousness,
as a bridegroom adorns his head like a
  priest,
  and as a bride adorns herself with her
  jewels.
¹¹For as the soil makes the young plant
  come up
  and a garden causes seeds to grow,
so the Sovereign LORD will make
  righteousness and praise
  spring up before all nations.

Zion's New Name

62 For Zion's sake I will not keep silent,
  for Jerusalem's sake I will not remain
  quiet,
till her righteousness shines out like the
  dawn,
  her salvation like a blazing torch.
²The nations will see your righteousness,
  and all kings your glory;
you will be called by a new name
  that the mouth of the LORD will bestow.
³You will be a crown of splendour in the
  LORD's hand,
  a royal diadem in the hand of your God.
⁴No longer will they call you Deserted,
  or name your land Desolate.
But you will be called Hephzibah,^a
  and your land Beulah;^b
for the LORD will take delight in you,
  and your land will be married.
⁵As a young man marries a maiden,
  so will your sons^c marry you;
as a bridegroom rejoices over his bride,
  so will your God rejoice over you.

⁶I have posted watchmen on your walls, O
  Jerusalem;
  they will never be silent day or night.
You who call on the LORD,
  give yourselves no rest,
⁷and give him no rest till he establishes
  Jerusalem
  and makes her the praise of the earth.

⁸The LORD has sworn by his right hand
  and by his mighty arm:
''Never again will I give your grain
  as food for your enemies,
and never again will foreigners drink the
  new wine
  for which you have toiled;
⁹but those who harvest it will eat it
  and praise the LORD,
and those who gather the grapes will
  drink it
  in the courts of my sanctuary.''

---

^a1 Hebrew; Septuagint *the blind*   ^a4 *Hephzibah* means *my delight is in her.*
^b4 *Beulah* means *married.*   ^c5 Or *Builder*

¹⁰Pass through, pass through the gates!
  Prepare the way for the people.
Build up, build up the highway!
  Remove the stones.
Raise a banner for the nations.

¹¹The LORD has made proclamation
  to the ends of the earth:
"Say to the Daughter of Zion,
  'See, your Saviour comes!
See, his reward is with him,
  and his recompense accompanies
  him.'"
¹²They will be called the Holy People,
  the Redeemed of the LORD;
and you will be called Sought After,
  the City No Longer Deserted.

God's Day of Vengeance and Redemption

63 Who is this coming from Edom,
  from Bozrah, with his garments
  stained crimson?
Who is this, robed in splendour,
  striding forward in the greatness of his
  strength?

"It is I, speaking in righteousness,
  mighty to save."

²Why are your garments red,
  like those of one treading the
  winepress?

³"I have trodden the winepress alone;
  from the nations no-one was with me.
I trampled them in my anger
  and trod them down in my wrath;
their blood spattered my garments,
  and I stained all my clothing.
⁴For the day of vengeance was in my heart,
  and the year of my redemption has
  come.
⁵I looked, but there was no-one to help,
  I was appalled that no-one gave support;
so my own arm worked salvation for me,
  and my own wrath sustained me.
⁶I trampled the nations in my anger;
  in my wrath I made them drunk
  and poured their blood on the ground."

Praise and Prayer

⁷I will tell of the kindnesses of the LORD,
  the deeds for which he is to be praised,
  according to all the LORD has done for
  us—
yes, the many good things he has done
  for the house of Israel,
  according to his compassion and many
  kindnesses.
⁸He said, "Surely they are my people,
  sons who will not be false to me";
  and so he became their Saviour.
⁹In all their distress he too was distressed,
  and the angel of his presence saved
  them.

In his love and mercy he redeemed them;
  he lifted them up and carried them
  all the days of old.
¹⁰Yet they rebelled
  and grieved his Holy Spirit.
So he turned and became their enemy
  and he himself fought against them.

¹¹Then his people recalled^a the days of old,
  the days of Moses and his people—
where is he who brought them through the
  sea,
  with the shepherd of his flock?
Where is he who set
  his Holy Spirit among them,
¹²who sent his glorious arm of power
  to be at Moses' right hand,
who divided the waters before them,
  to gain for himself everlasting renown,
¹³who led them through the depths?
Like a horse in open country,
  they did not stumble;
¹⁴like cattle that go down to the plain,
  they were given rest by the Spirit of the
  LORD.
This is how you guided your people
  to make for yourself a glorious name.

¹⁵Look down from heaven and see
  from your lofty throne, holy and
  glorious.
Where are your zeal and your might?
  Your tenderness and compassion are
  withheld from us.
¹⁶But you are our Father,
  though Abraham does not know us
  or Israel acknowledge us;
you, O LORD, are our Father,
  our Redeemer from of old is your name.
¹⁷Why, O LORD, do you make us wander
  from your ways
  and harden our hearts so that we do not
  revere you?
Return for the sake of your servants,
  the tribes that are your inheritance.
¹⁸For a little while your people possessed
  your holy place,
  but now our enemies have trampled
  down your sanctuary.
¹⁹We are yours from of old;
  but you have not ruled over them,
  they have not been called by your
  name.^b

64 Oh, that you would rend the
  heavens and come down,
  that the mountains would tremble before
  you!
²As when fire sets twigs ablaze
  and causes water to boil,
come down to make your name known to
  your enemies
  and cause the nations to quake before
  you!
³For when you did awesome things that we
  did not expect,
  you came down, and the mountains
  trembled before you.

---

^a11 Or *But may he recall*
^b19 Or *We are like those you have never ruled, / like those never called by your name*

⁴Since ancient times no-one has heard,
  no ear has perceived,
no eye has seen any God besides you,
  who acts on behalf of those who wait for
    him.
⁵You come to the help of those who gladly
    do right,
  who remember your ways.
But when we continued to sin against
    them,
  you were angry.
How then can we be saved?
⁶All of us have become like one who is
    unclean,
  and all our righteous acts are like filthy
    rags;
we all shrivel up like a leaf,
  and like the wind our sins sweep us
    away.
⁷No-one calls on your name
  or strives to lay hold of you;
for you have hidden your face from us
  and made us waste away because of our
    sins.

⁸Yet, O LORD, you are our Father.
  We are the clay, you are the potter;
  we are all the work of your hand.
⁹Do not be angry beyond measure, O LORD;
  do not remember our sins for ever.
Oh, look upon us we pray,
  for we are all your people.
¹⁰Your sacred cities have become a desert;
  even Zion is a desert, Jerusalem a
    desolation.
¹¹Our holy and glorious temple, where our
    fathers praised you,
  has been burned with fire,
  and all that we treasured lies in ruins.
¹²After all this, O LORD, will you hold
    yourself back?
  Will you keep silent and punish us
    beyond measure?

Judgment and Salvation

65 "I revealed myself to those who did
    not ask for me;
  I was found by those who did not seek
    me.
To a nation that did not call on my name,
  I said, 'Here am I, here am I.'
²All day long I have held out my hands
  to an obstinate people,
who walk in ways not good,
  pursuing their own imaginations—
³a people who continually provoke me
  to my very face,
offering sacrifices in gardens
  and burning incense on altars of brick;
⁴who sit among the graves
  and spend their nights keeping secret
    vigil;
who eat the flesh of pigs,
  and whose pots hold broth of unclean
    meat;
⁵who say, 'Keep away; don't come near
    me,
  for I am too sacred for you!'
Such people are smoke in my nostrils,
  a fire that keeps burning all day.

⁶"See, it stands written before me;
  I will not keep silent but will pay back in
    full;
I will pay it back into their laps—
⁷both your sins and the sins of your
    fathers,"
  says the LORD.
"Because they burned sacrifices on the
    mountains
  and defied me on the hills,
I will measure into their laps
  the full payment for their former
    deeds."

⁸This is what the LORD says:

"As when juice is still found in a cluster of
    grapes
  and men say, 'Don't destroy it,
    there is yet some good in it,'
so will I do on behalf of my servants;
  I will not destroy them all.
⁹I will bring forth descendants from Jacob,
  and from Judah those who will possess
    my mountains;
my chosen people will inherit them,
  and there will my servants live.
¹⁰Sharon will become a pasture for flocks,
  and the Valley of Achor a resting place
    for herds,
for my people who seek me.

¹¹"But as for you who forsake the LORD
  and forget my holy mountain,
who spread a table for Fortune
  and fill bowls of mixed wine for Destiny,
¹²I will destine you for the sword,
  and you will all bend down for the
    slaughter;
for I called but you did not answer,
  I spoke but you did not listen.
You did evil in my sight
  and chose what displeases me."

¹³Therefore this is what the Sovereign
LORD says:

"My servants will eat,
  but you will go hungry;
my servants will drink,
  but you will go thirsty;
my servants will rejoice,
  but you will be put to shame.
¹⁴My servants will sing
  out of the joy of their hearts,
but you will cry out
  from anguish of heart
  and wail in brokenness of spirit.
¹⁵You will leave your name
  to my chosen ones as a curse;
the Sovereign LORD will put you to death,
  but to his servants he will give another
    name.
¹⁶Whoever invokes a blessing in the land
  will do so by the God of truth;
he who takes an oath in the land
  will swear by the God of truth.
For the past troubles will be forgotten
  and hidden from my eyes.

New Heavens and a New Earth

17"Behold, I will create
    new heavens and a new earth.
The former things will not be remembered,
    nor will they come to mind.
18But be glad and rejoice for ever
    in what I will create,
for I will create Jerusalem to be a delight
    and its people a joy.
19I will rejoice over Jerusalem
    and take delight in my people;
the sound of weeping and of crying
    will be heard in it no more.

20"Never again will there be in it
    an infant who lives but a few days,
    or an old man who does not live out his
        years;
he who dies at a hundred
    will be thought a mere youth;
he who fails to reach*a* a hundred
    will be considered accursed.
21They will build houses and dwell in them;
    they will plant vineyards and eat their
        fruit.
22No longer will they build houses and
        others live in them,
    or plant and others eat.
For as the days of a tree,
    so will be the days of my people;
my chosen ones will long enjoy
    the works of their hands.
23They will not toil in vain
    or bear children doomed to misfortune;
for they will be a people blessed by the
        LORD,
    they and their descendants with them.
24Before they call I will answer;
    while they are still speaking I will hear.
25The wolf and the lamb will feed together,
    and the lion will eat straw like the ox,
    but dust will be the serpent's food.
They will neither harm nor destroy
    on all my holy mountain,"
                        says the LORD.

Judgment and Hope

66 This is what the LORD says:

"Heaven is my throne,
    and the earth is my footstool.
Where is the house you will build for me?
    Where will my resting place be?
2Has not my hand made all these things,
    and so they came into being?"
                        declares the LORD.

"This is the one I esteem:
    he who is humble and contrite in spirit,
    and trembles at my word.
3But whoever sacrifices a bull
    is like one who kills a man,
and whoever offers a lamb,
    like one who breaks a dog's neck;
whoever makes a grain offering
    is like one who presents pig's blood,
and whoever burns memorial incense,
    like one who worships an idol.

They have chosen their own ways,
    and their souls delight in their
        abominations;
4so I also will choose harsh treatment for
        them
    and will bring upon them what they
        dread.
For when I called, no-one answered,
    when I spoke, no-one listened.
They did evil in my sight
    and chose what displeases me."

5Hear the word of the LORD,
    you who tremble at his word;
"Your brothers who hate you,
    and exclude you because of my name,
        have said,
'Let the LORD be glorified,
    that we may see your joy!'
Yet they will be put to shame.
6Hear that uproar from the city,
    hear that noise from the temple!
It is the sound of the LORD
    repaying his enemies all they deserve.

7"Before she goes into labour,
    she gives birth;
before the pains come upon her,
    she delivers a son.
8Who has ever heard of such a thing?
    Who has ever seen such things?
Can a country be born in a day
    or a nation be brought forth in a
        moment?
Yet no sooner is Zion in labour
    than she gives birth to her children.
9Do I bring to the moment of birth
    and not give delivery?" says the LORD.
"Do I close up the womb
    when I bring to delivery?" says your
        God.

10"Rejoice with Jerusalem and be glad for
        her,
    all you who love her;
rejoice greatly with her,
    all you who mourn over her.
11For you will nurse and be satisfied
    at her comforting breasts;
you will drink deeply
    and delight in her overflowing
        abundance."

12For this is what the LORD says:

"I will extend peace to her like a river,
    and the wealth of nations like a flooding
        stream;
you will nurse and be carried on her arm
    and dandled on her knees.
13As a mother comforts her child,
    so will I comfort you;
and you will be comforted over
        Jerusalem."

14When you see this, your heart will rejoice
    and you will flourish like grass;
the hand of the LORD will be made known
    to his servants,
but his fury will be shown to his foes.

---

a20 Or / the sinner who reaches

¹⁵See, the LORD is coming with fire,
and his chariots are like a whirlwind;
he will bring down his anger with fury,
and his rebuke with flames of fire.
¹⁶For with fire and with his sword
the LORD will execute judgment upon all men,
and many will be those slain by the LORD.

¹⁷"Those who consecrate and purify themselves to go into the gardens, following the one in the midst of[a] those who eat the flesh of pigs and rats and other abominable things—they will meet their end together," declares the LORD.

¹⁸"And I, because of their actions and their imaginations, am about to come[b] and gather all nations and tongues, and they will come and see my glory.

¹⁹"I will set a sign among them, and I will send some of those who survive to the nations—to Tarshish, to the Libyans[c] and Lydians (famous as archers), to Tubal and Greece, and to the distant islands that have not heard of my fame or seen my glory. They will proclaim my glory among the nations. ²⁰And they will bring all your brothers, from all the nations, to my holy mountain in Jerusalem as an offering to the LORD—on horses, in chariots and wagons, and on mules and camels," says the LORD. "They will bring them, as the Israelites bring their grain offerings, to the temple of the LORD in ceremonially clean vessels. ²¹And I will select some of them also to be priests and Levites," says the LORD.

²²"As the new heavens and the new earth that I make will endure before me," declares the LORD, "so will your name and descendants endure. ²³From one New Moon to another and from one Sabbath to another, all mankind will come and bow down before me," says the LORD. ²⁴"And they will go out and look upon the dead bodies of those who rebelled against me; their worm will not die, nor will their fire be quenched, and they will be loathsome to all mankind."

---

a17 Or gardens behind one of your temples, and   b18 The meaning of the Hebrew for this clause is uncertain.
c19 Some Septuagint manuscripts Put (Libyans); Hebrew Pul

Jeremiah

1 The words of Jeremiah son of Hilkiah, one of the priests at Anathoth in the territory of Benjamin. ²The word of the LORD came to him in the thirteenth year of the reign of Josiah son of Amon king of Judah, ³and through the reign of Jehoiakim son of Josiah king of Judah, down to the fifth month of the eleventh year of Zedekiah son of Josiah king of Judah, when the people of Jerusalem went into exile.

The Call of Jeremiah

⁴The word of the LORD came to me, saying,

⁵"Before I formed you in the womb I
      knew*a* you,
   before you were born I set you apart;
   I appointed you as a prophet to the
      nations."

⁶"Ah, Sovereign LORD," I said, "I do not know how to speak; I am only a child."

⁷But the LORD said to me, "Do not say, 'I am only a child.' You must go to everyone I send you to and say whatever I command you. ⁸Do not be afraid of them, for I am with you and will rescue you," declares the LORD.

⁹Then the LORD reached out his hand and touched my mouth and said to me, "Now, I have put my words in your mouth. ¹⁰See, today I appoint you over nations and kingdoms to uproot and tear down, to destroy and overthrow, to build and to plant."

¹¹The word of the LORD came to me: "What do you see, Jeremiah?"

"I see the branch of an almond tree," I replied.

¹²The LORD said to me, "You have seen correctly, for I am watching*b* to see that my word is fulfilled."

¹³The word of the LORD came to me again: "What do you see?"

"I see a boiling pot, tilting away from the north," I answered.

¹⁴The LORD said to me, "From the north disaster will be poured out on all who live in the land. ¹⁵I am about to summon all the peoples of the northern kingdoms," declares the LORD.

"Their kings will come and set up their
      thrones
in the entrance of the gates of
      Jerusalem;
   they will come against all her surrounding
      walls
   and against all the towns of Judah.
¹⁶I will pronounce my judgments on my
      people
   because of their wickedness in forsaking
      me,
in burning incense to other gods
   and in worshipping what their hands
      have made.

¹⁷"Get yourself ready! Stand up and say to them whatever I command you. Do not be terrified by them, or I will terrify you before them. ¹⁸Today I have made you a fortified city, an iron pillar and a bronze wall to stand against the whole land—against the kings of Judah, its officials, its priests and the people of the land. ¹⁹They will fight against you but will not overcome you, for I am with you and will rescue you," declares the LORD.

Israel Forsakes God

2 The word of the LORD came to me: ²"Go and proclaim in the hearing of Jerusalem:

"'I remember the devotion of your youth,
   how as a bride you loved me
and followed me through the desert,
   through a land not sown.
³Israel was holy to the LORD,
   the firstfruits of his harvest;
all who devoured her were held guilty,
   and disaster overtook them,'"
                              declares the LORD.

⁴Hear the word of the LORD, O house of
      Jacob,
   all you clans of the house of Israel.

⁵This is what the LORD says:

"What fault did your fathers find in me,
   that they strayed so far from me?
They followed worthless idols
   and became worthless themselves.
⁶They did not ask, 'Where is the LORD,
   who brought us up out of Egypt

---

a5 Or *chose*   *b12* The Hebrew for *watching* sounds like the Hebrew for *almond tree*.

and led us through the barren wilderness,
    through a land of deserts and rifts,
a land of drought and darkness,[a]
    a land where no-one travels and no-one
        lives?'
[7]I brought you into a fertile land
    to eat its fruit and rich produce.
But you came and defiled my land
    and made my inheritance detestable.
[8]The priests did not ask,
    'Where is the LORD?'
Those who deal with the law did not know
        me;
    the leaders rebelled against me.
The prophets prophesied by Baal,
    following worthless idols.

[9]"Therefore I bring charges against you
        again,"
                        declares the LORD.
    "And I will bring charges against your
        children's children.
[10]Cross over to the coasts of Kittim[b] and
        look,
    send to Kedar[c] and observe closely;
    see if there has ever been anything like
        this:
[11]Has a nation ever changed its gods?
    (Yet they are not gods at all.)
But my people have exchanged their[d]
        Glory
    for worthless idols.
[12]Be appalled at this, O heavens,
    and shudder with great horror,"
                        declares the LORD.
[13]"My people have committed two sins:
They have forsaken me,
    the spring of living water,
and have dug their own cisterns,
    broken cisterns that cannot hold water.
[14]Is Israel a servant, a slave by birth?
    Why then has he become plunder?
[15]Lions have roared;
    they have growled at him.
They have laid waste his land;
    his towns are burned and deserted.
[16]Also, the men of Memphis[e] and
        Tahpanhes
    have shaved the crown of your head.[f]
[17]Have you not brought this on yourselves
    by forsaking the LORD your God
    when he led you in the way?
[18]Now why go to Egypt
    to drink water from the Shihor?[g]
And why go to Assyria
    to drink water from the River?[h]
[19]Your wickedness will punish you;
    your backsliding will rebuke you.
Consider then and realise
    how evil and bitter it is for you
when you forsake the LORD your God
    and have no awe of me,"
                declares the Lord,
            the LORD Almighty.

[20]"Long ago you broke off your yoke
    and tore off your bonds;

you said, 'I will not serve you!'
Indeed, on every high hill
    and under every spreading tree
    you lay down as a prostitute.
[21]I had planted you like a choice vine
    of sound and reliable stock.
How then did you turn against me
    into a corrupt, wild vine?
[22]Although you wash yourself with soda
    and use an abundance of soap,
    the stain of your guilt is still before me,"
                declares the Sovereign LORD.
[23]"How can you say, 'I am not defiled;
    I have not run after the Baals'?
See how you behaved in the valley;
    consider what you have done.
You are a swift she-camel
    running here and there,
[24]a wild donkey accustomed to the desert,
    sniffing the wind in her craving—
    in her heat who can restrain her?
Any males that pursue her need not tire
        themselves;
    at mating time they will find her.
[25]Do not run until your feet are bare
    and your throat is dry.
But you said, 'It's no use!
    I love foreign gods,
    and I must go after them.'

[26]"As a thief is disgraced when he is caught,
    so the house of Israel is disgraced—
they, their kings and their officials,
    their priests and their prophets.
[27]They say to wood, 'You are my father,'
    and to stone, 'You gave me birth.'
They have turned their backs to me
    and not their faces;
yet when they are in trouble, they say,
    'Come and save us!'
[28]Where then are the gods you made for
        yourselves?
    Let them come if they can save you
    when you are in trouble!
For you have as many gods
    as you have towns, O Judah.

[29]"Why do you bring charges against me?
    You have all rebelled against me,"
                        declares the LORD.
[30]"In vain I punished your people;
    they did not respond to correction.
Your sword has devoured your prophets
    like a ravening lion.

[31]"You of this generation, consider the
word of the LORD:

    "Have I been a desert to Israel
        or a land of great darkness?
Why do my people say, 'We are free to
        roam;
    we will come to you no more'?
[32]Does a maiden forget her jewellery,
    a bride her wedding ornaments?
Yet my people have forgotten me,
    days without number.

[a]6 Or and the shadow of death   [b]10 That is, Cyprus and western coastlands
[c]10 The home of Bedouin tribes in the Syro-Arabian desert
[d]11 Masoretic Text; an ancient Hebrew scribal tradition my   [e]16 Hebrew Noph
[f]16 Or have cracked your skull   [g]18 That is, a branch of the Nile   [h]18 That is, the Euphrates

³³How skilled you are at pursuing love!
　　Even the worst of women can learn from
　　　　your ways.
³⁴On your clothes men find
　　the lifeblood of the innocent poor,
　　though you did not catch them breaking
　　　　in.
Yet in spite of all this
³⁵　you say, 'I am innocent;
　　he is not angry with me.'
But I will pass judgment on you
　　because you say, 'I have not sinned.'
³⁶Why do you go about so much,
　　changing your ways?
You will be disappointed by Egypt
　　as you were by Assyria.
³⁷You will also leave that place
　　with your hands on your head,
for the LORD has rejected those you trust;
　　you will not be helped by them.

3   "If a man divorces his wife
　　and she leaves him and marries another
　　　　man,
　　should he return to her again?
　　Would not the land be completely
　　　　defiled?
But you have lived as a prostitute with
　　　　many lovers—
　　would you now return to me?"
　　　　　　　　　declares the LORD.
²"Look up to the barren heights and see.
　　Is there any place where you have not
　　　　been ravished?
By the roadside you sat waiting for lovers,
　　sat like a nomad^a in the desert.
You have defiled the land
　　with your prostitution and wickedness.
³Therefore the showers have been
　　　　withheld,
　　and no spring rains have fallen.
Yet you have the brazen look of a
　　　　prostitute;
　　you refuse to blush with shame.
⁴Have you not just called to me:
　　'My Father, my friend from my youth,
⁵will you always be angry?
　　Will your wrath continue for ever?'
This is how you talk,
　　but you do all the evil you can."

Unfaithful Israel

⁶During the reign of King Josiah, the LORD said to me, "Have you seen what faithless Israel has done? She has gone up on every high hill and under every spreading tree and has committed adultery there. ⁷I thought that after she had done all this she would return to me but she did not, and her unfaithful sister Judah saw it. ⁸I gave faithless Israel her certificate of divorce and sent her away because of all her adulteries. Yet I saw that her unfaithful sister Judah had no fear; she also went out and committed adultery. ⁹Because Israel's immorality mattered so little to her, she defiled the land and committed adultery with stone and wood. ¹⁰In spite of all this, her unfaithful sister Judah did not return to me

with all her heart, but only in pretence," declares the LORD.
¹¹The LORD said to me, "Faithless Israel is more righteous than unfaithful Judah. ¹²Go, proclaim this message towards the north:

　"'Return, faithless Israel,' declares the
　　　　LORD,
　　'I will frown on you no longer,
　for I am merciful,' declares the LORD,
　　'I will not be angry for ever.
¹³Only acknowledge your guilt—
　　you have rebelled against the LORD your
　　　　God,
　you have scattered your favours to foreign
　　　　gods
　　under every spreading tree,
　　and have not obeyed me,'"
　　　　　　　　　declares the LORD.

¹⁴"Return, faithless people," declares the LORD, "for I am your husband. I will choose you—one from a town and two from a clan —and bring you to Zion. ¹⁵Then I will give you shepherds after my own heart, who will lead you with knowledge and understanding. ¹⁶In those days, when your numbers have increased greatly in the land," declares the LORD, "men will no longer say, 'The ark of the covenant of the LORD.' It will never enter their minds or be remembered; it will not be missed, nor will another one be made. ¹⁷At that time they will call Jerusalem The Throne of the LORD, and all nations will gather in Jerusalem to honour the name of the LORD. No longer will they follow the stubbornness of their evil hearts. ¹⁸In those days the house of Judah will join the house of Israel, and together they will come from a northern land to the land I gave your forefathers as an inheritance.

¹⁹"I myself said,

　"'How gladly would I treat you like sons
　　and give you a desirable land,
　　the most beautiful inheritance of any
　　　　nation.'
　I thought you would call me 'Father'
　　and not turn away from following me.
²⁰But like a woman unfaithful to her
　　　　husband,
　so you have been unfaithful to me, O
　　　　house of Israel,"
　　　　　　　　　declares the LORD.

²¹A cry is heard on the barren heights,
　　the weeping and pleading of the people
　　　　of Israel,
　because they have perverted their ways
　　and have forgotten the LORD their God.

²²"Return, faithless people;
　　I will cure you of backsliding."

　"Yes, we will come to you,
　　for you are the LORD our God.
²³Surely the ⌊idolatrous⌋ commotion on the
　　　　hills
　　and mountains is a deception;

^a2 Or an Arab

surely in the LORD our God
   is the salvation of Israel.
24From our youth shameful gods have
   consumed
   the fruits of our fathers' labour—
their flocks and herds,
   their sons and daughters.
25Let us lie down in our shame,
   and let our disgrace cover us.
We have sinned against the LORD our God,
   both we and our fathers;
from our youth till this day
   we have not obeyed the LORD our God.''

4 "If you will return, O Israel,
   return to me,''
                    declares the LORD.
"If you put your detestable idols out of my
   sight
   and no longer go astray,
2and if in a truthful, just and righteous way
   you swear, 'As surely as the LORD
   lives,'
then the nations will be blessed by him
   and in him they will glory.''

3This is what the LORD says to the men of
Judah and to Jerusalem:

"Break up your unploughed ground
   and do not sow among thorns.
4Circumcise yourselves to the LORD,
   circumcise your hearts,
   you men of Judah and people of
      Jerusalem,
or my wrath will break out and burn like
   fire
   because of the evil you have done—
   burn with no-one to quench it.

Disaster From the North

5"Announce in Judah and proclaim in
   Jerusalem and say:
   'Sound the trumpet throughout the
      land!'
Cry aloud and say:
   'Gather together!
   Let us flee to the fortified cities!'
6Raise the signal to go to Zion!
   Flee for safety without delay!
For I am bringing disaster from the north,
   even terrible destruction.''

7A lion has come out of his lair;
   a destroyer of nations has set out.
He has left his place
   to lay waste your land.
Your towns will lie in ruins
   without inhabitant.
8So put on sackcloth,
   lament and wail,
for the fierce anger of the LORD
   has not turned away from us.

9"In that day,'' declares the LORD,
   "the king and the officials will lose
      heart,
the priests will be horrified,
   and the prophets will be appalled.''

10Then I said, "Ah, Sovereign LORD, how
completely you have deceived this people
and Jerusalem by saying, 'You will have
peace,' when the sword is at our throats.''

11At that time this people and Jerusalem
will be told, "A scorching wind from the
barren heights in the desert blows towards
my people, but not to winnow or cleanse; 12a
wind too strong for that comes from me.[a]
Now I pronounce my judgments against
them.''

13Look! He advances like the clouds,
   his chariots come like a whirlwind,
   his horses are swifter than eagles.
   Woe to us! We are ruined!
14O Jerusalem, wash the evil from your
      heart and be saved.
   How long will you harbour wicked
      thoughts?
15A voice is announcing from Dan,
   proclaiming disaster from the hills of
      Ephraim.
16"Tell this to the nations,
   proclaim it to Jerusalem:
'A besieging army is coming from a distant
      land,
   raising a war cry against the cities of
      Judah.
17They surround her like men guarding a
      field,
   because she has rebelled against me,' ''
                    declares the LORD.
18"Your own conduct and actions
   have brought this upon you.
This is your punishment.
   How bitter it is!
   How it pierces to the heart!''

19Oh, my anguish, my anguish!
   I writhe in pain.
Oh, the agony of my heart!
   My heart pounds within me,
   I cannot keep silent.
For I have heard the sound of the trumpet;
   I have heard the battle cry.
20Disaster follows disaster;
   the whole land lies in ruins.
In an instant my tents are destroyed,
   my shelter in a moment.
21How long must I see the battle standard
   and hear the sound of the trumpet?

22"My people are fools;
   they do not know me.
They are senseless children;
   they have no understanding.
They are skilled in doing evil;
   they know not how to do good.''

23I looked at the earth,
   and it was formless and empty;
and at the heavens,
   and their light was gone.
24I looked at the mountains,
   and they were quaking;
   all the hills were swaying.
25I looked, and there were no people;
   every bird in the sky had flown away.

[a]12 Or *comes at my command*

²⁶I looked, and the fruitful land was a desert;
    all its towns lay in ruins
    before the LORD, before his fierce anger.

²⁷This is what the LORD says:

"The whole land will be ruined,
    though I will not destroy it completely.
²⁸Therefore the earth will mourn
    and the heavens above grow dark,
because I have spoken and will not relent,
    I have decided and will not turn back."

²⁹At the sound of horsemen and archers
    every town takes to flight.
Some go into the thickets;
    some climb up among the rocks.
All the towns are deserted;
    no-one lives in them.

³⁰What are you doing, O devastated one?
    Why dress yourself in scarlet
    and put on jewels of gold?
Why shade your eyes with paint?
    You adorn yourself in vain.
Your lovers despise you;
    they seek your life.

³¹I hear a cry as of a woman in labour,
    a groan as of one bearing her first
        child—
the cry of the Daughter of Zion gasping for
        breath,
    stretching out her hands and saying,
"Alas! I am fainting;
    my life is given over to murderers."

Not One Is Upright

5 "Go up and down the streets of
        Jerusalem,
    look around and consider,
    search through her squares.
If you can find but one person
    who deals honestly and seeks the truth,
    I will forgive this city.
²Although they say, 'As surely as the LORD
        lives,'
    still they are swearing falsely."

³O LORD, do not your eyes look for truth?
    You struck them, but they felt no pain;
    you crushed them but they refused
        correction.
They made their faces harder than stone
    and refused to repent.
⁴I thought, "These are only the poor;
    they are foolish,
for they do not know the way of the LORD,
    the requirements of their God.
⁵So I will go to the leaders
    and speak to them;
surely they know the way of the LORD,
    the requirements of their God."
But with one accord they too had broken
        off the yoke
    and torn off the bonds.
⁶Therefore a lion from the forest will attack
        them,
    a wolf from the desert will ravage them,
    a leopard will lie in wait near their towns
to tear to pieces any who venture out,

for their rebellion is great
    and their backslidings many.

⁷"Why should I forgive you?
    Your children have forsaken me
    and sworn by gods that are not gods.
I supplied all their needs,
    yet they committed adultery
    and thronged to the houses of
        prostitutes.
⁸They are well-fed, lusty stallions,
    each neighing for another man's wife.
⁹Should I not punish them for this?"
    declares the LORD.
"Should I not avenge myself
    on such a nation as this?

¹⁰"Go through her vineyards and ravage
        them,
    but do not destroy them completely.
Strip off her branches,
    for these people do not belong to the
        LORD.
¹¹The house of Israel and the house of Judah
    have been utterly unfaithful to me,"
                declares the LORD.

¹²They have lied about the LORD;
    they said, "He will do nothing!
No harm will come to us;
    we will never see sword or famine.
¹³The prophets are but wind
    and the word is not in them;
    so let what they say be done to them."

¹⁴Therefore this is what the LORD God
Almighty says:

"Because the people have spoken these
        words,
    I will make my words in your mouth a
        fire
    and these people the wood it consumes.
¹⁵O house of Israel," declares the LORD,
    "I am bringing a distant nation against
        you—
an ancient and enduring nation,
    a people whose language you do not
        know,
    whose speech you do not understand.
¹⁶Their quivers are like an open grave;
    all of them are mighty warriors.
¹⁷They will devour your harvests and food,
    devour your sons and daughters;
they will devour your flocks and herds,
    devour your vines and fig-trees.
With the sword they will destroy
    the fortified cities in which you trust.

¹⁸"Yet even in those days," declares the
LORD, "I will not destroy you completely.
¹⁹And when the people ask, 'Why has the
LORD our God done all this to us?' you will
tell them, 'As you have forsaken me and
served foreign gods in your own land, so now
you will serve foreigners in a land not your
own.'

²⁰"Announce this to the house of Jacob
    and proclaim it in Judah:

JEREMIAH 4:1–4
'Break up your unploughed ground and do not sow among thorns' (v. 3).

UNLESS THE GROUND is prepared and the thorns are removed, sowing good seed is a pointless exercise. No farmer would expect to reap a harvest without the investment of time and effort. This predominantly rural people would know immediately what God was saying through Jeremiah. They were being encouraged to assess the hardness and bareness of their lives. With the same resources, others had produced a rich harvest in character and godliness, whereas they had produced nothing of worth. Breaking up the unploughed ground meant reviewing with concern the potential of their lives, and ruing the wilful disregard they had shown for achievement and fulfilment. It meant also considering the plans God had for them and how they had shamed him and shamed themselves. There are fruits in keeping with repentance, there is a sorrow which leads to repentance and salvation, and these the Israelites were invited to produce.

Today we benefit from the ministry of the Holy Spirit, part of whose mission is to produce conviction within us, but if we fail to examine the effects of our disobedience, our repentance will probably be shallow. God has such high hopes for his people. He sees our great potential and, even though many years may have been wasted, he has the grace and power to redeem them, bringing our lives to such fulfilment that we will rejoice, and his name will be glorified. Our God is a great God whose power and love have not diminished with the years.

> *Out of my darkness he called me,*
> *Out of my doubt, my despair,*
> *Out of the wastes of my winter,*
> *Into the spring of his care.*

(John Gowans)

→632

READING JEREMIAH 24; 29:4–7

'The LORD showed me two baskets of figs placed in front of the temple of the LORD. One basket had very good figs, like those that ripen early; the other basket had very poor figs, so bad that they could not be eaten' (24:1b, 2).

TALKING ABOUT 'THE EXILE' makes it seem that a single, great event occurred, when Jews were carried off to Babylon and Judah was devastated. That was not so. The exile occurred in dribs and drabs, over a period of years. On at least three occasions, perhaps more, Nebuchadnezzar carted people off to Babylon from Judah. He took mainly well-off members of society, princes, priests, landowners, merchants and so on. The Babylonians intended to leave Judah desolate, unable to rebel again. On the final occasion many escaped and fled to Egypt, taking Jeremiah with them.

The story is complex. Piecing events together requires careful reading of the account in Second Kings, as well as many references in Jeremiah. Further clues are found in Daniel and Ezekiel.

In the vision we read today, Jeremiah sees those who have been taken forcibly to Babylon as the 'good figs'. We might be tempted to think Jeremiah was under the common delusion that the grass is always greener on the other side of the fence. Those far away appear good. We see the faults of those close at hand.

But Jeremiah proved right. Strong religious and political leaders emerged in Babylon. The immigrants prospered.

The disaster of exile enabled the Jews to develop a new community and strengthen their faith, independently of the temple which had proved such a mixed blessing in the past.

→653

²¹Hear this, you foolish and senseless
    people,
  who have eyes but do not see,
  who have ears but do not hear:
²²Should you not fear me?'' declares the
    LORD.
  ''Should you not tremble in my
    presence?
I made the sand a boundary for the sea,
  an everlasting barrier it cannot cross.
The waves may roll, but they cannot
    prevail;
  they may roar, but they cannot cross it.
²³But these people have stubborn and
    rebellious hearts;
  they have turned aside and gone away.
²⁴They do not say to themselves,
  'Let us fear the LORD our God,
who gives autumn and spring rains in
    season,
  who assures us of the regular weeks of
    harvest.'
²⁵Your wrongdoings have kept these away;
  your sins have deprived you of good.

²⁶''Among my people are wicked men
  who lie in wait like men who snare birds
  and like those who set traps to catch
    men.
²⁷Like cages full of birds,
  their houses are full of deceit;
they have become rich and powerful
²⁸ and have grown fat and sleek.
  Their evil deeds have no limit;
  they do not plead the case of the
    fatherless to win it,
  they do not defend the rights of the
    poor.
²⁹Should I not punish them for this?''
    declares the LORD.
  ''Should I not avenge myself
  on such a nation as this?

³⁰''A horrible and shocking thing
  has happened in the land:
³¹The prophets prophesy lies,
  the priests rule by their own authority,
and my people love it this way.
  But what will you do in the end?

Jerusalem Under Siege

6 ''Flee for safety, people of Benjamin!
    Flee from Jerusalem!
Sound the trumpet in Tekoa!
  Raise the signal over Beth Hakkerem!
For disaster looms out of the north,
  even terrible destruction.
²I will destroy the Daughter of Zion,
  so beautiful and delicate.
³Shepherds with their flocks will come
    against her;
  they will pitch their tents round her,
  each tending his own portion.''

⁴''Prepare for battle against her!
  Arise, let us attack at noon!
But, alas, the daylight is fading,
  and the shadows of evening grow long.
⁵So arise, let us attack at night
  and destroy her fortresses!''

⁶This is what the LORD Almighty says:

''Cut down the trees
  and build siege ramps against Jerusalem.
This city must be punished;
  it is filled with oppression.
⁷As a well pours out its water,
  so she pours out her wickedness.
Violence and destruction resound in her;
  her sickness and wounds are ever before
    me.
⁸Take warning, O Jerusalem,
  or I will turn away from you
and make your land desolate
  so that no-one can live in it.''

⁹This is what the LORD Almighty says:

''Let them glean the remnant of Israel
  as thoroughly as a vine;
pass your hand over the branches again,
  like one gathering grapes.''

¹⁰To whom can I speak and give warning?
  Who will listen to me?
Their ears are closed[a]
  so that they cannot hear.
The word of the LORD is offensive to them;
  they find no pleasure in it.
¹¹But I am full of the wrath of the LORD,
  and I cannot hold it in.

''Pour it out on the children in the street
  and on the young men gathered
    together;
both husband and wife will be caught in it,
  and the old, those weighed down with
    years.
¹²Their houses will be turned over to others,
  together with their fields and their
    wives,
when I stretch out my hand
  against those who live in the land,''
                    declares the LORD.
¹³''From the least to the greatest,
  all are greedy for gain;
prophets and priests alike,
  all practise deceit.
¹⁴They dress the wound of my people
  as though it were not serious.
'Peace, peace,' they say,
  when there is no peace.
¹⁵Are they ashamed of their loathsome
    conduct?
No, they have no shame at all;
  they do not even know how to blush.
So they will fall among the fallen;
  they will be brought down when I punish
    them,''
                    says the LORD.

¹⁶This is what the LORD says:

''Stand at the crossroads and look;
  ask for the ancient paths,
ask where the good way is, and walk in it,
  and you will find rest for your souls.
  But you said, 'We will not walk in it.'
¹⁷I appointed watchmen over you and said,

ᵃ10 Hebrew *uncircumcised*

'Listen to the sound of the trumpet!'
But you said, 'We will not listen.'
18Therefore hear, O nations;
observe, O witnesses,
what will happen to them.
19Hear, O earth:
I am bringing disaster on this people,
the fruit of their schemes,
because they have not listened to my words
and have rejected my law.
20What do I care about incense from Sheba
or sweet calamus from a distant land?
Your burnt offerings are not acceptable;
your sacrifices do not please me.''

21Therefore this is what the LORD says:

''I will put obstacles before this people.
Fathers and sons alike will stumble over
them;
neighbours and friends will perish.''

22This is what the LORD says:

''Look, an army is coming
from the land of the north;
a great nation is being stirred up
from the ends of the earth.
23They are armed with bow and spear;
they are cruel and show no mercy.
They sound like the roaring sea
as they ride on their horses;
they come like men in battle formation
to attack you, O Daughter of Zion.''

24We have heard reports about them,
and our hands hang limp.
Anguish has gripped us,
pain like that of a woman in labour.
25Do not go out to the fields
or walk on the roads,
for the enemy has a sword,
and there is terror on every side.
26O my people, put on sackcloth
and roll in ashes;
mourn with bitter wailing
as for an only son,
for suddenly the destroyer
will come upon us.

27''I have made you a tester of metals
and my people the ore,
that you may observe
and test their ways.
28They are all hardened rebels,
going about to slander.
They are bronze and iron;
they all act corruptly.
29The bellows blow fiercely
to burn away the lead with fire,
but the refining goes on in vain;
the wicked are not purged out.
30They are called rejected silver,
because the LORD has rejected them.''

False Religion Worthless

7 This is the word that came to Jeremiah
from the LORD: 2''Stand at the gate of
the LORD's house and there proclaim this
message:

'''Hear the word of the LORD, all you
people of Judah who come through these
gates to worship the LORD. 3This is what the
LORD Almighty, the God of Israel, says: Reform your ways and your actions, and I will
let you live in this place. 4Do not trust in
deceptive words and say, ''This is the temple
of the LORD, the temple of the LORD, the
temple of the LORD!'' 5If you really change
your ways and your actions and deal with
each other justly, 6if you do not oppress the
alien, the fatherless or the widow and do not
shed innocent blood in this place, and if you
do not follow other gods to your own harm,
7then I will let you live in this place, in the
land I gave to your forefathers for ever and
ever. 8But look, you are trusting in deceptive
words that are worthless.

9'''Will you steal and murder, commit
adultery and perjury,a burn incense to Baal
and follow other gods you have not known,
10and then come and stand before me in this
house, which bears my Name, and say, ''We
are safe''—safe to do all these detestable
things? 11Has this house, which bears my
Name, become a den of robbers to you? But I
have been watching! declares the LORD.

12'''Go now to the place in Shiloh where I
first made a dwelling for my Name, and see
what I did to it because of the wickedness of
my people Israel. 13While you were doing all
these things, declares the LORD, I spoke to
you again and again, but you did not listen;
I called you, but you did not answer.
14Therefore, what I did to Shiloh I will now
do to the house that bears my Name, the
temple you trust in, the place I gave to you
and your fathers. 15I will thrust you from my
presence, just as I did all your brothers, the
people of Ephraim.'

16''So do not pray for this people nor offer
any plea or petition for them; do not plead
with me, for I will not listen to you. 17Do you
not see what they are doing in the towns of
Judah and in the streets of Jerusalem? 18The
children gather wood, the fathers light the
fire, and the women knead the dough and
make cakes of bread for the Queen of
Heaven. They pour out drink offerings to
other gods to provoke me to anger. 19But am I
the one they are provoking? declares the
LORD. Are they not rather harming themselves, to their own shame?

20'''Therefore this is what the Sovereign
LORD says: My anger and my wrath will be
poured out on this place, on man and beast,
on the trees of the field and on the fruit of the
ground, and it will burn and not be quenched.
21'''This is what the LORD Almighty, the
God of Israel, says: Go ahead, add your
burnt offerings to your other sacrifices and
eat the meat yourselves! 22For when I
brought your forefathers out of Egypt and
spoke to them, I did not just give them commands about burnt offerings and sacrifices,
23but I gave them this command: Obey me,
and I will be your God and you will be my
people. Walk in all the ways I command you,
that it may go well with you. 24But they did

a9 Or and swear by false gods

not listen or pay attention; instead, they followed the stubborn inclinations of their evil hearts. They went backward and not forward. 25From the time your forefathers left Egypt until now, day after day, again and again I sent you my servants the prophets. 26But they did not listen to me or pay attention. They were stiff-necked and did more evil than their forefathers.'

27"When you tell them all this, they will not listen to you; when you call to them, they will not answer. 28Therefore say to them, 'This is the nation that has not obeyed the LORD its God or responded to correction. Truth has perished; it has vanished from their lips. 29Cut off your hair and throw it away; take up a lament on the barren heights, for the LORD has rejected and abandoned this generation that is under his wrath.

The Valley of Slaughter

30"'The people of Judah have done evil in my eyes, declares the LORD. They have set up their detestable idols in the house that bears my Name and have defiled it. 31They have built the high places of Topheth in the Valley of Ben Hinnom to burn their sons and daughters in the fire—something I did not command, nor did it enter my mind. 32So beware, the days are coming, declares the LORD, when people will no longer call it Topheth or the Valley of Ben Hinnom, but the Valley of Slaughter, for they will bury the dead in Topheth until there is no more room. 33Then the carcasses of this people will become food for the birds of the air and the beasts of the earth, and there will be no-one to frighten them away. 34I will bring an end to the sounds of joy and gladness and to the voices of bride and bridegroom in the towns of Judah and the streets of Jerusalem, for the land will become desolate.

8 "'At that time, declares the LORD, the bones of the kings and officials of Judah, the bones of the priests and prophets, and the bones of the people of Jerusalem will be removed from their graves. 2They will be exposed to the sun and the moon and all the stars of the heavens, which they have loved and served and which they have followed and consulted and worshipped. They will not be gathered up or buried, but will be like refuse lying on the ground. 3Wherever I banish them, all the survivors of this evil nation will prefer death to life, declares the LORD Almighty.'

Sin and Punishment

4"Say to them, 'This is what the LORD says:

"'When men fall down, do they not get up?
  When a man turns away, does he not return?
5Why then have these people turned away?
  Why does Jerusalem always turn away?
They cling to deceit;
  they refuse to return.

6I have listened attentively,
  but they do not say what is right.
No-one repents of his wickedness,
  saying, "What have I done?"
Each pursues his own course
  like a horse charging into battle.
7Even the stork in the sky
  knows her appointed seasons,
and the dove, the swift and the thrush
  observe the time of their migration.
But my people do not know
  the requirements of the LORD.

8"'How can you say, "We are wise,
  for we have the law of the LORD,"
when actually the lying pen of the scribes
  has handled it falsely?
9The wise will be put to shame;
  they will be dismayed and trapped.
Since they have rejected the word of the LORD,
  what kind of wisdom do they have?
10Therefore I will give their wives to other men
  and their fields to new owners.
From the least to the greatest,
  all are greedy for gain;
prophets and priests alike,
  all practise deceit.
11They dress the wound of my people
  as though it were not serious.
"Peace, peace," they say,
  when there is no peace.
12Are they ashamed of their loathsome conduct?
No, they have no shame at all;
  they do not even know how to blush.
So they will fall among the fallen;
  they will be brought down when they are punished,
                                   says the LORD.

13"'I will take away their harvest,
                          declares the LORD.
There will be no grapes on the vine.
There will be no figs on the tree,
  and their leaves will wither.
What I have given them
  will be taken from them.'"a

14"Why are we sitting here?
  Gather together!
Let us flee to the fortified cities
  and perish there!
For the LORD our God has doomed us to perish
  and given us poisoned water to drink,
  because we have sinned against him.
15We hoped for peace
  but no good has come,
for a time of healing
  but there was only terror.
16The snorting of the enemy's horses
  is heard from Dan;
at the neighing of their stallions
  the whole land trembles.
They have come to devour
  the land and everything in it,
  the city and all who live there."

---

a13 The meaning of the Hebrew for this sentence is uncertain.

17"See, I will send venomous snakes among
    you,
  vipers that cannot be charmed,
  and they will bite you,"
                    declares the LORD.

18O my Comforter[b] in sorrow,
  my heart is faint within me.
19Listen to the cry of my people
  from a land far away:
  "Is the LORD not in Zion?
  Is her King no longer there?"

  "Why have they provoked me to anger
    with their images,
  with their worthless foreign idols?"

20"The harvest is past,
  the summer has ended,
  and we are not saved."

21Since my people are crushed, I am
    crushed;
  I mourn, and horror grips me.
22Is there no balm in Gilead?
  Is there no physician there?
  Why then is there no healing
  for the wound of my people?

9 1Oh, that my head were a spring of
    water
  and my eyes a fountain of tears!
  I would weep day and night
  for the slain of my people.
2Oh, that I had in the desert
  a lodging place for travellers,
  so that I might leave my people
  and go away from them;
  for they are all adulterers,
  a crowd of unfaithful people.

3"They make ready their tongue
  like a bow, to shoot lies;
  it is not by truth
  that they triumph[a] in the land.
  They go from one sin to another;
  they do not acknowledge me,"
                    declares the LORD.
4"Beware of your friends;
  do not trust your brothers.
  For every brother is a deceiver,[b]
  and every friend a slanderer.
5Friend deceives friend,
  and no-one speaks the truth.
  They have taught their tongues to lie;
  they weary themselves with sinning.
6You[c] live in the midst of deception;
  in their deceit they refuse to
    acknowledge me,"
                    declares the LORD.

7Therefore this is what the LORD Almighty
says:

  "See, I will refine and test them,
  for what else can I do
  because of the sin of my people?
8Their tongue is a deadly arrow;
  it speaks with deceit.

With his mouth each speaks cordially to
    his neighbour,
  but in his heart he sets a trap for him.
9Should I not punish them for this?"
    declares the LORD.
  "Should I not avenge myself
  on such a nation as this?"

10I will weep and wail for the mountains
  and take up a lament concerning the
    desert pastures.
  They are desolate and untravelled,
  and the lowing of cattle is not heard.
  The birds of the air have fled
  and the animals are gone.

11"I will make Jerusalem a heap of ruins,
  a haunt of jackals;
  and I will lay waste the towns of Judah
  so that no-one can live there."

12What man is wise enough to understand
this? Who has been instructed by the LORD
and can explain it? Why has the land been
ruined and laid waste like a desert that no-
one can cross?

13The LORD said, "It is because they have
forsaken my law, which I set before them;
they have not obeyed me or followed my law.
14Instead, they have followed the stubbornness of their hearts; they have followed the
Baals, as their fathers taught them."
15Therefore, this is what the LORD Almighty,
the God of Israel, says: "See, I will make this
people eat bitter food and drink poisoned
water. 16I will scatter them among nations
that neither they nor their fathers have
known, and I will pursue them with the
sword until I have destroyed them."

17This is what the LORD Almighty says:

  "Consider now! Call for the wailing
    women to come;
  send for the most skilful of them.
18Let them come quickly
  and wail over us
  till our eyes overflow with tears
  and water streams from our eyelids.
19The sound of wailing is heard from Zion:
  'How ruined we are!
  How great is our shame!
  We must leave our land
  because our houses are in ruins.'"

20Now, O women, hear the word of the
    LORD;
  open your ears to the words of his
    mouth.
  Teach your daughters how to wail;
  teach one another a lament.
21Death has climbed in through our windows
  and has entered our fortresses;
  it has cut off the children from the streets
  and the young men from the public
    squares.

b18 The meaning of the Hebrew for this word is uncertain.   *a3 Or lies; / they are not valiant for truth*
b4 Or a deceiving Jacob   *c6 That is, Jeremiah (the Hebrew is singular)*

22Say, "This is what the LORD declares:

"'The dead bodies of men will lie
like refuse on the open field,
like cut corn behind the reaper,
with no-one to gather them.'"

23This is what the LORD says:

"Let not the wise man boast of his wisdom
or the strong man boast of his strength
or the rich man boast of his riches,
24but let him who boasts boast about this:
that he understands and knows me,
that I am the LORD, who exercises
kindness,
justice and righteousness on earth,
for in these I delight,"
declares the LORD.

25"The days are coming," declares the LORD, "when I will punish all who are circumcised only in the flesh—26Egypt, Judah, Edom, Ammon, Moab and all who live in the desert in distant places.*d* For all these nations are really uncircumcised, and even the whole house of Israel is uncircumcised in heart."

God and Idols

10 Hear what the LORD says to you, O house of Israel. 2This is what the LORD says:

"Do not learn the ways of the nations
or be terrified by signs in the sky,
though the nations are terrified by them.
3For the customs of the peoples are
worthless;
they cut a tree out of the forest,
and a craftsman shapes it with his
chisel.
4They adorn it with silver and gold;
they fasten it with hammer and nails
so that it will not totter.
5Like a scarecrow in a melon patch,
their idols cannot speak;
they must be carried
because they cannot walk.
Do not fear them;
they can do no harm
nor can they do any good."

6No-one is like you, O LORD;
you are great,
and your name is mighty in power.
7Who should not revere you,
O King of the nations?
This is your due.
Among all the wise men of the nations
and in all their kingdoms,
there is no-one like you.
8They are all senseless and foolish;
they are taught by worthless wooden
idols.
9Hammered silver is brought from Tarshish
and gold from Uphaz.
What the craftsman and goldsmith have
made
is then dressed in blue and purple—

all made by skilled workers.
10But the LORD is the true God;
he is the living God, the eternal King.
When he is angry, the earth trembles;
the nations cannot endure his wrath.

11"Tell them this: 'These gods, who did not make the heavens and the earth, will perish from the earth and from under the heavens.'"*a*

12But God made the earth by his power;
he founded the world by his wisdom
and stretched out the heavens by his
understanding.
13When he thunders, the waters in the
heavens roar;
he makes clouds rise from the ends of
the earth.
He sends lightning with the rain
and brings out the wind from his
storehouses.

14Everyone is senseless and without
knowledge;
every goldsmith is shamed by his idols.
His images are a fraud;
they have no breath in them.
15They are worthless, the objects of
mockery;
when their judgment comes, they will
perish.
16He who is the Portion of Jacob is not like
these,
for he is the Maker of all things,
including Israel, the tribe of his
inheritance—
the LORD Almighty is his name.

Coming Destruction

17Gather up your belongings to leave the
land,
you who live under siege.
18For this is what the LORD says:
"At this time I will hurl out
those who live in this land;
I will bring distress on them
so that they may be captured."

19Woe to me because of my injury!
My wound is incurable!
Yet I said to myself,
"This is my sickness, and I must endure
it."
20My tent is destroyed;
all its ropes are snapped.
My sons are gone from me and are no
more;
no-one is left now to pitch my tent
or to set up my shelter.
21The shepherds are senseless
and do not enquire of the LORD;
so they do not prosper
and all their flock is scattered.
22Listen! The report is coming—
a great commotion from the land of the
north!
It will make the towns of Judah desolate,
a haunt of jackals.

---

d26 Or *desert and who clip the hair by their foreheads*   *a11* The text of this verse is in Aramaic.

Jeremiah's Prayer

23I know, O LORD, that a man's life is not his
    own;
  it is not for man to direct his steps.
24Correct me, LORD, but only with justice—
    not in your anger,
  lest you reduce me to nothing.
25Pour out your wrath on the nations
    that do not acknowledge you,
  on the peoples who do not call on your
    name.
For they have devoured Jacob;
  they have devoured him completely
    and destroyed his homeland.

The Covenant Is Broken

11 This is the word that came to Jeremiah from the LORD: 2"Listen to the
terms of this covenant and tell them to the
people of Judah and to those who live in
Jerusalem. 3Tell them that this is what the
LORD, the God of Israel, says: 'Cursed is the
man who does not obey the terms of this
covenant—4the terms I commanded your
forefathers when I brought them out of
Egypt, out of the iron-smelting furnace.' I
said, 'Obey me and do everything I command
you, and you will be my people, and I will be
your God. 5Then I will fulfil the oath I swore
to your forefathers, to give them a land
flowing with milk and honey'—the land you
possess today."

  I answered, "Amen, LORD."
  6The LORD said to me, "Proclaim all these
words in the towns of Judah and in the streets
of Jerusalem: 'Listen to the terms of this
covenant and follow them. 7From the time I
brought your forefathers up from Egypt until
today, I warned them again and again,
saying, "Obey me." 8But they did not listen
or pay attention; instead, they followed the
stubbornness of their evil hearts. So I
brought on them all the curses of the covenant I had commanded them to follow but
that they did not keep.'"

  9Then the LORD said to me, "There is a
conspiracy among the people of Judah and
those who live in Jerusalem. 10They have
returned to the sins of their forefathers, who
refused to listen to my words. They have
followed other gods to serve them. Both the
house of Israel and the house of Judah have
broken the covenant I made with their forefathers. 11Therefore this is what the LORD
says: 'I will bring on them a disaster they
cannot escape. Although they cry out to me,
I will not listen to them. 12The towns of Judah
and the people of Jerusalem will go and cry
out to the gods to whom they burn incense,
but they will not help them at all when disaster strikes. 13You have as many gods as you
have towns, O Judah; and the altars you have
set up to burn incense to that shameful god
Baal are as many as the streets of Jerusalem.'

  14"Do not pray for this people nor offer
any plea or petition for them, because I will
not listen when they call to me in the time of
their distress.

15"What is my beloved doing in my temple
    as she works out her evil schemes with
      many?
  Can consecrated meat avert ⌐your
    punishment⌐?
When you engage in your wickedness,
  then you rejoice." *a*

16The LORD called you a thriving olive tree
  with fruit beautiful in form.
But with the roar of a mighty storm
  he will set it on fire,
  and its branches will be broken.

17The LORD Almighty, who planted you, has
decreed disaster for you, because the house
of Israel and the house of Judah have done
evil and provoked me to anger by burning
incense to Baal.

Plot Against Jeremiah

18Because the LORD revealed their plot to
me, I knew it, for at that time he showed me
what they were doing. 19I had been like a
gentle lamb led to the slaughter; I did not realise that they had plotted against me, saying,

  "Let us destroy the tree and its fruit;
    let us cut him off from the land of the
      living,
    that his name be remembered no more."
20But, O LORD Almighty, you who judge
    righteously
  and test the heart and mind,
let me see your vengeance upon them,
  for to you I have committed my cause.

21"Therefore this is what the LORD says
about the men of Anathoth who are seeking
your life and saying, 'Do not prophesy in the
name of the LORD or you will die by our
hands'—22therefore this is what the LORD
Almighty says: 'I will punish them. Their
young men will die by the sword, their sons
and daughters by famine. 23Not even a remnant will be left to them, because I will bring
disaster on the men of Anathoth in the year of
their punishment.'"

Jeremiah's Complaint

12 You are always righteous, O LORD,
    when I bring a case before you.
Yet I would speak with you about your
    justice:
  Why does the way of the wicked prosper?
  Why do all the faithless live at ease?
2You have planted them, and they have
    taken root;
  they grow and bear fruit.
You are always on their lips
  but far from their hearts.
3Yet you know me, O LORD;
  you see me and test my thoughts about
    you.
Drag them off like sheep to be butchered!
  Set them apart for the day of slaughter!
4How long will the land lie parched*a*
  and the grass in every field be withered?
Because those who live in it are wicked,
  the animals and birds have perished.

---

*a*15 Or *Could consecrated meat avert your punishment? | Then you would rejoice*   *a*4 Or *land mourn*

Moreover, the people are saying,
   "He will not see what happens to us."

God's Answer

5"If you have raced with men on foot
    and they have worn you out,
    how can you compete with horses?
 If you stumble in safe country,*b*
    how will you manage in the thickets by*c*
      the Jordan?
6Your brothers, your own family—
    even they have betrayed you;
    they have raised a loud cry against you.
 Do not trust them,
    though they speak well of you.

7"I will forsake my house,
    abandon my inheritance;
 I will give the one I love
    into the hands of her enemies.
8My inheritance has become to me
    like a lion in the forest.
 She roars at me;
    therefore I hate her.
9Has not my inheritance become to me
    like a speckled bird of prey
    that other birds of prey surround and
      attack?
 Go and gather all the wild beasts;
    bring them to devour.
10Many shepherds will ruin my vineyard
    and trample down my field;
 they will turn my pleasant field
    into a desolate wasteland.
11It will be made a wasteland,
    parched and desolate before me;
 the whole land will be laid waste
    because there is no-one who cares.
12Over all the barren heights in the desert
    destroyers will swarm,
 for the sword of the LORD will devour
    from one end of the land to the other;
    no-one will be safe.
13They will sow wheat but reap thorns;
    they will wear themselves out but gain
      nothing.
 So bear the shame of your harvest
    because of the LORD's fierce anger."

14This is what the LORD says: "As for all
my wicked neighbours who seize the inheritance I gave to my people Israel, I will uproot
them from their lands and I will uproot the
house of Judah from among them. 15But after
I uproot them, I will again have compassion
and will bring each of them back to his own
inheritance and his own country. 16And if
they learn well the ways of my people and
swear by my name, saying, 'As surely as the
LORD lives'—even as they once taught my
people to swear by Baal—then they will be
established among my people. 17But if any
nation does not listen, I will completely uproot and destroy it," declares the LORD.

A Linen Belt

13 This is what the LORD said to me: "Go
    and buy a linen belt and put it round
your waist, but do not let it touch water." 2So

I bought a belt, as the LORD directed, and put
it round my waist.
   3Then the word of the LORD came to me a
second time: 4"Take the belt you bought and
are wearing round your waist, and go now to
Perath*a* and hide it there in a crevice in the
rocks." 5So I went and hid it at Perath, as the
LORD told me.
   6Many days later the LORD said to me, "Go
now to Perath and get the belt I told you to
hide there." 7So I went to Perath and dug up
the belt and took it from the place where I
had hidden it, but now it was ruined and
completely useless.
   8Then the word of the LORD came to me:
9"This is what the LORD says: 'In the same
way I will ruin the pride of Judah and the
great pride of Jerusalem. 10These wicked
people, who refuse to listen to my words,
who follow the stubbornness of their hearts
and go after other gods to serve and worship
them, will be like this belt—completely useless! 11For as a belt is bound round a man's
waist, so I bound the whole house of Israel
and the whole house of Judah to me,' declares the LORD, 'to be my people for my
renown and praise and honour. But they
have not listened.'

Wineskins

12"Say to them: 'This is what the LORD, the
God of Israel, says: Every wineskin should
be filled with wine.' And if they say to you,
'Don't we know that every wineskin should
be filled with wine?' 13then tell them, 'This is
what the LORD says: I am going to fill with
drunkenness all who live in this land, including the kings who sit on David's throne, the
priests, the prophets and all those living in
Jerusalem. 14I will smash them one against
the other, fathers and sons alike, declares the
LORD. I will allow no pity or mercy or compassion to keep me from destroying them.'"

Threat of Captivity

15Hear and pay attention,
    do not be arrogant,
    for the LORD has spoken.
16Give glory to the LORD your God
    before he brings the darkness,
 before your feet stumble
    on the darkening hills.
 You hope for light,
    but he will turn it to thick darkness
    and change it to deep gloom.
17But if you do not listen,
    I will weep in secret
    because of your pride;
 my eyes will weep bitterly,
    overflowing with tears,
    because the LORD's flock will be taken
      captive.

18Say to the king and to the queen mother,
    "Come down from your thrones,
 for your glorious crowns
    will fall from your heads."

---

b5 Or *If you put your trust in a land of safety*   *c5* Or *the flooding of*
a4 Or possibly *the Euphrates*; also in verses 5–7

¹⁹The cities in the Negev will be shut up,
  and there will be no-one to open them.
All Judah will be carried into exile,
  carried completely away.

²⁰Lift up your eyes and see
  those who are coming from the north.
Where is the flock that was entrusted to
    you,
  the sheep of which you boasted?
²¹What will you say when ⌊the Lord⌋ sets
    over you
  those you cultivated as your special
    allies?
Will not pain grip you
  like that of a woman in labour?
²²And if you ask yourself,
  "Why has this happened to me?"—
it is because of your many sins
  that your skirts have been torn off
  and your body ill-treated.
²³Can the Ethiopianᵇ change his skin
  or the leopard its spots?
Neither can you do good
  who are accustomed to doing evil.

²⁴"I will scatter you like chaff
  driven by the desert wind.
²⁵This is your lot,
  the portion I have decreed for you,"
                    declares the Lord,
"because you have forgotten me
  and trusted in false gods.
²⁶I will pull up your skirts over your face
  that your shame may be seen—
²⁷your adulteries and lustful neighings,
  your shameless prostitution!
I have seen your detestable acts
  on the hills and in the fields.
Woe to you, O Jerusalem!
  How long will you be unclean?"

Drought, Famine, Sword

14 This is the word of the Lord to Jere-
    miah concerning the drought:

²"Judah mourns,
  her cities languish;
they wail for the land,
  and a cry goes up from Jerusalem.
³The nobles send their servants for water;
  they go to the cisterns
  but find no water.
They return with their jars unfilled;
  dismayed and despairing,
  they cover their heads.
⁴The ground is cracked
  because there is no rain in the land;
the farmers are dismayed
  and cover their heads.
⁵Even the doe in the field
  deserts her newborn fawn
  because there is no grass.
⁶Wild donkeys stand on the barren heights
  and pant like jackals;
their eyesight fails
  for lack of pasture."

⁷Although our sins testify against us,
  O Lord, do something for the sake of
    your name.
For our backsliding is great;
  we have sinned against you.
⁸O Hope of Israel,
  its Saviour in times of distress,
why are you like a stranger in the land,
  like a traveller who stays only a night?
⁹Why are you like a man taken by surprise,
  like a warrior powerless to save?
You are among us, O Lord,
  and we bear your name;
  do not forsake us!

¹⁰This is what the Lord says about this
people:

"They greatly love to wander;
  they do not restrain their feet.
So the Lord does not accept them;
  he will now remember their wickedness
  and punish them for their sins."

¹¹Then the Lord said to me, "Do not pray
for the well-being of this people. ¹²Although
they fast, I will not listen to their cry; though
they offer burnt offerings and grain offerings,
I will not accept them. Instead, I will destroy
them with the sword, famine and plague."

¹³But I said, "Ah, Sovereign Lord, the
prophets keep telling them, 'You will not see
the sword or suffer famine. Indeed, I will give
you lasting peace in this place.'"

¹⁴Then the Lord said to me, "The prophets
are prophesying lies in my name. I have not
sent them or appointed them or spoken to
them. They are prophesying to you false
visions, divinations, idolatriesᵃ and the delusions of their own minds. ¹⁵Therefore, this is
what the Lord says about the prophets who
are prophesying in my name: I did not send
them, yet they are saying, 'No sword or
famine will touch this land.' Those same
prophets will perish by sword and famine.
¹⁶And the people they are prophesying to will
be thrown out into the streets of Jerusalem
because of the famine and sword. There will
be no-one to bury them or their wives, their
sons or their daughters. I will pour out on
them the calamity they deserve.

¹⁷"Speak this word to them:

"'Let my eyes overflow with tears
  night and day without ceasing;
for my virgin daughter—my people—
  has suffered a grievous wound,
  a crushing blow.
¹⁸If I go into the country,
  I see those slain by the sword;
if I go into the city,
  I see the ravages of famine.
Both prophet and priest
  have gone to a land they know not.'"

¹⁹Have you rejected Judah completely?
  Do you despise Zion?

ᵇ23 Hebrew *Cushite* (probably a person from the upper Nile region)   ᵃ14 Or *visions, worthless divinations*

Why have you afflicted us
　　so that we cannot be healed?
We hoped for peace
　　but no good has come,
for a time of healing
　　but there is only terror.
20O LORD, we acknowledge our wickedness
　　and the guilt of our fathers;
　　we have indeed sinned against you.
21For the sake of your name do not despise
　　us;
　　do not dishonour your glorious throne.
Remember your covenant with us
　　and do not break it.
22Do any of the worthless idols of the
　　nations bring rain?
Do the skies themselves send down
　　showers?
No, it is you, O LORD our God.
Therefore our hope is in you,
　　for you are the one who does all this.

15 Then the LORD said to me: "Even if
Moses and Samuel were to stand before me, my heart would not go out to this
people. Send them away from my presence!
Let them go! 2And if they ask you, 'Where
shall we go?' tell them, 'This is what the
LORD says:

"'Those destined for death, to death;
those for the sword, to the sword;
those for starvation, to starvation;
those for captivity, to captivity.'

3"I will send four kinds of destroyers
against them," declares the LORD, "the
sword to kill and the dogs to drag away and
the birds of the air and the beasts of the earth
to devour and destroy. 4I will make them
abhorrent to all the kingdoms of the earth
because of what Manasseh son of Hezekiah
king of Judah did in Jerusalem.

5"Who will have pity on you, O Jerusalem?
Who will mourn for you?
Who will stop to ask how you are?
6You have rejected me," declares the
　　LORD.
"You keep on backsliding.
So I will lay hands on you and destroy
　　you;
　　I can no longer show compassion.
7I will winnow them with a winnowing fork
　　at the city gates of the land.
I will bring bereavement and destruction
　　on my people,
　　for they have not changed their ways.
8I will make their widows more numerous
　　than the sand of the sea.
At midday I will bring a destroyer
　　against the mothers of their young men;
suddenly I will bring down on them
　　anguish and terror.
9The mother of seven will grow faint
　　and breathe her last.
Her sun will set while it is still day;
　　she will be disgraced and humiliated.

I will put the survivors to the sword
　　before their enemies,"
　　　　　　　　　　　declares the LORD.

10Alas, my mother, that you gave me birth,
　　a man with whom the whole land strives
　　　and contends!
I have neither lent nor borrowed,
　　yet everyone curses me.

11The LORD said,

"Surely I will deliver you for a good
　　purpose;
surely I will make your enemies plead
　　with you
　　in times of disaster and times of distress.

12"Can a man break iron—
　　iron from the north—or bronze?
13Your wealth and your treasures
　　I will give as plunder, without charge,
because of all your sins
　　throughout your country.
14I will enslave you to your enemies
　　ina a land you do not know,
for my anger will kindle a fire
　　that will burn against you."

15You understand, O LORD;
　　remember me and care for me.
Avenge me on my persecutors.
You are long-suffering—do not take me
　　away;
　　think of how I suffer reproach for your
　　sake.
16When your words came, I ate them;
　　they were my joy and my heart's
　　delight,
for I bear your name,
　　O LORD God Almighty.
17I never sat in the company of revellers,
　　never made merry with them;
I sat alone because your hand was on me
　　and you had filled me with indignation.
18Why is my pain unending
　　and my wound grievous and incurable?
Will you be to me like a deceptive brook,
　　like a spring that fails?

19Therefore this is what the LORD says:

"If you repent, I will restore you
　　that you may serve me;
if you utter worthy, not worthless, words,
　　you will be my spokesman.
Let this people turn to you,
　　but you must not turn to them.
20I will make you a wall to this people,
　　a fortified wall of bronze;
they will fight against you
　　but will not overcome you,
for I am with you
　　to rescue and save you,"
　　　　　　　　　　　declares the LORD.
21"I will save you from the hands of the
　　wicked
　　and redeem you from the grasp of the
　　cruel."

a14 Some Hebrew manuscripts, Septuagint and Syriac (see also Jer. 17:4); most Hebrew manuscripts I will cause
your enemies to bring you / into

Day of Disaster

16 Then the word of the LORD came to me: 2"You must not marry and have sons or daughters in this place." 3For this is what the LORD says about the sons and daughters born in this land and about the women who are their mothers and the men who are their fathers: 4"They will die of deadly diseases. They will not be mourned or buried but will be like refuse lying on the ground. They will perish by sword and famine, and their dead bodies will become food for the birds of the air and the beasts of the earth."

5For this is what the LORD says: "Do not enter a house where there is a funeral meal; do not go to mourn or show sympathy, because I have withdrawn my blessing, my love and my pity from this people," declares the LORD. 6"Both high and low will die in this land. They will not be buried or mourned, and no-one will cut himself or shave his head for them. 7No-one will offer food to comfort those who mourn for the dead—not even for a father or a mother—nor will anyone give them a drink to console them.

8"And do not enter a house where there is feasting and sit down to eat and drink. 9For this is what the LORD Almighty, the God of Israel, says: Before your eyes and in your days I will bring an end to the sounds of joy and gladness and to the voices of bride and bridegroom in this place.

10"When you tell these people all this and they ask you, 'Why has the LORD decreed such a great disaster against us? What wrong have we done? What sin have we committed against the LORD our God?' 11then say to them, 'It is because your fathers forsook me,' declares the LORD, 'and followed other gods and served and worshipped them. They forsook me and did not keep my law. 12But you have behaved more wickedly than your fathers. See how each of you is following the stubbornness of his evil heart instead of obeying me. 13So I will throw you out of this land into a land neither you nor your fathers have known, and there you will serve other gods day and night, for I will show you no favour.'

14"However, the days are coming," declares the LORD, "when men will no longer say, 'As surely as the LORD lives, who brought the Israelites up out of Egypt,' 15but they will say, 'As surely as the LORD lives, who brought the Israelites up out of the land of the north and out of all the countries where he had banished them.' For I will restore them to the land I gave to their forefathers.

16"But now I will send for many fishermen," declares the LORD, "and they will catch them. After that I will send for many hunters, and they will hunt them down on every mountain and hill and from the crevices of the rocks. 17My eyes are on all their ways; they are not hidden from me, nor is their sin concealed from my eyes. 18I will repay them double for their wickedness and their sin, because they have defiled my land

with the lifeless forms of their vile images and have filled my inheritance with their detestable idols."

19O LORD, my strength and my fortress,
     my refuge in time of distress,
to you the nations will come
     from the ends of the earth and say,
"Our fathers possessed nothing but false
          gods,
     worthless idols that did them no good.
20Do men make their own gods?
     Yes, but they are not gods!"

21"Therefore I will teach them—
     this time I will teach them
     my power and might.
Then they will know
     that my name is the LORD.

17 "Judah's sin is engraved with an iron tool,
     inscribed with a flint point,
on the tablets of their hearts
     and on the horns of their altars.
2Even their children remember
     their altars and Asherah poles*a*
beside the spreading trees
     and on the high hills.
3My mountain in the land
     and your*b* wealth and all your treasures
I will give away as plunder,
     together with your high places,
     because of sin throughout your country.
4Through your own fault you will lose
     the inheritance I gave you.
I will enslave you to your enemies
     in a land you do not know,
for you have kindled my anger,
     and it will burn for ever."

5This is what the LORD says:

"Cursed is the one who trusts in man,
     who depends on flesh for his strength
     and whose heart turns away from the
          LORD.
6He will be like a bush in the wastelands;
     he will not see prosperity when it
          comes.
He will dwell in the parched places of the
          desert,
     in a salt land where no-one lives.

7But blessed is the man who trusts in the
          LORD,
     whose confidence is in him.
8He will be like a tree planted by the water
     that sends out its roots by the stream.
It does not fear when heat comes;
     its leaves are always green.
It has no worries in a year of drought
     and never fails to bear fruit."

9The heart is deceitful above all things
     and beyond cure.
     Who can understand it?

10"I the LORD search the heart
     and examine the mind,

---

*a*2 That is, symbols of the goddess Asherah   *b*2, 3 Or *hills | *3*and the mountains of the land. | Your*

to reward a man according to his conduct,
   according to what his deeds deserve.''

11Like a partridge that hatches eggs it did
      not lay
   is the man who gains riches by unjust
      means.
When his life is half gone, they will desert
      him,
   and in the end he will prove to be a fool.

12A glorious throne, exalted from the
      beginning,
   is the place of our sanctuary.
13O LORD, the hope of Israel,
   all who forsake you will be put to
      shame.
Those who turn away from you will be
      written in the dust
   because they have forsaken the LORD,
      the spring of living water.

14Heal me, O LORD, and I shall be healed;
   save me and I shall be saved,
   for you are the one I praise.
15They keep saying to me,
   "Where is the word of the LORD?
   Let it now be fulfilled!"
16I have not run away from being your
      shepherd;
   you know I have not desired the day of
      despair.
   What passes my lips is open before you.
17Do not be a terror to me;
   you are my refuge in the day of disaster.
18Let my persecutors be put to shame,
   but keep me from shame;
   let them be terrified,
   but keep me from terror.
Bring on them the day of disaster;
   destroy them with double destruction.

Keeping the Sabbath Holy

19This is what the LORD said to me: "Go
and stand at the gate of the people, through
which the kings of Judah go in and out; stand
also at all the other gates of Jerusalem. 20Say
to them, 'Hear the word of the LORD, O kings
of Judah and all people of Judah and everyone living in Jerusalem who come through
these gates. 21This is what the LORD says: Be
careful not to carry a load on the Sabbath day
or bring it through the gates of Jerusalem.
22Do not bring a load out of your houses or do
any work on the Sabbath, but keep the Sabbath day holy, as I commanded your forefathers. 23Yet they did not listen or pay
attention; they were stiff-necked and would
not listen or respond to discipline. 24But if
you are careful to obey me, declares the
LORD, and bring no load through the gates of
this city on the Sabbath, but keep the Sabbath day holy by not doing any work on it,
25then kings who sit on David's throne will
come through the gates of this city with their
officials. They and their officials will come
riding in chariots and on horses, accompanied by the men of Judah and those living in
Jerusalem, and this city will be inhabited for
ever. 26People will come from the towns of
Judah and the villages around Jerusalem,
from the territory of Benjamin and the western foothills, from the hill country and the
Negev, bringing burnt offerings and sacrifices, grain offerings, incense and thank-
offerings to the house of the LORD. 27But if
you do not obey me to keep the Sabbath day
holy by not carrying any load as you come
through the gates of Jerusalem on the Sabbath day, then I will kindle an unquenchable
fire in the gates of Jerusalem that will consume her fortresses.'"

At the Potter's House

18 This is the word that came to Jere-
      miah from the LORD: 2"Go down to
the potter's house, and there I will give you
my message." 3So I went down to the potter's house, and I saw him working at the
wheel. 4But the pot he was shaping from the
clay was marred in his hands; so the potter
formed it into another pot, shaping it as
seemed best to him.

5Then the word of the LORD came to me:
6"O house of Israel, can I not do with you as
this potter does?" declares the LORD. "Like
clay in the hand of the potter, so are you in
my hand, O house of Israel. 7If at any time I
announce that a nation or kingdom is to be
uprooted, torn down and destroyed, 8and if
that nation I warned repents of its evil, then
I will relent and not inflict on it the disaster
I had planned. 9And if at another time I
announce that a nation or kingdom is to be
built up and planted, 10and if it does evil in my
sight and does not obey me, then I will reconsider the good I had intended to do for it.

11"Now therefore say to the people of
Judah and those living in Jerusalem, 'This is
what the LORD says: Look! I am preparing a
disaster for you and devising a plan against
you. So turn from your evil ways, each one of
you, and reform your ways and your actions.' 12But they will reply, 'It's no use. We
will continue with our own plans; each of us
will follow the stubbornness of his evil
heart.'"

13Therefore this is what the LORD says:

"Enquire among the nations:
   Who has ever heard anything like this?
A most horrible thing has been done
   by Virgin Israel.
14Does the snow of Lebanon
   ever vanish from its rocky slopes?
Do its cool waters from distant sources
   ever cease to flow?a
15Yet my people have forgotten me;
   they burn incense to worthless idols,
   which made them stumble in their ways
   and in the ancient paths.
They made them walk in bypaths
   and on roads not built up.
16Their land will be laid waste,
   an object of lasting scorn;
all who pass by will be appalled
   and will shake their heads.

a14 The meaning of the Hebrew for this sentence is uncertain.

¹⁷Like a wind from the east,
  I will scatter them before their enemies;
I will show them my back and not my face
  in the day of their disaster.''

¹⁸They said, "Come, let's make plans
against Jeremiah; for the teaching of the law
by the priest will not be lost, nor will counsel
from the wise, nor the word from the
prophets. So come, let's attack him with our
tongues and pay no attention to anything he
says.''

¹⁹Listen to me, O LORD;
  hear what my accusers are saying!
²⁰Should good be repaid with evil?
  Yet they have dug a pit for me.
Remember that I stood before you
  and spoke on their behalf
  to turn your wrath away from them.
²¹So give their children over to famine;
  hand them over to the power of the
    sword.
Let their wives be made childless and
    widows;
  let their men be put to death,
  their young men slain by the sword in
    battle.
²²Let a cry be heard from their houses
  when you suddenly bring invaders
    against them,
for they have dug a pit to capture me
  and have hidden snares for my feet.
²³But you know, O LORD,
  all their plots to kill me.
Do not forgive their crimes
  or blot out their sins from your sight.
Let them be overthrown before you;
  deal with them in the time of your anger.

19 This is what the LORD says: "Go and
buy a clay jar from a potter. Take
along some of the elders of the people and of
the priests ²and go out to the Valley of Ben
Hinnom, near the entrance of the Potsherd
Gate. There proclaim the words I tell you,
³and say, 'Hear the word of the LORD, O
kings of Judah and people of Jerusalem. This
is what the LORD Almighty, the God of Israel,
says: Listen! I am going to bring a disaster on
this place that will make the ears of everyone
who hears of it tingle. ⁴For they have forsaken me and made this a place of foreign
gods; they have burned sacrifices in it to gods
that neither they nor their fathers nor the
kings of Judah ever knew, and they have
filled this place with the blood of the innocent. ⁵They have built the high places of Baal
to burn their sons in the fire as offerings to
Baal—something I did not command or mention, nor did it enter my mind. ⁶So beware,
the days are coming, declares the LORD,
when people will no longer call this place
Topheth or the Valley of Ben Hinnom, but
the Valley of Slaughter.

⁷"'In this place I will ruin*ᵃ* the plans of
Judah and Jerusalem. I will make them fall by
the sword before their enemies, at the hands

of those who seek their lives, and I will give
their carcasses as food to the birds of the air
and the beasts of the earth. ⁸I will devastate
this city and make it an object of scorn; all
who pass by will be appalled and will scoff
because of all its wounds. ⁹I will make them
eat the flesh of their sons and daughters, and
they will eat one another's flesh during the
stress of the siege imposed on them by the
enemies who seek their lives.'

¹⁰"Then break the jar while those who go
with you are watching, ¹¹and say to them,
'This is what the LORD Almighty says: I will
smash this nation and this city just as this
potter's jar is smashed and cannot be repaired. They will bury the dead in Topheth
until there is no more room. ¹²This is what I
will do to this place and to those who live
here, declares the LORD. I will make this city
like Topheth. ¹³The houses in Jerusalem and
those of the kings of Judah will be defiled like
this place, Topheth—all the houses where
they burned incense on the roofs to all the
starry hosts and poured out drink offerings to
other gods.'''

¹⁴Jeremiah then returned from Topheth,
where the LORD had sent him to prophesy,
and stood in the court of the LORD's temple
and said to all the people, ¹⁵"This is what the
LORD Almighty, the God of Israel, says: 'Listen! I am going to bring on this city and the
villages around it every disaster I pronounced against them, because they were
stiff-necked and would not listen to my
words.'''

Jeremiah and Pashhur

20 When the priest Pashhur son of Immer, the chief officer in the temple of
the LORD, heard Jeremiah prophesying these
things, ²he had Jeremiah the prophet beaten
and put in the stocks at the Upper Gate of
Benjamin at the LORD's temple. ³The next
day, when Pashhur released him from the
stocks, Jeremiah said to him, "The LORD's
name for you is not Pashhur, but Magor-
Missabib.*ᵃ* ⁴For this is what the LORD says: 'I
will make you a terror to yourself and to all
your friends; with your own eyes you will see
them fall by the sword of their enemies. I will
hand all Judah over to the king of Babylon,
who will carry them away to Babylon or put
them to the sword. ⁵I will hand over to their
enemies all the wealth of this city—all its
products, all its valuables and all the treasures of the kings of Judah. They will take it
away as plunder and carry it off to Babylon.
⁶And you, Pashhur, and all who live in your
house will go into exile to Babylon. There
you will die and be buried, you and all your
friends to whom you have prophesied lies.'''

Jeremiah's Complaint

⁷O LORD, you deceived*ᵇ* me, and I was
    deceived;*ᵇ*
  you overpowered me and prevailed.
I am ridiculed all day long;
  everyone mocks me.

---

*ᵃ7 The Hebrew for *ruin* sounds like the Hebrew for *jar* (see verses 1 and 10).*
*ᵃ3 *Magor-Missabib* means *terror on every side.*   *ᵇ7 Or *persuaded**

[8]Whenever I speak, I cry out
  proclaiming violence and destruction.
So the word of the LORD has brought me
  insult and reproach all day long.
[9]But if I say, "I will not mention him
  or speak any more in his name,"
his word is in my heart like a fire,
  a fire shut up in my bones.
I am weary of holding it in;
  indeed, I cannot.
[10]I hear many whispering,
  "Terror on every side!
  Report him! Let's report him!"
All my friends
  are waiting for me to slip, saying,
"Perhaps he will be deceived;
  then we will prevail over him
  and take our revenge on him."

[11]But the LORD is with me like a mighty
    warrior;
so my persecutors will stumble and not
    prevail.
They will fail and be thoroughly disgraced;
  their dishonour will never be forgotten.
[12]O LORD Almighty, you who examine the
    righteous
  and probe the heart and mind,
let me see your vengeance upon them,
  for to you I have committed my cause.

[13]Sing to the LORD!
  Give praise to the LORD!
He rescues the life of the needy
  from the hands of the wicked.

[14]Cursed be the day I was born!
  May the day my mother bore me not be
    blessed!
[15]Cursed be the man who brought my father
    the news,
who made him very glad, saying,
  "A child is born to you—a son!"
[16]May that man be like the towns
  the LORD overthrew without pity.
May he hear wailing in the morning,
  a battle cry at noon.
[17]For he did not kill me in the womb,
  with my mother as my grave,
  her womb enlarged for ever.
[18]Why did I ever come out of the womb
  to see trouble and sorrow
  and to end my days in shame?

God Rejects Zedekiah's Request

21 The word came to Jeremiah from the
LORD when King Zedekiah sent to
him Pashhur son of Malkijah and the priest
Zephaniah son of Maaseiah. They said:
[2]"Enquire now of the LORD for us because
Nebuchadnezzar[a] king of Babylon is attacking us. Perhaps the LORD will perform wonders for us as in times past so that he will
withdraw from us."

[3]But Jeremiah answered them, "Tell
Zedekiah, [4]'This is what the LORD, the God
of Israel, says: I am about to turn against you
the weapons of war that are in your hands,

which you are using to fight the king of
Babylon and the Babylonians[b] who are outside the wall besieging you. And I will gather
them inside this city. [5]I myself will fight
against you with an outstretched hand and a
mighty arm in anger and fury and great
wrath. [6]I will strike down those who live in
this city—both men and animals—and they
will die of a terrible plague. [7]After that, declares the LORD, I will hand over Zedekiah
king of Judah, his officials and the people in
this city who survive the plague, sword and
famine, to Nebuchadnezzar king of Babylon
and to their enemies who seek their lives. He
will put them to the sword; he will show them
no mercy or pity or compassion.'

[8]"Furthermore, tell the people, 'This is
what the LORD says: See, I am setting before
you the way of life and the way of death.
[9]Whoever stays in this city will die by the
sword, famine or plague. But whoever goes
out and surrenders to the Babylonians who
are besieging you will live; he will escape
with his life. [10]I have determined to do this
city harm and not good, declares the LORD. It
will be given into the hands of the king of
Babylon, and he will destroy it with fire.'

[11]"Moreover, say to the royal house of
Judah, 'Hear the word of the LORD; [12]O
house of David, this is what the LORD says:

"'Administer justice every morning;
  rescue from the hand of his oppressor
  the one who has been robbed,
or my wrath will break out and burn like
    fire
because of the evil you have done—
  burn with no-one to quench it.
[13]I am against you, ˻Jerusalem,˼
  you who live above this valley
  on the rocky plateau,
            declares the LORD—
you who say, "Who can come against us?
  Who can enter our refuge?"
[14]I will punish you as your deeds deserve,
            declares the LORD.
I will kindle a fire in your forests
  that will consume everything around
    you.'"

Judgment Against Evil Kings

22 This is what the LORD says: "Go
down to the palace of the king of
Judah and proclaim this message there:
[2]'Hear the word of the LORD, O king of
Judah, you who sit on David's throne—you,
your officials and your people who come
through these gates. [3]This is what the LORD
says: Do what is just and right. Rescue from
the hand of his oppressor the one who has
been robbed. Do no wrong or violence to the
alien, the fatherless or the widow, and do not
shed innocent blood in this place. [4]For if you
are careful to carry out these commands,
then kings who sit on David's throne will
come through the gates of this palace, riding
in chariots and on horses, accompanied by
their officials and their people. [5]But if you do

[a]2 Hebrew Nebuchadrezzar, of which Nebuchadnezzar is a variant; here and often in Jeremiah and
Ezekiel   [b]4 Or Chaldeans; also in verse 9

not obey these commands, declares the LORD, I swear by myself that this palace will become a ruin.'''

⁶For this is what the LORD says about the palace of the king of Judah:

"Though you are like Gilead to me,
  like the summit of Lebanon,
I will surely make you like a desert,
  like towns not inhabited.
⁷I will send destroyers against you,
  each man with his weapons,
and they will cut up your fine cedar beams
  and throw them into the fire.

⁸"People from many nations will pass by this city and will ask one another, 'Why has the LORD done such a thing to this great city?' ⁹And the answer will be: 'Because they have forsaken the covenant of the LORD their God and have worshipped and served other gods.'"

¹⁰Do not weep for the dead ⸢king⸣ or mourn his loss;
  rather, weep bitterly for him who is exiled,
because he will never return
  nor see his native land again.

¹¹For this is what the LORD says about Shallumᵃ son of Josiah, who succeeded his father as king of Judah but has gone from this place: "He will never return. ¹²He will die in the place where they have led him captive; he will not see this land again."

¹³"Woe to him who builds his palace by unrighteousness,
  his upper rooms by injustice,
making his countrymen work for nothing,
  not paying them for their labour.
¹⁴He says, 'I will build myself a great palace
  with spacious upper rooms.'
So he makes large windows in it,
  panels it with cedar
  and decorates it in red.

¹⁵Does it make you a king
  to have more and more cedar?
Did not your father have food and drink?
  He did what was right and just,
  so all went well with him.
¹⁶He defended the cause of the poor and needy,
  and so all went well.
Is that not what it means to know me?"
  declares the LORD.
¹⁷"But your eyes and your heart
  are set only on dishonest gain,
on shedding innocent blood
  and on oppression and extortion."

¹⁸Therefore this is what the LORD says about Jehoiakim son of Josiah king of Judah:

"They will not mourn for him:
  'Alas, my brother! Alas, my sister!'

They will not mourn for him:
  'Alas, my master! Alas, his splendour!'
¹⁹He will have the burial of a donkey—
  dragged away and thrown
  outside the gates of Jerusalem."

²⁰"Go up to Lebanon and cry out,
  let your voice be heard in Bashan,
cry out from Abarim,
  for all your allies are crushed.
²¹I warned you when you felt secure,
  but you said, 'I will not listen!'
This has been your way from your youth;
  you have not obeyed me.
²²The wind will drive all your shepherds away,
  and your allies will go into exile.
Then you will be ashamed and disgraced
  because of all your wickedness.
²³You who live in 'Lebanon',ᵇ
  who are nestled in cedar buildings,
how you will groan when pangs come upon you,
  pain like that of a woman in labour!

²⁴"As surely as I live," declares the LORD, "even if you, Jehoiachinᶜ son of Jehoiakim king of Judah, were a signet ring on my right hand, I would still pull you off. ²⁵I will hand you over to those who seek your life, those you fear—to Nebuchadnezzar king of Babylon and to the Babylonians.ᵈ ²⁶I will hurl you and the mother who gave you birth into another country, where neither of you was born, and there you both will die. ²⁷You will never come back to the land you long to return to."

²⁸Is this man Jehoiachin a despised, broken pot,
  an object no-one wants?
Why will he and his children be hurled out,
  cast into a land they do not know?
²⁹O land, land, land,
  hear the word of the LORD!
³⁰This is what the LORD says:
"Record this man as if childless,
  a man who will not prosper in his lifetime,
for none of his offspring will prosper,
  none will sit on the throne of David
  or rule any more in Judah."

The Righteous Branch

23 "Woe to the shepherds who are destroying and scattering the sheep of my pasture!" declares the LORD. ²Therefore this is what the LORD, the God of Israel, says to the shepherds who tend my people: "Because you have scattered my flock and driven them away and have not bestowed care on them, I will bestow punishment on you for the evil you have done," declares the LORD. ³"I myself will gather the remnant of my flock out of all the countries where I have driven them and will bring them back to their pasture, where they will be fruitful and increase in number. ⁴I will place shepherds

---

ᵃ11 Also called *Jehoahaz*   ᵇ23 That is, the palace in Jerusalem (see 1 Kings 7:2)
ᶜ24 Hebrew *Coniah*, a variant of *Jehoiachin*; also in verse 28   ᵈ25 Or *Chaldeans*

over them who will tend them, and they will
no longer be afraid or terrified, nor will any
be missing,'' declares the LORD.

⁵''The days are coming,'' declares the
    LORD,
  ''when I will raise up to David*a* a
    righteous Branch,
a King who will reign wisely
  and do what is just and right in the land.
⁶In his days Judah will be saved
  and Israel will live in safety.
This is the name by which he will be
    called:
  The LORD Our Righteousness.

⁷''So then, the days are coming,'' declares
the LORD, ''when people will no longer say,
'As surely as the LORD lives, who brought the
Israelites up out of Egypt,' ⁸but they will say,
'As surely as the LORD lives, who brought the
descendants of Israel up out of the land of the
north and out of all the countries where he
had banished them.' Then they will live in
their own land.''

Lying Prophets

⁹Concerning the prophets:

My heart is broken within me;
  all my bones tremble.
I am like a drunken man,
  like a man overcome by wine,
because of the LORD
  and his holy words.
¹⁰The land is full of adulterers;
  because of the curse*b* the land lies
    parched*c*
  and the pastures in the desert are
    withered.
The ᵤprophetsᵤ follow an evil course
  and use their power unjustly.

¹¹''Both prophet and priest are godless;
  even in my temple I find their
    wickedness,''
                    declares the LORD.
¹²''Therefore their path will become
    slippery;
  they will be banished to darkness
  and there they will fall.
I will bring disaster on them
  in the year they are punished,''
                    declares the LORD.

¹³''Among the prophets of Samaria
  I saw this repulsive thing:
They prophesied by Baal
  and led my people Israel astray.
¹⁴And among the prophets of Jerusalem
  I have seen something horrible:
They commit adultery and live a lie.
They strengthen the hands of evildoers,
  so that no-one turns from his
    wickedness.
They are all like Sodom to me;
  the people of Jerusalem are like
    Gomorrah.''

¹⁵Therefore, this is what the LORD Almighty says concerning the prophets:

''I will make them eat bitter food
  and drink poisoned water,
because from the prophets of Jerusalem
  ungodliness has spread throughout the
    land.''

¹⁶This is what the LORD Almighty says:

''Do not listen to what the prophets are
    prophesying to you;
  they fill you with false hopes.
They speak visions from their own minds,
  not from the mouth of the LORD.
¹⁷They keep saying to those who despise
    me,
  'The LORD says: You will have peace.'
And to all who follow the stubbornness of
    their hearts
  they say, 'No harm will come to you.'
¹⁸But which of them has stood in the council
    of the LORD
  to see or to hear his word?
  Who has listened and heard his word?
¹⁹See, the storm of the LORD
  will burst out in wrath,
a whirlwind swirling down
  on the heads of the wicked.
²⁰The anger of the LORD will not turn back
  until he fully accomplishes
  the purposes of his heart.
In days to come
  you will understand it clearly.
²¹I did not send these prophets,
  yet they have run with their message;
I did not speak to them,
  yet they have prophesied.
²²But if they had stood in my council,
  they would have proclaimed my words
    to my people
and would have turned them from their
    evil ways
  and from their evil deeds.

²³''Am I only a God nearby,''
                    declares the LORD,
  ''and not a God far away?
²⁴Can anyone hide in secret places
  so that I cannot see him?''
                    declares the LORD.
  ''Do not I fill heaven and earth?''
                    declares the LORD.

²⁵''I have heard what the prophets say who
prophesy lies in my name. They say, 'I had a
dream! I had a dream!' ²⁶How long will this
continue in the hearts of these lying
prophets, who prophesy the delusions of
their own minds? ²⁷They think the dreams
they tell one another will make my people
forget my name, just as their fathers forgot
my name through Baal worship. ²⁸Let the
prophet who has a dream tell his dream, but
let the one who has my word speak it faithfully. For what has straw to do with grain?''
declares the LORD. ²⁹''Is not my word like

---

*a*5 Or *up from David's line*   *b*10 Or *because of these things*
*c*10 Or *land mourns*

fire,'' declares the LORD, ''and like a hammer that breaks a rock in pieces?

³⁰''Therefore,'' declares the LORD, ''I am against the prophets who steal from one another words supposedly from me. ³¹Yes,'' declares the LORD, ''I am against the prophets who wag their own tongues and yet declare, 'The LORD declares.' ³²Indeed, I am against those who prophesy false dreams,'' declares the LORD. ''They tell them and lead my people astray with their reckless lies, yet I did not send or appoint them. They do not benefit these people in the least,'' declares the LORD.

False Oracles and False Prophets

³³''When these people, or a prophet or a priest, ask you, 'What is the oracle*d* of the LORD?' say to them, 'What oracle?*e* I will forsake you, declares the LORD.' ³⁴If a prophet or a priest or anyone else claims, 'This is the oracle of the LORD,' I will punish that man and his household. ³⁵This is what each of you keeps on saying to his friend or relative: 'What is the LORD's answer?' or 'What has the LORD spoken?' ³⁶But you must not mention 'the oracle of the LORD' again, because every man's own word becomes his oracle and so you distort the words of the living God, the LORD Almighty, our God. ³⁷This is what you keep saying to a prophet: 'What is the LORD's answer to you?' or 'What has the LORD spoken?' ³⁸Although you claim, 'This is the oracle of the LORD,' this is what the LORD says: You used the words, 'This is the oracle of the LORD,' even though I told you that you must not claim, 'This is the oracle of the LORD.' ³⁹Therefore, I will surely forget you and cast you out of my presence along with the city I gave to you and your fathers. ⁴⁰I will bring upon you everlasting disgrace—everlasting shame that will not be forgotten.''

Two Baskets of Figs

24 After Jehoiachin*a* son of Jehoiakim king of Judah and the officials, the craftsmen and the artisans of Judah were carried into exile from Jerusalem to Babylon by Nebuchadnezzar king of Babylon, the LORD showed me two baskets of figs placed in front of the temple of the LORD. ²One basket had very good figs, like those that ripen early; the other basket had very poor figs, so bad that they could not be eaten.

³Then the LORD asked me, ''What do you see, Jeremiah?''

''Figs,'' I answered. ''The good ones are very good, but the poor ones are so bad that they cannot be eaten.''

⁴Then the word of the LORD came to me: ⁵''This is what the LORD, the God of Israel, says: 'Like these good figs, I regard as good the exiles from Judah, whom I sent away from this place to the land of the Babylonians.*b* ⁶My eyes will watch over them for

their good, and I will bring them back to this land. I will build them up and not tear them down; I will plant them and not uproot them. ⁷I will give them a heart to know me, that I am the LORD. They will be my people, and I will be their God, for they will return to me with all their heart.

⁸''But like the poor figs, which are so bad that they cannot be eaten,' says the LORD, 'so will I deal with Zedekiah king of Judah, his officials and the survivors from Jerusalem, whether they remain in this land or live in Egypt. ⁹I will make them abhorrent and an offence to all the kingdoms of the earth, a reproach and a byword, an object of ridicule and cursing, wherever I banish them. ¹⁰I will send the sword, famine and plague against them until they are destroyed from the land I gave to them and their fathers.' ''

Seventy Years of Captivity

25 The word came to Jeremiah concerning all the people of Judah in the fourth year of Jehoiakim son of Josiah king of Judah, which was the first year of Nebuchadnezzar king of Babylon. ²So Jeremiah the prophet said to all the people of Judah and to all those living in Jerusalem: ³For twenty-three years—from the thirteenth year of Josiah son of Amon king of Judah until this very day—the word of the LORD has come to me and I have spoken to you again and again, but you have not listened.

⁴And though the LORD has sent all his servants the prophets to you again and again, you have not listened or paid any attention. ⁵They said, ''Turn now, each of you, from your evil ways and your evil practices, and you can stay in the land the LORD gave to you and your fathers for ever and ever. ⁶Do not follow other gods to serve and worship them; do not provoke me to anger with what your hands have made. Then I will not harm you.''

⁷''But you did not listen to me,'' declares the LORD, ''and you have provoked me with what your hands have made, and you have brought harm to yourselves.''

⁸Therefore the LORD Almighty says this: ''Because you have not listened to my words, ⁹I will summon all the peoples of the north and my servant Nebuchadnezzar king of Babylon,'' declares the LORD, ''and I will bring them against this land and its inhabitants and against all the surrounding nations. I will completely destroy*a* them and make them an object of horror and scorn, and an everlasting ruin. ¹⁰I will banish from them the sounds of joy and gladness, the voices of bride and bridegroom, the sound of millstones and the light of the lamp. ¹¹This whole country will become a desolate wasteland, and these nations will serve the king of Babylon for seventy years.

¹²''But when the seventy years are fulfilled, I will punish the king of Babylon and his nation, the land of the Babylonians,*b* for

---

d33 Or *burden* (see Septuagint and Vulgate)
e33 Hebrew; Septuagint and Vulgate *'You are the burden*; the Hebrew for *oracle* and *burden* is the same.
a1 Hebrew *Jeconiah*, a variant of *Jehoiachin*   *b5* Or *Chaldeans*
a9 The Hebrew term refers to the irrevocable giving over of things or persons to the LORD, often by totally destroying them.   *b12* Or *Chaldeans*

their guilt," declares the LORD, "and will make it desolate for ever. 13I will bring upon that land all the things I have spoken against it, all that are written in this book and prophesied by Jeremiah against all the nations. 14They themselves will be enslaved by many nations and great kings; I will repay them according to their deeds and the work of their hands."

The Cup of God's Wrath

15This is what the LORD, the God of Israel, said to me: "Take from my hand this cup filled with the wine of my wrath and make all the nations to whom I send you drink it. 16When they drink it, they will stagger and go mad because of the sword I will send among them."

17So I took the cup from the LORD's hand and made all the nations to whom he sent me drink it: 18Jerusalem and the towns of Judah, its kings and officials, to make them a ruin and an object of horror and scorn and cursing, as they are today; 19Pharaoh king of Egypt, his attendants, his officials and all his people, 20and all the foreign people there; all the kings of Uz; all the kings of the Philistines (those of Ashkelon, Gaza, Ekron, and the people left at Ashdod); 21Edom, Moab and Ammon; 22all the kings of Tyre and Sidon; the kings of the coastlands across the sea; 23Dedan, Tema, Buz and all who are in distant places;c 24all the kings of Arabia and all the kings of the foreign people who live in the desert; 25all the kings of Zimri, Elam and Media; 26and all the kings of the north, near and far, one after the other—all the kingdoms on the face of the earth. And after all of them, the king of Sheshachd will drink it too.

27"Then tell them, 'This is what the LORD Almighty, the God of Israel, says: Drink, get drunk and vomit, and fall to rise no more because of the sword I will send among you.' 28But if they refuse to take the cup from your hand and drink, tell them, 'This is what the LORD Almighty says: You must drink it! 29See, I am beginning to bring disaster on the city that bears my Name, and will you indeed go unpunished? You will not go unpunished, for I am calling down a sword upon all who live on the earth, declares the LORD Almighty.'

30"Now prophesy all these words against them and say to them:

"'The LORD will roar from on high;
    he will thunder from his holy dwelling
    and roar mightily against his land.
He will shout like those who tread the
        grapes,
    shout against all who live on the earth.
31The tumult will resound to the ends of the
        earth,
    for the LORD will bring charges against
        the nations;
he will bring judgment on all mankind
    and put the wicked to the sword,'"
                    declares the LORD.

32This is what the LORD Almighty says:

"Look! Disaster is spreading
    from nation to nation;
a mighty storm is rising
    from the ends of the earth."

33At that time those slain by the LORD will be everywhere—from one end of the earth to the other. They will not be mourned or gathered up or buried, but will be like refuse lying on the ground.

34Weep and wail, you shepherds;
    roll in the dust, you leaders of the flock.
For your time to be slaughtered has come;
    you will fall and be shattered like fine
        pottery.
35The shepherds will have nowhere to flee,
    the leaders of the flock no place to
        escape.
36Hear the cry of the shepherds,
    the wailing of the leaders of the flock,
    for the LORD is destroying their pasture.
37The peaceful meadows will be laid waste
    because of the fierce anger of the LORD.
38Like a lion he will leave his lair,
    and their land will become desolate
because of the sworde of the oppressor
    and because of the LORD's fierce anger.

Jeremiah Threatened With Death

26 Early in the reign of Jehoiakim son of Josiah king of Judah, this word came from the LORD: 2"This is what the LORD says: Stand in the courtyard of the LORD's house and speak to all the people of the towns of Judah who come to worship in the house of the LORD. Tell them everything I command you; do not omit a word. 3Perhaps they will listen and each will turn from his evil way. Then I will relent and not bring on them the disaster I was planning because of the evil they have done. 4Say to them, 'This is what the LORD says: If you do not listen to me and follow my law, which I have set before you, 5and if you do not listen to the words of my servants the prophets, whom I have sent to you again and again (though you have not listened), 6then I will make this house like Shiloh and this city an object of cursing among all the nations of the earth.'"

7The priests, the prophets and all the people heard Jeremiah speak these words in the house of the LORD. 8But as soon as Jeremiah finished telling all the people everything the LORD had commanded him to say, the priests, the prophets and all the people seized him and said, "You must die! 9Why do you prophesy in the LORD's name that this house will be like Shiloh and this city will be desolate and deserted?" And all the people crowded around Jeremiah in the house of the LORD.

10When the officials of Judah heard about these things, they went up from the royal palace to the house of the LORD and took their places at the entrance of the New Gate of the

---

c23 Or *who clip the hair by their foreheads*   d26 *Sheshach* is a cryptogram for Babylon.
e38 Some Hebrew manuscripts and Septuagint (see also Jer. 46:16 and 50:16); most Hebrew manuscripts *anger*

LORD's house. [11]Then the priests and the prophets said to the officials and all the people, "This man should be sentenced to death because he has prophesied against this city. You have heard it with your own ears!"

[12]Then Jeremiah said to all the officials and all the people: "The LORD sent me to prophesy against this house and this city all the things you have heard. [13]Now reform your ways and your actions and obey the LORD your God. Then the LORD will relent and not bring the disaster he has pronounced against you. [14]As for me, I am in your hands; do with me whatever you think is good and right. [15]Be assured, however, that if you put me to death, you will bring the guilt of innocent blood on yourselves and on this city and on those who live in it, for in truth the LORD has sent me to you to speak all these words in your hearing."

[16]Then the officials and all the people said to the priests and the prophets, "This man should not be sentenced to death! He has spoken to us in the name of the LORD our God."

[17]Some of the elders of the land stepped forward and said to the entire assembly of people, [18]"Micah of Moresheth prophesied in the days of Hezekiah king of Judah. He told all the people of Judah, 'This is what the LORD Almighty says:

"'Zion will be ploughed like a field,
    Jerusalem will become a heap of rubble,
    the temple hill a mound overgrown with thickets.'[a]

[19]"Did Hezekiah king of Judah or anyone else in Judah put him to death? Did not Hezekiah fear the LORD and seek his favour? And did not the LORD relent, so that he did not bring the disaster he pronounced against them? We are about to bring a terrible disaster on ourselves!"

[20](Now Uriah son of Shemaiah from Kiriath Jearim was another man who prophesied in the name of the LORD; he prophesied the same things against this city and this land as Jeremiah did. [21]When King Jehoiakim and all his officers and officials heard his words, the king sought to put him to death. But Uriah heard of it and fled in fear to Egypt. [22]King Jehoiakim, however, sent Elnathan son of Acbor to Egypt, along with some other men. [23]They brought Uriah out of Egypt and took him to King Jehoiakim, who had him struck down with a sword and his body thrown into the burial place of the common people.)

[24]Furthermore, Ahikam son of Shaphan supported Jeremiah, and so he was not handed over to the people to be put to death.

Judah to Serve Nebuchadnezzar

27 Early in the reign of Zedekiah[a] son of Josiah king of Judah, this word came to Jeremiah from the LORD: [2]This is what the LORD said to me: "Make a yoke out of straps and crossbars and put it on your neck. [3]Then send word to the kings of Edom, Moab, Ammon, Tyre and Sidon through the envoys who have come to Jerusalem to Zedekiah king of Judah. [4]Give them a message for their masters and say, 'This is what the LORD Almighty, the God of Israel, says: "Tell this to your masters: [5]With my great power and outstretched arm I made the earth and its people and the animals that are on it, and I give it to anyone I please. [6]Now I will hand all your countries over to my servant Nebuchadnezzar king of Babylon; I will make even the wild animals subject to him. [7]All nations will serve him and his son and his grandson until the time for his land comes; then many nations and great kings will subjugate him.

[8]"'"If, however, any nation or kingdom will not serve Nebuchadnezzar king of Babylon or bow its neck under his yoke, I will punish that nation with the sword, famine and plague, declares the LORD, until I destroy it by his hand. [9]So do not listen to your prophets, your diviners, your interpreters of dreams, your mediums or your sorcerers who tell you, 'You will not serve the king of Babylon.' [10]They prophesy lies to you that will only serve to remove you far from your lands; I will banish you and you will perish. [11]But if any nation will bow its neck under the yoke of the king of Babylon and serve him, I will let that nation remain in its own land to till it and to live there, declares the LORD.'"'"

[12]I gave the same message to Zedekiah king of Judah. I said, "Bow your neck under the yoke of the king of Babylon; serve him and his people, and you will live. [13]Why will you and your people die by the sword, famine and plague with which the LORD has threatened any nation that will not serve the king of Babylon? [14]Do not listen to the words of the prophets who say to you, 'You will not serve the king of Babylon,' for they are prophesying lies to you. [15]'I have not sent them,' declares the LORD. 'They are prophesying lies in my name. Therefore, I will banish you and you will perish, both you and the prophets who prophesy to you.'"

[16]Then I said to the priests and all these people, "This is what the LORD says: Do not listen to the prophets who say, 'Very soon now the articles from the LORD's house will be brought back from Babylon.' They are prophesying lies to you. [17]Do not listen to them. Serve the king of Babylon, and you will live. Why should this city become a ruin? [18]If they are prophets and have the word of the LORD, let them plead with the LORD Almighty that the furnishings remaining in the house of the LORD and in the palace of the king of Judah and in Jerusalem not be taken to Babylon. [19]For this is what the LORD Almighty says about the pillars, the Sea, the movable stands and the other furnishings

---

[a]18 Micah 3:12
[a]1 A few Hebrew manuscripts and Syriac (see also Jer. 27:3, 12 and 28:1); most Hebrew manuscripts *Jehoiakim* (most Septuagint manuscripts do not have this verse.)

that are left in this city, 20which Nebuchadnezzar king of Babylon did not take away when he carried Jehoiachin*b* son of Jehoiakim king of Judah into exile from Jerusalem to Babylon, along with all the nobles of Judah and Jerusalem—21yes, this is what the LORD Almighty, the God of Israel, says about the things that are left in the house of the LORD and in the palace of the king of Judah and in Jerusalem: 22'They will be taken to Babylon and there they will remain until the day I come for them,' declares the LORD. 'Then I will bring them back and restore them to this place.'''

The False Prophet Hananiah

28 In the fifth month of that same year, the fourth year, early in the reign of Zedekiah king of Judah, the prophet Hananiah son of Azzur, who was from Gibeon, said to me in the house of the LORD in the presence of the priests and all the people: 2"This is what the LORD Almighty, the God of Israel, says: 'I will break the yoke of the king of Babylon. 3Within two years I will bring back to this place all the articles of the LORD's house that Nebuchadnezzar king of Babylon removed from here and took to Babylon. 4I will also bring back to this place Jehoiachin son of Jehoiakim king of Judah and all the other exiles from Judah who went to Babylon,' declares the LORD, 'for I will break the yoke of the king of Babylon.'''

5Then the prophet Jeremiah replied to the prophet Hananiah before the priests and all the people who were standing in the house of the LORD. 6He said, "Amen! May the LORD do so! May the LORD fulfil the words you have prophesied by bringing the articles of the LORD's house and all the exiles back to this place from Babylon. 7Nevertheless, listen to what I have to say in your hearing and in the hearing of all the people: 8From early times the prophets who preceded you and me have prophesied war, disaster and plague against many countries and great kingdoms. 9But the prophet who prophesies peace will be recognised as one truly sent by the LORD only if his prediction comes true."

10Then the prophet Hananiah took the yoke off the neck of the prophet Jeremiah and broke it, 11and he said before all the people, "This is what the LORD says: 'In the same way will I break the yoke of Nebuchadnezzar king of Babylon off the neck of all the nations within two years.'" At this, the prophet Jeremiah went on his way.

12Shortly after the prophet Hananiah had broken the yoke off the neck of the prophet Jeremiah, the word of the LORD came to Jeremiah: 13"Go and tell Hananiah, 'This is what the LORD says: You have broken a wooden yoke, but in its place you will get a yoke of iron. 14This is what the LORD Almighty, the God of Israel, says: I will put an iron yoke on the necks of all these nations to make them serve Nebuchadnezzar king of Babylon, and they will serve him. I will even give him control over the wild animals.'''

15Then the prophet Jeremiah said to Hananiah the prophet, "Listen, Hananiah! The LORD has not sent you, yet you have persuaded this nation to trust in lies. 16Therefore, this is what the LORD says: 'I am about to remove you from the face of the earth. This very year you are going to die, because you have preached rebellion against the LORD.'''

17In the seventh month of that same year, Hananiah the prophet died.

A Letter to the Exiles

29 This is the text of the letter that the prophet Jeremiah sent from Jerusalem to the surviving elders among the exiles and to the priests, the prophets and all the other people Nebuchadnezzar had carried into exile from Jerusalem to Babylon. 2(This was after King Jehoiachin and the queen mother, the court officials and the leaders of Judah and Jerusalem, the craftsmen and the artisans had gone into exile from Jerusalem.) 3He entrusted the letter to Elasah son of Shaphan and to Gemariah son of Hilkiah, whom Zedekiah king of Judah sent to King Nebuchadnezzar in Babylon. It said:

4This is what the LORD Almighty, the God of Israel, says to all those I carried into exile from Jerusalem to Babylon: 5"Build houses and settle down; plant gardens and eat what they produce. 6Marry and have sons and daughters; find wives for your sons and give your daughters in marriage, so that they too may have sons and daughters. Increase in number there; do not decrease. 7Also, seek the peace and prosperity of the city to which I have carried you into exile. Pray to the LORD for it, because if it prospers, you too will prosper." 8Yes, this is what the LORD Almighty, the God of Israel, says: "Do not let the prophets and diviners among you deceive you. Do not listen to the dreams you encourage them to have. 9They are prophesying lies to you in my name. I have not sent them," declares the LORD.

10This is what the LORD says: "When seventy years are completed for Babylon, I will come to you and fulfil my gracious promise to bring you back to this place. 11For I know the plans I have for you," declares the LORD, "plans to prosper you and not to harm you, plans to give you hope and a future. 12Then you will call upon me and come and pray to me, and I will listen to you. 13You will seek me and find me when you seek me with all your heart. 14I will be found by you," declares the LORD, "and will bring you back from captivity.*a* I will gather you from all the nations and places where I have banished you," declares the LORD, "and will bring you back to the place from which I carried you into exile."

15You may say, "The LORD has raised

---

*b*20 Hebrew *Jeconiah*, a variant of *Jehoiachin*; also in 28:4 and 29:2   *a*14 Or *will restore your fortunes* up prophets for us in Babylon," ¹⁶but this is what the LORD says about the king who sits on David's throne and all the people who remain in this city, your countrymen who did not go with you into exile—¹⁷yes, this is what the LORD Almighty says: "I will send the sword, famine and plague against them and I will make them like poor figs that are so bad they cannot be eaten. ¹⁸I will pursue them with the sword, famine and plague and will make them abhorrent to all the kingdoms of the earth and an object of cursing and horror, of scorn and reproach, among all the nations where I drive them. ¹⁹For they have not listened to my words," declares the LORD, "words that I sent to them again and again by my servants the prophets. And you exiles have not listened either," declares the LORD.

²⁰Therefore, hear the word of the LORD, all you exiles whom I have sent away from Jerusalem to Babylon. ²¹This is what the LORD Almighty, the God of Israel, says about Ahab son of Kolaiah and Zedekiah son of Maaseiah, who are prophesying lies to you in my name: "I will hand them over to Nebuchadnezzar king of Babylon, and he will put them to death before your very eyes. ²²Because of them, all the exiles from Judah who are in Babylon will use this curse: 'The LORD treat you like Zedekiah and Ahab, whom the king of Babylon burned in the fire.' ²³For they have done outrageous things in Israel; they have committed adultery with their neighbours' wives and in my name have spoken lies, which I did not tell them to do. I know it and am a witness to it," declares the LORD.

Message to Shemaiah

²⁴Tell Shemaiah the Nehelamite, ²⁵"This is what the LORD Almighty, the God of Israel, says: You sent letters in your own name to all the people in Jerusalem, to Zephaniah son of Maaseiah the priest, and to all the other priests. You said to Zephaniah, ²⁶'The LORD has appointed you priest in place of Jehoiada to be in charge of the house of the LORD; you should put any madman who acts like a prophet into the stocks and neck-irons. ²⁷So why have you not reprimanded Jeremiah from Anathoth, who poses as a prophet among you? ²⁸He has sent this message to us in Babylon: It will be a long time. Therefore build houses and settle down; plant gardens and eat what they produce.'"

²⁹Zephaniah the priest, however, read the letter to Jeremiah the prophet. ³⁰Then the word of the LORD came to Jeremiah: ³¹'Send this message to all the exiles: 'This is what the LORD says about Shemaiah the Nehelamite: Because Shemaiah has prophesied to you, even though I did not send him, and has led you to believe a lie, ³²this is what the LORD says: I will surely punish Shemaiah the Nehelamite and his descendants. He will

have no-one left among this people, nor will he see the good things I will do for my people, declares the LORD, because he has preached rebellion against me.'"

Restoration of Israel

30 This is the word that came to Jeremiah from the LORD: ²"This is what the LORD, the God of Israel, says: 'Write in a book all the words I have spoken to you. ³The days are coming,' declares the LORD, 'when I will bring my people Israel and Judah back from captivity*a* and restore them to the land I gave to their forefathers to possess,' says the LORD."

⁴These are the words the LORD spoke concerning Israel and Judah: ⁵"This is what the LORD says:

"'Cries of fear are heard—
    terror, not peace.
⁶Ask and see:
    Can a man bear children?
Then why do I see every strong man
    with his hands on his stomach like a
        woman in labour,
    every face turned deathly pale?
⁷How awful that day will be!
    None will be like it.
It will be a time of trouble for Jacob,
    but he will be saved out of it.

⁸"'In that day,' declares the LORD
        Almighty,
    'I will break the yoke off their necks
and will tear off their bonds;
    no longer will foreigners enslave them.
⁹Instead, they will serve the LORD their
        God
    and David their king,
    whom I will raise up for them.

¹⁰"'So do not fear, O Jacob my servant;
    do not be dismayed, O Israel,'
            declares the LORD.
'I will surely save you out of a distant
        place,
    your descendants from the land of their
        exile.
Jacob will again have peace and security,
    and no-one will make him afraid.
¹¹I am with you and will save you,'
    declares the LORD.
'Though I completely destroy all the
        nations
    among which I scatter you,
    I will not completely destroy you.
I will discipline you but only with justice;
    I will not let you go entirely
        unpunished.'

¹²"This is what the LORD says:

"'Your wound is incurable,
    your injury beyond healing.
¹³There is no-one to plead your cause,
    no remedy for your sore,
    no healing for you.

---

*a*3 Or will restore the fortunes of my people Israel and Judah

JEREMIAH 28:12–17

'Then the prophet Jeremiah said to Hananiah the prophet. "Listen, Hananiah! The LORD has not sent you, yet you have persuaded this nation to trust in lies" ' (v. 15).

SOME TIME ELAPSED before Jeremiah returned to Hananiah to renew this battle of the prophets. God did not give Jeremiah an immediate word with which to respond, but when it came, true to the prophetic tradition, it was comprehensive and devastating. Jeremiah's wooden yoke would be replaced by an iron yoke for the nations. Hananiah had prophesied freedom within two years, and Hananiah himself would die in the current year. If prophets are proved by the fulfilment of their prophecies, Jeremiah was dramatically and totally vindicated.

Influencing others to do wrong is a serious business. Hananiah had assumed an authority he did not possess, presenting his wishful thinking as a revelation and was therefore accountable for his own deception and the deception of others.

The problem is topical. There are those who speak with authority on the supreme rights of the individual. On these grounds euthanasia should be legalized; abortion be on demand; sexual deviancy be tolerated to a point of encouragement; drug-taking be decriminalized, and so on. Some of our false prophets have assumed the authority to set aside the Ten Commandments and the teaching of our Lord, greatly to the detriment of others. Without doubt, God will hold them accountable.

> *Lord,*
> *Let me but speak your will,*
> *And not my own desires.*
> *Let me your plans fulfil;*
> *Do all your love requires.*
> *This is my soul's prevailing choice*
> *To speak for you with loyal voice.*

→654

JEREMIAH 31:27–34; 32:1, 2, 9, 15

'I will put my law in their minds and write it on their hearts . . . they will all know me, from the least of them to the greatest, declares the LORD. For I will forgive their wickedness and will remember their sin no more' (31:33, 34).

JEREMIAH IS KNOWN as the prophet of personal religion. He seems to have been the first to appreciate fully how individuals, not just society as a whole, can relate closely to God. There are elements of personal faith and a personal calling in the experience of earlier prophetic figures, but Jeremiah's own personal relationship to God is something quite new in the history of Israel's religious pilgrimage.

Today we see Jeremiah's own experience reflected in the promise held out for the rest of us. He knew God personally. He had spoken to God in his despair, as well as in his triumph. He had argued with God. He had relied absolutely on God. He knew others could do the same.

Jeremiah knew God so well himself that he also believed a day would come when everyone would know God so clearly for themselves that no one would need to teach another about God. That state of affairs is still in the future! We all still rely on words mediated to us through reading, through exposition, and in worship, as well as on direct communion with God. But what a vision!

Jeremiah backed up his vision of a future with God by a practical action. He bought some land. At the time it must have seemed foolish. Judah was on the brink of invasion. Destruction was just round the corner. But after destruction comes construction. The immediate future may be bleak, but it is not without hope, both for society and for individuals within society.

I confess, Lord, that the things of this world sometimes cause me to doubt. Too often I rely on other people, instead of on you. Deepen my relationship with you. Give me Jeremiah's confidence to question you without losing the ability to rely on you completely.

→681

14All your allies have forgotten you;
    they care nothing for you.
I have struck you as an enemy would
    and punished as would the cruel,
because your guilt is so great
    and your sins so many.
15Why do you cry out over your wound,
    your pain that has no cure?
Because of your great guilt and many sins
    I have done these things to you.

16" 'But all who devour you will be
    devoured;
    all your enemies will go into exile.
Those who plunder you will be plundered;
    all who make spoil of you I will despoil.
17But I will restore you to health
    and heal your wounds,'
                        declares the LORD,
'because you are called an outcast,
    Zion for whom no-one cares.'

18"This is what the LORD says:

" 'I will restore the fortunes of Jacob's
    tents
    and have compassion on his dwellings;
the city will be rebuilt on her ruins,
    and the palace will stand in its proper
    place.
19From them will come songs of
    thanksgiving
    and the sound of rejoicing.
I will add to their numbers,
    and they will not be decreased;
I will bring them honour,
    and they will not be disdained.
20Their children will be as in days of old,
    and their community will be established
    before me;
I will punish all who oppress them.
21Their leader will be one of their own;
    their ruler will arise from among them.
I will bring him near and he will come
    close to me,
    for who is he who will devote himself
    to be close to me?'
                        declares the LORD.
22" 'So you will be my people,
    and I will be your God.' "

23See, the storm of the LORD
    will burst out in wrath,
a driving wind swirling down
    on the heads of the wicked.
24The fierce anger of the LORD will not turn
    back
    until he fully accomplishes
    the purposes of his heart.
In days to come
    you will understand this.

31 "At that time," declares the LORD, "I
    will be the God of all the clans of
Israel, and they will be my people."
2This is what the LORD says:

"The people who survive the sword
    will find favour in the desert;
    I will come to give rest to Israel."

3The LORD appeared to us in the past,[a]
saying:

"I have loved you with an everlasting
    love;
    I have drawn you with loving-kindness.
4I will build you up again
    and you will be rebuilt, O Virgin Israel.
Again you will take up your tambourines
    and go out to dance with the joyful.
5Again you will plant vineyards
    on the hills of Samaria;
the farmers will plant them
    and enjoy their fruit.
6There will be a day when watchmen cry
    out
    on the hills of Ephraim,
'Come, let us go up to Zion,
    to the LORD our God.' "

7This is what the LORD says:

"Sing with joy for Jacob;
    shout for the foremost of the nations.
Make your praises heard, and say,
    'O LORD, save your people,
    the remnant of Israel.'
8See, I will bring them from the land of the
    north
    and gather them from the ends of the
    earth.
Among them will be the blind and the
    lame,
    expectant mothers and women in
    labour;
    a great throng will return.
9They will come with weeping;
    they will pray as I bring them back.
I will lead them beside streams of water
    on a level path where they will not
    stumble,
because I am Israel's father,
    and Ephraim is my firstborn son.

10"Hear the word of the LORD, O nations;
    proclaim it in distant coastlands:
'He who scattered Israel will gather them
    and will watch over his flock like a
    shepherd.'
11For the LORD will ransom Jacob
    and redeem them from the hand of those
    stronger than they.
12They will come and shout for joy on the
    heights of Zion;
    they will rejoice in the bounty of the
    LORD—
the grain, the new wine and the oil,
    the young of the flocks and herds.
They will be like a well-watered garden,
    and they will sorrow no more.
13Then maidens will dance and be glad,
    young men and old as well.
I will turn their mourning into gladness;
    I will give them comfort and joy instead
    of sorrow.
14I will satisfy the priests with abundance,
    and my people will be filled with my
    bounty,"
                        declares the LORD.

a3 Or LORD has appeared to us from afar

¹⁵This is what the LORD says:

"A voice is heard in Ramah,
    mourning and great weeping,
Rachel weeping for her children
    and refusing to be comforted,
    because her children are no more."

¹⁶This is what the LORD says:

"Restrain your voice from weeping
    and your eyes from tears,
for your work will be rewarded,"
                    declares the LORD.
    "They will return from the land of the
        enemy.
¹⁷So there is hope for your future,"
                    declares the LORD.
    "Your children will return to their own
        land.

¹⁸"I have surely heard Ephraim's moaning:
    'You disciplined me like an unruly calf,
    and I have been disciplined.
Restore me, and I will return,
    because you are the LORD my God.
¹⁹After I strayed,
    I repented;
after I came to understand,
    I beat my breast.
I was ashamed and humiliated
    because I bore the disgrace of my
        youth.'
²⁰Is not Ephraim my dear son,
    the child in whom I delight?
Though I often speak against him,
    I still remember him.
Therefore my heart yearns for him;
    I have great compassion for him,"
                    declares the LORD.

²¹"Set up road signs;
    put up guideposts.
Take note of the highway,
    the road that you take.
Return, O Virgin Israel,
    return to your towns.
²²How long will you wander,
    O unfaithful daughter?
The LORD will create a new thing on
        earth—
    a woman will surround^b a man."

²³This is what the LORD Almighty, the God
of Israel, says: "When I bring them back
from captivity,^{c} the people in the land of
Judah and in its towns will once again use
these words: 'The LORD bless you, O righteous dwelling, O sacred mountain.' ²⁴People
will live together in Judah and all its towns
—farmers and those who move about with
their flocks. ²⁵I will refresh the weary and
satisfy the faint."

²⁶At this I awoke and looked around. My
sleep had been pleasant to me.

²⁷"The days are coming," declares the
LORD, "when I will plant the house of Israel
and the house of Judah with the offspring of

men and of animals. ²⁸Just as I watched over
them to uproot and tear down, and to overthrow, destroy and bring disaster, so I will
watch over them to build and to plant,"
declares the LORD. ²⁹"In those days people
will no longer say,

'The fathers have eaten sour grapes,
    and the children's teeth are set on edge.'

³⁰Instead, everyone will die for his own sin;
whoever eats sour grapes—his own teeth
will be set on edge.

³¹"The time is coming," declares the LORD,
    "when I will make a new covenant
with the house of Israel
    and with the house of Judah.
³²It will not be like the covenant
    I made with their forefathers
when I took them by the hand
    to lead them out of Egypt,
because they broke my covenant,
    though I was a husband to^d them,"^{e}
                    declares the LORD.
³³"This is the covenant that I will make with
        the house of Israel
    after that time," declares the LORD.
    "I will put my law in their minds
    and write it on their hearts.
I will be their God,
    and they will be my people.
³⁴No longer will a man teach his neighbour,
    or a man his brother, saying, 'Know the
        LORD,'
because they will all know me,
    from the least of them to the greatest,"
                    declares the LORD.
    "For I will forgive their wickedness
    and will remember their sins no more."

³⁵This is what the LORD says,

he who appoints the sun
    to shine by day,
who decrees the moon and stars
    to shine by night,
who stirs up the sea
    so that its waves roar—
    the LORD Almighty is his name:
³⁶"Only if these decrees vanish from my
        sight,"
    declares the LORD,
"will the descendants of Israel ever cease
    to be a nation before me."

³⁷This is what the LORD says:

"Only if the heavens above can be
        measured
    and the foundations of the earth below
        be searched out
will I reject all the descendants of Israel
    because of all they have done,"
                    declares the LORD.

³⁸"The days are coming," declares the
LORD, "when this city will be rebuilt for me

---

^{b}22 Or *will go about seeking*; or *will protect* ^{c}23 Or *I restore their fortunes*
^{d}32 Hebrew; Septuagint and Syriac *covenant, I and I turned away from* ^{e}32 Or *was their master*

from the Tower of Hananel to the Corner Gate. ³⁹The measuring line will stretch from there straight to the hill of Gareb and then turn to Goah. ⁴⁰The whole valley where dead bodies and ashes are thrown, and all the terraces out to the Kidron Valley on the east as far as the corner of the Horse Gate, will be holy to the LORD. The city will never again be uprooted or demolished."

Jeremiah Buys a Field

32 This is the word that came to Jeremiah from the LORD in the tenth year of Zedekiah king of Judah, which was the eighteenth year of Nebuchadnezzar. ²The army of the king of Babylon was then besieging Jerusalem, and Jeremiah the prophet was confined in the courtyard of the guard in the royal palace of Judah.

³Now Zedekiah king of Judah had imprisoned him there, saying, "Why do you prophesy as you do? You say, 'This is what the LORD says: I am about to hand this city over to the king of Babylon, and he will capture it. ⁴Zedekiah king of Judah will not escape out of the hands of the Babylonians*a* but will certainly be handed over to the king of Babylon, and will speak with him face to face and see him with his own eyes. ⁵He will take Zedekiah to Babylon, where he will remain until I deal with him, declares the LORD. If you fight against the Babylonians, you will not succeed.'"

⁶Jeremiah said, "The word of the LORD came to me: ⁷Hanamel son of Shallum your uncle is going to come to you and say, 'Buy my field at Anathoth, because as nearest relative it is your right and duty to buy it.'

⁸"Then, just as the LORD had said, my cousin Hanamel came to me in the courtyard of the guard and said, 'Buy my field at Anathoth in the territory of Benjamin. Since it is your right to redeem it and possess it, buy it for yourself.'

"I knew that this was the word of the LORD; ⁹so I bought the field at Anathoth from my cousin Hanamel and weighed out for him seventeen shekels*b* of silver. ¹⁰I signed and sealed the deed, had it witnessed, and weighed out the silver on the scales. ¹¹I took the deed of purchase—the sealed copy containing the terms and conditions, as well as the unsealed copy—¹²and I gave this deed to Baruch son of Neriah, the son of Mahseiah, in the presence of my cousin Hanamel and of the witnesses who had signed the deed and of all the Jews sitting in the courtyard of the guard.

¹³"In their presence I gave Baruch these instructions: ¹⁴'This is what the LORD Almighty, the God of Israel, says: Take these documents, both the sealed and unsealed copies of the deed of purchase, and put them in a clay jar so that they will last a long time. ¹⁵For this is what the LORD Almighty, the God of Israel, says: Houses, fields and vineyards will again be bought in this land.'

¹⁶"After I had given the deed of purchase to Baruch son of Neriah, I prayed to the LORD:

¹⁷"Ah, Sovereign LORD, you have made the heavens and the earth by your great power and outstretched arm. Nothing is too hard for you. ¹⁸You show love to thousands but bring the punishment for the fathers' sins into the laps of their children after them. O great and powerful God, whose name is the LORD Almighty, ¹⁹great are your purposes and mighty are your deeds. Your eyes are open to all the ways of men; you reward everyone according to his conduct and as his deeds deserve. ²⁰You performed miraculous signs and wonders in Egypt and have continued them to this day, both in Israel and among all mankind, and have gained the renown that is still yours. ²¹You brought your people Israel out of Egypt with signs and wonders, by a mighty hand and an outstretched arm and with great terror. ²²You gave them this land you had sworn to give to their forefathers, a land flowing with milk and honey. ²³They came in and took possession of it, but they did not obey you or follow your law; they did not do what you commanded them to do. So you brought all this disaster upon them.

²⁴"See how the siege ramps are built up to take the city. Because of the sword, famine and plague, the city will be handed over to the Babylonians who are attacking it. What you said has happened, as you now see. ²⁵And though the city will be handed over to the Babylonians, you, O Sovereign LORD, say to me, 'Buy the field with silver and have the transaction witnessed.'"

²⁶Then the word of the LORD came to Jeremiah: ²⁷"I am the LORD, the God of all mankind. Is anything too hard for me? ²⁸Therefore, this is what the LORD says: I am about to hand this city over to the Babylonians and to Nebuchadnezzar king of Babylon, who will capture it. ²⁹The Babylonians who are attacking this city will come in and set it on fire; they will burn it down, along with the houses where the people provoked me to anger by burning incense on the roofs to Baal and by pouring out drink offerings to other gods.

³⁰"The people of Israel and Judah have done nothing but evil in my sight from their youth; indeed, the people of Israel have done nothing but provoke me with what their hands have made, declares the LORD. ³¹From the day it was built until now, this city has so aroused my anger and wrath that I must remove it from my sight. ³²The people of Israel and Judah have provoked me by all the evil they have done—they, their kings and officials, their priests and prophets, the men of Judah and the people of Jerusalem. ³³They turned their backs to me and not their faces;

---

*a*4   Or *Chaldeans*; also in verses 5, 24, 25, 28, 29 and 43
*b*9   That is, about 7 ounces (about 200 grams)

though I taught them again and again, they would not listen or respond to discipline. ³⁴They set up their abominable idols in the house that bears my Name and defiled it. ³⁵They built high places for Baal in the Valley of Ben Hinnom to sacrifice their sons and daughters^c to Molech, though I never commanded, nor did it enter my mind, that they should do such a detestable thing and so make Judah sin.

³⁶"You are saying about this city, 'By the sword, famine and plague it will be handed over to the king of Babylon'; but this is what the LORD, the God of Israel, says: ³⁷I will surely gather them from all the lands where I banish them in my furious anger and great wrath; I will bring them back to this place and let them live in safety. ³⁸They will be my people, and I will be their God. ³⁹I will give them singleness of heart and action, so that they will always fear me for their own good and the good of their children after them. ⁴⁰I will make an everlasting covenant with them: I will never stop doing good to them, and I will inspire them to fear me, so that they will never turn away from me. ⁴¹I will rejoice in doing them good and will assuredly plant them in this land with all my heart and soul.

⁴²"This is what the LORD says: As I have brought all this great calamity on this people, so I will give them all the prosperity I have promised them. ⁴³Once more fields will be bought in this land of which you say, 'It is a desolate waste, without men or animals, for it has been handed over to the Babylonians.' ⁴⁴Fields will be bought for silver, and deeds will be signed, sealed and witnessed in the territory of Benjamin, in the villages around Jerusalem, in the towns of Judah and in the towns of the hill country, of the western foothills and of the Negev, because I will restore their fortunes,^d declares the LORD."

Promise of Restoration

33 While Jeremiah was still confined in the courtyard of the guard, the word of the LORD came to him a second time: ²"This is what the LORD says, he who made the earth, the LORD who formed it and established it—the LORD is his name: ³'Call to me and I will answer you and tell you great and unsearchable things you do not know.' ⁴For this is what the LORD, the God of Israel, says about the houses in this city and the royal palaces of Judah that have been torn down to be used against the siege ramps and the sword ⁵in the fight with the Babylonians:^a 'They will be filled with the dead bodies of the men I will slay in my anger and wrath. I will hide my face from this city because of all its wickedness.

⁶"'Nevertheless, I will bring health and healing to it; I will heal my people and will let them enjoy abundant peace and security. ⁷I will bring Judah and Israel back from captivity^b and will rebuild them as they were before. ⁸I will cleanse them from all the sin they have committed against me and will

forgive all their sins of rebellion against me. ⁹Then this city will bring me renown, joy, praise and honour before all nations on earth that hear of all the good things I do for it; and they will be in awe and will tremble at the abundant prosperity and peace I provide for it.'

¹⁰"This is what the LORD says: 'You say about this place, "It is a desolate waste, without men or animals." Yet in the towns of Judah and the streets of Jerusalem that are deserted, inhabited by neither men nor animals, there will be heard once more ¹¹the sounds of joy and gladness, the voices of bride and bridegroom, and the voices of those who bring thank-offerings to the house of the LORD, saying,

"Give thanks to the LORD Almighty,
    for the LORD is good;
    his love endures for ever."

For I will restore the fortunes of the land as they were before,' says the LORD. ¹²"This is what the LORD Almighty says: 'In this place, desolate and without men or animals—in all its towns there will again be pastures for shepherds to rest their flocks. ¹³In the towns of the hill country, of the western foothills and of the Negev, in the territory of Benjamin, in the villages around Jerusalem and in the towns of Judah, flocks will again pass under the hand of the one who counts them,' says the LORD.

¹⁴"'The days are coming,' declares the LORD, 'when I will fulfil the gracious promise I made to the house of Israel and to the house of Judah.

¹⁵"'In those days and at that time
    I will make a righteous Branch sprout
        from David's line;
    he will do what is just and right in the
        land.
¹⁶In those days Judah will be saved
    and Jerusalem will live in safety.
This is the name by which it^c will be called:
    The LORD Our Righteousness.'

¹⁷For this is what the LORD says: 'David will never fail to have a man to sit on the throne of the house of Israel, ¹⁸nor will the priests, who are Levites, ever fail to have a man to stand before me continually to offer burnt offerings, to burn grain offerings and to present sacrifices.'"

¹⁹The word of the LORD came to Jeremiah: ²⁰"This is what the LORD says: 'If you can break my covenant with the day and my covenant with the night, so that day and night no longer come at their appointed time, ²¹then my covenant with David my servant —and my covenant with the Levites who are priests ministering before me—can be broken and David will no longer have a descendant to reign on his throne. ²²I will make the descendants of David my servant and the Levites who minister before me as countless

---

^c35 Or *to make their sons and daughters pass through the fire*   ^d44 Or *will bring them back from captivity*
^a5 Or *Chaldeans*   ^b7 Or *will restore the fortunes of Judah and Israel*   ^c16 Or *he*

as the stars of the sky and as measureless as the sand on the seashore.'"

²³The word of the LORD came to Jeremiah: ²⁴"Have you not noticed that these people are saying, 'The LORD has rejected the two kingdoms[d] he chose'? So they despise my people and no longer regard them as a nation. ²⁵This is what the LORD says: 'If I have not established my covenant with day and night and the fixed laws of heaven and earth, ²⁶then I will reject the descendants of Jacob and David my servant and will not choose one of his sons to rule over the descendants of Abraham, Isaac and Jacob. For I will restore their fortunes[e] and have compassion on them.'"

Warning to Zedekiah

34 While Nebuchadnezzar king of Babylon and all his army and all the kingdoms and peoples in the empire he ruled were fighting against Jerusalem and all its surrounding towns, this word came to Jeremiah from the LORD: ²"This is what the LORD, the God of Israel, says: Go to Zedekiah king of Judah and tell him, 'This is what the LORD says: I am about to hand this city over to the king of Babylon, and he will burn it down. ³You will not escape from his grasp but will surely be captured and handed over to him. You will see the king of Babylon with your own eyes, and he will speak with you face to face. And you will go to Babylon.

⁴"'Yet hear the promise of the LORD, O Zedekiah king of Judah. This is what the LORD says concerning you: You will not die by the sword; ⁵you will die peacefully. As people made a funeral fire in honour of your fathers, the former kings who preceded you, so they will make a fire in your honour and lament, "Alas, O master!" I myself make this promise, declares the LORD.'"

⁶Then Jeremiah the prophet told all this to Zedekiah king of Judah, in Jerusalem, ⁷while the army of the king of Babylon was fighting against Jerusalem and the other cities of Judah that were still holding out—Lachish and Azekah. These were the only fortified cities left in Judah.

Freedom for Slaves

⁸The word came to Jeremiah from the LORD after King Zedekiah had made a covenant with all the people in Jerusalem to proclaim freedom for the slaves. ⁹Everyone was to free his Hebrew slaves, both male and female; no-one was to hold a fellow Jew in bondage. ¹⁰So all the officials and people who entered into this covenant agreed that they would free their male and female slaves and no longer hold them in bondage. They agreed, and set them free. ¹¹But afterwards they changed their minds and took back the slaves they had freed and enslaved them again.

¹²Then the word of the LORD came to Jeremiah: ¹³"This is what the LORD, the God of Israel, says: I made a covenant with your forefathers when I brought them out of Egypt, out of the land of slavery. I said, ¹⁴'Every seventh year each of you must free any fellow Hebrew who has sold himself to you. After he has served you for six years, you must let him go free.'[a] Your fathers, however, did not listen to me or pay attention to me. ¹⁵Recently you repented and did what is right in my sight: Each of you proclaimed freedom to his countrymen. You even made a covenant before me in the house that bears my Name. ¹⁶But now you have turned round and profaned my name; each of you has taken back the male and female slaves you had set free to go where they wished. You have forced them to become your slaves again.

¹⁷"Therefore, this is what the LORD says: You have not obeyed me; you have not proclaimed freedom for your fellow countrymen. So I now proclaim 'freedom' for you, declares the LORD—'freedom' to fall by the sword, plague and famine. I will make you abhorrent to all the kingdoms of the earth. ¹⁸The men who have violated my covenant and have not fulfilled the terms of the covenant they made before me, I will treat like the calf they cut in two and then walked between its pieces. ¹⁹The leaders of Judah and Jerusalem, the court officials, the priests and all the people of the land who walked between the pieces of the calf, ²⁰I will hand over to their enemies who seek their lives. Their dead bodies will become food for the birds of the air and the beasts of the earth.

²¹"I will hand Zedekiah king of Judah and his officials over to their enemies who seek their lives, to the army of the king of Babylon, which has withdrawn from you. ²²I am going to give the order, declares the LORD, and I will bring them back to this city. They will fight against it, take it and burn it down. And I will lay waste the towns of Judah so that no-one can live there."

The Recabites

35 This is the word that came to Jeremiah from the LORD during the reign of Jehoiakim son of Josiah king of Judah: ²"Go to the Recabite family and invite them to come to one of the side rooms of the house of the LORD and give them wine to drink."

³So I went to get Jaazaniah son of Jeremiah, the son of Habazziniah, and his brothers and all his sons—the whole family of the Recabites. ⁴I brought them into the house of the LORD, into the room of the sons of Hanan son of Igdaliah the man of God. It was next to the room of the officials, which was over that of Maaseiah son of Shallum the door-keeper. ⁵Then I set bowls full of wine and some cups before the men of the Recabite family and said to them, "Drink some wine."

⁶But they replied, "We do not drink wine, because our forefather Jonadab son of Recab gave us this command: 'Neither you nor your descendants must ever drink wine. ⁷Also you must never build houses, sow seed or plant vineyards; you must never have any of these

---

d24 Or *families*   *e26* Or *will bring them back from captivity*   *a14* Deut. 15:12

things, but must always live in tents. Then you will live a long time in the land where you are nomads.' ⁸We have obeyed everything our forefather Jonadab son of Recab commanded us. Neither we nor our wives nor our sons and daughters have ever drunk wine ⁹or built houses to live in or had vineyards, fields or crops. ¹⁰We have lived in tents and have fully obeyed everything our forefather Jonadab commanded us. ¹¹But when Nebuchadnezzar king of Babylon invaded this land, we said, 'Come, we must go to Jerusalem to escape the Babylonian*ᵃ* and Aramean armies.' So we have remained in Jerusalem.''

¹²Then the word of the LORD came to Jeremiah, saying: ¹³''This is what the LORD Almighty, the God of Israel, says: Go and tell the men of Judah and the people of Jerusalem, 'Will you not learn a lesson and obey my words?' declares the LORD. ¹⁴Jonadab son of Recab ordered his sons not to drink wine and this command has been kept. To this day they do not drink wine, because they obey their forefather's command. But I have spoken to you again and again, yet you have not obeyed me. ¹⁵Again and again I sent all my servants the prophets to you. They said, ''Each of you must turn from your wicked ways and reform your actions; do not follow other gods to serve them. Then you shall live in the land I have given to you and your fathers.'' But you have not paid attention or listened to me. ¹⁶The descendants of Jonadab son of Recab have carried out the command their forefather gave them, but these people have not obeyed me.'

¹⁷''Therefore, this is what the LORD God Almighty, the God of Israel, says: 'Listen! I am going to bring on Judah and on everyone living in Jerusalem every disaster I pronounced against them. I spoke to them, but they did not listen; I called to them, but they did not answer.' ''

¹⁸Then Jeremiah said to the family of the Recabites, ''This is what the LORD Almighty, the God of Israel, says: 'You have obeyed the command of your forefather Jonadab and have followed all his instructions and have done everything he ordered.' ¹⁹Therefore, this is what the LORD Almighty, the God of Israel, says: 'Jonadab son of Recab shall never fail to have a man to serve me.' ''

Jehoiakim Burns Jeremiah's Scroll

36 In the fourth year of Jehoiakim son of Josiah king of Judah, this word came to Jeremiah from the LORD: ²''Take a scroll and write on it all the words I have spoken to you concerning Israel, Judah and all the other nations from the time I began speaking to you in the reign of Josiah till now. ³Perhaps when the people of Judah hear about every disaster I plan to inflict on them, each of them will turn from his wicked way; then I will forgive their wickedness and their sin.''

⁴So Jeremiah called Baruch son of Neriah, and while Jeremiah dictated all the words the LORD had spoken to him, Baruch wrote them on the scroll. ⁵Then Jeremiah told Baruch, ''I am restricted; I cannot go to the LORD's temple. ⁶So you go to the house of the LORD on a day of fasting and read to the people from the scroll the words of the LORD that you wrote as I dictated. Read them to all the people of Judah who come in from their towns. ⁷Perhaps they will bring their petition before the LORD, and each will turn from his wicked ways, for the anger and wrath pronounced against this people by the LORD are great.''

⁸Baruch son of Neriah did everything Jeremiah the prophet told him to do; at the LORD's temple he read the words of the LORD from the scroll. ⁹In the ninth month of the fifth year of Jehoiakim son of Josiah king of Judah, a time of fasting before the LORD was proclaimed for all the people in Jerusalem and those who had come from the towns of Judah. ¹⁰From the room of Gemariah son of Shaphan the secretary, which was in the upper courtyard at the entrance of the New Gate of the temple, Baruch read to all the people at the LORD's temple the words of Jeremiah from the scroll.

¹¹When Micaiah son of Gemariah, the son of Shaphan, heard all the words of the LORD from the scroll, ¹²he went down to the secretary's room in the royal palace, where all the officials were sitting: Elishama the secretary, Delaiah son of Shemaiah, Elnathan son of Acbor, Gemariah son of Shaphan, Zedekiah son of Hananiah, and all the other officials. ¹³After Micaiah told them everything he had heard Baruch read to the people from the scroll, ¹⁴all the officials sent Jehudi son of Nethaniah, the son of Shelemiah, the son of Cushi, to say to Baruch, ''Bring the scroll from which you have read to the people and come.'' So Baruch son of Neriah went to them with the scroll in his hand. ¹⁵They said to him, ''Sit down, please, and read it to us.''

So Baruch read it to them. ¹⁶When they heard all these words, they looked at each other in fear and said to Baruch, ''We must report all these words to the king.'' ¹⁷Then they asked Baruch, ''Tell us, how did you come to write all this? Did Jeremiah dictate it?''

¹⁸''Yes,'' Baruch replied, ''he dictated all these words to me, and I wrote them in ink on the scroll.''

¹⁹Then the officials said to Baruch, ''You and Jeremiah, go and hide. Don't let anyone know where you are.''

²⁰After they put the scroll in the room of Elishama the secretary, they went to the king in the courtyard and reported everything to him. ²¹The king sent Jehudi to get the scroll, and Jehudi brought it from the room of Elishama the secretary and read it to the king and all the officials standing beside him. ²²It was the ninth month and the king was sitting in the winter apartment, with a fire burning in the brazier in front of him. ²³Whenever Jehudi had read three or four columns of the scroll, the king cut them off with a scribe's knife and threw them into the brazier, until

the entire scroll was burned in the fire. 24The king and all his attendants who heard all these words showed no fear, nor did they tear their clothes. 25Even though Elnathan, Delaiah and Gemariah urged the king not to burn the scroll, he would not listen to them. 26Instead, the king commanded Jerahmeel, a son of the king, Seraiah son of Azriel and Shelemiah son of Abdeel to arrest Baruch the scribe and Jeremiah the prophet. But the LORD had hidden them.

27After the king burned the scroll containing the words that Baruch had written at Jeremiah's dictation, the word of the LORD came to Jeremiah: 28"Take another scroll and write on it all the words that were on the first scroll, which Jehoiakim king of Judah burned up. 29Also tell Jehoiakim king of Judah, 'This is what the LORD says: You burned that scroll and said, "Why did you write on it that the king of Babylon would certainly come and destroy this land and cut off both men and animals from it?" 30Therefore, this is what the LORD says about Jehoiakim king of Judah: He will have no-one to sit on the throne of David; his body will be thrown out and exposed to the heat by day and the frost by night. 31I will punish him and his children and his attendants for their wickedness; I will bring on them and those living in Jerusalem and the people of Judah every disaster I pronounced against them, because they have not listened.'"

32So Jeremiah took another scroll and gave it to the scribe Baruch son of Neriah, and as Jeremiah dictated, Baruch wrote on it all the words of the scroll that Jehoiakim king of Judah had burned in the fire. And many similar words were added to them.

Jeremiah in Prison

37 Zedekiah son of Josiah was made king of Judah by Nebuchadnezzar king of Babylon; he reigned in place of Jehoiachin[a] son of Jehoiakim. 2Neither he nor his attendants nor the people of the land paid any attention to the words the LORD had spoken through Jeremiah the prophet.

3King Zedekiah, however, sent Jehucal son of Shelemiah with the priest Zephaniah son of Maaseiah to Jeremiah the prophet with this message: "Please pray to the LORD our God for us."

4Now Jeremiah was free to come and go among the people, for he had not yet been put in prison. 5Pharaoh's army had marched out of Egypt, and when the Babylonians[b] who were besieging Jerusalem heard the report about them, they withdrew from Jerusalem.

6Then the word of the LORD came to Jeremiah the prophet: 7"This is what the LORD, the God of Israel, says: Tell the king of Judah, who sent you to enquire of me, 'Pharaoh's army, which has marched out to support you, will go back to its own land, to Egypt. 8Then the Babylonians will return and

attack this city; they will capture it and burn it down.' 9"This is what the LORD says: Do not deceive yourselves, thinking, 'The Babylonians will surely leave us.' They will not! 10Even if you were to defeat the entire Babylonian[c] army that is attacking you and only wounded men were left in their tents, they would come out and burn this city down."

11After the Babylonian army had withdrawn from Jerusalem because of Pharaoh's army, 12Jeremiah started to leave the city to go to the territory of Benjamin to get his share of the property among the people there. 13But when he reached the Benjamin Gate, the captain of the guard, whose name was Irijah son of Shelemiah, the son of Hananiah, arrested him and said, "You are deserting to the Babylonians!"

14"That's not true!" Jeremiah said. "I am not deserting to the Babylonians." But Irijah would not listen to him; instead, he arrested Jeremiah and brought him to the officials. 15They were angry with Jeremiah and had him beaten and imprisoned in the house of Jonathan the secretary, which they had made into a prison.

16Jeremiah was put into a vaulted cell in a dungeon, where he remained a long time. 17Then King Zedekiah sent for him and had him brought to the palace, where he asked him privately, "Is there any word from the LORD?"

"Yes," Jeremiah replied, "you will be handed over to the king of Babylon."

18Then Jeremiah said to King Zedekiah, "What crime have I committed against you or your officials or this people, that you have put me in prison? 19Where are your prophets who prophesied to you, 'The king of Babylon will not attack you or this land'? 20But now, my lord the king, please listen. Let me bring my petition before you: Do not send me back to the house of Jonathan the secretary, or I shall die there."

21King Zedekiah then gave orders for Jeremiah to be placed in the courtyard of the guard and given bread from the street of the bakers each day until all the bread in the city was gone. So Jeremiah remained in the courtyard of the guard.

Jeremiah Thrown Into a Cistern

38 Shephatiah son of Mattan, Gedaliah son of Pashhur, Jehucal[a] son of Shelemiah, and Pashhur son of Malkijah heard what Jeremiah was telling all the people when he said, 2"This is what the LORD says: 'Whoever stays in this city will die by the sword, famine or plague, but whoever goes over to the Babylonians[b] will live. He will escape with his life; he will live.' 3And this is what the LORD says: 'This city will certainly be handed over to the army of the king of Babylon, who will capture it.'"

4Then the officials said to the king, "This

---

a1 Hebrew Coniah, a variant of Jehoiachin   b5 Or Chaldeans; also in verses 8, 9, 13 and 14
c10 Or Chaldean; also in verse 11   a1 Hebrew Jucal, a variant of Jehucal
b2 Or Chaldeans; also in verses 18, 19 and 23

man should be put to death. He is discouraging the soldiers who are left in this city, as well as all the people, by the things he is saying to them. This man is not seeking the good of these people but their ruin.''

5''He is in your hands,'' King Zedekiah answered. ''The king can do nothing to oppose you.''

6So they took Jeremiah and put him into the cistern of Malkijah, the king's son, which was in the courtyard of the guard. They lowered Jeremiah by ropes into the cistern; it had no water in it, only mud, and Jeremiah sank down into the mud.

7But Ebed-Melech, a Cushite,c an officiald in the royal palace, heard that they had put Jeremiah into the cistern. While the king was sitting in the Benjamin Gate, 8Ebed-Melech went out of the palace and said to him, 9''My lord the king, these men have acted wickedly in all they have done to Jeremiah the prophet. They have thrown him into a cistern, where he will starve to death when there is no longer any bread in the city.''

10Then the king commanded Ebed-Melech the Cushite, ''Take thirty men from here with you and lift Jeremiah the prophet out of the cistern before he dies.''

11So Ebed-Melech took the men with him and went to a room under the treasury in the palace. He took some old rags and worn-out clothes from there and let them down with ropes to Jeremiah in the cistern. 12Ebed-Melech the Cushite said to Jeremiah, ''Put these old rags and worn-out clothes under your arms to pad the ropes.'' Jeremiah did so, 13and they pulled him up with the ropes and lifted him out of the cistern. And Jeremiah remained in the courtyard of the guard.

Zedekiah Questions Jeremiah Again

14Then King Zedekiah sent for Jeremiah the prophet and had him brought to the third entrance to the temple of the Lord. ''I am going to ask you something,'' the king said to Jeremiah. ''Do not hide anything from me.''

15Jeremiah said to Zedekiah, ''If I give you an answer, will you not kill me? Even if I did give you counsel, you would not listen to me.''

16But King Zedekiah swore this oath secretly to Jeremiah: ''As surely as the Lord lives, who has given us breath, I will neither kill you nor hand you over to those who are seeking your life.''

17Then Jeremiah said to Zedekiah, ''This is what the Lord God Almighty, the God of Israel, says: 'If you surrender to the officers of the king of Babylon, your life will be spared and this city will not be burned down; you and your family will live. 18But if you will not surrender to the officers of the king of Babylon, this city will be handed over to the Babylonians and they will burn it down; you yourself will not escape from their hands.' ''

19King Zedekiah said to Jeremiah, ''I am afraid of the Jews who have gone over to the Babylonians, for the Babylonians may hand me over to them and they will ill-treat me.''

20''They will not hand you over,'' Jeremiah replied. ''Obey the Lord by doing what I tell you. Then it will go well with you, and your life will be spared. 21But if you refuse to surrender, this is what the Lord has revealed to me: 22All the women left in the palace of the king of Judah will be brought out to the officials of the king of Babylon. Those women will say to you:

'''They misled you and overcame you—
    those trusted friends of yours.
Your feet are sunk in the mud;
    your friends have deserted you.'

23''All your wives and children will be brought out to the Babylonians. You yourself will not escape from their hands but will be captured by the king of Babylon; and this city wille be burned down.''

24Then Zedekiah said to Jeremiah, ''Do not let anyone know about this conversation, or you may die. 25If the officials hear that I talked with you, and they come to you and say, 'Tell us what you said to the king and what the king said to you; do not hide it from us or we will kill you,' 26then tell them, 'I was pleading with the king not to send me back to Jonathan's house to die there.' ''

27All the officials did come to Jeremiah and question him, and he told them everything the king had ordered him to say. So they said no more to him, for no-one had heard his conversation with the king.

28And Jeremiah remained in the courtyard of the guard until the day Jerusalem was captured.

The Fall of Jerusalem

39 This is how Jerusalem was taken: 1In the ninth year of Zedekiah king of Judah, in the tenth month, Nebuchadnezzar king of Babylon marched against Jerusalem with his whole army and laid siege to it. 2And on the ninth day of the fourth month of Zedekiah's eleventh year, the city wall was broken through. 3Then all the officials of the king of Babylon came and took seats in the Middle Gate: Nergal-Sharezer of Samgar, Nebo-Sarsekima a chief officer, Nergal-Sharezer a high official and all the other officials of the king of Babylon. 4When Zedekiah king of Judah and all the soldiers saw them, they fled; they left the city at night by way of the king's garden, through the gate between the two walls, and headed towards the Arabah.b

5But the Babylonianc army pursued them and overtook Zedekiah in the plains of Jericho. They captured him and took him to Nebuchadnezzar king of Babylon at Riblah in the land of Hamath, where he pronounced sentence on him. 6There at Riblah the king of Babylon slaughtered the sons of Zedekiah before his eyes and also killed all the nobles of Judah. 7Then he put out Zedekiah's eyes

---

c7 Probably from the upper Nile region   d7 Or a eunuch   e23 Or and you will cause this city to
a3 Or Nergal-Sharezer, Samgar-Nebo, Sarsekim   b4 Or the Jordan Valley   c5 Or Chaldean

and bound him with bronze shackles to take him to Babylon.

[8]The Babylonians*d* set fire to the royal palace and the houses of the people and broke down the walls of Jerusalem. [9]Nebuzaradan commander of the imperial guard carried into exile to Babylon the people who remained in the city, along with those who had gone over to him, and the rest of the people. [10]But Nebuzaradan the commander of the guard left behind in the land of Judah some of the poor people, who owned nothing; and at that time he gave them vineyards and fields.

[11]Now Nebuchadnezzar king of Babylon had given these orders about Jeremiah through Nebuzaradan commander of the imperial guard: [12]"Take him and look after him; don't harm him but do for him whatever he asks." [13]So Nebuzaradan the commander of the guard, Nebushazban a chief officer, Nergal-Sharezer a high official and all the other officers of the king of Babylon [14]sent and had Jeremiah taken out of the courtyard of the guard. They handed him over to Gedaliah son of Ahikam, the son of Shaphan, to take him back to his home. So he remained among his own people.

[15]While Jeremiah had been confined in the courtyard of the guard, the word of the Lord came to him: [16]"Go and tell Ebed-Melech the Cushite, 'This is what the Lord Almighty, the God of Israel, says: I am about to fulfil my words against this city through disaster, not prosperity. At that time they will be fulfilled before your eyes. [17]But I will rescue you on that day, declares the Lord; you will not be handed over to those you fear. [18]I will save you; you will not fall by the sword but will escape with your life, because you trust in me, declares the Lord.'"

Jeremiah Freed

40 The word came to Jeremiah from the Lord after Nebuzaradan commander of the imperial guard had released him at Ramah. He had found Jeremiah bound in chains among all the captives from Jerusalem and Judah who were being carried into exile to Babylon. [2]When the commander of the guard found Jeremiah, he said to him, "The Lord your God decreed this disaster for this place. [3]And now the Lord has brought it about; he has done just as he said he would. All this happened because you people sinned against the Lord and did not obey him. [4]But today I am freeing you from the chains on your wrists. Come with me to Babylon, if you like, and I will look after you; but if you do not want to, then don't come. Look, the whole country lies before you; go wherever you please." [5]However, before Jeremiah turned to go,*a* Nebuzaradan added, "Go back to Gedaliah son of Ahikam, the son of Shaphan, whom the king of Babylon has appointed over the towns of Judah, and live with him among the people, or go anywhere else you please."

Then the commander gave him provisions and a present and let him go. [6]So Jeremiah went to Gedaliah son of Ahikam at Mizpah and stayed with him among the people who were left behind in the land.

Gedaliah Assassinated

[7]When all the army officers and their men who were still in the open country heard that the king of Babylon had appointed Gedaliah son of Ahikam as governor over the land and had put him in charge of the men, women and children who were the poorest in the land and who had not been carried into exile to Babylon, [8]they came to Gedaliah at Mizpah—Ishmael son of Nethaniah, Johanan and Jonathan the sons of Kareah, Seraiah son of Tanhumeth, the sons of Ephai the Netophathite, and Jaazaniah*b* the son of the Maacathite, and their men. [9]Gedaliah son of Ahikam, the son of Shaphan, took an oath to reassure them and their men. "Do not be afraid to serve the Babylonians,"*c* he said. "Settle down in the land and serve the king of Babylon, and it will go well with you. [10]I myself will stay in Mizpah to represent you before the Babylonians who come to us, but you are to harvest the wine, summer fruit and oil, and put them in your storage jars, and live in the towns you have taken over."

[11]When all the Jews in Moab, Ammon, Edom and all the other countries heard that the king of Babylon had left a remnant in Judah and had appointed Gedaliah son of Ahikam, the son of Shaphan, as governor over them, [12]they all came back to the land of Judah, to Gedaliah at Mizpah, from all the countries where they had been scattered. And they harvested an abundance of wine and summer fruit.

[13]Johanan son of Kareah and all the army officers still in the open country came to Gedaliah at Mizpah [14]and said to him, "Don't you know that Baalis king of the Ammonites has sent Ishmael son of Nethaniah to take your life?" But Gedaliah son of Ahikam did not believe them.

[15]Then Johanan son of Kareah said privately to Gedaliah in Mizpah, "Let me go and kill Ishmael son of Nethaniah, and no-one will know it. Why should he take your life and cause all the Jews who are gathered around you to be scattered and the remnant of Judah to perish?"

[16]But Gedaliah son of Ahikam said to Johanan son of Kareah, "Don't do such a thing! What you are saying about Ishmael is not true."

41 In the seventh month Ishmael son of Nethaniah, the son of Elishama, who was of royal blood and had been one of the king's officers, came with ten men to Gedaliah son of Ahikam at Mizpah. While they were eating together there, [2]Ishmael son of Nethaniah and the ten men who were with him got up and struck down Gedaliah son of Ahikam, the son of Shaphan, with the sword, killing the one whom the king of Babylon

*d*8 Or *Chaldeans*   *a*5 Or *Jeremiah answered*   *b*8 Hebrew *Jezaniah*, a variant of *Jaazaniah*
*c*9 Or *Chaldeans*; also in verse 10

had appointed as governor over the land. ³Ishmael also killed all the Jews who were with Gedaliah at Mizpah, as well as the Babylonian[a] soldiers who were there.

⁴The day after Gedaliah's assassination, before anyone knew about it, ⁵eighty men who had shaved off their beards, torn their clothes and cut themselves came from Shechem, Shiloh and Samaria, bringing grain offerings and incense with them to the house of the LORD. ⁶Ishmael son of Nethaniah went out from Mizpah to meet them, weeping as he went. When he met them, he said, "Come to Gedaliah son of Ahikam." ⁷When they went into the city, Ishmael son of Nethaniah and the men who were with him slaughtered them and threw them into a cistern. ⁸But ten of them said to Ishmael, "Don't kill us! We have wheat and barley, oil and honey, hidden in a field." So he let them alone and did not kill them with the others. ⁹Now the cistern where he threw all the bodies of the men he had killed along with Gedaliah was the one King Asa had made as part of his defence against Baasha king of Israel. Ishmael son of Nethaniah filled it with the dead.

¹⁰Ishmael made captives of all the rest of the people who were in Mizpah—the king's daughters along with all the others who were left there, over whom Nebuzaradan commander of the imperial guard had appointed Gedaliah son of Ahikam. Ishmael son of Nethaniah took them captive and set out to cross over to the Ammonites.

¹¹When Johanan son of Kareah and all the army officers who were with him heard about all the crimes Ishmael son of Nethaniah had committed, ¹²they took all their men and went to fight Ishmael son of Nethaniah. They caught up with him near the great pool in Gibeon. ¹³When all the people Ishmael had with him saw Johanan son of Kareah and the army officers who were with him, they were glad. ¹⁴All the people Ishmael had taken captive at Mizpah turned and went over to Johanan son of Kareah. ¹⁵But Ishmael son of Nethaniah and eight of his men escaped from Johanan and fled to the Ammonites.

Flight to Egypt

¹⁶Then Johanan son of Kareah and all the army officers who were with him led away all the survivors from Mizpah whom he had recovered from Ishmael son of Nethaniah after he had assassinated Gedaliah son of Ahikam: the soldiers, women, children and court officials he had brought from Gibeon. ¹⁷And they went on, stopping at Geruth Kimham near Bethlehem on their way to Egypt ¹⁸to escape the Babylonians.[b] They were afraid of them because Ishmael son of Nethaniah had killed Gedaliah son of Ahikam, whom the king of Babylon had appointed as governor over the land.

42 Then all the army officers, including Johanan son of Kareah and Jezaniah[a] son of Hoshaiah, and all the people from the least to the greatest approached ²Jeremiah the prophet and said to him, "Please hear our petition and pray to the LORD your God for this entire remnant. For as you now see, though we were once many, now only a few are left. ³Pray that the LORD your God will tell us where we should go and what we should do."

⁴"I have heard you," replied Jeremiah the prophet. "I will certainly pray to the LORD your God as you have requested; I will tell you everything the LORD says and will keep nothing back from you."

⁵Then they said to Jeremiah, "May the LORD be a true and faithful witness against us if we do not act in accordance with everything the LORD your God sends you to tell us. ⁶Whether it is favourable or unfavourable, we will obey the LORD our God, to whom we are sending you, so that it will go well with us, for we will obey the LORD our God."

⁷Ten days later the word of the LORD came to Jeremiah. ⁸So he called together Johanan son of Kareah and all the army officers who were with him and all the people from the least to the greatest. ⁹He said to them, "This is what the LORD, the God of Israel, to whom you sent me to present your petition, says: ¹⁰'If you stay in this land, I will build you up and not tear you down; I will plant you and not uproot you, for I am grieved over the disaster I have inflicted on you. ¹¹Do not be afraid of the king of Babylon, whom you now fear. Do not be afraid of him, declares the LORD, for I am with you and will save you and deliver you from his hands. ¹²I will show you compassion so that he will have compassion on you and restore you to your land.'

¹³"However, if you say, 'We will not stay in this land,' and so disobey the LORD your God, ¹⁴and if you say, 'No, we will go and live in Egypt, where we will not see war or hear the trumpet or be hungry for bread,' ¹⁵then hear the word of the LORD, O remnant of Judah. This is what the LORD Almighty, the God of Israel, says: 'If you are determined to go to Egypt and you do go to settle there, ¹⁶then the sword you fear will overtake you there, and the famine you dread will follow you into Egypt, and there you will die. ¹⁷Indeed, all who are determined to go to Egypt to settle there will die by the sword, famine and plague; not one of them will survive or escape the disaster I will bring on them.' ¹⁸This is what the LORD Almighty, the God of Israel, says: 'As my anger and wrath have been poured out on those who lived in Jerusalem, so will my wrath be poured out on you when you go to Egypt. You will be an object of cursing and horror, of condemnation and reproach; you will never see this place again.'

¹⁹"O remnant of Judah, the LORD has told you, 'Do not go to Egypt.' Be sure of this: I warn you today ²⁰that you made a fatal mistake[b] when you sent me to the LORD your God and said, 'Pray to the LORD our God for us; tell us everything he says and we will do it.' ²¹I have told you today, but you still have

---

[a]3 Or *Chaldean*   [b]18 Or *Chaldeans*   [a]1 Hebrew; Septuagint (see also 43:2) *Azariah*
[b]20 Or *you erred in your hearts*

not obeyed the LORD your God in all he sent me to tell you. ²²So now, be sure of this: You will die by the sword, famine and plague in the place where you want to go to settle.''

43 When Jeremiah finished telling the people all the words of the LORD their God—everything the LORD had sent him to tell them—²Azariah son of Hoshaiah and Johanan son of Kareah and all the arrogant men said to Jeremiah, ''You are lying! The LORD our God has not sent us to say, 'You must not go to Egypt to settle there.' ³But Baruch son of Neriah is inciting you against us to hand us over to the Babylonians,ᵃ so that they may kill us or carry us into exile to Babylon.''

⁴So Johanan son of Kareah and all the army officers and all the people disobeyed the LORD's command to stay in the land of Judah. ⁵Instead, Johanan son of Kareah and all the army officers led away all the remnant of Judah who had come back to live in the land of Judah from all the nations where they had been scattered. ⁶They also led away all the men, women and children and the king's daughters whom Nebuzaradan commander of the imperial guard had left with Gedaliah son of Ahikam, the son of Shaphan, and Jeremiah the prophet and Baruch son of Neriah. ⁷So they entered Egypt in disobedience to the LORD and went as far as Tahpanhes.

⁸In Tahpanhes the word of the LORD came to Jeremiah: ⁹''While the Jews are watching, take some large stones with you and bury them in clay in the brick pavement at the entrance to Pharaoh's palace in Tahpanhes. ¹⁰Then say to them, 'This is what the LORD Almighty, the God of Israel, says: I will send for my servant Nebuchadnezzar king of Babylon, and I will set his throne over these stones I have buried here; he will spread his royal canopy above them. ¹¹He will come and attack Egypt, bringing death to those destined for death, captivity to those destined for captivity, and the sword to those destined for the sword. ¹²Heᵇ will set fire to the temples of the gods of Egypt; he will burn their temples and take their gods captive. As a shepherd wraps his garment round him, so will he wrap Egypt round himself and depart from there unscathed. ¹³There in the temple of the sunᶜ in Egypt he will demolish the sacred pillars and will burn down the temples of the gods of Egypt.' ''

Disaster Because of Idolatry

44 This word came to Jeremiah concerning all the Jews living in Lower Egypt —in Migdol, Tahpanhes and Memphisᵃ— and in Upper Egypt:ᵇ ²''This is what the LORD Almighty, the God of Israel, says: You saw the great disaster I brought on Jerusalem and on all the towns of Judah. Today they lie deserted and in ruins ³because of the evil they have done. They provoked me to anger by burning incense and by worshipping other gods that neither they nor you nor your fathers ever knew. ⁴Again and again I sent my servants the prophets, who said, 'Do not do this detestable thing that I hate!' ⁵But they did not listen or pay attention; they did not turn from their wickedness or stop burning incense to other gods. ⁶Therefore, my fierce anger was poured out; it raged against the towns of Judah and the streets of Jerusalem and made them the desolate ruins they are today.

⁷''Now this is what the LORD God Almighty, the God of Israel, says: Why bring such great disaster on yourselves by cutting off from Judah the men and women, the children and infants, and so leave yourselves without a remnant? ⁸Why provoke me to anger with what your hands have made, burning incense to other gods in Egypt, where you have come to live? You will destroy yourselves and make yourselves an object of cursing and reproach among all the nations on earth. ⁹Have you forgotten the wickedness committed by your fathers and by the kings and queens of Judah and the wickedness committed by you and your wives in the land of Judah and the streets of Jerusalem? ¹⁰To this day they have not humbled themselves or shown reverence, nor have they followed my law and the decrees I set before you and your fathers.

¹¹''Therefore, this is what the LORD Almighty, the God of Israel, says: I am determined to bring disaster on you and to destroy all Judah. ¹²I will take away the remnant of Judah who were determined to go to Egypt to settle there. They will all perish in Egypt; they will fall by the sword or die from famine. From the least to the greatest, they will die by sword or famine. They will become an object of cursing and horror, of condemnation and reproach. ¹³I will punish those who live in Egypt with the sword, famine and plague, as I punished Jerusalem. ¹⁴None of the remnant of Judah who have gone to live in Egypt will escape or survive to return to the land of Judah, to which they long to return and live; none will return except a few fugitives.''

¹⁵Then all the men who knew that their wives were burning incense to other gods, along with all the women who were present —a large assembly—and all the people living in Lower and Upper Egypt,ᶜ said to Jeremiah, ¹⁶''We will not listen to the message you have spoken to us in the name of the LORD! ¹⁷We will certainly do everything we said we would: We will burn incense to the Queen of Heaven and will pour out drink offerings to her just as we and our fathers, our kings and our officials did in the towns of Judah and in the streets of Jerusalem. At that time we had plenty of food and were well off and suffered no harm. ¹⁸But ever since we stopped burning incense to the Queen of Heaven and pouring out drink offerings to her, we have had nothing and have been perishing by sword and famine.''

¹⁹The women added, ''When we burned incense to the Queen of Heaven and poured

ᵃ3 Or Chaldeans   ᵇ12 Or I   ᶜ13 Or in Heliopolis   ᵃ1 Hebrew Noph   ᵇ1 Hebrew in Pathros
ᶜ15 Hebrew in Egypt and Pathros

out drink offerings to her, did not our husbands know that we were making cakes like her image and pouring out drink offerings to her?''

²⁰Then Jeremiah said to all the people, both men and women, who were answering him, ²¹''Did not the LORD remember and think about the incense burned in the towns of Judah and the streets of Jerusalem by you and your fathers, your kings and your officials and the people of the land? ²²When the LORD could no longer endure your wicked actions and the detestable things you did, your land became an object of cursing and a desolate waste without inhabitants, as it is today. ²³Because you have burned incense and have sinned against the LORD and have not obeyed him or followed his law or his decrees or his stipulations, this disaster has come upon you, as you now see.''

²⁴Then Jeremiah said to all the people, including the women, ''Hear the word of the LORD, all you people of Judah in Egypt. ²⁵This is what the LORD Almighty, the God of Israel, says: You and your wives have shown by your actions what you promised when you said, 'We will certainly carry out the vows we made to burn incense and pour out drink offerings to the Queen of Heaven.'

''Go ahead then, do what you promised! Keep your vows! ²⁶But hear the word of the LORD, all Jews living in Egypt: 'I swear by my great name,' says the LORD, 'that no-one from Judah living anywhere in Egypt shall ever again invoke my name or swear, ''As surely as the Sovereign LORD lives.'' ²⁷For I am watching over them for harm, not for good; the Jews in Egypt will perish by sword and famine until they are all destroyed. ²⁸Those who escape the sword and return to the land of Judah from Egypt will be very few. Then the whole remnant of Judah who came to live in Egypt will know whose word will stand—mine or theirs.

²⁹'' 'This will be the sign to you that I will punish you in this place,' declares the LORD, 'so that you will know that my threats of harm against you will surely stand.' ³⁰This is what the LORD says: 'I am going to hand Pharaoh Hophra king of Egypt over to his enemies who seek his life, just as I handed Zedekiah king of Judah over to Nebuchadnezzar king of Babylon, the enemy who was seeking his life.' ''

A Message to Baruch

45 This is what Jeremiah the prophet told Baruch son of Neriah in the fourth year of Jehoiakim son of Josiah king of Judah, after Baruch had written on a scroll the words Jeremiah was then dictating: ²''This is what the LORD, the God of Israel, says to you, Baruch: ³You said, 'Woe to me! The LORD has added sorrow to my pain; I am worn out with groaning and find no rest.' ''

⁴ The LORD said, ''Say this to him: 'This is what the LORD says: I will overthrow what I have built and uproot what I have planted, throughout the land. ⁵Should you then seek great things for yourself? Seek them not. For I will bring disaster on all people, declares the LORD, but wherever you go I will let you escape with your life.' ''

A Message About Egypt

46 This is the word of the LORD that came to Jeremiah the prophet concerning the nations:

²Concerning Egypt:

This is the message against the army of Pharaoh Neco king of Egypt, which was defeated at Carchemish on the Euphrates River by Nebuchadnezzar king of Babylon in the fourth year of Jehoiakim son of Josiah king of Judah:

³''Prepare your shields, both large and
    small,
  and march out for battle!
⁴Harness the horses,
  mount the steeds!
Take your positions
  with helmets on!
Polish your spears,
  put on your armour!
⁵What do I see?
  They are terrified,
they are retreating,
  their warriors are defeated.
They flee in haste
  without looking back,
  and there is terror on every side,''
                              declares the LORD.
⁶''The swift cannot flee
  nor the strong escape.
In the north by the River Euphrates
  they stumble and fall.

⁷''Who is this that rises like the Nile,
  like rivers of surging waters?
⁸Egypt rises like the Nile,
  like rivers of surging waters.
She says, 'I will rise and cover the earth;
  I will destroy cities and their people.'
⁹Charge, O horses!
  Drive furiously, O charioteers!
March on, O warriors—
  men of Cush[a] and Put who carry shields,
  men of Lydia who draw the bow.
¹⁰But that day belongs to the Lord, the LORD
    Almighty—
  a day of vengeance, for vengeance on
    his foes.
The sword will devour till it is satisfied,
  till it has quenched its thirst with blood.
For the Lord, the LORD Almighty, will
    offer sacrifice
  in the land of the north by the River
    Euphrates.

¹¹''Go up to Gilead and get balm,
  O Virgin Daughter of Egypt.
But you multiply remedies in vain;
  there is no healing for you.
¹²The nations will hear of your shame;
  your cries will fill the earth.

ᵃ9 That is, the upper Nile region

One warrior will stumble over another;
    both will fall down together.''

[13]This is the message the LORD spoke to
Jeremiah the prophet about the coming of
Nebuchadnezzar king of Babylon to attack
Egypt:

[14]''Announce this in Egypt, and proclaim it
        in Migdol;
    proclaim it also in Memphis[b] and
        Tahpanhes:
'Take your positions and get ready,
    for the sword devours those around
        you.'
[15]Why will your warriors be laid low?
    They cannot stand, for the LORD will
        push them down.
[16]They will stumble repeatedly;
    they will fall over each other.
They will say, 'Get up, let us go back
    to our own people and our native lands,
    away from the sword of the oppressor.'
[17]There they will exclaim,
    'Pharaoh king of Egypt is only a loud
        noise;
    he has missed his opportunity.'

[18]''As surely as I live,'' declares the King,
    whose name is the LORD Almighty,
    ''one will come who is like Tabor among
        the mountains,
    like Carmel by the sea.
[19]Pack your belongings for exile,
    you who live in Egypt,
for Memphis will be laid waste
    and lie in ruins without inhabitant.

[20]''Egypt is a beautiful heifer,
    but a gadfly is coming
    against her from the north.
[21]The mercenaries in her ranks
    are like fattened calves.
They too will turn and flee together,
    they will not stand their ground,
for the day of disaster is coming upon
        them,
    the time for them to be punished.
[22]Egypt will hiss like a fleeing serpent
    as the enemy advances in force;
they will come against her with axes,
    like men who cut down trees.
[23]They will chop down her forest,''
                        declares the LORD,
    ''dense though it be.
They are more numerous than locusts,
    they cannot be counted.
[24]The Daughter of Egypt will be put to
        shame,
    handed over to the people of the north.''

[25]The LORD Almighty, the God of Israel,
says: ''I am about to bring punishment on
Amon god of Thebes,[c] on Pharaoh, on Egypt
and her gods and her kings, and on those who
rely on Pharaoh. [26]I will hand them over to
those who seek their lives, to Nebuchadnezzar king of Babylon and his officers. Later,
however, Egypt will be inhabited as in times
past,'' declares the LORD.

[27]''Do not fear, O Jacob my servant;
    do not be dismayed, O Israel.
I will surely save you out of a distant
        place,
    and your descendants from the land of
        their exile.
Jacob will again have peace and security,
    and no-one will make him afraid.
[28]Do not fear, O Jacob my servant,
    for I am with you,'' declares the LORD.
''Though I completely destroy all the
        nations
    among which I scatter you,
    I will not completely destroy you.
I will discipline you but only with justice;
    I will not let you go entirely
        unpunished.''

A Message About the Philistines

47 This is the word of the LORD that came
to Jeremiah the prophet concerning
the Philistines before Pharaoh attacked
Gaza:

[2]This is what the LORD says:

''See how the waters are rising in the
        north;
    they will become an overflowing torrent.
They will overflow the land and everything
        in it,
    the towns and those who live in them.
The people will cry out;
    all who dwell in the land will wail
[3]at the sound of the hoofs of galloping
        steeds,
    at the noise of enemy chariots
    and the rumble of their wheels.
Fathers will not turn to help their children;
    their hands will hang limp.
[4]For the day has come
    to destroy all the Philistines
and to cut off all survivors
    who could help Tyre and Sidon.
The LORD is about to destroy the
        Philistines,
    the remnant from the coasts of
        Caphtor.[a]
[5]Gaza will shave her head in mourning;
    Ashkelon will be silenced.
O remnant on the plain,
    how long will you cut yourselves?

[6]''Ah, sword of the LORD,' ⌊you cry,⌋
    'how long till you rest?
Return to your scabbard;
    cease and be still.'
[7]But how can it rest
    when the LORD has commanded it,
when he has ordered it
    to attack Ashkelon and the coast?''

A Message About Moab

48 Concerning Moab:

This is what the LORD Almighty, the God of
Israel, says:

[b]14 Hebrew Noph; also in verse 19   [c]25 Hebrew No   [a]4 That is, Crete

"Woe to Nebo, for it will be ruined.
Kiriathaim will be disgraced and
    captured;
  the stronghold[a] will be disgraced and
    shattered.
²Moab will be praised no more;
  in Heshbon[b] men will plot her downfall:
  'Come, let us put an end to that nation.'
You too, O Madmen,[c] will be silenced;
  the sword will pursue you.
³Listen to the cries from Horonaim,
  cries of great havoc and destruction.
⁴Moab will be broken;
  her little ones will cry out.[d]
⁵They go up the way to Luhith,
  weeping bitterly as they go;
on the road down to Horonaim
  anguished cries over the destruction are
    heard.
⁶Flee! Run for your lives;
  become like a bush[e] in the desert.
⁷Since you trust in your deeds and riches,
  you too will be taken captive,
and Chemosh will go into exile,
  together with his priests and officials.
⁸The destroyer will come against every
    town,
  and not a town will escape.
The valley will be ruined
  and the plateau destroyed,
because the LORD has spoken.
⁹Put salt on Moab,
  for she will be laid waste;[f]
her towns will become desolate,
  with no-one to live in them.

¹⁰"A curse on him who is lax in doing the
    LORD's work!
  A curse on him who keeps his sword
    from bloodshed!

¹¹"Moab has been at rest from youth,
  like wine left on its dregs,
not poured from one jar to another—
  she has not gone into exile.
So she tastes as she did,
  and her aroma is unchanged.
¹²But days are coming,"
    declares the LORD,
  "when I will send men who pour from jars,
  and they will pour her out;
they will empty her jars
  and smash her jugs.
¹³Then Moab will be ashamed of Chemosh,
  as the house of Israel was ashamed
when they trusted in Bethel.

¹⁴"How can you say, 'We are warriors,
  men valiant in battle'?
¹⁵Moab will be destroyed and her towns
    invaded;
  her finest young men will go down in the
    slaughter,"
  declares the King, whose name is the
    LORD Almighty.
¹⁶"The fall of Moab is at hand;
  her calamity will come quickly.

¹⁷Mourn for her, all who live around her,
  all who know her fame;
say, 'How broken is the mighty sceptre,
  how broken the glorious staff!'

¹⁸"Come down from your glory
  and sit on the parched ground,
  O inhabitants of the Daughter of Dibon,
for he who destroys Moab
  will come up against you
  and ruin your fortified cities.
¹⁹Stand by the road and watch,
  you who live in Aroer.
Ask the man fleeing and the woman
    escaping,
  ask them, 'What has happened?'
²⁰Moab is disgraced, for she is shattered.
  Wail and cry out!
Announce by the Arnon
  that Moab is destroyed.
²¹Judgment has come to the plateau—
  to Holon, Jahzah and Mephaath,
²² to Dibon, Nebo and Beth Diblathaim,
²³ to Kiriathaim, Beth Gamul and Beth
    Meon,
²⁴ to Kerioth and Bozrah—
  to all the towns of Moab, far and near.
²⁵Moab's horn[g] is cut off;
  her arm is broken,"
                    declares the LORD.

²⁶"Make her drunk,
  for she has defied the LORD.
Let Moab wallow in her vomit;
  let her be an object of ridicule.
²⁷Was not Israel the object of your ridicule?
  Was she caught among thieves,
that you shake your head in scorn
  whenever you speak of her?
²⁸Abandon your towns and dwell among the
    rocks,
  you who live in Moab.
Be like a dove that makes its nest
  at the mouth of a cave.

²⁹"We have heard of Moab's pride—
  her overweening pride and conceit,
her pride and arrogance
  and the haughtiness of her heart.
³⁰I know her insolence but it is futile,"
                    declares the LORD,
  "and her boasts accomplish nothing.
³¹Therefore I wail over Moab,
  for all Moab I cry out,
  I moan for the men of Kir Hareseth.
³²I weep for you, as Jazer weeps,
  O vines of Sibmah.
Your branches spread as far as the sea;
  they reached as far as the sea of Jazer.
The destroyer has fallen
  on your ripened fruit and grapes.
³³Joy and gladness are gone
  from the orchards and fields of Moab.
I have stopped the flow of wine from the
    presses;
  no-one treads them with shouts of joy.

---

[a]1 Or / Misgab   [b]2 The Hebrew for Heshbon sounds like the Hebrew for plot.
[c]2 The name of the Moabite town Madmen sounds like the Hebrew for be silenced.
[d]4 Hebrew; Septuagint / proclaim it to Zoar   [e]6 Or like Aroer
[f]9 Or Give wings to Moab, / for she will fly away   [g]25 Horn here symbolises strength.

Although there are shouts,
  they are not shouts of joy.

³⁴"The sound of their cry rises
  from Heshbon to Elealeh and Jahaz,
from Zoar as far as Horonaim and Eglath
  Shelishiyah,
for even the waters of Nimrim are dried
  up.
³⁵In Moab I will put an end
  to those who make offerings on the high
    places
  and burn incense to their gods,"
               declares the LORD.
³⁶"So my heart laments for Moab like a
    flute;
  it laments like a flute for the men of Kir
    Hareseth.
The wealth they acquired is gone.
³⁷Every head is shaved
  and every beard cut off;
every hand is slashed
  and every waist is covered with
    sackcloth.
³⁸On all the roofs in Moab
  and in the public squares
there is nothing but mourning,
  for I have broken Moab
  like a jar that no-one wants,"
              declares the LORD.
³⁹"How shattered she is! How they wail!
  How Moab turns her back in shame!
Moab has become an object of ridicule,
  an object of horror to all those around
    her."

⁴⁰This is what the LORD says:

"Look! An eagle is swooping down,
  spreading its wings over Moab.
⁴¹Kerioth^h will be captured
  and the strongholds taken.
In that day the hearts of Moab's warriors
  will be like the heart of a woman in
    labour.
⁴²Moab will be destroyed as a nation
  because she defied the LORD.
⁴³Terror and pit and snare await you,
  O people of Moab,"
              declares the LORD.
⁴⁴"Whoever flees from the terror
  will fall into a pit,
whoever climbs out of the pit
  will be caught in a snare;
for I will bring upon Moab
  the year of her punishment,"
              declares the LORD.

⁴⁵"In the shadow of Heshbon
  the fugitives stand helpless,
for a fire has gone out from Heshbon,
  a blaze from the midst of Sihon;
it burns the foreheads of Moab,
  the skulls of the noisy boasters.
⁴⁶Woe to you, O Moab!
  The people of Chemosh are destroyed;
your sons are taken into exile
  and your daughters into captivity.

⁴⁷"Yet I will restore the fortunes of Moab
  in days to come,"
              declares the LORD.

Here ends the judgment on Moab.

A Message About Ammon

49 Concerning the Ammonites:

This is what the LORD says:

"Has Israel no sons?
  Has she no heirs?
Why then has Molech^a taken possession of
    Gad?
  Why do his people live in its towns?
²But the days are coming,"
    declares the LORD,
"when I will sound the battle cry
  against Rabbah of the Ammonites;
it will become a mound of ruins,
  and its surrounding villages will be set
    on fire.
Then Israel will drive out
  those who drove her out,"
             says the LORD.
³"Wail, O Heshbon, for Ai is destroyed!
  Cry out, O inhabitants of Rabbah!
Put on sackcloth and mourn;
  rush here and there inside the walls,
for Molech will go into exile,
  together with his priests and officials.
⁴Why do you boast of your valleys,
  boast of your valleys so fruitful?
O unfaithful daughter,
  you trust in your riches and say,
  'Who will attack me?'
⁵I will bring terror on you
  from all those around you,"
          declares the Lord,
              the LORD Almighty.
"Every one of you will be driven away,
  and no-one will gather the fugitives.

⁶"Yet afterwards, I will restore the
  fortunes of the Ammonites,"
              declares the LORD.

A Message About Edom

⁷Concerning Edom:

This is what the LORD Almighty says:

"Is there no longer wisdom in Teman?
  Has counsel perished from the prudent?
  Has their wisdom decayed?
⁸Turn and flee, hide in deep caves,
  you who live in Dedan,
for I will bring disaster on Esau
  at the time I punish him.
⁹If grape-pickers came to you,
  would they not leave a few grapes?
If thieves came during the night,
  would they not steal only as much as
    they wanted?
¹⁰But I will strip Esau bare;
  I will uncover his hiding-places,
  so that he cannot conceal himself.

^h41 Or The cities   ^a1 Or their king; Hebrew malcam; also in verse 3

His children, relatives and neighbours will
    perish,
  and he will be no more.
¹¹Leave your orphans; I will protect their
    lives.
  Your widows too can trust in me.''

¹²This is what the LORD says: ''If those
who do not deserve to drink the cup must
drink it, why should you go unpunished? You
will not go unpunished, but must drink it. ¹³I
swear by myself,'' declares the LORD, ''that
Bozrah will become a ruin and an object of
horror, of reproach and of cursing; and all its
towns will be in ruins for ever.''

¹⁴I have heard a message from the LORD:
  An envoy was sent to the nations to say,
''Assemble yourselves to attack it!
  Rise up for battle!''

¹⁵''Now I will make you small among the
    nations,
  despised among men.
¹⁶The terror you inspire
  and the pride of your heart have
    deceived you,
  you who live in the clefts of the rocks,
  who occupy the heights of the hill.
Though you build your nest as high as the
    eagle's,
  from there I will bring you down,''
                    declares the LORD.
¹⁷''Edom will become an object of horror;
  all who pass by will be appalled and will
    scoff
  because of all its wounds.
¹⁸As Sodom and Gomorrah were
    overthrown,
  along with their neighbouring towns,''
                    says the LORD,
''so no-one will live there;
  no man will dwell in it.

¹⁹''Like a lion coming up from Jordan's
    thickets
  to a rich pasture-land,
I will chase Edom from its land in an
    instant.
  Who is the chosen one I will appoint for
    this?
Who is like me and who can challenge me?
  And what shepherd can stand against
    me?''
²⁰Therefore, hear what the LORD has
    planned against Edom,
  what he has purposed against those who
    live in Teman:
The young of the flock will be dragged
    away;
  he will completely destroy their pasture
    because of them.
²¹At the sound of their fall the earth will
    tremble;
  their cry will resound to the Red Sea.ᵇ
²²Look! An eagle will soar and swoop down,
  spreading its wings over Bozrah.

In that day the hearts of Edom's warriors
  will be like the heart of a woman in
    labour.

A Message About Damascus

²³Concerning Damascus:

''Hamath and Arpad are dismayed,
  for they have heard bad news.
They are disheartened,
  troubled likeᶜ the restless sea.
²⁴Damascus has become feeble,
  she has turned to flee
  and panic has gripped her;
anguish and pain have seized her,
  pain like that of a woman in labour.
²⁵Why has the city of renown not been
    abandoned,
  the town in which I delight?
²⁶Surely, her young men will fall in the
    streets;
  all her soldiers will be silenced in that
    day,''
                    declares the LORD Almighty.
²⁷''I will set fire to the walls of Damascus;
  it will consume the fortresses of
    Ben-Hadad.''

A Message About Kedar and Hazor

²⁸Concerning Kedar and the kingdoms of
Hazor, which Nebuchadnezzar king of
Babylon attacked:

This is what the LORD says:

''Arise, and attack Kedar
  and destroy the people of the East.
²⁹Their tents and their flocks will be taken;
  their shelters will be carried off
  with all their goods and camels.
Men will shout to them,
  'Terror on every side!'

³⁰''Flee quickly away!
  Stay in deep caves, you who live in
    Hazor,''
                    declares the LORD.
''Nebuchadnezzar king of Babylon has
    plotted against you;
  he has devised a plan against you.

³¹''Arise and attack a nation at ease,
  which lives in confidence,''
                    declares the LORD,
''a nation that has neither gates nor bars;
  its people live alone.
³²Their camels will become plunder,
  and their large herds will be booty.
I will scatter to the winds those who are in
    distant placesᵈ
  and will bring disaster on them from
    every side,''
                    declares the LORD.
³³''Hazor will become a haunt of jackals,
  a desolate place for ever.
No-one will live there;
  no man will dwell in it.''

ᵇ21 Hebrew *Yam Suph*; that is, Sea of Reeds   ᶜ23 Hebrew *on* or *by*
ᵈ32 Or *who clip the hair by their foreheads*

A Message About Elam

³⁴This is the word of the LORD that came to Jeremiah the prophet concerning Elam, early in the reign of Zedekiah king of Judah:

³⁵This is what the LORD Almighty says:

"See, I will break the bow of Elam,
  the mainstay of their might.
³⁶I will bring against Elam the four winds
  from the four quarters of the heavens;
I will scatter them to the four winds,
  and there will not be a nation
  where Elam's exiles do not go.
³⁷I will shatter Elam before their foes,
  before those who seek their lives;
I will bring disaster upon them,
  even my fierce anger,"
               declares the LORD.
"I will pursue them with the sword
  until I have made an end of them.
³⁸I will set my throne in Elam
  and destroy her king and officials,"
               declares the LORD.

³⁹"Yet I will restore the fortunes of Elam
  in days to come,"
               declares the LORD.

A Message About Babylon

50 This is the word the LORD spoke through Jeremiah the prophet concerning Babylon and the land of the Babylonians:^a

²"Announce and proclaim among the
  nations,
  lift up a banner and proclaim it;
  keep nothing back, but say,
'Babylon will be captured;
  Bel will be put to shame,
  Marduk filled with terror.
Her images will be put to shame
  and her idols filled with terror.'
³A nation from the north will attack her
  and lay waste her land.
No-one will live in it;
  both men and animals will flee away.

⁴"In those days, at that time,"
  declares the LORD,
"the people of Israel and the people of
  Judah together
will go in tears to seek the LORD their
  God.
⁵They will ask the way to Zion
  and turn their faces towards it.
They will come and bind themselves to the
  LORD
  in an everlasting covenant
  that will not be forgotten.

⁶"My people have been lost sheep;
  their shepherds have led them astray
  and caused them to roam on the
  mountains.
They wandered over mountain and hill
  and forgot their own resting place.

⁷Whoever found them devoured them;
  their enemies said, 'We are not guilty,
for they sinned against the LORD, their true
  pasture,
  the LORD, the hope of their fathers.'

⁸"Flee out of Babylon;
  leave the land of the Babylonians,
  and be like the goats that lead the flock.
⁹For I will stir up and bring against Babylon
  an alliance of great nations from the land
  of the north.
They will take up their positions against
  her,
  and from the north she will be captured.
Their arrows will be like skilled warriors
  who do not return empty-handed.
¹⁰So Babylonia^b will be plundered;
  all who plunder her will have their fill,"
               declares the LORD.

¹¹"Because you rejoice and are glad,
  you who pillage my inheritance,
because you frolic like a heifer threshing
  corn
  and neigh like stallions,
¹²your mother will be greatly ashamed;
  she who gave you birth will be
  disgraced.
She will be the least of the nations—
  a wilderness, a dry land, a desert.
¹³Because of the LORD's anger she will not
  be inhabited
but will be completely desolate.
All who pass Babylon will be horrified and
  scoff
  because of all her wounds.

¹⁴"Take up your positions round Babylon,
  all you who draw the bow.
Shoot at her! Spare no arrows,
  for she has sinned against the LORD.
¹⁵Shout against her on every side!
  She surrenders, her towers fall,
  her walls are torn down.
Since this is the vengeance of the LORD,
  take vengeance on her;
  do to her as she has done to others.
¹⁶Cut off from Babylon the sower,
  and the reaper with his sickle at harvest.
Because of the sword of the oppressor
  let everyone return to his own people,
  let everyone flee to his own land.

¹⁷"Israel is a scattered flock
  that lions have chased away.
The first to devour him
  was the king of Assyria;
the last to crush his bones
  was Nebuchadnezzar king of Babylon."

¹⁸Therefore this is what the LORD Almighty, the God of Israel, says:

"I will punish the king of Babylon and his
  land
  as I punished the king of Assyria.

---

^a1 Or *Chaldeans*; also in verses 8, 25, 35 and 45   ^b10 Or *Chaldea*

¹⁹But I will bring Israel back to his own
pasture
and he will graze on Carmel and Bashan;
his appetite will be satisfied
on the hills of Ephraim and Gilead.
²⁰In those days, at that time,"
declares the LORD,
"search will be made for Israel's guilt,
but there will be none,
and for the sins of Judah,
but none will be found,
for I will forgive the remnant I spare.

²¹"Attack the land of Merathaim
and those who live in Pekod.
Pursue, kill and completely destroy*c*
them,"
declares the LORD.
"Do everything I have commanded you.
²²The noise of battle is in the land,
the noise of great destruction!
²³How broken and shattered
is the hammer of the whole earth!
How desolate is Babylon
among the nations!
²⁴I set a trap for you, O Babylon,
and you were caught before you knew it;
you were found and captured
because you opposed the LORD.
²⁵The LORD has opened his arsenal
and brought out the weapons of his
wrath,
for the Sovereign LORD Almighty has work
to do
in the land of the Babylonians.
²⁶Come against her from afar.
Break open her granaries;
pile her up like heaps of grain.
Completely destroy her
and leave her no remnant.
²⁷Kill all her young bulls;
let them go down to the slaughter!
Woe to them! For their day has come,
the time for them to be punished.
²⁸Listen to the fugitives and refugees from
Babylon
declaring in Zion
how the LORD our God has taken
vengeance,
vengeance for his temple.

²⁹"Summon archers against Babylon,
all those who draw the bow.
Encamp all round her;
let no-one escape.
Repay her for her deeds;
do to her as she has done.
For she defied the LORD,
the Holy One of Israel.
³⁰Therefore, her young men will fall in the
streets;
all her soldiers will be silenced in that
day,"
declares the LORD.
³¹"See, I am against you, O arrogant one,"
declares the Lord, the LORD Almighty,
"for your day has come,
the time for you to be punished.

³²The arrogant one will stumble and fall
and no-one will help her up;
I will kindle a fire in her towns
that will consume all who are around
her."

³³This is what the LORD Almighty says:

"The people of Israel are oppressed,
and the people of Judah as well.
All their captors hold them fast,
refusing to let them go.
³⁴Yet their Redeemer is strong;
the LORD Almighty is his name.
He will vigorously defend their cause
so that he may bring rest to their land,
but unrest to those who live in Babylon.

³⁵"A sword against the Babylonians!"
declares the LORD—
"against those who live in Babylon
and against her officials and wise men!
³⁶A sword against her false prophets!
They will become fools.
A sword against her warriors!
They will be filled with terror.
³⁷A sword against her horses and chariots
and all the foreigners in her ranks!
They will become women.
A sword against her treasures!
They will be plundered.
³⁸A drought on*d* her waters!
They will dry up.
For it is a land of idols,
idols that will go mad with terror.

³⁹"So desert creatures and hyenas will live
there,
and there the owl will dwell.
It will never again be inhabited
or lived in from generation to
generation.
⁴⁰As God overthrew Sodom and Gomorrah
along with their neighbouring towns,"
declares the LORD,
"so no-one will live there;
no man will dwell in it.

⁴¹"Look! An army is coming from the north;
a great nation and many kings
are being stirred up from the ends of the
earth.
⁴²They are armed with bows and spears;
they are cruel and without mercy.
They sound like the roaring sea
as they ride on their horses;
they come like men in battle formation
to attack you, O Daughter of Babylon.
⁴³The king of Babylon has heard reports
about them,
and his hands hang limp.
Anguish has gripped him,
pain like that of a woman in labour.
⁴⁴Like a lion coming up from Jordan's
thickets
to a rich pasture-land,
I will chase Babylon from its land in an
instant.

---

c21 The Hebrew term refers to the irrevocable giving over of things or persons to the LORD, often by totally
destroying them; also in verse 26.   *d38* Or *A sword against*

Who is the chosen one I will appoint for
　　this?
Who is like me and who can challenge me?
　And what shepherd can stand against
　　me?''
⁴⁵Therefore, hear what the LORD has
　　planned against Babylon,
　what he has purposed against the land of
　　the Babylonians:
The young of the flock will be dragged
　　away;
　he will completely destroy their pasture
　　because of them.
⁴⁶At the sound of Babylon's capture the
　　earth will tremble;
　its cry will resound among the nations.

51　This is what the LORD says:

''See, I will stir up the spirit of a destroyer
　against Babylon and the people of Leb
　Kamai.ᵃ
²I will send foreigners to Babylon
　to winnow her and to devastate her
　　land;
they will oppose her on every side
　in the day of her disaster.
³Let not the archer string his bow,
　nor let him put on his armour.
Do not spare her young men;
　completely destroyᵇ her army.
⁴They will fall down slain in Babylon,ᶜ
　fatally wounded in her streets.
⁵For Israel and Judah have not been
　　forsaken
　by their God, the LORD Almighty,
though their landᵈ is full of guilt
　before the Holy One of Israel.

⁶''Flee from Babylon!
　Run for your lives!
　Do not be destroyed because of her sins.
It is time for the LORD's vengeance;
　he will pay her what she deserves.
⁷Babylon was a gold cup in the LORD's
　　hand;
　she made the whole earth drunk.
The nations drank her wine;
　therefore they have now gone mad.
⁸Babylon will suddenly fall and be broken.
　Wail over her!
Get balm for her pain;
　perhaps she can be healed.

⁹''We would have healed Babylon,
　but she cannot be healed;
let us leave her and each go to his own
　　land,
for her judgment reaches to the skies,
　it rises as high as the clouds.'

¹⁰''The LORD has vindicated us;
　come, let us tell in Zion
what the LORD our God has done.'

¹¹''Sharpen the arrows,
　take up the shields!

The LORD has stirred up the kings of the
　　Medes,
　because his purpose is to destroy
　　Babylon.
The LORD will take vengeance,
　vengeance for his temple.
¹²Lift up a banner against the walls of
　　Babylon!
Reinforce the guard,
station the watchmen,
　prepare an ambush!
The LORD will carry out his purpose,
　his decree against the people of
　　Babylon.
¹³You who live by many waters
　and are rich in treasures,
your end has come,
　the time for you to be cut off.
¹⁴The LORD Almighty has sworn by himself:
　I will surely fill you with men, as with a
　　swarm of locusts,
　and they will shout in triumph over you.

¹⁵''He made the earth by his power;
　he founded the world by his wisdom
　and stretched out the heavens by his
　　understanding.
¹⁶When he thunders, the waters in the
　　heavens roar;
　he makes clouds rise from the ends of
　　the earth.
He sends lightning with the rain
　and brings out the wind from his
　　storehouses.

¹⁷''Every man is senseless and without
　　knowledge;
　every goldsmith is shamed by his idols.
His images are a fraud;
　they have no breath in them.
¹⁸They are worthless, the objects of
　　mockery;
　when their judgment comes, they will
　　perish.
¹⁹He who is the Portion of Jacob is not like
　　these,
　for he is the Maker of all things,
including the tribe of his inheritance—
　the LORD Almighty is his name.

²⁰''You are my war club,
　my weapon for battle—
with you I shatter nations,
　with you I destroy kingdoms,
²¹with you I shatter horse and rider,
　with you I shatter chariot and driver,
²²with you I shatter man and woman,
　with you I shatter old man and youth,
　with you I shatter young man and
　　maiden,
²³with you I shatter shepherd and flock,
　with you I shatter farmer and oxen,
　with you I shatter governors and
　　officials.

²⁴''Before your eyes I will repay Babylon
and all who live in Babyloniaᵉ for all the

ᵃ1 *Leb Kamai* is a cryptogram for Chaldea, that is, Babylonia.
ᵇ3 The Hebrew term refers to the irrevocable giving over of things or persons to the LORD, often by totally destroying
them.　　ᶜ4 Or *Chaldea*　　ᵈ5 Or *I and the land ⸤of the Babylonians⸥*　　ᵉ24 Or *Chaldea*; also in verse 35

wrong they have done in Zion,'' declares the LORD.

25''I am against you, O destroying mountain,
    you who destroy the whole earth,''
                    declares the LORD.
''I will stretch out my hand against you,
    roll you off the cliffs,
    and make you a burnt-out mountain.
26No rock will be taken from you for a
        cornerstone,
    nor any stone for a foundation,
    for you will be desolate for ever,''
                    declares the LORD.

27''Lift up a banner in the land!
    Blow the trumpet among the nations!
Prepare the nations for battle against her;
    summon against her these kingdoms:
    Ararat, Minni and Ashkenaz.
Appoint a commander against her;
    send up horses like a swarm of locusts.
28Prepare the nations for battle against
        her—
    the kings of the Medes,
    their governors and all their officials,
    and all the countries they rule.
29The land trembles and writhes,
    for the LORD's purposes against Babylon
        stand—
to lay waste the land of Babylon
    so that no-one will live there.
30Babylon's warriors have stopped fighting;
    they remain in their strongholds.
Their strength is exhausted;
    they have become like women.
Her dwellings are set on fire;
    the bars of her gates are broken.
31One courier follows another
    and messenger follows messenger
to announce to the king of Babylon
    that his entire city is captured,
32the river crossings seized,
    the marshes set on fire,
    and the soldiers terrified.''

33This is what the LORD Almighty, the God
of Israel, says:

''The Daughter of Babylon is like a
        threshing-floor
    at the time it is trampled;
    the time to harvest her will soon
        come.''

34''Nebuchadnezzar king of Babylon has
        devoured us,
    he has thrown us into confusion,
    he has made us an empty jar.
Like a serpent he has swallowed us
    and filled his stomach with our
        delicacies,
    and then has spewed us out.
35May the violence done to our flesh/ be
        upon Babylon,''
    say the inhabitants of Zion.
''May our blood be on those who live in
        Babylonia,''
    says Jerusalem.

36Therefore, this is what the LORD says:

''See, I will defend your cause
    and avenge you;
I will dry up her sea
    and make her springs dry.
37Babylon will be a heap of ruins,
    a haunt of jackals,
    an object of horror and scorn,
    a place where no-one lives.
38Her people all roar like young lions,
    they growl like lion cubs.
39But while they are aroused,
    I will set out a feast for them
    and make them drunk,
so that they shout with laughter—
    then sleep for ever and not awake,''
                    declares the LORD.
40''I will bring them down
    like lambs to the slaughter,
    like rams and goats.

41''How Sheshach⁸ will be captured,
    the boast of the whole earth seized!
What a horror Babylon will be
    among the nations!
42The sea will rise over Babylon;
    its roaring waves will cover her.
43Her towns will be desolate,
    a dry and desert land,
a land where no-one lives,
    through which no man travels.
44I will punish Bel in Babylon
    and make him spew out what he has
        swallowed.
The nations will no longer stream to him.
    And the wall of Babylon will fall.

45''Come out of her, my people!
    Run for your lives!
    Run from the fierce anger of the LORD.
46Do not lose heart or be afraid
    when rumours are heard in the land;
one rumour comes this year, another the
        next,
    rumours of violence in the land
    and of ruler against ruler.
47For the time will surely come
    when I will punish the idols of Babylon;
her whole land will be disgraced
    and her slain will all lie fallen within her.
48Then heaven and earth and all that is in
        them
    will shout for joy over Babylon,
for out of the north
    destroyers will attack her,''
                    declares the LORD.

49''Babylon must fall because of Israel's
        slain,
    just as the slain in all the earth
    have fallen because of Babylon.
50You who have escaped the sword,
    leave and do not linger!
Remember the LORD in a distant land,
    and think on Jerusalem.''

51''We are disgraced,
    for we have been insulted
    and shame covers our faces,

ƒ35 Or done to us and to our children   ⁸41 Sheshach is a cryptogram for Babylon.

because foreigners have entered
the holy places of the Lord's house."

52"But days are coming," declares the
Lord,
"when I will punish her idols,
and throughout her land
the wounded will groan.
53Even if Babylon reaches the sky
and fortifies her lofty stronghold,
I will send destroyers against her,"
declares the Lord.

54"The sound of a cry comes from Babylon,
the sound of great destruction
from the land of the Babylonians.h
55The Lord will destroy Babylon;
he will silence her noisy din.
Waves ⌞of enemies⌟ will rage like great
waters;
the roar of their voices will resound.
56A destroyer will come against Babylon;
her warriors will be captured,
and their bows will be broken.
For the Lord is a God of retribution;
he will repay in full.
57I will make her officials and wise men
drunk,
her governors, officers and warriors as
well;
they will sleep for ever and not awake,"
declares the King, whose name is the
Lord Almighty.

58This is what the Lord Almighty says:

"Babylon's thick wall will be levelled
and her high gates set on fire;
the peoples exhaust themselves for
nothing,
the nations' labour is only fuel for the
flames."

59This is the message Jeremiah gave to the
staff officer Seraiah son of Neriah, the son of
Mahseiah, when he went to Babylon with
Zedekiah king of Judah in the fourth year of
his reign. 60Jeremiah had written on a scroll
about all the disasters that would come upon
Babylon—all that had been recorded concerning Babylon. 61He said to Seraiah,
"When you get to Babylon, see that you read
all these words aloud. 62Then say, 'O Lord,
you have said you will destroy this place, so
that neither man nor animal will live in it; it
will be desolate for ever.' 63When you finish
reading this scroll, tie a stone to it and throw
it into the Euphrates. 64Then say, 'So will
Babylon sink to rise no more because of the
disaster I will bring upon her. And her people
will fall.'"

The words of Jeremiah end here.

The Fall of Jerusalem

52 Zedekiah was twenty-one years old
when he became king, and he reigned
in Jerusalem for eleven years. His mother's
name was Hamutal daughter of Jeremiah;
she was from Libnah. 2He did evil in the eyes
of the Lord, just as Jehoiakim had done. 3It
was because of the Lord's anger that all this
happened to Jerusalem and Judah, and in the
end he thrust them from his presence.

Now Zedekiah rebelled against the king of
Babylon.

4So in the ninth year of Zedekiah's reign,
on the tenth day of the tenth month,
Nebuchadnezzar king of Babylon marched
against Jerusalem with his whole army. They
camped outside the city and built siege works
all around it. 5The city was kept under siege
until the eleventh year of King Zedekiah.

6By the ninth day of the fourth month the
famine in the city had become so severe that
there was no food for the people to eat. 7Then
the city wall was broken through, and the
whole army fled. They left the city at night
through the gate between the two walls near
the king's garden, though the Babyloniansa
were surrounding the city. They fled towards
the Arabah,b 8but the Babylonianc army pursued King Zedekiah and overtook him in the
plains of Jericho. All his soldiers were separated from him and scattered, 9and he was
captured.

He was taken to the king of Babylon at
Riblah in the land of Hamath, where he pronounced sentence on him. 10There at Riblah
the king of Babylon slaughtered the sons of
Zedekiah before his eyes; he also killed all
the officials of Judah. 11Then he put out Zedekiah's eyes, bound him with bronze shackles
and took him to Babylon, where he put him in
prison till the day of his death.

12On the tenth day of the fifth month, in the
nineteenth year of Nebuchadnezzar king of
Babylon, Nebuzaradan commander of the
imperial guard, who served the king of Babylon, came to Jerusalem. 13He set fire to the
temple of the Lord, the royal palace and all
the houses of Jerusalem. Every important
building he burned down. 14The whole
Babylonian army under the commander of
the imperial guard broke down all the walls
around Jerusalem. 15Nebuzaradan the commander of the guard carried into exile some
of the poorest people and those who remained in the city, along with the rest of the
craftsmend and those who had gone over to
the king of Babylon. 16But Nebuzaradan left
behind the rest of the poorest people of the
land to work the vineyards and fields.

17The Babylonians broke up the bronze
pillars, the movable stands and the bronze
Sea that were at the temple of the Lord and
they carried all the bronze to Babylon.
18They also took away the pots, shovels,
wick trimmers, sprinkling bowls, dishes and
all the bronze articles used in the temple
service. 19The commander of the imperial
guard took away the basins, censers, sprinkling bowls, pots, lampstands, dishes and
bowls used for drink offerings—all that were
made of pure gold or silver.

20The bronze from the two pillars, the Sea

h54 Or Chaldeans   a7 Or Chaldeans; also in verse 17   b7 Or the Jordan Valley
c8 Or Chaldean; also in verse 14   d15 Or populace

and the twelve bronze bulls under it, and the movable stands, which King Solomon had made for the temple of the LORD, was more than could be weighed. [21]Each of the pillars was eighteen cubits high and twelve cubits in circumference;[e] each was four fingers thick, and hollow. [22]The bronze capital on the top of the one pillar was five cubits[f] high and was decorated with a network and pomegranates of bronze all around. The other pillar, with its pomegranates, was similar. [23]There were ninety-six pomegranates on the sides; the total number of pomegranates above the surrounding network was a hundred.

[24]The commander of the guard took as prisoners Seraiah the chief priest, Zephaniah the priest next in rank and the three doorkeepers. [25]Of those still in the city, he took the officer in charge of the fighting men, and seven royal advisers. He also took the secretary who was chief officer in charge of conscripting the people of the land and sixty of his men who were found in the city. [26]Nebuzaradan the commander took them all and brought them to the king of Babylon at Riblah. [27]There at Riblah, in the land of Hamath, the king had them executed.

So Judah went into captivity, away from her land. [28]This is the number of the people Nebuchadnezzar carried into exile:

in the seventh year, 3,023 Jews;
[29]in Nebuchadnezzar's eighteenth year,
　　832 people from Jerusalem;
[30]in his twenty-third year,
　　745 Jews taken into exile by
　　　Nebuzaradan
the commander of the imperial guard.
There were 4,600 people in all.

Jehoiachin Released

[31]In the thirty-seventh year of the exile of Jehoiachin king of Judah, in the year Evil-Merodach[g] became king of Babylon, he released Jehoiachin king of Judah and freed him from prison on the twenty-fifth day of the twelfth month. [32]He spoke kindly to him and gave him a seat of honour higher than those of the other kings who were with him in Babylon. [33]So Jehoiachin put aside his prison clothes and for the rest of his life ate regularly at the king's table. [34]Day by day the king of Babylon gave Jehoiachin a regular allowance as long as he lived, till the day of his death.

---

[e]21 That is, about 27 feet (about 8.1 metres) high and 18 feet (about 5.5 metres) in circumference　[f]22 That is, about 7½ feet (about 2.3 metres)　[g]31 Also called Amel-Marduk

Lamentations

1 *a* How deserted lies the city,
  once so full of people!
How like a widow is she,
  who once was great among the nations!
She who was queen among the provinces
  has now become a slave.

²Bitterly she weeps at night,
  tears are upon her cheeks.
Among all her lovers
  there is none to comfort her.
All her friends have betrayed her;
  they have become her enemies.

³After affliction and harsh labour,
  Judah has gone into exile.
She dwells among the nations;
  she finds no resting place.
All who pursue her have overtaken her
  in the midst of her distress.

⁴The roads to Zion mourn,
  for no-one comes to her appointed
    feasts.
All her gateways are desolate,
  her priests groan,
her maidens grieve,
  and she is in bitter anguish.

⁵Her foes have become her masters;
  her enemies are at ease.
The LORD has brought her grief
  because of her many sins.
Her children have gone into exile,
  captive before the foe.

⁶All the splendour has departed
  from the Daughter of Zion.
Her princes are like deer
  that find no pasture;
in weakness they have fled
  before the pursuer.

⁷In the days of her affliction and wandering
  Jerusalem remembers all the treasures
  that were hers in days of old.
When her people fell into enemy hands,
  there was no-one to help her.
Her enemies looked at her
  and laughed at her destruction.

⁸Jerusalem has sinned greatly
  and so has become unclean.
All who honoured her despise her,
  for they have seen her nakedness;
she herself groans
  and turns away.

⁹Her filthiness clung to her skirts;
  she did not consider her future.
Her fall was astounding;
  there was none to comfort her.
"Look, O LORD, on my affliction,
  for the enemy has triumphed."

¹⁰The enemy laid hands
  on all her treasures;
she saw pagan nations
  enter her sanctuary—
those you had forbidden
  to enter your assembly.

¹¹All her people groan
  as they search for bread;
they barter their treasures for food
  to keep themselves alive.
"Look, O LORD, and consider,
  for I am despised."

¹²"Is it nothing to you, all you who pass by?
  Look around and see.
Is any suffering like my suffering
  that was inflicted on me,
that the LORD brought on me
  in the day of his fierce anger?

¹³"From on high he sent fire,
  sent it down into my bones.
He spread a net for my feet
  and turned me back.
He made me desolate,
  faint all the day long.

¹⁴"My sins have been bound into a yoke;*b*
  by his hands they were woven together.
They have come upon my neck
  and the Lord has sapped my strength.
He has handed me over
  to those I cannot withstand.

¹⁵"The Lord has rejected
  all the warriors in my midst;

---

*a*This chapter is an acrostic poem, the verses of which begin with the successive letters of the Hebrew alphabet.
*b*14 Most Hebrew manuscripts; Septuagint *He kept watch over my sins*

he has summoned an army against me
  to^c crush my young men.
In his winepress the Lord has trampled
  the Virgin Daughter of Judah.

16"This is why I weep
  and my eyes overflow with tears.
No-one is near to comfort me,
  no-one to restore my spirit.
My children are destitute
  because the enemy has prevailed."

17Zion stretches out her hands,
  but there is no-one to comfort her.
The LORD has decreed for Jacob
  that his neighbours become his foes;
Jerusalem has become
  an unclean thing among them.

18"The LORD is righteous,
  yet I rebelled against his command.
Listen, all you peoples;
  look upon my suffering.
My young men and maidens
  have gone into exile.

19"I called to my allies
  but they betrayed me.
My priests and my elders
  perished in the city
while they searched for food
  to keep themselves alive.

20"See, O LORD, how distressed I am!
  I am in torment within,
and in my heart I am disturbed,
  for I have been most rebellious.
Outside, the sword bereaves;
  inside, there is only death.

21"People have heard my groaning,
  but there is no-one to comfort me.
All my enemies have heard of my distress;
  they rejoice at what you have done.
May you bring the day you have
    announced
  so that they may become like me.

22"Let all their wickedness come before
    you;
  deal with them
as you have dealt with me
  because of all my sins.
My groans are many
  and my heart is faint."

2 ^{a} How the Lord has covered the
    Daughter of Zion
  with the cloud of his anger!^{b}
He has hurled down the splendour of
    Israel
  from heaven to earth;
he has not remembered his footstool
  in the day of his anger.

2Without pity the Lord has swallowed up
  all the dwellings of Jacob;

in his wrath he has torn down
  the strongholds of the Daughter of
    Judah.
He has brought her kingdom and its
    princes
  down to the ground in dishonour.

3In fierce anger he has cut off
  every horn^c of Israel.
He has withdrawn his right hand
  at the approach of the enemy.
He has burned in Jacob like a flaming fire
  that consumes everything around it.

4Like an enemy he has strung his bow;
  his right hand is ready.
Like a foe he has slain
  all who were pleasing to the eye;
he has poured out his wrath like fire
  on the tent of the Daughter of Zion.

5The Lord is like an enemy;
  he has swallowed up Israel.
He has swallowed up all her palaces
  and destroyed her strongholds.
He has multiplied mourning and
    lamentation
  for the Daughter of Judah.

6He has laid waste his dwelling like a
    garden;
  he has destroyed his place of meeting.
The LORD has made Zion forget
  her appointed feasts and her Sabbaths;
in his fierce anger he has spurned
  both king and priest.

7The Lord has rejected his altar
  and abandoned his sanctuary.
He has handed over to the enemy
  the walls of her palaces;
they have raised a shout in the house of
    the LORD
  as on the day of an appointed feast.

8The LORD determined to tear down
  the wall around the Daughter of Zion.
He stretched out a measuring line
  and did not withhold his hand from
    destroying.
He made ramparts and walls lament;
  together they wasted away.

9Her gates have sunk into the ground;
  their bars he has broken and destroyed.
Her king and her princes are exiled among
    the nations,
  the law is no more,
and her prophets no longer find
  visions from the LORD.

10The elders of the Daughter of Zion
  sit on the ground in silence;
they have sprinkled dust on their heads
  and put on sackcloth.
The young women of Jerusalem
  have bowed their heads to the ground.

---

^{c}15 Or *has set a time for me | when he will*
^{a}This chapter is an acrostic poem, the verses of which begin with the successive letters of the Hebrew alphabet.
^{b}1 Or *How the LORD in his anger | has treated the Daughter of Zion with contempt!*
^{c}3 Or *| all the strength*; or *every king; horn* here symbolises strength.

11My eyes fail from weeping,
  I am in torment within,
my heart is poured out on the ground
  because my people are destroyed,
because children and infants faint
  in the streets of the city.

12They say to their mothers,
  "Where is bread and wine?"
as they faint like wounded men
  in the streets of the city,
as their lives ebb away
  in their mothers' arms.

13What can I say for you?
  With what can I compare you,
  O Daughter of Jerusalem?
To what can I liken you,
  that I may comfort you,
  O Virgin Daughter of Zion?
Your wound is as deep as the sea.
  Who can heal you?

14The visions of your prophets
  were false and worthless;
they did not expose your sin
  to ward off your captivity.
The oracles they gave you
  were false and misleading.

15All who pass your way
  clap their hands at you;
they scoff and shake their heads
  at the Daughter of Jerusalem:
"Is this the city that was called
  the perfection of beauty,
  the joy of the whole earth?"

16All your enemies open their mouths
  wide against you;
they scoff and gnash their teeth
  and say, "We have swallowed her up.
This is the day we have waited for;
  we have lived to see it."

17The LORD has done what he planned;
  he has fulfilled his word,
  which he decreed long ago.
He has overthrown you without pity,
  he has let the enemy gloat over you,
  he has exalted the horn[d] of your foes.

18The hearts of the people
  cry out to the Lord.
O wall of the Daughter of Zion,
  let your tears flow like a river
  day and night;
give yourself no relief,
  your eyes no rest.

19Arise, cry out in the night,
  as the watches of the night begin;
pour out your heart like water
  in the presence of the Lord.
Lift up your hands to him
  for the lives of your children,
who faint from hunger
  at the head of every street.

20"Look, O LORD, and consider:
  Whom have you ever treated like this?
Should women eat their offspring,
  the children they have cared for?
Should priest and prophet be killed
  in the sanctuary of the Lord?

21"Young and old lie together
  in the dust of the streets;
my young men and maidens
  have fallen by the sword.
You have slain them in the day of your
    anger;
  you have slaughtered them without pity.

22"As you summon to a feast day,
  so you summoned against me terrors on
    every side.
In the day of the LORD's anger
  no-one escaped or survived;
those I cared for and reared,
  my enemy has destroyed."

3[a] I am the man who has seen affliction
     by the rod of his wrath.
2He has driven me away and made me walk
  in darkness rather than light;
3indeed, he has turned his hand against me
  again and again, all day long.

4He has made my skin and my flesh grow
    old
  and has broken my bones.
5He has besieged me and surrounded me
  with bitterness and hardship.
6He has made me dwell in darkness
  like those long dead.

7He has walled me in so that I cannot
    escape;
  he has weighed me down with chains.
8Even when I call out or cry for help,
  he shuts out my prayer.
9He has barred my way with blocks of
    stone;
  he has made my paths crooked.

10Like a bear lying in wait,
  like a lion in hiding,
11he dragged me from the path and mangled
    me
  and left me without help.
12He drew his bow
  and made me the target for his arrows.

13He pierced my heart
  with arrows from his quiver.
14I became the laughing-stock of all my
    people;
  they mock me in song all day long.
15He has filled me with bitter herbs
  and sated me with gall.

16He has broken my teeth with gravel;
  he has trampled me in the dust.
17I have been deprived of peace;
  I have forgotten what prosperity is.

d17 Horn here symbolises strength.
aThis chapter is an acrostic poem; the verses of each stanza begin with the successive letters of the Hebrew alphabet,
and the verses within each stanza begin with the same letter.

18So I say, "My splendour is gone
  and all that I had hoped from the
    LORD."

19I remember my affliction and my
    wandering,
  the bitterness and the gall.
20I well remember them,
  and my soul is downcast within me.
21Yet this I call to mind
  and therefore I have hope:

22Because of the LORD's great love we are
    not consumed,
  for his compassions never fail.
23They are new every morning;
  great is your faithfulness.
24I say to myself, "The LORD is my portion;
  therefore I will wait for him."

25The LORD is good to those whose hope is in
    him,
  to the one who seeks him;
26it is good to wait quietly
  for the salvation of the LORD.
27It is good for a man to bear the yoke
  while he is young.

28Let him sit alone in silence,
  for the LORD has laid it on him.
29Let him bury his face in the dust—
  there may yet be hope.
30Let him offer his cheek to one who would
    strike him,
  and let him be filled with disgrace.

31For men are not cast off
  by the Lord for ever.
32Though he brings grief, he will show
    compassion,
  so great is his unfailing love.
33For he does not willingly bring affliction
  or grief to the children of men.

34To crush underfoot
  all prisoners in the land,
35to deny a man his rights
  before the Most High,
36to deprive a man of justice—
  would not the Lord see such things?

37Who can speak and have it happen
  if the Lord has not decreed it?
38Is it not from the mouth of the Most High
  that both calamities and good things
    come?
39Why should any living man complain
  when punished for his sins?

40Let us examine our ways and test them,
  and let us return to the LORD.
41Let us lift up our hearts and our hands
  to God in heaven, and say:
42"We have sinned and rebelled
  and you have not forgiven.

43"You have covered yourself with anger
    and pursued us;
  you have slain without pity.

44You have covered yourself with a cloud
  so that no prayer can get through.
45You have made us scum and refuse
  among the nations.

46"All our enemies have opened their
    mouths
  wide against us.
47We have suffered terror and pitfalls,
  ruin and destruction."
48Streams of tears flow from my eyes
  because my people are destroyed.

49My eyes will flow unceasingly,
  without relief,
50until the LORD looks down
  from heaven and sees.
51What I see brings grief to my soul
  because of all the women of my city.

52Those who were my enemies without
    cause
  hunted me like a bird.
53They tried to end my life in a pit
  and threw stones at me;
54the waters closed over my head,
  and I thought I was about to be cut off.

55I called on your name, O LORD,
  from the depths of the pit.
56You heard my plea: "Do not close your
    ears
  to my cry for relief."
57You came near when I called you,
  and you said, "Do not fear."

58O Lord, you took up my case;
  you redeemed my life.
59You have seen, O LORD, the wrong done to
    me.
  Uphold my cause!
60You have seen the depth of their
    vengeance,
  all their plots against me.

61O LORD, you have heard their insults,
  all their plots against me—
62what my enemies whisper and mutter
  against me all day long.
63Look at them! Sitting or standing,
  they mock me in their songs.

64Pay them back what they deserve, O
    LORD,
  for what their hands have done.
65Put a veil over their hearts,
  and may your curse be on them!
66Pursue them in anger and destroy them
  from under the heavens of the LORD.

4*a* How the gold has lost its lustre,
  the fine gold become dull!
The sacred gems are scattered
  at the head of every street.

2How the precious sons of Zion,
  once worth their weight in gold,
are now considered as pots of clay,
  the work of a potter's hands!

*a*This chapter is an acrostic poem, the verses of which begin with the successive letters of the Hebrew alphabet.

LAMENTATIONS 3:22–27
'Because of the LORD's great love we are not consumed, for his compassions never fail. They are new every morning; great is your faithfulness' (vv. 22, 23).

EVERY NEW DAY is precisely that. God does not come to us with a weakening, time-worn compassion. He does not suffer from 'compassion fatigue'. Every morning bespeaks a new day and a new, fresh, energetic and innovative compassion. To him, each day is one of challenge and opportunity. It is, in fact, a day of grace. Although we may see today much as we see other days, the truth is that it can be, and God means it to be, marvellously different. In his compassion God does not hold our past errors and failings against us. We merit judgement. We receive mercy.

Hugh Redwood was the night editor of a British national daily newspaper. As he was returning home after his night's work the story broke concerning the River Thames overflowing its banks and flooding Westminster. Observing the sensitive yet practical way in which two Salvation Army officers handled the problems of the newly homeless, Redwood devoted his spare time to assisting the work in the slums of London. He visited a very poor home where there were so many needs because of a husband's desertion. To clarify the distraught woman's thinking, he asked, 'What is your greatest need?' She thought a while and replied, 'Shoes for the children.' Redwood was able to supply the need, of course.

It is a question which could help us. What is your greatest need? The compassions of God never fail. They are new every morning. They are new today, and available.

O Lord, grant me the mind to understand that it is your desire to be compassionate to me today. Help me to identify my needs and bring them to you in prayer. Amen.

> *Great is thy faithfulness!*
> *Great is thy faithfulness!*
> *Morning by morning new mercies I see.*

(Thomas O. Chisholm)

→682

EZEKIEL 1:13–21

'This was the appearance . . . a wheel intersecting a wheel . . . all four rims were full of eyes all around . . . Wherever the spirit would go, they would go, and the wheels would rise along with them, because the spirit of the living creatures was in the wheels' (vv. 16, 18b, 20).

'WHEELS WITHIN WHEELS' is a phrase, perhaps not so common these days as it once was, which conveys an atmosphere of something complicated, involved and probably a little underhand. It creates a picture of unseen workings, things happening which people do not wish to bring to the light of day.

The phrase originates from Ezekiel's vision of creatures moving every which way, on wheels which intersect each other. When you try to work out the physical possibility of wheels working in this manner, the mind whirls. Such a system, it seems to me, could not work in practice, though I stand to be corrected by some with more knowledge of mechanics.

But the physical possibility is not our main concern. Drawing pictures, or making models of Ezekiel's creatures is an interesting exercise, but not of great spiritual importance. Our concern is with the reality symbolized by the wheels. The reality is spiritual. Forces which motivated the human spirit can drive it in any direction at any moment. Such spiritual forces can be given over to the direction of God. Or they can be used by Satan. Ezekiel pictures creatures wholly given over to direction by God. They act almost like the arms and legs of God, able to go exactly where the spirit leads them without let or hindrance. They are all-seeing, all-powerful and fully open to God's will.

Ezekiel's visions seek to express the majesty, power and knowledge of God. Six centuries later, God expressed himself in the form of a single, vulnerable individual who was also fully open to his will.

³Even jackals offer their breasts
  to nurse their young,
but my people have become heartless
  like ostriches in the desert.

⁴Because of thirst the infant's tongue
  sticks to the roof of its mouth;
the children beg for bread,
  but no-one gives it to them.

⁵Those who once ate delicacies
  are destitute in the streets.
Those nurtured in purple
  now lie on ash heaps.

⁶The punishment of my people
  is greater than that of Sodom,
which was overthrown in a moment
  without a hand turned to help her.

⁷Their princes were brighter than snow
  and whiter than milk,
their bodies more ruddy than rubies,
  their appearance like sapphires.*b*

⁸But now they are blacker than soot;
  they are not recognised in the streets.
Their skin has shrivelled on their bones;
  it has become as dry as a stick.

⁹Those killed by the sword are better off
  than those who die of famine;
racked with hunger, they waste away
  for lack of food from the field.

¹⁰With their own hands compassionate
    women
  have cooked their own children,
who became their food
  when my people were destroyed.

¹¹The LORD has given full vent to his wrath;
  he has poured out his fierce anger.
He kindled a fire in Zion
  that consumed her foundations.

¹²The kings of the earth did not believe,
  nor did any of the world's people,
that enemies and foes could enter
  the gates of Jerusalem.

¹³But it happened because of the sins of her
    prophets
  and the iniquities of her priests,
who shed within her
  the blood of the righteous.

¹⁴Now they grope through the streets
  like men who are blind.
They are so defiled with blood
  that no-one dares to touch their
    garments.

¹⁵"Go away! You are unclean!" men cry to
    them.
  "Away! Away! Don't touch us!"
When they flee and wander about,
  people among the nations say,
  "They can stay here no longer."

¹⁶The LORD himself has scattered them;
  he no longer watches over them.
The priests are shown no honour,
  the elders no favour.

¹⁷Moreover, our eyes failed,
  looking in vain for help;
from our towers we watched
  for a nation that could not save us.

¹⁸Men stalked us at every step,
  so we could not walk in our streets.
Our end was near, our days were
    numbered,
  for our end had come.

¹⁹Our pursuers were swifter
  than eagles in the sky;
they chased us over the mountains
  and lay in wait for us in the desert.

²⁰The LORD's anointed, our very life breath,
  was caught in their traps.
We thought that under his shadow
  we would live among the nations.

²¹Rejoice and be glad, O Daughter of Edom,
  you who live in the land of Uz.
But to you also the cup will be passed;
  you will be drunk and stripped naked.

²²O Daughter of Zion, your punishment will
    end;
  he will not prolong your exile.
But, O Daughter of Edom, he will punish
    your sin
  and expose your wickedness.

5 Remember, O LORD, what has
    happened to us;
  look, and see our disgrace.
²Our inheritance has been turned over to
    aliens,
  our homes to foreigners.
³We have become orphans and fatherless,
  our mothers like widows.
⁴We must buy the water we drink;
  our wood can be had only at a price.
⁵Those who pursue us are at our heels;
  we are weary and find no rest.
⁶We submitted to Egypt and Assyria
  to get enough bread.
⁷Our fathers sinned and are no more,
  and we bear their punishment.
⁸Slaves rule over us,
  and there is none to free us from their
    hands.
⁹We get our bread at the risk of our lives
  because of the sword in the desert.
¹⁰Our skin is hot as an oven,
  feverish from hunger.
¹¹Women have been ravished in Zion,
  and virgins in the towns of Judah.
¹²Princes have been hung up by their hands;
  elders are shown no respect.
¹³Young men toil at the millstones;
  boys stagger under loads of wood.
¹⁴The elders are gone from the city gate;
  the young men have stopped their
    music.

b7 Or lapis lazuli

¹⁵Joy is gone from our hearts;
　our dancing has turned to
　mourning.
¹⁶The crown has fallen from our head.
　Woe to us, for we have sinned!
¹⁷Because of this our hearts are faint;
　because of these things our eyes grow
　dim
¹⁸for Mount Zion, which lies desolate,
　with jackals prowling over it.

¹⁹You, O Lord, reign for ever;
　your throne endures from generation to
　generation.
²⁰Why do you always forget us?
　Why do you forsake us so long?
²¹Restore us to yourself, O Lord, that we
　may return;
　renew our days as of old
²²unless you have utterly rejected us
　and are angry with us beyond measure.

Ezekiel

The Living Creatures and the Glory of the Lord

1 In the[a] thirtieth year, in the fourth month on the fifth day, while I was among the exiles by the Kebar River, the heavens were opened and I saw visions of God.

²On the fifth of the month—it was the fifth year of the exile of King Jehoiachin—³the word of the Lord came to Ezekiel the priest, the son of Buzi,[b] by the Kebar River in the land of the Babylonians.[c] There the hand of the Lord was upon him.

⁴I looked, and I saw a windstorm coming out of the north—an immense cloud with flashing lightning and surrounded by brilliant light. The centre of the fire looked like glowing metal, ⁵and in the fire was what looked like four living creatures. In appearance their form was that of a man, ⁶but each of them had four faces and four wings. ⁷Their legs were straight; their feet were like those of a calf and gleamed like burnished bronze. ⁸Under their wings on their four sides they had the hands of a man. All four of them had faces and wings, ⁹and their wings touched one another. Each one went straight ahead; they did not turn as they moved.

¹⁰Their faces looked like this: Each of the four had the face of a man, and on the right side each had the face of a lion, and on the left the face of an ox; each also had the face of an eagle. ¹¹Such were their faces. Their wings were spread out upwards; each had two wings, one touching the wing of another creature on either side, and two wings covering its body. ¹²Each one went straight ahead. Wherever the spirit would go, they would go, without turning as they went. ¹³The appearance of the living creatures was like burning coals of fire or like torches. Fire moved back and forth among the creatures; it was bright, and lightning flashed out of it. ¹⁴The creatures sped back and forth like flashes of lightning.

¹⁵As I looked at the living creatures, I saw a wheel on the ground beside each creature with its four faces. ¹⁶This was the appearance and structure of the wheels: They sparkled like chrysolite, and all four looked alike. Each appeared to be made like a wheel intersecting a wheel. ¹⁷As they moved, they would go in any one of the four directions the creatures faced; the wheels did not turn about[d] as the creatures went. ¹⁸Their rims were high and awesome, and all four rims were full of eyes all around.

¹⁹When the living creatures moved, the wheels beside them moved; and when the living creatures rose from the ground, the wheels also rose. ²⁰Wherever the spirit would go, they would go, and the wheels would rise along with them, because the spirit of the living creatures was in the wheels. ²¹When the creatures moved, they also moved; when the creatures stood still, they also stood still; and when the creatures rose from the ground, the wheels rose along with them, because the spirit of the living creatures was in the wheels.

²²Spread out above the heads of the living creatures was what looked like an expanse, sparkling like ice, and awesome. ²³Under the expanse their wings were stretched out towards the other, and each had two wings covering its body. ²⁴When the creatures moved, I heard the sound of their wings, like the roar of rushing waters, like the voice of the Almighty,[e] like the tumult of an army. When they stood still, they lowered their wings.

²⁵Then there came a voice from above the expanse over their heads as they stood with lowered wings. ²⁶Above the expanse over their heads was what looked like a throne of sapphire,[f] and high above on the throne was a figure like that of a man. ²⁷I saw that from what appeared to be his waist up he looked like glowing metal, as if full of fire, and that from there down he looked like fire; and brilliant light surrounded him. ²⁸Like the appearance of a rainbow in the clouds on a rainy day, so was the radiance around him.

This was the appearance of the likeness of the glory of the Lord. When I saw it, I fell face down, and I heard the voice of one speaking.

Ezekiel's Call

2 He said to me, "Son of man, stand up on your feet and I will speak to you." ²As he spoke, the Spirit came into me and raised

---

[a]1 Or ⌐my⌐   [b]3 Or Ezekiel son of Buzi the priest   [c]3 Or Chaldeans   [d]17 Or aside
[e]24 Hebrew Shaddai   [f]26 Or lapis lazuli

me to my feet, and I heard him speaking to me.

³He said: "Son of man, I am sending you to the Israelites, to a rebellious nation that has rebelled against me; they and their fathers have been in revolt against me to this very day. ⁴The people to whom I am sending you are obstinate and stubborn. Say to them, 'This is what the Sovereign LORD says.' ⁵And whether they listen or fail to listen—for they are a rebellious house—they will know that a prophet has been among them. ⁶And you, son of man, do not be afraid of them or their words. Do not be afraid, though briers and thorns are all around you and you live among scorpions. Do not be afraid of what they say or terrified by them, though they are a rebellious house. ⁷You must speak my words to them, whether they listen or fail to listen, for they are rebellious. ⁸But you, son of man, listen to what I say to you. Do not rebel like that rebellious house; open your mouth and eat what I give you."

⁹Then I looked, and I saw a hand stretched out to me. In it was a scroll, ¹⁰which he unrolled before me. On both sides of it were written words of lament and mourning and woe.

3 And he said to me, "Son of man, eat what is before you, eat this scroll; then go and speak to the house of Israel." ²So I opened my mouth, and he gave me the scroll to eat.

³Then he said to me, "Son of man, eat this scroll I am giving you and fill your stomach with it." So I ate it, and it tasted as sweet as honey in my mouth.

⁴He then said to me: "Son of man, go now to the house of Israel and speak my words to them. ⁵You are not being sent to a people of obscure speech and difficult language, but to the house of Israel—⁶not to many peoples of obscure speech and difficult language, whose words you cannot understand. Surely if I had sent you to them, they would have listened to you. ⁷But the house of Israel is not willing to listen to you because they are not willing to listen to me, for the whole house of Israel is hardened and obstinate. ⁸But I will make you as unyielding and hardened as they are. ⁹I will make your forehead like the hardest stone, harder than flint. Do not be afraid of them or terrified by them, though they are a rebellious house."

¹⁰And he said to me, "Son of man, listen carefully and take to heart all the words I speak to you. ¹¹Go now to your countrymen in exile and speak to them. Say to them, 'This is what the Sovereign LORD says,' whether they listen or fail to listen."

¹²Then the Spirit lifted me up, and I heard behind me a loud rumbling sound—May the glory of the LORD be praised in his dwelling-place!—¹³the sound of the wings of the living creatures brushing against each other and the sound of the wheels beside them, a loud rumbling sound. ¹⁴The Spirit then lifted me up and took me away, and I went in bitterness and in the anger of my spirit, with the strong hand of the LORD upon me. ¹⁵I came to the exiles who lived at Tel Abib near the Kebar River. And there, where they were living, I sat among them for seven days—overwhelmed.

Warning to Israel

¹⁶At the end of seven days the word of the LORD came to me. ¹⁷"Son of man, I have made you a watchman for the house of Israel; so hear the word I speak and give them warning from me. ¹⁸When I say to a wicked man, 'You will surely die,' and you do not warn him or speak out to dissuade him from his evil ways in order to save his life, that wicked man will die forᵃ his sin, and I will hold you accountable for his blood. ¹⁹But if you do warn the wicked man and he does not turn from his wickedness or from his evil ways, he will die for his sin; but you will have saved yourself.

²⁰"Again, when a righteous man turns from his righteousness and does evil, and I put a stumbling-block before him, he will die. Since you did not warn him, he will die for his sin. The righteous things he did will not be remembered, and I will hold you accountable for his blood. ²¹But if you do warn the righteous man not to sin and he does not sin, he will surely live because he took warning, and you will have saved yourself."

²²The hand of the LORD was upon me there, and he said to me, "Get up and go out to the plain, and there I will speak to you." ²³So I got up and went out to the plain. And the glory of the LORD was standing there, like the glory I had seen by the Kebar River, and I fell face down.

²⁴Then the Spirit came into me and raised me to my feet. He spoke to me and said: "Go, shut yourself inside your house. ²⁵And you, son of man, they will tie with ropes; you will be bound so that you cannot go out among the people. ²⁶I will make your tongue stick to the roof of your mouth so that you will be silent and unable to rebuke them, though they are a rebellious house. ²⁷But when I speak to you, I will open your mouth and you shall say to them, 'This is what the Sovereign LORD says.' Whoever will listen let him listen, and whoever will refuse let him refuse; for they are a rebellious house.

Siege of Jerusalem Symbolised

4 "Now, son of man, take a clay tablet, put it in front of you and draw the city of Jerusalem on it. ²Then lay siege to it: Erect siege works against it, build a ramp up to it, set up camps against it and put battering-rams around it. ³Then take an iron pan, place it as an iron wall between you and the city and turn your face towards it. It will be under siege, and you shall besiege it. This will be a sign to the house of Israel.

⁴"Then lie on your left side and put the sin of the house of Israel upon yourself.ᵃ You are to bear their sin for the number of days you lie on your side. ⁵I have assigned you the same number of days as the years of their sin.

ᵃ18 Or *in*; also in verses 19 and 20   ᵃ4 Or *your side*

EZEKIEL 3:16–21 (also 33:1–9)
'Son of man, I have made you a watchman for the house of Israel; so hear the word I speak and give them warning from me' (v. 17).

RESPONSIBILITY, claimed mathematician Charles Coulson, is what marks out a man from a machine. He said, nearly thirty years ago,

> There is no difficulty, in principle, in designing a machine that will invent new things, that will learn by its own mistakes, that will even be able to reproduce itself. But no one has suggested that we can design a machine that will consciously exercise responsibility . . . thinking about responsibility is ultimately thinking about what makes us really and truly human.

Ezekiel would agree with Coulson. Over and over again, sometimes one way, sometimes another, Ezekiel emphasizes the supreme importance of human responsibility. Jeremiah before him had said that an old proverb 'The fathers have eaten sour grapes, and the children's teeth are set on edge' would no longer apply. Up to that time people had taken refuge in thinking that their own misfortune, their own misdeeds were somehow related to the misdeeds of their ancestors. 'Instead, (says Jeremiah) everyone will die for his own sin; whoever eats sour grapes – his own teeth will be set on edge'.

Ezekiel, too, quotes this proverb but not until he has made it clear that responsibility means more than just taking care of one's own skin. The 'I'm-all-right-Jack-who-cares-about-you?' type of philosophy has no place in Ezekiel's thinking.

Ezekiel stresses the role of the watchman. His task is to warn of impending danger. If he doesn't, he becomes responsible, not just for his own fate, but also for the fate of his friends. A message repeated in Chapter 33.

True individual responsibility includes responsibility for others.

→688

EZEKIEL 18:1–9, 25–32

'For every living soul belong to me . . . the soul who sins is the one who will die. Suppose there is a righteous man who does what is just and right . . . that man is righteous; he will surely live, declares the Sovereign LORD' (vv. 4, 5a, 9b).

INDIVIDUAL RESPONSIBILITY was not a new idea in Ezekiel's day. It's there in the Ten Commandments. It is implied by the way God deals with individuals throughout the Old Testament. But equally a nagging thought remains that 'visiting the iniquity of the fathers upon the children to the third and fourth generation', might somehow outweigh the need to be careful about one's own actions.

The idea of sins being visited on future generations is meant to be a warning to us, here and now, to take care. Our sins will affect following generations. But how easily a warning becomes an excuse. Instead of taking the warning and thinking, 'I must not fail for my children's sake' we find an excuse to say 'My failure is my forebears' fault.'

Looking at our world today we see good reasons to think like that. How can we unravel the hurt of war previous generations left? How can we live at peace with those who killed our fathers, mothers, our brothers, sisters and cousins? Aren't their sins visited on us, leaving a trail of bitterness and recrimination which fate decrees that we follow?

No, says Ezekiel. Look to your own actions. Forget past failures. They need not weigh you down. Think of present and future. They are not decreed by fate, but created by your actions. If you are righteous, you will live. If you sin, you will die. Such statements are true – against a backcloth of eternity.

Individual responsibility means we are no longer at the mercy of blind fate, for we can 'get ourselves a new heart and a new spirit'.

→713

So for 390 days you will bear the sin of the house of Israel.

6"After you have finished this, lie down again, this time on your right side, and bear the sin of the house of Judah. I have assigned you 40 days, a day for each year. 7Turn your face towards the siege of Jerusalem and with bared arm prophesy against her. 8I will tie you up with ropes so that you cannot turn from one side to the other until you have finished the days of your siege.

9"Take wheat and barley, beans and lentils, millet and spelt; put them in a storage jar and use them to make bread for yourself. You are to eat it during the 390 days you lie on your side. 10Weigh out twenty shekels*b* of food to eat each day and eat it at set times. 11Also measure out a sixth of a hin*c* of water and drink it at set times. 12Eat the food as you would a barley cake; bake it in the sight of the people, using human excrement for fuel." 13The LORD said, "In this way the people of Israel will eat defiled food among the nations where I will drive them."

14Then I said, "Not so, Sovereign LORD! I have never defiled myself. From my youth until now I have never eaten anything found dead or torn by wild animals. No unclean meat has ever entered my mouth."

15"Very well," he said, "I will let you bake your bread over cow manure instead of human excrement."

16He then said to me: "Son of man, I will cut off the supply of food in Jerusalem. The people will eat rationed food in anxiety and drink rationed water in despair, 17for food and water will be scarce. They will be appalled at the sight of each other and will waste away because of*d* their sin.

5 "Now, son of man, take a sharp sword and use it as a barber's razor to shave your head and your beard. Then take a set of scales and divide up the hair. 2When the days of your siege come to an end, burn a third of the hair with fire inside the city. Take a third and strike it with the sword all around the city. And scatter a third to the wind. For I will pursue them with drawn sword. 3But take a few strands of hair and tuck them away in the folds of your garment. 4Again, take a few of these and throw them into the fire and burn them up. A fire will spread from there to the whole house of Israel.

5"This is what the Sovereign LORD says: This is Jerusalem, which I have set in the centre of the nations, with countries all around her. 6Yet in her wickedness she has rebelled against my laws and decrees more than the nations and countries around her. She has rejected my laws and has not followed my decrees.

7"Therefore this is what the Sovereign LORD says: You have been more unruly than the nations around you and have not followed my decrees or kept my laws. You have not even*a* conformed to the standards of the nations around you.

8"Therefore this is what the Sovereign LORD says: I myself am against you, Jerusalem, and I will inflict punishment on you in the sight of the nations. 9Because of all your detestable idols, I will do to you what I have never done before and will never do again. 10Therefore in your midst fathers will eat their children, and children will eat their fathers. I will inflict punishment on you and will scatter all your survivors to the winds. 11Therefore as surely as I live, declares the Sovereign LORD, because you have defiled my sanctuary with all your vile images and detestable practices, I myself will withdraw my favour; I will not look on you with pity or spare you. 12A third of your people will die of the plague or perish by famine inside you; a third will fall by the sword outside your walls; and a third I will scatter to the winds and pursue with drawn sword.

13"Then my anger will cease and my wrath against them will subside, and I will be avenged. And when I have spent my wrath upon them, they will know that I the LORD have spoken in my zeal.

14"I will make you a ruin and a reproach among the nations around you, in the sight of all who pass by. 15You will be a reproach and a taunt, a warning and an object of horror to the nations around you when I inflict punishment on you in anger and in wrath and with stinging rebuke. I the LORD have spoken. 16When I shoot at you with my deadly and destructive arrows of famine, I will shoot to destroy you. I will bring more and more famine upon you and cut off your supply of food. 17I will send famine and wild beasts against you, and they will leave you childless. Plague and bloodshed will sweep through you, and I will bring the sword against you. I the LORD have spoken."

A Prophecy Against the Mountains of Israel

6 The word of the LORD came to me: 2"Son of man, set your face against the mountains of Israel; prophesy against them 3and say: 'O mountains of Israel, hear the word of the Sovereign LORD. This is what the Sovereign LORD says to the mountains and hills, to the ravines and valleys: I am about to bring a sword against you, and I will destroy your high places. 4Your altars will be demolished and your incense altars will be smashed; and I will slay your people in front of your idols. 5I will lay the dead bodies of the Israelites in front of their idols, and I will scatter your bones around your altars. 6Wherever you live, the towns will be laid waste and the high places demolished, so that your altars will be laid waste and devastated, your idols smashed and ruined, your incense altars broken down, and what you have made wiped out. 7Your people will fall slain among you, and you will know that I am the LORD.

8"'But I will spare some, for some of you will escape the sword when you are scattered among the lands and nations. 9Then in the

b10 That is, about 8 ounces (about 0.2 kilogram)   *c11* That is, about 1 pint (about 0.6 litre)
d17 Or *away in*   *a7* Most Hebrew manuscripts; some Hebrew manuscripts and Syriac *You have*

nations where they have been carried captive, those who escape will remember me —how I have been grieved by their adulterous hearts, which have turned away from me, and by their eyes, which have lusted after their idols. They will loathe themselves for the evil they have done and for all their detestable practices. ¹⁰And they will know that I am the LORD; I did not threaten in vain to bring this calamity on them.

¹¹"'This is what the Sovereign LORD says: Strike your hands together and stamp your feet and cry out "Alas!" because of all the wicked and detestable practices of the house of Israel, for they will fall by the sword, famine and plague. ¹²He that is far away will die of the plague, and he that is near will fall by the sword, and he that survives and is spared will die of famine. So will I spend my wrath upon them. ¹³And they will know that I am the LORD, when their people lie slain among their idols around their altars, on every high hill and on all the mountaintops, under every spreading tree and every leafy oak—places where they offered fragrant incense to all their idols. ¹⁴And I will stretch out my hand against them and make the land a desolate waste from the desert to Diblah[a] —wherever they live. Then they will know that I am the LORD.'"

The End Has Come

7 The word of the LORD came to me: ²"Son of man, this is what the Sovereign LORD says to the land of Israel: The end! The end has come upon the four corners of the land. ³The end is now upon you and I will unleash my anger against you. I will judge you according to your conduct and repay you for all your detestable practices. ⁴I will not look on you with pity or spare you; I will surely repay you for your conduct and the detestable practices among you. Then you will know that I am the LORD.

⁵"This is what the Sovereign LORD says: Disaster! An unheard-of[a] disaster is coming. ⁶The end has come! The end has come! It has roused itself against you. It has come! ⁷Doom has come upon you—you who dwell in the land. The time has come, the day is near; there is panic, not joy, upon the mountains. ⁸I am about to pour out my wrath on you and spend my anger against you; I will judge you according to your conduct and repay you for all your detestable practices. ⁹I will not look on you with pity or spare you; I will repay you in accordance with your conduct and the detestable practices among you. Then you will know that it is I the LORD who strikes the blow.

¹⁰"The day is here! It has come! Doom has burst forth, the rod has budded, arrogance has blossomed! ¹¹Violence has grown into[b] a rod to punish wickedness; none of the people will be left, none of that crowd—no wealth, nothing of value. ¹²The time has come, the day has arrived. Let not the buyer rejoice nor the seller grieve, for wrath is upon the whole crowd. ¹³The seller will not recover the land he has sold as long as both of them live, for the vision concerning the whole crowd will not be reversed. Because of their sins, not one of them will preserve his life. ¹⁴Though they blow the trumpet and get everything ready, no-one will go into battle, for my wrath is upon the whole crowd.

¹⁵"Outside is the sword, inside are plague and famine; those in the country will die by the sword, and those in the city will be devoured by famine and plague. ¹⁶All who survive and escape will be in the mountains, moaning like doves of the valleys, each because of his sins. ¹⁷Every hand will go limp, and every knee will become as weak as water. ¹⁸They will put on sackcloth and be clothed with terror. Their faces will be covered with shame and their heads will be shaved. ¹⁹They will throw their silver into the streets, and their gold will be an unclean thing. Their silver and gold will not be able to save them in the day of the LORD's wrath. They will not satisfy their hunger or fill their stomachs with it, for it has made them stumble into sin. ²⁰They were proud of their beautiful jewellery and used it to make their detestable idols and vile images. Therefore I will turn these into an unclean thing for them. ²¹I will hand it all over as plunder to foreigners and as loot to the wicked of the earth, and they will defile it. ²²I will turn my face away from them, and they will desecrate my treasured place; robbers will enter it and desecrate it.

²³"Prepare chains, because the land is full of bloodshed and the city is full of violence. ²⁴I will bring the most wicked of the nations to take possession of their houses; I will put an end to the pride of the mighty, and their sanctuaries will be desecrated. ²⁵When terror comes, they will seek peace, but there will be none. ²⁶Calamity upon calamity will come, and rumour upon rumour. They will try to get a vision from the prophet; the teaching of the law by the priest will be lost, as will the counsel of the elders. ²⁷The king will mourn, the prince will be clothed with despair, and the hands of the people of the land will tremble. I will deal with them according to their conduct, and by their own standards I will judge them. Then they will know that I am the LORD."

Idolatry in the Temple

8 In the sixth year, in the sixth month on the fifth day, while I was sitting in my house and the elders of Judah were sitting before me, the hand of the Sovereign LORD came upon me there. ²I looked, and I saw a figure like that of a man.[a] From what appeared to be his waist down he was like fire, and from there up his appearance was as bright as glowing metal. ³He stretched out what looked like a hand and took me by the hair of my head. The Spirit lifted me up

---

[a]14 Most Hebrew manuscripts; a few Hebrew manuscripts *Riblah*
[a]5 Most Hebrew manuscripts; some Hebrew manuscripts and Syriac *Disaster after*
[b]11 Or *The violent one has become*　　[a]2 Or *saw a fiery figure*

between earth and heaven and in visions of God he took me to Jerusalem, to the entrance to the north gate of the inner court, where the idol that provokes to jealousy stood. ⁴And there before me was the glory of the God of Israel, as in the vision I had seen in the plain.

⁵Then he said to me, "Son of man, look towards the north." So I looked, and in the entrance north of the gate of the altar I saw this idol of jealousy.

⁶And he said to me, "Son of man, do you see what they are doing—the utterly detestable things the house of Israel is doing here, things that will drive me far from my sanctuary? But you will see things that are even more detestable."

⁷Then he brought me to the entrance to the court. I looked, and I saw a hole in the wall. ⁸He said to me, "Son of man, now dig into the wall." So I dug into the wall and saw a doorway there.

⁹And he said to me, "Go in and see the wicked and detestable things they are doing here." ¹⁰So I went in and looked, and I saw portrayed all over the walls all kinds of crawling things and detestable animals and all the idols of the house of Israel. ¹¹In front of them stood seventy elders of the house of Israel, and Jaazaniah son of Shaphan was standing among them. Each had a censer in his hand, and a fragrant cloud of incense was rising.

¹²He said to me, "Son of man, have you seen what the elders of the house of Israel are doing in the darkness, each at the shrine of his own idol? They say, 'The Lᴏʀᴅ does not see us; the Lᴏʀᴅ has forsaken the land.'" ¹³Again, he said, "You will see them doing things that are even more detestable."

¹⁴Then he brought me to the entrance to the north gate of the house of the Lᴏʀᴅ, and I saw women sitting there, mourning for Tammuz. ¹⁵He said to me, "Do you see this, son of man? You will see things that are even more detestable than this."

¹⁶He then brought me into the inner court of the house of the Lᴏʀᴅ, and there at the entrance to the temple, between the portico and the altar, were about twenty-five men. With their backs towards the temple of the Lᴏʀᴅ and their faces towards the east, they were bowing down to the sun in the east.

¹⁷He said to me, "Have you seen this, son of man? Is it a trivial matter for the house of Judah to do the detestable things they are doing here? Must they also fill the land with violence and continually provoke me to anger? Look at them putting the branch to their nose! ¹⁸Therefore I will deal with them in anger; I will not look on them with pity or spare them. Although they shout in my ears, I will not listen to them."

Idolaters Killed

9 Then I heard him call out in a loud voice, "Bring the guards of the city here, each with a weapon in his hand." ²And I saw six men coming from the direction of the upper gate, which faces north, each with a deadly weapon in his hand. With them was a man

clothed in linen who had a writing kit at his side. They came in and stood beside the bronze altar.

³Now the glory of the God of Israel went up from above the cherubim, where it had been, and moved to the threshold of the temple. Then the Lᴏʀᴅ called to the man clothed in linen who had the writing kit at his side ⁴and said to him, "Go throughout the city of Jerusalem and put a mark on the foreheads of those who grieve and lament over all the detestable things that are done in it."

⁵As I listened, he said to the others, "Follow him through the city and kill, without showing pity or compassion. ⁶Slaughter old men, young men and maidens, women and children, but do not touch anyone who has the mark. Begin at my sanctuary." So they began with the elders who were in front of the temple.

⁷Then he said to them, "Defile the temple and fill the courts with the slain. Go!" So they went out and began killing throughout the city. ⁸While they were killing and I was left alone, I fell face down, crying out, "Ah, Sovereign Lᴏʀᴅ! Are you going to destroy the entire remnant of Israel in this outpouring of your wrath on Jerusalem?"

⁹He answered me, "The sin of the house of Israel and Judah is exceedingly great; the land is full of bloodshed and the city is full of injustice. They say, 'The Lᴏʀᴅ has forsaken the land; the Lᴏʀᴅ does not see.' ¹⁰So I will not look on them with pity or spare them, but I will bring down on their own heads what they have done."

¹¹Then the man in linen with the writing kit at his side brought back word, saying, "I have done as you commanded."

The Glory Departs From the Temple

10 I looked, and I saw the likeness of a throne of sapphire[a] above the expanse that was over the heads of the cherubim. ²The Lᴏʀᴅ said to the man clothed in linen, "Go in among the wheels beneath the cherubim. Fill your hands with burning coals from among the cherubim and scatter them over the city." And as I watched, he went in.

³Now the cherubim were standing on the south side of the temple when the man went in, and a cloud filled the inner court. ⁴Then the glory of the Lᴏʀᴅ rose from above the cherubim and moved to the threshold of the temple. The cloud filled the temple, and the court was full of the radiance of the glory of the Lᴏʀᴅ. ⁵The sound of the wings of the cherubim could be heard as far away as the outer court, like the voice of God Almighty[b] when he speaks.

⁶When the Lᴏʀᴅ commanded the man in linen, "Take fire from among the wheels, from among the cherubim," the man went in and stood beside a wheel. ⁷Then one of the cherubim reached out his hand to the fire that was among them. He took up some of it and put it into the hands of the man in linen, who took it and went out. ⁸(Under the wings of the

cherubim could be seen what looked like the hands of a man.)

⁹I looked, and I saw beside the cherubim four wheels, one beside each of the cherubim; the wheels sparkled like chrysolite. ¹⁰As for their appearance, the four of them looked alike; each was like a wheel intersecting a wheel. ¹¹As they moved, they would go in any one of the four directions the cherubim faced; the wheels did not turn about[c] as the cherubim went. The cherubim went in whatever direction the head faced, without turning as they went. ¹²Their entire bodies, including their backs, their hands and their wings, were completely full of eyes, as were their four wheels. ¹³I heard the wheels being called "the whirling wheels". ¹⁴Each of the cherubim had four faces: One face was that of a cherub, the second the face of a man, the third the face of a lion, and the fourth the face of an eagle.

¹⁵Then the cherubim rose upwards. These were the living creatures I had seen by the Kebar River. ¹⁶When the cherubim moved, the wheels beside them moved; and when the cherubim spread their wings to rise from the ground, the wheels did not leave their side. ¹⁷When the cherubim stood still, they also stood still; and when the cherubim rose, they rose with them, because the spirit of the living creatures was in them.

¹⁸Then the glory of the LORD departed from over the threshold of the temple and stopped above the cherubim. ¹⁹While I watched, the cherubim spread their wings and rose from the ground, and as they went, the wheels went with them. They stopped at the entrance to the east gate of the LORD's house, and the glory of the God of Israel was above them.

²⁰These were the living creatures I had seen beneath the God of Israel by the Kebar River, and I realised that they were cherubim. ²¹Each had four faces and four wings, and under their wings were what looked like the hands of a man. ²²Their faces had the same appearance as those I had seen by the Kebar River. Each one went straight ahead.

Judgment on Israel's Leaders

11 Then the Spirit lifted me up and brought me to the gate of the house of the LORD that faces east. There at the entrance to the gate were twenty-five men, and I saw among them Jaazaniah son of Azzur and Pelatiah son of Benaiah, leaders of the people. ²The LORD said to me, "Son of man, these are the men who are plotting evil and giving wicked advice in this city. ³They say, 'Will it not soon be time to build houses?[a] This city is a cooking pot, and we are the meat.' ⁴Therefore prophesy against them; prophesy, son of man."

⁵Then the Spirit of the LORD came upon me, and he told me to say: "This is what the LORD says: That is what you are saying, O house of Israel, but I know what is going

through your mind. ⁶You have killed many people in this city and filled its streets with the dead.

⁷"Therefore this is what the Sovereign LORD says: The bodies you have thrown there are the meat and this city is the pot, but I will drive you out of it. ⁸You fear the sword, and the sword is what I will bring against you, declares the Sovereign LORD. ⁹I will drive you out of the city and hand you over to foreigners and inflict punishment on you. ¹⁰You will fall by the sword, and I will execute judgment on you at the borders of Israel. Then you will know that I am the LORD. ¹¹This city will not be a pot for you, nor will you be the meat in it; I will execute judgment on you at the borders of Israel. ¹²And you will know that I am the LORD, for you have not followed my decrees or kept my laws but have conformed to the standards of the nations around you."

¹³Now as I was prophesying, Pelatiah son of Benaiah died. Then I fell face down and cried out in a loud voice, "Ah, Sovereign LORD! Will you completely destroy the remnant of Israel?"

¹⁴The word of the LORD came to me: ¹⁵"Son of man, your brothers—your brothers who are your blood-relatives[b] and the whole house of Israel—are those of whom the people of Jerusalem have said, 'They are[c] far away from the LORD; this land was given to us as our possession.'

Promised Return of Israel

¹⁶"Therefore say: 'This is what the Sovereign LORD says: Although I sent them far away among the nations and scattered them among the countries, yet for a little while I have been a sanctuary for them in the countries where they have gone.'

¹⁷"Therefore say: 'This is what the Sovereign LORD says: I will gather you from the nations and bring you back from the countries where you have been scattered, and I will give you back the land of Israel again.'

¹⁸"They will return to it and remove all its vile images and detestable idols. ¹⁹I will give them an undivided heart and put a new spirit in them; I will remove from them their heart of stone and give them a heart of flesh. ²⁰Then they will follow my decrees and be careful to keep my laws. They will be my people, and I will be their God. ²¹But as for those whose hearts are devoted to their vile images and detestable idols, I will bring down on their own heads what they have done, declares the Sovereign LORD."

²²Then the cherubim, with the wheels beside them, spread their wings, and the glory of the God of Israel was above them. ²³The glory of the LORD went up from within the city and stopped above the mountain east of it. ²⁴The Spirit lifted me up and brought me to the exiles in Babylonia[d] in the vision given by the Spirit of God.

---

[c]11 Or aside   [a]3 Or This is not the time to build houses.
[b]15 Or are in exile with you (see Septuagint and Syriac)
[c]15 Or those to whom the people of Jerusalem have said, 'Stay   [d]24 Or Chaldea

Then the vision I had seen went up from me, ²⁵and I told the exiles everything the LORD had shown me.

The Exile Symbolised

12 The word of the LORD came to me: ²"Son of man, you are living among a rebellious people. They have eyes to see but do not see and ears to hear but do not hear, for they are a rebellious people.

³"Therefore, son of man, pack your belongings for exile and in the daytime, as they watch, set out and go from where you are to another place. Perhaps they will understand, though they are a rebellious house. ⁴During the daytime, while they watch, bring out your belongings packed for exile. Then in the evening, while they are watching, go out like those who go into exile. ⁵While they watch, dig through the wall and take your belongings out through it. ⁶Put them on your shoulder as they are watching and carry them out at dusk. Cover your face so that you cannot see the land, for I have made you a sign to the house of Israel."

⁷So I did as I was commanded. During the day I brought out my things packed for exile. Then in the evening I dug through the wall with my hands. I took my belongings out at dusk, carrying them on my shoulders while they watched.

⁸In the morning the word of the LORD came to me: ⁹"Son of man, did not that rebellious house of Israel ask you, 'What are you doing?'

¹⁰"Say to them, 'This is what the Sovereign LORD says: This oracle concerns the prince in Jerusalem and the whole house of Israel who are there.' ¹¹Say to them, 'I am a sign to you.'

"As I have done, so it will be done to them. They will go into exile as captives.

¹²"The prince among them will put his things on his shoulder at dusk and leave, and a hole will be dug in the wall for him to go through. He will cover his face so that he cannot see the land. ¹³I will spread my net for him, and he will be caught in my snare; I will bring him to Babylonia, the land of the Chaldeans, but he will not see it, and there he will die. ¹⁴I will scatter to the winds all those around him—his staff and all his troops—and I will pursue them with drawn sword.

¹⁵"They will know that I am the LORD, when I disperse them among the nations and scatter them through the countries. ¹⁶But I will spare a few of them from the sword, famine and plague, so that in the nations where they go they may acknowledge all their detestable practices. Then they will know that I am the LORD."

¹⁷The word of the LORD came to me: ¹⁸"Son of man, tremble as you eat your food, and shudder in fear as you drink your water. ¹⁹Say to the people of the land: 'This is what the Sovereign LORD says about those living in Jerusalem and in the land of Israel: They will eat their food in anxiety and drink their water in despair, for their land will be stripped of everything in it because of the violence of all who live there. ²⁰The inhabited towns will be laid waste and the land will be desolate. Then you will know that I am the LORD.'"

²¹The word of the LORD came to me: ²²"Son of man, what is this proverb you have in the land of Israel: 'The days go by and every vision comes to nothing'? ²³Say to them, 'This is what the Sovereign LORD says: I am going to put an end to this proverb, and they will no longer quote it in Israel.' Say to them, 'The days are near when every vision will be fulfilled. ²⁴For there will be no more false visions or flattering divinations among the people of Israel. ²⁵But I the LORD will speak what I will, and it shall be fulfilled without delay. For in your days, you rebellious house, I will fulfil whatever I say, declares the Sovereign LORD.'"

²⁶The word of the LORD came to me: ²⁷"Son of man, the house of Israel is saying, 'The vision he sees is for many years from now, and he prophesies about the distant future.'

²⁸"Therefore say to them, 'This is what the Sovereign LORD says: None of my words will be delayed any longer; whatever I say will be fulfilled, declares the Sovereign LORD.'"

False Prophets Condemned

13 The word of the LORD came to me: ²"Son of man, prophesy against the prophets of Israel who are now prophesying. Say to those who prophesy out of their own imagination: 'Hear the word of the LORD! ³This is what the Sovereign LORD says: Woe to the foolish[a] prophets who follow their own spirit and have seen nothing! ⁴Your prophets, O Israel, are like jackals among ruins. ⁵You have not gone up to the breaks in the wall to repair it for the house of Israel so that it will stand firm in the battle on the day of the LORD. ⁶Their visions are false and their divinations a lie. They say, "The LORD declares", when the LORD has not sent them; yet they expect their words to be fulfilled. ⁷Have you not seen false visions and uttered lying divinations when you say, "The LORD declares", though I have not spoken?

⁸"'Therefore this is what the Sovereign LORD says: Because of your false words and lying visions, I am against you, declares the Sovereign LORD. ⁹My hand will be against the prophets who see false visions and utter lying divinations. They will not belong to the council of my people or be listed in the records of the house of Israel, nor will they enter the land of Israel. Then you will know that I am the Sovereign LORD.

¹⁰"'Because they lead my people astray, saying, "Peace", when there is no peace, and because, when a flimsy wall is built, they cover it with whitewash, ¹¹therefore tell those who cover it with whitewash that it is going to fall. Rain will come in torrents, and I will send hailstones hurtling down, and violent winds will burst forth. ¹²When the wall collapses, will people not ask you, "Where is the whitewash you covered it with?"

---

^a3 Or *wicked*

13"'Therefore this is what the Sovereign LORD says: In my wrath I will unleash a violent wind, and in my anger hailstones and torrents of rain will fall with destructive fury. 14I will tear down the wall you have covered with whitewash and will level it to the ground so that its foundation will be laid bare. When it*b* falls, you will be destroyed in it; and you will know that I am the LORD. 15So I will spend my wrath against the wall and against those who covered it with whitewash. I will say to you, "The wall is gone and so are those who whitewashed it, 16those prophets of Israel who prophesied to Jerusalem and saw visions of peace for her when there was no peace, declares the Sovereign LORD."'

17"'Now, son of man, set your face against the daughters of your people who prophesy out of their own imagination. Prophesy against them 18and say, 'This is what the Sovereign LORD says: Woe to the women who sew magic charms on all their wrists and make veils of various lengths for their heads in order to ensnare people. Will you ensnare the lives of my people but preserve your own? 19You have profaned me among my people for a few handfuls of barley and scraps of bread. By lying to my people, who listen to lies, you have killed those who should not have died and have spared those who should not live.

20"'Therefore this is what the Sovereign LORD says: I am against your magic charms with which you ensnare people like birds and I will tear them from your arms; I will set free the people that you ensnare like birds. 21I will tear off your veils and save my people from your hands, and they will no longer fall prey to your power. Then you will know that I am the LORD. 22Because you disheartened the righteous with your lies, when I had brought them no grief, and because you encouraged the wicked not to turn from their evil ways and so save their lives, 23therefore you will no longer see false visions or practise divination. I will save my people from your hands. And then you will know that I am the LORD.'"

Idolaters Condemned

14 Some of the elders of Israel came to me and sat down in front of me. 2Then the word of the LORD came to me: 3"Son of man, these men have set up idols in their hearts and put wicked stumbling-blocks before their faces. Should I let them enquire of me at all? 4Therefore speak to them and tell them, 'This is what the Sovereign LORD says: When any Israelite sets up idols in his heart and puts a wicked stumbling-block before his face and then goes to a prophet, I the LORD will answer him myself in keeping with his great idolatry. 5I will do this to recapture the hearts of the people of Israel, who have all deserted me for their idols.'

6"Therefore say to the house of Israel, 'This is what the Sovereign LORD says:

Repent! Turn from your idols and renounce all your detestable practices!

7"'When any Israelite or any alien living in Israel separates himself from me and sets up idols in his heart and puts a wicked stumbling-block before his face and then goes to a prophet to enquire of me, I the LORD will answer him myself. 8I will set my face against that man and make him an example and a byword. I will cut him off from my people. Then you will know that I am the LORD.

9"'And if the prophet is enticed to utter a prophecy, I the LORD have enticed that prophet, and I will stretch out my hand against him and destroy him from among my people Israel. 10They will bear their guilt —the prophet will be as guilty as the one who consults him. 11Then the people of Israel will no longer stray from me, nor will they defile themselves any more with all their sins. They will be my people, and I will be their God, declares the Sovereign LORD.'"

Judgment Inescapable

12The word of the LORD came to me: 13"Son of man, if a country sins against me by being unfaithful and I stretch out my hand against it to cut off its food supply and send famine upon it and kill its men and their animals, 14even if these three men—Noah, Daniel*a* and Job—were in it, they could save only themselves by their righteousness, declares the Sovereign LORD.

15"Or if I send wild beasts through that country and they leave it childless and it becomes desolate so that no-one can pass through it because of the beasts, 16as surely as I live, declares the Sovereign LORD, even if these three men were in it, they could not save their own sons or daughters. They alone would be saved, but the land would be desolate.

17"Or if I bring a sword against that country and say, 'Let the sword pass throughout the land,' and I kill its men and their animals, 18as surely as I live, declares the Sovereign LORD, even if these three men were in it, they could not save their own sons or daughters. They alone would be saved.

19"Or if I send a plague into that land and pour out my wrath upon it through bloodshed, killing its men and their animals, 20as surely as I live, declares the Sovereign LORD, even if Noah, Daniel and Job were in it, they could save neither son nor daughter. They would save only themselves by their righteousness.

21"For this is what the Sovereign LORD says: How much worse will it be when I send against Jerusalem my four dreadful judgments—sword and famine and wild beasts and plague—to kill its men and their animals! 22Yet there will be some survivors—sons and daughters who will be brought out of it. They will come to you, and when you see their conduct and their actions, you will be consoled regarding the disaster I have brought upon Jerusalem—every disaster I have

---

*b*14 Or *the city*
*a*14 Or *Danel*; the Hebrew spelling may suggest a person other than the prophet Daniel; also in verse 20.

brought upon it. [23]You will be consoled when you see their conduct and their actions, for you will know that I have done nothing in it without cause, declares the Sovereign LORD.''

Jerusalem, a Useless Vine

15 The word of the LORD came to me: [2]''Son of man, how is the wood of a vine better than that of a branch on any of the trees in the forest? [3]Is wood ever taken from it to make anything useful? Do they make pegs from it to hang things on? [4]And after it is thrown on the fire as fuel and the fire burns both ends and chars the middle, is it then useful for anything? [5]If it was not useful for anything when it was whole, how much less can it be made into something useful when the fire has burned it and it is charred?

[6]''Therefore this is what the Sovereign LORD says: As I have given the wood of the vine among the trees of the forest as fuel for the fire, so will I treat the people living in Jerusalem. [7]I will set my face against them. Although they have come out of the fire, the fire will yet consume them. And when I set my face against them, you will know that I am the LORD. [8]I will make the land desolate because they have been unfaithful, declares the Sovereign LORD.''

An Allegory of Unfaithful Jerusalem

16 The word of the LORD came to me: [2]''Son of man, confront Jerusalem with her detestable practices [3]and say, 'This is what the Sovereign LORD says to Jerusalem: Your ancestry and birth were in the land of the Canaanites; your father was an Amorite and your mother a Hittite. [4]On the day you were born your cord was not cut, nor were you washed with water to make you clean, nor were you rubbed with salt or wrapped in cloths. [5]No-one looked on you with pity or had compassion enough to do any of these things for you. Rather, you were thrown out into the open field, for on the day you were born you were despised.

[6]''Then I passed by and saw you kicking about in your blood, and as you lay there in your blood I said to you, ''Live!''[a] [7]I made you grow like a plant of the field. You grew up and developed and became the most beautiful of jewels.[b] Your breasts were formed and your hair grew, you who were naked and bare.

[8]''Later I passed by, and when I looked at you and saw that you were old enough for love, I spread the corner of my garment over you and covered your nakedness. I gave you my solemn oath and entered into a covenant with you, declares the Sovereign LORD, and you became mine.

[9]''I bathed[c] you with water and washed the blood from you and put ointments on you. [10]I clothed you with an embroidered dress and put leather sandals on you. I dressed you in fine linen and covered you

with costly garments. [11]I adorned you with jewellery: I put bracelets on your arms and a necklace around your neck, [12]and I put a ring on your nose, ear-rings on your ears and a beautiful crown on your head. [13]So you were adorned with gold and silver; your clothes were of fine linen and costly fabric and embroidered cloth. Your food was fine flour, honey and olive oil. You became very beautiful and rose to be a queen. [14]And your fame spread among the nations on account of your beauty, because the splendour I had given you made your beauty perfect, declares the Sovereign LORD.

[15]''But you trusted in your beauty and used your fame to become a prostitute. You lavished your favours on anyone who passed by and your beauty became his.[d] [16]You took some of your garments to make gaudy high places, where you carried on your prostitution. Such things should not happen, nor should they ever occur. [17]You also took the fine jewellery I gave you, the jewellery made of my gold and silver, and you made for yourself male idols and engaged in prostitution with them. [18]And you took your embroidered clothes to put on them, and you offered my oil and incense before them. [19]Also the food I provided for you—the fine flour, olive oil and honey I gave you to eat —you offered as fragrant incense before them. That is what happened, declares the Sovereign LORD.

[20]''And you took your sons and daughters whom you bore to me and sacrificed them as food to the idols. Was your prostitution not enough? [21]You slaughtered my children and sacrificed them[e] to the idols. [22]In all your detestable practices and your prostitution you did not remember the days of your youth, when you were naked and bare, kicking about in your blood.

[23]''Woe! Woe to you, declares the Sovereign LORD. In addition to all your other wickedness, [24]you built a mound for yourself and made a lofty shrine in every public square. [25]At the head of every street you built your lofty shrines and degraded your beauty, offering your body with increasing promiscuity to anyone who passed by. [26]You engaged in prostitution with the Egyptians, your lustful neighbours, and provoked me to anger with your increasing promiscuity. [27]So I stretched out my hand against you and reduced your territory; I gave you over to the greed of your enemies, the daughters of the Philistines, who were shocked by your lewd conduct. [28]You engaged in prostitution with the Assyrians too, because you were insatiable; and even after that, you still were not satisfied. [29]Then you increased your promiscuity to include Babylonia,[f] a land of merchants, but even with this you were not satisfied.

[30]''How weak-willed you are, declares the Sovereign LORD, when you do all these things, acting like a brazen prostitute!

---

[a]6 A few Hebrew manuscripts, Septuagint and Syriac; most Hebrew manuscripts ''Live!'' And as you lay there in your blood I said to you, ''Live!''   [b]7 Or became mature   [c]9 Or I had bathed [d]15 Most Hebrew manuscripts; one Hebrew manuscript (see some Septuagint manuscripts) by. Such a thing should not happen   [e]21 Or and made them pass through ⌊the fire⌋   [f]29 Or Chaldea

³¹When you built your mounds at the head of every street and made your lofty shrines in every public square, you were unlike a prostitute, because you scorned payment.

³²"You adulterous wife! You prefer strangers to your own husband! ³³Every prostitute receives a fee, but you give gifts to all your lovers, bribing them to come to you from everywhere for your illicit favours. ³⁴So in your prostitution you are the opposite of others; no-one runs after you for your favours. You are the very opposite, for you give payment and none is given to you.

³⁵"Therefore, you prostitute, hear the word of the LORD! ³⁶This is what the Sovereign LORD says: Because you poured out your wealth^g and exposed your nakedness in your promiscuity with your lovers, and because of all your detestable idols, and because you gave them your children's blood, ³⁷therefore I am going to gather all your lovers, with whom you found pleasure, those you loved as well as those you hated. I will gather them against you from all around and will strip you in front of them, and they will see all your nakedness. ³⁸I will sentence you to the punishment of women who commit adultery and who shed blood; I will bring upon you the blood vengeance of my wrath and jealous anger. ³⁹Then I will hand you over to your lovers, and they will tear down your mounds and destroy your lofty shrines. They will strip you of your clothes and take your fine jewellery and leave you naked and bare. ⁴⁰They will bring a mob against you, who will stone you and hack you to pieces with their swords. ⁴¹They will burn down your houses and inflict punishment on you in the sight of many women. I will put a stop to your prostitution, and you will no longer pay your lovers. ⁴²Then my wrath against you will subside and my jealous anger will turn away from you; I will be calm and no longer angry.

⁴³"Because you did not remember the days of your youth but enraged me with all these things, I will surely bring down on your head what you have done, declares the Sovereign LORD. Did you not add lewdness to all your other detestable practices?

⁴⁴"Everyone who quotes proverbs will quote this proverb about you: "Like mother, like daughter." ⁴⁵You are a true daughter of your mother, who despised her husband and her children; and you are a true sister of your sisters, who despised their husbands and their children. Your mother was a Hittite and your father an Amorite. ⁴⁶Your older sister was Samaria, who lived to the north of you with her daughters; and your younger sister, who lived to the south of you with her daughters, was Sodom. ⁴⁷You not only walked in their ways and copied their detestable practices, but in all your ways you soon became more depraved than they. ⁴⁸As surely as I live, declares the Sovereign LORD, your sister Sodom and her daughters never did what you and your daughters have done.

⁴⁹"Now this was the sin of your sister Sodom: She and her daughters were arrogant, overfed and unconcerned; they did not help the poor and needy. ⁵⁰They were haughty and did detestable things before me. Therefore I did away with them as you have seen. ⁵¹Samaria did not commit half the sins you did. You have done more detestable things than they, and have made your sisters seem righteous by all these things you have done. ⁵²Bear your disgrace, for you have furnished some justification for your sisters. Because your sins were more vile than theirs, they appear more righteous than you. So then, be ashamed and bear your disgrace, for you have made your sisters appear righteous.

⁵³"However, I will restore the fortunes of Sodom and her daughters and of Samaria and her daughters, and your fortunes along with them, ⁵⁴so that you may bear your disgrace and be ashamed of all you have done in giving them comfort. ⁵⁵And your sisters, Sodom with her daughters and Samaria with her daughters, will return to what they were before; and you and your daughters will return to what you were before. ⁵⁶You would not even mention your sister Sodom in the day of your pride, ⁵⁷before your wickedness was uncovered. Even so, you are now scorned by the daughters of Edom^h and all her neighbours and the daughters of the Philistines—all those around you who despise you. ⁵⁸You will bear the consequences of your lewdness and your detestable practices, declares the LORD.

⁵⁹"This is what the Sovereign LORD says: I will deal with you as you deserve, because you have despised my oath by breaking the covenant. ⁶⁰Yet I will remember the covenant I made with you in the days of your youth, and I will establish an everlasting covenant with you. ⁶¹Then you will remember your ways and be ashamed when you receive your sisters, both those who are older than you and those who are younger. I will give them to you as daughters, but not on the basis of my covenant with you. ⁶²So I will establish my covenant with you, and you will know that I am the LORD. ⁶³Then, when I make atonement for you for all you have done, you will remember and be ashamed and never again open your mouth because of your humiliation, declares the Sovereign LORD.""

Two Eagles and a Vine

17 The word of the LORD came to me: ²"Son of man, set forth an allegory and tell the house of Israel a parable. ³Say to them, 'This is what the Sovereign LORD says: A great eagle with powerful wings, long feathers and full plumage of varied colours came to Lebanon. Taking hold of the top of a cedar, ⁴he broke off its topmost shoot and carried it away to a land of merchants, where he planted it in a city of traders.

⁵"'He took some of the seed of your land and put it in fertile soil. He planted it like a

---

^{g}36 Or lust
^{h}57 Many Hebrew manuscripts and Syriac; most Hebrew manuscripts, Septuagint and Vulgate *Aram*

willow by abundant water, ⁶and it sprouted and became a low, spreading vine. Its branches turned towards him, but its roots remained under it. So it became a vine and produced branches and put out leafy boughs.

⁷"'But there was another great eagle with powerful wings and full plumage. The vine now sent out its roots towards him from the plot where it was planted and stretched out its branches to him for water. ⁸It had been planted in good soil by abundant water so that it would produce branches, bear fruit and become a splendid vine.'

⁹"Say to them, 'This is what the Sovereign Lord says: Will it thrive? Will it not be uprooted and stripped of its fruit so that it withers? All its new growth will wither. It will not take a strong arm or many people to pull it up by the roots. ¹⁰Even if it is transplanted, will it thrive? Will it not wither completely when the east wind strikes it —wither away in the plot where it grew?'"

¹¹Then the word of the Lord came to me: ¹²"Say to this rebellious house, 'Do you not know what these things mean?' Say to them: 'The king of Babylon went to Jerusalem and carried off her king and her nobles, bringing them back with him to Babylon. ¹³Then he took a member of the royal family and made a treaty with him, putting him under oath. He also carried away the leading men of the land, ¹⁴so that the kingdom would be brought low, unable to rise again, surviving only by keeping his treaty. ¹⁵But the king rebelled against him by sending his envoys to Egypt to get horses and a large army. Will he succeed? Will he who does such things escape? Will he break the treaty and yet escape?

¹⁶"'As surely as I live, declares the Sovereign Lord, he shall die in Babylon, in the land of the king who put him on the throne, whose oath he despised and whose treaty he broke. ¹⁷Pharaoh with his mighty army and great horde will be of no help to him in war, when ramps are built and siege works erected to destroy many lives. ¹⁸He despised the oath by breaking the covenant. Because he had given his hand in pledge and yet did all these things, he shall not escape.

¹⁹"'Therefore this is what the Sovereign Lord says: As surely as I live, I will bring down on his head my oath that he despised and my covenant that he broke. ²⁰I will spread my net for him, and he will be caught in my snare. I will bring him to Babylon and execute judgment upon him there because he was unfaithful to me. ²¹All his fleeing troops will fall by the sword, and the survivors will be scattered to the winds. Then you will know that I the Lord have spoken.

²²"'This is what the Sovereign Lord says: I myself will take a shoot from the very top of a cedar and plant it; I will break off a tender sprig from its topmost shoots and plant it on a high and lofty mountain. ²³On the mountain heights of Israel I will plant it; it will produce branches and bear fruit and become a splendid cedar. Birds of every kind will nest in it; they will find shelter in the shade of its branches. ²⁴All the trees of the field will know that I the Lord bring down the tall tree and make the low tree grow tall. I dry up the green tree and make the dry tree flourish.

"'I the Lord have spoken, and I will do it.'"

The Soul Who Sins Will Die

18 The word of the Lord came to me: ²"What do you people mean by quoting this proverb about the land of Israel:

"'The fathers eat sour grapes,
    and the children's teeth are set on
        edge'?

³"As surely as I live, declares the Sovereign Lord, you will no longer quote this proverb in Israel. ⁴For every living soul belongs to me, the father as well as the son—both alike belong to me. The soul who sins is the one who will die.

⁵"Suppose there is a righteous man
    who does what is just and right.
⁶He does not eat at the mountain shrines
    or look to the idols of the house of
        Israel.
He does not defile his neighbour's wife
    or lie with a woman during her period.
⁷He does not oppress anyone,
    but returns what he took in pledge for a
        loan.
He does not commit robbery,
    but gives his food to the hungry
    and provides clothing for the naked.
⁸He does not lend at usury
    or take excessive interest.ᵃ
He withholds his hand from doing wrong
    and judges fairly between man and man.
⁹He follows my decrees
    and faithfully keeps my laws.
That man is righteous;
    he will surely live,
            declares the Sovereign Lord.

¹⁰"Suppose he has a violent son, who sheds blood or does any of these other thingsᵇ ¹¹(though the father has done none of them):

"He eats at the mountain shrines.
He defiles his neighbour's wife.
¹²He oppresses the poor and needy.
He commits robbery.
He does not return what he took in pledge.
He looks to the idols.
He does detestable things.
¹³He lends at usury and takes excessive
    interest.

Will such a man live? He will not! Because he has done all these detestable things, he will surely be put to death and his blood will be on his own head.

¹⁴"But suppose this son has a son who sees all the sins his father commits, and though he sees them, he does not do such things:

15"He does not eat at the mountain shrines
    or look to the idols of the house of
        Israel.
He does not defile his neighbour's wife.
16He does not oppress anyone
    or require a pledge for a loan.
He does not commit robbery,
    but gives his food to the hungry
    and provides clothing for the naked.
17He withholds his hand from sin*c*
    and takes no usury or excessive interest.
He keeps my laws and follows my decrees.

He will not die for his father's sin; he will
surely live. 18But his father will die for his
own sin, because he practised extortion,
robbed his brother and did what was wrong
among his people.
    19"Yet you ask, 'Why does the son not
share the guilt of his father?' Since the son
has done what is just and right and has been
careful to keep all my decrees, he will surely
live. 20The soul who sins is the one who will
die. The son will not share the guilt of the
father, nor will the father share the guilt of
the son. The righteousness of the righteous
man will be credited to him, and the wickedness of the wicked will be charged against
him.
    21"But if a wicked man turns away from all
the sins he has committed and keeps all my
decrees and does what is just and right, he
will surely live; he will not die. 22None of the
offences he has committed will be remembered against him. Because of the righteous
things he has done, he will live. 23Do I take
any pleasure in the death of the wicked?
declares the Sovereign LORD. Rather, am I
not pleased when they turn from their ways
and live?
    24"But if a righteous man turns from his
righteousness and commits sin and does the
same detestable things the wicked man does,
will he live? None of the righteous things he
has done will be remembered. Because of the
unfaithfulness he is guilty of and because of
the sins he has committed, he will die.
    25"Yet you say, 'The way of the Lord is
not just.' Hear, O house of Israel: Is my way
unjust? Is it not your ways that are unjust?
26If a righteous man turns from his righteousness and commits sin, he will die for it;
because of the sin he has committed he will
die. 27But if a wicked man turns away from
the wickedness he has committed and does
what is just and right, he will save his life.
28Because he considers all the offences he
has committed and turns away from them,
he will surely live; he will not die. 29Yet the
house of Israel says, 'The way of the Lord is
not just.' Are my ways unjust, O house of
Israel? Is it not your ways that are unjust?
    30"Therefore, O house of Israel, I will
judge you, each one according to his ways,
declares the Sovereign LORD. Repent! Turn
away from all your offences; then sin will not
be your downfall. 31Rid yourselves of all the
offences you have committed, and get a new

heart and a new spirit. Why will you die, O
house of Israel? 32For I take no pleasure in
the death of anyone, declares the Sovereign
LORD. Repent and live!

A Lament for Israel's Princes

19 "Take up a lament concerning the
    princes of Israel 2and say:

"'What a lioness was your mother
    among the lions!
She lay down among the young lions
    and reared her cubs.
3She brought up one of her cubs,
    and he became a strong lion.
He learned to tear the prey
    and he devoured men.
4The nations heard about him,
    and he was trapped in their pit.
They led him with hooks
    to the land of Egypt.

5"'When she saw her hope unfulfilled,
    her expectation gone,
she took another of her cubs
    and made him a strong lion.
6He prowled among the lions,
    for he was now a strong lion.
He learned to tear the prey
    and he devoured men.
7He broke down*a* their strongholds
    and devastated their towns.
The land and all who were in it
    were terrified by his roaring.
8Then the nations came against him,
    those from regions round about.
They spread their net for him,
    and he was trapped in their pit.
9With hooks they pulled him into a cage
    and brought him to the king of Babylon.
They put him in prison,
    so his roar was heard no longer
    on the mountains of Israel.

10"'Your mother was like a vine in your
        vineyard*b*
    planted by the water;
it was fruitful and full of branches
    because of abundant water.
11Its branches were strong,
    fit for a ruler's sceptre.
It towered high
    above the thick foliage,
conspicuous for its height
    and for its many branches.
12But it was uprooted in fury
    and thrown to the ground.
The east wind made it shrivel,
    it was stripped of its fruit;
its strong branches withered
    and fire consumed them.
13Now it is planted in the desert,
    in a dry and thirsty land.
14Fire spread from one of its main*c* branches
    and consumed its fruit.
No strong branch is left on it
    fit for a ruler's sceptre.'

---

*c*17 Septuagint (see also verse 8); Hebrew *from the poor*   *a*7 Targum (see Septuagint); Hebrew *He knew*
*b*10 Two Hebrew manuscripts; most Hebrew manuscripts *your blood*   *c*14 Or *from under its*

This is a lament and is to be used as a lament."

Rebellious Israel

20 In the seventh year, in the fifth month on the tenth day, some of the elders of Israel came to enquire of the LORD, and they sat down in front of me.

²Then the word of the LORD came to me: ³"Son of man, speak to the elders of Israel and say to them, 'This is what the Sovereign LORD says: Have you come to enquire of me? As surely as I live, I will not let you enquire of me, declares the Sovereign LORD.'

⁴"Will you judge them? Will you judge them, son of man? Then confront them with the detestable practices of their fathers ⁵and say to them: 'This is what the Sovereign LORD says: On the day I chose Israel, I swore with uplifted hand to the descendants of the house of Jacob and revealed myself to them in Egypt. With uplifted hand I said to them, "I am the LORD your God." ⁶On that day I swore to them that I would bring them out of Egypt into a land I had searched out for them, a land flowing with milk and honey, the most beautiful of all lands. ⁷And I said to them, "Each of you, get rid of the vile images you have set your eyes on, and do not defile yourselves with the idols of Egypt. I am the LORD your God."

⁸"'But they rebelled against me and would not listen to me; they did not get rid of the vile images they had set their eyes on, nor did they forsake the idols of Egypt. So I said I would pour out my wrath on them and spend my anger against them in Egypt. ⁹But for the sake of my name I did what would keep it from being profaned in the eyes of the nations they lived among and in whose sight I had revealed myself to the Israelites by bringing them out of Egypt. ¹⁰Therefore I led them out of Egypt and brought them into the desert. ¹¹I gave them my decrees and made known to them my laws, for the man who obeys them will live by them. ¹²Also I gave them my Sabbaths as a sign between us, so they would know that I the LORD made them holy.

¹³"'Yet the people of Israel rebelled against me in the desert. They did not follow my decrees but rejected my laws—although the man who obeys them will live by them —and they utterly desecrated my Sabbaths. So I said I would pour out my wrath on them and destroy them in the desert. ¹⁴But for the sake of my name I did what would keep it from being profaned in the eyes of the nations in whose sight I had brought them out. ¹⁵Also with uplifted hand I swore to them in the desert that I would not bring them into the land I had given them—a land flowing with milk and honey, most beautiful of all lands —¹⁶because they rejected my laws and did not follow my decrees and desecrated my Sabbaths. For their hearts were devoted to their idols. ¹⁷Yet I looked on them with pity and did not destroy them or put an end to them in the desert. ¹⁸I said to their children in

the desert, "Do not follow the statutes of your fathers or keep their laws or defile yourselves with their idols. ¹⁹I am the LORD your God; follow my decrees and be careful to keep my laws. ²⁰Keep my Sabbaths holy, that they may be a sign between us. Then you will know that I am the LORD your God."

²¹"'But the children rebelled against me: They did not follow my decrees, they were not careful to keep my laws—although the man who obeys them will live by them—and they desecrated my Sabbaths. So I said I would pour out my wrath on them and spend my anger against them in the desert. ²²But I withheld my hand, and for the sake of my name I did what would keep it from being profaned in the eyes of the nations in whose sight I had brought them out. ²³Also with uplifted hand I swore to them in the desert that I would disperse them among the nations and scatter them through the countries, ²⁴because they had not obeyed my laws but had rejected my decrees and desecrated my Sabbaths, and their eyes ˌlustedˌ after their fathers' idols. ²⁵I also gave them over to statutes that were not good and laws they could not live by; ²⁶I let them become defiled through their gifts—the sacrifice of every firstborn*ᵃ*—that I might fill them with horror so that they would know that I am the LORD.'

²⁷"Therefore, son of man, speak to the people of Israel and say to them, 'This is what the Sovereign LORD says: In this also your fathers blasphemed me by forsaking me: ²⁸When I brought them into the land I had sworn to give them and they saw any high hill or any leafy tree, there they offered their sacrifices, made offerings that provoked me to anger, presented their fragrant incense and poured out their drink offerings. ²⁹Then I said to them: What is this high place you go to?'" (It is called Bamah*ᵇ* to this day.)

Judgment and Restoration

³⁰"Therefore say to the house of Israel: 'This is what the Sovereign LORD says: Will you defile yourselves the way your fathers did and lust after their vile images? ³¹When you offer your gifts—the sacrifice of your sons in*ᶜ* the fire—you continue to defile yourselves with all your idols to this day. Am I to let you enquire of me, O house of Israel? As surely as I live, declares the Sovereign LORD, I will not let you enquire of me.

³²"'You say, "We want to be like the nations, like the peoples of the world, who serve wood and stone." But what you have in mind will never happen. ³³As surely as I live, declares the Sovereign LORD, I will rule over you with a mighty hand and an outstretched arm and with outpoured wrath. ³⁴I will bring you from the nations and gather you from the countries where you have been scattered—with a mighty hand and an outstretched arm and with outpoured wrath. ³⁵I will bring you into the desert of the nations and there, face to face, I will execute judgment upon you. ³⁶As I judged your fathers in

---

ᵃ26 Or —*making every firstborn pass through* ˌ*the fire*ˌ
ᶜ31 Or —*making your sons pass through*
ᵇ29 Bamah means *high place.*

the desert of the land of Egypt, so I will judge you, declares the Sovereign LORD. ³⁷I will take note of you as you pass under my rod, and I will bring you into the bond of the covenant. ³⁸I will purge you of those who revolt and rebel against me. Although I will bring them out of the land where they are living, yet they will not enter the land of Israel. Then you will know that I am the LORD.

³⁹"As for you, O house of Israel, this is what the Sovereign LORD says: Go and serve your idols, every one of you! But afterwards you will surely listen to me and no longer profane my holy name with your gifts and idols. ⁴⁰For on my holy mountain, the high mountain of Israel, declares the Sovereign LORD, there in the land the entire house of Israel will serve me, and there I will accept them. There I will require your offerings and your choice gifts,*d* along with all your holy sacrifices. ⁴¹I will accept you as fragrant incense when I bring you out from the nations and gather you from the countries where you have been scattered, and I will show myself holy among you in the sight of the nations. ⁴²Then you will know that I am the LORD, when I bring you into the land of Israel, the land I had sworn with uplifted hand to give to your fathers. ⁴³There you will remember your conduct and all the actions by which you have defiled yourselves, and you will loathe yourselves for all the evil you have done. ⁴⁴You will know that I am the LORD, when I deal with you for my name's sake and not according to your evil ways and your corrupt practices, O house of Israel, declares the Sovereign LORD.'"

Prophecy Against the South

⁴⁵The word of the LORD came to me: ⁴⁶"Son of man, set your face towards the south; preach against the south and prophesy against the forest of the southland. ⁴⁷Say to the southern forest: 'Hear the word of the LORD. This is what the Sovereign LORD says: I am about to set fire to you, and it will consume all your trees, both green and dry. The blazing flame will not be quenched, and every face from south to north will be scorched by it. ⁴⁸Everyone will see that I the LORD have kindled it; it will not be quenched.'"

⁴⁹Then I said, "Ah, Sovereign LORD! They are saying of me, 'Isn't he just telling parables?'"

Babylon, God's Sword of Judgment

21 The word of the LORD came to me: ²"Son of man, set your face against Jerusalem and preach against the sanctuary. Prophesy against the land of Israel ³and say to her: 'This is what the LORD says: I am against you. I will draw my sword from its scabbard and cut off from you both the righteous and the wicked. ⁴Because I am going to cut off the righteous and the wicked, my sword will be unsheathed against everyone from south to north. ⁵Then all people will

know that I the LORD have drawn my sword from its scabbard; it will not return again.'

⁶"Therefore groan, son of man! Groan before them with broken heart and bitter grief. ⁷And when they ask you, 'Why are you groaning?' you shall say, 'Because of the news that is coming. Every heart will melt and every hand go limp; every spirit will become faint and every knee become as weak as water.' It is coming! It will surely take place, declares the Sovereign LORD."

⁸The word of the LORD came to me: ⁹"Son of man, prophesy and say, 'This is what the Lord says:

"'A sword, a sword,
    sharpened and polished—
¹⁰sharpened for the slaughter,
    polished to flash like lightning!

"'Shall we rejoice in the sceptre of my son ⌊Judah⌋? The sword despises every such stick.

¹¹"'The sword is appointed to be polished,
    to be grasped with the hand;
it is sharpened and polished,
    made ready for the hand of the slayer.
¹²Cry out and wail, son of man,
    for it is against my people;
    it is against all the princes of Israel.
They are thrown to the sword
    along with my people.
Therefore beat your breast.

¹³"'Testing will surely come. And what if the sceptre ⌊of Judah⌋, which the sword despises, does not continue? declares the Sovereign LORD.'

¹⁴"So then, son of man, prophesy
    and strike your hands together.
Let the sword strike twice,
    even three times.
It is a sword for slaughter—
    a sword for great slaughter,
    closing in on them from every side.
¹⁵So that hearts may melt
    and the fallen be many,
I have stationed the sword for slaughter*a*
    at all their gates.
Oh! It is made to flash like lightning,
    it is grasped for slaughter.
¹⁶O sword, slash to the right,
    then to the left,
    wherever your blade is turned.
¹⁷I too will strike my hands together,
    and my wrath will subside.
I the LORD have spoken."

¹⁸The word of the LORD came to me: ¹⁹"Son of man, mark out two roads for the sword of the king of Babylon to take, both starting from the same country. Make a signpost where the road branches off to the city. ²⁰Mark out one road for the sword to come against Rabbah of the Ammonites and another against Judah and fortified Jerusalem. ²¹For the king of Babylon will stop at

---

*d*40 Or *and the gifts of your firstfruits*   *a*15 Septuagint; the meaning of the Hebrew for this word is uncertain.

the fork in the road, at the junction of the two roads, to seek an omen: He will cast lots with arrows, he will consult his idols, he will examine the liver. ²²Into his right hand will come the lot for Jerusalem, where he is to set up battering-rams, to give the command to slaughter, to sound the battle cry, to set battering-rams against the gates, to build a ramp and to erect siege works. ²³It will seem like a false omen to those who have sworn allegiance to him, but he will remind them of their guilt and take them captive.

²⁴"Therefore this is what the Sovereign LORD says: 'Because you people have brought to mind your guilt by your open rebellion, revealing your sins in all that you do—because you have done this, you will be taken captive.

²⁵"O profane and wicked prince of Israel, whose day has come, whose time of punishment has reached its climax, ²⁶this is what the Sovereign LORD says: Take off the turban, remove the crown. It will not be as it was: The lowly will be exalted and the exalted will be brought low. ²⁷A ruin! A ruin! I will make it a ruin! It will not be restored until he comes to whom it rightfully belongs; to him I will give it.'

²⁸"And you, son of man, prophesy and say, 'This is what the Sovereign LORD says about the Ammonites and their insults:

"'A sword, a sword,
    drawn for the slaughter,
polished to consume
    and to flash like lightning!
²⁹Despite false visions concerning you
    and lying divinations about you,
it will be laid on the necks
    of the wicked who are to be slain,
whose day has come,
    whose time of punishment has reached
      its climax.
³⁰Return the sword to its scabbard.
    In the place where you were created,
in the land of your ancestry,
    I will judge you.
³¹I will pour out my wrath upon you
    and breathe out my fiery anger against
      you;
I will hand you over to brutal men,
    men skilled in destruction.
³²You will be fuel for the fire,
    your blood will be shed in your land,
you will be remembered no more;
    for I the LORD have spoken.'"

Jerusalem's Sins

22 The word of the LORD came to me: ²"Son of man, will you judge her? Will you judge this city of bloodshed? Then confront her with all her detestable practices ³and say: 'This is what the Sovereign LORD says: O city that brings on herself doom by shedding blood in her midst and defiles herself by making idols, ⁴you have become guilty because of the blood you have shed and have become defiled by the idols you

have made. You have brought your days to a close, and the end of your years has come. Therefore I will make you an object of scorn to the nations and a laughing-stock to all the countries. ⁵Those who are near and those who are far away will mock you, O infamous city, full of turmoil.

⁶"'See how each of the princes of Israel who are in you uses his power to shed blood. ⁷In you they have treated father and mother with contempt; in you they have oppressed the alien and ill-treated the fatherless and the widow. ⁸You have despised my holy things and desecrated my Sabbaths. ⁹In you are slanderous men bent on shedding blood; in you are those who eat at the mountain shrines and commit lewd acts. ¹⁰In you are those who dishonour their fathers' bed; in you are those who violate women during their period, when they are ceremonially unclean. ¹¹In you one man commits a detestable offence with his neighbour's wife, another shamefully defiles his daughter-in-law, and another violates his sister, his own father's daughter. ¹²In you men accept bribes to shed blood; you take usury and excessive interest*a* and make unjust gain from your neighbours by extortion. And you have forgotten me, declares the Sovereign LORD.

¹³"'I will surely strike my hands together at the unjust gain you have made and at the blood you have shed in your midst. ¹⁴Will your courage endure or your hands be strong in the day I deal with you? I the LORD have spoken, and I will do it. ¹⁵I will disperse you among the nations and scatter you through the countries; and I will put an end to your uncleanness. ¹⁶When you have been defiled*b* in the eyes of the nations, you will know that I am the LORD.'"

¹⁷Then the word of the LORD came to me: ¹⁸"Son of man, the house of Israel has become dross to me; all of them are the copper, tin, iron and lead left inside a furnace. They are but the dross of silver. ¹⁹Therefore this is what the Sovereign LORD says: 'Because you have all become dross, I will gather you into Jerusalem. ²⁰As men gather silver, copper, iron, lead and tin into a furnace to melt it with a fiery blast, so will I gather you in my anger and my wrath and put you inside the city and melt you. ²¹I will gather you and I will blow on you with my fiery wrath, and you will be melted inside her. ²²As silver is melted in a furnace, so you will be melted inside her, and you will know that I the LORD have poured out my wrath upon you.'"

²³Again the word of the LORD came to me: ²⁴"Son of man, say to the land, 'You are a land that has had no rain or showers*c* in the day of wrath.' ²⁵There is a conspiracy of her princes*d* within her like a roaring lion tearing its prey; they devour people, take treasures and precious things and make many widows within her. ²⁶Her priests do violence to my law and profane my holy things; they do not distinguish between the holy and the common; they teach that there is no difference

---

*a*12 Or *usury and interest*   *b*16 Or *When I have allotted you your inheritance*
*c*24 Septuagint; Hebrew *has not been cleansed or rained on*   *d*25 Septuagint; Hebrew *prophets*

between the unclean and the clean; and they shut their eyes to the keeping of my Sabbaths, so that I am profaned among them. [27]Her officials within her are like wolves tearing their prey; they shed blood and kill people to make unjust gain. [28]Her prophets whitewash these deeds for them by false visions and lying divinations. They say, 'This is what the Sovereign LORD says'—when the LORD has not spoken. [29]The people of the land practise extortion and commit robbery; they oppress the poor and needy and ill-treat the alien, denying them justice.

[30]"I looked for a man among them who would build up the wall and stand before me in the gap on behalf of the land so that I would not have to destroy it, but I found none. [31]So I will pour out my wrath on them and consume them with my fiery anger, bringing down on their own heads all they have done, declares the Sovereign LORD."

Two Adulterous Sisters

23 The word of the LORD came to me: [2]"Son of man, there were two women, daughters of the same mother. [3]They became prostitutes in Egypt, engaging in prostitution from their youth. In that land their breasts were fondled and their virgin bosoms caressed. [4]The older was named Oholah, and her sister was Oholibah. They were mine and gave birth to sons and daughters. Oholah is Samaria, and Oholibah is Jerusalem.

[5]"Oholah engaged in prostitution while she was still mine; and she lusted after her lovers, the Assyrians—[6]warriors clothed in blue, governors and commanders, all of them handsome young men, and mounted horsemen. [7]She gave herself as a prostitute to all the elite of the Assyrians and defiled herself with all the idols of everyone she lusted after. [8]She did not give up the prostitution she began in Egypt, when during her youth men slept with her, caressed her virgin bosom and poured out their lust upon her.

[9]"Therefore I handed her over to her lovers, the Assyrians, for whom she lusted. [10]They stripped her naked, took away her sons and daughters and killed her with the sword. She became a byword among women, and punishment was inflicted on her.

[11]"Her sister Oholibah saw this, yet in her lust and prostitution she was more depraved than her sister. [12]She too lusted after the Assyrians—governors and commanders, warriors in full dress, mounted horsemen, all handsome young men. [13]I saw that she too defiled herself; both of them went the same way.

[14]"But she carried her prostitution still further. She saw men portrayed on a wall, figures of Chaldeans[a] portrayed in red, [15]with belts round their waists and flowing turbans on their heads; all of them looked like Babylonian chariot officers, natives of Chaldea.[b] [16]As soon as she saw them, she lusted

after them and sent messengers to them in Chaldea. [17]Then the Babylonians came to her, to the bed of love, and in their lust they defiled her. After she had been defiled by them, she turned away from them in disgust. [18]When she carried on her prostitution openly and exposed her nakedness, I turned away from her in disgust, just as I had turned away from her sister. [19]Yet she became more and more promiscuous as she recalled the days of her youth, when she was a prostitute in Egypt. [20]There she lusted after her lovers, whose genitals were like those of donkeys and whose emission was like that of horses. [21]So you longed for the lewdness of your youth, when in Egypt your bosom was caressed and your young breasts fondled.[c]

[22]"Therefore, Oholibah, this is what the Sovereign LORD says: I will stir up your lovers against you, those you turned away from in disgust, and I will bring them against you from every side—[23]the Babylonians and all the Chaldeans, the men of Pekod and Shoa and Koa, and all the Assyrians with them, handsome young men, all of them governors and commanders, chariot officers and men of high rank, all mounted on horses. [24]They will come against you with weapons,[d] chariots and wagons and with a throng of people; they will take up positions against you on every side with large and small shields and with helmets. I will turn you over to them for punishment, and they will punish you according to their standards. [25]I will direct my jealous anger against you, and they will deal with you in fury. They will cut off your noses and your ears, and those of you who are left will fall by the sword. They will take away your sons and daughters, and those of you who are left will be consumed by fire. [26]They will also strip you of your clothes and take your fine jewellery. [27]So I will put a stop to the lewdness and prostitution you began in Egypt. You will not look on these things with longing or remember Egypt any more.

[28]"For this is what the Sovereign LORD says: I am about to hand you over to those you hate, to those you turned away from in disgust. [29]They will deal with you in hatred and take away everything you have worked for. They will leave you naked and bare, and the shame of your prostitution will be exposed. Your lewdness and promiscuity [30]have brought this upon you, because you lusted after the nations and defiled yourself with their idols. [31]You have gone the way of your sister; so I will put her cup into your hand.

[32]"This is what the Sovereign LORD says:

"You will drink your sister's cup,
　a cup large and deep;
it will bring scorn and derision,
　for it holds so much.
[33]You will be filled with drunkenness and
　sorrow,

---

[a]14 Or Babylonians　[b]15 Or Babylonia; also in verse 16
[c]21 Syriac (see also verse 3); Hebrew caressed because of your young breasts
[d]24 The meaning of the Hebrew for this word is uncertain.

the cup of ruin and desolation,
the cup of your sister Samaria.
34You will drink it and drain it dry;
you will dash it to pieces
and tear your breasts.

I have spoken, declares the Sovereign LORD.

35"Therefore this is what the Sovereign
LORD says: Since you have forgotten me
and thrust me behind your back, you must
bear the consequences of your lewdness and
prostitution."

36The LORD said to me: "Son of man, will
you judge Oholah and Oholibah? Then confront them with their detestable practices,
37for they have committed adultery and
blood is on their hands. They committed
adultery with their idols; they even sacrificed
their children, whom they bore to me,e as
food for them. 38They have also done this to
me: At that same time they defiled my sanctuary and desecrated my Sabbaths. 39On the
very day they sacrificed their children to
their idols, they entered my sanctuary and
desecrated it. That is what they did in my
house.

40"They even sent messengers for men
who came from far away, and when they
arrived you bathed yourself for them,
painted your eyes and put on your jewellery.
41You sat on an elegant couch, with a table
spread before it on which you had placed my
incense and oil that belonged to me.

42"The noise of a carefree crowd was
around her; Sabeansf were brought from the
desert along with men from the rabble, and
they put bracelets on the arms of the woman
and her sister and beautiful crowns on their
heads. 43Then I said about the one worn out
by adultery, 'Now let them use her as a
prostitute, for that is all she is.' 44And they
slept with her. As men sleep with a prostitute, so they slept with those lewd women,
Oholah and Oholibah. 45But righteous men
will sentence them to the punishment of
women who commit adultery and shed
blood, because they are adulterous and blood
is on their hands.

46"This is what the Sovereign LORD says:
Bring a mob against them and give them over
to terror and plunder. 47The mob will stone
them and cut them down with their swords;
they will kill their sons and daughters and
burn down their houses.

48"So I will put an end to lewdness in the
land, that all women may take warning and
not imitate you. 49You will suffer the penalty
for your lewdness and bear the consequences
of your sins of idolatry. Then you will know
that I am the Sovereign LORD."

The Cooking Pot

24 In the ninth year, in the tenth month
on the tenth day, the word of the LORD
came to me: 2"Son of man, record this date,
this very date, because the king of Babylon
has laid siege to Jerusalem this very day.
3Tell this rebellious house a parable and say

to them: 'This is what the Sovereign LORD
says:

"'Put on the cooking pot; put it on
and pour water into it.
4Put into it the pieces of meat,
all the choice pieces—the leg and the
shoulder.
Fill it with the best of these bones;
5 take the pick of the flock.
Pile wood beneath it for the bones;
bring it to the boil
and cook the bones in it.

6"'For this is what the Sovereign LORD
says:

"'Woe to the city of bloodshed,
to the pot now encrusted,
whose deposit will not go away!
Empty it piece by piece
without casting lots for them.

7"'For the blood she shed is in her midst:
She poured it on the bare rock;
she did not pour it on the ground,
where the dust would cover it.
8To stir up wrath and take revenge
I put her blood on the bare rock,
so that it would not be covered.

9"'Therefore this is what the Sovereign
LORD says:

"'Woe to the city of bloodshed!
I, too, will pile the wood high.
10So heap on the wood
and kindle the fire.
Cook the meat well,
mixing in the spices;
and let the bones be charred.
11Then set the empty pot on the coals
till it becomes hot and its copper glows
so its impurities may be melted
and its deposit burned away.
12It has frustrated all efforts;
its heavy deposit has not been removed,
not even by fire.

13"'Now your impurity is lewdness. Because I tried to cleanse you but you would
not be cleansed from your impurity, you will
not be clean again until my wrath against you
has subsided.

14"'I the LORD have spoken. The time has
come for me to act. I will not hold back; I will
not have pity, nor will I relent. You will be
judged according to your conduct and your
actions, declares the Sovereign LORD.'"

Ezekiel's Wife Dies

15The word of the LORD came to me:
16"Son of man, with one blow I am about to
take away from you the delight of your eyes.
Yet do not lament or weep or shed any tears.
17Groan quietly; do not mourn for the dead.
Keep your turban fastened and your sandals
on your feet; do not cover the lower part

---

e37 Or even made the children they bore to me pass through ⌊the fire⌋   f42 Or drunkards of your face or eat the customary food ⌊of mourners⌋.''

¹⁸So I spoke to the people in the morning, and in the evening my wife died. The next morning I did as I had been commanded.

¹⁹Then the people asked me, "Won't you tell us what these things have to do with us?"

²⁰So I said to them, "The word of the LORD came to me: ²¹Say to the house of Israel, 'This is what the Sovereign LORD says: I am about to desecrate my sanctuary—the stronghold in which you take pride, the delight of your eyes, the object of your affection. The sons and daughters you left behind will fall by the sword. ²²And you will do as I have done. You will not cover the lower part of your face or eat the customary food ⌊of mourners⌋. ²³You will keep your turbans on your heads and your sandals on your feet. You will not mourn or weep but will waste away because of*ᵃ* your sins and groan among yourselves. ²⁴Ezekiel will be a sign to you; you will do just as he has done. When this happens, you will know that I am the Sovereign LORD.'

²⁵"And you, son of man, on the day I take away their stronghold, their joy and glory, the delight of their eyes, their heart's desire, and their sons and daughters as well—²⁶on that day a fugitive will come to tell you the news. ²⁷At that time your mouth will be opened; you will speak with him and will no longer be silent. So you will be a sign to them, and they will know that I am the LORD."

A Prophecy Against Ammon

25 The word of the LORD came to me: ²"Son of man, set your face against the Ammonites and prophesy against them. ³Say to them, 'Hear the word of the Sovereign LORD. This is what the Sovereign LORD says: Because you said "Aha!" over my sanctuary when it was desecrated and over the land of Israel when it was laid waste and over the people of Judah when they went into exile, ⁴therefore I am going to give you to the people of the East as a possession. They will set up their camps and pitch their tents among you; they will eat your fruit and drink your milk. ⁵I will turn Rabbah into a pasture for camels and Ammon into a resting place for sheep. Then you will know that I am the LORD. ⁶For this is what the Sovereign LORD says: Because you have clapped your hands and stamped your feet, rejoicing with all the malice of your heart against the land of Israel, ⁷therefore I will stretch out my hand against you and give you as plunder to the nations. I will cut you off from the nations and exterminate you from the countries. I will destroy you, and you will know that I am the LORD.'"

A Prophecy Against Moab

⁸"This is what the Sovereign LORD says: 'Because Moab and Seir said, "Look, the house of Judah has become like all the other nations," ⁹therefore I will expose the flank of Moab, beginning at its frontier towns—Beth Jeshimoth, Baal Meon and Kiriathaim—the glory of that land. ¹⁰I will give Moab along with the Ammonites to the people of the East as a possession, so that the Ammonites will not be remembered among the nations; ¹¹and I will inflict punishment on Moab. Then they will know that I am the LORD.'"

A Prophecy Against Edom

¹²"This is what the Sovereign LORD says: 'Because Edom took revenge on the house of Judah and became very guilty by doing so, ¹³therefore this is what the Sovereign LORD says: I will stretch out my hand against Edom and kill its men and their animals. I will lay it waste, and from Teman to Dedan they will fall by the sword. ¹⁴I will take vengeance on Edom by the hand of my people Israel, and they will deal with Edom in accordance with my anger and my wrath; they will know my vengeance, declares the Sovereign LORD.'"

A Prophecy Against Philistia

¹⁵"This is what the Sovereign LORD says: 'Because the Philistines acted in vengeance and took revenge with malice in their hearts, and with ancient hostility sought to destroy Judah, ¹⁶therefore this is what the Sovereign LORD says: I am about to stretch out my hand against the Philistines, and I will cut off the Kerethites and destroy those remaining along the coast. ¹⁷I will carry out great vengeance on them and punish them in my wrath. Then they will know that I am the LORD, when I take vengeance on them.'"

A Prophecy Against Tyre

26 In the eleventh year, on the first day of the month, the word of the LORD came to me: ²"Son of man, because Tyre has said of Jerusalem, 'Aha! The gate to the nations is broken, and its doors have swung open to me; now that she lies in ruins I will prosper,' ³therefore this is what the Sovereign LORD says: I am against you, O Tyre, and I will bring many nations against you, like the sea casting up its waves. ⁴They will destroy the walls of Tyre and pull down her towers; I will scrape away her rubble and make her a bare rock. ⁵Out in the sea she will become a place to spread fishing nets, for I have spoken, declares the Sovereign LORD. She will become plunder for the nations, ⁶and her settlements on the mainland will be ravaged by the sword. Then they will know that I am the LORD.

⁷"For this is what the Sovereign LORD says: From the north I am going to bring against Tyre Nebuchadnezzar*ᵃ* king of Babylon, king of kings, with horses and chariots, with horsemen and a great army. ⁸He will ravage your settlements on the mainland with the sword; he will set up siege works against you, build a ramp up to your walls and raise his shields against you. ⁹He will direct the blows of his battering-rams against your walls and demolish your towers with his

---

ᵃ23 Or away in
ᵃ7 Hebrew Nebuchadrezzar, of which Nebuchadnezzar is a variant; here and often in Ezekiel and Jeremiah

weapons. ¹⁰His horses will be so many that they will cover you with dust. Your walls will tremble at the noise of the war horses, wagons and chariots when he enters your gates as men enter a city whose walls have been broken through. ¹¹The hoofs of his horses will trample all your streets; he will kill your people with the sword, and your strong pillars will fall to the ground. ¹²They will plunder your wealth and loot your merchandise; they will break down your walls and demolish your fine houses and throw your stones, timber and rubble into the sea. ¹³I will put an end to your noisy songs, and the music of your harps will be heard no more. ¹⁴I will make you a bare rock, and you will become a place to spread fishing nets. You will never be rebuilt, for I the LORD have spoken, declares the Sovereign LORD.

¹⁵"This is what the Sovereign LORD says to Tyre: Will not the coastlands tremble at the sound of your fall, when the wounded groan and the slaughter takes place in you? ¹⁶Then all the princes of the coast will step down from their thrones and lay aside their robes and take off their embroidered garments. Clothed with terror, they will sit on the ground, trembling every moment, appalled at you. ¹⁷Then they will take up a lament concerning you and say to you:

"'How you are destroyed, O city of
      renown,
   peopled by men of the sea!
You were a power on the seas,
   you and your citizens;
you put your terror
   on all who lived there.
¹⁸Now the coastlands tremble
   on the day of your fall;
the islands in the sea
   are terrified at your collapse.'

¹⁹"This is what the Sovereign LORD says: When I make you a desolate city, like cities no longer inhabited, and when I bring the ocean depths over you and its vast waters cover you, ²⁰then I will bring you down with those who go down to the pit, to the people of long ago. I will make you dwell in the earth below, as in ancient ruins, with those who go down to the pit, and you will not return or take your place*b* in the land of the living. ²¹I will bring you to a horrible end and you will be no more. You will be sought, but you will never again be found, declares the Sovereign LORD."

A Lament for Tyre

27 The word of the LORD came to me: ²"Son of man, take up a lament concerning Tyre. ³Say to Tyre, situated at the gateway to the sea, merchant of peoples on many coasts, 'This is what the Sovereign LORD says:

"'You say, O Tyre,
   "I am perfect in beauty."
⁴Your domain was on the high seas;
   your builders brought your beauty to
      perfection.
⁵They made all your timbers
   of pine trees from Senir;*a*
they took a cedar from Lebanon
   to make a mast for you.
⁶Of oaks from Bashan
   they made your oars;
of cypress wood*b* from the coasts of
      Cyprus*c*
   they made your deck, inlaid with ivory.
⁷Fine embroidered linen from Egypt was
      your sail
   and served as your banner;
your awnings were of blue and purple
   from the coasts of Elishah.
⁸Men of Sidon and Arvad were your
      oarsmen;
   your skilled men, O Tyre, were aboard
      as your seamen.
⁹Veteran craftsmen of Gebal*d* were on
      board
   as shipwrights to caulk your seams.
All the ships of the sea and their sailors
   came alongside to trade for your wares.

¹⁰"'Men of Persia, Lydia and Put
   served as soldiers in your army.
They hung their shields and helmets on
      your walls,
   bringing you splendour.
¹¹Men of Arvad and Helech
   manned your walls on every side;
men of Gammad
   were in your towers.
They hung their shields around your walls;
   they brought your beauty to perfection.

¹²"'Tarshish did business with you because of your great wealth of goods; they exchanged silver, iron, tin and lead for your merchandise.

¹³"'Greece, Tubal and Meshech traded with you; they exchanged slaves and articles of bronze for your wares.

¹⁴"'Men of Beth Togarmah exchanged work horses, war horses and mules for your merchandise.

¹⁵"'The men of Rhodes*e* traded with you, and many coastlands were your customers; they paid you with ivory tusks and ebony.

¹⁶"'Aram*f* did business with you because of your many products; they exchanged turquoise, purple fabric, embroidered work, fine linen, coral and rubies for your merchandise.

¹⁷"'Judah and Israel traded with you; they exchanged wheat from Minnith and confections,*g* honey, oil and balm for your wares.

¹⁸"'Damascus, because of your many products and great wealth of goods, did business with you in wine from Helbon and wool from Zahar.

---

*b*20 Septuagint; Hebrew *return, and I will give glory*   *a*5 That is, Hermon
*b*6 Targum; the Masoretic Text has a different division of the consonants.   *c*6 Hebrew *Kittim*
*d*9 That is, Byblos   *e*15 Septuagint; Hebrew *Dedan*
*f*16 Most Hebrew manuscripts; some Hebrew manuscripts and Syriac *Edom*
*g*17 The meaning of the Hebrew for this word is uncertain.

19''Danites and Greeks from Uzal bought your merchandise; they exchanged wrought iron, cassia and calamus for your wares.
20''Dedan traded in saddle blankets with you.
21'''Arabia and all the princes of Kedar were your customers; they did business with you in lambs, rams and goats.
22'''The merchants of Sheba and Raamah traded with you; for your merchandise they exchanged the finest of all kinds of spices and precious stones, and gold.
23'''Haran, Canneh and Eden and merchants of Sheba, Asshur and Kilmad traded with you. 24In your market-place they traded with you beautiful garments, blue fabric, embroidered work and multicoloured rugs with cords twisted and tightly knotted.

25''' 'The ships of Tarshish serve
    as carriers for your wares.
You are filled with heavy cargo
    in the heart of the sea.
26Your oarsmen take you
    out to the high seas.
But the east wind will break you to pieces
    in the heart of the sea.
27Your wealth, merchandise and wares,
    your mariners, seamen and
        shipwrights,
your merchants and all your soldiers,
    and everyone else on board
will sink into the heart of the sea
    on the day of your shipwreck.
28The shorelands will quake
    when your seamen cry out.
29All who handle the oars
    will abandon their ships;
the mariners and all the seamen
    will stand on the shore.
30They will raise their voice
    and cry bitterly over you;
they will sprinkle dust on their heads
    and roll in ashes.
31They will shave their heads because of you
    and will put on sackcloth.
They will weep over you with anguish of
        soul
    and with bitter mourning.
32As they wail and mourn over you,
    they will take up a lament concerning
        you:
"Who was ever silenced like Tyre,
    surrounded by the sea?"
33When your merchandise went out on the
        seas,
    you satisfied many nations;
with your great wealth and your wares
    you enriched the kings of the earth.
34Now you are shattered by the sea
    in the depths of the waters;
your wares and all your company
    have gone down with you.
35All who live in the coastlands
    are appalled at you;
their kings shudder with horror
    and their faces are distorted with fear.

36The merchants among the nations hiss at
        you;
    you have come to a horrible end
    and will be no more.' ''

A Prophecy Against the King of Tyre

28 The word of the LORD came to me:
2''Son of man, say to the ruler of Tyre, 'This is what the Sovereign LORD says:

'' 'In the pride of your heart
    you say, "I am a god;
I sit on the throne of a god
    in the heart of the seas."
But you are a man and not a god,
    though you think you are as wise as a
        god.
3Are you wiser than Daniel?a
    Is no secret hidden from you?
4By your wisdom and understanding
    you have gained wealth for yourself
and amassed gold and silver
    in your treasuries.
5By your great skill in trading
    you have increased your wealth,
and because of your wealth
    your heart has grown proud.

6''' 'Therefore this is what the Sovereign
LORD says:

'' 'Because you think you are wise,
    as wise as a god,
7I am going to bring foreigners against you,
    the most ruthless of nations;
they will draw their swords against your
        beauty and wisdom
    and pierce your shining splendour.
8They will bring you down to the pit,
    and you will die a violent death
    in the heart of the seas.
9Will you then say, "I am a god,"
    in the presence of those who kill you?
You will be but a man, not a god,
    in the hands of those who slay you.
10You will die the death of the
        uncircumcised
    at the hands of foreigners.

I have spoken, declares the Sovereign
LORD.' ''

11The word of the LORD came to me:
12''Son of man, take up a lament concerning
the king of Tyre and say to him: 'This is what
the Sovereign LORD says:

'' 'You were the model of perfection,
    full of wisdom and perfect in beauty.
13You were in Eden,
    the garden of God;
every precious stone adorned you:
    ruby, topaz and emerald,
    chrysolite, onyx and jasper,
    sapphire,b turquoise and beryl.c
Your settings and mountingsd were made
    of gold;

---

a3 Or Danel; the Hebrew spelling may suggest a person other than the prophet Daniel.
b13 Or lapis lazuli   c13 The precise identification of some of these precious stones is uncertain.
d13 The meaning of the Hebrew for this phrase is uncertain.

on the day you were created they were
prepared.
[14]You were anointed as a guardian cherub,
for so I ordained you.
You were on the holy mount of God;
you walked among the fiery stones.
[15]You were blameless in your ways
from the day you were created
till wickedness was found in you.
[16]Through your widespread trade
you were filled with violence,
and you sinned.
So I drove you in disgrace from the mount
of God,
and I expelled you, O guardian cherub,
from among the fiery stones.
[17]Your heart became proud
on account of your beauty,
and you corrupted your wisdom
because of your splendour.
So I threw you to the earth;
I made a spectacle of you before kings.
[18]By your many sins and dishonest trade
you have desecrated your sanctuaries.
So I made a fire come out from you,
and it consumed you,
and I reduced you to ashes on the ground
in the sight of all who were watching.
[19]All the nations who knew you
are appalled at you;
you have come to a horrible end
and will be no more.' "

A Prophecy Against Sidon

[20]The word of the LORD came to me:
[21]"Son of man, set your face against Sidon;
prophesy against her [22]and say: 'This is what
the Sovereign LORD says:

" 'I am against you, O Sidon,
and I will gain glory within you.
They will know that I am the LORD,
when I inflict punishment on her
and show myself holy within her.
[23]I will send a plague upon her
and make blood flow in her streets.
The slain will fall within her,
with the sword against her on every
side.
Then they will know that I am the LORD.

[24]" 'No longer will the people of Israel
have malicious neighbours who are painful
briers and sharp thorns. Then they will know
that I am the Sovereign LORD.
[25]" 'This is what the Sovereign LORD says:
When I gather the people of Israel from the
nations where they have been scattered, I
will show myself holy among them in the
sight of the nations. Then they will live in
their own land, which I gave to my servant
Jacob. [26]They will live there in safety and will
build houses and plant vineyards; they will
live in safety when I inflict punishment on all
their neighbours who maligned them. Then
they will know that I am the LORD their
God.' "

A Prophecy Against Egypt

29 In the tenth year, in the tenth month
on the twelfth day, the word of the
LORD came to me: [2]"Son of man, set your
face against Pharaoh king of Egypt and
prophesy against him and against all Egypt.
[3]Speak to him and say: 'This is what the
Sovereign LORD says:

" 'I am against you, Pharaoh king of
Egypt,
you great monster lying among your
streams.
You say, "The Nile is mine;
I made it for myself."
[4]But I will put hooks in your jaws
and make the fish of your streams stick
to your scales.
I will pull you out from among your
streams,
with all the fish sticking to your scales.
[5]I will leave you in the desert,
you and all the fish of your streams.
You will fall on the open field
and not be gathered or picked up.
I will give you as food
to the beasts of the earth and the birds of
the air.

[6]Then all who live in Egypt will know that I
am the LORD.

" 'You have been a staff of reed for the
house of Israel. [7]When they grasped you with
their hands, you splintered and you tore open
their shoulders; when they leaned on you,
you broke and their backs were wrenched.[a]
[8]" 'Therefore this is what the Sovereign
LORD says: I will bring a sword against you
and kill your men and their animals. [9]Egypt
will become a desolate wasteland. Then they
will know that I am the LORD.
" 'Because you said, "The Nile is mine; I
made it," [10]therefore I am against you and
against your streams, and I will make the
land of Egypt a ruin and a desolate waste
from Migdol to Aswan, as far as the border of
Cush.[b] [11]No foot of man or animal will pass
through it; no-one will live there for forty
years. [12]I will make the land of Egypt desolate among devastated lands, and her cities
will lie desolate for forty years among ruined
cities. And I will disperse the Egyptians
among the nations and scatter them through
the countries.
[13]" 'Yet this is what the Sovereign LORD
says: At the end of forty years I will gather
the Egyptians from the nations where they
were scattered. [14]I will bring them back from
captivity and return them to Upper Egypt,[c]
the land of their ancestry. There they will be
a lowly kingdom. [15]It will be the lowliest of
kingdoms and will never again exalt itself
above the other nations. I will make it so
weak that it will never again rule over the
nations. [16]Egypt will no longer be a source of
confidence for the people of Israel but will be
a reminder of their sin in turning to her for

[a]7 Syriac (see also Septuagint and Vulgate); Hebrew *and you caused their backs to stand*
[b]10 That is, the upper Nile region   [c]14 Hebrew *to Pathros*

help. Then they will know that I am the
Sovereign LORD.'"

17In the twenty-seventh year, in the first
month on the first day, the word of the LORD
came to me. 18"Son of man, Nebuchadnezzar king of Babylon drove his army in a hard
campaign against Tyre; every head was
rubbed bare and every shoulder made raw.
Yet he and his army got no reward from the
campaign he led against Tyre. 19Therefore
this is what the Sovereign LORD says: I am
going to give Egypt to Nebuchadnezzar king
of Babylon, and he will carry off its wealth.
He will loot and plunder the land as pay for
his army. 20I have given him Egypt as a
reward for his efforts because he and his
army did it for me, declares the Sovereign
LORD.
21"On that day I will make a horn*d* grow for
the house of Israel, and I will open your
mouth among them. Then they will know that
I am the LORD."

A Lament for Egypt

30 The word of the LORD came to me:
2"Son of man, prophesy and say:
'This is what the Sovereign LORD says:

"'Wail and say,
"Alas for that day!"
3For the day is near,
the day of the LORD is near—
a day of clouds,
a time of doom for the nations.
4A sword will come against Egypt,
and anguish will come upon Cush.*a*
When the slain fall in Egypt,
her wealth will be carried away
and her foundations torn down.

5Cush and Put, Lydia and all Arabia, Libya*b*
and the people of the covenant land will fall
by the sword along with Egypt.
6"'This is what the LORD says:

"'The allies of Egypt will fall
and her proud strength will fail.
From Migdol to Aswan
they will fall by the sword within her,
declares the Sovereign LORD.
7"'They will be desolate
among desolate lands,
and their cities will lie
among ruined cities.
8Then they will know that I am the LORD,
when I set fire to Egypt
and all her helpers are crushed.

9"'On that day messengers will go out
from me in ships to frighten Cush out of her
complacency. Anguish will take hold of them
on the day of Egypt's doom, for it is sure to
come.

10"'This is what the Sovereign LORD says:

"'I will put an end to the hordes of Egypt
by the hand of Nebuchadnezzar king of
Babylon.
11He and his army—the most ruthless of
nations—
will be brought in to destroy the land.
They will draw their swords against Egypt
and fill the land with the slain.
12I will dry up the streams of the Nile
and sell the land to evil men;
by the hand of foreigners
I will lay waste the land and everything
in it.

I the LORD have spoken.

13"'This is what the Sovereign LORD says:

"'I will destroy the idols
and put an end to the images in
Memphis.*c*
No longer will there be a prince in Egypt,
and I will spread fear throughout the
land.
14I will lay waste Upper Egypt,*d*
set fire to Zoan
and inflict punishment on Thebes.*e*
15I will pour out my wrath on Pelusium,*f*
the stronghold of Egypt,
and cut off the hordes of Thebes.
16I will set fire to Egypt;
Pelusium will writhe in agony.
Thebes will be taken by storm;
Memphis will be in constant distress.
17The young men of Heliopolis*g* and
Bubastis*h*
will fall by the sword,
and the cities themselves will go into
captivity.
18Dark will be the day at Tahpanhes
when I break the yoke of Egypt;
there her proud strength will come to an
end.
She will be covered with clouds,
and her villages will go into captivity.
19So I will inflict punishment on Egypt,
and they will know that I am the
LORD.'"

20In the eleventh year, in the first month on
the seventh day, the word of the LORD came
to me: 21"Son of man, I have broken the arm
of Pharaoh king of Egypt. It has not been
bound up for healing or put in a splint so as to
become strong enough to hold a sword.
22Therefore this is what the Sovereign LORD
says: I am against Pharaoh king of Egypt. I
will break both his arms, the good arm as well
as the broken one, and make the sword fall
from his hand. 23I will disperse the Egyptians
among the nations and scatter them through
the countries. 24I will strengthen the arms of
the king of Babylon and put my sword in his
hand, but I will break the arms of Pharaoh,
and he will groan before him like a mortally
wounded man. 25I will strengthen the arms of
the king of Babylon, but the arms of Pharaoh

d21 Horn here symbolises strength.   a4 That is, the upper Nile region; also in verses 5 and 9
b5 Hebrew Cub   c13 Hebrew Noph; also in verse 16   d14 Hebrew waste Pathros
e14 Hebrew No; also in verses 15 and 16   f15 Hebrew Sin; also in verse 16   g17 Hebrew Awen (or On)
h17 Hebrew Pi Beseth

will fall limp. Then they will know that I am the LORD, when I put my sword into the hand of the king of Babylon and he brandishes it against Egypt. ²⁶I will disperse the Egyptians among the nations and scatter them through the countries. Then they will know that I am the LORD.''

A Cedar in Lebanon

31 In the eleventh year, in the third month on the first day, the word of the LORD came to me: ²''Son of man, say to Pharaoh king of Egypt and to his hordes:

'''Who can be compared with you in
    majesty?
³Consider Assyria, once a cedar in
    Lebanon,
  with beautiful branches overshadowing
    the forest;
it towered on high,
  its top above the thick foliage.
⁴The waters nourished it,
  deep springs made it grow tall;
their streams flowed
  all around its base
and sent their channels
  to all the trees of the field.
⁵So it towered higher
  than all the trees of the field;
its boughs increased
  and its branches grew long,
  spreading because of abundant waters.
⁶All the birds of the air
  nested in its boughs,
all the beasts of the field
  gave birth under its branches;
all the great nations
  lived in its shade.
⁷It was majestic in beauty,
  with its spreading boughs,
for its roots went down
  to abundant waters.
⁸The cedars in the garden of God
  could not rival it,
nor could the pine trees
  equal its boughs,
nor could the plane trees
  compare with its branches—
no tree in the garden of God
  could match its beauty.
⁹I made it beautiful
  with abundant branches,
the envy of all the trees of Eden
  in the garden of God.

¹⁰'''Therefore this is what the Sovereign LORD says: Because it towered on high, lifting its top above the thick foliage, and because it was proud of its height, ¹¹I handed it over to the ruler of the nations, for him to deal with according to its wickedness. I cast it aside, ¹²and the most ruthless of foreign nations cut it down and left it. Its boughs fell on the mountains and in all the valleys; its branches lay broken in all the ravines of the land. All the nations of the earth came out from under its shade and left it. ¹³All the birds of the air settled on the fallen tree, and all the

beasts of the field were among its branches. ¹⁴Therefore no other trees by the waters are ever to tower proudly on high, lifting their tops above the thick foliage. No other trees so well-watered are ever to reach such a height; they are all destined for death, for the earth below, among mortal men, with those who go down to the pit.

¹⁵'''This is what the Sovereign LORD says: On the day it was brought down to the grave[a] I covered the deep springs with mourning for it; I held back its streams, and its abundant waters were restrained. Because of it I clothed Lebanon with gloom, and all the trees of the field withered away. ¹⁶I made the nations tremble at the sound of its fall when I brought it down to the grave with those who go down to the pit. Then all the trees of Eden, the choicest and best of Lebanon, all the trees that were well-watered, were consoled in the earth below. ¹⁷Those who lived in its shade, its allies among the nations, had also gone down to the grave with it, joining those killed by the sword.

¹⁸'''Which of the trees of Eden can be compared with you in splendour and majesty? Yet you, too, will be brought down with the trees of Eden to the earth below; you will lie among the uncircumcised, with those killed by the sword.

'''This is Pharaoh and all his hordes, declares the Sovereign LORD.'''

A Lament for Pharaoh

32 In the twelfth year, in the twelfth month on the first day, the word of the LORD came to me: ²''Son of man, take up a lament concerning Pharaoh king of Egypt and say to him:

'''You are like a lion among the nations;
  you are like a monster in the seas
thrashing about in your streams,
  churning the water with your feet
  and muddying the streams.

³'''This is what the Sovereign LORD says:

'''With a great throng of people
  I will cast my net over you,
  and they will haul you up in my net.
⁴I will throw you on the land
  and hurl you on the open field.
I will let all the birds of the air settle on
    you
  and all the beasts of the earth gorge
    themselves on you.
⁵I will spread your flesh on the mountains
  and fill the valleys with your remains.
⁶I will drench the land with your flowing
    blood
  all the way to the mountains,
  and the ravines will be filled with your
    flesh.
⁷When I snuff you out, I will cover the
    heavens
  and darken their stars;
I will cover the sun with a cloud,
  and the moon will not give its light.

---

⁸All the shining lights in the heavens
  I will darken over you;
  I will bring darkness over your land,
          declares the Sovereign Lord.
⁹I will trouble the hearts of many peoples
  when I bring about your destruction
    among the nations,
  among*a* lands you have not known.
¹⁰I will cause many peoples to be appalled at
    you,
  and their kings will shudder with horror
    because of you
  when I brandish my sword before them.
On the day of your downfall
  each of them will tremble
  every moment for his life.

¹¹'For this is what the Sovereign Lord
says:

'The sword of the king of Babylon
  will come against you.
¹²I will cause your hordes to fall
  by the swords of mighty men—
    the most ruthless of all nations.
They will shatter the pride of Egypt,
  and all her hordes will be overthrown.
¹³I will destroy all her cattle
  from beside abundant waters
no longer to be stirred by the foot of man
  or muddied by the hoofs of cattle.
¹⁴Then I will let her waters settle
  and make her streams flow like oil,
          declares the Sovereign Lord.
¹⁵When I make Egypt desolate
  and strip the land of everything in it,
  when I strike down all who live there,
  then they will know that I am the Lord.'

¹⁶"This is the lament they will chant for
her. The daughters of the nations will chant
it; for Egypt and all her hordes they will chant
it, declares the Sovereign Lord."

¹⁷In the twelfth year, on the fifteenth day of
the month, the word of the Lord came to me:
¹⁸"Son of man, wail for the hordes of Egypt
and consign to the earth below both her and
the daughters of mighty nations, with those
who go down to the pit. ¹⁹Say to them, 'Are
you more favoured than others? Go down
and be laid among the uncircumcised.'
²⁰They will fall among those killed by the
sword. The sword is drawn; let her be
dragged off with all her hordes. ²¹From within the grave*b* the mighty leaders will say of
Egypt and her allies, 'They have come down
and they lie with the uncircumcised, with
those killed by the sword.'

²²"Assyria is there with her whole army;
she is surrounded by the graves of all her
slain, all who have fallen by the sword.
²³Their graves are in the depths of the pit and
her army lies around her grave. All who had
spread terror in the land of the living are
slain, fallen by the sword.
²⁴"Elam is there, with all her hordes
around her grave. All of them are slain, fallen
by the sword. All who had spread terror in

the land of the living went down uncircumcised to the earth below. They bear their
shame with those who go down to the pit. ²⁵A
bed is made for her among the slain, with all
her hordes around her grave. All of them are
uncircumcised, killed by the sword. Because
their terror had spread in the land of the
living, they bear their shame with those who
go down to the pit; they are laid among the
slain.

²⁶"Meshech and Tubal are there, with all
their hordes around their graves. All of them
are uncircumcised, killed by the sword because they spread their terror in the land of
the living. ²⁷Do they not lie with the other
uncircumcised warriors who have fallen,
who went down to the grave with their
weapons of war, whose swords were placed
under their heads? The punishment for their
sins rested on their bones, though the terror
of these warriors had stalked through the
land of the living.

²⁸"You too, O Pharaoh, will be broken and
will lie among the uncircumcised, with those
killed by the sword.

²⁹"Edom is there, her kings and all her
princes; despite their power, they are laid
with those killed by the sword. They lie with
the uncircumcised, with those who go down
to the pit.

³⁰"All the princes of the north and all the
Sidonians are there; they went down with the
slain in disgrace despite the terror caused by
their power. They lie uncircumcised with
those killed by the sword and bear their
shame with those who go down to the pit.

³¹"Pharaoh—he and all his army—will see
them and he will be consoled for all his
hordes that were killed by the sword, declares the Sovereign Lord. ³²Although I had
him spread terror in the land of the living,
Pharaoh and all his hordes will be laid among
the uncircumcised, with those killed by the
sword, declares the Sovereign Lord."

Ezekiel a Watchman

33 The word of the Lord came to me:
²"Son of man, speak to your countrymen and say to them: 'When I bring the
sword against a land, and the people of the
land choose one of their men and make him
their watchman, ³and he sees the sword coming against the land and blows the trumpet to
warn the people, ⁴then if anyone hears the
trumpet but does not take warning and the
sword comes and takes his life, his blood will
be on his own head. ⁵Since he heard the
sound of the trumpet but did not take warning, his blood will be on his own head. If he
had taken warning, he would have saved
himself. ⁶But if the watchman sees the sword
coming and does not blow the trumpet to
warn the people and the sword comes and
takes the life of one of them, that man will be
taken away because of his sin, but I will hold
the watchman accountable for his blood.'

⁷"Son of man, I have made you a watchman for the house of Israel; so hear the word

a9 Hebrew; Septuagint *bring you into captivity among the nations, / to*
b21 Hebrew *Sheol*; also in verse 27

I speak and give them warning from me. 8When I say to the wicked, 'O wicked man, you will surely die,' and you do not speak out to dissuade him from his ways, that wicked man will die for[a] his sin, and I will hold you accountable for his blood. 9But if you do warn the wicked man to turn from his ways and he does not do so, he will die for his sin, but you will be saved yourself.

10"Son of man, say to the house of Israel, 'This is what you are saying: "Our offences and sins weigh us down, and we are wasting away because of[b] them. How then can we live?"' 11Say to them, 'As surely as I live, declares the Sovereign LORD, I take no pleasure in the death of the wicked, but rather that they turn from their ways and live. Turn! Turn from your evil ways! Why will you die, O house of Israel?'

12"Therefore, son of man, say to your countrymen, 'The righteousness of the righteous man will not save him when he disobeys, and the wickedness of the wicked man will not cause him to fall when he turns from it. The righteous man, if he sins, will not be allowed to live because of his former righteousness.' 13If I tell the righteous man that he will surely live, but then he trusts in his righteousness and does evil, none of the righteous things he has done will be remembered; he will die for the evil he has done. 14And if I say to the wicked man, 'You will surely die,' but he then turns away from his sin and does what is just and right—15if he gives back what he took in pledge for a loan, returns what he has stolen, follows the decrees that give life, and does no evil, he will surely live; he will not die. 16None of the sins he has committed will be remembered against him. He has done what is just and right; he will surely live.

17"Yet your countrymen say, 'The way of the Lord is not just.' But it is their way that is not just. 18If a righteous man turns from his righteousness and does evil, he will die for it. 19And if a wicked man turns away from his wickedness and does what is just and right, he will live by doing so. 20Yet, O house of Israel, you say, 'The way of the Lord is not just.' But I will judge each of you according to his own ways."

Jerusalem's Fall Explained

21In the twelfth year of our exile, in the tenth month on the fifth day, a man who had escaped from Jerusalem came to me and said, "The city has fallen!" 22Now the evening before the man arrived, the hand of the LORD was upon me, and he opened my mouth before the man came to me in the morning. So my mouth was opened and I was no longer silent.

23Then the word of the LORD came to me: 24"Son of man, the people living in those ruins in the land of Israel are saying, 'Abraham was only one man, yet he possessed the land. But we are many; surely the land has been given to us as our possession.' 25Therefore say to them, 'This is what the Sovereign LORD says: Since you eat meat with the blood still in it and look to your idols and shed blood, should you then possess the land? 26You rely on your sword, you do detestable things, and each of you defiles his neighbour's wife. Should you then possess the land?'

27"Say this to them: 'This is what the Sovereign LORD says: As surely as I live, those who are left in the ruins will fall by the sword, those out in the country I will give to the wild animals to be devoured, and those in strongholds and caves will die of a plague. 28I will make the land a desolate waste, and her proud strength will come to an end, and the mountains of Israel will become desolate so that no-one will cross them. 29Then they will know that I am the LORD, when I have made the land a desolate waste because of all the detestable things they have done.'

30"As for you, son of man, your countrymen are talking together about you by the walls and at the doors of the houses, saying to each other, 'Come and hear the message that has come from the LORD.' 31My people come to you, as they usually do, and sit before you to listen to your words, but they do not put them into practice. With their mouths they express devotion, but their hearts are greedy for unjust gain. 32Indeed, to them you are nothing more than one who sings love songs with a beautiful voice and plays an instrument well, for they hear your words but do not put them into practice.

33"When all this comes true—and it surely will—then they will know that a prophet has been among them."

Shepherds and Sheep

34 The word of the LORD came to me: 2"Son of man, prophesy against the shepherds of Israel; prophesy and say to them: 'This is what the Sovereign LORD says: Woe to the shepherds of Israel who only take care of themselves! Should not shepherds take care of the flock? 3You eat the curds, clothe yourselves with the wool and slaughter the choice animals, but you do not take care of the flock. 4You have not strengthened the weak or healed the sick or bound up the injured. You have not brought back the strays or searched for the lost. You have ruled them harshly and brutally. 5So they were scattered because there was no shepherd, and when they were scattered they became food for all the wild animals. 6My sheep wandered over all the mountains and on every high hill. They were scattered over the whole earth, and no-one searched or looked for them.

7"'Therefore, you shepherds, hear the word of the LORD: 8As surely as I live, declares the Sovereign LORD, because my flock lacks a shepherd and so has been plundered and has become food for all the wild animals, and because my shepherds did not search for my flock but cared for themselves rather than for my flock, 9therefore, O shepherds, hear the word of the LORD: 10This is what

[a]8 Or in; also in verse 9   [b]10 Or away in

the Sovereign LORD says: I am against the shepherds and will hold them accountable for my flock. I will remove them from tending the flock so that the shepherds can no longer feed themselves. I will rescue my flock from their mouths, and it will no longer be food for them.

11"'For this is what the Sovereign LORD says: I myself will search for my sheep and look after them. 12As a shepherd looks after his scattered flock when he is with them, so will I look after my sheep. I will rescue them from all the places where they were scattered on a day of clouds and darkness. 13I will bring them out from the nations and gather them from the countries, and I will bring them into their own land. I will pasture them on the mountains of Israel, in the ravines and in all the settlements in the land. 14I will tend them in a good pasture, and the mountain heights of Israel will be their grazing land. There they will lie down in good grazing land, and there they will feed in a rich pasture on the mountains of Israel. 15I myself will tend my sheep and make them lie down, declares the Sovereign LORD. 16I will search for the lost and bring back the strays. I will bind up the injured and strengthen the weak, but the sleek and the strong I will destroy. I will shepherd the flock with justice.

17"'As for you, my flock, this is what the Sovereign LORD says: I will judge between one sheep and another, and between rams and goats. 18Is it not enough for you to feed on the good pasture? Must you also trample the rest of your pasture with your feet? Is it not enough for you to drink clear water? Must you also muddy the rest with your feet? 19Must my flock feed on what you have trampled and drink what you have muddied with your feet?

20"'Therefore this is what the Sovereign LORD says to them: See, I myself will judge between the fat sheep and the lean sheep. 21Because you shove with flank and shoulder, butting all the weak sheep with your horns until you have driven them away, 22I will save my flock, and they will no longer be plundered. I will judge between one sheep and another. 23I will place over them one shepherd, my servant David, and he will tend them; he will tend them and be their shepherd. 24I the LORD will be their God, and my servant David will be prince among them. I the LORD have spoken.

25"'I will make a covenant of peace with them and rid the land of wild beasts so that they may live in the desert and sleep in the forests in safety. 26I will bless them and the places surrounding my hill.a I will send down showers in season; there will be showers of blessing. 27The trees of the field will yield their fruit and the ground will yield its crops; the people will be secure in their land. They will know that I am the LORD, when I break the bars of their yoke and rescue them from the hands of those who enslaved them. 28They will no longer be plundered by the nations, nor will wild animals devour them.

They will live in safety, and no-one will make them afraid. 29I will provide for them a land renowned for its crops, and they will no longer be victims of famine in the land or bear the scorn of the nations. 30Then they will know that I, the LORD their God, am with them and that they, the house of Israel, are my people, declares the Sovereign LORD. 31You my sheep, the sheep of my pasture, are people, and I am your God, declares the Sovereign LORD.'"

A Prophecy Against Edom

35 The word of the LORD came to me: 2"Son of man, set your face against Mount Seir; prophesy against it 3and say: 'This is what the Sovereign LORD says: I am against you, Mount Seir, and I will stretch out my hand against you and make you a desolate waste. 4I will turn your towns into ruins and you will be desolate. Then you will know that I am the LORD.

5"'Because you harboured an ancient hostility and delivered the Israelites over to the sword at the time of their calamity, the time their punishment reached its climax, 6therefore as surely as I live, declares the Sovereign LORD, I will give you over to bloodshed and it will pursue you. Since you did not hate bloodshed, bloodshed will pursue you. 7I will make Mount Seir a desolate waste and cut off from it all who come and go. 8I will fill your mountains with the slain; those killed by the sword will fall on your hills and in your valleys and in all your ravines. 9I will make you desolate for ever; your towns will not be inhabited. Then you will know that I am the LORD.

10"'Because you have said, "These two nations and countries will be ours and we will take possession of them," even though I the LORD was there, 11therefore as surely as I live, declares the Sovereign LORD, I will treat you in accordance with the anger and jealousy you showed in your hatred of them and I will make myself known among them when I judge you. 12Then you will know that I the LORD have heard all the contemptible things you have said against the mountains of Israel. You said, "They have been laid waste and have been given over to us to devour." 13You boasted against me and spoke against me without restraint, and I heard it. 14This is what the Sovereign LORD says: While the whole earth rejoices, I will make you desolate. 15Because you rejoiced when the inheritance of the house of Israel became desolate, that is how I will treat you. You will be desolate, O Mount Seir, you and all of Edom. Then they will know that I am the LORD.'"

A Prophecy to the Mountains of Israel

36 "Son of man, prophesy to the mountains of Israel and say, 'O mountains of Israel, hear the word of the LORD. 2This is what the Sovereign LORD says: The enemy said of you, "Aha! The ancient heights have become our possession."' 3Therefore

a26 Or I will make them and the places surrounding my hill a blessing

EZEKIEL 34:1–16

'As a shepherd looks after his scattered flock . . . so will I look after my sheep . . . I will search for the lost and bring back the strays. I will bind up the injured and strengthen the weak, but the sleek and the strong I will destroy. I will shepherd the flock with justice' (vv. 12a, 16).

HOW COMFORTING! A fine preview of the New Testament good shepherd (John 10). The parallel is plain to all, but look carefully at the sleek and the strong being destroyed. The shepherd is suspicious of the sleek and the strong! How have they become strong? How has their prosperity come about? Has the fat sheep taken more than his share of nourishment, and pushed his weaker brother out? Does he need destroying to ensure he doesn't keep on doing it?

Yes, indeed, as other versions of v. 16 make clear. The KJV has 'I will destroy the fat and the strong,' and the Living Bible adds a different slant on feeding, 'I will feed them, yes – feed them punishment!' Comforting words have a sting in the tail. Throwing pounds, marks, dollars or yen at a problem while influenced by a pop concert may placate a conscience or two. It will make no long-term difference. Givers will remain rich, recipients poor; for proper long-term care of the weak would mean real pain and sacrifice for the strong, and that is unacceptable except to a small minority amongst whom are numbered earnest Christians of all kinds.

Jesus tells of a shepherd who left the ninety and nine to look after themselves, and sought the lost one (Matt. 18:12; Luke 15:4) over whom he rejoiced. This message is very close to that of Ezekiel. Both demand real priority for the weak, if anything like justice is to be done.

Lord, help all those who are weak – and help those of us who are strong not to complain when you do. Help us to work with you to achieve justice, even when it hurts us personally.

→714

DANIEL 1:17–21
'To these four young men God gave knowledge and understanding of all kinds of literature and learning. And Daniel could understand visions and dreams of all kinds' (v. 17).

WE HAVE ALL MET PEOPLE who seem to have a special understanding of those around them; the kind of people others start to talk to, and tell them their problems without any embarrassment. They are able to set others at ease, give them confidence, and help them to cope with the difficulties they face.

Some time ago I was speaking to a well-known TV personality. He had just been to a large Salvation Army gathering as a special guest. He had been very, very nervous but, he told me, one particular officer at that meeting had been able to put him at ease. 'That man,' he said, 'is priceless. He is worth his weight in gold. He could walk into any media job and name his salary.'

Today's passage gives me the impression that Daniel and his friends were like that. They had this immediate sense of harmony with people, and an ability to put them at their ease. Daniel's interview with the king is not described in detail, but we get an impression of Daniel holding the king's interest and putting him at ease, rather than the other way round. Part of the secret was certainly to be found in knowing the subject. The Hebrew boys had indeed learned well. But knowing a subject and being able to communicate it effectively to others are very different things.

Daniel's communication skill came from his strong reliance on God, coupled with his confident use of the abilities God had given him.

→733

prophesy and say, 'This is what the Sovereign Lord says: Because they ravaged and hounded you from every side so that you became the possession of the rest of the nations and the object of people's malicious talk and slander, 4therefore, O mountains of Israel, hear the word of the Sovereign Lord: This is what the Sovereign Lord says to the mountains and hills, to the ravines and valleys, to the desolate ruins and the deserted towns that have been plundered and ridiculed by the rest of the nations around you —5this is what the Sovereign Lord says: In my burning zeal I have spoken against the rest of the nations, and against Edom, for with glee and with malice in their hearts they made my land their own possession so that they might plunder its pasture-land.' 6Therefore prophesy concerning the land of Israel and say to the mountains and hills, to the ravines and valleys: 'This is what the Sovereign Lord says: I speak in my jealous wrath because you have suffered the scorn of the nations. 7Therefore this is what the Sovereign Lord says: I swear with uplifted hand that the nations around you will also suffer scorn.

8"'But you, O mountains of Israel, will produce branches and fruit for my people Israel, for they will soon come home. 9I am concerned for you and will look on you with favour; you will be ploughed and sown, 10and I will multiply the number of people upon you, even the whole house of Israel. The towns will be inhabited and the ruins rebuilt. 11I will increase the number of men and animals upon you, and they will be fruitful and become numerous. I will settle people on you as in the past and will make you prosper more than before. Then you will know that I am the Lord. 12I will cause people, my people Israel, to walk upon you. They will possess you, and you will be their inheritance; you will never again deprive them of their children.

13"'This is what the Sovereign Lord says: Because people say to you, "You devour men and deprive your nation of its children," 14therefore you will no longer devour men or make your nation childless, declares the Sovereign Lord. 15No longer will I make you hear the taunts of the nations, and no longer will you suffer the scorn of the peoples or cause your nation to fall, declares the Sovereign Lord.'"

16Again the word of the Lord came to me: 17"Son of man, when the people of Israel were living in their own land, they defiled it by their conduct and their actions. Their conduct was like a woman's monthly uncleanness in my sight. 18So I poured out my wrath on them because they had shed blood in the land and because they had defiled it with their idols. 19I dispersed them among the nations, and they were scattered through the countries; I judged them according to their conduct and their actions. 20And wherever they went among the nations they profaned my holy name, for it was said of them, 'These are the Lord's people, and yet they had to leave his land.' 21I had concern for my holy name, which the house of Israel profaned among the nations where they had gone.

22"Therefore say to the house of Israel, 'This is what the Sovereign Lord says: It is not for your sake, O house of Israel, that I am going to do these things, but for the sake of my holy name, which you have profaned among the nations where you have gone. 23I will show the holiness of my great name, which has been profaned among the nations, the name you have profaned among them. Then the nations will know that I am the Lord, declares the Sovereign Lord, when I show myself holy through you before their eyes.

24"'For I will take you out of the nations; I will gather you from all the countries and bring you back into your own land. 25I will sprinkle clean water on you, and you will be clean; I will cleanse you from all your impurities and from all your idols. 26I will give you a new heart and put a new spirit in you; I will remove from you your heart of stone and give you a heart of flesh. 27And I will put my Spirit in you and move you to follow my decrees and be careful to keep my laws. 28You will live in the land I gave your forefathers; you will be my people, and I will be your God. 29I will save you from all your uncleanness. I will call for the corn and make it plentiful and will not bring famine upon you. 30I will increase the fruit of the trees and the crops of the field, so that you will no longer suffer disgrace among the nations because of famine. 31Then you will remember your evil ways and wicked deeds, and you will loathe yourselves for your sins and detestable practices. 32I want you to know that I am not doing this for your sake, declares the Sovereign Lord. Be ashamed and disgraced for your conduct, O house of Israel!

33"'This is what the Sovereign Lord says: On the day I cleanse you from all your sins, I will resettle your towns, and the ruins will be rebuilt. 34The desolate land will be cultivated instead of lying desolate in the sight of all who pass through it. 35They will say, "This land that was laid waste has become like the garden of Eden; the cities that were lying in ruins, desolate and destroyed, are now fortified and inhabited." 36Then the nations around you that remain will know that I the Lord have rebuilt what was destroyed and have replanted what was desolate. I the Lord have spoken, and I will do it.'

37"This is what the Sovereign Lord says: Once again I will yield to the plea of the house of Israel and do this for them: I will make their people as numerous as sheep, 38as numerous as the flocks for offerings at Jerusalem during her appointed feasts. So will the ruined cities be filled with flocks of people. Then they will know that I am the Lord."

The Valley of Dry Bones

37 The hand of the Lord was upon me, and he brought me out by the Spirit of the Lord and set me in the middle of a valley; it was full of bones. 2He led me to and fro among them, and I saw a great many bones on the floor of the valley, bones that were very dry. ³He asked me, "Son of man, can these bones live?"

I said, "O Sovereign LORD, you alone know."

⁴Then he said to me, "Prophesy to these bones and say to them, 'Dry bones, hear the word of the LORD! ⁵This is what the Sovereign LORD says to these bones: I will make breath*ª* enter you, and you will come to life. ⁶I will attach tendons to you and make flesh come upon you and cover you with skin; I will put breath in you, and you will come to life. Then you will know that I am the LORD."

⁷So I prophesied as I was commanded. And as I was prophesying, there was a noise, a rattling sound, and the bones came together, bone to bone. ⁸I looked, and tendons and flesh appeared on them and skin covered them, but there was no breath in them.

⁹Then he said to me, "Prophesy to the breath; prophesy, son of man, and say to it, 'This is what the Sovereign LORD says: Come from the four winds, O breath, and breathe into these slain, that they may live.'" ¹⁰So I prophesied as he commanded me, and breath entered them; they came to life and stood up on their feet—a vast army.

¹¹Then he said to me: "Son of man, these bones are the whole house of Israel. They say, 'Our bones are dried up and our hope is gone; we are cut off.' ¹²Therefore prophesy and say to them: 'This is what the Sovereign LORD says: O my people, I am going to open your graves and bring you up from them; I will bring you back to the land of Israel. ¹³Then you, my people, will know that I am the LORD, when I open your graves and bring you up from them. ¹⁴I will put my Spirit in you and you will live, and I will settle you in your own land. Then you will know that I the LORD have spoken, and I have done it, declares the LORD.'"

One Nation Under One King

¹⁵The word of the LORD came to me: ¹⁶"Son of man, take a stick of wood and write on it, 'Belonging to Judah and the Israelites associated with him.' Then take another stick of wood, and write on it, 'Ephraim's stick, belonging to Joseph and all the house of Israel associated with him.' ¹⁷Join them together into one stick so that they will become one in your hand.

¹⁸"When your countrymen ask you, 'Won't you tell us what you mean by this?' ¹⁹say to them, 'This is what the Sovereign LORD says: I am going to take the stick of Joseph—which is in Ephraim's hand—and of the Israelite tribes associated with him, and join it to Judah's stick, making them a single stick of wood, and they will become one in my hand.' ²⁰Hold before their eyes the sticks you have written on ²¹and say to them, 'This is what the Sovereign LORD says: I will

take the Israelites out of the nations where they have gone. I will gather them from all around and bring them back into their own land. ²²I will make them one nation in the land, on the mountains of Israel. There will be one king over all of them and they will never again be two nations or be divided into two kingdoms. ²³They will no longer defile themselves with their idols and vile images or with any of their offences, for I will save them from all their sinful backsliding,*ᵇ* and I will cleanse them. They will be my people, and I will be their God.

²⁴"My servant David will be king over them, and they will all have one shepherd. They will follow my laws and be careful to keep my decrees. ²⁵They will live in the land I gave to my servant Jacob, the land where your fathers lived. They and their children and their children's children will live there for ever, and David my servant will be their prince for ever. ²⁶I will make a covenant of peace with them; it will be an everlasting covenant. I will establish them and increase their numbers, and I will put my sanctuary among them for ever. ²⁷My dwelling-place will be with them; I will be their God, and they will be my people. ²⁸Then the nations will know that I the LORD make Israel holy, when my sanctuary is among them for ever.'"

A Prophecy Against Gog

38 The word of the LORD came to me: ²"Son of man, set your face against Gog, of the land of Magog, the chief prince of*ª* Meshech and Tubal; prophesy against him ³and say: 'This is what the Sovereign LORD says: I am against you, O Gog, chief prince of*ᵇ* Meshech and Tubal. ⁴I will turn you around, put hooks in your jaws and bring you out with your whole army—your horses, your horsemen fully armed, and a great horde with large and small shields, all of them brandishing their swords. ⁵Persia, Cush*ᶜ* and Put will be with them, all with shields and helmets, ⁶also Gomer with all its troops, and Beth Togarmah from the far north with all its troops—the many nations with you.

⁷"Get ready; be prepared, you and all the hordes gathered about you, and take command of them. ⁸After many days you will be called to arms. In future years you will invade a land that has recovered from war, whose people were gathered from many nations to the mountains of Israel, which had long been desolate. They had been brought out from the nations, and now all of them live in safety. ⁹You and all your troops and the many nations with you will go up, advancing like a storm; you will be like a cloud covering the land.

¹⁰"This is what the Sovereign LORD says: On that day thoughts will come into your mind and you will devise an evil scheme. ¹¹You will say, "I will invade a land of unwalled villages; I will attack a peaceful and

ª5 The Hebrew for this word can also mean *wind* or *spirit* (see verses 6–14).
ᵇ23 Many Hebrew manuscripts (see also Septuagint); most Hebrew manuscripts *all their dwelling-places where they sinned*   *ª2* Or *the prince of Rosh,*   *ᵇ3* Or *Gog, prince of Rosh,*   *ᶜ5* That is, the upper Nile region

unsuspecting people—all of them living without walls and without gates and bars. ¹²I will plunder and loot and turn my hand against the resettled ruins and the people gathered from the nations, rich in livestock and goods, living at the centre of the land." ¹³Sheba and Dedan and the merchants of Tarshish and all her villages*d* will say to you, "Have you come to plunder? Have you gathered your hordes to loot, to carry off silver and gold, to take away livestock and goods and to seize much plunder?"'

¹⁴"Therefore, son of man, prophesy and say to Gog: 'This is what the Sovereign LORD says: In that day, when my people Israel are living in safety, will you not take notice of it? ¹⁵You will come from your place in the far north, you and many nations with you, all of them riding on horses, a great horde, a mighty army. ¹⁶You will advance against my people Israel like a cloud that covers the land. In days to come, O Gog, I will bring you against my land, so that the nations may know me when I show myself holy through you before their eyes.

¹⁷"'This is what the Sovereign LORD says: Are you not the one I spoke of in former days by my servants the prophets of Israel? At that time they prophesied for years that I would bring you against them. ¹⁸This is what will happen in that day: When Gog attacks the land of Israel, my hot anger will be aroused, declares the Sovereign LORD. ¹⁹In my zeal and fiery wrath I declare that at that time there shall be a great earthquake in the land of Israel. ²⁰The fish of the sea, the birds of the air, the beasts of the field, every creature that moves along the ground, and all the people on the face of the earth will tremble at my presence. The mountains will be overturned, the cliffs will crumble and every wall will fall to the ground. ²¹I will summon a sword against Gog on all my mountains, declares the Sovereign LORD. Every man's sword will be against his brother. ²²I will execute judgment upon him with plague and bloodshed; I will pour down torrents of rain, hailstones and burning sulphur on him and on his troops and on the many nations with him. ²³And so I will show my greatness and my holiness, and I will make myself known in the sight of many nations. Then they will know that I am the LORD.'

39 "Son of man, prophesy against Gog and say: 'This is what the Sovereign LORD says: I am against you, O Gog, chief prince of*ª* Meshech and Tubal. ²I will turn you around and drag you along. I will bring you from the far north and send you against the mountains of Israel. ³Then I will strike your bow from your left hand and make your arrows drop from your right hand. ⁴On the mountains of Israel you will fall, you and all your troops and the nations with you. I will give you as food to all kinds of carrion birds and to the wild animals. ⁵You will fall in the open field, for I have spoken, declares the Sovereign LORD. ⁶I will send fire on Magog

and on those who live in safety in the coastlands, and they will know that I am the LORD.

⁷"'I will make known my holy name among my people Israel. I will no longer let my holy name be profaned, and the nations will know that I the LORD am the Holy One in Israel. ⁸It is coming! It will surely take place, declares the Sovereign LORD. This is the day I have spoken of.

⁹"'Then those who live in the towns of Israel will go out and use the weapons for fuel and burn them up—the small and large shields, the bows and arrows, the war clubs and spears. For seven years they will use them for fuel. ¹⁰They will not need to gather wood from the fields or cut it from the forests, because they will use the weapons for fuel. And they will plunder those who plundered them and loot those who looted them, declares the Sovereign LORD.

¹¹"'On that day I will give Gog a burial place in Israel, in the valley of those who travel east towards*b* the Sea.*c* It will block the way of travellers, because Gog and all his hordes will be buried there. So it will be called the Valley of Hamon Gog.*d*

¹²"'For seven months the house of Israel will be burying them in order to cleanse the land. ¹³All the people of the land will bury them, and the day I am glorified will be a memorable day for them, declares the Sovereign LORD.

¹⁴"'Men will be regularly employed to cleanse the land. Some will go throughout the land and, in addition to them, others will bury those that remain on the ground. At the end of the seven months they will begin their search. ¹⁵As they go through the land and one of them sees a human bone, he will set up a marker beside it until the gravediggers have buried it in the Valley of Hamon Gog. ¹⁶(Also a town called Hamonah*e* will be there.) And so they will cleanse the land.'

¹⁷"Son of man, this is what the Sovereign LORD says: Call out to every kind of bird and all the wild animals: 'Assemble and come together from all around to the sacrifice I am preparing for you, the great sacrifice on the mountains of Israel. There you will eat flesh and drink blood. ¹⁸You will eat the flesh of mighty men and drink the blood of the princes of the earth as if they were rams and lambs, goats and bulls—all of them fattened animals from Bashan. ¹⁹At the sacrifice I am preparing for you, you will eat fat till you are glutted and drink blood till you are drunk. ²⁰At my table you will eat your fill of horses and riders, mighty men and soldiers of every kind,' declares the Sovereign LORD.

²¹"'I will display my glory among the nations, and all the nations will see the punishment I inflict and the hand I lay upon them. ²²From that day forward the house of Israel will know that I am the LORD their God. ²³And the nations will know that the people of Israel went into exile for their sin, because they were unfaithful to me. So I hid my face from them and handed them over to their

d13 Or her strong lions   ª1 Or Gog, prince of Rosh,   b11 Or of   c11 That is, the Dead Sea
d11 Hamon Gog means hordes of Gog.   e16 Hamonah means horde.

enemies, and they all fell by the sword. 24I dealt with them according to their uncleanness and their offences, and I hid my face from them.

25"Therefore this is what the Sovereign LORD says: I will now bring Jacob back from captivity*f* and will have compassion on all the people of Israel, and I will be zealous for my holy name. 26They will forget their shame and all the unfaithfulness they showed towards me when they lived in safety in their land with no-one to make them afraid. 27When I have brought them back from the nations and have gathered them from the countries of their enemies, I will show myself holy through them in the sight of many nations. 28Then they will know that I am the LORD their God, for though I sent them into exile among the nations, I will gather them to their own land, not leaving any behind. 29I will no longer hide my face from them, for I will pour out my Spirit on the house of Israel, declares the Sovereign LORD.''

The New Temple Area

40 In the twenty-fifth year of our exile, at the beginning of the year, on the tenth of the month, in the fourteenth year after the fall of the city—on that very day the hand of the LORD was upon me and he took me there. 2In visions of God he took me to the land of Israel and set me on a very high mountain, on whose south side were some buildings that looked like a city. 3He took me there, and I saw a man whose appearance was like bronze; he was standing in the gateway with a linen cord and a measuring rod in his hand. 4The man said to me, ''Son of man, look with your eyes and hear with your ears and pay attention to everything I am going to show you, for that is why you have been brought here. Tell the house of Israel everything you see.''

The East Gate to the Outer Court

5I saw a wall completely surrounding the temple area. The length of the measuring rod in the man's hand was six long cubits, each of which was a cubit*d* and a handbreadth.*b* He measured the wall; it was one measuring rod thick and one rod high.

6Then he went to the gate facing east. He climbed its steps and measured the threshold of the gate; it was one rod deep.*c* 7The alcoves for the guards were one rod long and one rod wide, and the projecting walls between the alcoves were five cubits thick. And the threshold of the gate next to the portico facing the temple was one rod deep.

8Then he measured the portico of the gateway; 9it*d* was eight cubits deep and its jambs were two cubits thick. The portico of the gateway faced the temple.

10Inside the east gate were three alcoves on each side; the three had the same measurements, and the faces of the projecting walls

on each side had the same measurements. 11Then he measured the width of the entrance to the gateway; it was ten cubits and its length was thirteen cubits. 12In front of each alcove was a wall one cubit high, and the alcoves were six cubits square. 13Then he measured the gateway from the top of the rear wall of one alcove to the top of the opposite one; the distance was twenty-five cubits from one parapet opening to the opposite one. 14He measured along the faces of the projecting walls all around the inside of the gateway—sixty cubits. The measurement was up to the portico*e* facing the courtyard.*f* 15The distance from the entrance of the gateway to the far end of its portico was fifty cubits. 16The alcoves and the projecting walls inside the gateway were surmounted by narrow parapet openings all round, as was the portico; the openings all round faced inward. The faces of the projecting walls were decorated with palm trees.

The Outer Court

17Then he brought me into the outer court. There I saw some rooms and a pavement that had been constructed all round the court; there were thirty rooms along the pavement. 18It abutted the sides of the gateways and was as wide as they were long; this was the lower pavement. 19Then he measured the distance from the inside of the lower gateway to the outside of the inner court; it was a hundred cubits on the east side as well as on the north.

The North Gate

20Then he measured the length and width of the gate facing north, leading into the outer court. 21Its alcoves—three on each side—its projecting walls and its portico had the same measurements as those of the first gateway. It was fifty cubits long and twenty-five cubits wide. 22Its openings, its portico and its palm tree decorations had the same measurements as those of the gate facing east. Seven steps led up to it, with its portico opposite them. 23There was a gate to the inner court facing the north gate, just as there was on the east. He measured from one gate to the opposite one; it was a hundred cubits.

The South Gate

24Then he led me to the south side and I saw a gate facing south. He measured its jambs and its portico, and they had the same measurements as the others. 25The gateway and its portico had narrow openings all round, like the openings of the others. It was fifty cubits long and twenty-five cubits wide. 26Seven steps led up to it, with its portico opposite them; it had palm tree decorations on the faces of the projecting walls on each side. 27The inner court also had a gate facing south, and he measured from this gate to the outer gate on the south side; it was a hundred cubits.

---

*f*25 Or *now restore the fortunes of Jacob*   *a*5 The common cubit was about 1½ feet (about 0.5 metre).
*b*5 That is, about 3 inches (about 8 centimetres)   *c*6 Septuagint; Hebrew *deep, the first threshold, one rod deep*
*d*8,9 Many Hebrew manuscripts, Septuagint, Vulgate and Syriac; most Hebrew manuscripts *gateway facing the temple; it was one rod deep.* *9Then he measured the portico of the gateway; it*
*e*14 Septuagint; Hebrew *projecting wall*   *f*14 The meaning of the Hebrew for this verse is uncertain.

Gates to the Inner Court

28Then he brought me into the inner court through the south gate, and he measured the south gate; it had the same measurements as the others. 29Its alcoves, its projecting walls and its portico had the same measurements as the others. The gateway and its portico had openings all round. It was fifty cubits long and twenty-five cubits wide. 30(The porticoes of the gateways around the inner court were twenty-five cubits wide and five cubits deep.) 31Its portico faced the outer court; palm trees decorated its jambs, and eight steps led up to it.

32Then he brought me to the inner court on the east side, and he measured the gateway; it had the same measurements as the others. 33Its alcoves, its projecting walls and its portico had the same measurements as the others. The gateway and its portico had openings all round. It was fifty cubits long and twenty-five cubits wide. 34Its portico faced the outer court; palm trees decorated the jambs on either side, and eight steps led up to it.

35Then he brought me to the north gate and measured it. It had the same measurements as the others, 36as did its alcoves, its projecting walls and its portico, and it had openings all round. It was fifty cubits long and twenty-five cubits wide. 37Its porticog faced the outer court; palm trees decorated the jambs on either side, and eight steps led up to it.

The Rooms for Preparing Sacrifices

38A room with a doorway was by the portico in each of the inner gateways, where the burnt offerings were washed. 39In the portico of the gateway were two tables on each side, on which the burnt offerings, sin offerings and guilt offerings were slaughtered. 40By the outside wall of the portico of the gateway, near the steps at the entrance to the north gateway were two tables, and on the other side of the steps were two tables. 41So there were four tables on one side of the gateway and four on the other—eight tables in all—on which the sacrifices were slaughtered. 42There were also four tables of dressed stone for the burnt offerings, each a cubit and a half long, a cubit and a half wide and a cubit high. On them were placed the utensils for slaughtering the burnt offerings and the other sacrifices. 43And double-pronged hooks, each a handbreadth long, were attached to the wall all around. The tables were for the flesh of the offerings.

Rooms for the Priests

44Outside the inner gate, within the inner court, were two rooms, oneh at the side of the north gate and facing south, and another at the side of the southi gate and facing north. 45He said to me, "The room facing south is for the priests who have charge of the temple, 46and the room facing north is for the priests

who have charge of the altar. These are the sons of Zadok, who are the only Levites who may draw near to the LORD to minister before him."

47Then he measured the court: It was square—a hundred cubits long and a hundred cubits wide. And the altar was in front of the temple.

The Temple

48He brought me to the portico of the temple and measured the jambs of the portico; they were five cubits wide on either side. The width of the entrance was fourteen cubits and its projecting walls werej three cubits wide on either side. 49The portico was twenty cubits wide, and twelvek cubits from front to back. It was reached by a flight of stairs,l and there were pillars on each side of the jambs.

41 Then the man brought me to the outer sanctuary and measured the jambs; the width of the jambs was six cubitsa on each side.b 2The entrance was ten cubits wide, and the projecting walls on each side of it were five cubits wide. He also measured the outer sanctuary; it was forty cubits long and twenty cubits wide.

3Then he went into the inner sanctuary and measured the jambs of the entrance; each was two cubits wide. The entrance was six cubits wide, and the projecting walls on each side of it were seven cubits wide. 4And he measured the length of the inner sanctuary; it was twenty cubits, and its width was twenty cubits across the end of the outer sanctuary. He said to me, "This is the Most Holy Place."

5Then he measured the wall of the temple; it was six cubits thick, and each side room round the temple was four cubits wide. 6The side rooms were on three levels, one above another, thirty on each level. There were ledges all round the wall of the temple to serve as supports for the side rooms, so that the supports were not inserted into the wall of the temple. 7The side rooms all round the temple were wider at each successive level. The structure surrounding the temple was built in ascending stages, so that the rooms widened as one went upward. A stairway went up from the lowest floor to the top floor through the middle floor.

8I saw that the temple had a raised base all round it, forming the foundation of the side rooms. It was the length of the rod, six long cubits. 9The outer wall of the side rooms was five cubits thick. The open area between the side rooms of the temple 10and the ⌊priests'⌋ rooms was twenty cubits wide all round the temple. 11There were entrances to the side rooms from the open area, one on the north and another on the south; and the base adjoining the open area was five cubits wide all round.

12The building facing the temple courtyard

---

g37 Septuagint (see also verses 31 and 34); Hebrew jambs
h44 Septuagint; Hebrew were rooms for singers, which were   i44 Septuagint; Hebrew east
j48 Septuagint; Hebrew entrance was   k49 Septuagint; Hebrew eleven
l49 Hebrew; Septuagint Ten steps led up to it   a1 The common cubit was about 1½ feet (about 0.5 metre)
b1 One Hebrew manuscript and Septuagint; most Hebrew manuscripts side, the width of the tent

on the west side was seventy cubits wide. The wall of the building was five cubits thick all round, and its length was ninety cubits.

¹³Then he measured the temple; it was a hundred cubits long, and the temple courtyard and the building with its walls were also a hundred cubits long. ¹⁴The width of the temple courtyard on the east, including the front of the temple, was a hundred cubits.

¹⁵Then he measured the length of the building facing the courtyard at the rear of the temple, including its galleries on each side; it was a hundred cubits.

The outer sanctuary, the inner sanctuary and the portico facing the court, ¹⁶as well as the thresholds and the narrow windows and galleries round the three of them—everything beyond and including the threshold was covered with wood. The floor, the wall up to the windows, and the windows were covered. ¹⁷In the space above the outside of the entrance to the inner sanctuary and on the walls at regular intervals all round the inner and outer sanctuary ¹⁸were carved cherubim and palm trees. Palm trees alternated with cherubim. Each cherub had two faces: ¹⁹the face of a man towards the palm tree on one side and the face of a lion towards the palm tree on the other. They were carved all round the whole temple. ²⁰From the floor to the area above the entrance, cherubim and palm trees were carved on the wall of the outer sanctuary.

²¹The outer sanctuary had a rectangular door-frame, and the one at the front of the Most Holy Place was similar. ²²There was a wooden altar three cubits high and two cubits square;ᶜ its corners, its baseᵈ and its sides were of wood. The man said to me, "This is the table that is before the LORD." ²³Both the outer sanctuary and the Most Holy Place had double doors. ²⁴Each door had two leaves—two hinged leaves for each door. ²⁵And on the doors of the outer sanctuary were carved cherubim and palm trees like those carved on the walls, and there was a wooden overhang on the front of the portico. ²⁶On the side walls of the portico were narrow windows with palm trees carved on each side. The side rooms of the temple also had overhangs.

Rooms for the Priests

42 Then the man led me northward into the outer court and brought me to the rooms opposite the temple courtyard and opposite the outer wall on the north side. ²The building whose door faced north was a hundred cubitsᵃ long and fifty cubits wide. ³Both in the section twenty cubits from the inner court and in the section opposite the pavement of the outer court, gallery faced gallery at the three levels. ⁴In front of the rooms was an inner passageway ten cubits wide and a hundred cubitsᵇ long. Their doors were on the north. ⁵Now the upper rooms were narrower, for the galleries took more

space from them than from the rooms on the lower and middle floors of the building. ⁶The rooms on the third floor had no pillars, as the courts had; so they were smaller in floor space than those on the lower and middle floors. ⁷There was an outer wall parallel to the rooms and the outer court; it extended in front of the rooms for fifty cubits. ⁸While the row of rooms on the side next to the outer court was fifty cubits long, the row on the side nearest the sanctuary was a hundred cubits long. ⁹The lower rooms had an entrance on the east side as one enters them from the outer court.

¹⁰On the south sideᶜ along the length of the wall of the outer court, adjoining the temple courtyard and opposite the outer wall, were rooms ¹¹with a passageway in front of them. These were like the rooms on the north; they had the same length and width, with similar exits and dimensions. Similar to the doorways on the north ¹²were the doorways of the rooms on the south. There was a doorway at the beginning of the passageway that was parallel to the corresponding wall extending eastward, by which one enters the rooms.

¹³Then he said to me, "The north and south rooms facing the temple courtyard are the priests' rooms, where the priests who approach the LORD will eat the most holy offerings. There they will put the most holy offerings—the grain offerings, the sin offerings and the guilt offerings—for the place is holy. ¹⁴Once the priests enter the holy precincts, they are not to go into the outer court until they leave behind the garments in which they minister, for these are holy. They are to put on other clothes before they go near the places that are for the people."

¹⁵When he had finished measuring what was inside the temple area, he led me out by the east gate and measured the area all around: ¹⁶He measured the east side with the measuring rod; it was five hundred cubits.ᵈ ¹⁷He measured the north side; it was five hundred cubitsᵉ by the measuring rod. ¹⁸He measured the south side; it was five hundred cubits by the measuring rod. ¹⁹Then he turned to the west side and measured; it was five hundred cubits by the measuring rod. ²⁰So he measured the area on all four sides. It had a wall round it, five hundred cubits long and five hundred cubits wide, to separate the holy from the common.

The Glory Returns to the Temple

43 Then the man brought me to the gate facing east, ²and I saw the glory of the God of Israel coming from the east. His voice was like the roar of rushing waters, and the land was radiant with his glory. ³The vision I saw was like the vision I had seen when heᵃ came to destroy the city and like the visions I had seen by the Kebar River, and I fell face down. ⁴The glory of the LORD entered the temple through the gate facing east. ⁵Then the Spirit lifted me up and brought me into

---

ᶜ22 Septuagint; Hebrew *long*   ᵈ22 Septuagint; Hebrew *length*
ᵃ2 The common cubit was about 1½ feet (about 0.5 metre).   ᵇ4 Septuagint and Syriac; Hebrew *and one cubit*
ᶜ10 Septuagint; Hebrew *Eastward*   ᵈ16 See Septuagint of verse 17; Hebrew *rods*; also in verses 18 and 19.
ᵉ17 Septuagint; Hebrew *rods*   ᵃ3 Some Hebrew manuscripts and Vulgate; most Hebrew manuscripts *I*

the inner court, and the glory of the LORD filled the temple.

6While the man was standing beside me, I heard someone speaking to me from inside the temple. 7He said: "Son of man, this is the place of my throne and the place for the soles of my feet. This is where I will live among the Israelites for ever. The house of Israel will never again defile my holy name—neither they nor their kings—by their prostitution*b* and the lifeless idols*c* of their kings at their high places. 8When they placed their threshold next to my threshold and their doorposts beside my doorposts, with only a wall between me and them, they defiled my holy name by their detestable practices. So I destroyed them in my anger. 9Now let them put away from me their prostitution and the lifeless idols of their kings, and I will live among them for ever.

10"Son of man, describe the temple to the people of Israel, that they may be ashamed of their sins. Let them consider the plan, 11and if they are ashamed of all they have done, make known to them the design of the temple —its arrangement, its exits and entrances —its whole design and all its regulations*d* and laws. Write these down before them so that they may be faithful to its design and follow all its regulations.

12"This is the law of the temple: All the surrounding area on top of the mountain will be most holy. Such is the law of the temple.

The Altar

13"These are the measurements of the altar in long cubits, that cubit being a cubit*e* and a handbreadth:*f* Its gutter is a cubit deep and a cubit wide, with a rim of one span*g* around the edge. And this is the height of the altar: 14From the gutter on the ground up to the lower edge it is two cubits high and a cubit wide, and from the smaller ledge up to the larger ledge it is four cubits high and a cubit wide. 15The altar hearth is four cubits high, and four horns project upward from the hearth. 16The altar hearth is square, twelve cubits long and twelve cubits wide. 17The upper ledge also is square, fourteen cubits long and fourteen cubits wide, with a rim of half a cubit and a gutter of a cubit all round. The steps of the altar face east."

18Then he said to me, "Son of man, this is what the Sovereign LORD says: These will be the regulations for sacrificing burnt offerings and sprinkling blood upon the altar when it is built: 19You are to give a young bull as a sin offering to the priests, who are Levites, of the family of Zadok, who come near to minister before me, declares the Sovereign LORD. 20You are to take some of its blood and put it on the four horns of the altar and on the four corners of the upper ledge and all round the rim, and so purify the altar and make atonement for it. 21You are to take the bull for the sin offering and burn it in the designated part of the temple area outside the sanctuary.

22"On the second day you are to offer a male goat without defect for a sin offering, and the altar is to be purified as it was purified with the bull. 23When you have finished purifying it, you are to offer a young bull and a ram from the flock, both without defect. 24You are to offer them before the LORD, and the priests are to sprinkle salt on them and sacrifice them as a burnt offering to the LORD.

25"For seven days you are to provide a male goat daily for a sin offering; you are also to provide a young bull and a ram from the flock, both without defect. 26For seven days they are to make atonement for the altar and cleanse it; thus they will dedicate it. 27At the end of these days, from the eighth day on, the priests are to present your burnt offerings and fellowship offerings*h* on the altar. Then I will accept you, declares the Sovereign LORD."

The Prince, the Levites, the Priests

44 Then the man brought me back to the outer gate of the sanctuary, the one facing east, and it was shut. 2The LORD said to me, "This gate is to remain shut. It must not be opened; no-one may enter through it. It is to remain shut because the LORD, the God of Israel, has entered through it. 3The prince himself is the only one who may sit inside the gateway to eat in the presence of the LORD. He is to enter by way of the portico of the gateway and go out the same way."

4Then the man brought me by way of the north gate to the front of the temple. I looked and saw the glory of the LORD filling the temple of the LORD, and I fell face down.

5The LORD said to me, "Son of man, look carefully, listen closely and give attention to everything I tell you concerning all the regulations regarding the temple of the LORD. Give attention to the entrance of the temple and all the exits of the sanctuary. 6Say to the rebellious house of Israel, 'This is what the Sovereign LORD says: Enough of your detestable practices, O house of Israel! 7In addition to all your other detestable practices, you brought foreigners uncircumcised in heart and flesh into my sanctuary, desecrating my temple while you offered me food, fat and blood, and you broke my covenant. 8Instead of carrying out your duty in regard to my holy things, you put others in charge of my sanctuary. 9This is what the Sovereign LORD says: No foreigner uncircumcised in heart and flesh is to enter my sanctuary, not even the foreigners who live among the Israelites.

10"The Levites who went far from me when Israel went astray and who wandered from me after their idols must bear the consequences of their sin. 11They may serve in my sanctuary, having charge of the gates of the temple and serving in it; they may slaughter the burnt offerings and sacrifices for the people and stand before the people and serve them. 12But because they served them in the presence of their idols and made the house of

---

b7 Or *their spiritual adultery*; also in verse 9   *c7* Or *the corpses*; also in verse 9
d11 Some Hebrew manuscripts and Septuagint; most Hebrew manuscripts *regulations and its whole design*
e13 The common cubit was about 1½ feet (about 0.5 metre).   *f13* That is, about 3 inches (about 8 centimetres)
g13 That is, about 9 inches (about 23 centimetres)   *h27* Traditionally *peace offerings*

Israel fall into sin, therefore I have sworn with uplifted hand that they must bear the consequences of their sin, declares the Sovereign LORD. [13]They are not to come near to serve me as priests or come near any of my holy things or my most holy offerings; they must bear the shame of their detestable practices. [14]Yet I will put them in charge of the duties of the temple and all the work that is to be done in it.

[15]"'But the priests, who are Levites and descendants of Zadok and who faithfully carried out the duties of my sanctuary when the Israelites went astray from me, are to come near to minister before me; they are to stand before me to offer sacrifices of fat and blood, declares the Sovereign LORD. [16]They alone are to enter my sanctuary; they alone are to come near my table to minister before me and perform my service.

[17]"'When they enter the gates of the inner court, they are to wear linen clothes; they must not wear any woollen garment while ministering at the gates of the inner court or inside the temple. [18]They are to wear linen turbans on their heads and linen undergarments round their waists. They must not wear anything that makes them perspire. [19]When they go out into the outer court where the people are, they are to take off the clothes they have been ministering in and leave them in the sacred rooms, and put on other clothes, so that they do not consecrate the people by means of their garments.

[20]"'They must not shave their heads or let their hair grow long, but they are to keep the hair of their heads trimmed. [21]No priest is to drink wine when he enters the inner court. [22]They must not marry widows or divorced women; they may marry only virgins of Israelite descent or widows of priests. [23]They are to teach my people the difference between the holy and the common and show them how to distinguish between the unclean and the clean.

[24]"'In any dispute, the priests are to serve as judges and decide it according to my ordinances. They are to keep my laws and my decrees for all my appointed feasts, and they are to keep my Sabbaths holy.

[25]"'A priest must not defile himself by going near a dead person; however, if the dead person was his father or mother, son or daughter, brother or unmarried sister, then he may defile himself. [26]After he is cleansed, he must wait seven days. [27]On the day he goes into the inner court of the sanctuary to minister in the sanctuary, he is to offer a sin offering for himself, declares the Sovereign LORD.

[28]"'I am to be the only inheritance the priests have. You are to give them no possession in Israel; I will be their possession. [29]They will eat the grain offerings, the sin

offerings and the guilt offerings; and everything in Israel devoted[a] to the LORD will belong to them. [30]The best of all the firstfruits and of all your special gifts will belong to the priests. You are to give them the first portion of your ground meal so that a blessing may rest on your household. [31]The priests must not eat anything, bird or animal, found dead or torn by wild animals.

Division of the Land

45 "'When you allot the land as an inheritance, you are to present to the LORD a portion of the land as a sacred district, 25,000 cubits long and 20,000[a] cubits wide; the entire area will be holy. [2]Of this, a section 500 cubits square is to be for the sanctuary, with 50 cubits around it for open land. [3]In the sacred district, measure off a section 25,000 cubits[b] long and 10,000 cubits[c] wide. In it will be the sanctuary, the Most Holy Place. [4]It will be the sacred portion of the land for the priests, who minister in the sanctuary and who draw near to minister before the LORD. It will be a place for their houses as well as a holy place for the sanctuary. [5]An area 25,000 cubits long and 10,000 cubits wide will belong to the Levites, who serve in the temple, as their possession for towns to live in.[d]

[6]"'You are to give the city as its property an area 5,000 cubits wide and 25,000 cubits long, adjoining the sacred portion; it will belong to the whole house of Israel.

[7]"'The prince will have the land bordering each side of the area formed by the sacred district and the property of the city. It will extend westward from the west side and eastward from the east side, running lengthwise from the western to the eastern border parallel to one of the tribal portions. [8]This land will be his possession in Israel. And my princes will no longer oppress my people but will allow the house of Israel to possess the land according to their tribes.

[9]"'This is what the Sovereign LORD says: You have gone far enough, O princes of Israel! Give up your violence and oppression and do what is just and right. Stop dispossessing my people, declares the Sovereign LORD. [10]You are to use accurate scales, an accurate ephah[e] and an accurate bath.[f] [11]The ephah and the bath are to be the same size, the bath containing a tenth of a homer[g] and the ephah a tenth of a homer; the homer is to be the standard measure for both. [12]The shekel[h] is to consist of twenty gerahs. Twenty shekels plus twenty-five shekels plus fifteen shekels equal one mina.[i]

Offerings and Holy Days

[13]"'This is the special gift you are to offer: a sixth of an ephah from each homer of wheat and a sixth of an ephah from each homer of barley. [14]The prescribed portion of oil,

---

[a]29 The Hebrew term refers to the irrevocable giving over of things or persons to the LORD.
[a]1 Septuagint (see also verses 3 and 5 and 48:9); Hebrew 10,000   [b]3 That is, about 7 miles (about 11 kilometres)
[c]3 That is, about 3 miles (about 5 kilometres)
[d]5 Septuagint; Hebrew temple; they will have as their possession 20 rooms   [e]10 An ephah was a dry measure.
[f]10 A bath was a liquid measure.   [g]11 A homer was a dry measure.
[h]12 A shekel weighed about ⅔ ounce (about 11.5 grams).
[i]12 That is, 60 shekels; the common mina was 50 shekels.

measured by the bath, is a tenth of a bath from each cor (which consists of ten baths or one homer, for ten baths are equivalent to a homer). ¹⁵Also one sheep is to be taken from every flock of two hundred from the well-watered pastures of Israel. These will be used for the grain offerings, burnt offerings and fellowship offerings*ʲ* to make atonement for the people, declares the Sovereign LORD. ¹⁶All the people of the land will participate in this special gift for the use of the prince in Israel. ¹⁷It will be the duty of the prince to provide the burnt offerings, grain offerings and drink offerings at the festivals, the New Moons and the Sabbaths—at all the appointed feasts of the house of Israel. He will provide the sin offerings, grain offerings, burnt offerings and fellowship offerings to make atonement for the house of Israel.

¹⁸"'This is what the Sovereign LORD says: In the first month on the first day you are to take a young bull without defect and purify the sanctuary. ¹⁹The priest is to take some of the blood of the sin offering and put it on the doorposts of the temple, on the four corners of the upper ledge of the altar and on the gateposts of the inner court. ²⁰You are to do the same on the seventh day of the month for anyone who sins unintentionally or through ignorance; so you are to make atonement for the temple.

²¹"'In the first month on the fourteenth day you are to observe the Passover, a feast lasting seven days, during which you shall eat bread made without yeast. ²²On that day the prince is to provide a bull as a sin offering for himself and for all the people of the land. ²³Every day during the seven days of the Feast he is to provide seven bulls and seven rams without defect as a burnt offering to the LORD, and a male goat for a sin offering. ²⁴He is to provide as a grain offering an ephah for each bull and an ephah for each ram, along with a hin*ᵏ* of oil for each ephah.

²⁵"'During the seven days of the Feast, which begins in the seventh month on the fifteenth day, he is to make the same provision for sin offerings, burnt offerings, grain offerings and oil.

46 "'This is what the Sovereign LORD says: The gate of the inner court facing east is to be shut on the six working days, but on the Sabbath day and on the day of the New Moon it is to be opened. ²The prince is to enter from the outside through the portico of the gateway and stand by the gatepost. The priests are to sacrifice his burnt offering and his fellowship offerings.*ᵃ* He is to worship at the threshold of the gateway and then go out, but the gate will not be shut until evening. ³On the Sabbaths and New Moons the people of the land are to worship in the presence of the LORD at the entrance to that gateway. ⁴The burnt offering the prince brings to the LORD on the Sabbath day is to be six male lambs and a ram, all without defect. ⁵The grain offering given with the ram is to be

an ephah,*ᵇ* and the grain offering with the lambs is to be as much as he pleases, along with a hin*ᶜ* of oil for each ephah. ⁶On the day of the New Moon he is to offer a young bull, six lambs and a ram, all without defect. ⁷He is to provide as a grain offering one ephah with the bull, one ephah with the ram, and with the lambs as much as he wants to give, along with a hin of oil with each ephah. ⁸When the prince enters, he is to go in through the portico of the gateway, and he is to come out the same way.

⁹"'When the people of the land come before the LORD at the appointed feasts, whoever enters by the north gate to worship is to go out by the south gate; and whoever enters by the south gate is to go out by the north gate. No-one is to return through the gate by which he entered, but each is to go out by the opposite gate. ¹⁰The prince is to be among them, going in when they go in and going out when they go out.

¹¹"'At the festivals and the appointed feasts, the grain offering is to be an ephah with a bull, an ephah with a ram, and with the lambs as much as one pleases, along with a hin of oil for each ephah. ¹²When the prince provides a freewill offering to the LORD—whether a burnt offering or fellowship offerings—the gate facing east is to be opened for him. He shall offer his burnt offering or his fellowship offerings as he does on the Sabbath day. Then he shall go out, and after he has gone out, the gate will be shut.

¹³"'Every day you are to provide a year-old lamb without defect for a burnt offering to the LORD; morning by morning you shall provide it. ¹⁴You are also to provide with it morning by morning a grain offering, consisting of a sixth of an ephah with a third of a hin of oil to moisten the flour. The presenting of this grain offering to the LORD is a lasting ordinance. ¹⁵So the lamb and the grain offering and the oil shall be provided morning by morning for a regular burnt offering.

¹⁶"'This is what the Sovereign LORD says: If the prince makes a gift from his inheritance to one of his sons, it will also belong to his descendants; it is to be their property by inheritance. ¹⁷If, however, he makes a gift from his inheritance to one of his servants, the servant may keep it until the year of freedom; then it will revert to the prince. His inheritance belongs to his sons only; it is theirs. ¹⁸The prince must not take any of the inheritance of the people, driving them off their property. He is to give his sons their inheritance out of his own property, so that none of my people will be separated from his property.'"

¹⁹Then the man brought me through the entrance at the side of the gate to the sacred rooms facing north, which belonged to the priests, and showed me a place at the western end. ²⁰He said to me, "This is the place where the priests will cook the guilt offering and the sin offering and bake the grain

ʲ15 Traditionally *peace offerings*; also in verse 17
ᵃ2 Traditionally *peace offerings*; also in verse 12
ᶜ5 That is, probably about 6 pints (about 4 litres)
ᵏ24 That is, probably about 6 pints (about 4 litres)
ᵇ5 That is, probably about ⅗ bushel (about 22 litres)

offering, to avoid bringing them into the outer court and consecrating the people."

21He then brought me to the outer court and led me round to its four corners, and I saw in each corner another court. 22In the four corners of the outer court were enclosed[d] courts, forty cubits long and thirty cubits wide; each of the courts in the four corners was the same size. 23Around the inside of each of the four courts was a ledge of stone, with places for fire built all round under the ledge. 24He said to me, "These are the kitchens where those who minister at the temple will cook the sacrifices of the people."

The River From the Temple

47 The man brought me back to the entrance of the temple, and I saw water coming out from under the threshold of the temple towards the east (for the temple faced east). The water was coming down from under the south side of the temple, south of the altar. 2He then brought me out through the north gate and led me round the outside to the outer gate facing east, and the water was flowing from the south side.

3As the man went eastward with a measuring line in his hand, he measured off a thousand cubits[a] and then led me through water that was ankle-deep. 4He measured off another thousand cubits and led me through water that was knee-deep. He measured off another thousand and led me through water that was up to the waist. 5He measured off another thousand, but now it was a river that I could not cross, because the water had risen and was deep enough to swim in—a river that no-one could cross. 6He asked me, "Son of man, do you see this?"

Then he led me back to the bank of the river. 7When I arrived there, I saw a great number of trees on each side of the river. 8He said to me, "This water flows towards the eastern region and goes down into the Arabah,[b] where it enters the Sea.[c] When it empties into the Sea,[c] the water there becomes fresh. 9Swarms of living creatures will live wherever the river flows. There will be large numbers of fish, because this water flows there and makes the salt water fresh; so where the river flows everything will live. 10Fishermen will stand along the shore; from En Gedi to En Eglaim there will be places for spreading nets. The fish will be of many kinds—like the fish of the Great Sea.[d] 11But the swamps and marshes will not become fresh; they will be left for salt. 12Fruit trees of all kinds will grow on both banks of the river. Their leaves will not wither, nor will their fruit fail. Every month they will bear, because the water from the sanctuary flows to them. Their fruit will serve for food and their leaves for healing."

The Boundaries of the Land

13This is what the Sovereign LORD says: "These are the boundaries by which you are to divide the land for an inheritance among the twelve tribes of Israel, with two portions for Joseph. 14You are to divide it equally among them. Because I swore with uplifted hand to give it to your forefathers, this land will become your inheritance.

15This is to be the boundary of the land:

"On the north side it will run from the Great Sea by the Hethlon road past Lebo[e] Hamath to Zedad, 16Berothah[f] and Sibraim (which lies on the border between Damascus and Hamath), as far as Hazer Hatticon, which is on the border of Hauran. 17The boundary will extend from the sea to Hazar Enan,[g] along the northern border of Damascus, with the border of Hamath to the north. This will be the north boundary.
18On the east side the boundary will run between Hauran and Damascus, along the Jordan between Gilead and the land of Israel, to the eastern sea and as far as Tamar.[h] This will be the east boundary.
19"On the south side it will run from Tamar as far as the waters of Meribah Kadesh, then along the Wadi ˌof Egyptˌ to the Great Sea. This will be the south boundary.
20"On the west side, the Great Sea will be the boundary to a point opposite Lebo[i] Hamath. This will be the west boundary.

21"You are to distribute this land among yourselves according to the tribes of Israel. 22You are to allot it as an inheritance for yourselves and for the aliens who have settled among you and who have children. You are to consider them as native-born Israelites; along with you they are to be allotted an inheritance among the tribes of Israel. 23In whatever tribe the alien settles, there you are to give him his inheritance," declares the Sovereign LORD.

The Division of the Land

48 "These are the tribes, listed by name: At the northern frontier, Dan will have one portion; it will follow the Hethlon road to Lebo[a] Hamath; Hazar Enan and the northern border of Damascus next to Hamath will be part of its border from the east side to the west side.

2"Asher will have one portion; it will border the territory of Dan from east to west.

3"Naphtali will have one portion; it will border the territory of Asher from east to west.

4"Manasseh will have one portion; it will

---

d22 The meaning of the Hebrew for this word is uncertain.　a3 That is, about 1,500 feet (about 460 metres)
b8 Or the Jordan Valley　c8 That is, the Dead Sea
d10 That is, the Mediterranean; also in verses 15, 19 and 20　e15 Or past the entrance to
f15,16 See Septuagint and Ezekiel 48:1; Hebrew road to go into Zedad, 16Hamath, Berothah
g17 Hebrew Enon, a variant of Enan
h18 Septuagint and Syriac; Hebrew Israel. You will measure to the eastern sea
i20 Or opposite the entrance to　a1 Or to the entrance to

border the territory of Naphtali from east to west.

5"Ephraim will have one portion; it will border the territory of Manasseh from east to west.

6"Reuben will have one portion; it will border the territory of Ephraim from east to west.

7"Judah will have one portion; it will border the territory of Reuben from east to west.

8"Bordering the territory of Judah from east to west will be the portion you are to present as a special gift. It will be 25,000 cubits^b wide, and its length from east to west will equal one of the tribal portions; the sanctuary will be in the centre of it.

9"The special portion you are to offer to the LORD will be 25,000 cubits long and 10,000 cubits^c wide. ¹⁰This will be the sacred portion for the priests. It will be 25,000 cubits long on the north side, 10,000 cubits wide on the west side, 10,000 cubits wide on the east side and 25,000 cubits long on the south side. In the centre of it will be the sanctuary of the LORD. ¹¹This will be for the consecrated priests, the Zadokites, who were faithful in serving me and did not go astray as the Levites did when the Israelites went astray. ¹²It will be a special gift to them from the sacred portion of the land, a most holy portion, bordering the territory of the Levites.

13"Alongside the territory of the priests, the Levites will have an allotment 25,000 cubits long and 10,000 cubits wide. Its total length will be 25,000 cubits and its width 10,000 cubits. ¹⁴They must not sell or exchange any of it. This is the best of the land, and must not pass into other hands, because it is holy to the LORD.

15"The remaining area, 5,000 cubits wide and 25,000 cubits long, will be for the common use of the city, for houses and for pasture-land. The city will be in the centre of it ¹⁶and will have these measurements: the north side 4,500 cubits, the south side 4,500 cubits, the east side 4,500 cubits, and the west side 4,500 cubits. ¹⁷The pasture-land for the city will be 250 cubits on the north, 250 cubits on the south, 250 cubits on the east, and 250 cubits on the west. ¹⁸What remains of the area, bordering on the sacred portion and running the length of it, will be 10,000 cubits on the east side and 10,000 cubits on the west side. Its produce will supply food for the workers of the city. ¹⁹The workers from the city who farm it will come from all the tribes of Israel. ²⁰The entire portion will be a square, 25,000 cubits on each side. As a special gift you will set aside the sacred portion, along with the property of the city.

21"What remains on both sides of the area formed by the sacred portion and the city property will belong to the prince. It will extend eastward from the 25,000 cubits of the sacred portion to the eastern border, and westward from the 25,000 cubits to the western border. Both these areas running the length of the tribal portions will belong to the prince, and the sacred portion with the temple sanctuary will be in the centre of them. ²²So the property of the Levites and the property of the city will lie in the centre of the area that belongs to the prince. The area belonging to the prince will lie between the border of Judah and the border of Benjamin.

23"As for the rest of the tribes: Benjamin will have one portion; it will extend from the east side to the west side.

24"Simeon will have one portion; it will border the territory of Benjamin from east to west.

25"Issachar will have one portion; it will border the territory of Simeon from east to west.

26"Zebulun will have one portion; it will border the territory of Issachar from east to west.

27"Gad will have one portion; it will border the territory of Zebulun from east to west.

28"The southern boundary of Gad will run south from Tamar to the waters of Meribah Kadesh, then along the Wadi ⌊of Egypt⌋ to the Great Sea.^d

29"This is the land you are to allot as an inheritance to the tribes of Israel, and these will be their portions," declares the Sovereign LORD.

The Gates of the City

30"These will be the exits of the city: Beginning on the north side, which is 4,500 cubits long, ³¹the gates of the city will be named after the tribes of Israel. The three gates on the north side will be the gate of Reuben, the gate of Judah and the gate of Levi.

32"On the east side, which is 4,500 cubits long, will be three gates: the gate of Joseph, the gate of Benjamin and the gate of Dan.

33"On the south side, which measures 4,500 cubits, will be three gates: the gate of Simeon, the gate of Issachar and the gate of Zebulun.

34"On the west side, which is 4,500 cubits long, will be three gates: the gate of Gad, the gate of Asher and the gate of Naphtali.

35"The distance all around will be 18,000 cubits.

"And the name of the city from that time on will be:

THE LORD IS THERE."

^b8 That is, about 7 miles (about 11 kilometres)   ^c9 That is, about 3 miles (about 5 kilometres)
^d28 That is, the Mediterranean

Daniel

Daniel's Training in Babylon

1 In the third year of the reign of
Jehoiakim king of Judah, Nebuchadnezzar king of Babylon came to Jerusalem
and besieged it. ²And the Lord delivered
Jehoiakim king of Judah into his hand, along
with some of the articles from the temple of
God. These he carried off to the temple of his
god in Babylonia*a* and put in the treasure-
house of his god.

³Then the king ordered Ashpenaz, chief of
his court officials, to bring in some of the
Israelites from the royal family and the nobility—⁴young men without any physical
defect, handsome, showing aptitude for
every kind of learning, well informed, quick
to understand, and qualified to serve in the
king's palace. He was to teach them the
language and literature of the Babylonians.*b*
⁵The king assigned them a daily amount of
food and wine from the king's table. They
were to be trained for three years, and after
that they were to enter the king's service.

⁶Among these were some from Judah:
Daniel, Hananiah, Mishael and Azariah.
⁷The chief official gave them new names: to
Daniel, the name Belteshazzar; to Hananiah,
Shadrach; to Mishael, Meshach; and to
Azariah, Abednego.

⁸But Daniel resolved not to defile himself
with the royal food and wine, and he asked
the chief official for permission not to defile
himself in this way. ⁹Now God had caused
the official to show favour and sympathy to
Daniel, ¹⁰but the official told Daniel, "I am
afraid of my lord the king, who has assigned
your*c* food and drink. Why should he see you
looking worse than the other young men of
your age? The king would then have my head
because of you."

¹¹Daniel then said to the guard whom the
chief official had appointed over Daniel,
Hananiah, Mishael and Azariah, ¹²"Please
test your servants for ten days: Give us
nothing but vegetables to eat and water
to drink. ¹³Then compare our appearance
with that of the young men who eat the royal
food, and treat your servants in accordance
with what you see." ¹⁴So he agreed to this
and tested them for ten days.

¹⁵At the end of the ten days they looked
healthier and better nourished than any of the
young men who ate the royal food. ¹⁶So
the guard took away their choice food and
the wine they were to drink and gave them
vegetables instead.

¹⁷To these four young men God gave
knowledge and understanding of all kinds of
literature and learning. And Daniel could
understand visions and dreams of all kinds.

¹⁸At the end of the time set by the king to
bring them in, the chief official presented
them to Nebuchadnezzar. ¹⁹The king talked
with them, and he found none equal to
Daniel, Hananiah, Mishael and Azariah; so
they entered the king's service. ²⁰In every
matter of wisdom and understanding about
which the king questioned them, he found
them ten times better than all the magicians
and enchanters in his whole kingdom.

²¹And Daniel remained there until the first
year of King Cyrus.

Nebuchadnezzar's Dream

2 In the second year of his reign, Nebuchadnezzar had dreams; his mind was
troubled and he could not sleep. ²So the king
summoned the magicians, enchanters,
sorcerers and astrologers*a* to tell him what he
had dreamed. When they came in and stood
before the king, ³he said to them, "I have had
a dream that troubles me and I want to know
what it means."*b*

⁴Then the astrologers answered the king in
Aramaic,*c* "O king, live for ever! Tell your
servants the dream, and we will interpret it."

⁵The king replied to the astrologers, "This
is what I have firmly decided: If you do not
tell me what my dream was and interpret it, I
will have you cut into pieces and your houses
turned into piles of rubble. ⁶But if you tell me
the dream and explain it, you will receive
from me gifts and rewards and great honour.
So tell me the dream and interpret it for me."

⁷Once more they replied, "Let the king tell
his servants the dream, and we will interpret
it."

⁸Then the king answered, "I am certain
that you are trying to gain time, because you
realise that this is what I have firmly decided:

---

a2 Hebrew *Shinar*   *b4* Or *Chaldeans*   *c10* The Hebrew for *your* and *you* in this verse is plural.
a2 Or *Chaldeans*; also in verses 4, 5 and 10   *b3* Or *was*
c4 The text from here through chapter 7 is in Aramaic.

9If you do not tell me the dream, there is just one penalty for you. You have conspired to tell me misleading and wicked things, hoping the situation will change. So then, tell me the dream, and I will know that you can interpret it for me."

10The astrologers answered the king, "There is not a man on earth who can do what the king asks! No king, however great and mighty, has ever asked such a thing of any magician or enchanter or astrologer. 11What the king asks is too difficult. No-one can reveal it to the king except the gods, and they do not live among men."

12This made the king so angry and furious that he ordered the execution of all the wise men of Babylon. 13So the decree was issued to put the wise men to death, and men were sent to look for Daniel and his friends to put them to death.

14When Arioch, the commander of the king's guard, had gone out to put to death the wise men of Babylon, Daniel spoke to him with wisdom and tact. 15He asked the king's officer, "Why did the king issue such a harsh decree?" Arioch then explained the matter to Daniel. 16At this, Daniel went in to the king and asked for time, so that he might interpret the dream for him.

17Then Daniel returned to his house and explained the matter to his friends Hananiah, Mishael and Azariah. 18He urged them to plead for mercy from the God of heaven concerning this mystery, so that he and his friends might not be executed with the rest of the wise men of Babylon. 19During the night the mystery was revealed to Daniel in a vision. Then Daniel praised the God of heaven 20and said:

"Praise be to the name of God for ever and ever;
    wisdom and power are his.
21He changes times and seasons;
    he sets up kings and deposes them.
He gives wisdom to the wise
    and knowledge to the discerning.
22He reveals deep and hidden things;
    he knows what lies in darkness,
    and light dwells with him.
23I thank and praise you, O God of my fathers:
You have given me wisdom and power,
you have made known to me what we asked of you,
    you have made known to us the dream of the king."

Daniel Interprets the Dream

24Then Daniel went to Arioch, whom the king had appointed to execute the wise men of Babylon, and said to him, "Do not execute the wise men of Babylon. Take me to the king, and I will interpret his dream for him." 25Arioch took Daniel to the king at once and said, "I have found a man among the exiles from Judah who can tell the king what his dream means."

26The king asked Daniel (also called Belteshazzar), "Are you able to tell me what I saw in my dream and interpret it?"

27Daniel replied, "No wise man, enchanter, magician or diviner can explain to the king the mystery he has asked about, 28but there is a God in heaven who reveals mysteries. He has shown King Nebuchadnezzar what will happen in days to come. Your dream and the visions that passed through your mind as you lay on your bed are these:

29"As you were lying there, O king, your mind turned to things to come, and the revealer of mysteries showed you what is going to happen. 30As for me, this mystery has been revealed to me, not because I have greater wisdom than other living men, but so that you, O king, may know the interpretation and that you may understand what went through your mind.

31"You looked, O king, and there before you stood a large statue—an enormous, dazzling statue, awesome in appearance. 32The head of the statue was made of pure gold, its chest and arms of silver, its belly and thighs of bronze, 33its legs of iron, its feet partly of iron and partly of baked clay. 34While you were watching, a rock was cut out, but not by human hands. It struck the statue on its feet of iron and clay and smashed them. 35Then the iron, the clay, the bronze, the silver and the gold were broken to pieces at the same time and became like chaff on a threshing-floor in the summer. The wind swept them away without leaving a trace. But the rock that struck the statue became a huge mountain and filled the whole earth.

36"This was the dream, and now we will interpret it to the king. 37You, O king, are the king of kings. The God of heaven has given you dominion and power and might and glory; 38in your hands he has placed mankind and the beasts of the field and the birds of the air. Wherever they live, he has made you ruler over them all. You are that head of gold.

39"After you, another kingdom will rise, inferior to yours. Next, a third kingdom, one of bronze, will rule over the whole earth. 40Finally, there will be a fourth kingdom, strong as iron—for iron breaks and smashes everything—and as iron breaks things to pieces, so it will crush and break all the others. 41Just as you saw that the feet and toes were partly of baked clay and partly of iron, so this will be a divided kingdom; yet it will have some of the strength of iron in it, even as you saw iron mixed with clay. 42As the toes were partly iron and partly clay, so this kingdom will be partly strong and partly brittle. 43And just as you saw the iron mixed with baked clay, so the people will be a mixture and will not remain united, any more than iron mixes with clay.

44"In the time of those kings, the God of heaven will set up a kingdom that will never be destroyed, nor will it be left to another people. It will crush all those kingdoms and bring them to an end, but it will itself endure for ever. 45This is the meaning of the vision of the rock cut out of a mountain, but not by human hands—a rock that broke the iron, the bronze, the clay, the silver and the gold to pieces.

"The great God has shown the king what will take place in the future. The dream is true and the interpretation is trustworthy."

46Then King Nebuchadnezzar fell prostrate before Daniel and paid him honour and ordered that an offering and incense be presented to him. 47The king said to Daniel, "Surely your God is the God of gods and the Lord of kings and a revealer of mysteries, for you were able to reveal this mystery."

48Then the king placed Daniel in a high position and lavished many gifts on him. He made him ruler over the entire province of Babylon and placed him in charge of all its wise men. 49Moreover, at Daniel's request the king appointed Shadrach, Meshach and Abednego administrators over the province of Babylon, while Daniel himself remained at the royal court.

The Image of Gold and the Fiery Furnace

3 King Nebuchadnezzar made an image of gold, ninety feet high and nine feet[a] wide, and set it up on the plain of Dura in the province of Babylon. 2He then summoned the satraps, prefects, governors, advisers, treasurers, judges, magistrates and all the other provincial officials to come to the dedication of the image he had set up. 3So the satraps, prefects, governors, advisers, treasurers, judges, magistrates and all the other provincial officials assembled for the dedication of the image that King Nebuchadnezzar had set up, and they stood before it.

4Then the herald loudly proclaimed, "This is what you are commanded to do, O peoples, nations and men of every language: 5As soon as you hear the sound of the horn, flute, zither, lyre, harp, pipes and all kinds of music, you must fall down and worship the image of gold that King Nebuchadnezzar has set up. 6Whoever does not fall down and worship will immediately be thrown into a blazing furnace."

7Therefore, as soon as they heard the sound of the horn, flute, zither, lyre, harp and all kinds of music, all the peoples, nations and men of every language fell down and worshipped the image of gold that King Nebuchadnezzar had set up.

8At this time some astrologers[b] came forward and denounced the Jews. 9They said to King Nebuchadnezzar, "O king, live for ever! 10You have issued a decree, O king, that everyone who hears the sound of the horn, flute, zither, lyre, harp, pipes and all kinds of music must fall down and worship the image of gold, 11and that whoever does not fall down and worship will be thrown into a blazing furnace. 12But there are some Jews whom you have set over the affairs of the province of Babylon—Shadrach, Meshach and Abednego—who pay no attention to you, O king. They neither serve your gods nor worship the image of gold you have set up."

13Furious with rage, Nebuchadnezzar

summoned Shadrach, Meshach and Abednego. So these men were brought before the king, 14and Nebuchadnezzar said to them, "Is it true, Shadrach, Meshach and Abednego, that you do not serve my gods or worship the image of gold I have set up? 15Now when you hear the sound of the horn, flute, zither, lyre, harp, pipes and all kinds of music, if you are ready to fall down and worship the image I made, very good. But if you do not worship it, you will be thrown immediately into a blazing furnace. Then what god will be able to rescue you from my hand?"

16Shadrach, Meshach and Abednego replied to the king, "O Nebuchadnezzar, we do not need to defend ourselves before you in this matter. 17If we are thrown into the blazing furnace, the God we serve is able to save us from it, and he will rescue us from your hand, O king. 18But even if he does not, we want you to know, O king, that we will not serve your gods or worship the image of gold you have set up."

19Then Nebuchadnezzar was furious with Shadrach, Meshach and Abednego, and his attitude towards them changed. He ordered the furnace to be heated seven times hotter than usual 20and commanded some of the strongest soldiers in his army to tie up Shadrach, Meshach and Abednego and throw them into the blazing furnace. 21So these men, wearing their robes, trousers, turbans and other clothes, were bound and thrown into the blazing furnace. 22The king's command was so urgent and the furnace so hot that the flames of the fire killed the soldiers who took up Shadrach, Meshach and Abednego, 23and these three men, firmly tied, fell into the blazing furnace.

24Then King Nebuchadnezzar leaped to his feet in amazement and asked his advisers, "Weren't there three men that we tied up and threw into the fire?"

They replied, "Certainly, O king."

25He said, "Look! I see four men walking around in the fire, unbound and unharmed, and the fourth looks like a son of the gods."

26Nebuchadnezzar then approached the opening of the blazing furnace and shouted, "Shadrach, Meshach and Abednego, servants of the Most High God, come out! Come here!"

So Shadrach, Meshach and Abednego came out of the fire, 27and the satraps, prefects, governors and royal advisers crowded around them. They saw that the fire had not harmed their bodies, nor was a hair of their heads singed; their robes were not scorched, and there was no smell of fire on them.

28Then Nebuchadnezzar said, "Praise be to the God of Shadrach, Meshach and Abednego, who has sent his angel and rescued his servants! They trusted in him and defied the king's command and were willing to give up their lives rather than serve or worship any god except their own God. 29Therefore I decree that the people of any nation or

[a]1 Aramaic sixty cubits high and six cubits wide (about 27 metres high and 2.7 metres wide)
[b]8 Or Chaldeans

language who say anything against the God of Shadrach, Meshach and Abednego be cut into pieces and their houses be turned into piles of rubble, for no other god can save in this way.''

³⁰Then the king promoted Shadrach, Meshach and Abednego in the province of Babylon.

Nebuchadnezzar's Dream of a Tree

4 King Nebuchadnezzar,

To the peoples, nations and men of every language, who live in all the world:

May you prosper greatly!

²It is my pleasure to tell you about the miraculous signs and wonders that the Most High God has performed for me.

³ How great are his signs,
   how mighty his wonders!
His kingdom is an eternal kingdom;
   his dominion endures from
      generation to generation.

⁴I, Nebuchadnezzar, was at home in my palace, contented and prosperous. ⁵I had a dream that made me afraid. As I was lying in my bed, the images and visions that passed through my mind terrified me. ⁶So I commanded that all the wise men of Babylon be brought before me to interpret the dream for me. ⁷When the magicians, enchanters, astrologers[a] and diviners came, I told them the dream, but they could not interpret it for me. ⁸Finally, Daniel came into my presence and I told him the dream. (He is called Belteshazzar, after the name of my god, and the spirit of the holy gods is in him.)

⁹I said, ''Belteshazzar, chief of the magicians, I know that the spirit of the holy gods is in you, and no mystery is too difficult for you. Here is my dream; interpret it for me. ¹⁰These are the visions I saw while lying in my bed: I looked, and there before me stood a tree in the middle of the land. Its height was enormous. ¹¹The tree grew large and strong and its top touched the sky; it was visible to the ends of the earth. ¹²Its leaves were beautiful, its fruit abundant, and on it was food for all. Under it the beasts of the field found shelter, and the birds of the air lived in its branches; from it every creature was fed.

¹³''In the visions I saw while lying in my bed, I looked, and there before me was a messenger,[b] a holy one, coming down from heaven. ¹⁴He called in a loud voice: 'Cut down the tree and trim off its branches; strip off its leaves and scatter its fruit. Let the animals flee from under it and the birds from its branches. ¹⁵But let the stump and its roots, bound with

iron and bronze, remain in the ground, in the grass of the field.

'''Let him be drenched with the dew of heaven, and let him live with the animals among the plants of the earth. ¹⁶Let his mind be changed from that of a man and let him be given the mind of an animal, till seven times[c] pass by for him.

¹⁷'''The decision is announced by messengers, the holy ones declare the verdict, so that the living may know that the Most High is sovereign over the kingdoms of men and gives them to anyone he wishes and sets over them the lowliest of men.'

¹⁸''This is the dream that I, King Nebuchadnezzar, had. Now, Belteshazzar, tell me what it means, for none of the wise men in my kingdom can interpret it for me. But you can, because the spirit of the holy gods is in you.''

Daniel Interprets the Dream

¹⁹Then Daniel (also called Belteshazzar) was greatly perplexed for a time, and his thoughts terrified him. So the king said, ''Belteshazzar, do not let the dream or its meaning alarm you.''

Belteshazzar answered, ''My lord, if only the dream applied to your enemies and its meaning to your adversaries! ²⁰The tree you saw, which grew large and strong, with its top touching the sky, visible to the whole earth, ²¹with beautiful leaves and abundant fruit, providing food for all, giving shelter to the beasts of the field, and having nesting places in its branches for the birds of the air— ²²you, O king, are that tree! You have become great and strong; your greatness has grown until it reaches the sky, and your dominion extends to distant parts of the earth.

²³''You, O king, saw a messenger, a holy one, coming down from heaven and saying, 'Cut down the tree and destroy it, but leave the stump, bound with iron and bronze, in the grass of the field, while its roots remain in the ground. Let him be drenched with the dew of heaven; let him live like the wild animals, until seven times pass by for him.'

²⁴''This is the interpretation, O king, and this is the decree the Most High has issued against my lord the king: ²⁵You will be driven away from people and will live with the wild animals; you will eat grass like cattle and be drenched with the dew of heaven. Seven times will pass by for you until you acknowledge that the Most High is sovereign over the kingdoms of men and gives them to anyone he wishes. ²⁶The command to leave the stump of the tree with its roots means that your kingdom will be restored to you when you acknowledge that Heaven rules. ²⁷Therefore, O king, be pleased to accept my advice: Renounce your sins by doing what is right,

and your wickedness by being kind to the oppressed. It may be that then your prosperity will continue.''

The Dream Is Fulfilled

28All this happened to King Nebuchadnezzar. 29Twelve months later, as the king was walking on the roof of the royal palace of Babylon, 30he said, ''Is not this the great Babylon I have built as the royal residence, by my mighty power and for the glory of my majesty?''

31The words were still on his lips when a voice came from heaven, ''This is what is decreed for you, King Nebuchadnezzar: Your royal authority has been taken from you. 32You will be driven away from people and will live with the wild animals; you will eat grass like cattle. Seven times will pass by for you until you acknowledge that the Most High is sovereign over the kingdoms of men and gives them to anyone he wishes.''

33Immediately what had been said about Nebuchadnezzar was fulfilled. He was driven away from people and ate grass like cattle. His body was drenched with the dew of heaven until his hair grew like the feathers of an eagle and his nails like the claws of a bird.

34At the end of that time, I, Nebuchadnezzar, raised my eyes towards heaven, and my sanity was restored. Then I praised the Most High; I honoured and glorified him who lives for ever.

His dominion is an eternal dominion;
　　his kingdom endures from generation
　　　to generation.
35 All the peoples of the earth
　　are regarded as nothing.
He does as he pleases
　　with the powers of heaven
　　and the peoples of the earth.
No-one can hold back his hand
　　or say to him: ''What have you
　　　done?''

36At the same time that my sanity was restored, my honour and splendour were returned to me for the glory of my kingdom. My advisers and nobles sought me out, and I was restored to my throne and became even greater than before. 37Now I, Nebuchadnezzar, praise and exalt and glorify the King of heaven, because everything he does is right and all his ways are just. And those who walk in pride he is able to humble.

The Writing on the Wall

5 King Belshazzar gave a great banquet for a thousand of his nobles and drank wine with them. 2While Belshazzar was drinking his wine, he gave orders to bring in the gold and silver goblets that Nebuchadnezzar his father*a* had taken from the temple in Jerusalem, so that the king and his nobles, his wives and his concubines might drink from them. 3So they brought in the gold goblets that had been taken from the temple of God in Jerusalem, and the king and his nobles, his wives and his concubines drank from them. 4As they drank the wine, they praised the gods of gold and silver, of bronze, iron, wood and stone.

5Suddenly the fingers of a human hand appeared and wrote on the plaster of the wall, near the lampstand in the royal palace. The king watched the hand as it wrote. 6His face turned pale and he was so frightened that his knees knocked together and his legs gave way.

7The king called out for the enchanters, astrologers*b* and diviners to be brought and said to these wise men of Babylon, ''Whoever reads this writing and tells me what it means will be clothed in purple and have a gold chain placed around his neck, and he will be made the third highest ruler in the kingdom.''

8Then all the king's wise men came in, but they could not read the writing or tell the king what it meant. 9So King Belshazzar became even more terrified and his face grew more pale. His nobles were baffled.

10The queen,*c* hearing the voices of the king and his nobles, came into the banquet hall. ''O king, live for ever!'' she said. ''Don't be alarmed! Don't look so pale! 11There is a man in your kingdom who has the spirit of the holy gods in him. In the time of your father he was found to have insight and intelligence and wisdom like that of the gods. King Nebuchadnezzar your father—your father the king, I say—appointed him chief of the magicians, enchanters, astrologers and diviners. 12This man Daniel, whom the king called Belteshazzar, was found to have a keen mind and knowledge and understanding, and also the ability to interpret dreams, explain riddles and solve difficult problems. Call for Daniel, and he will tell you what the writing means.''

13So Daniel was brought before the king, and the king said to him, ''Are you Daniel, one of the exiles my father the king brought from Judah? 14I have heard that the spirit of the gods is in you and that you have insight, intelligence and outstanding wisdom. 15The wise men and enchanters were brought before me to read this writing and tell me what it means, but they could not explain it. 16Now I have heard that you are able to give interpretations and to solve difficult problems. If you can read this writing and tell me what it means, you will be clothed in purple and have a gold chain placed around your neck, and you will be made the third highest ruler in the kingdom.''

17Then Daniel answered the king, ''You may keep your gifts for yourself and give your rewards to someone else. Nevertheless, I will read the writing for the king and tell him what it means.

---

*a*2 Or *ancestor*; or *predecessor*; also in verses 11, 13 and 18　　*b*7 Or *Chaldeans*; also in verse 11
*c*10 Or *queen mother*

18"O king, the Most High God gave your father Nebuchadnezzar sovereignty and greatness and glory and splendour. 19Because of the high position he gave him, all the peoples and nations and men of every language dreaded and feared him. Those the king wanted to put to death, he put to death; those he wanted to spare, he spared; those he wanted to promote, he promoted; and those he wanted to humble, he humbled. 20But when his heart became arrogant and hardened with pride, he was deposed from his royal throne and stripped of his glory. 21He was driven away from people and given the mind of an animal; he lived with the wild donkeys and ate grass like cattle; and his body was drenched with the dew of heaven, until he acknowledged that the Most High God is sovereign over the kingdoms of men and sets over them anyone he wishes.

22"But you his son,d O Belshazzar, have not humbled yourself, though you knew all this. 23Instead, you have set yourself up against the Lord of heaven. You had the goblets from his temple brought to you, and you and your nobles, your wives and your concubines drank wine from them. You praised the gods of silver and gold, of bronze, iron, wood and stone, which cannot see or hear or understand. But you did not honour the God who holds in his hand your life and all your ways. 24Therefore he sent the hand that wrote the inscription.

25"This is the inscription that was written:

MENE, MENE, TEKEL, PARSINe

26"This is what these words mean:

Menef: God has numbered the days of your reign and brought it to an end.
27*Tekelg*: You have been weighed on the scales and found wanting.
28*Peresh*: Your kingdom is divided and given to the Medes and Persians."

29Then at Belshazzar's command, Daniel was clothed in purple, a gold chain was placed around his neck, and he was proclaimed the third highest ruler in the kingdom. 30That very night Belshazzar, king of the Babylonians,i was slain, 31and Darius the Mede took over the kingdom, at the age of sixty-two.

Daniel in the Den of Lions

6 It pleased Darius to appoint 120 satraps to rule throughout the kingdom, 2with three administrators over them, one of whom was Daniel. The satraps were made accountable to them so that the king might not suffer loss. 3Now Daniel so distinguished himself among the administrators and the satraps by his exceptional qualities that the king

planned to set him over the whole kingdom. 4At this, the administrators and the satraps tried to find grounds for charges against Daniel in his conduct of government affairs, but they were unable to do so. They could find no corruption in him, because he was trustworthy and neither corrupt nor negligent. 5Finally these men said, "We will never find any basis for charges against this man Daniel unless it has something to do with the law of his God."

6So the administrators and the satraps went as a group to the king and said: "O King Darius, live for ever! 7The royal administrators, prefects, satraps, advisers and governors have all agreed that the king should issue an edict and enforce the decree that anyone who prays to any god or man during the next thirty days, except to you, O king, shall be thrown into the lions' den. 8Now, O king, issue the decree and put it in writing so that it cannot be altered—in accordance with the laws of the Medes and Persians, which cannot be repealed." 9So King Darius put the decree in writing.

10Now when Daniel learned that the decree had been published, he went home to his upstairs room where the windows opened towards Jerusalem. Three times a day he got down on his knees and prayed, giving thanks to his God, just as he had done before. 11Then these men went as a group and found Daniel praying and asking God for help. 12So they went to the king and spoke to him about his royal decree: "Did you not publish a decree that during the next thirty days anyone who prays to any god or man except to you, O king, would be thrown into the lions' den?"

The king answered, "The decree stands—in accordance with the laws of the Medes and Persians, which cannot be repealed."

13Then they said to the king, "Daniel, who is one of the exiles from Judah, pays no attention to you, O king, or to the decree you put in writing. He still prays three times a day." 14When the king heard this, he was greatly distressed; he was determined to rescue Daniel and made every effort until sundown to save him.

15Then the men went as a group to the king and said to him, "Remember, O king, that according to the law of the Medes and Persians no decree or edict that the king issues can be changed."

16So the king gave the order, and they brought Daniel and threw him into the lions' den. The king said to Daniel, "May your God, whom you serve continually, rescue you!"

17A stone was brought and placed over the mouth of the den, and the king sealed it with his own signet ring and with the rings of his nobles, so that Daniel's situation might not be changed. 18Then the king returned to his palace and spent the night without eating and without any entertainment being brought to him. And he could not sleep.

d22 Or *descendant*; or *successor*   e25 Aramaic *UPARSIN* (that is, *AND PARSIN*)
f26 *Mene* can mean *numbered* or *mina* (a unit of money).   g27 *Tekel* can mean *weighed* or *shekel*.
h28 *Peres* (the singular of *Parsin*) can mean *divided* or *Persia* or *a half mina* or *a half shekel*.
i30 Or *Chaldeans*

¹⁹At the first light of dawn, the king got up and hurried to the lions' den. ²⁰When he came near the den, he called to Daniel in an anguished voice, "Daniel, servant of the living God, has your God, whom you serve continually, been able to rescue you from the lions?"

²¹Daniel answered, "O king, live for ever! ²²My God sent his angel, and he shut the mouths of the lions. They have not hurt me, because I was found innocent in his sight. Nor have I ever done any wrong before you, O king."

²³The king was overjoyed and gave orders to lift Daniel out of the den. And when Daniel was lifted from the den, no wound was found on him, because he had trusted in his God.

²⁴At the king's command, the men who had falsely accused Daniel were brought in and thrown into the lions' den, along with their wives and children. And before they reached the floor of the den, the lions overpowered them and crushed all their bones.

²⁵Then King Darius wrote to all the peoples, nations and men of every language throughout the land:

"May you prosper greatly!

²⁶"I issue a decree that in every part of my kingdom people must fear and reverence the God of Daniel.

"For he is the living God
and he endures for ever;
his kingdom will not be destroyed,
his dominion will never end.
²⁷ He rescues and he saves;
he performs signs and wonders
in the heavens and on the earth.
He has rescued Daniel
from the power of the lions."

²⁸So Daniel prospered during the reign of Darius and the reign of Cyrus*a* the Persian.

Daniel's Dream of Four Beasts

7 In the first year of Belshazzar king of Babylon, Daniel had a dream, and visions passed through his mind as he was lying on his bed. He wrote down the substance of his dream.

²Daniel said: "In my vision at night I looked, and there before me were the four winds of heaven churning up the great sea. ³Four great beasts, each different from the others, came up out of the sea.

⁴"The first was like a lion, and it had the wings of an eagle. I watched until its wings were torn off and it was lifted from the ground so that it stood on two feet like a man, and the heart of a man was given to it.

⁵"And there before me was a second beast, which looked like a bear. It was raised up on one of its sides, and it had three ribs in its mouth between its teeth. It was told, 'Get up and eat your fill of flesh!'

⁶"After that, I looked, and there before me was another beast, one that looked like a leopard. And on its back it had four wings like those of a bird. This beast had four heads, and it was given authority to rule.

⁷"After that, in my vision at night I looked, and there before me was a fourth beast—terrifying and frightening and very powerful. It had large iron teeth; it crushed and devoured its victims and trampled underfoot whatever was left. It was different from all the former beasts, and it had ten horns.

⁸"While I was thinking about the horns, there before me was another horn, a little one, which came up among them; and three of the first horns were uprooted before it. This horn had eyes like the eyes of a man and a mouth that spoke boastfully.

⁹"As I looked,

"thrones were set in place,
and the Ancient of Days took his seat.
His clothing was as white as snow;
the hair of his head was white like wool.
His throne was flaming with fire,
and its wheels were all ablaze.
¹⁰A river of fire was flowing,
coming out from before him.
Thousands upon thousands attended him;
ten thousand times ten thousand stood
before him.
The court was seated,
and the books were opened.

¹¹"Then I continued to watch because of the boastful words the horn was speaking. I kept looking until the beast was slain and its body destroyed and thrown into the blazing fire. ¹²(The other beasts had been stripped of their authority, but were allowed to live for a period of time.)

¹³"In my vision at night I looked, and there before me was one like a son of man, coming with the clouds of heaven. He approached the Ancient of Days and was led into his presence. ¹⁴He was given authority, glory and sovereign power; all peoples, nations and men of every language worshipped him. His dominion is an everlasting dominion that will not pass away, and his kingdom is one that will never be destroyed.

The Interpretation of the Dream

¹⁵"I, Daniel, was troubled in spirit, and the visions that passed through my mind disturbed me. ¹⁶I approached one of those standing there and asked him the true meaning of all this.

"So he told me and gave me the interpretation of these things: ¹⁷'The four great beasts are four kingdoms that will rise from the earth. ¹⁸But the saints of the Most High will receive the kingdom and will possess it for ever—yes, for ever and ever.'

¹⁹"Then I wanted to know the true meaning of the fourth beast, which was different from all the others and most terrifying, with its iron teeth and bronze claws—the beast that crushed and devoured its victims and trampled underfoot whatever was left. ²⁰I also wanted to know about the ten horns on

*a*28 Or *Darius, that is, the reign of Cyrus*

DANIEL 6:16–23

'Daniel answered, "O king, live for ever! My God sent his angel, and he shut the mouths of the lions. They have not hurt me, because I was found innocent in his sight. Nor have I ever done any wrong before you, O king" ' (vv. 21, 22).

THE ACCOUNT OF DANIEL in the lion's den has much in common with the earlier story of Shadrach, Meshach and Abednego being thrown into the fiery furnace. The same message of fortitude and trust in God is being proclaimed in this story, as in the previous one.

There is a difference, though. The fiery furnace can never be explained away. If the story is anything more than a traditional tale or fable, then a miracle clearly occurred. But Daniel in the lions' den is different. It is indeed a strange, unusual occurrence. But lions are living creatures and there is always a faint possibility of interaction between them and human beings.

Some people have 'a way' with animals. They are able to establish contact with them. They possess a confidence to which the animals respond. The fiercest animal, faced with this kind of confident human being may behave in a way which seems completely out of character.

Daniel's deliverance was miraculous. Was it the miracle of a person, so confident in his master, God, that he was able to hold his ground, not just in human company but also with some of God's other creatures?

God uses people to further his purposes. Does he use his animal creation, too? Are animals just for humans to exploit, or also for them to relate to?

Thank God for the lion's smaller relatives the cats, and other pets, which relate so strongly to many lonely human beings.

→734

HOSEA 1

'Call him Jezreel, because I will soon punish . . . Call her [not loved] for I will no longer show love to the house of Israel . . . Call him [not my people] for . . . I am not your God' (vv. 4a, 6b, 9).

PUNISHMENT, HATE, REJECTION. What a way to start a relationship! Not only did Hosea marry a prostitute, but how he named his children makes it pretty clear what that involved. It is a very sordid story. It is astounding how such a story can illustrate God's relationship with his people – but it does.

Hosea is an ancient book, from an ancient culture. It speaks to a people almost as much Canaanite as Israelite. Cult prostitution was common. Sexual acts, fertility rites, were performed in temples with the idea that the land would follow suit and produce its crop. It was as much part of the social scene in Samaria as the football or sports stadium is in our modern world. Baal worship involved regarding the god as husband to the land. In contrast 'Hosea uses all his passion and poetry to make men see that the Lord is wedded to the *people* morally and spiritually, and not to the land' (J. B. Phillips).

Within human relationships where one partner is faithless or unreliable, punishment, hate and rejection are bound to surface somewhere. It may be the innocent partner who bears punishment. It could be the guilty one who hates the innocent. In Hosea's case Gomer rejected him, not the other way round. So, too, in our relationship with God. He suffers, he is vilified by faithless souls, and he is all too often rejected. When we reject him, however much he longs for us, God does not force himself on us.

God says, sorrowfully, 'you are not my people' until we ourselves return to his care.

→743

its head and about the other horn that came up, before which three of them fell—the horn that looked more imposing than the others and that had eyes and a mouth that spoke boastfully. [21]As I watched, this horn was waging war against the saints and defeating them, [22]until the Ancient of Days came and pronounced judgment in favour of the saints of the Most High, and the time came when they possessed the kingdom.

[23]"He gave me this explanation: 'The fourth beast is a fourth kingdom that will appear on earth. It will be different from all the other kingdoms and will devour the whole earth, trampling it down and crushing it. [24]The ten horns are ten kings who will come from this kingdom. After them another king will arise, different from the earlier ones; he will subdue three kings. [25]He will speak against the Most High and oppress his saints and try to change the set times and the laws. The saints will be handed over to him for a time, times and half a time.[a]

[26]"'But the court will sit, and his power will be taken away and completely destroyed for ever. [27]Then the sovereignty, power and greatness of the kingdoms under the whole heaven will be handed over to the saints, the people of the Most High. His kingdom will be an everlasting kingdom, and all rulers will worship and obey him.'

[28]"This is the end of the matter. I, Daniel, was deeply troubled by my thoughts, and my face turned pale, but I kept the matter to myself."

Daniel's Vision of a Ram and a Goat

8 In the third year of King Belshazzar's reign, I, Daniel, had a vision, after the one that had already appeared to me. [2]In my vision I saw myself in the citadel of Susa in the province of Elam; in the vision I was beside the Ulai Canal. [3]I looked up, and there before me was a ram with two horns, standing beside the canal, and the horns were long. One of the horns was longer than the other but grew up later. [4]I watched the ram as he charged towards the west and the north and the south. No animal could stand against him, and none could rescue from his power. He did as he pleased and became great.

[5]As I was thinking about this, suddenly a goat with a prominent horn between his eyes came from the west, crossing the whole earth without touching the ground. [6]He came towards the two-horned ram I had seen standing beside the canal and charged at him in great rage. [7]I saw him attack the ram furiously, striking the ram and shattering his two horns. The ram was powerless to stand against him; the goat knocked him to the ground and trampled on him, and none could rescue the ram from his power. [8]The goat became very great, but at the height of his power his large horn was broken off, and in its place four prominent horns grew up towards the four winds of heaven.

[9]Out of one of them came another horn, which started small but grew in power to the south and to the east and towards the Beautiful Land. [10]It grew until it reached the host of the heavens, and it threw some of the starry host down to the earth and trampled on them. [11]It set itself up to be as great as the Prince of the host; it took away the daily sacrifice from him, and the place of his sanctuary was brought low. [12]Because of rebellion, the host ˪of the saints˩[a] and the daily sacrifice were given over to it. It prospered in everything it did, and truth was thrown to the ground.

[13]Then I heard a holy one speaking, and another holy one said to him, "How long will it take for the vision to be fulfilled—the vision concerning the daily sacrifice, the rebellion that causes desolation, and the surrender of the sanctuary and of the host that will be trampled underfoot?"

[14]He said to me, "It will take 2,300 evenings and mornings; then the sanctuary will be reconsecrated."

The Interpretation of the Vision

[15]While I, Daniel, was watching the vision and trying to understand it, there before me stood one who looked like a man. [16]And I heard a man's voice from the Ulai calling, "Gabriel, tell this man the meaning of the vision."

[17]As he came near the place where I was standing, I was terrified and fell prostrate. "Son of man," he said to me, "understand that the vision concerns the time of the end."

[18]While he was speaking to me, I was in a deep sleep, with my face to the ground. Then he touched me and raised me to my feet.

[19]He said: "I am going to tell you what will happen later in the time of wrath, because the vision concerns the appointed time of the end.[b] [20]The two-horned ram that you saw represents the kings of Media and Persia. [21]The shaggy goat is the king of Greece, and the large horn between his eyes is the first king. [22]The four horns that replaced the one that was broken off represent four kingdoms that will emerge from his nation but will not have the same power.

[23]"In the latter part of their reign, when rebels have become completely wicked, a stern-faced king, a master of intrigue, will arise. [24]He will become very strong, but not by his own power. He will cause astounding devastation and will succeed in whatever he does. He will destroy the mighty men and the holy people. [25]He will cause deceit to prosper, and he will consider himself superior. When they feel secure, he will destroy many and take his stand against the Prince of princes. Yet he will be destroyed, but not by human power.

[26]"The vision of the evenings and mornings that has been given you is true, but seal up the vision, for it concerns the distant future."

[27]I, Daniel, was exhausted and lay ill for several days. Then I got up and went about

---

[a]25 Or for a year, two years and half a year   [a]12 Or rebellion, the armies
[b]19 Or because the end will be at the appointed time

the king's business. I was appalled by the vision; it was beyond understanding.

Daniel's Prayer

9 In the first year of Darius son of Xerxes*a* (a Mede by descent), who was made ruler over the Babylonian*b* kingdom—²in the first year of his reign, I, Daniel, understood from the Scriptures, according to the word of the LORD given to Jeremiah the prophet, that the desolation of Jerusalem would last seventy years. ³So I turned to the Lord God and pleaded with him in prayer and petition, in fasting, and in sackcloth and ashes.

⁴I prayed to the LORD my God and confessed:

"O Lord, the great and awesome God, who keeps his covenant of love with all who love him and obey his commands, ⁵we have sinned and done wrong. We have been wicked and have rebelled; we have turned away from your commands and laws. ⁶We have not listened to your servants the prophets, who spoke in your name to our kings, our princes and our fathers, and to all the people of the land.

⁷"Lord, you are righteous, but this day we are covered with shame—the men of Judah and people of Jerusalem and all Israel, both near and far, in all the countries where you have scattered us because of our unfaithfulness to you. ⁸O LORD, we and our kings, our princes and our fathers are covered with shame because we have sinned against you. ⁹The Lord our God is merciful and forgiving, even though we have rebelled against him; ¹⁰we have not obeyed the LORD our God or kept the laws he gave us through his servants the prophets. ¹¹All Israel has transgressed your law and turned away, refusing to obey you.

"Therefore the curses and sworn judgments written in the Law of Moses, the servant of God, have been poured out on us, because we have sinned against you. ¹²You have fulfilled the words spoken against us and against our rulers by bringing upon us great disaster. Under the whole heaven nothing has ever been done like what has been done to Jerusalem. ¹³Just as it is written in the Law of Moses, all this disaster has come upon us, yet we have not sought the favour of the LORD our God by turning from our sins and giving attention to your truth. ¹⁴The LORD did not hesitate to bring the disaster upon us, for the LORD our God is righteous in everything he does; yet we have not obeyed him.

¹⁵"Now, O Lord our God, who brought your people out of Egypt with a mighty hand and who made for yourself a name that endures to this day, we have

sinned, we have done wrong. ¹⁶O Lord, in keeping with all your righteous acts, turn away your anger and your wrath from Jerusalem, your city, your holy hill. Our sins and the iniquities of our fathers have made Jerusalem and your people an object of scorn to all those around us.

¹⁷"Now, our God, hear the prayers and petitions of your servant. For your sake, O Lord, look with favour on your desolate sanctuary. ¹⁸Give ear, O God, and hear; open your eyes and see the desolation of the city that bears your Name. We do not make requests of you because we are righteous, but because of your great mercy. ¹⁹O Lord, listen! O Lord, forgive! O Lord, hear and act! For your sake, O my God, do not delay, because your city and your people bear your Name."

The Seventy "Sevens"

²⁰While I was speaking and praying, confessing my sin and the sin of my people Israel and making my request to the LORD my God for his holy hill—²¹while I was still in prayer, Gabriel, the man I had seen in the earlier vision, came to me in swift flight about the time of the evening sacrifice. ²²He instructed me and said to me, "Daniel, I have now come to give you insight and understanding. ²³As soon as you began to pray, an answer was given, which I have come to tell you, for you are highly esteemed. Therefore, consider the message and understand the vision:

²⁴"Seventy 'sevens'*c* are decreed for your people and your holy city to finish*d* transgression, to put an end to sin, to atone for wickedness, to bring in everlasting righteousness, to seal up vision and prophecy and to anoint the most holy.*e*

²⁵"Know and understand this: From the issuing of the decree*f* to restore and rebuild Jerusalem until the Anointed One,*g* the ruler, comes, there will be seven 'sevens', and sixty-two 'sevens'. It will be rebuilt with streets and a trench, but in times of trouble. ²⁶After the sixty-two 'sevens', the Anointed One will be cut off and will have nothing.*h* The people of the ruler who will come will destroy the city and the sanctuary. The end will come like a flood: War will continue until the end, and desolations have been decreed. ²⁷He will confirm a covenant with many for one 'seven'.*i* In the middle of the 'seven'*i* he will put an end to sacrifice and offering. And on a wing ⌊of the temple⌋ he will set up an abomination that causes desolation, until the end that is decreed is poured out on him.*j*"*k*

Daniel's Vision of a Man

10 In the third year of Cyrus king of Persia, a revelation was given to Daniel (who was called Belteshazzar). Its

---

*a*1 Hebrew *Ahasuerus*   *b*1 Or *Chaldean*   *c*24 Or 'weeks'; also in verses 25 and 26
*d*24 Or *restrain*   *e*24 Or *Most Holy Place*; or *most holy One*   *f*25 Or *word*
*g*25 Or *an anointed one*; also in verse 26   *h*26 Or *off and will have no-one*; or *off, but not for himself*
*i*27 Or 'week'   *j*27 Or *it*
*k*27 Or *And one who causes desolation will come upon the pinnacle of the abominable ⌊temple⌋, until the end that is decreed is poured out on the desolated ⌊city⌋*

message was true and it concerned a great war.[a] The understanding of the message came to him in a vision.

[2]At that time I, Daniel, mourned for three weeks. [3]I ate no choice food; no meat or wine touched my lips; and I used no lotions at all until the three weeks were over.

[4]On the twenty-fourth day of the first month, as I was standing on the bank of the great river, the Tigris, [5]I looked up and there before me was a man dressed in linen, with a belt of the finest gold round his waist. [6]His body was like chrysolite, his face like lightning, his eyes like flaming torches, his arms and legs like the gleam of burnished bronze, and his voice like the sound of a multitude.

[7]I, Daniel, was the only one who saw the vision; the men with me did not see it, but such terror overwhelmed them that they fled and hid themselves. [8]So I was left alone, gazing at this great vision; I had no strength left, my face turned deathly pale and I was helpless. [9]Then I heard him speaking, and as I listened to him, I fell into a deep sleep, my face to the ground.

[10]A hand touched me and set me trembling on my hands and knees. [11]He said, "Daniel, you who are highly esteemed, consider carefully the words I am about to speak to you, and stand up, for I have now been sent to you." And when he said this to me, I stood up trembling.

[12]Then he continued, "Do not be afraid, Daniel. Since the first day that you set your mind to gain understanding and to humble yourself before your God, your words were heard, and I have come in response to them. [13]But the prince of the Persian kingdom resisted me twenty-one days. Then Michael, one of the chief princes, came to help me, because I was detained there with the king of Persia. [14]Now I have come to explain to you what will happen to your people in the future, for the vision concerns a time yet to come."

[15]While he was saying this to me, I bowed with my face towards the ground and was speechless. [16]Then one who looked like a man[b] touched my lips, and I opened my mouth and began to speak. I said to the one standing before me, "I am overcome with anguish because of the vision, my lord, and I am helpless. [17]How can I, your servant, talk with you, my lord? My strength is gone and I can hardly breathe."

[18]Again the one who looked like a man touched me and gave me strength. [19]"Do not be afraid, O man highly esteemed," he said. "Peace! Be strong now; be strong."

When he spoke to me, I was strengthened and said, "Speak, my lord, since you have given me strength."

[20]So he said, "Do you know why I have come to you? Soon I will return to fight against the prince of Persia, and when I go, the prince of Greece will come; [21]but first I will tell you what is written in the Book of

Truth. (No-one supports me against them except Michael, your prince. [1]And in the first year of Darius the Mede, I took my stand to support and protect him.)

11

The Kings of the South and the North

[2]"Now then, I tell you the truth: Three more kings will appear in Persia, and then a fourth, who will be far richer than all the others. When he has gained power by his wealth, he will stir up everyone against the kingdom of Greece. [3]Then a mighty king will appear, who will rule with great power and do as he pleases. [4]After he has appeared, his empire will be broken up and parcelled out towards the four winds of heaven. It will not go to his descendants, nor will it have the power he exercised, because his empire will be uprooted and given to others.

[5]"The king of the South will become strong, but one of his commanders will become even stronger than he and will rule his own kingdom with great power. [6]After some years, they will become allies. The daughter of the king of the South will go to the king of the North to make an alliance, but she will not retain her power, and he and his power[a] will not last. In those days she will be handed over, together with her royal escort and her father[b] and the one who supported her.

[7]"One from her family line will arise to take her place. He will attack the forces of the king of the North and enter his fortress; he will fight against them and be victorious. [8]He will also seize their gods, their metal images and their valuable articles of silver and gold and carry them off to Egypt. For some years he will leave the king of the North alone. [9]Then the king of the North will invade the realm of the king of the South but will retreat to his own country. [10]His sons will prepare for war and assemble a great army, which will sweep on like an irresistible flood and carry the battle as far as his fortress.

[11]"Then the king of the South will march out in rage and fight against the king of the North, who will raise a large army, but it will be defeated. [12]When the army is carried off, the king of the South will be filled with pride and will slaughter many thousands, yet he will not remain triumphant. [13]For the king of the North will muster another army, larger than the first; and after several years, he will advance with a huge army fully equipped.

[14]"In those times many will rise against the king of the South. The violent men among your own people will rebel in fulfilment of the vision, but without success. [15]Then the king of the North will come and build up siege ramps and will capture a fortified city. The forces of the South will be powerless to resist; even their best troops will not have the strength to stand. [16]The invader will do as he pleases; no-one will be able to stand against him. He will establish himself in the Beautiful

---

[a]1 Or *true and burdensome*
[b]16 Most manuscripts of the Masoretic Text; one manuscript of the Masoretic Text, Dead Sea Scrolls and Septuagint *Then something that looked like a man's hand*   [a]6 Or *offspring*
[b]6 Or *child* (see Vulgate and Syriac)

Land and will have the power to destroy it. [17]He will determine to come with the might of his entire kingdom and will make an alliance with the king of the South. And he will give him a daughter in marriage in order to overthrow the kingdom, but his plans*c* will not succeed or help him. [18]Then he will turn his attention to the coastlands and will take many of them, but a commander will put an end to his insolence and will turn his insolence back upon him. [19]After this, he will turn back towards the fortresses of his own country but will stumble and fall, to be seen no more.

[20]"His successor will send out a tax collector to maintain the royal splendour. In a few years, however, he will be destroyed, yet not in anger or in battle.

[21]"He will be succeeded by a contemptible person who has not been given the honour of royalty. He will invade the kingdom when its people feel secure, and he will seize it through intrigue. [22]Then an overwhelming army will be swept away before him; both it and a prince of the covenant will be destroyed. [23]After coming to an agreement with him, he will act deceitfully, and with only a few people he will rise to power. [24]When the richest provinces feel secure, he will invade them and will achieve what neither his fathers nor his forefathers did. He will distribute plunder, loot and wealth among his followers. He will plot the overthrow of fortresses—but only for a time.

[25]"With a large army he will stir up his strength and courage against the king of the South. The king of the South will wage war with a large and very powerful army, but he will not be able to stand because of the plots devised against him. [26]Those who eat from the king's provisions will try to destroy him; his army will be swept away, and many will fall in battle. [27]The two kings, with their hearts bent on evil, will sit at the same table and lie to each other, but to no avail, because an end will still come at the appointed time. [28]The king of the North will return to his own country with great wealth, but his heart will be set against the holy covenant. He will take action against it and then return to his own country.

[29]"At the appointed time he will invade the South again, but this time the outcome will be different from what it was before. [30]Ships of the western coastlands*d* will oppose him, and he will lose heart. Then he will turn back and vent his fury against the holy covenant. He will return and show favour to those who forsake the holy covenant.

[31]"His armed forces will rise up to desecrate the temple fortress and will abolish the daily sacrifice. Then they will set up the abomination that causes desolation. [32]With flattery he will corrupt those who have violated the covenant, but the people who know their God will firmly resist him.

[33]"Those who are wise will instruct many, though for a time they will fall by the sword or be burned or captured or plundered. [34]When they fall, they will receive a little help, and many who are not sincere will join them. [35]Some of the wise will stumble, so that they may be refined, purified and made spotless until the time of the end, for it will still come at the appointed time.

The King Who Exalts Himself

[36]"The king will do as he pleases. He will exalt and magnify himself above every god and will say unheard-of things against the God of gods. He will be successful until the time of wrath is completed, for what has been determined must take place. [37]He will show no regard for the gods of his fathers or for the one desired by women, nor will he regard any god, but will exalt himself above them all. [38]Instead of them, he will honour a god of fortresses; a god unknown to his fathers he will honour with gold and silver, with precious stones and costly gifts. [39]He will attack the mightiest fortresses with the help of a foreign god and will greatly honour those who acknowledge him. He will make them rulers over many people and will distribute the land at a price.*e*

[40]"At the time of the end the king of the South will engage him in battle, and the king of the North will storm out against him with chariots and cavalry and a great fleet of ships. He will invade many countries and sweep through them like a flood. [41]He will also invade the Beautiful Land. Many countries will fall, but Edom, Moab and the leaders of Ammon will be delivered from his hand. [42]He will extend his power over many countries; Egypt will not escape. [43]He will gain control of the treasures of gold and silver and all the riches of Egypt, with the Libyans and Nubians in submission. [44]But reports from the east and the north will alarm him, and he will set out in a great rage to destroy and annihilate many. [45]He will pitch his royal tents between the seas at*f* the beautiful holy mountain. Yet he will come to his end, and no-one will help him.

The End Times

12 "At that time Michael, the great prince who protects your people, will arise. There will be a time of distress such as has not happened from the beginning of nations until then. But at that time your people—everyone whose name is found written in the book—will be delivered. [2]Multitudes who sleep in the dust of the earth will awake: some to everlasting life, others to shame and everlasting contempt. [3]Those who are wise*a* will shine like the brightness of the heavens, and those who lead many to righteousness, like the stars for ever and ever. [4]But you, Daniel, close up and seal the words of the scroll until the time of the end. Many will go here and there to increase knowledge."

[5]Then I, Daniel, looked, and there before me stood two others, one on this bank of the

---

*c*17 Or *but she*   *d*30 Hebrew *of Kittim*   *e*39 Or *land for a reward*   *f*45 Or *the sea and*
*a*3 Or *who impart wisdom*

river and one on the opposite bank. ⁶One of them said to the man clothed in linen, who was above the waters of the river, "How long will it be before these astonishing things are fulfilled?"

⁷The man clothed in linen, who was above the waters of the river, lifted his right hand and his left hand towards heaven, and I heard him swear by him who lives for ever, saying, "It will be for a time, times and half a time.*b* When the power of the holy people has been finally broken, all these things will be completed."

⁸I heard, but I did not understand. So I asked, "My lord, what will the outcome of all this be?"

⁹He replied, "Go your way, Daniel, because the words are closed up and sealed until the time of the end. ¹⁰Many will be purified, made spotless and refined, but the wicked will continue to be wicked. None of the wicked will understand, but those who are wise will understand.

¹¹"From the time that the daily sacrifice is abolished and the abomination that causes desolation is set up, there will be 1,290 days. ¹²Blessed is the one who waits for and reaches the end of the 1,335 days.

¹³"As for you, go your way till the end. You will rest, and then at the end of the days you will rise to receive your allotted inheritance."

---

b7 Or a year, two years and half a year

Hosea

1

The word of the LORD that came to Hosea son of Beeri during the reigns of Uzziah, Jotham, Ahaz and Hezekiah, kings of Judah, and during the reign of Jeroboam son of Joash king of Israel:

Hosea's Wife and Children

²When the LORD began to speak through Hosea, the LORD said to him, "Go, take to yourself an adulterous wife and children of unfaithfulness, because the land is guilty of the vilest adultery in departing from the LORD." ³So he married Gomer daughter of Diblaim, and she conceived and bore him a son.

⁴Then the LORD said to Hosea, "Call him Jezreel, because I will soon punish the house of Jehu for the massacre at Jezreel, and I will put an end to the kingdom of Israel. ⁵In that day I will break Israel's bow in the Valley of Jezreel."

⁶Gomer conceived again and gave birth to a daughter. Then the LORD said to Hosea, "Call her Lo-Ruhamah,ᵃ for I will no longer show love to the house of Israel, that I should at all forgive them. ⁷Yet I will show love to the house of Judah; and I will save them —not by bow, sword or battle, or by horses and horsemen, but by the LORD their God."

⁸After she had weaned Lo-Ruhamah, Gomer had another son. ⁹Then the LORD said, "Call him Lo-Ammi,ᵇ for you are not my people, and I am not your God.

¹⁰"Yet the Israelites will be like the sand on the seashore, which cannot be measured or counted. In the place where it was said to them, 'You are not my people', they will be called 'sons of the living God'. ¹¹The people of Judah and the people of Israel will be reunited, and they will appoint one leader and will come up out of the land, for great will be the day of Jezreel.

2

"Say of your brothers, 'My people', and of your sisters, 'My loved one'.

Israel Punished and Restored

²"Rebuke your mother, rebuke her,
  for she is not my wife,
  and I am not her husband.
Let her remove the adulterous look from
    her face

and the unfaithfulness from between her
    breasts.
³Otherwise I will strip her naked
  and make her as bare as on the day she
    was born;
I will make her like a desert,
  turn her into a parched land,
  and slay her with thirst.
⁴I will not show my love to her children,
  because they are the children of
    adultery.
⁵Their mother has been unfaithful
  and has conceived them in disgrace.
She said, 'I will go after my lovers,
  who give me my food and my water,
  my wool and my linen, my oil and my
    drink.'
⁶Therefore I will block her path with
    thornbushes;
  I will wall her in so that she cannot find
    her way.
⁷She will chase after her lovers but not
    catch them;
  she will look for them but not find them.
Then she will say,
  'I will go back to my husband as at first,
  for then I was better off than now.'
⁸She has not acknowledged that I was the
    one
  who gave her the grain, the new wine
    and oil,
who lavished on her the silver and gold—
  which they used for Baal.

⁹"Therefore I will take away my grain
    when it ripens,
  and my new wine when it is ready.
I will take back my wool and my linen,
  intended to cover her nakedness.
¹⁰So now I will expose her lewdness
  before the eyes of her lovers;
  no-one will take her out of my hands.
¹¹I will stop all her celebrations:
  her yearly festivals, her New Moons,
  her Sabbath days—all her appointed
    feasts.
¹²I will ruin her vines and her fig-trees,
  which she said were her pay from her
    lovers;
I will make them a thicket,
  and wild animals will devour them.

ᵃ6 Lo-Ruhamah means not loved.   ᵇ9 Lo-Ammi means not my people.

¹³I will punish her for the days
   she burned incense to the Baals;
she decked herself with rings and
      jewellery,
   and went after her lovers,
   but me she forgot,"
                     declares the LORD.

¹⁴"Therefore I am now going to allure her;
   I will lead her into the desert
   and speak tenderly to her.
¹⁵There I will give her back her vineyards,
   and will make the Valley of Achor*ᵃ* a
      door of hope.
There she will sing*ᵇ* as in the days of her
      youth,
   as in the day she came up out of Egypt.

¹⁶"In that day," declares the LORD,
   "you will call me 'my husband';
   you will no longer call me 'my master'.*ᶜ*
¹⁷I will remove the names of the Baals from
      her lips;
   no longer will their names be invoked.
¹⁸In that day I will make a covenant for them
   with the beasts of the field and the birds
      of the air
   and the creatures that move along the
      ground.
Bow and sword and battle
   I will abolish from the land,
   so that all may lie down in safety.
¹⁹I will betroth you to me for ever;
   I will betroth you in*ᵈ* righteousness and
      justice,
   in*ᵉ* love and compassion.
²⁰I will betroth you in faithfulness,
   and you will acknowledge the LORD.

²¹"In that day I will respond,"
      declares the LORD—
   "I will respond to the skies,
   and they will respond to the earth;
²²and the earth will respond to the grain,
   the new wine and oil,
   and they will respond to Jezreel.*ᶠ*
²³I will plant her for myself in the land;
   I will show my love to the one I called
      'Not my loved one'.*ᵍ*
I will say to those called 'Not my people',*ʰ*
   'You are my people';
   and they will say, 'You are my God.' "

Hosea's Reconciliation With His Wife

3 The LORD said to me, "Go, show your
   love to your wife again, though she is
loved by another and is an adulteress. Love
her as the LORD loves the Israelites, though
they turn to other gods and love the sacred
raisin cakes."
   ²So I bought her for fifteen shekels*ᵃ* of
silver and about a homer and a lethek*ᵇ* of
barley. ³Then I told her, "You are to live
with*ᶜ* me for many days; you must not be a
prostitute or be intimate with any man, and I
will live with*ᶜ* you."

⁴For the Israelites will live for many days
without king or prince, without sacrifice or
sacred stones, without ephod or idol.
⁵Afterwards the Israelites will return and
seek the LORD their God and David their
king. They will come trembling to the LORD
and to his blessings in the last days.

The Charge Against Israel

4 Hear the word of the LORD, you
   Israelites,
   because the LORD has a charge to bring
      against you who live in the land:
"There is no faithfulness, no love,
   no acknowledgment of God in the land.
²There is only cursing,*ᵃ* lying and murder,
   stealing and adultery;
they break all bounds,
   and bloodshed follows bloodshed.
³Because of this the land mourns,*ᵇ*
   and all who live in it waste away;
the beasts of the field and the birds of the
      air
   and the fish of the sea are dying.

⁴"But let no man bring a charge,
   let no man accuse another,
for your people are like those
   who bring charges against a priest.
⁵You stumble day and night,
   and the prophets stumble with you.
So I will destroy your mother—
⁶   my people are destroyed from lack of
      knowledge.

"Because you have rejected knowledge,
   I also reject you as my priests;
because you have ignored the law of your
      God,
   I also will ignore your children.
⁷The more the priests increased,
   the more they sinned against me;
they exchanged*ᶜ* their*ᵈ* Glory for
      something disgraceful.
⁸They feed on the sins of my people
   and relish their wickedness.
⁹And it will be: Like people, like priests.
   I will punish both of them for their ways
   and repay them for their deeds.

¹⁰"They will eat but not have enough;
   they will engage in prostitution but not
      increase,
because they have deserted the LORD
   to give themselves ¹¹to prostitution,
to old wine and new,
   which take away the understanding ¹²of
      my people.
They consult a wooden idol
   and are answered by a stick of wood.
A spirit of prostitution leads them astray;
   they are unfaithful to their God.
¹³They sacrifice on the mountaintops
   and burn offerings on the hills,
under oak, poplar and terebinth,
   where the shade is pleasant.

---

*ᵃ*15 *Achor* means *trouble.*   *ᵇ*15 Or *respond*   *ᶜ*16 Hebrew *baal*   *ᵈ*19 Or *with*; also in verse 20
*ᵉ*19 Or *with*   *ᶠ*22 *Jezreel* means *God plants.*   *ᵍ*23 Hebrew *Lo-Ruhamah*   *ʰ*23 Hebrew *Lo-Ammi*
*ᵃ*2 That is, about 6 ounces (about 170 grams)   *ᵇ*2 That is, probably about 9 bushels (about 330 litres)
*ᶜ*3 Or *wait for*   *ᵃ*2 That is, to pronounce a curse upon   *ᵇ*3 Or *dries up*
*ᶜ*7 Syriac and an ancient Hebrew scribal tradition; Masoretic Text *I will exchange*
*ᵈ*7 Masoretic Text; an ancient Hebrew scribal tradition *my*

Therefore your daughters turn to
  prostitution
and your daughters-in-law to adultery.

14"I will not punish your daughters
  when they turn to prostitution,
nor your daughters-in-law
  when they commit adultery,
because the men themselves consort with
  harlots
and sacrifice with shrine-prostitutes—
a people without understanding will
  come to ruin!

15"Though you commit adultery, O Israel,
  let not Judah become guilty.

  "Do not go to Gilgal;
do not go up to Beth Aven.*e*
  And do not swear, 'As surely as the
  Lord lives!'
16The Israelites are stubborn,
  like a stubborn heifer.
How then can the Lord pasture them
  like lambs in a meadow?
17Ephraim is joined to idols;
  leave him alone!
18Even when their drinks are gone,
  they continue their prostitution;
  their rulers dearly love shameful ways.
19A whirlwind will sweep them away,
  and their sacrifices will bring them
  shame.

Judgment Against Israel

5 "Hear this, you priests!
  Pay attention, you Israelites!
Listen, O royal house!
  This judgment is against you:
You have been a snare at Mizpah,
  a net spread out on Tabor.
2The rebels are deep in slaughter.
  I will discipline all of them.
3I know all about Ephraim;
  Israel is not hidden from me.
Ephraim, you have now turned to
  prostitution;
  Israel is corrupt.

4"Their deeds do not permit them
  to return to their God.
A spirit of prostitution is in their heart;
  they do not acknowledge the Lord.
5Israel's arrogance testifies against them;
  the Israelites, even Ephraim, stumble in
  their sin;
  Judah also stumbles with them.
6When they go with their flocks and herds
  to seek the Lord,
they will not find him;
  he has withdrawn himself from them.
7They are unfaithful to the Lord;
  they give birth to illegitimate children.
Now their New Moon festivals
  will devour them and their fields.

8"Sound the trumpet in Gibeah,
  the horn in Ramah.

Raise the battle cry in Beth Aven;*a*
  lead on, O Benjamin.
9Ephraim will be laid waste
  on the day of reckoning.
Among the tribes of Israel
  I proclaim what is certain.
10Judah's leaders are like those
  who move boundary stones.
I will pour out my wrath on them
  like a flood of water.
11Ephraim is oppressed,
  trampled in judgment,
  intent on pursuing idols.*b*
12I am like a moth to Ephraim,
  like rot to the people of Judah.

13"When Ephraim saw his sickness,
  and Judah his sores,
then Ephraim turned to Assyria,
  and sent to the great king for help.
But he is not able to cure you,
  not able to heal your sores.
14For I will be like a lion to Ephraim,
  like a great lion to Judah.
I will tear them to pieces and go away;
  I will carry them off, with no-one to
  rescue them.
15Then I will go back to my place
  until they admit their guilt.
And they will seek my face;
  in their misery they will earnestly seek
  me."

Israel Unrepentant

6 "Come, let us return to the Lord.
  He has torn us to pieces
but he will heal us;
he has injured us
  but he will bind up our wounds.
2After two days he will revive us;
  on the third day he will restore us,
  that we may live in his presence.
3Let us acknowledge the Lord;
  let us press on to acknowledge him.
As surely as the sun rises,
  he will appear;
he will come to us like the winter rains,
  like the spring rains that water the
  earth."

4"What can I do with you, Ephraim?
  What can I do with you, Judah?
Your love is like the morning mist,
  like the early dew that disappears.
5Therefore I cut you in pieces with my
  prophets,
I killed you with the words of my
  mouth;
my judgments flashed like lightning
  upon you.
6For I desire mercy, not sacrifice,
  and acknowledgment of God rather than
  burnt offerings.
7Like Adam,*a* they have broken the
  covenant—
they were unfaithful to me there.
8Gilead is a city of wicked men,
  stained with footprints of blood.

---

e15 Beth Aven means house of wickedness (a name for Bethel, which means house of God).
a8 Beth Aven means house of wickedness (a name for Bethel, which means house of God).
b11 The meaning of the Hebrew for this word is uncertain.   a7 Or As at Adam; or Like men

HOSEA 6

'For I desire mercy, not sacrifice, and acknowledgement of God rather than burnt offerings' (v. 6).

A LANDMARK INDEED. Verse 6 is central to Hosea's message. It is like the highest mountain top in a range of peaks, standing out above the rest in majestic grandeur, visible from miles around. And when you stand on its lofty height you are overwhelmed by the breathtaking vision of God's world below.

There are other such peaks in the work of the 'minor' prophets:

Amos 5:24: 'Let justice roll on like a river, righteousness like a never-failing stream!'
Micah 6:8: 'What does the Lord require of you? To act justly and to love mercy and to walk humbly with your God.'
Habakkuk 2:4: 'The righteous will live by his faith.'
Zechariah 7:9: 'The Lord Almighty says: "Administer true justice, show mercy and compassion to one another." '

These peaks cannot be reached by the ancient equivalent of a helicopter. There is no short cut. We need to scale the lower slopes before we stand on the heights and look down. However, as we climb, as we try to come to grips with uncomfortable truths which stand out at various points lower down in the foothills, the peak is often visible. Sometimes it is covered in cloud. Sometimes we feel that we shall never reach it, but always we know it is there.

A fuller understanding of what is meant by 'mercy, not sacrifice' can be discovered by grappling with the full story of Hosea, and relating it to the ultimate loving sacrifice of Jesus, our Lord and Saviour.

→744

JOEL 2:28–32

'And afterwards, I will pour out my Spirit on all people . . . on my servants, both men and women, I will pour out my Spirit in those days . . . and everyone who calls on the name of the LORD will be saved' (vv. 28a, 29a, 32a).

THE ACTIVITY OF THE SPIRIT in the Old Testament was limited. Specially chosen, particular people – prophets, kings, sometimes even priests, were visited with a certain gift and moved by the Spirit. For instance Gideon, (Judg. 6:34) Samson, (Judg. 13:25). But there was no widespread manifestation.

Even today's promise spoken through Joel would be interpreted by most of his hearers, and certainly by later generations, as applying only to Jews. When Peter spoke on the day of Pentecost and related the unique Pentecost experience to this general outpouring prophesied in Joel (Acts 2:17–21) Peter himself assumed that the Spirit would only be given to Jews. He did not learn properly that the gift would be given to others until after his contact with Cornelius (Acts 10:47).

But as in so many other prophetic instances, Joel spoke truer than he knew. God would intervene, and act in a new way with his children. At the same time he would ensure that some Jews, and others closely connected with them, would be prepared just enough for them to move to an understanding of this new thing that God was doing in their midst. It is at our peril that almost 2,500 years after they were spoken, there are certain parts of Joel's unique vision that we still do not take on board fully. How many Christian communities, including Salvationist ones, accept fully and completely that the Spirit is poured out on men and women alike? How many of us take seriously the statement that all who call on the name of the Lord will be saved?

Lord, we are so immature. We find it so hard to accept that your Spirit is available to all. We find it so hard to accept in practice that we are of equal value to you. Develop in us the spiritual insight to see beyond outward appearances into the common sonship which we all share.

→757

9As marauders lie in ambush for a man,
    so do bands of priests;
they murder on the road to Shechem,
    committing shameful crimes.
10I have seen a horrible thing
    in the house of Israel.
There Ephraim is given to prostitution
    and Israel is defiled.

11"Also for you, Judah,
    a harvest is appointed.

"Whenever I would restore the fortunes of
    my people,
7 1whenever I would heal Israel,
    the sins of Ephraim are exposed
and the crimes of Samaria revealed.
They practise deceit,
    thieves break into houses,
    bandits rob in the streets;
2but they do not realise
    that I remember all their evil deeds.
Their sins engulf them;
    they are always before me.

3"They delight the king with their
    wickedness,
    the princes with their lies.
4They are all adulterers,
    burning like an oven
whose fire the baker need not stir
    from the kneading of the dough till it
    rises.
5On the day of the festival of our king
    the princes become inflamed with wine,
    and he joins hands with the mockers.
6Their hearts are like an oven;
    they approach him with intrigue.
Their passion smoulders all night;
    in the morning it blazes like a flaming
    fire.
7All of them are hot as an oven;
    they devour their rulers.
All their kings fall,
    and none of them calls on me.

8"Ephraim mixes with the nations;
    Ephraim is a flat cake not turned over.
9Foreigners sap his strength,
    but he does not realise it.
His hair is sprinkled with grey,
    but he does not notice.
10Israel's arrogance testifies against him,
    but despite all this
he does not return to the LORD his God
    or search for him.

11"Ephraim is like a dove,
    easily deceived and senseless—
now calling to Egypt,
    now turning to Assyria.
12When they go, I will throw my net over
    them;
    I will pull them down like birds of the
    air.
When I hear them flocking together,
    I will catch them.
13Woe to them,
    because they have strayed from me!

Destruction to them,
    because they have rebelled against me!
I long to redeem them
    but they speak lies against me.
14They do not cry out to me from their
    hearts
    but wail upon their beds.
They gather together*a* for grain and new
    wine
    but turn away from me.
15I trained them and strengthened them,
    but they plot evil against me.
16They do not turn to the Most High;
    they are like a faulty bow.
Their leaders will fall by the sword
    because of their insolent words.
For this they will be ridiculed
    in the land of Egypt.

Israel to Reap the Whirlwind

8 "Put the trumpet to your lips!
    An eagle is over the house of the LORD
because the people have broken my
    covenant
    and rebelled against my law.
2Israel cries out to me,
    'O our God, we acknowledge you!'
3But Israel has rejected what is good;
    an enemy will pursue him.
4They set up kings without my consent;
    they choose princes without my
    approval.
With their silver and gold
    they make idols for themselves
    to their own destruction.
5Throw out your calf-idol, O Samaria!
    My anger burns against them.
How long will they be incapable of purity?
6   They are from Israel!
This calf—a craftsman has made it;
    it is not God.
It will be broken in pieces,
    that calf of Samaria.

7"They sow the wind
    and reap the whirlwind.
The stalk has no head;
    it will produce no flour.
Were it to yield grain,
    foreigners would swallow it up.
8Israel is swallowed up;
    now she is among the nations
    like a worthless thing.
9For they have gone up to Assyria
    like a wild donkey wandering alone.
    Ephraim has sold herself to lovers.
10Although they have sold themselves
    among the nations,
    I will now gather them together.
They will begin to waste away
    under the oppression of the mighty king.

11"Though Ephraim built many altars for sin
    offerings,
    these have become altars for sinning.
12I wrote for them the many things of my
    law,
    but they regarded them as something
    alien.

*a*14 Most Hebrew manuscripts; some Hebrew manuscripts and Septuagint *They slash themselves*

¹³They offer sacrifices given to me
  and they eat the meat,
  but the LORD is not pleased with them.
Now he will remember their wickedness
  and punish their sins:
  They will return to Egypt.
¹⁴Israel has forgotten his Maker
  and built palaces;
  Judah has fortified many towns.
But I will send fire upon their cities
  that will consume their fortresses.''

Punishment for Israel

9 Do not rejoice, O Israel;
  do not be jubilant like the other nations.
For you have been unfaithful to your
    God;
  you love the wages of a prostitute
  at every threshing-floor.
²Threshing-floors and winepresses will not
    feed the people;
  the new wine will fail them.
³They will not remain in the LORD's land;
  Ephraim will return to Egypt
  and eat unclean*a* food in Assyria.
⁴They will not pour out wine offerings to
    the LORD,
  nor will their sacrifices please him.
Such sacrifices will be to them like the
    bread of mourners;
  all who eat them will be unclean.
This food will be for themselves;
  it will not come into the temple of the
    LORD.

⁵What will you do on the day of your
    appointed feasts,
  on the festival days of the LORD?
⁶Even if they escape from destruction,
  Egypt will gather them,
  and Memphis will bury them.
Their treasures of silver will be taken over
    by briers,
  and thorns will overrun their tents.
⁷The days of punishment are coming,
  the days of reckoning are at hand.
  Let Israel know this.
Because your sins are so many
  and your hostility so great,
  the prophet is considered a fool,
  the inspired man a maniac.
⁸The prophet, along with my God,
  is the watchman over Ephraim,*b*
yet snares await him on all his paths,
  and hostility in the house of his God.
⁹They have sunk deep into corruption,
  as in the days of Gibeah.
God will remember their wickedness
  and punish them for their sins.

¹⁰''When I found Israel,
  it was like finding grapes in the desert;
when I saw your fathers,
  it was like seeing the early fruit on the
    fig-tree.
But when they came to Baal Peor,
  they consecrated themselves to that
    shameful idol

and became as vile as the thing they
    loved.
¹¹Ephraim's glory will fly away like a bird—
  no birth, no pregnancy, no conception.
¹²Even if they bring up children,
  I will bereave them of every one.
Woe to them
  when I turn away from them!
¹³I have seen Ephraim, like Tyre,
  planted in a pleasant place.
But Ephraim will bring out
  their children to the slayer.''

¹⁴Give them, O LORD—
  what will you give them?
Give them wombs that miscarry
  and breasts that are dry.

¹⁵''Because of all their wickedness in Gilgal,
  I hated them there.
Because of their sinful deeds,
  I will drive them out of my house.
I will no longer love them;
  all their leaders are rebellious.
¹⁶Ephraim is blighted,
  their root is withered,
  they yield no fruit.
Even if they bear children,
  I will slay their cherished offspring.''

¹⁷My God will reject them
  because they have not obeyed him;
  they will be wanderers among the
    nations.

10 Israel was a spreading vine;
  he brought forth fruit for himself.
As his fruit increased,
  he built more altars;
as his land prospered,
  he adorned his sacred stones.
²Their heart is deceitful,
  and now they must bear their guilt.
The LORD will demolish their altars
  and destroy their sacred stones.

³Then they will say, ''We have no king
  because we did not revere the LORD.
But even if we had a king,
  what could he do for us?''
⁴They make many promises,
  take false oaths
  and make agreements;
therefore lawsuits spring up
  like poisonous weeds in a ploughed
    field.
⁵The people who live in Samaria fear
  for the calf-idol of Beth Aven.*a*
Its people will mourn over it,
  and so will its idolatrous priests,
those who had rejoiced over its splendour,
  because it is taken from them into exile.
⁶It will be carried to Assyria
  as tribute for the great king.
Ephraim will be disgraced;
  Israel will be ashamed of its wooden
    idols.*b*
⁷Samaria and its king will float away
  like a twig on the surface of the waters.

---

*a*3 That is, ceremonially unclean *b*8 Or *The prophet is the watchman over Ephraim, / the people of my God*
*a*5 *Beth Aven* means *house of wickedness* (a name for Bethel, which means *house of God*). *b*6 Or *its counsel*

8The high places of wickedness[c] will be
      destroyed—
  it is the sin of Israel.
Thorns and thistles will grow up
  and cover their altars.
Then they will say to the mountains,
  "Cover us!"
  and to the hills, "Fall on us!"

9"Since the days of Gibeah, you have
      sinned, O Israel,
  and there you have remained.[d]
  Did not war overtake
    the evildoers in Gibeah?
10When I please, I will punish them;
  nations will be gathered against them
  to put them in bonds for their double sin.
11Ephraim is a trained heifer
    that loves to thresh;
  so I will put a yoke
    on her fair neck.
  I will drive Ephraim,
    Judah must plough,
    and Jacob must break up the ground.
12Sow for yourselves righteousness,
    reap the fruit of unfailing love,
  and break up your unploughed ground;
    for it is time to seek the LORD,
  until he comes
    and showers righteousness on you.
13But you have planted wickedness,
    you have reaped evil,
  you have eaten the fruit of deception.
  Because you have depended on your own
      strength
    and on your many warriors,
14the roar of battle will rise against your
      people,
  so that all your fortresses will be
      devastated—
  as Shalman devastated Beth Arbel on the
      day of battle,
  when mothers were dashed to the
      ground with their children.
15Thus will it happen to you, O Bethel,
    because your wickedness is great.
  When that day dawns,
    the king of Israel will be completely
      destroyed.

God's Love for Israel

11 "When Israel was a child, I loved
      him,
  and out of Egypt I called my son.
2But the more I[a] called Israel,
    the further they went from me.[b]
  They sacrificed to the Baals
    and they burned incense to images.
3It was I who taught Ephraim to walk,
    taking them by the arms;
  but they did not realise
    it was I who healed them.
4I led them with cords of human kindness,
    with ties of love;
  I lifted the yoke from their neck
    and bent down to feed them.

5"Will they not return to Egypt
    and will not Assyria rule over them
    because they refuse to repent?
6Swords will flash in their cities,
    will destroy the bars of their gates
    and put an end to their plans.
7My people are determined to turn from
      me.
  Even if they call to the Most High,
    he will by no means exalt them.

8"How can I give you up, Ephraim?
    How can I hand you over, Israel?
  How can I treat you like Admah?
    How can I make you like Zeboiim?
  My heart is changed within me;
    all my compassion is aroused.
9I will not carry out my fierce anger,
    nor will I turn and devastate Ephraim.
  For I am God, and not man—
    the Holy One among you.
  I will not come in wrath.[c]
10They will follow the LORD;
    he will roar like a lion.
  When he roars,
    his children will come trembling from
      the west.
11They will come trembling
    like birds from Egypt,
    like doves from Assyria.
  I will settle them in their homes,"
    declares the LORD.

Israel's Sin

12Ephraim has surrounded me with lies,
    the house of Israel with deceit.
  And Judah is unruly against God,
    even against the faithful Holy One.

12 1Ephraim feeds on the wind;
      he pursues the east wind all day
    and multiplies lies and violence.
  He makes a treaty with Assyria
    and sends olive oil to Egypt.
2The LORD has a charge to bring against
      Judah;
  he will punish Jacob[a] according to his
      ways
    and repay him according to his deeds.
3In the womb he grasped his brother's heel;
    as a man he struggled with God.
4He struggled with the angel and overcame
      him;
  he wept and begged for his favour.
  He found him at Bethel
    and talked with him there—
5the LORD God Almighty,
    the LORD is his name of renown!
6But you must return to your God;
    maintain love and justice,
    and wait for your God always.

7The merchant uses dishonest scales;
    he loves to defraud.
8Ephraim boasts,
    "I am very rich; I have become
      wealthy.

---

[c]8 Hebrew aven, a reference to Beth Aven (a derogatory name for Bethel)   [d]9 Or there a stand was taken
[a]2 Some Septuagint manuscripts; Hebrew they   [b]2 Septuagint; Hebrew them   [c]9 Or come against any city
[a]2 Jacob means he grasps the heel (figuratively, he deceives).

With all my wealth they will not find in me
  any iniquity or sin.''

9''I am the LORD your God,
  ⌊who brought you⌋ out of[b] Egypt;
I will make you live in tents again,
  as in the days of your appointed
    feasts.
10I spoke to the prophets,
  gave them many visions
  and told parables through them.''

11Is Gilead wicked?
  Its people are worthless!
Do they sacrifice bulls in Gilgal?
  Their altars will be like piles of stones
  on a ploughed field.
12Jacob fled to the country of Aram;[c]
  Israel served to get a wife,
  and to pay for her he tended sheep.
13The LORD used a prophet to bring Israel up
  from Egypt,
  by a prophet he cared for him.
14But Ephraim has bitterly provoked him to
  anger;
  his Lord will leave upon him the guilt of
  his bloodshed
  and will repay him for his contempt.

The LORD's Anger Against Israel

13 When Ephraim spoke, men
  trembled;
  he was exalted in Israel.
  But he became guilty of Baal worship
    and died.
2Now they sin more and more;
  they make idols for themselves from
    their silver,
cleverly fashioned images,
  all of them the work of craftsmen.
It is said of these people,
  ''They offer human sacrifice
  and kiss[a] the calf-idols.''
3Therefore they will be like the morning
  mist,
  like the early dew that disappears,
  like chaff swirling from a
    threshing-floor,
  like smoke escaping through a
    window.

4''But I am the LORD your God,
  ⌊who brought you⌋ out of Egypt.
You shall acknowledge no God but me,
  no Saviour except me.
5I cared for you in the desert,
  in the land of burning heat.
6When I fed them, they were satisfied;
  when they were satisfied, they became
    proud;
  then they forgot me.
7So I will come upon them like a lion,
  like a leopard I will lurk by the path.
8Like a bear robbed of her cubs,
  I will attack them and rip them open.
Like a lion I will devour them;
  a wild animal will tear them apart.

9''You are destroyed, O Israel,
  because you are against me, against
    your helper.
10Where is your king, that he may save you?
  Where are your rulers in all your towns,
  of whom you said,
    'Give me a king and princes'?
11So in my anger I gave you a king,
  and in my wrath I took him away.
12The guilt of Ephraim is stored up,
  his sins are kept on record.
13Pains as of a woman in childbirth come to
  him,
  but he is a child without wisdom;
when the time arrives,
  he does not come to the opening of the
    womb.

14''I will ransom them from the power of the
  grave;[c]
  I will redeem them from death.
Where, O death, are your plagues?
  Where, O grave,[c] is your destruction?

  ''I will have no compassion,
15 even though he thrives among his
    brothers.
An east wind from the LORD will come,
  blowing in from the desert;
his spring will fail
  and his well dry up.
His storehouse will be plundered
  of all its treasures.
16The people of Samaria must bear their
  guilt,
  because they have rebelled against their
    God.
They will fall by the sword;
  their little ones will be dashed to the
    ground,
  their pregnant women ripped open.''

Repentance to Bring Blessing

14 Return, O Israel, to the LORD your
  God.
  Your sins have been your downfall!
2Take words with you
  and return to the LORD.
Say to him:
  ''Forgive all our sins
  and receive us graciously,
  that we may offer the fruit of our lips.[a]
3Assyria cannot save us;
  we will not mount war-horses.
We will never again say 'Our gods'
  to what our own hands have made,
  for in you the fatherless find
    compassion.''

4''I will heal their waywardness
  and love them freely,
  for my anger has turned away from
    them.
5I will be like the dew to Israel;
  he will blossom like a lily.
Like a cedar of Lebanon
  he will send down his roots;

---

[b]9 Or *God / ever since you were in*   [c]12 That is, North-west Mesopotamia
[a]2 Or *''Men who sacrifice / kiss*   [b]4 Or *God / ever since you were in*
[c]14 Hebrew *Sheol*   [a]2 Or *offer our lips as sacrifices of bulls*

6 his young shoots will grow.
His splendour will be like an olive tree,
  his fragrance like a cedar of Lebanon.
7Men will dwell again in his shade.
He will flourish like the corn.
He will blossom like a vine,
  and his fame will be like the wine from
    Lebanon.
8O Ephraim, what more have I*b* to do with
  idols?

I will answer him and care for him.
I am like a green pine tree;
  your fruitfulness comes from me.''

9Who is wise? He will realise these things.
  Who is discerning? He will understand
    them.
The ways of the LORD are right;
  the righteous walk in them,
  but the rebellious stumble in them.

Joel

1 The word of the LORD that came to Joel
son of Pethuel.

An Invasion of Locusts

²Hear this, you elders;
   listen, all who live in the land.
Has anything like this ever happened in
      your days
   or in the days of your forefathers?
³Tell it to your children,
   and let your children tell it to their
      children,
   and their children to the next
      generation.
⁴What the locust swarm has left
   the great locusts have eaten;
what the great locusts have left
   the young locusts have eaten;
what the young locusts have left
   other locusts*ᵃ* have eaten.

⁵Wake up, you drunkards, and weep!
   Wail, all you drinkers of wine;
wail because of the new wine,
   for it has been snatched from your lips.
⁶A nation has invaded my land,
   powerful and without number;
it has the teeth of a lion,
   the fangs of a lioness.
⁷It has laid waste my vines
   and ruined my fig-trees.
It has stripped off their bark
   and thrown it away,
   leaving their branches white.

⁸Mourn like a virginᵇ in sackcloth
   grieving for the husbandᶜ of her youth.
⁹Grain offerings and drink offerings
   are cut off from the house of the LORD.
The priests are in mourning,
   those who minister before the LORD.
¹⁰The fields are ruined,
   the ground is dried up;ᵈ
the grain is destroyed,
   the new wine is dried up,
   the oil fails.
¹¹Despair, you farmers,
   wail, you vine growers;
grieve for the wheat and the barley,
   because the harvest of the field is
      destroyed.

¹²The vine is dried up
   and the fig-tree is withered;
the pomegranate, the palm and the apple
      tree—
   all the trees of the field—are dried up.
Surely the joy of mankind
   is withered away.

A Call to Repentance

¹³Put on sackcloth, O priests, and mourn;
   wail, you who minister before the altar.
Come, spend the night in sackcloth,
   you who minister before my God;
for the grain offerings and drink offerings
   are withheld from the house of your
      God.
¹⁴Declare a holy fast;
   call a sacred assembly.
Summon the elders
   and all who live in the land
to the house of the LORD your God,
   and cry out to the LORD.

¹⁵Alas for that day!
   For the day of the LORD is near;
it will come like destruction from the
      Almighty.ᵉ

¹⁶Has not the food been cut off
   before our very eyes—
joy and gladness
   from the house of our God?
¹⁷The seeds are shrivelled
   beneath the clods.ᶠ
The storehouses are in ruins,
   the granaries have been broken down,
   for the grain has dried up.
¹⁸How the cattle moan!
   The herds mill about
because they have no pasture;
   even the flocks of sheep are suffering.

¹⁹To you, O LORD, I call,
   for fire has devoured the open pastures
   and flames have burned up all the trees
      of the field.
²⁰Even the wild animals pant for you;
   the streams of water have dried up
   and fire has devoured the open
      pastures.

ᵃ4 The precise meaning of the four Hebrew words used here for locusts is uncertain.   *ᵇ8* Or *young woman*
ᶜ8 Or *betrothed*   *ᵈ10* Or *ground mourns*   *ᵉ15* Hebrew *Shaddai*
ᶠ17 The meaning of the Hebrew for this word is uncertain.

An Army of Locusts

2 Blow the trumpet in Zion;
  sound the alarm on my holy hill.
Let all who live in the land tremble,
  for the day of the LORD is coming.
It is close at hand—
2 a day of darkness and gloom,
  a day of clouds and blackness.
Like dawn spreading across the mountains
  a large and mighty army comes,
such as never was of old
  nor ever will be in ages to come.

3Before them fire devours,
  behind them a flame blazes.
Before them the land is like the garden of
    Eden,
  behind them, a desert waste—
nothing escapes them.
4They have the appearance of horses;
  they gallop along like cavalry.
5With a noise like that of chariots
  they leap over the mountaintops,
like a crackling fire consuming stubble,
  like a mighty army drawn up for battle.

6At the sight of them, nations are in
    anguish;
  every face turns pale.
7They charge like warriors;
  they scale walls like soldiers.
They all march in line,
  not swerving from their course.
8They do not jostle each other;
  each marches straight ahead.
They plunge through defences
  without breaking ranks.
9They rush upon the city;
  they run along the wall.
They climb into the houses;
  like thieves they enter through the
    windows.

10Before them the earth shakes,
  the sky trembles,
the sun and moon are darkened,
  and the stars no longer shine.
11The LORD thunders
  at the head of his army;
his forces are beyond number,
  and mighty are those who obey his
    command.
The day of the LORD is great;
  it is dreadful.
Who can endure it?

Rend Your Heart

12"Even now," declares the LORD,
  "return to me with all your heart,
  with fasting and weeping and
    mourning."

13Rend your heart
  and not your garments.
Return to the LORD your God,
  for he is gracious and compassionate,
slow to anger and abounding in love,
  and he relents from sending calamity.
14Who knows? He may turn and have pity
  and leave behind a blessing—
grain offerings and drink offerings
  for the LORD your God.

15Blow the trumpet in Zion,
  declare a holy fast,
  call a sacred assembly.
16Gather the people,
  consecrate the assembly;
bring together the elders,
  gather the children,
  those nursing at the breast.
Let the bridegroom leave his room
  and the bride her chamber.
17Let the priests, who minister before the
    LORD,
  weep between the temple porch and the
    altar.
Let them say, "Spare your people, O
    LORD.
Do not make your inheritance an object
    of scorn,
  a byword among the nations.
Why should they say among the peoples,
  'Where is their God?'"

The LORD's Answer

18Then the LORD will be jealous for his land
  and take pity on his people.

19The LORD will reply[a] to them:

"I am sending you grain, new wine and oil,
  enough to satisfy you fully;
never again will I make you
  an object of scorn to the nations.

20"I will drive the northern army far from
    you,
  pushing it into a parched and barren
    land,
with its front columns going into the
    eastern sea[b]
  and those in the rear into the western
    sea.[c]
And its stench will go up;
  its smell will rise."

Surely he has done great things.[d]
21 Be not afraid, O land;
  be glad and rejoice.
Surely the LORD has done great things.
22 Be not afraid, O wild animals,
  for the open pastures are becoming
    green.
The trees are bearing their fruit;
  the fig-tree and the vine yield their
    riches.
23Be glad, O people of Zion,
  rejoice in the LORD your God,
for he has given you
  the autumn rains in righteousness.[e]
He sends you abundant showers,
  both autumn and spring rains, as before.

---

[a]18,19 Or LORD was jealous . . . / and took pity . . . / [a]19 The LORD replied   [b]20 That is, the Dead Sea
[c]20 That is, the Mediterranean   [d]20 Or rise. / Surely it has done great things."
[e]23 Or / the teacher for righteousness:

24The threshing-floors will be filled with
grain;
 the vats will overflow with new wine and
 oil.

25"I will repay you for the years the locusts
have eaten—
 the great locust and the young locust,
 the other locusts and the locust
 swarm*—
my great army that I sent among you.
26You will have plenty to eat, until you are
full,
 and you will praise the name of the LORD
 your God,
 who has worked wonders for you;
never again will my people be shamed.
27Then you will know that I am in Israel,
 that I am the LORD your God,
 and that there is no other;
never again will my people be shamed.

The Day of the LORD

28"And afterwards,
 I will pour out my Spirit on all people.
Your sons and daughters will prophesy,
 your old men will dream dreams,
 your young men will see visions.
29Even on my servants, both men and
 women,
 I will pour out my Spirit in those days.
30I will show wonders in the heavens
 and on the earth,
 blood and fire and billows of smoke.
31The sun will be turned to darkness
 and the moon to blood
 before the coming of the great and
 dreadful day of the LORD.
32And everyone who calls
 on the name of the LORD will be saved;
 for on Mount Zion and in Jerusalem
 there will be deliverance,
 as the LORD has said,
 among the survivors
 whom the LORD calls.

The Nations Judged

3 "In those days and at that time,
 when I restore the fortunes of Judah
 and Jerusalem,
 2I will gather all nations
 and bring them down to the Valley of
 Jehoshaphat.*a*
There I will enter into judgment against
them
 concerning my inheritance, my people
 Israel,
for they scattered my people among the
 nations
 and divided up my land.
3They cast lots for my people
 and traded boys for prostitutes;
 they sold girls for wine
 that they might drink.

4"Now what have you against me, O Tyre
and Sidon and all you regions of Philistia?
Are you repaying me for something I have

done? If you are paying me back, I will
swiftly and speedily return on your own
heads what you have done. 5For you took my
silver and my gold and carried off my finest
treasures to your temples. 6You sold the
people of Judah and Jerusalem to the Greeks,
that you might send them far from their
homeland.
 7"See, I am going to rouse them out of the
places to which you sold them, and I will
return on your own heads what you have
done. 8I will sell your sons and daughters to
the people of Judah, and they will sell them to
the Sabeans, a nation far away." The LORD
has spoken.

9Proclaim this among the nations:
 Prepare for war!
Rouse the warriors!
 Let all the fighting men draw near and
 attack.
10Beat your ploughshares into swords
 and your pruning hooks into spears.
Let the weakling say,
 "I am strong!"
11Come quickly, all you nations from every
 side,
 and assemble there.

Bring down your warriors, O LORD!

12"Let the nations be roused;
 let them advance into the Valley of
 Jehoshaphat,
for there I will sit
 to judge all the nations on every side.
13Swing the sickle,
 for the harvest is ripe.
Come, trample the grapes,
 for the winepress is full
 and the vats overflow—
so great is their wickedness!"

14Multitudes, multitudes
 in the valley of decision!
For the day of the LORD is near
 in the valley of decision.
15The sun and moon will be darkened,
 and the stars no longer shine.
16The LORD will roar from Zion
 and thunder from Jerusalem;
 the earth and the sky will tremble.
But the LORD will be a refuge for his
 people,
 a stronghold for the people of Israel.

Blessings for God's People

17"Then you will know that I, the LORD your
God,
 dwell in Zion, my holy hill.
Jerusalem will be holy;
 never again will foreigners invade her.

18"In that day the mountains will drip new
 wine,
 and the hills will flow with milk;
 all the ravines of Judah will run with
 water.

---

*25 The precise meaning of the four Hebrew words used here for locusts is uncertain.
*a2 Jehoshaphat means the LORD judges; also in verse 12.

A fountain will flow out of the LORD's
    house
  and will water the valley of acacias.*b*
¹⁹But Egypt will be desolate,
  Edom a desert waste,
because of violence done to the people of
    Judah,
  in whose land they shed innocent blood.

²⁰Judah will be inhabited for ever
  and Jerusalem through all
    generations.
²¹Their bloodguilt, which I have not
    pardoned,
  I will pardon.''

        The LORD dwells in Zion!

Amos

1 The words of Amos, one of the
shepherds of Tekoa—what he saw concerning Israel two years before the earthquake, when Uzziah was king of Judah and
Jeroboam son of Jehoash[a] was king of Israel.

[2]He said:

"The LORD roars from Zion
  and thunders from Jerusalem;
the pastures of the shepherds dry up,[b]
  and the top of Carmel withers."

Judgment on Israel's Neighbours

[3]This is what the LORD says:

"For three sins of Damascus,
  even for four, I will not turn back ⌊my
    wrath⌋.
Because she threshed Gilead
  with sledges having iron teeth,
[4]I will send fire upon the house of Hazael
  that will consume the fortresses of
    Ben-Hadad.
[5]I will break down the gate of Damascus;
  I will destroy the king who is in[c] the
    Valley of Aven[d]
and the one who holds the sceptre in Beth
    Eden.
The people of Aram will go into exile to
    Kir,"
                                      says the LORD.

[6]This is what the LORD says:

"For three sins of Gaza,
  even for four, I will not turn back ⌊my
    wrath⌋.
Because she took captive whole
    communities
  and sold them to Edom,
[7]I will send fire upon the walls of Gaza
  that will consume her fortresses.
[8]I will destroy the king[e] of Ashdod
  and the one who holds the sceptre in
    Ashkelon.
I will turn my hand against Ekron,
  till the last of the Philistines is dead,"
                            says the Sovereign LORD.

[9]This is what the LORD says:

"For three sins of Tyre,
  even for four, I will not turn back ⌊my
    wrath⌋.
Because she sold whole communities of
    captives to Edom,
  disregarding a treaty of brotherhood,
[10]I will send fire upon the walls of Tyre
  that will consume her fortresses."

[11]This is what the LORD says:

"For three sins of Edom,
  even for four, I will not turn back ⌊my
    wrath⌋.
Because he pursued his brother with a
    sword,
  stifling all compassion,[f]
because his anger raged continually
  and his fury flamed unchecked,
[12]I will send fire upon Teman
  that will consume the fortresses of
    Bozrah."

[13]This is what the LORD says:

"For three sins of Ammon,
  even for four, I will not turn back ⌊my
    wrath⌋.
Because he ripped open the pregnant
    women of Gilead
  in order to extend his borders,
[14]I will set fire to the walls of Rabbah
  that will consume her fortresses
amid war cries on the day of battle,
  amid violent winds on a stormy day.
[15]Her king[g] will go into exile,
  he and his officials together,"
                                      says the LORD.

2 This is what the LORD says:

"For three sins of Moab,
  even for four, I will not turn back ⌊my
    wrath⌋.
Because he burned, as if to lime,
  the bones of Edom's king,
[2]I will send fire upon Moab
  that will consume the fortresses of
    Kerioth.[a]

---

[a]1 Hebrew *Joash*, a variant of *Jehoash*   [b]2 Or *shepherds mourn*   [c]5 Or *the inhabitants of*
[d]5 *Aven* means *wickedness*.   [e]8 Or *inhabitants*   [f]11 Or *sword / and destroyed his allies*
[g]15 Or / *Molech*; Hebrew *malcam*   [a]2 Or *of her cities*

Moab will go down in great tumult
  amid war cries and the blast of the
  trumpet.
[3]I will destroy her ruler
  and kill all her officials with him,"
                          says the LORD.

[4]This is what the LORD says:

"For three sins of Judah,
  even for four, I will not turn back ⌐my
  wrath⌐.
Because they have rejected the law of the
  LORD
and have not kept his decrees,
because they have been led astray by false
  gods,[b]
  the gods[c] their ancestors followed,
[5]I will send fire upon Judah
  that will consume the fortresses of
  Jerusalem."

Judgment on Israel

[6]This is what the LORD says:

"For three sins of Israel,
  even for four, I will not turn back ⌐my
  wrath⌐.
They sell the righteous for silver,
  and the needy for a pair of sandals.
[7]They trample on the heads of the poor
  as upon the dust of the ground
  and deny justice to the oppressed.
Father and son use the same girl
  and so profane my holy name.
[8]They lie down beside every altar
  on garments taken in pledge.
In the house of their god
  they drink wine taken as fines.

[9]"I destroyed the Amorite before them,
  though he was tall as the cedars
  and strong as the oaks.
I destroyed his fruit above
  and his roots below.

[10]"I brought you up out of Egypt,
  and I led you for forty years in the desert
  to give you the land of the Amorites.
[11]I also raised up prophets from among your
  sons
  and Nazirites from among your young
  men.
Is this not true, people of Israel?"
                          declares the LORD.
[12]"But you made the Nazirites drink wine
  and commanded the prophets not to
  prophesy.

[13]"Now then, I will crush you
  as a cart crushes when loaded with
  grain.
[14]The swift will not escape,
  the strong will not muster their strength,
  and the warrior will not save his life.
[15]The archer will not stand his ground,
  the fleet-footed soldier will not get
  away,
  and the horseman will not save his life.

[16]Even the bravest warriors
  will flee naked on that day,"
                          declares the LORD.

Witnesses Summoned Against Israel

3 Hear this word the LORD has spoken
  against you, O people of Israel—against
the whole family I brought up out of Egypt:

[2]"You only have I chosen
  of all the families of the earth;
therefore I will punish you
  for all your sins."

[3]Do two walk together
  unless they have agreed to do so?
[4]Does a lion roar in the thicket
  when he has no prey?
Does he growl in his den
  when he has caught nothing?
[5]Does a bird fall into a trap on the ground
  where no snare has been set?
Does a trap spring up from the earth
  when there is nothing to catch?
[6]When a trumpet sounds in a city,
  do not the people tremble?
When disaster comes to a city,
  has not the LORD caused it?

[7]Surely the Sovereign LORD does nothing
  without revealing his plan
  to his servants the prophets.

[8]The lion has roared—
  who will not fear?
The Sovereign LORD has spoken—
  who can but prophesy?

[9]Proclaim to the fortresses of Ashdod
  and to the fortresses of Egypt:
"Assemble yourselves on the mountains
  of Samaria;
see the great unrest within her
  and the oppression among her people."

[10]"They do not know how to do right,"
                          declares the LORD,
"who hoard plunder and loot in their
  fortresses."

[11]Therefore this is what the Sovereign
LORD says:

"An enemy will overrun the land;
  he will pull down your strongholds
  and plunder your fortresses."

[12]This is what the LORD says:

"As a shepherd saves from the lion's
  mouth
  only two leg bones or a piece of an ear,
so will the Israelites be saved,
those who sit in Samaria
  on the edge of their beds
  and in Damascus on their couches."[a]

[13]"Hear this and testify against the house
of Jacob," declares the Lord, the LORD God
Almighty.

---

[b]4 Or by lies   [c]4 Or lies   [a]12 The meaning of the Hebrew for this line is uncertain.

14"On the day I punish Israel for her sins,
   I will destroy the altars of Bethel;
the horns of the altar will be cut off
   and fall to the ground.
15I will tear down the winter house
   along with the summer house;
the houses adorned with ivory will be
      destroyed
   and the mansions will be demolished,"
                              declares the LORD.

Israel Has Not Returned to God

4 Hear this word, you cows of Bashan on
   Mount Samaria,
you women who oppress the poor and
      crush the needy
   and say to your husbands, "Bring us
      some drinks!"
2The Sovereign LORD has sworn by his
      holiness:
"The time will surely come
when you will be taken away with hooks,
   the last of you with fish-hooks.
3You will each go straight out
   through breaks in the wall,
and you will be cast out towards
   Harmon,"ᵃ
                              declares the LORD.

4"Go to Bethel and sin;
   go to Gilgal and sin yet more.
Bring your sacrifices every morning,
   your tithes every three years.ᵇ
5Burn leavened bread as a thank-offering
   and brag about your freewill offerings—
boast about them, you Israelites,
   for this is what you love to do,"
                        declares the Sovereign LORD.

6"I gave you empty stomachsᶜ in every city
   and lack of bread in every town,
   yet you have not returned to me,"
                              declares the LORD.

7"I also withheld rain from you
   when the harvest was still three months
      away.
I sent rain on one town,
   but withheld it from another.
One field had rain;
   another had none and dried up.
8People staggered from town to town for
      water
   but did not get enough to drink,
   yet you have not returned to me,"
                              declares the LORD.

9"Many times I struck your gardens and
      vineyards,
   I struck them with blight and mildew.
Locusts devoured your fig and olive trees,
   yet you have not returned to me,"
                              declares the LORD.

10"I sent plagues among you
   as I did to Egypt.
I killed your young men with the sword,
   along with your captured horses.

I filled your nostrils with the stench of
      your camps,
   yet you have not returned to me,"
                              declares the LORD.

11"I overthrew some of you
   as Iᵈ overthrew Sodom and Gomorrah.
You were like a burning stick snatched
      from the fire,
   yet you have not returned to me,"
                              declares the LORD.

12"Therefore this is what I will do to you,
      Israel,
and because I will do this to you,
   prepare to meet your God, O Israel."

13He who forms the mountains,
   creates the wind,
   and reveals his thoughts to man,
he who turns dawn to darkness,
   and treads the high places of the earth—
   the LORD God Almighty is his name.

A Lament and Call to Repentance

5 Hear this word, O house of Israel, this
   lament I take up concerning you:

2"Fallen is Virgin Israel,
   never to rise again,
deserted in her own land,
   with no-one to lift her up."

3This is what the Sovereign LORD says:

"The city that marches out a thousand
      strong for Israel
   will have only a hundred left;
the town that marches out a hundred
      strong
   will have only ten left."

4This is what the LORD says to the house of
Israel:

"Seek me and live;
5   do not seek Bethel,
do not go to Gilgal,
   do not journey to Beersheba.
For Gilgal will surely go into exile,
   and Bethel will be reduced to nothing."ᵃ
6Seek the LORD and live,
   or he will sweep through the house of
      Joseph like a fire;
it will devour,
   and Bethel will have no-one to quench
      it.

7You who turn justice into bitterness
   and cast righteousness to the ground
8(he who made the Pleiades and Orion,
   who turns blackness into dawn
   and darkens day into night,
who calls for the waters of the sea
   and pours them out over the face of the
      land—
   the LORD is his name—

ᵃ3 Masoretic Text; with a different word division of the Hebrew (see Septuagint) out, O mountain of oppression
ᵇ4 Or tithes on the third day   ᶜ6 Hebrew you cleanness of teeth   ᵈ11 Hebrew God
ᵃ5 Or grief; or wickedness; Hebrew aven, a reference to Beth Aven (a derogatory name for Bethel)

AMOS 5:18–27
'I hate, I despise your religious feasts; I cannot stand your assemblies . . . Away with the noise of your songs! . . . But let justice roll on like a river, righteousness like a never-failing stream!' (vv. 21a, 23a, 24).

AMOS, LIKE JESUS centuries later, felt exasperated by the complacent, 'superior' people of his day. Those who upheld the establishment; who wanted order and ritual in their lives; who wanted stability instead of justice; who wanted to maintain their own position of advantage – all these were condemned, but those he particularly condemned were the religious people.

It is a difficult message. It seems to put a premium on being outside ordinary society, on being poor, on being outcast, on being despised. Once we are respectable, we seem to be doomed. And where would society be without the respectable pillars of the establishment who keep things well ordered and ticking along nicely? It would certainly be in a sorry state.

Perhaps hypocrisy is the price we must pay for order and calm in society. Yet Amos, like Jesus, demands that we face the unpleasant facts. He requires us not to hide behind the need for stability, comfort and order. He condemns religious rituals of the rich when the pleas of the poor around them are being ignored. He reminds us that we may be unpleasantly surprised when the longed for 'day of the Lord' comes upon us.

Amos' impassioned plea to rid religion of hypocrisy and bring about a just society is as impractical now as it was then. Yet every step that we take to expose hypocrisy and bring justice to the poor and oppressed is a step in favour of Amos, in favour of Christ who carried the protest further, and against the immoral, 'practical' standards of society.

Every step towards justice will soften the impact of the 'day of the Lord' which Amos warns us will be a day of unexpected darkness unless we change our ways.

→758

OBADIAH vv. 15–21
'But on Mount Zion will be deliverance; it will be holy, and the house of Jacob will possess its inheritance' (v. 17).

OBADIAH PRONOUNCED JUDGEMENT on Edom, largely because of the way in which Edom rejoiced when Jerusalem was sacked and its people deported (vv. 11–14). Edom was 'Esau' country (Gen. 36:1ff.). Esau was viewed as typical of the insensitive and ungodly who put material things first (Heb. 12:16). Edom and Israel were not good neighbours. Obadiah's prophecy related to the forthcoming destruction of Edom (v. 18), and Israel's repossession of its inheritance (v. 17). Older translators used the phrase 'possess their possessions' (AV, NKJV, RAV), which stirs the imagination a little more.

It is possible to have an inheritance, or possessions, and not to possess them! It was possible to be part of the chosen people living in Jerusalem, and not experience the blessings God had given them. We are the new Israel: it is equally possible for us to receive the gifts of God and yet not truly possess them.

Some wealthy people keep their jewellery in the bank, obviously and wisely for safety. But they are owners rather than possessors. To be possessed, in Obadiah's sense, an inheritance or possession needs to be cherished and nourished, its capacity for pleasure and service exploited to the full.

Because we are Christ's, we too have possessions. They are part of our glorious inheritance. Some will only be fulfilled at a future date, but some are meant for immediate use. Among our gifts we have joy, peace, assurance, comfort and the Holy Spirit himself. How important that we should actually possess those priceless gifts and that our lives should reveal the completeness of that possession.

> *Now let thy Spirit bring me in,*
> *And give thy servant to possess*
> *The land of rest from inbred sin,*
> *The land of perfect holiness.*

> *(Charles Wesley)*

→767

[9]he flashes destruction on the stronghold
  and brings the fortified city to ruin)
[10]you hate the one who reproves in court
  and despise him who tells the truth.

[11]You trample on the poor
  and force him to give you grain.
Therefore, though you have built stone
    mansions,
  you will not live in them;
though you have planted lush vineyards,
  you will not drink their wine.
[12]For I know how many are your offences
  and how great your sins.

You oppress the righteous and take bribes
  and you deprive the poor of justice in
    the courts.
[13]Therefore the prudent man keeps quiet in
    such times,
  for the times are evil.

[14]Seek good, not evil,
  that you may live.
Then the LORD God Almighty will be with
    you,
  just as you say he is.
[15]Hate evil, love good;
  maintain justice in the courts.
Perhaps the LORD God Almighty will have
    mercy
  on the remnant of Joseph.

[16]Therefore this is what the Lord, the LORD
God Almighty, says:

"There will be wailing in all the streets
  and cries of anguish in every public
    square.
The farmers will be summoned to weep
  and the mourners to wail.
[17]There will be wailing in all the vineyards,
  for I will pass through your midst,"
                                    says the LORD.

The Day of the LORD
[18]Woe to you who long
  for the day of the LORD!
Why do you long for the day of the LORD?
  That day will be darkness, not light.
[19]It will be as though a man fled from a lion
    only to meet a bear,
as though he entered his house
  and rested his hand on the wall
    only to have a snake bite him.
[20]Will not the day of the LORD be darkness,
    not light—
  pitch-dark, without a ray of brightness?

[21]"I hate, I despise your religious feasts;
  I cannot stand your assemblies.
[22]Even though you bring me burnt offerings
    and grain offerings,
  I will not accept them.
Though you bring choice fellowship
    offerings,[b]
  I will have no regard for them.

[23]Away with the noise of your songs!
  I will not listen to the music of your
    harps.
[24]But let justice roll on like a river,
  righteousness like a never-failing stream!

[25]"Did you bring me sacrifices and offerings
  for forty years in the desert, O house of
    Israel?
[26]You have lifted up the shrine of your king,
  the pedestal of your idols,
  the star of your god—[c]
  which you made for yourselves.
[27]Therefore I will send you into exile beyond
    Damascus,"
  says the LORD, whose name is God
    Almighty.

Woe to the Complacent
6 Woe to you who are complacent in Zion,
  and to you who feel secure on Mount
    Samaria,
you notable men of the foremost nation,
  to whom the people of Israel come!
[2]Go to Calneh and look at it;
  go from there to great Hamath,
  and then go down to Gath in Philistia.
Are they better off than your two
    kingdoms?
  Is their land larger than yours?
[3]You put off the evil day
  and bring near a reign of terror.
[4]You lie on beds inlaid with ivory
  and lounge on your couches.
You dine on choice lambs
  and fattened calves.
[5]You strum away on your harps like David
  and improvise on musical instruments.
[6]You drink wine by the bowlful
  and use the finest lotions,
  but you do not grieve over the ruin of
    Joseph.
[7]Therefore you will be among the first to go
    into exile;
  your feasting and lounging will end.

The LORD Abhors the Pride of Israel
[8]The Sovereign LORD has sworn by himself
—the LORD God Almighty declares:

"I abhor the pride of Jacob
  and detest his fortresses;
I will deliver up the city
  and everything in it."

[9]If ten men are left in one house, they too
will die. [10]And if a relative who is to burn the
bodies comes to carry them out of the house
and asks anyone still hiding there, "Is anyone with you?" and he says, "No," then he
will say, "Hush! We must not mention the
name of the LORD."

[11]For the LORD has given the command,
  and he will smash the great house into
    pieces
  and the small house into bits.

---

b22 Traditionally *peace offerings*
c26 Or *lifted up Sakkuth your king | and Kaiwan your idols, | your star-gods*; Septuagint *lifted up the shrine of Molech
| and the star of your god Rephan, | their idols*

12Do horses run on the rocky crags?
　Does one plough there with oxen?
But you have turned justice into poison
　and the fruit of righteousness into
　　bitterness—
13you who rejoice in the conquest of Lo
　Debar*a*
　and say, "Did we not take Karnaim*b* by
　　our own strength?"

14For the LORD God Almighty declares,
　"I will stir up a nation against you, O
　　house of Israel,
that will oppress you all the way
　from Lebo*c* Hamath to the valley of the
　　Arabah."

Locusts, Fire and a Plumb-Line

7 This is what the Sovereign LORD showed
　me: He was preparing swarms of locusts
after the king's share had been harvested and
just as the second crop was coming up.
2When they had stripped the land clean, I
cried out, "Sovereign LORD, forgive! How
can Jacob survive? He is so small!"

3So the LORD relented.

"This will not happen," the LORD said.

4This is what the Sovereign LORD showed
me: The Sovereign LORD was calling for judgment by fire; it dried up the great deep and
devoured the land. 5Then I cried out,
"Sovereign LORD, I beg you, stop! How can
Jacob survive? He is so small!"

6So the LORD relented.

"This will not happen either," the
Sovereign LORD said.

7This is what he showed me: The Lord was
standing by a wall that had been built true to
plumb, with a plumb-line in his hand. 8And
the LORD asked me, "What do you see,
Amos?"

"A plumb-line," I replied.

Then the Lord said, "Look, I am setting a
plumb-line among my people Israel; I will
spare them no longer.

9"The high places of Isaac will be
　　destroyed
　and the sanctuaries of Israel will be
　　ruined;
　with my sword I will rise against the
　　house of Jeroboam."

Amos and Amaziah

10Then Amaziah the priest of Bethel sent a
message to Jeroboam king of Israel: "Amos
is raising a conspiracy against you in the very
heart of Israel. The land cannot bear all his
words. 11For this is what Amos is saying:

　" 'Jeroboam will die by the sword,
　and Israel will surely go into exile,
　　away from their native land.' "

12Then Amaziah said to Amos, "Get out,
you seer! Go back to the land of Judah. Earn
your bread there and do your prophesying

there. 13Don't prophesy any more at Bethel,
because this is the king's sanctuary and the
temple of the kingdom."

14Amos answered Amaziah, "I was
neither a prophet nor a prophet's son, but
I was a shepherd, and I also took care of
sycamore-fig trees. 15But the LORD took me
from tending the flock and said to me, 'Go,
prophesy to my people Israel.' 16Now then,
hear the word of the LORD. You say,

　" 'Do not prophesy against Israel,
　and stop preaching against the house of
　　Isaac.'

17"Therefore this is what the LORD says:

　" 'Your wife will become a prostitute in
　　the city,
　and your sons and daughters will fall by
　　the sword.
Your land will be measured and divided
　up,
　and you yourself will die in a pagan*a*
　　country.
And Israel will certainly go into exile,
　away from their native land.' "

A Basket of Ripe Fruit

8 This is what the Sovereign LORD showed
　me: a basket of ripe fruit. 2"What do you
see, Amos?" he asked.

"A basket of ripe fruit," I answered.

Then the LORD said to me, "The time is
ripe for my people Israel; I will spare them no
longer.

3"In that day," declares the Sovereign
LORD, "the songs in the temple will turn to
wailing.*a* Many, many bodies—flung everywhere! Silence!"

4Hear this, you who trample the needy
　and do away with the poor of the land,

5saying,

"When will the New Moon be over
　that we may sell grain,
and the Sabbath be ended
　that we may market wheat?"—
skimping the measure,
　boosting the price
　and cheating with dishonest scales,
6buying the poor with silver
　and the needy for a pair of sandals,
　selling even the sweepings with the
　　wheat.

7The LORD has sworn by the Pride of
Jacob: "I will never forget anything they
have done.

8"Will not the land tremble for this,
　and all who live in it mourn?
The whole land will rise like the Nile;
　it will be stirred up and then sink
　like the river of Egypt.

---

a13 Lo Debar means nothing.　　*b13 Karnaim means horns; horn here symbolises strength.*
c14 Or from the entrance to　　*a17 Hebrew an unclean*　　*a3 Or "the temple singers will wail*

9"In that day," declares the Sovereign
LORD,

"I will make the sun go down at noon
  and darken the earth in broad daylight.
10I will turn your religious feasts into
    mourning
  and all your singing into weeping.
I will make all of you wear sackcloth
  and shave your heads.
I will make that time like mourning for an
    only son
  and the end of it like a bitter day.

11"The days are coming," declares the
    Sovereign LORD,
  "when I will send a famine through the
    land—
not a famine of food or a thirst for water,
  but a famine of hearing the words of the
    LORD.
12Men will stagger from sea to sea
  and wander from north to east,
searching for the word of the LORD,
  but they will not find it.

13"In that day

"the lovely young women and strong
    young men
  will faint because of thirst.
14They who swear by the shame[b] of
    Samaria,
  or say, 'As surely as your god lives, O
    Dan',
  or, 'As surely as the god[c] of Beersheba
    lives'—
they will fall,
  never to rise again."

Israel to Be Destroyed

9 I saw the Lord standing by the altar, and
  he said:

"Strike the tops of the pillars
  so that the thresholds shake.
Bring them down on the heads of all the
    people;
  those who are left I will kill with the
    sword.
Not one will get away,
  none will escape.
2Though they dig down to the depths of the
    grave,[a]
  from there my hand will take them.
Though they climb up to the heavens,
  from there I will bring them down.
3Though they hide themselves on the top of
    Carmel,
  there I will hunt them down and seize
    them.
Though they hide from me at the bottom of
    the sea,
  there I will command the serpent to bite
    them.

4Though they are driven into exile by their
    enemies,
  there I will command the sword to slay
    them.
I will fix my eyes upon them
  for evil and not for good."

5The Lord, the LORD Almighty,
  he who touches the earth and it melts,
  and all who live in it mourn—
the whole land rises like the Nile,
  then sinks like the river of Egypt—
6he who builds his lofty palace[b] in the
    heavens
  and sets its foundation[c] on the earth,
who calls for the waters of the sea
  and pours them out over the face of the
    land—
the LORD is his name.

7"Are not you Israelites
  the same to me as the Cushites?"[d]
                                declares the LORD.
"Did I not bring Israel up from Egypt,
  the Philistines from Caphtor[e]
  and the Arameans from Kir?

8"Surely the eyes of the Sovereign LORD
  are on the sinful kingdom.
I will destroy it
  from the face of the earth—
yet I will not totally destroy
  the house of Jacob,"
                                declares the LORD.
9"For I will give the command,
  and I will shake the house of Israel
    among all the nations
as grain is shaken in a sieve,
  and not a pebble will reach the ground.
10All the sinners among my people
  will die by the sword,
all those who say,
  'Disaster will not overtake or meet us.'

Israel's Restoration

11"In that day I will restore
  David's fallen tent.
I will repair its broken places,
  restore its ruins,
  and build it as it used to be,
12so that they may possess the remnant of
    Edom
  and all the nations that bear my name,"[f]
                declares the LORD,
                        who will do these things.

13"The days are coming," declares the
LORD,

"when the reaper will be overtaken by the
    ploughman
  and the planter by the one treading
    grapes.

---

b14 Or by Ashima; or by the idol   c14 Or power   a2 Hebrew to Sheol
b6 The meaning of the Hebrew for this phrase is uncertain.
c6 The meaning of the Hebrew for this word is uncertain.   d7 That is, people from the upper Nile region
e7 That is, Crete
f12 Hebrew; Septuagint so that the remnant of men / and all the nations that bear my name may seek ˌthe Lordˌ

New wine will drip from the mountains
and flow from all the hills.

[14] I will bring back my exiled[g] people Israel;
they will rebuild the ruined cities and
live in them.
They will plant vineyards and drink their
wine;

they will make gardens and eat their
fruit.

[15] I will plant Israel in their own land,
never again to be uprooted
from the land I have given them,''

says the Lord your God.

Obadiah

¹The vision of Obadiah.

This is what the Sovereign LORD says about Edom—

We have heard a message from the LORD:
An envoy was sent to the nations to say,
"Rise, and let us go against her for
battle"—

²"See, I will make you small among the
nations;
you will be utterly despised.
³The pride of your heart has deceived you,
you who live in the clefts of the rocks*ᵃ*
and make your home on the heights,
you who say to yourself,
'Who can bring me down to the
ground?'
⁴Though you soar like the eagle
and make your nest among the stars,
from there I will bring you down,"
declares the LORD.
⁵"If thieves came to you,
if robbers in the night—
Oh, what a disaster awaits you—
would they not steal only as much as
they wanted?
If grape pickers came to you,
would they not leave a few grapes?
⁶But how Esau will be ransacked,
his hidden treasures pillaged!
⁷All your allies will force you to the border;
your friends will deceive and overpower
you;
those who eat your bread will set a trap for
you,*ᵇ*
but you will not detect it.

⁸"In that day," declares the LORD,
"will I not destroy the wise men of
Edom,
men of understanding in the mountains
of Esau?
⁹Your warriors, O Teman, will be terrified,
and everyone in Esau's mountains
will be cut down in the slaughter.
¹⁰Because of the violence against your
brother Jacob,
you will be covered with shame;
you will be destroyed for ever.

¹¹On the day you stood aloof
while strangers carried off his wealth
and foreigners entered his gates
and cast lots for Jerusalem,
you were like one of them.
¹²You should not look down on your brother
in the day of his misfortune,
nor rejoice over the people of Judah
in the day of their destruction,
nor boast so much
in the day of their trouble.
¹³You should not march through the gates of
my people
in the day of their disaster,
nor look down on them in their calamity
in the day of their disaster,
nor seize their wealth
in the day of their disaster.
¹⁴You should not wait at the crossroads
to cut down their fugitives,
nor hand over their survivors
in the day of their trouble.

¹⁵"The day of the LORD is near
for all nations.
As you have done, it will be done to you;
your deeds will return upon your own
head.
¹⁶Just as you drank on my holy hill,
so all the nations will drink continually;
they will drink and drink
and be as if they had never been.
¹⁷But on Mount Zion will be deliverance;
it will be holy,
and the house of Jacob
will possess its inheritance.
¹⁸The house of Jacob will be a fire
and the house of Joseph a flame;
the house of Esau will be stubble,
and they will set it on fire and consume
it.
There will be no survivors
from the house of Esau."
The LORD has spoken.

¹⁹People from the Negev will occupy
the mountains of Esau,
and people from the foothills will possess
the land of the Philistines.
They will occupy the fields of Ephraim and
Samaria,
and Benjamin will possess Gilead.

---

*ᵃ*3 Or *of Sela*   *ᵇ*7 The meaning of the Hebrew for this clause is uncertain.

²⁰This company of Israelite exiles who are in
Canaan
will possess ⌊the land⌋ as far as
Zarephath;
the exiles from Jerusalem who are in
Sepharad
will possess the towns of the
Negev.
²¹Deliverers will go up onᶜ Mount Zion
to govern the mountains of Esau.
And the kingdom will be the
LORD's.

Jonah

Jonah Flees From the LORD

1 The word of the LORD came to Jonah son of Amittai: ²"Go to the great city of Nineveh and preach against it, because its wickedness has come up before me."

³But Jonah ran away from the LORD and headed for Tarshish. He went down to Joppa, where he found a ship bound for that port. After paying the fare, he went aboard and sailed for Tarshish to flee from the LORD.

⁴Then the LORD sent a great wind on the sea, and such a violent storm arose that the ship threatened to break up. ⁵All the sailors were afraid and each cried out to his own god. And they threw the cargo into the sea to lighten the ship.

But Jonah had gone below deck, where he lay down and fell into a deep sleep. ⁶The captain went to him and said, "How can you sleep? Get up and call on your god! Maybe he will take notice of us, and we will not perish."

⁷Then the sailors said to each other, "Come, let us cast lots to find out who is responsible for this calamity." They cast lots and the lot fell on Jonah.

⁸So they asked him, "Tell us, who is responsible for making all this trouble for us? What do you do? Where do you come from? What is your country? From what people are you?"

⁹He answered, "I am a Hebrew and I worship the LORD, the God of heaven, who made the sea and the land."

¹⁰This terrified them and they asked, "What have you done?" (They knew he was running away from the LORD, because he had already told them so.)

¹¹The sea was getting rougher and rougher. So they asked him, "What should we do to you to make the sea calm down for us?"

¹²"Pick me up and throw me into the sea," he replied, "and it will become calm. I know that it is my fault that this great storm has come upon you."

¹³Instead, the men did their best to row back to land. But they could not, for the sea grew even wilder than before. ¹⁴Then they cried to the LORD, "O LORD, please do not let us die for taking this man's life. Do not hold us accountable for killing an innocent man,

for you, O LORD, have done as you pleased." ¹⁵Then they took Jonah and threw him overboard, and the raging sea grew calm. ¹⁶At this the men greatly feared the LORD, and they offered a sacrifice to the LORD and made vows to him.

¹⁷But the LORD provided a great fish to swallow Jonah, and Jonah was inside the fish three days and three nights.

Jonah's Prayer

2 From inside the fish Jonah prayed to the LORD his God. ²He said:

"In my distress I called to the LORD,
  and he answered me.
From the depths of the grave*a* I called for
  help,
  and you listened to my cry.
³You hurled me into the deep,
  into the very heart of the seas,
  and the currents swirled about me;
all your waves and breakers
  swept over me.
⁴I said, 'I have been banished
  from your sight;
yet I will look again
  towards your holy temple.'
⁵The engulfing waters threatened me,*b*
  the deep surrounded me;
seaweed was wrapped around my
  head.
⁶To the roots of the mountains I sank
  down;
  the earth beneath barred me in for
  ever.
But you brought my life up from the pit,
  O LORD my God.

⁷"When my life was ebbing away,
  I remembered you, LORD,
and my prayer rose to you,
  to your holy temple.

⁸"Those who cling to worthless idols
  forfeit the grace that could be theirs.
⁹But I, with a song of thanksgiving,
  will sacrifice to you.
What I have vowed I will make good.
  Salvation comes from the LORD."

---

*a*2 Hebrew *Sheol*   *b*5 Or *waters were at my throat*

10And the LORD commanded the fish, and it vomited Jonah onto dry land.

Jonah Goes to Nineveh

3 Then the word of the LORD came to Jonah a second time: 2"Go to the great city of Nineveh and proclaim to it the message I give you."

3Jonah obeyed the word of the LORD and went to Nineveh. Now Nineveh was a very important city—a visit required three days. 4On the first day, Jonah started into the city. He proclaimed: "Forty more days and Nineveh will be overturned." 5The Ninevites believed God. They declared a fast, and all of them, from the greatest to the least, put on sackcloth.

6When the news reached the king of Nineveh, he rose from his throne, took off his royal robes, covered himself with sackcloth and sat down in the dust. 7Then he issued a proclamation in Nineveh:

"By the decree of the king and his nobles:

Do not let any man or beast, herd or flock, taste anything; do not let them eat or drink. 8But let man and beast be covered with sackcloth. Let everyone call urgently on God. Let them give up their evil ways and their violence. 9Who knows? God may yet relent and with compassion turn from his fierce anger so that we will not perish."

10When God saw what they did and how they turned from their evil ways, he had compassion and did not bring upon them the destruction he had threatened.

Jonah's Anger at the LORD's Compassion

4 But Jonah was greatly displeased and became angry. 2He prayed to the LORD, "O LORD, is this not what I said when I was still at home? That is why I was so quick to flee to Tarshish. I knew that you are a gracious and compassionate God, slow to anger and abounding in love, a God who relents from sending calamity. 3Now, O LORD, take away my life, for it is better for me to die than to live."

4But the LORD replied, "Have you any right to be angry?"

5Jonah went out and sat down at a place east of the city. There he made himself a shelter, sat in its shade and waited to see what would happen to the city. 6Then the LORD God provided a vine and made it grow up over Jonah to give shade for his head to ease his discomfort, and Jonah was very happy about the vine. 7But at dawn the next day God provided a worm, which chewed the vine so that it withered. 8When the sun rose, God provided a scorching east wind, and the sun blazed on Jonah's head so that he grew faint. He wanted to die, and said, "It would be better for me to die than to live."

9But God said to Jonah, "Do you have a right to be angry about the vine?"

"I do," he said. "I am angry enough to die."

10But the LORD said, "You have been concerned about this vine, though you did not tend it or make it grow. It sprang up overnight and died overnight. 11But Nineveh has more than a hundred and twenty thousand people who cannot tell their right hand from their left, and many cattle as well. Should I not be concerned about that great city?"

JONAH 4

'O LORD, is this not what I said when I was still at home? That is why I was so quick to flee to Tarshish. I knew that you are a gracious God, slow to anger and abounding in love, a God who relents from sending calamity' (v. 2).

POOR JONAH! God denied him his desire to see justice done. How many of us share Jonah's experience! We cannot stand seeing people 'get away' with their crimes. War criminals are still hounded in the name of justice, after over fifty years. Yet here we see God forgiving murderous tyrants with hardly more than a gentle warning from Jonah.

Law and Order lobbies demand tougher sentencing so that justice is seen to be done, often regardless of whether sentences are effective to protect the public and prevent further offences. In Britain we still use resources locking up petty criminals in appalling conditions. Any grudge they harbour against society receives massive reinforcement. In crowded conditions they are only likely to learn how to be effective criminals rather than to be rehabilitated.

Jonah's indignation at God's mercy was natural. We all share it to some degree. But that is one of the things about mercy. It is unnatural. It comes to us by the grace of God, not through our own natural inclinations.

Jonah in this chapter seems to be an irritable, cross and disagreeable fellow. So cross, indeed, over the gourd which God gave him as protection, that we might be tempted to laugh. But before we laugh, let us examine our own reactions to see whether we have received God's gracious gift of mercy, not just for ourselves, but in our attitudes towards other people.

Search me, O God, and know my heart; test me and know my anxious thoughts. See if there is any offensive way in me, and lead me in the way everlasting. (Psalm 139:23–24)

→768

MICAH 6:1–8
'With what shall I come before the LORD and bow down before the exalted God?'
(v. 6).

ACCEPTABLE WORSHIP. The first part of today's reading is in the form of a law court scene. God's people are summoned to appear to plead their case (vv. 1, 2). God asks two questions in which the people are challenged to show if he has failed them in any way (v. 3). Then, in a brief review of history, God shows how he has been faithful to the covenant made with the people and by implication exposes their faithlessness. This is calculated to stir them to recognize their sin and return in penitence and obedience to fulfil their part of the covenant with God.

The second part of the reading contains a series of questions in which the people ask what God wants. Should they go overboard in an outward display of religion? Should they come to worship with a multitude of sacrifices and with ten thousand rivers of oil? How is their sin to be expiated? Would human sacrifice be appropriate (vv. 6, 7)? Even in English translation the way these questions are built up leads us to expect the answer 'no' and in effect that is the answer which is given.

What God requires is more simple and more profound than that. He requires a close relationship with himself. 'Walk humbly with your God' would probably be better translated 'walk carefully' and this means: 'Walking with God with full insight into what he has done for his people' (Stoebe). For Christians that demands a living relationship with the risen Lord and the rejection of everything in worship and in life that would turn faith into an externalized religious observance.

Acceptable worship also requires a positive attitude to other people – justice and mercy (v. 8). This is echoed in Matthew 7:12, and the whole requirement of this passage is stressed in Mark 12:29–31. Where do we stand in our relationship of God? Are we offering that inner obedience to him or have we been diverted from that to offer external and unacceptable substitutes?

Lord, keep us aware of our responsibilities to live in obedience to your will for our lives. May our worship strengthen our living relationship with yourself. Save us from the peril of offering substitutes for true devotion and enable us to carry the essentials of Christian life and worship into the world in which we are called to live. Amen.

→773

Micah

1 The word of the LORD that came to
Micah of Moresheth during the reigns of
Jotham, Ahaz and Hezekiah, kings of Judah
—the vision he saw concerning Samaria and
Jerusalem.

²Hear, O peoples, all of you,
  listen, O earth and all who are in it,
that the Sovereign LORD may witness
    against you,
  the Lord from his holy temple.

Judgment Against Samaria and Jerusalem

³Look! The LORD is coming from his
    dwelling-place;
  he comes down and treads the high
    places of the earth.
⁴The mountains melt beneath him
  and the valleys split apart,
like wax before the fire,
  like water rushing down a slope.
⁵All this is because of Jacob's
    transgression,
  because of the sins of the house of
    Israel.
What is Jacob's transgression?
  Is it not Samaria?
What is Judah's high place?
  Is it not Jerusalem?

⁶"Therefore I will make Samaria a heap of
    rubble,
  a place for planting vineyards.
I will pour her stones into the valley
  and lay bare her foundations.
⁷All her idols will be broken to pieces;
  all her temple gifts will be burned with
    fire;
  I will destroy all her images.
Since she gathered her gifts from the
    wages of prostitutes,
  as the wages of prostitutes they will
    again be used."

Weeping and Mourning

⁸Because of this I will weep and wail;
  I will go about barefoot and naked.

I will howl like a jackal
  and moan like an owl.
⁹For her wound is incurable;
  it has come to Judah.
It*ᵃ* has reached the very gate of my people,
  even to Jerusalem itself.
¹⁰Tell it not in Gath;*ᵇ*
  weep not at all.*ᶜ*
In Beth Ophrah*ᵈ*
  roll in the dust.
¹¹Pass on in nakedness and shame,
  you who live in Shaphir.*ᵉ*
Those who live in Zaanan*ᶠ*
  will not come out.
Beth Ezel is in mourning;
  its protection is taken from you.
¹²Those who live in Maroth*ᵍ* writhe in pain,
    waiting for relief,
because disaster has come from the LORD,
  even to the gate of Jerusalem.
¹³You who live in Lachish,*ʰ*
  harness the team to the chariot.
You were the beginning of sin
  to the Daughter of Zion,
for the transgressions of Israel
  were found in you.
¹⁴Therefore you will give parting gifts
  to Moresheth Gath.
The town of Aczib*ⁱ* will prove deceptive
  to the kings of Israel.
¹⁵I will bring a conqueror against you
  who live in Mareshah.*ʲ*
He who is the glory of Israel
  will come to Adullam.
¹⁶Shave your heads in mourning
  for the children in whom you delight;
make yourselves as bald as the vulture,
  for they will go from you into exile.

Man's Plans and God's

2 Woe to those who plan iniquity,
  to those who plot evil on their beds!
At morning's light they carry it out
  because it is in their power to do it.
²They covet fields and seize them,
  and houses, and take them.
They defraud a man of his home,
  a fellow-man of his inheritance.

ᵃ9 Or *He*   *ᵇ10 Gath* sounds like the Hebrew for *tell.*
ᶜ10 Hebrew; Septuagint may suggest *not in Acco.* The Hebrew for *in Acco* sounds like the Hebrew for *weep.*
ᵈ10 Beth Ophrah means *house of dust.*   *ᵉ11 Shaphir* means *pleasant.*
ᶠ11 Zaanan sounds like the Hebrew for *come out.*   *ᵍ12 Maroth* sounds like the Hebrew for *bitter.*
ʰ13 Lachish sounds like the Hebrew for *team.*   *ⁱ14 Aczib* means *deception.*
ʲ15 Mareshah sounds like the Hebrew for *conqueror.*

[3]Therefore, the LORD says:

"I am planning disaster against this
     people,
  from which you cannot save yourselves.
You will no longer walk proudly,
  for it will be a time of calamity.
[4]In that day men will ridicule you;
  they will taunt you with this mournful
     song:
'We are utterly ruined;
  my people's possession is divided up.
He takes it from me!
  He assigns our fields to traitors.'"

[5]Therefore you will have no-one in the
     assembly of the LORD
  to divide the land by lot.

False Prophets

[6]"Do not prophesy," their prophets say.
  "Do not prophesy about these things;
     disgrace will not overtake us."
[7]Should it be said, O house of Jacob:
  "Is the Spirit of the LORD angry?
     Does he do such things?"

"Do not my words do good
  to him whose ways are upright?
[8]Lately my people have risen up
     like an enemy.
You strip off the rich robe
  from those who pass by without a care,
  like men returning from battle.
[9]You drive the women of my people
  from their pleasant homes.
You take away my blessing
  from their children for ever.
[10]Get up, go away!
  For this is not your resting place,
because it is defiled,
  it is ruined, beyond all remedy.
[11]If a liar and deceiver comes and says,
  'I will prophesy for you plenty of wine
     and beer,'
  he would be just the prophet for this
     people!

Deliverance Promised

[12]"I will surely gather all of you, O Jacob;
  I will surely bring together the remnant
     of Israel.
I will bring them together like sheep in a
     pen,
  like a flock in its pasture;
  the place will throng with people.
[13]One who breaks open the way will go up
     before them;
  they will break through the gate and go
     out.
Their king will pass through before them,
  the LORD at their head."

Leaders and Prophets Rebuked

3   Then I said,

"Listen, you leaders of Jacob,
  you rulers of the house of Israel.
Should you not know justice,
[2] you who hate good and love evil;

who tear the skin from my people
  and the flesh from their bones;
[3]who eat my people's flesh,
  strip off their skin
  and break their bones in pieces;
who chop them up like meat for the pan,
  like flesh for the pot."

[4]Then they will cry out to the LORD,
  but he will not answer them.
At that time he will hide his face from
     them
  because of the evil they have done.

[5]This is what the LORD says:

"As for the prophets
  who lead my people astray,
if one feeds them,
  they proclaim 'peace';
if he does not,
  they prepare to wage war against him.
[6]Therefore night will come over you,
     without visions,
  and darkness, without divination.
The sun will set for the prophets,
  and the day will go dark for them.
[7]The seers will be ashamed
  and the diviners disgraced.
They will all cover their faces
  because there is no answer from God."

[8]But as for me, I am filled with power,
  with the Spirit of the LORD,
  and with justice and might,
to declare to Jacob his transgression,
  to Israel his sin.
[9]Hear this, you leaders of the house of
     Jacob,
  you rulers of the house of Israel,
who despise justice
  and distort all that is right;
[10]who build Zion with bloodshed,
  and Jerusalem with wickedness.
[11]Her leaders judge for a bribe,
  her priests teach for a price,
  and her prophets tell fortunes for
     money.
Yet they lean upon the LORD and say,
  "Is not the LORD among us?
  No disaster will come upon us."
[12]Therefore because of you,
  Zion will be ploughed like a field,
Jerusalem will become a heap of rubble,
  the temple hill a mound overgrown with
     thickets.

The Mountain of the LORD

4   In the last days

the mountain of the LORD's temple will be
     established
  as chief among the mountains;
it will be raised above the hills,
  and peoples will stream to it.

[2]Many nations will come and say,

"Come, let us go up to the mountain of the
     LORD,
  to the house of the God of Jacob.

He will teach us his ways,
  so that we may walk in his paths.''
The law will go out from Zion,
  the word of the LORD from Jerusalem.
[3]He will judge between many peoples
  and will settle disputes for strong
    nations far and wide.
They will beat their swords into
    ploughshares
  and their spears into pruning hooks.
Nation will not take up sword against
    nation,
  nor will they train for war any more.
[4]Every man will sit under his own vine
  and under his own fig-tree,
and no-one will make them afraid,
  for the LORD Almighty has spoken.
[5]All the nations may walk
  in the name of their gods;
we will walk in the name of the LORD
  our God for ever and ever.

The LORD's Plan

[6]''In that day,'' declares the LORD,

''I will gather the lame;
  I will assemble the exiles
  and those I have brought to grief.
[7]I will make the lame a remnant,
  those driven away a strong nation.
The LORD will rule over them in Mount
    Zion
  from that day and for ever.
[8]As for you, O watchtower of the flock,
  O stronghold[a] of the Daughter of Zion,
the former dominion will be restored to
    you;
  kingship will come to the Daughter of
    Jerusalem.''

[9]Why do you now cry aloud—
  have you no king?
Has your counsellor perished,
  that pain seizes you like that of a woman
    in labour?
[10]Writhe in agony, O Daughter of Zion,
  like a woman in labour,
for now you must leave the city
  to camp in the open field.
You will go to Babylon;
  there you will be rescued.
There the LORD will redeem you
  out of the hand of your enemies.

[11]But now many nations
  are gathered against you.
They say, ''Let her be defiled,
  let our eyes gloat over Zion!''
[12]But they do not know
  the thoughts of the LORD;
they do not understand his plan,
  he who gathers them like sheaves to the
    threshing-floor.

[13]''Rise and thresh, O Daughter of Zion,
  for I will give you horns of iron;
I will give you hoofs of bronze
  and you will break to pieces many
    nations.''

You will devote their ill-gotten gains to the
    LORD,
  their wealth to the Lord of all the earth.

A Promised Ruler From Bethlehem

5 Marshal your troops, O city of troops,[a]
  for a siege is laid against us.
They will strike Israel's ruler
  on the cheek with a rod.

[2]''But you, Bethlehem Ephrathah,
  though you are small among the clans[b]
    of Judah,
out of you will come for me
  one who will be ruler over Israel,
whose origins[c] are from of old,
  from ancient times.''[d]

[3]Therefore Israel will be abandoned
  until the time when she who is in labour
    gives birth
and the rest of his brothers return
  to join the Israelites.

[4]He will stand and shepherd his flock
  in the strength of the LORD,
  in the majesty of the name of the LORD
    his God.
And they will live securely, for then his
    greatness
  will reach to the ends of the earth.
[5] And he will be their peace.

Deliverance and Destruction

When the Assyrian invades our land
  and marches through our fortresses,
we will raise against him seven shepherds,
  even eight leaders of men.
[6]They will rule[e] the land of Assyria with the
    sword,
  the land of Nimrod with drawn sword.[f]
He will deliver us from the Assyrian
  when he invades our land
  and marches into our borders.

[7]The remnant of Jacob will be
  in the midst of many peoples
like dew from the LORD,
  like showers on the grass,
which do not wait for man
  or linger for mankind.
[8]The remnant of Jacob will be among the
    nations,
  in the midst of many peoples,
like a lion among the beasts of the forest,
  like a young lion among flocks of sheep,
which mauls and mangles as it goes,
  and no-one can rescue.
[9]Your hand will be lifted up in triumph over
    your enemies,
  and all your foes will be destroyed.

[10]''In that day,'' declares the LORD,

''I will destroy your horses from among
    you
  and demolish your chariots.
[11]I will destroy the cities of your land
  and tear down all your strongholds.

[a8] Or hill   [a1] Or Strengthen your walls, O walled city   [b2] Or rulers   [c2] Hebrew goings out
[d2] Or from days of eternity   [e6] Or crush   [f6] Or Nimrod in its gates

¹²I will destroy your witchcraft
and you will no longer cast spells.
¹³I will destroy your carved images
and your sacred stones from among you;
you will no longer bow down
to the work of your hands.
¹⁴I will uproot from among you your
Asherah poles^g
and demolish your cities.
¹⁵I will take vengeance in anger and wrath
upon the nations that have not obeyed
me.''

The LORD's Case Against Israel

6 Listen to what the LORD says:

"Stand up, plead your case before the
mountains;
let the hills hear what you have to say.
²Hear, O mountains, the LORD's
accusation;
listen, you everlasting foundations of
the earth.
For the LORD has a case against his people;
he is lodging a charge against Israel.

³"My people, what have I done to you?
How have I burdened you? Answer me.
⁴I brought you up out of Egypt
and redeemed you from the land of
slavery.
I sent Moses to lead you,
also Aaron and Miriam.
⁵My people, remember
what Balak king of Moab counselled
and what Balaam son of Beor answered.
Remember ˌyour journeyˌ from Shittim to
Gilgal,
that you may know the righteous acts of
the LORD.''

⁶With what shall I come before the LORD
and bow down before the exalted God?
Shall I come before him with burnt
offerings,
with calves a year old?
⁷Will the LORD be pleased with thousands
of rams,
with ten thousand rivers of oil?
Shall I offer my firstborn for my
transgression,
the fruit of my body for the sin of my
soul?
⁸He has showed you, O man, what is good.
And what does the LORD require of you?
To act justly and to love mercy
and to walk humbly with your God.

Israel's Guilt and Punishment

⁹Listen! The LORD is calling to the city—
and to fear your name is wisdom—
"Heed the rod and the One who
appointed it.^a
¹⁰Am I still to forget, O wicked house,
your ill-gotten treasures
and the short ephah,^b which is
accursed?

¹¹Shall I acquit a man with dishonest scales,
with a bag of false weights?
¹²Her rich men are violent;
her people are liars
and their tongues speak deceitfully.
¹³Therefore, I have begun to destroy you,
to ruin you because of your sins.
¹⁴You will eat but not be satisfied;
your stomach will still be empty.^c
You will store up but save nothing,
because what you save I will give to the
sword.
¹⁵You will plant but not harvest;
you will press olives but not use the oil
on yourselves,
you will crush grapes but not drink the
wine.
¹⁶You have observed the statutes of Omri
and all the practices of Ahab's house,
and you have followed their traditions.
Therefore I will give you over to ruin
and your people to derision;
you will bear the scorn of the nations.''^d

Israel's Misery

7 What misery is mine!
I am like one who gathers summer fruit
at the gleaning of the vineyard;
there is no cluster of grapes to eat,
none of the early figs that I crave.
²The godly have been swept from the land;
not one upright man remains.
All men lie in wait to shed blood;
each hunts his brother with a net.
³Both hands are skilled in doing evil;
the ruler demands gifts,
the judge accepts bribes,
the powerful dictate what they desire—
they all conspire together.
⁴The best of them is like a brier,
the most upright worse than a thorn
hedge.
The day of your watchmen has come,
the day God visits you.
Now is the time of their confusion.
⁵Do not trust a neighbour;
put no confidence in a friend.
Even with her who lies in your embrace
be careful of your words.
⁶For a son dishonours his father,
a daughter rises up against her mother,
a daughter-in-law against her
mother-in-law—
a man's enemies are the members of his
own household.

⁷But as for me, I watch in hope for the
LORD,
I wait for God my Saviour;
my God will hear me.

Israel Will Rise

⁸Do not gloat over me, my enemy!
Though I have fallen, I will rise.
Though I sit in darkness,
the LORD will be my light.
⁹Because I have sinned against him,
I will bear the LORD's wrath,

---

^g14 That is, symbols of the goddess Asherah   ^a9 The meaning of the Hebrew for this line is uncertain.
^b10 An ephah was a dry measure.   ^c14 The meaning of the Hebrew for this word is uncertain.
^d16 Septuagint; Hebrew scorn due to my people

MICAH 7:18–20
'Who is a God like you, who pardons sin and forgives the transgression?' (v. 18).

DOXOLOGY. The concluding verses of the book of Micah are in the form of a hymn of devotion. The central theme of the writer's 'Praise God, from whom all blessings flow' is God's willingness to forgive (vv. 18, 19). This is a tremendous discovery for it moves away from some of those early concepts of God in which his nature was seen in the way he overcame Israel's enemies. Leslie C. Allen comments, 'With an insight born of richer experience, God's people have come to see that his majesty is most evident in his grace.'

There is much in our lives that should evoke a spirit of thankfulness to God but the grace of forgiveness is the greatest gift of all. To discover that we can do nothing to merit forgiveness could lead us to despair. To realize that our repentance does not initiate grace but rather opens up our lives to God's redeeming purpose, throws us back on the mercy of the pardoning God.

In that experience the guilt of our sin is removed, never to threaten us again (v. 19). God is as good as his promise. Spiritual disaster overtakes us when we break faith with God but he never forgets his promise to his people (v. 20). Any barrier to the healing of our relationship with God is built from our side and not from his.

Micah's final emphasis on God's steadfast love should encourage us to trust that love and to live responsibly in God's presence.

→774

NAHUM 1:1–15

'Look, there on the mountains, the feet of one who brings good news, who proclaims peace!' (v. 15).

GOOD NEWS FOR THE BIGOT. The words of today's text have become familiar through their use in Isaiah 52:7. In that context they are applied to the end of the Babylonian captivity. Isaiah combines nationalism and universalism, an element totally absent from Nahum. For this prophet, the good news is of the total destruction of the hated Assyrian enemy and of the capital city, Nineveh. In verse 14 we sense the mood of this whole book: 'The Lord has given a command concerning you, (Nineveh): "You will have no descendants to bear your name . . . I will prepare your grave for you are vile." ' Nahum has been described as 'the nearest thing to a hymn of hate in the whole Old Testament' and verse 15 shows the prophet calling on his hearers to rejoice in that hatred.

The Assyrians were regarded as the most cruel and tyrannical empire in the world and surrounding nations would shed no tears at her total destruction. In our Christian era we have to remember how easy it is to feel like that about tyrants. But that does not mean total hatred is justified. Nahum needs to be set alongside Jonah. Both believed that Nineveh came within the orbit of God's concern. Nahum rejoiced that Nineveh got what she deserved, whereas Jonah discovered that such people were the concern of God's missionary care. That is the really good news which is most effectively proclaimed in the coming of Jesus and it leaves no room for bigotry.

Lord, help me to see other people with your eyes.

→777

until he pleads my case
   and establishes my right.
He will bring me out into the light;
   I will see his righteousness.
[10]Then my enemy will see it
   and will be covered with shame,
she who said to me,
   "Where is the LORD your God?"
My eyes will see her downfall;
   even now she will be trampled underfoot
   like mire in the streets.

[11]The day for building your walls will come,
   the day for extending your boundaries.
[12]In that day people will come to you
   from Assyria and the cities of Egypt,
even from Egypt to the Euphrates
   and from sea to sea
   and from mountain to mountain.
[13]The earth will become desolate because of
   its inhabitants,
   as the result of their deeds.

Prayer and Praise

[14]Shepherd your people with your staff,
   the flock of your inheritance,
which lives by itself in a forest,
   in fertile pasture-lands.[a]
Let them feed in Bashan and Gilead
   as in days long ago.

[15]"As in the days when you came out of
      Egypt,
   I will show them my wonders."

[16]Nations will see and be ashamed,
   deprived of all their power.
They will lay their hands on their mouths
   and their ears will become deaf.
[17]They will lick dust like a snake,
   like creatures that crawl on the
      ground.
They will come trembling out of their
      dens;
   they will turn in fear to the LORD our
      God
   and will be afraid of you.
[18]Who is a God like you,
   who pardons sin and forgives the
      transgression
   of the remnant of his inheritance?
You do not stay angry for ever
   but delight to show mercy.
[19]You will again have compassion on us;
   you will tread our sins underfoot
   and hurl all our iniquities into the depths
      of the sea.
[20]You will be true to Jacob,
   and show mercy to Abraham,
as you pledged on oath to our fathers
   in days long ago.

---

[a]14 Or *in the middle of Carmel*

Nahum

1 An oracle concerning Nineveh. The book of the vision of Nahum the Elkoshite.

The LORD's Anger Against Nineveh

2 The LORD is a jealous and avenging God;
    the LORD takes vengeance and is filled
        with wrath.
The LORD takes vengeance on his foes
    and maintains his wrath against his
        enemies.
3 The LORD is slow to anger and great in
        power;
    the LORD will not leave the guilty
        unpunished.
His way is in the whirlwind and the storm,
    and clouds are the dust of his feet.
4 He rebukes the sea and dries it up;
    he makes all the rivers run dry.
Bashan and Carmel wither
    and the blossoms of Lebanon fade.
5 The mountains quake before him
    and the hills melt away.
The earth trembles at his presence,
    the world and all who live in it.
6 Who can withstand his indignation?
    Who can endure his fierce anger?
His wrath is poured out like fire;
    the rocks are shattered before him.

7 The LORD is good,
    a refuge in times of trouble.
He cares for those who trust in him,
8   but with an overwhelming flood
he will make an end of ₍Nineveh₎;
    he will pursue his foes into darkness.

9 Whatever they plot against the LORD
he*a* will bring to an end;
    trouble will not come a second time.
10 They will be entangled among thorns
    and drunk from their wine;
    they will be consumed like dry
        stubble.*b*
11 From you, ₍O Nineveh,₎ has one come
        forth
    who plots evil against the LORD
    and counsels wickedness.

12 This is what the LORD says:

"Although they have allies and are
        numerous,
    they will be cut off and pass away.
Although I have afflicted you, ₍O Judah,₎
    I will afflict you no more.
13 Now I will break their yoke from your
        neck
    and tear your shackles away."

14 The LORD has given a command
        concerning you, ₍Nineveh₎:
    "You will have no descendants to bear
        your name.
I will destroy the carved images and cast
        idols
    that are in the temple of your gods.
I will prepare your grave,
    for you are vile."

15 Look, there on the mountains,
    the feet of one who brings good news,
    who proclaims peace!
Celebrate your festivals, O Judah,
    and fulfil your vows.
No more will the wicked invade you;
    they will be completely destroyed.

Nineveh to Fall

2 An attacker advances against you,
        ₍Nineveh₎.
Guard the fortress,
    watch the road,
    brace yourselves,
    marshal all your strength!

2 The LORD will restore the splendour of
        Jacob
    like the splendour of Israel,
though destroyers have laid them waste
    and have ruined their vines.

3 The shields of his soldiers are red;
    the warriors are clad in scarlet.
The metal on the chariots flashes
    on the day they are made ready;
    the spears of pine are brandished.*a*
4 The chariots storm through the streets,
    rushing back and forth through the
        squares.
They look like flaming torches;
    they dart about like lightning.

---

*a*9 Or *What do you foes plot against the LORD? | He*
*a*3 Hebrew; Septuagint and Syriac / *the horsemen rush to and fro*
*b*10 The meaning of the Hebrew for this verse is uncertain.

'All who see you will flee from you and say, "Nineveh is in ruins – who will mourn for her?" ' (3:7).

THE ENEMY DESTROYED. The reading for today is rather longer than usual but it encompasses the whole poem which describes the destruction of Assyria. The poem consists of four main sections. First, the seige, capture and plunder of Nineveh (2:1–10), second, the end of the ferocious army (2:11–13), third, a further description of the attack on the city (3:1–4), and finally, Niveveh's humiliation and dishonour (3:5–7). In spite of the subject the poetic skill of the prophet is displayed to great effect in these verses.

Nahum obviously enjoyed his work. Is he, therefore, to be dismissed as a brilliant but misguided man? For all its intense nationalism, this book serves to remind us that callous militarism is a denial of true humanity and an affront to God. Jesus, with a compasion not found in Nahum, said, 'all who draw the sword will die by the sword' (Matt. 26:52). We do not gloat over the destruction of enemies but we do live in an era which would do well to hear Nahum's essential condemnation of inhumane oppression.

If we continue to solve our problems by the sword we stand in danger of destroying ourselves and the whole of civilization with us.

→778

HABAKKUK 3:1–16
'Lord, I have heard of your fame; I stand in awe of your deeds, Lord' (v. 2).

A VICTORIOUS GOD. There is no universal agreement among scholars about the authorship of this psalm, but it is assumed here that Habakkuk wrote it and it is based on his vision (see 2:2).

After the introduction in verses 1 and 2, we are given a vision of an active God. The whole section down to verse 16 uses the rich variety of Hebrew poetic idiom to describe the victorious God. Every verse speaks power, as the writer builds image upon image in his attempt to describe what is essentially indescribable.

Verses 13 and 14 point to deliverance from trouble and the overthrow of an oppressor. The writer stands in awe at the power and majesty of God (vv. 2 and 16). He is beginning to understand that God works on a bigger scale than time-bound minds can imagine.

How shall we think and speak of God's power? Like the prophet, we shall have to express the fact that God is totally opposed to sin. But as Christians we shall have to see God's creative power. His first action against sin is to seek to forgive it and to redeem the sinner. In that sense God's plan for us is creative. He is constantly at work perfecting his grace within us, and bringing fulfilment into our lives. That is the victory he seeks.

Thank you, Lord that you hate the sin but love the sinner.

→785

⁵He summons his picked troops,
  yet they stumble on their way.
They dash to the city wall;
  the protective shield is put in place.
⁶The river gates are thrown open
  and the palace collapses.
⁷It is decreed*b* that ⌊the city⌋
  be exiled and carried away.
Its slave girls moan like doves
  and beat upon their breasts.
⁸Nineveh is like a pool,
  and its water is draining away.
"Stop! Stop!" they cry,
  but no-one turns back.
⁹Plunder the silver!
  Plunder the gold!
The supply is endless,
  the wealth from all its treasures!
¹⁰She is pillaged, plundered, stripped!
  Hearts melt, knees give way,
  bodies tremble, every face grows pale.

¹¹Where now is the lions' den,
  the place where they fed their young,
where the lion and lioness went,
  and the cubs, with nothing to fear?
¹²The lion killed enough for his cubs
  and strangled the prey for his mate,
filling his lairs with the kill
  and his dens with the prey.

¹³"I am against you,"
  declares the LORD Almighty.
"I will burn up your chariots in smoke,
  and the sword will devour your young
    lions.
I will leave you no prey on the earth.
The voices of your messengers
  will no longer be heard."

Woe to Nineveh

3 Woe to the city of blood,
  full of lies,
full of plunder,
  never without victims!
²The crack of whips,
  the clatter of wheels,
galloping horses
  and jolting chariots!
³Charging cavalry,
  flashing swords
  and glittering spears!
Many casualties,
  piles of dead,
bodies without number,
  people stumbling over the corpses—
⁴all because of the wanton lust of a harlot,
  alluring, the mistress of sorceries,
who enslaved nations by her prostitution
  and peoples by her witchcraft.

⁵"I am against you," declares the LORD
    Almighty.
"I will lift your skirts over your face.
I will show the nations your nakedness
  and the kingdoms your shame.
⁶I will pelt you with filth,
  I will treat you with contempt
  and make you a spectacle.

⁷All who see you will flee from you and say,
  'Nineveh is in ruins—who will mourn
    for her?'
Where can I find anyone to comfort
  you?''

⁸Are you better than Thebes,*a*
  situated on the Nile,
  with water around her?
The river was her defence,
  the waters her wall.
⁹Cush*b* and Egypt were her boundless
    strength;
  Put and Libya were among her allies.
¹⁰Yet she was taken captive
  and went into exile.
Her infants were dashed to pieces
  at the head of every street.
Lots were cast for her nobles,
  and all her great men were put in chains.
¹¹You too will become drunk;
  you will go into hiding
  and seek refuge from the enemy.

¹²All your fortresses are like fig-trees
  with their first ripe fruit;
when they are shaken,
  the figs fall into the mouth of the eater.
¹³Look at your troops—
  they are all women!
The gates of your land
  are wide open to your enemies;
  fire has consumed their bars.

¹⁴Draw water for the siege,
  strengthen your defences!
Work the clay,
  tread the mortar,
  repair the brickwork!
¹⁵There the fire will devour you;
  the sword will cut you down
  and, like grasshoppers, consume you.
Multiply like grasshoppers,
  multiply like locusts!
¹⁶You have increased the number of your
    merchants
  till they are more than the stars of the
    sky,
but like locusts they strip the land
  and then fly away.
¹⁷Your guards are like locusts,
  your officials like swarms of locusts
  that settle in the walls on a cold day—
but when the sun appears they fly away,
  and no-one knows where.

¹⁸O king of Assyria, your shepherds*c*
    slumber;
  your nobles lie down to rest.
Your people are scattered on the
    mountains
  with no-one to gather them.
¹⁹Nothing can heal your wound;
  your injury is fatal.
Everyone who hears the news about you
  claps his hands at your fall,
for who has not felt
  your endless cruelty?

---

b7 The meaning of the Hebrew for this word is uncertain.
b9 That is, the upper Nile region   *c18* Or *rulers*
a8 Hebrew *No Amon*

Habakkuk

1

The oracle that Habakkuk the prophet received.

Habakkuk's Complaint

2How long, O LORD, must I call for help,
  but you do not listen?
Or cry out to you, "Violence!"
  but you do not save?
3Why do you make me look at injustice?
  Why do you tolerate wrong?
Destruction and violence are before me;
  there is strife, and conflict abounds.
4Therefore the law is paralysed,
  and justice never prevails.
The wicked hem in the righteous,
  so that justice is perverted.

The LORD's Answer

5"Look at the nations and watch—
  and be utterly amazed.
For I am going to do something in your
  days
    that you would not believe,
    even if you were told.
6I am raising up the Babylonians,[a]
  that ruthless and impetuous people,
who sweep across the whole earth
  to seize dwelling-places not their own.
7They are a feared and dreaded people;
  they are a law to themselves
  and promote their own honour.
8Their horses are swifter than leopards,
  fiercer than wolves at dusk.
Their cavalry gallops headlong;
  their horsemen come from afar.
They fly like a vulture swooping to
  devour;
9 they all come bent on violence.
Their hordes[b] advance like a desert wind
  and gather prisoners like sand.
10They deride kings
  and scoff at rulers.
They laugh at all fortified cities;
  they build earthen ramps and capture
    them.
11Then they sweep past like the wind and go
  on—
  guilty men, whose own strength is their
    god."

Habakkuk's Second Complaint

12O LORD, are you not from everlasting?
  My God, my Holy One, we will not die.
O LORD, you have appointed them to
  execute judgment;
O Rock, you have ordained them to
  punish.
13Your eyes are too pure to look on evil;
  you cannot tolerate wrong.
Why then do you tolerate the treacherous?
  Why are you silent while the wicked
  swallow up those more righteous than
    themselves?
14You have made men like fish in the sea,
  like sea creatures that have no ruler.
15The wicked foe pulls all of them up with
  hooks,
he catches them in his net,
he gathers them up in his drag-net;
  and so he rejoices and is glad.
16Therefore he sacrifices to his net
  and burns incense to his drag-net,
for by his net he lives in luxury
  and enjoys the choicest food.
17Is he to keep on emptying his net,
  destroying nations without mercy?

2

I will stand at my watch
  and station myself on the ramparts;
I will look to see what he will say to me,
  and what answer I am to give to this
    complaint.[a]

The LORD's Answer

2Then the LORD replied:

"Write down the revelation
  and make it plain on tablets
  so that a herald[b] may run with it.
3For the revelation awaits an appointed
  time;
  it speaks of the end
  and will not prove false.
Though it linger, wait for it;
  it[c] will certainly come and will not
    delay.

4"See, he is puffed up;
  his desires are not upright—
  but the righteous will live by his faith—[d]

---

a6 Or Chaldeans   b9 The meaning of the Hebrew for this word is uncertain.
a1 Or And what to answer when I am rebuked   b2 Or so that whoever reads it
c3 Or Though he linger, wait for him; I he   d4 Or faithfulness

⁵indeed, wine betrays him;
  he is arrogant and never at rest.
Because he is as greedy as the grave*e*
  and like death is never satisfied,
he gathers to himself all the nations
  and takes captive all the peoples.

⁶"Will not all of them taunt him with ridicule and scorn, saying,

" 'Woe to him who piles up stolen goods
  and makes himself wealthy by extortion!
How long must this go on?'
⁷Will not your debtors*f* suddenly arise?
  Will they not wake up and make you
    tremble?
  Then you will become their victim.
⁸Because you have plundered many
    nations,
  the peoples who are left will plunder
    you.
For you have shed man's blood;
  you have destroyed lands and cities and
    everyone in them.

⁹"Woe to him who builds his realm by
    unjust gain
  to set his nest on high,
  to escape the clutches of ruin!
¹⁰You have plotted the ruin of many
    peoples,
  shaming your own house and forfeiting
    your life.
¹¹The stones of the wall will cry out,
  and the beams of the woodwork will
    echo it.

¹²"Woe to him who builds a city with
    bloodshed
  and establishes a town by crime!
¹³Has not the LORD Almighty determined
  that the people's labour is only fuel for
    the fire,
  that nations exhaust themselves for
    nothing?
¹⁴For the earth will be filled with the
    knowledge of the glory of the LORD,
  as the waters cover the sea.

¹⁵"Woe to him who gives drink to his
    neighbours,
  pouring it from the wineskin till they are
    drunk,
  so that he can gaze on their naked
    bodies.
¹⁶You will be filled with shame instead of
    glory.
  Now it is your turn! Drink and be
    exposed!*g*
The cup from the LORD's right hand is
    coming round to you,
  and disgrace will cover your glory.
¹⁷The violence you have done to Lebanon
    will overwhelm you,
  and your destruction of animals will
    terrify you.

For you have shed man's blood;
  you have destroyed lands and cities and
    everyone in them.

¹⁸"Of what value is an idol, since a man has
    carved it?
  Or an image that teaches lies?
For he who makes it trusts in his own
    creation;
  he makes idols that cannot speak.
¹⁹Woe to him who says to wood, 'Come to
    life!'
  Or to lifeless stone, 'Wake up!'
Can it give guidance?
  It is covered with gold and silver;
  there is no breath in it.
²⁰But the LORD is in his holy temple;
  let all the earth be silent before him.''

Habakkuk's Prayer

3 A prayer of Habakkuk the prophet. On
    *shigionoth.*ᵃ

²LORD, I have heard of your fame;
  I stand in awe of your deeds, O LORD.
Renew them in our day,
  in our time make them known;
  in wrath remember mercy.

³God came from Teman,
  the Holy One from Mount Paran.
                                    *Selah*ᵇ

His glory covered the heavens
  and his praise filled the earth.
⁴His splendour was like the sunrise;
  rays flashed from his hand,
  where his power was hidden.
⁵Plague went before him;
  pestilence followed his steps.
⁶He stood, and shook the earth;
  he looked, and made the nations
    tremble.
The ancient mountains crumbled
  and the age-old hills collapsed.
  His ways are eternal.
⁷I saw the tents of Cushan in distress,
  the dwellings of Midian in anguish.

⁸Were you angry with the rivers, O LORD?
  Was your wrath against the streams?
Did you rage against the sea
  when you rode with your horses
  and your victorious chariots?
⁹You uncovered your bow,
  you called for many arrows.   *Selah*
You split the earth with rivers;
¹⁰   the mountains saw you and writhed.
  Torrents of water swept by;
  the deep roared
  and lifted its waves on high.

¹¹Sun and moon stood still in the heavens
  at the glint of your flying arrows,
  at the lightning of your flashing spear.
¹²In wrath you strode through the earth
  and in anger you threshed the nations.

e5 Hebrew *Sheol*   *f7* Or *creditors*
g16 Masoretic Text; Dead Sea Scrolls, Aquila, Vulgate and Syriac (see also Septuagint) *and stagger*
a1 Probably a literary or musical term
b3 A word of uncertain meaning; possibly a musical term; also in verses 9 and 13

¹³You came out to deliver your people,
  to save your anointed one.
You crushed the leader of the land of
  wickedness,
  you stripped him from head to foot.
                                    Selah
¹⁴With his own spear you pierced his head
  when his warriors stormed out to scatter
    us,
  gloating as though about to devour
  the wretched who were in hiding.
¹⁵You trampled the sea with your horses,
  churning the great waters.

¹⁶I heard and my heart pounded,
  my lips quivered at the sound;
decay crept into my bones,
  and my legs trembled.

Yet I will wait patiently for the day of
  calamity
  to come on the nation invading us.
¹⁷Though the fig-tree does not bud
  and there are no grapes on the vines,
though the olive crop fails
  and the fields produce no food,
though there are no sheep in the pen
  and no cattle in the stalls,
¹⁸yet I will rejoice in the LORD,
  I will be joyful in God my Saviour.

¹⁹The Sovereign LORD is my strength;
  he makes my feet like the feet of a deer,
  he enables me to go on the heights.

For the director of music. On my stringed
instruments.

Zephaniah

1 The word of the LORD that came to Zephaniah son of Cushi, the son of Gedaliah, the son of Amariah, the son of Hezekiah, during the reign of Josiah son of Amon king of Judah:

Warning of Coming Destruction

2 "I will sweep away everything
 from the face of the earth,"
 declares the LORD.
3 "I will sweep away both men and animals;
 I will sweep away the birds of the air
 and the fish of the sea.
 The wicked will have only heaps of
 rubble[a]
 when I cut off man from the face of the
 earth,"
 declares the LORD.

Against Judah

4 "I will stretch out my hand against Judah
 and against all who live in Jerusalem.
 I will cut off from this place every remnant
 of Baal,
 the names of the pagan and the
 idolatrous priests—
5 those who bow down on the roofs
 to worship the starry host,
 those who bow down and swear by the
 LORD
 and who also swear by Molech,[b]
6 those who turn back from following the
 LORD
 and neither seek the LORD nor enquire of
 him.
7 Be silent before the Sovereign LORD,
 for the day of the LORD is near.
 The LORD has prepared a sacrifice;
 he has consecrated those he has invited.
8 On the day of the LORD's sacrifice
 I will punish the princes
 and the king's sons
 and all those clad
 in foreign clothes.
9 On that day I will punish
 all who avoid stepping on the
 threshold,[c]
 who fill the temple of their gods
 with violence and deceit.
10 "On that day," declares the LORD,
 "a cry will go up from the Fish Gate,

wailing from the New Quarter,
 and a loud crash from the hills.
11 Wail, you who live in the market
 district;[d]
 all your merchants will be wiped out,
 all who trade with[e] silver will be ruined.
12 At that time I will search Jerusalem with
 lamps
 and punish those who are complacent,
 who are like wine left on its dregs,
 who think, 'The LORD will do nothing,
 either good or bad.'
13 Their wealth will be plundered,
 their houses demolished.
 They will build houses
 but not live in them;
 they will plant vineyards
 but not drink the wine.

The Great Day of the LORD

14 "The great day of the LORD is near—
 near and coming quickly.
 Listen! The cry on the day of the LORD will
 be bitter,
 the shouting of the warrior there.
15 That day will be a day of wrath,
 a day of distress and anguish,
 a day of trouble and ruin,
 a day of darkness and gloom,
 a day of clouds and blackness,
16 a day of trumpet and battle cry
 against the fortified cities
 and against the corner towers.
17 I will bring distress on the people
 and they will walk like blind men,
 because they have sinned against the
 LORD.
 Their blood will be poured out like dust
 and their entrails like filth.
18 Neither their silver nor their gold
 will be able to save them
 on the day of the LORD's wrath.
 In the fire of his jealousy
 the whole world will be consumed,
 for he will make a sudden end
 of all who live in the earth."

2 Gather together, gather together,
 O shameful nation,
2 before the appointed time arrives
 and that day sweeps on like chaff,

---

a3 The meaning of the Hebrew for this line is uncertain.   b5 Hebrew *Malcam*, that is, Milcom
c9 See 1 Samuel 5:5.   d11 Or *the Mortar*   e11 Or *in*

before the fierce anger of the LORD comes
   upon you,
  before the day of the LORD's wrath
    comes upon you.
³Seek the LORD, all you humble of the land,
  you who do what he commands.
Seek righteousness, seek humility;
  perhaps you will be sheltered
   on the day of the LORD's anger.

Against Philistia

⁴Gaza will be abandoned
  and Ashkelon left in ruins.
At midday Ashdod will be emptied
  and Ekron uprooted.
⁵Woe to you who live by the sea,
  O Kerethite people;
the word of the LORD is against you,
  O Canaan, land of the Philistines.

"I will destroy you,
  and none will be left."

⁶The land by the sea, where the Kerethites^a
  dwell,
will be a place for shepherds and sheep
  pens.
⁷It will belong to the remnant of the house
  of Judah;
  there they will find pasture.
In the evening they will lie down
  in the houses of Ashkelon.
The LORD their God will care for them;
  he will restore their fortunes.^b

Against Moab and Ammon

⁸"I have heard the insults of Moab
  and the taunts of the Ammonites,
who insulted my people
  and made threats against their land.
⁹Therefore, as surely as I live,"
  declares the LORD Almighty, the God of
   Israel,
"surely Moab will become like Sodom,
  the Ammonites like Gomorrah—
a place of weeds and salt pits,
  a wasteland for ever.
The remnant of my people will plunder
  them;
  the survivors of my nation will inherit
   their land."

¹⁰This is what they will get in return for their
  pride,
  for insulting and mocking the people of
   the LORD Almighty.
¹¹The LORD will be awesome to them
  when he destroys all the gods of the
   land.
The nations on every shore will worship
  him,
  every one in its own land.

Against Cush

¹²"You too, O Cushites,^c
  will be slain by my sword."

Against Assyria

¹³He will stretch out his hand against the
  north
  and destroy Assyria,
leaving Nineveh utterly desolate
  and dry as the desert.
¹⁴Flocks and herds will lie down there,
  creatures of every kind.
The desert owl and the screech owl
  will roost on her columns.
Their calls will echo through the
  windows,
  rubble will be in the doorways,
  the beams of cedar will be exposed.
¹⁵This is the carefree city
  that lived in safety.
She said to herself,
  "I am, and there is none besides me."
What a ruin she has become,
  a lair for wild beasts!
All who pass by her scoff
  and shake their fists.

The Future of Jerusalem

3 Woe to the city of oppressors,
  rebellious and defiled!
²She obeys no-one,
  she accepts no correction.
She does not trust in the LORD,
  she does not draw near to her God.
³Her officials are roaring lions,
  her rulers are evening wolves,
  who leave nothing for the morning.
⁴Her prophets are arrogant;
  they are treacherous men.
Her priests profane the sanctuary
  and do violence to the law.
⁵The LORD within her is righteous;
  he does no wrong.
Morning by morning he dispenses his
  justice,
  and every new day he does not fail,
  yet the unrighteous know no shame.

⁶"I have cut off nations;
  their strongholds are demolished.
I have left their streets deserted,
  with no-one passing through.
Their cities are destroyed;
  no-one will be left—no-one at all.
⁷I said to the city,
  'Surely you will fear me
  and accept correction!'
Then her dwelling would not be cut off,
  nor all my punishments come upon
   her.
But they were still eager
  to act corruptly in all they did.
⁸Therefore wait for me," declares the
  LORD,
  "for the day I will stand up to testify.^a
I have decided to assemble the nations,
  to gather the kingdoms
and to pour out my wrath on them—
  all my fierce anger.
The whole world will be consumed
  by the fire of my jealous anger.

---

^a6 The meaning of the Hebrew for this word is uncertain.   ^b7 Or *will bring back their captives*
^c12 That is, people from the upper Nile region   ^a8 Septuagint and Syriac; Hebrew *will rise up to plunder*

ZEPHANIAH 1:7–13

'I will . . . punish those who are complacent . . . who think, "The LORD will do nothing, either good or bad" ' (v. 12, GNB).

SINGLE-DIMENSION LIVING. Zephaniah continues his proclamation about forthcoming judgement by describing 'the day of the Lord' (vv. 7–13). The phrase expressed a popular idea that God would intervene and bring deliverance from enemies and a new prosperity to his people. For the prophets 'the day of the Lord' had a darker meaning. Amos stood the popular idea on its head and showed that it would be a day of judgement from which there would be no escape (Amos 5:18–20). Zephaniah followed the ideas of Amos but extended them to include other nations.

Among the scathing condemnations of Zephaniah, is one directed towards those who lived self-centred, self-satisfied lives; who left no room at all for a God-dimension (v. 12). They had dismissed God as irrelevant.

That is an up-to-date attitude if ever there was one. Many people believe that humanity is left to its own devices, that success or failure is exclusively the product of personal effort and that on a cosmic scale events are at the mercy of a kind of fatalism. It is possible for Christians to become infected by these attitudes, and for all practical purposes to live life without any sense of God-dimension.

We should remember the warnings of Zephaniah (v. 13) that what we build by human effort is subject to decay and offers no lasting hope

HAGGAI 2:15–19

'Give careful thought; Is there yet any seed left in the barn? Until now the vine and the fig-tree, the pomegranate and the olive tree have not borne fruit. From this day on I will bless you' (vv. 18b–19).

WORKING AND WAITING BY FAITH. For almost four months the people had been harangued by Haggai. For just over half that time Zechariah had been trumpeting out his message too. Reluctantly the people had responded, beginning to look away from their own concerns, beginning to cooperate with the temple building. But there was no sudden miracle. The fig-trees had not yet produced. Ezra (4:24 and 5:15) tells us the building took four years. At what point prosperity began to come, we do not know. The promise had been held out. The people had responded. They now had to wait and work by faith.

The impression given here is of a slight pause in the action. 'Give careful thought.' The pause is necessary. They need reminding that it is God who is going to bless them. They have been able to plant. That in itself is something of a minor miracle, considering the pressure they were under from their neighbours who did not wish to see the temple built (Ezra 4:4 and 5:3). Now they must wait. An earlier pause in the action had resulted in no progress being made for about seventeen years (Ezra 4:5). This time things are different. The waiting is waiting on God in faith, knowing that he will bless.

'*Faith is an act which is the negation of all activity, a moment of passivity out of which the strength for action comes, because in it* God *acts.*' (*C. H. Dodd*)

→793·

⁹"Then will I purify the lips of the peoples,
   that all of them may call on the name of
      the LORD
   and serve him shoulder to shoulder.
¹⁰From beyond the rivers of Cushᵇ
   my worshippers, my scattered people,
   will bring me offerings.
¹¹On that day you will not be put to shame
   for all the wrongs you have done to me,
because I will remove from this city
   those who rejoice in their pride.
Never again will you be haughty
   on my holy hill.
¹²But I will leave within you
   the meek and humble,
   who trust in the name of the LORD.
¹³The remnant of Israel will do no wrong;
   they will speak no lies,
   nor will deceit be found in their
      mouths.
They will eat and lie down
   and no-one will make them afraid."

¹⁴Sing, O Daughter of Zion;
   shout aloud, O Israel!
Be glad and rejoice with all your heart,
   O Daughter of Jerusalem!
¹⁵The LORD has taken away your
      punishment,
   he has turned back your enemy.

The LORD, the King of Israel, is with you;
   never again will you fear any harm.
¹⁶On that day they will say to Jerusalem,
   "Do not fear, O Zion;
   do not let your hands hang limp.
¹⁷The LORD your God is with you,
   he is mighty to save.
He will take great delight in you,
   he will quiet you with his love,
   he will rejoice over you with singing."

¹⁸"The sorrows for the appointed feasts
   I will remove from you;
   they are a burden and a reproach to
      you.ᶜ
¹⁹At that time I will deal
   with all who oppressed you;
I will rescue the lame
   and gather those who have been
      scattered.
I will give them praise and honour
   in every land where they were put to
      shame.
²⁰At that time I will gather you;
   at that time I will bring you home.
I will give you honour and praise
   among all the peoples of the earth
when I restore your fortunesᵈ
   before your very eyes,"
                              says the LORD.

ᵇ10 That is, the upper Nile region
ᶜ18 Or "I will gather you who mourn for the appointed feasts; / your reproach is a burden to you
ᵈ20 Or I bring back your captives

Haggai

A Call to Build the House of the LORD

1 In the second year of King Darius, on the first day of the sixth month, the word of the LORD came through the prophet Haggai to Zerubbabel son of Shealtiel, governor of Judah, and to Joshua*ᵃ* son of Jehozadak, the high priest:

2This is what the LORD Almighty says: "These people say, 'The time has not yet come for the LORD's house to be built.'"

3Then the word of the LORD came through the prophet Haggai: 4"Is it a time for you yourselves to be living in your panelled houses, while this house remains a ruin?"

5Now this is what the LORD Almighty says: "Give careful thought to your ways. 6You have planted much, but have harvested little. You eat, but never have enough. You drink, but never have your fill. You put on clothes, but are not warm. You earn wages, only to put them in a purse with holes in it."

7This is what the LORD Almighty says: "Give careful thought to your ways. 8Go up into the mountains and bring down timber and build the house, so that I may take pleasure in it and be honoured," says the LORD. 9"You expected much, but see, it turned out to be little. What you brought home, I blew away. Why?" declares the LORD Almighty. "Because of my house, which remains a ruin, while each of you is busy with his own house. 10Therefore, because of you the heavens have withheld their dew and the earth its crops. 11I called for a drought on the fields and the mountains, on the grain, the new wine, the oil and whatever the ground produces, on men and cattle, and on the labour of your hands."

12Then Zerubbabel son of Shealtiel, Joshua son of Jehozadak, the high priest, and the whole remnant of the people obeyed the voice of the LORD their God and the message of the prophet Haggai, because the LORD their God had sent him. And the people feared the LORD.

13Then Haggai, the LORD's messenger, gave this message of the LORD to the people: "I am with you," declares the LORD. 14So the LORD stirred up the spirit of Zerubbabel son of Shealtiel, governor of Judah, and the spirit of Joshua son of Jehozadak, the high priest, and the spirit of the whole remnant of the people. They came and began work on the house of the LORD Almighty, their God, 15on the twenty-fourth day of the sixth month in the second year of King Darius.

The Promised Glory of the New House

2 On the twenty-first day of the seventh month, the word of the LORD came through the prophet Haggai: 2"Speak to Zerubbabel son of Shealtiel, governor of Judah, to Joshua son of Jehozadak, the high priest, and to the remnant of the people. Ask them, 3'Who of you is left who saw this house in its former glory? How does it look to you now? Does it not seem to you like nothing? 4But now be strong, O Zerubbabel,' declares the LORD. 'Be strong, O Joshua son of Jehozadak, the high priest. Be strong, all you people of the land,' declares the LORD, 'and work. For I am with you,' declares the LORD Almighty. 5'This is what I covenanted with you when you came out of Egypt. And my Spirit remains among you. Do not fear.'

6"This is what the LORD Almighty says: 'In a little while I will once more shake the heavens and the earth, the sea and the dry land. 7I will shake all nations, and the desired of all nations will come, and I will fill this house with glory,' says the LORD Almighty. 8'The silver is mine and the gold is mine,' declares the LORD Almighty. 9'The glory of this present house will be greater than the glory of the former house,' says the LORD Almighty. 'And in this place I will grant peace,' declares the LORD Almighty."

Blessings for a Defiled People

10On the twenty-fourth day of the ninth month, in the second year of Darius, the word of the LORD came to the prophet Haggai: 11"This is what the LORD Almighty says: 'Ask the priests what the law says: 12If a person carries consecrated meat in the fold of his garment, and that fold touches some bread or stew, some wine, oil or other food, does it become consecrated?'"

The priests answered, "No."

13Then Haggai said, "If a person defiled by contact with a dead body touches one of these things, does it become defiled?"

ᵃ1 A variant of *Jeshua*; here and elsewhere in Haggai

"Yes," the priests replied, "it becomes defiled."

¹⁴Then Haggai said, "'So it is with this people and this nation in my sight,' declares the LORD. 'Whatever they do and whatever they offer there is defiled.

¹⁵"'Now give careful thought to this from this day onᵃ—consider how things were before one stone was laid on another in the LORD's temple. ¹⁶When anyone came to a heap of twenty measures, there were only ten. When anyone went to a wine vat to draw fifty measures, there were only twenty. ¹⁷I struck all the work of your hands with blight, mildew and hail, yet you did not turn to me,' declares the LORD. ¹⁸'From this day on, from this twenty-fourth day of the ninth month, give careful thought to the day when the foundation of the LORD's temple was laid. Give careful thought: ¹⁹Is there yet any seed left in the barn? Until now, the vine and the

fig-tree, the pomegranate and the olive tree have not borne fruit.

"'From this day on I will bless you.'"

Zerubbabel the LORD's Signet Ring

²⁰The word of the LORD came to Haggai a second time on the twenty-fourth day of the month: ²¹"Tell Zerubbabel governor of Judah that I will shake the heavens and the earth. ²²I will overturn royal thrones and shatter the power of the foreign kingdoms. I will overthrow chariots and their drivers; horses and their riders will fall, each by the sword of his brother.

²³"'On that day,' declares the LORD Almighty, 'I will take you, my servant Zerubbabel son of Shealtiel,' declares the LORD, 'and I will make you like my signet ring, for I have chosen you,' declares the LORD Almighty."

ᵃ15 Or *to the days past*

Zechariah

A Call to Return to the LORD

1 In the eighth month of the second year of Darius, the word of the LORD came to the prophet Zechariah son of Berekiah, the son of Iddo:

²"The LORD was very angry with your forefathers. ³Therefore tell the people: This is what the LORD Almighty says: 'Return to me,' declares the LORD Almighty, 'and I will return to you,' says the LORD Almighty. ⁴Do not be like your forefathers, to whom the earlier prophets proclaimed: This is what the LORD Almighty says: 'Turn from your evil ways and your evil practices.' But they would not listen or pay attention to me, declares the LORD. ⁵Where are your forefathers now? And the prophets, do they live for ever? ⁶But did not my words and my decrees, which I commanded my servants the prophets, overtake your forefathers?

"Then they repented and said, 'The LORD Almighty has done to us what our ways and practices deserve, just as he determined to do.'"

The Man Among the Myrtle Trees

⁷On the twenty-fourth day of the eleventh month, the month of Shebat, in the second year of Darius, the word of the LORD came to the prophet Zechariah son of Berekiah, the son of Iddo.

⁸During the night I had a vision—and there before me was a man riding a red horse! He was standing among the myrtle trees in a ravine. Behind him were red, brown and white horses.

⁹I asked, "What are these, my lord?"

The angel who was talking with me answered, "I will show you what they are."

¹⁰Then the man standing among the myrtle trees explained, "They are the ones the LORD has sent to go throughout the earth."

¹¹And they reported to the angel of the LORD, who was standing among the myrtle trees, "We have gone throughout the earth and found the whole world at rest and in peace."

¹²Then the angel of the LORD said, "LORD Almighty, how long will you withhold mercy from Jerusalem and from the towns of Judah, which you have been angry with these seventy years?" ¹³So the LORD spoke kind and comforting words to the angel who talked with me.

¹⁴Then the angel who was speaking to me said, "Proclaim this word: This is what the LORD Almighty says: 'I am very jealous for Jerusalem and Zion, ¹⁵but I am very angry with the nations that feel secure. I was only a little angry, but they added to the calamity.'

¹⁶"Therefore, this is what the LORD says: 'I will return to Jerusalem with mercy, and there my house will be rebuilt. And the measuring line will be stretched out over Jerusalem,' declares the LORD Almighty.

¹⁷"Proclaim further: This is what the LORD Almighty says: 'My towns will again overflow with prosperity, and the LORD will again comfort Zion and choose Jerusalem.'"

Four Horns and Four Craftsmen

¹⁸Then I looked up—and there before me were four horns! ¹⁹I asked the angel who was speaking to me, "What are these?"

He answered me, "These are the horns that scattered Judah, Israel and Jerusalem."

²⁰Then the LORD showed me four craftsmen. ²¹I asked, "What are these coming to do?"

He answered, "These are the horns that scattered Judah so that no-one could raise his head, but the craftsmen have come to terrify them and throw down these horns of the nations who lifted up their horns against the land of Judah to scatter its people."

A Man With a Measuring Line

2 Then I looked up—and there before me was a man with a measuring line in his hand! ²I asked, "Where are you going?"

He answered me, "To measure Jerusalem, to find out how wide and how long it is."

³Then the angel who was speaking to me left, and another angel came to meet him ⁴and said to him: "Run, tell that young man, 'Jerusalem will be a city without walls because of the great number of men and livestock in it. ⁵And I myself will be a wall of fire around it,' declares the LORD, 'and I will be its glory within.'

⁶"Come! Come! Flee from the land of the north," declares the LORD, "for I have scattered you to the four winds of heaven," declares the LORD.

⁷"Come, O Zion! Escape, you who live in the Daughter of Babylon!" ⁸For this is what

the LORD Almighty says: "After he has honoured me and has sent me against the nations that have plundered you—for whoever touches you touches the apple of his eye—[a]I will surely raise my hand against them so that their slaves will plunder them.[a] Then you will know that the LORD Almighty has sent me.

10"Shout and be glad, O Daughter of Zion. For I am coming, and I will live among you," declares the LORD. 11"Many nations will be joined with the LORD in that day and will become my people. I will live among you and you will know that the LORD Almighty has sent me to you. 12The LORD will inherit Judah as his portion in the holy land and will again choose Jerusalem. 13Be still before the LORD, all mankind, because he has roused himself from his holy dwelling."

Clean Garments for the High Priest

3 Then he showed me Joshua[a] the high priest standing before the angel of the LORD, and Satan[b] standing at his right side to accuse him. 2The LORD said to Satan, "The LORD rebuke you, Satan! The LORD, who has chosen Jerusalem, rebuke you! Is not this man a burning stick snatched from the fire?"

3Now Joshua was dressed in filthy clothes as he stood before the angel. 4The angel said to those who were standing before him, "Take off his filthy clothes."

Then he said to Joshua, "See, I have taken away your sin, and I will put rich garments on you."

5Then I said, "Put a clean turban on his head." So they put a clean turban on his head and clothed him, while the angel of the LORD stood by.

6The angel of the LORD gave this charge to Joshua: 7"This is what the LORD Almighty says: 'If you will walk in my ways and keep my requirements, then you will govern my house and have charge of my courts, and I will give you a place among these standing here.

8"'Listen, O high priest Joshua and your associates seated before you, who are men symbolic of things to come: I am going to bring my servant, the Branch. 9See, the stone I have set in front of Joshua! There are seven eyes[c] on that one stone, and I will engrave an inscription on it,' says the LORD Almighty, 'and I will remove the sin of this land in a single day.

10"'In that day each of you will invite his neighbour to sit under his vine and fig-tree,' declares the LORD Almighty."

The Gold Lampstand and the Two Olive Trees

4 Then the angel who talked with me returned and wakened me, as a man is wakened from his sleep. 2He asked me, "What do you see?"

I answered, "I see a solid gold lampstand with a bowl at the top and seven lights on it,

with seven channels to the lights. 3Also there are two olive trees by it, one on the right of the bowl and the other on its left."

4I asked the angel who talked with me, "What are these, my lord?"

5He answered, "Do you not know what these are?"

"No, my lord," I replied.

6So he said to me, "This is the word of the LORD to Zerubbabel: 'Not by might nor by power, but by my Spirit,' says the LORD Almighty.

7"What[a] are you, O mighty mountain? Before Zerubbabel you will become level ground. Then he will bring out the capstone to shouts of 'God bless it! God bless it!'"

8Then the word of the LORD came to me: 9"The hands of Zerubbabel have laid the foundation of this temple; his hands will also complete it. Then you will know that the LORD Almighty has sent me to you.

10"Who despises the day of small things? Men will rejoice when they see the plumbline in the hand of Zerubbabel.

"(These seven are the eyes of the LORD, which range throughout the earth.)"

11Then I asked the angel, "What are these two olive trees on the right and the left of the lampstand?"

12Again I asked him, "What are these two olive branches beside the two gold pipes that pour out golden oil?"

13He replied, "Do you not know what these are?"

"No, my lord," I said.

14So he said, "These are the two who are anointed to[b] serve the Lord of all the earth."

The Flying Scroll

5 I looked again—and there before me was a flying scroll!

2He asked me, "What do you see?"

I answered, "I see a flying scroll, thirty feet long and fifteen feet wide."[a]

3And he said to me, "This is the curse that is going out over the whole land; for according to what it says on one side, every thief will be banished, and according to what it says on the other, everyone who swears falsely will be banished. 4The LORD Almighty declares, 'I will send it out, and it will enter the house of the thief and the house of him who swears falsely by my name. It will remain in his house and destroy it, both its timbers and its stones.'"

The Woman in a Basket

5Then the angel who was speaking to me came forward and said to me, "Look up and see what this is that is appearing."

6I asked, "What is it?"

He replied, "It is a measuring basket."[b] And he added, "This is the iniquity[c] of the people throughout the land."

7Then the cover of lead was raised, and there in the basket sat a woman! 8He said, "This is wickedness," and he pushed her

---

[a]8,9 Or says after . . . eye: 9"I . . . plunder them."   [a]1 A variant of Jeshua; here and elsewhere in Zechariah
[b]1 Satan means accuser.   [c]9 Or facets   [a]7 Or Who   [b]14 Or two who bring oil and
[a]2 Hebrew twenty cubits long and ten cubits wide (about 9 metres long and 4.5 metres wide)
[b]6 Hebrew an ephah; also in verses 7–11   [c]6 Or appearance

back into the basket and pushed the lead cover down over its mouth.

9Then I looked up—and there before me were two women, with the wind in their wings! They had wings like those of a stork, and they lifted up the basket between heaven and earth.

10"Where are they taking the basket?" I asked the angel who was speaking to me.

11He replied, "To the country of Babylonia*d* to build a house for it. When it is ready, the basket will be set there in its place."

Four Chariots

6 I looked up again—and there before me were four chariots coming out from between two mountains—mountains of bronze! 2The first chariot had red horses, the second black, 3the third white, and the fourth dappled—all of them powerful. 4I asked the angel who was speaking to me, "What are these, my lord?"

5The angel answered me, "These are the four spirits*a* of heaven, going out from standing in the presence of the Lord of the whole world. 6The one with the black horses is going towards the north country, the one with the white horses towards the west,*b* and the one with the dappled horses towards the south."

7When the powerful horses went out, they were straining to go throughout the earth. And he said, "Go throughout the earth!" So they went throughout the earth.

8Then he called to me, "Look, those going towards the north country have given my Spirit*c* rest in the land of the north."

A Crown for Joshua

9The word of the Lord came to me: 10"Take ˻silver and gold˼ from the exiles Heldai, Tobijah and Jedaiah, who have arrived from Babylon. Go the same day to the house of Josiah son of Zephaniah. 11Take the silver and gold and make a crown, and set it on the head of the high priest, Joshua son of Jehozadak. 12Tell him this is what the Lord Almighty says: 'Here is the man whose name is the Branch, and he will branch out from his place and build the temple of the Lord. 13It is he who will build the temple of the Lord, and he will be clothed with majesty and will sit and rule on his throne. And he will be a priest on his throne. And there will be harmony between the two.' 14The crown will be given to Heldai,*d* Tobijah, Jedaiah and Hen*e* son of Zephaniah as a memorial in the temple of the Lord. 15Those who are far away will come and help to build the temple of the Lord, and you will know that the Lord Almighty has sent me to you. This will happen if you diligently obey the Lord your God."

Justice and Mercy, Not Fasting

7 In the fourth year of King Darius, the word of the Lord came to Zechariah on the fourth day of the ninth month, the month of Kislev. 2The people of Bethel had sent Sharezer and Regem-Melech, together with their men, to entreat the Lord 3by asking the priests of the house of the Lord Almighty and the prophets, "Should I mourn and fast in the fifth month, as I have done for so many years?"

4Then the word of the Lord Almighty came to me: 5"Ask all the people of the land and the priests, 'When you fasted and mourned in the fifth and seventh months for the past seventy years, was it really for me that you fasted? 6And when you were eating and drinking, were you not just feasting for yourselves? 7Are these not the words the Lord proclaimed through the earlier prophets when Jerusalem and its surrounding towns were at rest and prosperous, and the Negev and the western foothills were settled?'"

8And the word of the Lord came again to Zechariah: 9"This is what the Lord Almighty says: 'Administer true justice; show mercy and compassion to one another. 10Do not oppress the widow or the fatherless, the alien or the poor. In your hearts do not think evil of each other.'

11"But they refused to pay attention; stubbornly they turned their backs and stopped up their ears. 12They made their hearts as hard as flint and would not listen to the law or to the words that the Lord Almighty had sent by his Spirit through the earlier prophets. So the Lord Almighty was very angry.

13"'When I called, they did not listen; so when they called, I would not listen,' says the Lord Almighty. 14'I scattered them with a whirlwind among all the nations, where they were strangers. The land was left so desolate behind them that no-one could come or go. This is how they made the pleasant land desolate.'"

The Lord Promises to Bless Jerusalem

8 Again the word of the Lord Almighty came to me. 2This is what the Lord Almighty says: "I am very jealous for Zion; I am burning with jealousy for her."

3This is what the Lord says: "I will return to Zion and dwell in Jerusalem. Then Jerusalem will be called the City of Truth, and the mountain of the Lord Almighty will be called the Holy Mountain."

4This is what the Lord Almighty says: "Once again men and women of ripe old age will sit in the streets of Jerusalem, each with cane in hand because of his age. 5The city streets will be filled with boys and girls playing there."

6This is what the Lord Almighty says: "It may seem marvellous to the remnant of this people at that time, but will it seem marvellous to me?" declares the Lord Almighty.

7This is what the Lord Almighty says: "I will save my people from the countries of the east and the west. 8I will bring them back to live in Jerusalem; they will be my people, and I will be faithful and righteous to them as their God."

*d*11 Hebrew *Shinar*　　*a*5 Or *winds*　　*b*6 Or *horses after them*　　*c*8 Or *spirit*
*d*14 Syriac; Hebrew *Helem*　　*e*14 Or *and the gracious one, the*

ZECHARIAH 8:1–8

'Jerusalem will be called The City of Truth, and the mountain of the LORD Almighty will be called The Holy Mountain' (v. 3b).

A BEAUTIFUL PICTURE of peace, prosperity and truth is painted in this passage. Zechariah waxes lyrical about his vision of the future of Jerusalem. How saddened he would be to see that city today, torn apart by strife, wracked with rival perceptions of the truth so different from each other that it becomes impossible to assess the city's real condition; impossible even to guess what is fact and what is fiction.

Yet Jerusalem is still the city of truth. Jews, Muslims and Christians each venerate the city in their own way and associate it with the revelation of truth as they understand it. It was in Jerusalem that Christ's own perception of the truth brought about his condemnation and crucifixion. A city of truth, certainly, but how different from Zechariah's ideal!

Jesus talked in the upper room, in Jerusalem, about the 'Spirit of truth . . . who will guide you into all truth'. Spreading out from Jerusalem, from the cross, and from Jesus' resurrection, the Spirit of truth has burned in the hearts of generations of Christians. We pray today for that Spirit to come, not just to Jerusalem, but here, where we are in the rough and tumble of our everyday lives.

> *Come, gracious Spirit, heavenly dove,*
> *With light and comfort from above,*
> *Be thou our guardian, thou our guide;*
> *O'er every thought and step preside.*
>
> *The light of truth to us display*
> *That we may know and choose thy way;*
> *Plant holy fear in every heart*
> *That we from God may ne'er depart.*

(Simon Browne)

→794

MALACHI 3:6–16a

' "Test me in this," says the LORD Almighty, "and see if I will not throw open the floodgates of heaven and pour out so much blessing that you will not have room enough for it" ' (v. 10b).

THE STEP OF FAITH. The immediate reaction to our passage today is to think material blessings will always follow if our tithe is paid. But look more closely at v. 14. Promise of material blessing there may be, but that must never be the basis on which we serve the Lord. As soon as we say, 'What did we *gain* by carrying out his requirements . . .?' our primary motivation of loving God for his own sake is lost, and we go astray.

Some think that tithing will bring about material prosperity. A few churches even use this as part of their appeal, (the 'Cadillac syndrome'). It really is a distortion of the truth, for tithing will not solve all our financial problems, although disciplined giving is certainly a great blessing. If we give our tithe conscientiously, we are continually aware of our financial situation. This helps us live within our means, and brings a sense of freedom, knowing that our giving to the Lord is done well.

But just as the earthquake kills indiscriminately, floods destroy the homes of the righteous as well as the wicked, famine affects the godly and the ungodly alike, so too the terrors of unemployment, the collapse of long-standing businesses, the fluctuations of the economy, affect the population at random.

Bring your tithes certainly, but bring them because you love God, not because you want him to love you and make you prosperous.

→805

⁹This is what the LORD Almighty says: "You who now hear these words spoken by the prophets who were there when the foundation was laid for the house of the LORD Almighty, let your hands be strong so that the temple may be built. ¹⁰Before that time there were no wages for man or beast. No-one could go about his business safely because of his enemy, for I had turned every man against his neighbour. ¹¹But now I will not deal with the remnant of this people as I did in the past," declares the LORD Almighty.

¹²"The seed will grow well, the vine will yield its fruit, the ground will produce its crops, and the heavens will drop their dew. I will give all these things as an inheritance to the remnant of this people. ¹³As you have been an object of cursing among the nations, O Judah and Israel, so will I save you, and you will be a blessing. Do not be afraid, but let your hands be strong."

¹⁴This is what the LORD Almighty says: "Just as I had determined to bring disaster upon you and showed no pity when your fathers angered me," says the LORD Almighty, ¹⁵"so now I have determined to do good again to Jerusalem and Judah. Do not be afraid. ¹⁶These are the things you are to do: Speak the truth to each other, and render true and sound judgment in your courts; ¹⁷do not plot evil against your neighbour, and do not love to swear falsely. I hate all this," declares the LORD.

¹⁸Again the word of the LORD Almighty came to me. ¹⁹This is what the LORD Almighty says: "The fasts of the fourth, fifth, seventh and tenth months will become joyful and glad occasions and happy festivals for Judah. Therefore love truth and peace."

²⁰This is what the LORD Almighty says: "Many peoples and the inhabitants of many cities will yet come, ²¹and the inhabitants of one city will go to another and say, 'Let us go at once to entreat the LORD and seek the LORD Almighty. I myself am going.' ²²And many peoples and powerful nations will come to Jerusalem to seek the LORD Almighty and to entreat him."

²³This is what the LORD Almighty says: "In those days ten men from all languages and nations will take firm hold of one Jew by the hem of his robe and say, 'Let us go with you, because we have heard that God is with you.'"

Judgment on Israel's Enemies
An Oracle

9 The word of the LORD is against the land of Hadrach
and will rest upon Damascus—
for the eyes of men and all the tribes of Israel
are on the LORD—ᵃ
²and upon Hamath too, which borders on it,
and upon Tyre and Sidon, though they are very skilful.

³Tyre has built herself a stronghold;
she has heaped up silver like dust,
and gold like the dirt of the streets.
⁴But the Lord will take away her possessions
and destroy her power on the sea,
and she will be consumed by fire.
⁵Ashkelon will see it and fear;
Gaza will writhe in agony,
and Ekron too, for her hope will wither.
Gaza will lose her king
and Ashkelon will be deserted.
⁶Foreigners will occupy Ashdod,
and I will cut off the pride of the Philistines.
⁷I will take the blood from their mouths,
the forbidden food from between their teeth.
Those who are left will belong to our God
and become leaders in Judah,
and Ekron will be like the Jebusites.
⁸But I will defend my house
against marauding forces.
Never again will an oppressor overrun my people,
for now I am keeping watch.

The Coming of Zion's King

⁹Rejoice greatly, O Daughter of Zion!
Shout, Daughter of Jerusalem!
See, your kingᵇ comes to you,
righteous and having salvation,
gentle and riding on a donkey,
on a colt, the foal of a donkey.
¹⁰I will take away the chariots from Ephraim
and the war-horses from Jerusalem,
and the battle-bow will be broken.
He will proclaim peace to the nations.
His rule will extend from sea to sea
and from the Riverᶜ to the ends of the earth.ᵈ
¹¹As for you, because of the blood of my covenant with you,
I will free your prisoners from the waterless pit.
¹²Return to your fortress, O prisoners of hope;
even now I announce that I will restore twice as much to you.
¹³I will bend Judah as I bend my bow
and fill it with Ephraim.
I will rouse your sons, O Zion,
against your sons, O Greece,
and make you like a warrior's sword.

The LORD Will Appear

¹⁴Then the LORD will appear over them;
his arrow will flash like lightning.
The Sovereign LORD will sound the trumpet;
he will march in the storms of the south,
¹⁵ and the LORD Almighty will shield them.
They will destroy
and overcome with slingstones.
They will drink and roar as with wine;
they will be full like a bowl
used for sprinklingᵉ the corners of the altar.

ᵃ1 Or Damascus. / For the eye of the LORD is on all mankind, / as well as on the tribes of Israel.
ᵇ9 Or King   ᶜ10 That is, the Euphrates   ᵈ10 Or the end of the land   ᵉ15 Or bowl, / like

[16]The LORD their God will save them on that day
  as the flock of his people.
They will sparkle in his land
  like jewels in a crown.
[17]How attractive and beautiful they will be!
  Grain will make the young men thrive,
  and new wine the young women.

The LORD Will Care for Judah

10 Ask the LORD for rain in the springtime;
  it is the LORD who makes the storm clouds.
He gives showers of rain to men,
  and plants of the field to everyone.
[2]The idols speak deceit,
  diviners see visions that lie;
they tell dreams that are false,
  they give comfort in vain.
Therefore the people wander like sheep
  oppressed for lack of a shepherd.

[3]"My anger burns against the shepherds,
  and I will punish the leaders;
for the LORD Almighty will care
  for his flock, the house of Judah,
  and make them like a proud horse in battle.
[4]From Judah will come the cornerstone,
  from him the tent peg,
  from him the battle-bow,
  from him every ruler.
[5]Together they[a] will be like mighty men
  trampling the muddy streets in battle.
Because the LORD is with them,
  they will fight and overthrow the horsemen.

[6]"I will strengthen the house of Judah
  and save the house of Joseph.
I will restore them
  because I have compassion on them.
They will be as though
  I had not rejected them,
for I am the LORD their God
  and I will answer them.
[7]The Ephraimites will become like mighty men,
  and their hearts will be glad as with wine.
Their children will see it and be joyful;
  their hearts will rejoice in the LORD.
[8]I will signal for them
  and gather them in.
Surely I will redeem them;
  they will be as numerous as before.
[9]Though I scatter them among the peoples,
  yet in distant lands they will remember me.
They and their children will survive,
  and they will return.
[10]I will bring them back from Egypt
  and gather them from Assyria.
I will bring them to Gilead and Lebanon,
  and there will not be room enough for them.
[11]They will pass through the sea of trouble;
  the surging sea will be subdued

and all the depths of the Nile will dry up.
Assyria's pride will be brought down
  and Egypt's sceptre will pass away.
[12]I will strengthen them in the LORD
  and in his name they will walk,"
                    declares the LORD.

11 Open your doors, O Lebanon,
  so that fire may devour your cedars!
[2]Wail, O pine tree, for the cedar has fallen;
  the stately trees are ruined!
Wail, oaks of Bashan;
  the dense forest has been cut down!
[3]Listen to the wail of the shepherds:
  their rich pastures are destroyed!
Listen to the roar of the lions;
  the lush thicket of the Jordan is ruined!

Two Shepherds

[4]This is what the LORD my God says: "Pasture the flock marked for slaughter. [5]Their buyers slaughter them and go unpunished. Those who sell them say, 'Praise the LORD, I am rich!' Their own shepherds do not spare them. [6]For I will no longer have pity on the people of the land," declares the LORD. "I will hand everyone over to his neighbour and his king. They will oppress the land, and I will not rescue them from their hands."

[7]So I pastured the flock marked for slaughter, particularly the oppressed of the flock. Then I took two staffs and called one Favour and the other Union, and I pastured the flock. [8]In one month I got rid of the three shepherds.

The flock detested me, and I grew weary of them [9]and said, "I will not be your shepherd. Let the dying die, and the perishing perish. Let those who are left eat one another's flesh."

[10]Then I took my staff called Favour and broke it, revoking the covenant I had made with all the nations. [11]It was revoked on that day, and so the afflicted of the flock who were watching me knew it was the word of the LORD.

[12]I told them, "If you think it best, give me my pay; but if not, keep it." So they paid me thirty pieces of silver.

[13]And the LORD said to me, "Throw it to the potter"—the handsome price at which they priced me! So I took the thirty pieces of silver and threw them into the house of the LORD to the potter.

[14]Then I broke my second staff called Union, breaking the brotherhood between Judah and Israel.

[15]Then the LORD said to me, "Take again the equipment of a foolish shepherd. [16]For I am going to raise up a shepherd over the land who will not care for the lost, or seek the young, or heal the injured, or feed the healthy, but will eat the meat of the choice sheep, tearing off their hoofs.

[17]"Woe to the worthless shepherd,
  who deserts the flock!
May the sword strike his arm and his right eye!

---

[a]4,5 Or *ruler, all of them together.* | [5]*They*

May his arm be completely withered,
his right eye totally blinded!"

Jerusalem's Enemies to Be Destroyed
An Oracle

12 This is the word of the LORD concerning Israel. The LORD, who stretches out the heavens, who lays the foundation of the earth, and who forms the spirit of man within him, declares: ²"I am going to make Jerusalem a cup that sends all the surrounding peoples reeling. Judah will be besieged as well as Jerusalem. ³On that day, when all the nations of the earth are gathered against her, I will make Jerusalem an immovable rock for all the nations. All who try to move it will injure themselves. ⁴On that day I will strike every horse with panic and its rider with madness," declares the LORD. "I will keep a watchful eye over the house of Judah, but I will blind all the horses of the nations. ⁵Then the leaders of Judah will say in their hearts, 'The people of Jerusalem are strong, because the LORD Almighty is their God.'

⁶"On that day I will make the leaders of Judah like a brazier in a woodpile, like a flaming torch among sheaves. They will consume right and left all the surrounding peoples, but Jerusalem will remain intact in her place.

⁷"The LORD will save the dwellings of Judah first, so that the honour of the house of David and of Jerusalem's inhabitants may not be greater than that of Judah. ⁸On that day the LORD will shield those who live in Jerusalem, so that the feeblest among them will be like David, and the house of David will be like God, like the Angel of the LORD going before them. ⁹On that day I will set out to destroy all the nations that attack Jerusalem.

Mourning for the One They Pierced

¹⁰"And I will pour out on the house of David and the inhabitants of Jerusalem a spirit^a of grace and supplication. They will look on^b me, the one they have pierced, and they will mourn for him as one mourns for an only child, and grieve bitterly for him as one grieves for a firstborn son. ¹¹On that day the weeping in Jerusalem will be great, like the weeping of Hadad Rimmon in the plain of Megiddo. ¹²The land will mourn, each clan by itself, with their wives by themselves: the clan of the house of David and their wives, the clan of the house of Nathan and their wives, ¹³the clan of the house of Levi and their wives, the clan of Shimei and their wives, ¹⁴and all the rest of the clans and their wives.

Cleansing From Sin

13 "On that day a fountain will be opened to the house of David and the inhabitants of Jerusalem, to cleanse them from sin and impurity. ²"On that day, I will banish the names of the idols from the land, and they will be remembered no more," declares the LORD Almighty. "I will remove both the prophets and the spirit of impurity from the land. ³And if anyone still prophesies, his father and mother, to whom he was born, will say to him, 'You must die, because you have told lies in the LORD's name.' When he prophesies, his own parents will stab him.

⁴"On that day every prophet will be ashamed of his prophetic vision. He will not put on a prophet's garment of hair in order to deceive. ⁵He will say, 'I am not a prophet. I am a farmer; the land has been my livelihood since my youth.'^{a} ⁶If someone asks him, 'What are these wounds on your body?'^{b} he will answer, 'The wounds I was given at the house of my friends.'

The Shepherd Struck, the Sheep Scattered

⁷"Awake, O sword, against my shepherd,
    against the man who is close to me!"
    declares the LORD Almighty.
"Strike the shepherd,
    and the sheep will be scattered,
    and I will turn my hand against the little
        ones.
⁸In the whole land," declares the LORD,
    "two-thirds will be struck down and
        perish;
    yet one-third will be left in it.
⁹This third I will bring into the fire;
    I will refine them like silver
    and test them like gold.
They will call on my name
    and I will answer them;
I will say, 'They are my people,'
    and they will say, 'The LORD is our
        God.'"

The LORD Comes and Reigns

14 A day of the LORD is coming when your plunder will be divided among you.

²I will gather all the nations to Jerusalem to fight against it; the city will be captured, the houses ransacked, and the women raped. Half of the city will go into exile, but the rest of the people will not be taken from the city. ³Then the LORD will go out and fight against those nations, as he fights in the day of battle. ⁴On that day his feet will stand on the Mount of Olives, east of Jerusalem, and the Mount of Olives will be split in two from east to west, forming a great valley, with half of the mountain moving north and half moving south. ⁵You will flee by my mountain valley, for it will extend to Azel. You will flee as you fled from the earthquake^a in the days of Uzziah king of Judah. Then the LORD my God will come, and all the holy ones with him.

⁶On that day there will be no light, no cold or frost. ⁷It will be a unique day, without daytime or night-time—a day known to the LORD. When evening comes, there will be light.

---

^{a}10 Or *the Spirit* ^{b}10 Or *to* ^{a}5 Or *farmer; a man sold me in my youth*
^{b}6 Or *wounds between your hands*
^{a}5 Or ^{5}*My mountain valley will be blocked and will extend to Azel. It will be blocked as it was blocked because of the earthquake*

8On that day living water will flow out from Jerusalem, half to the eastern sea[b] and half to the western sea,[c] in summer and in winter.

9The LORD will be king over the whole earth. On that day there will be one LORD, and his name the only name.

10The whole land, from Geba to Rimmon, south of Jerusalem, will become like the Arabah. But Jerusalem will be raised up and remain in its place, from the Benjamin Gate to the site of the First Gate, to the Corner Gate, and from the Tower of Hananel to the royal winepresses. 11It will be inhabited; never again will it be destroyed. Jerusalem will be secure.

12This is the plague with which the LORD will strike all the nations that fought against Jerusalem: Their flesh will rot while they are still standing on their feet, their eyes will rot in their sockets, and their tongues will rot in their mouths. 13On that day men will be stricken by the LORD with great panic. Each man will seize the hand of another, and they will attack each other. 14Judah too will fight at Jerusalem. The wealth of all the surrounding nations will be collected—great quantities of gold and silver and clothing.

15A similar plague will strike the horses and mules, the camels and donkeys, and all the animals in those camps.

16Then the survivors from all the nations that have attacked Jerusalem will go up year after year to worship the King, the LORD Almighty, and to celebrate the Feast of Tabernacles. 17If any of the peoples of the earth do not go up to Jerusalem to worship the King, the LORD Almighty, they will have no rain. 18If the Egyptian people do not go up and take part, they will have no rain. The LORD[d] will bring on them the plague he inflicts on the nations that do not go up to celebrate the Feast of Tabernacles. 19This will be the punishment of Egypt and the punishment of all the nations that do not go up to celebrate the Feast of Tabernacles.

20On that day HOLY TO THE LORD will be inscribed on the bells of the horses, and the cooking pots in the LORD's house will be like the sacred bowls in front of the altar. 21Every pot in Jerusalem and Judah will be holy to the LORD Almighty, and all who come to sacrifice will take some of the pots and cook in them. And on that day there will no longer be a Canaanite[e] in the house of the LORD Almighty.

---

b8 That is, the Dead Sea   c8 That is, the Mediterranean   d18 Or part, then the LORD   e21 Or merchant

Malachi

1 An oracle: The word of the LORD to Israel through Malachi.*a*

Jacob Loved, Esau Hated

²"I have loved you," says the LORD.

"But you ask, 'How have you loved us?'

"Was not Esau Jacob's brother?" the LORD says. "Yet I have loved Jacob, ³but Esau I have hated, and I have turned his mountains into a wasteland and left his inheritance to the desert jackals."

⁴Edom may say, "Though we have been crushed, we will rebuild the ruins."

But this is what the LORD Almighty says: "They may build, but I will demolish. They will be called the Wicked Land, a people always under the wrath of the LORD. ⁵You will see it with your own eyes and say, 'Great is the LORD—even beyond the borders of Israel!'

Blemished Sacrifices

⁶"A son honours his father, and a servant his master. If I am a father, where is the honour due to me? If I am a master, where is the respect due to me?" says the LORD Almighty. "It is you, O priests, who show contempt for my name.

"But you ask, 'How have we shown contempt for your name?'

⁷"You place defiled food on my altar.

"But you ask, 'How have we defiled you?'

"By saying that the LORD's table is contemptible. ⁸When you bring blind animals for sacrifice, is that not wrong? When you sacrifice crippled or diseased animals, is that not wrong? Try offering them to your governor! Would he be pleased with you? Would he accept you?" says the LORD Almighty.

⁹"Now implore God to be gracious to us. With such offerings from your hands, will he accept you?"—says the LORD Almighty.

¹⁰"Oh, that one of you would shut the temple doors, so that you would not light useless fires on my altar! I am not pleased with you," says the LORD Almighty, "and I will accept no offering from your hands. ¹¹My name will be great among the nations, from the rising to the setting of the sun. In every place incense and pure offerings will be brought to my name, because my name will be great among the nations," says the LORD Almighty.

¹²"But you profane it by saying of the Lord's table, 'It is defiled', and of its food, 'It is contemptible.' ¹³And you say, 'What a burden!' and you sniff at it contemptuously," says the LORD Almighty.

"When you bring injured, crippled or diseased animals and offer them as sacrifices, should I accept them from your hands?" says the LORD. ¹⁴"Cursed is the cheat who has an acceptable male in his flock and vows to give it, but then sacrifices a blemished animal to the Lord. For I am a great king," says the LORD Almighty, "and my name is to be feared among the nations.

Admonition for the Priests

2 "And now this admonition is for you, O priests. ²If you do not listen, and if you do not set your heart to honour my name," says the LORD Almighty, "I will send a curse upon you, and I will curse your blessings. Yes, I have already cursed them, because you have not set your heart to honour me.

³"Because of you I will rebuke*a* your descendants;*b* I will spread on your faces the offal from your festival sacrifices, and you will be carried off with it. ⁴And you will know that I have sent you this admonition so that my covenant with Levi may continue," says the LORD Almighty. ⁵"My covenant was with him, a covenant of life and peace, and I gave them to him; this called for reverence and he revered me and stood in awe of my name. ⁶True instruction was in his mouth and nothing false was found on his lips. He walked with me in peace and uprightness, and turned many from sin.

⁷"For the lips of a priest ought to preserve knowledge, and from his mouth men should seek instruction—because he is the messenger of the LORD Almighty. ⁸But you have turned from the way and by your teaching have caused many to stumble; you have violated the covenant with Levi," says the LORD Almighty. ⁹"So I have caused you to be despised and humiliated before all the people, because you have not followed my ways but have shown partiality in matters of the law."

Judah Unfaithful

¹⁰Have we not all one Father?*c* Did not one God create us? Why do we profane the

---

a1 Malachi means *my messenger.*   *a3* Or *cut off* (see Septuagint)   *b3* Or *will blight your corn*   *c10* Or *father* covenant of our fathers by breaking faith with one another?

[11]Judah has broken faith. A detestable thing has been committed in Israel and in Jerusalem: Judah has desecrated the sanctuary the LORD loves, by marrying the daughter of a foreign god. [12]As for the man who does this, whoever he may be, may the LORD cut him off from the tents of Jacob[d]—even though he brings offerings to the LORD Almighty.

[13]Another thing you do: You flood the LORD's altar with tears. You weep and wail because he no longer pays attention to your offerings or accepts them with pleasure from your hands. [14]You ask, "Why?" It is because the LORD is acting as the witness between you and the wife of your youth, because you have broken faith with her, though she is your partner, the wife of your marriage covenant.

[15]Has not ⌊the LORD⌋ made them one? In flesh and spirit they are his. And why one? Because he was seeking godly offspring.[e] So guard yourself in your spirit, and do not break faith with the wife of your youth.

[16]"I hate divorce," says the LORD God of Israel, "and I hate a man's covering himself[f] with violence as well as with his garment," says the LORD Almighty.

So guard yourself in your spirit, and do not break faith.

The Day of Judgment

[17]You have wearied the LORD with your words.

"How have we wearied him?" you ask.

By saying, "All who do evil are good in the eyes of the LORD, and he is pleased with them" or "Where is the God of justice?"

3 "See, I will send my messenger, who will prepare the way before me. Then suddenly the Lord you are seeking will come to his temple; the messenger of the covenant, whom you desire, will come," says the Lord Almighty.

[2]But who can endure the day of his coming? Who can stand when he appears? For he will be like a refiner's fire or a launderer's soap. [3]He will sit as a refiner and purifier of silver; he will purify the Levites and refine them like gold and silver. Then the LORD will have men who will bring offerings in righteousness, [4]and the offerings of Judah and Jerusalem will be acceptable to the LORD, as in days gone by, as in former years.

[5]"So I will come near to you for judgment. I will be quick to testify against sorcerers, adulterers and perjurers, against those who defraud labourers of their wages, who oppress the widows and the fatherless, and deprive aliens of justice, but do not fear me," says the LORD Almighty.

Robbing God

[6]"I the LORD do not change. So you, O descendants of Jacob, are not destroyed. [7]Ever since the time of your forefathers you

have turned away from my decrees and have not kept them. Return to me, and I will return to you," says the LORD Almighty.

"But you ask, 'How are we to return?'

[8]"Will a man rob God? Yet you rob me.

"But you ask, 'How do we rob you?'

"In tithes and offerings. [9]You are under a curse—the whole nation of you—because you are robbing me. [10]Bring the whole tithe into the storehouse, that there may be food in my house. Test me in this," says the LORD Almighty, "and see if I will not throw open the floodgates of heaven and pour out so much blessing that you will not have room enough for it. [11]I will prevent pests from devouring your crops, and the vines in your fields will not cast their fruit," says the LORD Almighty. [12]"Then all the nations will call you blessed, for yours will be a delightful land," says the LORD Almighty.

[13]"You have said harsh things against me," says the LORD.

"Yet you ask, 'What have we said against you?'

[14]"You have said, 'It is futile to serve God. What did we gain by carrying out his requirements and going about like mourners before the LORD Almighty? [15]But now we call the arrogant blessed. Certainly the evildoers prosper, and even those who challenge God escape.'"

[16]Then those who feared the LORD talked with each other, and the LORD listened and heard. A scroll of remembrance was written in his presence concerning those who feared the LORD and honoured his name.

[17]"They will be mine," says the LORD Almighty, "in the day when I make up my treasured possession.[a] I will spare them, just as in compassion a man spares his son who serves him. [18]And you will again see the distinction between the righteous and the wicked, between those who serve God and those who do not.

The Day of the LORD

4 "Surely the day is coming; it will burn like a furnace. All the arrogant and every evildoer will be stubble, and that day that is coming will set them on fire," says the LORD Almighty. "Not a root or a branch will be left to them. [2]But for you who revere my name, the sun of righteousness will rise with healing in its wings. And you will go out and leap like calves released from the stall. [3]Then you will trample down the wicked; they will be ashes under the soles of your feet on the day when I do these things," says the LORD Almighty.

[4]"Remember the law of my servant Moses, the decrees and laws I gave him at Horeb for all Israel.

[5]"See, I will send you the prophet Elijah before that great and dreadful day of the LORD comes. [6]He will turn the hearts of the fathers to their children, and the hearts of the children to their fathers; or else I will come and strike the land with a curse."

---

d12 Or [12]May the LORD cut off from the tents of Jacob anyone who gives testimony on behalf of the man who does this
e15 Or [15]But the one ⌊who is our father⌋ did not do this, not as long as life remained in him. And what was he seeking?
An offspring from God   f16 Or his wife   a17 Or Almighty, "my treasured possession, in the day when I act

THE
NEW TESTAMENT

Matthew

The Genealogy of Jesus

1 A record of the genealogy of Jesus Christ the son of David, the son of Abraham:

²Abraham was the father of Isaac,
 Isaac the father of Jacob,
 Jacob the father of Judah and his brothers,
 ³Judah the father of Perez and Zerah, whose mother was Tamar,
 Perez the father of Hezron,
 Hezron the father of Ram,
 ⁴Ram the father of Amminadab,
 Amminadab the father of Nahshon,
 Nahshon the father of Salmon,
 ⁵Salmon the father of Boaz, whose mother was Rahab,
 Boaz the father of Obed, whose mother was Ruth,
 Obed the father of Jesse,
 ⁶and Jesse the father of King David.

 David was the father of Solomon, whose mother had been Uriah's wife,
 ⁷Solomon the father of Rehoboam,
 Rehoboam the father of Abijah,
 Abijah the father of Asa,
 ⁸Asa the father of Jehoshaphat,
 Jehoshaphat the father of Jehoram,
 Jehoram the father of Uzziah,
 ⁹Uzziah the father of Jotham,
 Jotham the father of Ahaz,
 Ahaz the father of Hezekiah,
 ¹⁰Hezekiah the father of Manasseh,
 Manasseh the father of Amon,
 Amon the father of Josiah,
 ¹¹and Josiah the father of Jeconiah*a* and his brothers at the time of the exile to Babylon.

 ¹²After the exile to Babylon:
 Jeconiah was the father of Shealtiel,
 Shealtiel the father of Zerubbabel,
 ¹³Zerubbabel the father of Abiud,
 Abiud the father of Eliakim,
 Eliakim the father of Azor,
 ¹⁴Azor the father of Zadok,
 Zadok the father of Akim,
 Akim the father of Eliud,
 ¹⁵Eliud the father of Eleazar,
 Eleazar the father of Matthan,
 Matthan the father of Jacob,
 ¹⁶and Jacob the father of Joseph, the husband of Mary, of whom was born Jesus, who is called Christ.

¹⁷Thus there were fourteen generations in all from Abraham to David, fourteen from David to the exile to Babylon, and fourteen from the exile to the Christ.*b*

The Birth of Jesus Christ

¹⁸This is how the birth of Jesus Christ came about: His mother Mary was pledged to be married to Joseph, but before they came together, she was found to be with child through the Holy Spirit. ¹⁹Because Joseph her husband was a righteous man and did not want to expose her to public disgrace, he had in mind to divorce her quietly.

²⁰But after he had considered this, an angel of the Lord appeared to him in a dream and said, "Joseph son of David, do not be afraid to take Mary home as your wife, because what is conceived in her is from the Holy Spirit. ²¹She will give birth to a son, and you are to give him the name Jesus,*c* because he will save his people from their sins."

²²All this took place to fulfil what the Lord had said through the prophet: ²³"The virgin will be with child and will give birth to a son, and they will call him Immanuel"*d*—which means, "God with us."

²⁴When Joseph woke up, he did what the angel of the Lord had commanded him and took Mary home as his wife. ²⁵But he had no union with her until she gave birth to a son. And he gave him the name Jesus.

The Visit of the Magi

2 After Jesus was born in Bethlehem in Judea, during the time of King Herod, Magi*a* from the east came to Jerusalem ²and asked, "Where is the one who has been born king of the Jews? We saw his star in the east*b* and have come to worship him."

³When King Herod heard this he was disturbed, and all Jerusalem with him. ⁴When he had called together all the people's chief

---

a11 That is, Jehoiachin; also in verse 12
b17 Or *Messiah*. "The Christ" (Greek) and "the Messiah" (Hebrew) both mean "the Anointed One".
c21 *Jesus* is the Greek form of *Joshua*, which means *the LORD saves*.   *d23* Isaiah 7:14
a1 Traditionally *Wise Men*   *b2* Or *star when it rose*

priests and teachers of the law, he asked them where the Christ[c] was to be born. 5"In Bethlehem in Judea," they replied, "for this is what the prophet has written:

6"'But you, Bethlehem, in the land of
    Judah,
  are by no means least among the rulers
    of Judah;
  for out of you will come a ruler
  who will be the shepherd of my people
    Israel.'[d]"

7Then Herod called the Magi secretly and found out from them the exact time the star had appeared. 8He sent them to Bethlehem and said, "Go and make a careful search for the child. As soon as you find him, report to me, so that I too may go and worship him."

9After they had heard the king, they went on their way, and the star they had seen in the east[e] went ahead of them until it stopped over the place where the child was. 10When they saw the star, they were overjoyed. 11On coming to the house, they saw the child with his mother Mary, and they bowed down and worshipped him. Then they opened their treasures and presented him with gifts of gold and of incense and of myrrh. 12And having been warned in a dream not to go back to Herod, they returned to their country by another route.

The Escape to Egypt

13When they had gone, an angel of the Lord appeared to Joseph in a dream. "Get up," he said, "take the child and his mother and escape to Egypt. Stay there until I tell you, for Herod is going to search for the child to kill him."

14So he got up, took the child and his mother during the night and left for Egypt, 15where he stayed until the death of Herod. And so was fulfilled what the Lord had said through the prophet: "Out of Egypt I called my son."[f]

16When Herod realised that he had been outwitted by the Magi, he was furious, and he gave orders to kill all the boys in Bethlehem and its vicinity who were two years old and under, in accordance with the time he had learned from the Magi. 17Then what was said through the prophet Jeremiah was fulfilled:

18"A voice is heard in Ramah,
    weeping and great mourning,
  Rachel weeping for her children
    and refusing to be comforted,
  because they are no more."[g]

The Return to Nazareth

19After Herod died, an angel of the Lord appeared in a dream to Joseph in Egypt 20and said, "Get up, take the child and his mother and go to the land of Israel, for those who were trying to take the child's life are dead."

21So he got up, took the child and his mother and went to the land of Israel. 22But when he heard that Archelaus was reigning in Judea in place of his father Herod, he was afraid to go there. Having been warned in a dream, he withdrew to the district of Galilee, 23and he went and lived in a town called Nazareth. So was fulfilled what was said through the prophets: "He will be called a Nazarene."

John the Baptist Prepares the Way

3 In those days John the Baptist came, preaching in the Desert of Judea 2and saying, "Repent, for the kingdom of heaven is near." 3This is he who was spoken of through the prophet Isaiah:

"A voice of one calling in the desert,
'Prepare the way for the Lord,
  make straight paths for him.'"[a]

4John's clothes were made of camel's hair, and he had a leather belt round his waist. His food was locusts and wild honey. 5People went out to him from Jerusalem and all Judea and the whole region of the Jordan. 6Confessing their sins, they were baptised by him in the Jordan River.

7But when he saw many of the Pharisees and Sadducees coming to where he was baptising, he said to them: "You brood of vipers! Who warned you to flee from the coming wrath? 8Produce fruit in keeping with repentance. 9And do not think you can say to yourselves, 'We have Abraham as our father.' I tell you that out of these stones God can raise up children for Abraham. 10The axe is already at the root of the trees, and every tree that does not produce good fruit will be cut down and thrown into the fire.

11"I baptise you with[b] water for repentance. But after me will come one who is more powerful than I, whose sandals I am not fit to carry. He will baptise you with the Holy Spirit and with fire. 12His winnowing fork is in his hand, and he will clear his threshing-floor, gathering his wheat into the barn and burning up the chaff with unquenchable fire."

The Baptism of Jesus

13Then Jesus came from Galilee to the Jordan to be baptised by John. 14But John tried to deter him, saying, "I need to be baptised by you, and do you come to me?"

15Jesus replied, "Let it be so now; it is proper for us to do this to fulfil all righteousness." Then John consented.

16As soon as Jesus was baptised, he went up out of the water. At that moment heaven was opened, and he saw the Spirit of God descending like a dove and lighting on him. 17And a voice from heaven said, "This is my Son, whom I love; with him I am well pleased."

The Temptation of Jesus

4 Then Jesus was led by the Spirit into the desert to be tempted by the devil. 2After fasting for forty days and forty nights, he was

c4 Or Messiah   d6 Micah 5:2   e9 Or seen when it rose   f15 Hosea 11:1   g18 Jer. 31:15
a3 Isaiah 40:3   b11 Or in

MATHEW 2:1–12
'They opened their treasures and presented him with gifts of gold and of incense and of myrrh' (v. 11).

GIVING PRESENTS TO CHILDREN at Christmas is, it seems, a fairly recent thing. It has become common practice only in the last two hundred years or so. Gifts are strange things. We wait for them with great excitement, and when we receive them it is often an anti-climax – not quite what we were expecting, or what we wanted.

Some people are great to give presents to, they appreciate them so much. Others, you hardly dare give them anything because it's never what they want. We have all seen the adverts 'FOR SALE – unwanted gift'. Some then even have the cheek to say 'would make ideal present!' And what about gift shops? 'The gift is almost by definition something you would want so little yourself that there's no sacrifice involved in giving it away,' said journalist Gerald Priestland.

The most precious gifts are not the most costly in money terms, but those which mean something. A child's first painting, a trinket from a special holiday, needlework painstakingly crafted by an invalid – the list could go on. The gifts the wise men brought were costly gifts, but they too meant something.

Gold for a king. Incense for a priest. Myrrh for burial. In terms of God's gift of himself, they are of incalculable worth. Christ the king takes a heavy responsibility for us. As priest he is the only mediator between us and God. In death he is our Saviour.

Jesus did not keep the wise men's gifts for himself. He shares them with us eternally.

→806

MATTHEW 2:13–23

'When Herod realised that he had been outwitted by the Magi, he was furious, and he gave orders to kill all the boys in Bethlehem and its vicinity who were two years old and under' (v. 16).

MARTYRDOM IS CLOSELY CONNECTED with Christmas. On 26 December is the feast of Stephen, the first Christian martyr. On 28 December is the feast of the Holy Innocents, the children butchered by Herod in order to try and get rid of Jesus.

It is no accident that Stephen's feast follows so closely on Christmas Day, for the very essence of Christ's coming is found in the martyrdom, not only of our Lord himself, but that of his people.

Martyrdom, today, is usually closer to the killing of the Holy Innocents, than it is to the stoning of Stephen. Few people – though probably more than any of us ever imagine – are directly killed on account of their Christian faith. Far more come to their deaths because men like Herod think they can show their power through the slaughter of the defenceless.

Remembering these two violent feast days, which follow so closely on the celebration of one who brings good tidings of peace on earth, let us remember all those who are the victims of terror; all those millions who still suffer from the loss of loved ones in war; all those who nurse injuries, physical, mental and spiritual, brought about by the violence of men of 'power'.

> *But with the woes of sin and strife*
> *The world has suffered long;*
> *Beneath the angel-strain have rolled*
> *Two thousand years of wrong.*
> *And man, at war with man, hears not*
> *The love song which they bring;*
> *O hush the noise, ye men of strife,*
> *And hear the angels sing.*

> *(Edmund Hamilton Sears)*

→809

hungry. [3]The tempter came to him and said, "If you are the Son of God, tell these stones to become bread."

[4]Jesus answered, "It is written: 'Man does not live on bread alone, but on every word that comes from the mouth of God.'[a]"

[5]Then the devil took him to the holy city and had him stand on the highest point of the temple. [6]"If you are the Son of God," he said, "throw yourself down. For it is written:

"'He will command his angels concerning
  you,
  and they will lift you up in their hands,
so that you will not strike your foot against
  a stone.'[b]"

[7]Jesus answered him, "It is also written: 'Do not put the Lord your God to the test.'[c]"

[8]Again, the devil took him to a very high mountain and showed him all the kingdoms of the world and their splendour. [9]"All this I will give you," he said, "if you will bow down and worship me."

[10]Jesus said to him, "Away from me, Satan! For it is written: 'Worship the Lord your God, and serve him only.'[d]"

[11]Then the devil left him, and angels came and attended him.

Jesus Begins to Preach

[12]When Jesus heard that John had been put in prison, he returned to Galilee. [13]Leaving Nazareth, he went and lived in Capernaum, which was by the lake in the area of Zebulun and Naphtali—[14]to fulfil what was said through the prophet Isaiah:

[15]"Land of Zebulun and land of Naphtali,
  the way to the sea, along the Jordan,
  Galilee of the Gentiles—
[16]the people living in darkness
  have seen a great light;
  on those living in the land of the shadow of
    death
  a light has dawned."[e]

[17]From that time on Jesus began to preach, "Repent, for the kingdom of heaven is near."

The Calling of the First Disciples

[18]As Jesus was walking beside the Sea of Galilee, he saw two brothers, Simon called Peter and his brother Andrew. They were casting a net into the lake, for they were fishermen. [19]"Come, follow me," Jesus said, "and I will make you fishers of men." [20]At once they left their nets and followed him.

[21]Going on from there, he saw two other brothers, James son of Zebedee and his brother John. They were in a boat with their father Zebedee, preparing their nets. Jesus called them, [22]and immediately they left the boat and their father and followed him.

Jesus Heals the Sick

[23]Jesus went throughout Galilee, teaching in their synagogues, preaching the good news of the kingdom, and healing every disease and sickness among the people. [24]News about him spread all over Syria, and people brought to him all who were ill with various diseases, those suffering severe pain, the demon-possessed, those having seizures, and the paralysed, and he healed them. [25]Large crowds from Galilee, the Decapolis,[f] Jerusalem, Judea and the region across the Jordan followed him.

The Beatitudes

5 Now when he saw the crowds, he went up on a mountainside and sat down. His disciples came to him, [2]and he began to teach them, saying:

[3]"Blessed are the poor in spirit,
  for theirs is the kingdom of heaven.
[4]Blessed are those who mourn,
  for they will be comforted.
[5]Blessed are the meek,
  for they will inherit the earth.
[6]Blessed are those who hunger and thirst
    for righteousness,
  for they will be filled.
[7]Blessed are the merciful,
  for they will be shown mercy.
[8]Blessed are the pure in heart,
  for they will see God.
[9]Blessed are the peacemakers,
  for they will be called sons of God.
[10]Blessed are those who are persecuted
    because of righteousness,
  for theirs is the kingdom of heaven.

[11]"Blessed are you when people insult you, persecute you and falsely say all kinds of evil against you because of me. [12]Rejoice and be glad, because great is your reward in heaven, for in the same way they persecuted the prophets who were before you.

Salt and Light

[13]"You are the salt of the earth. But if the salt loses its saltiness, how can it be made salty again? It is no longer good for anything, except to be thrown out and trampled by men.

[14]"You are the light of the world. A city on a hill cannot be hidden. [15]Neither do people light a lamp and put it under a bowl. Instead they put it on its stand, and it gives light to everyone in the house. [16]In the same way, let your light shine before men, that they may see your good deeds and praise your Father in heaven.

The Fulfilment of the Law

[17]"Do not think that I have come to abolish the Law or the Prophets; I have not come to abolish them but to fulfil them. [18]I tell you the truth, until heaven and earth disappear, not the smallest letter, not the least stroke of a pen, will by any means disappear from the Law until everything is accomplished. [19]Anyone who breaks one of the least of these commandments and teaches others to

a4 Deut. 8:3   *b6* Psalm 91:11,12   *c7* Deut. 6:16   *d10* Deut. 6:13   *e16* Isaiah 9:1,2
f25 That is, the Ten Cities

do the same will be called least in the kingdom of heaven, but whoever practises and teaches these commands will be called great in the kingdom of heaven. ²⁰For I tell you that unless your righteousness surpasses that of the Pharisees and the teachers of the law, you will certainly not enter the kingdom of heaven.

Murder

²¹"You have heard that it was said to the people long ago, 'Do not murder,ᵃ and anyone who murders will be subject to judgment.' ²²But I tell you that anyone who is angry with his brotherᵇ will be subject to judgment. Again, anyone who says to his brother, 'Raca,'ᶜ is answerable to the Sanhedrin. But anyone who says, 'You fool!' will be in danger of the fire of hell.

²³"Therefore, if you are offering your gift at the altar and there remember that your brother has something against you, ²⁴leave your gift there in front of the altar. First go and be reconciled to your brother; then come and offer your gift.

²⁵"Settle matters quickly with your adversary who is taking you to court. Do it while you are still with him on the way, or he may hand you over to the judge, and the judge may hand you over to the officer, and you may be thrown into prison. ²⁶I tell you the truth, you will not get out until you have paid the last penny.ᵈ

Adultery

²⁷"You have heard that it was said, 'Do not commit adultery.'ᵉ ²⁸But I tell you that anyone who looks at a woman lustfully has already committed adultery with her in his heart. ²⁹If your right eye causes you to sin, gouge it out and throw it away. It is better for you to lose one part of your body than for your whole body to be thrown into hell. ³⁰And if your right hand causes you to sin, cut it off and throw it away. It is better for you to lose one part of your body than for your whole body to go into hell.

Divorce

³¹"It has been said, 'Anyone who divorces his wife must give her a certificate of divorce.'ᶠ ³²But I tell you that anyone who divorces his wife, except for marital unfaithfulness, causes her to become an adulteress, and anyone who marries the divorced woman commits adultery.

Oaths

³³"Again, you have heard that it was said to the people long ago, 'Do not break your oath, but keep the oaths you have made to the Lord.' ³⁴But I tell you, Do not swear at all: either by heaven, for it is God's throne; ³⁵or by the earth, for it is his footstool; or by Jerusalem, for it is the city of the Great King. ³⁶And do not swear by your head, for you cannot make even one hair white or black.

³⁷Simply let your 'Yes' be 'Yes', and your 'No', 'No'; anything beyond this comes from the evil one.

An Eye for an Eye

³⁸"You have heard that it was said, 'Eye for eye, and tooth for tooth.'ᵍ ³⁹But I tell you, Do not resist an evil person. If someone strikes you on the right cheek, turn to him the other also. ⁴⁰And if someone wants to sue you and take your tunic, let him have your cloak as well. ⁴¹If someone forces you to go one mile, go with him two miles. ⁴²Give to the one who asks you, and do not turn away from the one who wants to borrow from you.

Love for Enemies

⁴³"You have heard that it was said, 'Love your neighbourʰ and hate your enemy.' ⁴⁴But I tell you: Love your enemiesⁱ and pray for those who persecute you, ⁴⁵that you may be sons of your Father in heaven. He causes his sun to rise on the evil and the good, and sends rain on the righteous and the unrighteous. ⁴⁶If you love those who love you, what reward will you get? Are not even the tax collectors doing that? ⁴⁷And if you greet only your brothers, what are you doing more than others? Do not even pagans do that? ⁴⁸Be perfect, therefore, as your heavenly Father is perfect.

Giving to the Needy

6 "Be careful not to do your 'acts of righteousness' before men, to be seen by them. If you do, you will have no reward from your Father in heaven.

²"So when you give to the needy, do not announce it with trumpets, as the hypocrites do in the synagogues and on the streets, to be honoured by men. I tell you the truth, they have received their reward in full. ³But when you give to the needy, do not let your left hand know what your right hand is doing, ⁴so that your giving may be in secret. Then your Father, who sees what is done in secret, will reward you.

Prayer

⁵"And when you pray, do not be like the hypocrites, for they love to pray standing in the synagogues and on the street corners to be seen by men. I tell you the truth, they have received their reward in full. ⁶But when you pray, go into your room, close the door and pray to your Father, who is unseen. Then your Father, who sees what is done in secret, will reward you. ⁷And when you pray, do not keep on babbling like pagans, for they think they will be heard because of their many words. ⁸Do not be like them, for your Father knows what you need before you ask him.

⁹"This, then, is how you should pray:

"'Our Father in heaven,
hallowed be your name,

ᵃ21 Exodus 20:13   ᵇ22 Some manuscripts brother without cause   ᶜ22 An Aramaic term of contempt
ᵈ26 Greek kodrantes   ᵉ27 Exodus 20:14   ᶠ31 Deut. 24:1   ᵍ38 Exodus 21:24; Lev. 24:20 and Deut. 19:21
ʰ43 Lev. 19:18   ⁱ44 Some late manuscripts enemies, bless those who curse you, do good to those who hate you

MATTHEW 5:1–12
'Rejoice and be glad, because great is your reward in heaven' (v. 12).

THE ESSENCE OF JESUS' TEACHING is summed up in these twelve verses. They are rounded off in Matthew's Gospel by a promise of reward in heaven. But the experience they describe is not merely for the future, it is a present experience. As Barclay puts it 'The Beatitudes are not promises of future happiness; they are congratulations on present bliss.'

Congratulations if you are poor in spirit. Congratulations if you mourn. Congratulations if you are meek. Congratulations if you long for righteousness. Congratulations if you are merciful. Congratulations if your heart is pure. Congratulations if you make peace. Congratulations if you are persecuted!

Few of these qualities are those the world values highly. Even making peace – which most people approve of in theory – is not highly valued unless, along with the peace, you get your own way! Otherwise, in this world's terms, peace spells defeat. J. B. Phillips, writing over thirty years ago, summed up the world's attitude to peacemaking with an anti-Beatitude 'Blessed are the trouble-makers: for they make people take notice of them.'

It is true that trouble-making often gets things in motion, and means that things get done. Jesus himself recognized that in his story of the importunate widow. But getting things done, making changes here and there, is not bringing in the kingdom. The kingdom only comes after a complete revolution in your heart and mine.

You know, Lord, how we like to be noticed. We need to feel valued. We love to be liked. Show us a better way. Your way.

→810

MATTHEW 6:1–6, 16–18
'When you pray, do not be like the hypocrites, for they love to pray standing in the synagogues and on the street corners to be seen by men' (v. 5).

SALVATIONISTS have a high profile. They wear uniform, march the streets, hold meetings on street corners, sell *The War Cry* in public houses, and do lots of other extrovert things. They need to ask themselves carefully *why* they do those things. Marching along Oxford Street in the West End of London, behind a band so musically efficient it can play in the forecourt of Buckingham Palace and not feel out of place – that can be an exhilarating experience, enough to turn the head of many a young person. Addressing a crowd in a market square in Santiago, or pressing the claims of Christ in the back streets of Nairobi; even holding forth in an apparently empty housing estate in inner-city Britain, can inflate one's ego.

It would be easy, in the light of today's passage, to condemn such outward show, say that Jesus told us not to parade our religion before men, and ask the Army to retire into its citadels, or the homes of its soldiers.

Balance is needed. There is a requirement to go into the highways and bring in those not already invited to the Christian banquet. But in doing so it must always be the invitation of Christ himself that is offered. The messenger bearing the invitation recedes into the background, so that the message can be heard. Striking that balance is not easy, especially when the invitation is offered with enthusiasm.

Father in heaven, we ask you to bless all open-air ministry. May those who invite others to the Lord's banquet, do so with enthusiasm but without egoism. Guard them against any form of hypocrisy in what they do.

→813

¹⁰your kingdom come,
  your will be done
    on earth as it is in heaven.
¹¹Give us today our daily bread.
¹²Forgive us our debts,
  as we also have forgiven our debtors.
¹³And lead us not into temptation,
  but deliver us from the evil one.'ᵃ

¹⁴For if you forgive men when they sin against you, your heavenly Father will also forgive you. ¹⁵But if you do not forgive men their sins, your Father will not forgive your sins.

Fasting

¹⁶"When you fast, do not look sombre as the hypocrites do, for they disfigure their faces to show men they are fasting. I tell you the truth, they have received their reward in full. ¹⁷But when you fast, put oil on your head and wash your face, ¹⁸so that it will not be obvious to men that you are fasting, but only to your Father, who is unseen; and your Father, who sees what is done in secret, will reward you.

Treasures in Heaven

¹⁹"Do not store up for yourselves treasures on earth, where moth and rust destroy, and where thieves break in and steal. ²⁰But store up for yourselves treasures in heaven, where moth and rust do not destroy, and where thieves do not break in and steal. ²¹For where your treasure is, there your heart will be also.

²²"The eye is the lamp of the body. If your eyes are good, your whole body will be full of light. ²³But if your eyes are bad, your whole body will be full of darkness. If then the light within you is darkness, how great is that darkness!

²⁴"No-one can serve two masters. Either he will hate the one and love the other, or he will be devoted to the one and despise the other. You cannot serve both God and Money.

Do Not Worry

²⁵"Therefore I tell you, do not worry about your life, what you will eat or drink; or about your body, what you will wear. Is not life more important than food, and the body more important than clothes? ²⁶Look at the birds of the air; they do not sow or reap or store away in barns, and yet your heavenly Father feeds them. Are you not much more valuable than they? ²⁷Who of you by worrying can add a single hour to his life?ᵇ

²⁸"And why do you worry about clothes? See how the lilies of the field grow. They do not labour or spin. ²⁹Yet I tell you that not even Solomon in all his splendour was dressed like one of these. ³⁰If that is how God clothes the grass of the field, which is here today and tomorrow is thrown into the fire, will he not much more clothe you, O you of little faith? ³¹So do not worry, saying, 'What

shall we eat?' or 'What shall we drink?' or 'What shall we wear?' ³²For the pagans run after all these things, and your heavenly Father knows that you need them. ³³But seek first his kingdom and his righteousness, and all these things will be given to you as well. ³⁴Therefore do not worry about tomorrow, for tomorrow will worry about itself. Each day has enough trouble of its own.

Judging Others

7 "Do not judge, or you too will be judged. ²For in the same way as you judge others, you will be judged, and with the measure you use, it will be measured to you.

³"Why do you look at the speck of sawdust in your brother's eye and pay no attention to the plank in your own eye? ⁴How can you say to your brother, 'Let me take the speck out of your eye,' when all the time there is a plank in your own eye? ⁵You hypocrite, first take the plank out of your own eye, and then you will see clearly to remove the speck from your brother's eye.

⁶"Do not give dogs what is sacred; do not throw your pearls to pigs. If you do, they may trample them under their feet, and then turn and tear you to pieces.

Ask, Seek, Knock

⁷"Ask and it will be given to you; seek and you will find; knock and the door will be opened to you. ⁸For everyone who asks receives; he who seeks finds; and to him who knocks, the door will be opened.

⁹"Which of you, if his son asks for bread, will give him a stone? ¹⁰Or if he asks for a fish, will give him a snake? ¹¹If you, then, though you are evil, know how to give good gifts to your children, how much more will your Father in heaven give good gifts to those who ask him! ¹²So in everything, do to others what you would have them do to you, for this sums up the Law and the Prophets.

The Narrow and Wide Gates

¹³"Enter through the narrow gate. For wide is the gate and broad is the road that leads to destruction, and many enter through it. ¹⁴But small is the gate and narrow the road that leads to life, and only a few find it.

A Tree and Its Fruit

¹⁵"Watch out for false prophets. They come to you in sheep's clothing, but inwardly they are ferocious wolves. ¹⁶By their fruit you will recognise them. Do people pick grapes from thornbushes, or figs from thistles? ¹⁷Likewise every good tree bears good fruit, but a bad tree bears bad fruit. ¹⁸A good tree cannot bear bad fruit, and a bad tree cannot bear good fruit. ¹⁹Every tree that does not bear good fruit is cut down and thrown into the fire. ²⁰Thus, by their fruit you will recognise them.

²¹"Not everyone who says to me, 'Lord, Lord,' will enter the kingdom of heaven, but only he who does the will of my Father who is

---

ᵃ13 Or *from evil*; some late manuscripts *one, | for yours is the kingdom and the power and the glory for ever. Amen.*
ᵇ27 Or *single cubit to his height*

in heaven. 22Many will say to me on that day, 'Lord, Lord, did we not prophesy in your name, and in your name drive out demons and perform many miracles?' 23Then I will tell them plainly, 'I never knew you. Away from me, you evildoers!'

The Wise and Foolish Builders

24"Therefore everyone who hears these words of mine and puts them into practice is like a wise man who built his house on the rock. 25The rain came down, the streams rose, and the winds blew and beat against that house; yet it did not fall, because it had its foundation on the rock. 26But everyone who hears these words of mine and does not put them into practice is like a foolish man who built his house on sand. 27The rain came down, the streams rose, and the winds blew and beat against that house, and it fell with a great crash."

28When Jesus had finished saying these things, the crowds were amazed at his teaching, 29because he taught as one who had authority, and not as their teachers of the law.

The Man With Leprosy

8 When he came down from the mountainside, large crowds followed him. 2A man with leprosy*a* came and knelt before him and said, "Lord, if you are willing, you can make me clean."

3Jesus reached out his hand and touched the man. "I am willing," he said. "Be clean!" Immediately he was cured*b* of his leprosy. 4Then Jesus said to him, "See that you don't tell anyone. But go, show yourself to the priest and offer the gift Moses commanded, as a testimony to them."

The Faith of the Centurion

5When Jesus had entered Capernaum, a centurion came to him, asking for help. 6"Lord," he said, "my servant lies at home paralysed and in terrible suffering."

7Jesus said to him, "I will go and heal him."

8The centurion replied, "Lord, I do not deserve to have you come under my roof. But just say the word, and my servant will be healed. 9For I myself am a man under authority, with soldiers under me. I tell this one, 'Go,' and he goes; and that one, 'Come,' and he comes. I say to my servant, 'Do this,' and he does it."

10When Jesus heard this, he was astonished and said to those following him, "I tell you the truth, I have not found anyone in Israel with such great faith. 11I say to you that many will come from the east and the west, and will take their places at the feast with Abraham, Isaac and Jacob in the kingdom of heaven. 12But the subjects of the kingdom will be thrown outside, into the darkness, where there will be weeping and gnashing of teeth."

13Then Jesus said to the centurion, "Go! It will be done just as you believed it would." And his servant was healed at that very hour.

Jesus Heals Many

14When Jesus came into Peter's house, he saw Peter's mother-in-law lying in bed with a fever. 15He touched her hand and the fever left her, and she got up and began to wait on him.

16When evening came, many who were demon-possessed were brought to him, and he drove out the spirits with a word and healed all the sick. 17This was to fulfil what was spoken through the prophet Isaiah:

"He took up our infirmities
    and carried our diseases."*c*

The Cost of Following Jesus

18When Jesus saw the crowd around him, he gave orders to cross to the other side of the lake. 19Then a teacher of the law came to him and said, "Teacher, I will follow you wherever you go."

20Jesus replied, "Foxes have holes and birds of the air have nests, but the Son of Man has nowhere to lay his head."

21Another disciple said to him, "Lord, first let me go and bury my father."

22But Jesus told him, "Follow me, and let the dead bury their own dead."

Jesus Calms the Storm

23Then he got into the boat and his disciples followed him. 24Without warning, a furious storm came up on the lake, so that the waves swept over the boat. But Jesus was sleeping. 25The disciples went and woke him, saying, "Lord, save us! We're going to drown!"

26He replied, "You of little faith, why are you so afraid?" Then he got up and rebuked the winds and the waves, and it was completely calm.

27The men were amazed and asked, "What kind of man is this? Even the winds and the waves obey him!"

The Healing of Two Demon-possessed Men

28When he arrived at the other side in the region of the Gadarenes,*d* two demon-possessed men coming from the tombs met him. They were so violent that no-one could pass that way. 29"What do you want with us, Son of God?" they shouted. "Have you come here to torture us before the appointed time?"

30Some distance from them a large herd of pigs was feeding. 31The demons begged Jesus, "If you drive us out, send us into the herd of pigs."

32He said to them, "Go!" So they came out and went into the pigs, and the whole herd rushed down the steep bank into the lake and died in the water. 33Those tending the pigs ran off, went into the town and reported all

---

*a2 The Greek word was used for various diseases affecting the skin—not necessarily leprosy.
*b3 Greek *made clean*   *c17 Isaiah 53:4   *d28 Some manuscripts *Gergesenes*; others *Gerasenes*

MATTHEW 7:7–11
'Ask and it will be given to you; seek and you will find; knock and the door will be opened to you' (v. 7).

WE ARE TO ASK! Jesus commanded us to do so, of course. He also commanded that we should ask in faith, and that we should ask in his name. According to the apostle James, by tradition identified as the brother of our Lord, we do not have, because we do not ask God for it, and sometimes, when we ask we do not receive because we have asked with the wrong motives.

We are to seek! The verb 'to seek' is strong and active. In the original Greek it includes the ideas of endeavour, of searching for something hidden, of desire, of resolute will. Such searching, according to Jesus, will be rewarded by finding. God has not made everything immediately available to his people. Paul, speaking to the Athenians, refers to the apparently slow-moving strategy of God and affirms that 'God did this so that men would seek him and perhaps reach out for him and find him.'

We are to knock! There are doors which do not always open at the first rap but which, when finally they yield, open the way to opportunities and glories undreamed of. Persistence is a requirement in prayer. Knocking persistently on doors is more than a mere human occupation. The book of Revelation gives us a picture of the Son of God himself knocking patiently and persistently at the door of the human heart. If he can do that for so meagre a reward, we can be persistent with a heavenly Father who is willing to give us our heart's desire.

> *O Lord, increase our faith and love,*
> *So shall we all thy goodness prove*
> *And gain from thine own boundless store*
> *The fruits of prayer for evermore.*

(William Cowper)

→814

MATTHEW 10:37–39
'Whoever finds his life will lose it, and whoever loses his life for my sake will find it' (v. 39).

GEORGE MATHESON expands on this paradox as powerfully as any other in his great hymn:

> *Make me a captive, Lord.*
> *And then I shall be free;*
> *Force me to render up my sword.*
> *And I shall conqueror be.*

The self-centred life is a life doomed to failure and destined for destruction. The cluster of sentiments, attitudes and desires which help to shape human personality in the unredeemed are anti-social and threaten the spiritual life. From earliest days this was foreseen: 'When your herds and flocks grow large and your silver and gold increase and all you have is multiplied, then your heart will become proud and you will forget the LORD your God.' Jesus also had much to say about accumulating riches. If we seek to satisfy our natural desires, ultimately we will lose our lives, but if we surrender our lives, seeking the abundant life which is found in Christ, we will be satisfied to the depths of our being.

It is by self-forgetfulness that we find life and fulfilment, and by self-centredness that we lose our lives. Only to the open, surrendered heart can the Lord Christ come and, by his Spirit, dwell within.

> *Lord, teach us in your only Son*
> *To reach the way we dream*
> *To follow truth as he knew truth.*
> *And find the life supreme.*

(*Miriam M. Richards*)

→817

;, including what had happened to the ~~'on~~-possessed men. ³⁴Then the whole town went out to meet Jesus. And when they saw him, they pleaded with him to leave their region.

Jesus Heals a Paralytic

9 Jesus stepped into a boat, crossed over and came to his own town. ²Some men brought to him a paralytic, lying on a mat. When Jesus saw their faith, he said to the paralytic, "Take heart, son; your sins are forgiven."

³At this, some of the teachers of the law said to themselves, "This fellow is blaspheming!"

⁴Knowing their thoughts, Jesus said, "Why do you entertain evil thoughts in your hearts? ⁵Which is easier: to say, 'Your sins are forgiven,' or to say, 'Get up and walk'? ⁶But so that you may know that the Son of Man has authority on earth to forgive sins. . . ." Then he said to the paralytic, "Get up, take your mat and go home." ⁷And the man got up and went home. ⁸When the crowd saw this, they were filled with awe; and they praised God, who had given such authority to men.

The Calling of Matthew

⁹As Jesus went on from there, he saw a man named Matthew sitting at the tax collector's booth. "Follow me," he told him, and Matthew got up and followed him.

¹⁰While Jesus was having dinner at Matthew's house, many tax collectors and "sinners" came and ate with him and his disciples. ¹¹When the Pharisees saw this, they asked his disciples, "Why does your teacher eat with tax collectors and 'sinners'?"

¹²On hearing this, Jesus said, "It is not the healthy who need a doctor, but the sick. ¹³But go and learn what this means: 'I desire mercy, not sacrifice.'ᵃ For I have not come to call the righteous, but sinners."

Jesus Questioned About Fasting

¹⁴Then John's disciples came and asked him, "How is it that we and the Pharisees fast, but your disciples do not fast?"

¹⁵Jesus answered, "How can the guests of the bridegroom mourn while he is with them? The time will come when the bridegroom will be taken from them; then they will fast.

¹⁶"No-one sews a patch of unshrunk cloth on an old garment, for the patch will pull away from the garment, making the tear worse. ¹⁷Neither do men pour new wine into old wineskins. If they do, the skins will burst, the wine will run out and the wineskins will be ruined. No, they pour new wine into new wineskins, and both are preserved."

A Dead Girl and a Sick Woman

¹⁸While he was saying this, a ruler came and knelt before him and said, "My daughter has just died. But come and put your hand on her, and she will live." ¹⁹Jesus got up and went with him, and so did his disciples.

²⁰Just then a woman who had been subject to bleeding for twelve years came up behind him and touched the edge of his cloak. ²¹She said to herself, "If I only touch his cloak, I will be healed."

²²Jesus turned and saw her. "Take heart, daughter," he said, "your faith has healed you." And the woman was healed from that moment.

²³When Jesus entered the ruler's house and saw the flute players and the noisy crowd, ²⁴he said, "Go away. The girl is not dead but asleep." But they laughed at him. ²⁵After the crowd had been put outside, he went in and took the girl by the hand, and she got up. ²⁶News of this spread through all that region.

Jesus Heals the Blind and Mute

²⁷As Jesus went on from there, two blind men followed him, calling out, "Have mercy on us, Son of David!"

²⁸When he had gone indoors, the blind men came to him, and he asked them, "Do you believe that I am able to do this?"

"Yes, Lord," they replied.

²⁹Then he touched their eyes and said, "According to your faith will it be done to you"; ³⁰and their sight was restored. Jesus warned them sternly, "See that no-one knows about this." ³¹But they went out and spread the news about him all over that region.

³²While they were going out, a man who was demon-possessed and could not talk was brought to Jesus. ³³And when the demon was driven out, the man who had been mute spoke. The crowd was amazed and said, "Nothing like this has ever been seen in Israel."

³⁴But the Pharisees said, "It is by the prince of demons that he drives out demons."

The Workers Are Few

³⁵Jesus went through all the towns and villages, teaching in their synagogues, preaching the good news of the kingdom and healing every disease and sickness. ³⁶When he saw the crowds, he had compassion on them, because they were harassed and helpless, like sheep without a shepherd. ³⁷Then he said to his disciples, "The harvest is plentiful but the workers are few. ³⁸Ask the Lord of the harvest, therefore, to send out workers into his harvest field."

Jesus Sends Out the Twelve

10 He called his twelve disciples to him and gave them authority to drive out evilᵃ spirits and to heal every disease and sickness.

²These are the names of the twelve apostles: first, Simon (who is called Peter) and his brother Andrew; James son of Zebedee, and his brother John; ³Philip and Bartholomew; Thomas and Matthew the tax

---

ᵃ13 Hosea 6:6   ᵃ1 Greek *unclean*

collector; James son of Alphaeus, and Thaddaeus; 4Simon the Zealot and Judas Iscariot, who betrayed him.

5These twelve Jesus sent out with the following instructions: "Do not go among the Gentiles or enter any town of the Samaritans. 6Go rather to the lost sheep of Israel. 7As you go, preach this message: 'The kingdom of heaven is near.' 8Heal the sick, raise the dead, cleanse those who have leprosy,b drive out demons. Freely you have received, freely give. 9Do not take along any gold or silver or copper in your belts; 10take no bag for the journey, or extra tunic, or sandals or a staff; for the worker is worth his keep.

11"Whatever town or village you enter, search for some worthy person there and stay at his house until you leave. 12As you enter the home, give it your greeting. 13If the home is deserving, let your peace rest on it; if it is not, let your peace return to you. 14If anyone will not welcome you or listen to your words, shake the dust off your feet when you leave that home or town. 15I tell you the truth, it will be more bearable for Sodom and Gomorrah on the day of judgment than for that town. 16I am sending you out like sheep among wolves. Therefore be as shrewd as snakes and as innocent as doves.

17"Be on your guard against men; they will hand you over to the local councils and flog you in their synagogues. 18On my account you will be brought before governors and kings as witnesses to them and to the Gentiles. 19But when they arrest you, do not worry about what to say or how to say it. At that time you will be given what to say, 20for it will not be you speaking, but the Spirit of your Father speaking through you.

21"Brother will betray brother to death, and a father his child; children will rebel against their parents and have them put to death. 22All men will hate you because of me, but he who stands firm to the end will be saved. 23When you are persecuted in one place, flee to another. I tell you the truth, you will not finish going through the cities of Israel before the Son of Man comes.

24"A student is not above his teacher, nor a servant above his master. 25It is enough for the student to be like his teacher, and the servant like his master. If the head of the house has been called Beelzebub,c how much more the members of his household!

26"So do not be afraid of them. There is nothing concealed that will not be disclosed, or hidden that will not be made known. 27What I tell you in the dark, speak in the daylight; what is whispered in your ear, proclaim from the roofs. 28Do not be afraid of those who kill the body but cannot kill the soul. Rather, be afraid of the One who can destroy both soul and body in hell. 29Are not two sparrows sold for a penny?d Yet not one of them will fall to the ground apart from the will of your Father. 30And even the very hairs of your head are all numbered. 31So don't

be afraid; you are worth more than many sparrows.

32"Whoever acknowledges me before men, I will also acknowledge him before my Father in heaven. 33But whoever disowns me before men, I will disown him before my Father in heaven.

34"Do not suppose that I have come to bring peace to the earth. I did not come to bring peace, but a sword. 35For I have come to turn

> " 'a man against his father,
>   a daughter against her mother,
> a daughter-in-law against her
>   mother-in-law—
36   a man's enemies will be the members of
>   his own household.'e

37"Anyone who loves his father or mother more than me is not worthy of me; anyone who loves his son or daughter more than me is not worthy of me; 38and anyone who does not take his cross and follow me is not worthy of me. 39Whoever finds his life will lose it, and whoever loses his life for my sake will find it.

40"He who receives you receives me, and he who receives me receives the one who sent me. 41Anyone who receives a prophet because he is a prophet will receive a prophet's reward, and anyone who receives a righteous man because he is a righteous man will receive a righteous man's reward. 42And if anyone gives even a cup of cold water to one of these little ones because he is my disciple, I tell you the truth, he will certainly not lose his reward."

Jesus and John the Baptist

11 After Jesus had finished instructing his twelve disciples, he went on from there to teach and preach in the towns of Galilee.a

2When John heard in prison what Christ was doing, he sent his disciples 3to ask him, "Are you the one who was to come, or should we expect someone else?"

4Jesus replied, "Go back and report to John what you hear and see: 5The blind receive sight, the lame walk, those who have leprosyb are cured, the deaf hear, the dead are raised, and the good news is preached to the poor. 6Blessed is the man who does not fall away on account of me."

7As John's disciples were leaving, Jesus began to speak to the crowd about John: "What did you go out into the desert to see? A reed swayed by the wind? 8If not, what did you go out to see? A man dressed in fine clothes? No, those who wear fine clothes are in kings' palaces. 9Then what did you go out to see? A prophet? Yes, I tell you, and more than a prophet. 10This is the one about whom it is written:

> " 'I will send my messenger ahead of you,
>   who will prepare your way before you.'c

---

b8 The Greek word was used for various diseases affecting the skin—not necessarily leprosy.
c25 Greek Beezeboul or Beelzeboul   d29 Greek an assarion   e36 Micah 7:6   a1 Greek in their towns
b5 The Greek word was used for various diseases affecting the skin—not necessarily leprosy.   c10 Mal. 3:1

MATTHEW 11:25–30
'Come to me, all you who are weary and burdened, and I will give you rest' (v. 28).

WHAT ENORMOUS BURDENS SOME PEOPLE CARRY. In this invitation which Jesus gave to burdened and wearied people, it is easy to assume that he was referring to those burdened by the demands of the Jewish Law. Undoubtedly the Law was a heavy weight pressing down upon most of his listeners, but his appeal is of universal application. Almost every group of people contains individuals for whom life has become wearisome. Burdens come with a wide variety of labels and in many instances with a great deal of distress, disillusionment and doubt. Burdens can also isolate people. Ella Wheeler Wilcox expressed it memorably:

> Laugh, and the world laughs with you,
> Weep and you weep alone,
> For the sad old earth must borrow its mirth,
> But has trouble enough of its own.

The verse has enough truth in it to make the invitation of Christ even more remarkable. He never distanced himself from the burdened and troubled. He was even prepared to take the entire city of Jerusalem to his heart. He is the great burden-bearer, as so many of us have proved.

His promised rest is not usually associated with a withdrawal from the demands and activities of life, but rather relates to the grace which enables us to cope, and to cope well. When Paul was under heavy stress he was conscious of the Lord standing by him.

Was not Jesus the best yoke-maker in Nazareth? His love ensures that his yokes fit well. His compassions ensure that such burdens as he allows us to bear are bearable.

No burden is too great for Christ to share and bear.

→818

MATTHEW 12:1–2
'When the Pharisees saw this, they said to him, "Look! Your disciples are doing what is unlawful on the Sabbath" ' (v. 2).

AT TIMES we are surprised by the censure in our Lord's words against the Pharisees. For one so gentle and loving, his unyielding judgement seems a little out of character, but it was the implacable opposition of the Scribes and Pharisees which made him conclude that they, the teachers and custodians of the Law, had perverted and devalued the Law – its wholesomeness was corrupted by their interpretation. Furthermore, Jesus was convinced that the Pharisees were largely governed by substandard motives. They used the authority of the Law to achieve personal ends. By contrast, Jesus brought the wholesomeness of heaven into human affairs, exercising a natural authority which the people found engaging – not so, however, the Pharisees.

The conflict recorded in our chosen Scripture emerged very simply. It was the Sabbath; Jesus and the disciples were walking through a cornfield; the disciples ran their hands through the corn stalks, rubbed the ears of corn together to expose the seeds and then ate them. The Pharisees had interpreted the law regarding not working on the Sabbath to mean that no one could reap, winnow the corn or prepare a meal on the Sabbath, and these three offences had just been committed by the disciples. Little wonder that Jesus was exasperated by them.

There is a magnitude about the gospel which rises above the pettiness of dogmatic, albeit well-meaning, people. Hallelujah!

> *For the love of God is broader*
> *Than the measure of man's mind;*
> *And the heart of the eternal*
> *Is most wonderfully kind.*

> (*Frederick William Faber*)

→821

[11]I tell you the truth: Among those born of women there has not risen anyone greater than John the Baptist; yet he who is least in the kingdom of heaven is greater than he. [12]From the days of John the Baptist until now, the kingdom of heaven has been forcefully advancing, and forceful men lay hold of it. [13]For all the Prophets and the Law prophesied until John. [14]And if you are willing to accept it, he is the Elijah who was to come. [15]He who has ears, let him hear.

[16]"To what can I compare this generation? They are like children sitting in the marketplaces and calling out to others:

[17]"'We played the flute for you,
    and you did not dance;
 we sang a dirge,
    and you did not mourn.'

[18]For John came neither eating nor drinking, and they say, 'He has a demon.' [19]The Son of Man came eating and drinking, and they say, 'Here is a glutton and a drunkard, a friend of tax collectors and "sinners".' But wisdom is proved right by her actions."

Woe on Unrepentant Cities

[20]Then Jesus began to denounce the cities in which most of his miracles had been performed, because they did not repent. [21]"Woe to you, Korazin! Woe to you, Bethsaida! If the miracles that were performed in you had been performed in Tyre and Sidon, they would have repented long ago in sackcloth and ashes. [22]But I tell you, it will be more bearable for Tyre and Sidon on the day of judgment than for you. [23]And you, Capernaum, will you be lifted up to the skies? No, you will go down to the depths.[d] If the miracles that were performed in you had been performed in Sodom, it would have remained to this day. [24]But I tell you that it will be more bearable for Sodom on the day of judgment than for you."

Rest for the Weary

[25]At that time Jesus said, "I praise you, Father, Lord of heaven and earth, because you have hidden these things from the wise and learned, and revealed them to little children. [26]Yes, Father, for this was your good pleasure.

[27]"All things have been committed to me by my Father. No-one knows the Son except the Father, and no-one knows the Father except the Son and those to whom the Son chooses to reveal him.

[28]"Come to me, all you who are weary and burdened, and I will give you rest. [29]Take my yoke upon you and learn from me, for I am gentle and humble in heart, and you will find rest for your souls. [30]For my yoke is easy and my burden is light."

Lord of the Sabbath

12 At that time Jesus went through the cornfields on the Sabbath. His disciples were hungry and began to pick some ears of corn and eat them. [2]When the Pharisees saw this, they said to him, "Look! Your disciples are doing what is unlawful on the Sabbath."

[3]He answered, "Haven't you read what David did when he and his companions were hungry? [4]He entered the house of God, and he and his companions ate the consecrated bread—which was not lawful for them to do, but only for the priests. [5]Or haven't you read in the Law that on the Sabbath the priests in the temple desecrate the day and yet are innocent? [6]I tell you that one[a] greater than the temple is here. [7]If you had known what these words mean, 'I desire mercy, not sacrifice,'[b] you would not have condemned the innocent. [8]For the Son of Man is Lord of the Sabbath."

[9]Going on from that place, he went into their synagogue, [10]a man with a shrivelled hand was there. Looking for a reason to accuse Jesus, they asked him, "Is it lawful to heal on the Sabbath?"

[11]He said to them, "If any of you has a sheep and it falls into a pit on the Sabbath, will you not take hold of it and lift it out? [12]How much more valuable is a man than a sheep! Therefore it is lawful to do good on the Sabbath."

[13]Then he said to the man, "Stretch out your hand." So he stretched it out and it was completely restored, just as sound as the other. [14]But the Pharisees went out and plotted how they might kill Jesus.

God's Chosen Servant

[15]Aware of this, Jesus withdrew from that place. Many followed him, and he healed all their sick, [16]warning them not to tell who he was. [17]This was to fulfil what was spoken through the prophet Isaiah:

[18]"Here is my servant whom I have chosen,
    the one I love, in whom I delight;
 I will put my Spirit on him,
    and he will proclaim justice to the
        nations.
[19]He will not quarrel or cry out;
    no-one will hear his voice in the streets.
[20]A bruised reed he will not break,
    and a smouldering wick he will not snuff
        out,
 till he leads justice to victory.
[21]   In his name the nations will put their
        hope."[c]

Jesus and Beelzebub

[22]Then they brought him a demon-possessed man who was blind and mute, and Jesus healed him, so that he could both talk and see. [23]All the people were astonished and said, "Could this be the Son of David?"

[24]But when the Pharisees heard this, they said, "It is only by Beelzebub,[d] the prince of demons, that this fellow drives out demons."

[25]Jesus knew their thoughts and said to them, "Every kingdom divided against itself will be ruined, and every city or household

d23 Greek *Hades*   *a6* Or *something*; also in verses 41 and 42   *b7* Hosea 6:6   *c21* Isaiah 42:1–4
d24 Greek *Beezeboul* or *Beelzeboul*; also in verse 27

divided against itself will not stand. ²⁶If Satan drives out Satan, he is divided against himself. How then can his kingdom stand? ²⁷And if I drive out demons by Beelzebub, by whom do your people drive them out? So then, they will be your judges. ²⁸But if I drive out demons by the Spirit of God, then the kingdom of God has come upon you.

²⁹"Or again, how can anyone enter a strong man's house and carry off his possessions unless he first ties up the strong man? Then he can rob his house.

³⁰"He who is not with me is against me, and he who does not gather with me scatters. ³¹And so I tell you, every sin and blasphemy will be forgiven men, but the blasphemy against the Spirit will not be forgiven. ³²Anyone who speaks a word against the Son of Man will be forgiven, but anyone who speaks against the Holy Spirit will not be forgiven, either in this age or in the age to come.

³³"Make a tree good and its fruit will be good, or make a tree bad and its fruit will be bad, for a tree is recognised by its fruit. ³⁴You brood of vipers, how can you who are evil say anything good? For out of the overflow of the heart the mouth speaks. ³⁵The good man brings good things out of the good stored up in him, and the evil man brings evil things out of the evil stored up in him. ³⁶But I tell you that men will have to give account on the day of judgment for every careless word they have spoken. ³⁷For by your words you will be acquitted, and by your words you will be condemned."

The Sign of Jonah

³⁸Then some of the Pharisees and teachers of the law said to him, "Teacher, we want to see a miraculous sign from you."

³⁹He answered, "A wicked and adulterous generation asks for a miraculous sign! But none will be given it except the sign of the prophet Jonah. ⁴⁰For as Jonah was three days and three nights in the belly of a huge fish, so the Son of Man will be three days and three nights in the heart of the earth. ⁴¹The men of Nineveh will stand up at the judgment with this generation and condemn it; for they repented at the preaching of Jonah, and now one[e] greater than Jonah is here. ⁴²The Queen of the South will rise at the judgment with this generation and condemn it; for she came from the ends of the earth to listen to Solomon's wisdom, and now one greater than Solomon is here.

⁴³"When an evil[f] spirit comes out of a man, it goes through arid places seeking rest and does not find it. ⁴⁴Then it says, 'I will return to the house I left.' When it arrives, it finds the house unoccupied, swept clean and put in order. ⁴⁵Then it goes and takes with it seven other spirits more wicked than itself, and they go in and live there. And the final condition of that man is worse than the first. That is how it will be with this wicked generation."

Jesus' Mother and Brothers

⁴⁶While Jesus was still talking to the crowd, his mother and brothers stood outside, wanting to speak to him. ⁴⁷Someone told him, "Your mother and brothers are standing outside, wanting to speak to you."[g]

⁴⁸He replied to him, "Who is my mother, and who are my brothers?" ⁴⁹Pointing to his disciples, he said, "Here are my mother and my brothers. ⁵⁰For whoever does the will of my Father in heaven is my brother and sister and mother."

The Parable of the Sower

13 That same day Jesus went out of the house and sat by the lake. ²Such large crowds gathered round him that he got into a boat and sat in it, while all the people stood on the shore. ³Then he told them many things in parables, saying: "A farmer went out to sow his seed. ⁴As he was scattering the seed, some fell along the path, and the birds came and ate it up. ⁵Some fell on rocky places, where it did not have much soil. It sprang up quickly, because the soil was shallow. ⁶But when the sun came up, the plants were scorched, and they withered because they had no root. ⁷Other seed fell among thorns, which grew up and choked the plants. ⁸Still other seed fell on good soil, where it produced a crop—a hundred, sixty or thirty times what was sown. ⁹He who has ears, let him hear."

¹⁰The disciples came to him and asked, "Why do you speak to the people in parables?"

¹¹He replied, "The knowledge of the secrets of the kingdom of heaven has been given to you, but not to them. ¹²Whoever has will be given more, and he will have an abundance. Whoever does not have, even what he has will be taken from him. ¹³This is why I speak to them in parables:

"Though seeing, they do not see;
    though hearing, they do not hear or
        understand.

¹⁴In them is fulfilled the prophecy of Isaiah:

"'You will be ever hearing but never
        understanding;
    you will be ever seeing but never
        perceiving.
¹⁵For this people's heart has become
        calloused;
    they hardly hear with their ears,
    and they have closed their eyes.
Otherwise they might see with their eyes,
    hear with their ears,
    understand with their hearts
and turn, and I would heal them.'[a]

¹⁶"But blessed are your eyes because they see, and your ears because they hear. ¹⁷For I tell you the truth, many prophets and righteous men longed to see what you see but did not see it, and to hear what you hear but did not hear it.

---

[e]41 Or *something*; also in verse 42   [f]43 Greek *unclean*   [g]47 Some manuscripts do not have verse 47.
[a]15 Isaiah 6:9,10

'The field is the world, and the good seed stands for the sons of the kingdom. The weeds are the sons of the evil one' (v. 38).

THE KINGDOM OF HEAVEN IS LIKE . . . So begin a number of parables, the first of which relates to the enemy who sowed bad seed in the field after the good seed had been sown. Our Lord's listeners would be only too aware of the problem. The bad seed was a weed known as 'bearded darnel'. In its early stages it was virtually indistinguishable from wheat. As it grew, its roots intertwined the roots of the wheat, making it impossible to separate without damaging the good seed. The only practical course to follow was to allow the good and bad seeds to grow together, harvest them together, separating them after they had been cut. The grain from each was alike in size but not in colour. Since darnel was slightly poisonous it had to be removed.

The parable relates to the problem of the existence of bad people in the world and the Church. It is not always easy for us to differentiate between the true and the counterfeit. There is a substantial grey area between those who are clearly good and those who are clearly bad.

Our Lord seems to be counselling us to be patient with other people. We are not to judge. We have neither knowledge enough nor wisdom enough to do so. It has been well said that when we point one finger at another, we point three at ourselves; but judgement there will be, and he will be the judge.

'We have not stopped praying for you and asking God to fill you with the knowledge of his will through all spiritual wisdom and understanding. And we pray this in order that you may live a life worthy of the Lord and may please him in every way: bearing fruit in every good work, growing in the knowledge of God.'

→822

MATTHEW 14:12, 13
'When Jesus heard what had happened, he withdrew by boat privately to a solitary place' (v. 13a).

IF JESUS needed a reminder that he had been sent into an evil and hostile world, he had it in the death of John the Baptist. That his forerunner should die was one thing, that he should die with such sickening violence, his head presented as a trophy to an incredibly evil woman, was quite another. Understandably, Jesus withdrew privately to a solitary place. He had much to think about.

We hardly dare intrude upon the possible thoughts racing through his mind, which stimulated his need for quiet reflection. He knew that the hostility of the Pharisees and Herod foreshadowed his own death, which would also be violent. John's death served to concentrate in one event the historic conflict between good and evil, highlighting the priority that if we are to fear at all, we must fear the one who can destroy the soul rather than the one who destroys the body. Jesus would be confident that John had fulfilled his destiny and would be praising God for his faithfulness and steadfastness. We also speculate that Jesus needed time in which to finetune his ministry, ensuring he had time to do all that was necessary before he, too, was killed.

The desire of Jesus for solitude finds an echo in our own hearts. Even though we walk daily with the Lord, we need those special times of rich and deep communion to centre our hearts more truly upon him.

> *O thou by whom we come to God,*
> *The life, the truth, the way!*
> *The path of prayer thyself has trod:*
> *Lord, teach us how to pray!*

(James Montgomery)

→825

18"Listen then to what the parable of the sower means: 19When anyone hears the message about the kingdom and does not understand it, the evil one comes and snatches away what was sown in his heart. This is the seed sown along the path. 20The one who received the seed that fell on rocky places is the man who hears the word and at once receives it with joy. 21But since he has no root, he lasts only a short time. When trouble or persecution comes because of the word, he quickly falls away. 22The one who received the seed that fell among the thorns is the man who hears the word, but the worries of this life and the deceitfulness of wealth choke it, making it unfruitful. 23But the one who received the seed that fell on good soil is the man who hears the word and understands it. He produces a crop, yielding a hundred, sixty or thirty times what was sown."

The Parable of the Weeds

24Jesus told them another parable: "The kingdom of heaven is like a man who sowed good seed in his field. 25But while everyone was sleeping, his enemy came and sowed weeds among the wheat, and went away. 26When the wheat sprouted and formed ears, then the weeds also appeared.

27"The owner's servants came to him and said, 'Sir, didn't you sow good seed in your field? Where then did the weeds come from?'

28"'An enemy did this,' he replied.

"The servants asked him, 'Do you want us to go and pull them up?'

29"'No,' he answered, 'because while you are pulling the weeds, you may root up the wheat with them. 30Let both grow together until the harvest. At that time I will tell the harvesters: First collect the weeds and tie them in bundles to be burned; then gather the wheat and bring it into my barn.'"

The Parables of the Mustard Seed and the Yeast

31He told them another parable: "The kingdom of heaven is like a mustard seed, which a man took and planted in his field. 32Though it is the smallest of all your seeds, yet when it grows, it is the largest of garden plants and becomes a tree, so that the birds of the air come and perch in its branches."

33He told them still another parable: "The kingdom of heaven is like yeast that a woman took and mixed into a large amount*b* of flour until it worked all through the dough."

34Jesus spoke all these things to the crowd in parables; he did not say anything to them without using a parable. 35So was fulfilled what was spoken through the prophet:

"I will open my mouth in parables,
   I will utter things hidden since the
      creation of the world."*c*

The Parable of the Weeds Explained

36Then he left the crowd and went into the house. His disciples came to him and said,

"Explain to us the parable of the weeds in the field."

37He answered, "The one who sowed the good seed is the Son of Man. 38The field is the world, and the good seed stands for the sons of the kingdom. The weeds are the sons of the evil one, 39and the enemy who sows them is the devil. The harvest is the end of the age, and the harvesters are angels.

40"As the weeds are pulled up and burned in the fire, so it will be at the end of the age. 41The Son of Man will send out his angels, and they will weed out of his kingdom everything that causes sin and all who do evil. 42They will throw them into the fiery furnace, where there will be weeping and gnashing of teeth. 43Then the righteous will shine like the sun in the kingdom of their Father. He who has ears, let him hear.

The Parables of the Hidden Treasure and the Pearl

44"The kingdom of heaven is like treasure hidden in a field. When a man found it, he hid it again, and then in his joy went and sold all he had and bought that field.

45"Again, the kingdom of heaven is like a merchant looking for fine pearls. 46When he found one of great value, he went away and sold everything he had and bought it.

The Parable of the Net

47"Once again, the kingdom of heaven is like a net that was let down into the lake and caught all kinds of fish. 48When it was full, the fishermen pulled it up on the shore. Then they sat down and collected the good fish in baskets, but threw the bad away. 49This is how it will be at the end of the age. The angels will come and separate the wicked from the righteous 50and throw them into the fiery furnace, where there will be weeping and gnashing of teeth.

51"Have you understood all these things?" Jesus asked.

"Yes," they replied.

52He said to them, "Therefore every teacher of the law who has been instructed about the kingdom of heaven is like the owner of a house who brings out of his storeroom new treasures as well as old."

A Prophet Without Honour

53When Jesus had finished these parables, he moved on from there. 54Coming to his home town, he began teaching the people in their synagogue, and they were amazed. "Where did this man get this wisdom and these miraculous powers?" they asked. 55"Isn't this the carpenter's son? Isn't his mother's name Mary, and aren't his brothers James, Joseph, Simon and Judas? 56Aren't all his sisters with us? Where then did this man get all these things?" 57And they took offence at him.

But Jesus said to them, "Only in his home town and in his own house is a prophet without honour."

---

*b*33 Greek *three satas* (probably about ⅗ bushel or 22 litres)   *c*35 Psalm 78:2

⁵⁸And he did not do many miracles there because of their lack of faith.

John the Baptist Beheaded

14 At that time Herod the tetrarch heard the reports about Jesus, ²and he said to his attendants, "This is John the Baptist; he has risen from the dead! That is why miraculous powers are at work in him."

³Now Herod had arrested John and bound him and put him in prison because of Herodias, his brother Philip's wife, ⁴for John had been saying to him: "It is not lawful for you to have her." ⁵Herod wanted to kill John, but he was afraid of the people, because they considered him a prophet.

⁶On Herod's birthday the daughter of Herodias danced for them and pleased Herod so much ⁷that he promised with an oath to give her whatever she asked. ⁸Prompted by her mother, she said, "Give me here on a platter the head of John the Baptist." ⁹The king was distressed, but because of his oaths and his dinner guests, he ordered that her request be granted ¹⁰and had John beheaded in the prison. ¹¹His head was brought in on a platter and given to the girl, who carried it to her mother. ¹²John's disciples came and took his body and buried it. Then they went and told Jesus.

Jesus Feeds the Five Thousand

¹³When Jesus heard what had happened, he withdrew by boat privately to a solitary place. Hearing of this, the crowds followed him on foot from the towns. ¹⁴When Jesus landed and saw a large crowd, he had compassion on them and healed their sick.

¹⁵As evening approached, the disciples came to him and said, "This is a remote place, and it's already getting late. Send the crowds away, so that they can go to the villages and buy themselves some food."

¹⁶Jesus replied, "They do not need to go away. You give them something to eat."

¹⁷"We have here only five loaves of bread and two fish," they answered.

¹⁸"Bring them here to me," he said. ¹⁹And he directed the people to sit down on the grass. Taking the five loaves and the two fish and looking up to heaven, he gave thanks and broke the loaves. Then he gave them to the disciples, and the disciples gave them to the people. ²⁰They all ate and were satisfied, and the disciples picked up twelve basketfuls of broken pieces that were left over. ²¹The number of those who ate was about five thousand men, besides women and children.

Jesus Walks on the Water

²²Immediately Jesus made the disciples get into the boat and go on ahead of him to the other side, while he dismissed the crowd. ²³After he had dismissed them, he went up on a mountainside by himself to pray. When evening came, he was there alone, ²⁴but the boat was already a considerable distance*ᵃ* from land, buffeted by the waves because the wind was against it.

²⁵During the fourth watch of the night Jesus went out to them, walking on the lake. ²⁶When the disciples saw him walking on the lake, they were terrified. "It's a ghost," they said, and cried out in fear.

²⁷But Jesus immediately said to them: "Take courage! It is I. Don't be afraid."

²⁸"Lord, if it's you," Peter replied, "tell me to come to you on the water."

²⁹"Come," he said.

Then Peter got down out of the boat, walked on the water and came towards Jesus. ³⁰But when he saw the wind, he was afraid and, beginning to sink, cried out, "Lord, save me!"

³¹Immediately Jesus reached out his hand and caught him. "You of little faith," he said, "why did you doubt?"

³²And when they climbed into the boat, the wind died down. ³³Then those who were in the boat worshipped him, saying, "Truly you are the Son of God."

³⁴When they had crossed over, they landed at Gennesaret. ³⁵And when the men of that place recognised Jesus, they sent word to all the surrounding country. People brought all their sick to him ³⁶and begged him to let the sick just touch the edge of his cloak, and all who touched him were healed.

Clean and Unclean

15 Then some Pharisees and teachers of the law came to Jesus from Jerusalem and asked, ²"Why do your disciples break the tradition of the elders? They don't wash their hands before they eat!"

³Jesus replied, "And why do you break the command of God for the sake of your tradition? ⁴For God said, 'Honour your father and mother'*ᵃ* and 'Anyone who curses his father or mother must be put to death.'*ᵇ* ⁵But you say that if a man says to his father or mother, 'Whatever help you might otherwise have received from me is a gift devoted to God,' ⁶he is not to 'honour his father'*ᶜ* with it. Thus you nullify the word of God for the sake of your tradition. ⁷You hypocrites! Isaiah was right when he prophesied about you:

⁸"'These people honour me with their lips,
   but their hearts are far from me.
⁹They worship me in vain;
   their teachings are but rules taught by
       men.'*ᵈ*"

¹⁰Jesus called the crowd to him and said, "Listen and understand. ¹¹What goes into a man's mouth does not make him 'unclean', but what comes out of his mouth, that is what makes him 'unclean'."

¹²Then the disciples came to him and asked, "Do you know that the Pharisees were offended when they heard this?"

¹³He replied, "Every plant that my heavenly Father has not planted will be pulled up by the roots. ¹⁴Leave them; they are blind guides.*ᵉ* If a blind man leads a blind man, both will fall into a pit."

¹⁵Peter said, "Explain the parable to us."

---

*ᵃ*24 Greek *many stadia*   *ᵃ*4 Exodus 20:12; Deut. 5:16
*ᶜ*6 Some manuscripts *father or his mother*   *ᵈ*9 Isaiah 29:13   *ᵇ*4 Exodus 21:17; Lev. 20:9   *ᵉ*14 Some manuscripts *guides of the blind*

MATTHEW 15:21–8

'A Canaanite woman from that vicinity came to him, crying out, "Lord, Son of David, have mercy on me! My daughter is suffering terribly from demon-possession" ' (v. 22).

AT THIS STAGE, the policy of Jesus was to concentrate on 'the lost sheep of Israel'. We assume that he and the disciples were in this region, north of Galilee, because he needed privacy and time to instruct his disciples. Somehow this woman, whose nation was one of Israel's sometime enemies, had heard of him and brought her daughter's need to him.

Jesus seemed disinclined to be helpful at first which was out of character with him, unless he was seeking to find and strengthen her faith. We note, for instance, that she qualified his lordship by his human title, but when she knelt before him (with her growing faith seeing beyond the human to the divine?), she called him Lord, in a more definitive sense. It almost seems as though Jesus handled her rather roughly with the reference to the dogs, but Barclay points out that the word used for dogs was not the word for the vicious, uncared for scavengers of the streets, but rather, the small, treasured, pet dog. We also assume that Jesus said it with a smile on his face, a twinkle in his eye, and a chuckle in his voice.

The mother, compassionate, cheerful and yet persistent, her faith growing by the moment, gave the answer which obviously delighted our Lord. And he who had difficulty in not rising to an obvious need, healed the girl from that moment.

> *Lowly paths our Lord has taken.*
> *And he proved by word and deed,*
> *For the lonely and forsaken*
> *There is grace beyond all need.*

> (*Albert Orsborn*)

→826

MATTHEW 16:17–20
'I will give you the keys of the kingdom of heaven' (v. 19a).

ONLY TWICE is the term 'Church' used in the Gospels, each time being recorded in Matthew's Gospel. In neither instance does our Lord have an institution in mind, but rather an assembly or congregation of people. In fact, the New Testament is remarkably consistent on this issue. The 'Church' is always people, a congregation 'called out' from the world to belong to Christ. Inevitably, with the passage of time and the need to accommodate the growing numbers of believers, venues had to be established, worship would evolve and service be regulated, but, even so, the Church is people, not buildings or an institution. It is an organism, not an organization.

The keys of the kingdom, although given to Peter and used by him, quickly passed to the worshipping and witnessing body of believers. Peter demonstrated his stewardship of the keys on the day of Pentecost. Following his sermon on that day, 3,000 people entered the kingdom. The Holy Spirit also used Peter in the house of Cornelius to open the door of the kingdom to the Gentiles, and his witness was crucial at the Council of Jerusalem which established the place of Gentiles in the Church. But others confirmed that they too held this all-important key, not least Philip, Paul and Barnabas.

It is true to say that opening the door of the kingdom, and responsibility for discipline within the Church (v. 19b) are the privileges of the Church, the people who are Christ's body.

> *O lead me, Lord, that I may lead*
> *The wandering and the wavering feet;*
> *O feed me, Lord, that I may feed*
> *Thy hungering ones with manna sweet.*

> *(Frances Ridley Havergal)*

→829

[16] "Are you still so dull?" Jesus asked them. [17] "Don't you see that whatever enters the mouth goes into the stomach and then out of the body? [18] But the things that come out of the mouth come from the heart, and these make a man 'unclean'. [19] For out of the heart come evil thoughts, murder, adultery, sexual immorality, theft, false testimony, slander. [20] These are what make a man 'unclean'; but eating with unwashed hands does not make him 'unclean'."

The Faith of the Canaanite Woman

[21] Leaving that place, Jesus withdrew to the region of Tyre and Sidon. [22] A Canaanite woman from that vicinity came to him, crying out, "Lord, Son of David, have mercy on me! My daughter is suffering terribly from demon-possession."

[23] Jesus did not answer a word. So his disciples came to him and urged him, "Send her away, for she keeps crying out after us."

[24] He answered, "I was sent only to the lost sheep of Israel."

[25] The woman came and knelt before him. "Lord, help me!" she said.

[26] He replied, "It is not right to take the children's bread and toss it to their dogs."

[27] "Yes, Lord," she said, "but even the dogs eat the crumbs that fall from their masters' table."

[28] Then Jesus answered, "Woman, you have great faith! Your request is granted." And her daughter was healed from that very hour.

Jesus Feeds the Four Thousand

[29] Jesus left there and went along the Sea of Galilee. Then he went up on a mountainside and sat down. [30] Great crowds came to him, bringing the lame, the blind, the crippled, the mute and many others, and laid them at his feet; and he healed them. [31] The people were amazed when they saw the mute speaking, the crippled made well, the lame walking and the blind seeing. And they praised the God of Israel.

[32] Jesus called his disciples to him and said, "I have compassion for these people; they have already been with me three days and have nothing to eat. I do not want to send them away hungry, or they may collapse on the way."

[33] His disciples answered, "Where could we get enough bread in this remote place to feed such a crowd?"

[34] "How many loaves do you have?" Jesus asked.

"Seven," they replied, "and a few small fish."

[35] He told the crowd to sit down on the ground. [36] Then he took the seven loaves and the fish, and when he had given thanks, he broke them and gave them to the disciples, and they in turn to the people. [37] They all ate and were satisfied. Afterwards the disciples picked up seven basketfuls of broken pieces that were left over. [38] The number of those who ate was four thousand, besides women and children. [39] After Jesus had sent the crowd away, he got into the boat and went to the vicinity of Magadan.

The Demand for a Sign

16 The Pharisees and Sadducees came to Jesus and tested him by asking him to show them a sign from heaven.

[2] He replied,[a] "When evening comes, you say, 'It will be fair weather, for the sky is red,' [3] and in the morning, 'Today it will be stormy, for the sky is red and overcast.' You know how to interpret the appearance of the sky, but you cannot interpret the signs of the times. [4] A wicked and adulterous generation looks for a miraculous sign, but none will be given it except the sign of Jonah." Jesus then left them and went away.

The Yeast of the Pharisees and Sadducees

[5] When they went across the lake, the disciples forgot to take bread. [6] "Be careful," Jesus said to them. "Be on your guard against the yeast of the Pharisees and Sadducees."

[7] They discussed this among themselves and said, "It is because we didn't bring any bread."

[8] Aware of their discussion, Jesus asked, "You of little faith, why are you talking among yourselves about having no bread? [9] Do you still not understand? Don't you remember the five loaves for the five thousand, and how many basketfuls you gathered? [10] Or the seven loaves for the four thousand, and how many basketfuls you gathered? [11] How is it you don't understand that I was not talking to you about bread? But be on your guard against the yeast of the Pharisees and Sadducees." [12] Then they understood that he was not telling them to guard against the yeast used in bread, but against the teaching of the Pharisees and Sadducees.

Peter's Confession of Christ

[13] When Jesus came to the region of Caesarea Philippi, he asked his disciples, "Who do people say the Son of Man is?"

[14] They replied, "Some say John the Baptist; others say Elijah; and still others, Jeremiah or one of the prophets."

[15] "But what about you?" he asked. "Who do you say I am?"

[16] Simon Peter answered, "You are the Christ,[b] the Son of the living God."

[17] Jesus replied, "Blessed are you, Simon son of Jonah, for this was not revealed to you by man, but by my Father in heaven. [18] And I tell you that you are Peter,[c] and on this rock I will build my church, and the gates of Hades[d] will not overcome it.[e] [19] I will give you the keys of the kingdom of heaven; whatever you bind on earth will be[f] bound in heaven, and whatever you loose on earth will be[f] loosed in heaven." [20] Then he warned his disciples not to tell anyone that he was the Christ.

---

[a]2 Some early manuscripts do not have the rest of verse 2 and all of verse 3.   [b]16 Or *Messiah*; also in verse 20   [c]18 *Peter* means *rock*.   [d]18 Or *hell*   [e]18 Or *not prove stronger than it*   [f]19 Or *have been*

Jesus Predicts His Death

21From that time on Jesus began to explain to his disciples that he must go to Jerusalem and suffer many things at the hands of the elders, chief priests and teachers of the law, and that he must be killed and on the third day be raised to life.

22Peter took him aside and began to rebuke him. "Never, Lord!" he said. "This shall never happen to you!"

23Jesus turned and said to Peter, "Get behind me, Satan! You are a stumbling-block to me; you do not have in mind the things of God, but the things of men."

24Then Jesus said to his disciples, "If anyone would come after me, he must deny himself and take up his cross and follow me. 25For whoever wants to save his life[g] will lose it, but whoever loses his life for me will find it. 26What good will it be for a man if he gains the whole world, yet forfeits his soul? Or what can a man give in exchange for his soul? 27For the Son of Man is going to come in his Father's glory with his angels, and then he will reward each person according to what he has done. 28I tell you the truth, some who are standing here will not taste death before they see the Son of Man coming in his kingdom."

The Transfiguration

17 After six days Jesus took with him Peter, James and John the brother of James, and led them up a high mountain by themselves. 2There he was transfigured before them. His face shone like the sun, and his clothes became as white as the light. 3Just then there appeared before them Moses and Elijah, talking with Jesus.

4Peter said to Jesus, "Lord, it is good for us to be here. If you wish, I will put up three shelters—one for you, one for Moses and one for Elijah."

5While he was still speaking, a bright cloud enveloped them, and a voice from the cloud said, "This is my Son, whom I love; with him I am well pleased. Listen to him!"

6When the disciples heard this, they fell face down to the ground, terrified. 7But Jesus came and touched them. "Get up," he said. "Don't be afraid." 8When they looked up, they saw no-one except Jesus.

9As they were coming down the mountain, Jesus instructed them, "Don't tell anyone what you have seen, until the Son of Man has been raised from the dead."

10The disciples asked him, "Why then do the teachers of the law say that Elijah must come first?"

11Jesus replied, "To be sure, Elijah comes and will restore all things. 12But I tell you, Elijah has already come, and they did not recognise him, but have done to him everything they wished. In the same way the Son of Man is going to suffer at their hands." 13Then the disciples understood that he was talking to them about John the Baptist.

The Healing of a Boy With a Demon

14When they came to the crowd, a man approached Jesus and knelt before him. 15"Lord, have mercy on my son," he said. "He has seizures and is suffering greatly. He often falls into the fire or into the water. 16I brought him to your disciples, but they could not heal him."

17"O unbelieving and perverse generation," Jesus replied, "how long shall I stay with you? How long shall I put up with you? Bring the boy here to me." 18Jesus rebuked the demon, and it came out of the boy, and he was healed from that moment.

19Then the disciples came to Jesus in private and asked, "Why couldn't we drive it out?"

20He replied, "Because you have so little faith. I tell you the truth, if you have faith as small as a mustard seed, you can say to this mountain, 'Move from here to there' and it will move. Nothing will be impossible for you."[a]

22When they came together in Galilee, he said to them, "The Son of Man is going to be betrayed into the hands of men. 23They will kill him, and on the third day he will be raised to life." And the disciples were filled with grief.

The Temple Tax

24After Jesus and his disciples arrived in Capernaum, the collectors of the two-drachma tax came to Peter and asked, "Doesn't your teacher pay the temple tax?"[b] 25"Yes, he does," he replied.

When Peter came into the house, Jesus was the first to speak. "What do you think, Simon?" he asked. "From whom do the kings of the earth collect duty and taxes —from their own sons or from others?"

26"From others," Peter answered.

"Then the sons are exempt," Jesus said to him. 27"But so that we may not offend them, go to the lake and throw out your line. Take the first fish you catch; open its mouth and you will find a four-drachma coin. Take it and give it to them for my tax and yours."

The Greatest in the Kingdom of Heaven

18 At that time the disciples came to Jesus and asked, "Who is the greatest in the kingdom of heaven?"

2He called a little child and had him stand among them. 3And he said: "I tell you the truth, unless you change and become like little children, you will never enter the kingdom of heaven. 4Therefore, whoever humbles himself like this child is the greatest in the kingdom of heaven.

5"And whoever welcomes a little child like this in my name welcomes me. 6But if anyone causes one of these little ones who believe in me to sin, it would be better for him to have a large millstone hung around his neck and to be drowned in the depths of the sea.

---

[g]25 The Greek word means either *life* or *soul*; also in verse 26.
[a]20 Some manuscripts *you.* 21*But this kind does not go out except by prayer and fasting.*
[b]24 Greek *the two drachmas*

MATTHEW 17:1–3
'Just then there appeared before them Moses and Elijah, talking with Jesus'
(v. 3).

TWO GREAT FIGURES from the past came from the eternal world to share these moments with Jesus. We can understand why Moses should be one because of his outstanding qualities of leadership and goodness. Moses had also prophesied of Christ, but we need to speculate a little more regarding the choice of Elijah. He was, of course, one of the earliest prophets, who holds an exalted place in Jewish history, but it was commonly believed that Elijah would appear to prepare the way for the Messiah. Jesus himself confirmed this, revealing that in John the Baptist the expectation had been fulfilled.

Moses and Elijah talked with Jesus about his 'decease' or his 'departure'. The Greek word used was the appropriate and imaginative word 'exodus'. Our Lord was to make no ordinary passage from this world. It is of interest that neither Moses nor Elijah went to heaven in an ordinary kind of way either.

Did these two men, standing with Jesus on a hillside tell him about that other hill where two quite different men would be with him? One who would verbally abuse him, and the other who would take a believing, almost prophetic, role by asking, 'Jesus, remember me when you come into your kingdom'? But Moses and Elijah would reassure Jesus that his heavenly Father would be with him, regardless of his feelings on that day.

> *God is not absent from this world of ours,*
> *Nor stands he on the sidelines of our field,*
> *But he is with us in our testing hours*
> *Combating evil; forcing it to yield.*
> *Our God is with us! Had we eyes to see*
> *We would perceive his glorious majesty.*

→830

MATTHEW 18:21–35
'Jesus answered, "I tell you , not seven times, but seventy-seven times" ' (v. 22).

ON THE AUTHORITY OF AMOS, the rabbis taught that forgiveness should not be extended more than three times. Peter was clearly concerned about brotherly relationships and, with the rabbinical figure of three forgivings in his mind, he no doubt thought that by doubling it and adding one for good measure, he would be somewhere near his generous Lord's standard. He must have been a surprised man to hear: 'not seven times, but seventy-seven times'. Our Lord then launched into another graphic parable about the unmerciful servant who received mercy from his king, but who then showed no mercy to a fellow-servant. The debt of which he was forgiven by the king was incredibly high and the debt of his fellow-servant which he refused to forgive was incredibly low.

The forgiven spirit must always be a forgiving spirit. We who stand alongside the servant, owing so much to our heavenly king and being forgiven for it, must not stand beside that same servant and refuse to forgive the relatively small debts which are owed to us. Of divine forgiveness there is no end. Likewise there should be no end to ours. No one can keep count of acts of forgiveness up to four hundred and ninety! Long before then their spirit would match that of their Saviour.

The principle appears to be that forgiveness begets 'forgiveness'. The forgiven becomes the forgiving. In our parable the servant is the exception to this rule and our Lord makes it clear that the unforgiving are those who cannot be forgiven.

> *For the peace of forgiveness,*
> *And the grace to forgive,*
> *I thank thee Lord.*

7"Woe to the world because of the things that cause people to sin! Such things must come, but woe to the man through whom they come! [8]If your hand or your foot causes you to sin, cut it off and throw it away. It is better for you to enter life maimed or crippled than to have two hands or two feet and be thrown into eternal fire. [9]And if your eye causes you to sin, gouge it out and throw it away. It is better for you to enter life with one eye than to have two eyes and be thrown into the fire of hell.

The Parable of the Lost Sheep

[10]"See that you do not look down on one of these little ones. For I tell you that their angels in heaven always see the face of my Father in heaven.[a]

[12]"What do you think? If a man owns a hundred sheep, and one of them wanders away, will he not leave the ninety-nine on the hills and go to look for the one that wandered off? [13]And if he finds it, I tell you the truth, he is happier about that one sheep than about the ninety-nine that did not wander off. [14]In the same way your Father in heaven is not willing that any of these little ones should be lost.

A Brother Who Sins Against You

[15]"If your brother sins against you,[b] go and show him his fault, just between the two of you. If he listens to you, you have won your brother over. [16]But if he will not listen, take one or two others along, so that 'every matter may be established by the testimony of two or three witnesses.'[c] [17]If he refuses to listen to them, tell it to the church; and if he refuses to listen even to the church, treat him as you would a pagan or a tax collector.

[18]"I tell you the truth, whatever you bind on earth will be[d] bound in heaven, and whatever you loose on earth will be[d] loosed in heaven.

[19]"Again, I tell you that if two of you on earth agree about anything you ask for, it will be done for you by my Father in heaven. [20]For where two or three come together in my name, there am I with them."

The Parable of the Unmerciful Servant

[21]Then Peter came to Jesus and asked, "Lord, how many times shall I forgive my brother when he sins against me? Up to seven times?"

[22]Jesus answered, "I tell you, not seven times, but seventy-seven times.[e]

[23]"Therefore, the kingdom of heaven is like a king who wanted to settle accounts with his servants. [24]As he began the settlement, a man who owed him ten thousand talents[f] was brought to him. [25]Since he was not able to pay, the master ordered that he and his wife and his children and all that he had be sold to repay the debt.

[26]"The servant fell on his knees before

him. 'Be patient with me,' he begged, 'and I will pay back everything.' [27]The servant's master took pity on him, cancelled the debt and let him go.

[28]"But when that servant went out, he found one of his fellow-servants who owed him a hundred denarii.[g] He grabbed him and began to choke him. 'Pay back what you owe me!' he demanded.

[29]"His fellow-servant fell to his knees and begged him, 'Be patient with me, and I will pay you back.'

[30]"But he refused. Instead, he went off and had the man thrown into prison until he could pay the debt. [31]When the other servants saw what had happened, they were greatly distressed and went and told their master everything that had happened.

[32]"Then the master called the servant in. 'You wicked servant,' he said, 'I cancelled all that debt of yours because you begged me to. [33]Shouldn't you have had mercy on your fellow-servant just as I had on you?' [34]In anger his master turned him over to the jailers to be tortured, until he should pay back all he owed.

[35]"This is how my heavenly Father will treat each of you unless you forgive your brother from your heart."

Divorce

19 When Jesus had finished saying these things, he left Galilee and went into the region of Judea to the other side of the Jordan. [2]Large crowds followed him, and he healed them there.

[3]Some Pharisees came to him to test him. They asked, "Is it lawful for a man to divorce his wife for any and every reason?"

[4]"Haven't you read," he replied, "that at the beginning the Creator 'made them male and female',[a] [5]and said, 'For this reason a man will leave his father and mother and be united to his wife, and the two will become one flesh'[b]? [6]So they are no longer two, but one. Therefore what God has joined together, let man not separate."

[7]"Why then," they asked, "did Moses command that a man give his wife a certificate of divorce and send her away?"

[8]Jesus replied, "Moses permitted you to divorce your wives because your hearts were hard. But it was not this way from the beginning. [9]I tell you that anyone who divorces his wife, except for marital unfaithfulness, and marries another woman commits adultery."

[10]The disciples said to him, "If this is the situation between a husband and wife, it is better not to marry."

[11]Jesus replied, "Not everyone can accept this word, but only those to whom it has been given. [12]For some are eunuchs because they were born that way; others were made that way by men; and others have renounced marriage[c] because of the kingdom of heaven. The one who can accept this should accept it."

---

[a]10 Some manuscripts *heaven.* [11]*The Son of Man came to save what was lost.*
[b]15 Some manuscripts do not have *against you.*   [c]16 Deut. 19:15   [d]18 Or *have been*
[e]22 Or *seventy times seven*   [f]24 That is, millions of pounds   [g]28 That is, a few pounds   [a]4 Gen. 1:27
[b]5 Gen. 2:24   [c]12 Or *have made themselves eunuchs*

The Little Children and Jesus

13Then little children were brought to Jesus for him to place his hands on them and pray for them. But the disciples rebuked those who brought them.

14Jesus said, "Let the little children come to me, and do not hinder them, for the kingdom of heaven belongs to such as these."
15When he had placed his hands on them, he went on from there.

The Rich Young Man

16Now a man came up to Jesus and asked, "Teacher, what good thing must I do to get eternal life?"

17"Why do you ask me about what is good?" Jesus replied. "There is only One who is good. If you want to enter life, obey the commandments."

18"Which ones?" the man enquired.

Jesus replied, "'Do not murder, do not commit adultery, do not steal, do not give false testimony, 19honour your father and mother,'d and 'love your neighbour as yourself.'e"

20"All these I have kept," the young man said. "What do I still lack?"

21Jesus answered, "If you want to be perfect, go, sell your possessions and give to the poor, and you will have treasure in heaven. Then come, follow me."

22When the young man heard this, he went away sad, because he had great wealth.

23Then Jesus said to his disciples, "I tell you the truth, it is hard for a rich man to enter the kingdom of heaven. 24Again I tell you, it is easier for a camel to go through the eye of a needle than for a rich man to enter the kingdom of God."

25When the disciples heard this, they were greatly astonished and asked, "Who then can be saved?"

26Jesus looked at them and said, "With man this is impossible, but with God all things are possible."

27Peter answered him, "We have left everything to follow you! What then will there be for us?"

28Jesus said to them, "I tell you the truth, at the renewal of all things, when the Son of Man sits on his glorious throne, you who have followed me will also sit on twelve thrones, judging the twelve tribes of Israel.
29And everyone who has left houses or brothers or sisters or father or motherf or children or fields for my sake will receive a hundred times as much and will inherit eternal life. 30But many who are first will be last, and many who are last will be first.

The Parable of the Workers in the Vineyard

20 "For the kingdom of heaven is like a landowner who went out early in the morning to hire men to work in his vineyard. 2He agreed to pay them a denarius for the day and sent them into his vineyard.

3"About the third hour he went out and saw others standing in the market-place doing nothing. 4He told them, 'You also go and work in my vineyard, and I will pay you whatever is right.' 5So they went.

"He went out again about the sixth hour and the ninth hour and did the same thing. 6About the eleventh hour he went out and found still others standing around. He asked them, 'Why have you been standing here all day long doing nothing?'

7"Because no-one has hired us,' they answered.

"He said to them, 'You also go and work in my vineyard.'

8"When evening came, the owner of the vineyard said to his foreman, 'Call the workers and pay them their wages, beginning with the last ones hired and going on to the first.'

9"The workers who were hired about the eleventh hour came and each received a denarius. 10So when those came who were hired first, they expected to receive more. But each one of them also received a denarius. 11When they received it, they began to grumble against the landowner. 12"These men who were hired last worked only one hour,' they said, 'and you have made them equal to us who have borne the burden of the work and the heat of the day.'

13"But he answered one of them, 'Friend, I am not being unfair to you. Didn't you agree to work for a denarius? 14Take your pay and go. I want to give the man who was hired last the same as I gave you. 15Don't I have the right to do what I want with my own money? Or are you envious because I am generous?'

16"So the last will be first, and the first will be last."

Jesus Again Predicts His Death

17Now as Jesus was going up to Jerusalem, he took the twelve disciples aside and said to them, 18"We are going up to Jerusalem, and the Son of Man will be betrayed to the chief priests and the teachers of the law. They will condemn him to death 19and will turn him over to the Gentiles to be mocked and flogged and crucified. On the third day he will be raised to life!"

A Mother's Request

20Then the mother of Zebedee's sons came to Jesus with her sons and, kneeling down, asked a favour of him.

21"What is it you want?" he asked.

She said, "Grant that one of these two sons of mine may sit at your right and the other at your left in your kingdom."

22"You don't know what you are asking," Jesus said to them. "Can you drink the cup I am going to drink?"

"We can," they answered.

23Jesus said to them, "You will indeed drink from my cup, but to sit at my right or left is not for me to grant. These places belong to those for whom they have been prepared by my Father."

24When the ten heard about this, they were

d19 Exodus 20:12–16; Deut. 5:16–20   e19 Lev. 19:18   f29 Some manuscripts mother or wife

MATTHEW 19:3–12
'Some Pharisees came to him to test him. They asked, "Is it lawful for a man to divorce his wife for any and every reason?" ' (v. 3).

JESUS TOOK THE CONCEPT of marriage back to first principles. From creation it was intended that a married couple would become as 'one flesh'. The union was designed by God to be inviolable. The Pharisees, perceiving a conflict between Jesus and the authority of Moses, promptly asked why Moses had initiated divorce if it was not right. Our Lord explained that the Mosaic permission to divorce was due to human hardness. He made it clear that divorce for 'any and every reason' trivialized a divine institution.

The majority of people, not least Christians, take marriage very seriously and infidelity remains the major cause for divorce. It is true that changing social conditions, including the equality of the sexes (in biblical days a woman could rarely divorce a man), greater expectations from marriage, help for single families, etc., have served to increase the number of, and reasons for, divorce. Nevertheless, except for a small number of people, most couples try hard to make their marriages work. A great deal of pain has been inflicted by those who, technically faithful, have, one way or another, abused their partners, thereby destroying the trust upon which a marriage depends. Some marriages have also been beset by an unendurable incompatibility. There are also those who, for one reason or another, should not engage in marriage.

More care is being shown these days for the quality of marriage. Increasingly, guidance is being given before marriage to ensure a good relationship, and more marriage enrichment courses are being held for those who want to experience an even better relationship.

Pray more for the enhancement of Christian marriages. They are crucial to us and to God.

→834

MATTHEW 21:1–11
'When Jesus entered Jerusalem, the whole city was stirred and asked, "Who is this?" ' (v. 10).

'WHO IS THIS?' The question reverberated through the streets of Jerusalem on that first Palm Sunday. The people had never seen a sight quite like this. It was not the traditional pattern of Israel's monarchs.

A donkey, not a war horse, was Jesus' means of entering Jerusalem. Palm branches, not spears, were his escort. The songs of children, not the shouts of soldiers, were his welcome. He entered no palace, commandeered no guards, signed no decrees. We read that the whole city was stirred and asked, 'Who is this?'

The answer to that question had been given centuries before by the prophet Zechariah, who predicted this very moment: 'Rejoice greatly, O Daughter of Zion! Shout, Daughter of Jerusalem! See, your king comes to you, righteous and having salvation, gentle and riding on a donkey' (Zech. 9:9).

This bronzed Galilean riding into the city of Jerusalem that day was the king. He was the king of the universe, the sovereign of the cosmos. He was the God who had flung galaxies into space. He was the astonishing composite of humanity and divinity. In him, heaven touched earth. Holiness and earthliness intertwined. In contrast, the mighty Roman emperor of that day became but a footnote in the chronicle of prophecy.

'Who is this?' is a question that confronts each life. May we in response to this central question of history answer: 'He is the king of my life. He is my Saviour and my sovereign who merits my deepest adoration and my highest praise.'

Lord Jesus, on this day, make a further triumphal entry in my life and rule supremely without a rival upon the throne of my heart.

indignant with the two brothers. 25Jesus called them together and said, "You know that the rulers of the Gentiles lord it over them, and their high officials exercise authority over them. 26Not so with you. Instead, whoever wants to become great among you must be your servant, 27and whoever wants to be first must be your slave—28just as the Son of Man did not come to be served, but to serve, and to give his life as a ransom for many."

Two Blind Men Receive Sight

29As Jesus and his disciples were leaving Jericho, a large crowd followed him. 30Two blind men were sitting by the roadside, and when they heard that Jesus was going by, they shouted, "Lord, Son of David, have mercy on us!"

31The crowd rebuked them and told them to be quiet, but they shouted all the louder, "Lord, Son of David, have mercy on us!"

32Jesus stopped and called them. "What do you want me to do for you?" he asked.

33"Lord," they answered, "we want our sight."

34Jesus had compassion on them and touched their eyes. Immediately they received their sight and followed him.

The Triumphal Entry

21 As they approached Jerusalem and came to Bethphage on the Mount of Olives, Jesus sent two disciples, 2saying to them, "Go to the village ahead of you, and at once you will find a donkey tied there, with her colt by her. Untie them and bring them to me. 3If anyone says anything to you, tell him that the Lord needs them, and he will send them right away."

4This took place to fulfil what was spoken through the prophet:

5"Say to the Daughter of Zion,
  'See, your king comes to you,
gentle and riding on a donkey,
  on a colt, the foal of a donkey.'"[a]

6The disciples went and did as Jesus had instructed them. 7They brought the donkey and the colt, placed their cloaks on them, and Jesus sat on them. 8A very large crowd spread their cloaks on the road, while others cut branches from the trees and spread them on the road. 9The crowds that went ahead of him and those that followed shouted,

"Hosanna[b] to the Son of David!"

"Blessed is he who comes in the name of the Lord!"[c]

"Hosanna[b] in the highest!"

10When Jesus entered Jerusalem, the whole city was stirred and asked, "Who is this?"

11The crowds answered, "This is Jesus, the prophet from Nazareth in Galilee."

Jesus at the Temple

12Jesus entered the temple area and drove out all who were buying and selling there. He overturned the tables of the money-changers and the benches of those selling doves. 13"It is written," he said to them, "'My house will be called a house of prayer,'[d] but you are making it a 'den of robbers'.[e]"

14The blind and the lame came to him at the temple, and he healed them. 15But when the chief priests and the teachers of the law saw the wonderful things he did and the children shouting in the temple area, "Hosanna to the Son of David," they were indignant.

16"Do you hear what these children are saying?" they asked him.

"Yes," replied Jesus, "have you never read,

"'From the lips of children and infants
  you have ordained praise'[f]?"

17And he left them and went out of the city to Bethany, where he spent the night.

The Fig-Tree Withers

18Early in the morning, as he was on his way back to the city, he was hungry. 19Seeing a fig-tree by the road, he went up to it but found nothing on it except leaves. Then he said to it, "May you never bear fruit again!" Immediately the tree withered.

20When the disciples saw this, they were amazed. "How did the fig-tree wither so quickly?" they asked.

21Jesus replied, "I tell you the truth, if you have faith and do not doubt, not only can you do what was done to the fig-tree, but also you can say to this mountain, 'Go, throw yourself into the sea,' and it will be done. 22If you believe, you will receive whatever you ask for in prayer."

The Authority of Jesus Questioned

23Jesus entered the temple courts, and, while he was teaching, the chief priests and the elders of the people came to him. "By what authority are you doing these things?" they asked. "And who gave you this authority?"

24Jesus replied, "I will also ask you one question. If you answer me, I will tell you by what authority I am doing these things. 25John's baptism—where did it come from? Was it from heaven, or from men?"

They discussed it among themselves and said, "If we say, 'From heaven', he will ask, 'Then why didn't you believe him?' 26But if we say, 'From men'—we are afraid of the people, for they all hold that John was a prophet."

27So they answered Jesus, "We don't know."

a5 Zech. 9:9
b9 A Hebrew expression meaning "Save!" which became an exclamation of praise; also in verse 15
c9 Psalm 118:26   d13 Isaiah 56:7   e13 Jer. 7:11   f16 Psalm 8:2

Then he said, "Neither will I tell you by what authority I am doing these things.

The Parable of the Two Sons

28"What do you think? There was a man who had two sons. He went to the first and said, 'Son, go and work today in the vineyard.'

29" 'I will not,' he answered, but later he changed his mind and went.

30"Then the father went to the other son and said the same thing. He answered, 'I will, sir,' but he did not go.

31"Which of the two did what his father wanted?"

"The first," they answered.

Jesus said to them, "I tell you the truth, the tax collectors and the prostitutes are entering the kingdom of God ahead of you. 32For John came to you to show you the way of righteousness, and you did not believe him, but the tax collectors and the prostitutes did. And even after you saw this, you did not repent and believe him.

The Parable of the Tenants

33"Listen to another parable: There was a landowner who planted a vineyard. He put a wall around it, dug a winepress in it and built a watchtower. Then he rented the vineyard to some farmers and went away on a journey. 34When the harvest time approached, he sent his servants to the tenants to collect his fruit.

35"The tenants seized his servants; they beat one, killed another, and stoned a third. 36Then he sent other servants to them, more than the first time, and the tenants treated them in the same way. 37Last of all, he sent his son to them. 'They will respect my son,' he said.

38"But when the tenants saw the son, they said to each other, 'This is the heir. Come, let's kill him and take his inheritance.' 39So they took him and threw him out of the vineyard and killed him.

40"Therefore, when the owner of the vineyard comes, what will he do to those tenants?"

41"He will bring those wretches to a wretched end," they replied, "and he will rent the vineyard to other tenants, who will give him his share of the crop at harvest time."

42Jesus said to them, "Have you never read in the Scriptures:

" 'The stone the builders rejected
has become the capstone;g
the Lord has done this,
and it is marvellous in our eyes'h?

43"Therefore I tell you that the kingdom of God will be taken away from you and given to a people who will produce its fruit. 44He who falls on this stone will be broken to pieces, but he on whom it falls will be crushed."i

45When the chief priests and the Pharisees heard Jesus' parables, they knew he was talking about them. 46They looked for a way

to arrest him, but they were afraid of the crowd because the people held that he was a prophet.

The Parable of the Wedding Banquet

22 Jesus spoke to them again in parables, saying: 2"The kingdom of heaven is like a king who prepared a wedding banquet for his son. 3He sent his servants to those who had been invited to the banquet to tell them to come, but they refused to come.

4"Then he sent some more servants and said, 'Tell those who have been invited that I have prepared my dinner: My oxen and fattened cattle have been slaughtered, and everything is ready. Come to the wedding banquet.'

5"But they paid no attention and went off—one to his field, another to his business. 6The rest seized his servants, ill-treated them and killed them. 7The king was enraged. He sent his army and destroyed those murderers and burned their city.

8"Then he said to his servants, 'The wedding banquet is ready, but those I invited did not deserve to come. 9Go to the street corners and invite to the banquet anyone you find.' 10So the servants went out into the streets and gathered all the people they could find, both good and bad, and the wedding hall was filled with guests.

11"But when the king came in to see the guests, he noticed a man there who was not wearing wedding clothes. 12'Friend,' he asked, 'how did you get in here without wedding clothes?' The man was speechless.

13"Then the king told the attendants, 'Tie him hand and foot, and throw him outside, into the darkness, where there will be weeping and gnashing of teeth.'

14"For many are invited, but few are chosen."

Paying Taxes to Caesar

15Then the Pharisees went out and laid plans to trap him in his words. 16They sent their disciples to him along with the Herodians. "Teacher," they said, "we know you are a man of integrity and that you teach the way of God in accordance with the truth. You aren't swayed by men, because you pay no attention to who they are. 17Tell us then, what is your opinion? Is it right to pay taxes to Caesar or not?"

18But Jesus, knowing their evil intent, said, "You hypocrites, why are you trying to trap me? 19Show me the coin used for paying the tax." They brought him a denarius, 20and he asked them, "Whose portrait is this? And whose inscription?"

21"Caesar's," they replied.

Then he said to them, "Give to Caesar what is Caesar's, and to God what is God's."

22When they heard this, they were amazed. So they left him and went away.

Marriage at the Resurrection

23That same day the Sadducees, who say there is no resurrection, came to him with a

g42 Or cornerstone   h42 Psalm 118:22,23   i44 Some manuscripts do not have verse 44.

MATTHEW 22:1–14

'The wedding banquet is ready, but those I invited did not deserve to come. Go to the street corners and invite to the banquet anyone you can find . . . "Friend," he asked, "how did you get in here without wedding clothes?" ' (vv. 8, 9, 12).

ONE PARABLE OR TWO? Today's passage reads like a single parable but as a single parable it is impossible to make sense of it. The king's action, expecting someone picked up off the street to be wearing a wedding garment, becomes so unreasonable, it requires all kinds of complicated manoeuvres to interpret it. Many have suggested that it was customary for the king to provide a wedding garment for his guests as they came in to the banquet, so only those who rejected the garment and rushed in to scoff the food were themselves rejected. But there is no hard evidence for such a custom.

More likely the first ten verses are one parable, and verses 11–14 come from a different parable. Evidence for this can be found by looking at Luke, where the parable does end at verse 10 (Luke 14:15–24). If we separate the two parables, we can make sense of them. The first warns us not to ignore God's invitation. The second tells us to be prepared, and reminds us of the part that we must play in responding to God.

God requires us to be prepared to enter his presence. It is a simple preparation, as simple as putting on a garment, yet so necessary if we are to enjoy to the full the privilege of worship, and respond fully to God's simple invitation to come into his presence.

> *In simple trust like theirs who heard,*
> *Beside the Syrian sea,*
> *The gracious calling of the Lord,*
> *Let us, like them, without a word*
> *Rise up and follow thee.*

(*John Greenleaf Whittier*)

→838

MATTHEW 25:1–13

'The kingdom of heaven will be like ten virgins who took their lamps and went out to meet the bridegroom . . . The foolish ones took their lamps but did not take any oil with them. The wise, however, took oil in jars along with their lamps' (vv. 1, 3, 4).

ADVENT, IN THE NORTHERN HEMISPHERE, is the darkest time of year, getting darker every day. But the lights of Advent, candles on the altar and the Advent wreath, fairy lights, illuminations in the street and on Christmas trees, make even the darkest day bright. It is a joy to anticipate the coming of the infant king in this profusion of light and colour. It heightens the excitement of the season. Soon we will be celebrating, the waiting will be over and we shall greet the infant Son of God in season, yet again.

This parable seems to fit such a scene. It breathes an air of anticipation. It does not, like many other parables, say 'The kingdom *is* like . . .' but 'The kingdom *will be* like . . .' Much of our life is spent anticipating, waiting for things about to happen. Sometimes we queue for a bus; look forward to a holiday; wait anxiously for exam results; worry about what the harvest is going to be; dread the reaction of a loved one when they find out what we have done, etc., etc. Small things and great, all involve some degree of waiting.

But waiting, in the end, may get us down. The bridegroom in this parable was a long time coming, and in spite of their excitement, sleep overcame the guests. Sometimes the Church suffers like that. After times of great expectation which appear to be a long time coming to fulfilment, lethargy can set in. At such times it is easy to end up unprepared for the coming of the king (bridegroom). At such times preparedness is more necessary than ever.

R. L. Stevenson said 'to travel hopefully is better than to arrive.' Is that true of the Christian way?

→841

question. 24"Teacher," they said, "Moses told us that if a man dies without having children, his brother must marry the widow and have children for him. 25Now there were seven brothers among us. The first one married and died, and since he had no children, he left his wife to his brother. 26The same thing happened to the second and third brother, right on down to the seventh. 27Finally, the woman died. 28Now then, at the resurrection, whose wife will she be of the seven, since all of them were married to her?"

29Jesus replied, "You are in error because you do not know the Scriptures or the power of God. 30At the resurrection people will neither marry nor be given in marriage; they will be like the angels in heaven. 31But about the resurrection of the dead—have you not read what God said to you, 32'I am the God of Abraham, the God of Isaac, and the God of Jacob'a? He is not the God of the dead but of the living."

33When the crowds heard this, they were astonished at his teaching.

The Greatest Commandment

34Hearing that Jesus had silenced the Sadducees, the Pharisees got together. 35One of them, an expert in the law, tested him with this question: 36"Teacher, which is the greatest commandment in the Law?"

37Jesus replied: "'Love the Lord your God with all your heart and with all your soul and with all your mind.'b 38This is the first and greatest commandment. 39And the second is like it: 'Love your neighbour as yourself.'c 40All the Law and the Prophets hang on these two commandments."

Whose Son Is the Christ?

41While the Pharisees were gathered together, Jesus asked them, 42"What do you think about the Christ?d Whose son is he?"

"The son of David," they replied.

43He said to them, "How is it then that David, speaking by the Spirit, calls him 'Lord'? For he says,

44"'The Lord said to my Lord:
"Sit at my right hand
until I put your enemies
under your feet."'e

45If then David calls him 'Lord', how can he be his son?" 46No-one could say a word in reply, and from that day on no-one dared to ask him any more questions.

Seven Woes

23 Then Jesus said to the crowds and to his disciples: 2"The teachers of the law and the Pharisees sit in Moses' seat. 3So you must obey them and do everything they tell you. But do not do what they do, for they do not practise what they preach. 4They tie up heavy loads and put them on men's shoulders, but they themselves are not willing to lift a finger to move them.

5"Everything they do is done for men to see: They make their phylacteriesa wide and the tassels on their garments long; 6they love the place of honour at banquets and the most important seats in the synagogues; 7they love to be greeted in the market-places and to have men call them 'Rabbi'.

8"But you are not to be called 'Rabbi', for you have only one Master and you are all brothers. 9And do not call anyone on earth 'father', for you have one Father, and he is in heaven. 10Nor are you to be called 'teacher', for you have one Teacher, the Christ.b 11The greatest among you will be your servant. 12For whoever exalts himself will be humbled, and whoever humbles himself will be exalted.

13"Woe to you, teachers of the law and Pharisees, you hypocrites! You shut the kingdom of heaven in men's faces. You yourselves do not enter, nor will you let those enter who are trying to.c

15"Woe to you, teachers of the law and Pharisees, you hypocrites! You travel over land and sea to win a single convert, and when he becomes one, you make him twice as much a son of hell as you are.

16"Woe to you, blind guides! You say, 'If anyone swears by the temple, it means nothing; but if anyone swears by the gold of the temple, he is bound by his oath.' 17You blind fools! Which is greater: the gold, or the temple that makes the gold sacred? 18You also say, 'If anyone swears by the altar, it means nothing; but if anyone swears by the gift on it, he is bound by his oath.' 19You blind men! Which is greater: the gift, or the altar that makes the gift sacred? 20Therefore, he who swears by the altar swears by it and by everything on it. 21And he who swears by the temple swears by it and by the one who dwells in it. 22And he who swears by heaven swears by God's throne and by the one who sits on it.

23"Woe to you, teachers of the law and Pharisees, you hypocrites! You give a tenth of your spices—mint, dill and cummin. But you have neglected the more important matters of the law—justice, mercy and faithfulness. You should have practised the latter, without neglecting the former. 24You blind guides! You strain out a gnat but swallow a camel.

25"Woe to you, teachers of the law and Pharisees, you hypocrites! You clean the outside of the cup and dish, but inside they are full of greed and self-indulgence. 26Blind Pharisee! First clean the inside of the cup and dish, and then the outside also will be clean.

27"Woe to you, teachers of the law and Pharisees, you hypocrites! You are like whitewashed tombs, which look beautiful on the outside but on the inside are full of dead men's bones and everything unclean. 28In the same way, on the outside you appear to

a32 Exodus 3:6   b37 Deut. 6:5   c39 Lev. 19:18   d42 Or Messiah   e44 Psalm 110:1
a5 That is, boxes containing Scripture verses, worn on forehead and arm   b10 Or Messiah
c13 Some manuscripts to. 14Woe to you, teachers of the Law and Pharisees, you hypocrites! You devour widows' houses and for a show make lengthy prayers. Therefore you will be punished more severely.

people as righteous but on the inside you are full of hypocrisy and wickedness.

29"Woe to you, teachers of the law and Pharisees, you hypocrites! You build tombs for the prophets and decorate the graves of the righteous. 30And you say, 'If we had lived in the days of our forefathers, we would not have taken part with them in shedding the blood of the prophets.' 31So you testify against yourselves that you are the descendants of those who murdered the prophets. 32Fill up, then, the measure of the sin of your forefathers!

33"You snakes! You brood of vipers! How will you escape being condemned to hell? 34Therefore I am sending you prophets and wise men and teachers. Some of them you will kill and crucify; others you will flog in your synagogues and pursue from town to town. 35And so upon you will come all the righteous blood that has been shed on earth, from the blood of righteous Abel to the blood of Zechariah son of Berakiah, whom you murdered between the temple and the altar. 36I tell you the truth, all this will come upon this generation.

37"O Jerusalem, Jerusalem, you who kill the prophets and stone those sent to you, how often I have longed to gather your children together, as a hen gathers her chicks under her wings, but you were not willing. 38Look, your house is left to you desolate. 39For I tell you, you will not see me again until you say, 'Blessed is he who comes in the name of the Lord.'*d*"

Signs of the End of the Age

24 Jesus left the temple and was walking away when his disciples came up to him to call his attention to its buildings. 2"Do you see all these things?" he asked. "I tell you the truth, not one stone here will be left on another; every one will be thrown down."

3As Jesus was sitting on the Mount of Olives, the disciples came to him privately. "Tell us," they said, "when will this happen, and what will be the sign of your coming and of the end of the age?"

4Jesus answered: "Watch out that no-one deceives you. 5For many will come in my name, claiming, 'I am the Christ,'*a* and will deceive many. 6You will hear of wars and rumours of wars, but see to it that you are not alarmed. Such things must happen, but the end is still to come. 7Nation will rise against nation, and kingdom against kingdom. There will be famines and earthquakes in various places. 8All these are the beginning of birth-pains.

9"Then you will be handed over to be persecuted and put to death, and you will be hated by all nations because of me. 10At that time many will turn away from the faith and will betray and hate each other, 11and many false prophets will appear and deceive many people. 12Because of the increase of wickedness, the love of most will grow cold, 13but he who stands firm to the end will be saved.

14And this gospel of the kingdom will be preached in the whole world as a testimony to all nations, and then the end will come.

15"So when you see standing in the holy place 'the abomination that causes desolation',*b* spoken of through the prophet Daniel—let the reader understand—16then let those who are in Judea flee to the mountains. 17Let no-one on the roof of his house go down to take anything out of the house. 18Let no-one in the field go back to get his cloak. 19How dreadful it will be in those days for pregnant women and nursing mothers! 20Pray that your flight will not take place in winter or on the Sabbath. 21For then there will be great distress, unequalled from the beginning of the world until now—and never to be equalled again. 22If those days had not been cut short, no-one would survive, but for the sake of the elect those days will be shortened. 23At that time if anyone says to you, 'Look, here is the Christ!' or, 'There he is!' do not believe it. 24For false Christs and false prophets will appear and perform great signs and miracles to deceive even the elect—if that were possible. 25See, I have told you ahead of time.

26"So if anyone tells you, 'There he is, out in the desert,' do not go out; or, 'Here he is, in the inner rooms,' do not believe it. 27For as lightning that comes from the east is visible even in the west, so will be the coming of the Son of Man. 28Wherever there is a carcass, there the vultures will gather.

29"Immediately after the distress of those days

"'the sun will be darkened,
    and the moon will not give its light;
the stars will fall from the sky,
    and the heavenly bodies will be
        shaken.'*c*

30"At that time the sign of the Son of Man will appear in the sky, and all the nations of the earth will mourn. They will see the Son of Man coming on the clouds of the sky, with power and great glory. 31And he will send his angels with a loud trumpet call, and they will gather his elect from the four winds, from one end of the heavens to the other.

32"Now learn this lesson from the fig-tree: As soon as its twigs get tender and its leaves come out, you know that summer is near. 33Even so, when you see all these things, you know that it*d* is near, right at the door. 34I tell you the truth, this generation*e* will certainly not pass away until all these things have happened. 35Heaven and earth will pass away, but my words will never pass away.

The Day and Hour Unknown

36"No-one knows about that day or hour, not even the angels in heaven, nor the Son,*f* but only the Father. 37As it was in the days of Noah, so it will be at the coming of the Son of Man. 38For in the days before the flood, people were eating and drinking, marrying

d39 Psalm 118:26   a5 Or *Messiah*; also in verse 23   b15 Daniel 9:27; 11:31; 12:11   c29 Isaiah 13:10; 34:4
d33 Or *he*   e34 Or *race*   f36 Some manuscripts do not have *nor the Son*.

MATTHEW 25:31–46
'The King will reply, "I tell you the truth, whatever you did for one of the least of these brothers of mine, you did for me" ' (v. 40).

NOT ONLY THE GREAT BUT ALSO THE HUMBLE, especially the humble, qualify for entry to this great kingdom. Those who over-project themselves and undervalue others have already had their reward. It is in fact the quality of our ordinary day-to-day relationships which determines how we stand before the Lord. Those unselfconscious acts of kindness and thoughtfulness indicate the kind of people we truly are, and he who sees beyond the obvious judges accordingly.

In accordance with his plan to rescue fallen humanity, our Lord fulfils the task to the utmost degree. He invests every human being, whether hungry, thirsty, a stranger, poor, sick or a felon, with his own dignity. When we serve them, we serve him. From start to finish of his earthly life our Lord was emphasizing humility and concern: a lowly birth, a carpenter's home, associating with outcasts and sinners, distress over the lost, warnings against the dangers of riches and possessions, even being buried in another man's tomb. We are slow learners of true humility.

Typically, those who had served others were unaware of the significance of their serving, and those who were careless were oblivious of their carelessness. Martin was a Roman soldier who gave a needy beggar half of his cloak to keep him warm. Subsequently, in a dream, he saw the Lord wearing that half cloak and heard an angel asking our Lord where it came from. Our Lord replied, 'My servant Martin gave it to me.'

Christ comes to us in many a different guise,
He walks our ordinary way, each day,
And we should see him, in each other's eyes.

→842

MATTHEW 26:36-45
'Watch and pray so that you will not fall into temptation. The spirit is willing, but the body is weak' (v. 41).

AMID THE SHADOWS and agonies of Gethsemane, Jesus fought a battle, the like of which there has never been. The salvation of the world was in the balance as the tempter sought to deflect him from the cross. Here, with the forces of good and evil locked in deadly combat, Christ took up his armour of prayer. There beneath the gnarled and twisted olive trees, in his moment of supreme trial, Jesus poured out his soul in prayer.

'Not my will, but yours be done,' is the final prayer of triumph we hear echoing from the garden. With that prayer of submission the greatest battle in the history of the world was won. There the victory of the cross and over the grave was assured in that prayer of consecration. In contrast, the disciples who slept reaped failure and defeat.

Prayer in the Christian life is not to be reserved for emergencies, but is to be a vital and regular part of our life. Prayer to the soul is as breathing is to the body. It sustains and invigorates the spiritual life. It is part and parcel of the Christian life, the intimate companion of consecration.

Prayer is pivotal for all of us. A prayerless life is a powerless life. A prayerful life is a powerful life. Most of the casualties in the spiritual life are found at the place of a weakened prayer life. In prayer, our weakness is linked to divine power, our foolishness to eternal wisdom, our need with the channel of infinite resources.

Let us watch and pray lest we fall into temptation, and lest the great opportunities for God's kingdom come and pass by, unseen and unseized.

Christ of Gethsemane, make me adequate for life's testings by the power of prayer.

→845

and giving in marriage, up to the day Noah entered the ark; 39and they knew nothing about what would happen until the flood came and took them all away. That is how it will be at the coming of the Son of Man. 40Two men will be in the field; one will be taken and the other left. 41Two women will be grinding with a hand mill; one will be taken and the other left.

42"Therefore keep watch, because you do not know on what day your Lord will come. 43But understand this: If the owner of the house had known at what time of night the thief was coming, he would have kept watch and would not have let his house be broken into. 44So you also must be ready, because the Son of Man will come at an hour when you do not expect him.

45"Who then is the faithful and wise servant, whom the master has put in charge of the servants in his household to give them their food at the proper time? 46It will be good for that servant whose master finds him doing so when he returns. 47I tell you the truth, he will put him in charge of all his possessions. 48But suppose that servant is wicked and says to himself, 'My master is staying away a long time,' 49and he then begins to beat his fellow-servants and to eat and drink with drunkards. 50The master of that servant will come on a day when he does not expect him and at an hour he is not aware of. 51He will cut him to pieces and assign him a place with the hypocrites, where there will be weeping and gnashing of teeth.

The Parable of the Ten Virgins

25 "At that time the kingdom of heaven will be like ten virgins who took their lamps and went out to meet the bridegroom. 2Five of them were foolish and five were wise. 3The foolish ones took their lamps but did not take any oil with them. 4The wise, however, took oil in jars along with their lamps. 5The bridegroom was a long time in coming, and they all became drowsy and fell asleep.

6"At midnight the cry rang out: 'Here's the bridegroom! Come out to meet him!'

7"Then all the virgins woke up and trimmed their lamps. 8The foolish ones said to the wise, 'Give us some of your oil; our lamps are going out.'

9"'No,' they replied, 'there may not be enough for both us and you. Instead, go to those who sell oil and buy some for yourselves.'

10"But while they were on their way to buy the oil, the bridegroom arrived. The virgins who were ready went in with him to the wedding banquet. And the door was shut.

11"Later the others also came. 'Sir! Sir!' they said. 'Open the door for us!'

12"But he replied, 'I tell you the truth, I don't know you.'

13"Therefore keep watch, because you do not know the day or the hour.

The Parable of the Talents

14"Again, it will be like a man going on a journey, who called his servants and entrusted his property to them. 15To one he gave five talents[a] of money, to another two talents, and to another one talent, each according to his ability. Then he went on his journey. 16The man who had received the five talents went at once and put his money to work and gained five more. 17So also, the one with the two talents gained two more. 18But the man who had received the one talent went off, dug a hole in the ground and hid his master's money.

19"After a long time the master of those servants returned and settled accounts with them. 20The man who had received the five talents brought the other five. 'Master,' he said, 'you entrusted me with five talents. See, I have gained five more.'

21"His master replied, 'Well done, good and faithful servant! You have been faithful with a few things; I will put you in charge of many things. Come and share your master's happiness!'

22"The man with the two talents also came. 'Master,' he said, 'you entrusted me with two talents; see, I have gained two more.'

23"His master replied, 'Well done, good and faithful servant! You have been faithful with a few things; I will put you in charge of many things. Come and share your master's happiness!'

24"Then the man who had received the one talent came. 'Master,' he said, 'I knew that you are a hard man, harvesting where you have not sown and gathering where you have not scattered seed. 25So I was afraid and went out and hid your talent in the ground. See, here is what belongs to you.'

26"His master replied, 'You wicked, lazy servant! So you knew that I harvest where I have not sown and gather where I have not scattered seed? 27Well then, you should have put my money on deposit with the bankers, so that when I returned I would have received it back with interest.

28"'Take the talent from him and give it to the one who has the ten talents. 29For everyone who has will be given more, and he will have an abundance. Whoever does not have, even what he has will be taken from him. 30And throw that worthless servant outside, into the darkness, where there will be weeping and gnashing of teeth.'

The Sheep and the Goats

31"When the Son of Man comes in his glory, and all the angels with him, he will sit on his throne in heavenly glory. 32All the nations will be gathered before him, and he will separate the people one from another as a shepherd separates the sheep from the goats. 33He will put the sheep on his right and the goats on his left.

34"Then the King will say to those on his right, 'Come, you who are blessed by my Father; take your inheritance, the kingdom

---

[a]15 A talent was worth several hundred pounds.

prepared for you since the creation of the world. ³⁵For I was hungry and you gave me something to eat, I was thirsty and you gave me something to drink, I was a stranger and you invited me in, ³⁶I needed clothes and you clothed me, I was sick and you looked after me, I was in prison and you came to visit me.'

³⁷"Then the righteous will answer him, 'Lord, when did we see you hungry and feed you, or thirsty and give you something to drink? ³⁸When did we see you a stranger and invite you in, or needing clothes and clothe you? ³⁹When did we see you sick or in prison and go to visit you?'

⁴⁰"The King will reply, 'I tell you the truth, whatever you did for one of the least of these brothers of mine, you did for me.'

⁴¹"Then he will say to those on his left, 'Depart from me, you who are cursed, into the eternal fire prepared for the devil and his angels. ⁴²For I was hungry and you gave me nothing to eat, I was thirsty and you gave me nothing to drink, ⁴³I was a stranger and you did not invite me in, I needed clothes and you did not clothe me, I was sick and in prison and you did not look after me.'

⁴⁴"They also will answer, 'Lord, when did we see you hungry or thirsty or a stranger or needing clothes or sick or in prison, and did not help you?'

⁴⁵"He will reply, 'I tell you the truth, whatever you did not do for one of the least of these, you did not do for me.'

⁴⁶"Then they will go away to eternal punishment, but the righteous to eternal life."

The Plot Against Jesus

26 When Jesus had finished saying all these things, he said to his disciples, ²"As you know, the Passover is two days away—and the Son of Man will be handed over to be crucified."

³Then the chief priests and the elders of the people assembled in the palace of the high priest, whose name was Caiaphas, ⁴and they plotted to arrest Jesus in some sly way and kill him. ⁵"But not during the Feast," they said, "or there may be a riot among the people."

Jesus Anointed at Bethany

⁶While Jesus was in Bethany in the home of a man known as Simon the Leper, ⁷a woman came to him with an alabaster jar of very expensive perfume, which she poured on his head as he was reclining at the table.

⁸When the disciples saw this, they were indignant. "Why this waste?" they asked. ⁹"This perfume could have been sold at a high price and the money given to the poor."

¹⁰Aware of this, Jesus said to them, "Why are you bothering this woman? She has done a beautiful thing to me. ¹¹The poor you will always have with you, but you will not always have me. ¹²When she poured this perfume on my body, she did it to prepare me for burial. ¹³I tell you the truth, wherever this gospel is preached throughout the

world, what she has done will also be told in memory of her."

Judas Agrees to Betray Jesus

¹⁴Then one of the Twelve—the one called Judas Iscariot—went to the chief priests ¹⁵and asked, "What are you willing to give me if I hand him over to you?" So they counted out for him thirty silver coins. ¹⁶From then on Judas watched for an opportunity to hand him over.

The Lord's Supper

¹⁷On the first day of the Feast of Unleavened Bread, the disciples came to Jesus and asked, "Where do you want us to make preparations for you to eat the Passover?"

¹⁸He replied, "Go into the city to a certain man and tell him, 'The Teacher says: My appointed time is near. I am going to celebrate the Passover with my disciples at your house.'" ¹⁹So the disciples did as Jesus had directed them and prepared the Passover.

²⁰When evening came, Jesus was reclining at the table with the Twelve. ²¹And while they were eating, he said, "I tell you the truth, one of you will betray me."

²²They were very sad and began to say to him one after the other, "Surely not I, Lord?"

²³Jesus replied, "The one who has dipped his hand into the bowl with me will betray me. ²⁴The Son of Man will go just as it is written about him. But woe to that man who betrays the Son of Man! It would be better for him if he had not been born."

²⁵Then Judas, the one who would betray him, said, "Surely not I, Rabbi?"

Jesus answered, "Yes, it is you."ᵃ

²⁶While they were eating, Jesus took bread, gave thanks and broke it, and gave it to his disciples, saying, "Take and eat; this is my body."

²⁷Then he took the cup, gave thanks and offered it to them, saying, "Drink from it, all of you. ²⁸This is my blood of theᵇ covenant, which is poured out for many for the forgiveness of sins. ²⁹I tell you, I will not drink of this fruit of the vine from now on until that day when I drink it anew with you in my Father's kingdom."

³⁰When they had sung a hymn, they went out to the Mount of Olives.

Jesus Predicts Peter's Denial

³¹Then Jesus told them, "This very night you will all fall away on account of me, for it is written:

" 'I will strike the shepherd,
    and the sheep of the flock will be
      scattered.'ᶜ

³²But after I have risen, I will go ahead of you into Galilee."

³³Peter replied, "Even if all fall away on account of you, I never will."

³⁴"I tell you the truth," Jesus answered,

ᵃ25 Or "You yourself have said it."   ᵇ28 Some manuscripts the new   ᶜ31 Zech. 13:7

THE GATHERING STORM now breaks in all its fury. Jesus rises from prayer in the garden and announces, 'Rise, let us go! Here comes my betrayer!' The words had not fallen from his lips but the silence, the solitude, the struggle of Gethsemane were ruthlessly invaded. The Gospel records, 'While he was still speaking, Judas, one of the Twelve, arrived. With him was a large crowd armed with swords and clubs' (v. 47).

The full moon was riding high at the Passover time. Yet John's account describes the multitude as coming with lanterns and torches (18:3). They must have thought that Jesus would be hiding and that they would have to search for him among the trees, shadows and rocks of the garden.

But when they came upon the company in the garden, far from hiding, Jesus steps forth and demands, 'Who is it you want?' When they said 'Jesus of Nazareth,' he replied 'I am he' (John 18:7, 8). The man they thought would be skulking and hiding now stood fearlessly before them.

Roles suddenly seemed reversed. The one to be captured is in command. An authority radiates from him that makes the attackers fall back. He says to the mob, 'Here I am. Let the others go their way.' His thought was not for his own safety but for that of his followers.

Crisis brings out the true quality of a person. It reveals the foundations of life. The crisis of the arrest in the garden brought forth the majesty and mercy, the poise and power of Christ. It demonstrated the power and adequacy that he found in prayer and in submission to the will of his heavenly Father.

We, too, will confront crises in life. We, too, will be assailed by forces that would overcome us unless we are fortified by the presence and power of God within. Only when enabled by the Holy Spirit will we, like the Master, be able to face calmly, courageously and victoriously the worst that life can throw at us.

Lord, who stood with calm and strength when hell's forces assailed, grant to me that inner strength that will enable me to triumph in the time of testing.

→846

MATTHEW 27:27–44

'Above his head they placed the written charge against him: THIS IS JESUS, THE KING OF THE JEWS' (v. 37).

WE OBSERVE OUR LORD ON CALVARY from three perspectives: the first looking forward, the second looking on and the third looking back.

> See, my servant will act wisely; he will be raised and lifted up and highly exalted . . . He was despised and rejected by men, a man of sorrows, and familiar with suffering . . . Surely, he took up our infirmities and carried our sorrows . . . He was pierced for our transgressions, he was crushed for our iniquities; the punishment that brought us peace was upon him, and by his wounds we are healed. We all, like sheep, have gone astray, each of us has turned to his own way; and the Lord has laid on him the iniquity of us all . . . He was led like a lamb to the slaughter, and as a sheep before her shearers is silent, so he did not open his mouth. (Isa. 52:13; 53:3–7).

Then he (one of the criminals crucified with Jesus) said, 'Jesus, remember me when you come into your kingdom.' Jesus answered him. 'I tell you the truth, today you will be with me in paradise.' (Luke 23:42, 43). The centurion . . . exclaimed, 'Surely, he was the Son of God!' (v. 54).

> 'He committed no sin, and no deceit was found in his mouth. When they hurled their insults at him, he did not retaliate; when he suffered he made no threats . . . He himself bore our sins in his body on the tree, so that we might die to sins and live for righteousness; by his wounds you have been healed' (1 Pet 2:22–24).

> *When I survey the wondrous cross*
> *On which the Prince of Glory died,*
> *My richest gain I count but loss,*
> *And pour contempt on all my pride.*

> (*Isaac Watts*)

→849

"this very night, before the cock crows, you will disown me three times."

35But Peter declared, "Even if I have to die with you, I will never disown you." And all the other disciples said the same.

Gethsemane

36Then Jesus went with his disciples to a place called Gethsemane, and he said to them, "Sit here while I go over there and pray." 37He took Peter and the two sons of Zebedee along with him, and he began to be sorrowful and troubled. 38Then he said to them, "My soul is overwhelmed with sorrow to the point of death. Stay here and keep watch with me."

39Going a little farther, he fell with his face to the ground and prayed, "My Father, if it is possible, may this cup be taken from me. Yet not as I will, but as you will."

40Then he returned to his disciples and found them sleeping. "Could you men not keep watch with me for one hour?" he asked Peter. 41"Watch and pray so that you will not fall into temptation. The spirit is willing, but the body is weak."

42He went away a second time and prayed, "My Father, if it is not possible for this cup to be taken away unless I drink it, may your will be done."

43When he came back, he again found them sleeping, because their eyes were heavy. 44So he left them and went away once more and prayed the third time, saying the same thing.

45Then he returned to the disciples and said to them, "Are you still sleeping and resting? Look, the hour is near, and the Son of Man is betrayed into the hands of sinners. 46Rise, let us go! Here comes my betrayer!"

Jesus Arrested

47While he was still speaking, Judas, one of the Twelve, arrived. With him was a large crowd armed with swords and clubs, sent from the chief priests and the elders of the people. 48Now the betrayer had arranged a signal with them: "The one I kiss is the man; arrest him." 49Going at once to Jesus, Judas said, "Greetings, Rabbi!" and kissed him.

50Jesus replied, "Friend, do what you came for."*d*

Then the men stepped forward, seized Jesus and arrested him. 51With that, one of Jesus' companions reached for his sword, drew it out and struck the servant of the high priest, cutting off his ear.

52"Put your sword back in its place," Jesus said to him, "for all who draw the sword will die by the sword. 53Do you think I cannot call on my Father, and he will at once put at my disposal more than twelve legions of angels? 54But how then would the Scriptures be fulfilled that say it must happen in this way?"

55At that time Jesus said to the crowd, "Am I leading a rebellion, that you have come out with swords and clubs to capture me? Every day I sat in the temple courts

teaching, and you did not arrest me. 56But this has all taken place that the writings of the prophets might be fulfilled." Then all the disciples deserted him and fled.

Before the Sanhedrin

57Those who had arrested Jesus took him to Caiaphas, the high priest, where the teachers of the law and the elders had assembled. 58But Peter followed him at a distance, right up to the courtyard of the high priest. He entered and sat down with the guards to see the outcome.

59The chief priests and the whole Sanhedrin were looking for false evidence against Jesus so that they could put him to death. 60But they did not find any, though many false witnesses came forward.

Finally two came forward 61and declared, "This fellow said, 'I am able to destroy the temple of God and rebuild it in three days.'"

62Then the high priest stood up and said to Jesus, "Are you not going to answer? What is this testimony that these men are bringing against you?" 63But Jesus remained silent.

The high priest said to him, "I charge you under oath by the living God: Tell us if you are the Christ,*e* the Son of God."

64"Yes, it is as you say," Jesus replied. "But I say to all of you: In the future you will see the Son of Man sitting at the right hand of the Mighty One and coming on the clouds of heaven."

65Then the high priest tore his clothes and said, "He has spoken blasphemy! Why do we need any more witnesses? Look, now you have heard the blasphemy. 66What do you think?"

"He is worthy of death," they answered.

67Then they spat in his face and struck him with their fists. Others slapped him 68and said, "Prophesy to us, Christ. Who hit you?"

Peter Disowns Jesus

69Now Peter was sitting out in the courtyard, and a servant girl came to him. "You also were with Jesus of Galilee," she said.

70But he denied it before them all. "I don't know what you're talking about," he said.

71Then he went out to the gateway, where another girl saw him and said to the people there, "This fellow was with Jesus of Nazareth."

72He denied it again, with an oath: "I don't know the man!"

73After a little while, those standing there went up to Peter and said, "Surely you are one of them, for your accent gives you away."

74Then he began to call down curses on himself and he swore to them, "I don't know the man!"

Immediately a cock crowed. 75Then Peter remembered the word Jesus had spoken: "Before the cock crows, you will disown me three times." And he went outside and wept bitterly.

*d*50 Or "Friend, why have you come?"   *e*63 Or Messiah; also in verse 68

Judas Hangs Himself

27 Early in the morning, all the chief priests and the elders of the people came to the decision to put Jesus to death. [2]They bound him, led him away and handed him over to Pilate, the governor.

[3]When Judas, who had betrayed him, saw that Jesus was condemned, he was seized with remorse and returned the thirty silver coins to the chief priests and the elders. [4]"I have sinned," he said, "for I have betrayed innocent blood."

"What is that to us?" they replied. "That's your responsibility."

[5]So Judas threw the money into the temple and left. Then he went away and hanged himself.

[6]The chief priests picked up the coins and said, "It is against the law to put this into the treasury, since it is blood money." [7]So they decided to use the money to buy the potter's field as a burial place for foreigners. [8]That is why it has been called the Field of Blood to this day. [9]Then what was spoken by Jeremiah the prophet was fulfilled: "They took the thirty silver coins, the price set on him by the people of Israel, [10]and they used them to buy the potter's field, as the Lord commanded me."[a]

Jesus Before Pilate

[11]Meanwhile Jesus stood before the governor, and the governor asked him, "Are you the king of the Jews?"

"Yes, it is as you say," Jesus replied.

[12]When he was accused by the chief priests and the elders, he gave no answer. [13]Then Pilate asked him, "Don't you hear the testimony they are bringing against you?" [14]But Jesus made no reply, not even to a single charge—to the great amazement of the governor.

[15]Now it was the governor's custom at the Feast to release a prisoner chosen by the crowd. [16]At that time they had a notorious prisoner, called Barabbas. [17]So when the crowd had gathered, Pilate asked them, "Which one do you want me to release to you: Barabbas, or Jesus who is called Christ?" [18]For he knew it was out of envy that they had handed Jesus over to him.

[19]While Pilate was sitting on the judge's seat, his wife sent him this message: "Don't have anything to do with that innocent man, for I have suffered a great deal today in a dream because of him."

[20]But the chief priests and the elders persuaded the crowd to ask for Barabbas and to have Jesus executed.

[21]"Which of the two do you want me to release to you?" asked the governor.

"Barabbas," they answered.

[22]"What shall I do, then, with Jesus who is called Christ?" Pilate asked.

They all answered, "Crucify him!"

[23]"Why? What crime has he committed?" asked Pilate.

But they shouted all the louder, "Crucify him!"

[24]When Pilate saw that he was getting nowhere, but that instead an uproar was starting, he took water and washed his hands in front of the crowd. "I am innocent of this man's blood," he said. "It is your responsibility!"

[25]All the people answered, "Let his blood be on us and on our children!"

[26]Then he released Barabbas to them. But he had Jesus flogged, and handed him over to be crucified.

The Soldiers Mock Jesus

[27]Then the governor's soldiers took Jesus into the Praetorium and gathered the whole company of soldiers round him. [28]They stripped him and put a scarlet robe on him, [29]and then twisted together a crown of thorns and set it on his head. They put a staff in his right hand and knelt in front of him and mocked him. "Hail, king of the Jews!" they said. [30]They spat on him, and took the staff and struck him on the head again and again. [31]After they had mocked him, they took off the robe and put his own clothes on him. Then they led him away to crucify him.

The Crucifixion

[32]As they were going out, they met a man from Cyrene, named Simon, and they forced him to carry the cross. [33]They came to a place called Golgotha (which means The Place of the Skull). [34]There they offered Jesus wine to drink, mixed with gall; but after tasting it, he refused to drink it. [35]When they had crucified him, they divided up his clothes by casting lots.[b] [36]And sitting down, they kept watch over him there. [37]Above his head they placed the written charge against him: THIS IS JESUS, THE KING OF THE JEWS. [38]Two robbers were crucified with him, one on his right and one on his left. [39]Those who passed by hurled insults at him, shaking their heads [40]and saying, "You who are going to destroy the temple and build it in three days, save yourself! Come down from the cross, if you are the Son of God!"

[41]In the same way the chief priests, the teachers of the law and the elders mocked him. [42]"He saved others," they said, "but he can't save himself! He's the King of Israel! Let him come down now from the cross, and we will believe in him. [43]He trusts in God. Let God rescue him now if he wants him, for he said, 'I am the Son of God.'" [44]In the same way the robbers who were crucified with him also heaped insults on him.

The Death of Jesus

[45]From the sixth hour until the ninth hour darkness came over all the land. [46]About the ninth hour Jesus cried out in a loud voice, "Eloi, Eloi,[c] lama sabachthani?"—which means, "My God, my God, why have you forsaken me?"[d]

[a]10 See Zech. 11:12,13; Jer. 19:1–13; 32:6–9.
[b]35 A few late manuscripts lots that the word spoken by the prophet might be fulfilled: 'They divided my garments among themselves and cast lots for my clothing.' (Psalm 22:18) [c]46 Some manuscripts Eli, Eli
[d]46 Psalm 22:1

MATTHEW 27:62–66

'. . . order for the tomb be made secure until the third day . . . (v. 64a).

WHILE SOME RELIGIOUS LEADERS did not believe in Christ, there was a fact they could not dismiss. Though corrupt, and as faithless as their Roman rulers, they could not ignore the fact of the empty tomb. An empty tomb would witness to the Messiah and fuel the flames of hope among a people desperately in search of a Saviour. So they tried to keep Christ in the tomb!

Today, followers of darkness labour no less passionately, no less subtly and craftily, to stop the proclamation of salvation through the shed blood of the man on the cross. In spite of all of the evidence of his life, death, and resurrection, people still dispute, and malign, all to keep Christ in the tomb. Satan labours unceasingly to keep the stone over the door, for if Christ is not risen then our faith is vain, and lost humanity is imprisoned within that tomb with Christ.

However, the effort is as futile today as it was long ago. Nothing could, or can, keep the risen Christ out of his world. Jesus holds the power of life and death, both spiritual and physical, in his hands. He will be the Saviour, no matter what unbelief does or says. He is the king of glory.

In league with the Holy Spirit, may our lives proclaim with great persuasion that the closed tomb is an illusion, implying power where there is no power. If we believe the word of Jesus; that death cannot hold the anointed one of God, then Christ and his eternal and abundant life will ours. The tomb was not the end, but a glorious beginning!

Death cannot keep his prey,
Jesus, my Saviour.

(*Robert Lowry*)

→850

MATTHEW 28:1–8
'He is not here; he has risen, just as he said' (v. 6a).

> *THE CROSS speaks for the futility of man's effort.*
> *Easter for the fulfilment of man's hope.*
> *The cross stands as the handiwork of man,*
> *Easter as the handiwork of God.*
> *Any man can build a cross,*
> *Only God can produce an Easter.*

(*Will Sessions, 'Week of the Cross', p. 89*)

Can it be true? Has he risen indeed? It is clear from the scriptural accounts of that first Easter morning, that hope in a living Christ had died with the crucifixion of Jesus (Luke 24:1). In spite of an empty tomb, and heavenly messengers proclaiming the resurrection, Matthew reports 'some doubted' (Matt. 28:17). Of Mary's account Mark says, 'they did not believe' (16:11). In response to the witness of the Emmaus travellers Mark writes: 'they did not believe them either' (16:13).

After the anguish of Friday, the Easter story seemed too good to be accepted on the word of a few people. In response to this doubt, and to doubt ever after, Luke reports that Jesus 'showed himself to these men and gave many convincing proofs that he was alive. He appeared to them over a period of forty days and spoke about the kingdom of God' (Acts 1:3). Dramatically, the hope of the followers again began to stir.

Even so, the new hope did not come easily, but come it did. And this new hope in Christ has ever stood as a testimony to the power of the gospel to accomplish all of the good that it has promised, throughout the whole of Christian history. It is on the basis of this new hope that Paul describes the gospel as 'the power of God to salvation for everyone who believes'. (Rom. 1:16)

Grant us to know in our hearts, as well as our minds that Jesus is alive –
alive for evermore! Amen.

47When some of those standing there heard this, they said, "He's calling Elijah."

48Immediately one of them ran and got a sponge. He filled it with wine vinegar, put it on a stick, and offered it to Jesus to drink. 49The rest said, "Now leave him alone. Let's see if Elijah comes to save him."

50And when Jesus had cried out again in a loud voice, he gave up his spirit.

51At that moment the curtain of the temple was torn in two from top to bottom. The earth shook and the rocks split. 52The tombs broke open and the bodies of many holy people who had died were raised to life. 53They came out of the tombs, and after Jesus' resurrection they went into the holy city and appeared to many people.

54When the centurion and those with him who were guarding Jesus saw the earthquake and all that had happened, they were terrified, and exclaimed, "Surely he was the Son*e* of God!"

55Many women were there, watching from a distance. They had followed Jesus from Galilee to care for his needs. 56Among them were Mary Magdalene, Mary the mother of James and Joses, and the mother of Zebedee's sons.

The Burial of Jesus

57As evening approached, there came a rich man from Arimathea, named Joseph, who had himself become a disciple of Jesus. 58Going to Pilate, he asked for Jesus' body, and Pilate ordered that it be given to him. 59Joseph took the body, wrapped it in a clean linen cloth, 60and placed it in his own new tomb that he had cut out of the rock. He rolled a big stone in front of the entrance to the tomb and went away. 61Mary Magdalene and the other Mary were sitting there opposite the tomb.

The Guard at the Tomb

62The next day, the one after Preparation Day, the chief priests and the Pharisees went to Pilate. 63"Sir," they said, "we remember that while he was still alive that deceiver said, 'After three days I will rise again.' 64So give the order for the tomb to be made secure until the third day. Otherwise, his disciples may come and steal the body and tell the people that he has been raised from the dead. This last deception will be worse than the first."

65"Take a guard," Pilate answered. "Go, make the tomb as secure as you know how." 66So they went and made the tomb secure by putting a seal on the stone and posting the guard.

The Resurrection

28 After the Sabbath, at dawn on the first day of the week, Mary Magdalene and the other Mary went to look at the tomb.

2There was a violent earthquake, for an angel of the Lord came down from heaven and, going to the tomb, rolled back the stone and sat on it. 3His appearance was like lightning, and his clothes were white as snow. 4The guards were so afraid of him that they shook and became like dead men.

5The angel said to the women, "Do not be afraid, for I know that you are looking for Jesus, who was crucified. 6He is not here; he has risen, just as he said. Come and see the place where he lay. 7Then go quickly and tell his disciples: 'He has risen from the dead and is going ahead of you into Galilee. There you will see him.' Now I have told you."

8So the women hurried away from the tomb, afraid yet filled with joy, and ran to tell his disciples. 9Suddenly Jesus met them. "Greetings," he said. They came to him, clasped his feet and worshipped him. 10Then Jesus said to them, "Do not be afraid. Go and tell my brothers to go to Galilee; there they will see me."

The Guards' Report

11While the women were on their way, some of the guards went into the city and reported to the chief priests everything that had happened. 12When the chief priests had met with the elders and devised a plan, they gave the soldiers a large sum of money, 13telling them, "You are to say, 'His disciples came during the night and stole him away while we were asleep.' 14If this report gets to the governor, we will satisfy him and keep you out of trouble." 15So the soldiers took the money and did as they were instructed. And this story has been widely circulated among the Jews to this very day.

The Great Commission

16Then the eleven disciples went to Galilee, to the mountain where Jesus had told them to go. 17When they saw him, they worshipped him; but some doubted. 18Then Jesus came to them and said, "All authority in heaven and on earth has been given to me. 19Therefore go and make disciples of all nations, baptising them in*a* the name of the Father and of the Son and of the Holy Spirit, 20and teaching them to obey everything I have commanded you. And surely I am with you always, to the very end of the age."

*e*54 Or *a son*   *a*19 Or *into*; see Acts 8:16; 19:5; Rom. 6:3; 1 Cor. 1:13; 10:2 and Gal. 3:27.

Mark

John the Baptist Prepares the Way

1 The beginning of the gospel about Jesus Christ, the Son of God.[a]

[2]It is written in Isaiah the prophet:

"I will send my messenger ahead of you,
    who will prepare your way"[b]—
[3]"a voice of one calling in the desert,
'Prepare the way for the Lord,
    make straight paths for him.'"[c]

[4]And so John came, baptising in the desert region and preaching a baptism of repentance for the forgiveness of sins. [5]The whole Judean countryside and all the people of Jerusalem went out to him. Confessing their sins, they were baptised by him in the Jordan River. [6]John wore clothing made of camel's hair, with a leather belt round his waist, and he ate locusts and wild honey. [7]And this was his message: "After me will come one more powerful than I, the thongs of whose sandals I am not worthy to stoop down and untie. [8]I baptise you with[d] water, but he will baptise you with the Holy Spirit."

The Baptism and Temptation of Jesus

[9]At that time Jesus came from Nazareth in Galilee and was baptised by John in the Jordan. [10]As Jesus was coming up out of the water, he saw heaven being torn open and the Spirit descending on him like a dove. [11]And a voice came from heaven: "You are my Son, whom I love; with you I am well pleased."

[12]At once the Spirit sent him out into the desert, [13]and he was in the desert for forty days, being tempted by Satan. He was with the wild animals, and angels attended him.

The Calling of the First Disciples

[14]After John was put in prison, Jesus went into Galilee, proclaiming the good news of God. [15]"The time has come," he said. "The kingdom of God is near. Repent and believe the good news!"

[16]As Jesus walked beside the Sea of Galilee, he saw Simon and his brother Andrew casting a net into the lake, for they were fishermen. [17]"Come, follow me," Jesus said, "and I will make you fishers of men." [18]At once they left their nets and followed him.

[19]When he had gone a little farther, he saw James son of Zebedee and his brother John in a boat, preparing their nets. [20]Without delay he called them, and they left their father Zebedee in the boat with the hired men and followed him.

Jesus Drives Out an Evil Spirit

[21]They went to Capernaum, and when the Sabbath came, Jesus went into the synagogue and began to teach. [22]The people were amazed at his teaching, because he taught them as one who had authority, not as the teachers of the law. [23]Just then a man in their synagogue who was possessed by an evil[e] spirit cried out, [24]"What do you want with us, Jesus of Nazareth? Have you come to destroy us? I know who you are—the Holy One of God!"

[25]"Be quiet!" said Jesus sternly. "Come out of him!" [26]The evil spirit shook the man violently and came out of him with a shriek.

[27]The people were all so amazed that they asked each other, "What is this? A new teaching—and with authority! He even gives orders to evil spirits and they obey him." [28]News about him spread quickly over the whole region of Galilee.

Jesus Heals Many

[29]As soon as they left the synagogue, they went with James and John to the home of Simon and Andrew. [30]Simon's mother-in-law was in bed with a fever, and they told Jesus about her. [31]So he went to her, took her hand and helped her up. The fever left her and she began to wait on them.

[32]That evening after sunset the people brought to Jesus all the sick and demon-possessed. [33]The whole town gathered at the door, [34]and Jesus healed many who had various diseases. He also drove out many demons, but he would not let the demons speak because they knew who he was.

Jesus Prays in a Solitary Place

[35]Very early in the morning, while it was still dark, Jesus got up, left the house and

---

[a]1 Some manuscripts do not have *the Son of God*.   [b]2 Mal. 3:1   [c]3 Isaiah 40:3   [d]8 Or *in*
[e]23 Greek *unclean*; also in verses 26 and 27

MARK 1:21-34

' "Be quiet!" said Jesus sternly. "Come out of him!" The evil spirit shook the man violently and came out of him with a shriek . . . that evening after sunset the people brought to Jesus all the sick and demon-possessed . . . and Jesus healed many' (vv. 25, 26, 32, 34a).

ONE MAN demanded the whole of Jesus' attention in the synagogue. The man was possessed by an evil spirit. What that means is very difficult to say. Spirit possession is almost impossible to define. Sometimes it seems to be used as a convenient label for violent mental disorders which could be described in other ways. But, however we define our terms, there are some situations where a person becomes detached from reality and has to be reached via an outside influence, that is to say the evil spirit.

No amount of reason will help. They are beyond the reach of normal conversation. The only way through is by prayer and by the authority of Christ himself. A clear distinction is made by Mark between casting out demons and the general run of Jesus' healing ministry. It is therefore tempting to think of casting out demons as something quite separate from other kinds of healing, however it takes place.

God's power is involved in exorcism, as when Jesus cast the evil spirit out of this man. God's power is involved in spiritual healing of all kinds. God's power is involved in physical healing, as when Jesus healed Peter's mother-in-law. God's power is involved in physical healing of all kinds.

The healing performed by Jesus was remarkable, visible, often instanta-neous, and usually we call it miraculous. But the same power is at work in all healing. What was available through Jesus is available to us, the healing power of God.

→854

'When Jesus saw their faith, he said to the paralytic. "Son, your sins are forgiven" ' (v. 5).

PETER COULD NEVER FORGET this incident. They were back at his home. Peter would be proud to be host to his master. As on a previous occasion that needy crowd gathered around the house. A sick man who had four special friends was brought to Jesus for healing, and they could not get to him because of the crowd. Being resourceful men, they went to the back of the house and, ascending the steps leading to the roof, they proceeded to tear a hole in the roof through which they lowered their friend. The action of the four friends represented the importunity which our Lord was happy to praise.

We are not sure whether he was praising the faith of the four friends only, or including that of the sick man, but certainly, our Lord was moved by their faith. It is noticeable, that Jesus in this instance first addressed the spiritual need and then addressed the man's physical need. We are left to assume that the sick man was made completely whole.

From this incident we observe that faith generates faith. The faith of the four inspired faith in the sick, man, or conversely, the faith of the sick man inspired faith in his four friends. The mood of the story, however, suggests that the initiative lay with the four. We also observe that faith is effective. Our Lord delights in our dependence upon him. Our faith seems to create the atmosphere in which he can work most positively. In his home town of Nazareth Jesus could do little because of their lack of faith. It seems incredible that we can affect others through our faith, but this story suggests that we can and must.

' *"If you can?" said Jesus. "Everything is possible for him who believes." Immediately the boy's father exclaimed. "I do believe: help me overcome my unbelief!"* '

went off to a solitary place, where he prayed. ³⁶Simon and his companions went to look for him, ³⁷and when they found him, they exclaimed: "Everyone is looking for you!"

³⁸Jesus replied, "Let us go somewhere else—to the nearby villages—so that I can preach there also. That is why I have come." ³⁹So he travelled throughout Galilee, preaching in their synagogues and driving out demons.

A Man With Leprosy

⁴⁰A man with leprosy*ᶠ* came to him and begged him on his knees, "If you are willing, you can make me clean."

⁴¹Filled with compassion, Jesus reached out his hand and touched the man. "I am willing," he said. "Be clean!" ⁴²Immediately the leprosy left him and he was cured.

⁴³Jesus sent him away at once with a strong warning: ⁴⁴"See that you don't tell this to anyone. But go, show yourself to the priest and offer the sacrifices that Moses commanded for your cleansing, as a testimony to them." ⁴⁵Instead he went out and began to talk freely, spreading the news. As a result, Jesus could no longer enter a town openly but stayed outside in lonely places. Yet the people still came to him from everywhere.

Jesus Heals a Paralytic

2 A few days later, when Jesus again entered Capernaum, the people heard that he had come home. ²So many gathered that there was no room left, not even outside the door, and he preached the word to them. ³Some men came, bringing to him a paralytic, carried by four of them. ⁴Since they could not get him to Jesus because of the crowd, they made an opening in the roof above Jesus and, after digging through it, lowered the mat the paralysed man was lying on. ⁵When Jesus saw their faith, he said to the paralytic, "Son, your sins are forgiven."

⁶Now some teachers of the law were sitting there, thinking to themselves, ⁷"Why does this fellow talk like that? He's blaspheming! Who can forgive sins but God alone?"

⁸Immediately Jesus knew in his spirit that this was what they were thinking in their hearts, and he said to them, "Why are you thinking these things? ⁹Which is easier: to say to the paralytic, 'Your sins are forgiven,' or to say, 'Get up, take your mat and walk'? ¹⁰But that you may know that the Son of Man has authority on earth to forgive sins. . . ." He said to the paralytic, ¹¹"I tell you, get up, take your mat and go home." ¹²He got up, took his mat and walked out in full view of them all. This amazed everyone and they praised God, saying, "We have never seen anything like this!"

The Calling of Levi

¹³Once again Jesus went out beside the lake. A large crowd came to him, and he began to teach them. ¹⁴As he walked along,

he saw Levi son of Alphaeus sitting at the tax collector's booth. "Follow me," Jesus told him, and Levi got up and followed him.

¹⁵While Jesus was having dinner at Levi's house, many tax collectors and "sinners" were eating with him and his disciples, for there were many who followed him. ¹⁶When the teachers of the law who were Pharisees saw him eating with the "sinners" and tax collectors, they asked his disciples: "Why does he eat with tax collectors and 'sinners'?"

¹⁷On hearing this, Jesus said to them, "It is not the healthy who need a doctor, but the sick. I have not come to call the righteous, but sinners."

Jesus Questioned About Fasting

¹⁸Now John's disciples and the Pharisees were fasting. Some people came and asked Jesus, "How is it that John's disciples and the disciples of the Pharisees are fasting, but yours are not?"

¹⁹Jesus answered, "How can the guests of the bridegroom fast while he is with them? They cannot, so long as they have him with them. ²⁰But the time will come when the bridegroom will be taken from them, and on that day they will fast.

²¹"No-one sews a patch of unshrunk cloth on an old garment. If he does, the new piece will pull away from the old, making the tear worse. ²²And no-one pours new wine into old wineskins. If he does, the wine will burst the skins, and both the wine and the wineskins will be ruined. No, he pours new wine into new wineskins."

Lord of the Sabbath

²³One Sabbath Jesus was going through the cornfields, and as his disciples walked along, they began to pick some ears of corn. ²⁴The Pharisees said to him, "Look, why are they doing what is unlawful on the Sabbath?"

²⁵He answered, "Have you never read what David did when he and his companions were hungry and in need? ²⁶In the days of Abiathar the high priest, he entered the house of God and ate the consecrated bread, which is lawful only for priests to eat. And he also gave some to his companions."

²⁷Then he said to them, "The Sabbath was made for man, not man for the Sabbath. ²⁸So the Son of Man is Lord even of the Sabbath."

3 Another time he went into the synagogue, and a man with a shrivelled hand was there. ²Some of them were looking for a reason to accuse Jesus, so they watched him closely to see if he would heal him on the Sabbath. ³Jesus said to the man with the shrivelled hand, "Stand up in front of everyone."

⁴Then Jesus asked them, "Which is lawful on the Sabbath: to do good or to do evil, to save life or to kill?" But they remained silent.

⁵He looked round at them in anger and, deeply distressed at their stubborn hearts,

---

ᶠ40 The Greek word was used for various diseases affecting the skin—not necessarily leprosy.

said to the man, "Stretch out your hand." He stretched it out, and his hand was completely restored. [6]Then the Pharisees went out and began to plot with the Herodians how they might kill Jesus.

Crowds Follow Jesus

[7]Jesus withdrew with his disciples to the lake, and a large crowd from Galilee followed. [8]When they heard all he was doing, many people came to him from Judea, Jerusalem, Idumea, and the regions across the Jordan and around Tyre and Sidon. [9]Because of the crowd he told his disciples to have a small boat ready for him, to keep the people from crowding him. [10]For he had healed many, so that those with diseases were pushing forward to touch him. [11]Whenever the evil[a] spirits saw him, they fell down before him and cried out, "You are the Son of God." [12]But he gave them strict orders not to tell who he was.

The Appointing of the Twelve Apostles

[13]Jesus went up on a mountainside and called to him those he wanted, and they came to him. [14]He appointed twelve—designating them apostles[b]—that they might be with him and that he might send them out to preach [15]and to have authority to drive out demons. [16]These are the twelve he appointed: Simon (to whom he gave the name Peter); [17]James son of Zebedee and his brother John (to them he gave the name Boanerges, which means Sons of Thunder); [18]Andrew, Philip, Bartholomew, Matthew, Thomas, James son of Alphaeus, Thaddaeus, Simon the Zealot [19]and Judas Iscariot, who betrayed him.

Jesus and Beelzebub

[20]Then Jesus entered a house, and again a crowd gathered, so that he and his disciples were not even able to eat. [21]When his family heard about this, they went to take charge of him, for they said, "He is out of his mind." [22]And the teachers of the law who came down from Jerusalem said, "He is possessed by Beelzebub![c] By the prince of demons he is driving out demons."

[23]So Jesus called them and spoke to them in parables: "How can Satan drive out Satan? [24]If a kingdom is divided against itself, that kingdom cannot stand. [25]If a house is divided against itself, that house cannot stand. [26]And if Satan opposes himself and is divided, he cannot stand; his end has come. [27]In fact, no-one can enter a strong man's house and carry off his possessions unless he first ties up the strong man. Then he can rob his house. [28]I tell you the truth, all the sins and blasphemies of men will be forgiven them. [29]But whoever blasphemes against the Holy Spirit will never be forgiven; he is guilty of an eternal sin."

[30]He said this because they were saying, "He has an evil spirit."

Jesus' Mother and Brothers

[31]Then Jesus' mother and brothers arrived. Standing outside, they sent someone in to call him. [32]A crowd was sitting around him, and they told him, "Your mother and brothers are outside looking for you."

[33]"Who are my mother and my brothers?" he asked.

[34]Then he looked at those seated in a circle around him and said, "Here are my mother and my brothers! [35]Whoever does God's will is my brother and sister and mother."

The Parable of the Sower

4 Again Jesus began to teach by the lake. The crowd that gathered round him was so large that he got into a boat and sat in it out on the lake, while all the people were along the shore at the water's edge. [2]He taught them many things by parables, and in his teaching said: [3]"Listen! A farmer went out to sow his seed. [4]As he was scattering the seed, some fell along the path, and the birds came and ate it up. [5]Some fell on rocky places, where it did not have much soil. It sprang up quickly, because the soil was shallow. [6]But when the sun came up, the plants were scorched, and they withered because they had no root. [7]Other seed fell among thorns, which grew up and choked the plants, so that they did not bear grain. [8]Still other seed fell on good soil. It came up, grew and produced a crop, multiplying thirty, sixty, or even a hundred times."

[9]Then Jesus said, "He who has ears to hear, let him hear."

[10]When he was alone, the Twelve and the others around him asked him about the parables. [11]He told them, "The secret of the kingdom of God has been given to you. But to those on the outside everything is said in parables [12]so that,

"'they may be ever seeing but never
    perceiving,
 and ever hearing but never
    understanding;
 otherwise they might turn and be
    forgiven!'[a]"

[13]Then Jesus said to them, "Don't you understand this parable? How then will you understand any parable? [14]The farmer sows the word. [15]Some people are like seed along the path, where the word is sown. As soon as they hear it, Satan comes and takes away the word that was sown in them. [16]Others, like seed sown on rocky places, hear the word and at once receive it with joy. [17]But since they have no root, they last only a short time. When trouble or persecution comes because of the word, they quickly fall away. [18]Still others, like seed sown among thorns, hear the word; [19]but the worries of this life, the deceitfulness of wealth and the desires for other things come in and choke the word, making it unfruitful. [20]Others, like seed sown on good soil, hear the word, accept it, and

---

[a]11 Greek *unclean*; also in verse 30   [b]14 Some manuscripts do not have *designating them apostles*.
[c]22 Greek *Beezeboul* or *Beelzeboul*   [a]12 Isaiah 6:9,10

MARK 3:22–30
'If a house is divided against itself, that house cannot stand . . . Whoever blasphemes against the Holy Spirit will never be forgiven' (vv. 25, 29a).

SCANDALOUS DIVISIONS within the Church weaken witness and dissipate energy. It is important to know what we believe. It is important to worship correctly 'in spirit and in truth'. But it is vital to remember that people have different perceptions of the truth. Fighting our own corner, trying to make people believe every detail of *our* belief, detracts from the urgent task of spreading the gospel of Jesus Christ. The gospel is not only belief, but encounter. It is meeting with Christ, relating to God who speaks to us through his Holy Spirit.

What, then, of the sin against the Holy Spirit? Such sin is not one act or even a series of acts. It is an attitude of mind. It creeps up on us gradually. We do something wrong, and pretend we haven't. We do it again, and it doesn't seem so bad. We continue to do it, and finally we may convince ourselves it is right! That is how we come to commit the unforgivable sin. We convince ourselves that right is wrong and wrong is right. We cannot be forgiven, for we no longer have any sense of sin.

The surest way to avoid committing the unforgivable sin is to keep Christ central in our thinking. When we concentrate on him we remain sensitive to right and wrong. Sometimes we will be puzzled as to which course of action to take. Sometimes we may have doubts. But we shall never reach the point where we blindly keep on doing wrong, deceiving ourselves into thinking it is right. Differences with our Christian neighbours may remain, but we will get them in proportion. We will fight the common enemy, Satan, instead of fighting each other.

Only those who no longer have a conscience can be guilty of the unforgivable sin.

→858

MARK 4:35–41

'He got up, rebuked the wind and said to the waves, "Quiet! Be still!" Then the wind died down and it was completely calm' (v. 39).

THE DAY HAD BEEN LONG and some break from the crowds was needed. What more restful than a journey across the lake? Jesus therefore proposed the crossing. Accompanied by other small boats, they set out. Exhausted, Jesus lay down to rest using the helmsman's cushion as a pillow. The Sea of Galilee is quite small but occasionally, and without warning, a storm can arise creating great danger. As fishermen, none would be more aware of the danger than Peter, Andrew, James and John who had won their living from this variable sea. The sleeping Jesus was oblivious of the danger until, in fear and panic, the disciples roused him. Peter alone recalls the reproach in their voices as they cry to him: 'Don't you care if we drown?' As though rebuking some wild, living creature, Jesus stood up and commanded peace. Only Mark's Gospel records the actual command given to the waves.

It was now the turn of the disciples to be rebuked for their lack of faith! Having been terrified of the storm, they were now terrified of Jesus. Who was this man who could control both winds and waves?

They had no cause for physical fear because Jesus was sharing their situation. No circumstance was, or is, beyond his power of control. His presence builds confidence, but they had cause for apprehension and awe. They had become accustomed to his healing miracles, but to be suddenly confronted by such a dramatic miracle over wind and sea was awesome.

> *Jesus, source of calm unfailing,*
> *With his peace my heart has filled.*
> *He abides, o'er all prevailing,*
> *And, in him, life's storms are stilled.*

> *(Charles Coller)*

→861

produce a crop—thirty, sixty or even a hundred times what was sown.''

A Lamp on a Stand

21He said to them, "Do you bring in a lamp to put it under a bowl or a bed? Instead, don't you put it on its stand? 22For whatever is hidden is meant to be disclosed, and whatever is concealed is meant to be brought out into the open. 23If anyone has ears to hear, let him hear.''

24"Consider carefully what you hear," he continued. "With the measure you use, it will be measured to you—and even more. 25Whoever has will be given more; whoever does not have, even what he has will be taken from him.''

The Parable of the Growing Seed

26He also said, "This is what the kingdom of God is like. A man scatters seed on the ground. 27Night and day, whether he sleeps or gets up, the seed sprouts and grows, though he does not know how. 28All by itself the soil produces corn—first the stalk, then the ear, then the full grain in the ear. 29As soon as the grain is ripe, he puts the sickle to it, because the harvest has come.''

The Parable of the Mustard Seed

30Again he said, "What shall we say the kingdom of God is like, or what parable shall we use to describe it? 31It is like a mustard seed, which is the smallest seed you plant in the ground. 32Yet when planted, it grows and becomes the largest of all garden plants, with such big branches that the birds of the air can perch in its shade.''

33With many similar parables Jesus spoke the word to them, as much as they could understand. 34He did not say anything to them without using a parable. But when he was alone with his own disciples, he explained everything.

Jesus Calms the Storm

35That day when evening came, he said to his disciples, "Let us go over to the other side." 36Leaving the crowd behind, they took him along, just as he was, in the boat. There were also other boats with him. 37A furious squall came up, and the waves broke over the boat, so that it was nearly swamped. 38Jesus was in the stern, sleeping on a cushion. The disciples woke him and said to him, "Teacher, don't you care if we drown?''

39He got up, rebuked the wind and said to the waves, "Quiet! Be still!" Then the wind died down and it was completely calm.

40He said to his disciples, "Why are you so afraid? Do you still have no faith?''

41They were terrified and asked each other, "Who is this? Even the wind and the waves obey him!''

The Healing of a Demon-possessed Man

5 They went across the lake to the region of the Gerasenes.[a] 2When Jesus got out of the boat, a man with an evil[b] spirit came from the tombs to meet him. 3This man lived in the tombs, and no-one could bind him any more, not even with a chain. 4For he had often been chained hand and foot, but he tore the chains apart and broke the irons on his feet. No-one was strong enough to subdue him. 5Night and day among the tombs and in the hills he would cry out and cut himself with stones.

6When he saw Jesus from a distance, he ran and fell on his knees in front of him. 7He shouted at the top of his voice, "What do you want with me, Jesus, Son of the Most High God? Swear to God that you won't torture me!'' 8For Jesus had said to him, "Come out of this man, you evil spirit!''

9Then Jesus asked him, "What is your name?''

"My name is Legion," he replied, "for we are many." 10And he begged Jesus again and again not to send them out of the area.

11A large herd of pigs was feeding on the nearby hillside. 12The demons begged Jesus, "Send us among the pigs; allow us to go into them." 13He gave them permission, and the evil spirits came out and went into the pigs. The herd, about two thousand in number, rushed down the steep bank into the lake and were drowned.

14Those tending the pigs ran off and reported this in the town and countryside, and the people went out to see what had happened. 15When they came to Jesus, they saw the man who had been possessed by the legion of demons, sitting there, dressed and in his right mind; and they were afraid. 16Those who had seen it told the people what had happened to the demon-possessed man —and told about the pigs as well. 17Then the people began to plead with Jesus to leave their region.

18As Jesus was getting into the boat, the man who had been demon-possessed begged to go with him. 19Jesus did not let him, but said, "Go home to your family and tell them how much the Lord has done for you, and how he has had mercy on you." 20So the man went away and began to tell in the Decapolis[c] how much Jesus had done for him. And all the people were amazed.

A Dead Girl and a Sick Woman

21When Jesus had again crossed over by boat to the other side of the lake, a large crowd gathered round him while he was by the lake. 22Then one of the synagogue rulers, named Jairus, came there. Seeing Jesus, he fell at his feet 23and pleaded earnestly with him, "My little daughter is dying. Please come and put your hands on her so that she will be healed and live." 24So Jesus went with him.

A large crowd followed and pressed

---

[a]1 Some manuscripts *Gadarenes*; other manuscripts *Gergesenes*　　　[b]2 Greek *unclean*; also in verses 8 and 13　　　[c]20 That is, the Ten Cities

around him. 25And a woman was there who had been subject to bleeding for twelve years. 26She had suffered a great deal under the care of many doctors and had spent all she had, yet instead of getting better she grew worse. 27When she heard about Jesus, she came up behind him in the crowd and touched his cloak, 28because she thought, "If I just touch his clothes, I will be healed." 29Immediately her bleeding stopped and she felt in her body that she was freed from her suffering.

30At once Jesus realised that power had gone out from him. He turned around in the crowd and asked, "Who touched my clothes?"

31"You see the people crowding against you," his disciples answered, "and yet you can ask, 'Who touched me?'"

32But Jesus kept looking around to see who had done it. 33Then the woman, knowing what had happened to her, came and fell at his feet and, trembling with fear, told him the whole truth. 34He said to her, "Daughter, your faith has healed you. Go in peace and be freed from your suffering."

35While Jesus was still speaking, some men came from the house of Jairus, the synagogue ruler. "Your daughter is dead," they said. "Why bother the teacher any more?"

36Ignoring what they said, Jesus told the synagogue ruler, "Don't be afraid; just believe."

37He did not let anyone follow him except Peter, James and John the brother of James. 38When they came to the home of the synagogue ruler, Jesus saw a commotion, with people crying and wailing loudly. 39He went in and said to them, "Why all this commotion and wailing? The child is not dead but asleep." 40But they laughed at him.

After he put them all out, he took the child's father and mother and the disciples who were with him, and went in where the child was. 41He took her by the hand and said to her, *"Talitha koum!"* (which means, "Little girl, I say to you, get up!"). 42Immediately the girl stood up and walked around (she was twelve years old). At this they were completely astonished. 43He gave strict orders not to let anyone know about this, and told them to give her something to eat.

A Prophet Without Honour

6 Jesus left there and went to his home town, accompanied by his disciples. 2When the Sabbath came, he began to teach in the synagogue, and many who heard him were amazed.

"Where did this man get these things?" they asked. "What's this wisdom that has been given him, that he even does miracles! 3Isn't this the carpenter? Isn't this Mary's son and the brother of James, Joseph,a Judas and Simon? Aren't his sisters here with us?" And they took offence at him.

4Jesus said to them, "Only in his home town, among his relatives and in his own house is a prophet without honour." 5He could not do any miracles there, except lay his hands on a few sick people and heal them. 6And he was amazed at their lack of faith.

Jesus Sends Out the Twelve

Then Jesus went round teaching from village to village. 7Calling the Twelve to him, he sent them out two by two and gave them authority over evilb spirits.

8These were his instructions: "Take nothing for the journey except a staff—no bread, no bag, no money in your belts. 9Wear sandals but not an extra tunic. 10Whenever you enter a house, stay there until you leave that town. 11And if any place will not welcome you or listen to you, shake the dust off your feet when you leave, as a testimony against them."

12They went out and preached that people should repent. 13They drove out many demons and anointed many sick people with oil and healed them.

John the Baptist Beheaded

14King Herod heard about this, for Jesus' name had become well known. Some were saying,c "John the Baptist has been raised from the dead, and that is why miraculous powers are at work in him."

15Others said, "He is Elijah."

And still others claimed, "He is a prophet, like one of the prophets of long ago."

16But when Herod heard this, he said, "John, the man I beheaded, has been raised from the dead!"

17For Herod himself had given orders to have John arrested, and he had him bound and put in prison. He did this because of Herodias, his brother Philip's wife, whom he had married. 18For John had been saying to Herod, "It is not lawful for you to have your brother's wife." 19So Herodias nursed a grudge against John and wanted to kill him. But she was not able to, 20because Herod feared John and protected him, knowing him to be a righteous and holy man. When Herod heard John, he was greatly puzzled;d yet he liked to listen to him.

21Finally the opportune time came. On his birthday Herod gave a banquet for his high officials and military commanders and the leading men of Galilee. 22When the daughter of Herodias came in and danced, she pleased Herod and his dinner guests.

The king said to the girl, "Ask me for anything you want, and I'll give it to you." 23And he promised her with an oath, "Whatever you ask I will give you, up to half my kingdom."

24She went out and said to her mother, "What shall I ask for?"

"The head of John the Baptist," she answered.

25At once the girl hurried in to the king with the request: "I want you to give me right now the head of John the Baptist on a platter."

---

a3 Greek *Joses*, a variant of *Joseph*   b7 Greek *unclean*   c14 Some early manuscripts *He was saying*
d20 Some early manuscripts *he did many things*

'Ignoring what they said, Jesus told the synagogue ruler, "Don't be afraid; just believe" ' (v. 36).

NEED MAKES FOR BOLDNESS. It also overcomes other scruples. Jairus, one of the rulers of the synagogue, whose voice might well have been one of support for Jesus among the antagonized synagogue rulers, broke with his colleagues when he came pleading with Jesus to save his little daughter from death. He was confident that Jesus had but to lay his hands on her and she would be healed. As Jesus moved towards Jairus' home, he was delayed by another needy person who, simply by touching him, was healed. At that point, messengers came to say that Jairus' daughter had died and the healer would not therefore be needed. It was in response to this that Jesus instructed Jairus to have faith rather than fear.

Every miracle recorded in Mark's Gospel is performed in the context of faith. One can imagine the simple, uncomplicated Peter, taking hold of this basic condition for a miracle and preaching it faithfully through the years. Supporting this statement, we note that in his first letter Peter puts a strong emphasis on faith. Clearly, Mark had observed this.

Some people seem to find faith comes more easily to them than certain others do. People who are sceptical by nature experience difficulties. Others who have been hurt and still carry wounds or even tender scars, may not find faith easy. But Jesus never asks for a specified quantity of faith, he simply asks for the faith we have. He will gladly make that the starting point!

> *My faith looks up to thee.*
> *My faith so small, so slow;*
> *It lifts its drooping eyes to thee,*
> *And claims the blessing now.*

(*Bramwell Booth*)

' "Why don't your disciples live according to the tradition of the elders instead of
eating their food with 'unclean' hands?" He replied, "Isaiah was right when he
prophesied about you hypocrites; as it is written, 'These people honour me with
their lips, but their hearts are far from me' " ' (vv. 5b, 6).

TEACHERS OF THE LAW get a bad press in Mark. Mark's Gospel
contains little, if anything, good about them. They were experts in
religion who controlled the day-to-day life of the people. Presumably
most were sincere, educated men who wanted to do the very best they
could with the knowledge they had. But, instead of looking at the
motives behind actions, like lawyers the world over they could only
look at the actions themselves.

When lawyers do start looking into motives things get difficult, for
no one can fully gauge what another person's intention is. In Britain,
for example, if a car kills someone on the road, the law requires a jury
to decide what the driver's intention was when they took the action
which caused death. That, of course, is almost impossible. So quite
often a driver who kills by careless driving is convicted of a minor
offence, and simply fined.

Recently the mother of a man who had been killed by a car saw this
car parked a few days later. In rage she took a hammer to it. She was
fined the same amount as the driver who had killed her son, but
additionally she received a suspended prison sentence! The car, she
claims, was looked on as more valuable than her son's life. Such are the
difficulties which will arise when intention is brought to bear upon the
legal system.

*In spite of the difficulties, Christ calls us to be more careful about
motives than about actions themselves.*

26The king was greatly distressed, but because of his oaths and his dinner guests, he did not want to refuse her. 27So he immediately sent an executioner with orders to bring John's head. The man went, beheaded John in the prison, 28and brought back his head on a platter. He presented it to the girl, and she gave it to her mother. 29On hearing of this, John's disciples came and took his body and laid it in a tomb.

Jesus Feeds the Five Thousand

30The apostles gathered round Jesus and reported to him all they had done and taught. 31Then, because so many people were coming and going that they did not even have a chance to eat, he said to them, "Come with me by yourselves to a quiet place and get some rest."

32So they went away by themselves in a boat to a solitary place. 33But many who saw them leaving recognised them and ran on foot from all the towns and got there ahead of them. 34When Jesus landed and saw a large crowd, he had compassion on them, because they were like sheep without a shepherd. So he began teaching them many things.

35By this time it was late in the day, so his disciples came to him. "This is a remote place," they said, "and it's already very late. 36Send the people away so that they can go to the surrounding countryside and villages and buy themselves something to eat."

37But he answered, "You give them something to eat."

They said to him, "That would take eight months of a man's wages!e Are we to go and spend that much on bread and give it to them to eat?"

38"How many loaves do you have?" he asked. "Go and see."

When they found out, they said, "Five —and two fish."

39Then Jesus directed them to have all the people sit down in groups on the green grass. 40So they sat down in groups of hundreds and fifties. 41Taking the five loaves and the two fish and looking up to heaven, he gave thanks and broke the loaves. Then he gave them to his disciples to set before the people. He also divided the two fish among them all. 42They all ate and were satisfied, 43and the disciples picked up twelve basketfuls of broken pieces of bread and fish. 44The number of the men who had eaten was five thousand.

Jesus Walks on the Water

45Immediately Jesus made his disciples get into the boat and go on ahead of him to Bethsaida, while he dismissed the crowd. 46After leaving them, he went up on a mountainside to pray.

47When evening came, the boat was in the middle of the lake, and he was alone on land. 48He saw the disciples straining at the oars, because the wind was against them. About the fourth watch of the night he went out to

them, walking on the lake. He was about to pass by them, 49but when they saw him walking on the lake, they thought he was a ghost. They cried out, 50because they all saw him and were terrified.

Immediately he spoke to them and said, "Take courage! It is I. Don't be afraid." 51Then he climbed into the boat with them, and the wind died down. They were completely amazed, 52for they had not understood about the loaves; their hearts were hardened.

53When they had crossed over, they landed at Gennesaret and anchored there. 54As soon as they got out of the boat, people recognised Jesus. 55They ran throughout that whole region and carried the sick on mats to wherever they heard he was. 56And wherever he went —into villages, towns or countryside—they placed the sick in the market-places. They begged him to let them touch even the edge of his cloak, and all who touched him were healed.

Clean and Unclean

7 The Pharisees and some of the teachers of the law who had come from Jerusalem gathered round Jesus and 2saw some of his disciples eating food with hands that were "unclean", that is, unwashed. 3(The Pharisees and all the Jews do not eat unless they give their hands a ceremonial washing, holding to the tradition of the elders. 4When they come from the market-place they do not eat unless they wash. And they observe many other traditions, such as the washing of cups, pitchers and kettles.a)

5So the Pharisees and teachers of the law asked Jesus, "Why don't your disciples live according to the tradition of the elders instead of eating their food with 'unclean' hands?"

6He replied, "Isaiah was right when he prophesied about you hypocrites; as it is written:

" 'These people honour me with their lips,
    but their hearts are far from me.
7They worship me in vain;
    their teachings are but rules taught by
        men.'b

8You have let go of the commands of God and are holding on to the traditions of men."

9And he said to them: "You have a fine way of setting aside the commands of Godc in order to observec your own traditions! 10For Moses said, 'Honour your father and your mother,'d and, 'Anyone who curses his father or mother must be put to death.'e 11But you say that if a man says to his father or mother: 'Whatever help you might otherwise have received from me is Corban' (that is, a gift devoted to God), 12then you no longer let him do anything for his father or mother. 13Thus you nullify the word of God by your

e37 Greek *take two hundred denarii*   a4 Some early manuscripts *pitchers, kettles and dining couches*
b6,7 Isaiah 29:13   c9 Some manuscripts *set up*   d10 Exodus 20:12; Deut. 5:16
e10 Exodus 21:17; Lev. 20:9

tradition that you have handed down. And you do many things like that."

14Again Jesus called the crowd to him and said, "Listen to me, everyone, and understand this. 15Nothing outside a man can make him 'unclean' by going into him. Rather, it is what comes out of a man that makes him 'unclean'."*f*

17After he had left the crowd and entered the house, his disciples asked him about this parable. 18"Are you so dull?" he asked. "Don't you see that nothing that enters a man from the outside can make him 'unclean'? 19For it doesn't go into his heart but into his stomach, and then out of his body." (In saying this, Jesus declared all foods "clean".)

20He went on: "What comes out of a man is what makes him 'unclean'. 21For from within, out of men's hearts, come evil thoughts, sexual immorality, theft, murder, adultery, 22greed, malice, deceit, lewdness, envy, slander, arrogance and folly. 23All these evils come from inside and make a man 'unclean'.

The Faith of a Syro-Phoenician Woman

24Jesus left that place and went to the vicinity of Tyre.*g* He entered a house and did not want anyone to know it; yet he could not keep his presence secret. 25In fact, as soon as she heard about him, a woman whose little daughter was possessed by an evil*h* spirit came and fell at his feet. 26The woman was a Greek, born in Syrian Phoenicia. She begged Jesus to drive the demon out of her daughter.

27"First let the children eat all they want," he told her, "for it is not right to take the children's bread and toss it to their dogs."

28"Yes, Lord," she replied, "but even the dogs under the table eat the children's crumbs."

29Then he told her, "For such a reply, you may go; the demon has left your daughter."

30She went home and found her child lying on the bed, and the demon gone.

The Healing of a Deaf and Mute Man

31Then Jesus left the vicinity of Tyre and went through Sidon, down to the Sea of Galilee and into the region of the Decapolis.*i* 32There some people brought to him a man who was deaf and could hardly talk, and they begged him to place his hand on the man.

33After he took him aside, away from the crowd, Jesus put his fingers into the man's ears. Then he spat and touched the man's tongue. 34He looked up to heaven and with a deep sigh said to him, "*Ephphatha!*" (which means, "Be opened!"). 35At this, the man's ears were opened, his tongue was loosened and he began to speak plainly.

36Jesus commanded them not to tell anyone. But the more he did so, the more they kept talking about it. 37People were overwhelmed with amazement. "He has done everything well," they said. "He even makes the deaf hear and the mute speak."

Jesus Feeds the Four Thousand

8 During those days another large crowd gathered. Since they had nothing to eat, Jesus called his disciples to him and said, 2"I have compassion for these people; they have already been with me three days and have nothing to eat. 3If I send them home hungry, they will collapse on the way, because some of them have come a long distance."

4His disciples answered, "But where in this remote place can anyone get enough bread to feed them?"

5"How many loaves do you have?" Jesus asked.

"Seven," they replied.

6He told the crowd to sit down on the ground. When he had taken the seven loaves and given thanks, he broke them and gave them to his disciples to set before the people, and they did so. 7They had a few small fish as well; he gave thanks for them also and told the disciples to distribute them. 8The people ate and were satisfied. Afterwards the disciples picked up seven basketfuls of broken pieces that were left over. 9About four thousand men were present. And having sent them away, 10he got into the boat with his disciples and went to the region of Dalmanutha.

11The Pharisees came and began to question Jesus. To test him, they asked him for a sign from heaven. 12He sighed deeply and said, "Why does this generation ask for a miraculous sign? I tell you the truth, no sign will be given to it." 13Then he left them, got back into the boat and crossed to the other side.

The Yeast of the Pharisees and Herod

14The disciples had forgotten to bring bread, except for one loaf they had with them in the boat. 15"Be careful," Jesus warned them. "Watch out for the yeast of the Pharisees and that of Herod."

16They discussed this with one another and said, "It is because we have no bread."

17Aware of their discussion, Jesus asked them: "Why are you talking about having no bread? Do you still not see or understand? Are your hearts hardened? 18Do you have eyes but fail to see, and ears but fail to hear? And don't you remember? 19When I broke the five loaves for the five thousand, how many basketfuls of pieces did you pick up?"

"Twelve," they replied.

20"And when I broke the seven loaves for the four thousand, how many basketfuls of pieces did you pick up?"

They answered, "Seven."

21He said to them, "Do you still not understand?"

The Healing of a Blind Man at Bethsaida

22They came to Bethsaida, and some people brought a blind man and begged Jesus to touch him. 23He took the blind man by the hand and led him outside the village. When he had spat on the man's eyes and put his

---

f15 Some early manuscripts *'unclean'*. *16If anyone has ears to hear, let him hear."*
g24 Many early manuscripts *Tyre and Sidon*   *h25* Greek *unclean*   *i31* That is, the Ten Cities

MARK 8:27–35

'For whoever wants to save his life will lose it, but whoever loses his life for me . . . will save it' (v. 35, NIV).

WITH WHICH apostle do you most readily identify? Perhaps it is Peter. Many scholars believe the Gospel of Mark comprises the big fisherman's memories and he doesn't lack candour in his self-disclosure. When questioned about Jesus' identity. Peter answered, 'You are the Christ.' It appeared to be the 'correct' answer, but Jesus then stunned his disciples with the first prediction of his imminent death. 'This can't be,' thought Peter, and he rebuked Jesus. But the tables were turned; Peter himself was soundly rebuked by Jesus: 'Out of my sight, Satan! You do not have in mind the things of God, but the things of men.'

On the eve of the passion events Peter revealed his appalling weakness when, faced with questioning by a servant girl, he reverted to language he hadn't used for three years, cursing and swearing that he knew nothing of Jesus.

The master's mission appeared in jeopardy. It always is – because Jesus has chosen to entrust it to us. Fortunately, ours is the God of the second chance. Peter discovered that immediately following the resurrection and again by the Sea of Tiberias when he and the other disciples went fishing together. And so can we. We too can pick ourselves up from our failures and hear the master's gracious words of challenge and reappointment: 'Do you truly love me? Feed my lambs.'

> *Follow thou me, he calls again,*
> *And I will make you fishers of men:*
> *As in the days by Galilee.*
> *Jesus is calling you and me.*

(*Sidney Edward Cox*)

→866

MARK 9:14–29

'After Jesus had gone indoors, his disciples asked him privately, "Why couldn't we drive it out?" He replied, "This kind can come out only by prayer" ' (vv. 28, 29).

WHEN WE HAVE BEEN on the mountain top, almost inevitably the valley awaits us. The transfiguration must have been one of the most glorious of our Lord's earthly experiences. The splendour of eternity had been glimpsed again. Jesus had communed with his Father, with Moses and Elijah. He had received the reassurances he needed in order to press on and achieve his objectives. He must have been well satisfied. Peter, James and John had also been uniquely blessed. They had been granted a vision of infinite value to their present faith and future leadership. Feelings of awe, privilege, and euphoria must have coursed through them. Following Jesus held remarkable surprises and blessings.

In the valley a crowd awaited them. A boy, probably an epileptic, having been brought to the disciples remained uncured in spite of their efforts. A large crowd had gathered which included teachers of the law, and an argument had developed. Again we observe the emphasis Jesus made on faith. He deplored the lack of faith in the generation, affirmed the illimitable power available to those who have faith, evoked the affirmation of faith from the father, and, in response to the disciples' later question, emphasized that this kind of healing only came as a result of prayer. This statement is not at variance with an emphasis on faith because true faith depends on our total reliance on God in prayer.

The problems of the valley are not unrelated to the glories of the mountain top. Exalted experiences are desirable, deeply satisfying and enriching, but the valleys and their problems need us. The glory of the one fits us for the demands of the other.

Help me, Lord, to have more faith. Amen.

hands on him, Jesus asked, "Do you see anything?"

[24]He looked up and said, "I see people; they look like trees walking around."

[25]Once more Jesus put his hands on the man's eyes. Then his eyes were opened, his sight was restored, and he saw everything clearly. [26]Jesus sent him home, saying, "Don't go into the village."[a]

Peter's Confession of Christ

[27]Jesus and his disciples went on to the villages around Caesarea Philippi. On the way he asked them, "Who do people say I am?"

[28]They replied, "Some say John the Baptist; others say Elijah; and still others, one of the prophets."

[29]"But what about you?" he asked. "Who do you say I am?"

Peter answered, "You are the Christ."[b]

[30]Jesus warned them not to tell anyone about him.

Jesus Predicts His Death

[31]He then began to teach them that the Son of Man must suffer many things and be rejected by the elders, chief priests and teachers of the law, and that he must be killed and after three days rise again. [32]He spoke plainly about this, and Peter took him aside and began to rebuke him.

[33]But when Jesus turned and looked at his disciples, he rebuked Peter. "Get behind me, Satan!" he said. "You do not have in mind the things of God, but the things of men."

[34]Then he called the crowd to him along with his disciples and said: "If anyone would come after me, he must deny himself and take up his cross and follow me. [35]For whoever wants to save his life[c] will lose it, but whoever loses his life for me and for the gospel will save it. [36]What good is it for a man to gain the whole world, yet forfeit his soul? [37]Or what can a man give in exchange for his soul? [38]If anyone is ashamed of me and my words in this adulterous and sinful generation, the Son of Man will be ashamed of him when he comes in his Father's glory with the holy angels."

9 And he said to them, "I tell you the truth, some who are standing here will not taste death before they see the kingdom of God come with power."

The Transfiguration

[2]After six days Jesus took Peter, James and John with him and led them up a high mountain, where they were all alone. There he was transfigured before them. [3]His clothes became dazzling white, whiter than anyone in the world could bleach them. [4]And there appeared before them Elijah and Moses, who were talking with Jesus.

[5]Peter said to Jesus, "Rabbi, it is good for us to be here. Let us put up three shelters —one for you, one for Moses and one for

Elijah." [6](He did not know what to say, they were so frightened.)

[7]Then a cloud appeared and enveloped them, and a voice came from the cloud: "This is my Son, whom I love. Listen to him!"

[8]Suddenly, when they looked round, they no longer saw anyone with them except Jesus.

[9]As they were coming down the mountain, Jesus gave them orders not to tell anyone what they had seen until the Son of Man had risen from the dead. [10]They kept the matter to themselves, discussing what "rising from the dead" meant.

[11]And they asked him, "Why do the teachers of the law say that Elijah must come first?"

[12]Jesus replied, "To be sure, Elijah does come first, and restores all things. Why then is it written that the Son of Man must suffer much and be rejected? [13]But I tell you, Elijah has come, and they have done to him everything they wished, just as it is written about him."

The Healing of a Boy With an Evil Spirit

[14]When they came to the other disciples, they saw a large crowd around them and the teachers of the law arguing with them. [15]As soon as all the people saw Jesus, they were overwhelmed with wonder and ran to greet him.

[16]"What are you arguing with them about?" he asked.

[17]A man in the crowd answered, "Teacher, I brought you my son, who is possessed by a spirit that has robbed him of speech. [18]Whenever it seizes him, it throws him to the ground. He foams at the mouth, gnashes his teeth and becomes rigid. I asked your disciples to drive out the spirit, but they could not."

[19]"O unbelieving generation," Jesus replied, "how long shall I stay with you? How long shall I put up with you? Bring the boy to me."

[20]So they brought him. When the spirit saw Jesus, it immediately threw the boy into a convulsion. He fell to the ground and rolled around, foaming at the mouth.

[21]Jesus asked the boy's father, "How long has he been like this?"

"From childhood," he answered. [22]"It has often thrown him into fire or water to kill him. But if you can do anything, take pity on us and help us."

[23]"'If you can'?" said Jesus. "Everything is possible for him who believes."

[24]Immediately the boy's father exclaimed, "I do believe; help me overcome my unbelief!"

[25]When Jesus saw that a crowd was running to the scene, he rebuked the evil[a] spirit. "You deaf and mute spirit," he said, "I command you, come out of him and never enter him again."

---

[a]26 Some manuscripts *Don't go and tell anyone in the village*
[b]29 Or *Messiah*. "The Christ" (Greek) and "the Messiah" (Hebrew) both mean "the Anointed One".
[c]35 The Greek word means either *life* or *soul*; also in verse 36.   [a]25 Greek *unclean*

26The spirit shrieked, convulsed him violently and came out. The boy looked so much like a corpse that many said, "He's dead." 27But Jesus took him by the hand and lifted him to his feet, and he stood up.

28After Jesus had gone indoors, his disciples asked him privately, "Why couldn't we drive it out?"

29He replied, "This kind can come out only by prayer."[b]

30They left that place and passed through Galilee. Jesus did not want anyone to know where they were, 31because he was teaching his disciples. He said to them, "The Son of Man is going to be betrayed into the hands of men. They will kill him, and after three days he will rise." 32But they did not understand what he meant and were afraid to ask him about it.

Who Is the Greatest?

33They came to Capernaum. When he was in the house, he asked them, "What were you arguing about on the road?" 34But they kept quiet because on the way they had argued about who was the greatest.

35Sitting down, Jesus called the Twelve and said, "If anyone wants to be first, he must be the very last, and the servant of all."

36He took a little child and had him stand among them. Taking him in his arms, he said to them, 37"Whoever welcomes one of these little children in my name welcomes me; and whoever welcomes me does not welcome me but the one who sent me."

Whoever Is Not Against Us Is for Us

38"Teacher," said John, "we saw a man driving out demons in your name and we told him to stop, because he was not one of us."

39"Do not stop him," Jesus said. "No-one who does a miracle in my name can in the next moment say anything bad about me, 40for whoever is not against us is for us. 41I tell you the truth, anyone who gives you a cup of water in my name because you belong to Christ will certainly not lose his reward.

Causing to Sin

42"And if anyone causes one of these little ones who believe in me to sin, it would be better for him to be thrown into the sea with a large millstone tied around his neck. 43If your hand causes you to sin, cut it off. It is better for you to enter life maimed than with two hands to go into hell, where the fire never goes out.[c] 45And if your foot causes you to sin, cut it off. It is better for you to enter life crippled than to have two feet and be thrown into hell.[d] 47And if your eye causes you to sin, pluck it out. It is better for you to enter the kingdom of God with one eye than to have two eyes and be thrown into hell, 48where

" 'their worm does not die,
and the fire is not quenched.'[e]

49Everyone will be salted with fire.

50"Salt is good, but if it loses its saltiness, how can you make it salty again? Have salt in yourselves, and be at peace with each other."

Divorce

10 Jesus then left that place and went into the region of Judea and across the Jordan. Again crowds of people came to him, and as was his custom, he taught them.

2Some Pharisees came and tested him by asking, "Is it lawful for a man to divorce his wife?"

3"What did Moses command you?" he replied.

4They said, "Moses permitted a man to write a certificate of divorce and send her away."

5"It was because your hearts were hard that Moses wrote you this law," Jesus replied. 6"But at the beginning of creation God 'made them male and female'.[a] 7'For this reason a man will leave his father and mother and be united to his wife,[b] 8and the two will become one flesh.'[c] So they are no longer two, but one. 9Therefore what God has joined together, let man not separate."

10When they were in the house again, the disciples asked Jesus about this. 11He answered, "Anyone who divorces his wife and marries another woman commits adultery against her. 12And if she divorces her husband and marries another man, she commits adultery."

The Little Children and Jesus

13People were bringing little children to Jesus to have him touch them, but the disciples rebuked them. 14When Jesus saw this, he was indignant. He said to them, "Let the little children come to me, and do not hinder them, for the kingdom of God belongs to such as these. 15I tell you the truth, anyone who will not receive the kingdom of God like a little child will never enter it." 16And he took the children in his arms, put his hands on them and blessed them.

The Rich Young Man

17As Jesus started on his way, a man ran up to him and fell on his knees before him. "Good teacher," he asked, "what must I do to inherit eternal life?"

18"Why do you call me good?" Jesus answered. "No-one is good—except God alone. 19You know the commandments: 'Do not murder, do not commit adultery, do not steal, do not give false testimony, do not defraud, honour your father and mother.'[d]"

20"Teacher," he declared, "all these I have kept since I was a boy."

21Jesus looked at him and loved him. "One thing you lack," he said. "Go, sell everything you have and give to the poor, and you

---

[b]29 Some manuscripts *prayer and fasting*
[c]43 Some manuscripts *out,* 44*where* / " *'their worm does not die,* / *and the fire is not quenched.'*
[d]45 Some manuscripts *hell,* 46*where* / " *'their worm does not die,* / *and the fire is not quenched.'*
[e]48 Isaiah 66:24   [a]6 Gen. 1:27   [b]7 Some early manuscripts *do not have and be united to his wife.*
[c]8 Gen. 2:24   [d]19 Exodus 20:12–16; Deut. 5:16–20

IN THE MORNING on the way to Jerusalem, Jesus and the disciples came upon the fig tree he cursed the day before, which had now withered. It is fitting that this day should begin with a display of Christ's authority, for it will be spent debating with Jewish leaders. Jesus is not merely trying to establish his authority. He is proclaiming it, and basing his teachings on that authority.

We can accept Christ or reject him. However, we cannot decide the outcome of these choices. Acceptance brings blessing; rejection, condemnation. This is a divine absolute. People have only one option if they are to be blessed of God, and Christ clearly establishes that option as his followers exclaim: 'Rabbi, look! The fig-tree you cursed has withered!' Jesus responds, 'Have faith in God.' At the very beginning of this day, Christ provides the answer to every dilemma, every problem, every concern, every difficulty, every question that will ever face any person, 'Have faith in God'.

In today's passage we are confronted by a people who stand at the very centre of a life-changing event. They are caught up to a greater or lesser degree in a major issue of the day, namely, has the Saviour, the Anointed One of God, come in the person of this carpenter's son from Nazareth? Could this be the day of their divine visitation? Could it be ours?

Jesus says, 'Yes, "Have faith in God." ' Trust the promises embodied in his only Son. Follow him, walk with him, talk with him, become his very own.

'Therefore keep watch . . . If he comes suddenly, do not let him find you sleeping. What I say to you, I say to everyone: "Watch!" '
(*Mark 13:35–37*).

' "My soul is overwhelmed with sorrow to the point of death," he said to them. "Stay here and keep watch" ' (v. 34).

THEY ARRIVED AT GETHSEMANE. Jesus needed to pray and felt the need for support as he prayed. He told the disciples to sit down but took Peter, James and John with him. This was the third time Mark records that the three had been with him in special circumstances. First, at the healing of Jairus' daughter, second at the transfiguration, and now in Gethsemane. Jesus was deeply moved in his spirit, and used words redolent of one of the most profound psalms to express himself. He knew what lay ahead of him, and his spirit, the most finely tuned in all history, shrank from the impending humiliation, pain, the weight of human sin, and death.

Our Lord's loneliness was to be intensified by the failure of his three closest disciples to share this time of distress with him. Even though they heard the stress and agony in the opening words of Jesus' prayer, they were overwhelmed by sleep rather than the sense of imminent disaster. How deep our Lord's need was for them we can only guess when he broke his prayer and returned to them, only to find them asleep. It was Peter who had professed his loyalty but hours before; it was Peter Jesus addressed with some reproach in his voice, 'Could you not keep watch for one hour?' But the ever gracious Jesus excused them on the grounds that 'the spirit is willing, but the body is weak'. Three times he found them sleeping. The last time coincided with the arrival of Judas and the armed guard.

Jesus had counselled the disciples to vigilance and prayer against temptation. The temptation is not specified. Was it an insensitivity to the person and mission of our Lord? We may never know, but the advice to the disciples remains valid today.

'Could you not keep watch for one hour?'

will have treasure in heaven. Then come, follow me.''

22At this the man's face fell. He went away sad, because he had great wealth.

23Jesus looked around and said to his disciples, ''How hard it is for the rich to enter the kingdom of God!''

24The disciples were amazed at his words. But Jesus said again, ''Children, how hard it is*e* to enter the kingdom of God! 25It is easier for a camel to go through the eye of a needle than for a rich man to enter the kingdom of God.''

26The disciples were even more amazed, and said to each other, ''Who then can be saved?''

27Jesus looked at them and said, ''With man this is impossible, but not with God; all things are possible with God.''

28Peter said to him, ''We have left everything to follow you!''

29''I tell you the truth,'' Jesus replied, ''no-one who has left home or brothers or sisters or mother or father or children or fields for me and the gospel 30will fail to receive a hundred times as much in this present age (homes, brothers, sisters, mothers, children and fields—and with them, persecutions) and in the age to come, eternal life. 31But many who are first will be last, and the last first.''

Jesus Again Predicts His Death

32They were on their way up to Jerusalem, with Jesus leading the way, and the disciples were astonished, while those who followed were afraid. Again he took the Twelve aside and told them what was going to happen to him. 33''We are going up to Jerusalem,'' he said, ''and the Son of Man will be betrayed to the chief priests and teachers of the law. They will condemn him to death and will hand him over to the Gentiles, 34who will mock him and spit on him, flog him and kill him. Three days later he will rise.''

The Request of James and John

35Then James and John, the sons of Zebedee, came to him. ''Teacher,'' they said, ''we want you to do for us whatever we ask.''

36''What do you want me to do for you?'' he asked.

37They replied, ''Let one of us sit at your right and the other at your left in your glory.''

38''You don't know what you are asking,'' Jesus said. ''Can you drink the cup I drink or be baptised with the baptism I am baptised with?''

39''We can,'' they answered.

Jesus said to them, ''You will drink the cup I drink and be baptised with the baptism I am baptised with, 40but to sit at my right or left is not for me to grant. These places belong to those for whom they have been prepared.''

41When the ten heard about this, they became indignant with James and John. 42Jesus called them together and said, ''You know that those who are regarded as rulers of the Gentiles lord it over them, and their high officials exercise authority over them. 43Not so with you. Instead, whoever wants to become great among you must be your servant, 44and whoever wants to be first must be slave of all. 45For even the Son of Man did not come to be served, but to serve, and to give his life as a ransom for many.''

Blind Bartimaeus Receives His Sight

46Then they came to Jericho. As Jesus and his disciples, together with a large crowd, were leaving the city, a blind man, Bartimaeus (that is, the Son of Timaeus), was sitting by the roadside begging. 47When he heard that it was Jesus of Nazareth, he began to shout, ''Jesus, Son of David, have mercy on me!''

48Many rebuked him and told him to be quiet, but he shouted all the more, ''Son of David, have mercy on me!''

49Jesus stopped and said, ''Call him.''

So they called to the blind man, ''Cheer up! On your feet! He's calling you.'' 50Throwing his cloak aside, he jumped to his feet and came to Jesus.

51''What do you want me to do for you?'' Jesus asked him.

The blind man said, ''Rabbi, I want to see.''

52''Go,'' said Jesus, ''your faith has healed you.'' Immediately he received his sight and followed Jesus along the road.

The Triumphal Entry

11 As they approached Jerusalem and came to Bethphage and Bethany at the Mount of Olives, Jesus sent two of his disciples, 2saying to them, ''Go to the village ahead of you, and just as you enter it, you will find a colt tied there, which no-one has ever ridden. Untie it and bring it here. 3If anyone asks you, 'Why are you doing this?' tell him, 'The Lord needs it and will send it back here shortly.' ''

4They went and found a colt outside in the street, tied at a doorway. As they untied it, 5some people standing there asked, ''What are you doing, untying that colt?'' 6They answered as Jesus had told them to, and the people let them go. 7When they brought the colt to Jesus and threw their cloaks over it, he sat on it. 8Many people spread their cloaks on the road, while others spread branches they had cut in the fields. 9Those who went ahead and those who followed shouted,

''Hosanna!''*a*

''Blessed is he who comes in the name of the Lord!''*b*

10''Blessed is the coming kingdom of our father David!''

''Hosanna in the highest!''

---

*e*24 Some manuscripts *is for those who trust in riches*
*a*9 A Hebrew expression meaning ''Save!'' which became an exclamation of praise; also in verse 10.
*b*9 Psalm 118:25,26

11Jesus entered Jerusalem and went to the temple. He looked around at everything, but since it was already late, he went out to Bethany with the Twelve.

Jesus Clears the Temple

12The next day as they were leaving Bethany, Jesus was hungry. 13Seeing in the distance a fig-tree in leaf, he went to find out if it had any fruit. When he reached it, he found nothing but leaves, because it was not the season for figs. 14Then he said to the tree, "May no-one ever eat fruit from you again." And his disciples heard him say it.

15On reaching Jerusalem, Jesus entered the temple area and began driving out those who were buying and selling there. He overturned the tables of the money-changers and the benches of those selling doves, 16and would not allow anyone to carry merchandise through the temple courts. 17And as he taught them, he said, "Is it not written:

"'My house will be called
  a house of prayer for all nations'c?

But you have made it 'a den of robbers'.d"

18The chief priests and the teachers of the law heard this and began looking for a way to kill him, for they feared him, because the whole crowd was amazed at his teaching.

19When evening came, theye went out of the city.

The Withered Fig-Tree

20In the morning, as they went along, they saw the fig-tree withered from the roots. 21Peter remembered and said to Jesus, "Rabbi, look! The fig-tree you cursed has withered!"

22"Havef faith in God," Jesus answered. 23"I tell you the truth, if anyone says to this mountain, 'Go, throw yourself into the sea,' and does not doubt in his heart but believes that what he says will happen, it will be done for him. 24Therefore I tell you, whatever you ask for in prayer, believe that you have received it, and it will be yours. 25And when you stand praying, if you hold anything against anyone, forgive him, so that your Father in heaven may forgive you your sins."g

The Authority of Jesus Questioned

27They arrived again in Jerusalem, and while Jesus was walking in the temple courts, the chief priests, the teachers of the law and the elders came to him. 28"By what authority are you doing these things?" they asked. "And who gave you authority to do this?"

29Jesus replied, "I will ask you one question. Answer me, and I will tell you by what authority I am doing these things. 30John's baptism—was it from heaven, or from men? Tell me!"

31They discussed it among themselves and said, "If we say, 'From heaven', he will ask, 'Then why didn't you believe him?' 32But if we say, 'From men'. . . ." (They feared the people, for everyone held that John really was a prophet.)

33So they answered Jesus, "We don't know."

Jesus said, "Neither will I tell you by what authority I am doing these things."

The Parable of the Tenants

12 He then began to speak to them in parables: "A man planted a vineyard. He put a wall around it, dug a pit for the winepress and built a watchtower. Then he rented the vineyard to some farmers and went away on a journey. 2At harvest time he sent a servant to the tenants to collect from them some of the fruit of the vineyard. 3But they seized him, beat him and sent him away empty-handed. 4Then he sent another servant to them; they struck this man on the head and treated him shamefully. 5He sent still another, and that one they killed. He sent many others; some of them they beat, others they killed.

6"He had one left to send, a son, whom he loved. He sent him last of all, saying, 'They will respect my son.'

7"But the tenants said to one another, 'This is the heir. Come, let's kill him, and the inheritance will be ours.' 8So they took him and killed him, and threw him out of the vineyard.

9"What then will the owner of the vineyard do? He will come and kill those tenants and give the vineyard to others. 10Haven't you read this scripture:

"'The stone the builders rejected
  has become the capstone;a
11the Lord has done this,
  and it is marvellous in our eyes'b?"

12Then they looked for a way to arrest him because they knew he had spoken the parable against them. But they were afraid of the crowd; so they left him and went away.

Paying Taxes to Caesar

13Later they sent some of the Pharisees and Herodians to Jesus to catch him in his words. 14They came to him and said, "Teacher, we know you are a man of integrity. You aren't swayed by men, because you pay no attention to who they are; but you teach the way of God in accordance with the truth. Is it right to pay taxes to Caesar or not? 15Should we pay or shouldn't we?"

But Jesus knew their hypocrisy. "Why are you trying to trap me?" he asked. "Bring me a denarius and let me look at it." 16They brought the coin, and he asked them, "Whose portrait is this? And whose inscription?"

"Caesar's," they replied.

17Then Jesus said to them, "Give to Caesar what is Caesar's and to God what is God's." And they were amazed at him.

---

c17 Isaiah 56:7   d17 Jer. 7:11   e19 Some early manuscripts he   f22 Some early manuscripts If you have
g25 Some manuscripts sins. 26But if you do not forgive, neither will your Father who is in heaven forgive your sins.
a10 Or cornerstone   b11 Psalm 118:22,23

Marriage at the Resurrection

18Then the Sadducees, who say there is no resurrection, came to him with a question. 19"Teacher," they said, "Moses wrote for us that if a man's brother dies and leaves a wife but no children, the man must marry the widow and have children for his brother. 20Now there were seven brothers. The first one married and died without leaving any children. 21The second one married the widow, but he also died, leaving no child. It was the same with the third. 22In fact, none of the seven left any children. Last of all, the woman died too. 23At the resurrection*c* whose wife will she be, since the seven were married to her?"

24Jesus replied, "Are you not in error because you do not know the Scriptures or the power of God? 25When the dead rise, they will neither marry nor be given in marriage; they will be like the angels in heaven. 26Now about the dead rising—have you not read in the book of Moses, in the account of the bush, how God said to him, 'I am the God of Abraham, the God of Isaac, and the God of Jacob'*d*? 27He is not the God of the dead, but of the living. You are badly mistaken!"

The Greatest Commandment

28One of the teachers of the law came and heard them debating. Noticing that Jesus had given them a good answer, he asked him, "Of all the commandments, which is the most important?"

29"The most important one," answered Jesus, "is this: 'Hear, O Israel, the Lord our God, the Lord is one.*e* 30Love the Lord your God with all your heart and with all your soul and with all your mind and with all your strength.'*f* 31The second is this: 'Love your neighbour as yourself.'*g* There is no commandment greater than these."

32"Well said, teacher," the man replied. "You are right in saying that God is one and there is no other but him. 33To love him with all your heart, with all your understanding and with all your strength, and to love your neighbour as yourself is more important than all burnt offerings and sacrifices."

34When Jesus saw that he had answered wisely, he said to him, "You are not far from the kingdom of God." And from then on no-one dared ask him any more questions.

Whose Son Is the Christ?

35While Jesus was teaching in the temple courts, he asked, "How is it that the teachers of the law say that the Christ*h* is the son of David? 36David himself, speaking by the Holy Spirit, declared:

" 'The Lord said to my Lord:
    "Sit at my right hand
until I put your enemies
    under your feet." '*i*

37David himself calls him 'Lord'. How then can he be his son?"

The large crowd listened to him with delight.

38As he taught, Jesus said, "Watch out for the teachers of the law. They like to walk around in flowing robes and be greeted in the market-places, 39and have the most important seats in the synagogues and the places of honour at banquets. 40They devour widows' houses and for a show make lengthy prayers. Such men will be punished most severely."

The Widow's Offering

41Jesus sat down opposite the place where the offerings were put and watched the crowd putting their money into the temple treasury. Many rich people threw in large amounts. 42But a poor widow came and put in two very small copper coins,*j* worth only a fraction of a penny.*k*

43Calling his disciples to him, Jesus said, "I tell you the truth, this poor widow has put more into the treasury than all the others. 44They all gave out of their wealth; but she, out of her poverty, put in everything—all she had to live on."

Signs of the End of the Age

13 As he was leaving the temple, one of his disciples said to him, "Look, Teacher! What massive stones! What magnificent buildings!"

2"Do you see all these great buildings?" replied Jesus. "Not one stone here will be left on another; every one will be thrown down."

3As Jesus was sitting on the Mount of Olives opposite the temple, Peter, James, John and Andrew asked him privately, 4"Tell us, when will these things happen? And what will be the sign that they are all about to be fulfilled?"

5Jesus said to them: "Watch out that no-one deceives you. 6Many will come in my name, claiming, 'I am he,' and will deceive many. 7When you hear of wars and rumours of wars, do not be alarmed. Such things must happen, but the end is still to come. 8Nation will rise against nation, and kingdom against kingdom. There will be earthquakes in various places, and famines. These are the beginning of birth-pains.

9"You must be on your guard. You will be handed over to the local councils and flogged in the synagogues. On account of me you will stand before governors and kings as witnesses to them. 10And the gospel must first be preached to all nations. 11Whenever you are arrested and brought to trial, do not worry beforehand about what to say. Just say whatever is given you at the time, for it is not you speaking, but the Holy Spirit.

12"Brother will betray brother to death, and a father his child. Children will rebel against their parents and have them put to death. 13All men will hate you because of me, but he who stands firm to the end will be saved.

*c*23 Some manuscripts *resurrection, when men rise from the dead,*   *d*26 Exodus 3:6
*e*29 Or *the Lord our God is one Lord*   *f*30 Deut. 6:4,5   *g*31 Lev. 19:18   *h*35 Or *Messiah*
*i*36 Psalm 110:1   *j*42 Greek *two lepta*   *k*42 Greek *kodrantes*

14"When you see 'the abomination that causes desolation'*a* standing where it*b* does not belong—let the reader understand—then let those who are in Judea flee to the mountains. 15Let no-one on the roof of his house go down or enter the house to take anything out. 16Let no-one in the field go back to get his cloak. 17How dreadful it will be in those days for pregnant women and nursing mothers! 18Pray that this will not take place in winter, 19because those will be days of distress unequalled from the beginning, when God created the world, until now—and never to be equalled again. 20If the Lord had not cut short those days, no-one would survive. But for the sake of the elect, whom he has chosen, he has shortened them. 21At that time if anyone says to you, 'Look, here is the Christ!'*c* or, 'Look, there he is!' do not believe it. 22For false Christs and false prophets will appear and perform signs and miracles to deceive the elect—if that were possible. 23So be on your guard; I have told you everything ahead of time.

24"But in those days, following that distress,

" 'the sun will be darkened,
    and the moon will not give its light;
25the stars will fall from the sky,
    and the heavenly bodies will be
      shaken.'*d*

26"At that time men will see the Son of Man coming in clouds with great power and glory. 27And he will send his angels and gather his elect from the four winds, from the ends of the earth to the ends of the heavens.

28"Now learn this lesson from the fig-tree: As soon as its twigs get tender and its leaves come out, you know that summer is near. 29Even so, when you see these things happening, you know that it is near, right at the door. 30I tell you the truth, this generation*e* will certainly not pass away until all these things have happened. 31Heaven and earth will pass away, but my words will never pass away.

The Day and Hour Unknown

32"No-one knows about that day or hour, not even the angels in heaven, nor the Son, but only the Father. 33Be on guard! Be alert!*f* You do not know when that time will come. 34It's like a man going away: He leaves his house and puts his servants in charge, each with his assigned task, and tells the one at the door to keep watch.

35"Therefore keep watch because you do not know when the owner of the house will come back—whether in the evening, or at midnight, or when the cock crows, or at dawn. 36If he comes suddenly, do not let him find you sleeping. 37What I say to you, I say to everyone: 'Watch!' "

Jesus Anointed at Bethany

14 Now the Passover and the Feast of Unleavened Bread were only two days away, and the chief priests and the teachers of the law were looking for some sly way to arrest Jesus and kill him. 2"But not during the Feast," they said, "or the people may riot."

3While he was in Bethany, reclining at the table in the home of a man known as Simon the Leper, a woman came with an alabaster jar of very expensive perfume, made of pure nard. She broke the jar and poured the perfume on his head.

4Some of those present were saying indignantly to one another, "Why this waste of perfume? 5It could have been sold for more than a year's wages*a* and the money given to the poor." And they rebuked her harshly.

6"Leave her alone," said Jesus. "Why are you bothering her? She has done a beautiful thing to me. 7The poor you will always have with you, and you can help them any time you want. But you will not always have me. 8She did what she could. She poured perfume on my body beforehand to prepare for my burial. 9I tell you the truth, wherever the gospel is preached throughout the world, what she has done will also be told, in memory of her."

10Then Judas Iscariot, one of the Twelve, went to the chief priests to betray Jesus to them. 11They were delighted to hear this and promised to give him money. So he watched for an opportunity to hand him over.

The Lord's Supper

12On the first day of the Feast of Unleavened Bread, when it was customary to sacrifice the Passover lamb, Jesus' disciples asked him, "Where do you want us to go and make preparations for you to eat the Passover?"

13So he sent two of his disciples, telling them, "Go into the city, and a man carrying a jar of water will meet you. Follow him. 14Say to the owner of the house he enters, 'The Teacher asks: Where is my guest room, where I may eat the Passover with my disciples?' 15He will show you a large upper room, furnished and ready. Make preparations for us there."

16The disciples left, went into the city and found things just as Jesus had told them. So they prepared the Passover.

17When evening came, Jesus arrived with the Twelve. 18While they were reclining at the table eating, he said, "I tell you the truth, one of you will betray me—one who is eating with me."

19They were saddened, and one by one they said to him, "Surely not I?"

20"It is one of the Twelve," he replied, "one who dips bread into the bowl with me. 21The Son of Man will go just as it is written about him. But woe to that man who betrays the Son of Man! It would be better for him if he had not been born."

---

a14 Daniel 9:27; 11:31; 12:11   *b14* Or *he;* also in verse 29   *c21* Or *Messiah*   *d25* Isaiah 13:10; 34:4   *e30* Or *race*   *f33* Some manuscripts *alert and pray*   *a5* Greek *than three hundred denarii*

22While they were eating, Jesus took bread, gave thanks and broke it, and gave it to his disciples, saying, "Take it; this is my body."

23Then he took the cup, gave thanks and offered it to them, and they all drank from it.

24"This is my blood of the[b] covenant, which is poured out for many," he said to them. 25"I tell you the truth, I will not drink again of the fruit of the vine until that day when I drink it anew in the kingdom of God."

26When they had sung a hymn, they went out to the Mount of Olives.

Jesus Predicts Peter's Denial

27"You will all fall away," Jesus told them, "for it is written:

" 'I will strike the shepherd,
    and the sheep will be scattered.'[c]

28But after I have risen, I will go ahead of you into Galilee."

29Peter declared, "Even if all fall away, I will not."

30"I tell you the truth," Jesus answered, "today—yes, tonight—before the cock crows twice[d] you yourself will disown me three times."

31But Peter insisted emphatically, "Even if I have to die with you, I will never disown you." And all the others said the same.

Gethsemane

32They went to a place called Gethsemane, and Jesus said to his disciples, "Sit here while I pray." 33He took Peter, James and John along with him, and he began to be deeply distressed and troubled. 34"My soul is overwhelmed with sorrow to the point of death," he said to them. "Stay here and keep watch."

35Going a little farther, he fell to the ground and prayed that if possible the hour might pass from him. 36"Abba,[e] Father," he said, "everything is possible for you. Take this cup from me. Yet not what I will, but what you will."

37Then he returned to his disciples and found them sleeping. "Simon," he said to Peter, "are you asleep? Could you not keep watch for one hour? 38Watch and pray so that you will not fall into temptation. The spirit is willing, but the body is weak."

39Once more he went away and prayed the same thing. 40When he came back, he again found them sleeping, because their eyes were heavy. They did not know what to say to him.

41Returning the third time, he said to them, "Are you still sleeping and resting? Enough! The hour has come. Look, the Son of Man is betrayed into the hands of sinners. 42Rise! Let us go! Here comes my betrayer!"

Jesus Arrested

43Just as he was speaking, Judas, one of the Twelve, appeared. With him was a crowd armed with swords and clubs, sent from the chief priests, the teachers of the law, and the elders.

44Now the betrayer had arranged a signal with them: "The one I kiss is the man; arrest him and lead him away under guard." 45Going at once to Jesus, Judas said, "Rabbi!" and kissed him. 46The men seized Jesus and arrested him. 47Then one of those standing near drew his sword and struck the servant of the high priest, cutting off his ear.

48"Am I leading a rebellion," said Jesus, "that you have come out with swords and clubs to capture me? 49Every day I was with you, teaching in the temple courts, and you did not arrest me. But the Scriptures must be fulfilled." 50Then everyone deserted him and fled.

51A young man, wearing nothing but a linen garment, was following Jesus. When they seized him, 52he fled naked, leaving his garment behind.

Before the Sanhedrin

53They took Jesus to the high priest, and all the chief priests, elders and teachers of the law came together. 54Peter followed him at a distance, right into the courtyard of the high priest. There he sat with the guards and warmed himself at the fire.

55The chief priests and the whole Sanhedrin were looking for evidence against Jesus so that they could put him to death, but they did not find any. 56Many testified falsely against him, but their statements did not agree.

57Then some stood up and gave this false testimony against him: 58"We heard him say, 'I will destroy this man-made temple and in three days will build another, not made by man.'" 59Yet even then their testimony did not agree.

60Then the high priest stood up before them and asked Jesus, "Are you not going to answer? What is this testimony that these men are bringing against you?" 61But Jesus remained silent and gave no answer.

Again the high priest asked him, "Are you the Christ,[f] the Son of the Blessed One?"

62"I am," said Jesus. "And you will see the Son of Man sitting at the right hand of the Mighty One and coming on the clouds of heaven."

63The high priest tore his clothes. "Why do we need any more witnesses?" he asked. 64"You have heard the blasphemy. What do you think?"

They all condemned him as worthy of death. 65Then some began to spit at him; they blindfolded him, struck him with their fists, and said, "Prophesy!" And the guards took him and beat him.

Peter Disowns Jesus

66While Peter was below in the courtyard, one of the servant girls of the high priest came by. 67When she saw Peter warming himself, she looked closely at him.

b24 Some manuscripts the new   c27 Zech. 13:7   d30 Some early manuscripts do not have twice.
e36 Aramaic for Father   f61 Or Messiah

"You also were with that Nazarene, Jesus," she said.

[68]But he denied it. "I don't know or understand what you're talking about," he said, and went out into the entrance.[g]

[69]When the servant girl saw him there, she said again to those standing around, "This fellow is one of them." [70]Again he denied it.

After a little while, those standing near said to Peter, "Surely you are one of them, for you are a Galilean."

[71]He began to call down curses on himself, and he swore to them, "I don't know this man you're talking about."

[72]Immediately the cock crowed the second time.[h] Then Peter remembered the word Jesus had spoken to him: "Before the cock crows twice[i] you will disown me three times." And he broke down and wept.

Jesus Before Pilate

15 Very early in the morning, the chief priests, with the elders, the teachers of the law and the whole Sanhedrin, reached a decision. They bound Jesus, led him away and turned him over to Pilate.

[2]"Are you the king of the Jews?" asked Pilate.

"Yes, it is as you say," Jesus replied.

[3]The chief priests accused him of many things. [4]So again Pilate asked him, "Aren't you going to answer? See how many things they are accusing you of."

[5]But Jesus still made no reply, and Pilate was amazed.

[6]Now it was the custom at the Feast to release a prisoner whom the people requested. [7]A man called Barabbas was in prison with the insurrectionists who had committed murder in the uprising. [8]The crowd came up and asked Pilate to do for them what he usually did.

[9]"Do you want me to release to you the king of the Jews?" asked Pilate, [10]knowing it was out of envy that the chief priests had handed Jesus over to him. [11]But the chief priests stirred up the crowd to have Pilate release Barabbas instead.

[12]"What shall I do, then, with the one you call the king of the Jews?" Pilate asked them.

[13]"Crucify him!" they shouted.

[14]"Why? What crime has he committed?" asked Pilate.

But they shouted all the louder, "Crucify him!"

[15]Wanting to satisfy the crowd, Pilate released Barabbas to them. He had Jesus flogged, and handed him over to be crucified.

The Soldiers Mock Jesus

[16]The soldiers led Jesus away into the palace (that is, the Praetorium) and called together the whole company of soldiers. [17]They put a purple robe on him, then twisted together a crown of thorns and set it on him. [18]And they began to call out to him, "Hail, king of the Jews!" [19]Again and again they struck him on the head with a staff and spat on him. Falling on their knees, they paid homage to him. [20]And when they had mocked him, they took off the purple robe and put his own clothes on him. Then they led him out to crucify him.

The Crucifixion

[21]A certain man from Cyrene, Simon, the father of Alexander and Rufus, was passing by on his way in from the country, and they forced him to carry the cross. [22]They brought Jesus to the place called Golgotha (which means The Place of the Skull). [23]Then they offered him wine mixed with myrrh, but he did not take it. [24]And they crucified him. Dividing up his clothes, they cast lots to see what each would get.

[25]It was the third hour when they crucified him. [26]The written notice of the charge against him read: THE KING OF THE JEWS. [27]They crucified two robbers with him, one on his right and one on his left.[a] [29]Those who passed by hurled insults at him, shaking their heads and saying, "So! You who are going to destroy the temple and build it in three days, [30]come down from the cross and save yourself!"

[31]In the same way the chief priests and the teachers of the law mocked him among themselves. "He saved others," they said, "but he can't save himself! [32]Let this Christ,[b] this King of Israel, come down now from the cross, that we may see and believe." Those crucified with him also heaped insults on him.

The Death of Jesus

[33]At the sixth hour darkness came over the whole land until the ninth hour. [34]And at the ninth hour Jesus cried out in a loud voice, "Eloi, Eloi, lama sabachthani?"—which means, "My God, my God, why have you forsaken me?"[c]

[35]When some of those standing near heard this, they said, "Listen, he's calling Elijah."

[36]One man ran, filled a sponge with wine vinegar, put it on a stick, and offered it to Jesus to drink. "Now leave him alone. Let's see if Elijah comes to take him down," he said.

[37]With a loud cry, Jesus breathed his last.

[38]The curtain of the temple was torn in two from top to bottom. [39]And when the centurion, who stood there in front of Jesus, heard his cry and[d] saw how he died, he said, "Surely this man was the Son[e] of God!"

[40]Some women were watching from a distance. Among them were Mary Magdalene, Mary the mother of James the younger and of Joses, and Salome. [41]In Galilee these women had followed him and cared for his needs. Many other women who had come up with him to Jerusalem were also there.

[g68] Some early manuscripts entrance and the cock crowed
[h72] Some early manuscripts do not have the second time.   [i72] Some early manuscripts do not have twice.
[a27] Some manuscripts left, [28]and the scripture was fulfilled which says, "He was counted with the lawless ones" (Isaiah 53:12)   [b32] Or Messiah   [c34] Psalm 22:1
[d39] Some manuscripts do not have heard his cry and.   [e39] Or a son

MARK 15:21–41
'And they crucified him' (v. 24a).

WE LOOK BACK AND WONDER why they crucified him. How could anyone look upon the Lord of glory and contemplate such action? He was not only good, he was transparently so. When he challenged his opponents to prove him guilty of sin (John 8:46) they were unable to do so. When the same opponents decided to have him arrested and charged they could produce only false witnesses (Matt. 26:60). Clearly there is a divisiveness in goodness which produces enemies. Jesus was a threat to the establishment because the establishment over many years had lost its way (John 11:49). If he was what he claimed to be then all they stood for socially, politically and materially was lost. The religious leaders had but two alternatives, they could either support him or oppose him. Merely to state the alternatives is to make their actions understandable.

That, however, simply expresses the crucifixion from the human angle and if that was a sufficient explanation we would never have heard of Jesus. Christ was crucified in order that human sin might be dealt with. Quite how he achieved this has exercised the minds and hearts of the most devout throughout the centuries and still there is no unanimity. Fortunately, it is through the cross and not through a theory of the cross that we have forgiveness. We only know that in some mysterious and glorious way the sins of all the world, all peoples and all generations, all the sins, the thinkable and the unthinkable, the foolish and the wilful, the simple and the utterly shameful were laid upon him as he hung upon the cross (2 Cor. 5:21; Gal. 3:13). And when we seek his forgiveness, for whatever kind of sin, then we are forgiven (1 John 1:9). We behold the mystery of Calvary with deepest awe and gratitude.

> *There was no other good enough*
> *To pay the price of sin;*
> *He only could unlock the gate*
> *Of heaven, and let us in.*

(Cecil F. Alexander)

→878

MARK 16:1–8
' "But go, tell his disciples and Peter" ' (v. 7a).

PETER STRESSED HIS FAULTS in recounting the gospel story to Mark. If the record was to be put straight, then others would have to do that, and since Mark's Gospel was the first written, he had no guarantee that others would do so. Peter seems to have spent the time after the crucifixion with the other disciples. Luke records Peter's going to the tomb and coming away very thoughtfully; John records both John and Peter going to the tomb. The younger John outran Peter, but stood at the entrance of the tomb, whereas the ever-impetuous Peter ran past him and observed the neat way in which the cloths had been folded.

After his denial of Jesus, Peter was wise not to separate himself from the others. Not that their behaviour, with the possible exception of John, and, of course, the women who were present at the crucifixion, was any better than his. His failure had actually come because his love had placed him in a vulnerable position, while the other disciples had remained at a safe distance. But the message from the angel to the women to tell the disciples, and Peter, revealed our Lord's special concern that Peter's wounds should be healed and that he should be restored. It is worthy of note that Luke records a special appearance of Jesus to Peter on that resurrection day. We assume that Peter's modesty compelled his silence on this meeting, but how precious it must have been.

No failure is too great, no sin is too great, to preclude a return into the fellowship of Christ. Easter Day is proof that our Lord can handle our failures and our sins.

> *He lifted sin's great burden.*
> *He saw my deep dismay.*
> *And graciously he pardoned me*
> *On that wonderful, wonderful day.*

(Sidney E. Cox)

The Burial of Jesus

42It was Preparation Day (that is, the day before the Sabbath). So as evening approached, 43Joseph of Arimathea, a prominent member of the Council, who was himself waiting for the kingdom of God, went boldly to Pilate and asked for Jesus' body. 44Pilate was surprised to hear that he was already dead. Summoning the centurion, he asked him if Jesus had already died. 45When he learned from the centurion that it was so, he gave the body to Joseph. 46So Joseph bought some linen cloth, took down the body, wrapped it in the linen, and placed it in a tomb cut out of rock. Then he rolled a stone against the entrance of the tomb. 47Mary Magdalene and Mary the mother of Joses saw where he was laid.

The Resurrection

16 When the Sabbath was over, Mary Magdalene, Mary the mother of James, and Salome bought spices so that they might go to anoint Jesus' body. 2Very early on the first day of the week, just after sunrise, they were on their way to the tomb 3and they asked each other, "Who will roll the stone away from the entrance of the tomb?"

4But when they looked up, they saw that the stone, which was very large, had been rolled away. 5As they entered the tomb, they saw a young man dressed in a white robe sitting on the right side, and they were alarmed.

6"Don't be alarmed," he said. "You are looking for Jesus the Nazarene, who was crucified. He has risen! He is not here. See the place where they laid him. 7But go, tell his disciples and Peter, 'He is going ahead of you into Galilee. There you will see him, just as he told you.'"

8Trembling and bewildered, the women went out and fled from the tomb. They said nothing to anyone, because they were afraid.

[The most reliable early manuscripts and other ancient witnesses do not have Mark 16:9–20.]

9When Jesus rose early on the first day of the week, he appeared first to Mary Magdalene, out of whom he had driven seven demons. 10She went and told those who had been with him and who were mourning and weeping. 11When they heard that Jesus was alive and that she had seen him, they did not believe it.

12Afterwards Jesus appeared in a different form to two of them while they were walking in the country. 13These returned and reported it to the rest; but they did not believe them either.

14Later Jesus appeared to the Eleven as they were eating; he rebuked them for their lack of faith and their stubborn refusal to believe those who had seen him after he had risen.

15He said to them, "Go into all the world and preach the good news to all creation. 16Whoever believes and is baptised will be saved, but whoever does not believe will be condemned. 17And these signs will accompany those who believe: In my name they will drive out demons; they will speak in new tongues; 18they will pick up snakes with their hands; and when they drink deadly poison, it will not hurt them at all; they will place their hands on sick people, and they will get well."

19After the Lord Jesus had spoken to them, he was taken up into heaven and he sat at the right hand of God. 20Then the disciples went out and preached everywhere, and the Lord worked with them and confirmed his word by the signs that accompanied it.

Luke

Introduction

1 Many have undertaken to draw up an account of the things that have been fulfilled[a] among us, ²just as they were handed down to us by those who from the first were eye-witnesses and servants of the word. ³Therefore, since I myself have carefully investigated everything from the beginning, it seemed good also to me to write an orderly account for you, most excellent Theophilus, ⁴so that you may know the certainty of the things you have been taught.

The Birth of John the Baptist Foretold

⁵In the time of Herod king of Judea there was a priest named Zechariah, who belonged to the priestly division of Abijah; his wife Elizabeth was also a descendant of Aaron. ⁶Both of them were upright in the sight of God, observing all the Lord's commandments and regulations blamelessly. ⁷But they had no children, because Elizabeth was barren; and they were both well on in years.

⁸Once when Zechariah's division was on duty and he was serving as priest before God, ⁹he was chosen by lot, according to the custom of the priesthood, to go into the temple of the Lord and burn incense. ¹⁰And when the time for the burning of incense came, all the assembled worshippers were praying outside.

¹¹Then an angel of the Lord appeared to him, standing at the right side of the altar of incense. ¹²When Zechariah saw him, he was startled and was gripped with fear. ¹³But the angel said to him: "Do not be afraid, Zechariah; your prayer has been heard. Your wife Elizabeth will bear you a son, and you are to give him the name John. ¹⁴He will be a joy and delight to you, and many will rejoice because of his birth, ¹⁵for he will be great in the sight of the Lord. He is never to take wine or other fermented drink, and he will be filled with the Holy Spirit even from birth.[b] ¹⁶Many of the people of Israel will he bring back to the Lord their God. ¹⁷And he will go on before the Lord, in the spirit and power of Elijah, to turn the hearts of the fathers to their children and the disobedient to the wisdom of the righteous—to make ready a people prepared for the Lord."

¹⁸Zechariah asked the angel, "How can I be sure of this? I am an old man and my wife is well on in years."

¹⁹The angel answered, "I am Gabriel. I stand in the presence of God, and I have been sent to speak to you and to tell you this good news. ²⁰And now you will be silent and not able to speak until the day this happens, because you did not believe my words, which will come true at their proper time."

²¹Meanwhile, the people were waiting for Zechariah and wondering why he stayed so long in the temple. ²²When he came out, he could not speak to them. They realised he had seen a vision in the temple, for he kept making signs to them but remained unable to speak.

²³When his time of service was completed, he returned home. ²⁴After this his wife Elizabeth became pregnant and for five months remained in seclusion. ²⁵"The Lord has done this for me," she said. "In these days he has shown his favour and taken away my disgrace among the people."

The Birth of Jesus Foretold

²⁶In the sixth month, God sent the angel Gabriel to Nazareth, a town in Galilee, ²⁷to a virgin pledged to be married to a man named Joseph, a descendant of David. The virgin's name was Mary. ²⁸The angel went to her and said, "Greetings, you who are highly favoured! The Lord is with you."

²⁹Mary was greatly troubled at his words and wondered what kind of greeting this might be. ³⁰But the angel said to her, "Do not be afraid, Mary, you have found favour with God. ³¹You will be with child and give birth to a son, and you are to give him the name Jesus. ³²He will be great and will be called the Son of the Most High. The Lord God will give him the throne of his father David, ³³and he will reign over the house of Jacob for ever; his kingdom will never end."

³⁴"How will this be," Mary asked the angel, "since I am a virgin?"

³⁵The angel answered, "The Holy Spirit will come upon you, and the power of the Most High will overshadow you. So the holy one to be born will be called[c] the Son of God. ³⁶Even Elizabeth your relative is going to

---

[a]1 Or *been surely believed* [b]15 Or *from his mother's womb*
[c]35 Or *So the child to be born will be called holy,*

LUKE 1:1–4

'Therefore, since I myself have carefully investigated everything from the beginning, it seemed good also to me to write an orderly account for you, most excellent Theophilus, so that you may know the certainty of the things you have been taught' (vv. 3, 4).

WHO WAS THEOPHILUS? Both the Gospel of Luke and the Acts of the Apostles were addressed to him. The fact that Luke addresses him as 'most excellent' seems to suggest that he was not a Christian, otherwise he would have been given the designation 'brother'. The name implies that he was a Greek and some have conjectured that 'most excellent' indicated that he had an official status. Apart from Luke's compulsion to record the events of our Lord's life and the beginnings of the Church, there is a strong possibility that by addressing his work to 'the most excellent Theophilus', Luke might be smoothing the way for a broader acceptance of the gospel itself. There was much misunderstanding of the faith in those days and the name and person of Theophilus could well be used to lift the general level of acceptance.

Although not intended by Luke, the very name of the addressee and our lack of knowledge of him have an interesting significance for us. Theophilus means 'loved of God', and as a person we cannot identify him. Neither in Luke's Gospel can we identify the prodigal son, nor the good Samaritan, nor the importunate friend, but down the years men and women have identified themselves in one or other of these roles and have found salvation.

Since we too are 'loved of God', can we not take this Gospel as one which is addressed to us, and let the Holy Spirit make of it a very personal and persuasive account of the life of Christ?

> *Lord, thy word abideth,*
> *And our footsteps guideth;*
> *Who its truth believeth*
> *Light and joy receiveth.*

(*Henry W. Baker*)

→882

LUKE 1:39–45, 57–66

'As soon as the sound of your greeting reached my ears, the baby in my womb leaped for joy . . . Her neighbours and relatives heard that the Lord had shown her great mercy, and they shared her joy' (vv. 44, 58).

A SORROW SHARED IS A SORROW HALVED. A joy shared is not halved but doubled. How strange! But how comforting! The power of sharing is strong indeed. It is a terrible thing to feel that you are alone.

Many areas of life are private, closed to the gaze of others. Because of this, it can seem to any one of us that an unusual trait, habit or difficulty is unique. Many are haunted by guilt for they fear no one else has the same feelings or instincts which are part of their mental and emotional state. The more we talk openly about feelings of anger, destructive urges, sexual drives, nightmares, insecurities, phobias, etc. the more we realize we are not alone. Others share our feelings and may understand them in greater or lesser degree.

Today's two passages are records of sharing. Mary and Elizabeth shared what was indeed a rare experience, being chosen by the Spirit for a special, unique task. But even such rare experiences could still be shared. Neither of them was alone.

The unique experience of Christmas, the divine presence coming into the world at a point in time, can be shared like any other. Let us pray that Christians everywhere will share their joy at the coming of the infant king, and so increase not only their own joy but the joy of others.

How often it is a relief just to know that there are other people who share the same oddity or difficulty. However hard they try, people find it almost impossible to understand the difficulties of others when they have not experienced them themselves.

→885

have a child in her old age, and she who was said to be barren is in her sixth month. [37]For nothing is impossible with God."

[38]"I am the Lord's servant," Mary answered. "May it be to me as you have said." Then the angel left her.

Mary Visits Elizabeth

[39]At that time Mary got ready and hurried to a town in the hill country of Judea, [40]where she entered Zechariah's home and greeted Elizabeth. [41]When Elizabeth heard Mary's greeting, the baby leaped in her womb, and Elizabeth was filled with the Holy Spirit. [42]In a loud voice she exclaimed: "Blessed are you among women, and blessed is the child you will bear! [43]But why am I so favoured, that the mother of my Lord should come to me? [44]As soon as the sound of your greeting reached my ears, the baby in my womb leaped for joy. [45]Blessed is she who has believed that what the Lord has said to her will be accomplished!"

Mary's Song

[46]And Mary said:

"My soul glorifies the Lord
[47]   and my spirit rejoices in God my Saviour,
[48]for he has been mindful
    of the humble state of his servant.
    From now on all generations will call me blessed,
[49]   for the Mighty One has done great things for me—
    holy is his name.
[50]His mercy extends to those who fear him,
    from generation to generation.
[51]He has performed mighty deeds with his arm;
    he has scattered those who are proud in their inmost thoughts.
[52]He has brought down rulers from their thrones
    but has lifted up the humble.
[53]He has filled the hungry with good things
    but has sent the rich away empty.
[54]He has helped his servant Israel,
    remembering to be merciful
[55]to Abraham and his descendants for ever,
    even as he said to our fathers."

[56]Mary stayed with Elizabeth for about three months and then returned home.

The Birth of John the Baptist

[57]When it was time for Elizabeth to have her baby, she gave birth to a son. [58]Her neighbours and relatives heard that the Lord had shown her great mercy, and they shared her joy.

[59]On the eighth day they came to circumcise the child, and they were going to name him after his father Zechariah, [60]but his mother spoke up and said, "No! He is to be called John."

[61]They said to her, "There is no-one among your relatives who has that name."

[62]Then they made signs to his father, to find out what he would like to name the child. [63]He asked for a writing tablet, and to everyone's astonishment he wrote, "His name is John." [64]Immediately his mouth was opened and his tongue was loosed, and he began to speak, praising God. [65]The neighbours were all filled with awe, and throughout the hill country of Judea people were talking about all these things. [66]Everyone who heard this wondered about it, asking, "What then is this child going to be?" For the Lord's hand was with him.

Zechariah's Song

[67]His father Zechariah was filled with the Holy Spirit and prophesied:

[68]"Praise be to the Lord, the God of Israel,
    because he has come and has redeemed his people.
[69]He has raised up a horn[d] of salvation for us
    in the house of his servant David
[70](as he said through his holy prophets of long ago),
[71]salvation from our enemies
    and from the hand of all who hate us—
[72]to show mercy to our fathers
    and to remember his holy covenant,
[73]   the oath he swore to our father Abraham:
[74]to rescue us from the hand of our enemies,
    and to enable us to serve him without fear
[75]   in holiness and righteousness before him all our days.

[76]And you, my child, will be called a prophet of the Most High;
    for you will go on before the Lord to prepare the way for him,
[77]to give his people the knowledge of salvation
    through the forgiveness of their sins,
[78]because of the tender mercy of our God,
    by which the rising sun will come to us from heaven
[79]to shine on those living in darkness
    and in the shadow of death,
    to guide our feet into the path of peace."

[80]And the child grew and became strong in spirit; and he lived in the desert until he appeared publicly to Israel.

The Birth of Jesus

2 In those days Caesar Augustus issued a decree that a census should be taken of the entire Roman world. ([2]This was the first census that took place while Quirinius was governor of Syria.) [3]And everyone went to his own town to register.

[4]So Joseph also went up from the town of Nazareth in Galilee to Judea, to Bethlehem the town of David, because he belonged to the house and line of David. [5]He went there to register with Mary, who was pledged to be married to him and was expecting a child. [6]While they were there, the time came for the

[d]69 *Horn* here symbolises strength.

baby to be born, 7and she gave birth to her firstborn, a son. She wrapped him in cloths and placed him in a manger, because there was no room for them in the inn.

The Shepherds and the Angels

8And there were shepherds living out in the fields near by, keeping watch over their flocks at night. 9An angel of the Lord appeared to them, and the glory of the Lord shone around them, and they were terrified. 10But the angel said to them, "Do not be afraid. I bring you good news of great joy that will be for all the people. 11Today in the town of David a Saviour has been born to you; he is Christ*a* the Lord. 12This will be a sign to you: You will find a baby wrapped in cloths and lying in a manger."

13Suddenly a great company of the heavenly host appeared with the angel, praising God and saying,

14"Glory to God in the highest,
    and on earth peace to men on whom his
      favour rests."

15When the angels had left them and gone into heaven, the shepherds said to one another, "Let's go to Bethlehem and see this thing that has happened, which the Lord has told us about."

16So they hurried off and found Mary and Joseph, and the baby, who was lying in the manger. 17When they had seen him, they spread the word concerning what had been told them about this child, 18and all who heard it were amazed at what the shepherds said to them. 19But Mary treasured up all these things and pondered them in her heart. 20The shepherds returned, glorifying and praising God for all the things they had heard and seen, which were just as they had been told.

Jesus Presented in the Temple

21On the eighth day, when it was time to circumcise him, he was named Jesus, the name the angel had given him before he had been conceived.

22When the time of their purification according to the Law of Moses had been completed, Joseph and Mary took him to Jerusalem to present him to the Lord 23(as it is written in the Law of the Lord, "Every firstborn male is to be consecrated to the Lord"*b*), 24and to offer a sacrifice in keeping with what is said in the Law of the Lord: "a pair of doves or two young pigeons".*c*

25Now there was a man in Jerusalem called Simeon, who was righteous and devout. He was waiting for the consolation of Israel, and the Holy Spirit was upon him. 26It had been revealed to him by the Holy Spirit that he would not die before he had seen the Lord's Christ. 27Moved by the Spirit, he went into the temple courts. When the parents brought

in the child Jesus to do for him what the custom of the Law required, 28Simeon took him in his arms and praised God, saying:

29"Sovereign Lord, as you have promised,
    you now dismiss*d* your servant in peace.
30For my eyes have seen your salvation,
31 which you have prepared in the sight of
      all people,
32a light for revelation to the Gentiles
    and for glory to your people Israel."

33The child's father and mother marvelled at what was said about him. 34Then Simeon blessed them and said to Mary, his mother: "This child is destined to cause the falling and rising of many in Israel, and to be a sign that will be spoken against, 35so that the thoughts of many hearts will be revealed. And a sword will pierce your own soul too."

36There was also a prophetess, Anna, the daughter of Phanuel, of the tribe of Asher. She was very old; she had lived with her husband seven years after her marriage, 37and then was a widow until she was eighty-four.*e* She never left the temple but worshipped night and day, fasting and praying. 38Coming up to them at that very moment, she gave thanks to God and spoke about the child to all who were looking forward to the redemption of Jerusalem.

39When Joseph and Mary had done everything required by the Law of the Lord, they returned to Galilee to their own town of Nazareth. 40And the child grew and became strong; he was filled with wisdom, and the grace of God was upon him.

The Boy Jesus at the Temple

41Every year his parents went to Jerusalem for the Feast of the Passover. 42When he was twelve years old, they went up to the Feast, according to the custom. 43After the Feast was over, while his parents were returning home, the boy Jesus stayed behind in Jerusalem, but they were unaware of it. 44Thinking he was in their company, they travelled on for a day. Then they began looking for him among their relatives and friends. 45When they did not find him, they went back to Jerusalem to look for him. 46After three days they found him in the temple courts, sitting among the teachers, listening to them and asking them questions. 47Everyone who heard him was amazed at his understanding and his answers. 48When his parents saw him, they were astonished. His mother said to him, "Son, why have you treated us like this? Your father and I have been anxiously searching for you."

49"Why were you searching for me?" he asked. "Didn't you know I had to be in my Father's house?" 50But they did not understand what he was saying to them.

51Then he went down to Nazareth with them and was obedient to them. But his mother treasured all these things in her heart.

a11 Or *Messiah.* "The Christ" (Greek) and "the Messiah" (Hebrew) both mean "the Anointed One"; also in verse 26. *b23* Exodus 13:2,12 *c24* Lev. 12:8 *d29* Or *promised, / now dismiss*
e37 Or *widow for eighty-four years*

LUKE 2:1–20

'She gave birth to her first-born, a son. She wrapped him in cloths and placed him in a manger . . . Mary treasured up all these things and pondered them in her heart (vv. 7a, 19).

CHRISTMAS IS A NOISY TIME. People celebrate with music and singing. Parties and feasting occur as at no other time of the year. Yet here and there, amid the jollity and fun, are little pockets of quietness and meditation – during a midnight vigil, or a morning service; the quietness of a deserted street, or the confines of one's own home; the silence of a lonely vigil at the bedside of a sick friend, or the stillness of a workplace where you are on duty alone.

Quietness can be physical, a real silence you can almost touch, or it may be spiritual, a peace which flows around you in the midst of the hurly burly of the celebration. That, surely, was Mary's experience.

Her Christmas was noisy. The warm breath of animals, lowing and bleating round the manger; people crowding into the inn; angels loudly praising God; shepherds coming excitedly to worship – the whole picture is of activity and noise. Yet something so peaceful, so quiet surrounds Mary's action, as she gently places Jesus in the manger, treasuring these things in her heart. We sense her mood of quietness and peace amidst the noisy reality.

> *Softly the night is sleeping*
> *On Bethlehem's peaceful hill;*
> *Silent the shepherds watching,*
> *The gentle flocks are still.*
> *But hark! The wondrous music*
> *Falls from the op'ning sky;*
> *Valley and cliff re-echo:*
> *Glory to God on high!*
> *Glory to God! It rings again;*
> *Peace on the earth, goodwill to men.*

(Anon)

→886

LUKE 2:21–35

'A light for revelation to the Gentiles and for glory to your people Israel . . . This child is destined to cause the falling and rising of many in Israel, and to be a sign that will be spoken against, so that the thoughts of many hearts will be revealed. And a sword will pierce your own soul too' (vv. 32, 34b, 35).

SIMEON'S EXPERIENCE was a narrow one, probably confined to Jerusalem, particularly the surroundings of the temple. Day in day out, month in month out, year in year out the old man waited to see his dream come true, to see the arrival of the anointed one of Israel, the Lord's Messiah or Christ who would be the bringer of salvation.

Simeon's experience was limited, but his vision was wide. He knew Israel was God's special choice. Many of his contemporaries simply left matters there. If God had chosen Israel, then so be it. They were content to bask in that glory, take the blessings God bestowed on them now, and wait for a brighter future. One day, perhaps, Rome would be overthrown and Israel would come into its own.

For Simeon it was different. God's choice of Israel was as a light to the Gentiles. God's covenant would only have meaning if it spread beyond the confines of Israel and Judaism, to encompass the whole Gentile world as well. How remarkable that Simeon should see such potential in the tiny baby that was brought to him, just like so many thousands of others, routinely presented for circumcision and dedication to the Lord.

How important for us each to realize the potential which exists in every tiny human being. Not all babies are potential Messiahs, but each has enormous possibilities for good or ill. Once that is recognized, it is possible to educate, to develop the child's gifts and capabilities and to bring out the potential for good.

→889

[52]And Jesus grew in wisdom and stature, and in favour with God and men.

John the Baptist Prepares the Way

3 In the fifteenth year of the reign of Tiberius Caesar—when Pontius Pilate was governor of Judea, Herod tetrarch of Galilee, his brother Philip tetrarch of Iturea and Traconitis, and Lysanias tetrarch of Abilene —[2]during the high priesthood of Annas and Caiaphas, the word of God came to John son of Zechariah in the desert. [3]He went into all the country around the Jordan, preaching a baptism of repentance for the forgiveness of sins. [4]As is written in the book of the words of Isaiah the prophet:

"A voice of one calling in the desert,
'Prepare the way for the Lord,
  make straight paths for him.
[5]Every valley shall be filled in,
  every mountain and hill made low.
The crooked roads shall become straight,
  the rough ways smooth.
[6]And all mankind will see God's
  salvation.'"[a]

[7]John said to the crowds coming out to be baptised by him, "You brood of vipers! Who warned you to flee from the coming wrath? [8]Produce fruit in keeping with repentance. And do not begin to say to yourselves, 'We have Abraham as our father.' For I tell you that out of these stones God can raise up children for Abraham. [9]The axe is already at the root of the trees, and every tree that does not produce good fruit will be cut down and thrown into the fire."

[10]"What should we do then?" the crowd asked.

[11]John answered, "The man with two tunics should share with him who has none, and the one who has food should do the same."

[12]Tax collectors also came to be baptised. "Teacher," they asked, "what should we do?"

[13]"Don't collect any more than you are required to," he told them.

[14]Then some soldiers asked him, "And what should we do?"

He replied, "Don't extort money and don't accuse people falsely—be content with your pay."

[15]The people were waiting expectantly and were all wondering in their hearts if John might possibly be the Christ.[b] [16]John answered them all, "I baptise you with[c] water. But one more powerful than I will come, the thongs of whose sandals I am not worthy to untie. He will baptise you with the Holy Spirit and with fire. [17]His winnowing fork is in his hand to clear his threshing-floor and to gather the wheat into his barn, but he will burn up the chaff with unquenchable fire." [18]And with many other words John exhorted the people and preached the good news to them.

[19]But when John rebuked Herod the tetrarch because of Herodias, his brother's wife, and all the other evil things he had done, [20]Herod added this to them all: He locked John up in prison.

The Baptism and Genealogy of Jesus

[21]When all the people were being baptised, Jesus was baptised too. And as he was praying, heaven was opened [22]and the Holy Spirit descended on him in bodily form like a dove. And a voice came from heaven: "You are my Son, whom I love; with you I am well pleased."

[23]Now Jesus himself was about thirty years old when he began his ministry. He was the son, so it was thought, of Joseph,

the son of Heli, [24]the son of Matthat,
the son of Levi, the son of Melki,
the son of Jannai, the son of Joseph,
[25]the son of Mattathias, the son of Amos,
the son of Nahum, the son of Esli,
the son of Naggai, [26]the son of Maath,
the son of Mattathias, the son of Semein,
the son of Josech, the son of Joda,
[27]the son of Joanan, the son of Rhesa,
the son of Zerubbabel, the son of Shealtiel,
the son of Neri, [28]the son of Melki,
the son of Addi, the son of Cosam,
the son of Elmadam, the son of Er,
[29]the son of Joshua, the son of Eliezer,
the son of Jorim, the son of Matthat,
the son of Levi, [30]the son of Simeon,
the son of Judah, the son of Joseph,
the son of Jonam, the son of Eliakim,
[31]the son of Melea, the son of Menna,
the son of Mattatha, the son of Nathan,
the son of David, [32]the son of Jesse,
the son of Obed, the son of Boaz,
the son of Salmon,[d] the son of Nahshon,
[33]the son of Amminadab, the son of Ram,[e]
the son of Hezron, the son of Perez,
the son of Judah, [34]the son of Jacob,
the son of Isaac, the son of Abraham,
the son of Terah, the son of Nahor,
[35]the son of Serug, the son of Reu,
the son of Peleg, the son of Eber,
the son of Shelah, [36]the son of Cainan,
the son of Arphaxad, the son of Shem,
the son of Noah, the son of Lamech,
[37]the son of Methuselah, the son of Enoch,
the son of Jared, the son of Mahalalel,
the son of Kenan, [38]the son of Enosh,
the son of Seth, the son of Adam,
the son of God.

The Temptation of Jesus

4 Jesus, full of the Holy Spirit, returned from the Jordan and was led by the Spirit in the desert, [2]where for forty days he was tempted by the devil. He ate nothing during those days, and at the end of them he was hungry.

[3]The devil said to him, "If you are the Son of God, tell this stone to become bread."

---

[a]6 Isaiah 40:3–5   [b]15 Or Messiah   [c]16 Or in   [d]32 Some early manuscripts Sala
[e]33 Some manuscripts Amminadab, the son of Admin, the son of Arni; other manuscripts vary widely.

⁴Jesus answered, "It is written: 'Man does not live on bread alone.'ᵃ"

⁵The devil led him up to a high place and showed him in an instant all the kingdoms of the world. ⁶And he said to him, "I will give you all their authority and splendour, for it has been given to me, and I can give it to anyone I want to. ⁷So if you worship me, it will all be yours."

⁸Jesus answered, "It is written: 'Worship the Lord your God and serve him only.'ᵇ"

⁹The devil led him to Jerusalem and had him stand on the highest point of the temple. "If you are the Son of God," he said, "throw yourself down from here. ¹⁰For it is written:

"'He will command his angels concerning you
    to guard you carefully;
¹¹they will lift you up in their hands,
    so that you will not strike your foot
        against a stone.'ᶜ"

¹²Jesus answered, "It says: 'Do not put the Lord your God to the test.'ᵈ"

¹³When the devil had finished all this tempting, he left him until an opportune time.

Jesus Rejected at Nazareth

¹⁴Jesus returned to Galilee in the power of the Spirit, and news about him spread through the whole countryside. ¹⁵He taught in their synagogues, and everyone praised him.

¹⁶He went to Nazareth, where he had been brought up, and on the Sabbath day he went into the synagogue, as was his custom. And he stood up to read. ¹⁷The scroll of the prophet Isaiah was handed to him. Unrolling it, he found the place where it is written:

¹⁸"The Spirit of the Lord is on me,
    because he has anointed me
    to preach good news to the poor.
He has sent me to proclaim freedom for
        the prisoners
    and recovery of sight for the blind,
to release the oppressed,
¹⁹   to proclaim the year of the Lord's
        favour."ᵉ

²⁰Then he rolled up the scroll, gave it back to the attendant and sat down. The eyes of everyone in the synagogue were fastened on him, ²¹and he began by saying to them, "Today this scripture is fulfilled in your hearing."

²²All spoke well of him and were amazed at the gracious words that came from his lips. "Isn't this Joseph's son?" they asked.

²³Jesus said to them, "Surely you will quote this proverb to me: 'Physician, heal yourself! Do here in your home town what we have heard that you did in Capernaum.'"

²⁴"I tell you the truth," he continued, "no prophet is accepted in his home town. ²⁵I assure you that there were many widows in

Israel in Elijah's time, when the sky was shut for three and a half years and there was a severe famine throughout the land. ²⁶Yet Elijah was not sent to any of them, but to a widow in Zarephath in the region of Sidon. ²⁷And there were many in Israel with leprosyᶠ in the time of Elisha the prophet, yet not one of them was cleansed—only Naaman the Syrian."

²⁸All the people in the synagogue were furious when they heard this. ²⁹They got up, drove him out of the town, and took him to the brow of the hill on which the town was built, in order to throw him down the cliff. ³⁰But he walked right through the crowd and went on his way.

Jesus Drives Out an Evil Spirit

³¹Then he went down to Capernaum, a town in Galilee, and on the Sabbath began to teach the people. ³²They were amazed at his teaching, because his message had authority.

³³In the synagogue there was a man possessed by a demon, an evilᵍ spirit. He cried out at the top of his voice, ³⁴"Ha! What do you want with us, Jesus of Nazareth? Have you come to destroy us? I know who you are—the Holy One of God!"

³⁵"Be quiet!" Jesus said sternly. "Come out of him!" Then the demon threw the man down before them all and came out without injuring him.

³⁶All the people were amazed and said to each other, "What is this teaching? With authority and power he gives orders to evil spirits and they come out!" ³⁷And the news about him spread throughout the surrounding area.

Jesus Heals Many

³⁸Jesus left the synagogue and went to the home of Simon. Now Simon's mother-in-law was suffering from a high fever, and they asked Jesus to help her. ³⁹So he bent over her and rebuked the fever, and it left her. She got up at once and began to wait on them.

⁴⁰When the sun was setting, the people brought to Jesus all who had various kinds of sickness, and laying his hands on each one, he healed them. ⁴¹Moreover, demons came out of many people, shouting, "You are the Son of God!" But he rebuked them and would not allow them to speak, because they knew he was the Christ.ʰ

⁴²At daybreak Jesus went out to a solitary place. The people were looking for him and when they came to where he was, they tried to keep him from leaving them. ⁴³But he said, "I must preach the good news of the kingdom of God to the other towns also, because that is why I was sent." ⁴⁴And he kept on preaching in the synagogues of Judea.ⁱ

The Calling of the First Disciples

5 One day as Jesus was standing by the Lake of Gennesaret,ᵃ with the people crowding round him and listening to the word

---

ᵃ4 Deut. 8:3   ᵇ8 Deut. 6:13   ᶜ11 Psalm 91:11,12   ᵈ12 Deut. 6:16   ᵉ19 Isaiah 61:1,2
ᶠ27 The Greek word was used for various diseases affecting the skin—not necessarily leprosy.
ᵍ33 Greek unclean; also in verse 36   ʰ41 Or Messiah
ⁱ44 Or the land of the Jews; some manuscripts Galilee   ᵃ1 That is, Sea of Galilee

LUKE 2:36–40

'There was also a prophetess, Anna . . . She never left the temple but worshipped night and day, fasting and praying' (vv. 36a, 37b).

YOUNG AND OLD, rich and poor, male and female, all alike have a share in the gospel. Scholars often stress the way Luke gives prominence to women who were associated with Jesus and the gospel. For instance, Mary herself, Elizabeth, the widow of Nain, the woman in Simon's house, Susanna and Joanna, Martha and Mary, and others.

Luke does not quite give Anna, the old prophetess, the prominence he accords to the old man, Simeon. But Anna *is* included. In a society where women were regarded as having no legal rights, and where they depended on a guardian to act for them throughout their life, it is a truly remarkable picture. Today the battle for women to be recognized as full human beings with equal rights and opportunities is still being fought. Some might feel it has already been won, but there is still a long way to go. Tragically there are still societies where women are regarded as inferior. In others they are treated as inferior, even where theoretically they enjoy 'equality'.

Still more tragically, the Christian Church has often failed to follow its Lord, and has treated women almost as though they were a different species. Jesus went far beyond the conventions of his day in the welcome that he accorded to women, and in the high regard which he gave to them. Let us pray that his Church today will do the same.

Instead of lagging behind society in recognizing the basic rights of man and woman alike, may the Church be in the vanguard, taking their example from our Lord Jesus Christ as Luke has portrayed him.

→890

LUKE 3:1–9, 15–18

'John answered them all, "I baptise you with water. But one more powerful than I will come, the thongs of whose sandals I am not worthy to untie" ' (v. 16).

GOD DOES NOT OFTEN interfere with the ordinary laws of nature, but when he does it is with powerful effect. The promise of a son to the aged Zechariah and Elizabeth (Luke 1:11ff.) was as startling as to Abraham and Sarah hundreds of years earlier (Gen. 17:15–17). The promise to Abraham was the beginning of a dynasty, the promise to Zechariah heralded the imminence of the kingdom of God.

Zechariah's encounter with the angel of the Lord and the subsequent encounter of Elizabeth with Mary, the mother of our Lord (Luke 1:39ff.), serve only to confirm that the inspired words of the prophets, and the hopes of the faithful, were about to be fulfilled by the incarnation of the Son of God.

Was there a ripple of excitement among the heavenly host as God began to draw in the strands of human history and prophetic revelation? Were there gasps of amazement and satisfaction on the part of the angelic choir when they learned of their special role above a Bethlehem field in the very near future? Certainly, there would be a gathering sense of awe in the minds of Zechariah and Elizabeth, and Mary and Joseph, as they became increasingly aware of their place in this unique event. And we, from our vantage point in history, tracing God's strategy, can only marvel at the glory of this divine intervention in human affairs.

John the Baptist seemed to match the expectations of the people for the Messiah (Luke 3:15). But he was only the messenger, the herald of Christ's coming, one who was more than a prophet and yet was the least in the kingdom he came to proclaim (Luke 7:26–28). The Christ was yet to be revealed.

Thank you, Lord, for loving us so much.

→893

of God, [2]he saw at the water's edge two boats, left there by the fishermen, who were washing their nets. [3]He got into one of the boats, the one belonging to Simon, and asked him to put out a little from shore. Then he sat down and taught the people from the boat.

[4]When he had finished speaking, he said to Simon, "Put out into deep water, and let down[b] the nets for a catch."

[5]Simon answered, "Master, we've worked hard all night and haven't caught anything. But because you say so, I will let down the nets."

[6]When they had done so, they caught such a large number of fish that their nets began to break. [7]So they signalled to their partners in the other boat to come and help them, and they came and filled both boats so full that they began to sink.

[8]When Simon Peter saw this, he fell at Jesus' knees and said, "Go away from me, Lord; I am a sinful man!" [9]For he and all his companions were astonished at the catch of fish they had taken, [10]and so were James and John, the sons of Zebedee, Simon's partners.

Then Jesus said to Simon, "Don't be afraid; from now on you will catch men." [11]So they pulled their boats up on shore, left everything and followed him.

The Man With Leprosy

[12]While Jesus was in one of the towns, a man came along who was covered with leprosy.[c] When he saw Jesus, he fell with his face to the ground and begged him, "Lord, if you are willing, you can make me clean."

[13]Jesus reached out his hand and touched the man. "I am willing," he said. "Be clean!" And immediately the leprosy left him.

[14]Then Jesus ordered him, "Don't tell anyone, but go, show yourself to the priest and offer the sacrifices that Moses commanded for your cleansing, as a testimony to them."

[15]Yet the news about him spread all the more, so that crowds of people came to hear him and to be healed of their sicknesses. [16]But Jesus often withdrew to lonely places and prayed.

Jesus Heals a Paralytic

[17]One day as he was teaching, Pharisees and teachers of the law, who had come from every village of Galilee and from Judea and Jerusalem, were sitting there. And the power of the Lord was present for him to heal the sick. [18]Some men came carrying a paralytic on a mat and tried to take him into the house to lay him before Jesus. [19]When they could not find a way to do this because of the crowd, they went up on the roof and lowered him on his mat through the tiles into the middle of the crowd, right in front of Jesus. [20]When Jesus saw their faith, he said, "Friend, your sins are forgiven."

[21]The Pharisees and the teachers of the law began thinking to themselves, "Who is this fellow who speaks blasphemy? Who can forgive sins but God alone?"

[22]Jesus knew what they were thinking and asked, "Why are you thinking these things in your hearts? [23]Which is easier: to say, 'Your sins are forgiven,' or to say, 'Get up and walk'? [24]But that you may know that the Son of Man has authority on earth to forgive sins. . . ." He said to the paralysed man, "I tell you, get up, take your mat and go home." [25]Immediately he stood up in front of them, took what he had been lying on and went home praising God. [26]Everyone was amazed and gave praise to God. They were filled with awe and said, "We have seen remarkable things today."

The Calling of Levi

[27]After this, Jesus went out and saw a tax collector by the name of Levi sitting at his tax booth. "Follow me," Jesus said to him, [28]and Levi got up, left everything and followed him.

[29]Then Levi held a great banquet for Jesus at his house, and a large crowd of tax collectors and others were eating with them. [30]But the Pharisees and the teachers of the law who belonged to their sect complained to his disciples, "Why do you eat and drink with tax collectors and 'sinners'?"

[31]Jesus answered them, "It is not the healthy who need a doctor, but the sick. [32]I have not come to call the righteous, but sinners to repentance."

Jesus Questioned About Fasting

[33]They said to him, "John's disciples often fast and pray, and so do the disciples of the Pharisees, but yours go on eating and drinking."

[34]Jesus answered, "Can you make the guests of the bridegroom fast while he is with them? [35]But the time will come when the bridegroom will be taken from them; in those days they will fast."

[36]He told them this parable: "No-one tears a patch from a new garment and sews it on an old one. If he does, he will have torn the new garment, and the patch from the new will not match the old. [37]And no-one pours new wine into old wineskins. If he does, the new wine will burst the skins, the wine will run out and the wineskins will be ruined. [38]No, new wine must be poured into new wineskins. [39]And no-one after drinking old wine wants the new, for he says, 'The old is better.'"

Lord of the Sabbath

6 One Sabbath Jesus was going through the cornfields, and his disciples began to pick some ears of corn, rub them in their hands and eat the grain. [2]Some of the Pharisees asked, "Why are you doing what is unlawful on the Sabbath?"

[3]Jesus answered them, "Have you never read what David did when he and his companions were hungry? [4]He entered the house of God, and taking the consecrated bread, he ate what is lawful only for priests to eat. And

---

[b]4 The Greek verb is plural.
[c]12 The Greek word was used for various diseases affecting the skin—not necessarily leprosy.

he also gave some to his companions.''
⁵Then Jesus said to them, "The Son of Man is
Lord of the Sabbath.''

⁶On another Sabbath he went into the
synagogue and was teaching, and a man was
there whose right hand was shrivelled. ⁷The
Pharisees and the teachers of the law were
looking for a reason to accuse Jesus, so they
watched him closely to see if he would heal
on the Sabbath. ⁸But Jesus knew what they
were thinking and said to the man with the
shrivelled hand, "Get up and stand in front of
everyone.'' So he got up and stood there.

⁹Then Jesus said to them, "I ask you,
which is lawful on the Sabbath: to do good or
to do evil, to save life or to destroy it?''

¹⁰He looked round at them all, and then
said to the man, "Stretch out your hand.'' He
did so, and his hand was completely restored. ¹¹But they were furious and began to
discuss with one another what they might do
to Jesus.

The Twelve Apostles

¹²One of those days Jesus went out to a
mountainside to pray, and spent the night
praying to God. ¹³When morning came, he
called his disciples to him and chose twelve
of them, whom he also designated apostles:
¹⁴Simon (whom he named Peter), his brother
Andrew, James, John, Philip, Bartholomew,
¹⁵Matthew, Thomas, James son of Alphaeus,
Simon who was called the Zealot, ¹⁶Judas
son of James, and Judas Iscariot, who became a traitor.

Blessings and Woes

¹⁷He went down with them and stood on a
level place. A large crowd of his disciples
was there and a great number of people from
all over Judea, from Jerusalem, and from the
coast of Tyre and Sidon, ¹⁸who had come to
hear him and to be healed of their diseases.
Those troubled by evilᵃ spirits were cured,
¹⁹and the people all tried to touch him,
because power was coming from him and
healing them all.

²⁰Looking at his disciples, he said:

"Blessed are you who are poor,
    for yours is the kingdom of God.
²¹Blessed are you who hunger now,
    for you will be satisfied.
Blessed are you who weep now,
    for you will laugh.
²²Blessed are you when men hate you,
    when they exclude you and insult you
    and reject your name as evil,
    because of the Son of Man.

²³"Rejoice in that day and leap for joy,
because great is your reward in heaven. For
that is how their fathers treated the prophets.

²⁴"But woe to you who are rich,
    for you have already received your
        comfort.
²⁵Woe to you who are well fed now,
    for you will go hungry.

Woe to you who laugh now,
    for you will mourn and weep.
²⁶Woe to you when all men speak well of
        you,
    for that is how their fathers treated the
        false prophets.

Love for Enemies

²⁷"But I tell you who hear me: Love your
enemies, do good to those who hate you,
²⁸bless those who curse you, pray for those
who ill-treat you. ²⁹If someone strikes you on
one cheek, turn to him the other also. If
someone takes your cloak, do not stop him
from taking your tunic. ³⁰Give to everyone
who asks you, and if anyone takes what
belongs to you, do not demand it back. ³¹Do
to others as you would have them do to you.

³²"If you love those who love you, what
credit is that to you? Even 'sinners' love
those who love them. ³³And if you do good to
those who are good to you, what credit is that
to you? Even 'sinners' do that. ³⁴And if you
lend to those from whom you expect repay-
ment, what credit is that to you? Even 'sinners' lend to 'sinners', expecting to be repaid
in full. ³⁵But love your enemies, do good to
them, and lend to them without expecting to
get anything back. Then your reward will be
great, and you will be sons of the Most High,
because he is kind to the ungrateful and
wicked. ³⁶Be merciful, just as your Father is
merciful.

Judging Others

³⁷"Do not judge, and you will not be
judged. Do not condemn, and you will not be
condemned. Forgive, and you will be forgiven. ³⁸Give, and it will be given to you. A
good measure, pressed down, shaken
together and running over, will be poured
into your lap. For with the measure you use,
it will be measured to you.''

³⁹He also told them this parable: "Can a
blind man lead a blind man? Will they not
both fall into a pit? ⁴⁰A student is not above
his teacher, but everyone who is fully trained
will be like his teacher.

⁴¹"Why do you look at the speck of sawdust in your brother's eye and pay no attention to the plank in your own eye? ⁴²How can
you say to your brother, 'Brother, let me take
the speck out of your eye,' when you yourself fail to see the plank in your own eye? You
hypocrite, first take the plank out of your
eye, and then you will see clearly to remove
the speck from your brother's eye.

A Tree and Its Fruit

⁴³"No good tree bears bad fruit, nor does a
bad tree bear good fruit. ⁴⁴Each tree is recognised by its own fruit. People do not pick figs
from thorn-bushes, or grapes from briers.
⁴⁵The good man brings good things out of the
good stored up in his heart, and the evil man
brings evil things out of the evil stored up in
his heart. For out of the overflow of his heart
his mouth speaks.

ᵃ18 Greek unclean

Luke 5:1–11
'Put out into deep water, and let down the nets for a catch' (v. 4b).

LUKE INCLUDES A UNIQUE MIRACLE as he describes Jesus calling his first disciples. The story is quite different from the simple, matter-of-fact accounts in Mark and Matthew. They give the impression that perhaps Peter, Andrew, James and John already knew Jesus and were half expecting him to call them. Just a word from the Lord, and they left their nets to follow him.

Luke, on the other hand, describes a miraculous catch of fish which convinced them they should follow. The incident is remarkably like an incident in John's Gospel after the resurrection, where Jesus directed operations from the shore. Both feature Peter's reaction. At the beginning Peter could only see his sin, feel his inadequacy, and ask the Lord to keep his distance. At the end, Peter jumps out of the boat to be with his Lord. How typical that Jesus should do something as practical as helping his disciples in their everyday work, both before and after his ministry.

In today's passage, Peter and his partners had to push the boat out. They had to get into deep water. In other words they had to take a risk. We may just wonder whether their whole night of toil had been in the shallows. Not until Jesus encouraged, or rather ordered, them out into the deep did they make their catch. And Jesus did not call them until he saw that they were prepared to take that risk.

> *Launch out into the deep,*
> *O let the shoreline go!*
> *Launch out, launch out in the ocean divine,*
> *Out where the full tides flow*

> *(Albert B. Simpson)*

→894

LUKE 6:1–11

'Which is lawful on the Sabbath: to do good or to do evil, to save life or to destroy it?' (v. 9b).

LAW AND JUSTICE do not always go hand in hand. Many laws affect people unfairly. Some laws contravene basic human rights. Such injustice is usually easier to see at a distance, than on one's own doorstep. It is easier to encourage law-breaking somewhere else, than to do so in your own back yard. For example, it is easy for some politicians to encourage political strikes in other countries, in the interests of justice, and to condemn them in Britain on the basis that they are against the law.

In Jesus' time the Sabbath had become so sacred and hedged about with legal restriction that Luke cannot even bring himself to record – as Mark does – the saying that 'The Sabbath was made for the good of man'. What had started off as a good, reasonable and highly desirable attempt to give space for worship, rest and recreation, had become a strait-jacket preventing reasonable actions of mercy and compassion. Because the Sabbath was seen as a sacred institution, reason was hardly applied to it.

The disciples plucked ears of corn. According to the law that was harvesting on the Sabbath. Jesus healed a paralysed man in the synagogue. That, too, was work and only allowed if life was in danger. Jesus opposed such restrictions on humane activity. He himself broke the law, and defended his disciples' illegal actions on the basis of reason and sound common sense.

As a general rule we use the law to fight injustice. But we may, at any time, be called upon to decide whether to challenge a sacred institution, an unjust or stupid law. Jesus was not afraid to cut through legal and religious prejudice, and to apply reason to the most sacred matters.

→897

The Wise and Foolish Builders

46"Why do you call me, 'Lord, Lord,' and do not do what I say? 47I will show you what he is like who comes to me and hears my words and puts them into practice. 48He is like a man building a house, who dug down deep and laid the foundation on rock. When the flood came, the torrent struck that house but could not shake it, because it was well built. 49But the one who hears my words and does not put them into practice is like a man who built a house on the ground without a foundation. The moment the torrent struck that house, it collapsed and its destruction was complete."

The Faith of the Centurion

7 When Jesus had finished saying all this in the hearing of the people, he entered Capernaum. 2There a centurion's servant, whom his master valued highly, was sick and about to die. 3The centurion heard of Jesus and sent some elders of the Jews to him, asking him to come and heal his servant. 4When they came to Jesus, they pleaded earnestly with him, "This man deserves to have you do this, 5because he loves our nation and has built our synagogue." 6So Jesus went with them.

He was not far from the house when the centurion sent friends to say to him: "Lord, don't trouble yourself, for I do not deserve to have you come under my roof. 7That is why I did not even consider myself worthy to come to you. But say the word, and my servant will be healed. 8For I myself am a man under authority, with soldiers under me. I tell this one, 'Go', and he goes; and that one, 'Come', and he comes. I say to my servant, 'Do this', and he does it."

9When Jesus heard this, he was amazed at him, and turning to the crowd following him, he said, "I tell you, I have not found such great faith even in Israel." 10Then the men who had been sent returned to the house and found the servant well.

Jesus Raises a Widow's Son

11Soon afterwards, Jesus went to a town called Nain, and his disciples and a large crowd went along with him. 12As he approached the town gate, a dead person was being carried out—the only son of his mother, and she was a widow. And a large crowd from the town was with her. 13When the Lord saw her, his heart went out to her and he said, "Don't cry."

14Then he went up and touched the coffin, and those carrying it stood still. He said, "Young man, I say to you, get up!" 15The dead man sat up and began to talk, and Jesus gave him back to his mother.

16They were all filled with awe and praised God. "A great prophet has appeared among us," they said. "God has come to help his people." 17This news about Jesus spread throughout Judea[a] and the surrounding country.

Jesus and John the Baptist

18John's disciples told him about all these things. Calling two of them, 19he sent them to the Lord to ask, "Are you the one who was to come, or should we expect someone else?"

20When the men came to Jesus, they said, "John the Baptist sent us to you to ask, 'Are you the one who was to come, or should we expect someone else?'"

21At that very time Jesus cured many who had diseases, sicknesses and evil spirits, and gave sight to many who were blind. 22So he replied to the messengers, "Go back and report to John what you have seen and heard: The blind receive sight, the lame walk, those who have leprosy[b] are cured, the deaf hear, the dead are raised, and the good news is preached to the poor. 23Blessed is the man who does not fall away on account of me."

24After John's messengers left, Jesus began to speak to the crowd about John: "What did you go out into the desert to see? A reed swayed by the wind? 25If not, what did you go out to see? A man dressed in fine clothes? No, those who wear expensive clothes and indulge in luxury are in palaces. 26But what did you go out to see? A prophet? Yes, I tell you, and more than a prophet. 27This is the one about whom it is written:

"'I will send my messenger ahead of you,
who will prepare your way before you.'[c]

28I tell you, among those born of women there is no-one greater than John; yet the one who is least in the kingdom of God is greater than he."

(29All the people, even the tax collectors, when they heard Jesus' words, acknowledged that God's way was right, because they had been baptised by John. 30But the Pharisees and experts in the law rejected God's purpose for themselves, because they had not been baptised by John.)

31"To what, then, can I compare the people of this generation? What are they like? 32They are like children sitting in the market-place and calling out to each other:

"'We played the flute for you,
and you did not dance;
we sang a dirge,
and you did not cry.'

33For John the Baptist came neither eating bread nor drinking wine, and you say, 'He has a demon.' 34The Son of Man came eating and drinking, and you say, 'Here is a glutton and a drunkard, a friend of tax collectors and "sinners".' 35But wisdom is proved right by all her children."

Jesus Anointed by a Sinful Woman

36Now one of the Pharisees invited Jesus to have dinner with him, so he went to the Pharisee's house and reclined at the table. 37When a woman who had lived a sinful life in that town learned that Jesus was eating at the Pharisee's house, she brought an alabaster jar of perfume, 38and as she stood behind him at his feet weeping, she began to wet his feet with her tears. Then she wiped them with her hair, kissed them and poured perfume on them.

39When the Pharisee who had invited him saw this, he said to himself, "If this man were a prophet, he would know who is touching him and what kind of woman she is—that she is a sinner."

40Jesus answered him, "Simon, I have something to tell you."

"Tell me, teacher," he said.

41"Two men owed money to a certain money-lender. One owed him five hundred denarii,d and the other fifty. 42Neither of them had the money to pay him back, so he cancelled the debts of both. Now which of them will love him more?"

43Simon replied, "I suppose the one who had the bigger debt cancelled."

"You have judged correctly," Jesus said.

44Then he turned towards the woman and said to Simon, "Do you see this woman? I came into your house. You did not give me any water for my feet, but she wet my feet with her tears and wiped them with her hair. 45You did not give me a kiss, but this woman, from the time I entered, has not stopped kissing my feet. 46You did not put oil on my head, but she has poured perfume on my feet. 47Therefore, I tell you, her many sins have been forgiven—for she loved much. But he who has been forgiven little loves little."

48Then Jesus said to her, "Your sins are forgiven."

49The other guests began to say among themselves, "Who is this who even forgives sins?"

50Jesus said to the woman, "Your faith has saved you; go in peace."

The Parable of the Sower

8 After this, Jesus travelled about from one town and village to another, proclaiming the good news of the kingdom of God. The Twelve were with him, 2and also some women who had been cured of evil spirits and diseases: Mary (called Magdalene) from whom seven demons had come out; 3Joanna the wife of Chuza, the manager of Herod's household; Susanna; and many others. These women were helping to support them out of their own means.

4While a large crowd was gathering and people were coming to Jesus from town after town, he told this parable: 5"A farmer went out to sow his seed. As he was scattering the seed, some fell along the path; it was trampled on, and the birds of the air ate it up. 6Some fell on rock, and when it came up, the plants withered because they had no moisture. 7Other seed fell among thorns, which grew up with it and choked the plants. 8Still other seed fell on good soil. It came up and yielded a crop, a hundred times more than was sown."

When he said this, he called out, "He who has ears to hear, let him hear."

9His disciples asked him what this parable meant. 10He said, "The knowledge of the secrets of the kingdom of God has been given to you, but to others I speak in parables, so that,

" 'though seeing, they may not see;
    though hearing, they may not
        understand.'a

11"This is the meaning of the parable: The seed is the word of God. 12Those along the path are the ones who hear, and then the devil comes and takes away the word from their hearts, so that they may not believe and be saved. 13Those on the rock are the ones who receive the word with joy when they hear it, but they have no root. They believe for a while, but in the time of testing they fall away. 14The seed that fell among thorns stands for those who hear, but as they go on their way they are choked by life's worries, riches and pleasures, and they do not mature. 15But the seed on good soil stands for those with a noble and good heart, who hear the word, retain it, and by persevering produce a crop.

A Lamp on a Stand

16"No-one lights a lamp and hides it in a jar or puts it under a bed. Instead, he puts it on a stand, so that those who come in can see the light. 17For there is nothing hidden that will not be disclosed, and nothing concealed that will not be known or brought out into the open. 18Therefore consider carefully how you listen. Whoever has will be given more; whoever does not have, even what he thinks he has will be taken from him."

Jesus' Mother and Brothers

19Now Jesus' mother and brothers came to see him, but they were not able to get near him because of the crowd. 20Someone told him, "Your mother and brothers are standing outside, wanting to see you."

21He replied, "My mother and brothers are those who hear God's word and put it into practice."

Jesus Calms the Storm

22One day Jesus said to his disciples, "Let's go over to the other side of the lake." So they got into a boat and set out. 23As they sailed, he fell asleep. A squall came down on the lake, so that the boat was being swamped, and they were in great danger.

24The disciples went and woke him, saying, "Master, Master, we're going to drown!"

He got up and rebuked the wind and the raging waters; the storm subsided, and all was calm. 25"Where is your faith?" he asked his disciples.

In fear and amazement they asked one another, "Who is this? He commands even the winds and the water, and they obey him."

d41 A denarius was a coin worth about a day's wages.   a10 Isaiah 6:9

LUKE 7:11–17

'When the Lord saw her, his heart went out to her and he said, "Don't cry." Then he went up and touched the coffin, and . . . said, "Young man, I say to you, get up!" The dead man sat up and began to talk, and Jesus gave him back to his mother' (vv. 13–15).

JESUS' CONCERN, throughout this story, is for the woman rather than for her son. It is one of the rare occasions when Jesus performed a miracle without being asked. He saw the situation, was moved by it, and acted. Luke has recorded this story as an act of compassion, rather than just a portrayal of power. How well it illustrates Luke's interest in Jesus as the friend of the poor and the helpless.

Nowhere are we humans more helpless than in the face of death. It seems so final, completely irreversible. Once that boundary has been passed there is nothing we can do about it. Yet death does not obliterate everything. It cannot take away the memories of loved ones. It cannot undo the things that have been done in life, and sometimes on rare occasions death itself appears to be a person's greatest achievement.

John Brown was executed in 1859. Despite his violent anti-slavery activity, it is his death, rather than his life, which is remembered and immortalized in Charles S. Hall's words

> *John Brown's body lies a mould'ring in the grave.*
> *His soul goes marching on!*

Jesus conquered death. But there are more ways of conquering death than by physical resurrection. Restoration of the widow's son, Jairus' daughter (Luke 8) and Lazarus (John 11) were merely temporary. The memory of a figure like John Brown will also pass in time. But what Jesus offers us is to share his own eternal conquest of death, in the life of the kingdom.

Lord, we praise you for your victory over death. Thank you for sharing that victory with us.

→898

LUKE 8:19–21

' "My mother and brothers are those who hear God's word and put it into practice" ' (v. 21).

THE PICTURE OF JESUS that many of us have is a comforting picture. We dwell on words which invite us to come and ease our heavy burden to find rest, peace and salvation for our souls. But awkward, difficult sayings have a habit of hitting us between the eyes and shaking us out of our complacency.

This is one of those sayings. It is not as extreme as the later, similar saying where Jesus talks of hating one's father and mother and brothers. But it is still the kind of thing which brings us up with a jolt. Jesus is deliberately provoking those who wish to follow him, deliberately provoking his friends and family, and deliberately rejecting any idea of a popular, mass following.

Jesus consistently refused to use any kind of mass influence. He refused to accept offers of political leadership. We have no record of him setting up communities of Christians in the places where he preached. He even failed to keep the sympathy of the crowd which hailed him as he entered Jerusalem in triumph, shortly before his death.

Instead he offered a way of sacrifice and rejection, a way where Christians would have to be as close to each other as members of their own family, a way where even close friends and relatives will mock, misunderstand and possibly reject those who become fully committed to the Lord Jesus Christ.

Jesus has no illusions about the hardness of the Christian way. But at the same time he offers each of us his close friendship and brotherly love. Do we do the same for our fellow Christians of all kinds?

→901

The Healing of a Demon-possessed Man

26They sailed to the region of the Gerasenes,*b* which is across the lake from Galilee. 27When Jesus stepped ashore, he was met by a demon-possessed man from the town. For a long time this man had not worn clothes or lived in a house, but had lived in the tombs. 28When he saw Jesus, he cried out and fell at his feet, shouting at the top of his voice, "What do you want with me, Jesus, Son of the Most High God? I beg you, don't torture me!" 29For Jesus had commanded the evil*c* spirit to come out of the man. Many times it had seized him, and though he was chained hand and foot and kept under guard, he had broken his chains and had been driven by the demon into solitary places.

30Jesus asked him, "What is your name?"

"Legion," he replied, because many demons had gone into him. 31And they begged him repeatedly not to order them to go into the Abyss.

32A large herd of pigs was feeding there on the hillside. The demons begged Jesus to let them go into them, and he gave them permission. 33When the demons came out of the man, they went into the pigs, and the herd rushed down the steep bank into the lake and was drowned.

34When those tending the pigs saw what had happened, they ran off and reported this in the town and countryside, 35and the people went out to see what had happened. When they came to Jesus, they found the man from whom the demons had gone out, sitting at Jesus' feet, dressed and in his right mind; and they were afraid. 36Those who had seen it told the people how the demon-possessed man had been cured. 37Then all the people of the region of the Gerasenes asked Jesus to leave them, because they were overcome with fear. So he got into the boat and left.

38The man from whom the demons had gone out begged to go with him, but Jesus sent him away, saying, 39"Return home and tell how much God has done for you." So the man went away and told all over the town how much Jesus had done for him.

A Dead Girl and a Sick Woman

40Now when Jesus returned, a crowd welcomed him, for they were all expecting him. 41Then a man named Jairus, a ruler of the synagogue, came and fell at Jesus' feet, pleading with him to come to his house 42because his only daughter, a girl of about twelve, was dying.

As Jesus was on his way, the crowds almost crushed him. 43And a woman was there who had been subject to bleeding for twelve years,*d* but no-one could heal her. 44She came up behind him and touched the edge of his cloak, and immediately her bleeding stopped.

45"Who touched me?" Jesus asked.

When they all denied it, Peter said, "Master, the people are crowding and pressing against you."

46But Jesus said, "Someone touched me; I know that power has gone out from me."

47Then the woman, seeing that she could not go unnoticed, came trembling and fell at his feet. In the presence of all the people, she told why she had touched him and how she had been instantly healed. 48Then he said to her, "Daughter, your faith has healed you. Go in peace."

49While Jesus was still speaking, someone came from the house of Jairus, the synagogue ruler. "Your daughter is dead," he said. "Don't bother the teacher any more."

50Hearing this, Jesus said to Jairus, "Don't be afraid; just believe, and she will be healed."

51When he arrived at the house of Jairus, he did not let anyone go in with him except Peter, John and James, and the child's father and mother. 52Meanwhile, all the people were wailing and mourning for her. "Stop wailing," Jesus said. "She is not dead but asleep."

53They laughed at him, knowing that she was dead. 54But he took her by the hand and said, "My child, get up!" 55Her spirit returned, and at once she stood up. Then Jesus told them to give her something to eat. 56Her parents were astonished, but he ordered them not to tell anyone what had happened.

Jesus Sends Out the Twelve

9 When Jesus had called the Twelve together, he gave them power and authority to drive out all demons and to cure diseases, 2and he sent them out to preach the kingdom of God and to heal the sick. 3He told them: "Take nothing for the journey—no staff, no bag, no bread, no money, no extra tunic. 4Whatever house you enter, stay there until you leave that town. 5If people do not welcome you, shake the dust off your feet when you leave their town, as a testimony against them." 6So they set out and went from village to village, preaching the gospel and healing people everywhere.

7Now Herod the tetrarch heard about all that was going on. And he was perplexed, because some were saying that John had been raised from the dead, 8others that Elijah had appeared, and still others that one of the prophets of long ago had come back to life. 9But Herod said, "I beheaded John. Who, then, is this I hear such things about?" And he tried to see him.

Jesus Feeds the Five Thousand

10When the apostles returned, they reported to Jesus what they had done. Then he took them with him and they withdrew by themselves to a town called Bethsaida, 11but the crowds learned about it and followed him. He welcomed them and spoke to them about the kingdom of God, and healed those who needed healing.

12Late in the afternoon the Twelve came to him and said, "Send the crowd away so they

---

b26 Some manuscripts Gadarenes; *other manuscripts* Gergesenes; *also in verse 37*   *c29 Greek* unclean
d43 Many manuscripts years, and she had spent all she had on doctors

can go to the surrounding villages and countryside and find food and lodging, because we are in a remote place here."

13He replied, "You give them something to eat."

They answered, "We have only five loaves of bread and two fish—unless we go and buy food for all this crowd." 14(About five thousand men were there.)

But he said to his disciples, "Make them sit down in groups of about fifty each." 15The disciples did so, and everybody sat down. 16Taking the five loaves and the two fish and looking up to heaven, he gave thanks and broke them. Then he gave them to the disciples to set before the people. 17They all ate and were satisfied, and the disciples picked up twelve basketfuls of broken pieces that were left over.

Peter's Confession of Christ

18Once when Jesus was praying in private and his disciples were with him, he asked them, "Who do the crowds say I am?"

19They replied, "Some say John the Baptist; others say Elijah; and still others, that one of the prophets of long ago has come back to life."

20"But what about you?" he asked. "Who do you say I am?"

Peter answered, "The Christ*a* of God."

21Jesus strictly warned them not to tell this to anyone. 22And he said, "The Son of Man must suffer many things and be rejected by the elders, chief priests and teachers of the law, and he must be killed and on the third day be raised to life."

23Then he said to them all: "If anyone would come after me, he must deny himself and take up his cross daily and follow me. 24For whoever wants to save his life will lose it, but whoever loses his life for me will save it. 25What good is it for a man to gain the whole world, and yet lose or forfeit his very self? 26If anyone is ashamed of me and my words, the Son of Man will be ashamed of him when he comes in his glory and in the glory of the Father and of the holy angels. 27I tell you the truth, some who are standing here will not taste death before they see the kingdom of God."

The Transfiguration

28About eight days after Jesus said this, he took Peter, John and James with him and went up onto a mountain to pray. 29As he was praying, the appearance of his face changed, and his clothes became as bright as a flash of lightning. 30Two men, Moses and Elijah, 31appeared in glorious splendour, talking with Jesus. They spoke about his departure, which he was about to bring to fulfilment at Jerusalem. 32Peter and his companions were very sleepy, but when they became fully awake, they saw his glory and the two men standing with him. 33As the men were leaving Jesus, Peter said to him, "Master, it is good for us to be here. Let us put up three shelters —one for you, one for Moses and one for

Elijah." (He did not know what he was saying.)

34While he was speaking, a cloud appeared and enveloped them, and they were afraid as they entered the cloud. 35A voice came from the cloud, saying, "This is my Son, whom I have chosen; listen to him." 36When the voice had spoken, they found that Jesus was alone. The disciples kept this to themselves, and told no-one at that time what they had seen.

The Healing of a Boy With an Evil Spirit

37The next day, when they came down from the mountain, a large crowd met him. 38A man in the crowd called out, "Teacher, I beg you to look at my son, for he is my only child. 39A spirit seizes him and he suddenly screams; it throws him into convulsions so that he foams at the mouth. It scarcely ever leaves him and is destroying him. 40I begged your disciples to drive it out, but they could not."

41"O unbelieving and perverse generation," Jesus replied, "how long shall I stay with you and put up with you? Bring your son here."

42Even while the boy was coming, the demon threw him to the ground in a convulsion. But Jesus rebuked the evil*b* spirit, healed the boy and gave him back to his father. 43And they were all amazed at the greatness of God.

While everyone was marvelling at all that Jesus did, he said to his disciples, "Listen carefully to what I am about to tell you: The Son of Man is going to be betrayed into the hands of men." 45But they did not understand what this meant. It was hidden from them, so that they did not grasp it, and they were afraid to ask him about it.

Who Will Be the Greatest?

46An argument started among the disciples as to which of them would be the greatest. 47Jesus, knowing their thoughts, took a little child and made him stand beside him. 48Then he said to them, "Whoever welcomes this little child in my name welcomes me; and whoever welcomes me welcomes the one who sent me. For he who is least among you all—he is the greatest."

49"Master," said John, "we saw a man driving out demons in your name and we tried to stop him, because he is not one of us."

50"Do not stop him," Jesus said, "for whoever is not against you is for you."

Samaritan Opposition

51As the time approached for him to be taken up to heaven, Jesus resolutely set out for Jerusalem. 52And he sent messengers on ahead, who went into a Samaritan village to get things ready for him; 53but the people there did not welcome him, because he was heading for Jerusalem. 54When the disciples James and John saw this, they asked, "Lord, do you want us to call fire down from heaven to destroy them?"*c* 55But Jesus turned and

*a*20 Or *Messiah*   *b*42 Greek *unclean*   *c*54 Some manuscripts *them, even as Elijah did*

LUKE 9:46–50

' "Master," said John, "we saw a man driving out demons in your name and we tried to stop him, because he is not one of us" ' (v. 49).

THE DISCIPLES WANTED TO PROTECT JESUS and his message from harm. They did not want his reputation to suffer by association with people who might misuse the gospel. They were proud of their master – and probably a little proud of being chosen, being considered good enough to be his followers.

They seem to have forgotten that we are all sinners, with odd quirks and customs. We all have weaknesses. We all suffer from failings likely to turn people away from our Lord. Well-meaning people who restrict the message do more harm to the cause of Christ than those who open up the gospel without fully understanding it.

Furthermore, those with attractive, magnetic personalities are just as likely to harm the cause by relying on their human skills, instead of sticking to the simple gospel message. Whatever our background, whatever our faults and failings, we are all capable of ministering in Christ's name. And Christ can use that ministry. Christ will not reject us because we attempt to minister in his name. He is likely to reject us if we kid ourselves that we are better than other people and have some special claim on grace.

> *I have no claim on grace; I have no right to plead;*
> *I stand before my maker's face condemned in thought and deed.*
> *But since there died a Lamb who, guiltless, my guilt bore,*
> *I lay fast hold on Jesus' name, and sin is mine no more.*

> (*Albert Orsborn*)

We confess, Lord, that our understanding is limited. We are apt to reject some whose understanding of the gospel is different from our own. Convince us, Lord, that the gospel is for everyone, not just in theory but in practice too.

→902

'But he wanted to justify himself, so he asked Jesus, "And who is my neighbour?" ' (v. 29).

THE LAWYER PLAYED into Jesus' hands. Having failed to confound Jesus, he persisted by seeking a definition of the word neighbour. The exercise commenced with a lawyer seeking to make our Lord look a little foolish and ended with one of the greatest stories of all time. Jesus made the pomposity of the lawyer serve a great end.

It matters not at all whether the story is based on a real incident. Our Lord's hearers would be familiar with the hazards of the Jerusalem to Jericho road. They would also be aware of the natural tendency not to become involved in other people's problems. The priest would have suffered ceremonial defilement had he touched a bleeding person or a corpse. Therefore, with no observers present it was easy to pass by on the other side. The Levite had a similar, although not quite so pressing constraint, but the Jericho road allows occasional views of the way ahead and possibly the Levite knew that the priest had ignored the man. Whatever the reason, either of example or personal predisposition, the Levite also passed by.

Possibly the hearers would be enjoying the commentary on priestly and levitical conduct, and would half expect that the next on the road would be a Jewish layman who would make the right response. But Jesus chose a Samaritan, a despised outsider, to show that whoever is merciful is a neighbour and also very near to the heart of God. And he made the lawyer virtually say so. Our Lord must have had a twinkle in his eye that day.

'I tell you the truth, whatever you did for one of the least of these brothers of mine, you did for me' (Matt. 25:40).

rebuked them, [56]and[d] they went to another village.

The Cost of Following Jesus

[57]As they were walking along the road, a man said to him, "I will follow you wherever you go."

[58]Jesus replied, "Foxes have holes and birds of the air have nests, but the Son of Man has nowhere to lay his head."

[59]He said to another man, "Follow me."

But the man replied, "Lord, first let me go and bury my father."

[60]Jesus said to him, "Let the dead bury their own dead, but you go and proclaim the kingdom of God."

[61]Still another said, "I will follow you, Lord; but first let me go back and say good-bye to my family."

[62]Jesus replied, "No-one who puts his hand to the plough and looks back is fit for service in the kingdom of God."

Jesus Sends Out the Seventy-two

10 After this the Lord appointed seventy-two[a] others and sent them two by two ahead of him to every town and place where he was about to go. [2]He told them, "The harvest is plentiful, but the workers are few. Ask the Lord of the harvest, therefore, to send out workers into his harvest field. [3]Go! I am sending you out like lambs among wolves. [4]Do not take a purse or bag or sandals; and do not greet anyone on the road.

[5]"When you enter a house, first say, 'Peace to this house.' [6]If a man of peace is there, your peace will rest on him; if not, it will return to you. [7]Stay in that house, eating and drinking whatever they give you, for the worker deserves his wages. Do not move around from house to house.

[8]"When you enter a town and are welcomed, eat what is set before you. [9]Heal the sick who are there and tell them, 'The kingdom of God is near you.' [10]But when you enter a town and are not welcomed, go into its streets and say, [11]'Even the dust of your town that sticks to our feet we wipe off against you. Yet be sure of this: The kingdom of God is near.' [12]I tell you, it will be more bearable on that day for Sodom than for that town.

[13]"Woe to you, Korazin! Woe to you, Bethsaida! For if the miracles that were performed in you had been performed in Tyre and Sidon, they would have repented long ago, sitting in sackcloth and ashes. [14]But it will be more bearable for Tyre and Sidon at the judgment than for you. [15]And you, Capernaum, will you be lifted up to the skies? No, you will go down to the depths.[b]

[16]"He who listens to you listens to me; he who rejects you rejects me; but he who rejects me rejects him who sent me."

[17]The seventy-two returned with joy and said, "Lord, even the demons submit to us in your name."

[18]He replied, "I saw Satan fall like lightning from heaven. [19]I have given you authority to trample on snakes and scorpions and to overcome all the power of the enemy; nothing will harm you. [20]However, do not rejoice that the spirits submit to you, but rejoice that your names are written in heaven."

[21]At that time Jesus, full of joy through the Holy Spirit, said, "I praise you, Father, Lord of heaven and earth, because you have hidden these things from the wise and learned, and revealed them to little children. Yes, Father, for this was your good pleasure.

[22]"All things have been committed to me by my Father. No-one knows who the Son is except the Father, and no-one knows who the Father is except the Son and those to whom the Son chooses to reveal him."

[23]Then he turned to his disciples and said privately, "Blessed are the eyes that see what you see. [24]For I tell you that many prophets and kings wanted to see what you see but did not see it, and to hear what you hear but did not hear it."

The Parable of the Good Samaritan

[25]On one occasion an expert in the law stood up to test Jesus. "Teacher," he asked, "what must I do to inherit eternal life?"

[26]"What is written in the Law?" he replied. "How do you read it?"

[27]He answered: "'Love the Lord your God with all your heart and with all your soul and with all your strength and with all your mind';[c] and, 'Love your neighbour as yourself.'[d]"

[28]"You have answered correctly," Jesus replied. "Do this and you will live."

[29]But he wanted to justify himself, so he asked Jesus, "And who is my neighbour?"

[30]In reply Jesus said: "A man was going down from Jerusalem to Jericho, when he fell into the hands of robbers. They stripped him of his clothes, beat him and went away, leaving him half-dead. [31]A priest happened to be going down the same road, and when he saw the man, he passed by on the other side. [32]So too, a Levite, when he came to the place and saw him, passed by on the other side. [33]But a Samaritan, as he travelled, came where the man was; and when he saw him, he took pity on him. [34]He went to him and bandaged his wounds, pouring on oil and wine. Then he put the man on his own donkey, brought him to an inn and took care of him. [35]The next day he took out two silver coins[e] and gave them to the innkeeper. 'Look after him,' he said, 'and when I return, I will reimburse you for any extra expense you may have.'

[36]"Which of these three do you think was a neighbour to the man who fell into the hands of robbers?"

[37]The expert in the law replied, "The one who had mercy on him."

Jesus told him, "Go and do likewise."

---

[d]55,56 Some manuscripts them. And he said, "You do not know what kind of spirit you are of, for the Son of Man did not come to destroy men's lives, but to save them." [56]And   [a]1 Some manuscripts seventy; also in verse 17
[b]15 Greek Hades   [c]27 Deut. 6:5   [d]27 Lev. 19:18   [e]35 Greek two denarii

At the Home of Martha and Mary

38As Jesus and his disciples were on their way, he came to a village where a woman named Martha opened her home to him. 39She had a sister called Mary, who sat at the Lord's feet listening to what he said. 40But Martha was distracted by all the preparations that had to be made. She came to him and asked, "Lord, don't you care that my sister has left me to do the work by myself? Tell her to help me!"

41"Martha, Martha," the Lord answered, "you are worried and upset about many things, 42but only one thing is needed.ƒ Mary has chosen what is better, and it will not be taken away from her."

Jesus' Teaching on Prayer

11 One day Jesus was praying in a certain place. When he finished, one of his disciples said to him, "Lord, teach us to pray, just as John taught his disciples."

2He said to them, "When you pray, say:

"'Father,ᵃ
hallowed be your name,
your kingdom come.ᵇ
3Give us each day our daily bread.
4Forgive us our sins,
for we also forgive everyone who sins against us.ᶜ
And lead us not into temptation.'"ᵈ

5Then he said to them, "Suppose one of you has a friend, and he goes to him at midnight and says, 'Friend, lend me three loaves of bread, 6because a friend of mine on a journey has come to me, and I have nothing to set before him.'

7"Then the one inside answers, 'Don't bother me. The door is already locked, and my children are with me in bed. I can't get up and give you anything.' 8I tell you, though he will not get up and give him the bread because he is his friend, yet because of the man's boldnessᵉ he will get up and give him as much as he needs.

9"So I say to you: Ask and it will be given to you; seek and you will find; knock and the door will be opened to you. 10For everyone who asks receives; he who seeks finds; and to him who knocks, the door will be opened.

11"Which of you fathers, if your son asks forƒ a fish, will give him a snake instead? 12Or if he asks for an egg, will give him a scorpion? 13If you then, though you are evil, know how to give good gifts to your children, how much more will your Father in heaven give the Holy Spirit to those who ask him!"

Jesus and Beelzebub

14Jesus was driving out a demon that was mute. When the demon left, the man who had been mute spoke, and the crowd was amazed. 15But some of them said, "By Beelzebub,ᵍ the prince of demons, he is driving out demons." 16Others tested him by asking for a sign from heaven.

17Jesus knew their thoughts and said to them: "Any kingdom divided against itself will be ruined, and a house divided against itself will fall. 18If Satan is divided against himself, how can his kingdom stand? I say this because you claim that I drive out demons by Beelzebub. 19Now if I drive out demons by Beelzebub, by whom do your followers drive them out? So then, they will be your judges. 20But if I drive out demons by the finger of God, then the kingdom of God has come to you.

21"When a strong man, fully armed, guards his own house, his possessions are safe. 22But when someone stronger attacks and overpowers him, he takes away the armour in which the man trusted and divides up the spoils.

23"He who is not with me is against me, and he who does not gather with me, scatters.

24"When an evilʰ spirit comes out of a man, it goes through arid places seeking rest and does not find it. Then it says, 'I will return to the house I left.' 25When it arrives, it finds the house swept clean and put in order. 26Then it goes and takes seven other spirits more wicked than itself, and they go in and live there. And the final condition of that man is worse than the first."

27As Jesus was saying these things, a woman in the crowd called out, "Blessed is the mother who gave you birth and nursed you."

28He replied, "Blessed rather are those who hear the word of God and obey it."

The Sign of Jonah

29As the crowds increased, Jesus said, "This is a wicked generation. It asks for a miraculous sign, but none will be given it except the sign of Jonah. 30For as Jonah was a sign to the Ninevites, so also will the Son of Man be to this generation. 31The Queen of the South will rise at the judgment with the men of this generation and condemn them; for she came from the ends of the earth to listen to Solomon's wisdom, and now oneⁱ greater than Solomon is here. 32The men of Nineveh will stand up at the judgment with this generation and condemn it; for they repented at the preaching of Jonah, and now one greater than Jonah is here.

The Lamp of the Body

33"No-one lights a lamp and puts it in a place where it will be hidden, or under a bowl. Instead he puts it on its stand, so that those who come in may see the light. 34Your eye is the lamp of your body. When your eyes are good, your whole body also is full of light. But when they are bad, your body also is full of darkness. 35See to it, then, that the light

---

ƒ42 Some manuscripts *but few things are needed—or only one*   ᵃ2 Some manuscripts *Our Father in heaven*
ᵇ2 Some manuscripts *come. May your will be done on earth as it is in heaven.*
ᶜ4 Greek *everyone who is indebted to us*   ᵈ4 Some manuscripts *temptation but deliver us from the evil one*
ᵉ8 Or *persistence*   ƒ11 Some manuscripts *for bread, will give him a stone; or if he asks for*
ᵍ15 Greek *Beezeboul* or *Beelzeboul*; also in verses 18 and 19   ʰ24 Greek *unclean*
ⁱ31 Or *something*; also in verse 32

LUKE 11:1–13
'If you then, though you are evil, know how to give good gifts to your children, how much more will your Father in heaven give the Holy Spirit to those who ask him!' (v. 13).

IT IS THE CUSTOM rather than the exception for parents to be generous, even over-generous to their children. When we observe harshness or meanness we are disturbed, because parents are not expected to act in that way. Our Lord took this basic concept of a parent who wants only the best for his children and used it to illustrate our heavenly Father's generosity towards us.

Would a man give his son a snake when he asks for fish? Or a stone when he asks for bread? Or a scorpion when he asks for an egg? Simply to ask the question is to provide the answer. Of course a parent would not do that. It is unthinkable! The disciples were carried by our Lord's perceptive questions, and he went on to make the equally unassailable point that if we who are evil know how to give to our children, how much more will our heavenly Father give to us. The corresponding verse in Matthew's Gospel says that God will give 'good gifts', but Luke specifies the 'Holy Spirit'. With and through the Holy Spirit come all of God's good gifts.

We have but to ask. But the asking must be related to the intensities of desire and intention which lie behind the asking, seeking and knocking, referred to by Jesus in this Scripture.

At Pentecost we celebrate the time when God met human aspirations for a God-centred life. He is more willing to give than sometimes we are willing to ask.

> *Come, Holy Ghost, all sacred fire!*
> *Come, fill this earthly temple now*
> *Emptied of every base desire,*
> *Reign thou within, and only thou.*

(Francis Bottome)

→906

'But when you give a banquet, invite the poor, the crippled, the lame, the blind, and you will be blessed. Although they cannot repay you, you will be repaid at the resurrection of the righteous' (vv. 13, 14).

THE BABY WAS an economic liability. His severely deformed legs meant that he would need undue care and would probably never work. His parents therefore placed him on the village rubbish dump to die. No doubt they were disappointed, but they could always have another baby. A passing nurse heard the weakening cries of the child and turned to investigate. She took the child into care with a number of other such children who were also economic liabilities, and had the joy of seeing him, and the others, grow into bright, happy, clever and able young people.

Our Lord was familiar with the plight of severely disabled people in a society which had no social security support. He was also at that moment at the banqueting table of a prominent Pharisee. He had noted the quality of the guests and their search for the better places at the table, and had a further word of counsel to give. Clearly, there is nothing wrong in having friends and associates for a meal. That is a good thing to do, as Jesus himself well knew and approved. Such invitations are delightfully reciprocal, and the reward is immediate, with no eternal significance. Jesus proposes that to such normal hospitality we should add an unselfish generosity and invite those who cannot reciprocate. That represents a higher level of hospitality because it is truly altruistic, the reward being found in the joy of exercising care.

Our Lord had, and has, a tremendous concern for those who, for one reason or another find themselves on the fringe, or even beyond that, of ordinary friendship and associations.

'The Son of Man came to seek and to save what was lost' (Luke 19:10).

→911

within you is not darkness. ³⁶Therefore, if your whole body is full of light, and no part of it dark, it will be completely lighted, as when the light of a lamp shines on you.''

Six Woes

³⁷When Jesus had finished speaking, a Pharisee invited him to eat with him; so he went in and reclined at the table. ³⁸But the Pharisee, noticing that Jesus did not first wash before the meal, was surprised.

³⁹Then the Lord said to him, ''Now then, you Pharisees clean the outside of the cup and dish, but inside you are full of greed and wickedness. ⁴⁰You foolish people! Did not the one who made the outside make the inside also? ⁴¹But give what is inside ᴸthe dish ʲ to the poor, and everything will be clean for you.

⁴²''Woe to you Pharisees, because you give God a tenth of your mint, rue and all other kinds of garden herbs, but you neglect justice and the love of God. You should have practised the latter without leaving the former undone.

⁴³''Woe to you Pharisees, because you love the most important seats in the synagogues and greetings in the market-places.

⁴⁴''Woe to you, because you are like unmarked graves, which men walk over without knowing it.''

⁴⁵One of the experts in the law answered him, ''Teacher, when you say these things, you insult us also.''

⁴⁶Jesus replied, ''And you experts in the law, woe to you, because you load people down with burdens they can hardly carry, and you yourselves will not lift one finger to help them.

⁴⁷''Woe to you, because you build tombs for the prophets, and it was your forefathers who killed them. ⁴⁸So you testify that you approve of what your forefathers did; they killed the prophets, and you build their tombs. ⁴⁹Because of this, God in his wisdom said, 'I will send them prophets and apostles, some of whom they will kill and others they will persecute.' ⁵⁰Therefore this generation will be held responsible for the blood of all the prophets that has been shed since the beginning of the world, ⁵¹from the blood of Abel to the blood of Zechariah, who was killed between the altar and the sanctuary. Yes, I tell you, this generation will be held responsible for it all.

⁵²''Woe to you experts in the law, because you have taken away the key to knowledge. You yourselves have not entered, and you have hindered those who were entering.''

⁵³When Jesus left there, the Pharisees and the teachers of the law began to oppose him fiercely and to besiege him with questions, ⁵⁴waiting to catch him in something he might say.

Warnings and Encouragements

12 Meanwhile, when a crowd of many thousands had gathered, so that they were trampling on one another, Jesus began to speak first to his disciples, saying: ''Be on your guard against the yeast of the Pharisees, which is hypocrisy. ²There is nothing concealed that will not be disclosed, or hidden that will not be made known. ³What you have said in the dark will be heard in the daylight, and what you have whispered in the ear in the inner rooms will be proclaimed from the roofs.

⁴''I tell you, my friends, do not be afraid of those who kill the body and after that can do no more. ⁵But I will show you whom you should fear: Fear him who, after the killing of the body, has power to throw you into hell. Yes, I tell you, fear him. ⁶Are not five sparrows sold for two pennies?ᵃ Yet not one of them is forgotten by God. ⁷Indeed, the very hairs of your head are all numbered. Don't be afraid; you are worth more than many sparrows.

⁸''I tell you, whoever acknowledges me before men, the Son of Man will also acknowledge him before the angels of God. ⁹But he who disowns me before men will be disowned before the angels of God. ¹⁰And everyone who speaks a word against the Son of Man will be forgiven, but anyone who blasphemes against the Holy Spirit will not be forgiven.

¹¹''When you are brought before synagogues, rulers and authorities, do not worry about how you will defend yourselves or what you will say, ¹²for the Holy Spirit will teach you at that time what you should say.''

The Parable of the Rich Fool

¹³Someone in the crowd said to him, ''Teacher, tell my brother to divide the inheritance with me.''

¹⁴Jesus replied, ''Man, who appointed me a judge or an arbiter between you?'' ¹⁵Then he said to them, ''Watch out! Be on your guard against all kinds of greed; a man's life does not consist in the abundance of his possessions.''

¹⁶And he told them this parable: ''The ground of a certain rich man produced a good crop. ¹⁷He thought to himself, 'What shall I do? I have no place to store my crops.'

¹⁸''Then he said, 'This is what I'll do. I will tear down my barns and build bigger ones, and there I will store all my grain and my goods. ¹⁹And I'll say to myself, ''You have plenty of good things laid up for many years. Take life easy; eat, drink and be merry.'''

²⁰''But God said to him, 'You fool! This very night your life will be demanded from you. Then who will get what you have prepared for yourself?'

²¹''This is how it will be with anyone who stores up things for himself but is not rich towards God.''

Do Not Worry

²²Then Jesus said to his disciples: ''Therefore I tell you, do not worry about your life, what you will eat; or about your body, what you will wear. ²³Life is more than food, and the body more than clothes. ²⁴Consider the

---

ʲ41 Or *what you have*   ᵃ6 Greek *two assaria*

ravens: They do not sow or reap, they have no storeroom or barn; yet God feeds them. And how much more valuable you are than birds! 25Who of you by worrying can add a single hour to his life?*b* 26Since you cannot do this very little thing, why do you worry about the rest?'

27''Consider how the lilies grow. They do not labour or spin. Yet I tell you, not even Solomon in all his splendour was dressed like one of these. 28If that is how God clothes the grass of the field, which is here today, and tomorrow is thrown into the fire, how much more will he clothe you, O you of little faith! 29And do not set your heart on what you will eat or drink; do not worry about it. 30For the pagan world runs after all such things, and your Father knows that you need them. 31But seek his kingdom, and these things will be given to you as well.

32''Do not be afraid, little flock, for your Father has been pleased to give you the kingdom. 33Sell your possessions and give to the poor. Provide purses for yourselves that will not wear out, a treasure in heaven that will not be exhausted, where no thief comes near and no moth destroys. 34For where your treasure is, there your heart will be also.

Watchfulness

35''Be dressed ready for service and keep your lamps burning, 36like men waiting for their master to return from a wedding banquet, so that when he comes and knocks they can immediately open the door for him. 37It will be good for those servants whose master finds them watching when he comes. I tell you the truth, he will dress himself to serve, will have them recline at the table and will come and wait on them. 38It will be good for those servants whose master finds them ready, even if he comes in the second or third watch of the night. 39But understand this: If the owner of the house had known at what hour the thief was coming, he would not have let his house be broken into. 40You also must be ready, because the Son of Man will come at an hour when you do not expect him.''

41Peter asked, ''Lord, are you telling this parable to us, or to everyone?''

42The Lord answered, ''Who then is the faithful and wise manager, whom the master puts in charge of his servants to give them their food allowance at the proper time? 43It will be good for that servant whom the master finds doing so when he returns. 44I tell you the truth, he will put him in charge of all his possessions. 45But suppose the servant says to himself, 'My master is taking a long time in coming,' and he then begins to beat the menservants and maidservants and to eat and drink and get drunk. 46The master of that servant will come on a day when he does not expect him and at an hour he is not aware of. He will cut him to pieces and assign him a place with the unbelievers.

47''That servant who knows his master's will and does not get ready or does not do what his master wants will be beaten with many blows. 48But the one who does not know and does things deserving punishment will be beaten with few blows. From everyone who has been given much, much will be demanded; and from the one who has been entrusted with much, much more will be asked.

Not Peace but Division

49''I have come to bring fire on the earth, and how I wish it were already kindled! 50But I have a baptism to undergo, and how distressed I am until it is completed! 51Do you think I came to bring peace on earth? No, I tell you, but division. 52From now on there will be five in one family divided against each other, three against two and two against three. 53They will be divided, father against son and son against father, mother against daughter and daughter against mother, mother-in-law against daughter-in-law and daughter-in-law against mother-in-law.''

Interpreting the Times

54He said to the crowd: ''When you see a cloud rising in the west, immediately you say, 'It's going to rain,' and it does. 55And when the south wind blows, you say, 'It's going to be hot,' and it is. 56Hypocrites! You know how to interpret the appearance of the earth and the sky. How is it that you don't know how to interpret this present time?

57''Why don't you judge for yourselves what is right? 58As you are going with your adversary to the magistrate, try hard to be reconciled to him on the way, or he may drag you off to the judge, and the judge turn you over to the officer, and the officer throw you into prison. 59I tell you, you will not get out until you have paid the last penny.''*c*

Repent or Perish

13 Now there were some present at that time who told Jesus about the Galileans whose blood Pilate had mixed with their sacrifices. 2Jesus answered, ''Do you think that these Galileans were worse sinners than all the other Galileans because they suffered this way? 3I tell you, no! But unless you repent, you too will all perish. 4Or those eighteen who died when the tower in Siloam fell on them—do you think they were more guilty than all the others living in Jerusalem? 5I tell you, no! But unless you repent, you too will all perish.''

6Then he told this parable: ''A man had a fig-tree, planted in his vineyard, and he went to look for fruit on it, but did not find any. 7So he said to the man who took care of the vineyard, 'For three years now I've been coming to look for fruit on this fig-tree and haven't found any. Cut it down! Why should it use up the soil?'

8'''Sir,' the man replied, 'leave it alone for one more year, and I'll dig round it and fertilise it. 9If it bears fruit next year, fine! If not, then cut it down.'''

A Crippled Woman Healed on the Sabbath

[10]On a Sabbath Jesus was teaching in one of the synagogues, [11]and a woman was there who had been crippled by a spirit for eighteen years. She was bent over and could not straighten up at all. [12]When Jesus saw her, he called her forward and said to her, "Woman, you are set free from your infirmity." [13]Then he put his hands on her, and immediately she straightened up and praised God.

[14]Indignant because Jesus had healed on the Sabbath, the synagogue ruler said to the people, "There are six days for work. So come and be healed on those days, not on the Sabbath."

[15]The Lord answered him, "You hypocrites! Doesn't each of you on the Sabbath untie his ox or donkey from the stall and lead it out to give it water? [16]Then should not this woman, a daughter of Abraham, whom Satan has kept bound for eighteen long years, be set free on the Sabbath day from what bound her?"

[17]When he said this, all his opponents were humiliated, but the people were delighted with all the wonderful things he was doing.

The Parables of the Mustard Seed and the Yeast

[18]Then Jesus asked, "What is the kingdom of God like? What shall I compare it to? [19]It is like a mustard seed, which a man took and planted in his garden. It grew and became a tree, and the birds of the air perched in its branches."

[20]Again he asked, "What shall I compare the kingdom of God to? [21]It is like yeast that a woman took and mixed into a large amount[a] of flour until it worked all through the dough."

The Narrow Door

[22]Then Jesus went through the towns and villages, teaching as he made his way to Jerusalem. [23]Someone asked him, "Lord, are only a few people going to be saved?"

He said to them, [24]"Make every effort to enter through the narrow door, because many, I tell you, will try to enter and will not be able to. [25]Once the owner of the house gets up and closes the door, you will stand outside knocking and pleading, 'Sir, open the door for us.'

"But he will answer, 'I don't know you or where you come from.'

[26]"Then you will say, 'We ate and drank with you, and you taught in our streets.'

[27]"But he will reply, 'I don't know you or where you come from. Away from me, all you evildoers!'

[28]"There will be weeping there, and gnashing of teeth, when you see Abraham, Isaac and Jacob and all the prophets in the kingdom of God, but you yourselves thrown out. [29]People will come from east and west and north and south, and will take their places at the feast in the kingdom of God.

[30]Indeed there are those who are last who will be first, and first who will be last."

Jesus' Sorrow for Jerusalem

[31]At that time some Pharisees came to Jesus and said to him, "Leave this place and go somewhere else. Herod wants to kill you."

[32]He replied, "Go tell that fox, 'I will drive out demons and heal people today and tomorrow, and on the third day I will reach my goal.' [33]In any case, I must keep going today and tomorrow and the next day—for surely no prophet can die outside Jerusalem!

[34]"O Jerusalem, Jerusalem, you who kill the prophets and stone those sent to you, how often I have longed to gather your children together, as a hen gathers her chicks under her wings, but you were not willing! [35]Look, your house is left to you desolate. I tell you, you will not see me again until you say, 'Blessed is he who comes in the name of the Lord.'[b]"

Jesus at a Pharisee's House

14 One Sabbath, when Jesus went to eat in the house of a prominent Pharisee, he was being carefully watched. [2]There in front of him was a man suffering from dropsy. [3]Jesus asked the Pharisees and experts in the law, "Is it lawful to heal on the Sabbath or not?" [4]But they remained silent. So taking hold of the man, he healed him and sent him away.

[5]Then he asked them, "If one of you has a son[a] or an ox that falls into a well on the Sabbath day, will you not immediately pull him out?" [6]And they had nothing to say.

[7]When he noticed how the guests picked the places of honour at the table, he told them this parable: [8]"When someone invites you to a wedding feast, do not take the place of honour, for a person more distinguished than you may have been invited. [9]If so, the host who invited both of you will come and say to you, 'Give this man your seat.' Then, humiliated, you will have to take the least important place. [10]But when you are invited, take the lowest place, so that when your host comes, he will say to you, 'Friend, move up to a better place.' Then you will be honoured in the presence of all your fellow guests. [11]For everyone who exalts himself will be humbled, and he who humbles himself will be exalted."

[12]Then Jesus said to his host, "When you give a luncheon or dinner, do not invite your friends, your brothers or relatives, or your rich neighbours; if you do, they may invite you back and so you will be repaid. [13]But when you give a banquet, invite the poor, the crippled, the lame, the blind, [14]and you will be blessed. Although they cannot repay you, you will be repaid at the resurrection of the righteous."

The Parable of the Great Banquet

[15]When one of those at the table with him heard this, he said to Jesus, "Blessed is the

---

[a]21 Greek three satas (probably about ⅔ bushel or 22 litres) [b]35 Psalm 118:26 [a]5 Some manuscripts donkey

man who will eat at the feast in the kingdom of God.''

16Jesus replied: ''A certain man was preparing a great banquet and invited many guests. 17At the time of the banquet he sent his servant to tell those who had been invited, 'Come, for everything is now ready.'

18''But they all alike began to make excuses. The first said, 'I have just bought a field, and I must go and see it. Please excuse me.'

19''Another said, 'I have just bought five yoke of oxen, and I'm on my way to try them out. Please excuse me.'

20''Still another said, 'I have just got married, so I can't come.'

21''The servant came back and reported this to his master. Then the owner of the house became angry and ordered his servant, 'Go out quickly into the streets and alleys of the town and bring in the poor, the crippled, the blind and the lame.'

22'' 'Sir,' the servant said, 'what you ordered has been done, but there is still room.'

23''Then the master told his servant, 'Go out to the roads and country lanes and make them come in, so that my house will be full. 24I tell you, not one of those men who were invited will get a taste of my banquet.' ''

The Cost of Being a Disciple

25Large crowds were travelling with Jesus, and turning to them he said: 26''If anyone comes to me and does not hate his father and mother, his wife and children, his brothers and sisters—yes, even his own life—he cannot be my disciple. 27And anyone who does not carry his cross and follow me cannot be my disciple.

28''Suppose one of you wants to build a tower. Will he not first sit down and estimate the cost to see if he has enough money to complete it? 29For if he lays the foundation and is not able to finish it, everyone who sees it will ridicule him, 30saying, 'This fellow began to build and was not able to finish.'

31''Or suppose a king is about to go to war against another king. Will he not first sit down and consider whether he is able with ten thousand men to oppose the one coming against him with twenty thousand? 32If he is not able, he will send a delegation while the other is still a long way off and will ask for terms of peace. 33In the same way, any of you who does not give up everything he has cannot be my disciple.

34''Salt is good, but if it loses its saltiness, how can it be made salty again? 35It is fit neither for the soil nor for the manure heap; it is thrown out.

''He who has ears to hear, let him hear.''

The Parable of the Lost Sheep

15 Now the tax collectors and ''sinners'' were all gathering round to hear him. 2But the Pharisees and the teachers of the law

muttered, ''This man welcomes sinners, and eats with them.''

3Then Jesus told them this parable: 4''Suppose one of you has a hundred sheep and loses one of them. Does he not leave the ninety-nine in the open country and go after the lost sheep until he finds it? 5And when he finds it, he joyfully puts it on his shoulders 6and goes home. Then he calls his friends and neighbours together and says, 'Rejoice with me; I have found my lost sheep.' 7I tell you that in the same way there will be more rejoicing in heaven over one sinner who repents than over ninety-nine righteous persons who do not need to repent.

The Parable of the Lost Coin

8''Or suppose a woman has ten silver coins*a* and loses one. Does she not light a lamp, sweep the house and search carefully until she finds it? 9And when she finds it, she calls her friends and neighbours together and says, 'Rejoice with me; I have found my lost coin.' 10In the same way, I tell you, there is rejoicing in the presence of the angels of God over one sinner who repents.''

The Parable of the Lost Son

11Jesus continued: ''There was a man who had two sons. 12The younger one said to his father, 'Father, give me my share of the estate.' So he divided his property between them.

13''Not long after that, the younger son got together all he had, set off for a distant country and there squandered his wealth in wild living. 14After he had spent everything, there was a severe famine in that whole country, and he began to be in need. 15So he went and hired himself out to a citizen of that country, who sent him to his fields to feed pigs. 16He longed to fill his stomach with the pods that the pigs were eating, but no-one gave him anything.

17''When he came to his senses, he said, 'How many of my father's hired men have food to spare, and here I am starving to death! 18I will set out and go back to my father and say to him: Father, I have sinned against heaven and against you. 19I am no longer worthy to be called your son; make me like one of your hired men.' 20So he got up and went to his father.

''But while he was still a long way off, his father saw him and was filled with compassion for him; he ran to his son, threw his arms around him and kissed him.

21''The son said to him, 'Father, I have sinned against heaven and against you. I am no longer worthy to be called your son.'*b*

22''But the father said to his servants, 'Quick! Bring the best robe and put it on him. Put a ring on his finger and sandals on his feet. 23Bring the fattened calf and kill it. Let's have a feast and celebrate. 24For this son of mine was dead and is alive again; he was lost and is found.' So they began to celebrate.

25''Meanwhile, the older son was in the

---

a8 Greek *ten drachmas*, each worth about a day's wages
b21 Some early manuscripts *son. Make me like one of your hired men.*

LUKE 15:17–21
'I will set out and go back to my father and say to him: "Father, I have sinned against heaven and against you" ' (v. 18).

EXPERIENCE IS a hard taskmaster at times. With his dream-world of freedom shattered amid the unpleasant realities of his plight, the prodigal 'came to his senses'. Scratch below the surface of any person and there, albeit at times beneath layers of sinfulness, lies the signature of God. When we 'come to our senses' we are not too far from the Father's home.

Hardship and suffering frequently have the effect of concentrating the mind on life's true meaning. Prosperity and ease tend to cushion us against reality. A storm at sea triggered the processes which led to the conversion of John Newton. It was his spiritual bankruptcy which led that even more distinguished prodigal, Augustine, back to God. 'I sank away from thee,' he prayed, 'and I wandered, O my God, too much astray from thee, in these days of my youth, and I became to myself a barren land.'

This parable shows clearly the effects of human sin. It isolates us, erodes the finer feelings, deprives us of a rightful heritage and destroys self-worth. The parable also shows the meaning of repentance with its realistic review of the situation, a reorientation of the mind and heart, and the return to the Father.

All sin, whether directed against another, or against oneself, ultimately is against God. He has planned so much for us, given us so much, and has such great expectations of us, that our Lord's insight revealed through the prodigal must be right: 'Father, I have sinned against heaven and against you.'

> *I once was lost, but now am found,*
> *Was blind, but now I see.*

(John Newton)

Thank you, Lord. Amen.

→912

'Just as it was in the days of Noah . . . It was the same in the days of Lot. People were eating and drinking, buying and selling, planting and building. But the day Lot left Sodom, fire and sulphur rained down from heaven and destroyed them all. It will be just like this on the day the Son of Man is revealed' (vv. 26a, 28–30).

LIFE GOES ON . . . OR DOES IT? Very little changes. The scale of things may change, but disaster is still disaster. We become accustomed to disasters on a grand scale. The destruction of Sodom, today, would quickly be pushed off the front pages by news of greater disasters. Even Noah's flood, which probably affected the world known then, rather than the whole globe, would merit front page coverage only for a limited time.

Great strides have been made in environmental control in recent years. New crops, new medicines, new processes, new machinery, new building of dams, roads, airports, skyscapers, houses by the million – the list of new things is almost endless. Yet basic problems remain. Desert grows worldwide at an ever-increasing rate. Third world mortality remains high. In the 'developed' world, localized poverty increases as the majority become richer.

Conflict and scepticism are still the same as in the time of Noah. Greed and ambition are no different from the greed and ambition of Lot. People still try to forecast the future. They are still concerned about when – and where – the end will be. But life goes on. Though particular lives are lost, life itself continues. People build, and build and attempt to rebuild. And so it must be.

Though the ideal society seems as far away today as it did in the days before Christ, we each have a part to play, building for a better world until the day when the Son of Man will be revealed.

→917

field. When he came near the house, he heard music and dancing. 26So he called one of the servants and asked him what was going on. 27'Your brother has come,' he replied, 'and your father has killed the fattened calf because he has him back safe and sound.'

28"The older brother became angry and refused to go in. So his father went out and pleaded with him. 29But he answered his father, 'Look! All these years I've been slaving for you and never disobeyed your orders. Yet you never gave me even a young goat so I could celebrate with my friends. 30But when this son of yours who has squandered your property with prostitutes comes home, you kill the fattened calf for him!'

31"'My son,' the father said, 'you are always with me, and everything I have is yours. 32But we had to celebrate and be glad, because this brother of yours was dead and is alive again; he was lost and is found.'"

The Parable of the Shrewd Manager

16 Jesus told his disciples: "There was a rich man whose manager was accused of wasting his possessions. 2So he called him in and asked him, 'What is this I hear about you? Give an account of your management, because you cannot be manager any longer.'

3"The manager said to himself, 'What shall I do now? My master is taking away my job. I'm not strong enough to dig, and I'm ashamed to beg—4I know what I'll do so that, when I lose my job here, people will welcome me into their houses.'

5"So he called in each one of his master's debtors. He asked the first, 'How much do you owe my master?'

6"'Eight hundred gallonsª of olive oil,' he replied.

"The manager told him, 'Take your bill, sit down quickly, and make it four hundred.'

7"Then he asked the second, 'And how much do you owe?'

"'A thousand bushelsᵇ of wheat,' he replied.

"He told him, 'Take your bill and make it eight hundred.'

8"The master commended the dishonest manager because he had acted shrewdly. For the people of this world are more shrewd in dealing with their own kind than are the people of the light. 9I tell you, use worldly wealth to gain friends for yourselves, so that when it is gone, you will be welcomed into eternal dwellings.

10"Whoever can be trusted with very little can also be trusted with much, and whoever is dishonest with very little will also be dishonest with much. 11So if you have not been trustworthy in handling worldly wealth, who will trust you with true riches? 12And if you have not been trustworthy with someone else's property, who will give you property of your own?

13"No servant can serve two masters. Either he will hate the one and love the other, or he will be devoted to the one and despise

the other. You cannot serve both God and Money."

14The Pharisees, who loved money, heard all this and were sneering at Jesus. 15He said to them, "You are the ones who justify yourselves in the eyes of men, but God knows your hearts. What is highly valued among men is detestable in God's sight.

Additional Teachings

16"The Law and the Prophets were proclaimed until John. Since that time, the good news of the kingdom of God is being preached, and everyone is forcing his way into it. 17It is easier for heaven and earth to disappear than for the least stroke of a pen to drop out of the Law.

18"Anyone who divorces his wife and marries another woman commits adultery, and the man who marries a divorced woman commits adultery.

The Rich Man and Lazarus

19"There was a rich man who was dressed in purple and fine linen and lived in luxury every day. 20At his gate was laid a beggar named Lazarus, covered with sores 21and longing to eat what fell from the rich man's table. Even the dogs came and licked his sores.

22"The time came when the beggar died and the angels carried him to Abraham's side. The rich man also died and was buried. 23In hell,ᶜ where he was in torment, he looked up and saw Abraham far away, with Lazarus by his side. 24So he called to him, 'Father Abraham, have pity on me and send Lazarus to dip the tip of his finger in water and cool my tongue, because I am in agony in this fire.'

25"But Abraham replied, 'Son, remember that in your lifetime you received your good things, while Lazarus received bad things, but now he is comforted here and you are in agony. 26And besides all this, between us and you a great chasm has been fixed, so that those who want to go from here to you cannot, nor can anyone cross over from there to us.'

27"He answered, 'Then I beg you, father, send Lazarus to my father's house, 28for I have five brothers. Let him warn them, so that they will not also come to this place of torment.'

29"Abraham replied, 'They have Moses and the Prophets; let them listen to them.'

30"'No, father Abraham,' he said, 'but if someone from the dead goes to them, they will repent.'

31"He said to him, 'If they do not listen to Moses and the Prophets, they will not be convinced even if someone rises from the dead.'"

Sin, Faith, Duty

17 Jesus said to his disciples: "Things that cause people to sin are bound to come, but woe to that person through whom

ª6 Greek one hundred batous (probably about 3 kilolitres)
ᵇ7 Greek one hundred korous (probably about 35 kilolitres)   ᶜ23 Greek Hades

they come. ²It would be better for him to be thrown into the sea with a millstone tied round his neck than for him to cause one of these little ones to sin. ³So watch yourselves.

"If your brother sins, rebuke him, and if he repents, forgive him. ⁴If he sins against you seven times in a day, and seven times comes back to you and says, 'I repent,' forgive him."

⁵The apostles said to the Lord, "Increase our faith!"

⁶He replied, "If you have faith as small as a mustard seed, you can say to this mulberry tree, 'Be uprooted and planted in the sea,' and it will obey you.

⁷"Suppose one of you had a servant ploughing or looking after the sheep. Would he say to the servant when he comes in from the field, 'Come along now and sit down to eat'? ⁸Would he not rather say, 'Prepare my supper, get yourself ready and wait on me while I eat and drink; after that you may eat and drink'? ⁹Would he thank the servant because he did what he was told to do? ¹⁰So you also, when you have done everything you were told to do, should say, 'We are unworthy servants; we have only done our duty.'"

Ten Healed of Leprosy

¹¹Now on his way to Jerusalem, Jesus travelled along the border between Samaria and Galilee. ¹²As he was going into a village, ten men who had leprosy*ᵃ* met him. They stood at a distance ¹³and called out in a loud voice, "Jesus, Master, have pity on us!"

¹⁴When he saw them, he said, "Go, show yourselves to the priests." And as they went, they were cleansed.

¹⁵One of them, when he saw he was healed, came back, praising God in a loud voice. ¹⁶He threw himself at Jesus' feet and thanked him—and he was a Samaritan.

¹⁷Jesus asked, "Were not all ten cleansed? Where are the other nine? ¹⁸Was no-one found to return and give praise to God except this foreigner?" ¹⁹Then he said to him, "Rise and go; your faith has made you well."

The Coming of the Kingdom of God

²⁰Once, having been asked by the Pharisees when the kingdom of God would come, Jesus replied, "The kingdom of God does not come with your careful observation, ²¹nor will people say, 'Here it is,' or 'There it is,' because the kingdom of God is within*ᵇ* you."

²²Then he said to his disciples, "The time is coming when you will long to see one of the days of the Son of Man, but you will not see it. ²³Men will tell you, 'There he is!' or 'Here he is!' Do not go running off after them. ²⁴For the Son of Man in his day*ᶜ* will be like the lightning, which flashes and lights up the sky from one end to the other. ²⁵But first he must suffer many things and be rejected by this generation.

²⁶"Just as it was in the days of Noah, so also will it be in the days of the Son of Man. ²⁷People were eating, drinking, marrying and being given in marriage up to the day Noah entered the ark. Then the flood came and destroyed them all.

²⁸"It was the same in the days of Lot. People were eating and drinking, buying and selling, planting and building. ²⁹But the day Lot left Sodom, fire and sulphur rained down from heaven and destroyed them all.

³⁰"It will be just like this on the day the Son of Man is revealed. ³¹On that day no-one who is on the roof of his house, with his goods inside, should go down to get them. Likewise, no-one in the field should go back for anything. ³²Remember Lot's wife! ³³Whoever tries to keep his life will lose it, and whoever loses his life will preserve it. ³⁴I tell you, on that night two people will be in one bed; one will be taken and the other left. ³⁵Two women will be grinding grain together; one will be taken and the other left."*ᵈ*

³⁷"Where, Lord?" they asked.

He replied, "Where there is a dead body, there the vultures will gather."

The Parable of the Persistent Widow

18 Then Jesus told his disciples a parable to show them that they should always pray and not give up. ²He said: "In a certain town there was a judge who neither feared God nor cared about men. ³And there was a widow in that town who kept coming to him with the plea, 'Grant me justice against my adversary.'

⁴"For some time he refused. But finally he said to himself, 'Even though I don't fear God or care about men, ⁵yet because this widow keeps bothering me, I will see that she gets justice, so that she won't eventually wear me out with her coming!'"

⁶And the Lord said, "Listen to what the unjust judge says. ⁷And will not God bring about justice for his chosen ones, who cry out to him day and night? Will he keep putting them off? ⁸I tell you, he will see that they get justice, and quickly. However, when the Son of Man comes, will he find faith on the earth?"

The Parable of the Pharisee and the Tax Collector

⁹To some who were confident of their own righteousness and looked down on everybody else, Jesus told this parable: ¹⁰"Two men went up to the temple to pray, one a Pharisee and the other a tax collector. ¹¹The Pharisee stood up and prayed about*ᵃ* himself: 'God, I thank you that I am not like other men—robbers, evildoers, adulterers—or even like this tax collector. ¹²I fast twice a week and give a tenth of all I get.'

¹³"But the tax collector stood at a distance. He would not even look up to heaven, but beat his breast and said, 'God, have mercy on me, a sinner.'

¹⁴"I tell you that this man, rather than the

ᵃ12 The Greek word was used for various diseases affecting the skin—not necessarily leprosy.
ᵇ21 Or among   ᶜ24 Some manuscripts do not have in his day.
ᵈ35 Some manuscripts left. ³⁶Two men will be in the field; one will be taken and the other left.   ᵃ11 Or to

other, went home justified before God. For everyone who exalts himself will be humbled, and he who humbles himself will be exalted."

The Little Children and Jesus

15People were also bringing babies to Jesus to have him touch them. When the disciples saw this, they rebuked them. 16But Jesus called the children to him and said, "Let the little children come to me, and do not hinder them, for the kingdom of God belongs to such as these. 17I tell you the truth, anyone who will not receive the kingdom of God like a little child will never enter it."

The Rich Ruler

18A certain ruler asked him, "Good teacher, what must I do to inherit eternal life?"

19"Why do you call me good?" Jesus answered. "No-one is good—except God alone. 20You know the commandments: 'Do not commit adultery, do not murder, do not steal, do not give false testimony, honour your father and mother.'*b*"

21"All these I have kept since I was a boy," he said.

22When Jesus heard this, he said to him, "You still lack one thing. Sell everything you have and give to the poor, and you will have treasure in heaven. Then come, follow me."

23When he heard this, he became very sad, because he was a man of great wealth. 24Jesus looked at him and said, "How hard it is for the rich to enter the kingdom of God! 25Indeed, it is easier for a camel to go through the eye of a needle than for a rich man to enter the kingdom of God."

26Those who heard this asked, "Who then can be saved?"

27Jesus replied, "What is impossible with men is possible with God."

28Peter said to him, "We have left all we had to follow you!"

29"I tell you the truth," Jesus said to them, "no-one who has left home or wife or brothers or parents or children for the sake of the kingdom of God 30will fail to receive many times as much in this age and, in the age to come, eternal life."

Jesus Again Predicts His Death

31Jesus took the Twelve aside and told them, "We are going up to Jerusalem, and everything that is written by the prophets about the Son of Man will be fulfilled. 32He will be turned over to the Gentiles. They will mock him, insult him, spit on him, flog him and kill him. 33On the third day he will rise again."

34The disciples did not understand any of this. Its meaning was hidden from them, and they did not know what he was talking about.

A Blind Beggar Receives His Sight

35As Jesus approached Jericho, a blind man was sitting by the roadside begging. 36When he heard the crowd going by, he asked what was happening. 37They told him, "Jesus of Nazareth is passing by."

38He called out, "Jesus, Son of David, have mercy on me!"

39Those who led the way rebuked him and told him to be quiet, but he shouted all the more, "Son of David, have mercy on me!"

40Jesus stopped and ordered the man to be brought to him. When he came near, Jesus asked him, 41"What do you want me to do for you?"

"Lord, I want to see," he replied.

42Jesus said to him, "Receive your sight; your faith has healed you." 43Immediately he received his sight and followed Jesus, praising God. When all the people saw it, they also praised God.

Zacchaeus the Tax Collector

19 Jesus entered Jericho and was passing through. 2A man was there by the name of Zacchaeus; he was a chief tax collector and was wealthy. 3He wanted to see who Jesus was, but being a short man he could not, because of the crowd. 4So he ran ahead and climbed a sycamore-fig tree to see him, since Jesus was coming that way.

5When Jesus reached the spot, he looked up and said to him, "Zacchaeus, come down immediately. I must stay at your house today." 6So he came down at once and welcomed him gladly.

7All the people saw this and began to mutter, "He has gone to be the guest of a 'sinner'."

8But Zacchaeus stood up and said to the Lord, "Look, Lord! Here and now I give half of my possessions to the poor, and if I have cheated anybody out of anything, I will pay back four times the amount."

9Jesus said to him, "Today salvation has come to this house, because this man, too, is a son of Abraham. 10For the Son of Man came to seek and to save what was lost."

The Parable of the Ten Minas

11While they were listening to this, he went on to tell them a parable, because he was near Jerusalem and the people thought that the kingdom of God was going to appear at once. 12He said: "A man of noble birth went to a distant country to have himself appointed king and then to return. 13So he called ten of his servants and gave them ten minas.*a* 'Put this money to work,' he said, 'until I come back.'

14"But his subjects hated him and sent a delegation after him to say, 'We don't want this man to be our king.'

15"He was made king, however, and returned home. Then he sent for the servants to whom he had given the money, in order to find out what they had gained with it.

16"The first one came and said, 'Sir, your mina has earned ten more.'

17"'Well done, my good servant!' his master replied. 'Because you have been trustworthy in a very small matter, take charge of ten cities.'

---

*b*20 Exodus 20:12–16; Deut. 5:16–20   *a*13 A mina was about three months' wages.

18"The second came and said, 'Sir, your mina has earned five more.'

19"His master answered, 'You take charge of five cities.'

20"Then another servant came and said, 'Sir, here is your mina; I have kept it laid away in a piece of cloth. 21I was afraid of you, because you are a hard man. You take out what you did not put in and reap what you did not sow.'

22"His master replied, 'I will judge you by your own words, you wicked servant! You knew, did you, that I am a hard man, taking out what I did not put in, and reaping what I did not sow? 23Why then didn't you put my money on deposit, so that when I came back, I could have collected it with interest?'

24"Then he said to those standing by, 'Take his mina away from him and give it to the one who has ten minas.'

25"'Sir,' they said, 'he already has ten!'

26"He replied, 'I tell you that to everyone who has, more will be given, but as for the one who has nothing, even what he has will be taken away. 27But those enemies of mine who did not want me to be a king over them—bring them here and kill them in front of me.'"

The Triumphal Entry

28After Jesus had said this, he went on ahead, going up to Jerusalem. 29As he approached Bethphage and Bethany at the hill called the Mount of Olives, he sent two of his disciples, saying to them, 30"Go to the village ahead of you, and as you enter it, you will find a colt tied there, which no-one has ever ridden. Untie it and bring it here. 31If anyone asks you, 'Why are you untying it?' tell him, 'The Lord needs it.'"

32Those who were sent ahead went and found it just as he had told them. 33As they were untying the colt, its owners asked them, "Why are you untying the colt?"

34They replied, "The Lord needs it."

35They brought it to Jesus, threw their cloaks on the colt and put Jesus on it. 36As he went along, people spread their cloaks on the road.

37When he came near the place where the road goes down the Mount of Olives, the whole crowd of disciples began joyfully to praise God in loud voices for all the miracles they had seen:

38"Blessed is the king who comes in the name of the Lord!"[b]

"Peace in heaven and glory in the highest!"

39Some of the Pharisees in the crowd said to Jesus, "Teacher, rebuke your disciples!"

40"I tell you," he replied, "if they keep quiet, the stones will cry out."

41As he approached Jerusalem and saw the city, he wept over it 42and said, "If you, even you, had only known on this day what would bring you peace—but now it is hidden from your eyes. 43The days will come upon you when your enemies will build an embankment against you and encircle you and hem you in on every side. 44They will dash you to the ground, you and the children within your walls. They will not leave one stone on another, because you did not recognise the time of God's coming to you."

Jesus at the Temple

45Then he entered the temple area and began driving out those who were selling. 46"It is written," he said to them, "'My house will be a house of prayer';[c] but you have made it 'a den of robbers'.[d]"

47Every day he was teaching at the temple. But the chief priests, the teachers of the law and the leaders among the people were trying to kill him. 48Yet they could not find any way to do it, because all the people hung on his words.

The Authority of Jesus Questioned

20 One day as he was teaching the people in the temple courts and preaching the gospel, the chief priests and the teachers of the law, together with the elders, came up to him. 2"Tell us by what authority you are doing these things," they said. "Who gave you this authority?"

3He replied, "I will also ask you a question. Tell me, 4John's baptism—was it from heaven, or from men?"

5They discussed it among themselves and said, "If we say, 'From heaven,' he will ask, 'Why didn't you believe him?' 6But if we say, 'From men,' all the people will stone us, because they are persuaded that John was a prophet."

7So they answered, "We don't know where it was from."

8Jesus said, "Neither will I tell you by what authority I am doing these things."

The Parable of the Tenants

9He went on to tell the people this parable: "A man planted a vineyard, rented it to some farmers and went away for a long time. 10At harvest time he sent a servant to the tenants so they would give him some of the fruit of the vineyard. But the tenants beat him and sent him away empty-handed. 11He sent another servant, but that one also they beat and treated shamefully and sent away empty-handed. 12He sent still a third, and they wounded him and threw him out.

13"Then the owner of the vineyard said, 'What shall I do? I will send my son, whom I love; perhaps they will respect him.'

14"But when the tenants saw him, they talked the matter over. 'This is the heir,' they said. 'Let's kill him, and the inheritance will be ours.' 15So they threw him out of the vineyard and killed him.

"What then will the owner of the vineyard do to them? 16He will come and kill those tenants and give the vineyard to others."

When the people heard this, they said, "May this never be!"

b38 Psalm 118:26   c46 Isaiah 56:7   d46 Jer. 7:11

LUKE 20:9–13

'Then the owner of the vineyard said, "What shall I do? I will send my son, whom I love, perhaps they will respect him" ' (v. 13).

THE JEWISH SCHOLAR C. G. Montefiore once pointed out the main difference between Judaism and Christianity, as he saw it, by saying 'The Rabbis had said that if the sinner returns to God, God will receive him: they had not said that the love of God goes out to seek the sinner where he is. But in the Gospels it is so.'

Such statements are over-simplified, but this one highlights an important point in the controversy between Jesus and the authorities. It would be easy to dwell on the final part of today's story, and say that judgement will fall on the tenants, but there is a striking lesson to be learnt before that. Even the story of the lost son does not go so far as this story. The son had already decided to go back to his father before the waiting father saw him far off and came to meet him. In today's parable (or allegory if you want to be more precise) there is a succession of messengers, each coming from the owner (God), each seeking what rightly belongs to the owner.

This idea of a seeking God is hard for us to accept. Most people seem to want to go out and find God. A lot of Christian terminology reinforces that idea. We talk, rightly, of Christianity as 'the Way'. We emphasize Jesus' words 'Seek and you shall find,' and that is good and proper. But we must not forget that God seeks us, too.

In the Salvation Army a simple chorus is often sung:

> *Meet my need, Lord; Meet my need, Lord;*
> *Meet my need, just now.*
> *I am waiting, and thou art coming,*
> *To meet my need just now.*

Note particularly line three: I am waiting, and *thou* art coming. *Resist the temptation to change the order!*

→918

LUKE 21:5–28 (especially vv. 20–28)
'When these things begin to take place, stand up and lift up your heads, because your redemption is drawing near' (v. 28).

WHEN FACED BY DANGER the natural tendency is to duck. Some animals even freeze and play 'dead'. On holiday in Norfolk we saw a frog, floating on the surface, all one-sided and apparently lifeless. I had accidentally touched it with a stick trailing in the water. We watched a long time, sorry the frog had been killed by such a little accident. Suddenly, when he felt the danger was over, he kicked and zoomed away into the depths. In a game park in Kenya we saw a dead jackal cub by the roadside, apparently run down by a passing car. Again we stopped. Again, when the danger seemed to be over, mother jackal came along and the 'dead' baby exploded into life, and trotted off after mum.

Faced by danger, Jesus' advice is exactly the opposite. Even the advice to flee, involves risk, actually being seen by the enemy running away. When danger threatens we need to stand up and be counted. It goes against every instinct of self-preservation. It is folly by any worldly standard, in the face of the dangers talked about in this chapter ranging from invasion by a ruthless enemy to vast, cosmic dangers which herald the coming End.

Persecution leads to opportunities for witness. In all such conditions we have the support and the power of God with us.

> Oft in danger, oft in woe,
>   Onward, Christian, onward go:
> Let not fears your cause impede,
>   Great your strength if great your need.

> (H. K. White and F. Fuller-Maitland, alt.)

This chapter does not tell us when the end will be, but gives strength to face the end whenever it comes.

→921

17Jesus looked directly at them and asked, "Then what is the meaning of that which is written:

" 'The stone the builders rejected
    has become the capstone'*a,b*?

18Everyone who falls on that stone will be broken to pieces, but he on whom it falls will be crushed."

19The teachers of the law and the chief priests looked for a way to arrest him immediately, because they knew he had spoken this parable against them. But they were afraid of the people.

Paying Taxes to Caesar

20Keeping a close watch on him, they sent spies, who pretended to be honest. They hoped to catch Jesus in something he said so that they might hand him over to the power and authority of the governor. 21So the spies questioned him: "Teacher, we know that you speak and teach what is right, and that you do not show partiality but teach the way of God in accordance with the truth. 22Is it right for us to pay taxes to Caesar or not?"

23He saw through their duplicity and said to them, 24"Show me a denarius. Whose portrait and inscription are on it?"

25"Caesar's," they replied.

He said to them, "Then give to Caesar what is Caesar's, and to God what is God's."

26They were unable to trap him in what he had said there in public. And astonished by his answer, they became silent.

The Resurrection and Marriage

27Some of the Sadducees, who say there is no resurrection, came to Jesus with a question. 28"Teacher," they said, "Moses wrote for us that if a man's brother dies and leaves a wife but no children, the man must marry the widow and have children for his brother. 29Now there were seven brothers. The first one married a woman and died childless. 30The second 31and then the third married her, and in the same way the seven died, leaving no children. 32Finally, the woman died too. 33Now then, at the resurrection whose wife will she be, since the seven were married to her?"

34Jesus replied, "The people of this age marry and are given in marriage. 35But those who are considered worthy of taking part in that age and in the resurrection from the dead will neither marry nor be given in marriage, 36and they can no longer die; for they are like the angels. They are God's children, since they are children of the resurrection. 37But in the account of the bush, even Moses showed that the dead rise, for he calls the Lord 'the God of Abraham, and the God of Isaac, and the God of Jacob'.*c* 38He is not the God of the dead, but of the living, for to him all are alive."

39Some of the teachers of the law responded, "Well said, teacher!" 40And no-one dared to ask him any more questions.

Whose Son Is the Christ?

41Then Jesus said to them, "How is it that they say the Christ*d* is the Son of David? 42David himself declares in the Book of Psalms:

" 'The Lord said to my Lord:
    "Sit at my right hand
43until I make your enemies
    a footstool for your feet." '*e*

44David calls him 'Lord'. How then can he be his son?"

45While all the people were listening, Jesus said to his disciples, 46"Beware of the teachers of the law. They like to walk around in flowing robes and love to be greeted in the market-places and have the most important seats in the synagogues and the places of honour at banquets. 47They devour widows' houses and for a show make lengthy prayers. Such men will be punished most severely."

The Widow's Offering

21 As he looked up, Jesus saw the rich putting their gifts into the temple treasury. 2He also saw a poor widow put in two very small copper coins.*a* 3"I tell you the truth," he said, "this poor widow has put in more than all the others. 4All these people gave their gifts out of their wealth; but she out of her poverty put in all she had to live on."

Signs of the End of the Age

5Some of his disciples were remarking about how the temple was adorned with beautiful stones and with gifts dedicated to God. But Jesus said, 6"As for what you see here, the time will come when not one stone will be left on another; every one of them will be thrown down."

7"Teacher," they asked, "when will these things happen? And what will be the sign that they are about to take place?"

8He replied: "Watch out that you are not deceived. For many will come in my name, claiming, 'I am he,' and 'The time is near.' Do not follow them. 9When you hear of wars and revolutions, do not be frightened. These things must happen first, but the end will not come right away."

10Then he said to them: "Nation will rise against nation, and kingdom against kingdom. 11There will be great earthquakes, famines and pestilences in various places, and fearful events and great signs from heaven.

12"But before all this, they will lay hands on you and persecute you. They will deliver you to synagogues and prisons, and you will be brought before kings and governors, and all on account of my name. 13This will result in your being witnesses to them. 14But make up your mind not to worry beforehand how you will defend yourselves. 15For I will give you words and wisdom that none of your adversaries will be able to resist or contradict. 16You will be betrayed even by parents,

---

*a17 Or cornerstone   b17 Psalm 118:22   c37 Exodus 3:6   d41 Or Messiah   e43 Psalm 110:1
a2 Greek two lepta*

brothers, relatives and friends, and they will put some of you to death. [17]All men will hate you because of me. [18]But not a hair of your head will perish. [19]By standing firm you will gain life.

[20]"When you see Jerusalem being surrounded by armies, you will know that its desolation is near. [21]Then let those who are in Judea flee to the mountains, let those in the city get out, and let those in the country not enter the city. [22]For this is the time of punishment in fulfilment of all that has been written. [23]How dreadful it will be in those days for pregnant women and nursing mothers! There will be great distress in the land and wrath against this people. [24]They will fall by the sword and will be taken as prisoners to all the nations. Jerusalem will be trampled on by the Gentiles until the times of the Gentiles are fulfilled.

[25]"There will be signs in the sun, moon and stars. On the earth, nations will be in anguish and perplexity at the roaring and tossing of the sea. [26]Men will faint from terror, apprehensive of what is coming on the world, for the heavenly bodies will be shaken. [27]At that time they will see the Son of Man coming in a cloud with power and great glory. [28]When these things begin to take place, stand up and lift up your heads, because your redemption is drawing near."

[29]He told them this parable: "Look at the fig-tree and all the trees. [30]When they sprout leaves, you can see for yourselves and know that summer is near. [31]Even so, when you see these things happening, you know that the kingdom of God is near.

[32]"I tell you the truth, this generation[b] will certainly not pass away until all these things have happened. [33]Heaven and earth will pass away, but my words will never pass away.

[34]"Be careful, or your hearts will be weighed down with dissipation, drunkenness and the anxieties of life, and that day will close on you unexpectedly like a trap. [35]For it will come upon all those who live on the face of the whole earth. [36]Be always on the watch, and pray that you may be able to escape all that is about to happen, and that you may be able to stand before the Son of Man."

[37]Each day Jesus was teaching at the temple, and each evening he went out to spend the night on the hill called the Mount of Olives, [38]and all the people came early in the morning to hear him at the temple.

Judas Agrees to Betray Jesus

22 Now the Feast of Unleavened Bread, called the Passover, was approaching, [2]and the chief priests and the teachers of the law were looking for some way to get rid of Jesus, for they were afraid of the people. [3]Then Satan entered Judas, called Iscariot, one of the Twelve. [4]And Judas went to the chief priests and the officers of the temple guard and discussed with them how he might betray Jesus. [5]They were delighted and agreed to give him money. [6]He consented, and watched for an opportunity to hand Jesus over to them when no crowd was present.

The Last Supper

[7]Then came the day of Unleavened Bread on which the Passover lamb had to be sacrificed. [8]Jesus sent Peter and John, saying, "Go and make preparations for us to eat the Passover."

[9]"Where do you want us to prepare for it?" they asked.

[10]He replied, "As you enter the city, a man carrying a jar of water will meet you. Follow him to the house that he enters, [11]and say to the owner of the house, 'The Teacher asks: Where is the guest room, where I may eat the Passover with my disciples?' [12]He will show you a large upper room, all furnished. Make preparations there."

[13]They left and found things just as Jesus had told them. So they prepared the Passover.

[14]When the hour came, Jesus and his apostles reclined at the table. [15]And he said to them, "I have eagerly desired to eat this Passover with you before I suffer. [16]For I tell you, I will not eat it again until it finds fulfilment in the kingdom of God."

[17]After taking the cup, he gave thanks and said, "Take this and divide it among you. [18]For I tell you I will not drink again of the fruit of the vine until the kingdom of God comes."

[19]And he took bread, gave thanks and broke it, and gave it to them, saying, "This is my body given for you; do this in remembrance of me."

[20]In the same way, after the supper he took the cup, saying, "This cup is the new covenant in my blood, which is poured out for you. [21]But the hand of him who is going to betray me is with mine on the table. [22]The Son of Man will go as it has been decreed, but woe to that man who betrays him." [23]They began to question among themselves which of them it might be who would do this.

[24]Also a dispute arose among them as to which of them was considered to be greatest. [25]Jesus said to them, "The kings of the Gentiles lord it over them; and those who exercise authority over them call themselves Benefactors. [26]But you are not to be like that. Instead, the greatest among you should be like the youngest, and the one who rules like the one who serves. [27]For who is greater, the one who is at the table or the one who serves? Is it not the one who is at the table? But I am among you as one who serves. [28]You are those who have stood by me in my trials. [29]And I confer on you a kingdom, just as my Father conferred one on me, [30]so that you may eat and drink at my table in my kingdom and sit on thrones, judging the twelve tribes of Israel.

[31]"Simon, Simon, Satan has asked to sift you[a] as wheat. [32]But I have prayed for you, Simon, that your faith may not fail. And when you have turned back, strengthen your brothers."

LUKE 22:7–19

' "I tell you, I will not eat it again until it finds fulfilment in the kingdom of God" . . . And he took bread, gave thanks and broke it, and gave it to them, saying "This is my body given for you; do this in remembrance of me" ' (vv. 16, 19).

TODAY WE LOOK AGAIN at the difficult concept of the kingdom of God. Jesus has told his disciples it is just round the corner, but no one knows exactly when it will come. Now he is saying he won't eat or drink again until the kingdom has come.

In a real sense the kingdom arrived with the death and resurrection of Christ. Every Christian is a citizen of the kingdom of heaven, not just a citizen of some future kingdom, but of one which now exists here in the Church, and in the hearts and lives of individual Christians. That kingdom was brought in by the submissive death of Jesus. That kingdom is one we all have the opportunity to be part of.

Being part of that kingdom involves sacrifice. Jesus says, 'This is my body given for you, do this in remembrance of me.' Every act of breaking bread reminds us of the sacrifice of Jesus. Salvationists witness to the fact that the sacrifice is paramount. Even formal remembrance by breaking bread can sometimes overshadow the real intention, which is that Christians should participate fully in Jesus' sacrifice.

'Do this in remembrance of me' involves sharing in the breaking of Jesus' body; being prepared to make the sacrifice he makes. When we forget that we exclude ourselves from the kingdom.

> *Dear Saviour, I can ne'er repay*
> *The debt of love I owe.*
> *Here, Lord, I give myself away,*
> *'Tis all that I can do.*

> *(Isaac Watts)*

→922

LUKE 23:26–31

'As they led him away, they seized Simon from Cyrene . . . and put the cross on him and made him carry it behind Jesus' (v. 26).

OUR HOLY WEEK PILGRIMAGE now leads to the *Via Dolorosa*, the road of sorrows. It is the most sacred road of history. It is the road on which love travelled the farthest. It is the road on which Jesus carried his cross to Calvary.

Many a man died from the scourging of the dreaded cat-o'-nine-tails. But Jesus survived that, as well as the sleepless night, the quick succession of interrogations and the travesty of the trials. Weakened from the torture, he sank beneath the weight of the death beam on his trek to Calvary.

The soldiers, impatient of the delay and wanting to get this wretched business over with, grab hold of Simon, an onlooker, and press him into service. To Simon it must have been an extreme annoyance, a terrible indignity as he gets caught up in the divine drama of the ages.

Mark's account describes Simon as the father of Alexander and Rufus (15:21), suggesting they must have been well known in the church at Rome to whom Mark's Gospel was addressed. In the apostle Paul's letter to the church at Rome, he extends greeting to 'Rufus, chosen in the Lord, and his mother, who has been a mother to me, too' (Rom. 16:13). It seems very plausible that this refers to Simon's family. And could the Simeon (another form of Simon) of Acts 13:1 be this same Simon of the road of sorrows? In that message he is called Niger, which meant one with a swarthy skin from Africa. Thus it is not at all improbable that Simon was a black man.

Simon of Cyrene is typical of the Christian life. All of us sooner or later are called upon to carry our cross for Christ. Because Simon carried the cross that day, he, his wife and sons, and others found Christ and eternal life. And we too find life's true meaning in the carrying of our cross for Christ.

Christ of the road of sorrows, give me a willingness to pay the cost of true discipleship.

→925

33But he replied, "Lord, I am ready to go with you to prison and to death."

34Jesus answered, "I tell you, Peter, before the cock crows today, you will deny three times that you know me."

35Then Jesus asked them, "When I sent you without purse, bag or sandals, did you lack anything?"

"Nothing," they answered.

36He said to them, "But now if you have a purse, take it, and also a bag; and if you don't have a sword, sell your cloak and buy one. 37It is written: 'And he was numbered with the transgressors';b and I tell you that this must be fulfilled in me. Yes, what is written about me is reaching its fulfilment."

38The disciples said, "See, Lord, here are two swords."

"That is enough," he replied.

Jesus Prays on the Mount of Olives

39Jesus went out as usual to the Mount of Olives, and his disciples followed him. 40On reaching the place, he said to them, "Pray that you will not fall into temptation." 41He withdrew about a stone's throw beyond them, knelt down and prayed, 42"Father, if you are willing, take this cup from me; yet not my will, but yours be done." 43An angel from heaven appeared to him and strengthened him. 44And being in anguish, he prayed more earnestly, and his sweat was like drops of blood falling to the ground.c

45When he rose from prayer and went back to the disciples, he found them asleep, exhausted from sorrow. 46"Why are you sleeping?" he asked them. "Get up and pray so that you will not fall into temptation."

Jesus Arrested

47While he was still speaking a crowd came up, and the man who was called Judas, one of the Twelve, was leading them. He approached Jesus to kiss him, 48but Jesus asked him, "Judas, are you betraying the Son of Man with a kiss?"

49When Jesus' followers saw what was going to happen, they said, "Lord, should we strike with our swords?" 50And one of them struck the servant of the high priest, cutting off his right ear.

51But Jesus answered, "No more of this!" And he touched the man's ear and healed him.

52Then Jesus said to the chief priests, the officers of the temple guard, and the elders, who had come for him, "Am I leading a rebellion, that you have come with swords and clubs? 53Every day I was with you in the temple courts, and you did not lay a hand on me. But this is your hour—when darkness reigns."

Peter Disowns Jesus

54Then seizing him, they led him away and took him into the house of the high priest. Peter followed at a distance. 55But when they had kindled a fire in the middle of the courtyard and had sat down together, Peter sat down with them. 56A servant girl saw him seated there in the firelight. She looked closely at him and said, "This man was with him."

57But he denied it. "Woman, I don't know him," he said.

58A little later someone else saw him and said, "You also are one of them."

"Man, I am not!" Peter replied.

59About an hour later another asserted, "Certainly this fellow was with him, for he is a Galilean."

60Peter replied, "Man, I don't know what you're talking about!" Just as he was speaking, the cock crowed. 61The Lord turned and looked straight at Peter. Then Peter remembered the word the Lord had spoken to him: "Before the cock crows today, you will disown me three times." 62And he went outside and wept bitterly.

The Guards Mock Jesus

63The men who were guarding Jesus began mocking and beating him. 64They blindfolded him and demanded, "Prophesy! Who hit you?" 65And they said many other insulting things to him.

Jesus Before Pilate and Herod

66At daybreak the council of the elders of the people, both the chief priests and teachers of the law, met together, and Jesus was led before them. 67"If you are the Christ,"d they said, "tell us."

Jesus answered, "If I tell you, you will not believe me, 68and if I asked you, you would not answer. 69But from now on, the Son of Man will be seated at the right hand of the mighty God."

70They all asked, "Are you then the Son of God?"

He replied, "You are right in saying I am."

71Then they said, "Why do we need any more testimony? We have heard it from his own lips."

23 Then the whole assembly rose and led him off to Pilate. 2And they began to accuse him, saying, "We have found this man subverting our nation. He opposes payment of taxes to Caesar and claims to be Christ,a a king."

3So Pilate asked Jesus, "Are you the king of the Jews?"

"Yes, it is as you say," Jesus replied.

4Then Pilate announced to the chief priests and the crowd, "I find no basis for a charge against this man."

5But they insisted, "He stirs up the people all over Judeab by his teaching. He started in Galilee and has come all the way here."

6On hearing this, Pilate asked if the man was a Galilean. 7When he learned that Jesus was under Herod's jurisdiction, he sent him to Herod, who was also in Jerusalem at that time.

8When Herod saw Jesus, he was greatly

---

b37 Isaiah 53:12   c44 Some early manuscripts do not have verses 43 and 44.   d67 Or Messiah
a2 Or Messiah; also in verses 35 and 39   b5 Or over the land of the Jews

pleased, because for a long time he had been wanting to see him. From what he had heard about him, he hoped to see him perform some miracle. 9He plied him with many questions, but Jesus gave him no answer. 10The chief priests and the teachers of the law were standing there, vehemently accusing him. 11Then Herod and his soldiers ridiculed and mocked him. Dressing him in an elegant robe, they sent him back to Pilate. 12That day Herod and Pilate became friends—before this they had been enemies.

13Pilate called together the chief priests, the rulers and the people, 14and said to them, "You brought me this man as one who was inciting the people to rebellion. I have examined him in your presence and have found no basis for your charges against him. 15Neither has Herod, for he sent him back to us; as you can see, he has done nothing to deserve death. 16Therefore, I will punish him and then release him."*c*

18With one voice they cried out, "Away with this man! Release Barabbas to us!" (19Barabbas had been thrown into prison for an insurrection in the city, and for murder.)

20Wanting to release Jesus, Pilate appealed to them again. 21But they kept shouting, "Crucify him! Crucify him!"

22For the third time he spoke to them: "Why? What crime has this man committed? I have found in him no grounds for the death penalty. Therefore I will have him punished and then release him."

23But with loud shouts they insistently demanded that he be crucified, and their shouts prevailed. 24So Pilate decided to grant their demand. 25He released the man who had been thrown into prison for insurrection and murder, the one they asked for, and surrendered Jesus to their will.

The Crucifixion

26As they led him away, they seized Simon from Cyrene, who was on his way in from the country, and put the cross on him and made him carry it behind Jesus. 27A large number of people followed him, including women who mourned and wailed for him. 28Jesus turned and said to them, "Daughters of Jerusalem, do not weep for me; weep for yourselves and for your children. 29For the time will come when you will say, 'Blessed are the barren women, the wombs that never bore and the breasts that never nursed!' 30Then

"'they will say to the mountains, "Fall on us!"
and to the hills "Cover us!"'*d*

31For if men do these things when the tree is green, what will happen when it is dry?"

32Two other men, both criminals, were also led out with him to be executed. 33When they came to the place called the Skull, there they crucified him, along with the criminals —one on his right, the other on his left. 34Jesus said, "Father, forgive them, for they

do not know what they are doing."*e* And they divided up his clothes by casting lots.

35The people stood watching, and the rulers even sneered at him. They said, "He saved others; let him save himself if he is the Christ of God, the Chosen One."

36The soldiers also came up and mocked him. They offered him wine vinegar 37and said, "If you are the king of the Jews, save yourself."

38There was a written notice above him, which read: THIS IS THE KING OF THE JEWS.

39One of the criminals who hung there hurled insults at him: "Aren't you the Christ? Save yourself and us!"

40But the other criminal rebuked him. "Don't you fear God," he said, "since you are under the same sentence? 41We are punished justly, for we are getting what our deeds deserve. But this man has done nothing wrong."

42Then he said, "Jesus, remember me when you come into your kingdom.*f*"

43Jesus answered him, "I tell you the truth, today you will be with me in paradise."

Jesus' Death

44It was now about the sixth hour, and darkness came over the whole land until the ninth hour, 45for the sun stopped shining. And the curtain of the temple was torn in two. 46Jesus called out with a loud voice, "Father, into your hands I commit my spirit." When he had said this, he breathed his last.

47The centurion, seeing what had happened, praised God and said, "Surely this was a righteous man." 48When all the people who had gathered to witness this sight saw what took place, they beat their breasts and went away. 49But all those who knew him, including the women who had followed him from Galilee, stood at a distance, watching these things.

Jesus' Burial

50Now there was a man named Joseph, a member of the Council, a good and upright man, 51who had not consented to their decision and action. He came from the Judean town of Arimathea and he was waiting for the kingdom of God. 52Going to Pilate, he asked for Jesus' body. 53Then he took it down, wrapped it in linen cloth and placed it in a tomb cut in the rock, one in which no-one had yet been laid. 54It was Preparation Day, and the Sabbath was about to begin.

55The women who had come with Jesus from Galilee followed Joseph and saw the tomb and how his body was laid in it. 56Then they went home and prepared spices and perfumes. But they rested on the Sabbath in obedience to the commandment.

The Resurrection

24 On the first day of the week, very early in the morning, the women took the spices they had prepared and went to the

---

c16 Some manuscripts *him."* *17Now he was obliged to release one man to them at the Feast.*   *d30* Hosea 10:8
e34 Some early manuscripts do not have this sentence.   *f42* Some manuscripts *come with your kingly power*

LUKE 23:33–49
'When they came to the place called the Skull, there they crucified him' (v. 33).

THE SON OF GOD, nailed to a felon's cross on a skull-shaped hill before a howling mob! A strange place and incredible way indeed for God Incarnate to end his earthly mission.

No other event in all history has made such an impact upon us as Calvary. We feel very much a part of Calvary and the cross and all that happened there. When Rembrandt painted the crucifixion, among the faces in the crowd the great artist painted himself, knowing he was a part of that divine drama of the ages.

Yes, we were there. Our sins were the tongues that jeered him, the hard palms that slapped him, the knuckled fists that pummelled his face. Our sins were the scourges that cut his back to shreds, the thorns that punctured his brow, the nails that pierced his sacred hands. In the immortal words of Isaiah, 'He was pierced for our transgressions, he was crushed for our iniquities . . . by his wounds we are healed' (Isa. 53:5).

Calvary was the bulletin-board on which God nailed his amnesty for sinful men. At Adam's fall, sin entered into the bloodstream of humanity and brought the condemnation of eternal death. On Calvary the scarlet payment was made for our salvation.

That humble tree that supported Jesus' limbs on its common, broken bark has become man's highest symbol of hope. Today it 'towers o'er the wrecks of time'. It has been carved into every form of beauty, emblazoned on flags of nations, engraved on sceptres and diadems of kings. At Calvary our Lord turned the tragedy of the cross into a triumph of our salvation.

With Isaac Watts, we are constrained to say:

> *When I survey the wondrous cross*
> *On which the Prince of Glory died,*
> *My richest gain I count but loss,*
> *And pour contempt on all my pride.*

Divine love, upon a cross impaled, I am moved to a holy hush and a deeper devotion as I contemplate your unspeakable love on Calvary.

→926

LUKE 24:13–35

'Were not our hearts burning within us while he talked with us on the road and opened the Scriptures to us?' (v. 32)

IN THINKING OF EMMAUS, we picture two disciples, sad and disillusioned. Across their loftiest dreams is written the word 'failure'. With hope gone, were they not heading back to the old life, the old friendships, the old ruts? If there is anything redeeming about this event, it is that in the midst of this tragedy they talked together of all these things which had happened. While the testimonies of those early visitors to the tomb did not convince these two travellers that Jesus had risen from the grave, on that road to Emmaus they thought about those events and their meaning. As they thought and talked, 'Jesus himself drew near and went with them.' Unknowingly these despondent disciples had kept a channel of communication open between themselves and God.

Someone has said, 'The winds of God are always blowing, but we must hoist the sails.' It is up to us to keep the lines of communication open between ourselves and God. Even when times are difficult, if we keep our thoughts on the kingdom, we can always be in touch with Christ. All is never lost if our minds and hearts are open to him.

And this truth applies not only to us but to others whom we know. As we live in the Spirit, we will help another make that vital contact. Someone else will find encouragement in spirit as Christ draws near to them and ministers to their need.

O Lord Jesus, speak to us that your truth might burn within us, rekindling the flame of zeal for the things of God. We are your people. Fill us with your fullness. It is in Jerusalem, our Jerusalem, that we wish to stand, right in the centre of your will, fully indwelt by your Spirit. Amen.

→929

tomb. ²They found the stone rolled away from the tomb, ³but when they entered, they did not find the body of the Lord Jesus. ⁴While they were wondering about this, suddenly two men in clothes that gleamed like lightning stood beside them. ⁵In their fright the women bowed down with their faces to the ground, but the men said to them, "Why do you look for the living among the dead? ⁶He is not here; he has risen! Remember how he told you, while he was still with you in Galilee: ⁷'The Son of Man must be delivered into the hands of sinful men, be crucified and on the third day be raised again.'" ⁸Then they remembered his words.

⁹When they came back from the tomb, they told all these things to the Eleven and to all the others. ¹⁰It was Mary Magdalene, Joanna, Mary the mother of James, and the others with them who told this to the apostles. ¹¹But they did not believe the women, because their words seemed to them like nonsense. ¹²Peter, however, got up and ran to the tomb. Bending over, he saw the strips of linen lying by themselves, and he went away, wondering to himself what had happened.

On the Road to Emmaus

¹³Now that same day two of them were going to a village called Emmaus, about seven miles*a* from Jerusalem. ¹⁴They were talking with each other about everything that had happened. ¹⁵As they talked and discussed these things with each other, Jesus himself came up and walked along with them; ¹⁶but they were kept from recognising him.

¹⁷He asked them, "What are you discussing together as you walk along?"

They stood still, their faces downcast. ¹⁸One of them, named Cleopas, asked him, "Are you only a visitor to Jerusalem and do not know the things that have happened there in these days?"

¹⁹"What things?" he asked.

"About Jesus of Nazareth," they replied. "He was a prophet, powerful in word and deed before God and all the people. ²⁰The chief priests and our rulers handed him over to be sentenced to death, and they crucified him; ²¹but we had hoped that he was the one who was going to redeem Israel. And what is more, it is the third day since all this took place. ²²In addition, some of our women amazed us. They went to the tomb early this morning ²³but didn't find his body. They came and told us that they had seen a vision of angels, who said he was alive. ²⁴Then some of our companions went to the tomb and found it just as the women had said, but him they did not see."

²⁵He said to them, "How foolish you are, and how slow of heart to believe all that the prophets have spoken! ²⁶Did not the Christ*b* have to suffer these things and then enter his glory?" ²⁷And beginning with Moses and all the Prophets, he explained to them what was said in all the Scriptures concerning himself.

²⁸As they approached the village to which they were going, Jesus acted as if he were going further. ²⁹But they urged him strongly, "Stay with us, for it is nearly evening; the day is almost over." So he went in to stay with them.

³⁰When he was at the table with them, he took bread, gave thanks, broke it and began to give it to them. ³¹Then their eyes were opened and they recognised him, and he disappeared from their sight. ³²They asked each other, "Were not our hearts burning within us while he talked with us on the road and opened the Scriptures to us?"

³³They got up and returned at once to Jerusalem. There they found the Eleven and those with them, assembled together ³⁴and saying, "It is true! The Lord has risen and has appeared to Simon." ³⁵Then the two told what had happened on the way, and how Jesus was recognised by them when he broke the bread.

Jesus Appears to the Disciples

³⁶While they were still talking about this, Jesus himself stood among them and said to them, "Peace be with you."

³⁷They were startled and frightened, thinking they saw a ghost. ³⁸He said to them, "Why are you troubled, and why do doubts rise in your minds? ³⁹Look at my hands and my feet. It is I myself! Touch me and see; a ghost does not have flesh and bones, as you see I have."

⁴⁰When he had said this, he showed them his hands and feet. ⁴¹And while they still did not believe it because of joy and amazement, he asked them, "Do you have anything here to eat?" ⁴²They gave him a piece of broiled fish, ⁴³and he took it and ate it in their presence.

⁴⁴He said to them, "This is what I told you while I was still with you: Everything must be fulfilled that is written about me in the Law of Moses, the Prophets and the Psalms."

⁴⁵Then he opened their minds so they could understand the Scriptures. ⁴⁶He told them, "This is what is written: The Christ will suffer and rise from the dead on the third day, ⁴⁷and repentance and forgiveness of sins will be preached in his name to all nations, beginning at Jerusalem. ⁴⁸You are witnesses of these things. ⁴⁹I am going to send you what my Father has promised; but stay in the city until you have been clothed with power from on high."

The Ascension

⁵⁰When he had led them out to the vicinity of Bethany, he lifted up his hands and blessed them. ⁵¹While he was blessing them, he left them and was taken up into heaven. ⁵²Then they worshipped him and returned to Jerusalem with great joy. ⁵³And they stayed continually at the temple, praising God.

---

*a*13 Greek *sixty stadia* (about 11 kilometres)   *b*26 Or *Messiah*; also in verse 46

John

The Word Became Flesh

1 In the beginning was the Word, and the Word was with God, and the Word was God. [2]He was with God in the beginning. [3]Through him all things were made; without him nothing was made that has been made. [4]In him was life, and that life was the light of men. [5]The light shines in the darkness, but the darkness has not understood[d] it.

[6]There came a man who was sent from God; his name was John. [7]He came as a witness to testify concerning that light, so that through him all men might believe. [8]He himself was not the light; he came only as a witness to the light. [9]The true light that gives light to every man was coming into the world.[b]

[10]He was in the world, and though the world was made through him, the world did not recognise him. [11]He came to that which was his own, but his own did not receive him. [12]Yet to all who received him, to those who believed in his name, he gave the right to become children of God—[13]children born not of natural descent,[c] nor of human decision or a husband's will, but born of God.

[14]The Word became flesh and made his dwelling among us. We have seen his glory, the glory of the One and Only,[d] who came from the Father, full of grace and truth. [15]John testifies concerning him. He cries out, saying, "This was he of whom I said, 'He who comes after me has surpassed me because he was before me.'" [16]From the fulness of his grace we have all received one blessing after another. [17]For the law was given through Moses; grace and truth came through Jesus Christ. [18]No-one has ever seen God, but God the One and Only,[e,f] who is at the Father's side, has made him known.

John the Baptist Denies Being the Christ

[19]Now this was John's testimony when the Jews of Jerusalem sent priests and Levites to ask him who he was. [20]He did not fail to confess, but confessed freely, "I am not the Christ."[g]

[21]They asked him, "Then who are you? Are you Elijah?"

He said, "I am not."

"Are you the Prophet?"

He answered, "No."

[22]Finally they said, "Who are you? Give us an answer to take back to those who sent us. What do you say about yourself?"

[23]John replied in the words of Isaiah the prophet, "I am the voice of one calling in the desert, 'Make straight the way for the Lord.'[h]"

[24]Now some Pharisees who had been sent [25]questioned him, "Why then do you baptise if you are not the Christ, nor Elijah, nor the Prophet?"

[26]"I baptise with[i] water," John replied, "but among you stands one you do not know. [27]He is the one who comes after me, the thongs of whose sandals I am not worthy to untie."

[28]This all happened at Bethany on the other side of the Jordan, where John was baptising.

Jesus the Lamb of God

[29]The next day John saw Jesus coming towards him and said, "Look, the Lamb of God, who takes away the sin of the world! [30]This is the one I meant when I said, 'A man who comes after me has surpassed me because he was before me.' [31]I myself did not know him, but the reason I came baptising with water was that he might be revealed to Israel."

[32]Then John gave this testimony: "I saw the Spirit come down from heaven as a dove and remain on him. [33]I would not have known him, except that the one who sent me to baptise with water told me, 'The man on whom you see the Spirit come down and remain is he who will baptise with the Holy Spirit.' [34]I have seen and I testify that this is the Son of God."

Jesus' First Disciples

[35]The next day John was there again with two of his disciples. [36]When he saw Jesus

---

[a]5 Or *darkness, and the darkness has not overcome*
[b]9 Or *This was the true light that gives light to every man who comes into the world*   [c]13 Greek *of bloods*
[d]14 Or *the Only Begotten*   [e]18 Or *the Only Begotten*
[f]18 Some manuscripts *but the only* (or *only begotten*) *Son*
[g]20 Or *Messiah.* "The Christ" (Greek) and "the Messiah" (Hebrew) both mean "the Anointed One"; also in verse 25.   [h]23 Isaiah 40:3   [i]26 Or *in*; also in verses 31 and 33

JOHN 1:1–5

'In the beginning was the Word . . . In him life was and that life was the light of men. The light shines in the darkness, but the darkness has not understood it' (vv. 1, 4, 5).

'GOD EXPRESSED HIMSELF'. This phrase from J. B. Phillips' translation is quite different from saying 'In the beginning was the Word', or 'When all things began, the word already was' but it does make us catch our breath and take another look at the meaning of John's familiar introduction to the Gospel.

In J. B. Phillips' language, Jesus is God expressing himself. A few years ago self-expression was all the rage. Recently its value has been questioned. We have begun to realize that undisciplined self-expression is not the answer to everything. But God's self-expression in the form of Jesus is disciplined as well as free.

God limited himself in time and space. He accepted the discipline of expressing himself in a particular way which could be understood by us, his creatures. He did this voluntarily for our sakes.

God's self-expression in Jesus still gives light to a very dark world. Many try to extinguish that light. Sometimes, in some areas, it seems to be almost extinguished. Preaching and teaching about Christ is forbidden in many places. It is merely ignored in others. But wherever Christians serve their fellow men, in humility and sincerity, there the light shines.

In some areas of the world, Christian social service is tolerated, only if the serving Christians agree not to preach. Should scarce Christian resources be used in such a way? Read verses four and five again before you answer.

→930

JOHN 1:35–51

'Andrew, Simon Peter's brother, was one of the two who heard what John had said and who had followed Jesus . . . Philip found Nathanael and told him' (vv. 40, 45).

ANDREW, PETER, PHILIP, NATHANAEL, are named in this section. Andrew brought Peter, Philip brought Nathanael: a fine missionary story. The most effective witness, often the hardest to make, is to our close family. They know our faults. Both Andrew and Philip made that witness fearlessly from the start.

But who was the other disciple? One who hid his light under a bushel? Perhaps. But tradition says the other disciple was John the gospel-writer himself. That makes sense. Parallel accounts in Matthew, Mark and Luke show Andrew and Peter, James and John were called together. We cannot reconcile the accounts completely, but it is clear that John, Zebedee's son, was one of Jesus' first disciples.

We shall not know for certain this side of eternity, if John Zebedee or another John wrote the Gospel. John is not mentioned by name within the Gospel that bears his name. References to 'the disciple whom Jesus loved', probably mean John. Most of us like our name to be recognized. We dislike anonymity. Even when reluctant to put ourselves forward, we still crave recognition. John was content to remain unnamed. His only need was to know Jesus loved him.

Jesus loves me! This I know, for the Bible tells me so.
Little ones to him belong. They are weak but he is strong.

Is such a simple statement sufficient for me? Or do I still crave human recognition?

→933

passing by, he said, "Look, the Lamb of God!"

37When the two disciples heard him say this, they followed Jesus. 38Turning round, Jesus saw them following and asked, "What do you want?"

They said, "Rabbi" (which means Teacher), "where are you staying?"

39"Come," he replied, "and you will see."

So they went and saw where he was staying, and spent that day with him. It was about the tenth hour.

40Andrew, Simon Peter's brother, was one of the two who heard what John had said and who had followed Jesus. 41The first thing Andrew did was to find his brother Simon and tell him, "We have found the Messiah" (that is, the Christ). 42And he brought him to Jesus.

Jesus looked at him and said, "You are Simon son of John. You will be called Cephas" (which, when translated, is Peter*j*).

Jesus Calls Philip and Nathanael

43The next day Jesus decided to leave for Galilee. Finding Philip, he said to him, "Follow me."

44Philip, like Andrew and Peter, was from the town of Bethsaida. 45Philip found Nathanael and told him, "We have found the one Moses wrote about in the Law, and about whom the prophets also wrote—Jesus of Nazareth, the son of Joseph."

46"Nazareth! Can anything good come from there?" Nathanael asked.

"Come and see," said Philip.

47When Jesus saw Nathanael approaching, he said of him, "Here is a true Israelite, in whom there is nothing false."

48"How do you know me?" Nathanael asked.

Jesus answered, "I saw you while you were still under the fig-tree before Philip called you."

49Then Nathanael declared, "Rabbi, you are the Son of God; you are the King of Israel."

50Jesus said, "You believe*k* because I told you I saw you under the fig-tree. You shall see greater things than that." 51He then added, "I tell you*l* the truth, you*l* shall see heaven open, and the angels of God ascending and descending on the Son of Man."

Jesus Changes Water to Wine

2 On the third day a wedding took place at Cana in Galilee. Jesus' mother was there, 2and Jesus and his disciples had also been invited to the wedding. 3When the wine was gone, Jesus' mother said to him, "They have no more wine."

4"Dear woman, why do you involve me?" Jesus replied, "My time has not yet come."

5His mother said to the servants, "Do whatever he tells you."

6Nearby stood six stone water jars, the kind used by the Jews for ceremonial washing, each holding from twenty to thirty gallons.*a*

7Jesus said to the servants, "Fill the jars with water"; so they filled them to the brim.

8Then he told them, "Now draw some out and take it to the master of the banquet."

They did so, 9and the master of the banquet tasted the water that had been turned into wine. He did not realise where it had come from, though the servants who had drawn the water knew. Then he called the bridegroom aside 10and said, "Everyone brings out the choice wine first and then the cheaper wine after the guests have had too much to drink; but you have saved the best till now."

11This, the first of his miraculous signs, Jesus performed at Cana in Galilee. He thus revealed his glory, and his disciples put their faith in him.

Jesus Clears the Temple

12After this he went down to Capernaum with his mother and brothers and his disciples. There they stayed for a few days.

13When it was almost time for the Jewish Passover, Jesus went up to Jerusalem. 14In the temple courts he found men selling cattle, sheep and doves, and others sitting at tables exchanging money. 15So he made a whip out of cords, and drove all from the temple area, both sheep and cattle; he scattered the coins of the money-changers and overturned their tables. 16To those who sold doves he said, "Get these out of here! How dare you turn my Father's house into a market!"

17His disciples remembered that it is written, "Zeal for your house will consume me."*b*

18Then the Jews demanded of him, "What miraculous sign can you show us to prove your authority to do all this?"

19Jesus answered them, "Destroy this temple, and I will raise it again in three days."

20The Jews replied, "It has taken forty-six years to build this temple, and you are going to raise it in three days?" 21But the temple he had spoken of was his body. 22After he was raised from the dead, his disciples recalled what he had said. Then they believed the Scripture and the words that Jesus had spoken.

23Now while he was in Jerusalem at the Passover Feast, many people saw the miraculous signs he was doing and believed in his name.*c* 24But Jesus would not entrust himself to them, for he knew all men. 25He did not need man's testimony about man, for he knew what was in a man.

Jesus Teaches Nicodemus

3 Now there was a man of the Pharisees named Nicodemus, a member of the Jewish ruling council. 2He came to Jesus at night and said, "Rabbi, we know you are a teacher who has come from God. For no-one

---

j42 Both *Cephas* (Aramaic) and *Peter* (Greek) mean *rock*.   *k50* Or *Do you believe . . .* ?
l51 The Greek is plural.   *a6* Greek *two to three metretes* (probably about 75 to 115 litres)
b17 Psalm 69:9   *c23* Or *and believed in him*

could perform the miraculous signs you are doing if God were not with him."

[3]In reply Jesus declared, "I tell you the truth, no-one can see the kingdom of God unless he is born again."[a]

[4]"How can a man be born when he is old?" Nicodemus asked. "Surely he cannot enter a second time into his mother's womb to be born!"

[5]Jesus answered, "I tell you the truth, no-one can enter the kingdom of God unless he is born of water and the Spirit. [6]Flesh gives birth to flesh, but the Spirit[b] gives birth to spirit. [7]You should not be surprised at my saying, 'You[c] must be born again.' [8]The wind blows wherever it pleases. You hear its sound, but you cannot tell where it comes from or where it is going. So it is with everyone born of the Spirit."

[9]"How can this be?" Nicodemus asked.

[10]"You are Israel's teacher," said Jesus, "and do you not understand these things? [11]I tell you the truth, we speak of what we know, and we testify to what we have seen, but still you people do not accept our testimony. [12]I have spoken to you of earthly things and you do not believe; how then will you believe if I speak of heavenly things? [13]No-one has ever gone into heaven except the one who came from heaven—the Son of Man.[d] [14]Just as Moses lifted up the snake in the desert, so the Son of Man must be lifted up, [15]that everyone who believes in him may have eternal life.[e]

[16]"For God so loved the world that he gave his one and only Son,[f] that whoever believes in him shall not perish but have eternal life. [17]For God did not send his Son into the world to condemn the world, but to save the world through him. [18]Whoever believes in him is not condemned, but whoever does not believe stands condemned already because he has not believed in the name of God's one and only Son.[g] [19]This is the verdict: Light has come into the world, but men loved darkness instead of light because their deeds were evil. [20]Everyone who does evil hates the light, and will not come into the light for fear that his deeds will be exposed. [21]But whoever lives by the truth comes into the light, so that it may be seen plainly that what he has done has been done through God."[h]

John the Baptist's Testimony About Jesus

[22]After this, Jesus and his disciples went out into the Judean countryside, where he spent some time with them, and baptised. [23]Now John also was baptising at Aenon near Salim, because there was plenty of water, and people were constantly coming to be baptised. [24](This was before John was put in prison.) [25]An argument developed between some of John's disciples and a certain Jew[i] over the matter of ceremonial washing. [26]They came to John and said to him,

"Rabbi, that man who was with you on the other side of the Jordan—the one you testified about—well, he is baptising, and everyone is going to him."

[27]To this John replied, "A man can receive only what is given him from heaven. [28]You yourselves can testify that I said, 'I am not the Christ[j] but am sent ahead of him.' [29]The bride belongs to the bridegroom. The friend who attends the bridegroom waits and listens for him, and is full of joy when he hears the bridegroom's voice. That joy is mine, and it is now complete. [30]He must become greater; I must become less.

[31]"The one who comes from above is above all; the one who is from the earth belongs to the earth, and speaks as one from the earth. The one who comes from heaven is above all. [32]He testifies to what he has seen and heard, but no-one accepts his testimony. [33]The man who has accepted it has certified that God is truthful. [34]For the one whom God has sent speaks the words of God, for God[k] gives the Spirit without limit. [35]The Father loves the Son and has placed everything in his hands. [36]Whoever believes in the Son has eternal life, but whoever rejects the Son will not see life, for God's wrath remains on him."[l]

Jesus Talks With a Samaritan Woman

4 The Pharisees heard that Jesus was gaining and baptising more disciples than John, [2]although in fact it was not Jesus who baptised, but his disciples. [3]When the Lord learned of this, he left Judea and went back once more to Galilee.

[4]Now he had to go through Samaria. [5]So he came to a town in Samaria called Sychar, near the plot of ground Jacob had given to his son Joseph. [6]Jacob's well was there, and Jesus, tired as he was from the journey, sat down by the well. It was about the sixth hour.

[7]When a Samaritan woman came to draw water, Jesus said to her, "Will you give me a drink?" [8](His disciples had gone into the town to buy food.)

[9]The Samaritan woman said to him, "You are a Jew and I am a Samaritan woman. How can you ask me for a drink?" (For Jews do not associate with Samaritans.[a])

[10]Jesus answered her, "If you knew the gift of God and who it is that asks you for a drink, you would have asked him and he would have given you living water."

[11]"Sir," the woman said, "you have nothing to draw with and the well is deep. Where can you get this living water? [12]Are you greater than our father Jacob, who gave us the well and drank from it himself, as did also his sons and his flocks and herds?"

[13]Jesus answered, "Everyone who drinks this water will be thirsty again, [14]but whoever drinks the water I give him will never thirst. Indeed, the water I give him will become in

---

[a]3 Or *born from above*; also in verse 7   [b]6 Or *but spirit*   [c]7 The Greek is plural.
[d]13 Some manuscripts *Man, who is in heaven*   [e]15 Or *believes may have eternal life in him*
[f]16 Or *his only begotten Son*   [g]18 Or *God's only begotten Son*
[h]21 Some interpreters end the quotation after verse 15.   [i]25 Some manuscripts *and certain Jews*
[j]28 Or *Messiah*   [k]34 Greek *he*   [l]36 Some interpreters end the quotation after verse 30.
[a]9 Or *do not use dishes Samaritans have used*

JOHN 2:1–11

'This, the first of his miraculous signs, Jesus performed in Cana of Galilee. He thus revealed his glory and his disciples put their faith in him' (v. 11).

CONFORMING TO THE PATTERN. John's Gospel contains few miracles. Matthew, Mark and Luke contain many. Yet the miraculous element in Jesus' ministry is as important to John as it is to the other gospel-writers. Every miracle he records has a special significance, and whole sections of his Gospel are introduced by a miracle story. The pattern is usually

ACTION (Miracle)		DIALOGUE (Conversation)		MONOLOGUE (Sermon)	
5:1–9	Healing the palsied man	5:10–18	About Sabbath healing	5:19–40	On God the Father and the Son
9:1–7	Blind man healed	9:8–41	About who Jesus is	10:1–18	On the good shepherd

The pattern is not so clear in Chapter 2, but it is there. The water is turned to wine, a conversation with Nicodemus follows, and this turns almost unnoticed into a discourse about the difference between earthly and heavenly things. Thus we see, not only the miracle, but the meaning of the miracle. Jesus, turning the water into wine is illustrating the change which takes place when a person is born again. The old goes, the new comes. The earthly vanishes, the heavenly appears.

What happened is important, the meaning *behind what happened is often more important.*

→934

JOHN 3:1–21
'For God so loved the world that he gave his one and only Son' (v. 16a).

NICODEMUS WAS FIRST TO HEAR these most familiar words. These words have been proclaimed openly; shouted from the house-tops; declaimed from pulpits; written on tracts; used as the spearhead of Christian evangelistic activity. But they were first spoken in secret at dead of night to one frightened Pharisee.

What a description of the spread of the gospel – a secret meeting – a congregation of one – no visible result! Nicodemus hardly came over to the Christian cause. He continued to sit in the Jewish councils. John describes one occasion where Nicodemus defused a nasty situation, but there was no open confession of Christian commitment until after Jesus' death.

Jesus did not condemn Nicodemus for his fear. He chided him gently for his lack of understanding. He ended the conversation with a reminder that anyone concerned about the truth must in the end declare it openly. *The person who lives by the truth comes out into the light.* He does not say to Nicodemus, 'You must come out into the light, here and now.' Jesus allows the truth to do its own work in Nicodemus' heart. Inevitably, if we live by the truth, it will come out into the open. We cannot hide the truth. If it is in us, it will shine through.

> *God gave his Son for me,*
> *O wondrous love!*
> *From sin to set me free,*
> *O wondrous love!*
> *A guilty rebel I,*
> *Bound and condemned to die,*
> *He did not pass me by;*
> *O wondrous love!*

(Charles Fry)

→937

him a spring of water welling up to eternal life.''

¹⁵The woman said to him, "Sir, give me this water so that I won't get thirsty and have to keep coming here to draw water."

¹⁶He told her, "Go, call your husband and come back."

¹⁷"I have no husband," she replied.

Jesus said to her, "You are right when you say you have no husband. ¹⁸The fact is, you have had five husbands, and the man you now have is not your husband. What you have just said is quite true."

¹⁹"Sir," the woman said, "I can see that you are a prophet. ²⁰Our fathers worshipped on this mountain, but you Jews claim that the place where we must worship is in Jerusalem."

²¹Jesus declared, "Believe me, woman, a time is coming when you will worship the Father neither on this mountain nor in Jerusalem. ²²You Samaritans worship what you do not know; we worship what we do know, for salvation is from the Jews. ²³Yet a time is coming and has now come when the true worshippers will worship the Father in spirit and truth, for they are the kind of worshippers the Father seeks. ²⁴God is spirit, and his worshippers must worship in spirit and in truth."

²⁵The woman said, "I know that Messiah" (called Christ) "is coming. When he comes, he will explain everything to us."

²⁶Then Jesus declared, "I who speak to you am he."

The Disciples Rejoin Jesus

²⁷Just then his disciples returned and were surprised to find him talking with a woman. But no-one asked, "What do you want?" or "Why are you talking with her?"

²⁸Then, leaving her water jar, the woman went back to the town and said to the people, ²⁹"Come, see a man who told me everything I ever did. Could this be the Christ?"[b] ³⁰They came out of the town and made their way towards him.

³¹Meanwhile his disciples urged him, "Rabbi, eat something."

³²But he said to them, "I have food to eat that you know nothing about."

³³Then his disciples said to each other, "Could someone have brought him food?"

³⁴"My food," said Jesus, "is to do the will of him who sent me and to finish his work. ³⁵Do you not say, 'Four months more and then the harvest'? I tell you, open your eyes and look at the fields! They are ripe for harvest. ³⁶Even now the reaper draws his wages, even now he harvests the crop for eternal life, so that the sower and the reaper may be glad together. ³⁷Thus the saying 'One sows and another reaps' is true. ³⁸I sent you to reap what you have not worked for. Others have done the hard work, and you have reaped the benefits of their labour."

Many Samaritans Believe

³⁹Many of the Samaritans from that town believed in him because of the woman's testimony, "He told me everything I ever did." ⁴⁰So when the Samaritans came to him, they urged him to stay with them, and he stayed two days. ⁴¹And because of his words many more became believers.

⁴²They said to the woman, "We no longer believe just because of what you said; now we have heard for ourselves, and we know that this man really is the Saviour of the world."

Jesus Heals the Official's Son

⁴³After the two days he left for Galilee. ⁴⁴(Now Jesus himself had pointed out that a prophet has no honour in his own country.) ⁴⁵When he arrived in Galilee, the Galileans welcomed him. They had seen all that he had done in Jerusalem at the Passover Feast, for they also had been there.

⁴⁶Once more he visited Cana in Galilee, where he had turned the water into wine. And there was a certain royal official whose son lay sick at Capernaum. ⁴⁷When this man heard that Jesus had arrived in Galilee from Judea, he went to him and begged him to come and heal his son, who was close to death.

⁴⁸"Unless you people see miraculous signs and wonders," Jesus told him, "you will never believe."

⁴⁹The royal official said, "Sir, come down before my child dies."

⁵⁰Jesus replied, "You may go. Your son will live."

The man took Jesus at his word and departed. ⁵¹While he was still on the way, his servants met him with the news that his boy was living. ⁵²When he enquired as to the time when his son got better, they said to him, "The fever left him yesterday at the seventh hour."

⁵³Then the father realised that this was the exact time at which Jesus had said to him, "Your son will live." So he and all his household believed.

⁵⁴This was the second miraculous sign that Jesus performed, having come from Judea to Galilee.

The Healing at the Pool

5 Some time later, Jesus went up to Jerusalem for a feast of the Jews. ²Now there is in Jerusalem near the Sheep Gate a pool, which in Aramaic is called Bethesda[a] and which is surrounded by five covered colonnades. ³Here a great number of disabled people used to lie—the blind, the lame, the paralysed.[b] ⁵One who was there had been an invalid for thirty-eight years. ⁶When Jesus saw him lying there and learned that he had been in this condition for a long time, he asked him, "Do you want to get well?"

---

[b]29 Or *Messiah*

[a]2 Some manuscripts *Bethzatha*; other manuscripts *Bethsaida*   [b]3 Some less important manuscripts *paralysed* —*and they waited for the moving of the waters.* ⁴*From time to time an angel of the Lord would come down and stir up the waters. The first one into the pool after each such disturbance would be cured of whatever disease he had.*

7"Sir," the invalid replied, "I have no-one to help me into the pool when the water is stirred. While I am trying to get in, someone else goes down ahead of me."

8Then Jesus said to him, "Get up! Pick up your mat and walk." 9At once the man was cured; he picked up his mat and walked.

The day on which this took place was a Sabbath, 10and so the Jews said to the man who had been healed, "It is the Sabbath; the law forbids you to carry your mat."

11But he replied, "The man who made me well said to me, 'Pick up your mat and walk.'"

12So they asked him, "Who is this fellow who told you to pick it up and walk?"

13The man who was healed had no idea who it was, for Jesus had slipped away into the crowd that was there.

14Later Jesus found him at the temple and said to him, "See, you are well again. Stop sinning or something worse may happen to you." 15The man went away and told the Jews that it was Jesus who had made him well.

Life Through the Son

16So, because Jesus was doing these things on the Sabbath, the Jews persecuted him. 17Jesus said to them, "My Father is always at his work to this very day, and I, too, am working." 18For this reason the Jews tried all the harder to kill him; not only was he breaking the Sabbath, but he was even calling God his own Father, making himself equal with God.

19Jesus gave them this answer: "I tell you the truth, the Son can do nothing by himself; he can do only what he sees his Father doing, because whatever the Father does the Son also does. 20For the Father loves the Son and shows him all he does. Yes, to your amazement he will show him even greater things than these. 21For just as the Father raises the dead and gives them life, even so the Son gives life to whom he is pleased to give it. 22Moreover, the Father judges no-one, but has entrusted all judgment to the Son, 23that all may honour the Son just as they honour the Father. He who does not honour the Son does not honour the Father, who sent him.

24"I tell you the truth, whoever hears my word and believes him who sent me has eternal life and will not be condemned; he has crossed over from death to life. 25I tell you the truth, a time is coming and has now come when the dead will hear the voice of the Son of God and those who hear will live. 26For as the Father has life in himself, so he has granted the Son to have life in himself. 27And he has given him authority to judge because he is the Son of Man.

28"Do not be amazed at this, for a time is coming when all who are in their graves will hear his voice 29and come out—those who have done good will rise to live, and those who have done evil will rise to be condemned. 30By myself I can do nothing; I judge only as I hear, and my judgment is just, for I seek not to please myself but him who sent me.

Testimonies About Jesus

31"If I testify about myself, my testimony is not valid. 32There is another who testifies in my favour, and I know that his testimony about me is valid.

33"You have sent to John and he has testified to the truth. 34Not that I accept human testimony; but I mention it that you may be saved. 35John was a lamp that burned and gave light, and you chose for a time to enjoy his light.

36"I have testimony weightier than that of John. For the very work that the Father has given me to finish, and which I am doing, testifies that the Father has sent me. 37And the Father who sent me has himself testified concerning me. You have never heard his voice nor seen his form, 38nor does his word dwell in you, for you do not believe the one he sent. 39You diligently study^c the Scriptures because you think that by them you possess eternal life. These are the Scriptures that testify about me, 40yet you refuse to come to me to have life.

41"I do not accept praise from men, 42but I know you. I know that you do not have the love of God in your hearts. 43I have come in my Father's name, and you do not accept me; but if someone else comes in his own name, you will accept him. 44How can you believe if you accept praise from one another, yet make no effort to obtain the praise that comes from the only God?^{d}

45"But do not think I will accuse you before the Father. Your accuser is Moses, on whom your hopes are set. 46If you believed Moses, you would believe me, for he wrote about me. 47But since you do not believe what he wrote, how are you going to believe what I say?"

Jesus Feeds the Five Thousand

6 Some time after this, Jesus crossed to the far shore of the Sea of Galilee (that is, the Sea of Tiberias), 2and a great crowd of people followed him because they saw the miraculous signs he had performed on the sick. 3Then Jesus went up on a mountainside and sat down with his disciples. 4The Jewish Passover Feast was near.

5When Jesus looked up and saw a great crowd coming towards him, he said to Philip, "Where shall we buy bread for these people to eat?" 6He asked this only to test him, for he already had in mind what he was going to do.

7Philip answered him, "Eight months' wages^a would not buy enough bread for each one to have a bite!"

8Another of his disciples, Andrew, Simon Peter's brother, spoke up, 9"Here is a boy with five small barley loaves and two small fish, but how far will they go among so many?"

---

^{c}39 Or Study diligently (the imperative) ^{d}44 Some early manuscripts the Only One
^{a}7 Greek two hundred denarii

JOHN 4:1–30

'Whoever drinks the water I give him will never thirst. Indeed, the water I give him will become in him a spring of water welling up to eternal life' (v. 14).

CONSERVATIONISTS search continually for renewable energy sources. Harnessing tides, wind, and sun to provide energy on a massive scale at the touch of a switch is still a dream for the future. Hydroelectric power nearly does so, but it needs special conditions, great dams, high mountains, and much rain. As yet it can only supplement other sources of energy. It has its own environmental hazards. Valleys are flooded and climates are changed.

Modern conservation needs may seem a far cry from the woman at the well confronted by Jesus. But there is a connection. We are surrounded by power from sun, wind and tides – yet we cannot harness them properly. She was surrounded by spiritual power – yet had no means of using it for her benefit until Jesus came along.

Her ancestors, the Samaritans, had worshipped on Mount Gerizim (Deut. 11:29; 27:12) ever since northern Israel had been destroyed. (722 BC) But the available power had not filtered down to her. It had made no difference to her life. She was undoubtedly a sinner (v. 18). Moral and religious convention simply thrust her aside, and condemned her to a life of rejection, drawing water from the well at midday, when no one else was around.

Jesus broke through that convention. He offered her spiritual power, not condemnation. He offers the same to you and to me – a renewable source of spiritual energy which will never dry up or be exhausted.

David prayed 'Create in me a pure heart, O God, and renew a steadfast spirit within me.' We praise you, Lord, that in Jesus you give the power for that to happen – not just in the lives of the saints, but in the lives of sinners like ourselves.

→938

'You diligently study the Scriptures because you think that by them you possess eternal life. These are the Scriptures that testify about me, yet you refuse to come to me to have life' (vv. 39, 40).

A WORD OF WARNING. What we do when we study the Scriptures together each day may bring comfort; it may bring challenge; it may even open up the way to salvation. But it can never take the place of a close, personal relationship with the Lord Jesus Christ.

A study book on John's Gospel, by Donald Guthrie, is called *Exploring God's Word*. In it he sets out main headings and short comments which help to guide the reader through this beautiful Gospel. About John 5:39 he writes:

Jesus acknowledged the importance of Scripture

He frequently cited it or alluded to it. He clearly regarded it as the word of God. In this he would have agreed with his Jewish contemporaries.

He recognised the possibility of missing its message

In spite of their diligent searching, the hearers had never found the secret of eternal life. This suggests that searching is not enough. It must be done in the right way.

He affirmed the witness they bore to him

It is certainly possible to miss this. Some read the Scriptures with blinkers. But the early Church had no doubt that they spoke of Christ. The message of the Old Testament must be interpreted in this light. (Compare v. 46, 'Moses wrote about me.')

Scripture is a constant witness to Jesus Christ for those who search with the aim of finding him.

(*Donald Guthrie*)

→941

10Jesus said, "Make the people sit down." There was plenty of grass in that place, and the men sat down, about five thousand of them. 11Jesus then took the loaves, gave thanks, and distributed to those who were seated as much as they wanted. He did the same with the fish.

12When they had all had enough to eat, he said to his disciples, "Gather the pieces that are left over. Let nothing be wasted." 13So they gathered them and filled twelve baskets with the pieces of the five barley loaves left over by those who had eaten.

14After the people saw the miraculous sign that Jesus did, they began to say, "Surely this is the Prophet who is to come into the world." 15Jesus, knowing that they intended to come and make him king by force, withdrew again to a mountain by himself.

Jesus Walks on the Water

16When evening came, his disciples went down to the lake, 17where they got into a boat and set off across the lake for Capernaum. By now it was dark, and Jesus had not yet joined them. 18A strong wind was blowing and the waters grew rough. 19When they had rowed three or three and a half miles,b they saw Jesus approaching the boat, walking on the water; and they were terrified. 20But he said to them, "It is I; don't be afraid." 21Then they were willing to take him into the boat, and immediately the boat reached the shore where they were heading.

22The next day the crowd that had stayed on the opposite shore of the lake realised that only one boat had been there, and that Jesus had not entered it with his disciples, but that they had gone away alone. 23Then some boats from Tiberias landed near the place where the people had eaten the bread after the Lord had given thanks. 24Once the crowd realised that neither Jesus nor his disciples were there, they got into the boats and went to Capernaum in search of Jesus.

Jesus the Bread of Life

25When they found him on the other side of the lake, they asked him, "Rabbi, when did you get here?"

26Jesus answered, "I tell you the truth, you are looking for me, not because you saw miraculous signs but because you ate the loaves and had your fill. 27Do not work for food that spoils, but for food that endures to eternal life, which the Son of Man will give you. On him God the Father has placed his seal of approval."

28Then they asked him, "What must we do to do the works God requires?"

29Jesus answered, "The work of God is this: to believe in the one he has sent."

30So they asked him, "What miraculous sign then will you give that we may see it and believe you? What will you do? 31Our forefathers ate the manna in the desert; as it is written: 'He gave them bread from heaven to eat.'c"

32Jesus said to them, "I tell you the truth, it is not Moses who has given you the bread from heaven, but it is my Father who gives you the true bread from heaven. 33For the bread of God is he who comes down from heaven and gives life to the world."

34"Sir," they said, "from now on give us this bread."

35Then Jesus declared, "I am the bread of life. He who comes to me will never go hungry, and he who believes in me will never be thirsty. 36But as I told you, you have seen me and still you do not believe. 37All that the Father gives me will come to me, and whoever comes to me I will never drive away. 38For I have come down from heaven not to do my will but to do the will of him who sent me. 39And this is the will of him who sent me, that I shall lose none of all that he has given me, but raise them up at the last day. 40For my Father's will is that everyone who looks to the Son and believes in him shall have eternal life, and I will raise him up at the last day."

41At this the Jews began to grumble about him because he said, "I am the bread that came down from heaven." 42They said, "Is this not Jesus, the son of Joseph, whose father and mother we know? How can he now say, 'I came down from heaven'?"

43"Stop grumbling among yourselves," Jesus answered. 44"No-one can come to me unless the Father who sent me draws him, and I will raise him up at the last day. 45It is written in the Prophets: 'They will all be taught by God.'d Everyone who listens to the Father and learns from him comes to me. 46No-one has seen the Father except the one who is from God; only he has seen the Father. 47I tell you the truth, he who believes has everlasting life. 48I am the bread of life. 49Your forefathers ate the manna in the desert, yet they died. 50But here is the bread that comes down from heaven, which a man may eat and not die. 51I am the living bread that came down from heaven. If anyone eats of this bread, he will live for ever. This bread is my flesh, which I will give for the life of the world."

52Then the Jews began to argue sharply among themselves, "How can this man give us his flesh to eat?"

53Jesus said to them, "I tell you the truth, unless you can eat the flesh of the Son of Man and drink his blood, you have no life in you. 54Whoever eats my flesh and drinks my blood has eternal life, and I will raise him up at the last day. 55For my flesh is real food and my blood is real drink. 56Whoever eats my flesh and drinks my blood remains in me, and I in him. 57Just as the living Father sent me and I live because of the Father, so the one who feeds on me will live because of me. 58This is the bread that came down from heaven. Your forefathers ate manna and died, but he who feeds on this bread will live for ever." 59He said this while teaching in the synagogue in Capernaum.

b19 Greek rowed twenty-five or thirty stadia (about 5 or 6 kilometres)
c31 Exodus 16:4; Neh. 9:15; Psalm 78:24,25   d45 Isaiah 54:13

Many Disciples Desert Jesus

⁶⁰On hearing it, many of his disciples said, "This is a hard teaching. Who can accept it?"

⁶¹Aware that his disciples were grumbling about this, Jesus said to them, "Does this offend you? ⁶²What if you see the Son of Man ascend to where he was before! ⁶³The Spirit gives life; the flesh counts for nothing. The words I have spoken to you are spirit*ᵉ* and they are life. ⁶⁴Yet there are some of you who do not believe." For Jesus had known from the beginning which of them did not believe and who would betray him. ⁶⁵He went on to say, "This is why I told you that no-one can come to me unless the Father has enabled him."

⁶⁶From this time many of his disciples turned back and no longer followed him.

⁶⁷"You do not want to leave too, do you?" Jesus asked the Twelve.

⁶⁸Simon Peter answered him, "Lord, to whom shall we go? You have the words of :ternal life. ⁶⁹We believe and know that you ire the Holy One of God."

⁷⁰Then Jesus replied, "Have I not chosen you, the Twelve? Yet one of you is a devil!" ⁷¹(He meant Judas, the son of Simon Iscariot, who, though one of the Twelve, was later to betray him.)

Jesus Goes to the Feast of Tabernacles

7 After this, Jesus went around in Galilee, purposely staying away from Judea because the Jews there were waiting to take his life. ²But when the Jewish Feast of Tabernacles was near, ³Jesus' brothers said to him, "You ought to leave here and go to Judea, so that your disciples may see the miracles you do. ⁴No-one who wants to become a public figure acts in secret. Since you are doing these things, show yourself to the world." ⁵For even his own brothers did not believe in him.

⁶Therefore Jesus told them, "The right time for me has not yet come; for you any time is right. ⁷The world cannot hate you, but it hates me because I testify that what it does is evil. ⁸You go to the Feast. I am not yet*ᵃ* going up to this Feast, because for me the right time has not yet come." ⁹Having said this, he stayed in Galilee.

¹⁰However, after his brothers had left for the Feast, he went also, not publicly, but in secret. ¹¹Now at the Feast the Jews were watching for him and asking, "Where is that man?"

¹²Among the crowds there was widespread whispering about him. Some said, "He is a good man."

Others replied, "No, he deceives the people." ¹³But no-one would say anything publicly about him for fear of the Jews.

Jesus Teaches at the Feast

¹⁴Not until halfway through the Feast did Jesus go up to the temple courts and begin to teach. ¹⁵The Jews were amazed and asked, "How did this man get such learning without having studied?"

¹⁶Jesus answered, "My teaching is not my own. It comes from him who sent me. ¹⁷If anyone chooses to do God's will, he will find out whether my teaching comes from God or whether I speak on my own. ¹⁸He who speaks on his own does so to gain honour for himself, but he who works for the honour of the one who sent him is a man of truth; there is nothing false about him. ¹⁹Has not Moses given you the law? Yet not one of you keeps the law. Why are you trying to kill me?"

²⁰"You are demon-possessed," the crowd answered. "Who is trying to kill you?"

²¹Jesus said to them, "I did one miracle, and you are all astonished. ²²Yet, because Moses gave you circumcision (though actually it did not come from Moses, but from the patriarchs), you circumcise a child on the Sabbath. ²³Now if a child can be circumcised on the Sabbath so that the law of Moses may not be broken, why are you angry with me for healing the whole man on the Sabbath? ²⁴Stop judging by mere appearances, and make a right judgment."

Is Jesus the Christ?

²⁵At that point some of the people of Jerusalem began to ask, "Isn't this the man they are trying to kill? ²⁶Here he is, speaking publicly, and they are not saying a word to him. Have the authorities really concluded that he is the Christ?*ᵇ* ²⁷But we know where this man is from; when the Christ comes, no-one will know where he is from."

²⁸Then Jesus, still teaching in the temple courts, cried out, "Yes, you know me, and you know where I am from. I am not here on my own, but he who sent me is true. You do not know him, ²⁹but I know him because I am from him and he sent me."

³⁰At this they tried to seize him, but no-one laid a hand on him, because his time had not yet come. ³¹Still, many in the crowd put their faith in him. They said, "When the Christ comes, will he do more miraculous signs than this man?"

³²The Pharisees heard the crowd whispering such things about him. Then the chief priests and the Pharisees sent temple guards to arrest him.

³³Jesus said, "I am with you for only a short time, and then I go to the one who sent me. ³⁴You will look for me, but you will not find me; and where I am, you cannot come."

³⁵The Jews said to one another, "Where does this man intend to go that we cannot find him? Will he go where our people live scattered among the Greeks, and teach the Greeks? ³⁶What did he mean when he said, 'You will look for me, but you will not find me,' and 'Where I am, you cannot come'?"

³⁷On the last and greatest day of the Feast, Jesus stood and said in a loud voice, "If anyone is thirsty, let him come to me and drink. ³⁸Whoever believes in me, as*ᶜ* the Scripture has said, streams of living water

*ᵉ63 Or Spirit   ᵃ8 Some early manuscripts do not have yet.   ᵇ26 Or Messiah; also in verses 27, 31, 41 and 42
ᶜ37,38 Or If anyone is thirsty, let him come to me. / And let him drink, ³⁸who believes in me. / As*

JOHN 6:1–21
'Jesus, knowing that they intended to come and make him king by force, withdrew again to a mountain by himself' (v. 15). 'He said to them "It is I; don't be afraid" ' (v. 20).

EGO EIMI is a phrase of slightly odd Greek (*Eimi* would be enough, without the *Ego*), characteristic of John's Gospel. It means 'I am' – one of the most basic, most common, yet most significant statements that can be made.

Usually the 'I am' is followed by another well-known phrase, describing something of the nature of Jesus – and of God.

I am the bread of life	6:35
I am the light of the world	8:12 (9:5)
I am one who testifies for myself	8:18
I am who I am	8:28
I am the gate	10:9
I am the good shepherd	10:11
I am the resurrection and the life	11:25
I am the way and the truth and the life	14:6
I am the true vine	15:1

All these simple affirmations taken together remind us of God revealing himself to Moses in the desert, saying 'I AM WHO I AM'.

Today's phrase 'It is I' also reads *EGO EIMI* in Greek. Unlike the other uses listed above, no description of Jesus follows it. It stands alone. But there is a command attached to it. 'Don't be afraid.' Sometimes fear does catch hold of us. Sometimes we are like the disciples caught up in the storm. In those cases we are bound to feel deep, strong emotion. Sometimes everything will be black and we will despise ourselves for feeling the way that we do. But always the promise is there. Jesus says to us

'It is I; don't be afraid.' (v. 20)

→942

JOHN 7:37–43: 8:12–20

'When Jesus spoke again to the people, he said, "I am the light of the world. Whoever follows me will never walk in darkness, but will have the light of life" ' (v. 12).

THIS IS THE SECOND of the 'I am' statements of our Lord. The occasion was the Feast of the Tabernacles, an annual celebration relating to the wilderness days following the Exodus. For seven days the people lived in makeshift booths of branches and leaves to remind them of those demanding pilgrim days. Daily, morning and evening, water was processed up to the temple from the Pool of Siloam by a priest and was poured out beside the altar. This symbolized the water Moses drew from the rock. In the evening, golden candelabra, reminders of the guiding light of Exodus, were lit in the court of the women. Such was the intensity of those lights that the whole area was illuminated. It is assumed that on the seventh and climactic day of the feast, after Jesus had declared, 'if any man is thirsty, let him come to me and drink', he used the strong lights as an illustration and announced, 'I am the light of the world.'

This was another Messianic claim by Jesus. There was a tradition that 'Light' was one of the names of the Messiah. John also contrasts the darkness and light. In his prologue John refers to the Word as the source of life which brought light to mankind, an ever-shining light which the darkness cannot extinguish.

Christ as light illuminates and guides. He reveals God himself. He reveals our own true nature and needs, and because he is life as well as light, he is able to meet our needs – and not our needs only, but the needs of the whole world.

'There will be no more night. They will not need the light of a lamp or the light of the sun, for the Lord God will give them light. And they will reign for ever and ever.' (*Rev. 22:5*)

→945

will flow from within him." [39]By this he meant the Spirit, whom those who believed in him were later to receive. Up to that time the Spirit had not been given, since Jesus had not yet been glorified.

[40]On hearing his words, some of the people said, "Surely this man is the Prophet."

[41]Others said, "He is the Christ."

Still others asked, "How can the Christ come from Galilee? [42]Does not the Scripture say that the Christ will come from David's family[d] and from Bethlehem, the town where David lived?" [43]Thus the people were divided because of Jesus. [44]Some wanted to seize him, but no-one laid a hand on him.

Unbelief of the Jewish Leaders

[45]Finally the temple guards went back to the chief priests and Pharisees, who asked them, "Why didn't you bring him in?"

[46]"No-one ever spoke the way this man does," the guards declared.

[47]"You mean he has deceived you also?" the Pharisees retorted. [48]"Has any of the rulers or of the Pharisees believed in him? [49]No! But this mob that knows nothing of the law—there is a curse on them."

[50]Nicodemus, who had gone to Jesus earlier and who was one of their own number, asked, [51]"Does our law condemn a man without first hearing him to find out what he is doing?"

[52]They replied, "Are you from Galilee, too? Look into it, and you will find that a prophet[e] does not come out of Galilee."

[The earliest and most reliable manuscripts and other ancient witnesses do not have John 7:53–8:11]

---

[53]Then each went to his own home.

8 But Jesus went to the Mount of Olives. [2]At dawn he appeared again in the temple courts, where all the people gathered round him, and he sat down to teach them. [3]The teachers of the law and the Pharisees brought in a woman caught in adultery. They made her stand before the group [4]and said to Jesus, "Teacher, this woman was caught in the act of adultery. [5]In the Law Moses commanded us to stone such women. Now what do you say?" [6]They were using this question as a trap, in order to have a basis for accusing him.

But Jesus bent down and started to write on the ground with his finger. [7]When they kept on questioning him, he straightened up and said to them, "If any one of you is without sin, let him be the first to throw a stone at her." [8]Again he stooped down and wrote on the ground.

[9]At this, those who heard began to go away one at a time, the older ones first, until only Jesus was left, with the woman still standing there. [10]Jesus straightened up and asked her, "Woman, where are they? Has no-one condemned you?"

[11]"No-one, sir," she said.

"Then neither do I condemn you," Jesus declared. "Go now and leave your life of sin."

The Validity of Jesus' Testimony

[12]When Jesus spoke again to the people, he said, "I am the light of the world. Whoever follows me will never walk in darkness, but will have the light of life."

[13]The Pharisees challenged him, "Here you are, appearing as your own witness; your testimony is not valid."

[14]Jesus answered, "Even if I testify on my own behalf, my testimony is valid, for I know where I came from and where I am going. But you have no idea where I come from or where I am going. [15]You judge by human standards; I pass judgment on no-one. [16]But if I do judge, my decisions are right, because I am not alone. I stand with the Father, who sent me. [17]In your own Law it is written that the testimony of two men is valid. [18]I am one who testifies for myself; my other witness is the Father, who sent me."

[19]Then they asked him, "Where is your father?"

"You do not know me or my Father," Jesus replied. "If you knew me, you would know my Father also." [20]He spoke these words while teaching in the temple area near the place where the offerings were put. Yet no-one seized him, because his time had not yet come.

[21]Once more Jesus said to them, "I am going away, and you will look for me, and you will die in your sin. Where I go, you cannot come."

[22]This made the Jews ask, "Will he kill himself? Is that why he says, 'Where I go, you cannot come'?"

[23]But he continued, "You are from below; I am from above. You are of this world; I am not of this world. [24]I told you that you would die in your sins; if you do not believe that I am ʟthe one I claim to be⏌,[a] you will indeed die in your sins."

[25]"Who are you?" they asked.

"Just what I have been claiming all along," Jesus replied. [26]"I have much to say in judgment of you. But he who sent me is reliable, and what I have heard from him I tell the world."

[27]They did not understand that he was telling them about his Father. [28]So Jesus said, "When you have lifted up the Son of Man, then you will know that I am ʟthe one I claim to be⏌ and that I do nothing on my own but speak just what the Father has taught me. [29]The one who sent me is with me; he has not left me alone, for I always do what pleases him." [30]Even as he spoke, many put their faith in him.

The Children of Abraham

[31]To the Jews who had believed him, Jesus said, "If you hold to my teaching, you are really my disciples. [32]Then you will know the truth, and the truth will set you free."

---

[d]42 Greek *seed*   [e]52 Two early manuscripts *the Prophet*   [a]24 Or *I am he*; also in verse 28

33They answered him, "We are Abraham's descendants*b* and have never been slaves of anyone. How can you say that we shall be set free?"

34Jesus replied, "I tell you the truth, everyone who sins is a slave to sin. 35Now a slave has no permanent place in the family, but a son belongs to it for ever. 36So if the Son sets you free, you will be free indeed. 37I know you are Abraham's descendants. Yet you are ready to kill me, because you have no room for my word. 38I am telling you what I have seen in the Father's presence, and you do what you have heard from your father."*c*

39"Abraham is our father," they answered.

"If you were Abraham's children," said Jesus, "then you would*d* do the things Abraham did. 40As it is, you are determined to kill me, a man who has told you the truth that I heard from God. Abraham did not do such things. 41You are doing the things your own father does."

"We are not illegitimate children," they protested. "The only Father we have is God himself."

The Children of the Devil

42Jesus said to them, "If God were your Father, you would love me, for I came from God and now am here. I have not come on my own; but he sent me. 43Why is my language not clear to you? Because you are unable to hear what I say. 44You belong to your father, the devil, and you want to carry out your father's desire. He was a murderer from the beginning, not holding to the truth, for there is no truth in him. When he lies, he speaks his native language, for he is a liar and the father of lies. 45Yet because I tell the truth, you do not believe me! 46Can any of you prove me guilty of sin? If I am telling the truth, why don't you believe me? 47He who belongs to God hears what God says. The reason you do not hear is that you do not belong to God."

The Claims of Jesus About Himself

48The Jews answered him, "Aren't we right in saying that you are a Samaritan and demon-possessed?"

49"I am not possessed by a demon," said Jesus, "but I honour my Father and you dishonour me. 50I am not seeking glory for myself; but there is one who seeks it, and he is the judge. 51I tell you the truth, if anyone keeps my word, he will never see death."

52At this the Jews exclaimed, "Now we know that you are demon-possessed! Abraham died and so did the prophets, yet you say that if anyone keeps your word, he will never taste death. 53Are you greater than our father Abraham? He died, and so did the prophets. Who do you think you are?"

54Jesus replied, "If I glorify myself, my glory means nothing. My Father, whom you claim as your God, is the one who glorifies me. 55Though you do not know him, I know him. If I said I did not, I would be a liar like you, but I do know him and keep his word. 56Your father Abraham rejoiced at the thought of seeing my day; he saw it and was glad."

57"You are not yet fifty years old," the Jews said to him, "and you have seen Abraham!"

58"I tell you the truth," Jesus answered, "before Abraham was born, I am!" 59At this, they picked up stones to stone him, but Jesus hid himself, slipping away from the temple grounds.

Jesus Heals a Man Born Blind

9 As he went along, he saw a man blind from birth. 2His disciples asked him, "Rabbi, who sinned, this man or his parents, that he was born blind?"

3"Neither this man nor his parents sinned," said Jesus, "but this happened so that the work of God might be displayed in his life. 4As long as it is day, we must do the work of him who sent me. Night is coming, when no-one can work. 5While I am in the world, I am the light of the world."

6Having said this, he spat on the ground, made some mud with the saliva, and put it on the man's eyes. 7"Go," he told him, "wash in the Pool of Siloam" (this word means Sent). So the man went and washed, and came home seeing.

8His neighbours and those who had formerly seen him begging asked, "Isn't this the same man who used to sit and beg?" 9Some claimed that he was.

Others said, "No, he only looks like him."

But he himself insisted, "I am the man."

10"How then were your eyes opened?" they demanded.

11He replied, "The man they call Jesus made some mud and put it on my eyes. He told me to go to Siloam and wash. So I went and washed, and then I could see."

12"Where is this man?" they asked him.

"I don't know," he said.

The Pharisees Investigate the Healing

13They brought to the Pharisees the man who had been blind. 14Now the day on which Jesus had made the mud and opened the man's eyes was a Sabbath. 15Therefore the Pharisees also asked him how he had received his sight. "He put mud on my eyes," the man replied, "and I washed, and now I see."

16Some of the Pharisees said, "This man is not from God, for he does not keep the Sabbath."

But others asked, "How can a sinner do such miraculous signs?" So they were divided.

17Finally they turned again to the blind man, "What have you to say about him? It was your eyes he opened."

The man replied, "He is a prophet."

18The Jews still did not believe that he had been blind and had received his sight until they sent for the man's parents. 19"Is this

---

b33 Greek *seed*; also in verse 37   *c38* Or *presence. Therefore do what you have heard from the Father.*
d39 Some early manuscripts *"If you are Abraham's children," said Jesus, "then*

JOHN 8:32
'Then you will know the truth, and the truth will set you free' (v. 32).

WE NEED NOT argue the case for freedom. Men and women in every generation have died either to win it or to preserve it. Those who live in free societies tend to take freedom for granted, and many of those who live under authoritarian regimes continue to dream of it. However, the reality is that whilst freedom owes much to political and economic systems, it is possible to be without real freedom in a free society. Conversely, it is possible to be free in a captive society. True freedom is of the spirit. Jesus said that freedom comes from truth. But truth is not abstract! When he came into our world Jesus embodied truth. As John's Gospel says, 'Grace and truth came through Jesus Christ' (1:17). Even more specifically Jesus described himself as 'the way and the truth and the life' (John 14:6). He also stated that the Spirit whom he and the Father would send would be the Spirit of truth (John 15:26). Truth, to Jesus and his followers, is a refreshing, releasing and empowering reality. We sing of this truth with glorious abandon in Charles Wesley's words:

> *My chains fell off, my heart was free,*
> *I rose, went forth, and followed thee.*

Because truth is Christ and Christ sets us free (v. 36), untruth, as displayed in any way in any society, cannot enslave us. Neither can the untruths that come to our hearts through doubt, discouragement, or the onslaught of Satan. In his temptations Jesus defended himself with truth (Matt. 4:1–11), and John the Baptist, once he had been reassured by Jesus (Matt. 11:4–14), was totally free again, even though he was in prison facing death.

> *Thy loving Spirit, Christ, alone*
> *Can lead me forth and make me free,*
> *Burst every bond through which I groan*
> *And set my heart at liberty.*

> *(Charles Wesley)*

→946

JOHN 9:1–12

'His disciples asked him, "Rabbi, who sinned, this man or his parents, that he was born blind?" ' (v. 2).

IN THE CONTEXT of that day, the question as to whose sin produced the blindness was understandable. Indeed, even today, with our more developed concept of the love of God, the question tracks through the minds of many asking whether or not the illness they face is a judgement of God. Our Lord's reply that it was neither the blind man's sin nor his parents' sin (v. 3) reassures us as it reassured them. God has not set a quota of disabilities to be roughly distributed across our world. Sadly, the disabilities are a fact, but the power of God can be displayed through them.

In this case, our Lord granted the experience of healing. This happens today, of course, though as often as we pray for it in faith, and that makes problems for us. Even so, the power of the Lord can be experienced healingly. There is a healing of the mind and spirit which is not due to human endeavour but to the grace of God. Thomas Moore's words say it so well:

> *Here bring your wounded hearts, here tell your anguish,*
> *Earth has no sorrow that Heaven cannot heal.*

There is healing of spirit for both the sufferer and those who share the suffering, resulting in a show of courage, fortitude, grace and contentment, the qualities of which are truly eternal. The widow of Bishop John Robinson wrote of the 'curious grace of God' which had sustained both of them during those precious months while his illness took its course. Clearly there was no healing because he died; equally clearly there was healing because, in spirit, both were healed. Is that not a great miracle? God's power was wonderfully displayed in them (v. 3b).

> *Lord, come to me with healing for my soul.*
> *My needs, my deepest needs, to thee are known.*
> *Do thou but touch and make me fully whole.*
> *And let thy glory through my life be shown.*

→949

your son?" they asked. "Is this the one you say was born blind? How is it that now he can see?"

20"We know he is our son," the parents answered, "and we know he was born blind. 21But how he can see now, or who opened his eyes, we don't know. Ask him. He is of age; he will speak for himself." 22His parents said this because they were afraid of the Jews, for already the Jews had decided that anyone who acknowledged that Jesus was the Christ*a* would be put out of the synagogue. 23That was why his parents said, "He is of age; ask him."

24A second time they summoned the man who had been blind. "Give glory to God,"*b* they said. "We know this man is a sinner."

25He replied, "Whether he is a sinner or not, I don't know. One thing I do know. I was blind but now I see!"

26Then they asked him, "What did he do to you? How did he open your eyes?"

27He answered, "I have told you already and you did not listen. Why do you want to hear it again? Do you want to become his disciples, too?"

28Then they hurled insults at him and said, "You are this fellow's disciple! We are disciples of Moses! 29We know that God spoke to Moses, but as for this fellow, we don't even know where he comes from."

30The man answered, "Now that is remarkable! You don't know where he comes from, yet he opened my eyes. 31We know that God does not listen to sinners. He listens to the godly man who does his will. 32Nobody has ever heard of opening the eyes of a man born blind. 33If this man were not from God, he could do nothing."

34To this they replied, "You were steeped in sin at birth; how dare you lecture us!" And they threw him out.

Spiritual Blindness

35Jesus heard that they had thrown him out, and when he found him, he said, "Do you believe in the Son of Man?"

36"Who is he, sir?" the man asked. "Tell me so that I may believe in him."

37Jesus said, "You have now seen him; in fact, he is the one speaking with you."

38Then the man said, "Lord, I believe," and he worshipped him.

39Jesus said, "For judgment I have come into this world, so that the blind will see and those who see will become blind."

40Some Pharisees who were with him heard him say this and asked, "What? Are we blind too?"

41Jesus said, "If you were blind, you would not be guilty of sin; but now that you claim you can see, your guilt remains.

The Shepherd and His Flock

10 "I tell you the truth, the man who does not enter the sheep pen by the gate, but climbs in by some other way, is a thief and a robber. 2The man who enters by the gate is the shepherd of his sheep. 3The watchman opens the gate for him, and the sheep listen to his voice. He calls his own sheep by name and leads them out. 4When he has brought out all his own, he goes on ahead of them, and his sheep follow him because they know his voice. 5But they will never follow a stranger; in fact, they will run away from him because they do not recognise a stranger's voice." 6Jesus used this figure of speech, but they did not understand what he was telling them.

7Therefore Jesus said again, "I tell you the truth, I am the gate for the sheep. 8All who ever came before me were thieves and robbers, but the sheep did not listen to them. 9I am the gate; whoever enters through me will be saved.*a* He will come in and go out, and find pasture. 10The thief comes only to steal and kill and destroy; I have come that they may have life, and have it to the full.

11"I am the good shepherd. The good shepherd lays down his life for the sheep. 12The hired hand is not the shepherd who owns the sheep. So when he sees the wolf coming, he abandons the sheep and runs away. Then the wolf attacks the flock and scatters it. 13The man runs away because he is a hired hand and cares nothing for the sheep.

14"I am the good shepherd; I know my sheep and my sheep know me—15just as the Father knows me and I know the Father—and I lay down my life for the sheep. 16I have other sheep that are not of this sheep pen. I must bring them also. They too will listen to my voice, and there shall be one flock and one shepherd. 17The reason my Father loves me is that I lay down my life—only to take it up again. 18No-one takes it from me, but I lay it down of my own accord. I have authority to lay it down and authority to take it up again. This command I received from my Father."

19At these words the Jews were again divided. 20Many of them said, "He is demon-possessed and raving mad. Why listen to him?"

21But others said, "These are not the sayings of a man possessed by a demon. Can a demon open the eyes of the blind?"

The Unbelief of the Jews

22Then came the Feast of Dedication*b* at Jerusalem. It was winter, 23and Jesus was in the temple area walking in Solomon's Colonnade. 24The Jews gathered round him, saying, "How long will you keep us in suspense? If you are the Christ,*c* tell us plainly."

25Jesus answered, "I did tell you, but you do not believe. The miracles I do in my Father's name speak for me, 26but you do not believe because you are not my sheep. 27My sheep listen to my voice; I know them, and they follow me. 28I give them eternal life, and they shall never perish; no-one can snatch

---

*a*22 Or *Messiah*　　*b*24 A solemn charge to tell the truth (see Joshua 7:19)　　*a*9 Or *kept safe*
*b*22 That is, Hanukkah　　*c*24 Or *Messiah*

them out of my hand. 29My Father, who has given them to me, is greater than all;*d* no-one can snatch them out of my Father's hand. 30I and the Father are one.''

31Again the Jews picked up stones to stone him, 32but Jesus said to them, ''I have shown you many great miracles from the Father. For which of these do you stone me?''

33''We are not stoning you for any of these,'' replied the Jews, ''but for blasphemy, because you, a mere man, claim to be God.''

34Jesus answered them, ''Is it not written in your Law, 'I have said you are gods'*e*? 35If he called them 'gods', to whom the word of God came—and the Scripture cannot be broken—36what about the one whom the Father set apart as his very own and sent into the world? Why then do you accuse me of blasphemy because I said, 'I am God's Son'? 37Do not believe me unless I do what my Father does. 38But if I do it, even though you do not believe me, believe the miracles, that you may know and understand that the Father is in me, and I in the Father.'' 39Again they tried to seize him, but he escaped their grasp.

40Then Jesus went back across the Jordan to the place where John had been baptising in the early days. Here he stayed 41and many people came to him. They said, ''Though John never performed a miraculous sign, all that John said about this man was true.'' 42And in that place many believed in Jesus.

The Death of Lazarus

11 Now a man named Lazarus was sick. He was from Bethany, the village of Mary and her sister Martha. 2This Mary, whose brother Lazarus now lay sick, was the same one who poured perfume on the Lord and wiped his feet with her hair. 3So the sisters sent word to Jesus, ''Lord, the one you love is sick.''

4When he heard this, Jesus said, ''This sickness will not end in death. No, it is for God's glory so that God's Son may be glorified through it.'' 5Jesus loved Martha and her sister and Lazarus. 6Yet when he heard that Lazarus was sick, he stayed where he was two more days.

7Then he said to his disciples, ''Let us go back to Judea.''

8''But Rabbi,'' they said, ''a short while ago the Jews tried to stone you, and yet you are going back there?''

9Jesus answered, ''Are there not twelve hours of daylight? A man who walks by day will not stumble, for he sees by this world's light. 10It is when he walks by night that he stumbles, for he has no light.''

11After he had said this, he went on to tell them, ''Our friend Lazarus has fallen asleep; but I am going there to wake him up.''

12His disciples replied, ''Lord, if he sleeps, he will get better.'' 13Jesus had been speaking of his death, but his disciples thought he meant natural sleep.

14So then he told them plainly, ''Lazarus is dead, 15and for your sake I am glad I was not there, so that you may believe. But let us go to him.''

16Then Thomas (called Didymus) said to the rest of the disciples, ''Let us also go, that we may die with him.''

Jesus Comforts the Sisters

17On his arrival, Jesus found that Lazarus had already been in the tomb for four days. 18Bethany was less than two miles*a* from Jerusalem, 19and many Jews had come to Martha and Mary to comfort them in the loss of their brother. 20When Martha heard that Jesus was coming, she went out to meet him, but Mary stayed at home.

21''Lord,'' Martha said to Jesus, ''if you had been here, my brother would not have died. 22But I know that even now God will give you whatever you ask.''

23Jesus said to her, ''Your brother will rise again.''

24Martha answered, ''I know he will rise again in the resurrection at the last day.''

25Jesus said to her, ''I am the resurrection and the life. He who believes in me will live, even though he dies; 26and whoever lives and believes in me will never die. Do you believe this?''

27''Yes, Lord,'' she told him, ''I believe that you are the Christ,*b* the Son of God, who was to come into the world.''

28And after she had said this, she went back and called her sister Mary aside. ''The Teacher is here,'' she said, ''and is asking for you.'' 29When Mary heard this, she got up quickly and went to him. 30Now Jesus had not yet entered the village, but was still at the place where Martha had met him. 31When the Jews who had been with Mary in the house, comforting her, noticed how quickly she got up and went out, they followed her, supposing she was going to the tomb to mourn there.

32When Mary reached the place where Jesus was and saw him, she fell at his feet and said, ''Lord, if you had been here, my brother would not have died.''

33When Jesus saw her weeping, and the Jews who had come along with her also weeping, he was deeply moved in spirit and troubled. 34''Where have you laid him?'' he asked.

''Come and see, Lord,'' they replied.

35Jesus wept.

36Then the Jews said, ''See how he loved him!''

37But some of them said, ''Could not he who opened the eyes of the blind man have kept this man from dying?''

Jesus Raises Lazarus From the Dead

38Jesus, once more deeply moved, came to the tomb. It was a cave with a stone laid across the entrance. 39''Take away the stone,'' he said.

''But, Lord,'' said Martha, the sister of the

---

*d*29 Many early manuscripts *What my Father has given me is greater than all*   *e*34 Psalm 82:6
*a*18 Greek *fifteen stadia* (about 3 kilometres)   *b*27 Or *Messiah*

JOHN 10:1–10

'I am the gate; whoever enters through me will be saved. He will come in and go out, and find pasture' (v. 9).

THERE WERE TWO KINDS of sheepfold. One could be an enclosure in front of a house, the other, a walled area on the hillside offering shelter from the natural hazards of exposed places. Frequently, the sheep from a number of flocks were sheltered in the same fold. This created no problems of identity because the sheep were well known to the shepherd and they responded to his call. The fold had but one entrance. When the sheep were inside it was customary for the shepherd to sit across the narrow doorway. Quite literally, the shepherd was the door.

The illustration was appropriate for our Lord. He came, not to indicate a door to God's fold, but to be the door. It is through him, and him alone, that we become part of God's flock. 'For through him we both have access to the Father by one Spirit.' Those who do not enter the fold by him, he describes as thieves and robbers.

Whoever enters the fold through him will 'come in and go out, and find pasture'. The promise is heavy with safety, freedom, fulfilment and opportunity. His concern is to give us as much security as we need in order that we might have the challenge and satisfaction which come from living a full life. He is the door of opportunity. A world of new experiences and achievements awaits us as we step out in faith in the name of Jesus. He is the door to a greater spiritual maturity as we explore the paths of contemplation, prayer and faith.

> *Is he a door? I'll enter in;*
> *Behold the pastures large and green!*
> *A paradise divinely fair;*
> *None but the sheep have freedom there.*

(Isaac Watts)

→950

'Jesus said to her, "I am the resurrection and the life. He who believes in me will live, even though he dies; and whoever lives and believes in me will never die. Do you believe this?" ' (vv. 25, 26).

A CLOSE AFFINITY EXISTED between Jesus and Mary, Martha and Lazarus. They had opened their home to him and he was happy to be with them. It was understandable that when Lazarus became ill the sisters should send word to Jesus, expecting him to return immediately and heal their brother. But Jesus had a larger scenario before him, a greater glory in mind.

Because Christ is life, he is also the means of new life. When the believer surrenders his hold upon this life he enters into the full reality of eternal life. 'Because I live, you also will live.' To the bereaved, the grief of loss and separation is real, but the loved one, being in Christ, has embarked upon life's greatest adventure.

Many of us have experienced the resurrection ourselves: we who 'were dead in trespasses and sins. God made us alive with Christ'. We know the guilt, the despair, the lostness of our condition before we came to Christ, and now we know the joy of resurrection. Because of Jesus, eternal life is now. 'Trophies of grace' is an old term used to describe people who seemed irredeemably lost, but who, through the miracle-working power of Jesus' grace, have become new people. 'If anyone is in Christ, he is a new creation; the old has gone, the new has come!' Happily and gloriously, there are many trophies of grace today. Christ is the resurrection and life.

> *It was indeed more miracles than one:*
> *I was not blind and yet he gave me sight:*
> *I was not deaf and yet he gave me hearing;*
> *Nor was I dead, yet me he raised to life.*

(Andrew Young)

→953

dead man, "by this time there is a bad odour, for he has been there four days."

40Then Jesus said, "Did I not tell you that if you believed, you would see the glory of God?"

41So they took away the stone. Then Jesus looked up and said, "Father, I thank you that you have heard me. 42I knew that you always hear me, but I said this for the benefit of the people standing here, that they may believe that you sent me."

43When he had said this, Jesus called in a loud voice, "Lazarus, come out!" 44The dead man came out, his hands and feet wrapped with strips of linen, and a cloth around his face.

Jesus said to them, "Take off the grave clothes and let him go."

The Plot to Kill Jesus

45Therefore many of the Jews who had come to visit Mary, and had seen what Jesus did, put their faith in him. 46But some of them went to the Pharisees and told them what Jesus had done. 47Then the chief priests and the Pharisees called a meeting of the Sanhedrin.

"What are we accomplishing?" they asked. "Here is this man performing many miraculous signs. 48If we let him go on like this, everyone will believe in him, and then the Romans will come and take away both our place[c] and our nation."

49Then one of them, named Caiaphas, who was high priest that year, spoke up, "You know nothing at all! 50You do not realise that it is better for you that one man die for the people than that the whole nation perish."

51He did not say this on his own, but as high priest that year he prophesied that Jesus would die for the Jewish nation, 52and not only for that nation but also for the scattered children of God, to bring them together and make them one. 53So from that day on they plotted to take his life.

54Therefore Jesus no longer moved about publicly among the Jews. Instead he withdrew to a region near the desert, to a village called Ephraim, where he stayed with his disciples.

55When it was almost time for the Jewish Passover, many went up from the country to Jerusalem for their ceremonial cleansing before the Passover. 56They kept looking for Jesus, and as they stood in the temple area they asked one another, "What do you think? Isn't he coming to the Feast at all?" 57But the chief priests and Pharisees had given orders that if anyone found out where Jesus was, he should report it so that they might arrest him.

Jesus Anointed at Bethany

12 Six days before the Passover, Jesus arrived at Bethany, where Lazarus lived, whom Jesus had raised from the dead. 2Here a dinner was given in Jesus' honour.

Martha served, while Lazarus was among those reclining at the table with him. 3Then Mary took about a pint[a] of pure nard, an expensive perfume; she poured it on Jesus' feet and wiped his feet with her hair. And the house was filled with the fragrance of the perfume.

4But one of his disciples, Judas Iscariot, who was later to betray him, objected, 5"Why wasn't this perfume sold and the money given to the poor? It was worth a year's wages."[b] 6He did not say this because he cared about the poor but because he was a thief; as keeper of the money bag, he used to help himself to what was put into it.

7"Leave her alone," Jesus replied. "⌐It was intended⌐ that she should save this perfume for the day of my burial. 8You will always have the poor among you, but you will not always have me."

9Meanwhile a large crowd of Jews found out that Jesus was there and came, not only because of him but also to see Lazarus, whom he had raised from the dead. 10So the chief priests made plans to kill Lazarus as well, 11for on account of him many of the Jews were going over to Jesus and putting their faith in him.

The Triumphal Entry

12The next day the great crowd that had come for the Feast heard that Jesus was on his way to Jerusalem. 13They took palm branches and went out to meet him, shouting,

"Hosanna!"[c]

"Blessed is he who comes in the name of
    the Lord!"[d]

"Blessed is the King of Israel!"

14Jesus found a young donkey and sat upon it, as it is written,

15"Do not be afraid, O Daughter of Zion;
    see, your king is coming,
    seated on a donkey's colt."[e]

16At first his disciples did not understand all this. Only after Jesus was glorified did they realise that these things had been written about him and that they had done these things to him.

17Now the crowd that was with him when he called Lazarus from the tomb and raised him from the dead continued to spread the word. 18Many people, because they had heard that he had given this miraculous sign, went out to meet him. 19So the Pharisees said to one another, "See, this is getting us nowhere. Look how the whole world has gone after him!"

Jesus Predicts His Death

20Now there were some Greeks among those who went up to worship at the Feast.

---

c48 Or temple   a3 Greek a litra (probably about 0.5 litre)   b5 Greek three hundred denarii
c13 A Hebrew expression meaning "Save!" which became an exclamation of praise   d13 Psalm 118:25,26
e15 Zech. 9:9

²¹They came to Philip, who was from Bethsaida in Galilee, with a request. "Sir," they said, "we would like to see Jesus." ²²Philip went to tell Andrew; Andrew and Philip in turn told Jesus.

²³Jesus replied, "The hour has come for the Son of Man to be glorified. ²⁴I tell you the truth, unless a grain of wheat falls to the ground and dies, it remains only a single seed. But if it dies, it produces many seeds. ²⁵The man who loves his life will lose it, while the man who hates his life in this world will keep it for eternal life. ²⁶Whoever serves me must follow me; and where I am, my servant also will be. My Father will honour the one who serves me.

²⁷"Now my heart is troubled, and what shall I say? 'Father, save me from this hour'? No, it was for this very reason I came to this hour. ²⁸Father, glorify your name!"

Then a voice came from heaven, "I have glorified it, and will glorify it again." ²⁹The crowd that was there and heard it said it had thundered; others said an angel had spoken to him.

³⁰Jesus said, "This voice was for your benefit, not mine. ³¹Now is the time for judgment on this world; now the prince of this world will be driven out. ³²But I, when I am lifted up from the earth, will draw all men to myself." ³³He said this to show the kind of death he was going to die.

³⁴The crowd spoke up, "We have heard from the Law that the Christ⁄ will remain for ever, so how can you say, 'The Son of Man must be lifted up'? Who is this 'Son of Man'?"

³⁵Then Jesus told them, "You are going to have the light just a little while longer. Walk while you have the light, before darkness overtakes you. The man who walks in the dark does not know where he is going. ³⁶Put your trust in the light while you have it, so that you may become sons of light." When he had finished speaking, Jesus left and hid himself from them.

The Jews Continue in Their Unbelief

³⁷Even after Jesus had done all these miraculous signs in their presence, they still would not believe in him. ³⁸This was to fulfil the word of Isaiah the prophet:

"Lord, who has believed our message
 and to whom has the arm of the Lord
  been revealed?"ᵍ

³⁹For this reason they could not believe, because, as Isaiah says elsewhere:

⁴⁰"He has blinded their eyes
 and deadened their hearts,
so they can neither see with their eyes,
 nor understand with their hearts,
 nor turn—and I would heal them."ʰ

⁴¹Isaiah said this because he saw Jesus' glory and spoke about him.

⁴²Yet at the same time many even among the leaders believed in him. But because of the Pharisees they would not confess their faith for fear they would be put out of the synagogue; ⁴³for they loved praise from men more than praise from God.

⁴⁴Then Jesus cried out, "When a man believes in me, he does not believe in me only, but in the one who sent me. ⁴⁵When he looks at me, he sees the one who sent me. ⁴⁶I have come into the world as a light, so that no-one who believes in me should stay in darkness.

⁴⁷"As for the person who hears my words but does not keep them, I do not judge him. For I did not come to judge the world, but to save it. ⁴⁸There is a judge for the one who rejects me and does not accept my words; that very word which I spoke will condemn him at the last day. ⁴⁹For I did not speak of my own accord, but the Father who sent me commanded me what to say and how to say it. ⁵⁰I know that his command leads to eternal life. So whatever I say is just what the Father has told me to say."

Jesus Washes His Disciples' Feet

13 It was just before the Passover Feast. Jesus knew that the time had come for him to leave this world and go to the Father. Having loved his own who were in the world, he now showed them the full extent of his love.ᵃ

²The evening meal was being served, and the devil had already prompted Judas Iscariot, son of Simon, to betray Jesus. ³Jesus knew that the Father had put all things under his power, and that he had come from God and was returning to God; ⁴so he got up from the meal, took off his outer clothing, and wrapped a towel round his waist. ⁵After that, he poured water into a basin and began to wash his disciples' feet, drying them with the towel that was wrapped round him.

⁶He came to Simon Peter, who said to him, "Lord, are you going to wash my feet?"

⁷Jesus replied, "You do not realise now what I am doing, but later you will understand."

⁸"No," said Peter, "you shall never wash my feet."

Jesus answered, "Unless I wash you, you have no part with me."

⁹"Then, Lord," Simon Peter replied, "not just my feet but my hands and my head as well!"

¹⁰Jesus answered, "A person who has had a bath needs only to wash his feet; his whole body is clean. And you are clean, though not every one of you." ¹¹For he knew who was going to betray him, and that was why he said not every one was clean.

¹²When he had finished washing their feet, he put on his clothes and returned to his place. "Do you understand what I have done for you?" he asked them. ¹³"You call me 'Teacher' and 'Lord', and rightly so, for that is what I am. ¹⁴Now that I, your Lord and Teacher, have washed your feet, you also should wash one another's feet. ¹⁵I have set you an example that you should do as I have

---

ʲ34 Or Messiah   ᵍ38 Isaiah 53:1   ʰ40 Isaiah 6:10   ᵃ1 Or he loved them to the last

JOHN 12:1–11

'One of his disciples, Judas Iscariot, who was later to betray him, objected, "Why wasn't this perfume sold and the money given to the poor? It was worth a year's wages" ' (vv. 4, 5).

EXTRAVAGANT GESTURES have an important place in human life. Without them, life could be very dull indeed. In the context of one dinner party, Mary's impulsive act was extravagant in the extreme. Yet in the context of the world history of Christianity, the value of that one bottle of ointment is a tiny, tiny sum, compared to the value of the memory of Mary's action which has penetrated into the minds of millions of Christians over the centuries. Readers of *Words of Life* pay over a penny per page. Twenty five thousand pennies come to two hundred and fifty pounds. Possibly about the value of the bottle of ointment that Mary wasted! (Remember that a year's wages in many parts of the world even today is less than two hundred and fifty pounds).

Such attempts to value the gesture are in one way meaningless, in another they indicate how one simple action can have a continuing impact. One thoughtless word in a comment can wound for ever. One simple statement can inspire again and again and again.

Extravagant gestures are fine, but Judas had a point as well! This passage shows that the Christian Church has been engaged in social action right from the start. While Jesus was still with them in the flesh, there was a purse used for the common good – not just the good of the disciples, but for the good of the poor. Perhaps it was administered by a scoundrel, but it was there nevertheless.

Shouldn't the Church's extravagant gestures today be directed to the poor? Giving generously to the poor is the closest we can get to Mary's extravagant gesture towards her Lord.

→954

' "Lord, are you going to wash my feet?" Jesus replied, "You do not realise now what I am doing, but later you will understand." "No," said Peter, "you shall never wash my feet." ' (vv. 6b–8).

PETER WAS JUST LIKE THE CROWD, he wanted Jesus to conform to his pattern. He longed for Jesus to be the Lord and master of the universe, to take control. Peter was willing to follow him right to the death, to serve him and be obedient to him. But only on condition that Jesus acted in the way Peter thought he should. In Peter's eyes it was not proper for a lord to wash a servant's feet. That was turning Peter's whole world upside down.

We still feel that way today. Criticism is still levelled at those who are too familiar with the people they are supposed to lead. In theory leaders claim to want to have the 'common touch'. In practice they have to remain aloof and protected. They know how vulnerable they are. They surround themselves with advisers who can be blamed when things go wrong. Secretaries answer their phones and deal with their correspondence. The most prominent may even have bodyguards to protect them from physical assault.

'All these things are necessary', I can hear you say. 'Without such arrangements efficient administration would be impossible.' That is true. But Jesus shows us that there are occasions when the red tape must be broken, when the Lord and master must set an example.

The great sacrifice of going to the cross is memorable. It was, of course, necessary. But equally necessary was the tiny gesture with the towel.

done for you. 16I tell you the truth, no servant is greater than his master, nor is a messenger greater than the one who sent him. 17Now that you know these things, you will be blessed if you do them.

Jesus Predicts His Betrayal

18"I am not referring to all of you; I know those I have chosen. But this is to fulfil the scripture: 'He who shares my bread has lifted up his heel against me.'*b*

19"I am telling you now before it happens, so that when it does happen you will believe that I am He. 20I tell you the truth, whoever accepts anyone I send accepts me; and whoever accepts me accepts the one who sent me."

21After he had said this, Jesus was troubled in spirit and testified, "I tell you the truth, one of you is going to betray me."

22His disciples stared at one another, at a loss to know which of them he meant. 23One of them, the disciple whom Jesus loved, was reclining next to him. 24Simon Peter motioned to this disciple and said, "Ask him which one he means."

25Leaning back against Jesus, he asked him, "Lord, who is it?"

26Jesus answered, "It is the one to whom I will give this piece of bread when I have dipped it in the dish." Then, dipping the piece of bread, he gave it to Judas Iscariot, son of Simon. 27As soon as Judas took the bread, Satan entered into him.

"What you are about to do, do quickly," Jesus told him, 28but no-one at the meal understood why Jesus said this to him. 29Since Judas had charge of the money, some thought Jesus was telling him to buy what was needed for the Feast, or to give something to the poor. 30As soon as Judas had taken the bread, he went out. And it was night.

Jesus Predicts Peter's Denial

31When he was gone, Jesus said, "Now is the Son of Man glorified and God is glorified in him. 32If God is glorified in him,*c* God will glorify the Son in himself, and will glorify him at once.

33"My children, I will be with you only a little longer. You will look for me, and just as I told the Jews, so I tell you now: Where I am going, you cannot come.

34"A new command I give you: Love one another. As I have loved you, so you must love one another. 35By this all men will know that you are my disciples, if you love one another."

36Simon Peter asked him, "Lord, where are you going?"

Jesus replied, "Where I am going, you cannot follow now, but you will follow later."

37Peter asked, "Lord, why can't I follow you now? I will lay down my life for you."

38Then Jesus answered, "Will you really lay down your life for me? I tell you the truth,

before the cock crows, you will disown me three times!

Jesus Comforts His Disciples

14 "Do not let your hearts be troubled. Trust in God;*a* trust also in me. 2In my Father's house are many rooms; if it were not so, I would have told you. I am going there to prepare a place for you. 3And if I go and prepare a place for you, I will come back and take you to be with me that you also may be where I am. 4You know the way to the place where I am going."

Jesus the Way to the Father

5Thomas said to him, "Lord, we don't know where you are going, so how can we know the way?"

6Jesus answered, "I am the way and the truth and the life. No-one comes to the Father except through me. 7If you really knew me, you would know*b* my Father as well. From now on, you do know him and have seen him."

8Philip said, "Lord, show us the Father and that will be enough for us."

9Jesus answered: "Don't you know me, Philip, even after I have been among you such a long time? Anyone who has seen me has seen the Father. How can you say, 'Show us the Father'? 10Don't you believe that I am in the Father, and that the Father is in me? The words I say to you are not just my own. Rather, it is the Father, living in me, who is doing his work. 11Believe me when I say that I am in the Father and the Father is in me; or at least believe on the evidence of the miracles themselves. 12I tell you the truth, anyone who has faith in me will do what I have been doing. He will do even greater things than these, because I am going to the Father. 13And I will do whatever you ask in my name, so that the Son may bring glory to the Father. 14You may ask me for anything in my name, and I will do it.

Jesus Promises the Holy Spirit

15"If you love me, you will obey what I command. 16And I will ask the Father, and he will give you another Counsellor to be with you for ever—17the Spirit of truth. The world cannot accept him, because it neither sees him nor knows him. But you know him, for he lives with you and will be*c* in you. 18I will not leave you as orphans; I will come to you. 19Before long, the world will not see me any more, but you will see me. Because I live, you also will live. 20On that day you will realise that I am in my Father, and you are in me, and I am in you. 21Whoever has my commands and obeys them, he is the one who loves me. He who loves me will be loved by my Father, and I too will love him and show myself to him."

22Then Judas (not Judas Iscariot) said, "But, Lord, why do you intend to show yourself to us and not to the world?"

23Jesus replied, "If anyone loves me, he

b18 Psalm 41:9   *c32* Many early manuscripts do not have *If God is glorified in him.*   *a1* Or *You trust in God*
b7 Some early manuscripts *If you really have known me, you will know*   *c17* Some early manuscripts *and is*

will obey my teaching. My Father will love him, and we will come to him and make our home with him. 24He who does not love me will not obey my teaching. These words you hear are not my own; they belong to the Father who sent me.

25"All this I have spoken while still with you. 26But the Counsellor, the Holy Spirit, whom the Father will send in my name, will teach you all things and will remind you of everything I have said to you. 27Peace I leave with you; my peace I give you. I do not give to you as the world gives. Do not let your hearts be troubled and do not be afraid.

28"You heard me say, 'I am going away and I am coming back to you.' If you loved me, you would be glad that I am going to the Father, for the Father is greater than I. 29I have told you now before it happens, so that when it does happen you will believe. 30I will not speak with you much longer, for the prince of this world is coming. He has no hold on me, 31but the world must learn that I love the Father and that I do exactly what my Father has commanded me.

"Come now; let us leave.

The Vine and the Branches

15 "I am the true vine, and my Father is the gardener. 2He cuts off every branch in me that bears no fruit, while every branch that does bear fruit he prunes*a* so that it will be even more fruitful. 3You are already clean because of the word I have spoken to you. 4Remain in me, and I will remain in you. No branch can bear fruit by itself; it must remain in the vine. Neither can you bear fruit unless you remain in me.

5"I am the vine; you are the branches. If a man remains in me and I in him, he will bear much fruit; apart from me you can do nothing. 6If anyone does not remain in me, he is like a branch that is thrown away and withers; such branches are picked up, thrown into the fire and burned. 7If you remain in me and my words remain in you, ask whatever you wish, and it will be given you. 8This is to my Father's glory, that you bear much fruit, showing yourselves to be my disciples.

9"As the Father has loved me, so have I loved you. Now remain in my love. 10If you obey my commands, you will remain in my love, just as I have obeyed my Father's commands and remain in his love. 11I have told you this so that my joy may be in you and that your joy may be complete. 12My command is this: Love each other as I have loved you. 13Greater love has no-one than this, that he lay down his life for his friends. 14You are my friends if you do what I command. 15I no longer call you servants, because a servant does not know his master's business. Instead, I have called you friends, for everything that I learned from my Father I have made known to you. 16You did not choose me, but I chose you and appointed you to go and bear fruit—fruit that will last. Then the

Father will give you whatever you ask in my name. 17This is my command: Love each other.

The World Hates the Disciples

18"If the world hates you, keep in mind that it hated me first. 19If you belonged to the world, it would love you as its own. As it is, you do not belong to the world, but I have chosen you out of the world. That is why the world hates you. 20Remember the words I spoke to you: 'No servant is greater than his master.'*b* If they persecuted me, they will persecute you also. If they obeyed my teaching, they will obey yours also. 21They will treat you this way because of my name, for they do not know the One who sent me. 22If I had not come and spoken to them, they would not be guilty of sin. Now, however, they have no excuse for their sin. 23He who hates me hates my Father as well. 24If I had not done among them what no-one else did, they would not be guilty of sin. But now they have seen these miracles, and yet they have hated both me and my Father. 25But this is to fulfil what is written in their Law: 'They hated me without reason.'*c*

26"When the Counsellor comes, whom I will send to you from the Father, the Spirit of truth who goes out from the Father, he will testify about me. 27And you also must testify, for you have been with me from the beginning.

16 "All this I have told you so that you will not go astray. 2They will put you out of the synagogue; in fact, a time is coming when anyone who kills you will think he is offering a service to God. 3They will do such things because they have not known the Father or me. 4I have told you this, so that when the time comes you will remember that I warned you. I did not tell you this at first because I was with you.

The Work of the Holy Spirit

5"Now I am going to him who sent me, yet none of you asks me, 'Where are you going?' 6Because I have said these things, you are filled with grief. 7But I tell you the truth: It is for your good that I am going away. Unless I go away, the Counsellor will not come to you; but if I go, I will send him to you. 8When he comes, he will convict the world of guilt*a* in regard to sin and righteousness and judgment: 9in regard to sin, because men do not believe in me; 10in regard to righteousness, because I am going to the Father, where you can see me no longer; 11and in regard to judgment, because the prince of this world now stands condemned.

12"I have much more to say to you, more than you can now bear. 13But when he, the Spirit of truth, comes, he will guide you into all truth. He will not speak on his own; he will speak only what he hears, and he will tell you what is yet to come. 14He will bring glory to me by taking from what is mine and making it known to you. 15All that belongs to the

---

*a2 The Greek for *prunes* also means *cleans*.   *b20 John 13:16   *c25 Psalms 35:19; 69:4
*a8 Or *will expose the guilt of the world*

JOHN 15:26, 27

'When the Counsellor comes, whom I will send to you from the Father, the Spirit of truth who goes out from the Father, he will testify about me. And you also must testify, for you have been with me from the beginning' (vv. 26, 27).

THE SPIRIT POINTS TO JESUS. Today's reading is unusually short. It is also unusually important. Sometimes the central point of verse 26 has been lost through attention to less important detail. This is always a danger when we closely interpret small portions of Scripture, think about them deeply, and bring them to the centre of attention. And that is exactly what we are doing today! It is dangerous, but sometimes danger must be faced. A lifeboat which only went to sea in calm weather would be a very odd lifeboat indeed.

Over the centuries the Church has been divided into two great camps, the Eastern (Orthodox) and Western (Catholic). Verse 26 has, to some extent, been the basis of that division. The Eastern (Orthodox) Church takes this verse literally and speaks of the Spirit 'proceeding' from the Father. The Western (Catholic) talks of the Spirit proceeding from the Father *and the Son*. The East never adopted this idea. The attempt to understand the nature of the Holy Spirit split the Church into East and West.

Understanding the nature of the Holy Spirit is important, like understanding the nature of atomic power is important. How much more important it is to understand what the Spirit, or atomic power, *does*. The Spirit witnesses to Jesus; atomic power releases enormous physical energy with lasting side effects. We forget either at our peril.

We may not fully understand the relationship between Father, Son and Spirit, but we must never forget the prime function of the Spirit. The Spirit witnesses to Jesus, not to himself. What an example for all to follow!

→958

JOHN 16:17–33

'I have told you these things, so that in me you may have peace. In this world you will have trouble. But take heart! I have overcome the world' (16:33).

JESUS' MEETING WITH HIS DISCIPLES in the upper room signals the beginning of our Lord's passion. It was there that, as the Gospel narrator records: 'Jesus was troubled in spirit' (13:21).

The immortal words of our Master in the upper room, floating like soft music through the night air, resonate with timeless truths through the centuries. Here we find the eleventh commandment of love, the incomparable 'Do not let your hearts be troubled,' the instructive parable of the vine, our Lord's intimation of his atoning sacrifice, his promise of his coming again, and the vital teaching on the Holy Spirit.

Our Lord's farewell within those walls is his longest recorded discourse in Scripture, comprising five chapters in the Gospel of John. This sublime meditation is the last will and testament of Jesus Christ to his followers. It contains the quintessence of the gospel, the essentials of our theology.

An 'upper room' experience in our day has come to be synonymous with one of great blessing and fellowship with the Lord. We cannot roll back the centuries and enter into the divine communion of that upper room as did those early disciples. But we too can know the fellowship and presence of our Lord. We too can hear his word and precious promises to us. We too can affirm our love and loyalty to him.

As with the disciples of old, so we must come to the cross by way of the upper room. To understand Calvary, we need to know our Lord's presence, listen to his word, and obey his commands. He waits to speak his immortal words to our listening hearts.

Lord Jesus, come to me in a new and special way. Lead me to an upper room experience of divine communion and deeper consecration.

→961

Father is mine. That is why I said the Spirit will take from what is mine and make it known to you.

16"In a little while you will see me no more, and then after a little while you will see me."

The Disciples' Grief Will Turn to Joy

17Some of his disciples said to one another, "What does he mean by saying, 'In a little while you will see me no more, and then after a little while you will see me,' and 'Because I am going to the Father'?" 18They kept asking, "What does he mean by 'a little while'? We don't understand what he is saying."

19Jesus saw that they wanted to ask him about this, so he said to them, "Are you asking one another what I meant when I said, 'In a little while you will see me no more, and then after a little while you will see me'? 20I tell you the truth, you will weep and mourn while the world rejoices. You will grieve, but your grief will turn to joy. 21A woman giving birth to a child has pain because her time has come; but when her baby is born she forgets the anguish because of her joy that a child is born into the world. 22So with you: Now is your time of grief, but I will see you again and you will rejoice, and no-one will take away your joy. 23In that day you will no longer ask me anything. I tell you the truth, my Father will give you whatever you ask in my name. 24Until now you have not asked for anything in my name. Ask and you will receive, and your joy will be complete.

25"Though I have been speaking figuratively, a time is coming when I will no longer use this kind of language but will tell you plainly about my Father. 26In that day you will ask in my name. I am not saying that I will ask the Father on your behalf. 27No, the Father himself loves you because you have loved me and have believed that I came from God. 28I came from the Father and entered the world; now I am leaving the world and going back to the Father."

29Then Jesus' disciples said, "Now you are speaking clearly and without figures of speech. 30Now we can see that you know all things and that you do not even need to have anyone ask you questions. This makes us believe that you came from God."

31"You believe at last!"*b* Jesus answered. 32"But a time is coming, and has come, when you will be scattered, each to his own home. You will leave me all alone. Yet I am not alone, for my Father is with me.

33"I have told you these things, so that in me you may have peace. In this world you will have trouble. But take heart! I have overcome the world."

Jesus Prays for Himself

17 After Jesus said this, he looked towards heaven and prayed:

"Father, the time has come. Glorify your Son, that your Son may glorify

you. 2For you granted him authority over all people that he might give eternal life to all those you have given him. 3Now this is eternal life: that they may know you, the only true God, and Jesus Christ, whom you have sent. 4I have brought you glory on earth by completing the work you gave me to do. 5And now, Father, glorify me in your presence with the glory I had with you before the world began.

Jesus Prays for His Disciples

6"I have revealed you*a* to those whom you gave me out of the world. They were yours; you gave them to me and they have obeyed your word. 7Now they know that everything you have given me comes from you. 8For I gave them the words you gave me and they accepted them. They knew with certainty that I came from you, and they believed that you sent me. 9I pray for them. I am not praying for the world, but for those you have given me, for they are yours. 10All I have is yours, and all you have is mine. And glory has come to me through them. 11I will remain in the world no longer, but they are still in the world, and I am coming to you. Holy Father, protect them by the power of your name—the name you gave me—so that they may be one as we are one. 12While I was with them, I protected them and kept them safe by that name you gave me. None has been lost except the one doomed to destruction so that Scripture would be fulfilled.

13"I am coming to you now, but I say these things while I am still in the world, so that they may have the full measure of my joy within them. 14I have given them your word and the world has hated them, for they are not of the world any more than I am of the world. 15My prayer is not that you take them out of the world but that you protect them from the evil one. 16They are not of the world, even as I am not of it. 17Sanctify*b* them by the truth; your word is truth. 18As you sent me into the world, I have sent them into the world. 19For them I sanctify myself, that they too may be truly sanctified.

Jesus Prays for All Believers

20"My prayer is not for them alone. I pray also for those who will believe in me through their message, 21that all of them may be one, Father, just as you are in me and I am in you. May they also be in us so that the world may believe that you have sent me. 22I have given them the glory that you gave me, that they may be one as we are one: 23I in them and you in me. May they be brought to complete unity to let the world know

---

*b*31 Or *"Do you now believe?"* *a*6 Greek *your name*; also in verse 26
*b*17 Greek *hagiazo (set apart for sacred use* or *make holy)*; also in verse 19

that you sent me and have loved them even as you have loved me.

²⁴"Father, I want those you have given me to be with me where I am, and to see my glory, the glory you have given me because you loved me before the creation of the world.

²⁵"Righteous Father, though the world does not know you, I know you, and they know that you have sent me. ²⁶I have made you known to them, and will continue to make you known in order that the love you have for me may be in them and that I myself may be in them."

Jesus Arrested

18 When he had finished praying, Jesus left with his disciples and crossed the Kidron Valley. On the other side there was an olive grove, and he and his disciples went into it.

²Now Judas, who betrayed him, knew the place, because Jesus had often met there with his disciples. ³So Judas came to the grove, guiding a detachment of soldiers and some officials from the chief priests and Pharisees. They were carrying torches, lanterns and weapons.

⁴Jesus, knowing all that was going to happen to him, went out and asked them, "Who is it you want?"

⁵"Jesus of Nazareth," they replied.

"I am he," Jesus said. (And Judas the traitor was standing there with them.) ⁶When Jesus said, "I am he," they drew back and fell to the ground.

⁷Again he asked them, "Who is it you want?"

And they said, "Jesus of Nazareth."

⁸"I told you that I am he," Jesus answered. "If you are looking for me, then let these men go." ⁹This happened so that the words he had spoken would be fulfilled: "I have not lost one of those you gave me."ᵃ

¹⁰Then Simon Peter, who had a sword, drew it and struck the high priest's servant, cutting off his right ear. (The servant's name was Malchus.)

¹¹Jesus commanded Peter, "Put your sword away! Shall I not drink the cup the Father has given me?"

Jesus Taken to Annas

¹²Then the detachment of soldiers with its commander and the Jewish officials arrested Jesus. They bound him ¹³and brought him first to Annas, who was the father-in-law of Caiaphas, the high priest that year. ¹⁴Caiaphas was the one who had advised the Jews that it would be good if one man died for the people.

Peter's First Denial

¹⁵Simon Peter and another disciple were following Jesus. Because this disciple was known to the high priest, he went with Jesus into the high priest's courtyard, ¹⁶but Peter had to wait outside at the door. The other disciple, who was known to the high priest,

came back, spoke to the girl on duty there and brought Peter in.

¹⁷"You are not one of his disciples, are you?" the girl at the door asked Peter.

He replied, "I am not."

¹⁸It was cold, and the servants and officials stood round a fire they had made to keep warm. Peter also was standing with them, warming himself.

The High Priest Questions Jesus

¹⁹Meanwhile, the high priest questioned Jesus about his disciples and his teaching.

²⁰"I have spoken openly to the world," Jesus replied. "I always taught in synagogues or at the temple, where all the Jews come together. I said nothing in secret. ²¹Why question me? Ask those who heard me. Surely they know what I said."

²²When Jesus said this, one of the officials near by struck him in the face. "Is this the way you answer the high priest?" he demanded.

²³"If I said something wrong," Jesus replied, "testify as to what is wrong. But if I spoke the truth, why did you strike me?" ²⁴Then Annas sent him, still bound, to Caiaphas the high priest.ᵇ

Peter's Second and Third Denials

²⁵As Simon Peter stood warming himself, he was asked, "You are not one of his disciples, are you?"

He denied it, saying, "I am not."

²⁶One of the high priest's servants, a relative of the man whose ear Peter had cut off, challenged him, "Didn't I see you with him in the olive grove?" ²⁷Again Peter denied it, and at that moment a cock began to crow.

Jesus Before Pilate

²⁸Then the Jews led Jesus from Caiaphas to the palace of the Roman governor. By now it was early morning, and to avoid ceremonial uncleanness the Jews did not enter the palace; they wanted to be able to eat the Passover. ²⁹So Pilate came out to them and asked, "What charges are you bringing against this man?"

³⁰"If he were not a criminal," they replied, "we would not have handed him over to you."

³¹Pilate said, "Take him yourselves and judge him by your own law."

"But we have no right to execute anyone," the Jews objected. ³²This happened so that the words Jesus had spoken indicating the kind of death he was going to die would be fulfilled.

³³Pilate then went back inside the palace, summoned Jesus and asked him, "Are you the king of the Jews?"

³⁴"Is that your own idea," Jesus asked, "or did others talk to you about me?"

³⁵"Am I a Jew?" Pilate replied. "It was your people and your chief priests who handed you over to me. What is it you have done?"

³⁶Jesus said, "My kingdom is not of this

ᵃ9 John 6:39   ᵇ24 Or (*Now Annas had sent him, still bound, to Caiaphas the high priest.*)

JOHN 17:1–8
'Father, the time has come. Glorify your Son, that your Son may glorify you' (vv. 1b, 2a).

JESUS' FINAL WORDS to his disciples, as recorded in John 16, were 'I have overcome the world.' That conquest was achieved by means of the cross.

This great prayer of Jesus, called by some his 'High Priestly prayer', was uttered in full knowledge of the terrible fate that awaited him. Its earnest passion reflects the urgency of the situation. Jesus sympathized strongly with his disciples. He knew they would be lonely and isolated. They were no longer part of 'the world'. They might, perhaps, feel that he too had abandoned them.

His concern was more for them than it was for himself. He knew his agony was inevitable. He knew they would suffer mental anguish, too – and he wanted their suffering to be eased, while he faced his own fierce pain. Their agony would continue into the future, long after his physical pain had ended.

We cannot know exactly in what sense the suffering of Jesus continues eternally. We do know that the suffering of his followers is a present reality, and that he, Jesus, shares it with us.

In a similar fashion, he prays this prayer with us, too. He holds before us all the time the goal of glorifying God. Jesus' willingness to go to the cross was God-glorifying. Our willingness to follow the demands of Christ is also God-glorifying.

Christ's work on the cross is finished and our redemption is complete. Yet Christ's suffering continues, for by our sin we still frustrate his love.

→962

JOHN 19:1–27

'We have no king but Caesar,' the chief priests answered. (v. 15) 'When Jesus saw his mother there, and the disciple whom he loved standing near by, he said to his mother, "Dear woman, here is your son," and to the disciple, "Here is your mother." From that time on, this disciple took her into his home' (vv. 26, 27).

MATTHEW, MARK AND LUKE all say how, a few days before, the Pharisees and Herodians ganged up and tried to trick Jesus, asking 'Is it right for us to pay taxes to Caesar?' John omits that incident, but he alone records the chief priests chanting at the trial so shortly after, 'We have no king but Caesar.'

They condemn themselves out of their own mouths. They are not tricked into it. Eager to condemn another, they condemn themselves. Just like any other chanting mob, thoughtless and careless of the monstrous nature of their chant, they are caught up in the excitement of the moment and the crowd.

Jesus was almost isolated on the cross. But not completely alone. His mother was there. Only John tells of Jesus instructing the beloved disciple to look after Mary. In a sea of anger and blasphemy washing over him from the crowd, in the middle of Jesus' agony, comes a moment of calm. Jesus commits Mary to the care of his friend. Jesus has not let family loyalty displace his loyalty to God. But family loyalty shines out from the heart of the cross.

We may not know the physical pain of the cross, but many of us know the pain of parting from family and friends.

> *When we asunder part,*
> *It gives us inward pain;*
> *But we shall still be joined in heart*
> *And hope to meet again.*

(John Fawcett)

→965

world. If it were, my servants would fight to prevent my arrest by the Jews. But now my kingdom is from another place.''

37''You are a king, then!'' said Pilate.

Jesus answered, ''You are right in saying I am a king. In fact, for this reason I was born, and for this I came into the world, to testify to the truth. Everyone on the side of truth listens to me.''

38''What is truth?'' Pilate asked. With this he went out again to the Jews and said, ''I find no basis for a charge against him. 39But it is your custom for me to release to you one prisoner at the time of the Passover. Do you want me to release 'the king of the Jews'?''

40They shouted back, ''No, not him! Give us Barabbas!'' Now Barabbas had taken part in a rebellion.

Jesus Sentenced to be Crucified

19 Then Pilate took Jesus and had him flogged. 2The soldiers twisted together a crown of thorns and put it on his head. They clothed him in a purple robe 3and went up to him again and again, saying, ''Hail, king of the Jews!'' And they struck him in the face.

4Once more Pilate came out and said to the Jews, ''Look, I am bringing him out to you to let you know that I find no basis for a charge against him.'' 5When Jesus came out wearing the crown of thorns and the purple robe, Pilate said to them, ''Here is the man!''

6As soon as the chief priests and their officials saw him, they shouted, ''Crucify! Crucify!''

But Pilate answered, ''You take him and crucify him. As for me, I find no basis for a charge against him.''

7The Jews insisted, ''We have a law, and according to that law he must die, because he claimed to be the Son of God.''

8When Pilate heard this, he was even more afraid, 9and he went back inside the palace. ''Where do you come from?'' he asked Jesus, but Jesus gave him no answer. 10''Do you refuse to speak to me?'' Pilate said. ''Don't you realise I have power either to free you or to crucify you?''

11Jesus answered, ''You would have no power over me if it were not given to you from above. Therefore the one who handed me over to you is guilty of a greater sin.''

12From then on, Pilate tried to set Jesus free, but the Jews kept shouting, ''If you let this man go, you are no friend of Caesar. Anyone who claims to be a king opposes Caesar.''

13When Pilate heard this, he brought Jesus out and sat down on the judge's seat at a place known as the Stone Pavement (which in Aramaic is Gabbatha). 14It was the day of Preparation of Passover Week, about the sixth hour.

''Here is your king,'' Pilate said to the Jews.

15But they shouted, ''Take him away! Take him away! Crucify him!''

''Shall I crucify your king?'' Pilate asked.

''We have no king but Caesar,'' the chief priests answered.

16Finally Pilate handed him over to them to be crucified.

The Crucifixion

So the soldiers took charge of Jesus. 17Carrying his own cross, he went out to the place of the Skull (which in Aramaic is called Golgotha). 18Here they crucified him, and with him two others—one on each side and Jesus in the middle.

19Pilate had a notice prepared and fastened to the cross. It read: JESUS OF NAZARETH, THE KING OF THE JEWS. 20Many of the Jews read this sign, for the place where Jesus was crucified was near the city, and the sign was written in Aramaic, Latin and Greek. 21The chief priests of the Jews protested to Pilate, ''Do not write 'The King of the Jews,' but that this man claimed to be king of the Jews.''

22Pilate answered, ''What I have written, I have written.''

23When the soldiers crucified Jesus, they took his clothes, dividing them into four shares, one for each of them, with the undergarment remaining. This garment was seamless, woven in one piece from top to bottom.

24''Let's not tear it,'' they said to one another. ''Let's decide by lot who will get it.''

This happened that the scripture might be fulfilled which said,

''They divided my garments among them
    and cast lots for my clothing.''[a]

So this is what the soldiers did.

25Near the cross of Jesus stood his mother, his mother's sister, Mary the wife of Clopas, and Mary Magdalene. 26When Jesus saw his mother there, and the disciple whom he loved standing near by, he said to his mother, ''Dear woman, here is your son,'' 27and to the disciple, ''Here is your mother.'' From that time on, this disciple took her into his home.

The Death of Jesus

28Later, knowing that all was now completed, and so that the Scripture would be fulfilled, Jesus said, ''I am thirsty.'' 29A jar of wine vinegar was there, so they soaked a sponge in it, put the sponge on a stalk of the hyssop plant, and lifted it to Jesus' lips. 30When he had received the drink, Jesus said, ''It is finished.'' With that, he bowed his head and gave up his spirit.

31Now it was the day of Preparation, and the next day was to be a special Sabbath. Because the Jews did not want the bodies left on the crosses during the Sabbath, they asked Pilate to have the legs broken and the bodies taken down. 32The soldiers therefore came and broke the legs of the first man who had been crucified with Jesus, and then those of the other. 33But when they came to Jesus and found that he was already dead, they did

a24 Psalm 22:18

not break his legs. [34]Instead, one of the soldiers pierced Jesus' side with a spear, bringing a sudden flow of blood and water. [35]The man who saw it has given testimony, and his testimony is true. He knows that he tells the truth, and he testifies so that you also may believe. [36]These things happened so that the scripture would be fulfilled: "Not one of his bones will be broken,"[b] [37]and, as another scripture says, "They will look on the one they have pierced."[c]

The Burial of Jesus

[38]Later, Joseph of Arimathea asked Pilate for the body of Jesus. Now Joseph was a disciple of Jesus, but secretly because he feared the Jews. With Pilate's permission, he came and took the body away. [39]He was accompanied by Nicodemus, the man who earlier had visited Jesus at night. Nicodemus brought a mixture of myrrh and aloes, about seventy-five pounds.[d] [40]Taking Jesus' body, the two of them wrapped it, with the spices, in strips of linen. This was in accordance with Jewish burial customs. [41]At the place where Jesus was crucified, there was a garden, and in the garden a new tomb, in which no-one had ever been laid. [42]Because it was the Jewish day of Preparation and since the tomb was near by, they laid Jesus there.

The Empty Tomb

20 Early on the first day of the week, while it was still dark, Mary Magdalene went to the tomb and saw that the stone had been removed from the entrance. [2]So she came running to Simon Peter and the other disciple, the one Jesus loved, and said, "They have taken the Lord out of the tomb, and we don't know where they have put him!"

[3]So Peter and the other disciple started for the tomb. [4]Both were running, but the other disciple outran Peter and reached the tomb first. [5]He bent over and looked in at the strips of linen lying there but did not go in. [6]Then Simon Peter, who was behind him, arrived and went into the tomb. He saw the strips of linen lying there, [7]as well as the burial cloth that had been around Jesus' head. The cloth was folded up by itself, separate from the linen. [8]Finally the other disciple, who had reached the tomb first, also went inside. He saw and believed. [9](They still did not understand from Scripture that Jesus had to rise from the dead.)

Jesus Appears to Mary Magdalene

[10]Then the disciples went back to their homes, [11]but Mary stood outside the tomb crying. As she wept, she bent over to look into the tomb [12]and saw two angels in white, seated where Jesus' body had been, one at the head and the other at the foot.

[13]They asked her, "Woman, why are you crying?"

"They have taken my Lord away," she said, "and I don't know where they have put

him." [14]At this, she turned round and saw Jesus standing there, but she did not realise that it was Jesus.

[15]"Woman," he said, "why are you crying? Who is it you are looking for?"

Thinking he was the gardener, she said, "Sir, if you have carried him away, tell me where you have put him, and I will get him."

[16]Jesus said to her, "Mary."

She turned towards him and cried out in Aramaic, "Rabboni!" (which means Teacher).

[17]Jesus said, "Do not hold on to me, for I have not yet returned to the Father. Go instead to my brothers and tell them, 'I am returning to my Father and your Father, to my God and your God.'"

[18]Mary Magdalene went to the disciples with the news: "I have seen the Lord!" And she told them that he had said these things to her.

Jesus Appears to His Disciples

[19]On the evening of that first day of the week, when the disciples were together, with the doors locked for fear of the Jews, Jesus came and stood among them and said, "Peace be with you!" [20]After he said this, he showed them his hands and side. The disciples were overjoyed when they saw the Lord.

[21]Again Jesus said, "Peace be with you! As the Father has sent me, I am sending you." [22]And with that he breathed on them and said, "Receive the Holy Spirit. [23]If you forgive anyone his sins, they are forgiven; if you do not forgive them, they are not forgiven."

Jesus Appears to Thomas

[24]Now Thomas (called Didymus), one of the Twelve, was not with the disciples when Jesus came. [25]So the other disciples told him, "We have seen the Lord!"

But he said to them, "Unless I see the nail marks in his hands and put my finger where the nails were, and put my hand into his side, I will not believe it."

[26]A week later his disciples were in the house again, and Thomas was with them. Though the doors were locked, Jesus came and stood among them and said, "Peace be with you!" [27]Then he said to Thomas, "Put your finger here; see my hands. Reach out your hand and put it into my side. Stop doubting and believe."

[28]Thomas said to him, "My Lord and my God!"

[29]Then Jesus told him, "Because you have seen me, you have believed; blessed are those who have not seen and yet have believed."

[30]Jesus did many other miraculous signs in the presence of his disciples, which are not recorded in this book. [31]But these are written that you may[a] believe that Jesus is the Christ, the Son of God, and that by believing you may have life in his name.

[b]36 Exodus 12:46; Num. 9:12; Psalm 34:20　[c]37 Zech. 12:10　[d]39 Greek *a hundred litrai* (about 34 kilograms)　[a]31 Some manuscripts *may continue to*

JOHN 19:38–20:18
'At the place where Jesus was crucified, there was a garden, and in the garden a new tomb' (v. 41).

'COME, SEE THE PLACE WHERE THE LORD LAY,' (Matt. 28:6, NKJV) was the invitation of the angel to the women at the tomb on that first Easter morning. The narrative of John's Gospel tells us that there was a garden at the place of crucifixion and burial. Still today, flowers bloom at the site of the resurrection tomb.

On Easter day and every day we rejoice, for the resurrection turns graves into gardens, fears into faith, brokenness into blessing, adversities into advantages, scars into stars. Easter turns life's stresses into strengths, its tragedies into triumphs, its death into life and its Good Fridays into Easter Sundays.

Let exhilaration abound, let exultation resound, let jubilation echo, let music fill the air and let our radiant witness resonate with praise and thanksgiving! Today we rejoice, for he is risen! He is risen, indeed!

Because he lives – there is hope! Because he lives – there is salvation! Because he lives – there is power! Because he lives – there is peace! Because he lives – there is life eternal! Because he lives – we can face tomorrow!

'He is risen' is the grand and glorious message we celebrate again this Easter. There is no message more needed by our troubled and tortured world. For the message of Easter is that Jesus Christ is alive! He is in the world today! He would live in our hearts! And he is coming again in mighty triumph! No wonder Christians celebrate with joy at Easter.

The resurrection of Jesus Christ, as a majestic Matterhorn, towers over the landscape of human history. It is for each of us the singularly most important event that ever happened. Let us turn away from the temporal and look to the one who is eternal. Let us know and share the inexpressible joy of the one who floods our prosaic paths with his peerless glory! For we commemorate not a crucifixion but a coronation.

Risen Lord, keep me ever under the spell of your mighty resurrection.

→966

JOHN 20:24-31
'Blessed are those who have not seen and yet have believed' (v. 29).

JOHN ALONE RECORDS the account of Thomas, referred to as the 'doubter'. But Thomas is not alone in doubting. Many of us are like him. We want to see for ourselves. We are not entirely satisfied with another person's account of an important event. Others might be duped but we would not be fooled. Doubting is not to be excused. Our chosen Scripture makes this abundantly clear. However, honest doubting is understandable. Our Lord had so much patience, he must have taught his followers over and over again to change doubt into faith.

What is the essence of this saving faith? It is not blind trust in whatever we are told, certainly not when it comes to our salvation. It is to believe the witness of those whose testimony corresponds with the truth of Scripture. Jesus often confronted the doubts of his followers with the truth of Scripture, frequently quoting the prophets.

Becoming students of God's word is not for preachers and teachers alone. It is for all of us who would bear the name of Christ as his followers. Weak faith results from lack of biblical knowledge, or uncertainty about the whole of salvation history in which the scriptural word is embedded. Strong faith comes from a growing knowledge of the word of God, and a willingness to accept the testimony of the great cloud of witnesses, whose lives give credibility to that word. The word and the people of the word nurture those in search of truth.

> *A glory gilds the sacred page,*
> *Majestic, like the sun;*
> *It gives a light to every age;*
> *It gives, but borrows none.*

(William Cowper)

→969

Jesus and the Miraculous Catch of Fish

21 Afterwards Jesus appeared again to his disciples, by the Sea of Tiberias.[a] It happened this way: [2]Simon Peter, Thomas (called Didymus), Nathanael from Cana in Galilee, the sons of Zebedee, and two other disciples were together. [3]"I'm going out to fish," Simon Peter told them, and they said, "We'll go with you." So they went out and got into the boat, but that night they caught nothing.

[4]Early in the morning, Jesus stood on the shore, but the disciples did not realise that it was Jesus.

[5]He called out to them, "Friends, haven't you any fish?"

"No," they answered.

[6]He said, "Throw your net on the right side of the boat and you will find some." When they did, they were unable to haul the net in because of the large number of fish.

[7]Then the disciple whom Jesus loved said to Peter, "It is the Lord!" As soon as Simon Peter heard him say, "It is the Lord," he wrapped his outer garment around him (for he had taken it off) and jumped into the water. [8]The other disciples followed in the boat, towing the net full of fish, for they were not far from shore, about a hundred yards.[b] [9]When they landed, they saw a fire of burning coals there with fish on it, and some bread.

[10]Jesus said to them, "Bring some of the fish you have just caught."

[11]Simon Peter climbed aboard and dragged the net ashore. It was full of large fish, 153, but even with so many the net was not torn. [12]Jesus said to them, "Come and have breakfast." None of the disciples dared ask him, "Who are you?" They knew it was the Lord. [13]Jesus came, took the bread and gave it to them, and did the same with the fish. [14]This was now the third time Jesus appeared to his disciples after he was raised from the dead.

Jesus Reinstates Peter

[15]When they had finished eating, Jesus said to Simon Peter, "Simon son of John, do you truly love me more than these?"

"Yes, Lord," he said, "you know that I love you."

Jesus said, "Feed my lambs."

[16]Again Jesus said, "Simon son of John, do you truly love me?"

He answered, "Yes, Lord, you know that I love you."

Jesus said, "Take care of my sheep."

[17]The third time he said to him, "Simon son of John, do you love me?"

Peter was hurt because Jesus asked him the third time, "Do you love me?" He said, "Lord, you know all things; you know that I love you."

Jesus said, "Feed my sheep. [18]I tell you the truth, when you were younger you dressed yourself and went where you wanted; but when you are old you will stretch out your hands, and someone else will dress you and lead you where you do not want to go." [19]Jesus said this to indicate the kind of death by which Peter would glorify God. Then he said to him, "Follow me!"

[20]Peter turned and saw that the disciple whom Jesus loved was following them. (This was the one who had leaned back against Jesus at the supper and had said, "Lord, who is going to betray you?") [21]When Peter saw him, he asked, "Lord, what about him?"

[22]Jesus answered, "If I want him to remain alive until I return, what is that to you? You must follow me." [23]Because of this, the rumour spread among the brothers that this disciple would not die. But Jesus did not say that he would not die; he only said, "If I want him to remain alive until I return, what is that to you?"

[24]This is the disciple who testifies to these things and who wrote them down. We know that his testimony is true.

[25]Jesus did many other things as well. If every one of them were written down, I suppose that even the whole world would not have room for the books that would be written.

Acts

Jesus Taken Up Into Heaven

1 In my former book, Theophilus, I wrote about all that Jesus began to do and to teach ²until the day he was taken up to heaven, after giving instructions through the Holy Spirit to the apostles he had chosen. ³After his suffering, he showed himself to these men and gave many convincing proofs that he was alive. He appeared to them over a period of forty days and spoke about the kingdom of God. ⁴On one occasion, while he was eating with them, he gave them this command: "Do not leave Jerusalem, but wait for the gift my Father promised, which you have heard me speak about. ⁵For John baptised with*a* water, but in a few days you will be baptised with the Holy Spirit."

⁶So when they met together, they asked him, "Lord, are you at this time going to restore the kingdom to Israel?"

⁷He said to them: "It is not for you to know the times or dates the Father has set by his own authority. ⁸But you will receive power when the Holy Spirit comes on you; and you will be my witnesses in Jerusalem, and in all Judea and Samaria, and to the ends of the earth."

⁹After he said this, he was taken up before their very eyes, and a cloud hid him from their sight.

¹⁰They were looking intently up into the sky as he was going, when suddenly two men dressed in white stood beside them. ¹¹"Men of Galilee," they said, "why do you stand here looking into the sky? This same Jesus, who has been taken from you into heaven, will come back in the same way you have seen him go into heaven."

Matthias Chosen to Replace Judas

¹²Then they returned to Jerusalem from the hill called the Mount of Olives, a Sabbath day's walk*b* from the city. ¹³When they arrived, they went upstairs to the room where they were staying. Those present were Peter, John, James and Andrew; Philip and Thomas, Bartholomew and Matthew; James son of Alphaeus and Simon the Zealot, and Judas son of James. ¹⁴They all joined together constantly in prayer, along with the women and Mary the mother of Jesus, and with his brothers.

¹⁵In those days Peter stood up among the believers*c* (a group numbering about a hundred and twenty) ¹⁶and said, "Brothers, the Scripture had to be fulfilled which the Holy Spirit spoke long ago through the mouth of David concerning Judas, who served as guide for those who arrested Jesus—¹⁷he was one of our number and shared in this ministry."

¹⁸(With the reward he got for his wickedness, Judas bought a field; there he fell headlong, his body burst open and all his intestines spilled out. ¹⁹Everyone in Jerusalem heard about this, so they called that field in their language Akeldama, that is, Field of Blood.)

²⁰"For," said Peter, "it is written in the Book of Psalms,

" 'May his place be deserted;
    let there be no-one to dwell in it,'*d*

and,

" 'May another take his place of
      leadership.'*e*

²¹Therefore it is necessary to choose one of the men who have been with us the whole time the Lord Jesus went in and out among us, ²²beginning from John's baptism to the time when Jesus was taken up from us. For one of these must become a witness with us of his resurrection."

²³So they proposed two men: Joseph called Barsabbas (also known as Justus) and Matthias. ²⁴Then they prayed, "Lord, you know everyone's heart. Show us which of these two you have chosen ²⁵to take over this apostolic ministry, which Judas left to go where he belongs." ²⁶Then they cast lots, and the lot fell to Matthias; so he was added to the eleven apostles.

The Holy Spirit Comes at Pentecost

2 When the day of Pentecost came, they were all together in one place. ²Suddenly a sound like the blowing of a violent wind came from heaven and filled the

---

*a*5 Or *in* *b*12 That is, about ¾ of a mile (about 1,100 metres) *c*15 Greek *brothers* *d*20 Psalm 69:25
*e*20 Psalm 109:8

JOHN 21:15–23
'Then he said to him [Peter], "Follow me!"' (v. 19).

WHILE ALL THE GOSPELS record Peter's denial of the Lord, John alone records Peter's restoration. John reports that Christ asks Peter three times, 'do you love me?' Why ask Peter three times? Wasn't Peter sure of his love for the Master? Although nothing is more apparent from the scriptural record than the fact that Peter loved Jesus.

But perhaps Peter didn't understand what loving Jesus really meant. Jesus said, 'Simon . . . do you love me more than these?' Jesus had just finished feeding the disciples. 'Do you love me more than the others?' Or, perhaps, 'Do you love me more than the ordinary things of life?' Or, 'Do you realize that there is something special about loving me? When I'm gone from your sight again, are you going back to the old way, which is not the way at all? Instead of feeding my lambs will you again go back fishing? Because, if you really love me, Peter, it's going to cost you your very life. Do you love me more than this very life you possess?'

Love is the final and ultimate ingredient in the mix of disciple preparation. As the light begins to dawn on a new day of promise, this special ingredient is held up, and we begin to understand that only love with integrity, perseverance, humility and compassion, can fit us to break the bonds of time and space to fulfil our divine calling in Christ. It is so easy to say, 'I love you Jesus.' But love needs to be nurtured through his word, faithful service, and the intimate discipline of prayer to make it strong and sure.

> *Let love be first, let love be last,*
> *Its light o'er all my life be cast.*

(Thomas C. Marshall)

→970

ACTS 1:1–8

'But you will receive power when the Holy Spirit comes on you; and you will be my witnesses in Jerusalem, and in all Judea and Samaria, and to the ends of the earth' (v. 8).

THERE ARE MANY times when we feel that we lack the strength and ability to be a strong witness for Christ, but the promise of Scripture is that we have the necessary power when we have the Holy Spirit. ' "Not by might nor by power, but by my Spirit," says the LORD Almighty'. With the Holy Spirit comes the power and the enablement to witness and live for God.

Mrs General Bramwell Booth wrote,

> We need, and must seek after, a more adequate perception of God's almighty power, a truer conception of the part that he is willing to play in our lives. Oh! let each finally know that we are called to go to war not at our own charge, not in reliance upon our own strength, not to conquer by our wisdom, or thought, or knowledge, or attention, or even by our experience. All true work will be done, and every victory attained, by the power of God working in and through us.

'I am not ashamed of the gospel, because it is the power of God for the salvation of everyone who believes.' The Spirit gives us this confidence in the power of the gospel to change lives, and with this confident faith, we boldly witness. We all cry out at times, 'O God, help me . . . enable me . . . strengthen me!' And God answers, 'I will . . . I can . . . I did.' Call upon the Holy Spirit for all the courage, strength and power you need. We can claim God's promise, 'You will receive power!'

> *Spirit divine, attend our prayers,*
> *And make this house thy home;*
> *Descend with all thy gracious powers;*
> *O come, great Spirit, come.*

(Andrew Reed)

→971

ACTS 2:1–4

'Suddenly a sound like the blowing of a violent wind came from heaven and filled the whole house where they were sitting. They saw what seemed to be tongues of fire that separated and came to rest on each of them' (vv. 2, 3).

ANOTHER CELEBRATION DAY! The prophecies made by Isaiah (Isa. 32:15) and Joel (Joel 2:28–32), and promises made by Jesus about the Holy Spirit (John 14:16–26; 15:26; 16:7–11; Luke 24:49; Acts 1:4,5) became gloriously real on the day of Pentecost. The Spirit came, not just for specific men and specific tasks (Judg. 6:34, 14:6), but for all people, for all generations and for all time. His coming was the unfolding of a further vital element in God's strategy for mankind.

The ascension of Christ only ten days earlier, with his promise concerning the Spirit (1:7–9), must have given the disciples enormous expectations. They were not to be disappointed, either with the mysterious manner of his coming or the dramatic events which immediately followed. With a sound like that of a violent wind, the Spirit invaded that room of praying disciples. He could have come differently, but since both the Greek and Hebrew words for Spirit are also used for wind, it was most appropriate that he should come in that manner. And he came with fire!

We celebrate the day chosen by God for the realization of human hopes for purity. A day when men and women should have the power to be the people of God. A day when the Holy Spirit would be actively at work within human hearts: teaching, guiding, inspiring, comforting, preparing for mission and, above all, producing Christlikeness. We thank God for that day when he, the Holy Spirit, came, and that he, the Holy Spirit, is with us still, undiminished in presence, power and purpose.

O Holy Spirit, let me celebrate with joy and thanksgiving your coming into the world. Through your power, I can be what God the Father wants me to be. Amen.

→972

ACTS 2:5–13

'Utterly amazed, they asked: "Are not all these men who are speaking Galileans? Then how is it that each of us hears them in his own native language?" ' (vv. 7, 8).

THE HOLY SPIRIT represents power, a power great enough to break through all man-made barriers. We must remember that the disciples fled in fear when Jesus was captured. Even after the resurrection they met behind locked doors 'for fear of the Jews'. But after receiving the Holy Spirit they emerged from their hiding place and began witnessing courageously for Christ before the very people from whom they had been hiding. The Holy Spirit breaks down those personal barriers of timidity and fear which prevent us from declaring ourselves as believers. Released from inhibitions, many a basically shy person has become an articulate and tenacious witness to the gospel.

The barriers preventing communication were broken. Scholars seem to be divided as to whether the communication gift was one of languages, or whether it was the gift of tongues referred to elsewhere in Acts and in Corinthians. The fact that no interpreter was needed seems to suggest that it was a gift of language rather than glossolalia. The point being made is that through the power of the Spirit, both in the disciples and in the hearers, there was communication of such quality that not only did the crowd hear, but they were disposed to respond. The natural barriers of their culture and faith crumbled under the hammer blows of the Spirit.

It had to be a mighty show of spiritual energy to move across a crowd so large and produce a conviction so deep that 3,000 were converted that very day.

'When he, the Spirit of truth, comes, he will guide you into all truth. He will not speak on his own; he will speak only what he hears, and he will tell you what is yet to come.'

whole house where they were sitting. ³They saw what seemed to be tongues of fire that separated and came to rest on each of them. ⁴All of them were filled with the Holy Spirit and began to speak in other tongues*ᵃ* as the Spirit enabled them.

⁵Now there were staying in Jerusalem God-fearing Jews from every nation under heaven. ⁶When they heard this sound, a crowd came together in bewilderment, because each one heard them speaking in his own language. ⁷Utterly amazed, they asked: "Are not all these men who are speaking Galileans? ⁸Then how is it that each of us hears them in his own native language? ⁹Parthians, Medes and Elamites; residents of Mesopotamia, Judea and Cappadocia, Pontus and Asia, ¹⁰Phrygia and Pamphylia, Egypt and the parts of Libya near Cyrene; visitors from Rome ¹¹(both Jews and converts to Judaism); Cretans and Arabs—we hear them declaring the wonders of God in our own tongues!" ¹²Amazed and perplexed, they asked one another, "What does this mean?"

¹³Some, however, made fun of them and said, "They have had too much wine."*ᵇ*

Peter Addresses the Crowd

¹⁴Then Peter stood up with the Eleven, raised his voice and addressed the crowd: "Fellow Jews and all of you who live in Jerusalem, let me explain this to you; listen carefully to what I say. ¹⁵These men are not drunk, as you suppose. It's only nine in the morning! ¹⁶No, this is what was spoken by the prophet Joel:

¹⁷" 'In the last days, God says,
     I will pour out my Spirit on all people.
   Your sons and daughters will prophesy,
     your young men will see visions,
     your old men will dream dreams.
¹⁸Even on my servants, both men and
        women,
     I will pour out my Spirit in those days,
        and they will prophesy.
¹⁹I will show wonders in the heaven above
        and signs on the earth below,
        blood and fire and billows of smoke.
²⁰The sun will be turned to darkness
        and the moon to blood
     before the coming of the great and
        glorious day of the Lord.
²¹And everyone who calls
     on the name of the Lord will be saved.'*ᶜ*

²²"Men of Israel, listen to this: Jesus of Nazareth was a man accredited by God to you by miracles, wonders and signs, which God did among you through him, as you yourselves know. ²³This man was handed over to you by God's set purpose and foreknowledge; and you, with the help of wicked men,*ᵈ* put him to death by nailing him to the cross. ²⁴But God raised him from the dead, freeing him from the agony of death, because

it was impossible for death to keep its hold on him. ²⁵David said about him:

" 'I saw the Lord always before me.
   Because he is at my right hand,
     I will not be shaken.
²⁶Therefore my heart is glad and my tongue
        rejoices;
     my body also will live in hope,
²⁷because you will not abandon me to the
        grave,
     nor will you let your Holy One see
        decay.
²⁸You have made known to me the paths of
        life;
     you will fill me with joy in your
        presence.'*ᵉ*

²⁹"Brothers, I can tell you confidently that the patriarch David died and was buried, and his tomb is here to this day. ³⁰But he was a prophet and knew that God had promised him on oath that he would place one of his descendants on his throne. ³¹Seeing what was ahead, he spoke of the resurrection of the Christ,*ᶠ* that he was not abandoned to the grave, nor did his body see decay. ³²God has raised this Jesus to life, and we are all witnesses of the fact. ³³Exalted to the right hand of God, he has received from the Father the promised Holy Spirit and has poured out what you now see and hear. ³⁴For David did not ascend to heaven, and yet he said,

" 'The Lord said to my Lord:
     "Sit at my right hand
³⁵until I make your enemies
     a footstool for your feet." '*ᵍ*

³⁶"Therefore let all Israel be assured of this: God has made this Jesus, whom you crucified, both Lord and Christ."

³⁷When the people heard this, they were cut to the heart and said to Peter and the other apostles, "Brothers, what shall we do?"

³⁸Peter replied, "Repent and be baptised, every one of you, in the name of Jesus Christ for the forgiveness of your sins. And you will receive the gift of the Holy Spirit. ³⁹The promise is for you and your children and for all who are far off—for all whom the Lord our God will call."

⁴⁰With many other words he warned them; and he pleaded with them, "Save yourselves from this corrupt generation." ⁴¹Those who accepted his message were baptised, and about three thousand were added to their number that day.

The Fellowship of the Believers

⁴²They devoted themselves to the apostles' teaching and to the fellowship, to the breaking of bread and to prayer. ⁴³Everyone was filled with awe, and many wonders and miraculous signs were done by the apostles. ⁴⁴All the believers were together and had

---

ᵃ4 Or *languages;* also in verse 11   *ᵇ13* Or *sweet wine*   *ᶜ21* Joel 2:28–32
ᵈ23 Or *of those not having the law* (that is, Gentiles)   *ᵉ28* Psalm 16:8–11
ᶠ31 Or *Messiah.* "The Christ" (Greek) and "the Messiah" (Hebrew) both mean "the Anointed One"; also in verse 36.   *ᵍ35* Psalm 110:1

everything in common. [45]Selling their possessions and goods, they gave to anyone as he had need. [46]Every day they continued to meet together in the temple courts. They broke bread in their homes and ate together with glad and sincere hearts, [47]praising God and enjoying the favour of all the people. And the Lord added to their number daily those who were being saved.

Peter Heals the Crippled Beggar

3 One day Peter and John were going up to the temple at the time of prayer—at three in the afternoon. [2]Now a man crippled from birth was being carried to the temple gate called Beautiful, where he was put every day to beg from those going into the temple courts. [3]When he saw Peter and John about to enter, he asked them for money. [4]Peter looked straight at him, as did John. Then Peter said, "Look at us!" [5]So the man gave them his attention, expecting to get something from them.

[6]Then Peter said, "Silver or gold I do not have, but what I have I give you. In the name of Jesus Christ of Nazareth, walk." [7]Taking him by the right hand, he helped him up, and instantly the man's feet and ankles became strong. [8]He jumped to his feet and began to walk. Then he went with them into the temple courts, walking and jumping, and praising God. [9]When all the people saw him walking and praising God, [10]they recognised him as the same man who used to sit begging at the temple gate called Beautiful, and they were filled with wonder and amazement at what had happened to him.

Peter Speaks to the Onlookers

[11]While the beggar held on to Peter and John, all the people were astonished and came running to them in the place called Solomon's Colonnade. [12]When Peter saw this, he said to them: "Men of Israel, why does this surprise you? Why do you stare at us as if by our own power or godliness we had made this man walk? [13]The God of Abraham, Isaac and Jacob, the God of our fathers, has glorified his servant Jesus. You handed him over to be killed, and you disowned him before Pilate, though he had decided to let him go. [14]You disowned the Holy and Righteous One and asked that a murderer be released to you. [15]You killed the author of life, but God raised him from the dead. We are witnesses of this. [16]By faith in the name of Jesus, this man whom you see and know was made strong. It is Jesus' name and the faith that comes through him that has given this complete healing to him, as you can all see.

[17]"Now, brothers, I know that you acted in ignorance, as did your leaders. [18]But this is how God fulfilled what he had foretold through all the prophets, saying that his Christ[a] would suffer. [19]Repent, then, and turn to God, so that your sins may be wiped out, that times of refreshing may come from the Lord, [20]and that he may send the Christ,

who has been appointed for you—even Jesus. [21]He must remain in heaven until the time comes for God to restore everything, as he promised long ago through his holy prophets. [22]For Moses said, 'The Lord your God will raise up for you a prophet like me from among your own people; you must listen to everything he tells you. [23]Anyone who does not listen to him will be completely cut off from among his people.'[b]

[24]"Indeed, all the prophets from Samuel on, as many as have spoken, have foretold these days. [25]And you are heirs of the prophets and of the covenant God made with your fathers. He said to Abraham, 'Through your offspring all peoples on earth will be blessed.'[c] [26]When God raised up his servant, he sent him first to you to bless you by turning each of you from your wicked ways."

Peter and John Before the Sanhedrin

4 The priests and the captain of the temple guard and the Sadducees came up to Peter and John while they were speaking to the people. [2]They were greatly disturbed because the apostles were teaching the people and proclaiming in Jesus the resurrection of the dead. [3]They seized Peter and John, and because it was evening, they put them in jail until the next day. [4]But many who heard the message believed, and the number of men grew to about five thousand.

[5]The next day the rulers, elders and teachers of the law met in Jerusalem. [6]Annas the high priest was there, and so were Caiaphas, John, Alexander and the other men of the high priest's family. [7]They had Peter and John brought before them and began to question them: "By what power or what name did you do this?"

[8]Then Peter, filled with the Holy Spirit, said to them: "Rulers and elders of the people! [9]If we are being called to account today for an act of kindness shown to a cripple and are asked how he was healed, [10]then know this, you and all the people of Israel: It is by the name of Jesus Christ of Nazareth, whom you crucified but whom God raised from the dead, that this man stands before you healed. [11]He is

"'the stone you builders rejected,
which has become the capstone.'[a, b]

[12]Salvation is found in no-one else, for there is no other name under heaven given to men by which we must be saved."

[13]When they saw the courage of Peter and John and realised that they were unschooled, ordinary men, they were astonished and they took note that these men had been with Jesus. [14]But since they could see the man who had been healed standing there with them, there was nothing they could say. [15]So they ordered them to withdraw from the Sanhedrin and then conferred together. [16]"What are we going to do with these men?"

[a]18 Or Messiah; also in verse 20　　[b]23 Deut. 18:15,18,19　　[c]25 Gen. 22:18; 26:4
[a]11 Or cornerstone　　[b]11 Psalm 118:22

Acts 2:36–47
'And the Lord added to their number daily those who were being saved' (v. 47b).

THE DYNAMIC POWER of the Spirit could not be contained. The disciples were totally transformed people. They were spearheading a mission which was to prove irresistible to growing numbers of people. They had run through a gamut of experiences in a few short weeks. They had seen their leader crucified as a felon. They had been shocked to the depths of their hearts by his appearance before them as a risen Saviour. They had met him now here, now there, over forty days, and had seen him rise into the heavens, and, remaining in Jerusalem, sensitized by prayer, they had become infilled by the Holy Spirit whom Jesus had promised and for whom they had waited.

From being an insignificant minority, they had become a force to be reckoned with in Jerusalem. The future was theirs to claim through the Holy Spirit.

A strong sense of destiny, of mission, comes through Luke's accounts of those early days. Some of those who had shouted 'crucify him', must have been numbered among those who began to call him 'Lord'. There must have been an exhilaration about those early days of instant spiritual success which made the disciples take advantage of every occasion to consolidate the work of grace. A tidal wave of wonder and acceptance swept across the city and daily there were more converts.

To you, and to me, the doctrine of the Holy Ghost should come as revelation straight from the eternal throne. To know that God himself wants to help us by his own operation directly and indirectly upon the hearts of men, should inspire us with hope and with courage. And send us into the fight more confident of victory than ever.

(*William Booth*)

→976

ACTS 3:1–12

'Men of Israel, why does this surprise you? Why do you stare at us as if by our own power or godliness we had made this man walk?' (v. 12b).

PETER HAD HIMSELF passed through the surprise barrier. He had run into the empty tomb on Easter Day. Jesus had sought him out on that same day, presumably to reassure him. He had been one of the group in the upper room on the evening of Easter Day, and had been the subject of a searching encounter by Jesus at the lakeside. He had also been present at the ascension of Jesus and was in the upper room when the Spirit came. Peter knew that an entirely new element had come into human experience. He was prepared to be surprised by God and not be over-surprised by the event. God was present with people in a way in which he had never been present before. Inevitably, unusual, even miraculous, events would occur.

The crippled man at the gate of the temple was a case in point. He asked for help from Peter and John, hoping for and expecting money, instead of which he received a miracle. Understandably, the people gathered in amazement and Peter, who by now was becoming used to the gloriously unexpected, tried to help them through the surprise barrier.

Since Pentecost, the Holy Spirit has made our partnership with God a reality. That same Holy Spirit is not only at work in our hearts but in the hearts of others, prompting, convicting and convincing them. He is also seeking to reproduce the life of Jesus within each of us. There is no reason why we should be surprised if feared and adverse circumstances seem to improve; if we have strength to endure; if relationships ease; if the ungodly become godly and if we ourselves become better people. The Holy Spirit makes miraculous things happen!

Increase the level of my expectations, Lord. Amen.

→977

ACTS 4:1–14

'They seized Peter and John, and because it was evening, they put them in jail until the next day' (v. 3).

THESE MOMENTOUS EVENTS began quite simply. Peter and John had only gone to the temple for afternoon prayer. They were unaware of the fact that a miracle was lying in wait for them. In ordinary day-to-day events the Holy Spirit seeks opportunity to express the ministries of the Lord Jesus.

Such was the excitement created by the miracle and Peter's declarations to the gathered crowd, that the temple guard appeared. The Sadducees with them were disturbed at the preaching because they did not believe in the resurrection of the dead. It was too late for reference to the Sanhedrin that day, so the apostles were put in prison for the night.

The meeting with the Sanhedrin next morning had dramatic elements. Caiaphas, the High Priest, was the one who had said of Jesus, 'It is better . . . that one man die for the people than that the whole nation perish': the very same Caiaphas who had organized the capture, trial and death of Jesus. What were his thoughts now, with Jesus alive, and unlearned men proclaiming his resurrection? With their new-found boldness and eloquence through the Holy Spirit, the apostles confounded the Sanhedrin. But the Sanhedrin noted they had been with Jesus. The Holy Spirit had already begun to mark them as Christ's men.

Dullness and boredom are not traits of the Spirit-filled life. Always, there is something new to discover and to experience, some test of faith, truth to find, strength to gain, or service to give. God has a challenge for us just round the next corner.

'Pentecost with its challenge is normal Christianity.'

(*Dick Sheppard*)

→978

ACTS 4:13–22
'We cannot help speaking about what we have seen and heard' (v. 20).

LIFE IN THE SPIRIT reduces our options. We have no alternative but to speak of the things God has done for us. The Sanhedrin wondered what they should do with Peter and John so they ordered them from their meeting in order to determine their own course of action. The Sanhedrin could not refute the facts: a man had been healed, and Peter and John had courage and authority. They therefore decided to command them to be silent. The Pharisees had forgotten there are some things we cannot withhold. They had themselves asked Christ to rebuke his disciples on Palm Sunday when they hailed him as the coming king, only to hear Jesus say, 'If they keep quiet, the stones will cry out.' How could Peter and John remain silent? The compulsion of God was upon them.

Jeremiah knew the experience: 'His word is in my heart like a burning fire, shut up in my bones.' Paul was to express it, 'Woe to me if I do not preach the gospel!' Peter and John knew they were to obey God rather than men.

The Holy Spirit gives boldness, wisdom and even the words we need to match the demands of the occasion. So it was in those early days of faith, and so it is today. It is usually the simple but authoritative account of what God has done or is doing for us that proves to be so helpful to others. New converts are so full of the joy of the Lord that they cannot remain silent. This is why they so often bring other new people to Christ. They have the compulsion of gratitude and joy within them.

Thank you, Lord, for all you have done for me. Give me the wisdom and the courage to share this, and the faith to believe that you will use my simple witness. Amen.

→981

they asked. "Everybody living in Jerusalem knows they have done an outstanding miracle, and we cannot deny it. [17]But to stop this thing from spreading any further among the people, we must warn these men to speak no longer to anyone in this name."

[18]Then they called them in again and commanded them not to speak or teach at all in the name of Jesus. [19]But Peter and John replied, "Judge for yourselves whether it is right in God's sight to obey you rather than God. [20]For we cannot help speaking about what we have seen and heard."

[21]After further threats they let them go. They could not decide how to punish them, because all the people were praising God for what had happened. [22]For the man who was miraculously healed was over forty years old.

The Believers' Prayer

[23]On their release, Peter and John went back to their own people and reported all that the chief priests and elders had said to them. [24]When they heard this, they raised their voices together in prayer to God. "Sovereign Lord," they said, "you made the heaven and the earth and the sea, and everything in them. [25]You spoke by the Holy Spirit through the mouth of your servant, our father David:

" 'Why do the nations rage
    and the peoples plot in vain?
[26]The kings of the earth take their stand
    and the rulers gather together
against the Lord
    and against his Anointed One.'[c, d]

[27]Indeed Herod and Pontius Pilate met together with the Gentiles and the people[e] of Israel in this city to conspire against your holy servant Jesus, whom you anointed. [28]They did what your power and will had decided beforehand should happen. [29]Now, Lord, consider their threats and enable your servants to speak your word with great boldness. [30]Stretch out your hand to heal and perform miraculous signs and wonders through the name of your holy servant Jesus."

[31]After they prayed, the place where they were meeting was shaken. And they were all filled with the Holy Spirit and spoke the word of God boldly.

The Believers Share Their Possessions

[32]All the believers were one in heart and mind. No-one claimed that any of his possessions was his own, but they shared everything they had. [33]With great power the apostles continued to testify to the resurrection of the Lord Jesus, and much grace was upon them all. [34]There were no needy persons among them. For from time to time those who owned lands or houses sold them, brought the money from the sales [35]and put it at the apostles' feet, and it was distributed to anyone as he had need.

[36]Joseph, a Levite from Cyprus, whom the apostles called Barnabas (which means Son of Encouragement), [37]sold a field he owned and brought the money and put it at the apostles' feet.

Ananias and Sapphira

5 Now a man named Ananias, together with his wife Sapphira, also sold a piece of property. [2]With his wife's full knowledge he kept back part of the money for himself, but brought the rest and put it at the apostles' feet.

[3]Then Peter said, "Ananias, how is it that Satan has so filled your heart that you have lied to the Holy Spirit and kept for yourself some of the money you received for the land? [4]Didn't it belong to you before it was sold? And after it was sold, wasn't the money at your disposal? What made you think of doing such a thing? You have not lied to men but to God."

[5]When Ananias heard this, he fell down and died. And great fear seized all who heard what had happened. [6]Then the young men came forward, wrapped up his body, and carried him out and buried him.

[7]About three hours later his wife came in, not knowing what had happened. [8]Peter asked her, "Tell me, is this the price you and Ananias got for the land?"

"Yes," she said, "that is the price."

[9]Peter said to her, "How could you agree to test the Spirit of the Lord? Look! The feet of the men who buried your husband are at the door, and they will carry you out also."

[10]At that moment she fell down at his feet and died. Then the young men came in and, finding her dead, carried her out and buried her beside her husband. [11]Great fear seized the whole church and all who heard about these events.

The Apostles Heal Many

[12]The apostles performed many miraculous signs and wonders among the people. And all the believers used to meet together in Solomon's Colonnade. [13]No-one else dared join them, even though they were highly regarded by the people. [14]Nevertheless, more and more men and women believed in the Lord and were added to their number. [15]As a result, people brought the sick into the streets and laid them on beds and mats so that at least Peter's shadow might fall on some of them as he passed by. [16]Crowds gathered also from the towns around Jerusalem, bringing their sick and those tormented by evil[a] spirits, and all of them were healed.

The Apostles Persecuted

[17]Then the high priest and all his associates, who were members of the party of the Sadducees, were filled with jealousy. [18]They arrested the apostles and put them in the public jail. [19]But during the night an angel of the Lord opened the doors of the jail and brought them out. [20]"Go, stand in the temple courts," he said, "and tell the people the full message of this new life."

---

[c]26 That is, Christ or Messiah   [d]26 Psalm 2:1,2   [e]27 The Greek is plural.   [a]16 Greek *unclean*

²¹At daybreak they entered the temple courts, as they had been told, and began to teach the people.

When the high priest and his associates arrived, they called together the Sanhedrin—the full assembly of the elders of Israel—and sent to the jail for the apostles. ²²But on arriving at the jail, the officers did not find them there. So they went back and reported, ²³"We found the jail securely locked, with the guards standing at the doors; but when we opened them, we found no-one inside." ²⁴On hearing this report, the captain of the temple guard and the chief priests were puzzled, wondering what would come of this.

²⁵Then someone came and said, "Look! The men you put in jail are standing in the temple courts teaching the people." ²⁶At that, the captain went with his officers and brought the apostles. They did not use force, because they feared that the people would stone them.

²⁷Having brought the apostles, they made them appear before the Sanhedrin to be questioned by the high priest. ²⁸"We gave you strict orders not to teach in this name," he said. "Yet you have filled Jerusalem with your teaching and are determined to make us guilty of this man's blood."

²⁹Peter and the other apostles replied: "We must obey God rather than men! ³⁰The God of our fathers raised Jesus from the dead—whom you had killed by hanging him on a tree. ³¹God exalted him to his own right hand as Prince and Saviour that he might give repentance and forgiveness of sins to Israel. ³²We are witnesses of these things, and so is the Holy Spirit, whom God has given to those who obey him."

³³When they heard this, they were furious and wanted to put them to death. ³⁴But a Pharisee named Gamaliel, a teacher of the law, who was honoured by all the people, stood up in the Sanhedrin and ordered that the men be put outside for a little while. ³⁵Then he addressed them: "Men of Israel, consider carefully what you intend to do to these men. ³⁶Some time ago Theudas appeared, claiming to be somebody, and about four hundred men rallied to him. He was killed, all his followers were dispersed, and it all came to nothing. ³⁷After him, Judas the Galilean appeared in the days of the census and led a band of people in revolt. He too was killed, and all his followers were scattered. ³⁸Therefore, in the present case I advise you: Leave these men alone! Let them go! For if their purpose or activity is of human origin, it will fail. ³⁹But if it is from God, you will not be able to stop these men; you will only find yourselves fighting against God."

⁴⁰His speech persuaded them. They called the apostles in and had them flogged. Then they ordered them not to speak in the name of Jesus, and let them go.

⁴¹The apostles left the Sanhedrin, rejoicing because they had been counted worthy of suffering disgrace for the Name. ⁴²Day after day, in the temple courts and from house to house, they never stopped teaching and proclaiming the good news that Jesus is the Christ.*b*

The Choosing of the Seven

6 In those days when the number of disciples was increasing, the Grecian Jews among them complained against the Hebraic Jews because their widows were being overlooked in the daily distribution of food. ²So the Twelve gathered all the disciples together and said, "It would not be right for us to neglect the ministry of the word of God in order to wait on tables. ³Brothers, choose seven men from among you who are known to be full of the Spirit and wisdom. We will turn this responsibility over to them ⁴and will give our attention to prayer and the ministry of the word."

⁵This proposal pleased the whole group. They chose Stephen, a man full of faith and of the Holy Spirit; also Philip, Procorus, Nicanor, Timon, Parmenas, and Nicolas from Antioch, a convert to Judaism. ⁶They presented these men to the apostles, who prayed and laid their hands on them.

⁷So the word of God spread. The number of disciples in Jerusalem increased rapidly, and a large number of priests became obedient to the faith.

Stephen Seized

⁸Now Stephen, a man full of God's grace and power, did great wonders and miraculous signs among the people. ⁹Opposition arose, however, from members of the Synagogue of the Freedmen (as it was called)—Jews of Cyrene and Alexandria as well as the provinces of Cilicia and Asia. These men began to argue with Stephen, ¹⁰but they could not stand up against his wisdom or the Spirit by whom he spoke.

¹¹Then they secretly persuaded some men to say, "We have heard Stephen speak words of blasphemy against Moses and against God."

¹²So they stirred up the people and the elders and the teachers of the law. They seized Stephen and brought him before the Sanhedrin. ¹³They produced false witnesses, who testified, "This fellow never stops speaking against this holy place and against the law. ¹⁴For we have heard him say that this Jesus of Nazareth will destroy this place and change the customs Moses handed down to us."

¹⁵All who were sitting in the Sanhedrin looked intently at Stephen, and they saw that his face was like the face of an angel.

Stephen's Speech to the Sanhedrin

7 Then the high priest asked him, "Are these charges true?"

²To this he replied: "Brothers and fathers, listen to me! The God of glory appeared to our father Abraham while he was still in Mesopotamia, before he lived in Haran.

ACTS 4:23–31
'On their release, Peter and John went back to their own people and reported all that the chief priests and elders had said to them' (v. 23).

PETER AND JOHN returned to base. They had a great story to tell, although probably their friends knew much of it already. Certainly, they needed to reassure their friends and equally certainly, they needed reassurance themselves. The value of Christian community must never be underestimated. We belong to each other. We suffer and rejoice with each other. We build each other up.

We can imagine the excited statements from Peter and John and the eager questions from the fellowship. When the Church is under attack the bonding between its members is deepened, and these followers of Jesus were experiencing their first real brush with the authorities. The experience of Peter and John today could be the experience of others tomorrow.

Occasionally, some Christians are called to work and witness in isolation and they are afforded the essential grace to do this. But God has made of us social beings. We find our true identity as we relate to others, and faith itself is more easily maintained in a creative community of believers. Later, Paul was to extend sublimely the concept of Christian community. He visualized us as being part of each other's inheritance and wrote of the 'wealth and glory of the share he offers you among his people in their heritage'. Note the description, 'wealth and glory!' A devalued 'share' can always be nurtured and enhanced to the glory of the fellowship, and the greater glory of God.

Help us to build each other up,
Our little stock improve;
Increase our faith, confirm our hope,
And perfect us in love.

(*Charles Wesley*)

→982

ACTS 5: 12–16

'The apostles performed many miraculous signs and wonders among the people. And all the believers used to meet together in Solomon's Colonnade (v. 12).

THE UNFORTUNATE episode in the early verses of this chapter does not preclude a continuing atmosphere of the miraculous. The believers met in a public section of the temple where all could see them, obviously obeying God rather than men. Verses 13 and 14 appear to contradict each other and we are left to make conjecture as to their meaning. Possibly many believed in the Lord but few were prepared to join in a public leadership role. (And we think that is a modern problem!)

One thing is certain, however. The Spirit-filled and directed apostles were having an enormous impact on Jerusalem. Their influence was such that people laid their sick in the streets where Peter was expected to pass, so that his shadow might fall on them. Something similar had happened at one stage in the gospel account of Jesus' ministry. Peter would have been the first to say that healing virtue was not inherent in him, and certainly none in his shadow! It was the power of the risen Christ conveyed by the the Holy Spirit indwelling Peter who performed the miracles and healed the sick. But Peter was the conduit through whom the healing influence flowed.

God is still looking for people through whom he can work. Education, prestige or talents, are not factors. A personal encounter with Christ and willingness to be a channel of his power are what makes the difference.

> *In thy steps I will follow, come joy or come sorrow,*
> *Dear Saviour, I will follow thee.*

> (*Herbert Howard Booth*)

→985

3'Leave your country and your people,' God said, 'and go to the land I will show you.'[a]

4''So he left the land of the Chaldeans and settled in Haran. After the death of his father, God sent him to this land where you are now living. 5He gave him no inheritance here, not even a foot of ground. But God promised him that he and his descendants after him would possess the land, even though at that time Abraham had no child. 6God spoke to him in this way: 'Your descendants will be strangers in a country not their own, and they will be enslaved and ill-treated for four hundred years. 7But I will punish the nation they serve as slaves,' God said, 'and afterwards they will come out of that country and worship me in this place.'[b] 8Then he gave Abraham the covenant of circumcision. And Abraham became the father of Isaac and circumcised him eight days after his birth. Later Isaac became the father of Jacob, and Jacob became the father of the twelve patriarchs.

9''Because the patriarchs were jealous of Joseph, they sold him as a slave into Egypt. But God was with him 10and rescued him from all his troubles. He gave Joseph wisdom and enabled him to gain the goodwill of Pharaoh king of Egypt; so he made him ruler over Egypt and all his palace.

11''Then a famine struck all Egypt and Canaan, bringing great suffering, and our fathers could not find food. 12When Jacob heard that there was grain in Egypt, he sent our fathers on their first visit. 13On their second visit, Joseph told his brothers who he was, and Pharaoh learned about Joseph's family. 14After this, Joseph sent for his father Jacob and his whole family, seventy-five in all. 15Then Jacob went down to Egypt, where he and our fathers died. 16Their bodies were brought back to Shechem and placed in the tomb that Abraham had bought from the sons of Hamor at Shechem for a certain sum of money.

17''As the time drew near for God to fulfil his promise to Abraham, the number of our people in Egypt greatly increased. 18Then another king, who knew nothing about Joseph, became ruler of Egypt. 19He dealt treacherously with our people and oppressed our forefathers by forcing them to throw out their newborn babies so that they would die.

20''At that time Moses was born, and he was no ordinary child.[c] For three months he was cared for in his father's house. 21When he was placed outside, Pharaoh's daughter took him and brought him up as her own son. 22Moses was educated in all the wisdom of the Egyptians and was powerful in speech and action.

23''When Moses was forty years old, he decided to visit his fellow Israelites. 24He saw one of them being ill-treated by an Egyptian, so he went to his defence and avenged him by killing the Egyptian. 25Moses thought that his own people would realise that God

was using him to rescue them, but they did not. 26The next day Moses came upon two Israelites who were fighting. He tried to reconcile them by saying, 'Men, you are brothers; why do you want to hurt each other?'

27''But the man who was ill-treating the other pushed Moses aside and said, 'Who made you ruler and judge over us? 28Do you want to kill me as you killed the Egyptian yesterday?'[d] 29When Moses heard this, he fled to Midian, where he settled as a foreigner and had two sons.

30''After forty years had passed, an angel appeared to Moses in the flames of a burning bush in the desert near Mount Sinai. 31When he saw this, he was amazed at the sight. As he went over to look more closely, he heard the Lord's voice: 32'I am the God of your fathers, the God of Abraham, Isaac and Jacob.'[e] Moses trembled with fear and did not dare to look.

33''Then the Lord said to him, 'Take off your sandals; the place where you are standing is holy ground. 34I have indeed seen the oppression of my people in Egypt. I have heard their groaning and have come down to set them free. Now come, I will send you back to Egypt.'[f]

35''This is the same Moses whom they had rejected with the words, 'Who made you ruler and judge?' He was sent to be their ruler and deliverer by God himself, through the angel who appeared to him in the bush. 36He led them out of Egypt and did wonders and miraculous signs in Egypt, at the Red Sea[g] and for forty years in the desert.

37''This is that Moses who told the Israelites, 'God will send you a prophet like me from your own people.'[h] 38He was in the assembly in the desert, with the angel who spoke to him on Mount Sinai, and with our fathers; and he received living words to pass on to us.

39''But our fathers refused to obey him. Instead, they rejected him and in their hearts turned back to Egypt. 40They told Aaron, 'Make us gods who will go before us. As for this fellow Moses who led us out of Egypt —we don't know what has happened to him!'[i] 41That was the time they made an idol in the form of a calf. They brought sacrifices to it and held a celebration in honour of what their hands had made. 42But God turned away and gave them over to the worship of the heavenly bodies. This agrees with what is written in the book of the prophets:

'' 'Did you bring me sacrifices and
      offerings
      for forty years in the desert, O house of
      Israel?
43You have lifted up the shrine of Molech
      and the star of your god Rephan,
      the idols you made to worship.
Therefore I will send you into exile'[j]
      beyond Babylon.

*a*3 Gen. 12:1   *b*7 Gen. 15:13,14   *c*20 Or *was fair in the sight of God*   *d*28 Exodus 2:14
*e*32 Exodus 3:6   *f*34 Exodus 3:5,7,8,10   *g*36 That is, Sea of Reeds   *h*37 Deut. 18:15
*i*40 Exodus 32:1   *j*43 Amos 5:25–27

44"Our forefathers had the tabernacle of the Testimony with them in the desert. It had been made as God directed Moses, according to the pattern he had seen. 45Having received the tabernacle, our fathers under Joshua brought it with them when they took the land from the nations God drove out before them. It remained in the land until the time of David, 46who enjoyed God's favour and asked that he might provide a dwelling-place for the God of Jacob.*k* 47But it was Solomon who built the house for him.

48"However, the Most High does not live in houses made by men. As the prophet says:

49"'Heaven is my throne,
    and the earth is my footstool.
What kind of house will you build for me?
                        says the Lord.
    Or where will my resting place be?
50Has not my hand made all these things?'*l*

51"You stiff-necked people, with uncircumcised hearts and ears! You are just like your fathers: You always resist the Holy Spirit! 52Was there ever a prophet your fathers did not persecute? They even killed those who predicted the coming of the Righteous One. And now you have betrayed and murdered him—53you who have received the law that was put into effect through angels but have not obeyed it."

The Stoning of Stephen

54When they heard this, they were furious and gnashed their teeth at him. 55But Stephen, full of the Holy Spirit, looked up to heaven and saw the glory of God, and Jesus standing at the right hand of God. 56"Look," he said, "I see heaven open and the Son of Man standing at the right hand of God."

57At this they covered their ears and, yelling at the top of their voices, they all rushed at him, 58dragged him out of the city and began to stone him. Meanwhile, the witnesses laid their clothes at the feet of a young man named Saul.

59While they were stoning him, Stephen prayed, "Lord Jesus, receive my spirit." 60Then he fell on his knees and cried out, "Lord, do not hold this sin against them." When he had said this, he fell asleep.

8 And Saul was there, giving approval to his death.

The Church Persecuted and Scattered

On that day a great persecution broke out against the church at Jerusalem, and all except the apostles were scattered throughout Judea and Samaria. 2Godly men buried Stephen and mourned deeply for him. 3But Saul began to destroy the church. Going from house to house, he dragged off men and women and put them in prison.

Philip in Samaria

4Those who had been scattered preached the word wherever they went. 5Philip went down to a city in Samaria and proclaimed the Christ*a* there. 6When the crowds heard Philip and saw the miraculous signs he did, they all paid close attention to what he said. 7With shrieks, evil*b* spirits came out of many, and many paralytics and cripples were healed. 8So there was great joy in that city.

Simon the Sorcerer

9Now for some time a man named Simon had practised sorcery in the city and amazed all the people of Samaria. He boasted that he was someone great, 10and all the people, both high and low, gave him their attention and exclaimed, "This man is the divine power known as the Great Power." 11They followed him because he had amazed them for a long time with his magic. 12But when they believed Philip as he preached the good news of the kingdom of God and the name of Jesus Christ, they were baptised, both men and women. 13Simon himself believed and was baptised. And he followed Philip everywhere, astonished by the great signs and miracles he saw.

14When the apostles in Jerusalem heard that Samaria had accepted the word of God, they sent Peter and John to them. 15When they arrived, they prayed for them that they might receive the Holy Spirit, 16because the Holy Spirit had not yet come upon any of them; they had simply been baptised into*c* the name of the Lord Jesus. 17Then Peter and John placed their hands on them, and they received the Holy Spirit.

18When Simon saw that the Spirit was given at the laying on of the apostles' hands, he offered them money 19and said, "Give me also this ability so that everyone on whom I lay my hands may receive the Holy Spirit."

20Peter answered: "May your money perish with you, because you thought you could buy the gift of God with money! 21You have no part or share in this ministry, because your heart is not right before God. 22Repent of this wickedness and pray to the Lord. Perhaps he will forgive you for having such a thought in your heart. 23For I see that you are full of bitterness and captive to sin."

24Then Simon answered, "Pray to the Lord for me so that nothing you have said may happen to me."

25When they had testified and proclaimed the word of the Lord, Peter and John returned to Jerusalem, preaching the gospel in many Samaritan villages.

Philip and the Ethiopian

26Now an angel of the Lord said to Philip, "Go south to the road—the desert road—that goes down from Jerusalem to Gaza." 27So he started out, and on his way he met an Ethiopian*d* eunuch, an important official in charge of all the treasury of Candace, queen of the Ethiopians. This man had gone to Jerusalem to worship, 28and on his way home was sitting in his chariot reading the book of

k46 Some early manuscripts *the house of Jacob*   *l50* Isaiah 66:1,2   *a5* Or *Messiah*   *b7* Greek *unclean*
c16 Or *in*   *d27* That is, from the upper Nile region

ACTS 7:17–34

'Moses thought that his own people would recognise that God was using him to rescue them' (v. 25).

MISSION MISUNDERSTOOD. Luke's artistry – or is it Stephen's? – is shown here. The basis of the accusation against Stephen is a misunderstanding of his intention. His approach indicates he realized they would not understand. Stephen does not dwell on the Law and its requirements, but speaks of his own personal experience, which he illustrates by reference to Moses, and feeling the full force of misunderstanding, throws it back at his accusers.

They should have understood. There is no excuse for them not to understand. Their prophets had already said (e.g. Isa 49:6), Gentiles would be brought into the community of God's own people. Stephen's intention was not to destroy the Hebrew community, but to widen it to embrace the whole world. In the mission and sacrifice of Jesus a new world of deliverance was opening up to those crying out for Stephen's blood. But they could not see it.

We marvel at Stephen's ability to say, like his master, when being slain by the mob, 'Lord, do not hold this sin against them' (v. 60), but his whole speech shows he was prepared for what was going to happen. He had counted the cost of his actions. His destruction was no passive surrender. He went down fighting and his final words were shouted. His mission was based on the example of Moses, as well as Jesus.

In Stephen we see progressive Christianity at its very highest.

→986

ACTS 8:4–13
'Those who had been scattered preached the word wherever they went' (v. 4).

RESISTANCE OR RETREAT? A small boy came home rather bedraggled. 'What have you been doing?' asked mother. 'Fighting,' came the obvious reply. 'Who won?' said Mum. 'O, I did – I ran away and hid!'

It is hard to get the right balance between preaching and serving (Acts 6:2). It is just as hard to get the right balance between resistance and retreat. Stephen was effective in standing his ground. His resistance influenced Saul, yet Saul himself later appears to have been criticized for too easily running away.

Acts 17:10 describes his flight from Thessalonica. 1 Thessalonians 2:1, 2 could be construed as Saul's defence of his actions when writing to those who knew that on one occasion at least he had regarded discretion as the better part of valour. 1 Corinthians 9:19–23, where Paul tells us that he became all things to all men, makes the same point about the need for a flexible approach.

Philip fled and lived to fight another day. How strange that his flight led to Samaria, the heart of enemy country. For a Jew, it was like going from the frying-pan into the fire! But as often in the story of the spread of the gospel, apparent defeat turned into victory.

What seemed to be stony ground, turned out to be fruitful soil.

→989

Isaiah the prophet. 29The Spirit told Philip, "Go to that chariot and stay near it."

30Then Philip ran up to the chariot and heard the man reading Isaiah the prophet. "Do you understand what you are reading?" Philip asked.

31"How can I," he said, "unless someone explains it to me?" So he invited Philip to come up and sit with him.

32The eunuch was reading this passage of Scripture:

"He was led like a sheep to the slaughter,
and as a lamb before the shearer is
silent,
so he did not open his mouth.
33In his humiliation he was deprived of
justice.
Who can speak of his descendants?
For his life was taken from the earth."*e*

34The eunuch asked Philip, "Tell me, please, who is the prophet talking about, himself or someone else?" 35Then Philip began with that very passage of Scripture and told him the good news about Jesus.

36As they travelled along the road, they came to some water and the eunuch said, "Look, here is water. Why shouldn't I be baptised?"*f* 38And he gave orders to stop the chariot. Then both Philip and the eunuch went down into the water and Philip baptised him. 39When they came up out of the water, the Spirit of the Lord suddenly took Philip away, and the eunuch did not see him again, but went on his way rejoicing. 40Philip, however, appeared at Azotus and travelled about, preaching the gospel in all the towns until he reached Caesarea.

Saul's Conversion

9 Meanwhile, Saul was still breathing out murderous threats against the Lord's disciples. He went to the high priest 2and asked him for letters to the synagogues in Damascus, so that if he found any there who belonged to the Way, whether men or women, he might take them as prisoners to Jerusalem. 3As he neared Damascus on his journey, suddenly a light from heaven flashed around him. 4He fell to the ground and heard a voice say to him, "Saul, Saul, why do you persecute me?"

5"Who are you, Lord?" Saul asked.

"I am Jesus, whom you are persecuting," he replied. 6"Now get up and go into the city, and you will be told what you must do."

7The men travelling with Saul stood there speechless; they heard the sound but did not see anyone. 8Saul got up from the ground, but when he opened his eyes he could see nothing. So they led him by the hand into Damascus. 9For three days he was blind, and did not eat or drink anything.

10In Damascus there was a disciple named Ananias. The Lord called to him in a vision, "Ananias!"

"Yes, Lord," he answered.

11The Lord told him, "Go to the house of Judas on Straight Street and ask for a man from Tarsus named Saul, for he is praying. 12In a vision he has seen a man named Ananias come and place his hands on him to restore his sight."

13"Lord," Ananias answered, "I have heard many reports about this man and all the harm he has done to your saints in Jerusalem. 14And he has come here with authority from the chief priests to arrest all who call on your name."

15But the Lord said to Ananias, "Go! This man is my chosen instrument to carry my name before the Gentiles and their kings and before the people of Israel. 16I will show him how much he must suffer for my name."

17Then Ananias went to the house and entered it. Placing his hands on Saul, he said, "Brother Saul, the Lord—Jesus, who appeared to you on the road as you were coming here—has sent me so that you may see again and be filled with the Holy Spirit." 18Immediately, something like scales fell from Saul's eyes, and he could see again. He got up and was baptised, 19and after taking some food, he regained his strength.

Saul in Damascus and Jerusalem

Saul spent several days with the disciples in Damascus. 20At once he began to preach in the synagogues that Jesus is the Son of God. 21All those who heard him were astonished and asked, "Isn't he the man who caused havoc in Jerusalem among those who call on this name? And hasn't he come here to take them as prisoners to the chief priests?" 22Yet Saul grew more and more powerful and baffled the Jews living in Damascus by proving that Jesus is the Christ.*a*

23After many days had gone by, the Jews conspired to kill him, 24but Saul learned of their plan. Day and night they kept close watch on the city gates in order to kill him. 25But his followers took him by night and lowered him in a basket through an opening in the wall.

26When he came to Jerusalem, he tried to join the disciples, but they were all afraid of him, not believing that he really was a disciple. 27But Barnabas took him and brought him to the apostles. He told them how Saul on his journey had seen the Lord and that the Lord had spoken to him, and how in Damascus he had preached fearlessly in the name of Jesus. 28So Saul stayed with them and moved about freely in Jerusalem, speaking boldly in the name of the Lord. 29He talked and debated with the Grecian Jews, but they tried to kill him. 30When the brothers learned of this, they took him down to Caesarea and sent him off to Tarsus.

31Then the church throughout Judea, Galilee and Samaria enjoyed a time of peace. It was strengthened; and encouraged by the

e33 Isaiah 53:7,8   f36 Some late manuscripts baptised?" 37Philip said, "If you believe with all your heart, you may." The eunuch answered, "I believe that Jesus Christ is the Son of God."   a22 Or Messiah

Holy Spirit, it grew in numbers, living in the fear of the Lord.

Aeneas and Dorcas

³²As Peter travelled about the country, he went to visit the saints in Lydda. ³³There he found a man named Aeneas, a paralytic who had been bedridden for eight years. ³⁴"Aeneas," Peter said to him, "Jesus Christ heals you. Get up and tidy up your mat." Immediately Aeneas got up. ³⁵All those who lived in Lydda and Sharon saw him and turned to the Lord.

³⁶In Joppa there was a disciple named Tabitha (which, when translated, is Dorcas[b]), who was always doing good and helping the poor. ³⁷About that time she became sick and died, and her body was washed and placed in an upstairs room. ³⁸Lydda was near Joppa; so when the disciples heard that Peter was in Lydda, they sent two men to him and urged him, "Please come at once!"

³⁹Peter went with them, and when he arrived he was taken upstairs to the room. All the widows stood around him, crying and showing him the robes and other clothing that Dorcas had made while she was still with them.

⁴⁰Peter sent them all out of the room; then he got down on his knees and prayed. Turning towards the dead woman, he said, "Tabitha, get up." She opened her eyes, and seeing Peter she sat up. ⁴¹He took her by the hand and helped her to her feet. Then he called the believers and the widows and presented her to them alive. ⁴²This became known all over Joppa, and many people believed in the Lord. ⁴³Peter stayed in Joppa for some time with a tanner named Simon.

Cornelius Calls for Peter

10 At Caesarea there was a man named Cornelius, a centurion in what was known as the Italian Regiment. ²He and all his family were devout and God-fearing; he gave generously to those in need and prayed to God regularly. ³One day at about three in the afternoon he had a vision. He distinctly saw an angel of God, who came to him and said, "Cornelius!"

⁴Cornelius stared at him in fear. "What is it, Lord?" he asked.

The angel answered, "Your prayers and gifts to the poor have come up as a memorial offering before God. ⁵Now send men to Joppa to bring back a man named Simon who is called Peter. ⁶He is staying with Simon the tanner, whose house is by the sea."

⁷When the angel who spoke to him had gone, Cornelius called two of his servants and a devout soldier who was one of his attendants. ⁸He told them everything that had happened and sent them to Joppa.

Peter's Vision

⁹About noon the following day as they were on their journey and approaching the city, Peter went up on the roof to pray. ¹⁰He became hungry and wanted something to eat, and while the meal was being prepared, he fell into a trance. ¹¹He saw heaven opened and something like a large sheet being let down to earth by its four corners. ¹²It contained all kinds of four-footed animals, as well as reptiles of the earth and birds of the air. ¹³Then a voice told him, "Get up, Peter. Kill and eat."

¹⁴"Surely not, Lord!" Peter replied. "I have never eaten anything impure or unclean."

¹⁵The voice spoke to him a second time, "Do not call anything impure that God has made clean."

¹⁶This happened three times, and immediately the sheet was taken back to heaven.

¹⁷While Peter was wondering about the meaning of the vision, the men sent by Cornelius found out where Simon's house was and stopped at the gate. ¹⁸They called out, asking if Simon who was known as Peter was staying there.

¹⁹While Peter was still thinking about the vision, the Spirit said to him, "Simon, three[a] men are looking for you. ²⁰So get up and go downstairs. Do not hesitate to go with them, for I have sent them."

²¹Peter went down and said to the men, "I'm the one you're looking for. Why have you come?"

²²The men replied, "We have come from Cornelius the centurion. He is a righteous and God-fearing man, who is respected by all the Jewish people. A holy angel told him to have you come to his house so that he could hear what you have to say." ²³Then Peter invited the men into the house to be his guests.

Peter at Cornelius' House

The next day Peter started out with them, and some of the brothers from Joppa went along. ²⁴The following day he arrived in Caesarea. Cornelius was expecting them and had called together his relatives and close friends. ²⁵As Peter entered the house, Cornelius met him and fell at his feet in reverence. ²⁶But Peter made him get up. "Stand up," he said, "I am only a man myself."

²⁷Talking with him, Peter went inside and found a large gathering of people. ²⁸He said to them: "You are well aware that it is against our law for a Jew to associate with a Gentile or visit him. But God has shown me that I should not call any man impure or unclean. ²⁹So when I was sent for, I came without raising any objection. May I ask why you sent for me?"

³⁰Cornelius answered: "Four days ago I was in my house praying at this hour, at three in the afternoon. Suddenly a man in shining clothes stood before me ³¹and said, 'Cornelius, God has heard your prayer and remembered your gifts to the poor. ³²Send to Joppa for Simon who is called Peter. He is a guest in the home of Simon the tanner, who lives by

---

b36 Both *Tabitha* (Aramaic) and *Dorcas* (Greek) mean *gazelle*.
a19 One early manuscript *two*; other manuscripts do not have the number.

ACTS 10:23b–35
'Then Peter began to speak: "I now realise how true it is that God does not show favouritism but accepts men from every nation who fear him and do what is right" ' (vv. 34.35).

PETER HAD rightly interpreted his vision. Anything, or anyone that God had made was neither impure nor unclean. Peter's reference to the law forbidding Jews to associate with Gentiles was possibly meant more for the Jewish Christians who accompanied him than for Cornelius. Although bold new thoughts and actions were becoming the norm. the breaking down of this barrier would need explanation and defence. Peter had been wise to take witnesses along with him.

Cornelius was unaware of the great significance of his vision until the divine strategy became apparent. He simply shared it with Peter and the others as an explanation of his action in sending for Peter. Now that they were together, no doubt marvelling at this remarkable intervention in their affairs by God, Cornelius, with the perception of the devout, knew that they were in the presence of God and should listen to all that God had in mind for them.

Did Cornelius' mature statement of the presence of God remind Peter of our Lord's words, 'Where two or three come together in my name, there am I with them'? Although the whole of life is lived in the presence of God. there is a special sense in which the Lord is present when we are together, because, even as the smallest group, we take on the characteristics of his Church.

> *Jesus. we look to thee.*
> *Thy promised presence claim:*
> *Thou in the midst of us shalt be.*
> *Assembled in thy name.*

(*Charles Wesley*)

→990

ACTS 12:1–5

'It was about this time that King Herod arrested some who belonged to the church, intending to persecute them' (v. 1).

THE SAFETY provided by the gospel is not of a physical order. While illustrations can be produced to show the protection of God, the facts of history show that privation, suffering and even death have to be endured by some. Jesus warned us all, 'No servant is greater than his master. If they persecuted me, they will persecute you also.' The apostle James, brother of John, was among those arrested, and became the first of the apostolic group to die for his faith. By his death James fulfilled our Lord's prophecy concerning him. Having given satisfaction to the Jews by this action, Herod moved to take Peter prisoner with a view to a show trial later.

The prisoner, Peter, was the subject of much earnest prayer by the Church, but presumably, James, the martyr, had been also the subject of much earnest prayer by the same people in the same fellowship. Quite why Peter was spared and James was not is one of the mysteries of prayer and faith. We all know the problem. We pray with equal faith for two people: one is spared and the other is not. One goes into remission, or is healed, while with the other the illness runs its course.

There is no easy answer to this searching, and sometimes painful, problem. Perhaps this is where faith surrenders to a mystery beyond our capacity to understand and trusts in the proven love of God. His love, in sad times or joyful times, continues to hold us and grant us peace.

> *O Lord, how great this mystery,*
> *Beyond our power to understand:*
> *But this we know, in life or death*
> *Our times are firmly in thy hand.*

→993

the sea.' ³³So I sent for you immediately, and it was good of you to come. Now we are all here in the presence of God to listen to everything the Lord has commanded you to tell us.''

³⁴Then Peter began to speak: ''I now realise how true it is that God does not show favouritism ³⁵but accepts men from every nation who fear him and do what is right. ³⁶You know the message God sent to the people of Israel, telling the good news of peace through Jesus Christ, who is Lord of all. ³⁷You know what has happened throughout Judea, beginning in Galilee after the baptism that John preached—³⁸how God anointed Jesus of Nazareth with the Holy Spirit and power, and how he went around doing good and healing all who were under the power of the devil, because God was with him.

³⁹''We are witnesses of everything he did in the country of the Jews and in Jerusalem. They killed him by hanging him on a tree, ⁴⁰but God raised him from the dead on the third day and caused him to be seen. ⁴¹He was not seen by all the people, but by witnesses whom God had already chosen—by us who ate and drank with him after he rose from the dead. ⁴²He commanded us to preach to the people and to testify that he is the one whom God appointed as judge of the living and the dead. ⁴³All the prophets testify about him that everyone who believes in him receives forgiveness of sins through his name.''

⁴⁴While Peter was still speaking these words, the Holy Spirit came on all who heard the message. ⁴⁵The circumcised believers who had come with Peter were astonished that the gift of the Holy Spirit had been poured out even on the Gentiles. ⁴⁶For they heard them speaking in tongues^b and praising God.

Then Peter said, ⁴⁷''Can anyone keep these people from being baptised with water? They have received the Holy Spirit just as we have.'' ⁴⁸So he ordered that they be baptised in the name of Jesus Christ. Then they asked Peter to stay with them for a few days.

Peter Explains His Actions

11 The apostles and the brothers throughout Judea heard that the Gentiles also had received the word of God. ²So when Peter went up to Jerusalem, the circumcised believers criticised him ³and said, ''You went into the house of uncircumcised men and ate with them.''

⁴Peter began and explained everything to them precisely as it had happened: ⁵''I was in the city of Joppa praying, and in a trance I saw a vision. I saw something like a large sheet being let down from heaven by its four corners, and it came down to where I was. ⁶I looked into it and saw four-footed animals of the earth, wild beasts, reptiles, and birds of the air. ⁷Then I heard a voice telling me, 'Get up, Peter. Kill and eat.'

⁸''I replied, 'Surely not, Lord! Nothing impure or unclean has ever entered my mouth.'

⁹''The voice spoke from heaven a second time, 'Do not call anything impure that God has made clean.' ¹⁰This happened three times, and then it was pulled up to heaven again.

¹¹''Right then three men who had been sent to me from Caesarea stopped at the house where I was staying. ¹²The Spirit told me to have no hesitation about going with them. These six brothers also went with me, and we entered the man's house. ¹³He told us how he had seen an angel appear in his house and say, 'Send to Joppa for Simon who is called Peter. ¹⁴He will bring you a message through which you and all your household will be saved.'

¹⁵''As I began to speak, the Holy Spirit came on them as he had come on us at the beginning. ¹⁶Then I remembered what the Lord had said: 'John baptised with^a water, but you will be baptised with the Holy Spirit.' ¹⁷So if God gave them the same gift as he gave us, who believed in the Lord Jesus Christ, who was I to think that I could oppose God?''

¹⁸When they heard this, they had no further objections and praised God, saying, ''So then, God has granted even the Gentiles repentance unto life.''

The Church in Antioch

¹⁹Now those who had been scattered by the persecution in connection with Stephen travelled as far as Phoenicia, Cyprus and Antioch, telling the message only to Jews. ²⁰Some of them, however, men from Cyprus and Cyrene, went to Antioch and began to speak to Greeks also, telling them the good news about the Lord Jesus. ²¹The Lord's hand was with them, and a great number of people believed and turned to the Lord.

²²News of this reached the ears of the church at Jerusalem, and they sent Barnabas to Antioch. ²³When he arrived and saw the evidence of the grace of God, he was glad and encouraged them all to remain true to the Lord with all their hearts. ²⁴He was a good man, full of the Holy Spirit and faith, and a great number of people were brought to the Lord.

²⁵Then Barnabas went to Tarsus to look for Saul, ²⁶and when he found him, he brought him to Antioch. So for a whole year Barnabas and Saul met with the church and taught great numbers of people. The disciples were called Christians first at Antioch.

²⁷During this time some prophets came down from Jerusalem to Antioch. ²⁸One of them, named Agabus, stood up and through the Spirit predicted that a severe famine would spread over the entire Roman world. (This happened during the reign of Claudius.) ²⁹The disciples, each according to his ability, decided to provide help for the brothers living in Judea. ³⁰This they did, sending their gift to the elders by Barnabas and Saul.

^b46 Or *other languages*   ^a16 Or *in*

Peter's Miraculous Escape From Prison

12 It was about this time that King Herod arrested some who belonged to the church, intending to persecute them. [2]He had James, the brother of John, put to death with the sword. [3]When he saw that this pleased the Jews, he proceeded to seize Peter also. This happened during the Feast of Unleavened Bread. [4]After arresting him, he put him in prison, handing him over to be guarded by four squads of four soldiers each. Herod intended to bring him out for public trial after the Passover.

[5]So Peter was kept in prison, but the church was earnestly praying to God for him.

[6]The night before Herod was to bring him to trial, Peter was sleeping between two soldiers, bound with two chains, and sentries stood guard at the entrance. [7]Suddenly an angel of the Lord appeared and a light shone in the cell. He struck Peter on the side and woke him up. "Quick, get up!" he said, and the chains fell off Peter's wrists.

[8]Then the angel said to him, "Put on your clothes and sandals." And Peter did so. "Wrap your cloak around you and follow me," the angel told him. [9]Peter followed him out of the prison, but he had no idea that what the angel was doing was really happening; he thought he was seeing a vision. [10]They passed the first and second guards and came to the iron gate leading to the city. It opened for them by itself, and they went through it. When they had walked the length of one street, suddenly the angel left him.

[11]Then Peter came to himself and said, "Now I know without a doubt that the Lord sent his angel and rescued me from Herod's clutches and from everything the Jewish people were anticipating."

[12]When this had dawned on him, he went to the house of Mary the mother of John, also called Mark, where many people had gathered and were praying. [13]Peter knocked at the outer entrance, and a servant girl named Rhoda came to answer the door. [14]When she recognised Peter's voice, she was so overjoyed she ran back without opening it and exclaimed, "Peter is at the door!"

[15]"You're out of your mind," they told her. When she kept insisting that it was so, they said, "It must be his angel."

[16]But Peter kept on knocking, and when they opened the door and saw him, they were astonished. [17]Peter motioned with his hand for them to be quiet and described how the Lord had brought him out of prison. "Tell James and the brothers about this," he said, and then he left for another place.

[18]In the morning, there was no small commotion among the soldiers as to what had become of Peter. [19]After Herod had a thorough search made for him and did not find him, he cross-examined the guards and ordered that they be executed.

Herod's Death

Then Herod went from Judea to Caesarea and stayed there a while. [20]He had been quarrelling with the people of Tyre and Sidon; they now joined together and sought an audience with him. Having secured the support of Blastus, a trusted personal servant of the king, they asked for peace, because they depended on the king's country for their food supply.

[21]On the appointed day Herod, wearing his royal robes, sat on his throne and delivered a public address to the people. [22]They shouted, "This is the voice of a god, not of a man." [23]Immediately, because Herod did not give praise to God, an angel of the Lord struck him down, and he was eaten by worms and died.

[24]But the word of God continued to increase and spread.

[25]When Barnabas and Saul had finished their mission, they returned from[a] Jerusalem, taking with them John, also called Mark.

Barnabas and Saul Sent Off

13 In the church at Antioch there were prophets and teachers: Barnabas, Simeon called Niger, Lucius of Cyrene, Manaen (who had been brought up with Herod the tetrarch) and Saul. [2]While they were worshipping the Lord and fasting, the Holy Spirit said, "Set apart for me Barnabas and Saul for the work to which I have called them." [3]So after they had fasted and prayed, they placed their hands on them and sent them off.

On Cyprus

[4]The two of them, sent on their way by the Holy Spirit, went down to Seleucia and sailed from there to Cyprus. [5]When they arrived at Salamis, they proclaimed the word of God in the Jewish synagogues. John was with them as their helper.

[6]They travelled through the whole island until they came to Paphos. There they met a Jewish sorcerer and false prophet named Bar-Jesus, [7]who was an attendant of the proconsul, Sergius Paulus. The proconsul, an intelligent man, sent for Barnabas and Saul because he wanted to hear the word of God. [8]But Elymas the sorcerer (for that is what his name means) opposed them and tried to turn the proconsul from the faith. [9]Then Saul, who was also called Paul, filled with the Holy Spirit, looked straight at Elymas and said, [10]"You are a child of the devil and an enemy of everything that is right! You are full of all kinds of deceit and trickery. Will you never stop perverting the right ways of the Lord? [11]Now the hand of the Lord is against you. You are going to be blind, and for a time you will be unable to see the light of the sun."

Immediately mist and darkness came over him, and he groped about, seeking someone to lead him by the hand. [12]When the proconsul saw what had happened, he believed, for he was amazed at the teaching about the Lord.

a25 Some manuscripts to

ACTS 13:1–3
'While they were worshipping the Lord and fasting, the Holy Spirit said, "Set apart for me Barnabas and Saul for the work to which I have called them" ' (v. 2).

A STRATEGY for growth in the early Church was emerging. Previously, growth had been due to unique events, or persecution, but now the Church was moving to a deliberate policy of church planting. Luke does not make it clear that the entire Church was involved, but since previous decisions had been made by the entire Church, and on Barnabas's and Paul's return the whole Church came together for a report, we assume that the full company was present. We further assume that those named were the members most eligible for special service.

Under given circumstances it is possible for a group to determine the will of God. The premise is not without danger, but if God's people are deeply concerned about his work, and under mature leadership seek his will, there is no reason why the divine guidance should not be given and received. Especially if they are earnest and patient enough to surrender their need of food.

It will be noticed that the Holy Spirit asked for, and received, the best the Church had to offer. Barnabas, a long-established disciple, was a man of rich spiritual and social skills, while Saul, also called Paul, had already proved his abilities as prophet and teacher. With such openness and obedience, the company waiting on God could hardly fail to make the right decision.

> *Be it ours, then, while we're here,*
> *Him to follow without fear,*
> *Where he calls us, there to go,*
> *What he bids us, that to do.*

(Thomas Kelly)

→994

ACTS 15:5–12

'Now then, why do you try to test God by putting on the necks of the disciples a yoke that neither we nor our fathers have been able to bear?' (v. 10).

APPROPRIATELY, though probably not deliberately, this summary of the Council in Jerusalem takes the central place in the Acts of the Apostles. Without doubt, it was one of the most significant events of the early Church. Had it not taken place, the new faith would have foundered. Since the Law of Moses had not been cancelled, believers who had been Pharisees held that the Law must be kept. Equally clearly, Simon Peter, who had led Cornelius and his household to faith, believed that the old conditions of membership of the people of God had been superseded, not by human objections, or by default, but by the Holy Spirit himself. Peter, therefore, presented the case for the Gentiles powerfully. In five short verses, he widened the door through which millions of people would pass into the kingdom, further exercising the keys of the kingdom given him by Christ.

As far as the party of the Pharisees was concerned, Paul may well have been a more persuasive advocate for freedom from the Jewish Law than Peter. Himself a Pharisee, dramatically converted to the faith, Paul, with Barnabas, told of the mighty deeds done by Christ, of the gift of the Holy Spirit without any condition other than faith in the Lord Christ. On the very practical grounds of experience the case was made that Christians should not be subjected to the Law, the yoke of which was as ineffective as it was burdensome.

> E'en now by faith I claim him mine,
> The risen Son of God;
> Redemption by his death I find,
> And cleansing through the blood.

(*Martha M. Stockton*)

→999

In Pisidian Antioch

[13]From Paphos, Paul and his companions sailed to Perga in Pamphylia, where John left them to return to Jerusalem. [14]From Perga they went on to Pisidian Antioch. On the Sabbath they entered the synagogue and sat down. [15]After the reading from the Law and the Prophets, the synagogue rulers sent word to them, saying, "Brothers, if you have a message of encouragement for the people, please speak."

[16]Standing up, Paul motioned with his hand and said: "Men of Israel and you Gentiles who worship God, listen to me! [17]The God of the people of Israel chose our fathers; he made the people prosper during their stay in Egypt, with mighty power he led them out of that country, [18]he endured their conduct[a] for about forty years in the desert, [19]he overthrew seven nations in Canaan and gave their land to his people as their inheritance. [20]All this took about 450 years.

"After this, God gave them judges until the time of Samuel the prophet. [21]Then the people asked for a king, and he gave them Saul son of Kish, of the tribe of Benjamin, who ruled for forty years. [22]After removing Saul, he made David their king. He testified concerning him: 'I have found David son of Jesse a man after my own heart; he will do everything I want him to do.'

[23]"From this man's descendants God has brought to Israel the Saviour Jesus, as he promised. [24]Before the coming of Jesus, John preached repentance and baptism to all the people of Israel. [25]As John was completing his work, he said: 'Who do you think I am? I am not that one. No, but he is coming after me, whose sandals I am not worthy to untie.'

[26]"Brothers, children of Abraham, and you God-fearing Gentiles, it is to us that this message of salvation has been sent. [27]The people of Jerusalem and their rulers did not recognise Jesus, yet in condemning him they fulfilled the words of the prophets that are read every Sabbath. [28]Though they found no proper ground for a death sentence, they asked Pilate to have him executed. [29]When they had carried out all that was written about him, they took him down from the tree and laid him in a tomb. [30]But God raised him from the dead, [31]and for many days he was seen by those who had travelled with him from Galilee to Jerusalem. They are now his witnesses to our people.

[32]"We tell you the good news: What God promised our fathers [33]he has fulfilled for us, their children, by raising up Jesus. As it is written in the second Psalm:

" 'You are my Son;
    today I have become your Father.'[b, c]

[34]The fact that God raised him from the dead, never to decay, is stated in these words:

" 'I will give you the holy and sure
    blessings promised to David.'[d]

[35]So it is stated elsewhere:

" 'You will not let your Holy One see
    decay.'[e]

[36]"For when David had served God's purpose in his own generation, he fell asleep; he was buried with his fathers and his body decayed. [37]But the one whom God raised from the dead did not see decay.

[38]"Therefore, my brothers, I want you to know that through Jesus the forgiveness of sins is proclaimed to you. [39]Through him everyone who believes is justified from everything you could not be justified from by the law of Moses. [40]Take care that what the prophets have said does not happen to you:

[41]" 'Look, you scoffers,
    wonder and perish,
for I am going to do something in your
    days
    that you would never believe,
    even if someone told you.'[f]"

[42]As Paul and Barnabas were leaving the synagogue, the people invited them to speak further about these things on the next Sabbath. [43]When the congregation was dismissed, many of the Jews and devout converts to Judaism followed Paul and Barnabas, who talked with them and urged them to continue in the grace of God.

[44]On the next Sabbath almost the whole city gathered to hear the word of the Lord. [45]When the Jews saw the crowds, they were filled with jealousy and talked abusively against what Paul was saying.

[46]Then Paul and Barnabas answered them boldly: "We had to speak the word of God to you first. Since you reject it and do not consider yourselves worthy of eternal life, we now turn to the Gentiles. [47]For this is what the Lord has commanded us:

" 'I have made you[g] a light for the
    Gentiles,
    that you[g] may bring salvation to the
    ends of the earth.'[h]"

[48]When the Gentiles heard this, they were glad and honoured the word of the Lord; and all who were appointed for eternal life believed.

[49]The word of the Lord spread through the whole region. [50]But the Jews incited the God-fearing women of high standing and the leading men of the city. They stirred up persecution against Paul and Barnabas, and expelled them from their region. [51]So they shook the dust from their feet in protest against them and went to Iconium. [52]And the disciples were filled with joy and with the Holy Spirit.

In Iconium

14 At Iconium Paul and Barnabas went as usual into the Jewish synagogue. There they spoke so effectively that a great

---

[a]18 Some manuscripts *and cared for them*   [b]33 Or *have begotten you*   [c]33 Psalm 2:7   [d]34 Isaiah 55:3   [e]35 Psalm 16:10   [f]41 Hab. 1:5   [g]47 The Greek is singular.   [h]47 Isaiah 49:6

number of Jews and Gentiles believed. ²But the Jews who refused to believe stirred up the Gentiles and poisoned their minds against the brothers. ³So Paul and Barnabas spent considerable time there, speaking boldly for the Lord, who confirmed the message of his grace by enabling them to do miraculous signs and wonders. ⁴The people of the city were divided; some sided with the Jews, others with the apostles. ⁵There was a plot afoot among the Gentiles and Jews, together with their leaders, to ill-treat them and stone them. ⁶But they found out about it and fled to the Lycaonian cities of Lystra and Derbe and to the surrounding country, ⁷where they continued to preach the good news.

In Lystra and Derbe

⁸In Lystra there sat a man crippled in his feet, who was lame from birth and had never walked. ⁹He listened to Paul as he was speaking. Paul looked directly at him, saw that he had faith to be healed ¹⁰and called out, "Stand up on your feet!" At that, the man jumped up and began to walk.

¹¹When the crowd saw what Paul had done, they shouted in the Lycaonian language, "The gods have come down to us in human form!" ¹²Barnabas they called Zeus, and Paul they called Hermes because he was the chief speaker. ¹³The priest of Zeus, whose temple was just outside the city, brought bulls and wreaths to the city gates because he and the crowd wanted to offer sacrifices to them.

¹⁴But when the apostles Barnabas and Paul heard of this, they tore their clothes and rushed out into the crowd, shouting: ¹⁵"Men, why are you doing this? We too are only men, human like you. We are bringing you good news, telling you to turn from these worthless things to the living God, who made heaven and earth and sea and everything in them. ¹⁶In the past, he let all nations go their own way. ¹⁷Yet he has not left himself without testimony: He has shown kindness by giving you rain from heaven and crops in their seasons; he provides you with plenty of food and fills your hearts with joy." ¹⁸Even with these words, they had difficulty keeping the crowd from sacrificing to them.

¹⁹Then some Jews came from Antioch and Iconium and won the crowd over. They stoned Paul and dragged him outside the city, thinking he was dead. ²⁰But after the disciples had gathered round him, he got up and went back into the city. The next day he and Barnabas left for Derbe.

The Return to Antioch in Syria

²¹They preached the good news in that city and won a large number of disciples. Then they returned to Lystra, Iconium and Antioch, ²²strengthening the disciples and encouraging them to remain true to the faith. "We must go through many hardships to enter the kingdom of God," they said. ²³Paul and Barnabas appointed elders[a] for them in each church and, with prayer and fasting,

committed them to the Lord, in whom they had put their trust. ²⁴After going through Pisidia, they came into Pamphylia, ²⁵and when they had preached the word in Perga, they went down to Attalia.

²⁶From Attalia they sailed back to Antioch, where they had been committed to the grace of God for the work they had now completed. ²⁷On arriving there, they gathered the church together and reported all that God had done through them and how he had opened the door of faith to the Gentiles. ²⁸And they stayed there a long time with the disciples.

The Council at Jerusalem

15 Some men came down from Judea to Antioch and were teaching the brothers: "Unless you are circumcised, according to the custom taught by Moses, you cannot be saved." ²This brought Paul and Barnabas into sharp dispute and debate with them. So Paul and Barnabas were appointed, along with some other believers, to go up to Jerusalem to see the apostles and elders about this question. ³The church sent them on their way, and as they travelled through Phoenicia and Samaria, they told how the Gentiles had been converted. This news made all the brothers very glad. ⁴When they came to Jerusalem, they were welcomed by the church and the apostles and elders, to whom they reported everything God had done through them.

⁵Then some of the believers who belonged to the party of the Pharisees stood up and said, "The Gentiles must be circumcised and required to obey the law of Moses."

⁶The apostles and elders met to consider this question. ⁷After much discussion, Peter got up and addressed them: "Brothers, you know that some time ago God made a choice among you that the Gentiles might hear from my lips the message of the gospel and believe. ⁸God, who knows the heart, showed that he accepted them by giving the Holy Spirit to them, just as he did to us. ⁹He made no distinction between us and them, for he purified their hearts by faith. ¹⁰Now then, why do you try to test God by putting on the necks of the disciples a yoke that neither we nor our fathers have been able to bear? ¹¹No! We believe it is through the grace of our Lord Jesus that we are saved, just as they are."

¹²The whole assembly became silent as they listened to Barnabas and Paul telling about the miraculous signs and wonders God had done among the Gentiles through them. ¹³When they finished, James spoke up: "Brothers, listen to me. ¹⁴Simon[a] has described to us how God at first showed his concern by taking from the Gentiles a people for himself. ¹⁵The words of the prophets are in agreement with this, as it is written:

¹⁶"'After this I will return
    and rebuild David's fallen tent.
   Its ruins I will rebuild,
    and I will restore it,

---

[a]23 Or *Barnabas ordained elders*; or *Barnabas had elders elected*
[a]14 Greek *Simeon*, a variant of *Simon*; that is, Peter

[17]that the remnant of men may seek the
Lord,
and all the Gentiles who bear my name,
says the Lord, who does these things'[b]
[18] that have been known for ages.[c]

[19]"It is my judgment, therefore, that we
should not make it difficult for the Gentiles
who are turning to God. [20]Instead we should
write to them, telling them to abstain from
food polluted by idols, from sexual immorality, from the meat of strangled animals and
from blood. [21]For Moses has been preached
in every city from the earliest times and is
read in the synagogues on every Sabbath."

The Council's Letter to Gentile Believers

[22]Then the apostles and elders, with the
whole church, decided to choose some of
their own men and send them to Antioch with
Paul and Barnabas. They chose Judas (called
Barsabbas) and Silas, two men who were
leaders among the brothers. [23]With them
they sent the following letter:

The apostles and elders, your brothers,

To the Gentile believers in Antioch,
Syria and Cilicia:

Greetings.

[24]We have heard that some went out
from us without our authorisation and
disturbed you, troubling your minds by
what they said. [25]So we all agreed to
choose some men and send them to you
with our dear friends Barnabas and Paul
—[26]men who have risked their lives for
the name of our Lord Jesus Christ.
[27]Therefore we are sending Judas and
Silas to confirm by word of mouth what
we are writing. [28]It seemed good to the
Holy Spirit and to us not to burden you
with anything beyond the following requirements: [29]You are to abstain from
food sacrificed to idols, from blood,
from the meat of strangled animals and
from sexual immorality. You will do
well to avoid these things.

Farewell.

[30]The men were sent off and went down to
Antioch, where they gathered the church
together and delivered the letter. [31]The
people read it and were glad for its encouraging message. [32]Judas and Silas, who themselves were prophets, said much to encourage and strengthen the brothers. [33]After
spending some time there, they were sent off
by the brothers with the blessing of peace to
return to those who had sent them.[d] [35]But
Paul and Barnabas remained in Antioch,
where they and many others taught and
preached the word of the Lord.

Disagreement Between Paul and Barnabas

[36]Some time later Paul said to Barnabas,
"Let us go back and visit the brothers in all
the towns where we preached the word of
the Lord and see how they are doing."
[37]Barnabas wanted to take John, also called
Mark, with them, [38]but Paul did not think it
wise to take him, because he had deserted
them in Pamphylia and had not continued
with them in the work. [39]They had such a
sharp disagreement that they parted company. Barnabas took Mark and sailed for
Cyprus, [40]but Paul chose Silas and left, commended by the brothers to the grace of the
Lord. [41]He went through Syria and Cilicia,
strengthening the churches.

Timothy Joins Paul and Silas

16 He came to Derbe and then to Lystra,
where a disciple named Timothy
lived, whose mother was a Jewess and a
believer, but whose father was a Greek. [2]The
brothers at Lystra and Iconium spoke well of
him. [3]Paul wanted to take him along on the
journey, so he circumcised him because of
the Jews who lived in that area, for they all
knew that his father was a Greek. [4]As they
travelled from town to town, they delivered
the decisions reached by the apostles and
elders in Jerusalem for the people to obey.
[5]So the churches were strengthened in the
faith and grew daily in numbers.

Paul's Vision of the Man of Macedonia

[6]Paul and his companions travelled
throughout the region of Phrygia and Galatia,
having been kept by the Holy Spirit from
preaching the word in the province of Asia.
[7]When they came to the border of Mysia,
they tried to enter Bithynia, but the Spirit of
Jesus would not allow them to. [8]So they
passed by Mysia and went down to Troas.
[9]During the night Paul had a vision of a man
of Macedonia standing and begging him,
"Come over to Macedonia and help us."
[10]After Paul had seen the vision, we got ready
at once to leave for Macedonia, concluding
that God had called us to preach the gospel to
them.

Lydia's Conversion in Philippi

[11]From Troas we put out to sea and sailed
straight for Samothrace, and the next day on
to Neapolis. [12]From there we travelled to
Philippi, a Roman colony and the leading city
of that district of Macedonia. And we stayed
there several days.

[13]On the Sabbath we went outside the city
gate to the river, where we expected to find a
place of prayer. We sat down and began to
speak to the women who had gathered there.
[14]One of those listening was a woman named
Lydia, a dealer in purple cloth from the city
of Thyatira, who was a worshipper of God.
The Lord opened her heart to respond to
Paul's message. [15]When she and the members of her household were baptised, she
invited us to her home. "If you consider me a
believer in the Lord," she said, "come and
stay at my house." And she persuaded us.

Paul and Silas in Prison

[16]Once when we were going to the place of
prayer, we were met by a slave girl who had a

[b]17 Amos 9:11,12   [c]17,18 Some manuscripts things'— / [18]known to the Lord for ages is his work
[d]33 Some manuscripts them, [34] but Silas decided to remain there

spirit by which she predicted the future. She earned a great deal of money for her owners by fortune-telling. [17]This girl followed Paul and the rest of us, shouting, "These men are servants of the Most High God, who are telling you the way to be saved." [18]She kept this up for many days. Finally Paul became so troubled that he turned round and said to the spirit, "In the name of Jesus Christ I command you to come out of her!" At that moment the spirit left her.

[19]When the owners of the slave girl realised that their hope of making money was gone, they seized Paul and Silas and dragged them into the market-place to face the authorities. [20]They brought them before the magistrates and said, "These men are Jews, and are throwing our city into an uproar [21]by advocating customs unlawful for us Romans to accept or practise."

[22]The crowd joined in the attack against Paul and Silas, and the magistrates ordered them to be stripped and beaten. [23]After they had been severely flogged, they were thrown into prison, and the jailer was commanded to guard them carefully. [24]Upon receiving such orders, he put them in the inner cell and fastened their feet in the stocks.

[25]About midnight Paul and Silas were praying and singing hymns to God, and the other prisoners were listening to them. [26]Suddenly there was such a violent earthquake that the foundations of the prison were shaken. At once all the prison doors flew open, and everybody's chains came loose. [27]The jailer woke up, and when he saw the prison doors open, he drew his sword and was about to kill himself because he thought the prisoners had escaped. [28]But Paul shouted, "Don't harm yourself! We are all here!"

[29]The jailer called for lights, rushed in and fell trembling before Paul and Silas. [30]He then brought them out and asked, "Sirs, what must I do to be saved?"

[31]They replied, "Believe in the Lord Jesus, and you will be saved—you and your household." [32]Then they spoke the word of the Lord to him and to all the others in his house. [33]At that hour of the night the jailer took them and washed their wounds; then immediately he and all his family were baptised. [34]The jailer brought them into his house and set a meal before them; he was filled with joy because he had come to believe in God—he and his whole family.

[35]When it was daylight, the magistrates sent their officers to the jailer with the order: "Release those men." [36]The jailer told Paul, "The magistrates have ordered that you and Silas be released. Now you can leave. Go in peace."

[37]But Paul said to the officers: "They beat us publicly without a trial, even though we are Roman citizens, and threw us into prison. And now do they want to get rid of us quietly? No! Let them come themselves and escort us out."

[38]The officers reported this to the magistrates, and when they heard that Paul and Silas were Roman citizens, they were alarmed. [39]They came to appease them and escorted them from the prison, requesting them to leave the city. [40]After Paul and Silas came out of the prison, they went to Lydia's house, where they met with the brothers and encouraged them. Then they left.

In Thessalonica

17 When they had passed through Amphipolis and Apollonia, they came to Thessalonica, where there was a Jewish synagogue. [2]As his custom was, Paul went into the synagogue, and on three Sabbath days he reasoned with them from the Scriptures, [3]explaining and proving that the Christ[a] had to suffer and rise from the dead. "This Jesus I am proclaiming to you is the Christ,"[a] he said. [4]Some of the Jews were persuaded and joined Paul and Silas, as did a large number of God-fearing Greeks and not a few prominent women.

[5]But the Jews were jealous; so they rounded up some bad characters from the market-place, formed a mob and started a riot in the city. They rushed to Jason's house in search of Paul and Silas in order to bring them out to the crowd.[b] [6]But when they did not find them, they dragged Jason and some other brothers before the city officials, shouting: "These men who have caused trouble all over the world have now come here, [7]and Jason has welcomed them into his house. They are all defying Caesar's decrees, saying that there is another king, one called Jesus." [8]When they heard this, the crowd and the city officials were thrown into turmoil. [9]Then they put Jason and the others on bail and let them go.

In Berea

[10]As soon as it was night, the brothers sent Paul and Silas away to Berea. On arriving there, they went to the Jewish synagogue. [11]Now the Bereans were of more noble character than the Thessalonians, for they received the message with great eagerness and examined the Scriptures every day to see if what Paul said was true. [12]Many of the Jews believed, as did also a number of prominent Greek women and many Greek men.

[13]When the Jews in Thessalonica learned that Paul was preaching the word of God at Berea, they went there too, agitating the crowds and stirring them up. [14]The brothers immediately sent Paul to the coast, but Silas and Timothy stayed at Berea. [15]The men who escorted Paul brought him to Athens and then left with instructions for Silas and Timothy to join him as soon as possible.

In Athens

[16]While Paul was waiting for them in Athens, he was greatly distressed to see that the city was full of idols. [17]So he reasoned in the synagogue with the Jews and the God-fearing Greeks, as well as in the market-place

---

a3 Or Messiah   b5 Or the assembly of the people

ACTS 16:6–15

'After Paul had seen the vision, we got ready at once to leave for Macedonia, concluding that God had called us to preach the gospel to them' (v. 10).

THREE TIMES in the Acts of the Apostles we note the change from the third person plural to the first person plural: from 'they' to 'we'. By this we assume that Luke was no longer using other sources, having himself become a member of Paul's group. Luke's personal faith, therefore, like that of so many others, was formed and tested on the battlefield.

Luke's portrait of Christ in his Gospel is sensitive, tender and comprehensive. He portrays Jesus as the universal Saviour but he also makes a stronger emphasis upon the work of the Holy Spirit than either Matthew or Mark. The fact that Luke had not met the human Jesus, but had seen the dynamic work of the Holy Spirit, perhaps helps to account for this emphasis.

In his first recorded experience of missionary work Luke had a realistic introduction to its thrills and hazards. Firstly, there was the positive response to the gospel of the relatively well-to-do Lydia, whose religious background no doubt helped her to faith. Second, there was the deliverance of a young slave girl from a fortune-telling spirit. It was the anger of the girl's owners at their loss through this deliverance that caused them to start the riot which resulted in Paul and Silas being imprisoned and punished. Third, Luke learned of the conversion of the gaoler and witnessed his joy in the faith.

These diverse and dramatic examples of the Holy Spirit's power evidently did much for Luke. It seems that he stayed on at Philippi to build the church as Paul, Silas and Timothy moved on.

'You will receive power when the Holy Spirit comes on you; and you will be my witnesses in Jerusalem, and in all Judaea and Samaria, and to the ends of the earth.'

(Acts 1:8)

→1000

ACTS 18:1–4

'There he met a Jew named Aquila, a native of Pontus, who had recently come from Italy with his wife Priscilla, because Claudius had ordered all the Jews to leave Rome. Paul went to see them' (v. 2).

PAUL NEEDED ALLIES after his lonely, frustrating and somewhat disappointing ministry in Athens and he found them in Aquila and Priscilla. They too probably needed allies, having been banished from Rome. Apparently there had been rioting in Rome over the preaching of a man called 'Christus'. Scholars assume that the conflict was similar to that experienced in Thessalonica between the Jews and Christians. Those who preached about Christ provoked the Jews as they won converts. It is also assumed that Aquila and Priscilla were already Christians, otherwise Luke would most certainly have recorded their conversion. Possibly they were numbered among the 'visitors from Rome' present in Jerusalem at the Feast of Pentecost when the Holy Spirit descended.

Aquila and Priscilla would share Paul's view of an active providence at work. Paul left Athens a downcast man; Aquila and Priscilla left Rome with reluctance; they met in Corinth to their own benefit and that of the future Church. Adding further to the idea of providence is that they were all tentmakers. Even affluent Jews ensured their children had a trade to support them should adversity come; these three people, therefore, were able to work together, maintaining themselves by making tents, which gave them the opportunity to declare the gospel. It is of interest that those who believed life to be a pilgrimage made only mobile dwellings.

> *God gently works through providence:*
> *A problem here; a hazard there;*
> *Till, with strategic consequence,*
> *We see his wisdom in his care*

day by day with those who happened to be there. [18]A group of Epicurean and Stoic philosophers began to dispute with him. Some of them asked, "What is this babbler trying to say?" Others remarked, "He seems to be advocating foreign gods." They said this because Paul was preaching the good news about Jesus and the resurrection. [19]Then they took him and brought him to a meeting of the Areopagus, where they said to him, "May we know what this new teaching is that you are presenting? [20]You are bringing some strange ideas to our ears, and we want to know what they mean." [21](All the Athenians and the foreigners who lived there spent their time doing nothing but talking about and listening to the latest ideas.)

[22]Paul then stood up in the meeting of the Areopagus and said: "Men of Athens! I see that in every way you are very religious. [23]For as I walked around and looked carefully at your objects of worship, I even found an altar with this inscription: TO AN UNKNOWN GOD. Now what you worship as something unknown I am going to proclaim to you.

[24]"The God who made the world and everything in it is the Lord of heaven and earth and does not live in temples built by hands. [25]And he is not served by human hands, as if he needed anything, because he himself gives all men life and breath and everything else. [26]From one man he made every nation of men, that they should inhabit the whole earth; and he determined the times set for them and the exact places where they should live. [27]God did this so that men would seek him and perhaps reach out for him and find him, though he is not far from each one of us. [28]'For in him we live and move and have our being.' As some of your own poets have said, 'We are his offspring.'

[29]"Therefore since we are God's offspring, we should not think that the divine being is like gold or silver or stone—an image made by man's design and skill. [30]In the past God overlooked such ignorance, but now he commands all people everywhere to repent. [31]For he has set a day when he will judge the world with justice by the man he has appointed. He has given proof of this to all men by raising him from the dead."

[32]When they heard about the resurrection of the dead, some of them sneered, but others said, "We want to hear you again on this subject." [33]At that, Paul left the Council. [34]A few men became followers of Paul and believed. Among them was Dionysius, a member of the Areopagus, also a woman named Damaris, and a number of others.

In Corinth

18 After this, Paul left Athens and went to Corinth. [2]There he met a Jew named Aquila, a native of Pontus, who had recently come from Italy with his wife Priscilla, because Claudius had ordered all the Jews to leave Rome. Paul went to see them, [3]and because he was a tentmaker as they were, he stayed and worked with them.

[4]Every Sabbath he reasoned in the synagogue, trying to persuade Jews and Greeks.

[5]When Silas and Timothy came from Macedonia, Paul devoted himself exclusively to preaching, testifying to the Jews that Jesus was the Christ.[a] [6]But when the Jews opposed Paul and became abusive, he shook out his clothes in protest and said to them, "Your blood be on your own heads! I am clear of my responsibility. From now on I will go to the Gentiles."

[7]Then Paul left the synagogue and went next door to the house of Titius Justus, a worshipper of God. [8]Crispus, the synagogue ruler, and his entire household believed in the Lord; and many of the Corinthians who heard him believed and were baptised.

[9]One night the Lord spoke to Paul in a vision: "Do not be afraid; keep on speaking, do not be silent. [10]For I am with you, and no-one is going to attack and harm you, because I have many people in this city." [11]So Paul stayed for a year and a half, teaching them the word of God.

[12]While Gallio was proconsul of Achaia, the Jews made a united attack on Paul and brought him into court. [13]"This man," they charged, "is persuading the people to worship God in ways contrary to the law."

[14]Just as Paul was about to speak, Gallio said to the Jews, "If you Jews were making a complaint about some misdemeanour or serious crime, it would be reasonable for me to listen to you. [15]But since it involves questions about words and names and your own law—settle the matter yourselves. I will not be a judge of such things." [16]So he had them ejected from the court. [17]Then they all turned on Sosthenes the synagogue ruler and beat him in front of the court. But Gallio showed no concern whatever.

Priscilla, Aquila and Apollos

[18]Paul stayed on in Corinth for some time. Then he left the brothers and sailed for Syria, accompanied by Priscilla and Aquila. Before he sailed, he had his hair cut off at Cenchrea because of a vow he had taken. [19]They arrived at Ephesus, where Paul left Priscilla and Aquila. He himself went into the synagogue and reasoned with the Jews. [20]When they asked him to spend more time with them, he declined. [21]But as he left, he promised, "I will come back if it is God's will." Then he set sail from Ephesus. [22]When he landed at Caesarea, he went up and greeted the church and then went down to Antioch.

[23]After spending some time in Antioch, Paul set out from there and travelled from place to place throughout the region of Galatia and Phrygia, strengthening all the disciples.

[24]Meanwhile a Jew named Apollos, a native of Alexandria, came to Ephesus. He was a learned man, with a thorough knowledge of the Scriptures. [25]He had been instructed in the way of the Lord, and he spoke with great fervour[b] and taught about Jesus accurately, though he knew only the baptism of John.

---

[a]5 Or *Messiah*; also in verse 28   [b]25 Or *with fervour in the Spirit*

26He began to speak boldly in the synagogue. When Priscilla and Aquila heard him, they invited him to their home and explained to him the way of God more adequately.

27When Apollos wanted to go to Achaia, the brothers encouraged him and wrote to the disciples there to welcome him. On arriving, he was a great help to those who by grace had believed. 28For he vigorously refuted the Jews in public debate, proving from the Scriptures that Jesus was the Christ.

Paul in Ephesus

19 While Apollos was at Corinth, Paul took the road through the interior and arrived at Ephesus. There he found some disciples 2and asked them, "Did you receive the Holy Spirit when*a* you believed?"

They answered, "No, we have not even heard that there is a Holy Spirit."

3So Paul asked, "Then what baptism did you receive?"

"John's baptism," they replied.

4Paul said, "John's baptism was a baptism of repentance. He told the people to believe in the one coming after him, that is, in Jesus." 5On hearing this, they were baptised into*b* the name of the Lord Jesus. 6When Paul placed his hands on them, the Holy Spirit came on them, and they spoke in tongues*c* and prophesied. 7There were about twelve men in all.

8Paul entered the synagogue and spoke boldly there for three months, arguing persuasively about the kingdom of God. 9But some of them became obstinate; they refused to believe and publicly maligned the Way. So Paul left them. He took the disciples with him and had discussions daily in the lecture hall of Tyrannus. 10This went on for two years, so that all the Jews and Greeks who lived in the province of Asia heard the word of the Lord.

11God did extraordinary miracles through Paul, 12so that even handkerchiefs and aprons that had touched him were taken to the sick, and their illnesses were cured and the evil spirits left them.

13Some Jews who went around driving out evil spirits tried to invoke the name of the Lord Jesus over those who were demon-possessed. They would say, "In the name of Jesus, whom Paul preaches, I command you to come out." 14Seven sons of Sceva, a Jewish chief priest, were doing this. 15One day the evil spirit answered them, "Jesus I know, and I know about Paul, but who are you?" 16Then the man who had the evil spirit jumped on them and overpowered them all. He gave them such a beating that they ran out of the house naked and bleeding.

17When this became known to the Jews and Greeks living in Ephesus, they were all seized with fear, and the name of the Lord Jesus was held in high honour. 18Many of those who believed now came and openly confessed their evil deeds. 19A number who had practised sorcery brought their scrolls together and burned them publicly. When they calculated the value of the scrolls, the total came to fifty thousand drachmas.*d* 20In this way the word of the Lord spread widely and grew in power.

21After all this had happened, Paul decided to go to Jerusalem, passing through Macedonia and Achaia. "After I have been there," he said, "I must visit Rome also." 22He sent two of his helpers, Timothy and Erastus, to Macedonia, while he stayed in the province of Asia a little longer.

The Riot in Ephesus

23About that time there arose a great disturbance about the Way. 24A silversmith named Demetrius, who made silver shrines of Artemis, brought in no little business for the craftsmen. 25He called them together, along with the workmen in related trades, and said: "Men, you know we receive a good income from this business. 26And you see and hear how this fellow Paul has convinced and led astray large numbers of people here in Ephesus and in practically the whole province of Asia. He says that man-made gods are no gods at all. 27There is danger not only that our trade will lose its good name, but also that the temple of the great goddess Artemis will be discredited, and the goddess herself, who is worshipped throughout the province of Asia and the world, will be robbed of her divine majesty."

28When they heard this, they were furious and began shouting: "Great is Artemis of the Ephesians!" 29Soon the whole city was in an uproar. The people seized Gaius and Aristarchus, Paul's travelling companions from Macedonia, and rushed as one man into the theatre. 30Paul wanted to appear before the crowd, but the disciples would not let him. 31Even some of the officials of the province, friends of Paul, sent him a message begging him not to venture into the theatre.

32The assembly was in confusion: Some were shouting one thing, some another. Most of the people did not even know why they were there. 33The Jews pushed Alexander to the front, and some of the crowd shouted instructions to him. He motioned for silence in order to make a defence before the people. 34But when they realised he was a Jew, they all shouted in unison for about two hours: "Great is Artemis of the Ephesians!"

35The city clerk quietened the crowd and said: "Men of Ephesus, doesn't all the world know that the city of Ephesus is the guardian of the temple of the great Artemis and of her image, which fell from heaven? 36Therefore, since these facts are undeniable, you ought to be quiet and not do anything rash. 37You have brought these men here, though they have neither robbed temples nor blasphemed our goddess. 38If, then, Demetrius and his fellow craftsmen have a grievance against anybody, the courts are open and there are proconsuls. They can press charges. 39If there is anything further you want to bring up, it must be settled in a legal assembly. 40As it is, we are in danger of being charged with rioting because of today's events. In that

---

a2 Or after   b5 Or in   c6 Or other languages
d19 A drachma was a silver coin worth about a day's wages.

ACTS 19:23–27
'About that time there arose a great disturbance about the Way' (v. 23).

CONFLICT is virtually inescapable once Christ has been proclaimed as Lord. As we have seen, Christianity is a way of life in its own right. As such, it threatens every other way. A great industry had been developed in Ephesus in connection with the temple of the goddess Artemis. The temple was one of the seven wonders of the world; if the goddess was discredited and devotees from the provinces and other parts of the world ceased to come for worship, then Demetrius and his fellow silversmiths would be out of work. Their concern was understandable.

It was impossible for Christianity to live comfortably with the worship of any god, not least a goddess like Artemis. She was a fertility goddess; her worship encouraged and legitimized sexual excess, her regular festivals being orgies which inflamed and degraded the participants. Although the first Ephesian temple to Artemis had been built in Jeremiah's day, the new faith with its emphasis on purity, discipline and the nobility of humankind threatened it and those who profited by its existence.

The site of the once proud temple is now most appropriately a swamp; even so, Artemis is not dead. Her followers, many of whom have become rich by promoting pornography and sexual perversion, pursue their evil courses with freedom, and many others suffer in mind and body because of their obsessive 'worship'. The way of Christ will always be in conflict with the way of 'Artemis'.

> *We go forth not to fight 'gainst the sinner, but sin;*
> *The lost and the outcast we love:*
> *And the claims of our King we before them will bring*
> *As we urge them his mercy to prove.*

(*Frederick William Fry*)

→1004

ACTS 22:17–22

'The Lord . . . said to me. "Leave Jerusalem immediately, because they will not accept your testimony about me" . . . When the blood of your martyr Stephen was shed, I stood there giving my approval' (vv. 18b, 20a).

PAUL HAD LEARNT over the years how to hold a crowd's attention. He was used to opposition. Previously, he had taken the Lord's advice to flee from Jerusalem to avoid the wrath of his former friends, but he was now ready to stand against the crowd whatever the consequences. He had no illusions about what those consequences might be. He had himself seen Stephen's stoning.

The reaction of the crowd, indeed, was so predictable that 'martyr', which simply means 'witness', very soon became the common expression for those who died because of their uncompromising testimony to the Lordship of Jesus Christ. Stephen was the first Christian martyr, in the sense of dying for his faith, but each of us is called to witness in that same way, with uncompromising sincerity.

There is room for compromise over actions and activities. There is room for compromise over administrative decisions, over forms of worship, over acceptance of the finer points of doctrine. But the *witness* of the Church can never be a matter of compromise. Unless we are prepared to witness to the point of martyrdom, the Church will weaken and wither away. Witness is simple, yet effective. It will create tension, opposition and accusation, but we cannot allow our voice to be muted because of that. The example in these pages of Acts is one for us all to follow. We recognize, with Paul, the need to witness to all what we have seen and heard – that Jesus Christ is Lord.

Thank you, Father, for the witness of the Church today. We praise you for courageous Christians who maintain faithful witness in difficult conditions. May the Church never flinch from its primary task of witnessing to the saving power of the Lord Jesus Christ: Give us the courage to play our full part in that witness.

→1009

case we would not be able to account for this commotion, since there is no reason for it." ⁴¹After he had said this, he dismissed the assembly.

Through Macedonia and Greece

20 When the uproar had ended, Paul sent for the disciples and, after encouraging them, said good-bye and set out for Macedonia. ²He travelled through that area, speaking many words of encouragement to the people, and finally arrived in Greece, ³where he stayed three months. Because the Jews made a plot against him just as he was about to sail for Syria, he decided to go back through Macedonia. ⁴He was accompanied by Sopater son of Pyrrhus from Berea, Aristarchus and Secundus from Thessalonica, Gaius from Derbe, Timothy also, and Tychicus and Trophimus from the province of Asia. ⁵These men went on ahead and waited for us at Troas. ⁶But we sailed from Philippi after the Feast of Unleavened Bread, and five days later joined the others at Troas, where we stayed seven days.

Eutychus Raised From the Dead at Troas

⁷On the first day of the week we came together to break bread. Paul spoke to the people and, because he intended to leave the next day, kept on talking until midnight. ⁸There were many lamps in the upstairs room where we were meeting. ⁹Seated in a window was a young man named Eutychus, who was sinking into a deep sleep as Paul talked on and on. When he was sound asleep, he fell to the ground from the third storey and was picked up dead. ¹⁰Paul went down, threw himself on the young man and put his arms around him. "Don't be alarmed," he said. "He's alive!" ¹¹Then he went upstairs again and broke bread and ate. After talking until daylight, he left. ¹²The people took the young man home alive and were greatly comforted.

Paul's Farewell to the Ephesian Elders

¹³We went on ahead to the ship and sailed for Assos, where we were going to take Paul aboard. He had made this arrangement because he was going there on foot. ¹⁴When he met us at Assos, we took him aboard and went on to Mitylene. ¹⁵The next day we set sail from there and arrived off Kios. The day after that we crossed over to Samos, and on the following day arrived at Miletus. ¹⁶Paul had decided to sail past Ephesus to avoid spending time in the province of Asia, for he was in a hurry to reach Jerusalem, if possible, by the day of Pentecost.

¹⁷From Miletus, Paul sent to Ephesus for the elders of the church. ¹⁸When they arrived, he said to them: "You know how I lived the whole time I was with you, from the first day I came into the province of Asia. ¹⁹I served the Lord with great humility and with tears, although I was severely tested by the plots of the Jews. ²⁰You know that I have not hesitated to preach anything that would be helpful to you but have taught you publicly and from house to house. ²¹I have declared to both Jews and Greeks that they must turn to God in repentance and have faith in our Lord Jesus.

²²"And now, compelled by the Spirit, I am going to Jerusalem, not knowing what will happen to me there. ²³I only know that in every city the Holy Spirit warns me that prison and hardships are facing me. ²⁴However, I consider my life worth nothing to me, if only I may finish the race and complete the task the Lord Jesus has given me—the task of testifying to the gospel of God's grace.

²⁵"Now I know that none of you among whom I have gone about preaching the kingdom will ever see me again. ²⁶Therefore, I declare to you today that I am innocent of the blood of all men. ²⁷For I have not hesitated to proclaim to you the whole will of God. ²⁸Keep watch over yourselves and all the flock of which the Holy Spirit has made you overseers.ᵃ Be shepherds of the church of God,ᵇ which he bought with his own blood. ²⁹I know that after I leave, savage wolves will come in among you and will not spare the flock. ³⁰Even from your own number men will arise and distort the truth in order to draw away disciples after them. ³¹So be on your guard! Remember that for three years I never stopped warning each of you night and day with tears.

³²"Now I commit you to God and to the word of his grace, which can build you up and give you an inheritance among all those who are sanctified. ³³I have not coveted anyone's silver or gold or clothing. ³⁴You yourselves know that these hands of mine have supplied my own needs and the needs of my companions. ³⁵In everything I did, I showed you that by this kind of hard work we must help the weak, remembering the words the Lord Jesus himself said: 'It is more blessed to give than to receive.'"

³⁶When he had said this, he knelt down with all of them and prayed. ³⁷They all wept as they embraced him and kissed him. ³⁸What grieved them most was his statement that they would never see his face again. Then they accompanied him to the ship.

On to Jerusalem

21 After we had torn ourselves away from them, we put out to sea and sailed straight to Cos. The next day we went to Rhodes and from there to Patara. ²We found a ship crossing over to Phoenicia, went on board and set sail. ³After sighting Cyprus and passing to the south of it, we sailed on to Syria. We landed at Tyre, where our ship was to unload its cargo. ⁴Finding the disciples there, we stayed with them seven days. Through the Spirit they urged Paul not to go on to Jerusalem. ⁵But when our time was up, we left and continued on our way. All the disciples and their wives and children accompanied us out of the city, and there on the beach we knelt to pray. ⁶After saying goodbye to each other, we went aboard the ship, and they returned home.

[7]We continued our voyage from Tyre and landed at Ptolemais, where we greeted the brothers and stayed with them for a day. [8]Leaving the next day, we reached Caesarea and stayed at the house of Philip the evangelist, one of the Seven. [9]He had four unmarried daughters who prophesied.

[10]After we had been there a number of days, a prophet named Agabus came down from Judea. [11]Coming over to us, he took Paul's belt, tied his own hands and feet with it and said, "The Holy Spirit says, 'In this way the Jews of Jerusalem will bind the owner of this belt and will hand him over to the Gentiles.'"

[12]When we heard this, we and the people there pleaded with Paul not to go up to Jerusalem. [13]Then Paul answered, "Why are you weeping and breaking my heart? I am ready not only to be bound, but also to die in Jerusalem for the name of the Lord Jesus." [14]When he would not be dissuaded, we gave up and said, "The Lord's will be done."

[15]After this, we got ready and went up to Jerusalem. [16]Some of the disciples from Caesarea accompanied us and brought us to the home of Mnason, where we were to stay. He was a man from Cyprus and one of the early disciples.

Paul's Arrival at Jerusalem

[17]When we arrived at Jerusalem, the brothers received us warmly. [18]The next day Paul and the rest of us went to see James, and all the elders were present. [19]Paul greeted them and reported in detail what God had done among the Gentiles through his ministry.

[20]When they heard this, they praised God. Then they said to Paul: "You see, brother, how many thousands of Jews have believed, and all of them are zealous for the law. [21]They have been informed that you teach all the Jews who live among the Gentiles to turn away from Moses, telling them not to circumcise their children or live according to our customs. [22]What shall we do? They will certainly hear that you have come, [23]so do what we tell you. There are four men with us who have made a vow. [24]Take these men, join in their purification rites and pay their expenses, so that they can have their heads shaved. Then everybody will know there is no truth in these reports about you, but that you yourself are living in obedience to the law. [25]As for the Gentile believers, we have written to them our decision that they should abstain from food sacrificed to idols, from blood, from the meat of strangled animals and from sexual immorality."

[26]The next day Paul took the men and purified himself along with them. Then he went to the temple to give notice of the date when the days of purification would end and the offering would be made for each of them.

Paul Arrested

[27]When the seven days were nearly over, some Jews from the province of Asia saw Paul at the temple. They stirred up the whole crowd and seized him, [28]shouting, "Men of Israel, help us! This is the man who teaches all men everywhere against our people and our law and this place. And besides, he has brought Greeks into the temple area and defiled this holy place." [29](They had previously seen Trophimus the Ephesian in the city with Paul and assumed that Paul had brought him into the temple area.)

[30]The whole city was aroused, and the people came running from all directions. Seizing Paul, they dragged him from the temple, and immediately the gates were shut. [31]While they were trying to kill him, news reached the commander of the Roman troops that the whole city of Jerusalem was in an uproar. [32]He at once took some officers and soldiers and ran down to the crowd. When the rioters saw the commander and his soldiers, they stopped beating Paul.

[33]The commander came up and arrested him and ordered him to be bound with two chains. Then he asked who he was and what he had done. [34]Some in the crowd shouted one thing and some another, and since the commander could not get at the truth because of the uproar, he ordered that Paul be taken into the barracks. [35]When Paul reached the steps, the violence of the mob was so great he had to be carried by the soldiers. [36]The crowd that followed kept shouting, "Away with him!"

Paul Speaks to the Crowd

[37]As the soldiers were about to take Paul into the barracks, he asked the commander, "May I say something to you?"

"Do you speak Greek?" he replied. [38]"Aren't you the Egyptian who started a revolt and led four thousand terrorists out into the desert some time ago?"

[39]Paul answered, "I am a Jew, from Tarsus in Cilicia, a citizen of no ordinary city. Please let me speak to the people."

[40]Having received the commander's permission, Paul stood on the steps and motioned to the crowd. When they were all silent, he said to them in Aramaic[a]:

22 [1]"Brothers and fathers, listen now to my defence."

[2]When they heard him speak to them in Aramaic, they became very quiet.

Then Paul said: [3]"I am a Jew, born in Tarsus of Cilicia, but brought up in this city. Under Gamaliel I was thoroughly trained in the law of our fathers and was just as zealous for God as any of you are today. [4]I persecuted the followers of this Way to their death, arresting both men and women and throwing them into prison, [5]as also the high priest and all the Council can testify. I even obtained letters from them to their brothers in Damascus, and went there to bring these people as prisoners to Jerusalem to be punished.

[a]40 Or possibly *Hebrew*; also in 22:2

6"About noon as I came near Damascus, suddenly a bright light from heaven flashed around me. 7I fell to the ground and heard a voice say to me, 'Saul! Saul! Why do you persecute me?'

8"'Who are you, Lord?' I asked.

"'I am Jesus of Nazareth, whom you are persecuting,' he replied. 9My companions saw the light, but they did not understand the voice of him who was speaking to me.

10"'What shall I do, Lord?' I asked.

"'Get up,' the Lord said, 'and go into Damascus. There you will be told all that you have been assigned to do.' 11My companions led me by the hand into Damascus, because the brilliance of the light had blinded me.

12"A man named Ananias came to see me. He was a devout observer of the law and highly respected by all the Jews living there. 13He stood beside me and said, 'Brother Saul, receive your sight!' And at that very moment I was able to see him.

14"Then he said: 'The God of our fathers has chosen you to know his will and to see the Righteous One and to hear words from his mouth. 15You will be his witness to all men of what you have seen and heard. 16And now what are you waiting for? Get up, be baptised and wash your sins away, calling on his name.'

17"When I returned to Jerusalem and was praying at the temple, I fell into a trance 18and saw the Lord speaking. 'Quick!' he said to me. 'Leave Jerusalem immediately, because they will not accept your testimony about me.'

19"'Lord,' I replied, 'these men know that I went from one synagogue to another to imprison and beat those who believe in you. 20And when the blood of your martyr[a] Stephen was shed, I stood there giving my approval and guarding the clothes of those who were killing him.'

21"Then the Lord said to me, 'Go; I will send you far away to the Gentiles.'"

Paul the Roman Citizen

22The crowd listened to Paul until he said this. Then they raised their voices and shouted, "Rid the earth of him! He's not fit to live!"

23As they were shouting and throwing off their cloaks and flinging dust into the air, 24the commander ordered Paul to be taken into the barracks. He directed that he be flogged and questioned in order to find out why the people were shouting at him like this. 25As they stretched him out to flog him, Paul said to the centurion standing there, "Is it legal for you to flog a Roman citizen who hasn't even been found guilty?"

26When the centurion heard this, he went to the commander and reported it. "What are you going to do?" he asked. "This man is a Roman citizen."

27The commander went to Paul and asked, "Tell me, are you a Roman citizen?"

"Yes, I am," he answered.

28Then the commander said, "I had to pay a big price for my citizenship."

"But I was born a citizen," Paul replied.

29Those who were about to question him withdrew immediately. The commander himself was alarmed when he realised that he had put Paul, a Roman citizen, in chains.

Before the Sanhedrin

30The next day, since the commander wanted to find out exactly why Paul was being accused by the Jews, he released him and ordered the chief priests and all the Sanhedrin to assemble. Then he brought Paul and had him stand before them.

23 Paul looked straight at the Sanhedrin and said, "My brothers, I have fulfilled my duty to God in all good conscience to this day." 2At this the high priest Ananias ordered those standing near Paul to strike him on the mouth. 3Then Paul said to him, "God will strike you, you whitewashed wall! You sit there to judge me according to the law, yet you yourself violate the law by commanding that I be struck!"

4Those who were standing near Paul said, "You dare to insult God's high priest?"

5Paul replied, "Brothers, I did not realise that he was the high priest; for it is written: 'Do not speak evil about the ruler of your people.'[a]"

6Then Paul, knowing that some of them were Sadducees and the others Pharisees, called out in the Sanhedrin, "My brothers, I am a Pharisee, the son of a Pharisee. I stand on trial because of my hope in the resurrection of the dead." 7When he said this, a dispute broke out between the Pharisees and the Sadducees, and the assembly was divided. 8(The Sadducees say that there is no resurrection, and that there are neither angels nor spirits, but the Pharisees acknowledge them all.)

9There was a great uproar, and some of the teachers of the law who were Pharisees stood up and argued vigorously. "We find nothing wrong with this man," they said. "What if a spirit or an angel has spoken to him?" 10The dispute became so violent that the commander was afraid Paul would be torn to pieces by them. He ordered the troops to go down and take him away from them by force and bring him into the barracks.

11The following night the Lord stood near Paul and said, "Take courage! As you have testified about me in Jerusalem, so you must also testify in Rome."

The Plot to Kill Paul

12The next morning the Jews formed a conspiracy and bound themselves with an oath not to eat or drink until they had killed Paul. 13More than forty men were involved in this plot. 14They went to the chief priests and elders and said, "We have taken a solemn oath not to eat anything until we have killed Paul. 15Now then, you and the Sanhedrin petition the commander to bring him before you on the pretext of wanting more accurate

---

[a]20 Or witness   [a]5 Exodus 22:28

information about his case. We are ready to kill him before he gets here.''

16But when the son of Paul's sister heard of this plot, he went into the barracks and told Paul.

17Then Paul called one of the centurions and said, "Take this young man to the commander; he has something to tell him." 18So he took him to the commander.

The centurion said, "Paul, the prisoner, sent for me and asked me to bring this young man to you because he has something to tell you.''

19The commander took the young man by the hand, drew him aside and asked, "What is it you want to tell me?''

20He said: "The Jews have agreed to ask you to bring Paul before the Sanhedrin tomorrow on the pretext of wanting more accurate information about him. 21Don't give in to them, because more than forty of them are waiting in ambush for him. They have taken an oath not to eat or drink until they have killed him. They are ready now, waiting for your consent to their request.''

22The commander dismissed the young man and cautioned him, "Don't tell anyone that you have reported this to me.''

Paul Transferred to Caesarea

23Then he called two of his centurions and ordered them, "Get ready a detachment of two hundred soldiers, seventy horsemen and two hundred spearmen*b* to go to Caesarea at nine tonight. 24Provide mounts for Paul so that he may be taken safely to Governor Felix.''

25He wrote a letter as follows:

26Claudius Lysias,

To His Excellency, Governor Felix:

Greetings.

27This man was seized by the Jews and they were about to kill him, but I came with my troops and rescued him, for I had learned that he is a Roman citizen. 28I wanted to know why they were accusing him, so I brought him to their Sanhedrin. 29I found that the accusation had to do with questions about their law, but there was no charge against him that deserved death or imprisonment. 30When I was informed of a plot to be carried out against the man, I sent him to you at once. I also ordered his accusers to present to you their case against him.

31So the soldiers, carrying out their orders, took Paul with them during the night and brought him as far as Antipatris. 32The next day they let the cavalry go on with him, while they returned to the barracks. 33When the cavalry arrived in Caesarea, they delivered the letter to the governor and handed Paul over to him. 34The governor read the letter

and asked what province he was from. Learning that he was from Cilicia, 35he said, "I will hear your case when your accusers get here." Then he ordered that Paul be kept under guard in Herod's palace.

The Trial Before Felix

24 Five days later the high priest Ananias went down to Caesarea with some of the elders and a lawyer named Tertullus, and they brought their charges against Paul before the governor. 2When Paul was called in, Tertullus presented his case before Felix: "We have enjoyed a long period of peace under you, and your foresight has brought about reforms in this nation. 3Everywhere and in every way, most excellent Felix, we acknowledge this with profound gratitude. 4But in order not to weary you further, I would request that you be kind enough to hear us briefly.

5"We have found this man to be a troublemaker, stirring up riots among the Jews all over the world. He is a ringleader of the Nazarene sect 6and even tried to desecrate the temple; so we seized him. 8By*a* examining him yourself you will be able to learn the truth about all these charges we are bringing against him.''

9The Jews joined in the accusation, asserting that these things were true.

10When the governor motioned for him to speak, Paul replied: "I know that for a number of years you have been a judge over this nation; so I gladly make my defence. 11You can easily verify that no more than twelve days ago I went up to Jerusalem to worship. 12My accusers did not find me arguing with anyone at the temple, or stirring up a crowd in the synagogues or anywhere else in the city. 13And they cannot prove to you the charges they are now making against me. 14However, I admit that I worship the God of our fathers as a follower of the Way, which they call a sect. I believe everything that agrees with the Law and that is written in the Prophets, 15and I have the same hope in God as these men, that there will be a resurrection of both the righteous and the wicked. 16So I strive always to keep my conscience clear before God and man.

17"After an absence of several years, I came to Jerusalem to bring my people gifts for the poor and to present offerings. 18I was ceremonially clean when they found me in the temple courts doing this. There was no crowd with me, nor was I involved in any disturbance. 19But there are some Jews from the province of Asia, who ought to be here before you and bring charges if they have anything against me. 20Or these who are here should state what crime they found in me when I stood before the Sanhedrin—21unless it was this one thing I shouted as I stood in their presence: 'It is concerning the resurrection of the dead that I am on trial before you today.' ''

22Then Felix, who was well acquainted

b23 The meaning of the Greek for this word is uncertain.
a6–8 Some manuscripts him and wanted to judge him according to our law. 7But the commander, Lysias, came and with the use of much force snatched him from our hands 8and ordered his accusers to come before you. By

ACTS 23:11

'The following night the Lord stood near Paul and said, "Take courage! As you have testified about me in Jerusalem, so you must also testify in Rome" ' (v.11).

THE GUARD COMMANDER had Paul removed from the court and from this moment onwards he was completely in Roman custody. As he had done on a previous occasion when danger threatened, the Lord came to Paul with his reassuring presence.

If ever a man needed spiritual reinforcement, surely that man was Paul. His ministry up to this time had been largely the building and strengthening of the churches. Although he had faced angry mobs, had been subjected to attack, even imprisonment, he had usually been accompanied by like-minded men, and was exposed to the joys of winning people for Christ, instructing them in the faith, becoming a father in God to them. But now he was on his own. The future, clouded surely by his own conviction that he would never see his treasured colleagues again, and the prayers of his Spirit-led people pleading with him not to proceed to Jerusalem, stretched ahead. How gracious of the Lord to visit him.

Christ's visitation was to give him both courage and direction. In spite of the fears of his colleagues, our Lord's message revealed that Paul was in Jerusalem within the divine will, and that his ultimate destination was Rome. Paul had longed to visit Rome, but never dreamed he would do so as a prisoner. However, if the Lord was going to be with him, prisoner or not, he would remain a free soul.

> *His presence my steps shall attend,*
> *His fullness my wants shall supply;*
> *On him, till my journey shall end,*
> *My unwavering faith shall rely.*

> (*Edward Turney*)

→1010

ACTS 26:6-8

'And now it is because of my hope in what God has promised our fathers that I am on trial today' (v. 6,).

IN THESE SIMPLE STATEMENTS Paul gives expression to his years of study of Scripture and the teaching he received from our Lord and the Holy Spirit, following his conversion. Appointed by God to be the apostle to the Gentiles, Paul's major success was his total grasp of the purposes of God as they were expressed through the people of Israel.

Paul saw, with great clarity, that Judaism was more than the creation of a people, it was the creation of a means whereby the rest of the world would come to know God. All the peoples of the earth were to be blessed through Abraham. Abraham is the father of all who believe; the father of many nations. But it was also the promise of the Messiah running like a golden cord through the Scriptures which captured him. In those revelations he received directly from the Lord, we wonder if Jesus tutored him about the messianic promises as he tutored the two disciples on the Emmaus road. Whatever the revelations were, Paul was left in no doubt that Jesus was the hope of Israel and the true fulfilment of the twelve tribes of Israel.

Part of Paul's persuasiveness resided in his unshaken conviction that the present and future of Christianity was bound up in the past of Israel. He discarded only Israel's insularity and bigotry as he pressed the claims of Christ, the Messiah who was to be the Saviour of the entire world.

Is it not reasonable to believe
That God who planned the bud, should plan the flower?
Who planned the womb should plan the child and man?
Who gave the promise should redeem his word?

→1015

with the Way, adjourned the proceedings. "When Lysias the commander comes," he said, "I will decide your case." 23He ordered the centurion to keep Paul under guard but to give him some freedom and permit his friends to take care of his needs.

24Several days later Felix came with his wife Drusilla, who was a Jewess. He sent for Paul and listened to him as he spoke about faith in Christ Jesus. 25As Paul discoursed on righteousness, self-control and the judgment to come, Felix was afraid and said, "That's enough for now! You may leave. When I find it convenient, I will send for you." 26At the same time he was hoping that Paul would offer him a bribe, so he sent for him frequently and talked with him.

27When two years had passed, Felix was succeeded by Porcius Festus, but because Felix wanted to grant a favour to the Jews, he left Paul in prison.

The Trial Before Festus

25 Three days after arriving in the province, Festus went up from Caesarea to Jerusalem, 2where the chief priests and Jewish leaders appeared before him and presented the charges against Paul. 3They urgently requested Festus, as a favour to them, to have Paul transferred to Jerusalem, for they were preparing an ambush to kill him along the way. 4Festus answered, "Paul is being held at Caesarea, and I myself am going there soon. 5Let some of your leaders come with me and press charges against the man there, if he has done anything wrong."

6After spending eight or ten days with them, he went down to Caesarea, and the next day he convened the court and ordered that Paul be brought before him. 7When Paul appeared, the Jews who had come down from Jerusalem stood around him, bringing many serious charges against him, which they could not prove.

8Then Paul made his defence: "I have done nothing wrong against the law of the Jews or against the temple or against Caesar."

9Festus, wishing to do the Jews a favour, said to Paul, "Are you willing to go up to Jerusalem and stand trial before me there on these charges?"

10Paul answered: "I am now standing before Caesar's court, where I ought to be tried. I have not done any wrong to the Jews, as you yourself know very well. 11If, however, I am guilty of doing anything deserving death, I do not refuse to die. But if the charges brought against me by these Jews are not true, no-one has the right to hand me over to them. I appeal to Caesar!"

12After Festus had conferred with his council, he declared: "You have appealed to Caesar. To Caesar you will go!"

Festus Consults King Agrippa

13A few days later King Agrippa and Bernice arrived at Caesarea to pay their respects to Festus. 14Since they were spending many days there, Festus discussed Paul's case with the king. He said: "There is a man here whom Felix left as a prisoner. 15When I went to Jerusalem, the chief priests and elders of the Jews brought charges against him and asked that he be condemned.

16"I told them that it is not the Roman custom to hand over any man before he has faced his accusers and has had an opportunity to defend himself against their charges. 17When they came here with me, I did not delay the case, but convened the court the next day and ordered the man to be brought in. 18When his accusers got up to speak, they did not charge him with any of the crimes I had expected. 19Instead, they had some points of dispute with him about their own religion and about a dead man named Jesus whom Paul claimed was alive. 20I was at a loss how to investigate such matters; so I asked if he would be willing to go to Jerusalem and stand trial there on these charges. 21When Paul made his appeal to be held over for the Emperor's decision, I ordered him to be held until I could send him to Caesar."

22Then Agrippa said to Festus, "I would like to hear this man myself."

He replied, "Tomorrow you will hear him."

Paul Before Agrippa

23The next day Agrippa and Bernice came with great pomp and entered the audience room with the high ranking officers and the leading men of the city. At the command of Festus, Paul was brought in. 24Festus said: "King Agrippa, and all who are present with us, you see this man! The whole Jewish community has petitioned me about him in Jerusalem and here in Caesarea, shouting that he ought not to live any longer. 25I found he had done nothing deserving of death, but because he made his appeal to the Emperor I decided to send him to Rome. 26But I have nothing definite to write to His Majesty about him. Therefore I have brought him before all of you, and especially before you, King Agrippa, so that as a result of this investigation I may have something to write. 27For I think it is unreasonable to send on a prisoner without specifying the charges against him."

26 Then Agrippa said to Paul, "You have permission to speak for yourself."

So Paul motioned with his hand and began his defence: 2"King Agrippa, I consider myself fortunate to stand before you today as I make my defence against all the accusations of the Jews, 3and especially so because you are well acquainted with all the Jewish customs and controversies. Therefore, I beg you to listen to me patiently.

4"The Jews all know the way I have lived ever since I was a child, from the beginning of my life in my own country, and also in Jerusalem. 5They have known me for a long time and can testify, if they are willing, that according to the strictest sect of our religion, I lived as a Pharisee. 6And now it is because of my hope in what God has promised our fathers that I am on trial today. 7This is the promise our twelve tribes are hoping to see fulfilled as they earnestly serve God day and night. O King, it is because of this hope that the Jews are accusing me. [8]Why should any of you consider it incredible that God raises the dead?

[9]"I too was convinced that I ought to do all that was possible to oppose the name of Jesus of Nazareth. [10]And that is just what I did in Jerusalem. On the authority of the chief priests I put many of the saints in prison, and when they were put to death, I cast my vote against them. [11]Many a time I went from one synagogue to another to have them punished, and I tried to force them to blaspheme. In my obsession against them, I even went to foreign cities to persecute them.

[12]"On one of these journeys I was going to Damascus with the authority and commission of the chief priests. [13]About noon, O King, as I was on the road, I saw a light from heaven, brighter than the sun, blazing around me and my companions. [14]We all fell to the ground, and I heard a voice saying to me in Aramaic,[a] 'Saul, Saul, why do you persecute me? It is hard for you to kick against the goads.'

[15]"Then I asked, 'Who are you, Lord?'

"'I am Jesus, whom you are persecuting,' the Lord replied. [16]'Now get up and stand on your feet. I have appeared to you to appoint you as a servant and as a witness of what you have seen of me and what I will show you. [17]I will rescue you from your own people and from the Gentiles. I am sending you to them [18]to open their eyes and turn them from darkness to light, and from the power of Satan to God, so that they may receive forgiveness of sins and a place among those who are sanctified by faith in me.'

[19]"So then, King Agrippa, I was not disobedient to the vision from heaven. [20]First to those in Damascus, then to those in Jerusalem and in all Judea, and to the Gentiles also, I preached that they should repent and turn to God and prove their repentance by their deeds. [21]That is why the Jews seized me in the temple courts and tried to kill me. [22]But I have had God's help to this very day, and so I stand here and testify to small and great alike. I am saying nothing beyond what the prophets and Moses said would happen— [23]that the Christ[b] would suffer and, as the first to rise from the dead, would proclaim light to his own people and to the Gentiles."

[24]At this point Festus interrupted Paul's defence. "You are out of your mind, Paul!" he shouted. "Your great learning is driving you insane."

[25]"I am not insane, most excellent Festus," Paul replied. "What I am saying is true and reasonable. [26]The king is familiar with these things, and I can speak freely to him. I am convinced that none of this has escaped his notice, because it was not done in a corner. [27]King Agrippa, do you believe the prophets? I know you do."

[28]Then Agrippa said to Paul, "Do you think that in such a short time you can persuade me to be a Christian?"

[29]Paul replied, "Short time or long—I pray God that not only you but all who are listening to me today may become what I am, except for these chains."

[30]The king rose, and with him the governor and Bernice and those sitting with them. [31]They left the room, and while talking with one another, they said, "This man is not doing anything that deserves death or imprisonment."

[32]Agrippa said to Festus, "This man could have been set free if he had not appealed to Caesar."

Paul Sails for Rome

27 When it was decided that we would sail for Italy, Paul and some other prisoners were handed over to a centurion named Julius, who belonged to the Imperial Regiment. [2]We boarded a ship from Adramyttium about to sail for ports along the coast of the province of Asia, and we put out to sea. Aristarchus, a Macedonian from Thessalonica, was with us.

[3]The next day we landed at Sidon; and Julius, in kindness to Paul, allowed him to go to his friends so they might provide for his needs. [4]From there we put out to sea again and passed to the lee of Cyprus because the winds were against us. [5]When we had sailed across the open sea off the coast of Cilicia and Pamphylia, we landed at Myra in Lycia. [6]There the centurion found an Alexandrian ship sailing for Italy and put us on board. [7]We made slow headway for many days and had difficulty arriving off Cnidus. When the wind did not allow us to hold our course, we sailed to the lee of Crete, opposite Salmone. [8]We moved along the coast with difficulty and came to a place called Fair Havens, near the town of Lasea.

[9]Much time had been lost, and sailing had already become dangerous because by now it was after the Fast.[a] So Paul warned them, [10]"Men, I can see that our voyage is going to be disastrous and bring great loss to ship and cargo, and to our own lives also." [11]But the centurion, instead of listening to what Paul said, followed the advice of the pilot and of the owner of the ship. [12]Since the harbour was unsuitable to winter in, the majority decided that we should sail on, hoping to reach Phoenix and winter there. This was a harbour in Crete, facing both south-west and north-west.

The Storm

[13]When a gentle south wind began to blow, they thought they had obtained what they wanted; so they weighed anchor and sailed along the shore of Crete. [14]Before very long, a wind of hurricane force, called the "north-easter", swept down from the island. [15]The ship was caught by the storm and could not head into the wind; so we gave way to it and were driven along. [16]As we passed to the lee of a small island called Cauda, we were hardly able to make the lifeboat secure. [17]When the men had hoisted it aboard, they

---

[a]14 Or Hebrew   [b]23 Or Messiah   [a]9 That is, the Day of Atonement (Yom Kippur)

passed ropes under the ship itself to hold it together. Fearing that they would run aground on the sand-bars of Syrtis, they lowered the sea anchor and let the ship be driven along. [18]We took such a violent battering from the storm that the next day they began to throw the cargo overboard. [19]On the third day, they threw the ship's tackle overboard with their own hands. [20]When neither sun nor stars appeared for many days and the storm continued raging, we finally gave up all hope of being saved.

[21]After the men had gone a long time without food, Paul stood up before them and said: "Men, you should have taken my advice not to sail from Crete; then you would have spared yourselves this damage and loss. [22]But now I urge you to keep up your courage, because not one of you will be lost; only the ship will be destroyed. [23]Last night an angel of the God whose I am and whom I serve stood beside me [24]and said, 'Do not be afraid, Paul. You must stand trial before Caesar; and God has graciously given you the lives of all who sail with you.' [25]So keep up your courage, men, for I have faith in God that it will happen just as he told me. [26]Nevertheless, we must run aground on some island."

The Shipwreck

[27]On the fourteenth night we were still being driven across the Adriatic[b] Sea, when about midnight the sailors sensed they were approaching land. [28]They took soundings and found that the water was one hundred and twenty feet[c] deep. A short time later they took soundings again and found it was ninety feet[d] deep. [29]Fearing that we would be dashed against the rocks, they dropped four anchors from the stern and prayed for daylight. [30]In an attempt to escape from the ship, the sailors let the lifeboat down into the sea, pretending they were going to lower some anchors from the bow. [31]Then Paul said to the centurion and the soldiers, "Unless these men stay with the ship, you cannot be saved." [32]So the soldiers cut the ropes that held the lifeboat and let it fall away.

[33]Just before dawn Paul urged them all to eat. "For the last fourteen days," he said, "you have been in constant suspense and have gone without food—you haven't eaten anything. [34]Now I urge you to take some food. You need it to survive. Not one of you will lose a single hair from his head." [35]After he said this, he took some bread and gave thanks to God in front of them all. Then he broke it and began to eat. [36]They were all encouraged and ate some food themselves. [37]Altogether there were 276 of us on board. [38]When they had eaten as much as they wanted, they lightened the ship by throwing the grain into the sea.

[39]When daylight came, they did not recognise the land, but they saw a bay with a sandy beach, where they decided to run the ship aground if they could. [40]Cutting loose the anchors, they left them in the sea and at the same time untied the ropes that held the rudders. Then they hoisted the foresail to the wind and made for the beach. [41]But the ship struck a sand-bar and ran aground. The bow stuck fast and would not move, and the stern was broken to pieces by the pounding of the surf.

[42]The soldiers planned to kill the prisoners to prevent any of them from swimming away and escaping. [43]But the centurion wanted to spare Paul's life and kept them from carrying out their plan. He ordered those who could swim to jump overboard first and get to land. [44]The rest were to get there on planks or on pieces of the ship. In this way everyone reached land in safety.

Ashore on Malta

28 Once safely on shore, we found out that the island was called Malta. [2]The islanders showed us unusual kindness. They built a fire and welcomed us all because it was raining and cold. [3]Paul gathered a pile of brushwood and, as he put it on the fire, a viper, driven out by the heat, fastened itself on his hand. [4]When the islanders saw the snake hanging from his hand, they said to each other, "This man must be a murderer; for though he escaped from the sea, Justice has not allowed him to live." [5]But Paul shook the snake off into the fire and suffered no ill effects. [6]The people expected him to swell up or suddenly fall dead, but after waiting a long time and seeing nothing unusual happen to him, they changed their minds and said he was a god.

[7]There was an estate near by that belonged to Publius, the chief official of the island. He welcomed us to his home and for three days entertained us hospitably. [8]His father was sick in bed, suffering from fever and dysentery. Paul went in to see him and, after prayer, placed his hands on him and healed him. [9]When this had happened, the rest of the sick on the island came and were cured. [10]They honoured us in many ways and when we were ready to sail, they furnished us with the supplies we needed.

Arrival at Rome

[11]After three months we put out to sea in a ship that had wintered in the island. It was an Alexandrian ship with the figurehead of the twin gods Castor and Pollux. [12]We put in at Syracuse and stayed there three days. [13]From there we set sail and arrived at Rhegium. The next day the south wind came up, and on the following day we reached Puteoli. [14]There we found some brothers who invited us to spend a week with them. And so we came to Rome. [15]The brothers there had heard that we were coming, and they travelled as far as the Forum of Appius and the Three Taverns to meet us. At the sight of these men Paul thanked God and was encouraged. [16]When we got to Rome, Paul was

---

[b]27 In ancient times the name referred to an area extending well south of Italy.
[c]28 Greek twenty orguias (about 37 metres)　　　[d]28 Greek fifteen orguias (about 27 metres)

allowed to live by himself, with a soldier to guard him.

Paul Preaches at Rome Under Guard

¹⁷Three days later he called together the leaders of the Jews. When they had assembled, Paul said to them: "My brothers, although I have done nothing against our people or against the customs of our ancestors, I was arrested in Jerusalem and handed over to the Romans. ¹⁸They examined me and wanted to release me, because I was not guilty of any crime deserving death. ¹⁹But when the Jews objected, I was compelled to appeal to Caesar—not that I had any charge to bring against my own people. ²⁰For this reason I have asked to see you and talk with you. It is because of the hope of Israel that I am bound with this chain."

²¹They replied, "We have not received any letters from Judea concerning you, and none of the brothers who have come from there has reported or said anything bad about you. ²²But we want to hear what your views are, for we know that people everywhere are talking against this sect."

²³They arranged to meet Paul on a certain day, and came in even larger numbers to the place where he was staying. From morning till evening he explained and declared to them the kingdom of God and tried to convince them about Jesus from the Law of Moses and from the Prophets. ²⁴Some were convinced by what he said, but others would not believe. ²⁵They disagreed among themselves and began to leave after Paul had made this final statement: "The Holy Spirit spoke the truth to your forefathers when he said through Isaiah the prophet:

²⁶" 'Go to this people and say,
"You will be ever hearing but never
      understanding;
   you will be ever seeing but never
      perceiving."
²⁷For this people's heart has become
      calloused;
   they hardly hear with their ears,
   and they have closed their eyes.
Otherwise they might see with their eyes,
   hear with their ears,
   understand with their hearts
and turn, and I would heal them.'ᵃ

²⁸"Therefore I want you to know that God's salvation has been sent to the Gentiles, and they will listen!"ᵇ

³⁰For two whole years Paul stayed there in his own rented house and welcomed all who came to see him. ³¹Boldly and without hindrance he preached the kingdom of God and taught about the Lord Jesus Christ.

ᵃ27 Isaiah 6:9,10
ᵇ28 Some manuscripts listen!" ²⁹After he said this, the Jews left, arguing vigorously among themselves.

ACTS 27:21–6

'Last night an angel of the God whose I am and whom I serve stood beside me and said, "Do not be afraid Paul. You must stand trial before Caesar; and God has graciously given you the lives of all who sail with you" ' (vv. 23, 24).

ALTHOUGH THE SHIP'S CREW HAD BEHAVED improvidently by leaving Fair Havens against the advice of Paul, God still had his purposes to work out through Paul. As the major character in this drama whose work was incomplete, Paul could not be lost, but as an act of grace, God had given the assurance that not one person would be lost. The ship's company had the perfect antidote for despair: the Lord was with them. The Lord's messenger who stood beside Paul during the previous night gives cause for us to repeat Newton's words:

> *With Christ in the vessel,*
> *I smile at the storm.*

In these most frightening circumstances Paul's faith in God, and his providence, remained intact. He never forgot who he was and to whom he belonged, 'whose I am and whom I serve', are key words.

Paul was assured he would face Caesar according to the promise given earlier, but great dangers still lay ahead. Although the men would be saved, the prospect had some unattractive elements: the ship would be lost and they would run aground on some unspecified island. At least, every life would be saved, which must have exceeded their recent expectations.

> *The storm may roar without me,*
> *My heart may low be laid;*
> *But God is round about me,*
> *And can I be dismayed?*

> (*Anna Laetitia Waring*)

→1016

ROMANS 1:8–17

'I am not ashamed of the gospel, because it is the power of God for the salvation of everyone who believes: first for the Jew, then for the Gentile. For in the gospel a righteousness from God is revealed' (vv. 16, 17a).

POWER AND RIGHTEOUSNESS. Romans knew the meaning of power. Their emperor was the most powerful man in the world. But as the Roman writer Epictetus said so rightly 'While the Emperor has power to give peace from war on land and sea, he is unable to give peace from passion, grief, and envy. He cannot give peace of heart, for which man longs even more than outward peace.' What human power cannot do, above all, is bring men to salvation.

The gospel of Christ, declares Paul, can do just that. But salvation requires righteousness, that is *being made right* with God. How is that to be achieved? God alone can do it and he chooses to do it by means of the gospel. The gospel depends on a man of whom, by ordinary standards, many people would be ashamed. After all, he died on a cross – to Roman thinking the despicable death of a common, non-Roman criminal – to Jewish thought a death which involved a terrible curse (Deut. 21:22, 23). Just as God had used a tiny and insignificant people, the Jews, to reveal himself initially, so he now uses a single, individual, representative man, one of society's rejects, to reveal his power fully.

When we realize that, we begin to understand how righteousness depends on faith. We cannot earn a right relationship with God. We cannot become good enough. We can only identify with Christ in faith. That means letting go of all we hold dear, letting go everything we depend on, and accepting. That is faith.

Faith is not something we achieve, but a gift open for all to accept from God.

→1019

Romans

1 Paul, a servant of Christ Jesus, called to be an apostle and set apart for the gospel of God—²the gospel he promised beforehand through his prophets in the Holy Scriptures ³regarding his Son, who as to his human nature was a descendant of David, ⁴and who through the Spirit*a* of holiness was declared with power to be the Son of God,*b* by his resurrection from the dead: Jesus Christ our Lord. ⁵Through him and for his name's sake, we received grace and apostleship to call people from among all the Gentiles to the obedience that comes from faith. ⁶And you also are among those who are called to belong to Jesus Christ.

⁷To all in Rome who are loved by God and called to be saints:

Grace and peace to you from God our Father and from the Lord Jesus Christ.

Paul's Longing to Visit Rome

⁸First, I thank my God through Jesus Christ for all of you, because your faith is being reported all over the world. ⁹God, whom I serve with my whole heart in preaching the gospel of his Son, is my witness how constantly I remember you ¹⁰in my prayers at all times; and I pray that now at last by God's will the way may be opened for me to come to you.

¹¹I long to see you so that I may impart to you some spiritual gift to make you strong —¹²that is, that you and I may be mutually encouraged by each other's faith. ¹³I do not want you to be unaware, brothers, that I planned many times to come to you (but have been prevented from doing so until now) in order that I might have a harvest among you, just as I have had among the other Gentiles.

¹⁴I am bound both to Greeks and non-Greeks, both to the wise and the foolish. ¹⁵That is why I am so eager to preach the gospel also to you who are at Rome.

¹⁶I am not ashamed of the gospel, because it is the power of God for the salvation of everyone who believes: first for the Jew, then for the Gentile. ¹⁷For in the gospel a righteousness from God is revealed, a righteousness that is by faith from first to last,*c* just as it is written: "The righteous will live by faith."*d*

God's Wrath Against Mankind

¹⁸The wrath of God is being revealed from heaven against all the godlessness and wickedness of men who suppress the truth by their wickedness, ¹⁹since what may be known about God is plain to them, because God has made it plain to them. ²⁰For since the creation of the world God's invisible qualities—his eternal power and divine nature —have been clearly seen, being understood from what has been made, so that men are without excuse.

²¹For although they knew God, they neither glorified him as God nor gave thanks to him, but their thinking became futile and their foolish hearts were darkened. ²²Although they claimed to be wise, they became fools ²³and exchanged the glory of the immortal God for images made to look like mortal man and birds and animals and reptiles.

²⁴Therefore God gave them over in the sinful desires of their hearts to sexual impurity for the degrading of their bodies with one another. ²⁵They exchanged the truth of God for a lie, and worshipped and served created things rather than the Creator—who is for ever praised. Amen.

²⁶Because of this, God gave them over to shameful lusts. Even their women exchanged natural relations for unnatural ones. ²⁷In the same way the men also abandoned natural relations with women and were inflamed with lust for one another. Men committed indecent acts with other men, and received in themselves the due penalty for their perversion.

²⁸Furthermore, since they did not think it worth while to retain the knowledge of God, he gave them over to a depraved mind, to do what ought not to be done. ²⁹They have become filled with every kind of wickedness, evil, greed and depravity. They are full of envy, murder, strife, deceit and malice. They are gossips, ³⁰slanderers, God-haters, insolent, arrogant and boastful; they invent ways of doing evil; they disobey their parents; ³¹they are senseless, faithless, heartless,

---

a4 Or *who as to his spirit*   *b4* Or *was appointed to be the Son of God with power*
c17 Or *is from faith to faith*   *d17* Hab. 2:4

ruthless. [32]Although they know God's righteous decree that those who do such things deserve death, they not only continue to do these very things but also approve of those who practise them.

God's Righteous Judgment

2 You, therefore, have no excuse, you who pass judgment on someone else, for at whatever point you judge the other, you are condemning yourself, because you who pass judgment do the same things. [2]Now we know that God's judgment against those who do such things is based on truth. [3]So when you, a mere man, pass judgment on them and yet do the same things, do you think you will escape God's judgment? [4]Or do you show contempt for the riches of his kindness, tolerance and patience, not realising that God's kindness leads you towards repentance?

[5]But because of your stubbornness and your unrepentant heart, you are storing up wrath against yourself for the day of God's wrath, when his righteous judgment will be revealed. [6]God "will give to each person according to what he has done".[a] [7]To those who by persistence in doing good seek glory, honour and immortality, he will give eternal life. [8]But for those who are self-seeking and who reject the truth and follow evil, there will be wrath and anger. [9]There will be trouble and distress for every human being who does evil: first for the Jew, then for the Gentile; [10]but glory, honour and peace for everyone who does good: first for the Jew, then for the Gentile. [11]For God does not show favouritism.

[12]All who sin apart from the law will also perish apart from the law, and all who sin under the law will be judged by the law. [13]For it is not those who hear the law who are righteous in God's sight, but it is those who obey the law who will be declared righteous. [14](Indeed, when Gentiles, who do not have the law, do by nature things required by the law, they are a law for themselves, even though they do not have the law, [15]since they show that the requirements of the law are written on their hearts, their consciences also bearing witness, and their thoughts now accusing, now even defending them.) [16]This will take place on the day when God will judge men's secrets through Jesus Christ, as my gospel declares.

The Jews and the Law

[17]Now you, if you call yourself a Jew; if you rely on the law and brag about your relationship to God; [18]if you know his will and approve of what is superior because you are instructed by the law; [19]if you are convinced that you are a guide for the blind, a light for those who are in the dark, [20]an instructor of the foolish, a teacher of infants, because you have in the law the embodiment of knowledge and truth—[21]you, then, who teach others, do you not teach yourself? You who preach against stealing, do you steal?

[22]You who say that people should not commit adultery, do you commit adultery? You who abhor idols, do you rob temples? [23]You who brag about the law, do you dishonour God by breaking the law? [24]As it is written: "God's name is blasphemed among the Gentiles because of you."[b]

[25]Circumcision has value if you observe the law, but if you break the law, you have become as though you had not been circumcised. [26]If those who are not circumcised keep the law's requirements, will they not be regarded as though they were circumcised? [27]The one who is not circumcised physically and yet obeys the law will condemn you who, even though you have the[c] written code and circumcision, are a law-breaker.

[28]A man is not a Jew if he is only one outwardly, nor is circumcision merely outward and physical. [29]No, a man is a Jew if he is one inwardly; and circumcision is circumcision of the heart, by the Spirit, not by the written code. Such a man's praise is not from men, but from God.

God's Faithfulness

3 What advantage, then, is there in being a Jew, or what value is there in circumcision? [2]Much in every way! First of all, they have been entrusted with the very words of God.

[3]What if some did not have faith? Will their lack of faith nullify God's faithfulness? [4]Not at all! Let God be true, and every man a liar. As it is written:

"So that you may be proved right when
    you speak
    and prevail when you judge."[a]

[5]But if our unrighteousness brings out God's righteousness more clearly, what shall we say? That God is unjust in bringing his wrath on us? (I am using a human argument.) [6]Certainly not! If that were so, how could God judge the world? [7]Someone might argue, "If my falsehood enhances God's truthfulness and so increases his glory, why am I still condemned as a sinner?" [8]Why not say—as we are being slanderously reported as saying and as some claim that we say—"Let us do evil that good may result"? Their condemnation is deserved.

No-one Is Righteous

[9]What shall we conclude then? Are we any better?[b] Not at all! We have already made the charge that Jews and Gentiles alike are all under sin. [10]As it is written:

"There is no-one righteous, not even one;
[11]   there is no-one who understands,
    no-one who seeks God.
[12]All have turned away,
    they have together become worthless;
there is no-one who does good,
    not even one."

---

[a]6 Psalm 62:12; Prov. 24:12   [b]24 Isaiah 52:5; Ezek. 36:22   [c]27 Or who, by means of a   [a]4 Psalm 51:4
[b]9 Or worse   [c]12 Psalms 14:1–3; 53:1–3; Eccles. 7:20

ROMANS 3:21–31
'All . . . are justified freely by his grace through the redemption that came by Christ Jesus. God presented him as a sacrifice of atonement, through faith in his blood (vv. 24, 25).

Three illustrations:

1. The law court. God has *justified* the sinner. He has counted him as righteous. This is our Roman letter's main theme (1:16, 17). It is a costly decision on God's part, for it involves redemption, demonstrated by

2. The slave market, where the *redemption* of slaves, their emancipation, could be made by payment of a price on their behalf. The price paid by God was to let go his only Son, Christ Jesus, to suffer and die for us. This transaction is set against the background of

3. The temple, where *atonement* had been made through animal sacrifice for many centuries. Jesus became the one sacrifice valid for all time and in eternity.

Each picture has value. None tells the whole story. But what a story! The law court, with its trembling defendants; the slave market, with its welter of human misery; the temple, with its oceans of slaughtered beasts can all be used to illustrate the pain involved in the greatest action of love the world has ever know. They are, in Paul's own words, speaking about the things of God in a human way (3:5).

But even the human can come very close to the heart of God.

→1020

ROMANS 5:1–11

'And hope does not disappoint us, because God has poured out his love into our hearts by the Holy Spirit whom he has given us' (v. 5).

FAITH, HOPE, LOVE. These verses are of central importance. Not only do they begin to state important differences Christ makes to the life of the Christian, they bring together three concepts which Paul has already detailed in 1 Corinthians 13. The three ideas are also found in 1 Peter 1:21, 22 and 1 Thessalonians 1:3.

These ideas belong to the very earliest proclamations of the Christian Church. They are completely intertwined and it is impossible to enjoy one fully without the others. We would not suggest they are like the three monkeys which used to be seen in the parlours of an older generation – one with eyes covered 'See no evil' – one with ears covered 'hear no evil' – one with mouth covered 'speak no evil' – but they belong together as closely as those three monkeys.

Faith is the initial response, as well as being a gift from God. Hope springs to life immediately we begin our response in faith. It is part and parcel of our new, God-ward direction, the 'turning round' which is called by the technical term 'repentance'. But none of this is real or even useful unless it issues in love; love towards our fellows which springs from our love of God.

'My command is this: Love each other as I have loved you.' (John 15:12)

¹³"Their throats are open graves;
    their tongues practise deceit."*d*
"The poison of vipers is on their lips."*e*
¹⁴   "Their mouths are full of cursing and
        bitterness."*f*
¹⁵"Their feet are swift to shed blood;
¹⁶   ruin and misery mark their ways,
¹⁷and the way of peace they do not
        know."*g*
¹⁸   "There is no fear of God before their
        eyes."*h*

¹⁹Now we know that whatever the law
says, it says to those who are under the law,
so that every mouth may be silenced and the
whole world held accountable to God.
²⁰Therefore no-one will be declared right-
eous in his sight by observing the law; rather,
through the law we become conscious of
sin.

Righteousness Through Faith

²¹But now a righteousness from God, apart
from law, has been made known, to which
the Law and the Prophets testify. ²²This
righteousness from God comes through faith
in Jesus Christ to all who believe. There is no
difference, ²³for all have sinned and fall short
of the glory of God, ²⁴and are justified freely
by his grace through the redemption that
came by Christ Jesus. ²⁵God presented him
as a sacrifice of atonement,*i* through faith in
his blood. He did this to demonstrate his
justice, because in his forbearance he had left
the sins committed beforehand unpunished
²⁶—he did it to demonstrate his justice at the
present time, so as to be just and the one who
justifies those who have faith in Jesus.

²⁷Where, then, is boasting? It is excluded.
On what principle? On that of observing the
law? No, but on that of faith. ²⁸For we maintain that a man is justified by faith apart from
observing the law. ²⁹Is God the God of Jews
only? Is he not the God of Gentiles too?
Yes, of Gentiles too, ³⁰since there is only one
God, who will justify the circumcised by
faith and the uncircumcised through that
same faith. ³¹Do we, then, nullify the law
by this faith? Not at all! Rather, we uphold
the law.

Abraham Justified by Faith

4 What then shall we say that Abraham,
    our forefather, discovered in this mat-
ter? ²If, in fact, Abraham was justified by
works, he had something to boast about—
but not before God. ³What does the Scripture
say? "Abraham believed God, and it was
credited to him as righteousness."*a*

⁴Now when a man works, his wages are
not credited to him as a gift, but as an obligation. ⁵However, to the man who does not
work but trusts God who justifies the wicked,
his faith is credited as righteousness. ⁶David
says the same thing when he speaks of the
blessedness of the man to whom God credits
righteousness apart from works:

⁷"Blessed are they
    whose transgressions are forgiven,
    whose sins are covered.
⁸Blessed is the man
    whose sin the Lord will never count
        against him."*b*

⁹Is this blessedness only for the circum-
cised, or also for the uncircumcised? We
have been saying that Abraham's faith was
credited to him as righteousness. ¹⁰Under
what circumstances was it credited? Was it
after he was circumcised, or before? It was
not after, but before! ¹¹And he received the
sign of circumcision, a seal of the righteousness that he had by faith while he was still
uncircumcised. So then, he is the father of all
who believe but have not been circumcised,
in order that righteousness might be credited
to them. ¹²And he is also the father of the
circumcised who not only are circumcised
but who also walk in the footsteps of the faith
that our father Abraham had before he was
circumcised.

¹³It was not through law that Abraham and
his offspring received the promise that he
would be heir of the world, but through the
righteousness that comes by faith. ¹⁴For if
those who live by law are heirs, faith has
no value and the promise is worthless,
¹⁵because law brings wrath. And where there
is no law there is no transgression.

¹⁶Therefore, the promise comes by faith,
so that it may be by grace and may be guaran-
teed to all Abraham's offspring—not only to
those who are of the law but also to those
who are of the faith of Abraham. He is the
father of us all. ¹⁷As it is written: "I have
made you a father of many nations."*c* He is
our father in the sight of God, in whom he believed—the God who gives life to the dead and
calls things that are not as though they were.

¹⁸Against all hope, Abraham in hope be-
lieved and so became the father of many
nations, just as it had been said to him, "So
shall your offspring be."*d* ¹⁹Without weakening in his faith, he faced the fact that his body
was as good as dead—since he was about a
hundred years old—and that Sarah's womb
was also dead. ²⁰Yet he did not waver
through unbelief regarding the promise of
God, but was strengthened in his faith and
gave glory to God, ²¹being fully persuaded
that God had power to do what he had prom-
ised. ²²This is why "it was credited to him as
righteousness." ²³The words "it was credited to him" were written not for him alone,
²⁴but also for us, to whom God will credit
righteousness—for us who believe in him
who raised Jesus our Lord from the dead.
²⁵He was delivered over to death for our sins
and was raised to life for our justification.

Peace and Joy

5 Therefore, since we have been justified
    through faith, we*a* have peace with God
through our Lord Jesus Christ, ²through

---

d13 Psalm 5:9   *e13* Psalm 140:3   *f14* Psalm 10:7   *g17* Isaiah 59:7,8   *h18* Psalm 36:1
i25 Or *as the one who would turn aside his wrath, taking away sin*
a3 Gen. 15:6; also in verse 22   *b8* Psalm 32:1,2   *c17* Gen. 17:5   *d18* Gen. 15:5   *a1* Or *let us*

whom we have gained access by faith into this grace in which we now stand. And we[a] rejoice in the hope of the glory of God. ³Not only so, but we[a] also rejoice in our sufferings, because we know that suffering produces perseverance; ⁴perseverance, character; and character, hope. ⁵And hope does not disappoint us, because God has poured out his love into our hearts by the Holy Spirit, whom he has given us.

⁶You see, at just the right time, when we were still powerless, Christ died for the ungodly. ⁷Very rarely will anyone die for a righteous man, though for a good man someone might possibly dare to die. ⁸But God demonstrates his own love for us in this: While we were still sinners, Christ died for us.

⁹Since we have now been justified by his blood, how much more shall we be saved from God's wrath through him! ¹⁰For if, when we were God's enemies, we were reconciled to him through the death of his Son, how much more, having been reconciled, shall we be saved through his life! ¹¹Not only is this so, but we also rejoice in God through our Lord Jesus Christ, through whom we have now received reconciliation.

Death Through Adam, Life Through Christ

¹²Therefore, just as sin entered the world through one man, and death through sin, and in this way death came to all men, because all sinned—¹³for before the law was given, sin was in the world. But sin is not taken into account when there is no law. ¹⁴Nevertheless, death reigned from the time of Adam to the time of Moses, even over those who did not sin by breaking a command, as did Adam, who was a pattern of the one to come.

¹⁵But the gift is not like the trespass. For if the many died by the trespass of the one man, how much more did God's grace and the gift that came by the grace of the one man, Jesus Christ, overflow to the many! ¹⁶Again, the gift of God is not like the result of the one man's sin: The judgment followed one sin and brought condemnation, but the gift followed many trespasses and brought justification. ¹⁷For if, by the trespass of the one man, death reigned through that one man, how much more will those who receive God's abundant provision of grace and of the gift of righteousness reign in life through the one man, Jesus Christ.

¹⁸Consequently, just as the result of one trespass was condemnation for all men, so also the result of one act of righteousness was justification that brings life for all men. ¹⁹For just as through the disobedience of the one man the many were made sinners, so also through the obedience of the one man the many will be made righteous.

²⁰The law was added so that the trespass might increase. But where sin increased, grace increased all the more, ²¹so that, just as sin reigned in death, so also grace might reign

through righteousness to bring eternal life through Jesus Christ our Lord.

Dead to Sin, Alive in Christ

6 What shall we say, then? Shall we go on sinning, so that grace may increase? ²By no means! We died to sin; how can we live in it any longer? ³Or don't you know that all of us who were baptised into Christ Jesus were baptised into his death? ⁴We were therefore buried with him through baptism into death in order that, just as Christ was raised from the dead through the glory of the Father, we too may live a new life.

⁵If we have been united with him like this in his death, we will certainly also be united with him in his resurrection. ⁶For we know that our old self was crucified with him so that the body of sin might be done away with,[a] that we should no longer be slaves to sin—⁷because anyone who has died has been freed from sin.

⁸Now if we died with Christ, we believe that we will also live with him. ⁹For we know that since Christ was raised from the dead, he cannot die again; death no longer has mastery over him. ¹⁰The death he died, he died to sin once for all; but the life he lives, he lives to God.

¹¹In the same way, count yourselves dead to sin but alive to God in Christ Jesus. ¹²Therefore do not let sin reign in your mortal body so that you obey its evil desires. ¹³Do not offer the parts of your body to sin, as instruments of wickedness, but rather offer yourselves to God, as those who have been brought from death to life; and offer the parts of your body to him as instruments of righteousness. ¹⁴For sin shall not be your master, because you are not under law, but under grace.

Slaves to Righteousness

¹⁵What then? Shall we sin because we are not under law but under grace? By no means! ¹⁶Don't you know that when you offer yourselves to someone to obey him as slaves, you are slaves to the one whom you obey —whether you are slaves to sin, which leads to death, or to obedience, which leads to righteousness? ¹⁷But thanks be to God that, though you used to be slaves to sin, you wholeheartedly obeyed the form of teaching to which you were entrusted. ¹⁸You have been set free from sin and have become slaves to righteousness.

¹⁹I put this in human terms because you are weak in your natural selves. Just as you used to offer the parts of your body in slavery to impurity and to ever-increasing wickedness, so now offer them in slavery to righteousness leading to holiness. ²⁰When you were slaves to sin, you were free from the control of righteousness. ²¹What benefit did you reap at that time from the things you are now ashamed of? Those things result in death! ²²But now that you have been set free from sin and have become slaves to God, the benefit you reap leads to holiness, and the

---

[a]2,3 Or let us   [a]6 Or be rendered powerless

result is eternal life. ²³For the wages of sin is death, but the gift of God is eternal life in*b* Christ Jesus our Lord.

An Illustration From Marriage

7 Do you not know, brothers—for I am speaking to men who know the law—that the law has authority over a man only as long as he lives? ²For example, by law a married woman is bound to her husband as long as he is alive, but if her husband dies, she is released from the law of marriage. ³So then, if she marries another man while her husband is still alive, she is called an adulteress. But if her husband dies, she is released from that law and is not an adulteress, even though she marries another man.

⁴So, my brothers, you also died to the law through the body of Christ, that you might belong to another, to him who was raised from the dead, in order that we might bear fruit to God. ⁵For when we were controlled by the sinful nature,*a* the sinful passions aroused by the law were at work in our bodies, so that we bore fruit for death. ⁶But now, by dying to what once bound us, we have been released from the law so that we serve in the new way of the Spirit, and not in the old way of the written code.

Struggling With Sin

⁷What shall we say, then? Is the law sin? Certainly not! Indeed I would not have known what sin was except through the law. For I would not have known what coveting really was if the law had not said, "Do not covet."*b* ⁸But sin, seizing the opportunity afforded by the commandment, produced in me every kind of covetous desire. For apart from law, sin is dead. ⁹Once I was alive apart from law; but when the commandment came, sin sprang to life and I died. ¹⁰I found that the very commandment that was intended to bring life actually brought death. ¹¹For sin, seizing the opportunity afforded by the commandment, deceived me, and through the commandment put me to death. ¹²So then, the law is holy, and the commandment is holy, righteous and good.

¹³Did that which is good, then, become death to me? By no means! But in order that sin might be recognised as sin, it produced death in me through what was good, so that through the commandment sin might become utterly sinful.

¹⁴We know that the law is spiritual; but I am unspiritual, sold as a slave to sin. ¹⁵I do not understand what I do. For what I want to do I do not do, but what I hate I do. ¹⁶And if I do what I do not want to do, I agree that the law is good. ¹⁷As it is, it is no longer I myself who do it, but it is sin living in me. ¹⁸I know that nothing good lives in me, that is, in my sinful nature.*c* For I have the desire to do what is good, but I cannot carry it out. ¹⁹For what I do is not the good I want to do; no, the

evil I do not want to do—this I keep on doing. ²⁰Now if I do what I do not want to do, it is no longer I who do it, but it is sin living in me that does it.

²¹So I find this law at work: When I want to do good, evil is right there with me. ²²For in my inner being I delight in God's law; ²³but I see another law at work in the members of my body, waging war against the law of my mind and making me a prisoner of the law of sin at work within my members. ²⁴What a wretched man I am! Who will rescue me from this body of death? ²⁵Thanks be to God— through Jesus Christ our Lord!

So then, I myself in my mind am a slave to God's law, but in the sinful nature a slave to the law of sin.

Life Through the Spirit

8 Therefore, there is now no condemnation for those who are in Christ Jesus,*a* ²because through Christ Jesus the law of the Spirit of life set me free from the law of sin and death. ³For what the law was powerless to do in that it was weakened by the sinful nature,*b* God did by sending his own Son in the likeness of sinful man to be a sin offering.*c* And so he condemned sin in sinful man,*d* ⁴in order that the righteous requirements of the law might be fully met in us, who do not live according to the sinful nature but according to the Spirit.

⁵Those who live according to the sinful nature have their minds set on what that nature desires; but those who live in accordance with the Spirit have their minds set on what the Spirit desires. ⁶The mind of sinful man*e* is death, but the mind controlled by the Spirit is life and peace; ⁷the sinful mind*f* is hostile to God. It does not submit to God's law, nor can it do so. ⁸Those controlled by the sinful nature cannot please God.

⁹You, however, are controlled not by the sinful nature but by the Spirit, if the Spirit of God lives in you. And if anyone does not have the Spirit of Christ, he does not belong to Christ. ¹⁰But if Christ is in you, your body is dead because of sin, yet your spirit is alive because of righteousness. ¹¹And if the Spirit of him who raised Jesus from the dead is living in you, he who raised Christ from the dead will also give life to your mortal bodies through his Spirit, who lives in you.

¹²Therefore, brothers, we have an obligation—but it is not to the sinful nature, to live according to it. ¹³For if you live according to the sinful nature, you will die; but if by the Spirit you put to death the misdeeds of the body, you will live, ¹⁴because those who are led by the Spirit of God are sons of God. ¹⁵For you did not receive a spirit that makes you a slave again to fear, but you received the Spirit of sonship.*g* And by him we cry, "*Abba*,*h* Father." ¹⁶The Spirit himself testifies with our spirit that we are God's children. ¹⁷Now if we are children, then we are heirs—heirs of God and co-heirs with Christ,

---

*b*23 Or *through*   *a*5 Or *the flesh*; also in verse 25   *b*7 Exodus 20:17; Deut. 5:21   *c*18 Or *my flesh*
*a*1 Some later manuscripts *Jesus, who do not live according to the sinful nature but according to the Spirit,*
*b*3 Or *the flesh*; also in verses 4, 5, 8, 9, 12 and 13   *c*3 Or *man, for sin*   *d*3 Or *in the flesh*
*e*6 Or *mind set on the flesh*   *f*7 Or *the mind set on the flesh*   *g*15 Or *adoption*   *h*15 Aramaic for *Father*

if indeed we share in his sufferings in order that we may also share in his glory.

Future Glory

[18]I consider that our present sufferings are not worth comparing with the glory that will be revealed in us. [19]The creation waits in eager expectation for the sons of God to be revealed. [20]For the creation was subjected to frustration, not by its own choice, but by the will of the one who subjected it, in hope [21]that[i] the creation itself will be liberated from its bondage to decay and brought into the glorious freedom of the children of God.

[22]We know that the whole creation has been groaning as in the pains of childbirth right up to the present time. [23]Not only so, but we ourselves, who have the firstfruits of the Spirit, groan inwardly as we wait eagerly for our adoption as sons, the redemption of our bodies. [24]For in this hope we were saved. But hope that is seen is no hope at all. Who hopes for what he already has? [25]But if we hope for what we do not yet have, we wait for it patiently.

[26]In the same way, the Spirit helps us in our weakness. We do not know what we ought to pray for, but the Spirit himself intercedes for us with groans that words cannot express. [27]And he who searches our hearts knows the mind of the Spirit, because the Spirit intercedes for the saints in accordance with God's will.

More Than Conquerors

[28]And we know that in all things God works for the good of those who love him,[j] who[k] have been called according to his purpose. [29]For those God foreknew he also predestined to be conformed to the likeness of his Son, that he might be the firstborn among many brothers. [30]And those he predestined, he also called; those he called, he also justified; those he justified, he also glorified.

[31]What, then, shall we say in response to this? If God is for us, who can be against us? [32]He who did not spare his own Son, but gave him up for us all—how will he not also, along with him, graciously give us all things? [33]Who will bring any charge against those whom God has chosen? It is God who justifies. [34]Who is he that condemns? Christ Jesus, who died—more than that, who was raised to life—is at the right hand of God and is also interceding for us. [35]Who shall separate us from the love of Christ? Shall trouble or hardship or persecution or famine or nakedness or danger or sword? [36]As it is written:

"For your sake we face death all day long;
    we are considered as sheep to be
        slaughtered."[l]

[37]No, in all these things we are more than conquerors through him who loved us. [38]For I am convinced that neither death nor life, neither angels nor demons,[m] neither the present nor the future, nor any powers, [39]neither height nor depth, nor anything else in all creation, will be able to separate us from the love of God that is in Christ Jesus our Lord.

God's Sovereign Choice

9 I speak the truth in Christ—I am not lying, my conscience confirms it in the Holy Spirit—[2]I have great sorrow and unceasing anguish in my heart. [3]For I could wish that I myself were cursed and cut off from Christ for the sake of my brothers, those of my own race, [4]the people of Israel. Theirs is the adoption as sons; theirs the divine glory, the covenants, the receiving of the law, the temple worship and the promises. [5]Theirs are the patriarchs, and from them is traced the human ancestry of Christ, who is God over all, for ever praised![a] Amen.

[6]It is not as though God's word had failed. For not all who are descended from Israel are Israel. [7]Nor because they are his descendants are they all Abraham's children. On the contrary, "It is through Isaac that your offspring will be reckoned."[b] [8]In other words, it is not the natural children who are God's children, but it is the children of the promise who are regarded as Abraham's offspring. [9]For this was how the promise was stated: "At the appointed time I will return, and Sarah will have a son."[c]

[10]Not only that, but Rebekah's children had one and the same father, our father Isaac. [11]Yet, before the twins were born or had done anything good or bad—in order that God's purpose in election might stand: [12]not by works but by him who calls—she was told, "The older will serve the younger."[d] [13]Just as it is written: "Jacob I loved, but Esau I hated."[e]

[14]What then shall we say? Is God unjust? Not at all! [15]For he says to Moses,

"I will have mercy on whom I have mercy,
    and I will have compassion on whom I
        have compassion."[f]

[16]It does not, therefore, depend on man's desire or effort, but on God's mercy. [17]For the Scripture says to Pharaoh: "I raised you up for this very purpose, that I might display my power in you and that my name might be proclaimed in all the earth."[g] [18]Therefore God has mercy on whom he wants to have mercy, and he hardens whom he wants to harden.

[19]One of you will say to me: "Then why does God still blame us? For who resists his will?" [20]But who are you, O man, to talk

[i]20,21 Or subjected it in hope. [21]For
[j]28 Some manuscripts And we know that all things work together for good to those who love God
[k]28 Or works together with those who love him to bring about what is good—with those who
[l]36 Psalm 44:22   [m]38 Or not heavenly rulers
[a]5 Or Christ, who is over all. God be for ever praised! Or Christ. God who is over all be for ever praised!
[b]7 Gen. 21:12   [c]9 Gen. 18:10,14   [d]12 Gen. 25:23   [e]13 Mal. 1:2,3   [f]15 Exodus 33:19
[g]17 Exodus 9:16

ROMANS 7:14–25

'We know that the law is spiritual; but I am unspiritual, sold as a slave to sin. I do not understand what I do. For what I want to do I do not do, but what I hate I do' (vv. 14, 15).

SOLD AS A SLAVE TO SIN describes our earthly condition. This applies to all, redeemed or not. Redemption does not release us from bodily limitations. We still cannot be in more than one place at once. We cannot do everything we want to. We cannot always convince everyone of the wonder of Jesus. We cannot get rid of all sickness, and death, and disaster – and so we could go on.

Many have discussed whether these verses talk about Paul before or after he was redeemed. That is to miss the point. He is describing man's natural state, not just himself. We can then make sense of verses 24 and 25, and need not follow translators such as Moffatt and Phillips, who change their order. Is it not true that conflict always exists between the spiritual and material, even though spiritual life cannot be divorced from the material body in which it is lived?

Roger Bowen says,

A Christian belongs to two worlds (or, two ages) at the same time. He belongs to *this world* where evil, suffering, and death are present, even in his own life – he is *not yet* saved from these things. On the other hand, he belongs to the *new world* where Christ is King – he *already has* righteousness, life, and peace; he is a new man. This is why Paul wrote, 'I do not understand my own actions'; this is why there is this conflict in the life of every Christian. The new and the old fight against one another, and this fact should not surprise us . . . Those who only belong to the old age do not experience this conflict; and we shall not experience it in the age to come. But Christians should expect to experience this conflict now, as Paul did, because they live in both ages. They belong to God, but around them and in them are things which hinder them from serving him as they want to.

Who will rescue me? Thanks be to God – Jesus Christ our Lord!

→1026

ROMANS 9:1-5

'I have great sorrow and unceasing anguish in my heart. For I could wish that I myself were cursed and cut off from Christ for the sake of my brothers, those of my own race, the people of Israel' (vv. 2, 3).

TAKE HOLD OF LIFE. Paul is desperate. He wants above all to convince his own people of the claims of Christ. Like Moses (Exod. 32:32) he is willing to be cut off from the promise himself, if it means his own people will be saved.

The Jews, Paul's people, had many advantages – wonderful traditions, including the Scriptures (covenant, law and promise, v. 4), the temple, fine worship and a whole lot more. All this was theirs for they had become the adopted children of God. They were the heirs of the promise made to Abraham.

Through the life and ministry, death and resurrection of Jesus, these gifts were now being extended to a wider company. Rather like the elder brother in Jesus' parable of the prodigal (Luke 15) the Jews would feel left out and unjustly treated, as well as having natural suspicion which a radical new movement always arouses.

If this comparison is fair, then Paul is willing to sacrifice himself for the sake of the 'elder brother'. Such a quality is rare. There may be glamour attached to rescuing the prodigal, but laying down your life for the 'elder brother' who has enjoyed all the advantages up to now, that is sacrifice indeed.

'Greater love has no-one than this, that he lay down his life for his friends.' (John 15:13)

→1029

back to God? "Shall what is formed say to him who formed it, 'Why did you make me like this?'"*h* 21Does not the potter have the right to make out of the same lump of clay some pottery for noble purposes and some for common use?

22What if God, choosing to show his wrath and make his power known, bore with great patience the objects of his wrath—prepared for destruction? 23What if he did this to make the riches of his glory known to the objects of his mercy, whom he prepared in advance for glory—24even us, whom he also called, not only from the Jews but also from the Gentiles? 25As he says in Hosea:

"I will call them 'my people' who are not
    my people;
and I will call her 'my loved one' who is
    not my loved one,"*i*

26and,

"It will happen that in the very place
    where it was said to them,
    'You are not my people,'
they will be called 'sons of the living
    God'."*j*

27Isaiah cries out concerning Israel:

"Though the number of the Israelites be
    like the sand by the sea,
only the remnant will be saved.
28For the Lord will carry out
    his sentence on earth with speed and
    finality."*k*

29It is just as Isaiah said previously:

"Unless the Lord Almighty
    had left us descendants,
we would have become like Sodom,
    we would have been like Gomorrah."*l*

Israel's Unbelief

30What then shall we say? That the Gentiles, who did not pursue righteousness, have obtained it, a righteousness that is by faith; 31but Israel, who pursued a law of righteousness, has not attained it. 32Why not? Because they pursued it not by faith but as if it were by works. They stumbled over the "stumbling-stone". 33As it is written:

"See, I lay in Zion a stone that causes men
    to stumble
    and a rock that makes them fall,
and the one who trusts in him will never be
    put to shame."*m*

10 Brothers, my heart's desire and prayer to God for the Israelites is that they may be saved. 2For I can testify about them that they are zealous for God, but their zeal is not based on knowledge. 3Since they did not know the righteousness that comes

from God and sought to establish their own, they did not submit to God's righteousness. 4Christ is the end of the law so that there may be righteousness for everyone who believes.

5Moses describes in this way the righteousness that is by the law: "The man who does these things will live by them."*a* 6But the righteousness that is by faith says: "Do not say in your heart, 'Who will ascend into heaven?'*b*" (that is, to bring Christ down) 7"or 'Who will descend into the deep?'*c*" (that is, to bring Christ up from the dead). 8But what does it say? "The word is near you; it is in your mouth and in your heart,"*d* that is, the word of faith we are proclaiming: 9That if you confess with your mouth, "Jesus is Lord," and believe in your heart that God raised him from the dead, you will be saved. 10For it is with your heart that you believe and are justified, and it is with your mouth that you confess and are saved. 11As the Scripture says, "Anyone who trusts in him will never be put to shame."*e* 12For there is no difference between Jew and Gentile—the same Lord is Lord of all and richly blesses all who call on him, 13for, "Everyone who calls on the name of the Lord will be saved."*f*

14How, then, can they call on the one they have not believed in? And how can they believe in the one of whom they have not heard? And how can they hear without someone preaching to them? 15And how can they preach unless they are sent? As it is written, "How beautiful are the feet of those who bring good news!"*g*

16But not all the Israelites accepted the good news. For Isaiah says, "Lord, who has believed our message?"*h* 17Consequently, faith comes from hearing the message, and the message is heard through the word of Christ. 18But I ask: Did they not hear? Of course they did:

"Their voice has gone out into all the
    earth,
    their words to the ends of the world."*i*

19Again I ask: Did Israel not understand? First, Moses says,

"I will make you envious by those who are
    not a nation;
I will make you angry by a nation that
    has no understanding."*j*

20And Isaiah boldly says,

"I was found by those who did not seek
    me;
I revealed myself to those who did not
    ask for me."*k*

21But concerning Israel he says,

"All day long I have held out my hands
    to a disobedient and obstinate
    people."*l*

---

h20 Isaiah 29:16; 45:9   *i25* Hosea 2:23   *j26* Hosea 1:10   *k28* Isaiah 10:22,23   *l29* Isaiah 1:9
m33 Isaiah 8:14; 28:16   *a5* Lev. 18:5   *b6* Deut. 30:12   *c7* Deut. 30:13   *d8* Deut. 30:14
e11 Isaiah 28:16   *f13* Joel 2:32   *g15* Isaiah 52:7   *h16* Isaiah 53:1   *i18* Psalm 19:4
j19 Deut. 32:21   *k20* Isaiah 65:1   *l21* Isaiah 65:2

The Remnant of Israel

11 I ask then: Did God reject his people? By no means! I am an Israelite myself, a descendant of Abraham, from the tribe of Benjamin. [2]God did not reject his people, whom he foreknew. Don't you know what the Scripture says in the passage about Elijah —how he appealed to God against Israel: [3]"Lord, they have killed your prophets and torn down your altars; I am the only one left, and they are trying to kill me"[a]? [4]And what was God's answer to him? "I have reserved for myself seven thousand who have not bowed the knee to Baal."[b] [5]So too, at the present time there is a remnant chosen by grace. [6]And if by grace, then it is no longer by works; if it were, grace would no longer be grace.[c]

[7]What then? What Israel sought so earnestly it did not obtain, but the elect did. The others were hardened, [8]as it is written:

"God gave them a spirit of stupor,
    eyes so that they could not see
    and ears so that they could not hear,
to this very day."[d]

[9]And David says:

"May their table become a snare and a
        trap,
    a stumbling-block and a retribution for
        them.
[10]May their eyes be darkened so they cannot
        see,
    and their backs be bent for ever."[e]

Ingrafted Branches

[11]Again I ask: Did they stumble so as to fall beyond recovery? Not at all! Rather, because of their transgression, salvation has come to the Gentiles to make Israel envious. [12]But if their transgression means riches for the world, and their loss means riches for the Gentiles, how much greater riches will their fulness bring!

[13]I am talking to you Gentiles. Inasmuch as I am the apostle to the Gentiles, I make much of my ministry [14]in the hope that I may somehow arouse my own people to envy and save some of them. [15]For if their rejection is the reconciliation of the world, what will their acceptance be but life from the dead? [16]If the part of the dough offered as firstfruits is holy, then the whole batch is holy; if the root is holy, so are the branches.

[17]If some of the branches have been broken off, and you, though a wild olive shoot, have been grafted in among the others and now share in the nourishing sap from the olive root, [18]do not boast over those branches. If you do, consider this: You do not support the root, but the root supports you. [19]You will say then, "Branches were broken off so that I could be grafted in." [20]Granted.

But they were broken off because of unbelief, and you stand by faith. Do not be arrogant, but be afraid. [21]For if God did not spare the natural branches, he will not spare you either.

[22]Consider therefore the kindness and sternness of God: sternness to those who fell, but kindness to you, provided that you continue in his kindness. Otherwise, you also will be cut off. [23]And if they do not persist in unbelief, they will be grafted in, for God is able to graft them in again. [24]After all, if you were cut out of an olive tree that is wild by nature, and contrary to nature were grafted into a cultivated olive tree, how much more readily will these, the natural branches, be grafted into their own olive tree!

All Israel Will Be Saved

[25]I do not want you to be ignorant of this mystery, brothers, so that you may not be conceited: Israel has experienced a hardening in part until the full number of the Gentiles has come in. [26]And so all Israel will be saved, as it is written:

"The deliverer will come from Zion;
    he will turn godlessness away from
        Jacob.
[27]And this is[f] my covenant with them
    when I take away their sins."[g]

[28]As far as the gospel is concerned, they are enemies on your account; but as far as election is concerned, they are loved on account of the patriarchs, [29]for God's gifts and his call are irrevocable. [30]Just as you who were at one time disobedient to God have now received mercy as a result of their disobedience, [31]so they too have now become disobedient in order that they too may now[h] receive mercy as a result of God's mercy to you. [32]For God has bound all men over to disobedience so that he may have mercy on them all.

Doxology

[33]Oh, the depth of the riches of the wisdom
        and[i] knowledge of God!
    How unsearchable his judgments,
        and his paths beyond tracing out!
[34]"Who has known the mind of the Lord?
        Or who has been his counsellor?"[j]
[35]"Who has ever given to God,
        that God should repay him?"[k]
[36]For from him and through him and to him
        are all things.
    To him be the glory for ever! Amen.

Living Sacrifices

12 Therefore, I urge you, brothers, in view of God's mercy, to offer your bodies as living sacrifices, holy and pleasing to God—this is your spiritual[a] act of worship. [2]Do not conform any longer to the pattern of this world, but be transformed by

[a]3 1 Kings 19:10,14   [b]4 1 Kings 19:18
[c]6 Some manuscripts by grace. But if by works, then it is no longer grace; if it were, work would no longer be work.
[d]8 Deut. 29:4; Isaiah 29:10   [e]10 Psalm 69:22,23   [f]27 Or will be   [g]27 Isaiah 59:20,21; 27:9; Jer. 31:33,34
[h]31 Some manuscripts do not have now.   [i]33 Or riches and the wisdom and the   [j]34 Isaiah 40:13
[k]35 Job 41:11   [a]1 Or reasonable

ROMANS 10:14–17

'How, then, can they call on the one they have not believed in? And how can they believe in the one of whom they have not heard? And how can they hear without someone preaching to them?' (v. 14).

WHOSOEVER HEARETH! SHOUT SHOUT THE SOUND is the first line of an old gospel hymn by Philip Bliss. It is sung heartily by Christian congregations of many denominations, but it has contributed especially to the joyful worship of Sunday evening salvation meetings in the Salvation Army. Such boisterous, communal activity is a form of preaching just as surely as the carefully thought-out exposition of Scripture from the highest pulpit in the land. It causes people to hear, and come in contact with the gospel of Christ.

This is, indeed, one of the great mysteries of the faith. God makes all the running. He makes the effort. He provides us with salvation. He 'predestinates,' if you like. Yet he also allows us a part in the effort. He gives us the joy of telling others about himself. He uses *us* to spread knowledge of his truth. We cannot save anyone, but we can be instruments through which God's saving activity is channelled. The same Albert Orsborn who wrote 'I have no claim on grace, I have no right to plead' wrote:

> *O is not the Christ midst the crowd of today*
> *Whose questioning cries do not cease?*
> *And will he not show to the hearts that would know*
> *The things that belong to their peace?*
> *But how shall they hear if the preacher forebear*
> *Or lack in compassionate zeal?*

What better comment could there be on Paul's words in Romans 10:14?

→1030

ROMANS 12:17–21

'Do not take revenge, my friends, but leave room for God's wrath, for it is written: "It is mine to avenge: I will repay," says the Lord . . . Do not be overcome by evil, but overcome evil with good' (vv. 19, 21).

OVERCOME EVIL WITH GOOD. It's a tall order. Our natural reaction is exactly the opposite, to overcome evil with yet more evil. When we are attacked we wish to retaliate. Meet violence with violence is the natural way. In v. 20 Paul quotes Proverbs 25: 21, 22.

A Christian pastor was once attacked by an English national newspaper. Using inaccurate information from one of his flock, the newspaper printed a story about his private life, which was highly damaging. The pastor had in his possession evidence which would have been even more damaging about the informer. His first reaction was to use this information and expose the informer publicly. However, that would involve hurting not only the man who had slandered him, but also other members of his flock. His natural reaction remained, and even now he would probably love the other fellow to 'get what he deserves'. But pastoral concern for others involved, restrained his reaction and enabled him to take the hurt himself without personal, vindictive retaliation. His training as a pastor, and personal Christian concern for the flock provide a powerful example of overcoming evil with good.

We may not have to face the same devastating opportunity of putting Paul's words into action, but when we experience similar feelings Christ can enable our concern for others to overcome the desire to get even.

→1033

the renewing of your mind. Then you will be able to test and approve what God's will is—his good, pleasing and perfect will.

[3]For by the grace given me I say to every one of you: Do not think of yourself more highly than you ought, but rather think of yourself with sober judgment, in accordance with the measure of faith God has given you. [4]Just as each of us has one body with many members, and these members do not all have the same function, [5]so in Christ we who are many form one body, and each member belongs to all the others. [6]We have different gifts, according to the grace given us. If a man's gift is prophesying, let him use it in proportion to his[b] faith. [7]If it is serving, let him serve; if it is teaching, let him teach; [8]if it is encouraging, let him encourage; if it is contributing to the needs of others, let him give generously; if it is leadership, let him govern diligently; if it is showing mercy, let him do it cheerfully.

Love

[9]Love must be sincere. Hate what is evil; cling to what is good. [10]Be devoted to one another in brotherly love. Honour one another above yourselves. [11]Never be lacking in zeal, but keep your spiritual fervour, serving the Lord. [12]Be joyful in hope, patient in affliction, faithful in prayer. [13]Share with God's people who are in need. Practise hospitality.

[14]Bless those who persecute you; bless and do not curse. [15]Rejoice with those who rejoice; mourn with those who mourn. [16]Live in harmony with one another. Do not be proud, but be willing to associate with people of low position.[c] Do not be conceited.

[17]Do not repay anyone evil for evil. Be careful to do what is right in the eyes of everybody. [18]If it is possible, as far as it depends on you, live at peace with everyone. [19]Do not take revenge, my friends, but leave room for God's wrath, for it is written: "It is mine to avenge; I will repay,"[d] says the Lord. [20]On the contrary:

"If your enemy is hungry, feed him;
     if he is thirsty, give him something to
          drink.
In doing this, you will heap burning coals
     on his head."[e]

[21]Do not be overcome by evil, but overcome evil with good.

Submission to the Authorities

13 Everyone must submit himself to the governing authorities, for there is no authority except that which God has established. The authorities that exist have been established by God. [2]Consequently, he who rebels against the authority is rebelling against what God has instituted, and those who do so will bring judgment on themselves. [3]For rulers hold no terror for those who do right, but for those who do wrong. Do

you want to be free from fear of the one in authority? Then do what is right and he will commend you. [4]For he is God's servant to do you good. But if you do wrong, be afraid, for he does not bear the sword for nothing. He is God's servant, an agent of wrath to bring punishment on the wrongdoer. [5]Therefore, it is necessary to submit to the authorities, not only because of possible punishment but also because of conscience.

[6]This is also why you pay taxes, for the authorities are God's servants, who give their full time to governing. [7]Give everyone what you owe him: If you owe taxes, pay taxes; if revenue, then revenue; if respect, then respect; if honour, then honour.

Love, for the Day Is Near

[8]Let no debt remain outstanding, except the continuing debt to love one another, for he who loves his fellow-man has fulfilled the law. [9]The commandments, "Do not commit adultery," "Do not murder," "Do not steal," "Do not covet,"[a] and whatever other commandment there may be, are summed up in this one rule: "Love your neighbour as yourself."[b] [10]Love does no harm to its neighbour. Therefore love is the fulfilment of the law.

[11]And do this, understanding the present time. The hour has come for you to wake up from your slumber, because our salvation is nearer now than when we first believed. [12]The night is nearly over; the day is almost here. So let us put aside the deeds of darkness and put on the armour of light. [13]Let us behave decently, as in the daytime, not in orgies and drunkenness, not in sexual immorality and debauchery, not in dissension and jealousy. [14]Rather, clothe yourselves with the Lord Jesus Christ, and do not think about how to gratify the desires of the sinful nature.[c]

The Weak and the Strong

14 Accept him whose faith is weak, without passing judgment on disputable matters. [2]One man's faith allows him to eat everything, but another man, whose faith is weak, eats only vegetables. [3]The man who eats everything must not look down on him who does not, and the man who does not eat everything must not condemn the man who does, for God has accepted him. [4]Who are you to judge someone else's servant? To his own master he stands or falls. And he will stand, for the Lord is able to make him stand.

[5]One man considers one day more sacred than another; another man considers every day alike. Each one should be fully convinced in his own mind. [6]He who regards one day as special, does so to the Lord. He who eats meat, eats to the Lord, for he gives thanks to God; and he who abstains, does so to the Lord and gives thanks to God. [7]For none of us lives to himself alone and none of us dies to himself alone. [8]If we live, we live to the Lord; and if we die, we die to the Lord.

[b]6 Or in agreement with the   [c]16 Or willing to do menial work   [d]19 Deut. 32:35   [e]20 Prov. 25:21,22
[a]9 Exodus 20:13–15,17; Deut. 5:17–19,21   [b]9 Lev. 19:18   [c]14 Or the flesh

So, whether we live or die, we belong to the Lord.

⁹For this very reason, Christ died and returned to life so that he might be Lord of both the dead and the living. ¹⁰You, then, why do you judge your brother? Or why do you look down on your brother? For we will all stand before God's judgment seat. ¹¹It is written:

"'As surely as I live,' says the Lord,
'Every knee will bow before me;
   every tongue will confess to God.'"*a*

¹²So then, each of us will give an account of himself to God.

¹³Therefore let us stop passing judgment on one another. Instead, make up your mind not to put any stumbling-block or obstacle in your brother's way. ¹⁴As one who is in the Lord Jesus, I am fully convinced that no food*b* is unclean in itself. But if anyone regards something as unclean, then for him it is unclean. ¹⁵If your brother is distressed because of what you eat, you are no longer acting in love. Do not by your eating destroy your brother for whom Christ died. ¹⁶Do not allow what you consider good to be spoken of as evil. ¹⁷For the kingdom of God is not a matter of eating and drinking, but of righteousness, peace and joy in the Holy Spirit, ¹⁸because anyone who serves Christ in this way is pleasing to God and approved by men.

¹⁹Let us therefore make every effort to do what leads to peace and to mutual edification. ²⁰Do not destroy the work of God for the sake of food. All food is clean, but it is wrong for a man to eat anything that causes someone else to stumble. ²¹It is better not to eat meat or drink wine or to do anything else that will cause your brother to fall.

²²So whatever you believe about these things keep between yourself and God. Blessed is the man who does not condemn himself by what he approves. ²³But the man who has doubts is condemned if he eats, because his eating is not from faith; and everything that does not come from faith is sin.

15 We who are strong ought to bear with the failings of the weak and not to please ourselves. ²Each of us should please his neighbour for his good, to build him up. ³For even Christ did not please himself but, as it is written: "The insults of those who insult you have fallen on me."*a* ⁴For everything that was written in the past was written to teach us, so that through endurance and the encouragement of the Scriptures we might have hope.

⁵May the God who gives endurance and encouragement give you a spirit of unity among yourselves as you follow Christ Jesus, ⁶so that with one heart and mouth you may glorify the God and Father of our Lord Jesus Christ.

⁷Accept one another, then, just as Christ accepted you, in order to bring praise to God. ⁸For I tell you that Christ has become a servant of the Jews*b* on behalf of God's truth, to confirm the promises made to the patriarchs ⁹so that the Gentiles may glorify God for his mercy, as it is written:

"Therefore I will praise you among the
   Gentiles;
I will sing hymns to your name."*c*

¹⁰Again, it says,

"Rejoice, O Gentiles, with his people."*d*

¹¹And again,

"Praise the Lord, all you Gentiles,
   and sing praises to him, all you
   peoples."*e*

¹²And again, Isaiah says,

"The Root of Jesse will spring up,
   one who will arise to rule over the
   nations;
the Gentiles will hope in him."*f*

¹³May the God of hope fill you with all joy and peace as you trust in him, so that you may overflow with hope by the power of the Holy Spirit.

Paul the Minister to the Gentiles

¹⁴I myself am convinced, my brothers, that you yourselves are full of goodness, complete in knowledge and competent to instruct one another. ¹⁵I have written to you quite boldly on some points, as if to remind you of them again, because of the grace God gave me ¹⁶to be a minister of Christ Jesus to the Gentiles with the priestly duty of proclaiming the gospel of God, so that the Gentiles might become an offering acceptable to God, sanctified by the Holy Spirit.

¹⁷Therefore I glory in Christ Jesus in my service to God. ¹⁸I will not venture to speak of anything except what Christ has accomplished through me in leading the Gentiles to obey God by what I have said and done —¹⁹by the power of signs and miracles, through the power of the Spirit. So from Jerusalem all the way around to Illyricum, I have fully proclaimed the gospel of Christ. ²⁰It has always been my ambition to preach the gospel where Christ was not known, so that I would not be building on someone else's foundation. ²¹Rather, as it is written:

"Those who were not told about him will
   see,
   and those who have not heard will
   understand."*g*

²²This is why I have often been hindered from coming to you.

---

a11 Isaiah 45:23   *b14* Or *that nothing*   *a3* Psalm 69:9   *b8* Greek *circumcision*
c9 2 Samuel 22:50; Psalm 18:49   *d10* Deut. 32:43   *e11* Psalm 117:1   *f12* Isaiah 11:10
g21 Isaiah 52:15

**"Let no debt remain outstanding, except the continuing debt to love one another
. . . Love does no harm to its neighbour' (vv. 8, 10).**

THE DEBT OF MUTUAL LOVE. Paul rarely quotes Jesus directly.
Even here, Paul's quotation is in turn quoted by Jesus from the Old
Testament. But Paul's thoughts and feelings are entirely those of this
Lord.

Our modern world confuses love with lust. 'Love your neighbour,'
says the comedian, 'but hope her husband doesn't find out.' This
confusion is most serious when it affects relationships, but it also
occurs in the realm of things. Credit booms come about, not just
because people want things for themselves, but also from their desire
to give things to others. They confuse loving with material giving.

Again, take Paul's advice too literally and society would collapse.
Paul is not condemning young couples seeking a mortgage to buy a
house. Even if changes of circumstance mean that arrears occur and
the bank forecloses, usually Paul's sympathy would lie with the couple
rather than the bank. Paul would encourage enterprise. He was a
tentmaker, and who knows, perhaps he had to borrow to restart his
business after study in Jerusalem.

But Paul does condemn irresponsible, thoughtless actions taken at
our neighbour's expense. He makes it clear that his religion, the
religion of Christ, is one where normal, everyday obligations must
be recognized. They can all be summed up in the 'law of love,' the same
law which Jesus gives to us.

'Love one another as I have loved you.'

→1034

'We who are strong ought to bear with the failings of the weak and not to please ourselves' (v. 1).

SO EASY TO SAY, SO HARD TO DO. Bearing with the failings of the weak sounds very nice in theory. It can give a glow of righteous warmth to believe we are tolerating someone who is just that little bit less able than ourselves, spiritually. But who are we to judge?

In the physical realm it is not too difficult – for we can tell if someone has lost an arm, or is blind, or if they cannot talk. We can make allowances for that in our relationships with them. Surely, we do everything possible to make things easier for them: put pressure on authorities to provide ramps; avoid parking our car on the pavement (a severe hazard for the blind); take time to listen and communicate and so on.

Even in the physical realm, however, appearances are deceptive. A person with one leg and a well-made artificial one may be very mobile. Few people will realize their difficulties, so few will make any concession. A person's deafness is undetectable by appearance. Pain, too, is invisible.

But how much harder in realms of the spirit! We cannot tell a person's spiritual handicaps. We don't know how much they understand, how much they feel, how much they suffer. All we know is the look in the eye, the brave face, the almost-hidden grimace of spiritual pain, the hurt look when a Christian friend fails to reach the standard expected.

Let us dwell on such matters before we risk anything that 'causes someone else to stumble' (v. 20).

→1037

Paul's Plan to Visit Rome

23But now that there is no more place for me to work in these regions, and since I have been longing for many years to see you, 24I plan to do so when I go to Spain. I hope to visit you while passing through and to have you assist me on my journey there, after I have enjoyed your company for a while. 25Now, however, I am on my way to Jerusalem in the service of the saints there. 26For Macedonia and Achaia were pleased to make a contribution for the poor among the saints in Jerusalem. 27They were pleased to do it, and indeed they owe it to them. For if the Gentiles have shared in the Jews' spiritual blessings, they owe it to the Jews to share with them their material blessings. 28So after I have completed this task and have made sure that they have received this fruit, I will go to Spain and visit you on the way. 29I know that when I come to you, I will come in the full measure of the blessing of Christ.

30I urge you, brothers, by our Lord Jesus Christ and by the love of the Spirit, to join me in my struggle by praying to God for me. 31Pray that I may be rescued from the unbelievers in Judea and that my service in Jerusalem may be acceptable to the saints there, 32so that by God's will I may come to you with joy and together with you be refreshed. 33The God of peace be with you all. Amen.

Personal Greetings

16 I commend to you our sister Phoebe, a servant[a] of the church in Cenchrea. 2I ask you to receive her in the Lord in a way worthy of the saints and to give her any help she may need from you, for she has been a great help to many people, including me.

3Greet Priscilla[b] and Aquila, my fellow-workers in Christ Jesus. 4They risked their lives for me. Not only I but all the churches of the Gentiles are grateful to them. 5Greet also the church that meets at their house.

Greet my dear friend Epenetus, who was the first convert to Christ in the province of Asia. 6Greet Mary, who worked very hard for you. 7Greet Andronicus and Junias, my relatives who have been in prison with me. They are outstanding among the apostles, and they were in Christ before I was. 8Greet Ampliatus, whom I love in the Lord.

9Greet Urbanus, our fellow-worker in Christ, and my dear friend Stachys. 10Greet Apelles, tested and approved in Christ.

Greet those who belong to the household of Aristobulus. 11Greet Herodion, my relative.

Greet those in the household of Narcissus who are in the Lord. 12Greet Tryphena and Tryphosa, those women who work hard in the Lord.

Greet my dear friend Persis, another woman who has worked very hard in the Lord. 13Greet Rufus, chosen in the Lord, and his mother, who has been a mother to me, too. 14Greet Asyncritus, Phlegon, Hermes, Patrobas, Hermas and the brothers with them. 15Greet Philologus, Julia, Nereus and his sister, and Olympas and all the saints with them.

16Greet one another with a holy kiss.

All the churches of Christ send greetings.

17I urge you, brothers, to watch out for those who cause divisions and put obstacles in your way that are contrary to the teaching you have learned. Keep away from them. 18For such people are not serving our Lord Christ, but their own appetites. By smooth talk and flattery they deceive the minds of naïve people. 19Everyone has heard about your obedience, so I am full of joy over you; but I want you to be wise about what is good, and innocent about what is evil.

20The God of peace will soon crush Satan under your feet.

The grace of our Lord Jesus be with you.

21Timothy, my fellow-worker, sends his greetings to you, as do Lucius, Jason and Sosipater, my relatives.

22I, Tertius, who wrote down this letter, greet you in the Lord.

23Gaius, whose hospitality I and the whole church here enjoy, sends you his greetings. Erastus, who is the city's director of public works, and our brother Quartus send you their greetings.[c]

25Now to him who is able to establish you by my gospel and the proclamation of Jesus Christ, according to the revelation of the mystery hidden for long ages past, 26but now revealed and made known through the prophetic writings by the command of the eternal God, so that all nations might believe and obey him—27to the only wise God be glory for ever through Jesus Christ! Amen.

---

[a]1 Or deaconess   [b]3 Greek Prisca, a variant of Priscilla
[c]23 Some manuscripts their greetings. 24May the grace of our Lord Jesus Christ be with all of you. Amen.

1 Corinthians

1 Paul, called to be an apostle of Christ Jesus by the will of God, and our brother Sosthenes,

²To the church of God in Corinth, to those sanctified in Christ Jesus and called to be holy, together with all those everywhere who call on the name of our Lord Jesus Christ —their Lord and ours:

³Grace and peace to you from God our Father and the Lord Jesus Christ.

Thanksgiving

⁴I always thank God for you because of his grace given you in Christ Jesus. ⁵For in him you have been enriched in every way—in all your speaking and in all your knowledge —⁶because our testimony about Christ was confirmed in you. ⁷Therefore you do not lack any spiritual gift as you eagerly wait for our Lord Jesus Christ to be revealed. ⁸He will keep you strong to the end, so that you will be blameless on the day of our Lord Jesus Christ. ⁹God, who has called you into fellowship with his Son Jesus Christ our Lord, is faithful.

Divisions in the Church

¹⁰I appeal to you, brothers, in the name of our Lord Jesus Christ, that all of you agree with one another so that there may be no divisions among you and that you may be perfectly united in mind and thought. ¹¹My brothers, some from Chloe's household have informed me that there are quarrels among you. ¹²What I mean is this: One of you says, "I follow Paul"; another, "I follow Apollos"; another, "I follow Cephas";ᵃ still another, "I follow Christ."

¹³Is Christ divided? Was Paul crucified for you? Were you baptised intoᵇ the name of Paul? ¹⁴I am thankful that I did not baptise any of you except Crispus and Gaius, ¹⁵so no-one can say that you were baptised into my name. (¹⁶Yes, I also baptised the household of Stephanas; beyond that, I don't remember if I baptised anyone else.) ¹⁷For Christ did not send me to baptise, but to preach the gospel—not with words of human wisdom, lest the cross of Christ be emptied of its power.

Christ the Wisdom and Power of God

¹⁸For the message of the cross is foolishness to those who are perishing, but to us who are being saved it is the power of God. ¹⁹For it is written:

"I will destroy the wisdom of the wise;
    the intelligence of the intelligent I will
        frustrate."ᶜ

²⁰Where is the wise man? Where is the scholar? Where is the philosopher of this age? Has not God made foolish the wisdom of the world? ²¹For since in the wisdom of God the world through its wisdom did not know him, God was pleased through the foolishness of what was preached to save those who believe. ²²Jews demand miraculous signs and Greeks look for wisdom, ²³but we preach Christ crucified: a stumblingblock to Jews and foolishness to Gentiles, ²⁴but to those whom God has called, both Jews and Greeks, Christ the power of God and the wisdom of God. ²⁵For the foolishness of God is wiser than man's wisdom, and the weakness of God is stronger than man's strength.

²⁶Brothers, think of what you were when you were called. Not many of you were wise by human standards; not many were influential; not many were of noble birth. ²⁷But God chose the foolish things of the world to shame the wise; God chose the weak things of the world to shame the strong. ²⁸He chose the lowly things of this world and the despised things—and the things that are not—to nullify the things that are, ²⁹so that no-one may boast before him. ³⁰It is because of him that you are in Christ Jesus, who has become for us wisdom from God—that is, our righteousness, holiness and redemption. ³¹Therefore, as it is written: "Let him who boasts boast in the Lord."ᵈ

2 When I came to you, brothers, I did not come with eloquence or superior wisdom as I proclaimed to you the testimony about God.ᵃ ²For I resolved to know nothing while I was with you except Jesus Christ and him crucified. ³I came to you in weakness and fear, and with much trembling. ⁴My message and my preaching were not with

---

ᵃ12 That is, Peter   ᵇ13 Or in; also in verse 15   ᶜ19 Isaiah 29:14   ᵈ31 Jer. 9:24
ᵃ1 Some manuscripts as I proclaimed to you God's mystery

ROMANS 16:1–6, 12–16
'I commend to you our sister Phoebe, a deaconess of the church . . . I ask you to receive her in the Lord in a way worthy of the saints' (vv. 1, 2).

> *Partakers of the Saviour's grace,*
> *The same in mind and heart*
> *Nor joy, nor grief, nor time, nor place*
> *Nor life, nor death can part.*

> (*Charles Wesley*)

FEMINISM – NEW TESTAMENT STYLE. Paul is often charged with being anti-woman. He did tell women not to gossip or question in church (1 Corinthians 15:34), but wait to ask their husbands at home! Such words, and growing Church tradition through the centuries, often combined to push women into a background role. Proverbs 31 assigns women a more public role than appears at first. So, too, does Paul here.

Phoebe is a deaconess. In addition to domestic matters, visiting and so on, she probably took the eucharist to those who could not make it to church. Many deacons prophesied – a role open to women, as we know from Paul himself (1 Corinthians 11:5). And here Paul entrusts Phoebe with the same job he gave Timothy and others, taking a vital letter to its destined church. This was particularly important with the Roman letter as Paul had not yet been to Rome. Phoebe was even more of an ambassador than her male brethren. We could parody the verse above in the light of Galatians 3:28:

> *All groups alike shall toil with Thee*
> *And in Thy kingdom share,*
> *Both male and female, bond or free*
> *There's no distinction there.*

Lord Jesus Christ who united all groups within your earthly ministry, help us to break down barriers between the different groups in society. May we accord to all people, men, women, and children their rightful place in the Church, and never prevent anyone from fulfilling the role to which you have called them.

→1038

1 CORINTHIANS 1:10–15

'My brothers, some from Chloe's household have informed me that there are quarrels among you' (v. 11).

IT IS A MISTAKE to consider church disunity a new phenomenon. Here (AD 55), at least four rival groups existed within the Corinthian church.

1. 'I follow Paul' (v. 12a) LIBERTINES, probably a few among the first believers in Corinth. After hearing Paul talk of abolishing the law, they thought if they just believed the gospel they could do as they liked.

2. 'I follow Apollos' (v. 12b) PHILOSOPHERS. Apollos was a learned Alexandrian Jew who knew Greek philosophy. This group probably thought themselves a little better intellectually than other Corinthian Christians.

3. 'I follow Cephas' (v. 12c) LEGALISTS probably a group who thought Christian life required strict adherence to Jewish Law.

4. 'I follow Christ' (v. 12d) MYSTICS. They probably thought themselves superior to the others, following Christ alone.

Each preserves an element of the truth.
1. We have *freedom* in Christ;
2. Depth of spiritual life can be helped through using our *intellect*;
3. The Jewish *Law* is of value to Christians;
4. We can have *direct* communion with our Lord.

Together, each could learn from the other and profit from the other's emphasis on one aspect of the truth. None has the whole truth. As rivals they are a scandal and only serve to place a stumbling block in the path of seekers after truth.

I would follow Christ – if it were not for the Christians. (Mahatma Gandhi)

→1041

wise and persuasive words, but with a demonstration of the Spirit's power, ⁵so that your faith might not rest on men's wisdom, but on God's power.

Wisdom From the Spirit

⁶We do, however, speak a message of wisdom among the mature, but not the wisdom of this age or of the rulers of this age, who are coming to nothing. ⁷No, we speak of God's secret wisdom, a wisdom that has been hidden and that God destined for our glory before time began. ⁸None of the rulers of this age understood it, for if they had, they would not have crucified the Lord of glory. ⁹However, as it is written:

"No eye has seen,
    no ear has heard,
no mind has conceived
    what God has prepared for those who
        love him"ᵇ—

¹⁰but God has revealed it to us by his Spirit.

The Spirit searches all things, even the deep things of God. ¹¹For who among men knows the thoughts of a man except the man's spirit within him? In the same way no-one knows the thoughts of God except the Spirit of God. ¹²We have not received the spirit of the world but the Spirit who is from God, that we may understand what God has freely given us. ¹³This is what we speak, not in words taught us by human wisdom but in words taught by the Spirit, expressing spiritual truths in spiritual words.ᶜ ¹⁴The man without the Spirit does not accept the things that come from the Spirit of God, for they are foolishness to him, and he cannot understand them, because they are spiritually discerned. ¹⁵The spiritual man makes judgments about all things, but he himself is not subject to any man's judgment:

¹⁶"For who has known the mind of the Lord
    that he may instruct him?"ᵈ

But we have the mind of Christ.

On Divisions in the Church

3 Brothers, I could not address you as spiritual but as worldly—mere infants in Christ. ²I gave you milk, not solid food, for you were not yet ready for it. Indeed, you are still not ready. ³You are still worldly. For since there is jealousy and quarrelling among you, are you not worldly? Are you not acting like mere men? ⁴For when one says, "I follow Paul," and another, "I follow Apollos," are you not mere men?

⁵What, after all, is Apollos? And what is Paul? Only servants, through whom you came to believe—as the Lord has assigned to each his task. ⁶I planted the seed, Apollos watered it, but God made it grow. ⁷So neither he who plants nor he who waters is anything, but only God, who makes things grow. ⁸The man who plants and the man who waters

have one purpose, and each will be rewarded according to his own labour. ⁹For we are God's fellow-workers; you are God's field, God's building.

¹⁰By the grace God has given me, I laid a foundation as an expert builder, and someone else is building on it. But each one should be careful how he builds. ¹¹For no-one can lay any foundation other than the one already laid, which is Jesus Christ. ¹²If any man builds on this foundation using gold, silver, costly stones, wood, hay or straw, ¹³his work will be shown for what it is, because the Day will bring it to light. It will be revealed with fire, and the fire will test the quality of each man's work. ¹⁴If what he has built survives, he will receive his reward. ¹⁵If it is burned up, he will suffer loss; he himself will be saved, but only as one escaping through the flames.

¹⁶Don't you know that you yourselves are God's temple and that God's Spirit lives in you? ¹⁷If anyone destroys God's temple, God will destroy him; for God's temple is sacred, and you are that temple.

¹⁸Do not deceive yourselves. If any one of you thinks he is wise by the standards of this age, he should become a "fool" so that he may become wise. ¹⁹For the wisdom of this world is foolishness in God's sight. As it is written: "He catches the wise in their craftiness";ᵃ ²⁰and again, "The Lord knows that the thoughts of the wise are futile."ᵇ ²¹So then, no more boasting about men! All things are yours, ²²whether Paul or Apollos or Cephasᶜ or the world or life or death or the present or the future—all are yours, ²³and you are of Christ, and Christ is of God.

Apostles of Christ

4 So then, men ought to regard us as servants of Christ and as those entrusted with the secret things of God. ²Now it is required that those who have been given a trust must prove faithful. ³I care very little if I am judged by you or by any human court; indeed, I do not even judge myself. ⁴My conscience is clear, but that does not make me innocent. It is the Lord who judges me. ⁵Therefore judge nothing before the appointed time; wait till the Lord comes. He will bring to light what is hidden in darkness and will expose the motives of men's hearts. At that time each will receive his praise from God.

⁶Now, brothers, I have applied these things to myself and Apollos for your benefit, so that you may learn from us the meaning of the saying, "Do not go beyond what is written." Then you will not take pride in one man over against another. ⁷For who makes you different from anyone else? What do you have that you did not receive? And if you did receive it, why do you boast as though you did not?

⁸Already you have all you want! Already you have become rich! You have become kings—and that without us! How I wish that you really had become kings so that we might

ᵇ9 Isaiah 64:4   ᶜ13 Or Spirit, interpreting spiritual truths to spiritual men
ᵈ16 Isaiah 40:13   ᵃ19 Job 5:13   ᵇ20 Psalm 94:11   ᶜ22 That is, Peter

be kings with you! 9For it seems to me that God has put us apostles on display at the end of the procession, like men condemned to die in the arena. We have been made a spectacle to the whole universe, to angels as well as to men. 10We are fools for Christ, but you are so wise in Christ! We are weak, but you are strong! You are honoured, we are dishonoured! 11To this very hour we go hungry and thirsty, we are in rags, we are brutally treated, we are homeless. 12We work hard with our own hands. When we are cursed, we bless; when we are persecuted, we endure it; 13when we are slandered, we answer kindly. Up to this moment we have become the scum of the earth, the refuse of the world.

14I am not writing this to shame you, but to warn you, as my dear children. 15Even though you have ten thousand guardians in Christ, you do not have many fathers, for in Christ Jesus I became your father through the gospel. 16Therefore I urge you to imitate me. 17For this reason I am sending to you Timothy, my son whom I love, who is faithful in the Lord. He will remind you of my way of life in Christ Jesus, which agrees with what I teach everywhere in every church.

18Some of you have become arrogant, as if I were not coming to you. 19But I will come to you very soon, if the Lord is willing, and then I will find out not only how these arrogant people are talking, but what power they have. 20For the kingdom of God is not a matter of talk but of power. 21What do you prefer? Shall I come to you with a whip, or in love and with a gentle spirit?

Expel the Immoral Brother!

5 It is actually reported that there is sexual immorality among you, and of a kind that does not occur even among pagans: A man has his father's wife. 2And you are proud! Shouldn't you rather have been filled with grief and have put out of your fellowship the man who did this? 3Even though I am not physically present, I am with you in spirit. And I have already passed judgment on the one who did this, just as if I were present. 4When you are assembled in the name of our Lord Jesus and I am with you in spirit, and the power of our Lord Jesus is present, 5hand this man over to Satan, so that the sinful naturea may be destroyed and his spirit saved on the day of the Lord.

6Your boasting is not good. Don't you know that a little yeast works through the whole batch of dough? 7Get rid of the old yeast that you may be a new batch without yeast—as you really are. For Christ, our Passover lamb, has been sacrificed. 8Therefore let us keep the Festival, not with the old yeast, the yeast of malice and wickedness, but with bread without yeast, the bread of sincerity and truth.

9I have written to you in my letter not to associate with sexually immoral people— 10not at all meaning the people of this world

who are immoral, or the greedy and swindlers, or idolaters. In that case you would have to leave this world. 11But now I am writing to you that you must not associate with anyone who calls himself a brother but is sexually immoral or greedy, an idolater or a slanderer, a drunkard or a swindler. With such a man do not even eat.

12What business is it of mine to judge those outside the church? Are you not to judge those inside? 13God will judge those outside. "Expel the wicked man from among you."b

Lawsuits Among Believers

6 If any of you has a dispute with another, dare he take it before the ungodly for judgment instead of before the saints? 2Do you not know that the saints will judge the world? And if you are to judge the world, are you not competent to judge trivial cases? 3Do you not know that we will judge angels? How much more the things of this life! 4Therefore, if you have disputes about such matters, appoint as judges even men of little account in the church!a 5I say this to shame you. Is it possible that there is nobody among you wise enough to judge a dispute between believers? 6But instead, one brother goes to law against another—and this in front of unbelievers!

7The very fact that you have lawsuits among you means you have been completely defeated already. Why not rather be wronged? Why not rather be cheated? 8Instead, you yourselves cheat and do wrong, and you do this to your brothers.

9Do you not know that the wicked will not inherit the kingdom of God? Do not be deceived: Neither the sexually immoral nor idolaters nor adulterers nor male prostitutes nor homosexual offenders 10nor thieves nor the greedy nor drunkards nor slanderers nor swindlers will inherit the kingdom of God. 11And that is what some of you were. But you were washed, you were sanctified, you were justified in the name of the Lord Jesus Christ and by the Spirit of our God.

Sexual Immorality

12"Everything is permissible for me"— but not everything is beneficial. "Everything is permissible for me"—but I will not be mastered by anything. 13"Food for the stomach and the stomach for food"—but God will destroy them both. The body is not meant for sexual immorality, but for the Lord, and the Lord for the body. 14By his power God raised the Lord from the dead, and he will raise us also. 15Do you not know that your bodies are members of Christ himself? Shall I then take the members of Christ and unite them with a prostitute? Never! 16Do you not know that he who unites himself with a prostitute is one with her in body? For it is said, "The two will become one flesh."b 17But he who unites himself with the Lord is one with him in spirit.

18Flee from sexual immorality. All other

a5 Or that his body; or that the flesh   b13 Deut. 17:7; 19:19; 21:21; 22:21,24; 24:7
a4 Or matters, do you appoint as judges men of little account in the church?
b16 Gen. 2:24

1 CORINTHIANS 3:7–17

'For we are God's fellow-workers; you are God's field, God's building . . . you are God's temple and . . . God's Spirit lives in you' (vv. 9, 16).

PAUL DOES NOT TELL STORIES like Jesus did. The most we get is a vivid comparison of the Christian with some specific object, a little word picture perhaps, which illustrates some aspect of the Christian life. We have three of them in this passage: field, building and temple (a particular kind of building). None is a complete picture, but each contributes something to the appreciation of the Christian's life and task.

The field picture may reflect Paul's knowledge of the parable of the sower, in which Jesus compares the people with different kinds of soil. Paul complicates the picture slightly, by comparing himself with a sower, and Apollos with one who waters the field, respectively. But notice how he describes the two tasks as equal.

The evangelist's task, the spectacular preaching, may be more glamorous. The pastor's task, the everyday care, is of equal importance.

His building illustration is a little harder, for he gives the impression that we are responsible for our own building upon the Christian foundation which is laid. There is, however, a little let-out clause (v. 15), which shows that whatever our *works* are, they do not earn us our salvation. Paul's special contribution is to make us aware that we are God's temple, his special dwelling place, holy and usable.

> *I would be thy holy temple,*
> *Sacred and indwelt by thee.*
>
> (*Brindley Boon*)

Lord, make me fit to be your temple. Help me to value my body, however frail it may be, so that others may see your Spirit, shining out from your own creation.

→1042

1 CORINTHIANS 6:12–20

' "Everything is permissible for me," but not everything is beneficial . . . Do you not know that your bodies are members of Christ himself?' (vv. 12, 15).

SEXUAL SCANDALS, especially if they involve members of the body of Christ, are part and parcel of the world's entertainment. Drives and instincts, to which we are all subject, are the raw material of much of the world's drama. We study the incredible insights which certain playwrights and artists have into the deepest recesses of the human mind, and find them entertaining at the same time.

Sometimes this is a valuable exercise. Sometimes it helps reassure us we are not alone in experiencing deep physical and emotional feelings. Sometimes it may enable us to appreciate that others feel in ways very different from our own instinctive orientations. However, all too often it becomes mere titillation, pandering to the lowest common denominator of physical desires.

What care we must take over how we channel bodily desires and instincts! All are God-given, and can be used in his service, but each one of them can also be corrupted. Sexual desire and its fulfilment are an integral part of the closest human relationship, marriage – but uncontrolled sexuality causes some of the most bestial crimes against those least able to defend themselves, particularly women and children. Paul's picture of the body as a temple of the Holy Spirit will not eradicate every sexual abuse overnight.

Christians should think carefully, and read 1 Corinthians 6 even more carefully, before embarking on any sexual relationship with another, within or without the Church.

→1045

sins a man commits are outside his body, but he who sins sexually sins against his own body. 19Do you not know that your body is a temple of the Holy Spirit, who is in you, whom you have received from God? You are not your own; 20you were bought at a price. Therefore honour God with your body.

Marriage

7 Now for the matters you wrote about: It is good for a man not to marry.*a* 2But since there is so much immorality, each man should have his own wife, and each woman her own husband. 3The husband should fulfil his marital duty to his wife, and likewise the wife to her husband. 4The wife's body does not belong to her alone but also to her husband. In the same way, the husband's body does not belong to him alone but also to his wife. 5Do not deprive each other except by mutual consent and for a time, so that you may devote yourselves to prayer. Then come together again so that Satan will not tempt you because of your lack of self-control. 6I say this as a concession, not as a command. 7I wish that all men were as I am. But each man has his own gift from God; one has this gift, another has that.

8Now to the unmarried and the widows I say: It is good for them to stay unmarried, as I am. 9But if they cannot control themselves, they should marry, for it is better to marry than to burn with passion.

10To the married I give this command (not I, but the Lord): A wife must not separate from her husband. 11But if she does, she must remain unmarried or else be reconciled to her husband. And a husband must not divorce his wife.

12To the rest I say this (I, not the Lord): If any brother has a wife who is not a believer and she is willing to live with him, he must not divorce her. 13And if a woman has a husband who is not a believer and he is willing to live with her, she must not divorce him. 14For the unbelieving husband has been sanctified through his wife, and the unbelieving wife has been sanctified through her believing husband. Otherwise your children would be unclean, but as it is, they are holy. 15But if the unbeliever leaves, let him do so. A believing man or woman is not bound in such circumstances; God has called us to live in peace. 16How do you know, wife, whether you will save your husband? Or, how do you know, husband, whether you will save your wife?

17Nevertheless, each one should retain the place in life that the Lord assigned to him and to which God has called him. This is the rule I lay down in all the churches. 18Was a man already circumcised when he was called? He should not become uncircumcised. Was a man uncircumcised when he was called? He should not be circumcised. 19Circumcision is

nothing and uncircumcision is nothing. Keeping God's commands is what counts. 20Each one should remain in the situation which he was in when God called him. 21Were you a slave when you were called? Don't let it trouble you—although if you can gain your freedom, do so. 22For he who was a slave when he was called by the Lord is the Lord's freedman; similarly, he who was a free man when he was called is Christ's slave. 23You were bought at a price; do not become slaves of men. 24Brothers, each man, as responsible to God, should remain in the situation God called him to.

25Now about virgins: I have no command from the Lord, but I give a judgment as one who by the Lord's mercy is trustworthy. 26Because of the present crisis, I think that it is good for you to remain as you are. 27Are you married? Do not seek a divorce. Are you unmarried? Do not look for a wife. 28But if you do marry, you have not sinned; and if a virgin marries, she has not sinned. But those who marry will face many troubles in this life, and I want to spare you this.

29What I mean, brothers, is that the time is short. From now on those who have wives should live as if they had none; 30those who mourn, as if they did not; those who are happy, as if they were not; those who buy something, as if it were not theirs to keep; 31those who use the things of the world, as if not engrossed in them. For this world in its present form is passing away.

32I would like you to be free from concern. An unmarried man is concerned about the Lord's affairs—how he can please the Lord. 33But a married man is concerned about the affairs of this world—how he can please his wife—34and his interests are divided. An unmarried woman or virgin is concerned about the Lord's affairs: Her aim is to be devoted to the Lord in both body and spirit. But a married woman is concerned about the affairs of this world—how she can please her husband. 35I am saying this for your own good, not to restrict you, but that you may live in a right way in undivided devotion to the Lord.

36If anyone thinks he is acting improperly towards the virgin he is engaged to, and if she is getting on in years and he feels he ought to marry, he should do as he wants. He is not sinning. They should get married. 37But the man who has settled the matter in his own mind, who is under no compulsion but has control over his own will, and who has made up his mind not to marry the virgin—this man also does the right thing. 38So then, he who marries the virgin does right, but he who does not marry her does even better.*b*

39A woman is bound to her husband as long as he lives. But if her husband dies, she is free to marry anyone she wishes, but he must belong to the Lord. 40In my judgment, she is

a1 Or "It is good for a man not to have sexual relations with a woman."
b36–38 Or 36If anyone thinks he is not treating his daughter properly, and if she is getting on in years, and he feels she ought to marry, he should do as he wants. He is not sinning. He should let her get married. 37But the man who has settled the matter in his own mind, who is under no compulsion but has control over his own will, and who has made up his mind to keep the virgin unmarried—this man also does the right thing. 38So then, he who gives his virgin in marriage does right, but he who does not give her in marriage does even better.

happier if she stays as she is—and I think that I too have the Spirit of God.

Food Sacrificed to Idols

8 Now about food sacrificed to idols: We know that we all possess knowledge.[a] Knowledge puffs up, but love builds up. [2]The man who thinks he knows something does not yet know as he ought to know. [3]But the man who loves God is known by God.

[4]So then, about eating food sacrificed to idols: We know that an idol is nothing at all in the world and that there is no God but one. [5]For even if there are so-called gods, whether in heaven or on earth (as indeed there are many "gods" and many "lords"), [6]yet for us there is but one God, the Father, from whom all things came and for whom we live; and there is but one Lord, Jesus Christ, through whom all things came and through whom we live.

[7]But not everyone knows this. Some people are still so accustomed to idols that when they eat such food they think of it as having been sacrificed to an idol, and since their conscience is weak, it is defiled. [8]But food does not bring us near to God; we are no worse if we do not eat, and no better if we do.

[9]Be careful, however, that the exercise of your freedom does not become a stumbling-block to the weak. [10]For if anyone with a weak conscience sees you who have this knowledge eating in an idol's temple, won't he be emboldened to eat what has been sacrificed to idols? [11]So this weak brother, for whom Christ died, is destroyed by your knowledge. [12]When you sin against your brothers in this way and wound their weak conscience, you sin against Christ. [13]Therefore, if what I eat causes my brother to fall into sin, I will never eat meat again, so that I will not cause him to fall.

The Rights of an Apostle

9 Am I not free? Am I not an apostle? Have I not seen Jesus our Lord? Are you not the result of my work in the Lord? [2]Even though I may not be an apostle to others, surely I am to you! For you are the seal of my apostleship in the Lord.

[3]This is my defence to those who sit in judgment on me. [4]Don't we have the right to food and drink? [5]Don't we have the right to take a believing wife along with us, as do the other apostles and the Lord's brothers and Cephas?[a] [6]Or is it only I and Barnabas who must work for a living?

[7]Who serves as a soldier at his own expense? Who plants a vineyard and does not eat of its grapes? Who tends a flock and does not drink of the milk? [8]Do I say this merely from a human point of view? Doesn't the Law say the same thing? [9]For it is written in the Law of Moses: "Do not muzzle an ox while it is treading out the grain."[b] Is it about oxen that God is concerned? [10]Surely he says this for us, doesn't he? Yes, this was written for us, because when the ploughman ploughs

and the thresher threshes, they ought to do so in the hope of sharing in the harvest. [11]If we have sown spiritual seed among you, is it too much if we reap a material harvest from you? [12]If others have this right of support from you, shouldn't we have it all the more?

But we did not use this right. On the contrary, we put up with anything rather than hinder the gospel of Christ. [13]Don't you know that those who work in the temple get their food from the temple, and those who serve at the altar share in what is offered on the altar? [14]In the same way, the Lord has commanded that those who preach the gospel should receive their living from the gospel.

[15]But I have not used any of these rights. And I am not writing this in the hope that you will do such things for me. I would rather die than have anyone deprive me of this boast. [16]Yet when I preach the gospel, I cannot boast, for I am compelled to preach. Woe to me if I do not preach the gospel! [17]If I preach voluntarily, I have a reward; if not voluntarily, I am simply discharging the trust committed to me. [18]What then is my reward? Just this: that in preaching the gospel I may offer it free of charge, and so not make use of my rights in preaching it.

[19]Though I am free and belong to no man, I make myself a slave to everyone, to win as many as possible. [20]To the Jews I became like a Jew, to win the Jews. To those under the law I became like one under the law (though I myself am not under the law), so as to win those under the law. [21]To those not having the law I became like one not having the law (though I am not free from God's law but am under Christ's law), so as to win those not having the law. [22]To the weak I became weak, to win the weak. I have become all things to all men so that by all possible means I might save some. [23]I do all this for the sake of the gospel, that I may share in its blessings.

[24]Do you not know that in a race all the runners run, but only one gets the prize? Run in such a way as to get the prize. [25]Everyone who competes in the games goes into strict training. They do it to get a crown that will not last; but we do it to get a crown that will last for ever. [26]Therefore I do not run like a man running aimlessly; I do not fight like a man beating the air. [27]No, I beat my body and make it my slave so that after I have preached to others, I myself will not be disqualified for the prize.

Warnings From Israel's History

10 For I do not want you to be ignorant of the fact, brothers, that our forefathers were all under the cloud and that they all passed through the sea. [2]They were all baptised into Moses in the cloud and in the sea. [3]They all ate the same spiritual food [4]and drank the same spiritual drink; for they drank from the spiritual rock that accompanied them, and that rock was Christ. [5]Nevertheless, God was not pleased with most of

---

[a]1 Or "We all possess knowledge," as you say   [a]5 That is, Peter   [b]9 Deut. 25:4

1 CORINTHIANS 7:1–16, 29–31
'The wife's body does not belong to her alone but also to her husband. In the same way, the husband's body does not belong to him alone but also to his wife' (v. 4).

TIMOTHY AND TITUS are usually called the 'pastoral epistles'. First Corinthians is also pastoral, in great part written to answer specific difficulties outlined by the young church. Five times Paul answers with the words *Peri de* 'now concerning'. The infant church's first question was concerning physical relationships within marriage, then

7:25	'Now about virgins . . .'
8:1	'Now about food sacrificed to idols'
12:1	'Now about spiritual gifts'
16:1	'Now about the collection for God's people . . .'

Each was a pressing problem. Today's problems are different, but Paul's principles still apply. In keeping with the views of his Jewish contemporaries, Paul takes a very physical view of marriage. 'It is better to marry than to burn with passion' (7:9). When he wrote that he probably still believed the end of all things was close at hand (see 7:26, 29). Only in such a context do some of his words make sense.

But note carefully his words in v. 4. The NIV brings out the sense most clearly. However physical or spiritual a marriage relationship may be, it is a relationship of equals. Each has equal responsibility to make it work.

We confess, Lord, it is hard for us not to put value judgements on differences. Help us never to regard anyone different from ourselves as inferior. Enable us to value the contributions made by people of both sexes to the common life of humanity. Guard us from extremes of both male chauvinism and militant feminism.

→1046

1 CORINTHIANS 9:19–23

'I have become all things to all men so that by all possible means I might save some' (v. 20).

THIS IS ONE of those Scripture passages which can be misused to excuse all manner of injustice, double-dealing, compromise, dishonesty, hypocrisy, and hosts of other vices, on the grounds of 'identifying with the people I am working to save'. It is therefore doubly important to interpret it in the light of other passages, and not in isolation.

Paul is not committed to any one group within or without the Church. He is free to act according to his own conscience, without glancing over his shoulder to his paymasters, or having all the time to think of the reaction of his friends. Before we can be 'all things to all men' we have to free ourselves of undue commitment to any particular group of people. Jesus loved the Samaritans, and pleaded their cause, but he did not claim to be one.

Freedom in the gospel is not licence. We may become Jews to win Jews, or weak to win the weak – even perhaps strong to win the strong, but can we become thieves to win the thief? Only in so far as we share their suffering. Jesus himself went to the cross with thieves, without himself being one. We may endure the conditions of the sinner as Jesus did, and risk being tainted by the sin. But we also have God's assurance that, whenever we act from love of our fellows, then he is there. He identifies with us, saving us in the world, amongst both weak and strong.

> *O Christ, who died with arms outstretched in love*
> *For all who lift their faces to thy cross,*
> *Fill, thou, our lives with charity divine,*
> *Till thou and thine are all, and self is lost.*

(Catherine Bonnell Arnott)

→1049

them; their bodies were scattered over the desert.

[6]Now these things occurred as examples[a] to keep us from setting our hearts on evil things as they did. [7]Do not be idolaters, as some of them were; as it is written: "The people sat down to eat and drink and got up to indulge in pagan revelry."[b] [8]We should not commit sexual immorality, as some of them did—and in one day twenty-three thousand of them died. [9]We should not test the Lord, as some of them did—and were killed by snakes. [10]And do not grumble, as some of them did—and were killed by the destroying angel.

[11]These things happened to them as examples and were written down as warnings for us, on whom the fulfilment of the ages has come. [12]So, if you think you are standing firm, be careful that you don't fall! [13]No temptation has seized you except what is common to man. And God is faithful; he will not let you be tempted beyond what you can bear. But when you are tempted, he will also provide a way out so that you can stand up under it.

Idol Feasts and the Lord's Supper

[14]Therefore, my dear friends, flee from idolatry. [15]I speak to sensible people; judge for yourselves what I say. [16]Is not the cup of thanksgiving for which we give thanks a participation in the blood of Christ? And is not the bread that we break a participation in the body of Christ? [17]Because there is one loaf, we, who are many, are one body, for we all partake of the one loaf.

[18]Consider the people of Israel: Do not those who eat the sacrifices participate in the altar? [19]Do I mean then that a sacrifice offered to an idol is anything, or that an idol is anything? [20]No, but the sacrifices of pagans are offered to demons, not to God, and I do not want you to be participants with demons. [21]You cannot drink the cup of the Lord and the cup of demons too; you cannot have a part in both the Lord's table and the table of demons. [22]Are we trying to arouse the Lord's jealousy? Are we stronger than he?

The Believer's Freedom

[23]"Everything is permissible"—but not everything is beneficial. "Everything is permissible"—but not everything is constructive. [24]Nobody should seek his own good, but the good of others.

[25]Eat anything sold in the meat market without raising questions of conscience, [26]for, "The earth is the Lord's, and everything in it."[c]

[27]If some unbeliever invites you to a meal and you want to go, eat whatever is put before you without raising questions of conscience. [28]But if anyone says to you, "This has been offered in sacrifice," then do not eat

it, both for the sake of the man who told you and for conscience' sake[d]—[29]the other man's conscience, I mean, not yours. For why should my freedom be judged by another's conscience? [30]If I take part in the meal with thankfulness, why am I denounced because of something I thank God for?

[31]So whether you eat or drink or whatever you do, do it all for the glory of God. [32]Do not cause anyone to stumble, whether Jews, Greeks or the church of God—[33]even as I try to please everybody in every way. For I am not seeking my own good but the good of many, so that they may be saved. [11] [1]Follow my example, as I follow the example of Christ.

Propriety in Worship

[2]I praise you for remembering me in everything and for holding to the teachings,[a] just as I passed them on to you.

[3]Now I want you to realise that the head of every man is Christ, and the head of the woman is man, and the head of Christ is God. [4]Every man who prays or prophesies with his head covered dishonours his head. [5]And every woman who prays or prophesies with her head uncovered dishonours her head—it is just as though her head were shaved. [6]If a woman does not cover her head, she should have her hair cut off; and if it is a disgrace for a woman to have her hair cut or shaved off, she should cover her head. [7]A man ought not to cover his head,[b] since he is the image and glory of God; but the woman is the glory of man. [8]For man did not come from woman, but woman from man; [9]neither was man created for woman, but woman for man. [10]For this reason, and because of the angels, the woman ought to have a sign of authority on her head.

[11]In the Lord, however, woman is not independent of man, nor is man independent of woman. [12]For as woman came from man, so also man is born of woman. But everything comes from God. [13]Judge for yourselves: Is it proper for a woman to pray to God with her head uncovered? [14]Does not the very nature of things teach you that if a man has long hair, it is a disgrace to him, [15]but that if a woman has long hair, it is her glory? For long hair is given to her as a covering. [16]If anyone wants to be contentious about this, we have no other practice—nor do the churches of God.

The Lord's Supper

[17]In the following directives I have no praise for you, for your meetings do more harm than good. [18]In the first place, I hear that when you come together as a church, there are divisions among you, and to some extent I believe it. [19]No doubt there have to be differences among you to show which of you have God's approval. [20]When you come together, it is not the Lord's Supper you eat,

---

[a]6 Or types; also in verse 11   [b]7 Exodus 32:6   [c]26 Psalm 24:1
[d]28 Some manuscripts conscience' sake, for "the earth is the Lord's and everything in it"   [a]2 Or traditions
[b]4-7 Or [4]Every man who prays or prophesies with long hair dishonours his head. [5]And every woman who prays or prophesies with no covering ₃of hair₃ on her head dishonours her head—she is just like one of the "shorn women". [6]If a woman has no covering, let her be for now with short hair, but since it is a disgrace for a woman to have her hair shorn or shaved, she should grow it again. [7]A man ought not to have long hair

²¹for as you eat, each of you goes ahead without waiting for anybody else. One remains hungry, another gets drunk. ²²Don't you have homes to eat and drink in? Or do you despise the church of God and humiliate those who have nothing? What shall I say to you? Shall I praise you for this? Certainly not!

²³For I received from the Lord what I also passed on to you: The Lord Jesus, on the night he was betrayed, took bread, ²⁴and when he had given thanks, he broke it and said, "This is my body, which is for you; do this in remembrance of me." ²⁵In the same way, after supper he took the cup, saying, "This cup is the new covenant in my blood; do this, whenever you drink it, in remembrance of me." ²⁶For whenever you eat this bread and drink this cup, you proclaim the Lord's death until he comes.

²⁷Therefore, whoever eats the bread or drinks the cup of the Lord in an unworthy manner will be guilty of sinning against the body and blood of the Lord. ²⁸A man ought to examine himself before he eats of the bread and drinks of the cup. ²⁹For anyone who eats and drinks without recognising the body of the Lord eats and drinks judgment on himself. ³⁰That is why many among you are weak and sick, and a number of you have fallen asleep. ³¹But if we judged ourselves, we would not come under judgment. ³²When we are judged by the Lord, we are being disciplined so that we will not be condemned with the world.

³³So then, my brothers, when you come together to eat, wait for each other. ³⁴If anyone is hungry, he should eat at home, so that when you meet together it may not result in judgment.

And when I come I will give further directions.

Spiritual Gifts

12 Now about spiritual gifts, brothers, I do not want you to be ignorant. ²You know that when you were pagans, somehow or other you were influenced and led astray to mute idols. ³Therefore I tell you that no-one who is speaking by the Spirit of God says, "Jesus be cursed," and no-one can say, "Jesus is Lord," except by the Holy Spirit.

⁴There are different kinds of gifts, but the same Spirit. ⁵There are different kinds of service, but the same Lord. ⁶There are different kinds of working, but the same God works all of them in all men.

⁷Now to each one the manifestation of the Spirit is given for the common good. ⁸To one there is given through the Spirit the message of wisdom, to another the message of knowledge by means of the same Spirit, ⁹to another faith by the same Spirit, to another gifts of healing by that one Spirit, ¹⁰to another miraculous powers, to another prophecy, to another distinguishing between spirits, to another speaking in different kinds of

tongues,ᵃ and to still another the interpretation of tongues.ᵃ ¹¹All these are the work of one and the same Spirit, and he gives them to each one, just as he determines.

One Body, Many Parts

¹²The body is a unit, though it is made up of many parts; and though all its parts are many, they form one body. So it is with Christ. ¹³For we were all baptised byᵇ one Spirit into one body—whether Jews or Greeks, slave or free—and we were all given the one Spirit to drink.

¹⁴Now the body is not made up of one part but of many. ¹⁵If the foot should say, "Because I am not a hand, I do not belong to the body," it would not for that reason cease to be part of the body. ¹⁶And if the ear should say, "Because I am not an eye, I do not belong to the body," it would not for that reason cease to be part of the body. ¹⁷If the whole body were an eye, where would the sense of hearing be? If the whole body were an ear, where would the sense of smell be? ¹⁸But in fact God has arranged the parts in the body, every one of them, just as he wanted them to be. ¹⁹If they were all one part, where would the body be? ²⁰As it is, there are many parts, but one body.

²¹The eye cannot say to the hand, "I don't need you!" And the head cannot say to the feet, "I don't need you!" ²²On the contrary, those parts of the body that seem to be weaker are indispensable, ²³and the parts that we think are less honourable we treat with special honour. And the parts that are unpresentable are treated with special modesty, ²⁴while our presentable parts need no special treatment. But God has combined the members of the body and has given greater honour to the parts that lacked it, ²⁵so that there should be no division in the body, but that its parts should have equal concern for each other. ²⁶If one part suffers, every part suffers with it; if one part is honoured, every part rejoices with it.

²⁷Now you are the body of Christ, and each one of you is a part of it. ²⁸And in the church God has appointed first of all apostles, second prophets, third teachers, then workers of miracles, also those having gifts of healing, those able to help others, those with gifts of administration, and those speaking in different kinds of tongues. ²⁹Are all apostles? Are all prophets? Are all teachers? Do all work miracles? ³⁰Do all have gifts of healing? Do all speak in tongues?ᶜ Do all interpret? ³¹But eagerly desireᵈ the greater gifts.

Love

And now I will show you the most excellent way.

13 If I speak in the tonguesᵃ of men and of angels, but have not love, I am only a resounding gong or a clanging cymbal. ²If I have the gift of prophecy and can fathom all mysteries and all knowledge, and if I have a faith that can move mountains, but have not

---

ᵃ10 Or languages; also in verse 28   ᵇ13 Or with; or in   ᶜ30 Or other languages
ᵈ31 Or But you are eagerly desiring   ᵃ1 Or languages

1 CORINTHIANS 11:17–22, 33, 34
'When you come together, it is not the Lord's Supperyou eat' (v. 20).

IT WOULD APPEAR that the custom at Corinth, at least before they received Paul's letter, was to celebrate the communion service as a full meal, just as the Last Supper was a full meal. The church at Corinth was poor. Presumably it was difficult to provide a set meal for everyone, so the congregation brought their own.

Unfortunately this highlighted economic divisions within the community. Some had plenty, others little or nothing. What an opportunity to share! But the opportunity was missed. Paul in his wisdom probably realized such sharing was practically impossible. Instead he advised them to celebrate communion as a symbolic meal, simply remembering Jesus' actions at the last supper.

Paul's advice to the Corinthian Christians solved the outward problem of scandalous division between rich and poor at the communion table. It did not solve the wider problem of the scandalous difference between rich and poor in the Christian community at large. That is still a scandal which should weigh heavily on the heart of each and every Christian.

Nor did Paul anticipate later theological divisions which would divide Christians of different backgrounds (denominations), making some unwelcome to partake of the bread and wine because of those differences. Although there is a long way to go before full intercommunion exists between all churches, those differences are now being overcome, slowly but surely.

At a time when the scandalous gap between rich and poor countries is causing increasing concern, numbers of rich countries are reducing the tax 'burden' of rich individuals – thus increasing the gap between rich and poor in their own lands. Christians who remain silent about this are 'passing by on the other side'.

→1050

1 CORINTHIANS 12:26–13:3
'Eagerly desire the greater gifts. And now I will show you the most excellent way' (v. 31).

GIFTS ARE A BY-PRODUCT of the Christian life, fine and desirable, but never the main aim. It's a hard lesson to learn. It can make Christianity unpopular, for many crave the gifts rather than the giver. Craving spiritual gifts is not wrong in itself, any more than sex is wrong in itself. But a wrongly directed urge to acquire even spiritual gifts can be as damaging as a wrongly directed sexual urge. If our desire to acquire spiritual gifts makes us envy those who already have them, it is being wrongly directed. Such desire is only healthy within a lasting, steady relationship with Jesus.

If the gift takes your mind away from the giver, something is wrong. If it brings injury to other members of the body, something is wrong.

Follow the more excellent way, the way of love – the way of relationship with Jesus above all else – and the gifts will fall into place. Michael Green's book *I Believe in the Holy Spirit* says

We shall expect to see the work of the Spirit in the interdependence of the church membership, where love controls attitudes, and where gifts are used for the good of the community, not for the gratification of the individual . . . In the church where the Spirit is given freedom, the charismatic will not obtrude his gift, and the settled ministry will not fear it. Both strands need each other in the corporateness of the body of Christ; and both will, in the church where the Spirit is obeyed, resist the temptation of seceding from their sometimes awkward bedfellows.

Thou Christ of burning, cleansing flame, send the fire!
Thy Blood-bought gift today we claim. Send the fire!
Look down and see this waiting host,
Give us the promised Holy Ghost.
We want another Pentecost. Send the fire!

(*William Booth*)

→1053

love, I am nothing. ³If I give all I possess to the poor and surrender my body to the flames,*b* but have not love, I gain nothing.

⁴Love is patient, love is kind. It does not envy, it does not boast, it is not proud. ⁵It is not rude, it is not self-seeking, it is not easily angered, it keeps no record of wrongs. ⁶Love does not delight in evil but rejoices with the truth. ⁷It always protects, always trusts, always hopes, always perseveres.

⁸Love never fails. But where there are prophecies, they will cease; where there are tongues, they will be stilled; where there is knowledge, it will pass away. ⁹For we know in part and we prophesy in part, ¹⁰but when perfection comes, the imperfect disappears. ¹¹When I was a child, I talked like a child, I thought like a child, I reasoned like a child. When I became a man, I put childish ways behind me. ¹²Now we see but a poor reflection as in a mirror; then we shall see face to face. Now I know in part; then I shall know fully, even as I am fully known.

¹³And now these three remain: faith, hope and love. But the greatest of these is love.

Gifts of Prophecy and Tongues

14 Follow the way of love and eagerly desire spiritual gifts, especially the gift of prophecy. ²For anyone who speaks in a tongue*a* does not speak to men but to God. Indeed, no-one understands him; he utters mysteries with his spirit.*b* ³But everyone who prophesies speaks to men for their strengthening, encouragement and comfort. ⁴He who speaks in a tongue edifies himself, but he who prophesies edifies the church. ⁵I would like every one of you to speak in tongues,*c* but I would rather have you prophesy. He who prophesies is greater than one who speaks in tongues,*c* unless he interprets, so that the church may be edified.

⁶Now, brothers, if I come to you and speak in tongues, what good will I be to you, unless I bring you some revelation or knowledge or prophecy or word of instruction? ⁷Even in the case of lifeless things that make sounds, such as the flute or harp, how will anyone know what tune is being played unless there is a distinction in the notes? ⁸Again, if the trumpet does not sound a clear call, who will get ready for battle? ⁹So it is with you. Unless you speak intelligible words with your tongue, how will anyone know what you are saying? You will just be speaking into the air. ¹⁰Undoubtedly there are all sorts of languages in the world, yet none of them is without meaning. ¹¹If then I do not grasp the meaning of what someone is saying, I am a foreigner to the speaker, and he is a foreigner to me. ¹²So it is with you. Since you are eager to have spiritual gifts, try to excel in gifts that build up the church.

¹³For this reason anyone who speaks in a tongue should pray that he may interpret what he says. ¹⁴For if I pray in a tongue, my spirit prays, but my mind is unfruitful. ¹⁵So

what shall I do? I will pray with my spirit, but I will also pray with my mind; I will sing with my spirit, but I will also sing with my mind. ¹⁶If you are praising God with your spirit, how can one who finds himself among those who do not understand*d* say "Amen" to your thanksgiving, since he does not know what you are saying? ¹⁷You may be giving thanks well enough, but the other man is not edified.

¹⁸I thank God that I speak in tongues more than all of you. ¹⁹But in the church I would rather speak five intelligible words to instruct others than ten thousand words in a tongue.

²⁰Brothers, stop thinking like children. In regard to evil be infants, but in your thinking be adults. ²¹In the Law it is written:

"Through men of strange tongues
  and through the lips of foreigners
I will speak to this people,
  but even then they will not listen to
    me,"*e*

says the Lord.

²²Tongues, then, are a sign, not for believers but for unbelievers; prophecy, however, is for believers, not for unbelievers. ²³So if the whole church comes together and everyone speaks in tongues, and some who do not understand*f* or some unbelievers come in, will they not say that you are out of your mind? ²⁴But if an unbeliever or someone who does not understand*g* comes in while everybody is prophesying, he will be convinced by all that he is a sinner and will be judged by all, ²⁵and the secrets of his heart will be laid bare. So he will fall down and worship God, exclaiming, "God is really among you!"

Orderly Worship

²⁶What then shall we say, brothers? When you come together, everyone has a hymn, or a word of instruction, a revelation, a tongue or an interpretation. All of these must be done for the strengthening of the church. ²⁷If anyone speaks in a tongue, two—or at the most three—should speak, one at a time, and someone must interpret. ²⁸If there is no interpreter, the speaker should keep quiet in the church and speak to himself and God.

²⁹Two or three prophets should speak, and the others should weigh carefully what is said. ³⁰And if a revelation comes to someone who is sitting down, the first speaker should stop. ³¹For you can all prophesy in turn so that everyone may be instructed and encouraged. ³²The spirits of prophets are subject to the control of prophets. ³³For God is not a God of disorder but of peace.

As in all the congregations of the saints, ³⁴women should remain silent in the churches. They are not allowed to speak, but must be in submission, as the Law says. ³⁵If they want to enquire about something, they should ask their own husbands at home; for it is disgraceful for a woman to speak in the church.

---

b3 Some early manuscripts *body that I may boast*   *a2* Or *another language*; also in verses 4, 13, 14, 19, 26 and 27
b2 Or *by the Spirit*   *c5* Or *other languages*; also in verses 6, 18, 22, 23 and 39   *d16* Or *among the enquirers*
e21 Isaiah 28:11,12   *f23* Or *some enquirers*   *g24* Or *or some enquirer*

36Did the word of God originate with you? Or are you the only people it has reached? 37If anybody thinks he is a prophet or spiritually gifted, let him acknowledge that what I am writing to you is the Lord's command. 38If he ignores this, he himself will be ignored.*h*

39Therefore, my brothers, be eager to prophesy, and do not forbid speaking in tongues. 40But everything should be done in a fitting and orderly way.

The Resurrection of Christ

15 Now, brothers, I want to remind you of the gospel I preached to you, which you received and on which you have taken your stand. 2By this gospel you are saved, if you hold firmly to the word I preached to you. Otherwise, you have believed in vain.

3For what I received I passed on to you as of first importance:*a* that Christ died for our sins according to the Scriptures, 4that he was buried, that he was raised on the third day according to the Scriptures, 5and that he appeared to Peter,*b* and then to the Twelve. 6After that, he appeared to more than five hundred of the brothers at the same time, most of whom are still living, though some have fallen asleep. 7Then he appeared to James, then to all the apostles, 8and last of all he appeared to me also, as to one abnormally born.

9For I am the least of the apostles and do not even deserve to be called an apostle, because I persecuted the church of God. 10But by the grace of God I am what I am, and his grace to me was not without effect. No, I worked harder than all of them—yet not I, but the grace of God that was with me. 11Whether, then, it was I or they, this is what we preach, and this is what you believed.

The Resurrection of the Dead

12But if it is preached that Christ has been raised from the dead, how can some of you say that there is no resurrection of the dead? 13If there is no resurrection of the dead, then not even Christ has been raised. 14And if Christ has not been raised, our preaching is useless and so is your faith. 15More than that, we are then found to be false witnesses about God, for we have testified about God that he raised Christ from the dead. But he did not raise him if in fact the dead are not raised. 16For if the dead are not raised, then Christ has not been raised either. 17And if Christ has not been raised, your faith is futile; you are still in your sins. 18Then those also who have fallen asleep in Christ are lost. 19If only for this life we have hope in Christ, we are to be pitied more than all men.

20But Christ has indeed been raised from the dead, the firstfruits of those who have fallen asleep. 21For since death came through a man, the resurrection of the dead comes also through a man. 22For as in Adam all die, so in Christ all will be made alive. 23But each in his own turn: Christ, the firstfruits; then,

when he comes, those who belong to him. 24Then the end will come, when he hands over the kingdom to God the Father after he has destroyed all dominion, authority and power. 25For he must reign until he has put all his enemies under his feet. 26The last enemy to be destroyed is death. 27For he "has put everything under his feet".*c* Now when it says that "everything" has been put under him, it is clear that this does not include God himself, who put everything under Christ. 28When he has done this, then the Son himself will be made subject to him who put everything under him, so that God may be all in all.

29Now if there is no resurrection, what will those do who are baptised for the dead? If the dead are not raised at all, why are people baptised for them? 30And as for us, why do we endanger ourselves every hour? 31I die every day—I mean that, brothers—just as surely as I glory over you in Christ Jesus our Lord. 32If I fought wild beasts in Ephesus for merely human reasons, what have I gained? If the dead are not raised,

> "Let us eat and drink,
>   for tomorrow we die."*d*

33Do not be misled: "Bad company corrupts good character." 34Come back to your senses as you ought, and stop sinning; for there are some who are ignorant of God—I say this to your shame.

The Resurrection Body

35But someone may ask, "How are the dead raised? With what kind of body will they come?" 36How foolish! What you sow does not come to life unless it dies. 37When you sow, you do not plant the body that will be, but just a seed, perhaps of wheat or of something else. 38But God gives it a body as he has determined, and to each kind of seed he gives its own body. 39All flesh is not the same: Men have one kind of flesh, animals have another, birds another and fish another. 40There are also heavenly bodies and there are earthly bodies; but the splendour of the heavenly bodies is one kind, and the splendour of the earthly bodies is another. 41The sun has one kind of splendour, the moon another and the stars another; and star differs from star in splendour.

42So will it be with the resurrection of the dead. The body that is sown is perishable, it is raised imperishable; 43it is sown in dishonour, it is raised in glory; it is sown in weakness, it is raised in power; 44it is sown a natural body, it is raised a spiritual body.

If there is a natural body, there is also a spiritual body. 45So it is written: "The first man Adam became a living being";*e* the last Adam, a life-giving spirit. 46The spiritual did not come first, but the natural, and after that the spiritual. 47The first man was of the dust of the earth, the second man from heaven. 48As was the earthly man, so are those who

---

*h*38 Some manuscripts *If he is ignorant of this, let him be ignorant*   *a*3 Or *you at the first*
*b*5 Greek *Cephas*   *c*27 Psalm 8:6   *d*32 Isaiah 22:13   *e*45 Gen. 2:7

1 CORINTHIANS 13:4–13
'Now we see but a poor reflection as in a mirror, then we shall see face to face'
(v. 12).

FAITH, HOPE AND LOVE are the three gifts which will remain, which are carried over from time into eternity. They are the supreme virtues. And they are closely interwoven with each other.

What is faith without hope and love?
    Just a cold, intellectual conviction with no saving power at all.
What is hope without faith and love?
    Just a dream, a bubble that will burst one day.
What is love without faith and hope?
    Just passion, just feeling, just emotion, without any principle or any foundation.

            (*Alan Redpath*)

If all three remain, what is it about love which causes it to surpass the others, and to be the supreme virtue? Surely it is *the* virtue which involves others. We can have our own faith. We can hold to our own hope in spite of everything around us. But love requires another. We cannot just love ourselves. It is also the virtue which, above all, we share with God himself. God does not have faith, he is the object of faith. God does not have hope, for he already knows. But he does have love. Indeed he is love.

    Love suffereth patiently, Love worketh silently,
        Love seeketh not her own.
    Love never faileth, Love still prevaileth,
        Lord, in me thy love enthrone!

           (*Arch R. Wiggins*)

→1054

1 CORINTHIANS 14:33b–40
'As in all the congregations of the saints, women should remain silent in the churches' (v. 33b, 34a).

PAUL SPEAKS ABOUT WOMEN prophesying as an ordinary and accepted part of the well-ordered service in church. In Corinth they should pray or prophesy with their heads covered.

How then can Paul at the same time deny women the possibility of speaking in church? The answer is that he doesn't. By speaking, in this instance, he means either gossiping or public dissent. In the synagogue it was normal for a speaker to be challenged about his interpretation of the Law. Paul asks that such questioning should not be carried over into the Christian church service, at least not by the women. It is still very much a matter of culture. Women in Paul's day should not question the authority of men. But even in Paul's day they were not forbidden to prophesy or preach!

Catherine Booth, writing over a century ago states

Whether the Church will allow women to speak in *her* assemblies can only be a question of time; common sense, public opinion and the blessed results of female agency will force her to give us an honest and impartial rendering of the solitary text on which she grounds her prohibitions. Then, when the true light shines and God's works take the place of man's traditions, the doctor of divinity who shall teach that Paul commands woman to be silent when God's spirit urges her to speak will be regarded much the same as we should regard an astronomer who should teach that the sun is the earth's satellite.

Mrs Booth's prophecies are being fulfilled, but there is still a long way to go!

Pray for women preachers who still have to overcome prejudice against them from within their own congregations.

→1057

are of the earth; and as is the man from heaven, so also are those who are of heaven. ⁴⁹And just as we have borne the likeness of the earthly man, so shall we*f* bear the likeness of the man from heaven.

⁵⁰I declare to you, brothers, that flesh and blood cannot inherit the kingdom of God, nor does the perishable inherit the imperishable. ⁵¹Listen, I tell you a mystery: We will not all sleep, but we will all be changed—⁵²in a flash, in the twinkling of an eye, at the last trumpet. For the trumpet will sound, the dead will be raised imperishable, and we will be changed. ⁵³For the perishable must clothe itself with the imperishable, and the mortal with immortality. ⁵⁴When the perishable has been clothed with the imperishable, and the mortal with immortality, then the saying that is written will come true: "Death has been swallowed up in victory."*g*

⁵⁵"Where, O death, is your victory?
    Where, O death, is your sting?"*h*

⁵⁶The sting of death is sin, and the power of sin is the law. ⁵⁷But thanks be to God! He gives us the victory through our Lord Jesus Christ.

⁵⁸Therefore, my dear brothers, stand firm. Let nothing move you. Always give yourselves fully to the work of the Lord, because you know that your labour in the Lord is not in vain.

The Collection for God's People

16 Now about the collection for God's people: Do what I told the Galatian churches to do. ²On the first day of every week, each one of you should set aside a sum of money in keeping with his income, saving it up, so that when I come no collections will have to be made. ³Then, when I arrive, I will give letters of introduction to the men you approve and send them with your gift to Jerusalem. ⁴If it seems advisable for me to go also, they will accompany me.

Personal Requests

⁵After I go through Macedonia, I will come to you—for I will be going through Macedonia. ⁶Perhaps I will stay with you awhile, or even spend the winter, so that you can help me on my journey, wherever I go. ⁷I do not want to see you now and make only a passing visit; I hope to spend some time with you, if the Lord permits. ⁸But I will stay on at Ephesus until Pentecost, ⁹because a great door for effective work has opened to me, and there are many who oppose me.

¹⁰If Timothy comes, see to it that he has nothing to fear while he is with you, for he is carrying on the work of the Lord, just as I am. ¹¹No-one, then, should refuse to accept him. Send him on his way in peace so that he may return to me. I am expecting him along with the brothers.

¹²Now about our brother Apollos: I strongly urged him to go to you with the brothers. He was quite unwilling to go now, but he will go when he has the opportunity.

¹³Be on your guard; stand firm in the faith; be men of courage; be strong. ¹⁴Do everything in love.

¹⁵You know that the household of Stephanas were the first converts in Achaia, and they have devoted themselves to the service of the saints. I urge you, brothers, ¹⁶to submit to such as these and to everyone who joins in the work, and labours at it. ¹⁷I was glad when Stephanas, Fortunatus and Achaicus arrived, because they have supplied what was lacking from you. ¹⁸For they refreshed my spirit and yours also. Such men deserve recognition.

Final Greetings

¹⁹The churches in the province of Asia*a* send you greetings. Aquila and Priscilla*a* greet you warmly in the Lord, and so does the church that meets at their house. ²⁰All the brothers here send you greetings. Greet one another with a holy kiss.

²¹I, Paul, write this greeting in my own hand.

²²If anyone does not love the Lord—a curse be on him. Come, O Lord!*b* ²³The grace of the Lord Jesus be with you. ²⁴My love to all of you in Christ Jesus. Amen.*c*

---

*f*49 Some early manuscripts *so let us*   *g*54 Isaiah 25:8   *h*55 Hosea 13:14
*a*19 Greek *Prisca*, a variant of *Priscilla*   *b*22 In Aramaic the expression *Come, O Lord* is *Marana tha*.
*c*24 Some manuscripts do not have *Amen*.

2 Corinthians

1 Paul, an apostle of Christ Jesus by the will of God, and Timothy our brother,

To the church of God in Corinth, together with all the saints throughout Achaia:

²Grace and peace to you from God our Father and the Lord Jesus Christ.

The God of All Comfort

³Praise be to the God and Father of our Lord Jesus Christ, the Father of compassion and the God of all comfort, ⁴who comforts us in all our troubles, so that we can comfort those in any trouble with the comfort we ourselves have received from God. ⁵For just as the sufferings of Christ flow over into our lives, so also through Christ our comfort overflows. ⁶If we are distressed, it is for your comfort and salvation; if we are comforted, it is for your comfort, which produces in you patient endurance of the same sufferings we suffer. ⁷And our hope for you is firm, because we know that just as you share in our sufferings, so also you share in our comfort.

⁸We do not want you to be uninformed, brothers, about the hardships we suffered in the province of Asia. We were under great pressure, far beyond our ability to endure, so that we despaired even of life. ⁹Indeed, in our hearts we felt the sentence of death. But this happened that we might not rely on ourselves but on God, who raises the dead. ¹⁰He has delivered us from such a deadly peril, and he will deliver us. On him we have set our hope that he will continue to deliver us, ¹¹as you help us by your prayers. Then many will give thanks on our*a* behalf for the gracious favour granted us in answer to the prayers of many.

Paul's Change of Plans

¹²Now this is our boast: Our conscience testifies that we have conducted ourselves in the world, and especially in our relations with you, in the holiness and sincerity that are from God. We have done so not according to worldly wisdom but according to God's grace. ¹³For we do not write to you anything you cannot read or understand. And I hope that, ¹⁴as you have understood us in part, you will come to understand fully that

you can boast of us just as we will boast of you in the day of the Lord Jesus.

¹⁵Because I was confident of this, I planned to visit you first so that you might benefit twice. ¹⁶I planned to visit you on my way to Macedonia and to come back to you from Macedonia, and then to have you send me on my way to Judea. ¹⁷When I planned this, did I do it lightly? Or do I make my plans in a worldly manner so that in the same breath I say, "Yes, yes" and "No, no"?

¹⁸But as surely as God is faithful, our message to you is not "Yes" and "No". ¹⁹For the Son of God, Jesus Christ, who was preached among you by me and Silas*b* and Timothy, was not "Yes" and "No", but in him it has always been "Yes". ²⁰For no matter how many promises God has made, they are "Yes" in Christ. And so through him the "Amen" is spoken by us to the glory of God. ²¹Now it is God who makes both us and you stand firm in Christ. He anointed us, ²²set his seal of ownership on us, and put his Spirit in our hearts as a deposit, guaranteeing what is to come.

²³I call God as my witness that it was in order to spare you that I did not return to Corinth. ²⁴Not that we lord it over your faith, but we work with you for your joy, because it **2** is by faith you stand firm. ¹So I made up my mind that I would not make another painful visit to you. ²For if I grieve you, who is left to make me glad but you whom I have grieved? ³I wrote as I did so that when I came I should not be distressed by those who ought to make me rejoice. I had confidence in all of you, that you would all share my joy. ⁴For I wrote to you out of great distress and anguish of heart and with many tears, not to grieve you but to let you know the depth of my love for you.

Forgiveness for the Sinner

⁵If anyone has caused grief, he has not so much grieved me as he has grieved all of you, to some extent—not to put it too severely. ⁶The punishment inflicted on him by the majority is sufficient for him. ⁷Now instead, you ought to forgive and comfort him, so that he will not be overwhelmed by excessive sorrow. ⁸I urge you, therefore, to reaffirm your love for him. ⁹The reason I wrote to you

THE CHURCH as the body of Christ is central to Paul's thinking. Of course he recognizes our individuality. Our salvation is strongly connected to individual belief and acceptance of Christ's way, the way of the cross. But Christian life is lived in community. That community, the Church in all its varied forms, is an imperfect body which is continually being transformed through the work of the Holy Spirit, and through the Spirit's transformation of the lives of individual Christians.

Such transformation continues beyond the point of death. It is not complete here on earth. Denis Duncan writes 'it is clear that death is part of the journey to that wholeness which is completed in God's presence.' In more technical language, John Robinson writes

> The habit of treating 1 Corinthians 15 in isolation from the rest of Paul's writing has tended to obscure its connection with the very much larger number of passages which depict this gradual transformation and glorification of the body from baptism onwards. The result is that the final change has become mistakenly conceived as quasi-magical and unrelated to anything that has gone before.

We can now begin to understand v. 19 which appears so mournful at first. It seems to say Christians are miserable souls. Pity them if their hope of the next life is in vain, because their life here on earth is so miserable! But it is not saying that at all. It's saying Christians should be pitied if the transformation they experience here on earth does not continue. That is quite a different matter.

Death is a natural end and a natural beginning, part of a continual process of transformation which will be complete only after the day of judgement.

→1058

2 CORINTHIANS 1:1–7
'To the church of God in Corinth, together with all the saints throughout Achaia
. . . just as the sufferings of Christ flow over into our lives so also through Christ
our comfort overflows' (v. 1b, 5).

BEING A CHRISTIAN is not an easy option. Time and again Paul
reminds us of this. Nowhere did he need to do so more than in Corinth.
Corinth was a wealthy city, with many highly educated citizens. The
people attracted to the church in Corinth were not amongst them. Of
the Christians at Corinth 'not many . . . were wise . . . not many were
influential; not many were of noble birth. But God chose the foolish
things of the world to shame the wise.'

Christian fellowship works wonders. It brings people together. It
gives them a common purpose. It makes them aware of each other's
needs. It produces trust. It inspires confidence. The power of a
Christian community, even a community of Christians belonging to
the powerless classes, very quickly becomes evident to its members.
Material prosperity often follows. Christians help each other, and it is
not long before some of them begin to enjoy the fruits of material
success.

How easy it is to start to rely on this mutual prosperity. The joys of
the Christian life are emphasized, and suffering quickly becomes
forgotten as the community grows from strength to strength. Something like that seems to have happened in Corinth. Time and again
Paul has to remind them that suffering is an essential part of the
Christian experience. Without suffering, the true strength of community in Christ cannot be experienced.

*Unless we are thrown back on to divine resources we may deceive
ourselves into thinking that our own resources are sufficient.*

→1061

was to see if you would stand the test and be obedient in everything. ¹⁰If you forgive anyone, I also forgive him. And what I have forgiven—if there was anything to forgive—I have forgiven in the sight of Christ for your sake, ¹¹in order that Satan might not outwit us. For we are not unaware of his schemes.

Ministers of the New Covenant

¹²Now when I went to Troas to preach the gospel of Christ and found that the Lord had opened a door for me, ¹³I still had no peace of mind, because I did not find my brother Titus there. So I said good-bye to them and went on to Macedonia.

¹⁴But thanks be to God, who always leads us in triumphal procession in Christ and through us spreads everywhere the fragrance of the knowledge of him. ¹⁵For we are to God the aroma of Christ among those who are being saved and those who are perishing. ¹⁶To the one we are the smell of death; to the other, the fragrance of life. And who is equal to such a task? ¹⁷Unlike so many, we do not peddle the word of God for profit. On the contrary, in Christ we speak before God with sincerity, like men sent from God.

3 Are we beginning to commend ourselves again? Or do we need, like some people, letters of recommendation to you or from you? ²You yourselves are our letter, written on our hearts, known and read by everybody. ³You show that you are a letter from Christ, the result of our ministry, written not with ink but with the Spirit of the living God, not on tablets of stone but on tablets of human hearts.

⁴Such confidence as this is ours through Christ before God. ⁵Not that we are competent in ourselves to claim anything for ourselves, but our competence comes from God. ⁶He has made us competent as ministers of a new covenant—not of the letter but of the Spirit; for the letter kills, but the Spirit gives life.

The Glory of the New Covenant

⁷Now if the ministry that brought death, which was engraved in letters on stone, came with glory, so that the Israelites could not look steadily at the face of Moses because of its glory, fading though it was, ⁸will not the ministry of the Spirit be even more glorious? ⁹If the ministry that condemns men is glorious, how much more glorious is the ministry that brings righteousness! ¹⁰For what was glorious has no glory now in comparison with the surpassing glory. ¹¹And if what was fading away came with glory, how much greater is the glory of that which lasts!

¹²Therefore, since we have such a hope, we are very bold. ¹³We are not like Moses, who would put a veil over his face to keep the Israelites from gazing at it while the radiance was fading away. ¹⁴But their minds were made dull, for to this day the same veil remains when the old covenant is read. It has not been removed, because only in Christ is it

taken away. ¹⁵Even to this day when Moses is read, a veil covers their hearts. ¹⁶But whenever anyone turns to the Lord, the veil is taken away. ¹⁷Now the Lord is the Spirit, and where the Spirit of the Lord is, there is freedom. ¹⁸And we, who with unveiled faces all reflect[a] the Lord's glory, are being transformed into his likeness with ever-increasing glory, which comes from the Lord, who is the Spirit.

Treasures in Jars of Clay

4 Therefore, since through God's mercy we have this ministry, we do not lose heart. ²Rather, we have renounced secret and shameful ways; we do not use deception, nor do we distort the word of God. On the contrary, by setting forth the truth plainly we commend ourselves to every man's conscience in the sight of God. ³And even if our gospel is veiled, it is veiled to those who are perishing. ⁴The god of this age has blinded the minds of unbelievers, so that they cannot see the light of the gospel of the glory of Christ, who is the image of God. ⁵For we do not preach ourselves, but Jesus Christ as Lord, and ourselves as your servants for Jesus' sake. ⁶For God, who said, "Let light shine out of darkness,"[a] made his light shine in our hearts to give us the light of the knowledge of the glory of God in the face of Christ.

⁷But we have this treasure in jars of clay to show that this all-surpassing power is from God and not from us. ⁸We are hard pressed on every side, but not crushed; perplexed, but not in despair; ⁹persecuted, but not abandoned; struck down, but not destroyed. ¹⁰We always carry around in our body the death of Jesus, so that the life of Jesus may also be revealed in our body. ¹¹For we who are alive are always being given over to death for Jesus' sake, so that his life may be revealed in our mortal body. ¹²So then, death is at work in us, but life is at work in you.

¹³It is written: "I believed; therefore I have spoken."[b] With that same spirit of faith we also believe and therefore speak, ¹⁴because we know that the one who raised the Lord Jesus from the dead will also raise us with Jesus and present us with you in his presence. ¹⁵All this is for your benefit, so that the grace that is reaching more and more people may cause thanksgiving to overflow to the glory of God.

¹⁶Therefore we do not lose heart. Though outwardly we are wasting away, yet inwardly we are being renewed day by day. ¹⁷For our light and momentary troubles are achieving for us an eternal glory that far outweighs them all. ¹⁸So we fix our eyes not on what is seen, but on what is unseen. For what is seen is temporary, but what is unseen is eternal.

Our Heavenly Dwelling

5 Now we know that if the earthly tent we live in is destroyed, we have a building from God, an eternal house in heaven, not built by human hands. ²Meanwhile we groan,

---

*a18 Or contemplate   a6 Gen. 1:3   b13 Psalm 116:10

longing to be clothed with our heavenly dwelling, 3because when we are clothed, we will not be found naked. 4For while we are in this tent, we groan and are burdened, because we do not wish to be unclothed but to be clothed with our heavenly dwelling, so that what is mortal may be swallowed up by life. 5Now it is God who has made us for this very purpose and has given us the Spirit as a deposit, guaranteeing what is to come.

6Therefore we are always confident and know that as long as we are at home in the body we are away from the Lord. 7We live by faith, not by sight. 8We are confident, I say, and would prefer to be away from the body and at home with the Lord. 9So we make it our goal to please him, whether we are at home in the body or away from it. 10For we must all appear before the judgment seat of Christ, that each one may receive what is due to him for the things done while in the body, whether good or bad.

The Ministry of Reconciliation

11Since, then, we know what it is to fear the Lord, we try to persuade men. What we are is plain to God, and I hope it is also plain to your conscience. 12We are not trying to commend ourselves to you again, but are giving you an opportunity to take pride in us, so that you can answer those who take pride in what is seen rather than in what is in the heart. 13If we are out of our mind, it is for the sake of God; if we are in our right mind, it is for you. 14For Christ's love compels us, because we are convinced that one died for all, and therefore all died. 15And he died for all, that those who live should no longer live for themselves but for him who died for them and was raised again.

16So from now on we regard no-one from a worldly point of view. Though we once regarded Christ in this way, we do so no longer. 17Therefore, if anyone is in Christ, he is a new creation; the old has gone, the new has come! 18All this is from God, who reconciled us to himself through Christ and gave us the ministry of reconciliation: 19that God was reconciling the world to himself in Christ, not counting men's sins against them. And he has committed to us the message of reconciliation. 20We are therefore Christ's ambassadors, as though God were making his appeal through us. We implore you on Christ's behalf: Be reconciled to God. 21God made him who had no sin to be sin[a] for us, so that in him we might become the righteousness of God.

6 As God's fellow-workers we urge you not to receive God's grace in vain. 2For he says,

"In the time of my favour I heard you,
and in the day of salvation I helped
you."[a]

I tell you, now is the time of God's favour, now is the day of salvation.

Paul's Hardships

3We put no stumbling-block in anyone's path, so that our ministry will not be discredited. 4Rather, as servants of God we commend ourselves in every way: in great endurance; in troubles, hardships and distresses; 5in beatings, imprisonments and riots; in hard work, sleepless nights and hunger; 6in purity, understanding, patience and kindness; in the Holy Spirit and in sincere love; 7in truthful speech and in the power of God; with weapons of righteousness in the right hand and in the left; 8through glory and dishonour, bad report and good report; genuine, yet regarded as impostors; 9known, yet regarded as unknown; dying, and yet we live on; beaten, and yet not killed; 10sorrowful, yet always rejoicing; poor, yet making many rich; having nothing, and yet possessing everything.

11We have spoken freely to you, Corinthians, and opened wide our hearts to you. 12We are not withholding our affection from you, but you are withholding yours from us. 13As a fair exchange—I speak as to my children—open wide your hearts also.

Do Not Be Yoked With Unbelievers

14Do not be yoked together with unbelievers. For what do righteousness and wickedness have in common? Or what fellowship can light have with darkness? 15What harmony is there between Christ and Belial?[b] What does a believer have in common with an unbeliever? 16What agreement is there between the temple of God and idols? For we are the temple of the living God. As God has said: "I will live with them and walk among them, and I will be their God, and they will be my people."[c]

17"Therefore come out from them
and be separate,
says the Lord.
Touch no unclean thing,
and I will receive you."[d]
18"I will be a Father to you,
and you will be my sons and daughters,
says the Lord Almighty."[e]

7 Since we have these promises, dear friends, let us purify ourselves from everything that contaminates body and spirit, perfecting holiness out of reverence for God.

Paul's Joy

2Make room for us in your hearts. We have wronged no-one, we have corrupted no-one, we have exploited no-one. 3I do not say this to condemn you; I have said before that you have such a place in our hearts that we would live or die with you. 4I have great confidence in you; I take great pride in you. I am greatly encouraged; in all our troubles my joy knows no bounds.

5For when we came into Macedonia, this

---

*a21 Or be a sin offering   *a2 Isaiah 49:8   *b15 Greek Beliar, a variant of Belial
*c16 Lev. 26:12; Jer. 32:38; Ezek. 37:27   *d17 Isaiah 52:11; Ezek. 20:34,41   *e18 2 Samuel 7:14; 7:8

2 CORINTHIANS 3:1–6

'You are a letter from Christ, the result of our ministry, written not with ink but with the Spirit of the living God, not on tablets of stone but on tablets of human hearts' (v. 3).

TWO OLD TESTAMENT PICTURES combine here; first, Jeremiah's picture of a new covenant written on the heart; second, the picture of Moses with the stone tablets of the Law in his hands. They were emotive pictures for Paul. They meant something, too, to his readers in Corinth.

Christianity's roots are in the Old Testament. Most of those attracted to Christ came either from the ranks of Judaism or from the ranks of the God-fearers, people who followed the ethical codes of Judaism and who were on the fringes of the synagogue although they did not accept all the ritual requirements of full adherence to Judaism. Even those from a completely pagan background would still be introduced to the Old Testament Scriptures for as yet there were no Christian Scriptures to introduce them to!

Paul was convinced that the Old Testament pointed directly and clearly to Christ. But where the old covenant is static, solid and limited, the new covenant is living, developing and free. The new covenant does not depend on adherence to laws and codes of conduct. It depends on a living, spiritual relationship with the Lord. Every Christian individual, every Christian community is meant to be a living advertisement for the gospel.

What a responsibility! To reflect the very nature of God in our everyday lives. Yet the imperfect church at Corinth is achieving it. Paul builds up their confidence by telling them that they are the living proof of Christ.

Am I a living advertisement for the gospel? Is my Christian community living proof of the effectiveness of the new covenant in Christ?

→1062

2 CORINTHIANS 5:11–21

'Therefore, if anyone is in Christ, he is a new creation, the old has gone, the new has come! All this is from God, who reconciled us to himself through Christ and gave us the ministry of reconciliation' (vv. 17, 19).

PAUL'S PICTURES ARE VARIED. He describes salvation in three different ways. In Romans, he speaks about freedom, a picture from the slave market. But that can give rise to misunderstanding, as if God buys our freedom from Satan the slave master. He also speaks about justification, a picture from the law court. But that can give rise to misunderstanding, as though God acquits us and pretends we're righteous when we aren't. Here, Paul speaks of reconciliation. He uses the third picture less than the others, but it is at the centre of his Corinthian letters. Paul stresses the need for good personal relationships in building up the Church. His own pastoral care and concern for the Corinthians surfaces many times over.

In Christ, God has reconciled the world to himself. God himself has brought us into a new relationship, a relationship where the veil has been taken away. Now we come face to face with his reality, face to face with our Saviour, Christ Jesus. Nothing we do can bring about reconciliation. There is nothing we can offer to God to atone for our sins. No sacrifice of ours can atone for sin. All we can do is to accept with praise the work that God has done for us.

But when we accept God's gift of reconciliation we become, in a wonderful way, a part of the reconciling process. Christians who trust completely in the work that God has done in Christ become part of a great 'ministry of reconciliation'.

Individual Christians and the Church as a community of Christians receive from God power to be at peace with God, and power to communicate that peace to others.

→1065

body of ours had no rest, but we were harassed at every turn—conflicts on the outside, fears within. [6]But God, who comforts the downcast, comforted us by the coming of Titus, [7]and not only by his coming but also by the comfort you had given him. He told us about your longing for me, your deep sorrow, your ardent concern for me, so that my joy was greater than ever.

[8]Even if I caused you sorrow by my letter, I do not regret it. Though I did regret it—I see that my letter hurt you, but only for a little while—[9]yet now I am happy, not because you were made sorry, but because your sorrow led you to repentance. For you became sorrowful as God intended and so were not harmed in any way by us. [10]Godly sorrow brings repentance that leads to salvation and leaves no regret, but worldly sorrow brings death. [11]See what this godly sorrow has produced in you: what earnestness, what eagerness to clear yourselves, what indignation, what alarm, what longing, what concern, what readiness to see justice done. At every point you have proved yourselves to be innocent in this matter. [12]So even though I wrote to you, it was not on account of the one who did the wrong or of the injured party, but rather that before God you could see for yourselves how devoted to us you are. [13]By all this we are encouraged.

In addition to our own encouragement, we were especially delighted to see how happy Titus was, because his spirit has been refreshed by all of you. [14]I had boasted to him about you, and you have not embarrassed me. But just as everything we said to you was true, so our boasting about you to Titus has proved to be true as well. [15]And his affection for you is all the greater when he remembers that you were all obedient, receiving him with fear and trembling. [16]I am glad I can have complete confidence in you.

Generosity Encouraged

8 And now, brothers, we want you to know about the grace that God has given the Macedonian churches. [2]Out of the most severe trial, their overflowing joy and their extreme poverty welled up in rich generosity. [3]For I testify that they gave as much as they were able, and even beyond their ability. Entirely on their own, [4]they urgently pleaded with us for the privilege of sharing in this service to the saints. [5]And they did not do as we expected, but they gave themselves first to the Lord and then to us in keeping with God's will. [6]So we urged Titus, since he had earlier made a beginning, to bring also to completion this act of grace on your part. [7]But just as you excel in everything—in faith, in speech, in knowledge, in complete earnestness and in your love for us[a]—see that you also excel in this grace of giving.

[8]I am not commanding you, but I want to test the sincerity of your love by comparing it with the earnestness of others. [9]For you know the grace of our Lord Jesus Christ, that though he was rich, yet for your sakes he became poor, so that you through his poverty might become rich.

[10]And here is my advice about what is best for you in this matter: Last year you were the first not only to give but also to have the desire to do so. [11]Now finish the work, so that your eager willingness to do it may be matched by your completion of it, according to your means. [12]For if the willingness is there, the gift is acceptable according to what one has, not according to what he does not have.

[13]Our desire is not that others might be relieved while you are hard pressed, but that there might be equality. [14]At the present time your plenty will supply what they need, so that in turn their plenty will supply what you need. Then there will be equality, [15]as it is written: "He who gathered much did not have too much, and he who gathered little did not have too little."[b]

Titus Sent to Corinth

[16]I thank God, who put into the heart of Titus the same concern I have for you. [17]For Titus not only welcomed our appeal, but he is coming to you with much enthusiasm and on his own initiative. [18]And we are sending along with him the brother who is praised by all the churches for his service to the gospel. [19]What is more, he was chosen by the churches to accompany us as we carry the offering, which we administer in order to honour the Lord himself and to show our eagerness to help. [20]We want to avoid any criticism of the way we administer this liberal gift. [21]For we are taking pains to do what is right, not only in the eyes of the Lord but also in the eyes of men.

[22]In addition, we are sending with them our brother who has often proved to us in many ways that he is zealous, and now even more so because of his great confidence in you. [23]As for Titus, he is my partner and fellow-worker among you; as for our brothers, they are representatives of the churches and an honour to Christ. [24]Therefore show these men the proof of your love and the reason for our pride in you, so that the churches can see it.

9 There is no need for me to write to you about this service to the saints. [2]For I know your eagerness to help, and I have been boasting about it to the Macedonians, telling them that since last year you in Achaia were ready to give; and your enthusiasm has stirred most of them to action. [3]But I am sending the brothers in order that our boasting about you in this matter should not prove hollow, but that you may be ready, as I said you would be. [4]For if any Macedonians come with me and find you unprepared, we—not to say anything about you—would be ashamed of having been so confident. [5]So I thought it necessary to urge the brothers to visit you in advance and finish the arrangements for the generous gift you had promised. Then it will be ready as a generous gift, not as one grudgingly given.

---

[a]7 Some manuscripts *in our love for you*   [b]15 Exodus 16:18

Sowing Generously

6Remember this: Whoever sows sparingly will also reap sparingly, and whoever sows generously will also reap generously. 7Each man should give what he has decided in his heart to give, not reluctantly or under compulsion, for God loves a cheerful giver. 8And God is able to make all grace abound to you, so that in all things at all times, having all that you need, you will abound in every good work. 9As it is written:

"He has scattered abroad his gifts to the
  poor;
  his righteousness endures for ever."[a]

10Now he who supplies seed to the sower and bread for food will also supply and increase your store of seed and will enlarge the harvest of your righteousness. 11You will be made rich in every way so that you can be generous on every occasion, and through us your generosity will result in thanksgiving to God.

12This service that you perform is not only supplying the needs of God's people but is also overflowing in many expressions of thanks to God. 13Because of the service by which you have proved yourselves, men will praise God for the obedience that accompanies your confession of the gospel of Christ, and for your generosity in sharing with them and with everyone else. 14And in their prayers for you their hearts will go out to you, because of the surpassing grace God has given you. 15Thanks be to God for his indescribable gift!

Paul's Defence of His Ministry

10 By the meekness and gentleness of Christ, I appeal to you—I, Paul, who am "timid" when face to face with you, but "bold" when away! 2I beg you that when I come I may not have to be as bold as I expect to be towards some people who think that we live by the standards of this world. 3For though we live in the world, we do not wage war as the world does. 4The weapons we fight with are not the weapons of the world. On the contrary, they have divine power to demolish strongholds. 5We demolish arguments and every pretension that sets itself up against the knowledge of God, and we take captive every thought to make it obedient to Christ. 6And we will be ready to punish every act of disobedience, once your obedience is complete.

7You are looking only on the surface of things.[a] If anyone is confident that he belongs to Christ, he should consider again that we belong to Christ just as much as he. 8For even if I boast somewhat freely about the authority the Lord gave us for building you up rather than pulling you down, I will not be ashamed of it. 9I do not want to seem to be trying to frighten you with my letters. 10For

some say, "His letters are weighty and forceful, but in person he is unimpressive and his speaking amounts to nothing." 11Such people should realise that what we are in our letters when we are absent, we will be in our actions when we are present.

12We do not dare to classify or compare ourselves with some who commend themselves. When they measure themselves by themselves and compare themselves with themselves, they are not wise. 13We, however, will not boast beyond proper limits, but will confine our boasting to the field God has assigned to us, a field that reaches even to you. 14We are not going too far in our boasting, as would be the case if we had not come to you, for we did get as far as you with the gospel of Christ. 15Neither do we go beyond our limits by boasting of work done by others.[b] Our hope is that, as your faith continues to grow, our area of activity among you will greatly expand, 16so that we can preach the gospel in the regions beyond you. For we do not want to boast about work already done in another man's territory. 17But, "Let him who boasts boast in the Lord."[c] 18For it is not the one who commends himself who is approved, but the one whom the Lord commends.

Paul and the False Apostles

11 I hope you will put up with a little of my foolishness; but you are already doing that. 2I am jealous for you with a godly jealousy. I promised you to one husband, to Christ, so that I might present you as a pure virgin to him. 3But I am afraid that just as Eve was deceived by the serpent's cunning, your minds may somehow be led astray from your sincere and pure devotion to Christ. 4For if someone comes to you and preaches a Jesus other than the Jesus we preached, or if you receive a different spirit from the one you received, or a different gospel from the one you accepted, you put up with it easily enough. 5But I do not think I am in the least inferior to those "super-apostles". 6I may not be a trained speaker, but I do have knowledge. We have made this perfectly clear to you in every way.

7Was it a sin for me to lower myself in order to elevate you by preaching the gospel of God to you free of charge? 8I robbed other churches by receiving support from them so as to serve you. 9And when I was with you and needed something, I was not a burden to anyone, for the brothers who came from Macedonia supplied what I needed. I have kept myself from being a burden to you in any way, and will continue to do so. 10As surely as the truth of Christ is in me, nobody in the regions of Achaia will stop this boasting of mine. 11Why? Because I do not love you? God knows I do! 12And I will keep on doing what I am doing in order to cut the ground from under those who want an opportunity to

---

[a]9 Psalm 112:9   [a]7 Or Look at the obvious facts
[b]13–15 Or 13We, however, will not boast about things that cannot be measured, but we will boast according to the standard of measurement that the God of measure has assigned us—a measurement that relates even to you. 14. . . 15Neither do we boast about things that cannot be measured in regard to the work done by others.
[c]17 Jer. 9:24

2 CORINTHIANS 8:8–15

'If the willingness is there, the gift is acceptable according to what one has, not according to what he does not have. Our desire is not that others might be relieved while you are hard pressed, but that there might be equality' (vv. 12, 13).

TWO WHOLE CHAPTERS are devoted to giving in this letter. No Christian church at this time seems to have been wealthy. But Paul was very concerned about the Christians in Jerusalem. Their first experiment with pooling resources soon used up the assets of the few wealthy people who joined their ranks. There were few large legacies or gifts of income-producing land. They could not support charitable projects by selling off valuable real estate, as they had none. A poor and struggling minority, they had to live from hand to mouth, never quite sure where their income would come from.

Paul felt some responsibility towards them. His strong Jewish background would have filled him with the notion that Jerusalem was a special place. There was a long tradition of providing resources for Jerusalem. We saw how, centuries earlier, the people had been happy to support those who were willing to remain in Jerusalem. Paul must have felt similarly that Christians who held out there despite the persecution deserved support.

We saw yesterday how he prepared the ground. But his appeal was never by way of exploiting the good nature of the givers. He used no psychological blackmail in order to maximize the appeal. Instead he started off with the clear, Christian principle that 'if the willingness is there, the gift is acceptable according to what one has, not according to what he does not have'. It is the principle of the widow's mite simply stated from another viewpoint.

In Christian giving motives are more important than amounts.

→1066

'We are not going too far in our boasting, as would be the case if we had not come to you; but we did get as far as you with the gospel of Christ' (v. 14).

CHRISTIAN MISSION ACTIVITY has always caused debate. To-day some question the whole concept of missionary work. Last century in the 'scramble for Africa' Christian missions sometimes competed with each other for converts, thus sowing confusion. In other areas, more sensibly, but not without argument, missions negotiated with each other the areas they would concentrate on.

The first century was like that too. Some questioned whether Gentiles should receive the gospel at all (Acts 15:1). Paul received a commission to preach to the Gentiles (implying he ought to leave the Jews alone) while Peter's mission was to evangelize his own people, the Jews (Gal. 2:8, 9).

Paul himself decided he would preach only in areas where the gospel had not yet been heard. Yet soon his mission encountered difficulties because others came, preaching a different message from the one he had given (Gal. 1:6 etc.) sowing discontent in the new congregations. This happened in Corinth too.

Paul claimed he evangelized Corinth first, so he was not over-stretching his authority by giving continued pastoral advice. He hoped Corinth, being soundly founded and run, would help him in his task of extending the gospel. It should not get bogged down in purposeless argument about who had authority where. To further the work, Paul lets himself be dragged into controversy and fighting his own corner, but he hopes that in doing so controversy will be ended, and the borders of Christendom extended beyond his own 'corner'.

Christ Jesus, we thank you for all the areas where churches are working together to preach the gospel to others. We pray that such cooperation will continue without rivalry, jealousy, or squabbles over differences of approach. Help all who have the task of defining areas of mission. Give them broad visions of the power and scope of the gospel message.

be considered equal with us in the things they boast about.

13For such men are false apostles, deceitful workmen, masquerading as apostles of Christ. 14And no wonder, for Satan himself masquerades as an angel of light. 15It is not surprising, then, if his servants masquerade as servants of righteousness. Their end will be what their actions deserve.

Paul Boasts About His Sufferings

16I repeat: Let no-one take me for a fool. But if you do, then receive me just as you would a fool, so that I may do a little boasting. 17In this self-confident boasting I am not talking as the Lord would, but as a fool. 18Since many are boasting in the way the world does, I too will boast. 19You gladly put up with fools since you are so wise! 20In fact, you even put up with anyone who enslaves you or exploits you or takes advantage of you or pushes himself forward or slaps you in the face. 21To my shame I admit that we were too weak for that!

What anyone else dares to boast about—I am speaking as a fool—I also dare to boast about. 22Are they Hebrews? So am I. Are they Israelites? So am I. Are they Abraham's descendants? So am I. 23Are they servants of Christ? (I am out of my mind to talk like this.) I am more. I have worked much harder, been in prison more frequently, been flogged more severely, and been exposed to death again and again. 24Five times I received from the Jews the forty lashes minus one. 25Three times I was beaten with rods, once I was stoned, three times I was shipwrecked, I spent a night and a day in the open sea, 26I have been constantly on the move. I have been in danger from rivers, in danger from bandits, in danger from my own countrymen, in danger from Gentiles; in danger in the city, in danger in the country, in danger at sea; and in danger from false brothers. 27I have laboured and toiled and have often gone without sleep; I have known hunger and thirst and have often gone without food; I have been cold and naked. 28Besides everything else, I face daily the pressure of my concern for all the churches. 29Who is weak, and I do not feel weak? Who is led into sin, and I do not inwardly burn?

30If I must boast, I will boast of the things that show my weakness. 31The God and Father of the Lord Jesus, who is to be praised for ever, knows that I am not lying. 32In Damascus the governor under King Aretas had the city of the Damascenes guarded in order to arrest me. 33But I was lowered in a basket from a window in the wall and slipped through his hands.

Paul's Vision and His Thorn

12 I must go on boasting. Although there is nothing to be gained, I will go on to visions and revelations from the Lord. 2I know a man in Christ who fourteen years ago was caught up to the third heaven. Whether it was in the body or out of the body I do not

know—God knows. 3And I know that this man—whether in the body or apart from the body I do not know, but God knows—4was caught up to paradise. He heard inexpressible things, things that man is not permitted to tell. 5I will boast about a man like that, but I will not boast about myself, except about my weaknesses. 6Even if I should choose to boast, I would not be a fool, because I would be speaking the truth. But I refrain, so no-one will think more of me than is warranted by what I do or say.

7To keep me from becoming conceited because of these surpassingly great revelations, there was given me a thorn in my flesh, a messenger of Satan, to torment me. 8Three times I pleaded with the Lord to take it away from me. 9But he said to me, "My grace is sufficient for you, for my power is made perfect in weakness." Therefore I will boast all the more gladly about my weaknesses, so that Christ's power may rest on me. 10That is why, for Christ's sake, I delight in weaknesses, in insults, in hardships, in persecutions, in difficulties. For when I am weak, then I am strong.

Paul's Concern for the Corinthians

11I have made a fool of myself, but you drove me to it. I ought to have been commended by you, for I am not in the least inferior to the "super-apostles", even though I am nothing. 12The things that mark an apostle—signs, wonders and miracles—were done among you with great perseverance. 13How were you inferior to the other churches, except that I was never a burden to you? Forgive me this wrong!

14Now I am ready to visit you for the third time, and I will not be a burden to you, because what I want is not your possessions but you. After all, children should not have to save up for their parents, but parents for their children. 15So I will very gladly spend for you everything I have and expend myself as well. If I love you more, will you love me less? 16Be that as it may, I have not been a burden to you. Yet, crafty fellow that I am, I caught you by trickery! 17Did I exploit you through any of the men I sent you? 18I urged Titus to go to you and I sent our brother with him. Titus did not exploit you, did he? Did we not act in the same spirit and follow the same course?

19Have you been thinking all along that we have been defending ourselves to you? We have been speaking in the sight of God as those in Christ; and everything we do, dear friends, is for your strengthening. 20For I am afraid that when I come I may not find you as I want you to be, and you may not find me as you want me to be. I fear that there may be quarrelling, jealousy, outbursts of anger, factions, slander, gossip, arrogance and disorder. 21I am afraid that when I come again my God will humble me before you, and I will be grieved over many who have sinned earlier and have not repented of the impurity, sexual sin and debauchery in which they have indulged.

Final Warnings

13 This will be my third visit to you. "Every matter must be established by the testimony of two or three witnesses."[a] [2]I already gave you a warning when I was with you the second time. I now repeat it while absent: On my return I will not spare those who sinned earlier or any of the others, [3]since you are demanding proof that Christ is speaking through me. He is not weak in dealing with you, but is powerful among you. [4]For to be sure, he was crucified in weakness, yet he lives by God's power. Likewise, we are weak in him, yet by God's power we will live with him to serve you.

[5]Examine yourselves to see whether you are in the faith; test yourselves. Do you not realise that Christ Jesus is in you—unless, of course, you fail the test? [6]And I trust that you will discover that we have not failed the test. [7]Now we pray to God that you will not do anything wrong. Not that people will see that we have stood the test but that you will do what is right even though we may seem to have failed. [8]For we cannot do anything against the truth, but only for the truth. [9]We are glad whenever we are weak but you are strong; and our prayer is for your perfection. [10]This is why I write these things when I am absent, that when I come I may not have to be harsh in my use of authority—the authority the Lord gave me for building you up, not for tearing you down.

Final Greetings

[11]Finally, brothers, good-bye. Aim for perfection, listen to my appeal, be of one mind, live in peace. And the God of love and peace will be with you.

[12]Greet one another with a holy kiss. [13]All the saints send their greetings.

[14]May the grace of the Lord Jesus Christ, and the love of God, and the fellowship of the Holy Spirit be with you all.

---

[a]1 Deut. 19:15

2 CORINTHIANS 12:11–18

'The things that mark an apostle – signs, wonders and miracles – were done among you with great perseverance. How were you inferior to the other churches, except that I was never a burden to you? Forgive me this wrong!' (vv. 12, 13).

THE GRASS IS ALWAYS GREENER on the other side of the fence. The Corinthians were feeling inferior. They seem to have been jealous of other churches who appeared to be doing better than they were, or who had had a more sensational start than they had. After all, Paul stayed with them for eighteen months, whereas he had only stayed possibly a matter of weeks in some of the places he evangelized earlier. It looked as if they were being singled out as difficult.

And now, to add insult to injury, not only had they needed Paul's presence so much longer than other churches, but Paul was accepting support from the Macedonian churches, while he didn't ask the Corinthians to help him! You can't please some people!

Paul makes a great effort to point out to them that everything they heard about happening in other churches had also happened in Corinth. The apostles, Paul himself, Titus and Timothy had performed wonders amongst them. But when things happen close at hand, it never seems quite as sensational as hearing about what has happened in distant places. We quickly get used to the extraordinary. The most beautiful place we visit on holiday, and where we would love to be able to live is often just another boring old area to its inhabitants. We fail to see beauty on our own doorstep.

What wonderful things are happening around me which I have hardly noticed before?

→1070

2 CORINTHIANS 13:5–10

'Examine yourselves to see whether you are in the faith; test yourselves. Do you not realise that Christ Jesus is in you – unless, of course, you fail the test?' (v. 5).

SALVATIONISTS ARE EXTROVERT in expression of their love for God, and their desire to win the world to Jesus. But much of their worship, their poetry and literature is introvert, concerned with personal salvation, concerned with whether they pass the test of commitment to our Lord and Saviour.

It is not fashionable to look inward in such a way today. The fashion is to look inward, but not to test oneself against a standard, let alone against the highest standard of all, Jesus Christ. Fashionable followers of meditation techniques look inward and expect to find the divine, not without effort, but without the need for conversion. The Christian who looks inward expects to find, and does find, a sinful soul which can be transformed by grace.

The test is how far the transformation has really taken place. How far can we stand in the sight of God, not looking over our shoulder to those around us, and say that though we are weak, in Christ we are strong?

We may, of course, fail the test. If we do there is still hope, for our strength does not depend on finding goodness, divinity, unity, force or peace within ourselves. Our strength depends on God. Christ has opened up access to the divine. We latch on to that. We do not find it merely in ourselves.

> *Have I worked for hireling wages,*
> *Or as one with vows to keep,*
> *With a heart whose love engages*
> *Life or death, to save the sheep?*
> *All is known to thee, my Master,*
> *All is known, and that is why*
> *I can work and wait the verdict*
> *Of thy kind but searching eye.*

(*Albert Orsborn*)

→1073

Galatians

1 Paul, an apostle—sent not from men nor by man, but by Jesus Christ and God the Father, who raised him from the dead—²and all the brothers with me,

To the churches in Galatia:

³Grace and peace to you from God our Father and the Lord Jesus Christ, ⁴who gave himself for our sins to rescue us from the present evil age, according to the will of our God and Father, ⁵to whom be glory for ever and ever. Amen.

No Other Gospel

⁶I am astonished that you are so quickly deserting the one who called you by the grace of Christ and are turning to a different gospel —⁷which is really no gospel at all. Evidently some people are throwing you into confusion and are trying to pervert the gospel of Christ. ⁸But even if we or an angel from heaven should preach a gospel other than the one we preached to you, let him be eternally condemned! ⁹As we have already said, so now I say again: If anybody is preaching to you a gospel other than what you accepted, let him be eternally condemned!

¹⁰Am I now trying to win the approval of men, or of God? Or am I trying to please men? If I were still trying to please men, I would not be a servant of Christ.

Paul Called by God

¹¹I want you to know, brothers, that the gospel I preached is not something that man made up. ¹²I did not receive it from any man, nor was I taught it; rather, I received it by revelation from Jesus Christ.

¹³For you have heard of my previous way of life in Judaism, how intensely I persecuted the church of God and tried to destroy it. ¹⁴I was advancing in Judaism beyond many Jews of my own age and was extremely zealous for the traditions of my fathers. ¹⁵But when God, who set me apart from birth[a] and called me by his grace, was pleased ¹⁶to reveal his Son in me so that I might preach him among the Gentiles, I did not consult any man, ¹⁷nor did I go up to Jerusalem to see those who were apostles before I was, but I went immediately into Arabia and later returned to Damascus.

¹⁸Then after three years, I went up to Jerusalem to get acquainted with Peter[b] and stayed with him fifteen days. ¹⁹I saw none of the other apostles—only James, the Lord's brother. ²⁰I assure you before God that what I am writing to you is no lie. ²¹Later I went to Syria and Cilicia. ²²I was personally unknown to the churches of Judea that are in Christ. ²³They only heard the report: "The man who formerly persecuted us is now preaching the faith he once tried to destroy." ²⁴And they praised God because of me.

Paul Accepted by the Apostles

2 Fourteen years later I went up again to Jerusalem, this time with Barnabas. I took Titus along also. ²I went in response to a revelation and set before them the gospel that I preach among the Gentiles. But I did this privately to those who seemed to be leaders, for fear that I was running or had run my race in vain. ³Yet not even Titus, who was with me, was compelled to be circumcised, even though he was a Greek. ⁴This matter arose₎ because some false brothers had infiltrated our ranks to spy on the freedom we have in Christ Jesus and to make us slaves. ⁵We did not give in to them for a moment, so that the truth of the gospel might remain with you.

⁶As for those who seemed to be important —whatever they were makes no difference to me; God does not judge by external appearance—those men added nothing to my message. ⁷On the contrary, they saw that I had been entrusted with the task of preaching the gospel to the Gentiles,[a] just as Peter had been to the Jews.[b] ⁸For God, who was at work in the ministry of Peter as an apostle to the Jews, was also at work in my ministry as an apostle to the Gentiles. ⁹James, Peter[c] and John, those reputed to be pillars, gave me and Barnabas the right hand of fellowship when they recognised the grace given to me. They agreed that we should go to the Gentiles, and they to the Jews. ¹⁰All they asked was that we should continue to remember the poor, the very thing I was eager to do.

---

[a]15 Or from my mother's womb   [b]18 Greek Cephas   [a]7 Greek uncircumcised
[b]7 Greek circumcised; also in verses 8 and 9   [c]9 Greek Cephas; also in verses 11 and 14

Paul Opposes Peter

[11]When Peter came to Antioch, I opposed him to his face, because he was clearly in the wrong. [12]Before certain men came from James, he used to eat with the Gentiles. But when they arrived, he began to draw back and separate himself from the Gentiles because he was afraid of those who belonged to the circumcision group. [13]The other Jews joined him in his hypocrisy, so that by their hypocrisy even Barnabas was led astray.

[14]When I saw that they were not acting in line with the truth of the gospel, I said to Peter in front of them all, "You are a Jew, yet you live like a Gentile and not like a Jew. How is it, then, that you force Gentiles to follow Jewish customs?

[15]"We who are Jews by birth and not 'Gentile sinners' [16]know that a man is not justified by observing the law, but by faith in Jesus Christ. So we, too, have put our faith in Christ Jesus that we may be justified by faith in Christ and not by observing the law, because by observing the law no-one will be justified.

[17]"If, while we seek to be justified in Christ, it becomes evident that we ourselves are sinners, does that mean that Christ promotes sin? Absolutely not! [18]If I rebuild what I destroyed, I prove that I am a law-breaker. [19]For through the law I died to the law so that I might live for God. [20]I have been crucified with Christ and I no longer live, but Christ lives in me. The life I live in the body, I live by faith in the Son of God, who loved me and gave himself for me. [21]I do not set aside the grace of God, for if righteousness could be gained through the law, Christ died for nothing!"[d]

Faith or Observance of the Law

3 You foolish Galatians! Who has bewitched you? Before your very eyes Jesus Christ was clearly portrayed as crucified. [2]I would like to learn just one thing from you: Did you receive the Spirit by observing the law, or by believing what you heard? [3]Are you so foolish? After beginning with the Spirit, are you now trying to attain your goal by human effort? [4]Have you suffered so much for nothing—if it really was for nothing? [5]Does God give you his Spirit and work miracles among you because you observe the law, or because you believe what you heard?

[6]Consider Abraham: "He believed God, and it was credited to him as righteousness."[a] [7]Understand, then, that those who believe are children of Abraham. [8]The Scripture foresaw that God would justify the Gentiles by faith, and announced the gospel in advance to Abraham: "All nations will be blessed through you."[b] [9]So those who have faith are blessed along with Abraham, the man of faith.

[10]All who rely on observing the law are under a curse, for it is written: "Cursed is everyone who does not continue to do everything written in the Book of the Law."[c] [11]Clearly no-one is justified before God by the law, because, "The righteous will live by faith."[d] [12]The law is not based on faith; on the contrary, "The man who does these things will live by them."[e] [13]Christ redeemed us from the curse of the law by becoming a curse for us, for it is written: "Cursed is everyone who is hung on a tree."[f] [14]He redeemed us in order that the blessing given to Abraham might come to the Gentiles through Christ Jesus, so that by faith we might receive the promise of the Spirit.

The Law and the Promise

[15]Brothers, let me take an example from everyday life. Just as no-one can set aside or add to a human covenant that has been duly established, so it is in this case. [16]The promises were spoken to Abraham and to his seed. The Scripture does not say "and to seeds", meaning many people, but "and to your seed",[g] meaning one person, who is Christ. [17]What I mean is this: The law, introduced 430 years later, does not set aside the covenant previously established by God and thus do away with the promise. [18]For if the inheritance depends on the law, then it no longer depends on a promise; but God in his grace gave it to Abraham through a promise.

[19]What, then, was the purpose of the law? It was added because of transgressions until the Seed to whom the promise referred had come. The law was put into effect through angels by a mediator. [20]A mediator, however, does not represent just one party; but God is one.

[21]Is the law, therefore, opposed to the promises of God? Absolutely not! For if a law had been given that could impart life, then righteousness would certainly have come by the law. [22]But the Scripture declares that the whole world is a prisoner of sin, so that what was promised, being given through faith in Jesus Christ, might be given to those who believe.

[23]Before this faith came, we were held prisoners by the law, locked up until faith should be revealed. [24]So the law was put in charge to lead us to Christ[h] that we might be justified by faith. [25]Now that faith has come, we are no longer under the supervision of the law.

Sons of God

[26]You are all sons of God through faith in Christ Jesus, [27]for all of you who were baptised into Christ have clothed yourselves with Christ. [28]There is neither Jew nor Greek, slave nor free, male nor female, for you are all one in Christ Jesus. [29]If you belong to Christ, then you are Abraham's seed, and heirs according to the promise.

4 What I am saying is that as long as the heir is a child, he is no different from a slave, although he owns the whole estate.

---

*d*21 Some interpreters end the quotation after verse 14.   *a*6 Gen. 15:6   *b*8 Gen. 12:3; 18:18; 22:18
*c*10 Deut. 27:26   *d*11 Hab. 2:4   *e*12 Lev. 18:5   *f*13 Deut. 21:23   *g*16 Gen. 12:7; 13:15; 24:7
*h*24 Or *charge until Christ came*

'Even if we or an angel from heaven should preach a gospel other than the one we preached to you, let him be eternally condemned!' (v. 8).

NOTHING IS MORE IMPORTANT than the gospel of Jesus Christ. The truth of that statement is plain for all to see. After even the shallowest reading of Paul's letter to the Galatians, you could not possibly mistake the importance of keeping to the truth of the gospel.

Paul may be misrepresented. People may revile him and hurt him. They may persecute him and imprison him. All that is of little account to him. Only when the truth of the gospel is threatened does Paul really react strongly.

Paul obviously expected things to be difficult after he left his flock to fend for themselves. Before he wrote this letter, he had already had to tell the Galatians to ignore those who preached a different gospel to the one which he proclaimed. But Paul is astonished that the Galatians have so quickly deserted the true faith – the gospel which states salvation comes through Christ and Christ alone – and gone back to Jewish and/or pagan ways.

Paul wonders where he has gone wrong. Has he given the impression that he was speaking under the authority of the Jerusalem church? Has he let them think that, by not insisting on circumcision, he was watering down the gospel to make it easier for his pagan congregation to accept? Surely they can see that neither of these is the case. Paul's authority is from God. His gospel involves complete commitment and sacrifice – otherwise he himself would have chosen the easy path, and stuck to his own strong Jewish tradition.

Paul seems to blame himself as much as the false teachers for the fact that the Galatians have strayed. In our keenness to guard the gospel do we, like Paul, sometimes blame ourselves too much for other people's failings?

→1074

GALATIANS 3:26–4:7

'There is neither Jew nor Greek, slave nor free, male nor female, for you are all one in Christ Jesus' (v. 28).

EVERY CHRISTIAN should have this verse engraved in their heart. It is a logical conclusion of Paul's argument. It is a sign of full maturity in Christ. When barriers are broken down; when there is true communion at every level of life, then Christ is really present.

Through the centuries it has hardly been possible for this verse to be taken seriously. Poverty, ignorance, pagan cultures and Old Testament influences have all conspired to keep women in the home, and require men to function in the world outside. Paul himself had to bow to cultural pressure and ask women to keep their heads covered when they prayed.

Today that has changed. How glad Paul would be! Affluence, technology and the possibility of communicating Christ to the general population in a way previously undreamed of, mean that it is now possible to put into practice, here and now on earth, a foretaste of what is to come in the heavenly realms, the unity in Christ portrayed here by Paul.

Effective contraception limiting families; industrial and office organization enabling job sharing; compulsory education for children; and a host of other measures make it possible for women to undertake virtually every task previously reserved for men.

How Paul would rejoice – and how saddened he would be that he himself is often quoted in support of restricting the ministerial and other activities of women.

²He is subject to guardians and trustees until the time set by his father. ³So also, when we were children, we were in slavery under the basic principles of the world. ⁴But when the time had fully come, God sent his Son, born of a woman, born under law, ⁵to redeem those under law, that we might receive the full rights of sons. ⁶Because you are sons, God sent the Spirit of his Son into our hearts, the Spirit who calls out, "*Abba*,ᵃ Father." ⁷So you are no longer a slave, but a son; and since you are a son, God has made you also an heir.

Paul's Concern for the Galatians

⁸Formerly, when you did not know God, you were slaves to those who by nature are not gods. ⁹But now that you know God—or rather are known by God—how is it that you are turning back to those weak and miserable principles? Do you wish to be enslaved by them all over again? ¹⁰You are observing special days and months and seasons and years! ¹¹I fear for you, that somehow I have wasted my efforts on you.

¹²I plead with you, brothers, become like me, for I became like you. You have done me no wrong. ¹³As you know, it was because of an illness that I first preached the gospel to you. ¹⁴Even though my illness was a trial to you, you did not treat me with contempt or scorn. Instead, you welcomed me as if I were an angel of God, as if I were Christ Jesus himself. ¹⁵What has happened to all your joy? I can testify that, if you could have done so, you would have torn out your eyes and given them to me. ¹⁶Have I now become your enemy by telling you the truth?

¹⁷Those people are zealous to win you over, but for no good. What they want is to alienate you ₁from us₁, so that you may be zealous for them. ¹⁸It is fine to be zealous, provided the purpose is good, and to be so always and not just when I am with you. ¹⁹My dear children, for whom I am again in the pains of childbirth until Christ is formed in you, ²⁰how I wish I could be with you now and change my tone, because I am perplexed about you!

Hagar and Sarah

²¹Tell me, you who want to be under the law, are you not aware of what the law says? ²²For it is written that Abraham had two sons, one by the slave woman and the other by the free woman. ²³His son by the slave woman was born in the ordinary way; but his son by the free woman was born as the result of a promise.

²⁴These things may be taken figuratively, for the women represent two covenants. One covenant is from Mount Sinai and bears children who are to be slaves: This is Hagar. ²⁵Now Hagar stands for Mount Sinai in Arabia and corresponds to the present city of Jerusalem, because she is in slavery with her children. ²⁶But the Jerusalem that is above is free, and she is our mother. ²⁷For it is written:

"Be glad, O barren woman,
    who bears no children;
break forth and cry aloud,
    you who have no labour pains;
because more are the children of the
        desolate woman
    than of her who has a husband."ᵇ

²⁸Now you, brothers, like Isaac, are children of promise. ²⁹At that time the son born in the ordinary way persecuted the son born by the power of the Spirit. It is the same now. ³⁰But what does the Scripture say? "Get rid of the slave woman and her son, for the slave woman's son will never share in the inheritance with the free woman's son."ᶜ ³¹Therefore, brothers, we are not children of the slave woman, but of the free woman.

Freedom in Christ

5 It is for freedom that Christ has set us free. Stand firm, then, and do not let yourselves be burdened again by a yoke of slavery.

²Mark my words! I, Paul, tell you that if you let yourselves be circumcised, Christ will be of no value to you at all. ³Again I declare to every man who lets himself be circumcised that he is required to obey the whole law. ⁴You who are trying to be justified by law have been alienated from Christ; you have fallen away from grace. ⁵But by faith we eagerly await through the Spirit the righteousness for which we hope. ⁶For in Christ Jesus neither circumcision nor uncircumcision has any value. The only thing that counts is faith expressing itself through love.

⁷You were running a good race. Who cut in on you and kept you from obeying the truth? ⁸That kind of persuasion does not come from the one who calls you. ⁹"A little yeast works through the whole batch of dough." ¹⁰I am confident in the Lord that you will take no other view. The one who is throwing you into confusion will pay the penalty, whoever he may be. ¹¹Brothers, if I am still preaching circumcision, why am I still being persecuted? In that case the offence of the cross has been abolished. ¹²As for those agitators, I wish they would go the whole way and emasculate themselves!

¹³You, my brothers, were called to be free. But do not use your freedom to indulge the sinful natureᵃ; rather, serve one another in love. ¹⁴The entire law is summed up in a single command: "Love your neighbour as yourself."ᵇ ¹⁵If you keep on biting and devouring each other, watch out or you will be destroyed by each other.

Life by the Spirit

¹⁶So I say, live by the Spirit, and you will not gratify the desires of the sinful nature. ¹⁷For the sinful nature desires what is contrary to the Spirit, and the Spirit what is

---

ᵃ6 Aramaic for *Father*   ᵇ27 Isaiah 54:1   ᶜ30 Gen. 21:10
ᵃ13 Or *the flesh*; also in verses 16, 17, 19 and 24   ᵇ14 Lev. 19:18

contrary to the sinful nature. They are in conflict with each other, so that you do not do what you want. 18But if you are led by the Spirit, you are not under law.

19The acts of the sinful nature are obvious: sexual immorality, impurity and debauchery; 20idolatry and witchcraft; hatred, discord, jealousy, fits of rage, selfish ambition, dissensions, factions 21and envy; drunkenness, orgies, and the like. I warn you, as I did before, that those who live like this will not inherit the kingdom of God.

22But the fruit of the Spirit is love, joy, peace, patience, kindness, goodness, faithfulness, 23gentleness and self-control. Against such things there is no law. 24Those who belong to Christ Jesus have crucified the sinful nature with its passions and desires. 25Since we live by the Spirit, let us keep in step with the Spirit. 26Let us not become conceited, provoking and envying each other.

Doing Good to All

6 Brothers, if someone is caught in a sin, you who are spiritual should restore him gently. But watch yourself, or you also may be tempted. 2Carry each other's burdens, and in this way you will fulfil the law of Christ. 3If anyone thinks he is something when he is nothing, he deceives himself. 4Each one should test his own actions. Then he can take pride in himself, without comparing himself to somebody else, 5for each one should carry his own load.

6Anyone who receives instruction in the word must share all good things with his instructor.

7Do not be deceived: God cannot be mocked. A man reaps what he sows. 8The one who sows to please his sinful nature, from that nature[a] will reap destruction; the one who sows to please the Spirit, from the Spirit will reap eternal life. 9Let us not become weary in doing good, for at the proper time we will reap a harvest if we do not give up. 10Therefore, as we have opportunity, let us do good to all people, especially to those who belong to the family of believers.

Not Circumcision but a New Creation

11See what large letters I use as I write to you with my own hand!

12Those who want to make a good impression outwardly are trying to compel you to be circumcised. The only reason they do this is to avoid being persecuted for the cross of Christ. 13Not even those who are circumcised obey the law, yet they want you to be circumcised that they may boast about your flesh. 14May I never boast except in the cross of our Lord Jesus Christ, through which[b] the world has been crucified to me, and I to the world. 15Neither circumcision nor uncircumcision means anything; what counts is a new creation. 16Peace and mercy to all who follow this rule, even to the Israel of God.

17Finally, let no-one cause me trouble, for I bear on my body the marks of Jesus.

18The grace of our Lord Jesus Christ be with your spirit, brothers. Amen.

[a]8 Or his flesh, from the flesh   [b]14 Or whom

GALATIANS 4:21–31

'One covenant is from Mount Sinai and bears children who are to be slaves: This is Hagar . . . You, brothers, like Isaac, are children of promise. At that time the son born in the ordinary way persecuted the son born by the power of the Spirit. It is the same now' (vv. 24b, 28, 29).

THE PICTURE PAUL USES to illustrate the difference between freedom in Christ and slavery to the law is a difficult one, a story from Genesis which he uses as an allegory.

Abraham's wife, Sarah, was barren and old. In accordance with ancient custom she asked Hagar, a slave girl, to have a child by Abraham for her. Hagar had a son called Ishmael. For a while Hagar must have thought her son would inherit everything of Abraham's, including his special covenant relationship with God. Later on, Sarah had a son, Isaac. God's covenant continued through Isaac, the free-born son, not through Ishmael, the slave girl's son.

Hagar stands for the old covenant, the Law, which was given on Mount Sinai. She was a slave. Her children were slaves, and the covenant based on Law makes men slaves of the Law. It hardly seems just, Hagar's descendants being condemned to eternal slavery nor, at the same time, Isaac's descendants being for ever free. Paul is not commenting on the justice of the situation. He simply uses a Jew's own perception of how things then stood, to highlight the importance of freedom, of the new covenant, of grace rather than Law.

Strange as this may seem to us, there remains in it the one great fact. The man who makes law the principle of his life is in the position of a slave; all his life he is seeking to satisfy his master the law. Whereas the man who makes grace the principle of his life has made love his dominant principle. He is the free man . . . love is always more powerful than law.

(*William Barclay*)

→1078

GALATIANS 6:1–6

'if someone is caught in a sin, you who are spiritual should restore him gently. Watch yourself , or you also may be tempted' (v. 1).

RESTORE HIM GENTLY . . . BUT WATCH YOURSELF. Jesus sets us a clear example. He himself was never afraid to eat with sinners, or to associate with them in any way at all. His parables tend to show sinners in a favourable light, compared with those who claim to be righteous. There seems to be no warning in the Gospels against associating with sinners.

Paul, however, is acutely aware of the dangers facing his infant flock. He knows how easy it is to be influenced by the people you associate with. He knows how easy it is for the policeman to turn criminal; for the doctor to take drugs and alcohol; for the psychiatrist to become mad; and for the priest to commit the same sins as are confessed to him.

Faced with a wrongdoer, Paul says, the Christian must 'restore him gently'. Loudmouthed condemnation is out. Patient persuasion is in. It is a lesson that Paul knows he has to learn himself. He found it easy to condemn. We only need to read the first chapters of Galatians to see that. Paul easily took on the same tone as those who opposed him.

> *O let me feel thee near me; the world is ever near;*
> *I see the sights that dazzle, the tempting sounds I hear.*
> *My foes are ever near me, around me and within;*
> *But, Jesus, draw thou nearer and shield my soul from sin.*

(John Ernest Bode)

The first verses of Chapter 6 are addressed to Paul himself as much as to anyone else. And that makes them all the more effective.

→1081

Ephesians

1 Paul, an apostle of Christ Jesus by the will of God,

To the saints in Ephesus,[a] the faithful[b] in Christ Jesus:

²Grace and peace to you from God our Father and the Lord Jesus Christ.

Spiritual Blessings in Christ

³Praise be to the God and Father of our Lord Jesus Christ, who has blessed us in the heavenly realms with every spiritual blessing in Christ. ⁴For he chose us in him before the creation of the world to be holy and blameless in his sight. In love ⁵he[c] predestined us to be adopted as his sons through Jesus Christ, in accordance with his pleasure and will—⁶to the praise of his glorious grace, which he has freely given us in the One he loves. ⁷In him we have redemption through his blood, the forgiveness of sins, in accordance with the riches of God's grace ⁸that he lavished on us with all wisdom and understanding. ⁹And he[d] made known to us the mystery of his will according to his good pleasure, which he purposed in Christ, ¹⁰to be put into effect when the times will have reached their fulfilment—to bring all things in heaven and on earth together under one head, even Christ.

¹¹In him we were also chosen,[e] having been predestined according to the plan of him who works out everything in conformity with the purpose of his will, ¹²in order that we, who were the first to hope in Christ, might be for the praise of his glory. ¹³And you also were included in Christ when you heard the word of truth, the gospel of your salvation. Having believed, you were marked in him with a seal, the promised Holy Spirit, ¹⁴who is a deposit guaranteeing our inheritance until the redemption of those who are God's possession—to the praise of his glory.

Thanksgiving and Prayer

¹⁵For this reason, ever since I heard about your faith in the Lord Jesus and your love for all the saints, ¹⁶I have not stopped giving thanks for you, remembering you in my prayers. ¹⁷I keep asking that the God of our Lord Jesus Christ, the glorious Father, may give you the Spirit[f] of wisdom and revelation, so that you may know him better. ¹⁸I pray also that the eyes of your heart may be enlightened in order that you may know the hope to which he has called you, the riches of his glorious inheritance in the saints, ¹⁹and his incomparably great power for us who believe. That power is like the working of his mighty strength, ²⁰which he exerted in Christ when he raised him from the dead and seated him at his right hand in the heavenly realms, ²¹far above all rule and authority, power and dominion, and every title that can be given, not only in the present age but also in the one to come. ²²And God placed all things under his feet and appointed him to be head over everything for the church, ²³which is his body, the fulness of him who fills everything in every way.

Made Alive in Christ

2 As for you, you were dead in your transgressions and sins, ²in which you used to live when you followed the ways of this world and of the ruler of the kingdom of the air, the spirit who is now at work in those who are disobedient. ³All of us also lived among them at one time, gratifying the cravings of our sinful nature[a] and following its desires and thoughts. Like the rest, we were by nature objects of wrath. ⁴But because of his great love for us, God, who is rich in mercy, ⁵made us alive with Christ even when we were dead in transgressions—it is by grace you have been saved. ⁶And God raised us up with Christ and seated us with him in the heavenly realms in Christ Jesus, ⁷in order that in the coming ages he might show the incomparable riches of his grace, expressed in his kindness to us in Christ Jesus. ⁸For it is by grace you have been saved, through faith —and this not from yourselves, it is the gift of God—⁹not by works, so that no-one can boast. ¹⁰For we are God's workmanship, created in Christ Jesus to do good works, which God prepared in advance for us to do.

One in Christ

¹¹Therefore, remember that formerly you who are Gentiles by birth and called

---

a1 Some early manuscripts do not have *in Ephesus*. *b1* Or *believers who are* *c4, 5* Or *sight in love.* *⁵He* *d8, 9* Or *us. With all wisdom and understanding,* *⁹he* *e11* Or *were made heirs* *f17* Or *a spirit* *a3* Or *our flesh* "uncircumcised" by those who call themselves "the circumcision" (that done in the body by the hands of men)—[12]remember that at that time you were separate from Christ, excluded from citizenship in Israel and foreigners to the covenants of the promise, without hope and without God in the world. [13]But now in Christ Jesus you who once were far away have been brought near through the blood of Christ.

[14]For he himself is our peace, who has made the two one and has destroyed the barrier, the dividing wall of hostility, [15]by abolishing in his flesh the law with its commandments and regulations. His purpose was to create in himself one new man out of the two, thus making peace, [16]and in this one body to reconcile both of them to God through the cross, by which he put to death their hostility. [17]He came and preached peace to you who were far away and peace to those who were near. [18]For through him we both have access to the Father by one Spirit.

[19]Consequently, you are no longer foreigners and aliens, but fellow-citizens with God's people and members of God's household, [20]built on the foundation of the apostles and prophets, with Christ Jesus himself as the chief cornerstone. [21]In him the whole building is joined together and rises to become a holy temple in the Lord. [22]And in him you too are being built together to become a dwelling in which God lives by his Spirit.

Paul the Preacher to the Gentiles

3 For this reason I, Paul, the prisoner of Christ Jesus for the sake of you Gentiles—

[2]Surely you have heard about the administration of God's grace that was given to me for you, [3]that is, the mystery made known to me by revelation, as I have already written briefly. [4]In reading this, then, you will be able to understand my insight into the mystery of Christ, [5]which was not made known to men in other generations as it has now been revealed by the Spirit to God's holy apostles and prophets. [6]This mystery is that through the gospel the Gentiles are heirs together with Israel, members together of one body, and sharers together in the promise in Christ Jesus.

[7]I became a servant of this gospel by the gift of God's grace given me through the working of his power. [8]Although I am less than the least of all God's people, this grace was given me: to preach to the Gentiles the unsearchable riches of Christ, [9]and to make plain to everyone the administration of this mystery, which for ages past was kept hidden in God, who created all things. [10]His intent was that now, through the church, the manifold wisdom of God should be made known to the rulers and authorities in the heavenly realms, [11]according to his eternal purpose which he accomplished in Christ Jesus our Lord. [12]In him and through faith in him we

may approach God with freedom and confidence. [13]I ask you, therefore, not to be discouraged because of my sufferings for you, which are your glory.

A Prayer for the Ephesians

[14]For this reason I kneel before the Father, [15]from whom his whole family[a] in heaven and on earth derives its name. [16]I pray that out of his glorious riches he may strengthen you with power through his Spirit in your inner being, [17]so that Christ may dwell in your hearts through faith. And I pray that you, being rooted and established in love, [18]may have power, together with all the saints, to grasp how wide and long and high and deep is the love of Christ, [19]and to know this love that surpasses knowledge—that you may be filled to the measure of all the fulness of God.

[20]Now to him who is able to do immeasurably more than all we ask or imagine, according to his power that is at work within us, [21]to him be glory in the church and in Christ Jesus throughout all generations, for ever and ever! Amen.

Unity in the Body of Christ

4 As a prisoner for the Lord, then, I urge you to live a life worthy of the calling you have received. [2]Be completely humble and gentle; be patient, bearing with one another in love. [3]Make every effort to keep the unity of the Spirit through the bond of peace. [4]There is one body and one Spirit —just as you were called to one hope when you were called—[5]one Lord, one faith, one baptism; [6]one God and Father of all, who is over all and through all and in all.

[7]But to each one of us grace has been given as Christ apportioned it. [8]This is why it[a] says:

"When he ascended on high,
    he led captives in his train
    and gave gifts to men."[b]

[9](What does "he ascended" mean except that he also descended to the lower, earthly regions?[c] [10]He who descended is the very one who ascended higher than all the heavens, in order to fill the whole universe.) [11]It was he who gave some to be apostles, some to be prophets, some to be evangelists, and some to be pastors and teachers, [12]to prepare God's people for works of service, so that the body of Christ may be built up [13]until we all reach unity in the faith and in the knowledge of the Son of God and become mature, attaining to the whole measure of the fulness of Christ.

[14]Then we will no longer be infants, tossed back and forth by the waves, and blown here and there by every wind of teaching and by the cunning and craftiness of men in their deceitful scheming. [15]Instead, speaking the truth in love, we will in all things grow up into him who is the Head, that is, Christ. [16]From him the whole body, joined and held together by every supporting ligament, grows and

---

[a]15 Or whom all fatherhood   [a]8 Or God   [b]8 Psalm 68:18
[c]9 Or the depths of the earth

EPHESIANS 2:8–10

'For it is by grace that you have been saved, through faith – and this is not from yourselves, it is the gift of God' (v. 8).

GRACE IS GOD'S INITIATIVE, faith is man's response. Paul's teaching is summed up in Ephesians, nowhere more clearly than here. Grace is God's free gift. But grace is much more than a free offer that you could pick up on a supermarket shelf. It is more than an extravagant gift from an indulgent father who spoils his children. It is more than a simple matter of disregarding sin and offering blind forgiveness.

Grace brings power, God's power, to do those good deeds which he planned for us to do. It was God's grace which enabled Paul to work. It was God's grace that empowered him to overcome, even to glory in his personal weaknesses. It was God's grace that permitted him to lay the foundations of the churches. Paul was controlled by grace, the power of which is so strong that some have been led to think that God's grace is irresistible. But that is not so.

God's grace does not take away man's freedom. Man can 'make nonsense' of God's grace. Man can fail to use God's grace. Man can even put himself outside the range of God's grace. Without the response of faith God's grace can be ineffective. John Newton resisted God's grace for years before he responded in faith and was able to write

'Twas grace that taught my heart to fear,
And grace my fears relieved;
How precious did that grace appear
The hour I first believed!

Through many dangers, toils and snares
I have already come;
'Tis grace has brought me safe thus far,
And grace will lead me home.

→1082

EPHESIANS 4:8–16
'When he ascended on high, he led captives in his train and gave gifts to men . . .
Speaking the truth in love, we will in all things grow up into him who is the Head,
that is, Christ' (v. 8, 15).

PAUL QUOTES PSALM 68 to stress that the ascension is not remote
and unimportant, but relevant to us today (Ps. 68:16). By it, Christ
gives gifts to men.

In Britain the ascension goes by almost unnoticed. It is hardly
discussed. In contrast to emotive, almost materialist discussion of the
bodily nature of the resurrection, any discussion of the ascension of
Jesus must take account of the spiritual nature of the event.

It matters supremely how we understand our relationship to the
ascended Lord, the glorified Christ, to Jesus – *as he is now*. William
Barclay writes 'The ascension stands for the final liberation of Jesus
from all limitations of time and space.' That is true, but it's only half
the story. Jesus is free of time and space. That freedom enables him to
relate to us in time and space.

He does this through the ministry of the Holy Spirit. The ascended
Christ descends to us now, not just as a baby in a manger, but as a
Spirit, holy, full of fire and activity. He disturbs our consciences, and
strengthens our resolve. He produces revival in our hearts, and speaks
to us clearly about the needs of this present generation. He gives gifts
to each of us so that the body of Christ may be built up in great variety
but with an overriding unity.

Let us debate the nature of the ascended Lord, by all means – but
only if we are then prepared to listen to the Spirit which descends.

> *O holy child of Bethlehem,*
> *Descend to us, we pray;*
> *Cast out our sin, and enter in,*
> *Be born in us today.*

> *(Phillips Brooks)*

The true wonder of the ascension is that the ascended Lord is ever
present, with us – today.

→1085

builds itself up in love, as each part does its work.

Living as Children of Light

17So I tell you this, and insist on it in the Lord, that you must no longer live as the Gentiles do, in the futility of their thinking. 18They are darkened in their understanding and separated from the life of God because of the ignorance that is in them due to the hardening of their hearts. 19Having lost all sensitivity, they have given themselves over to sensuality so as to indulge in every kind of impurity, with a continual lust for more.

20You, however, did not come to know Christ that way. 21Surely you heard of him and were taught in him in accordance with the truth that is in Jesus. 22You were taught, with regard to your former way of life, to put off your old self, which is being corrupted by its deceitful desires; 23to be made new in the attitude of your minds; 24and to put on the new self, created to be like God in true righteousness and holiness.

25Therefore each of you must put off falsehood and speak truthfully to his neighbour, for we are all members of one body. 26"In your anger do not sin"d: Do not let the sun go down while you are still angry, 27and do not give the devil a foothold. 28He who has been stealing must steal no longer, but must work, doing something useful with his own hands, that he may have something to share with those in need.

29Do not let any unwholesome talk come out of your mouths, but only what is helpful for building others up according to their needs, that it may benefit those who listen. 30And do not grieve the Holy Spirit of God, with whom you were sealed for the day of redemption. 31Get rid of all bitterness, rage and anger, brawling and slander, along with every form of malice. 32Be kind and compassionate to one another, forgiving each other, just as in Christ God forgave you.

5 Be imitators of God, therefore, as dearly loved children 2and live a life of love, just as Christ loved us and gave himself up for us as a fragrant offering and sacrifice to God.

3But among you there must not be even a hint of sexual immorality, or of any kind of impurity, or of greed, because these are improper for God's holy people. 4Nor should there be obscenity, foolish talk or coarse joking, which are out of place, but rather thanksgiving. 5For of this you can be sure: No immoral, impure or greedy person—such a man is an idolater—has any inheritance in the kingdom of Christ and of God.a 6Let no-one deceive you with empty words, for because of such things God's wrath comes on those who are disobedient. 7Therefore do not be partners with them.

8For you were once darkness, but now you are light in the Lord. Live as children of light 9(for the fruit of the light consists in all goodness, righteousness and truth) 10and find out what pleases the Lord. 11Have nothing to do with the fruitless deeds of darkness, but rather expose them. 12For it is shameful even to mention what the disobedient do in secret. 13But everything exposed by the light becomes visible, 14for it is light that makes everything visible. This is why it is said:

"Wake up, O sleeper,
    rise from the dead,
and Christ will shine on you."

15Be very careful, then, how you live—not as unwise but as wise, 16making the most of every opportunity, because the days are evil. 17Therefore do not be foolish, but understand what the Lord's will is. 18Do not get drunk on wine, which leads to debauchery. Instead, be filled with the Spirit. 19Speak to one another with psalms, hymns and spiritual songs. Sing and make music in your heart to the Lord, 20always giving thanks to God the Father for everything, in the name of our Lord Jesus Christ.

21Submit to one another out of reverence for Christ.

Wives and Husbands

22Wives, submit to your husbands as to the Lord. 23For the husband is the head of the wife as Christ is the head of the church, his body, of which he is the Saviour. 24Now as the church submits to Christ, so also wives should submit to their husbands in everything.

25Husbands, love your wives, just as Christ loved the church and gave himself up for her 26to make her holy, cleansingb her by the washing with water through the word, 27and to present her to himself as a radiant church, without stain or wrinkle or any other blemish, but holy and blameless. 28In this same way, husbands ought to love their wives as their own bodies. He who loves his wife loves himself. 29After all, no-one ever hated his own body, but he feeds and cares for it, just as Christ does the church—30for we are members of his body. 31"For this reason a man will leave his father and mother and be united to his wife, and the two will become one flesh."c 32This is a profound mystery—but I am talking about Christ and the church. 33However, each one of you also must love his wife as he loves himself, and the wife must respect her husband.

Children and Parents

6 Children, obey your parents in the Lord, for this is right. 2"Honour your father and mother"—which is the first commandment with a promise—3"that it may go well with you and that you may enjoy long life on the earth."a

4Fathers, do not exasperate your children; instead, bring them up in the training and instruction of the Lord.

Slaves and Masters

5Slaves, obey your earthly masters with respect and fear, and with sincerity of heart,

d26 Psalm 4:4   a5 Or kingdom of the Christ and God   b26 Or having cleansed
c31 Gen. 2:24   a3 Deut. 5:16

just as you would obey Christ. 6Obey them not only to win their favour when their eye is on you, but like slaves of Christ, doing the will of God from your heart. 7Serve wholeheartedly, as if you were serving the Lord, not men, 8because you know that the Lord will reward everyone for whatever good he does, whether he is slave or free.

9And masters, treat your slaves in the same way. Do not threaten them, since you know that he who is both their Master and yours is in heaven, and there is no favouritism with him.

The Armour of God

10Finally, be strong in the Lord and in his mighty power. 11Put on the full armour of God so that you can take your stand against the devil's schemes. 12For our struggle is not against flesh and blood, but against the rulers, against the authorities, against the powers of this dark world and against the spiritual forces of evil in the heavenly realms. 13Therefore put on the full armour of God, so that when the day of evil comes, you may be able to stand your ground, and after you have done everything, to stand. 14Stand firm then, with the belt of truth buckled round your waist, with the breastplate of righteousness

in place, 15and with your feet fitted with the readiness that comes from the gospel of peace. 16In addition to all this, take up the shield of faith, with which you can extinguish all the flaming arrows of the evil one. 17Take the helmet of salvation and the sword of the Spirit, which is the word of God. 18And pray in the Spirit on all occasions with all kinds of prayers and requests. With this in mind, be alert and always keep on praying for all the saints.

19Pray also for me, that whenever I open my mouth, words may be given me so that I will fearlessly make known the mystery of the gospel, 20for which I am an ambassador in chains. Pray that I may declare it fearlessly, as I should.

Final Greetings

21Tychicus, the dear brother and faithful servant in the Lord, will tell you everything, so that you also may know how I am and what I am doing. 22I am sending him to you for this very purpose, that you may know how we are, and that he may encourage you.

23Peace to the brothers, and love with faith from God the Father and the Lord Jesus Christ. 24Grace to all who love our Lord Jesus Christ with an undying love.

EPHESIANS 5:21–33
'Submit to one another out of reverence for Christ. Wives, submit to your husbands as to the Lord' (vv. 21, 22).

PAUL'S IDEAS ON MARRIAGE cause much needless controversy, partly because:
1. A single, memorable phrase can affect the reading of a whole passage.
2. It is hard to keep the context continually in mind.
3. Paul compares husband-wife relations and Christ-Church relations.

1. 'Wives submit to your husbands' is memorable, clear, and convenient for men – who still wield power in most societies. It is tempting to think Paul intends things to be ordered like that for ever, regardless of particular situations and changes in society. But set it against 'Submit to one another out of reverence for Christ' and the picture changes completely. That means husbands also submitting to wives! How many of us take that seriously?

2. The context of Paul's words was a world where he had to make it clear that Christianity would not mean the break up of family life. It would not mean all responsibilities being renounced.

3. There is a tendency for us to feel that the relationship between Christ and the Church should be one where Christ controls absolutely. He is, after all, the head. However, Christ's own concern is not so much control as love. Christ himself would rather his Church make its own way in the world through understanding what the love of Christ means, instead of expecting to be rescued by outside control all the time. In any loving relationship the emphasis on control must give way to an emphasis on mutual dependence.

The mystery of the marriage relationship is much deeper than any discussion of who should control whom. As Paul says 'This is a profound mystery.'

→1086

EPHESIANS 6:10–13

'Put on the full armour of God so that you can take your stand against the devil's schemes. For our struggle is not against flesh and blood, but against the rulers, against the authorities, against the powers of this dark world' (vv. 11, 12).

THE ARMED STRUGGLE of the Christian is real. It is a continual fight against wickedness of all kinds. Paul mentions no specific sin, no particular offence in this section. It would be easy if we could single out one particularly unpleasant sinful act, concentrate our attention on that, and hope that everything else will fall into place.

Things don't work like that. We can't fight sin by concentrating on sins. We can only fight sin by concentrating on the powerful forces which create sin. That is what Paul means by arming ourselves against the spiritual forces of evil in the heavenly realms. That is what Paul means by struggle against the authorities and powers of this dark world. He doesn't mean we should take up a particular issue, run a campaign and then rest content with our achievement.

An example: Paul would surely approve of the fight against racism in modern society. He would, however, never dream of thinking that getting racial attitudes right would make everything else come right, too. Conquest of racism would improve our world, but it could not redeem our world.

> *O may I love like thee,*
> *In all thy footsteps tread!*
> *Thou hatest all iniquity,*
> *But nothing thou hast made.*
> *O may I learn the art*
> *With meekness to reprove*
> *To hate the sin with all my heart,*
> *But still the sinner love!*

(*Charles Wesley*)

→1089

Philippians

1 Paul and Timothy, servants of Christ Jesus,

To all the saints in Christ Jesus at Philippi, together with the overseers[a] and deacons:

2Grace and peace to you from God our Father and the Lord Jesus Christ.

Thanksgiving and Prayer

3I thank my God every time I remember you. 4In all my prayers for all of you, I always pray with joy 5because of your partnership in the gospel from the first day until now, 6being confident of this, that he who began a good work in you will carry it on to completion until the day of Christ Jesus.

7It is right for me to feel this way about all of you, since I have you in my heart; for whether I am in chains or defending and confirming the gospel, all of you share in God's grace with me. 8God can testify how I long for all of you with the affection of Christ Jesus.

9And this is my prayer: that your love may abound more and more in knowledge and depth of insight, 10so that you may be able to discern what is best and may be pure and blameless until the day of Christ, 11filled with the fruit of righteousness that comes through Jesus Christ—to the glory and praise of God.

Paul's Chains Advance the Gospel

12Now I want you to know, brothers, that what has happened to me has really served to advance the gospel. 13As a result, it has become clear throughout the whole palace guard[b] and to everyone else that I am in chains for Christ. 14Because of my chains, most of the brothers in the Lord have been encouraged to speak the word of God more courageously and fearlessly.

15It is true that some preach Christ out of envy and rivalry, but others out of goodwill. 16The latter do so in love, knowing that I am put here for the defence of the gospel. 17The former preach Christ out of selfish ambition, not sincerely, supposing that they can stir up trouble for me while I am in chains.[c] 18But what does it matter? The important thing is that in every way, whether from false motives or true, Christ is preached. And because of this I rejoice.

Yes, and I will continue to rejoice, 19for I know that through your prayers and the help given by the Spirit of Jesus Christ, what has happened to me will turn out for my deliverance.[d] 20I eagerly expect and hope that I will in no way be ashamed, but will have sufficient courage so that now as always Christ will be exalted in my body, whether by life or by death. 21For to me, to live is Christ and to die is gain. 22If I am to go on living in the body, this will mean fruitful labour for me. Yet what shall I choose? I do not know! 23I am torn between the two: I desire to depart and be with Christ, which is better by far; 24but it is more necessary for you that I remain in the body. 25Convinced of this, I know that I will remain, and I will continue with all of you for your progress and joy in the faith, 26so that through my being with you again your joy in Christ Jesus will overflow on account of me.

27Whatever happens, conduct yourselves in a manner worthy of the gospel of Christ. Then, whether I come and see you or only hear about you in my absence, I will know that you stand firm in one spirit, contending as one man for the faith of the gospel 28without being frightened in any way by those who oppose you. This is a sign to them that they will be destroyed, but that you will be saved—and that by God. 29For it has been granted to you on behalf of Christ not only to believe on him, but also to suffer for him, 30since you are going through the same struggle you saw I had, and now hear that I still have.

Imitating Christ's Humility

2 If you have any encouragement from being united with Christ, if any comfort from his love, if any fellowship with the Spirit, if any tenderness and compassion, 2then make my joy complete by being like-minded, having the same love, being one in spirit and purpose. 3Do nothing out of selfish ambition or vain conceit, but in humility consider others better than yourselves. 4Each of you should look not only to your

a1 Traditionally bishops   b13 Or whole palace
c16, 17 Some late manuscripts have verses 16 and 17 in reverse order.   d19 Or salvation

own interests, but also to the interests of others.

⁵Your attitude should be the same as that of Christ Jesus:

⁶Who, being in very nature*a* God,
did not consider equality with God
something to be grasped,
⁷but made himself nothing,
taking the very nature*b* of a servant,
being made in human likeness.
⁸And being found in appearance as a man,
he humbled himself
and became obedient to death—even
death on a cross!
⁹Therefore God exalted him to the highest place
and gave him the name that is above
every name,
¹⁰that at the name of Jesus every knee
should bow,
in heaven and on earth and under the earth,
¹¹and every tongue confess that Jesus Christ
is Lord,
to the glory of God the Father.

Shining as Stars

¹²Therefore, my dear friends, as you have always obeyed—not only in my presence, but now much more in my absence —continue to work out your salvation with fear and trembling, ¹³for it is God who works in you to will and to act according to his good purpose.

¹⁴Do everything without complaining or arguing, ¹⁵so that you may become blameless and pure, children of God without fault in a crooked and depraved generation, in which you shine like stars in the universe ¹⁶as you hold out*c* the word of life—in order that I may boast on the day of Christ that I did not run or labour for nothing. ¹⁷But even if I am being poured out like a drink offering on the sacrifice and service coming from your faith, I am glad and rejoice with all of you. ¹⁸So you too should be glad and rejoice with me.

Timothy and Epaphroditus

¹⁹I hope in the Lord Jesus to send Timothy to you soon, that I also may be cheered when I receive news about you. ²⁰I have no-one else like him, who takes a genuine interest in your welfare. ²¹For everyone looks out for his own interests, not those of Jesus Christ. ²²But you know that Timothy has proved himself, because as a son with his father he has served with me in the work of the gospel. ²³I hope, therefore, to send him as soon as I see how things go with me. ²⁴And I am confident in the Lord that I myself will come soon.

²⁵But I think it is necessary to send back to you Epaphroditus, my brother, fellow-worker and fellow-soldier, who is also your messenger, whom you sent to take care of my needs. ²⁶For he longs for all of you and is distressed because you heard he was ill.

²⁷Indeed he was ill, and almost died. But God had mercy on him, and not on him only but also on me, to spare me sorrow upon sorrow. ²⁸Therefore I am all the more eager to send him, so that when you see him again you may be glad and I may have less anxiety. ²⁹Welcome him in the Lord with great joy, and honour men like him, ³⁰because he almost died for the work of Christ, risking his life to make up for the help you could not give me.

No Confidence in the Flesh

3 Finally, my brothers, rejoice in the Lord! It is no trouble for me to write the same things to you again, and it is a safeguard for you.

²Watch out for those dogs, those men who do evil, those mutilators of the flesh. ³For it is we who are the circumcision, we who worship by the Spirit of God, who glory in Christ Jesus, and who put no confidence in the flesh—⁴though I myself have reasons for such confidence.

If anyone else thinks he has reasons to put confidence in the flesh, I have more: ⁵circumcised on the eighth day, of the people of Israel, of the tribe of Benjamin, a Hebrew of Hebrews; in regard to the law, a Pharisee; ⁶as for zeal, persecuting the church; as for legalistic righteousness, faultless.

⁷But whatever was to my profit I now consider loss for the sake of Christ. ⁸What is more, I consider everything a loss compared to the surpassing greatness of knowing Christ Jesus my Lord, for whose sake I have lost all things. I consider them rubbish, that I may gain Christ ⁹and be found in him, not having a righteousness of my own that comes from the law, but that which is through faith in Christ —the righteousness that comes from God and is by faith. ¹⁰I want to know Christ and the power of his resurrection and the fellowship of sharing in his sufferings, becoming like him in his death, ¹¹and so, somehow, to attain to the resurrection from the dead.

Pressing on Towards the Goal

¹²Not that I have already obtained all this, or have already been made perfect, but I press on to take hold of that for which Christ Jesus took hold of me. ¹³Brothers, I do not consider myself yet to have taken hold of it. But one thing I do: Forgetting what is behind and straining towards what is ahead, ¹⁴I press on towards the goal to win the prize for which God has called me heavenwards in Christ Jesus.

¹⁵All of us who are mature should take such a view of things. And if on some point you think differently, that too God will make clear to you. ¹⁶Only let us live up to what we have already attained.

¹⁷Join with others in following my example, brothers, and take note of those who live according to the pattern we gave you. ¹⁸For, as I have often told you before and now say again even with tears, many live

PHILIPPIANS 1:1–6
'Being confident of this, that he who began a good work in you will carry it on to completion until the day of Christ Jesus' (v. 6).

GOD WOULD NOT engage himself in a doomed enterprise. Occasionally we meet someone who seems to specialize in supporting lost causes, but usually we give our energies to causes which we believe will succeed. In sporting contests the 'underdog' believes he can win, and there are precedents enough to indicate that his confidence has merit. However, God, the Almighty God, who knows the end from the beginning, does not undertake a task which is lost before it is begun (1 Cor. 1:8).

When malevolent men rejoiced in the fact that Christ had died through crucifixion, and that his dream of kingship had died with him, the reply of God was the overwhelming victory of resurrection. More than that, the cross itself, that shameful instrument of death, conceived, fashioned and raised by evil men, became the means and symbol of that victory, being raised high in triumph by the Church ever since (Col 12:13–15).

Paul's common sense, his simple, matter-of-fact statement to the Philippians, is a source of encouragement to us today. Having commenced a work of grace within us, God will see that work through to fulfilment. The only real impediment to that determination is found within the human will. God believes in us! He will help us to keep trusting him. God's intention for us is nothing less than likeness to Jesus (Rom. 8:29). It is an incredible aspiration, totally beyond our human striving, but in the plan of God and by his grace, it is an aspiration destined to be fully realized (Col. 3:1–4).

> *Not might, nor power, thyself hast said,*
> *Can vice destroy or virtue spread;*
> *Thy Spirit, Lord, this work must do.*
> *Who only can our hearts renew.*

> (*Edward Boaden*)

→1090

PHILIPPIANS 2:1–11

'Therefore God exalted him to the highest place and gave him the name that is above every name' (v. 9).

> *JESUS, name above all names,*
> *Beautiful Saviour, glorious Lord,*
> *Emmanuel, God is with us,*
> *Blessed redeemer, Living Word.*

As we extol the Christ by singing Naida Hearn's chorus we move into one of the most remarkable revelations in Scripture. Only by the power and inspiration of the Holy Spirit could Paul so sensitively and accurately, define the nature and role of Christ, affirming the special glory which God bestowed upon him. God gave him the name which is above every name.

It was by divine decree that the name Jesus was given (Matt. 1:20, 21). The name comes to us via Greek and Latin from the Hebrew name Joshua, meaning 'Jehovah is salvation', or as Matthew puts it, 'he will save his people from their sins'. A most appropriate name, loved increasingly through all generations since.

There seems little doubt that God as part of his overwhelming approval of the work of Christ, not only 'seated him at his right hand in the heavenly realms, far above all rule and authority, power and dominion, and every title that can be given, not only in the present age but also in the one to come' (Eph. 1:20, 21), but also gave him his own name of Lord. God named his Son after himself! He could confer no greater honour. 'Lord' equals YHWH, the four letters used by the Jews to indicate the sacred name of the God most high, from which letters we take the name either as Jehovah or Yahweh. It is the name above all names.

> *Jesus is worthy to receive*
> *Honour and power divine;*
> *And blessings more than we can give*
> *Be, Lord, for ever thine.*

(Isaac Watts)

→1093

as enemies of the cross of Christ. [19]Their destiny is destruction, their god is their stomach, and their glory is in their shame. Their mind is on earthly things. [20]But our citizenship is in heaven. And we eagerly await a Saviour from there, the Lord Jesus Christ, [21]who, by the power that enables him to bring everything under his control, will transform our lowly bodies so that they will be like his glorious body.

4 Therefore, my brothers, you whom I love and long for, my joy and crown, that is how you should stand firm in the Lord, dear friends!

Exhortations

[2]I plead with Euodia and I plead with Syntyche to agree with each other in the Lord. [3]Yes, and I ask you, loyal yoke-fellow,[a] help these women who have contended at my side in the cause of the gospel, along with Clement and the rest of my fellow-workers, whose names are in the book of life.

[4]Rejoice in the Lord always. I will say it again: Rejoice! [5]Let your gentleness be evident to all. The Lord is near. [6]Do not be anxious about anything, but in everything, by prayer and petition, with thanksgiving, present your requests to God. [7]And the peace of God, which transcends all understanding, will guard your hearts and your minds in Christ Jesus.

[8]Finally, brothers, whatever is true, whatever is noble, whatever is right, whatever is pure, whatever is lovely, whatever is admirable—if anything is excellent or praiseworthy—think about such things. [9]Whatever you have learned or received or heard from me, or seen in me—put it into practice. And the God of peace will be with you.

Thanks for Their Gifts

[10]I rejoice greatly in the Lord that at last you have renewed your concern for me. Indeed, you have been concerned, but you had no opportunity to show it. [11]I am not saying this because I am in need, for I have learned to be content whatever the circumstances. [12]I know what it is to be in need, and I know what it is to have plenty. I have learned the secret of being content in any and every situation, whether well fed or hungry, whether living in plenty or in want. [13]I can do everything through him who gives me strength.

[14]Yet it was good of you to share in my troubles. [15]Moreover, as you Philippians know, in the early days of your acquaintance with the gospel, when I set out from Macedonia, not one church shared with me in the matter of giving and receiving, except you only; [16]for even when I was in Thessalonica, you sent me aid again and again when I was in need. [17]Not that I am looking for a gift, but I am looking for what may be credited to your account. [18]I have received full payment and even more; I am amply supplied, now that I have received from Epaphroditus the gifts you sent. They are a fragrant offering, an acceptable sacrifice, pleasing to God. [19]And my God will meet all your needs according to his glorious riches in Christ Jesus.

[20]To our God and Father be glory for ever and ever. Amen.

Final Greetings

[21]Greet all the saints in Christ Jesus. The brothers who are with me send greetings. [22]All the saints send you greetings, especially those who belong to Caesar's household.

[23]The grace of the Lord Jesus Christ be with your spirit. Amen.[b]

---

[a]3 Or loyal Syzygus   [b]23 Some manuscripts do not have *Amen*.

Colossians

1 Paul, an apostle of Christ Jesus by the will of God, and Timothy our brother,

[2]To the holy and faithful[a] brothers in Christ at Colosse:

Grace and peace to you from God our Father.[b]

Thanksgiving and Prayer

[3]We always thank God, the Father of our Lord Jesus Christ, when we pray for you, [4]because we have heard of your faith in Christ Jesus and of the love you have for all the saints—[5]the faith and love that spring from the hope that is stored up for you in heaven and that you have already heard about in the word of truth, the gospel [6]that has come to you. All over the world this gospel is bearing fruit and growing, just as it has been doing among you since the day you heard it and understood God's grace in all its truth. [7]You learned it from Epaphras, our dear fellow-servant, who is a faithful minister of Christ on our[c] behalf, [8]and who also told us of your love in the Spirit.

[9]For this reason, since the day we heard about you, we have not stopped praying for you and asking God to fill you with the knowledge of his will through all spiritual wisdom and understanding. [10]And we pray this in order that you may live a life worthy of the Lord and may please him in every way: bearing fruit in every good work, growing in the knowledge of God, [11]being strengthened with all power according to his glorious might so that you may have great endurance and patience, and joyfully [12]giving thanks to the Father, who has qualified you[d] to share in the inheritance of the saints in the kingdom of light. [13]For he has rescued us from the dominion of darkness and brought us into the kingdom of the Son he loves, [14]in whom we have redemption,[e] the forgiveness of sins.

The Supremacy of Christ

[15]He is the image of the invisible God, the firstborn over all creation. [16]For by him all things were created: things in heaven and on earth, visible and invisible, whether thrones or powers or rulers or authorities; all things were created by him and for him. [17]He is before all things, and in him all things hold together. [18]And he is the head of the body, the church; he is the beginning and the firstborn from among the dead, so that in everything he might have the supremacy. [19]For God was pleased to have all his fulness dwell in him, [20]and through him to reconcile to himself all things, whether things on earth or things in heaven, by making peace through his blood, shed on the cross.

[21]Once you were alienated from God and were enemies in your minds because of[f] your evil behaviour. [22]But now he has reconciled you by Christ's physical body through death to present you holy in his sight, without blemish and free from accusation—[23]if you continue in your faith, established and firm, not moved from the hope held out in the gospel. This is the gospel that you heard and that has been proclaimed to every creature under heaven, and of which I, Paul, have become a servant.

Paul's Labour for the Church

[24]Now I rejoice in what was suffered for you, and I fill up in my flesh what is still lacking in regard to Christ's afflictions, for the sake of his body, which is the church. [25]I have become its servant by the commission God gave me to present to you the word of God in its fulness—[26]the mystery that has been kept hidden for ages and generations, but is now disclosed to the saints. [27]To them God has chosen to make known among the Gentiles the glorious riches of this mystery, which is Christ in you, the hope of glory. [28]We proclaim him, admonishing and teaching everyone with all wisdom, so that we may present everyone perfect in Christ. [29]To this end I labour, struggling with all his energy, which so powerfully works in me.

2 I want you to know how much I am struggling for you and for those at Laodicea, and for all who have not met me personally. [2]My purpose is that they may be encouraged in heart and united in love, so that they may have the full riches of complete understanding, in order that they may know

---

a2 Or *believing*   *b2* Some manuscripts *Father and the Lord Jesus Christ*   *c7* Some manuscripts *your*
d12 Some manuscripts *us*   *e14* A few late manuscripts *redemption through his blood*
f21 Or *minds, as shown by*

COLOSSIANS 1:1–8

'All over the world this gospel is producing fruit and growing, just as it has been doing among you since the day you heard it and understood God's grace in all its truth' (v. 6).

REASSURANCE IS a key factor in Paul's letters. Firstly, he disarms those who might have expected some rebuff, by expressing his deep thankfulness to God for them, making it clear that he prays for them. Paul refers to their faith and love, key elements in their relationship with God and his people, and then proceeds to indicate the dynamic nature of the gospel they have accepted. The spread of the gospel is no mere local phenomenon. Wherever the gospel is preached it takes root, growing, bearing fruit and seeding itself afresh. The Colossians would be aware of the founding of the Church in Ephesus and its spread across Asia. They would know that in spite of opposition, sometimes from the Jews, sometimes from the authorities, sometimes from people with vested interests, the Church still multiplied its numbers.

Against the background of a growing, multi-national, multi-racial movement, local problems acquire a clearer perspective. Paul could write with the authority of one who knew the faith thoroughly and could therefore correct errors. His handling of the Colossians was warm, sensitive and masterly.

The word to the Colossians is true today. The gospel is still bearing fruit and growing. In the developing world, the growth continues to be dramatic, but even in our materialistic, sophisticated and self-reliant Western world, there is clear evidence that the tide of godliness is turning, and that the tide of the Spirit is flowing strongly and freely.

> *O what amazing words of grace*
> *Are in the gospel found,*
> *Suited to every sinner's case*
> *Who hears the joyful sound.*

(*Samuel Medley*)

→1097

PHILIPPIANS 4:10–13
'I can do everything through him who gives me strength' (v. 13).

THERE IS an unwritten limitation in our key verse. Paul was claiming, not that he could literally do everything, but that he could do everything God wanted him to do. Such was Paul's dedication that he seemed not to want to do anything other than the will of God, therefore, his statement was correct for him, but it probably would not be correct for those of us who are less single-minded.

From his earliest days of faith, Paul seemed to have confidence in God's ability to equip and empower him. When his ministry was being strongly challenged by certain members of the Corinthian church, part of his defence included the affirmation that his ministry was competent, because his competence came from God (2 Cor. 3:5). Later, in the same letter, he returned to an acknowledgement of his weakness, using it to indicate his strength: 'When I am weak, then I am strong' (2 Cor. 12:9, 10). We can be no other than strong when life is lived in total dependence on God.

When we are confident in our God-given wisdom, skills and resources, we have the confidence to declare that we, too, can do everything through him who gives us strength. Confidence, say the competitors in sport, industry and politics, is essential to success. In the business of living, coping with the unforeseen challenges of health, family life, employment or non-employment, endeavouring to be a faithful witness and fruitful servant for Christ, we need much confidence. Not an unrealistic self-confidence, but a confidence based on the victory of Christ and our essential place as members of his body. We are destined for victory because Christ has planned it that way.

> *Lord, turn my weakness into strength,*
> *Help me, each day's demands to face.*
> *Give to my heart that confidence*
> *Which comes from all-sufficient grace.*

→1094

the mystery of God, namely, Christ, ³in whom are hidden all the treasures of wisdom and knowledge. ⁴I tell you this so that no-one may deceive you by fine-sounding arguments. ⁵For though I am absent from you in body, I am present with you in spirit and delight to see how orderly you are and how firm your faith in Christ is.

Freedom From Human Regulations Through Life With Christ

⁶So then, just as you received Christ Jesus as Lord, continue to live in him, ⁷rooted and built up in him, strengthened in the faith as you were taught, and overflowing with thankfulness.

⁸See to it that no-one takes you captive through hollow and deceptive philosophy, which depends on human tradition and the basic principles of this world rather than on Christ.

⁹For in Christ all the fulness of the Deity lives in bodily form, ¹⁰and you have been given fulness in Christ, who is the Head over every power and authority. ¹¹In him you were also circumcised, in the putting off of the sinful nature,ᵃ not with a circumcision done by the hands of men but with the circumcision done by Christ, ¹²having been buried with him in baptism and raised with him through your faith in the power of God, who raised him from the dead.

¹³When you were dead in your sins and in the uncircumcision of your sinful nature,ᵇ God made youᶜ alive with Christ. He forgave us all our sins, ¹⁴having cancelled the written code, with its regulations, that was against us and that stood opposed to us; he took it away, nailing it to the cross. ¹⁵And having disarmed the powers and authorities, he made a public spectacle of them, triumphing over them by the cross.ᵈ

¹⁶Therefore do not let anyone judge you by what you eat or drink, or with regard to a religious festival, a New Moon celebration or a Sabbath day. ¹⁷These are a shadow of the things that were to come; the reality, however, is found in Christ. ¹⁸Do not let anyone who delights in false humility and the worship of angels disqualify you for the prize. Such a person goes into great detail about what he has seen, and his unspiritual mind puffs him up with idle notions. ¹⁹He has lost connection with the Head, from whom the whole body, supported and held together by its ligaments and sinews, grows as God causes it to grow.

²⁰Since you died with Christ to the basic principles of this world, why, as though you still belonged to it, do you submit to its rules: ²¹"Do not handle! Do not taste! Do not touch!"? ²²These are all destined to perish with use, because they are based on human commands and teachings. ²³Such regulations indeed have an appearance of wisdom, with their self-imposed worship, their false humility and their harsh treatment of the body, but they lack any value in restraining sensual indulgence.

Rules for Holy Living

3 Since, then, you have been raised with Christ, set your hearts on things above, where Christ is seated at the right hand of God. ²Set your minds on things above, not on earthly things. ³For you died, and your life is now hidden with Christ in God. ⁴When Christ, who is yourᵃ life, appears, then you also will appear with him in glory.

⁵Put to death, therefore, whatever belongs to your earthly nature: sexual immorality, impurity, lust, evil desires and greed, which is idolatry. ⁶Because of these, the wrath of God is coming.ᵇ ⁷You used to walk in these ways, in the life you once lived. ⁸But now you must rid yourselves of all such things as these: anger, rage, malice, slander and filthy language from your lips. ⁹Do not lie to each other, since you have taken off your old self with its practices ¹⁰and have put on the new self, which is being renewed in knowledge in the image of its Creator. ¹¹Here there is no Greek or Jew, circumcised or uncircumcised, barbarian, Scythian, slave or free, but Christ is all, and is in all.

¹²Therefore, as God's chosen people, holy and dearly loved, clothe yourselves with compassion, kindness, humility, gentleness and patience. ¹³Bear with each other and forgive whatever grievances you may have against one another. Forgive as the Lord forgave you. ¹⁴And over all these virtues put on love, which binds them all together in perfect unity.

¹⁵Let the peace of Christ rule in your hearts, since as members of one body you were called to peace. And be thankful. ¹⁶Let the word of Christ dwell in you richly as you teach and admonish one another with all wisdom, and as you sing psalms, hymns and spiritual songs with gratitude in your hearts to God. ¹⁷And whatever you do, whether in word or deed, do it all in the name of the Lord Jesus, giving thanks to God the Father through him.

Rules for Christian Households

¹⁸Wives, submit to your husbands, as is fitting in the Lord.

¹⁹Husbands, love your wives and do not be harsh with them.

²⁰Children, obey your parents in everything, for this pleases the Lord.

²¹Fathers, do not embitter your children, or they will become discouraged.

²²Slaves, obey your earthly masters in everything; and do it, not only when their eye is on you and to win their favour, but with sincerity of heart and reverence for the Lord. ²³Whatever you do, work at it with all your heart, as working for the Lord, not for men, ²⁴since you know that you will receive an inheritance from the Lord as a reward. It is the Lord Christ you are serving. ²⁵Anyone

---

ᵃ11 Or the flesh   ᵇ13 Or your flesh   ᶜ13 Some manuscripts us   ᵈ15 Or them in him
ᵃ4 Some manuscripts our   ᵇ6 Some early manuscripts coming on those who are disobedient

who does wrong will be repaid for his wrong, and there is no favouritism.

4 Masters, provide your slaves with what is right and fair, because you know that you also have a Master in heaven.

Further Instructions

²Devote yourselves to prayer, being watchful and thankful. ³And pray for us, too, that God may open a door for our message, so that we may proclaim the mystery of Christ, for which I am in chains. ⁴Pray that I may proclaim it clearly, as I should. ⁵Be wise in the way you act towards outsiders; make the most of every opportunity. ⁶Let your conversation be always full of grace, seasoned with salt, so that you may know how to answer everyone.

Final Greetings

⁷Tychicus will tell you all the news about me. He is a dear brother, a faithful minister and fellow-servant in the Lord. ⁸I am sending him to you for the express purpose that you may know about our[a] circumstances and that he may encourage your hearts. ⁹He is coming with Onesimus, our faithful and dear brother, who is one of you. They will tell you everything that is happening here.

¹⁰My fellow-prisoner Aristarchus sends you his greetings, as does Mark, the cousin of Barnabas. (You have received instructions about him; if he comes to you, welcome him.) ¹¹Jesus, who is called Justus, also sends greetings. These are the only Jews among my fellow-workers for the kingdom of God, and they have proved a comfort to me. ¹²Epaphras, who is one of you and a servant of Christ Jesus, sends greetings. He is always wrestling in prayer for you, that you may stand firm in all the will of God, mature and fully assured. ¹³I vouch for him that he is working hard for you and for those at Laodicea and Hierapolis. ¹⁴Our dear friend Luke, the doctor, and Demas send greetings. ¹⁵Give my greetings to the brothers at Laodicea, and to Nympha and the church in her house.

¹⁶After this letter has been read to you, see that it is also read in the church of the Laodiceans and that you in turn read the letter from Laodicea.

¹⁷Tell Archippus: ''See to it that you complete the work you have received in the Lord.''

¹⁸I, Paul, write this greeting in my own hand. Remember my chains. Grace be with you.

COLOSSIANS 3:1–3

'Since, then, you have been raised with Christ, set your hearts on things above, where Christ is seated at the right hand of God. Set your minds on things above, not on earthly things' (vv. 1, 2).

PAUL BELIEVED that the redeemed are completely identified with Christ. For him, the rite of baptism was a symbolic identification of the believer with the death and resurrection of our Lord. Baptism is a symbol. Faith is the reality. As the believer went under the water, symbolically he died with Christ; as he rose up, symbolically he rose with Christ. In Paul's judgment, we have a right to assume that as Christ died to sin, so we, having died with him, should no longer be enslaved by sin. Clearly, we are forgetful of the work of grace Christ performed on our behalf. 'Sin shall not be our master.' So often, and always to our cost, we fail to make that assumption.

Since we have been raised with Christ, we are to set our hearts and minds on those things which belong to Christ. We are to 'aspire' to the realm above. It is the aspiring soul which is the growing, maturing, achieving soul. We are at our best when we are reaching outwards and upwards towards the grace which has been secured for us by Christ. How he must rejoice when we look up beyond the things which keep us earthbound and vulnerable to evil. We are to set our affections and our minds – the warmth of feeling and the power of thought – on higher things. And, precious affirmation indeed, our lives are 'hidden with Christ in God'. This truth is hidden from a blinkered world, but it is a glorious fact none the less.

> *Be heaven, e'en now, our soul's abode,*
> *Hid be our life with Christ in God.*
> *Our spirit Lord, be one with thine;*
> *Let all our works in thee be wrought,*
> *And filled with thee be all our thought,*
> *Until in us thy likeness shine.*

(trs. John Wesley)

→1098

COLOSSIANS 4:10–18

'I, Paul, write this greeting in my own hand. Remember my chains. Grace be with you' (v. 18).

PAUL PROBABLY DICTATED this letter to a scribe. We see him, therefore, taking the pen and writing the final greeting. Obviously being very conscious of the chains which hamper him, he makes the plea, 'remember my chains'. But after reading this letter and allowing its great thoughts to move us, this act of remembrance is not easy. We are more conscious of his strength than of his hardships. He does not impress us as a man who was the victim of the Roman judicial system. The atmosphere of his letter, the grandeur of his concepts, his perceptions of the supremacy of Christ, marked him as a man essentially free. He had been rescued and was a member of another kingdom. He had died with Christ and risen with him, and his sights were set on a greater destiny than Rome could afford. He had been strengthened with that glorious might which enabled him to meet whatever came with fortitude, patience and joyful thanks. The word of Christ dwelt within him richly, and those are the things we remember, certainly not his chains!

Similarly, when we read *The Pilgrim's Progress*, we do not see Bunyan in Bedford Jail. With Dietrich Bonhoeffer, although we are aware of the Nazi concentration camp as we read his *Letters and Papers from Prison*, we are much more conscious of the risen Lord. Pam Ridgers was severely paralysed by polio, but such was her faith and her gift to organize and communicate, that even though she was confined to her wheelchair, you hardly noticed it!

Our Lord enables us to transcend our circumstances, and he is risen and dwells within us, 'the hope of glory'.

> *O for a thousand tongues to sing*
> *My great redeemer's praise;*
> *The glories of my God and King,*
> *The triumphs of his grace!*

(*Charles Wesley*)

→1101

1 Thessalonians

1

Paul, Silas[a] and Timothy,

To the church of the Thessalonians in God the Father and the Lord Jesus Christ:

Grace and peace to you.[b]

Thanksgiving for the Thessalonians' Faith

[2]We always thank God for all of you, mentioning you in our prayers. [3]We continually remember before our God and Father your work produced by faith, your labour prompted by love, and your endurance inspired by hope in our Lord Jesus Christ.

[4]For we know, brothers loved by God, that he has chosen you, [5]because our gospel came to you not simply with words, but also with power, with the Holy Spirit and with deep conviction. You know how we lived among you for your sake. [6]You became imitators of us and of the Lord; in spite of severe suffering, you welcomed the message with the joy given by the Holy Spirit. [7]And so you became a model to all the believers in Macedonia and Achaia. [8]The Lord's message rang out from you not only in Macedonia and Achaia—your faith in God has become known everywhere. Therefore we do not need to say anything about it, [9]for they themselves report what kind of reception you gave us. They tell how you turned to God from idols to serve the living and true God, [10]and to wait for his Son from heaven, whom he raised from the dead—Jesus, who rescues us from the coming wrath.

Paul's Ministry in Thessalonica

2

You know, brothers, that our visit to you was not a failure. [2]We had previously suffered and been insulted in Philippi, as you know, but with the help of our God we dared to tell you his gospel in spite of strong opposition. [3]For the appeal we make does not spring from error or impure motives, nor are we trying to trick you. [4]On the contrary, we speak as men approved by God to be entrusted with the gospel. We are not trying to please men but God, who tests our hearts. [5]You know we never used flattery, nor did we put on a mask to cover up greed—God is our witness. [6]We were not looking for praise from men, not from you or anyone else.

As apostles of Christ we could have been a burden to you, [7]but we were gentle among you, like a mother caring for her little children. [8]We loved you so much that we were delighted to share with you not only the gospel of God but our lives as well, because you had become so dear to us. [9]Surely you remember, brothers, our toil and hardship; we worked night and day in order not to be a burden to anyone while we preached the gospel of God to you.

[10]You are witnesses, and so is God, of how holy, righteous and blameless we were among you who believed. [11]For you know that we dealt with each of you as a father deals with his own children, [12]encouraging, comforting and urging you to live lives worthy of God, who calls you into his kingdom and glory.

[13]And we also thank God continually because, when you received the word of God, which you heard from us, you accepted it not as the word of men, but as it actually is, the word of God, which is at work in you who believe. [14]For you, brothers, became imitators of God's churches in Judea, which are in Christ Jesus: You suffered from your own countrymen the same things those churches suffered from the Jews, [15]who killed the Lord Jesus and the prophets and also drove us out. They displease God and are hostile to all men [16]in their effort to keep us from speaking to the Gentiles so that they may be saved. In this way they always heap up their sins to the limit. The wrath of God has come upon them at last.[a]

Paul's Longing to See the Thessalonians

[17]But, brothers, when we were torn away from you for a short time (in person, not in thought), out of our intense longing we made every effort to see you. [18]For we wanted to come to you—certainly I, Paul, did, again and again—but Satan stopped us. [19]For what is our hope, our joy, or the crown in which we will glory in the presence of our Lord Jesus

---

[a]1 Greek *Silvanus*, a variant of *Silas*
[b]1 Some early manuscripts *you from God our Father and the Lord Jesus Christ*
[a]16 Or *them fully*

Christ when he comes? Is it not you? ²⁰Indeed, you are our glory and joy.

3 So when we could stand it no longer, we thought it best to be left by ourselves in Athens. ²We sent Timothy, who is our brother and God's fellow-worker^a in spreading the gospel of Christ, to strengthen and encourage you in your faith, ³so that no-one would be unsettled by these trials. You know quite well that we were destined for them. ⁴In fact, when we were with you, we kept telling you that we would be persecuted. And it turned out that way, as you well know. ⁵For this reason, when I could stand it no longer, I sent to find out about your faith. I was afraid that in some way the tempter might have tempted you and our efforts might have been useless.

Timothy's Encouraging Report

⁶But Timothy has just now come to us from you and has brought good news about your faith and love. He has told us that you always have pleasant memories of us and that you long to see us, just as we also long to see you. ⁷Therefore, brothers, in all our distress and persecution we were encouraged about you because of your faith. ⁸For now we really live, since you are standing firm in the Lord. ⁹How can we thank God enough for you in return for all the joy we have in the presence of our God because of you? ¹⁰Night and day we pray most earnestly that we may see you again and supply what is lacking in your faith.

¹¹Now may our God and Father himself and our Lord Jesus clear the way for us to come to you. ¹²May the Lord make your love increase and overflow for each other and for everyone else, just as ours does for you. ¹³May he strengthen your hearts so that you will be blameless and holy in the presence of our God and Father when our Lord Jesus comes with all his holy ones.

Living to Please God

4 Finally, brothers, we instructed you how to live in order to please God, as in fact you are living. Now we ask you and urge you in the Lord Jesus to do this more and more. ²For you know what instructions we gave you by the authority of the Lord Jesus. ³It is God's will that you should be sanctified: that you should avoid sexual immorality; ⁴that each of you should learn to control his own body^a in a way that is holy and honourable, ⁵not in passionate lust like the heathen, who do not know God; ⁶and that in this matter no-one should wrong his brother or take advantage of him. The Lord will punish men for all such sins, as we have already told you and warned you. ⁷For God did not call us to be impure, but to live a holy life. ⁸Therefore, he who rejects this instruction does not reject man but God, who gives you his Holy Spirit.

⁹Now about brotherly love we do not need to write to you, for you yourselves have been taught by God to love each other. ¹⁰And in fact, you do love all the brothers throughout Macedonia. Yet we urge you, brothers, to do so more and more.

¹¹Make it your ambition to lead a quiet life, to mind your own business and to work with your hands, just as we told you, ¹²so that your daily life may win the respect of outsiders and so that you will not be dependent on anybody.

The Coming of the Lord

¹³Brothers, we do not want you to be ignorant about those who fall asleep, or to grieve like the rest of men, who have no hope. ¹⁴We believe that Jesus died and rose again and so we believe that God will bring with Jesus those who have fallen asleep in him. ¹⁵According to the Lord's own word, we tell you that we who are still alive, who are left till the coming of the Lord, will certainly not precede those who have fallen asleep. ¹⁶For the Lord himself will come down from heaven, with a loud command, with the voice of the archangel and with the trumpet call of God, and the dead in Christ will rise first. ¹⁷After that, we who are still alive and are left will be caught up together with them in the clouds to meet the Lord in the air. And so we will be with the Lord for ever. ¹⁸Therefore encourage each other with these words.

5 Now, brothers, about times and dates we do not need to write to you, ²for you know very well that the day of the Lord will come like a thief in the night. ³While people are saying, "Peace and safety", destruction will come on them suddenly, as labour pains on a pregnant woman, and they will not escape.

⁴But you, brothers, are not in darkness so that this day should surprise you like a thief. ⁵You are all sons of the light and sons of the day. We do not belong to the night or to the darkness. ⁶So then, let us not be like others, who are asleep, but let us be alert and self-controlled. ⁷For those who sleep, sleep at night, and those who get drunk, get drunk at night. ⁸But since we belong to the day, let us be self-controlled, putting on faith and love as a breastplate, and the hope of salvation as a helmet. ⁹For God did not appoint us to suffer wrath but to receive salvation through our Lord Jesus Christ. ¹⁰He died for us so that, whether we are awake or asleep, we may live together with him. ¹¹Therefore encourage one another and build each other up, just as in fact you are doing.

Final Instructions

¹²Now we ask you, brothers, to respect those who work hard among you, who are over you in the Lord and who admonish you. ¹³Hold them in the highest regard in love because of their work. Live in peace with each other. ¹⁴And we urge you, brothers, warn those who are idle, encourage the timid, help the weak, be patient with everyone. ¹⁵Make sure that nobody pays back

^a2 Some manuscripts *brother and fellow-worker*; other manuscripts *brother and God's servant*
^a4 Or *learn to live with his own wife*; or *learn to acquire a wife*

I THESSALONIANS 1:2–5

'We continually remember before our God and Father your **work** produced by **faith**, your **labour** prompted by **love**, and your **endurance** inspired by **hope** in our Lord Jesus Christ' (v. 3).

FAITH, LOVE, HOPE are the supreme Christian virtues. First Thessalonians may be an early letter, but it has the same stress on these three qualities that is found in First Corinthians 13, Romans 5, and also in the writings of Peter. Indeed, First Thessalonians goes further in one way than any of these other examples, for it associates a particular activity with each of these virtues.

Faith produces work. Is this Paul's way of saying very positively, 'faith by itself, if it is not accompanied by action, is dead'? A clear indication, if we needed it, that he is in agreement with James. There is no contradiction between them.

Love goes further, and *generates labour, kopos* in Greek, which means work so tough that it can be wearisome. This same word is actually translated 'weariness' in one case in AV. If the hallmark of faith is work, then the hallmark of love is continuing toil.

Hope inspires endurance. What a different complexion this puts on the other two! Producing work and toil sounds so ordinary, but inspiring endurance – that is something else! That sounds noble. It is high, and lifts work and labour away from everyday, humdrum existence into the realms of light.

How should Christians view Samuel Johnson's remark that 'Hope is itself a species of happiness and, perhaps, the chief happiness which the world affords'?

→1102

'How can we thank God enough for you in return for all the joy we have in the presence of our God because of you?' (v. 9).

THE REASON FOR PAUL'S LETTER is to express joy at Timothy's news. Timothy had come back from Thessalonica, bubbling over with delight at the progress being made, and at the steadfast faith of the new church. The Thessalonians were not yet perfect. They still needed further instruction, and Paul hoped to return to give that instruction to 'supply what is lacking in [their] faith'.

Paul had preached the good news in Thessalonica. Now Timothy brought back good news of progress. That, too, was proclamation, a proclamation of encouragement.

We badly need such proclamation today. When the motives of Christian missionaries in the past are often questioned, we need to see and hear news of the growth of the gospel. That can, and does occur when Christian communities are left to develop without the 'missionary' input. For twenty years, Salvationist missionaries have been barred from Burma. At first it seemed the very existence of The Salvation Army in Burma was threatened, but recently our hearts have been warmed by news of remarkable progress, and the recommencement of Salvation Army officer training without any missionary involvement. In East Africa, as missionaries have withdrawn, so the Church has gone from strength to strength, adapting to present needs and doubling, sometimes trebling in numbers.

We confess, Lord, we are sometimes unwilling to let go of cherished projects, and unwilling to allow those for whom we feel responsible develop independently. Guide us, so that we know how much guidance to give to others, and when to leave them to find their own guidance from you.

wrong for wrong, but always try to be kind to each other and to everyone else.

¹⁶Be joyful always; ¹⁷pray continually; ¹⁸give thanks in all circumstances, for this is God's will for you in Christ Jesus.

¹⁹Do not put out the Spirit's fire; ²⁰do not treat prophecies with contempt. ²¹Test everything. Hold on to the good. ²²Avoid every kind of evil.

²³May God himself, the God of peace, sanctify you through and through. May your whole spirit, soul and body be kept blameless at the coming of our Lord Jesus Christ. ²⁴The one who calls you is faithful and he will do it.

²⁵Brothers, pray for us. ²⁶Greet all the brothers with a holy kiss. ²⁷I charge you before the Lord to have this letter read to all the brothers.

²⁸The grace of our Lord Jesus Christ be with you.

2 Thessalonians

1 Paul, Silas[a] and Timothy,

To the church of the Thessalonians in God our Father and the Lord Jesus Christ:

²Grace and peace to you from God the Father and the Lord Jesus Christ.

Thanksgiving and Prayer

³We ought always to thank God for you, brothers, and rightly so, because your faith is growing more and more, and the love every one of you has for each other is increasing. ⁴Therefore, among God's churches we boast about your perseverance and faith in all the persecutions and trials you are enduring.

⁵All this is evidence that God's judgment is right, and as a result you will be counted worthy of the kingdom of God, for which you are suffering. ⁶God is just: He will pay back trouble to those who trouble you ⁷and give relief to you who are troubled, and to us as well. This will happen when the Lord Jesus is revealed from heaven in blazing fire with his powerful angels. ⁸He will punish those who do not know God and do not obey the gospel of our Lord Jesus. ⁹They will be punished with everlasting destruction and shut out from the presence of the Lord and from the majesty of his power ¹⁰on the day he comes to be glorified in his holy people and to be marvelled at among all those who have believed. This includes you, because you believed our testimony to you.

¹¹With this in mind, we constantly pray for you, that our God may count you worthy of his calling, and that by his power he may fulfil every good purpose of yours and every act prompted by your faith. ¹²We pray this so that the name of our Lord Jesus may be glorified in you, and you in him, according to the grace of our God and the Lord Jesus Christ.[b]

The Man of Lawlessness

2 Concerning the coming of our Lord Jesus Christ and our being gathered to him, we ask you, brothers, ²not to become easily unsettled or alarmed by some prophecy, report or letter supposed to have come from us, saying that the day of the Lord has already come. ³Don't let anyone deceive you in any way, for ⌊that day will not come⌋ until the rebellion occurs and the man of lawlessness[a] is revealed, the man doomed to destruction. ⁴He will oppose and will exalt himself over everything that is called God or is worshipped, so that he sets himself up in God's temple, proclaiming himself to be God.

⁵Don't you remember that when I was with you I used to tell you these things? ⁶And now you know what is holding him back, so that he may be revealed at the proper time. ⁷For the secret power of lawlessness is already at work; but the one who now holds it back will continue to do so till he is taken out of the way. ⁸And then the lawless one will be revealed, whom the Lord Jesus will overthrow with the breath of his mouth and destroy by the splendour of his coming. ⁹The coming of the lawless one will be in accordance with the work of Satan displayed in all kinds of counterfeit miracles, signs and wonders, ¹⁰and in every sort of evil that deceives those who are perishing. They perish because they refused to love the truth and so be saved. ¹¹For this reason God sends them a powerful delusion so that they will believe the lie ¹²and so that all will be condemned who have not believed the truth but have delighted in wickedness.

Stand Firm

¹³But we ought always to thank God for you, brothers loved by the Lord, because from the beginning God chose you[b] to be saved through the sanctifying work of the Spirit and through belief in the truth. ¹⁴He called you to this through our gospel, that you might share in the glory of our Lord Jesus Christ. ¹⁵So then, brothers, stand firm and hold to the teachings[c] we passed on to you, whether by word of mouth or by letter.

¹⁶May our Lord Jesus Christ himself and God our Father, who loved us and by his grace gave us eternal encouragement and good hope, ¹⁷encourage your hearts and strengthen you in every good deed and word.

Request for Prayer

3 Finally, brothers, pray for us that the message of the Lord may spread rapidly and be honoured, just as it was with you.

*a*1 Greek *Silvanus*, a variant of *Silas*   *b*12 Or *God and Lord, Jesus Christ*   *a*3 Some manuscripts *sin*
*b*13 Some manuscripts *because God chose you as his firstfruits*   *c*15 Or *traditions*

'Now, brothers, about times and dates we do not need to write to you ... while people are saying, "Peace and safety", destruction will come on them suddenly' (vv. 1, 3).

WE UNDERSTAND EASILY that there is 'life' and 'quality of life'. It is less easy to understand that for biblical writers there was 'time' and 'quality of time'. RSV keeps the distinction by talking of 'times' and 'seasons', when translating the two different Greek words for time. The first refers simply to the *length* of time, the second to the *kind* of time that it is. An hour is an hour, whatever we are doing. But how long an hour seems when we are sitting with a blank mind in an exam room, waiting for the clock to tick by! How short when we are full of ideas, and are writing furiously against the clock!

We may wonder when the second coming will happen. This is natural, both because we are inquisitive by nature, and also we feel a basic insecurity. Speculation about when it will happen is fruitless. No one knows.

But the *kind* of time it will be, that is different. It will be a time of great trouble and turbulence which is quite unexpected. So preparation for it needs to be made, not just when the foundations of everything seem to be shaken, but even more so in the times when we appear to have peace and security. I am reminded of the rich fool's words (Luke 12:19) 'I'll say to myself, "You have plenty of good things laid up for many years. Take life easy; eat, drink and be merry." ' It is when we feel like that, that the time is ripe for us to rethink, to consider what kind of time it is that we live in, and that the unexpected is just around the corner.

We praise you, Lord, for the gift of time. Thank you for the order and system which it brings to our lives. Thank you for the human ability to measure it accurately. Help us never to misuse it, never to take it for granted. May every moment lead to quietness and inner tranquillity, without idleness or apathy.

→1106

2 THESSALONIANS 1:5–10

'This will happen when the Lord Jesus is revealed from heaven in blazing fire with his powerful angels. He will punish those who do not know God and do not obey the gospel of our Lord Jesus' (vv. 7b, 8).

LEITH SAMUEL has written a small commentary on Thessalonians, entitled *Awaiting Christ's Return*. Study of this letter is often undertaken when looking at the idea of the second coming. Yet we need to remind ourselves continually that Christ is here with us. He comes over and over again to us. The Holy Spirit is given so that we can enjoy a taste of the presence of Christ here and now.

Rather than talk about the second coming of Christ, isn't it better to refer to his final appearance? Then we won't fall into the trap of thinking he is now absent.

But however we describe it, the appearance of Christ in his glory is associated with the end of the world, and with final judgement. This is a sensitive subject. Few of us like to dwell on the horrors of hell, or even consider the dreadful fate of being completely separated from God, suffering torment. We cannot get away from the fact that there will be judgement. We are told this over and over again in the New Testament. But before we become over-burdened let us take comfort from the fact that God's judgement is completely just. It is based on a knowledge of all the facts. It is based, not simply on our actions, but on our response to God's leadings.

We may feel very weak, inadequate and unworthy. We may feel we have not responded as we should. But God makes us holy and fit for his presence. For that, above all, we are morally obliged to thank him.

→1109

2And pray that we may be delivered from wicked and evil men, for not everyone has faith. 3But the Lord is faithful, and he will strengthen and protect you from the evil one. 4We have confidence in the Lord that you are doing and will continue to do the things we command. 5May the Lord direct your hearts into God's love and Christ's perseverance.

Warning Against Idleness

6In the name of the Lord Jesus Christ, we command you, brothers, to keep away from every brother who is idle and does not live according to the teaching*a* you received from us. 7For you yourselves know how you ought to follow our example. We were not idle when we were with you, 8nor did we eat anyone's food without paying for it. On the contrary, we worked night and day, labouring and toiling so that we would not be a burden to any of you. 9We did this, not because we do not have the right to such help, but in order to make ourselves a model for you to follow. 10For even when we were with you, we gave you this rule: "If a man will not work, he shall not eat."

11We hear that some among you are idle. They are not busy; they are busybodies. 12Such people we command and urge in the Lord Jesus Christ to settle down and earn the bread they eat. 13And as for you, brothers, never tire of doing what is right.

14If anyone does not obey our instruction in this letter, take special note of him. Do not associate with him, in order that he may feel ashamed. 15Yet do not regard him as an enemy, but warn him as a brother.

Final Greetings

16Now may the Lord of peace himself give you peace at all times and in every way. The Lord be with all of you.

17I, Paul, write this greeting in my own hand, which is the distinguishing mark in all my letters. This is how I write.

18The grace of our Lord Jesus Christ be with you all.

*a*6 Or *tradition*

1 Timothy

1

Paul, an apostle of Christ Jesus by the command of God our Saviour and of Christ Jesus our hope,

²To Timothy my true son in the faith:

Grace, mercy and peace from God the Father and Christ Jesus our Lord.

Warning Against False Teachers of the Law

³As I urged you when I went into Macedonia, stay there in Ephesus so that you may command certain men not to teach false doctrines any longer ⁴nor to devote themselves to myths and endless genealogies. These promote controversies rather than God's work—which is by faith. ⁵The goal of this command is love, which comes from a pure heart and a good conscience and a sincere faith. ⁶Some have wandered away from these and turned to meaningless talk. ⁷They want to be teachers of the law, but they do not know what they are talking about or what they so confidently affirm.

⁸We know that the law is good if one uses it properly. ⁹We also know that law*ᵃ* is made not for the righteous but for lawbreakers and rebels, the ungodly and sinful, the unholy and irreligious; for those who kill their fathers or mothers, for murderers, ¹⁰for adulterers and perverts, for slave traders and liars and perjurers—and for whatever else is contrary to the sound doctrine ¹¹that conforms to the glorious gospel of the blessed God, which he entrusted to me.

The Lord's Grace to Paul

¹²I thank Christ Jesus our Lord, who has given me strength, that he considered me faithful, appointing me to his service. ¹³Even though I was once a blasphemer and a persecutor and a violent man, I was shown mercy because I acted in ignorance and unbelief. ¹⁴The grace of our Lord was poured out on me abundantly, along with the faith and love that are in Christ Jesus.

¹⁵Here is a trustworthy saying that deserves full acceptance: Christ Jesus came into the world to save sinners—of whom I am the worst. ¹⁶But for that very reason I was shown mercy so that in me, the worst of sinners, Christ Jesus might display his unlimited patience as an example for those who would believe on him and receive eternal life. ¹⁷Now to the King eternal, immortal, invisible, the only God, be honour and glory for ever and ever. Amen.

¹⁸Timothy, my son, I give you this instruction in keeping with the prophecies once made about you, so that by following them you may fight the good fight, ¹⁹holding on to faith and a good conscience. Some have rejected these and so have shipwrecked their faith. ²⁰Among them are Hymenaeus and Alexander, whom I have handed over to Satan to be taught not to blaspheme.

Instructions on Worship

2

I urge, then, first of all, that requests, prayers, intercession and thanksgiving be made for everyone—²for kings and all those in authority, that we may live peaceful and quiet lives in all godliness and holiness. ³This is good, and pleases God our Saviour, ⁴who wants all men to be saved and to come to a knowledge of the truth. ⁵For there is one God and one mediator between God and men, the man Christ Jesus, ⁶who gave himself as a ransom for all men—the testimony given in its proper time. ⁷And for this purpose I was appointed a herald and an apostle —I am telling the truth, I am not lying—and a teacher of the true faith to the Gentiles.

⁸I want men everywhere to lift up holy hands in prayer, without anger or disputing. ⁹I also want women to dress modestly, with decency and propriety, not with braided hair or gold or pearls or expensive clothes, ¹⁰but with good deeds, appropriate for women who profess to worship God.

¹¹A woman should learn in quietness and full submission. ¹²I do not permit a woman to teach or to have authority over a man; she must be silent. ¹³For Adam was formed first, then Eve. ¹⁴And Adam was not the one deceived; it was the woman who was deceived and became a sinner. ¹⁵But women*ᵃ* will be saved*ᵇ* through childbearing—if they continue in faith, love and holiness with propriety.

*ᵃ*9 Or *that the law*   *ᵃ*15 Greek *she*   *ᵇ*15 Or *restored*

2 THESSALONIANS 3:6–12
'If a man will not work, he shall not eat' (v. 10).

WORK is one of the blessings of God. It has always been necessary. Before the Fall, God gave Adam work to do. Work is not a curse. Only man's sin makes it so. Sin creates differences between people. Sin causes one person to exploit another for his own 'gain'. Sin emphasizes self instead of others.

Our own age is an age of unprecedented leisure. The busiest of us still have more time off than our forebears did. If we don't, we are overworking. Overworking is theft – stealing another's opportunity to work, and turning what should be a blessing into a curse.

Refusing to work is just as bad as overworking. Paul's statement that the one who will not work 'shall not eat' has to be handled carefully, though. Work is more than paid employment. The 'unemployed' person who takes pride in keeping the family together, actively pursuing education or other 'leisure' activities, deserves to eat just as much and just as well as those who (often mistakenly) think that they provide for his support.

A greedy society where poverty for the unemployed is used to spur people on to work, may have total wealth far greater than another where resources are more equally shared. But it will be poorer, morally and socially. Injustice will mar relationships. People will fear for their property and their own safety. A 'fortress' mentality will appear, and ultimately the only way to restore the community may be through catastrophe.

Questions for the employed: What does my work contribute to the community? Is it of as much value as the contribution of my 'unemployed' neighbour?

A question for the unemployed: How can I best use my resources of time, talent and even money, not just for myself, but for the benefit of others?

→1110

1 TIMOTHY 1:3–6

'Command certain men not to teach false doctrines any longer nor to devote themselves to myths and endless genealogies. These promote controversies rather than God's work – which is by faith' (vv. 3b, 4).

FALSE DOCTRINE concerns Paul greatly. But even in Galatians, the sternest of his church letters, he does not plunge into condemnation quite as he does here. However, he immediately qualifies the stern order, saying 'The goal of this command is love, which comes from a pure heart.'

The myths causing trouble in the Church, taking people away from true doctrine, were not simply little fairy stories. The genealogies weren't lists of Jewish ancestors, like those in the Gospels. They were probably complicated 'Gnostic' genealogies which claimed to show how a series of forms emanated from God, becoming more and more material until at last one was found far enough removed from God to make contact with matter possible. The 'Gnostics' tried to fit Jesus into such schemes. Instead of Christ being the only mediator between God and man, they saw him as one among many.

Similar problems face the Church today. New movements want to honour Christ as one among many. As Christians we have a duty to listen to, to love and respect those with different views from our own. But we must never allow ourselves to be deflected from the worship of Christ, one and only. Any religion which denies Christ complete pre-eminence, is not Christian.

> *My Christ, he is the Heaven of heavens,*
> *My Christ, what shall I call?*
> *My Christ is first, my Christ is last,*
> *My Christ is all-in-all.*

(John Mason)

Overseers and Deacons

3 Here is a trustworthy saying: If anyone sets his heart on being an overseer,[a] he desires a noble task. [2]Now the overseer must be above reproach, the husband of but one wife, temperate, self-controlled, respectable, hospitable, able to teach, [3]not given to drunkenness, not violent but gentle, not quarrelsome, not a lover of money. [4]He must manage his own family well and see that his children obey him with proper respect. [5](If anyone does not know how to manage his own family, how can he take care of God's church?) [6]He must not be a recent convert, or he may become conceited and fall under the same judgment as the devil. [7]He must also have a good reputation with outsiders, so that he will not fall into disgrace and into the devil's trap.

[8]Deacons, likewise, are to be men worthy of respect, sincere, not indulging in much wine, and not pursuing dishonest gain. [9]They must keep hold of the deep truths of the faith with a clear conscience. [10]They must first be tested; and then if there is nothing against them, let them serve as deacons.

[11]In the same way, their wives[b] are to be women worthy of respect, not malicious talkers but temperate and trustworthy in everything.

[12]A deacon must be the husband of but one wife and must manage his children and his household well. [13]Those who have served well gain an excellent standing and great assurance in their faith in Christ Jesus.

[14]Although I hope to come to you soon, I am writing you these instructions so that, [15]if I am delayed, you will know how people ought to conduct themselves in God's household, which is the church of the living God, the pillar and foundation of the truth. [16]Beyond all question, the mystery of godliness is great:

He[c] appeared in a body,[d]
    was vindicated by the Spirit,
was seen by angels,
    was preached among the nations,
was believed on in the world,
    was taken up in glory.

Instructions to Timothy

4 The Spirit clearly says that in later times some will abandon the faith and follow deceiving spirits and things taught by demons. [2]Such teachings come through hypocritical liars, whose consciences have been seared as with a hot iron. [3]They forbid people to marry and order them to abstain from certain foods, which God created to be received with thanksgiving by those who believe and who know the truth. [4]For everything God created is good, and nothing is to be rejected if it is received with thanksgiving, [5]because it is consecrated by the word of God and prayer.

[6]If you point these things out to the brothers, you will be a good minister of Christ Jesus, brought up in the truths of the faith and of the good teaching that you have followed. [7]Have nothing to do with godless myths and old wives' tales; rather, train yourself to be godly. [8]For physical training is of some value, but godliness has value for all things, holding promise for both the present life and the life to come.

[9]This is a trustworthy saying that deserves full acceptance [10](and for this we labour and strive), that we have put our hope in the living God, who is the Saviour of all men, and especially of those who believe.

[11]Command and teach these things. [12]Don't let anyone look down on you because you are young, but set an example for the believers in speech, in life, in love, in faith and in purity. [13]Until I come, devote yourself to the public reading of Scripture, to preaching and to teaching. [14]Do not neglect your gift, which was given you through a prophetic message when the body of elders laid their hands on you.

[15]Be diligent in these matters; give yourself wholly to them, so that everyone may see your progress. [16]Watch your life and doctrine closely. Persevere in them, because if you do, you will save both yourself and your hearers.

Advice About Widows, Elders and Slaves

5 Do not rebuke an older man harshly, but exhort him as if he were your father. Treat younger men as brothers, [2]older women as mothers, and younger women as sisters, with absolute purity.

[3]Give proper recognition to those widows who are really in need. [4]But if a widow has children or grandchildren, these should learn first of all to put their religion into practice by caring for their own family and so repaying their parents and grandparents, for this is pleasing to God. [5]The widow who is really in need and left all alone puts her hope in God and continues night and day to pray and to ask God for help. [6]But the widow who lives for pleasure is dead even while she lives. [7]Give the people these instructions, too, so that no-one may be open to blame. [8]If anyone does not provide for his relatives, and especially for his immediate family, he has denied the faith and is worse than an unbeliever.

[9]No widow may be put on the list of widows unless she is over sixty, has been faithful to her husband,[a] [10]and is well known for her good deeds, such as bringing up children, showing hospitality, washing the feet of the saints, helping those in trouble and devoting herself to all kinds of good deeds.

[11]As for younger widows, do not put them on such a list. For when their sensual desires overcome their dedication to Christ, they want to marry. [12]Thus they bring judgment on themselves, because they have broken their first pledge. [13]Besides, they get into the habit of being idle and going about from

---

[a]1 Traditionally *bishop*; also in verse 2   [b]11 Or *way, deaconesses*   [c]16 Some manuscripts *God*
[d]16 Or *in the flesh*   [a]9 Or *has had but one husband*

house to house. And not only do they become idlers, but also gossips and busybodies, saying things they ought not to. [14]So I counsel younger widows to marry, to have children, to manage their homes and to give the enemy no opportunity for slander. [15]Some have in fact already turned away to follow Satan.

[16]If any woman who is a believer has widows in her family, she should help them and not let the church be burdened with them, so that the church can help those widows who are really in need.

[17]The elders who direct the affairs of the church well are worthy of double honour, especially those whose work is preaching and teaching. [18]For the Scripture says, "Do not muzzle the ox while it is treading out the grain,"[b] and "The worker deserves his wages."[c] [19]Do not entertain an accusation against an elder unless it is brought by two or three witnesses. [20]Those who sin are to be rebuked publicly, so that the others may take warning.

[21]I charge you, in the sight of God and Christ Jesus and the elect angels, to keep these instructions without partiality, and to do nothing out of favouritism.

[22]Do not be hasty in the laying on of hands, and do not share in the sins of others. Keep yourself pure.

[23]Stop drinking only water, and use a little wine because of your stomach and your frequent illnesses.

[24]The sins of some men are obvious, reaching the place of judgment ahead of them; the sins of others trail behind them. [25]In the same way, good deeds are obvious, and even those that are not cannot be hidden.

6 All who are under the yoke of slavery should consider their masters worthy of full respect, so that God's name and our teaching may not be slandered. [2]Those who have believing masters are not to show less respect for them because they are brothers. Instead, they are to serve them even better, because those who benefit from their service are believers, and dear to them. These are the things you are to teach and urge on them.

Love of Money

[3]If anyone teaches false doctrines and does not agree to the sound instruction of our Lord Jesus Christ and to godly teaching, [4]he is conceited and understands nothing. He has an unhealthy interest in controversies and quarrels about words that result in envy, strife, malicious talk, evil suspicions [5]and constant friction between men of corrupt mind, who have been robbed of the truth and who think that godliness is a means to financial gain.

[6]But godliness with contentment is great gain. [7]For we brought nothing into the world, and we can take nothing out of it. [8]But if we have food and clothing, we will be content with that. [9]People who want to get rich fall into temptation and a trap and into many foolish and harmful desires that plunge men into ruin and destruction. [10]For the love of money is a root of all kinds of evil. Some people, eager for money, have wandered from the faith and pierced themselves with many griefs.

Paul's Charge to Timothy

[11]But you, man of God, flee from all this, and pursue righteousness, godliness, faith, love, endurance and gentleness. [12]Fight the good fight of the faith. Take hold of the eternal life to which you were called when you made your good confession in the presence of many witnesses. [13]In the sight of God, who gives life to everything, and of Christ Jesus, who while testifying before Pontius Pilate made the good confession, I charge you [14]to keep this command without spot or blame until the appearing of our Lord Jesus Christ, [15]which God will bring about in his own time—God, the blessed and only Ruler, the King of kings and Lord of lords, [16]who alone is immortal and who lives in unapproachable light, whom no-one has seen or can see. To him be honour and might for ever. Amen.

[17]Command those who are rich in this present world not to be arrogant nor to put their hope in wealth, which is so uncertain, but to put their hope in God, who richly provides us with everything for our enjoyment. [18]Command them to do good, to be rich in good deeds, and to be generous and willing to share. [19]In this way they will lay up treasure for themselves as a firm foundation for the coming age, so that they may take hold of the life that is truly life.

[20]Timothy, guard what has been entrusted to your care. Turn away from godless chatter and the opposing ideas of what is falsely called knowledge, [21]which some have professed and in so doing have wandered from the faith.

Grace be with you.

1 TIMOTHY 2:5–7

'For there is one God and one mediator between God and men, the man Christ Jesus, who gave himself as a ransom for all men' (vv. 5, 6).

THE WAY was one of the earliest descriptions of Christianity. It is a very fitting description, for it puts over the idea that Christianity is a living, moving, vital experience. We go along a way.

It also highlights the uniqueness of Christianity. Both those elements come out in today's short passage. It is of such vital importance that we do well to read it over and over again. Not only is Christianity living, moving, vital; not only is it unique; it is for all.

This simple statement that salvation is for all has led to enormous controversy. It seems to fly in the face of the idea of an elect who will be saved. It seems to deny the possibility that some will be excluded. It has led to awful contortions on the part of Christian theologians, from Augustine's peculiar statement that 'all' means 'all the predestined, because every type of man is amongst them' to Origen's claim that even the devil himself will be saved.

We do well to stick by Paul's simple statement, that God *wants* everyone to be saved.

1. It is God's will that all should be saved. Christianity is not just for a spiritual elite.
2. God has given us freedom and responsibility. People can exclude themselves from that salvation.

→1114

1 TIMOTHY 6:11-16

'Pursue righteousness, godliness, faith, love, endurance and gentleness . . . Take hold of the eternal life to which you were called when you made your confession in the presence of many witnesses' (vv. 11b, 12b).

POSITIVE THINKING is a mark of this letter throughout.

The writer encourages Timothy to strive for high standards in every area of conduct. He warns him not to be despondent when some reject the gospel. He gives him positive advice on how to handle his congregation. In this final chapter he places in front of Timothy the positive values of righteousness, godliness, faith, love, endurance and gentleness.

All these qualities are easier to achieve when the faith is confessed publicly. It is important that coming into the Christian community should be a public matter. The Christian way is indeed a mystery, but it is a public mystery. There is nothing secretive about it.

It is important that the congregation comes together and invites others to attend when young people are confirmed in the faith. It is important that the baptism of an adult should be an occasion of public rejoicing. It is important that the enrolment of a Salvationist should be in a gathering open to all. The new Christian should be encouraged to witness, whether or not their witness seems to be appreciated. Paul reminds Timothy that our Lord witnessed even in front of Pilate.

In order to proclaim our faith effectively, we need first to make public profession of our faith.

→1117

2 Timothy

1

Paul, an apostle of Christ Jesus by the will of God, according to the promise of life that is in Christ Jesus,

²To Timothy, my dear son:

Grace, mercy and peace from God the Father and Christ Jesus our Lord.

Encouragement to Be Faithful

³I thank God, whom I serve, as my forefathers did, with a clear conscience, as night and day I constantly remember you in my prayers. ⁴Recalling your tears, I long to see you, so that I may be filled with joy. ⁵I have been reminded of your sincere faith, which first lived in your grandmother Lois and in your mother Eunice and, I am persuaded, now lives in you also. ⁶For this reason I remind you to fan into flame the gift of God, which is in you through the laying on of my hands. ⁷For God did not give us a spirit of timidity, but a spirit of power, of love and of self-discipline.

⁸So do not be ashamed to testify about our Lord, or ashamed of me his prisoner. But join with me in suffering for the gospel, by the power of God, ⁹who has saved us and called us to a holy life—not because of anything we have done but because of his own purpose and grace. This grace was given us in Christ Jesus before the beginning of time, ¹⁰but it has now been revealed through the appearing of our Saviour, Christ Jesus, who has destroyed death and has brought life and immortality to light through the gospel. ¹¹And of this gospel I was appointed a herald and an apostle and a teacher. ¹²That is why I am suffering as I am. Yet I am not ashamed, because I know whom I have believed, and am convinced that he is able to guard what I have entrusted to him for that day.

¹³What you heard from me, keep as the pattern of sound teaching, with faith and love in Christ Jesus. ¹⁴Guard the good deposit that was entrusted to you—guard it with the help of the Holy Spirit who lives in us.

¹⁵You know that everyone in the province of Asia has deserted me, including Phygelus and Hermogenes.

¹⁶May the Lord show mercy to the household of Onesiphorus, because he often refreshed me and was not ashamed of my chains. ¹⁷On the contrary, when he was in Rome, he searched hard for me until he found me. ¹⁸May the Lord grant that he will find mercy from the Lord on that day! You know very well in how many ways he helped me in Ephesus.

2

You then, my son, be strong in the grace that is in Christ Jesus. ²And the things you have heard me say in the presence of many witnesses entrust to reliable men who will also be qualified to teach others. ³Endure hardship with us like a good soldier of Christ Jesus. ⁴No-one serving as a soldier gets involved in civilian affairs—he wants to please his commanding officer. ⁵Similarly, if anyone competes as an athlete, he does not receive the victor's crown unless he competes according to the rules. ⁶The hardworking farmer should be the first to receive a share of the crops. ⁷Reflect on what I am saying, for the Lord will give you insight into all this.

⁸Remember Jesus Christ, raised from the dead, descended from David. This is my gospel, ⁹for which I am suffering even to the point of being chained like a criminal. But God's word is not chained. ¹⁰Therefore I endure everything for the sake of the elect, that they too may obtain the salvation that is in Christ Jesus, with eternal glory.

¹¹Here is a trustworthy saying:

If we died with him,
 we will also live with him;
¹²if we endure,
 we will also reign with him.
If we disown him,
 he will also disown us;
¹³if we are faithless,
 he will remain faithful,
 for he cannot disown himself.

A Workman Approved by God

¹⁴Keep reminding them of these things. Warn them before God against quarrelling about words; it is of no value, and only ruins those who listen. ¹⁵Do your best to present yourself to God as one approved, a workman who does not need to be ashamed and who correctly handles the word of truth. ¹⁶Avoid godless chatter, because those who indulge in it will become more and more ungodly. ¹⁷Their teaching will spread like gangrene. Among them are Hymenaeus and Philetus, ¹⁸who have wandered away from the truth. They say that the resurrection has already taken place, and they destroy the faith of

some. [19]Nevertheless, God's solid foundation stands firm, sealed with this inscription: "The Lord knows those who are his,"[a] and, "Everyone who confesses the name of the Lord must turn away from wickedness."

[20]In a large house there are articles not only of gold and silver, but also of wood and clay; some are for noble purposes and some for ignoble. [21]If a man cleanses himself from the latter, he will be an instrument for noble purposes, made holy, useful to the Master and prepared to do any good work.

[22]Flee the evil desires of youth, and pursue righteousness, faith, love and peace, along with those who call on the Lord out of a pure heart. [23]Don't have anything to do with foolish and stupid arguments, because you know they produce quarrels. [24]And the Lord's servant must not quarrel; instead, he must be kind to everyone, able to teach, not resentful. [25]Those who oppose him he must gently instruct, in the hope that God will grant them repentance leading them to a knowledge of the truth, [26]and that they will come to their senses and escape from the trap of the devil, who has taken them captive to do his will.

Godlessness in the Last Days

3 But mark this: There will be terrible times in the last days. [2]People will be lovers of themselves, lovers of money, boastful, proud, abusive, disobedient to their parents, ungrateful, unholy, [3]without love, unforgiving, slanderous, without self-control, brutal, not lovers of the good, [4]treacherous, rash, conceited, lovers of pleasure rather than lovers of God—[5]having a form of godliness but denying its power. Have nothing to do with them.

[6]They are the kind who worm their way into homes and gain control over weak-willed women, who are loaded down with sins and are swayed by all kinds of evil desires, [7]always learning but never able to acknowledge the truth. [8]Just as Jannes and Jambres opposed Moses, so also these men oppose the truth—men of depraved minds, who, as far as the faith is concerned, are rejected. [9]But they will not get very far because, as in the case of those men, their folly will be clear to everyone.

Paul's Charge to Timothy

[10]You, however, know all about my teaching, my way of life, my purpose, faith, patience, love, endurance, [11]persecutions, sufferings—what kinds of things happened to me in Antioch, Iconium and Lystra, the persecutions I endured. Yet the Lord rescued me from all of them. [12]In fact, everyone who wants to live a godly life in Christ Jesus will be persecuted, [13]while evil men and impostors will go from bad to worse, deceiving and being deceived. [14]But as for you, continue in what you have learned and have become convinced of, because you know those from whom you learned it, [15]and how from infancy you have known the holy Scriptures, which are able to make you wise for

salvation through faith in Christ Jesus. [16]All Scripture is God-breathed and is useful for teaching, rebuking, correcting and training in righteousness, [17]so that the man of God may be thoroughly equipped for every good work.

4 In the presence of God and of Christ Jesus, who will judge the living and the dead, and in view of his appearing and his kingdom, I give you this charge: [2]Preach the Word; be prepared in season and out of season; correct, rebuke and encourage—with great patience and careful instruction. [3]For the time will come when men will not put up with sound doctrine. Instead, to suit their own desires, they will gather around them a great number of teachers to say what their itching ears want to hear. [4]They will turn their ears away from the truth and turn aside to myths. [5]But you, keep your head in all situations, endure hardship, do the work of an evangelist, discharge all the duties of your ministry.

[6]For I am already being poured out like a drink offering, and the time has come for my departure. [7]I have fought the good fight, I have finished the race, I have kept the faith. [8]Now there is in store for me the crown of righteousness, which the Lord, the righteous Judge, will award to me on that day—and not only to me, but also to all who have longed for his appearing.

Personal Remarks

[9]Do your best to come to me quickly, [10]for Demas, because he loved this world, has deserted me and has gone to Thessalonica. Crescens has gone to Galatia, and Titus to Dalmatia. [11]Only Luke is with me. Get Mark and bring him with you, because he is helpful to me in my ministry. [12]I sent Tychicus to Ephesus. [13]When you come, bring the cloak that I left with Carpus at Troas, and my scrolls, especially the parchments.

[14]Alexander the metalworker did me a great deal of harm. The Lord will repay him for what he has done. [15]You too should be on your guard against him, because he strongly opposed our message.

[16]At my first defence, no-one came to my support, but everyone deserted me. May it not be held against them. [17]But the Lord stood at my side and gave me strength, so that through me the message might be fully proclaimed and all the Gentiles might hear it. And I was delivered from the lion's mouth. [18]The Lord will rescue me from every evil attack and will bring me safely to his heavenly kingdom. To him be glory for ever and ever. Amen.

Final Greetings

[19]Greet Priscilla[a] and Aquila and the household of Onesiphorus. [20]Erastus stayed in Corinth, and I left Trophimus sick in Miletus. [21]Do your best to get here before winter. Eubulus greets you, and so do Pudens, Linus, Claudia and all the brothers. [22]The Lord be with your spirit. Grace be with you.

---

[a]19 Num. 16:5 (see Septuagint)　　[a]19 Greek Prisca, a variant of Priscilla

2 TIMOTHY 1:1–2
'Paul . . . to Timothy, my dear son: Grace, mercy and peace from God the Father and Christ Jesus our Lord' (v. 2).

GRACE, MERCY AND PEACE. Paul starts most of his letters with the simple greeting 'Grace' and 'Peace'. A tiny alteration to the normal form of words at the beginning of a Greek letter makes it read 'Grace' – the kind of change which would make 'hello' read 'hallow'.

'Peace' was the normal Hebrew form of address. Paul's letters span two worlds, Hebrew and Greek, right from their very first words. But in the two letters to Timothy, Paul adds the word 'mercy' to his greeting.

I like that. Not only does Paul join the opposing worlds of Greek and Hebrew thinking, he joins them by talking of the mercy of God. Everything is made different when mercy is added. The sternest rebuke is softened when it is tempered with a merciful action.

Sometimes Paul sounds stern. Sometimes he appears to be unbending. But always he stresses the fact of God's mercy.

Verses by Annie Johnson Flint remind us of God's mercy:

> *He giveth more grace as our burdens grow greater,*
> *He sendeth more strength as our labours increase,*
> *To added afflictions he addeth his mercy,*
> *To multiplied trials he multiplies peace.*
>
> *When we have exhausted our store of endurance,*
> *When our strength has failed ere the day is half-done,*
> *When we reach the end of our hoarded resources*
> *Our Father's full giving is only begun.*

→1118

2 TIMOTHY 3:10–17

'All Scripture is God-breathed and is useful for teaching, rebuking, correcting and training in righteousness' (v. 16).

PAUL'S BIBLE was the Old Testament. It has always caused difficulty, that Christians regard the Old Testament as part of their Scriptures. Right from the beginning, some people have wanted to deny the Old Testament its rightful place as the record of God's early dealings with his people.

In the earliest days of the Church, many felt that certain Old Testament stories were unworthy. So in order to see Christ as the fulfilment of the Old Testament, you had to treat Old Testament stories as allegories. In other words, they hardly liked to think the Old Testament referred to real events at all. They thought most of it was merely symbolic.

Paul refutes this idea strongly. He knows the old covenant has been replaced, yet he clings strongly to its value for the Christian. Compare this passage with Romans 15:4. 'For everything that was written in the past was written to *teach* us, so that through *endurance* and the *encouragement* of the Scriptures we might have hope.'

Here again the importance of teaching. Endurance is equivalent to training – the *ongoing* teaching. Where Romans talks of encouragement, Timothy talks of correction – and all that is really added in Timothy is the element of reproof.

The Old Testament Scriptures are able to instruct one for salvation, but they will not necessarily do so unless interpreted by faith and with Christ as the clue.

(*A. T. Hanson*)

→1121

Titus

1 Paul, a servant of God and an apostle of Jesus Christ for the faith of God's elect and the knowledge of the truth that leads to godliness—[2]a faith and knowledge resting on the hope of eternal life, which God, who does not lie, promised before the beginning of time, [3]and at his appointed season he brought his word to light through the preaching entrusted to me by the command of God our Saviour,

[4]To Titus, my true son in our common faith:

Grace and peace from God the Father and Christ Jesus our Saviour.

Titus' Task on Crete

[5]The reason I left you in Crete was that you might straighten out what was left unfinished and appoint[a] elders in every town, as I directed you. [6]An elder must be blameless, the husband of but one wife, a man whose children believe and are not open to the charge of being wild and disobedient. [7]Since an overseer[b] is entrusted with God's work, he must be blameless—not overbearing, not quick-tempered, not given to drunkenness, not violent, not pursuing dishonest gain. [8]Rather he must be hospitable, one who loves what is good, who is self-controlled, upright, holy and disciplined. [9]He must hold firmly to the trustworthy message as it has been taught, so that he can encourage others by sound doctrine and refute those who oppose it.

[10]For there are many rebellious people, mere talkers and deceivers, especially those of the circumcision group. [11]They must be silenced, because they are ruining whole households by teaching things they ought not to teach—and that for the sake of dishonest gain. [12]Even one of their own prophets has said, "Cretans are always liars, evil brutes, lazy gluttons." [13]This testimony is true. Therefore, rebuke them sharply, so that they will be sound in the faith [14]and will pay no attention to Jewish myths or to the commands of those who reject the truth. [15]To the pure, all things are pure, but to those who are corrupted and do not believe, nothing is pure. In fact, both their minds and consciences are corrupted. [16]They claim to know God, but by their actions they deny him. They are detestable, disobedient and unfit for doing anything good.

What Must Be Taught to Various Groups

2 You must teach what is in accord with sound doctrine. [2]Teach the older men to be temperate, worthy of respect, self-controlled, and sound in faith, in love and in endurance.

[3]Likewise, teach the older women to be reverent in the way they live, not to be slanderers or addicted to much wine, but to teach what is good. [4]Then they can train the younger women to love their husbands and children, [5]to be self-controlled and pure, to be busy at home, to be kind, and to be subject to their husbands, so that no-one will malign the word of God.

[6]Similarly, encourage the young men to be self-controlled. [7]In everything set them an example by doing what is good. In your teaching show integrity, seriousness [8]and soundness of speech that cannot be condemned, so that those who oppose you may be ashamed because they have nothing bad to say about us.

[9]Teach slaves to be subject to their masters in everything, to try to please them, not to talk back to them, [10]and not to steal from them, but to show that they can be fully trusted, so that in every way they will make the teaching about God our Saviour attractive.

[11]For the grace of God that brings salvation has appeared to all men. [12]It teaches us to say "No" to ungodliness and worldly passions, and to live self-controlled, upright and godly lives in this present age, [13]while we wait for the blessed hope—the glorious appearing of our great God and Saviour, Jesus Christ, [14]who gave himself for us to redeem us from all wickedness and to purify for himself a people that are his very own, eager to do what is good.

[15]These, then, are the things you should teach. Encourage and rebuke with all authority. Do not let anyone despise you.

Doing What is Good

3 Remind the people to be subject to rulers and authorities, to be obedient, to be ready to do whatever is good, ²to slander no-one, to be peaceable and considerate, and to show true humility towards all men.

³At one time we too were foolish, disobedient, deceived and enslaved by all kinds of passions and pleasures. We lived in malice and envy, being hated and hating one another. ⁴But when the kindness and love of God our Saviour appeared, ⁵he saved us, not because of righteous things we had done, but because of his mercy. He saved us through the washing of rebirth and renewal by the Holy Spirit, ⁶whom he poured out on us generously through Jesus Christ our Saviour, ⁷so that, having been justified by his grace, we might become heirs having the hope of eternal life. ⁸This is a trustworthy saying. And I want you to stress these things, so that those who have trusted in God may be careful to devote themselves to doing what is good. These things are excellent and profitable for everyone.

⁹But avoid foolish controversies and genealogies and arguments and quarrels about the law, because these are unprofitable and useless. ¹⁰Warn a divisive person once, and then warn him a second time. After that, have nothing to do with him. ¹¹You may be sure that such a man is warped and sinful; he is self-condemned.

Final Remarks

¹²As soon as I send Artemas or Tychicus to you, do your best to come to me at Nicopolis, because I have decided to winter there. ¹³Do everything you can to help Zenas the lawyer and Apollos on their way and see that they have everything they need. ¹⁴Our people must learn to devote themselves to doing what is good, in order that they may provide for daily necessities and not live unproductive lives.

¹⁵Everyone with me sends you greetings. Greet those who love us in the faith.

Grace be with you all.

2 TIMOTHY 4

'I am already being poured out like a drink offering, and the time has come for my departure. I have fought the good fight, I have finished the race, I have kept the faith' (vv. 6, 7).

PAUL IS SATISFIED. He has had a long life. He has lived it to the full. There have been disasters along the way, and many victories too. But he can look back with satisfaction because he himself has taken his own advice to Timothy. He has taught with patience. He has kept his head in all situations. He has encouraged, corrected and rebuked.

In prison, awaiting death, Paul is calm and forward-looking. He speaks about his departure. A departure comes at the beginning of a journey. The word he uses is used for untying a boat at the start of a voyage. He is loosing the moorings, letting go and launching out into the deep. For him it will be a calm yet exciting voyage. What a lovely picture of death!

There is, naturally, some fear in setting out on a journey. We never quite know what lies at the end of the voyage. And that is true of the voyage into the next world. The New Testament uses a number of pictures to describe death. It talks of sleep. It talks of 'moving house'. It speaks of closer fellowship with Christ. In today's passage Paul also describes it as a coronation. But there is no literal description of life after death. What comes at the end of the voyage is unknown. We take that journey in faith, knowing only that at its end we shall indeed be in fellowship with our Lord and Saviour.

> *Teach me to live, that I may dread*
> *The grave as little as my bed;*
> *Teach me to die, that so I may*
> *Rise glorious at the awful day.*

(Thomas Ken)

→1122

'In your teaching show integrity, seriousness and soundness of speech that cannot be condemned' (vv. 7, 8).

THE HOUSEHOLD OF FAITH. The instructions given in today's passage are similar to the rules given for the ordering of a Christian household in Colossians 3:18–41; Ephesians 5:22–6:9; 1 Peter 2:18–3:7. This concern with domestic Christianity may seem somewhat surprising in view of the instructions to Titus to set church government in order (1:5).

Perhaps we need to recognize the importance of carrying Christian principles into our homes. First, making sure that they are places where faith, ethical teaching, and self-control are all taught. This is important for the Church in every age. Church-centred Christian education is important among all ages in the community. However, it should not become a substitute for teaching in the home.

Second, Christianity should also be demonstrated in our homes, thus the teaching is set side-by-side with an example.

We also need to recognize that as Christians we are part of a larger family – the Church. The qualities of the personal family unit should be evident in the larger community. Non-Christians should not be given opportunity to accuse us of naivety or insincerity (v. 8).

Lord, help us to teach your way, by the grace of God. Amen.

→1125

Philemon

1Paul, a prisoner of Christ Jesus, and Timothy our brother,

To Philemon our dear friend and fellow-worker, 2to Apphia our sister, to Archippus our fellow-soldier and to the church that meets in your home:

3Grace to you and peace from God our Father and the Lord Jesus Christ.

Thanksgiving and Prayer

4I always thank my God as I remember you in my prayers, 5because I hear about your faith in the Lord Jesus and your love for all the saints. 6I pray that you may be active in sharing your faith, so that you will have a full understanding of every good thing we have in Christ. 7Your love has given me great joy and encouragement, because you, brother, have refreshed the hearts of the saints.

Paul's Plea for Onesimus

8Therefore, although in Christ I could be bold and order you to do what you ought to do, 9yet I appeal to you on the basis of love. I then, as Paul—an old man and now also a prisoner of Christ Jesus—10I appeal to you for my son Onesimus,*a* who became my son while I was in chains. 11Formerly he was useless to you, but now he has become useful both to you and to me.

12I am sending him—who is my very heart —back to you. 13I would have liked to keep him with me so that he could take your place in helping me while I am in chains for the gospel. 14But I did not want to do anything without your consent, so that any favour you do will be spontaneous and not forced. 15Perhaps the reason he was separated from you for a little while was that you might have him back for good—16no longer as a slave, but better than a slave, as a dear brother. He is very dear to me but even dearer to you, both as a man and as a brother in the Lord.

17So if you consider me a partner, welcome him as you would welcome me. 18If he has done you any wrong or owes you anything, charge it to me. 19I, Paul, am writing this with my own hand. I will pay it back—not to mention that you owe me your very self. 20I do wish, brother, that I may have some benefit from you in the Lord; refresh my heart in Christ. 21Confident of your obedience, I write to you, knowing that you will do even more than I ask.

22And one thing more: Prepare a guest room for me, because I hope to be restored to you in answer to your prayers.

23Epaphras, my fellow-prisoner in Christ Jesus, sends you greetings. 24And so do Mark, Aristarchus, Demas and Luke, my fellow-workers.

25The grace of the Lord Jesus Christ be with your spirit.

---

a10 Onesimus means useful.

Hebrews

The Son Superior to Angels

1 In the past God spoke to our forefathers through the prophets at many times and in various ways, ²but in these last days he has spoken to us by his Son, whom he appointed heir of all things, and through whom he made the universe. ³The Son is the radiance of God's glory and the exact representation of his being, sustaining all things by his powerful word. After he had provided purification for sins, he sat down at the right hand of the Majesty in heaven. ⁴So he became as much superior to the angels as the name he has inherited is superior to theirs.

⁵For to which of the angels did God ever say,

"You are my Son;
today I have become your Father"*a,b*?

Or again,

"I will be his Father,
and he will be my Son"*c*?

⁶And again, when God brings his firstborn into the world, he says,

"Let all God's angels worship him."*d*

⁷In speaking of the angels he says,

"He makes his angels winds,
his servants flames of fire."*e*

⁸But about the Son he says,

"Your throne, O God, will last for ever
and ever,
and righteousness will be the sceptre of
your kingdom.
⁹You have loved righteousness and hated
wickedness;
therefore God, your God, has set you
above your companions
by anointing you with the oil of joy."*f*

¹⁰He also says,

"In the beginning, O Lord, you laid the
foundations of the earth,
and the heavens are the work of your
hands.
¹¹They will perish, but you remain;
they will all wear out like a garment.
¹²You will roll them up like a robe;
like a garment they will be changed.
But you remain the same,
and your years will never end."*g*

¹³To which of the angels did God ever say,

"Sit at my right hand
until I make your enemies
a footstool for your feet"*h*?

¹⁴Are not all angels ministering spirits sent to serve those who will inherit salvation?

Warning to Pay Attention

2 We must pay more careful attention, therefore, to what we have heard, so that we do not drift away. ²For if the message spoken by angels was binding, and every violation and disobedience received its just punishment, ³how shall we escape if we ignore such a great salvation? This salvation, which was first announced by the Lord, was confirmed to us by those who heard him. ⁴God also testified to it by signs, wonders and various miracles, and gifts of the Holy Spirit distributed according to his will.

Jesus Made Like His Brothers

⁵It is not to angels that he has subjected the world to come, about which we are speaking. ⁶But there is a place where someone has testified:

"What is man that you are mindful of him,
the son of man that you care for him?
⁷You made him a little*a* lower than the
angels;
you crowned him with glory and honour
⁸ and put everything under his feet."*b*

In putting everything under him, God left nothing that is not subject to him. Yet at present we do not see everything subject to him. ⁹But we see Jesus, who was made a little lower than the angels, now crowned with

---

a5 Or *have begotten you*   *b5* Psalm 2:7   *c5* 2 Samuel 7:14; 1 Chron. 17:13
d6 Deut. 32:43 (see Dead Sea Scrolls and Septuagint)   *e7* Psalm 104:4   *f9* Psalm 45:6,7
g12 Psalm 102:25–27   *h13* Psalm 110:1   *a7* Or *him for a little while*; also in verse 9   *b8* Psalm 8:4–6

PHILEMON vv. 1–3

'Grace to you and peace from God our Father and the Lord Jesus Christ' (v. 3).

THIS VERY BRIEF LETTER breathes the Spirit of God the Father and God the Son. Only a man whose heart was truly oriented on Christ could write such a tender, generous and confident letter (Gal. 2:20). No reference to his own personal hardship creeps into the letter: rather, with becoming acceptance and pride, he describes himself as a 'prisoner of Christ Jesus' (vv. 1a, 13b). He was, of course, a prisoner of the Roman Empire, suffering for his faith in Christ, but his insights told him that in reality he was a prisoner of the Lord Jesus. His insight was correct.

Onesimus was a runaway slave who had received Christ through Paul's ministry (v. 10). How Onesimus made contact with Paul is a mystery. Perhaps he had heard of Paul and sought him out, perhaps it was one of those simple sequences of events which confirm our belief in providence. Whatever it was, two men who in different ways were prisoners of the system came together, and Onesimus the slave became a free man in Christ. Regrettably, that freedom did not free him from his legal master. Paul therefore wrote to Philemon (v. 1b), asking him to honour his own standing in Christ and grant Onesimus freedom (vv. 8, 16, 20).

It was Paul's custom to include a benediction in the early part of his letters (see Titus 1:4). Gracious words are easy to write when circumstances are favourable, but to write them from prison presupposes a heart of grace, and such was Paul's heart. Grace and peace are active, not passive, elements in our world. Peace guards our hearts and minds (Phil. 4:7), grace enables us to mature in Christ (1 Cor. 15:10). Paul therefore expected that Philemon would rise to the challenge this letter gave him.

> *O let my spirit rise above my circumstance.*
> *And let my words be always words of grace.*
> *Let others see your light upon my countenance.*
> *Your light of love reflecting from my face.*

→1126

HEBREWS 1:1–4

'In the past God spoke to our forefathers through the prophets at many times and in various ways, but in these last days he has spoken to us by his Son' (vv. 1, 2).

CONTINUITY AND CHANGE march together through the Epistle to the Hebrews. From the opening verse the author makes clear how God's new revelation is rooted in the past. God spoke through the prophets.

The infinitely varied experience recorded in the Old Testament is, indeed, God speaking. Different voices shout or whisper through its pages. From Moses' thundering, to the 'still, small voice' calling Elijah; from Samson's brute force, to the guile of Gideon; from the burning coals searing through Isaiah's prophecy, to the introvert silences of Ezekiel; God speaks through them all. Gradually, so gradually, his people begin to hear.

Hebrews uses Old Testament arguments to proclaim the completeness of the new revelation. There is continuity between old and new, yet God's revelation through the Son is also entirely new and superior to the old. So in Hebrews massive tension builds up. The author accepts this tension. He doesn't engage in agonized questioning about the link between old and new as Paul does. Paul and Hebrews do have much in common.

There are strong links, too, between Hebrews and John. For example, Hebrews says God speaks through the Son. John tells us 'The Word became flesh'. They are saying the same thing from different angles. God's Word as revealed in Christ is complete. It belongs to 'now', not just to 'then'.

The story of divine revelation is a story of progression up to Christ, but there is no progression beyond him.

(F. F. Bruce)

→1129

glory and honour because he suffered death, so that by the grace of God he might taste death for everyone. ¹⁰In bringing many sons to glory, it was fitting that God, for whom and through whom everything exists, should make the author of their salvation perfect through suffering. ¹¹Both the one who makes men holy and those who are made holy are of the same family. So Jesus is not ashamed to call them brothers. ¹²He says,

"I will declare your name to my brothers;
   in the presence of the congregation I will
      sing your praises."*c*

¹³And again,

"I will put my trust in him."*d*

And again he says,

"Here am I, and the children God has
   given me."*e*

¹⁴Since the children have flesh and blood, he too shared in their humanity so that by his death he might destroy him who holds the power of death—that is, the devil—¹⁵and free those who all their lives were held in slavery by their fear of death. ¹⁶For surely it is not angels he helps, but Abraham's descendants. ¹⁷For this reason he had to be made like his brothers in every way, in order that he might become a merciful and faithful high priest in service to God, and that he might make atonement for*f* the sins of the people. ¹⁸Because he himself suffered when he was tempted, he is able to help those who are being tempted.

Jesus Greater Than Moses

3 Therefore, holy brothers, who share in the heavenly calling, fix your thoughts on Jesus, the apostle and high priest whom we confess. ²He was faithful to the one who appointed him, just as Moses was faithful in all God's house. ³Jesus has been found worthy of greater honour than Moses, just as the builder of a house has greater honour than the house itself. ⁴For every house is built by someone, but God is the builder of everything. ⁵Moses was faithful as a servant in all God's house, testifying to what would be said in the future. ⁶But Christ is faithful as a son over God's house. And we are his house, if we hold on to our courage and the hope of which we boast.

Warning Against Unbelief

⁷So, as the Holy Spirit says:

"Today, if you hear his voice,
⁸   do not harden your hearts
   as you did in the rebellion,
      during the time of testing in the desert,
⁹where your fathers tested and tried me
   and for forty years saw what I did.

¹⁰That is why I was angry with that
      generation,
   and I said, 'Their hearts are always
      going astray,
   and they have not known my ways.'
¹¹So I declared on oath in my anger,
   'They shall never enter my rest.' "*a*

¹²See to it, brothers, that none of you has a sinful, unbelieving heart that turns away from the living God. ¹³But encourage one another daily, as long as it is called Today, so that none of you may be hardened by sin's deceitfulness. ¹⁴We have come to share in Christ if we hold firmly till the end the confidence we had at first. ¹⁵As has just been said:

"Today, if you hear his voice,
   do not harden your hearts
   as you did in the rebellion."*b*

¹⁶Who were they who heard and rebelled? Were they not all those Moses led out of Egypt? ¹⁷And with whom was he angry for forty years? Was it not with those who sinned, whose bodies fell in the desert? ¹⁸And to whom did God swear that they would never enter his rest if not to those who disobeyed?*c* ¹⁹So we see that they were not able to enter, because of their unbelief.

A Sabbath-rest for the People of God

4 Therefore, since the promise of entering his rest still stands, let us be careful that none of you be found to have fallen short of it. ²For we also have had the gospel preached to us, just as they did; but the message they heard was of no value to them, because those who heard did not combine it with faith.*a* ³Now we who have believed enter that rest, just as God has said,

"So I declared on oath in my anger,
   'They shall never enter my rest.' "*b*

And yet his work has been finished since the creation of the world. ⁴For somewhere he has spoken about the seventh day in these words: "And on the seventh day God rested from all his work."*c* ⁵And again in the passage above he says, "They shall never enter my rest."

⁶It still remains that some will enter that rest, and those who formerly had the gospel preached to them did not go in, because of their disobedience. ⁷Therefore God again set a certain day, calling it Today, when a long time later he spoke through David, as was said before:

"Today, if you hear his voice,
   do not harden your hearts."*d*

⁸For if Joshua had given them rest, God would not have spoken later about another day. ⁹There remains, then, a Sabbath-rest for

---

*c*12 Psalm 22:22   *d*13 Isaiah 8:17   *e*13 Isaiah 8:18
*f*17 Or *and that he might turn aside God's wrath, taking away*   *a*11 Psalm 95:7-11   *b*15 Psalm 95:7,8
*c*18 Or *disbelieved*   *a*2 Many manuscripts *because they did not share in the faith of those who obeyed*
*b*3 Psalm 95:11; also in verse 5   *c*4 Gen. 2:2   *d*7 Psalm 95:7,8

the people of God; [10]for anyone who enters God's rest also rests from his own work, just as God did from his. [11]Let us, therefore, make every effort to enter that rest, so that no-one will fall by following their example of disobedience.

[12]For the word of God is living and active. Sharper than any double-edged sword, it penetrates even to dividing soul and spirit, joints and marrow; it judges the thoughts and attitudes of the heart. [13]Nothing in all creation is hidden from God's sight. Everything is uncovered and laid bare before the eyes of him to whom we must give account.

Jesus the Great High Priest

[14]Therefore, since we have a great high priest who has gone through the heavens,[e] Jesus the Son of God, let us hold firmly to the faith we profess. [15]For we do not have a high priest who is unable to sympathise with our weaknesses, but we have one who has been tempted in every way, just as we are—yet was without sin. [16]Let us then approach the throne of grace with confidence, so that we may receive mercy and find grace to help us in our time of need.

5 Every high priest is selected from among men and is appointed to represent them in matters related to God, to offer gifts and sacrifices for sins. [2]He is able to deal gently with those who are ignorant and are going astray, since he himself is subject to weakness. [3]This is why he has to offer sacrifices for his own sins, as well as for the sins of the people.

[4]No-one takes this honour upon himself; he must be called by God, just as Aaron was. [5]So Christ also did not take upon himself the glory of becoming a high priest. But God said to him,

"You are my Son;
today I have become your Father."[a,b]

[6]And he says in another place,

"You are a priest for ever,
in the order of Melchizedek."[c]

[7]During the days of Jesus' life on earth, he offered up prayers and petitions with loud cries and tears to the one who could save him from death, and he was heard because of his reverent submission. [8]Although he was a son, he learned obedience from what he suffered [9]and, once made perfect, he became the source of eternal salvation for all who obey him [10]and was designated by God to be high priest in the order of Melchizedek.

Warning Against Falling Away

[11]We have much to say about this, but it is hard to explain because you are slow to learn. [12]In fact, though by this time you ought to be teachers, you need someone to teach you the elementary truths of God's word all over again. You need milk, not solid food! [13]Anyone who lives on milk, being still an infant, is not acquainted with the teaching about righteousness. [14]But solid food is for the mature, who by constant use have trained themselves to distinguish good from evil.

6 Therefore let us leave the elementary teachings about Christ and go on to maturity, not laying again the foundation of repentance from acts that lead to death,[a] and of faith in God, [2]instruction about baptisms, the laying on of hands, the resurrection of the dead, and eternal judgment. [3]And God permitting, we will do so.

[4]It is impossible for those who have once been enlightened, who have tasted the heavenly gift, who have shared in the Holy Spirit, [5]who have tasted the goodness of the word of God and the powers of the coming age, [6]if they fall away, to be brought back to repentance, because[b] to their loss they are crucifying the Son of God all over again and subjecting him to public disgrace.

[7]Land that drinks in the rain often falling on it and that produces a crop useful to those for whom it is farmed receives the blessing of God. [8]But land that produces thorns and thistles is worthless and is in danger of being cursed. In the end it will be burned.

[9]Even though we speak like this, dear friends, we are confident of better things in your case—things that accompany salvation. [10]God is not unjust; he will not forget your work and the love you have shown him as you have helped his people and continue to help them. [11]We want each of you to show this same diligence to the very end, in order to make your hope sure. [12]We do not want you to become lazy, but to imitate those who through faith and patience inherit what has been promised.

The Certainty of God's Promise

[13]When God made his promise to Abraham, since there was no-one greater for him to swear by, he swore by himself, [14]saying, "I will surely bless you and give you many descendants."[c] [15]And so after waiting patiently, Abraham received what was promised.

[16]Men swear by someone greater than themselves, and the oath confirms what is said and puts an end to all argument. [17]Because God wanted to make the unchanging nature of his purpose very clear to the heirs of what was promised, he confirmed it with an oath. [18]God did this so that, by two unchangeable things in which it is impossible for God to lie, we who have fled to take hold of the hope offered to us may be greatly encouraged. [19]We have this hope as an anchor for the soul, firm and secure. It enters the inner sanctuary behind the curtain, [20]where Jesus, who went before us, has entered on our behalf. He has become a high priest for ever, in the order of Melchizedek.

---

[e]14 Or gone into heaven   [a]5 Or have begotten you   [b]5 Psalm 2:7   [c]6 Psalm 110:4
[a]1 Or from useless rituals   [b]6 Or repentance while   [c]14 Gen. 22:17

HEBREWS 4:1–11

'Those who heard did not combine it with faith . . . those who formerly had the gospel preached to them did not go in, because of their disobedience' (vv. 2b, 6b).

DISOBEDIENCE. Without faith, we cannot obey. Without obedience faith is hollow, and we cannot enter into God's rest. The connection between faith and obedience, unbelief and disobedience is clearly outlined in Hebrews. They are so close that some translations make 'unbelief' and 'disobedience' appear interchangeable, as in the verse quoted above.

In the Gospels, particularly in John, the link between faith and obedience is more distant. It is mediated through love. Jesus says 'Anyone who has faith in me will do what I have been doing' but when calling for obedience he stresses that the first essential element is love. 'If you love me you will obey what I command.'

In Hebrews the harsh connection between faith and obedience is softened, not by stressing the need for love, but by holding out the promise of rest. Rest means being in a state of harmony with God. This world is one of discord and strife. The next is one of harmony and rest, a rest like that which God enjoyed at the accomplishment of creation. It is not a state of idleness and inactivity, but of worshipful harmony with our maker.

No soul can have rest until it finds created things are empty. When the soul gives up all for love, so that it can have Him that is all, then it finds true rest.

(*Julian of Norwich*)

→1130

'For the word of God is living and active. Sharper than any double-edged sword, it penetrates even to dividing soul and spirit' (v. 12a).

THE LIVING WORD of God, sharper than any sword, is, in this context, not Christ himself, nor even the New Testament, but the Old Testament. Perhaps the writer to Hebrews knew Paul's works. He may have known one or more Gospels – but he did not yet regard them as Scripture. We tend to re-interpret his words to mean the Scriptures of the Old *and* New Testaments. We make them relevant to *our* situation, in the same way that Hebrews re-interpreted the Old Testament, making it relevant to *his* situation.

It is because the Scriptures, both Old and New Testaments, are living and active, usable and adaptable, that we can re-interpret them in this way. They are not like the tablets of stone on which the Law was written, fixed and immutable for ever more. Instead their words live. They take on new meanings as we understand them better. They speak to us in different situations. Sometimes they cut us to the heart, at others they build us up, regenerate our spiritual life and inspire us to greater achievement than we ever thought possible.

The writer can hardly mention the living word without thinking of Christ in person, so he passes quickly from talking of the Scriptures as a sword, to talk about Jesus as high priest. The writer's view, once more, is coloured by his Old Testament background. Paul almost entirely ignores the priestly system of the Old Testament, but Hebrews uses it to illustrate Jesus' complete identification with us.

Hebrews 4:15 'We do not have a high priest who is unable to sympathise with our weaknesses.'

→1133

Melchizedek the Priest

7 This Melchizedek was king of Salem and priest of God Most High. He met Abraham returning from the defeat of the kings and blessed him, ²and Abraham gave him a tenth of everything. First, his name means "king of righteousness"; then also, "king of Salem" means "king of peace". ³Without father or mother, without genealogy, without beginning of days or end of life, like the Son of God he remains a priest for ever.

⁴Just think how great he was: Even the patriarch Abraham gave him a tenth of the plunder! ⁵Now the law requires the descendants of Levi who become priests to collect a tenth from the people—that is, their brothers—even though their brothers are descended from Abraham. ⁶This man, however, did not trace his descent from Levi, yet he collected a tenth from Abraham and blessed him who had the promises. ⁷And without doubt the lesser person is blessed by the greater. ⁸In the one case, the tenth is collected by men who die; but in the other case, by him who is declared to be living. ⁹One might even say that Levi, who collects the tenth, paid the tenth through Abraham, ¹⁰because when Melchizedek met Abraham, Levi was still in the body of his ancestor.

Jesus Like Melchizedek

¹¹If perfection could have been attained through the Levitical priesthood (for on the basis of it the law was given to the people), why was there still need for another priest to come—one in the order of Melchizedek, not in the order of Aaron? ¹²For when there is a change of the priesthood, there must also be a change of the law. ¹³He of whom these things are said belonged to a different tribe, and no-one from that tribe has ever served at the altar. ¹⁴For it is clear that our Lord descended from Judah, and in regard to that tribe Moses said nothing about priests. ¹⁵And what we have said is even more clear if another priest like Melchizedek appears, ¹⁶one who has become a priest not on the basis of a regulation as to his ancestry but on the basis of the power of an indestructible life. ¹⁷For it is declared:

"You are a priest for ever,
  in the order of Melchizedek."ᵃ

¹⁸The former regulation is set aside because it was weak and useless ¹⁹(for the law made nothing perfect), and a better hope is introduced, by which we draw near to God.

²⁰And it was not without an oath! Others became priests without any oath; ²¹but he became a priest with an oath when God said to him:

"The Lord has sworn
  and will not change his mind:
'You are a priest for ever.'"ᵇ

²²Because of this oath, Jesus has become the guarantee of a better covenant.

²³Now there have been many of those priests, since death prevented them from continuing in office; ²⁴but because Jesus lives for ever, he has a permanent priesthood. ²⁵Therefore he is able to save completelyᶜ those who come to God through him, because he always lives to intercede for them.

²⁶Such a high priest meets our need—one who is holy, blameless, pure, set apart from sinners, exalted above the heavens. ²⁷Unlike the other high priests, he does not need to offer sacrifices day after day, first for his own sins, and then for the sins of the people. He sacrificed for their sins once for all when he offered himself. ²⁸For the law appoints as high priests men who are weak; but the oath, which came after the law, appointed the Son, who has been made perfect for ever.

The High Priest of a New Covenant

8 The point of what we are saying is this: We do have such a high priest, who sat down at the right hand of the throne of the Majesty in heaven, ²and who serves in the sanctuary, the true tabernacle set up by the Lord, not by man.

³Every high priest is appointed to offer both gifts and sacrifices, and so it was necessary for this one also to have something to offer. ⁴If he were on earth, he would not be a priest, for there are already men who offer the gifts prescribed by the law. ⁵They serve at a sanctuary that is a copy and shadow of what is in heaven. This is why Moses was warned when he was about to build the tabernacle: "See to it that you make everything according to the pattern shown you on the mountain."ᵃ ⁶But the ministry Jesus has received is as superior to theirs as the covenant of which he is mediator is superior to the old one, and it is founded on better promises.

⁷For if there had been nothing wrong with that first covenant, no place would have been sought for another. ⁸But God found fault with the people and said:ᵇ

"The time is coming, declares the Lord,
  when I will make a new covenant
with the house of Israel
  and with the house of Judah.
⁹It will not be like the covenant
  I made with their forefathers
when I took them by the hand
  to lead them out of Egypt,
because they did not remain faithful to my
  covenant,
  and I turned away from them,
    declares the Lord.
¹⁰This is the covenant I will make with the
  house of Israel
  after that time, declares the Lord.
I will put my laws in their minds
  and write them on their hearts.
I will be their God,
  and they will be my people.
¹¹No longer will a man teach his neighbour,

ᵃ17 Psalm 110:4   ᵇ21 Psalm 110:4   ᶜ25 Or for ever   ᵃ5 Exodus 25:40
ᵇ8 Some manuscripts may be translated fault and said to the people.

or a man his brother, saying, 'Know the Lord,'
because they will all know me,
    from the least of them to the greatest.
¹²For I will forgive their wickedness
    and will remember their sins no more.''*c*

¹³By calling this covenant ''new'', he has made the first one obsolete; and what is obsolete and ageing will soon disappear.

Worship in the Earthly Tabernacle

9 Now the first covenant had regulations for worship and also an earthly sanctuary. ²A tabernacle was set up. In its first room were the lampstand, the table and the consecrated bread; this was called the Holy Place. ³Behind the second curtain was a room called the Most Holy Place, ⁴which had the golden altar of incense and the gold-covered ark of the covenant. This ark contained the gold jar of manna, Aaron's staff that had budded, and the stone tablets of the covenant. ⁵Above the ark were the cherubim of the Glory, overshadowing the atonement cover*a*. But we cannot discuss these things in detail now.

⁶When everything had been arranged like this, the priests entered regularly into the outer room to carry on their ministry. ⁷But only the high priest entered the inner room, and that only once a year, and never without blood, which he offered for himself and for the sins the people had committed in ignorance. ⁸The Holy Spirit was showing by this that the way into the Most Holy Place had not yet been disclosed as long as the first tabernacle was still standing. ⁹This is an illustration for the present time, indicating that the gifts and sacrifices being offered were not able to clear the conscience of the worshipper. ¹⁰They are only a matter of food and drink and various ceremonial washings—external regulations applying until the time of the new order.

The Blood of Christ

¹¹When Christ came as high priest of the good things that are already here,*b* he went through the greater and more perfect tabernacle that is not man-made, that is to say, not a part of this creation. ¹²He did not enter by means of the blood of goats and calves; but he entered the Most Holy Place once for all by his own blood, having obtained eternal redemption. ¹³The blood of goats and bulls and the ashes of a heifer sprinkled on those who are ceremonially unclean sanctify them so that they are outwardly clean. ¹⁴How much more, then, will the blood of Christ, who through the eternal Spirit offered himself unblemished to God, cleanse our consciences from acts that lead to death,*c* so that we may serve the living God! ¹⁵For this reason Christ is the mediator of a new covenant, that those who are called may receive the promised eternal inheritance—

now that he has died as a ransom to set them free from the sins committed under the first covenant.

¹⁶In the case of a will,*d* it is necessary to prove the death of the one who made it, ¹⁷because a will is in force only when somebody has died; it never takes effect while the one who made it is living. ¹⁸This is why even the first covenant was not put into effect without blood. ¹⁹When Moses had proclaimed every commandment of the law to all the people, he took the blood of calves, together with water, scarlet wool and branches of hyssop, and sprinkled the scroll and all the people. ²⁰He said, ''This is the blood of the covenant, which God has commanded you to keep.''*e* ²¹In the same way, he sprinkled with the blood both the tabernacle and everything used in its ceremonies. ²²In fact, the law requires that nearly everything be cleansed with blood, and without the shedding of blood there is no forgiveness.

²³It was necessary, then, for the copies of the heavenly things to be purified with these sacrifices, but the heavenly things themselves with better sacrifices than these. ²⁴For Christ did not enter a man-made sanctuary that was only a copy of the true one; he entered heaven itself, now to appear for us in God's presence. ²⁵Nor did he enter heaven to offer himself again and again, the way the high priest enters the Most Holy Place every year with blood that is not his own. ²⁶Then Christ would have had to suffer many times since the creation of the world. But now he has appeared once for all at the end of the ages to do away with sin by the sacrifice of himself. ²⁷Just as man is destined to die once, and after that to face judgment, ²⁸so Christ was sacrificed once to take away the sins of many people; and he will appear a second time, not to bear sin, but to bring salvation to those who are waiting for him.

Christ's Sacrifice Once for All

10 The law is only a shadow of the good things that are coming—not the realities themselves. For this reason it can never, by the same sacrifices repeated endlessly year after year, make perfect those who draw near to worship. ²If it could, would they not have stopped being offered? For the worshippers would have been cleansed once for all, and would no longer have felt guilty for their sins. ³But those sacrifices are an annual reminder of sins, ⁴because it is impossible for the blood of bulls and goats to take away sins.

⁵Therefore, when Christ came into the world, he said:

''Sacrifice and offering you did not desire,
    but a body you prepared for me;
⁶with burnt offerings and sin offerings
    you were not pleased.
⁷Then I said, 'Here I am—it is written
    about me in the scroll—
I have come to do your will, O God.' ''*a*

---

c12 Jer. 31:31–34   *a5* Traditionally *the mercy seat*   *b11* Some early manuscripts *are to come*
c14 Or *from useless rituals*   *d16* Same Greek word as *covenant*; also in verse 17   *e20* Exodus 24:8
a7 Psalm 40:6–8 (see Septuagint)

HEBREWS 7:20–28

'Because Jesus lives for ever, he has a permanent priesthood. Therefore he is able to save completely those who come to God through him, because he always lives to intercede for them. Such a high priest meets our need – one who is holy, blameless, pure' (vv. 24–26a).

THE NAME OF JESUS is used in Hebrews quite deliberately. Jesus means Saviour. The purpose of Jesus' priesthood is not only to mediate, but to save. Earlier channels of communication had their uses. Priests and prophets could let the people know what God required. But they could not offer eternal salvation. Their ministry was limited in time and space. Each generation produced new priests and prophets. They lived and died, and their office died with them.

With Jesus things are different. His priesthood is permanent. He has offered himself. The offering has been accepted by God for eternity. There is no need to repeat it. In a sense it is going on all the time, for the life, death and resurrection of Jesus is the meeting place of time and eternity. The eternal has flooded in to history.

We participate in that meeting. His holiness, his blameless purity are mediated to us. He meets our need for a life that is higher, nobler and greater than we dare even to think about without him. He transforms our sinful, hellish existence here below into life with a heavenly perspective. We, too, can be holy, blameless and pure, through the single and complete sacrifice of Jesus. It is Jesus himself who guarantees this.

> *Jesus, the name to sinners dear,*
> *The name to sinners given;*
> *He scatters all their guilty fear;*
> *He turns their Hell to Heaven.*

> (*Charles Wesley*)

→1134

HEBREWS 10:26–39

'If we deliberately keep on sinning after we have received the knowledge of the truth, no sacrifice for sins is left . . . You need to persevere so that when you have done the will of God, you will receive what he has promised' (vv. 26, 36).

WE HAVE FREEDOM IN CHRIST, a freedom no one can take from us. Hebrews pleads with us not to reject that freedom. But what does it mean to deliberately keep on sinning? Surely, no one who has received the light of Christ could go on deliberately sinning. It seems a contradiction in terms.

Perhaps the author has in mind the people Paul talks about, who felt that the more they sinned, the more grace would abound. That was a popular attitude. Hebrews' call to holiness, and its stress on an upright, ethical lifestyle, may reflect the presence of a similar attitude in some members of the Hebrew congregation which received this letter. Hebrews makes very clear the dreadful fate awaiting those who 'trample the Son of God under foot' in that manner.

But for most of us, deliberate sin is simply closing our minds to the leading of God. We take refuge in rules and regulations. We order our lives as though the old dispensation was still in force, rather than launch out into the depths of life in Christ. Such an attitude may seem less serious but that only makes it more dangerous. It is easy to see when someone commits a gross sin. It is hard for us within the Church to tell when someone has 'insulted the Spirit of grace'. Those outside the Church often see it more clearly.

The greatest handicap the Church has is the unsatisfactory lives of professing Christians.

(*Dick Sheppard*)

→1137

[8]First he said, "Sacrifices and offerings, burnt offerings and sin offerings you did not desire, nor were you pleased with them" (although the law required them to be made). [9]Then he said, "Here I am, I have come to do your will." He sets aside the first to establish the second. [10]And by that will, we have been made holy through the sacrifice of the body of Jesus Christ once for all.

[11]Day after day every priest stands and performs his religious duties; again and again he offers the same sacrifices, which can never take away sins. [12]But when this priest had offered for all time one sacrifice for sins, he sat down at the right hand of God. [13]Since that time he waits for his enemies to be made his footstool, [14]because by one sacrifice he has made perfect for ever those who are being made holy.

[15]The Holy Spirit also testifies to us about this. First he says:

[16]"This is the covenant I will make with them
     after that time, says the Lord.
I will put my laws in their hearts,
     and I will write them on their minds."[b]

[17]Then he adds:

"Their sins and lawless acts
     I will remember no more."[c]

[18]And where these have been forgiven, there is no longer any sacrifice for sin.

A Call to Persevere

[19]Therefore, brothers, since we have confidence to enter the Most Holy Place by the blood of Jesus, [20]by a new and living way opened for us through the curtain, that is, his body, [21]and since we have a great priest over the house of God, [22]let us draw near to God with a sincere heart in full assurance of faith, having our hearts sprinkled to cleanse us from a guilty conscience and having our bodies washed with pure water. [23]Let us hold unswervingly to the hope we profess, for he who promised is faithful. [24]And let us consider how we may spur one another on towards love and good deeds. [25]Let us not give up meeting together, as some are in the habit of doing, but let us encourage one another —and all the more as you see the Day approaching.

[26]If we deliberately keep on sinning after we have received the knowledge of the truth, no sacrifice for sins is left, [27]but only a fearful expectation of judgment and of raging fire that will consume the enemies of God. [28]Anyone who rejected the law of Moses died without mercy on the testimony of two or three witnesses. [29]How much more severely do you think a man deserves to be punished who has trampled the Son of God under foot, who has treated as an unholy thing the blood of the covenant that sanctified him, and who has insulted the Spirit of grace? [30]For we know him who said, "It is mine to avenge; I will repay,"[d] and again, "The Lord will judge his people."[e] [31]It is a dreadful thing to fall into the hands of the living God.

[32]Remember those earlier days after you had received the light, when you stood your ground in a great contest in the face of suffering. [33]Sometimes you were publicly exposed to insult and persecution; at other times you stood side by side with those who were so treated. [34]You sympathised with those in prison and joyfully accepted the confiscation of your property, because you knew that you yourselves had better and lasting possessions.

[35]So do not throw away your confidence; it will be richly rewarded. [36]You need to persevere so that when you have done the will of God, you will receive what he has promised. [37]For in just a very little while,

"He who is coming will come and will not delay.
[38] But my righteous one[f] will live by faith.
     And if he shrinks back,
     I will not be pleased with him."[g]

[39]But we are not of those who shrink back and are destroyed, but of those who believe and are saved.

By Faith

11 Now faith is being sure of what we hope for and certain of what we do not see. [2]This is what the ancients were commended for.

[3]By faith we understand that the universe was formed at God's command, so that what is seen was not made out of what was visible.

[4]By faith Abel offered God a better sacrifice than Cain did. By faith he was commended as a righteous man, when God spoke well of his offerings. And by faith he still speaks, even though he is dead.

[5]By faith Enoch was taken from this life, so that he did not experience death; he could not be found, because God had taken him away. For before he was taken, he was commended as one who pleased God. [6]And without faith it is impossible to please God, because anyone who comes to him must believe that he exists and that he rewards those who earnestly seek him.

[7]By faith Noah, when warned about things not yet seen, in holy fear built an ark to save his family. By his faith he condemned the world and became heir of the righteousness that comes by faith.

[8]By faith Abraham, when called to go to a place he would later receive as his inheritance, obeyed and went, even though he did not know where he was going. [9]By faith he made his home in the promised land like a stranger in a foreign country; he lived in tents, as did Isaac and Jacob, who were heirs with him of the same promise. [10]For he was looking forward to the city with foundations, whose architect and builder is God.

[11]By faith Abraham, even though he was

[b]16 Jer. 31:33   [c]17 Jer. 31:34   [d]30 Deut. 32:35   [e]30 Deut. 32:36; Psalm 135:14
[f]38 One early manuscript But the righteous   [g]38 Hab. 2:3,4

past age—and Sarah herself was barren—was enabled to become a father because he[a] considered him faithful who had made the promise. [12]And so from this one man, and he as good as dead, came descendants as numerous as the stars in the sky and as countless as the sand on the seashore.

[13]All these people were still living by faith when they died. They did not receive the things promised; they only saw them and welcomed them from a distance. And they admitted that they were aliens and strangers on earth. [14]People who say such things show that they are looking for a country of their own. [15]If they had been thinking of the country they had left, they would have had opportunity to return. [16]Instead, they were longing for a better country—a heavenly one. Therefore God is not ashamed to be called their God, for he has prepared a city for them.

[17]By faith Abraham, when God tested him, offered Isaac as a sacrifice. He who had received the promises was about to sacrifice his one and only son, [18]even though God had said to him, "It is through Isaac that your offspring[b] will be reckoned."[c] [19]Abraham reasoned that God could raise the dead, and figuratively speaking, he did receive Isaac back from death.

[20]By faith Isaac blessed Jacob and Esau in regard to their future.

[21]By faith Jacob, when he was dying, blessed each of Joseph's sons, and worshipped as he leaned on the top of his staff.

[22]By faith Joseph, when his end was near, spoke about the exodus of the Israelites from Egypt and gave instructions about his bones.

[23]By faith Moses' parents hid him for three months after he was born, because they saw he was no ordinary child, and they were not afraid of the king's edict.

[24]By faith Moses, when he had grown up, refused to be known as the son of Pharaoh's daughter. [25]He chose to be ill-treated along with the people of God rather than to enjoy the pleasures of sin for a short time. [26]He regarded disgrace for the sake of Christ as of greater value than the treasures of Egypt, because he was looking ahead to his reward. [27]By faith he left Egypt, not fearing the king's anger; he persevered because he saw him who is invisible. [28]By faith he kept the Passover and the sprinkling of blood, so that the destroyer of the firstborn would not touch the firstborn of Israel.

[29]By faith the people passed through the Red Sea[d] as on dry land; but when the Egyptians tried to do so, they were drowned.

[30]By faith the walls of Jericho fell, after the people had marched around them for seven days.

[31]By faith the prostitute Rahab, because she welcomed the spies, was not killed with those who were disobedient.[e]

[32]And what more shall I say? I do not have time to tell about Gideon, Barak, Samson, Jephthah, David, Samuel and the prophets, [33]who through faith conquered kingdoms, administered justice, and gained what was promised; who shut the mouths of lions, [34]quenched the fury of the flames, and escaped the edge of the sword; whose weakness was turned to strength; and who became powerful in battle and routed foreign armies. [35]Women received back their dead, raised to life again. Others were tortured and refused to be released, so that they might gain a better resurrection. [36]Some faced jeers and flogging, while still others were chained and put in prison. [37]They were stoned;[f] they were sawn in two; they were put to death by the sword. They went about in sheepskins and goatskins, destitute, persecuted and ill-treated—[38]the world was not worthy of them. They wandered in deserts and mountains, and in caves and holes in the ground.

[39]These were all commended for their faith, yet none of them received what had been promised. [40]God had planned something better for us so that only together with us would they be made perfect.

God Disciplines His Sons

12 Therefore, since we are surrounded by such a great cloud of witnesses, let us throw off everything that hinders and the sin that so easily entangles, and let us run with perseverance the race marked out for us. [2]Let us fix our eyes on Jesus, the author and perfecter of our faith, who for the joy set before him endured the cross, scorning its shame, and sat down at the right hand of the throne of God. [3]Consider him who endured such opposition from sinful men, so that you will not grow weary and lose heart.

[4]In your struggle against sin, you have not yet resisted to the point of shedding your blood. [5]And you have forgotten that word of encouragement that addresses you as sons:

"My son, do not make light of the Lord's discipline,
 and do not lose heart when he rebukes you,
[6]because the Lord disciplines those he loves,
 and he punishes everyone he accepts as a son."[a]

[7]Endure hardship as discipline; God is treating you as sons. For what son is not disciplined by his father? [8]If you are not disciplined (and everyone undergoes discipline), then you are illegitimate children and not true sons. [9]Moreover, we have all had human fathers who disciplined us and we respected them for it. How much more should we submit to the Father of our spirits and live! [10]Our fathers disciplined us for a little while as they thought best; but God disciplines us for our good, that we may share in his holiness. [11]No discipline seems pleasant at the time, but painful. Later on, however, it produces a harvest of

[a]11 Or By faith even Sarah, who was past age, was enabled to bear children because she
[b]18 Greek seed   [c]18 Gen. 21:12   [d]29 That is, Sea of Reeds   [e]31 Or unbelieving
[f]37 Some early manuscripts stoned; they were put to the test;   [a]6 Prov. 3:11,12

HEBREWS 11:32–40

'And what more shall I say? I do not have time to tell about Gideon, Barak, Samson, Jephthah, David, Samuel and the prophets, who through faith conquered kingdoms, administered justice, and gained what was promised' (vv. 32, 33).

MOSES WAS THE SUPREME FIGURE in Israel's history. He led the people and communed with God in a unique manner. He was the Law-giver, and looked on as the first of the prophets. He brought his wandering, desert tribes right to the promised land – even though he never settled there with them.

But Hebrews does not simply offer the example of the patriarchs and Moses. The writer names others, some well known, some less famous. There seems little to link their experience. They had varying degrees of ability. Their moral character differed. Some were upright, true and noble. Others were downright deceitful and corrupt.

What do they have in common? Faith, certainly, for that is the whole message of this chapter. And something else, too; all faced enormous odds against them. Each at some stage experienced a situation which seemed completely hopeless; Gideon with his three hundred; Barak facing chariots; Samson against the Philistines; Jephthah once an outlaw; David against Goliath; Samuel guiding the people, protesting, into the era of kingship.

The message for us is simple. Hebrews teaches us that faith is not something passive, not merely a matter of belief. Faith spurs us on to act for God, even against the odds.

> *Faith, mighty faith, the promise sees,*
> *And looks to that alone;*
> *Laughs at impossibilities*
> *And cries: It shall be done!*

(Charles Wesley)

→1138

HEBREWS 12:1–3

'Let us fix our eyes on Jesus, the author and perfector of our faith, who for the joy set before him endured the cross' (v. 2).

A MAN STANDING on the deck of a ship suddenly heard a deafening rumble as a nearby volcano burst into flame. The whole countryside was lit up and then the flame died. In those moments he said that he saw the fire that is ever burning in the heart of that mountain.

When we contemplate the passion of our Lord, his suffering and death on Calvary, we have a glimpse of the love that is forever in the heart of God for each of us. Calvary is the supreme articulation of God's love for the world. As we ponder the stupendous scene of the Son of God impaled on a felon's cross for us, we are constrained with Charles Wesley to exclaim:

> *Amazing love! How can it be*
> *That thou, my God, shouldst die for me?*

Let us make a pilgrimage of the soul to Calvary, journeying through the suffering and sacrifice of our Lord in his final week upon earth. Such a journey ushers us into the Holy of Holies in the sanctuary of Christ's life. The writer of Hebrews invokes just such a contemplation, to 'fix our eyes on Jesus' and to consider his enduring the cross for us.

'The cross transforms everything,' writes John Stott in his seminal book, *The Cross of Christ*. The tiny hill of Calvary has become the pinnacle of history that towers over all other events. The destiny of every soul lies in what took place on the cross.

The cost of Christian discipleship has never been lowered. Christ still calls: 'If anyone would come after me, he must deny himself and take up his cross and follow me' (Matt. 16:24). It is still true that 'the way of the cross leads home' – home to God and to our eternal destiny.

Eternal God, lest I forget your love to me, lead me these days to Calvary.

righteousness and peace for those who have been trained by it.

12Therefore, strengthen your feeble arms and weak knees! 13"Make level paths for your feet,"*b* so that the lame may not be disabled, but rather healed.

Warning Against Refusing God

14Make every effort to live in peace with all men and to be holy; without holiness no-one will see the Lord. 15See to it that no-one misses the grace of God and that no bitter root grows up to cause trouble and defile many. 16See that no-one is sexually immoral, or is godless like Esau, who for a single meal sold his inheritance rights as the oldest son. 17Afterwards, as you know, when he wanted to inherit this blessing, he was rejected. He could bring about no change of mind, though he sought the blessing with tears.

18You have not come to a mountain that can be touched and that is burning with fire; to darkness, gloom and storm; 19to a trumpet blast or to such a voice speaking words that those who heard it begged that no further word be spoken to them, 20because they could not bear what was commanded: "If even an animal touches the mountain, it must be stoned."*c* 21The sight was so terrifying that Moses said, "I am trembling with fear."*d*

22But you have come to Mount Zion, to the heavenly Jerusalem, the city of the living God. You have come to thousands upon thousands of angels in joyful assembly, 23to the church of the firstborn, whose names are written in heaven. You have come to God, the judge of all men, to the spirits of righteous men made perfect, 24to Jesus the mediator of a new covenant, and to the sprinkled blood that speaks a better word than the blood of Abel.

25See to it that you do not refuse him who speaks. If they did not escape when they refused him who warned them on earth, how much less will we, if we turn away from him who warns us from heaven? 26At that time his voice shook the earth, but now he has promised, "Once more I will shake not only the earth but also the heavens."*e* 27The words "once more" indicate the removing of what can be shaken—that is, created things—so that what cannot be shaken may remain.

28Therefore, since we are receiving a kingdom that cannot be shaken, let us be thankful, and so worship God acceptably with reverence and awe, 29for our "God is a consuming fire."*f*

Concluding Exhortations

13 Keep on loving each other as brothers. 2Do not forget to entertain strangers, for by so doing some people have entertained angels without knowing it. 3Remember those in prison as if you were their fellow-prisoners, and those who are ill-treated as if you yourselves were suffering.

4Marriage should be honoured by all, and the marriage bed kept pure, for God will judge the adulterer and all the sexually immoral. 5Keep your lives free from the love of money and be content with what you have, because God has said,

"Never will I leave you;
 never will I forsake you."*a*

6So we say with confidence,

"The Lord is my helper; I will not be
  afraid.
 What can man do to me?"*b*

7Remember your leaders, who spoke the word of God to you. Consider the outcome of their way of life and imitate their faith. 8Jesus Christ is the same yesterday and today and for ever. 9Do not be carried away by all kinds of strange teachings. It is good for our hearts to be strengthened by grace, not by ceremonial foods, which are of no value to those who eat them. 10We have an altar from which those who minister at the tabernacle have no right to eat.

11The high priest carries the blood of animals into the Most Holy Place as a sin offering, but the bodies are burned outside the camp. 12And so Jesus also suffered outside the city gate to make the people holy through his own blood. 13Let us, then, go to him outside the camp, bearing the disgrace he bore. 14For here we do not have an enduring city, but we are looking for the city that is to come.

15Through Jesus, therefore, let us continually offer to God a sacrifice of praise—the fruit of lips that confess his name. 16And do not forget to do good and to share with others, for with such sacrifices God is pleased.

17Obey your leaders and submit to their authority. They keep watch over you as men who must give an account. Obey them so that their work will be a joy, not a burden, for that would be of no advantage to you.

18Pray for us. We are sure that we have a clear conscience and desire to live honourably in every way. 19I particularly urge you to pray so that I may be restored to you soon.

20May the God of peace, who through the blood of the eternal covenant brought back from the dead our Lord Jesus, that great Shepherd of the sheep, 21equip you with everything good for doing his will, and may he work in us what is pleasing to him, through Jesus Christ, to whom be glory for ever and ever. Amen.

22Brothers, I urge you to bear with my word of exhortation, for I have written you only a short letter.

23I want you to know that our brother Timothy has been released. If he arrives soon, I will come with him to see you.

24Greet all your leaders and all God's people. Those from Italy send you their greetings.

25Grace be with you all.

b13 Prov. 4:26   *c20* Exodus 19:12,13   *d21* Deut. 9:19   *e26* Haggai 2:6   *f29* Deut. 4:24
a5 Deut. 31:6   *b6* Psalm 118:6,7

James

1

James, a servant of God and of the Lord Jesus Christ,

To the twelve tribes scattered among the nations:

Greetings.

Trials and Temptations

²Consider it pure joy, my brothers, whenever you face trials of many kinds, ³because you know that the testing of your faith develops perseverance. ⁴Perseverance must finish its work so that you may be mature and complete, not lacking anything. ⁵If any of you lacks wisdom, he should ask God, who gives generously to all without finding fault, and it will be given to him. ⁶But when he asks, he must believe and not doubt, because he who doubts is like a wave of the sea, blown and tossed by the wind. ⁷That man should not think he will receive anything from the Lord; ⁸he is a double-minded man, unstable in all he does.

⁹The brother in humble circumstances ought to take pride in his high position. ¹⁰But the one who is rich should take pride in his low position, because he will pass away like a wild flower. ¹¹For the sun rises with scorching heat and withers the plant; its blossom falls and its beauty is destroyed. In the same way, the rich man will fade away even while he goes about his business.

¹²Blessed is the man who perseveres under trial, because when he has stood the test, he will receive the crown of life that God has promised to those who love him.

¹³When tempted, no-one should say, "God is tempting me." For God cannot be tempted by evil, nor does he tempt anyone; ¹⁴but each one is tempted when, by his own evil desire, he is dragged away and enticed. ¹⁵Then, after desire has conceived, it gives birth to sin; and sin, when it is full-grown, gives birth to death.

¹⁶Don't be deceived, my dear brothers. ¹⁷Every good and perfect gift is from above, coming down from the Father of the heavenly lights, who does not change like shifting shadows. ¹⁸He chose to give us birth through the word of truth, that we might be a kind of firstfruits of all he created.

Listening and Doing

¹⁹My dear brothers, take note of this: Everyone should be quick to listen, slow to speak and slow to become angry, ²⁰for man's anger does not bring about the righteous life that God desires. ²¹Therefore, get rid of all moral filth and the evil that is so prevalent, and humbly accept the word planted in you, which can save you.

²²Do not merely listen to the word, and so deceive yourselves. Do what it says. ²³Anyone who listens to the word but does not do what it says is like a man who looks at his face in a mirror ²⁴and, after looking at himself, goes away and immediately forgets what he looks like. ²⁵But the man who looks intently into the perfect law that gives freedom, and continues to do this, not forgetting what he has heard, but doing it—he will be blessed in what he does.

²⁶If anyone considers himself religious and yet does not keep a tight rein on his tongue, he deceives himself and his religion is worthless. ²⁷Religion that God our Father accepts as pure and faultless is this: to look after orphans and widows in their distress and to keep oneself from being polluted by the world.

Favouritism Forbidden

2

My brothers, as believers in our glorious Lord Jesus Christ, don't show favouritism. ²Suppose a man comes into your meeting wearing a gold ring and fine clothes, and a poor man in shabby clothes also comes in. ³If you show special attention to the man wearing fine clothes and say, "Here's a good seat for you," but say to the poor man, "You stand there" or "Sit on the floor by my feet," ⁴have you not discriminated among yourselves and become judges with evil thoughts?

⁵Listen, my dear brothers: Has not God chosen those who are poor in the eyes of the world to be rich in faith and to inherit the kingdom he promised those who love him? ⁶But you have insulted the poor. Is it not the rich who are exploiting you? Are they not the ones who are dragging you into court? ⁷Are they not the ones who are slandering the noble name of him to whom you belong?

⁸If you really keep the royal law found in Scripture, "Love your neighbour as

HEBREWS 13:1–14
'Jesus Christ is the same yesterday and today and for ever' (v. 8).

DOCTRINE COMES FIRST in Hebrews. Most of the teaching about the person and nature of Christ comes in the first chapters, mingled with just a few verses containing practical advice and ethical statements.

Similarly, interspersed amongst the ethical teaching at the end of the letter, we find a verse or two of doctrine to remind us of the basis for the practical commands Hebrews contains. In today's passage the exhortations to love each other as brothers; to offer hospitality; to remember prisoners; to maintain sexual purity; to refrain from greed; and to support leaders, are followed by a little verse so important that it is often isolated and quoted out of context.

It is, indeed, a jewel which reflects a truth lying at the heart of the gospel. Jesus is eternally the same. He does not change. Our perceptions of him may change, but he does not. This then leads us to the further truth that God does not change. He is, always has been, and always will be just like we see him reflected in the life, ministry and death of Jesus. God has always given of himself to us completely, to suffer with us, to die for us, to impart his grace to us and bring us into fellowship with him.

> *O love, invisible before,*
> *I see thee now, desire thee more;*
> *When Jesus speaks thy word is clear;*
> *I search his face and find thee near.*
>
> *I come to thee with quiet mind,*
> *Thyself to know thy will to find;*
> *In Jesus' steps my steps must be,*
> *I follow him to follow thee.*

(*Catherine Baird*)

→1142

JAMES 2:13–26

'His faith and his actions were working together, and his faith was made complete by what he did' (v. 22).

WHAT A WONDERFUL TESTIMONY to the quality of Abraham's life. We know that Abraham was not perfect. His misdeeds were many and serious, but he practised what he believed. He believed God wanted the sacrifice of his son, Isaac. He acted upon that belief.

Happily, however, he also remained open to be convinced that his belief was wrong. His commitment was still absolute, but the content of his belief changed. When our minds become so closed that we can no longer take hold of new revelation, we are indeed lost. Without new revelation (which means a change in our beliefs) we would still be practising child sacrifice! Without new revelation the gospel of Christ could never have been preached!

So faith is not the acceptance of a set of doctines which we promise to adhere to throughout our lives. In some ways it would be much easier if that were the case. Sign your name; be loyal; put up the barriers against outsiders and construct your own little world with a few, a few hundreds, or thousands of others. Many do it. They commit themselves to all kinds of organizations (including a church or The Salvation Army) and hope that blind acceptance of their doctrines will save them. Acceptance of doctrine is helpful, but only as a pointer on the way to God in Christ. Of itself it cannot save.

Good deeds are helpful. But of themselves they cannot save. The only route to salvation is commitment to Christ – which involves belief, and acting upon that belief.

We act in humility using the understanding which we have at that moment reached, assured that more understanding will be given as we keep our attention fixed on Jesus.

→1145

yourself,"*a* you are doing right. 9But if you show favouritism, you sin and are convicted by the law as law-breakers. 10For whoever keeps the whole law and yet stumbles at just one point is guilty of breaking all of it. 11For he who said, "Do not commit adultery,"*b* also said, "Do not murder."*c* If you do not commit adultery but do commit murder, you have become a law-breaker.

12Speak and act as those who are going to be judged by the law that gives freedom, 13because judgment without mercy will be shown to anyone who has not been merciful. Mercy triumphs over judgment!

Faith and Deeds

14What good is it, my brothers, if a man claims to have faith but has no deeds? Can such faith save him? 15Suppose a brother or sister is without clothes and daily food. 16If one of you says to him, "Go, I wish you well; keep warm and well fed," but does nothing about his physical needs, what good is it? 17In the same way, faith by itself, if it is not accompanied by action, is dead.

18But someone will say, "You have faith; I have deeds."

Show me your faith without deeds, and I will show you my faith by what I do. 19You believe that there is one God. Good! Even the demons believe that—and shudder.

20You foolish man, do you want evidence that faith without deeds is useless?*d* 21Was not our ancestor Abraham considered righteous for what he did when he offered his son Isaac on the altar? 22You see that his faith and his actions were working together, and his faith was made complete by what he did. 23And the scripture was fulfilled that says, "Abraham believed God, and it was credited to him as righteousness,"*e* and he was called God's friend. 24You see that a person is justified by what he does and not by faith alone.

25In the same way, was not even Rahab the prostitute considered righteous for what she did when she gave lodging to the spies and sent them off in a different direction? 26As the body without the spirit is dead, so faith without deeds is dead.

Taming the Tongue

3 Not many of you should presume to be teachers, my brothers, because you know that we who teach will be judged more strictly. 2We all stumble in many ways. If anyone is never at fault in what he says, he is a perfect man, able to keep his whole body in check.

3When we put bits into the mouths of horses to make them obey us, we can turn the whole animal. 4Or take ships as an example. Although they are so large and are driven by strong winds, they are steered by a very small rudder wherever the pilot wants to go. 5Likewise the tongue is a small part of the body, but it makes great boasts. Consider what a great forest is set on fire by a small

spark. 6The tongue also is a fire, a world of evil among the parts of the body. It corrupts the whole person, sets the whole course of his life on fire, and is itself set on fire by hell.

7All kinds of animals, birds, reptiles and creatures of the sea are being tamed and have been tamed by man, 8but no man can tame the tongue. It is a restless evil, full of deadly poison.

9With the tongue we praise our Lord and Father, and with it we curse men, who have been made in God's likeness. 10Out of the same mouth come praise and cursing. My brothers, this should not be. 11Can both fresh water and salt*a* water flow from the same spring? 12My brothers, can a fig-tree bear olives, or a grapevine bear figs? Neither can a salt spring produce fresh water.

Two Kinds of Wisdom

13Who is wise and understanding among you? Let him show it by his good life, by deeds done in the humility that comes from wisdom. 14But if you harbour bitter envy and selfish ambition in your hearts, do not boast about it or deny the truth. 15Such "wisdom" does not come down from heaven but is earthly, unspiritual, of the devil. 16For where you have envy and selfish ambition, there you find disorder and every evil practice.

17But the wisdom that comes from heaven is first of all pure; then peace-loving, considerate, submissive, full of mercy and good fruit, impartial and sincere. 18Peacemakers who sow in peace raise a harvest of righteousness.

Submit Yourselves to God

4 What causes fights and quarrels among you? Don't they come from your desires that battle within you? 2You want something but don't get it. You kill and covet, but you cannot have what you want. You quarrel and fight. You do not have, because you do not ask God. 3When you ask, you do not receive, because you ask with wrong motives, that you may spend what you get on your pleasures.

4You adulterous people, don't you know that friendship with the world is hatred towards God? Anyone who chooses to be a friend of the world becomes an enemy of God. 5Or do you think Scripture says without reason that the spirit he caused to live in us envies intensely?*a* 6But he gives us more grace. That is why Scripture says:

"God opposes the proud
but gives grace to the humble."*b*

7Submit yourselves, then, to God. Resist the devil, and he will flee from you. 8Come near to God and he will come near to you. Wash your hands, you sinners, and purify your hearts, you double-minded. 9Grieve, mourn and wail. Change your laughter to mourning and your joy to gloom. 10Humble

---

*a*8 Lev. 19:18   *b*11 Exodus 20:14; Deut. 5:18   *c*11 Exodus 20:13; Deut. 5:17
*d*20 Some early manuscripts *dead*   *e*23 Gen. 15:6   *a*11 Greek *bitter* (see also verse 14)
*a*5 Or *that God jealously longs for the spirit that he made to live in us; or that the Spirit he caused to live in us longs jealously*   *b*6 Prov. 3:34

yourselves before the Lord, and he will lift you up.

[11]Brothers, do not slander one another. Anyone who speaks against his brother or judges him speaks against the law and judges it. When you judge the law, you are not keeping it, but sitting in judgment on it. [12]There is only one Lawgiver and Judge, the one who is able to save and destroy. But you—who are you to judge your neighbour?

Boasting About Tomorrow

[13]Now listen, you who say, "Today or tomorrow we will go to this or that city, spend a year there, carry on business and make money." [14]Why, you do not even know what will happen tomorrow. What is your life? You are a mist that appears for a little while and then vanishes. [15]Instead, you ought to say, "If it is the Lord's will, we will live and do this or that." [16]As it is, you boast and brag. All such boasting is evil. [17]Anyone, then, who knows the good he ought to do and doesn't do it, sins.

Warning to Rich Oppressors

5 Now listen, you rich people, weep and wail because of the misery that is coming upon you. [2]Your wealth has rotted, and moths have eaten your clothes. [3]Your gold and silver are corroded. Their corrosion will testify against you and eat your flesh like fire. You have hoarded wealth in the last days. [4]Look! The wages you failed to pay the workmen who mowed your fields are crying out against you. The cries of the harvesters have reached the ears of the Lord Almighty. [5]You have lived on earth in luxury and self-indulgence. You have fattened yourselves in the day of slaughter.[a] [6]You have condemned and murdered innocent men, who were not opposing you.

Patience in Suffering

[7]Be patient, then, brothers, until the Lord's coming. See how the farmer waits for the land to yield its valuable crop and how patient he is for the autumn and spring rains. [8]You too, be patient and stand firm, because the Lord's coming is near. [9]Don't grumble against each other, brothers, or you will be judged. The Judge is standing at the door!

[10]Brothers, as an example of patience in the face of suffering, take the prophets who spoke in the name of the Lord. [11]As you know, we consider blessed those who have persevered. You have heard of Job's perseverance and have seen what the Lord finally brought about. The Lord is full of compassion and mercy.

[12]Above all, my brothers, do not swear —not by heaven or by earth or by anything else. Let your "Yes" be yes, and your "No", no, or you will be condemned.

The Prayer of Faith

[13]Is any one of you in trouble? He should pray. Is anyone happy? Let him sing songs of praise. [14]Is any one of you sick? He should call the elders of the church to pray over him and anoint him with oil in the name of the Lord. [15]And the prayer offered in faith will make the sick person well; the Lord will raise him up. If he has sinned, he will be forgiven. [16]Therefore confess your sins to each other and pray for each other so that you may be healed. The prayer of a righteous man is powerful and effective.

[17]Elijah was a man just like us. He prayed earnestly that it would not rain, and it did not rain on the land for three and a half years. [18]Again he prayed, and the heavens gave rain, and the earth produced its crops.

[19]My brothers, if one of you should wander from the truth and someone should bring him back, [20]remember this: Whoever turns a sinner from the error of his way will save him from death and cover over a multitude of sins.

---

[a]5 Or yourselves as in a day of feasting

'Brothers, do not slander one another. Anyone who speaks against his brother or judges him speaks against the law and judges it . . . There is only one Lawgiver and Judge, the one who is able to save and destroy' (vv. 11a, 12a).

THE BASIC REQUIREMENT of God's law is to love one another, that is, to seek the other person's good. Today we see that slander is at the root of man's denial of God's law. Whenever we condemn another person unjustly; whenever we seek to 'put them down' with sarcasm or cruel comment; whenever we talk without full knowledge of the facts, we are denying God's law. By taking upon ourselves the task of condemnation, we are seizing hold of what belongs to God.

No judge worthy of the name attempts to pass judgement until all the facts are known. Human knowledge of course is limited, so a judge has to make the best possible decision in the circumstances, always aware that a ruling may be imperfect, always recognizing with humility the defects of human wisdom.

Slander bypasses all these limitations. It is deceitful, claiming knowledge where knowledge is lacking. It is malicious, making no attempt to look for the good. It is harmful to the slanderer as well as to his victim, for it blunts the edge of compassion. It makes people blind to the feelings of others. Slanderous comment is eagerly sought by those who wish to feel more righteous than their betters. Slander sells newspapers, but it eats away at the heart of human society. It destroys, instead of building, and cheapens us all by its insidious influence.

Slander involves others in sin. Those who hear become tainted as much as those who speak.

→1146

'Is any one of you in trouble? He should pray. Is anyone happy? Let him sing songs of praise. Is any one of you sick? He should call the elders of the church to pray over him' (vv. 13, 14a).

JACOB'S BLESSING ON JOSEPH is too long to quote here as it stands. It has in it many of the elements of prayer. Jacob describes the help which comes from God in times of trouble. He states that Joseph will remain steady and strong because his mind is fixed on God who is the mighty one, the shepherd and the rock of Israel. And Jacob praises God for the blessings which will come to Joseph against the background of his trouble.

Here in James, too, we are encouraged to pray in times of trouble. Sometimes trouble embitters people and prevents them calling on God at all. But in many cases trouble leads people to call on God who would not normally do so – even if the calling is sometimes more by way of abuse than of request for strength to cope with the trouble. Whether we praise or complain, the main thing is to focus our attention on God.

When we are happy, too, we must pray. Praise is prayer. That is often harder for many people. They tend to think, albeit sometimes subconsciously, that happiness comes from their own achievement. The truly prayerful person realizes this is not so and praises God for happiness too.

Finally, in sickness, prayer is imperative. It may be a prayer for healing. It may be a prayer for spiritual strength to cope with illness. It may be the tortured prayer of the mentally ill. Whatever it is, sharing in prayer with the one who is sick is part of the ministry of every Christian, and of the Church as a whole.

Trouble, joy and sickness are all incentives to pray.

→1149

1 Peter

1 Peter, an apostle of Jesus Christ,

To God's elect, strangers in the world, scattered throughout Pontus, Galatia, Cappadocia, Asia and Bithynia, ²who have been chosen according to the foreknowledge of God the Father, through the sanctifying work of the Spirit, for obedience to Jesus Christ and sprinkling by his blood:

Grace and peace be yours in abundance.

Praise to God for a Living Hope

³Praise be to the God and Father of our Lord Jesus Christ! In his great mercy he has given us new birth into a living hope through the resurrection of Jesus Christ from the dead, ⁴and into an inheritance that can never perish, spoil or fade—kept in heaven for you, ⁵who through faith are shielded by God's power until the coming of the salvation that is ready to be revealed in the last time. ⁶In this you greatly rejoice, though now for a little while you may have had to suffer grief in all kinds of trials. ⁷These have come so that your faith—of greater worth than gold, which perishes even though refined by fire—may be proved genuine and may result in praise, glory and honour when Jesus Christ is revealed. ⁸Though you have not seen him, you love him; and even though you do not see him now, you believe in him and are filled with an inexpressible and glorious joy, ⁹for you are receiving the goal of your faith, the salvation of your souls.

¹⁰Concerning this salvation, the prophets, who spoke of the grace that was to come to you, searched intently and with the greatest care, ¹¹trying to find out the time and circumstances to which the Spirit of Christ in them was pointing when he predicted the sufferings of Christ and the glories that would follow. ¹²It was revealed to them that they were not serving themselves but you, when they spoke of the things that have now been told you by those who have preached the gospel to you by the Holy Spirit sent from heaven. Even angels long to look into these things.

Be Holy

¹³Therefore, prepare your minds for action; be self-controlled; set your hope fully on the grace to be given you when Jesus Christ is revealed. ¹⁴As obedient children, do not conform to the evil desires you had when you lived in ignorance. ¹⁵But just as he who called you is holy, so be holy in all you do; ¹⁶for it is written: "Be holy, because I am holy."ᵃ

¹⁷Since you call on a Father who judges each man's work impartially, live your lives as strangers here in reverent fear. ¹⁸For you know that it was not with perishable things such as silver or gold that you were redeemed from the empty way of life handed down to you from your forefathers, ¹⁹but with the precious blood of Christ, a lamb without blemish or defect. ²⁰He was chosen before the creation of the world, but was revealed in these last times for your sake. ²¹Through him you believe in God, who raised him from the dead and glorified him, and so your faith and hope are in God.

²²Now that you have purified yourselves by obeying the truth so that you have sincere love for your brothers, love one another deeply, from the heart.ᵇ ²³For you have been born again, not of perishable seed, but of imperishable, through the living and enduring word of God. ²⁴For,

"All men are like grass,
    and all their glory is like the flowers of
        the field;
the grass withers and the flowers fall,
25   but the word of the Lord stands for
        ever."ᶜ

And this is the word that was preached to you.

2 Therefore, rid yourselves of all malice and all deceit, hypocrisy, envy, and slander of every kind. ²Like newborn babies, crave pure spiritual milk, so that by it you may grow up in your salvation, ³now that you have tasted that the Lord is good.

The Living Stone and a Chosen People

⁴As you come to him, the living Stone —rejected by men but chosen by God and precious to him—⁵you also, like living stones, are being built into a spiritual house to be a holy priesthood, offering spiritual sacrifices acceptable to God through Jesus Christ. ⁶For in Scripture it says:

ᵃ16 Lev. 11:44,45; 19:2; 20:7   ᵇ22 Some early manuscripts *from a pure heart*   ᶜ25 Isaiah 40:6–8

"See, I lay a stone in Zion,
  a chosen and precious cornerstone,
and the one who trusts in him
  will never be put to shame."[a]

7Now to you who believe, this stone is
precious. But to those who do not believe,

"The stone the builders rejected
  has become the capstone,"[b,c]

8and,

"A stone that causes men to stumble
  and a rock that makes them fall."[d]

They stumble because they disobey the
message—which is also what they were destined for.

9But you are a chosen people, a royal
priesthood, a holy nation, a people belonging
to God, that you may declare the praises
of him who called you out of darkness into
his wonderful light. 10Once you were not a
people, but now you are the people of God;
once you had not received mercy, but now
you have received mercy.

11Dear friends, I urge you, as aliens and
strangers in the world, to abstain from sinful
desires, which war against your soul. 12Live
such good lives among the pagans that,
though they accuse you of doing wrong, they
may see your good deeds and glorify God on
the day he visits us.

Submission to Rulers and Masters

13Submit yourselves for the Lord's sake to
every authority instituted among men:
whether to the king, as the supreme authority, 14or to governors, who are sent by him to
punish those who do wrong and to commend
those who do right. 15For it is God's will that
by doing good you should silence the ignorant talk of foolish men. 16Live as free men,
but do not use your freedom as a cover-up for
evil; live as servants of God. 17Show proper
respect to everyone: Love the brotherhood
of believers, fear God, honour the king.

18Slaves, submit yourselves to your masters with all respect, not only to those who
are good and considerate, but also to those
who are harsh. 19For it is commendable if a
man bears up under the pain of unjust suffering because he is conscious of God. 20But
how is it to your credit if you receive a
beating for doing wrong and endure it? But if
you suffer for doing good and you endure it,
this is commendable before God. 21To this
you were called, because Christ suffered for
you, leaving you an example, that you should
follow in his steps.

22"He committed no sin,
  and no deceit was found in his mouth."[e]

23When they hurled their insults at him, he
did not retaliate; when he suffered, he made
no threats. Instead, he entrusted himself to

him who judges justly. 24He himself bore our
sins in his body on the tree, so that we might
die to sins and live for righteousness; by his
wounds you have been healed. 25For you
were like sheep going astray, but now you
have returned to the Shepherd and Overseer
of your souls.

Wives and Husbands

3 Wives, in the same way be submissive to
  your husbands so that, if any of them do
not believe the word, they may be won over
without words by the behaviour of their
wives, 2when they see the purity and reverence of your lives. 3Your beauty should not
come from outward adornment, such as
braided hair and the wearing of gold jewellery and fine clothes. 4Instead, it should be
that of your inner self, the unfading beauty of
a gentle and quiet spirit, which is of great
worth in God's sight. 5For this is the way the
holy women of the past who put their hope in
God used to make themselves beautiful.
They were submissive to their own husbands, 6like Sarah, who obeyed Abraham
and called him her master. You are her
daughters if you do what is right and do not
give way to fear.

7Husbands, in the same way be considerate as you live with your wives, and treat
them with respect as the weaker partner and
as heirs with you of the gracious gift of life, so
that nothing will hinder your prayers.

Suffering for Doing Good

8Finally, all of you, live in harmony with
one another; be sympathetic, love as
brothers, be compassionate and humble. 9Do
not repay evil with evil or insult with insult,
but with blessing, because to this you were
called so that you may inherit a blessing.
10For,

"Whoever would love life
  and see good days
must keep his tongue from evil
  and his lips from deceitful speech.
11He must turn from evil and do good;
  he must seek peace and pursue it.
12For the eyes of the Lord are on the
  righteous
  and his ears are attentive to their prayer,
but the face of the Lord is against those
  who do evil."[a]

13Who is going to harm you if you are eager
to do good? 14But even if you should suffer
for what is right, you are blessed. "Do not
fear what they fear[b]; do not be frightened."[c]
15But in your hearts set apart Christ as Lord.
Always be prepared to give an answer to
everyone who asks you to give the reason for
the hope that you have. But do this with
gentleness and respect, 16keeping a clear
conscience, so that those who speak maliciously against your good behaviour in
Christ may be ashamed of their slander. 17It
is better, if it is God's will, to suffer for doing

---

[a]6 Isaiah 28:16   [b]7 Or cornerstone   [c]7 Psalm 118:22   [d]8 Isaiah 8:14   [e]22 Isaiah 53:9
[a]12 Psalm 34:12–16   [b]14 Or not fear their threats   [c]14 Isaiah 8:12

'Just as he who called you is holy, so be holy in all you do; for it is written: "Be holy, because I am holy" ' (v. 15).

CHRISTIANITY is a matter of relationship, rather than one of authority. God does not simply say to us 'Do what I say, because I say so.' Instead he calls us into relationship with him and asks us to be holy, because he is holy. He identified with us by sending his Son to die for us. In turn, he asks us to identify with him completely, and commit ourselves to him.

Being holy is a matter of relationship, not in mindless fashion, but with careful thought. Peter calls on his readers to prepare their minds. Reasoned argument is no substitute for a close relationship with God – but close relationship does not rule out argument. We use our minds as well as our emotions in this commitment to our Lord. We react to him. We question him. We entreat him. We may even, like the prophets of old, argue with him. But whatever else we do, being holy means committing ourselves to him alone.

Tim Lenton writes

If commitment is not first and only to God, it is worse than useless. Indeed, a commitment to something else – *even if it is something closely associated to God* – is a block and a substitute. It is not only traditionalists who fall prey to it. We can be equally wrongly committed to, say, using guitars in worship, to much speaking in tongues, to dance or drama. It is not a question of old and new, tradition and innovations. It is not, as many churchmen seem to think, a question of adding or taking away, and so losing the essence of worship. It is a question of idolatry. If we commit ourselves to anything less than God, we are not nearly there. We are very, very far away.

Lord, keep us close to you in every way. Keep our spirits sensitive to your leading, and our minds alert to your demands.

→1150

1 PETER 2:1–5

'Like newborn babes, crave pure spiritual milk . . . like living stones, are being built into a spiritual house to be a holy priesthood, offering spiritual sacrifices acceptable to God through Jesus Christ' (vv. 2a, 5b).

TOGETHERNESS IN THE GOSPEL would be a fitting title for Peter's letter. Over and again he stresses the need for Christians to work together, and his illustrations often spell out the fact that solitary Christianity is a contradiction in terms.

The initial craving for spiritual milk may appear to be a solitary process – but milk can only come where someone is on hand to provide it. As the spiritual experience of the Christian grows, the metaphors of togetherness increase. One stone on its own is useless. To build a spiritual house it is necessary for the bricks, the living stones, to come together. Only then can a vital structure, a vibrant community, be built.

A priest is one who mediates. Priesthood implies bringing together. The Latin word for priest, *pontifex*, means a bridge builder. That sums up the priestly function – to build a bridge between people and God. Every Christian is a priest. Every Christian has the spiritual responsibility to be a bridge between others and God. It is not something we can leave to a select few. We are all in it together. There is no longer a separate caste of priests, as under the old dispensation. Peter teaches that the holy priesthood is a spiritual priesthood, involving the whole Christian community.

The spiritual sacrifice we offer to God involves sacrificing our own desires, our own ambitions, our own thoughts and feelings. It involves handing them over to God, for him to use on behalf of others. This spiritual sacrifice is made by men and women alike. All are priests.

→1153

good than for doing evil. [18]For Christ died for sins once for all, the righteous for the unrighteous, to bring you to God. He was put to death in the body but made alive by the Spirit, [19]through whom[d] also he went and preached to the spirits in prison [20]who disobeyed long ago when God waited patiently in the days of Noah while the ark was being built. In it only a few people, eight in all, were saved through water, [21]and this water symbolises baptism that now saves you also—not the removal of dirt from the body but the pledge[e] of a good conscience towards God. It saves you by the resurrection of Jesus Christ, [22]who has gone into heaven and is at God's right hand—with angels, authorities and powers in submission to him.

Living for God

4 Therefore, since Christ suffered in his body, arm yourselves also with the same attitude, because he who has suffered in his body is done with sin. [2]As a result, he does not live the rest of his earthly life for evil human desires, but rather for the will of God. [3]For you have spent enough time in the past doing what pagans choose to do—living in debauchery, lust, drunkenness, orgies, carousing and detestable idolatry. [4]They think it strange that you do not plunge with them into the same flood of dissipation, and they heap abuse on you. [5]But they will have to give account to him who is ready to judge the living and the dead. [6]For this is the reason the gospel was preached even to those who are now dead, so that they might be judged according to men in regard to the body, but live according to God in regard to the spirit.

[7]The end of all things is near. Therefore be clear minded and self-controlled so that you can pray. [8]Above all, love each other deeply, because love covers over a multitude of sins. [9]Offer hospitality to one another without grumbling. [10]Each one should use whatever gift he has received to serve others, faithfully administering God's grace in its various forms. [11]If anyone speaks, he should do it as one speaking the very words of God. If anyone serves, he should do it with the strength God provides, so that in all things God may be praised through Jesus Christ. To him be the glory and the power for ever and ever. Amen.

Suffering for Being a Christian

[12]Dear friends, do not be surprised at the painful trial you are suffering, as though something strange were happening to you. [13]But rejoice that you participate in the sufferings of Christ, so that you may be overjoyed when his glory is revealed. [14]If you are insulted because of the name of Christ, you are blessed, for the Spirit of glory and of God rests on you. [15]If you suffer, it should not be as a murderer or thief or any other kind of criminal, or even as a meddler. [16]However, if you suffer as a Christian, do not be ashamed, but praise God that you bear that name. [17]For it is time for judgment to begin with the family of God; and if it begins with us, what will the outcome be for those who do not obey the gospel of God? [18]And,

"If it is hard for the righteous to be saved,
　　what will become of the ungodly and the
　　　sinner?"[a]

[19]So then, those who suffer according to God's will should commit themselves to their faithful Creator and continue to do good.

To Elders and Young Men

5 To the elders among you, I appeal as a fellow-elder, a witness of Christ's sufferings and one who also will share in the glory to be revealed: [2]Be shepherds of God's flock that is under your care, serving as overseers—not because you must, but because you are willing, as God wants you to be; not greedy for money, but eager to serve; [3]not lording it over those entrusted to you, but being examples to the flock. [4]And when the Chief Shepherd appears, you will receive the crown of glory that will never fade away.

[5]Young men, in the same way be submissive to those who are older. All of you, clothe yourselves with humility towards one another, because,

"God opposes the proud
　　but gives grace to the humble."[a]

[6]Humble yourselves, therefore, under God's mighty hand, that he may lift you up in due time. [7]Cast all your anxiety on him because he cares for you.

[8]Be self-controlled and alert. Your enemy the devil prowls around like a roaring lion looking for someone to devour. [9]Resist him, standing firm in the faith, because you know that your brothers throughout the world are undergoing the same kind of sufferings.

[10]And the God of all grace, who called you to his eternal glory in Christ, after you have suffered a little while, will himself restore you and make you strong, firm and steadfast. [11]To him be the power for ever and ever. Amen.

Final Greetings

[12]With the help of Silas,[b] whom I regard as a faithful brother, I have written to you briefly, encouraging you and testifying that this is the true grace of God. Stand fast in it.

[13]She who is in Babylon, chosen together with you, sends you her greetings, and so does my son Mark. [14]Greet one another with a kiss of love.

Peace to all of you who are in Christ.

---

d18,19 Or alive in the spirit, [19]*through which*　　*e21 Or response*
[a]*18 Prov. 11:31*　　[a]*5 Prov. 3:34*　　[b]*12 Greek Silvanus, a variant of Silas*

2 Peter

1 Simon Peter, a servant and apostle of Jesus Christ,

To those who through the righteousness of our God and Saviour Jesus Christ have received a faith as precious as ours:

²Grace and peace be yours in abundance through the knowledge of God and of Jesus our Lord.

Making One's Calling and Election Sure

³His divine power has given us everything we need for life and godliness through our knowledge of him who called us by his own glory and goodness. ⁴Through these he has given us his very great and precious promises, so that through them you may participate in the divine nature and escape the corruption in the world caused by evil desires.

⁵For this very reason, make every effort to add to your faith goodness; and to goodness, knowledge; ⁶and to knowledge, self-control; and to self-control, perseverance; and to perseverance, godliness; ⁷and to godliness, brotherly kindness; and to brotherly kindness, love. ⁸For if you possess these qualities in increasing measure, they will keep you from being ineffective and unproductive in your knowledge of our Lord Jesus Christ. ⁹But if anyone does not have them, he is short-sighted and blind, and has forgotten that he has been cleansed from his past sins.

¹⁰Therefore, my brothers, be all the more eager to make your calling and election sure. For if you do these things, you will never fall, ¹¹and you will receive a rich welcome into the eternal kingdom of our Lord and Saviour Jesus Christ.

Prophecy of Scripture

¹²So I will always remind you of these things, even though you know them and are firmly established in the truth you now have. ¹³I think it is right to refresh your memory as long as I live in the tent of this body, ¹⁴because I know that I will soon put it aside, as our Lord Jesus Christ has made clear to me. ¹⁵And I will make every effort to see that after my departure you will always be able to remember these things.

¹⁶We did not follow cleverly invented stories when we told you about the power and coming of our Lord Jesus Christ, but we were eye-witnesses of his majesty. ¹⁷For he received honour and glory from God the Father when the voice came to him from the Majestic Glory, saying, "This is my Son, whom I love; with him I am well pleased."[a] ¹⁸We ourselves heard this voice that came from heaven when we were with him on the sacred mountain.

¹⁹And we have the word of the prophets made more certain, and you will do well to pay attention to it, as to a light shining in a dark place, until the day dawns and the morning star rises in your hearts. ²⁰Above all, you must understand that no prophecy of Scripture came about by the prophet's own interpretation. ²¹For prophecy never had its origin in the will of man, but men spoke from God as they were carried along by the Holy Spirit.

False Teachers and Their Destruction

2 But there were also false prophets among the people, just as there will be false teachers among you. They will secretly introduce destructive heresies, even denying the sovereign Lord who bought them—bringing swift destruction on themselves. ²Many will follow their shameful ways and will bring the way of truth into disrepute. ³In their greed these teachers will exploit you with stories they have made up. Their condemnation has long been hanging over them, and their destruction has not been sleeping.

⁴For if God did not spare angels when they sinned, but sent them to hell,[a] putting them into gloomy dungeons[b] to be held for judgment; ⁵if he did not spare the ancient world when he brought the flood on its ungodly people, but protected Noah, a preacher of righteousness, and seven others; ⁶if he condemned the cities of Sodom and Gomorrah by burning them to ashes, and made them an example of what is going to happen to the ungodly; ⁷and if he rescued Lot, a righteous man, who was distressed by the filthy lives of lawless men ⁸(for that righteous man, living among them day after day, was tormented in his righteous soul by the lawless deeds he saw and heard)—⁹if this is so, then the Lord

---

a17 Matt. 17:5; Mark 9:7; Luke 9:35   *a4* Greek *Tartarus*   *b4* Some manuscripts *into chains of darkness*

1 PETER 5:8–11

'Your enemy the devil prowls around like a roaring lion . . . Resist him, standing firm in the faith, because you know that your brothers throughout the world are undergoing the same kind of sufferings' (vv. 8b, 9).

REMEMBER, THERE'S ALWAYS somebody worse off than you are. How annoying those words can be. Very often we want to feel that we're badly done to, and that our problems really are greater than those of other people. Sometimes it is a comfort to think that we are coping with more than the next person has to endure. We get a kind of inverted pride in managing our adverse circumstances, sometimes even in managing them alone.

Yet how comforting it is also to know that we are not suffering alone. When we suffer, isolation makes our suffering much, much worse. Many people find strength by joining with other victims. Hence the mushrooming of societies for sufferers of all kinds: battered wives, abused children, victims of cancer, the limbless, the hard of hearing, the aged – the list is endless.

Overcoming isolation was one of the main values of the letters written by early Christians. People like Peter, Paul, the writer to the Hebrews, and others, were able to reassure those who suffered that they were not alone. It was a comfort to know God, in Jesus, was with them – but equally it was a comfort to know that others were holding firm to the faith, despite enormous hardship.

> *Join hands then, brothers of the faith,*
> *Whate'er your race may be;*
> *Who serves my Father as a son*
> *Is surely kin to me.*

(John Oxenham)

→1154

2 PETER 1:12–19

'We did not follow cleverly invented stories when we told you about the power and coming of our Lord Jesus Christ, but we were eye-witnesses of his majesty' (v. 16).

THIS WRITER HAS GOOD REASON to underline some fundamentals of the faith. He lived in an era when some Christians had heard the gospel from those who had known Jesus in the flesh. Those memories shone for them in the darkness of persecution which beset the early Church – though what sustained them was not a distant memory of his physical presence, but the present experience of the Holy Spirit in their lives.

The writer wants his readers to be very clear about the reality of Christ. Jesus had belonged to the world around them; he had been a man of blood and flesh like any other. He had shed real blood when he died, choking for breath just as any other crucified man would. Yet he had been a man unlike any other, a man wholly pleasing to God, a man who rose from the dead. The gospel was no invention. It was the record of eye-witnesses who had seen the Son of God walking and talking with men and women. It was not make-believe.

Today it is equally important that Christians are clear about their faith in Jesus. They must know him, and his suffering and his triumph over death because it is their triumph too (Phil. 3:10).

O God our maker, help us to realize the things that are essential to our faith; the fundamentals to which we must hold at all costs. Yet, even as we determine to be adamant on these, help us also to deal gently with those who shout loudest to hide their own doubts. As we grow stronger, Lord, give us the courage to be meek. Amen.

knows how to rescue godly men from trials and to hold the unrighteous for the day of judgment, while continuing their punishment.*c* ¹⁰This is especially true of those who follow the corrupt desire of the sinful nature*d* and despise authority.

Bold and arrogant, these men are not afraid to slander celestial beings; ¹¹yet even angels, although they are stronger and more powerful, do not bring slanderous accusations against such beings in the presence of the Lord. ¹²But these men blaspheme in matters they do not understand. They are like brute beasts, creatures of instinct, born only to be caught and destroyed, and like beasts they too will perish.

¹³They will be paid back with harm for the harm they have done. Their idea of pleasure is to carouse in broad daylight. They are blots and blemishes, revelling in their pleasures while they feast with you.*e* ¹⁴With eyes full of adultery, they never stop sinning; they seduce the unstable; they are experts in greed—an accursed brood! ¹⁵They have left the straight way and wandered off to follow the way of Balaam son of Beor, who loved the wages of wickedness. ¹⁶But he was rebuked for his wrongdoing by a donkey—a beast without speech—who spoke with a man's voice and restrained the prophet's madness.

¹⁷These men are springs without water and mists driven by a storm. Blackest darkness is reserved for them. ¹⁸For they mouth empty, boastful words and, by appealing to the lustful desires of sinful human nature, they entice people who are just escaping from those who live in error. ¹⁹They promise them freedom, while they themselves are slaves of depravity—for a man is a slave to whatever has mastered him. ²⁰If they have escaped the corruption of the world by knowing our Lord and Saviour Jesus Christ and are again entangled in it and overcome, they are worse off at the end than they were at the beginning. ²¹It would have been better for them not to have known the way of righteousness, than to have known it and then to turn their backs on the sacred command that was passed on to them. ²²Of them the proverbs are true: "A dog returns to its vomit,"*f* and, "A sow that is washed goes back to her wallowing in the mud."

The Day of the Lord

3 Dear friends, this is now my second letter to you. I have written both of them as reminders to stimulate you to wholesome thinking. ²I want you to recall the words spoken in the past by the holy prophets and the command given by our Lord and Saviour through your apostles.

³First of all, you must understand that in the last days scoffers will come, scoffing and following their own evil desires. ⁴They will say, "Where is this 'coming' he promised? Ever since our fathers died, everything goes on as it has since the beginning of creation." ⁵But they deliberately forget that long ago by God's word the heavens existed and the earth was formed out of water and by water. ⁶By these waters also the world of that time was deluged and destroyed. ⁷By the same word the present heavens and earth are reserved for fire, being kept for the day of judgment and destruction of ungodly men.

⁸But do not forget this one thing, dear friends: With the Lord a day is like a thousand years, and a thousand years are like a day. ⁹The Lord is not slow in keeping his promise, as some understand slowness. He is patient with you, not wanting anyone to perish, but everyone to come to repentance.

¹⁰But the day of the Lord will come like a thief. The heavens will disappear with a roar; the elements will be destroyed by fire, and the earth and everything in it will be laid bare.*a*

¹¹Since everything will be destroyed in this way, what kind of people ought you to be? You ought to live holy and godly lives ¹²as you look forward to the day of God and speed its coming.*b* That day will bring about the destruction of the heavens by fire, and the elements will melt in the heat. ¹³But in keeping with his promise we are looking forward to a new heaven and a new earth, the home of righteousness.

¹⁴So then, dear friends, since you are looking forward to this, make every effort to be found spotless, blameless and at peace with him. ¹⁵Bear in mind that our Lord's patience means salvation, just as our dear brother Paul also wrote to you with the wisdom that God gave him. ¹⁶He writes the same way in all his letters, speaking in them of these matters. His letters contain some things that are hard to understand, which ignorant and unstable people distort, as they do the other Scriptures, to their own destruction.

¹⁷Therefore, dear friends, since you already know this, be on your guard so that you may not be carried away by the error of lawless men and fall from your secure position. ¹⁸But grow in the grace and knowledge of our Lord and Saviour Jesus Christ. To him be glory both now and for ever! Amen.

---

*c*9 Or *unrighteous for punishment until the day of judgment*   *d*10 Or *the flesh*
*e*13 Some manuscripts *in their love feasts*   *f*22 Prov. 26:11
*a*10 Some manuscripts *be burned up*   *b*12 Or *as you wait eagerly for the day of God to come*

1 John

The Word of Life

1 That which was from the beginning, which we have heard, which we have seen with our eyes, which we have looked at and our hands have touched—this we proclaim concerning the Word of life. [2]The life appeared; we have seen it and testify to it, and we proclaim to you the eternal life, which was with the Father and has appeared to us. [3]We proclaim to you what we have seen and heard, so that you also may have fellowship with us. And our fellowship is with the Father and with his Son, Jesus Christ. [4]We write this to make our[a] joy complete.

Walking in the Light

[5]This is the message we have heard from him and declare to you: God is light; in him there is no darkness at all. [6]If we claim to have fellowship with him yet walk in the darkness, we lie and do not live by the truth. [7]But if we walk in the light, as he is in the light, we have fellowship with one another, and the blood of Jesus, his Son, purifies us from all[b] sin.

[8]If we claim to be without sin, we deceive ourselves and the truth is not in us. [9]If we confess our sins, he is faithful and just and will forgive us our sins and purify us from all unrighteousness. [10]If we claim we have not sinned, we make him out to be a liar and his word has no place in our lives.

2 My dear children, I write this to you so that you will not sin. But if anybody does sin, we have one who speaks to the Father in our defence—Jesus Christ, the Righteous One. [2]He is the atoning sacrifice for our sins, and not only for ours but also for[a] the sins of the whole world.

[3]We know that we have come to know him if we obey his commands. [4]The man who says, "I know him," but does not do what he commands is a liar, and the truth is not in him. [5]But if anyone obeys his word, God's love[b] is truly made complete in him. This is how we know we are in him: [6]Whoever claims to live in him must walk as Jesus did.

[7]Dear friends, I am not writing you a new command but an old one, which you have had since the beginning. This old command is the message you have heard. [8]Yet I am writing you a new command; its truth is seen in him and you, because the darkness is passing and the true light is already shining.

[9]Anyone who claims to be in the light but hates his brother is still in the darkness. [10]Whoever loves his brother lives in the light, and there is nothing in him[c] to make him stumble. [11]But whoever hates his brother is in the darkness and walks around in the darkness; he does not know where he is going, because the darkness has blinded him.

[12]I write to you, dear children,
    because your sins have been forgiven on
        account of his name.
[13]I write to you, fathers,
    because you have known him who is
        from the beginning.
I write to you, young men,
    because you have overcome the evil
        one.
I write to you, dear children,
    because you have known the Father.
[14]I write to you, fathers,
    because you have known him who is
        from the beginning.
I write to you, young men,
    because you are strong,
    and the word of God lives in you,
    and you have overcome the evil one.

Do Not Love the World

[15]Do not love the world or anything in the world. If anyone loves the world, the love of the Father is not in him. [16]For everything in the world—the cravings of sinful man, the lust of his eyes and the boasting of what he has and does—comes not from the Father but from the world. [17]The world and its desires pass away, but the man who does the will of God lives for ever.

Warning Against Antichrists

[18]Dear children, this is the last hour; and as you have heard that the antichrist is coming, even now many antichrists have come. This is how we know it is the last hour. [19]They went out from us, but they did not really belong to us. For if they had belonged to us,

---

a4 Some manuscripts *your*   *b7* Or *every*
a2 Or *He is the one who turns aside God's wrath, taking away our sins, and not only ours but also*
b5 Or *word, love for God*   *c10* Or *it*

2 PETER 3:17, 18
'Grow in the grace and knowledge of our Lord and Saviour Jesus Christ' (v. 18).

EASTERN CHRISTIANS make icons of Jesus. The pictorial representations of the Saviour are works of art and making them takes many hours of hard work.

Growing in holiness requires the dedication that an artist gives to his work. The Christian is trying, by God's grace, to create an icon of Jesus in living flesh. The representation will never be what the original is, but it will bear a likeness to the original. That likeness comes only after many hours of living for God, of constantly asking, 'What would Jesus do here? What would he say?'

Yet, without the touch of the Holy Spirit, and the indwelling of the Holy Spirit, all the labour and love will be in vain. Human beings cannot make *themselves* holy. They need the creative power of the Holy Spirit in their lives if they are to achieve Christ–likeness. So they must seek the Spirit's presence in their lives if they are to grow to be like Jesus. The Spirit will not force himself on anyone. He goes only where he is invited, and stays only where he is wanted and as long as he is wanted.

His work is both instant and constant. In a moment he cleanses and makes holy; yet at the end of the longest lifetime the believer still has more to learn of Jesus.

> *To be like Jesus!*
> *This hope possesses me.*
> *His Spirit helping me,*
> *Like him I'll be.*

(John Gowans)

→1158

1 JOHN 1:5–10; 2:9

'God is light . . . if we walk in the light, as he is in the light, we have fellowship with one another, and the blood of Jesus, his Son, purifies us from all sin' (vv. 5b, 7).

KOINONIA, FELLOWSHIP, is a beautiful word. It means sharing together in love, sharing the gospel, sharing friendship, sharing resources – all are covered by the word *koinonia*. It is one of those words which a number of Christians use in its Greek original to indicate a depth of feeling that they think the simple English word 'fellowship' lacks. *Koinonia* is also the word used for the relationship of marriage. Husband and wife share together completely.

We don't need to go round using Greek words, but we do need to practise the kind of deep, caring love which this word conveys. That is only possible when we walk in the light of God. God sheds light on the Christian community and on each individual Christian. It is not just an intellectual light. It is not an idea which simply stays in the mind. It is a practical light which results in fellowship between Christians, then flows outwards into the community at large.

A recent survey in Norway showed that people who claimed to be Christian were more likely to condemn the lifestyle of their neighbours, and they were less likely to accept anyone with a criminal record as a neighbour, than those who did not claim allegiance to Christ. Either there was something very wrong with the survey, or very wrong with the 'Christians' they interviewed.

Theoretical Christianity is no Christianity at all.

'Anyone who claims to be in the light but hates his brother is still in the darkness' (2:9).

→1161

they would have remained with us; but their going showed that none of them belonged to us. ²⁰But you have an anointing from the Holy One, and all of you know the truth.*d* ²¹I do not write to you because you do not know the truth, but because you do know it and because no lie comes from the truth. ²²Who is the liar? It is the man who denies that Jesus is the Christ. Such a man is the antichrist—he denies the Father and the Son. ²³No-one who denies the Son has the Father; whoever acknowledges the Son has the Father also.

²⁴See that what you have heard from the beginning remains in you. If it does, you also will remain in the Son and in the Father. ²⁵And this is what he promised us—even eternal life.

²⁶I am writing these things to you about those who are trying to lead you astray. ²⁷As for you, the anointing you received from him remains in you, and you do not need anyone to teach you. But as his anointing teaches you about all things and as that anointing is real, not counterfeit—just as it has taught you, remain in him.

Children of God

²⁸And now, dear children, continue in him, so that when he appears we may be confident and unashamed before him at his coming.

²⁹If you know that he is righteous, you know that everyone who does what is right has been born of him.

3 How great is the love the Father has lavished on us, that we should be called children of God! And that is what we are! The reason the world does not know us is that it did not know him. ²Dear friends, now we are children of God, and what we will be has not yet been made known. But we know that when he appears,*a* we shall be like him, for we shall see him as he is. ³Everyone who has this hope in him purifies himself, just as he is pure.

⁴Everyone who sins breaks the law; in fact, sin is lawlessness. ⁵But you know that he appeared so that he might take away our sins. And in him is no sin. ⁶No-one who lives in him keeps on sinning. No-one who continues to sin has either seen him or known him.

⁷Dear children, do not let anyone lead you astray. He who does what is right is righteous, just as he is righteous. ⁸He who does what is sinful is of the devil, because the devil has been sinning from the beginning. The reason the Son of God appeared was to destroy the devil's work. ⁹No-one who is born of God will continue to sin, because God's seed remains in him; he cannot go on sinning, because he has been born of God. ¹⁰This is how we know who the children of God are and who the children of the devil are: Anyone who does not do what is right is not a child of God; nor is anyone who does not love his brother.

Love One Another

¹¹This is the message you heard from the beginning: We should love one another. ¹²Do not be like Cain, who belonged to the evil one and murdered his brother. And why did he murder him? Because his own actions were evil and his brother's were righteous. ¹³Do not be surprised, my brothers, if the world hates you. ¹⁴We know that we have passed from death to life, because we love our brothers. Anyone who does not love remains in death. ¹⁵Anyone who hates his brother is a murderer, and you know that no murderer has eternal life in him.

¹⁶This is how we know what love is: Jesus Christ laid down his life for us. And we ought to lay down our lives for our brothers. ¹⁷If anyone has material possessions and sees his brother in need but has no pity on him, how can the love of God be in him? ¹⁸Dear children, let us not love with words or tongue but with actions and in truth. ¹⁹This then is how we know that we belong to the truth, and how we set our hearts at rest in his presence ²⁰whenever our hearts condemn us. For God is greater than our hearts, and he knows everything.

²¹Dear friends, if our hearts do not condemn us, we have confidence before God ²²and receive from him anything we ask, because we obey his commands and do what pleases him. ²³And this is his command: to believe in the name of his Son, Jesus Christ, and to love one another as he commanded us. ²⁴Those who obey his commands live in him, and he in them. And this is how we know that he lives in us: We know it by the Spirit he gave us.

Test the Spirits

4 Dear friends, do not believe every spirit, but test the spirits to see whether they are from God, because many false prophets have gone out into the world. ²This is how you can recognise the Spirit of God: Every spirit that acknowledges that Jesus Christ has come in the flesh is from God, ³but every spirit that does not acknowledge Jesus is not from God. This is the spirit of the antichrist, which you have heard is coming and even now is already in the world.

⁴You, dear children, are from God and have overcome them, because the one who is in you is greater than the one who is in the world. ⁵They are from the world and therefore speak from the viewpoint of the world, and the world listens to them. ⁶We are from God, and whoever knows God listens to us; but whoever is not from God does not listen to us. This is how we recognise the Spirit*a* of truth and the spirit of falsehood.

God's Love and Ours

⁷Dear friends, let us love one another, for love comes from God. Everyone who loves has been born of God and knows God. ⁸Whoever does not love does not know God, because God is love. ⁹This is how God showed his love among us: He sent his one

---

*d*20 Some manuscripts *and you know all things*   *a*2 Or *when it is made known*   *a*6 Or *spirit* and only Son[b] into the world that we might live through him. [10]This is love: not that we loved God, but that he loved us and sent his Son as an atoning sacrifice for[c] our sins. [11]Dear friends, since God so loved us, we also ought to love one another. [12]No-one has ever seen God; but if we love one another, God lives in us and his love is made complete in us.

[13]We know that we live in him and he in us, because he has given us of his Spirit. [14]And we have seen and testify that the Father has sent his Son to be the Saviour of the world. [15]If anyone acknowledges that Jesus is the Son of God, God lives in him and he in God. [16]And so we know and rely on the love God has for us.

God is love. Whoever lives in love lives in God, and God in him. [17]In this way, love is made complete among us so that we will have confidence on the day of judgment, because in this world we are like him. [18]There is no fear in love. But perfect love drives out fear, because fear has to do with punishment. The one who fears is not made perfect in love.

[19]We love because he first loved us. [20]If anyone says, "I love God," yet hates his brother, he is a liar. For anyone who does not love his brother, whom he has seen, cannot love God, whom he has not seen. [21]And he has given us this command: Whoever loves God must also love his brother.

Faith in the Son of God

5 Everyone who believes that Jesus is the Christ is born of God, and everyone who loves the father loves his child as well. [2]This is how we know that we love the children of God: by loving God and carrying out his commands. [3]This is love for God: to obey his commands. And his commands are not burdensome, [4]for everyone born of God overcomes the world. This is the victory that has overcome the world, even our faith. [5]Who is it that overcomes the world? Only he who believes that Jesus is the Son of God.

[6]This is the one who came by water and blood—Jesus Christ. He did not come by water only, but by water and blood. And it is the Spirit who testifies, because the Spirit is the truth. [7]For there are three that testify: [8]the[a] Spirit, the water and the blood; and the three are in agreement. [9]We accept man's testimony, but God's testimony is greater because it is the testimony of God, which he has given about his Son. [10]Anyone who believes in the Son of God has this testimony in his heart. Anyone who does not believe God has made him out to be a liar, because he has not believed the testimony God has given about his Son. [11]And this is the testimony: God has given us eternal life, and this life is in his Son. [12]He who has the Son has life; he who does not have the Son of God does not have life.

Concluding Remarks

[13]I write these things to you who believe in the name of the Son of God so that you may know that you have eternal life. [14]This is the confidence we have in approaching God: that if we ask anything according to his will, he hears us. [15]And if we know that he hears us—whatever we ask—we know that we have what we asked of him.

[16]If anyone sees his brother commit a sin that does not lead to death, he should pray and God will give him life. I refer to those whose sin does not lead to death. There is a sin that leads to death. I am not saying that he should pray about that. [17]All wrongdoing is sin, and there is sin that does not lead to death.

[18]We know that anyone born of God does not continue to sin; the one who was born of God keeps him safe, and the evil one cannot harm him. [19]We know that we are children of God, and that the whole world is under the control of the evil one. [20]We know also that the Son of God has come and has given us understanding, so that we may know him who is true. And we are in him who is true —even in his Son Jesus Christ. He is the true God and eternal life.

[21]Dear children, keep yourselves from idols.

---

[b]9 Or *his only begotten Son*   [c]10 Or *as the one who would turn aside his wrath, taking away*
[a]7, 8 Late manuscripts of the Vulgate *testify in heaven: the Father, the Word and the Holy Spirit, and these three are one.* [8]*And there are three that testify on earth: the* (not found in any Greek manuscript before the sixteenth century)

1 JOHN 3:11-18
'Dear children, let us not love with words or tongue but with actions and in truth' (v. 18).

DOING THE TRUTH, not just speaking it, is characteristic of John. His favourite words are about ideas like 'word' and 'knowledge,' but ideas are only of value if they help us to cope with the reality around us. Doing the truth, acting sincerely with a pure motivation, is so much more important than making sure that every idea is grammatically defined and exactly expressed.

Truth for its own sake has little place in John's world. Truth is there in order to bring us into relationship with God and with our fellows. For all its poetic beauty, for all the power of its ideas, John's work is very practical.

It is as practical as the work of someone like Einstein whose complicated theories look like mathematical truth for its own sake. But their practical applications are felt over and over and over again with every new exploration into space. If truth is present it is not usually long before it becomes apparent in practice. However, the human mind is so intricate, and reality itself is so complex, that words and ideas can often be used to deceive. This is as true in the field of morality and religion as anywhere else. How urgently we need the truthful spirit of Christ.

> *Truthful Spirit, dwell with me;*
> *I myself would truthful be,*
> *And with wisdom kind and clear*
> *Let thy life in mine appear;*
> *And with actions brotherly*
> *Speak my Lord's sincerity.*

> (*Thomas Toke Lynch*)

→1162

1 JOHN 4:19–21
'If anyone says, "I love God," yet hates his brother, he is a liar' (v. 20a).

THIS IS A DIFFICULT PASSAGE. It sounds so simple. If you don't love your brother, who you can see, how can you love God, who is unseen? But do things actually work like that? Isn't it often easier to love something unseen than to love something we are in contact with all the time?

When we see things, or people, we see their imperfections. Their annoying ways grate on us. The sounds they make, particularly in these days of powerful hi-fi, may drive us to distraction. The hurt they inflict by unkind comment may drive us to tears. The litter they throw may disgust us. The greed that they show may disillusion us. Their violence may terrify us.

All manner of unpleasant characteristics, real or imagined, may turn me off my fellows. How, then, can John say we can't love God unless we love our brother also? Surely it can't mean that God is like these unpleasant people that we are supposed to love?

That would be getting things the wrong way round. We love God *because* God first loved us. So if we say we love God, the love we claim to have must surely be something like his love. That love is shown to us in spite of everything that we do and did to him. However unpleasant we are, God still loves us. He is still concerned for us. He still reaches out to us. If we have any understanding of what that love is like, then we will do the same to other people, no matter how wicked, unpleasant or downright disgusting they are.

Our love for God is unseen. The only way it can be made visible is by the way that we treat others.

→1163

1 JOHN 5:1–8

'He did not come by water only, but by water and blood . . . For there are three that testify: the Spirit, the water and the blood; and the three are in agreement' (vv. 6b, 7, 8).

FALSE DOCTRINE was never far away in the early Church. One of the commonest heresies involved believing that it was impossible for God to suffer.

This led people to consider that divinity descended on Jesus at his baptism, and left him *before* his crucifixion. John insists such a view is mistaken. The blood, that is the suffering of Jesus, is as necessary as the water, which is associated with the descent of the Spirit on Jesus.

If God in Christ Jesus did not suffer, how can he share in and redeem our suffering? Bernard Mobbs writes 'A remote, impassive deity can be of no help to suffering, struggling man.'

There are three witnesses to Jesus' divinity: the Spirit, the water and the blood. Jesus shares the Spirit of God. That is evident, but it does not necessarily connect Jesus with us. So John is concerned to emphasize the reality of Jesus' experience. The water reminds us of this. The water indicates not only the rite of baptism, but the fact that Christ shares our real humanity. He was born of water, that is to say, the waters broke at his birth – he experienced real physical birth just like each one of us. And the blood witnesses to the fact that God in Christ suffers with us.

Only the God who enters into man's suffering can redeem it from meaninglessness.

(*Bernard Mobbs*)

→1164

2 JOHN

'And now, dear lady, I am not writing you a new command but one we have had from the beginning. I ask that we love one another' (v. 5).

DEAR LADY, makes this tiny letter sound like a love letter. It could be! In one sense, of course it is. But it is unlikely that John is writing to one individual female. More probably he is writing to a specific church.

We don't know which church. We don't know the occasion. But we do know that there was a particular pastoral difficulty to be dealt with. Fraudulent teachers were going round preaching doctrines which were not true. 2 John is a simple warning not to be taken in by those deceivers.

This letter is written by the same person as 1 John. It is a rare instance where we can all be our own New Testament scholars, and accept with confidence the rightness of our findings. This short, personal letter has all the marks of John's style, vocabulary and method of expression.

But it is not just the second letter of John. It is also second best. I think John wrote it in a hurry, probably just putting down what he could get on one sheet of paper. That would do for the time being. A letter is better than nothing. But how much better to meet the person behind the letter! All writers know that writing is second best. A person's real presence, their true personality, can only be appreciated when we meet them face to face.

We praise you, Lord, for the letters of the New Testament, and for what they reveal to us of the character of your Son. Yet we recognize that they are just second best, not to be compared with the overwhelming experience that awaits us when we meet him face to face.

→1167

2 John

¹The elder,

To the chosen lady and her children, whom I love in the truth—and not I only, but also all who know the truth—²because of the truth, which lives in us and will be with us for ever:

³Grace, mercy and peace from God the Father and from Jesus Christ, the Father's Son, will be with us in truth and love.

⁴It has given me great joy to find some of your children walking in the truth, just as the Father commanded us. ⁵And now, dear lady, I am not writing you a new command but one we have had from the beginning. I ask that we love one another. ⁶And this is love: that we walk in obedience to his commands. As you have heard from the beginning, his command is that you walk in love.

⁷Many deceivers, who do not acknowledge Jesus Christ as coming in the flesh, have gone out into the world. Any such person is the deceiver and the antichrist. ⁸Watch out that you do not lose what you have worked for, but that you may be rewarded fully. ⁹Anyone who runs ahead and does not continue in the teaching of Christ does not have God; whoever continues in the teaching has both the Father and the Son. ¹⁰If anyone comes to you and does not bring this teaching, do not take him into your house or welcome him. ¹¹Anyone who welcomes him shares in his wicked work.

¹²I have much to write to you, but I do not want to use paper and ink. Instead, I hope to visit you and talk with you face to face, so that our joy may be complete.

¹³The children of your chosen sister send their greetings.

3 John

¹The elder,

To my dear friend Gaius, whom I love in the truth.

²Dear friend, I pray that you may enjoy good health and that all may go well with you, even as your soul is getting along well. ³It gave me great joy to have some brothers come and tell about your faithfulness to the truth and how you continue to walk in the truth. ⁴I have no greater joy than to hear that my children are walking in the truth.

⁵Dear friend, you are faithful in what you are doing for the brothers, even though they are strangers to you. ⁶They have told the church about your love. You will do well to send them on their way in a manner worthy of God. ⁷It was for the sake of the Name that they went out, receiving no help from the pagans. ⁸We ought therefore to show hospitality to such men so that we may work together for the truth.

⁹I wrote to the church, but Diotrephes, who loves to be first, will have nothing to do with us. ¹⁰So if I come, I will call attention to what he is doing, gossiping maliciously about us. Not satisfied with that, he refuses to welcome the brothers. He also stops those who want to do so and puts them out of the church.

¹¹Dear friend, do not imitate what is evil but what is good. Anyone who does what is good is from God. Anyone who does what is evil has not seen God. ¹²Demetrius is well spoken of by everyone—and even by the truth itself. We also speak well of him, and you know that our testimony is true.

¹³I have much to write to you, but I do not want to do so with pen and ink. ¹⁴I hope to see you soon, and we will talk face to face.

Peace to you. The friends here send their greetings. Greet the friends there by name.

3 JOHN 1–8
'Dear friend, you are faithful in what you are doing for the brothers, even though they are strangers to you' (v. 5).

GAIUS WAS AN INDIVIDUAL. We know less about him than about other recipients of New Testament letters. We can get a fair picture of Timothy, of Philemon and of Titus, but Gaius is comparatively unknown. He could just be the Gaius mentioned by Paul, but Gaius was a common name and there is nothing else at all to link them.

We do know he was loyal, concerned about the truth, and hospitable. He looked after some 'brothers' who were complete strangers. These 'brothers' are also an interesting unknown quantity. Were they wandering preachers set apart to evangelize in places where the Church was already established? A bit like early-day friars? Whoever they were, they depended entirely on the Church for support. Gaius is commended for giving that support.

Now, as then, Christians should be known for the way we support and help each other, as well as for charitable efforts outwith our own community. In small denominations with a clear identity, like The Salvation Army, hospitality within the community can be very remarkable. A Salvationist feels at home in other SA settings right round the world – and is accepted as one of the community. But such a recognizable identity carries the risk of identifying with the denomination, rather than with the Church as a whole.

Let us pray for similar feelings of care and being 'at home' to extend, not just within denominational boundaries, but throughout the Church.

Does membership of my own denomination or sect within the Church help or hinder my relationship to the whole Church?

→1168

JUDE vv. 17–25

'To him who is able to keep you from falling and to present you before his glorious presence without fault and with great joy – to the only God our Saviour be glory, majesty, power and authority, through Jesus Christ our Lord, before all ages, now and for evermore! Amen' (vv. 24, 25).

HOW VERY BEAUTIFULLY Jude, in one glorious sentence, links human frailty and destiny with the authority, power and majesty of our heavenly Father. Clearly, our preservation from evil and presentation before God in heaven are entirely dependent upon the grace of God. We are inclined to be 'accident prone' and there are sufficient obstacles on our pilgrim way to cause us to fall, but we have a God who can keep us from falling! God, in whom we trust, is a reliable and constant companion!

> *Courage, brother, do not stumble,*
> *Though thy path be dark as night;*
> *There's a star to guide the humble:*
> *Trust in God and do the right.*

(Norman Macleod)

If Jude was the brother of James (v. 1), and there is no good reason to doubt it, then he was also the brother of our Lord (Matt. 13:55; Mark 6:3). Jude is the English form of Judas. Intially our Lord's brothers did not believe in him, but they gathered in the upper room after the resurrection (Acts 1:14), James becoming a leader in the Church (Gal. 1:19) and writer of the Epistle. It was humility which made both James and Jude claim to be only servants of the Lord Jesus (James 1:1; Jude v. 1).

Jude must often have reproached himself for failing to follow Christ from the beginning (John 7:5), and his experience probably lies behind the affirmation of God's ability to support and guide us to our journey's end. Experience also gave rise to the adoration which lies behind the closing, glorious doxology.

Lord, guide thou my steps today. Amen.

Jude

¹Jude, a servant of Jesus Christ and a brother of James,

To those who have been called, who are loved by God the Father and kept by^a Jesus Christ:

²Mercy, peace and love be yours in abundance.

The Sin and Doom of Godless Men

³Dear friends, although I was very eager to write to you about the salvation we share, I felt I had to write and urge you to contend for the faith that was once for all entrusted to the saints. ⁴For certain men whose condemnation was written about^b long ago have secretly slipped in among you. They are godless men, who change the grace of our God into a licence for immorality and deny Jesus Christ our only Sovereign and Lord.

⁵Though you already know all this, I want to remind you that the Lord^c delivered his people out of Egypt, but later destroyed those who did not believe. ⁶And the angels who did not keep their positions of authority but abandoned their own home—these he has kept in darkness, bound with everlasting chains for judgment on the great Day. ⁷In a similar way, Sodom and Gomorrah and the surrounding towns gave themselves up to sexual immorality and perversion. They serve as an example of those who suffer the punishment of eternal fire.

⁸In the very same way, these dreamers pollute their own bodies, reject authority and slander celestial beings. ⁹But even the archangel Michael, when he was disputing with the devil about the body of Moses, did not dare to bring a slanderous accusation against him, but said, "The Lord rebuke you!" ¹⁰Yet these men speak abusively against whatever they do not understand; and what things they do understand by instinct, like unreasoning animals—these are the very things that destroy them.

¹¹Woe to them! They have taken the way of Cain; they have rushed for profit into Balaam's error; they have been destroyed in Korah's rebellion.

¹²These men are blemishes at your love feasts, eating with you without the slightest qualm—shepherds who feed only themselves. They are clouds without rain, blown along by the wind; autumn trees, without fruit and uprooted—twice dead. ¹³They are wild waves of the sea, foaming up their shame; wandering stars, for whom blackest darkness has been reserved for ever.

¹⁴Enoch, the seventh from Adam, prophesied about these men: "See, the Lord is coming with thousands upon thousands of his holy ones ¹⁵to judge everyone, and to convict all the ungodly of all the ungodly acts they have done in the ungodly way, and of all the harsh words ungodly sinners have spoken against him." ¹⁶These men are grumblers and fault-finders; they follow their own evil desires; they boast about themselves and flatter others for their own advantage.

A Call to Persevere

¹⁷But, dear friends, remember what the apostles of our Lord Jesus Christ foretold. ¹⁸They said to you, "In the last times there will be scoffers who will follow their own ungodly desires." ¹⁹These are the men who divide you, who follow mere natural instincts and do not have the Spirit.

²⁰But you, dear friends, build yourselves up in your most holy faith and pray in the Holy Spirit. ²¹Keep yourselves in God's love as you wait for the mercy of our Lord Jesus Christ to bring you to eternal life.

²²Be merciful to those who doubt; ²³snatch others from the fire and save them; to others show mercy, mixed with fear—hating even the clothing stained by corrupted flesh.

Doxology

²⁴To him who is able to keep you from falling and to present you before his glorious presence without fault and with great joy —²⁵to the only God our Saviour be glory, majesty, power and authority, through Jesus Christ our Lord, before all ages, now and for evermore! Amen.

^a1 Or for; or in   ^b4 Or men who were marked out for condemnation
^c5 Some early manuscripts Jesus

Revelation

Prologue

1 The revelation of Jesus Christ, which God gave him to show his servants what must soon take place. He made it known by sending his angel to his servant John, ²who testifies to everything he saw—that is, the word of God and the testimony of Jesus Christ. ³Blessed is the one who reads the words of this prophecy, and blessed are those who hear it and take to heart what is written in it, because the time is near.

Greetings and Doxology

⁴John,

To the seven churches in the province of Asia:

Grace and peace to you from him who is, and who was, and who is to come, and from the seven spirits*a* before his throne, ⁵and from Jesus Christ, who is the faithful witness, the firstborn from the dead, and the ruler of the kings of the earth.

To him who loves us and has freed us from our sins by his blood, ⁶and has made us to be a kingdom and priests to serve his God and Father—to him be glory and power for ever and ever! Amen.

⁷Look, he is coming with the clouds,
 and every eye will see him,
 even those who pierced him;
 and all the peoples of the earth will
 mourn because of him.
 So shall it be! Amen.

⁸"I am the Alpha and the Omega," says the Lord God, "who is, and who was, and who is to come, the Almighty."

One Like a Son of Man

⁹I, John, your brother and companion in the suffering and kingdom and patient endurance that are ours in Jesus, was on the island of Patmos because of the word of God and the testimony of Jesus. ¹⁰On the Lord's Day I was in the Spirit, and I heard behind me a loud voice like a trumpet, ¹¹which said: "Write on a scroll what you see and send it to the seven churches: to Ephesus, Smyrna, Pergamum, Thyatira, Sardis, Philadelphia and Laodicea."

¹²I turned round to see the voice that was speaking to me. And when I turned I saw seven golden lampstands, ¹³and among the lampstands was someone "like a son of man",*b* dressed in a robe reaching down to his feet and with a golden sash round his chest. ¹⁴His head and hair were white like wool, as white as snow, and his eyes were like blazing fire. ¹⁵His feet were like bronze glowing in a furnace, and his voice was like the sound of rushing waters. ¹⁶In his right hand he held seven stars, and out of his mouth came a sharp double-edged sword. His face was like the sun shining in all its brilliance.

¹⁷When I saw him, I fell at his feet as though dead. Then he placed his right hand on me and said: "Do not be afraid. I am the First and the Last. ¹⁸I am the Living One; I was dead, and behold I am alive for ever and ever! And I hold the keys of death and Hades.

¹⁹"Write, therefore, what you have seen, what is now and what will take place later. ²⁰The mystery of the seven stars that you saw in my right hand and of the seven golden lampstands is this: The seven stars are the angels*c* of the seven churches, and the seven lampstands are the seven churches.

To the Church in Ephesus

2 "To the angel*a* of the church in Ephesus write:

These are the words of him who holds the seven stars in his right hand and walks among the seven golden lampstands: ²I know your deeds, your hard work and your perseverance. I know that you cannot tolerate wicked men, that you have tested those who claim to be apostles but are not, and have found them false. ³You have persevered and have endured hardships for my name, and have not grown weary.

⁴Yet I hold this against you: You have forsaken your first love. ⁵Remember the height from which you have fallen!

---

a4 Or *the sevenfold Spirit*   *b13* Daniel 7:13   *c20* Or *messengers*
a1 Or *messenger*; also in verses 8, 12 and 18

REVELATION 1:1–3
'The revelation of Jesus Christ . . . He made it known by sending his angel to his servant John, who testifies to everything he saw' (vv. 1, 2a).

REVELATION, OR THE APOCALYPSE, is the New Testament's most difficult book, yet for many it is the most fascinating. When written, it was a very modern book. Being 'modern' has its pitfalls. For example, the language of Revelation is special, stylized language. It possibly sounded as strange to educated Greeks as the words accompanying 'rap' music sound to the older generation today. Yet its purpose is to 'reveal', to make clear – not to confuse.

Revelation draws vivid pictures of the world as it was then, and as it would become. The pictures are like political cartoons where each 'beast' has a recognizable identity (rather like Low's carthorse?). To understand the word pictures in Revelation today we need to know the history and circumstances of their writing. Sometimes such knowledge is available, sometimes not. (Similarly, to young or non-English readers Low's carthorse is probably meaningless. Older Englishmen may know it well.)

Other 'apocalypses' were written at that time. Most were Jewish, a few Christian. Revelation's Jewishness is so marked, some Christian interpreters (e.g. Luther and Calvin) thought it shouldn't be in the New Testament at all.

We disagree. But because John put in everything he saw, we need to extract what we find most helpful. We try to understand what helped past generations, what will help future generations and what, with effort, may help our generation gain new insight to the gospel – a 'visual', to use modern jargon.

'Blessed is the one who reads the words of this prophesy' (v. 3). May that be the experience of all who undertake this study of the present and the future.

→1172

REVELATION 3:7–13

'See, I have placed before you an open door that no-one can shut. I know that you have little strength, yet you have kept my word and have not denied my name' (v. 8).

OPPORTUNITY UNLIMITED! So often human plans are frustrated. We cannot accomplish what we would like to achieve. Our opinions differ from those around us. We cannot convince others our beliefs are right. Yet we share this promise to the Philadelphian church. An open door is set before us which no one can shut.

This is possibly my favourite verse from Revelation. Doors speak of access, of opportunity, of the ability to change from one set of circumstances to another. A permanently closed door is a dreadful thing. It denotes imprisonment, restriction, decay or dereliction.

But an open door speaks of freedom and opportunity. The opportunity put before us in Revelation is an opportunity for those of little strength. They cannot open the door themselves. It has to be opened for them. Yet no one can shut it in their face.

That, to me, is the message of Christ. Access to God through an open door – unlimited opportunity for the weak, the helpless, the powerless, all in the strength of God.

It is lovely to belong to a strong, growing, powerful church and to feel the strength of like-minded people around us. But today's word is for those who are few in number, struggling, yet remaining faithful.

Remember today all those who work and witness on their own, or with just a handful of other Christians around them. Remember those who remain faithful in larger situations where most are simply comfortable and taking their ease.

→1175

Repent and do the things you did at first. If you do not repent, I will come to you and remove your lampstand from its place. ⁶But you have this in your favour: You hate the practices of Nicolaitans, which I also hate.

⁷He who has an ear, let him hear what the Spirit says to the churches. To him who overcomes, I will give the right to eat from the tree of life, which is in the paradise of God.

To the Church in Smyrna

⁸"To the angel of the church in Smyrna write:

These are the words of him who is the First and the Last, who died and came to life again. ⁹I know your afflictions and your poverty—yet you are rich! I know the slander of those who say they are Jews and are not, but are a synagogue of Satan. ¹⁰Do not be afraid of what you are about to suffer. I tell you, the devil will put some of you in prison to test you, and you will suffer persecution for ten days. Be faithful, even to the point of death, and I will give you the crown of life.

¹¹He who has an ear, let him hear what the Spirit says to the churches. He who overcomes will not be hurt at all by the second death.

To the Church in Pergamum

¹²"To the angel of the church in Pergamum write:

These are the words of him who has the sharp, double-edged sword. ¹³I know where you live—where Satan has his throne. Yet you remain true to my name. You did not renounce your faith in me, even in the days of Antipas, my faithful witness, who was put to death in your city—where Satan lives.

¹⁴Nevertheless, I have a few things against you: You have people there who hold to the teaching of Balaam, who taught Balak to entice the Israelites to sin by eating food sacrificed to idols and by committing sexual immorality. ¹⁵Likewise you also have those who hold to the teaching of the Nicolaitans. ¹⁶Repent therefore! Otherwise, I will soon come to you and will fight against them with the sword of my mouth.

¹⁷He who has an ear, let him hear what the Spirit says to the churches. To him who overcomes, I will give some of the hidden manna. I will also give him a white stone with a new name written on it, known only to him who receives it.

To the Church in Thyatira

¹⁸"To the angel of the church in Thyatira write:

These are the words of the Son of God, whose eyes are like blazing fire and whose feet are like burnished bronze. ¹⁹I know your deeds, your love and faith, your service and perseverance, and that you are now doing more than you did at first.

²⁰Nevertheless, I have this against you: You tolerate that woman Jezebel, who calls herself a prophetess. By her teaching she misleads my servants into sexual immorality and the eating of food sacrificed to idols. ²¹I have given her time to repent of her immorality, but she is unwilling. ²²So I will cast her on a bed of suffering, and I will make those who commit adultery with her suffer intensely, unless they repent of her ways. ²³I will strike her children dead. Then all the churches will know that I am he who searches hearts and minds, and I will repay each of you according to your deeds. ²⁴Now I say to the rest of you in Thyatira, to you who do not hold to her teaching and have not learned Satan's so-called deep secrets (I will not impose any other burden on you): ²⁵Only hold on to what you have until I come.

²⁶To him who overcomes and does my will to the end, I will give authority over the nations—

²⁷'He will rule them with an iron
       sceptre;
   he will dash them to pieces like
       pottery'ᵇ—

just as I have received authority from my Father. ²⁸I will also give him the morning star. ²⁹He who has an ear, let him hear what the Spirit says to the churches.

To the Church in Sardis

3 "To the angelᵃ of the church in Sardis write:

These are the words of him who holds the seven spiritsᵇ of God and the seven stars. I know your deeds; you have a reputation of being alive, but you are dead. ²Wake up! Strengthen what remains and is about to die, for I have not found your deeds complete in the sight of my God. ³Remember, therefore, what you have received and heard; obey it, and repent. But if you do not wake up, I will come like a thief, and you will not know at what time I will come to you.

⁴Yet you have a few people in Sardis who have not soiled their clothes. They will walk with me, dressed in white, for they are worthy. ⁵He who overcomes will, like them, be dressed in white. I will never blot out his name from the book of life, but will acknowledge his name before my Father and his angels. ⁶He who has an ear, let him hear what the Spirit says to the churches.

ᵇ27 Psalm 2:9   ᵃ1 Or *messenger*; also in verses 7 and 14   ᵇ1 Or *the sevenfold Spirit*

To the Church in Philadelphia

7"To the angel of the church in Philadelphia write:

These are the words of him who is holy and true, who holds the key of David. What he opens no-one can shut, and what he shuts no-one can open. 8I know your deeds. See, I have placed before you an open door that no-one can shut. I know that you have little strength, yet you have kept my word and have not denied my name. 9I will make those who are of the synagogue of Satan, who claim to be Jews though they are not, but are liars—I will make them come and fall down at your feet and acknowledge that I have loved you. 10Since you have kept my command to endure patiently, I will also keep you from the hour of trial that is going to come upon the whole world to test those who live on the earth.

11I am coming soon. Hold on to what you have, so that no-one will take your crown. 12Him who overcomes I will make a pillar in the temple of my God. Never again will he leave it. I will write on him the name of my God and the name of the city of my God, the new Jerusalem, which is coming down out of heaven from my God; and I will also write on him my new name. 13He who has an ear, let him hear what the Spirit says to the churches.

To the Church in Laodicea

14"To the angel of the church in Laodicea write:

These are the words of the Amen, the faithful and true witness, the ruler of God's creation. 15I know your deeds, that you are neither cold nor hot. I wish you were either one or the other! 16So, because you are lukewarm—neither hot nor cold—I am about to spit you out of my mouth. 17You say, 'I am rich; I have acquired wealth and do not need a thing.' But you do not realise that you are wretched, pitiful, poor, blind and naked. 18I counsel you to buy from me gold refined in the fire, so that you can become rich; and white clothes to wear, so that you can cover your shameful nakedness; and salve to put on your eyes, so that you can see.

19Those whom I love I rebuke and discipline. So be earnest, and repent. 20Here I am! I stand at the door and knock. If anyone hears my voice and opens the door, I will come in and eat with him, and he with me. 21To him who overcomes, I will give the right to sit with me on my throne, just as I overcame and sat down with my Father on his throne. 22He who has an ear, let him hear what the Spirit says to the churches."

The Throne in Heaven

4 After this I looked, and there before me was a door standing open in heaven. And the voice I had first heard speaking to me like a trumpet said, "Come up here, and I will show you what must take place after this." 2At once I was in the Spirit, and there before me was a throne in heaven with someone sitting on it. 3And the one who sat there had the appearance of jasper and carnelian. A rainbow, resembling an emerald, encircled the throne. 4Surrounding the throne were twenty-four other thrones, and seated on them were twenty-four elders. They were dressed in white and had crowns of gold on their heads. 5From the throne came flashes of lightning, rumblings and peals of thunder. Before the throne, seven lamps were blazing. These are the seven spirits*a* of God. 6Also before the throne there was what looked like a sea of glass, clear as crystal.

In the centre, around the throne, were four living creatures, and they were covered with eyes, in front and behind. 7The first living creature was like a lion, the second was like an ox, the third had a face like a man, the fourth was like a flying eagle. 8Each of the four living creatures had six wings and was covered with eyes all around, even under his wings. Day and night they never stop saying:

"Holy, holy, holy
is the Lord God Almighty,
who was, and is, and is to come."

9Whenever the living creatures give glory, honour and thanks to him who sits on the throne and who lives for ever and ever, 10the twenty-four elders fall down before him who sits on the throne, and worship him who lives for ever and ever. They lay their crowns before the throne and say:

11"You are worthy, our Lord and God,
to receive glory and honour and power,
for you created all things,
and by your will they were created
and have their being."

The Scroll and the Lamb

5 Then I saw in the right hand of him who sat on the throne a scroll with writing on both sides and sealed with seven seals. 2And I saw a mighty angel proclaiming in a loud voice, "Who is worthy to break the seals and open the scroll?" 3But no-one in heaven or on earth or under the earth could open the scroll or even look inside it. 4I wept and wept because no-one was found who was worthy to open the scroll or look inside. 5Then one of the elders said to me, "Do not weep! See, the Lion of the tribe of Judah, the Root of David, has triumphed. He is able to open the scroll and its seven seals."

6Then I saw a Lamb, looking as if it had been slain, standing in the centre of the throne, encircled by the four living creatures and the elders. He had seven horns and seven eyes, which are the seven spirits*a* of God sent

a5 Or the sevenfold Spirit　　a6 Or the sevenfold Spirit

REVELATION 4:6b-11

'Around the throne were four living creatres, and they were covered with eyes, in front and behind. The first living creature was like a lion, the second was like an ox, the third had a face like a man, the fourth was like a flying eagle' (vv. 6b, 7).

THE FOUR CREATURES relate to the four 'cherubim' in Ezekiel, which each had the face of a man, a lion, a bull and an eagle. In Genesis the cherubim guarded the way to the Garden of Eden after Adam and Eve's banishment. In later works like the book of Enoch, the cherubim became known as the guardians of the throne of God, rather in the way that they appear here.

Each creature represents the foremost in its class. Each fulfils its function in the best possible way. Christian interpreters use these pictures to symbolize the four evangelists. Interpretations vary, but Augustine identifies:

Matthew	The Lion	The Gospel which shows Jesus as the Lion of Judah, fulfilling all the prophets' expectations
Mark	The Man	The Gospel which shows the true humanity of Jesus
Luke	The Ox	The Gospel which shows Jesus as the sacrifice for all men and women everywhere
John	The Eagle	The Gospel which soars above the others in its range of thought about Jesus

The important point for us, though, is that these ideal creatures, along with the twenty-four elders and others, worship God supremely.

> *Holy, holy, holy; all the saints adore thee,*
> *Casting down their golden crowns around the glassy sea;*
> *Cherubim and seraphim falling down before thee,*
> *Who wert, and art, and evermore shalt be!*

> *(Reginald Heber)*

→1176

REVELATION 5:1–14

'Then I saw a Lamb, looking as if it had been slain, standing in the centre of the throne . . . He had seven horns and seven eyes, which are the seven spirits of God sent out into all the earth' (v. 6).

THE LION OF JUDAH of verse 5 quickly fades from sight to be replaced by a Lamb. What a difference! No longer the foremost of beasts. No longer the strong, the aggressive, the warlike, but the meek, the humble, the peaceful.

'The Lamb' is still saturated with symbolism. It is perfect, with seven horns, and seven eyes which are the seven spirits of God. One spirit for each of seven churches? We can see John is telling us something very important. He is emphasizing the complete change produced by the advent of Christ, the Lamb 'slain from the foundation of the world'. Power and might may seem the way, but God's plan from before the world's creation, was that salvation should come from Christ. Christ, treated like a sacrificial lamb, was crucified but then crowned as Lord of life.

John is making a strong christological statement here. The Lamb, Christ, is not merely the source of salvation – he is also worthy of the same praise, the same expressions of worth that belong to God himself. 'Every creature in heaven, on earth, in the world below, and in the sea – all living beings in the universe,' sing the same song that has been sung already to the Lord of all things.

> *Come, let us join our cheerful songs*
> *With angels round the throne;*
> *Ten thousand thousand are their tongues,*
> *But all their joys are one.*
>
> *Worthy the Lamb that died, they cry,*
> *To be exalted thus!*
> *Worthy the Lamb, our hearts reply,*
> *For he was slain for us!*

(Isaac Watts)

→1179

out into all the earth. [7]He came and took the scroll from the right hand of him who sat on the throne. [8]And when he had taken it, the four living creatures and the twenty-four elders fell down before the Lamb. Each one had a harp and they were holding golden bowls full of incense, which are the prayers of the saints. [9]And they sang a new song:

"You are worthy to take the scroll
  and to open its seals,
because you were slain,
  and with your blood you purchased men
    for God
  from every tribe and language and
    people and nation.
[10]You have made them to be a kingdom and
    priests to serve our God,
  and they will reign on the earth."

[11]Then I looked and heard the voice of many angels, numbering thousands upon thousands, and ten thousand times ten thousand. They encircled the throne and the living creatures and the elders. [12]In a loud voice they sang:

"Worthy is the Lamb, who was slain,
  to receive power and wealth and wisdom
    and strength
  and honour and glory and praise!"

[13]Then I heard every creature in heaven and on earth and under the earth and on the sea, and all that is in them, singing:

"To him who sits on the throne and to the
    Lamb
  be praise and honour and glory and power,
    for ever and ever!"

[14]The four living creatures said, "Amen", and the elders fell down and worshipped.

The Seals

6 I watched as the Lamb opened the first of the seven seals. Then I heard one of the four living creatures say in a voice like thunder, "Come!" [2]I looked, and there before me was a white horse! Its rider held a bow, and he was given a crown, and he rode out as a conqueror bent on conquest.

[3]When the Lamb opened the second seal, I heard the second living creature say, "Come!" [4]Then another horse came out, a fiery red one. Its rider was given power to take peace from the earth and to make men slay each other. To him was given a large sword.

[5]When the Lamb opened the third seal, I heard the third living creature say, "Come!" I looked, and there before me was a black horse! Its rider was holding a pair of scales in his hand. [6]Then I heard what sounded like a voice among the four living creatures, saying, "A quart[a] of wheat for a day's wages,[b] and three quarts of barley for a day's wages,[b] and do not damage the oil and the wine!"

[7]When the Lamb opened the fourth seal, I heard the voice of the fourth living creature say, "Come!" [8]I looked, and there before me was a pale horse! Its rider was named Death, and Hades was following close behind him. They were given power over a fourth of the earth to kill by sword, famine and plague, and by the wild beasts of the earth.

[9]When the Lamb opened the fifth seal, I saw under the altar the souls of those who had been slain because of the word of God and the testimony they had maintained. [10]They called out in a loud voice, "How long, Sovereign Lord, holy and true, until you judge the inhabitants of the earth and avenge our blood?" [11]Then each of them was given a white robe, and they were told to wait a little longer, until the number of their fellow-servants and brothers who were to be killed as they had been was completed.

[12]I watched as he opened the sixth seal. There was a great earthquake. The sun turned black like sackcloth made of goat hair, the whole moon turned blood red, [13]and the stars in the sky fell to earth, as late figs drop from a fig-tree when shaken by a strong wind. [14]The sky receded like a scroll, rolling up, and every mountain and island was removed from its place.

[15]Then the kings of the earth, the princes, the generals, the rich, the mighty, and every slave and every free man hid in caves and among the rocks of the mountains. [16]They called to the mountains and the rocks, "Fall on us and hide us from the face of him who sits on the throne and from the wrath of the Lamb! [17]For the great day of their wrath has come, and who can stand?"

144,000 Sealed

7 After this I saw four angels standing at the four corners of the earth, holding back the four winds of the earth to prevent any wind from blowing on the land or on the sea or on any tree. [2]Then I saw another angel coming up from the east, having the seal of the living God. He called out in a loud voice to the four angels who had been given power to harm the land and the sea: [3]"Do not harm the land or the sea or the trees until we put a seal on the foreheads of the servants of our God." [4]Then I heard the number of those who were sealed: 144,000 from all the tribes of Israel.

[5]From the tribe of Judah 12,000 were
    sealed,
  from the tribe of Reuben 12,000,
  from the tribe of Gad 12,000,
[6]from the tribe of Asher 12,000,
  from the tribe of Naphtali 12,000,
  from the tribe of Manasseh 12,000,
[7]from the tribe of Simeon 12,000,
  from the tribe of Levi 12,000,
  from the tribe of Issachar 12,000,
[8]from the tribe of Zebulun 12,000,
  from the tribe of Joseph 12,000,
  from the tribe of Benjamin 12,000.

---

[a]6 Greek a choinix (probably about a litre)   [b]6 Greek a denarius

The Great Multitude in White Robes

⁹After this I looked and there before me was a great multitude that no-one could count, from every nation, tribe, people and language, standing before the throne and in front of the Lamb. They were wearing white robes and were holding palm branches in their hands. ¹⁰And they cried out in a loud voice:

"Salvation belongs to our God,
who sits on the throne,
and to the Lamb."

¹¹All the angels were standing round the throne and around the elders and the four living creatures. They fell down on their faces before the throne and worshipped God, ¹²saying:

"Amen!
Praise and glory
and wisdom and thanks and honour
and power and strength
be to our God for ever and ever.
Amen!"

¹³Then one of the elders asked me, "These in white robes—who are they, and where did they come from?"

¹⁴I answered, "Sir, you know."

And he said, "These are they who have come out of the great tribulation; they have washed their robes and made them white in the blood of the Lamb. ¹⁵Therefore,

"they are before the throne of God
and serve him day and night in his
temple;
and he who sits on the throne will spread
his tent over them.
¹⁶Never again will they hunger;
never again will they thirst.
The sun will not beat upon them,
nor any scorching heat.
¹⁷For the Lamb at the centre of the throne
will be their shepherd;
he will lead them to springs of living
water.
And God will wipe away every tear from
their eyes."

The Seventh Seal and the Golden Censer

8 When he opened the seventh seal, there was silence in heaven for about half an hour.

²And I saw the seven angels who stand before God, and to them were given seven trumpets.

³Another angel, who had a golden censer, came and stood at the altar. He was given much incense to offer, with the prayers of all the saints, on the golden altar before the throne. ⁴The smoke of the incense, together with the prayers of the saints, went up before God from the angel's hand. ⁵Then the angel took the censer, filled it with fire from the altar, and hurled it on the earth; and there came peals of thunder, rumblings, flashes of lightning and an earthquake.

The Trumpets

⁶Then the seven angels who had the seven trumpets prepared to sound them.

⁷The first angel sounded his trumpet, and there came hail and fire mixed with blood, and it was hurled down upon the earth. A third of the earth was burned up, a third of the trees were burned up, and all the green grass was burned up.

⁸The second angel sounded his trumpet, and something like a huge mountain, all ablaze, was thrown into the sea. A third of the sea turned into blood, ⁹a third of the living creatures in the sea died, and a third of the ships were destroyed.

¹⁰The third angel sounded his trumpet, and a great star, blazing like a torch, fell from the sky on a third of the rivers and on the springs of water—¹¹the name of the star is Wormwood.ᵃ A third of the waters turned bitter, and many people died from the waters that had become bitter.

¹²The fourth angel sounded his trumpet, and a third of the sun was struck, a third of the moon, and a third of the stars, so that a third of them turned dark. A third of the day was without light, and also a third of the night.

¹³As I watched, I heard an eagle that was flying in mid-air call out in a loud voice: "Woe! Woe! Woe to the inhabitants of the earth, because of the trumpet blasts about to be sounded by the other three angels!"

9 The fifth angel sounded his trumpet, and I saw a star that had fallen from the sky to the earth. The star was given the key to the shaft of the Abyss. ²When he opened the Abyss, smoke rose from it like the smoke from a gigantic furnace. The sun and sky were darkened by the smoke from the Abyss. ³And out of the smoke locusts came down upon the earth and were given power like that of scorpions of the earth. ⁴They were told not to harm the grass of the earth or any plant or tree, but only those people who did not have the seal of God on their foreheads. ⁵They were not given power to kill them, but only to torture them for five months. And the agony they suffered was like that of the sting of a scorpion when it strikes a man. ⁶During those days men will seek death, but will not find it; they will long to die, but death will elude them.

⁷The locusts looked like horses prepared for battle. On their heads they wore something like crowns of gold, and their faces resembled human faces. ⁸Their hair was like women's hair, and their teeth were like lions' teeth. ⁹They had breastplates like breastplates of iron, and the sound of their wings was like the thundering of many horses and chariots rushing into battle. ¹⁰They had tails and stings like scorpions, and in their tails they had power to torment people for five months. ¹¹They had as king over them the angel of the Abyss, whose name in Hebrew is Abaddon, and in Greek, Apollyon.ᵃ

¹²The first woe is past; two other woes are yet to come.

ᵃ11 That is, Bitterness   ᵃ11 *Abaddon* and *Apollyon* mean *Destroyer*.

REVELATION 7:1-4, 9-17

'After this I looked and there before me was a great multitude that no-one could count . . . wearing white robes . . . And they cried out in a loud voice: "Salvation belongs to our God, who sits on the throne, and to the Lamb" ' (vv. 9, 10).

BIBLICAL NUMBERS are often symbolic, conveying ideas of perfection, imperfection, good and evil. Twelve is a good number, associated with the twelve tribes of Israel, twelve apostles and so on. 144,000 is twelve multiplied by twelve – goodness upon goodness – multiplied a thousandfold to emphasize ideas of limitless goodness and perfection.

It is a number used in the same way that Jesus did when he told Peter to forgive, not seven times but seventy times seven. None of us, I hope, would say 'Right then, add up the occasions of forgiveness. When you reach 490, that's it!' No, Jesus is telling us forgiveness is infinite.

So, too, we should see the symbolism in John's use of number. He is not saying 144,000 will be saved. He is emphasizing the perfection of a group amongst the saved. That becomes plain when he pictures the numberless multitude who worship God and cry 'Salvation!' having come through the great persecution. The elder who speaks to John tells him it is the numberless multitude, not just the 144,000, who have come through and who now enjoy the glorious bliss, which he describes in forceful Old Testament phrases.

> *When we gather at last over Jordan,*
> *And the ransomed in glory we see,*
> *As the numberless sands of the seashore,*
> *What a wonderful sight that will be!*
>
> *Numberless as the sands of the seashore,*
> *Numberless as the sands of the shore!*
>   *O what a sight 'twill be*
>   *When the ransomed host we see,*
> *As numberless as the sands of the seashore*

(F. A. Blackmer)

→1180

THE SEVENTH SEAL IS OPENED. A dramatic silence follows. Silence is solemn. Silence can be tense. Silence can be emotional. The pause before the trumpet sound encompasses them all, solemnity, drama, tension and emotion. It also enables the prayers of the faithful to be heard, rising from the earth.

The Jews had a picturesque idea that during the day the angels' song in heaven prevented prayer being heard. In this tense moment, the song must have been interrupted, allowing souls on earth to communicate with God. Today we would stress that God is always able to hear. He is always communicating with us through the Son. Today, we would hardly use the same picture John used, but it helps us understand a little of how John's mind was working, saturated with the cultural images of his day. Though they come from a different time and culture, when they are interpreted, these pictures can still show us something of God.

Following the silence, at the sound of the seven trumpets, one after the other, John sees powerful visions. The trumpet sound is associated with the 'parousia', the coming of Christ. It is also an Old Testament image, reminding us of the conquest of Jericho. But more than that, the trumpet is a warning. The watchman's trumpet told of impending danger. It had to be heeded, or disaster would strike. The responsibility of the one who blew the trumpet, the watchman, was to avert disaster, yet in John's vision the trumpet heralds disaster.

Past warnings have gone unheeded. The disasters John outlines do not produce repentance. Yet throughout John's visions we find hints that repentance may turn disaster away (9:20, 21 etc.).

→1183

[13]The sixth angel sounded his trumpet, and I heard a voice coming from the horns[b] of the golden altar that is before God. [14]It said to the sixth angel who had the trumpet, "Release the four angels who are bound at the great river Euphrates." [15]And the four angels who had been kept ready for this very hour and day and month and year were released to kill a third of mankind. [16]The number of the mounted troops was two hundred million. I heard their number.

[17]The horses and riders I saw in my vision looked like this: Their breastplates were fiery red, dark blue, and yellow as sulphur. The heads of the horses resembled the heads of lions, and out of their mouths came fire, smoke and sulphur. [18]A third of mankind was killed by the three plagues of fire, smoke and sulphur that came out of their mouths. [19]The power of the horses was in their mouths and in their tails; for their tails were like snakes, having heads with which they inflict injury.

[20]The rest of mankind that were not killed by these plagues still did not repent of the work of their hands; they did not stop worshipping demons, and idols of gold, silver, bronze, stone and wood—idols that cannot see or hear or walk. [21]Nor did they repent of their murders, their magic arts, their sexual immorality or their thefts.

The Angel and the Little Scroll

10 Then I saw another mighty angel coming down from heaven. He was robed in a cloud, with a rainbow above his head; his face was like the sun, and his legs were like fiery pillars. [2]He was holding a little scroll, which lay open in his hand. He planted his right foot on the sea and his left foot on the land, [3]and he gave a loud shout like the roar of a lion. When he shouted, the voices of the seven thunders spoke. [4]And when the seven thunders spoke, I was about to write; but I heard a voice from heaven say, "Seal up what the seven thunders have said and do not write it down."

[5]Then the angel I had seen standing on the sea and on the land raised his right hand to heaven. [6]And he swore by him who lives for ever and ever, who created the heavens and all that is in them, the earth and all that is in it, and the sea and all that is in it, and said, "There will be no more delay! [7]But in the days when the seventh angel is about to sound his trumpet, the mystery of God will be accomplished, just as he announced to his servants the prophets."

[8]Then the voice that I had heard from heaven spoke to me once more: "Go, take the scroll that lies open in the hand of the angel who is standing on the sea and on the land."

[9]So I went to the angel and asked him to give me the little scroll. He said to me, "Take it and eat it. It will turn your stomach sour, but in your mouth it will be as sweet as honey." [10]I took the little scroll from the angel's hand and ate it. It tasted as sweet as honey in my mouth, but when I had eaten it,

my stomach turned sour. [11]Then I was told, "You must prophesy again about many peoples, nations, languages and kings."

The Two Witnesses

11 I was given a reed like a measuring rod and was told, "Go and measure the temple of God and the altar, and count the worshippers there. [2]But exclude the outer court; do not measure it, because it has been given to the Gentiles. They will trample on the holy city for 42 months. [3]And I will give power to my two witnesses, and they will prophesy for 1,260 days, clothed in sackcloth." [4]These are the two olive trees and the two lampstands that stand before the Lord of the earth. [5]If anyone tries to harm them, fire comes from their mouths and devours their enemies. This is how anyone who wants to harm them must die. [6]These men have power to shut up the sky so that it will not rain during the time they are prophesying; and they have power to turn the waters into blood and to strike the earth with every kind of plague as often as they want.

[7]Now when they have finished their testimony, the beast that comes up from the Abyss will attack them, and overpower and kill them. [8]Their bodies will lie in the street of the great city, which is figuratively called Sodom and Egypt, where also their Lord was crucified. [9]For three and a half days men from every people, tribe, language and nation will gaze on their bodies and refuse them burial. [10]The inhabitants of the earth will gloat over them and will celebrate by sending each other gifts, because these two prophets had tormented those who live on earth.

[11]But after the three and a half days a breath of life from God entered them, and they stood on their feet, and terror struck those who saw them. [12]Then they heard a loud voice from heaven saying to them, "Come up here." And they went up to heaven in a cloud, while their enemies looked on.

[13]At that very hour there was a severe earthquake and a tenth of the city collapsed. Seven thousand people were killed in the earthquake, and the survivors were terrified and gave glory to the God of heaven.

[14]The second woe has passed; the third woe is coming soon.

The Seventh Trumpet

[15]The seventh angel sounded his trumpet, and there were loud voices in heaven, which said:

"The kingdom of the world has become
    the kingdom of our Lord and of his
    Christ,
  and he will reign for ever and ever."

[16]And the twenty-four elders, who were seated on their thrones before God, fell on their faces and worshipped God, [17]saying:

"We give thanks to you, Lord God
　Almighty,
　the One who is and who was,
because you have taken your great power
　and have begun to reign.
[18]The nations were angry;
　and your wrath has come.
The time has come for judging the dead,
　and for rewarding your servants the
　　prophets
and your saints and those who reverence
　your name,
　both small and great—
and for destroying those who destroy the
　earth."

[19]Then God's temple in heaven was
opened, and within his temple was seen the
ark of his covenant. And there came flashes
of lightning, rumblings, peals of thunder, an
earthquake and a great hailstorm.

The Woman and the Dragon

12 A great and wondrous sign appeared
in heaven: a woman clothed with the
sun, with the moon under her feet and a
crown of twelve stars on her head. [2]She was
pregnant and cried out in pain as she was
about to give birth. [3]Then another sign
appeared in heaven: an enormous red dragon
with seven heads and ten horns and seven
crowns on his heads. [4]His tail swept a third of
the stars out of the sky and flung them to the
earth. The dragon stood in front of the
woman who was about to give birth, so that
he might devour her child the moment it was
born. [5]She gave birth to a son, a male child,
who will rule all the nations with an iron
sceptre. And her child was snatched up to
God and to his throne. [6]The woman fled into
the desert to a place prepared for her by God,
where she might be taken care of for 1,260
days.
[7]And there was war in heaven. Michael
and his angels fought against the dragon, and
the dragon and his angels fought back. [8]But
he was not strong enough, and they lost their
place in heaven. [9]The great dragon was
hurled down—that ancient serpent called the
devil, or Satan, who leads the whole world
astray. He was hurled to the earth, and his
angels with him.
[10]Then I heard a loud voice in heaven say:

"Now have come the salvation and the
　power and the kingdom of our God,
　and the authority of his Christ.
For the accuser of our brothers,
　who accuses them before our God day
　　and night,
　has been hurled down.
[11]They overcame him
　by the blood of the Lamb
　and by the word of their testimony;
they did not love their lives so much
　as to shrink from death.

[12]Therefore rejoice, you heavens
　and you who dwell in them!
But woe to the earth and the sea,
　because the devil has gone down to you!
He is filled with fury,
　because he knows that his time is
　　short."

[13]When the dragon saw that he had been
hurled to the earth, he pursued the woman
who had given birth to the male child. [14]The
woman was given the two wings of a great
eagle, so that she might fly to the place
prepared for her in the desert, where she
would be taken care of for a time, times and
half a time, out of the serpent's reach. [15]Then
from his mouth the serpent spewed water like
a river, to overtake the woman and sweep her
away with the torrent. [16]But the earth helped
the woman by opening its mouth and swal-
lowing the river that the dragon had spewed
out of his mouth. [17]Then the dragon was
enraged at the woman and went off to make
war against the rest of her offspring—those
who obey God's commandments and hold to

13 the testimony of Jesus. [1]And the
dragon[a] stood on the shore of the sea.

The Beast out of the Sea

And I saw a beast coming out of the sea.
He had ten horns and seven heads, with ten
crowns on his horns, and on each head a
blasphemous name. [2]The beast I saw resembled a leopard, but had feet like those of a
bear and a mouth like that of a lion. The
dragon gave the beast his power and his
throne and great authority. [3]One of the heads
of the beast seemed to have had a fatal
wound, but the fatal wound had been healed.
The whole world was astonished and followed the beast. [4]Men worshipped the
dragon because he had given authority to the
beast, and they also worshipped the beast
and asked, "Who is like the beast? Who can
make war against him?"
[5]The beast was given a mouth to utter
proud words and blasphemies and to exercise his authority for forty-two months. [6]He
opened his mouth to blaspheme God, and to
slander his name and his dwelling-place and
those who live in heaven. [7]He was given
power to make war against the saints and to
conquer them. And he was given authority
over every tribe, people, language and
nation. [8]All inhabitants of the earth will
worship the beast—all whose names have
not been written in the book of life belonging
to the Lamb that was slain from the creation
of the world.[b]
[9]He who has an ear, let him hear.

[10]If anyone is to go into captivity,
　into captivity he will go.
If anyone is to be killed[c] with the sword,
　with the sword he will be killed.

This calls for patient endurance and faithfulness on the part of the saints.

---

[a]1 Some late manuscripts *And I*
[b]8 Or *written from the creation of the world in the book of life belonging to the Lamb that was slain*
[c]10 Some manuscripts *anyone kills*

REVELATION 12

'And there was war in heaven. Michael and his angels fought against the dragon, and the dragon and his angels fought back' (v. 7).

THE TEN HORNED BEAST reminds us strongly of Daniel's visions (Dan. 7:7, 8, 10). The woman giving birth is a picture of the birth of the Church. The woman should be understood as representing Israel, rather than Mary the mother of Jesus. These visions are set against a background of Psalm 2 (Ps. 2:7, 9, Rev. 12:5). We also find echoes of the ancient Babylonian creation myth, as described in Isaiah and the Psalms (Isa. 27:1, 51:9; Ps. 74: 14).

There was a strong belief in John's day that events on earth were simply a mirror of what went on in heaven. They believed the traumas of earth were due to conflict in heaven. That is why, later in his work, John is concerned to emphasize that there will be a new heaven as well as a new earth (Rev. 21).

The multitude of influences at work upon John's vision, makes it difficult for us to focus on one particular point. However, we can see clearly that the dragon, Satan, the Devil, the personification of evil, is a persistent fighter who will pursue the Church to the very gates of heaven itself in his desire to confound the will of God. We cannot fight him on our own. We need all the forces of heaven at our disposal to conquer him.

And finally, he comes with the greatest ferocity just when we think the battle has been won. It is no accident that the fierce, heavenly battle (v. 7) follows so shortly on the blowing of the seventh trumpet when all seemed to be well (11:15). Constant vigilance is needed in the fight against evil.

Dear Father in heaven, it is so easy to forget the immense power of evil when things seem to be going well for us. Help us never to become complacent, but to campaign energetically against the evil one in order to hasten the final victory over Satan.

→1184

REVELATION 14
'The 144,000 who had been redeemed . . . and offered as firstfruits to God and the Lamb' (vv. 3b, 4b).

'Blessed are the dead who die in the Lord from now on (v. 13b).

OVER-EMPHASIS can be dangerous. We previously mentioned the 144,000. Two other points from this chapter have sometimes been over-emphasized.

1. The 144,000 'firstfruits' are described as men who have never 'defiled' themselves with women. This can give a false sense that celibacy is the Christian ideal, and marriage second-best. Such ideas can do untold damage.

2. Martyrdom. Martyrdom was going to come to many of John's readers. He had to encourage them to stand firm against every threat from Rome. He reminded them that against a backdrop of eternity, Rome (Babylon) had already fallen. He reminded them that their rewards were eternal, while the rewards Rome could offer were only temporary. But John's words should not lead Christians to seek martyrdom, nor should his words about the firstfruits of the re-deemed lead Christians to seek celibacy as a 'better' state.

Some may be called to celibacy, others to face martyrdom. Neither challenge will make anyone a 'better' Christian than others, but neither need prove impossible when encountered. They are not to be regarded as restraints, but like so many other experiences, as possible paths to Christian freedom.

> *In service which thy love appoints*
> *There are no bonds for me*
> *My secret heart is taught the truth*
> *That makes thy children free:*
> *A life of self-renouncing love*
> *Is one of liberty.*

(*Anna L. Waring*)

→1187

The Beast out of the Earth

¹¹Then I saw another beast, coming out of the earth. He had two horns like a lamb, but he spoke like a dragon. ¹²He exercised all the authority of the first beast on his behalf, and made the earth and its inhabitants worship the first beast, whose fatal wound had been healed. ¹³And he performed great and miraculous signs, even causing fire to come down from heaven to earth in full view of men. ¹⁴Because of the signs he was given power to do on behalf of the first beast, he deceived the inhabitants of the earth. He ordered them to set up an image in honour of the beast who was wounded by the sword and yet lived. ¹⁵He was given power to give breath to the image of the first beast, so that it could speak and cause all who refused to worship the image to be killed. ¹⁶He also forced everyone, small and great, rich and poor, free and slave, to receive a mark on his right hand or on his forehead, ¹⁷so that no-one could buy or sell unless he had the mark, which is the name of the beast or the number of his name.

¹⁸This calls for wisdom. If anyone has insight, let him calculate the number of the beast, for it is man's number. His number is 666.

The Lamb and the 144,000

14 Then I looked, and there before me was the Lamb, standing on Mount Zion, and with him 144,000 who had his name and his Father's name written on their foreheads. ²And I heard a sound from heaven like the roar of rushing waters and like a loud peal of thunder. The sound I heard was like that of harpists playing their harps. ³And they sang a new song before the throne and before the four living creatures and the elders. No-one could learn the song except the 144,000 who had been redeemed from the earth. ⁴These are those who did not defile themselves with women, for they kept themselves pure. They follow the Lamb wherever he goes. They were purchased from among men and offered as firstfruits to God and the Lamb. ⁵No lie was found in their mouths; they are blameless.

The Three Angels

⁶Then I saw another angel flying in mid-air, and he had the eternal gospel to proclaim to those who live on the earth—to every nation, tribe, language and people. ⁷He said in a loud voice, "Fear God and give him glory, because the hour of his judgment has come. Worship him who made the heavens, the earth, the sea and the springs of water."

⁸A second angel followed and⁄ said, "Fallen! Fallen is Babylon the Great, which made all the nations drink the maddening wine of her adulteries."

⁹A third angel followed them and said in a loud voice: "If anyone worships the beast and his image and receives his mark on the forehead or on the hand, ¹⁰he, too, will drink of the wine of God's fury, which has been poured full strength into the cup of his wrath. He will be tormented with burning sulphur in the presence of the holy angels and of the Lamb. ¹¹And the smoke of their torment rises for ever and ever. There is no rest day or night for those who worship the beast and his image, or for anyone who receives the mark of his name." ¹²This calls for patient endurance on the part of the saints who obey God's commandments and remain faithful to Jesus.

¹³Then I heard a voice from heaven say, "Write: Blessed are the dead who die in the Lord from now on."

"Yes," says the Spirit, "they will rest from their labour, for their deeds will follow them."

The Harvest of the Earth

¹⁴I looked, and there before me was a white cloud, and seated on the cloud was one "like a son of man"ᵃ with a crown of gold on his head and a sharp sickle in his hand. ¹⁵Then another angel came out of the temple and called in a loud voice to him who was sitting on the cloud, "Take your sickle and reap, because the time to reap has come, for the harvest of the earth is ripe." ¹⁶So he who was seated on the cloud swung his sickle over the earth, and the earth was harvested.

¹⁷Another angel came out of the temple in heaven, and he too had a sharp sickle. ¹⁸Still another angel, who had charge of the fire, came from the altar and called in a loud voice to him who had the sharp sickle, "Take your sharp sickle and gather the clusters of grapes from the earth's vine, because its grapes are ripe." ¹⁹The angel swung his sickle on the earth, gathered its grapes and threw them into the great winepress of God's wrath. ²⁰They were trampled in the winepress outside the city, and blood flowed out of the press, rising as high as the horses' bridles for a distance of 1,600 stadia.ᵇ

Seven Angels With Seven Plagues

15 I saw in heaven another great and marvellous sign: seven angels with the seven last plagues—last, because with them God's wrath is completed. ²And I saw what looked like a sea of glass mixed with fire and, standing beside the sea, those who had been victorious over the beast and his image and over the number of his name. They held harps given them by God ³and sang the song of Moses the servant of God and the song of the Lamb:

"Great and marvellous are your deeds,
    Lord God Almighty.
Just and true are your ways,
    King of the ages.
⁴Who will not fear you, O Lord,
    and bring glory to your name?
For you alone are holy.
All nations will come
    and worship before you,
for your righteous acts have been
    revealed."

ᵃ14 Daniel 7:13   ᵇ20 That is, about 180 miles (about 300 kilometres)

⁵After this I looked and in heaven the temple, that is, the tabernacle of the Testimony, was opened. ⁶Out of the temple came the seven angels with the seven plagues. They were dressed in clean, shining linen and wore golden sashes round their chests. ⁷Then one of the four living creatures gave to the seven angels seven golden bowls filled with the wrath of God, who lives for ever and ever. ⁸And the temple was filled with smoke from the glory of God and from his power, and no-one could enter the temple until the seven plagues of the seven angels were completed.

The Seven Bowls of God's Wrath

16 Then I heard a loud voice from the temple saying to the seven angels, "Go, pour out the seven bowls of God's wrath on the earth."

²The first angel went and poured out his bowl on the land, and ugly and painful sores broke out on the people who had the mark of the beast and worshipped his image.

³The second angel poured out his bowl on the sea, and it turned into blood like that of a dead man, and every living thing in the sea died.

⁴The third angel poured out his bowl on the rivers and springs of water, and they became blood. ⁵Then I heard the angel in charge of the waters say:

"You are just in these judgments,
    you who are and who were, the Holy
        One,
    because you have so judged;
⁶for they have shed the blood of your saints
        and prophets,
    and you have given them blood to drink
        as they deserve."

⁷And I heard the altar respond:

"Yes, Lord God Almighty,
    true and just are your judgments."

⁸The fourth angel poured out his bowl on the sun, and the sun was given power to scorch people with fire. ⁹They were seared by the intense heat and they cursed the name of God, who had control over these plagues, but they refused to repent and glorify him.

¹⁰The fifth angel poured out his bowl on the throne of the beast, and his kingdom was plunged into darkness. Men gnawed their tongues in agony ¹¹and cursed the God of heaven because of their pains and their sores, but they refused to repent of what they had done.

¹²The sixth angel poured out his bowl on the great river Euphrates, and its water was dried up to prepare the way for the kings from 'the East. ¹³Then I saw three evil^a spirits that looked like frogs; they came out of the mouth of the dragon, out of the mouth of the beast and out of the mouth of the false prophet. ¹⁴They are spirits of demons performing miraculous signs, and they go out to the kings

of the whole world, to gather them for the battle on the great day of God Almighty.

¹⁵"Behold, I come like a thief! Blessed is he who stays awake and keeps his clothes with him, so that he may not go naked and be shamefully exposed."

¹⁶Then they gathered the kings together to the place that in Hebrew is called Armageddon.

¹⁷The seventh angel poured out his bowl into the air, and out of the temple came a loud voice from the throne, saying, "It is done!" ¹⁸Then there came flashes of lightning, rumblings, peals of thunder and a severe earthquake. No earthquake like it has ever occurred since man has been on earth, so tremendous was the quake. ¹⁹The great city split into three parts, and the cities of the nations collapsed. God remembered Babylon the Great and gave her the cup filled with the wine of the fury of his wrath. ²⁰Every island fled away and the mountains could not be found. ²¹From the sky huge hailstones of about a hundred pounds each fell upon men. And they cursed God on account of the plague of hail, because the plague was so terrible.

The Woman on the Beast

17 One of the seven angels who had the seven bowls came and said to me, "Come, I will show you the punishment of the great prostitute, who sits on many waters. ²With her the kings of the earth committed adultery and the inhabitants of the earth were intoxicated with the wine of her adulteries."

³Then the angel carried me away in the Spirit into a desert. There I saw a woman sitting on a scarlet beast that was covered with blasphemous names and had seven heads and ten horns. ⁴The woman was dressed in purple and scarlet, and was glittering with gold, precious stones and pearls. She held a golden cup in her hand, filled with abominable things and the filth of her adulteries. ⁵This title was written on her forehead:

MYSTERY
BABYLON THE GREAT
THE MOTHER OF PROSTITUTES
AND OF THE ABOMINATIONS
OF THE EARTH.

⁶I saw that the woman was drunk with the blood of the saints, the blood of those who bore testimony to Jesus.

When I saw her, I was greatly astonished. ⁷Then the angel said to me: "Why are you astonished? I will explain to you the mystery of the woman and of the beast she rides, which has the seven heads and ten horns. ⁸The beast, which you saw, once was, now is not, and will come up out of the Abyss and go to his destruction. The inhabitants of the earth whose names have not been written in the book of life from the creation of the world will be astonished when they see the beast,

^a13 Greek unclean

REVELATION 16

'Then I heard a loud voice speaking from the temple saying to the seven angels: "Go, pour out the seven bowls of God's wrath on the earth." . . . but they refused to repent and glorify him' (vv. 1, 9b).

WILL WE EVER LEARN? John describes the increasing momentum of disaster, through each set of seven. With this final set, disaster becomes universal, not limited in the way that it has been previously. John has gone beyond condemnation of Rome (to which he returns in the next chapter) to talk about a more general outpouring of God's wrath. Wrath is no longer an impersonal force which is naturally opposed to evil, but a passionate, personal anger from God involving itself in the whole process.

All kinds of pointers might lead us to think the seven plagues are nearly upon us in our present day. We could relate the water becoming like blood to pollution of the seas. We could relate the destruction of God's people to the holocaust a generation ago. We could relate the sun, burning people with its fiery heat, to global warming and destruction of the ozone layer which until now protected us from the worst effects of the sun. But the thing which strikes home most strongly to me is not the anger, wrath or disaster, but the people's reaction.

Just this week I heard people ask the question, 'Can we afford measures needed to protect the environment?' Faced with the possibility of disaster on the scale of the plagues of Revelation 16, where the planet faces poisoning and life itself grinding to a terrible halt, the first question people ask is 'What will it cost?' They can hardly think beyond their own pockets, or beyond the limits set by our materialist society.

If ever we doubt the reality of John's visions, we only need to think of people faced with destruction asking 'What will it cost?' to realize that he is right. Disaster alone will not make people learn the lessons of the past.

→1188

REVELATION 18
'When the kings of the earth . . . see the smoke of her burning, they will weep and mourn over her . . . The merchants who sold these things and gained their wealth from her will stand far off, terrified at her torment' (vv. 9, 15).

CHAPTER 18 almost repeats the images of Chapter 17. Repetition of the picture of depravity and debauchery, however, makes a very important point.

We could read Chapter 17 and think no one was sorry to see the oppressor destroyed. We cannot read Chapter 18 without realizing that the struggle to destroy oppression will meet much opposition. Merril C. Tenney suggests Chapter 17 refers to religious power. Few outside the priestly caste mourn the passing of a decadent religious authority like Rome's religious dictatorship. Tenney further suggests Chapter 18 refers to social, cultural and commercial power in general.

This interpretation may not convince us totally, but we must admit that those who have held the reigns of government; those who have underpinned its economic structures; those who have participated in its trade and picked up the crumbs of prosperity on the borders of its luxurious vanity – all these and many others will watch with horror when anything arises to destroy those things that they have built up.

In individual terms too, before God can reign, religious, commercial and cultural idols must be broken down.

> *The dearest idol I have known,*
> *Whate'er that idol be,*
> *Help me to tear it from thy throne,*
> *And worship only thee.*

> *So shall my walk be close with God,*
> *Calm and serene my frame;*
> *So purer light shall mark the road,*
> *That leads me to the Lamb.*

(William Cowper)

because he once was, now is not, and yet will come. ⁹"This calls for a mind with wisdom. The seven heads are seven hills on which the woman sits. ¹⁰They are also seven kings. Five have fallen, one is, the other has not yet come; but when he does come, he must remain for a little while. ¹¹The beast who once was, and now is not, is an eighth king. He belongs to the seven and is going to his destruction.

¹²"The ten horns you saw are ten kings who have not yet received a kingdom, but who for one hour will receive authority as kings along with the beast. ¹³They have one purpose and will give their power and authority to the beast. ¹⁴They will make war against the Lamb, but the Lamb will overcome them because he is Lord of lords and King of kings—and with him will be his called, chosen and faithful followers."

¹⁵Then the angel said to me, "The waters you saw, where the prostitute sits, are peoples, multitudes, nations and languages. ¹⁶The beast and the ten horns you saw will hate the prostitute. They will bring her to ruin and leave her naked; they will eat her flesh and burn her with fire. ¹⁷For God has put it into their hearts to accomplish his purpose by agreeing to give the beast their power to rule, until God's words are fulfilled. ¹⁸The woman you saw is the great city that rules over the kings of the earth."

The Fall of Babylon

18 After this I saw another angel coming down from heaven. He had great authority, and the earth was illuminated by his splendour. ²With a mighty voice he shouted:

"Fallen! Fallen is Babylon the Great!
 She has become a home for demons
and a haunt for every evil^a spirit,
 a haunt for every unclean and detestable
  bird.
³For all the nations have drunk
 the maddening wine of her adulteries.
The kings of the earth committed adultery
 with her,
 and the merchants of the earth grew rich
  from her excessive luxuries."

⁴Then I heard another voice from heaven say:

"Come out of her, my people,
 so that you will not share in her sins,
 so that you will not receive any of her
  plagues;
⁵for her sins are piled up to heaven,
 and God has remembered her crimes.
⁶Give back to her as she has given;
 pay her back double for what she has
  done.
Mix her a double portion from her own
  cup.
⁷Give her as much torture and grief
 as the glory and luxury she gave herself.

In her heart she boasts,
 'I sit as queen; I am not a widow,
 and I will never mourn.'
⁸Therefore in one day her plagues will
  overtake her:
 death, mourning and famine.
She will be consumed by fire,
 for mighty is the Lord God who judges
  her.

⁹"When the kings of the earth who committed adultery with her and shared her luxury see the smoke of her burning, they will weep and mourn over her. ¹⁰Terrified at her torment, they will stand far off and cry:

"'Woe! Woe, O great city,
 O Babylon, city of power!
In one hour your doom has come!'

¹¹"The merchants of the earth will weep and mourn over her because no-one buys their cargoes any more—¹²cargoes of gold, silver, precious stones and pearls; fine linen, purple, silk and scarlet cloth; every sort of citron wood, and articles of every kind made of ivory, costly wood, bronze, iron and marble; ¹³cargoes of cinnamon and spice, of incense, myrrh and frankincense, of wine and olive oil, of fine flour and wheat; cattle and sheep; horses and carriages; and bodies and souls of men.

¹⁴"They will say, 'The fruit you longed for is gone from you. All your riches and splendour have vanished, never to be recovered.' ¹⁵The merchants who sold these things and gained their wealth from her will stand far off, terrified at her torment. They will weep and mourn ¹⁶and cry out:

"'Woe! Woe, O great city,
 dressed in fine linen, purple and scarlet,
 and glittering with gold, precious stones
  and pearls!
¹⁷In one hour such great wealth has been
  brought to ruin!'

"Every sea captain, and all who travel by ship, the sailors, and all who earn their living from the sea, will stand far off. ¹⁸When they see the smoke of her burning, they will exclaim, 'Was there ever a city like this great city?' ¹⁹They will throw dust on their heads, and with weeping and mourning cry out:

"'Woe! Woe, O great city,
 where all who had ships on the sea
 became rich through her wealth!
In one hour she has been brought to ruin!
²⁰Rejoice over her, O heaven!
 Rejoice, saints and apostles and
  prophets!
God has judged her for the way she treated
  you.'"

²¹Then a mighty angel picked up a boulder the size of a large millstone and threw it into the sea, and said:

^a2 Greek *unclean*

"With such violence
the great city of Babylon will be thrown
down,
never to be found again.
²²The music of harpists and musicians, flute
players and trumpeters,
will never be heard in you again.
No workman of any trade
will ever be found in you again.
The sound of a millstone
will never be heard in you again.
²³The light of a lamp
will never shine in you again.
The voice of bridegroom and bride
will never be heard in you again.
Your merchants were the world's great
men.
By your magic spell all the nations were
led astray.
²⁴In her was found the blood of prophets and
of the saints,
and of all who have been killed on the
earth.''

Hallelujah!

19 After this I heard what sounded like
the roar of a great multitude in heaven
shouting:

"Hallelujah!
Salvation and glory and power belong to
our God,
² for true and just are his judgments.
He has condemned the great prostitute
who corrupted the earth by her
adulteries.
He has avenged on her the blood of his
servants.''

³And again they shouted:

"Hallelujah!
The smoke from her goes up for ever and
ever.''

⁴The twenty-four elders and the four living
creatures fell down and worshipped God,
who was seated on the throne. And they
cried:

"Amen, Hallelujah!''

⁵Then a voice came from the throne,
saying:

"Praise our God,
all you his servants,
you who fear him,
both small and great!''

⁶Then I heard what sounded like a great
multitude, like the roar of rushing waters and
like loud peals of thunder, shouting:

"Hallelujah!
For our Lord God Almighty reigns.
⁷Let us rejoice and be glad
and give him glory!

For the wedding of the Lamb has come,
and his bride has made herself ready.
⁸Fine linen, bright and clean,
was given her to wear.''

(Fine linen stands for the righteous acts of the
saints.)

⁹Then the angel said to me, "Write:
'Blessed are those who are invited to the
wedding supper of the Lamb!''' And he
added, "These are the true words of God.''

¹⁰At this I fell at his feet to worship him.
But he said to me, "Do not do it! I am a
fellow-servant with you and with your
brothers who hold to the testimony of Jesus.
Worship God! For the testimony of Jesus is
the spirit of prophecy.''

The Rider on the White Horse

¹¹I saw heaven standing open and there
before me was a white horse, whose rider is
called Faithful and True. With justice he
judges and makes war. ¹²His eyes are like
blazing fire, and on his head are many
crowns. He has a name written on him that
no-one knows but he himself. ¹³He is dressed
in a robe dipped in blood, and his name is the
Word of God. ¹⁴The armies of heaven were
following him, riding on white horses and
dressed in fine linen, white and clean. ¹⁵Out
of his mouth comes a sharp sword with which
to strike down the nations. "He will rule
them with an iron sceptre.''ᵃ He treads the
winepress of the fury of the wrath of God
Almighty. ¹⁶On his robe and on his thigh he
has this name written:

KING OF KINGS AND LORD OF LORDS.

¹⁷And I saw an angel standing in the sun,
who cried in a loud voice to all the birds flying
in mid-air, "Come, gather together for the
great supper of God, ¹⁸so that you may eat
the flesh of kings, generals, and mighty men,
of horses and their riders, and the flesh of all
people, free and slave, small and great.''

¹⁹Then I saw the beast and the kings of the
earth and their armies gathered together to
make war against the rider on the horse and
his army. ²⁰But the beast was captured, and
with him the false prophet who had performed the miraculous signs on his behalf.
With these signs he had deluded those who
had received the mark of the beast and worshipped his image. The two of them were
thrown alive into the fiery lake of burning
sulphur. ²¹The rest of them were killed with
the sword that came out of the mouth of the
rider on the horse, and all the birds gorged
themselves on their flesh.

The Thousand Years

20 And I saw an angel coming down out
of heaven, having the key to the
Abyss and holding in his hand a great chain.
²He seized the dragon, that ancient serpent,
who is the devil, or Satan, and bound him for
a thousand years. ³He threw him into the

ᵃ15 Psalm 2:9

REVELATION 20:1–6

'He seized the dragon, that ancient serpent, who is the devil, or Satan, and bound him for a thousand years . . . After that, he must be set free for a short time' (vv. 2, 3b).

JOHN'S IDEA OF A MILLENNIUM, a thousand-year reign of Christ and the saints, has brought untold puzzlement to scores of generations of Christians. It raises all kinds of questions in Christian minds. It sounds so simple. The Devil will be bound for a thousand years, then loosed upon the earth once more. However, no generation of Christians has been satisfied just to take this passage at its face value and leave it in the hands of the Lord.

Since earliest times some have believed that the millennium is already here, that Satan is bound and Christ is triumphant in the hearts of individual Christians. Others, like Augustine, have denied that there will be any literal reign of Christ on earth, and have claimed that John's thoughts should be considered on an entirely spiritual plain. Some have felt that the millennium did not apply to earth at all, but referred to Christ's reign in heaven. There have, too, always been some who believe the millennium is just about to arrive.

Nineteenth-century hopes of inevitable progress towards the millennium were shaken by two world wars in this century. On the other hand we cannot deny that our environment is a thousand times different from that of even two generations ago, let alone that of the last century. We can be pretty sure the millennium has not yet arrived, but we cannot simply dismiss John's vision of a thousand-year reign of Christ. It may be just round the corner, or thousands of years away.

We cannot simply dismiss a literal interpretation of John's words. In practice we should live as though the millennium is upon us.

→1192

REVELATION 21:1–8

'I saw the Holy City, the new Jerusalem, coming down out of heaven from God, prepared as a bride beautifully dressed for her husband' (v. 2).

HOW WE LOVE NEW THINGS. Something as simple as a new page in an exercise book can give a child great pleasure, a chance to start again. How often we resolve to treat something new better than we treated the old one. A new car, perhaps, or a new bike. We start doing all the right things, keeping to the service plan, or oiling the chain correctly.

Then something goes wrong. What was new is new no longer. It suffers the same drawbacks as the old one. The page in the exercise book has things crossed out; the car gets scratched or the engine starts to knock; the bicycle wheels buckle – and so on, for there is nothing essentially new about these things. They are newly fashioned. They may even be better fashioned than the articles they replaced, but they are still man's artefacts, with the same drawbacks, the same tendency to wear out and become shabby. We also become bored with them as we did with their predecessors.

The new Jerusalem is different. It is not just a different one of the same. It is a city of a new order entirely. It is not even just a heavenly city of the present order, for heaven itself has been recreated in John's vision.

We can hardly describe this newness without using pictures very similar to those that John uses. Pictures of what we know now, recreated. Yet somehow I cannot get away from the thought that what we shall experience in the new Jerusalem will be so utterly different from our experience now that even the beautiful, haunting visions of these final chapters of Revelation cannot do it justice.

Our hope is not just for more of the same, but for something so new that John himself can hardly picture it.

→1195

Abyss, and locked and sealed it over him, to keep him from deceiving the nations any more until the thousand years were ended. After that, he must be set free for a short time.

⁴I saw thrones on which were seated those who had been given authority to judge. And I saw the souls of those who had been beheaded because of their testimony for Jesus and because of the word of God. They had not worshipped the beast or his image and had not received his mark on their foreheads or their hands. They came to life and reigned with Christ for a thousand years. ⁵(The rest of the dead did not come to life until the thousand years were ended.) This is the first resurrection. ⁶Blessed and holy are those who have part in the first resurrection. The second death has no power over them, but they will be priests of God and of Christ and will reign with him for a thousand years.

Satan's Doom

⁷When the thousand years are over, Satan will be released from his prison ⁸and will go out to deceive the nations in the four corners of the earth—Gog and Magog—to gather them for battle. In number they are like the sand on the seashore. ⁹They marched across the breadth of the earth and surrounded the camp of God's people, the city he loves. But fire came down from heaven and devoured them. ¹⁰And the devil, who deceived them, was thrown into the lake of burning sulphur, where the beast and the false prophet had been thrown. They will be tormented day and night for ever and ever.

The Dead Are Judged

¹¹Then I saw a great white throne and him who was seated on it. Earth and sky fled from his presence, and there was no place for them. ¹²And I saw the dead, great and small, standing before the throne, and books were opened. Another book was opened, which is the book of life. The dead were judged according to what they had done as recorded in the books. ¹³The sea gave up the dead that were in it, and death and Hades gave up the dead that were in them, and each person was judged according to what he had done. ¹⁴Then death and Hades were thrown into the lake of fire. The lake of fire is the second death. ¹⁵If anyone's name was not found written in the book of life, he was thrown into the lake of fire.

The New Jerusalem

21 Then I saw a new heaven and a new earth, for the first heaven and the first earth had passed away, and there was no longer any sea. ²I saw the Holy City, the new Jerusalem, coming down out of heaven from God, prepared as a bride beautifully dressed for her husband. ³And I heard a loud voice from the throne saying, "Now the dwelling of God is with men, and he will live with

them. They will be his people, and God himself will be with them and be their God. ⁴He will wipe every tear from their eyes. There will be no more death or mourning or crying or pain, for the old order of things has passed away."

⁵He who was seated on the throne said, "I am making everything new!" Then he said, "Write this down, for these words are trustworthy and true."

⁶He said to me: "It is done. I am the Alpha and the Omega, the Beginning and the End. To him who is thirsty I will give to drink without cost from the spring of the water of life. ⁷He who overcomes will inherit all this, and I will be his God and he will be my son. ⁸But the cowardly, the unbelieving, the vile, the murderers, the sexually immoral, those who practise magic arts, the idolaters and all liars—their place will be in the fiery lake of burning sulphur. This is the second death."

⁹One of the seven angels who had the seven bowls full of the seven last plagues came and said to me, "Come, I will show you the bride, the wife of the Lamb." ¹⁰And he carried me away in the Spirit to a mountain great and high, and showed me the Holy City, Jerusalem, coming down out of heaven from God. ¹¹It shone with the glory of God, and its brilliance was like that of a very precious jewel, like a jasper, clear as crystal. ¹²It had a great, high wall with twelve gates, and with twelve angels at the gates. On the gates were written the names of the twelve tribes of Israel. ¹³There were three gates on the east, three on the north, three on the south and three on the west. ¹⁴The wall of the city had twelve foundations, and on them were the names of the twelve apostles of the Lamb.

¹⁵The angel who talked with me had a measuring rod of gold to measure the city, its gates and its walls. ¹⁶The city was laid out like a square, as long as it was wide. He measured the city with the rod and found it to be 12,000 stadia[a] in length, and as wide and high as it is long. ¹⁷He measured its wall and it was 144 cubits[b] by man's measurement, which the angel was using. ¹⁸The wall was made of jasper, and the city of pure gold, as pure as glass. ¹⁹The foundations of the city walls were decorated with every kind of precious stone. The first foundation was jasper, the second sapphire, the third chalcedony, the fourth emerald, ²⁰the fifth sardonyx, the sixth carnelian, the seventh chrysolite, the eighth beryl, the ninth topaz, the tenth chrysoprase, the eleventh jacinth, and the twelfth amethyst.[d] ²¹The twelve gates were twelve pearls, each gate made of a single pearl. The great street of the city was of pure gold, like transparent glass.

²²I did not see a temple in the city, because the Lord God Almighty and the Lamb are its temple. ²³The city does not need the sun or the moon to shine on it, for the glory of God gives it light, and the Lamb is its lamp. ²⁴The nations will walk by its light, and the kings of

---

[a]16 That is, about 1,400 miles (about 2,200 kilometres)   [b]17 That is, about 200 feet (about 65 metres)
[c]17 Or high   [d]20 The precise identification of some of these precious stones is uncertain.

the earth will bring their splendour into it. 25On no day will its gates ever be shut, for there will be no night there. 26The glory and honour of the nations will be brought into it. 27Nothing impure will ever enter it, nor will anyone who does what is shameful or deceitful, but only those whose names are written in the Lamb's book of life.

The River of Life

22 Then the angel showed me the river of the water of life, as clear as crystal, flowing from the throne of God and of the Lamb 2down the middle of the great street of the city. On each side of the river stood the tree of life, bearing twelve crops of fruit, yielding its fruit every month. And the leaves of the tree are for the healing of the nations. 3No longer will there be any curse. The throne of God and of the Lamb will be in the city, and his servants will serve him. 4They will see his face, and his name will be on their foreheads. 5There will be no more night. They will not need the light of a lamp or the light of the sun, for the Lord God will give them light. And they will reign for ever and ever.

6The angel said to me, "These words are trustworthy and true. The Lord, the God of the spirits of the prophets, sent his angel to show his servants the things that must soon take place."

Jesus Is Coming

7"Behold, I am coming soon! Blessed is he who keeps the words of the prophecy in this book."

8I, John, am the one who heard and saw these things. And when I had heard and seen them, I fell down to worship at the feet of the angel who had been showing them to me. 9But he said to me, "Do not do it! I am a fellow-servant with you and with your brothers the prophets and of all who keep the words of this book. Worship God!"

10Then he told me, "Do not seal up the words of the prophecy of this book, because the time is near. 11Let him who does wrong continue to do wrong; let him who is vile continue to be vile; let him who does right continue to do right; and let him who is holy continue to be holy."

12"Behold, I am coming soon! My reward is with me, and I will give to everyone according to what he has done. 13I am the Alpha and the Omega, the First and the Last, the Beginning and the End.

14"Blessed are those who wash their robes, that they may have the right to the tree of life and may go through the gates into the city. 15Outside are the dogs, those who practise magic arts, the sexually immoral, the murderers, the idolaters and everyone who loves and practises falsehood.

16"I, Jesus, have sent my angel to give youª this testimony for the churches. I am the Root and the Offspring of David, and the bright Morning Star."

17The Spirit and the bride say, "Come!" And let him who hears say, "Come!" Whoever is thirsty, let him come; and whoever wishes, let him take the free gift of the water of life.

18I warn everyone who hears the words of the prophecy of this book: If anyone adds anything to them, God will add to him the plagues described in this book. 19And if anyone takes words away from this book of prophecy, God will take away from him his share in the tree of life and in the holy city, which are described in this book.

20He who testifies to these things says, "Yes, I am coming soon."

Amen. Come, Lord Jesus.

21The grace of the Lord Jesus be with God's people. Amen.

ª16 The Greek is plural.

Table
of Weights
and
Measures

Table of Weights and Measures

	BIBLICAL UNIT	APPROXIMATE IMPERIAL EQUIVALENT	APPROXIMATE METRIC EQUIVALENT
WEIGHTS			
talent	*(60 minas)*	75 pounds	34 kilograms
mina	*(50 shekels)*	1¼ pounds	0.6 kilogram
shekel	*(2 bekas)*	⅖ ounce	11.5 grams
pim	*(⅔ shekel)*	¼ ounce	7.7 grams
beka	*(10 gerahs)*	⅕ ounce	5.8 grams
gerah		¹⁄₅₀ ounce	0.6 gram
LENGTH			
cubit		18 inches	0.5 metre
span		9 inches	23 centimetres
handbreadth		3 inches	8 centimetres
CAPACITY			
Dry Measure			
cor [homer]	*(10 ephahs)*	6 bushels	220 litres
lethek	*(5 ephahs)*	3 bushels	110 litres
ephah	*(10 omers)*	⅗ bushel	22 litres
seah	*(⅓ ephah)*	13 pints	7.3 litres
omer	*(¹⁄₁₀ ephah)*	4 pints	2 litres
cab	*(¹⁄₁₈ ephah)*	2 pints	1 litre
Liquid Measure			
bath	*(1 ephah)*	5 gallons	22 litres
hin	*(⅙ bath)*	7 pints	4 litres
log	*(¹⁄₇₂ bath)*	½ pint	0.3 litre

The figures of the table are calculated on the basis of a shekel equalling 11.5 grams, a cubit equalling 18 inches and an ephah equalling 22 litres. It is based upon the best available information, but it is not intended to be mathematically precise; like the measurement equivalents in the footnotes, it merely gives approximate amounts and distances. Weights and measures differed somewhat at various times and places in the ancient world. There is uncertainty particularly about the ephah and the bath; further discoveries may give more light on these units of capacity.

Special Seasons of the Year Reading Plan

Advent

1 Luke 3:1–9, 15–18
2 Matthew 25:1–13
3 1 Thessalonians 5:1–5
4 Isaiah 7:10–17

5 Isaiah 9:2–7
6 Isaiah 11:1–9
7 Isaiah 12:1–6

Christmas

1 Luke 1:39–45, 57–66
2 Luke 2:1–20
3 John 1:1–5
4 Luke 2:21–35

5 Luke 2:36–40
6 Matthew 2:1–12
7 Matthew 2:13–23

Easter

1 Matthew 21:1–11
2 Hebrews 12:1–13
3 John 16:17–33
4 Matthew 26:36–45
5 Matthew 26:46–56

6 Luke 23:26–31
7 Luke 23:33–49
8 John 19:38–20:18
9 Luke 24:13–35
10 John 20:24–31

Pentecost

1 Acts 2:1–4
2 Acts 2:5–13
3 Acts 2:36–47
4 Acts 3:1–12

5 Acts 4:1–14
6 Acts 4:13–22
7 Acts 4:23–31

The Bible in One Year

One Year Bible Reading Plan

This reading plan divides the complete Bible into 365 portions, dated for every day of the year. Each section offers a reading from the Old Testament, the New Testament, and from Psalms or Proverbs. The Old Testament is in broadly chronological order; otherwise, traditional Bible order is maintained.

January

1	Ge 1:1–2:17	Mt 1:1–17	Ps 1:1–6
2	Ge 2:18–4:16	Mt 1:18–2:18	Ps 2:1–12
3	Ge 4:17–6:22	Mt 2:19–3:17	Ps 3:1–8
4	Ge 7:1–9:17	Mt 4:1–22	Pr 1:1–7
5	Ge 9:18–11:9	Mt 4:23–5:20	Ps 4:1–8
6	Ge 11:10–13:18	Mt 5:21–42	Ps 5:1–12
7	Ge 14:1–16:16	Mt 5:43–6:24	Ps 6:1–10
8	Ge 17:1–18:33	Mt 6:25–7:23	Pr 1:8–19
9	Ge 19:1–20:18	Mt 7:24–8:22	Ps 7:1–9
10	Ge 21:1–23:20	Mt 8:23–9:13	Ps 7:10–17
11	Ge 24:1–67	Mt 9:14–38	Ps 8:1–9
12	Ge 25:1–26:35	Mt 10:1–31	Pr 1:20–33
13	Ge 27:1–28:22	Mt 10:32–11:10	Ps 9:1–6
14	Ge 29:1–30:43	Mt 11:11–30	Ps 9:7–12
15	Ge 31:1–55	Mt 12:1–21	Ps 9:13–20
16	Ge 32:1–33:20	Mt 12:22–45	Pr 2:1–11
17	Ge 34:1–35:29	Mt 12:46–13:17	Ps 10:1–11
18	Ge 36:1–37:36	Mt 13:18–35	Ps 10:12–18
19	Ge 38:1–39:23	Mt 13:36–58	Ps 11:1–7
20	Ge 40:1–41:40	Mt 14:1–21	Pr 2:12–22
21	Ge 41:41–42:38	Mt 14:22–15:9	Ps 12:1–8
22	Ge 43:1–44:34	Mt 15:10–39	Ps 13:1–6
23	Ge 45:1–46:34	Mt 16:1–20	Ps 14:1–7
24	Ge 47:1–48:22	Mt 16:21–17:13	Pr 3:1–10
25	Ge 49:1–50:26	Mt 17:14–18:9	Ps 15:1–5
26	Job 1:1–4:11	Mt 18:10–35	Ps 16:1–11
27	Job 4:12–7:21	Mt 19:1–15	Ps 17:1–5
28	Job 8:1–10:22	Mt 19:16–30	Pr 3:11–20
29	Job 11:1–14:22	Mt 20:1–19	Ps 17:6–12
30	Job 15:1–18:21	Mt 20:20–34	Ps 17:13–15
31	Job 19:1–21:34	Mt 21:1–17	Ps 18:1–6

February

1	Job 22:1–24:25	Mt 21:18–32	Pr 3:21–35
2	Job 25:1–29:25	Mt 21:33–22:14	Ps 18:7–15
3	Job 30:1–32:22	Mt 22:15–45	Ps 18:16–24
4	Job 33:1–35:16	Mt 23:1–39	Ps 18:25–36
5	Job 36:1–38:41	Mt 24:1–31	Pr 4:1–9
6	Job 39:1–42:17	Mt 24:32–25:13	Ps 18:37–42
7	Ex 1:1–2:25	Mt 25:14–46	Ps 18:43–50
8	Ex 3:1–4:31	Mt 26:1–30	Ps 19:1–6
9	Ex 5:1–6:27	Mt 26:31–46	Pr 4:10–19
10	Ex 6:28–8:32	Mt 26:47–68	Ps 19:7–14
11	Ex 9:1–10:29	Mt 26:69–27:10	Ps 20:1–9
12	Ex 11:1–12:51	Mt 27:11–44	Ps 21:1–7
13	Ex 13:1–14:31	Mt 27:45–66	Pr 4:20–27

14	Ex 15:1–16:36	Mt 28:1–20	Ps 21:8–13
15	Ex 17:1–18:27	Mk 1:1–28	Ps 22:1–11
16	Ex 19:1–20:26	Mk 1:29–2:17	Ps 22:12–21
17	Ex 21:1–22:31	Mk 2:18–3:30	Pr 5:1–14
18	Ex 23:1–24:18	Mk 3:31–4:29	Ps 22:22–31
19	Ex 25:1–26:37	Mk 4:30–5:20	Ps 23:1–6
20	Ex 27:1–28:43	Mk 5:21–6:6a	Ps 24:1–10
21	Ex 29:1–30:38	Mk 6:6b–29	Pr 5:15–23
22	Ex 31:1–33:6	Mk 6:30–56	Ps 25:1–7
23	Ex 33:7–34:35	Mk 7:1–30	Ps 25:8–15
24	Ex 35:1–36:38	Mk 7:31–8:13	Ps 25:16–22
25	Ex 37:1–38:31	Mk 8:14–9:1	Pr 6:1–11
26	Ex 39:1–40:38	Mk 9:2–32	Ps 26:1–12
27	Lev 1:1–2:16	Mk 9:33–10:12	Ps 27:1–6
28	Lev 3:1–4:35	Mk 10:13–31	Ps 27:7–14

March

1	Lev 5:1–7:10	Mk 10:32–52	Pr 6:12–19
2	Lev 7:11–8:36	Mk 11:1–26	Ps 28:1–9
3	Lev 9:1–10:20	Mk 11:27–12:12	Ps 29:1–11
4	Lev 11:1–12:9	Mk 12:13–27	Ps 30:1–7
5	Lev 13:1–59	Mk 12:28–44	Pr 6:20–29
6	Lev 14:1–57	Mk 13:1–31	Ps 30:8–12
7	Lev 15:1–16:34	Mk 13:32–14:16	Ps 31:1–8
8	Lev 17:1–18:30	Mk 14:17–42	Ps 31:9–18
9	Lev 19:1–20:27	Mk 14:43–72	Pr 6:30–35
10	Lev 21:1–22:33	Mk 15:1–32	Ps 31:19–24
11	Lev 23:1–24:23	Mk 15:33–47	Ps 32:1–11
12	Lev 25:1–26:13	Mk 16:1–20	Ps 33:1–11
13	Lev 26:14–27:34	Lk 1:1–25	Pr 7:1–9
14	Nu 1:1–2:9	Lk 1:26–38	Ps 33:12–22
15	Nu 2:10–3:51	Lk 1:39–56	Ps 34:1–10
16	Nu 4:1–5:10	Lk 1:57–80	Ps 34:11–22
17	Nu 5:11–6:27	Lk 2:1–20	Pr 7:10–20
18	Nu 7:1–65	Lk 2:21–40	Ps 35:1–10
19	Nu 7:66–9:14	Lk 2:41–52	Ps 35:11–18
20	Nu 9:15–11:23	Lk 3:1–22	Ps 35:19–28
21	Nu 11:24–13:33	Lk 3:23–4:13	Pr 7:21–27
22	Nu 14:1–15:21	Lk 4:14–37	Ps 36:1–12
23	Nu 15:22–16:35	Lk 4:38–5:16	Ps 37:1–9
24	Nu 16:36–18:32	Lk 5:17–32	Ps 37:10–20
25	Nu 19:1–21:3	Lk 5:33–6:11	Pr 8:1–11
26	Nu 21:4–22:20	Lk 6:12–36	Ps 37:21–31
27	Nu 22:21–23:30	Lk 6:37–7:10	Ps 37:32–40
28	Nu 24:1–26:11	Lk 7:11–35	Ps 38:1–12
29	Nu 26:12–27:11	Lk 7:36–50	Pr 8:12–21
30	Nu 27:12–29:11	Lk 8:1–18	Ps 38:13–22
31	Nu 29:12–31:24	Lk 8:19–39	Ps 39:1–13

April

1	Nu 31:25–32:42	Lk 8:40–9:9	Ps 40:1–8
2	Nu 33:1–34:29	Lk 9:10–27	Pr 8:22–31
3	Nu 35:1–36:13	Lk 9:28–56	Ps 40:9–17
4	Dt 1:1–2:37	Lk 9:57–10:24	Ps 41:1–6
5	Dt 3:1–4:49	Lk 10:25–11:4	Ps 41:7–13
6	Dt 5:1–6:25	Lk 11:5–32	Pr 8:32–36
7	Dt 7:1–8:20	Lk 11:33–54	Ps 42:1–6a
8	Dt 9:1–10:22	Lk 12:1–34	Ps 42:6b–11
9	Dt 11:1–12:32	Lk 12:35–59	Ps 43:1–5
10	Dt 13:1–14:29	Lk 13:1–30	Pr 9:1–12
11	Dt 15:1–16:20	Lk 13:31–14:14	Ps 44:1–12
12	Dt 16:21–18:22	Lk 14:15–35	Ps 44:13–26
13	Dt 19:1–20:20	Lk 15:1–32	Ps 45:1–9
14	Dt 21:1–22:30	Lk 16:1–18	Pr 9:13–18
15	Dt 23:1–25:19	Lk 16:19–17:10	Ps 45:10–17
16	Dt 26:1–28:14	Lk 17:11–37	Ps 46:1–11
17	Dt 28:15–68	Lk 18:1–30	Ps 47:1–9
18	Dt 29:1–30:10	Lk 18:31–19:10	Pr 10:1–10
19	Dt 30:11–31:30	Lk 19:11–44	Ps 48:1–8
20	Dt 32:1–52	Lk 19:45–20:26	Ps 48:9–14
21	Dt 33:1–34:12	Lk 20:27–21:4	Ps 49:1–20
22	Jos 1:1–2:24	Lk 21:5–38	Pr 10:11–20
23	Jos 3:1–5:12	Lk 22:1–38	Ps 50:1–15
24	Jos 5:13–7:26	Lk 22:39–62	Ps 50:16–23
25	Jos 8:1–9:15	Lk 22:63–23:25	Ps 51:1–9
26	Jos 9:16–10:43	Lk 23:26–56	Pr 10:21–30
27	Jos 11:1–12:24	Lk 24:1–35	Ps 51:10–19
28	Jos 13:1–14:15	Lk 24:36–53	Ps 52:1–9
29	Jos 15:1–63	Jn 1:1–28	Ps 53:1–6
30	Jos 16:1–18:28	Jn 1:29–51	Pr 10:31–11:8

May

1	Jos 19:1–20:9	Jn 2:1–25	Ps 54:1–7
2	Jos 21:1–22:34	Jn 3:1–21	Ps 55:1–11
3	Jos 23:1–24:33	Jn 3:22–36	Ps 55:12–23
4	Jdg 1:1–2:5	Jn 4:1–26	Pr 11:9–18
5	Jdg 2:6–3:31	Jn 4:27–42	Ps 56:1–13
6	Jdg 4:1–5:31	Jn 4:43–5:15	Ps 57:1–6
7	Jdg 6:1–7:8a	Jn 5:16–30	Ps 57:7–11
8	Jdg 7:8b–8:35	Jn 5:31–47	Pr 11:19–28
9	Jdg 9:1–57	Jn 6:1–24	Ps 58:1–11
10	Jdg 10:1–11:28	Jn 6:25–59	Ps 59:1–8
11	Jdg 11:29–13:25	Jn 6:60–7:13	Ps 59:9–17
12	Jdg 14:1–15:20	Jn 7:14–44	Pr 11:29–12:7
13	Jdg 16:1–17:13	Jn 7:45–8:11	Ps 60:1–4
14	Jdg 18:1–19:30	Jn 8:12–30	Ps 60:5–12
15	Jdg 20:1–21:25	Jn 8:31–59	Ps 61:1–8
16	Ru 1:1–2:23	Jn 9:1–34	Pr 12:8–17

17	Ru 3:1–4:22	Jn 9:35–10:21	Ps 62:1–12
18	1Sa 1:1–2:26	Jn 10:22–42	Ps 63:1–11
19	1Sa 2:27–4:22	Jn 11:1–44	Ps 64:1–10
20	1Sa 5:1–7:17	Jn 11:45–12:11	Pr 12:18–27
21	1Sa 8:1–10:8	Jn 12:12–36	Ps 65:1–13
22	1Sa 10:9–12:25	Jn 12:37–13:17	Ps 66:1–12
23	1Sa 13:1–14:23	Jn 13:18–38	Ps 66:13–20
24	1Sa 14:24–15:35	Jn 14:1–31	Pr 12:28–13:9
25	1Sa 16:1–17:37	Jn 15:1–16:4	Ps 67:1–7
26	1Sa 17:38–18:30	Jn 16:5–17:5	Ps 68:1–6
27	1Sa 19:1–20:42	Jn 17:6–26	Ps 68:7–14
28	1Sa 21:1–23:29	Jn 18:1–24	Pr 13:10–19
29	1Sa 24:1–25:44	Jn 18:25–40	Ps 68:15–20
30	1Sa 26:1–28:25	Jn 19:1–27	Ps 68:21–27
31	1Sa 29:1–31:13	Jn 19:28–20:9	Ps 68:28–35

June

1	2Sa 1:1–2:7	Jn 20:10–31	Pr 13:20–14:4
2	2Sa 2:8–3:21	Jn 21:1–25	Ps 69:1–12
3	2Sa 3:22–5:16	Ac 1:1–22	Ps 69:13–28
4	2Sa 5:17–6:23	Ac 1:23–2:21	Ps 69:29–36
5	2Sa 7:1–8:18	Ac 2:22–47	Pr 14:5–14
6	2Sa 9:1–10:19	Ac 3:1–26	Ps 70:1–5
7	2Sa 11:1–12:31	Ac 4:1–22	Ps 71:1–8
8	2Sa 13:1–39	Ac 4:23–5:11	Ps 71:9–18
9	2Sa 14:1–15:12	Ac 5:12–42	Pr 14:15–24
10	2Sa 15:13–16:23	Ac 6:1–7:19	Ps 71:19–24
11	2Sa 17:1–18:18	Ac 7:20–43	Ps 72:1–20
12	2Sa 18:19–19:43	Ac 7:44–8:3	Ps 73:1–14
13	2Sa 20:1–21:22	Ac 8:4–40	Pr 14:25–35
14	2Sa 22:1–23:7	Ac 9:1–31	Ps 73:15–28
15	2Sa 23:8–24:25	Ac 9:32–10:23a	Ps 74:1–9
16	1Ki 1:1–2:12	Ac 10:23b–11:18	Ps 74:10–17
17	1Ki 2:13–3:15	Ac 11:19–12:19a	Pr 15:1–10
18	1Ki 3:16–5:18	Ac 12:19b–13:15	Ps 74:18–23
19	1Ki 6:1–7:22	Ac 13:16–41	Ps 75:1–10
20	1Ki 7:23–8:21	Ac 13:42–14:7	Ps 76:1–12
21	1Ki 8:22–9:9	Ac 14:8–28	Pr 15:11–20
22	1Ki 9:10–11:13	Ac 15:1–21	Ps 77:1–9
23	1Ki 11:14–12:24	Ac 15:22–41	Ps 77:10–20
24	1Ki 12:25–14:20	Ac 16:1–15	Ps 78:1–8
25	1Ki 14:21–16:7	Ac 16:16–40	Pr 15:21–30
26	1Ki 16:8–18:15	Ac 17:1–21	Ps 78:9–16
27	1Ki 18:16–19:21	Ac 17:22–18:8	Ps 78:17–31
28	1Ki 20:1–21:29	Ac 18:9–28	Ps 78:32–39
29	1Ki 22:1–53	Ac 19:1–41	Pr 15:31–16:7
30	2Ki 1:1–2:25	Ac 20:1–38	Ps 78:40–55

July

1	2Ki 3:1–4:37	Ac 21:1–26	Ps 78:56–72
2	2Ki 4:38–6:23	Ac 21:27–22:16	Ps 79:1–13
3	2Ki 6:24–8:15	Ac 22:17–23:11	Pr 16:8–17
4	2Ki 8:16–9:37	Ac 23:12–35	Ps 80:1–7
5	2Ki 10:1–11:21	Ac 24:1–27	Ps 80:8–19
6	2Ki 12:1–14:22	Ac 25:1–22	Ps 81:1–7
7	2Ki 14:23–15:38	Ac 25:23–26:23	Pr 16:18–27
8	2Ki 16:1–17:41	Ac 26:24–27:12	Ps 81:8–16
9	2Ki 18:1–19:13	Ac 27:13–32	Ps 82:1–8
10	2Ki 19:14–20:21	Ac 27:33–28:16	Ps 83:1–18
11	2Ki 21:1–23:7	Ac 28:17–31	Pr 16:28–17:4
12	2Ki 23:8–24:17	Ro 1:1–17	Ps 84:1–7
13	2Ki 24:18–25:30	Ro 1:18–32	Ps 84:8–12
14	Jnh 1:1–4:11	Ro 2:1–24	Ps 85:1–7
15	Am 1:1–2:16	Ro 2:25–3:8	Pr 17:5–14
16	Am 3:1–4:13	Ro 3:9–31	Ps 85:8–13
17	Am 5:1–27	Ro 4:1–15	Ps 86:1–10
18	Am 6:1–7:17	Ro 4:16–5:11	Ps 86:11–17
19	Am 8:1–9:15	Ro 5:12–6:10	Pr 17:15–24
20	Hos 1:1–2:23	Ro 6:11–23	Ps 87:1–7
21	Hos 3:1–5:15	Ro 7:1–13	Ps 88:1–9a
22	Hos 6:1–7:16	Ro 7:14–8:8	Ps 88:9b–18
23	Hos 8:1–9:17	Ro 8:9–27	Pr 17:25–18:6
24	Hos 10:1–11:11	Ro 8:28–39	Ps 89:1–8
25	Hos 11:12–14:9	Ro 9:1–21	Ps 89:9–13
26	1Ch 1:1–2:17	Ro 9:22–10:4	Ps 89:14–18
27	1Ch 2:18–4:8	Ro 10:5–11:10	Pr 18:7–16
28	1Ch 4:9–5:26	Ro 11:11–32	Ps 89:19–29
29	1Ch 6:1–81	Ro 11:33–12:21	Ps 89:30–37
30	1Ch 7:1–8:28	Ro 13:1–14	Ps 89:38–45
31	1Ch 8:29–10:14	Ro 14:1–18	Pr 18:17–19:2

August

1	1Ch 11:1–12:18	Ro 14:19–15:13	Ps 89:46–52
2	1Ch 12:19–14:17	Ro 15:14–33	Ps 90:1–10
3	1Ch 15:1–16:36	Ro 16:1–27	Ps 90:11–17
4	1Ch 16:37–18:17	1Co 1:1–17	Pr 19:3–12
5	1Ch 19:1–22:1	1Co 1:18–2:5	Ps 91:1–8
6	1Ch 22:2–23:32	1Co 2:6–16	Ps 91:9–16
7	1Ch 24:1–26:13	1Co 3:1–23	Ps 92:1–15
8	1Ch 26:14–27:34	1Co 4:1–21	Pr 19:13–22
9	1Ch 28:1–29:30	1Co 5:1–13	Ps 93:1–5
10	2Ch 1:1–17	1Co 6:1–20	Ps 94:1–11
11	Ecc 1:1–3:22	1Co 7:1–16	Ps 94:12–23
12	Ecc 4:1–6:12	1Co 7:17–31	Pr 19:23–20:4
13	Ecc 7:1–9:12	1Co 7:32–8:13	Ps 95:1–11

14	Ecc 9:13–12:14	1Co 9:1–18	Ps 96:1–13
15	2Ch 2:1–5:1	1Co 9:19–10:13	Ps 97:1–12
16	2Ch 5:2–7:10	1Co 10:14–11:1	Pr 20:5–14
17	2Ch 7:11–9:31	1Co 11:2–34	Ps 98:1–9
18	SS 1:1–4:16	1Co 12:1–26	Ps 99:1–9
19	SS 5:1–8:14	1Co 12:27–13:13	Ps 100:1–5
20	2Ch 10:1–12:16	1Co 14:1–17	Pr 20:15–24
21	2Ch 13:1–15:19	1Co 14:18–40	Ps 101:1–8
22	2Ch 16:1–18:27	1Co 15:1–34	Ps 102:1–11
23	2Ch 18:28–21:3	1Co 15:35–49	Ps 102:12–17
24	2Ch 21:4–23:21	1Co 15:50–16:4	Pr 20:25–21:4
25	2Ch 24:1–25:28	1Co 16:5–24	Ps 102:18–28
26	2Ch 26:1–28:27	2Co 1:1–11	Ps 103:1–12
27	2Ch 29:1–31:1	2Co 1:12–22	Ps 103:13–22
28	2Ch 31:2–33:20	2Co 1:23–2:11	Pr 21:5–16
29	2Ch 33:21–35:19	2Co 2:12–3:6	Ps 104:1–18
30	2Ch 35:20–36:23	2Co 3:7–18	Ps 104:19–30
31	Mic 1:1–4:13	2Co 4:1–18	Ps 104:31–35

September

1	Mic 5:1–7:20	2Co 5:1–10	Pr 21:17–26
2	Isa 1:1–2:22	2Co 5:11–6:2	Ps 105:1–11
3	Isa 3:1–5:7	2Co 6:3–7:1	Ps 105:12–22
4	Isa 5:8–8:10	2Co 7:2–16	Ps 105:23–36
5	Isa 8:11–10:19	2Co 8:1–15	Pr 21:27–22:6
6	Isa 10:20–13:22	2Co 8:16–9:5	Ps 105:37–45
7	Isa 14:1–16:14	2Co 9:6–15	Ps 106:1–15
8	Isa 17:1–19:25	2Co 10:1–18	Ps 106:16–31
9	Isa 20:1–23:18	2Co 11:1–15	Pr 22:7–16
10	Isa 24:1–26:21	2Co 11:16–33	Ps 106:32–39
11	Isa 27:1–28:29	2Co 12:1–10	Ps 106:40–48
12	Isa 29:1–30:18	2Co 12:11–21	Ps 107:1–9
13	Isa 30:19–32:20	2Co 13:1–14	Pr 22:17–27
14	Isa 33:1–35:10	Gal 1:1–24	Ps 107:10–22
15	Isa 36:1–37:38	Gal 2:1–10	Ps 107:23–32
16	Isa 38:1–40:31	Gal 2:11–3:9	Ps 107:33–43
17	Isa 41:1–42:25	Gal 3:10–25	Pr 22:28–23:9
18	Isa 43:1–44:23	Gal 3:26–4:20	Ps 108:1–5
19	Isa 44:24–46:13	Gal 4:21–5:6	Ps 108:6–13
20	Isa 47:1–49:7	Gal 5:7–26	Ps 109:1–20
21	Isa 49:8–51:16	Gal 6:1–18	Pr 23:10–18
22	Isa 51:17–54:17	Eph 1:1–23	Ps 109:21–31
23	Isa 55:1–57:13	Eph 2:1–22	Ps 110:1–7
24	Isa 57:14–59:21	Eph 3:1–21	Ps 111:1–10
25	Isa 60:1–62:12	Eph 4:1–16	Pr 23:19–28
26	Isa 63:1–65:16	Eph 4:17–5:7	Ps 112:1–10
27	Isa 65:17–66:24	Eph 5:8–33	Ps 113:1–9
28	Na 1:1–3:19	Eph 6:1–24	Ps 114:1–8
29	Zep 1:1–3:20	Php 1:1–26	Pr 23:29–24:4
30	Jer 1:1–2:30	Php 1:27–2:11	Ps 115:1–11

October

1	Jer 2:31–4:9	Php 2:12–30	Ps 115:12–18
2	Jer 4:10–5:31	Php 3:1–4:1	Ps 116:1–11
3	Jer 6:1–7:29	Php 4:2–23	Pr 24:5–14
4	Jer 7:30–9:16	Col 1:1–23	Ps 116:12–19
5	Jer 9:17–11:13	Col 1:24–2:5	Ps 117:1–2
6	Jer 11:14–13:27	Col 2:6–23	Ps 118:1–16
7	Jer 14:1–15:21	Col 3:1–4:1	Pr 24:15–22
8	Jer 16:1–17:27	Col 4:2–18	Ps 118:17–29
9	Jer 18:1–20:18	1Th 1:1–2:16	Ps 119:1–8
10	Jer 21:1–23:8	1Th 2:17–3:13	Ps 119:9–16
11	Jer 23:9–25:14	1Th 4:1–18	Pr 24:23–34
12	Jer 25:15–26:24	1Th 5:1–28	Ps 119:17–24
13	Jer 27:1–29:23	2Th 1:1–12	Ps 119:25–32
14	Jer 29:24–31:14	2Th 2:1–17	Ps 119:33–40
15	Jer 31:15–32:25	2Th 3:1–18	Pr 25:1–10
16	Jer 32:26–34:22	1Ti 1:1–20	Ps 119:41–48
17	Jer 35:1–37:21	1Ti 2:1–15	Ps 119:49–56
18	Jer 38:1–40:6	1Ti 3:1–16	Ps 119:57–64
19	Jer 40:7–42:22	1Ti 4:1–16	Pr 25:11–20
20	Jer 43:1–45:5	1Ti 5:1–6:2	Ps 119:65–72
21	Jer 46:1–47:7	1Ti 6:3–21	Ps 119:73–80
22	Jer 48:1–49:6	2Ti 1:1–18	Ps 119:81–88
23	Jer 49:7–50:10	2Ti 2:1–26	Pr 25:21–26:2
24	Jer 50:11–51:14	2Ti 3:1–17	Ps 119:89–96
25	Jer 51:15–64	2Ti 4:1–22	Ps 119:97–104
26	Jer 52:1–34	Tit 1:1–16	Ps 119:105–112
27	Hab 1:1–3:19	Tit 2:1–15	Pr 26:3–12
28	La 1:1–2:6	Tit 3:1–15	Ps 119:113–120
29	La 2:7–3:39	Phm 1–25	Ps 119:21–128
30	La 3:40–5:22	Heb 1:1–14	Ps 119:129–136
31	Ob 1–21	Heb 2:1–18	Pr 26:13–22

November

1	Joel 1:1–2:17	Heb 3:1–19	Ps 119:137–144
2	Joel 2:18–3:21	Heb 4:1–13	Ps 119:145–152
3	Eze 1:1–3:27	Heb 4:14–5:10	Ps 119:153–160
4	Eze 4:1–6:14	Heb 5:11–6:12	Pr 26:23–27:4
5	Eze 7:1–9:11	Heb 6:13–7:10	Ps 119:161–168
6	Eze 10:1–12:28	Heb 7:11–28	Ps 119:169–176
7	Eze 13:1–15:8	Heb 8:1–13	Ps 120:1–7
8	Eze 16:1–63	Heb 9:1–15	Pr 27:5–14
9	Eze 17:1–18:32	Heb 9:16–28	Ps 121:1–8
10	Eze 19:1–20:44	Heb 10:1–18	Ps 122:1–9
11	Eze 20:45–22:22	Heb 10:19–39	Ps 123:1–4
12	Eze 22:23–23:49	Heb 11:1–16	Pr 27:15–22
13	Eze 24:1–25:17	Heb 11:17–40	Ps 124:1–8
14	Eze 26:1–27:36	Heb 12:1–13	Ps 125:1–5
15	Eze 28:1–29:21	Heb 12:14–29	Ps 126:1–6
16	Eze 30:1–31:18	Heb 13:1–25	Pr 27:23–28:6
17	Eze 32:1–33:20	Jas 1:1–27	Ps 127:1–5

December

Subject Index

NEW INTERNATIONAL VERSION

Bible Guide

INTRODUCTION

HOW TO USE THE BIBLE GUIDE

These 'Helps' are intended to help you to study and understand your Bible. You will want to refer to them from time to time whenever you study your Bible and although they can't possibly tell you all you want to know because they are a brief guide only, they will provide you with a lot of background information.

First, a word about using Bible references. What does 1 Corinthians 1:18 mean? If you look in the Index at the beginning of your Bible you will see the books of the Bible listed. Notice that several books have two parts: Samuel and Kings in the Old Testament for example. Corinthians is in the New Testament and so our reference is to the first book of Corinthians. After the name of the book comes the chapter of the book and then the verse—in this case, chapter one, verse eighteen.

INDEX TO THE BIBLE GUIDE

THE BIBLE AT A GLANCE

BIBLE REFERENCE	SETTING AND IMPORTANT CHARACTERS	IMPORTANT EVENTS	APPROXIMATE DATE
Genesis 1-11	*'Eden'* *Mesopotamia* Adam & Eve Noah	Creation Flood	
Genesis 12-36	*'Israel'* Abraham Isaac Jacob		1800 B.C.
Genesis 37 – Exodus 12	*Egypt* Joseph Moses	'Exodus' Giving of the Law	1400 B.C.
Exodus 13 – Deuteronomy 34	*Desert Wanderings* Moses		
Joshua – 1 Samuel 7 Ruth	*Israel* Joshua Samuel	Conquest Settlement	1200 B.C.
1 Samuel 8 – 1 Kings 11 1 Chronicles – 2 Chronicles 11	*Israel* Saul David Solomon	Founding of the monarchy	1000 B.C.
1 Kings 12 – 2 Kings 25 2 Chronicles 12-36 Jonah Joel Nahum Zephaniah Lamentations Habakkuk Obadiah	*Israel* Elijah Elisha — Amos Hosea Isaiah Micah	Kingdom of Israel divided into Israel and Judah	900 B.C.
	Babylon Jeremiah Ezekiel Daniel	Israel 'ended' Judah exiled	587 B.C.
Ezra Nehemiah Esther	*Israel* Haggai Zechariah Malachi	'Return'	400 B.C.
Matthew Mark Luke John	*Israel* Jesus Christ	Birth, death, resurrection	
Acts Letters Revelation	*'All the World'* Peter John Paul	Birth & growth of the churches	100 A.D.

Psalms, Proverbs, Job, Song of Songs, Ecclesiastes

PLAN OF THE BIBLE

GENESIS

As its name implies this book is about origins or beginnings—of the universe, of the different nations, of sin, and of the Jewish people. The first eleven chapters reach back to the beginning of time and deal with questions that we all ask: who made the world? where did we come from? why is there suffering and evil in the world?

In chapters 12–50 we move from the general (the human race) to the particular as we learn how God moved into the chaos and confusion and chose one man, Abraham. God directed him to settle in the land of Israel and he and his descendants, Isaac and Jacob, are known as the patriarchs (fathers) or founders of Israel. Jacob's twelve sons are the beginnings of the twelve tribes. Through Joseph, one of his sons, the whole family settle in Egypt.

EXODUS

The centre-piece of this book is God's deliverance of emergent Israel from Egypt and the book's name means 'going out'. Some four hundred years separate Genesis and Exodus, during which time Egyptian attitudes to the settlers changed from peaceful co-existence to hostility and oppression. Moses emerged to lead God's people out of Egypt, their destination being the land of Israel. At the mountain of Sinai God gave Moses the laws which were to form the basis of the newly-formed nation's life. These are summed up in the Ten Commandments.

LEVITICUS

This is a book of further laws or rules, mainly for Israel's worship, and in particular about sacrifice and the priesthood. A keyword is 'holiness', for the intention of the laws was to help the people relate to God and in so doing to reflect his character in daily life.

NUMBERS

The first ten chapters continue in the legal atmosphere of Leviticus. The name of the book arises from the various censuses or numberings taken prior to breaking camp and leaving Sinai. The remaining chapters are a sad record of almost forty years wandering in the desert and of complaints and rebellion against Moses and God.

DEUTERONOMY

The setting of the book is the border of the land of Israel. It is presented as three sermons of Moses in which he surveys the journey from Egypt, the people's rebellion and God's patient loyalty. He restates and underlines some of the laws of Exodus, Leviticus and Numbers (thus the book's title, which means 'second law-giving'), and stresses the need for obedience after they have settled in Israel. The book closes with some final words of Moses and his death.

JOSHUA

The first twelve chapters tell us about the initial occupation of Israel under its new leader, Joshua. The remaining chapters outline the planned territorial division among the twelve tribes. Many of the native people still had to be conquered.

JUDGES

This book continues the story of the conquest of the land of Israel which involved conflict with various tribes both in and around Israel. Interwoven in the account is the constant disobedience to God alternating with a turning back to him, and his patient loyalty which is demonstrated in various leaders (called 'judges') who emerged to rally the tribes to fight their enemies.

RUTH

This is a story of family loyalty and loyalty to God and to his laws. It is set in the same period as Judges. The central character, Ruth, was not an Israelite but came to believe in God and, through her marriage to an Israelite called Boaz, became the great-grandmother of David and an ancestor of Jesus.

1 SAMUEL

The first and second books of Samuel recount Israel's history in the crucial transition from intermittent leadership to monarchy. The books take their name from the prophet who appointed the first two kings, Saul and David.

1 Samuel picks up from the book of Judges and shows how the continued harassment from neighbouring tribes made the people ask for a king.

2 SAMUEL

This is about Israel's second, and best known king, David. The book opens against a background of civil war following the death of Saul in battle. Later in the book we read of intrigue among David's sons over the succession. It was David who established Jerusalem as Israel's capital.

1 KINGS

The two books of Kings cover the history of Israel over a period of almost four hundred years.

The first eleven chapters of 1 Kings concern David's son, Solomon, the third king of Israel. His importance centres on his building of the Jerusalem Temple, the focal point of Israel's worship. His son, Rehoboam, inherited a dissatisfied nation and due to his foolish attitude ten of the tribes formed themselves into a separate state under a former official of Solomon's called Jeroboam. Subsequently this state is known as Israel, or the Northern Kingdom, and the remaining two tribes as Judah, or the Southern Kingdom. The history of these two states is recounted in interwoven accounts in the remaining chapters of 1 and 2 Kings. Elijah, an important prophet, dominates the end of 1 Kings.

2 KINGS

The death of Elijah and the emergence of the prophet Elisha occupy the early chapters of 2 Kings. The remaining sweep of the history covers some three hundred years, and from a religious point of view is all downhill apart from one or two religious revivals promoted by the reigning monarch. The end of the Northern Kingdom comes a century and a half before that of Judah, but in both cases it is understood as the inevitable punishment for turning away from God.

1 CHRONICLES

The two books of Chronicles cover the same period as Samuel and Kings but from a particular point of view. The writer, known as 'The Chronicler', shows that David laid the foundations of Israel's worship even though he did not build the Temple. In the first nine chapters he uses family trees to trace the history of Israel from Adam to the return from Exile to show that Judah is the true people of God.

2 CHRONICLES

Solomon, the builder of the Temple, is the subject of chapters 1–9. It becomes obvious in the remaining chapters that interest lies only in the history of Judah, through whom God would continue his purpose. Special attention is also given to kings who promoted religious reform. The end of the book goes beyond 2 Kings as it hints that the period in exile in Babylon is about to end. Persia has taken over the Babylonian empire.

EZRA

This follows on in time immediately from 2 Chronicles. The Persian king has issued a decree which allows the Jews to return to Israel and to rebuild the Jerusalem Temple. In chapters 3–6 we learn that initially the altar was rebuilt and sacrifices resumed but opposition halted the temple rebuilding for many years. Finally, it was completed and dedicated. Some time later (chapters 7–10) Ezra, an expert on the Jewish law, was sent from Babylon to help and guide the newly-established community. The main problem was that the Jews were intermarrying with other nations, thereby threatening the survival of national identity.

NEHEMIAH

Another leader in establishing the new community, Nehemiah organised the rebuilding of the walls round Jerusalem, so vital to its security (chapters 1–7). Once this was done Ezra read the law (from the first five books of the Bible) to the people and led them in a confession of their disobedience to God and then to a promise to obey him in the future (chapters 8–10). Nehemiah also carried through several social reforms (chapters 11–13).

ESTHER

The setting of this story is the Persian king's palace in the same period as Ezra–Nehemiah. Esther, a Jew, became a Persian queen and was able to save the Jews in the Persian empire from a plot to exterminate them.

JOB

The story of Job is found in the first two and the last chapter of the book. Satan is allowed to bring several major tragedies into the life of this good and religious man. The main section of the book is a discussion between Job and three friends (a fourth makes a brief appearance) as to why Job has suffered so much trouble. The questions raised are not only about human suffering but about God: is he fair? is he even good? Traditional, trite answers are shown to be inadequate.

PSALMS

Here are sacred songs, poems and prayers which originated in Israel's worship and her experience of God. They are traditionally associated with David but reflect centuries of individual and corporate responses to God. Human emotions of anger, despair, sadness, guilt, doubt, joy, praise and adoration are expressed. Themes include the Law, Jerusalem and its Temple, Israel's history, the natural world, human suffering and God's justice.

PROVERBS

The first nine chapters are written as though a father, or perhaps a teacher, is giving advice to a son or student. After this each verse presents a proverb as we know proverbs today—concise, common sense and often witty statements about wise, successful living. Dominant themes include: poverty, justice, pride, self-control, drunkenness, anger, speaking wisely.

ECCLESIASTES

The name of this book means something like 'The Teacher' and the central word is 'meaningless'. The writer examines every aspect of life: wealth, social position, professional success and pleasure and concludes that they are futile because of the fact of death which comes to everyone. The only positive suggestion is that we should enjoy whatever God has given us, and in 12:13 the Teacher states his conclusion: 'Fear God and keep his Commandments'.

SONG OF SONGS

This is presented in poetic form as a 'song' about the wonder of sexual love. There are at least two individual speakers, a man and a woman, and a group called 'friends'. There are conversations between them, but also thoughts of each lover about the other. Many see the Song as a symbol of God's love for his people.

ISAIAH

This book relates to a period of some three hundred years. Chapters 1–39 are set in the closing years of the Northern Kingdom when Judah was still relatively safe. Isaiah worked in Jerusalem warning its people that God's judgment must fall on them because of social injustice and religious hypocrisy. To successive kings of Judah he advised dependence on God's guidance and protection rather than on political alliances with foreign nations. Jerusalem is spared the same fate as the Northern Kingdom for the time being.

Chapters 40–55 are concerned with the Jewish exiles in Babylon. The message is one of comfort: God is about to do something new and the punishment and pain of the past are over. The return to the land of Israel will recall the deliverance from Egypt.

In the final section of the book, which is set in the period after the temple had been re-built, there is evidence that the new community is in danger of slipping back into old patterns of behaviour. Alongside warnings is a vision of the greatness of God and his plans for the blessing of the Jews, and through them, of all nations.

JEREMIAH

This prophet worked in the closing years of Judah. His message was one of warning: God's judgment must come if the people persist in rebelling against him. Indeed, judgment has become inevitable and they would be wise to recognise that God was using Babylon to punish them. When the ruling classes were exiled to Babylon Jeremiah told them that God would work out his plans through the exiles. At the same time he tried to encourage those who remained in Judah to accept their fate, but his words fell on deaf ears. Within the book we have several insights into what this unpopular prophet was thinking and feeling.

LAMENTATIONS

This is a funeral song about the devastated city of Jerusalem, possibly written by Jeremiah. Each chapter is a complete poem and in each the mood changes from anguish and despair in the recognition that punishment was deserved, to hope in God's love and mercy. Prayer is made that God will once again show these to his people.

EZEKIEL

This prophet was exiled to Babylon and his work was among the exiles there. He may have been a priest and a key theme of the book is God's holiness. The book is full of strange symbolism, visions and accounts of how the prophet often presented his message through drama. Roughly, the first thirty-three chapters convey a similar message to that of Jeremiah and at a similar period: Jerusalem will be captured by Babylon and the temple will be destroyed. Once this had

taken place Ezekiel's message was one of comfort (chapters 33–39): God will bring back his people to their own country one day. Meanwhile, in Babylon they will learn that God can be worshipped even though there is no temple or they cannot offer sacrifice. Chapters 40–48 are a detailed vision of the future which centres on the Temple.

DANIEL

Daniel was also an exile in Babylon but was chosen to live in the Babylonian court and to train for the civil service. Despite this privilege we learn that Daniel, and later three of his friends, refused to give up their Jewish faith. God blessed their loyalty and Daniel was respected and consulted by the Babylonian, and later the Persian kings, particularly because of his ability to interpret dreams. The second part of the book (chapters 7–12) includes some detailed visions full of strange symbols and not always easy to interpret.

HOSEA

This prophet lived and worked in the Northern Kingdom in the closing years of its existence. Through his own experience of a broken marriage Hosea gained a deep insight into Israel's relationship to God. The covenant made at Sinai was like a marriage, but like Hosea's own wife Israel had left God to worship Canaanite gods. Hosea speaks movingly of the sadness God feels because of his love for Israel even though she deserves to be punished.

JOEL

We are not sure when Joel lived. In chapter 1 he speaks of the devastation caused by a plague of locusts. This may have been a real event or a vision but in either case it is a symbol of the invading army which God will use to punish his people (2:1–11). Joel calls the people to turn back to God while there is still time and speaks of a special outpouring of God's Spirit (2:12–32). Chapter 3 concerns a final and universal judgment.

AMOS

This prophet came from the Southern Kingdom but worked in the Northern Kingdom slightly earlier than Hosea. In chapters 1–2 he speaks of God's judgment on the surrounding nations but also on the complacent Northern Kingdom. In chapter 3 he announces that God has broken off the covenant agreement with his people in the Northern Kingdom and the next few chapters show why: oppression, social injustice, religious hypocrisy. Five visions (chapters 7–9) show that there is still time to turn back to God, but in the last two visions punishment is inevitable. A hope for something beyond God's judgment is expressed in the last few verses.

OBADIAH

This is the shortest Old Testament book and we know nothing about the prophet. The theme is the punishment of Edom, which lay to the south-east of the Dead Sea. The

Edomites were descendants of Esau and thus related to the Israelites, yet they were long-standing enemies. The reference in this book suggests that when Jerusalem fell to the Babylonian army in 587 B.C. the Edomites did nothing to help and maybe even took some advantage of Judah's fate. While Edom disappeared from history Obadiah foretells the return of Israel to her own land.

JONAH

God told the prophet Jonah to go and warn the people of Nineveh, capital of Assyria (a cruel enemy of Israel) that God was going to punish her. After attempts to evade God's orders Jonah reluctantly preached in the city and the Ninevites turned to God. Jonah was furious with God for showing mercy to such wicked people and God tries to demonstrate to the prophet that he feels compassion even for Israel's enemies.

MICAH

This prophet lived and worked a little later than Amos and Hosea and about the same time as Isaiah and what he has to say is very similar to them. He worked in the Southern Kingdom and condemned social injustice and inequality, and corruption among the political and religious leaders. God must punish his people but beyond that Micah speaks of a future which will centre on the Jerusalem temple when a descendant of David will emerge to lead God's people against her enemies (chapters 4–7). 6:6–8 seems to sum up the message, not only of Micah, but of all the prophets of this period.

NAHUM

This prophet announces the destruction of Nineveh, capital of Assyria. In the opening verses Nahum speaks of God as 'slow to anger' but also that he will 'not leave the guilty unpunished'. It is for this reason that God must now punish Nineveh for extreme cruelty. Chapters 2 and 3 are a poem about the siege of Nineveh. This took place in 612 B.C.

HABAKKUK

Because Habakkuk mentions Babylon (1:6) it is assumed that he worked at the end of the seventh century B.C. The prophet questions God about his justice: why does he turn a blind eye to cruelty and wickedness? how can he use wicked people to punish people who are better than them? God gives no direct answer (chapter 2) but promises that one day he will punish all oppression and injustice. Chapter 3 is a poem about God coming to punish all wickedness and concludes with a statement by the prophet of his trust in God, no matter what happens.

ZEPHANIAH

Zephaniah worked just before Jeremiah. The theme of the book is God's universal judgment. Chapter 1 deals with the judgment of Israel but 2:1–3 promises that this may be averted if they turn back to God. The remainder of chapter 2 foretells the punishment of

some of Israel's neighbours. Beyond the judgment of Jerusalem the prophet sees hope (chapter 3).

HAGGAI

Haggai and Zechariah belong to the same period (520 B.C.). Many Jews had returned to Israel to rebuild their national life. Initially they worked with enthusiasm but opposition brought the work of rebuilding the Temple to a standstill. Haggai rallied the people, showing that the economic difficulties they were experiencing were because they had their priorities wrong. The important thing for their national life was God's 'house' and God had greater things in store if they would only learn to put him first.

ZECHARIAH

Like Haggai, this prophet encouraged the people to take up the work they had left off and complete the Temple building. His messages are given in a series of visions in chapters 1–8 and concern other issues as well as the rebuilding. Chapters 9–14 are in a different form, more typical of prophetic messages. Their theme is the future age: Israel's deliverance, God's triumph and the work of the Messiah.

MALACHI

This book indicates that after the time of Haggai and Zechariah things deteriorated again. The people felt disappointed with God (1:2–5), the religious leaders were corrupt and slipshod in their duties (1:6–2:9), and everybody disobedient to God's laws (2:10–16) while at the same time treating him with contempt (2:17–3:18). Chapter 4 looks forward to the time when injustice will be dealt with and those who are loyal to God will be restored.

MATTHEW

The first three Gospels follow a similar pattern and are often known as the 'Synoptic Gospels' because they 'see together' the life of Jesus. Yet each has its own particular emphasis.

Matthew begins by tracing Jesus' family history back to Abraham and recounts various incidents concerned with Jesus' birth (chapters 1–2). His is a carefully organised Gospel and he is especially interested in what Jesus said: the Sermon on the Mount (chapters 5–7), parables about the kingdom of heaven (chapter 13) and parables about the end of time (chapter 25). He also shows that Jesus is the Messiah spoken of in the Old Testament.

MARK

This Gospel concentrates mainly on what Jesus did, although the writer does include some of Jesus' teaching. Within the first few chapters several miracles are recorded. He does not speak about Jesus' birth but begins with John the Baptist's work and Jesus' baptism and temptations. Chapters 1–9 are about Jesus' work in Galilee, chapters 10–15 his journey to Jerusalem ending in his death, and chapter 16 about his resurrection. 16:9–20 was added later, probably by the early church.

LUKE

The first two chapters of this Gospel contain several unique incidents related to Jesus' birth and early life. Luke traces Jesus' family tree to Adam, which underlines the emphasis on Jesus as the Saviour of the whole world. He stresses that Jesus is concerned for minority groups, for the poor and the oppressed. Other prominent themes are prayer, joy and the Holy Spirit. He often cross-references events to dates in secular history. He is also the author of Acts.

JOHN

It is obvious from the first verse that this Gospel is very different in atmosphere to the other three. Jesus' miracles are called 'signs', Jesus does not speak of the 'kingdom' but of 'eternal life'. There are no parables but several long, rather complex sermons which are usually linked to one of the signs. Thus when Jesus heals a blind man he speaks of himself as 'the light of the world'. These 'I am' sayings are quite distinctive to this Gospel and the accounts of Jesus' appearances after his resurrection are also unique.

ACTS

This is the 'second instalment' of the story begun in Luke's Gospel and tells us what happened in the early church in the first thirty years or so. It begins with the ascension of Jesus (chapter 1) and the coming of the Holy Spirit at Pentecost (chapter 2). The next ten chapters show how the gospel spread beyond the locality of Jerusalem as far as Samaria. Peter, Stephen and James are the main characters. Chapters 13–28 centre on Paul and his three missionary tours taking the gospel to Greece and Europe. The whole book shows that the main source of opposition to the 'new religion' came from the Jews, not the Roman government.

ROMANS

This is the first of twenty-one letters found in the New Testament. They are very important because they give us an inside view of life in the earliest Christian churches and the teaching of their leaders. Paul had not been to Rome when he wrote this letter. It is the most detailed account of an important part of his teaching: that the only way to be accepted by God was to rely on what Jesus did through his death and resurrection (chapters 1–8). In chapters 9–11 Paul expresses the hope that although the Jews have largely refused this teaching they will one day accept it. Romans follows the pattern of most of Paul's letters: the first part is teaching and the second practical application in real life. Thus chapters 12–16 speak of how Christians should behave in the church and in the world.

1 CORINTHIANS

This and the following letter were written to a church in the Greek city of Corinth which Paul had visited (Acts 18:1–21). Paul had heard that there were various problems in the church: party politics (chapters 1–4), moral problems (chapter 5), Christians taking each other to court (chapter 6), marriage (chapter 7), special difficulties arising from living in a city full of temples to various gods (chapters 8–10), the organisation of worship (chapters 11–14) and intellectual problems with life after death (chapter 15).

2 CORINTHIANS

Between this and the previous letter Paul visited the church. There had been a lot of criticism and even hostility shown to him, and his authority as a leader had been called into question. Relationships had improved but Paul finds it necessary to stress the genuineness of his authority as an apostle (chapters 2–3, 10–13). The letter shows how deeply Paul felt (chapter 7). Chapter 5 contains further teaching on life after death, and chapters 8–9 give details about an appeal for financial help for a group of churches facing hardship.

GALATIANS

This is probably the first of Paul's letters and its theme is similar to that of Romans. It is apparent that many Jews felt that non-Jews becoming Christians should keep the Jewish law and in particular the food laws, and be circumcised. (Acts also tells us this.) The heart of Paul's teaching on this view is found in 2:14–21: a right relationship with God is possible only through Jesus, and nothing else is required. Chapters 5–6 show that this does not mean we can do as we like. Christians are called to 'serve one another in love' and the Holy Spirit is given to help them do this.

EPHESIANS

This letter may have been written to several churches in and around the important city of Ephesus. Paul founded this church on his third missionary tour (Acts 18:23–20:1). The clear theme of the letter is unity: God's plan is to bring to an end all that divides men and women, social classes, cultures, nations and religions. Jesus Christ is the unifying force, as the head 'unites' the human body. Chapters 4–6 show that this unity is very practical: it is worked out in good relationships in the family, the church and the work place.

PHILIPPIANS

Paul established this church on his second missionary tour (Acts 16:6–40), and this letter was written some ten or twelve years after that visit. It is a warm, personal letter to a church for which he felt a deep affection. He speaks of his imprisonment which has resulted in the gospel being preached to Roman personnel (chapter 1). Chapter 2 contains an important statement about Jesus as the servant who was willing to give up his rights for the good of others, and Paul encourages the church to follow that example.

COLOSSIANS

The church was founded by Epaphras, one of Paul's converts. The contents of the letter make it clear that wrong teaching was creeping into the church. In the face of this Paul stresses the true gospel: Jesus is absolutely central. He existed before time began and he is the one who brings God and the human race together again (chapter 1). Rituals, regulations, philosophical reasonings and self-denial are not what is required (chapter 2) but right relationships and attitudes in the church, the family, the work place and the world (chapters 3–4).

1 THESSALONIANS

Paul founded this church on his second missionary tour (Acts 17:1–9) amid a lot of opposition from Jews. This and 2 Thessalonians are among Paul's earliest letters. No doubt because the Jews had continued to undermine his reputation Paul begins by insisting that he is a true apostle (chapters 1–2). From chapter 3 we learn that Timothy had been sent to the church and had returned to Paul with an encouraging report. In chapters 4 and 5 Paul deals with two questions: what happens to Christians when they die? and when will Jesus return?

2 THESSALONIANS

The Thessalonian church did not fully understand what Paul had said in his first letter (1 Thessalonians) about Jesus' return. They had also been confused by other teachers who said that Jesus had already returned. Furthermore, some church members had even opted out of responsibilities on the basis that if Jesus was about to return there was not much point in going to work! Paul deals with all these difficulties.

1 TIMOTHY

Paul had met Timothy on his second missionary tour (Acts 16:1–3) and Timothy had worked with him. Now he was a leader in the church at Ephesus and Paul writes to encourage him and give him advice about organising the church there. He writes about public prayer, the appointment of leaders, help for widows and attitudes to slaves (chapters 2–5). He warns about those who teach differently to what has been taught by recognised leaders.

2 TIMOTHY

This is more personal than 1 Timothy and was written at the end of Paul's life. He warns Timothy that wrong teaching is on the increase and people will easily be deceived. In the face of this Timothy must stand by the truth, which will take courage.

TITUS

In a similar way to Timothy, Titus was a leader in the church on the island of Crete. Paul writes as he did in 1 Timothy, about the organisation and leadership of the church, correct teaching in the face of error and right attitudes in the church, the work place and the world.

PHILEMON

Philemon was probably a convert of Paul's and now a church worker. Onesimus, one of his slaves, had run away but had met Paul and become a Christian. Paul writes to Philemon to say that he is sending Onesimus back to his master and appeals to Philemon to do what would have been unusual in those days—to forgive and reinstate Onesimus.

HEBREWS

We do not know who wrote this letter, nor who the readers were. Since the writer's theme is that the Temple and its ceremonies were temporary pointers to Christianity it is probable that the original readers were Jews. The keyword for this letter is 'better'. Jesus has offered a better (and the last) sacrifice (chapters 4–7). He is 'better' than all that has gone before: greater than the angels (chapters 1–2), greater than Moses (chapter 3). The New Covenant has replaced the Old (chapters 8–10). In the closing chapters he writes to encourage his readers to keep going in the face of difficulties and hostility. The people of the Old Testament did wonderful things because they relied on God (chapter 11). Christians must follow their example and the example of Jesus (chapter 12).

JAMES

James may have been Jesus' brother who was also the first leader of the church in Jerusalem. It could be the first of the New Testament letters to be written, and it is very practical. The main themes are: if we say we are Christians we must also live like Christians; discrimination of any kind is wrong, as is oppression of the poor and the weak; Christians should be self-controlled, especially in what they say.

1 PETER

This letter was written to Christians in the Black Sea coastal area, probably in the early 60s A.D. The theme is suffering, and probably the readers were facing real persecution because they were Christians. Christians must not be surprised if they experience opposition and persecution; Jesus, their example, certainly did! Indeed, they may be full of hope and joy because they are sharing with Jesus in this way. Throughout the letter there are also practical guidelines on Christian behaviour.

2 PETER

The letter opens with the same emphasis as in 1 Peter on Christian behaviour. Chapters 2 and 3 are a strong onslaught against those who mislead by wrong teaching and the writer speaks in detail of their future punishment. This leads him to speak of the return of Jesus.

1 JOHN

It is probable that the writer of this letter and 2 and 3 John was also the writer of the Gospel of John and the book of Revelation. It is clear that the Christians to whom he wrote 1 John were worried by teachers of strange ideas. They were saying they had special understanding of spiritual matters. This meant that they were claiming to be perfect on the one hand, and that Jesus could not have been a real man on the other. In reply John stresses the certainty that Christians have: 'we know' is a favourite phrase. One of the clear proofs that people are Christians is that they love other Christians.

2 JOHN

This letter is written to 'the chosen lady' which probably refers to a church, not an individual. Some of the themes found in 1 John are taken up here: loving God means doing what he has told us to do and loving others. The writer warns about teachers of wrong ideas.

3 JOHN

This letter is addressed to someone called Gaius who is praised for the way he is standing by the truth. A man called Diotrephes is setting himself up as a leader and turning away representatives of the writer.

JUDE

Many believe that Jude was a brother of Jesus. His letter uses almost the same words as 2 Peter 2:1–3:3 to condemn all who mislead by their wrong teaching. He too writes of their future punishment and encourages his readers to keep to the teaching they were given originally.

REVELATION

This letter was written to seven churches in Asia Minor which are named in the course of messages to them from Jesus in chapters 2–3. John had a vision of Jesus which he describes in chapter 1. In chapters 4–5 he has another vision of Jesus and in the course of this Jesus takes a scroll from the hand 'of him who sat on the throne'. The rest of the book recounts what happens as Jesus opens this scroll. These chapters are full of difficult symbols which we do not fully understand and we cannot be certain of their meaning. But the basic message of the book is that God is in control and all evil will eventually be destroyed.

THE LAND AND PEOPLE OF THE BIBLE

GEOGRAPHY

NAME: The place in which the story of the Bible is set has been known by different names in its history:

Canaan is the earliest reference to the country (Genesis 10:19; 11:31). As Genesis 12:6 shows, the name is associated with the people who lived there: Canaanites.

Israel or 'the land of Israel', is the name used as the Old Testament progresses (e.g. 1 Samuel 13:19). When the nation was divided the northern part was called **'Israel'**, and the southern area **'Judah'**. In the New Testament period under the Romans, the land was divided into provinces such as 'Judea' and 'Galilee'.

Palestine has also been used, as for example, in the earlier part of this century. It is associated with the **'Philistines'** who once occupied the coastal area to the west of Israel—the 'land of the Philistines' or 'Philistia'.

Today, the whole area is so divided that the various titles only confuse!

PHYSICAL FEATURES: The land of Israel is small, roughly the size of Wales, 150–200 miles long and 100 miles at its widest point. It is a land of great contrasts. Travelling in an easterly direction from the Mediterranean Sea there is a coastal plain from which the land slopes gently at first, then more steeply to the central highlands of Judea. It then drops sharply to the Jordan rift valley and rises again to a mountainous plateau in the Trans-Jordan area. Travelling from north to south the land descends steadily from Mount Hermon (9000 feet) to the Dead Sea (1275 feet below sea level).

LANDSCAPE: The present landscape is very different from what it was in the early Old Testament period. Then the northern central area and Trans-Jordan were covered by lush forest, and the plains nearer the coast were sand dunes, lagoons, swamp and forest. In the northwest and central areas (where most of the Bible story is set) there were fertile plains. The southern area was desert scrub.

CLIMATE: There are great variations in the climate which falls roughly between temperate and tropical, with wet winters and hot, dry summers (May/June–September/October). Climate varies with the height above sea level, distance from the coast, etc. **Rainfall** is vital and while the rainy season is predictable there are great variations from year to year. In the Bible there are references to:

'the early rains'–mid-October: (Autumn) which make ploughing possible. This is followed by the rainy season proper, November–March, with most rain falling in December and January.

'the latter rains' or 'spring rains'—vital to mature the grain.

Rainfall averages lessen from north to south and from west to east. During the summer, dew and morning mist bring moisture to the coastal areas and the plains, and this is of vital importance. Drought and famine were constant factors which had to be reckoned with.

OCCUPATIONS:

Agriculture. The people of the Bible, and particularly of Old Testament times, were farmers. Almost everyone would have had their own smallholding, growing what was needed for food, and keeping sheep, goats and cattle. Goats provided milk, and their skins were used to make tents. Sheep provided milk and wool, and occasionally meat. By New Testament times it was fairly common to keep chickens.

Though a large part of the land was desert and rock, and therefore unsuitable for farming, the areas of lower Galilee were fertile. Barley was grown in the fertile valleys (such as the Jordan valley), and wheat in the Plain of Jezreel. Flax for making linen, and millet were also grown. Pomegranates, melons, dates, cucumbers, figs and nuts were important crops providing a supplement to water in the long hot season. On the lower hills there were vineyards—the vine is an important symbol in the Bible (e.g. Isaiah 5:7; John 15:1). Olives were eaten for food, and their oil was used for lighting, cooking, medicine, and soap for washing. **Harvesting** began in March (Flax) and proceeded with barley (April/May), wheat (May/June), grapes (July–October), figs (August/September) and olives (October/November).

Other Occupations

FISHING: Whole communities made their living from fishing, as the New Testament Gospels show. Lake Galilee was the focus for this.

MINING: The mining of iron and copper in the area of Ezion Geber began around 1000 B.C. Chemical salts and pitch were found in the Dead Sea area.

POTTERY: Although there are several references to potters and their craft in the Bible, there was nothing distinctive about Israelite pottery.

FROM TENTS TO TOWNS

THE TRIBE: The story of Israel begins with Abraham. He lived a 'semi-nomadic' life (i.e. travelling from place to place and living in tents) much as the modern Bedouin today. The tribe would include the entire family, from the head of the family/tribe, through the various generations to the youngest member. Servants and large numbers of animals would be included.

EARLY COMMUNITIES: After the settlement in Canaan under Joshua's leadership, the twelve tribes gradually settled into small farming communities or villages, which later became walled towns and cities. Towns were small with about 150–200 houses.

LATER DEVELOPMENTS: Under the kings, and especially Solomon, towns became larger and the gap between rich and poor widened as farms were taken over, and even tenant farmers were forced off their land.

NEW TESTAMENT TIMES: By New Testament times towns were planned more carefully, though life was still quite rural. Jerusalem probably had a quarter of a million inhabitants in the time of Jesus. The Romans, famed for their civil engineering, did much to improve conditions by building drainage schemes, aqueducts etc. They also created 'provinces', some of which were governed by a governor or pro-consul, and others (where troops were stationed) by a procurator. Some cities were given special status as Roman colonies and were governed by magistrates. Philippi was one of these. Roman citizenship was another privilege and Paul was proud of his.

HOW PEOPLE LIVED

The Bible covers a period of some 2000 years so there were changes in some customs and in the way people lived. It is only possible to look at a few of these customs in this section.

FAMILY LIFE:

Circumcision. Eight days after birth a boy was circumcised. Other races practised circumcision but it had religious meaning for the Jews. It reminded them that God had chosen them and that they were different from other people.

Education. Learning was based on 'the Scriptures', particularly the Laws in the Pentateuch. The many festivals helped children to learn about the history of Israel. Children were taught at home, but by New Testament times boys would go to the synagogue school.

The eldest son succeeded his father. While both boys and girls would help on the farm, girls would also help in the home. Women did all the food preparation, water carrying, spinning, weaving, and the making of clothes.

Marriage. This was arranged by parents, and throughout biblical times there was an insistence that marriage should take place only between fellow Israelites, though many disregarded this, as the Old Testament shows. The **engagement** was binding and a 'bride price' (mohar) would be paid to the bride's father, and a dowry by the bride's father. These could be paid in servants, land, property or work, not only in money. **Divorce** was allowed, but the actual grounds for this were not

clear and were still being debated in Jesus' time.

Death. There were clear mourning rites which lasted seven days. The body had to be buried within 24 hours, either in a cave, or for the rich, a specially prepared tomb. There was no clear understanding of a **life beyond death** in the Old Testament. It was believed that the dead went to a 'place of shadows' called 'Sheol'. By the New Testament period the Pharisees believed in a physical resurrection, and certainly many of the ordinary people did as well (see John 11).

JUSTICE AND ADMINISTRATION:

Early period. After the settlement, when towns began to be established, the entrance ('the gate') became the meeting place and a kind of law-court, where cases were heard and judgment given. Under Solomon an organised administration and government began to emerge, and community and military service was introduced.

Later period. Towards the end of the Old Testament period families of priests began to emerge with wide powers and influence. Together with 'elders' these priests formed a central governing body called **'the Sanhedrin'** or 'the Council'. It had wide civil and administrative powers and its own police force. It was this court that tried Jesus, and later, some of his followers.

ISRAEL AND HER NEIGHBOURS

Although Israel was a tiny country its position in relation to the nations which surround it gave it a strategic importance. This is because it formed a kind of land bridge between powerful nations: Egypt in the south and Mesopotamia in the north were constantly struggling with each other for possession, influence and control of vital trade routes. An understanding of this helps us to see why, in the Old Testament in particular, there was constant warfare and threat of invasion.

SUMERIA. This probably forms the background culture to Genesis 1–11. It is the oldest culture of which we know, and dates to at least 4500 B.C., so that Sumeria is often called 'the cradle of civilisation'. It lay near the Persian Gulf, between the Tigris and Euphrates rivers (modern S. Iraq). Its largest city was **Ur** from which Abraham's family came. Sumerians were scientists, mathematicians and astronomers, but their greatest contribution to civilisation was **writing**, which they seem to have invented. The earliest understandable writing dates from 3200 B.C., and many later languages developed from this. Sumeria had been finally absorbed by the Semites by 1750 B.C., but its legacy of writings lived on.

EGYPT. In Genesis and Exodus the founding fathers of Israel (Abraham, Isaac etc.) travelled constantly to and from Egypt. Egyptian civilisation is very old and reaches back at least to 3000 B.C. It was an advanced culture and Egyptians had special interest in dreams and their interpretation, as well as in poetry, proverbs and story-writing. Their king was called 'Pharaoh' (his Majesty) and was regarded as a god.

At the end of the Old Testament period Egypt's power had dwindled so that she often tried to form political alliances with other nations, including Israel, to keep herself going.

CANAANITES. These were the main racial group in Palestine at the time of the Conquest. They lived in small 'city-states' or 'fortress towns', built on hill summits. Other tribal groups lived alongside them, such as Amorites, Perizzites, etc. (see Exodus 33:2). The significance of the Canaanites for Israel's history is in their religion. This was a nature religion, its chief god being Baal, the storm god, and provider (or withholder) of rain.

PHILISTINES. They appear to have been part of a general movement of tribes known as 'Sea People', who came to the coastal areas of Palestine from Crete, Cyprus and the Aegean Islands. The territory was known as 'the land of the Philistines' or 'Philistia'. They had five settlements or 'city-states': Gaza, Ashkelon, Gath, Ashdod and Ekron which formed a closely knit and very efficient social and military unit. Their chief god was Dagon.

There was constant border warfare between Israel and the Philistines throughout the period of the Judges and until King David finally defeated them.

SYRIA. Also called Aram (after the Aramean tribes who settled here), Syria lay to the north of Israel. Its chief city was Damascus. Aramaic was probably the language of these early settlers. Relationships between Israel and Syria varied between border warfare, independent existence and alliance.

In the New Testament Antioch in Syria was an important centre of early Christianity, and it was there that the followers of Jesus were first called Christians.

ASSYRIA. This lay in north Mesopotamia (the northern part of modern Iraq). It was an ancient nation, settled at least by *c.* 2300 B.C., but its importance for the history of Israel spans a period of some 200 years (850–650 B.C.) during which Israel became part of the Assyrian empire. Their capital city was Asshur (their chief god had the same name), but later Nineveh became the capital city until Assyria fell to the Babylonians in 612 B.C. Assyria was a cruel, but very efficient, military nation who resettled conquered peoples away from their own land, thus breaking their national identity. This fate befell the Northern Kingdom of Israel in 722 B.C. Kings mentioned in the OT are **Tiglath-Pileser III** (744–727 B.C.—2 Ki 15:29), **Shalmaneser V** (726–722 B.C.—2 Ki 17:3), **Sargon II** (721–705 B.C.—Isa 20:1), **Sennacherib** (704–681 B.C.—2 Ki 18:13), **Esarhaddon** (681–669 B.C.—2 Ki 19:37) and **Ashurbanipal** (660–627 B.C.—Ezr 4:10).

BABYLON. Babylonian history reaches back to the Sumerian period from which it derives many of its cultural traditions. It lay in what is now Southern Iraq. The Assyrian Empire passed to Babylon under king Nebuchadnezzar. Both Ezekiel and Daniel were exiled to Babylon, and Ezra the scribe returned to Israel from Babylon, although by then Babylon had itself fallen to the Persian king, Cyrus, in 539 B.C.

PERSIA. Persians were originally travelling Indo-Europeans from Southern Russia, who settled in what is now modern Iran about 1000 B.C. Their capital was Susa, where Nehemiah was based, while the book of Esther gives an inside view of life in the royal palace there. We learn about Persian policy towards conquered peoples from 2 Chronicles and Ezra, both of which contain a decree of king Cyrus. It shows that Persia encouraged subject nations to continue their own religion and culture. Kings mentioned in the OT are **Cyrus II**, the Great (or Darius the Mede, 559–530 B.C.; 2 Ch 36:22–23; Ezr 1:1–4; Da 1:21); **Darius I**, the Great (522–486 B.C.; Ezr 4:5; Ne 12:22; Hag 1:1; Zec 1:1), **Artaxerxes** (465–424 B.C.; Ezr 7:1, 21–26; Ne 2:1–8), **Darius II** (424–404 B.C.; Ne 12:22).

Persian power was overthrown by Alexander the Great of Greece in 331 B.C.

GREECE. It was Alexander the Great who was responsible for the spread of Greek civilisation throughout the vast Greek empire. Greek cities were established all over the empire, and Greek philosophy, science, morality, customs and language spread everywhere (including Israel) even after Alexander's death when his empire was divided between his four generals.

ROME. In 63 B.C. much of Israel was incorporated into the Roman province of Syria when Pompey marched into Jerusalem. Over the next few decades there was a lot of rivalry among Roman leaders, but in 31 B.C. Octavian emerged as sole ruler of the Empire. In 27 B.C. he took the name Augustus and it was during his rule that Jesus was born (Luke 2:1). Rome brought many benefits to the world: for example, roads which made travelling and trade so much easier. Latin and Greek were the official language throughout the empire and this helped the early Christian missionaries as they went everywhere preaching.

Despite the fact that subject nations were allowed to follow their own customs and religion, the Jews hated Rome. In the time of Jesus Roman troops were stationed in Judea, and Jewish hopes that God would intervene and deliver them became very strong. Resistance to Roman rule increased during the period A.D. 60–70 and in A.D. 70. Rome retaliated by destroying the Temple in Jerusalem.

Persecution of Christians seems to have been unusual, but the book of Revelation may indicate a firmer line being taken against the Christian church.

WELL-KNOWN EVENTS IN THE BIBLE

Creation   **Genesis** 1–2
The first sin   **Genesis** 3
Cain kills Abel   **Genesis** 4
Noah and the Ark   **Genesis** 6–9
Sodom and Gomorrah   **Genesis** 18–19
Abraham sacrifices Isaac   **Genesis** 22
Jacob's Dream   **Genesis** 28:10–22
Joseph's coat of many colours   **Genesis** 37
Moses in the bullrushes   **Exodus** 2
Moses and the burning bush   **Exodus** 3
Plagues on Egypt   **Exodus** 7–11
The first Passover   **Exodus** 12
The Exodus   **Exodus** 12–13
Crossing the Red Sea   **Exodus** 13–14
Manna and quail   **Exodus** 16
Water from the rock   **Exodus** 17
The Ten Commandments   **Exodus** 20
Balaam's donkey   **Numbers** 22
Death of Moses   **Deuteronomy** 34
Crossing the Jordan   **Joshua** 3
The Battle of Jericho   **Joshua** 6
Gideon and the fleece   **Judges** 6–7
Samson and Delilah   **Judges** 13–16
Samuel called by God   **1 Samuel** 1–3
David and Goliath   **1 Samuel** 17
David and Bathsheba   **2 Samuel**
Solomon builds the Temple   **1 Kings** 6–7, **2 Chronicles** 3–4
Elijah and the priests of Baal   **1 Kings** 18
The miracles of Elisha   **2 Kings** 4–5
'The Lord is my Shepherd'   **Psalm** 23
Benefits of Wisdom   **Proverbs** 3
Sayings of the wise   **Proverbs** 22
The Wife of noble character   **Proverbs** 31
'To us a child is born'   **Isaiah** 9
Ezekiel and the dry bones   **Ezekiel** 37
The fiery furnace   **Daniel** 3
Writing on the wall   **Daniel** 5
Daniel in the lions' den   **Daniel** 6
Hosea and his adulterous wife   **Hosea** 1–3
Jonah and the fish   **Jonah** 1
Coming of the Holy Spirit at Pentecost   **Acts** 2
Death of Stephen   **Acts** 6–7
Conversion of Saul   **Acts** 9:1–31
Paul's shipwreck   **Acts** 27–28

WELL-KNOWN EVENTS IN THE LIFE OF JESUS

Birth   **Matthew** 1–2; **Luke** 1–2
Baptism   **Matthew** 3:13–17; **Mark** 1:9–11; **Luke** 3:21–22
Temptation   **Matthew** 4:1–11; **Mark** 1:12–13; **Luke** 4:1–13
The transfiguration   **Matthew** 17:1–13; **Mark** 9:2–13; **Luke** 9:28–36
The triumphal entry into Jerusalem   **Matthew** 21:1–11; **Mark** 11:1–11; **Luke** 19:28–44;
   John 12:12–19
Jesus clears the temple   **Matthew** 21:12–13; **Mark** 11:15–19; **Luke** 19:45–48;
   John 2:12–25
The widow's offering   **Mark** 12:41–44; **Luke** 21:1–4
The last supper   **Matthew** 26:17–30; **Mark** 14:12–26; **Luke** 22:7–38; **John** 13:21–30
Jesus washes his disciples' feet   **John** 13:1–17
Jesus at Gethsemane   **Matthew** 26:36–46; **Mark** 14:32–42; **Luke** 22:39–46
Judas betrays Jesus   **Matthew** 26:47–56; **Mark** 14:43–50; **Luke** 22:1–6, 47–53;
   John 18:1–11
Peter denies Jesus   **Matthew** 26:69–75; **Mark** 14:66–72; **Luke** 22:54–62;
   John 18:15–18, 25–27
The trial and crucifixion   **Matthew** 26:57–27:66; **Mark** 15:1–47; **Luke** 22:66–23:56;
   John 18:28–19:42
Resurrection and ascension   **Matthew** 28:1–20; **Mark** 16:1–20; **Luke** 24:1–53;
   John 20:1–21:25

SELECTED MIRACLES OF JESUS

Man with leprosy   **Matthew 8:2–4; Mark 1:40–42; Luke 5:12–13**
Roman centurion's servant   **Matthew 8:5–13; Luke 7:1–10**
Calming the storm   **Matthew 8:23–27; Mark 4:37–41; Luke 8:22–25**
Two demon-possessed men   **Matthew 8:28–34; Mark 5:1–15; Luke 8:26–39**
Paralysed man   **Matthew 9:2–7; Mark 2:3–12; Luke 5:18–25**
Jairus's daughter   **Matthew 9:18–19, 23–25; Mark 5:22–24, 38–42; Luke 8:41–42, 49–56**
Woman with bleeding   **Matthew 9:20–22; Mark 5:25–29; Luke 8:43–48**
Walking on water   **Matthew 14:25; Mark 6:48–51; John 6:19–21**
5000 people fed   **Matthew 14:15–21; Mark 6:35–44; Luke 9:12–17; John 6:5–13**
Canaanite woman's daughter   **Matthew 15:21–28; Mark 7:24–30**
4000 people fed   **Matthew 15:32–38; Mark 8:1–9**
Boy with a demon   **Matthew 17:14–18; Mark 9:17–29; Luke 9:38–43**
Fig-tree withered   **Matthew 21:18–22; Mark 11:12–14, 20–25**
Man possessed (in synagogue)   **Mark 1:23–26; Luke 4:33–35**
Catch of fish   **Luke 5:4–11**
Widow's son at Nain   **Luke 7:11–15**
Crippled woman   **Luke 13:11–13**
Ten men with leprosy   **Luke 17:11–19**
The high-priest's servant   **Luke 22:50–51**
Water turned to wine   **John 2:1–11**
Official's son at Capernaum   **John 4:46–54**
Sick man at pool of Bethesda   **John 5:1–9**
Man born blind   **John 9:1–7**
Lazarus   **John 11:1–44**
Another catch of fish   **John 21:1–11**

SELECTED PARABLES OF JESUS

Lamp under a bowl   **Matthew 5:14–15; Mark 4:21–22; Luke 8:16; 11:33**
House on the rock   **Matthew 7:24–27; Luke 6:47–49**
New cloth   **Matthew 9:16; Mark 2:21; Luke 5:36**
New wine in old wineskins   **Matthew 9:17; Mark 2:22; Luke 5:37–38**
Sower   **Matthew 13:3–8, 18–23; Mark 4:3–8, 14–20; Luke 8:5–8, 11–15**
Weeds   **Matthew 13:24–30, 36–43**
Mustard seed   **Matthew 13:31–32; Mark 4:30–32; Luke 13:18–19**
Yeast   **Matthew 13:33; Luke 13:20–21**
Hidden treasure   **Matthew 13:44**
Valuable pearl   **Matthew 13:45–46**
Owner of a house   **Matthew 13:52**
Lost sheep   **Matthew 18:12–14; Luke 15:4–7**
Unforgiving servant   **Matthew 18:23–34**
Workers in the vineyard   **Matthew 20:1–16**
Wicked tenants   **Matthew 21:33–44; Mark 12:1–11; Luke 20:9–18**
Wedding feast   **Matthew 22:2–14**
Faithful and wise servant   **Matthew 24:45–51; Luke 12:42–48**
Ten virgins   **Matthew 25:1–13**
Talents   **Matthew 25:14–30; Luke 19:12–27**
Sheep and goats   **Matthew 25:31–46**
Watchful servants   **Mark 13:35–37; Luke 12:35–40**
Good samaritan   **Luke 10:30–37**
Friend at midnight   **Luke 11:5–8**
Rich fool   **Luke 12:16–21**
Wedding feast   **Luke 14:7–14**
Great banquet   **Luke 14:16–24**
Cost of discipleship   **Luke 14:28–33**
Lost coin   **Luke 15:8–10**
Lost (prodigal) son   **Luke 15:11–32**
Rich man and Lazarus   **Luke 16:19–31**
Pharisee and tax collector   **Luke 18:10–14**

The Division of Canaan

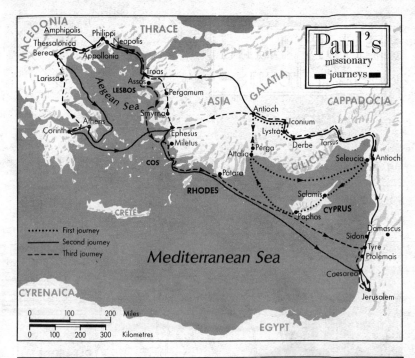

Paul's missionary journeys

- - - First journey
—— Second journey
- - - Third journey

Paul's journey to Rome